150306

Footprint South American Handbook 2008

Ben Box
84th edition

"At Lake Grey we walked across ribbed sand towards the icebergs, and in the woods behind them we ate box-leafed barberry fruits, the elixir of Patagonia, which cast their spell if you taste them and compel you to return."

Sara Wheelerl, Travels in a Thin Country (Little, Brown and Co, 1994)

WITHDRAWN

South American Highlights

See colour maps at back of book

❶ Cartagena
Beautiful colonial city, with a dark history, page 812

❷ The Galápagos Islands
The greatest wildlife show on earth, page 1017

❸ Cotopaxi
Herds of wild horses and llamas beneath a perfect, snow-capped volcano, page 935

❹ Machu Picchu and the Sacred Valley of the Incas
South America's top attraction, with the continent's gringo capital close by, page 1240

❺ Manu National Park
Home to jaguars and giant otters, page 1277

❻ Lake Titicaca
The world's highest navigable lake, home to ancient island communities, page 1196

❼ Salar de Uyuni
Blinding white salt flats, scarlet lakes, and volcanoes, page 284

❽ The Lake District
Beautiful lakes, forests and volcanoes, page 684

❾ Los Llanos
Venezuela's Wild West, with lots of wildlife, page 1379

❿ Canaima and the Angel Falls
Table-top mountains, 'lost worlds' and the world's highest waterfall, page 1408

11 Iwokrama
One of the best places to see the Amazon rainforest, page 1434

12 The Amazon
The world's largest river system and jungle, and a once-in-a-lifetime experience, page 532

13 Brazil's northeastern beaches
Idyllic sands and palm trees, giant sand dunes, and all-night lambada parties, page 509

14 Salvador
Brazil's party city, with colonial architecture and an African soul, page 463

15 Iguazú Falls
So vast they make Niagara look like a dripping tap, page 172

16 Buenos Aires
The city of tango, fashion, steak, nostalgia and wine, page 70

17 Península Valdés
Where Patagonia meets the Atlantic and whales come to breed, page 202

18 Torres del Paine
Hardcore trekking at the end of the Andes, page 753

19 Falklands/ Malvinas
The South Atlantic's answer to the Galápagos, with amazing marine birds and mammals, page 1467

Contents

Introducing
Highlights   2
A foot in the door   9

Planning your trip
First-time travel guide   18
Sport & activities   20
Ways to escape   30
Finding out more   32

Essentials
Before you travel   34
Getting there   34
Getting around   42
Health   45
Essentials A-Z   49

Argentina

Essentials   64
Buenos Aires &
   the Pampas   **70**
Sights   72
Around Buenos Aires   98
The Pampas   98
Atlantic Coast   103
West of
   Buenos Aires   **110**
Córdoba   110
Around Córdoba   114
Mendoza & around   119
South of Mendoza   125
Mendoza to Chile   126
San Juan & around   129
La Rioja & Catamarca   133
Northwest
   Argentina   **137**
Santiago del Estero   137
Tucumán & around   138
Cafayate   143

Salta   146
Jujuy   152
Jujuy to the Chilean
   & Bolivian borders   154
The Northeast   **160**
Up the Río Uruguay   160
Up the Río Paraná   162
The Chaco   167
Misiones   169
Iguazú Falls   172
Lake District   **177**
Nuequén & around   177
Parque Nacional Lanín   179
Parque Nacional
   Nahuel Huapi   182
Bariloche & around   185
South of Bariloche   193
Patagonia   **200**
Viedma, Carmen de
   Patagones & around   201
Puerto Madryn
   & around   202
Trelew & the
   Chubut Valley   206
Comodoro Rivadavia
   & inland   209
Río Gallegos & around   212
Ruta 40 to the glaciers   215
Parque Nacional
   Los Glaciares   217
Tierra del Fuego   **225**
Ushuaia & around   226

Bolivia

Essentials   236
La Paz & around   **242**
Sights   243
Around La Paz   248
Lake Titicaca   **264**

The Yungas   **274**
Southwest Bolivia   **277**
Oruro   277
Uyuni   283
Tupiza   289
Central & Southern
   Highlands   **292**
Potosí   292
Sucre   297
Tarija   303
Cochabamba & around   306
Northern Lowlands   **313**
Madidi &
   Rurrenabaque   314
Riberalta to Brazil   317
Cochabamba
   to Trinidad   319
Santa Cruz &
   Eastern Lowlands   **321**
Santa Cruz   321
Southeastern Brazil   326
Eastern Bolivia   331

Brazil

Essentials   340
Rio de Janeiro   **348**
Sights   350
East of Rio   378
West of Rio   385
São Paulo   **391**
Sights   395
São Paulo coast   406
Minas Gerais
   & Espírito Santo   **411**
Belo Horizonte   411
East & south
   of Belo Horizonte   416
Espírito Santo   426

North of
  Belo Horizonte   430
Southern Brazil   **432**
  Curitiba & around   432
  Paranaguá & the coast   437
  Santa Catarina   440
  Rio Grande do Sul   448
  Porto Alegre   448
  Rio Grande do Sul state 453
Foz do Iguaçu   **458**
Salvador de Bahia   **463**
  Sights   465
  Inland from Salvador   478
  South of Salvador   481
  North of Salvador   488
Recife & the
  northeast coast   **490**
  Recife   490
  Around Recife   499
  South of Recife   504
  João Pessoa   507
  Natal   509
Fortaleza & the
  north coast   **516**
  Fortaleza   516
  Coast east of Fortaleza 523
  Coast west of Fortaleza 524
  West of Fortaleza   530
The Amazon   **532**
  Travel up the
    Amazon River   532
  Belém & around   535
  Belém to Manaus   542
  Manaus   545
Amazon frontiers   **555**
  Manaus to Colombia,
    Peru, Venezuela
    & Guyana   555
  Southern Amazônia   559
Brasília & Goiás   **564**
  Brasília   565
  Goiás   571
  Tocantins   576
The Pantanal   **577**
  Campo Grande
    & around   579
  Corumbá   586
  Cuibá   588

Chile

Essentials   **598**
Santiago & around   **605**
  Around Santiago   623
Valparaíso & around   **626**
  Valparaíso   625
  Viña del Mar & around   633
North of Santiago   **637**
  Ovalle to La Serena   637
  North of La Serena   644
Far north   **648**
  Antofagasta   648
  North of Antofagasta   652
  San Pedro de Atacama   656
  Iquique & around   660
  Arica & Lauca   665
Central Valley   **673**
  Rancagua to Chillán   673
  Concepción & around   678
Lake District   **684**
  Temuco & around   684
  Lagos Villarica, Calafquén
    & Panguipulli   691
  Valdivia & Osorno   701
  Southern lakes   706
Puerto Montt
  & Chiloé   **713**
  Puerto Montt   713
  Chiloé   718
Carretera Austral   **726**
  Puerto Montt
    to Chaitén   727
  Chaitén to Coyhaique   729
  Lago General Carrera
    & around   737
Far south   **742**
  Punta Arenas & around   742
  Puerto Natales
    & around   748

Parque Nacional
  Torres del Paine   753
  Tierra del Fuego   758
Chilean Pacific
  Islands   **761**
  Juan Fernández Islands   761
  Rapa Nui/Easter Island   762

Colombia

Essentials   **772**
Bogotá   **780**
  Sights   782
  Around Bogotá   796
Bogotá to the
  Venezuelan
  border   **799**
  Bogotá to Villa de Leiva   799
  Tunja to Cocuy   804
  To Bucaramanga
    & Cúcuta   806
Cartagena & the
  north coast   **812**
  Cartagena   812
  To Panama   823
  Barranquilla   827
  Santa Marta, Tayrona
    & Ciudad Perdida   828
  To Venezuela   835
  San Andrés
    & Providencia   838
Medellín & Chocó   **842**
  Medellín   842
  Around Medellín   848
  Department of Chocó   849
La Zona Cafetera   **852**
  Manizales & around   852
  Pereira to Cartago   855
Cali & the
  Cauca Valley   **859**

Cali	859	
Cauca & the coast	863	
Popayán, Tierradentro		
& San Agustín	**865**	
Popayán &		
Tierradentro	865	
Popayán to		
San Agustín	869	
Southern Colombia	**876**	
South to Ecuador	876	
Leticia & the Amazon	880	

Ecuador

Essentials	**886**
Quito & around	**893**
Sights	896
Around Quito	916
Northern Ecuador	**921**
Quito to Otavalo	922
Otavalo & around	923
Otavalo to the	
Colombian border	928
Cotopaxi, Latacunga	
& Quilotoa	**935**
Cotopaxi & Latagunga	935
Quiltoa circuit	940
Ambato	943
Baños & Riobamba	**946**
Baños & around	948
Riobamba & around	952
Cuenca & around	**959**
Cuenca to the	
Peruvian border	**968**
Vilcabamba to Peru	974
Guayaquil & south	
to Peru	**976**
Guayaquil	978
South to Peru	984
Pacific lowlands	**987**

Guayaquil to	
Puerto López	987
Manta & Bahia	
de Caráquez	993
Northern lowlands	999
The Oriente	**1004**
Northern Oriente	1005
Central &	
southern Oriente	1010
Galápagos Islands	**1017**
Background	1017
Ins & outs	1018
The islands	1020

Paraguay

Essentials	**1036**
Asunción	**1039**
Sights	1040
East of Asunción	**1050**
South of Asunción	**1056**
North of Asunción	**1061**
The Chaco	**1063**

Peru

Essentials	**1070**
Lima	**1079**
Sights	1081
Huaraz & the	
Cordilleras	**1107**
Huarez	1107

Cordillera Blanca	1115
Cordillera	
Huayhuash	1123
North coast	**1124**
Trujillo & around	1127
Chiclayo & around	1137
Piura & around	1143
North to Ecuador	1146
Northern	
Highlands	**1151**
Trujillo to Cajamarca	1152
Chachapoyas Region	1158
Chachapoyas	
to the Amazon	1163
Chachapoyas to Ecuador	
& the coast	1166
South coast	**1167**
South from Lima	1167
Nazca & around	1172
Arequipa &	
the far south	**1178**
Arequipa	1178
Colca Canyon	1188
Cotahuasi Canyon	1192
South to Chile	1193
Lake Titicaca	**1196**
The islands	1203
To Cuzco	1204
Border with Bolivia	1206
Cuzco	**1208**
Southeast from Cuzco	1232
Sacred Valley	
of the Incas	**1234**
Machu Picchu	1240
Inca trails	1243
Vitcos & Vilcabamba	1246
West of Cuzco	1247
Central Highlands	**1248**
Lima to Huancayo	1248
Huancayo & around	1250
Huancavelica	1254
Ayacucho	1256
Ayacucho to Cuzco	1260
East & north of	
La Oroya	1262
Amazon Basin	**1266**
North from Huánuco	
to Pucallpa	1266

Yurimaguas &
  Pacaya-Samiria   1269
Iquitos & around   1271
Southeastern jungle   1277

Uruguay

Essentials   **1288**
Montevideo   **1292**
Sights   1293
Western Uruguay   **1304**
Eastern Uruguay   **1314**
East from
  Montevideo   1314
Montevideo north
  to Brazil   1322

Venezuela

Essentials   **1328**
Caracas   **1334**
Sights   1335
Around Caracas   1347
West from Caracas   **1349**
Maracay & around   1349
Valencia & around   1353
Coro & around   1357
From Maracaibo
  to Colombia   1360
Barquisimeto
  & around   1363

Valera to Mérida   1364
Mérida & around   **1366**
Mérida   1366
Sierra Nevada
  de Mérida   1372
**Los Llanos
  & Amazonas**   **1378**
Los Llanos   1379
Amazonas   1381
East coast   **1383**
Caracas to Puerto
  La Cruz   1384
Parque Nacional
  Mochima   1387
Cumaná   1389
Araya to Paria   1391
Isla de Margarita   1390
Los Roques   1403
**Canaima & the
  Orinoco Delta**   **1404**
Ciudad Bolívar   1405
Canaima &
  Angel Falls   1408
Ciudad Guayana & the
  Orinoco Delta   1411
Ciudad Guayana to
  Santa Elena
  de Uairén   1414
Mount Roraima   1421

Guianas

Guyana   **1426**
Essentials   1426
Georgetown   1429
Outside
  Georgetown   1431
Suriname   **1444**
Essentials   1444

Paramaribo   1447
Outside Paramaribo   1449
Guyane   **1456**
Essentials   1456
Cayenne   1459
Outside Cayenne   1460

Falkland Islands/
Islas Malvinas

Essentials   **1468**
Stanley & around   **1471**
**Beyond the
  Falklands**   **1477**
South Georgia   1477
Antarctica   1478

Background

Pre-independence
  history   1480
Post-independence
  history   1486
Culture   1508
Land & environment   1524

Footnotes

Useful words and phrases
                           1532
Spanish and Portuguese
  pronunciation   1534
Index   1537
Advertisers' index   1547
Acknowledgements   1549
About the author   1551
Credits   1552
Map symbols   1553
Colour maps   1563

Mountain high, tunnel deep
Towering over the city of Potosí like a giant headstone is
Cerro Rico, whose vast silver lodes helped finance the Spanish
Empire and which claimed the lives of millions of slaves.

A foot in the door

If your system is jaded, South America will uplift your senses with the tropical sun rising over a palm-fringed beach, or a bracing wind blowing off the southern ice fields. Light can be blinding on the high altitude salt flats, or dense and green in the rainforest. The gentle scent of ripe guava fills the countryside, but the fire of chilli from that innocent-looking jar will electrify your taste buds.

As capybara wade through wetland shallows in the Pantanal, the spectacled bear struggles for survival in secret places in the Andes. Penguins congregate in the lee of glaciers, while tiny swifts dart through mighty waterfalls and their eternal rainbows. Volcanoes come to life and the earth trembles, yet elsewhere there are ancient, immovable tabletop plateaux. But above all is the Amazon Basin, the earth's greatest jungle, where the immensity of the trees and the smallest details of the wildlife are truly amazing.

You can explore the cities of prehispanic civilizations and the churches of colonial times, or you can immerse yourself in the present with its celebrations and its social dilemmas. Where past and present mix, there are festivals, crafts and gastronomy, from the humble potato in its umpteen varieties to the most sophisticated of wines.

If you are looking for something more active, throw yourself off a giant sand dune into a lake, or climb the highest mountain. Walk in the treetops of the rainforest, at eye level with birds and monkeys. Help homeless street kids gain a better life, or teach traumatized animals to return to the wild. Whatever South America inspires you to do, you will find that there is no limit to the passion that it fires within you.

Contemporary South America

When the Spaniard, Francisco de Orellana, floated across the South American continent via the Amazon in 1542, he and his crew brought back tales of royal highways, grand cities and ferocious women warriors (who gave the river its name). Soon European explorers were seeking the fabulous El Dorado in what they called the 'Green Hell', but the myths gradually evaporated as scientists began to uncover the Amazon's mysteries. The indigenous cultures who survive in this vast tissue of waterways have a knowledge of the environment unmatched by science. But the threats of tree-felling, mineral exploitation and burning for unsustainable agriculture lead many to fear that, before this immense plant repository is fully understood, it will have disappeared.

Loss of the rainforest is one of many powerful symbols of rapid change in South America. Others include retreating glaciers from global warming, and the displacement of people because of civil unrest or unequal distribution of land. In parts of South America there are still a few indigenous peoples who are ignorant of technological and social

Worth its salt
Driving across the Salar de Uyuni, the highest and largest salt lake in the world, is one of the strangest, most fantastic experiences you will have, especially during June and July when the bright blue skies contrast with the blinding-white salt crust.

developments. Others shun them and lament the changes they have brought. For good or ill, South America is growing closer to the rest of the world as the demands of trade and communications create a growing interdependence between countries. At the same time, the global call to make poverty history has as much urgency in South America as elsewhere. Hunger and marginalization are seen as the root of civil strife. Recent elections have introduced a new alignment in politics and an eagerness among some politicians to work with their Latin neighbours and others to confront shared problems.

Real successors to the mythical do exist, from prehispanic Caral, in Peru, to megalopolises like São Paulo. The Incas' royal highway, Capaq Ñan, has been replaced by the Panamericana. And, yes, there are female warriors, not just guerrillas, but activists campaigning alongside their male colleagues for human, land and other rights. As a major contributor to many economies, tourism has its part to play, for travellers to this marvellous continent must take responsibility for putting something back, not plundering like the *conquistadores* of the past.

Sight for sore feet
No amount of hype can detract from the sheer magnificence of seeing Machu Picchu. The ancient Inca citadel straddles the saddle of a high mountain with steep terraced slopes falling away to the fast-flowing Río Urubamba snaking its hairpin course far below.

1   Nothing prepares you for the spectacular beauty of the Torres del Paine National Park, in the far south of Chile, renowned for its challenging treks. ▶▶ See page 753.

2   Best seen from sea, the origins of the giant pre-Columbian candelabra at Paracas remain a mystery. ▶▶ See page 1169.

3   The remains of the Jesuit Mission settlements are still very much in evidence near the banks of the Río Paraná in Paraguay. ▶▶ See page 1057.

4   The Caribbean island of Isla de Margarita is one of Venezuela's main centres for pottery production. ▶▶ See page 1396.

5   One of the most distinctive of jungle sounds is the full-throated roar of the howler monkey.

6   The sun sets on the Brazilian Pantanal, a vast wetland, half the size of France, and home to a staggering array of wildlife. ▶▶ See page 577.

7   Textiles continue to play an important part in society in many parts of Bolivia.

8   Easter Island is famous for its numerous (600 or so) huge stone figures (moai) that stand up to 9 m in height. ▶▶ See page 762.

9   Lying on the equator, nearly 1,000 km west of the Ecuadorian coast, the Galápagos Islands are world-renowned for their fearless wildlife. ▶▶ See page 1017.

10 The Iguazú Falls, on the Argentina-Brazil border, may not be the highest in South America, but they are a magnificent sight. ▶▶ See page 172.

11 In the town of Silvia, in Colombia, you'll see the colourful Guambiano people going about their business at the famous market. ▶▶ See page 866.

12. The empty spaces of Patagonia are home to cattle farms and great sheep estancias, and very few people. ▶▶ See page 200.

The Andes

Down the length of South America runs the Andean mountain chain, which starts in the north overlooking the Caribbean and ends in the south in the fabulous towers and spires of the Chaitén Massif and the Torres del Paine National Park. Condors patrol its deep canyons and strata of rocks display colours you never knew existed in stone. Out of Lake Titicaca, the highest navigable lake in the world, strode the Inca dynasty, founding Cuzco, which has metamorphosed into the gringo capital of South America. Further south, beautiful lakes in Chile and Argentina shelter beneath snowcapped peaks. On their shores are resorts for summer watersports, fishing and winter skiing. Unlike its treeless Argentine counterpart, Chilean Patagonia is a wet and windy confusion of fjords, channels and ancient woodlands.

Forests and wetlands

In the heart of the continent, the Amazon Basin contains 20% of the world's plant and bird species, 10% of the mammals and an inestimable number of insects. In the waters live some 2,000 species of fish, plus shy giant otters, caiman and two species of freshwater dolphin. There are trees that strangle their neighbours, palms with a million thorns, plants that heal and vines that will blow your mind. Stalking in the undergrowth is the mythical jaguar, whose influence has spread through almost every religion that has come into contact with the rainforest. On its perimeter, cattle and cowboys share the land with wild birds and animals in the *llanos* of the Orinoco and the wetlands of the Brazilian/Bolivian Pantanal, while mysterious ecosystems hide on table-top mountains on the Venezuela/Brazil border and in Bolivia.

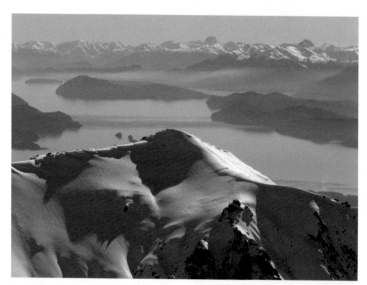

Lago Nahuel Huapi, in the Argentine Lake District, is a vast body of water, with long arms of water (brazos) stretching far into the surrounding land, and best explored by boat.

The Oruro Carnival, one of the continent's great festivals, is a manic mix of music, dancing, drinking and water throwing.

Islands and beaches

On the Pacific, at islands such as the Ballestas (Peru) and Isla de la Plata (Ecuador) you can see much marine life, but the destination *par excellence* is the Galápagos. On the peaks of massive volcanoes, which jut into the ocean, albatross, boobies, giant tortoises and iguanas have evolved with little instinctive fear of man, a paradise for naturalists. Meanwhile, the Atlantic coast of Brazil, all 7,408 km of it, is an endless succession of beaches, in wooded coves, dotted with islands in the south, palm tree and dune-fringed in the north.

Down through the years

When the Spanish *conquistadores* and the Portuguese colonizers arrived in South America over 500 years ago, many civilizations had risen and fallen. Most had thrived in the apparently inhospitable deserts of the Pacific coast. They left their monuments in sculptures etched into the surface of the desert, most famously at Nazca in Peru. The Incas and their contemporaries were soon overthrown and the European dominance altered every aspect of the continent. But against the odds, traditions have survived and native languages are still spoken, adapting like everything else by taking old ideas into new settings. The best way to see these processes at work is in the festivals, where Christian and indigenous religious symbols merge, brass bands blare, masqueraders represent mythical and real figures and the age-old desire to have a good time is taken to its limit.

Rhythm of life
Dubbed 'Africa in exile', Salvador (or Bahia as it is also known), is home to a heady mix of colonial buildings, beautiful beaches, African culture and pulsating musical rhythms.

First-time travel guide	18
Sport and activities	20
Ways to escape	30
Finding out more	32

Footprint features

Cost of travelling	19
Key events	20

Uruguay Birdwatching is best in the east of the country, where a number of national parks have been set up in a variety of habitats. These include coastal zones, such as the sand dunes at Cabo Polonio, lakes, marshes and forest reserves on the Atlantic, Santa Teresa (which also contains important historical sites) and offshore islands. In Uruguay, though, nature tourism seldom means being in the wilderness as most land is farmed and nature reserves are small. For birdwatching information, contact **Aves Uruguay** ① *Canelones 1164, Montevideo, T02-902 8642, www.avesuruguay.org.uy* (in Spanish) or the Ministry of Tourism.

Venezuela The *llanos* are a prime wildlife destination, and if you intend to go there, you should plan the timing carefully to make the most of your trip. Amazonas and the Orinoco delta also offer wildlife possibilities, but in the latter case tours can be expensive and poorly organized, so choose with caution. The Gran Sabana does not have quite the extent of wildlife that you will find in the *llanos*, but is unmatched for open landscapes. In the Andes, too, the scenery is the key, and throughout the *páramo* (open grasslands with small pockets of cloud forest above 2,500-3,000 m), the unusual *frailejón* plant (felt-leaved and with a yellow bloom) is a common sight. You may also be lucky enough to see the condor. Another significant birdwatching site is the Parque Nacional Henri Pittier in the coastal mountains between Maracay and the Caribbean. For marine birdlife, the Cuare Wildlife Sanctuary is an important nesting area. Finally, a much visited attraction is the Cueva del Guácharo, a cave near Caripe in the east.

Guyana, Suriname and Guyane In Guyana, habitats range from undisturbed rain- and other types of forest to savannahs, wetlands and coastal areas. The country's checklist of birds numbers over 815, with new ones being added frequently. Guyana features a fantastic range of Guianan Shield endemics and Amazon species including Harpy Eagle, Red Siskin and Guianan cock-of-the-rock. See the website of the **Guyana Birding Tourism Program** ① *www.guyana birding.com*, which has comprehensive lists and details. This is a joint initiative of the Guyana Tourism Authority and the Guyana Trade Investment Support Program and is funded by the United States Agency for International Development (USAID). There are many excellent birding sites in Guyana, including the Iwokrama Centre for Rain Forest Conservation and Development (which also has a high incidence of jaguar sightings), Surama, various ranches in the Rupununi, Shanklands Rainforest Resort, Woweta Cock-of-the-Rock Trail and Kaieteur Falls. In addition Shell Beach is famous for its nesting grounds for marine turtles and colonies of scarlet ibis. In all three countries, the rivers lead to landscapes which combine savannahs and tropical forests, with excellent opportunities to see wildlife beside the waterways, on lakes and in the jungle. The 1.6 million-ha Central Suriname Nature Reserve, a relatively new protected area, is just opening up to tourism. It has a variety of pristine ecosystems with a high diversity of plant life, significant populations of jaguar, giant armadillo, giant river otter, tapir, sloths, eight species of primates, and 400 of the 576 bird species recorde in the country.

The Falkland Islands/Islas Malvinas Although remote, the islands are a mecca for wildlife watchers. Five types of penguins are the main attraction, but albatross, giant petrels, geese, ducks and many other species can be seen close to. Marine mammals, too, are easy to see: sea lions and elephant seals on the beaches, orca and other whales and dolphins off shore.

Climbing

When planning climbs or treks in the Andes you should be aware of the effects and dangers of acute mountain sickness and cerebral and pulmonary oedema. These can be avoided by spending a few days acclimatizing to the altitude before starting your walk, and by climbing slowly. The recommended maximum altitude gain is 300 m per day. Be wary of agencies wanting to sell you trips with very fast ascents; they should ask if you are acclimatized. See the Health section, page 45, for the dangers of altitude sickness.

Argentina The Andes offer great climbing opportunities. Among the most popular peaks are Aconcagua, in Mendoza province, Pissis in Catamarca, and Lanín and Tronador, reached from the Lake District. The northern part of Los Glaciares national park, around El Chaltén, has some spectacular peaks with very difficult mountaineering. Climbing clubs (**Club Andino**) can be found in Mendoza, Bariloche, Esquel, Junín de los Andes, Ushuaia and other cities and in some places equipment can be hired.

Bolivia Some of the world's best mountaineering can be found in Bolivia, but infrastructure is not well developed, so don't expect to be rescued if you get into trouble. With a dozen peaks at or above 6,000 m and almost a thousand over 5,000 m, most levels of skill can find something to tempt them. The season is May to September, with usually stable conditions June to August. Proper technical equipment, experience and/or a competent guide are

23

essential to cross glaciers and climb snow and ice safely. The four ranges in which to climb are: the Cordillera Real, which has 600 5,000 m plus mountains, including six at 6,000 m or above: Illimani 6,439 m, Ancohuma 6,427 m, Illampu 6,368 m, Chearoco 6,104 m, Huayna Potosí 6,088 m (the most popular) and Chachacomani 6,000 m. A week's acclimatization at the height of La Paz or equivalent is necessary before attempting to climb above 5,000 m. Access is easy from the flat Altiplano, but public transport is not always possible. Quimza Cruz, southeast of La Paz, is hard to get to but offers some excellent possibilities. The volcanic Cordillera Occidental contains Bolivia's highest peak, Sajama (6,542 m), plus Parinacota and Pomerape. The Apolobamba range, northwest of La Paz, has many 5,000-m-plus peaks.

Brazil The most popular form of climbing (*escalada*) is rock-face climbing. In the heart of Rio, you can see, or join, climbers scaling the rocks at the base of Pão de Açúcar and on the Sugar Loaf itself. Not too far away, the Serra dos Órgãos provides plenty of challenges, not least the Dedo de Deus (God's Finger). Rio de Janeiro is the state where the sport is most fully developed, but not far behind are Paraná, Minas Gerais, São Paulo and Rio Grande do Sul.

Chile There are four different terrains: rock climbing; high mountains; ice climbing; and volcanoes. Some volcanoes and high mountains are difficult to get to and you need permission to climb. Other volcanoes, like Villarrica and Osomo are popular excursions, although access is controlled by Conaf (see page 599). The **Federación de Andinismo de Chile** and the **Escuela Nacional de Montaña** are both at Almirante Simpson 77A in Santiago.

Colombia The best possibilities for mountaineers are the national parks of Los Nevados (eg Nevado del Ruiz, Nevado de Tolima) and Sierra Nevada del Cocuy (eg Ritacuba Blanca and Ritacuba Negra check security situation and conditions before setting out). For rock and ice climbing, the Nevados and Cocuy offer some technical challenges and Suesca, north of Bogotá near Nemocón, is considered the most important centre for rock climbing in the country. The best source of information is **Mauricio Afanador**, who can be contacted at *Café y Crepes* (see Bogotá, Eating). The climbing clubs at the **Universidad Nacional** and Germán Escobar at the **Platypus Hotel** in Bogotá are also excellent sources of information. Try also **Roca Solida** ① *Diagonal 127A No 28-28, Bogotá, T600 7480*, for information on climbing opportunities in and around Bogotá. Maps can be obtained at the **Instituto Geográfico Agustín Codazzi**. If you intend to climb, bring all your own equipment. It may be hard to find in Colombia. Equipment available at **Almacén Aventura** ① *Cra 13, No 67-26, Bogotá, T/F313 3219* and *Cra 7, No 121-53, T213 5001*, includes rope, boots, etc; light equipment, rucksacks, tents, etc, of reasonable quality, can be bought in markets and **Exito** and **Carrefour** supermarkets.

Ecuador The country offers some exceptional high-altitude climbing, with 10 mountains over 5,000 m – most with easy access. The four most frequently climbed are Cotopaxi (technically easy with a guide and equipment), Tungurahua (an active volcano, enquire about the level of volcanic activity before climbing), Chimborazo (a long, demanding climb, with at times impassable *penitentes* – conical ice formations – near the summit) and Iliniza Norte (the only one of the 'big 10' without a glacier, but a rope is needed). The other six, Iliniza Sur, Antisana, El Altar, Sangay, Carihuairazo and Cayambe vary in degree of difficulty and/or danger. Sangay is technically easy, but extremely dangerous from the falling rocks being ejected from the volcano. Many other mountains can be climbed and climbing clubs, guiding agencies and tour operators will give advice. Proper equipment and good guidance are essential. The dangers of inadequate acclimatization, snow blindness, climbing without a qualified guide or adequate equipment must be taken very seriously, especially on the 'easier' mountains which may lure the less experienced. Deglaciation reshapes high-altitude landscapes and alters climbing routes. Inform yourself of current conditions before undertaking an ascent. There are two climbing seasons: June to August and December to February. Allegedly, the eastern cordillera is drier December to February and the western cordillera June to August (though it is often windy in August), and Cotopaxi has more clear days than any other peak. It is best to avoid the wetter seasons from March to May and September to November. Bad weather is only predominant for the mountains on the eastern side of the eastern cordillera. Being on the equator, days and nights are 12 hours long. As a result, climbs are attempted all year round all over the country.

Mountain rescue facilities in Ecuador are rudimentary and poorly organized, so you must be as self-sufficient as possible. There's no helicopter rescue and little cooperation from the army, police or government. If you will be climbing extensively in Ecuador, it's a good idea to register with your embassy or consulate and advise them of any insurance you may have to cover the costs of rescue or repatriation by air ambulance. The first place the authorities usually contact in the event of an emergency involving a foreign climber is the embassy of their home country. Cellular phones can be used from some mountains. In an emergency contact **Safari Tours** or **Compañía de Guías de Montaña**, see under Quito, Activities and tours.

Peru The Cordillera Blanca, with Huaraz as a base, is an ice climber's paradise. Over 50 summits are between 5,000 and 6,000 m and over 20 exceed 6,000 m. There is a wide range of difficulty and no peak fees are charged (although national park entrance has to paid in the Cordillera Blanca). The **Peruvian Mountain Guide Association** (AGMP) is located in the *Casa de Guías*, Huaraz. The Cordillera Huayhuash, southeast of Huaraz, is a bit more remote, with fewer facilities, but has some of the most spectacular ice walls in Peru. In the south of the country, the Cordilleras Vilcabamba and Vilcanota are the main destinations, but Cuzco is not developed for climbing. Elsewhere in the Sierras are other peaks which are rarely climbed. Rock climbing is becoming popular in the Huaraz area, at Monterrey (for beginners) and Quebrada de Llaca. Climbing equipment can be hired in Huaraz quite easily, but the quality can be poor.

Venezuela Although there are some opportunities for climbing in the Gran Sabana, these are mostly hard to get to and are technically very challenging. The heart of Venezuelan mountaineering and trekking is the Andes, with Mérida as the base. A number of important peaks can be scaled and there are some superb hikes in the highlands. Bear in mind that high altitudes will be reached and acclimatization is essential. Similarly, suitable equipment is necessary and you may wish to consider bringing your own. For more details on climbing and mountaineering, contact **Asociación Venezolana de Instructores y Guías de Montaña**, AVIGM, T0416-217 0392 (mob, Henry Guerra, secretary), www.avigm.com.

Diving and snorkelling

Brazil The best diving in Brazil is the Atol das Rocas; only available through private charter through www.dehouche.com; very expensive but completely unspoilt, with visibility up to 40 m and with one of the highest levels of biodiversity in the tropical southern Atlantic. Fernando de Noronha has coral gardens, drop offs and wrecks which include a 50-m Brazilian navy destroyer with full armament. Visibility is up to 50 m, safe, current-free and drift diving. Amongst others, divers see at least two species of turtle, spinner dolphins, more than three species of shark, huge snapper and vast shoals of goatfish and jack. Arraial de Cabo is interesting because of the meeting of a southerly cold and northerly warm current and has the best marine life in southeast Brazil.

Colombia There are dive sites on both the Caribbean and Pacific coasts, but the former is more developed. Caribbean diving centres are Cartagena, Santa Marta and nearby Taganga, San Andrés and Providencia, the Islas de San Bernardo off the coast of Sucre, Isla Fuerte off Córdoba department and Capurganá, near the Panamanian border. On the Pacific, Bahía Solano and Gorgana Island offer excellent diving opportunities. There are dive shops in most of these places (see text). You can also contact Pedro Roa (helpful) of **Aqua Sub Diving** ⓘ *Av Suba No 122-20 (inside the shopping centre) T613 8038, Bogotá, aquasub_dive@uole.com,* who can direct you to diving instructors belonging to the **Asociación Colombiana de Instructores de Buceo** (ACIB). A five-day PADI course costs about US$200 (2007 prices). Most of the upmarket hotels in the resorts arrange diving and snorkelling trips.

Ecuador The prime spot is the Galápagos, with more than 20 dive sites: each island has its own unique underwater environment. Off the mainland, the best place to dive is the Parque Nacional Machalilla, at Isla La Plata. Colonies of sea lions can be seen here and migrating humpback whales pass this stretch of coast between late June and September.

Venezuela Venezuela's waters are not as famous as those off neighbouring Bonaire, but they have excellent opportunities for seeing underwater flora, fauna and shipwrecks. The main areas are the national parks of Mochima and Islas Los Roques (more currents, so best for experienced divers), a number of sites to the east and west of Caracas, and in the waters off Isla de Margarita.

Fishing

Argentina The three main areas for fishing are the Northern Zone, around Junín de los Andes, extending south to Bariloche; the Central Zone around Esquel; the Southern Zone around Río Gallegos and Río Grande. The first two of these areas are in the lake district. Among the best lakes are: Lagos Traful, Gutiérrez, Mascardi, Futalaufquen (in Los Alerces National Park), Meliquina, Falkner, Villarino, Nuevo, Lacar, Lolog, Curruhué, Chico, Huechulafquen, Paimún, Epulafquen, Tromen (all in Lanín National Park), and, in the far north, Quillén. The Río Limay has good trout fishing, as do the rivers further north, the Quilquihue, Malle, Chimehuín, Collón-Curá, Hermoso, Meliquina and Caleufú. The southern

Rafting and kayaking

Argentina There are some good whitewater rafting runs in Mendoza province, near the provincial capital and near San Rafael and Malargüe. In the Lake District there are possibilities in the Lanín, Nahuel Huapi and Los Alerces national parks.

Brazil Companies offer whitewater rafting trips in São Paulo state (eg on the Rios Juquiá, Jaguarí, do Peixe, Paraibuna), in Rio de Janeiro (also on the Paraibuna, at Três Rios in the Serra dos Órgões), Paraná (Rio Ribeira), Santa Catarina (Rio Itajaí) and Rio Grande do Sul (Três Coroas). The Rio Novo, Jalapão, Tocantins, is an excellent, new destination. Canoeing is supervised by the **Confederação Brasileira de Canoagem** (CBCa). It covers all aspects of the sport, speed racing, slalom, downriver, surfing and ocean kayaking. For downriver canoeing, go to Visconde de Mauá (Rio de Janeiro state) where the Rio Preto is famous for the sport; also the Rio Formoso at Bonito (Mato Grosso do Sul). A recommended river for slalom is the Pranhana, Três Coroas, Rio Grande do Sul. For kayak surfing the best places are Rio, the Ilha de Santa Catarina and Ubatuba, while ocean kayaking is popular in Rio, Búzios and Santos (São Paulo).

Chile Over 20 rivers between Santiago and Tierra del Fuego are excellent for whitewater rafting. Some run through spectacular mountain scenery, such as the Río Petrohué, which flows through temperate rainforest beneath the Osorno and Calbuco volcanoes. Rafting is generally well organized and equipment is usually of a high standard. Access to headwaters of most rivers is easy. For beginners, many agencies in Santiago, Puerto Varas and Pucón offer half-day trips on Grade 3 rivers. The best Grade 4 and 5 rafting is in Futaleufú, near Chaitén. Sea kayaking is best enjoyed in the waters between Chiloé and the mainland and in the sheltered fjords off the northernmost section of the Carretera Austral. Kayaking and other watersports such as windsurfing take place in many lakes in the Lake District, notably Lagos Villarrica and Llanquihue, which holds an annual kayaking regatta.

Colombia Whitewater rafting is growing in popularity and is at present based at San Gil (Santander), Villeta and Utica (Cundinamarca) and less developed in St Agustin (Huila).

Ecuador A whitewater paradise with dozens of accessible rivers, warm waters and tropical rainforest; regional rainy seasons differ so that throughout the year there is always a river to run. The majority of Ecuador's whitewater rivers share a number of characteristics. Plunging off the Andes, the upper sections are very steep creeks offering, if they're runnable at all, serious technical Grade 5, suitable for expert kayakers only. As the creeks join on the lower slopes they form rivers navigable by both raft and kayak (ie less steep, more volume). Some of these rivers offer up to 100 km of continuous Grade 3-4 whitewater, before flattening out to rush towards the Pacific Ocean on one side of the ranges or deep into the Amazon Basin on the other. As a general rule the rivers running straight off the eastern and western slopes of the Andes are less subject to pollution than the highland rivers which drain some of the most densely populated regions of the country. Ask about water quality before signing up for a trip. Of the rivers descending to the Pacific coast, the Blanco and its tributaries are the most frequently run. They are within easy reach of Quito, as is the Quijos on the eastern side of the Sierra. In the Oriente, the main rafting and kayaking rivers are the Aguarico and its tributary the Dué, the Napo, Pastaza and Upano. See the relevant paragraphs under Quito Activities and tours, Baños and Tena.

Peru Yet more claims to some of the finest whitewater rivers in the world, Peru has some spectacular places only accessible by this type of craft: desert canyons, jungle gorges and exotic rock formations. Availability is almost year-round and all levels of difficulty can be enjoyed. Cuzco is probably the rafting capital and the Río Urubamba has some very popular trips. Further afield is the Río Apurímac, which has some of the best whitewater rafting, including a trip at the source of the Amazon. In the southeastern jungle, a trip on the Río Tambopata to the Tambopata-Candamo Reserved Zone involves four days of whitewater followed by two of drifting through virgin forest; an excellent adventure which must be booked up in advance. Around Arequipa is some first-class, technical rafting in the Cotahuasi and Colca canyons and some less-demanding trips on the Río Majes. Other destinations are the Río Santa near Huaraz and the Río Cañete, south of Lima.

Skiing

Argentina The season is from May to October, depending on the weather and the resort. Las Leñas, south of Mendoza, is of international standard. Major resorts exist on Cerro Catedral and Cerro Otto near Bariloche and Chapelco near San Martín de los Andes. Smaller resorts, with fewer facilities, can be found near Mendoza (Los Penitentes, Vallecitos and Manantiales), in the Lake

District (Caviahue, Cerro Bayo; La Hoya – near Esquel) and near Ushuaia (Cerro Martial, Wallner).

Chile The season is from June to September, weather permitting. The major international ski resorts are in the Andes near Santiago, Farellones, El Colorado, La Parva, Valle Nevado, Portillo and Lagunillas. South of Santiago, skiing is mostly on the slopes of volcanoes. The larger resorts are Termas de Chillán, Villarrica/Pucón and Antillanca, but there are a great many smaller places with limited facilities which are worth the effort to get to for some adventurous fun. Details of the major resorts and some smaller ones are given in the text. Addresses of ski federations, clubs and operators are given under Santiago, Activities and tours.

Surfing

Brazil This can be enjoyed in just about every coastal state. It does not require permits; all you need is a board and the right type of wave. Best waves in the country are at Cacimba do Padre beach, Fernando de Noronha, the archipelago, 345 km out in the Atlantic. International surf championships are held here annually. Other good waves are found in the south, where long stretches of the Atlantic, often facing the swell head-on, give some excellent and varied breaks. Many Brazilian mainland surf spots are firmly on the international championship circuit, including Saquarema, in Rio de Janeiro state. Best waves in Rio de Janeiro city are at Joatinga, Prainha or Grumari beaches. One of the best states for surfing is Santa Catarina. See the website www.brazilsurftravel.com, based in Santa Catarina but with lots of info and links.

Ecuador There are a few, select surfing spots, such as Mompiche (Esmeraldas), San Mateo (Manabí), Montañita (Guayas) and Playas, near Guayaquil. Waves are generally best December to March, except at Playas where the season is June to September. In the Galápagos there is good surfing at Playa Punta Carola, outside Puerto Baquerizo Moreno on San Cristóbal.

Peru Peru is a top international surfing destination. Its main draws are the variety of wave and the year-round action. The main seasons are September to February in the north and March to December in the south, though May is often ideal south of Lima. The biggest wave is at Pico Alto (sometimes 6 m in May), south of Lima, and the largest break is 800 m at Chicama, near Trujillo. There are more than 30 top surfing beaches. For information, see www.bodyboardperu.com, www.peruazul.com.pe and www.wannasurf.com; enter Peru in the search box.

Trekking

A network of paths and tracks covers much of South America and is in constant use by the local people. In countries with a large indigenous population – Ecuador, Peru and Bolivia, for instance – you can walk just about anywhere, but in the more European countries, such as Venezuela, Chile, and Argentina, you must usually limit yourself to the many excellent national parks with hiking trails. When planning treks in the Andes you should be aware of the effects and dangers of acute mountain sickness; see above under Climbing, page 22. Also be aware that the weather can deteriorate rapidly, so equip yourself accordingly. Hiking and backpacking should not be approached casually. Even if you only plan to be out a couple of hours you should have comfortable, safe footwear (which can cope with the wet) and a daypack to carry your sweater and waterproof (which must be more than showerproof). At high altitudes the difference in temperature between sun and shade is remarkable. Longer trips require basic backpacking equipment. Essential items are: backpack with frame, sleeping bag, closed cell foam mat for insulation, stove, tent or tarpaulin, dried food (not tins), water bottle, compass/GPS. Some, but not all of these things, are available locally. Hikers have little to fear from the animal kingdom apart from insects (although it's best to avoid actually stepping on a snake). You are much more of a threat to the environment than vice versa. Leave no evidence of your passing. Respect their system of reciprocity; if they give you hospitality or food, then is the time to reciprocate with presents. **South American Explorers** have good information and advice on trekking and sells books.

Argentina There is ample scope for short and long-distance trekking. The best locations are in the foothills and higher up in the Andes. Some suggestions are the valleys around Salta; San Juan and La Rioja; Mendoza and Malargüe; in the national parks of the Lake District. Around El Chaltén in Los Glaciares national park there is some of the best trekking on the continent.

Bolivia There are many opportunities for trekking in Bolivia, from gentle one-day hikes in foothills and valleys to challenging walks of several days from highlands to lowlands on Inca or gold-diggers trails. The best known are: the Choro, Takesi and Yunga Cruz hikes, all of whose starting points can be reached from La Paz; the Mapiri Trail and the Illampu Circuit, both approached from Sorata; and the Apolobamba treks in the northwest. None of these should be attempted without full planning and equipment. Various treks are outlined in the text, especially near La Paz and from Sorata. **Warning** All these trails are in remote places and robbery and violent attacks have been made on tourists and Bolivians alike. It is advisable to hike these trails in large, organized groups. The local tourist office also produces leaflets with sketch maps on walks in the vicinity of La Paz. There are also some excellent guides available through local clubs.

Brazil This is very popular, especially in Rio de Janeiro, São Paulo, Minas Gerais, Paraná and Rio Grande do Sul. There are plenty of hiking agencies which handle tours. Trails are frequently graded according to difficulty; this is noticeably so in areas where *trilhas ecológicas* have been laid out in forests or other sites close to busy tourist areas. Many national parks and protected areas provide good opportunities for trekking (eg the Chapada Diamantina in Bahia) and local information can easily be found to get you on the right track. The latest area to come under the trekker's gaze is Jalapão in Tocantins.

Chile Trekking possibilities are endless, ranging from short, signposted trails in national parks to hikes of several days, such as the circuit of the Parque Nacional Torres del Paine. The Sendero de Chile aims to link the whole country by footpath, stretching 8,500 km by 2010. The path is complete in the metropolitan region. See www.senderodechile.cl (in Spanish).

Colombia Trekking is popular with walks ranging from one-day excursions out of Bogotá, or at San Agustín, to three to four-day hikes. Good places for longer treks include the national parks of Los Nevados (from Ibagué, Manizales or Pereira), Sierra Nevada del Cocuy in the northeast, and Puracé (between Popayán and San Agustín). Well-trodden is the path to the Ciudad Perdida in the Sierra Nevada de Santa Marta, which has one of the country's main archaeological sites. In the departments of Boyacá and Santander there are many colonial *caminos reales*. Sources of information include tourist offices and Ministerio del Medio Ambiente (see National parks, in Colombia Essentials). See also Bogotá, Activities and tours.

Ecuador The varied landscape, diverse ecological environments and friendly villages within a compact area make travelling on foot a refreshing change from crowded buses. Hiking in the Sierra is mostly across high elevation *páramo*, through agricultural lands and past indigenous communities. There are outstanding views of glaciated peaks in the north and pre-Columbian ruins in the south. On the coast there are only a few areas developed for hiking ranging from dry forest to coastal rainforest. In the tropical rainforests of the Oriente, local guides are often required because of the difficulty in navigation and because you will be walking on land owned by local indigenous tribes. The Andean slopes are steep and often covered by virtually impenetrable cloud forests and it rains a lot. Many ancient trading routes head down the river valleys. Some of these trails are still used. Others may be overgrown and difficult to follow but offer the reward of intact ecosystems. You may be travelling across land that is either owned outright by indigenous people or jointly managed with the Ministry of the Environment. It is important to be respectful of the people and request permission to pass through or camp. Sometimes a fee may be charged by locals but it is usually minimal. The Quito Activities and tours section lists companies which rent equipment and give advice. A recommended book is *Trekking in Ecuador*, by Robert and Daisy Kunstaetter (The Mountaineers, Seattle, 2002); also www.trekkinginecuador.com.

Peru Most walking is on trails well-trodden by local people, but some of the more popular routes are becoming damaged. Little is done to maintain the trails and no guards control them; a few conservation groups are trying to remedy this. If camping, ask permission from the landowner first, and do not leave litter anywhere. There are some outstanding circuits around the peaks of the Cordilleras Blanca (eg Llanganuco to Santa Cruz, and the treks out of Caraz) and Huayhuash. The Ausangate trek near Cuzco is also good. A second type of trek is walking among, or to, ruins. The prime example is the Inca Trail to Machu Picchu, but others include those to Vilcabamba (the Incas' last home) and Choquequirao, and the treks in the Chachapoyas region. The Colca and Cotahuasi canyons also offer superb trekking.

Ways to escape

Wild landscapes

The Amazon Rainforest, covering some 6 million sq km and spilling across the borders of nine countries, is arguably the world's greatest remaining wilderness. Huge areas of the Amazon remain unexplored, but in South America, still a continent dominated by the forces of nature, there is even more, from the sweeping plains of Los Llanos in Venezuela and Colombia to the temperate rainforests of Chilean Patagonia. **Guyana** is one of the final frontiers of Latin America, with few visitors. The Iwokrama Rainforest Program is a pioneering project for research and sustainable development, one of the best places to catch a glimpse of the elusive jaguar. Alternatively there's the Rupununi Savanna for cowboy fantasies and wildlife watching. Imagine a tropical version of the American Wild West and add the chance to meet some of South America's few remaining giant otters and harpy eagles. Recently created and largely unexplored, the **Central Suriname Game Reserve** covers 10% of Suriname, deep in the country's green heart. If your ambition is to discover an unknown species or ten, this could be the place. Jewels of Brazil's endangered cerrado ecosystem, the **Chapada dos Veadeiros** and **Emas National Parks** present excellent wildlife viewing opportunities and remain strongholds of the seldom seen maned wolf and giant anteater. Emas also possesses the greatest concentration of termite mounds on the planet, which is paradise if you're an anteater! At the beginning of the rainy season (September-October) the termite larvae glow and the night time savanna lights up with it's own bioluminescent response to the Manhattan skyline. In **Noel Kempff Mercado National Park**, Bolivia's northeastern wilderness, waterfalls cascade from the cliffs of the ancient Huanchaca Plateau. This could have been another model for Conan Doyle's "Lost World" and even today reaching Noel Kempff is an adventure. Inaccessibility has preserved some of South America's rarest and most impressive flora and fauna, truly, the land that time forgot. **Esteros do Iberá**, Argentina's little known rival to the Pantanal (Brazil and Bolivia's great wetland), is a wildlife haven of marshes, forests and palm savanna providing nature's antidote to the turbulence of Buenos Aires. Experience a close encounter with the largest mammals on the planet, whale watching off Argentina's **Valdés Peninsula**. Southern Right whales breed in the Patagonian waters every year, and the almost uninhabited area is home to a host of other wildlife. You may be able to get closer still – wildlife census are carried out by willing participants using sea kayaks to collect information.

Islands and beaches

With thousands of kilometres of unspoiled coastline, South America is the ideal place to find an untouched patch of sand – a far cry from Rio's Copacabana. Good diving and beautiful beaches divided by rocky headlands, **Tayrona National Park** is little visited in troubled Colombia. This is what the Americas looked like when Columbus first gazed upon its shores – give or take the occasional hammock. On the coast of **Rio Grande do Norte and Ceará**, in Brazil, you can blast along hundreds of kilometres of undeveloped beaches in an open-topped buggy, explore the region's giant sand dunes that rise above an emerald ocean, and absorb the traditional Afro-Brazilian culture of the tiny fishing villages that dot the coastline. A far-flung Colombian Caribbean island, **Providencia** boasts gorgeous coral reefs and a distinctive English-speaking Caribbean culture. On this former hideaway of pirate Henry Morgan, who knows, you could even come upon some buried treasure! Exploring the reefs and inquisitive sea life of the **Galápagos Islands** from underwater is a truly memorable experience. Snorkelling and diving around the islands is strictly controlled for minimum impact on wildlife, although sea lions, turtles, dolphins and numerous sea bird species seem impervious to the potential threat of man. Diving in the waters of **Fernando de Noronha Islands**, Brazil, you may be accompanied by spinner dolphins, but very few tourists. Access to the islands is restricted and their waters are a protected nature reserve. Afterwards, back on the mainland, join the local party and celebrate carnival in the colonial town of Olinda.

Lost worlds and ancient cultures

South America's human history began thousands of years before Pizarro crushed the Inca Empire with horses and Spanish steel. The remains of hundreds of pre-Inca cultures litter the continent. **San Agustín**, set in flowering valleys and canyons of the upper Río Magdalena in Colombia, was once home to a great, but enigmatic civilization. Their legacy, painted burial tombs and hundreds of intricately carved statues of men and beasts, lie scattered throughout the region and can be reached on foot, horseback, or by jeep. The **Vilcabamba Mountains** of Peru were the last refuge of Manco Inca's rebellion against the Conquistadors, Vilcabamba's frozen peaks and jungled river canyons are still shrouded in mystery. The **Jesuit Missions Circuit** in Bolivia is a reminder of an idealistic past. The ornate decoration of the Mission churches stands in vivid contrast to the empty landscape that surrounds them. Millions of years before the first humans stepped onto the South American continent, the earth trembled under the weight of very different masters.

Roads to nowhere

South America is the land of the road (or river!) less travelled, a continent where opportunity beckons at every turn. Here are a couple to whet your appetite. The **Carreterra Austral** in Chile is the South's wild road, passing snow capped volcanoes, raging rivers, glacial fjords and isolated communities. Take a step off the road and there's all the windswept isolation you can handle. One of the least travelled roads into Bolivia is the route across the **Gran Chaco** in Paraguay. This peculiar area of marshland and thorn scrub has only 100,000 inhabitants in an area of 24 million ha. When it's hot, it's very hot (temperatures can reach 45°C) and when it's wet is impassable. But the bus will get through, somehow. The bizarre scenery of the **Salar de Uyuni** can be explored on four-day jeep trips from Uyuni, Bolivia. The dazzling expanse of the world's largest salt flat and the surrounding desert are full of weird and wonderful scenery: lunar landscapes and cactus-covered islands. It's also possible by bike, but expert assistance is advised – losing your sense of direction is easy when crossing the salt.

Finding out more

Travel and safety information Local sources of information, eg tourist offices, are given in the country chapters, below. **South American Explorers** ① *126 Indian Creek Rd, Ithaca, NY, 14850, T607 277 0488, ithacaclub@saexplorers.org, www.saexplorers.org,* is a non-profit educational organization staffed by volunteers, widely recognized as the best place to go for information on South America. Highly recommended as a source for specialized information, trip reports, maps, lectures, library resources. SAE publishes a 64-page quarterly journal, helps members plan trips and expeditions, stores gear, holds post, hosts book exchanges, provides expert travel advice, etc. Annual membership fee US$50 individual (US$80 couple) plus US$10 for overseas postage of its quarterly journal, The South American Explorer. The SAE membership card is good for many discounts throughout Ecuador, Peru, Argentina and, to a lesser extent, Bolivia and Uruguay. The Clubhouses in Quito, Lima, Cuzco and Buenos Aires are attractive and friendly. SAE will sell used equipment on consignment (donations of used equipment, unused medicines, etc are welcome).

See also Ron Mader's website **www.planeta.com**, which contains masses of useful information on ecotourism, conservation, travel, news, links, language schools and articles.

It is better to seek security advice before you leave from your own consulate than from travel agencies. You can contact: **British Foreign and Commonwealth Office** ① *Travel Advice Unit, T0845 850 2829.* Footprint is a partner in the Foreign and Commonwealth Office's Know before you go campaign www.fco.gov.uk/travel. US State Department's **Bureau of Consular Affairs** ① *Overseas Citizens Services, T1-888-407-4747, www.travel.state.gov.* **Australian Department of Foreign Affairs** ① *T+61-2-6261 3305, www.smartraveller.gov.au/.*

Useful websites

Website addresses for individual countries are given in the relevant chapters' Essentials sections and throughout the text. The following is a selection of sites, which may be of interest:
www.bootsnall.com/samericatravelguides/index.shtml Online travel guides for South America, updated monthly.
http://gosouthamerica.about.com/ Articles and links on sights, planning, countries, culture, gay and lesbian travel.
www.lanic.utexas.edu The Latin American Network Information Center: loads of information on everything.
www.lata.org Lists tour operators, hotels, airlines, etc. Has a useful (free) guide which can also be ordered by phoning T020-8715 2913.

www.oanda.com Currency converter and for all your financial needs.
www.oas.org The Organization of American States site, with its magazine *Americas*.
www.southamericadaily.com From the World News Network, links to newspapers, plus environment, health, business and travel sites.
www.virtualtourist.com/f/4/ South America travel forum, which can take you down some interesting alleyways, lots of links, trips, etc; good exploring here.
www.putumayo.com For the lowdown on the latest Latin sounds.
www.whatsonwhen.com and **www.national-holidays.com** for worldwide information on festivals and events.

Essentials

Before you travel   34
Getting there   34
Getting around   42
Health   45
Essentials A-Z   49

⁑ Footprint features

Carnet de passages   43
Second languages and anomalies   52
Sleeping and eating   58

except for the **Qantas** route to Sydney which connects with **LAN** to Buenos Aires. From **Japan** there are direct flights to Brazil and from **South Africa** to Argentina and Brazil. Within **Latin America** there is plenty of choice on local carriers and some connections on US or European airlines. For airpasses, see below. To Guyana, the main routes are via the Caribbean (Port of Spain, Trinidad and Barbados) or New York, Miami and Toronto. Suriname is served by flights from Amsterdam, Miami, Port of Spain, Curaçao and Aruba, while Guyane has flights from Paris and the French-speaking Caribbean. All three have air connections with northern Brazil.

Baggage
There is no standard baggage allowance to Latin America. If you fly via the USA you are allowed two pieces of luggage up to 32 kg per case. Brazil has adopted this system, but it is not uniformly applied by all airlines. On flights from Europe there is a weight allowance of 20-23 kg, although some carriers use the two-piece system, but may not apply it in both directions. The two-piece system is gaining wider acceptance, but check in advance. Excess baggage charges can be high. Weight limits for internal flights are often lower; enquire beforehand.

Prices and discounts
From the UK, flights to Bogotá, Buenos Aires, Caracas, Lima, Rio and São Paulo start at between US$800-1,580 (in low season, May 2007 exchange rates). Prices rise in July and at Christmas. **From the USA**, Caracas and Bogotá are generally the cheapest destinations (around US$430-570); Lima fares are US$600-665 and Buenos Aires US$735-855 (all from Miami, low season). **From Australia**, flights to Rio de Janeiro start at about US$1,600-1,700, and Buenos Aires US$1,400-1,500. Most airlines offer discounted fares on scheduled flights through agencies who specialize in this type of fare. For a list of these agencies see page 38. If you buy discounted air tickets always check the reservation with the airline concerned to make sure the flight still exists. Also remember the IATA airlines' schedules change in March and

October each year, so if you're going to be away a long time it's best to leave return flight coupons open. Peak times are 7 December-15 January and 10 July-10 September. If you intend travelling during those times, book as far ahead as possible. Between February and May and September and November special offers may be available.

Air passes

The **Mercosur Airpass** for Brazil, Argentina, Chile, Uruguay and Paraguay, using several local carriers, is available to any passenger with a return ticket to a participating country. It must be bought in conjunction with an international flight; minimum stay is seven days, maximum 45; and a minimum of two countries must be visited. Maximum number of coupons is eight, the maximum number of stops per country is three. Fares are worked out on a mileage basis and cost US$295-1,195. **TAM** also has an airpass which links Brazil with the other Mercosur countries (not valid if you arrived on **Lan**). You must include at least two of those countries with a maximum of two stops per country (three in

Brazil); minimum stay five days, maximum 30; maximum eight coupons, which range from US$280-1,021. The **Aerolíneas Argentinas/Austral** air pass links Argentina, Brazil, Chile and Uruguay, with a minimum of two countries, maximum stay 45 days, maximum number of coupons 10, fares based on mileage: US$300-1,800. Two stopovers are allowed in Argentina, one in the other countries. **Lan** has an airpass valid for travel on any of its routes in South America, on any part of its network in South America, available to anyone who has purchased a transatlantic ticket with **Lan**. It's valid for six months. Coupons range from US$86-199 (257 to Easter Island), but cost more if you entered South America by a carrier other than Lan. The **All America Airpass**, a multi-carrier, multi-country facility from Germany's **Hahn Air**, is built up from individual sectors at specially negotiated rates that can be bought just as a single journey, or a multi-sector trip, as required and according to cost. There is no minimum or maximum stay; see *www.allairpass.com*. See the respective countries for airpasses operated by national airlines.

Discount flight agents
UK and Ireland

STA Travel, T0870 163 0026, www.statravel.co.uk. 65 branches in the UK, including many university campuses. Specialists in low-cost flights and tours, good for student IDs and insurance.

Trailfinders, 194 Kensington High St, London, W8 7RG, T020-7938 3939, www.trailfinders.com. 18 branches in London and throughout the UK. Also 1 branch in Dublin and 5 travel centres in Australia.

North America

Air Brokers International, 685 Market St, Suite 400, San Francisco, CA94105, T01-800-883 3273, www.airbrokers.com. Consolidator and specialist on RTW and Circle Pacific tickets.

Discount Airfares Worldwide On-Line, www.etn.nl/discount.htm. A hub of consolidator and discount agent links.

STA Travel, 1-800-781-4040, www.statravel.com. Over 100 branches in the USA and Canada, including many university campuses.

Travel CUTS, in major Canadian cities and on university campuses, T1-866-246-9762, www.travelcuts.com. Specialist in student discount fares, IDs and other travel services. Also in California, USA.

Travelocity, www.travelocity.com. Consolidator.

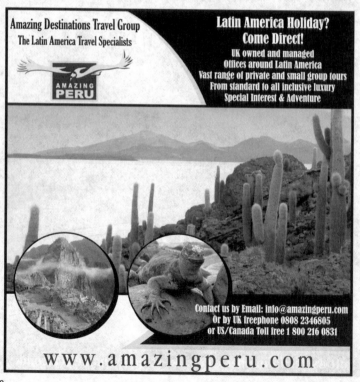

Ladatco, 2200 S Dixie Highway, Suite 704, Coconut Grove, FL 33133, USA, T1-800 327 6162, www.ladatco.com.

Last Frontiers, Fleet Marston Farm, Aylesbury HP18 0QT, UK, T01296-653000, www.lastfrontiers.com. South American specialists offering tailor-made itineraries plus specialist themed tours.

Latin American Travel Association, c/o Travel PR, 133a St Margaret's Rd, Twickenham, TW1 1RG, UK, T020-8715 2913, www.lata.org.

Lost World Adventures, 337 Shadowmoor Dr, Decatur GA 30030, USA, T800-999 0558, www.lostworld.com.

MILA Tours, 100 S Greenleaf, Gurnee, IL 60031, USA, T1-800-367 7378, www.milatours.com.

Myths and Mountains, 976 Tee Court, Incline Village, NV 89451, USA, T800-670 6984, 775-832 5454, www.mythsandmountains.com.

Nature Expeditions International, 7860 Peters Rd, suite F-103, Plantation, FL 33324, USA, T1-800-869 0639, www.naturexp.com.

New Worlds, Northway House, 1379 High Rd, London, N20 9LP, T020-8445 8444, www.newworlds.co.uk. Tailor-made itineraries.

Nouveaux Mondes, Rte Suisse 7, CH-1295 Mies, Switzerland, T+41-22-950 9660, info@nouveauxmondes.com.

Oasis Overland, The Marsh, Henstridge, BA8 0TF, UK, T01963-363400, www.oasisoverland.co.uk. Small group trips to Peru and overland tours.

Peru For Less, US office: T1-877-269 0309; UK office: T0203 002 0571; Peru (Lima) office: T272 0542, www.peruforless.com.

Reef and Rainforest Tours Ltd, Dart Marine Park, Steamer Quay, Totnes, Devon TQ9 5AL, UK, T01803-866965, www.reefandrainforest.co.uk.

Responsible Travel.com, www.responsibletravel.com.

Select Latin America, 79 Maltings Pl, 169 Tower Bridge Rd, London SE1 3LJ, UK, T020-7407 1478, www.selectlatinamerica.com. Tailor-made holidays and small group tours.

South American Experience, 47 Causton St, London SW1P 4AT, UK, T020-7676 5511, www.southamericanexperience.co.uk.

South American Tours, Stephanstrasse 13, D-60313, Frankfurt, Germany, T+49-69-405 8970, www.southamericantours.de.

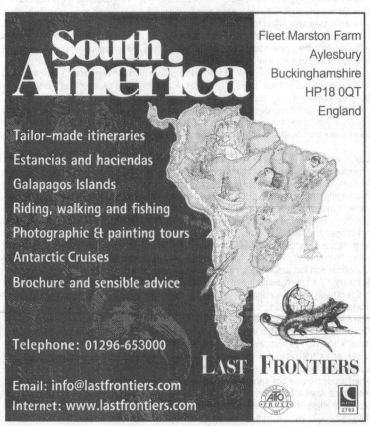

Steppes Latin America, 51 Castle St, Cirencester, Glos GL7 1QD, T01285-885333, www.steppes latinAmerica.co.uk. Tailor-made itineraries for destinations throughout Latin America.

Tambo Tours, 4405 Spring Cypress Rd, Suite #210, Spring, TX 77388, USA, T1-888-2-GO-PERU (246-7378), T001-281 528 9448, www.2GOPERU.com. Long-established adventure and tour specialist with offices in Peru and the USA. Customized trips to the Amazon and archaeological sites of Peru, Bolivia and Ecuador.

Travelbag, 3-5 High St, Alton, Hants GU13 1TL, UK, T0870-814 4440, www.travelbag.co.uk.

TrekAmerica Travel Ltd, Grange Mills, Weir Rd, London SW12 0NE, UK, T0870-444 8735, www.trekamerica.co.uk.

Tribes Travel, 12 The Business Centre, Earl Soham, Woodbridge, Suffolk, IP13 7SA, UK, T01728-685971, www.tribes.co.uk.

Trips Worldwide, 14 Frederick Pl, Bristol BS8 1AS, UK, T0117-311 4400, www.tripsworldwide.co.uk.

Tropical Nature Travel, www.tropicalnature travel.com. Ecotour company with itineraries to Ecuador, Peru and Brazil.

Tucan, 316 Uxbridge Rd, Acton, London W3 9QP, T020-8896 1600, and 217 Alison Rd, Randwick, NSW 2031, Sydney, T02-9326 6633, www.tucantravel.com.

Veloso Tours, 34 Warple Way, London W3 0RG, UK, T020-8762 0616, www.veloso.com.

World Expeditions, T020-8870 2600 (UK), www.worldexpeditions.co.uk, with offices in Australia, New Zealand, USA and Canada.

Getting around → *See Getting there, above, for details of air transport including air passes.*

Buses and trains

The continent has an extensive road system with frequent bus services. The buses are often comfortable; the difficulties of Andean terrain affect the quality of vehicles. In mountainous country do not expect buses to get to their destination after long journeys anywhere near on time. Do not turn up for a bus at the last minute; if it is full it may depart early. Tall travellers are advised to take aisle rather than window seats on long journeys as this allows more leg room. When the journey takes more than three or four hours, meal stops at roadside restaurants (usually with toilets), good and bad, are the rule. Usually, no announcement is made on the duration of a stop; ask the driver and follow him, if he eats, eat. See what the locals are eating – and buy likewise, or make sure you're stocked up well on food and drink at the start. For drinks, stick to bottled water or soft drinks or coffee (black). The food sold by vendors at bus stops may be all right; watch if locals are buying, though unpeeled fruit is, of course, reliable.

Where they still run, trains are slower than buses. They tend to provide finer scenery and you can normally see much more wildlife than from the road – it is less disturbed by one or two trains a day than by the more frequent road traffic.

Car

The car A normal car will reach most places of interest, but high ground clearance is useful for badly surfaced or unsurfaced roads and for fording rivers. For greater flexibility in mountain and jungle territory 4WD vehicles are recommended. In Patagonia, main roads are gravel rather than paved: perfectly passable without 4WD, just rough and dusty. Consider fitting wire guards for headlamps, and for windscreens too. Diesel cars are much cheaper to run than petrol ones and the fuel is easily available, although in Venezuela you may have to look hard for it outside Caracas. Standard European and Japanese cars run on fuel with a higher octane rating than is commonly available in North, South or Central America, and in Brazil petrol (*gasolina*) is in fact gasohol, with a 12% admixture of alcohol.

Security Spare no ingenuity in making your car secure, inside and out (even wing mirrors, spot lamps, wheels without locking nuts can be stolen). Try never to leave the car unattended except in a locked garage or guarded parking space. Lock the clutch or accelerator to the steering wheel with a heavy, obvious chain or lock. Street children will generally protect your car for a tip.

Documents To drive your own vehicle in South America, you must have an international driver's licence. You must also have the vehicle's registration document in the name of the driver, or, in the case of a car registered in someone else's name, a notarized letter of authorization. Be very careful to keep **all** the papers you are given when you enter, to produce when you leave (see box opposite).

Insurance Insurance for the vehicle against accident, damage or theft is best arranged in the country of origin. In Latin American countries it is very expensive to insure against accident and theft, especially as you should take into account the value of the car increased by duties

❖ Carnet de passages

There are two recognized documents for taking a vehicle through customs in South America: a *carnet de passages* issued jointly by the *Fedération Internationale de l'Automobile* (FIA – Paris) and the Alliance Internationale de Tourisme (AIT-Geneva), and the *Libreta de Pasos por Aduana* issued by the *Federación Interamericana de Touring y Automóvil Clubs* (FITAC). The *carnet de passages* is recognized by all South American customs authorities but is not required by any. The *libreta*, a 10-page book of three-part passes for customs, should be available from any South American automobile club member of FITAC, but in practice it is only available to non-residents from the *Touring y Automóvil Club de Venezuela*. At US$400, it is not worth the effort or expense, not is it needed to enter Venezuela. If you wish to purchase one of these documents, get

a *carnet de passages*, issued in the country where the vehicle is registered. In the UK it costs £150 for 25 pages, available from the *RAC*, www.rac.co.uk/web/knowhow/going_ on_a_journey/driving_abroad/carnet_ de_passages. In Canada the fee is CAN$450, but in all cases you have to add on administration fees, deposits and insurance premiums, which can take the cost into the thousands, depending on the value of the car. In the USA the *AAA* does not issue the *carnet*, although the HQ in Washington DC may give advice. It is available from the *Canadian Automobile Association*, 1145 Hunt Club Road, suite 200, Ottawa K1V 0Y3, T613-247 0117, www.caa.ca, who can give full details. Also from the *AAA* of Australia, details at www.aaa .asn.au/touring/overseas.htm. Ask the motoring organization in your home country about availability of the *carnet*.

calculated in real (ie non-devaluing) terms. If the car is stolen or written off you will be required to pay very high import duty on its value. Third-party insurance can be very difficult to find. Some countries may insist that it be bought at the border (Venezuela seems to be the only country where it is easy to obtain). If you can get the legally required minimum cover, so much the better. If not, drive with extreme caution and very defensively. If involved in an accident and you're uninsured, your car could be confiscated. If anyone is hurt, do not pick them up (you may become liable). Try to seek assistance from the nearest police station or hospital.

Shipping a vehicle From Europe or the USA you can go to Panama and shop around for the best value sailing to whichever port best suits your travelling plans. There are, however, no roll-on/roll-off (RORO) services from Panama to west coast South America. You may find a RORO service from Panama to Colombia, Venezuela or Brazil, but the best bet would be to ship RORO from the USA. Otherwise find a container service if your vehicle is low enough. It is also possible to ship a vehicle from Costa Rica. Alternatively, you can ship a vehicle direct from Europe (eg Grimaldi Lines from Antwerp, T0032-3-545 8808, V.Vanstechelman@grimaldi.be) or the USA.

Driving to Heaven, by Derek Stansfield (write to: Ropley, Broad Oak, Sturminster Newton, DT10 2HG, UK, T01258-472534, £4.95 plus postage, or www.amazon.co.uk), is recommended for information on South American motoring conditions and requirements.

Car hire The main international car hire companies operate in all countries, but they tend to be very expensive, reflecting the high costs and accident rates. Hotels and tourist agencies will tell you where to find cheaper rates, but you will need to check that you have such basics as spare wheel, toolkit and functioning lights, etc. You'll probably have more fun if you drive yourself, although it's always possible to hire a car with driver. If you plan to do a lot of driving and will have time at the end to dispose of it, investigate the possibility of buying a second-hand car locally; since hiring is so expensive it may well work out cheaper and will probably do you just as well.

Car hire insurance Check exactly what the hirer's insurance policy covers. In many cases it only protects you against minor bumps and scrapes, not major accidents, nor 'natural' damage (eg flooding). Ask if extra cover is available. Also find out, if using a credit card, whether the card automatically includes insurance. Beware of being billed for scratches which were already on the vehicle. Also check the windscreen and ask what procedures are involved if a new one is needed.

for more than a month), know your own blood group and if you suffer a long-term condition such as diabetes or epilepsy make sure someone knows or that you have a Medic Alert bracelet/necklace with this information on it.

Vaccinations The following are commonly recommended for South America. The final decision, however, should be based on a consultation with your GP or travel clinic. **Polio** Recommended if nil in last 10 years. **Tetanus** Recommended if nil in last 10 years (but after five doses you have had enough for life). **Typhoid** Recommended if nil in last three years. **Yellow fever** Obligatory for most areas except Chile, Paraguay, Argentina and Uruguay. However, if you are travelling around South America it is best to get this vaccine since you will need it for the northern areas. **Rabies** Recommended if going to jungle and/or remote areas. **Hepatitis A** Recommended – the disease can be caught easily from food and water.

A-Z of health risks

Altitude sickness Acute mountain sickness can strike from about 3,000 m upwards and in general is more likely to affect those who ascend rapidly (for example by plane) and those who over-exert themselves. Acute mountain sickness takes a few hours or days to come on and presents with headache, lassitude, dizziness, loss of appetite, nausea and vomiting. Insomnia is common and often associated with a suffocating feeling when lying down in bed. You may notice that your breathing tends to wax and wane at night and your face is puffy in the mornings; all part of the syndrome. If the symptoms are mild, the treatment is rest and painkillers (preferably not aspirin-based) for the headaches. Should symptoms be severe and prolonged it is best to descend to a lower altitude immediately and reascend, if necessary, slowly and in stages. The symptoms disappear very quickly, even after a few hundred metres of descent.

The best way of preventing acute mountain sickness is a relatively slow ascent. When trekking to high altitude, some time spent walking at medium altitude, getting fit and acclimatizing is beneficial. When flying to places over 3,000 m, a few hours' rest and the avoidance of alcohol, cigarettes and heavy food will help prevent acute mountain sickness.

Bites and stings This is a very rare event indeed for travellers, but if you are unlucky (or careless) enough to be bitten by a venomous snake, spider, scorpion or sea creature, try to identify the culprit, without putting yourself in further danger (do not try to catch a live snake). Snake bites in particular are very frightening, but in fact rarely poisonous – even venomous snakes can bite without injecting venom. Victims should be taken to a hospital or a doctor without delay. It is not advised for travellers to carry snake bite antivenom as it can do more harm than good in inexperienced hands. Reassure and comfort the victim frequently. Immobilize the limb with a bandage or a splint and get the patient to lie still. Do not slash the bite area and try to suck out the poison. This also does more harm than good. You should apply a tourniquet in these circumstances, but don't attempt this if you are not experienced.

Certain tropical fish inject venom into feet when trodden on, which can be exceptionally painful. Wear plastic shoes if such creatures are reported. The pain can be relieved by immersing the foot in hot water (as hot as you can bear) for as long as the pain persists.

Chagas' disease The disease occurs throughout South America, affects locals more than travellers, but travellers can be exposed by sleeping in mud-constructed huts where the bug that carries the parasite bites and defecates on an exposed part of skin. You may notice nothing at all or a local swelling, with fever, tiredness and enlargement of lymph glands, spleen and liver. The seriousness of the parasite infection is caused by the long-term effects which include gross enlargement of the heart and/or guts. Early treatment is required with toxic drugs. Prevention: always keep a light burning at night. Never scratch the bite, but swab it with disinfectant. Sleep under a permethrin-treated bed net and use insect repellents.

Dengue fever This is a viral disease spread by mosquitoes that tend to bite during the day. The symptoms are fever and often intense joint pains, also some people develop a rash. Symptoms last about a week but it can take a few weeks to recover fully. Dengue can be difficult to distinguish from malaria as both diseases tend to occur in the same countries. There are no effective vaccines or antiviral drugs though, fortunately, travellers rarely develop the more severe forms of the disease (these can prove fatal). Rest, plenty of fluids and paracetamol (not aspirin) is the recommended treatment.

Diarrhoea and intestinal upset Diarrhoea can refer either to loose stools or an increased frequency of bowel movement, both of which can be a nuisance. Symptoms should be relatively short lived but if they persist beyond two weeks specialist medical attention should be sought. Also seek medical help if there is blood in the stools and/or fever.

Adults can use an antidiarrhoeal medication such as loperamide to control the symptoms but only for up to 24 hours. In addition keep well hydrated by drinking plenty of fluids and eat bland foods. Oral rehydration sachets taken after each loose stool are a useful way to keep well hydrated. These should always be used when treating children and the elderly.

Bacterial traveller's diarrhoea is the most common form. Ciproxin (Ciprofloxacin) is a useful antibiotic and can be obtained by private prescription in the UK. You need to take one 500 mg tablet when the diarrhoea starts. If there are so signs of improvement after 24 hours the diarrhoea is likely to be viral and not bacterial. If it is due to other organisms such as those causing giardia or amoebic dysentery, different antibiotics will be required.

The standard advice to prevent problems is to be careful with water and ice for drinking. Ask yourself where the water came from. If you have any doubts then boil it or filter and treat it. There are many filter/treatment devices available. Food can also transmit disease. Be wary of salads (what were they washed in, who handled them), re-heated foods or food that has been left out in the sun having been cooked earlier in the day. There is a simple adage that says wash it, peel it, boil it or forget it. Also be wary of unpasteurised dairy products as they too can transmit diseases.

Hanta virus Some forest and riverine rodents carry hanta virus, epidemics of which have occurred in Argentina and Chile, but do occur worldwide. Symptoms are a flu-like illness which can lead to complications. Try as far as possible to avoid rodent-infested areas, especially close contact with rodent droppings. Campers and parents with small children should be especially careful.

Hepatitis Hepatitis means inflammation of the liver. Viral causes of the disease can be acquired anywhere in the world. The most obvious symptom is a yellowing of your skin or the whites of your eyes. However, prior to this all that you may notice is itching and tiredness. Pre-travel hepatitis A vaccine is the best bet. Hepatitis B (for which there is a vaccine) is spread through blood and unprotected sexual intercourse, both of which can be avoided.

Leishmaniasis A skin form of this disease occurs in all countries of South America except Chile and Uruguay. The main disease areas are in Bolivia, Brazil and Peru. If infected, you may notice a raised lump, which leads to a purplish discoloration on white skin and a possible ulcer. The parasite is transmitted by the bite of a sandfly. Sandflies do not fly very far and the greatest risk is at ground levels, so if you can sleep above ground, under a permethrin treated net, do so. In addition, use insect repellent. Seek advice for any persistent skin lesion or nasal symptom. Several weeks treatment is required under specialist supervision. The drugs themselves are toxic but if not taken in sufficient amounts recurrence of the disease is more likely.

Leptospirosis Various forms of leptospirosis occur throughout Latin America, transmitted by a bacterium which is excreted in rodent urine. Fresh water and moist soil harbour the organisms, which enter the body through cuts and scratches. If you suffer from any form of prolonged fever consult a doctor.

Malaria Malaria can cause death within 24 hours and can start as something resembling an attack of flu. You may feel tired, lethargic, headachy, feverish; or more seriously, develop fits, followed by coma and then death. Have a low index of suspicion because it is very easy to write off vague symptoms, which may actually be malaria. If you have a temperature, visit a doctor as soon as you can and ask for a malaria test. On your return home, if you suffer any of these symptoms, have a test as soon as possible. Even if a previous test proved negative, this could save your life.

Treatment is with drugs and may be oral or into a vein depending on the seriousness of the infection. Remember ABCD: Awareness (of whether the disease is present in the area you are travelling in), Bite avoidance, Chemoprohylaxis, Diagnosis.

To prevent mosquito bites wear clothes that cover arms and legs, use effective insect repellents in areas with known risks of insect-spread disease and use a mosquito net treated with an insecticide. Repellents containing 30-50% DEET (Di-ethyltoluamide) are recommended when visiting malaria endemic areas; lemon eucalyptus (Mosiguard) is a reasonable alternative. The key advice is to guard against contracting malaria by taking the correct anti-malarials and finishing the recommended course. If you are A popular target for insect bites or develop lumps quite soon after being bitten use antihistamine tablets and apply a cream such as hydrocortisone.

Remember that it is risky to buy medicine, and in particular anti-malarials, in some developing countries. These may be sub-standard or part of a trade in counterfeit drugs.

Rabies Rabies is endemic throughout Latin America so be aware of the dangers of the bite from any animal. Rabies vaccination before travel can be considered but if bitten always seek urgent medical attention – whether or not you have been previously vaccinated – after first cleaning the wound and treating with an iodine-base disinfectant or alcohol.

Schistosomiasis (bilharzia) The mansoni form of this flat worm occurs in Suriname and Venezuela (check the CDC, WHO websites and a travel clinic specialist for up to date information for affected locations). The form that penetrates the skin after you have swum or waded through snail infested water can cause a local itch soon after, fever after a few weeks and much later diarrhoea, abdominal pain and spleen or liver enlargement. A single drug cures this disease.

Sun Take good heed of advice regarding protecting yourself against the sun. Overexposure can lead to sunburn and, in the longer term, skin cancers and premature skin aging. The best advice is simply to avoid exposure to the sun by covering exposed skin, wearing a hat and staying out of the sun if possible, especially between late morning and early afternoon. Apply a high-factor sunscreen (greater than SPF15) and also make sure it screens against UVB. A further danger in tropical climates is heat exhaustion or more seriously heatstroke. This can be avoided by good hydration, which means drinking water past the point of simply quenching thirst. Also when first exposed to tropical heat take time to acclimatize by avoiding strenuous activity in the middle of the day. If you cannot avoid heavy exercise it is also a good idea to increase salt intake.

Ticks Ticks usually attach themselves to the lower parts of the body often when walking in areas where cattle have grazed. They take a while to attach themselves strongly, but swell up as they start to suck blood. The important thing is to remove them gently, so that they do not leave their head parts in your skin because this can cause a nasty allergic reaction some days later. Do not use petrol, vaseline, lighted cigarettes, etc to remove the tick, but, with a pair of tweezers remove the beast gently by gripping it at the attached (head) end and rock it out in very much the same way that a tooth is extracted. **Typhus,** carried by ticks, can also occur. There is usually a reaction at the site of the bite and a fever. Certain tropical flies which lay their eggs under the skin of sheep and cattle also occasionally do the same thing to humans with the unpleasant result that a maggot grows under the skin and pops up as a boil or pimple. The best way to remove these is to cover the boil with oil, vaseline or nail varnish so as to stop the maggot breathing, then to squeeze it out gently the next day.

Underwater health If you plan to dive make sure that you are fit do so. The **British Sub-Aqua Club** (BSAC), Telford's Quay, South Pier Road, Ellesmere Port, Cheshire CH65 4FL, UK, T01513-506200, F01513-506215, www.bsac.com, can put you in touch with doctors who will carry out medical examinations. Check that any dive company you use are reputable and have the appropriate certification from the **Professional Association of Diving Instructors** (PADI), Unit 7, St Philips Central, Albert Rd, St Philips, Bristol, BS2 OTD, T0117-3007234, www.padi.com.

Water There are a number of ways of purifying water. Dirty water should first be strained through a filter bag and then boiled or treated. Bring water to a rolling boil for several minutes. There are sterilizing methods that can be used and products generally contain chlorine (eg Puritabs) or iodine (eg Pota Aqua) compounds. There are a number of water sterilizers now on the market available in personal and expedition size. Make sure you take the spare parts or spare chemicals with you and do not believe everything the manufacturers say.

Other diseases and risks There are a range of other insect-borne diseases that are quite rare in travellers, but worth finding out about if going to particular destinations. One example is river blindness (Onchocerciasis), carried by blackflies found in parts of Venezuela. Also

48

remember that unprotected sex always carries a risk. You can lessen this by using condoms, a femidom or if you want to be completely safe, by avoiding sex altogether.

Websites

www.cdc.gov Centres for Disease Control and Prevention (USA).

www.dh.gov.uk/en/Policyandguidance/Heal thadvicefortravellers/index.htm Department of Health advice for travellers.

www.fitfortravel.scot.nhs.uk Fit for Travel (UK), a site from Scotland providing a quick A-Z of vaccine and travel health advice requirements for each country.

www.fco.gov.uk Foreign and Commonwealth Office (FCO), UK.

www.itg.be Prince Leopold Institute for Tropical Medicine.

www.nathnac.org National Travel Health Network and Centre (NaTHNaC).

www.who.int World Health Organisation.

Books

Dawood, R, editor, *Travellers' health*, 3rd ed, Oxford: Oxford University Press, 2002.

Warrell, David, and Sarah Anderson, editors, *Expedition Medicine*, The Royal Geographic Society, ISBN 1 86197 040-4.

Essentials A-Z

Children → *For health matters, see page 45. Visit www.babygoes2.com.*
Travel with children can bring you into closer contact with South American families and, generally, presents no special problems – in fact the path is often smoother for family groups. Officials tend to be more amenable where children are concerned and they are pleased if your child knows a little Spanish or Portuguese. Moreover, thieves and pickpockets seem to have some traditional respect for families, and may leave you alone because of it! **Note** Buy nappies/diapers at every available opportunity, in case of short supply later on.

People contemplating overland travel in South America with children should remember that a lot of time can be spent waiting for public transport. Even then, buses can de delayed on the journey by bad weather. Travel on trains, while not as fast or at times as comfortable as buses, allows more scope for moving about. Beware of doors left open for ventilation especially if air-conditioning is not working. If hiring a car, check that it has rear seat belts.

On all long-distance buses you pay for each seat, and there are no half-fares if the children occupy a seat each. For shorter trips it is cheaper, if less comfortable, to seat small children on your knee. Often there are spare seats which children can occupy after tickets have been collected. In city and local excursion buses, small children generally do not pay a fare, but are not entitled to a seat when paying customers are standing. On sightseeing tours you should always bargain for a family rate – often children can go free. All civil airlines charge half for children under 12, but some military services don't have half-fares, or have younger age limits. Children's fares on Lloyd Aéreo Boliviano are considerably more than half, and there is only a 7 kg baggage allowance. (LAB also checks children's ages on passports.) Note that a child travelling free on a long excursion is not always covered by the operator's travel insurance; it is advisable to pay a small premium to arrange cover.

Food can be a problem if the children are picky eaters. It is easier to take food such as biscuits, drinks and bread with you on longer trips than to rely on meal stops. Avocados are safe and nutritious; they can be fed to babies as young as six months and most older children like them. A small immersion heater and jug for making hot drinks is invaluable, but remember that electric current varies. Try and get a dual-voltage one (110v and 220v).

In all **hotels**, try to negotiate family rates. If charges are per person, always insist that two children will occupy one bed only, therefore counting as one tariff. If rates are per bed, the same applies. In either case you can almost always get a reduced rate at cheaper hotels. Occasionally when travelling with a child you will be refused a room in a hotel that is 'unsuitable'. On river boat trips, unless you have very large hammocks, it may be more comfortable and cost effective to hire a two-berth cabin for two adults and a child. (In restaurants, you can normally buy children's helpings, or divide one full-size helping between two children.)

Disabled travellers

In most of South America, facilities for the disabled are severely lacking. For those in wheelchairs, ramps and toilet access are limited to some of the more upmarket, or most restrict traditional rights and activities), but individual choice and awareness can make a difference in many instances, and collectively, travellers are having a significant effect in shaping a more responsible and sustainable industry.

Of course travel can have beneficial impacts and this is something to which every traveller can contribute. Many national parks are part funded by receipts from visitors. Similarly, travellers can promote patronage and protection of important archaeological sites and heritage through their interest and contributions via entrance and performance fees. They can also support small-scale enterprises by staying in locally run hotels and hostels, eating in local restaurants and by purchasing local goods, supplies and arts and crafts. In fact, since the early 1990s there has been a phenomenal growth in tourism that promotes and supports the conservation of natural environments and is also fair and equitable to local communities. This 'ecotourism' segment is probably the fastest-growing sector of the travel industry and provides a vast and growing range of destinations and activities in South America.

While the authenticity of some ecotourism operators' claims needs to be interpreted with care, there is clearly both a huge demand for this type of activity and also significant opportunities to support worthwhile conservation and social development initiatives. Organizations such as **Conservation International** ① T001-202-912 1000, www.ecotour .org, the **International Ecotourism society** ① T001-202-347 9203, www.eco tourism.org, Planeta ① www.planeta.com, and **Tourism Concern** ① T44-20-7133 3330, www.tourism concern .org.uk, have begun to develop and/or promote ecotourism projects and destinations and their websites are an excellent source of information for sites and initiatives throughout South America. Both **Earthwatch** ① T44-1865 318838 (UK), T978-461 0081 (US), www.earthwatch.org, and **Discovery Initiatives** ① T44-1285-643333, www.discovery initiatives.com, offer a chance to participate directly in scientific research and development projects.

South America offers unique and unforgettable experiences – often based on the natural environment, cultural heritage and local society. These are the reasons many of us choose to travel and why many more will want to do so in the future. Shouldn't we provide an opportunity for future travellers and hosts to enjoy the quality of experience and interaction that we take for granted?

Safety → For specific local problems, see under the individual countries in the text.

Drugs Users of drugs, even of soft ones, without medical prescription should be particularly careful, as some countries impose heavy penalties – up to 10 years' imprisonment – for even the simple possession of such substances. In this connection, the planting of drugs on travellers, by traffickers or the police, is not unknown. If offered drugs on the street, make no response at all and keep walking. Note that people who roll their own cigarettes are often suspected of carrying drugs and subjected to intensive searches.

Keeping safe Generally speaking, most places in South America are no more dangerous than any major city in Europe or North America. In provincial towns, main places of interest, on daytime buses and in ordinary restaurants the visitor should be quite safe. Nevertheless, in large cities (particularly in crowded places, eg bus stations, markets), crime exists, most of which is opportunistic. If you are aware of the dangers, act confidently and use your common sense, you will lessen many of the risks. The following tips are all endorsed by travellers. Keep all documents secure; hide your main cash supply in different places or under your clothes: extra pockets sewn inside shirts and trousers, pockets closed with a zip or safety pin, moneybelts (best worn under rather than outside your clothes at the waist), neck or leg pouches, a thin chain for attaching a purse to your bag or under your clothes and elasticated support bandages for keeping money and cheques above the elbow or below the knee have been repeatedly recommended. Be extra vigilant when withdrawing cash from an ATM: make sure you are not being watched; never give your card to anyone, however smart he may look or plausible he may sound as a 'bank employee' wishing to swipe your card to check for problems. Keep cameras in bags; take spare spectacles (eyeglasses); don't wear expensive wrist-watches or jewellery. If you wear a shoulder-bag in a market, carry it in front of you.

Ignore mustard smearers and paint or shampoo sprayers, and strangers' remarks like "what's that on your shoulder?" or "have you seen that dirt on your shoe?" Furthermore, don't bend over to pick up money or other items in the street. These are all ruses intended to distract your attention and make you easy prey for an accomplice to steal from. Take local advice about being out at night and, if walking after dark, walk in the road, not on the pavement/sidewalk.

Ruses involving plainclothes policemen are infrequent, but it is worth knowing that the real police only have the right to see your passport (not your money, tickets or hotel room). Before handing anything over, ask why they need to see it and make sure you understand the reason. Insist on seeing identification and on going to the police station by main roads. On no account take them directly back to your lodgings. Be even more suspicious if he seeks confirmation of his status from a passer-by. A related scam is for a 'tourist' to gain your confidence, then accomplices create a reason to check your documents. If someone tries to bribe you, insist on a receipt. If attacked, remember your assailants may well be armed, and try not to resist.

Leave any valuables you don't need in safe-deposit in your hotel when sightseeing locally. Always keep an inventory of what you have deposited. If there is no safe, lock your bags and secure them in your room (some people take eyelet-screws for padlocking cupboards or drawers). Hostels with shared rooms should provide secure, clean lockers for guests. If you lose valuables, always report to the police and note details of the report – for insurance purposes.

When you have all your luggage with you, be careful. From airports take official taxis or special airport buses. Take a taxi between bus station/railway station and hotel. Keep your bags with you in the taxi and pay only when you and your luggage are safely out of the vehicle. Make sure the taxi has inner door handles and do not share the ride with a stranger. Avoid night buses; never arrive at night; and watch your belongings whether they are stowed inside or outside the cabin (roof top luggage racks create extra problems, which are sometimes unavoidable – make sure your bag is waterproof). Major bus lines often issue a luggage ticket when bags are stored in the hold of the bus. Finally, never accept food, drink, sweets or cigarettes from unknown fellow travellers on buses or trains. They may be drugged, and you would wake up hours later without your belongings.

Rape This can happen anywhere. If you are the victim of a sexual assault, you are advised to contact a doctor (this can be your home doctor if you prefer). You will need tests to determine whether you have contracted any sexually-transmitted diseases; you may also need advice on post-coital contraception. You should also contact your embassy, where consular staff are very willing to help in such cases.

Police Whereas in Europe and North America we are accustomed to law enforcement on a systematic basis, in general, enforcement in Latin America is achieved by periodic campaigns. The most typical is a round-up of criminals in the cities just before Christmas. In December, therefore, you may well be asked for identification at any time, and if you cannot produce it, you will be jailed. If a visitor is jailed his or her friends should provide food every day. This is especially important for people on a diet, such as diabetics. In the event of a vehicle accident in which anyone is injured, all drivers involved are automatically detained until blame has been established, and this does not usually take less than two weeks. Never offer a bribe unless you are fully conversant with the customs of the country. (In Chile, for instance, it would land you in serious trouble if you tried to bribe a *carabinero*.) Wait until the official makes the suggestion, or offer money in some form which is apparently not bribery, for example "In our country we have a system of on-the-spot fines (*multas de inmediato*). Is there a similar system here?" Do not assume that an official who accepts a bribe is prepared to do anything else than is illegal. You bribe him to persuade him to do his job, or to persuade him not to do it, or to do it more quickly, or more slowly. You do not bribe him to do something which is illegal. The mere suggestion would make him very upset. If an official suggests that a bribe must be paid before you can proceed on your way, be patient (assuming you have the time) and he may relent.

Shopping

Handicrafts, like food, enjoy regional distinctiveness, especially in items such as textiles. Each region, even every village, has its own characteristic pattern or style of cloth, so the choice is enormous. In the Andes, weaving has a spiritual significance, as well as a practical one. Reproductions of pre-Columbian designs can be found in pottery and jewellery and many artisans make delightful gold and silver items. Musical instruments (eg from Bolivia), gaucho wear, the mate drinking gourd and silver straw (*bombilla*), soapstone carvings and ceramics are just some of the things you can bring home with you. Remember that handicrafts can almost invariably be bought more cheaply away from the capital, though there may be less choice. **Gemstones** are good in Brazil; emeralds in Colombia. Leather goods are best in Argentina, Uruguay, Brazil and Colombia, while Peru is now marketing native cotton. Buy **beachwear** in Brazil; it is matchless. **Bargaining** seems to be the general rule in most countries' street markets, but don't make a fool of yourself by bargaining over what, to you, is a small amount of money.

can usually be locked in the hold. It is easier for men to take the friendliness of locals at face value; women may be subject to much unwanted attention. To help minimize this, do not wear suggestive clothing and do not flirt. By wearing a wedding ring, carrying a photograph of your 'husband' and 'children', and saying that your 'husband' is close at hand, you may dissuade an aspiring suitor. When asked how long you are travelling, say only for a short time because a long journey may give the impression that you are wealthy (even if you are not). If politeness fails, do not feel bad about showing offence and departing. When accepting a social invitation, make sure that someone knows the address and the time you left. Ask if you can bring a friend (even if you do not intend to do so). A good rule is always to act with confidence, as though you know where you are going, even if you do not. Someone who looks lost is more likely to attract unwanted attention. Do not tell strangers where you are staying.

Working/volunteering in South America

If you are seeking more than casual work in any South American country, there will be income tax implications which you should research at the relevant consulate before leaving home. **Voluntary work** falls generally into three main categories: community projects, conservation and teaching. A number of organizations can arrange a 'voluntourism' package for you, in which you will probably have to pay for your airfare and raise money before you go. You will probably be working at grassroots level and conditions may be harsh. But at the same time you will be contributing to the local community or its environment and gaining a new perspective on travelling.

Gap year/career breaks There is some overlap between volunteering and gap year or career break tourism as many people who make this type of trip do some form of work. There is an increasing amount of help for students on a gap year and, in the UK at least, a well-planned and productive gap year can be an advantage when it comes to university and job application. The career-break market is growing fast and there is help online to guide you. Some organizations help from planning to finding something to do; others are quite specific in the type of project or country in which they operate. See www.gapyear.com, www.gap.org.uk and www.yearoutgroup.org. For a range of options, try www.gvi.co.uk (Global Vision International), or www.i-to-i.com. More specific (but not limited to South America) are www.raleigh.org.uk (Raleigh International), www.rainforest concern.org (Rainforest Concern), with environmental projects in Bolivia, Brazil, Chile, Colombia, Ecuador and Peru, www.handsupholidays.com, with projects in Argentina, Brazil and Peru, www.madventurer.com, www.questoverseas.com (Quest Overseas, which also organizes expeditions) and www.thepodsite.co.uk (Personal Overseas Development), with projects in Peru, www.outreachinternational.co.uk (Outreach), with projects in Ecuador, www.teaching-abroad.co.uk, for more than teaching, located in Argentina, Bolivia, Chile and Peru, and www.vso.org.uk (Voluntary Service Overseas), working in Guyana.

An excellent place to start for low and zero-cost volunteer programmes in South America is Steve McElhinney's website, www.volunteersouthamerica.net. In Bolivia, see www.volunteer bolivia.org. In Brazil, there are two websites with information on volunteering: www.portaldo voluntario.org.br and www.voluntarios.com.br, both in Portuguese. Catalytic Communities, www.comcat.org, also has projects in Brazil. In Colombia, Peace Brigades International, www.peacebrigades.org/index.html, which protects human rights and promotes nonviolent transformation of conflicts, employs foreign nationals who often work as human rights monitors and observers. Fluent Spanish is essential. 'Voluntourism' in Ecuador attracts many visitors. Several language schools operate volunteering schemes in conjunction with Spanish classes. Environmental conservation: www.arcoiris.org.ec (Fundación Arcoiris), works with a variety of nature conservation and sustainable community development projects in the far south of the country; www.jatunsacha.org (Fundación Jatun Sacha), has many different sites at which volunteers can work, all in exceptional natural areas; www.fnatura.org (Fundación Natura), a large Ecuadorean NGO, promotes environmental awareness and education. For other options in the continent, contact South American Explorers, see above.

If looking for a paying job, visit the **International Career and Employment Center**, www.internationaljobs.org. To teach in international Baccalaureate (IB) schools, you need to be a qualified subject teacher (primary or secondary level) with one to two years' experience. See www.ibo.org/ for a list of bilingual schools. You don't have to speak Spanish to work in a bilingual school. Most schools offer private health care packages and annual flights home.

Another resource is Vacation Work's www.vacationwork.co.uk, who publish a number of books, including Susan Griffith's *Work your Way around the World*, 12th edition, 2005.

Argentina

Essentials	**64**	Bariloche and around	185
Buenos Aires and the Pampas	**70**	South of Bariloche	193
Sights	72	**Patagonia**	**200**
Around Buenos Aires	98	Ins and outs	200
The Pampas	98	Viedma, Carmen de Patagones	
Atlantic Coast	103	and around	201
West of Buenos Aires	**110**	Puerto Madryn and around	202
Córdoba	110	Trelew and the Chubut Valley	206
Around Córdoba	114	Comodoro Rivadavia and inland	209
Mendoza and around	119	Río Gallegos and around	212
South of Mendoza	125	Ruta 40 to the glaciers	215
Mendoza to Chile	126	Parque Nacional Los Glaciares	217
San Juan and around	129	**Tierra del Fuego**	**225**
La Rioja and Catamarca	133	Ushuaia and around	226
Northwest Argentina	**137**		
Santiago del Estero	137		
Tucumán and around	138		
Cafayate	143		
Salta	146		
Jujuy	152		
Jujuy to the Chilean and			
Bolivian borders	154	**❖ Footprint features**	
The Northeast	**160**		
Up the Río Uruguay	160	Don't miss …	63
Up the Río Paraná	163	Touching down	66
The Chaco	167	Driving in Argentina	68
Misiones	169	Cloud line	148
Iguazú Falls	172	True brew	161
Lake District	**177**	Walks around Bariloche	188
Nuequén and around	177	The Old Patagonian Express	195
Parque Nacional Lanín	179	Keeping up with the Joneses	205
Parque Nacional Nahuel Huapi	182		

Essentials

Planning your trip

The capital, **Buenos Aires**, has a distinctly European feel, its architecture mostly 20th-century, though earlier buildings can be found in San Telmo district. The central docklands have been reclaimed as an upmarket restaurant zone and the Palermo district, with its large parks, has become increasingly popular for eating out. Across the Río de la Plata is Uruguay; just northwest is Tigre, on the Paraná delta, a popular spot for escaping the city; to the southeast are coastal resorts which lead round to the most famous, Mar del Plata. West and south of Buenos Aires stretch the grasslands of the pampas, home of the *gaucho* (cowboy) and large *estancias*.

Through **Northwest Argentina** a string of cities gives access to the Andean foothills and the higher peaks. On the way to the mountains are Córdoba, an important industrial centre close to resorts in the Sierras de Córdoba, and Santiago del Estero, Argentina's oldest city. From Tucumán, surrounded by sugar cane but in view of the Andes, there is a beautiful route through desert foothills around Cafayate and the Valles Calchaquíes to the fine city of Salta. This is the ideal centre for exploring this wonderful part of the country with its remote valleys and high-altitude mining communities. From Salta there are routes to Bolivia, through an area of isolated villages, to Chile over lonely passes and to Paraguay across the Chaco.

In the **Northeast**, the wetlands of Mesopotamia have some interesting wildlife zones, such as the Iberá Marshes, and in Misiones province, sandwiched between Brazil and Paraguay, are ruined Jesuit missions, principally San Ignacio Miní. The highlight of this region are the magnificent Iguazú Falls, usually included on any itinerary to the country.

Back in the Northwest, **Ruta 40** starts its long, frequently remote journey beside the Andes to the far south. Among the many attractions it passes are the city of Mendoza, on the main Buenos Aires-Santiago road, with its vineyards, climbing and skiing centres, and the strange lunar landscapes of San Juan province. It traverses the **Lake District**, renowned for its lovely scenery and good fishing. The main centres are San Martín de los Andes and Bariloche, but there are many smaller places to visit, like Esquel, the terminus of the Old Patagonian Express. From Bariloche and other points, there are crossings to Chile. Ruta 40 continues south to the stunning peaks and glaciers of Los Glaciares national park.

On the Atlantic side of **Patagonia**, a good place to break the journey is Puerto Madryn and the Península Valdés. Here you can see whales, elephant seals and guanaco at close quarters. Just south of here are the Welsh communities of the Chubut Valley and, south again, three areas of petrified forest. Río Gallegos is the most southerly town of any size on the mainland. One road goes west to the most visited part of Los Glaciares, El Calafate, near where the Perito Moreno glacier tumbles into Lago Argentino. Just north of here, El Chaltén at the foot of the jagged FitzRoy massif has some of the most spectacular trekking in the country. This increasingly popular area now forms part of the circuit which includes the Torres del Paine national park in Chile. Beyond Río Gallegos is Tierra del Fuego, shared with Chile; on the Argentine side is what claims to be the southernmost town in the world, Ushuaia, on the shores of the Beagle Channel.

When to go Climate ranges from sub-tropical in the north to cold temperate in Tierra del Fuego. The densely populated central zone is temperate. From mid-December to the end of February, Buenos Aires can be oppressively hot and humid, with temperatures of 27-35°C (80-95°F) and an average humidity of 70%. The city virtually shuts down in late December and early January as people escape on holiday. Autumn can be a good time to visit and spring in Buenos Aires (September-October) is often very pleasant. The Northeast is best visited in winter when it is cooler and drier. Corrientes and Misiones provinces are increasingly wet from September. The winter is also a good time to visit the Northwest, but routes to Chile across the Andes may be closed by snow at this time and spring and autumn may be better: summer rains, especially in Jujuy, can make roads impassable. In the winter (June-August) establishments may close in the far south, transport can be restricted and routes across the Andes to Chile may be blocked by snow. Spring and autumn are the best seasons for visiting the Lake District. Ideally Patagonia should be visited in December or February-April, avoiding the winter months when the weather is cold and many services are closed. There are also school holidays in July when some facilities such as youth hostels may be heavily booked. Note that Bariloche is very popular with for school groups in July and December/early January.

Finding out more The national office of the **Secretaría de Turismo** ① *Av Santa Fe 883, Buenos Aires, T0800-5550016, www.turismo.gov.ar*. For free tourist information anywhere in the country T0800-555 0016 (0800-2000). Addresses of other tourist offices are given in the text. For tourist information abroad, contact Argentine embassies and consulates.

National parks Administración de Parques Nacionales ① *Santa Fe 690, opposite Plaza San Martín, T4311 0303, Mon-Fri 1000-1700*, has leaflets on national parks. Also library **(Biblioteca Perito Moreno)** ① *public Tue-Fri 1000-1300, 1400-1700*. The website **www.patri monionatural.com** has information on Argentina's national parks and monuments.

Tourist offices

Each province has a tourist office, Casa de Provincia, in Buenos Aires, Mon-Fri 1000-1630/1730.
Buenos Aires Province, Av Callao 237, T4371 7046, www.casaprov.gba.gov.ar, www.bue.gov.ar.
Catamarca, Av Córdoba 2080, T/F4374 6891, www.catamarca.gov.ar.
Chaco, Av Callao 322, T4372 5209, www.ecomchaco.com.ar.
Chubut, Sarmiento 1172, T4382 2009, www.chubut.com.ar.
Córdoba, Av Callao 332, T4373 4277, www.cba.gov.ar.
Corrientes, San Martín 333, p 4, T/F4394 2808, www.corrientes.gov.ar.
Entre Ríos, Suipacha 844, T4326 2573, www.turismo.entrerios.gov.ar.
Formosa, Hipólito Yrigoyen 1429, T4381 2037, www.casadeformosa.gov.ar.
Jujuy, Av Santa Fe 967, T4393 6096, www.casadejujuy.gov.ar.
La Pampa, Suipacha 346, T4326 1145, www.turismolapampa.gov.ar.
La Rioja, Av Callao 745, T4815 1929, www.larioja.gov.ar/turismo.
Mar del Plata, Av Corrientes 1660, local 16, T4384 5658, www.mardelplata.gov.ar.
Mendoza, Av Callao 445, T4374 1105, www.mendoza.gov.ar.
Misiones, Santa Fe 989, T4322 1097, www.misiones.gov.ar/turismo.
Municipalidad de la Costa, B Mitre 737, T4394 2330, www.lacostaturismo.com.ar.
Neuquén, Maipú 48, T4343 2324, www.neuquen.gov.ar.
Río Negro, Tucumán 1916, T4371 7078, www.rionegrotur.com.ar.
Salta, Diagonal Norte 933, T4326 2456, www.turismosalta.gov.ar.

San Juan, Sarmiento 1251, T4382 9241, www.sanjuan.gov.ar.
San Luis, Azcuénaga 1083, T5778 1621, www.sanluis.gov.ar.
Santa Cruz, 25 de Mayo 279, T4325 3102, www.epatagonia.gov.ar.
Santa Fé, Montevideo 373, p 2, T5811 4327, www.mercotur.com/santiagodelestero.
Santiago del Estero, Florida 274, T4326 9418, www.mercotur.com/santiagodelestero.
Tierra del Fuego, Sarmiento 745, T4311 0233, www.tierradelfuego.org.ar.
Tucumán, Suipacha 140, T4322 0010, www.tucumanturismo.gov.ar.
 For **Patagonia**, see www.patagonia.com.ar or http://patagonia-argentina.com. For youth hostels, contact **Asatej**, see Useful addresses, page 97.

Websites

www.liveargentina.com Tourist information for the whole country. In several languages.
www.museosargentinos.org.ar/museos Argentina's museums.
http://ar.yahoo.com, www.grippo.com.ar, www.google.com.ar Argentine search engines.
www.terra.com.ar News, entertainment, weather, tourism and Spanish phone directory.
www.mercotour.com Information on travel in Spanish, English and Portuguese.
www.guiaypf.com.ar Site of the YPF fuel company, with travel and tourist information.
www.meteonet.com.ar Useful web site for forecasts and weather satellite images.
www.alojar.com.ar Accommodation search engine and tourist information in Spanish.
www.tageblatt.com.ar *Argentinisches Tageblatt*, German-language weekly, very informative.
www.buenosairesherald.com *Buenos Aires Herald*, English language daily.

Maps Several road maps are available including those of the **ACA** (best and most up-to-date), **Firestone**, and **Automapa**, www.automapa.com.ar (regional maps, Michelin-style, high quality). Topographical maps are issued by the **Instituto Geográfico Militar** ① *Av Cabildo 381, Buenos Aires, T4576 5578 (one block from Subte Ministro Carranza, Line D, or take bus 152), Mon-Fri 0800-1300, www.igm.gov.ar*. 1:500,000 sheets cost US$3 each and are 'years old'; better coverage of 1:100,000 and 1:250,000, but no city plans. Take passport if buying maps. For walkers, the **Sendas y Bosques** series is recommended: 1:200,000, laminated and easy to read, with good books containing English summaries; www.guiasendasybosques.com.ar.

Touching down

Airport taxes US$28 for all flights, payable in pesos, dollars or euros (check with the agent selling your flight ticket if these charges have been included in the price). Montevideo and Punta del Este from Aeroparque are subject to US$14 tax. All internal taxes, US$12, are payable only in pesos when not included in the ticket. When in transit from one international flight to another, you may be obliged to pass through immigration and customs, have your passport stamped and be made to pay an airport tax on departure. There is a 5% tax on the purchase of air tickets.

Business hours Banks, government offices, insurance offices and business houses are not open on Saturday; normal office hours are 0900-1200, 1400-1900. **Banks**: 1000-1500 but time varies according to the city, and sometimes according to the season. **Government offices**: 1230-1930 (winter) and 0730-1300 (summer). **Post offices**: stamps on sale during working days 0800-2000 but 0900-1300 on Saturday. **Shops**: 0900-2000, many close at 1300 on Saturday. Outside the main cities many close for the daily afternoon siesta, reopening at about 1700. 24-hour opening is allowed except on Monday.

In an emergency Police T101. If robbed or attacked, call the tourist police, **Comisaría del Turista**, Av Corrientes 436, Buenos Aires, T011-4346 5748 (24 hrs) or T0800-999 5000, English spoken, turista@policiafederal.gov.ar.

Urgent medical service T107.

International phone code +54. Ringing: equal tones with long pauses. Engaged: equal tones with equal pauses.

Official time GMT -3.

Tipping 10% in restaurants and cafés. Porters and ushers are usually tipped.

VAT/IVA 21%; VAT is not levied on medicines, books and some foodstuffs.

Voltage 220 volts (and 110 too in some hotels), 50 cycles, AC, European Continental-type plugs in old buildings, Australian three-pin flat-type in the new. Adaptors can be purchased locally for either type (ie from new three-pin to old two-pin and vice-versa).

Weights and measures Metric.

Visas and immigration Passports are not required by citizens of South American countries who hold identity cards issued by their own governments. No visa is necessary for British citizens and nationals of western European, Central American and Caribbean countries, plus citizens of Australia, Canada, Croatia, Czech Republic, Hungary, Israel, Japan, Malaysia, New Zealand, Poland, Singapore, Slovenia, South Africa, Turkey and USA, who are given a tourist card ('tarjeta de entrada') on entry and may stay for three months, which can be renewed only once for another three months (fee US$35) at the **Dirección Nacional de Migraciones** ① *Av Antártida Argentina 1365 (Retiro), Buenos Aires, T4312 8663, open 0800-1300*. For all others there are three forms of visa: a tourist visa (multiple entry, valid for three months; onward ticket and proof of adequate funds must be provided; fees vary depending on the country of origin; can be extended 30 days), a business visa (US$35, valid for one year) and a transit visa. If leaving Argentina on a short trip, check on re-entry that border officials look at the correct expiry date on your visa, otherwise they will give only 30 days. Carry your passport at all times; backpackers are often targets for thorough searches – just stay calm; it is illegal not to have identification to hand.

At land borders if you don't need a visa, 90 days' permission to stay is usually given without proof of transportation out of Argentina. Make sure you are given a tourist card, otherwise you will have to obtain one before leaving the country. If you need a 90-day extension for your stay then leave the country (eg at Iguazú), and 90 further days will be given on return. Visa extensions may also be obtained from the address above, ask for 'Prorrogas de Permanencia'. No renewals are given after the expiry date. To authorize an exit stamp if your visa or tourist stamp has expired, go to Dirección Nacional de Migraciones and a 10-day authorization will be given for US$17, providing a proof of transportation out of the country. Alternatively, you can forego all the paperwork by paying a US$50 fine at a border immigration post.

Argentine embassies and consulates Visit www.mrecic.gov.ar for a full list of addresses.

Money The currency is the Argentine peso (ARS or $, we use AR$), divided into 100 centavos. Peso notes in circulation: 2, 5, 10, 20, 50 and 100. Coins in circulation: 1, 5, 10, 25 and 50 centavos and 1 peso. Exchange rate July 2007: US$1 = 3.09 pesos, €1 = 4.2 pesos. Foreigners are advised to use credit cards to withdraw cash, where possible, and for making payments. If paying in cash, do so in pesos because, away from the capital, dollars are often not accepted for fear of forgeries. ATMs (known as *cajeros automáticos*) can be found in every town and city (with the notable exception of El Chaltén in the south). They are usually Banelco or Link, accepting international cards. Changing TCs can involve lengthy bureaucracy and high commission charges, usually 10%. When crossing a land border into Argentina, make sure you have some Argentine currency as there are normally no facilities at the border.

Credit cards American Express, Diners Club, Visa and MasterCard cards are all widely accepted in the major cities and provincial capitals, though less so outside these. There is a high surcharge on credit card transactions in many establishments; many hotels offer reductions for cash. For lost or stolen cards: **MasterCard** T0800-555 0507, **Visa** T4379 3333 (T0810-666 3368 from outside Buenos Aires).

Cost of travelling Budget travellers should allow about US$30 a day for food, accommodation and travel. This takes into account spending time in Patagonia, which is more expensive than the centre and north, and having to stay in hotels on those occasions where there is no hostel. Hotel prices in 2007 started at about US$7-10 pp in uncategorized establishments (US$7-8 pp in a double room), with many good rooms available from US$20-40 pp. Breakfast will cost about US$2-3, while cheap meals range from US$5-8 (US$2-3 for sandwich or pizza). The average cost of internet use is US$1 per hour.

Getting around

Air Internal air services are run by **Aerolíneas Argentinas** (AR) *www.aerolineas.com.ar*, **Austral** (part of AR), **LAN Argentina**, www.lan.com, and the army airline **LADE** (in Patagonia, Buenos Aires and Paraná) *www.lade.com.ar*, which provides a good extended schedule with new Fokker F-28 jets. Some airlines operate during the high season, or are air taxis on a semi-regular schedule. Children under three travel free. **LADE** flights are heavily booked in advance, especially for travel during December and January. It also operates discount tickets: spouse (75%) and children (37.5%). Check in two hours before flight to avoid being 'bumped off' from over-booking. Meals are rarely served on internal flights.

Under the banner **Visit Argentina**, **Aerolíneas Argentinas** sell coupons for **AR/Austral** domestic flights at a reduced rate in conjunction with any international **AR** flight ticket. These fares range from US$25 (some flights from Salta or Mendoza) to US$260 (some flights from Bariloche), plus taxes. The coupon for the first flight must be booked before the international departure and all coupons must be booked within the valid period of the international ticket. Tickets are not refundable, changes of route are not possible but changes of date are free. For children under two years the Visit Argentina fare is 10%. It is unwise to set up too tight a schedule because of delays which may be caused by bad weather. Flights between Buenos Aires and El Calafate are often fully booked two to three weeks ahead, and there may be similar difficulties on the routes to Bariloche and Iguazú. If you are 'wait-listed' they cannot ensure a seat. Reconfirmation at least 24 hours ahead of a flight is essential.

Buenos Aires centre

N

0 metres 100
0 yards 100

Sleeping

Aspen Towers **1** *B3*
Aventura Inn **36** *C4*
BA Stop **34** *D2*
Bisonte Palace **2** *B3*
Castelar **3** *E2*
Che Lagarto **20** *F3*
Colón **4** *C3*
Colonial Youth Hostel **6** *C4*
Crillon **5** *B3*
Dolmen **28** *B3*
Dorá **12** *B3*
El Cachafaz **7** *C3*
El Conquistador **29** *B3*
El Hostal de Granados **33** *F4*
Embajador **8** *B3*
España **9** *E3*
Faena Universe **27** *C5*
Frossard **10** *C4*
Goya **11** *C3*
Hilton **27** *C5*
Hostel-Inn Tango **23** *F3*
Hostel Suites Obelisco **37** *D3*
Kilca Hostel &
  Backpacker **35** *F1*
La Casa de Etty **13** *F1*
La Giralda **14** *D3*
Marbella **15** *E2*
Marriott Plaza **16** *B4*
Milhouse Hostel **17** *E3*
NH City **31** *E4*
O'Rei **18** *C3*
Orly **19** *B4*
Panamericano **12** *C3*
Pestana **30** *B3*
Plaza San Martín
  Suites **32** *B3*
St Nicholas **21** *D1*
Suipacha Inn **22** *C3*
Uruguay **24** *E3*
V&S **25** *C3*
Waldorf **26** *B4*

Eating

Abril **1** *B3*
Aroma **27** *B4*
Broccolino **2** *C3*
Café de la Biblioteca **3** *B2*
Café Tortoni **4** *D3*
Capataz **28** *C3*
Chiquilín **6** *D1*
Clásica y Moderna **29** *B1*
Confitería Ideal **8** *D3*
Desiderio **5** *B3*
El Gato Negro **11** *C1*
El Palacio de la Papa
  Frita **13** *C3/D1*

El Querandí **14** *E4*
Empire Bar **15** *B4*
Exedra **30** *B3*
Florida Garden **16** *B4*
Fratello **31** *C4*
Gianni's **25** *B4/C3*
Gran Victoria **32** *C3*
Güerrín **17** *D2*
La Casona del
  Nonno **18** *C3*
La Chacra **33** *B3*
La Estancia **19** *C3*
La Pipeta **20** *C4*
La Trastienda **35** *E5*
Los Inmortales **22** *C3*
Morizono **23** *B4*
Palacio Español **7** *E3*
Richmond **24** *C4*
Saint Moritz **39** *B3*
Sorrento **36** *C4*
Tancat **34** *B4*
Tomo 1 **26** *C3*

Bars & clubs

Celta Bar **40** *D1*
Druid In **38** *B4*
El Living **41** *B1*
Kilkenny **37** *B4*
La Cigale **42** *C4*
Porto Pirata **38** *B4*
Temple Bar **44** *B3*

Museums

Casa de Gobierno
  (Casa Rosada) &
  Museo de los
  Presidentes **1** *D5*
Museo de Armas **2** *B3*
Museo de Arte
  Hispanoamericano
  Isaac Fernández
  Blanco **3** *A3*
Museo de Arte
  Moderno & Teatro
  General San
  Martín **4** *D1*
Museo de la
  Ciudad **5** *E4*
Museo del Cabildo
  y la Revolución
  de Mayo **6** *E4*
Museo del
  Holocausto **12** *B1*
Museo del Teatro
  Nacional Cervantes **7** *B2*
Museo Etnográfico
  JB Ambrosetti **8** *E4*
Museo Judío **9** *C2*
Museo y Biblioteca
  Mitre **10** *D4*
Museo Nacional
  Ferroviario at Retiro
  Station **11** *A3*

Argentina Buenos Aires Sights

75

donated by the Canadian government. Behind Retiro station is **Museo Nacional Ferroviario** ① *ring the bell, free, Av del Libertador 405, T4318 3343, Mon-Fri 1000-1600, archives 1000-1400, free.* For railway fans: locomotives, machinery, documents of the Argentine system's history, the building is in very poor condition. In a warehouse beside is the workshop of the sculptor Carlos Regazzoni who recycles refuse material from railways.

Museo de Arte Hispanoamericano Isaac Fernández Blanco ① *Suipacha 1422 (3 blocks west of Retiro), T4326 3396, Tue-Sun, 1400-1900, Thu free, US$0.35, for guided visits in English contact Marina at T4327 0272, tours in Spanish Sat, Sun 1500,* is one of the city's best museums. It contains a fascinating collection of colonial art, especially paintings and silver, also temporary exhibitions of Latin American art, in a beautiful neocolonial mansion (Palacio Noel, 1920s) with Spanish gardens; free concerts and tango lessons on Monday and Thursday.

Recoleta and Palermo

Nuestra Señora del Pilar, Junín 1898, is a jewel of colonial architecture dating from 1732 (renovated in later centuries), facing onto the public gardens of Recoleta. A fine wooden image of San Pedro de Alcántara, attributed to the famous 17th-century Spanish sculptor Alonso Cano, is preserved in a side chapel on the left, and there are stunning gold altars. Upstairs is an interesting museum of religious art.

Next to it, the **Cemetery of the Recoleta** ① *entrance at Junín 1790, near Museo de Bellas Artes (see below), T4804 7040, 0700-1800, free tours in Spanish 1100, 1500 (on Tue and Thu 1100 in English), check times as they may change* is one of the sights of Buenos Aires. With its streets and alleys separating family mausoleums built in every imaginable architectural style, La Recoleta is often compared to a miniature city. Among the famous names from Argentine history is Evita Perón who lies in the Duarte family mausoleum: to find it from the entrance go to the first tree-filled plaza; turn left and where this avenue meets a main avenue (go just beyond the Turriaca tomb), turn right; then take the third passage on the left. On Saturday and Sunday there is a good craft market in the park on Plaza Francia outside the cemetery (1100-1800), with street artists and performers. Next to the cemetery, the **Centro Cultural Recoleta** ① *T4803 0358, www.centroculturalrecoleta.org, Tue-Fri 1400-2100, Sat, Sun, holidays 1000-2100, buses 110, 102, 17, 60 (walk from corner of Las Heras y Junín, 2 blocks) from downtown, eg Correo Central, 61/62, 93, 130 to Av del Libertador y Av Pueyrredón,* specializes in contemporary local art. Next door, the Buenos Aires Design Centre has good design and handicraft shops. This area has many good restaurants, recommended for a drink at sunset.

Museo de Bellas Artes (National Gallery) ① *Av del Libertador 1473, T4803 0802, www.mnba.org.ar, Tue-Fri 1230-1930, Sat-Sun 0930-1930, guided tours Tue-Sun 1600, 1700, 1800, tours for children in summer Tue-Fri 1100, 1700, Sat-Sun 1700, free.* This excellent museum gives a taste of Argentine art, as well as a fine collection of European works, particularly post-Impressionist. Superb Argentine 19th and 20th-century paintings, sculpture and wooden carvings; also films, classical music concerts and art courses. **Biblioteca Nacional** (National Library) ① *Av del Libertador 1600 y Agüero 2502, T4806 6155, www.bibnal.edu.ar, Mon-Fri 0900-2000, Sat and Sun 1200-1900, closed Jan.* Housed in a modern building, only a fraction of the extensive stock can be seen. Art gallery, periodical archives; cultural events held. **Museo Nacional de Arte Decorativo** ① *Av del Libertador 1902, T4802 6606, www.mnad.org, Tue-Sun 1400-1900 (Jan-Feb, closed Mon and Sun), US$0.70, guided visits Wed-Fri 1630 (ask in advance for tours in English).* It contains collections of painting, furniture, porcelain, crystal, sculpture exhibited in sumptuous halls, once a family residence.

Palermo Chico is a delightful residential area with several houses of once wealthy families, dating from the early 20th-century. The predominant French style of the district was broken in 1929 by the rationalist lines of the **Casa de la Cultura** ① *Rufino de Elizalde 2831, T4804 0553, Tue-Fri 1500-1900, Sat-Sun 1300-1900.* The original residence of the writer Victoria Ocampo was a gathering place for artists and intellectuals and is now an attractive cultural centre with art exhibitions and occasional concerts.

Museo de Motivos Populares Argentinos José Hernández ① *Av del Libertador 2373, T4802 7294, www.mujose.org.ar, Wed-Sun 1300-1900, US$0.35, free Sun, closed Feb; for guided tours in English call in advance.* The widest collection of Argentine folkloric art, with rooms dedicated to indigenous, colonial and Gaucho artefacts; handicraft shop and library. **Museo de Arte Latinoamericano (MALBA)** ① *Av Figueroa Alcorta 3415, T4808 6500, www.malba.org.ar, daily 1200-1930 (Wed free, open till 2100; Tue closed), US$3.40 (free for ISIC holders), guided tours in Spanish or English can be booked a week in advance,*

Recoleta & Palermo

To Las Cañitas

To Belgrano, Museo Histórico
Sarmiento, Museo de Arte
Español Enrique Larreta &
Museo Casa Yrurtia

To Museo de Artes Plásticas
Eduardo Sívori

Planetarium

To 5, 6, 7, 8

Colombia

Show Grounds

Av Sarmiento

To Aeroparque

Plaza Italia

PALERMO

Japanese
Garden

A Berro

Av Casares

Palermo Parks
(Parque Tres de Febrero)

Botanical
Gardens

Zoological
Gardens

Rep India

Av del Libertador

To Plaza Cortázar, Malas
Artes, Palermo Viejo &
Palermo Restaurants

J M Gutiérrez

La Finur

Cabello

República Árabe Siria

Cervino

E Seguí

Av Casares

Av Pte F Alcorta

Gelly

Cavia

Paseo Alcorta
Shopping Mall

To Aeroparque

To 4

S Ortiz

Av Scalabrini Ortiz

Araoz

Av Gral las Heras

Ugarteche

J M Gutiérrez

Cabello

Cervino

E Seguí

J Salguero

M Coronado

Av Pte F Alcorta

Av Santa Fe

Arenales

Juncal

French

Paunero

S Ruggeri

MALBA

S Martín de Tours

Casros

Ombú

Juez Pedro

J Álvarez

Bulnes

Museo de Motivos
Populares
Argentinos
José Hernández

Av Ocampo

Aguado

Elizalde

M R Castilla

Estrada

Sevilla

J Salguero

Vidt

Bulnes

Bulnes

Av Cnel Diaz

Pacheco de Melo

Peña

Tagle

Guise-An

Alto Palermo
Shopping Mall

Billinghurst

S de Bustamante

Bollini

Museo
Nacional
de Arte
Decorativo

P Lucena

V López

Austria

Austria

Aguero

Arenales

Berutti

Juncal

French

Aguero

Av Gral las Heras

Coper

Galileo

Gelly y Obés

Guido

Biblioteca
Nacional

Libres del Sur

Bibiloni

RECOLETA

Laprida

Anchorena

Gutiérrez

Guemes

Dr Agote

Av del Libertador

Museo de
Bellas Artes

Ecuador

Barrientos

Cantilo

Vicente López

Av Pte F Alcorta

González

Pueyrredón

Av Pueyrredón

Av Pueyrredón

Leven

Mansilla

Larrea

Azcuénaga

Centro
Cultural
Recoleta

Buenos Aires
Design Centre

Marcelo T de Alvear

Pte J E Uriburu

Peña

Pte de Melo

Junín

Cemetery
of the
Recoleta

Nuestra
Señora
del Pilar

Palais
de Glace

R M Ortiz

Quintana

Av Alvear

Schiafino

To Retiro Station & City Centre

Facultad de
Medicina

Av Santa Fe

Charcas

Paraguay

Juncal

Arenales

Ayacucho

Av Callao

Rodríguez Peña

Patio
Bullrich
Shopping
Centre

Posadas

Av del Libertador

Viamonte

Río Bamba

Av Córdoba

Ayacucho

Paraguay

Plaza R Peña

Plaza V
López

Montevideo

Parera

Av Quintana

Libertad

Juncal

Tucuman

Callao

Rodríguez Peña

Montevideo

Paraná

Uruguay

Arenales

Arroyo

Cerrito

A

C Pelegrini

Av 9 de Julio

Argentina Buenos Aires Sights

0 metres 200
0 yards 200

N

Sleeping
Alvear Palace **1**
Art **6**
Bo Bo **7**

Che Lulu **8**
Etoile **2**
Four Seasons **3**
Malabia House **4**
Tango Backpackers Hostel **5**

Eating
Café Victoria **1**
El Mirasol **8**

El Sanjuanino **7**
Ice Cream Freddo **2**
Juana M **15**
La Cabaña **20**
La Madeleine **10**
La Tasca de Plaza Mayor **8**
Lola & Buller Brewing
  Company **4**
Milion **3**

Notorious **19**
Persicco **5**
Piegari **8**
Rodi Bar **6**
Shamrock **21**
Sirop **14**
Un' Altra Volta **16**
Winery **12**

old house attractively restored with all the usual facilities of any hostel. In Congreso district, not too far from the centre, 15 blocks west of San Telmo, but having its own barrio life. Good for stays of a week or so. There is a dorm for girls only and rooms with private bath (**C**).

F pp **El Cachafaz**, Viamonte 982, T4328 1445, www.elcachafaz.com. A renovated old house, central with dorms and **D** double rooms, breakfast and free internet access, laundry facilities.

F-G pp **Hostel Aguila**, Espinosa 1628, T4581 6663, www.delaguilahostel.com. Good value, owned by a tango teacher (free classes), welcoming, large terrace. Free transfers to/from transport terminals. Far from centre, by corner of San Martín and Juan B Justo, where the areas of Caballito, Villa Crespo and Paternal meet (buses 24, 34, 57, 109, 110).

Palermo *p76, map p77*

L-B La Otra Orilla, Julián Alvarez 1779, Palermo Viejo, T4867 4070, www.otraorilla.com.ar. Homely, quiet, French-style 1930s residence with seven very different rooms, from a great suite to a cute single. Some have a balcony or street views, others are more secluded. The patio is delightful for having breakfast in summer. Very good value.

AL Malabia House, Malabia 1555, Palermo Viejo, T4833 2410, www.malabiahouse.com.ar. Elegant but expensive B&B with individually designed bedrooms and calm sitting rooms, great breakfast, reliable and welcoming. Recommended.

AL-A Bo Bo, Guatemala 4882, T4774 0505, www.bobohotel.com. On a leafy street, 7 rooms decorated in contemporary style, some with with private balconies, excellent restaurant.

C Che Lulu, Emilio Zola 5185, T4772 0289, www.chelulu.com. Some double rooms and more hostel-style accommodation in this rambling, laid-back house on a quiet quaint street just a few blocks from Palermo subte. Not luxurious, but great value and very welcoming. Often recommended.

Youth hostels

F pp **Casa Esmeralda**, Honduras 5765, T4772 2446, www.casaesmeralda.com.ar. Laid-back, dorms and **D** doubles, neat garden with hammocks and pond. Sebastián, offers basic comfort with great charm.

F pp **Tango Backpackers Hostel**, Paraguay 4601, T4776 6871, www.tangobp.com. Well situated for Palermo's nightlife, lots of activities, free internet access and Wi-Fi, open terrace with outdoor showers. HI discount.

San Telmo and around *p79, maps p74 and p83*

A Mansión Dandi Royal, Piedras 922, T4307 7623, www.hotelmansiondandiroyal.com. A wonderfully restored 1903 residence, small upmarket hotel with an elegant tango atmosphere, small pool, good value. Daily tango lessons and *milonga* every Wed.

C La Casita de San Telmo, Cochabamba 286 T/F4307 5073, www.lacasitadesantelmo.com. 7 rooms in restored 1840's house, most open onto a garden with a beautiful fig tree, owners are tango fans; rooms rented by day, week or month.

D Victoria, Chacabuco 726, T/F4361 2135. Rooms with bath, fan, kitchen and laundry facilities.

Youth hostels

E-F pp **Kilca Hostel & Backpacker**, Mexico 1545, between Saenz Peña and Virrey Cevallos, T4381 1966, www.kilcabackpacker.com. Lovingly restored 19th-century house with very attractive landscaped patios. The 5 rooms can be shared by up to 6, or used as a double. Wi-Fi, breakfast included.

F pp **El Hostal de Granados**, Chile 374, T43625600, www.hostaldegranados.com.ar. Small, light, well-equipped rooms in an interesting building on a popular street, rooms for 2 (**D**) to 4, with bath, breakfast included, kitchen, free internet, laundry.

F pp **Hostel-Inn Buenos Aires**, Humberto Primo 820, T4300 7992, www.hibuenosaires.com. An old 2-storey mansion with an outdoors terrace, activities, free internet and wifi, breakfast included and individual lockers in every room. HI discount.

F pp **Hostel-Inn Tango City**, Piedras 680, T4300 5764, www.hitangocity.com. Well organized in renovated house, popular, lively, lots of activities, breakfast, free internet access and Wi-Fi. HI discount.
F pp **Sandanzas**, Balcarce 1351, T4300 7375, www.sandanzas.com.ar. Arty hostel run by a group of friends. Small but with a light airy feel, D in double with bath, lounge and patio, free internet, breakfast and use of bikes, DVDs, kitchen.

Homestays and student residences
Argentina B&B, www.argentinabandb.com.ar. Arranges reliable accommodation with host families in Buenos Aires and other towns; rooms from US$40 per night. Many hosts speak English.
B&T Argentina, T4821 6057, www.bytarg entina.com. Accommodation in student residences and host families; also furnished flats.
La Casa de Etty, Luis Sáenz Peña 617, T4384 6378, coret@ciudad.com.ar. Run by Esther Corcias, manager of **Organización Coret**, www.angel fire.com/pq/coret. Host families or furnished flats.

Apartments/self catering
Apartments cost from US$40 per night.
Bahouse, T4815 7602, www.bahouse.com.ar. Very good flats, all furnished and well-located in Retiro, Recoleta, Belgrano, Palermo and the centre.
Tu Casa Argentina, Esmeralda 980, p 2B, T4312 4127, www.tucasargentina.com. Furnished flats by the day, week, month (from US$400 per month).

⑦ Eating

Eating out in Buenos Aires is one of the city's great pleasures, with a huge variety of restaurants from the chic to the cheap. To try some of Argentina's excellent steak, choose from one of the many *parrillas*, where your huge slab of lean meat will be expertly cooked over a wood fire. If in doubt about where to eat, head for Puerto Madero, where there are lots of good places serving international as well as local cuisine. In many mid- to upper-range restaurants, lunch is far cheaper than dinner. A portion at a *comidas para llevar* (take away) place costs US$2-3. Many cheaper restaurants are *tenedor libre*: eat as much as you like for a fixed price. Most cafés serve tea or coffee plus *facturas*, or pastries, for breakfast, US$0.80-1.20.

Retiro, and the area between Plaza de Mayo and Plaza San Martín
p72, map p74
¶¶¶ **La Chacra**, Av Córdoba 941 (just off 9 de Julio). A superb traditional *parrilla* with excellent steaks (US$16 for parrilla and salads for 2), impeccable old-fashioned service, lively atmosphere.
¶¶¶ **Morizono**, Reconquista 899. Japanese sushi and sashami, as well as other dishes.
¶¶¶ **Sorrento**, Corrientes 668 (just off Florida). Intimate, elegant atmosphere, traditional menu with good fish dishes and steak.

San Telmo

Sleeping ⊖
El Hostal de Granados **7**
Garden House **8**
Hostel-Inn Buenos Aires **2**
La Casita de San Telmo **3**
Mansión Dandi Royal **4**
Sandanzas **5**

Victoria **6**

Eating ⑦
El Desnivel **1**
La Brigada **3**
La Casa de Esteban de Luca **2**

La Vieja Rotiseria **4**
Lezama **6**
Mi Tío **8**

Bars & clubs ⑦
Boquitas Pintadas **5**

83

♥♥♥ **Tomo 1**, Panamericano Hotel, Carlos Pellegrini 521, T4326 6695. Argentine regional dishes and international cuisine of a high standard in a sophisticated atmosphere. Very expensive.

♥♥ **Broccolino**, Esmeralda 776. Good Italian food, very popular, try *pechuguitas*.

♥♥ **Chiquilín**, Sarmiento 1599. *Parrilla* and pasta, good value.

♥♥ **El Palacio de la Papa Frita**, Lavalle 735 and 954, Corrientes 1620. Great place for a filling feed, with a large menu, and quite atmospheric, despite the bright lighting.

♥♥ **El Querandí**, Perú 302 y Moreno. Good food in an intimate atmosphere in this place that was opened in the 1920s. Popular café, lively, well known for its Gin Fizz, now a tango venue, too.

♥♥ **Empire Bar**, Tres Sargentos 427. Serves Thai food in a tasteful atmosphere.

♥♥ **Fratello**, Tucumán 688. Pastas and other Italian dishes in attractive Italian-style surroundings.

♥♥ **La Estancia**, Lavalle 941. A slightly touristy but reliable *parrilla*, popular with business people at lunchtime, good grills, US$14 for 2.

♥♥ **La Pipeta**, San Martín 498. Downstairs, a traditional place, established 40 years, for good food in a noisy atmosphere, closed Sun.

♥♥ **Los Inmortales**, Lavalle 746. Specializes in pizza, tasty and good value, great salads, good service.

♥♥ **Palacio Español** at the Club Español, B de Irigoyen 180 (on Av 9 de Julio, near Av de Mayo). Luxurious ambience in a fine building, recommended for a quiet dinner, with very good food, basically Spanish dishes.

♥♥ **Tancat**, Paraguay 645. Delicious Spanish food.

♥ **Abril**, Suipacha y Arenales. Very good pasta; best choice of its category in the area.

♥ **Capataz**, Maipú 529, T4326 6086. Argentine food, *empanadas* and steak and vegetables on the *parrilla*, in a bright trendy atmosphere, good value. Delivers to home or hostel. Recommended.

♥ **Exedra**, Carlos Pellegrini and Córdoba. A welcoming traditional café right on Av 9 de Julio, set menu US$5-8, with a glass of wine.

♥ **Gianni´s**, Viamonte 834 and 25 de Mayo 757 (open 0900-1700). The set menu with the meal-of-the-day makes an ideal lunch in a renovated old house. Good Risottos and salads.

♥ **Gran Victoria**, Suipacha 783. Good value *tenedor libre*, including parrilla, in a cheery atmosphere, also cheap set meals.

♥ **Güerrín**, Corrientes 1368. A Buenos Aires institution. Serves incredibly cheap and filling pizza and *faina* (chick pea polenta) which you eat standing up at a bar, or at tables, though you miss out on the colourful local life that way. Wonderful.

♥ **La Casona del Nonno**, Lavalle 827. Popular with tourists for its cheap set price menu, Italian-style food, cheap pastas and *parrilla*.
Tea rooms, café-bars and ice cream

Cafés

Aroma, Florida y M T de Alvear. A great place to relax, with a huge space upstairs, comfortable chairs for watching the world go by.

Café de la Biblioteca, M T de Alvear 1155 (Asociación Biblioteca de Mujeres). Coffee and light snacks, evening shows.

Café Tortoni, Av de Mayo 825-9. This most famous Buenos Aires café has been the elegant haunt of artists and writers for over 100 years, with marble columns, stained glass ceilings, old leather chairs, and photographs of its famous clientele on the walls. Excellent coffee and cakes, good tea, excellent tango, live jazz in evenings, all rather pricey, but worth a visit.

Clásica y Moderna, Callao 892. One of the city's most welcoming cafés, with a bookshop, great atmosphere, good breakfast through to drinks at night, live music Thu-Sat. Highly recommended.

Confitería Ideal, Suipacha 384. One of the most atmospheric cafés in the city. Wonderfully old-fashioned 1930's interior, serving good coffee and excellent cakes with good service. Upstairs, tango is taught and there's tango dancing at a *milonga* here. Highly recommended.

Desiderio, Av Santa Fe y Esmeralda. Good coffee and drinks, in a nice, though noisy corner on plaza San Martín.

El Gato Negro, Av Corrientes 1669. An old pharmacy, serving a choice of coffees and teas, and good cakes. Wide range of spices on sale.

Florida Garden, Florida y Paraguay. Another well-known café, popular for lunch, and tea.

Munchi's, Florida y MT de Alvear. New ice cream vendors in the centre where Italian tradition has been marked for decades by 'heladerías' such as **Cadore**, Av Corrientes 1695 or **El Vesuvio**, Av Corrientes 1181, the oldest of all.

Richmond, Florida 468, between Lavalle and Corrientes. Genteel, old fashioned and charming place for tea with cakes, and a basement where chess is played between 1200-2400 daily.

Saint Moritz, Esmeralda y Paraguay. Original late 1950s decor with a particularly calm atmosphere on a very busy corner.

La Recova *map p77*

Three blocks west of Plaza San Martín, under the flyover at the northern end of Av 9 de Julio, between Arroyo and Av del Libertador, are several recommended restaurants.

♥♥♥ **El Mirasol**, Posadas 1032. Serves top quality parrilla in an elegant atmosphere.

♥♥♥ **Piegari**, Posadas 1042. Great for Italian food.

♥♥♥ **La Tasca de Plaza Mayor**, Posadas 1052. Good Spanish food.

♥♥ **Juana M**, Carlos Pellegrini 1535 (downstairs). Excellent choice, popular with locals for its good range of dishes, and very good salads.

♟ **Winery**, Paseo La Recova, off Libertador 500. A chic wine bar where you can sample the best of Argentina's fine wines, light dishes such as salads and gourmet sandwiches. Also at Av Alem 880.

Recoleta *p76, map p77*
♟♟♟ **La Cabaña**, Rodríguez Peña 1967, T4814 0001, www.lacabanabuenosaires.com.ar. Historic steak-house, recreated by Orient-Express, classic beef and new cuisine, also offers cookery classes. Very elegant; connected to new Duhau-Hyatt Hotel.
♟♟♟ **Lola**, Roberto M Ortiz 1805. Well known for superb pasta dishes, lamb and fish.
♟♟♟ **Prima Fila**, Av Pueyrredón y Av del Libertador (inside Buenos Aires Design Mall), T4804 0055. Refined place for very good Italian-style food, also tables outside on a terrace by the park.
♟♟♟ **Sirop**, Pasaje del Correo, Vte Lopez 1661, T4813 5900. Delightful chic design, delicious French-inspired food, superb patisserie too. Highly recommended.
♟♟ **El Sanjuanino**, Posadas 1515. Atmospheric place offering typical dishes from the northwest: *humitas, tamales,* and *empanadas,* as well as unusual game dishes.
♟♟ **Rodi Bar**, Vicente López 1900. Excellent *bife* and other dishes in this typical *bodegón,* welcoming and unpretentious.
♟ **La Madeleine**, Av Santa Fe 1726. Great for cheap and delicious pastas, bright and cheerful, open 24 hrs. Recommended.

Tea rooms, café-bars and ice cream
Café Victoria, Roberto M Ortiz 1865. Wonderful old-fashioned café, popular and refined, great cakes.
Ice Cream Freddo, Pacheco de Melo y Callao, Ayacucho y Quintana, Arenales y Callao, Roberto M Ortiz y Guido and at shopping malls. Known for the best ice cream.
Milion, Paraná 1048. Stylish bar and café in an elegant mansion with marble stairs and a garden, young and cool clientèle.
Un'Altra Volta, Santa Fe y Callao. Great ice creams too. Try delicious mascarpone.

San Telmo *p79, maps p74 and p83*
There are many restaurants along C Defensa, and in the surrounding streets.
♟♟♟ **La Brigada**, Estados Unidos 461, T4361 5557. Atmospheric *parrilla,* serving excellent Argentine cuisine and wines. Very popular, not cheap, but recommended. Always reserve.
♟♟ **La Casa de Esteban de Luca**, Defensa 1000. *Parrilla* and pastas in a lively café atmosphere, attentive service, good.
♟ **El Desnivel**, Defensa 855. Popular for cheap, basic food, packed at weekends, good atmosphere.
♟ **La Trastienda**, Balcarce 460. Theatre café with lots of live events, also serving meals and drinks

from breakfast to dinner, great music, relaxed and cool, but busy lunchtime. Recommended.
♟ **La Vieja Rotiseria**, Defensa 963. Cheap café with bargain *parrilla,* packed at weekends, so go early.
♟ **Lezama**, Brasil 359 (on Parque Lezama). A typical *bodegón,* popular with families, typical Argentine menu, huge portions, service is rather slow.
♟ **Mi Tío**, Defensa 900. A small pizza place, beloved by San Telmo locals.

Puerto Madero *p79*
The revamped docks area is an attractive place to eat, and to stroll along the waterfront before dinner. There are many good places here, generally in stylish interiors and with good service: along Av Alicia Moreau de Justo (from north to south), these are recommended.
♟♟♟ **Bice**, No 192, T4315 6216. Italian-influenced, traditional pastas with Argentine meat and fish.
♟♟♟ **El Mirasol del Puerto**, No 202. well known and loved for a broad menu.
♟♟♟ **Katrine**, No 138. Delicious fish and pasta.
♟♟♟ **Las Lilas**, No 516. Excellent *parrilla,* popular with tourists.
♟♟♟ **La Parolaccia**, Nos 1052 and 1170. Pasta and seafood, executive lunch US$8 Mon-Fri, popular.
♟♟ **Siga La Vaca**, Av Alicia Moreau de Justo 1714, T4315 6801. Huge variety of meats, tenedor libre, price includes wine, good desserts.
♟ The cheapest places are next to the boat, **Fragata Sarmiento** on Dique 3.

Palermo *p76, map p77*
This area of Buenos Aires is very popular, with many chic restaurants and bars in Palermo Viejo (referred to as 'Palermo Soho' for the area next to Plaza Cortázar and 'Palermo Hollywood' for the area beyond the railways and Av Juan B Justo) and the Las Cañitas district (see below). It's a sprawling district, so you could take a taxi to one of these restaurants, and walk around before deciding where to eat. It's also a great place to stop for lunch, with cobbled streets, and 1900s buildings, now housing chic clothes shops.
♟♟♟ **Dominga**, Honduras 5618, T4771 4443, www.domingarestaurant.com. Elegant, excellent Asian influenced food, professional service, good wine list, ideal for a romantic evening or treat, lunch Mon-Fri US$7, closed Sun.
♟♟♟ **Lomo**, Costa Rica 4661, T4833 3200. The best steak in Palermo, very stylish.
♟♟ **Bio**, Humboldt 2199, T4774 3880. Delicious gourmet oragnic food, on a sunny corner, open daily, but closed Mon for dinner.
♟♟ **Cluny**, El Salvador 4618, T4831 7176. Very classy, a great place for lunch, fish and pasta with great sauces, mellow music.
♟♟ **El Manto**, Costa Rica 5801, T4774 2409. Genuine Armenian dishes, relaxed, good for a quiet evening.

♥♥ **El Preferido de Palermo**, Serrano y Guatemala, T4778 7101. Excellent for fish and seafood, very popular.

♥♥ **Eterna Cadencia**, Honduras 5574, T4774 4100. A small bookshop with a café which is perfect for lunch, open 0900-2400, closed Mon.

♥♥ **Janio**, Malabia 1805, T4833 6540. One of Palermo's first restaurants, open for breakfast through to the early hours, lunch US$5, sophisticated Argentine cuisine in the evening.

♥♥ **Omm**, Honduras 5656, T4774 4224. Cosy wine and tapas bar with good food, open from 1800. Also **Omm Carnes**, Costa Rica 5198, T4773 0954, for meat dishes and steak, open from 1100, closed Mon evening.

♥♥ **Social Paraíso**, Honduras 5182. Simple delicious dishes in a relaxed chic atmosphere, with a lovely patio at the back. Good fish and tasty salads.

Tea rooms, café-bars and ice cream

Palermo has good cafés opposite the park on Av del Libertador, including the fabulous ice creams at **Un'Altra Volta**, Av del Libertador 3060 (another branch at Echeverría 2302, Belgrano). **Persicco**, Salguero y Cabello, Maure y Migueletes and Av Rivadavia 4933 (Caballito). The grandsons of **Freddo**'s founders also offer excellent ice cream.

Las Cañitas p76, map p77

This area of Palermo is fashionable for a wide range of interesting restaurants mostly along C Baez, and most opening at around 2000, though only open for lunch at weekends:

♥♥♥ **Baez**, Baez 240. Very trendy, with lots of orange neon, serving sophisticated Italian-style food.

♥♥ **Campo Bravo**, Baez y Arevalo. Stylish, minimalist, superb steaks and vegetables on the *parrilla*. Popular and recommended.

♥♥ **De la Ostia**, Baez 212. A small, chic bistro for tapas and Spanish-style food, good atmosphere.

♥♥ **Eh! Santino**, Baez 194. Trendy, small, Italian-style food, dark and cosy with lots of mirrors.

♥♥ **Morelia**, Baez 260. Cooks superb pizzas on the *parrilla* or in wood ovens, and has a lovely roof terrace for summer.

♥♥ **Novecento**, across the road from De la Ostia. A lively French-style bistro, stylish but unpretentious and cosy, good fish dishes among a broad menu.

♥ **El Primo**, opposite corner from **Campo Bravo**. A popular *parrilla* for slightly older crowd. Cheap set menus in a relaxed atmosphere with fairy lights.

Cheap eats

For quick cheap snacks the markets are recommended. Also huge choice in basement of **Galerías Pacífico**, Florida y Viamonte. Some supermarkets have good, cheap restaurants: **Coto** supermarket, Viamonte y Paraná, upstairs. Many supermarkets have very good deli counters and

other shops sell *fiambres* (smoked, cured meats) and cheeses for quick, cheap eating. Good snacks all day and night at **Retiro and Constitución** railway termini. The snack bars in underground stations are also cheap. **Delicity** bakeries, several branches, have very fresh *facturas* (pastries), cakes, breads, and American donuts. Another good bakery for breakfasts and salads is **Bonpler**, Florida 481, 0730-2300, with the daily papers, classical music. Other branches throughout the city.

🟠 Bars and clubs

Generally it is not worth going to clubs before 0230 at weekends. Dress is usually smart.

Bars

Boquitas Pintadas, Estados Unidos 1393 (Constitución), T4381 6064. Bar and hotel.

Buller Brewing Company, Roberto M Ortiz 1827 (Recoleta). Brew pub. Happy hour till 2100.

La Cigale, 25 de Mayo 722, T4312 8275. Popular after office hours, good music, guest DJs on Tue.

Irish pubs abound. St Patrick's Day, 17 Mar, has become a new reason to celebrate, especially in the pub district (corner of Reconquista and MT de Alvear). **Celta Bar**, Rodríguez Peña y Sarmiento. **Druid Inn**, Reconquista 1040. Live music weekly, English spoken, good for lunch. **The Kilkenny**, MT de Alvear 399 esq Reconquista. Open 1730-0600 (Sat 2000-0600), happy hour 1800-2000, popular. **Porto Pirata**, next to Druid Inn. **The Shamrock**, Rodríguez Peña 1220. Irish-run, popular, happy hour 1800-2400. **The Temple Bar**, MT de Alvear 945.

There are good bars in San Telmo around Plaza Dorrego.

In Palermo Viejo, live music usually begins 2330-2400. Las Cañitas is best on Thu night; not so appealing at weekends. Good and popular are: **Bar 6**, Armenia 1676, T4833 6807, chic modern bar, good lunches, friendly atmosphere, closed Sun. **Mundo Bizarro**, Guatemala 4802, shows bizarre films on big screen, American-style food, electronic music Fri-Sat, 1960s and 1980s the rest of the week.

Clubs

El Living, M T de Alvear 1540, T4811 4730. Relaxed bar and small club.

Maluco Beleza, Sarmiento 1728. Brazilian flavour, entertaining, popular.

Niceto Club and **Club 69**, Niceto Vega 5510, T4779 9396, www.nicetoclub.com, www.club69.com.ar. Early live shows and funk or electronic music for dancing afterwards.

Pacha, Av Costanera Rafael Obligado y Pampa, T4788 4280. Electronic music.

Opera Bay, Cecilia Grierson 225 (Puerto Madero, on dock 4), www.operabay.com. Best on Wed after office hours and Fri-Sat after 0200.

Camping equipment

Good equipment from **Buenos Aires Sports**, Panamericana y Paraná, Martínez (Shopping Unicenter, 2nd level). **Eurocamping**, Paraná 761. **Fugate** (no sign), Gascón 238 (off Rivadavia 4000 block), T4982 0203. Also repairs equipment. **Outside Mountain Equipment**, Otero 172 (Chacarita), T4856 6204, www.outside.com.ar. Camping gas available at **Britam**, B Mitre 1111, **Todo Gas**, Sarmiento 1540, and **El Pescador**, Paraguay y Libertad. **Cacique Camping**, Esteban Echeverría 3360, Munro, T4762 4475, caciquenet@ciudad.com.ar. Manufactured clothing and equipment. **Ecrin**, Mendoza 1679, T4784 4799, www.ecrin.com.ar. Imported climbing equipment. **Angel Baraldo**, Av Belgrano 270, www.baraldo.com.ar. Imported and national stock. **Montagne**, Florida 719, Paraná 834, www.montagneoutdoors.com.ar, and **Camping Center**, Esmeralda 945, www.camping-center.com.ar. Good selection of outdoor sports articles. **Costanera Uno**, at the southern end of Costanera Norte, 4312 4545, www.costanerauno.com.ar. For nautical sports, very good. GPS repair service, **Jorge Gallo**, Liniers 1522, Tigre, T4731 0323.

Handicrafts

Alhué, Juncal 1625. Very good aboriginal-style crafts. **Arte y Esperanza**, Balcarce 234. Crafts made by aboriginal communities, sold by a Fair Trade organization. **Artesanías Argentinas**, Montevideo 1386. Aboriginal crafts and other traditional items. **El Boyero**, Galería Larreta, Florida 953, T4312 3564. High quality silver, leather, woodwork and other typical Argentine handicrafts. **Martín Fierro**, Santa Fe 992. Good handicrafts, stonework etc. Recommended. **Plata Nativa**, Galería del Sol, Florida 860, local 41. For Latin American folk handicrafts; **Puna**, **Arte Indígena**, Galería Promenade Alvear, Av Alvear 1883, local 41, T4801 6589. Authentic hand-woven pure llama wool rugs and carpets made by Northwest Argentina aboriginal communities. Also delicate handmade silver jewellery, pottery and wooden gifts from Bolivia and Argentine Puna region.

Leather goods

Several shops are concentrated along Florida next to Plaza San Martín and also in Suipacha (900 block). **Aida**, Galería de la Flor, local 30, Florida 670. Quality, inexpensive leather products, can make a leather jacket to measure in the same day. **All Horses**, Suipacha 1350. Quality leather clothing. **Campanera Dalla Fontana**, Reconquista 735. Leather factory, fast, efficient and reasonably priced for made-to-measure clothes. **Casa López**, MT de Alvear 640/658. The most traditional and finest leather shop, expensive but worth it. **Fortín**, Santa Fe 1245. Excellent items. **Galería del Caminante**, Florida 844. Has a variety of good shops with leather goods, arts and crafts, souvenirs, etc. **King's Game**, Maipú 984. Another good shop. **La Curtiembre**, Juncal 1173, Paraguay 670. Affordable prices for good quality articles. **Prüne**, Florida 963. Fashionable designs, many options in leather and not very expensive. **Uma**, in shopping malls and at Honduras 5225 (Palermo Viejo). The trendiest of all.

Markets

Caminito, Vuelta de Rocha (Boca), 1000-1700. Plastic arts and local crafts. **Costanera Sur**, next to the Fuente de las Nereidas. Weekends 1100-2000. Crafts, books, coins, stamps. **Feria Hippie**, in Recoleta, near cemetery. Big craft and jewellery market, Sat and Sun 1000-2200, good street atmosphere, expensive. **Feria de Mataderos**, Lisandro de la Torre y Av de los Corrales 6436, T4687 1949, subte E to end of line then taxi (US$3.50), or buses 36, 92, 97, 126, 141. Long way but few tourists, fair of Argentine handicrafts and traditions, music and dance festivals, gaucho horsemanship skills, every Sun 1200-1800 (Sat 1800-2400 in summer); nearby *Museo de los Corrales*, Av de los Corrales 6436, T4687 1949, Sun 1200-1800 (in summer, Sat 1800-2300), US$0.35. **Mercado de las Luces**, Manzana de las Luces, Perú y Alsina, Mon-Fri 1100-1900, Sun 1400-1900. Handicrafts, second-hand books, plastic arts. **Parque Centenario**, Díaz Vélez y L Marechal. Sat market, 1000-2200, local crafts, cheap handmade clothes, used items of all sorts. **Parque Lezama**, Brasil y Defensa, San Telmo. Handicraft market at weekends, 1000-2200. **Parque Rivadavia**, Av Rivadavia 4900. Second-hand books and magazines (daily), records, tapes, Cds and coins (Sun 0900-1400, under a big ombú tree). **Plaza Belgrano**, near Belgrano Barrancas station on Juramento, between Cuba y Obligado. Sat-Sun, 1000-2200 craft, jewellery, etc market. **Plaza Dorrego**, San Telmo. For souvenirs, antiques, etc, with free tango performances and live music, Sun 1000-1700, wonderfully atmospheric, and interesting array of 'antiques'. **Plaza Italia**, Santa Fe y Uriarte (Palermo). Second hand textbooks and magazines (daily), handicrafts market on Sat-Sun 1000-2200.

Shopping malls

Abasto de Buenos Aires, Av Corrientes 3247, T4959 3400. In the former city's fruit and vegetable market building: cheaper clothes, good choice, cinemas. **Alto Palermo**, Col Díaz y Santa Fe, T5777 8000, nearest Subte: opposite Bulnes, line D. Great for all the main clothes chain stores, and about 10 blocks' walk from Palermo's boutiques.

Urban biking, Moliere 2801 (Villa Devoto), T4568 4321, www.urbanbiking.com. 4-hr tours starting next to the English clock tower in Retiro, US$24. Night city tours, US$18, tours to San Isidro and Tigre, US$33, or the pampas. Also rents bikes. **What's Up BA**, www.wubatourism.com. For a wide variety of cultural experiences around the city, including finding accommodation.

⊙ Transport

Air

Ezeiza (officially Ministro Pistarini, T5480 6111, www.aa2000.com.ar), the international airport, is 35 km southwest of the centre (also handles domestic flights to El Calafate and Ushuaia in high season). The airport has 2 terminals: 'A' for all airlines except **Aerolíneas Argentinas**, which uses 'B'. 'A' has a very modern check-in hall. There are duty free shops (expensive), exchange facilities (**Banco de la Nación; Banco Piano; Global Exchange** – rates of exchange in baggage reclaim are poorer than elsewhere) and ATMs (Visa and MasterCard), post office (open 0800-2000) and a left luggage office (US$2 per piece). No hotels nearby. There is a **Devolución IVA/Tax Free** desk (return of VAT) for purchases over the value of AR$90/US$100 (ask for a TAX FREE refund form at the shop when you buy). Reports of pilfering from luggage. To discourage this have your bags sealed by Secure Bag in the check-in hall. Hotel booking service at Tourist Information desk – helpful, but prices are higher if booked in this way. A display in immigration shows choices and prices of transport into the city.

Airport buses Special buses to/from the centre are run by **Manuel Tienda León** (office in front of you as you arrive), company office and terminal at Av Madero 1299 y San Martín, behind Sheraton Hotel in Retiro, T4315 5115, www.tiendaleon.com. To **Ezeiza**: 0400, 0500, then every 30 mins till 2100 and 2200, 2230 (be 15 mins early); from Ezeiza: 0600-2400 regular buses, then also for night arrivals, US$8.50 (US$15 return), 40-min journey, pay by pesos, dollars, euros or credit card. **Manuel Tienda León** will also collect passengers from addresses in centre for US$0.35 extra, book the previous day. Bus from Ezeiza to Aeroparque, 1 hr, US$8.50. Remise taxis to town or to Aeroparque, US$24. Services on request with **Transfer Express**, T0800-444 4872, reservas@transfer-express.com.ar, airport office in front of you as you arrive, remise taxi from Ezeiza to town or to Aeroparque, US$23. **Aeroparque** (Jorge Newbery Airport), 4 km north of the centre, T4576 5111, www.aa2000.com.ar, handles all internal flights, and **AR** and **Pluna** flights to Montevideo and Punta del Este. The terminal is divided into 2 sections, 'A' for all arrivals and **AR/Austral** and **LAN** check-in desks, 'B' for **Pluna** and **LADE** check-in desks. On the 1st floor

there is a **patio de comidas**, many shops and the airport tax counter. At the airport also tourist information, car rental, bus companies, bank, ATMs, exchange facilities, post office, public phones, Secure Bag (US$5 per piece) and luggage deposit (between sections A-B at the information point), US$4 per piece a day. **Manuel Tienda León** buses to Aeroparque (see above for address), 0710-0255, every hour; from Aeroparque (departs from sector B, stops at AR), 0900-2000 every hour, and 2130, 20-min journey, US$3. Local buses 33 and 45 run from outside the airport to the Retiro railway station, then to **La Boca** and **Constitución** respectively. No 37 goes to **Palermo** and **Recoleta** and No 160 to **Palermo** and **Almagro**. If going to the airport, make sure it goes to Aeroparque by asking the driver, US$0.27. **Remise taxis**: are operated by **Transfer Express** and **Manuel Tienda León**, US$8 to centre, US$23-24 to Ezeiza. Taxi to centre US$4. **Manuel Tienda León** operates buses between Ezeiza and Aeroparque airports, stopping in city centre, US$8.50. **AR/Austral** offer daily flights to the main cities, for details see text under intended destination. **LADE** offers weekly flights to **Trelew** and **Bariloche** with several stops in Patagonia.

Bus

Local City buses are called *colectivos* and cover a very wide radius. They are clean, frequent, efficient and very fast. The basic fare is US$0.27, US$0.45 to the suburbs. Have coins ready for ticket machine as drivers do not sell tickets, but may give change. The bus number is not always sufficient indication of destination, as each number may have a variety of routes, but bus stops display routes of buses stopping there and little plaques are displayed in the driver's window. No 86 (white and blue, **Empresa Duvi**, T4302 6067) runs to the centre from outside the airport terminal to the left as you leave the building, 2 hrs, US$0.45, coins only, runs all day, every 20 mins during the day. To travel to Ezeiza, catch the bus at Av de Mayo y Perú, 1 block from Plaza de Mayo (many other stops, but this is central) – make sure it has 'Aeropuerto' red sign in the window as many 86s stop short of Ezeiza. See **Information** in **Ins and outs**, above, for city guides listing bus routes.

Long distance Bus terminal at Ramos Mejía y Antártida Argentina (Subte Line C), behind Retiro station, for information and booking with credit card, T4310 0700, www.tebasa.com.ar. Information desk is at the top of long ramp to your left. All ticket offices are upstairs, even numbers to the left, foreign companies at the very end (full list at the top of the escalator). International services operate from platforms 67-75. Buenos Aires city information desk on ground floor, beside an ATM;

another ATM and a bank (with exchange facilities for US$ and euros) upstairs. Locutorios with internet on ground floor. Remise taxis hiring points next to the platforms. At the basement and ground levels there are left-luggage lockers, US$2.50 for 1 day with tokens sold in kiosks; for large baggage, there's a *guarda equipaje* in the basement. Fares vary according to time of year and comfort: advance booking is essential Dec-Mar, Easter, Jul and long weekends. **Coche cama** is advisable for overnight journeys: seats fully recline and food is served for just a few pesos more. Travellers have reported getting student discounts without showing evidence of status, so it's always worth asking. For further details of bus services and fares, look under proposed destinations. There are no direct buses to either of the airports.

International buses International services are run by both local and foreign companies; heavily booked Dec-Mar, especially at weekends. Do not buy Uruguayan bus tickets in Buenos Aires; wait till you get to Colonia. To **Montevideo** Bus de la Carrera, 1000, 2200 and 2300 daily, US$27, 8 hrs, with a *coche cama* at 2230 (US$29), via Zárate-Gualeguaychú-Puerto Unzué-Fray Bentos-Mercedes. CAUVI goes also to Montevideo and to **Punta del Este** (10 hrs, US$35). Direct buses to **Santiago** (Chile), 1,400 km, 20-22 hrs, US$50. To **Bolivia**: Ormeño, T4313 2259, runs 2 weekly services (Tue, Sat 1500) to **La Paz**, 55 hrs, US$74 (via Santa Cruz and Cochabamba) and **Potosí** Buses goes across the border to **Villazón**, US$56. Argentine companies only reach the border, where you can change buses: to **La Quiaca** (US$48-53), to **Aguas Blancas** (US$53), or to **Pocitos** (US$53-57, cheaper via Tucumán). To **Asunción** (Paraguay), 1,370 km via Clorinda (toll bridge): about 15 bus companies, with executive (luxury service, 16 hrs, US$53), *diferencial* (with food, drinks, 17-18 hrs, US$33-40) and *común* (without food, but a/c, toilet, 17-18 hrs, US$27-30). Also to **Ciudad del Este** (18 hrs, US$27-33), **Encarnación** (12 hrs, US$27-33) and minor destinations in Paraguay. To **Peru** Ormeño (T4313 2259) and El Rápido Internacional (T4315 0804), direct service to **Lima** (only stops for meals, not included in the price), Mon, Wed, Sat 1800 or Tue, Fri, Sun 1800 respectively, 3 days, US$140. **La Veloz del Norte**, T0800-444 8356, goes to **Lima** via Paso de Jama and San Pedro de Atacama, Wed, Sun 0900, 3 days, US$150 (first meal included), if you need a visa for Chile, get one before travelling. Direct buses to **Brazil** by Pluma, T4313 3880: **São Paulo** via Paso de los Libres, 36 hrs, US$84, **Rio de Janeiro**, 42 hrs, US$91 (via **Foz do Iguaçu**, 18 hrs, US$38), **Porto Alegre**, 20 hrs, US$64, **Florianópolis**, 26 hrs, US$75, **Curitiba**, 30 hrs, US$82. To **Rio de Janeiro**, changing buses at

Posadas and Foz do Iguaçu is almost half price, 50 hrs. A third route across the Río de la Plata and through Uruguay is a bit cheaper and offers a variety of transport and journey breaks.

Driving
Driving in Buenos Aires is no problem, provided you have eyes in the back of your head and good nerves. Note that traffic fines are high and police increasingly on the lookout for drivers without the correct papers. Car hire is cheaper if you arrange it when you arrive rather than from home. See also Essentials, page 43, for international rental agencies. **Europcar**, Maipú 965, T4311 1000, www.europcar.com.ar. **Thrifty**, Carlos Pellegrini 1576, T0810-999 8500, www.thriftyar.com.ar. There are several national rental agencies, eg **Serra Lima**, Av Córdoba 3121, T4962 8508 or T0800-777 5462, or **Dietrich**, Av Las Heras 2277, T0810-345 3438, www.dietrichrentacar.com. **Ruta Sur**, Lavalle 482, p 5, T5238 4072, www.rutasur.com. Rents 4WDs and motorhomes. **Motoring Associations**: see ACA, page 68.

Ferry
To **Montevideo** and **Colonia** from Terminal Dársena Norte, Av Antártida Argentina 821 (two blocks from Av Córdoba y Alem). **Buquebus**, T4316 6500/6550, www.buquebus.com (tickets from Terminal or from offices at Av Córdoba 879 and Posadas 1452): 1) Direct to **Montevideo**, 2-3 a day, 3 hrs, US$63 tourist class, US$75 1st class one way, vehicles US$87-97, motorcycles US$68, bus connection to Punta del Este, US$8 extra. 2) To **Colonia**, services by 2 companies: **Buquebus**: 10 crossings a day, from 45 mins to 3 hrs, US$19.60 tourist class, US$26 1st class one way, US$34.50-45.20 on fast vessels, with bus connection to **Montevideo** (US$7.30 extra). Motorcycles US$23.60-35.60, cars US$36-42 and 57-63 (depending on size of vehicle and boat). **Colonia Express**, www.coloniaexpress.com, makes 2 crossings a day between Buenos and Aires Colonia in a fast catamaran (no vehicles carried) with bus connections to/from Montevideo, Punta del Este and other Uruguay towns. Fares, including Montevideo-Colonia bus: US$33 (US$22 on Wed). Office is at Av Córdoba 753, T4313-5100; ferries leave from the cruise ship terminal at Puerto Nuevo, not far from Retiro bus terminal. You must go there by taxi. See under Tigre, page 102, for services to Carmelo and Nueva Palmira.

Metro (Subte)
Five lines link the outer parts of the city to the centre. Line 'A' runs under Av Rivadavia, from Plaza de Mayo to Primera Junta. Line 'B' from central Post Office, on Av L N Alem, under Av Corrientes to Federico Lacroze railway station at

Chacarita, ending at Los Incas. **Line 'C'** links Plaza Constitución with the Retiro railway station, and provides connections with all the other lines. **Line 'D'** runs from Plaza de Mayo (Catedral), under Av Roque Sáenz Peña (Diagonal Norte), Córdoba, Santa Fe and Palermo to Congreso de Tucumán (Belgrano). **Line 'E'** runs from Plaza de Mayo (Cabildo, on C Bolívar) through San Juan to Plaza de los Virreyes (connection to Premetro train service to the southwest end of the city). Note that 3 stations, 9 de Julio (Line 'D'), Diagonal Norte (Line 'C') and Carlos Pellegrini (Line 'B') are linked by pedestrian tunnels. The fare is US$0.25, the same for any direct trip or combination between lines; magnetic cards (for 1, 2, 5, 10 or 30 journeys) must be bought at the station before boarding; only pesos accepted. Trains are operated by **Metrovías**, T4555 1616, and run Mon-Sat 0500-2250 (Sun 0800-2200). Line A, the oldest was built in 1913, the earliest in South America; it starts running Mon-Fri at 0600. Backpacks and luggage allowed. Free map (if available) from stations and tourist office.

Taxi

Taxis are painted yellow and black, and carry Taxi flags. Fares are shown in pesos. The meter starts at US$0.65 when the flag goes down; make sure it isn't running when you get in. A fixed rate of US$0.07 for every 200 m or 1-min wait is charged thereafter. A charge is sometimes made for each piece of hand baggage (ask first). About 10% tip expected. Phone a radio taxi from a phone box or locutorio, giving the address of where you are, and you'll usually be collected within 5 mins. Taxis from official rank in bus terminal are registered with police and safe. For extra security, take a remise taxi booked from a booth on the bus platform itself, more expensive but very secure (to Ezeiza US$18; to Aeroparque US$5.50). Taxis from a registered company are safer, and some 'Radio Taxis' you see on the street are false. Check that the driver's licence is displayed. Lock doors on the inside. Worst places are the two airports and Retiro; make sure you know roughly what the fare should be before the journey: eg from Aeroparque to: Ezeiza US$15 (plus toll), Congreso US$5, Plaza de Mayo US$5, Retiro US$4, La Boca US$6. In theory fares double for journeys outside city limits (Gen Paz circular highway), but you can often negotiate. Radio Taxis (same colours and fares) are managed by several different companies (eg **Del Plata**, T4504 7776; **Pídalo**, T4956 1200; **Llámenos**, T4815 3333) and are recommended as a safer alternative; minimum fare is US$1.70.

Remise taxis operate all over the city, run from an office and have no meter. The companies are identified by signs on the pavement. Fares, which are fixed and can be cheaper than regular taxis,

can be verified by phoning the office, and items left in the car can easily be reclaimed. **La Terminal**, T4312 0711 is recommended, particularly from Retiro bus station.

From centre to **Ezeiza** US$18. Fixed-price *remise taxis* for up to 4 passengers can be booked from the **Manuel Tienda León** or **Transfer Express** counter at Ezeiza, prices above. Avoid unmarked cars at Ezeiza no matter how attractive the fare may sound; drivers are adept at separating you from far more money than you can possibly owe them. Always ask to see the taxi driver's licence. If you take an ordinary taxi the Policía de Seguridad Aeroportuaria on duty notes down the car's licence and time of departure. There have been recent reports of taxi drivers taking Ezeiza airport-bound passengers to remote places, stealing all their luggage and leaving them there. If in doubt, take a *remise* or airport bus.

Tram

Old-fashioned street cars operate Mar-Nov on Sat and holidays 1600-1930 and Sun 1000-1300, 1600-1930 and Dec-Feb on Sat and holidays 1700-2030, Sun 1000-1300, 1700-2030, free, on a circular route along the streets of Caballito district, from C Emilio Mitre 500, Subte Primera Junta (Line A) or Emilio Mitre (Line E), no stops en route. Operated by **Asociación Amigos del Tranvía**, T4431 1073, www.tranvia.org.ar.

Train

There are 4 main terminals: 1) **Retiro** (3 lines: **Mitre**, **Belgrano** and **San Martín** in separate buildings). Train information T4311 8704. Mitre line (run by **TBA**, T4317 4407 or T0800-333 3822, www.tbanet.com.ar). Urban and suburban services include: **Belgrano**, **Mitre** (connection to Tren de la Costa, see below), **Olivos**, **San Isidro**, and **Tigre** (see below); long distance services to **Rosario Norte**, 1 weekly on Fri evening, 6 hrs, US$4; to **Tucumán** via Rosario, Mon and Fri, 2100, returning Mon and Thu 1000, 26 hrs, US$20 sleeper, US$16 pullman, US$13 1st class (run by **NOA Ferrocarriles**, T4893 2244). Belgrano line to northwestern suburbs, including Villa Rosa, run by **Ferrovías**, T4511 8833. San Martín line for services to Pilar.

2) **Constitución**, train information T4304 0028: Roca line (run by **Metropolitano**, www.metropolitano.com.ar). Urban and suburban services to La Plata (US$ 0.50), Ezeiza (US$0.35), Ranelagh (US$0.27) and Quilmes (US$0.20). Long distance services (run by **Ferrobaires**, T4304 0028 or T0800-222 8736, www.ferrobaires.gba.gov.ar): Bahía Blanca, 5 weekly, 12½ hrs, US$7-13, food mediocre; to Mar del Plata daily, 5½-6 hrs, US$7-10; to Pinamar, 2 weekly, 6 hrs, US$9-11; to Miramar, summer only, 7 hrs, US$8-13; to Tandil, weekly, 7½ hrs, US$5-8.

3) **Federico Lacroze** Urquiza line and Metro headquarters (run by **Metrovías**, T4555 1616, www.metrovias.com.ar). Suburban services: to General Lemos. **Trenes Especiales Argentinos**, T4551 1634, runs twice a week a train to **Posadas**, minimum 26 hrs, US$13-41, from Lacroze via the towns along Río Uruguay.

4) **Once**: Sarmiento line (run by *TBA*, see above). Urban and suburban services include **Luján** (connection at Moreno, US$0.70), **Mercedes** (US$1) and **Lobos**. A fast service runs Mon-Fri between Puerto Madero (station at Av Alicia Moreau de Justo y Perón) and Castelar. Tickets checked before boarding and on train and collected at the end of the journey; urban and suburban fares are charged according different sections of each line; fares vary depending on the company, cheapest is about US$0.15.

⊙ Directory

Airline offices Aerolíneas Argentinas (AR) and **Austral**, Perú y Rivadavia, Av LN Alem 1134 and Av Cabildo 2900, T0810-2228 6527. **Air Canada**, Av Córdoba 656, T4327 3640. **Air France-KLM**, San Martín 344 p 23, T4317 4700. **Alitalia**, Av Santa Fe 887, T4787 7848. **American Airlines**, Av Santa Fe 881, T4318 1111, Av Pueyrredón 1997 and branches in Belgrano and Acassuso. **Avianca**, Carlos Pellegrini 1163 p 4, T4394 5990. **British Airways**, Av del Libertador 498 p 13, T0800-666 1459. **Copa**, Carlos Pellegrini 989 p 2, T0810-222 2672. **Cubana**, Sarmiento 552 p 11, T4325 0691. **Delta**, Carlos Pellegrini 1141, T0800-666 0133. **Iberia**, Carlos Pellegrini, 1163 p 1/3, T4131 1000. **LAB**, Carlos Pellegrini 141, T4323 1900. **Lan**, Cerrito y Paraguay, T0810-999 9526. **Líneas Aéreas del Estado (LADE)**, Perú 710, T5129 9000, Aeroparque T4514 1524. **Lufthansa**, M T Alvear 590, p 6, T4319 0600. **Malaysia Airlines**, Suipacha 1111 p 14, T4312 6971. Mexicana, Av Córdoba 1131. **Pluna**, Florida 1, T4342 7000. **TAM**, Cerrito 1030, T4819 4800 or T0810 333 3333. **United**, Av Madero 900, T0810-777 8648. **Banks** ATMs are widespread for MasterCard or Visa (look for Link ATMs). The financial district lies within a small area north of Plaza de Mayo, between Rivadavia, 25 de Mayo, Av Corrientes and Florida. In non-central areas find banks/ATMs along the main avenues. Banks open Mon-Fri 1000-1500. Use credit or debit cards for withdrawing cash rather than carrying TCs. Most banks charge commission especially on TCs (as much as US$10). US dollar bills are often scanned electronically for forgeries, while TCs are sometimes very difficult to change and you may be asked for proof of purchase. Major credit cards usually accepted but check for surcharges. General MasterCard office at Perú 151, T4348

7000, www.mastercard.com/ar, open 0930-1800. Visa, Corrientes 1437 p 2, T4379 3400, www.visa.com.ar. **American Express** offices are at Arenales 707 y Maipú, by Plaza San Martín, T4310 3000 or T0810-555 2639, www.american express.com.ar, where you can apply for a card, get financial services and change Amex TCs (1000-1500 only, T0810-444 2437, no commission into US$ or pesos); no commission either at Banco de la Provincia de Buenos Aires, several branches, or at Banco Columbia, Perón 350. Citibank, B Mitre 502, T0810-444 2484, changes only Citicorps TCs cheques, no commission; branch at Florida 199. *Casas de cambio* include Banco Piano, San Martín 345, T4321 9200 (has exchange facility at Ezeiza airport, 0500-2400), www.bancopiano.com.ar, changes all TCs (commission 2%). **Forex**, MT de Alvear 540, T4311 5543. **Eves**, Tucumán 702. Banco Ciudad at Av Córdoba 675 branch is open to tourists (with passport) for currency exchange and TCs, Mon 1000-1800, Tue-Fri 1000-1700, Sat-Sun 1100-1800. Other South American currencies can only be exchanged in *casas de cambio*. Western Union, branches in Correo Argentino post offices (for transfers within Argentina) and at Av Córdoba 975 (for all transfers), T0800-800 3030. **Cultural centres** British Council, M T de Alvear 590, p 4, T4311 9814, F4311 7747 (Mon-Thu 0830-1700, Fri 0830-1330). British Arts Centre (BAC), Suipacha 1333, T4393 6941, www.britishartscentre.org.ar. English plays and films, music concerts, photography exhibitions (closed Jan). Goethe Institut, Corrientes 319/43, T4311 8964, German library and newspapers (Mon, Tue, Thu 1230-1930, Fri 1230-1600, closed Jan), free German films shown, cultural programmes, German language courses. In the same building, upstairs, is the German Club, Corrientes 327. Alliance Française, Córdoba 946, T4322 0068, www.alianza francesa.org.ar. French library, temporary film and art exhibitions. Instituto Cultural Argentino Norteamericano (ICANA), Maipú 672, T5382 1500, www.icana.org.ar. Biblioteca Centro Lincoln, Maipú 672, T5382 1536, www.bcl.edu.ar, Mon-Wed 1000-2000, Thu and Fri 1000-1800 (Jan and Feb Mon-Fri 1300-1900), library (borrowing for members only), English/US newspapers. **Embassies and consulates** All open Mon-Fri unless stated otherwise. Australia, Villanueva y Zabala, T4779 3500, www.argentina.embassy. gov.au. 0830-1100, ticket queuing system; take bus 29 along Av Luis María Campos to Zabala. Austria, French 3671, T4802 1400, www.austria. org.ar. Mon-Fri 0900-1200. Belgium, Defensa 113 p 8, T4331 0066, 0800-1300, www.diplobel.org/ argentina. Bolivia, Consulate, Alsina 1886, T4381 4171, www.embajadade bolivia.com.ar, 0830-1530, visa while you wait or a month wait (depending on the country of origin), tourist bureau. **Brazil**, Consulate, C Pellegrini 1363, p 5, T4515 6500, www.conbrasil.org.ar. 1000-1300, tourist visa takes at least 48 hrs, US$25-110. **Canada**, Tagle 2828, T4808 1000, www.dfait-maeci.gc.ca/argentina. Mon-Thu 0830-1230, 1330-1730, tourist visa Mon-Thu 0845-1130. **Chile**, Consulate, San Martín 439, p 9, T4394 6582, www.embajadadechile.com.ar, 0900-1330. **Denmark**, Consulate, Alem 1074, p 9, T4312 6901, www.dinamarca.org.ar. Mon-Thu 0930-1200. **Finland**, Av Santa Fe 846, p 5, T4312 0600. **France**, Santa Fe 846, p 4, T4312 2409, www.con sulatfrance.int.ar, 0900-1230, 1400-1600 (by appointment). **Germany**, Villanueva 1055, T4778 2500, www.embajada-alemana.org.ar. 0830-1100. **Ireland**, Av Del Libertador 1068 p 6, T5787 0801, www.irlanda.org.ar. 0900-1300, 1400-1530. **Israel**, Av de Mayo 701, p 10, T4338 2500, Mon-Thu 0900-1200, Fri 0900-1100. **Italy**, consulate at M T de Alvear 1125/49, T4816 6133/36, www.consitalia-bsas.org.ar, Mon, Tue, Thu, Fri 0800-1100. **Japanese Consulate**, Bouchard 547 p 17, T4318 8200, www.ar.emb-japan.go.jp, 0900-1230, 1430-1700. **Netherlands**, Olga Cossettini 831 p 3, Puerto Madero, T4338 0050, www.embajadaholanda.int.ar, Mon-Thu 0900-1300, Fri 0900-1230. **New Zealand**, C Pellegrini 1427 p 5, T4328 0747, www.nzembassy.com/buenosaires. Mon-Thu 0900-1300, 1400-1730, Fri 0900-1300. **Norway**, Esmeralda 909, p 3 B, T4312 2204, www.noruega.org.ar, 0930-1400. **Paraguay**, Consulate, Viamonte 1851, T4814 4803, 0800-1330. **South Africa**, MT de Alvear 590, p 8, T4317 2900, www.embajadasudafrica.org.ar, Mon-Thu 0815-1230, 1315-1715, Fri 0815-1415. **Spain**, Consulate, Guido 1760, T4811 0070, www.mae.es/consulados/buenosaires. 0815-1430. **Sweden**, Tacuarí 147 p 6, T4329 0800, www.sweden abroad.com/buenosaires, 1000-1200. **Switzerland**, Santa Fe 846, p10, T4311 6491, www.eda.admin.ch/buenosaires_emb, open 0900-1200. **UK**, Luis Agote 2412 (near corner Pueyrredón y Guido), T4808 2200 (call T15-5114 1036 for emergencies only out of normal office hours), www.britain.org.ar. 0900-1300 (Jan-Feb 0900-1200). **Uruguay**, Consulate, Av Las Heras 1907, T4807 3045, www.embajadadeluru guay.com.ar. 0930-1730, visa takes up to 72 hrs. **US Embassy and Consulate General**, Colombia 4300, T5777 4533 (for emergencies involving US citizens, T5777 4354 or T5777 4873 after office hours), http://buenosaires.us embassy.gov. **Internet** Prices range from US$0.50 to US$1 per hr, shop around. Most *locutorios* (phone offices) have internet access. **Language schools** All-Spanish, Talcahuano 77 p 1, T4381 3914, www.all-spanish.com.ar. One to one classes. **Argentina I.L.E.E**, Av Callao 339, p 3, T4782 7173,

www.argentinailee.com. Recommended by individuals and organizations alike. **Cedic**, Reconquista 715, p 11 E, T/F4315 1156, www.cedic.com.ar. Recommended. **International Bureau of Language**, Florida 165, 3rd floor, T4331 4250, www.ibl.com.ar. Group and one-to-one lessons, all levels, recommended. **PLS**, Carabelas 241 p 1, T4394 0543, www.pls. com.ar. Recommended for travellers and executives and their families; also translation and interpreting services. **Universidad de Buenos Aires**, 25 de Mayo 221, T4334 7512 or T4343 1196, www.idiomas.filo.uba.ar. Offers cheap, coherent courses, including summer intensive courses. For other schools teaching Spanish, and for private tutors look in *Buenos Aires Herald* in the classified advertisements. Enquire also at *Asatej* (see Useful addresses). **Medical services** Urgent medical service: for free municipal ambulance service to an emergency hospital department (day and night) **Casualty ward, Sala de guardia**, T107 or T4923 1051/58 (SAME). Inoculations: **Hospital Rivadavia**, Av Las Heras 2670, T4809 2000, Mon-Fri, 0700-1300 (bus 10, 37, 59, 60, 62, 92, 93 or 102 from Plaza Constitución), or **Dirección de Sanidad de Fronteras y Terminales de Transporte**, Ing Huergo 690, T4343 1190, Mon 1400-1500, Tue-Wed 1100-1200, Thu and Fri 1600-1700, bus 20 from Retiro, no appointment required (yellow fever only; take passport). If not provided, buy the vaccines in **Laboratorio Biol**, Uriburu 153, T4953 7215, or in larger chemists. Many chemists have signs indicating that they give injections. Any hospital with an infectology department will give hepatitis A. **Travel Medicine Service (Centros Médicos Stamboulian)**, 25 de Mayo 464, T4311 3000, French 3085, T5236 7772, also in Belgrano and Flores, www.viajeros.cei.com.ar. Private health advice for travellers and inoculations centre. Public Hospitals: **Hospital Argerich**, Almte Brown esq Pi y Margall 750, T4121 0700. **Hospital Juan A Fernández**, Cerviño y Bulnes, T4808 2600/2650, good medical attention. **British Hospital**, Perdriel 74, T4309 6400, www.hospitalbritanico.org.ar. US$24 a visit. **German Hospital**, Av Pueyrredón 1640, between Beruti and Juncal, T4827 7000, www.hospitalale man.com.ar Both maintain first-aid centres (*centros asistenciales*) as do the other main hospitals. Dental treatment at Solís 2180, T4305 2530/ 2110. Excellent dental treatment centre at **Carroll Forest**, Vuelta de Obligado 1551 (Belgrano), T4781 9037, info@carroll-forest.com.ar. **Post offices** Correo Central, Correos Argentinos, Sarmiento y Alem, T4891 9191, www.correoargentino.com.ar, Mon-Fri, 0800-2000, Sat 1000-1300. *Poste Restante* (only to/from national destinations) on ground floor

(US$0.25 per letter). Philatelic section open Mon-Fri 1000-1700, T5550 5176. **Centro Postal Internacional**, for all parcels over 2 kg for mailing abroad, at Av Comodoro Py y Antártida Argentina, near Retiro station, helpful, many languages spoken, packaging materials available, Mon-Fri 1000-1700. Post office at Montevideo 1408 near Plaza V López, friendly staff, Spanish only. Also at Santa Fe 945 and many others. UPS, T0800-2222 877, www.ups.com. DHL, T0810-2222 345, www.dhl.com.ar. FedEx, T0810-3333 339, www.fedex.com. **Telephone** International and local calls, internet and fax from phone offices (*locutorios* or *telecentros*), of which there are many in the city centre. **Useful addresses** Migraciones: (Immigration), Antártida Argentina 1355, edificio 4 (visas extended mornings only), T4317 0200, www.migraciones.gov.ar, 0730-1330 (see also Visas and immigration in Essentials). **Central Police Station**: Moreno 1550, Virrey Cevallos 362, T4370 5911/5800 (emergency, T101 from any phone, free). See page 66 for **Comisaría del Turista** (tourist police). **Aves Argentinas/AOP** (a BirdLife International partner), 25 de Mayo 749 p 2, T4312 8958, for information on birdwatching and specialist tours, good library open Wed and Fri 1500-2000 (closed Jan). Student organizations: **Asatej**: Helpful

Argentine Youth and Student Travel Organization, runs a Student Flight Centre, Florida 835, p 3, oficina 320, T4114 7600, www.asatej.com, Mon-Fri 0900-1900 (and other branches in BA: Belgrano, Monserrat, Palermo, Recoleta, Caballito), www.asatej.net. Offering booking for flights (student discounts) including cheap one-way flights (long waiting lists), hotels and travel; information for all South America, notice board for travellers, ISIC cards sold (giving extensive discounts; Argentine ISIC guide available here), English and French spoken; also runs: **Red Argentino de Alojamiento Para Jovenes** (affiliated to HI); **Asatej Travel Store**, at the same office, selling widerange of travel goods. **Oviajes**, Uruguay 385, p 6, T4371 6137, Lavalle 477 p 1, T5199 0831 and Echeverría 2498 p 1, T4785 7840, www.oviajes.com.ar. Tickets and information, also issues cards for Hostels of Americas, Nomads and Hostels of Europe, ISIC, ITIC and G0 25 cards, aimed at students, teachers and independent travellers. Cheap fares also at **TIJE**, San Martín 640 p 6, T4326 2036 or branches at Paraguay 1178, p 7, T5218 2800 and Zabala 1736, p 1, T4770 9500, www.tije.com, and at STB (STA representative), Viamonte 577 p 3, T5217 2727, www.stb.com.ar. **YMCA**: (Central), Reconquista 439, T4311 4785. **YWCA**: Tucumán 844, T4322 1550.

Around Buenos Aires

Tigre → *Population: 31,000 (Partido de Tigre -Tigre county- 301,000).*
This touristy little town, 32 km northwest of Buenos Aires, is a popular weekend destination lying on the lush jungly banks of the Río Luján, with a fun fair and an excellent fruit and handicrafts market (Puerto de Frutos) daily 1100-2000 with access from Calles Sarmiento or Perú. There are restaurants on the waterfront in Tigre across the Río Tigre from the railway line, along Lavalle and Paseo Victorica; cheaper places can be found on Italia and Cazón on the near side. North of the town is the delta of the Río Paraná: innumerable canals and rivulets, with holiday homes and restaurants on the banks and a fruit-growing centre. The fishing is excellent and the peace is only disturbed by motor-boats at weekends. Regattas are held in November. Take a trip on one of the regular launch services (*lanchas colectivas*) which run to all parts of the delta, including taxi launches – watch prices for these – from the wharf (*Estación Fluvial*). Tourist catamarans, five services daily, 1-2 hour trips, US$4-7, from Lavalle 499 on Río Tigre, T4731 0261/63, www.tigreencatamaran.com.ar, and *Río Tur* (from Puerto de Frutos, T4731 0280, www.rioturcatamaranes.com.ar). *Sturla* (Estación Fluvial, oficina 10, T4731 1300, www.sturlaviajes.com.ar) runs three 1-hour trips a day, US$4, to which can be added a barbecue at an island with a daily half-day tour (US$18); also full-day tours that include lunch and kayak excursions for US$48. Trips to the open Río de la Plata estuary are available with *Catamarán Libertad* (T4799 6030) from Puerto de Olivos on Sunday to the delta (US$4) or to Buenos Aires coasts (US$2.70), and on Saturday to the delta, US$5.

    Museo Naval ① *Paseo Victorica 602, T4749 0608, Mon-Thu 0830-1230, Fri 0830-1730, Sat-Sun 1030-1830, US$1.* Worth a visit to see the displays on the Argentine navy. There are also relics of the 1982 Falklands/Malvinas War. **Museo de Arte** ① *Paseo Victoria 972, T4512 4528, Wed-Fri 0900-1900, Sat-Sun 1200-1900, US$1.50*, new art museum opened late 2006.

Isla Martín García
This island in the Río de la Plata (Juan Díaz de Solís' landfall in 1516) used to be a military base. Now it is an ecological/historical centre and an ideal excursion from the capital, with many trails through the cane brakes, trees and rocky outcrops – interesting birds and flowers. Boat trips: four weekly from Tigre at 0900, returning 2000, three-hour journey, US$16 return (US$33 including lunch and guide; US$60 pp including weekend overnight at inn, full board). Reservations only through *Cacciola* (address under Ferries to Uruguay, above), who also handle bookings for the inn and restaurant on the island. There is also a campsite.

The Pampas

South and west of Buenos Aires the flat, fertile lands of the pampa húmeda stretch seemingly without end, the horizon broken only by a lonely windpump or a line of poplar trees. This is home to the gaucho, whose traditions of music and fine craftsmanship remain alive. Argentina's agricultural heartland is punctuated by quiet pioneer towns, like Chascomús, and the houses of grand estancias. Argentina's former wealth lay in these splendid places, where you can stay as a guest, go horse riding, and get a great insight into the country's history and gaucho culture. The mountain range at Tandil offers great walking and marvellous views.

Luján → *Phone code: 02323. Population: 65,000.*
This is a place of pilgrimage for devout Catholics throughout Argentina. In 1630 an image of the Virgin brought by ship from Brazil was being transported to its new owner in Santiago del Estero by ox cart, when the cart got stuck, despite strenuous efforts by men and oxen to move it. This was taken as a sign that the Virgin willed she should stay there, A chapel was built for the image, and around it grew Luján. The chapel has long since been superseded by an impressive neo-Gothic basilica and the Virgin now stands on the High Altar. Each arch of the church is dedicated to an Argentine province, and the transepts to Uruguay, Paraguay and Ireland. Behind the Cabildo is the river, with river walks, cruises and restaurants (an excellent one is L'*Eau Vive* on the road to Buenos Aires at Constitución 2112, run by nuns, pleasant surroundings). Luján is a very popular spot at weekends, and there are huge pilgrimages on 5 October, 8 May and 8 December, when the town is completely packed.

Museo Histórico Colonial ① *Wed-Fri 1215-1800, Sat, Sun 1015-1800, closed Jan, US$0.30*, in the old Cabildo building, is one of the most interesting museums in the country. Exhibits illustrate its historical and political development. General Beresford, the commander of the British troops which seized Buenos Aires in 1806, was a prisoner here, as were Generals Mitre, Paz and Belgrano in later years. Next to it are museums devoted to transport and to motor vehicles and there is also a poor **Museo de Bellas Artes.**

San Antonio de Areco → *Phone code: 02326. Colour map 8, grid B5.*

San Antonio de Areco, 113 km northwest of Buenos Aires, is a completely authentic, late 19th-century town, with crumbling single-storey buildings around a plaza filled with palms and plane trees, streets lined with orange trees, and an attractive *costanera* along the river bank. There are several *estancias* nearby and the town itself has historical *boliches* (combined bar and provisions store). The gaucho traditions are maintained in silver, textiles and leather handicrafts of the highest quality, as well as frequent gaucho activities, the most important of which is the **Day of Tradition** in the second week of November (book accommodation ahead), with traditional parades, gaucho games, events on horseback, music and dance. **Museo Gauchesco Ricardo Güiraldes** ① *on Camino Güiraldes, daily except Tue, 1100-1700, US$0.70*, is a replica of a typical *estancia* of the late 19th century, with impressive *gaucho* artefacts and displays on the life of Güiraldes, the writer whose best-known book, *Don Segundo Sombra*, celebrates the gaucho. He wrote the book in the **Estancia La Porteña** ① *8 km from town, www.sanantoniodeareco.com/turismo/historia/historia/laportena/index.htm*, which dates from 1823. Superb gaucho **silverwork** for sale at the workshop and museum of **Juan José Draghi** ① *Alvear 345, T454219, 0900-2000*. Excellent **chocolates** at **La Olla de Cobre** ① *Matheu 433, T453105*, with a charming little café for drinking chocolate and the most amazing home-made *alfajores*. There is a large park spanning the river near the **tourist information centre** (address above). The **Centro Cultural y Museo Usina Vieja,** ① *Alsina 66, Tue-Fri 0800-1400, Sat, Sun, holidays 1100-1700, free*, is the city museum. There are ATMs on the plaza, but nowhere to change TCs. The **tourist office** is at ① *Zerboni y Arellano, Parque San Martín, T453165, www.sanantoniodeareco.com*.

La Plata → *Phone code: 0221. Colour map 8, grid B5. Population: 545,000.*

La Plata, on the Río de la Plata, was founded in 1882 as capital of Buenos Aires province and is now an important administrative centre, with an excellent university. It's a well-planned city, reminiscent of Paris in places, with the French-style **legislature** and the elegant **Casa de Gobierno** on **Plaza San Martín**, central in a series of plazas along the spine of the city. On **Plaza Moreno** to the south there's an impressive Italianate palace housing the **Municipalidad**, and the **Cathedral,** a striking neo-Gothic brick construction. North of Plaza San Martín is La Plata's splendid park, the **Paseo del Bosque**, with mature trees, a boating lake and the **Museo de La Plata** ① *T425 7744, www.fcnym.unlp.edu.ar, daily 1000-1800, closed 1 Jan, 1 May, 25 Dec, US$1.50, free guided tours, weekdays 1400, 1600, Sat-Sun hourly, in Spanish and in English (phone first), highly recommended.* This museum houses an outstanding collection of stuffed animals, wonderful dinosaur skeletons and artefacts from pre-Columbian peoples throughout the Americas. 8 km northwest of the city is the **República de los Niños** ① *Col Gral Belgrano y Calle 501, daily 1000-2200, US$1, getting there: take a train from La Plata or Buenos Aires to Gonnet station, US$0.30, or bus 338, car park US$1.* This is Eva Peron's legacy, a delightful children's village with scaled-down castles, oriental palaces, a train, boat lake and restaurant. Fun for a picnic. The **Parque Ecológico** ① *Camino Centenario y San Luis, Villa Elisa, T473-2449, 0900-1930, free, getting there: take bus 273 D or E*, is another good place for families, with native forest and llamas, armadillos and ñandú roaming around.

The small municipal **tourist office** ① *Pasaje Dardo Rocha, T427 1535, Mon-Fri 1000-1700, and long weekends only*, in an Italianate palace, also houses a gallery of contemporary **Latin American art** ① *C 50 entre 6 y 7, T427 1843, www.cultura. laplata.gov.ar, 1000-1300, 1500-1800, weekends 1500-1800, free.*

Chascomús, Dolores and Tandil

To get to the heart of the pampas, stay in one of many estancias scattered over the plains. There are several accessible from the main roads to the coast, fast Ruta 2 (be prepared for tolls) and Ruta 11, near two well-preserved historic towns, Chasomús and Dolores. At Punta Indio, 165 km from Buenos Aires, is 1920s Tudor style **Estancia Juan Gerónimo** ① *T011-493 74326, US$15pp* *for the day, (L) full board, activities included, English and French spoken.* Set on the coast in a beautiful nature reserve which protects a huge variety of fauna, the estancia offers walks and horse rides in 4,000 ha. Accommodation is simple and elegant, and the food exquisite.

Chascomús is a beautifully preserved town from the 1900's, with a rather Wild West feel to it, Chascomús is a lively place built on a huge lake, perfect for fishing and water sports. There's a great little museum **Museo Pampeano** ① *Muñoz y Lastra, T425110, Tue-Fri 0800-1400, Sat-Sun 0900-1300, 1730-1930, free,* with gaucho artefacts, old maps and fabulous antique furniture. **Tourist office** ① *Libres del Sur 242,1st floor, or on the laguna. T430405, 0900-19000 daily, www.chas comus.com.ar.* Dolores is a delightful small town, like stepping back in time to the 1900's, very tranquil. **Museo Libres del Sur** ① *daily 1000-1700, US$0.30,* is an old house in Parque Libres del Sur, full of gaucho silver, plaited leather *tablero,* branding irons, and a huge cart from 1868. The **Sierras de Tandil** are 2,000 million years old, among the world's oldest mountains, beautiful curved hills of granite and basalt, offering wonderful walking and riding. Tandil itself is an attractive, breezy town, a good base for exploring the sierras, with a couple of marvellous estancias close by. There's a park, **Parque Independencia,** with great views from the hill with its Moorish-style castle, and an amphitheatre, where there's a famous community theatre event throughout Easter week (book hotels ahead). The nearest peak, 5 km away, **Cerro El Centinela,** offers wild countryside for riding, climbing, walking, ascent by 1.2-km cable car ride, and regional delicacies at the restaurants. Very helpful **tourist information** at ① *Av Espora 1120, on the way into town, T02293-432073, or at the bus terminal, www.tandil.gov.ar.* Look up estancias on the Las Pampas province's website: www.vivalaspampas.com.ar and www.caminodel gaucho.com.ar, T0221-425 7482.

● Sleeping

Tigre *p98*
AL La Pascuala, Arroyo Las Cañas (Tigre Delta second section), T4378 0982, www.lapas cuala.com. One of Argentina's most delightful places to stay, an hour by launch from Tigre, buried deep from the outside world, with 15 individual lodges on stilts in the water, connected by wooden walkways, all comforts and luxuries provided and very tasteful décor, with intimate dining room, jacuzzi and pool amidst the trees. Full board, excellent food and service. Recommended.
AL Villa Julia, Paseo Victoria 800, in Tigre itself, T4749 0642, www.villajulia.com.ar. Part of the New Age Town and Country group, www.newage-hotels.com. A 1906 villa converted into a chic hotel, beautifully-restored fittings, comfortable, good restaurant open to non-residents.
C TAMET Tigre Delta Youth Hostel, Río Lujan y Abra Vieja, T4728-0396. For a relaxing stay on an island with sandy beaches and quite comfortable premises, hot showers, with breakfast, games and canoes, basic cooking facilities, restaurant.

San Antonio de Areco *p99*
C Paradores Draghi, Lavalle 385, T454219, paradores@sanantoniodeareco.com. Renovated colonial buildingg, traditional style, very comfortable, with kitchen and bathroom.
D Los Abuelos, Zerboni y Zapiola T456390. In a renovated 1900s house, breakfast included, good, simple but comfortable rooms and a small pool.
D Hostal de Areco, Zapiola 25, T456118, info@hostaldeareco.com.ar. A popular place offering a warm welcome, good value.

D Posada del Ceibo, Irigoyen y Smith, T454614, www.laposadadelceibo.com.ar. 1950s-style motel, family friendly, basic rooms, cable TV, small pool.
Camping Three sites in the park by the river: best is **Club River Plate**, Av del Valle y Alvear, T452744, sports club, shady sites with all facilities, pool. Also **Auto-camping La Porteña**, a beautiful spot 12 km from town on the Güiraldes *estancia*.

Estancias
Some of the province's finest *estancias* are within easy reach for day visits, offering horse riding, an *asado* lunch, and other activities. Stay overnight to really appreciate the peace and beauty of these historical places. Look online at: www.sanantoniode areco.com/turismo/estancias/index.htm, or www.turismo.gov.ar/eng/menu.htm (go to Active Tourism, Rural Tourism).
LL El Ombú, T492080, T011-4710 2795 (BsAs office), www.estanciaelombu.com. Fine house with magnificent terrace dating from 1890, comfortable rooms, horse riding, English-speaking owners; price includes full board and activities but not transfer. Recommended.
L La Bamba, T456293, T011-4732 1269 (BsAs office), www.la-bamba.com.ar. Dating from 1830, in grand parkland, charming rooms, English-speaking owners who have lived here for generations, superb meals. Recommended.

La Plata *p99*
B Hotel Corregidor, C 6 No 1026, T425 6800. Upmarket, modern business hotel, well furnished, pleasant public rooms, good value.

D Catedral, C 49 No.965, T483 0091. Modest but welcoming, modern, with fan, breakfast included.
D La Plata Hotel, Av 51 No 783, T/F422 9090. Modern, well furnished, comfortable, spacious rooms and nice bathrooms.

Estancias
A Casa de Campo La China, 60 km from La Plata on Ruta 11, T0221-421 2931, www.casadecamp olachina.com.ar. A charming 1930s adobe house set in eucalyptus woods, with beautifully decorated spacious rooms off an open gallery, with open views, day visits (US$25) to ride horses, or in carriages, eat *asado*, or stay the night, guests of charming Cecilia and Marcelo, who speak perfect English. Delicious food. Highly recommended.

Chascomús *p99*
A La Posada, Costanera España, T423503, on the laguna, delightful, very comfortable.
A Torre Azul, Mercedes y Tandil, T422984, torre_azul@topmail.com.ar. Pool and spa, also with classy accommodation.
D Laguna, Libres del Sur y Maipú, T426113. Best in town, good value, pleasant quiet rooms.

Estancias
Both *estancias* will collect you from Chascomús.
LL Haras La Viviana, 45 km from Chascomús, T011-4702 9633, http://haraslaviviana.com.ar. Perfect for horse riding, since fine polo ponies are bred here. Tiny cabins in gardens by a huge laguna where you can kayak or fish, very peaceful, good service, lady novelist owner is quite a character, fluent English spoken.
AL La Horqueta, 3 km from Chascomús on Ruta 20, T011-4813 1910, www.la horqueta.com. Full board, 1898 Tudor style mansion in lovely grounds with laguna for fishing, horse riding, bikes to borrow, English-speaking hosts, safe gardens especially good for children, plain food.

Dolores *p99*
L Dos Talas, 10 km from town, T443020, 155 13282, www.dostalas.ar. The most beautiful *estancia* in the pampas, and one of the oldest. An elegant house in grand parkland designed by Charles Thays, with fascinating history, visible in all the family photos, artefacts and the vast library. This is one of the few *estancias* where you are truly the owners' guests. The rooms and the service are impeccable, the food exquisite; stay for days, completely relax. Pool, riding, English spoken.

Tandil *p99*
A Las Acacias, Av Brasil 642, T02293-423373, www.posadalasacacias.com.ar. Attractive modern hostería in restored 1890s dairy farm near golf club, good service, Italian and English spoken.

D Bed and Breakfast, Belgrano 39, T02293-426989, www.cybertandil. com.ar/byb. One of the best places to stay, comfortable double room or large apartment, in an idyllic walled garden with small pool, charming English hosts, phone in advance. Recommended.

Estancias
L Siempre Verde, T02292-498555, lasiempre verde@dilhard.com.ar. A 1900's house 45 km southwest of Tandil (next to Barker) with traditional-style rooms, good views. The owners, descendants of one of Argentina's most important families, are very hospitable and helpful. Wonderful horse riding and walking among the sierras, fishing, *asados* on the hillside, camping. Highly recommended.
AL Ave María, 16 km from Tandil, past Cerro El Centinela, T02293-422843, www.avemaria tandil.com.ar. In beautiful gardens overlooking the rocky summits of the sierras. You're encouraged to feel at home and relax, swim in the pool or walk in the grounds, hills and woodland. Impeccable rooms, superb food and discreet staff who speak English. Highly recommended.

🍴 Eating

San Antonio de Areco *p99*
Many *parrillas* on the bank of the Río Areco.
🍴 **El Almacén**, Bolivar 66. Original 1900s store and place to eat, popular.
🍴 **El Almacén de Ramos Generales**, Zapiola 143, T456376. Perfect place to try regional dishes such as *locro*, also superb *asados*.
🍴 **La Costa Reyes**, Zerboni y Belgrano, on the *costanera* near the park. Delicious *parrilla*.
🍴 **La Filomena**, Vieytes 395. Elegant, modern, delicious food, with live music at weekends.
🍴 **La Vuelta del Gato** opposite the park. Good pizzas and salami, with traditional *patero* wine.

La Plata *p99*
🍴 **El Modelo**, C 54 y C5. Traditional German-style *cervecería*, with good menu and great beer.
🍴 **Don Quijote**, Plaza Paso. Delicious food in lovely surroundings, well known.
🍴 **El Gran Chaparral**, C 60 y C 117 (Paseo del Bosque). Good basic *parrilla* in the park, great steaks.
🍴 **La Aguada**, C 50 entre 7 y 8. Oldest restaurant in town, good for *minutas* (light meals), famous for its *papas fritas* (chips – the chip soufflé is amazing).
Confitería París, C 7 y 49. The best croissants, and a lovely place for coffee.

Chascomús *p99*
🍴 **El Viejo Lobo**, Mitre y Dolores. Very good fish.
🍴 **El Colonial**, Lastra y Belgrano. Great food, and very cheap, at this traditional *parrilla*.

Tandil *p99*

Plenty of *pizzerías*, also good locally-made sausages and cheeses served in *picadas* (nibbles) with drinks.

†† 1905, Av Santamarina y San Martín. Charming old house serving excellent, elaborate meals.

†† Epoca de Quesos, San Martín y 14 de Julio, T448750. Atmospheric, delicious local produce, wines and *picadas*.

† El Molino, Juncal 936. Broad menu, meat cooked *al disco*, on an open fire, delicious.

† Parador del Sol in the *balneario* by Lago del Fuerte, Zarini s/n, T435697. Great pasta and salad.

† Taberna Pizuela, Paz y Pinto. Attractive old place serving good simple dishes, including pizza, their speciality.

▲ Activities and tours

Horse riding Contact an approved guide who will take you to otherwise inaccessible privately owned land for trekking. **Eco de las Sierras**, Tandil, T442741, T156 21083, Lucrecia Ballesteros. Highly recommended guide, young, friendly and knowledgeable. **Las Patronas** stables, near Mercedes, T02324-430421, laspatronas@ yahoo.com.ar. US$35 for a complete day in the ranch with horse riding and lunch. Recommended.

Trekking and mountain biking Horizonte Vertical, T432762, climbing and walking. Tandil Aventuro, T421836, trekking and mountain biking.

☉ Transport

Tigre *p98*

Bus From central **Buenos Aires**: take No 60 from Constitución: the 60 'bajo' takes a little longer than the 60 'alto' but is more interesting for sightseeing.

Ferry To **Carmelo** (Uruguay) from Terminal Internacional, Lavalle 520, Tigre. **Cacciola**, T4749 0931, www.cacciolaviajes.com (in Buenos Aires at Florida 520, p 1, of 113, T4393 6100), 0830, 1630, 3½ hrs, US$15 (US$25 return). Bus connection to Montevideo, 3 hrs, US$20, US$35 return. Other bus destinations in Uruguay and overnight stays in Carmelo (from US$50 including accommodation). Connecting bus to Tigre from Carlos Pellegrini y Av Córdoba, 0635, 1445.

To **Nueva Palmira** (Uruguay) from Estación Fluvial de Tigre. **Líneas Delta Argentino**, oficina 6 at Estación Fluvial, T4731 1236, www.lineas delta.com.ar. Daily at 0730 plus 1700 on Fri, 3 hrs, US$13 (US$25 return). Bus connection to Colonia, 5 hrs from Tigre, US$16, US$28 return.

Note Argentine port taxes are generally included in the fares for Argentine departures.

Train From **Buenos Aires**: take train from Retiro station (FC Mitre section) to Tigre or to Bartolomé Mitre and change to the Maipú station (the stations are linked) for the **Tren de la Costa**, T4002 6000, www.trendelacosta.com.ar, US$2 one way, every 20 mins from Maipú Mon-Thu 0710-2300, Fri 0710-2400, Sat-Sun 0830-0010, 25 mins journey. (Buses to Tren de la Costa are 60 from Constitución, 19 or 71 from Once, 152 from centre.) Several stations on this line have shopping centres (eg San Isidro), and the terminus, Estación Delta, has the huge fun fair, El Parque de la Costa, and a casino. You can get off the train as many times as you want on the same ticket.

Luján *p98*

Bus From **Buenos Aires** (Plaza Once) Bus 52 and (Plaza Italia at Palermo) bus 57, frequent, 1 hr 50 mins with direct service, US$1.50. To **San Antonio de Areco**, 3 a day, US$1.20, Empresa Argentina, 1 hr. Train to Once station, US$0.60 (change at Moreno).

San Antonio de Areco *p99*

Bus From **Buenos Aires** (Retiro bus terminal), 2 hrs, US$5, every hour with Chevallier or Pullman General Belgrano. For connections to northern Argentina go to Pilar.

La Plata *p99*

Bus Terminal at Calle 4 and Diagonal 74. Information T427 3186/427 3198. To **Buenos Aires**, 1½ hrs, US$2, every 30 mins, all through the night from Retiro terminal, daytime only from Plaza Constitución. To **San Clemente del Tuyú**, US$5. **Train** To/from **Buenos Aires** (Constitución), frequent, US$2, 1 hr 10 mins (ticket office hidden behind shops opposite platform 6).

Chascomús *p99*

Bus Frequent service, several per day to **Buenos Aires**, US$4.50, **La Plata**, Mar del Plata, and daily to **Bahía Blanca**, **Tandil** and **Villa Gesell**; terminal T422595. **Train** Station T422220. Daily to **Buenos Aires** (Constitución), 2 daily, US$5 1st class, **Tandil** and **Mar del Plata**.

Tandil *p99*

Bus Frequent from **Buenos Aires** (5-6 hrs, US$12-14), **Bahía Blanca** (6 hrs, US$10), **Mar del Plata** (4 hrs, US$4), **Necochea**. Bus terminal Av Buzón 650, travel information T432092. **Train** Station at Av Machado y Colón, T423002. From **Buenos Aires** (US$5-8, one a week) and **Bahía Blanca**, station T423002.

Atlantic Coast

Among the 500 km of resorts stretching from to San Clemente de Tuyú to Monte Hermoso, the most attractive is upmarket Pinamar, with the chic Cariló next door. Villa Gesell is relaxed and friendly, while, next to it are the quiet, beautiful Mar Azul and Mar de las Pampas. Mar del Plata, Argentina's most famous resort, is a huge city with packed beaches, popular for its lively nightlife and casino; much more appealing in winter. Next to it, tranquil Miramar is great for young families, and Necochea has wild expanses of dunes to explore. Near the port of Bahía Blanca is the Sierra de la Ventana, the highest range of hills in the pampas, a great place for hiking.

Partido de la Costa

San Clemente del Tuyú is closest to the capital, the first of a string of identical small resorts known as **Partido de la Costa**, not worth a detour unless you're keen on fishing. They're old-fashioned towns, cheaper than the more popular resorts further southwest, but rather run down. There's excellent sea fishing, for shark, *pejerrey* and *brotola* from pier or boats, and fish can often be bought on the beach from local fishermen, but since the Río de la Plata flows here, the water is poor for bathing. San Clemente's main attraction is **Mundo Marino** ① *signposted from road into town, T430300, www.mundomarino.com.ar, US$11, children US$7*, the biggest sea life centre in South America, with performing seals and dolphins, all totally unnatural but undeniably fun for small children. Plenty of small hotels and campsites. At **Punta Rasa**, 9 km north, there is a lighthouse and a private nature reserve run by the **Fundación Vida Silvestre**, which, in summer, is home to thousands of migratory birds from the northern hemisphere. www.vidasilvestre.org.ar. There's a beautiful stretch of empty beach 15 km south of **Mar de Ajó,** the southernmost of these resorts, which belongs to one of the few *estancias* to offer horse riding on the sands, **Palantelén** ① *T02257-420983, www.palantelen.com.ar*. A peaceful place to walk and relax, delightful house, private tango lessons on a terrace under the stars, charming English-speaking hosts. Highly recommended. **Tourist information** ① *Mar del Tuyú, T02246-433035, www.lacostaturismo.com.ar.*

Pinamar and Cariló → *Phone code: 02254.*

The two most desirable resorts on the coast, 340 km from Buenos Aires, via Ruta 11, are next to each other, with the quiet old fashioned Belgian pioneer town Ostende in between. **Pinamar** is one of the most attractive resorts on the whole coast, with stylish architecture and mature trees lining its avenues. It is great for young people and families, with smart *balnearios* ranging from chic, quiet places with superb restaurants, to very trendy spots with loud music, beach parties and live bands at night. There are golf courses and tennis courts, and fine hotels and smart restaurants all along the main street, Avenida Bunge, running perpendicular to the sea. It's a stylish and well-maintained resort, slightly pricey. Explore the dunes at **Reserva Dunícola**, 13 km north, by horse or 4WD. **Tourist office** ① *Av Bunge 654, T491680, www.pina mar.gov.ar, www.pinamarturismo.com.ar*, English spoken, helpful, can book accommodation.

Cariló, the most exclusive beach resort in Argentina, has a huge area of mature woodland, where its luxury apart-hotels and *cabañas* are all tastefully concealed. The *balnearios* are neat and exclusive – of which *Hemingway* is *the* place, full of wealthy Porteños – and there are good restaurants and shops around the tiny centre. The tourist office is at Boyero y Castaño, T570773.

Villa Gesell → *Phone code: 02255. Population: 40,000.*

In contrast to the rather elite Cariló, Villa Gesell, 22 km south of Pinamar, is warm, welcoming and very laid-back. Set amid thousands of trees planted by its German founder, it has grown in recent years into a thriving tourist town, but retains its village feel. The beaches are safe and there's plenty of nightlife. In January, it's overrun by Argentine youth, far quieter in late February and March. Next to it are the two of the most tranquil and charming beach retreats: idyllic and wooded **Mar de las Pampas** and **Mar Azul** are both still underdeveloped, with fine *cabañas* to choose from. Get a map from the tourist office in Villa Gesell, or as you enter Mar de las Pampas. There's no grid system and it can be tricky finding your way around. Villa Gesell's main street is Avenida 3, pedestrianized in the evenings, full of cafés, restaurants and bars. The main **tourist office** is *at the bus terminal, T477253*, or on the right as you drive into town ① *Av de los Pioneros, 1921, T458596, open 0800-2200 daily in summer, off season 0900-1900, www.villagesell.gov.ar*, very helpful, English spoken.

Mar del Plata → *Phone code: 0223. Colour map 8, grid C5. Population: 560,000.*

The oldest and most famous Argentine resort has lost much of its charm since it was built in 1874. It's now a huge city offering great nightlife in summer, but if you like some space on the beach, it's best to go elsewhere as there are plenty of better beaches on this stretch of coast. There are hundreds of hotels, all busy (and double the price) in January-February; winter can be pleasantly warm, and much quieter. **Tourist offices** ⓘ *San Luís 1949, T494 4140 (ext 130/ 131), 0800-1500, or, more conveniently, next to the Casino Central on Blvd Marítimo, 0800-2000, www.mardelplata.gov.ar.* English spoken, good leaflets on daily events with bus routes. Also lists of hotels and apartment/chalet letting agents. For what's on, see *www.todomar delplata.com*. Out of season offices may be closed, or only open mornings.

The city centre is around **Playa Bristol**, with the huge casino, and **Plaza San Martín**, with pedestrian streets Rivadavia and San Martín full of shops and restaurants. 10 blocks southwest, the area of Los Troncos contains some remarkable mansions dating from Mar del Plata's heyday, from mock Tudor **Villa Blaquier** to **Villa Ortiz Basualdo** (1909), inspired by Loire chateaux, now the **Museo Municipal de Arte** ⓘ *Av Colón 1189, daily in summer 1700-2200, winter Wed-Mon 1200-1700, US$1, including guided tour.* Rooms furnished in period style. Nearby is the splendid **Museo del Mar** ⓘ *Av Colón 1114, T451 3553, www.museodelmar.org, summer daily 1000-2300, winter Mon-Thu 1000-1800, Fri-Sun 1000-2000, US$1.50.* It has a vast collection of 30,000 sea shells, a small aquarium, café and roof terrace. The **Centro Cultural Victoria Ocampo** ⓘ *Matheu 1851, T492 2193, daily in summer, off season closed Tue and mornings, US$1.* This beautiful 1900's wooden house in lovely gardens was where the famous author entertained illustrious literary figures; concerts held in grounds in summer. Nearby is the **Villa Mitre** ⓘ *Lamadrid 3870, Mon-Fri 0900-2000 Sat-Sun 1600-2000, closes at 1700 in winter, US$0.70.* Owned by a descendent of Bartolomé Mitre, it has a collection of old photos and artefacts. Beaches are filled with hundreds of tiny beach huts, *carpas*, rented by the day US$5-7, entitling you to use the balneario's showers, toilets, restaurants.

Beaches include fashionable **Playa Grande**, where the best hotels and shops are, as well as the famous golf course, with private *balnearios* for wealthy *porteños*, a small area open to the public; **Playa La Perla**, now packed and pretty grim, but **Playa Punta Mogotes**, further west, is by far the most appealing. The **port area**, south of Playa Grande, is interesting when the old orange fishing boats come in, and at night, for its wonderful seafood restaurants. A sea lion colony basks on rusting wrecks by the Escollera Sur (southern breakwater) and fishing is good all along the coast, where *pejerrey, corvina* and *pescadilla* abound. Lots of theatres, cinemas, and the **Casino** ⓘ *Dec to end-Apr, 1600-0330; 1600-0400 on Sat; May-Dec, Mon-Fri 1500-0230; weekends 1500-0300; free; minimum bet US$0.50.* Lively festivals are 17 November, Day of Tradition, with gaucho-related events, the national fishing festival in mid to late January, and the international film festival in mid-March.

Inland, 68 km west of Mar de la Plata is the town of **Balcarce** with some splendid art deco buildings and a leafy central plaza. You're most likely to visit the **Museo Juan Manuel Fangio** ⓘ *Dardo Rocha 639, T425540, daily in summer 0900-1900, winter 1000-1700, US$3.30, children US$1.70.* Argentina's best-loved racing driver was born here, and the Municipalidad on the plaza has been turned into a great museum, housing his trophies, and many of the racing cars he drove. There are excellent *parrillas* on the outskirts. The **Laguna Brava**, 38 km away, at the foot of the Balcarce hills, offers *pejerrey* fishing, and plentiful birdlife in lovely wooded surroundings. Visit **Estancia Laguna Brava** ⓘ *RN 226 Km 37.5, T0223-460 8002,* for horse riding, trekking, mountain biking and water sports on the lake with fine views of Sierra Brava. **Tourist information** ⓘ *C 17 No 671, T02266-425758.* For fishing, contact the **Club de Pesca Balcarce** ⓘ *Villa Laguna Brava, T460 8019.* Frequent buses from Mar de la Plata.

Miramar → *Phone code: 02291. Colour map 8, grid C5. Population: 22,000.*

Miramar, 53 km southwest of Mar del Plata, along the coast road, is a charming small resort, known as the 'city of bicycles', and orientated towards families with small children. It has a big leafy plaza at its centre, a good stretch of beach with soft sand, and a relaxed atmosphere; a quieter, low-key alternative to Mar del Plata. The most attractive area of the town is away from the high rise buildings on the sea front, at the **Vivero Dunícola Florentino Ameghino**, a 502-ha forest park on the beach, with lots of walks, restaurants and picnic places for *asado* among the mature trees. In town there are lots of restaurants along Calle 21, and good cafés at *balnearios* on the seafront. **Tourist office** ⓘ *central plaza, C 28 No 1086, T02291-420190, www.miramar-digital.com, Mon-Fri 0700-2100, Sat-Sun in summer 0900-2100.* Helpful, listings and maps.

Necochea → *Phone code: 02262. Colour map 8, grid C5. Population: 65,000.*

Necochea is a well-established resort, famous for its long stretch of beach, and while the central area is built up and busy in the summer, further west there are beautiful empty beaches and high sand dunes. There's also a fine golf club and rafting nearby on the river Quequén. **Tourist offices**① *on the beach front at Av 79 y Av 2, T438333, www.necochea.gov.ar; also upstairs at the Municipalidad, C 56 No 2945, T431153,* English spoken, list of apartments for rent. There are banks with ATMs and *locutorios* along the pedestrianized C 83.

The **Parque Miguel Lillo** (named after the Argentine botanist) starts three blocks west of Plaza San Martín and stretches along the seafront, a wonderful dense forest of over 600 ha. There are lovely walks along paths, many campsites and picnic spots, a swan lake with paddle boats, an amphitheatre, lots of restaurants, and places to practise various sports. West of Necochea, there's a natural arch of rock at the **Cueva del Tigre**, and beyond it stretches a vast empty beach, separated from the land by sand dunes up to 100 m high, the **Médano Blanco**. This is an exhilarating area for walking or horse riding and the dunes are popular for 4WD riding. Vehicles and buses stop where the road ends at Parador Médano Blanco (a good place for lunch) where you can rent 4WDs for US$50 (4 people), T155 68931.

Bahía Blanca and around → *Phone code: 0291. Colour map 8, grid C4. Pop: 300,000.*

The province's most important port and naval base, Bahía Blanca is a quiet, attractive city. It's a good starting point for exploring **Sierra de la Ventana**, 100 km north, or relaxing on beaches an hour to the east. The architecture is remarkable with many fine buildings especially around the central **Plaza Rivadavia**, notably the ornate, Italianate **Municipalidad** of 1904 and the French-style **Banco de la Nación** (1927). Three blocks north on the main shopping street, Alsina, there's the classical **Teatro Colón** (1922). Northwest of the plaza, there's the attractive **Parque de Mayo** with a fine golf course and sports centre nearby. The **Museo Histórico**① *at the side of the Teatro Municipal, Dorrego 116, T456 3117, Tue-Sun 1500-2000,* has sections on the pre-Hispanic period and interesting photos of early Bahía Blanca. Not to be missed, though, is the **Museo del Puerto** ① *Torres y Carrega, 7 km away in the port area at* Ingeniero White, *weekends, 1700-2030 summer, 1500-2000 winter, and week days by arrangement, free; getting there: bus 500A or 504 from plaza, taxi US$3.* It houses entertaining and imaginative displays on immigrant life in the early 20th century, and a quaint *confitería* on Sunday. **Tourist office**① *in the Municipalidad on the main plaza, Alsina 65 (small door outside to the right), T459 4007, www.bahiablanca.gov.ar, Mon-Fri 0730-1900, Sat 1000-1300.* Very helpful.

At **Pehuén-Có**, 84 km east of Bahía Blanca, there's a long stretch of sandy beaches, with dunes, relatively empty and unspoilt (beware of jellyfish when wind is in the south), signposted from the main road 24 km from Bahía Blanca. It has a wild and untouristy feel, with a single hotel, several campsites well shaded, and a couple of places to eat. There's a more established resort at **Monte Hermoso**, 106 km east, with more hotels and a better organized campsite, but quiet, with a family feel, and wonderful beaches. One of the few places on the coast where the sun rises and sets over the sea.

Sierra de la Ventana → *Phone code 0291.*

The magnificent Sierra de la Ventana, the highest range of hills in the pampas, lies within easy reach of Bahía for a day or weekend visit (100 km north of Bahía Blanca). They're as old as those in Tandil, but much more accessible for long hikes, with stunning views from their craggy peaks. There are daily buses and *combis* from Bahía Blanca, but you could stop at **Tornquist**, 70 km north of Bahía Blanca by Ruta 33, a quaint place, with an attractive park in the central plaza.

The sierras are accessed within the **Parque Provincial Ernesto Tornquist** ① *US$1,* 25 km northeast of Tornquist on Ruta 76. There are two main points of entry, one at the foot of Cerro Ventana and the other, further east, at the foot of Cerro Bahía Blanca. To enter the Cerro Ventana section, turn left (signposted) after the massive ornate gates from the Tornquist family home. Nearby is *Campamento Base*, T0291-491 0067, camping, basic dormitory, hot showers. At the entrance to the park itself, there's a car park and interpretation centre with *guardaparques* ① *Dec-Apr 0800-1700,* who can advise on walks. From here it's a two to three-hour walk to the summit of **Cerro de la Ventana**, which has fantastic views from the 'window' (which gives the range its name), in the summit ridge; clearly marked path but with no shade. To enter the Cerro Bahía Blanca section, continue 4 km further along Ruta 76. There's a car park and **interpretation centre**① *T491 0039, Dec-Easter 0800-1800,* with *guardaparques* who can advise on walks. From here you can go on a guided visit (only with own vehicle, four to five hours), to natural caves, and the **Cueva de las Pinturas**, which contains petroglyphs. Also from here, an hour-long trail goes to Cerro Bahía Blanca. **Villa Ventana**, 10 km further, is a pretty, wooded settlement with excellent teashop, *Casa de Heidi*, and good food at *Las Golondrinas*. Helpful **tourist office** ⓘ *entrance to Village Ventana, T491 0095, www.sierradelaventana.org.ar*.

The town of **Sierra de la Ventana**, further east, is a good centre for exploring the hills, with a greater choice of hotels than Villa Ventana, and wonderful open landscapes all around. There is a 18-hole golf course, and good trout fishing in the Río Sauce Grande. Excellent **tourist office** ⓘ *Av Roca, just before railway track, T491 5303 (same website as Villa Ventana)*.

● Sleeping

Atlantic Coast *p103*
Since accommodation is plentiful all along the coast, only a small selection is listed here. Most resorts have *balnearios*, private beaches, where you pay US$15-20 per day for family/group use of a sunshade or beach hut, showers, toilets and restaurants. Avoid January when the whole coast is packed out.

Pinamar *p103*
There are plenty of hotels in Pinamar, of a high standard, all 4-stars have a pool. Some hotels are a long way from the beach. Book ahead in Jan and Feb. All those listed are recommended.
AL Del Bosque, Av Bunge 1550, T482480, elbosque@telpin.com.ar. Very attractive, in woods, not on the beach, a smart 4 star with pool, tennis courts, nice restaurant, good service.
AL Reviens, Burriquetas 79, T497010, www.hotel reviens.com. Modern, luxurious hotel, international style, right on the beach. Recommended.
B La Posada, Del Odiseo 324, T482267, www.pinamar.com.ar/laposada. Good value, more old-fashioned style, comfortable, next to sea and town centre, pretty gardens where breakfast is served.
B Las Araucarias, Av Bunge 1411, T480812. Attractive, smaller hotel with gardens.
B Playas, Av Bunge 140, T482236, www.pina marsa.com.ar. A lovely setting with stylish rooms, and comfortable lounge, small pool, good service, a couple of blocks from the beach. Recommended.
B Soleado Hotel, Sarmiento y Nuestras Malvinas, T490304, www.pinamarturismo.com.ar. Bright, beachfront hotel, cosy spacious rooms.
Camping Several well-equipped sites (US$11-13 per day for 4 in 2 tents), all by the beach at Ostende.

Villa Gesell *p103*
AL Terrazas Club, Av 2 entre 104 y 105, T462181, www.terrazasclubhotel.com.ar. The smartest in town, great service, huge breakfasts, pool and access to the *Azulmarina* Spa, T461245, www.spaazulmarina.com.ar, closed off season.
B Playa, Alameda 205 y C 303, T458027. The first ever hotel, in the wooded old part of town, renovated, comfortable, closed off season.

D Hostería Gran Chalet, Paseo 105 No 447 y Av 4-5, T462913. Warm welcome, comfortable large rooms, good breakfast. Recommended.
E pp Hospedaje Aguas Verdes, Av 5, entre 104 y 105, T462040, clo@terra.com.ar. Airy, with a little garden, rooms for 2-6, some English spoken by very welcoming owners.

Mar del Plata *p104*
Busy traffic makes it impossible to move along the coast in summer: choose a hotel near the beach you want.
L Costa Galana, Bv Marítimo 5725, T486 0000, reservas@hotelcostagalana.com.ar. The best by far, stylish, 5 star, all luxury facilities, at Playa Grandet.
AL Hermitage, Bv Marítimo 2657, T451 9081, www.lacapitalnet.com.ar/hermitag. Charming old-fashioned 4 star on the seafront.
AL Spa República, Córdoba 1968, T492 1142, hosparep@statics.com.ar. Modern, with pool and spa, good restaurant. Recommended.
B-C Argentino, Belgrano 2225 y Entre Ríos, T493 2223, www.argentinohotel-mdp.com.ar. Modern rooms in this traditional 4 star in the city, also apartments, very good value.
C Selent, Arenales 2347, T494 0878, www.hotelselent.com.ar. Quiet with neat rooms, warm welcome, great value.
C Los Troncos, Rodríguez Peña 156, T451 8882. Small, chalet-style hotel in quiet residential area, handy for Güemes bars and restaurants, garden.
D Costa Mogotes, Martínez de Hoz 2401, T484 3140. Tidy, modern, with airy confitería, near Playa Punta Mogotes. Closed off season.

Balcarce *p104*
D Balcarce, C 16 y 17, T422055. Next to the museum, the most comfortable option, good.
Camping Complejo Polideportivo, Ruta 55, Km 63.5, T420251, with pools and good facilities, all kinds of sports too. **Club de Pesca de Balcarce**, RN 226, Km 38.5 at Laguna Brava, T460 8019, well organized site, with all facilities, and good fishing.

Miramar *p104*
B América, Diag Rosende Mitre 1114, T420847. One of the most attractive places in Spanish

colonial style, surrounded by trees, lots of games for children, bikes for hire, lovely gardens.
D Brisas del Mar, C 29 No 557, T420334. Sea front, family-run, neat rooms, cheery restaurant, attentive, good value.
Camping Lots of sites including **F** pp El Durazno, 2 km from town, T431984, with good facilities , including shops, restaurant and cabañas. Take bus 501 marked 'Playas'.

Necochea *p105*
Most hotels are in the seafront area just north of Av 2. There are at least 100 within 700 m of the beach. Many close off season, when you can bargain with those still open.
A Ñikén, C 87 No 335, T432323, 2 blocks from the sea. Very comfortable, 4 star, pool, good facilities, good restaurant, excellent service.
B Bahía, Diagonal San Martín 731, T423353. Really kind owners, comfortable rooms, pool in neat gardens. Recommended.
B España, C 89 No 215, T422896 (ACA affiliated). Modern, well suited to families, attentive staff. Recommended.
B Hostería del Bosque, C 89 No 350, T/F420002. 5 blocks from beach, quiet, comfortable, lovely atmosphere, great restaurant. Recommended.
B Presidente, C 4 No 4040, T423800. Also 4 star and recommended for excellent service, comfortable rooms and pool.
B San Miguel, C 85 No 301, T/F425155 (ACA). Good service and value, comfortable, open all year.
C Marino, Av 79 No 253, T524140, summer only. One of the first hotels, in an historic 1920s building with a wonderful staircase and patios, faded grandeur, but full of character.
Camping Camping UATRE, Av 10 y 187, T438278, the best site, a few km west of town towards Médano Blanco, great facilities, beautifully situated *cabañas*. US$2 pp per day. Campsites on beach US$1 pp in season.

Bahía Blanca *p105*
B Austral, Colón 159, T011-4326 0746, www.hoteles-austral.com.ar. Plain but spacious rooms, very good, fine views, attentive service, decent restaurant.
B Argos, España 149, T455 0404, www.hotel argos.com. 3 blocks from plaza, 4-star business hotel, smart rooms, good breakfast, restaurant.
B Bahía, Chiclana 251, T455 0601, www.bahia-hotel.com.ar. New business hotel, good value, well-equipped comfortable rooms, bright bar and *confitería*. Recommended.
C Barne, H Yrigoyen 270, T453 0294. Family-run, low-key, good value, welcoming.
D-E Hospedaje Bayón, Chiclana 487, T452 2504. Quite basic but OK, cheaper without bath, friendly.

Camping A couple of options in town, but far better to head for Pehuen Có, see below.

Monte Hermoso *p105*
B La Goleta, Av Pte Perón y C 10, T481142. Modern, upmarket, lovely rooms with sea views and balconies, central.
C Petit Hotel, Av Argentina 244, T491818. Simple, modernized 1940's style, family-run, on the beach, breakfast extra. Cheap restaurant, *El Faro*, on the beach (breakfast extra). Recommended.
Camping There are many sites around Monte Hermoso, with good facilities, including: **Americano**, T481149 signposted from main road 5 km before town (bus or taxi from town). Lovely shady site by beach, US$11 per group of 4 per day, hot showers, pool, restaurant, food shop, *locutorio*. Recommended. Many others, most with good facilities.

Tornquist *p105*
D San José, Güemes 138, T0291-494 0152. Small, central, modern hotel with good, simple rooms, quiet.
Camping Parque Norte, just north on Ruta 76, T494 0661. Popular lakeside park to bathe/picnic.

Sierra de la Ventana *p105*
AL Estancia Cerro de la Cruz, just outside Sierra town (phone for directions) T156-486957. Luxurious *estancia* with beautiful views, charming hosts. Recommended.
B Cabañas La Caledonia, Los Robles y Ombúes in **Villa Arcadia**, a couple of blocks over the railway track, T156-462003. Well equipped in pretty gardens.
B Las Vertientes, RP 76, Km 221, signposted to the left just before the turning to Sierra de la Ventana town, T491 0064, lasvertientes@ ba.net. Very welcoming ranch in lovely surroundings, relaxing, horse riding, day visits, US$10pp.
C Provincial, Drago y Malvinas, T491 5025. Old 1940s place, quaint rather than comfy, fabulous views, restaurant, pool, good value.
Camping Sierra Aventura, Av San Martín y Camino a la Hoya, T452 4787, pretty site with eucalyptus trees, hot showers.

Villa Ventana *p106*
Lots of accommodation in *cabañas*; municipal campsite by river with all facilities.
C Hotel El Mirador, before you reach the Villa, great location right at the foot of Cerro de la Ventana, T494 1338, comfortable rooms, some with tremendous views, very peaceful, good restaurant.

🍴 Eating

Mar del Plata *p104*

2 areas have become popular for smaller shops
bars and restaurants: Around C Güemes:
♙♙ Tisiano, San Lorenzo 1332. Good
pasta restaurant in leafy patio.
♙ Almacén El Condal, charming old street-
corner bar, serving *picadas* and drinks,
popular with young crowd.
♙ La Bodeguita, Castelli 1252. Cuban bar with food.
   Around Alem, next to cemetery, lots of pubs
and bars. Traditional favourites:
♙ Confitería Manolo, famous for *churros*
and hot chocolate in the early hours, popular
with post-party people.
♙ Parrilla Trenque Lauken, Mitre 2807,
traditional *parrillada*.
   Seafood restaurants in the Centro Comercial
Puerto, many brightly lit and not atmospheric.
♙♙ Taberna Baska, 12 de Octubre 3301. Seafood.
♙♙ El Viejo Pop, T480 1632. The best place, ship
design, candlelit, superb paella.
   Tenedor libre restaurants of all kinds along San
Martín, and cheap restaurants along Rivadavia.

Necochea *p105*

There are some excellent seafood restaurants.
♙ Cantina Venezia, near the port at Av 59 No
259. The most famous, delicious fish, first class.
♙ Chimichurri, C 83 No 345. Recommended
for *parrilla*.
♙ Parrilla El Loco, C 56 No 3202, T437094. A classic
parrilla, deservedly popular for superb steaks.

Bahía Blanca *p105*

♙♙ Lola Mora, Av Alem y Sarmiento. Elegant,
delicious Mediterranean food, in a colonial-style
house. Excellent and good value set meal.
♙ Micho, Guillermo Torres 3875, T457 0346.
A superb chic fish restaurant at the port (take
bus 500 or 501, but go there by taxi at night,
as it's in an insalubrious area).
♙ El Mundo de la Pizza, Dorrego 53. Fabulous
pizzas, lots of choice, the city's favourite.
♙ Santino, Dorrego 38. Italian-influenced, quiet
sophisticated atmosphere, good value and a
welcoming glass of champagne. US$6 for
2 courses and wine. Recommended.
El Cofre, Dorrego 2 e Yrigoyen. Laid back, good
for a coffee during the day with internet access
and live music at weekends, young crowd.
La Piazza, on the corner of the plaza at O'Higgins
y Chiclana. Great coffee, buzzing atmosphere,
good salads, and cakes too.

Muñoz, O'Higgins y Drago. Sophisticated
café, good for reading the papers.

Monte Hermoso *p105*

♙♙ Marfil, Valle Encantado 91. The smartest,
delicious fish and pastas.
♙ Pizza Jet, Valle Encantado e Int Majluf.
Hugely popular for all kinds of food, arrive
before 2130 to get a table.

🍸 Bars and clubs

Mar del Plata *p104*

Many bars and nightclubs are on Alem or its
surroundings and start at around 0200. **Mr Jones**,
Alem 3738, for the under 25s. **La Llorona**, on
Olavarria, near Blvd Marítimo, for the over 25s.

Bahía Blanca *p105*

Lots of discos on **Fuerte Argentino**
(along the stream leading to the park) mainly
catering for under 25's: **Chocolate**, **Bonito**.
Sobremonte, No 6690, huge complex of bars
and dance floors (it's fine to be over 25 here!).

🚍 Transport

San Clemente del Tuyú *p103*

Bus To **Mar del Plata** (and to resorts in
between) are frequent, **Rápido del Sud**,
El Rápido Argentino, US$6, 5 hrs. To **Buenos
Aires**, several companies, US$12-16.

Pinamar *p103*

Bus Terminal 4 blocks north of main plaza at
Av Bunge e Intermédanos, T403500. To **Buenos
Aires**, US$12-16, 4-5hrs, several companies.
Trains The station is a few kilometres away,
free bus transfers from town. See page 102.

Villa Gesell *p103*

Air Regular flights (in summer) from Buenos
Aires to airport, 5 km away, taxi US$3, usually
minibuses meet each flight. Several companies,
book in advance at weekends.
Bus Direct to **Buenos Aires**, many companies,
5 hrs, US$12-15. To **Mar del Plata** 2 hrs, US$3.30.
Also buses from Mendoza, Córdoba. Terminal at
Av 3 y Paseo 140.

Mar del Plata *p104*

Air Camet airport, T478 3990, 10 km north
of town. Several flights daily to **Buenos Aires**,
LADE (T493 8220), AR/Austral (T496 0101). LADE
also to many Patagonian towns once a week.

🔴 *For an explanation of the sleeping and eating price codes used in this guide, see page 58.*
● *Other relevant information is found in Essentials pages 68-69.*

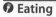

Remise taxi from airport to town, US$5, mini bus US$2, also bus 542 (signed Aeropuerto) US$0.40.

Boat 1-hr boat trips along the city coast on the **Anamora**, several times daily in summer, weekends only in winter, from Dársena B, Muelle de Guardacostas in the port, US$7, T489 0310.

Bus For information T451 5406. The bus terminal, in a former railway station, is central at Alberti y Las Heras, but squalid and short on services. Not a place to hang around at night. **El Rápido**, T451 0600, **Flecha bus**, T486 0512, **TAC**, T4510014, **Chevalier**, T451 8447. **La Estrella**, T486 0915. To **Buenos Aires**, 5-6 hrs, US$11-16, many companies; **Chevalier**, and **Costera Criolla**, also have *coche cama*. To **La Plata**, 6 hrs, US$15. **El Cóndor** and Rápido Argentino. To **San Clemente del Tuyú**, El Rápido, frequent, 5 hrs, US$8. To **Bahía Blanca**, only **Pampa**, 6 daily, US$12, 7 hrs. Change there for buses to **Bariloche** (Vía Bariloche, 20 hrs, US$48) and **Puerto Madryn**. To all Patagonian towns, ending at Río Gallegos, 36 hrs, US$80, with Transportadora Patagónica. To **Mendoza**, **Andesmar**, daily 19-22 hrs, US$43-57.

Train To **Buenos Aires** (Constitución) from Estación Norte, Luro 4599, T475 6076, 13 blocks from the centre. Buses to/from centre 511, 512, 512B, 541. See page 102. Also services to Miramar.

Miramar *p104*

Bus Terminal at C 34 y Av 23, T423359. 8 daily to **Buenos Aires**, many companies, 6 hrs, US$12-16. To/from **Mar del Plata**, US$1.40, Rápido del Sud, from C 23 y 24, T423359. To **Necochea**, El Rápido, US$3.

Train See page 102. Station at Av 40 y C 15, T420657.

Necochea *p105*

Bus Terminal at Av 58 y Jesuita Cardiel, T422470, 3 km from the beach area; bus 513, 517 from outside the terminal to the beach. Taxi to beach area US$2. To **Buenos Aires**, 8 hrs, US$15, **La Estrella**, **El Cóndor** and few others. To **Mar del Plata**, El Rápido, US$4. To **Bahía Blanca**, El Rápido US$10.

Bahía Blanca *p105*

Air Airport Comandante Espora, lies 11 km northeast of centre, US$3 in a taxi. Airport information T486 1456. Daily flights to **Buenos Aires** with AR/Austral (T456 0561/ 0810-2228 6527) and LADE (T452 1063). LADE has weekly flights to **Bariloche**, **Mar del Plata**, **Neuquén**, **Puerto Madryn**, **San Antonio Oeste**, **San Martín de los Andes** (may involve changes).

Bus Terminal in old railway station 2 km from centre, at Estados Unidos y Brown, T481 9615, connected by buses 512, 514, or taxi US$3, no hotels nearby. To **Buenos Aires** frequent, several

companies, 8½ hrs, US$15-18, shop around. Most comfortable by far is **Plusmar** suite bus, with flat beds US$25 (T456 0616). To **Mar del Plata**, El Rápido, US$12, 7 hrs. To **Córdoba**, US$21, 12 hrs. To **Neuquén**, 6 a day, 8 hrs, US$12. To **Necochea**, El Rápido, 5 hrs, US$10. To **Viedma** Ceferino, Plusmar and Río Paraná (to Carmen de Patagones), 4 hrs, US$6-8. To **Trelew**, **Don Otto** and others, US$30, 10½ hrs (9½ hrs to Puerto Madryn, US$26). To **Río Gallegos**, Don Otto US$36. To **Tornquist**, US$3, Río Paraná and La Estrella/El Cóndor, 1 hr 20 min; to **Sierra de la Ventana** (town) La Estrella/El Cóndor and Expreso Cabildo, US$5. Also *combi* (shared taxi) with Geotur T450 1190, terminal at San Martín 455.

Train Station at Av Gral Cerri 750, T452 9196. To/from **Buenos Aires**, see page 102.

Pehuén-Có and Monte Hermoso *p105*

Bus Combis Ariber minibus taxi service from Bahía Blanca to either town, ring to be collected from anywhere in town, T4565523, Combibus, T155-700400.

Sierra de la Ventana *p105*

Bus Geotur, San Martín 193, T491 5355. Operates a minibus a few times a day along RP 76 from Sierra de la Ventana to Tornquist, dropping off hikers at the entrance to the park. Also specializes in mountain biking, trekking and horse riding trips.

ⓘ Directory

Mar del Plata *p104*

Banks Many ATMs all around the central area, along Peatonal San Martín, at Santa Fe y Rivadavia and two close together by the casino. *Casas de Cambio* Jonestur, San Martín 2574, and Av Luro 3181, best rates for TCs and cash. Amex, at *Oti Internacional*, San Luis 1630, T494 5414. **La Moneta**, Rivadavia 2615. **Cultural centres** Cultural events: reduced price tickets are often available from **Cartelera Baires**, Santa Fe 1844, local 33, or from **Galería de los Teatros**, Santa Fe 1751. Asociación Argentina de Cultura Inglesa, San Luis 2498, friendly, extensive library. **Internet** Broadband internet can be found everywhere. **Telephones** Many *locutorios* around the town. **Useful addresses** Immigration Office: Rivadavia 3820, T492 4271, open morning.

Bahía Blanca *p105*

Banks Many ATMs on plaza for all major cards. *Casas de Cambio*: Pullman, San Martín 171. **Internet** Many places along Zelarrayan and Estomba near plaza. **Post offices** Moreno 34. **Telephones** Big *locutorio* at Alsina 108, also internet.

West of Buenos Aires

Rising out of the flat arid Pampa, the Sierras of Córdoba and San Luis give a dramatic setting to popular holiday towns and mountain retreats. Beyond the plains, fertile valleys stretch along the length of the Andean precordillera and climb up to the heights of Aconcagua and its neighbours. The western provinces of Mendoza, San Juan, La Rioja and Catamarca cover extreme contrasts, but Mendoza and the surrounding area to the south is popular for its excellent wines, climbing and superb ski and adventure resorts such as Malargüe.

Córdoba

→ *Phone code: 0351. Colour map 8, grid A3. Population: 1.4 million. Altitude: 440 m.*

Córdoba, the second city in the country, has some fine historic buildings and a lively university population. It is also an important route centre. Córdoba the city, capital of Córdoba Province, was founded in 1573. The site of the first university in the country, established in 1613 by the Jesuits, it now has two universities. It is an important industrial centre, the home of Argentina's motor industry, and a busy modern city with a flourishing shopping centre.

Ins and outs

Getting there Pajas Blancas airport, 12 km northwest of city, T475 0392, has shops, post office, a good restaurant and a *casa de cambio* (open Monday-Friday 1000-1500). The bus service (US$0.30) can be unreliable; a regular or *remise* taxi charges around US$5. Bus terminal at Blvd Perón 250, 8 blocks east of main Plaza, T434 1700. Left luggage lockers, US$0.65 per day, *remise* taxi desk, ATM, tourist office at the lower level, where the ticket offices are. Taxi US$0.65 to Plaza San Martín. Minibuses, *diferenciales*, have better services to the sierras and depart from nearby platform; tickets on bus or from offices at terminal, first floor. ►► *For further information, see Transport, page 113.*

Tourist offices **Municipal tourist office** ① *old Cabildo, Deán Funes 15, T428 5856.* Also at **Centro Obispo Mercadillo** ① *Plaza San Martín, Rosario de Santa Fe 39, T428 5600,* or in **Patio Olmos Shopping Mall** ① *Av San Juan y Vélez Sarsfield, T420 4100,* as well as at the bus terminal and at the airport. All open early morning to late at night, with useful city maps and information on guided walks and cycle tours. The municipality runs good, daily city tours leaving from the Centro Obispo Mercadillo; tourist offices have details. **Provincial tourist information** at the **Complejo Ferial** ① *8 km from the city centre, Av Carcano, Chateau Carreras, T434 8260, dacyt.turismo@cba.gov.ar.* See also: www.cordobatrip.com and www.cordoba.net. Both hane information in Spanish.

Sights

At the city's heart is **Plaza San Martín**, with a statue of the Liberator. On the west side is the old **Cabildo** ① *Independencia 30, free, except for entry to exhibitions, 0900-2100 (Mon 1400-2100).* Built around two internal patios, the building now houses the tourist office, a small gallery, a restaurant and a bookshop. Next to it stands the **Cathedral** ① *0800-1200, 1630-2000,* the oldest in Argentina (begun 1640, consecrated 1671), with attractive stained glass windows and a richly-decorated ceiling. Look out for statues of angels resembling native Americans. Behind the cathedral is the pleasant **Plaza del Fundador**, with a statue to the city founder Jerónimo Luis de Cabrera. One of the features of this part of the city is its old churches. Near Plaza San Martín at Independencia 122 is the 16th-century **Carmelo Convent** and chapel of **Santa Teresa**, whose rooms and beautiful patio form the **Museo de Arte Religioso Juan de Tejeda** ① *Wed-Sat 0930-1230, US$0.35, guided visits also in English and French.* This houses one of the finest collections of religious art in the country. The **Manzana Jesuítica** ① *contained within Av Vélez Sarsfield, Caseros, Duarte Quirós and Obispo Trejo, Tue-Sun 0900-1300, 1600-2000, US$1, T4332075,* has been declared a world heritage site by Unesco. **La Compañía** (Obispo Trejo y Caseros, built between 1640 and 1676) has a vaulted ceiling reminiscent of a ship's hull. Behind it, on Caseros, is the beautiful **Capilla Doméstica**, a private 17th century Jesuit chapel (guided visits only). Next to it are two former Jesuit institutions: the main building of the **Universidad Nacional de Córdoba** ⓘ *T4332075, Tue-Sun 0900-1300, 1600-2000, US$1*, housing one of the most valuable libraries in the country; and the **Colegio Nacional de Montserrat**, the most traditional high school in the province. Guided tours of the church, chapel, university (called Museo Histórico) and school leave from Obispo Trejo 242 ⓘ *Tue-Sun 1000, 1100, 1700 and 1800, available in English*. The **Basicilica de La Merced** ⓘ *25 de Mayo 83*, was built in the early 19th century, though its fine gilt wooden pulpit dates from the colonial period. On its exterior, overlooking Rivadavia, are fine murals in ceramic by local artist Armando Sica. Further east, at Blvd J D Perón, is the magnificent late 19th-century **Mitre railway station**, with its beautiful tiled *confitería*, still used for Sunday evening tango shows.

Museo Marqués de Sobremonte ⓘ *Rosario de Santa Fe 218, 1 block east of San Martin, T4331661, Tue-Sat 1000-1600 (in summer Mon-Fri 0900-1500), US$0.35, texts in English and German*. Formerly the house of Rafael Núñez, governor of Córdoba, and now the only surviving colonial family residence in the city, the museum displays 18th and 19th provincial history. **Museo Municipal de Bellas Artes** ⓘ *Av General Paz 33, T433 1512, Tue-Sun 0900-2100, US$0.35*. Has a permanent collection of contemporary art by celebrated Argentine artists in an early 20th-century mansion.

Córdoba

Córdoba
  Backpackers 14 *A1*
Córdoba Hostel 2 *C2*
Cristal 3 *B2*
Entre Ríos 5 *B3*
Heydi 8 *B3*

Sleeping 🛏
Alex 4 *B3*
Alto Paraná 1 *B3*
American Córdoba Park 6 *B1*

Hostel Joven 16 *A1*
NH Panorama 10 *A1*
Quetzal 11 *B3*
Sussex 12 *A2*

Windsor 13 *B2*

Eating 🍴
Alfonsina 1 *B2*
Betos 2 *B1*
El Anden 5 *B2*
El Arrabal 3 *C1*
El Ruedo 4 *A2*
La Cocina de Osés 7 *B1*
L'América 6 *B2*

La Vieja Casa
  del Francés 7 *B1*
Mandarina 9 *A2*
Puerto Illia 10 *B3*
Sorocabana 13 *A2*
Upacanejo 14 *A2*

Bars & clubs 🍸
Reina Alba 11 *C1*

⊜ Sleeping

Córdoba p110, map p111

A Amerian Córdoba Park, Bv San Juan 165, T420 7000, www.amerian.com. Swish, modern hotel with marbled foyer and professional service. Comfortable, superb breakfast, convenient and reliable. Also has a business centre, spa and pool.

A NH Panorama, Alvear 251, T410 3900, www.nh-hoteles.com. Comfortable, functional, small pool, gym, restaurant, views of Sierra from upper floors.

A Windsor, Buenos Aires 214, T422 4012, www.windsortower.com. Small, smart, warm, large breakfast, sauna, gym, pool.

C Cristal, Entre Ríos 58, T424 5000, www.hotel cristal.com.ar. Good, comfortable, well maintained, large breakfast, good service, a/c, welcoming.

C Sussex, San Jerónimo 125, T422 9070, hotelsussex@arnet.com. A/c, with breakfast, well kept, small pool, family welcome.

D Alto Paraná, Paraná 230, T428 1625, hotelal toparana@arnet.com.ar. Close to bus terminal, hot shower, TV, breakfast, very nice, good value.

D Heydi, Bv Illia 615, T421 8906, www.hotelheydi.com.ar. The best value in town, quiet, 3 star, pleasant rooms, breakfast included.

D Quetzal, San Jerónimo 579, T/F422 9106. Refurbished, spotless, good value, breakfast extra.

D-F Baluch Backpackers Hostel. San Martin 338, www.baluchbackpackers.com. From US$6 pp in dormitory. Organizes various activities.

E Alex, Bv Illia 742, T421 4350, www.alexhotel.com.ar. Good value, modern, cosy despitre a slightly off-putting exterior. All rooms include breakfast and a mate kit, helpful staff, close to the bus station.

E Córdoba Backpackers, Deán Funes 285, T422 0593, www.cordobabackpackers.com.ar. Cheaper with shared bath, new hostel, family atmosphere, very helpful. Recommended.

E Entre Ríos, Entre Ríos 567, T/F423 0311. Basic, welcoming, some rooms a/c, 1 room has wheelchair accessbreakfast, 10% discount for ISIC members.

F pp Córdoba Hostel, Ituzaingó 1070, T468 7359, www.cordobahostel.com.ar. In Nueva Córdoba district, small but decent rooms (**D** in double), cooking and relaxing with private lockers in rooms and large breakfast. Small discount for HI members.

F pp Hostel Joven, Tablada 414. Kitchen, internet, laundry, very good, helpful.

Estancias

Estancia Los Potreros, Sierras Chicas, Casilla de correo 4, La Cumbre, T452121, www.ride-americas.com. An exclusive 6,000-acre working cattle farm in the wild and scenic Cordoba hills. High standard of accommodation, with attention to detail in keeping with a time past. The "riders' estancia"... unrivalled in its fabulous horses (impeccably trained and calm polo horses). Even

for non-equestrians you can relax by the pool, go birdwatching or just enjoy the peaceful hilltop setting and savour the delicious food and wines - all included in the price. 3 nights minimum stay. Highly recommended (either take a bus to the nearest town, Río Ceballos, or the owners will arrange a taxi from Córdoba city or airport, 1 hr).

❷ Eating

Córdoba p110, map p111

♈ L'América, Caseros 67, T4271734. Designer restaurant with imaginative menu, from traditional to sushi to French, large selection of wines, home-made bread, great service, also cheap set menus.

♈ Betos, San Juan 450, T469 2774. Best *lomitos* in town at this large, popular *parrilla*. Recommended.

♈ La Cocina de Osés, Independencia 512. Nicely decorated if rather formal, good for fish, meat dishes and homemade pastas.

♈ Novecento, at the Cabildo, T423 0660. Smart and lively, in an airy patio, superb Mediterranean-style cooking, excellent service. Lunch only, bar open 0800-2000. Recommended.

♈ Upacanejo, San Jerónimo 171. Based on a popular comic character (staff dressed accordingly), *parrilla* serving excellent beef and chicken.

♈ La Vieja Casa del Francés, Independencia 508. Delicious grills, inviting atmosphere, expat owners happy to chat with diners. Recommended.

♈ Alfonsina, Duarte Quirós 66. Rural style in an old house, simple meals, pizzas and *empanadas* or breakfasts with homemade bread, piano and guitar music, popular with the city's young crowd.

Cafés

El Anden, Buenos Aires y Entre Ríos. Tasty *facturas*, croissants and good music.

El Ruedo, Obispo Trejo y 27 de Abril. A lively *confitería*, also serving light meals.

Mandarina, Obispo Trejo 171, T0351-426 4909. Central, welcoming, leafy, lots of great breakfasts, good for lunch and dinner. Highly recommended.

Puerto Illia, Bv Illia 555. By bus terminal, and open 24 hrs for breakfasts and simple meals – great if you arrive at night or have a long wait.

Sorocabana, Buenos Aires y San Jerónimo. Great breakfasts, popular, good views of Plaza San Martín.

❶ Bars and clubs

Cerro Las Rosas, Northwest of town, locally referred just as *Cerro*, has a lively area of bars and clubs (US$3.50 pp) along Av Rafael Núñez, including **Arcimboldo**, No 4567. **Factory**, No 3964, popular club for all ages, playing a mix of electronic and Latin dance music. **Villa Agur**, José

Roque Funes y Tristán Malbrán, is more rock and roll with food and live music.

Chateau Carreras, further northwest is another popular area. **Carreras**, on Av Ramón J Cárcano. The most popular club.

El Abasto district, on the river (about 8 blocks north of Plaza San Martín) has several good places for lower budgets: **Casa Babylon**, Bv Las Heras 48, very popular disco night Fri, rock Sat. **Dvino**, Pasaje Agustín Pérez 32 (behind Puente Alvear). Before 1900, taste wines. There are many affordable options around Bv San Juan and Av Vélez Sarsfield, along La Cañada or south of Bv Illia at Nueva Córdoba district. **Reina Alba**, Obispo Trejo y F Rivera, is a redesigned old house with a chic bar. **Rita**, Independencia 1162, is a refurbished old house with a trendy clientele.

Studenty bars on Rondeau between Av H Yrigoyen and Chacabuco. Less noisy are: **Johnny B Good**, H Yrigoyen 320, and **Posh**, H Yrigoyen 464, for jazz, blues and bossa nova after 2400. *Cuarteto* music, a Cordobés invention, is hugely popular.

⊙ Entertainment

See free listings magazines *La Cova* and *Ocio en Córdoba*, local newspaper *La Voz del Interior*, and *www.cordoba.net*, for events.

Cinema Many cinemas including **Cineclub Municipal**, Bv Illia 49, **Teatro Córdoba**, 27 de Abril 275, both showing independent and foreign language films, and the new theatre in **Shopping Patio Olmos** (see below), with new releases.

Dance **Confitería Mitre**, Bv Perón 101 (in railway station), tango class before *milonga* (public place to dance) begins, US$1.30. The patio at the Cabildo on Fri has tango lessons and dance. **El Arrabal**, Belgrano y Fructuoso Rivera, restaurant with a tango show after 2400, Fri and Sat, US$1.70 extra.

Theatre The Festival of Latinamerican Theatre is held every Oct. **Teatro del Libertador**, Av Vélez Sarsfield 367, T433 2312, is traditional and sumptuous, with a rich history.

⊙ Shopping

Bookshops Librería Blackpool, Deán Funes 395, for imported English books. **Yenny-El Ateneo**, Av Gral Paz 180. Has some English titles.

Handicrafts Mundo Aborigen, Rivadavia 155. **Paseo de las Artes**, Achával Rodríguez y La Cañada. Handicraft market, Sat-Sun 1600-2200 (in summer 1800-2300), ceramics, leather, wood and metalware. **Unión de Artesanos**, San Martín 42 (Galería San Martín, local 22).

Shopping malls Córdoba Shopping, José de Goyechea 2851 (Villa Cabrera). **Nuevocentro**, Av Duarte Quirós 1400. **Patio Olmos**, Av Vélez Sarsfield y Bv San Juan. Central.

⊙ Transport

Córdoba *p110, map p111*

Air AR/Austral run a shuttle service several times a day to/from **Buenos Aires**, about 2 hrs. LAN also flies to Buenos Aires. Most major Argentine cities are served by AR, usually via BsAs. International flights to **Bolivia** (Santa Cruz), **Brazil** and **Chile** direct, others via BsAs.

Bus Municipal buses and electric buses (trolleys) do not accept cash. You have to buy tokens (*cospeles*) or cards from kiosks, normal US$0.30.

The terminal at Bvd Perón 250 has restaurants, supermarket, internet, left-luggage lockers. ATM and tourist office. To **Buenos Aires**, several companies, 9-11 hrs, US$12 *común*, US$17-22 *coche cama*. To **Salta**, 12 hrs, US$20-28. To **Jujuy**, US$24, 13-14 hrs. To **Mendoza**, 9-12 hrs, frequent, US$12-18. To **La Rioja**, 6-7 hrs, US$7. To **Catamarca**, 6 hrs, US$10-12. To **San Luis**, Andesmar, Autotransportes San Juan-Mar del Plata, TAC, 7 hrs, US$6-8. TAC and Andesmar have connecting services to several destinations in **Patagonia**. See towns below for buses to the Sierras de Córdoba. To **Santiago** (Chile), US$20, 17-19 hrs, CATA, TAC. To **Bolivia** take Balut or Andesmar services to the border at La Quiaca (19 hrs, US$20) or Pocitos (17 hrs, US$20-23).

⊙ Directory

Airline offices Aerolíneas Argentinas/ Austral, Colón 520, T410 7600. **LAB**, Colón 166, T421 6458. **LAN**, Figueroa Alcorta 206, T475 9555.

Banks Open in the morning. There are many Link and Banelco ATMs; all accept international credit cards. **Citibank**, Ituzaingó 238, changes Citicorp and Visa TCs (no commission). **Exprinter**, Rivadavia 47. Cash and Amex TCs (low commission). **Barujel**, Rivadavia y 25 de Mayo. Cash, Amex TCs (15% commission), Visa TCs; also Western Union branch. **Cultural centres** Asociación Argentina de Cultura Británica, Av H Yrigoyen 496, T468 1995. Good library with books and magazines, English teaching materials, videos and a reading room, Mon-Fri 0900-2000. **Consulates** Bolivia, San Jeronimo 167, p 6, T424 5650. Chile, Crisol 280, T469 0432. **Internet** Many places, US$0.35 per hr. Mega Cyber, MT de Alvear 229, open til 0500. **Language schools** ILEE, T4824829, www.ilee.com.ar. Spanish courses and lodging arranged. **Medical services** Emergencies, T107. Hospital Córdoba, Av Patria 656, T434 9000. Hospital Clínicas, Santa Rosa 1564, T433 7010. **Post offices** Colón 210, parcel service on the ground floor by the customs office. **Telephones** There are plenty of *locutorios*, many with post office and internet. **Useful addresses** Dirección Nacional de Migraciones, Caseros 676, T422 2740. Police, T101. Fire department, T100.

Around Córdoba

Sierras de Córdoba

The Sierras de Córdoba offer beautiful mountain landscapes with many rivers and streams, plus the advantage of good infrastructure and accessibility. Adventure tourism has really taken off here, so there's something for everyone in the hills and valleys. San Luis, too, has pleasant hills and is a good place to buy onyx. Popular for tourism among the upper classes in the late 19th century, the Sierras de Córdoba were opened up for mass tourism in the 1940's with the building of lots of hotels. The most visited sights lie along the valleys of **Punilla**, **Traslasierra** and **Calamuchita**, and on the east side of the **Sierra Chica**, north of Córdoba, all forming itineraries of about 70 km long each. There's a useful network of dirt roads (usually used for rally competitions!). Summer rainstorms may cause sudden floods along riversides. Beware when choosing a campsite.

Villa Carlos Paz In the Punilla Valley is this large modern town (*Phone code 03541, Population 56,000, Altitude 642 m*) on an artificial lake Lago San Roque, 36 km west of Córdoba. It is the nearest resort to Córdoba and is therefore often crowded. Trips on the lake are offered in all kinds of water-vehicles, from amphibious trucks to catamarans (stalls along Avenida San Martín, opposite bus station, US$3.30). A chair-lift runs from the Complejo Aerosilla to the summit of the Cerro de la Cruz, which offers splendid views (US$3.30). North of Villa Carlos Paz, on Ruta 38, a road branches west to Tanti from where local buses go to **Los Gigantes**, a paradise for climbers, two-day treks possible (entry US$1). Club Andino has several *refugios*; contact **Club Andino Córdoba** *T0351-480 5126.* **Tourist information** ① *San Martín 400 and No 1000, T0810-888 2729, open 0700-2100, www.sierrascordobesas.com.ar.*

Cosquín On the banks of the Río Cosquín, 26 km north of Villa Carlos Paz, Cosquín (*Phone code: 03541, Population 18,800, Altitude 708 m*) is the site of the most important **folklore festival**, in the last two weeks in January. A popular rock festival is held in early February so that accommodation is almost impossible to find between 10 January and 10 February. **Museo Camín Cosquín** ① *at Km 760, out of town, T451184, 0900-1230, 1400-1800 (closes later in summer), US$0.65.* Minerals, fossils and archaeology, recommended. Take a *remise* taxi from the town centre, US$5 (or walk two hours) to the **Pan de Azúcar** hill (1,260 m), from where there is a good view over the Punilla valley. Chairlift to top (all year round). **Tourist office** ① *Av San Martín 560, Plaza Próspero Molino, T453701.*

North from Córdoba

La Falda (*Phone code: 03548, Population 16,000, Altitude 934 m*), 82 km north of Córdoba, is a good base for walking, if not an attractive town. Visit the **Trenshow** ① *Las Murallas 200, T423041, 0930-2000, US$2,* a model railway museum. **Camino de El Cuadrado** crosses the sierras eastward to Río Ceballos, passing an excellent vantage point at *Balcón de las Nubes* and the 18th-century *Estancia El Silencio*, 11 km from La Falda, where is a small museum and outdoor activities are organized. To the west, an 80-km rough winding road goes to La Higuera, across the Cumbres de Gaspar. It crosses the vast **Pampa de Olaén**, a 1,100-m high grass-covered plateau with the tiny, 18th-century chapel of **Santa Bárbara** (20 km from La Falda) and the **Cascadas de Olaén**, with three waterfalls, 2 km south of the chapel. **Tourist office** ① *Av España 50 (at the former railway station), T423007.*

North of La Falda is **La Cumbre** (*Phone code: 03548, Population 7,200, Altitude 1141 m*), at the highest point in the Punilla Valley, Founded by British engineers and workers who built the railway here in 1900, it is an attractive place with tree-lined avenues. It has classy shops, good places to eat and have tea, a golf course and, nearby, the paragliding centre of **Cuchi Corral** (see Activities and tours, below).

Capilla del Monte About 106 km north of Córdoba and set in the heart of the Sierras, Capilla del Monte (*Phone code 03458, Altitude 979 m*) is a good centre for trekking, paragliding and exploring this area. Excursions in the hills, particularly to Cerro Uritorco, 1,979 m, a four-hour climb (no shade, entry US$2) via La Toma where there are medicinal waters and from where there are further walking opportunities. There is horse riding and tours to meditation and 'energy' centres: the location of many sightings of UFOs, the area is popular for 'mystical tourism'. **Tourist office** ① *in the old railway station at the end of the diagonal Calle Buenos Aires, open daily 0830-2030, some English spoken, T481903.*

Jesús María (*Colour map 8, grid A3. Population: 27,000. Altitude: 533 m. 51 km north of Córdoba on Ruta 9*) **Estancia de Jesús María** ① *T420126, Mon-Fri 0800-1900, Sat-Sun 1000-1200, 1400-1800 (1500-1900 in summer and spring), US$0.65, Mon free, easy 15-min walk from bus station: take Av Juan B Justo, north, turn left at Av Cleto Peña, cross bridge on river and follow a dirt road right about 300 m.* Dating from the 17th century, the estancia has the remains of its once famous winery, reputed to have produced the first wine in the Americas, which was served to the Spanish royal family. In the cloister is an excellent **Museo Jesuítico**, where Cuzco-style paintings, religious objects and a curious collection of plates are exhibited. **Estancia de Caroya**, ① *T426701, daily 0900-1300, 1400-1800 (1500-1900 in spring and summer), US$1, 20-min walk from bus station, taxi US$1.50.* A rather more humble place in the southern suburbs, this estancia also dates from the 17th century; a large white building around a lovely patio, with a quaint stone chapel beside it. **Estancia de Santa Catalina** ①*T424467, winter Tue-Fri 1000-1300, 1400-1800 (summer Tue-Sat 1000-1300, 1500-1930, Sun 1000-1800), weekends-only Jan, Feb, Jul, Easter and bank holidays), US$2. From the bus station, remise taxis US$8-10 return including 2-hr stay.* Still in private hands, beautifully located in the countryside northwest of Jesús María, this is the largest of the *estancias* and has the most splendid buildings, well preserved and containing some fine religious art. Each January there is a gaucho and folklore festival, lasting 10 nights from second week; very popular. Some 4 km north of Jesús María is **Sinsacate**, a fine colonial posting inn, now a museum, with chapel attached.

At Rayo Cortado, 114 km north of Jesús María, a turning leads west to **Cerro Colorado**, 160 km north of Córdoba, the former home of the late Argentine folklore singer and composer Atahualpa Yupanqui. His house is a **museum** ① *T155-198715, daily 0900-1300, 1600-2000, at the end of the winding road to Agua Escondida, also offers guided tours*, lush grounds, with chance of spotting armadillos. There are about 35,000 rock paintings by the indigenous Comechingones in the nearby **Reserva Natural y Cultural Cerro Colorado** ① *at the foot of Cerro Intihuasi, daily in summer 0700-1300, 1400-2000, winter daily 0800-1900, US$1, only with guide, 1-1½ hr tour*, and a small **archaeological museum** ① *daily 0700-1300, 1400-2000, tours at 0830, 1030, 1600 and 1800*. There is a cheap hostería, T03522-422180, and campsite; an unpaved road, 12 km, branches off Ruta 9 at Santa Elena, 104 km north of Jesús María. To get there: Ciudad de Córdoba bus goes to/from Córdoba 3 times weekly, 4½ hours, US$5.

Southwest of Córdoba

A scenic road southwest from Villa Carlos Paz passes **Icho Cruz**, before climbing into the Sierra Grande and crossing the Pampa de Achala, a huge granite plateau at 2,000 m. At La Pampilla, 55 km from Villa Carlos Paz, is the entrance to the **Parque Nacional Quebrada del Condorito** ① *administration at Sabattini 33, of 2, T433371, Villa Carlos Paz, www.carlospaz.gov.ar/pn condorito*, covering 40,000 ha of the Pampa de Achala and surrounding slopes. This is the easternmost habitat of the condor and an ideal flying school for the younger birds. Sightings are not guaranteed (Balcón Sur is a likely spot), but there's great trekking on the *pastizal de altura* (sierran grassland). Several camping places. Tours from Villa Carlos Paz. If you have your own car, park it at the NGO Fundación Cóndor (9 km before La Pampilla), beside a handicraft shop (1 km before La Pampilla) or at El Cóndor (7 km after La Pampilla). Ciudad de Córdoba and TAC buses can stop at La Pampilla on their way to Mina Clavero (from Villa Carlos Paz: 1 hr, US$1.90).

Mina Clavero This is a good centre, 40 km west of Córdoba, for exploring the high *sierra* and the Traslasierra Valley (*Phone code: 03544, Colour map 8, grid A3, Population: 6,800, Altitude: 915 m*). There is an intriguing museum, **Museo Rocsen** ① *13 km south and about 5 km east of the village of Nono, T498218, www.museorocsen.org; daily 0900 till sunset, US$1, getting there: taxi, US$1.30*. The personal collection of Sr Bouchón, it is a wonderfully bizarre mix of subjects, including furniture, minerals, instruments, archaeology and animals ('by far the best natural history and cultural museum, a whole day is needed to visit', Federico Kirbus). There are many hotels, *hosterías hospedajes*, campsites and restaurants around Mina Clavero; others at Cura Brochero and Nono. **Tourist office** (with ATM) ① *Av San Martín y Av Mitre, T470171, mclavero.turismo@traslasierra.com, open 0900 till very late.*

South from Córdoba

Alta Gracia (*Phone code 03547, Colour map 8, grid A3, Population 42,600, Altitude 580 m*). Beside Lago Tajamar, Alta Gracia, 39 km southwest of Córdoba, has an interesting **Estancia Jesuítica Alta Gracia** (a UNESCO World Heritage Site) ① *T421303, winter Tue-Fri 0900-1300,*

C **Gran San Luis**, Av Illia 470,
T425049, hotelsanluis@hotmail.com. 3-star
traditional hotel, with breakfast, restaurant
(closed weekends), good pool, parking.
D **Aiello**, Av Illia 431, T425609. With breakfast,
a/c, spacious, garage, restaurant open weekdays.
Recommended as best value in town.
D **Grand Palace**, Rivadavia 657, T422059.
With breakfast, some rooms with a/c, parking,
central, spacious, good lunches, lively
with friendly staff.
E **Belgrano**, Belgrano 1440, T435923.
With breakfast, probably the best budget
option, rooms with bath and fan.

Camping There are a few campsites in
El Volcán, on the riverbank (20 km from
San Luís). Also C **Campo la Sierra**, T494171,
www.campola sierra.com.ar, Swiss-owned
7-ha farm, warm welcome, with German-style
cooking, breakfast, pool and archery, dorms in
cabins also available.

Sierras de San Luis *p116*
D pp **Hostería Las Verbenas**, 10 km south of
Carolina, T02652-430918, www.lasverbenas.com.ar.
In the beautiful Pancata Valley, ideal place for
exploring the area, price is full board.
D **La Posta del Caminante**, RP 9 Km 83, Carolina,
T02652-490223, www.lapostadelcaminante.com.ar.
Comfortable rooms in former mining engineers'
residence, with breakfast, cheaper with shared
bath, restaurant next door, pool in natural setting,
trips to mines and horse-riding excursions.

Libertador General San Martín *p116*
D **Hostería San Martín**, with bath and
breakfast, meals served, good value.

Merlo *p117*
There are many hotels, *hosterías* and *residenciales*
both in the town and nearby. Book in advance
Jan-Feb, Easter, Jul-Aug and long weekends.
B **Villa de Merlo**, Pedernera y Av del Sol,
T475335. Nice rooms, good views, quiet,
relaxing, gardens with pool, sports facilities.
D **Colonial**, Av Dos Venados y P Tisera, T475388,
hotelcolonial@hotmail.com. Good value, quiet
residential area not far from centre, simple rooms,
with breakfast, internet, tiny pool on patio.

🍴 Eating

La Falda *p114*
🍴 **El Cristal**, San Lorenzo 39. Very good
cooking, where the locals eat.
🍴 **Pachamama**, Av Edén 127. Health food
shop with cheap organic vegetable pies, or
wholemeal pizzas and *empanadas*.

Alta Gracia *p115*
🍴🍴🍴 **Morena**, Av Sarmiento 413. Good,
imaginative contemporary Argentine cuisine,
in welcoming atmosphere of nice old house.
🍴 **Alta Gracia Golf Club**, Av Carlos Pellegrini
1000, T422922. Superb food in elegant
surroundings in this charming neighbourhood
golf club. Recommended.
🍴 **Hispania**, Urquiza 90. Same owners as *Hotel
Hispania*, an excellent and moderately priced
place serving fish and seafood, delicious desserts.
🍴 **Leyendas**, Bv Pellegrini 797, T429042.
American-style, sport-inspired bar, cosy,
good hamburgers and snacks, buzzing
atmosphere. Recommended.

San Luis *p116*
🍴🍴 **Rotisería La Porteña**, Junín y Gral Paz,
T431722. Good simple food, huge portions,
enjoyable atmosphere, popular.
🍴🍴 **Los Robles**, Colón 684, T436767. *Parrilla* with
good food, wide choice, formal. Recommended.
🍴 **Crocantes**, San Martín 630. Excellent bakery
with good choice of freshly-made sandwiches.
🍴 **La Pulpería del Arriero**, 9 de Julio 753,
T432446. Regional specialities with live folk
music in the evening. Also has good value
set menus.

▲ Activities and tours

La Falda *p114*
Tour operators
Turismo Talampaya, T470412 or T15630384,
turismotalampaya@yahoo.com.ar. 4WD
full-day trips to the Pampa de Olaén and
Jesuit Estancia La Candelaria for US$15 pp.
VH, T424831 or 15562740, vhcabalgatas@
hotmail.com. One-hour horse horse rides to
nearby hills US$5 pp.

La Cumbre *p114*
Paragliding The world-renowned paragliding
site of Cuchi Corral is 9 km west of La Cumbre
on an unpaved road; operators include **Fechu**,
T155-70951, **Toti López**, T494017, **Mariano
Baccola**, T0351-156 548009, or **Andy Hediger** at
Aero Club La Cumbre, T452544. The tourist office
in La Falda also has a list of instructors; prices
start at US$50 for a first flight with instructor.

⊖ Transport

Villa Carlos Paz *p114*
Bus Villa Carlos Paz is a transport hub and there
are frequent buses to **Buenos Aires** and other
main destinations, as well as to the towns in
the Punilla and Traslasierra valleys. To the
Calamuchita Valley the only option is

Sarmiento bus to Alta Gracia, 1 hr, US$0.85, several daily. To/from **Córdoba**, Ciudad de Córdoba, also Car-Cor and El Serra minibus services, 45 mins, US$0.80.

Cosquín *p114*
Bus La Calera, TAC and Ciudad de Córdoba run frequently along the Punilla valley and to Córdoba, 1½ hrs, US$2.

La Falda *p114*
Bus To **Córdoba** from La Falda US$2, **La Calera** and Ciudad de Córdoba, also minibuses. Daily buses to **Buenos Aires**.

Capilla del Monte *p114*
Bus To **Córdoba**, 3 hrs, US$3; to **Buenos Aires**, many companies daily.

Mina Clavero *p115*
Bus To **Córdoba**, US$4-6 depending on route 3-6 hrs; to **Buenos Aires**, TAC and others, US$17, 12 hrs; to **Mendoza**, 9 hrs, US$11.

Alta Gracia *p115*
Bus To **Córdoba**, US$0.70, every 15 mins, 1 hr; to **Buenos Aires**, several companies, 10-11 hrs, US$20.

Villa General Belgrano *p116*
Bus To/from **Córdoba**, 1½-2 hrs, US$5. To **Buenos Aires**, 10-11 hrs, US$20. To **La Cumbrecita** with Pájaro Blanco, Av San Martín 105, T461709, every 2-4 hrs, 1 hr 20 mins, US$5.50 return.

San Luis *p116*
Bus Terminal at Av España 990 between San Martín y Rivadavia, T424021. To **Buenos Aires**, US$15-20. To **Mendoza**, US$6, 3-4 hrs.

Merlo *p117*
Bus Terminal on R1, next to roundabout, 3 blocks from plaza, 10-min walk. Frequent services to **San Luis**, 3 hrs, US$3; to **Buenos Aires**, TAC, Sierras Cordobesas and Chevallier, US$15-18, 10-12 hrs; to Córdoba, TAC, 5 hrs, US$6.

Mendoza and around

→ *Phone code: 0261. Colour map 8, grid B2. Population: city 148,000. Altitude: 756 m.*
At the foot of the Andes, Mendoza is a dynamic and attractive city, surrounded by vineyards and *bodegas*. The city was colonized from Chile in 1561 and it played an important role in gaining independence from Spain when the Liberator José de San Martín set out to cross the Andes from here, to help in the liberation of Chile. Mendoza was completely destroyed by fire and earthquake in 1861, so today it is essentially a modern city of low buildings and wide avenues (as a precaution against earthquakes), thickly planted with trees and gardens.

Ins and outs
Information Main **tourist office** ① *San Martín, opposite Peatonal Sarmiento, T0810-666 6363, or 0261-420 2800*, very helpful, English and French spoken. At airport, *T448 0017*; at bus station, *T431 3001*. **Provincial office** ① *San Martín 1143, T420 2800*. All open 0900-2100. Very helpful office at the entrance to **Parque San Martín** ① *open daily 0800-1800*. All hand out maps and accommodation lists, with economical apartments for short lets, private lodgings in high season, also lists of bodegas and advice on buses; Aconcagua mountaineering information and permits. Useful websites include: www.turismo.mendoza.gov.ar, www.mendoza.gov.ar.

Sights
In the centre of the city is the **Plaza Independencia**, in the middle of which is the small **Museo Municipal de Arte Moderno** ① *Mon-Sat 0900-2100, Sun 1600-2100, US$1*, with temporary exhibitions, and on the east side, leafy streets lined with cafés. Among the other pleasant squares nearby is **Plaza España**, attractively tiled and with a mural illustrating the epic gaucho poem, *Martín Fierro*. **Plaza Pellegrini** (Avenida Alem y Av San Juan) is a beautiful small square where wedding photos are taken on Friday and Saturday nights, and a small antiques market.

On the west side of the city is the great **Parque San Martín** ① *0900-0200 daily, the entrance is 10 blocks west of the Plaza Independencia, reached by bus 110 'Zoo' from the centre, or the trolley from Sarmiento y 9 de Julio*. It is beautifully designed, with a famous zoo ① *Tue-Sun 0900-1800, US$1.50*, many areas for sports and picnics, and a large lake, where regattas are held. There is also a good restaurant. The **Museo de Ciencias Naturales y Antropológicas** ① *T428 7666, Tue-Sun 0830-1300, Tue-Fri 1400-1900, weekends 1500-1900*, has an ancient female mummy among its fossils and stuffed animals. There are views of the Andes rising in a blue-black perpendicular wall, topped off in winter with dazzling snow, into a china-blue sky. On a hill in the park is the **Cerro de la Gloria**, crowned by an astonishing monument to San Martín, with bas-reliefs depicting various episodes in the equipping of the Army of the Andes and the actual crossing. An hourly bus ('Oro Negro') runs to the top of the Cerro de la Gloria from the information office at the entrance, US$1, otherwise it's a 45-minute walk.

Mendoza's interesting history can be traced through two good museums: **Museo del Pasado Cuyano** ① *Montevideo 544, T4236031, Mon-Fri 0900-1230, US$0.50*, housed in a beautiful 1873 mansion, with lots of San Martín memorabilia and an exquisite Spanish 15th-century carved altarpiece; excellent tours. Also recommended is **Museo del Area Fundacional** ① *Beltrán y Videla Castillo, T425 6927, Tue-Sat 0800-2000, Sun 1500-2000 US$0.70 (interesting underground chamber with glass floor, extra US$0.20), children under 6 free, getting there: buses 1 (line 13) and 3 (line 112).* It contains displays of the city pre-earthquake, with original foundations revealed, and the ruins of Jesuit church **San Francisco** opposite; informative free tour. The small **Acuario Municipal** (aquarium) ① *underground at Buenos Aires e Ituzaingó, daily 0900-1230, 1500-2030, US$0.50*, is fun for kids.

In the nearby suburb of Luján de Cuyo, the city's best art gallery, with a small collection of Argentine paintings, is in the house where Fernando Fader painted decorative murals, at the **Museo Provincial de Bellas Artes, Casa de Fader** ① *Carril San Martín 36571, Mayor*

Mendoza

Sleeping
Andino **4** C1
Campo Base **1** B1
Campo Base II **2** C2
Carollo **2** B1
Churrasqueras del
  Parque **3** B1
Damajuana **5** C1
Dam-sire **6** B3
Gran Hotel Balbi **8** A1
Gran Hotel
  Mendoza **9** B2
Gran Hotel Ritz **10** B1
Hostel Internacional
  Mendoza **11** C2
Monterrey **14** A2
Nutibara **16** C1
Palace **17** A2
Park Hyatt **18** B1

RJ Hotel del Sol **19** A2
Savigliano Hostel **7** B3
Winca's Hostel **13** B1

Eating ⊙
Anna **1** A1
Azafrán **3** B1
Boccadoro **2** A1
Don Otto **4** A2
Comida de Campo **5** B2
Facundo **6** B1
Ferruccio Soppelsa **18** A2

Francesco **7** B1
Il Dolce **8** B2
La Marchigiana **10** A2
Mesón Español **11** C2
Mi Tierra **9** C1
Montecatini **12** A1
Mr Dog **13** A2
Por Acá, 390 **14** C1
Quinta Norte **17** B1
Sr Cheff **15** B2
Vía Civit **16** B1

Drummond, T496 0224, Tue-Fri 0800-1800, Sat-Sun 1400-1900. US$0.50, getting there: bus 200, 40 mins, in the gardens are sculptures.

A few other recommended trips are to the pretty village of **Cacheuta**, 29 km west, with thermal springs, to **Potrerillos**, **Puenta del Inca** and **Los Penitentes** (see Mendoza to Chile below) and to **Villavicencio**, 47 km north, good walks and a restaurant in the mountains.

Wine tours Many bodegas welcome visitors and offer tastings without pressure to buy (grape harvesting season March/April). If you've only time for one, make it **Bodega La Rural (San Felipe)** ① *at Montecaseros 2625, Coquimbito, Maipú, T497 2013, www.bodegala rural.com.ar; getting there: bus 170 (subnumber 173) from La Rioja y Garibaldi*. Small, traditional with a marvellous **Museo del Vino** ① *Mon-Sat 0900-1700, Sun and holidays 1000-1400*. South of Maipú is **Carinae** ① *Videla Aranda 2899, Cruz de Piedra, T499 0470, www.carinaevinos.com, 1000-1800*. French owners with an interest in astronomy as well as producing fine wines. (In Maipú itself, 15 km south of Mendoza, see the lovely plaza and eat good simple food at the Club Social.) In the suburb of Godoy Cruz are the beautiful **Bodegas Escorihuela** ① *Belgrano 1188, T424 2282, www.escorihuela.com.ar, tours Mon-Fri 0930, 1030, 1130, 1230, 1430, 1530, getting there: bus 'T' G Cruz from centre 9 de Julio, Godoy Cruz, or bus 170 subnumbers 174, 200, from Rioja, or 40 from the Plaza*, has an excellent restaurant run by renowned Francis Mallman (see Eating, below).

In or near **Luján de Cuyo** ① *T498 1912, www.lujandecuyo.gov.ar for tourist information*, there are several bodegas. Larger ones include **Norton** ① *T490 9760, www.norton.com.ar*, hourly visits Monday-Friday, book in advance, **Catena Zapata** ① *T490 0214, www.catena wines.com*, and **Séptima** ① *T498 5164, www.bodegasseptima.com.ar, Mon-Fri 1000-1700*, with sunset tastings on Tuesday and Thursday. **Tapiz** ① *C Pedro Molina, Russell, T496 3433, www.tapiz.com*, is not only a winery, but also a 1890s house converted into a superb hotel (**AL**) with restaurant to match. (See also **Cavas Wine Lodge**, below.) Also with an excellent restaurant (*La Bourgogne*) is **Carlos Pulenta-Vistalba** ① *RS Peña 3135, Vistalba, T498 9400, www.carlospulentawines.com*. Famed for its Malbec is **Renacer** ① *Brandsen 1863, Perdriel, T488 1247, www.bodegarenacer.com.ar*. Also in Perdriel is **Achával Ferrer** ① *C Cobos, T498 4874, www.achaval-ferrer.com*, a boutique bodega which has won many prizes. **El Lagar de Carmelo Patti** ① *Av San Martín 2614, Mayor Drummond, T498 1379*, has tours and tastings led by the owner (in Spanish only). For general information on wines of the region, visit: www.turismo.mendoza.gov.ar; www.vendimia.mendoza.gov.ar on the annual wine festival; www.welcometomendoza.com.ar (expat site, more than just wine); www.bestof mendoza.com (bodegas, restaurants and tours); and www.welcomeargentina.com/vino/index_i.html.

● Sleeping

Mendoza and around *p119, map p120*
Breakfast is included, unless specified otherwise.
the **Hyatt** (www.mendoza.park.hyatt.com) and **NH** (www.nh-hotels.com) chains have good hotels in the city.
LL Cavas Wine Lodge, Costaflores, Alto Agrelo, Luján de Cuyo, T410 6927, www.cavaswine lodge.com. A pricey but heavenly experience, ideal for a romantic and wonderfully relaxing stay. 14 spacious rooms in a beautifully restored rural mansion, with restaurant and spa. Each room has a fireplace and terrace, swimming pool, wonderful views. Highly recommended.
A Parador del Angel, 100m from main plaza, Chacras de Coria, Luján de Cuyo, T496 2201, www.paradordelangel.com.ar. Restored 100-year old house, tastefully decorated, very relaxing, gardens, pool, owner is an experienced mountain climber.
B Gran Hotel Mendoza, España 1210 y Espejo, T425 2000, www.hotelmendoza.com. Spacious

rooms, stylish decor, central, family rooms too, overpriced, but splendid views from its small restaurant.
B Gran Hotel Ritz, Perú 1008, T423 5115, aristo@infovia.com.ar. Very comfortable, reliable, central but quiet location, excellent service. Highly recommended.
B Nutibara, Mitre 867, T429 5428. Welcoming, eclectic decor if a bit outdated, lovely pool in a leafy patio, comfortable rooms, quiet, central. Recommended.
C Palace, Las Heras 70, T/F423 4200. A lovely quiet, central place, modern rooms, good value, Italian owned, popular restaurant.
D RJ Hotel Del Sol, Las Heras 212, T438 0218. Comfortable basic rooms, central. Highly recommended.
D Winca's Hostel, Sarmiento 717, T425 3804, www.wincashostel.com.ar. Nice, big rooms, **F** per bed, central, garden, internet, Spanish lessons, safe, pool.

D-F **Savigliano Hostel**, Pedro Palacios 944, T423 7746, www.savigliano.com.ar. Rooms with bath, without (**E**) and dorms (**F**), kitchen, opposite bus station, internet, kitchen facilities, washing machine, luggage stored, helpful, tours arranged. AHC Argentina Hostels Club.

E-F pp **Confluencia**, España 1512, T429 0430, www.hostalconfluencia.com.ar. Central, quiet, tidy, rooms for 2-4, with bath and breakfast, internet, cooking facilities, helpful, good budget choice.

E-F pp **Damajuana**, Arístides Villanueva 282, T425 5858, www.damajuanahostel.com.ar. A great hostel, very comfortable stylish dorms also double rooms (**C**), central, pool in lovely garden, restaurant. Recommended.

F **Andino** (or **Arístides**), Arístides Villanueva 470, T420 2486, www.mendozahostel.com. The quietest of the 3 hostels run by Campo Base (see below), in the lively bar area, basic, large garden which separates some rooms at the back from their bathrooms.

F pp **Campo Base**, Mitre 946, T429 0707, www.campo-base.com.ar. A lively place, discounts for HI members, cramped rooms, but lots of parties and barbecues, popular with mountain climbers, owned by expert mountain guide Roger Cangiani, who also runs a travel agency in town. Similar is **Campo Base II**, P Mendocinas 876, T429 0775, larger, rooms with own bath, small pool.

F pp **Dam-sire**, Viamonte 410, San José Guaymallén, T431 5142, 5 mins from terminal. Family run, spotless, breakfast included.

F pp **Hostel Internacional Mendoza**, España 343, T424 0018, www.hostelmendoza.net. The most comfortable hostel, HI discount, short walk south of the plaza, small rooms with bath, warm atmosphere, great food, barbecues on Fri, huge range of excursions. Warmly recommended.

E-F pp **Confluencia**, España 1512, T429 0430, www.hostalconfluencia.com.ar. Central, quiet, tidy, rooms for 2-4, with bath and breakfast, internet, cooking facilities, helpful, good budget choice.

Camping Camping Suizo, Av Champagnat, 9½ km from city, T444 1991, US$2 pp, modern, shady, with pool, barbecues, hot showers. Recommended. **Churrasqueras del Parque** in centre of Parque General San Martin, at Bajada del Cerro, T452 6016, 155-123124. There are 2 other sites at El Challao, 6 km west of the city centre, reached by Bus 110 (El Challao) leaving hourly from C Rioja. **Saucelandia**, at Guaymallén, 9 km east, Tirasso s/n, T451 1409. Take insect repellent.

● Eating

Mendoza and around *p119, map p120*
There are many open-air cafés for lunch on Peatonal Sarmiento and restaurants around Las Heras. The atmospheric indoor market on

Las Heras has cheap, delicious pizza, *parrilla* and pasta. Open late.

††† 1884 Francis Mallman, Bodega Escorihuela, Belgrano 1188, Godoy Cruz, T424 2698. The place to go for a really special dinner. Mallman is one of the country's great chefs, exotic and imaginative menu. Open for lunch and dinner, but reservation is advisable. Highly recommended.

†† Azafrán, Sarmiento 765. Wine lover's heaven, excellent *bodegas*, superb *picadas*, seasonally changing menu. Recommended.

†† Boccadoro, Mitre 1976. *Parrilla*, popular, locally renowned.

†† Casa de Campo, Urquiza 1516, Coquimbito, T481 1605. Delicious food, with local specialities including rabbit and suckling pig (*lechón*), also good local wine. Highly recommended.

†† Facundo, Sarmiento 641, T420 2866. Good modern *parrilla*, lots of other choices including Italian, good salad bar.

†† Francesco, Chile 1268, T425 3912. Smart old town house with a wonderful garden, excellent Italian food, prepared by the Barbera family, choose from over 350 different wines.

†† La Marchigiana, P Mendocinas 1550. Deservedly popular as one of Mendoza's best restaurants, wonderful Italian food in traditional style, also *parrillas* and delicious desserts, charming service.

†† Mesón Español, Montevideo 244. Spanish food, including great paella, live music at weekends. Cheap lunch menus.

†† Mi Tierra, Mitre y San Lorenzo. Recommended for wine tasting with expert advice, elegantly restored 1890's house, each room devoted to a different *bodega*: Norton, Catena Zapata, Chandon and Terrazas de los Andes. A limited menu with traditionally cooked meat-based dishes.

†† Montecatini, Gral Paz 370. Good Italian food, seafood and *parrilla*, more tourist oriented, popular with families.

†† Sr Cheff, Primitivo de la Reta 1071. Long-established, good *parrilla* and fish.

† Anna, Av Juan B Justo 161, T425 1818. One of the most attractive restaurants in town, informal, French-owned, very welcoming, good food and drink, French and Italian flavours, open for lunch and dinner, excellent value, open till late. Recommended.

† Comida de Campo, Sarmiento 55. Good set menu lunches and a vast range from *pastas caseras* to great traditional *Mendocino* steaks. Recommended.

† Don Otto, Las Heras 242. Cheap and cheerful, small and central place.

† Il Dolce, Sarmiento 81. Good vegetarian options, inexpensive swet lunches and dinners.

† Quinta Norte, Mitre y Espejo. Attractively set in an old family mansion, this is a great

informal place for good cheap meals that come in generous portions. Very good service.
❦ **Vía Civit**, Emilio Civit 277. For first class sandwiches, tarts and pastries in a relaxed but elegant traditional bakery. Open from breakfast time onwards.

Calle Arístides Villanueva, the extension of Colón heading west, has excellent restaurants and bars.
❦ **Por Acá**, Arístides Villanueva 557. Cosy bohemian living room for pizzas and drinks till late, popular, noisy.
❦ **3 90 (Tres con Noventa)**, Arístides Villanueva 451. Delicious pastas, incredibly cheap, studenty, warm cosy atmosphere. Highly recommended.
Ferruccio Soppelsa, Las Heras y España. The best place for ice cream (even wine flavours!). Recommended.
Mr Dog, Av Las Heras y P Mendocinas, popular fastfood chain, better than most.

❂ Festivals and events

Mendoza and around *p119, map p120*
The riotous wine harvesting festival, **Fiesta de la Vendimia**, is held in the amphitheatre of the Parque San Martín from **mid-Feb to mid-Mar**. A parallel event is the less-promoted but equally entertaining **Gay Vendimia Festival**, featuring parties, shows and the crowning of the Festival Queen. Hotels fill up fast and prices rise; also in Jul (the ski season) and around **21 Sep** (the **spring** festival).

◯ Shopping

Mendoza and around *p119, map p120*
Handicrafts The main shopping area is along San Martín and Las Heras, with good clothes, souvenir, leather and handicraft shops as well as vast sports emporia. **Mercado Artesanal**, San Martín 1133, 0830-1930 daily, for traditional leather, baskets, weaving; also weekend market on Plaza Independencia. Cheap shops include: **El Turista**, Las Heras 351, and **Las Viñas**, Las Heras 399. For higher quality head to **Raíces**, España 1092, just off Peatonal Sarmiento. Good choice of wines at *vinotecas*, eg **Central**, Mitre y Espejo, T459 0658, www.centralvinoteca.com, English spoken; **Marcelino**, T Benegas y M Zapata, T429 3648, Mon-Fri, offers tasting courses; **Puracepa**, Av Sarmiento 644, T423 8282, English spoken, stocks a huge range; **The Vines**, Espejo 567, T438 1031, www.vinesofmendoza.com, tasteful, if pricey, wine-tasting and shopping experience in a lovely restored house, presenting the best of the region's boutique bodegas, international orders only.
Supermarkets Super Vea, San Martín y Santiago del Estero, **Metro**, Colón 324.

▲▲ Activities and tours

Mendoza and around *p119, map p120*
Climbing Information from tourist office. Aconcagua permits from the Cuba building, Parque San Martín (aconcagua@mendoza.gov.ar), in summer, and directly from the park itself at Horcones, Puente del Inca, in winter. **Club Andinista**, F L Beltrán 357, Guaymallén, T431 9870, www.clubandinista.com.ar. See also page 127 for Aconcagua.
Whitewater rafting Popular on the Río Mendoza; ask agencies for details, eg **Ríos Andinos**, Sarmiento 717, T429 5030, www.riosandinos.com, also offers horse riding and some rock climbing.

Tour operators
Many agencies, especially on Paseo Sarmiento, run trekking, riding and rafting expeditions, as well as traditional tours to Alta Montaña, US$25, and bodegas, US$10.
Asatej, Peatonal Sarmiento 223, T429 0029, mendoza@asatej.com.ar. Very helpful, trips, cheap travel deals.
Bikes and Wines, Plazoleta Rutini, Maipú, T410 6686, www.bikesandwines.com. Cycle tours to Maipú wineries including lunch; also bike rental, 1000-1800.
Campo Base, Peatonal Sarmiento 229, T425 5511, www.youthtravelargentina.com. The same company that owns the youth hostels (see above) runs good expeditions, and has a helpful website in English: www.cerroaconcagua.com. Expert guide Roger Cangiani leads trips and gives advice on permits.
The Grapevine, Peatonal Sarmiento 133, Galería San Marcos local 12, T429 7522, www.thegrapevine-winetours.com.ar. British and Irish owned, organizes personalised tours in the wine region, including flights combined with visits and lunch. They also have their own wine club meetings and publish a very informative free magazine available everywhere.
Huentata, Las Heras 699, loc 7, T425 7444, www.huentata.com.ar. Conventional tours, plus Villavicencio, Cañon del Atuel, horse riding, Aconcagua. Recommended.
Inka Expediciones, Juan B Justo 343, Ciudad 5500, T429 8494, www.inka.com.ar. Climbing expeditions, including Aconcagua, highly professional, fixed departure dates, mules for hire.
Mancagua, España 967, T429 7398, www.manca guaviajes.com.ar. Many options in wine tours, combining different bodegas with optional lunches where wine is included. Recommended.
Mendoza Viajes Peatonal Sarmiento 129, T461 0210. Imaginative tours in comfortable coaches, professional, cheap deals available.

Postales del Plata, Tabanera s/n, Colonia Las Rosas, Tunayán (some 80 km south of Mendoza), T429-6210, www.postalesdelplata.com. Specializes in wine tours in Mendoza and Chile, cultural tours, fly fishing, has its own very good lodges at Chacras de Coria and Valle de Uco. **Trekking Travel**, Adolfo Calle 4171, T421 0450, www.trekking-travel.com.ar. For mountain biking and climbing.

⊖ Transport

Mendoza and around *p119, map p120*
Air El Plumerillo airport, 8 km north of centre, T430 7837, has a bank, tourist information, shops, restaurant and *locutorio*, but no left luggage. Reached from the centre by bus No 60 (subnumber 68) from Alem y Salta, every hour at 35 mins past the hour, 40 mins journey; make sure there is an 'Aeropuerto' sign on the front window. Taxi to/from centre US$5. Daily flights to **Buenos Aires**: 1 hr 50 mins, AR only. **AR/Austral** to **Córdoba**. LAN to **Santiago**.
Bus Most local services have 2 numbers, a general number and a 'subnumber' in brackets which indicates the specific route. Buses within and near the city are slightly cheaper with prepaid card which go into a machine on the bus, sold in shops, the bus terminal and **Mendobus** ticket offices everywhere. US$0.60 for minimum of two trips, US$1.75 ten. From 2007, the card is being replaced by a magnetic card, which can be topped up, like a phone card. There are 2 trolley bus routes, red and blue, US$0.25.
Long distance The huge bus terminal is on the east side of Av Videla, 15 mins' walk from centre (go via Av Alem, which has pedestrian tunnel), with shops, post office, *locutorio*, tourist information and supermarket (open till 2130), a good café, left luggage lockers and toilets (between platforms 38 and 39). It's not a place to linger at night. To **Buenos Aires**, 13-17 hrs, US$24-45, many companies including **Andesmar**, **La Estrella**, **Sendas** (*coche-cama* with meals and wine). To **Bariloche**, Andesmar one daily, US$38, 19 hrs, book well ahead (alternatively **TAC** go to Neuquén and change). To **Córdoba**, 9-12 hrs, US$12-18, several companies. To **San Rafael**, many daily 3½ hrs, US$5-6. To/from **San Juan**, Andesmar, and others, US$5, 2-2½ hrs. To **Tucumán**, US$26-34, 13-14 hrs, Andesmar, Autotransportes Mendoza, TAC, all via San Juan, **La Rioja** (US$17, 6-7 hrs), and **Catamarca** 10 hrs, US$18-35. To **Salta**, via Tucumán, several companies daily, US$35-60, 16-18 hrs. To **Uspallata**, 5 a day with Expreso Uspallata, US$4, 2¼ hrs. To **Potrerillos**, 1 hr, US$1.30.
Transport to Santiago, Chile Minibuses (US$15-20, 6-7 hrs) run by **Chi-Ar**, **Nevada** and

Radio Móvil daily leave when they have 10 passengers. When booking, ensure that the receipt states that you will be picked up and dropped at your hotel; if not you will be dropped at the bus station. Buses to Santiago daily, 10 companies, **Chile Bus**, **Cata**, **Tur Bus** and **Tas Choapa** have been recommended, **Ahumada** has a *coche cama* at 0845. Most buses are comfortable, with similar rates and journey times to minibuses, those with a/c and hostess service (includes breakfast) charge more, worth it when crossing the border as waiting time can be several hours. Almost all these companies also go daily to **Viña del Mar** and **Valparaíso**, US$10. Information at Mendoza bus terminal: shop around. Book at least 1 day ahead. Passport required, tourist cards given on bus. The ride is spectacular. If you want to return, it's cheaper to buy an undated return ticket Santiago-Mendoza.
Other International buses To **La Serena**, 3 a week, 12-16 hrs, US$27-30, **Covalle**, **Cata** and others. To **Lima**, 3-4 a week, **El Rápido**, and Ormeño, T431 4913, 2½ days, US$125-150.

⊕ Directory

Mendoza and around *p119, map p120*
Airline offices Aerolíneas Argentinas/ Austral, Peatonal Sarmiento 82, T420 4100. LAN, España y Rivadavia 135, T425 7900. **Banks** Many ATMs on and around Plaza San Martín taking all cards. Many *casas de cambio* along San Martín, corner of Espejo/Catamarca. Most open till 2000 Mon-Fri, and some open Sat morning. **Bike rental** Cycles El Túnel, at the exit of the subway coming from the bus terminal. Buys and sells cycles, also repairs. Indiana Aventuras, Espejo 65, T429 0002, info@indianaventuras.com.ar. Adventure World, Sarmineto 231, T429 0206. **Cultural centres** Alianza Francesa, Chile 1754. Instituto Dante Alighieri (Italy), Espejo 638. Instituto Cultural Argentino- Norteamericano, Chile 985. Instituto Cuyano de Cultura Hispánica (Spain), Villanueva 389. Goethe Institut, Morón 265, Mon-Fri, 0800-1200, 1600-2230, German newspapers, Spanish classes, very good. **Internet** Several internet cafés in the centre and a number of *locutorios*: a huge one on San Martín y Garibaldi, with internet. **Medical facilities** Central hospital near bus terminal at Alem y Salta, T420 0600. Lagomaggiore, public general hospital (with good reputation) at Timoteo Gordillo s/n, T425 9700. Hospital Materno y Infantil Humberto Notti, Bandera de los Andes 2683, T445 0045. Medical emergencies T428 0000. **Post Office** San Martín y Colón, T429 0848, Mon-Fri 0800-2000, Sat 1000-1300. **Useful addresses** ACA, Avenida San Martín 985, T420 2900, and Avenida Bandera de los Andes y Gdor Videla, T431 3510. Migraciones, San Martín 1859, T424 3512.

South of Mendoza

San Rafael → *Phone code: 02627. Colour map 8, grid B2. Population: 107,000.*
San Rafael, 236 km south of Mendoza, is a tranquil, leafy small town in the heart of fertile land which is irrigated by snow melt from the Andes to produce fine wines and fruit. A road runs west over El Pehuenche pass to Talca (Chile). Several bodegas can be visited: the impressive champagnerie at **Bianchi** ① *T422 046 www.vbianchi.com*. Some 5 km west on Hpólito Yrigoyen, is the more intimate **Jean Rivier** ① *H Yrigoyen 2385, T432675, bodega@jrivier.com*. Excellent wine. A small but interesting **natural history museum** ① *Tue-Sun 0800-2000, free; Iselin bus along Av JA Balloffet*, is 6 km southeast of town at Isla Río Diamante. **Tourist office** ① *Av H Yrigoyen y Balloffet, T437860, www.sanrafael.gov.ar, www.sanrafael-tour.com.*

Southwest of San Rafael, 35 km, is the **Cañon de Atuel**, a spectacular gorge 20 km long with strange polychrome rock formations. It is famous as a rafting centre. Daily buses, *Iselin* (T435998), go to the Valle Grande dam at the near end of the canyon, returning in the evening, US$2. Here there is plenty of accommodation, campsites, river rafting and horse riding. San Rafael tour operators run day tours. **Raffeish** ① *T436996, www.raffeish.com.ar.* Recommended as most professional rafting company. There is no public transport through the gorge to El Nihuel.

Las Leñas → *Altitude: 2,250 m. Season: mid-Jun to end-Oct. www.laslenas.com.*
At 182 km southwest of San Rafael, RN40 heads west into the Andes, and from it the road to the famous, chic (ie expensive) and internationally renowned ski resort of Las Leñas. It passes **Los Molles**, at Km 30, where there is simple accommodation: Further along the Las Leñas road is the **Pozo de las Animas**, two natural pits filled with water where the wind makes a ghostly wail, hence the name (Well of the Spirits). At the end of Valle Los Molles is Las Leñas, in a spectacular setting with excellent skiing over 64 km on 27 pistes, with a maximum drop of 1,200 m. Beyond Las Leñas the road continues into Valle Hermoso, accessible December-March only.

Malargüe → *Phone code: 02627. Colour map 8, grid B2. Population: 18,100.*
Further south on Ruta 40, Malargüe is developing as a centre for hiking and horse riding in stunning open landscape nearby. Most remarkable, **La Payunia Reserve**, 208 km south, has vast grasslands and stark volcanoes where thousands of guanacos roam, best enjoyed on horseback. **Laguna Llancanelo**, 75 km southeast, is filled with a great variety of birdlife in spring, when Chilean flamingoes come to nest. In addition, **Caverna de las Brujas** has extraordinary underground cave formations. Helpful **tourist office** on the main street (right hand side as you drive in from north), next to conference centre, *T471659 (open 0800-2300).*

⬤ Sleeping

San Rafael *p125*
B Kalton, Yrigoyen 120, T430047, kalton@ satlink.com. Charming, long-established, excellent service, comfortable, parking. Highly recommended.
B Family Inn, Av Yrigoyen 5501, T431451, www.familyinnsanrafael.com.ar. Modern roadside hotel, convenient, next to the airport, spacious, functional, neat gardens, pool, restaurant and gym.
C Regine, Independencia 623, T430274, www.reginehotel.com.ar. Delightful, rustic, pool in garden, popular with older guests, relaxing, good value. Also has a *quincho* for *parrillas*.
D Rex, H Yrirgoyen 56, T422177, hotelrex@ speedy.com.ar. Central, large comfortable rooms, heating, good value. Recommended.
D Tonin, Pellegrini 330, T422499, www.sanrafael-tour.com/tonin. A lovely quiet family-run place, modern spacious rooms, TV, next to the plaza.
E Tierrasoles Hostel, Alsina 245, T433449, www.tierrasoles.com.ar. HI member. Close to bus

station, lively, welcoming, basic dorms and double, shared bath; activities organized, bikes for hire.
Camping El Parador, in the park on Isla Río Diamante, 5 km southeast, T420492. There are more sites at Valle Grande in the Cañón del Atuel.

Los Molles *p125*
Cheaper options than Las Leñas, but all basic.
B Hotel Termas Lahuen-Có, T499700. The best, dating from 1930's, and now rather kitsch, with thermal baths, meals.

Las Leñas *p125*
There are several plush hotels, all **L-A** (phone number for all, T471100), and most with pool, including **Piscis, Aries, Escorpio** (great views), **Acuario** (right in the thick of the action), and **Geminis** (apart-hotel), and a disco, shop renting equipment and several restaurants. For cheaper accommodation stay in Los Molles or Malargüe.

Malargüe *p125*

Hotels issue 50% discount for Las Leñas lift pass, minimum 2 nights' stay. Accommodation is not of a high standard, with some very poor *cabañas*.

B Microhotel Inn, Ruta 40 Norte (north of centre), T472300, www.microtelinn.com.ar. The best, with comfortable rooms and well-equipped cabins, functional, heated pool, sauna, large restaurant.

B Río Grande, Ruta 40 Norte (north of centre), T471589, hotelriogrande@infovia.com.ar. Good value, renovated rooms.

E La Posta, San Martín 646, T472079, laposta_malargue@yahoo.com.ar. Welcoming wood-lined rooms, also has *parrilla* at Roca 374.

F pp Campo Base, Telles Meneses 897, T471534, www.backpackersmalargue.com.ar. Lively, basic dorms and doubles, shared bath, trips arranged.

F pp Internacional, Prol Constitución Nacional (Finca No65), 2 blocks from R40 Norte, south of centre, T470391, www.hostelmalargue.net. Eco-hostel in rural surroundings, on dairy farm with organic fruit and veg, good meals, basic, comfortable dorms and rooms, with travel agency.

● Eating

San Rafael *p125*

❖ **La Fusta**, Yrigoyen 538. Smart restaurant, serving a good value *parrilla* and delicious Italian food.

▲ Activities and tours

Malargüe *p125*

The tourist office can arrange indepedent visits to Llancanelo and La Payunia. Good tours with

Choique, Av San Martín y Rodríguez, T470391, www.choique.net, and **Karen Travel**, San Martín 54, T470342, www.karen travel.com.ar. Horse riding, Cueva de las Brujas, and nearby reserves.

Horse riding Kiñe, T02627-155 88635, www.kinie.com.ar. Horse riding in La Payunia Reserve and lodging at the **D pp Puesto La Agüita**, a lovely country houe offering full-board. Recommended.

Rafting Tero Aventura, T156-00182, teroaventura@hotmail.com. Rafting and inflatiables trips on Ríos Malargüe and Atuel, run by Frenchman Sylvain Maisonneuve.

❸ Transport

San Rafael *p125*

Bus To **Mendoza**, 3-3½ hrs, US$5-6; **Neuquén**, US$18-23, 8-9 hrs.

Las Leñas *p125*

Bus From **San Rafael**, US$15, with **Isolin** and **Butini**, winter only (check first, service changes from year to year).

Malargüe *p125*

Air Weekly flights **Buenos Aires** to Malargüe airport (T471600), on southern edge of town, more charter flights in the skiing season.

Bus Terminal at Aldao y Beltrán. Daily from Mendoza with Expreso Uspallata, 6 hrs, mini buses with Transporte Viento Sur, 4½ hrs, U$10. Several a day from **San Rafael**. Daily buses in ski season to **Las Leñas**.

Mendoza to Chile

The route to Chile is sometimes blocked by snow in winter: if travelling by car in June-October enquire about road conditions from *ACA* in Mendoza (T431 3510). Driving without snow chains and a shovel is prohibited between Uspallata and the border, but this can be resolved in a friendly way with border police. *ACA* and Chilean Automobile Club sell, but do not rent, chains.

Potrerillos and Uspallata → *Phone code: 02624. Colour map 8, grid A1.*

Fruta 7 is the only route for motorists to the Chilean border, via **Potrerillos** and **Uspallata**. Leave the city south by Avenida J Vicente Zapata, Access Ruta 7, leading to Ruta 40. Follow signs to Potrerillos, Uspallata and Chile. From Mendoza to the Chilean border is 204 km. The construction of a dam has forced a detour around **Cacheuta**, though it's worth a side trip for its relaxing hot springs, and very comfortable hotel (see below).

Potrerillos is a pretty village for horse riding, walking and rafting. In summer you can hike from Potrerillos to Vallecitos over two days, passing from desert steppe to scenic peaks. **Vallecitos** (season July-September, T488810, www.skivallecitos.com) is a tiny ski resort 21 km from Potrerillos (see below) along a winding *ripio* road. It has a basic ski-lodge, ski school and snack bar. **Refugio San Bernado** (T154-183857), cosy place run by mountain guides; the area is used as a base camp by climbers acclimatising and training before atttempting Aconcagua. **Los Penitentes** is a much better ski resort, 165 km west of Mendoza, on the road to Chile, named after its majestic mass of pinnacled rocks, looking like a horde of cowled monks. Good skiing on 28 pistes, very reasonably priced, with few people on slopes. For **Puente del Inca** see below.

Another recommended stopping point is the picturesque village of **Uspallata**, 52 km from Potrerillos. From here you can explore the mysterious white, egg-shaped domes of Las Bóvedas (2 km on RN39 north; entry US$0.30), built by the Huarpe Indians under the Jesuits to melt silver, where there is a small, interesting museum. The RN39 leads north to Barreal and Calingasta (see page 130), unpaved for its first part, rough and tricky when the snow melts and floods it in summer. The tourist office in Uspallata keeps unreliable hours. There are two food shops, bakeries, a post office and a Shell station with motel, restaurant, shop and *locutorio* open 0900-2200.

Puente del Inca → *Colour map 8, grid B2. Altitude: 2,718 m.*

The road that leads from Uspallata to cross the border to Chile is one of the most dramatic in Argentina, climbing through a gorge of richly coloured rock. Surrounded by mountains of great grandeur, Puente del Inca, 72 km west of Uspallata, is a good base for trekking or exploring on horseback. The natural bridge after which the place is named is one of the wonders of South America. Bright ochre yellow, it crosses the Río Mendoza at a height of 19 m, has a span of 21 m, and is 27 m wide, and seems to have been formed by sulphur-bearing hot springs. The bridge itself cannot be crossed. There are the remains of a thermal bath complex at the river just under the bridge. Horse treks go to Los Penitentes. Los Horcones, the Argentine customs post, is 1 km west: from here you can visit the green lake of Laguna los Horcones: follow signs to Parque Provincial Aconcagua, 2 km, where there is a Ranger station, excellent views of Aconcagua, especially morning; free camping, open climbing season only. From here a trail continues to the Plaza de Mulas base camp.

Aconcagua → *Colour map 8, grid B1. Altitude: 6,959 m.*

West of Puente del Inca on the right, there is a good view of Aconcagua, the highest peak in the Americas, sharply silhouetted against the blue sky. In 1985, a complete Inca mummy was discovered at 5,300 m on the mountain. The best time for climbing Aconcagua is from end-December to February. For camping, trekking or climbing it is first necessary to obtain a **permit**: These vary in price for high, mid or low season, and depending on the number of days. In high season (15 December to 31 January), a permit to climb Aconcagua (lasting 20 consecutive days from the date it is stamped at the park entrance) costs US$330 (US$500 via Plaza Guanacos) in high season, to US$400 (for any route) in winter; short treks cost from US$10 for day permits, to US$70 for seven-day treks to base camps. Permits must be bought, in person only, in summer (15 November to 15 March) at **Dirección de Recursos Naturales Renovables** ① *The Cuba Building, Av Los Robles y Rotonda de Rosedal, in the Parque San Martín in Mendoza, T425 2090, Mon-Fri 0800-1800, weekends and holidays 0900-1300.* In winter permits are bought directly from the *guardería* at Laguna Horcones, at the entrance to Parque Nacional Aconcagua. Places selling the permits, and fees, may change, so it's vital to check the official website: www.aconcagua.mendoza.gov.ar/.

There are two access routes: Río Horcones and Río Vacas, which lead to the two main base camps, Plaza de Mulas and Plaza Argentina respectively. Río Horcones starts a few kilometres from Puente del Inca, at the Horcones ranger station. About 80% of climbers use this route. From here you can go to Plaza de Mulas (4,370 m) for the North Face, or Plaza Francia (4,200 m) for the South Face. The intermediate camp for either is Confluencia (3,300 m), four hours from Horcones. Río Vacas is the access for those wishing to climb the Polish Glacier. The Plaza Argentina base camp (200 m) is three hours from Horcones and the intermediate camps are Pampa de Leñas and Casa de Piedra. From Puente del Inca, mules are available (list at the **Dirección de Recursos Naturales Renovables** ① *Parque Gral San Martín, Mendoza*, about US$120 per day for 60 kg of gear). This only takes you to Plaza de Mulas, near which is the highest hotel in the world (see below) and an accident prevention and medical assistance service (climbing season only); crowded in summer. The same service is offered at Plaza Argentina in high season (US$240 per day for mule 60 kg load). Climbers should make use of this service to check for early symptoms of mountain sickness and oedema. Take a tent able to withstand 100 mph/160 kph winds, and clothing and sleeping gear for temperatures below -40°C. Allow at least 8-10 days for acclimatization at lower altitudes before attempting the summit (four days from Plaza de Mulas). Hotel *Plaza de Mulas*, **AL** pp full board, **B** without meals, good food, information, medical treatment, recommended, also camping area; closed in winter.

In Mendoza you can book *refugio* reservations and programmes which include trekking, or climbing to the summit, with all equipment and accommodation or camping included (see Tour operators, above). Try to agree all contract terms in advance, such as the number of members of a group, so that they aren't changed before your expedition leaves. Treks and climbs are also organized by the famous climber **Sr Fernando Grajales** ① *Moreno 898, 5500 Mendoza, T493830, www.grajales.net (or T421 4330 and ask for Eduardo Ibarra at Hotel Plaza de Mulas for further information)*, and by **Roger Cangiani** of Campo Base (see Mendoza Activities and tours). Near the Cementerio is **Los Puquios** *T461-317603*, camping, mules, guides. Further information from **Dirección de Recursos Naturales Renovables** *(see also under Mendoza, www.mendoza.gov.ar)*.

Border with Chile

The road to the Chilean border, fully paved, goes through the 3.2-km Cristo Redentor toll road tunnel to Chile (open 24 hours; US$3 for cars, cyclists are not allowed to ride through, ask the officials to help you get a lift). The last settlement before the tunnel is tiny forlorn **Las Cuevas**, 16 km from Puente del Inca, with hostel accommodation, a basic café and a *kiosko*. In summer you can take the old road over La Cumbre pass to the statue of El Cristo Redentor (Christ the Redeemer), an 8-m statue erected jointly by Chile and Argentina in 1904 to celebrate the settlement of their boundary dispute. Take an all day excursion from Mendoza, drive in a 4WD, after snow has melted, or walk from Las Cuevas (4½ hours up, two hours down – only to be attempted by the fit, in good weather). **Expreso Uspallata** runs buses to Mendoza.

The Chilean border is beyond Las Cuevas, but all Argentine entry and exit formalities for cars and buses are dealt with at the Argentine customs post, Ingeniero Roque Carranza at Laguna Los Horcones, 2 km west of Puente del Inca. Customs are open 0730-2300. Car drivers can undertake all formalities in advance at *migraciones* in Mendoza, or Uspallata while refuelling. You can hitchhike, or possibly bargain with bus drivers for a seat, from Los Horcones to Santiago, but if you are dropped at the entrance to the tunnel, you cannot walk through. Customs officers may help to arrange a lift through to Chile.

● Sleeping

Cacheuta *p126*

AL Hotel and Spa Termas Cacheuta, Ruta 82, Km 38, T490152, www.termascacheuta.com. Price is full board, warm and inviting rustic-style rooms, lovely spa for day visits. Recommended.

Potrerillos *p126*

B Gran Hotel Potrerillos, Ruta Nacional 7, Km 50, T02624-482130. With breakfast, faded 1940s resort hotel, nice location, simple rooms, pool.
Camping There is also the excellent **ACA** site, T482013, shady, hot water after 1800, pool, clean.

Los Penitentes *p126*

AL Hostería Penitentes, Villa Los Penitentes T155-090432, penitentehosteria@hotmail.com. Cheery place near slopes, good café, cheaper for several nights. Recommended.
E pp Campo Base Penitentes, T0261-425 5511, www.penitentes.com.ar. A cheap ski resort option, lively, slightly cramped dorms, shared bath, restaurant, bar, minibus service to Mendoza. Hostel is open all year, offers ski programmes in season.

Uspallata *p127*

A Valle Andino, Ruta 7, T420095, www.hotel valleandino.com. Modern airy place with good rooms, pool and restaurant, breakfast included.

B Hotel Uspallata, on RN 7, Km 1149, towards Chile, T420 066. Lovely location, spacious and modern in big gardens away from the centre, pool, good value, comfortable rooms, cheap restaurant.
D Los Cóndores, T420002. Great value, bright, neat rooms, good restaurant, set menus and tasty pasta dishes. Highly recommended.
E pp Viena, Las Heras 240, T420046. Small family-run place, good little rooms, breakfast included.
F pp Hostel Uspallata, RN 7, Km 1141.5, T154-667240, www.hosteluspallata.com.ar. Basic rooms sleep 4-8, some with bath, discounts for HI members, bar, restaurant, tours arranged, attractive surroundings.

Puente del Inca *p127*

C Hostería Puente del Inca, RN7, Km 175, T4205304. Next to the small ski centre at Los Puquios. Doubles and rooms for 4-8, full-board option, huge cosy dining room, advice on Aconcagua, helpful owners, great atmosphere. Warmly recommended.
F pp Hostel La Vieja Estación, 100 m off the road, next to the Puente, T4521103. Basic but cheery hostel, cheap meals provided, kitchen.
Camping Possible next to the church (but windy), also at Los Puquios and Lago Horcones inside the park.

Border with Chile

F pp Arco de las Cuevas, Las Cuevas, T426 5273, www.arcodelascuevas.com.ar. Above the old road to Cristo Redentor. Spartan but comfortable dorms, restaurant and bar. Transfer to Aconcagua park.

℗ Eating

Potrerillos *p126*

ǁ **El Futre**, opposite the ACA campsite. Typical Cuyo food, vegetarian dishes and homemade pizzas. Open all day, summer only.

ǁ **Los Pinos**, Av Los Cóndores, on the left hand side as you go up the hill. Recommended for trout.

ǁ **Tomillo**, Av Los Cóndores, El Salto. Open all day. Excellent homemade cooking, welcoming.

Uspallata *p127*

ǁǁ **Bodega del Gato**, centre. Good *parrilla*.

ǁ **La Estancia de Elias**, Km 1146. Opposite Shell station, good cheap food but crowded.

ǁ **Pub Tibet**, at the crossroads. Bar with photos from *Seven Years in Tibet*, 1997 movie which was shot here, welcoming with warm atmosphere.

▲ Activities and tours

Potrerillos *p126*

Argentina Rafting, T02624-482037, www.argentinarafting.com. Reliable company, organizes good trips with climbing, hiking, kayaking and other adventure sports.

Uspallata *p127*

Desnivel Turismo Aventura, C Ejército de los Andes, T420275, desnivelturismoaventura@ yahoo.com.ar. Offers rafting, riding, mountain biking, trekking, climbing, skiing.

⊖ Transport

Puente del Inca *p127*

Bus Expreso Uspallata from Mendoza for **Uspallata** (6 a day) and **Puente del Inca** (3 a day) , US$5, 3½ hrs. Uspallata-Puente del Inca US$2. Local buses also go on from Puente del Inca to **Las Cuevas**, Expreso Uspallata, US$5 return (**Note** take passport). Buses going to Chile do not pick up passengers on the way.

San Juan and around

➜ *Phone code: 0264. Colour map 8, grid A2. Population: 122,000. Altitude: 650 m.*

San Juan, 177 km north of Mendoza, was founded in 1562 and is capital of its namesake province. Nearly destroyed by a 1944 earthquake, the modern centre is well laid-out, but lacks Mendoza's charm and sophistication. **Tourist office** ① *Sarmiento Sur 24 y San Martín, T421 0004, www.ischigualasto.com, daily 0800-2000 (in theory).*

Sights

You're most likely to visit on the way to the national parks further north, but there are some *bodegas* worth visiting. One of the country's largest wine producers, *Bodegas Bragagnolo*, is on the outskirts of town at Ruta 40 y Avenida Benavídez, Chimbas (bus 20 from terminal; guided tours daily 0830-1330, 1530-1930, not Sunday). The most interesting of the museums is **Museo de Ciencias Naturales** ① *Predio Ferial, Av España y Maipú, daily 0930-1330, US$2*. It includes fossils from Ischigualasto Provincial Park (see below). **Museo Casa Natal de Sarmiento** ① *Sarmiento Sur 21, summer daily 0900-1300, also Tue-Fri and Sun 1700-2000; winter Tue-Fri and Sun 0900-1900, Mon, Sat 0900-1400, US$1, free Sun.* This is the birthplace of Domingo Sarmiento (President of the Republic, 1868-1874). **Museo Histórico Celda de San Martín** ① *Laprida 57 Este, Mon-Sat 0900-1400, US$1*, includes the restored cloisters and two cells of the Convent of Santo Domingo. San Martín slept in one of these cells on his way to lead the crossing of the Andes.

The **Museo Arqueológico** of the University of San Juan ① *Acceso Sur entre C 5 y Progreso, Rawson, a few km south of the centre, T424 1424, Mon-Fri 0800-2000, Sat-Sun 1000-1800, US$0.70, getting there: buses 15, 49, 50 from centre*, contains an outstanding collection of prehispanic indigenous artefacts, including several well-preserved mummies. **Vallecito**, 64 km east, has a famous shrine to the **Difunta Correa**, Argentina's most loved pagan saint whose infant, according to legend, survived at her breast even after the mother's death from thirst in the desert. At roadsides everywhere you'll see mounds of plastic bottles left as offerings to ask for safe journeys, and during Holy Week 100,000 pilgrims visit the site. See the remarkable collection of personal items left in tribute in several elaborate shrines, including number plates from all over the world: photographs, stuffed animals, tea sets, hair (in plaits), plastic flowers, trophies, tennis rackets and guitars. There are cafés, toilets and souvenir stalls. Buses from San Juan to La Rioja stop here for five minutes, or **Vallecitos** runs a couple of services a day.

West of San Juan → *Phone code: 02648.*

Calingasta, 135 km west of San Juan, is an idyllic, secluded village in a green valley with stunning striped rocks (cider festival in April). Ruta 12 west from San Juan along the canyon of the Río San Juan has been closed by work on two dams, so to reach Calingasta you go north of San Juan to Talacasto, then take the paved Quebrada de las Burras road to Pachaco, where a bridge crosses the Río San Juan. After the bridge, police control alternating one-way traffic to/from Calingasta for 12 km. Cyclists should note that there is no shade on these roads, fill up with water at every opportunity. Consult the police before cycling from Calingasta to San Juan. **Tourist information** ⓘ Av Argentina s/n, T421066, or *Municipalidad, Lavalle y Sarmiento, Tamberías, T492005.*

Barreal, 40 km south of Calingasta on the road to Uspallata, is a tranquil place between the Andes and the precordillera, with great horse riding, trekking to Cerro Mercedaria, and wind-car racing (*carrovelismo*). **Tourist office** ⓘ *Calle Las Heras s/n, T02648-441066.* At **El Leoncito** (2,348 m), 26 km from Barreal there are two observatories ⓘ *T441088, www.casleo.gov.ar, US$3, daily 1000-1200, 1400-1800,* (no buses; tours from San Juan, or *Hotel Barreal*) and a nature reserve with a semi-arid environment and interesting wildlife, ranger post but no facilities.

North of San Juan

Ruta 40, the principal tourist route on the east Andean slope, heads north toward Cafayate and Salta, via San José de Jáchal. At Talacasto, 55 km from San Juan, Ruta 436 branches toward Las Flores (Km 180) and the Chilean border at Agua Negra pass (4,600 m; January-April, immigration, customs and ACA at Los Flores). **San José de Jáchal**, 99 km north of Talacasto is a wine and olive-growing centre with many adobe buildings. From here, the undulating Ruta 40, paved but for the first 25 km to the La Rioja border, crosses dozens of dry watercourses. It continues to Villa Unión (see below), paved but for the last 15 km. The town has hotels, a campsite behind the ACA station and places to eat. Expreso Argentino bus from San Juan at 0730 arrives at 0940.

Ischigualasto and Talampaya parks → *Phone code: 02646. Colour map 8, grid A2.*

Ruta 141 runs across the south of the province towards La Rioja province and Córdoba. Just after Marayes (133 km), paved Ruta 510 (poor in parts) goes north 135 km to **San Agustín del Valle Fértil**, the best base for exploring Ischigualasto. **Tourist information** ⓘ *on plaza, T420104.*

North of San Agustín, at a police checkpoint, 56 km by paved road, a side road goes northwest for 17 km to the 62,000 ha **Parque Provincial Ischigualasto** (a UNESCO World

Heritage Site), also known as **Valle de la Luna** for its bizarre sculptural desert landforms. Here the skeletons of the oldest known dinosaurs have been found (230 million years), though you'll have to visit the museum at San Juan to see their bones and fossils (US$2). **Tours and access** There is one tour route, lasting 2½ hours, visiting part of the park but encompassing the most interesting sites. You have to go with a ranger in your own vehicle and it can be crowded at holiday times. Tours from San Juan, US$50 (including breakfast, lunch and tour), 14 hours; from San Agustín US$15-20 for a guide (in both towns, ask at tourist office). Taxi to park US$30 from San Agustín (recommended if there are 4-5 people), more expensive out of season. You can camp opposite the ranger station, which has a small museum, but bring all food and water; expensive confitería next to ranger station. See also Activities and tours page 132.

Just beyond the police checkpoint, near Los Baldecitos, paved Ruta 150 heads east to Patquía and then to La Rioja or Chilecito. From the junction Ruta 76 heads north to Villa Unión. 61 km north of Los Baldecitos a paved road goes 14 km east to the 215,000-ha **Parque Nacional Talampaya** ① *T03825-470397, 0800-1800, (winter 0830-1730), US$4 for foreigners*, another collection of spectacular desert landforms and a UNESCO World Heritage Site. The park occupies the site of an ancient lake, where sediments have been eroded by water and wind for some 200 million years, forming a dramatic landscape of pale red hills. Numerous fossils have been found and some 600 year-old petroglyphs can be seen not far from the access to the gorge. Along the *cañón* of the Río Talampaya, extraordinary structures have been given popular names such as 'the balconies', 'the lift', 'the crib' or 'the owl'. At one point, the gorge narrows to 80 m and rises to 143 m. A refreshing leafy spot in the centre of the gorge, 'the botanical garden', has amazing diverse plants and trees. The end of the *cañón* is marked by the imposing cliffs of 'the cathedral' and the curious 'king on a camel'. 'The chessboard' and 'the monk', 53 m high, lie not far beyond the gorge, marking the end of the so-called **Circuito El Monje**. Only accessible with 4WD vehicles, **Circuito Los Cajones** continues in the same direction up to 'los pizarrones', an enormous wall of rock, covered with petroglyphs, and then to 'los cajones', a narrow pass between rock walls. **Circuito Ciudad Perdida** is another possible excursion in the park, southeast of the gorge, accessible only with 4WD vehicles, leading to an area of high cliffs and a large number of breathtaking rock formations. **Tours and access** Tour operators from La Rioja and Chilecito sometimes combine a visit with nearby Ischigualasto, otherwise access is difficult (check guide's fee and entrance included). Independent access is possible: buses/combis linking La Rioja and Villa Unión stop at the park entrance (a long walk to the *administración*), or better, at Pagancillo (village 30 km north), as most of the park wardens live there and offer free transfer to the park early in the morning (contact Adolfo Páez). Excursions arranged at the *administración*: guided walks to Quebrado Don Eduardo, a secondary gorge, next to the canyon (3 hours, US$10 pp); guided bike rides (3 hours, US$10 pp, cycle/helmet provided). Vehicle guided visits for Circuito El Monje (2 hours, US$12 pp), Circuito Los Cajones (4 hours, US$15 pp), and Circuitos Ciudad Perdida and Arco Iris (each 4½ hours, US$8 pp); no private vehicles allowed beyond the administration; apart from the organized tours, the options are walking or cycling. Best time to visit is in the morning, for natural light and avoiding strong afternoon winds. *Administración* has small restaurant, toilets, public telephones.

◉ Sleeping

San Juan *p129, map p130*
A-C hotels all include breakfast and parking.
A Alkázar, Laprida 82 Este, T421 4965, www.alkazar hotel.com.ar. Comfortable rooms, pool and gym, well run, central, excellent restaurant.
C Alkristal, Av de Circunvalación 1055 Sur, T425 4145, alkristal@alkazarhotel.com.ar. Comfortable, well-equipped rooms, modern, on outskirts, poor breakfast, but otherwise recommended, good value. Also smart apartments, good for groups.
C Capayán, Mitre 31 Este, T421 4222, hcapayan@ infovia.com.ar. Next to cinema on plaza, welcoming, comfortable, good service, restaurant.
D América, 9 de Julio 1052 Oeste, T427 2701, www.hotel-america.com.ar. Modern,

and very comfortable, good service, free internet, excursions arranged.
E Triásico Hostel, Pedro Echagüe 538 Este, Rawson, T421 9528, www.triasicohostel.com.ar. AHC member. Homely atmosphere, simple dorms/doubles, some with private bath, large patio with pool, tours offered.
F Zonda, Laprida 572 Oeste, T420 1009, www.zonda hostel.com.ar. Central, spotless hostel with a neat backyard, simple, light rooms, for 2-6, shared bath, breakfast, kitchen, dinner on request. Trips arranged.

Calingasta *p130*
E Hotel de Campo Calingasta, T421220, restored old colonial-style building, airy rooms, colonnaded patio, pool, lovely views, very tranquil.

Barreal *p130*

B Posada de Campo La Querencia, T0264- 1543 64699. With breakfast, comfy rooms, homely, attentive owners, lots of adventure opportunities.
C Posada San Eduardo, Av San Martín s/n, T441046. Charming colonial-style house, rooms around a courtyard, relaxing, good restaurant.
E Hotel Turismo Barreal, San Martín s/n, T441090, hotelbarreal@yahoo.com.ar. Nicely refurbished 1940s hotel, spartan rooms, and some hostel space, good restaurant, pool, riding.
Camping Municipal site in C Belgrano, T441241, shady, well-maintained, pool, open all year.

San Agustín del Valle Fértil *p130*

C Hostería Valle Fértil, Rivadavia s/n, T420015, www.alkazarhotel.com.ar. Good, a/c, smart, very comfortable, with fine views, also has *cabañas* and good restaurant open to non-residents.
F pp Campo Base, Tucumán entre Libertador y San Luis y, T420063, www.hostelvalledela luna.com.ar. Hl affiliated, cheerful, basic dorms, shared bath, tours.
F pp Los Olivos, Santa Fe y Tucumán, T420115. Welcoming and simple hostel accommodation, excellent value, with restaurant.
Camping La Majadita, lovely campsite on river 8 km west of town, hot showers, great views. **Municipal campsite**, Calle Rivadavia, 5 blocks from plaza, T420104.

Parque Nacional Talampaya *p131*

F Hotel Pagancillo, Pagancillo, T03825-156 66828. Shared bath, breakfast, comfortable.
Camping Basic site next to *administración*, US$1.

❶ Eating

San Juan *p129, map p130*

Ⅶ Las Leñas, San Martín 1670 Oeste. Huge, popular *parrilla*. Vegetarian restaurant next door.
Ⅶ Remolacha, Santa Fe 1232 Oeste. Stylish, warm atmosphere, superb Italian-inspired menu, delicious steaks and pastas. Recommended.
Ⅶ Soychú, Av de la Roza 223 Oeste, T422 1939. Great value vegetarian food. Highly recommended.
Ⅶ-Ⅶ Club Sirio Libanés 'El Palito', Entre Ríos 33 Sur. Pleasant, long-established, tasty food with some Middle Eastern dishes, buffet. Recommended.

❍ Shopping

San Juan *p129, map p130*

San Juan is known for its fine bedspreads, blankets, saddle cloths and other items made from sheep, llama and guanaco wool, fine leather, wooden plates and mortars and, of course, its wines.
Mercado Artesanal, España y San Luis, sells woven blankets/saddlebags. For wine stores try: **La Reja**, Jujuy 424 Sur and **La Bodega**, 25 de Mayo 957 Este.

▲ Activities and tours

San Juan *p129, map p130*

Nerja Tours, Entre Ríos 178 Sur, T421 5214, www.nerja-tours.com.ar. Good for local day trips and adventure tourism inside the national parks.
Valley Moon, Rivadavia 414 Oeste, T421 4868, www.valleymoon.com. Good local alternatives to conventional tours, also rafting, windsurfing at Rodeo, horse riding, climbing, experienced guides.

Barreal *p130*

Fortuna, C Mariano Moreno, T404 0913, www.fortunaviajes.com.ar. Sr Ramón Luis Ossa is an expert guide, running 4WD expedition and horse or mule treks crossing the foothills of the Andes in summer, 1-15 days. Highly recommended.

❸ Transport

San Juan *p129, map p130*

Air Chacritas Airport, 11 km southeast on RN 20. Daily to/from **Buenos Aires**, 1½ hrs with AR/ Austral (Av San Martín 215 Oeste, T0810-2228 6527, or 425 0487), also to Mendoza.
Bus Terminal at Estados Unidos y Santa Fe, 9 blocks east of centre (buses 33 and 35 go through the centre). T422 1604. To **La Rioja**, 5-6 hrs, US$10-15, 6 companies. **Catamarca**, 6 companies, 7-8 hrs, US$14-20. **Tucumán**, 6 companies, 10-12 hrs, US$20-30. **Córdoba**, Socasa, 20 de Julio, Autotransportes San Juan (T422 1870), 8-9 hrs, US$13-18. **Buenos Aires**, 14-16 hrs, US$25-40. To **San Agustín** with **Vallecito**, 3 a day, 4 hrs, US$6. Hourly departures to and from **Mendoza**, fares above. Also services to **Barreal** and **Calingasta** 4 hrs with El Triunfo, T421 4532.

Barreal *p130*

Bus From San Juan daily at 1900, **El Triunfo**, 5 hrs, US$8. Returning to San Juan at 2100. Also minibus run by José Luis Sosa, T441095.

San Agustín del Valle Fértil *p130*

Bus Empresa Vallecito runs a few services a day to **San Juan**, 4 hrs, US$6; 3 buses a week to **La Rioja**, 3 hrs, US$5.

❶ Directory

San Juan *p129, map p130*

Banks Banks 0800-1300. *Banelco* and *Link* ATMs accept international credit cards. **Cambio Santiago**, Gen Acha 52 Sur, T421 2232, Mon-Fri until 2100, Sat until 1300. **Internet** Several *locutorios* have internet, those at Rivadavia y Acha, on the plaza, and Mendoza 139 Sur are open on Sun. **Useful addresses** ACA, 9 de Julio y Rawson, T421 4205, helpful.

La Rioja and Catamarca

La Rioja → *Phone code: 03822. Colour map 8, grid A2. Population: 147,000.*

Founded 1591, at the edge of the plains, with views of Sierra de Velasco, La Rioja can be oppressively hot from November to March. But the town comes alive after the daily siesta and during the annual carnival, *Chaya* (in February), and the *Tinkunaco* festival (beginning on New Year's Eve and lasting four days). The city's main buildings and plazas date from the late 19th century, while the recent government of Carlos Menem, born in a little town 90 km north, has left a certain affluence. The **Church and Convent of San Francisco** ① *25 de Mayo y Bazán y Bustos, Tue-Sun 0900-1200, 1830-2100, free,* contains the Niño Alcalde, a remarkable image of the infant Jesus. You can also see the cell (*celda*) in which San Francisco Solano lived and the orange tree, now dead, which he planted in 1592 (25 de Mayo 218). San Francisco helped to bring peace between the Spaniards and the indigenous people in 1593, an event celebrated at Tinkunaco. The **Convent of Santo Domingo** ① *Luna y Lamadrid,* dates from 1623, said to be the oldest surviving church in Argentina. **Museo Arqueológico Inca Huasi** ① *Alberdi 650, Tue-Sat, 0900-1300, US$0.50,* owned by the Franciscan Order, contains a huge collection of fine Diaguita Indian ceramics, considered among the most important pre-Hispanic artefacts in the country. The **Mercado Artesanal** ① *Luna 790, Tue-Fri 0800-1200, 1600-2000, Sat-Sun 0900- 1300,* has expensive handicrafts. The **Museo de Arte Sacro** ① *in the same building Tue-Sat 0800-1200,* has 18th- and 19th-century images and Cusqueña school paintings. In a beautiful and well kept house at the opposite corner, the **Museo Folklórico** ① *Luna 811, T428500, Tue-Sun 0900-1200, 1600-2000 (Tue-Sat 0900-1200 in summer), US$0.35, free guided visits,* gives a fascinating insight into traditional La Rioja life, with a superb collection of native deities, rustic wine-making machinery and delicate silver *mates.* Well worth a visit too for its leafy patio. There are good views of La Rioja from Cerro de la Cruz (1,648 m), 23 km west, now a centre for hang-gliding. **Tourist office** ① *Luna 345, T426384, www.larioja.gov.ar/turismo.*

Chilecito → *Phone code: 03825. Colour map 8, grid A2. Population: 30,000.*

Chilecito, 129 km northwest of Patquía, is La Rioja province's second town. Founded in 1715, it has good views of Sierra de Famatina, especially from the top of El Portezuelo, an easy climb from the end of Calle El Maestro. The region is famous for its wines, olives and walnuts. **Finca Samay Huasi** ① *3 km south, T422629, Mon-Fri 0800-1300, 1330-1930, Sat-Sun 0800-1200, 1500-1900 (closed 22 Dec-6 Jan), US$0.35,* was the house of Joaquín V González, founder of La Plata University. He designed the gardens with native trees and strange stone monoliths expressing his love of ancient cultures; there's also a small natural history museum. It's an attractive place for a relaxing day; overnight guests welcome (**F** pp, **E** pp full board, book in advance). **Molino San Francisco y Museo de Chilecito** ① *J de Ocampo 50, Mon-Fri 0800-1200, 1600-2100, Sat-Sun 0830-1230, 1530-2000, US$0.35,* has archaeological, historical and artistic exhibits. At the **Cooperativa La Riojana** ① *La Plata 646, T423150,* there are free guided visits (45 minutes), you can watch local grapes being processed to make a wide variety of wines, including organic products; also a smart wine shop open in the mornings. At **Santa Florentina** (8 km northwest), there are the impressive remains of a huge early 20th century foundry, linked to Chilecito and La Mejicana mine by cable car. **Tourist office** ① *Castro y Bazán 52, T422688, daily 0800-1230, 1530-2100.* Also see www.chilecitotour.com.

Reserva Natural Laguna Brava

At Nonogasta 16 km south of Chilecito, the partly paved Ruta 40 heads west climbing through a deep narrow canyon in a series of hairpins to the Cuesta de Miranda (2,020 m). After the Cuesta is **Villa Unión**, 92 km from Nonogasta. From here excursions can be made by four-wheel drive vehicle to the Reserva Natural Laguna Brava, 150 km north. The road goes through **Vinchina** and Jagüe (basic facilities). Further on, as you climb the Portezuelo del Peñón, the salt lake of Laguna Brava becomes visible with some of the mightiest volcanoes on earth in the background. From the left these are the perfect cone Veladero (6,436 m), Reclus (6,335 m), Los Gemelos (6,130 m), Pissis (6,882 m) the highest volcano in the world, though inactive, and Bonete (6,759 m) which is visible from Villa Unión and Talampaya. For tours in this area see under Chilecito and La Rioja. **Access:** From Jagüe 4WD and going with two vehicles is essential; otherwise only by mountain bike. Summer rainfalls and winter snow may limit the access to only a short period in the year; usually in April or early May is best. Park entry US$2.

Catamarca → *Phone code: 03833. Colour map 8, grid A2. Population: 130,000. Altitude: 490 m.*

Officially San Fernando del Valle de Catamarca, the city is capital of its province, on the Río del Valle, between the Sierra de Ambato (to the west) and Ancasti (to the east), 153 km northeast of La Rioja and 240 km south of Tucumán. Now rather run-down, Catamarca is most famous for its textiles, and unless you're here for the poncho festival in mid-July (*feria* with quality handicrafts, food and live music), there's little to keep you. Summers are unbearably hot with temperatures up to 45°C. Some 37 km north is the much more appealing and prettier weekend retreat of **El Rodeo** with its cooler microclimate, good walks and charming *hosterías* (tourist information T490043, helpful). In the vast open puna to the northwest, there are traces of sophisticated ancient civilizations, and the finest of the city's six museums has an outstanding collection of indigenous artefacts. **Museo Arqueológico Adán Quiroga** ① *Sarmiento 446, T437413, Mon-Fri 0700-1300, 1430-2030, Sat-Sun 0830-1230, 1530-1830, US$0.50.* **Tourist office** ① *Av República 446, www.catamarca.com, www.catamarca.gov.ar, 0800-2100.* Helpful leaflets with bus times and prices. **Provincial office** ① *Roca y Virgen del Valle, T437594, Mon-Fri 0800-1300, 1500-2000,* and kiosks in airport and Terminal Shopping by bus station, Av Güemes.

Puna west of Catamarca

The high altitude desert of the puna is spectacular, with a distinct culture and remote untouristy towns. It's most easily reached by the paved road to **Aimogasta** and on to the small settlements of Tinogasta and Fiambalá, useful staging posts if taking the Paso San Fransisco to Chile, or north to Andagalá, or to Belén, where the rough road to Antofagasta de la Sierra begins. The *Zonda*, a strong, dry mountain wind, can cause dramatic temperature increases.

Tinogasta (*Phone code 03837*) is in an oasis of vineyards, olive groves, and poplars. It is the starting point for expeditions to **Pissis** the second highest mountain in South America, 6,882 m. To get there, take Ruta 60 which crosses Tinogasta in the direction of the San Francisco pass. You have to register at the police station outside Fiambalá, take passport. Expeditions organized and horse riding with Omar Monuey, La Espiga de Oro, 25 de Mayo 436 or *Varela Viajes*, T420428. At Fiambalá, contact Jonson and Ruth Reynoso, T496214.

Fiambalá is 49 km north of Tinogasta, a peaceful place in a vine-filled valley, with **Termas de Fiambalá**, hot springs, situated 14 km east (take a taxi; make sure fare includes wait and return). 4WD vehicles may be hired for approaching the Pissis-Ojos region; ask at the Intendencia.

Border with Chile – Paso San Francisco

Fiambalá is the starting-point for the crossing to Chile via Paso San Francisco (4,726 m), 203 km northwest along a paved road. The border is open 0830-1930, T498001. On the Chilean side roads run to El Salvador and Copiapó. This route is closed by snow June-October; take enough fuel for at least 400 km as there are no service stations from Fiambalá to just before Copiapó.

Belén → *Phone code 03835. Colour map 6, grid C3. Population: 8,800. Altitude: 1,000 m.*

A quiet intimate little town, Belén is famous for its ponchos, saddlebags and rugs, which you can see being woven. The museum, **Cóndor Huasi** ① *San Martín y Belgrano, 1st floor, daily,* contains fascinating Diaguita artefacts, and there is a newly constructed Virgen (the last one was struck by lightning) on the Cerro de Nuestra Señora de Belén above town; good views. Important festival: Nuestra Señora de Belén, 24 December-6 January. **Tourist information** ① *bus terminal, near plaza, Rivadavia y Lavalle, T461539, alpamicuna@cotelbelen.com.ar.*

South of Belén, Ruta 40 is paved to Chilecito via **Londres**, a quiet, pretty village. North of Belén Ruta 40 runs another 176 km, largely unpaved, to Santa María at the provincial border with Tucumán (see page 139), and on to Cafayate (page 143), or 260 km north to tiny remote **Antofagasta de la Sierra** and onwards to San Antonio de los Cobres in Salta. East of Belén, a rough and sandy road goes to **Andalgalá**, a former copper-mining town with a handicraft market, two archaeological museums and a decent hotel D Aquasol. For tours and information contact **Andalgalá Turismo**, T03835-422405, turandalgala@cotelbelen.com.ar. Very helpful.

● Sleeping

La Rioja *p133*
A/c or fan are essential for summer nights. High season is during Jul winter holidays.
B King's, Av Quiroga 1070, T422122. 4-star,

buffet breakfast included, a/c gym, pool and fine rooms, also car rental.
B Plaza, San Nicolás de Bari y 9 de Julio (on Plaza 25 de Mayo), T425215, www.plazahotel-

larioja.com.ar. Functional 4-star, pool on top floor, breakfast included, a/c.
C Vincent Apart Hotel, Santiago del Estero y San Nicolás de Bari, T432326. Spotless flats for up to 4, a/c, with dining room, kitchen and fridge, breakfast included, excellent value.
D Savoy, San Nicolás de Bari y Roque A Luna, T426894, hotelsavoy@infovia.com.ar. In a quiet residential area, tidy, comfortable, with breakfast and a/c, second floor best.
Camping Several sites along Av Ramírez de Velasco, in northwest suburbs on the way to Las Padercitas and Dique Los Sauces, but the best is **Camping de la Sociedad Sirio Libanesa**, at Balneario Los Sauces, 13 km west on Ruta 75, with hot showers and pool.

Chilecito p133
C Chilecito (ACA), T Gordillo y A G Ocampo, T422201, T15-666358. A/c, comfortable, with breakfast, safe parking, pool, cheap set menus.
D Finca del Paimán, Mariano Moreno y Santa Rosa (San Miguel, 3 km southeast of town), T425102, www.fincadelpaiman.com.ar. Delightful 4½-ha farm, spacious rooms, kitchen, breakfast and transport to/from Chilecito included. You can help with fruit harvesting or jam cooking! Warmly recommended, book in advance. Also has a hostel in Chilecito, **Hostel del Paimán**, El Maestro 188 y A Marasso (same T), old house in town centre, with rooms **E**, or dorms **F** pp, HI affiliated, lovely garden.
D Hostal Mary Pérez, Florencio Dávila 280, T/F423156, hostal_mp@hotmail.com. Best value, comfortable, welcoming atmosphere, good breakfast. Recommended.
Camping 3 sites at Santa Florentina and Las Talas, 8 km northwest (remise taxi US$2-2.50).

Reserva Natural Laguna Brava and Villa Unión p133
B Hotel Pircas Negras, on Ruta 76, Villa Unión, T03825-470611, www.hotelpircasnegras.com. Large modern building, the best in the area, comfortable rooms, restaurant and pool, excursions organized.
D Hotel Noryanepat, JVGonzález 150, Villa Unión, T470133. Small rooms with a/c, good.
E Dayton, Nicolás Dávila 115, Villa Unión, T470640. Basic but decent, with breakfast. There are several basic *hospedajes* in Vinchina.

Catamarca p134
Hotels are mostly unmodernized, overpriced and business-oriented.
C Arenales, Sarmiento 542, T431329, www.hotel-arenales.com.ar. Comfortable plain rooms, good bathrooms, restaurant.
C Hostería El Rodeo, El Rodeo, 37 km north on RP4, T490296, www.hotelguia.com/elrodeo. Daily

minibus from centre. Lovely spacious rooms, great views, tours organized. Highly recommended.
D Casino Catamarca, Pasaje César Carman s/n (behind the ACA service station), T432928, inforcentral@hotelcasinocatamarca.com. Smart, modern and bright, well decorated rooms, discreetly hidden casino, large pool, good value.
D Grand Hotel, Camilo Melet 41, T426715. Delightful, helpful owners, simple spacious rooms, a/c, TV, discounts for cash. Recommended.
D La Casa de Chicha, Los Gladiolos s/n, El Rodeo, T490082, la_casa_de_chicha@yahoo.com.ar. Idyllic setting in the mountains, antique furniture, excellent restaurant for lunch and dinner, or have tea in the beautiful garden, filled with pear trees.
D Pucara, Caseros 501, T431569. Boldly decorated entrance lounge, comfortable bedrooms with pink satin bedspreads and flamenco prints.
E Residencial Shinkal, Vicario Segura 1120, T421083. The best and newest residencial. Not recommended for single women. No breakfast.

Tinogasta p134
D Hostería Novel, Córdoba 200, T420009, near airport, friendly.
D Viñas del Sol, Perón 231, T420028.
E Res Don Alberto, A del Pino y Rivadavia, T420323.

Fiambalá p134
D Hostería Municipal, Almagro s/n, T03837-496016. Good value, also restaurant.
E pp Complejo Turístico, at the Termas, T496016. With cabins, also camping.

Belén p134
D Belén, Belgrano y Cubas, T461501, www.belencat.com.ar. Comfortable, also tour operator.
E Samay, Urquiza 349, T461320. Old fashioned but welcoming, homely little rooms with bath and fan.

🍴 Eating

La Rioja p133
🍴🍴 **El Corral**, Av Quiroga y Rivadavia. Traditional rustic *comidas de campo* and good local wines.
🍴🍴 **La Vieja Casona**, Rivadavia 427. Smart *parrilla*.
🍴 **La Aldea de la Virgen de Luján**, Rivadavia 756. Lively atmosphere, cheap and popular small place, including some Middle Eastern dishes.

Chilecito p133
🍴 **Club Arabe**, 25 de Mayo entre Zelada y Dávila and Famatina. Middle Eastern food only on request, served outside under grapevines.
🍴 **El Rancho de Ferrito**, PB Luna 647, T422481. Popular *parrilla*, with local wines.
🍴 **La Rosa**, Ocampo 149, T424693. Relaxing atmosphere, huge variety of pizzas, more extensive menu Fri and Sat.

Catamarca *p134*

¶¶ La Tinaja, Sarmiento 533, T435853. Delicious *parrilla* and excellent pastas, worth the price.

¶¶ Salsa Criolla, República 546 on the plaza. Traditional popular *parrilla*, sloppy service, but the beef is good. **Trattoria Montecarlo**, next door, same owner, Italian style.

¶ Richmond, the best café on the plaza, stylish.

¶ Sociedad Española, Virgen del Valle 725, T431897. Recommended for quality and variety, paella and other Spanish specialities, friendly service; worth the 5 block walk from the plaza.

Tinogasta *p134*

The water is notoriously bad in this region: avoid salads and ice, drink mineral water.
Restaurant Casa Grande, Constitución y Moreno. Good meals, try local wines.

Belén *p134*

Bar El Seminario, on the plaza. Great for beer and sandwiches, spills over onto the plaza at weekends, popular local meeting place.

◎ Shopping

Catamarca *p134*

Local specialities Cuesta del Portezuelo, Sarmiento 571 and **Valdez**, Sarmiento 578. You can see carpets being woven at **Mercado Artesanal**, Virgen del Valle 945, wide range of handicrafts, daily 0800-1330, 1500-2100; carpet factory Mon-Fri 0800-1200, 1500-2030.

▲ Activities and tours

La Rioja *p133*

For excursions to Talampaya, Valle de la Luna, Laguna Brava and Corona del Inca crater (high season only) and horse riding in Velasco mountains:
Aguada, D Vélez Sarsfield 742, T433695 or 15-675699, talampaya_aguada@ciudad.com.ar. Helpful agency with good tours, some English and French spoken.
Corona del Inca, PB Luna 914, T450054 or 15-663811, www.coronadelinca.com.ar. Wide range of tours, English spoken.
Néstor Pantaleo, Ecuador 813, T422103. Experienced photographer, runs 4WD trips, several languages spoken.

Chilecito *p133*

This is an excellent base for amazing treks in the Famatina mountains and 1-day trips to Talampaya and Valle de la Luna.
Alejo Piehl, T/F425102, 15672612, www.fincadel paiman.com.ar. Experienced guide (see Sleeping, above), all inclusive 1-day tours to Talampaya and Valle de la Luna, US$60pp, and unforgettable

2-3 day treks (US$35-130 pp) to Famatina, visiting abandoned cable car stations on the way to the summit. 4WD trips. Recommended.
Inka Ñan, T423641. Leopoldo Badoul organizes excursions to the province's main attractions.

Catamarca *p134*

Mountaineering Aníbal Vázquez, T03835-471001, trekking in Antofagasta de la Sierra.

◎ Transport

La Rioja *p133*

Air Airport 5 km northeast, via San Nicolás de Bari, RP5, T427239. To **Buenos Aires**, AR, T426307, flights often stop at Catamarca or Córdoba.
Bus Terminal 7 blocks south of the Cathedral at Artigas y España (T425453). To **Buenos Aires**, Gen Urquiza and **Chevallier** US$40-45, 15-17 hrs. To **Mendoza**, US$17, 6-7 hrs, many companies, and **San Juan** US$10-15, 5-6 hrs, same companies. To **Tucumán**, US$10-14, 5-6 hrs. To **Salta**, Andesmar, 10-11 hrs, US$18-26. Also provincial services.

Chilecito *p133*

Bus Terminal on Av Perón, on south access to town. To **San Juan** and Mendoza with **Vallecito**, US$15-17; to **La Rioja**, several times daily, US$4, 3 hrs. To **Córdoba**, US$12, 7 hrs, and **Buenos Aires**, US$35, 17 hrs, El Práctico, General Urquiza (T423279).

Catamarca *p134*

Air Airport, 20 km south, T430080. AR/Austral (Sarmiento 589, T424460) to/from **Buenos Aires**.
Bus Terminal 5 blocks southeast of plaza at Güemes y Tucumán T437578, with shops, café, ATM and locutorio. Taxi to/from Plaza 25 de Mayo US$0.50. To **Tucumán**, several companies, 3½-4hrs, US$6. To **Buenos Aires**, 4 companies daily, 14-18 hrs, US$25-53. To **Córdoba**, 4 companies daily, 6 hrs, US$10-12. To **Santiago del Estero**, 1 daily, 3 hrs, US$5; Mendoza, La Estrella, 4 hrs, US$5. To **Mendoza**, several companies daily, 10 hrs, US$18-35. To **La Rioja**, several companies daily, US$4, 2 hrs. To **Tinogasta**, see below. To **Belén** via Londres, two companies, 5 hrs, US$5-7; **Marín** (via Aconquija).

Tinogasta *p134*

Bus To **Tucumán**, Empresa Gutiérrez, 3 weekly (daily in high season). To **Catamarca**, Empresa Gutiérrez (connection to Buenos Aires), Robledo and Rubimar, US$6; to/from **La Rioja**, El Cóndor, daily, US$4-5.

Fiambalá *p134*

Bus Empresa Gutiérrez to **Catamarca** via Tinogasta. For Belén, change at Aimogasta.

Belén *p134*

Bus From Belén to **Santa María**, **San Cayetano** and **Parra** (connection there with other companies to Cafayate and Salta), daily, 5 hrs, US$7. To **Tinogasta**, **Robledo**, 4 weekly, 2-3 hrs, US$4. To **Antofagasta de la Sierra**, El Antofagasteño, 2 weekly, 11 hrs, US$15. For more frequent services to **Catamarca** or **La Rioja**, take bus to Aimogasta, 1 hr, US$2.

ⓞ Directory

La Rioja *p133*

Banks US$ cash changed at Banco de Galicia, Buenos Aires y San Nicolás de Bari, and at Daniel, exchange facilities at Rivadavia 525. **Internet** A handful of places in and around Plaza 25 de Mayo,

all charge about US$0.50-1 per hr. **Post offices** Av Perón 258; Western Union branch. **Telephones** Several *locutorios* in the centre and at Av Quiroga e Hipólito Yrigoyen, with internet access (US$0.60 per hr) near bus terminal.

Catamarca *p134*

Banks Many ATMs for all major cards, along Rivadavia and at bus terminal, BBVA Banco Francés, Rivadavia 520. **Banco de la Nación** San Martín 632. **Internet** Cedecc, Esquiú 414. Taraj Net, San Martín y Ayacucho. **Post offices** San Martín 753, slow, open 0800-1300, 1600-2000. **Telephones** Most *telecentros* around Plaza 25 de Mayo, also at República 845 and Rivadavia 758, open 0700-2400, daily.

Northwest Argentina

Two of the oldest cities in Argentina, Santiago del Estero and Tucumán, are at the start of the route to the fascinating Northwest. Both have some good museums and other sites of interest, but the summer heat may urge you to press on to the mountains. You can break the journey between the two cities at the rather worn, but much-visited spa of Termas de Río Hondo. Of the two routes to the atmospheric city of Salta, the more beautiful is via Tafí del Valle, the wine-producing town of Cafayate and the dramatic canyon of the Quebrada de las Conchas or the equally enchanting Valles Calchaquíes. Pretty towns in arid landscapes, archaeological remains and the Andes in the distance make for a memorable journey.

Santiago del Estero → *Phone code: 0385. Colour map 6, grid C4. Population: 328,000.*

Founded in 1553 by conquistadores pushing south from Peru, this is the oldest Argentine city, though little of its history is visible today. It's rather run down, but the people are relaxed and welcoming (*Altitude 200 m, 395 km north of Córdoba, 159 km southeast of Tucumán*). On the **Plaza Libertad** stand the **Municipalidad** and the **Cathedral** (the fifth on the site, dating from 1877), with the Cabildo-like Prefectura of Police. The fine **Casa de Gobierno** is on Plaza San Martín, three blocks north. In the convent of **Santo Domingo**, Urquiza y 25 de Mayo, is one of two copies of the 'Turin Shroud', given by Philip II to his 'beloved colonies of America'. On Plaza Lugones is the church of **San Francisco**, the oldest surviving church in the city, founded in 1565, with the cell of San Francisco Solano, patron saint of Tucumán, who stayed here in 1593. Beyond it is the pleasant **Parque Francisco de Aguirre**. A highly recommended museum, **Museo de Ciencias Antropológicas** ① *Avellaneda 353, T421 1380, Tue-Sun 0800-2000, free,* has an eclectic collection of prehispanic artefacts, exquisitely painted funerary urns, flattened skulls, anthropomorphic ceramics and musical instruments; fascinating, if poorly presented. Also interesting is the **Museo Histórico Provincial** ① *Urquiza 354, Mon-Fri 0700-1300, 1400-2000, Sat-Sun 1000-1200, free.* In a 200-year old mansion, it has 18th- and 19th-century artefacts from wealthy local families. **Carnival** is in February. **Tourist office** ① *Plaza Libertad, T421 4243.*

Some 65 km north of Santiago del Estero is **Termas de Río Hondo** (*phone code: 03858*), Argentina's most popular spa town which has its warm mineral-laden waters piped into every hotel in the city (160 of them), making it a mecca (or Lourdes) for older visitors with arthritic or skin conditions in July and August, when you'll need to book in advance. The hotels aside, the town is mostly run down, with a cream-coloured casino dominating the scruffy plaza and scores of *alfajores* shops. There are shops and banks all around the plaza. **Tourist office** ① *Caseros 132, T422143, or www.lastermasteriohondo.com,* helpful for accommodation advice.

● Sleeping

Santiago del Estero *p137*

B Carlos V, Independencia 110, T424 0303, hotelcarlosv@arnet.com.ar. Corner of the plaza, the city's most luxurious hotel, elegant rooms, pool, good restaurant, still good value for its range.
C Centro, 9 de Julio 131, T422 4350. Nice décor, very comfortable, airy restaurant. Recommended.
C Libertador, Catamarca 47, T421 9252. Smart and relaxing, spacious lounge, plain rooms, patio with pool (summer only), elegant restaurant, 5 blocks south of plaza in the better part of town.
D Savoy, Peatonal Tucumán 39, T421 2344. Good budget option, full of character and faded art nouveau grandeur, swirling stairwell, large airy rooms, very simple, a good choice.
F Res Alaska, Santa Fe 279, T422 1360. Close to bus station, hot water, TV, fan, good value.
Camping Las Casuarinas, Parque Aguirre, T421 1390. Insect repellent essential.

Termas de Río Hondo *p137*

L De los Pinos, Caseros y Maipú, T421043. The best option, attractive Spanish style, a little removed from the centre, huge park, pool, very comfortable rooms, with private thermal baths. Rates are all-inclusive.
B Termal Río Hondo, T421455, www.hotel termalriohondo.com.ar. Most comfortable in centre, modern rooms, pool, good restaurant.
Camping Two sites near river: **Del Río**, Av Yrigoyen y Ruta 9; **La Olla**, Av Yrigoyen y Lascano. Also **ACA**, on access to Dique Frontal (4 km from town), T421648; **El Mirador**, Ruta 9 y Urquiza.

● Eating

Santiago del Estero *p137*

♥♥ **Mia Mamma**, on the main plaza at 24 de Septiembre 15. A cheery place for *parrilla* and tasty pastas, with good salad starters.
♥♥ **Periko's** on the plaza, lively, popular, for *lomitos* and pizzas.
♥ **Don Pelachi**, Urquiza y Belgrano. Good value, large choice of dishes.

Termas de Río Hondo *p137*

For dinner, try *parrilla* at **San Cayetano**, or homely **Renacimiento**, both on Sarmiento (main street), reasonably priced. Cheaper still, on Alberdi y Sarmiento is **El Chorizo Loco**, a lively pizzería.

● Transport

Santiago del Estero *p137*

Air Airport on northwest outskirts. **AR/Austral** to **Buenos Aires** and **Tucumán**.
Bus Bus information, T421 3746. Terminal, Gallo 480, has toilets, a *locutorio*, basic café and kiosks, as well as stalls selling food. Taxi US$0.80 into town, or 8 blocks' walk. **Córdoba**, 6 hrs, US$8-10; **Jujuy**, 8 hrs, US$13; **Salta**, 6 hrs, US$16. To **Catamarca**, 1 daily, 3 hrs, US$5.

Termas de Río Hondo *p137*

Bus To **Santiago del Estero**, 1 hr, US$2 and to **Tucumán**, 2 hrs, US$3. The bus terminal is 8 blocks north of the centre, but buses will drop you at the plaza, opposite the casino, if asked.

Tucumán and around

→ *Phone code: 0381. Colour map 6, grid C4. Population: 740,000. Altitude: 450 m.*

San Miguel de Tucumán was founded by Spaniards coming south from Peru in 1565. Capital of a province rich in sugar, tobacco and citrus fruits, it is the biggest and busiest city in the north. It stands on a plain and is sweltering hot in summer (siesta from 1230-1630 is strictly observed), when you might prefer to retreat to the cooler mountain town of **Tafí del Valle** in the Sierra de Aconquija to the west. **Tourist office** ① *on the plaza, 24 de Septiembre 484, T430 3644, www.turismoentucuman.com, and www.tucumanturismo.gov.ar, Mon-Fri 0800-2200, Sat-Sun 0900-2100.* Also in the bus terminal and airport.

Sights

Casa Padilla (Museo de la Ciudad) ① *25 de Mayo 36, on the west side of the main Plaza Independencia, Mon-Sat 0900-1230, 1600-1900,* has a small collection of art and antiques in a historical house. Also on this side of the plaza is the ornate **Casa de Gobierno** and, nearby, the church of **San Francisco**, with a picturesque façade. A block north, the **Museo Arqueológico** ① *25 de Mayo 265, in university building, T422 1692, Mon-Fri 0800-1200, 1700-1900, US$0.50,* has a fine small collection. On the south side of Plaza Independencia is the **Cathedral** and, two blocks south, the interesting **Casa Histórica** ① *T431 0826, Mon-Fri 1000-1800, Sat-Sun 1300-1900, US$1; son et lumière show in garden nightly (not Thu, except in Jul) at 2030, adults US$2, children US$1, tickets also from tourist office on Plaza Independencia, no seats.* Here, in 1816, the country's Declaration of Independence was drawn up.

East of the centre is the **Parque de Julio**, one of the finest urban parks in Argentina. Extending over 400 ha, it contains a wide range of sub-tropical trees as well as a lake and sports facilities. The **Museo de la Industria Azucarera** ① *daily 0830-1230, free*, traces the development of the local sugar industry. There are good views over the city from **Cerro San Javier**, 27 km west of the city (*Empresa Ber Bus*, US$1.50 from bus terminal).

Tafí del Valle → *Phone code: 03867. Population: 3,300. Altitude: 1,976 m.*

South of Tucumán at Acheral on RN38, Ruta 307 heads northwest out of the sugar cane fields to zigzag up through forested hills to a treeless plateau, before El Mollar and the Embalse La Angostura. Here the valley is greener and you descend gradually to Tafí del Valle, a small town and popular weekend retreat from the heat of Tucumán in the summer (106 km). It has a cool microclimate, and makes a good base for walking, with several peaks of the Sierra de Aconquija providing satisfying day-hikes. There's some excellent, if pricey, accommodation and a **cheese festival** in early February, with live music. **Tourist information** to the south of semi-circular plaza, 0800-2200 daily, no phone. Map US$1.40. Visit the **Capilla Jesuítica y Museo de La Banda**, southwest of town across bridge over Rio Tafi, 500 m on left, ① *T421685, Mon-Sat 0900-1900, Sun 0900-1600 (closing early off season), US$0.70, includes a guided tour*, an 18th-century chapel and 19th-century *estancia*, with museum of archaeology and religious art. **Museo Los Tesoros de Tafí** ① *at La Banda, T421563*, is a small archaeological museum. The owner, Juan Carlos Yapura, offers guided walks to aboriginal sites in the mountains. ATM at Banco de Tucumán, Miguel Critto 311, T421033. Internet on Av Perón and one on Av Critto.

About 5km from the main road, across the Dique La Angostura, **El Mollar** is another weekend village with campsites and *cabañas*, popular with teenagers and students. Boating and fishing trips are offered on the reservoir, US$3.15 half day, US$10 full day.

Amaicha, Quilmes and Santa María

From Tafí the road runs 56 km northwest over the 3,040 m Infiernillo Pass (Km 85) with spectacular views and through grand arid landscape to sunny **Amaicha del Valle** (*Population 5,000; Altitude 1,997 m*) with the popular **Complejo Pachamama museum** ① *T421004, daily 0830-1200, 1400-1830 (closed Sun off season), US$2*, highly recommended, with overview of the Calchaquí culture, geology, tapestry for sale by Héctor Cruz, well-known Argentine sculptor and artist. From Amaicha the paved road continues north 15 km to the junction with Ruta 40.

Some 35 km north, and 5 km off the main road, are the striking ruins of **Quilmes** ① *0800-1830, US$1, includes guided tour and museum, with café, huge gift shop, hotel.* The setting is amazing, an intricate web of walls built into the mountain side, where 5,000 members of a Diaguita tribe lived, resisting Inca, and then Spanish domination, before being marched off to Córdoba and to the Quilmes in Buenos Aires where the beer comes from. For a day's visit take 0600 Aconquija bus from Cafayate to Santa María, alight after an hour at stop 5 km from site, or take 0700 **El Indio** bus (not on Thursday) from Santa María; take 1130 bus back to Cafayate, US$2; otherwise tours run from Cafayate.

Santa María (*Population 11,000*), 22 km south of Amaicha by paved road, is a delightful, untouristy small town with an interesting archaeology museum at the **Centro Cultural Yokavil** ① *corner of plaza, Mon-Fri 0900-2000, Sat 1000-2000, donation requested*, pleasant hotels and a municipal campsite. A helpful tourist kiosk is on the plaza, T421083, with map and list of accommodation; also a *locutorio* and internet places, ATM on Mitre at Banco de la Nación (only one for miles). South of Santa María, Ruta 40 goes to Belén, see page 134. Instead of going to Amaicha to get to Quilmes, you can take the Ruta 40 up the west bank of the Río Santa María: ask for the bridge over the river and turn right. The road is paved to the Catamarca/Tucumán border, thereafter *ripio*. After 15 km, you pass **Fuerte Quemado** ① *free*, an archaeological site of low-walled structures amid a variety of cactus. It's 10 km further to the Quilmes turn off.

Tucumán to Salta

The speedy route to Salta is via Rosario de la Frontera and Güemes. **Rosario de la Frontera** (*Phone code 03876, Altitude 769 m*), 130 km north of Tucumán, is a convenient place for a stop, with thermal springs 8 km away. About 20 km north is the historical post house, **Posta de Yatasto**, with museum, 2 km east of the main road; campsite. About 70 km north of Rosario de la Frontera, at Lumbreras, a road branches off Ruta 9 and runs 90 km northeast to the **Parque Nacional El Rey**, one of three cloudforest parks in the northwest. Stretching from heights of over 2,300m through jungle to the flat arid Chaco in the east, it contains a variety of animal and plant life. There's free camping and marked trails, but accessible only on foot or horseback with a guide; insects are a problem. Federico Norte, **Norte Trekking** ① *T0387-436 11844, www.nortetrekking.com*, runs the best expeditions, US$60 pp per day, all inclusive, camping, trekking, rafting, 4WD, also into Bolivia and Chile. Highly recommended. The park office is in Salta, at España 366, T4312683. Although drier in winter, the access road is poor, not recommended for ordinary vehicles. Park roads are impassable in the wet, November to May. There is no public transport to the park; it's best to go on an organized expedition. More information on National Parks website: www.parquesnacionales.gov.ar.

😴 Sleeping

Tucumán *p138, map p140*
All hotels include breakfast and have fans or a/c.
A Catalinas Park, Av Soldati 380, T450 2250. The city's most comfortable, good value, luxurious, minimalist hotel, overlooking Parque 9 de Julio, outstanding food and service, pool (open to non-residents), sauna, gym. Highly recommended.
A Suites Garden Park, Av Soldati 330, T431 0700, www.gardenparkhotel.com.ar. Smart, welcoming 4-star, views over Parque 9 de Julio, pool, gym, sauna, restaurant. Also apartments.
B Mediterráneo, 24 de Septiembre 364, T431 0025, www.hotelmediterraneo.com.ar. Good rooms, TV, a/c. 20-30% discount for *Footprint* owners.

C Carlos V, 25 de Mayo 330, T431 1666, www.redcarlosv.com.ar. Central, good service, with elegant restaurant.
C Premier, Crisóstomo Alvarez 510, T431 0381, info@redcarlosv.com.ar. Spacious comfortable rooms, modern bathrooms. Recommended.
C Dallas, Corrientes 985, T421 8500. Welcoming, nicely furnished large rooms, good bathrooms. Recommended, though far from centre.
C Francia, Crisóstomo Alvarez 467, T/F431 0781. Cheap apartments for 5, plain but comfortable high-ceilinged rooms, central, good budget option.
C Miami, Junín 580, 8 blocks from plaza, T431 0265, F422 2405. Good modern hotel, rooms

Tucumán

To Airport

To Train Station (2 blocks)

Salta · Maipú · Muñecas · 25 de Mayo

Corrientes · Honduras · Haiti · Pasaje Celedonio Gutiérrez · Av Soldati

To Museo de la Industria Azucarera

Junín · Santiago del Estero

San Juan · Guatemala · Cuba

To Fundación Miguel Lillo · *To San Javier*

Córdoba · Mercado del Norte · Museo Arqueológico · Lapridá · Rivadavia · Monteagudo · Balcarce · Av Avellaneda · **Parque 9 de Julio**

Mendoza · Norte Supermarket · San Francisco

A Jacques · Río de Janeiro · Francia

San Martín · Casa de Gobierno · Museo de la Ciudad · Plaza Independencia · **Cathedral** · 24 de Septiembre · Av B Aráoz · Moreno · Av Sáenz Peña · Charcas · Díaz Vélez

Ruta 9 To Santiago de Estero & Buenos Aires

Shopping del Jardín

C Alvarez · Ayacucho · Chacabuco · Buenos Aires · 9 de Julio · Museo Iramain · Congreso · Las Heras · Entre Ríos · Av Brígido · Av Mitre

To · *To* · Casa Histórica · *To*

San Lorenzo

N

0 metres 200
0 yards 200

Sleeping 😴
Argentina Norte 1
Carlos V 2
Catalinas Park 9
Dallas 4
Francia 5
Mediterráneo 7
Miami 8

Catalinas Park 9
Petit 10
Premier 11
Suites Garden Park 6
Tucumán Hostel 3
Versailles 5

Eating 🍴
Café de París 6
Cosas del Campo 7
El Fondo 1
Filipo 2
Il Postino 3
Klo y Klo 4
La Leñita 5

Panadería Villecco 8
Sir Harris 9
Superpanchería 10

Bars & clubs 🍸
Costumbres
Argentinos 11

with a/c and TV, though a little overpriced, discounts for HI members, pool.
C Versailles, Crisóstomo Alvarez 481, T422 9760, F422 9763. A touch of class, comfortable beds though rooms a bit small, and good service. Recommended.
E Hostería Aconquija, Av Aconquija 2530, T425-6901, Yerba Buena. Youth hostel. AHC member.
E Petit, Crisóstomo Alvarez 765, T431 3902, hotelpetit@redcarlosv.com.ar. Spacious old house with patio, small rooms at the back, pretty basic but quiet, cheaper without bath or fan.
E pp La Estrella, Av B Araoz 38, T421 4186. Near to the bus station, cheaper without bath, clean, helpful.
G pp Argentina Norte, Laprida 456, T430 2716, www.argentinanorte.com/hostel. Youth hostel in restored house with quiet atmosphere and lovely patio, basic dorms, well-equipped kitchen, internet, English spoken, good. Plus **E** double room with bath.
G Tucumán Hostel, Buenos Aires 669, T420 1584, www.tucumanhostel.com. The striking point of this old and quiet house is its beautiful Parador Tafinisto, at the bottom of Av Perón. Recommended for parrilla with plenty of regional dishes, and live folklore music at the weekends.

Tafí del Valle p139
Many places, including hotels, close out of season.
B Hostería Tafí del Valle, Av San Martín y Gdor Campero, T421027, www.soldelvalle.com.ar. Right at the top of the town, with splendid views, good restaurant, luxurious small rooms, pool.
B La Rosada, Belgrano 322, T421323/146, miguel_torres@sinectis.com.ar. Spacious rooms, well decorated, plenty of hot water, comfortable, excellent breakfast included, helpful staff, lots of expeditions on offer and free use of cycles.
B Lunahuana, Av Critto 540, T421330, www.lunahuana.com.ar. Stylish comfortable rooms with good views, spacious duplexes for families.
B Mirador del Tafí, T/F421219, www.mirador deltafi.com.ar. Warm attractive rooms and spacious lounge, superb restaurant, excellent views. Highly recommended.
D Los Cuartos, Av Gob Critto y Av Juan Calchaquí s/n, T0381-15587 4230, www.turismoen tucuman.com/loscuartos. Old *estancia*, rooms full of character, charming hosts. Recommended. Also offer a day at the *estancia*, lunch, horse riding. Delicious *té criollo*, and farm cheese can be bought here or at cheese shop on Av Miguel Critto.

E Hospedaje El Valle, above the big souvenir emporium at Perón 56, T421641. Basic but clean, some rooms with bath.
F pp La Cumbre, Av Perón 120, T421768, www.lacumbretafidelvalle.com. Basic, cramped rooms, but central, helpful owner is a tour operator with wide range of activities.
Camping Los Sauzales. Run down, US$2 pp plus tent. Better sites at El Mollar, such as **La Mutual**.

Quilmes p139
B Parador Ruinas de Quilmes, T03892-421075. Peaceful, very comfortable, boldly designed with weavings and ceramics, great views of Quilmes, good restaurant (residents only), free camping. Recommended.

Rosario de la Frontera p139
B Termas, Ruta 34 (6 km from bus station), T481004, hoteltermas@hotmail.com. Rambling place, good food, and thermal pool, horse riding, and golf. Baths US$2.
C ACA hostería, T481143. About 1 km from *Hotel Termas*, more comfortable.

Eating

Tucumán p138, map p140
Many popular restaurants and cafés along 25 de Mayo, north from Plaza Independencia, and on Plaza Hipólito Yrigoyen.
El Fondo, San Martín 848, T422 2161. Superb renowned steak house.
Klo y Klo, Junín 657. Delightful, welcoming and charming atmosphere, good range of seafood and pastas (closed Sun evening and Mon).
La Leñita, 25 de Mayo 377. Recommended for *parrilla*, superb salads, live folk music at weekends.
Sir Harris, Laprida y Mendoza. A Tucumán institution, cosy with good quality *tenedor libre*, some veggie dishes. Recommended.
Il Postino, 25 de Mayo y Córdoba. Attractive buzzing pizza place, plus *tapas* and *tortillas* too, stylish décor. Recommended.

Cafés
Café de París, Santiago del Estero 502 y 25 de Mayo. *Tapas* bar and stylish little restaurant.
Cosas del Campo, Lavalle 857 (south of centre, next to Plaza San Martín), T420 1758. Renowned for its *empanadas*, also for take-away.
Filipo, Mendoza y 25 de Mayo. Good for a coffee or drinks, a popular smart café, good atmosphere.
Panadería Villecco, Corrientes 751. Exceptional bread, also wholemeal (*integral*) and pastries.

● *For an explanation of the sleeping and eating price codes used in this guide, see page 58.*
● *Other relevant information is found in Essentials pages 68-69.*

Superpanchería, 25 de Mayo. Bright busy hot dog place with huge range of salads and toppings.

Tafí del Valle *p139*
Many places along Av Perón.
♥-♥ El Portal de la Villa, Av Perón 221, T421834, www.elportaldelavilla.com. Big with lots local dishes and *parrilla*, excellent *empanadas*.

❶ Bars and clubs

Tucumán *p138, map p140*
Costumbres Argentinos, San Juan 666 y Maipú. An intimate place with a good atmosphere, for late drinks.

❀ Festivals and events

Tucumán *p138, map p140*
9 Jul, Independence Day and **24 Sep**, Battle of Tucumán, both with huge processions/parties.

❂ Shopping

Tucumán *p138, map p140*
Handicrafts Mercado Artesanal, 24 de Septiembre 565. Small, but nice selection of lace, wood and leatherwork. Daily 0800-1300, 1700-2200 (in summer, mornings only). **Norte** supermarket, Muñecas 137. **Regionales del Jardín**, Congreso 18. Good selection of local jams, *alfajores* etc.

▲ Activities and tours

Tafí del Valle *p139*
La Cumbre, see Sleeping, above. Energetic and helpful company, offering full day walks to nearby peaks, waterfalls and ruins, or to Cerro Muñoz, with an *asado* at the summit (4,437 m), has open-sided truck.

❂ Transport

Tucumán *p138, map p140*
Air Airport at Benjamín Matienzo, 10 km east of town. Bus No 120 from terminal (*cospeles* required, sold in kiosks, US$0.35). Taxi US$4. **Cielos del Norte**, T426 5555, minibuses to/from airport to/from any place in town, US$1.50. To **Buenos Aires** via **Córdoba**, AR/ Austral (T431 1030).
Bus Bus terminal has 70 ticket offices, best to ask information kiosk opposite Disco T430 4696/422 2221. Local buses operate on *cospeles*, US$0.35, which you have to buy in advance in kiosks.

For long distance buses, the modern terminal is 6 blocks east of Plaza Independencia on Av Brigido Terán, with huge shopping complex, left luggage lockers (US$1), tourist information office (by *bolietería* 1), lots of *locutorios*, toilets and banks (with ATM). Bus 4 from outside terminal to San Lorenzo y 9 de Julio in centre. Taxi to centre US$0.50-1. To **Buenos Aires**, many companies, 14-16 hrs, US$28-50.
To **Salta** direct (not via Cafayate), 4-4½ hrs, several companies US$10-14. To **Cafayate** from Tafí del Valle: see below. To **Posadas**, Vosa, 16 hrs, US$27. To **Mendoza**, 13-14 hrs, US$26-34, via Catamarca, La Rioja, and San Juan. To **Catamarca**, Aconquija and other companies, 4 hrs, US$6. To **Andalgalá**, Gutiérrez, one daily, US$7. To **Córdoba**, 8 hrs, US$13-17. To/from **Santiago del Estero**, 2 hrs, US$5. To **La Quiaca** (border with Bolivia), Balut and Andesmar, 10 hrs, US$12. To **Santiago** (Chile) via Mendoza, Andesmar and El Rápido Internacional, daily, 22-24 hrs, US$35-50.

Tafí del Valle *p139*
Bus Smart new **Aconquija** terminal on Av Critto, with café, toilets, helpful information, T421025. To/from **Tucumán**, Aconquija, 8 daily, 2½ hrs (stop at El Mollar on request), US$4. To **Cafayate**, 3 a day, 2½ hrs, US$6. To **Salta**, 6 daily, 8 hrs, US$4.

❶ Directory

Tucumán *p138, map p140*
Banks Most banks along San Martín especially 700 block between Junín and Maipú. **Maguitur**, San Martín 765, T431 0127, accepts TCs. **Maxicambio**, San Martín 779, T431 0020, currency exchange. **Car hire** Avis, at airport, T426 7777, avis@ tucuman.com. **Donde Rent a Car**, Gob Gutiérrez 1384, T428 3626. **Movil Renta**, San Lorenzo 370, T431 0550, www.movilrenta.com.ar, and at airport. 20% discount for Footprint book owners. **Cultural centres** Alliance Française, Laprida 456, T421 9651, free events in French. **Internet** Cyber Noa, 9 de Julio y San Lorenzo and Centro Digital, Chacabuco 32. **Post office** Córdoba y 25 de Mayo, Mon-Fri 0800-1400, 1700-2000. **Telephone** Lots of *locutorios* including Telecentros, at 24 de Septiembre 612, Buenos Aires y Lavalle, San Lorenzo 704, offering broadband internet access, US$0.50-0.75 per hr.

A Finca Santana, take the road to Cachi Adentro, and ask for Camino to Finca San Miguel, on right at top, T1563 8762, www.fincasantana.net. Just 2 rooms in this boutique B&B in the heart of the valley, spectacular views, and complete sense of privacy and silence. Most welcoming, spacious living room, terrace and garden, gourmet breakfast, trekking can be arranged. Wonderful.

B Casa de Campo La Paya, 12 km south of Cachi at La Paya, clearly signposted from the road, T491139, www.casadecampo lapaya.com.ar. A restored 18th-century house with pool, elegant rooms, excellent dinners, very hospitable. Recommended.

B El Cortijo, opposite the ACA hotel, on Av Automóvil Club s/n, T491034, www.hostal elcortijo.com.ar. Lovely peaceful rooms, warm hospitality. Highly recommended.

C ACA Hostería Cachi, at the top of Juan Manuel Castilla, T491904, www.soldelvalle.com.ar. Smart modern rooms (with wheelchair access), great views, pool, good restaurant, non-residents can use the pool if they eat lunch.

C Llaqta Mawka, Ruiz de Los Llanos s/n, up from Plaza, T491016, www.hotelllaqtamawka.todoweb salta.com.ar. Traditional frontage hides a modern block, with garden-cum-terrace, view of the Nevado de Cachi, swimming pool. Comfortable rooms, ample breakfast, internet, TV, good value and popular with tourists (parking on street).

E Hospedaje Don Arturo, Bustamente s/n, T491087. Homely, small rooms on quiet street, charming owners.

G Hospedaje El Nevado de Cachi, Ruiz de los Llanos y F Suárez, T491912. Impeccable small rooms with bath around a central courtyard, hot water, *comedor*.

Camping Municipal campsite at Av Automóvil Club Argentina s/n, T491902, with pool and sports complex, also *cabañas* and *albergue*.

🍴 Eating

Cafayate *p143*
🍴 **Baco**, Güemes Norte y Rivadavia, T154-028366. Parrilla, *pasta casera*, pizzas, regional dishes, *empanadas* and *picadas*. Seating inside and on street, attractive corner, lively atmosphere. Wine a bit pricier than elsewhere, but all local, good selection, good meat dishes.

🍴🍴 **La Carreta de Don Olegario**, Güemes, on Plaza. Huge and brightly lit, good set menus including the usual meat dishes and pastas.

🍴🍴 **El Rancho**, Toscano 3, T421256. On plaza, meats, regional dishes. Best mid-range option.

🍴 **El Comedor Criollo**, Güemes Norte 254. A *parrilla*, also serving pasta, with *peña* at night. Recommended.

🍴 **Café de las Viñas**, Güemes Sur 58. Open all day, everything from breakfasts to cheap *lomitos*.

🍴 **Las Dos Marías**, San Martín 27 on Plaza. Small, serves excellent food, loved by locals.

🍴 **El Rincón del Amigo**, San Martín 25 on Plaza. Small place for great set menus and *empanadas*.

Cafés

Helados Miranda, Güemes Norte 170. Fabulous homemade ice cream, including wine flavour.

Cachi *p143*
🍴 **Confitería El Sol**, Ruiz de Los Llanos on the plaza. Regional food, limited menu, popular with groups in summer, also offers horse riding, contact delsol_cachi@hotmail.com or T03868-156 38690.

🍴 **Oliver Café**, Ruiz de Los Llanos on the plaza. Tiny café for ice creams, coffee, breakfasts, fruit juices, sandwiches and pizza.

⊙ Shopping

Cafayate *p143*
Handicrafts Apart from the rather general souvenir shops, there are some fine handicrafts. Visit Calchaquí tapestry exhibition of **Miguel Nanni** on the main plaza, silver work at **Jorge Barraco**, Colón 157, T421244. Paintings by **Calixto Mamaní**, Rivadavia 452. Local pottery, woollen goods, etc are sold in the **Mercado de Artesanos Cafayetanos** on the plaza (small, pricey).

▲▲ Activities and tours

Cafayate *p143*
Turismo Cordillerana, Quintana de Niño 59. Tours, horses, bike hire.
MulaNegra Expedition & Adventure, San Martín 83 on Plaza, T421739. Alternative tourism, mountain bikes, excursions, riding, trekking.
Cycle hire Many places, ask tourist office for list. **Horse riding** Horses can be hired from **La Florida**, Bodega Etchart, 2 km south of Cafayate.

⊙ Transport

Cafayate *p143*
Bus 2 bus terminals: With **El Indio** on Belgrano, ½ block from plaza, to **Santa María** (for Quilmes) 4 daily. To **Angastaco**, El Indio, one daily Mon-Fri, US$3, 1½ hrs (but does not continue to Molinos and Cachi). To/from **Tucumán**, Aconquija (Güemes Norte y Alvarado, Cafayate, T422175, open only when buses due), 3 daily, 5½ hrs, US$9; and to **Tafí del Valle**, 3 daily, US$5.50, 3 hrs (more via **Santa María**, 5½ hrs) with Aconquija.

Salta → *Phone code: 0387. Colour map 6, grid C3. Population: 470,000. Altitude: 1,190 m.*

Founded in 1582, Salta, 1,600 km north of Buenos Aires, is an atmospheric city, with many fine colonial buildings, elegant plazas, stirring folkloric music and fabulous food. It lies in the broad Lerma valley, surrounded by steep and forested mountains, and is a good base for exploring the Andean regions, Cachi in the Calchaquí valleys to the south (described above) and the Quebrada de Humahuaca north of Jujuy (described in the next section).

Salta is a fascinating city to explore on foot; in a couple of hours you can get a feel for its wonderful architecture. Good maps are available from the **Provincial Tourist Office** ① *Buenos Aires 93 (1 block from main plaza), T431 0950, www.turismosalta.gov.ar. Open weekdays 0800-2100, weekends 0900-2000.* Very helpful, gives free maps, advice on tours and arranges accommodation in private houses in high season (July), only when hotels are fully booked. Other websites: www.turismoensalta.com of the Cámara de Turismo, Alvarado 455, p 1, T401 1002; www.iruya.com and www.redsalta.com. Local buses in the city charge US$0.25.

Sights

The heart of Salta, is **Plaza 9 de Julio**, planted with tall palms and surrounded by colonial buildings. On the plaza, the **Cabildo**, 1783, one of the few to be found intact in the country, houses the impressive **Museo Histórico del Norte** ① *Caseros 549, Tue-Sat 0930-1330, Tue-Fri 1530-2030 (Sat 1630-2000), Sun 0930-1300, US$0.80.* The museum has displays on pre-Columbian and colonial history, independence wars, and a fine 18th-century pulpit. Opposite the Cabildo, is the 19th-century **Cathedral** (open mornings and evenings), painted pink and cream and reflected in the blue plate glass of a bank next door. It contains a huge late baroque altar (1807) and the much venerated images of the Virgin Mary and of the Cristo del Milagro, sent from Spain in 1592. The miracle was the sudden cessation of a terrifying series of earthquakes when the images were paraded through the streets on 15 September 1692. They still are, each September. Salta's newest museum, **Museo de Arqueología de Alta Montaña** (MAAM), ① *Mitre 77, T437 0499, www.maam.org.ar, Tue-Sun 0900-1300, 1600-2100, US$3.15, free Wed*, has a superb collection of exhibits from Inca high-altitude shrines, including mummies of child sacrifices, video material in Spanish and English, also temporary exhibits. Despite controversy over the display of the mummies, from 2007 they were expected to be on show to the public, albeit with respectful sensitivity. A block southwest of the Plaza is the **Museo de la Ciudad 'Casa de Hernández'** ① *Florida 97 y Alvarado, T4373352, Mon-Fri 0900-1300, 1530-2030, closed Sun, U$0.30.* This fine 18th-century mansion includes furniture and dull portraits, but a marvellous painting of Güemes. The magnificent façade of **San Francisco** church ① *on Caseros, 0730-1200, 1700-2100,* rises above the skyline with its splendid tower, ornately decorated in plum red and gold. Further along Caseros, the Convent of **San Bernardo**, rebuilt in colonial style in the mid-19th century, has a beautifully carved wooden portal of 1762, but is not open to visitors as nuns still live there. They will open up the small shop for you, selling quaint handicrafts.

At the end of Caseros is the **Cerro San Bernardo** (1,458 m) ① *accessible by cable car (teleférico from Parque San Martín), daily 1000-1930, US$2.70 return, US$1.35 children, fine views, 45 mins' walk to return.* At the summit are gardens, waterfalls, a café, a silver collection and playground. Further along Avenida H Yrigoyen is an impressive **statue to General Güemes**, whose *gaucho* troops repelled seven powerful Spanish invasions from Bolivia between 1814 and 1821.

Up beyond the Güemes statue is the **Museo Antropológico**, ① *Paseo Güemes, www.antropologico.gov.ar, Mon-Fri 0830-1830, Sat 0900-1300, 1500-1800, helpful and knowledgeable staff, US$0.70.* Fascinating displays on pre-Inca cultures include painted urns, intriguing board-flattened skulls (meant to confer superiority), a mummy discovered high in the Andes and many objects from Tastil (see page 147). **Museo de Ciencias Naturales** ① *Parque San Martín, Tue-Sun 1530-1930, US$0.30,* displays a bewildering number of stuffed animals and birds; the armadillo collection is interesting.

San Antonio de los Cobres → *Phone code 0387, Population 4,000, Altitude 3,775 m.*

Sitting in the vast emptiness of the puna, San Antonio de los Cobres, 168 km by road from Salta, is a simple, remote mining town of adobe houses with a friendly Coya community. Ruta 51 leads to La Polvorilla railway viaduct (see below), 20 km, ask in town for details and beware sudden changes in the weather. Try the *quesillo de cabra* (goat's cheese) from Estancia Las Cuevas. The *Huaira Huasi* restaurant, used by tour groups, has a good menu. At **Santa Rosa de Tastil** there are important prehispanic ruins and a small **museum** ① *daily 1000-1800, US$1*, recommended. Basic accommodation next door to the museum, no electricity or heating, take food, water and candles. Take El Quebradeño bus (see below), a tour from Salta, or share a taxi.

The famous **Tren a las Nubes** is a 570 km, narrow gauge railway running from Salta through the town of San Antonio de los Cobres to Socompa, on the Chilean border. San Antonio can also be reached by Ruta 51 from Salta. From **Campo Quijano**, the road runs along the floor of the Quebrada del Toro before climbing to Alto Blanco (paved section).

Ruta 51 from San Antonio de los Cobres to **San Pedro de Atacama**, Chile uses the **Sico** Pass (4,079 m). It's a spectacular route, crossing white salt lakes dotted with flamingoes and vast expanses of desert. Most of it is unpaved and the route has been replaced by that over Jama Pass (see page 155). There is a customs post at Paso Sico (you may be allowed to spend

Salta

El Correcaminos **5** *B2*
El Lagar **6** *A1*
Gran Hotel Presidente **8** *C2*
Hostal del Cerro **9** *D2*
Las Rejas **22** *B1*
Las Marías **10** *D2*
Munay **11** *D1*
Papyrus **7** *B3*
Petit **12** *D3*
Posada del Sol **14** *C1*
Regidor **15** *C1*

Residencial Elena **16** *D1*
Salta **18** *C1*
Solar de la Plaza **19** *B1*
Terra Oculta **20** *D2*
The Cottage **4** *C2*

Eating 🍴
Café del Paseo **2** *C1*
Doña Salta **1** *C2*
El Corredor de
  las Empanadas **3** *C2*

El Solar del Convento **4** *C1*
Frida **6** *A1*
La Casa de Güemes **5** *C1*
La Chueca **9** *C1*
La Criollita **12** *B1*
La Terraza de la Posta **7** *C1*
Madre Maíz **11** *C2*
Plaza Café **10** *C1*

Bars & clubs 🍸
La Vieja Estación **8** *A1*

Sleeping 🛏
Alejandro I **1** *C1*
Apart Ilusión **23** *D3*
Backpackers **2** *D2*
Del Antiguo Convento **3** *C2*

Cloud line

One of the great railway journeys of South America is the Tren a las Nubes (Train to the Clouds). Engineered by Richard Maury, of Pennsylvania (who is commemorated by the station at Km 78 which bears his name) this remarkable project was built in stages between 1921 and 1948, by which time developments in road and air transport had already reduced its importance. The line includes 21 tunnels, 13 viaducts, 31 bridges, 2 loops and 2 zig-zags. From Salta the line climbs gently to Campo Quijano (Km 40, 1,520 m), where it enters the Quebrada del Toro, an impressive rock-strewn gorge. At El Alisal (Km 50) and Chorrillos (Km 66) there are zig-zags as the line climbs the side of the gorge before turning north into the valley of the Río Rosario near Puerto Tastil (Km 101, 2,675 m), missing the archaeological areas around Santa Rosa de Tastil. At Km 122 and Km 129 the line goes into 360° loops before reaching Diego de Almagro (3,304 m). At Abra Muñano (3,952 m) the road to San Antonio can be seen zig-zagging its way up the end-wall of the Quebrada del Toro below. From Muñano (3,936 m) the line drops slightly to San Antonio, Km 196. The spectacular viaduct at La Polvorilla is 21 km further at 4,190 m, just beyond the branch line to the mines at La Concordia. The highest point on the line is reached at Abra Chorrillos (4,475 m, Km 231). From here the line runs on another 335 km across a rocky barren plateau 3,500-4,300 m above sea level before reaching Socompa (3,865 m).

Note For safety reasons the Tren a las Nubes was suspended in 2005 but it was due to repoen in 2007, see page 152.

the night here, T498 2001), hours 0800-2000: check first in San Antonio de los Cobres if it is open. On the Chilean side continue via Mina Laco and Socaire to Toconao (road may be bad between these two points). Customs and immigration are in San Pedro de Atacama. Note that fruit, vegetables and dairy products may not be taken into Chile (search 20 km after Paso Sico). Gasoline is available in San Pedro and Calama. Obtain sufficient drinking water for the trip in San Antonio and do not underestimate the effects of altitude.

Sleeping

Salta *p146, map p147*
Book ahead in Jul holidays and around 10-16 Sep during celebrations of Cristo del Milagro. Among Salta's most desirable places to stay are its colonial-style *estancias*, known locally as *fincas*.
L Finca El Bordo de las Lanzas, 45 km east of Salta, T490 3070, www.estanciaelbordo.com. Formal and luxurious, a taste of aristocratic life, with splendid horse riding and charming hosts. Highly recommended.
AL Alejandro I, Balcarce 252, T400 0000, www.alejandro1hotel.com.ar. A new business hotel on Plaza Belgrano, with absolute comfort in its minimalist rooms, elegant handmade touches. Splendid views from the top floors.
AL Solar de la Plaza, Juan M Leguizamon 669, T431 5111, www.solardelaplaza.com.ar. Elegant old former Salteño family home, faultless service, sumptuous rooms, great restaurant and a pool.

A El Lagar, 20 de Febrero 877, T431 9439/ 421 7943, ellagar@arnet.com.ar. An intimate boutique hotel owned by wine-making Etchart family, beautifully furnished rooms full of fine paintings, excellent restaurant, gardens (guests only). Highly recommended.
A Finca Los Los, Chicoana, 40 km from Salta at the entrance to the Valles Calchaquíes, T431 7258, www.redsalta.com/loslos. Open Mar to Dec. Great hilltop views, charming rooms, beautiful gardens, pool, unforgettable horse riding to *asados* in the mountains. Handy for the airport and Cachi. Highly recommended.
A Gran Hotel Presidente, Av Belgrano 353, T/F431 2022, reservas@grhotelpresidente.com.ar. Chic and ultra-modern, very plush rooms, good restaurant with great value fixed price menu (US$7), pool, gym.

A Hostería de Chicoana, in Chicoana, 47 km south, T490 7009, martinpek@salnet.com.ar. Bohemian but faded colonial style, English and German spoken, expert guide Martin Pekarek offers adventure excursions and horses for hire. Recommended.

A Papyrus, Pasaje Luis Linares 237 (no sign on this street, turn right at Repsol, top of hill), T422 7067, www.hotelpapyrus.com.ar. A luxury boutique hotel offering peace and comfort (ask for the modern bedrooms), small pool, excellent restaurant (by arrangement). Recommended.

A Portezuelo, Av Turística 1, T431 0104, www.portezuelohotel.com. Good views over the city, comfortable modern rooms, pool, fine restaurant, parking, also offers cheap deals (see website) and excellent excursions.

A Salta, Buenos Aires 1, in main plaza, T431 0740, www.hotelsalta.com. A Salta institution with neo-colonial public rooms, refurbished bedrooms, marvellous suites overlooking plaza, *confitería* and honorary membership of the Polo and Golf Club.

A-B pp Finca El Manantial, La Silleta, 25 km from Salta, T439 5506 or T156-858480, elmanantial@arnet.com.ar. Formal style in historical estancia, beautiful views, lovely rooms, marvellous food, swimming, farming activities ,riding and walking around the estate.

A-B Finca Santa Anita, Coronel Moldes, 60 km from Salta, on the way to Cafayate T/F490 5050, www.santaanita.com.ar. Family welcome at this prize-winning organic farm on a traditional colonial-style finca: great food and all activities included in the price. Beautiful views, swimming, guided walks to prehistoric rock paintings, and horse riding. Highly recommended.

C Hostal Selva Montana, C Alfonsina Storni 2315, T492 1184, www.iruya.com/ent/selva montana. At San Lorenzo, 11 km northwest of centre, extremely comfortable and relaxing modern hotel in traditional style, in forested hills, pool, horses and walks on offer. Highly recommended. Take a taxi or bus El Indio interurbano from terminal.

C Petit, H Yrigoyen 225, T4213012, www.todoweb salta.com.ar/petithotelsalta. Handy for the bus terminal and Cerro San Bernardo, plain pleasant rooms around a patio with pool and garden.

C Posada del Sol, Alvarado 646, T431 7300, www.hotelposadadelsol.com. With good service though dated rooms, popular with groups.

C Regidor, Buenos Aires 8, T431 1305. Smart wood panelling everywhere, small rooms, welcoming, good restaurant (no breakfast), good value.

C Del Antiguo Convento, Caseros 113, T422 7267, www.hoteldelconvento.com.ar. Small, new,

convenient, with old-fashioned rooms around a neat patio and more functional modern rooms, very helpful, a good choice.

C Apart Ilusión (Sweet Dreams), José Luis Fuentes 743, Portezuelo Norte, T432 1081, www.aparthotel ilusion.com.ar. On the slopes of Cerro San Bernardo, beautiful views, new, well-equipped self-catering apartments for 2-4, decorated with local handicrafts, English-speaking owner Sonia Alvarez, welcoming, breakfast and parking available, very good value.

D Hostal del Cerro, Santa Fe 456, T431 8572, hostaldelcerro@hotmail.com. On Parque San Martín, close to bus terminal, some rooms are a bit small, but comfortable and good value, hot water, with TV, very helpful, breakfast extra, parking at nearby service station US$1.50.

D Las Marías, Lerma 255, T422 4193, www.saltaguia.com/lasmarias. Central hostel, with breakfast, kitchen, close to Parque San Martín.

D Munay, San Martín 656, T4224936, www.munay hotel.jujuy.com. Excellent budget option, new, smart rooms with good bathrooms, warm welcome, breakfast included. Highly recommended.

E pp Backpackers, Buenos Aires 930, T4235910, www.backpackerssalta.com. 30 mins' walk from the plaza or Bus 12 from terminal. Well-run, busy, popular, HI affiliated, dorms, laundry, kitchen, travel information, dinner, parties and tours arranged.

E The Cottage, Juramento 54, T421 3668, hostal thecottage@hotmail.com. Hot water, kitchen facilities, internet, library and information, new.

E pp El Correcaminos, Vicente López 353, T422 0731, www.correcaminos.com.ar. 4 blocks from plaza, modern dorms, 2 doubles, shared bath, laundry, kitchen, free internet and pleasant garden, good, lively.

E Res Elena, Buenos Aires 256, T421 1529. Quiet, 'charming', safe, a nice old doorway leads to high-ceilinged passages and rooms, courtyard with trees and plants, rooms with bath, hot water, no breakfast, free water for coffee, free medical service, run by a charming old gentleman, book in advance by phone.

E pp Terra Oculta, Córdoba 361, T421 8769, www.terraoculta.com. Party atmosphere, laid-back place with small dorms, homely, kitchen, TV, email, laundry, great roof terrace bar, good annex at Av San Martín y Córdoba, very popular.

F pp Las Rejas, General Güemes 569, T421 5971, www.lasrejashostel.com.ar. Very good, well-located, rooms for 2-6 with bath, free internet and cooking facilities, welcoming owners, English spoken, breakfast US$1. AHC Argentina Hostels Club.

● *For an explanation of the sleeping and eating price codes used in this guide, see page 58.*
● *Other relevant information is found in Essentials pages 68-69.*

San Antonio de los Cobres *p146*
C **Hostería de las Nubes**, T0387-490 9059, edge of San Antonio on Salta road. Smart, includes breakfast, comfortable, modern and spacious. Recommended.
F **El Palenque**, Belgrano s/n, T490 9019. Also a café, family run.
F **Hospedaje Belgrano**, T490 9025. Welcoming, basic, hot showers, evening meals.

Campo Quijano *p147*
B **Hostería Punta Callejas**, T0387-490 4086. Bath, a/c, with breakfast, very clean and comfortable, pool, tennis, riding, excursions.
Camping Several sites, including municipal campsite, at entrance to Quebrada del Toro gorge, lovely spot with good facilities, hot showers, bungalows.

🍴 Eating

Salta *p146, map p147*
Salta has delicious and distinctive cuisine: try the *Locro, Humitas* and *Tamales*, served in the municipal market at San Martín y Florida.
🍴🍴 **El Solar del Convento**, Caseros 444, half a block from plaza. Elegant and not expensive, champagne when you arrive, delicious steaks. Recommended.
🍴 **La Casa de Güemes**, España 730. Popular, local dishes and *parrilla*, traditionally cooked in the house where General Güemes lived.
🍴 **Doña Salta**, Córdoba 46 (opposite San Francisco convent library). Excellent regional dishes and pleasant, rustic atmosphere, good value.
🍴 **La Terraza de la Posta**, España 456. Huge menu, great steak and *empanadas*. Recommended.
🍴 **El Corredor de las Empanadas**, Caseros 117 and Zuviría 913. Delicious *empanadas* and tasty local dishes in airy surroundings.
🍴 **Frida**, Balcarce 935, T432 0771. Great place for a drink or dinner, with vaguely Mexican-inspired food, plus local dishes, superb wine list, cosy interior with sofas and booths. Recommended.
🍴 **La Chueca**, España 476, T422 0653. Regional food, excellent *empanadas*, cheap and cheerful.
🍴 **La Criollita**, Zuviría 306. Small and unpretentious, a traditional place for tasty *empanadas*.
🍴 **Madre Maiz**, Alvarado 508. Very good vegetarian cooking, varied menu.
Lots of good places around the Plaza 9 de Julio for *empanadas*.

Cafés
Café del Paseo at *Hotel Colonial*, Zuviría 6. Open 24 hrs, superb breakfast, good value.
Plaza Café next to *Hotel Salta* is more popular with Salteños, good for coffee or breakfast.
150

🎵 Bars and clubs

Salta *p146, map p147*
Visit a *peña* to hear passionate folklore music live. There are many bars, called *peñas*, with excellent live bands on Balcarce towards railway station. **Balderrama**, T421 1542, is much touted but touristy (2200-0200). Head instead for: **La Casona del Molino**, Caseros 2600, T434 2835. Most authentic, in a crumbling old colonial house, good food and drink. **Gauchos de Güemes**, Uruguay 750, T492 1621, popular, delicious regional food. **La Vieja Estación**, Balcarce 885, T421 7727. Great atmosphere, good food, highly recommended.

🎉 Festivals and events

Salta *p146, map p147*
16-17 Jun, commemoration of the death of General Martín Güemes: folk music in evening and *gaucho* parade in morning around the Güemes statue. Salta celebrates **Carnival** with processions on the 4 weekends before Ash Wednesday at 2200 in Ciudad de Salta Stadium, 4 km south of town (US$0.50); also **Mardi Gras** (Shrove Tuesday) with a procession of decorated floats and dancers with intricate masks of feathers and mirrors. Water is squirted at passers-by and *bombas de agua* (small balloons filled with water) are sold for dropping from balconies.
15 Sep, Cristo del Milagro (see above);
24 Sep, Battles of Tucumán and Salta.

🛍 Shopping

Salta *p146, map p147*
Bookshops Feria del Libro, Buenos Aires 83. Huge shop, some in English. **Librería Rayuela**, Alvarado 570. Excellent, with some foreign-language books and magazines.
Handicrafts Arts and handicrafts are often cheaper in surrounding villages. **Mercado Artesanal** on the western outskirts, in the Casa El Alto Molino, San Martín 2555, T434 2808, daily 0900-2100, take bus 2, 3, or 7 from Av San Martín in centre and get off as bus crosses the railway line. Excellent range and high quality in lovely 18th-century mansion. **Siwok Crafts**, Zuviría 30. Quality wood carvings by the Wichi indigenous people, and typical *yika* woven bags.
Markets and supermarkets Mercado Municipal, San Martín y Florida, for meat, fish, vegetables, *empanadas, humitas* and other produce and handicrafts, closed 1300-1700 and Sun. **Norte**, 20 de Febrero y Caseros. Good supermarket. **San Francisco**, Deán Funes 596, T421 2984. 24-hr pharmacy. **Vea** supermarkets at Florida y Caseros, Mitre y Leguizamon and Mendoza entre Lerma y Catamarca.

⚑ Activities and tours

Salta *p146, map p147*

There are many tour operators, mostly on Buenos Aires, offering adventure trips and excursions; staff give out flyers on the street (likewise car hire companies). Out of season, tours often run only if there is sufficient demand; check carefully that tour will run on the day you want. All agencies charge similar prices for tours (though some charge extra for credit card payments): Salta city US$13; Quebrada del Toro and San Antonio de las Cobres US$42; Cachi US$35; Quebrada de Humahuaca US$40; San Antonio de las Cobres US$30; Cafayate (1 day) US$35; 2-day tour to Cafayate, Angastaco, Molinos, Cachi, US$70. The tourist office gives reports on agencies and their service.

Bici tours, T4394887, 15683 8067, www.bicinorte.com.ar. Specialists in cycle tours.

Hernán Uriburu (HRU), Leguizamon 446, T431 0605, www.nortetrekking.com/hru.htm. Well known and highly regarded for his horse- or mule-riding expeditions to the mountains, sleeping at locals' houses, very professional.

Movitrack, Buenos Aires 28, T431 6749, and a desk at airport, www.movitrack.com.ar. Entertaining safaris in a 4WD truck, to San Antonio de los Cobres, Humahuaca, Cafayate and Iruya, also over Paso de Sico to Chile, German, English spoken, expensive. They also have an OxyBus for high-altitude journeys.

Norte Trekking, Av del Libertador 1151, Barrio Grand Bourg, T436 1844, www.norte trekking.com. Excellent tours all over Salta and Jujuy, to Iruya, over Jama Pass to San Pedro de Atacama, hiking, horse riding, excursions to El Rey national park with experienced guide Federico Norte, knowledgeable, speaks English. Tailors tours to your interest and budget. Highly recommended.

Puna Expediciones, Agustín Usandivaras 230, T434 1875 or T154-030263, www.puna expeditions .com.ar. Qualified and experienced guide Luis H Aguilar organizes treks in remote areas of Salta and Jujuy (US$25 a day, all inclusive). Recommended.

Ricardo Clark Expeditions, Caseros 121, T/F421 5390, www.clarkexpediciones.com. Specialist birding tours for twitchers, plus eco-safaris and treks. English spoken.

Saltur, Caseros 485, T421 2012, F432 1111, saltursalta@arnet.com.ar. 4WD expeditions to national parks, Calchaquí valley, horse riding, efficient and recommended for local tours.

Turismo San Lorenzo, Dávalos 960, San Lorenzo. T492 1757, www.turismosanlorenzo.com. For horse riding, trekking and mountain biking, well run. Recommended.

⊙ Transport

Salta *p146, map p147*

Air The airport (T424 3115) is 12 km southwest, served by vans run by **Transfer del Pino**, US$3. Bus 22 to access to airport from San Martín, US$0.35; don't be fooled by taxi touts who tell you there is no bus. Taxi from bus station, US$5. LAB to **Santa Cruz** (Bolivia). AR flies to **Bs As** (2 hrs), and **Andes**, 1 a day. AR, LAB to **Córdoba**.

Bus Terminal is 8 blocks east of the main plaza, T401 1143 for information. Toilets, *locutorio*, café, *panadería*, kiosks. To **Buenos Aires**, several companies daily, US$35-63, 17-20 hrs (TAC – T431 6600). To **Córdoba**, several companies daily, 12 hrs, US$20-28. To **Santiago del Estero**, 6-7 hrs, US$16. To **Tucumán**, 4½ hrs, several companies, US$10-14. To **Mendoza** via Tucumán, several companies daily, US$35-60, 16-18 hrs. To **Jujuy**, several companies hourly between 0600 and 2200, 'directo', US$4, 2 hrs. To **La Rioja**, US$18-26, 10-11 hrs. To **Puerto Iguazú**, Andesmar, US$48-60, 25 hrs, daily. To **Cafayate**, US$7, 3½ hrs, 3-4 daily, with El Indio, T431 9389. To **Cachi** 1-2 daily at 0700, US$7, 4-4½ hrs, with Marcos Rueda, and usually continues to **Molinos**, every 2 days, US$10, 6½ hrs. To **Belén**, US$18, Wed 0700 with El Indio, via Angastaco (US$10), San Carlos, Cafayate (US$7) and Santa María (US$10). To **Rosario de la Frontera**, US$6, 2½-3 hrs. To **San Antonio de Los Cobres**, 5 hrs, El Quebradeño, daily, US$6.

International buses: To **Paraguay**: Flecha Bus (www.flechabus.com.ar) daily to Clorinda (at the border), 16 hrs, and La Nueva Estrella, T422 4048, 3 services weekly, US$27; buses or taxis will take you from there to Paraguay for a small fee. Alternatively travel to **Resistencia**, daily, US$19 with La Veloz del Norte, Flecha Bus, La Nueva Estrella, Autotransportes Mendoza or to **Formosa**, with *La Nueva Estrella*, US$25, 15 hrs, changing then, to a direct bus to Asunción. To **Chile**: Services to **Calama, San Pedro de Atacama, Antofagasta, Iquique** and **Arica** with **Géminis** and **Pullman**, T422 1366, pullmansalta@yahoo.com.ar, via Jujuy and the Jama Pass, three times a week, US$40 to **San Pedro** (Géminis, 11 hrs) and US$54-60 to **Arica**. Géminis and Pullman offices are outside the back of the terminal, across the street, at Dionisio Puch 117. To **Bolivia**: To **La Quiaca**, on Bolivian border, **Balut** and others, 7½ hrs, US$7-10. To **Aguas Blancas** or **Pocitos** (both on the Bolivian border, see page 157), several companies daily, US$10-15, 6 hrs; for **Santa Cruz**, La Veloz del Norte/Leal Bus, US$30.

Car hire Avis, at the airport, Ruta 51, T424 2289, salta@avis.com.ar. Efficient and very helpful, recommended. **Europe Rent A Car**, Buenos Aires 186, T422 3609. **Ruiz Moreno**, Buenos Aires 1,

T431 8049, in *Hotel Salta*, helpful. **Semisa Renta Truck 4x4**, Buenos Aires 1, Local 6, T423 6295, febearzi@salnet.com.ar. **Integral**, Buenos Aires 189, T155-016451. Many others.

Train Station at 20 de February y Ameghino, 9 blocks north of Plaza 9 de Julio, taxi US$1. The only train running is the **Tren a las Nubes** (Train to the Clouds, see page 148), which usually runs between Salta and La Polvorilla viaduct once a week from Apr to Nov, weather permitting, and on additional days in the high season (Jan/Feb and Jul/Aug). It departs promptly at 0705, returning to Salta 2200. At the time of writing, services were suspended, but it was due to reopen in 2007. The price may come down from the previous US$120 for foreigners. To **Socompa** (Chilean border): there is currently no information available about the cargo train with 2 passenger carriages leaving Salta once a week. You should ask at the ticket office, opens 0800, if it is running. Beyond Socompa there are irregular freight trains into Chile (Augusta Victoria, Baquedano or Antofagasta), but officially the Chilean railway authorities do not permit passengers to travel on this line. To travel on by train or truck may involve a wait of several days. There are only 4 buildings in Socompa: no food or lodging, but try the Chilean customs building.

Cachi *p143*
Bus To **Salta**, Marcos Rueda, T491063, daily (except Sun) at 0900, and Mon, Thu, Fri, Sun at 1500, 4½ hrs, US$7. To **Molinos** daily at 1200.

● Directory

Salta *p146, map p147*
Airline offices Andes, España 478, T437 3516. AR, Caseros 475, T431 1331/ 0862. LAB, Caseros 529, T431 1389. **Banks** Banks, open 0900-1400, all have ATMs (many on España). Banco de la Nación, Mitre y Belgrano. Banco de Salta, España 550 on main plaza. Cashes TCs. Amex, Chicoana Turismo, Zuviría 255, changes TCs. Dinar, Mitre 101/109; street changers opposite. Masventas, España 610, T431 0298, Changes dollars, euros, Chilean pesos and Tcs. You can get Chilean pesos at good rates. **Cultural centres** Alliance Française, Santa Fe 20, T431 2403. **Embassies and consulates** Bolivia, Mariano Boedo 34, T421 1040, open Mon-Fri, 0900-1400 (unhelpful, better to go to Jujuy). Chile, Santiago del Estero 965, T431 1857. Belgium, Pellegrini 835, T423 4252. Spain, República de Israel 137, T431 2296, F431 0206. Italy, Santiago del Estero 497, T432 1532. France, Santa Fe 156, T431 2403. Germany, Urquiza 409, T421 6525, F431 1772, consul Juan C Kühl, helpful. **Internet** Many fast and cheap places around the centre, some 24 hrs. **Medical Services** Hospital San Bernardo, Tobias 69. Emergencies T911. **Post offices** Deán Funes 160, between España and Belgrano. **Telephones** Several *locutorios* in town, some offer internet access. **Useful addresses** Immigration: Maipú 35, 0730-1230.

Jujuy → *Colour map 6, grid C4. Population: 237,000. Phone code: 0388. Altitude: 1,260 m.*

Though it lacks Salta's elegance, since there are few colonial buildings remaining, the historical city of Jujuy is the starting point for some of the country's most spectacular scenery and it has a distinctly Andean feel, evident in its food and music. With extremely varied landscapes, the area is rich in both contemporary and ancient culture, with prehispanic ruins at Tilcara, delightful villages and excursions. The **tourist office** on the plaza ① *Gorriti y Belgrano, Mon-Fri 0700-2200, Sat-Sun 0900-2100, www.jujuy.gov.ar*, accommodation leaflet and map. Also at bus terminal, T422 1343, 0700-2100.

Sights
San Salvador de Jujuy (pronounced Choo-Chooey, with *ch* as in Scottish loch) often referred to by locals as San Salvador, is the capital of Jujuy province and sits in a bowl ringed by lushly wooded mountains. The city was finally established in 1593, after earlier attempts met resistance from local indigenous groups, but the city was plagued by earthquakes, sacking and the Calchaquíes Wars for the next 200 years. It struggled to prosper, then in August 1812 Gen Belgrano, commanding the republican troops, ordered the city to be evacuated and destroyed before the advancing Spanish army. This extraordinary sacrifice is marked on 23-24 August by festivities known as El Exodo Jujeño with gaucho processions and military parades.

Away from the busy shopping streets, in the eastern part of the city, is the **Plaza Belgrano**, a wide square planted with tall palms and orange trees. It's lined with impressive buildings, including the elaborate French baroque-style **Casa de Gobierno** ① *daily 0900-2100*, containing the famous flag Belgrano presented to the city. On the west side is the late 19th-century **Cathedral** (the original, 1598-1653, was destroyed by earthquake in 1843) containing one of Argentina's finest colonial treasures: a gold-plated wooden pulpit, carved by *indígenas* in the Jesuit missions, depicting gilded angels mounting the stairs. The modern church of **San Francisco** ① *Belgrano y Lavalle, 2 blocks west of the plaza, daily 0730-1200, 1730-2100 (Thu till 2000)*, contains another fine gilded colonial pulpit, with ceramic angels around it, like that at Yavi. The **Museo Histórico Franciscano** ① *daily 0900-1300, 1600-2100*, at the church, includes 17th-century paintings and other artefacts from Cuzco. There are several other museums; don't miss the **Museo Arqueológico Provincial** ① *Lavalle 434, Mon-Fri 0800-2100, Sat-Sun 0900-1300, 1500-1900, US$0.35*, with beautiful ceramics from the Yavi and Humahuaca cultures, haphazardly displayed, a mummified infant, and a 2500-year old sculpture of a goddess giving birth.

There are hot springs 19 km west at **Termas de Reyes** ① *1 hr by bus Empresa 19 de Abril (línea 14) from bus terminal, 6 daily, last return bus 2040, US$1*, municipal baths US$0.50 and pool US$1; also cabins with thermal water. This resort (**Hotel Termas de Reyes** ① *T0388-492 2522, info@termasdereyes.com.ar*) is set among magnificent mountains.

● Sleeping

Jujuy *p152*
B Fenicia, 19 de Abril 427, T/F423 1800, www.quturismo.com.ar/fenicia/fenicia.html. A welcoming place, 1980's chic, spacious rooms (ask for the ones with swish bathrooms), some with great views. Recommended.
B Internacional, Belgrano 501 (Plaza Belgrano), T423 1599, www.hinternacionaljujuy.com.ar. On north west corner of the Plaza, quiet, smart, good value. Great views over city.
B Jujuy Palace, Belgrano 1060, T/F423 0433, jpalace@imagine.com.ar. Conference hotel, well-equipped rooms, restaurant has good reputation.
B La Aguada, Otero 170, T4232034, www.laaguada hosteria.com.ar. A charming family-owned hotel with 3 rooms, decorated with paintings by the owner's father, central, excellent choice.
B Norte, Alvear 444, T424 0903, www.hotel norte.com. A tastefully restored colonial house, with an old palm-tree in the patio, extremely comfortable, with wonderful attention to detail.
C Panorama, Belgrano 1295, T423 2533, hotel panorama@imagine.com.ar. Business hotel, more appealing than most, good value, stylish rooms.
D Sumay, Otero 232, T423 5065, www.sumay hotel.com.ar. Rather dark, but clean, very central, helpful staff.
F Yok Wahi, Lamadrid 168, T422 9608, www.yokwahi.com.ar. An attractive, central hostel with tidy dorms and one double with bath, quiet atmosphere. Discounts to HI members. The same owners run **Club Hostel**, a new larger hostel with a pool, next to the plaza, San Martín 155, T423 7565.

There are a number of cheap places near the bus terminal, of which the following are safe and comfortable, including:
F pp Rany's, Dorrego 327 next to bus station, T423 0042. Cheaper rooms without TV, basic, but clean and the lady owner is very kind, no breakfast, but loads of cafés around.
F Res San Carlos, República de Siria 459, T422 2286. With bath and TV, nicely maintained, comfortable, car park.
Camping E pp El Refugio is closest, Yala, Km 14, T490 9344, pretty spot on riverbank 14 km north of city, also has youth hostel, pool, and restaurant, horse riding and treks organized. Highly recommended, great place to relax.

● Eating

Jujuy *p152*
ⵏ **Chung King**, Alvear 627. Atmospheric, regional food. Sister restaurant next door, '50 kinds of pizza'.
ⵏ **Krysys**, Balcarce 272. Popular bistro-style *parrilla*, excellent steaks. Also has accommodation upstairs but not recommended.
ⵏ **La Candelaria**, Alvear 1346, some way out of town. Recommended *parrilla*, good service.
ⵏ **Madre Tierra**, Belgrano 619, behind the wholemeal bakery of same name. For vegetarians (or for a break from all the meat), delicious food (open 0700-1430, 1600-2130).
ⵏ **Manos Jujeños**, Sen Pérez 222. Regional specialities, the best *humitas*, charming, good for the *peña* at weekends.
ⵏ **Ruta 9**, Belgrano 743. Another great place, slightly cheaper, for *locro* and *tamales*, also a few Bolivian dishes.
ⵏ Following Lavalle across the bridge to the bus terminal (where it becomes Dorrego) there are lots of cheap *empanada* places.

Several good cafés, all on the same block of Belgrano between Lavalle and Necochea, including **Pingüino**, the best *heladería* in town.
Color Esperanza, Necochea 376. Bright café serving cheap *lomitos* and burgers.

● *For an explanation of the sleeping and eating price codes used in this guide, see page 58.*
● *Other relevant information is found in Essentials pages 68-69.*

Confitería La Royal Belgrano 770. A classic
café, good coffee and pastries.
Sociedad Española, opposite Tía Bigote.
Good cheap set menus with a Spanish flavour.
Tía Bigote, Pérez y Belgrano. Very popular
café and pizzería.

O Shopping

Jujuy p152
Handicrafts There are stalls near the cathedral.
Centro de Arte y Artesanías, Balcarce 427. **Paseo
de las Artesanías**, on the west side of the plaza.
Maps and travel guides Librería Belgrano,
Belgrano 602. English language magazines and
some books. **Librería Rayuela**, Belgrano 636.
Markets For food, you can't beat the Municipal
market at Dorrego y Alem, near the bus terminal.
Outside, women sell home-baked *empanadas*
and *tamales*, and delicious goat's cheese,
and all kinds of herbal cures.
Supermarkets Norte, Belgrano 825 and a
bigger branch at 19 de Abril y Necochea.

▲ Activities and tours

Jujuy p152
De Bor Turismo, Lavalle 295, T402 0241. 10%
discount for ISIC members on local excursions.
Horus Turismo, Belgrano 722, T422 7247,
horus@imgine.com.ar.
NASA, Senador Pérez 154, T422 3938. Guided tour
to Quebrada de Humahuaca (US$30 pp, min 4
people); 4WD for rent. For information on bird
watching, contact Mario Daniel Cheronaza, Peatonal
38, No 848-830, Viviendas 'El Arenal', Jujuy.

⊖ Transport

Jujuy p152
Air Airport at El Cadillal, 32 km southeast, T491
1505, taxi US$10. AR flights to **Córdoba** and
Buenos Aires. Bus terminal at Iguazú y Dorrego,
6 blocks south of the centre, T422 2134, T491 1101.

Bus To **Buenos Aires**, 19-23 hrs, US$45-63,
several daily with many companies. Via Tucumán
to **Córdoba**, Panamericano and **La Veloz del
Norte**, daily to **Tucumán**, 5 hrs, US$10, and
Córdoba, 13-14 hrs US$24. To **Salta**, see above.
To **La Quiaca**, 5-6 hrs, US$5-7, Panamericano,
Balut, El Quiaqueño. Several rigorous luggage
checks en route for drugs, including coca leaves.
To **Humahuaca**, Evelia and others, US$4, 3 hrs,
several daily, via Tilcara 2 hrs, US$2.50. To **Orán**
and **Aguas Blancas** (border with Bolivia), daily
with **Balut** and **Brown**, via San Pedro and
Ledesma. To **Purmamarca**, take buses to
Susques or to Humahuaca (those calling at
Purmamarca village). To **Susques**, Purmamarca
and Andes Bus, US$6, 4-6½ hrs, daily (except
Mon). To **Calilegua**: various companies to
Libertador Gral San Martín almost every hour,
eg **Balut**, from there take **Empresa 23 de
Agosto** or **Empresa 24 de Setiembre**,
leaving 0830 to **Valle Grande**, across Parque
Nacional Calilegua. All Pocitos or Orán buses
pass through Libertador San Martín.
To Chile: via the **Jama** pass (4,200 m), the route
taken by most traffic, including trucks, crossing to
northern Chile; hours 0900-1900. Géminis bus
tickets sold at **Ortiz Viajes**, L N Alem 917,
ortizviajes@latinmail.com.

⊕ Directory

Jujuy p152
Banks ATMs at: Banco de Jujuy, Balcarce y
Belgrano, changes dollars. TCs can be changed
at tour operators, **De Bor** and **Horus**, Belgrano
722. **Banco Francés**, Alvear y Lamadrid; **Banco
Salta**, San Martín 785. **Consulates** Bolivia,
Senador Pérez e Independencia, T424 0501,
0900-1300. **Internet** Cyber Explora, Güemes
1049; Ciber Nob, Otero 317; HVA, Lavalle 390 (all
US$0.50 per hr). **Telecom** centres at Alvear 870,
Belgrano 730 and elsewhere. **Post offices**
Independencia y Lamadrid. **Useful addresses**
Immigration: 19 de Abril 1057, T422 2638.

Jujuy to the Chilean and Bolivian borders

Ruta 9, the Pan-American Highway, runs through the beautiful **Quebrada de Humahuaca**, a
vast gorge of vividly coloured rock, with giant cacti in the higher parts, and emerald green
oasis villages on the river below. (January-March ask highway police about flooding on the
roads.) The whole area is very rich culturally: there are pre-Inca ruins at Tilcara (see below),
and throughout the Quebrada there are fine 16th-century churches and riotous pre-Lent
carnival celebrations. In Tilcara, pictures of the Passion are made of flowers and seeds at
Easter and a traditional procession on Holy Thursday at night is joined by thousands of
pan-pipe musicians.

For drivers heading off main roads in this area, note that service stations are far apart: at
Jujuy, Tilcara, Humahuaca, Abra Pampa and La Quiaca. Spare fuel and water must be carried.

Jujuy to Chile

Beyond Tumbaya, where there's a restored 17th-century church, Ruta 52 runs 3 km west to **Purmamarca**, a quiet, picturesque village, much visited for its spectacular mountain of seven colours, striped strata from terracotta to green (best seen in the morning), a lovely church with remarkable paintings and a good handicrafts market. (Buses to Jujuy 1½ hrs, US$1.35; to Tilcara US$0.65. Salta-San Pedro de Atacama buses can be boarded here, book at Hotel Manantial del Silencio one day in advance.) It's worth staying the night in Purmamarca to appreciate the town's quiet rhythm. There's a helpful, tiny tourist office on the plaza with list of accommodation, maps and bus tickets, open 0700-1800.

From Purmamarca paved Ruta 52 leads through another *quebrada* over the 4,164 m Abra Potrerillos to the **Salinas Grandes** salt flats at about 3,400 m on the Altiplano (fantastic views especially at sunset). From here roads lead southwest past spectacular rock formations along the east side of the salt flats to San Antonio de los Cobres, and west across the salt flats via Susques to the Paso de Jama (4,400m) and Chile. The only accommodation beyond Purmamarca is at **Susques**, opposite the outstanding church (see below). There are no services or money exchange at the border. This is the route taken by most passenger and truck traffic going from Salta or Jujuy to San Pedro de Atacama.

Jujuy to Bolivia

About 7 km north of the Purmamarca turning is **La Posta de Hornillos** ① *open, in theory, Wed-Mon 0900-1800, free,* a museum in a restored colonial posting house where Belgrano stayed, also the scene of several battles. About 2 km further is **Maimará** with its brightly striped rock, known as the 'Artist's Palette', and huge cemetery, decorated with flowers at Easter.

Tilcara → *Phone code: 0388. Colour map 6, grid C3. Population: 4,400. Altitude: 2,460 m.*

Tilcara lies 22 km north of the turn-off to Purmamarca. It's the liveliest Quebrada village, the best base for exploring the area. It has an excellent handicrafts market around its pleasant plaza and plenty of places to stay and to eat. The little tourist office on Belgrano, next to *Hotel de Turismo.* Daily 0800-2130, very helpful staff (no phone), www.tilcarajujuy.com.ar. Visit the Pucará, a restored prehispanic hilltop settlement, with panoramic views of the gorge, and the superb **Museo Arqueológico** ① *daily 0900-1230, 1400-1800, US$2 for both,* with a fine collection of pre-Columbian ceramics, masks and mummies. There are four art museums in town and good walks in all directions. Recommended guide for informative trips to the puna, Iruya, Salinas Grandes, and archaeological sites, is historian **Ariel Mosca** ① *T495 5119, arielpuna@hotmail.com.* English spoken. There are fiestas at weekends in January, carnival and Holy Week. There's an ATM on the plaza, taking most international cards.

At **Uquía** is one of the most impressive churches in the valley, with extraordinary Cuzqueño paintings of angels in 17th-century battle dress.

Humahuaca → *Phone code: 03887. Colour map 6, grid B3. Population: 8,000. Altitude: 2,940 m.*

Although Humahuaca, 129 km north of Jujuy, dates from 1591, it was almost entirely rebuilt in the mid-19th century. Now it is visited by daily coach trips. It still has a distinctive culture of its own, though, and is a useful stopping point for travelling north up to the puna, or to Iruya. On 2 February is *La Candelaria* festival. *Jueves de Comadres, Festival de las Coplas y de la Chicha,* at the beginning of carnival is famously animated, lots of drinking and throwing flour and water around. Book accommodation ahead. ATM at *Banco de Jujuy* on main plaza, all major credit cards. On the little plaza is the church, **La Candelaria**, originally of 1631, rebuilt 1873-80, containing gaudy gold retables and 12 fine Cuzqueño paintings. Also on the plaza, tourists gather to watch a mechanical figure of San Francisco Solano blessing the town from **El Cabildo**, the neo-colonial town hall, at 1200 daily. Overlooking the town is the massive **Monumento a la Independencia Argentina**, commemorating the heaviest fighting in the country during the Wars of Independence. At **Coctaca**, 10 km northeast, there is an impressive and extensive (40 ha) series of pre-colonial agricultural terraces. To Iruya (see below). **Humahuaca**: tourist information available from the town hall, office hours.

Iruya → *Colour map 6, grid B3. Altitude: 2,600 m.*

A rough *ripio* road 25 km north of Humahuaca runs northeast from the Panamericana (RN9) 8 km to Iturbe (also called Hipólito Irigoyen), and then up over the 4,000 m Abra del Cóndor before dropping steeply, around many hairpin bends, into the Quebrada de Iruya. The road is very rough and unsuited to small hire cars, but is one of Argentina's most amazing drives. Iruya, 66 km from Humahuaca, is a beautiful hamlet wedged on a hillside, like a hide-away. Its warm, friendly inhabitants hold a colourful Rosario festival on first Sunday in October and at Easter. It is worth spending a few days here to go horse riding or walking: the hike (seven hours return) to the remote **San Isidro** is unforgettable. At Titiconte 4 km away, there are unrestored pre-Inca ruins (guide necessary). Iruya has no ATM or tourist information, but a public phone, post office and a few food and handicraft shops.

Tres Cruces and Abra Pampa
Some 62 km north of Humahuaca on the Panamericana is Tres Cruces, where customs searches are made on vehicles from Bolivia. **Abra Pampa** (*Population 6,000*), 91 km north of Humahuaca, is a mining town. At 15 km southwest of Abra Pampa is the vicuña farm at **Miraflores**, the largest in Argentina. Information offered, photography permitted; buses go morning Monday-Saturday Abra Pampa-Miraflores.

Monumento Natural Laguna de los Pozuelos ① *50 km northwest of Abra Pampa, park office in Abra Pampa, T03887-491048*, is a nature reserve with a lake at its centre visited by huge colonies of flamingoes. There is a ranger station at the southern end of the park, with a campsite nearby. There is no bus transport, so it's best to go with a guide; the Laguna is 5 km from the road, very tough, high clearance recommended, walk last 800 m to reach the edge of the lagoon. Check with the park office before going – the lake can be dry with no birds, eg in September. (Altitude 3,650 m, temperatures can drop to -25°C in winter.) *Diego Bach* leads excellent, well-informed excursions, including panning for gold as the Jesuits did. Also five-day treks on horseback to the pristine cloudforest of **Parque Nacional Baritú** ① *T03885-422797, punatours@hotmail.com*, are highly recommended.

From a point 4 km north of Abra Pampa roads branch west to Cochinoca (25 km) and southwest to **Casabindo** (62 km). On 15 August at Casabindo, the local saint's day, the last and only *corrida de toros* (running with bulls) in Argentina is held, amidst a colourful popular celebration. *El Toreo de la Vincha* takes place in front of the church, where a bull defies onlookers to take a ribbon and medal which it carries. The church itself is a magnificent building, with twin bell towers, and inside a superb series of 16th century angels in armour paintings. The only place to stay is an **Albergue** at the village school, T03887-491129 (**F** per person in dorms), otherwise most visitors go on day-trips from Tilcara.

La Quiaca and Yavi → *Phone code: 03885. Altitude: 3,442 m. 5,121 km from Ushuaia. Colour map 6, grid B3.*
On the border with Bolivia, a concrete bridge links this typical border town with Villazón on the Bolivian side. Warm clothing is essential particularly in winter when temperatures can drop to -15°C, though care should be taken against sunburn during the day. On the third Sunday in October, villagers from the far reaches of the remote *altiplano* come to sell ceramic pots, sheepskins and vegetables, in the colourful three-day *Fiesta de la Olla.*, which also involves much high-spirited dancing and drinking. Two ATMs, but no facilities for changing cash or TCs, but plenty of *cambios* in Villazón. *Farmacia Nueva*, half a block from Church, has remedies for altitude sickness. **Yavi** is 16 km east of La Quiaca. Its **church of San Francisco** (1690) ① *Mon 1500-1800, Tue-Fri 0900-1200, 1500-1800, Sat-Sun 0900-1200*, is one of Argentina's treasures, with a magnificent gold retable and pulpit and windows of onyx. Caretaker Lydia lives opposite the police station and will show you round the church. Opposite the church is the 18th-century house of the Marqués Campero y Tojo, empty, but for a small selection of handicrafts.

Border with Bolivia → *Argentine time is 1 hr later than Bolivia. Do not photograph the border area.*
The border bridge is 10 blocks from La Quiaca bus terminal, 15 minutes walk (taxi US$1). Argentine office open 0700-2400; on Saturday, Sunday, and holidays there is a special fee of US$1.50 which may or may not be charged. If leaving Argentina for a short stroll into Villazón, show your passport, but do not let it be stamped by Migración, otherwise you will have to wait 24 hours before being allowed back into Argentina. Formalities on entering Argentina are usually very brief at the border but thorough customs searches are made 100 km south at Tres Cruces. Leaving Argentina is very straightforward, but travellers who need a visa to enter Bolivia are advised to get it before arriving in La Quiaca.

Parque Nacional Calilegua → *Colour map 6, grid C3.*

① *Park office: San Lorenzo s/n, Calilegua, T03886-422046, pncalilegua@cooperlib.com.ar.*
Reached by Ruta 83, via Ruta 34, from just north of Libertador, the park entrance is at Aguas
Negras, 12 km along the dirt road (4WD essential when wet, hitching from Libertador
possible), which climbs through the park and beyond to Valle Grande (basic accommodation
and shops), 90 km from Libertador.

Libertador General San Martín, a sugar town 113 km northeast of Jujuy on Ruta 34 to
southeastern Bolivia, is the closest base for exploring the park, an area of peaks over 3,000 m
and deep valleys covered in cloud forest, with a huge variety of wildlife, including 260 species of
bird and 60 species of mammals (you may spot tapirs, pumas, tarucas, Andean deer and even
jaguars here) There are six marked trails of various lengths. The best trek is to the summit of
Cerro Amarillo (3,720 m), five days round trip from Aguas Negras, or three days from the village
of San Francisco (*hospedaje* and *comedores*). There is a ranger's house at Aguas Negras, with
camping; drinking water from river nearby, and some cooking facilities and tables. Ask rangers
for directions and advice. Best time for visiting is November-March, the warmest but also the
wettest. **Tourist office**① *at the bus terminal.*

Routes to Bolivia

From Libertador, Ruta 34 runs northeast 244 km, to the Bolivian border at Pocitos (also called
Salvador Mazza) and Yacuiba (see Eastern Bolivia, page 328). It passes through **Embarcación**
and **Tartagal** (good regional museum, director Ramón Ramos very informative). In **Pocitos**, the
border town, is **G Hotel Buen Gusto**, just tolerable. There are no *casas de cambio* here. From
Yacuiba, across the border, buses go to Santa Cruz de la Sierra. Customs at Pocitos is not to be
trusted (theft reported) and overcharging for 'excess baggage' on buses occurs. Several bus
companies including Atahualpa have services from the border to Salta and Tucumán.

An alternative route is via Aguas Blancas. At Pichanal, 85 km northeast of Libertador, Ruta
50 heads north via **Orán,** an uninteresting place (*Population 60,000*).

Aguas Blancas on the border is 53 km from Orán (restaurants, shops, no accommodation,
nowhere to change money and Bolivianos are not accepted south of Aguas Blancas; fill up with
fuel here, or in Orán). The passport office is open from 0700 to 1200 and 1500 to 1900. Insist on an
exit stamp. Buses run from Bermejo, across the river (ferry US$0.50), to Tarija. Northwest of Aguas
Blancas is the **Parque Nacional Baritú,** see above, under Abra Pampa. There are no facilities.

● Sleeping

Jujuy to Chile: Purmamarca *p155*
A El Manantial del Silencio, Ruta 52 Km 3.5,
T0388-490 8080, www.hotelmanantial.com.ar.
Signposted from the road into Purmamarca.
Luxurious rooms in old estancia, wonderful
views, spacious living rooms with huge fire,
charming hosts, includes breakfast, heating,
riding, pool, superb restaurant (guests only).
C La Posta, C Santa Rosa de Lima 4 blocks up from
plaza, T4908029, www.postadepurmamarca
.com.ar. Breakfast, heating, helpful owner. Beautiful
elevated setting by the mountain, comfortable
rooms. Its restaurant at the plaza, serves delicious
local fare (♦). Highly recommended.
D El Pequeño Inti, C Florida 10 m from plaza,
T4908089, elintidepurmamarca@hotmail.com.
Small, modern rooms around a little courtyard,
breakfast, hot water, good value. Recommended.
D El Viejo Algarrobo, C Salta behind the church,
T/F490 8286, elviejoalgarrobo@hotmail.com.
Small but pleasant rooms, cheaper with shared
bath, good value and quality regional dishes
in its restaurant (♦).

E Hospedaje Familia García, C Lavalle ½ block
from the Plaza, T4908016, jhosep03@yahoo.com.ar.
Basic, shared bath, hot water, kitchen, family run.

Jujuy to Chile: Susques *p155*
D Pastos Chicos, R52, Km 220 (at Casas Quemadas,
3 km west of Susques), T03887-423 5387,
www.pastoschicos.com.ar. Rustic, comfortable,
good value, restaurant with regional specialities,
open to non-residents. Phone for pick-up.
D El Unquillar, R52, Km 219 (2 km west of
Susques), T03887-490201, www.elunquillar.com.ar.
Attractive, with local weavings, good rooms.
Restaurant open to public. Phone for pick-up.
F Res Las Vicuñitas, San Martín, Susques,
T03887-490207, opposite the church. Without
bath, hot water, breakfast available, very basic.

Jujuy to Bolivia: Maimará *p155*
C Posta del Sol, Martín Rodríguez y San Martín,
T499 7156, posta_del_sol@hotmail.com.
Comfortable, with good restaurant, owner is
tourist guide and has helpful information.

Tilcara *p155*

Book ahead in carnival and around Easter
when Tilcara is very busy.

B-C Quinta La Paceña, Padilla y Ambosetti,
T495 5098, quintalapacena@yahoo.com.ar.
Peaceful, architect-designed traditional adobe
house, with comfortable, stylish rooms for 2-4
(some cheaper rooms in old farmhouse),
gorgeous, well-kept garden, the nicest
place to stay in town.

C Los Establos, Gorrito s/n (next to *con los
Angeles*), T495 5379. Pretty, rustic rooms and
well equipped *cabañas* for 2-6 people.

C Posada con los Angeles, Gorriti 153
(signposted from access to town), T495 5153.
Charming individually designed rooms, garden
with views of mountains, relaxed atmosphere,
excursions organized. Warmly recommended.

D Hostal La Granja, at Huacalera, Km 90,
T0388-426 1766. A lovely rustic place with pool,
outstanding food and service, a good base for
exploring the region.

E pp Malka, San Martín s/n, 5 blocks from plaza up
steep hill, T495 5197. Beautifully located *cabañas*,
and an outstanding hostel, **F pp**, very comfortable
rustic dorms, all with kitchen and laundry facilities,
HI affiliated. Owner and guide Juan organizes a
great range of trips, including several days' trek to
Calilegua, horse riding, bike hire. Recommended.

E La Morada, Debenedetti s/n, T/F495 5118,
lamorada@imagine.cm.ar. Good rooms for 2 to 5
people with bath, cooking facilities, good option.

E Res El Antigal, Rivadavia s/n, ½ block from
plaza, T495 5020. Comfortable, good beds,
sunny patio, good value.

Camping Camping El Jardín, access on
Belgrano, T495 5128, US$2 pp, hot showers,
also **E pp** basic hostel accommodation.

Uquía *p155*

C Hostal de Uquía, next to the church,
T03387-490523, hostaluquia@yahoo.com.ar.
Comfortable place to stay, simple rooms around
a courtyard, also serves dinner, very good food.

Humahuaca *p155*

B Camino del Inca, on the other side of the river,
T421136, hosteriainca@imagine.com.ar. Smart,
well built modern place with good restaurant,
pool, excursions, a bit overpriced.

D Hostal Azul, B Medalla Milagrosa, La Banda,
T421107, www.hostalazulhumahuaca.com.ar.
Across the river, smart, welcoming, pleasant,
simple rooms with bath, good restaurant and
wine list, parking.

F pp Cabaña El Cardón, T421625,
www.elcardon.8K.com. Rural *cabaña* for
2-5 with all facilities, also regional foods,
excursions and riding, charming family.

F pp Posada El Sol, over bridge from
terminal, then 520 m, follow signs, T421466,
www.posadaelsol.com.ar. Quiet rural area, rooms
for 2-4 in a warm welcoming place, kitchen, also
laundry, horse riding, owner will collect from bus
station if called in advance. AHC Argentina Hostels
Club. Recommended.

E pp Res El Portillo, Tucumán 69, T421288.
Dormitories are cramped, **D** rooms, nice place,
shared bath, simple bar/restaurant.

Iruya *p155*

A Hostería de Iruya, T03887-482002,
www.hosteria deiruya.com.ar. A special place,
extremely comfortable, with good food,
and great views from the top of the village.
Highly recommended.

D Hostal Federico Tercero, at *Café del Hostal*,
bottom of the steep main street, T03887-156
29152. Owned by the delightful singer Jesús,
with simple rooms, some with bath, good food
from breakfast to dinner, frequent live music.

F pp Hosp Tacacho, on the Plaza, T03887-156
29350. Family welcome, simple rooms, great
views, *comedor*.

Abra Pampa *p156*

E Residencial El Norte, Sarmiento 530, shared
room, hot water, good food. *Res y restaurante
Cesarito*, 1 block from main plaza.

La Quiaca *p156*

D Turismo, Siria y San Martín, T422243,
intenmun@laquiaca.com.ar. The best place to
stay: modern, comfortable rooms with TV,
breakfast, pool, restaurant.

E Cristal, Sarmiento 539, T422255. Basic
functional rooms, shared bath.

E Hostería Munay, Belgrano 51, T423924,
www.munayhotel.jujuy.com. Very pleasant,
with comfortable rooms.

F La Frontera hotel and restaurant, Belgrano y
Siria, downhill from *Atahualpa* bus stop,
T422269. Good cheap food, basic but decent
rooms, hospitable owner.

Yavi *p156*

D Hostal de Yavi, Güemes 222,
T03887-490523, hostaldeyavi@hotmail.com.
Simple rooms but cosy sitting room, good
food, relaxed atmosphere. Recommended.

E La Casona 'Jatum Huasi', Sen Pérez y
San Martín, T03887-422316, mccailsaya@
laquiaca.com.ar. Welcoming.

Parque Nacional Calilegua *p157*

A-B Finca Portal de Piedra, Villa Monte, Santa
Bárbara, T03886-156 820564, www.portalde
piedra.netfirms.com. 17 km north of Libertador

General San Martín. Eco-run finca in its own reserve (Las Lancitas), convenient for PNs Calilegua andEl Rey, guesthouse and cabin, simple food, horse riding, trekking, birdwatching and other excursions, from Jujuy take a bus via San Pedro and Palma Sola (which is 12 km north of the finca).
C Posada del Sol, Los Ceibo y Pucará, Libertador General San Martín, T03886-424900, www.posada delsoljujuy.com.ar. Comfortable, functional hotel, with gardens and pool, has advice on local trips.

Orán *p157*
C Alto Verde, Pellegrini 671, T421214. Parking, pool, a/c.
D Res Crisol, López y Planes. Hot water. Recommended.

● Eating

Tilcara *p155*
♥♥ **Pucará**, up the hill towards the Pucará, T495 5721. Exquisite, posh Andean food and hearty puddings by renowned chef Garo Jurisic, intimate, rustic atmosphere.
♥ **El Patio Comidas** Lavalle 352. Great range, lovely patio at the back, popular, very good.
♥ **Música Esperanza (Bar del Centro)**, Belgrano 547, T495 5462. Small restaurant/café serving local dishes in the patio. Not always open. Both the restaurant and crafts shop next door sustain an NGO that organizes free art and music workshops for local children.

Cafés
El Cafecito on the plaza. For a taste of Tilcara's culture, don't miss this place, good coffee and locally-grown herbal teas, peña at weekends from celebrated local musicians.
La Peña de Carlitos, on the plaza. With music from the charismatic and delightful Carlitos, also cheap *menú del día*, *empanadas*, and drinks.

Humahuaca *p155*
♥ **El Portillo**, Tucumán 69. A simply decorated room, serving slightly more elaborate regional meals than the usual.
♥ **La Cacharpaya**, Jujuy 295. Good and lively, often filled with parties at lunch time, Andean music. Recommended.

● Transport

Tilcara *p155*
El Quiaqueño combines with **Andesmar/ Brown**, passes Tilcara en route to **Jujuy** 4 times a day from 1340, and en route to **La Quiaca** 6 times a day from 1110. **Jama Bus** runs between Tilcara, Humahuaca and La Quiaca.

Humahuaca *p155*
Bus Buses to all places along the Quebrada from the terminal (toilets, *confitería*, fruit and sandwich sellers outside), to **Iruya** (see below) and to **La Quiaca**, with **Balut** and **La Quiaqueña** (more comfortable), several daily, 3-3½ hrs, US$3-4. Rigorous police checks for drugs can cause delays on buses to La Quiaca. Keep passport with you.

Iruya *p155*
Bus Daily service from **Humahuaca** Empresa Mendoza, T03887-421016, 1030 daily, 3 hrs, US$5.50 return, returning 0600 (not on Sun) and 1515. Also excursions of several days organized by tour operators.

Yavi *p156*
No buses go to Yavi. You can hitchhike from the exit to R5 (US$1 pp is expected) or take a remise taxi for US$9 return, including ½ hr stay. **Remises La Quiaca**, Belgrano 169 (round the corner from terminal, La Quiaca), T03887-423344.

La Quiaca *p156*
Bus Bus terminal, **España y Belgrano**, luggage storage. several buses daily to **Salta** (US$8-10) with **Balut** (7½ hrs), **Atahualpa** and others. Several daily to **Humahuaca** and **Jujuy**, schedules above. Take own food, as sometimes long delays. Buses are stopped for routine border police controls and searched for coca leaves. **Note** Buses from Jujuy may arrive in the early morning when no restaurants are open and it is freezing cold outside.

Parque Nacional Calilegua *p157*
Bus From Libertador daily at 0830 going across the park to **Valle Grande** (US$4, 5 hrs), returning the same day. Also Tue, Thu, Sat to **Santa Ana** at 0600, US$4, 5 hrs, return 1430. *Remise* charges about US$2 from Libertador to Park entrance. All Pocitos or Orán buses pass through Libertador General San Martín.

Aguas Blancas *p157*
Bus Between Aguas Blancas and **Orán** buses run every 45 mins, US$1, luggage checks on bus. Direct buses to **Güemes**, 8 a day, US$5; through buses to **Salta**, La Veloz del Norte, Panamericano and Atahualpa, several daily, US$15, 7-10 hrs. To **Tucumán**, *La Veloz del Norte, Panamericano* and **La Estrella**, 1 a day each company. To **Jujuy** with **Balut** and **Brown**, 3 daily. To **Embarcación**, US$2; some services from Salta and Jujuy call at **Orán** en route to **Tartagal** and **Pocitos**. Note that buses are subject to slow searches for drugs and contraband.

The Northeast

The river systems of the Paraná, Paraguay and Uruguay, with hundreds of minor tributaries, small lakes and marshlands, dominate the Northeast. Between the Paraná and Uruguay rivers is Argentine Mesopotamia containing the provinces of Entre Ríos, Corrientes and Misiones, this last named after Jesuit foundations, whose red stone ruins have been rescued from the jungle. The great attraction of this region is undoubtedly the Iguazú Falls, which tumble into a gorge on a tributary of the Alto Paraná on the border with Brazil. But the region offers other opportunities for wildlife watching, such as the national parks of the Wet Chaco and the amazing flooded plains of the Esteros del Iberá. This is also the region of mate tea, sentimental chamamé music and tiny chipá bread.

Up the Río Uruguay

This river forms the frontier with Uruguay and there are many crossings as you head upstream to the point where Argentina, Uruguay and Brazil meet. On the way, you'll find riverside promenades, sandy beaches and palm forests.

Gualeguaychú → *Phone code: 03446. Colour map 8, grid B5. Population: 74,700.*
On the Río Gualeguaychú, 19 km above its confluence with the Río Paraná and 220 km north of Buenos Aires, this is a pleasant town with a lively pre-Lenten carnival. Some 33 km southeast the Libertador Gral San Martín Bridge (5.4 km long) provides the most southerly route across the Río Uruguay, to Fray Bentos (vehicles US$4; pedestrians and cyclists may cross only on vehicles, officials may arrange lifts). **Tourist office** ① *Plazoleta de los Artesanos, T423668, www.gualeguaychuturismo.com, 0800-2000 (later in summer).* The **Uruguayan consulate** is at Rivadavia 510, T426168. **Note** This crossing was frequently closed in 2007 owing to a the construction of a disputed paper mill across the river in Uruguay.

Nice walks can be taken along the *costanera* between the bridge and the small port, from where short boat excursions and city tours leave (also from the *balneario municipal*), T423248, high season only. **El Patio del Mate** ① *G Méndez y Costanera, T424371, www.elpatiodel mate.com.ar, daily 0800-2100.* A workshop dedicated to the *mate* gourd.

Concepción del Uruguay → *Phone code: 03442. Colour map 8, grid B5. Pop: 64,500.*
The first Argentine port of any size on the Río Uruguay was founded in 1783. Overlooking Plaza Ramírez is the church of the Immaculate Conception which contains the remains of Gen Urquiza. **Palacio San José** ① *32 km west of town, www.palacios anjose.com.ar, Mon-Fri 0830-1230, 1400-1830, Sat-Sun 0900-1745, US$1, free guided visits 1000, 1100, 1500, 1600.* Urquiza's former mansion, set in beautiful grounds with a lake, is now a museum, with artefacts from Urquiza's life and a collection of period furniture, recommended. Take Ruta 39 west and turn right after Caseros train station. Buses to Paraná or Rosario del Tala stop at El Cruce or Caseros, 4 or 8 km away respectively, US$0.80 (take *remise* taxi from Caseros). *Remise* taxis charge about US$8 with 1½ hour wait. Tour operators run *combis* in high season US$5 including entry. **Tourist office** ① *Galarza y Daniel Elía, T440812, www.concepcion entrerios.com.ar, Mon-Fri 0700-1300, 1400-2000, weekends 0700-2200 in high season.*

Colón → *Phone code: 03447. Colour map 8, grid A5. Population: 19,200.*
Founded in 1863, Colón is 45 km north of Concepción del Uruguay. It has shady streets, an attractive *costanera* and long sandy beaches, with cliffs visible from a considerable distance. At Avenida 12 de Abril y Paso is **La Casona** (1868), with a handicraft exhibition and shop. North of the port, Calle Belgrano leads to the **Complejo Termal** ① *T424717, daily 0900-2100, US$2,* with 10 thermal pools (34-40°C). **Tourist office** ① *Av Costanera Quirós y Gouchón, T421233, www.colonentrerios.com.ar. Mon-Fri 0630-2100, Sat 0700-2100, Sun 0800-2100.* The **Uruguayan consulate** is at San Martín 417, T421999.

✗ True brew

Yerba mate (*ilex paraguayensis*) is made into a tea which is widely drunk in Argentina, Paraguay, Brazil and Uruguay. Traditionally associated with the gauchos, the modern mate paraphernalia is a common sight anywhere: the gourd (*un mate*) in which the tea leaves are steeped, the straw (usually silver) and a thermos of hot water to top up the gourd. It was the Jesuits who first grew *yerba mate* in plantations, inspiring one of the drink's names: *té de jesuitas*. Also used has been *té de Paraguay*, but now just *mate* or *yerba* will do. In southern Brazil it is called *ximarão*; in Paraguay *tereré*, when drunk cold with digestive herbs.

Parque Nacional El Palmar

ⓘ *51 km north of Colón, T493049. US$4 (Argentines US$2). Buses from Colón, 1 hr, US$1.50, will drop you at the entrance and it is easy to hitch the last 12 km to the park administration. Remise taxis from Colón or Ubajay offer tours, eg from Colón: US$15 for a 4-hr return trip, including tour or waiting time. There are camping facilities (electricity, hot water), with restaurant opposite, and a small shop.*

This park of 8,500 ha is on the Río Uruguay, entrance gates off Ruta 14, where you'll be given a map and information on walks. The park contains varied scenery with a mature palm forest, sandy beaches on the Uruguay river, indigenous tombs and the remains of an 18th-century quarry and port, a good museum and many rheas and other birds. The Yatay palms grow up to 12 m and some are hundreds of years old. It is best to stay overnight as wildlife is more easily seen in the early morning or at sunset. Very popular at weekends in summer.

Refugio de Vida Silvestre La Aurora del Palmar ⓘ *T03447-154 31689, www.aurora delpalmar.com.ar, free*, is opposite the Parque Nacional El Palmar, 3 km south of Ubajay at Km 202 Ruta 14. A private reserve protecting a similar environment to that of its neighbour, La Aurora covers 1,150 ha, of which 200 are covered with a mature palm forest. There are also gallery forests along the streams and patches of *espinal* or scrub. Birds are easily seen, as are capybaras along the streams. The administration centre is only 500 m from Ruta 14 and services are well organized. There are guided excursions on horseback, on foot or canoe, two hours, US$5 per person, minimum two people. Camping US$2 pp a day plus US$1.50 per tent, or **D** in old railway carriages. Buses from Colón or those coming from the north will drop you at the entrance. Tell the driver you are going to La Aurora del Palmar, to avoid confusion with the national park. *Remise* taxi from Ubajay US$2. Book in advance or check availability for excursions.

Concordia → *Colour map 8, grid A5. Population: 93,800.*

Just downriver from Salto, Uruguay, Concordia, 104 km north of Colón, is a prosperous city. The Río Uruguay is impassable for large vessels beyond the rapids of Salto Chico near the city, and Salto Grande 32 km upriver, where there is a large international hydro electric dam, providing a crossing to Uruguay. In the streets around the main **Plaza 25 de Mayo** there are some fine public buildings. The city has a range of hotels and restaurants. **Tourist office** ⓘ *Plaza 25 de Mayo, daily 0700-2400*. The **Uruguayan consulate** is at Pellegrini 709, of 1 C, T421 0380. Above Salto Grande the river is generally known as the Alto Uruguay. About 153 km upstream from Concordia is the small port of **Monte Caseros**, with the Uruguayan town of Bella Unión, on the Brazilian border, almost opposite.

Paso de los Libres → *Colour map 8, grid A5. Population: 25,000. 336 km north of Concordia.*

Linked to the larger Brazilian town of Uruguaiana by a bridge over the Alto Uruguay, Paso de los Libres was founded in 1843 by General Madariaga. It was here that he crossed the river from Brazil with his 100 men and annexed Corrientes province for Argentina. The town is not regarded as a safe border crossing.

⊜ Sleeping

Gualeguaychú *p160*

Accommodation is scarce during carnival. Prices double Dec-Mar, Easter and long weekends. The tourist office has a list of family accommodation.
C Puerto Sol, San Lorenzo 477, T/F434017. Good rooms, a/c, next to the port, has a small resort on a nearby island (transfer included) for relaxing drink.
C Tykuá, Luis N Palma 150, T422625, hotel tykua@arnet.com.ar. Breakfast included, 3 blocks from the bridge (**D** in low season).
F pp Top Maló, T495255, topmalo@infovia.com.ar. HI affiliated, discounts for members. **E** in houses on stilts for 2 and 4 people with cooking facilities, shared rooms for up to 5, kitchen and linen included, campsite with hot showers and electricity for US$3.50 a day plus US$0.35 pp on first day. Attractive rustic style, warm atmosphere. Short boat excursions from US$2 pp, half-day fishing trips. German, Danish and some English spoken.
Camping Several sites on riverside, next to the bridge and north of it. **El Ñandubaysal**, T423298, www.nandu baysal.com.ar. The smartest, on the Río Uruguay, 15 km southeast (US$7.50 per tent).

Concepción del Uruguay *p160*

D Grand Hotel, Eva Perón 114, T422851, www.palaciotexier.com.ar. Originally a French-style mansion with adjacent theatre, superior rooms have a/c and TV but not much difference from standard, both include breakfast, no restaurant.

Colón *p160*

C Holimasú, Belgrano 28, T421305, www.hotel holimasu.com.ar. Nice patio, breakfast included, a/c extra, **D** in low season.
D Hostería Restaurant del Puerto, Alejo Peyret 158, T422698, hosteriadelpuerto@ciudad.com.ar. Great value, lovely atmosphere in old house, breakfast included.
D La Posada de David, Alejo Peyret 97, T423930, www.colontrerios.com.ar/posadadedavid/ubicacion.htm. Pleasant family house with garden, welcoming, good rooms with breakfast, great value.
F pp Sophie Hostel, Laprida 128, T424136, sophiehostel@yahoo.com.ar. HI affiliated, renovated house with large garden, cooking facilities, comfortable rooms for 2-8, welcoming owner Marcela, German and English spoken, homemade meals, great breakfast (free on your first morning), excellent information. Highly recommended.
Camping Several sites on river bank, US$3 daily.

⊘ Eating

Concepción del Uruguay *p160*

⫙ El Remanso, Rocamora y Eva Perón. Popular, moderately priced *parrilla*.

Colón *p160*

⫙ La Cosquilla de Angel, Alejo Peyret 180. The smartest place in town, meals include fish, set menu, live piano music in evenings.
⫙ El Viejo Almacén, Gral Urquiza y Paso. Cosy, very good cooking and excellent service.

⊖ Transport

Gualeguaychú *p160*

Bus Bus terminal at Bv Artigas y Bv Jurado, T440 688 (30-min walk to centre, *remise* taxi US$1.20). To **Concepción del Uruguay**, 1 hr, US$1.50. To **Fray Bentos**, 1¼ hrs, US$2.30, 2 a day (1 on Sun), arrive 30 mins before departure for immigration. To **Buenos Aires**, US$7-8, 3½ hrs, several daily.

Concepción del Uruguay *p160*

Bus Terminal at Rocamora y Los Constituyentes, T422352 (remise, US$0.40). To **Buenos Aires**, frequent, 4 hrs, US$8-9. To **Colón**, 45 mins, US$1.

Colón *p160*

Bus Terminal at Paysandú y Sourigues (10 blocks north of main plaza), T421716, left luggage at 24-hr bar. Not all long distance buses enter Colón. To **Buenos Aires**, US$8-10, 5-6 hrs. To **Mercedes** (for Iberá), several companies, 6-7 hrs, US$6-8. To **Paraná**, 4-5 hrs, US$7.
To Uruguay: via the Artigas Bridge (US$4 toll) all formalities are dealt with on the Uruguayan side. *Migraciones* officials board the bus, but non-Argentines/Uruguayans should get off bus for stamp. Bus to **Paysandú**, US$2-2.30, 45 mins.

Concordia *p161*

Bus Terminal at Justo y Yrigoyen, 13 blocks north-west of Plaza 25 de Mayo (reached by No 2 bus). To **Buenos Aires**, US$11, 6½ hrs. To **Paraná** 5 a day.
  To Uruguay Take No 4 bus from terminal, marked 'Puerto', for the **ferry** crossing to Salto, US$2, 15 mins. Tickets obtainable at a small kiosk, which shuts 15 mins before departure, outside immigration in the building marked 'Resguardo'. 5 departures Mon-Fri, 4 departures Sat, 2 departures (0800, 1800) Sun, 20 mins, passengers only. The **bus** service via the Salto Grande dam is run by Flecha Bus and Chadre, 2 day each, not Sun (taxi only), US$2, 1 hr, all formalities on the Argentine side, passports checked on bus. **Bicycles** are not allowed to cross the international bridge but officials will help cyclists find a lift.

Paso de los Libres *p161*

Bus Terminal is 1 km from town centre, near border. To **Brazil**: taxi or bus US$2.50. No bus service on Sun.

Up the Río Paraná

Several historic cities stand on the banks of the Paraná, which flows south from its confluence with the Río Paraguay. National parks protecting endangered marshes, especially at Iberá, are the highlight of the zone.

Rosario → *Phone code: 0341. Colour map 8, grid B5. Population: 1.2 million.*

The largest city in the province of Santa Fe and the third largest city in Argentina, Rosario, 295 km northwest of Buenos Aires, is a great industrial and export centre. It has a lively cultural scene with several theatres and bars where there are daily shows. The **tourist office** is on the riverside park next to the Monumento a la Bandera ① *Av Belgrano y Buenos Aires, T480 2230, www.rosarioturismo.com.* See www.viarosario.com, for the latest events information.

The old city centre is Plaza 25 de Mayo. Around it are the **cathedral** and the **Palacio Municipal**. On the north side is the **Museo de Arte Decorativo** ① *Santa Fe 748, T480 2547, Thu-Sun 1600-2000, free.* This sumptuous former residence houses a valuable private collection of paintings, furniture, tapestries sculptures and silverwork, brought mainly from Europe. Left of the cathedral, the *Pasaje Juramento* opens the pedestrian way to the imposing **Monumento a la Bandera** ① *T/F480 2238, Mon 1400-1800, Tue-Sun 0900-1800 (in summer till 1900), US$0.35 (tower), free (Salón de las Banderas).* This commemorates the site on which, in 1812, General Belgrano, on his way to fight the Spaniards in Jujuy, raised the Argentine flag for the first time. A 70 m-tower has excellent panoramic views. In the first half of November in the Parque a la Bandera (opposite the monument) *Fiesta de las Colectividades* lasts 10 nights, with stalls offering typical dishes and a stage for folk music and dances. From plaza 25 de Mayo, Córdoba leads west towards plaza San Martín and beyond, the Boulevard Oroño. These 14 blocks are known as the **Paseo del Siglo** and have the largest concentration of late 19th- and early 20th-century buildings in the city. **Museo de Bellas Artes J B Castagnino** ① *Av Pellegrini 2202, T480 2542, Wed-Mon 1400-2000, US$0.35.* Just outside, the 126-ha Parque Independencia has an impressive collection of French impressionist, Italian baroque and Flemish works, and one of best collections of Argentine paintings and sculpture.

Che Guevara was born here in 1928. The large white house at Entre Ríos y Urquiza where he lived for the first two years of his life before his family moved to Alta Gracia, near Córdoba (see page 115), is now an insurance company office. There are dozens of riverside resorts on the islands and sandbars opposite Rosario. Boats depart daily in summer (otherwise just at weekends) from *La Fluvial* or from *Costa Alta* to the resorts.

Paraná → *Phone code: 0343. Colour map 8, grid A5. Population: 247,600.*

About 30 km southeast of Santa Fe, the capital of Entre Ríos was, from 1854-61, capital of the Republic. The centre is on a hill offering views over the Río Paraná and beyond to Santa Fe. In the centre is the **Plaza Primero de Mayo**, around which are the **Municipalidad**, the large **Cathedral** and the **Colegio del Huerto**, seat of the Senate of the Argentine Confederation between 1854 and 1861. The **Casa de Gobierno** at Santa Fe y Laprida has a grand façade. Take pedestrianized San Martín and half block west of the corner with 25 de Junio is the fine **Teatro 3 de Febrero** (1908). Two blocks north is the **Plaza Alvear**; on the west side of which is the **Museo de Bellas Artes** ① *Buenos Aires 355, T420 7868, Tue-Fri 0700-1300, 1500-1900, Sat 1000-1400, 1700-2000, Sun 1000-1300, US$0.35.* It houses a vast collection of Argentine artists' work, with many by painter Cesario Bernaldo de Quirós. The city's glory is **Parque Urquiza**, along the cliffs above the Río Paraná. It has a statue to Gen Urquiza, and a bas-relief showing the battle of Caseros, at which he finally defeated Rosas. **Tourist offices**, in the centre at ① *Buenos Aires 132, T4230183*; at Parque Urquiza ① *Av Laurencena y Juan de San Martín, T4201837*; at the bus terminal, T4201862; and at the Hernandarias tunnel, www.turismoenparana.com.

Santa Fe → *Phone code: 0342. Colour map 8, grid A4. Population: 451,600.*

From Paraná to Santa Fe, the road goes under the Río Paraná by the Herandarias tunnel, toll US$1 per car, and then crosses a number of bridges (bus service by Etacer and Fluviales, US$1, 50 minutes). Santa Fe, capital of its province, was founded by settlers from Asunción in 1573, though its present site was not occupied until 1653. The south part of the city, around the **Plaza 25 de Mayo** is the historic centre. On the Plaza itself is the majestic **Casa de Gobierno**, built in 1911-1917 in French style on the site of the historic Cabildo, in which the 1853 constitution was drafted. Opposite is the **Cathedral**, and on the east side is the **Colegio de la Inmaculada Concepción**, including the **Iglesia de Nuestra Señora de los Milagros**, dating from 1694, with an ornate dome. **Museo Histórico Provincial** ① *3 de Febrero 2553, T457 3529, all year 0830-1200, afternoon hours change frequently, closed Mon, free.* The building, dating from 1690, is one of the oldest surviving civil buildings in the country. You can swim in the river at Guadalupe beach, on the Costanera Oeste. Take bus 16 from the centre to the Costanera. **Tourist offices**, at the bus terminal ① *T457 4123, 0700-1300, 1500-2100,* at Paseo del Restaurador ① *Bv Pellegrini y Rivadavia, T457 1881, 0700-1900* and at Boca del Tigre ① *Av Paso y Zavalía, 0700-1900,* all good, www.santaficiudad.gov.ar.

Esteros del Iberá

The **Reserva Natural del Iberá** protects nearly 13,000 sq km of wetlands known as the **Esteros del Iberá**, similar to the Pantanal in Brazil. Over sixty small lakes, no more than a few metres deep, cover 20-30% of the protected area, which is rich in aquatic plants. Like islands in the *lagunas, embalsados* are floating vegetation, thick enough to support large animals and trees. Wildlife includes black caiman, marsh deer, capybara and about 300 species of bird, among them the *yabirú* or *Juan Grande*, the largest stork in the western hemisphere. More difficult to see are the endangered maned wolf, the 3-m long yellow anaconda, the *yacaré ñato* and the river otter. There is a visitors' centre by the bridge at the access to Carlos Pellegrini (see below), open 0730-1200, 1400-1800, helpful and informative park rangers. **Mercedes** (*Phone code 03773, Population 30,900*), 250 km southeast of Corrientes, gives the best access and is the only point for getting regular transport to Carlos Pellegrini. There are a couple of decent places to stay, a few restaurants, ATMs and internet facilities; also a small tourist office on the plaza. The surrounding countryside is mostly grassy *pampas*, where rheas can be seen, with rocks emerging from the plains from time to time. **Carlos Pellegrini**, 120 km northeast of Mercedes (rough road), stands on beautiful *Laguna Iberá*. A one-day visit allows for a three-hour boat excursion (US$8-12 pp if not included in hotel rates), but some hotels offer more activities for longer stays, eg horse rides or guided walks.

Parque Nacional Mburucuyá

① *12 km east of the town of Mburucuyá, T03782-498022, free, 2 hotels. Buses San Antonio from Corrientes go daily to Mburucuyá, 2½ hrs, US$2.30; remises to the park, US$5.*

West of the Esteros del Iberá and 180 km southeast of Corrientes, this park covers 17,660 ha, stretching north from the marshes of the Río Santa Lucía. It includes savanna with *yatay* palms, 'islands' of wet Chaco forest, and *esteros*. The *mburucuyá* or passionflower gives the name to the park. Wildlife is easy to see. Formerly two *estancias*, Santa María and Santa Teresa, the land was donated by their owner, the Danish botanist Troels Pedersen, who identified 1,300 different plants here. Provincial route 86 (unpaved) crosses the park for 18 km leading to the information centre and free campsite (hot water and electricity).

Corrientes → *Phone code: 03783. Colour map 6, grid C6. Population: 316,500.*

Corrientes, founded in 1588 is some 30 km below the confluence of the Ríos Paraguay and Alto Paraná. The 2¾ km General Belgrano bridge across the Río Paraná (toll US$1 per car) links the city with Resistencia (25 km), from where Ruta 11 goes north to Formosa and Asunción. East of Corrientes, Ruta 12 follows the Alto Paraná to Posadas and Iguazú. The river can make the air heavy, moist and oppressive, but in winter the climate is pleasant. The city is capital of Corrientes province and the setting for Graham Greene's novel, *The Honorary Consul*. **Tourist offices**, city tourist office at ① *Plaza Cabral, daily 0700-2100,* good map. Provincial office ① *25 de Mayo 1330, T327200, province and city information, Mon-Fri 0700-1300, www.planetacorrientes.com.ar.*

On the **Plaza 25 de Mayo**, one of the best-preserved in Argentina, the **Jefatura de Policía,**built in 19th-century French style, the Italianate **Casa de Gobierno** and the church of **La Merced**. Six blocks south is the leafy Plaza de la Cruz, on which the church of **La Cruz de los Milagros** (1897) houses a cross, the Santo Madero, placed there by the founder of the city, Juan Torres de Vera – *indígenas* who tried to burn it were killed by lightning from a cloudless sky. The **Museo de Ciencias Naturales 'Amadeo Bonpland'** ① *San Martín 850, Mon-Sat 0900-1200, 1600-2000,* contains botanical, zoological, archaeological and mineralogical collections including 5,800 insects and huge wasp nest. A beautiful walk eastwards, along the Avenida Costanera, beside the Paraná river leads to **Parque Mitre**, from where there are views of sunset.

😴 Sleeping

Rosario *p163*

A-B Riviera, San Lorenzo 1460, T/F424 2058, www.solans.com. 4-star, business hotel with good rooms, large breakfast, sauna, gym and restaurant. 3 similar hotels in the same chain.
C Garden, Callao 39, T0341-4370025, www.hotel gardensa.com. Good option a little way from the centre, in the Pichincha district (next to Blv Oroño) with **B** superior rooms and comfortable standard rooms. Also restaurant and children's play area.
C Plaza del Sol, San Juan 1055, T/F421 9899, plaza@satlink.com.ar. Comfortable, spacious rooms, pool on the 11th floor with splendid views, with large breakfast.
D Rosario, Cortada Ricardone 1365 (access from Entre Ríos 900 block), T/F424 2170, hrosario@ infovia.com.ar. Central, good rooms with a/c and breakfast. Larger **C** rooms in annex.
E Savoy, San Lorenzo 1022, T448 0071. Early 20th-century mansion, once Rosario's best, faded grandeur, great value, attentive service, breakfast.

Paraná *p163*

B Mayorazgo, Etchevehere y Miranda, Costanera Alta, T423 0333, www.mayorazgo hotel.com. Upmarket, overlooking Parque Urquiza, casino, pool, gym, restaurant and fine views of the river.
C Gran Hotel Paraná, Urquiza 976, T422 3900, www.hotelesparana.com.ar. Overlooking Plaza Primero de Mayo, 3 room categories (breakfast included), smart restaurant *La Fourchette*, gym.
D San Jorge, Belgrano 368, T/F422 1685, www.san jorgehotel.com.ar. Renovated house, helpful staff, older rooms are cheaper than the modern ones at the back with TV, breakfast, kitchen.

Santa Fe *p163*

C Riogrande, San Gerónimo 2580, T450 0700, riogrande@santafe.com.ar. Santa Fe's best hotel, very good rooms, includes large breakfast.
D Castelar, 25 de Mayo y Peatonal Falucho, T/F456 0999. On a small plaza, 1930's hotel, good value, comfortable, breakfast included, restaurant.
D Hostal Santa Fe de la Veracruz, San Martín 2954, T/F455 1740, hostal_santafe@ciudad.com.ar. Traditional favourite, **C** superior rooms, all good value, large breakfast, restaurant, sauna (extra).
E Emperatriz, Irigoyen Freyre 2440, T/F453 0061. Attractive Hispanic-style building, plain rooms, spacious, comfortable, breakfast and a/c extra.

Esteros del Iberá *p164*
Mercedes

D La Casa de China, call for directions, T03773-156 27269. A delightful historical old house with clean rooms and a lovely patio, breakfast included. Recommended.

E World, Pujol 1162, T422508, 3 blocks from bus station. With fan and breakfast, shared bath, other meals available, Iberá information.
F pp Delicias del Iberá, Pujol 1162, T422508. Next to the *combis* to Pellegrini, excellent, shared bath, breakfast, good meals, garden.

Carlos Pellegrini

AL Rincón del Socorro, T03782-497073, T011-48112005 (in Buenos Aires), www.rincondelsocorro.com. Incredibly luxurious, this estancia is part of an impressive conservation project by North American millionaire Douglas Tompkins. Beautifully set in its own 12,000 hectares 35 km south of Carlos Pellegrini, with 6 spacious bedrooms, each with bathroom and little sitting room, 3 cabañas, and elegant sitting rooms and dining rooms. Delicious home-produced organic food, hosts Leslie and Valeria speak English, excellent trips on the lagunas with bilingual guides, *asados* at lunchtime, night safaris and wonderful horse riding. Gorgeous gardens, pool with superb views all around. Highly recommended.
A pp Hostería Ñandé Retá, T03773-499411, T011-4811 2005 (Buenos Aires), www.nandereta.com. Large old wooden house in a shady grove, play room, full board, home cooking, excursions.
A pp Posada Aguapé, T03773-499412, T/F011-4742 3015 (Buenos Aires), www.iberaesteros.com.ar. On a lagoon with a garden and pool, comfortable rooms, attractive dining room, rates are for full board and include 2 excursions. Recommended.
A pp Posada de la Laguna, T03773-499413, www.posadadelalaguna.com. A beautiful place run by Elsa Güiraldes (grand-daughter of famous Argentine novelist, Ricardo Güiraldes) and set on the lake, very comfortable, large neat garden and a swimming pool, full board and all excursions included, English and some French spoken, excellent country cooking. Highly recommended.
B pp Irupé Lodge, T03773-1540 2193, www.irupelodge.com.ar. Rustic, simple rooms, great views of the laguna from dining room, offers conventional and alternative trips, camping on islands, diving, fishing, several languages spoken.
B pp San Juan Poriahú, at Loreto, T03781-156 08674, T011-4791 9511 (Buenos Aires). An old estancia run by Marcos García Rams, at the northwest edge of the Esteros, full board, horse rides and boat trips to see wildlife on a property where there has been no hunting at all. Closed Jan, Feb and Jul. Access from Ruta 12. Recommended.
B pp San Lorenzo, at Galarza, T03756-481292. Next to 2 lakes on the northeast edge of the region, splendid for wildlife watching, full

board, only 3 rooms, horse rides, walks, boat trips all included. Boat excursions by night are charged separately. Access from Gobernador Virasoro (90 km), via Rutas 37 and 41. Transfer can be arranged to/from Gobernador Virasoro or Posadas for an extra charge. Closed Jan-Feb.
D pp Posada Ypa Sapukai, Sarmiento 212, T03773-420155, www.argentinahostels.com. Rates are for full-board and include two 3-hrs boat trips. Good value, nice atmosphere, excellent staff, excursion to the *laguna* is very well guided (US$8 pp), lunch or dinner US$4. AHC Argentina Hostels Club. Recommended.
F pp San Cayetano, T03773-156 28763. Very basic, run by local guide Roque Pera, also has campsite.

Corrientes *p164*
No good value, inexpensive accommodation in the city. All those listed have a/c.
C Gran Hotel Guaraní, Mendoza 970, T433800, www.hguarani.com.ar. 4-star, business-oriented with restaurant, pool and gym, parking, breakfast.
D Hostal del Río, Plácido Martínez 1098, T436100, www.hotelguia.com/hostaldelrio. In apartment tower overlooking the port, fine rooms, pleasantly decorated, pool, restaurant, breakfast.
D Turismo, Entre Ríos 650, T/F433174. Riverside location, nice style but a bit outdated, smart restaurant, breakfast, large pool, adjacent casino.

🍴 Eating

Rosario *p163*
⍦ Amarra, Av Belgrano y Buenos Aires. Good food, including fish and seafood, quite formal, cheap set menus Mon-Fri noon.
⍦ Club Español, Rioja 1052. Typical menu with some Iberian touches, old-fashioned, pleasant.
⍦ Gigante, San Martín 946. Large popular restaurant offering generous helpings of good food at incredibly low prices.
⍦ Pampa, Moreno y Mendoza. A good *parrilla* with attractive 1940s decor.
⍦ Rich, San Juan 1031. A classic, widely varied menu, superb food, reputed to be one of the best restaurants in the whole country. Set meals including pastas, meats and salads, closed Mon. Recommended.

Cafés
Café de la Opera, Mendoza y Laprida (next to *Teatro El Círculo*). Jazz, tango, Russian folk music and food, poetry or story-telling, pretty café.
Kaffa, Córdoba 1473. Good coffee in *El Ateneo* bookshop.
La Sede, San Lorenzo y Entre Ríos. Very popular café, especially at weekday lunchtime.
Victoria, Jujuy y Bvd Oroño. One of the oldest cafés in town and most traditional.

Santa Fe *p163*
Many good eating places, with excellent meals with wine. Many places in the centre close on Sun.
⍦ Baviera San Martín, San Martín 2941. Traditional, central, good varied menu.
⍦ Club Sirio Libanés, 25 de Mayo 2740. Very good Middle Eastern food, popular Sun lunch for families.
⍦ El Quincho de Chiquito, Av Almirante Brown y Obispo Príncipe (Costanera Oeste). Classic fish restaurant, excellent food, generous helpings and good value.

Cafés
Don Ernesto, San Martín y General López. A traditional café in the civic centre.
Las Delicias, Hipólito Yrigoyen y San Martín. Café and bakery with beautiful decor from early 20th century, good for coffees and pastries, fruit juices, sandwiches and alcohol.

Corrientes *p164*
⍦ El Solar, San Lorenzo 830. Informal, busy at lunchtime, meals by weight.
⍦ Martha de Bianchetti, 9 de Julio y Mendoza. Smart café and bakery.
Panambí, Junín near Córdoba. A traditional, central *confitería*, good pastries and regional breads.

⊖ Transport

Rosario *p163*
Air Airport at Fisherton, 15 km west of centre, T451 1226. *Remises* charge US$4-5. Daily flights to Buenos Aires with **AR** and **Aerovip**, 45 mins.
Bus Terminal at Santa Fe y Cafferata, about 30 blocks west of the *Monumento de la Bandera*, T437 2384. For local buses you must buy magnetic card sold at kiosks in the centre or near bus-stops (US$0.25 per journey), several bus lines to centre with stops on Córdoba (eg 101, 103, 115), US$0.25; from centre, take buses on Plaza 25 de Mayo, going via C Santa Fe. *Remise* US$1.50. To **Buenos Aires**, 4 hrs, US$7. To **Córdoba**, 6 hrs, US$8.50. To **Santa Fe**, 2½ hrs, US$5.
Train Rosario Norte station, Av del Valle y Av Ovidio Lagos. The Buenos Aires-Tucumán service operated by **TBA**, T0800-3333822, stops weekly in Rosario, though at inconvenient times in the day and tickets are only sold just before departures, at the station. To **Tucumán**, US$12; to **Buenos Aires**, US$3.50. Taxis charge US$0.80.

Paraná *p163*
Bus Terminal at Av Ramírez 2598 (10 blocks southeast of Plaza Primero de Mayo), T422 1282. Buses 1, 6 to/from centre, US$0.40. *Remise* US$2-2.50. To **Colón** on Río Uruguay, 4-5 hrs, US$8. To **Buenos Aires**, 6-7 hrs, US$15-22.

Santa Fe *p163*
Air Airport at Sauce Viejo, 17 km south. T499
5064. Taxi US$4 from bus terminal. Daily **AR**
and **Aerovip** to and from **Buenos Aires**.
Bus Terminal near the centre, Gen M Belgrano
2910, T457 4124. To **Córdoba**, US$8.50, 5 hrs.
Many buses to **Buenos Aires** US$11-13, 6 hrs;
to **Paraná** frequent service US$1, 50 mins; to
Rosario, 2½ hrs, US$4-5.

Esteros del Iberá *p164*
Bus Mercedes to **Carlos Pellegrini**: Itatí II
combis daily 1130 (schedules change frequently)
from Pujol 1166, T420184, T156 29598, 3 hrs,
US$3.30. Combi spends an hour picking up
passengers all around Mercedes after leaving the
office. Returns from Pellegrini at 0400, book by
2200 the night before at the local grocery (ask for
directions). Mercedes to **Buenos Aires**, 9-10 hrs,
US$12-14. Mercedes to **Corrientes**, 3 hrs, US$4.
To **Puerto Iguazú**, best to go via Corrientes,
otherwise via any important town along Ruta 14,
eg Paso de los Libres, 130 km southeast. There is a
direct bus from Carlos Pellegrini to **Posadas**.

Corrientes *p164*
Air Camba Punta Airport, 10 km east of city,
T458684. (Minibus picks up passengers from
hotels, T450072, US$1.30, US$2.70 to Resistencia
airport.) AR (T424647) to/from Buenos Aires.
Bus To **Resistencia**, Chaco–Corrientes, every

15 mins from Av Costanera y La Rioja at the port,
40 mins, US$0.70 return. Main terminal on
Av Maipú, 5 km southeast of centre, bus No 103
(be sure to ask the driver if goes to terminal as
same line has many different routes), 20 mins,
US$0.35 To **Posadas** US$8-13, 3½-4 hrs, several
companies, road paved. To **Buenos Aires**,
several companies, 11-12 hrs, US$20-30.
To **Asunción** (Paraguay), **Crucero del Norte**,
El Pulqui, 5-7 hrs, US$7-8.

⊙ Directory

Rosario *p163*
Airline offices Aerolíneas Argentinas, Santa
Fe 1410, T424 9517. **Banks** Many banks along
C Córdoba, east of plaza San Martín. Exchange at
Transatlántica, Mitre y Rioja. TCs exchanged at
Banex, Mitre y Santa Fe. 2% or US$10 commission.
Internet Several places in centre, US$0.50 per hr.
Post offices Córdoba y Buenos Aires.

Santa Fe *p163*
Banks Banking district around San Martín y
Tucumán. Exchange money and TCs at Tourfé,
San Martín 2500, or at **Columbia**, San Martín 2275.

Corrientes *p164*
Internet Many in centre. **Post offices** San
Juan y San Martín. **Telephones** Several
telecentros in centre.

The Chaco

Much of the Chaco is inaccessible because of poor roads (many of them impassable during
summer rains) and lack of public transport, but it has two attractive national parks which are
reachable all year round. Resistencia and Formosa are the main cities at the eastern rim, from
where Rutas 16 and 81 respectively go west almost straight across the plains to the hills in Salta
province. Buses to Salta take Ruta 16, while Ruta 81 has long unpaved sections west of Las
Lomitas, which make for a very hard journey after heavy rains. Presidencia Roque Sáenz Peña,
170 km northwest of Resistencia, is a reasonable place to stop over. The Chaco is one of the
main centres of indigenous population in Argentina: the Toba are settled in towns by the Río
Paraná and the semi-nomadic Wichi, or Mataco, live in the western region. Less numerous are
the Mocoví in Chaco and the Pilagá in central Formosa. The Chaco has two distinct natural
zones. The Wet Chaco spreads along the Ríos Paraná and Paraguay covered mainly by marshlands with savanna and groves of caranday palms, where birdwatching is excellent. Further west,
as rainfall diminishes, scrubland of algarrobo, white quebracho, palo borracho and various types
of cacti characterise the Dry Chaco, where South America's highest temperatures, exceeding 45°C,
have been recorded. Winters are mild, with only an occasional touch of frost in the south.

Resistencia → *Phone code: 03722. Colour map 6, grid C6. Population: 359,100.*

The hot and energetic capital of the Province of Chaco, Resistencia is 6½ km up the
Barranqueras stream on the west bank of the Paraná and 544 km north of Santa Fe. On the
Paraná itself is the little port of Barranqueras. Resistencia is known as the 'city of the statues',
there being over 200 of these in the streets. Four blocks from the central Plaza 25 de Mayo is the
Fogón de los Arrieros ⓘ *Brown 350 (between López y Planes and French), T426418, open to
non-members Mon-Sat 0900-1200, Mon-Fri 2100-2300, US$1.70.* This famous club and

informal cultural centre deserves a visit, for its occasional exhibitions and meetings. The **Museo Del Hombre Chaqueño**ⓘ *Juan B Justo 280, Mon-Fri 0800-1200, 1600-2000, free,* is a small anthropological museum with an exhibition of handicrafts by native Wichi, Toba and Mocoví people. It has a fascinating mythology section in which small statues represent Guaraní beliefs (still found in rural areas). There are banks and *cambios* in the centre for exchange. **Tourist office** ⓘ *Plaza 25 de Mayo, T458289, Mon-Fri 0800-2000.* **Provincial tourist office** ⓘ *Santa Fe 178, T423547, www.chaco.gov.ar/turismo, Mon-Fri 0630-2000, Sat 0800-1200,* .

Parque Nacional Chaco

ⓘ *T03725-496166, 24 hrs, free, 115 km northwest of Resistencia, best visited between Apr-Oct to avoid intense summer heat and voracious mosquitoes.*

The park extends over 15,000 ha and protects one of the last remaining untouched areas of the Wet Chaco with exceptional *quebracho colorado* trees, *caranday* palms and dense riverine forests with orchids along the banks of the Río Negro. Some 340 species of bird have been sighted in the park. Mammals include *caraya* monkeys and, much harder to see, collared peccary, puma and jaguarundi. 300 m from the entrance is the visitors' centre and a free campsite with hot showers and electricity. There you can hire bicycles or horses for US$1.30 per hour. The paved Ruta 16 goes northwest from Resistencia and after about 60 km Ruta 9 branches off, leading north to Colonia Elisa and Capitán Solari, 5 km east of the park entrance, via a dirt road. If in a group, call the park in advance to be picked up at Capitán Solari. *La Estrella* run daily buses Resistencia-Capitán Solari, where *remise* taxis should not charge more than US$1 to the park, a short journey that can also be done on foot. Tour operators run day-long excursions to the park from Resistencia.

Formosa → *Phone code: 03717. Colour map 6, grid C6. Population: 198,100.*

The capital of Formosa Province, 186 km above Corrientes, is the only Argentine port of any note on the Río Paraguay. It is oppressively hot from November to March. **Tourist office** ⓘ *José M Uriburu 820 (Plaza San Martín), 1600-2000, T420442, www.formosa.gov.ar, Mon-Fri 0730-1300.* Ask about guided excursions and accommodation at *estancias*.

Border with Paraguay

The easiest crossing is by road via the Puente Loyola, 4 km north of **Clorinda** (*Phone code 03718, Colour map 6, grid C6*). From Puerto Falcón, at the Paraguayan end of the bridge, the road runs 40 km northeast, crossing the Río Paraguay, before reaching Asunción. **Immigration** formalities for entering Argentina are dealt with at the Argentine end, those for leaving Argentina at the Paraguayan end. Crossing, open 24 hours. **Buses** from Puerto Falcón to Asunción run every hour, *Empresa Falcón* US$0.50, last bus to the centre of Asunción 1830.

A second route is by ferry from Puerto Pilcomayo, close to Clorinda, to Itá Enramada (Paraguay), US$0.50, five minutes, every 30 minutes. Then take bus 9 to Asunción. Argentine **immigration** is at Puerto Pilcomayo, closed at weekends for tourists. Paraguayan immigration at Itá Enramada, 24 hrs.

Parque Nacional Río Pilcomayo

ⓘ *Access to the park is free, 24 hrs, administration centre in Laguna Blanca, Av Pueyrredón y Ruta 86, T03718-470045, Mon-Fri 0700-1430.*

Some 48,000 ha, 65 km northwest of Clorinda is this national park is recognised as a natural wetland, with lakes, marshes and low-lying parts which flood during the rainy season. The remainder is grassland with caranday palm forests and Chaco woodland. Among the protected species are aguará-guazú, giant anteaters and coatis. Caimans, black howler monkeys, rheas and a variety of birds can also be seen. The park has two entrances leading to different areas. Easiest to reach on foot is Laguna Blanca, where there is an information point and a free campsite with electricity and cold water. From there, a footpath goes to the Laguna Blanca, the biggest lake in the park. A bit further is the second entrance, leading to the area of Estero Poí, with another information point and a campsite without facilities. **Godoy** buses run from Formosa or Resistencia to the small towns of Laguna Naick-Neck, 5 km from the park (for going to Laguna Blanca) and Laguna Blanca, 8 km from the park (for going to Estero Poí). **Remise** taxis from both towns should charge no more than US$3 for these short journeys. There are police controls on the way to the park because of the proximity to the Paraguay border.

● Sleeping

Resistencia *p167*
C Covadonga, Güemes 200, T444444, hotel covadonga@infovia.com.ar. The city's top hotel, comfortable, a/c, breakfast, pool, sauna and gym.
D Gran Hotel Royal, Obligado 211, T443666, www.granhotelroyal.com.ar. Good value, comfortable, a/c, breakfast included.
E Bariloche, Obligado 239, T421412, jag@cps arg.com. Best value, welcoming, good rooms, a/c, no breakfast but café at nearby *Gran Hotel Royal*.

Formosa *p168*
B Turismo, San Martín 759, T431122, hotelde turismoformosa@arnet.com.ar. Large building by the river, good views, a/c and breakfast.
C Casa Grande Apart-Hotel, Av González Lelong 185, T431573, www.casagrande apart.com.ar. 8 blocks north of Av 25 de Mayo, by river, good 1 and 2-room apartments with kitchenette, a/c and breakfast, gym and pool.
D Plaza, José M Uriburu 920, T426767. On Plaza, good, pool, with breakfast, very helpful, some English spoken, secure parking.
F El Extranjero, Av Gutnisky 2660, T452276. Opposite bus terminal, OK, with a/c.

❼ Eating

Resistencia *p167*
♈♈ Charly, Güemes 213, T434019. *Parrilla* and international food, excellent, a/c, popular.
♈ San José, Roca y Av Alberdi. A popular café and *confitería* on Plaza 25 de Mayo with excellent pastries and ice creams.

Formosa *p168*
♈ El Fortín, Mitre 602. Traditional, good for fish.
♈ El Tano Marino, Av 25 de Mayo 55. Italian, pastas are the speciality.
♈ Yayita, Belgrano 926. Central, serves regional dishes, such as *soyo*, or *sopa paraguaya*.

❀ Festivals and events

Resistencia *p167*
Fiesta Nacional de Pescado de los Grandes is celebrated **10-12 Oct**, Río Antequeros, 14 km away.

Formosa *p168*
The world's longest **Via Crucis** pilgrimage with 14 stops along Ruta 81 (registered in the Guinness Book of Records) takes place every Easter week, starting in Formosa and ending at the border with the province of Salta, 501 km northwest. **Festival de la caña con ruda** is held on the last night of **Jul**, when Paraguayan *caña* flavoured by the *ruda* plant is drunk as a protection against the mid-winter blues. A good chance to try regional dishes.

❸ Transport

Resistencia *p167*
Air Airport 8 km west of town (taxi US$3), T446 009. **AR**, T445550, to/from **Buenos Aires**, 1¼ hrs.
Bus To **Corrientes**, Chaco-Corrientes buses stop opposite *Norte* supermarket on Av Alberdi e Illia, 40 mins, US$0.40 return. Modern terminal on Av Malvinas Argentinas y Av Maclean in western outskirts (bus 3 or 10 from Oro y Perón, 1 block west of plaza, 20 mins, US$0.25; *remise* US$1.70). To **Buenos Aires** 12-13 hrs, US$15-30 several companies. To **Formosa** 2-2½ hrs, US$3-4. To **Iguazú**, 8-10½ hrs, US$12-15, several companies, some require change of bus in **Posadas**, 5½ hrs. To **Salta**, FlechaBus, La Nueva Estrella, 12½ hrs, US$18-20. To **Asunción** several companies, 5-5½ hrs, US$5-6.

Formosa *p168*
Air El Pucu airport, 5 km southwest, T452490; *remise*, US$2. **AR** (T429314) to **Buenos Aires** 1½ hrs.
Bus Terminal at Av Gutnisky y Antartida, 15 blocks west of Plaza San Martín, T430817 (*remise* US$1). To **Asunción**, 3 hrs, US$6. To **Resistencia**, 2½ hrs, US$3-4; to **Buenos Aires** 15-17 hrs, US$20-30.

Misiones

While Posadas is one of the main crossing points to Paraguay, most people will head northeast, through the province of the Jesuit Missions, towards Iguazú. This is a land of ruined religious establishments, gemstones and waterfalls.

Posadas → *Phone code: 03752. Population: 280,500.*

This is the main Argentine port on the south bank of the Alto Paraná, 377 km above Corrientes, and the capital of the province of Misiones. On the opposite bank of the river lies the Paraguayan town of Encarnación, reached by the San Roque bridge. The city's centre is **Plaza 9 de Julio**, on which stand the **Cathedral** and the **Gobernación**, in imitation French style. The riverside and adjacent districts are good for a stroll. Follow Rivadavia or Buenos Aires north to Avenida Andrés Guaçurarí (referred also to as Roque Pérez), a pleasant boulevard, lively at night with several bars. Immediately north of it is the small and hilly

Bajada Vieja or old port district. There is a good **Museo Regional Aníbal Cambas**ⓘ *Alberdi 600 in the Parque República del Paraguay, 11 blocks north of Plaza 9 de Julio, T447539, Mon-Fri 0700-1900*, its permanent exhibition of Guaraní artefacts and pieces collected from the nearby Jesuit missions is worth seeing. **Tourist office** ⓘ *Colón 1987, T447540, www.conozcamisiones.com, daily 0800-2000.* Also visit www.turismo.misiones.gov.ar.

Border with Paraguay

Argentine immigration and customs are on the Argentine side of the bridge to Encarnación. Buses across the bridge (see Transport page 172) do not stop for formalities; you must get exit stamps. Get off the bus, keep your ticket and luggage, and catch a later bus. Pedestrians and cyclists are not allowed to cross; cyclists must ask officials for assistance. Boats cross to Encarnación, 6-8 minutes, hourly Monday-Friday 0800-1800, US$1. Formalities and ticket office at main building. Port access from Av Costanera y Av Andrés Guaçurarí, T425044 (*Prefectura*).

San Ignacio Miní → *Phone code: 03752. Colour map 7, grid C1.*

ⓘ *0700-1900, US$4 with tour (ask for English version), leaves from entrance every 20 mins. Allow 1½ hrs. Go early to avoid crowds and the best light for pictures (also late afternoon); good birdwatching. Son et lumière show at the ruins, daily after sunset, Spanish only, US$0.80.*
The little town of San Ignacio is the site of the most impressive Jesuit ruins in the region, 63 km northeast of Posadas. It is a good base for visiting the other Jesuit ruins and for walking. San Ignacio, together with the missions of Santa Ana and Loreto, is a UNESCO World Heritage Site. There are heavy rains in February. Mosquitoes can be a problem. The local festival is 30-31 July.

San Ignacio Miní was founded on its present site in 1696. The 100 sq-m, grass-covered plaza is flanked north, east and west by 30 parallel blocks of stone buildings with four to 10 small, one-room dwellings in each block. The roofs have gone, but the massive metre-thick walls are still standing except where they have been torn down by the *ibapoi* trees. The public buildings, some of them 10 m high, are on the south side of the plaza. In the centre are the ruins of a large church finished about 1724. The masonry, sandstone from the Río Paraná, was held together by mud. Inside the entrance, 200 m from the ruins, is the **Centro de Interpretación Jesuítico-Guaraní**, with displays on the lives of the Guaraníes before the arrival of the Spanish, the work of the Jesuits and the consequences of their expulsion, as well as a fine model of the mission. **Museo Provincial** contains a small collection of artefacts from Jesuit reducciones.

The ruins of two other Jesuit missions are worth visiting (US$1 each, free with ticket to San Ignacio). **Loreto**ⓘ *0700-1830*, can be reached by a 3-km dirt road (signposted) which turns off Ruta 12, 10 km south of San Ignacio. Little remains other than a few walls; excavations are in progress. There are no buses to Loreto; the bus drops you off on Ruta 12, or take a tour from Posadas or a *remise*. **Santa Ana**ⓘ *16 km south, 0700-1900, buses stop on Ruta 12,* was the site of the Jesuit iron foundry. Impressive high walls still stand and beautiful steps lead from the church to the wide open plaza The ruins are 700 m along a path from Ruta 12 (signposted).

Near San Ignacio, is the **Casa de Horacio Quiroga** ⓘ *T470124, 0800-1900, US$0.65 (includes 40-min guided tour; ask in advance for English).* Take Calle San Martín (opposite direction to the ruins) to the Gendarmería HQ. Turn right and on your right are 2 attractive wood and stone houses. After 200 m the road turns left and 300 m later, a signposted narrow road branches off. The house of this Uruguayan writer, who lived part of his tragic life here as a farmer and carpenter between 1910 and 1916 and in the 1930s, is worth a visit. Many of his short stories were inspired by the subtropical environment and its inhabitants.

San Ignacio to Puerto Iguazú

Ruta 12 continues northeast, running parallel to Río Alto Paraná, towards Puerto Iguazú. With its bright red soil and lush vegetation, this attractive route is known as the Región de las Flores. You get a good view of the local economy: plantations of *yerba mate*, manioc and citrus fruits, timber yards, manioc mills and *yerba mate* factories. The road passes through several small modern towns including Jardín America, Puerto Rico, Montecarlo and Eldorado, with accommodation, campsites, places to eat and regular bus services. Just outside Eldorado, **Estancia Las Mercedes**ⓘ *Av San Martín Km 4, T03751-431511*, is an old *yerba mate* farm with period furnishings, open for day visits with activities like riding, boating, and for overnight stays with full board (**A**). **Wanda**, 50 km north of Eldorado, was named after a Polish princess and is famous as the site of open-cast amethyst and quartz mines which sell gems. There are guided tours to two of them, **Tierra Colorada** and **Compañía Minera Wanda**ⓘ *daily 0700-1900.*

Gran Salto del Moconá

For 3 km the waters of the Río Uruguay in a remote part of Misiones create magnificent falls (known in Brazil as Yucuma) up to 20 m high. They are surrounded by dense woodland protected by the Parque Estadual do Turvo (Brazil) and the Parque Provincial Moconá, the Reserva Provincial Esmeralda and the Reserva de la Biósfera Yabotí (Argentina). Moconá has roads and footpaths, accommodation where outdoor activities can be arranged, such as excursions to the falls, trekking in the forests, kayaking, birdwatching and 4WD trips. Alternative bases are El Soberbio (70 km southwest) or San Pedro (92 km northwest). Roads from both towns to Moconá are impassable after heavy rain. Regular bus service from Posadas to El Soberbio or San Pedro, and from Puerto Iguazú to San Pedro, but no bus all the way to the falls.

⊜ Sleeping

Posadas *p169*

B Julio César, Entre Ríos 1951, T427930, www.juliocesarhotel.com.ar. 4-star hotel with pool and gym, spacious reasonably-priced rooms, some with river views, breakfast included. Recommended.

C Continental, Bolívar 1879 (on Plaza 9 de Julio), T440990, www.hoteleramisiones.com.ar. Standard rooms and more spacious **B** VIP rooms, some have river views, restaurant on 1st floor.

C Posadas, Bolívar 1949, T440888, www.hotelposadas.com.ar. Business hotel with good standard rooms and bigger *especial* rooms, restaurant, free internet access for guests.

D City, Colón 1754, T433901, citysa@arnet.com.ar. Gloomy reception, but very good rooms, some overlooking plaza, with breakfast and a/c, restaurant on first floor, parking.

D Le Petit, Santiago del Estero 1630, T436031. Good value, small, a short walk from centre on a quiet street, a/c, with breakfast.

E Residencial Misiones, Félix de Azara 1960, T430133. Very hospitable, good rooms with fan, central, old house with a patio, no breakfast, cooking and laundry facilities, popular.

San Ignacio Miní *p170*

D El Descanso, Pellegrini 270, T470207. Small detached house, 5 blocks southwest of main Av Sarmiento, Comfortable. Also with campsite.

D San Ignacio, San Martín 823, T470047, hotelsanignacio@arnet.com.ar. Welcoming and very informative owner Beatriz offers very good rooms with a/c and apartments for 4-5, breakfast US$2, evening meals.

G pp La Casa de Inés y Juan, San Martín 1291 (no sign and no phone). Laid-back artist and writer's house, 2 rooms, small library and a backyard for pitching tents, where is also a small but delightful pool and a curious bathroom. Meals on request. Recommended.

E pp Res Doka, Alberdi 518, T470131, recidoka@yahoo.com.ar. Simple but comfortable rooms, handy for the ruins.

Camping Two sites on the river splendidly set and very well-kept on a small sandy bay, reached after 45-min walk from town at the end of the road leading to Quiroga's house. **Club de Pesca y Deportes Náuticos**, on a hilly ground with lush vegetation, US$1.50 pp per day plus US$1 per tent. **Playa del Sol**, T470207, on the beach side of the bay, same prices.

Gran Salto del Moconá *p171*

D Hostería Puesta del Sol, C Suipacha, El Soberbio, T03755-495161 (T4300 1377 in Buenos Aires). Great views, pool, restaurant, comfortable, with breakfast, a/c. For full board add US$6.50 pp. Boat excursions arranged to the falls, 7 to 8 hrs, US$20 pp (minimum 4 people). A less tiring journey to the falls is by an easy boat crossing to Brazil, then by vehicle to the Parque do Turvo, 7 hrs, meal included, US$20 pp. Otherwise, a 4WD journey on the Argentine side with more opportunities for trekking also takes 7 hrs, with a meal, US$20 pp. Also act as tour operators.

D pp Refugio Moconá, 3 km from access to the reserve, 8 km from the falls (or contact at Pasaje Dornelles 450, San Pedro), T03751-470022. Rooms for 4 to 5 people with shared bath, campsite for US$4.30 a day per tent, tents for rent (US$8.50 a day), meals, boat trips and activities. Runs various boat trips and excursions, such as transfer with sightseeing to/from San Pedro, 2 hrs, US$85 for up to 8 people. Also act as tour operators.

❶ Eating

Posadas *p169*

Most places offer *espeto corrido*, eat as much as you can *parrilla* with meat brought to the table.

↑↑ De La Costa, Av Costanera. Very popular with locals, on the river bank, with great views from the upper floor, and a cheerful buzz on Sat.

↑↑ El Mensú, Fleming y Coronel Reguera (at Bajada Vieja district). Attractive house offering a varied menu with fish, pastas and a large selection of wines, closed Mon.

↑↑ Diletto, Bolívar 1729. Good for fish, such as *surubí*, and, curiously, rabbit as their speciality.

↑↑ Espeto del Rey, Ayacucho y Tucumán. *Parrilla*, good food. Try *mandioca frita* (fried manioc).

¶ **La Querencia**, on Bolívar 322 (on Plaza 9 de Julio). Traditional large restaurant offering *parrilla*, *surubí* and pastas, good service.
¶ **La Rueda**, Av Costanera. A quiet smart place on the banks of the river.

San Ignacio Miní *p170*
¶ **La Aldea**, Rivadavia y Lanusse. An attractive house serving good and cheap pizzas, *empanadas* or other simple meals.

▲ Activities and tours

Posadas *p169*
Abra, Colón 1975, T422221, abramisiones@ arnet.com.ar. Tours to San Ignacio, including Santa Ana Jesuit ruins (US$20 pp), also those in Paraguay (US$23 pp) and in Brazil (US$48 pp), plus tours to waterfalls (US$47).
Guayrá, San Lorenzo 2208, T433415, www.guayra.com.ar. Tours to Iberá (US$50-65 pp if 4 people), to Saltos del Moconá (US$80 pp if 4 people), both sites in a 5-day excursion for US$240 pp (for 4), also car rental and transfer to Carlos Pellegrini (for Iberá).

● Transport

Posadas *p169*
Air Gen San Martín Airport, 12 km west, T457413, reached by Bus No 8 or 28 in 40 mins, US$0.25, *remise* US$8. To **Buenos Aires**, AR (Ayacucho 1728, T432889), direct 1 hr 25 mins, some flights call at Corrientes or Formosa, 1 hr 50 mins.
Bus Terminal about 5 km out of the city at Av Santa Catalina y Av Quaranta (T456106), on the road to Corrientes. Buses No 4, 8, 15, 21, to/from centre, 20 mins, US$0.25, *remise* US$2. Travel agencies in the centre can book bus tickets in advance. To **Buenos Aires**, 12-13 hrs, US$17-25. Frequent services to **San Ignacio Miní**, 1 hr, US$2.50, and **Puerto Iguazú**, US$10, 5-6 hrs *expreso*. To **Tucumán**, La Nueva Estrella, **Autotransportes Mendoza**, 16-18 hrs, US$18-21.
International To **Encarnación** (Paraguay), Servicio Internacional, 50 mins, US$0.65, leaving at least every 30 mins from platforms 11 and 12 (lower level), tickets on bus.

San Ignacio Miní *p170*
Bus Stop in front of the church, leaving almost hourly to **Posadas** (US$2.50) or to **Puerto Iguazú** (US$9). Do not rely on bus terminal at the end of Av Sarmiento, only a few stop there. More buses stop on Ruta 12 at the access road (Av Sarmiento).

● Directory

Posadas *p169*
Banks Banco de La Nación, Bolívar 1799. Round corner on Félix de Azara are Banco Río and HSBC. Citibank, San Martín y Colón. Mazza, Bolívar 1932. For money exchange, TCs accepted. **Consulates** Paraguay, San Lorenzo 179, T423858. Mon-Fri 0730-1400. Same-day visas. **Immigration** Dirección Nacional de Migraciones, Buenos Aires 1633, T427414. **Internet** Many places, average US$050 per hr (usually cheaper evenings and weekends). **Medical services** Hospital Dr Ramón Madariaga, Av L Torres 1177, T447000.
Post offices Bolívar y Ayacucho.

Iguazú Falls → *Colour map 7, grid C1.*

The mighty Iguazú Falls are the most overwhelmingly magnificent in all of South America. So impressive are they that Eleanor Roosevelt remarked "poor Niagara" on witnessing them (they are four times wider). Viewed from below, the tumbling water is majestically beautiful in its setting of begonias, orchids, ferns and palms. Toucans, flocks of parrots and cacique birds and great dusky swifts dodge in and out along with myriad butterflies (there are at least 500 different species). Above the impact of the water, upon basalt rock, hovers a perpetual 30-m high cloud of mist in which the sun creates blazing rainbows.

Ins and outs Information Entry is US$10, payable in pesos, reais or dollars (guests at Hotel Sheraton should pay and get tickets stamped at the hotel to avoid paying again). Argentines pay US$4. Entry next 3 days is half price with the same ticket. Open daily 0800-1900 (1800 in winter). Visitor Centre includes information and photographs of the flora and fauna, as well as books for sale. There are places to eat, toilets, shops and a locutorio in the park. In the rainy season, when water levels are high, waterproof coats or swimming costumes are advisable for some of the lower catwalks and for boat trips. Cameras should be carried in a plastic bag. **Tourist office** ① *Aguirre 396, Puerto Iguazú, T420800, www.iguazuargentina.com, also try www.iguazu turismo.gov.ar and www.turismo.misiones.gov.ar. Open 0900-2200.* They have a basic map of area with local information, only Spanish spoken.

The falls, on the Argentina-Brazil border, are 19 km upstream from the confluence of the Río Iguazú with the Río Alto Paraná. The Río Iguazú (I is Guaraní for water and guazú is Guaraní for big), which rises in the Brazilian hills near Curitiba, receives the waters of some 30 rivers as it crosses the plateau. Above the main falls, the river, sown with wooded islets, opens out to a width of 4 km. There are rapids for 3½ km above the 74 m precipice over which the water plunges in 275 falls over a frontage of 2,470 m, at a rate of 1,750 cu m a second (rising to 12,750 cu m in the rainy season).

Around the falls

→ *In Oct-Feb (daylight saving dates change each year) Brazil is 1 hr ahead.*

On both sides of the falls there are National Parks. Transport between the two parks is via the Ponte Tancredo Neves as there is no crossing at the falls themselves. The Brazilian park offers a superb panoramic view of the whole falls and is best visited in the morning when the light is better for photography. The Argentine park (which requires a day to explore properly) offers closer views of the individual falls in their forest setting with its wildlife and butterflies, though to appreciate these properly you need to go early and get well away from the visitors areas. Busiest times are holiday periods and on Sunday. Both parks have visitors' centres and tourist facilities on both sides are constantly being improved.

Parque Nacional Iguazú covers an area of 67,620 ha. The fauna includes jaguars, tapirs, brown capuchin monkeys, collared anteaters and coatimundis, but these are rarely seen around the falls. There is a huge variety of birds; among the butterflies are shiny blue morphos and red/black heliconius. From the Visitor Centre a small gas-run train (free), the **Tren de la Selva**, whisks visitors on a 25-minute trip through the jungle to the Estación del Diablo, where it's a 1-km walk along catwalks across the Río Iguazú to the park's centrepiece, the **Garanta del Diablo**. A visit here is particularly recommended in the evening when the light is best and the swifts are returning to roost on the cliffs, some behind the water (look out for full-moon tours run

Puerto Iguazú

Sleeping
El Güembe 1
Hostel Iguazú Falls 17
Hostel Park Iguazú 4
Hostería Casa Blanca 5
Hostería Los Helechos 6
Iguazú Jungle Lodge 7

Lilian 15
Noelia 8
Pirayú Resort 3
Residencial Paquita 10
Residencial San Fernando 11
Saint George 12

Eating
El Quincho del Tío
  Querido 5
La Esquina 6
La Rueda 3
Panificadora Real 4
Pizza Color 7

0 metres   200
0 yards   200

N

by the park office, US$5). Trains leave on the hour and 30 minutes past the hour. However, it's best to see the falls from a distance first, with excellent views from the two well-organized trails along the **Circuito Superior** and **Circuito Inferior**, each taking around an hour and a half. To reach these, get off the train at the **Estación Cataratas** (after 10 minutes' journey) and walk down the **Sendero Verde**. The Circuito Superior is a level path which takes you along the easternmost line of falls, Bossetti, Bernabé Mandez, Mbiguá (Guaraní for cormorant) and San Martín, allowing you to see these falls from above. This path is safe for those with walking difficulties, wheelchairs and pushchairs, though you should wear supportive non-slippery shoes. The Circuito Inferior takes you down to the water's edge via a series of steep stairs and walkways with superb views of both San Martín falls and the Gaganta del Diablo from a distance. Wheelchair users, pram pushers, and those who aren't good with steps should go down by the exit route for a smooth and easy descent. You could then return to the Estación Cataratas to take the train to Estación Garganta, 10 and 40 minutes past the hour, and see the falls close up. Every month on the five nights of full moon, there are 1½-hour guided walks (bilingual) that may include or not a dinner afterwards or before the walk, at the Restaurant La Selva, depending on the time of departure. See the website www.iguazuargentina.com for the dates and times. Bookings must be in person at the park or through agencies (the Park does not take reservations via email): US$27 with dinner; US$17 without.

At the very bottom of the Circuito Inferior, a free ferry crosses on demand to the small, hilly **Isla San Martín** where trails lead to *miradores* with good close views of the San Martín falls. The park has two further trails: **Sendero Macuco**, 7 km return (allow 7 hours), starting from near the Visitor Centre and leading to the river via a natural pool (El Pozón) fed by a slender waterfall, **Salto Arrechea** (a good place for bathing and the only permitted place in the park). **Sendero Yacaratiá** starts from the same place, but reaches the river by a different route, and ends at Puerto Macuco, where you could take the *Jungle Explorer* boat to the see the Falls themselves (see below). This trail is really for vehicles and less pleasant to walk along; better to visit on an organized safari, see Activities and Tours, below.

Around the Iguazú Falls

Puerto Iguazú → *Phone code: 03757. Colour map 7, grid C1. Population: 19,000.*

This modern town is 18 km northwest of the falls high above the river on the Argentine side near the confluence of the Ríos Iguazú and Alto Paraná. It serves mainly as a centre for visitors to the falls. The port lies to the north of the town centre at the foot of a hill: from the port you can follow the Río Iguazú downstream towards HitoTres Fronteras, a *mirador* with views over the point where the Ríos Iguazú and Alto Paraná meet and over neighbouring Brazil and Paraguay. There are souvenir shops, toilets and *La Reserva* and *La Barranca* pubs are here; bus US$0.25. **La Aripuca** ① *T423488, www.aripuca.com.ar, US$1.30, turn off Ruta 12 just after Hotel Cataratas, entrance after 250 m, English and German spoken*, is a large wooden structure housing a centre for the appreciation of the native tree species and their environment. **Güira Oga** (Casa de los Pájaros) ① *US$1, daily 0830-1800, turn off Ruta 12 at Hotel Orquídeas Palace, entrance is 800 m further along the road from Aripuca; T423980 (mob 156-70684)*, is a sanctuary for birds that have been injured, where they are treated and reintroduced to the wild; exquisite parrots and magnificent birds of prey. There is also a trail in the forest and a breeding centre for endangered species.

● Sleeping

Puerto Iguazú *p175, maps p173 and p174*
LL Yacutinga Lodge, 30 km from town, pick up by jeep, www.yacutinga.com. A beautiful lodge in the middle of the rainforest, with activities, learning about the bird and plant life and Guaraní culture. Accommodation is in rustic adobe houses in tropical gardens, superb food and drinks included, as well as boat trips and walks. Recommended.

LL-L Sheraton Internacional Iguazú Resort, T491800, www.sheraton.com/iguazu. Fine position overlooking the falls, excellent, good restaurant (dinner buffet US$12) and breakfast, sports facilities and bikes for hire (US$2.50 ½ day). Taxi to airport US$12. Recommended.
A Iguazú Jungle Lodge, Hipólito Iyrigoyen y San Lorenzo, T420600, www.iguazujungle lodge.com. The most luxurious place in the town, *cabañas* and loft apartments, 7 blocks from the centre, by a river, with lovely pool. Comfortable and stylish, a/c, Wi-Fi, DVDs, great service, lofts are US$80 for 2, breakfast included. Houses sleep 7, good value if full. Warmly recommended.
A Saint George, Córdoba 148, T420633, www.hotelsaintgeorge.com. With good breakfast, comfortable, attentive service, pool and garden, good restaurant with buffet dinner, close to bus station, parking. Recommended.
C Pirayú Resort, Av Tres Fronteras 550, on the way to the Hito, T420393, www.pirayu.com.ar. Beautiful complex, comfortable *cabañas*, lovely river views, sports and games, pool, entertainment.
C Hostería Los Helechos, Amarante 76, T420338, www.argentinahostels.com. AHC Argentina Hostels Club. Easy-going, popular, well maintained, a/c, with breakfast, pool, good, welcoming.
C-D Hostel-inn Iguazú, Ruta 12, Km 5, T420156. Great atmosphere, huge outdoors recreation area and the largest pool in town, restaurant and poolside bar. Backpacker tours. HI discount.
C-D Hostería Casa Blanca, Guaraní 121, near bus station, T421320. With breakfast, family run, spotless, large rooms, good showers, beautifully maintained.
D Lilian, Beltrán 183, T420968. Bright modern rooms, quiet, 2 blocks from bus terminal, breakfast, helpful owners, a charming option.
D Noelia, Fray Luis Beltrán 119, T420729. Not far from bus terminal, neat and tidy, family-run, good value, with breakfast. Recommended.

D Res Paquita, Córdoba 731, opposite terminal, T420434. Some rooms with balcony, a/c, a bit dated but nice setting. No breakfast but bakery next door.
D Res San Fernando, Córdoba y Guaraní, near terminal, T421429. Breakfast, popular, good value.
E-F pp Hostel Iguazú Falls, Guaraní 70, T421295, www.hosteliguazufalls.com. 1 block from terminal, HI affiliated, cheaper for members, also double rooms (**D**), more expensive with breakfast and a/c, kitchen, BBQ, luggage store, laundry, internet, lovely garden, good.
F pp El Güembe, El Urú 120, T421035, www.elguembe.com.ar. 3 blocks from the bus station this is the nicer and quieter of 2 hostels owned by the same people, welcoming and appealing. The other, **El Güembe House**, is much noisier, but still recommended for its friendly atmosphere, parties and music. Breakfast included in both places. Double rooms **D**.
F pp Hostel Park Iguazú, Amarante 111, T424342, www.hostelparkiguazu.com.ar. New, 2 blocks from bus station, neat rooms for 2-4, with bath, breakfast, small pool, helpful.
Camping El Viejo Americano, Ruta 12, Km 3.5, T420190, www.viejoamericano.com.ar. 3 pools, wooded gardens, *cabañas* and a hostel, camping US$3 pp, food shop, electricity, barbecue.

● Eating

Puerto Iguazú *p175, maps p173 and p174*
♥♥ El Quincho del Tío Querido, Bompland 110, T420151. Recommended for *parrilla* and local fish, very popular, great value.
♥♥ La Esquina, Córdoba 148, next to **St George**. Extensive buffet, beef, fish, salads, friendly service.
♥♥ La Rueda, Córdoba 28. The best in town. Good food and prices, fish, steaks and pastas, often with mellow live music. Highly recommended.
♥ Pizza Color, Córdoba y Amarante. Popular for pizza and *parrilla*.
♥ Pizzería La Costa, Av Río Iguazú, on costanera. Popular, informal, high above the river on the coast road, looks basic, but the pizzas are superb.
Panificadora Real, Córdoba y Guaraní. Good bread, open Sun evening; another branch at Victoria y Brasil in the centre.

▲ Activities and tours

Iguazú Falls *p173, map p174*
Explorador Expediciones, T421600, T15 673318, www.hotelguia.com/ turismo/explorador-expediciones, and at the Sheraton Hotel. Run by expert guide Daniel Somay, they offer two small-group tours: *Safari a la Cascada* which takes you by jeep to the Arrechea waterfall, stopping along the way to look at wildlife, with a short walk to the falls, 2 hrs, US$15. And *Safari en la Selva*, more

in-depth interpretation of the wildlife all around, in open jeeps, 2 hrs, US$25. Highly recommended. There are also night walking tours to the falls when the moon is full; on clear nights the moon casts a blue halo over the falls. Explorador also run recommended 2-day expeditions in 4WDs to the Salto de Moconá. Recommended guide: Miguel Castelino, Apartado Postal 22, Puerto Iguazú (3370), Misiones, T420157, focustours@aol.com.
Jungle Explorer, T421696, www.iguazu junglexplorer.com. On *Paseo Ecológico* you float silently 3 km down the river from Estación Garganta to appreciate the wildlife on its banks, 30 mins, US$8. *Aventura Náutica* is a journey by launch to give you a soaking under the Falls, great fun, not for the faint-hearted, 12 mins, US$15. *Gran Aventura* combines the Aventura Náutica with a longer boat trip and a jeep trip along the Yacaratiá trail, 1 hr, US$30. Tickets available at all embarkation points or at Sheraton Hotel.

Puerto Iguazú *p175, maps p173 and p174*
Aguas Grandes, Mariano Moreno 58, T421140, www.aguasgrandes.com. Tours to both sides of the falls and further afield, activities in the forest, including half-day for US$20, abseiling down waterfalls, good fun.
Cabalgatas por la Selva, Ruta 12, just after the Rotonda for the road to the international bridge, T155-42180 (mob). For horse riding, 3-hr trips, US$12. Agencies arrange day tours to the Brazilian side (lunch in Foz), Itaipú and Ciudad del Este. Some include the new Duty Free mall on the Argentine side. Also to a gem mine at Wanda, US$10, and the Jesuit ruins at San Ignació Miní, US$20 (better from Posadas, less driving time).

● Transport

Iguazú Falls *p173, map p174*
Bus Transportes El Práctico run every 45 mins from Puerto Iguazú bus terminal, stopping at the park entrance for the purchase of entry tickets, continuing to the Visitor Centre, US$1.50. First bus 0630, last 1910, journey time 30 mins; return buses from the park: 0750-2020. You can get on or off the bus at any point en route. **Cars** are not allowed beyond visitor centre (car entry US$3).

Puerto Iguazú *p175, maps p173 and p174*
Air Airport is 20 km southeast of Puerto Iguazú near the Falls, T420595. A bus service between airport and bus terminal connects with plane arrivals and departures, US$3, will also drop off/collect you from your hotel. **AR/Austral** fly direct to **Buenos Aires**, 1 hr 40 mins.
Bus The bus terminal, at Av Córdoba y Av Misiones, T423006, has a phone office, restaurant, various tour company desks and bus offices. To

Buenos Aires, 16-18 hrs, Tigre Iguazú, Vía Bariloche, daily, US$35 *semi cama*, US$45 *cama*. To **Posadas**, stopping at San Ignacio Miní, frequent, 5-6 hrs, US$10, *expreso*; to **San Ignacio Miní**, US$9, *servicio común*. Agencia de Pasajes Noelia, local 3, T422722, can book tickets beyond Posadas for other destinations in Argentina, ISIC discounts available.

Taxi T420973/421707. Fares: from **airport** to Sheraton Hotel US$10, to **Argentine falls** US$16, to **Brazilian falls**, US$18, to centre of **Foz** US$116, to **Brazilian airport**, US$25, to **Ciudad del Este** US$20, to **Tierra Colorada** mine US$30 with wait.

Border with Brazil

Crossing via the Puente Tancredo Neves is straight-forward. When leaving Argentina, Argentine immigration is at the Brazilian end of the bridge. **Brazilian consulate**, Av Córdoba 264, T421348.

Bus Leave Puerto Iguazú terminal for Foz do Iguaçu every 20 mins, US$1. The bus stops at the Argentine border post, but not the Brazilian. Argentine officials stamp you in and out, but Brazilian immigration does not for a day visit (useful if otherwise you may need an expensive visa) but if you are entering Brazil for the first time, or leaving, you must insist on getting off the bus. Buses also stop at the Duty Free mall. The bus does not wait for those who need stamps, just catch the next one, of whatever company. **Taxis** Between the border and Puerto Iguazú US$3.

Border with Paraguay

Crossing to Paraguay is via Puente Tancredo Neves to Brazil and then via the Puente de la Amistad to Ciudad del Este. Brazilian entry and exit stamps are not required unless you are stopping in Brazil. US$3 charge to enter Paraguay. The **Paraguayan consulate** is at Bompland 355.

Bus Direct buses (non-stop in Brazil), leave Puerto Iguazú terminal every 30 mins, US$2.50, 45 mins, liable to delays especially in crossing the bridge to Ciudad del Este. Only one bus on Sun, no schedule, better to go to Foz and change buses there.

● Directory

Puerto Iguazú *p175, maps p173 and p174*
Airline offices Aerolíneas Argentinas, Brasil y Aguirre, T420168. **Banks** ATMs at Macro Misiones and Banco de la Nación, Av Aguirre 179. *Sheraton* has an ATM. TCs can only be changed at **Cambio Libre** in the Hito Tres Fronteras, 0800-2200. Good exchange rates at the Brazilian border. **Internet** Generally expensive, US$1-1.20 per hr. Several places in towm.

Lake District

The Lake District contains a series of great lakes strung along the foot of the Andes from above 40°S to below 50°S in the Parque Nacional Los Glaciares area. This section covers the northern lakes; for convenience the southernmost lakes, including those in the Los Glaciares park area, are described under Patagonia (see page 200). The area is dramatic, beautiful and unspoilt, offering superb trekking, fishing, watersports, climbing and skiing. See the Chilean chapter, The Lake District (page 684), for map and details of the system of lakes on the far side of the Andes. These can be visited through various passes. Off season, from mid-April to June and mid-August to mid-November, many excursions, boat trips etc, run on a limited schedule, if at all. Public transport is also limited.

Neuquén and around

→ *Phone code: 0299. Colour map 8, grid C2. Population: Greater Neuquén: 290,000.*

Founded in 1904 on the west side of the confluence of the Ríos Limay and Neuquén, Neuquén is a pleasant provincial capital and a major stop en route from the east coast to the northern lakes and Bariloche. It serves both the oilfields to the west and the surrounding fruit orchards. There are also many wine *bodegas* nearby. At the Parque Centenario (be sure *not* to take the bus to Centenario industrial suburb), is a *mirador* with good views of the city and the confluence of the rivers, where they become the Negro. Visit **Museo de la Ciudad Paraje Confluencia** ① *Independencia y Córdoba*, interesting display on the Campaign of the Desert (19th-century annihilation of indigenous groups). Facing Neuquén and connected by bridge is Cipolletti, a prosperous centre of the fruit-growing region. **Tourist office** ① *Félix San Martín 182, T0299-442 4089, www.neuquentur.gov.ar. Mon-Fri 0700-2200, Sat-Sun 0800-2000* (don't confuse the streets Félix San Martín and General San Martín).

Villa El Chocón

The area around Villa El Chocón is rich in dinosaur fossils. Red sedimentary rocks have preserved, in relatively good condition, bones and footprints of the animals which lived in this region during the Cretaceous period about 100 million years ago. The **Museo Paleontológico Ernesto Bachmann** ① *civic centre, T0299-4901230, daily 0800-2100, 0900-1900 in low season, US$0.70*, displays the fossils of a giant carnivore (*Giganotosaurus carolinii*), guides in museum give good tours. The tourist office organizes guided tours to the 20-km long, 80-m high Cañón Escondido (or Coria) to see dinosaur footprints, three hours, US$5.

Zapala → *Phone code: 02942. Colour map 8, grid C2. Population: 35,000.*

Zapala, 185 km west of Neuquén, has an excellent geology museum, **Museo Mineralógico Dr Juan Olsacher**① *Etcheluz 52 (by bus terminal), 0900-1500, Sat-Sun 1600-2000, free*. Among the collections of minerals, fossils, shells and rocks, is a complete crocodile jaw, believed to be 80 million years old, and the largest ever turtle shell found from the Jurassic. There is an airport, an *ACA* service station, Km 1399 Ruta 22. **Tourist office** ① *Av Mayor Torres y San Martín, T02942-421132, summer Mon-Fri 0700-1930, Sat-Sun 0800-1300, 1600-1900.*

● Sleeping

Neuquén *p177*

AL Del Comahue, Av Argentina 377, T443 2040, www.hoteldelcomahue.com. 4-star, extremely comfortable, spa, pool, good service, excellent restaurant, 1900 Cuatro.

A Hostal del Caminante, Ruta 22, Km 1227, 13 km southwest of Neuquén, towards Zapala, T444 0118, www.hostaldelcaminante.com. A comfortable suburban place among fruit plantations with garden, pool and restaurant.

C Alcorta, Alcorta 84, T442 2652. Breakfast, TV in rooms, also flats for 4, good value.

C Royal, Av Argentina 143, T448 8902, www.royalhotel.com.ar. Modern, with parking, breakfast,.

D Res Inglés, Félix San Martín 534, T442 2252. Convenient, no breakfast, good value.

El Chocón *p178*

B La Posada del Dinosaurio, lakeshore, Villa El Chocón, Costa del Lago, Barrio 1, T0299-490 1200, www.posadadinosaurio.com.ar. With breakfast, comfortable, modern, all rooms with lake view.

Zapala *p178*

C Hue Melén, Brown 929, T422414. Good value, decent rooms, restaurant with best food in town.

D Coliqueo, Etcheluz 159, opposite bus terminal, T421308. Convenient and good.

D Pehuén, Elena de la Vega y Etcheluz, 1 block from bus terminal, T423135. Comfortable, recommended. There's also a municipal campsite.

● Eating

Neuquén *p177*

¶ **Anónima**, Av Olascoaga y Félix San Martín. Supermarket with *patio de comidas* (food hall).

¶ **El Reencuentro**, Alaska 6451. Delicious *parrilla*, popular, warm atmosphere.

¶ **La Birra**, Santa Fe 23. Lots of choice,

welcoming, chic, modern.

¶ **Tutto al Dente**, Alberdi 49. Tasty homemade pasta and good value set meals.

● Transport

Neuquén *p177*

Air Airport 7 km west of centre, T444 0244, www.anqn.com.ar. Bus **Centenario**, US$0.40 (with bus card), taxi US$4. AR/Austral flies to **Buenos Aires** and **Comodoro Rivadavia**; LADE flies to **Bariloche, Chapelco** and **Zapala**. Schedules change frequently.

Bus Terminal at Planas y Solalique, on Ruta 22, 4 km west of town. Buses US$0.35-0.70; taxi US$2.70. About a dozen companies to **Buenos Aires** daily, 12-16 hrs, US$25-35. To **Zapala** daily, 3 hrs, US$5. To **Junín de los Andes**, 5 hrs, US$9, many companies. To **San Martín de los Andes**, 6 hrs, US$12. To **Bariloche**, 7 companies, 5-6 hrs, US$13-16, sit on left. To **Mendoza**, TAC, daily, 12-13 hrs, US$23-31. To **Chile**: to **Temuco**, Igi-Llaima and El Valle, 12-14 hrs, US$25.

Zapala *p178*

Bus 3 companies to **San Martín de los Andes**, 3-4 hrs, US$10, via Junín de los Andes. To **Bariloche**, change at San Martín. To **Temuco** (Chile) all year, various companies, 10 hrs, daily between them, US$20. Buy Chilean pesos before leaving.

● Directory

Neuquén *p177*

Airline offices AR/Austral, Santa Fe 52, T442 2409/0810-2228 6527. **Banks** Lots of ATMs on Av Argentina. *Casas de Cambio*: Pullman, Alcorta 144, Exterior, San Martín 23. **Internet and telephones** At lots of *locutorios* everywhere in centre. **Post offices** Rivadavia y Santa Fe.

Parque Nacional Lanín

ⓘ US$4 to enter park (discount with student/teacher card). Helpful advice on walks from guardaparques at the entrance and at Puerto Canoa. Lanín National Park office, Frey 749, San Martín de los Andes, on main plaza, T429004, Mon-Fri 0800-1300, helpful but maps poor. Helpful information in Spanish is available from www.parque nacionallanin.gov.ar. Bus transport into the park is tricky, with services usually running to Lago Huechulafquen from San Martín de los Andes with Ko Ko Bus, but the timetable varies from year to year.

This beautiful, large park has sparkling lakes, wooded mountain valleys and one of Argentina's most striking peaks, the snow capped Lanín Volcano. The lakes of **Huechulafquen** and **Paimún** are unspoilt, beautiful, and easily accessible for superb walking and fishing, with three *hosterías* and blissful free camping all along the lakeside. From Puerto Canoa there is a boat excursion to **Lago Epulafquen** on the catamaran **José Julián** ⓘ T421038, www.cata maranjosejulian.com.ar, summer only (Dec-Mar), several daily, US$8, some refreshments available on board. Geologically, Lanín Volcano is one of the youngest of the Andes; it is extinct and one of the world's most beautiful mountains. It's a challenging and popular climb, starting near Seccional de Guardaparques (VHF 155675 or T491270) at Tromen pass where you must register and all climbing equipment and experience are checked. Crampons and ice-axe are essential, as is protection against strong, cold winds. There are three *refugios*, the first of which is a 5-hour walk. It's a 6-7 hour walk to the base of the volcano and back. Before setting off, seek advice from Lanín National Park office.

Border with Chile: the Tromen Pass

Formalities are carried out at the Argentine side of the Tromen Pass (Chileans call it Mamuil Malal). This route runs through glorious scenery to Pucón (135 km) on Lago Villarrica (Chile). It is less developed than the Huahum and Samoré (Puyehue) routes further south, and definitely not usable during heavy rain or snow (June to mid-November, phone to check: gendarmería, T491270, or customs, T492163). Parts are narrow and steep; it is unsuitable for bicycles. (Details of the Chilean side are given under Puesco, The Lake District) There is a campsite at Puesto Tromen (though very windy), but take food as there is only one basic shop at the pass. The international bus may not pick up passengers at Tromen or on the Chilean part of the route.

Junín de los Andes → Phone code: 02972. Colour map 8, grid B4. Population: 9,000.

Known as the trout capital of Argentina, Junín de los Andes is a relaxed, pretty town on the broad Río Chimehuín, a less touristy option than San Martín, with many trout-filled rivers and lakes nearby, and the best base for trekking in Parque Nacional Lanín. Its small **Museo Salesiano** ⓘ Ginés Ponte y Nogueira, Mon-Fri 0900-1230, 1430-1930, Sat 0900-1230, has a collection of items from the Mapuche culture and there are impressive sculptures at **Vía Christi** on the hill opposite ⓘ US$0.65. **Tourist office** ⓘ Plaza at Col Suárez y Padre Milanesio, T02972-491160, turismo@jdeandes.com.ar. Open summer 0800-2200, Mar-Nov 0800-2100.

San Martín de los Andes → Phone code: 02972 .Colour map 8, grid C1. Pop: 22,000.

This picturesque and upmarket tourist town, 40 km southwest of Junín, with its chocolate-box, chalet-style architecture, is spectacularly set at the east end of Lago Lacar. Mirador Bandurrias, 45-minute walk from the centre offers good views. There is excellent skiing on Cerro Chapelco (with varied summer activities for kids), and facilities for water skiing, windsurfing and sailing on Lago Lácar. The **tourist office** ⓘ main plaza, San Martín y Rosas 790, T02972-427347, www.smandes.gov.ar, 0800-2100 all year, has maps, accommodation lists, prices on wall board, very busy in summer, advisable to go early. Surrounded by lakes and mountains to explore, the most popular excursions are south along the **Seven Lakes Drive** (see below), north to the thermal baths at **Termas de Lahuen-Co** (also reached on foot after two days from Lagos Huechulafquen and Paimún) and to **Lagos Lolog** and **Lácar**. There's a *ripio* track along the north side of Lago Lácar with beaches and rafting at **Hua Hum**, and along the south to quieter and beautiful **Quila Quina**. Two good walks from Quila Quina: along a nature trail to a lovely waterfall, or a two-hour walk to a quiet Mapuche community in the hills above the lake. Boats from San Martín's pier, T428427, to Hua Hum three daily in season, US$18 return; to Quila Quina, hourly, 30 minutes, US$8 return. Cyclists can complete a circuit around Lago Lácar, or take the cable car up to Chapelco and come back down the paths.

Border with Chile: the Hua Hum Pass

A *ripio* road along the north shore of Lago Lácar through the Lanín National Park crosses the border to Puerto Pirihueico, where a boat crosses Lago Pirihueico; bikes can be taken (for vehicle reservations and information, www.panguipulli.cl/pasohuahum/index.html). Border open 0800-2100 in summer, 0800-2000 winter. *Ko Ko* bus goes to the pass (usually open all year round), two hours, and *Lafit* goes up to Panguipulli (Chile), weekly off-season, US$15, check terminal for schedule. For connections from Puerto Pirihueico to Panguipulli and beyond, see Chile chapter.

● Sleeping

Lago Huechulafquen *p179*

A Huechulafquen, Ruta 61, Km 55, T02972-427598. Best, half board, comfortable cabin-like rooms, gardens, expert fishing guide, restaurant open to non-residents in high season.

Camping Several sites in beautiful surroundings on Lagos Huechulafquen and Paimún in Parque Nacional Lanín. The most recommended are: **Bahía Canicul** (48 km from Junín), **Camping Lafquen-co** (53 km from Junín) and **Piedra Mala** (65 km from Junín).

Junín de los Andes *p179*

L Río Dorado Lodge & Fly shop, Pedro Illera 448, T491548, www.riodorado.com.ar. Comfortable rooms in log cabin-style fishing lodge, big American breakfast, pricey, great for anglers, good fly shop, lovely gardens, attentive service.

B Caleufu Travel Lodge, JA Roca 1323 (on Ruta 234), T492757, www.caleufutravellodge.com.ar. Excellent value, welcoming, very good rooms, neat garden, also comfortable apartments for up to 5 people. Owner Jorge speaks English. Recommended.

C Hostería Chimehuín, Col Suárez y 25 de Mayo, T491132, www.interpatagonia.com/hosteriachimehuin. Cosy, quaint old fishing lodge by the river, closed May. Recommended.

C Milla Piuké, Av Los Pehuenes y JA Roca (on Ruta 234), T492378, millapiuke@fronteradigital.net.ar. Most delightful and welcoming, comfortable, stylish rooms and apartments for families. Good breakfast included. Highly recommended.

D Posada Pehuén, Col Suárez 560, T491569, posadapehuen@fronteradigital.net.ar. A peaceful bed and breakfast with comfortable rooms, pretty garden, charming owners, good value.

D Res Marisa, JM de Rosas 360 (on Ruta 234), T491175, residencialmarisa@deandes.com.ar. A simple place with helpful owners, with bath, TV, breakfast US$1 extra, very good value.

E pp La Casa de Marita y Aldo, 25 de Mayo 371, T491042, casademaritayaldo@hotmail.com. A cheery and popular family house with basic accommodation.

Camping There are many sites in the area with two good ones in town, both by the river: **Mallín Laura Vicuña**, T491149, and **La Isla**, T492029, both good.

San Martín de los Andes *p179*

Single rooms are scarce. There are 2 high seasons, when rates are much higher: Jan/Feb and Jul/Aug. There are many excellent *cabañas* for families on the hill at the top of Perito Moreno. **Inmobiliaria Stordiau**, San Martín 1344, T421220, www.rohde turismo.com.ar. Recommended estate agent for renting houses, cabins and apartments per day. When everywhere else is full, Tourist Office provides a list of private addresses in high season.

L La Casa de Eugenia, Coronel Díaz, T427206, www.lacasadeeugenia.com.ar. B&B in a beautifuly renovated 1900s house, very welcoming and relaxing, cosy rooms, huge breakfast, charming hosts. Highly recommended.

L Las Lengas, Col Pérez 1175, T427659, www.hosterialaslengas.com.ar. Attractive spacious rooms, warm relaxing atmosphere with pool in nice garden, peaceful part of town.

AL La Cheminée, Gral Roca y Mariano Moreno, T427617, www.hosterialacheminee.com.ar. Cosy cottage-like rooms, breakfast included, but no restaurant, overpriced in high season but otherwise good, English spoken.

A Del Viejo Esquiador, San Martín 1242, T427690, www.delviejoesquiador.com. Very comfortable, good beds, in traditional hunting lodge style, excellent service. Recommended.

A Hostal del Esquiador, Col Rhode 975, T427674. Well decorated rooms, lovely sitting room, good service, free internet. Great value low season.

B La Masía, Obeid 811, T427879, www.hosterialamasia.com.ar. Spacious, high-ceilinged chalet-style rooms, cosy bar and lounge.

C Anay, Capitán Drury 841, T427514, www.interpatagonia.com/anay. Excellent value, central, cosy house with welcoming owners. No credit cards; closed in Dec.

C Casa Alta, Obeid 659, T427456. The home of charming multilingual owners, 'beyond comparison and fantastic' (closed in low season), lovely gardens, delicious breakfast. Book in advance.

C Hostería Las Lucarnas, Col Pérez 632, T427085, hosterialaslucarnas@hotmail.com. Central, pretty, simple comfortable rooms, English spoken, good value.

D Hostal del Lago, Col Rhode 854, T427598, www.hostal-del-lago.com.ar. Relaxed homely place, basic bathrooms, good breakfast included, pretty garden.

D Rukalhue, Juez del Valle 682 (3 blocks from terminal), T427431, www.rukalhue.com.ar. Budget choice with a rather institutional atmosphere, comfortable, well-heated, though thin-walled dorms and **C** double rooms with a poor breakfast, basic kitchen.

D-E pp Hosteria Bärenhaus, Los Alamos 156, Barrio Chapelco (8370), T/F422775, www.baerenhaus.com. 5 km outside town, free pick-up from bus terminal and airport. Welcoming young owners, very comfortable rooms with heating, English and German spoken. Recommended.

E pp Puma, A Fosbery 535 (north along Rivadavia, 2 blocks beyond bridge), T422443, www.pumahostel.com.ar. Discount for HI and ISIC members, small dorms with bath and **C** double room with view, laundry, kitchen facilities, bikes for hire, very well run by mountain guide owner, very nice, good value. Recommended.

Camping ACA Camping, Av Koessler 2176, T429430, with hot water and laundry facilities, also *cabañas*. **Camping Quila Quina**, T426919. Lovely site on a stream near Lago Lácar, 18 km from San Martín, with beaches, immaculate toilet blocks, restaurant and shop, access to boats and treks. Open only in summer and Easter.

🍴 Eating

Junín de los Andes *p179*
🍴 **Ruca Hueney**, Col Suárez y Milanesio, T491113. Good steak, trout and pasta dishes.
🍴 **La Posta de Junín**, JM de Rosas 160 (on Ruta 234), T492303. A recommended *parrilla* with good service and wine list; also trout, pizza and pastas.

San Martín de los Andes *p179*
🍴 **Avataras**, Tte Ramayón 765, T427104. Open only Thu-Sat from 2030, inspired, imaginative menu with cuisine from all over the world, from fondue to satay, fine wines, elegant surroundings. An excellent treat. Cheaper meals at its pub.
🍴 **El Regional**, Villegas 965, T425326. Popular for regional specialities – smoked trout, venison,

wild boar, pâtés and hams, El Bolsón's homemade beer, cheerful German-style decor.
🍴 **La Tasca**, Mariano Moreno 866, T428663. Recommended for its venison, trout and home made pastas with a varied wine list.
🍴 **Pura Vida**, Villegas 745. Small and welcoming, the only vegetarian place, serving tasty soups, also fish and chicken dishes, including a delicious chop suey with brown rice. For non-smokers and no credit cards.
🍴 **Ku**, San Martín 1053, T427039. Intimate atmosphere for *parrilla*, pastas and delicious mountain specialities, excellent service and wine list.
🍴 **La Costa del Pueblo**, Costanera opposite pier, T429289. Overlooking the lake, huge range of pastas, chicken and trout dishes, generous portions, good service, cheerful. Meal of the day for US$4 for 2 courses. Recommended.
🍴 **Tío Pico**, San Martín y Capitán Drury. Good lunches and drinks at this great bar/café.

🛍 Shopping

San Martín de los Andes *p179*
Abuela Goye, San Martín 807, sells delicious chocolates and runs a good café serving gorgeous cakes and delicious ice creams.
Mamusia, San Martín 601, is also a recommended chocolate shop, also sells home-made jams.

⛰ Activities and tours

San Martín de los Andes *p179*
Cycling
Many places in the centre rent mountain and normal bikes, reasonable prices, maps provided.
HG Rodados, San Martín 1061, T427345, hgrodados@smandes.com.ar. Arranges excursions, rents mountain bikes, US$8 per day, also spare parts and expertise.

Fishing
In addition to licence, US$3.50 extra per day for trolling and US$1.70 for fishing in Boca del Chimehuin or Río Correntoso. Contact the tourist office for a list of fishing guides or the National Park office.
Jorge Cardillo Pesca, Villegas 1061, T428372. Fly shop, sells equipment, fishing licences and offers excursions.
Flotadas Chimehuin, at Junín de los Andes, T491313. Offers fully inclusive fishing packages with expert bilingual guides.
Orvis, Gral Villegas 835, T425892, www.sanmartinorvis.com.ar. Fly shop, sells equipment and offer fishing excursions.
Juan Carlos Aráuz, M Moreno 1193, T427376. Fishing guide.

Skiing

Chapelco has 29 km of pistes, many of them challenging, with an overall drop of 730 m. Very good slopes and snow conditions from Jul to Sep make this a popular resort with foreigners and wealthier Argentines. To get to the slopes, take the bus from San Martín, US$2 return. Details, passes, equipment hire from office at San Martín y Elordi, T427845, www.chapelco.com. At the foot of the mountain are a restaurant and a café, with 4 more restaurants and a lodge on the mountain and a small café at the top.

Tours

Prices for conventional tours are similar in most agencies: one day's rafting at Hua Hum, US$33 ; Villa la Angostura via Seven Lakes, US$18; Lakes Huechulafquen and Paimún, US$18, and many other options. Most tours operate from 2 Jan.
El Claro, Col Díaz 751, T429363, www.elclaro turismo.com.ar. For conventional tours, horse riding, mountain biking and trekking.
El Refugio, Pérez 830, just off San Martín, upstairs, T425140, www.elrefugioturismo.com.ar. Bilingual guides, conventional tours, boat trips, also mountain bike hire, rafting, horse riding and trekking. Recommended.
Lanín Expediciones, San Martín 851, oficina 5, T429799, www.laninexpediciones.com. Adventure tourism for beginners or experts, from a 3-hr walk near San Martín, winter night walks in the forest, rafting in Aluminé, trekking in Lanín area, a 3-day ascent of the volcano, and climbs to 4,700-m Domuyo peak.

⊙ Transport

Junín de los Andes *p179*
Air Chapelco airport 19 km southwest towards San Martín, served by **AR** from Buenos Aires and

LADE (office in bus terminal, San Martín de los Andes, T427672) from Buenos Aires, Esquel, Neuquén and Bariloche.
Bus Terminal at Olavarría y F San Martín, T492038. To **San Martín**, **Centenario**, **Castelli** and others, 30 mins, US$2. To **Buenos Aires**, 19-21 hrs, US$35, US$50 *coche cama*. To **Temuco** (5 hrs) and **Valdivia** (via Paso Tromen), 6-7 hrs, US$20, **Igi Llaima** and **Empresa San Martín**. **Castelli** goes daily in Jan-Feb (Sun, Mon, Wed, Fri in Dec) to **Lago Paimún** (Parque Nacional Lanín), 2 hrs, US$4, also **Cooperativa Litrán** daily in summer.

San Martín de los Andes *p179*
Air Chapelco airport, 23 km away.
See under Junín de los Andes above.
Bus Terminal at Villegas 251 y Juez del Valle, T427044. Café, left luggage (US$0.70), toilet facilities, *kiosko*, *locutorio*. To **Buenos Aires**, 20 hrs, US$55 *coche cama*, daily, 6 companies. To **Villa La Angostura**, Albus 3 a day, US$6.75. To **Bariloche**, 3½-4 hrs, US$10 (not via 7 Lagos), several companies. **To Chile**: Temuco with **Empresa San Martín**, T427294 (Mon, Wed, Fri) and **Igi Llaima**, T427750 (Tue, Thu, Sat), US$15, heavily booked in summer.

❶ Directory

San Martín de los Andes *p179*
Banks Many ATMs on San Martín. Exchange at Banco de la Nación, San Martín 687, Banco Francés, San Martín y Sarmiento and Andina, Capitán Drury 876, which also changes TCs (3% commission) Banco de la Provincia de Neuquén, Obeid y Belgrano. **Medical Services** Hospital Ramón Carrillo, San Martín y Coronel Rodhe, T427211. **Police station** Belgrano 635, T427300, or T101. **Post Office** Gral Roca y Pérez, Mon-Fri 0800-1300, Sat 0900-1300.

Parque Nacional Nahuel Huapi

ⓘ *US$4 payable at Nahuel Huapi National Park office, at San Martín 24, Bariloche, T02944-423111, daily 0900-1400, www.parquesnacionales.gov.ar.*
Covering 709,000 ha and stretching along the Chilean border, this is the oldest National Park in Argentina. With lakes, rivers, glaciers, waterfalls, torrents, rapids, valleys, forest, bare mountains and snow-clad peaks, there are many kinds of wild animals living in the region, including the pudú, the endangered huemul (both deer) as well as river otters, cougars and guanacos. Bird life, particularly swans, geese and ducks, is abundant. The outstanding feature is the splendour of the lakes. The largest is **Lago Nahuel Huapi** (*Altitude 767 m*), 531 sq km and 460 m deep in places, particularly magnificent to explore by boat since the lake is very irregular in shape and long arms of water, or *brazos*, stretch far into the land. On a peninsula in the lake is exquisite **Parque Nacional Los Arrayanes** (see below). There are many islands: the largest is **Isla Victoria**, with its idyllic hotel. Trout and salmon have been introduced.

North of Villa La Angostura, Lagos Correntoso and Espejo both offer stunning scenery, and tranquil places to stay and walk. Navy blue Lago Traful, a short distance to the northeast, can be reached by a road which follows the Río Limay through the Valle Encantado, with its fantastic rock formations or directly from Villa La Angostura. **Villa Traful** is the perfect place to escape to, with fishing, camping, and walking. There's a tourist office at the eastern edge of town, T02944-479019, www.villatraful.info. Spectacular mountains surround the city of Bariloche, great trekking and skiing country. The most popular walks are described in the Bariloche section. South of Lago Nahuel Huapi, Lagos Mascardi, Guillelmo and Gutiérrez offer horse riding, trekking and rafting along the Río Manso. See page 195 for accommodation along their shores.

The well-maintained *ripio* road known as the **'Seven Lakes Drive'** runs south from San Martín to Bariloche via Lago Hermoso and Villa La Angostura and passes beautiful unspoilt stretches of water, framed by steep, forested mountains. There are several places to stay, open summer only. An alternative route, fully paved and faster, but less scenic is via Junín de los Andes and **Confluencia** on Ruta 40 (ACA service station and a hotel, also motel *El Rancho* just before Confluencia). Round-trip excursions along the Seven Lakes route, 5 hours, are operated by several companies, but it's better in your own transport.

Villa La Angostura → *Phone code 02944. Colour map 8, grid C1. Population: 7,000.*

This pretty town, 80 km northwest of Bariloche on Lago Nahuel Huapi, is a popular holiday resort with wealthier Argentines and there are countless restaurants, hotels and *cabaña* complexes around the centre, **El Cruce** and along Ruta 231 between Correntoso and Puerto Manzano. The picturesque port, known as **La Villa**, is 3 km away at the neck of the Quetrihué Peninsula. At its end is **Parque Nacional Los Arrayanes**, with 300 year old specimens of the rare *arrayán* tree, whose flaky bark is cinnamon coloured. The park can be reached on foot or by bike (12 km each way; for a return walk start from 0900 to 1400), or you could take the boat back. Catamarans run at least twice daily in summer from Bahía Mansa and Bahía Brava, down at La Villa, US$8 one way (plus the US$4 National Park entry fee); tickets sold at Hotel Angostura. See also below for tours by boat from Bariloche. There is a small ski resort at **Cerro Bayo** (www.cerrobayoweb.com) with summer activities too. The **tourist office** is opposite the bus terminal ① *Av Siete Lagos 93, T02944-494124, www.villalaangostura.gov.ar. Open high season 0800-2100, low season 0800-2000.* Good maps with accommodation marked.

● Sleeping

Parque Nacional Nahuel Huapi *p182*
B pp Hostería Los Siete Lagos (27 km north of Villa La Angostura), T02944-15497152, a charming, simple place run by very knowledgeable people about the region, on the shore of Lago Correntoso, great views and the best *tortas fritas* in the region, with the breakfast, excellent restaurant, home-made bread for sale.
Camping Several free campsites without facilities along the route, including the lovely Lago Espejo Camping, open all year, US$1 pp, no showers but toilets, drinking water and fireplaces. Recommended.

Villa Traful
D Cabañas Aiken, T02944-479048, www.aiken.com.ar.Well-decorated *cabañas* in beautiful surroundings near the lake (close to the tourist office), each with its own *parrillada*, also has a restaurant. Recommended.
D Hostería Villa Traful, T479005, www.hosteria villatraful.com. A cosy house with a tea room by the lake, also *cabañas* for 4-6 people, pretty

gardens, good value. The owner's son, Andrés organizes fishing and boat trips.
F Vulcanche Hostel, T02944-494015, www.vul canche.com. Chaelt-style hostel in gardens with good views, with good dorms and **D** cabins, including breakfast, large park for camping (US$4 pp), also cabins. Discounts to HI members.

Villa La Angostura *p183*
There are many pricey hotels and *cabañas* here; www.villalaangostura.gov.ar has an extensive list.
L Las Balsas, on Bahía Las Balsas (signposted from Av Arrayanes), T494308, www.las balsas.com. Reputed to be one of the best hotels in the country, lakeside, warm, relaxed, impeccable service, fine cuisine in the restaurant using local produce, indoor and outdoor pools, spa, trips arranged. Highly recommended.
A Hostal Las Nieves, Av Siete Lagos 980 (1.5 km west of El Cruce), T494573, www.las nieves.com. Small, good location with garden, very comfortable, heated swimming pool and sauna, good restaurant, English spoken, helpful.

A **Portal de Piedra**, Ruta 231, Km 56 y Río Bonito (at Puerto Manzano), T494278, www.portal depiedra.com. Small, attractive *hostería* and tea room in the woods, with heated pool and a small restaurant (guests only) open in high season.

A **Hotel Angostura**, Nahuel Huapi 1911, at La Villa, T494224. Built in 1938, this traditional hotel run by Familia Cilley since then has a lovely lakeside setting and a good restaurant and tea room, *Viejo Coihue*. There is a cabin for 6 (L) that has probably the most beautiful setting in the region. Boat excursions along the nearby shore are arranged.

C **Río Bonito**, Topa Topa 260, T494110, riobonito@ciudad.com.ar. 2 blocks from terminal, homely, quiet, comfortable, great breakfasts. Recommended.

C **Verena's Haus**, Los Taiques 268, T494467, www.verenashaus.com.ar. Adults and non-smokers only, German and English spoken, cosy, garden. Recommended.

F pp **Bajo Cero**, Av 7 Lagos al 1200, T495454, www.bajocerohostel.com. HI affiliated, well-situated, rooms for 2-4 with bath, linen, breakfast included.

F pp **Hostel La Angostura**, Barbagelata 157, 150 m up road behind tourist office, T494834, www.hostellaangostura.com.ar. A warm, luxurious hostel, all small dorms have bathrooms, breakfast included, good **C** doubles, young welcoming owners organize trips and rent bikes for US$6 a day too. HI discounts. Recommended.

F pp **Italian Hostel**, Los Maquis 215 (5 blocks from terminal), T494376, www.italian hostel.com.ar. Welcoming, small, with dorms and **D** doubles, rustic, functional and nice, run by a biker who closes the place in May-Jun. Fireplace and orchard from where you can pick berries and herbs for your meals. Recommended.

Camping **Osa Mayor**, signposted off main road, close to town, T494304, www.camping osamayor.com.ar. Well designed leafy and level site, all facilities, also rustic *cabañas* and dorms, helpful owner.

Eating

Parque Nacional Nahuel Huapi *p182*
Villa Traful

¶ **Aiken**, Villa Traful. Simple meals, excellent sandwiches with home-made bread and more expensive trout dishes. Open all year round.

¶ **Ñancu Lahuen**, Villa Traful. A chocolate shop, tea room, and restaurant serving local trout. Delightful and cosy, with big open fire, delicious food and reasonably priced.

Villa La Angostura *p183*

¶¶¶ **Tinto Bistró**, Blv Nahuel Huapi 34, T494924. An interesting, eclectic menu, very chic and trendy, great wine list. Good fun people-watching in season.

¶¶ **Los Troncos**, Av Arrayanes 67, T495035. Great local dishes, fabulous cakes and puddings. Warm atmosphere and cosy setting, live music at weekends.

¶¶ **Nativa Café**, Av Arrayanes 198. Relaxed and welcoming, excellent pizzas, huge salads, good place to hang out. Recommended.

¶¶ **Rincón Suizo**, Av Arrayanes 44. High season only, delicious regional specialities with a Swiss twist.

¶ **El Esquiador**, Las Retamas 146. If on a budget, this good, popular *parrilla* has an all-you-can-eat choice of cold starters, a main meal and a dessert.

¶ **Gran Nevada**, Av Arrayanes opposite Nativa. Jolly place for cheap *parrilla*, and *ñoquis*.

¶ **Hora Cero**, Av Arrayanes 45. Warm atmosphere and live music at weekends, popular, big range of excellent pizzas, *pizza libre* (as much as you can eat for US$2) on Wed and Sat is a great deal.

¶ **TemaTyCo**, Ruta 231 y Mirlo, T475211. Chic tearoom with an amazing range of teas and delicious cakes.

▲▲ Activities and tours

Villa La Angostura *p183*
There is lots to do here: bicycle hire (US$7 per day) and mountain biking (**Free Bikes**, Las Fucsias y Los Notros, T495047, info@free bikes.com.ar), boat trips, canopying (**Canopy Villa la Angostura**, Curruhué y Melinquina, T1541 7817, www.canopyargentina.com.ar), climbing, fishing, horse riding (US$10 per hr) and trekking (**Alma Sur**, T1556 4724, www.almasur.com).

⊖ Transport

Villa La Angostura *p183*
Bus Terminal at Av 7 Lagos y Av Arrayanes, opposite ACA service station. Urban buses **15 de Mayo**, US$0.35, link El Cruce (main bus stop on main road, 50 m from tourist office), La Villa, Correntoso and Puerto Manzano, and go up to Lago Espejo (US$0.85) and Cerro Bayo (US$1) in high season. To/from **Bariloche**, 1 hr, US$4, several companies. To **San Martín de los Andes**, 2½ hrs, US$7-9. Via Bariloche/El Valle goes to **Osorno**, 3½ hrs, and **Puerto Montt** (Chile), 5½ hrs, US$20; **Andesmar** and **Tas Choapa** go to **Valdivia**, US$18.

Bariloche and around → *Phone code: 02944. Colour map 8, grid C1. Population: 89,000.*

Beautifully situated on the south shore of Lago Nahuel Huapi, at the foot of Cerro Otto, San Carlos de Bariloche is an attractive tourist town and the best centre for exploring the National Park. There are many good hotels, restaurants and chocolate shops among its chalet-style stone and wooden buildings. Others along the lake shore have splendid views. Heaving with visitors in summer months, it's less busy in March-April when the forests are in their glory.

Ins and outs
Getting there and around The airport is 15 km east of town, the bus and train stations 3 km east. At peak holiday times (July and December-January), Bariloche is very busy with holidaymakers and students. The best times to visit are in the spring (September-November) and autumn (March-April), or February for camping and walking and August for skiing.
▶▶ *For more detailed information see Transport, page 192.*

Tourist information Oficina Municipal de Turismo, Centro Cívico, p 6, T429850, www.barilochepatagonia.info. Daily 0900-2100. Has full list of city buses, and details of hikes and campsites in the area and is helpful in finding accommodation. Very useful for information on hiking is *Club Andino Bariloche* (*CAB*), 20 de Febrero 30, T422266, www.clubandino.org. 0900-1300, plus 1600-2100 high season. Good *Infotrekking* maps (1:50,000, US$4.50), *Guía de Sendas y Picadas* maps (1:100,000, US$3.50 and 1:50,000, US$1.70) and a guidebook of paths, US$5, for sale. When Club Andino is closed, obtain more general information at the Nahuel Huapi National Park office (see address under Parque Nacional Nahuel Huapi, above). The *Traveller's Guru* is a free paper available at many points throughout Patagonia, written in English by travellers with valuable information for backpackers.

Sights
At the heart of the city is the **Centro Cívico**, built in 'Bariloche Alpine style' and separated from the lake by Avenida Rosas. It includes the **Museo de La Patagonia** which, apart from the region's fauna (stuffed), has indigenous artefacts and material from the lives of the first white settlers. ① *Tue-Fri 1000-1230, 1400-1900, Mon and Sat 1000-1300, US$1.* Next to it is

Bariloche

Sleeping ●
1004 1 *A1*
Albergue El Gaucho 2 *B1*
Cristal 6 *A2*
Edelweiss 4 *A1*
Familia Arko 19 *B1*
Hostel 41 Below 22 *A1*
Hostería Güemes 9 *B1*
Hostería Tirol 7 *A1*
La Bolsa 11 *B2*
La Pastorella 12 *B1*
Marco Polo Inn 10 *A1*
Patagonia Andina 15 *B1*
Periko's 16 *B1*
Piuké 17 *A3*
Premier 18 *A2*
Ruca Hueney 20 *B2*
Tres Reyes 21 *A2*

Eating ●
El Boliche de Alberto 1 *B2*
Familia Weiss 3 *A2*
Friends 4 *A2*
Jauja 5 *B2*
Kandahar 6 *B1*
La Alpina 2 *A2*
La Jirafa 7 *A2*
La Marmite 8 *A2*
Pilgrim 9 *A2*
Rock Chicken 10 *A2*
Simoca 11 *A2*
Vegetariano 12 *B1*

Biblioteca Sarmiento ① *Mon-Fri, 0900-1900 (closed 1-15 Jan)*, a library and cultural centre. The **cathedral**, built in 1946, lies six blocks east of here, with the main commercial area on Mitre in between. Opposite the main entrance to the cathedral there is a huge rock left in this spot by a glacier during the last glacial period. On the lakeshore is the **Museo Paleontológico** ① *12 de Octubre y Sarmiento, Mon-Sat 1600-1900, US$0.70*, which displays fossils mainly from Patagonia, including an ichthyosaur and replicas of a giant spider and shark's jaws.

Around Bariloche

One of South America's most important ski centres is just a few kilometres southwest from Bariloche, at **Cerro Catedral** (see Activities and tours, page 191). You can take a boat trip from Puerto Pañuelo (Km 25.5, bus 10, 20 or 21, or transfer arranged with tour operator, US$5.50) across Lago Nahuel Huapi to **Isla Victoria** and **Bosque de Arrayanes**, on the Quetrihué Peninsula; full or a half-day excursion (fewer options in low season), US$25 plus National Park entry (with **Turisur**, see address below, on the 1937 boat *Modesta Victoria*) or US$18 plus Park entry (with **Espacio**, on modern *Cau Cau*, T431372, www.islavictoriayarrayanes.com), take picnic lunch if you don't want to buy food sold on board. The all-day boat trip to **Puerto Blest**, in native Valdivian rainforest, is highly recommended. From Puerto Pañuelo, sail down to Puerto Blest (hotel, restaurant), continuing by short bus ride to Puerto Alegre and again by launch to Puerto Frías. From Puerto Blest, walk through forest to the Cascada and Laguna de los Cántaros (1½ hrs). Transfer to Puerto Pañuelo can be arranged from the agency; **Catedral Turismo** (see address below), US$18 plus Park entry and US$5 extra if going to Puerto Frías.

An old train (1912) leaves three times a week in summer from Bariloche railway station for an eight-hour excursion with two stops at Ñirihuau and Los Juncos (for birdwatching) and a walk up to **Cerro Elefante**, US$16-23 (lunch optional), T423858, www.trenhistoricoavapor.com.ar. Some tour operators offer an excursion to El Maitén, from where the Old Patagonian Express (La Trochita) runs a tourist service a few days a week (see under El Bolsón and Esquel).

Avenida Bustillo runs parallel to the lakeshore west of Bariloche, with access to the mountains above. At Km 5, a cable car (teleférico) goes up to **Cerro Otto** (1,405 m) with its revolving restaurant and splendid views. Transport and other details under Activities and tours (page 191). At Km 17.7 a chairlift goes up to **Cerro Campanario** (1,049 m) ① *daily 0900-1800, 7 mins, US$5*, with fine views of Isla Victoria and Puerto Pañuelo. At Km 18.3 **Circuito Chico** begins – a 60-km circular route around Lago Moreno Oeste, past Punto Panorámico and through Puerto Pañuelo to **Llao Llao**, Argentina's most famous hotel (details on this and others

Bariloche - the road to Llao Llao

Sleeping 😴
Alaska **6**
Aldebaran **19**

El Yeti **4**
Hostería Santa Rita **8**
Katy **10**

La Caleta **11**
Llao-Llao **20**
Petunia **14**

on Avenida Bustillo in Sleeping, below.) Take bus No 20, 45 mins, US$1, a half-day drive or tour with agency, or full day's cycle. You could also extend this circuit, returning via **Colonia Suiza** and **Cerro Catedral** (2,388 m) one of South America's most important ski centres. Whole-day trip to **Lagos Gutiérrez** and **Mascardi** and beautiful **Pampa Linda** at the base of mighty **Cerro Tronador** (3,478 m), visiting the strange **Ventisquero Negro** (black glacier), highly recommended. Several companies run 12-hour minibus excursions to San Martín de los Andes along the famous **Seven Lakes Drive**, returning via Paso Córdoba and the Valle Encantado, but these involve few stops.

Border with Chile

The Samoré (formerly Puyehue) Pass   A spectacular six-hour drive through the pass 125 km northwest of Bariloche. A good broad paved road, RN 40 then RN 231, goes around the east end of Lago Nahuel Huapi, then follows the north side of the lake through Villa La Angostura. The road is rough *ripio* from there on, with the occasional paved stretch. It passes the junction with 'Ruta de Los Siete Lagos' for San Martín at Km 90, Argentine customs (T494996) at El Rincón, Km 105, and the pass at Km 122 at an elevation of about 1,314 m. Chilean customs (T00566-4236284) is at Pajarito, Km 145, in the middle of a forest. The border is open from the second Saturday of October to 1 May, 0800-2100, winter 0900-2000 but liable to be closed after snowfalls. Chilean currency can be bought at Samoré pass customs at a reasonable rate.

Four bus companies (**El Valle, Bus Norte, Andesmar, Tas Choapa**) run daily services from Bariloche via Samoré pass to Osorno (4-6 hours, US$30) and Puerto Montt (6-7½ hours, same fare); **Andesmar** goes to Valdivia via Osorno (see Bariloche Transport below and take passport when booking). Sit on left side for best views. You can buy a ticket to the Chilean border, then another to Puerto Montt, or pay in stages in Chile, but there is little advantage in doing this.

Via Lake Todos Los Santos   The route is Bariloche to Puerto Pañuelo by road, Puerto Pañuelo to Puerto Blest by boat (1¼ hours), Puerto Blest to Puerto Alegre on Lago Frías by bus, cross the lake to Puerto Frías by boat (20 minutes), then 2 hours by road to Peulla. Leave for Petrohué in the afternoon by boat (1 hour 40 minutes), cross Lago Todos Los Santos, passing the Osorno volcano, then by bus to Puerto Montt (2 hours). This route is beautiful, but the weather is often wet. In summer a one-day journey option (*rápida*) is added to the regular two-day crossing (*normal*) that runs all-year round. **Cruce de Lagos** has the monopoly on the famous Three Lakes Crossing to Puerto Montt in Chile, US$165, and their representatives in Argentina are **Turismo Catedral** (see address below) and in Chile, **Andina del Sud**; credit

Related map
A Bariloche, p185

Lago Nahuel Huapi

Isla Huemul

Km 5

Centro Cívico
Moreno
Belgrano
Gallardo

Av Bustillo
Av de Los Pioneros

Supermarket Todo
Refugio Berghof

Cable Car
Cerro Otto
(1405m)

Onelli

To Cerro Catedral   To Lago Gutiérrez   To Lago Gutiérrez

Selva Negra 16
Tunquelén 17

Eating
Cervecería Blest 1
Il Gabbiano 4

Meli Hue 5

Walks around Bariloche

There's a network of paths in the mountains, and several refugios allowing for treks over several days. Refugios are leased by Club Andino Bariloche. On treks to refugios remember to add costs of ski lifts, buses, food at refugios and lodging (in Club Andino refugios: US$3-7 per night, plus US$1-1.70 for cooking, or US$2-4 for breakfast, US$4-7 for dinner). Take a good sleeping bag. Horseflies (*tábanos*) infest the lake shores and lower areas in summer. Among the many great treks possible here, these are recommended: From **Llao Llao** ① *getting there: bus 20 to Llao Llao*, delightful easy circuit in Valdivian (temperate) rainforest (two hours), also climb the small hill for wonderful views. Up to **Refugio López** (2,076 m) ① *getting there: bus 10 to Colonia Suiza and López, US$0.75 (check return times)*, five hours return, from southeastern tip of Lago Moreno up Arroyo López, for fabulous views. From Refugio López, extend this to 3-4 day trek via Refugio Italia, on Laguna Negra, to **Laguna Jacob** and **Refugio**

San Martín (poorly signposted, need experience). From Cerro Catedral to **Refugio Frey** (1,700 m, F pp, meals extra, camping), beautiful setting on small lake, via Arroyo Piedritas (four hours each way), or via cable car to *Refugio Lynch* and via Punta Nevada (only experienced walkers). To beautiful **Lago Gutiérrez**, 2 km downhill from Cerro Catedral, along lake shore to the road from El Bolsón and walk back to Bariloche (four hours), or Bus 50. From **Pampa Linda**, idyllic (*hosterías*, campsite), walk up to Refugio Otto Meiling (4-5 hours each way), to tranquil Laguna Ilon (5½ hrs each way), or across Paso de las Nubes to **Puerto Frías**, boat back to Bariloche (two days, check if open: closed when boggy). Bus to Pampa Linda from outside Club Andino Bariloche 0830 in summer, **Expreso Meiling**, T529875, US$10 one way or from **Transitando lo Natural** ① *20 de Febrero 25, T527926, 2¼ hours. Contact CAB for maps, guidebooks and to check walks are open (see under Tourist information).*

cards accepted. Book in advance during the high season, and beware the hard sell. For a two-day crossing, there is an overnight stop not included in the price, in Puerto Blest (**B** accommodation, half board) or in Peulla (**L** accommodation with breakfast). Details of accommodation under Peulla, Chile. Full price is charged even if only taking sections of the crossing. The only cheaper option, recommended to cyclists, is to pay US$60 for the boat trips. Summer crossing Monday-Saturday; rest of the year Monday-Friday.

The Argentine and Chilean border posts are open every day. There is an absolute ban in Chile on importing any fresh food – meat, cheese, fruit – from Argentina. Further information on border crossings in the Lake District will be found in the Chile chapter. You are strongly advised to get rid of all your Argentine pesos before leaving Argentina; it is useful to have some Chilean pesos before you cross into Chile from Bariloche, though you can buy them at a reasonable rate at the Chilean border post.

● Sleeping

Bariloche *p185, maps p185 and p186*
Prices rise in 2 peak seasons: Jul-Aug for skiing, and mid-Dec to Mar for summer holidays. If you arrive in the high season without a reservation, consult the listing published by the tourist office (address above). This selection gives lake-view, high-season prices where applicable. In low season you pay half of these prices in most cases. All those listed are recommended.

LL Llao-Llao, Av Bustillo Km 25, T448530 (in BsAs, Maipú 1300, T011-5776 7450), www.llaollao.com. Deservedly famous, superb location, complete luxury, golf course, pool, spa, water sports, restaurant.
LL Pire-Hue, Cerro Catedral, T011-4807 8200 (in Buenos Aires), www.pire-hue.com.ar. Exclusive 5-star hotel in ski resort with beautiful rooms and all facilities.

L Aldebaran, on Península San Pedro, reached from Av Bustillo Km 20.4, T465132, www.aldebaran patagonia.com. Not in chalet style, but tasteful rooms in this modern boutique hotel on the lake shore, superb views. Rustic-style restaurant, sauna and spa with outdoor pool, so you can bask under the stars. Great service from helpful bilingual staff.

L Edelweiss, San Martín 202, T445500, www.edel weiss.com.ar. 5-star with real attention to detail, excellent service, spacious comfortable rooms, indoor pool and beauty salon, Wi-Fi. *La Tavola* restaurant is excellent.

L Tunquelén, Av Bustillo, Km 24.5, T448400, www.maresur.com. 4-star, comfortable, splendid views, feels more secluded than its neighbour *Llao-Llao*, superb restaurant, attentive service.

A Cristal Mitre 355, T422002, hotelcristalres@ ciudad.com.ar. Central, charming, 60s style, TV and minibar (the superior rooms are best).

A-C Hostería Tirol, Libertad 175, T02944-426152, www.hosteriatirol.com.ar. Very neat family-run hotel just a block from the Civic Centre, with nice Tirolean touches, warm attention from the owners, Wi-Fi. Excellent value in low season.

B Tres Reyes, 12 de Octubre 135, T426121, reservas@hoteltresreyes.com. Traditional lake side hotel with spacious rooms, a bit dated, but with splendid views, cheaper to reserve on the spot than by email.

B La Caleta, Av Bustillo, Km 1.9, T443444, bungalows@bariloche.com.ar. *Cabañas* sleep 4, open fire, excellent value.

B La Pastorella, Belgrano 127, T424656, www.lapastorella.com.ar. Quaint hostería, whose hospitable owners speak English, good value, safe.

C Hostería Santa Rita, Av Bustillo, Km 7.2, T/F461028, www.santarita.com.ar. Bus 10, 20, 21, to Km 7.5. Close to the centre, peaceful lakeside views, comfortable, lovely terrace, great service.

C Premier, Rolando 263, T426168, www.hotel premier.com. Good central choice (very good value in low season), small rooms with TV and larger superior rooms, big breakfast, English spoken.

C Katy, Av Bustillo, Km 24.3, T448023, gringos patagonia@yahoo.de. Delightful, peaceful, garden full of flowers, charming Slovenian family Kastelic, breakfast included (also half-board). Also offers adventure tourism www.gringospatagonia.com.

D Refugio Neumeyer, 20 de Junio 728, 12 km south of Bariloche, T428995, www.eco-family.com. Not quite as luxurious as an estancia, but with many of the benefits, this mountain lodge has comfortable shared accommodation and rooms for families, all kinds of activities, with bilingual guides, regional restaurant.

D Piuké, Beschtedt 136, T423044. Delightful, simple, nicely decorated, breakfast included, excellent value, owner Martin Walter speaks German, Hungarian and Italian.

D Familia Arko, Güemes 691, T423109. English and German spoken, cooking facilities (no breakfast), helpful, good trekking information, beautiful garden, camping.

D Hostería Güemes, Güemes 715, T424785. Lovely, quiet, lots of space in living areas, very pleasant, big breakfast included, owner is a fishing expert and very knowledgeable about the area.

E Res No Me Olvides, Av Los Pioneros Km 1, T429140, 30 mins' walk or Bus 50/51 to corner of C Videla then follow signs. Beautiful house in quiet surroundings, use of kitchen, camping.

E pp Alaska, Lilinquen 328 (buses 10, 20, 21, get off at La Florida, Av Bustillo Km 7.5), T/F461564, www.alaska-hostel.com. Well run, cosy with shared rustic rooms for 4, all with bath, also double without bath (**D**), nice garden, kitchen facilities, washing machine, free internet, organizes horse riding and rafting, rents mountain bikes. machine, free internet, organizes horse riding and rafting, rents mountain bikes. Recommended. Also cabañas for 6. HI discounts. Owners run **Overland Patagonia** (see below) for trips along Ruta 40.

E pp Hostel 41 below, Pasaje Juramento 94, T436433, www.hostel41below.com. Central, quiet, relaxing atmosphere, good light rooms for 4 and **C** doubles, some with lake views.

E pp La Morada, Cerro Otto Km 5 (free transfer), T441711, www.lamoradahostel.com. Ideal place to chill out from the slopes of Cerro Otto, amazing views, very good doubles with bath (**D**), dorms, kitchen, laundry, English spoken. Also has **1004**, San Martín y Pagano, T432228, penthouse1004@yahoo.com.ar, central, on 10th floor, shared rooms, use of kitchen, very helpful.

E pp Patagonia Andina, Morales 564, T421861, www.elpatagoniaandina.com.ar. Comfortable dorms, doubles (**E**) with shared bath, small kitchen, TV area, sheets included, breakfast extra, internet, advice on trekking, double-check bookings.

E pp Periko's, Morales 555, T522326, www.perikos.com. Welcoming, quiet and nice atmosphere, same owners as Alaska Hostel, dorms and **D** doubles with bath, breakfast extra, kitchen, washing machine, *asado* every Fri, excellent service. Discounts on tours, contact with **Overland Patagonia**.

E pp Ruca Hueney, Elflein 396, T433986, www.rucahueney.com. Lovely, calm, comfortable beds with duvets, fabulous double room (**D**) with extra bunk beds, bathroom and great view, spotless kitchen, very kind owners, Spanish school. Recommended. AHC Argentina Hostels Club.

F pp Albergue El Gaucho, Belgrano 209, T522464, www.hostelelgaucho.com.ar. Welcoming, modern place in quiet part of town, some doubles with own bath (**E** pp), breakfast extra, English, Italian and German spoken.

F pp **La Bolsa**, Palacios 405 y Elflein, T423529. Relaxed atmosphere, rustic rooms with duvets, 1 double with bath **D**, some rooms with views, deck to sit out on, free internet. Recommended.

F pp **Marco Polo Inn**, Salta 422, T400105, www.marcopoloinn.com.ar. Central location, breakfast included, HI discount, **C** in doubles with bath, Wi-Fi, bar and restaurant, basic kitchen.

Camping List of sites from tourist office. These are recommended among the many along Bustillo. They charge US$2.50-3.50 pp. **Petunia**, Km 13.5, T461969, www.camping petunia.com. A lovely shady site going down to lakeside with all facilities. Shops and restaurants on most sites; these are closed outside Jan-Mar. **Selva Negra**, Km 2.95, T441013, camping selvanegra@ infovia.com.ar. Very good, discounts for long stay. **El Yeti**, Km 5.7, T442073, gerezjc@ bariloche.com.ar. All facilities, also *cabañas*.

● Eating

Bariloche *p185, map p185*

Bariloche is blessed with superb food, much of it locally produced, including smoked trout and salmon, wild boar and other delicacies, not least fine chocolate and, in season, delicious berries. There are many good delicatessens.

₹₹₹ **Chez Philippe**, Primera Junta 1080, T427291. Delicious local delicacies and fondue, fine French-influenced cuisine.

₹ **El Boliche de Alberto**, Villegas 347, T431433. Very good steak, huge portions, popular after 2000 (queues in summer), *peña*.

₹₹ **Familia Weiss**, Palacios y VA O'Connor. Excellent local specialities, live music. Wild boar and salmon-filled pasta particularly recommended.

₹₹ **Jauja**, Quaglia 366. Recommended for delicious local dishes, quiet and welcoming, good value (also take-away round the corner at Elflein 128, T429986, with legendary ice creams).

₹₹ **Kandahar**, 20 de Febrero 698, T424702. Atmospheric, warm and intimate, with exquisite food, run by ski champion Marta Peirono de Barber, superb wines and pisco sour. Dinner only, reserve in high season. Highly recommended.

₹₹ **La Marmite**, Mitre 329. Cosy, good service, huge range of fondues, good wild boar, delicious cakes for tea too. Recommended.

₹₹ **Pilgrim**, Palacios 167. Irish pub, serves a good range of beers, reasonable meals too.

₹₹ **Vegetariano**, 20 de Febrero 730, T421820. Also fish, excellent food, beautifully served, warm atmosphere, also take-away. Highly recommended.

₹ **Friends**, Mitre 302. A varied menu, including pizzas in a lively atmosphere, seething with gringos in summer, open 24 hrs.

₹ **La Jirafa**, Palacios 288. Cheery family-run place for good food, good value.

₹ **Rock Chicken**, Rolando 245. Small, busy, good value fast food (also take-away).

₹ **Simoca**, Palacios 264. Recommended for cheap cheap Tucumán specialities, huge empanadas.

La Alpina, Moreno 98. Old-fashioned café serving delicious cakes, good for tea.

Around Bariloche *p186, map p186*

₹₹₹ **Il Gabbiano**, Av Bustillo Km 24.3, T448346. Delicious Italian lunches and dinners. Booking essential (no credit cards).

₹₹ **La Raclette**, Cerro Catedral ski resort. Highly recommended, family place, open in winter.

₹₹ **Tasca Brava**, Av Bustillo Km 7, T462599. On lakeside, intimate atmosphere, Patagonian and superb Spanish cooking.

₹ **Cerveceria Blest**, Av Bustillo Km 11.6, T461026. Wonderful brewery with delicious beers, serving imaginative local and German dishes and steak and kidney pie. Recommended.

Refugio Lynch has restaurant and *confitería* up the slopes of Cerro Catedral. In Cerro Otto there's a revolving *confitería*, craft shop, great views. Also **Club Andino confitería**, at Refugio Berghof, 20 mins' walk from main *confitería* on summit.

Tea rooms

Meli Hue, Av Bustillo Km 24.7 (Colonia Suiza), T448029. Also recommended; also has B&B in a lavender garden and sells sweet-smelling produce.

● Shopping

Bariloche *p185, map p185*

The main shopping area is on Mitre between the Centro Cívico and Beschtedt, also on San Martín.

Chocolate The local stuff is excellent: several shops on Mitre. Local wines, from the Alto Río Negro, are also good. **Abuela Goye**, Mitre 258 and Quaglia 221. First rate chocolatier, also with café in the Quaglia branch. **Fenoglio**, Mitre 301 y Rolando. Very good chocolate and superb chocolate ice cream. **Mamushka**, opposite *El Turista*. Considered the best chocolate here, also with café. **El Turista**, Mitre 231/39. Aptly-named, you can watch chocolates being made here.

Outdoor Arbol, Mitre 263. Sells good quality outdoor gear, lovely clothes and gifts. **Feria Artesanal Municipal**, Moreno y Villegas.

Supermarkets Todo, Mitre 281, good selection, cheap. **Uno**, Moreno 350. **La Anónima**, Quaglia 331 and a huge **Norte** at Moreno y Onelli.

▲ Activities and tours

Bariloche *p185, map p185*
Climbing

Note that at higher levels, winter snow storms can begin as early as Apr, making climbing dangerous.

Club Andino Bariloche, see Tourist information and Walks, above. The club can contact mountain guides and provide information.

Cycling

Bikes can be hired at many places in high season. **Dirty Bikes**, V O'Connor 681, T425616, www.dirty bikes.com.ar. Very helpful for repairs, but pricey.

Fishing

Martín Pescador, Rolando 257, also in Cerro Catedral in winter, at Shopping Mall Las Terrazas, T422275. Fishing, camping and skiing equipment.

Horse riding

At the **Estancia Fortín Chacabuco**, T441766, www.estanciaspatagonicas.com (also offers lodging, **A**), catering for all levels, bilingual guides. **Tom Wesley**, in country ranch by the lake at Km 15.5, office at Mitre 385, T448193, www.tom wesley.com. Tuition and full day's riding offered.

Paragliding

Parapente Bariloche, T462234, parapente@ bariloche.com.ar. At Cerro Otto, US$45 (transfer included).

Skiing

Cerro Catedral, T423776, www.catedralalta patagonia.com, mid-Jun to end-Sep, busiest from mid-Jun to mid-Aug for school holidays, ski lifts: 0900-1700, ski lift pass: adults US$20 per day, ski school, US$30 per hr pp. It has 100 km of slopes of all grades, allowing a total drop of 1,010 m, and 52 km of cross country skiing routes. There are also snowboarding areas and a well-equipped base with hotels, restaurants and equipment hire, ski schools and nursery care for children. Bus are run by **3 de Mayo**, 'Catedral', leaves Moreno 480 every 90 mins (via Av Pioneros or via Av Bustillo), T425648, US$1. Cable car for Catedral T423776. **Cerro Otto**, cable car passengers can take free bus leaving from huts opposite National Park office, city buses US$0.40, or at Mitre y Villegas, hourly 1030-1730 in summer, returning hourly 1115-1915. Ticket for cable car US$10 pp, T441031. Ski gear can be rented by the day from **Cebron**, Mitre 171, or **Milenium**, Mitre 125. See also **Martín Pescador**, above.

Trekking

See Walks, on page 188. **Andescross**, T467502, 156 33581, www.andescross.com. Expert guides, all included. Trekking to Chile across the Andes, via Pampa Linda, Lago Frías, Peulla.

Tours

Check what your tour includes; cable cars and chair lifts are usually charged as extras. Tours get very booked up in season. Most travel agencies will pick you up from your hotel, and all charge roughly the same prices: Circuito Chico US$7-9, half-day; Isla Victoria and Bosque de Arrayanes US$18-25, full-day boat trip; Tronador, Ventisquero Negro and Pampa Linda , US$15 (US$26 plus National Park entry via Lago Mascardi by boat); Puerto Blest boat trip full-day including Cascada de los Cantaros and Lago Frías, US$22; El Bolsón US$22, full-day, including Lago Puelo.

Aguas Blancas, Morales 564, T432799, www.aguasblancas.com.ar. Rafting on the Río Manso, all grades, with expert guides, and all equipment provided (US$37-50), also 'duckies' - inflatable kayaks for beginners, bikes and horse riding, traditional lunches included.

Catedral Turismo, Palacios 263, T425444, cattur@bariloche.com.ar. Representatives for the famous Three Lakes Crossing to Chile, boat trips to Puerto Blest and conventional tours.

Del Lago Turismo, Villegas 222, T430056, www.dellagoturismo.com.ar. Very helpful, staff speak fluent English, all conventional tours, plus horse riding, rafting. Also recommended, a combined trip by boat along Lago Mascardi to Tronador.

Diversidad, 20 de Junio 728, T428995, www.eco-family.com. Riding, walking, skiing and other adventures, based at Refugio Neumeyer (see Sleeping, above), bilinggual guides. Highly Recommended.

Extremo Sur, Morales 765, T427301, www.extremo sur.com. Rafting and kayaking, all levels, full day all inclusive packages and longer trips to Chile.

Huala, San Martín 66, T522438, www.huala.com.ar. Offers rafting, riding, climbing, biking and more, English-speaking guides. Recommended.

Infinito Sur, T156 39624, www.infinito-sur.com. For climbing, trekking, mountain skiing, rafting, expeditions on the *estepa* in Argentine and Chilean Patagonia, highly experienced from Peru, Bolivia and all points south.

Overland Patagonia, Morales 555, T437654, www.overlandpatagonia.com. For a 4-day trip along Ruta 40 to El Calafate, with English-speaking guides and stops en route at Río Mayo, Estancia Los Toldos (for Cueva de las Manos) and Estancia Menelik (for Parque Nacional Perito Moreno), US$315, meals not included. Also other trips across Patagonia.

Tronador Turismo, Quaglia 283, T425644, www.tronadorturismo.com.ar. Conventional tours, trekking and rafting. Also to Refugio Neumeyer, and to Chilean border. Great adventurous wintersports options.

Turisur, Mitre 219, T426109, www.bariloche.com/ turisur. Boat trips to Bosque de Arrayanes, Isla Victoria on a 1937 ship and to Tronador via Lago Mascardi. Always reserve 1 day ahead.

Guides

Martín Angaut, T156 19829, fishing_
bariloche@hotmail.com. Professional fly-fishing
guide, English spoken; contact at **Martín
Pescador** (see above).
Daniel Feinstein, T442259, T155 05387,
defeinstein@bariloche.com.ar. For trekking, biking,
kayaking, natural history expeditions. Speaks
English. Experienced in Argentina and Chile.
Angel Fernández, T524609, 156 09799,
angel_e_fernandez@hotmail.com. For trekking,
biking, kayaking, natural history expeditions.
Extremely knowledgeable and charming, speaks
English. Recommended.

⊝ Transport

Bariloche *p185, map p185*

Air Airport is 15 km east of town, with access from
Ruta 40, 7 km east of centre, T426162; bus service
from town centre meets AR flights, US$2.60; also
colectivos and taxis (US$6). If staying on the road
to Llao Llao, west of town, expect to pay more for
transport to your hotel; a taxi charges US$11 from
town to Llao Llao. Car rental agencies, internet,
exchange, ATM, café at the airport. Many flights a
day to **Buenos Aires**, with **AR/Austral**. *AR* also
flies to **Esquel, Trelew, El Calafate** (summer only)
and **Ushuaia**. **LADE** to **Buenos Aires, Esquel** and
several other destinations in Patagonia. **LAN** Chile
flies to **Puerto Montt** and **Santiago**.
Bus Bus station 3 km east of centre; urban buses
70 and 71, to/from centre, Moreno y Rolando; also
bus 10, 20, 21, 72, US$1. Taxi US$3. Bus
information at terminal T432860. Toilets, small
confitería, kiosko, locutorio with internet, tourist
information desk. Left luggage US$2 per day. Bus
company offices in town (tickets can be purchased
there or at terminal): **Vía Bariloche/El Valle/Don
Otto/Transportadora Patagónica**, Mitre 321,
T429012; **Andesmar/Albus**, Mitre 385, T430211;
Chevallier/La Estrella/Ko Ko, Moreno 105,
T425914; **TAC**, Moreno 138, T434727; **Flechabus**,
T423090. **3 de Mayo**, for local services and
Viedma, Moreno 480, T425648. Prices rise in
summer. To **Buenos Aires**, 5 companies daily,
19-22 hrs, US$60 *coche cama* (recommended with
Via Bariloche). To **Bahía Blanca**, El Valle and El
Crucero del Norte, 14 hrs, US$38. To **Mendoza**,
US$38, *Andesmar*, 19 hrs, via Piedra del Aguila,
Neuquén, Cipolletti and San Rafael. To **Esquel**, via
El Bolsón, fares and schedules given below. To
Puerto Madryn, 13-14 hrs, US$35, with **Don Otto**.
To **Viedma** (along Ruta 23), **3 de Mayo**, 14 hrs,
US$21. To **San Martín de los Andes**, Ko Ko,
Albus, Via Bariloche/Turismo Algarrobal, US$10,
3½-4 hrs. To **Villa Traful** (via Confluencia), **Via
Bariloche/Turismo Algarrobal** and Albus, 1½-
2 hrs, US$4. To Chilean destinations, see under

Border with Chile, above. To **Río Gallegos**, no
direct bus, you have to overnight in Comodoro
Rivadavia en route: daily with **Don Otto**, US$55,
14-15 hrs; change same day to **Taqsa** bus to El
Calafate or following day to **Tecni Austral** bus to
Ushuaia. To **El Calafate**, take bus to Río Gallegos
and change there; take **Chaltén Travel**'s 2-4 day
trips on Ruta 40, www.chaltentravel.com (see page
223); or contact **Overland Patagonia** (see address
under Activities and tours) for a trip along Ruta 40.
Car hire Rates for all agencies are around
US$40 per day. **Localiza**, Frey y VA O'Connor,
T435374, localiza@autosurpatagonia.com.ar,
reliable. **Open**, Mitre 171 local 15, T/F426325,
www.opencar.com.ar, is cheaper. Likewise **Lagos**,
Mitre 83, T428880, www.lagosrentacar.com.ar. To
enter Chile, a permit is necessary; it's generally
included in the price. State when booking car,
allow 24 hrs. For international car rental
agencies, see Essentials, page 44.
Train To **Viedma**, Fri 1800 in Jan-Feb, **Tren
Patagónico**, www.trenpatagonico-sa.com.ar,
leaving in the afternoon, 17-hr journey mostly
at night, dusty, nice views only in the first few
hours, US$28 *pullman*, also with sleeper section,
US$48, and carries cars. To **Jacobacci**, 4½ hrs,
US$22-40. In Carmen de Patagones (across river
from Viedma), train to Buenos Aires; check first.
Booking office at station, 3 km east of centre
(T423172), same as bus station, closed 1200-
1500, Mon-Fri, Sat afternoon and all day Sun.

⊕ Directory

Bariloche *p185, map p185*
Airline offices Aerolíneas Argentinas/
Austral, Mitre 185y Villegas, T423682 (in airport,
T422144). LADE, Mitre 531, p 1, T423562 (in
airport, T423161) . LAN, Moreno 234, p 1,
T431043. **Banks** Banks and exchange shops
buy and sell virtually all European and South
American currencies, besides US dollars. Best
rates from **Sudamérica**, Mitre 63, T434555; all
TCs (3% commission). ATMs on Mitre at 158,
427, Moreno y Quaglia, San Martin 336.
Consulates Chile, JM de Rosas 180, T527468,
helpful. **Internet** Several cybercafés and at
locutorios in the centre, all with similar rates.
Medical facilities Emergencies: Dial 107.
Clinic: Hospital Zonal, Moreno 601, T426100.
Post offices Moreno 175, closed Sat
afternoon and Sun. **Telephones** Many
locutorios in the centre, along Mitre and 1st
block of Quaglia. **Useful addresses**
Customs: 24 de Septiembre 12, T425216.
Immigration office: Libertad 175, T423043.
Policía Federal (for tourist orientation),
Tiscornia y Morales, open 24 hrs,
T423789/423430, English spoken.

South of Bariloche

More wild and beautiful scenery can be explored along the Andes, with a few tourist centres like El Bolsón and Esquel giving access to lakes and national parks. There is trekking, rafting, skiing and fishing on offer, a train ride on the famous La Trochita and the magnificent Los Alerces national park to explore.

Bariloche to El Bolsón

Ruta 258, the paved road from Bariloche to El Bolsón, 126 km south, passes the beautiful lakes Gutiérrez, Mascardi and Guillelmo. From the southern end of Lago Mascardi, 35 km south of Bariloche, a *ripio* road (note one-way system) runs west towards Cerro Tronador and **Pampa Linda**, the starting point for excellent trekking including the two-day walk over Paso de los Nubes to Laguna Frías (see Walks page 188 and Sleeping page 195). **Río Villegas**, about 70 km south of Bariloche, is very beautiful, and there's world class rafting to be done on the **Río Manso**.

El Bolsón and around → *Population: 40,000. Phone code: 02944. Colour map 8, grid C1.*

El Bolsón is an attractive town in a broad fertile valley, surrounded by the mountains of the cordillera and dominated by the dramatic peak of Cerro Piltriquitrón 2,284 m (hence its name: the big bag). It's a magical setting which attracted thousands of hippies to create an ideological community here in the 1970's; they now produce the handicrafts, beers, fruit and jams, sold at the market on Tuesday, Thursday, Saturday, 1000-1700. There are many mountain walks and waterfalls nearby, and good fishing at Lagos Puelo (see below) and Epuyén (shops and petrol available) – both within easy access. **Tourist office** ① *Av San Martín y Roca, T492604, www.elbolson.gov.ar or www.bolsonturistico.com.ar. 0900-2100 all year, until 2400 in high summer. Extremely helpful with maps, treks to refugios and accommodation, English spoken.*

There are waterfalls at **Cascada Escondida**, 10 km northwest of town (2-hour dusty walk, ask for short-cut through woods), a good place for a picnic. There are fine views from **Cerro Piltriquitrón** – drive or taxi 10 km, then walk one hour through the sculptures of the **BosqueTallado** (or 6-7 hour round trip walk), food and shelter at *refugio* (1,400 m; US$3.50), then 3-hour walk from there to the summit. Views of the valley from **Cabeza del Indio**, a good 6 km drive or bike ride from the centre, and a pleasant one hour walk up to **Cerro Amigo**: follow Gral Roca east until it becomes Islas Malvinas and continue up the hill. There is wonderful trekking in the mountains and valleys west of town on an excellent network of trails with well equipped and staffed *refugios* in superb locations; at least 8 shelters were operating in 2006-2007, most open October-March. Most shelters offer simple accommodation (US$5 pp, sleeping bag required), some meals (US$4), basic supplies including home-baked bread and home-brewed beer, camping (US$1.50 pp), and hot showers (US$1). They have radio communication with each other and with town. Additional information and compulsory registration at the Club Andino or tourist office in El Bolsón. In high season there are minibuses to the trailheads, at other times hitch or take a remise taxi for US$5.

Cholila and around → *Phone code: 02945. Population: 1,300.*

A peaceful sprawling village, 76 km south of El Bolsón, with superb views at Lago Cholila (17 km west), crowned by the Matterhorn-like mountains of Cerros Dos and Tres Picos (campsite and expensive *Hostería El Pedregoso*). Excellent fishing, canoeing and kayaking on rivers nearby. Along Valle de Cholila (Ruta 71) are several lovely old brick and wooden houses and barns. Among them are the **wooden cabins**, where Butch Cassidy, the Sundance Kid and Etta Place lived between 1901 and 1905; the cabins have been badly renovated, sadly, so not worth the considerable effort to visit them (officially US$1 entry, if anyone's around to charge you). They are 13 km north, east of the road, opposite a police station. One km west of the road is the *Casa de Piedra* teahouse serving *té galés* and offering basic accommodation. **Villa Lago Rivadavia**, 15 km south of Cholila lies next to the northern gates of Parque Nacional Los Alerces, with an increasing number of *cabañas*. Tourist information hut open in summer only, opposite petrol station at El Rincón; also basic information at Municipalidad in Cholila, T498040.

At **Lago Puelo** in the **Parque Nacional Lago Puelo** there are gentle walks on marked paths, boat trips across the lake on a 1931 boat, and canoes for rent. Wardens at the park entrance (US$4) can advise on these and a 3-day trek through magnificent scenery to Chilean border. Gorgeous homemade *alfajores* in fairy tale setting at *El Bolsonero* on the old road to Lago Puelo.

Regular buses, US$2, from Avenida San Martín y Dorrego in El Bolsón go to the lake via Villa Lago Puelo. Boats: *Juana de Arco* ① *T493415, www.interpatagonia.com/juanadearco. Information in summer from hut in Avenida San Martín y Pellegrini*, 30-minute trip, US$5; to the Chilean border, 3 hours, US$15.

Esquel → *Phone code: 02945. Colour map 9, grid A1. Population: 30,000.*

Esquel, 293 km south of Bariloche, was originally an offshoot of the Welsh colony at Chubut, 650 km to the east, and still has a pioneer feel. A breezy open town in a fertile valley, with a backdrop of mountains, Esquel is the base for visiting the Parque Nacional Los Alerces and for skiing at **La Hoya** in winter (15 km, good 6½-hour trek in summer). Good walks from the town to Laguna La Zeta, 5 km, and to Cerro La Cruz, two hours (one way). It's also the departure point for the famous narrow gauge railway, **La Trochita** (see box, page 195). **Tourist office** ① *Av Alvear y Sarmiento, T451927, www.esquel.gov.ar. Daily 0800-2000, summer 0730-2200.*

Trevelin → *Colour map 9, grid A1. Population: 5,000.*

An offshoot of the Welsh Chubut colony (see box in Patagonia section, page 205), where Welsh is still spoken, the pretty village of Trevelin, 24 km southwest of Esquel, has a Welsh chapel (built 1910, closed) and tea rooms. The **Museo Regional** ① *US$1.50, 0900-2100*, in the old mill (1918) includes artefacts from the Welsh colony. The **Museo Cartref Taid** (ask for directions in the tourist office) is the house of John Evans, one of Trevelin's first pioneers, full of his belongings, another great insight into the local Welsh history. There's also a touching memorial of Evans' life at **El Tumbo del Caballo Malacara**, 200 m from the main plaza; a private garden containing the remains of Evans' horse, Malacara, who once saved his life; guided tours US$2. **Nant-y-fall Falls** ① *17 km southwest on the road to the border, US$1 pp including guide to 3 falls (1½-hr walk)*, are a series of impressive cascades in lovely forest. Helpful tourist office in the central plaza, *T480120, www.trevelin.org.* Has maps, accommodation booking service and English is spoken.

Parque Nacional Los Alerces → *Colour map 9, grid A1.*

① *33 km west of Esquel, US$4, December-Easter.* One of the most appealing and untouched expanses of the Andes region, this national park has several lakes including **Lago Futalaufquen**, with some of the best fishing in the area, **Lago Menéndez** which can be crossed by boat to visit rare and impressive *alerce* trees (Fitzroya cupressoides), some of which are over 2000 years old, and the green waters of **Lago Verde**. Relatively undeveloped, access is possible only to the east side of the park, via a *ripio* road (which is an alternative way from Esquel to El Bolsón) with many camping spots and *hosterías*. Helpful *guardaparques* give out maps and advice on walks at the visitor centre (T471020 ext 23) in Villa Futalaufquen (southern end of Lago Futulaufquen); also a service station, two food shops, *locutorio* and a restaurant *El Abuelo Monje*. Fishing licences from food shops, the *kiosko* or *Hosterías Cume Hué* and *Futalaufquen*, or petrol stations in Esquel.

Trekking and tours The west half of the park is inaccessible, but there are splendid walks along footpaths on the southern shore of Lago Futalaufquen, with several waterfalls, and near Lago Verde further north. Treks at Los Alerces range from an hour to two or three days. All long treks require previous registration with the *guardaparques*; some paths are closed in autumn and winter. For longer options or when trails here are closed, try the El Bolsón area, Parque Nacional Nahuel Huapi or Parque Nacional Lanín. At Lago Futalaufquen's northern end, walk across the bridge over Río Arrayanes to Lago Verde. A longer more difficult trek is to **Cerro El Dedal** (1,916 m), either returning the way you came from Villa Futalaufquen, 7½ hours, or making an 8 to 10 hour loop through Puerto Limonao. Walkers must register with the *guardaparques* and you're required to start before 1000. Carry plenty of water. Also a two- to three-day hike through *coihue* forest to the tip of beautiful, secluded **Lago Krügger** ① *refugio, open only Jan-Feb, campsite, US$5 pp and guardaparques' office*, where you can take a boat back to Puerto Limonao. On Lago Futalaufquen is a free campsite at Playa Blanca. **Cerros Alto El Petiso** and **La Torta** can be climbed and there is a trekkers' shelter at the base of **Cerro Cocinero. Boat trips:** US$43 to El Alerzal, from Puerto Limonao, across Lago Futalaufquen along the pea-green Río Arrayanes, lined with the extraordinary cinnamon-barked trees, to Puerto Mermoud on Lago Verde. A short walk leads to Puerto Chucao, on Lago Menéndez, where another boat makes the unforgettable trip to see the majestic 2600-year old alerce trees,

The Old Patagonian Express

Esquel is the terminus of a 402-km branch-line from Ingeniero Jacobacci, a junction on the old Buenos Aires-Bariloche mainline, 194 km east of Bariloche. This narrow-gauge line (0.75 m wide) took 23 years to build, being finally opened in 1945. It was made famous outside Argentina by Paul Theroux who described it in his book *The Old Patagonian Express*. The 1922 Henschel and Baldwin steam locomotives (from Germany and USA respectively) are powered by fuel oil and use 100 litres of water every km. Water has to be taken on at least every 40 km along the route. Most of the coaches are Belgian and also date from 1922. If you want to see the engines, go to El Maitén where the workshops are.

Until the Argentine government handed responsibility for railways over to the provincial governments in 1994, regular services ran the length of the line. Since then, services have been maintained between Esquel and El Maitén by the provincial government of Chubut.

walking to silent Lago Cisne, past the white waters of Río Cisne. A cheaper alternative is to get to Puerto Chucao on your own and take the boat there (US$25). Boats run frequently in high season. Book through **Patagonia Verde** ① *Esquel*, T454396, or **Safari Lacustre** ① *T471008, www.brazosur.com*.

Border with Chile: Paso Futaleufú → *Colour map 9, grid A1.*

There is a campsite (**Camping Puerto Ciprés**) on the Argentine side of river, 70 km southwest of Equel, via Trevelin. Cross the border river by the bridge after passing Argentine customs; Chilean customs is 1 km on the other side of river (one hour for all formalities). The Chilean town of Futaleufú is 9 km from the border. See page 199 for buses to the border.

South of Esquel, Ruta 40 is paved through the towns of **Tecka** and **Gobernador Costa** in Chubut province. At 38 km south of Gobernador Costa, gravelled Ruta 40 forks southwest through the town of Alto Río Senguer, while provincial Ruta 20 heads almost directly south for 141 km, before turning east towards Sarmiento and Comodoro Rivadavia. At La Puerta del Diablo, in the valley of the lower Río Senguer, Ruta 20 intersects provincial Ruta 22, which joins with Ruta 40 at the town of Río Mayo (see page 215). This latter route is completely paved and preferable to Ruta 40 for long-distance motorists; good informal campsites on the west side of the bridge across the Río Senguer.

● Sleeping

Bariloche to El Bolsón *p193*
AL Estancia Peuma Hue, 3 km off Ruta 40 (ex-Ruta 258 Km 25, T02944-15501030, www.peuma-hue.com. Best comfort in a homely environment, on the southern shores of Lago Gutiérrez, below Cerro Catedral Sur. Charming owner Evelyn Hoter and dedicated staff make it all work perfectly, tasty home-made food, superb horse riding and other activities, health treatments, yoga, meditation, etc, candlelit concerts. All inclusive, varied accommodation. Highly recommended.
AL El Retorno, Villa Los Coihues, on the shore of Lago Gutiérrez, T467333, www.hosteriael retorno.com. Stunning lakeside position, comfortable hunting lodge style, family run, with a beach, tennis, very comfortable rooms and self-catering apartments (Bus 50, follow signs from the road to El Bolsón).

A pp Hotel Tronador, T441062, www.hotel tronador.com. 37 km from Bariloche, on the narrow road from Villa Mascardi to Pampa Linda (there are restricted times for going in each direction: check with tourist office), open Nov-Apr, full board, lakeside paradise, lovely rooms with lake view, beautiful gardens, charming owner, also riding, fishing and lake excursions. Also camping *La Querencia*.
B Mascardi, T490518, www.mascardi.com. Luxurious hotel with a delightful setting along Lago Mascardi.
D Hostería Pampa Linda, T442038. A wonderfully comfortable, peaceful base for climbing Tronador and many other treks (plus horse riding, trekking and climbing courses), simple rooms, all with stunning views, restaurant, full board optional, packed lunches available for hikes. Charming owners, Sebastián de la Cruz is

one of the area's most experienced mountaineers. Highly recommended. Nearby is **Refugio Pampa Linda** (F pp, T424531) and **Camping Río Manso**.

Camping Camping Las Carpitas, 33 km from Bariloche, T490527. Summer only, great location, all facilities, also *cabañas*. **Camping Pampa Linda**, T424531. Idyllic spacious lakeside site with trees, good meals, food shop. **Camping Los Rápidos**, after crossing the Río Manso to Pampa Linda, T461861. All facilities, attractive shaded site going down to lake, *confitería*, open all year.

El Bolsón *p193*

Difficult to find accommodation in the high season: book ahead.

C La Casona de Odile, Barrio Luján, T492753, www.interpatagonia.com/odile. Rustic wooden cabins in idyllic lavender farm by stream, delicious French cooking, reserve ahead, English, French and German spoken. A really special place to stay; charismatic owner. Recommended.

D Amancay, Av San Martín 3207, T492222, www.hotelamancaybolson.com.ar. Good, comfortable and light rooms, though small and a bit old-fashioned, breakfast included.

D La Posada de Hamelin, Int Granollers 2179, T492030, gcapece@elbolson.com. Charming rooms, welcoming atmosphere, huge breakfasts with homemade jams and cakes, German spoken. Highly recommended.

D Refugio del Lago, at Lago Epuyén, T02945-499025, a.sophie@epuyen.net.ar. Relaxed place with breakfast, also good meals, trekking, riding, canoes for hiring, also camping and *cabañas*. Recommended. Owners are mountain guides. Book in advance.

D Hostería Steiner, San Martín 670, T492224. Another peaceful place surrounded by a lovely park, wood fire, restaurant, breakfast extra, German spoken. Recommended.

D Valle Nuevo, 25 de Mayo y Belgrano, T1560 2325. Small rooms, quiet place, cooking facilities, breakfast not included, but good value. Also runs nice **Albergue Sol del Valle** next door, T492087 (D double, E pp in dorm), cooking facilities. Also rents a few good value apartments with cooking facilities.

E pp Refugio Patagónico, Islas Malvinas y Pastorino, T156 35463, www.refugio patagonico.com.ar. High quality, small dorms with bath, breakfast US$1.40, in a spacious house in open fields, great views of Piltriquitrón, also camping. Recommended.

F Altos del Sur, Villa Turismo, T498730, www.altosdelsur.bolsonweb.com. Peaceful hostel in a lovely setting, shared rooms, one double (D) with bath, with breakfast, dinner

available, will collect from bus station if you call ahead. Recommended.

F pp El Pueblito, 4 km north in Barrio Luján, 1 km off Ruta 258 (now Ruta 40; take northbound bus along Av San Martín, US$0.50), T493560, www.elpueblitohostel.com.ar. Cosy wooden building in open country, doubles with bath (E), also has cabins, cooking and laundry facilities, shop, open fire. HI discounts.

Camping Arco Iris, T155 58330. Blissful wooded setting near Río Azul, helpful owners. **La Chacra**, Av Belgrano 1128, T492111, campinglachacra@yahoo.com.ar, 15 mins walk from town, well shaded, good facilities, lively atmosphere in season. **Quem Quem**, on river bank Río Quemquemtreu, T493550, quemquem@elbolson.com. Lovely site, hot showers, good walks, free pickup from town. There are many *cabañas* in picturesque settings with lovely views in the Villa Turismo, about US$40 for up to 5 people.

Cholila and around *p193*

AL La Rinconada, Villa Lago Rivadavia, T498091. Offers tours, horse riding, kayaking, American-owned.

B El Trébol, T/F498055, eltrebol@ar.inter.net. With breakfast, comfortable rooms with stoves, meals and half board also available, family-run, large garden, popular with fishing expeditions, reservations advised, bus stops in Cholila 4 km away.

D Cumelen Huenti, in Cholila village, T496031. With bath, heating, restaurant with good home cooking, helpful.

D pp La Pasarela, 2 km from town, T499061, www.lpuelo.com.ar. Dorms, camping, shops, fuel. **Cabañas Cerro La Momia**, Villa Lago Rivadavia, T011-4522 0617, www.cabanas cerrolamomia.com.ar. Very good *cabañas* for up to 6, picturesque setting among fruit orchards and wooded slopes. Restaurant, excursions arranged.

Camping F Autocamping Carlos Pellegrini, next to El Trébol, T498030. Free municipal camping in El Morro park, next to Cholila. **Camping El Abuelo**, 13 km south, at Villa Lago Rivadavia, T491013.

Esquel *p194*

Hotels are often full in Jan-Feb. Ask at tourist office for lodgings in private houses.

A-B Cumbres Blancas, Av Ameghino 1683, T/F455100, www.cumbresblancas.com.ar. Attractive modern building, a little out of centre, very comfortable, spacious rooms, sauna, gym, airy restaurant. Recommended.

B Angelina, Av Alvear 758, T452763. Good value, welcoming, big breakfast, English and Italian spoken, open high season only.

B Canela, Los Notros y Los Radales, Villa Ayelén, on road to Trevelin, T/F453890. Bed and breakfast and tea room in a lovely, quiet residential area, English spoken, owner knowledgeable about Patagonia.

C La Tour D'Argent, San Martín 1063, T454612, www.cpatagonia.com/esq/latour. With breakfast, bright, comfortable, family-run, very good value, traditional restaurant.

D La Chacra, Km 5 on Ruta 259 towards Trevelin, T452802, rinilachacra@ciudad.com.ar. Relaxing, spacious rooms, huge breakfast, Welsh and English spoken.

D La Posada, Chacabuco 905, T454095, laposada@art.inter.net. Tasteful B&B in quiet part of town, lovely lounge, very comfortable, breakfast included, excellent value.

D El Arrayán, Antártida Argentina 767, T451051. Comfortable carpeted rooms, with heating, reliable hot water, good value.

D Las Mutisias, Av Alvear 1021, T452083, lasmutisias@ciudad.com.ar. Spotless place run by Emma Cleri, helpful and very hospitable, no breakfast.

E Res El Cisne, Chacabuco 778, T452256. Basic small rooms, hot water, quiet, well kept, good value, breakfast extra.

E Lago Verde, Volta 1081, T452251, patagoniaverde@ciudad.com.ar. Breakfast extra, modern, comfortable, run by tour guides, same owners as **Patagonia Verde**, rooms for 2 and 3 with bath, near bus terminal, 2 blocks from La Trochita. Recommended.

E pp Casa del Pueblo, San Martín 661, T450581, www.epaadventure.com.ar. Smallish rooms but good atmosphere (**D** double with bath), kitchen, laundry. HI discounts, organizes adventure activities.

F pp Planeta Hostel, Av Alvear 2833, T456846, www.planetahostel.com. 4-6 bed dorms, with breakfast, internet, simple kitcehn facilities, English spoken.

G pp Hospedaje Rowlands, behind Rivadavia 330, T452578. Warm family welcome, Welsh spoken, breakfast extra, basic rooms with shared bath and a double with bath (**E**).

Camping El Hogar del Mochilero, Roca 1028 (statue of backpacker at entrance), T452166. Summer only, laundry facilities, 24-hr hot water, friendly owner, internet, free firewood for cooking. Also a basic large dorm (**F** pp). La Rural, 1 km on road to Trevelin, T1568 1429. Well organized and shady site with facilities. Millalen, Av Ameghino 2063 (5 blocks from bus terminal), T456164, good services and a dorm.

Trevelin p194
D Familia Pezzi, Sarmiento 353, T480146, hpezzi@intramed.com.ar. Charming family house with a beautiful garden, open Jan-Mar only, English spoken. Recommended.

D-E pp Casa Verde Hostal, Los Alerces s/n, T480091, www.casaverdehostel.com.ar. 'The best hostel in Argentina', by many reckonings. Charming owners Bibiana and Charly, spacious log cabin with panoramic views of wooded mountains, comfortable dorms for 4-6, all with bath, kitchen facilities, laundry, HI member, breakfast extra. Also a lovely rustic cabin for up to 7. English and Welsh spoken, excursions into Los Alerces, bikes for hire US$10 per day. Highly recommended.

Camping many sites, especially on the road to Futaleufú and Chile, charging about US$2-3 pp; also many *cabañas*; ask for full list at Tourist office.

Parque Nacional Los Alerces p194
East side of Lago Futalaufquen
L El Aura: Lago Verde Wilderness Resort, T011-4522 7754 (Buenos Aires), www.tenriverstenlakes.com/elaura-i.htm. Exquisite taste in these 3 stone cabins and a guest house on the shore of Lago Verde. Luxury in every respect, attention to detail, ecologically friendly. Impressive place.

A Hostería Quimé Quipan, T454134. Comfortable rooms with lake views, dinner included. Recommended.

C Bahía Rosales, T471044. Comfortable *cabaña* for 6 with kitchenette and bath, **F** pp in small basic cabin without bath, and camping in open ground, hot showers, restaurant, all recommended.

D Cabañas Tejas Negras, next to Pucón Pai, T471046. Really comfortable cabañas for 4, also good camp site, and tea room.

C Motel Pucón Pai, T451425, puconpai@ ciudad.com.ar. Slightly spartan rooms, but good restaurant, recommended for fishing; campsite with hot showers, US$2 pp.

Camping Los Maitenes, Villa Futalaufquen, excellent, US$1.50 pp, plus US$2 per tent. Several campsites at Lagos Rivadavia, Verde and Río Arrayanes, from free to US$3 depending on facilities.

Gobernador Costa p195
F Hotels Jair, good value, and *Vega*.
Camping Municipal site, all services, US$1.

❶ Eating

El Bolsón p193
Arcimbaldo, Av San Martin 2790, T492137. Good value *tenedor libre*, smoked fish and draft beer, open for breakfast.

Amancay, San Martín 3217. Good *parrilla* and homemade pastas.

¶¶ Cerro Lindo, Av San Martín 2524, T492899. Elegant, delicious pastas, vegetarian dishes and regional specialities.

¶¶ Jauja, Av San Martín 2867, T492448. Great meeting place, delicious fish and pasta, outstanding ice cream, English spoken. Recommended.

¶¶ Parrilla El Quincho, 10 mins north of town, signposted from Route 258, near Cataratas del Mallín, T492870. Excellent *asado* and lamb, charming rustic parrilla with garden going down to the river, tables in the open air. Recommended.

¶ La Calabaza, Av San Martín y Hube. Good inexpensive food including vegetarian dishes, relaxed atmosphere.

¶ Morena, Av San Martín y Hube. Small and unpretentious café/restaurant; for pizzas, pastas and some very good vegetarian meals.

Cafés

Cerveza El Bolsón, RN 258, Km 123.9, T492595, www.cervezaselbolson.com. Microbrewery where you can see how the beer is made and sample the 18 varieties. *Picadas* served with beer, sitting outside in the gardens. Highly recommended.

Dulcinea, on RN 258 to El Hoyo at Km 137.5, Debbie_dulcinea@ yahoo.com.ar. Delightful tea room, owner Debbie speaks English, famous for cakes and rose hip tea, fondue and *asado* in the evenings in season.

La Saltenita, Av Belgrano 515. For a great selection of *empanadas*.

La Tosca, Perito Moreno y Roca (behind Tourist office). A very agreeable café, atmospheric restaurant in summer, good sandwiches.

Esquel *p194*

¶¶ Dionisio, Av Fontana 656. Good value crêpes with the most varied fillings, *picadas* with beer or wine and meat dishes in a nice house. Also a café open in the late afternoon.

¶¶ Don Chiquito, behind Av Ameghino 1641, T450035. Delicious pastas in a fun atmosphere with plenty of games brought to the tables by magician owner Tito. Recommended.

¶¶ Tío Vicente, Av Ameghino y Av Fontana. Very good food; *parrilla* and pastas with varied sauces.

¶¶ Vascongada, 9 de Julio y Mitre, T452229. Traditional style, trout and other local specialities.

¶ Casa Grande, Roca 441. Popular for its varied menu (such as lamb and trout), reasonable prices.

¶ Tío Canuto, Av Alvear 949. Restaurant/bar with live music, tango shows and lessons, open Tue-Sun 1900-0300.

Cafés

María Castaña, Rivadavia y 25 de Mayo. Popular, good coffee.

Melys, Miguens 346, off Ameghino 2000. Plentiful Welsh teas and a good breakfast.

Trevelin *p194*

¶¶ Patagonia Celta, 25 de Mayo s/n, T480722. Delicious local specialities, trout and vegetarian dishes, best in town. Recommended.

¶ Parrilla Oregon, Av San Martín y Laprida, T480408. Large meals (particularly breakfasts), set menus based on *parrilla* and pastas.

¶ Parrilla del Club, Av San Martín y Libertad. Simple, cheap, good meals.

¶ Nain Maggie, Perito Moreno 179, T480232. Tea room, offering *té galés* and *torta negra*, expensive but good.

O Shopping

Esquel *p194*

Casa de Esquel (Robert Müller), 25 de Mayo 415. Wide range of new and secondhand books on Patagonia, also local crafts.

La Anónima, 9 de Julio y Belgrano. Big supermarket.

Los Vascos, 25 de Mayo y 9 de Julio. Traditional store founded in 1926, worth seeing.

▲▲ Activities and tours

El Bolsón *p193*

Grado 42, Av. Belgrano 406, T493124, www.grado42.com. Tours to El Maitén to take La Trochita, 7 hrs, US$25; also short excursions in the surroundings (US$10) and day trips to Parque Nacional Los Alerces (US$32), as well as wide range of adventure activities. Sells **Chaltén Travel** bus tickets (see p 223). Recommended.

Maputur, Perito Moreno 2331, T491139, www.maputur.com.ar. Horse rides, paragliding and mountain bikes for hire (US$7 per day).

Patagonia Adventures, Hube 418, T492513, www.argentinachileflyfishing.com. Rafting, paragliding, fishing, boat trip on Lago Puelo to remote forest lodge, horse riding to Chile.

Esquel *p194*
Fishing
Tourist office has a list of guides and companies hiring out equipment.

Skiing
One of Argentina's cheapest, with laid back family atmosphere, **La Hoya**, 15 km north, has 22 km of pistes, 8 ski-lifts. For skiing information ask at **Club Andino Esquel**, Pellegrini 787, T453248; travel agencies run 3 daily minibuses to La Hoya from Esquel, US$5 return, ski pass US$15. Equipment hire from US$6 a day.

Tours
Frontera Sur, Av Alvear y Sarmiento, T450505, www.fronterasur.net. Good company offering

adventure tourism of all sorts, as well as more traditional excursions, ski equipment and trekking.

Patagonia Verde, 9 de Julio 926, T454396, www.patagonia-verde.com.ar. Boat trips to El Alerzal on Lago Menéndez, rafting on Río Corcovado, tickets for 'La Trochita' and for Ruta 40 to El Calafate. Also range of adventure activities, horse riding, short local excursions and ski passes. English spoken. Excellent company, very professional.

Trevelin *p194*

Gales al Sur, Patagonia 186, T480427, www.gale salsur.com.ar. Another office in Esquel bus station, T455757. Adventure tours with mountain bikes, horses, canoes or a good pair of boots. Also bikes for rent (US$10 per day) and transfer to/from airport for all flights. English spoken.

⊘ Transport

El Bolsón *p193*

Bus Several daily from **Bariloche** and **Esquel**, with **Don Otto**, **Vía Bariloche**. Check with Vía Bariloche/El Valle, Mitre 321, T429012, or Bariloche bus station T432444, www.via bariloche.com, for timings. Heavily, even over-booked in high season. US$7.50, 2 hrs. Other destinations from these 2 towns. Buses to **Lago Puelo** with **Vía Bariloche** every 2 hrs, 4 on Sun, 45 mins, US$1.30. To **Parque Nacional Los Alerces** (highly recommended route), with **Transportes Esquel** (from ACA service station), once a day, US$5, 4-5 hrs, via Cholila and Epuyen.

Esquel *p194*

Air Airport, 20 km east of Esquel, by paved road, US$9 by taxi, US$3 by **Gales al Sur** minibus (see Activities and tours, above). To **Buenos Aires** and **Trelew** with AR (Av Fontana 408, T453614). LADE (Av Alvear 1085, T452124) to **Bariloche**, **Comodoro Rivadavia**, **El Bolsón**, **El Calafate**, **El Maitén**, **Mar del Plata**, **Puerto Madryn** and several other destinations in Patagonia; weekly departures.

Bus Smart terminal at Av Alvear 1871, T451584, US$1 by taxi from centre, it has toilets, *kiosko*, *locutorio* with internet, café, tourist information desk, left luggage (US$2 per day). To Buenos Aires change in Bariloche, with **Andesmar**, T450143, or Vía Bariloche, T453528, (US$55 *coche cama*). To Bariloche, (via El Bolsón, 2½ hrs), 4-5hrs, US$8-12, Don Otto (T453012), Vía Bariloche. To **Puerto Madryn**, Don Otto, 9 hrs, US$17-27. To **Trelew** US$23-30, 8 hrs nightly or 0800 Tue and Sat. To **Río Gallegos** (for connections to El Calafate or Ushuaia), Don Otto/Transportadora Patagónica runs a direct service daily (2 hrs stop at Comodoro

Rivadavia), 22 hrs, US$32, *semi cama*. To **Trevelin**, **Vía Trevelin** (T455222) and **Jacobsen** (T453528), Mon-Fri, hourly 0600-2300, every 2 hrs weekends, 30 mins, US$2. To **Paso Futaleufú** (Chilean border) via Trevelin, **Jacobsen** 0800 daily Jan/Feb, otherwise Mon, Wed (sometimes) and Fri, US$5. Buses connect there for Chaitén.

Train La Trochita (the Old Patagonian Express) generally runs from Esquel to **Nahuel Pan** (19 km) 5 times a week, and up to twice a day in high season (much less frequent in winter), taking 2½ hrs, US$5, children under 6 free. At wild and remote Nahuel Pan, there's just a small terrace of houses, home to a Mapuche community, who sell delicious cakes and display their knitwear, some of it very fine quality. Sometimes there's an extra service from **El Maitén** at the northernmost end of the line on Sat, taking 6 hrs, US$10, with a dining car. Information, in English including schedules in El Maitén, T02945-495190, and in Esquel T02945- 451403, www.latrochita.com.ar. Tickets from tour operators, or from Esquel station office, Urquiza y Roggero.

Parque Nacional Los Alerces *p194*

Bus From Esquel (Transportes Esquel, T453529) runs daily in Jan-Feb and 2-3 weekly off season at 0800 from Esquel to Lago Puelo, 6 hrs, US$4 one way, along the east side of Lago Futalaufquen, passing **Villa Futalaufquen** 0915, **Lago Verde** 1030, **Lago Rivadavia** 1045 and Cholila (sit on left). On the return it passes Lago Rivadavia at 1830, Lago Verde 1845 and Villa Futalaufquen 1945, back in Esquel 2100-2130; driver will stop anywhere en route if asked, and at your hotel on return. Extra frequencies in high summer from Esquel up to Lago Verde and from Lago Puelo up to Lago Verde (Bus La Golondrina), US$3.50 and year round from Esquel up to Villa Futalaufquen.

Border with Chile: Paso Futaleufú *p195*

Buses from Esquel via Trevelin to **Paso Futaleufú** (La Balsa), see above. Very little traffic for hitching.

❶ Directory

Esquel *p194*

Banks Banco de la Nación, Av Alvear y Roca, open 0730-1300; changes US$ and euros. ATM accepts all cards. ATMs also at Banco del Chubut, Av Alvear 1147, Banco Patagonia, 25 de Mayo 739, Bansud, 25 de Mayo 752. Exchange also at Finan City, Av Fontana 673. **Internet** Many places in centre. **Post offices** Av Alvear 1192 y Fontana, Mon-Fri and Sat mornings. **Telephones** Many *locutorios* in centre, including Cordillera, 25 de Mayo 526. El Alerce, 9 de Julio y 25 de Mayo.

Patagonia

Patagonia is the vast, windy, mostly treeless plateau covering all of southern Argentina south of the Río Colorado. The Atlantic coast is rich in marine life; penguins, whales and seals can all be seen around Puerto Madryn. The far south offers spectacular scenery in the Parque Nacional Los Glaciares, with the mighty Moreno and Upsala glaciers, as well as challenging trekking around Mount Fitz Roy. The contrasts are extreme: thousands of prehistoric handprints can be found in the Cueva de las Manos, but in most of Patagonia there's less than one person to each sq km; far from the densely wooded Andes, there are petrified forests in the deserts; and the legacy of brave early pioneers is the over-abundance of tea and cakes served up by Argentina's Welsh community in the Chubut valley.

Patagonia's appeal lies in its emptiness. Vegetation is sparse, since a relentless dry wind blows continually from the west, raising a haze of dust in summer, which can turn to mud in winter. Rainfall is high only in the foothills of the Andes, where dense virgin beech forests run from Neuquén to Tierra del Fuego. During a brief period in spring, after the snow melt, there is grass on the plateau, but in the desert-like expanses of eastern Patagonia, water can be pumped only in the deep crevices which intersect the land from west to east. This is where the great sheep estancias lie, sheltered from the wind. There is little agriculture except in the north, in the valleys of the Colorado and Negro rivers, where alfalfa is grown and cattle are raised. Centres of population are tiny and most of the towns are small ports on the Atlantic coast. Only Comodoro Rivadavia has a population over 100,000, thanks to its oil industry. Patagonia has attracted many generations of people getting away from it all, from Welsh religious pioneers to Butch Cassidy and the Sundance Kid, and tourism is an increasingly important source of income.

Ins and outs

Getting there

Air There are daily flights from Buenos Aires to Viedma, Trelew, Comodoro Rivadavia, Río Gallegos, El Calafate's airport, Lago Argentino, and Ushuaia. It is vital that you book these flights well ahead in the summer (December to February) and the winter ski season for Ushuaia (July and August). **Aerolíneas Argentinas** (AR) ① *Freephone (from within Argentina) 0810-222 86527, www.aerolineas.com.ar*, is now the only Argentine airline flying these routes and flights get booked up very quickly. At other times of the year, flights can be booked with just a few days' warning. The Chilean airline, **LAN** ① *freephone (within Chile) To800-9999 526, www.lan.com*, flies to Ushuaia from Argentine destinations as well as Punta Arenas, Puerto Montt and Santiago.

Air Force **LADE** flights in the region south of Bariloche go weekly and must be booked in advance from the flight's departure point. The baggage allowance is 15 kg. Flights are often heavily booked, but check again on the day of the flight even if it is sold out. **LADE** ① *To11-5129-9000, or 0810-810 5233, www.lade.com.ar*, tickets are much cheaper for a long flight with stops than buying separate segments. Overnight buses may be more convenient.

Road The principal roads in Patagonia are the Ruta 3, which runs down the Atlantic coast, and the Ruta 40 on the west. One of Argentina's main arteries, Ruta 3 runs from Buenos Aires to Ushuaia, interrupted by the car ferry crossing through Chilean territory across the Magellan Strait to Tierra del Fuego. It is mostly paved, except between Río Gallegos and San Sebastián (80 km north of Río Grande) and for 65 km south of Tolhuin. Regular buses run along the whole stretch, more frequently between October and April, and there are towns with services and accommodation every few hundred km. However, Ruta 40 is a wide unpaved *ripio* track which zigzags across the moors from Zapala to Lago Argentino, near El Calafate, ending at Cabo Vírgenes. It's by far the more interesting road, lonely and bleak, with little traffic even in the tourist summer season, offering fine views of the Andes and plenty of wildlife as well as giving access to many National Parks. The east-west road across Patagonia, from south of Esquel in the Lake District to Comodoro Rivadavia, is paved, and there's a good paved highway running from Bariloche through Neuquén to San Antonio Oeste.

Many of the roads in southern Argentina are *ripio* – gravelled – limiting maximum speeds to 60 km per hour, or less where surfaces are poor, very hard on low-clearance vehicles. Strong winds can also be a hazard. Windscreen and headlight protection is a good idea (expensive to buy, but can be improvised with wire mesh for windscreen, strips cut from plastic bottles for lights). There are cattle grids (*guardaganados*), even on main highways, usually signposted; cross them very slowly. Always carry plenty of fuel, as service stations may be as much as 300 km apart and as a precaution in case of a breakdown, carry warm clothing and make sure your car has anti-freeze. Petrol prices in Chubut, Santa Cruz and Tierra del Fuego provinces are 40% cheaper than in the rest of the country (10-15% for diesel).

There are good hotels at Perito Moreno and El Calafate, and basic accommodation at Gobernador Gregores and Río Mayo. In summer hotel prices are very high, especially in El Calafate and El Chaltén. From November onwards you must reserve hotels a week or more in advance. Camping is increasingly popular and *estancias* may be hospitable to travellers who are stuck for a bed. Many *estancias*, especially in Santa Cruz province, offer transport, excursions and food as well as accommodation: see www.estanciasdesantacruz.com. **ACA** establishments, which charge roughly the same prices all over Argentina, are good value in Patagonia. As very few hotels and restaurants have a/c or even fans, it can get uncomfortably hot in January.

Viedma, Carmen de Patagones and around

These two pleasant towns (*Phone code 02920, Colour map 8, grid C4*) lie on opposite banks of the Río Negro, about 27 km from its mouth and 270 km south of Bahía Blanca. Patagones is older and charming, but most services are in Viedma (*Population: 50,000*), capital of Río Negro Province. A quiet place, its main attraction is the perfect bathing area along the shaded south bank of the river. **El Cóndor** is a beautiful beach 30 km south of Viedma, three buses a day from Viedma in summer, with hotels open January-February, restaurants and shops, free camping on beach 2 km south. And 30 km further southwest is the sealion colony, **Lobería Punta Bermeja**, daily bus in summer from Viedma; hitching easy in summer. **Tourist office** ① *Av Villarino y Urquiza, T427171, www.rionegrotur.com.ar, 0900-2100*; there is another office on the Costanera.

Carmen de Patagones (*Population 16,000*) was founded in 1779 and many early pioneer buildings remain in the pretty streets winding down to the river. There's a fascinating museum, **Museo Histórico** ① *JJ Biedma 64, T462729, daily 0930-1230, 1900-2100, Sun afternoon only*, with artifacts of the indigenous inhabitants, missionaries and gauchos; good guided tours. Helpful **tourist office** at ① *Bynon 186, T462054* is more dynamic than Viedma's. The two towns are linked by two bridges and a four-minute frequent ferry crossing (US$0.20).

Bahía San Blas is an attractive small resort and renowned shark fishing area, 100 km from Patagones (tourist information at www.bahiasanblas.com); plentiful accommodation. Almost due west and 180 km along the coast, on the Gulf of San Matías, is **San Antonio Oeste** (*Phone code: 02934. Population: 14,000*), and 17 km south, the popular beach resort, **Las Grutas**. The caves themselves are not really worth visiting; but the water is famously warm. Las Grutas is closed in the winter, but very crowded in the summer; accessible by bus from San Antonio hourly US$1. San Antonio is on the bus routes north to Bahía Blanca and south as far as Río Gallegos and Punta Arenas.

● Sleeping

Viedma *p201*
C Austral, 25 de Mayo y Villarino, T422615, viedma@hoteles-austral.com.ar. Modern, with well-equipped if rather old-fashioned rooms.
C Nijar, Mitre 490, T422833. Most comfortable, smart, modern, good service.
D Peumayen, Buenos Aires 334, T425222. Old-fashioned friendly place on the plaza.
E Spa, 25 de Mayo 174, T430459. Good value, lovely and quiet, with steam baths, helpful staff.

Camping Good municipal site near the river, US$2 per person, all facilities including hot showers.
Estancias **AL La Luisa** and San Juan, both 40 km away in wilder country, T02920-463725, eleri@rnonline.com.ar. Traditional Patagonia *estancias*, with English speaking owners, riding, cattle mustering, good hospitality, all meals, transfers and activities included, open Dec-Mar. Highly recommended.

❷ Eating

Viedma *p201*

♦♦ **La Ochava**, Alsina y 25 de Mayo.
Good food and atmosphere.

♦ **La Balsa**, on the river at Colón y Villarino.
The best restaurant, cheap but delicious
seafood, good wines.

❸ Transport

Viedma *p201*

Air Airport 5 km south. LADE (Saavedra 403,
T/F424420) fly to **Buenos Aires**, **Mar del Plata**,

Bahía Blanca, **Neuquén**, **San Martín de Los
Andes**, **Trelew** and **Comodoro Rivadavia**.

Bus Terminal in Viedma at Av Pte Perón y Guido,
15 blocks from plaza; taxi US$1. To **Buenos Aires**
14 hrs, 3 daily, US$20, **Don Otto/La Estrella/
Cóndor**. To **San Antonio Oeste**, 2½ hrs, several
daily, US$4, **Don Otto**. To **Bahía Blanca**,
4 hrs, 4 daily, US$5.

Train A comfortable sleeper train, which also
carries cars, goes from Viedma to **Bariloche**
overnight Fri 1800. On board there's a restaurant
and a cinema car showing videos. US$48 for a
bed, US$28 for a reclining seat. T02944-431777,
www.trenpatagonico.com.ar. Book ahead.

Puerto Madryn and around

→ *Phone code: 02965. Colour map 9, grid A3. Population: 60,000.*

Puerto Madryn is a pleasant, breezy seaside town 250 km south of San Antonio Oeste. It stands
on the wide bay of Golfo Nuevo, the perfect base for the Península Valdés and its extraordinary
array of wildlife, just 70 km east. It was the site of the first Welsh landing in 1865 and is named
after the Welsh home of the colonist, Jones Parry. Popular for skin diving and the nature
reserves, the town's main industries are a huge aluminium plant and fish processing plants.
You can often spot whales directly from the coast at the long beach of **Playa El Doradillo**, 16 km
northeast (October-December). **EcoCentro** ① *Julio Verne 3784, T457470, www.eco
centro.org.ar, daily 1000-1800 (usually closed Tue in winter), US$6, reductions for students.*
An inspired interactive sea life information centre, art gallery, reading room and café, it is
perched on a cliff at the south end of town, with fantastic views of the whole bay. **Museo de
Ciencias Naturales y Oceanográfico** ① *Domecq García y J Menéndez, Mon-Fri 0900-1200,
1430-1900, Sat 1430-1900, US$1.* This informative museum has displays of local flora and
fauna. The **tourist office** is at ① *Av Roca 223, T/F453504, www.madryn.gov.ar, Mon-Fri
0700-2300, Sat-Sun 0830-2300,* extremely helpful. On 7 March the Battle of Patagones (1827)
is celebrated in a week-long colourful fiesta of horse displays and fine food.

Around Puerto Madryn

With **elephant seal** and **sea lion** colonies at the base of chalky cliffs, breeding grounds for
Southern right whales in the sheltered Golfo Nuevo and the Golfo San José, and **guanacos**,
rheas, **patagonian hares** and **armadillos** everywhere on land, the area around Puerto
Madryn, especially the Península Valdés, is a spectacular region for wildlife. Whales can be
seen from June to mid December, particularly interesting with their young September-October.
The sea lion breeding season runs from late December to late January, but visiting is good up
to late April. Bull elephant seals begin to claim their territory in the first half of August and the
breeding season is late September/early October. Orcas can be seen attacking seals at Punta
Norte in February/March. Conservation officials can be found at the main viewpoints,
informative but only Spanish spoken. The *EcoCentro* in Puerto Madryn, studies the marine
ecosystems. **Punta Loma** ① *0800-1200, 1430-1930; US$4, children US$2 (free with
Península Valdés ticket), information and video, many companies offer tours, taxi US$15
($8.30 one way, walk back).* This is a sea lion reserve 15 km southeast of Puerto Madryn, best
visited at low tide; sea lions can even be seen in Puerto Madryn harbour. See also Puerto
Deseado, page 210 and Punta Tombo, page 208.

Península Valdés

① *Entry US$12 for foreigners, children US$6 (US$3 Mercosur, US$1.65 Argentines).*

The Península Valdés, near Puerto Madryn, in Chubut province, has an amazing array of wildlife:
marine mammals including Southern Right Whales, penguins and guanacos. There are other
penguin colonies on the coast, a fine palaeontological museum in Trelew and villages where
Welsh settlers set up home. Several estancias offer excellent hospitality for those who wish to

get to know the vastness of this land. The best way to see the wildlife is by car. See Puerto Madryn for car hire; fuel will cost about US$10 for the return trip. A taxi costs US$70 per vehicle for the day. Take your time, roads are all unpaved except the road from Puerto Madryn to Puerto Pirámide. In summer there are several shops, but take sun protection and drinking water.

The Golfos Nuevo and San José are separated by the Istmo Carlos Ameghino, which leads to **Península Valdés**, a bleak, but beautiful treeless splay of land. In depressions in the heart of the peninsula are large salt flats; Salina Grande is 42 m below sea level. At the entrance to the peninsula, on the isthmus, there is an interesting Visitors' Centre with wonderful whale skeleton. Five km from the entrance, Isla de los Pájaros can be seen in Golfo San José, though its seabirds can only be viewed through fixed telescopes (at 400 m distance); best time is September to April. The main tourist centre of the Peninsula is **Puerto Pirámide** (*Population 400*), 107 km east of Puerto Madryn, where boat trips leave to see the whales in season (sailings controlled by Prefectura, according to weather). There's plentiful accommodation and eating places here (tourist information, T495084, www.puertopiramides.gov.ar).

Punta Norte (176 km) at the north end of the Valdés Peninsula, isn't usually included in tours, but has elephant seals and penguins (September-March) below its high, white cliffs, best seen at low tide, also, occasionally, orcas. There are several reasonably priced restaurants. At **Caleta Valdés**, 45 km south of Punta Norte, you can see huge colonies of elephant seals at close quarters, and there are three marked walks. At **Punta Delgada** (at the south of the peninsula) elephant seals and other wildlife can be seen. The beach on the entire coast is out of bounds; this is strictly enforced.

Puerto Madryn

Sleeping
ACA Camping 2
Bahía Nueva 1
Casa de Pueblo 12
El Gualicho 3
Hostel Viajeros 14
Hostería
  Torremolinos 4
La Tosca Hostel 16
Marina 5
Muelle Viejo 6
Península Valdés 7
Playa 8
Residencial J'Os 15
Residencial Verona 18
Santa Rita 9
Tierra del Sur 17
Tolosa 10
Villa Pirén 11

Eating
Cantina El Náutico 1
Centro de Difusión de la
  Pescada Artesanal 2
Halloween 3
Havanna 6
La Casona de Golfo 5
La Vaca y el Pollito 7
Mitos 10
Placido 11
Taska Beltza 12
Yoaquina 13

● Sleeping

Puerto Madryn *p202, map p203*
Book ahead in summer, and whale season.
Note that non-Argentines will often be
charged more in the pricier hotels.
A Marina, Av Roca 7, T/F454915, www.marina
madryn.com.ar. Great value little seafront
apartments for up to 5 people, book ahead.
A Península Valdés, Av Roca 155, T471292,
www.hotelpeninsula.com.ar. Luxurious minimalist
sea front hotel with great views. Spa, sauna, gym.
A Playa, Av Roca 187, T451446, www.playa
hotel.com.ar. Good sea front location, the slightly
pricier more modern rooms are worth it.
A Tolosa, Roque Sáenz Peña 253,
T471850, www.hoteltolosa.com.ar.
Extremely comfortable, modern, great
breakfasts. Disabled access. Recommended.
B Bahía Nueva, Av Roca 67, T451677,
www.bahianueva.com.ar. One of the best sea
front hotels, quite small but comfortable rooms,
professional staff, cheaper in low season.
B-C Villa Pirén, Av Roca 439, T/F456272,
www.piren.com.ar. Excellent modern rooms
and apartments in smart seafront place.
C Casa de Pueblo, Av Roca 475, T472500,
www.madryncasadepueblo.com.ar. Reputed
to be the first brothel in town, now a
charming seafront chalet hotel with
homely atmosphere, good value.
C Hostería Torremolinos, Marcos A Zar 64,
T453215. Nice, modern, well decorated rooms.
C Muelle Viejo, H Yrigoyen 38, T471284,
www.muelleviejo.com. Ask for the comfortable
modernized rooms in this funny old place. Rooms
for 4 are excellent value, kitchen facilities.
C-D Res Verona, 25 de Mayo 874, T451509,
hotel_verona@hotmail.com. New, with breakfast,
also has 3 apartments, excellent value.
D Residencial J'Os, Bolívar 75, T471433.
Nice little place, breakfast included.
D Hostal Santa Rita, Gob Maiz 370, T471050.
Welcoming, comfy, wash basins in rooms, few
bathrooms, dorm **E**, also kitchen facilities,
breakfast extra. Recommended.
E Tierra del Sur, 9 de Julio 57, T471379,
tierradelsuralojamiento@yahoo.com.ar. New,
good breakfast, kitchen very helpful.
E-F pp El Gualicho, Marcos A Zar 480, T454163,
http://elgualicho.com.ar. Best budget option,
HI discounts, nicely designed, enthusiastic
owner, free pick up from bus terminal, *parrilla*,
garden, some double rooms, bikes for hire.
Highly recommended.
F pp Hostel Viajeros, Gob Maíz 545, T456457,
www.hostelviajeros.com. With basic breakfast,
small rooms with 4 beds or doubles (**C**), big
kitchen/dining room, lawn, TV, helpful.

F pp La Tosca Hostel, Sarmiento 437,
Chubut, T456133, www.argentinahostels.com.
Also has doubles (**C**), AHC member.
Camping ACA, Blvd Brown, 3.5 km south of
town at Punta Cuevas, T452952. Open Sep-Apr,
hot showers, café, shop, no kitchen facilities, shady
trees, close to the sea. Closed out of season.

Península Valdés *p202*
Puerto Pirámide
L Las Restingas, 1ra Bajada al Mar, T495101,
www.lasrestingas.com. Exclusive, sea views,
very comfortable, with sophisticated
regional restaurant.
A Cabañas en el Mar, T495049,
www.piramides.net. Comfortable, well-
equipped 2-6 bed *cabañas*.
A The Paradise, 2da Bajada al Mar, T495030,
www.hosteriaparadise.com.ar. Large comfortable
rooms, suites with jacuzzis, fine seafood restaurant.
C ACA Motel, T495004, www.piramides.net.
Welcoming, handy for the beach, with good
seafood restaurant (you might spot whales from
its terrace), camping. There is also an ACA service
station (daily) with good café and shop.
Camping Municipal campsite by the black
sand beach, T495084, hot showers in evening,
good, get there early to secure a place. Do not
camp on the beach: people have been swept
away by the incoming tide.

Estancias

Several, including:
L Faro Punta Delgada, Punta Delgada, T15
406303, www.puntadelgada.com. Next to a
lighthouse, amazing setting, half and full board,
excellent food, very helpful. Recommended;
book in advance.
L Rincón Chico, near Punta Delgada, T156 88303
(T471733 in Puerto Madryn), www.rincon
chico.com.ar. A working sheep farm with luxurious
accommodation, walking and cycling circuits, half
and full board available. Recommended.
AL La Elvira, Caleta Valdés, near Punta Cantor,
T15 669153 (office in Puerto Madryn T474248),
www.laelvira.com. Traditional Patagonian dishes
and comfortable accommodation (B&B, half and
full board available).

● Eating

Puerto Madryn *p202, map p203*
Excellent seafood restaurants, mostly chargin
similar prices, but quality varies. You should
try at least one plate of *arroz con mariscos*
(rice with a whole selection of squid, prawns,
mussels and clams).

Keeping up with the Joneses

On 28 July 1865, 153 Welsh immigrants landed at Puerto Madryn, then a deserted beach deep in *indígena* country. After three weeks they pushed, on foot, across the parched pampa and into the Chubut river valley, where there is flat cultivable land along the riverside for a distance of 80 km upstream. Here, maintained in part by the Argentine Government, they settled, but it was three years before they realized the land was barren unless watered. They drew water from the river, which is higher than the surrounding flats, and built a fine system of irrigation canals. The colony, reinforced later by immigrants from Wales and from the US, prospered, but in 1899 a great flood drowned the valley and some of the immigrants left for Canada. The last Welsh contingent arrived in 1911. The object of the colony had been to create a 'Little Wales beyond Wales', and for four generations they kept the Welsh language alive. The language is, however, dying out in the fifth generation. There is an offshoot of the colony of Chubut at Trevelin, at the foot of the Andes nearly 650 km to the west, settled in 1888 (see page 194). It is interesting that this distant land gave to the Welsh language one of its most endearing classics: *Dringo'r Andes* (Climbing the Andes), written by one of the early women settlers.

♥♥♥ Placido, Av Roca 508, T455991. On the beach, stylish, intimate, excellent service, seafood and vegetarian options, also cheaper pasta dishes.
♥♥ Taska Beltza, 9 de Julio 345, T15 668085. Excellent food, chef 'El Negro' cooks superb paella, with Basque influence – book ahead, closed Mon. Highly recommended.
♥♥ Centro de Difusión de la Pescada Artesanal, Brown, 7th roundabout, no sign, T15 538085. Authentic cantina, where the fishermen's families cook meals with their catch, very popular, go early.
♥♥ La Vaca y el Pollito, Av Roca y A Storni, T458486. Built into the wooden hull of a boat, cosy, *parrilla*, seafood and pastas. Ideal for families, with soft play area.
♥♥ Yoaquina, Blvd Brown between 1st and 2nd roundabouts, T456058. Relaxed. Beachfront, eat outside in summer, good seafood, open from breakfast to after dinner, cheap lunch menu.
♥ Cantina El Náutico, Av Julio Roca y Albarracín, T471404. Long-established, good food (though set meal not great, go for individual dishes) and service, mainly fish, always full of locals.
♥ La Casona de Golfo, Av Roca 349. Good value *tenedor libre parrilla*, seafood, and 'helados libre', as much ice cream as you can eat. Great for families.
♥ Halloween, Av Roca 1355. Pizza and *empanadas*.

Cafés
Havanna, Av Roca y 28 de Julio. Smart, buzzing.
Mitos, 28 de Julio 80. Stylish café with good atmosphere. Recommended.
París 43, RS Peña y 25 de Mayo, T458166. Good place for coffees.

▲ Activities and tours
Puerto Madryn *p202, map p203*
Diving
Puerto Madryn is a diving centre, with several shipwrecked boats in the Golfo Nuevo. A 1st dive ('bautismo') for beginners costs about US$30 pp.
Lobo Larsen, Av H Yrigiyen 144, T15 516314, www.lobolarsen.com. Good equipment and boat, guide speaks English, professional, US$48 for 2 open-water dives.
Madryn Buceo, Blvd Brown, 3rd round-about in Balneario Nativo Sur, T155 13997, www.madrynbuceo.com. Offer courses of all kinds from beginners' dives to the week-long PADI course, around US$160, or US$30 for a day excursion.
Ocean Divers, Blvd Brown (between 1st and 2nd roundabout), T472569; advanced courses (PADI) and courses on video, photography and underwater communication.

Mountain bike hire
US$5 for 3 hrs, US$8.50 all day. See
El Gualicho, under Sleeping, above.
XT Mountain Bike, Av Roca 742, T472232.

Tours
Many agencies do similar 12-hr tours to the Península Valdés, about US$40, plus US$12 entrance to the Peninsula. They include the interpretation centre, Puerto Pirámides (the whales boat trip is US$25 extra), Punta Delgada and Caleta Valdés. Shop around to find out how long you'll spend at each place, how big the group is, and if your guide speaks English. On all

excursions take drink, food if you don't want to eat in the expensive restaurants, and binoculars. Most tour companies stay about 1 hr on location. Tours to see the penguins at Punta Tombo and Welsh villages are better from Trelew. Tours do not run after heavy rain in the low season. Recommended for Península Valdés:

Argentina Visión, Av Roca 536, T451427, www.argentinavision.com. Also 4WD adventure trips and *estancia* accommodation at Punta Delgada, English and French spoken.

Hydrosport, near the ACA in Puerto Pirámide, T495065, hysport@infovia.com.ar. Rents scuba equipment and boats, and organizes land and sea wildlife tours to see whales and dolphins.

Ryan's Travel, Yrigoyen 257, loc 4, www.ryanstravel.com.ar. Very helpful (also have offices in El Calafate and Ushuaia).

Jorge Schmidt, Puerto Pirámide, T495012. Recommended for whale watching.

Tito Botazzi, Blvd Brown 1070, T474110. Small groups and good bilingual guides, very popular for whale watching.

⊕ Transport

Puerto Madryn *p202, map p203*

Air Airport 10 km west; LADE to **Buenos Aires, Bahía Blanca, Viedma, Trelew, Comodoro Rivadavia** and other Patagonian airports. More flights to **Bariloche**, Buenos Aires, and El Calafate from Trelew. Buses to Trelew stop at entrance to airport if asked. Taxi US$30. Direct bus to Trelew airport, **Puma**, US$3.50, leaves 1½ hrs before flight and takes arriving passengers to Puerto Madryn.

Bus Terminal at Irigoyen y San Martín (behind old railway station), T451789, with café, clean toilets, locutorio, drinks and sweets kiosk. To **Buenos Aires**, 18 hrs, several companies,

US$50-65 (eg QueBus service with meals included). To **Bahía Blanca**, 9 ½ hrs with Don Otto, 2000, US$23. To **Comodoro Rivadavia**, 6 hrs, US$16-20. To **Río Gallegos**, 18 hrs; US$38, El Pingüino (connecting to El Calafate, Punta Arenas, Puerto Natales), Andesmar, TAC, Don Otto. To **Trelew**, 1 hr, every hr, US$3 with 28 de Julio, Mar y Valle. To **Bariloche**, 15 hrs, US$35, daily, except Wed, Don Otto.

Car hire Expensive, and note large excess for turning car over. Drive slowly on unpaved *ripio* roads; best to hire 4WD! **Madryn**, Roca 624, T452355. **Localiza** has an office (see Car Hire in Essentials). **Sigma**, T471739, or 15-699465 (24 hrs), www.sigmarentacar.com. Will deliver car to your hotel.

Taxi There are taxis outside the bus terminal, T452966/474177, and on the main plaza.

Península Valdés *p202*
28 de Julio **bus** company from Puerto Madryn to Puerto Pirámide, daily at 1000, returns 1800, US$3.50 each way, 1½ hrs.

⊕ Directory

Puerto Madryn *p202, map p203*
Airline offices Aerolíneas Argentinas, Roca 427, T450938. LADE, Roca 119, T451256.
Banks Lots of ATMs at the following: Banco Nación, 9 de Julio 117. Banco del Chubut, 25 de Mayo 154 and Río, Mitre 102. **Internet** Internet Centro Madryn, 25 de Mayo y Belgrano. US$0.60 per hr. Re Creo, Roque Sáenz Peña 101.
Medical services For emergencies call 107 or 451240. Late-night pharmacy at on Belgrano y 25 de Mayo. **Post offices** Belgrano y Maiz, 0900-1200, 1500-1900. **Telephones** Many *locutorios* in the centre.

Trelew and the Chubut Valley

→ *Phone code: 02965. Colour map 9, grid A3. Population: 90,000.*

Pronounced 'Trel-ay-Oo', Trelew is a busy town, with an excellent museum and a shady plaza, which hosts a small handicraft market at weekends. Visit mid-October to see the Eisteddfod (Welsh festival of arts). Evidence of Welsh settlement remains only in a few brick buildings: the 1889 **Capilla Tabernacl**, on Belgrano, between San Martín and 25 de Mayo, and the **Salón San David**, a 1913 Welsh meeting hall. On the road to Rawson, 3 km south, is one of the oldest standing Welsh chapels, **Capilla Moriah**, from 1880, with a simple interior and graves of many original settlers in the cemetery. **Museo Paleontológico Egidio Feruglio** ① *Fontana 140, T432100, www.mef.org.ar, Sep-Mar daily, 0900-2000, otherwise Mon-Fri 1000-1800, Sat-Sun 1000-2000, US$5, full disabled access and guides for the blind.* This is an excellent museum, which presents the origins of life and dynamically poised dinosaur skeletons. It has good information in Spanish and free tours in English, German and Italian; also a café and shop. Also has information about **Parque Paleontológico Bryn-Gwyn**, 8 km from Gaiman (see below). **Museo Regional Pueblo de Luis** ① *Fontana y 9 de Julio, T424062, Mon-Fri 0800-2000, Sat closed, Sun 1700-2000, US$0.65.* In the old 1889 railway station, it has displays on indigenous societies, failed Spanish attempts at settlement and on Welsh colonization. **Tourist office** on the plaza ① *Mitre 387, T420139, Mon-Fri 0800-1400, 1500-2100, Sat-Sun 0900-1300, 1500-2000. Www.trelew.gov.ar*, map available.

Gaiman and around → *Colour map 9, grid A3. Population: 4,400.*

A small pretty place with old brick houses retaining the Welsh pioneer feel, Gaiman hosts the annual Eisteddfod (Welsh festival of arts) in October. It's renowned for delicious, and excessive 'traditional' Welsh teas and its fascinating, tiny museum, **Museo Histórico Regional Galés** ① *Sarmiento y 28 de Julio, T491007, US$1, Tue-Sun 1500-1900*, revealing the spartan lives of the idealistic Welsh pioneers. Curator Mrs Roberts is very knowledgeable. **Geoparque Bryn Gwyn** ① *8 km south of town, T432100, www.mef.org.ar, open daily 0900-1600, closed 25 Dec and 1 Jan, US$2.50, getting there: taxi from Gaiman US$2*. Fossil beds 40 million years old are shown on a good guided tour; there is a visitor centre offering try-outs in paleontology fieldwork. **El Desafío** ① *2 blocks west of plaza, US$2.50, tickets valid 2 months*, is a quaint, if weatherbeaten private theme-park comprising pergolas and dinosaurs made of rubbish. The **tourist office** ① *Av Eugenio Tello, T491571, www.gaiman.gov.ar, Mon-Sat 0900-2000, Sun 1100-1800*, is on the plaza.

Dolavon, founded in 1919, is a quiet settlement, with a few buildings reminiscent of the Welsh past. The main street, Avenida Roca, runs parallel to the irrigation canal built by the settlers, where willow trees now trail into the water, and there's a Welsh chapel, **Capilla Carmel** at one end. The old flour mill at Maipú y Roca dates from 1927 and can be visited – ask for the key during office hours at the Municipalidad, Roca 188 (next to *Banco Provincial del Chubut*). There's *Autoservicio Belgrano* at the far end of San Martin, for food supplies, but no tea rooms, and nowhere to stay. The **municipal campsite**, two blocks north of the river, is free, with good facilities.

In the irrigated valley between Dolavon and Gaiman, you'll see more Welsh chapels tucked away among fringes of tall *alamo* (poplar) trees and silver birches (best if you're in your own transport). The **San David chapel** (1917) is a beautifully preserved brick construction, with an elegant bell tower, and sturdy oak-studded door, in a quiet spot surrounded by birches.

Paved Ruta 25 runs from Dolavon west to the upper Chubut Valley, passing near the **Florentino Ameghino** dam, a good leafy spot for a picnic. From Ameghino to Tecka on Ruta 40 (south of Trevelin) is one of the most beautiful routes across Patagonia from the coast to the

Trelew

Sleeping
Galicia 1
Libertador 2
Rayentray 3
Rivadavia 4
Touring Club 5

Eating
Café de mi Ciudad 5
Delikatesse 1
El Quijote 2
El Viejo Molino 3
La Bodeguita 4

Andes, lots of wildlife to be seen. It goes through Las Plumas (mind the bridge if driving), Los Altares, which has an ACA motel, camping, fuel and some shops, and Paso Los Indios.

South of Trelew

Punta Tombo ① *Park entrance US$7. Tours from Trelew and Puerto Madryn, US$25; 45 mins at the site, café and toilets. Access from Ruta 1, a ripio road between Trelew and Camarones. Closed late Mar-Sep.* This nature reserve is 107 km south of Trelew, open from September, when huge numbers of Magellanic penguins come here to breed, the largest single penguin colony on the South American subcontinent. Chicks can be seen from mid- November; they take to the water January to February. It's fascinating to see these creatures up close, but noisy colonies of tourists dominate in the morning; it's quieter in the afternoon. You'll see guanacos, hares and rheas on the way. Another large **penguin colony** ① *all year, US$5* – with lots of other marine life, including whales and orcas – is at Cabo Dos Bahías, easily reached from the town of **Camarones** 275 km north of Comodoro Rivadavia. The Guarda Fauna is 25 km from town.

● Sleeping

Trelew *p206, map p207*
B **Rayentray**, San Martín y Belgrano, T434702, www.cadenarayentray.com.ar. Large, modernized, comfortable rooms, professional staff, breakfast included, pool.
C **Libertador**, Rivadavia 31, T/F420220, www.hotellibertadortw.com. Modern, highly recommended for service and comfortable rooms, breakfast included.
D **Galicia**, 9 de Julio 214, T433802, www.hotelgalicia.com.ar. Central, grand entrance, comfortable rooms, excellent value. Recommended.
D **Rivadavia**, Rivadavia 55, T434472, hotelriv@infovia.com.ar. Simple, comfortable rooms with TV, breakfast extra, the cheapest recommendable place.
D **Touring Club**, Fontana 240, T/F433997, htouring@internet.siscotel.com. Gorgeous 1920's bar, faded elegance, simple rooms, great value, breakfast extra. Open from breakfast to the small hours for sandwiches and drinks. Recommended.

Gaiman *p207*
C **Posada Los Mimbres**, Chacra 211, 6 km west of Gaiman, T491299, www.posadalos mimbres.com.ar. Rooms in the old farmhouse or in modern building, good food, very relaxing.
D **Plas y Coed**, Yrigoyen 320, T155 85219. Marta Rees' delightful tea shop has double and twin rooms in an annex next door, with bath and TV, includes breakfast. Highly recommended.
D **Ty Gwyn**, 9 de Julio 111, T491009, tygwyn@ cpsarg.com. Neat, comfortable, with TV, above the tea rooms, excellent value.
E **Gwesty Tywi**, Jones 342, T491292, gwestywi@ infovia.com.ar. Pretty, well-kept bed and breakfast.

Camping **Los Doce Nogales** is an attractive site south of the river at Chacra 202, close to **Ty Te Caerdydd** tea room, T155 18030, with showers.

● Eating

Trelew *p206, map p207*
† **La Bodeguita**, Belgrano 374. Delicious pastas and pizzas, with interesting art on the walls, lively atmosphere. Recommended.
† **Delikatesse**, Belgrano y San Martin. Best pizzas in town, cheery place, popular with families.
† **El Quijote**, Rivadavia 463. Recommended *parrilla*, popular with locals.
† **El Viejo Molino** Gales 250, T428019. Open 1130-0030 (closed Mon), best in town, in renovated 1886 flour mill, for Patagonian lamb, pastas, good value set menu with wine included.
† **Supermercado Anónima**, Av Belgrano, 1 block north of Av Colombia, has a good food hall.
† **Supermercado Norte**, Soberanía y Belgrano. Cheap takeaway food.

Cafés
Café de mi Ciudad, Belgrano y San Martin. Smart café serving great coffee; read the papers here.

Gaiman *p207*
El Angel, Rivadavia 241. Stylish small restaurant serving excellent food.
La Colonia, on the main street. Quality *panadería*.
Siop Bara, Tello y 9 de Julio, sells cakes and ice creams.
Tavern Las, small pub at Tello y Miguel Jones.

● *For an explanation of the sleeping and eating price codes used in this guide, see page 58.*
● *Other relevant information is found in Essentials pages 68-69.*

🛏 Sleeping

Comodoro Rivadavia *p209*

B Lucania Palazzo, Moreno 676, T449 9338, www.lucania-palazzo.com. Most luxurious business hotel, superb rooms, sea views, good value, huge American breakfast, sauna and gym included. Recommended.

C Comodoro, 9 de Julio 770, T447 2300, info@comodorohotel.com.ar. Buffet breakfast included, pay extra for larger rooms.

D Azul, Sarmiento 724, T447 4628, Breakfast extra, quiet old place with lovely bright rooms, kind, great views from the *confitería*.

D Rua Marina, Belgrano 738, T447 6877. With TV and breakfast, recommended budget choice, owners are backpacker-friendly.

E Hospedaje Cari Hué, Belgrano 563, T447 2946. Excellent budget choice, breakfast extra, shared bath, nice owners who like backpackers!

Sarmiento *p210*

C Chacra Labrador, 10 km from Sarmiento, T0297-489 3329, agna@coopsar.com.ar. Excellent small *estancia*, breakfast included, other meals extra and available for non-residents, English and Dutch spoken, runs tours to petrified forests at good prices, will collect guests from Sarmiento (same price as taxi).

E Colón, Perito Moreno 650, T489 4212. One of the better cheap places in town.

E Hostería Los Lagos, Roca y Alberdi, T493046. Good, heating, restaurant.

Camping Club Deportivo Sarmiento, 25 de Mayo y Ruta 20, T4893103. **Municipal site** near Río Senguer, 2 km north of centre on Route 243, basic, no shower, US$3 for tent, US$1 pp.

Puerto Deseado *p210*

L Estancia La Madrugada, T155 94123, lwalker@caminosturismo.com.ar, or ats@caminosturismo.com.ar. Comfortable accommodation and good Patagonian home cooking, excursions to sea lion colony and cormorant nesting area, English spoken. Highly recommended.

C Isla Chaffers, San Martín y Mariano Moreno, T4872246. Modern, central.

C Los Acantilados, Pueyrredón y España, T4872167, www.pdeseado.com.ar/acantour. Beautifully located, good breakfast.

Puerto San Julián *p210*

B Bahía, San Martín 1075, T454028, nico@sanjulian.com.ar. Modern, comfortable, good value. Recommended.

B Estancia La María, 150 km northwest of Puerto San Julián, offers transport, lodging and meals and visits to fascinating caves with paintings of human hands, guanacos etc 4,000-12,000 years old, less visited than Cueva de las Manos. Contact Fernando Behm in San Julián, Saavedra 1163, T452328.

C Municipal, 25 de Mayo 917, T452300. Very nice, well run, good value, no restaurant.

C Res Sada, San Martín 1112, T452013. Fine, hot water, on busy main road, poor breakfast.

Camping Good municipal campsite Magallanes 650 y M Moreno, T452806. US$2 pp plus US$1 for the use of shower, repeatedly recommended, all facilities.

🍴 Eating

Comodoro Rivadavia *p209*

🍴 **La Barra**, San Martín 686. Good for breakfast, coffee or lunch.

🍴 **Cayo Coco**, Rivadavia 102. Excellent pizzas, good service.

🍴 **Dionisius**, 9 de Julio y Rivadavia. Elegant *parrilla*, set menu US$5.

🍴 **La Nueva Rosada**, Belgrano 861. Good for beef or chicken.

🍴 **Peperoni**, Rivadavia 348. Cheerful, modern, pastas.

🍴 **La Barca**, Belgrano 935. Good *tenedor libre*.

🍴 **Superquick** in *La Anónima* supermarket, San Martín y Güemes. Cheap food.

Café El Sol, Av Rivadavia y 25 de Mayo. Good café to hang out in.

Puerto Deseado *p210*

🍴 **La Casa de Don Ernesto**, San Martín 1245. Seafood and *parrilla*.

🍴 **El Pingüino**, Piedrabuena 958. *Parrilla*.

🍴 **El Viejo Marino**, Pueyrredón 224. Considered the in town best by locals.

Puerto San Julián *p210*

🍴 **Rural**, Ameghino y Vieytes. Good, but not before 2100. A number of others. Also bars and tearooms.

🍴 **Sportsman**, Mitre y 25 de Mayo. Excellent value.

● *For an explanation of the sleeping and eating price codes used in this guide, see page 58.*
● *Other relevant information is found in Essentials pages 68-69.*

▲ Activities and tours

Puerto Deseado *p210*
Darwin Expediciones, España 2601,
T156 247554, www.darwin-expeditions.com.
Los Vikingos, Estrada 1275, T156 245141/ 487
0020, vikingo@puertodeseado.com.ar. Both offer
excursions by boat to Ría Deseado reserve and
Reserva Provincial Isla Pingüino; also trips to the
Monumento Natural Bosques Petrificados.

◉ Transport

Comodoro Rivadavia *p209*
Air Airport, 13 km north. Bus No 6 from bus
terminal, hourly (45 mins), US$0.50. Taxi to airport,
US$3-5. To **Buenos Aires**, AR/Austral. LADE flies
to all Patagonian destinations once or twice a
week, plus **Bariloche**, **El Bolsón** and **Esquel**.
Bus Terminal in centre at Pellegrini 730,
T446 7305; has luggage store, *confitería*, toilets,
excellent tourist information office 0800-2100,
some kiosks. In summer buses usually arrive full;
book ahead. Services to **Buenos Aires** 2 daily,
28 hrs, US$45. To **Bariloche**, 14½ hrs, US$19,
Don Otto, T447 0450. To **Esquel** (paved road) 8
hrs direct with ETAP, T447 4841, and *Don Otto*,
US$18. To **Río Gallegos**, daily, 10-12 hrs,
US$17-21 (see below for companies). To **Puerto
Madryn**, US$16-20, and **Trelew**, 3 daily, 4 hrs,
US$12, several companies. To/from **Sarmiento**
and **Caleta Olivia**, see below. To **Coyhaique**
(Chile), US$35, 12 hrs, Giobbi twice a week.

Sarmiento *p210*
Bus 3 daily to/from **Comodoro Rivadavia**,
US$5, 2½ hrs. To **Chile** via **Río Mayo**, 0200,

twice weekly; seats are scarce in Río Mayo.
From Sarmiento you can reach **Esquel**
(448 km north along Rutas 20 and 40);
overnight buses on Sun stop at Río Mayo,
take food for journey.

Caleta Olivia *p210*
Bus To **Río Gallegos**, Andesmar, Sportman
(overnight) and **El Pingüino** (overnight, US$8),
US$8-16, 9½ hrs. Many buses to/from **Comodoro
Rivadavia**, 1 hr, US$2.50-3 (La Unión and
Sportman at terminal, T0297-485 1134), and
3 daily to **Puerto Deseado**, La Unión and
Sportman, 2½-3 hrs, US$6-8. To **Perito Moreno**
and **Los Antiguos**, 5-6 hrs, US$7, several daily.

Puerto San Julián *p210*
Air LADE (Berutti 985, T452137) flies
weekly to **Comodoro Rivadavia**, **El Calafate**,
Gobernador Gregores, **Puerto Deseado**,
Río Turbio and **Río Gallegos**.
Bus To/from **Río Gallegos**, El Pingüino,
6 hrs, US$8.

◉ Directory

Comodoro Rivadavia *p209*
Airline offices Aerolineas Argentinas,
9 de Julio 870, T444 0050. LADE, Rivadavia
360, T447 6565. **Banks** Many ATMs and
major banks along San Martín. Change money
at **Thaler**, San Martín 270, Mon-Sat 1000-
1300, or at weekends ETAP in bus terminal.
Consulates Chile, Almte Brown 456, Edif.
Torraca VIII, p 1, T447 1043. **Internet** Several
places on San Martín, and at Rivadavia 201.
Post offices San Martín y Moreno.

Río Gallegos and around

→ *Phone code: 02966. Colour map 9, grid C2. Population: 75,000.*

The capital of Santa Cruz Province, 232 km south of Piedrabuena, on the estuary of the Río
Gallegos, this pleasant open town was founded in 1885 as a centre for the trade in wool and
sheepskins, and boasts a few smart shops and some excellent restaurants. The delightful
Plaza San Martín, 2 blocks south of the main street, Avenida Roca, has an interesting
collection of trees, many planted by the early pioneers, and a tiny corrugated iron cathedral,
with a wood-panelled ceiling in the chancel and stained glass windows. The small **Museo de
los Pioneros** ⓘ *Elcano y Alberdi, daily 1000-2000, free,* is worth a visit. Interesting tour
given by the English-speaking owner, a descendent of the Scottish pioneers; great photos of
the first sheep-farming settlers, who came here in 1884 from the Malvinas/Falkland Islands.
Museo de Arte Eduardo Minichelli ⓘ *Maipú 13, Mon-Fri 0800-1900, Sat-Sun and holidays
1400-1800 (closed Jan/Feb),* has work by local artists. **Museo Regional Provincial Manuel
José Molina** ⓘ *in the Complejo Cultural Santa Cruz, Av San Martín y Ramón y Cajal 51,
Mon-Fri 1000-1800, Sat 1500-2000,* has rather dull rocks and fossils and a couple of dusty
dinosaur skeletons. **Museo Malvinas Argentinas** ⓘ *Pasteur 74, Mon and Thu 0800-1300,
Tue and Fri 1300-1730, 3rd Sun of month 1530-1830.* More stimulating, it aims to inform
visitors, with historical and geographical reasons, why the Malvinas are Argentine. The
provincial **tourist office** is at ⓘ *Roca 863, T438725, www.epatagonia.gov.ar, Mon-Fri*

Ruta 40 to the glaciers

Río Mayo (*Phone code 02903*; fuel and hotels **D-E**) is reached by Ruta 22 (paved) which branches southwest 74 km west of Sarmiento. Every November, it holds the **Fiesta Nacional de la Esquila** (national sheep-shearing competition). From Río Mayo, a road continues west 140 km to the Chilean border at Coyhaique Alto for Coyhaique in Chile. **South of Río Mayo** Ruta 40 is unpaved as far as Perito Moreno (124 km, high-clearance advised). There is no public transport and very few other vehicles even in mid-summer. At Km 31 on this road a turning leads west to Lago Blanco, to Chile via Paso Huemules and Balmaceda.

Perito Moreno (*Phone code 02963. Colour map 9, grid B2. Population: 3,000. Altitude: 400 m*), not to be confused with the famous glacier of the same name near El Calafate, nor with nearby Parque Nacional Perito Moreno, is a spruce little town, 25 km east of Lago Buenos Aires, the second largest lake in South America. Southwest is Parque Laguna, with varied bird life and fishing. But you're most likely to stop off here to see the **Cueva de las Manos** (see below). Two ATMs, but nowhere to change travellers cheques. **Tourist office** ① *in the bus terminal, low season 0800-2000, high season 0700-2300, T432222/020,* can advise on tours. Also has information on Patagonian *estancias*, in English.

Ruta 40 is unpaved and rough south of Perito Moreno; 124 km south, a marked road runs 46 km northeast to the famous **Cueva de las Manos** ① *US$5, under 12 free, a ranger at the site gives information.* In a beautiful volcanic canyon is an intriguing series of galleries with 10,000-year-old paintings of human hands and animals in red, orange, black, white and green. Worth the trip for the setting, especially early morning or evening. Road difficult after rain.

After hours of spectacular emptiness, even tiny **Bajo Caracoles** (*Population 100*) is a relief: a few houses with an expensive grocery store and very expensive fuel. From here Ruta 41 goes 99 km northwest to **Paso Roballos**, continuing to Cochrane in Chile.

Parque Nacional Perito Moreno

① *Free. Park office in Gobernador Gregores, Av San Martín 409, T02962-491477, www.parquesnacionales.com. Accessible only by own transport, Nov-Mar.*

South of Bajo Caracoles, 101 km, is a crossroads. Ruta 40 heads southeast while the turning northwest goes to remote Parque Nacional Perito Moreno (free), at the end of a 90-km *ripio* track. There is trekking and abundant wildlife among the large, interconnected system of lakes below glaciated peaks, though much of the park is dedicated to scientific study only. Lago Belgrano, the biggest lake, is a vivid turquoise, its surrounding mountains streaked with a mass of differing colours. Ammonite fossils can be found. The Park ranger, 10 km beyond the park entrance, has maps and information on walks and wildlife, none in English. Camping is free: no facilities, no fires. There is no public transport into the park but it may be possible to arrange a lift with estancia workers from Hotel Las Horquetas.

From the Parque Moreno junction to Tres Lagos, Ruta 40 improves considerably. East of the junction (7 km) is *Hotel Las Horquetas* (closed) and 15 km beyond is Tamel Aike village (police station, water). After another 34 km Ruta 40 turns sharply southwest, but if you need fuel before Tres Lagos, you must make a 72 km detour to Gobernador Gregores (always carry spare). At **Tres Lagos** a road turns off northwest to Lago San Martín. From Tres Lagos Ruta 40 deteriorates again and remains very rugged until the turnoff to the Fitz Roy sector of Parque Nacional Los Glaciares. 21 km beyond is the bridge over Río La Leona, with delightful *Hotel La Leona* whose café serves good cakes. Near here are petrified tree trunks 30 m long, protected in a natural reserve.

Border with Chile: Los Antiguos: from Perito Moreno Ruta 43 (paved) runs south of Lago Buenos Aires to **Los Antiguos**, 60 km west, 2 km from the Chilean border (*Phone code 02963*). ATM on Av 11 de Julio. **Tourist office** ① *Av 11 de Julio 446, T491261, 0800-2200 in summer, morning only other times. www.losantiguos.gov.ar.*

🔵 **Sleeping**

Río Mayo *p215*
L Estancia Don José, 2.5 km west of Río Mayo, T420015 or 0297-156 249155, www.guenguel.com.ar. Excellent *estancia*

accommodation, with superb food, rooms and cabins. The family business involves sustainable production of guanaco fibre.

Perito Moreno *p215*

D **Americano**, San Martín 1327, T432538. With breakfast, has a decent restaurant, new ownership.
D **Belgrano**, San Martín 1001, T432019. This hotel is often booked by Ruta 40 long-distance bus companies, basic, one key fits all rooms, helpful owner, breakfast extra, restaurant.
E pp **Santa Cruz**, Belgrano 1565. Simple rooms.
Camping Municipal site 2 km at Laguna de los Cisnes, T432072. Also 2 *cabaña* places.
Estancias 2 estancias on RN40: 28 km south:
AL pp **Telken**, sheep station of the Nauta family, T02963-432079, telkenpatagonia@argentina.com or jarinauta@yahoo.com.ar. Comfortable rooms, all meals available shared with family, English and Dutch spoken, horse treks and excursions (Cueva de las Manos US$80). Highly recommended.
B **Hostería Cueva de Las Manos**, 20 km from the cave at Estancia Las Toldos, 60 km south, 7 km off the road to Bajo Caracoles, T02963-432856/839 (Buenos Aires 49010436, F4903 7161). Open 1 Nov-5 Apr, closed Christmas and New Year, runs tours to the caves, horse riding.
E **Estancia Turística Casa de Piedra**, 75 km south of Perito Moreno on Ruta 40, in Perito Moreno ask for Sr Sabella, Av Perón 941, T02963-432199. Price is for rooms, camping G, hot showers, homemade bread, use of kitchen, excursions to Cueva de las Manos and volcanoes by car or horse.

Bajo Caracoles *p215*

L **Hostería Lagos del Furioso**, on the peninsula between Lagos Posadas and Pueyrredón, take Ruta 39, T02963-490253, www.lagosdel furioso.com. Open mid-Oct-Easter. Comfortable in cabins by the lake shore, offering Patagonian cooking with home produced food and good wines. Also offers horse riding, trekking and excursions in 4WD vehicles. 2 nights minimum.
D **Hotel Bajo Caracoles**, T434963. Old-fashioned but hospitable, meals.

Parque Nacional Perito Moreno *p215*

Nearest accommodation is B full board **Estancia La Oriental**, T02962-452196, elada@uvc.com.ar. Splendid setting, with comfortable rooms. Nov-Mar, with horse riding, trekking. See www.cielos patagonicos.com or www.estanciasdesantacruz.com, for other *estancias* in Santa Cruz: *Menelik* near PN Perito Moreno, and *El Cóndor*, on the southern shore of Lago San Martín, 135 km from Tres Lagos.

Tres Lagos *p215*

E **Restaurant Ahoniken**, Av San Martín, has rooms.
Camping At Estancia La Lucia, US$2.50, water, barbecue, 'a little, green paradise'; supermarket, fuel.

Los Antiguos *p215*

A **Hostería La Serena**, Km 29, details from Geraldine des Cressonières, T02963-432340. Very comfortable accommodation, excellent home-grown food, organizes fishing and trips in Chilean and Argentine Lake Districts, open Oct-Jun.
B **Antigua Patagonia**, Ruta 43, T491055, www.antiguapatagonia.com.ar. Luxurious rooms with beautiful views, excellent restaurant. Tours to Cueva de las Manos and nearby Monte Cevallos.
D **Argentino**, Av 11 de Julio 850, T491132, comfortable, decent restaurant.
F pp **Albergue Padilla**, San Martín 44 (just off main street) T491140. Comfortable dorms, *quincho* and garden. Also camping. El Chaltén travel tickets.
Camping An outstanding Camping Municipal, 2 km from centre on Ruta Provincial 43, T491265, with hot showers, F pp.

❶ Eating

Perito Moreno *p215*

Good food at **Pipach**, next to *Hotel Austral*, *Parador Bajo Caracoles*, or pizzas at **Nono's**, 9 de Julio y Saavedra.

❸ Transport

Río Mayo *p215*

Bus To **Sarmiento** and **Coyhaique** from bus office in the centre. Mon-Fri at 0300 **Giobbi** buses take Ruta 40 north from Río Mayo direct to Esquel.

Perito Moreno *p215*

Bus Terminal on edge of town next to petrol station, T432072, open only when buses arrive or depart . If crossing from Chile at Los Antiguos, 2 buses daily in summer, 1 hr, US$3, **La Unión** T432133. To **El Chaltén** and **El Calafate**, Chaltén Travel, see next paragraph, at 0800. To **Comodoro Rivadavia**, with La Unión, 0630, 1700 and **Sportman**, 1700, 6 hrs, US$9-10.

Los Antiguos *p215*

It is nearly impossible to hitchhike between Perito Moreno and El Calafate. Hardly any traffic and few services.
Bus To **Comodoro Rivadavia**, US$9-12, **La Unión** (T491093, at Turismo Toscas Bayas) and **Sportman** (11 de Julio 445, T491333), daily, 7½ hrs, via **Perito Moreno** and **Caleta Olivia**. *Albergue Padilla* sells tickets. To **El Chaltén** and **El Calafate**, via Perito Moreno, every other (odd) day at 0800, US$66, also north to **Bariloche**, every even day, US$65, **Chaltén Travel**, www.chalten travel.com, mid-Nov-Apr. To **Chile**, La Unión to **Chile Chico**, 8 km west, US$1, 45 mins (for routes from Chile Chico to Coyhaique, see Chile chapter).

Parque Nacional Los Glaciares

This park, the second largest in Argentina, extends over 724,000 ha. 40% of it is covered by ice fields (*hielos continentales*) from which 13 major glaciers descend into two great lakes, Lago Argentino and, further north, Lago Viedma, linked by the Río La Leona, flowing south from Lago Viedma. The only accessible areas of the park are the southern area around Lago Argentino, accessible from El Calafate, and the northern area around Cerro El Chaltén (Fitz Roy). Access to the central area is difficult and there are no tourist facilities.

Ins and outs
Access to the southern part of the park is 50 km west of El Calafate, US$10. **National Park Office** in Calafate ① *Av del Libertador 1302, T491005, www.losglaciares.com*, helpful, English spoken; in El Chaltén ① *across the bridge at the entrance to the town, T493004, Jan-Feb 0700-2200, low season: 0900-1600.* An informative talk about the National Park and its paths is given to all incoming bus passengers. Both hand out helpful trekking maps of the area, with paths and campsites marked, distances and walking times. Note that the hotel, restaurant and transport situation in this region changes greatly from year to year.

El Calafate and around → *Phone code: 02902. Colour map 9, grid B1. Population: 8,000.*
This town sits on the south shore of **Lago Argentino** and exists almost entirely as a tourist centre for the **Parque Nacional los Glaciares**, 50 km away. An ever-growing number of hotels, hostels and *cabañas* can't quite accommodate the hordes at times in January and February, but the town is empty and quiet all winter. It's neither cheap nor attractive, but the Lago Argentino is beautiful, and the shallow part at Bahía Redonda is good for birdwatching in the evenings. **Tourist office** ① *in the bus terminal, T491090, www.elcalafate.gov.ar. Helpful staff speak several languages. Summer: Oct-Apr daily 0800-2300; low season: daily 0800-2200. See also www.calafate.com.*

For the main excursions to the glaciers, see below. At **Punta Gualicho** (or Walichu) on the shores of Lago Argentino 7 km east of town, there are cave paintings (badly deteriorated); 6-hour horse ride (US$40 pp). A recommended 15-minute walk is from the Intendencia del Parque, following Calle Bustillo up the road towards the lake through a quiet residential area to **Laguna Nímez** ① *US$0.70, guides at the entrance in summer (likely to be closed in low season, though still a nice area away from busy centre)*, a bird reserve (fenced in), with flamingos, ducks, black-necked swans and abundant birdlife. **Centro de Interpretación Histórica** ① *Av Brown y Bonarelli, US$3*, has a very informative anthropological and historical exhibition about the region, with pictures and bilingual texts, also a very relaxing café/library. There are several *estancias* within reach, offering a day on a working farm, *asado al palo,* horse riding and accommodation. **Estancia Alice 'El Galpón del Glaciar'** ① *T492509, Buenos Aires T011-4311 8614, www.estanciaalice.com.ar.* **Estancia Nibepo Aike** ① *on Brazo Sur of Lago Argentino in the National Park, 55 km southwest (book at Av Libertador 1215 p 1, T02966-436010, www.nibepoaike.com.ar)*, beautiful setting in a more remote area, traditional 'estancia' style with original furniture, delightful meals served and an optional boat trip on Brazo Sur. **'Cerro Frías'** ① *25 km west, T492808, www.cerrofrias.com*, excursion includes one meal and an ascent of Cerro Frías (1,030 m) for great views; options are by horse, on 4WD vehicles or on foot, US$38. See also **Helsingfors**, in Sleeping below, or visit www.estanciasdesantacruz.com.

Glaciar Perito Moreno
At the western end of Lago Argentino (80 km from El Calafate) the major attraction is the Glaciar Perito Moreno, one of the few glaciers in the world that is moving. It descends to the surface of the water over a 5-km frontage and a height of about 60 m. Several times in the past, it advanced across the lake, cutting the Brazo Rico off from the Canal de los Témpanos; then the pressure of water in the Brazo Rico broke through the ice and reopened the channel. This spectacular rupture last occurred in March 2006. The glacier can be seen close up from a series of wooden walkways descending from the car park. Weather may be rough. The vivid blue hues of the ice floes, with the dull roar as pieces break off and float away as icebergs from the snout, are spectacular, especially at sunset. ▸▸ *See Transport, page 224, for further details.*

Glaciar Upsala

At the northwest end of Lago Argentino, 60 km long and 4 km wide, Upsala Glacier is a stunning expanse of untouched beauty. It can be reached by motor-boat from Punta Bandera, 50 km west of El Calafate, on a trip that also goes to Lago Onelli and Spegazzini glaciers (with **Fernández Campbell**, see under Activities and tours). Small Lago Onelli is quiet and very beautiful, beech trees on one side, and ice-covered mountains on the other. The lake is full of icebergs of every size and sculpted shape. **Mar Patag** runs a two-day boat trip to Upsala, Spegazzini and Moreno glaciers. **Upsala Explorer** is another boat excursion that reaches Upsala glacier (see under Activities and tours for both).

El Chaltén and around

(*Phone code 02962*) This small tourist town lies 217 km northwest of El Calafate in the north of the park, at the foot of the jagged peaks of the spectacular Fitz Roy massif, which soars steeply from the Patagonian steppe, its sides too steep for snow to stick. Chaltén is the Tehuelche name meaning the 'smoking mountain', and occasionally at sunrise the mountains are briefly lit up bright red for a few seconds, a phenomenon known as the 'sunrise of fire', or '*amanecer de fuego*'. The town is windy, expensive and unattractive, but offers amazing views of the nearby peaks and it's the base for some of the country's finest trekking. If you haven't got a tent, you can easily rent all you'll need. **Tourist office** ① *Güemes 21, T493011, www.elchalten.com, excellent site with accommodation listed, Mon-Fri 0900-2000, Sat-Sun 1300-2000*. Take cash as there are no banks or ATMs. Credit cards are not accepted. Internet is available at US$2 for 30 minutes.

The **Lago del Desierto**, 37 km north of El Chaltén, is surrounded by forests, a stunning virgin landscape. A short walk to a mirador at the end of the road gives fine views. Excursions from El Chaltén by **Chaltén Travel** daily in summer, US$12; also transfer from **Restaurant Las Lengas** (see below), T493023, US$10, with 2-hour waiting time. Campsite at the southern end of Lago del Desierto, and refugios at its northern end. To get to **Villa O'Higgins** (Chile), the southernmost town on the Carretera Austral, take a bus from El Chaltén to Lago del Desierto (1¾ hours, US$12). A 45-minute boat trip goes to the northern end (US$20), or walk up a path alongside the east shores 4½ hours to reach the northern end. From there you can trek or go on horseback (7 hours with guide, US$30) to Puerto Candelario Mancilla on Lago O'Higgins (lodging at estancia). Next day, take a boat from Candelario Mancilla to Bahía Bahamóndez (2¾ hours, US$35), then a bus to Villa O'Higgins, 7 km, US$3. The border is closed from May to November (check at www.villaohiggins.com for tours and boat availability).

Also daily boat trips on Lago Viedma to pass Glaciar Viedma, with ice trekking optional in the day-long tour. The *estancia Hostería El Pilar* (see Sleeping) is a base for trekking up Río Blanco or Río Eléctrico, or try the multi activity adventure circuit. Highly recommended.

Trekking and climbing

Trekking The two most popular walks are to **1) Laguna Torre** (three hours each way). After 1-1½ hours you'll come to Mirador Laguna Torre with great view of Cerro Torre and Fitz Roy, and 1¼ hours more to busy Camping De Agostini near the lake, where you have fantastic views. **2) Laguna de Los Tres** (four hours each way). Walk 1¼ hours up to Camping Capri, great views of Fitz Roy, then another hour to Camping Poincenot. Just beyond it is Camping Río Blanco (only for climbers, registration at the National Park office required). From Río Blanco you can walk another hour, very steep, to Laguna de los Tres where you'll get a spectacular view (not a good walk if it's cloudy). You can connect the two paths by taking one that takes about two hours and branches off south, northwest of Laguna Capri, passes by Lagunas Madre e Hija and reaches the path to Laguna Torre, west of the Mirador. This may be too long for a day. From El Chaltén to Laguna Torre along this route takes about seven hours. **3) Loma del Pliegue Tumbado** (four hours each way). To a viewpoint where you can see both cordons and Lago Viedma: marked path from Park Ranger's office, a good day walk, best in clear weather. **4) Laguna Toro** (seven hours each way). For more experienced trekkers, to wild glacial lake across the ice cap. **5) Up Río Blanco to Piedra del Fraile** (seven hours each way, two hours each way from the road to Lago del Desierto). A beautiful walk out of the National Park to campsite with facilities, and Refugio Piedra del Fraile, neither is free. Recommended. The best day walks are Laguna Capri, Mirador Laguna Torre, both of which have great views after an hour or so. Most paths are very clear and well worn, but a map is essential, even on short walks: the park information centre gives helpful maps of treks. If you wish to buy maps, the

66 99 Chaltén is the Tehuelche name meaning the 'smoking mountain', and occasionally at sunrise the mountains are briefly lit up bright red for a few seconds, a phenomenon known as the 'sunrise of fire'...

best are by *Zagier and Urruty*, www.patagoniashop.net, 1:50,000 (US$5-10); 1:100,000 (US$7.50), updated quite regularly and available in shops in El Calafate and El Chaltén. For trekking on horseback with guides: **Rodolfo Guerra** *T493020* (also hires animals to carry equipment, but can be poorly planned); **El Relincho** *T493007*. In summer **Restaurant Las Lengas** (see below) runs a regular minibus to Lago del Desierto passing by some starting points for treks and by Hostería El Pilar.

Climbing Base camp for Fitz Roy (3,405 m) is Campamento Río Blanco (see above). Other peaks include Cerro Torre (3,102 m), Torre Egger (2,900 m), Cerro Solo (2,121 m), Poincenot (3,002 m), Guillaumet (2,579 m), Saint-Exupery (2,558 m), Aguja Bífida (2,394 m) and Cordón Adela (2,938 m): most of these are for very experienced climbers. Generally the best time is mid February to end March; November-December is very windy; January is fair; winter is extremely cold, but weather is unpredictable and it all depends on the specific route being climbed. Permits for climbing are available at the national park information office. Guides are available in El Chaltén. **Fitz Roy Expediciones** ① *L Terray 212, T493107, www.fitzroyexpediciones.com.ar*. Owned by experienced guide Alberto del Castillo, organizes trekking and adventure trips including on the *Campo de Hielo Continental*, ice climbing schools, and fabulous longer trips. Climbers must be fit, but no technical experience required; equipment provided. Email with lots of notice to reserve. Highly recommended. **Casa De Guías** ① *Av Costanera Sur, T493118, www.casadeguias.com.ar*, are experienced climbers who lead groups to nearby peaks, to the Campo de Hielo Continental and easier treks. **Mermoz** ① *San Martín 493, T493098, mermoz@ infovia.com.ar*, for trips across Lago del Desierto, with bus transfer, English spoken, helpful.

El Calafate to Chile
If travelling from El Calafate to Torres del Paine by car or bike, you'll cross this bleak area of steppe. About 40 km before reaching the border there are small lagoons and salt flats with flamingoes (between El Calafate to Punta Arenas it is also possible to see guanacos and condors). From Calafate you can take the paved combination of Ruta 11, RN 40 and RN 5 to La Esperanza (165 km), where there's fuel, a campsite and a large but expensive *confitería* (lodging **D** with bath). From La Esperanza, Ruta 7 heads west (not completely paved) along the valley of the Río Coyle. A shorter route (closed in winter) missing La Esperanza, goes via El Cerrito and joins Ruta 7 at *Estancia Tapi Aike*. Ruta 7 continues to the border crossing at Cancha Carrera and then at Cerro Castillo meets the good *ripio* road between Torres del Paine (20 km north) and Puerto Natales (63 km south). For bus services along this route see under El Calafate.

Río Turbio → *Phone code 02902. Colour map 9, grid C2. Population: 6,600.*
A charmless place, 267 km west of Río Gallegos, 30 km from Puerto Natales (Chile), you're most likely to visit en route to or from Torres del Paine in Chile. The site of Argentina's largest coalfield hasn't recovered from the depression hitting the industry in the 1990s. It has a cargo railway, connecting it with Punta Loyola; Mina 1 is where the first mine was opened. There is a ski centre: **Valdelén** has six pistes and is ideal for beginners, also scope for cross-country skiing between early June and late September. **Tourist information** in the municipality ① *Juan José Paso 237, T421679, www.rioturbio.gov.ar*.

Border with Chile
1) Paso Mina Uno/Dorotea is 5 km south of Río Turbio. Open all year, 0800-2400. On the Chilean side this runs south to join the main Puerto Natales-Punta Arenas road. **2) Paso Casas**

Viejas is 33 km south of Río Turbio via 28 de Noviembre. Open all year, 0800-2400 (2200 in winter). On the Chilean side this runs west to join the main Puerto Natales-Punta Arenas road. **3) Paso Río Don Guillermo (or Cancha Carrera)** is 48 km north of Río Turbio, this is the most convenient crossing for Parque Nacional Torres del Paine. Open all year, 0800-2400 (2200 in winter). Argentine customs are fast and friendly. On the Chilean side the road continues 7 km to the border post at Cerro Castillo, where it joins the road from Puerto Natales to Torres del Paine.

● Sleeping

Parque Nacional los Glaciares *p217*
LL Estancia Helsingfors, 73 km northwest of La Leona, on Lago Viedma, T/F02966-420719 (in Bs As: T011-4315 1222), www.helsingfors.com.ar. Fabulous place in splendid position on Lago Viedma, stylish rooms, welcoming lounge, delicious food (full board), and excursions directly to glaciers and to Laguna Azul, by horse or trekking, plus boat trips. Open Oct-Apr.
LL Los Notros, 70 km west of Calafate on the road to the Moreno glacier, T/F499510 (in Bs As: T011-4814 3934), www.losnotros.com. Exclusive retreat with wonderful views of the glacier, spacious rooms, all-inclusive packages.

Camping AMSA, Olavarría 65 (50 m off the main road, turning south at the fire station), T492247. Hot water, open in summer, US$3.50 pp. **El Huala**, 42 km from El Calafate, on the road to Lago Roca. Free with basic facilities, open all year round. **Lago Roca**, 50 km from El Calafate, T499500, beautifully situated, US$4 pp, bike hire, fishing licences, restaurant/confitería, open Oct-Apr. (Ferretería Chuar, 1 block from bus terminal, sells gas for camping.)

El Calafate *p217, map p220*
Prepare to pay far more for accommodation here than elsewhere in Argentina. El Calafate is very popular in Jan-Feb, so book all transport and accommodation in advance. Best months to visit

El Calafate

N

0 metres 100
0 yards 100

Sleeping ●
Albergue & Hostal Lago Argentino 12
Alto Verde 1
América del Sur 22
Ariel 13

Cabañas Nevis 3
Calafate Hostel 4
Camping AMSA 25
Casa de Grillos 1
Cerro Cristal 6
El Quijote 8
Hostel Buenos Aires 2
Hostel del Glaciar Libertador 24
Hostel del Glaciar Pioneros 21
Hostería del Calafate

Hostel 4
Kosten Aike 14
Kau Yatún 23
Lago Azul 5
Los Alamos 15
Michelangelo 17
Patagonia Rebelde 7
Sir Thomas 11
Vientos del Sur 20

Eating ●
Borges y Alvarez 2

Casablanca 1
El Puesto 3
Heladería Aquarela 4
La Cocina 5
La Vaca Atada 10
Mi Viejo 7
Pura Vida 6
Rick's Café 7

are Oct, Nov and Mar, Apr when it is less crowded and less overpriced. Many hotels open only from Sep/Oct to Apr/May.

LL Kau Yatún, Estancia 25 de Mayo (10 blocks from centre, east of arroyo Calafate), T491059, www.kauyatun.com. Renovated main house of a former estancia, well-kept grounds, 2 excellent restaurants, only half board or all inclusive packages that include excursions in the National Park.

L Kosten Aike, Gob Moyano 1243, T492424, www.kostenaike.com.ar. Relaxed yet stylish, elegant spacious rooms, jacuzzi, gym, excellent restaurant, *Ariskaiken* (open to non residents), cosy bar, garden, English spoken. Recommended.

AL El Quijote, Gob Gregores 1155 , T491017, www.quijotehotel.com.ar. A very good hotel, spacious, well-designed with traditional touches, tasteful rooms with TV, restaurant *Sancho* (from US$10 for 3 courses), English and Italian spoken.

AL Los Alamos, Gob Moyano y Bustillo, T491144, www.posadalosalamos.com. Very comfortable, charming rooms, good service, lovely gardens and without doubt the best restaurant in town.

AL Patagonia Rebelde, José Haro 442, T494495, www.patagonia rebelde.com. Charming new building in traditional Patagonian style, resembling an old inn with rustic decor, good comfort with well-heated bedrooms and comfy sitting-rooms.

A Cabañas Nevis, Av del Libertador 1696, T493180, www.cabanasnevis.com.ar. Owner Mr Patterson offers very nice cabins for 5 and 8 (price quoted is for 5), some with lake view, great value. Recommended.

A Hostería del Calafate Hostel, 25 de Mayo y Gob Moyano, T491256, www.calafate hostels.com. Same owners as Calafate Hostel round the corner, small, extremely functional, plainly decorated, with TV, PC with internet and minibar in every room.

A Vientos del Sur, up the hill at Río Santa Cruz 2317, T493563, www.vientosdelsur.com. Very hospitable, calm, comfortable, TV, good views, kind family attention.

B Michelangelo, Espora y Gob Moyano, T491045, www.michelangelohotel.com.ar. Lovely, quiet, welcoming, TV, breakfast included, superb restaurant. Recommended.

B Ariel, Av Libertador 1693, T493131, www.hotelariel.com.ar. Modern, functional, well maintained, TV, with breakfast.

B Cerro Cristal, Gob Gregores 989, T491088, www.cerrocristalhotel.com.ar. Comfortable, quiet, free internet and TV, breakfast included, very good value in low season.

B-C Alto Verde, Zupic 138, T491326, www.welcomeargentina.com/altoverde. Top quality, spotless, spacious, helpful, breakfast included, also with apartments for 4.

C Casa de Grillos, Pasaje Las Bandurrias, T491160, www.casadegrillos.com.ar. Welcoming B&B in the calm green area, next to Nímez nature reserve. It has all the comfort and charm of a family house.

C Sir Thomas, Espora 257, T492220, www.sirthomas.com.ar. Modern, comfortable wood-lined rooms, breakfast extra.

C-F pp Albergue y Hostal Lago Argentino, Campaña del Desierto 1050-61 (near bus terminal), T491423, hostellagoargentino@ cotecal.com.ar. **F** pp shared dorms with kitchen facilities, too few showers when full, nice atmosphere, good flats and **B** doubles with breakfast on a neat garden.

D Posada Nakel Yenú, Pto. San Julian 244, T493711. Price includes breakfast, also has apartments (**B**), AHC member, www.argentinahotels.com.

E pp América del Sur, up the hill on C Puerto Deseado, access from Col Rosales east of Arroyo Calafate, T493525, www.americahostel.com.ar. Panoramic views from this comfortable, relaxed hostel, welcoming, well-heated rooms, with breakfast (**E** pp dorms for 4, **C** doubles with views, one room adapted for wheelchair users), chill-out area, fireplace, internet access, kitchen facilities. Warmly recommended.

E-F Hostel Buenos Aires, Buenos Aires 296, 200 m from terminal, T491147, www.glaciares calafate.com. Homely, quiet, kind owner, comfortable with doubles with bath and breakfast, doubles without bath, and dorms for up to 8, breakfast extra, kitchen facilities, helpful, good hot showers, luggage store, bikes for hire.

E-F pp Hostel del Glaciar 'Libertador', Av del Libertador 587 (next to the bridge), T491792, www.glaciar.com. HI discounts, open year round. Smaller and pricier than 'Pioneros', rooms are good and well-heated, all with own bath (**E** pp dorms for 4 and **AL** doubles), breakfast extra, cooking facilities, internet access. Free transfer from bus terminal. Owners run **Patagonia Backpackers** (see below under Activities and tours).

F pp Calafate Hostel, Gob Moyano 1226, 400 m from bus terminal, T492450, www.calafate hostels.com. A huge log cabin with good rooms: **E** pp dorms with or without bath, breakfast extra, **B-C** doubles with bath and breakfast. Kitchen facilities, internet access, lively sitting area. Book a month ahead for Jan-Feb and call ahead

⬤ *For an explanation of the sleeping and eating price codes used in this guide, see page 58.*
⬤ *Other relevant information is found in Essentials pages 68-69.*

for free shuttle from airport, HI discounts, helpful travel agency, Chaltén Travel (see below).

F pp Hostel del Glaciar 'Pioneros', Los Pioneros 251, T/F491243, www.glaciar.com. Discount for HI members, open mid Sep to mid Apr. Accommodation for all budgets: standard **C** doubles (also for 3 and 4) with bath, superior **B** doubles with bath, shared dorms up to 4 beds, **E** pp. Many languages spoken, lots of bathrooms, internet access, kitchen facilities, no breakfast, free shuttle from bus terminal. Very popular, so book well in advance and double-check. *Punto de Encuentro* restaurant with some vegetarian options. Owners run **Patagonia Backpackers** (see below under Activities and tours).

F pp Lago Azul, Perito Moreno 83, T491419. Charming Sra Echeverría and her husband Horacio, a Calafate pioneer, offer traditional Patagonian hospitality, 2 rooms for 3, shared bath. Highly recommended.

El Chaltén *p218*

In high season places are likely to be full: book ahead. Most places close in low season.

AL Hostería El Puma, Lionel Terray 212, T493095, www.elchalten.com/elpuma. A little apart, splendid views, lounge with log fire, tasteful stylish furnishings, comfortable, transfers and big American breakfast included. Can also arrange tours through their excellent agency Fitz Roy Expeditions, see Climbing, above. Recommended.

AL Hostería Posada Lunajuim, Trevisán s/n, T/F493047, www.elchalten.com/lunajuim. Stylish yet relaxed, comfortable (duvets on the beds), lounge with wood fire, with full American breakfast. Recommended.

A El Pilar (see above), T/F493002, www.hosteria elpilar.com.ar. Country house in a spectacular setting at the meeting of Ríos Blanco and de las Vueltas, with clear views of Fitz Roy. A chance to sample the simple life with access to less-visited northern part of the park. Simple comfortable rooms, great food, very special. Owner Marcelo Pagani is an experienced mountain guide.

B-C Nothofagus, Hensen s/n, T493087, www.elchalten.com/nothofagus. Cosy bed and breakfast, simple rooms with and without bath, good value. Recommended. AHC Argentina Hostels Club, www.argentinahostels.com.

C Hospedaje La Base, Lago del Desierto s/n, T493031. Good rooms for 2, 3 and 4, all with bath, tiny kitchen, self service breakfast included, great video lounge. Recommended.

E pp Albergue Patagonia, Av San Martín 493, T/F493019, www.elchalten.com/patagonia. HI-affiliated, small and cosy with rooms for 2 with own bath (**A**) or for 2 (**C**), 4, 5 or 6 with shared bath, kitchen, video room, bike hire, laundry,

very welcoming. Helpful information on Chaltén, also run excursions to Lago del Desierto.

E pp Albergue Rancho Grande, San Martín s/n, T493005, chaltenrancho@yahoo.com.ar. HI-affiliated, in a great position at the end of town with good open views and attractive restaurant and lounge, accommodates huge numbers of trekkers in rooms for 4, with shared bath, breakfast extra. Also **C** doubles, breakfast extra. Helpful, internet, English spoken. Recommended. Reservations in Calafate Hostel/Chaltén Travel, Calafate.

F pp Cóndor de los Andes, Av Río de las Vueltas y Halvorsen, T493101, www.condordelos andes.com. Nice little rooms for up to 6 with bath, sheets included, breakfast US$2, laundry service, library, kitchen, quiet.

Camping del Lago, Lago del Desierto 135, T493010, centrally located with hot showers. **El Refugio**, off San Martín just before Rancho Grande (US$3 pp plus US$2 for hot shower). A gas/alcohol stove is essential for camping as open fires are prohibited in campsites in of the National Park. Take plenty of warm clothes and a good sleeping bag. It is possible to rent equipment in El Chaltén, ask at park office or Rancho Grande.

In the National Park Poincenot, Capri, Laguna Toro, De Agostini. None has services, all river water is drinkable. Pack up all rubbish and take it back to town, do not wash within 70 m of rivers. **Camping Piedra del Fraile** on Río Eléctrico is behind park boundary, privately owned, has facilities.

Río Turbio *p219*

C De La Frontera, 4 km from Rio Turbio, Paraje Mina 1, T421979. The most recommendable. **D Hostería Capipe**, Dufour, 9 km from town, T482935, www.hosteriacapipe.com.ar. Simple, with restaurant.

❷ Eating

El Calafate *p217, map p220*

† **El Puesto**, Gob Moyano y 9 de Julio, T491620. Tasty thin-crust pizzas in a cosy old house. Pricier regional meals and takeaway. Recommended.

† **La Cocina**, Av del Libertador 1245. Good pizza and pasta, including a large variety of pancakes. **RR La Tablita**, Coronel Rosales 28 (near the bridge). The best place for a typical *parrilla* with generous portions and quality beef.

† **La Vaca Atada**, Av del Libertador 1176. Good homemade pastas and more elaborate and expensive dishes based on trout and king crab.

† **Mi Viejo**, Av del Libertador 1111. Popular *parrilla*, US$5.50 for grilled lamb.

Pura Vida, Av Libertador 2000 block, near C 17. Comfortable sofas, homemade Argentine food, vegetarian options, lovely atmosphere, lake view. Recommended.

Rick's Café, Av del Libertador 1091. Lively *parrilla* with good atmosphere.

Universo, Av del Libertador y 9 de Julio. Unpretentious and modest as El Calafate used to be. Good basic meals.

Cafés

Borges y Alvarez, Av del Libertador 1015 (Galería de los Gnomos). A lively café/bookshop, open till 0100, good place to hang out.

Casablanca, 25 de Mayo y Av del Libertador. Jolly place for omelettes, hamburgers, vegetarian, US$7 for steak and chips.

Heladería Aquarela, Av del Libertador 1177. The best ice cream – try the *calafate*.

El Chaltén *p218*

Estepa, Cerro Solo y Antonio Rojo. Small, intimate place with good, varied meals.

Fuegia, San Martín s/n. Pastas, trout, meat and vegetarian dishes. Dinner only, recommended.

Pangea, Lago del Desierto y San Martín. Open for lunch and dinner, drinks and coffee, calm, good music, varied menu. Recommended.

Patagonicus, Güemes y Madsen. Lovely warm place with salads, *pastas caseras* and fabulous pizzas for 2, US$3-8, open midday to midnight. Recommended.

Ruca Mahuida, Lionel Terray s/n. Widely regarded as the best restaurant with imaginative and well prepared food.

Zaffarancho (behind Rancho Grande), bar-restaurant, good range and reasonably priced.

Josh Aike, Lago de Desierto 105. Excellent *confitería*, homemade food, beautiful building. Recommended.

Las Lengas, Viedma y Güemes, opposite tourist office, cheaper than most. Plentiful meals, basic pastas and meat dishes. US$3 for meal of the day. Owner runs a minibus to Lago del Desierto.

Domo Blanco, Costanera y De Agostini, and Güemes y Río de las Vueltas. Delicious ice cream.

🎵 Bars and clubs

El Chaltén *p218*

Cervecería Bodegón El Chaltén, San Martín s/n. Brews its own excellent beer, also pizzas, *empanadas*, coffee and cakes.

🛍 Shopping

El Calafate *p217, map p220*

La Anónima. There is a supermarket on Av del Libertador y Perito Moreno.

El Chaltén *p218*

Several supermarkets, all expensive, and little fresh food available: **El Gringuito**, Av Antonio Rojo, has the best choice. Fuel is available next to the bridge.

▲ Activities and tours

El Calafate *p217, map p220*

Most agencies charge the same rates and run similar excursions.

Chaltén Travel, Av del Libertador 1174, T492212 (in Bs As T011-4326 7282), also Av Güemes y Lago del Desierto, El Chaltén, www.chalten travel.com. Most helpful, huge range of tours: glaciers, *estancias*, trekking, and bus to El Chaltén. Also sell tickets along the Ruta 40 to Perito Moreno, Los Antiguos, US$66, and Bariloche, US$130, departures 0800 (0830 from El Chaltén) mid-Nov-Apr on even days, either as a 2-day trip, overnight in Perito Moreno (chaper to book your own accommodation), 12-14 hrs travelling each day, poor ventialtion, or as a 4-day tour with stops at attractions on the way, English spoken.

Fernández Campbell, Av del Libertador 867, T491298, www.solopatagonia.com.ar. Memorable day-boat excursions to Upsala glacier and Lago Onelli (and Spegazzini glacier in summer); lunch extra in summer at restaurant on Bahía Onelli, US$60 plus transfer to Punta Bandera departure point. Recommended. Also 45-min boat trip to the front of Moreno glacier from a pier 1 km away from walkways, US$8.50 plus transfer from El Calafate.

Hielo y Aventura, Av del Libertador 935, T492205, www.hieloyaventura.com. Minitrekking includes walk through forests and 2-hr trek on Moreno glacier (crampons included), US$110. Also half-day boat excursion to Brazo Sur for a view of spectacular glaciers, including Moreno, US$40. Recommended.

Lago San Martín, Av del Libertador 1215, p 1, T492858, lagosanmartin@cotecal.com.ar. Operates with Estancias Turísticas de Santa Cruz, specializing in arranging estancia visits, helpful.

Mar Patag, T011-5031 0756, www.cruceros marpatag.com. Exclusive 2-day boat excursion to Upsala, Spegazzini and Moreno glaciers, US$350 pp, full board.

Mil Outdoor Adventure, Av del Libertador 1029, T491437, www.miloutdoor.com. Excursions in 4WD to panoramic views, 3-6 hrs, US$42-70.

Mundo Austral, Av del Libertador 1114, T492365, F492116. For all bus travel and cheaper trips to the glaciers, helpful bilingual guides.

Patagonia Backpackers, at Hosteles del Glaciar, T491243, www.glaciar.com. Alternative Glacier tour, entertaining, informative, includes walking, US$30. Recommended constantly. Also

Supertrekking en Chaltén, Oct-Apr, 2-day hiking trip, featuring the best treks in the Fitz Roy massif, including camping and ice trekking, US$180. Highly recommended. Also sells tickets for **Navimag** ferries (Puerto Natales-Puerto Montt).
Upsala Explorer, 9 de Julio 69, T491133, www.upsalaexplorer.com.ar. Spectacular full-day experience visiting Upsala glacier by boat, superb lunch at remote Estancia Cristina (vegetarians catered for on request), and excursions to Mirador del Upsala, weather permitting, US$150.

⊖ Transport

El Calafate *p217, map p220*
Air Airport, T491230, 22 km east of town, **Transpatagonia Expeditions**, T493766, runs service from town to meet flights, US$7 open return. Taxi (T491655/492655), US$10. **AR/Austral** flies daily to/from **Buenos Aires**. Many more flights in summer to **Bariloche**, **Ushuaia** and **Trelew** (office at 9 de Julio 57, T492815). **LADE** flies to **Ushuaia**, **Comodoro Rivadavia**, **Río Gallegos** and **Esquel** (office at Julio A Roca 1004, Loc 4, T491262). To **Puerto Natales** Aerovías Dap Nov-Mar only, representatives at **Aventura Andina**, Av del Libertador 761, T491726. Airport tax US$6.
Bus Terminal on Roca 1004, 1 block up stairs from Av del Libertador. To **Perito Moreno** glacier daily with **Taqsa** (T491843) or **Cal-Tur** (T491842), 1½ hrs, US$10. To **El Chaltén** daily with **Taqsa**, Chaltén Travel (T492212, at 0800), Los Glaciares, Cal-Tur, 4-5 hrs, US$35 return. To **Río Gallegos** daily with **Sportman** (T02966-15 464841), Taqsa, **Interlagos/Pingüino** (T491179), 4 hrs, US$7-10. To **Ushuaia** and **Bariloche** take bus to Río Gallegos for connections: **Taqsa** runs a 0300 service for the best connections; check first. See above for Chaltén Travel's buses to Los Antiguos via Perito Moreno and Bariloche, page 223.
Taxi (*remise*) to **Río Gallegos**, with Remises Perito Moreno, T491745, 4 hrs, US$135 irrespective of number of passengers, up to 4 people.
Direct bus services to Chile (Take passport when booking bus tickets to Chile.) To **Puerto Natales**, daily in summer with **Cootra** (T491444), via Río Turbio, 7 hrs, or with **Turismo Zaahj** (T491631), Wed, Fri, Sun, or **Bus Sur**, 1 a week, US$20 (advance booking recommended, tedious border crossing). **Note** Argentine pesos cannot be exchanged in Torres del Paine.
Car hire Average price about US$50 per day for small car with insurance. **Cristina**, Av del Libertador 1711, T491674, crisrenta@rnet.com.ar. **Localiza**, Av del Libertador 687, T491398, localizacalafate@hotmail.com. **ON Rent a Car**,

Av del Libertador 1831, T493788 or T02966-15629985, onrentacar@cotecal.com.ar. All their vehicles have a permit for crossing to Chile, included in the fee. Bikes for hire, US$17 per day.

Glaciar Perito Moreno *p217*
Boat A 1-hr boat trip departs from a pier 1 km away from walkways and gets closer to the glacier's face, US$8.50; can be arranged independently through **Fernández Campbell** (see above) or is offered with the regular excursions. Another boat trip and a mini-trekking on the glacier are organized by **Hielo y Aventura** (see Activities and tours for both). In all cases go early.
Bus From El Calafate with **Taqsa**, **Cal-Tur**, US$16 return; also guided excursions. Many agencies in El Calafate also run minibus tours (park entry not included). Out of season trips to the glacier may be difficult to arrange. Taxis US$80 for 4 passengers round trip including wait at the glacier.

El Chaltén *p218*
Bus In summer, buses fill quickly: book ahead. Fewer services off season. Daily buses to **El Calafate**, 4-5 hrs, US$18 one way, companies given above, El Chaltén phone numbers: **Chaltén Travel** T493005, **Cal Tur** T493062. **Overland Patagonia** does trips to **Bariloche** in 4 days, staying at *estancias* and visiting **Cueva de las Manos**, www.overland patagonia.com. See above for Chaltén Travel to Los Antiguos and Bariloche, page 223.

Río Turbio *p219*
Bus To **Puerto Natales**, 2 hrs, US$5, several daily with **Cootra** (Tte del Castillo 01, T421448, cootra@oyikil.com.ar), **Bus Sur**, **Lagoper** (Av de Los Mineros 262, T411831). To **El Calafate**, **Cootra**, 4 hrs, US$10. **Río Gallegos**, 5 hrs, US$10 (**Taqsa**).

❶ Directory

El Calafate *p217, map p220*
Banks Best to take cash as high commission is charged on exchange, but there are ATMs at airport, **Banco de la Provincia de Santa Cruz**, Av del Libertador 1285, and at **Banco de Tierra del Fuego**, 25 de Mayo 34. **Thaler**, Av del Libertador 1242 changes money and TCs. **Post office** Av del Libertador 1133. **Telephone** Open Calafate, Av del Libertador 996, huge locutorio for phone and also 20 fast internet places, central but expensive. More convenient, also big and with a café is **Centro Integral de Comunicaciones**, Av del Libertador 1486.

Tierra del Fuego → *Colour map 9, grid C3.*

The island at the extreme south of South America is divided between Argentina and Chile, with the tail end of the Andes cordillera providing dramatic mountain scenery along the southern fringe of both countries. There are lakes and forests, mostly still wild and undeveloped, offering good trekking in summer and downhill or cross-country skiing in winter. Until a century ago, the island was inhabited by four ethnic groups, Selknam (Onas), Alcaluf, Haush and Yamana. They were removed by settlers who occupied their land to introduce sheep and many died from disease. Their descendants (except for the extinct Haush) are very few in number and live on the islands. Many of the sheep farming estancias which replaced the indigenous people can be visited. Ushuaia, the island's main city, is an attractive base for exploring the southwest's small national park, and for boat trips along the Beagle channel to Harberton, a fascinating pioneer estancia. There's good trout and salmon fishing, and a tremendous variety of bird life in summer. Autumn colours are spectacular in March and April.

Ins and outs

Getting there There are no road/ferry crossings between the Argentine mainland and Argentine Tierra del Fuego. You have to go through Chilean territory. (Accommodation is sparse and planes and buses fill up quickly from Nov to Mar. Essential to book ahead.) From Río Gallegos, Ruta 3 reaches the Chilean border at Monte Aymond (67 km; open 24 hours summer, 0900-2300 April-October), passing Laguna Azul. For bus passengers the border crossing is easy; hire cars need a document for permission to cross. 30 km into Chile is **Punta Delgada**, with a dock 23 km beyond for the 20-minute Magellan Strait ferry-crossing over the Primera Angostura (First Narrows) to **Bahía Azul** (cosy tea room). Boats run every 90 minutes, 0830-2215, in low season, more frequently in summer, US$25 per vehicle, foot passengers US$4, www.tabsa.cl. Some 140 km southeast is Chilean San Sebastián, and then 14 km east, across the border (24 hours), is Argentine San Sebastián, with a basic ACA motel (**D**), T02964-425542; service station open 0700-2300. From here the road is paved to Río Grande (see below). The other ferry crossing is **Punta Arenas-Porvenir**. RN255 from Punta Delgada goes west 113 km to the intersection with the Punta Arenas-Puerto Natales road. 5 km north of Punta Arenas centre, at Tres Puentes, there is a ferry crossing to Porvenir (Tuesday-Sunday, 2 hours 20 minutes, US$50 per vehicle, bike US$12, foot passengers US$8, www.tabsa.cl – check timetable, subject to tides), from where a 234 km road runs east to Río Grande (six hours) via San Sebastián. The main road from San Sebastián (Argentina) to Ushuaia is paved, apart from the 65km from **Tolhuin** to Rancho Hambre. All other roads are *ripio* (unsurfaced). **Note** Fruit and meat may not be taken onto the island, nor between Argentina and Chile. ▸▸ *For further details, see Transport, page 232. For details of transport and hotels on Chilean territory, see the Chile chapter.*

Río Grande → *Population: 53,000. Phone code: 02964. Colour map 9, grid C2.*

Río Grande is a sprawling modern town in windy, dust-laden sheep-grazing and oil-bearing plains. (The oil is refined at San Sebastián in the smallest and most southerly refinery in the world.) The *frigorífico* (frozen meat) plant and sheep-shearing shed are among the largest in South America. Government tax incentives to companies in the 1970s led to a rapid growth in population; the subsequent withdrawal of incentives has produced increasing unemployment and emigration. The city was founded by Fagnano's Salesian mission in 1893; you can visit the original building **La Candelaria** ① *11 km north, T430667, Mon-Sat 1000-1200, 1500-1900, Sun 1500-1900, US$1.50, afternoon teas, US$3, getting there: taxi US$6 with wait.* The museum has displays of indigenous artefacts and natural history. Río Grande's **Museo de la Ciudad** ① *Alberdi 555, T430414, Mon-Fri 0900-1700, Sat 1500-1900* is also recommended for its history of the pioneers, missions and oil. **Local festivals**: Sheep shearing in January. Rural exhibition and handicrafts 2nd week February. Shepherd's day, with impressive sheepdog display first week March. **Tourist office**, Instituto Fueguino de Turismo office ① *Espora 533, T422887, www.tierradelfuego.org.ar, Mon-Fri 0900-2100, Sat 1000-2000, till 1700 in winter.*

● Sleeping

Río Grande *p225*

Book ahead, as there are few decent choices.
Several estancias offer full board and some,
mainly on the northern rivers, have expensive
fishing lodges: see www.tierradelfuego.org.ar.
L Estancia Viamonte, 40 km southeast
on the coast, T430861, www.estanciavia
monte.com. For an authentic experience
of Tierra del Fuego, built in 1902 by pioneer
Lucas Bridges, writer of *Uttermost Part of the
Earth*, to protect the indigenous Ona peoples,
this working *estancia* has simple and beautifully
furnished rooms in a spacious cottage.
Reserve a week ahead, riding and trekking
also arranged. Delicious meals.
B Posada de los Sauces, Elcano 839, T430868,
www.posadadelossauces.com.ar. Best by far,
with breakfast, beautifully decorated,
comfortable, good restaurant, cosy bar.
C Atlántida, Belgrano 582, T431915, atlantida@
netcombbs.com.ar. Modern, uninspiring but
good value, with breakfast, cable TV.
D Isla del Mar, Güemes 963, T422883,
www.hotelguia.com/hoteles/isladelmar.
On sea shore, bleak and a bit run down,
but breakfast included and staff are friendly.
F pp Argentino, San Martín 64, T422546,
hotelargentino@yahoo.com. Cheap place
with thin walls, also has doubles (**C**) and
rooms with or without bath, poor
breakfast, kitchen.

Camping
Refugio Camping Club Náutico, T420536,
nauticorg@speedy.com.ar, Rita and Carlos
Hansen. Very helpful.

● Eating

Río Grande *p225*

♯ **La Nueva Colonial**, Av Belgrano y Lasserre.
Delicious pasta, warm family atmosphere.
♯ **La Nueva Piamontesa**, restaurant and 24-hr
grocery store at Av Belgrano y Mackinlay,
T426332. Cheap set menus and take away.
♯ **La Rueda**, Islas Malvinas 998. Excellent *parrilla*.

● Transport

Río Grande *p225*

Air Airport 4 km west of town, T420600.
Taxi US$2. To **Buenos Aires**, AR daily, 3½ hrs
direct. LADE flies to **Río Gallegos**.
Bus To **Punta Arenas**, Chile, via Punta Delgada,
7-9 hrs, **Pacheco** (T425611) and **Tecni Austral**
(Moyano 516, T430610), US$25. To **Río Gallegos**,
Tecni Austral, Mon-Sat, 8 hrs, US$20. To **Ushuaia**,
3½-4 hrs, **Tecni Austral**, Mon-Sat 1800, US$8.50,
Pacheco, **Montiel** (25 de Mayo 712, T420997) and
Líder (Perito Moreno 635, T420003), US$10.
Car hire Europcar, Av Belgrano 423, T430365.
Localiza, San Martín 642, T430191.

● Directory

Río Grande *p225*

Airline offices Aerolineas Argentinas, San
Martín 607, T424467. LADE, Lasserre 447, T422968.
Banks ATMs: 4 banks on San Martín entre 100 y
300. Exchange is difficult: if coming from Chile, buy
Argentine pesos there. **Post offices** Rivadavia
968. **Supermarkets** La Nueva Piamontesa,
see Eating, above. **Norte**, San Martín y Piedrabuena,
good selection; also **La Anónima** on San Martín.
Telephone *Locutorios* all along San Martín.

Ushuaia and around → *Phone code: 02901. Colour map 9, grid C2. Population: 45,000.*

Situated 212 km southwest of Río Grande on new road via Paso Garibaldi, the most southerly
town in Argentina and growing fast, Ushuaia is beautifully positioned on the northern shore of
the Beagle Channel, which is named after the ship in which Darwin sailed here in 1832. Its
streets climb steeply towards snow-covered Cerro Martial and there are fine views over the
Beagle Channel to the jagged peaks of Isla Navarino (Chile). **Tourist offices** ⓘ *San Martín 674,
esq Fadul, T/F432001, www.e-ushuaia.com. Mon-Fri 0800-2000, Sat-Sun 0900-2000.* 'Best
in Argentina', very helpful English speaking staff, who will find you accommodation in summer.
Information available in English, French, German and Portuguese. There is also a tourist office at
the port and a desk at the airport. **Oficina Antártica**, at Muelle Turístico, T421423 (ext 33), daily
in summer 0800-1900; Monday-Friday 0900-1700 in low season, provides general information
on Antarctica with a small library with navigational charts.

Sights

First settled in 1884 by missionary Thomas Bridges, whose son Lucas became a great defender
of the indigenous peoples here, Ushuaia's fascinating history is still visible in its old buildings
and at **Estancia Harberton**, 85 km west (see below). A penal colony for many years, the old
prison, **Presidio** ⓘ *Yaganes y Gob Paz, at the back of the Naval Base, Mon-Sun 1000-2000,*

US$8.50 for foreigners, houses the small **Museo Marítimo**, with models and artefacts from seafaring days, and, in the cells of most of the huge five wings, the **Museo Penitenciario**, which details the history of the prison (be prisoner for an hour, Monday-Friday evenings in high season, to book T436321, US$8.50, not for under 15s). There is also an art gallery and an Antarctic hall. During the excellent guided visits (in Spanish only) a replica of the lighthouse that inspired Jules Verne's novel is seen from inside. Highly recommended. **Museo del Fin del Mundo** ① *Maipú y Rivadavia, T421863, www.tierradelfuego.org.ar/museo, daily 0900-2000 (Nov-Apr), 1200-1900 (May-Oct, Mon-Sat), US$3.50, students US$1.70.* In the 1912 bank building, it has small displays on indigenous peoples, missionaries and first settlers, as well as nearly all the birds of Tierra del Fuego (stuffed). Recommended. The building also contains an excellent library with helpful staff. **Museo Yámana** ① *Rivadavia 56, T422874, www.tierradelfuego.org.ar/mundoyamana, daily 1000-2000 high season, 1200-1900 low season, US$1.70.* Scale models depicting the geological evolution of the island and the everyday life of Yamana people, texts in English. Centro Beagle ① *Luis Pedro Fique 121, T432090, www.centrobeagle.com, Oct-Mar 1200-2400, closed Mon*, is a representation of Fitzroy's ship, with a model Yámana village where meals are served. Its main attraction is a dramatisation of Darwin's visit to Tierra del Fuego, *La Aventura del Beagle*, one-hour show, full of humour, in English and Spanish. Local events: winter solstice, the longest night with a torch-light procession and fireworks, 20-21 June.

Tren del Fin del Mundo ① *T431600, www.trendelfindelmundo.com.ar, 3 departures daily in summer, 1 in winter, US$20 tourist, US$35 1st class return, plus US$7 park entrance and US$2.50 for taxi to the station, tickets at station, travel agencies, or from Tranex kiosk in the port, sit on left outbound for the best views,* is the world's southernmost steam train, running new locomotives and carriages on track first laid by prisoners to carry wood to Ushuaia. A totally touristy experience with relentless commentary in English and Spanish, 50-minute ride from the Fin del Mundo station, 8 km west of Ushuaia, into Tierra del Fuego National Park (one way of starting a hike).

Cerro Martial, about 7 km behind the town, offers fine views down the Beagle Channel and to the north. Take a chairlift (*aerosilla*), daily 1000-1800 (1030-1630 in winter), US$3.50. To reach the chairlift, follow Magallanes out of town, allow 1½ hours. Several companies run minibus services from the corner of Maipú and Roca, frequent departures daily in summer, US$3-4 return. Taxis charge US$5 to the base, from where you can walk down all the way back. From the top you can walk 90 minutes to **Glaciar Martial**. Splendid tea shop and *cabañas* at the base, *refugio* up at the Cerro. Excursions can also be made to **Lagos Fagnano** and **Escondido**.

The **Estancia Harberton** ① *T422742, ngoodall@tierradelfuego.org.ar, US$5, daily 15 Oct-15 Apr, except 25 Dec, 1 Jan and Easter, museum: US$2,* the oldest on the island and run by descendants of British missionary, Thomas Bridges, whose family protected the indigenous peoples here, is 85 km from Ushuaia on Ruta J. It's a beautiful place, offering guided walks through protected forest and delicious teas or lunch (reserve ahead), in the *Mánakatush casa de té* overlooking the bay. The impressive **Museo Acatushún** ① *www.aca tushun.org,* has skeletons of South American sea mammals and birds, the result of 23 years' scientific investigation in Tierra del Fuego, with excellent tours in English. You can camp free, with permission from the owners, or stay in cottages. Access is from a good unpaved road which branches off Ruta 3, 40 km east of Ushuaia and runs 25 km through forest before the open country around Harberton; marvellous views, about two hours (no petrol outside of Ushuaia and Tolhuin). Boat trips to Harberton, twice weekly in summer, allow 1-2 hours on the estancia. Regular daily minibus service with **Ebenezer** from Maipú y 25 de Mayo, US$20 return.

Short boat excursions from Ushuaia are highly recommended, though the Beagle Channel can be very rough. These can be booked through most agencies, and most leave from the **Muelle Turístico**, where all operators have ticket booths, with a few using the **Muelle AFASYN** (next to old airport). Trip to the sea lion colony at Isla de los Lobos, Isla de los Pájaros and Les Eclaireurs lighthouse: 2½-3 hours on catamaran, US$30; 4½ hours on the *Patagonian Adventure*, US$40 including 1 hour trekking on Bridges island and hot drink; on the lovely old sailing boat *Barracuda*, excellent commentary, US$25; or on a sailing boat *Patagonia Explorer* in summer, 4½ hours, US$40. To Isla de los Lobos, Isla de los Pájaros, Les Eclaireurs lighthouse, and the Isla Martillo penguin colony (Oct-Mar only): 4½-6½ hours, US$44. To Isla de los Lobos, Isla de los Pájaros, Isla Martillo penguin colony, Les Eclaireurs lighthouse and Estancia Harberton: 6-9 hours round trip on catamaran, US$60, includes packed lunch and entrance fee, summer only. To the National Park, 5-5½ hrs, US$35-60, includes lunch.

Sea trips Cruceros Australis ① *www.australis.com*, operates two luxury cruise ships (one weekly each) from Ushuaia to Punta Arenas, via Puerto Williams and around Cabo de Hornos, 4-5 days, from US$1,244 pp in summer (book through agencies); frequently recommended. Ushuaia is also the starting point, or the last stop en route to Antarctica for several cruises from October to March that usually sail for 10-20 days along the western shores of the Antarctic peninsula and the South Shetland Islands. Other trips include stops at Falkland/Malvinas archipelago and at South Georgia. Cheapest fare to Antarctica with ship *Ushuaia* ① *www.antarpply.com, every 10 days Nov-Feb, around US$3,000-4,000 pp in advance in a twin cabin (small discount, if available, if booked a few days before departure). Book through travel agencies.* **Ushuaia Boating** ① *Gob Paz 190 (or at the Muelle Turístico), T436193, www.ushuaiaboating.com.ar,* operates all year round a channel crossing to Puerto Navarino, 30 minutes, and then bus to Puerto Williams, 90 minutes, US$100 one way. From Puerto Williams there are frequent ferries to Punta Arenas. At **Muelle AFASYN**, near the old airport, T435805, ask about possible crossings with a club member to Puerto Williams, about 4 hours, from US$80, or if any foreign sailing boat is going to Cabo de Hornos or Antarctica.

Parque Nacional Tierra del Fuego

① *US$8, getting there: in summer buses and minibuses, US$5 return to Lago Roca and to Lapataia, US$7, several companies, leaving from the tourist pier at Maipú y Roca and from Maipú y 25 de Mayo; last bus back 2000, 2100 in summer. Tierra del Fuego National Park Office, San Martín 1395, Ushuaia, T421315, Mon-Fri 0900-1600, has a basic map. Tourist office and National Park office have details and a map of park, with walks. See below for Camping.*
Covering 63,000 ha of mountains, lakes, rivers and deep valleys, this small but beautiful park stretches west to the Chilean border and north to Lago Fagnano, though large areas are closed to tourists. Public access is allowed from the park entrance 12 km west of Ushuaia, where you'll be given a basic map with marked walks. **1) Senda Costera**, 6.5 km, three hours each way. Along the shore from Ensenada (where boat trips start). From Lago Roca, continue along to Bahía Lapataia, crossing the broad green river, where there are more short paths to follow. **2) Senda Hito XXIV**, along Lago Roca, 4 km, 90 minutes one way, lots of birdlife. **3) Cerro Guanaco** (1,106 m), 4 km, four hours one way. Challenging hike up through forest to splendid views. Campsite in a good spot at Lago Roca, with *confitería*, it's best to go early morning or afternoon to avoid the tour buses.

Ushuaia

Sleeping 😴
Albergue Cruz del Sur **1**
Amanecer de la Bahía **4**
Antarctica **2**
Cabo San Diego **6**

Canal Beagle **7**
Cap Polonio &
  Marcopolo Restaurant **8**
Familia Velásquez **11**
Galeazzi-Basily **12**

Hostal Malvinas **13**
Hostería Posada Fin
  del Mundo **14**
Los Troncos **16**
Nahuel **5**

0 metres 200
0 yards 200

You'll see geese, the torrent duck, Magellanic woodpeckers and austral parakeets. There are no legal crossing points to Chile. Helpful *guardaparque* (ranger) at Lago Roca. Remember that the weather can be cold, damp and unpredictable, even in summer; winter days are short.

Sleeping

Ushuaia *p226, map p228*
The tourist office has a comprehensive list of all officially registered accommodation and will help with rooms in private homes, campsites etc. An excellent choice is to stay with Ushuaia families on a B&B basis.
LL Las Hayas, Camino Glaciar Martial, Km 3, T430710, www.lashayashotel.com.ar. Ushuaia's only 5 star, spectacular setting high up on the mountain, breakfast included, pool, sauna, gym, sports, shuttle from town and transfer from airport. Recommended.
L Cumbres del Martial, Luis F Martial 3560, 7 km from town, T424779, www.cumbresdel martial.com.ar. Charming cottage, very comfortable rooms with balconies, small, relaxed, secluded, also 4 *cabañas*, all with fireplace, also has **La Cabaña** restaurant and tea room.
L Tierra de Leyendas, Tierra de Vientos 2448, T443565, www.tierradeleyendas.com.ar. In the western suburbs. Five very comfortable rooms with incredible views of the Beagle Channel, or the snowy mountains at the back, excellent restaurant serving regional specialties. Only for non smokers. Recommended.

AL Canal Beagle, Maipú y 25 de Mayo, T432303, www.hotelcanalbeagle.com.ar. Good value ACA hotel (discounts for members), with a small pool, gym, sauna and clear views over the channel from some rooms, good restaurant.
A Hostería Posada Fin del Mundo, Gob Valdez 281, T437345, www.posadafindelmundo.com.ar. Family atmosphere, comfortable rooms, good value.
B Cabo San Diego, 25 de Mayo 368, T435600, www.cabosandiego.com.ar. Apart-hotel with spacious apartments, equipped for cooking, comfortable, with breakfast. Excellent value.
B Cap Polonio, San Martín 746, T422140, www.hotelcappolonio.com.ar. Smart, central, modern, comfortable, TV, free internet, chic restaurant/café *Marcopolo*.
B Hostal Malvinas, Gob Deloqui 615, T/F422626, www.hostalmalvinas.net. Comfortable but small rooms, small breakfast, free tea and coffee.
B Nahuel, 25 de Mayo 440, T423068, byb_nahuel@yahoo.com.ar. Charming and talkative Sra Navarrete has a comfortable B&B with channel views from the upper rooms and the terrace, good value, but noisy street.

Yakush **3**

Eating
Bodegón Fueguino **9**
Café Tante Sara **2**

El Turco **4**
Kaupé **5**
La Baguette **6**
La Estancia **7**
Martinica **14**

Moustacchio **10**
Parrilla La Rueda **11**
Tante Sara
  Pizzas & Pastas **12**
Tía Elvira **13**

Volver **15**

Bars & clubs
Lennon Pub **8**

D pp Familia Velásquez, Juana Fadul 361, T421719, almayo@arnet.com.ar. Cosy, welcoming house of a pioneer, with basic rooms, breakfast, cooking and laundry facilities, good.

D Galeazzi-Basily, Gdor Valdez 323, T423213, www.avesdelsur.com.ar. Easily the best, beautiful family home, incredible welcome, in pleasant area 5 blocks from centre, breakfast included, free internet. Also excellent value *cabañas* in the backyard. Recommended.

D Los Troncos, Gob Paz 1344, T/F421895. Comfortable house owned by Clarisa Ulloa, breakfast, cable TV and free internet.

E-F pp Amanecer de la Bahía, Magallanes 594, T424405, www.ushuaiahostel.com.ar. Light, spacious, impeccable, shared rooms for 4, but cramped for 6, also good double and triples **C** with shared bath, kitchen facilities, with breakfast, luggage store and own parking, AHC Argentina Hostel Club, www.argentinahostels.com.

F pp Albergue Cruz del Sur, Deloqui 636, T434099, www.xdelsur.com.ar. Welcoming Italian owner Luca, a nice, relaxed and small house with library, kitchen facilities and free tea, coffee and mate, book in advance, good for smokers. Recommended.

F pp Antarctica, Antártida Argentina 270, T435774, www.antarcticahostel.com. Central, welcoming, spacious chill-out room, excellent 24-hr bar, dorms for 6 and large **C** doubles, breakfast and internet included, bike rental (US$8.50 per day) and the omnipresence of Tino, the dog. Recommended.

F pp Yakush, Piedrabuena 118 y San Martín, T435807, www.hostelyakush.com.ar. Very-well run, central with spacious dorms, with breakfast, free internet, light kitchen and dining room and a steep garden with views. Recommended.

Camping La Pista del Andino, Leandro N Alem 2873, T435890, www.lapistadel andino.com.ar. Set in the Club Andino ski premises in a woodland area, it has wonderful views over the channel. Electricity, hot showers, tea room and grocery store, US$3 pp.

Around Ushuaia *p226*

LL Estancia Harberton, T422742, harberton@ tierradelfuego.org.ar. 2 restored buildings on the channel 90 km east of Ushuaia, very simple rooms, wonderful views, heating. Open mid-Oct-mid-Apr. Price given for 6 people.

A Hostería Petrel, RN 3, Km 3186, T02901-433569, hpetrel@infovia.com.ar. Secluded position in forest on the fjord-like

Lago Escondido, 50 km from Ushuaia towards Río Grande. Decent rooms with bath, good restaurant overlooking lake, and tiny basic *cabañas*. Idyllic but pricey.

C Cabañas Khami, on Lago Fagnano, 8 km from Tolhuin, T422296, www.cabaniaskhami.com.ar. Well-equipped, rustic cabins, good value with linen. Price given for 6 people.

D Parador Kawi Shiken, 4 km south of Tolhuin on RN3, Km 2945, TT156 11505, www.hotelguia.com/hoteles/kawi-shiken/. Rustic, 3 rooms, shared bath, *salón de té* and restaurant, horse riding.

D pp Refugio Solar del Bosque, 19 km from Ushuaia, RN3, Km 3020, T156 06176, www.solar-del-bosque.com.ar. A basic hostel for walkers, arranges excursions. Also has camping, US$2.50 pp, hot showers.

Camping Camping Haruwen, in the Haruwen Winter Sports complex (Km 36), T431099, US$3 per tent, electricity, shop, bar, restaurant, winter and summer activities.

Camping inside the Parque Nacional Tierra del Fuego Camping Lago Roca, T433313, 21 km from Ushuaia, by forested shore of Lago Roca, a beautiful site with good facilities, reached by bus Jan-Feb, expensive small shop, cafetería. There are also various sites with no facilities, eg **Bahía Ensenada** 14 km from Ushuaia; **Río Pipo** 16 km; **Las Bandurrias**, **Cauquenes** and **Laguna Verde**, 20 km from Ushuaia.

● Eating

Ushuaia *p226, map p228*

Lots of restaurants along San Martín and Maipú. Ask around for currently available seafood, especially *centolla* (king crab; US$14 on average) and *cholga* (giant mussels). Much cheaper if prepare your own meal; **Pesquera del Beagle**, Maipú 227, sells *centollón* (US$3 per kg; US$11 per kg ready to eat) and *centolla* (US$9 per kg; US$18 per kg ready to eat, just add lemon).

TTT Bodegón Fueguino, San Martín 859. Tapas, homemade pastas and good roast lamb with varied sauces in a renovated 1896 house.

TTT Kaupé, Roca 470 y Magallanes, T437396. Best restaurant in town, dishes, eg king crab, meat.

TTT Tía Elvira, Maipú 349. Excellent seafood.

TTT Volver, Maipú 37. Delicious seafood and fish in atmospheric 1898 house, with ancient newspaper all over the walls.

● *For an explanation of the sleeping and eating price codes used in this guide, see page 58.*
● *Other relevant information is found in Essentials pages 68-69.*

La Estancia, San Martín 253. A cheery and good value *parrilla*. Packed in high season. All-you-can-eat for US$7.

Moustacchio, San Martín y Gdor Godoy. Long established, good for seafood. On San Martín 272, there is a cheaper all-you-can-eat branch.

Parrilla La Rueda, San Martín y Rivadavia. Good *tenedor libre* (US$7) for beef, lamb and great salads.

Tante Sara Pizzas and Pastas, San Martín 137. Tasty filling food. Also takeaway.

El Turco, San Martín 1410. One of the few good cheap places, serving generous milanesas, pastas, pizzas and beef. Very popular with locals.

Martinica, San Martín entre Antártida Argentina y Yaganes. Cheap, small, busy, sit at the bar facing the *parrilla* and point to your favourite beef cut. Takeaway (T432134) and good meals of the day.

Cafés

Café Tante Sara, San Martin y Fadul. Opposite the tourist office, is the best, smart, good coffee, tasty sandwiches.

La Baguette, Don Bosco y San Martín. Best fresh takeaway sandwiches, also delicious *empanadas* and *facturas* (pastries).

Bars and clubs

Ushuaia *p226, map p228*
Küar, Av Perito Moreno 2232, east of town. Wonderful setting by the Beagle channel; restaurant/bar/brewery open from 1500.

Lennon Pub, Maipú y Gob Godoy. Good place for a late night drink, with live music.

Shopping

Ushuaia *p226, map p228*
Ushuaia's tax free status doesn't produce as many bargains as you might hope. Lots of souvenir shops on San Martín and several offering good quality leather and silver ware.

Atlántico Sur, San Martín 627, is the (not especially cheap) duty free shop.

Boutique del Libro, 25 de Mayo 62. A good range of books on Patagonia and Antarctica.

La Anónima, Gob Paz y Rivadavia and San Martín y Onas. Large supermarket.

Norte, 12 de Octubre y Karukinka. Supermarket, takeaway, fresh food, and fast-food diner.

Popper, San Martín 740. Sells outdoor clothes, camping and fishing gear.

Vraie, San Martín y 25 de Mayo. Lots of clothes.

World's End, San Martín y Lasserre. Books on the area, as well as T shirts and key rings.

Activities and tours

Ushuaia *p226, map p228*
Sports Centre on Malvinas Argentinas on west side of town (close to seafront). Swimming pool.

Fishing

Trout season is Nov-mid Apr, licences US$10 per day (an extra fee is charged for some rivers and lakes). **Asociación de Caza y Pesca** at Maipú 822, T423168, cazapescush@infovia.com.ar, Mon-Fri 1800-2100, sells licences.

Hiking and, climbing

Club Andino, Fadul 50, T422335, www.club andinoushuaia.com.ar. For advice, Mon-Fri 1000-1230, 1400-2130; Sat 1000-1400. Sells maps and trekking guidebooks; free guided walks once in a month in summer. The winter sports resorts along Ruta 3 (see below) are an excellent base for summer trekking and many arrange excursions. **Nunatak**, 19.5 km from Ushuaia, nunatak@ tierradelfuego.org.ar, is a small centre run by Gustavo Giró, who organizes eg day-treks to Glaciar Ojo de Albino past Laguna Perdida, US$40.

Skiing

Ushuaia is becoming popular as a winter resort with several centres for skiing, snowboarding and husky sledging. By far the best is **Cerro Castor complex**, 27 km from town, T499302, www.cerrocastor.com. 20 km of pistes, a vertical drop of 772 m and powder snow. Attractive centre with complete equipment rental for snowboarding and snowshoeing. Ski pass US$35 per day. Excellent cross country skiing, with various new centres along Ruta 3 at 18-36 km east of Ushuaia, of which **Tierra Mayor**, 21 km from town, T423240, or 155 13463, is the largest and recommended. In a beautiful wide valley between steep-sided mountains, offering half and full day excursions on sledges with huskies for hire, as well as cross country skiing and snowshoeing. Equipment hire and restaurant.

Tours

Lots of companies offer imaginative adventure tourism expeditions. All agencies charge the same fees for excursions; ask tourist office for a complete list: Tierra del Fuego National Park, 4 hrs, US$17 (entry fee US$8 extra); Lagos Escondido and Fagnano, 7 hrs, US$25 with lunch. With 3 or 4 people it might be worth hiring a *remise* taxi.
All Patagonia, Juana Fadul 48, T433622, www.allpatagonia.com. Trekking, ice climbing, and tours; trips to Cabo de Hornos and Antarctica.

Canal, Rivadavia 82, T437395, www.canal
fun.com. Huge range of activities, trekking,
canoeing, riding, 4WD excursions. Recommended.
Comapa, San Martín 245, T430727,
www.comapa.com. Conventional tours and
adventure tourism, bus tickets to Punta Arenas and
Puerto Natales, trips to Antarctica, Cabo de Hornos
and Navimag ferries for Puerto Natales-Puerto
Montt (10% ISIC discount for Navimag tickets).
Compañía de Guías de Patagonia, Gob Campos
795, T437753, www.companiadeguias.com.ar. The
best agency for walking guides, expeditions for all
levels, rock and ice climbing (training provided),
US$55 pp for a day-trek and climb on ice,
including equipment, transport. Recommended.
Rumbo Sur, San Martín 350, T421139,
www.rumbosur.com.ar. Flights, buses,
conventional tours, plus Antarctic expeditions,
mid-Nov to mid-Mar, English spoken.
Tolkar, Roca 157, T431412, www.tolkar
turismo.com.ar. Flights, bus tickets to Argentina
and Chile, trips to Cabo de Hornos and to
Antarctica, conventional and adventure tourism,
canoeing and mountain biking to Lago Fagnano.
Travel Lab, San Martín y 9 de Julio, T436555,
travellabush@speedy.com.ar. Tren del Fin del
Mundo, unconventional tours, mountain biking,
trekking etc, trips to Cabo de Hornos and Antarctica,
Navimag ferries, English and French spoken, helpful.
Turismo de Campo, Fuegia Basket 414,
T/F437351, www.turismodecampo.com.
Adventure tourism, English/French speaking
guides, boat and trekking trips in the National Park,
bird watching, sailing and trips to Antarctica.

⊖ Transport

Ushuaia *p226, map p228*
Air Airport 4 km from town. Book ahead in
summer; flights fill up fast. In winter flights often
delayed. Taxi to airport US$3 (no bus). Schedules
tend to change from season to season. Airport
tourist information only at flight times, T423970.
To **Buenos Aires** (Aeroparque or Ezeiza), 3½ hrs,
El Calafate, 1 hr, and **Río Gallegos**, 1 hr, with
AR/Austral and LADE (longer flights); also to **Río
Grande**, 1 hr, several a week (but check with
agents). In summer **Aerovías DAP** and **LAN** fly to
Punta Arenas. The Aeroclub de Ushuaia flies
Mon, Wed, Fri to **Puerto Williams**, US$100 one
way from the downtown airport.
Bus Urban buses from west to east across town,
most stops along Maipú, US$0.45. Tourist office

provides a list of minibus companies that run
daily from town (stops along Maipú) to nearby
attractions, eg Harberton, Lago Fagnano,
National Park. Passport needed when booking
international bus tickets. Buses always booked up
Dec-Mar; buy your ticket to leave as soon as you
arrive. To **Río Grande**, 3½-4 hrs, bus **Tecni
Austral**, Mon-Sat 0530, US$8.50, leaves from
Roca y Deloqui, book through **Tolkar** (address
above), and combis **Líder** (Gob Paz 921, T436421),
and **Montiel** (San Martín 1547, T421366), US$10.

To **Río Gallegos**, **Tecni Austral**, 11½ hrs,
US$30 (through Tolkar). To **Punta Arenas**, **Tecni
Austral**, Mon, Wed, Fri 0530, 11½ hrs (through
Tolkar); also Oct-Apr, **Pacheco**, 12-13 hrs, US$34
(book through **Comapa**, address above). To
Puerto Natales, Oct-Apr, **Bus Sur**, 15 hrs, US$38.
Car hire Most companies charge about US$45
per day, including insurance and 150 km per day,
special promotions available. **Localiza**, San Martín
1222, T430739. **Europcar**, Maipú 857, T430786.
Taxi Cheaper than *remises*, T422007, T440225.
Remises Carlitos, T422222; **Bahía Hermosa**,
T422233.

⊕ Directory

Ushuaia *p226, map p228*
Airline offices Aerolíneas Argentinas,
Roca 116, T421218. **Aerovías DAP**, Deloqui 555,
p 4, T431110. **LADE**, San Martín 542, shop 5,
T/F421123. **Banks** Banks open 1000-1500 in
summer. ATMs are plentiful all along San Martín,
using credit cards is easiest (but Sat, Sun and
holidays machines can be empty), changing
TCs is difficult and expensive. **Banco de Tierra
del Fuego**, San Martín 396 (also open on
summer weekends 1000-1300 for exchange
only), **Agencia de Cambio Thaler**, San
Martín 788, also open weekends, 1000-1300,
1700-2030. **Consulates** Chile, Jainen 50,
T430909. Germany, Rosas 516. **Internet**
Many broadband cyber cafés and *locutorios*
along San Martín. **Post offices** San Martín
y Godoy, Mon-Fri 0900-1900, Sat 0900-1300.
Telephones *Locutorios* all along San Martín.
Useful addresses Dirección Nacional
de Migraciones, Beauvoir 1536, T422334.
Biblioteca Popular Sarmiento, San Martín
1589, www.bpsarmiento.com.ar. Mon-Fri
1000-1800, library with a good range of
books about the area.

Bolivia

Essentials	**236**
La Paz and around	**242**
Ins and outs	242
Sights	243
Around La Paz	248
Lake Titicaca	**264**
The Yungas	**274**
Southwest Bolivia	**277**
Oruro	277
Uyuni	283
Tupiza	289
Central and Southern Highlands	**292**
Potosí	292
Sucre	297
Tarija	303
Cochabamba and around	306
Northern Lowlands	**313**
Madidi and Rurrenabaque	314
Riberalta to Brazil	317
Cochabamba to Trinidad	319
Santa Cruz and Eastern Lowlands	**321**
Santa Cruz	321
Southeastern Bolivia	326
Eastern Bolivia	331

☃ Footprint features

Don't miss …	235
Touching down	238
Driving in Bolivia	239
Tiny treats	247
La Diablada festival	279
Fiesta de la Virgen de Urkupiña,	
Quillacollo	311

Introduction

On Bolivia's Altiplano you are so far up it will make your head spin. Every day, the highest capital in the world transforms itself from a melée of indigenous markets and modern business into a canyon of glittering stars as the lights come on at nightfall.

Bolivia has some of the most bio-diverse conservation areas in South America: Madidi, Amboró and Noel Kempff Mercado all have an incredible range of habitats and variety of flora and fauna and you should visit at least one on your journey. If you fancy a trek, there are adventurous trails within a day of the capital, while anyone nostalgic for the revolutionary days of the 60s can retrace the final steps of Che Guevara. For a fun bike ride, try one of the most dangerous roads in the world, from the mountain heights to the lush Yungas valleys, through waterfalls and round hairpins – but do go with an expert.

In Bolivia you learn to expect the unexpected. On the largest salt flat on earth, a vast blinding-white expanse, you lose track of what is land and what is sky. At La Diablada festival in Oruro, dancers wear masks of the scariest monsters you could ever dream of. To visit the mines at Potosí, once the silver lode for the Spanish Empire, you buy dynamite and coca leaves as presents for the labourers. Flamingoes feed from red and green lakes rimmed by volcanoes. Dalí-esque rock structures dot the Altiplano. Turn the corner and you can swim with pink river dolphins in jungle waters, or fish for piranhas in the pampas. Before you go home, you can fill your bags with everything from the beautiful autumnal colours of the textiles, to packs of dried llama foetuses, which protect homes from evil spirits.

★ Don't miss ...

1 **Isla del Sol** Take a boat trip on Lake Titicaca to the fabled birthplace of the Incas, the Island of the Sun, and spend a few days walking through tiny villages that seem to belong to another age, page 265.

2 **Coroico** It's only a short run from the breathless altitudes of La Paz to the subtropical, flower and fruit-filled Yungas, but what a run. It's a hair-raising, tortuous 70-km ride to the town of Coroico, and the best way to go is on a mountain bike, page 274.

3 **La Diablada** At Oruro, in the southern Altiplano, a major mining town becomes the scene of one of Latin America's greatest carnivals. Fearsome devils with gruesome masks dance through the streets, page 279.

4 **Salar de Uyuni** The mining town of Uyuni is the gateway to the world's highest, largest salt flats. Beyond are the bright red Laguna Colorada and the jade green Laguna Verde, soda lakes where flamingos feed, page 284.

5 **Madidi** This national park is one of the most bio-diverse regions on earth, stretching from savannahs to cloud forest and providing habitats for some 1,000 bird species, monkeys, jaguar and other cats, page 314.

6 **Chiquitano Missions** Six exceptional Jesuit missions, among Bolivia's finest examples of colonial art and craftsmanship, page 331.

Bolivia

Essentials

Planning your trip

Where to go La Paz is the best place to start, as many international flights land here and it is closest to the well-travelled overland routes from Peru and Chile. The capital is easy to explore, but you do need to adjust to the altitude, which will leave you temporarily breathless. La Paz is, after all, the highest capital city in the world. There are some good museums and churches, and an indigenous market area. Daytrips include the pre-Inca city of **Tiahuanaco**, which is close to the beautiful **Lake Titicaca**. To appreciate the lake, a night or more on its shores is recommended. Northeast of La Paz, over the cordillera, are the **Yungas**, deep subtropical valleys, rich in vegetation, where a town like **Coroico** can provide welcome relief from the rigours of the Altiplano. Equally pleasant and lower than La Paz is **Sorata**, a good base for trekking and climbing.

South of La Paz is the mining city of **Oruro**, which hosts one of the most famous Latin American carnival celebrations, including the **Diablada** dance, usually held in mid- to late February. Southeast are the colonial cities of **Potosí**, where Spain garnered much of its imperial wealth from abundant silver deposits and present-day miners scour the mountain for meagre pickings, and **Sucre**, Bolivia's official capital, with an array of fine buildings. **Uyuni** and **Tupiza**, further south again, are the jumping-off places for trips to high-altitude puna with stunning salt flats, coloured lakes, flamingoes and horizons of volcanoes. **Tarija**, southeast of Potosí, is best known for its fruits and wine, dinosaur remains and Mediterranean climate (and thus its nickname 'the Andalucía of Bolivia'). Continuing beyond here you come to the Argentine border.

East of La Paz is **Cochabamba**, Bolivia's fourth largest city and centre of one of the country's main agricultural zones. The **Parque Nacional Toro Toro**, with its dinosaur tracks, rock paintings, canyons and waterfalls, is a tough but stunning excursion. Further east is **Santa Cruz de la Sierra**, now the country's most economically important (and largest) city, from where you can visit **Amboró**, **Noel Kempff Mercado** and other national parks, as well as follow in the footsteps of Che Guevara, take in **Samaipata**, the country's second most important archaeological site, see the beautiful **Jesuit missions** of the Chiquitania, or take the train to Corumbá in Brazil. Like its eastern neighbour, Bolivia has a **Pantanal** wetland, just now opening up to tourism, with opportunities to see a magnificent range of wildlife.

From La Paz you can fly into the Beni region, in the heart of the Bolivian Amazon. **Rurrenabaque** is the chief destination and starting point for the fantastic Chalalán Ecolodge in the **Parque Nacional Madidi**, which claims a greater bio-diversity than anywhere else on earth. Outside of Rurrenabaque, the further north you go the fewer tourists you will meet. April to October are the months to visit, although insects are year-round tenants.

When to go The most popular season for visitors is June to August, while some of the best festivals, eg Carnival and Holy Week, fall during the wet season, which is considered to be from December to March. The country has four climatic zones: (1) The Puna and Altiplano; average temperature, 10° C, but above 4000 m may drop as low as -25°C at night from June to August. By day, the tropical sun raises temperatures to above 20°C. Rainfall on the northern Altiplano is 400-700 mm, much less further south. Little rain falls upon the western plateau between May and November, but the rest of the year can be wet. (2) The Yungas north of La Paz and Cochabamba, among the spurs of the Cordillera; altitude, 750-1500 m; average temperature 24°C. (3) The Valles, or high valleys and basins gouged out by the rivers of the Puna; average temperature 19° C. Rainfall in the Yungas valleys is 700-800 mm a year, with high humidity. (4) The tropical lowlands; altitude 150m to 750 m; rainfall is high but seasonal (heaviest November to March, but can fall at any season); large areas suffer from alternate flooding and drought. The climate is hot, ranging from 23° to 25°C in the south and to 30°C in the north. Occasional cold, dust-laden winds from the south, the *surazos*, lower the temperature considerably.

Finding out more Tourism is under the control of the **Viceministerio de Turismo** ① *Av Mariscal Santa Cruz (El Prado) y Loayza, Edificio Cámara de Comercio, p 11, T02-237 5129, www.turismobolivia.bo, Mon-Fri 0830-1630.* They have Centros de Información Turística, **InfoTur**, at international arrivals in El Alto airport (T02-285 2543) and Viru Viru (Santa Cruz, T03-336 9595) ① *0600-2200, English spoken*. They are planning other information centres. See under each city for addresses of tourist offices.

National parks For information: **Servicio Nacional de Areas Protegidas** ① *Sernap, Loayza 178, Edif La Papelera, La Paz, T231 7742*, a purely administrative office. It is best to go to Sernap's regional offices: see ① *www.sernap.gov.bo*. Also **Fundación para el Desarrollo del Sistema Nacional de Áreas Protegidas** ① *Fundesnap, Prolongación Cordero 127, La Paz, T211 3364, www.fundesnap.org*.

Websites

Tourism, culture and general information
www.bolivia.com (Spanish) News, tourism, entertainment and information on regions.
www.presidencia.gov.bo Presidential website.
www.boliviahostels.com (English, French, German and Spanish) An independent network offering budget accommodation in Bolivia.
www.bolivian.com (Spanish and English) A comprehensive tourist guide to the country.
www.boliviaweb.com is the best English-language portal.
http://lanic.utexas.edu/la/sa/bolivia/ An excellent database on various topics indigenous to Bolivia, maintained by the University of Texas, USA.
www.noticiasbolivianas.com Here you'll find all the Bolivian news in one place. The best sources for daily news, in Spanish, are www.eldeber.com.bo (*El Deber*) and www.eldiario.net (*El Diario*).

www.andes-mesili.com The site of climbing guide and author Alain Mesili, with lots of interesting links to more than just adventure.
www.chiquitania.com The best site for information on the Chiquitania.

Wildlife and nature
www.fobomade.org.bo (Spanish) website of the Foro Boliviano Sobre Medio Ambiente y Desarrollo. For environmental issues.
www.redesma.org site of the Red de Desarrollo Sostenible y Medio Ambiente (Spanish and English) has lots of links to sustainable development topics and organizations.
www.wcs.org/international/latinamerica/am azon_andes World Conservation Society site with information on the Gran Chaco and on Northwestern Bolivia.

Maps Instituto Geográfico Militar (see page 256, www.igmsantacruz.com). IGM map prices for detailed political maps start at US$5 original, US$4 photocopy. IGM maps were prepared some 20 years ago and do not show trails or passes for trekking. **Liam P O'Brien** has a 1:135,000, full colour, shaded relief topographic map of the Cordillera Real, US$12.95 per copy (very hard to find, 2007), also a 1:2,200,000 full colour travel map of Bolivia (US$12.95) highlighting the National Parks from map distributors (**Bradt, Stanfords**, etc). **Walter Guzmán Córdova** colour maps, 1:150,000, of Choro-Takesi-Yunga Cruz, Mururata-Illimani, Huayna Potosí Oruro-Potosi-Salar de Uyuni, Illampu-Ancohuma, Titicaca-Tiwanaku-Yungas, Nigruni-Condoriri, La Paz department, Santa Cruz department, Sajama and Mapa Físico-Político-Vial (1:2,250,000, road map), available from bookshops in La Paz (see Shopping), US$6.70-7.50. The **German Alpine Club (Deutscher Alpenverein)** produces two maps of Sorata-Ancohuma-Illampu and Illimani, but are not available in La Paz.

Visas and immigration A passport only, valid for one year beyond date of visit, is needed for citizens of almost all Western European countries (except Ireland, Liechtenstein and Malta), Israel, Poland, Czech Republic, Japan, South Africa, Canada, South American countries (except Venezuela), Australia and New Zealand. Many are granted 90 days on entry, others are entitled to only 30. Two extensions of 30 days can be arranged at immigration at a cost of US$21 each. Nationals of all other countries (including USA, as of March 2007, US$100) require a visa. Some nationalities must gain authorization from the Bolivian Ministry of Foreign Affairs, which can take six weeks. Other countries which require a visa do not need authorisation (visas in this case take one to two working days). **Note** In 2007 the Bolivian authorites were reviewing **all** visa requirements. Do not leave home without first checking with a Bolivian consulate, or your home country's embassy in Bolvia, if you need a visa (checking online will not give the latest situation). Visa extensions and costs vary depending on your nationality. Extensions are granted in immigration offices in La Paz, Cochabamba and Santa Cruz. There should be a statutory 72 hours period outside Bolivia before renewing a visa but 24 hours is usually acceptable. On arrival ensure that visas and passports are stamped with the same, correct date of entry or this can lead to 'fines' later. If you outstay your visa the current fine is US$1.25 per day. Business visitors (unless passing through as tourists) are required to obtain a visa from a Bolivian consulate. This costs £61.50 (or equivalent); applicants should check all requirements

┇ Touching down

Airport taxes A departure tax of US$25, payable in dollars or bolivianos, cash only, is levied on leaving by air. On internal flights an airport tax of US$2.25 must be paid. Tax on airline tickets 14.9%.

Business hours 0900-1200 (sometimes 1230 in La Paz), and 1400-1800 (sometimes 1900 in La Paz). Sat is a half day. Opening and closing in the afternoon are several hours later in the provinces. **Banks**: 0900-1600 (*BCP* 0900-1800) some open 0900-1200, or 1300 on Saturday.

In an emergency Robberies should be reported to the *Policía Turística*, they will issue a report for insurance purposes but stolen goods are rarely recovered. In La Paz: Calle Hugo Estrada 1354, Plaza Tejada Sorzano frente al estadio, Miraflores, next to Love City Chinese restaurant, T222 5016. In cities which do not have a Policía Turística report robberies to the *Policía Técnica Judicial* (PTJ), Departamento de Robos. Police T110. Ambulance T118.

International phone code +591.

Equal tones with long pauses: ringing. Equal tones with equal pauses: engaged.

IDD prefix 0010 (Entel), 0011 (AES Communications Bolivia), 0012 (Teledata), 0013 (Bolivaitel).

Official time GMT -4.

Tipping Up to 10% in restaurants is generous, Bolivians seldom leave more than a few coins; otherwise give a tip for a service provided, eg, to a taxi driver who has been helpful (an extra Bs 0.50-1), to someone who has looked after a car or carried bags (usual tip Bs 0.50-1).

VAT/IVA 13%. Ask for an official receipt if you want it documented.

Voltage Varies considerably. Generally 110 volts, 50 cycles AC in La Paz, but newer districts and buildings have 220 volts; 220 volts 50 cycles AC elsewhere, but check before using any appliance. (You may even find 110 and 220 in the same room.) Sockets usually accept both continental European (round) and US-type (flat) 2-pin plugs.

Weights and measures Metric.

and regulations on length of stay and extensions in advance. A student visa costs £31, or equivalent.

Bolivian embassies and consulates For a full list, see www.rree.gov.bo/inimin.htm

Money The currency is the boliviano (Bs), divided into 100 centavos. There are notes for 200, 100, 50, 20 and 10 bolivianos, and 5, 2 and 1 boliviano coins, as well as 50, 20 and 10 centavos. Bolivianos are often referred to as pesos; expensive items, including hotel rooms, are often quoted in dollars. **Exchange rate** in February 2007: US$1 = Bs 8.34; 1 euro = Bs 10.82.

Many *casas de cambio* and street changers accept euros as well as dollars. When changing money, try to get notes in small denominations. Bs 100 notes are very difficult to change in La Paz and impossible elsewhere. Small change is often given in forms other than money: eg, cigarettes, sweets, or razor blades. Some larger *casas de cambio* will give US$ cash in exchange for travellers' cheques, usually with a commission (3-5%). *Banco Unión* (at the main branch in cities where they have more than one) gives US$ cash for TCs at 1% commission, minimum US$5, efficient service. *Banco Santa Cruz* and *BISA* also ask which currency you would prefer for TCs; *Citibank* gives US$ cash in La Paz. If arriving on Fri night, bring bolivianos or US dollars cash as it is difficult to change travellers' cheques at the weekend (in La Paz, try *El Lobo* restaurant, usually changes TCs at any time, good rates, or *Hotel Gloria*, good rates for most western currencies). American Express cards are not as useful as Visa, or, to a lesser extent, MasterCard. In all cities and large towns there are plenty of 24-hour cash machines (ATMs); they offer bolivianos or dollars. Those displaying the red *Enlace* sign are the best, accepting pretty much every foreign card. Next best are *BISA* ATMs. See Ins and outs, La Paz, **Safety**, on ATM scams; these are worst in La Paz, but may occur elsewhere.

Driving in Bolivia

Road A small percentage of Bolivian roads are paved and under 25% are gravel-surfaced. All roads, whatever their surface, may be closed in the rainy season (November- March). Road tolls vary from US$0.25 to US$1.25 for journeys up to 100 km. On toll roads you receive a stamped receipt at the first toll; don't lose it as it is stamped at subsequent toll posts.

Safety Take great care on the roads, especially at night. Too many truck drivers are drunk, almost never dip their headlights, and many private vehicles drive with faulty headlights.

Documents To bring a private vehicle into Bolivia temporary admission must be sought, but is not easily obtainable; a *carnet de passages* is not required. You must have an International Driving Permit. Always carry your passport, driving licence and registration documents. Bureaucracy regulations are tight and police checks frequent. If you are asked for a 'contribution' to the police force (*colaboración*), always ask for a receipt (*factura*).

Organizations Automóvil Club Boliviano, Av 6 de Agosto y Arce, La Paz, T243 2231. Check here for any special documents or permits that may be required.

Car hire The minimum age for hiring a car is 25. Rates tend to be very expensive. The rental company may only require a national licence, but a policeman may ask to see an international licence.

Fuel 85 and 92 octane; both contain lead. *Especial* (85) US$0.50, *premium* (92) US$0.60. Diesel costs US$0.46 per litre. Petrol is cheapest in Tarija and Santa Cruz, most expensive in Pando and La Paz.

Cost of travelling Bolivia is cheaper to visit than most neighbouring countries. Food, accommodation and transport are all cheap. Budget travellers can get by on US$20-25 per person per day for two travelling together. A basic hotel costs as little as US$3-5 per person, breakfast US$1-2, and a set lunch (*almuerzo*) costs around US$1.50-2.50. For just a few dollars more, though, you can find much better accommodation, more comfortable transport and a wider choice in food without breaking the bank. Prices are higher in the east, especially in Santa Cruz and Tarija, and in Pando and the upper reaches of the Beni. The average cost of using the internet is US$0.40 per hour.

Getting around

Air Internal air services are run by **Aero Sur** *www.aerosur.com* (the principal carrier), **Lloyd Aéreo Boliviano (LAB)** *www.labairlines.com.bo* (do not book through its website, only use agencies), and **Amazonas** *www.amaszonas.com*. LAB offers a 45-day domestic airpass, **Vibolpass**, for US$155-250 (3-5 coupons) for four flights between the main cities. It must be bought outside Bolivia. **Amazonas** also offers a 5-coupon airpass. Many flights radiate from La Paz, Santa Cruz or Cochabamba. Note that a 'through' flight may require a change of plane, or be delayed waiting for a connecting flight coming from elsewhere. Insure your bags heavily as they tend to get left around and LAB is reluctant to give compensation. If your internal flight is delayed keep your baggage with you and do not check it in until the flight is definitely announced. There have been reports of theft.

Bus Buses ply most of the roads (inter-urban buses are called *flotas*, urban ones *micros*, also minibuses and *trufis* – shared taxis). Many bus companies run frequent services and offer a/c, TV and other mod cons, all this despite the poor state of the roads. You should always try to reserve, and pay for, a seat as far as possible in advance and arrive in good time, but substantial savings can be made by buying tickets just before departure, as there is fierce competition to fill seats. In many cases, buses do not leave at the scheduled time as they try to fill seats and depart up to an hour late. A small charge is made for use of major bus terminals; payment is before departure. In the wet season, bus travel is subject to long delays and detours, at extra cost, and cancellations are not uncommon. Conversely, in the dry season journeys can be very dusty. On all journeys, take food and toilet wipes. It is best to travel by day, not just so you can see the scenery and avoid arriving at your destination at night, but also because drivers work long hours and there is less chance of them falling asleep in daylight. Bus companies are responsible for any luggage packed on the roof.

Note: On election day no public transport runs whatsoever; only cars with a special permit may be on the road. Civil disturbance is not uncommon in Bolivia, taking the form of strikes, demonstrations in major cities and frequent road blocks (*paros*) throughout the country, some lasting a few hours, others weeks. Try to be flexible in your travel plans if you encounter such disruptions and make the most of the attractions where you are staying if overland transport is not running.

Train There are passenger trains to the Argentine border at Villazón from Oruro, via Uyuni and Tupiza. Another line runs from Uyuni to Calama in Chile. The only other public railways of significance run from Santa Cruz to the Brazil border and southward. The new Santa Cruz terminal is amazingly efficient, and has connections with bus lines as well. Always check departure times in advance.

Sleeping → *See page 58 for our hotel grade price guide.*

Hotels and hostales Hotels must display prices by law (prices listed in this book include 20% tax and service charge). The number of stars awarded each hotel is regulated by law as well and is a fairly accurate assessment of an establishment's relative status.

Camping Camping is safe almost anywhere except near settlements (unless unavoidable). Warm sleeping gear essential, even in the lowlands in the winter. Sleeping bags are also useful for keeping warm on buses in the Andes.

Youth hostels Youth hostels are not necessarily cheaper: many middle range *residenciales* are affiliated to the HI. For information: **Hostelling International Bolivia** ① *C Guillermo Loayza 119, Sucre, T644 0471, www.HostellingBolivia.org.* In La Paz ① *Socabaya 457, p1, Hotel Torino, T240 9569.* In Santa Cruz ① *Junín 217, Hotel Copacabana, T336 2770.* At affiliated establishments, members usually receive a 10% discount. They also sell the HI card, US$40 and the ISIC card, US$20. Another website listing hostels is http://boliviahostels.com, but they are not necessarily affiliated.

Eating → *See page 58 for our Eating price guide.*

Eating out In the *pensiones* and cheaper restaurants a basic lunch (*almuerzo* – usually finished by 1300) and dinner (*cena*) are normally available. The *comida del día* is the best value in any class of restaurant. Lunch can also be obtained in many of the modern market buildings in the main towns; eat only what is cooked in front of you. Dishes cooked in the street are not safe. Llama meat contains parasites similar to those in pork, so make sure it has been cooked for a long time and is hot when you eat it. Be very careful of salads, which may carry a multitude of amoebic life and bacteria.

Food Bolivian highland cooking is usually very tasty and often *picante*. Recommended local specialities include *empanadas* (cheese pasties) and *humitas* (maize pies); *pukacapas* are *picante* cheese pies. Recommended main dishes include *sajta de pollo*, hot spicy chicken with onion, fresh potatoes and *chuño* (dehydrated potatoes), *parrillada* (a Bolivian kind of mixed grill), *fricase* (juicy pork dish served with *chuño*), *silpancho* (fried breaded meat with eggs, rice and bananas), *saice*, a dish of minced meat with picante sauce, served with rice, potatoes, onions and tomatoes, *pique macho*, roast meat with chips, onion and pepper, and *ají de lengua*, ox-tongue with chilis, potatoes and *chuño* or *tunta* (another kind of dehydrated potato). The soups are also good, especially a *chairo* soup made of meat, vegetables, *chuño* and *ají* (hot pepper) to which the locals like to add *llajua* or *halpahuayca* (hot sauces always set on restaurant tables) to make it even more *picante*. *Salteñas* are meat or chicken pasties (originating from Salta, Argentina), eaten regularly by Bolivians, mostly in the morning. Some are *muy picante* (very hot) with red chili peppers, but *medio picante* and *poco picante* ones can normally be obtained.

In the lowland Oriente region, the food usually comes with cooked banana, yucca and rice. The bread in this region is often sweet with cheese on top, and the rice bread is also unusual. In the north lowlands, many types of wild meat are served in tourist restaurants and on jungle tours. Bear in mind that the turtles whose eggs are eaten are endangered and that other species not endangered soon will be if they stay on the tourist menu.

Standard international cuisine is found at most good hotels and restaurants. Big cities and popular tourist destinations have an increasing number of cafés and restaurants which offer decent international cuisine at reasonable prices aimed at the traveller market. The best cheap option is always the *comida del día*, served in any class of restaurant for about US$1.50 and up. Markets are often the only choice for breakfast where restaurants do not open early, but check hygiene conditions. Dishes cooked on the street are not safe.

Drink The several makes of local, lager-type **beer** are recommendable; *Paceña* and *Ducal* are the best-selling brands. *El Inca* is a dark beer, sweet, like a stout, while *singani*, the national spirit, is distilled from grapes, and is cheap and strong. *Chuflay* is *singani* and a fizzy mixer, usually 7 Up. Good **wines** are produced by La Concepción and Kolhberg vineyards, near Tarija (tours are available and both wineries have on-site shops). *Chicha* is a fermented maize drink, popular in Cochabamba; it is not always alcoholic. In the countryside, look for the white flag outside the houses selling *chicha*. The hot maize drink, *api* (with cloves, cinnamon, lemon and sugar), is good on cold mornings. Bottled **water** is easily available but make sure the seal is unbroken (rain water is sometimes offered as an alternative). Outside the major cities, tap water should not be drunk without first being sterilized. Local water purifier is 'Lugol Fuerte Solución', an iodine-based product, US$1.75 per small bottle; also *iodo* from *farmacias*, US$0.50. For milk, try sachets of *Leche Pil* (plain, chocolate or strawberry-flavoured), at US$0.45 each.

Festivals and events
In Andean regions, **Carnaval Campesino** begins on **Ash Wednesday** and lasts for five days, ending with **Domingo de Tentación** in many small towns. Two weeks before Carnaval is **Jueves de Compadres** and one week before Jueves de Compadres, **Shrove Tuesday** is celebrated as **Martes de Challa**, when house owners make offerings to Pachamama and give drinks to passers-by. Carnaval is celebrated in many cities and towns usually with a *corso* parade with floats and folkloric dances, parties and water throwing. **2 February**: **Virgen de la Candelaria**, in rural communities, Copacabana, Santa Cruz. **Palm Sunday** (Domingo de Ramos) is the occasion for parades to the church throughout Bolivia; the devout carry woven palm fronds, then hang them outside their houses. **Semana Santa** in the eastern Chiquitania is especially interesting, with many processions, dances, and games not found outside the region. Most of these date back several hundred years. **Corpus Christi** is also a colourful festival. **3 May**: **Fiesta de la Invención de la Santa Cruz**, various parts. **2 June**: **Santísima Trinidad** in Beni Department. **24 June**: **San Juan**, all Bolivia. **29 June**: **San Pedro y San Pablo**, at Tiquina, Tihuanaco and throughout the Chiquitania. **25 July**: **Fiesta de Santiago** (St James), Altiplano and lake region. **16 August**: **San Roque**, patron saint of dogs; the animals are adorned with ribbons and other decorations. **1 and 2 November**: **All Saints and All Souls**, any local cemetery. **18 November**: **Beni's Departmental anniversary**, especially in Trinidad. For other festivals on the Altiplano enquire at hotels or tourist office in La Paz. Remember cities are very quiet on national holidays, but colourful celebrations will be going on in the villages. Beware of water-filled balloons thrown during carnival in even the coldest weather. Hotels are often full at the most popular places, for instance Copacabana on Good Friday; worth booking in advance.

Public holidays 1 January, New Year's Day; Carnival Week, Monday, Shrove Tuesday, Ash Wednesday; Holy Week: Thursday, Friday and Saturday; 1 May, Labour Day; Corpus Christi (movable); 16 July, La Paz Municipal Holiday; 5-7 August, Independence; 24 September, Santa Cruz Municipal Holiday; 2 November, Day of the Dead; Christmas Day.

La Paz and around → Phone code: 02. Colour map 6, grid A2. Population: 1.2 million.

The minute you arrive in La Paz, the highest capital city in the world, you realize this is no ordinary place. La Paz's airport is at a staggering 4,000 m above sea level. The sight of the city, lying 500 m below, at the bottom of a steep canyon and ringed by snow-peaked mountains, takes your breath away – literally. For at this altitude breathing can be a problem.

The Spaniards chose this odd place for a city on 20 October 1548, to avoid the chill winds of the plateau, and because they had found gold in the Río Choqueyapu, which runs through the canyon. The centre of the city, Plaza Murillo, is at 3,636 m, about 400 m below the level of the Altiplano and the new city of El Alto, perched dramatically on the rim of the canyon.

Ins and outs

Getting there La Paz has the highest commercial **airport** in the world, at El Alto, high above the city at 4,058 m; T281 0122. A taxi from the airport to the centre takes about 30 minutes, US$5. There are 3 main **bus terminals**; the bus station at Plaza Antofagasta, the cemetery district for Sorata, Copacabana and Tiahuanaco, and Villa Fátima for Coroico and the Yungas.
▶▶ *For more detailed information see Transport, page 260.*

Getting around There are two types of city bus: *micros* (small, old buses), which charge US$0.15 in the centre, US$0.20 from outside centre; and the faster minibuses (small vans), US$0.20 in the centre, US$0.30 outside. *Trufis* are fixed route collective taxis, with a sign with their route on the windscreen, US$0.30 in the centre, US$0.40 pp outside. Prices vary with demand, they are slightly higher at rush hour. Taxis are often, but not always, white. There are three types: regular honest taxis which may take several passengers at once, fake taxis which have been involved in robberies (see below), and radio taxis which take only one group of passengers at a time. Since it is impossible to distinguish between the first two, it is best to pay a bit more for a radio taxi which has a sign and number on the roof and can be ordered by phone; note the number when getting in. Radio taxis charge US$1 in the centre, US$2 outside.

Orientation The city's main street runs from **Plaza San Francisco** as Avenida Mcal Santa Cruz, then changes to Avenida 16 de Julio (more commonly known as the Prado) and ends at **Plaza del Estudiante**. The business quarter, government offices, central university (UMSA) and many of the main hotels and restaurants are in this area. From the Plaza del Estudiante, Avenida Villazón splits into Avenida Arce, which runs southeast towards the wealthier residential districts of **Zona Sur** and Avenida 6 de Agosto which runs through **Sopocachi**, an area full of restaurants, bars and clubs. In the valley, 15 minutes south of the centre, is Zona Sur, home to the resident foreign community. It has international shopping centres, supermarkets with imported items and some of the best restaurants and bars in La Paz (see page 254). Zona Sur begins after the bridge at La Florida beside the attractive Plaza Humboldt. The main road, Avenida Ballivián, begins at Calle 8 and continues up the hill to San Miguel on Calle 21 (about a 20-minute walk). Sprawled around the rim of the canyon is **El Alto**, now a city in its own right and reputedly the fastest growing in South America. Its population of 1 million is mostly indigenous immigrants from the countryside. El Alto is connected to La Paz by motorway (toll US$0.25, motorbikes and cycles free) and by a new road to Obrajes and the Zona Sur. Buses from Plaza Eguino and Pérez Velasco leave regularly for Plaza 16 de Julio, El Alto. Buses to and from La Paz always stop at El Alto in an area called *terminal*, off Avenida 6 de Marzo, where transport companies have small offices. If not staying in La Paz, you can change buses here and save a couple of hours. There is ample accommodation in the area.

Best time to visit Because of the altitude, nights are cold the year round. In the day, the sun is strong, but the moment you go into the shade or enter a building, the temperature falls. From December-March, the summer, it rains most afternoons, making it feel colder than it actually is. The two most important festivals, when the city gets particularly busy, are **Alasitas** (last week of January and first week of February) and **Festividad del Señor del Gran Poder** (end May/early June). See Festivals, page 255.

Tourist offices The **Alcaldía Municipal de La Paz** has information centres at: ① *Plaza del Estudiante at the lower end of El Prado between 16 de Julio and México, T237 1044, Mon-Fri 0900-1900, Sat-Sun 0930-1300*, very helpful, English and French spoken. There is an office at the airport and there are small municipal kiosks in Zona Sur and along Calles Jaén and Sucre. See www.lapaz.bo/paginas/turismo. A private office is at Linares 932, which has a good selection of guide books for reference, purchase or exchange.

Safety Fake police, narcotics police and immigration officers – usually plain-clothed but carrying forged ID – have been known to take people to their 'office' and ask to see documents and money; they then rob them. Legitimate police do not ask people for documents in the street unless they are involved in an accident, fight, etc. If approached, walk away and seek assistance from as many bystanders as possible. Never get in a vehicle with the 'officer' nor follow them to their 'office'. Many of the robberies are very slick, involving taxis and various accomplices. Take only radio taxis, identified by their dome lights and phone numbers. Lock the doors and never allow other passengers to share your cab, the extra security is well worth the extra cost. If someone else gets in, get out at once. The scams often include a fake tourist who first shares the taxi; when the fake police officer arrives he shows his money and has it returned, all to reassure the real tourist who is then robbed. Also if smeared or spat-on, walk away, don't let the good Samaritan clean you up, they will clean you out instead. The worst areas for all the above are the Cemetery neighbourhood where all the local buses arrive, and around Plaza Murillo. Other areas, eg Sopocachi, are generally safer.

Warning for ATM users: scams to get card numbers and PINs have flourished, especially in La Paz. The tourist police post warnings in hotels. See **Touching down**, page 238 for what to do in an emergency.

Sights

There are few colonial buildings left in La Paz; probably the best examples are in **Calle Jaén** (see below). Late 19th-, early 20th-century architecture, often displaying European influence, can be found in the streets around Plaza Murillo, but much of La Paz is modern. The **Plaza del Estudiante** (Plaza Franz Tamayo), or a bit above it, marks a contrast between old and new styles, between the commercial and the more elegant. The **Prado** itself is lined with high-rise blocks dating from the 1960s and 1970s.

Around Plaza Murillo

Plaza Murillo, three blocks north of the Prado, is the traditional centre. Facing its formal gardens are the huge, graceful **Cathedral**, the **Palacio Presidencial** in Italian renaissance style, usually known as the **Palacio Quemado** (burnt palace) twice gutted by fire in its stormy 130-year history, and, on the east side, the **Congreso Nacional**. In front of the Palacio Quemado is a statue of former President Gualberto Villarroel who was dragged into the plaza by an angry mob and hanged in 1946. Across from the Cathedral on Calle Socabaya is the **Palacio de los Condes de Arana** (built 1775), with beautiful exterior and patio. It houses the **Museo Nacional de Arte** ① *T240 8600, www.mna.org.bo, Tue-Sat 0900-1230, 1500-1900, Sun 0900-1230, US$1.25.* It has a fine collection of colonial paintings including many works by Melchor Pérez Holguín, considered one of the masters of Andean colonial art, and which also exhibits the works of contemporary local artists. Calle Comercio, running east-west across the Plaza, has most of the stores and shops. West of Plaza Murillo, at Ingavi 916, in the palace of the Marqueses de Villaverde, and undergoing renovation since 2005, is the **Museo Nacional de Etnografía y Folklore** ① *T240 8640, Tue-Fri 0900-1230, 1500-1700, Sat-Sun 0930-1300, US$1.25.* Various sections show the cultural richness of Bolivia by geographic region through textiles and other items. It has a *videoteca*.

Northwest of Plaza Murillo is **Calle Jaén**, a picturesque colonial street with a restaurant/peña, a café, craft shops, good views and four museums (known as Museos Municipales) housed in colonial buildings ① *Tue-Fri 0900-1230, 1500-1900, Sat-Sun 1000-1300, US$0.15 each.* **Museo Costumbrista** ① *on Plaza Riosinio, at the top of Jaén, T228 0758*, has miniature displays depicting incidents in the history of La Paz and well-known Paceños, as well as miniature replicas of reed rafts used by the Norwegian Thor Heyerdahl, and the Spaniard Kitin

243

La Paz

To **1 26**, Bus Station, El Alto, Airport, Titicaca,
Tiwanaku & Oruro

Plaza Riosinio

Museo Costumbrista, Casa Murillo, Metales Preciosos, del Litoral Boliviano & de Instrumentos Musicales

N

0 metres 100
0 yards 100

Sleeping

Adventure Brew
  Hostel **1** A2
Alcalá Aparthotel **18** F4
Columbus Palace **7** C5
Continental **28** A2
El Rey Palace **29** D4
Estrella Andina **8** B2
Europa **9** C4
Galería Virgen de
  Rosario **30** B2
Hostal Copacabana **22** B2
Hostal República **13** B4
La Joya **16** B1
Plaza **20** D4
Radisson Plaza **21** D5
Residencial Sucre **23** C3
Rosario **24** B2
Tambo de Oro **26** A2

Eating

Alexander
  Coffee **28** C4, E5
Andrómeda **1** D5
Armonía **11** E4
Bistrot **3** E5
Club de la Prensa **2** C4
El Arriero **29** E6
Kuchen Stube **30** E5
La Comedie **12** E5
La Quebecoise **18** E5
La Terraza **8** C4
Lu Qing **14** D4
Mongo's **19** E5
Reineke Fuchs **24** E5
Surucachi **13** C4
Vienna **7** D4
Wagamama **10** E6

Bars & clubs

Deadstroke **27** E5
Diesel Nacional **26** E5
Equinoccio **21** E4
RamJam **31** F5
Thelonius Jazz **25** E4

Related map
A La Paz centre,
page 246

Muñoz, to prove their theories of ancient migrations. **Museo del Litoral Boliviano** (T228 0758), has artefacts of the War of the Pacific, and interesting selection of old maps. **Museo de Metales Preciosos** (T228 0329), is well set out with Inca gold artefacts in basement vaults, also ceramics and archaeological exhibits, and **Museo Casa Murillo** (T228 0553), the erstwhile home of Pedro Domingo Murillo, one of the martyrs of the La Paz independence movement of 16 July 1809, has a good collection of paintings, furniture and national costumes. In addition to the Museos Municipales is the **Museo de Instrumentos Musicales** ① *Jaén 711 e Indaburo, T240 8177, Tue-Fri 0930-1230, 1530-1900, Sat-Sun 1000-1300, US$0.50*, in a refurbished colonial house. **Museo Tambo Quirquincho** ① *C Evaristo Valle, south of Jaén, near Plaza Mendoza, T239 0869, Tue-Fri, 0930-1230, 1530-1900, Sat-Sun, 1000-1300, US$0.50*, displays modern painting and sculpture, carnival masks, silver, early 20th century photography and city plans, and is recommended.

La Paz centre

Sleeping 🛏
Alojamiento París **8** *A3*
Arcabucero **1** *C1*
Austria **2** *B2*
El Solario **3** *B1*
El Viajero **4** *C1*
Fuentes **6** *C1*
Gloria **5** *B2*
Hospedaje Milenio **19** *A3*
Hostal Cactus **12** *B1*
Hostal Maya **18** *C1*
Hostal Naira **7** *C2*
Ingavi **9** *A2*
Majestic **11** *B1*
Milton **17** *D1*
Presidente & La Kantuta **13** *B2*
Residencial Latino **10** *A3*
Sagárnaga **15** *C1*
Torino **16** *B3*

Eating 🍴
100% Natural **1** *C1*
Alexander Coffee **2** *B3*
Angelo Colonial **3** *C1*
Banais **12** *B2*
Café Confitería de la Paz **4** *C2*
Casa del Corregidor **16** *D2*
Dumbos **18** *D3*
El Calicanto **17** *B2*
El Lobo **5** *B1*
Eli's Pizza Express **18** *D3*
Jackie Chan **6** *C2*
La Casa de Los Paceños **19** *A3*
Le Pot-Pourri
  des Gourmets **7** *C1*
O Mundo **7** *C1*
Pepe's **14** *C1*
Pizzas & Pastas **8** *C1*
Pizzería Italia **9** *C1*
Pizzería Romana **21** *B1*
Yussef **22** *C1*

Bars & clubs 🍸
Oliver's Travels **20** *C2*
Peña El Parnaso **15** *C2*
Sol y Luna **23** *C2*

Bolivia La Paz Sights

246

Tiny treats

One of the most intriguing items for sale in Andean markets is *Ekeko*, the god of good fortune and plenty and one of the most endearing of the Aymara folk legends. He is a cheery, avuncular little chap, with a happy face, a pot belly and short legs. His image, usually in plaster of Paris, is laden with various household items, as well as sweets, confetti and streamers, food, and with a cigarette dangling cheekily from his lower lip. Believers say that

these statues only bring luck if they are received as gifts. The *Ekeko* occupies a central role in the festival of Alacitas, the Feast of Plenty, which takes place in La Paz at the end of January. Everything under the sun can be bought in miniature: houses, trucks, buses, suitcases, university diplomas; you name it, you'll find it here. The idea is to have your mini-purchase blessed by a *Yatiri*, an Aymara priest, and the real thing will be yours within the year.

Plaza San Francisco up to the cemetery district

At the upper end of Avenida Mcal Santa Cruz is the **Plaza San Francisco** with the **church and monastery of San Francisco** ① *local weddings can be seen on Sat 1000-1200, the church opens for Mass at 0700, 0900, 1100 and 1900, Mon-Sat, and also at 0800, 1000 and 1200 on Sun*. Dating from 1549, this is one of the finest examples of colonial religious architecture in South America and well worth seeing. The **Cultural Museo San Francisco** ① *Plaza San Francisco 503, T231 8472, www.centrocultural-museosanfrancisco.org, daily 0900-2100, US$2.50, allow 1½-2 hrs, guides available free but tip appreciated, some speak English and French*, offers access to various areas of the church and convent which were previously off limits, including the choir, crypt (open 1400-1730), roof, various chapels and gardens. Fine art includes religious paintings from the 17th, 18th and 19th centuries, plus visiting exhibits and a hall devoted to the works of Tito Yupanqui, the indigenous sculptor of the Virgen de Copacabana. There is a pricey but good café at entrance. Behind the San Francisco church a network of narrow cobbled streets rise steeply up the canyon walls. Much of this area is a permanent street market. Handicraft shops, travel agencies, hotels and restaurants line the lower part of **Calle Sagárnaga** (here you find the highest concentration of tourists and pick-pockets). The amazing **Mercado de Hechicería**, 'witchcraft market', on Calles Melchor Jiménez and Linares, which cross Santa Cruz above San Francisco, sells fascinating charms, herbs and more gruesome items like llama foetuses. The excellent **Museo de la Coca** ① *Linares 914, daily 1000-1900, US$1, shop with coca sweets for sale,* is devoted to the coca plant, its history, cultural significance, medical values and political implications, with explanations in Spanish and English. In the same building is the **Museo de Arte Texil Andino Boliviano** ① *Mon-Sat 1000-1930, Sun 100-1700, US$1*, a small collection of old traditional weavings (not to be confused with the larger Museo de Textiles Andinos Bolivianos in Miraflores).

Further up, from Illampu to Rodríguez and in neighbouring streets, is the produce-based **Rodríguez market** ① *daily, but best on Sun morning*. Turning right on Max Paredes, heading north, is **Avenida Buenos Aires**, where small workshops turn out the costumes and masks for the Gran Poder festival, and with great views of Illimani, especially at sunset. Continuing west along Max Paredes towards the **cemetery district**, the streets are crammed with stalls selling every imaginable item. Transport converges on the cemetery district (for more information see page 260). See also Safety, above, page 243.

The Prado, Sopocachi, Miraflores and Zona Sur

Museo de Arte Contemporáneo Plaza ① *Av 16 de Julio 1698, T233 5905, Mon-Fri 0900-2100, US$1*. In a 19th-century house which has been declared a national monument, there is an excellent selection of contemporary art from national and international artists. Rotating exhibits, some work for sale. The new **Museo Fotográfico Nuñez de Arco** ① *16 de Julio 1615, Mon-Fri 1000-1300, 1500-2000, Sat 10-1300, US$1.90* has an interesting photo collection of the early excavations of Tiawanaku and old photos of La Paz and surroundings. Just off the Prado (go down the flight of stairs by the Hotel Plaza) is **Museo Nacional de Arqueología** or

Tiahuanaco (Tiwanaku) ① *Tiwanacu 93 entre Bravo y F Zuazo, T231 1621, www.bolivian.com/arqueologia, Mon-Fri 0900-1200, 1400-1800, US$1.25*. It contains good collections of the arts and crafts of ancient Tiwanaku and items from the eastern jungles. It also has a two-room exhibition of gold statuettes and objects found in Lake Titicaca. In Sopocachi district, above Avenida 6 de Agosto, is **Casa Museo Marina Núñez del Prado** ① *Ecuador 2034, T242 4175, www.bolivian.com/cmnp, daily 0930-1300, Tue-Fri 1500-1900 (may be closed afternoons and weekends), US$0.75, students US$0.30*, which houses an excellent collection of Marina Núñez's sculptures in the family mansion. By Plaza España, is **El Montículo**, a lovely park with great views of the city. On Avenida Libertador Simón Bolívar, from where there are great views of Mt Illimani, is the indigenous produce **Central Market** (called **Mercado Camacho**). Further east is the residential district of Miraflores where you'll find **Museo de Textiles Andinos Bolivianos** ① *Plaza Benito Juárez 488, Miraflores, T224 3601, Mon-Sat 0930-1200, 1500- 1800, Sun 1000-1230, US$1.25*, with good displays of textiles from around the country, detailed explanations and a knowledgeable owner. Outside the Hernan Siles national football stadium, on Plaza Tejada Sorzano, is the **Museo Semisubterráneo**, a sunken garden full of restored statues and other artefacts from Tiahuanaco, some of them badly eroded from traffic pollution. The **Kusillo Cultural Complex** ① *Av del Ejército, T222 6371, www.kusillo.org, museum hours Tue-Sun 0930-1830, US$0.65 midweek, US$1.25 weekends,* features interactive exhibits on Bolivian culture, shops selling native crafts, and a Museum of Science and Play.

Around La Paz

South of La Paz

To the south of the city are dry hills of many colours, topped by the **Muela del Diablo**, a striking outcrop. Here is the **Valle de la Luna**, or 'Moon Valley', which has a nice terraced cactus garden worth walking through; the climate in this valley is always much warmer than in the city. About 3 km from the bridge at Calacoto the road forks. For transport details see page 261. Most of the local travel agents organize tours to the Valle de la Luna. These are very brief, 5 minutes stop for photos in a US$15 tour of La Paz and surroundings; taxis cost US$6. Get out of the minibus at the turning and walk a few minutes east to the Valle entrance, or get out at the football field which is by the entrance. Take good shoes and water. Just past the Valle de la Luna is **Mallasa** where there are several small roadside restaurants and cafés and the **Hotel Oberland** (see page 252). The **zoo** ① *on the road to Río Abajo, entrance just past Mallasa after Valle de la Luna, daily 0900-1700, US$0.50 adults, US$0.25 children.* In a beautiful, wide open park-like setting, conditions for the animals and birds are relatively good, but the public is allowed to feed the animals. Quad biking is available behind the zoo.

Tiahuanaco

① *The site is open 0900-1700, US$10 for foreigners, including entry to museums. Allow 4 hrs to see the ruins and village. See also Transport, page 261.*

This remarkable archaeological site, 72 km west of La Paz, near the southern end of Lake Titicaca, takes its name from one of the most important pre-Columbian civilizations in South America. It is now the most popular excursion from La Paz, with facilities being improved as a result. Many archaeologists believe that Tiahuanaco existed as early as 1600 BC, while the complex visible today probably dates from the eight to the 10th centuries AD. The site may have been a ceremonial complex at the centre of an empire which covered almost half Bolivia, south Peru, north Chile and northwest Argentina. It was also a hub of trans-Andean trade. The demise of the Tiahuanaco civilization, according to studies by Alan Kolata of the University of Illinois, could have been precipitated by the flooding of the area's extensive system of raised fields (*Sukakollu*), which were capable of sustaining a population of 20,000. The Pumapunka section, 1 km south of the main complex may have been a port, as the waters of the lake used to be much higher than they are today. The raised field system is being reutilized in the Titicaca area.

One of the main structures is the **Kalasasaya**, meaning 'standing stones', referring to the statues found in that part: two of them, the Ponce monolith (centre of inner patio) and the Fraile monolith (southwest corner), have been re-erected. In the northwest corner is the Puerta del Sol, originally at Pumapunku. Its carvings, interrupted by being out of context, are thought to be either a depiction of the creator God, or a calendar. The motifs are exactly the same as those around the Ponce monolith. The **Templo Semisubterráneo** is a sunken temple whose walls are lined with faces, all different, according to some theories depicting states of health, the temple being a house of healing; another theory is that the faces display all the ethnicities of the world. The **Akapana**, originally a pyramid (said to have been the second largest in the world, covering over 28,000 sq m), still has some ruins on it. At **Pumapunku**, some of whose blocks weigh between 100 and 150 tonnes, a natural disaster may have put a sudden end to the construction before it was finished. Most of the best statues are in the **Museo Tiahuanaco** or the **Museo Semisubterráneo** in La Paz (see page 248). There is a small museum at the ticket office, the **Museo Regional Arqueológico de Tiahuanaco**, containing a well-illustrated explanation of the raised field system of agriculture. Next to the site museum is La Cabaña del Puma restaurant where lunch costs about US$2.

Written guide material is difficult to come by; hiring a good guide costs US$10. A map of the site with a historical explanation in English (published by Quipus) is sold at the ticket office, US$2.50. Locals sell copies of Tiahuanaco figures; cheaper here than from La Paz.

The nearby **Tiahuanaco village** still has remnants from the time of independence and the 16th-century church used pre-Columbian masonry. In fact, Tiahuanaco for a long while was the 'quarry' for the altiplano. For the festival on 21 June, before sunrise, there are colourful dances and llama sacrifices. On the 8th day of carnival (Sunday), there is a colourful carnival. Souvenirs for sale, bargain hard, do not take photographs.

By road to Chile

The main route to Chile is via Tambo Quemado (see page 280), but an alternative route, on which there are no trucks, is to go by good road direct from La Paz via Viacha to Santiago de Machaco (130 km, petrol); then 120 km to the border at Charaña (G Alojamiento Aranda; immigration behind railway station), very bad road. In Visviri (Chile) there is no fuel, accommodation, electricity, ask for restaurant and bargain price. From Visviri a regular road runs to Putre, see Chile chapter.

Trekking and climbing near La Paz

Four so-called 'Inca Trails' link the Altiplano with the Yungas, taking you from the high Andes to the sub-tropics, with dramatic changes in weather, temperature and vegetation. Each has excellent sections of stonework and they vary in difficulty from relatively straightforward to quite hard-going. In the rainy season going can be particularly tough. For details of how to reach the starting point of each trail, see Transport sections on page 262

Takesi Trail Start at **Ventilla** (see below), walk up the valley for about three hours passing the village of Choquekhota until the track crosses the river and to the right of the road, there is a falling-down brick wall with a map painted on it. The Takesi and Alto Takesi trails start here, following the path to the right of the wall. The road continues to Mina San Francisco. In the first hour's climb from the wall is excellent stone paving which is Inca or pre-Inca, depending on who you believe, either side of the pass at 4,630 m. There are camping possibilities at *Estancia Takesi* and in the village of Kakapi you can sleep at the **G Kakapi Tourist Lodge**, 10 beds with good mattresses, solar shower and toilet. It is run by the local community and sponsored by Fundación Pueblo. It is also possible to camp. You also have to pass the unpleasant mining settlement of Chojlla, between which and Yanakachi is a gate where it is necessary to register and often pay a small 'fee'. Yanakachi has a number of good places to stay, several good hikes and an orphanage you can help at. The Fundación Pueblo office on the plaza has information. Buy a minibus ticket on arrival in Yanakachi or walk 45 minutes down to the La Paz-Chulumani road for transport. The trek can be done in one long day, especially if you organize a jeep to the start of the trail, but is more relaxing in two or three. If you take it slowly, though, you'll have to carry camping kit. Hire mules in Choquekhota for US$8 per day plus up to US$8 for the muleteer. A 2-3 day alternative is from Mina San Francisco to El Castillo and the village of Chaco on the La Paz-Chulumani road. This trek is called La Reconquistada and has the distinction of including a 200 m disused mining tunnel.

Choro Trail (La Cumbre to Coroico) Immediately before the road drops down from La Cumbre to start the descent to Las Yungas, there is a good dirt road leading up to the *apacheta* (narrow pass) where the trail starts properly. Cloud and bad weather are normal at La Cumbre (4,660 m): you have to sign in at the Guardaparque post on the way to the pass.

The trail passes Samaña Pampa (small shop, sign in again, camping US$0.60), Chucura (pay US$1.20 fee, another shop, camping), Challapampa (camping possible, US$0.60, small shop), the Choro bridge and the Río Jacun-Manini (fill up with water at both river crossings). At Sandillani it is possible to stay at the lodge or camp in the carefully-tended garden of a Japanese man, Tamiji Hanamura, who keeps a book with the names of every passing traveller. He likes to see postcards and pictures from other countries. There is good paving down to Villa Esmeralda, after which is Chairo (lodging and camping), then to Yolosa. It takes three days to trek from La Cumbre to Chairo, from where you can take a truck to Yolosa (it runs when there are enough people: US$2.25 each). From Yolosa it is 8 km uphill to Coroico with regular transport for US$1.20 per person. The Choro Trail has a reputation for unfriendliness and occasional robbery, take care.

Yunga Cruz (Chuñavi to Chulumani) The best, but hardest of the four 'Inca' trails: from Chuñavi follow the path left (east) and contour gently up. Camping possible after two hours. Continue along the path staying on left hand side of the ridge to reach Cerro Khala Ciudad (literally, Stone City Mountain, you'll see why). Good paving brings you round the hill to join a path coming from Quircoma (on your right); continue, heading north, to Cerro Cuchillatuca and then Cerro Yunga Cruz, where there is water and camping is possible. After this point water and camping are difficult and normally impossible until you get down to Sikilini. The last water and camping possibilities are all within the next hour, take advantage of them. Each person should have at least two litres of water in bottles. For water purification, only use iodine-based preparations (iodine tincture, *iodo* in *farmacias* costs US$0.50: use five drops per litre.) There are some clearances on the way down but no water. Colectivos run from Sikilini to Chulumani. Starting in Chuñavi the trek takes three days. The Yunga Cruz trail is badly littered; clean up after yourself.

Huayna Potosí Huayna Potosí is normally climbed in two days, with one night camped on a glacier at 5,600 m. There is a refugio *Huayna Potosí*, which costs US$10 per night, plus food. Contact at Illampu 626, T/F02-245 6717, bolclimb@mail.megalink.com or La Paz agencies for further information. Average cost is US$140 for two-day tour including all equipment except sleeping bag. The starting point for the normal route is at Zongo, whose valley used to have a famous ice cave (now destroyed by global warming). See Climbing, hiking and trekking page 257, for details of guides.

● Sleeping

Around Plaza Murillo *p243, maps p244 and p246*

L-AL Presidente, Potosí y Sanjines 920, T240 6666, www.hotelpresidente-bo.com. The 'highest 5-star in the world'. Includes breakfast, gym and sauna, pool, all open to non-residents, internet, bar, excellent service, comfortable, good food.
B Gloria, Potosí 909, T240 7070, www.hotel gloria.com.bo. Modern, central, cable TV, price includes buffet breakfast, 2 restaurants, one is vegetarian, excellent food and service, run **Gloria Tours** (www.gloriatours.com.bo). Recommended.
D Hostal República, Comercio 1455, T220 2742, marynela@ceibo.entelnet.bo. **E** with shared bath, old house of former president, hot water, luggage stored, helpful, laundry service, good café, quiet garden, free internet, book ahead.
E The Adventure Brew Hostel, Av Montes 533, T246 1614, www.theadventurebrewhostel.com. With solar-heated showers, **F** pp in dorm, on-site

microbrewery, includes breakfast, rooftop terrace with great views of the city and Illimani, nightly BBQs, use of kitchen, convenient to the bus station, associated with **Gravity Assisted Mountain Biking** (see Activiites and Tours, below).
F Alojamiento París, Av Sucre 949, T228 5029. Electric shower, **F-G** shared bath, good value.
F Ingavi, Ingavi 727, T232 3645. Nice rooms with infrequent hot water, good value, poor service.
F Residencial Latino, Junín 857 y Sucre, T228 5463. With hot water, cheaper without bath, in a refurbished colonial house with patios, a pleasant simple hostel, good value.
F Tambo de Oro, Armentia 367, T228 1565, F228 2181. Near bus station, hot showers, TV, good value, safe for luggage.
F Torino, Socabaya 457, T240 6003. Ask for better rooms in new section, with or without bath, run-down rooms in old section, HI member, popular with backpackers, prices go up in high season, free

● For an explanation of the sleeping and eating price codes used in this guide, see page 58. Other
● relevant information is found in Essentials pages 240-241.

250

book exchange, good service, internet café (pricey) and good restaurant next door for breakfast and good value lunch (weekdays 1200-1500).

F-G Austria, Yanacocha 531, T240 8540, hotelaustria@acelerate.com. Without bath, cheaper in shared room, basic, hot water but only three showers, safe deposit, laundry, TV lounge, use of kitchen, book in advance, bus to Copacabana leaves here 0800-0830.

F-G Hospedaje Milenio, Yanacocha 860, T228 1263. Electric shower, basic, good value, family house, homely, helpful owner, quiet, kitchen.

Plaza San Francisco up to the cemetery district *p247, maps p244 and p246*
C Hostal Naira, Sagárnaga 161, T235 5645, www.hostalnaira.com. Hot water, comfortable but pricey, rooms around courtyard, some are dark, price includes buffet breakfast in **Café Banais**, safety deposit boxes.

C Rosario, Illampu 704, T245 1658, www.hotel rosario.com. 3-star, excellent buffet breakfast, cable TV, modem connection, sauna, laundry, internet café **Jiwhaki** (free for guests, great view), good restaurant, stores luggage, very helpful staff, no smoking. Highly recommended. **Turisbus** travel agency downstairs (see Tour operators, page 258), Cultural Interpretation Centre explains items for sale in nearby 'witches' market'.

D Continental, Illampu 626, T/F245 1176, hotelcontinental626@hotmail.com. **F** without bath, nice rooms, stores luggage, member of Hostelling International Bolivia.

D Galería Virgen de Rosario, C Santa Cruz 583, p 4, T246 1015, hgaleria@ceibo.entelnet.bo. Great rooms, lots of daylight, includes breakfast, cable TV, safety boxes, quiet, helpful, good value.

D La Joya, Max Paredes 541, T245 3841, www.hotelajoya.com. **E** without bath or breakfast, TV, modern and comfy, lift, laundry, popular area with free pickup from town centre, close to bus and train station.

D Sagárnaga, Sagárnaga 326, T235 0252, www.hotel-sagarnaga.com. Cheaper in plain rooms without TV, includes breakfast, solar-powered hot water, laundry, English spoken, *peña*, ATM.

E Arcabucero, C Viluyo 307, Linares (close to Museo de Coca), T/F231 3473. Pleasant new rooms in converted colonial house, excellent value but check the beds, breakfast extra.

D Estrella Andina, Illampu 716, T245 6421, juapame_2000@hotmail.com. Price includes breakfast, all rooms have a safe, English spoken, family run, comfortable, tidy, helpful, internet access, roof terrace, very nice.

D-E Fuentes, Linares 888, T231 3966, www.hotelf uentesbolivia.com. Cheaper without

bath, hot water, variety of rooms, includes breakfast, nice colonial style, comfortable, TV, interent, sauna, good value, family run, slow laundry service.

E Hostal Maya, Sagárnaga 339, T231 1970, mayahost_in@hotmail.com. **E-F** with shared bath, some rooms spacious, with balconies, others windowless and small, internet, money exchange, laundry, safe deposit, massage, luggage store, cable TV in living room.

E Majestic, Santa Cruz 359, T245 1628. Simple rooms, comfortable, laundry, safe, breakfast.

E Milton, Illampu y Calderón 1124, T236 8003, F236 5849. **F** without bath, hot water, includes breakfast, restaurant, expensive laundry, safe parking around corner, popular, will store luggage, excellent views from roof.

E Hostal Copacabana, Illampu 734, T245 1626, www.hostalcopacabana.com. Hot water, good showers, **F** without bath, soft beds, includes breakfast, changes TCs, basic but OK.

E Res Sucre, Colombia 340, on Plaza Sucre, T249 2038, F248 6723. **F** without bath, quiet area, hot water, big rooms, no double beds, luggage stored, helpful.

F El Viajero, Illampu 807, T245 3465, www.viajero.LoboPages.com. **F-G** without bath, **G** pp in dorm, a reasonable hostel, decorated

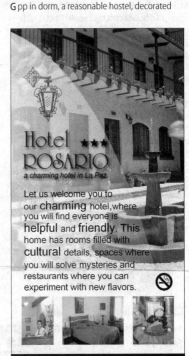

with plants, dorm has lockers.

F-G El Solario, Murillo 776, T236 7963, elsolario
hotel@yahoo.com. Central, shared bath, luggage
store, kitchen, internet, international phone calls,
laundry and medical services, taxi and travel
agency, good value, gets crowded.

F-G Hostal Cactus, Jiménez 818 y Santa Cruz,
T245 1421. Shared showers (electric), helpful,
kitchen facilities, luggage store, poor beds and
plunbing but peaceful and quiet.

The Prado, Sopocachi, Miraflores and Zona Sur *p247, map p244*

L Europa, Tiahuanacu 64, T231 5656, www.hotel
europa.com.bo. Next to the Museo Nacional de
ArqueologíaExcellent facilities and plenty of frills,
internet in rooms, health club, several restaurants
including a good café. Recommended.

L Radisson Plaza, Av Arce 2177, T244 1111,
www.radisson.com/lapazbo. 5-star hotel with all
facilities, excellent buffet in restaurant (see Eating
below), still referred to as the Sheraton.

AL Casa Grande, Av Ballivian 1000 y C 17,
Calacoto, T279 5511, www.casa-grande.com.bo.
Beautiful, top quality apartments, includes buffet
breakfast, Wi-Fi, airport pickup, restaurant, very
good service, discounts or longer stays.

AL Plaza, Av 16 de Julio 1789, T237 8311,
www.plazabolivia.com.bo. Excellent hotel with
good value restaurant (see below), peña show on
Fri, includes breakfast, internet, pool.

A El Rey Palace, Av 20 de Octubre 1947, T241
8541, www.hotel-rey-palace-bolivia.com.
Includes breakfast, large suites with bath tub,
internet, excellent restaurant, stylish, modern.

B Alcalá Aparthotel, Sanjinés 2662 at Plaza
España, Sopocachi, T241 2336, alcapt@zuper.net.
Nice, comfortable, spacious, furnished apartments,
includes breakfast, 20% discount per month.

B-D A La Maison, Pasaje Muñoz Cornejo15,
Sopocachi, T241 3704, www.alamaison-lapaz.
com. Apart-hotel, brightly decorated, breakfast,

laundry service, ADSL connection, TV, kitchens in
the larger flats, meals and tourist services can be
arranged, daily and monthly rates available.

C Columbus Palace, Illimani 1990 by Plaza
Tejada Sorzano, Miraflores, T224 2444,
www.hotel-columbus.com. Includes buffet
breakfast, internet, comfortable modern
rooms, restaurant with buffet lunch.

C EHT Sopocachi, Macario Pinilla 580 at
the base of El Montículo, T241 0312,
ehtsop@datacom-bo.net. Spacious furnished
apartments with kitchenette, good location
and views, US$750 per month.

South of La Paz *p248*

A-B Oberland, C 2 y 3, Mallasa, PO Box 9392,
12 km from centre, T274 5040, www.h-oberland.
com. A Swiss-owned, chalet-style restaurant
(excellent, not cheap) and hotel (also good) with
older resort facilities, gardens, cabañas, sauna, pool
(open to public – US$2 - very hot water), beach
volley, tennis. Permits camping with vehicle.

B Gloria Urmiri, Urmiri, T237 0010,
www.hotelgloria.com.bo. At hot springs
2 hrs from La Paz, price for weekend (wide
range of choices depending on the type of tub),
cheaper weekdays; B full board shared bath,
cheaper Mon-Fri. Transport US$5.60 pp
return. Entry to pools: US$2.50 pp small pool,
US$3.15 large pool, includes use of sauna.
Massage available, camping US$1.50,
reservations required.

C Allkamari, Pampa Koani in Valle de las
Animas, 30 mins from town on the road to
Palca, T279 1742, allkamari@ casalunaspa.com.
Reservations required, cabins in a lovely valley
between the Palca and La Animas canyons, a
retreat with nice views of Illimani and Huayna
Potosí, a place to relax and star-gaze, **A** cabin for
up to 8, **E** pp in dorm, includes breakfast, solar
heating, jacuzzi included, meals on request, use
of kitchen, horse and bike rentals, massage,

shamanic rituals, taxi from Calacoto US$4.50, bus No 42 from the cemetery to Uni (7 daily weekdays, hourly weekends), get off at Iglesia de las Animas and walk 1 km.

🍽 Eating

Around Plaza Murillo *p243, maps p244 and p246*
🍴 **La Casa de los Paceños**, Sucre 856, T228 0955, also at Los Pinos 200 in Calacoto. Tourist restaurant, excellent Bolivian food, à la carte only.
🍴 **El Calicanto**, Sanjines 467, T240 8008. Good food including regional specialities, renovated colonial house, live music at weekends.
🍴 **Club de la Prensa**, C Campero 52. Pleasant garden, limited menu – meat and fish only, in copious quantities – lively company.
🍴 **Hotel Gloria**, Potosí 909. Vegetarian, popular for *almuerzo*, US$3, buffet lunch or dinner US$2.15; international restaurant, daily 1200-1500, 1800-2230.
🍴 **La Kantuta**, in *Hotel Presidente*, Potosí 920. Excellent food, good service.

Cafés
Alexander Coffee, Potosí 1091. Part of a chain, sandwiches, salads, coffee, pastries.
Café Berlín, Mercado 1377 y Loayza and at Av Montenegro 5, Calacoto. Coffee, sweets, omelettes, breakfast, popular with locals, 0800-2300.
Café Confitería de la Paz, Camacho 1202, on the corner where Ayacucho joins Av Mcal Santa Cruz. Good if expensive tea room, traditional, meeting place for businessmen and politicians, great coffee and cakes.

Plaza San Francisco up to the cemetery district *p247, maps p244 and p246*
🍴 **Casa del Corregidor**, Murillo 1040, T236 3633. Centrally heated, Spanish colonial restaurant with mainly Bolivian dishes, excellent food, bar, Mon-Sat 1730-2300, peña from 2100.
🍴 **Tambo Colonial**, in *Hotel Rosario* (see above). Excellent local and international cuisine, good salad bar, huge buffet breakfast, peña at weekend. Recommended.
🍴🍴 **Pizzería Romana**, Santa Cruz 260. Good pizzas and pastas, good value.
🍴 **100% Natural**, Sagárnaga 345. Range of healthy, tasty fast foods ranging from salads to burgers and llama meat, good breakfasts, closed Sun.
🍴 **Angelo Colonial**, Linares 922. Excellent food, vegetarian options, and ambience, candlelight, antiques, good music, internet access, open early for breakfast, can get very busy. Has a hostal at Av Santa Cruz 1058, with hot water, safe, convenient.
🍴 **El Lobo**, Santa Cruz 441. Huge portions, Israeli dishes, good meeting place, noticeboard, popular.
🍴 **Jackie Chan**, Cochabamba 100 (just south of

Av Mcal Santa Cruz). Good Chinese, excellent value, popular with locals.
🍴 **Le Pot-Pourri des Gourmets**, Linares 906, close to Sagárnaga. Bolivian and a variety of main courses including vegetarian, *almuerzo* US$2.20, pastries, snacks, hot and cold drinks, quiet, homely, music, exceptional value, great atmosphere but slow service.
🍴 **Pizzas & Pastas**, Galería Sagárnaga 339, Sagárnaga (enter from Illampu and Linares). Homemade pizza and pasta, large variety, small place so may have to queue, good value, open 1530-2200.
🍴 **Pizzería Italia**, Illampu 840 and 809, 2nd floor, T712 1234. Thin-crust pizza, pasta and international food.
🍴 **Yussef**, Sagárnaga 380, second floor (poorly signed). Lebanese, great mezze, good for vegetarians, good value and relaxed atmosphere.

Cafés
Banais, Sagárnaga 161, same entrance as *Hostal Naira*. Coffee, sandwiches and juices, buffet breakfast, laid-back music and computer room downstairs.
O Mundo, Linares 906. Open only until 1500, below *Le Pot Pourri des Gourmets*, from which you can order food, good range of drinks.
Pepe's, Pasaje Jiménez 894, off Linares. Welcoming little café with good all-day breakfasts, sandwiches, omelettes, tables outside, cards and dominoes, magazines and guidebooks.

The Prado, Sopocachi, Miraflores and Zona Sur *p247, map p244*
🍴🍴 **Chalet la Suisse**, C 23, on the main avenue between Cs 24 and 25, Zona Sur, T279 3160. Serves excellent fondue, steaks, booking essential on Fri evening.
🍴🍴 **El Arriero**, Av 6 de Agosto 2535 (Casa Argentina), Sopocachi, also on C 17, Zona Sur. The best barbecue in the city with large portions.
🍴🍴 **Bistrot**, Fernando Guachalla 399, Sopocachi, in Alliance Française. Swish new restaurant with French menu, vegetarian options, sandwiches.
🍴🍴 **High Lander's**, Final Sánchez Lima 2667, Sopocachi, T243 0023. Very good Tex-Mex fare, nice atmosphere, good views from the end of the street, Mon-Fri 1200-1500, 1700-2300, Sat 1800-2330.
🍴🍴 **La Comedie**, Pasaje Medinacelli 2234, Sopocachi, T242 3561. 'Art café restaurant', contemporary, with a mainly French menu, good salads and cocktails.
🍴🍴 **La Tranquera**, Capitán Ravelo 2123 next to Hotel Camino Real, T244 1103. Good international food, grill and salad bar, daily 1200-1600, 1900-2300.
🍴🍴 **Radisson Plaza Hotel**, Av Arce 2177, T244 1111. Excellent buffet in 5-star setting, daily 1200-1500, delicious, friendly to backpackers.

♥♥ **Reineke Fuchs**, Jáuregui 2241, Sopocachi. Many European beers and food in a German-style bar. Renovation in mid-2006.

♥♥ **The Lounge**, Presbitero Medina 2527, T241 0585. American/Bolivian run, chilled atmosphere, western and Latin food, art exhibitions, excellent toilets, popular.

♥♥ **Utama**, in *Plaza* hotel, Av 16 de Julio 1789). 2 restaurants: **Utama** on the top floor, with the views, 1700-2300, à la carte, and **Uma**, on the ground floor, for breakfast and lunch, buffet lunch US$6.15. Recommended.

♥♥ **Vienna**, Federico Zuazo 1905, T244 1660, www.restaurantvienna.com. German, Austrian and local food, excellent food, atmosphere and service, live piano music, popular, open Mon-Fri 1200-1400, 1830-2200, Sun 1200-1430. Frequently recommended.

♥♥ **Wagamama**, just behind *Jalapeños*, Pasaje Pinilla 2557, T243 4911. Open Tue-Sat 1200-1430, 1900-2000 (closed Sun and Mon) serving huge plates of sushi, complimentary tea, excellent service, popular with ex-pats.

♥ **Andrómeda**, Av Arce 2116, T244 0726. Renowned for superb-value lunches, closing at time of going to press and reopening after as French bistro.

♥ **Armonía**, Ecuador 2286 y Quito. Nice vegetarian buffet lunch, Mon-Sat 1200-1430.

♥ **Eli's Pizza Express**, Av 16 de Julio 1400 block. English spoken, open daily including holidays (also at Comercio 914), very popular, maybe not the best pizza in La Paz, but certainly the largest omelettes.

♥ **La Quebecoise**, 20 de Octubre 2387, Sopocachi, T212 1682, Mon-Fri 1200-1500, 1900-2300, Sat 1900-2300. French Canadian, good value for buffet, grill and take-away, pleasant atmosphere.

♥ **Lu Qing**, 20 de Octubre 2090 y Aspiazu, T242 4188. Chinese food, large choice of dishes, set meals on weekdays, Mon-Sat 1130-1500, 1830-2300, Sun 1100-1530.

♥ **Mongo's**, Hnos Manchego 2444, near Plaza Isabela la Católica, T244 0714. Open 1900-0300, live music Mon and Tue, Mexican and Bolivian dishes, burgers, snacks, open fires, bar, club after midnight, popular with gringos and locals.

♥ **The Olive Tree**, Campos 334 y 6 de Agosto, Edificio Iturri. Closed Sat evening and Sun, good salads, soups and sandwiches.

♥ **Surucachi**, 16 de Julio 1598 (El Prado), T231 2135. Bolivian specialties, good value set lunches on weekdays, plus à la carte.

Cafés

Alexander Coffee (Café Alex), Av 16 de Julio 1832, T231 2790, also at 20 de Octubre 2463 Plaza Avaroa, Av Montenegro 1336, Calacoto, and the airport. Excellent coffee, smoothies, muffins, cakes and good, salads and sandwiches, open 0730-0000. Recommended.

Dumbos, Av 16 de Julio, near *Eli's* and Cinema. For meat and chicken *salteñas*, ice creams, look for the dancing furry animals outside.

Fridolin, Av 6 de Agosto 2415, T215 3188, and Comercial La Chiwiña, San Miguel, Calacoto. *Empanadas*, *tamales*, savoury and sweet (Austrian) pastries, coffee, breakfast.

Kuchen Stube, Rosendo Gutiérrez 461, Sopocachi. Excellent cakes, coffee and German specialities, Mon -Fri 0930-1230, 1500-1900.

La Terraza, 16 de Julio 1615, T231 0701, 0630-0000; 20 de Octubre 2171 y Gutierrez; and Av Montenegro y C 8, Calacoto, both 0730-0000. Excellent sandwiches and coffee, pancakes, breakfasts, make your own salads, in modern, US-style cafés.

⬡ Bars and clubs

The epicentre for nightlife in La Paz is currently Plaza Avaroa in Sopocachi. Clubs are clustered around here and crowds gather Fri and Sat nights.

San Francisco up to the cemetery district
p247, maps p244 and p246
Oliver's Travels, Murillo 1014. Fake English

VIENNA

RESTAURANT BAR

European style restaurant offering traditional cuisine and dining amid antiques, old prints and wood.

English and German spoken.

Our kitchen is open
Monday-Friday
12:00-14:00 18:30-22:00
Sundays
12:00-14:30

Federico Zuazo 1905 Casilla 56
Tel: 244 1660·Fax: 244 1572
La Paz - Bolivia

www.restaurantvienna.com
info@restaurantvienna.com

pub serving breakfasts, PG Tips, curries, fish and chips, pasta, sports channels, music, travel agency, very good book exchange, popular meeting place.
Sol y Luna, Murillo 999 y Cochabamba. Opens 1800. Dutch run, good breakfasts, snacks and cocktails, nice atmosphere, guide books for sale. Recommended.

The Prado, Sopocachi, Miraflores and Zona Sur *p247, map p244*
The Britannia, Av Ballivián on the left between C 15 y 16, Calaçoto, Zona Sur, T279 3070. Mon-Sat from 1700, cosy, popular with expats, bar snacks, designed as English pub, also Asian restaurant.
Deadstroke, Av 6 de Agosto 2460, Sopocachi. US-style pub, café and billiards bar, food, drinks (good value for beer), billiards, pool and other games, opens 1700.
Diesel Nacional, Av 20 de Octubre entre Gutiérrez y Guachalla, Sopocachi. A hip, modern club with an industrial theme.
Equinoccio, Sánchez Lima 2191, Sopocachi. Top venue for live music and bar, Thu-Sat.
Fak'n Tacos, Belisario Salinas opposite Presbitero Medina. Bizarre upstairs bar with a boxing ring for patrons' use, potent drinks, including the 'fishbowl'.
Ja Ron, 20 de Octubre esq Pasaje Medinacelli, Sopacachi. Bright bar with a bohemian feel, tree trunks for tables, potent cocktails, happy hour 1800-2100, stays open till 0200.
RamJam, C Presbitero Medina 2421, Sopocachi, T242 2295. Above Plaza Avaroa, open 1900-0300 or later, energetic place aimed at gringos and moneyed locals, with coffee, curry, Sun evening roasts, microbrewery beer and cable TV, dancing, packed Fri and Sat nights. Also **Ozone**, an oxygen bar, on the premises.
Theolonius Jazz Bar, 20 de Octubre 2172, Sopocachi, T233 7806. Tue-Sat from 1700. Renowned for jazz (what else?), but it is expensive, with an extra charge to see the jazz.

◉ Entertainment

For up-to-the-minute information on cinemas and shows, check *La Prensa* or *La Razón* on Fri, or visit www.la-razon.com.

Around Plaza Murillo *p243, maps p244 and p246*
Bocaisapo, Indaburo 654 y Jaén. Live music in a bar; no cover charge.
Marka Tambo, Junín 710, T228 0041. Wed-Sat 2000-0100, US$7 all inclusive, repeatedly recommended (also sells woven goods and serves lunch Mon-Sat 1200-1500).

Above Plaza San Francisco
p247, maps p244 and p246
Casa del Corregidor, see under Eating above. Good dinner show Mon-Thu, no cover charge, Fri and Sat *peña* US$4, both 2100, good, colonial atmosphere, traditional music and dance.
El Parnaso, Sagárnaga 189, T231 6827. Daily starting at 2030, meals available, purely for tourists but a good way to see local costumes and dancing.
Cinemas Films mainly in English with Spanish subtitles. Expect to pay around US$3.15.
Theatre Teatro Municipal Alberto Saavedra Pérez has a regular schedule of plays, opera, ballet and classical concerts, at Sanjines y Indaburo, T240 6183. The National Symphony Orchestra is very good and gives inexpensive concerts. Next door is the **Teatro Municipal de Cámara**, which shows dance, drama, music and poetry. **Casa Municipal de la Cultura 'Franz Tamayo'**, almost opposite Plaza San Francisco, hosts a variety of exhibitions, paintings, sculpture, photography, etc, mostly free. Free monthly guide to cultural events at information desk at entrance. The **Palacio Chico**, Ayacucho y Potosí, in old Correo, operated by the Secretaría Nacional de Cultura, also has exhibitions (good for modern art), concerts and ballet, Mon-Fri 0900-1230, 1500-1900, closed at weekends, free.

✦ Festivals and events

La Paz *p242, maps p244 and p246*
Jan/Feb: the Alasitas Fair, from 24 Jan to first week of Feb, in Parque Central up from Av del Ejército, also in Plaza Sucre/San Pedro (see box).
End May/early Jun Festividad del Señor de Gran Poder, the most important festival of the year, with a huge procession of costumed and masked dancers on the 3rd Sat after Trinity.
Jul Fiestas de Julio, a month of concerts and performances at the Teatro Municipal, with a variety of music, including the University Folkloric Festival. **8 Dec**, festival around Plaza España, not very large, but colourful and noisy. On New Year's Eve there are spectacular fireworks displays; view from higher up. See page 241 for national holidays and festivals outside La Paz.

○ Shopping

La Paz *p242, maps p244 and p246*
Bookshops Los Amigos del Libro, Mercado 1315, T220 4321, also Av Montenegro y C 18 (San Miguel) and El Alto airport. Expensive, but they sell a few tourist guide books and will also ship books. Gisbert, Comercio 1270, libgis@entelnet.bo. Books, stationery, will ship overseas. Yachaywasi, just below Plaza del Estudiante, opposite *Hotel Eldorado*. Large

selection, popular with students.

Camping equipment Kerosene for pressure stoves is available from a pump in Plaza Alexander, Pando e Inca. **Caza y Pesca**, Edif Handal Center, no 9, Av Mcal Santa Cruz y Socabaya, T240 9209. English spoken. **The Base Adventure Store**, Av 16 de Julio 1490, Edif Avenida, basement. Camping gear and clothing, head lamps, no rentals.

Handicrafts Above Plaza San Francisco (see page 247), up Sagárnaga, by the side of San Francisco church (behind which are many handicraft stalls in the Mercado Artesanal), are booths and small stores with interesting local items of all sorts, best value on Sun morning when prices are reduced. The lower end of Sagárnaga is best for antiques. At Sagárnaga 177 is an entire gallery of handicraft shops. On Linares, between Sagárnaga and Santa Cruz, high quality alpaca goods are priced in US$. Also in this area are many places making fleece jackets, gloves and hats, but shop around for value and service. **Artesanía Sorata**, Linares 862, and Sagárnaga 311. Mon-Sat 0930-1900 (and Sun 1000-1800 high season), specializes in dolls, sweaters and weavings. **Ayni**, Illampu 704, www.hotelrosario.com/ayni. Fair trade shop in Hotel Rosario, featuring Aymara work. **Comart Tukuypi**, Linares 958, T/F231 2686. High-quality textiles from an artisan community association. **Comercio Doryan**, Sagárnaga y Murillo, eg **Wari**, unit 12, Comercio Doryan, closed Sun. High quality alpaca goods, will make to measure very quickly, English spoken, prices reasonable. **Kunturi**, Nicolás Acosta 783, T249 4350. You will find wonderful handicrafts produced by the Institute for the Handicapped, including embroidered cards. **LAM** shops on Sagárnaga. Good quality alpaca goods. **Millma**, Sagárnaga 225, and Claudio Aliaga 1202, San Miguel, Zona Sur, closed Sat afternoon and Sun. Alpaca sweaters (made in their own factory) and antique and rare textiles. **Mother Earth**, Linares 870.

High-quality alpaca sweaters with natural dyes. **Toshy** on Sagárnaga. Top quality knitwear (closed Sat afternoon).

Jewellery There are good jewellery stores throughout the city: for example **Joyería King's**, Loayza 261, T232 8178, www.bolivia.com/empresas/kings/index.html. **Torre Ketal**, C 15, Calacoto, T277 2542. Gold and silver jewellery and souvenirs using native, Andean designs.

Maps IGM: head office at Estado Mayor General, Av Saavedra 2303, Miraflores (far from the centre), T222 0513, igmsmg@unete.com, Mon-Thu 0830-1630, Fri 0830-1200, take passport to buy maps. IGM's Oficina 5, Juan XXIII 100 (mud track between Rodríguez y Linares), Mon-Thu 0800-1200 and 1430-1800, Fri 0800-1400, will order maps from HQ. **Librería IMAS**, Av Mcal Santa Cruz entre Loayza y Colón, T235 8234. Ask for the map collection and check what is in stock. Maps are also sold in the Post Office on the stalls opposite the Poste Restante counter.

Markets In addition to those mentioned in the Sights section (page 247), the 5-km sq **El Alto** market is on Thu and Sun (the latter is bigger). Take a Ceja bus from along the Prado to Desvío. At the toll plaza on the autopista, change buses for one marked 16 de Julio; most other passengers will be doing the same, follow them. Arrive around 1000 and stay to 1600. Goods are cheap. Don't take anything of value, just a bin liner to carry your purchases. **Mercado Sopocachi**, Guachala y Ecuador, a well-stocked covered market selling foodstuffs, kitchen supplies, etc.

Musical instruments Many shops on Sagárnaga/Linares, for example **El Guitarrón**, Sagárnaga 303 esq Linares, and **Marka 'Wi**, Sagárnaga 851. **Pasaje Linares**, the stairs off C Linares, has a number of shops selling just instruments.

Shopping malls and supermarkets **Hipermaxi**, Cuba y Brazil, Miraflores. An out-of-centre mall. **Shopping Norte**, Potosí y Socabaya. Modern mall with restaurants and expensive merchandise. **Supermercado Ketal**, C 21, San Miguel, and Av Arce y Pinillo, near Plaza Isabel la Católica. Regular supermarket. **Supermercado Zatt**, Av Sánchez Lima 2362 near Plaza Avaroa. Has the best selection of dried foods etc for trekking.

▲ Activities and tours

La Paz *p242, maps p244 and p246*
City tours
Sightseeing, T279 1440, city tours on a double-decker bus, 2 circuits, downtown and Zona Sur with Valle de la Luna (1 morning and 1 afternoon departure to each), departs from Plaza Isabel la Católica and can hop on at Plaza San Francisco, tour recorded in 7 languages, US$6 for both circuits, daily except first Mon of each month.

Climbing, hiking and trekking
Guides must be hired through a tour company.
Ricardo Albert at *Inca Travel*, Av Arce 2116, Edif Santa Teresa.
Alberth Bolivia Tours, Illampu 773, T245 8018, alberthbolivia@hotmail.com. Good for climbing and trekking, good value, helpful, Juan speaks English, equipment rental.
Andean Summits, Aranzaes 2974, Sopocachi, T242 2106, www.andeansummits.com. For mountaineering and other adventure trips off the beaten track.
Azimut Explorer, Sagárnaga 213, Galería Chuquiago, of 11, T233 3809. Guide Juan Villarroel is one of the best.
Iván Blanco Alba, *Asociación de Guías de Montaña y Trekking*, Chaco 1063.
Bolivian Mountains, Murillo 929, T231 3197, www.bolivianmountains.com. A high-quality mountaineering outfit, with experienced guides

and good equipment, not cheap.
Club Andino Boliviano, C México 1638, T231 0863, can provide a list of guides and works with the Bolivian association of mountain guides.
Trek Bolivia, C Sagárnaga 392, T/F231 7106. Organizes expeditions in the Cordillera.
For Maps, see Essentials, page 237 and Shopping, above.

Football
Popular and played on Wed and Sun at the **Siles Stadium** in Miraflores (Micro A), which is shared by both La Paz's main teams, Bolívar and The Strongest. There are reserved seats.

Golf
Mallasilla is the world's highest golf course, at 3,318 m. Non-members can play at Mallasilla on weekdays, when the course is empty; no need to book. Club hire, green fee, balls and a caddy (compulsory, and you'll need one) also costs US$37.

Snooker/pool/other
Picco's, Edif 16 de Julio, Av 16 de Julio 1566. Good tables and friendly atmosphere.
San Luis, Edif México, 2do Sótano, C México 1411. Friendly atmosphere.
YMCA sportsground and gymnasium: opposite the University of San Andrés, Av Villazón, and clubhouse open to the public, Av 20 de Octubre 1839 (table tennis, billiards, etc).

Tour operators
Adventure Planet, Ramón Arias 100, Achumani, T271 0755, www.planetaventura.com. Adventure travel, including mountaineering, trekking and climbing, plus 4WD tours.
America Tours SRL, Av 16 de Julio 1490 (El Prado), Edificio Avenida PB, No 9, T237 4204, www.america-ecotours.com. Cultural and

ecotourism trips to many parts of the country (including the renowned Chalalán Lodge near Rurrenabaque, the Che Guevara Trail and Parque Nacional Noel Kempff Mercado), rafting, trekking and horse-riding, English spoken. Highly professional and recommended. Basic book exchange.

Bolivian Journeys, Sagárnaga 363, p 1, T/F235 7848. Camping, mountain bike tours, equipment rental (with large shoe sizes), maps, English and French spoken, very helpful.

Carmoar Tours, C Bueno 159, headed by Günther Ruttger T231 7202, carmoar@zuper.net. Has information for the Inca Trail to Coroico, rents trekking gear.

Crillon Tours, Av Camacho 1223, T233 7533, PO Box 4785, www.titicaca.com. With 24-hr ATM for cash on credit cards. In USA, 1450 South Bayshore Dr, suite 815, Miami, FL 33131, T305-358 5353, darius@titicaca.com. A very experienced company. Joint scheduled tours with Lima arranged. Fixed departures to Salar de Uyuni and much more. Full details of their Lake Titicaca services can be found on page 270.

Deep Rainforest, Illampu esp Plaza Eguino, Hotel Continental pb, T215 0385, www.deep-rainforest.com. Off the beaten track trekking tours, climbing, trips to the rainforest and pampas, good reports on all aspects, good English, manager Raúl Mendoza.

Detour, Av Mariscal Santa Cruz, Edif Camara Nacional de Comercio, T236 1626. Good for flight tickets, very professional, English spoken.

Explore Bolivia, Sagárnaga 339, Galería Sagárnaga of 1, T/F239 1810, explobol@ ceibo.entelnet.bo. Adventure sports, good bikes (Trek).

Et-n-ic, A Villamil 5136, Obrajes, T7064 3566, www.visitabolivia.com. Overland tours throughout Bolivia, Swiss staff, good reports.

Fremen, Edif Handal, Av Mariscal Santa Cruz y Socabaya, pb, of 13, T240 8200, www.andes-amazonia.com. Also offices in Cochabamba, Santa Cruz, Uyuni, Trinidad and Atlanta (GA). Run the *Flotel Reina de Enín* on the Río Mamoré (US$423pp double occupancy for 5 day trip), *El Puente* Hotel in Villa Tunari (C) and are involved with *Proyecto Tayka*, Red de Hoteles de los Andes, a chain of hotels in the Salar de Uyuni-Reserva Avaroa area (see page 288).

Gloria tours/Hotel Gloria, Potosí 909, T240 7070, www.gloriatours.com.bo. See Sleeping.

Gravity Assisted Mountain Biking, Av 16 de Julio 1490, Edificio Avenida, PB, of 10 (across the hall from, and part of, América Tours), T231 3849, www.gravitybolivia.com. A wide variety of mountain biking tours throughout Bolivia, including the world- famous downhill ride to Coroico (US$50). Also offers rides more challenging than the Coroico ride, including technical single-track and high-speed abandoned dirt roads, complete with coaching and all the safety equipment needed. Highly professional and recommended. Quality book exchange, sells new and used guidebooks, and gives a free T-shirt with every ride. Often full so worth booking on their web site in advance.

Magri Turismo, Capitán Ravelo 2101, T244 2727, www.magriturismo.com. Amex representative, gives TCs against American Express card but doesn't change TCs, offers Amex emergency services and clients' mail. Recommended for tours in Bolivia, travel services.

Nuevo Continente, at *Hotel Alem*, Sagárnaga 344, T237 3423, quiquisimo@mixmail.com. Recommended for trip to Zongo, Clemente is a good driver, cheap service to airport, very helpful.

Pachamama Tours, Sagárnaga 189 y Murillo Shopping Doryan p 2, of 35, T/F211 3179, www.magicbolivia.com. Cheap air fares within South America, very knowledgeable and professional for local tours, English spoken, also arranges cultural tours to indigenous groups.

Tauro Tours, Mercado 1362, Galería Paladium Mezz, local 'M', T220 1846, F220 1881. Top end adventure tours, jeep trips everywhere, run by the highly experienced and trained Carlos Aguilar.

Toñito Tours, Sagárnaga 189, Comercio Doryan, of 18, T233 6250, www.bolivian expeditions.com. Tours of the **Salar de Uyuni**, also book bus and train tickets, very helpful, hire out sleeping bags.

Topas Adventure Bolivia, Illampu 707, T211 1082, www.topas.bo. Joint venture of Akhamani Trek (Bolivia), Topas (Denmark) and the Royal Danish embassy, offering trekking, overland truck trips, jungle trips and climbing, English spoken, café and *pensión* to open.

Transturin, C Alfredo Ascarrunz 2518, Sopocachi, PO Box 5311, T242 2222, www.travelbolivia.com. Full travel services with this long-standing company, with tours ranging from La Paz to the whole country. Details of their Lake Titicaca services will be found on page 272.

Tupiza Tours, Av Tejada Sorzano 855, Edif Dica, entre Puerto Rico y Costa Rica, Zona Miraflores, T224 4282 (7206 0026, mob, out of office hours), hmitru@hotmail.com. For La Paz tours and tours to the southwest from Uyuni or Tupiza.

Turisbus, Illampu 704, T245 1341, www.turisbus.com. Helpful, trekking equipment rented, agent for PeruRail, tickets to Puno and Cuzco, also local and Bolivian tours. Recommended.

Turismo Balsa, Capitán Rvelo 2104, T235 4049, info@turismobalsa.com. City and tours throughout Bolivia (recommended), see also under Puerto Pérez, page 267. Also international flight deals.

Bolivia La Paz Listings

⊖ Transport

La Paz *p242, maps p244 and p246*
Air
Cotranstur minibuses, white with 'Cotranstur' and 'Aeropuerto' written on the side and back, go from Plaza Isabel La Católica, anywhere on the Prado and Av Mcal Santa Cruz to the airport between 0800-0830 to 1900-2000, US$0.50 (allow about 1 hr), best to have little luggage, departures from the airport every 5 mins or so. Colectivos from Plaza Isabel La Católica charge US$3 pp, carrying 4 passengers. Radio-taxi is US$5 to airport, US$6.50 from Zona Sur. There is an *Enlace* ATM for Cirrus, Plus, Visa and MasterCard credit/debit cards in the international departures hall for taking out local cash and a bank which changes cash, OK rates. To change money when bank is closed, ask at the departure tax window near information. The international departures hall is the main concourse, with all check-in desks, and is the hall for all domestic arrivals and departures. Tourist office at Arrivals. Bar/restaurant and café (cheaper) upstairs. For details of services, see under destinations.

Bus
For information, TT228 0551. Buses to: **Oruro**, **Potosí**, **Sucre**, **Cochabamba**, **Santa Cruz**, **Tarija** and **Villazón**, leave from the main terminal at Plaza Antofagasta (micros 2, M, CH or 130), see under each destination for details. Taxi to central hotels, US$1. The terminal (open 0700-2300) has a tourist booth by the main entrance, internet, a post office, **Entel**, restaurant, luggage store, near the main entrance and several private kiosks at the rear, US$0.30 per bag (0530-2200) and agencies,

such as **Turisbus**, **Diana**, **Vicuña** (cheaper than their offices in town). Touts find passengers the most convenient bus and are paid commission by the bus company.

To **Copacabana**, several bus companies (tourist service) pick-up travellers in their hotels (in the centre) and also stop at the main terminal, tickets from booths at the terminal (cheaper) or agencies in town. They all leave about 0800, 3½ hrs, US$2.50, return from Copacabana about 1100. When there are not enough passengers for each company, they pool them. **Diana Tours** T228 2809, **Nuevo Continente** T228 5191, **Turisbus** T245 1341 (more expensive). You can also book this service all the way to Puno, US$6.25.

Public buses to **Sorata**, **Copacabana** and **Tiahuanaco** leave from the Cemetery district. Companies include **Flota Copacabana**, **Manco Kapac**, **2 de Febrero**, **Ingavi**, **Trans Perla Andina**. To get to the Cemetery district, take any bus or minibus marked 'Cementerio' going up C Santa Cruz (US$0.17). On Plaza Reyes Ortiz are **Manco Kapac**, recommended, and **2 de Febrero** for **Copacabana** and **Tiquina**. From the Plaza go up Av Kollasuyo and at the 2nd street on the right (Manuel Bustillos) is the terminal for minibuses to **Achacachi**, **Huatajata** and **Huarina**, and buses for **Sorata**. Several micros (20, J, 10) and minibuses (223, 252, 270, 7) go up Kollasuyo; look for 'Kollasuyo' on the windscreen in most, but not all cases. Taxi US$1. Buses to **Coroico and the Yungas** leave from Villa Fátima (25 mins by micros B, V, X, K, 131, 135, or 136, or *trufis* 2 or 9, which pass Pérez Velasco coming down from Plaza Mendoza, and get off at the service station, C Yanacachi 1434). See Safety, page 243.

PETITA   RENT A CAR
LA PAZ   BOLIVIA

info@rentacarpetita.com
www.rentacarpetita.com
++5912 242 0329 / ++591 7722 6481

International buses From Plaza Antofagasta terminal: to **Buenos Aires**, US$85, Mon and Fri with **Ormeño**, 54 hrs. Alternatively, go to Villazón and change buses in Argentina. To **Arica** via the frontier at Tambo Quemado and Chungará **Pullmanbus** at 0630 (good), **Cuevas** at 0700, **Zuleeta** at 0600, 1200 and 1300, **Nuevo Continente** at 0815, US$11.25-12.50. Connecting service for Iquique and Santiago. To **Cuzco**: colectivos and agencies to **Puno** daily with different companies, most easily booked through travel agencies, US$15, 10 hrs. **Note**: Of the various La Paz-Puno services, only **Transturin** does not make you change to a Peruvian bus once over the border. International buses are run by Ormeño and Litoral. For luxury and other services to Peru see under Lake Titicaca below. To **Lima**, Ormeño daily at 1630, **Nuevo Continente** at 0800, US$70, 26 hrs.

Car hire

Imbex, Av Montes 522, T245 5432, www.imbex.com. Well-maintained Suzuki jeeps from US$60 per day, including 200 km free for 4-person 4WD. Highly recommended. **Kolla Motors**, Rosendo Gutierrez 502 entre Sánchez Lima y Ecuador, T241 9141, www.kollamotors.com. Well-maintained 6-seater 4WD Toyota jeeps, insurance and gasoline extra. **Petita Rent-a-car**, Valentín Abecia 2031, Sopocachi Alto, T242 0329, www.rentacarpetita.com. Swiss owners Ernesto Hug and Aldo Rezzonico. Recommended for well-maintained 4WD jeeps, etc, also offer adventure tours, German, French, English spoken. Recommended. Also arranges fishing trips. Ernesto also has garage for VW and other makes, Av Jaimes Freyre 2326, T241 5264. Highly recommended. See page 44 in Essentials for multinational car hire websites.

Taxi

Standard taxis charge US$0.75 pp for short trips within city limits. A *trufi* US$0.30 in the centre, US$0.40 pp beyond the centre. Taxi drivers are not tipped. At night, for safety, only take **radio taxis** (radio móvil), which are named as such, have a unique number and radio communication (e.g. **Alfa** T241 2525, **Latino** T231 1616). They charge US$1 in centre and US$2 to suburbs. Also good value for tours for 3 people, negotiate price. **Eduardo Figueroa**, T278 6281, taxi driver and travel agent. Recommended. **Adolfo Monje Palacios**, in front of *Hotel El Dorado* or T235 4384. Highly recommended for short or long trips. **Oscar Vera**, Simón Aguirre 2158, Villa Copacabana, La Paz, T223 0453, specializes in trips to the Salar de Uyuni and the Western Cordillera, speaks English. Recommended.

South of La Paz *p248*

Minibus A can be caught on the Prado. If you do not want to walk in the valley, stay on the bus to the end of the line and take a return bus, 2 hrs in all. Alternatively take Micro 11 ('Aranjuez' large, not small bus) from C Sagárnaga, near Plaza San Francisco, US$0.65, and ask driver where to get off. Most of the local travel agents organize tours to the Valle de la Luna. These are very brief, 5 mins stop for photos in a US$15 tour of La Paz and surroundings; taxis cost US$6.

Tiahuanaco *p248*

To get to Tiahuanaco, **Cooperativa Turismo** has tourist service with pick up from central hotels, or the terminal, at 0830, return at 1400, US$7.50. Otherwise take any **Micro** marked 'Cementerio' in La Paz, get out at Plaza Félix Reyes Ortiz, on Mariano Bautista (north side of cemetery), go north up Aliaga, 1 block east of Asín to find Tiahuanaco micros, US$1, 1½ hrs, every 30 mins, 0600 to 1700. Tickets can be bought in advance. **Taxi** for 2 costs about US$20-25 (can be shared), return, with unlimited time at site (US$30-40 including El Valle de la Luna). Some **buses** go on from Tiahuanaco to Desaguadero; virtually all Desaguadero buses stop at Tiahuanaco. Return buses (last back 1730-1800) leave from south side of the Plaza in village. Most tours from La Paz start at US$6.50 pp (not including site entrance or lunch) stopping at Laja and the highest point on the road before Tiahuanaco. Some tours include El Valle de la Luna. Minibuses (vans) to **Desaguadero**, from José María Asín y P Eyzaguirre (Cemetery district) US$1.25, 2 hrs, most movement on Tue and Fri when there is a market at the border.

Note When returning from Tiahuanaco (ruins or village) to La Paz, do not take a minibus if it has no other passengers. We have received reports of travellers being taken to El Alto and robbed at gun point. Wait for a public bus with paying passengers in it.

Takesi Trail *p249*

Take a Palca/Ventilla **bus** from outside *comedor popular* in C Max Paredes above junction with C Rodríguez, daily at 0530, US$1; or take any bus going to Bolsa Negra, Tres Ríos or Pariguaya (see Yunga Cruz below). Alternatively, take any **micro** or minibus to Chasquipampa or Ovejuyo and try hitching a lift with anything heading out of La Paz. If there isn't any transport, haggle with drivers of empty minibuses in Ovejuyo; you should be able to get one to go to Ventilla for about US$4. To **Mina San Francisco**: hire a **jeep** from La Paz; US$70, takes about 2 hrs. **Veloz del Norte** (T02-221 8279) leaves from Cocabaya 495 in Villa Fátima, 0900 and 1400; 3½ hrs, continuing to Chojlla. Buses to La Paz (US$2.85) leave from Yanakachi at 0545 and 1245-1300 or 1400 daily. Buses to **Yanakachi** leave from a street just off Plaza 24 de Septiembre, La Paz, at 0800 and 1500, 3-4 hrs.

Choro Trail *p249*

To the *apacheta* pass beyond **La Cumbre**, take a radio **taxi** from central La Paz for US$10, stopping to register at the Guardaparque hut. Or take a taxi to Villa Fátima in La Paz (US$1) then a bus to La Cumbre (US$1), 30 mins; make sure the drive knows you want to get off at La Cumbre.

Yunga Cruz Trail *p250*

Take the **bus** to **Pariguaya** between 0730-0830 Mon-Sat, from C Gral Luis Lara esq Venacio Burgoa near Plaza Líbano, San Pedro, US$2, 6 hrs to Chuñavi, US$2.25; 6½ hrs to Lambate (3 km further on). Buses to **Tres Ríos** and **Barro Negro/Tabacaya** depart at same time but stop well before Chuñavi. It's not possible to buy tickets in advance, be there at 0700.

Huayna Potosí *p250*

The mountain can be reached by transport arranged through tourist agencies (US$70) or the refugio. **Camión** from Plaza Ballivián in El Alto early morning or midday Mon, Wed, Fri (return next day), **taxi** (US$30), or **minibus** in the high season. If camping in the Zongo Pass area, stay at the site maintained by Miguel and family near the white house above the cross.

◑ Directory

La Paz *p242, maps p244 and p246*

Airline offices Aerolíneas Argentinas, Edif Petrolero, El Prado, Mezanine, of 13, T235 1624, F239 1059. **Aero Sur**, Av 16 de Julio 1616, p 11, T231 2244. **Amaszonas**, Av Saavedra 1649, T222 0848. **American Airlines**, Av 16 de Julio 1440, Edif Herman, T235 5384, www.aa.com. **British Airways** and **Iberia**, Ayacucho 378, Edif Credinform p 5, T220 3885 (BA), 220 2869 (Iberia). **Lan**, Av 16 de Julio 1566, p 1, T235 8377, www.lan.com. **Lloyd Aéreo Boliviano (LAB)**, Camacho 1460, T236 7707. **KLM**, Plaza del Estudiante 1931, T244 1595. **Lufthansa**, Av 6 de Agosto 2512 y P Salazar, T243 1717, F243 1267. **TACA**, El Prado 1479, Of 401, T231 3132, toll free T800-108222. **TAM** (Mercosur), Plaza del Estudiante 1931, T244 3442. **Transportes Aéreo Militar (TAM)**, Av Montes 738 esq Serrano, T212 1585, Mon-Fri 0830-1200 and 1430- 1830.

Banks *Enlace* ATMs at many sites in the city. **Bisa**, Av Gral Camacho 1233, open 0830-1200, 1430-1800, Sat 1000-1300, good service, changes US$ cash. Cash advance (in bolivianos) on Visa at **Banco Santa Cruz**, also known as *BSCH* (branch in Shopping Norte is open Sat afternoon), **Banco Mercantil**, Mercado 1190 (good, quick service), and **Banco Nacional**. **BCP**, Comercio y Yancocha, long hours Mon-Fri 0830-1800, Sat 0900-1200, US$ cash only. **Prodem**, Av Camacho esq Colón 1277, T215 0297, Illampu 784 y Santa Cruz, T214 7723, Sánchez Lima y Salinas and other branches, changes US$ cash. **Amex**, see *Magri Turismo* under Tour operators. **Visa**, Av Camacho 1448, p 11 y 12, T231 8585 (24 hrs), F211 6525, for cancelling lost or stolen credit cards. **Exchange houses**: Sudamer, Colón 256 y Camacho, open Mon-Fri till 1800, Sat till 1200. Good rates for currencies other than US$ including euros, 2% commission on US$ or euro TCs into dollars, and US$ TCs into bolivianos, frequently recommended. Unitours, Mercado y Loayza. Good rates for US$ cash. Very few deal in Argentine and Chilean pesos. Street changers on corners around Plaza del Estudiante, Camacho, Colón and Prado, OK rates. **Cultural centres** Alliance Française, Guachalla 399 esq Av 20 de Octubre T242 5005, www.afbolivia.org,

French-Spanish library, videos, newspapers, and cultural gatherings information. Call for opening hours. **Centro Boliviano Americano (CBA)**, Parque Zenón Iturralde 121, T243 0107 (10 mins walk from Plaza Estudiante down Av Arce), www.cba.edu.bo. Has public library and recent US papers. **Goethe-Institut**, Av Arce 2708 esq Campos, T243 1916, www.goethe.de. Excellent library, recent papers in German, CDs, cassettes and videos free on loan, German books for sale.

Cycle spares See Gravity Assisted Mountain Biking under Tour operators, page 258, very knowledgeable, www.gravity bolivia.com. In Calacoto: **Nosiglia Sport**, Av Costanera 28, T274 9904, nossport@ ceibo.entelnet.bo. **Embassies and consulates** Argentina, Aspiazú 497, Sopocachi, T241 7737, embarbol@ caoba.entelnet.bo. 24 hrs for visa, 0900-1330. **Brazil**, Av Arce, Edif Multicentro, T244 0202, embajadabrasil@acelerate.com. 0830-1700, Mon-Fri (visas take 2 days). **Canadian Consulate**, Edif Barcelona p 2, Victor Sanjinez 2678, Plaza España, T241 5021, 0900-1200. **Danish Consulate**, Av Arce 2799 and Cordero, Edif Fortaleza, p 9, T243 2070, lpbamb@um.dk. Mon-Fri, 0800-1600. **France**, Av Hernando Siles y C 8 No 5390, Obrajes, T278 6114, amfrabo@ ceibo.entelnet.bo. Take microbus N, A or L down Av 16 de Julio, Mon-Thu 0800-1300, 1430-1730, Fri 0800-1230. **Germany**, Av Arce 2395, T244 0066, info@embajada-alemana-bolivia.org. Mon-Fri 0900-1200. **Italy**, Av 6 de Agosto 2575, T243 4955, ambitlap@ceibo.entelnet.bo. Mon-Fri 0830-1300. **Netherlands Consulate**, Av 6 de Agosto 2455, Edif Hilda, p 7, T244 4040, nllap@caoba. entelnet.bo. 0900-1200. **Paraguayan Consulate**, Edif Illimani, p 1, Av 6 de Agosto y P Salazar, T243 3176, embapar@acelerate.com, good visa service. Mon-Fri 0830-1100. **Peru**, F Guachalla 300, Sopocachi, T244 1250, embbol@ caoba.entelnet.bo. Mon-Fri 0900-1600, visa US$10 in US$, issued same day if you go early. **Spanish Consulate**, Av 6 de Agosto 2827 y Cordero, T243 0118, embespa@ ceibo. entelnet.bo. Mon-Fri 0830-1500. **Sweden**, Pasaje Villegas s/n, entre 20 de Octubre y 6 de Agosto, T/F243 4943, open 0900-1200. **Switzerland**, C 13 No 455, Obrajes, T275 1001, vertretung@ paz.rep.admin.ch. Mon-Fri 0900-1200. **UK**, Av Arce 2732, T243 3424, ppa@megalink.com. Mon-Thu 0830-1330, Fri 0830-1200, visa section open 0900-1200. **USA**, Av Arce 2780 y Cordero, T216 8000, http://bolivia.usembassy.gov, Mon-Fri 0800-1730. **Internet** There are many internet cafés in the centre of La Paz, opening and shutting all the time. Cost US$0.40 per hr, fast connections, long hours, but many closed Sun.

Language schools Alliance Française (see also above). **Centro Boliviano Americano** (address under Cultural centres above), US$140 for 2 months, 1½ hrs tuition each afternoon. **Instituto de La Lengua Española**, María TeresaTejada, C Aviador esq final 14, No 180, Achumani, T279 6074, T715-56735 (mob), sicbol@caoba. entelnet.bo. One-to-one lessons US$7 per hr. Recommended. **Speak Easy Institute**, Av Arce 2047, between Goitia and Montevideo, just down from Plaza del Estudiante, T/F244 1779, speakeasy institute@yahoo.com. US$6 for one-to-one private lessons, cheaper for groups and couples, Spanish and English taught, very good. Private Spanish lessons from: Cecilia Corrales, José María Camacho 1664, San Pedro, T248 7458, besteaching75@hotmail.com. **Isabel Daza Vivado**, Murillo 1046, p 3, T231 1471, T706-28016 (mob), maria_daza@hotmail.com. US$3 per hr. **Enrique Eduardo Patzy**, Mendez Arcos 1060, Sopocachi, T241 5501 or 776-22210, epatzy@hotmail.com. US$6 an hr one-to-one tuition, speaks English and Japanese. Recommended. **Medical services** For hospitals, doctors and dentists, contact your consulate or the tourist office for recommendations. Health and hygiene: **Unidad Sanitaria La Paz**, on Ravelo behind *Hotel Radisson Plaza*, yellow fever shot and certificate for US$12. **Ministerio de Desarollo Humano, Secretaría Nacional de Salud**, Av Arce, near *Radisson Plaza*, yellow fever shot and certificate, rabies and cholera shots, malaria pills, bring own syringe (US$0.20 from any pharmacy). **Centro Piloto de Salva**, Av Montes y Basces, T236 9141, 10 mins walk from Plaza San Francisco, for malaria pills, helpful. **Laboratorios Illanani**, Edif Alborada p 3, of 304, Loayza y Juan de la Riva, T231 7290, open 0900-1230, 1430-1700, fast, efficient, hygienic. Tampons may be bought at most *farmacias* and supermarkets. Daily papers list pharmacies on duty (*de turno*). For contact lenses, **Optaluis**, Comercio 1089. **Post offices** Correo Central, Av Mcal Santa Cruz y Oruro, Mon-Fri 0800-2000, Sat 0830-1800, Sun 0900-1200. Another on Linares next to Museo de Coca, 0830-2000. Stamps are sold only at the post offices. *Poste Restante* keeps letters for 2 months, no charge. Check the letters filed under all parts of your name. For the procedure for sending parcels and for mailing prices, see page 55. To collect parcels costs US$0.15. Express postal service (top floor) is expensive. **DHL**, Av Mcal Santa Cruz 1297, T0800-4020, expensive and slow. **FedEx**, Rosendo Gutiérrez 113 esq Capitán Ravelo, T244 3537. **UPS**, Av 16 de Julio 1479, p 10. **Telephones** There are *cabinas* for competing phone companies everywhere. **Useful addresses** Immigration: to renew a visa go to **Migración Bolivia**, Av Camacho 1433, T211 0960. Mon-Fri 0830-1600, go early. Drop passport and tourist card at the booth on the right as you walk into the office in the morning and collect stamped passport in the afternoon.

Tourist Police: C Hugo Estrada 1354, Plaza Tejada Sorzano frente al estadio, Miraflores, next to *Love City* Chinese restaurant, T222 5016. Open 24 hrs, for insurance claims after theft, helpful.

Lake Titicaca

Lake Titicaca is two lakes joined by the Straits of Tiquina: the larger, northern lake (Lago Mayor, or Chucuito) contains the Islas del Sol and de la Luna; the smaller lake (Lago Menor, or Huiñamarca) has several small islands. The waters are a beautiful blue, reflecting the hills and the distant cordillera in the shallows of Huiñamarca, mirroring the sky in the rarified air and changing colour when it is cloudy or raining. A boat trip on the lake is a must.

Ins and outs
Getting there A paved road runs from La Paz to the Straits of Tiquina (114 km El Alto-San Pablo). ►► *See Transport page 272 for more details.*

La Paz to Copacabana
Puerto Pérez The closest point to the capital on Lake Titicaca, Puerto Pérez, 72 km from La Paz, was the original harbour for La Paz. It was founded in the 19th century by British navigators as a harbour for the first steam boat on the lake (the vessel was assembled piece by piece in Puno). Colourful fiestas are held on New Year's Day, Carnival, 3 May and 16 July (days may change each year). There are superb views of the lake and mountains.

Huatajata Further north along the east shore of the lake is Huatajata, with *Yacht Club Boliviano* (restaurant open to non-members, Saturday, Sunday lunch only, sailing for members only) and *Crillon Tours' International Hydroharbour* and *Inca Utama Hotel* (see below). Beyond here is **Chúa**, where there is fishing, sailing and *Transturin's* catamaran dock (see below). The public telephone office, *Cotel*, is on the plaza just off the main road.

Islands of Lake Huiñamarca
On **Suriqui** (1½ hours from Huatajata) in Lake Huiñamarca, a southeasterly extension of Lake Titicaca, you can visit the museum/craft shops of the Limachi brothers (now living at the *Inca Utama* cultural complex). The late Thor Heyerdahl's *Ra II*, which sailed from Morocco to Barbados in 1970, his *Tigris* reed boat, and the balloon gondola for the Nasca (Peru) flight experiment (see page 1173), were also constructed by the craftsmen of Suriqui. Reed boats are still made on Suriqui, probably the last place where the art survives. On **Kalahuta** there are *chullpas* (burial towers), old buildings and the uninhabited town of Kewaya. On **Pariti** there is Inca terracing and very good examples of weaving.

From Chúa the main road reaches the east side of the Straits at **San Pablo** (clean restaurant in blue building, with good toilets). On the west side is San Pedro, the main Bolivian naval base, from where a paved road goes to Copacabana. Vehicles are transported across on barges, US$4. Passengers cross separately, US$0.35 (not included in bus fares) and passports are checked. Expect delays during rough weather, when it can get very cold.

Copacabana → *Phone code: 02. Colour map 6, grid A2.*
A little town on Lake Titicaca 158 km from La Paz by paved road, Copacabana has a heavily restored, Moorish-style **cathedral**. ① *Mon-Fri 1100-1200, 1400-1800, Sat-Sun, 0800-1200, 1400-1800, only groups of 8 or more, US$0.20.* It contains a famous 16th century miracle-working Dark Virgin of the Lake, also known as the Virgin of Candelaria, one of the patron saints of Bolivia. If going during Carnival or on a religious holiday, arrive early and be prepared to hold onto your place, as things tend to get very crowded. The cathedral itself is notable for its spacious atrium with four small chapels; the main chapel has one of the finest gilt altars in Bolivia. The basilica is clean, white, with coloured tiles decorating the exterior arches, cupolas and chapels. Vehicles are blessed in front of the church daily, especially on Sunday.

There are 17th and 18th century paintings and statues in the sanctuary. Entrance at side of Basilica opposite *Entel*. **Tourist office** ⓘ *kiosk on Plaza 2 de Febrero*, is helpful when open.

On the headland which overlooks the town and port, Cerro Calvario, are the Stations of the Cross (a steep climb – leave plenty of time if going to see the sunset). On the hill behind the town (Cerro Sancollani) overlooking the lake, roughly southeast of the Basilica, is the **Horca del Inca**, two pillars of rock with another laid across them (probably a sun clock, now covered in graffiti), US$3. There is a path marked by arrows. Boys will offer to guide you: fix price in advance if you want their help. There's a lovely walk along the lakeside north to Yampupata, 17 km (allow 6 hours), through unspoilt countryside. At the village, or at Sicuani ask for a rowing boat to Isla del Sol, or trip on the lake (US$3.50). Motor boats cost more but are quicker. There are *alojamientos* and places to eat in Sicuani and Yumpapata.

Isla del Sol

The site of the main Inca creation myth (there are other versions) is a short distance by boat from Copacabana. Legend has it that Viracocha, the creator god, had his children, Manco Kapac and Mama Ocllo, spring from the waters of the lake to found Cuzco and the Inca dynasty. A sacred rock at the island's northwest end is worshipped as their birthplace. On the east shore near the jetty for *Crillon Tours'* hydrofoils and other craft is the Fuente del Inca, a pure spring, and Inca steps leading up from the water. A 2 km walk from the landing stage takes one to the main ruins of Pilcocaina, a two storey building with false domes and superb views. The community-run **Museo Comunitario de Etnografía** (or Mueso Templo del Sol) ⓘ *daily 0900-1200, 1300-1800, multi-site ticket US$0.60,* celebrates costumes used in sacred dances. Southeast of the Isla del Sol is the Isla de la Luna (or Coati), which also may be visited – the best ruins are an Inca temple and nunnery, both sadly neglected.

Border with Peru

West side of Lake Titicaca The road goes from La Paz 91 km west to the former port of **Guaqui**. The road crosses the border at **Desaguadero** 22 km further west and runs along the shore of the lake to Puno. (There are three La Paz-Puno routes, see also page 1196.) Bolivian immigration is just before the bridge, open 0830-1230 and 1400- 2030. Get exit stamp, walk a 200 m across the bridge then get entrance stamp on the other side. Get Peruvian visas in La Paz.

Copacabana

Lake
Titicaca

N

| 0 metres | 100 |
| 0 yards | 100 |

Sleeping 🛏
Ambassador 2
Boston 3
Chasqui de Oro 4
Colonial del Lago 5
El Mirador 15
Emperador 6

Gloria 7
Hostal La Luna 8
Hostal La Sonia 1
Kota Kahuaña 16
La Cúpula 9
Residencial Aransaya 11
Residencial Sucre 13

Rosario del Lago 14
Utama 9

Eating 🍴
Kala U'ta 1
La Orilla 2
Mankha Uta 4

Puerta del Sol 6
Snack 6 de Agosto 3
Sujma Wasi 5

There are a few basic hotels and restaurants on both sides of the bridge. Money changers on Peruvian side give reasonable rates. Market day is Friday: the streets and crossing are very busy.

Via Copacabana From Copacabana a new, paved road leads south to the Bolivian frontier at Kasani, then to Yunguyo. Do not photograph the border area. For La Paz tourist agency services on this route see under International Buses (page 261) and under Activities and tours page 270. The border is open 0830-1930 (Bolivian time). Buses/colectivos stop here and at the Peruvian side; or you can walk, 500 m, between the two posts. If crossing into Bolivia with a motorcycle, do not be fooled into paying any unnecessary charges to police or immigration. Going to Peru, money can be changed in Yunguyo but better rates are to be found in Puno. Coming into Bolivia, the best rates are at Copacabana.

East side of Lake Titicaca
From Huarina, a road heads northwest to Achacachi (market Sunday; fiesta 14 September). Here, one road goes north across a tremendous marsh to **Warisata**, then crosses the altiplano to Sorata (see below). At Achacachi, another road runs roughly parallel to the shore of Lake Titicaca, through **Ancoraimes** (Sunday market), **Carabuco** (with colonial church), **Escoma**, which has an Aymara market every Sunday morning, to **Puerto Acosta**, 10 km from the Peruvian border. It is a pleasant, friendly town with a large plaza and several simple places to stay and eat. The area around Puerto Acosta is good walking country. From La Paz to Puerto Acosta the road is paved as far as Escoma, then good until Puerto Acosta (best in the dry season, approximately May to October). North of Puerto Acosta towards Peru the road deteriorates and should not be attempted except in the dry season. An obelisk marks the international frontier at Cerro Janko Janko, on a promontory high above the lake with magnificent views. Here are hundreds of small stone storerooms, deserted except during the busy Wednesday and Saturday smugglers' market, the only days when transport is plentiful. You should get an exit stamp in La Paz before heading to this border (only preliminary entrance stamps are given here). There is a Peruvian customs post 2 km from the border and 2 km before Tilali, but Peruvian immigration is in Puno.

Sorata → *Phone code: 02. Colour map 6, grid A2. Population: 8,000. Altitude: 2,578 m.*
Sorata, 163 km from La Paz, is a beautiful colonial town nestled at the foot of Mount Illampu; around it are views over lush, alpine-like valleys. The climate is delightful. Nearby are some challenging long-distance hikes and, closer to the Peruvian border is more adventurous hiking and climbing country in the Cordillera de Apolobamba. The town has a charming plaza, with views of the snow-capped summit of Illampu on a clear day. The market area is near the plaza, half block down Muñecas on the right. Market day is Sunday; fiesta 14 September. There are lots of walking possibilities, including day hikes. The most popular is to **San Pedro cave** ① *0800-1700, US$1, toilets at entrance*, beyond the village of San Pedro. The walk is more interesting than the cave itself, which is formed in gypsum, has an underground 'lake' and is lit. It's best not to go alone. It is reached either by road, a 12 km walk (2½ hours) each way, or by a path along the Río San Cristóbal (about 3½ hours one way). Get clear directions before setting out. Take water, at least 1 litre per person, or else take sterilizing tablets and fill up at the tap in San Pedro. There are also drinks for sale. Taxi trucks also go there from the plaza, with a 30-minute wait, for US$5, most on Sunday.

Trekking and climbing from Sorata
Sorata is the starting point for climbing **Illampu** and Ancohuma but all routes out of the town are difficult, owing to the number of paths in the area and the very steep ascent. Experience and full equipment necessary and it's best to hire mules (see below). The 2-4 day trek to **Lagunas Chillata and Glaciar** is the most common route and gets busy during high season. Laguna Chillata can also be reached in a day-hike with light gear, but mind the difficult navigation and take warm clothing, food, water, sun protection, etc. Laguna Chillata has been heavily impacted by tourism (remove all trash, do not throw it in the pits around the lake) and many groups frequently camp there. The Inka Marka ruins are on the back of the rock looking towards Illampu from Laguna Chillata. The structures nearest the lake are in a sad state and unfortunately many have been converted to latrines. The **Circuito Illampu**, a 8-10 day high-altitude trek (five passes over 4,500 m) around Illampu, is excellent. It can get very cold and it is a hard walk, though very

beautiful with nice campsites on the way. Some food can be bought in Cocoyo on the third day. You must be acclimatized before setting out. A new option is the **Trans-Cordillera Trek**, 12 days from Sorata to Huayna Potosí, or 20 days all the way to Illimani at the opposite (south) end of the Cordillera Real. **Note:** Laguna San Francisco, along the Illampu Circuit, has for many years been the scene of repeated armed holdups. In late 2005 this was the only place in the Sorata area not considered safe and guided trekking parties were passing though in the small hours of the night to avoid contact with the local population.

Cordillera Apolobamba

The Area Protegida Apolobamba forms part of the Cordillera Apolobamba, the north extension of the Cordillera Real. The range itself has many 5,000 m-plus peaks, while the conservation area of 483,744 ha protects herds of vicuña, huge flocks of flamingoes and many condors. The area adjoins the Parque Nacional Madidi (see page 314). This is great trekking country and the five-day **Charazani to Pelechuco** mountain trek is one of the best in the country (see *Footprint Bolivia* for details). It passes traditional villages and the peaks of the southern Cordillera Apolobamba. **Charazani**, the main starting point, is the biggest village in the region (3,200 m). Its three-day fiesta is around 16 July. There are some **G** *alojamientos*, restaurants and shops. **Pelechuco** (3,600 m) is a basic village, also with **G** *alojamientos*, cafés and shops. The road to Pelechuco goes through the Area Protegida, passing La Cabaña, 5 km outside of which are the reserve's HQ. Visitors are welcome to see the vicuñas and there is accommodation and food.

⬤ Sleeping

La Paz to Copacabana *p264*
Puerto Pérez
AL **Hotel Las Balsas**, run by *Turismo Balsa* (see page 258, or T/F02-281 3226). In beautiful lakeside setting, with views of the cordillera, all rooms have balcony over the lake, willing to negotiate out of season, fitness facilities including pool, jacuzzi, sauna. Excellent restaurant with fixed price lunch or dinner good value at US$12.
D **Hostería Las Islas**, nearby on the Plaza. Shared bath, hot water, heated rooms, comfortable but can get crowded, *Blue Note* jazz bar next door.

Huatajata
C **Hotel Titicaca**, between Huatajata and Huarina, Km 80 from La Paz, T02-237 4877, F239 1225 (address in La Paz, Potosí y Ayacucho 1220, p 2). Beautiful views, sauna, pool, good

restaurant, very quiet during the week.
G **Máximo Catari's Inti Karka hotel**, waterfront, T0811 5058, and restaurant on the road. Full menu, open daily, average prices, good fish.

Copacabana *p264, map p265*
B-C **Rosario del Lago**, Rigoberto Paredes y Av Costanera, T862 2141, www.hotelrosario.com/lago. Same ownership as *Rosario*, La Paz, includes breakfast, hot water, *Turisbus* office (see below), small rooms with lake view, colonial style, beautifully furnished, internet café US$0.75/hr, handicrafts display, restaurant. Recommended.
C **Gloria**, 16 de Julio, T/F862 2094, www.hotelgloria.com.bo. Same group as *Gloria* in La Paz, price is full board (**B** at weekends) hot water, bar, café and restaurant with international and vegetarian food, gardens, money exchange.
C-D **Chasqui de Oro**, Av Costanera 55,

T862 2343. Includes breakfast, lakeside hotel, café/breakfast room has great views, trips organized, video room.

C-E La Cúpula, C Michel Pérez 1-3, T862 2029, www.hotelcupula.com. 5 mins' walk from centre, price depends on room (most expensive have kitchen and bath), sitting room with TV and video, fully- equipped kitchen, library, hot water, book exchange, excellent restaurant (with vegetarian options), great breakfast (extra), car parking, offer local tours, German owners. Very warmly recommended.

E Utama, Michel Pérez, T862 2013. With breakfast, hot water, good showers, comfy, book exchange.

F Boston, Conde de Lemos, near Basilica, T862 2231. **F** without bath, good, quiet.

F Colonial del Lago, Av 6 de Agosto y Av 16 de Julio, T862 2270. Bright rooms, some with lake view, **F** without bath, breakfast included, garden, good restaurant and peña.

F Res Sucre, Murillo 228, T862 2080. Hot water, parking, quiet, good cheap breakfast, laundry US$1.20, offers tours of lake.

F-G Ambassador, Bolívar y Jáuregui, T/F862 2216. Comfortable, rooms downstairs around courtyard, dorms upstairs, heater US$2 per day, hot water, rooftop restaurant, reduction for more than 1 night or with IH card, 10% with student card, luggage store, parking. Recommended.

G El Mirador, Av Costanera y Busch, T862 2289, elmiradorhotel@hotmail.com. In a pink building with lake views, breakfast included, hot water, mixed reports on service.

G Emperador, C Murillo 235, behind the Cathedral, T862 2083. Breakfast served in room for US$2, popular, laundry service and facilities, shared hot showers, helpful for trips to Isla del Sol. Repeatedly recommended.

G Hostal La Luna, José P Mejía 260, T862 2051. Very basic but very cheap, warm showers, laundry, breakfast in room on request (US$1), can arrange discounts on trips to Isla del Sol.

G Hostal La Sonia, Murillo 253, T7196 8441 (mobile). Some rooms with shared bath, good beds, big windows, roof terrace, laundry and kitchen facilities, breakfast in bed on request, helpful, good value but can be noisy.

G pp Kota Kahuaña, Av Busch 15. Shared hot showers, some rooms with bath, others with lake view, quiet, kitchen facilities, very hospitable. Recommended.

G Res Aransaya, Av 6 de Agosto 121, T862 2229. With hot shower, simple but comfortable, good restaurant and café.

Isla del Sol *p265*
It is worthwhile staying overnight for the many

beautiful walks through villages and Inca terraces, some still in use. Rooms are offered by many families on the island.

Yumani

Most of the dozen *posadas* on the island are at Yumani, on the south side near the Inca steps. They take advantage of the daily arrival of tourists, but do not always provide what they advertise (hot water, clean sheets, etc). Shop araound.

D Puerta del Sol, at the peak of the hill above the village. Very popular. (**G** without bath). Nearby is the owner's father's hostel, **G Templo del Sol**, with clean rooms, comfy beds, electric showers and a good restaurant.

F El Imperio del Sol, peach-coloured house. Comfortable, no running water.

F Inti Kala, opposite *Templo del Sol*. Shared electric showers, fantastic views, great value, serves good meals.

Pilcocaina

G Albergue Inca Sama, next to Pilcocaina ruins. Sleep on mattresses on floor, good food, also camping in typical tents (contact via *Hotel Playa Azul*, Copacabana, T862 2228, or La Paz T235 6566), Sr Pusari, offers boat service from Copacabana and trips to the north of island.

Challa

G Posada del Inca, at Challa, on the northeast coast, right on the beach. 8 double rooms, very basic outside toilets, no showers, contact Juan Mamani Ramos through *Entel* office, food is provided and beer or *refrescos* are for sale.

G pp Qhumphuri, mid-island on the east coast, 1 hr from the Inca Steps, 1 hr from the Inca ruins in the north. Simple but comfortable rooms with bath, local furniture, great views, restaurant serves all meals (extra cost), tasty food, cooking facilities, owner Juan Ramos Ticona interested in sustainable development.

Challapampa

Several places to stay around the Plaza in Challapampa, at the north end of the island.
G Posada Manco Kapac, one of 2 basic hostales owned by Lucio Arias and his father, Francisco (Lucio can also arrange boat tickets). Price depends on whether you have a shower or a bucket. Room for 35 people and a garden for camping, hot showers and views of Illampu. The second hostel has the same name but is further up the beach.

La Posada del Inca, a restored colonial hacienda, owned by *Crillon Tours* and only available as part of a tour with *Crillon*, see page 270. *Magri Turismo* also owns a hotel on the island. See La Paz, Tour operators on page 257.

See also *Transturin*'s overnight options on page 272.

Sorata *p266*

E-F Altai Oasis, T7151 9856 (mobile), resaltai@hotmail.com. At the bottom of the valley in a beautiful setting, with cabins (**C**), rooms with bath and camping (US$1.25 pp), transport to town US$3 for 5 people, quiet, well-designed, with good restaurant, owners Johnny and Roxana Resnikowski. Recommended.

E-F Gran Hotel Sorata (Ex-*Prefectural*), on the outskirts immediately above the police checkpoint, T281 7378, call from Plaza for free pick-up. Spacious although bathrooms (electric showers) a bit tired, breakfast included, free filtered water, large garden with great views, swimming pool (open to non-residents for US$0.50), games room, good restaurant, internet café, accepts credit cards. Not always open.

G Hostal El Mirador, Muñecas 400, T289 5008. With showers and toilets, kitchen, laundry facilities, sun terrace.

G Hostal Las Piedras, just off Ascarrunz, T7191 6341 (mobile). New, well-designed and mellow, European run, cheaper with shared bath, very helpful, good breakfasts. Recommended.

G Hostal Panchita, on plaza, T813 5038. Shared bath, large rooms, hot water, basic but good value, sunny courtyard and good restaurant.

G pp Paraíso, Villavicencio 117, T213 6671. Pleasant, fairly modern, American breakfast US$1.80, hot water, restaurant.

G Res Sorata, just off plaza, T213 6672, resorata@entelnet.bo. Administrator Louis Demers, from Quebec, and the German/Bolivian proprietors are helpful. The garden is lovely, older rooms (with shared bath) are basic, newer ones (with private bath) are adequate and good value, good showers. Restaurant with good

Sorata

Old Spanish Trail to Lakathiya

To San Pedro Caves

To San Pedro Caves

To Lakathiya & Lagunas Chillata & Glaciar

To La Paz

Swimming Pool

Shortcut to caves

Av 9 de Abril

Ascarrunz

Junín

Ayacucho

Abaroa

Libertad

Av E Gunther

Villavicencio

Catacora

Adrian Velasco

Ingavi

Abaroa

Calama

Muñecas

Entel

Plaza General Peñaranda

Cotel

Buho's Internet Café

Alcaldía

Farmacia Illampu

Esquivel

14 de Septiembre

Illampu

Sucre

Sorata Guides & Porters

Prodem

Bolívar

Murillo

Entel

Guías Illampu

Fernando Guachalla

Pasoskanqui

Plaza Obispo Bosque

Fco Camargo

Av Samuel Tejerina

Villami de Rada

Junín

To La Paz

Tranca

N

0 metres   100
0 yards   100

Sleeping
Altai Oasis & Restaurant **6**
Gran Hotel Sorata **3**
Hostal Las Piedras **12**
Hostal Mirador **4**

Hostal Panchita **5**
Paraíso **8**
Residencial Sorata **10**
Santa Lucia **13**
Villa Sorata **14**

Eating
Café Illampu **3**
La Gruta **2**
Nano's Pastelería **1**
Pete's Place **2**

lunch/dinner US$2.75, breakfast US$2, good service, washing machine US$1.50, DVDs to watch, slow internet access US$3.60 per hr.
G Santa Lucía, Ascarrunz, T213 6686, santa_lucia@yahoo.com. Modern, carpeted rooms, comfortable, cheaper with shared bath, patio, helpful.
G Villa Sorata, F Guachalla, T213 5241. Large, well-furnished rooms, electric shower, terrace with lovely views, nice small courtyard, good value but the owner lives abroad and staff are often absent.

🍴 Eating

Huatajata *p264*
Inti Raymi. With fresh fish and boat trips (US$22 per boat). There are other restaurants of varying standard, most lively at weekends and in the high season.

Copacabana *p264, map p265*
🍽 **La Orilla**, Av 6 de Agosto, close to lake. Open daily 1000-2200, usually warm, atmospheric, tasty food with local and international choices. Recommended.
🍽 **Kala U'ta**, Av 6 de Agosto. Nice atmosphere, good vegetarian food, coffee and chocolate.
🍽 **Mankha Uta**, lake end of Av 6 de Agosto. Warm, good service, cheap but uninspiring set meals, movies, Play Station and big sound system.
🍽 **Puerta del Sol**, Av 6 de Agosto. Similar to others on this avenue, excellent trout, eat in or takeaway.
🍽 **Snack 6 de Agosto**, Av 6 de Agosto. 2 branches, good trout, big portions, some vegetarian dishes, serves breakfast. Also has good rooms for rent, **D** with bath, **E** without, breakfast extra, laundry.
🍽 **Sujma Wasi**, Jáuregui 127. Open 0730-2300, excellent food and atmosphere, good breakfasts, vegetarian lunch, wide range of books on Bolivia.
    Good breakfasts and other meals, especially fish, in the market on C Abaroa.

Sorata *p266, map p269*
There are several Italian restaurants on the plaza, all quite similar (🍽-🍽), none is outstanding.
🍽-🍽 **Altai Oasis** (see Sleeping, above). Good breakfasts and other meals, home-gown vegetables, local honey, regarded as best in town.
🍽-🍽 **Café Illampu**, on the way to San Pedro cave. Swiss-run, excellent sandwiches, bread and cakes, camping US$1 (an extra US$0.50 to hire tent), mountain bikes for hire, closed Tue and Feb-Mar.
🍽-🍽 **Pete's Place**, Esquivel y 14 de Septiembre, 2nd floor. Vegetarian dishes

and set menus, also meat, `English tea', very good, British owner Pete is a good source of information, local maps and guide books, open Tue-Sat 0830-2200.
🍽 **La Gruta**, next to Pete's Place. Serves a cheap, large *comida del día*, fairly clean.
🍽 **Nano's Pastelería**, Muñecas on the plaza. Thu-Sat 1700-2200, Sun 0930-1200, good sweets and snacks.
🍽 **Royal House**, off Muñecas by the market. For set meals.

✣ Festivals and events

Copacabana *p264, map p265*
Note: At these times hotel prices quadruple.
1-3 Feb Virgen de la Candelaria, massive procession, dancing, fireworks, bullfights. **Easter**, with candlelight procession on Good Friday.
23 Jun, San Juan, also on Isla del Sol. **4-6 Aug**, La Virgen de Copacabana.

Sorata *p266, map p269*
Fiesta San Pedro, **7 days after Easter**. Feria Agro-Eco-Turística in **Jun**. Fiesta Patronal del Señor de la Columna, **14 Sep**, is the main festival.

▲ Activities and tours

Lake Titicaca *p264*
Crillon Tours (address under La Paz, Tour operators, page 257) run a hydrofoil service on Lake Titicaca with excellent bilingual guides. Tours stop at their Andean Roots cultural complex at *Inca Utama*: the Bolivian History Museum includes a recorded commentary; a 15-min video precedes the evening visit to the Kallawaya (Native Medicine) museum. The Inca Utama Hotel (**AL**) has a health spa based on natural remedies; the rooms are comfortable, with heating, electric blankets, good service, bar, good food in restaurant, reservations through *Crillon Tours* in La Paz. *Crillon* is Bolivia's oldest travel agency and is consistently highly recommended. Also at *Inca Utama* is an observatory (*Alajpacha*) with two telescopes and retractable thatched roof for viewing the night sky, a floating restaurant and bar on the lake (*La Choza Náutica*), a 252-sq m floating island, a colonial-style tower with 15 deluxe suites, panoramic elevator and 2 conference rooms. Health, astronomical, mystic and ecological programmes are offered. The hydrofoil trips include visits to Andean Roots complex, Copacabana, Islas del Sol and de la Luna, Straits of Tiquina and past reed fishing boats. See Isla del Sol, Sleeping, for *La Posada del Inca*. Crillon has a sustainable tourism project with Urus-Iruitos people on floating islands by the Isla Queweya.

INTENSIVE TITICACA

NEW

Discover the Hidden Pre-Inca treasures in the Southern part of Lake Titicaca, unknown today for the traditional Tourism Nature, Adventure & Mysticism:

Pariti Island & Local Museum, Urus Iruitos Floating Islands & Quewaya Sustainable Tourism Project, Kalauta Island & Largest Lake Necropolis.

COMPLETE PERU · BOLIVIA DAILY TITICACA CRUISES

Puno / Juli / Sun & Moon Islands / Urus Iruitos Authentic Floating Islands / Andean Roots Eco-Village - Huatajata / La Paz or vice versa

Crillon Tours s.a.
Bolivia
since 1958

www.titicaca.com

· LA PAZ, BOLIVIA: Casilla 4785 / Av. Camacho 1223 / Teléfono: (591-2) 2337533 o 2339047
Fax: (591-2) 211-6481 o (591-2) 211-6482 / E-mail: titicaca@entelnet.bo - andes@entelnet.bo

Trips can be arranged to/from Puno (bus and hydrofoil excursion to Isla del Sol) and from Copacabana via Isla del Sol to Cuzco and Machu Picchu. Other combinations of hydrofoil and land-based excursions can be arranged (also jungle and adventure tours). All facilities and modes of transport connected by radio.
Transturin (see also La Paz, Tour operators, page 257) run catamarans on Lake Titicaca, either for sightseeing or on the La Paz-Puno route. The catamarans are more leisurely than the hydrofoils of *Crillon* so there is more room and time for on-board entertainment, with bar, video and sun deck. From their dock at Chúa, catamarans run day and day/night cruises starting either in La Paz or Copacabana. Puno may also be the starting point for trips. Overnight cruises involve staying in a cabin on the catamaran, moored at the Isla del Sol, with lots of activities. On the island, Transturin has the *Inti Wata* cultural complex which has restored Inca terraces, an Aymara house and the underground *Ekako* museum. There is also a 50-passenger totora reed boat for trips to the Polkokaina Inca palace. All island-based activities are for catamaran clients only. Transturin runs through services to Puno without a change of bus, and without many of the formalities at the border.
Transturin offers last minute, half-price deals for drop-in travellers (24-48 hrs in advance, take passport): sold in Copacabana only, half-day tour on the lake, continuing to Puno by bus, or La Paz; overnight Copacabana-Isla del Sol- Copacabana with possible extension to La Paz. Sold in La Paz only: La Paz-Isla del Sol-La Paz, or with overnight stay (extension to Puno possible on request).
Turisbus (see La Paz, Tour operators page 257 and *Hoteles Rosario*, La Paz, and *Rosario del Lago*, Copacabana) offer guided tours in the fast launches *Titicaca Explorer I* (28 passengers) and *II* (8 passengers) to the Isla del Sol, returning to Copacabana via the Bahía de Sicuani for trips on traditional reed boats. Also La Paz-Puno, with

boat excursion to Isla del Sol, boxed lunch and road transport, or with additional overnight at *Hotel Rosario del Lago*.

Sorata *p266map p269*
Mountain biking
Hoodoo Tours, Plaza Gral Peñeranda, T7127 6685 (in La Paz, *Oliver's Travels*, Murillo y Tarija). Plenty of good routes, including multi-day trips (eg to Rurrenabaque) with emphasis on the fairly extreme.

Trekking guides
It is much cheaper to go to Sorata and ask about trekking there than to book up a trek with an agency in La Paz. Conversely, buy all your trekking food in La Paz as Sorata shops are poorly supplied. Asociación de Guías y Porteadores, T213 6698. Another guiding association is **Asociación de Guías Illampu**, Murillo entre Guachalla y Bolívar. Both offer similar services, quality and prices. Louis at *Residencial Sorata* can arrange guides and mules. Daily prices: guide prices start at US$12, porters and mules extra, remember you have to feed your guide/porter. When trekking avoid sedimented glacier melt water for drinking and treat with iodine all other water.

⊖ Transport

La Paz to Copacabana *p264*
Puerto Pérez
Bus Regular minibus service from **La Paz** Cementerio district: across from the cemetery, above the flower market, ask for buses to Batallas, price US$0.75.

Huatajata
Bus **La Paz**-Huatajata/Tiquina, US$0.85, **Transportes Titikaka**, Av Kollasuyo 16, daily from 0400, returning between 0700 and 1800.

Islands in Lago Huiñamarca *p264*
Ferry Máximo Catari (see Huatajata, Sleeping, above) arranges boats to the islands in Lago Huiñamarca, Pariti, Kalahuta and Suriqui: prices from US$25-US$40, 1 hr boat trip US$7.50, sailing boat for 3 US$16-20 for a day (boat trips recommended). Boats can also be hired in Tiquina for trips to Suriqui, US$3 per person in a group.

Copacabana *p264, map p265*
If arriving in Bolivia at Copacabana and going to La Paz, see Safety on page 243, for scams in the Cemetery district, where public transport arrives.
Bus Agency buses: several agencies go from La Paz to **Puno**, stopping at Copacabana for lunch, or with an open ticket for continuing to Puno later. They charge US$12-15 and depart La Paz 0800; La Paz- Copacabana takes 4½ hrs. They continue to the Peruvian border at Kasani and on to Puno, stopping for immigration formalities and changing money (better rates in Copacabana or Puno). 3½ hrs to Puno, US$2.50-4 depending on season, depart Copacabana around 1200-1400. It's also possible to catch a tour bus to **Cuzco**, usually depart around 1400, tickets US$17-20, change bus in Puno, tour company arranges connection. Tour buses Copacabana-La Paz charge US$3. To/from **La Paz**, US$2 plus US$0.35 for Tiquina crossing, 3½ hrs, several departures daily between 0700-1800 with **Manco Capac**, T862 2234, or 245 3035, La Paz or **2 de Febrero**, T862 2233, or 237 7181, La Paz. Both have offices on Copacabana's main plaza and in La Paz at Plaza Reyes Ortiz, opposite entrance to cemetery. Buses also from main terminal, US$3. Buy bus tickets as soon as possible as all buses are usually full by day of travel, especially Sun. 1-day trips from La Paz are not recommended as they allow only 1½-2 hrs in Copacabana. (See also Frontier via Copacabana page 266.) Bus to **Huatajata**, US$2 and to **Huarina**, US$2.50.
Car From **La Paz** to Copacabana (direct), 4 hrs, take exit to 'Río Seco' in El Alto.

Isla del Sol *p265*
Ferry Inca Tours and Titicaca Tours run motor boats to the island; both have offices on Av 6 de Agosto in Copacabana, as do other companies. Boats leave Copacabana at 0800, 1100 and 1300, US$1.20 pp. To hire a private boat for 12 costs US$70. Boats go to the north and south end: check on the day for return times. If you go to the north end, you have enough time to walk the length of the island (take food and water, allow 3 hrs). With the same ticket you can stay on the island and return another day. Other options are: half-day tours and tours which include north and south of Isla del Sol and Isla de La Luna in one day (not recommended, too short). Full-day tour US$4-5 pp

(more if you stay overnight). Expensive express boats may also be taken to Isla del Sol from Yampupata (see page 265), but none returns to Yampupata.

Border with Peru *p265*
Via Guaqui and Desaguadero
Bus Road paved all the way to Peru. Buses from La Paz to Guaqui and Desaguadero depart from same location as micros for Tiahuanaco (see above) every 30 mins, US$1.55, 1½-2 hrs. From Desaguadero to **La Paz** last bus departs 1700, buses may leave later if enough passengers, but charge a lot more.

Via Copacabana
Bus In Peru, bus starts at **Yunguyo**. *Colectivo* Copacabana-Kasani US$0.50 pp, Kasani- Yunguyo US$0.60 pp. Make sure, if arranging a through ticket La Paz-Puno, that you get all the necessary stamps en route, and find out if your journey involves a change of bus. Note the common complaint that through services La Paz-Puno (or vice versa) deteriorate once the border has been crossed, eg smaller buses are used, extra passengers taken on, passengers left stranded if the onward bus is already full, drivers won't drop you where the company says they will.

East side of Lake Titicaca *p266*
Bus **La Paz** (Reyes Cardona 772, Cancha Tejar, Cementerio district, T238 2239)-Puerto Acosta, 5 hrs, US$3.75, daily 0600, more on Sun. Transport past Puerto Acosta only operates on market days, Wed and Sat, and is mostly cargo trucks. Bus Puerto Acosta-La Paz at about 1400. There are frequent minivans to La Paz from **Escoma**, 25 km from Puerto Acosta; trucks from the border may take you this far.

Sorata *p266*
Bus From **La Paz** with Trans Unificada Sorata (from C Manuel Bustillos 683, 2 blocks up from Cementerio in La Paz), 0500-1600, 4½ hrs, US$1.65; from Sorata every hour daily 0400-1400 (till 1700 Fri and Sun). To **Rurrenabaque**: jeeps run between Sorata and **Santa Rosa**, down the valley past Consata. From Santa Rosa transport can be arranged to Mapiri and all the way to Rurrenabaque (a very long rough ride with interesting vegetation and views). To, or from **Peru**, change buses at Huarina for Copacabana.

Cordillera Apolobamba *p267*
Charazani
Bus From Calle Reyes Cardona, Cemetery district, La Paz, daily, 10 hrs, US$4.40, very crowded.

Pelechuco

Bus From **La Paz** (same street as for Charazani) leave on Wed and Thu, 1100, US$6, 18-24 hrs, returning Fri 2000 and Sat 1600. Jeeps charge US$250 to Charazani and US$300 to Pelechuco.

☉ Directory

Copacabana *p264, map p265*

Banks Banco Unión, 6 de Agosto opposite Oruro, reasonable rates of exchange, TCs at US$2 commission, cash advance on Visa and MasterCard 3% commission. **Prodem**, Av 6 de Agosto entre Oruro y Pando, for cash advances on Visa or MasterCard only (no debit cards), 5% commission, changes US$ cash. No ATM in town. Several *artesanías* on Av 6 de Agosto buy and sell US$ and Peruvian soles. **Internet** Alcadi, next to post office, opposite cathedral, US$2.40 per hr. Alf@Net, Av 6 de Agosto, next to *Hostal Colonial*, 0830-2200, US$2, has book exchange. In Municipal building, Plaza 2 de Febrero, US$2.95

per hr. Ifa-Internet, Av 16 de Julio y Jáuregui, Plaza Sucre. US$3.50 per hr. **Post offices** Plaza 2 de Febrero, open Tue-Sat 0900- 1200, 1430-1830, Sun 0900-1500, *poste restante*. **Telephones** Entel, open 0800-1230, 1330 -2000, international phone and fax, accept US$.

Sorata *p266*

Banks Prodem, on main plaza, variable hours Tue-Sun, changes US$ cash at fair rates, 5% commission on Visa/MasterCard cash advances only (no debit cards). Nowhere in town to change TCs. **Internet** Buho's Internet Café, on the plaza, 0900-1800. US$3 per hr, very slow connection but a cosy place. **Medical services** Hospital: Villamil de Rada e Illampu. Has oxygen and X-ray. There is an adequately equipped **pharmacy. Post offices** On the plaza, 0830-1230, 1500-1800, but La Paz **Correo** is more reliable. **Telephones** Several around the plaza, rates vary considerably from place to place, so shop around.

The Yungas

Only a few hours from La Paz are the subtropical valleys known as The Yungas. These steep, forested slopes, squeezed in between the Cordillera and the Amazon Lowlands, provide a welcome escape from the chill of the capital. The warm climate of The Yungas is also ideal for growing citrus fruit, bananas, coffee and coca leaves for the capital.

La Paz to the Yungas

The most commonly-used route to the Yungas is via **La Cumbre**, northeast of La Paz. The road out of La Paz circles cloudwards over La Cumbre pass at 4,660 m; the highest point is reached in half an hour; all around are towering snowcapped peaks. Soon after **Unduavi** the paving ends, the road becomes 'all-weather' and drops over 3,400 m to the green subtropical forest in 80 km. The roads to Chulumani and Coroico divide just after Unduavi, where there is a *garita* (check point), the only petrol station, and lots of roadside stalls. From Unduavi leading to Yolosa, the junction 8 km from Coroico, is steep, twisting, clinging to the side of sheer cliffs, and it is slippery in the wet. It is a breathtaking descent (best not to look over the edge if you don't like heights) and its reputation for danger is more than matched by the beauty of the scenery (sections have recently been upgraded with IMF funding). A new road from La Paz, including a 2½-km tunnel, has been built to Coroico via Chuspipata and Yolosa. For the La Cumbre-Coroico hike (Choro), see page 249. **Gravity Assisted Mountain Biking** (address under La Paz, Tour operators) run La Cumbre-Coroico down the so-called "World's Most Dangerous Road" with top quality bikes (with hydraulic disc brakes), English speaking guides, helmet, gloves, vehicle support throughout the day, four hours La Cumbre-Yolosa, then transport to Coroico and/or back to La Paz. Free next day transport back to La Paz. Recommended. Other companies do this trip too, but quality varies, and going with a reputable company is a sensible option. Many bike companies take riders back to La Paz the same day, but Coroico is worth more of your time. The road is especially dangerous mid-December to mid-February and many companies will not run bike tours at this time.

Coroico → *Phone code: 02. Colour map 6, grid A3.*

The little town of Coroico is perched on a hill at 1,760 m amid beautiful scenery. The hillside is covered with orange and banana groves; coffee is also grown and condors circle overhead. Coroico is a first-class place to relax with several good walks. A colourful four-day festival is held

19-22 October. On 2 November, All Souls' Day, the cemetery is festooned with black ribbons. A good walk is up to the waterfalls, starting from **El Calvario**. Follow the stations of the cross by the cemetery, off Calle Julio Zuazo Cuenca, which leads steeply uphill from the plaza. Facing the chapel at El Calvario, with your back to the town, look for the path on your left. This leads to the falls which are the town's water supply (Toma de Agua) and, beyond, to two more falls. **Cerro Uchumachi**, the mountain behind El Calvario, can be climbed following the same stations of the cross, but then look for the faded red and white antenna behind the chapel. From there it's about 1½ hours' steep walk to the top (take water). A third walk goes to the pools in the **Río Vagante**, 7 km off the road to Coripata; it takes about three hours. The **Cámara Hotelera** on the plaza functions as a **tourist information centre**. It has maps and information on trails, but they are not very accurate. There have been several incidents of young women being raped or attacked in this area; do not hike alone.

Caranavi → *Phone code: 02. Colour map 6, grid A2. Altitude: 600 m.*
From the road junction at Yolosa the lower fork follows the river northeast 75 km to Caranavi, an uninspiring town 156 km from La Paz. From here the road continues towards the settled area of the Alto Beni, at times following a picturesque gorge. Market days are Friday and Saturday. There is a range of hotels and *alojamientos* and buses from La Paz (Villa Fátima) to Rurrenabaque pass through. Beyond Caranavi, 70 km, is **Guanay** at the junction of the Tipuani and Mapiri rivers (basic lodging). From here there is river transport to Rurrenabaque.

Chulumani and around → *Phone code: 02. Colour map 6, grid A2. Altitude: 1,640 m.*
The capital of Sud Yungas, 124 km from La Paz, is a charming, relaxed little town with beautiful views and many hikes. There's a **fiesta** on 24 August (lasts 10 days) and a lively market every weekend. The road from Unduavi goes through **Puente Villa**, where a road branches north to Coroico through Coripata. The **tourist office** ⓘ *main plaza, Mon-Fri 0900-1330, 1500-2200, Sat, Sun 0700-2200, but frequently shut*, sells locally grown coffee, teas, jams and honey. **Apa Apa Ecological Park** ⓘ *10 km away, US$25 for up to 5 people fee including transport and hiking guide (no reduction for fewer people)*, is the last area of original Yungas forest with lots of interesting wildlife. The road to **Irupana**, a colonial village 1½ hours from Chulumani, passes the turn-off to the park. Ask to get off and walk 15 minutes up to the *hacienda* of Ramiro Portugal and his wife, Tildi (both speak English), who manage the park; you can use their pool after trek (3 rooms, full-board accommodation and campsite with bathrooms, US$10 per tent). Or T213 6106 to arrange transport from town, taxi US$3 one way; or T279 0381 (La Paz), or write to Casilla 10109, Miraflores, La Paz.

Bolivia The Yungas Listings

◉ Sleeping

Coroico *p274*
Hotel rooms are hard to find at holiday weekends and prices are higher.
C **El Viejo Molino**, T/F213 6004, valmar@

waranet.com. 2 km on road to Caranavi, 5-star, pool, jacuzzi, games room etc.
C **Gloria**, C Kennedy 1, T/F213 6020, www.hotel gloria.com.bo. Full board with bath (**B-C** at

weekend), cheaper Mon-Fri. Spacious, large pool and a kiddies' pool, breakfast extra, restaurant, internet, free transport from plaza.

C-E Esmeralda, reservations: Casilla PO Box 92 25, La Paz, T221 36017, www.hotelesmeralda.com, www.coroico-info.com. 10 mins uphill from plaza. Renovated suites with great views, de luxe rooms, **E** pp without private bath, dormitories **F** pp, hot showers, satellite TV and DVD, free pick-up (ring from *Totai Tours*), German owned, English spoken, hikes arranged, and tours by open-sided truck to coca fields and waterfalls, TCs (no commission), credit cards accepted, phones, book exchange, cinema room, breakfast US$2, buffet restaurant, Finnish sauna, garden, good pool, laundry, high-speed internet access US$1/hr, Wi-Fi zone, welding facilities for overland drivers, express van to La Paz on the new road, book ahead.

D-G pp **Sol y Luna**, 15-20 mins beyond *Hotel Esmeralda*, T7156 1626 (or Maison de la Bolivie, 6 de Agosto 2464, Ed Jardines, La Paz, T244 0588, lamaisontour@acelerate.com), www.solyluna-bolivia.com. 7 *cabañas* with bath and kitchen, splendid views, 2 apartments for 4 people, 2 rooms with bath, 7 rooms with shared bath for 1-4 people, meals available, vegetarian specialities and Indonesian banquet, camping US$2 pp (not suitable for cars), garden, pool, laundry service, and shiatsu massage (US$15-20), very good value, Sigrid, the owner, speaks English, French, German and Spanish. Recommended.

E Bella Vista, C Héroes del Chaco (2 blocks from main plaza), T7156 9237 (mob). Beautiful rooms and views, **F** without bath, 2 racquetball courts, terrace, bike hire, restaurant, pool.

E Don Quijote, 500 m out of town, on road to Coripata, T213 6007, quijote@mpoint.com.bo. With bath, pool, quiet, English spoken.

E Hostal Kory, at top of steps leading down from the plaza, T243 1311. Huge pool, terrace, **F** without bath, hot showers, kitchen, restaurant, snacks, laundry, good value, helpful.

G pp **El Cafetal**, Miranda, 10-min walk from town, T719-33979 (mob). French-run, very nice, restaurant with excellent French/Indian/vegetarian cuisine, good value. Highly recommended.

G Residencial de la Torre, Julio Zuazo Cuenca. Welcoming place with a flowery courtyard, sparse rooms, no alcoholic drinks allowed.

Chulumani *p275*
E Huayrani, just off Junín, T213 6351. Lovely views, garden, more expensive in winter.
F Country House, 400 m out of town. Bed and breakfast, pool, good value but rock hard beds, restaurant with home cooking.
F Hostal Familiar Dion, Alianza, just off the plaza, T213 6070. Modern, roof terrace, includes breakfast, laundry and use of kitchen, **F** without

bathroom and breakfast, very good.
F Panorama, top of hill on Murillo, T213 6109. Some rooms with view, garden, breakfast, pool.
G Alojamiento Danielito, Bolívar. Hot water extra, laundry facilities, good view.
G El Mirador, on Plaza Libertad, T213 6117. Cheaper without bath, good beds, restaurant, noisy at weekends from disco.

Puente Villa *p275*
D Hotel Tamapaya, T02-270 6099, just outside town, beautiful setting, shower, good rooms, pool.

🍽 Eating

Coroico *p274*
🍴 **Bamboo**, Iturralde. Good Mexican food and pleasant atmosphere, live music some nights with cover charge. Happy hour 1800-1900.
🍴 **Back-stube**, opposite *Hostal Kory*. German owned, set lunch (including vegetarian), wiener schnitzels, breakfasts, nice atmosphere.
🍴 **Pizzería Italia**, on the plaza. Best in town.
Café de la Senda Verde, Plazuela Julio Zuazo Cuenca. Open daily 0630-1900. Home roasted Yungas coffee, healthy breakfasts, toasted sandwiches and more, very nice.
Snack Hawaii, Plaza M V García Lanza. Basic snack bar on the plaza, open all-day, breakfast, burgers, sandwiches, juices, also has money exchange.

Chulumani *p275*
🍴 **La Hostería** on Junín close to the *tranca*. Pizzas and hamburgers.
🍴 **El Mesón**, on Plaza. Open 1200-1330 only, good cheap lunches.

▲ Activities and tours

Coroico *p274*
Cycling
CXC, Pacheco 79. Good bikes, US$20 for 6 hrs including packed lunch, a bit disorganized but good fun and helpful.

Horse riding
El Relincho, Don Reynaldo, T719-13675/23814 (mob), 100 m past *Hotel Esmeralda* (enquire here, ask for Fernando), US$25 for 4 hrs with lunch.

Tour operators
Eco Adventuras and Inca Land Tours, on main plaza. Bala Tours, T03-892 2527, balatours@yahoo.com, and Enin Tours, T03-892 2487, enintours@yahoo.com, of Rurrenabaque, run tours to Guanay by 4WD then boat to Rurrenabaque, with 2 camps along the way, all inclusive, guide and cook, US$140 for 4-6 people.

⊝ Transport

Coroico *p274*

Bus From La Paz all companies are on
C Yanacachi, beside YPFB station in Villa Fátima:
Turbus Totai (T221 8385), US$2.25, 3 hrs, several
daily from 0730-1630 each way; **Flota Yungueña**
(T221 3513); worth booking in advance. Best views
on left hand side on the descent to Yungas. Extra
services run on Sun. It can be difficult to book
journeys to La Paz on holidays and on Sun
evenings/Mon mornings (these are good times for
hitching). Pick-ups from La Paz may drop you at
Yolosa, 7 km from Coroico; there is usually
transport Yolosa-Coroico, US$1, or walk, uphill all
the way, 2 hrs. To **Caranavi**, direct bus at 1300,
continues to Rurrenabaque arriving at 0700 next
day, US$8. Buses and pick-ups run from Yolosa to
Rurrenabaque via Caranavi, daily at 1500 with
Yungueña, except Sun at 1730, with **Turbus
Totai**, US$8.75, 13-15 hrs, they will take you down
to Yolosa to catch the bus from La Paz.

Chulumani *p275*

Bus From **La Paz**: **Trans San Bartolomé**, Virgen
del Carmen 1750, Villa Fátima, T221 1674, daily at
0800-1600 or when full, 4 hrs, US$2.50. **Trans
Arenas**, daily at 0730-1800, US$2.25. **Trans 24 de
Agosto micros**, 15 de Abril 408 y San Borja, T221
0607, 0600-1600, when full. Buses return to La
Paz from the plaza, micros from the *tranca*.

❶ Directory

Coroico *p274*

Banks **Banco Mercantil**, on Central Plaza.
Mon-Fri 0830-1230, 1430-1830, Sat 0900- 1230,
cash advances (no commission) on MasterCard
and Visa. **Prodem**, J Suazo Cuenca, on main plaza,
changes US$ cash, cash advance on Visa or
MasterCard only (no debit cards), 5% commission.
Internet Carlos, who lives on C Caja de Agua,
T/F213 6041, has an internet café, will exchange
Spanish for English lessons. **Language**
classes Siria León Domínguez, Julio Zuazo
Cuenca 062, T7195 5431, siria_leon@
yahoo.com.es. US$3.60 per hr, also has rooms for
rent and makes silver jewellery, excellent English.
Medical services Hospital: T213 6002, the
best in the Yungas, good malaria advice.
Police East side of main plaza. **Post offices** on
plaza. **Telephones** Entel, on Sagárnaga next to
Flota Yungueña, for international and local calls.
Cotel, next to church, phones, public TV.

Chulumani *p275*

Banks On Plaza Libertad, **Banco Unión**, changes
US$100 or more only in cash and TCs (5%
commission), Mon-Fri 0830-1200, 1430- 1800.
Cooperativa San Bartolomé, changes cash
Mon-Fri 0800-1200, 1400-1700, Sat-Sun 0700-
1200. **Internet** In tourist office, US$1.05 per hr.

Southwest Bolivia

*The mining town of Oruro, with one of South America's greatest folkloric traditions, shimmering
salt flats, coloured lakes and surrealistic rock formations combine to make this one of the
most fascinating regions of Bolivia. Add some of the country's most celebrated festivals and
the last hide-out of Butch Cassidy and the Sundance Kid and you have the elements for some
great and varied adventures. The journey across the altiplano from Uyuni to San Pedro de
Atacama is now a popular route to Chile and there are other routes south to Argentina.*

Oruro

→ *Phone code: 02. 30 km southeast of La Paz. Colour map 6, grid A2. Population: 236,110. Altitude: 3,706 m.*

The mining town of Oruro is the gateway to the altiplano of southwest Bolivia. It's a functional
place which explodes into life once a year with its famous carnival, symbolised by La
Diablada. Not far to the west is the national park encompassing Bolivia's highest peak,
Sajama. The **tourist office**, ① *Montes 6072, Plaza 10 de Febrero, T/F525 0144. Mon-Fri
0800-1200, 1400-1800* is very helpful and informative. Another kiosk is outside *Entel* on
C Bolívar (same hours). Colour map and guide (Spanish only), US$1.

Although Oruro became famous as a mining town, there are no longer any working
mines of importance. It is, however, a major railway junction and the commercial centre for
the mining communities of the altiplano, as well as hosting the country's best-known
carnival (see page 279). Several fine buildings in the centre hint at the city's former
importance, notably the baroque concert hall (now a cinema) on Plaza 10 de Febrero and the

Casa de la Cultura (Museo Simón I Patiño) ① *Soria Galvarro 5755, Mon-Fri 0900-1200, 1400-1830, US$0.30.* Built as a mansion by the tin baron Simón Patiño, it is now run by the Universidad Técnica de Oruro, and contains European furniture and a carriage imported from France, also houses temporary exhibitions. There is a good view from the Cerro Corazón de Jesús, near the church of the Virgen del Socavón, five blocks west of Plaza 10 de Febrero at the end of Calle Mier.

The **Museo Etnográfico Minero** ① *inside the Church of the Virgen del Socavón, entry via the church 0900-1200, 1500-1800, US$0.50,* contains mining equipment and other artefacts from the beginning of the century as well as a representation of *El Tío* (in Catholic terminology the devil.) **Museo Antropológico** ① *south of centre on Av España, Mon-Fri 0900-1200, 1400-1800, Sat-Sun 1000-2000, 1500-1800, US$0.50, good guides, getting there: take micro A heading south or any trufi going south.* It has a unique collection of stone llama heads as well as impressive carnival masks.

The **Museo Mineralógico** ① *part of the University, Mon-Fri 0800-1200, 1430-1700, US$0.60, getting there: take micro A south to the Ciudad Universitaria,* has over 5,500 mineral specimens. **Casa Arte Taller Cardozo Velásquez,** ① *Junín 738 y Arica, east of the*

Oruro

N

0 metres 200
0 yards 200

Sleeping 🛏
Alojamiento La Paz 1 3 *C3*

Bernal 4 *A3*
Gran Sucre 6 *D2*
International Park 8 *A3*
Max Plaza 1 *C2*
Repostero 10 *D3*
Residencial Gran Boston 7 *C3*
Residencial Gloria 5 *D2*
Residencial San Salvador 12 *D3*

Samay Wasi 11 *A3*
Terminal 9 *A3*
Villa Real San Felipe 2 *D2*

Eating 🍴
Café Sur 1 *D2*
Chifa Jackie Chan 12 *D2*
Cocos Hard Rock 3 *D2*
El Fogón 13 *A3*

El Huerto 9 *D2*
El Nochero 5 *C2*
Govinda 6 *D2*
La Cabaña 7 *C2*
La Casona 8 *C2*
Las Retamas 2 *D1*
Nayjama 11 *D3*
Panadería Doña Filo 4 *D2*

La Diablada festival

On the **Saturday before Ash Wednesday**, Los Carnavales de Oruro include the famous **Diablada** ceremony in homage to the miraculous Virgen del Socavón, patroness of miners, and in gratitude to Pachamama, the Earth Mother. The entire procession starts its 5 km route through the town at 0700, reaching the Sanctuary of the Virgen del Socavón at 0400 on Sunday. There the dancers invoke her blessing and ask for pardon. The company then proceeds to the Av Cívica amphitheatre, where the dancers perform two masques. Afterwards, the dancers all enter the sanctuary, chant a hymn in Quechua and pray for pardon.

The **Diablada** was traditionally performed by indigenous miners, but several other guilds have taken up the custom. The Carnival is especially notable for its fantastically imaginative costumes. The working- class Oruro district known as La Ranchería is particularly famous for the excellence of its costumes.

The **Gran Corso del Carnaval** takes place on the Sunday, a very spectacular display. Monday is **El Día del Diablo y del Moreno** in which the Diablos and Morenos, with their bands, compete against each other on Avenida Cívica in demonstrations of dancing. Every group seems to join in, in 'total marvellous chaos'. The action usually parades out of the amphitheatre, ending up at the Plaza de Armas. At dusk dancers and musicians go their separate ways, serenading until the early hours. By Tuesday the main touristic events have ended.

Carnaval del Sur takes place, with ch'alla rituals to invoke ancestors, unite with Pachamama and bless personal possessions. This is also the día del agua on which everyone throws water and sprays foam at everyone else (though this goes on throughout carnival; plastic tunics are sold for US$0.20 by street vendors).

The Friday before carnival, traditional miners' ceremonies are held at mines, including the sacrifice of a llama. Visitors may only attend with a guide and permission from Comibol, via the tourist office. The Sunday before carnival the groups practise and make their final pledges. In honour of its syncretism of Andean, pre-Columbian tradition and Catholic faith, the Oruro Carnaval has been included on UNESCO's Heritage of Humanity list.

Seating Around the Plaza de Armas, along Avenida 6 de Agosto and on Avenida Cívica, seats cost US$5-10 a day, bought from the Alcaldía in the plaza, or whichever business has erected stands outside its building. Seats on Avenida Bolívar, etc, cost US$5 a day from the shops which built stands. You can wander freely among the dancers and take photographs.

Sleeping For the hotel of your choice it's essential to book in advance for carnival; prices range from US$10 per person without bath, to US$20 per person with, to US$100 per person per day in the better places. The tourist office has list of all householders willing to let rooms; host and guest arrange the price, at least US$10 per person. Most hotels sell only three-night packages. If you leave it till the last minute you'll pay grossly inflated prices.

Transport Prices from La Paz triple. Organized day trips from La Paz cost US$30-45, including transport departing 0430, food and a seat in the main plaza, returning at 1600-1700 (missing the last eight to nine hours).

centre, T527 5245, www.catcarve.org, Mon-Sat 0930-1200, US$0.45. Contemporary Bolivian painting and sculpture is displayed in the Cardozo Velásquez home, a family of seven artists.

Parque Nacional Sajama

A one-day drive to the west of Oruro is the **Parque Nacional Sajama** ① *park headquarters in Sajama village, To132-513 5526 (in La Paz To2-211 1360), www.sajamabolivia.com, US$2.50*, established in 1939 and covering 100,517 ha. The park contains the world's highest forest, consisting mainly of the rare queñual tree (Polylepis tarapacana) which grows up to an altitude of 5,200 m. The scenery is wonderful and includes views of three volcanoes (Sajama – Bolivia's highest peak at 6,542 m – Parinacota and Pomerape). The road is paved and leads across the border into the Parque Nacional Lauca in Chile. You can trek in the park, with or without porters and mules, but once you move away from the Río Sajama or its major tributaries, lack of water is a problem.

Sajama village → *Population: 500. Altitude: 4,200 m.*

In Sajama village, visitors are billeted with family-run *alojamientos* (**G**) on a rotatating basis. All are basic to very basic, especially the sanitary facilities; no showers or electricity, solar power for lighting only. There are many small *comedores* but food supplies are limited. It can be very windy and cold at night; a good sleeping bag, gloves and hat are essential. Crampons, ice axe and rope are needed for climbing the volcanoes and can be hired in the village. Local guides charge US$50 per day. Horses can be hired, US$8 per day including guide. Good bathing in hot springs 7 km northwest of village; jeeps can be rented to visit, US$5-6. Many villagers sell alpaca woolen items.

By road to Chile

The shortest and most widely used route from La Paz to Chile is the road to **Arica** via the border at Tambo Quemado (Bolivia) and **Chungará** (Chile). From La Paz take the highway south towards Oruro. Immediately before Patacamaya, turn right at green road sign to Puerto Japonés on the Río Desaguadero, then on to Tambo Quemado. Take extra petrol (none available after Chilean border until Arica), food and water. The journey is worthwhile for the breathtaking views.

Bolivian **customs and immigration** are at Tambo Quemado, where there are a couple of very basic places to stay and eat. Border control is open daily 0800-2000. Shops change bolivianos, pesos chilenos and dollars. From Tambo Quemado there is a stretch of about 7 km of 'no-man's land' before you reach the Chilean frontier at Chungará. Here the border crossing, which is set against the most spectacular scenic backdrop of Lago Chungará and Volcán Parinacota, is thorough but efficient; open 0800-2100. Expect a long wait behind lines of lorries. Drivers must fill in 'Relaciones de Pasajeros', US$0.25 from kiosk at border, giving details of driver, vehicle and passengers. Do not take any livestock, plants, fruit, vegetables, or dairy products into Chile.

An alternative crossing from Oruro: several bus companies travel southwest to Iquique, via the border posts of **Pisiga** (Bolivia) and **Colchane** (Chile). The road is paved 40 km to Toledo and in 2007 an 18-km section near the border had been paved. Work is in progress on other parts. There is also service from Oruro to Arica via Patacamaya and Tambo Quemado.

South of Oruro

Machacamarca, about 30 minutes south of Oruro, has a good railway museum. Further south, the road runs between the flat plain of Lago Poopó and the Cordillera Azanaque, a very scenic ride. There are thermal baths at **Pazña**, about 1 hour from Oruro. About 65 km south is the **Santuario de Aves Lago Poopó** (a Ramsar site since 2003), an excellent bird reserve on the lake of the same name. The lake dries up completely in winter. The closest place to Oruro to see flamingos and other birds is **Lago Uru Uru** (the northern section of the Poopó lake system), go to Villa Challacollo on the road to Pisiga (minibuses 102, 10, 5 or blue micros) and walk from there. Birds start arriving with the first rains in October or November. Further along, at Km 10 is Chusakeri, where chullpas can be seen on the hillside.

Access to the lake is a little closer from **Huari**, 15 minutes south of Challapata along a paved road. Huari (124 km south of Oruro) is a pleasant little town with a large brewery; there is a small museum and Mirador Tatacuchunita, a lookout on nearby Cerro Sullka. Sunsets over the lake are superb. There are a couple of basic *alojamientos*, eg **G** 25 de Mayo, 2 blocks from the plaza towards Challapata, shared bath, cold water in morning only. It is about 8 km walk from Huari to the lake, depending on the water level. Near the lake is the Uru-Muratos community of **Llapallapani** with circular adobe homes, those with straw roofs are known as *chillas* and those with conical adobe roofs are *putukus*. Cabins in *putuku* style form part of a community tourism programme. Boats can be hired when the water level is high, at other times Poopó is an unattainable mirage. There is good walking in the Cordillera Azanaque behind Huari; take food, water, warm clothing and all gear. **Challapata** (*fiesta* 15-17 July) has several places to stay, eg *Res Virgen del Carmen*, by main plaza, and a gas station.

Atlantis in the Andes Jim Allen's theory of Atlantis is well known around Oruro and a video about it is on display at the bus station (see www.geocities.com/webatlantis). **Pampa Aullagas**, the alleged Atlantis site, is 196 km from Oruro, southwest of Lago Poopó. Access is from the town of **Quillacas** along a road which branches west from the road to Uyuni just south of Huari. It can also be reached from the west through Toledo and Andamarca. A visit here can be combined with visits to the Salar de Coipasa.

Southwest of Lago Poopó, off the Oruro-Pisiga-Iquique road (turn off at **Sabaya**), is the **Salar de Coipasa**, 225 km from Oruro. It is smaller and less visited than the Salar de Uyuni, and has a turquoise lake in the middle of the salt pan surrounded by mountains with gorgeous views and large cacti. At the edge of the Salar is **Coquesa** (lodging available), which has a mirador and tombs with mummies ① *US$1.25* entry to each site. Coipasa is northwest of the Salar de Uyuni and travel from one to the other is possible with a private vehicle along the impressive **Ruta Intersalar**. Along the way are tombs, terracing and ancient irrigation canals at the archaeological site of **Alcaya** ① *US$1.25*, gradually being developed by the local community (near **Salinas de Garci Mendoza**, locally known as Salinas). Nearby are the towering volcanic cones of Cora Cora and Tunupa. Access to the north end of the Salar de Uyuni is at **Jirira**.

Note: Getting stranded out on the altiplano or, worse yet on the salar itself, is dangerous because of extreme temperatures and total lack of drinking water. It is best to visit this area with a tour operator that can take you, for example, from Oruro through the salares to Uyuni. Travellers with their own vehicles should only attempt this route following extensive local inquiry or after taking on a guide to avoid becoming lost or bogged. The edges of the salares are soft and only established entry points or ramps should be used to cross onto or off the salt.

● Sleeping

Oruro *p277, map 278*

C Gran Sucre, Sucre 510 esq 6 de Octubre, T527 6800, www.hotebol.com. Nicely refurbished old building, includes buffet breakfast, cheaper rooms on the ground floor, heaters on request. Recommended.

C Max Plaza, Adolfo Mier at Plaza 10 de Febrero, T525 2561. Includes breakfast, comfortable carpeted rooms, good central location.

C Villa Real San Felipe, San Felipe 678 y La Plata, south of the centre, T525 4993, www.villarealsanfelipe.com. Quaint small hotel with nicely furnished but small rooms, heating, includes buffet breakfast, sauna and whirlpool, restaurant, tour operator, best hotel in town.

D Samay Huasi, Av Brasil 232 opposite the terminal, T527 6737. Modern, includes breakfast, bright rooms, hot water, internet, 30% discount for IYHF members. Recommended.

E Repostero, Sucre 370 y Pagador, T525 8001. Hot water, includes breakfast, renovated carpeted rooms are pricier but better value than the old rooms, secure parking.

F Bernal, Brasil 701, opposite bus terminal, T527 9468. Modern, good value, excellent hot showers, cheaper with shared bath, heaters on request, restaurant, tours arranged. Recommended.

F Res Gran Boston, Pagador 1159 y Cochabamba, T527 4708. Recently refurbished

house, internal rooms around a covered patio, cheaper with shared bath, good value.

F Res San Salvador, V Galvarro 6325 near train station, T527 6771. Hot water, **G** with shared bath, electric shower, best in this area.

F Terminal, 21 de Enero y Bakovic opposite the terminal, T527 3431. Modern, hot water, cheaper with shared bath.

G Res Gloria, Potosí 6059, T527 6250. 19th century building, private toilet, shared electric shower, cheaper with shared toilet, basic but clean.

G Alojamiento La Paz I, Cochabamba 180, T527 4882. Shared bath, basic, clean, hot shower extra.

Sajama *p280*

A Tomarapi Ecolodge, north of Sajama in Tomarapi community, near Caripe, T02-241 4753, ecotomarapi@hotmail.com. Including full board (good food) and guiding service with climbing shelter at 4,900 m, helpful staff, simple but comfortable, with bath, hot water, heating.

South of Oruro *p280*

F Posada Doña Lupe, Jirira, T527 2094-Oruro. Hot water, cheaper without bath, use of kitchen but bring your own food, no meals available, caters to tour groups, pleasant, comfortable.

G **Alojamiento Paraíso**, Sabaya. Take sleeping bag, shared bath, cold water, meals on request or take own food, sells petrol.

G **Doña Wadi**, Salinas de Garci Mendoza, 1½ blocks from main plaza. Shared bath, hot water, basic but clean, meals available

⑦ Eating

Oruro *p277, map 278*

℡ **La Cabaña**, Junín 609. Comfortable, smart, good international food, bar, Sun and Mon 1200-1530 only.

℡ **Nayjama**, Aldana esq Pagador. Best in town, huge portions.

℡-℡ **Chifa Jackie Chan**, Bolívar 615 esq S Galvarro. Good Chinese, 1100-2300.

℡-℡ **El Fogón**, Brasil y 21 de Enero. Best of a poor lot by the bus terminal. The many greasy chicken places by the terminal are best avoided.

℡-℡ **Las Retamas**, Murguía 930 esq Washington. Excellent set lunches (℡), Bolivian and international dishes à la carte, very good pastries, pleasant atmosphere, out of the way but worth the trip. Recommended.

℡ **Cocos Hard Rock**, 6 de Octubre y Sucre. Set meals, local and international dishes.

℡ **La Casona**, Pres Montes 5970, opposite Post Office. A good *pizzería*.

℡ **Govinda**, 6 de Octubre 6071. Excellent vegetarian, Mon-Sat 0900-2130.

℡ **El Huerto**, Bolívar 359. Good, vegetarian options, open Sun.

Cafés

Café Sur, Arce 163, near train station. Live entertainment, seminars, films, Tue-Sat, good place to meet local students.

El Nochero, Av 6 de Octubre 1454, open 1700-2400, good coffee.

Jordan's Café Net, Bolívar 394 entre Potosí y Pagador. Coffee, breakfasts, Wi-fi and ADSL.

Panadería Doña Filo, 6 de Octubre esq Sucre. Excellent savoury snacks and sweets, closed Sun, takeaway only.

⑦ Bars and clubs

Oruro *p277, map 278*

Bravos, Montesinos y Pagador. Varied music.

Imagine, 6 de Octubre y Junín. Latin and other music.

⑦ Shopping

Oruro *p277, map 278*

Crafts On Av La Paz the 4 blocks between León and Belzu, 48-51, are largely given over to workshops producing masks and costumes for Carnival. **Artesanías Oruro**, A Mier 599, esq S Galvarro. Lovely selection of regional handicrafts produced by 6 rural community cooperatives; nice sweaters, carpets, wall-hangings.

Markets Mercado Campero, V Galvarro esq Bolívar. Sells everything, also *brujería* section for magical concoctions. **Mercado Fermín López**, C Ayacucho y Montes. Food and hardware. C Bolívar is the main shopping street. **Irupana**, S Galvarra y A Mier. Good selection of natural foods and snacks.

⑦ Activities and tours

Oruro *p277, map 278*

Charlie Tours, Brasil 232 at *Hotel Samay Huasi*, T527 6737, charlietours@yahoo.com. Regional tours including Salares de Coipasa and Uyuni, transport service.

Freddy Barrón, T527 6776, lufba@hotmail.com. Tours and transport, speaks German.

Viajeros del Tiempo, Soria Galvarro 1232, T527 1166. Offers trips to the nearby mines, hot pools and other attractions, open Mon-Fri 0900-1230, 1500-1930, Sat 0900-1200, phone in advance.

⑦ Transport

Oruro *p277, map 278*

Bus Bus terminal 10 blocks north of centre at Bakovic and Aroma, T525 3535, US$0.20 terminal tax to get on bus. Micro No 2 to centre, or any saying 'Plaza 10 de Febrero'. To **Challapata** and **Huari**: several companies go from the Oruro terminal to Challapata, about every hour, US$1, 1¾ hrs, and Huari, US$1.25, 2 hrs, last bus back leaves Huari about 1630. You can also take a bus to Challapata and a shared taxi from there to Huari, US$0.30. Daily services to: **La Paz** at least every hour 0400-2200, US$1.25-1.90, 3½ hrs;. **Cochabamba**, US$2.50, 4 hrs, 9 daily with **Copacabana**, more with other companies. **Potosí**, US$2.50 day bus, US$3.75 at night, 5 hrs, several daily, **Copacabana** *bus cama* at 2345 US$10. **Sucre** Bustillo 1100 and 2000, US$5, **Copacabana** at 2230, *semi-cama* US$10, *bus cama* US$15, 10 hrs. **Tarija**, Belgrano at 2030, US$7.50-10, 16 hrs. **Uyuni**, several companies, all depart 1900-2100, US$2.50, US$3.75 on Wed, 7 hrs. **Todo Turismo**, Rodríguez 134 entre 6 de Agosto y Bakovic (next to bus station), T511 1889, www.touringbolivia.com, offers a tourist bus departing from La Paz, stopping in Oruro, night departures only, US$20. To **Tupiza**, via Potosí, **Boquerón** at 1230, **Illimani** at 1630, US$9.75, 11-12 hrs, continuing to Villazón, US$10, 13-14 hrs. **Santa Cruz**, Bolívar at 2000, US$7.50, *bus cama* at 2130, US$11.25, 11 hrs. **Pisiga** (Chilean border), **Trans Pisiga**, Av Dehene y España, T526 2241, at 2000 and 2030, or with

Bolivia Southwest Bolivia Listings

Iquique bound buses, US$3.75, 4-5 hrs.
International buses (US$2 to cross border): to **Iquique** via Pisiga, several companies at 0100, Interbus at 0500 and 1200, **Bernal** at 1230, US$11.25, *bus cama* US$13.75, 10 hrs. **Arica** via Patacamaya and **Tambo Quemado** (US$3.75, 4 hrs), several companies between 1200 and 1300, US$11.25, 10 hrs.
Radio-taxis Sajama, T528 0801, provide transport to regional attractions.
Train Two companies run services from Oruro to **Uyuni** and on to **Villazón** via Tupiza. Each has an executive and two other classes of seat: Expreso del Sur, Mon and Fri at 1530, arriving in Uyuni at 2200 ; Wara Wara del Sur Sun and Wed at 1900, arriving in Uyuni at 0200. Fares: Expreso del Sur to Uyuni: *Ejecutivo* US$10, *Salón* US$5.50, *Popular* US$3.75; Tupiza: US$20.75, US$10.25 and US$ 6.70 respectively: Villazón: US$23.30, US$11.60 and US$8.20. Wara Wara del Sur to Uyuni: *Ejecutivo* US$8.40, *Salón* US$4.25, *Popular* US$3.55; Tupiza: US$15.15, US$7.30 and US$ 6.10 respectively: Villazón: US$18.30, US$9.15 and US$7.30. For details of trains from Uyuni to Villazón and for trains from Uyuni to Oruro, see Uyuni. For return times from Villazón, see page 291. Passengers with tickets Villazón-La Paz are transferred to a bus at Oruro. To check train times, T527 4605 (or La Paz 02-241 6545). In Nov-Jan and Jul you must have a lot of patience to get a ticket; demand is very high.

Sajama *p280*
To get to the park, take a La Paz-Oruro bus and change at Patacamaya. Mini-vans from Patacamaya (in front of **Restaurant Capitol**) to Sajama Sun-Fri 1300, 3 hrs, US$2. Sajama to Patacamaya Mon-Fri 0600-0700, some days via **Tambo Quemado**, confirm details and weekend schedule locally. From Tambo Quemado to Sajama about 1530 daily, 1 hr, US$0.65. Or take a La Paz-Arica bus, ask for Sajama, try to pay half the fare, but you may be charged full fare.

South of Oruro *p280*
Public transport to **Coipasa** is very scarce. Trans Pisiga, address above, goes every second Tue to Copaisa, US$3, 6 hrs. You can also ride with one of the buses to Iquique and get off at the turnoff, but it is difficult to hire a private vehicle for onward transportation in this sparsely populated area. There is transport going around the southern end of Poopó. Oruro to **Salinas**, 5 per week (different schedule every day), from Avs Caro y Ejército, US$2.60, 7 hrs.

⑩ Directory

Oruro *p277, map 278*
Banks Banco Bisa, Bolívar at Plaza 10 de Febrero, fair rates for US$ cash, US$6 flat rate for TCs (max US$500), cash advances on Visa and Mastercard, Mon-Fri 0900-1600, Sat 0900-1300. BCP, Bolívar esq Montes at Plaza 10 de Febrero, fair rates for US$ cash, Visa and Mastercard ATM, Mon-Fri 0900-1800, Sat 0900-1300. **Casa de Cambio** at the Terminal Terrestre, US$, euros, pesos chilenos and argentinos, soles, cash only, fair rates, daily 0800-2000. **Internet** Many in town, rates US$0.30-0.35. **Post offices** Presidente Montes 1456, half block from plaza. **Telephones** Many *cabinas* in town. **Useful addresses** Immigration, S Galvarro entre Ayacucho y Cochabamba.

Uyuni → *Phone code: 02. Colour map 6, grid B3. Population: 11,320. Altitude: 3,665 m.*

Uyuni lies near the eastern edge of the Salar de Uyuni and is one of the jumping-off points for trips to the salt flats, volcanoes and multi-coloured lakes of southwest Bolivia. Still a commercial and communication centre, Uyuni was, for much of the 20th century, important as a major railway junction. A statue of an armed railway worker, erected after the 1952 Revolution, dominates Avenida Ferroviaria. Most services are near the station. **Museo Arqueológico and Antropológico de los Andes Meridionales** ① *Arce y Potosí, Mon-Fri 1000-1200, 1400- 1800, Sat-Sun 0900-1300, US$0.35.* A small museum with local artifacts. Market on Avenida Potosí between the clock and Avaroa sells everything almost every day. Fiesta 11 July. There is a Railway Cemetery outside town with engines from 1907-1950s, now rusting hulks.

Pulacayo, 30 minutes ride from Uyuni, is a town at the site of a 19th-century silver mine. Here you can see the first locomotive in Bolivia and the train robbed by Butch Cassidy and the Sundance Kid. Information and tours from the Uyuni clock tower, Arce at Avenida Potosí.

Tourist office ① *Av Potosí 13, Mon-Fri 0830-1200, 1400-1830, Sat-Sun 0830-1200, T693 2060 and ask for the tourist office.* **Ranking Bolivia** ① *Potosí 9 y Arce, T693 2102, rankingbolivia@hotmail.com, daily 0830-2000.* Good source of local and regional information, database of tour operators based on traveller's reports, café, crafts, books and other products, video room, a place to hang out while waiting for transport, English spoken. Part of an internationally funded project which ended in 2005 and is continuing independently.

Salar de Uyuni

Crossing the Salar de Uyuni, the largest and highest salt lake in the world, is one of the great Bolivian trips. Driving across it is a fantastic experience, especially during June and July when the bright blue skies contrast with the blinding white salt crust. Farther south, and included on tours of the region, are the towering volcanoes, multi-coloured lakes (including Colorada and Verde) with abundant birdlife, weird rock formations, thermal activity and endless puna that make up some of most fabulous landscapes in South America.

Trips to the Salar de Uyuni enter via the *terraplén* (ramp) at Colchani and include stops to see traditional salt mining techniques and the Ojos del Agua, where salt water bubbles to the surface of the slat flat, perhaps a call at a salt hotel (see Sleeping, below) and a visit to the **Isla del Pescado** ① *entry US$1*, so-called because of its shape (also known as Incahuasi – Inca House). This is a coral island, raised up from the ocean bed, covered in tall cactii. There is a walking trail with superb views, a *Mongo's* café, basic lodging and toilets. If on an extended tour (see below), you may leave the Salar by another *terraplén*, eg Puerto Chupica in the southwest.

San Cristóbal

The original village of **San Cristóbal**, southwest of Uyuni, was relocated in 2002 to make way for a Canadian-owned open-pit mine, said to be one of the largest silver deposits in South America. The original church (1650) had been declared a national monument and was therefore rebuilt in its entirety. Ask at the Fundación San Cristóbal Office for the church to be opened as the interior artwork, restored by Italian techniques, is worth seeing. The fiesta is 27-28 July. San Cristóbal and other towns in the area, eg Alota (see below) and Culpina K, were offered tourism projects by the company in exchange for permission to allow the mine to proceed. Dubbed *pueblos auténticos* (authentic towns), they have yet to escape the look of the new money spent on them. The road San Cristóbal-Uyuni is paved to start with, then becomes good gravel (watch out for stones flung up by speeding trucks).

Reserva Nacional de Fauna Andina Eduardo Avaroa

① *Office at Avaroa entre Potosí y Colón, Uyuni, T693 2225/693 2400, and C Sen Aramayo y 7 de Noviembre, Tupiza, T694 4677, www.bolivia-rea.com, excellent map for sale, US$3.75 (not included in tour price; pay in bolivianos). Park ranger/entry points are near Laguna Colorada, Lagunas Verde and Blanca, close to the Chilean border, and at Sol de Mañana, near Quetena Chico. See http://delipez.org/turismo.*

In the far southwest of Bolivia, in the Lípez region, is the 714,000-ha **Reserva Nacional Eduardo Avaroa** (REA). There are two access routes from Uyuni (one via the Salar) and one from Tupiza. Until recently the Reserve's wonders were quite isolated, but tours now criss-cross the puna, many on the route from Uyuni to San Pedro de Atacama. Roads are unmarked, rugged truck tracks and may be impassable in the wet season. **Laguna Colorada**, at 4,270 m, 346 km southwest of Uyuni, is just one of the highlights of the reserve, its shores and shallows encrusted with borax and salt, an arctic white counterpoint to the flaming red, algae-coloured waters in which the rare James flamingoes, along with the more common Chilean and Andean flamingoes, breed and live. The sparkling jade **Laguna Verde** (lifeless because it is laden with arsenic) and its neighbour Laguna Blanca, near the Chilean border, are at the foot of Volcán Licancábur, 5,868 m. Between Lagunas Colorada and Verde there are thermal pools at Laguna Blanca (blissful water, a challenge to get out into the bitter wind - no facilities) and at Polques, on the shores of Río Amargo/Laguna Salada by the Salar de Chalviri. An *hospedaje* is being built at Polques (with luck it will have public toilets). All these places are on the `classic' tour route, across the Salar de Uyuni to **San Juan**, which has a museum of local *chullpas*, and is where most tour companies stop: plenty of lodgings. Other tours stop at **Culpina K**. Then you go to the Salar de Chiguana, Mirador del Volcán de Ollagüe, Cinco Lagunas, a chain of small, flamingo-specked lagoons, the much-photographed Arbol de Piedra in the Siloli desert, then Laguna Colorada (spend the second night here: *Hospedaje Laguna Colorada*, the newer and better *Huayllajara* – six-bed dorms, lots of blankets, take own food and stove, and *Campamento Ende*). From Colorada you go over the Cuesta del Pabellón, 4,850 m, to the Sol de Mañana geysers (not to be confused with the Sol de Mañana entry point), the Desierto de Dalí, a pure sandy desert as much Daliesque for the spacing of the rocks, with snow-covered peaks

284

behind, as for the shape of the rocks themselves, and Laguna Verde (4,400 m).

Jurisdiction of the reserve belongs to the villages of **Quetena Chico** and Quetena Grande (the smaller of the two), to the east of Laguna Colorada. The villagers are entitled to run lodging in the reserve: Quetena Chico runs *hospedajes* at Laguna Colorada. Quetena Grande runs *La Cabaña* at Hito Cajónes (see below). In Quetena Chico is the reserve's visitors information centre, **Centro Ecológico Ch'aska** ① *daily 0730-1800*, informative displays about the region's geology, vulcanology, fauna, flora, natural and human history; a worthwhile stop. The village has two *hospedajes* (*Piedra Preciosa* and *Hostal Quetena*, both **G**, hot water extra), and places to eat.

From Tupiza Tour operators in Tupiza run trips to the REA and Salar de Uyuni and go to places not included on tours from Uyuni. These include the beautiful Lagunas Celeste and Negra below Cerro Uturunco, which is near Quetena Chico; the **Valle de las Rocas**, 4,260 m, between the villages of **Alota** and Villa Mar (a vast extension of rocks eroded into fantastic configurations, with polylepis trees in sheltered corners); and isolated communities in the puna. The high altitude scenery is out of this world. *Alojamientos* in the villages on the tour routes cannot be booked. You turn up and search for a room. All provide kitchen space for the tour's cook or independent traveller to prepare meals, take your own stove, though. See also Tayka/Fremen in Uyuni, Activities and tours, below. There is public transport from Uyuni into the region, but rarely more than one bus a week, with several hours rough travelling. If travelling independently, note that there are countless tracks and no signposts.

Crossing into Chile

There is a REA ranger station near Lagunas Blanca and Verde: if coming from Bolivia, have your park entry receipt at hand, if crossing from Chile pay the entry fee. Alongside is a *refugio*, *La Cabaña*; US$5 pp in comfortable but very cold dorms, solar-powered lighting, hot water seldom works, cooking facilities but bring your own food (in high season book in advance – tour agencies can do this by radio). There is good climbing and hiking in the area with outstanding views. You must register at the ranger station before heading out and they may insist that you take a guide (eg to climb Licancábur, US$30 for guide plus US$40 for transport). Mind the altitude, intense solar radiation and lack of drinking water.

From the ranger station it's 5 km to the border at Hito Cajones (on the Chilean side called

Uyuni

To Post Office & Bus Offices
To Colchani & El Salar
Av Acre
Av Colón
To Buses to San Cristóbal
Museo Arqueológico y Antropológico de los Andes Meridionales
Andes Salt Expeditions
Colque Tours
Bolívar
Clock Tower
Entel
Av Potosí
Reli Tour
Prodem
Plaza Arce
Immigration
Sucre
To 7, 9 & Todo Turismo Buses
Kantuta Tours
To Military Base
Lavarap Laundry
Comert Craft Co-op
Toñito Tours
Esmeralda Tours
Av Ferroviaria
Armed Railway Workers' Monument
Railworker's Monument
To Tupiza

0 metres 20
0 yards 20

Sleeping
Avenida 1
Hostal Marith 10
Hostelling
  International 2
Jardines de Uyuni 9
Julia 11
Kory Wasy 3
Kutimuy 4
Los Girasoles 7

Mágia de Uyuni 6
Residencial Sucre 8
Toñito &
  Minuteman Pizza 5

Eating
16 de Julio 5
Arco Iris 2
Kactus 3

Hito Cajón), 4,500 m. Bolivian immigration open 0800-2100, charges US$2 in any currency (no other border crossing makes this charge). There are no services or facilities at the border. A further 6 km along a good dirt road into Chile is the intersection with the fully paved road from San Pedro de Atacama to Paso de Jama, the border between Chile and Argentina. From here it's 40 km (2,000 m downhill) to San Pedro. Chilean customs and immigration are just outside San Pedro and can take 45 minutes at busy times. See Transport, page 288.

● Sleeping

Uyuni *p283, map p285*
Water is frequently cut off and may only be available between 0600 and 1200.

B Los Girasoles, Santa Cruz 155, 3½ blocks from clock tower, T693 3323, www.girasoleshotel.com. Buffet breakfast, bright and warm (especially 2nd floor), comfortable, nicely decorated, heaters available, best in town. Recommended.

C Jardines de Uyuni, Potosí 133, T693 2989. Includes breakfast, rustic style but comfortable, hot water, heaters available, open fire in lounge, parking.

D Kory Wasy, Av Potosí, entre Arce y Sucre, T693 2670, kory_wasy@hotmail.com. **D** low season, overpriced but breakfast is included, good fun, sunny lobby but many dark rooms, restaurant, tour agency.

D Mágia de Uyuni, Av Colón 432, T693 2541, Magia_Uyuni@yahoo.es. All rooms have bath, Includes breakfast. Recommended.

D Toñito, Av Ferroviaria 60, T693 3186, www.bolivian expeditions.com. Spacious rooms with good beds, good breakfast included, TV, solar-powered showers and new annex in 2007, **F** with shared bath and no breakfast, very helpful, laundry, internet, tours.

E-F Hostelling International, Potosí y Sucre, T693 2228. Hot water, cheaper without bath, kitchen facilities, modern and popular, discount for IYHF members.

E-F Julia, Ferroviaria 314 y Arce, T693 2134. Spacious comfortable rooms, unreliable hot water.

F Avenida, Av Ferroviaria 11, opposite train station, T693 2078. **G** with shared bath, basic, limited water and shower facilities, basic, quite old, frequently used by travellers, parking.

G pp Hostal Marith, Av Potosí 61, T693 2174. Good budget option (better value without private bath), hot showers from 0830, simple, sunny patio with laundry sinks.

G Kutimuy, Avaroa esq Av Potosí, near market, T693 2391 (owned by Colque Tours, so often full of groups). Includes continental breakfast, warm rooms, electric showers, cheaper without bath.

G Residencial Sucre, Sucre 132, T693 2047, residencial.sucre.uyuni@gmail.com. Hot water, cheaper without bath, basic but adequate, warm and welcoming but 3 stars is optimistic!

Salar de Uyuni *p284*
These *hoteles de sal* are generally visited on tours, seldom independently.

AL Palacio de Sal, on the edge of the salar, near the ramp outside Colchani (book through **Jardines de Uyuni**, see above, operated by **Hidalgo Tours**, Junín esq Bolívar, T622 5186, Potosí, uyusalht@ceibo.entelnet.bo). Price is half-board. Spacious, comfortable luxury salt hotel, decorated with large salt sculptures, heating, hot water, sauna, lookout on second storey with views of the salar. It was relocated from its original location on the salar.

A Luna Salada, north of Colchani near entrance to the salar, T2693 22423 (mob), rodri_lara@yahoo.com. Half-board, private bath, hot water. **A** (high season).

D Playa Blanca, on the Salar de Uyuni, about 10 km from the Colchani access and 70 km from Isla del Pescado, T693 2115 (Uyuni). **E** in low season, half-board, all furnishings made of salt blocks, shared bath, no showers, single beds only, all solid and liquid waste is removed in barrels. This is the only hotel left on the salar and it is not clear if it will remain here, hotels were asked to leave for environmental reasons. A stop for most tours, day visitors must consume something in order to take photos, use of toilet US$0.60.
Playa Blanca has a second salt hotel in Colchani, same price, half-board, private bath, no shower.
See also **Tayka/Fremen** in Activites and tours on facing page.

San Cristóbal *p284*
C Hotel San Cristóbal, purpose-built, owned by the community, in centre. The bar is inside a huge oil drum, all metal furnishings. The rest is comfortable if simple, very hot water, good breakfast included, evening meal extra.

G pp Alojamiento behind the internet office. Basic rooms with several beds, separate bath, hot water extra. Owners keep ñandúes.

G pp Alojamiento Ali, a bit more expensive, but not much difference, rooms with 3 beds, hot water extra.

🍴 Eating

Uyuni p283, map p285
Avoid the market: this is not the place to get ill.
16 de Julio, Arce entre Avs Ferroviaria y Potosí. Opens 0700, good value breakfast and set lunch, à la carte in the evening, veggie options, meeting place.
Kactus, Arce y Potosí, p2. International food, homemade pasta, good pancakes, slow service.
Arco Iris, Plaza Arce. Good Italian food, pizza, and atmosphere, occasional live music.
La Loco, Av Potosí. Gringo food, with music and drinks till late, open fire, popular.
Minuteman, pizza restaurant attached to *Toñito Hotel* (see above), good pizzas and soups.
Café Den Danske, Quijarro y Matos. Tiny Danish-run café with genuinely international cuisine, good reports. The owner speaks English as well.

⛰ Activities and tours

Uyuni p283, map p285
Organization of tours from Uyuni to the Salar is much improved, but even good companies have their off days. Travel is in 4WD Landcruisers, cramped for those on the back seat, but the staggering scenery makes up for any discomfort. Always check the itinerary, the vehicle, the menu (vegetarians should be prepared for an egg-based diet), what is included in the price and what is not (accommodation is normally not included – add US$3-4.50 pp per night). Prices are based on a 6-person group – it is easy to find other people in Uyuni, especially in high season, Apr-Sep. If there are fewer than 6 you each pay more. Trips are usually 3 to 4 days: Salar de Uyuni, Lagunas Colorada and Verde, back to Uyuni; Uyuni-San Pedro de Atacama, including the Salar and lakes;

and Uyuni to Tupiza via all the sights. Prices range from US$65-220 pp depending on agency, departure point and season. Agencies in Potosí and La Paz also organize tours, but in some cases this may involve putting you on a bus to Uyuni where you meet up with one of the Uyuni agencies and get the same quality tour for a higher price. If the tour seriously fails to match the contract and the operator refuses any redress, complaints can be taken to the tourism office in Uyuni (see above) and then to the **Director Regional de Turismo**, La Prefectura del Departamento de Potosí, C La Paz, Potosí (T02-622 7477). Speak to travellers who have just returned from a tour, and try the following:

Tour operators
Andes Salt Expeditions, 56 Arce (main plaza), T693 2116, www.andes-salt-uyuni.com.bo. Company with a good reputation, especially for their tours of the salar and lagunas. But mixed reports received in 2007. Also have office in Potosí.
Andes Travel Office, Ayacucho 222, T693 2227. Good reports, run by Belgian Isabelle and Iver.
Colque Tours, Av Potosí 54, T/F693 2199, www.colquetours.com. Well-known but consistently mixed reports, has its own hostals on the edge of the Salar and by Laguna Verde and a branch in San Pedro de Atacama.
Esmeralda, Av Ferroviaria esq Arce, T693 2130, esmeraldaivan@hotmail.com. Good tours – cheaper end of market (good laundry next door).
Kantuta, Av Arce y Av Potosí, T693 3084, kantutatours@hotmail.com. Run by 3 eager brothers, also volcano-climbing tours, good food.
Oasis Odyssey, Av Ferroviaria, T693 3175. Good vehicles for salar tours, excellent guide (Javier Canaza and his wife, Liset, as cook).
Reli Tours, Av Arce 42, T693 3209, www.reli

tours.com. Reliable, good vehicles and food.
Tayka/Fremen, Sucre entre Uruguay y México,
T693 2987, www.andes-amazonia.com.
Proyecto Tayka, Red de Hoteles de los Andes,
a chain of hotels being built in the Salar de
Uyuni-Reserva Avaroa area, is a joint venture
between Fremen, Fundación Prodem and 4
local communities. Hotels have rooms with
private bath, hot water, heating, restaurant,
price in A range.
Toñito Tours, Av Ferroviaria 152, T693 3186,
www.bolivianexpeditions.com. Offers a variety
of good tours (also in La Paz, see page 257), with
their own hotel at Bella Vista on the edge of the
Salar.

San Cristóbal *p284*
Llama Mama. 60 km of exclusive bicycle trails
descending 2-3 or 4 hrs, depending on skill, 3
grades, US$200, all inclusive, taken up by car,
with guide and communication.

⊝ Transport

Uyuni *p283, map p285*
Bus Offices are on Av Arce, north of Colón. To
La Paz, 16 de Julio daily at 2000 (La Paz-Uyuni,
daily 1530), **Panasur** Wed and Sun at 1800 (La
Paz-Uyuni Tue and Fri 1730), US$6.25, 12 hrs, or
transfer in Oruro. Tourist buses with **Todo
Turismo**, C Santa Cruz 155 next to *Hotel Los
Girasoles*, T693 3337, www.touringbolivia.com,
Tue and Sun at 2000, Fri at 2330, US$25, 11 hrs, 1
additional departure in high season (La Paz office,
Plaza Antofagasta 504, Edif Paula, p1, opposite
the bus terminal, T211 9418, depart Mon, Wed
and Sat, 2100). **Oruro**, several companies
2000-2130, US$2.50-3.75; **Todo Turismo** (see
above), US$20. To **Potosí** several companies
0930-1000 and 1900-2000, US$3.10, 6 hrs,
spectacular scenery. To **Sucre** 6 de Octubre at
1900, or transfer in Potosí, US$5, 9 hrs. To **Tupiza**
with **11 de Julio**, Wed, Fri and Sun 0900, US$4.40,
8 hrs, ramshackle buses. 6-8 passenger jeeps with
12 de Octubre or **11 de Julio**, daily 0600,
US$6.25, 5 hrs. For **Tarija** change in Potosí or
Tupiza.

  Regional services To **San Cristóbal**, from
Av Potosí y Ayacucho, next to *Hostal Marith*, daily
1400, US$1.90, returns 0600. To **Vila Vila, San
Cristóbal, Culpina K, Serena, Alota, Villa Mar,
Soniquera, Quetena**, Trans Nor Lípez, Sun
1000, US$5 to Quetena, 10 hrs, return Wed 0300.
To **Alota** and **Colcha K**, 11 de Julio, Fri 1100,
US$2.50, return Wed 1100. To **Soniquera**
(between Villa Mar and Quetena), Sun 1100,
US$3.15, 5 hrs, return Wed 0700.
Road and train A road and railway line run
south from Oruro, through Río Mulato, to Uyuni

(323 km). The road is sandy and, after rain, very
bad, especially south of Río Mulato. The train
journey is quicker and more scenic. Check services
on arrival, T693 2153. **Expreso del Sur** leaves for
Oruro on Tue and Fri at 0000, arriving 0630. **Wara
Wara del Sur** service leaves on Mon and Fri at
0140, arriving 0840 (prices for both under Oruro).
To **Atocha, Tupiza** and **Villazón** Expreso del Sur
leaves Uyuni on Mon and Fri at 2220, arriving,
respectively, at 0045, 0315 and 0630. **Wara Wara**
leaves on Mon and Thu at 0220, arriving 0500,
0810 and 1200. The ticket office opens at 0830 and
1430 each day and one hour before the trains
leave. It closes once tickets are sold – get there
early or buy through a tour agent.
Travelling to Chile Chile is 1 hr ahead of
Bolivia from mid-Oct to Mar. Do not attempt to
take coca leaves across the border; it is an
arrestable offence. Also Chile does not allow dairy
produce, tea bags (of any description), fruit or
vegetables to be brought in.

  The easiest way is to go to San Pedro de
Atacama as part of your jeep trip to the Salar and
lagunas (see above). **Colque Tours**, address
above, as well as running Salar and Lagunas tours
that take you to **San Pedro de Atacama**, has a
direct jeep leaving their office every day at 1900,
US$25 pp, 16 hrs. They also run 2 mini-buses
daily from their camp near the ranger station at
Hito Cajones to San Pedro de Atacama, departing
1000 and 1700, US$5, 1 hr including stop at
immigration. There is another vehicle from Hito
Cajones to San Pedro de Atacama (*tránsito
público*), most days at about 1000, same price. At
other times onward transport to San Pedro must
be arranged by your agency, this can cost up to
US$60 if it is not included in your tour. The ranger
station may be able to assist in an emergency.
The *tránsito público* leaves San Pedro for Hito
Cajones at 0800 or 0830. It is usually booked
through an agency in town. Occasionally it runs
in the afternoon.

  There is a train service to **Calama** leaving 0330
Mon, US$13.20. Tickets are sold Fri-Sun. It should
take 16 hrs but involves a 1-hr change of trains at
Avaroa (arrives at Avaroa at 0800), then it's 40
mins to Ollagüe, where Chilean customs take 2-4
hrs. All passports are collected and stamped in
the rear carriage and should be ready for
collection after 1-2 hrs; queue for your passport,
no names are called out. After that it is an
uncomfortable 8 hrs to Calama. Train
Avaroa-Uyuni Thu 1200, arrives 1630. **Predilecto**
has a bus to Calama which leaves from the
terminal (T694 2330) Wed and Sun 0300, US$11,
15 hrs (depending on border crossing).

  If driving your own vehicle, from **Colchani** it is
about 60 km across to the southern shore of the
Salar. Follow the tracks made by other vehicles in

the dry season. The salt is soft and wet for about 2 km around the edges so only use established ramps. It is 20 km from the southern shore to Colcha K military checkpoint. From there, a poor gravel road leads 28 km to San Juan then the road enters the Salar de Chiguana, a mix of salt and mud which is often wet and soft with deep tracks which are easy to follow; 35 km away is Chiguana, another military post, then 45 km to the end of this Salar, a few kilometres before border at Ollagüe. This latter part is the most dangerous; very slippery with little traffic. Alternatively, take the route that tours use to Laguna Colorada and continue to Hito Cajones. **Toñito Tours** of Uyuni will let you follow one of their groups and even promise help in the event of a breakdown. There is no fuel between Uyuni and Calama (Chile) if going via Ollagüe, or San Pedro de Atacama. Keep to the road at all times; the road is impassable after rain, and there are still a few unmarked sections along the border that are mined!

❶ Directory

Uyuni *p283, map p285*
Banks Banco de Crédito, Av Potosí, entre Bolívar y Arce, changes cash occasionally. **Prodem**, Arce near Av Potosí, US$ cash at fair rates, Visa and Mastercard cash advances 5% comission, Mon-Fri 0830-1230 and 1430-1800, Sat 0830-1130. Several casas de cambio along Av Potosí, rates vary greatly, shop around, poor rates for TCs. **Internet** Many places in town, US$0.55 per hr. **Post offices** Av Arce esq C Cabrera. **Telephones** Several offices in town. **Useful addresses** Immigration: Av Sucre 94, corner of Av Potosí, T693 2062, open daily 0830-1200, 1400-1900 for visa extensions.

San Cristóbal *p284*
Bank For exchange at weekends only.
Internet By satellite, US$1.20 per hr.
Telephones Public phone in entrance to Hotel San Cristóbal.

Tupiza → *Phone code: 02. Colour map 6, grid B3. Population: 20,000. Altitude: 2,990 m.*

Set in a landscape of colourful, eroded mountains and stands of huge cactii, Tupiza, 200 km south of Uyuni, is a pleasant town with a lower altitude and warmer climate than Uyuni, making it a good alternative for visits to the Reserva Nacional Eduardo Avaroa and the Salar. There are also many things to do in the area and is best known as the place from which to take **Butch Cassidy and the Sundance Kid tours**. You can take bike rides, horse and jeep tours in the surroundings, eg the Quebrada Palala with the nearby 'Stone Forest', the Valle de los Machos and the Quebrada Seca. The Cañón del Inca is another site well worth visiting and there is a difficult and beautiful full-day trek: Tupiza-Cañón del Inca-Palala-Tupiza (guides or detailed route description available from Tupiza Tours). Another local option is *turismo rural*, staying in nearby rural communities, arranged by local agencies usually in conjunction with horse riding tours. The statue in the main plaza is to **Avelino Aramayo** (1802-1882), of the Aramayo mining dynasty, pre-eminent in the late 19th, early 20th centuries. **Chajra Huasi**, a palazzo-style, abandoned home of the Aramayo family across the Río Tupiza, may be visited. Beautiful sunsets over the fertile Tupiza valley can be seen from the foot of a statue of Christ on a hill behind the plaza. Market days are Monday, Thursday and Saturday, with local produce sold in the northern part of town; there is also a daily market at the north end of Avenida Chichas. **IGM office** ① *ground floor of Sub-Prefectura, next to the church, Mon-Fri 0800-1200 and 1500-1800*, topographic maps of southern Departamento de Potosí (including Salar de Uyuni and Lípez regions).

San Vicente → *Population: 400. Altitude: 4,500 m.*

Tupiza is the centre of Butch Cassidy and the Sundance Kid country and there are tours following their last few days. On 4 November 1908, they held up an Aramayo company payroll north of Salo. (**Aramayo hacienda** in Salo, one hour north of Tupiza, still stands. One-day tours from Tupiza go to the site of the hold-up, Huaca Huañusca.) Two days later they were killed by a four-man military police patrol in San Vicente, a silver and antimony mining camp. (Shoot out site off main street – ask locals.) Butch and Sundance are buried in the cemetery, but the grave has yet to be identified (ask around for the keyholder). An investigation of the supposed grave by the Nova project in 1991 proved negative, but see *Digging Up Butch and Sundance*, by Anne Meadows (Bison Books, 1996). There is no lodging, but ask at the mine office, who may find you a room. To get to San Vicente there are tours from hotels and agencies in Tupiza (see Listings, below); there is public transport once or twice a week from Tupiza or Atocha.

South to Argentine border → *Bolivian time is 1 hr behind Argentina.*

Villazón (81 km south of Tupiza) The Argentine border is here at Villazón (Phone code: 02; Cotevi phone company prefix 596, Entel 597, Population: 13,000, Altitude: 3,443 m). There is not much to see (good indoor market). Although not humid, Villazón and Bermejo, further east, are nonetheless widely considered the hottest towns in Bolivia, so dress accordingly. The border area must not be photographed.

Border with Argentina Bolivian immigration office is on Avenida República de Argentina just before bridge; open daily 0600-2000. They issue entry and exit stamps. Officials are efficient. For Argentine immigration see page 156. Once in Bolivia, boys offer to wheel your bags uphill to the bus stations, US$0.65, but they will ask for more. Change all your bolivianos into dollars or pesos, because there are no exchange facilities in La Quiaca and bolivianos are not accepted in Argentina. The Argentine consulate is at Plaza 6 de Agosto 117, upstairs; open Monday-Thursday 1000-1300.

● Sleeping

Tupiza *p289*
E Mitru, Av Chichas 187, T/F694 3001, www.tupiza tours.com. In new rooms with bath, **F** in older rooms with bath, **F** with shared bath (only 4 rooms left), **B** for suite with sitting room. All include breakfast. Very good, hot water, pool, games room, cable TV, parking, use of kitchen, luggage store, safes, book exchange, laundry (discount for hotel guests) and clothes-washing facilities, surcharge on credit card payments and TCs.
E Hostal Valle Hermoso, Av Pedro Araya 478, T694 2592, www.bolivia.freehosting.net. Good hot showers, breakfast included (**G** with shared bath and no breakfast), pleasant TV/breakfast room, breakfast extra, book exchange, tourist advice, *Butch Cassidy* video, firm beds, motorbikes can be parked in restaurant, accepts credit cards and TCs (5% extra). Second location, **Valle Hermoso 2**, Av Pedro Araya 585, T694 3441, near the bus station, refurbished house, 3 simple rooms with bath, several dorms for 6 or 8 with bunk beds, same prices as No 1, 10% discount for IYHF members in both locations.
F Mitru Anexo, Abaroa 20, T694 3002. **G** with shared bath, includes breakfast, restaurant, use of kitchen, use of pool and games room at Hotel Mitru.
E-F La Torre, Av Chichas 220, T694 2633, latorrehotel@yahoo.es. **G** with shared bath and no TV, includes breakfast, lovely refurbished house, comfortable rooms, good value, great service, use of kitchen. Recommended.
F Hostal Pedro Araya, Av P Araya 494, T694 2734, hostalarraya@hotmail.com. Convenient to bus and train stations, **G** with shared bath, hot water, includes small breakfast, modern comfortable rooms, use of kitchen, laundry, terrace. Check bill and confirm arrangements carefully.
G Renacer Chicheño, Barrio Ferroviario, Casa 18, T694 2718, hostalrenacer-ch@hotmail.com. Cheaper with shared bath, includes basic

breakfast, family home, use of kitchen.
G Res Centro, Av Santa Cruz 287, 2 blocks from station, T694 2705. Nice patio, motorbike and car parking, couple rooms with bath, most shared, basic but clean, hot water on request, parking, helpful owner, good value.

South to Argentine border: Villazón *p290*
E-F Res El Cortijo, 20 de Mayo 338, behind post office, T596 2093. Breakfast included, some rooms with bath, intermittent hot water, restaurant.
F Grand Palace, 25 de Mayo 52, 1 block southwest of bus terminal, T596 5333. Safe, hot water, **G** without bath, no breakfast, was recommended but since changed hands.
F Hostal Plaza, Plaza 6 de Agosto 138, T597 3535. Modern, smart, **G** without bath, TV, comfortable, good restaurant, *La Perla*, underneath hotel.
G Hostal Buena Vista, Av Antofagasta 508, T596 3055. Good rooms, shared bath, hot showers US$1.05, close to the train and bus stations, above reasonable restaurant.
G Res Panamericano, C 20 de Mayo 384, T596 2612. Shared bath, risky electric showers, sagging beds, laundry facilities, parking.

❼ Eating

Tupiza *p289*
ŤŤ-Ť Two places outside town serve speciality meals in rural surrounds on weekends only: La Estancia, 2 km north in Villa Remedios, best on Sun, *picante de cabrito* (spicy goat); La Campiña, in Tambillo Alto, 45 mins' walk north along the river, *cordero a la cruz* (lamb on the spit) and *lechón* (suckling pig).
Ť California, Cochabamba on main plaza, daily 0800-2300. Breakfast, pizza, vegetarian and regional dishes, popular with gringos.
Ť El Escorial, Chichas esq Abaroa. Good value set meal at midday, à la carte in the evening.
Ť Il Bambino, Florida y Santa Cruz. Recommended,

especially for *salteñas*, closed Sat and Sun evenings.

☕ La Casa de Irma, in supermarket *Frial Castro*, Florida. Only prepares meals for groups with several hours advance notice, lasagnes, chicken, meat and vegetarian dishes.

☕ Los Helechos, next door to *Mitru Anexo* on Abaroa. Burgers and main courses, vegetarian options, good salad bar, closed alternate Suns.

South to Argentine border: Villazón *p290*
Better to cross the border to La Quiaca to eat.
☕ El Repostero, opposite market. Serves good breakfasts and lunches.
☕ Snack El Turista, Edificio de Turismo. Open at 0900 for breakfast.

▲ Activities and tours

Tupiza *p289*
One-day jeep tours US$11-12; horse riding US$2-2.50 per hr; 2-day San Vicente plus colonial town of Portugalete US$55; Salar de Uyuni and Reserva Avaroa, 4 days with Spanish speaking guide, US$85-100 low season, US$90-120 high season (tours out of Tupiza are more expensive than those out of Uyuni because of the additional 400 km travelled). Prices per person based on groups of 6, add US$10 per day for English speaking guide. Some agencies include in their price entrance fees to Reserva Avaroa and Isla del Pescado.
Tupiza Tours, in *Hotel Mitru* (address above), are the most experienced and are at the higher end of the market. They have additional tours: 'triathlon' of riding, biking and jeep in the surroundings, US$22 pp (frequently recommended), and extensions to the Uyuni tour.
Valle Hermoso Tours, inside *Hostal Valle Hermoso 1*, T/F694 2592. Also recommended, offers similar tours, as do several new agencies. Most hotels listed have an agency.

◉ Transport

Tupiza *p289*
Bus There is small, well-organized, bus terminal at the south end of Av Pedro Arraya. To **Villazón** 0400, 1430, US$1.50, 2½ hrs. To **Potosí**, 1000, 2000, US$5.25, 7 hrs (change here for **Sucre**). Road from Potosí which goes on south to Villazón is 2-way, dirt, with a bridge over the Río Suipacha. To **Tarija**, 1930, 2000, US$5, 8 hrs (change here for **Santa Cruz**). To **Uyuni**, 11 de Julio, Mon, Thu, Sat at 1000, US$4.40, 8 hrs, poor vehicles; also 6-8 passenger jeeps daily at 0600 and 1030 (**12 de Octubre**) US$6.25, 5 hrs. To **Oruro**, 1200, 2030, US$6.25, 13 hrs (change here for **Cochabamba**). Expreso Tupiza has a direct

bus to **La Paz** at 1000 (La Paz-Tupiza at 1930, 15 hrs), otherwise via Potosí, 17 hrs, US$7.50.
Train Train station ticket office open Mon-Sat 0800-1100, 1530-1730, and in the early morning half an hour before trains arrive. To **Villazón**: Expreso del Sur Tue and Sat 0330, arriving 0630; Wara Wara Mon and Thu at 0830, arriving 1200. To **Atocha**, **Uyuni** and **Oruro**, *Expreso del Sur* Tue and Fri at 1840; *Wara Wara* Mon and Thu at 1850. Fares are given under Oruro.

South to Argentine border: Villazón *p290*
Bus Bus terminal is near plaza, 5 blocks from the border. There are lots of company offices jumbled together. Taxi to border, US$0.35 or hire porter, US$0.65, and walk across. From **La Paz**, several companies, 18 hrs, US$8.75 (even though buses are called 'direct', you may have to change in Potosí, perhaps to another company), depart La Paz 1630, depart **Villazón** 0800-0830. To **Potosí** several between 0800-0830 and 1800-1900, 10 hrs by day, 12 hrs at night, US$6 (terrible in the wet, can take 24 hrs; freezing at night). To **Tupiza**, several daily, US$1.50. To **Tarija**, beautiful journey but most buses overnight only, daily at 2000-2030, US$3, 6½ hrs, very cold on arrival but passengers can sleep on bus until daybreak.
Road An unpaved road goes to Tarija, improved for the last 16 km. The road linking Potosí with Villazón via Camargo is in poor condition and about 100 km longer than the border road via Tupiza.
Train Station about 1 km north of border on main road, taxi US$2.35. To **Tupiza**, **Atocha**, **Uyuni** and **Oruro**: Expreso del Sur Tue, Fri, 1530, **Wara Wara del Sur** Mon, Thu 1530. Ticket office opens 0800; take a number and wait till you are called.

◉ Directory

Tupiza *p289*
Banks No ATM in town. Banco de Crédito, on main plaza, Mon-Fri 0830-1230, 1430-1700, fair rates for cash, US$5 commission for Visa/MasterCard cash advances. **Prodem**, Cochabamba on main plaza, Mon-Fri 0830-1230, 1430-1800, Sat 0900-1200, fair rates for cash, 5% commission for Visa/MasterCard cash advances (no debit cards). **Cooperativa El Chorolque**, Av Santa Cruz 300 y Abaroa, Mon-Fri 0900-1600, Sat 0900-1100, cash only. **Cambios Latin America**, Abaroa y Santa Cruz, open daily or knock on door (long hours), bargain for best cash rate, 6% commission for TCs. **Tupiza Tours** gives cash against Visa, Mastercard and Tcs.
Internet Many internet places, US$0.70 per hr.
Post offices On Abaroa, northwest of plaza, Mon-Fri 0830-1800, Sat 0900-1700, Sun 0900-1200.
Telephones Several Entel offices, including

one on the plaza and another across the street from the bus station.

South to Argentine border: Villazón *p290*
Banks Banco de Crédito, Oruro 111, changes cash only; try the *casas de cambio* on Av República de Argentina, uphill from the border. **Internet** Several internet places, US$1.50 per hour. **Post offices** Av Independencia, opposite side to bus station. **Telephones** Entel office on the corner of Plaza 6 de Agosto and Gilberto Cortez.

Central and Southern Highlands

This region boasts two World Cultural Heritage sites, the mining city of Potosí, the source of great wealth for colonial Spain and of indescribable hardship for many Bolivians, and Sucre, the white city and Bolivia's official capital. In the south, Tarija is known for its fruit and wines and its traditions which set it apart from the rest of the country.

Potosí → *Phone code: 02. Colour map 6, grid B3. Population: 112,000. Altitude: 4,070 m.*

Potosí is the highest city of its size in the world. It was founded by the Spaniards on 10 April 1545, after they had discovered indigenous mine workings at Cerro Rico, which dominates the city. Immense amounts of silver were once extracted. In Spain 'es un Potosí' (it's a Potosí) is still used for anything superlatively rich. By the early 17th century Potosí was the largest city in the Americas, but over the next two centuries, as its lodes began to deteriorate and silver was found elsewhere, Potosí became little more than a ghost town. It was the demand for tin – a metal the Spaniards ignored – that saved the city from absolute poverty in the early 20th century, until the price slumped because of over-supply. Mining continues in Cerro Rico – mainly tin, zinc, lead, antimony and wolfram.

Ins and outs

Getting there The airport, the world's highest, is 5 km out of town on the Sucre road. There are no scheduled flights. The bus terminal is 20 minutes downhill walk or a short taxi or micro ride from the centre of town on Avenida Universitaria below rail station, T624 3361. **Entel,** post office, police, US$0.10 terminal tax. ▸▸ *For more detailed information see Transport, page 296.*

Tourist office On Plaza 6 de Agosto, T622 7405, gobmupoi@cedro.pts.entelnet.bo. Town maps US$0.40 (English, French, German and Spanish), better than glossy US$0.60 map (Spanish only), helpful. Open Monday-Friday 0800-1200, 1400-1800 (allegedly). The police station by the Alcaldía has a photo album showing common scams. Beware fake "plainclothes policemen", usually preceded by someone asking you for the time. The official police wear green uniforms and work in pairs. ▸▸ *See La Paz, page 243 for Safety hints.*

Sights

Large parts of Potosí are colonial, with twisting streets and an occasional great mansion with its coat of arms over the doorway. UNESCO has declared the city to be 'Patrimonio de la Humanidad' (World Cultural Heritage site). Some of the best buildings are grouped round the Plaza 10 de Noviembre. The old Cabildo and the Royal Treasury – Las Cajas Reales – are both here, converted to other uses. The **Cathedral** ① *faces Plaza 10 de Noviembre, Mon-Fri 0930-1000, 1500-1730, Sat 0930-1000, guided tour only, US$1.*

The **Casa Nacional de Moneda**, or Mint, is nearby ① *on C Ayacucho, T622 2777, Tue-Sat 0900-1200, 1400-1830, Sun 0900-1200, US$3, US$3 to take photos, US$3 for video, entry by regular, 2-hr guided tour only (in English at 0900, usually for 10 or more people).* Founded in 1572, rebuilt 1759-1773, it is one of the chief monuments of civil building in Hispanic America. Thirty of its 160 rooms are a museum with sections on mineralogy, and an art gallery in a splendid salon on the first floor. One section is dedicated to the works of the acclaimed 17th-18th century religious painter Melchor Pérez de Holguín. Elsewhere are coin dies and huge wooden presses which made the silver strips from which coins were cut. The smelting houses have carved altar pieces from Potosí's ruined churches.

You cannot fail to notice the huge, grinning mask of Bacchus over an archway between two principal courtyards. Erected in 1865, its smile is said to be ironic and aimed at the departing Spanish. Wear warm clothes, as it is cold inside.

Convento y Museo de Santa Teresa ① *Chicas y Ayacucho, T622 3847, 0900-1100, 1500-1700, only by guided tour in Spanish or English, US$3.15, US$1.50 to take photos, US$25(!) for video*. A guide is obligatory to this interesting collection of colonial and religious art. Among Potosí's baroque churches, typical of 18th-century Andean or 'mestizo' architecture, are the Jesuit **Compañía** church ① *on Ayacucho, 0800-1200, 1400-1800*, with an impressive bell-gable. **San Francisco** ① *Tarija y Nogales, T622 2539, Mon-Fri 0900-1700, 1430-1700, Sat 0900-1200, US$1.50, US$1.50 to take photos, US$3 for video*, with a fine organ, worthwhile for the views from the tower and roof, museum of ecclesiastical art, underground tunnel system. Also **San Lorenzo** (1728-1744) *on Héroes del Chaco*, with a rich portal and fine views from the tower. **San Martín**, on Hoyos, with an uninviting exterior, is beautiful inside, but is normally closed for fear of theft. Ask the German Redemptorist Fathers to show you around; their office is

Potosí

Sleeping 🛏
Backpackers Potosí **1** *D3*
Carlos V **2** *C3*
Casa de María Victoria **3** *D2*
Claudia **4** *A1*
El Turista **5** *D2*
Hostal Cerro Rico **7** *D3*
Hostal Colonial **8** *C3*
Hostal Compañía de Jesús **16** *C3*
Hostal Felimar **9** *B2*
Hostal Libertador **10** *D3*
Hostal Santa María **11** *A1*
Jerusalem **12** *B1*

Koala Den **19** *B3*
Posada San Lorenzo **13** *B2*
Residencial Copacabana **14** *A2*
Residencial Felcar **15** *A2*
Residencial Sumaj **17** *B1*
Tarija **18** *A2*

Eating 🍴
4060 Café **6** *C3*

Café La Plata **10** *C2*
Café Tokyo **9** *C2*
Chaplin **1** *C2*
Confitería Cherry's **2** *C3*
El Fogón **3** *C2*
El Mesón **11** *C3*
Kaypichu **4** *C3*
La Casona Pub **5** *C2*
Potocchi **7** *C3*
Sumaj Orcko **8** *C2*

just to the left of their church. Other churches to visit include **Jerusalén** ① *Plaza del Estudiante, Mon-Sat 1430-1830, US$0.75*, with **Museo Sacro** displaying gold work and painting. On the opposite side of Plaza del Estudiante is **San Bernardo** ① *Mon-Fri 0800-1200, 1400-1800*, which houses the Escuela Taller Potosí where you can see a display of restoration work. **San Agustín**, Bolívar y Quijarro, with crypts and catacombs (the whole city was interconnected by tunnels in colonial times) is open only by prior arrangement with the tourist office. Tour starts at 1700, US$0.10.

Teatro Omiste (1753) *on Plaza 6 de Agosto*, has a fine façade. The **Museo Universitario** ① *C Bolívar 698, Mon-Fri, 0800-1200, 1400-1800, US$0.75*, displays archaeology and some good modern Bolivian painting. **Museo del Ingenio de San Marcos** ① *Betanzos y La Paz, T622 2781, 1000-2300; restaurant 1200-2300, information office 1130-1230, 1430-1530, exhibition Mon-Sat 1300-2000*. This is a well-preserved example of the city's industrial past, with machinery used in grinding down the silver ore. It also has a restaurant, cultural activities and an exhibition of Calcha textiles. **Museo Etno-indumentario** (also known as **Fletes**) ① *Av Serrudo 152, T622 3258, Mon-Fri 0900-1200, 1400-1800, Sat 0900-1200, US$1.10, includes tour in Spanish and German*. This very interesting museum has a thorough display of the different dress and customs and their histories of Potosí department's 16 provinces.

In Potosí, 2,000 colonial buildings have been catalogued. At Quijarro and Omiste is the Esquina de las Cuatro Portadas (two houses with double doors), or Balcón de Llamacancha. Off Junín, see the Pasaje de Siete Vueltas (the passage of the seven turns). There is a fine stone doorway (house of the Marqués de Otavi, now a bank) in Junín between Matos and Bolívar. At Lanza 8 was the house of José de Quiroz and of Antonio López de Quiroga (now a school). Turn up Chuquisaca from Lanza and after three blocks right into Millares; here on the left is a sculpted stone doorway and on the right a doorway with two rampant lions in low relief on the lintel. Turning left up Nogales you come to an old mansion in a little plaza. Turn left along La Paz and one block along there is another stone doorway with suns in relief. At La Paz y Bolívar is the Casa del Balcón de la Horca. Turn left for the Casa de las Tres Portadas.

Mine tours

For many, the main reason for being in Potosí is to visit the mines of Cerro Rico. The state mines were closed in the 1980s and are now worked as cooperatives by small groups of miners. A 4½-hour morning tour to the mines and ore-processing plant involves meeting miners and seeing them at work in medieval conditions. Cerro Rico was described by one Spanish chronicler in the mid-16th century as 'the mouth of hell', and visitors should be aware that descending into its bowels is both physically and emotionally draining. The tour, as *Koala Tours* proclaim, is 'not for wimps or woosies'. The mine entrances are above 4,000 m and you will be walking, or rather crouching, around breathing in noxious gases and seeing people working in appalling conditions in temperatures up to 40°C. You should be acclimatized, fit and not have any heart or breathing problems, such as asthma. The guided tours run by Potosí agencies are conducted by former miners; by law all guides have to work with a travel agency and carry an ID card issued by the Prefectura. Essential equipment is provided: helmet, lamp and usually protective clothing (check when booking and ask about the level of difficulty of the tour). Wear old clothes and take torch and a handkerchief to filter the dusty air. The size of tour groups varies – some are as large as 20 people, which is excessive. The smaller the group the better. The price of tours is US$14 per person and includes transport. A contribution to the miners' cooperative is appreciated, as are medicines for the health centre (*Posta Sanitaria*) on Cerro Rico. Saturday and Sunday are the quietest days (Sunday is the miners' day off).

Tarapaya

A good place to freshen up after visiting the mines (or to spend a day relaxing) is Tarapaya, where there are thermal baths, Tarapaya itself (in poor condition) and Miraflores (public, US$0.30, private, US$0.60). On the other side of the river from Tarapaya is a 50 m diameter crater lake, whose temperature is 30° C; take sun protection. Below the crater lake are boiling ponds but on no account swim in the lake. Several people have drowned in the boiling waters and agencies do not warn of the dangers. Buses, micros and colectivos go from the bus terminal, outside Chuquimia market on Avenida Universitaria, every 30 minutes, 0700-1700, US$0.55. Taxi US$7.50 for a group. Last colectivo back to Potosí at 1800. Camping by the lake is possible and there is accommodation at Balneario Tarapaya.

Sleeping

Potosí p292, map p293
Unless otherwise stated hotels have no heating.
C Claudia, Av Maestro 322, T622 2242, claudia_hotel@hotmail.com. This modern hotel is away from the centre. Helpful staff. Recommended.
C Hostal Colonial, Hoyos 8, T622 4809, F622 7146. A pretty colonial house near the main plaza, with heating and basic breakfast, TV, has names and telephone numbers of guides, very helpful, even if you're not staying there, safe parking, best hotel in centre. Book in advance.
C Hostal Libertador, Millares 58, T622 7877, hostalib@cedro.pts.entelnet.bo. Central heating, quiet, helpful, comfortable, parking.
D Hostal Cerro Rico, Ramos 123 entre La Paz y Millares, T/F622 3539. Very good rooms upstairs, heating, hot water, **D** without bath, cable TV, internet, helpful, parking.
D Jerusalem, Oruro 143, T/F622 2600, hoteljer@cedro.pts.entelnet.bo. Pleasant, with breakfast, **F** without bath, helpful, *comedor*, parking, laundry, good value.
E Hostal Compañía de Jesús, Chuquisaca 445, T622 3173. Central, attractive, good value, includes breakfast.
E Hostal Felimar, Junín 14, T622 4357. Hot water, includes breakfast, very good, 2 roof-top suites, basement rooms have no exterior windows but warm, quiet.
F Carlos V, Linares 42 on Plaza 6 de Agosto, T622 5121. With breakfast, **G** without bath, occasional hot water 0700-1200, luggage store, 2400 curfew.
F Hostal Santa María, Av Serrudo 244, T622 3255. Hot water, cold rooms, cafetería, popular.
F El Turista, Lanza 19, T622 2492, F622 2517. Also *LAB* office, helpful, hot showers, breakfast (US$1), great view from top rooms, good value. Recommended but poor beds.
F Koala Den, Junín 56, T622 6467, see *Koala Tours*, below, but book separately. Refurbished, with heated dormitory (**F**) and shared showers, private rooms with bath and breakfast, TV and video and use of kitchen.
G pp Backpackers Potosí, Chuquisaca 460 y Padilla, T04-644 0889, potosi@boliviahostels.com. Recent addition to the network of budget hostels.
G Casa de María Victoria, Chuquisaca 148, T622 2132. All rooms open onto colonial courtyard, cheaper without bath, hot water, stores luggage, popular as budget choice, arranges mine tours, owner speaks English, good breakfast, leave nothing unattended.
G Posada San Lorenzo, C Bustillos 967, opposite market. Colonial building, courtyard, no showers.
G Res Copacabana, Av Serrudo 319, T622 2712. Single or shared rooms, restaurant, separate hot showers, will change $ cash, safe car park.
G Res Felcar, Serrudo 345 y Bustillos, T622 4966. Shared bath, hot water 0800-1600, popular, nice patio garden.
G Res Sumaj, Gumiel 12, T622 2336, hoteljer@cedro.pts.entelnet.bo. Small dark rooms with shared bath, kitchen, laundry, TV lounge, helpful, popular with travellers.
G Tarija, Av Serrudo 252, T622 2711. Poorly signed but the more expensive rooms are good, cheaper without bath, helpful, large courtyard for parking.

Eating

Potosí p292, map p293
♥♥ El Mesón, Plaza 10 de Noviembre, T622 3087. Excellent food, upmarket but good value.
♥♥-♥ La Casona Pub, Frías 34, T622 2954. Good food (meat fondue and trout recommended) and beer, nice atmosphere and service, open Mon-Sat 1000-1230, 1815-2400.
♥♥-♥ El Fogón, Oruro y Frías, T622 4969. Upmarket pub-restaurant, good food and atmosphere, open 1200-1500, 1800-2400.
♥♥-♥ Potocchi, Millares 24, T622 2467. Great traditional food, opens 0800, *peña* most nights.
♥ Chaplin, Quijarro y Matos 10. Pleasant, good breakfasts and fast food, vegetarian options, best *tucumanos*, closed 1200-1500 and Sun.
♥ Kaypichu, Millares 24. Vegetarian, stylish, good breakfasts, open 0700-1300 and 1600-2100, closed Mon.
♥ Sumaj Orcko, Quijarro 46. Large portions, cheap set lunch, reasonably priced, very popular with travellers, heating.

Cafés
4060 Café, Hoyos entre Padilla y Millares. 'Hip' place serving interesting food, more upmarket surroundings and pricier than others.
Café La Plata, Plaza 10 de Noviembre at Linares. For breakfast and then 1500-2200, closed Sun, good for coffee, cookies and cakes, wine and beer. English and French spoken. **Confitería Cherry's**, Padilla 8. Good cakes, popular, good breakfast, cheap, slow service, open 0800.
Café Tokyo, Oruro y Cobija. Good food, good value and service.

Festivals and events

Potosí p292, map p293
8-10 Mar is San Juan de Dios, with music, dancing, parades etc. In **May** there is a market on C Gumiel every Sun, with lotteries and lots of fun things for sale. **Fiesta de Manquiri**: on 3 consecutive Sat at the **end of May/beginning of Jun** llama sacrifices are

made at the cooperative mines in honour of *Pachamama*; the same occurs on **1 Aug**, the **Ritual del Espíritu**. Carnaval Minero, 2 weeks before carnival in Oruro, includes Tata Ckascho, when miners dance down Cerro Rico and El Tío (the *Dios Minero*) is paraded. **San Bartolomé**, or the **Fiesta de Chutillos**, is held from the middle of **Aug**, with the main event being processions of dancers on the weekend closest to the **24th-26th**; Sat features Potosino, and Sun national, groups. Costumes can be hired in *artesanía* market on C Sucre. Hotel and transport prices go up by 30% for the whole of that weekend. In **Oct**, Festival Internacional de la Cultura, in Potosí and Sucre. **10 Nov**, Fiesta Aniversiario de Potosí. Potosí is sometimes called the 'Ciudad de las Costumbres', especially at Corpus Cristi, Todos Santos and Carnaval, when special cakes are baked, families go visiting friends, etc.

Shopping

Potosí *p292, map p293*
Germán Laime, Sucre 38. Tailor, will make items (jackets, bags, etc) to customers' wishes.
Mercado Artesanal, at Sucre y Omiste, sells handwoven cloth and regional handicrafts. Some Fridays the merchants organize music, food and drink (*ponche*), not to be missed.
Mercado Central (see address above), sells mainly food and produce but silver is sold near the C Oruro entrance.

Activities and tours

Potosí *p292, map p293*
Trips to the Salar de Uyuni, Laguna Colorada and Laguna Verde are expensive here. See page 284 for advice on booking a trip.
The following have been recommended:
Amauta Expediciones, Ayacucho 17, T622 5515. For trips to Uyuni, the lagoons and the mines. Gerónimo Fuentes has been recommended and speaks English. 15% of income goes to the miners.
Andes Salt Expeditions, Plaza Alonso de Ibáñez 3, T622 5175, www.bolivia-travel.com.bo. Recommended guides. Run by Braulio Mamani, who speaks English. Daily city tours, bus and flight tickets, also have an office in Uyuni.
Carola Tours, Lanza y Chuquisaca. Guide and owner Santos Mamani is recommended.
Cerro Rico Travel, Bolívar 853, T622 7044, T718-35083 (mob), jacky_gc@yahoo.com. Jaqueline knows the mines well and speaks good English. Also English and French guides for trips to village *artesanía* markets north of the city and to colonial *haciendas*, horse and

mountain bike hire, treks, trips to Toro Toro.
Hidalgo Tours, Junín y Bolívar 19, T622 5186, uyusalht@ceibo.entelnet.bo. Upmarket and specialized services within the city and to Salar de Uyuni. Efraín Huanca has been recommended for mine tours.
Koala Tours, Ayacucho 5, T/F622 2092, frontpoi@cedro.pts.entelnet.bo. Run by Eduardo Garnica Fajardo who speaks English and French. Excellent mine tours by former miners, Juan Mamani Choque and Pedro Montes Caria have been recommended. The company donates 15% of its fees to support on-site health-care facilities. Frequently recommended. They also have a hostal, *The Koala Den*, see Sleeping, and an internet café, see below.
Silver Tours, Quijarro 12, Edif Minero, T622 3600, www.silvertours.8m.com. One of the cheaper firms, guide Fredi recommended.

Transport

Potosí *p292, map p293*
Bus When you buy your ticket you check your luggage into the operator's office and it is then loaded directly onto your bus. Daily services: to **La Paz** 1830-1930, US$5, 10 hrs by paved road, *bus cama* with **Flota Copacabana** US$7.50 (all departures from La Paz 1830-2030). To travel by day, go to **Oruro**, 0700 and 1900, US$2.50, 5 hrs. To **Cochabamba** 1830 and 1900, US$4.50, 12 hrs. To **Sucre** 4 daily 0700-1800, US$3, 3 hrs. Cars run to Sucre, taking 5 passengers, 2½ hrs, US$3.75 pp, drop-off at your hotel. To **Santa Cruz** 1900 (change in Sucre or Cochabamba), US$12, 18 hrs. To **Villazón** 0800, 1900, US$6, 10-12 hrs. To **Tarija** 1800, US$6.70-7.45, 12 hrs, spectacular journey but crowded bus. Buses to **Uyuni** leave from either side of the railway line (uphill the road is called Av Antofagasta or 9 de Abril, downhill it is Av Universitaria), 5 daily 1030 to 1930, US$3.10, 6 hrs, superb scenery; book in advance.
A **taxi** in town costs US$1.

Directory

Potosí *p292, map p293*
Banks There are ATMs around the centre. Banco Nacional, Junín 4-6. Exchange for US$ TCs and cash. Banco Mercantil, Sucre y Ayacucho. 1% commision on US$ TCs, no commission on Visa cash withdrawals. Almost opposite is Casa Fernández for cash exchange. Banco de Crédito, Bolívar y Sucre. Cash withdrawals on Visa. Prodem, Bolívar y Junín. Cash advances on Visa and MasterCard, 5% commission, also changes US$ cash. Many shops on Plaza Alonso de Ibáñez and on Bolívar, Sucre and Padilla

display 'compro dólares' signs. **Internet** All
US$0.75 per hr. Café Candelaria, Ayacucho 5,
T622 8050, also crafts, postcards, book exchange
(see *Koala Tours*, above). Tuko's Café, Junín 9,
p 3, T622 5489, tuco25@hotmail.com.
Open 0800-2300, 'the highest net café
in the world'; lots of information, English spoken,
popular music, videos, good food. Another
opposite bus terminal. **Post offices** Lanza 3,
Mon-Fri 0800-2000, Sat 0800-1800, Sun

0900-1200. **Telephones** Entel, on Plaza Arce
at end of Av Camacho, T624 3496. Also at Av
Universitaria near bus terminal, and on Padilla,
opposite *Confitería Cherys*. **Useful**
addresses Migración: Linares esq Padilla, T622
5989. Mon-Fri 0830-1630, closed lunchtime,
beware unnecessary charges for extensions.
Police station: on Plaza 10 de Noviembre.

Sucre → *Phone code: 04. Colour map 6, grid B3. Population: 131,769. Altitude: 2,790 m.*

Sucre has grown rapidly since the mid-1980s following severe drought which drove campesinos
from the countryside and the collapse of tin mining in 1985. Founded in 1538 as La Plata, it
became capital of the audiencia of Charcas in 1559. Its name was later changed to Chuquisaca
before the present name was adopted in 1825 in honour of the second president of the new
republic. Sucre is sometimes referred to as La Ciudad Blanca, owing to the tradition that all
buildings in the centre are painted in their original colonial white. This works to beautiful effect
and in 1992 UNESCO declared the city a 'Patrimonio Histórico y Cultural de la Humanidad'
(World Cultural Heritage site). There are two universities, the older dating from 1624.

Ins and outs
Getting there Juana Azurduy de Padilla airport is 5 km northwest of town (T645 4445). **Bus
terminal** is on north outskirts of town, 2 km from centre on Ostria Gutiérrez, T645 2029; taxi
US$0.75; Micro A or *trufi* No 8. Taxis cost US$0.45 per person within city limits. ▸▸ *For more
detailed information see Transport, page 302.*

Information Tourist office, Estudiantes 25, T644 7644, open Mon-Fri 0900-1200, 1500-1830,
very helpful, English and French spoken, sells copies of town map, US$0.15; also at the bus
station, allegedly open Monday-Friday 1000-1230, 1500-1730, Saturday 0800-1200; and at the
airport, to coincide with incoming flights. For country maps try Instituto Geográfico Militar, Arce
172, 1st floor, T645 5514. Open Monday-Friday 0830-1200, 1430-1800. As in Potosí and La Paz,
beware fake police and immigration officials and gangs of youths by the market.

Sights in the centre
Plaza 25 de Mayo is large, spacious, full of trees and surrounded by elegant buildings. Among
these are the **Casa de la Libertad** ① *T645 4200, Tue-Fri 0900-1115, 1430-1745, Sat 0930-1115,
US$1.50 with tour; US$1.50 photos, US$3 video.* Formerly the Assembly Hall of the Jesuit
University, where the country's Declaration of Independence was signed, this house contains a
famous portrait of Simón Bolívar by the Peruvian artist Gil de Castro, admired for its likeness.
Also on the Plaza is the beautiful 17th century **Cathedral** ① *entrance through the museum in
Calle Ortiz, if the door is locked wait for the guide, Mon-Fri 1000-1200, 1500-1700, Sat
1000-1200, US$1.50.* Worth seeing are the famous jewel-encrusted Virgin of Guadalupe, 1601,
and works by Viti, the first great painter of the New World, who studied under Raphael.
  San Felipe Neri ① *Azurduy y Ortiz, T645 4333, US$1 (extra charge for photos) with a free
guide from Universidad de Turismo office on Plaza 25 de Mayo.* The neoclassical church is
closed but ask the guide to gain access. The roof (note the penitents' benches), which
offers fine views over the city, is only open for an hour between 1630 and 1800 (times change).
The monastery is used as a school. Diagonally opposite is the church of **La Merced**, which is
notable for its gilded central and side altars. **San Miguel** (1130-1200), completed in 1628, has
been restored and is very beautiful with Moorish-style carved and painted ceilings, *alfarjes*
(early 17th century), pure-white walls and gold and silver altar. In the Sacristy some early
sculpture can be seen. Entry is not allowed if you are wearing shorts, short skirts or short
sleeves. **Santa Mónica**, Arenales y Junín, is perhaps one of the finest gems of Spanish
architecture in the Americas, but has been converted into a *salón multiuso* (multipurpose
space). **San Francisco** (1581) ① *in C Ravelo, 0700-1200, 1500-1900,* has altars coated in
gold leaf and 17th century ceilings; the bell is the one that summoned the people of Sucre to

struggle for independence. **San Lázaro** (1538) ⓘ *Calvo y Padilla, daily for mass 0630-0730, 1830-1930.* This is regarded as the first cathedral of La Plata (Sucre). On the nave walls are six paintings attributed to Zurbarán; it has fine silverwork and alabaster in the Baptistery.

Museo Textil-Etnográfico ⓘ *San Alberto 413 (Casa Capellánica), between San Lázaro and Plaza 25 de Mayo, T645 3841, www.bolivianet.com/asur, Mon-Fri 0830-1200, 1430-1800, Sat 0930-1200 (and Sat afternoon Jul/Aug/Sep), US$2, English, German and French-speaking guide.* Run by *Antropológicas del Surandino (ASUR)*, this excellent museum displays of regional textiles and traditional techniques, shop sells crafts. **Museo de Santa Clara** ⓘ *Calvo 212, Mon-Fri 0900-1200, 1500-1800, Sat 0900-1200, US$0.75.* As well as displays of paintings, books, vestments, some silver and musical instruments (including a 1664 organ), there is a window to view the church. Small items made by the nuns on sale. A few blocks away, the **Museo Universitario Charcas** ⓘ *Bolívar 698, Mon-Fri 0800-2000, Sat 0900-1200, 1500-1800, Sun 0900-1200, US$1.50, photos US$1.50,* has anthropological, archaeological and folkloric exhibits, and colonial collections and presidential and modern-art galleries.

Four blocks northwest of Plaza 25 de Mayo is the **Corte Suprema de Justicia** (free) the seat of Bolivia's national judiciary, and rationale behind the city's official status as being one of Bolivia's two capitals. To enter you must be smartly dressed and leave your passport with the guard; guides can be found in library. The nearby **Parque Bolívar** contains a monument and a miniature of the Eiffel tower in honour of one of Bolivia's richest 20th-century tin barons, Francisco Argandoña, who created much of Sucre's splendour. The **obelisk** opposite the Teatro Gran Mariscal, in Plaza Libertad, was erected with money raised by fining bakers who cheated on the size and weight of their bread. Also on this plaza is the Hospital Santa Bárbara (1574).

Sights outside the centre

Southeast of the city, at the top of Dalence, lies the Franciscan convent of **La Recoleta** with good views over the city and the **Museo de la Recoleta** ⓘ *C Pedro de Anzúrez, Mon-Fri 0900-1130, 1430-1630, US$1.20 for entrance to all collections, guided tours only.* It is notable for the beauty of its cloisters and gardens; the carved wooden choir stalls above the nave of the church are especially fine (see the martyrs transfixed by lances). In the grounds is the Cedro Milenario, a 1,400-year-old cedar. **Tanga Tanga** ⓘ *Iturricha 297, La Recoleta, T644 0299, Tue-Sun 0900-1200, 1430-1800,* is an interactive children's museum with art, music, theatre, dance and books (the excellent *Café Mirador* is in the garden). Behind Recoleta monastery a road flanked by Stations of the Cross ascends an attractive hill, **Cerro Churuquella**, with large eucalyptus trees on its flank, to a statue of Christ at the top. In the cemetery are mausoleums of presidents and other famous people, boys give guided tours; take Calle Junín south to its end, 7 to 8 blocks from main plaza.

About 5 km south on the Potosí road is the **Castillo de la Glorieta** ⓘ *daily 0830-1200, 1400-1800, US$1.* The former mansion of the Argandoña family, built in a mixture of contrasting European styles with painted ceilings, is in the military compound. Ask to see the paintings of the visit of the pope, in a locked room. Take any bus marked 'Liceo Militar' from the Plaza, or bus or trufi 4 or E. Some 7 km north of Sucre is **Cal Orcko** ⓘ *T645 1863, guided tours at 1000 and 1230, tours in English are available for US$2.* At this extensive area of dinosaur footprints, found in the Fancesa cement works, tracks from three types of dinosaur have been identified. Recommended, but don't expect any high-tech explanations or tourist facilities. Tour agencies charge US$10 per person as do taxi drivers who have trained as guides (untrained drivers charge US$7); ask tourist office for approved drivers. The wonderfully cheesy **Dino Truck** leaves daily 0930, 1200, 1430 from main plaza, US$4, minimum five people, good explanations in English.

Tarabuco → *Colour map 6, grid B4. Altitude: 3,295 m.*

Tarabuco, 64 km southeast of Sucre, is best known for its colourful ndigenous market on Sunday, with local people in traditional dress. It starts around 0930-1000 and is very popular with tourists, but still an enjoyable experience. Those in search of a bargain should have an idea about the quality on offer. The *Phujllay* independence celebration in mid-March is very colourful and lively. No one sleeps during this fiesta. There is budget accommodation. Try the Plaza or food stalls in market offering tasty local dishes. A good guide is *Alberto* from Sucre tourist office, US$45 for a full day in a car for four people. The market is not held at Carnival (when all Tarabuco is dancing in Sucre), Easter Sunday or on the holiday weekend in November.

Sucre to Paraguay

A road runs southeast from Sucre, through Tarabuco, to **Monteagudo** where there are several hotels including **E Fortín** ① *Plaza 20 de Agosto 1-2, T647 2135*, with bath, TV, includes breakfast, **F Alojamiento los Naranjos**, on road to bus terminal, hot showers, and a few restaurants. There are daily buses from Monteagudo to **Santa Cruz** (book early), US$8, 14 hours. The road then joins the road south from Santa Cruz to **Camiri** and **Boyuibe** (see page 328), from where a road heads east to the border with Paraguay at **Hito Villazón** (not to be confused with Villazón on the border with Argentina, see page 290). Most public transport goes south through Villamontes and a new road east to Paraguay, or continues south to **Yacuiba** on the border with Argentina (see page 328). The journey is beautiful through mountains. The easiest way to reach **Paraguay** from Sucre is to take a bus to Santa Cruz, then an international bus or flight to **Asunción**. Alternatively, take the bus to Camiri

Sucre

To Mercado Campesino

To Plaza Huallparimachi & Buses to Tarabuco & southeast

To Plaza Huallparimachi & Buses to Tarabuco & southeast

To La Recoleta Monastery

To La Paz   To Cemetery   To Potosí

To Museo Tanga Tanga & Tarabuco

Bolivia Sucre

0 metres   100
0 yards   100

Sleeping 🛏
Alojamiento La Plata **3** *C2*
Austria **4** *B3*
Avenida **17** *B1*
Backpackers Sucre
  Hostel **2** *C1*
Casa de Huéspedes
  Finita **22** *D3*
Casa de Huéspedes
  San Marcos **1** *B2*

Colonial **6** *C2*
El Hostal de Su Merced **7** *D2*
Gloria **8** *B3*
Grand **9** *C2*
Hostal Colón **5** *D1*
Hostal Cruz de Popayán **2** *C1*
Hostal Libertad **10** *C2*
Hostal Los Piños **11** *D1*
Hostal San Francisco **12** *B2*
Hostal Sucre **13** *D1*
La Posada **20** *D2*
Municipal Simón
  Bolívar **14** *A1*
Paola Hostal **21** *D1*

Potosí **15** *B1*
Real Audiencia **16** *D3*
Residencial Bolivia **18** *C2*
Residencial Charcas **19** *C2*

Eating 🍴
Arco Iris **1** *D2*
Bibliocafé **2** *D2*
Café Hacheh **4** *B1*
Café Mirador **5** *D3*
El Germen **6** *C3*
Joy Ride Café **8** *D2*
Kultur-Café Berlin **10** *D3*
La Casona **11** *B3*

La Plaza **13** *C2*
La Repizza **14** *D2*
La Taverne **15** *C2*
La Vieja Bodega **7** *D2*
Locot's Café
  Aventura **3** *C3*
Penco Penquito **16** *C2*
Pizzería
  Napolitano **13** *C2*
Salon de Té
  Las Delicias **17** *C2*

Bars & clubs 🍸
La Luna **12** *D2*

299

(*Emperador* at 1730 or *Andes Bus*, 1800, on alternate days, 18 hours, US$4.30). From Camiri take a colectivo to **Villamontes** (three hours, US$5), but stop in Boyuibe to get an exit stamp. In Villamontes, catch the Santa-Cruz-Asunción bus around 0600. Bargain hard not to pay the full Santa Cruz-Asunción fare. (See also page 328.)

● Sleeping

Sucre *p297, map p299*

B Real Audiencia, Potosí 142, T/F646 0823, realaudiencia2000@hotmail.com. Modern, large rooms, excellent restaurant, heated pool. Recommended.

C El Hostal de Su Merced, Azurday 16, T644 2706, sumerced@mara.scr.entelnet.bo. Beautifully-restored colonial building, more character than any other hotel in the city, owner and staff speak French and English, good breakfast buffet, internet, sun terrace, restaurant. Recommended.

C Paola Hostal, C Colón 138, T645 4978, paolahostal@pelicano.cnb.net. Comfortable, helpful hotel, with bath and jacuzzi, laundry, cafetería for snacks, internet, airport transfer.

C La Posada, Audiencia 92, T646 0101, www.laposadahostal.com. Smart, colonial-style, comfortable, ADSL internet, good courtyard restaurant.

C Refugio Andino Bramadero, 30 km from the city, details from Raul y Mabel Cagigao, Avaroa 472, T645 5592, bramader@yahoo.com. Cabins or rooms, well-furnished, full board, drinks and transport included, excellent value, owner Raul is an astronomer and advises on hikes, book in advance. Recommended.

D Colonial, Plaza 25 de Mayo 3, T645 4079, hoscol@mara.scr.entelnet.bo. Some rooms noisy, but generally recommended, good breakfast included.

D Hostal Cruz de Popayán, Loa 881 y Colón, T644 0889, popayan@boliviahostels.com. **F** without bath, also has dorms (**G** pp), breakfast included, free internet, in a colonial building, rooms around 3 courtyards, use of kitchen, coffee shop, laundry service, book exchange, can arrange transport and language classes, many good reports.

D Hostal Libertad, Arce y San Alberto, p 1, T645 3101, T646 0128. Spacious comfortable rooms, hot water and heating, TV, some rooms with good views.

D Hostal Sucre, Bustillos 113, T645 1411, hostalsucre@hotmail.com/hosucre@mara.scr.ent elnet.bo. Comfortable if plain rooms around 2 patios, TV, room service, breakfast included.

D Kantu Nucchu, 21 km southwest of Sucre, details from Augusto Marion, San Alberto 237, T438 0312, tursucre@mara.scr.entelnet.bo. With bath, kitchen, full board, **G** pp without meals, peaceful, colonial hacienda, hiking, swimming. Recommended.

D-E Municipal Simón Bolívar, Av Venezuela 1052, T645 5508, F645 1216. Including breakfast in patio, helpful and comfortable, restaurant.

E Austria, Av Ostria Gutiérrez 506, near bus station, T645 4202. Hot showers, redecorated, great beds and carpeted rooms, some cable TV, cafetería, parking, **G** rooms available and, next door, **G** in the *Alojamiento* (parking extra).

E Grand, Arce 61, T645 1704, granhot@mara.scr.entelnet.bo. Comfortable (ask for room 18), ground floor at the back is noisy, hot showers, includes poor breakfast in room, good value lunch in *Arcos* restaurant, laundry, safe, motorcycle parking. Recommended.

E Hostal los Piños, Colón 502, T645 4403, H-Pinos@mara.scr.entelnet.bo. Comfortable, hot showers, nice garden, quiet, peaceful, includes breakfast, laundry, kitchen, parking.

E Res Charcas, Ravelo 62, T645 3972, hostalcharcas@latinmail.com. **F** without bath, good value, huge breakfast extra, hot showers, runs bus to Tarabuco on Sun.

F Casa de huéspedes Finita, Padilla 233, T645 3220, delfi_eguez@hotmail.com. 2 rooms with bath, others without, breakfast included, hot water, heaters, **E** with full board for long stay, works with students studying Spanish.

F Hostal Colón, Colón 220, T645 5823, colon220@bolivia.com. Clean, laundry, helpful owner speaks English and German and has tourist information, breakfast included, coffee room, very nice.

F Hostal San Francisco, Av Arce 191 y Camargo, T645 2117, hostalsf@cotes.net.bo. Breakfast and other meals available, quiet, patio, laundry, excellent value.

F Res Bolivia, San Alberto 42, T645 4346, F645 3239. **G** without bath, spacious rooms, electric showers, fair beds, includes breakfast, clothes washing not allowed, safe and helpful.

G Alojamiento La Plata, Ravelo 32, T645 2102. Without bath, limited shower facilities, basic, noisy, good beds, popular with backpackers (lock rooms at all times).

● *For an explanation of the sleeping and eating price codes used in this guide, see page 58. Other*
● *relevant information is found in Essentials pages 240-241.*

G Avenida, Av H Siles 942, T645 1245. Hot showers, breakfast US$1, laundry, helpful, use of kitchen.

G pp Backpackers Sucre Hostel, Loa 891 esq Colón, T644 0889, sucre@ boliviahostels.com. A good bet for travellers, includes breakfast, safe, internet, laundry, luggage store, travel information. Recommended.

G Casa de Huéspedes San Marcos, Arce 223, T646 2087. Cheaper without bath, flower-filled patio, use of kitchen, quiet. Recommended.

G Gloria, Av Ostria Gutiérrez 438, T645 2847, opposite bus station. Great value.

G Potosí, Ravelo 262, T/F645 1975, castro@sucre.bo.net. Basic rooms around courtyard, popular, helpful, internet, good value, better rooms at the front.

Eating

Sucre p297, map p299
Many fruit juice and snack stalls in the central market; clean stalls also sell cheap meals (US$0.75-1.40). The local sausages and chocolate are recommended.

₩ Arco Iris, Bolívar 567. Swiss restaurant, good service and food, *peña* on Sat, excellent *rösti*, live music some nights.

₩ El Huerto, Ladislao Cabrera 86, T645 1538. International food with salad bar, good *almuerzo*, in a beautiful garden. Take a taxi there at night.

₩ La Casona, Ostria Guitiérrez 401, near bus terminal. Stylish, *platos típicos*, good value.

₩ El Germen, San Alberto 231. Vegetarian, set lunches (US1.80), excellent breakfast, US$1.05-2.10, open Mon-Sat 0800-2200, book exchange, German magazines. Recommended.

₩ Pizzería Napolitano, Plaza 25 de Mayo 30. Pizzas and pasta, home-made ice cream, good lunch options till 1700.

₩ La Plaza, Plaza 25 de Mayo 33. Good food, popular with locals, set lunch US$2.10, open 1200-2400.

₩ La Repizza, N Ortiz 78. Good value lunches, good pizzas in evening.

₩ La Taverne of the *Alliance Française*, Aniceto Arce 35, ½ block from plaza. Closed Sun evening, *peñas* Fri-Sat in Jul and Aug, good French food, also regular cultural events.

Cafés

Amanecer, Junín 855, German *pastelería*, run by social project supporting disabled children, opens 1530.

Bibliocafé, N Ortiz 50, near plaza. Good pasta and light meals, *almuerzo* US$3 1100-1600, closes 2000 (opens 1800 on Sun), music and drinks.

Café Hacheh, Pastor Sainz 233. Great coffee bar with art gallery, tasty lunch and fresh juices, open

1100-2400 (at 1700 on Sun), '70s style. Highly recommended.

Café Mirador, Iturricha 297 in Tanga Tanga museum garden, La Recoleta. Not cheap, but great coffee, fine views, good snacks and music.

Joy Ride Café, N Ortiz 14, same Dutch owner as *Joy Ride Bolivia* (see Tour operators). Great food and drink, good salads, open 0730 till late (0900 at weekends), very popular, upstairs lounge shows films Sun-Thu. Recommended.

Kultur-Café Berlin, Avaroa 326, open 0800-2400 (except Sun). Good breakfasts, computer with internet access, German newspapers, *peña* every other Fri (in same building as *Instituto Cultural Boliviano Alemán – ICBA*), popular meeting place.

Locot's Café Aventura, Bolívar 465, T691 5958, www.locotsbolivia.com. Open 0800 till late, fun, bright café serving international, Mexican and Bolivian food, live music and theatre, wireless internet, European/Bolivian owned, also has agency offering 'adrenaline activities', mountain biking, hiking, riding, paragliding.

Penco Penquito, Arenales 108. Excellent coffee and cakes.

Salon de Té Las Delicias, Estudiantes 50. Great cakes and snacks, open 1600-1900.

Tertulias, Plaza 25 de Mayo 59. Italian and other dishes, breakfasts, poor service.

La Vieja Bodega, N Ortiz 38. Good value, cheapish wine.

Bars and clubs

Sucre p297, map p299
La Luna, Argentina 65, back of Casa de la Cultura. Video pub with occasional live music, popular.

Mitsubanía, Av del Maestro y Av Venezuela. Club popular with local, younger, fashionable crowd, mixture of music with lots of *cumbia*, US$3 for men, women do not pay.

Rock Bar Chatarra, Junín esq Colón. Popular bar, open late, well-decorated.

Festivals and events

Sucre p297, map p299
24-26 May: Independence celebrations, most services, museums and restaurants closed on 25. **8 Sep**: Virgen de Guadalupe, 2-day fiesta. **Sep:** Festival Internacional de la Cultura, 2nd week, shared with Potosí. **21 Sep**: Día del Estudiante, music around main plaza.

Shopping

Sucre p297, map p299
Handicrafts Antropológicos del Surandino, *ASUR*, San Alberto 413, T642 3841 (in the *Museo*

Textil-Etnográfico). Weavings from around Tarabuco and from the Jalq'a. Weavings are more expensive, but of higher quality than elsewhere. **Artesanías Calcha**, Arce 103, opposite San Francisco church. Recommended, knowledgeable proprietor. **Chocolates para Tí**, San Alberto, just off Plaza, T 645 4260, www.chocolates-para-ti.com. One of the best chocolate shops in Sucre. Others can be found on Arce and Arenales. **Fundación Aprecia**, Raul F de Córdova 49, just off Colón, T642 4718. A workshop for blind weavers making beautiful rugs (they can make to order with advance notice).

Markets The central market is clean and colourful with many stalls selling *artesanía*, but beware theft. A bus from the central market will take you to the **Mercado Campesino** near football stadium.

▲ Activities and tours

Sucre *p297, map p299*
Bolivia Specialist, Bolívar 525, www.boliviaspecialist.com. Dutchman Dirk Dekker's agency for local hikes, horse riding and 4WD trips, tours throughout Bolivia and Peru, loads of information and connections.
Candelaria Tours, Audiencia No 1, C 322, T646 1661, F646 0289. Organizes excursions and also organizes Bolivian textile fashion shows, English spoken.
Joy Ride Bolivia, N Ortiz 14, T642 5544, www.joyridebol.com. Mountain biking and hiking tours. Sign up and get information at Joy Ride Café (see above).
Locot's Adventure, see Locot's Café Aventura under Eating, above. For many types of adventure sport.
Seatur, Plaza 25 de Mayo 24, T/F646 2425, seatur@latinmail.com. Local tours, English, German, French spoken.
Sur Andes, N Ortiz 6, T645 3212, F645 2632. Organizes trekking from half a day to 5 days, eg to pre-Columbian sites such as **Pumamachay** and the **Camino Prehispánico** (take sleeping bag and good shoes, all else provided, but no porters).

❷ Transport

Sucre *p297, map p299*
Air Aero Sur flies to **La Paz**, **Santa Cruz** and **Tarija**, LAB flies to **Cochabamba**. Few flights are daily. Aero Sur, Arenales 31, T645 4895. **LAB**, Bustillos 121, T645 2666 (Toll free 0800 3001). Airport minibus goes from entrance and will drop you off on Siles y Junín, and returns from here, 1½ hrs before flight (not always), US$0.70, 20-30

mins. Taxi US$4-5. *Trufis* No 1 and F go from entrance to H Siles y Loa, 1 block from main plaza, US$0.55, 25 mins.
Bus Daily to/from **La Paz** at 1830-2000, 13 hrs, US$7.50-10 (**Flota Copacabana** and **Trans Copacabana** have *bus-cama*). To **Cochabamba**: several companies daily at 1830, arriving 0630, US$4.50-5.25 (Trans Copacabana *bus-cama*, US$7.50). To **Potosí**: 3 hrs on a paved road, frequent departures between 0630 and 1800, US$3. **Silito Lindo** taxis take 4 people to Potosí for US$3.75; T644 1014. To **Tarija**: several companies, 16hrs, US$5.25-6. To **Uyuni**: 0700 (**Emperador**), 0800 (**Trans Capital**), 9 hrs, US$5. Or catch a bus to Potosí and change; try to book the connecting bus in advance – see *Trans Real Audencia*. To **Oruro**: 1700 with **Emperador** via Potosí, arrives 0300, US$5 (*bus-cama*, US$15). To **Santa Cruz**: many companies go between 1600 and 1730, 15 hrs, US$6-7.50. To **Villazón**: at 1300 (**Transtin Dilrey**, direct) and 1400 (**Villa Imperial**, via Potosí) both 15 hrs, US$8.20. **Trans Real Audencia**, Arce 99 y San Alberto (same entrance as Hostal Libertad), T644 3119, for hassle-free bus tickets reservations to: **Potosí** (US$3), **Uyuni** (US$6.70), **Villazón** and **Tupiza** (US$7.45), **Tarabuco** (Sun 0700 from outside office, US$3 return).
To Tarabuco Buses (US$1.25) leave 0630 or when full from Plaza Huallparimachi, Av Manco Capac, or across the railway (take micro B or C from opposite Mercado), 2½ hrs (or taxi, US$45). On Sunday only, at least one bus will wait on Ravelo by the market for travellers, charging US$3 return to Tarabuco. Shared trufi taxis can be arranged by hotels, with pick-up service, starting at 0700, US$3.25 return. First bus back 1300; you must return on the bus you went on. *Andes Bus* run tourist services, departing 0800 (or when full), returning 1430, US$3, book at office, take food and drink. Transport more difficult on weekdays; take an early bus and return by truck.
Car hire Imbex, Serrano 165, T646 1222, www.imbex.com. Recommended.
Road 164 km from **Potosí** (fully paved) 366 km to **Cochabamba** (for 1st hr from Sucre road is OK, terrible to **Epizana**, then paved).

❶ Directory

Sucre *p297, map p299*
Banks There are many *Enlace* 24hr ATMs around town. **Banco Nacional**, España esq San Alberto. Cash given on Visa and MasterCard US$3 commission, good rates for dollars, TCs changed, 5% commission. Diagonally opposite is **Banco Santa Cruz**. Good rates for cash, advances on Visa, MasterCard and Amex, US$10 fee. Travel agencies' rates are good and at **España**, España 134, T646 0189, changes for TCs, 3% commission

into US$, free into bolivianos, 9% commission on euro TCs. **Casa de Cambio Ambar**, San Alberto 7, T645 1339. Good rates for TCs. Stalls at corner of Camargo and Arce buy and sell cash $ as well as Argentine, Chilean and Brazilian currency, but not as good rates as *cambios*. Many shops and street changers on Hernando Siles/Camargo buy and sell $ cash. **Cultural centres** The Instituto Cultural Boliviano-Alemán (Goethe Institute), Avaroa 326, T645 2091, www.icba-sucre.edu.bo. Shows films, has German newspapers and books to lend (0930-1230 and 1500-2100), runs Spanish, German, Portuguese and Quechua courses and has the *Kulturcafé Berlín* (see above). Spanish lessons cost from US$6 for 45 mins for 1 person, with reductions the more students there are in the class. The *ICBA* also runs a folk music *peña* on Fri. **Centro Cultural Masis**, Bolívar 561, T645 3403. Promotes the Yampara culture through textiles, ceramics, figurines and music. Instruction in Quechua, traditional Bolivian music (3 hrs a week for US$15 a month, recommended) and handicrafts; stages musical events and exhibitions; items for sale. Open Mon-Sat 1430-2000 (knock if door closed); contact the director, Roberto Sahonero Gutierres at the centre Mon, Wed and Fri. **Alianza Francesa**, Aniceto Arce 35, T645 3599, www.afbolivia.org/_es/sucre.php. Offers Spanish classes. **Centro Boliviano Americano**, Calvo 301, T644 1608, http://lapaz.usembassy.gov/cbasucre/cba.htm. Library open Mon-Fri 0900-1200, 1500-2000 (good for reference works). Recommended for language courses. The **Centro Cultural Hacheh** (see address for *Café Hacheh* above), run by Felix Arciénega, Bolivian artist who organizes folk and jazz concerts, conferences, exhibitions and discussions, and is the editor of an art and poetry journal 'Hacheh'. **Casa de la Cultura**, Argentina 65, presents art exhibitions, concerts, folk dancing etc. **Embassies and consulates** Germany, Eva Kasewitz de Vilar, Rosendo Villa 54, T645 1369, ekvilar@mara.scr.entelnet.bo. Italy, Vice Consul, Martín Cruz 51, T645 5858. Paraguay, Plaza 25 de Mayo 28, T642 2999. Perú, Avaroa 472, T645 5592. **Internet** Many around town, generally slow connections, average US$0.60 per hr. **Language schools** Academia Latinoamericana de Español, Dalence 109, T646 0537, www.latinoschools.com. Professional, good extracurricular activities, US$90 for 5 full days (US$120 for private teacher – higher prices if you book by phone or email). Bolivian Language School, C Kilómetro 7 250, T644 3841, www.bolivianspanishschool.com. Near Parque Bolívar, pleasant school, good value, excellent teachers. Margot Macias Machicado, Olañeta 345, T642 3567, www.spanish-classes.8m.net. US$5 per hr. Recommended. Sofia Sauma, Loa 779, T645 1687, sadra@mara.scr.entelnet.bo. US$5 per hr. Private teachers advertise in bars etc. **Medical services** For hospitals, doctors and dentists, contact your consulate or the tourist office for recommendations. **Post offices** Ayacucho 100 y Junín, open till 2000 (1600 Sat, 1200 Sun), good service. *Poste Restante* is organized separately for men and women. **Telephones** Entel, España 252. 0730-2300. **Useful addresses** Immigration: Pastor Sáenz 117, T645 3647, Mon-Fri 0830-1630. Police radio patrol: T110 if in doubt about police or security matters.

Tarija → *Phone code: 04. Colour map 6, grid B4. Population: 109,000. Altitude: 1,840 m.*

Tarija, a pleasant, small city, with a delightful climate and streets and plazas planted with flowering trees, is often called the 'Andalucía of Bolivia' for its resemblance to that region of Spain. It is known for its fruit and wines and its traditions which set it apart from the rest of the country. The best time to visit is from January onwards, when the fruit is in season. The *indígena* strain is less evident here than elsewhere in Bolivia, but Tarija has a strong cultural heritage. Founded 4 July 1574 in the rich valley of the Río Guadalquivir, the city declared itself independent of Spain in 1807, and for a short time existed as an independent republic before joining Bolivia. In Plaza Luis de Fuentes there is a statue to the city's founder, Capitán Luis de Fuentes Vargas. The **tourist office** ① *on the main plaza in the Prefectura, T663 1000, Mon-Fri 0800-1200, 1430-1830*, is helpful, city map and guide for US$0.20 each. Also at Sucre y Bolívar.

Sights The oldest and most interesting church in the city is the **Basílica de San Francisco** ① *corner of La Madrid y Daniel Campos, 0700-1000, 1800-2000, Sun 0630-1200, 1800-2000*. It is beautifully painted inside, with praying angels depicted on the ceiling and the four evangelists at the four corners below the dome. The library is divided into old and new sections, the old containing some 15,000 volumes, the new a further 5,000. The oldest book is a 1501 *Iliad* incorporating other works. There are also old manuscripts and 19th century photograph albums. To see the library, go to the door at Ingavi 0137. Tarija's **university museum** ⓘ *Trigo y Lema, Mon-Fri 0800-1200, 1500-1800 (Sat opens at 0900), free, small donation appreciated,* contains a palaeontological collection (dinosaur bones, fossils, remains of an Andean elephant), as well as smaller mineralogical, ethnographic and anthropological collections. **Casa Dorada** ⓘ *Trigo y Ingavi (entrance on Ingavi), Mon-Fri 0900-1200, 1500-1800, Sat 0900-1200, guided tours only; donation (minimum US$0.30).* Also known as Maison d'Or, it is now the Casa de Cultura, begun in 1886. It belonged to importer/exporter Moisés Narvajas and his wife Esperanza Morales and has been beautifully restored inside and out; the photography room contains pictures of Tarijan history and the restoration of the house. Near Parque Bolívar (shady, pleasant) is another of Narvajas' houses, the **Castillo de Beatriz**, Bolívar between Junín and O'Connor; much of house is off-limits, but ask the owner if it is possible to visit. If no answer, enquire at the museum. The outskirts of the city can be a good place to look for **fossils**: take a micro or taxi in the direction of the airport. 5 km out of town, before the police control (*garita*), you see lovely structures of sand looking like a small canyon (*barrancos*). Here have been found bones, teeth, parts of saurian spines, etc; things come to the surface each year after the rains. You may have to go a long way from the city. About 15 km from the centre is the charming village of **San Lorenzo**. Just off the plaza is the **Museo Méndez** ⓘ *0900-1230, 1500-1830, minimum US$0.30 entry,* the house of the independence hero Eustaquio Méndez, 'El Moto'. The small museum exhibits his weapons, his bed, his 'testimonio'. At lunchtime on Sunday, many courtyards serve cheap meals. Take a trufi from Barrio del Carmen, at the roundabout just north of San Juan Church. They return from San Lorenzo plaza; 45 mins, US$0.45.The road to San Lorenzo passes **Tomatitas** (5 km) a popular picnic and river bathing area.

Bodegas Aranjuez bodega is a short walk across the river at Avenida Los Sauces 1976 (shop at 15 de Abril O-0241): ask Sr Milton Castellanos at the Agrochemical shop at Trigo 789 (Monday-Friday 1000-1200, 1500-1730, Saturday 0900-1200); he can also arrange visits to *Campos de Solana* (shop 15 de Abril E-0259). Farther afield is the **Rugero Singani** bodega at **El Valle de Concepción**, 36 km south of Tarija. An appointment must be made at Bodegas y Viñedos de la Concepción, La Madrid y Suipacha s/n, T664 3763. Visitors are given guided tours of the vineyards and the bodega. *Trufis* go from Parada del Chaco every 20-30 minutes, US$0.75, return from plaza. Note that all *bodegas* are closed on Sunday. See also Activities and tours page 305.

To Argentina → *Bolivia is 1 hr behind Argentina.*
The road to Villazón, 189 km, is the shortest route to Argentina, but a tiring seven hours in all (only the first 15 km is paved). The alternative route via Bermejo is the most easily reached from Tarija, 210 km, the views are spectacular (sit on right); not recommended in the rainy season or a month or so after. The first 50 km out of Tarija, and the last 20 km to Bermejo are paved. Many buses daily, usually at night, some early morning, 4-5 hours, US$7.75. At **Bermejo** (Population 13,000, Altitude: 415 m) there a few hotels and two *casas de cambio* on main street. Note there are thorough customs searches here and it's very hot. (Expect to spend up to 4 hours at customs and immigration. Electronic goods must be entered in your passport for later checks.) Cross river by ferry to Aguas Blancas, in Argentina. From Tarija to Yacuiba/Pocitos border is 290 km (see page 157). Daily buses to Yacuiba 0700-1800, 12 hours, US$5-8, mostly old buses, *Expresos Tarija* and *Narváez* are best.

⊖ Sleeping

Tarija *p303*
Blocks west of C Colón have a small O before number (oeste), and all blocks east have an E (este); blocks are numbered from Colón outwards. All streets north of Av Las Américas are preceded by N.
AL Los Parrales Resort, Urb Carmen de Aranjuez Km 3.5, T664 8444 (ask for Lic Miguel Piaggio), parrales@mail.com. Only 5-star accommodation in southern Bolivia and worth it,

European style amenities, can arrange city and vineyard tours and to Argentina, phone in advance for off-season discounts.
B Los Ceibos, Av Víctor Paz Estenssoro y La Madrid, T663 4430, ceibhot@cosett.com.bo. Including excellent buffet breakfast, large rooms, mini-bar, good restaurant, pool and cocktail bar.
C Hostal Loma de San Juan, Bolívar s/n (opposite Capela Loma de San Juan), T664 4206. Comfortable, pool, buffet breakfast included.

C **La Pasarela**, 10 km north of Tarija near the village of Coimata, T666 1333, info@lapasarelahotel.com. Belgian-owned hotel/restaurant/bar, includes breakfast, country views, tranquil, family atmosphere, living room, jacuzzi, swimming pool, internet, mountain bikes, laundry and camping.

D **Gran Hostal Baldiviezo**, La Madrid O-0443, T/F663 7711, administracion@ghb.htmlplanet.com. New hotel, central, good beds and facilities.

E **Hostal Carmen**, Ingavi O-0784 y R Rojas, T664 3372, vtb@olivo.tja.entelnet.bo. Shower, good value, F without cable TV, some ground floor rooms without exterior windows, good breakfast, transfer stand at airport, tour agency, book in advance.

F **Amancayas**, Ingavi 0-0777, residen_rosario@latinmail.com. F without bath, showers, cable TV, quiet, good value. Recommended but for the laundry.

F **Hostería España**, Alejandro Corrado O-0546, T664 1790. Hot showers, G without bath, pleasant.

F **Zeballos**, Sucre 0966, T664 2068. Nice atmosphere, G without bath, with breakfast, cable TV, quiet, safe, laundry, 5 mins from plaza.

G **Alojamiento Familiar**, Rana S 0231 y Navajas, T664 0832. Shared hot shower, no breakfast, modern, helpful, close to bus terminal, traffic noise.

🍴 Eating

Tarija *p303*
Many restaurants (and much else in town) close between 1400 and 1600.

🍴 **La Taberna Gattopardo**, on main plaza. Pizza, *parrillada* with Argentine beef, local wines, snacks, excellent salads, good value, opens 0700-0200 daily.

🍴 **Cabaña Don Pepe**, D Campos N-0138, near Av Las Américas. Excellent steaks at moderate prices, *peña* at weekends with local folk music.

🍴 **Chingo's**, on Plaza Sucre, is popular and serves cheap local food.

🍴 **Club Social Tarija**, east side of the plaza. Pleasant, old-fashioned, haunt of Tarija's business community, excellent *almuerzo* for US$1.80. Recommended.

🍴 **El Solar**, Campero y V Lema. Vegetarian, set lunch, Mon-Sat 0800-1400 only.

🍴 **Mateo's**, Trigo N-0610. Excellent *almuerzo* US$3 (includes salad bar), good value dinner, local and international dishes, pasta a speciality, closed 1530-1900 and Sun.

🍴 **Pizzería Europa**, main plaza west side. Internet (US$0.90 per hr), good *salteñas*.

La Fontana, La Madrid y Campos, is good for ice cream, snacks and coffee. For a cheap breakfast try the market. Try the local wines, eg Aranjuez,

La Concepción, Santa Ana de Casa Real or Kohlberg, the singani (a clear brandy, San Pedro de Oro and Rugero are recommended labels), also local beer, Astra.

✹ Festivals and events

Tarija *p303*
The city is famous for its colourful niño (child) processions on **15 Mar**, Día de Tarija. In **late Apr**, **Exposur** is held, approximately 20 km northwest of city; admission free; local and regional crafts, cuisine, and dances; much commercial activity as well. In the 3-day **San Roque** festival from the **1st Sun in Sep** the richly-dressed saint's statue is paraded through the streets; wearing lively colours, cloth turbans and cloth veils, the people dance before it and women throw flowers from the balconies. Dogs are decorated with ribbons for the day.
On **2nd Sun in Oct** the flower festival commemorates the **Virgen del Rosario** (celebrations in the surrounding towns are recommended, eg San Lorenzo and Padcaya). Another flower festival takes place in San Lorenzo in **Easter** week. Also in **Oct**, on 2 weekends mid-month, there is a **beer festival** on Av de las Américas. **La Virgen de Chaguaya**, **15 Aug**, people walk from Tarija to Santuario Chaguaya, south of El Valle, 60 km south of the city. For less devoted souls, Línea P *trufi* from Plaza Sucre, Tarija, to Padcaya, US$1; bus to Chaguaya and Padcaya from terminal daily, 0700, returns 1700, US$1.35.

▲ Activities and tours

Tarija *p303*
Internacional Tarija, Sucre 721, T664 4446, F664 5017. Flights and tours, helpful.
Mara Tours, Gral Trigo N-739, T664 3490, marvin@olivo.tja.entelnet.bo. Helpful.
VTB, at *Hostal Carmen* (see Sleeping above). All tours include a free city tour; 4-6 hr trips including singani bodegas, US$19 pp; comprehensive 10 hr "Tarija and surroundings in 1 Day", US$27; can also try your hand at an excavation with their palaeontology specialist!
Viva Tours, Sucre 0615, T663 8325, vivatour@cosett.com.bo. Vineyard tours US$30 with lunch.

✇ Transport

Tarija *p303*
Air Aero Sur flies to **La Paz**, **Sucre** and **Santa Cruz**. LAB flies to **Cochabamba**. Schedules change frequently; also flights are frequently cancelled and/or delayed. **Aero Sur** office: 15 de Abril entre Daniel Campos y Colón, T663 0893. LAB

office: Trigo N-0319, T644 2473. Taxi to airport, US$3.75, or *micro* A from Mercado Central which drops you 1 block away. Some hotels have free transport to town, you may have to call them. On arrival at Tarija, reconfirm your return flight immediately. Airport information T664 3135.

Bus The bus station is in the outskirts on Av de Las Américas (30 min walk from centre), T663 6508. **Potosí-Oruro-La Paz** (935 km) buses depeart daily at 0700 and 1700 (20 hrs, US$11.25; check which company operates the best buses, eg **San Lorenzo** has heating). To **Potosí** (386 km), daily at 1630, 12 hrs, US$6.70-7.45 with **AndesBus**, **San Lorenzo**, **San Jorge** and **Emperador**. To **Sucre**, direct with **Andesbus** (recommended), **Emperador** and **Villa Imperial**, depart 1600-1630, 17-18 hrs, US$5.25-6, check if you have to change buses in Potosí. To **Villazón**, several companies daily, depart morning and afternoon, 7 hrs, US$4.50, unpaved road. To **Santa Cruz**, several companies, US$10.45-12, 24 hrs over rough roads, last 140 km from Abapó is paved (between Entre Ríos and Villamontes is spectacular).

Directory

Tarija *p303*

Banks Many ATMs accept foreign cards. Banco Mercantil, Sucre y 15 de Abril. Exchanges cash and gives cash against Visa and MasterCard (US$5 authorization charge). **Banco de Crédito**, Trigo N-0784, **Banco Nacional**, Av Trigo, all change TCs. Dollars and Argentine pesos can be changed at a number of casas de cambio on Bolívar between Campos and Sucre. **Embassies and consulates** Argentina, Ballivián N-0699 y Bolívar, T664 4273, Mon-Fri, 0830-1230. Germany, Campero 321 , T664 2062, methfess@olivo.tja.entelnet.bo, helpful. **Internet** Café Internet Tarija On-Line, Campos N-0488, US$0.75 per hr. Pizzería Europa (see above), US$0.90 per hr. 2 on Plaza Sucre. **Language classes** Julia Gutiérrez Márquez, T663 2857, gringo108@hotmail.com. Recommended for language classes and information. **Post offices** V Lema y Sucre. Also at bus terminal. **Telephone** Entel, on main plaza, at V Lema y D Campos and at terminal.

Cochabamba and around

→ *Phone code: 04. Colour map 6, grid A3. Population: 594,790. Altitude: 2,570 m.*

Set in a bowl of rolling hills at a comfortable altitude, Cochabamba's unofficial title is 'City of Eternal Spring'. Its inhabitants enjoy a wonderfully warm, dry and sunny climate. Its parks and plazas are a riot of colour, from the striking purple of the bougainvillaea to the subtler tones of jasmin, magnolia and jacaranda. Bolivia's fourth largest city was founded in 1571. Today it is an important commercial and communications centre, while retaining a small-town, rural feel.

The fertile foothills surrounding the city provide much of the country's grain, fruit and coca. Markets, colonial towns and archaeological sites are all close by too. Further afield, the dinosaur tracks and great scenery at Torotoro National Park are worth an exhausting trip. The lowland route to Santa Cruz de la Sierra, now preferred to the old road over the mountains, has great birdwatching and the animal refuge in Villa Tunari deserves your support.

Ins and outs

Getting there and around The city is 394 km from La Paz by road, now completely paved. Neither airport, nor bus station are far from the centre. Buses and taxis serve both. The city is divided into four quadrants based on the intersection of Avenida Las Heroínas running west to east, and Avenida Ayacucho running north to south. In all longitudinal streets north of Heroínas the letter N precedes the four numbers. South of Heroínas the numbers are preceded by S. In all transversal streets west of Ayacucho the letter O (Oeste) precedes the numbers and all streets running east are preceded by E (Este). The first two numbers refer to the block, 01 being closest to Ayacucho or Heroínas; the last two refer to the building's number. ▶ *For more detailed information see Transport, page 312.*

Information The central **tourist office** is at Colombia E-0340, between 25 de Mayo y España, T422 1793, helpful, excellent city map and free guide; Monday-Friday 0830-1630. The tourist police are here for complaints, also at Jorge Wilstermann airport. Be careful around the markets and Plaza San Antonio and don't climb San Sebastián and La Coronilla hills.

Sights

At the heart of the old city is the arcaded **Plaza 14 de Septiembre** with the **Cathedral** dating from 1571, but much added to. Nearby are several colonial churches: **Santo Domingo**, Santiváñez y Ayacucho, begun in 1778 and still unfinished; **San Francisco**, 25 de Mayo y Bolívar, 1581, but heavily modernized in 1926; the **Convent of Santa Teresa**, Baptista y Ecuador, original construction 1760-90; and **La Compañía**, Baptista y Achá, whose whitewashed interior is completely devoid of the usual riot of late Baroque decoration.

Museo Arqueológico ① *Jordán between Aguirre and Ayacucho, Mon-Sun 0800-1700, US$2, free student guide (in Spanish, sometimes French or English).* Part of the Universidad de San Simón, this small but interesting display of artefacts includes amerindian hieroglyphic scripts and pre-Inca textiles, good 1½ hours tour. **Casa de la Cultura** ① *25 de Mayo y Av Las Heroínas, T425 9788, Mon-Fri 0800-1200, 1430-1830, free,* has a library and first editions of newspapers. Its **museum** ① *Casona Santiváñez, Santiváñez O-0156,* has exhibitions of paintings colonial and modern.

From Plaza Colón, at the north end of the old town, the wide **Avenida Ballivián** (known as **El Prado**) runs northwest to the wealthy modern residential areas. To the north of Plaza Colón lies the Patiño family's **Palacio de Portales** ① *Av Potosí 1450, T424 3137, Guided tours in Spanish Mon-Fri 1700, 1730 (in English), 1800, Sat at 1100, US$1.50, don't be late, useful library. The art gallery and gardens are open Mon-Fri 1700-1800, Sat-Sun 1000-1200.* Built in French renaissance style, furnished from Europe and set in 10 ha of gardens inspired by Versailles, the Patiño mansion was finished in 1927 but never occupied. It is now the *Centro Cultural Pedagógico Simón J Patiño*, with an excellent art gallery in the basement. Take micro G from Avenida San Martín.

To the south of the old town lie the bus and train stations and some of the best markets in Bolivia. These are very good for tourist items and souvenirs, but beware pickpockets. The huge **La Cancha market** ① *San Martín, Punata, República y Pulacayo,* is packed on Wednesday and Saturday with campesinos and well worth a visit. Woollen items are expensive but high quality (US$35-50 for an alpaca sweater). The nearby **Incallacta market** is for fruit and vegetables but also sells tourist souvenirs. There is also a Saturday market at Avenida América y Libertador, best before 0900. Overlooking the bus station is the **San Sebastián hill**, offering grand views of the city. The adjoining **La Coronilla hill** is topped by an imposing monument commemorating the defence of Cochabamba by its womenfolk against Spanish troops in 1812 (neither hill is safe to visit). At the east end of Avenida Heroínas is another hill, the **Cerro de San Pedro** ① *cable car Sun 0900-1900, Mon-Sat 1000-1800, US$1 return; US$0.15 to climb inside the statue for viewpoint,* with a statue to Cristo de la Concordia.

Around Cochabamba

Quillacollo, 13 km west of the city, has a good Sunday market and famous festival (see page 311). A few km beyond Quillacollo is a turn-off to the beautiful **Pairumani** *hacienda* ① *T426 0083 to check if it is open, Mon-Fri 1500-1600, Sat 0900-1130,* centre of the Patiño agricultural foundation, also known as **Villa Albina**, built in 1925-1932, furnished from Europe and inhabited by Patiño's wife, Albina. Take bus 7 or 38, or trufi 211 from Cochabamba. Some 27 km west of Cochabamba, near Sipe-Sipe, are **Inka-Rakay** ruins. The main attraction is the view from the site of the Cochabamba valley and the mountains around the ruins. **Tarata**, 33 km southeast of Cochabamba, is a colonial town with a traditional arcaded plaza on which stand the church (daily 0800-1300), the Casa Consistorial, and the Municipalidad. Inside the **Franciscan Convent** overlooking the town are the remains of the martyr, San Severino, patron saint of the town, more commonly known as the 'Saint of Rain'; festival, on the last Sunday of November, attracts thousands of people. Large procession on 3 May, day of La Santa Cruz, with fireworks and brass band. Market day Thursday (bus US$0.65, one hour, last return 1800). **Punata**, 48 km to the east, has a very lively market on Tuesday. It is famous for its Señor de los Milagros festival on 24 September. Behind the main church, which has many baroque/mestizo works of art, new vehicles are lined up to be blessed by the priest.

Parque Nacional Torotoro

① *US$3, local guide US$5 per day, plus his food for trips of over a day; tourist information is available at the national park office, open daily, ask here about all tours, guides, etc. In Cochabamba, Parque Portales entre Av G Villarroel y Trinidad 353, T448 6452,* *bichocu@hotmail.com*. In the province of Potosí, but best reached from Cochabamba (135 km), is **Torotoro**, a small village, set amid beautiful rocky landscape in the centre of the Parque Nacional Torotoro, covering an area of 16,570 ha and declared a National Park in 1989. Attractions include caves, a canyon, waterfalls, pictographs, ruins, fossilized dinosaur tracks and rock paintings, some of which can be seen by the Río Toro Toro just outside the village (ask directions, or take a young guide). This trip is highly recommended and tour operators now offer packages there. You should be able to speak Spanish.

Umajalanta cave, which has many stalactites and a lake with blind fish, is about 1½ hrs' walk northwest of Torotoro, with an hour's caving; a guide is necessary from the park office, US$5 per person in a group of 2-5 (take a head torch if possible). **El Vergel** waterfall can be reached without a guide, but you need good directions. The falls are fantastic, and the walk along the river bed is great fun if you like rock-hopping and skipping over pools. Fossils can be seen at Siete Vueltas, an afternoon's walk, but you need a guide. Mario Jaldín (Spanish speaking only) is knowledgeable. He lives two doors to the right of *Alojamiento Charcas*. He also leads a four-day trek to see canyons, condors, orchids, many birds and, if lucky, the Andean Bear and pumas; $80-100 per person, depending on the size of the group, includes camping gear and food, bring your own sleeping bag.

Cochabamba to Santa Cruz

The road via Chapare descends to the lowlands, with superb birdwatching on the way. The roads are manned by army and police and foreigners are subject to scrutiny. In the coca-growing territory around Villa Tunari the police advise not to stray from the main road.

The lowland road from Cochabamba to Santa Cruz runs through Villa Tunari, Sinahota and Chimoré (a centre for DEA operations; three hotels). The road is paved Villa Tunari-Santa Cruz. **Villa Tunari** is a relaxing place and holds an annual Fish Fair 5 and 6 August, with music, dancing and food. **Parque Ecoturístico Machía** ① *just outside town, free, but donations welcome*, offers good trails through semi-tropical forest. Beside the park is **Inti Wara Yassi** ① *Villa Tunari, T04-413 6572, or www.intiwarayassi.org for full information, donations welcome, to take photos US$2.25 and videos US$3.75*. This project rehabilitates animals back into the wild. Volunteering involves building rehabilitation facilities, and feeding and carrying out basic animal husbandry on a variety of monkeys, birds, wild cats and small land mammals. Living accommodation is basic, work is challenging but if you're lucky affords fascinating up-close encounters with native wildlife. A new park, Parque Ambue Ari, between Santa Cruz and Trinidad, is around 600 ha of jungle teeming with wildlife, rehabilitating pumas, monkeys, birds and bears. There is much to do and few volunteers, so lots of flexibility and opportunities, and a freer routine to allow for yoga or a morning nap after the animals' breakfast! Delicious food is provided. For transport from Cochabamba see page 312.

The mountain road The 500 km road via the mountains and Epizana to Santa Cruz is not paved and the new lowland route is preferred by most transport. Before the Siberia pass, 5 km beyond Montepunco (Km 119), the 23 km road to Pocona and Inkallajta turns off. The Inca ruins of **Inkallajta** (1463-1472, rebuilt 1525), on a flat spur of land at the mouth of a steep valley, are extensive and the main building of the fortress is said to have been the largest roofed Inca building. There are several good camping sites. The Cochabamba Archaeological Museum has some huts where visitors can stay, free, but take sleeping bag and food. Water available at nearby waterfall. The mountain road continues to Epizana, the junction for the road to Sucre, and on to Samaipata (see page 326).

● Sleeping

Cochabamba *p306, map p309*
There are many cheap places to stay near the bus station but most are short-stay and unsafe.
A Aranjuez, Av Buenos Aires E-0563, T428 0076, www.aranjuezhotel.com. 4-star, small, colonial style, good restaurant, jazz in the bar Fri-Sat night, small pool open to public (US$1). Recommended.
B Ambassador, España N-0349, T425 9001, ambassrv@comteco.entelnet.bo. Modern, central

and reasonable, includes breakfast, good restaurant.
B Gran Hotel Cochabamba, Plaza Ubaldo Anze, T428 2551, cbbhotel@bo.net. Beautifully set in the north part of the city (2 blocks from Los Portales at La Recoleta), with garden, swimming pool (US$3 for non-guests) and tennis courts, popular with tour groups. Recommended.
C Americana, Esteban Arce S-788, T425 0554, americana@mail.infornetcbba.com.bo. Fan,

Cochabamba

Bolivia Cochabamba & around Listings

N

0 metres 100
0 yards 100

Sleeping 🛏
Alojamiento Escobar **2** *E2*
Ambassador **1** *B2*
Americana **3** *E2*
Aranjuez **21** *A3*
Boston **4** *C2*
Cochabamba
  Backpackers **20** *E2*
Gran Hotel
  Cochabamba **22** *A3*
Hostal Buenos Aires **14** *B2*
Hostal Elisa **7** *E1*
Hostal Florida **8** *D2*
Hostal Ossil **11** *E1*
Hostería Jardín **9** *C1*
Ideal **10** *B2*

Maracaibo **11** *E1*
Regina **12** *B2*
Residencial Familiar **15** *D2*
Residencial Familiar
  Annex **16** *C2*
Residencial Jordán **17** *D3*
Residencial Jordán
  Annex **18** *D2*
Virgen de Copacabana **19** *E2*

Eating 🍴
Brazilian Coffee Bar **4** *B2*
Bufalo **5** *A3*
Café Express Bolivar **6** *C2*
Casablanca **23** *B2*
Comida Vegetariana **7** *B2*

Dumbo **8** *C2*
El Griego **21** *B2*
Eli's Pizza **9** *C2*
Gopal **11** *C2*
Habana Café **12** *B2*
La Cantonata **14** *B2*
Marco's **16** *D3*
Metrópolis &
  Metrópolis Pizza **17** *B2*
Picasso **18** *B2*
Snack Uno **19** *C2*
Souvenir **1** *B2*
Suiza **20** *A2*

Bars & clubs 🍸
Wunderbar **22** *B3*

309

helpful, lift, laundry, parking, *Rodizio* grill next door, good service.

D Boston, C 25 de Mayo 0167, T422 8530, hboston@supernet.com.bo. Restaurant, luggage deposit, quiet rooms at back, safe parking. Recommended but cheaper rooms not so good.

D Ideal, España N-0329, T423 5175. Includes breakfast, TV, restaurant, comfortable, good value but noisy at weekends from bar below.

D Regina, Reza 0359, T425 7382, hregina@supernet.com.bo. Spacious, efficient, breakfast extra, restaurant.

F Alojamiento Escobar, Aguirre S-0749, T422 5812. Recently upgraded, good value (not to be confused with *Residencial* at Uruguay E-0213).

F Hostal Buenos Aires, 25 de Mayo N-0329, T425 4005. **G** without bath, pleasant, clean communal baths, breakfast US$1.35.

F Hostal Elisa, Agustín López S-0834, T425 4404, F423 5102. **G** without bath, good showers, hot water, good breakfast US$2.25, modern, garden, 2 blocks from bus station, laundry service, very popular with travellers, helpful owner, but small single rooms and area is a bit dodgy at night.

F Hostal Florida, 25 de Mayo S-0583, T425 7911, floridah@elsito.com. **G** without bath or cable TV, hot water, noisy, popular, laundry service, safe deposit box, internet, breakfast.

E Hostería Jardín, Hamiraya N-0248, T424 7844, jaguirre@latinmail.com. **F** without bath, garden, safe car and motorcycle parking, good breakfast included, basic but good value, in a nice area.

F Res Jordán, C Antesana S-0671, T422 9294. Youth hostel, *ABAJ* affiliate, modern, basic, with cable TV and small pool. Annex (**F**) at 25 de Mayo S-0651, T422 5010.

G pp **Cochabamba Backpackers**, Av Aroma E-437 entre 25 de Mayo y San Martín, T425 7131, backpackers-cochabamba@boliviahostels.com. Close to bus station, a member of this network of Bolivian hostels.

G Hostal Ossil, Agustín López S-0915, close to bus terminal, T425 4476. New, good rooms, cooking facilities, helpful, good value.

G Maracaibo, Agustín López S-0925, T422 7110. Close to bus terminal, popular, safe.

G Res Familiar, Sucre E-0554, T422 7988. Pleasant, secure, good showers. Its annex at 25 de Mayo N-0234 (entre Colombia y Ecuador), T422 7986, is also pleasant, with a big courtyard, shared bath, hot water, comfortable.

G Virgen de Copacabana, Av Arce S-0875 y Brasil, T422 7929, near bus station. Electric showers, shared bath, good breakfast US$0.75, motorcycle parking, stores luggage, noisy TV, otherwise recommended.

Parque Nacional Torotoro *p307*

Several hostales have opened recently in Torotoro

and there is electricity in some.

G Alojamiento Charcas, near bus terminal, with very good restaurant serving hot, filling meals, US$1 pp (order dinner in the morning).

G De Los Hermanos, very basic rooms, supposedly running water, delightful owner with friendly pets.

Cochabamba to Santa Cruz *p308*
Villa Tunari

C Los Araras, across bridge on main road to Santa Cruz, T413 4116, hisc_marco@yahoo.com. **C** midweek, large rooms, nice gardens, good breakfast, HI affiliated.

C-D Las Palmas, T411 4103, 1 km out of town. With breakfast, pool and good restaurant, changes US$ cash, a bit run down.

D Bibosi, Plaza Principal, T428 0814. Pleasant, with gardens and pool.

D El Puente, Av de la Integración, 3 km from town, T425 9322 (book in advance at offices of *Fremen* Travel Agency). With breakfast and bath, cabins from 2 people to family-size, pool, tours to Carrasco national park, the hotel has a stream and natural pools.

G La Querencia, Beni 700, T413 6548. Pleasant terrace on river front, avoid noisy rooms at front, good cheap food, clothes-washing facilities.

G Las Palmas 2, corner of plaza. With bath, breakfast, fan, swimming pool (not very clean).

G San Mateo, opposite *Baviera* restaurant, by the river. Shared bath, choice of beds (hard or soft), helpful. Several other hotels; also 2 internet cafés, *Entel* office and post office.

⑦ Eating

Cochabamba *p306, map p309*

The bars and restaurants centre around España, Ecuador and Colombia, Plaza Colón and Av Ballivián and north of Río Rocha near Av Santa Cruz. A few km north of the city, in the village of Tiquipaya, are many comida criolla restaurants, eg **El Diente**, recommended.

♥♥♥♥ **La Cantonata**, España N-0409, T425 9222. Among the best Italian restaurants in Bolivia. Highly recommended.

♥♥♥♥ **Suiza**, Av Ballivián 820, T425 7103. International cuisine, good value, recommended.

♥♥ **Bufalo**, Torres Sofer, p 2, Av Oquendo N-0654. Brazilian *rodizio* grill, all-you-can-eat buffet for US$7.50, great service. Highly recommended.

♥♥ **Comida Vegetariana**, M Rocha E-0375. Good filling food, buffet lunch and breakfast, mostly soy-protein based dishes, but also serves chicken, closed Sun.

♥♥ **El Griego**, España N-0386. Good kebabs and lots of pasta dishes, colourful walls and modern art.

♥♥ **Habana Café**, M Rocha E-0348. Genuine

Fiesta de la Virgen de Urkupiña, Quillacollo

The festival lasts four days with much dancing and religious ceremony; its date varies each year between June and August. Plenty of transport from Cochabamba, hotels all full. Be there before 0900 to be sure of a seat, as you are not allowed to stand in the street. The first day is the most colourful with all the groups in costumes and masks, parading and dancing in the streets till late at night. Many groups have left by the second day and dancing stops earlier. The third day is dedicated to the pilgrimage. (Many buses, micros and *trufis* from Heroínas y Ayacucho, 20 minutes, US$0.30.)

Cuban food and drinks, can get lively at night, open 1200-last person leaves.

Marco's, Av Oquenda entre Cabrera y Uruguay. Good Peruvian ceviche, Sat-Sun 1200-1500.

Metrópolis, España N-0299. Good pasta dishes, huge portions, good vegetarian options, noisy. **Metrópolis Pizza** next door is good value.

Picasso, España 327, entre Ecuador y Mayor Rocha. Good value Italian and Mexican.

Eli's Pizza, 25 de Mayo N-0254 y Colombia. Son of the famous La Paz branch, great pizzas and serves Mexican fast food.

Gopal, C España 250, Galería Olimpia. Hare-krishna, US$1.50 for vegetarian lunch 1200-1500 only, closed Sun, English spoken, very good.

Incallacta market (see page 307) has excellent food for under US$1.

Snack Uno, Av Heroínas E-0562. Good lunches and dinners including vegetarian.

Cafés

Brazilian Coffee Bar, Av Ballivián just off Plaza Colón. Upmarket, tables on pavement.

Café Express Bolívar, Bolívar entre San Martín y 25 de Mayo. Great coffee in a delightful old-fashioned café.

Casablanca, 25 de Mayo entre Venezuela y Ecuador. Next to Google internet café, attractive, buzzing, good food and a wide selection of coffee, popular for wine and cocktails in the evening.

Dumbo, Av Heroínas 0440. Good ice-cream parlour, popular eating and meeting spot, also does cheap meals.

Souvenir, 25 de Mayo N-0391. *Salteñas*, crêpes and *confitería*, popular in the early evening.

Parque Nacional Torotoro *p307*

Salón de Té, Torotoro, run by Lydia García, provides good meals with prior notice, good breakfasts, bakes bread and cakes, welcoming.

Cochabamba to Santa Cruz:
Villa Tunari *p308*

El Bosque, west end of town, 1 km past toll booth. German, run by botanists, with orchid garden, one of the best in town.

Surubi, also known as Cuqui, 1 km west of town. A good restaurant with fish specialities, also has tents for camping.

Baviera, near the bridge on main road. Good steak and fish, good value, tourist information, also has rooms to let with hot water.

El Jazmín, opposite *Las Palmas*. Gringo hangout serving good pizza.

Bars and clubs

Cochabamba *p306, map p309*
Chilimania, M Rocha E-0333. Good for drinking and dancing.

D'Mons, Tarija y América. Mix of Latin, contemporary and classic American music, open 2300, US$4 including first drink.

Lujos, Beni E-0330. Nice atmosphere. Mix of Latin, contemporary and classic American music, open 2300, US$4 including first drink.

Wunderbar, Venezuela E-0635. Cable TV sports on Mon, music, darts upstairs, ribs, wings, subs, opens 1930.

Entertainment

Cochabamba *p306, map p309*
Peñas Totos, M Rocha y Ayacucho, T452 2460. Fri night 2000-0300; may open on Sat. Free entry.
Theatre Tra La La, Plazuela 4 de Noviembre, T428 5030. Popular productions, comedy, music and dance.

Festivals and events

Cochabamba *p306, map p309*
Carnival is celebrated 15 days before **Lent**. Rival groups (*comparsas*) compete in music, dancing, and fancy dress, culminating in El Corso on the last Sat of the Carnival. **Mascaritas** balls also take

place in the carnival season, when the young women wear long hooded satin masks. **14 Sep**: Day of Cochabamba.

O Shopping

Cochabamba *p306, map p309*
Bookshops Los Amigos del Libro, Ayacucho S-0156, T450 4150, in *Hotel Portales*, Av Pando 1271, and *Gran Hotel Cochabamba*, in the Torres Sofer shopping centre and at Jorge Wilsterman airport. Good, stocks US and English magazines as well as *South American Handbook*. City map and guide in colour for US$2.50.

▲ Activities and tours

Cochabamba *p306, map p309*
Adventure sports
Cochabamba is growing in popularity for parapenting, with several outfits offering tamdem jumps and courses more cheaply than other places, starting at US$30-35 and US$200-250 respectively; eg tornadojohn@hotmail.com (experienced, Spanish only; his brother speaks a bit of English).
AndesXtremo, La Paz 138 entre Ayacucho y Junín, T452 3392, www.andesxtremo.com. Adventure sports company offering parapenting, climbing, rafting, trekking and bungee-jumps, good value, professional staff.
Todo Turismo, Jordán 280, T450 5384, www.touringbolivia.com. With offices in La Paz, Oruro and Uyuni. Many local tours, including Totororo, tours to other parts of the coutnry and reservations.
Vicuñita Tours, Av Ayacucho 350, T452 0194, vicunitatours@hotmail.com. Specializes in local and regional travel, also overseas reservations (T03-334 0591 for Santa Cruz office).

◉ Transport

Cochabamba *p306, map p309*
Air Jorge Wilstermann airport, T459 1820. Airport bus is Micro B from Plaza 14 de Septiembre, US$0.40; taxis from airport to centre US$3.10. Reconfirm all flights (and obtain reconfirmation number), and arrive early for international flights. Several flights daily to/from **La Paz** (35 mins) and **Santa Cruz** (45 mins) with **LAB** and **Aero Sur** (book early for morning flights). *LAB* also to **Sucre**, **Trinidad** and **Tarija**. International flights to **Buenos Aires** with Aero Sur. LAB, Salamanca 675, open 0800, T423 0325. **Aero Sur**, Av Villarroel 105, esq Av Oblitos (Pando), T440 0910.
Bus *Micros* and *colectivos*, US$0.20; *trufis*, US$0.30. Anything marked 'San Antonio' goes to the market. *Trufis* C and 10 go from bus terminal

312

to the city centre. The main bus terminal is on Av Ayacucho on opposite side from Montes and Punata (T155). To **Santa Cruz**, 10 hrs, 0530-2200, US$3-4.50 (*buscama* US$7.50); only minibuses take the old mountain road via Epizana, from Av 9 de Abril y Av Oquendo, all day. See page 308. To/from **La Paz** many companies, shop around for best times, services and prices (about US$2.50, *buscama* US$4.50-6), by night or day, 7 hrs on paved road. Bus to **Oruro**, US$2.50, 4 hrs, buses hourly. To **Potosí**, US$4.50- 5.25 via Oruro, several companies 1830-2000. Daily to **Sucre**, US$4.50-5.25, 10 hrs, several companies between 1930 and 2030 (**Flota Copacabana** and **Trans Copacabana** recommended; latter *buscama* US$8.90). To **Sucre** by day; take a bus to Aiquile (see below), then a bus at 2400-0100 passing en route to Sucre. Local buses leave from Av Barrientos y Av 6 de Agosto, near La Coronilla for **Tarata**, **Punata** and **Cliza**. Av República y Av 6 de Agosto to **Epizana** and **Totora**. Av Oquendo y 9 de Abril (be careful in this area), to **Villa Tunari**, US$2.70, 4-5 hrs, several daily; **Chimoré**, US$5.75; **Eterazama**, US$5.75; **Puerto Villarroel**, US$4, 6-8 hrs (from 0800 when full, daily); **Puerto San Francisco**, US$6.50.
Taxi About US$0.50 from anywhere to the Plaza, more expensive to cross the river; double after dark.

Parque Nacional Torotoro *p307*
Air Travel to Torotoro is sometimes impossible overland in the wet season (end Nov-Mar), as flooded rivers wash out roads, but it is possible to fly quite cheaply as a group. Swiss pilot **Eugenio Arbinsona** charges US$120 for up to 5 passengers in his Cessna. It takes only 25 mins, but he may be persuaded to lengthen the journey by flying you through a canyon or two on the way. T424 6289 or T0717-23779 (mob).
Bus Check schedules with Gonzalo Milán, **Comercial El Dorado**, Honduras 646, Cochabamba, T422 0207, also very helpful on accommodation and activities. Transport to Torotoro goes in convoy from Av República y 6 de Agosto at 0600 Sun and Thu, be there at 0530, US$4 in a bus or the cab of a truck, US$3 in the back, 8 hrs on an improved dirt road via Aiquile, with stops at Cliza market and for lunch. Transport returns to **Cochabamba** every Mon and Fri, 0600. Groups can arrange with Gonzalo Milán to be picked up at a hotel. Alternatively, pay in advance and arrange to be picked up in Cliza where buses/trucks stop at 0800.

Cochabamba to Santa Cruz *p308*
Inkallajta
Best to go Thu or Sat when **micros** leave when full from 0700 from 6 de Agosto y República, Cochabamba, passing the sign to the ruins, from

where it's a 12 km walk. Otherwise take a micro to the checkpoint 10 km from Cochabamba, then a truck to Km 119 sign, walk towards Pocona or take a truck for 15 km, to where a large yellow sign indicates the trail. After 10 km the trail divides, take the downhill path and the ruins are a further 2 km.

⊙ Directory

Cochabamba *p306, map p309*
Banks Visa and MasterCard at *Enlace* ATMs all over the town (especially on Av Ballivián) and next to the bus terminal. Cash on Visa or MasterCard from many banks; no commission on bolivianos. **Bisa**, Aguirre y Calama. Best rates for cash and Amex TCs, changes euro TCs at 5% commission. **Ef€c**, Plaza 14 de Septiembre S-0262, changes TCs into dollars at 2% commission. Money changers congregate at most major intersections, especially outside *Entel*, and on Plaza Colón, poor rates. **Cultural centres** Centro Boliviano Americano, 25 de Mayo N-0365, T422 1288, www.cbacoch.org. Library of English-language books, open 0900-1200 and 1430-1900; also offers language classes. **Alianza Francesa**, Santiváñez O-0187, T422 1009, afcbba@ afbolivia.org. **Instituto Cultural Boliviano- Alemán**, Lanza 727, T412 323, icbacbba@ supernet.com.bo. Spanish classes. **Embassies and consulates Argentina**, F Blanco E-0929, T425 5859, consuladoar@ entelnet.bo. Visa applications 0830-1300. **Brazil**, Edif Los Tiempos Dos, Av Oquendo, p 9, T425 5860, cchbrvc14@ supernet.com.bo. Open 0830-1130, 1430-1730. **Germany**, España esq Av Heroínas, Edif La Promotora, p 6, of 602, T425 4024, coricba@ pino.cbb.entelnet.bo. **Italy**, Av Humboldt 932, T424 5809. **Netherlands**, Av Oquendo 654, Torres Sofer p 7, T423 0888. 0830-1200, 1400-1630 Mon-Fri. **Paraguay**, Av Gral Achá O-0107, Edif América p 6, T458 1801. 0830-1230, 1430-

1830 Mon-Fri. **Peru**, Pedro Blanco y Santa Cruz, edif Continental of 3H, T448 6157, conbba@ acelerate.com. 0800-1200, 1400- 1800 Mon-Fri. **Spain**, Colombia O-655, T458 2281, Mon-Fri 0900-1200, 1430-1730. **Sweden**, Barquisimeto, Villa La Glorieta, T/F424 5358, arvidsson@ comteco.entelnet.bo, Mon- Fri 0930-1200. **USA**, Av Oquendo, Torres Sofer p 6, T425 6714. 0900-1200 (will also attend to Britons and Canadians). **Internet** Many cybercafés all over town, charging US$0.60 per hr. **Language classes** Sra Blanca de La Rosa Villareal, Av Libertador Simón Bolívar 1108, esq Oblitas (T424 4298). US$5 per hr. **Runawasi**, J Hinojosa, Barrio Juan XXIII s/n, T/F424 8923, www.runawasi.org. Spanish and Quechua, also has accommodation. **Sra Alicia Ferrufino**, JQ Mendoza N-0349, T428 1006. US$10 per hr, **Elizabeth Siles Salas**, T423 2278, silessalas@latinmail.com. **Reginaldo Rojo**, T424 2322, frojo@supernet.com.bo. US$5 per hr. **María Pardo**, Pasaje El Rosal 20, Zona Queru Queru behind Burger King on Av América, T428 4615. US$5 per hr, also teaches Quechua. **Carmen Galinda Benavides**, Parque Lincoln N-0272, T424 7072. **Maricruz Almanzal**, Av San Martín 456, T422 7923, maricruz_almanza@ hotmail.com. US$5 for 50 mins, special offers. **Voluntarios Bolivia**, Casilla 2411, www.volunteerbolivia.org. Bolivian/US-run organization which offers language classes, homestays and a recommended volunteer programme. See also Cultural centres, above. **Medical facilities** For hospitals, doctors and dentists, contact your consulate or the tourist office for advice. **Post offices** Av Heroínas y Ayacucho, Mon-Fri 0800- 2000, Sat 0800-1800, Sun 0800-1200. **Telephones** Entel, Gral Achá y Ayacucho, international phone, fax (not possible to make AT&T credit card calls), open till 2300. **Useful addresses** Immigration Office:, Jordán y Arce, p 2, T422 5553, Mon-Fri 0830-1630.

Northern Lowlands

Bolivia's Northern lowlands account for about 70% of national territory. From scrubby east lowlands to dense tropical jungle in the north, this is pioneer country; home to missionaries, rubber tappers and cocaine refiners. Improved roads and frequent flights, particularly to Rurrenabaque and Trinidad, are opening up the area and wildlife and rainforest expeditions are becoming increasingly popular. Most people head to Rurrenabaque. If seeking hard travel and adventure, head for Cobija or Riberalta. Beni department has 53% of the country's birds and 50% of its mammals, but destruction of forest and habitat is proceeding at an alarming rate.

Madidi and Rurrenabaque

Caranavi to San Borja

From Caranavi, a road runs north to Sapecho, where a bridge crosses the Río Beni. Beyond Sapecho (7 km from the bridge), the road passes through Palos Blancos (several cheap lodgings). The road between Sapecho and Yucumo, three hours from Sapecho *tránsito*, is now a very good all-weather gravel surface. There are *hospedajes* (**G**) and restaurants in **Yucumo** where a road branches northwest, fording rivers several times on its way to Rurrenabaque. Taking the eastern branch from Yucumo it is 50 km (1-2 hours) to **San Borja**, a small, relatively wealthy cattle-raising centre with hotels (**E-G**) and restaurants clustered near the plaza. From San Borja the road goes east to Trinidad via **San Ignacio de Moxos**; see page 319. The road passes through part of the Pilón Lajas Reserve (see below).

Parque Nacional Madidi

ⓘ *Director: Ivan Arnold, C Libertad s/n junto a orillas del río Beni, San Buenaventura, T03-892-2540, www.sernap.gov.bo/madidi/. Visit also www.ecobolivia.org for information on Madidi. Insect repellent and sun protection are essential.*

Parque Nacional Madidi is quite possibly the most bio-diverse of all protected areas on the planet. It is the variety of habitats, from the freezing Andean peaks of the Cordillera Apolobamba in the southwest (reaching nearly 6,000 m), through cloud, elfin and dry forest to steaming tropical jungle and pampas (neo-tropical savannah) in the north and east, that account for the array of flora and fauna within the park's boundaries. In an area roughly the size of Wales or El Salvador are an estimated 1,000 bird species, 10 species of primates, five species of cat (with healthy populations of jaguar and puma), giant anteaters and many reptiles. Madidi is at the centre of a bi-national system of parks that spans the Bolivia-Peru border. The Heath river on the park's north-western border forms the two countries' frontier and links with the Tambopata National Reserve in Peru. To the southwest the Area Protegida Apolobamba protects extensive mountain ecosystems. It is easiest to visit the lowland areas of Madidi through Rurrenabaque; book in advance.

Pilón Lajas Biosphere Reserve and Indigenous Territory

ⓘ *Official HQ at the park's northernmost point, 1 km south of Rurrenabaque, US$6 pp. Contact Sernap, C Campero esq C Busch, Rurrenabaque, www.sernap.gov.bo.*

Beyond the Beni River in the southeast runs the Pilón Lajas Biosphere Reserve and Indigenous Territory, home to several native groups. Together with Madidi, it constitutes approximately 60,000 sq km, one of the largest systems of protected land in the neotropics. Unfortunately, much of this land is under pressure from logging interests, and the government has allocated precious little resources to combat encroachment. The Pilón Lajas Biosphere Reserve and Indigenous Territory, set up under the auspices of UNESCO, has one of the continent's most intact Amazonian rainforest ecosystems, as well as an incredible array of tropical forest animal life. NGOs have been working with the people of La Unión, Playa Ancha, Nuevos Horizontes and El Cebó to develop sustainable forestry, fish farming, cattle ranching and *artesanía*; tours are run by **Donato Tours** (see Activities and tours, below), which include lunch and transport.

Rurrenabaque → *Phone code: 03. Population: 15,000.*

The charming, picturesque jungle town of Rurre (as the locals call it), on the Río Beni, is the main jumping off point for tours in the Bolivian Amazon and pampas, from 2-4 day trips through to full expeditions. Across the river is San Buenaventura. Despite its growth as a trading, transport and ecotourism centre, Rurre is a pleasant town to walk around, although the climate is usually humid. Market day is Sunday.

An hour upstream from Rurre is **San Miguel del Bala**, in a beautiful setting on the edge of Madidi. Opened in 2004, it gives a good taste of the jungle, offers day trips and has en suite cabins where you can stay, bars and a plunge pool.

⏺ Sleeping

Madidi *p314*
A pp **Chalalán Ecolodge** is 5 hrs up-river from

Rurrenabaque, at San José de Uchupiamonas, in Madidi National Park. Addresses: C Sagárnaga

189 esq Murillo, Edif Shopping Doryan, p 2, of 35, T/F02-231 1451, or in Rurrenabaque C Comercio s/n, Zona Central (1/2 block from Plaza), T03-892 2419, info@chalalan.com. This is Bolivia's top ecotourism project, founded by the local community, Conservation International and the Interamerican Development Bank, and now has a well-deserved international reputation. Accommodation is in thatched cabins, and activities include fantastic wildlife-spotting and birdwatching, guided and self-guided trails, river and lake activities, and relaxing in pristine jungle surroundings. A 5-day trip includes travel time from La Paz; tours cost about US$100 per person per night, 3-night stay US$290, discounts for larger groups and longer stays. Air fares are an extra US$110.

A Wizard's Mountain Jungle Lodge (Cerro del Brujo), near Madidi and the Tacana community, T02-279 1742, www.boliviamistica.com. Ecolodge offering jungle and pampas tours, wide range of therapies, shamanic rituals, and a good canopy walkway, price is for 2 days, 1 night pp, many other options available, including community tourism at **Villa Alcira** in the Tacana community.

B per day San Miguel del Bala, 45-min boat trip up river from Rurre, T/F03-892 2394, info@ sanmigueldelbala.com. 7 cabins in delightful setting, good bathrooms, nice public areas, attentive staff. Highly recommended.

Pilón Lajas *p314*
Mapajo, Mapajo Ecoturismo Indígena, C Comercio, Rurrenabaque, T03-892 2317, www.mapajo.com. A community-run ecolodge 2 hrs by boat from Rurrenebaque has 4 *cabañas* without electricity (take a torch and batteries), cold showers and a dining room serving traditional meals. Minimum stay is 4 days/3 nights (prices start at US$220). You can visit the local community, walk in the forest, go birdwatching, etc. Take insect repellent, wear long trousers and strong footwear. Recommended.

Rurrenabaque *p314*
In high season hotels fill up very quickly.
C Hotel Safari, Comercio on the outskirts by the river (a hot walk), T892 2410, hotel-safari@hotmail.com. A peaceful spot with beautiful garden and comfortable rooms, pool, terrace and a good restaurant. Recommended.
F Asaí, C Vaca Díez, T892 2439. Electric showers, quiet, laundry area, courtyard and hammocks, luggage store, breakfast extra.
F Beni, Comercio, by ferry, T892 2408. Best rooms have a/c and TV, hot showers extra, cheaper without bath or a/c (but with fan). Spacious,

pleasant, good service.
F Oriental, on plaza, T892 2401. Hot showers, cheaper without bath, small breakfast included, quiet, hammocks in peaceful garden. A good option.
F Rurrenabaque, Vaca Díez y Bolívar, T892 2481. Safe, hot water, cooking and laundry facilities, good.
F Hostal Eden, southern end of C Bolívar, T892 2452. G without bath, hot water, breakfast available, has hammocks and kitchen, laundry, family run, helpful and good value.
G El Porteño, Comercio y Vaca Díez, T892 2558. Some big rooms with TV, bath, fan, comfortable beds, courtyard with hammocks, quite good.
G Jazmín, Comercio entre Aniceto Arce y Av Santa Cruz, T892 2337. Variety of rooms, some with bath, good value, fan, cold showers, hammock space. Recommended.
G pp Hostal El Curichal, Comercio 1490, T892 2647, elcurichal@hotmail.com. Nice courtyard, hammocks, laundry and small kitchen facilities, helpful staff, will change TCs and money.
G Hostal Turístico Santa Ana, 1 block north of plaza on Avaroa, T892 2399. Electric showers, poor water pressure, thin mattresses, laundry, luggage store, pretty courtyard, car park, basic, mixed reports.
G pp Jislene, C Comercio, T892 2526. Erlan Caldera and family very hospitable, hot water, fan, basic, good breakfast if booked in advance, information, helpful.
G pp Toucan, Aniceto Arce entre Avaroa y Bolívar. Rooms with electric fan and shower (hot water for 10 mins pp), includes breakfast, clean, pleasant.
G Tuichi, C Avaroa y Santa Cruz, T7198 3582. Cheaper without bath (but shared bathrooms are dirty), cold showers, luggage storage, kitchen and laundry facilities, fan, a sad reflection of its former reputation.

🍴 Eating

Rurrenabaque *p314*
🍴🍴 **Casa del Campo**, Vaca Díez y Avaroa. Good international and Bolivian food, ceviche, delicious desserts, hospitable staff.
🍴🍴 **Butterfly Pub**, C Comercio. Good pasta and fish dishes, friendly atmosphere and bar outside.
🍴🍴 **La Perla de Rurre**, Bolívar y Díez. Smartest place in town, for meat and fish under a shady tree.
🍴🍴 **Pizzería Italia**, Avaroa, T892 2611. Big pizzas, imaginative pastas, lively crowd and pool tables.
🍴 **Camila's**, Santa Cruz. Good breakfasts and snacks throughout the day, ideal when waiting for the Amazonas bus to the airport. Fast service.
🍴 **La Chocita**, on the main path to the river, great spot for people watching. Simple fish restaurant, popular, especially for the *almuerzo*. La Cabaña, another riverside restaurant, is next door.

¶ **Club Social Rurrenabaque**, on Comercio
1 block north of Santa Cruz. Vegetarian dishes on
request, good juices, fishburgers.
¶ **El Tacuara**, opposite *Camila's*. Good range of
dishes, also for breakfast. Good *almuerzos* and
fruit juices in the market.

Cafés
Café Bar Madidi, C Comercio. Coffees, juices,
some vegetarian dishes.
Moskkito Bar, cool bar for tall jungle tales. Good
meals, ½-price cocktails 1900-2100.
Pachamama, Avaroa sud, at south end of town.
English/Bolivian café/bar, snacks, river view, films,
playstation, internet and a book exchange.

▲ Activities and tours

Rurrenabaque *p314*
There are two types of tours to choose from, jungle
or pampas. Jungle tours normally last 4 days and 3
nights, US$20-30 per day all inclusive. The jungle is
very hot and humid in the rainy season with many
more biting insects and far fewer animals to be
seen. It's pretty basic and long enough for most
people to get a real sense of life in the jungle. You
will see a lot more wildlife on a 3-day Pampas tour
(US$25-35 per day), which involves a 4-hr jeep ride
to the Río Yacuma, then a series of boat trips. You
see howler, squirrel and capuchin monkeys,
caiman, capybara, pink dolphins, possibly
anacondas and a huge variety of birds. The
weather and general conditions are more pleasant
than in the jungle; season Jul to Oct. For pampas
and jungle tours, 1-day trips are a waste of time as
you would spend most of the time travellling. It is
recommended to go with an established company
as competition is forcing down prices and,
consequently, quality and standards of guiding.
Some agencies offer ecologically unsound
practices such as fishing, feeding monkeys,
catching caiman; before signing up for a tour ask if
the operator respects the environment. Pampas
tours may involve wading through knee-deep
water; wear appropriate shoes. It is cheaper to
book tours in Rurrenabaque than La Paz.

Tour operators
Agencia Fluvial, at *Hotel Tuichi*, T892 2372, runs
jungle tours on the Río Tuichi, normally 4 days, but
shorter by arrangement, US$25 pp per day
(payable in dollars) including food, transport and
mosquito nets. Take swimming costume and
insect repellent. Also 3-day 'Pampas Tours' on a
boat to Río Yacuma, US$30 pp per day. Tico Tudela
has opened *Hotel de la Pampa* near Lago Bravo,
2½ hrs from Rurrenabaque, as a base for visiting
Lago Rogagua (birds) and Río Yacuma. Fully
inclusive tours (including meals and

accommodation) US$40 pp per day.
Aguila Tours, Av Avaroa, T892 2478, jungle and
pampas tours (can be booked through *Eco Jungle
Tours*, C Sagárnaga, La Paz).
Bala Tours, Av Santa Cruz, T892 2527, www.bala
tours.com. Arranges Pampas and jungle tours,
good base camp in the Pampas. Recommended.
Donato Tours, C A Arce, T892 2571,
donatotours@hotmail.com. For regular tours and A
Day for the Community with trips to Pilón Lajas.
Indígena Tours, Abaroa s/n, T892 2091. Good
value tours, food and accommodation, helpful.
Mashaquipe Tours, Comercio s/n entre Santa
Cruz y Vaca, www.mashaquipe.com. Run by an
indigenous, Tacana family, with a camp in
Madidi, knowledgeable guides (including
women guides), US$25 per day.
Turismo Ecológico Social (TES), Av Santa
Cruz, next to tourist information office,
T7128 9664, turismoecologicosocial@
hotmail.com. Day tours to 4 local communities
and the Pilón Lajas buffer zone, US$25 pp
including lunch, water and guides.

⊝ Transport

Caranavi to San Borja *p314*
Bus Flota Yungueña daily except Thu at 1300

BALA TOURS
ECOLÓGICO
RURRENABAQUE

Jungle & Pampas

" AMAZONIAN DREAM TREKKING "

**An exciting and unforgetable adventure in
the most beautiful Bolivian jungle in
Madidi National Park**

Accommodation at Eco Lodge "Tacuarales"
· Trekking (1 up to 12 days)
· Birdwatching
· Fishing and relaxing

Pampas "Grassland"
· Accommodation at Eco Lodge "Caracoles"
· Wildlife viewing
· Boat riding
· Excellent & knowledgeable tour guides

Main office:
Av. Santa Cruz s/n Rurrenabaque-Beni
Phone/fax 591-3-892-2527
Mobile: 591-71247790, 591-71122053
balatours@yahoo.com www.balatours.com
General Manager: Alcides Santalla L.

from San Borja to **La Paz**, 19 hrs via Caranavi. **Yucumo** is on the La Paz-Caranavi-Rurrenabaque and San Borja bus routes. Rurrenabaque-La Paz bus passes through about 1800. If travelling to Rurrenabaque by bus take extra food in case there is a delay for river levels to fall. The road surface Caranavi-San Borja is good; San Borja-San Ignacio poor, long stretches are rutted and pot-holed; San Ignacio- Trinidad is good. Also San Borja to **Rurrenabaque** (Buses 1 de Mayo, T03-895 3467, US$4.40), **Santa Rosa**, **Riberalta**, **Guayaramerín** Thu, Sat, Sun. Minibuses and *camionetas* run daily between San Borja and **Trinidad** throughout the year, US$15, about 7 hrs including 20 mins crossing of Río Mamoré on ferry barge (up to 14 hrs in wet season); **1 de Mayo** to **San Ignacio** (US$8), **Trinidad** and **Santa Cruz**. Gasoline available at Yolosa, Caranavi, Yucumo, San Borja and San Ignacio.

Rurrenabaque *p314*
Air New airport. Flights with **Amaszonas** (C Santa Cruz, T892 2472), 3 a day from **La Paz** (US$62), also to **Trinidad, Santa Cruz, Riberalta, Guayaramerín, San Borja** and **Cobija**. Book all flights as early as possible and buy onward ticket on arrival. Check flight times in advance; they change frequently. Airport tax US$2. Motorcycle taxi from town, US$1.
Bus To/from **La Paz** via Caranavi daily at 1100

with **Flota Yungueña** and **Totai**; 18-20 hrs, US$8.20. Returns at 1100. **Flota Unificada** leaves La Paz (also from Villa Fátima) on Tue, Thu, Fri, Sat at 1030, same price. Continues to **Riberalta** and **Guayaramerín**; return departure time depends on road conditions. **Flota Yungueña** also has a 1030 bus which leaves Villa Fátima and continues to Riberalta and Guayaramerín.
Rurrenebaque-**Riberalta** should take 14-16 hrs, but can take 6 days or more in the wet. Take lots of food, torch and be prepared to work. To **Trinidad**, Tue, Thu, Sat, Sun at 2230 with **Trans Guaya** via **Yucumo** and **San Borja**, US$18.

❶ Directory

Rurrenabaque *p314*
Banks Prodem, Av Comercio 21 entre Vaca Díez y Santa Cruz, T892 2616. Changes US$ cash at fair rates, cash advance on Visa or MasterCard, 5% commission. **Bala Tours** will give cash advance against credit cards at 7.5% commission. Try hotels or agencies for small amounts. TCs can be used as payment for tours, but are difficult to cash. Try **Agencia Fluvial**, 5% commission. Most agencies accept credit cards for tours. **Internet** *Camila's*, next to restaurant of same name on Santa Cruz, US$3 per hr. **Post offices** On C Bolívar. Open Sat. **Telephones** Entel, on C Comercio, 2 blocks north of plaza, and Santa Cruz y Bolívar. Also email.

Riberalta to Brazil

Riberalta → *Phone code: 03. Colour map 3, grid B6. Population: 60,000. Altitude: 175 m.*
This town, at the confluence of the Madre de Dios and Beni rivers, is off the beaten track and a centre for brazil nut production. Change cash in shops and on street. Recent reports indicate an increase in theft and rape – worth knowing when the bus drops you in the middle of the night and everything is closed. Some 25 km away is Tumi-Chucua situated on a lovely lake. Nearby are the **Nature Gardens**. Here you can fish in the lake, good for birdwatching. They also have lots of information on the rainforest, the rubber boom and brazil nut production. Contact **Dr Willy Noack**, T/F352 2497 for further information.

Guayaramerín and border with Brazil → *Phone code: 03. Colour map 4, grid C1.*
Guayaramerín is a cheerful, prosperous little town on the bank of the Río Mamoré, opposite the Brazilian town of Guajará-Mirim. It has an important *Zona Libre*. Passage between the two towns is unrestricted; boat trip US$1.65 (more at night).

Bolivian immigration Avenida Costanera near port; open 0800-1100, 1400-1800. Passports must be stamped here when leaving, or entering Bolivia. On entering Bolivia, passports must also be stamped at the Bolivian consulate in Guajará-Mirim. For Brazilian immigration, see page 560. The Brazilian consulate is on 24 de Septiembre, Guayaramerín, T855 3766, open 0900-1300, 1400-1700; visas for entering Brazil are given here. To enter Brazil you must have a yellow fever certificate, or be inoculated at the health ministry (free). Exchange cash at the dock on the Bolivian side where rates are written up on blackboards (no travellers' cheques), although there is an ATM at the Banco do Brasil in Guajará-Mirim; no facilities for cash.

Cobija → *Phone code: 03. Colour map 3, grid B5. Population: 15,000.*

The capital of the lowland Department of Pando lies on the Río Acre which forms the frontier with Brazil. A new, single-tower suspension bridge has been built across the river to Brasiléia. As a duty-free zone, shops in centre have a huge selection of imported consumer goods at bargain prices. Brazilians and Peruvians flock here to stock up. As this is a this border area, watch out for scams and cons.

● Sleeping

Riberalta *p317*

Ask for a fan and check the water supply.
E Comercial Lazo, NG Salvatierra, T852 8326.
F without a/c, comfortable, laundry facilities, good value.
E-F Colonial, Plácido Méndez 1. Charming colonial casona, large, well-furnished rooms, no singles, nice gardens and courtyard, comfortable, good beds, helpful owners. Recommended.
G Res El Pauro, Salvatierra 157. Basic, shared baths, good café.
G Res Los Reyes, near airport, T852 8018. With fan, safe, pleasant but noisy disco nearby on Sat and Sun.

Guayaramerín *p317*

C Esperanza out of town in nearby Cachuela Esperanza, reserve through **America Tours** in La Paz, T02-237 4204, www.america-ecoturs.com. Eco-friendly.
D San Carlos, 6 de Agosto, 4 blocks from port, T855 2152/3. With a/c (**E** without), hot showers, changes dollars cash, TCs and reais, swimming pool, reasonable restaurant.

Cobija *p318*

F Prefectural Pando, Av 9 de Febrero, T842 2230. Includes breakfast, *comedor* does good lunch, manager Sr Angel Gil, helpful.
G Res Cocodrilo, Av Molina, T842 2215. Comfortable, good atmosphere, rooms with fan.
G Res Frontera, 9 de Febrero, T842 2740. Good location, basic but clean, fan.

● Eating

Riberalta *p317*

♥ **Club Social Progreso**, on plaza. Good value *almuerzo*, excellent fish.
♥ **Tucunare**, M Chávez/Martínez.Recommended. Good lunch at *comedor popular* in market for US$1.50.

Guayaramerín *p317*

There area several places on the plaza:
♥ **Gipsy**, good *almuerzo*; ♥ **Los Bibosis**, popular with visiting Brazilians; ♥ **Made in Brazil**, good coffee. Also ♥ **Only**, 25 de Mayo/Beni, good *almuerzo* for US$2.50, plus Chinese.

Cobija *p318*

♥♥-♥ **La Esquina de la Abuela**, opposite *Res Cocodrilo*, good food, not cheap.
♥ Good cheap meals in *comedor popular* in central market.

● Transport

Riberalta *p317*

Air Expect delays in the wet season. **Amaszonas** (Chuquisaca y Sucre, T852 3933) flies from **La Paz**, with connections to **Rurrenabaque, Trinidad** and **San Borja**. LAB office at M Chávez 77, T852 2239 (901-10-5000). Check all flight details in advance.
Bus Several companies (including **Yungueña**) to **La Paz**, via **Rurrenabaque** and **Caranavi** Tue-Sat at 1100, also Tue, Thu, Sat at 1000; US$22.40 (same price to Rurrenebaque, 18 hrs). To **Trinidad** with **8 de Diciembre** Mon, Wed, Thu, Sat, Sun at 0830, also **Trans Guaya** daily at 0930, via Rurrenabaque; to **Guayaramerín** several daily, US$3, 3 hrs. To **Cobija** several companies, none with daily service.
Ferry Cargo boats carry passengers along the **Río Madre de Dios**, but they are infrequent. There are not many boats to Rurrenabaque.

Guayaramerín *p317*

Air Frequent cheap flights have made air worth considering. **Amaszonas** (F Román y Mamoré, T855 3731) flies from **La Paz** with connections to **Rurrenabaque, Trinidad** and **San Borja**. LAB office at 25 de Mayo 652, T855 3540.
Bus Terminal is 2½ km from centre, Bs 5-10 on a motorcycle taxi. To/from **La Paz**, Flota **Yungueña**, daily 0830 (1030 from La Paz), 36 hrs, US$22.40. Also **Flota Unificada**, leaving La Paz Tue, Thu, Fri, Sat 1030, US$26.90. To **Riberalta** 3 hrs, US$3, daily 0700-1730. To **Trinidad** Fri, 30 hrs, US$23. To **Rurrenabaque**, US$18. To **Cobija** on Tue, Sat, Sun at 0600, US$17, 24 hrs. To **Santa Cruz** via Trinidad, 1-2 a week, 2½ days. Buses depart from Gral Federico Román. Roads are very difficult in wet season.
Ferry Check the notice of boats leaving port on the Port Captain's board, prominently displayed near the immigration post on the riverbank.

Boats up the Mamoré to **Trinidad** are fairly frequent – a 3-day wait at the most.

Cobija *p318*
Air Aero Sur, Coronel Cornejo 123, T812 3598, flies 3 days a week to **La Paz**. Also **Amaszonas**, Cornejo 121, T842 3844, to **La Paz** and **Trinidad**. LAB office at F Molina 139, T842 2170.
Bus Flota Yungueña to **La Paz** via Riberalta and Rurrenabaque Sat at 0700 (check times first, T842 2318). To **Riberalta** with several bus companies, depart from 2 de Febrero, most on Wed, Fri, Sun at 0600; good all-weather surface; 5 river crossings on pontoon rafts, takes 10-11 hrs.
Taxi These are very expensive, charging according to time and distance, eg US$10 to the outskirts, US$12 over the international bridge to Brasiléia. Besides taxis there are motorbike taxis

(much cheaper). **Brasiléia** can also be reached by **canoe**, US$0.35. The bridge can be crossed on foot as well, although one should be dressed neatly in any case when approaching Brazilian customs. Entry/exit stamps (free) are necessary and yellow fever vaccination certificate also (in theory), when crossing into Brazil.

● Directory

Cobija *p318*
Banks Lots of money changers along Av 2 de Febrero. Most shops will accept dollars or reais, or exchange money.
Internet Internet place near the university, 100 m from the plaza. **Post offices** on plaza.
Telephones Entel, on C Sucre, for telephone calls internal and abroad and fax, much cheaper than from Brazil.

Cochabamba to Trinidad

Villa Tunari to the Lowlands
Another route into Beni Department is via the lowland road between Cochabamba and Santa Cruz. At Ivirgazama, east of Villa Tunari, the road passes the turn-off to **Puerto Villarroel**, 27 km further north, from where cargo boats ply irregularly to Trinidad in about four to 10 days. You can get information from the Capitanía del Puerto notice board, or ask at docks. **F-G Amazonas Eco-hotel** *T/F04-423 5105*, with restaurant, boat trips arranged. There are very few stores in Villarroel. Sr Arturo Linares at the Cede office organizes boat trips to the jungle – not cheap.

Trinidad → *Phone code: 03. Colour map 6, grid A3. Population: 86,000. Altitude: 237 m.*
The hot and humid capital of the lowland Beni Department is a dusty city in the dry season, with many streets unpaved. Primarily a service centre for the surrounding ranches and communities, most travellers find themselves in the area for boats up and down the Río Mamoré. There are two ports, Almacén and Varador, check which one your boat is docking at. Puerto Varador is 13 km from town on the Río Mamoré on the road between Trinidad and San Borja; cross the river over the main bridge by the market, walk down to the service station by the police checkpoint and take a truck, US$1.70. Almacén is 8 km from the city. The main mode of transport in Trinidad is the motorbike (even for taxis, US$0.40 in city); rental on plaza from US$2 per hour, US$8 per half day. Transport can be arranged from the airport. The **tourist office** ① *in the Prefectura building at Joaquín de Sierra y La Paz, ground floor, T462 1305, ext 116*, is very helpful, sells guide and city map, US$2.

About 8 km from town is the Laguna Suárez, with plenty of wildlife; swimming is safe where the locals swim, near the café with the jetty (elsewhere there are stingrays and alligators). Motorbike taxi from Trinidad, US$1.30.

San Ignacio de Moxos → *Electricity is supplied in town from 1200- 2400.*
San Ignacio de Moxos, 90 km west of Trinidad, is known as the folklore capital of the Beni Department. It's a quiet town with a mainly indigenous population; 60% are *Macheteros*, who speak their own language. San Ignacio still maintains the traditions of the Jesuit missions with big *fiestas*, especially during Holy Week and the **Fiesta del Santo Patrono de Moxos**, the largest festival in the lowlands, at the end of July.

Magdalena and Bella Vista
Magdalena, northeast of Trinidad, stands on the banks of the Río Itonama. There is an abundance of wildlife and birds in the surrounding area. The city's main festival, Santa María Magdalena, is on 22 July attracting many visitors from all over. Drinking water is available and

electricity runs from 1800-2400. There is a bank (changes travellers' cheques), an *Entel* office and Post Office on the plaza. East of Magdalena, **Bella Vista** on the Río Blanco is considered by many to be one of the prettiest spots in northeast Bolivia. Lovely white sandbanks line the Río San Martín, 10 minutes' paddling by canoe from the boat moorings below town (boatmen will take you, returning later by arrangement; also accessible by motorcycle). Check that the sand is not covered by water after heavy rain. Other activities are swimming in the Río San Martín, canoeing, good country for cycling. Three well-stocked shops on plaza, but none sells mosquito repellent or spray/coils (bring your own, especially at the beginning of the wet season). The nearest bank is in Magdalena.

◎ Sleeping

Trinidad *p319*

B **Gran Moxos**, Av 6 de Agosto y Santa Cruz, T462 3305, F462 2240. Includes breakfast, a/c, fridge bar, cable TV, phone, good restaurant, accepts credit cards.

D-E **Hostal Aguahi**, Bolívar y Santa Cruz, T462 5570, F462 5569. A/c, fridge, comfortable, swimming pool in pleasant garden.

D-E **Monte Verde**, 6 de Agosto 76, T462 2750. With or without a/c, fridge bar, includes breakfast, owner speaks English. Recommended.

E **Copacabana**, Matías Carrasco 627, 3 blocks from plaza, T462 2811, copabeni@yahoo.com. Good value, though some beds uncomfortable, F pp without bath, helpful staff.

E-F **Hostal Jarajorechi**, Av 6 de Agosto y 27 de Mayo, T462 1716. With bath and breakfast, comfortable, ecotourism centre offering jungle expeditions, equipment and transport hire.

G **Paulista**, Av 6 de Agosto 36, T462 0018. Cheaper without bath, comfortable, good restaurant.

San Ignacio de Moxos *p319*

There are a several cheap *residencias* (**F-G**) on and around the main plaza.

Magdalena *p319*

C **Internacional**, T03-886 2210, info@hwzinc.com. With breakfast, pools, beautiful setting. Also basic hotels.

Bella Vista *p320*

G **Hotel Pescador**, owner Guillermo Esero Gómez very helpful and knowledgeable about the area, shared bath, provides meals for guests, offers excursions.

◍ Eating

Trinidad *p319*

♯♯ **Club Social 18 de Noviembre**, N Suárez y Vaca Díez on plaza. Good lunch for US$1.35, lively, popular with locals.

♯♯ **Pescadería El Moro**, Bolívar 707 y Natusch. Excellent fish. Also several good fish restaurants in Barrio Pompeya, south of plaza across river.

♯ **La Casona**, Plaza Ballivián. Good pizzas and set lunch, closed Tue.

♯ **La Estancia**, Barrio Pompeya, on Ibare entre Muibe y Velarde. Excellent steaks.

Heladería Oriental, on plaza. Good coffee, ice-cream, cakes, popular with locals.

▲ Activities and tours

Trinidad *p319*

Most agents offer excursions to local *estancias* and jungle tours down river to **Amazonia**. Most *estancias* can also be reached independently in 1 hr by hiring a motorbike.

Amazonia Holiday, 6 de Agosto 680, T462 5732, F462 2806. Good service.

Fremen, Cipriano Barace 332, T462 2276, www.andes-amazonia.com. Run speed boat trips along the **Mamoré** and **Ibare** rivers and to **Parque Nacional Isiboro Sécure**, US$80 per day; their *Flotel Reina de Enin* offers tours of more than 1 day, US$80 pp per day, good food.

Moxos, 6 de Agosto 114, T462 1141, turmoxos@ sauce.ben.entelnet.bo. Recommended.

Tarope Tours, 6 de Agosto 57, T/F462 1468. For flights.

◎ Transport

Villa Tunari to the Lowlands: Puerto Villarroel *p319*

From Cochabamba you can get a bus to **Puerto Villarroel** (see Cochabamba Transport, Bus), **Puerto San Francisco**, or **Todos Santos** on the Río Chapare.

Trinidad *p319*

Air Daily flights with **Amaszonas** (18 de Noviembre 267, T462 2426) to **La Paz, Rurrenabaque, San Borja, Riberalta, Guayaramerín, Cobija** and **Santa Cruz**. LAB (Santa Cruz 322, T462 1277) flies to **Cochabamba**. Airport, T462 0678. Taxi to airport US$1.20.

Bus Bus station is on Rómulo Mendoza, between Beni and Pinto, 9 blocks east of main plaza. Motorbike taxis will take people with backpacks from bus station to centre for US$0.45.

Several *flotas* daily to/from **La Paz** via San Borja and Caranavi, 20-21 hrs, depart 1730, US$17.50 (see also under San Borja, Transport). To **Santa Cruz** (12 hrs in dry season, US$5.80) and **Cochabamba** (US$11.60), with **Copacabana**, **Mopar** and **Bolívar** at 1700, 1730 and 1800; irregular morning service (generally 0900). Trinidad to Casarabe is paved and Santa Cruz to El Puente; otherwise gravel surface on all sections of unpaved road. To **Rurrenabaque** (US$18), **Riberalta** (US$21.15) and **Guayaramerín** (US$23), connecting with bus to **Cobija**; Guaya Tours Sun, Mon, Thu, Fri at 1030; road often impassable in wet season, at least 24 hrs to **Rurrenabaque**.
Ferry Cargo boats down the Río Mamoré to **Guayaramerín** take passengers, 3-4 days, assuming no breakdowns, best organized from Puerto Varador (speak to the Port Captain). **Argos** is recommended as friendly, US$22 pp, take water, fresh fruit, toilet paper and ear-plugs; only for the hardy traveller.

San Ignacio de Moxos *p319*
Bus The Trinidad to San Borja bus stops at the *Donchanta* restaurant for lunch, otherwise difficult to find transport to San Borja. Minibus to Trinidad daily at 0730 from plaza, also *camionetas*, check times before.

Magdalena *p319*
Road An unpaved road goes to Trinidad via San Ramón (pick-up US$10.50), passable only in the dry season. San Ramón to Magdalena takes 6 hrs on motorbike taxi, US$16.

Bella Vista *p320*
Bus There are daily buses from **Magdalena** (except in the rainy season), 2½ hrs, US$2.

❶ Directory

Trinidad *p319*
Banks Banco Mercantil, J de Sierra, near plaza. Changes cash and TCs, cash on Visa. **Banco Ganadero**, Plaza Ballivián. Visa agent. Street changers on 6 de Agosto (US dollars only). **Post offices and telephones** (Open daily till 1930) in same building at Av Barace, just off plaza.

Santa Cruz and Eastern Lowlands

In contrast to the highlands of the Andes and the gorges of the Yungas, eastern Bolivia is made up of vast plains stretching to the Chaco of Paraguay and the Pantanal wetlands of Brazil. Agriculture is well-developed and other natural resources are fully exploited, bringing prosperity to the region. There are a number of national parks with great biodiversity, such as Amboró and Noel Kempff Mercado. Historical interest lies in the pre-Inca ceremonial site at Samaipata, the beautiful Chiquitano Jesuit missions and, of much more recent date, the trails and villages where Che Guevara made his final attempt to bring revolution to Bolivia.

Santa Cruz → *Phone code: 03. Colour map 6, grid A4. Population: 1,465,305. Altitude: 416 m.*

A little over 50 years ago, what is now Bolivia's largest city was a remote backwater, but rail and road links ended its isolation and the exploitation of oil and gas in the Department of Santa Cruz helped fuel the city's rapid development. Santa Cruz is far removed from most travellers' perceptions of Bolivia. Formerly a haven for narcotraficantes, it is now less opulent, although agribusiness is an important economic concern. The city centre still retains much of its colonial air and during the lunchtime hiatus when the locals (who like to call themselves cambas) take refuge from the overwhelming heat, it can almost seem like its original self.

Ins and outs
Getting there The international **airport** is at **Viru-Viru**, about 13 km north of the city. Airport bus every 20 minutes from the bus terminal, 25 minutes (US$0.70), also *colectivos*. Taxi, US$7.50. From airport take bus to bus terminal then taxi to centre. Long distance and local **buses** leave from the new combined bus/train terminal, **Terminal Bimodal**, Avenida Montes on the southeastern edge of the city between Avenida Brasil and Tres Pasos, between the second and third *anillos*. T348 8382. No 12 bus to/from the centre, taxi US$1.50. The city has ten ring roads, Anillos 1, 2, 3, 4 and so on. Equipetrol suburb, where many hotels and bars are situated, is northwest of the heart of the city between Anillos 2 and 3.

Tourist office Prefectura del Departamento (Direcciones), on the north side of the main plaza, T333 2770 ext 144, with videos, guided tours. Information kiosk at the airport. The **Organización y Gestión del Destino Turístico Santa Cruz** (www.destinochiquitos.com), publishes a tourist guide (English/Spanish) entitled *Destino Turístico Santa Cruz – Bolivia* (US$10, available at most bookstores); also *Santa Cruz y Sus Provincias*, a wonderful, free little guide. **APAC**, Beni 228, T333 2287 (see Festivals and events, below) publishes *Santa Cruz Turístico*, US$5, which covers the city and the Jesuit missions, and is very knowledgeable about the region.

Sights

The Plaza 24 de Septiembre is the city's main square with the huge **Cathedral** (now also a basilica after the late Pope John Paul II's visit) ① *museum Tue, Thu, Sun 1000-1200, 1600-1800, US$0.75*, the Casa de Cultura and the Palacio Prefectural set around it. **Casa de la Cultura** has occasional exhibitions, a museum, giftshop and also an archaeological display;

Bolivia Santa Cruz

Santa Cruz

Sleeping
Alojamiento Santa
  Bárbara **1** *B1*
Asturias **14** *D2*
Backpackers
  Santa Cruz **16** *D1*
Bibosi **2** *B1*
Colonial **3** *B2*
Copacabana **4** *B1*
Crismar **15** *C1*
Excelsior **5** *B2*
House Inn **6** *D1*
Jodanga **9** *D3*
Las Américas **7** *B2*
Posada El Turista **8** *B1*
Residencial 26
  de Enero **12** *C1*
Residencial Bolívar **10** *B2*
Residencial Sands **11** *B3*
Viru-Viru **13** *B1*

Eating
Capri **1** *D1*
El Boliche **2** *B2*
El Patito Pekín **3** *B2*
Il Gatto **5** *B2*
Kivón **16** *B1*
La Casona **15** *B2*
La Esquina
  del Pescado **6** *B1*
Las Palmeras **7** *B1*
Michelangelo **9** *D2*
Pizzería Marguerita **10** *B2*
Rincón Brasil **17** *B2*
Sabor Brasil **11** *B1*
Su Salud **18** *B3*
Tía Lía **12** *B2*
Vegetariano **13** *B1*

Bars & clubs
Irlandés **14** *B2*

0 metres 200
0 yards 200

also plays, recitals, concerts and folk dancing. The heart of the city, with its arcaded streets and buildings with low, red-tiled roofs and overhanging eaves, retains a colonial feel, despite the profusion of modern, air-conditioned shops and restaurants. Five blocks north of the Plaza is **Parque El Arenal** in which is a mural by the celebrated painter, Lorgio Vaca, depicting the city's history. **Museo de Historia Natural de Noel Kempff Mercado** ① *Av Irala 565 entre Velasco e Independencia, T/F337 1216, www.museonoelkempff.org, Mon-Fri 0800- 1200, also Mon-Tue 1500-1830, US$0.15.* It has a video library. Contact this museum for trips and information to Parque Nacional Noel Kempff Mercado (see page 332). Some 12 km on the road to Cotoca are the **Botanical Gardens** (micro or colectivo from C Suárez Arana, 15 minutes).

● Sleeping

Santa Cruz *p321, map p322*

AL House Inn, Colón 643, T336 2323, www.houseinn.com.bo. 5-star suites with computer in each room, unlimited internet use, price includes taxes and breakfast, 2 pools, sauna, restaurant, a/c, parking, modern, Best Western.

B Las Américas, 21 de Mayo esq Seoane, T336 8778, lasamericas@cotas.com.bo. A/c, discount for longer stay, parking, arranges tours and car rental, restaurant, bar, 5-star service.

C Asturias, Moldes 154, T333 9611, www.hotel asturias.net. A/c, quiet, nice pool and gardens, internet, bar and restaurant, a good choice.

C Colonial, Buenos Aires 57, T333 3156, F333 9223. A/c, breakfast, restaurant, comfortable.

C Viru-Viru, Junín 338, T333 5298, F336 7500. Includes breakfast, a/c, cheaper with fan, pleasant, central.

D Copacabana, Junín 217, T332 1843, hotelcopacabanascz@hotmail.com. TV, laundry service, includes breakfast, restaurant, very good, popular with European tour groups.

D Excelsior, René Moreno 70, T334 0664, excelsior@cotas.net. Includes breakfast, good rooms, good lunches.

E Bibosi, Junín 218, T334 8548, htlbibosi@hotmail.com. Cheaper with shared bath, breakfast included, internet. Recommended.

E Crismar, Vallegrande 285 entre Pari y Camiri, by the '7 Calles' market (area not safe after 2100), T337 1918. With a/c, F with fan, cheaper with shared bath, breakfast served in rooms, basic but clean and good value.

E-F Jodanga, C El Fuerte 1380, Zona Parque Urbano, Barrio Los Chóferes, T339 6542, 7082 8202 (mob), www.jodanga.com. Good new backpacker option 10 mins' walk from Terminal Bimodal, **G** in dorm, kitchen, bar, swimming pool, billiards, DVDs, nice communal areas, internet, laundry, helpful owner and multilingual staff, can arrange voluntary work.

E-F Res 26 de Enero, Camiri 32, T332 1818, F333 7518. **G** without bath, very clean.

F Res Sands, Arenales 749, 7 blocks east of the main plaza, T337 7776. Unbelievable value, better

than many in much higher price brackets, cable TV, fan, very comfortable beds, pool.

F-G pp Res Bolívar, Sucre 131, T334 2500. Hot showers, some rooms with bath, others very small, lovely courtyard with hammocks, alcohol prohibited, excellent breakfast US$2.10. Recommended.

G Alojamiento Santa Bárbara, Santa Bárbara 151, T332 1817. Hot showers, shared bath, basic, helpful, popular, will store luggage, good value. Recommended.

G pp Backpackers Santa Cruz, Salvatierra 555 y Izozog, T312 0033, backpackers-santacruz@ boliviahostels.com. Budget place in the Backpackers network.

G Posada El Turista, Junín 455, T336 2870. Small basic rooms, central, quiet.

● Eating

Santa Cruz *p321, map p322*

Barrio Equipetrol is the area for the poshest restaurants and nightlife. Most restaurants close Mon. The bakeries on Junín, Los Manzanos and España sell the local specialities.

₸₸₸ **El Boliche**, Arenales 135. Open 1930 onwards, serves good crêpes, fondues and salads.

₸₸₸ **Il Gatto**, 24 de Septiembre 285. Bright and clean, good pizzas, US$2.25 buffet 1200-1500.

₸₸₸ **Michelangelo**, Chuquisaca 502. Excellent Italian. Mon-Fri 1200-1400, 1900-2330, Sat evenings only.

₸₸ **Capri**, Irala 634, "The best pizzas in town".

₸₸ **La Casona**, Arenales 222. German-run restaurant, very good food, open Mon 1600-2000, Tue-Fri 1030-1430, 1600-2000, Sat 1000-1400.

₸₸ **Pizzería Marguerita**, northwest corner of the plaza, T337 0285. A/c, truly superb filet mignon, good service, coffee, bar, also recommended, Mon-Fri 0900-2400, Sat-Sun 1600-2400. Finnish owner, speaks English, German.

₸ **El Patito Pekín**, 24 de Septiembre 307. Basic Chinese food, Mon-Sun 1100-1400, 1800-2000.

₸ **La Esquina del Pescado**, Sara y Florida. For fish, US$1.60 a plate.

₸ **Las Palmeras**, Ayacucho y Callali. Typical *camba*

food, large portions. Also at Junín 381.

Los Pozos market, taking up the whole block between 6 de Agosto, Suárez Arana, Quijarro and Campero, is open daily, clean, good for midday meals, food aisles serve local and Chinese food.

Rincón Brasil, Libertad 358. Brazilian-style *por kilo* place, popular, open every day 1130-1500, also (à la carte only) Tue-Sat from 1800.

Sabor Brasil, off Buenos Aires, entre Santa Bárbara y España, No 20. Another popular Brazilian-style *por kilo* place.

Su Salud, Quijarro 115. Tasty vegetarian food, filling lunches, huge portions. Recommended.

Tía Lía, Murillo 40. US$1.50 (US$2.25 weekends) for all the beef, chorizos, pork and chicken you want from a *parrillada*, huge selection of salads, pasta and bean dishes, Mon-Fri 1100-1500, Sat-Sun 1100-1600.

Vegetariano, Ayacucho 444. Breakfast, lunch and dinner, good.

Cafés

There are lots of very pleasant a/c cafés and ice cream parlours, where you can get coffee, ice cream, drinks, snacks and reasonably-priced meals.
Alexander's Coffee at Av Monseñor Rivero 400 in Zona El Cristo, T337 8653. For good coffee and people watching.
Fridolin, Pari 254 and Av Cañoto y Florida. Two good places for coffee and pastries.
Kivón, Ayacucho 267. Highly recommended for ice cream; also at Quijarro 409 in Mercado Los Pozos.

☊ Bars and clubs

Santa Cruz *p321, map p322*
Bar Irlandés Irish Pub, 3o Anillo Interno 1216 (between Av Cristo Redentor and Zoológico), T343 0671. Irish-themed pub, food available, English-speaking owner. Also *Café Irlandés*, Plaza 24 de Septiembre, Edificio Shopping Bolívar No 157 overlooking main plaza, T333 8118, live music Wed and Sat evening. Recommended.
M@D, Av San Martín 155, T336 0333. One of the best known and most popular clubs.
Moosehead, next to Bar Iralndés on 3o Anillo. Canadian bar/restaurant.

✿ Festivals and events

Santa Cruz *p321, map p322*
Cruceños are famous as fun-lovers and their music, the *carnavalitos*, can be heard all over South America. Of the various festivals, the brightest is **Carnival**, renowned for riotous behaviour, celebrated for the **15 days before Lent**: music in the streets, dancing, fancy dress

and the coronation of a queen. Beware the following day when youths run wild with buckets and balloons filled with water – no one is exempt. The *mascaritas* balls also take place during the pre-Lent season at *Caballo Blanco* when girls have the right to demand that men dance with them, and wear satin masks covering their heads completely, thus ensuring anonymity. **24 Sep** is a holiday.

The **Festival de Música Renacentista y Barroca Americana** is held in **April** every two years (next in 2008) in Santa Cruz and the Jesuit mission towns of the Chiquitania (San Javier, Concepción, among other places). It is organized by **Asociación Pro Arte y Cultura** (APAC), Beni 228, Santa Cruz, T333 2287, www.festivalesapac.com, and celebrates the wealth of sacred music written by Europeans and indigenous composers in the 17th and 18th centuries. APAC sells books, CDs, and videos of these extravaganzas and also offers – in both Santa Cruz and the mission towns – a schedule of continuous musical programmes. Every odd year in same locales APAC holds the **Festival Internacional de Teatro "Santa Cruz de la Sierra"**, next in 2009.

◎ Shopping

Santa Cruz *p321, map p322*
Bookshops El Ateno, Cañoto y 21 de Mayo, T333 3338. Books in English, access to internet. Los Amigos del Libro, Igavi 14, T332 7937, sells foreign language books and magazines. International magazines and newspapers often on sale in kiosks on main Plaza, eg *Miami Herald*, after arrival of daily Miami flight.
Handicrafts Idepe Usaka, Suaréz de Figueroa near Independencia, open Mon-Fri, 0900-1200, 1500-1800. Brilliant non-profit store specializing in colourful ceramics, fabrics, and mobiles. **Manos Indígenas**, Cuéllar 16, T337 2042. For fabrics and weavings from a number of indigenous groups. **Museo de Historia** in the Casa de Cultura. Best local crafts; hours are sporadic, call ahead, T355 0611. All proceeds go to *La Mancomunidad*, a local outfit that supports indigenous craftsmen and their families. **Uniarte**at Charagua 37 and 24 de Septiembre esq Seoane, T330 2995, 708-86942 (mob). Open 0900-1200, 1500-1830. Another first-rate non-profit store specializing in colourful ceramics, fabrics, and mobiles. **Vicuñita Handicrafts**, Ingavi e Independencia, T333 4711. By far the best and biggest selection from altiplano and lowlands. Very honest, will ship. Artesanía shops on Libertad and on Plaza 24 de Septiembre y Bolívar.
Jewellery RC Joyas, Bolívar 262, T333 2725.

Jewellery and Bolivian gems, the manager produces and sells good maps of Santa Cruz City and department.

Markets Bazar Siete Calles, mainly for clothing, but food and fruit is sold outside, main entrance is in 100 block of Isabel La Católica, also on Camiri and Vallegrande, past Ingavi. **Los Pozos**, see under Eating. Open daily; in summer it's full of exotic fruits. Beware of bag-snatching. There is a fruit and vegetable market at Sucre y Cochabamba, and a large indigenous market on Sun near the bus terminal.

▲ Activities and tours

Santa Cruz *p321, map p322*
Jean Paul Ayala,
jpdakidd@roble.scz.entelnet.bo. Recommended for birdwatching trips, speaks English.
Mario Berndt, T342 0340,
tauk@em.daitec-bo.com. Does large-scale tailored tours off the beaten track, mostly to the Altiplano, requires approx 3 months notice, speaks English, German and Spanish and is very knowledgeable about the area.
Forest Tour Operator, Cuéllar 22, T337 2042, www.forestbolivia.com. Environmentally sensitive tours to most national parks, Beni and Chiquitania. Works with local indigenous groups.
Fremen, Beni 79, T333 8535, F336 0265. Local tours, also jungle river cruises.
Magri Turismo, Warnes esq Potosí, T334 5663, www.magri-amexpress.com.bo. American Express agent. Recommended.
Ruta Verde, 21 de Mayo 332, T339 6470, www.rutaverdebolivia.com. Dutch/Bolivian owned operator running tours to national parks (Amboró, Noel Kempff Mercado), Jesuit missions, Amazonian boat trips, and tailor-made tours in Bolivia; well-organized, uses local guides, English and German spoken, good value. Also offers Spanish classses.

⊖ Transport

Santa Cruz *p321, map p322*
Air Airport information T181; the terminal has Emigration/Immigration office, **Entel** office, luggage lockers, duty free shop, restaurant (expensive), bank open 0830-1830, changes cash and TCs, withdrawal on Visa and MasterCard (when closed try **AASANA** desk, where you pay airport tax). LAB flies at least twice daily to **La Paz** and **Cochabamba**. Aero Sur flies to **La Paz** (several daily), **Cochabamba**, **Sucre**, **Tarija** and **Puerto Suárez**, plus Madrid, Asunción, Buenos Aires, Lima, São Paulo and Miami. Flights also with **Amazonas** to **Trinidad** for onward connections. International destinations include most South

American capitals, as well as **Salta**, **Tucumán** and **Córdoba**, **São Paulo** and some US gateways and cities in Mexico and Central America.
Bus Daily buses to **Cochabamba** (US$3-4.50, 10 hrs), many *flotas* leave between 0600-0900 and 1630-2100. Direct to **Sucre** daily between 1700-1800, 14 hrs, US$6-7.50. **Oruro** and **La Paz** 17 hrs, US$10-12.50, between 1700-2200 (some are *buscama*); change in Cochabamba for daytime travel. To **Camiri** (US$3.75), **Yacuiba** and **Tarija**, daily, several companies; 26-32 hrs to Tarija. To **Trinidad**, several daily, 12 hrs, US$4.50, all depart 1700 or 1900. **International**: Empresa Yacyretá, Mon, Tue, Thu, Sat, 2030 **Santa Cruz- Asunción**, US$45, minimum 24 hrs via Villamontes and the Chaco, for information T362 5557. **Stel Turismo**, T349 7762, runs the same route 2000 daily. See page 328 for the route to Paraguay across the Chaco.
Taxi About US$1.15 inside 1st Anillo (US$1.50 at night), US$1.30 inside 3rd Anillo, fix fare in advance.
Train Ferroviaria Oriental, T7164 8421. To **Quijarro** (for Brazil), see page 333, and **Yacuiba** (for Argentina), see page 328.

❶ Directory

Santa Cruz *p321, map p322*
Airline offices Aerolíneas Argentinas, Edif Banco de la Nación Argentina, on main Plaza, T333 9776. Aero Sur, Irala 616, T336 4446. Amaszonas, Aeropuerto El Trompillo, of 10, T357 8988. American Airlines, Beni 167, T334 1314. LAB, Warnes y Chuquisaca, T334 4596, or 901-10-5000.
Banks Enlace ATMs in airport departure lounge and throughout downtown; also in Equipetrol. Banco Mercantil, René Moreno y Suárez de Figueroa. Cash advance on Visa, changes cash and TCs. Medicambio on Plaza 24 de Septiembre will change TCs into dollars at 3% commission, excellent reputation. Menno Credit Union, 10 de Agosto 15, T332 8800, small office in Mennonite area of town, open 0900-1600, changes TCs, 1% commission, English, German and Dutch spoken. Street money changers on Plaza 24 de Septiembre and around bus terminal; they exchange guaraníes. **Car hire** Aby's, 3rd Anillo 1038, esq Pasaje Muralto 1038 (opposite zoo), T345 1560. Across, 4th Anillo, esq Radial 27 (400 m from Av Banzer Oeste), T344 1717. US$70 per day for basic Suzuki 4x4 (200 km per day) with insurance. Barron's, Av Alemana 50 y Tajibos, T342 0160, www.rentacarbolivia.com. Outstanding service and completely trustworthy; clean vehicles, fully equipped. **Cultural centres** See Asociación Pro Arte y Cultura under **Festivals and events**, above. Centro Boliviano Americano, Cochabamba 66, T334 2299, www.cba.com.bo.

Library with US papers and magazines, English classes, some cultural events. **Centro Cultural Franco Alemán**, Av Velarde 200, T332 9906, www.ccfranco aleman.org. Joint cultural institute with language courses, cultural events, library (internet access), both open Mon-Fri 0900-1200, 1530-2000. **Centro de Formación de la Cooperación Española**, Arenales 583, T335 1322, www.aeci.org.bo (concerts, films, art exhibitions, lectures, etc), very good. **Centro Simón I Patiño**, Independencia y Suárez de Figueroa 89, T 337 5726, www.fundacionpatino.org/. Exhibitions, galleries, and bookstore on Bolivian cultures.

Embassies and consulates Argentina, in Edif Banco de la Nación Argentina, Plaza 24 de Septiembre, Junín 22, T332 8291, Mon-Fri 0800-1300. Brazil, Av Busch 330, T337 1961, Mon-Fri 0900-1500. It takes 24 hrs to process visa applications, reported as unhelpful. Chile, Av San Martín, Edif Equipetrol Tower, p 9, T353 1796. Denmark, Landívar 401, T343 5540, Mon-Fri, 0900-1200, 1500-1800. Germany, Ñuflo de Chávez 437, T332 4153, Mon-Fri 0800-1200. Israel, Av Banzer 171, T342 4777, hobsch@infonet.bo. Italy, El Trompillo, Edif Honnen p 1, T336 6113, Mon-Fri

0830-1230. Japan, Cochabamba y Saavedra, T332 4197. Netherlands, Av Roque Aguilera 300, 3rd ring, between Grigotá and Paraí, T353 8799, ludo@alke.net, Mon-Fri 0900-1230. Paraguay, Manuel Ignacio Salvatierra 99, Edif Victoria, of 1A, T336 7585. Colour photo required for visa, Mon-Fri 0730-1400. Peru, Av La Salle 2327, T333 6344. Spain, Monseñor Santiesteban 237, T352 5200, Mon-Fri 0900-1200. Switzerland, Los Gomeros 98, T343 5540. USA, Güemes Este 6, Equipetrol, T335 4498, Mon-Fri 0900-1130 (very limited services offered; best to go to La Paz).

Internet cybercafés everywhere, US$0.40-0.80 per hr. **Medical services** For hospitals, doctors and dentists, contact your consulate or the tourist office for advice. **Post office** C Junín 146. **Telephone** Entel, Warnes 36 (entre Moreno y Chuquisaca), T332 5526, local and international calls and fax, open Mon-Fri 0730-2330, Sat, Sun and holidays 0730-2200. Also small *Entel* office at Quijarro 267. **Useful addresses** Immigration: 3er Anillo Interno esq Av Cronenbold, opposite the zoo, T333 6442/2136, Mon-Fri 0830-1200, 1430-1800, service can be very slow.

Southeastern Bolivia

The highlights of this area are southwest of Santa Cruz: the pre-Inca ruins of Samaipata, the nearby Parque Nacional Amboró and the newly-developed Che Guevara Trail, on which you can follow in the final, fatal footsteps of the revolutionary.

Samaipata → *Phone code: 03. Colour map M6, grid A4. Altitude: 1,650 m.*

From Santa Cruz the spectacular old mountain road to Cochabamba runs along the Piray gorge and up into the highlands. Some 120 km from Santa Cruz is Samaipata, a great place to relax midweek, with good lodging, restaurants, hikes and riding, and a helpful ex-pat community. Local *artesanías* include ceramics. At weekends the town bursts into life as crowds of Cruceños come to escape the city heat and to party. See www.samaipata.info.

The **Centro de Investigaciones Arqueológicas y Antropológicas Samaipata** has a collection of pots and vases with anthropomorphic designs, dating from 200 BC to 200 AD and, most importantly, provides information on the nearby pre-Inca ceremonial site commonly called **El Fuerte** ① *daily 0900-1700, Centro 0930-1230, 1430-1830; US$4 for El Fuerte and Centro de Investigaciones, US$0.75 for Centro only, ticket valid 4 days. Guides available at El Fuerte, US$5.* This sacred structure (1,970 m) consists of a complex system of channels, basins, high-relief sculptures, etc, carved out of one vast slab of rock. Latest research on dates is conflicting. Some suggests that Amazonian people created it around 1500 BC, but it could be later. There is evidence of subsequent occupations and that it was the eastern outpost of the Incas' Kollasuyo (their Bolivian Empire). It is no longer permitted to walk on the rock, so visit the museum first to see the excellent model. El Fuerte is 9 km from the town; 3 km along the highway, then 6 km up a rough, signposted road (taxi US$4.50); two hours' walk one way, or drive to the entrance. Pleasant bathing is possible in a river on the way to El Fuerte.

In addition to tours to El Fuerte, Amboró and the Ruta del Che (see below), many other tours are offered in the Samaipata area. These include **Cuevas**, 20 km east of town, with waterfalls and pools; the beautiful **Laguna Volcán** region, further east; forest and sandstone mountains at **Bella Vista/Codo de los Andes**; the 40-m high **La Pajcha** waterfall (40 km south), which can be combined with the **Cerro de los Cóndores**, where condors can regularly be seen. Tour operators arrange trips, often with guides who specialize in wildlife-watching.

Vallegrande and La Higuera

Some 115 km south of the Santa Cruz-Cochabamba road is La Higuera, where Che Guevara was killed. On 8 October each year, people gather there to celebrate his memory. La Higuera is reached through the colonial town of **Vallegrande** where, at **Hospital Nuestro Señor de Malta** ① *no fee, but voluntary donation to the health station*, you can see the old laundry building where Che's body was shown to the international press on 9 October 1967. Near Vallegrande's air strip you can see the results of excavations carried out in 1997 which finally unearthed his physical remains (now in Cuba), ask an airport attendant to see the site. Vallegrande has a small archaeological museum, above which is the **Che Guevara Room** *US$0.30*.

The schoolhouse in La Higuera where Che was executed is now a museum. Another **museum** (T03-942 2003), owned by René Villegas, is open when he is in town. Guides, including Pedro Calzadillo, headmaster of the school, will show visitors to the ravine of El Churo, where Che was captured on 8 October 1967. In 2004 the **Ruta del Che** (Che Guevara Trail) was opened, following the route of Che and his band as they feld the Bolivian army. It takes three to six days, depending on how much you do and how you travel. The trail is run by the Bolivian government, CARE International and local communities. Tour operators offer packages. See www.southamericanpictures.com/collections/che-guevara-trail/che-trail.htm.

Parque Nacional Amboró

This vast (442,500 ha) protected area lies only three hours west of Santa Cruz. Amboró encompasses three distinct major ecosystems and 11 life zones and is home to thousands of animal, plant and insect species (it is reputed to contain more butterflies than anywhere else on earth). The park is home to 820 species of birds, including the blue-horned curassow, the very rare quetzal and cock-of-the-rock, red and chestnut-fronted macaws, hoatzin and cuvier toucans, and most mammals native to Amazonia, such as capybaras, peccaries, tapirs, several species of monkey, and jungle cats like the jaguar, ocelot and margay, and the increasingly rare spectacled bear. There are also numerous waterfalls and cool, green swimming pools, moss-ridden caves and large tracts of virgin rainforest. The park itself is largely inaccessible and much wading is required to get around, but there is good trekking in the surrounding buffer zone which is where most tours operate. There are two places to base yourself: Samaipata (see also page 326) and Buena Vista. The park is administered by **SERNAP**. The park's main office is in Santa Cruz ① *Igmiri 210, Barrio Urbari, T355 5053, www.amboro-bo.org*. There are subsidiary offices in Samaipata and Buena Vista. Topographic maps of the area can be obtained at the IGM in Santa Cruz ① *Av Tres Pasos al Frente near the Tercer Anillo, Barrio Petrolero Sur, T346 3040, 0830-1230, 1500-1800*. Note that there are many biting insects so take repellent.

Access from Buena Vista Northwest of Santa Cruz by paved road is the sleepy town of Buena Vista. Most entrances to the park involve crossing the Río Surutú, which is usually in flood in the wet season (November-March). The most popular entrance to the park is Las Cruces, 35 km away, reached by a daily morning bus whose route runs alongside the Río Surutú for several km. From Las Cruces, the trail leads directly to the settlement of Villa Amboró, in the park's buffer zone. Also in the buffer zone is Macañucú, 50 km from Buena Vista, which has the best services in the park, with horse riding, hiking trails, guides, camping, kitchens and showers (US$20 pp per day), radio contact with the park office. There is a national park office just over a block from the plaza in Buena Vista, T932 2032 (permit free). Office is closed Sunday and siesta time. They can help with guides and suggestions.

Access from Samaipata Many agencies in Samaipata offer excursions. If going on your own, access is via **Mairana**, 17 km by minibus from Samaipata over a bad, but beautiful road (several basic hotels and roadside eateries), the meal stop for long distance buses between Santa Cruz and Sucre; you can catch these if there are seats available. Shared taxis from Santa Cruz to Mairana with **Cotrama** ① *Humberto Vásquez y Primer Anillo*, leave when full throughout the day, 3 hours, US$3.50, or minibus from Av Grigotá at Plaza Oruro. Shared taxis from Mairana to La Yunga, US$1.50 per person, more for an *expreso*. At **La Yunga** (US$2 entry fee), there are community-run cabins, **E**, with shared bath, no shower, basic, lovely views, meals available with advance notice. Guides from La Yunga charge US$15 per day to explore the buffer zone; take all your own trekking gear and provisions. Taxi Samaipata-La Yunga, 30 km, US$12 one way. The village of **Quirusillas** is 1½-2 hours by minibus from Mairana. As the area is close to the mountains, there is more rain than further east, with plenty of greenery and cloud forest. Quirusillas has two basic places to stay and a cemetery set on a hill overlooking a small valley. Lago Quirusillas is about 6 km away via a steep dirt road.

There is a minibus service from Mairana to Vallegrande (see above) and overnight buses to Cochabamba along the old road with **Expreso Surumi** on Tuesday, Friday and Sunday, 1530, 12 hours, US$4.50 (passengers sleep in the locked bus in a Cochabamba market area until dawn).

To Paraguay

South of Santa Cruz the road passes through Abapó and Camiri. A paved road heads south from Camiri, through Boyuibe, Villamontes and Yacuiba to Argentina (see below). At Boyuibe another road heads east to Paraguay, used less now than a new road from Villamontes (see below) to Mariscal Estigarribia in the Paraguayan Chaco. It is possible, albeit foolish, to drive from Boyuibe into Paraguay direct on the old road in a truck or 4WD, high clearance vehicle, carry insect repellent, food and water for a week. No help can be relied on in case of a breakdown; a winch is advisable, especially after rain. There are some rivers to ford and although they are dry in the dry season they can be impassable if there is rain in the area. The new route, once you leave the paved road at Villamontes, should be treated with the same respect. At Boyuibe (*Alojamiento Boyuibe*, has hot showers, restaurant, and two others, all **G**) all buses stop at Parador-Restaurante Yacyretá, on main road, owners are helpful, sell bus tickets to Asunción and have rooms to rent; change cash here (poor rates). Fuel and water are available.

Villamontes → *Phone code: 04. Colour map 6, grid B4.*

South of Boyuibe is Villamontes (280 km east of Tarija) renowned for fishing. It holds a Fiesta del Pescado in August. It is a friendly town on the edge of the Gran Chaco and is on the road and rail route from Santa Cruz to the Argentine border at Yacuiba. You can change buses here to/from Paraguay on the Santa Cruz-Yacuiba bus route, or to/from Tarija, or if coming from Sucre. There are two banks (no ATM, exchange limited) and an internet café (next to *El Arriero* restaurant) on Plaza 15 de Abril. *Entel* is one block northeast of this plaza.

The road to Paraguay runs east to **Ibibobo**. The first 80 km is an all-weather gravel surface. Bolivian exit stamps are given at Ibibobo. If travelling by bus, passports are collected by driver and returned on arrival at Mcal Estigarribia, Paraguay, with Bolivian exit stamp. Paraguayan immigration and thorough drugs searches take place in Mcal Estigarribia. See under Santa Cruz, page 325, for international bus services, and see the Chaco section of the Paraguay chapter for road conditions, etc. From Ibibobo to the frontier at Picada Sucre is 75 km, then it's 15 km to the border and another 8 km to the Paraguayan frontier post at **Fortín Infante Rivarola**. There are no police or immigration officials at the border.

To Argentina (Yacuiba) → *Colour map 6, grid B4. Population: 11,000.*

From Santa Cruz the route goes Boyuibe, Villamontes and Yacuiba, a prosperous city at the crossing to Pocitos in Argentina. From Villamontes to Yacuiba road is paved, but no bridges; river crossings tricky in wet season. In Yacuiba, there are **Entel** and Correos. Argentine consul at Comercio y Sucre. The border crossing is straightforward. Passengers leaving Bolivia must disembark at Yacuiba, take a taxi to Pocitos on the border (US$0.40, beware unscrupulous drivers) and walk across to Argentina.

● Sleeping

Samaipata *p326*
Rooms may be hard to find at weekends in high season. Most cabins listed have kitchen, bathroom, barbecue and hammocks.
D Cabañas de Traudi, across the road from *La Víspera*, T944 6094, traudiar@cotas.com.bo. Cabins for 2-8, also **F** lovely rooms (**G** with shared bathroom), heated pool US$1.50 for non residents, sitting area with open fire, TV and music system, ceramics shop, great place.
D Landhaus, C Murillo, T944 6033, www.samaipata-landhaus.com. Most central of all

the *cabañas*, beautiful place with a small pool, sun loungers, garden, hammocks, parking, internet and sauna (US$20 for up to 8 people), also rooms only with shared bathroom **F** pp; excellent restaurant and café.
C-D La Víspera, 1.2 km south of town, T944 6082, www.lavispera.org. Dutch-owned organic farm with accommodation in 4 cosy cabins, camping US$4-5, delicious local produce for breakfast, US$3 pp. Very peaceful; Margarita and Pieter know pretty much everything about the local area and can arrange all excursions

through *Bolviajes*. Highly recommended.

E Andoriña, Arte y Cultura, C Campero s/n frente *El Deber*, 2½ blocks from plaza, T944 6333, www.andorinasamaipata.com. **G** in dorm, **C** for cabin, includes breakfast with fruit and juices, tastefully decorated, kitchen, bar, public areas, garden, good views, picture library, cultural events and films. Enthusiastic owners Andrés and Doriña are very helpful and knowledgeable, English spoken.

G Alojamiento Vargas, around corner from museum. Clothes-washing facilities, use of kitchen, breakfast, owner Teresa is helpful. Recommended.

G Aranjuez, on the main road at the entrance to town, T944 6223. Upstairs terrace, clothes washing area, food available, includes breakfast, good value.

G Don Jorge, Bolívar, T944 6086. Cheaper with shared bath, hot showers, good beds, large shaded patio, good set lunch.

G Paola, western corner of plaza, T944 6093. Family-run, breakfast extra, good beds, warm showers, use of kitchen, good restaurant, can arrange guides to Amboró and El Fuerte and book microbus to Santa Cruz, rents mountain bikes US$1.25 per hr.

G Residencial Kim, near the plaza, T944 6161. Use of kitchen, cheaper with shared bath, family-run, spotless, good value. Recommended.

Vallegrande and La Higuera *p327*

G pp Alojamiento Teresita, Escalante y Mendoza. Has good rooms. In La Higuera you can camp in the school, but ask permission, US$0.30.

G La Sede de los Ganaderos, 1 block from plaz, T942 2176. Includes breakfast, hot water, large rooms, comfortable, parking.

Parque Nacional Amboró *p327*

AL Flora y Fauna, known as '*Doble F*', Buena Vista, T03-333 8118, Santa Cruz. Hilltop cabins, viewing platforms for birdwatchers, well-planned trails (same owner as *Café Irlandés* in Santa Cruz).

C Pozoazul, on the bypass, Buena Vista, T03-932 2091. A/c, kitchen, pool, good restaurant, helpful, also camping US$14 including showers and pool.

E Sumuqué, Av 6 de Agosto 250, Buena Vista, T03-932 2080. Cabins in pleasant gardens, trails.

G Nadia, Buena Vista, T03-932 2049. Central, small, family run.

CARE has funded cabins on the far bank of the Río Surutú just past Villa Aguiles on the road from Buena Vista to the river. Good trails, well located in the multiple-use area with lots of flora and fauna.

To Paraguay
Haciendas del Chaco, based in Camiri, T03-952

4155, http://haciendasdelchaco.com (under construction 2007), haciendasdelchaco@cidis.ws. A new group of 6 farms offering full board, hot showers, activities such as horse riding, cheese making, wildlife trails, trips to the Ruta del Che and Guaraní communities.

Villamontes *p328*

D Gran Hotel Avenida, 3 blocks east of Plaza 15 de Abril, T672 2297, F672 2412. A/c, includes breakfast, helpful owner, parking.

D pp El Rancho, 3 km from centre opposite station (taxi US$0.45) T672 2059, F672 2985. Lovely rooms, a/c, TV, excellent restaurant, also annexe **F** pp. Recommended.

To Argentina: Yacuiba *p328*

C Hotel París, Comercio y Campero, T682 2182. The best.

E Valentín, Avenida San Martín 1462, opposite rail station, T682 2645, F682 2317. **F** without bath, excellent value

🍴 Eating

Samaipata *p326*

🍴🍴🍴 **El Descanso en Los Alturas**. Wide choice including excellent steaks and pizzas.

🍴🍴 **Café Hamburg**, Bolívar. Laid back, bar, food (including vegetarian), well stocked book exchange, internet US$2.25 per hr (only after 1900), see *Roadrunners* tour agency below.

Cafés

Café Baden, 1 km towards Santa Cruz, good for ice cream and tortes as well as steak and *schweizer würstsalat*.

Chakana bar/restaurant/café open every day 0900-late, Dutch-owned, relaxing, *almuerzos* for US$2.25, good snacks and salads, seats outside, a book exchange, cakes and ice cream.

Panadería Gerlinde, near the Santa Cruz-Cochabamba main road. For superb biscuits, bread, homemade pastas, herbs, cheese, yoghurts and cold meats, Swiss-run, open daily 0700-2200. Also has a weekend stall in the market.

Vallegrande and La Higuera *p327*

🍴 **Café Santa Clara**, on the plaza. Decent food and beer, Che-inspired work, helpful staff.

🍴 **El Mirador**. Huge portions of meat, good.

Villamontes *p328*

🍴 **Churrasquería Argentina**, ½ block from Plaza 15 de Abril. For pizzas and grilled meat.

🍴 **Parillada El Arriero**, Plaza 15 de Abril. Good, cheap meals.

▲ Activities and tours

Samaipata *p326*
Those listed here are recommended. Expect to pay US$10-12 pp in a group of 4, up to US$30 for smaller groups.
Gilberto Aguilera, T944 6050, considered the most knowledgeable local guide, good value tours.
Amboró Tours, Bolívar 43, T/F944 6293, erickamboro@ cotas.com.bo. Run by Erick Prado who speaks only Spanish.
Michael Blendinger, C Bolívar opposite the museum, T944 6227, www.discoveringbolivia. com. German guide raised in Argentina who speaks English, runs fully- equipped 4WD tours, short and long treks, horse rides, specialist in nature and archaeology. Accommodation in cabins available, also inclusive packages.
Roadrunners, Olaf and Frank, T944 6193, www.samaipata.info/roadrunners/. Speak English and German, enthusiastic, lots of information and advice, recommended tour of El Fuerte.
See **La Víspera**, above, Margarita and Pieter, Bolviajes.

Parque Nacional Amboró *p327*
Amboró Adventures, on the plaza in Buena Vista, T03-932 2090. Excursions include guide and transportation, but not food.
Amboró Tours, near the park office in Buena Vista, T03-932 2093, 716 33990 (mob), rodosoto@ hotmail.com. Tours with very basic accommodation, simple food and include transport and guides, about US$50 pp per day, expensive for what's offered. Independent guides cost US$10 per day in Buena Vista.

⊕ Transport

Samaipata *p326*
Bus From **Santa Cruz** to Samaipata, only Sucre-bound buses leave from the new bus station. Shared taxis leave when full from the vicinity of the old bus station, at the junction of Av Omar Chávez Ortiz and Solís de Olguín: **Taxi Florida**, T333 5067 (in Samaipata T944 6133), 2½ hrs, US$3.50. **Expreso Samaipata** minibus, Av Omar Chávez Ortiz 1111, T336 2312 (Samaipata 944 6199), US$2, at 1700. Other minibuses from Av Grigotá y Tercer Anillo, **Montenegro** daily 1630, **Rojas** 0415, but not Mon, Wed, Fri. They return from Samaipata weekdays 0415-0430, Sun 1300 (Rojas), 1500 (Montenegro, from *Heladería Dany* on the plaza; buy tickets here the day before), 3 hrs, US$2. *Colectivos* in Samaipata will pick you up from your hotel, or else take you from the petrol station. Buses leaving Santa Cruz for **Sucre** pass through

Samaipata between 1800 and 2000. To get to Samaipata from **Sucre**, buses leave at night and arrive 0500-0600 (set your alarm in case the driver forgets to stop for you), stopping in Mairana or Mataral for breakfast, about ½ hr before Samaipata. Mini-bus from Mairana passes through Samaipata daily at 0445 near *Residencial Kim*, goes to Terminal Bimodal, T334 0772 .

Vallegrande and La Higuera *p327*
Bus Trans Vallegrande and others from Av Grigotá y 3o Anillo, daily buses at 0900, 1400, 1930 from Santa Cruz to **Vallegrande** via **Samaipata**, 5 hrs, US$4.30. Best to book in advance. From Vallegrande market, a daily bus departs 0815 to **Pucará** (45 km), from where there is transport (12 km) to **La Higuera**. Taxi Vallegrande-La Higuera US$25-30.

Parque Nacional Amboró *p327*
Bus Leave regularly from beside Santa Cruz terminal hourly from 0500-1500 (also minibuses from Montero, US$1, and buses from Villa Tunari, US$5) to **Buena Vista**. See page 327 for how to get to **Mairana** and **La Yunga**.

Villamontes *p328*
Bus To **Tarija** via Entre Ríos (unpaved road, 10 hrs) daily 1800, US$7.50. To **Santa Cruz** at 1030, 12 hrs, US$4.50, **Sucre** at 1930, US$7.50, and **La Paz** at 2000, US$9. Also to **Camiri**, **Tupiza**, **Villazón**.
Train The **Santa Cruz-Yacuiba** tren mixto stops here: Wed and Fri at 0515, returning to Santa Cruz on Wed and Fri at 1950. To Santa Cruz: Pullman US$10.50, 1st class US$4.50, 2nd class US$3.50; to Yacuiba, Pullman US$6, 1st class US$1.50, 2nd class US$1.10.

To Argentina: Yacuiba *p328*
Bus To **Santa Cruz**, about 20 companies run daily services, mostly at night, 14 hrs, US$13. To **Tarija**, daily morning and evening. To **Potosí-Oruro-La Paz**, with Trans Yacuiba and Expreso Tarija. Daily to **Sucre** with Flota Copacabana.
Train Santa Cruz-Yacuiba tren mixto Tue and Thu, 1530, 17 hrs, returning from Yacuiba Wed and Fri, 1700, Pullman US$12.50, 1st class US$6, 2nd class US$4.50.

⊕ Directory

Samaipata *p326*
Banks No ATMs. The Cooperativa near plaza changes US$ cash at fair rates. **Internet** At Entel on the plaza, slow and expensive, US$1.50-2 per hr. **Telephone** Several cabinas around the plaza.

Eastern Bolivia

The vast and rapidly-developing plains to the east of the Eastern Cordillera are Bolivia's richest area in natural resources. For the visitor, the beautiful churches of former Jesuit Chiquitano missions east of Santa Cruz are worth a visit and further east is Bolivia's portion of the Pantanal. The Noel Kempff Mercado national park, meanwhile, is one of the natural wonders of South America.

Chiquitano Jesuit Missions

Ten Jesuit missions survive east of Santa Cruz, six of which – San Javier, Concepción, San Rafael, Santa Ana, San Miguel and San José de Chiquitos – have churches which are UNESCO World Heritage Sites. The first three were built by the Swiss Jesuit, Padre Martin Schmidt, the other two (plus the one at San Ignacio de Velasco, demolished in 1948, see below) were built by other priests. Besides organizing *reducciones* and constructing churches, for each of which he built an organ, Padre Schmidt wrote music (some is still played today on traditional instruments) and he published a Spanish-Idioma Chiquitano dictionary based on his knowledge of all the dialects of the region. He worked in this part of the then-Viceroyalty of Peru until the expulsion of the Jesuits in 1767 by order of Charles III of Spain.

Access to the mission area is by bus or train from **Santa Cruz**: a paved highway runs north to San Ramón (139 km) and on north, to San Javier (45 km), turning east here to Concepción (68 km), then, unpaved, to San Ignacio (171 km). One road continues east to San Matías and the Brazilian border (good gravel part of the way); others head south either through San Miguel, or Santa Ana to meet at San Rafael for the continuation south to San José de Chiquitos. By rail, leave the Santa Cruz-Quijarro train at San José and from there travel north. The most comfortable way to visit is by jeep, in five days. The route is straightforward and fuel is available. For jeep hire, see page 325 . For information on the Chiquitano dry forest, visit www.fcbcinfo.org, the site (in Spanish and English) of the **Fundación para la Conservación del Bosque Chiquitano** (FCBC) ① *C Fortín Platanillos 190, Santa Cruz, T/F03-334 1017*. See also **www.chiquitania.com** for extensive historical and practical information, and **www.mancochiquitana.org**, the site of the **Mancomunidad de Municipios de la Gran Chiquitania**, a non-profit organization dedicated to the economic improvement of the region, including through handicraft workshops.

San Javier (or San Xavier) The first Jesuit mission in Chiquitos (1691), its church built by Padre Schmidt between 1749 and 1752 ① *US$0.45*. The original wooden structure has survived more or less intact and restoration was undertaken between 1987 and 1992 by the Swiss Hans Roth, himself a former Jesuit. Subtle designs and floral patterns cover the ceiling, walls and carved columns. One of the bas-relief paintings on the high altar depicts Martin Schmidt playing the piano for his indigenous choir. On the Plaza are the **Museo Misiones de Chiquitos** and the **Museo Yarítú** (on the pre-Jesuit Yaritús culture). The modern town prospers from extensive cattle ranching. Many fine walks in the surrounding countryside; also good for cycling with an all-terrain bike. Patron saint's *fiesta*, 3 December. Tourist guides' association has an office in the **Alcaldía** ① *T963 5001, or 963 5149 for a guide to the church*.

Concepción The village is dominated by its magnificent cathedral, completed by Padre Schmidt in 1756 and totally restored by the late Hans Roth 1975-1982 ① *entry US$1*. The interior of this beautiful church has an altar of laminated silver. In front of the church is a bell-cum-clock tower housing the original bells and behind it are well-restored cloisters. On the plaza, forming part of the Jesuit complex, is the **Museo Misional** ① *Mon-Sat 0800-1200, 1430-1830, Sun 1000-1230, US$0.45*. The ticket also gives entry to the **Hans Roth Museum**, dedicated to the restoration process. Visit also the **Museo Antropológico de la Chiquitania** ① *16 de Septiembre y Tte Capoblanco, 0800-1200, 1400-1800, free*, which explains the life of the indigenous peoples of the region. It has a café and guesthouse. Fiesta de la Inmaculada Concepción: 8 December. An orchid festival is held in the second week of October. There is a tourist office ① *T964 3057*, which can arrange trips to nearby recreational areas, ranches and communities. Various restaurants in town. Many places sell wood carvings and leather goods.

San Ignacio de Velasco A lack of funds for restoration led to the demolition of San Ignacio's replacement Jesuit church in 1948, the original having burnt down in 1808. A modern replica contains the elaborate high altar, pulpit and paintings and statues of saints. A museum in the Casa de la Cultura on the plaza has a few musical instruments from the old church (there is a tourist office here, open weekdays). Patron saint's day, preceded by a cattle fair, 31 July. The town is the main transport and commericial hub for the region. Laguna Guapomó on the outskirts is good for swimming, boating and fishing. *Entel* two blocks from plaza.

Santa Ana, San Rafael and San Miguel de Velasco The church in **Santa Ana** (founded 1755, constructed after the expulsion of the Jesuits), is a lovely wooden building, the most authentic of all the Jesuit *templos*. It is currently being restored, albeit sporadically. Sr Luis Rocha or his children will show you inside; ask for his house at the shop on the plaza where the bus stops. Fiesta de Santa Ana: 26 July. Two *alojamientos* in town and meals at Sra Silva's *Pensión El Tacú*, next to church, or the *Club Social*. **San Rafael's** church was completed by Padre Schmidt in 1748. It is one of the most beautifully restored (Concepción's also vying for this title), with mica-covered interior walls and frescoes in beige paint over the exterior. Patron saint's day, with traditional dancing, 24 October; Christmas pageant is worth seeing (*Hotel Paradita*, T962 4008, **G**, two others; four restaurants near the plaza). The frescoes on the façade of the church (1766) at **San Miguel** depict St Peter and St Paul; designs in brown and yellow cover all the interior and the exterior side walls. The mission runs three schools and workshop; the sisters are very welcoming and will gladly show tourists around. There is a **Museo Etnofolclórico**, off the Plaza at C Betania; next door is the Municipalidad/Casa de la Cultura, with a tourist information office ① *T962 4222*. San Miguel rivals San Ignacio for the quality of its Chiquitano art. Patron saint's day: 29 September. Some 4 km away is the **Santuario de Cotoca**, beside a lake where you can swim; ask at *La Pascana* for transport. (*Alojamiento y Restaurant La Pascana*, on plaza, T962 4220, basic, cheap meals; there are various other places to stay and eat and a public phone office.) Most traffic from San Ignacio goes via San Miguel, not Santa Ana, to San Rafael. If visiting these places from San Ignacio, it's probably better to go to San Rafael first, then go back via San Miguel. A day trip by taxi from San Ignacio to these villages costs US$35-40 (negotiate).

San José de Chiquitos → *Phone code: 03. Colour map 6, grid B5.*
One complete side of the plaza of this dusty little town is occupied by the superb frontage of the Jesuit mission, begun in the mid-1740s. The stone buildings, in Baroque style, are connected by a wall. They are the restored 18th century chapel (closed, although the German Franciscan missionary priest may open it if asked ahead of time), the church (1747) with its triangular façade; the four-storey bell-tower (1748, under repair in 2007) and the mortuary (*la bóveda* – 1750), with one central window but no entrance in its severe frontage (also closed for reapir, 2007). Behind are the *colegio* and workshops, which are being transformed into study and practice rooms for the town's young musicians. The **Museo Ayoreo-Chiquitano**, across the plaza, funded by FCBC (see above) and Hombre y Naturaleza, deals with the local indigenous culture. The **Oficina Mayor de Cultura y Turismo** is on the Plaza ① *T972 2084*. There is an *Entel* office and a hospital. On Monday, Mennonites bring their produce to sell to shops and to buy provisions. The colonies are 50 km west and the Mennonites, who speak English, German, plattdeutsch and Spanish, are happy to talk about their way of life. Fiesta de San José is 1 May, preceded by a week of folkloric and other events.

About 2 km south from San José is the **Parque Nacional Histórico Santa Cruz la Vieja** ① *daily US$2.50, pool US$0.75*. This includes a monument to the original site of Santa Cruz (about 1540), a *mirador* giving views over the jungle and, 5 km into the park, a religious shrine. The park's heavily-forested hills contain much animal and bird life; various trails with grand views; guides available from the small village in the park (take insect repellent). It gets very hot so start early and take plenty of water. The **Cascadas del Suruquizo**, 3½ km south of the park, are three beautiful waterfalls and springs, which are great for cooling off in. The park and falls are best visited by car or taxi because it is a very hot, dusty walk there (allow over one hour on foot).

Parque Nacional Noel Kempff Mercado
In the far northeast corner of Santa Cruz Department, **Parque Nacional Noel Kempff Mercado** (named after a pioneer of conservation in Bolivia) ① *US$30, in theory a guide is compulsory, at extra cost*, is one of the world's most diverse natural habitats. It covers 1,523,446 ha (roughly the same size as Massachusetts) and encompasses seven ecosystems, within which are 139

species of mammals (including black jaguars), 617 species of birds (including nine types of macaw), 74 species of reptiles and 110 species of orchid. Highlights include the **Huanchaca** or **Caparú Plateau**, which with its 200-500 m sheer cliffs and tumbling waterfalls is another candidate for Sir Arthur Conan Doyle's *Lost World* (Colonel Percy Fawcett, who discovered the plateau in 1910, was a friend of the writer). The three best-known waterfalls are Arco Iris, Federico Ahlfeld on the Río Paucerna and the 150-m high Catarata del Encanto. The **Reserva Biológica Laguna Bahía**, in the southwest quadrant, has some tremendous hiking across the high plateau, through breathtaking scenery. For information on the park, contact the **Fundación de Amigos de la Naturaleza** ① *FAN, Km 7.5 Doble Vía La Guardia, Santa Cruz, T355 6800, www.fan-bo.org*, which manages the park (ask for Richard Vaca). Also visit www.noelkempff.com (Proyecto de Acción Climática).

To Brazil

There are three routes from Santa Cruz: by air to Puerto Suárez, by rail to Quijarro, or by road via San Matías. Puerto Suárez is near Quijarro and these two routes lead to Corumbá on the Brazilian side, from where there is access to the southern Pantanal. The San Matías road links to Cáceres, Cuiabá and the northern Pantanal in Brazil.

Puerto Suárez → *Phone code: 03. Colour map 6, grid B6. Population: 21,000.*

On the shore of Laguna Cáceres, this is a friendly, quiet, small town, with a shady main plaza. There is a nice view of the lake from the park at the north end of Avenida Bolívar. The area around the train station is known as *Paradero*. Do not venture into the market area unless you are looking to contract any one of innumerable intestinal illnesses, and/or have your pockets picked. Fishing and photo tours to the ecologically-astonishing Pantanal can be arranged more cheaply than on the Brazilian side. You can also arrange river tours and day trips to Brazil; these are generally most easily done through a hotel, although they will add a 10-15% service charge (see below). For information on the province, see www.gbusch.info.

Quijarro → *Phone code: 03. Colour map 6, grid B6. Population: 15,000.*

The eastern terminus of the Bolivian railway, and the gateway to Brazil, is Quijarro, a growing town with a new railway station (in 2005). It is quite safe by day, but caution is recommended at night. The water supply is often unreliable, try the tap before checking in to a hotel. Prices are much lower than in neighbouring Brazil and there are some decent places to stay, in particular the five-star **Hotel El Pantanal** in nearby Arroyo Concepción.

Border with Brazil

The municipality by the border is known as Arroyo Concepción. You need not have your passport stamped if you visit Corumbá for the day. Otherwise get your exit stamp at Bolivian immigration (see below), formalities are straightforward. There are no formalities on the Brazilian side, you must get your entry stamp in the Corumbá bus station/*rodoviária* (see page 586). Yellow Fever vaccination is compulsory to enter Bolivia and Brazil, have your certificate at hand when you go for your entry stamp, otherwise you may be sent to get revaccinated. Bolivian immigration is at the border at Arroyo Concepción, on right just before bridge (open 0800-1200, 1400-1730 daily), or at Puerto Suárez airport, where Bolivian exit/entry stamps are issued. Money changers right at the border offer the worst rates. Ask around in the small shops past the bridge and check the rate with several of them before changing. The Brazilian consulate is in Santa Cruz, or in Puerto Suárez. See Transport, below, for taxis from the border.

Via San Matías to Cáceres

The road route from Santa Cruz is via San Ignacio de Velasco to San Matías, a busy little town with hotels and restaurants then on to Cáceres and Cuiabá. From Santa Cruz it is a three-day trip, roads permitting: there are two roads: San Ignacio, Espíritu, San Vicente (with petrol station), San Matías, and the more southerly San Rafael de Velasco, Arica, Mercedes, Torno, fork left after 120 km to Cerrito, San Matías. The northerly route tends to be in better condition, but check before setting out. See under San Ignacio, page 335, for bus information. Get your passport stamped in San Ignacio as there is no passport control in San Matías, but plenty of military checks en route. Once in Brazil go to immigration in Cáceres or, on Sunday, to Polícia Federal in Cuiabá.

Sleeping

Chiquitano Jesuit Missions *p331*
San Javier
D **Momoqui**, Av Santa Cruz before plaza, T963 5095, hotelmomoqui@hotmail.com. Cabins in nice garden, with pool, pleasant, no restaurant.
D **Gran Hotel El Reposo del Guerrero**, C Tte Busch Becerra, T963 5022. Cheaper Mon-Fri and with shared bath, includes breakfast, comfortable, restaurant, bar.
F-G **Alojamiento Ame-Tauná**, on plaza opposite church, T963 5018. Cheaper with shared bath, hot showers, clean.

Concepción
C **Gran Hotel Concepción**, on plaza, T964 3031, granhotelconcepcion@ hotmail.com. Excellent service, including buffet breakfast, pool, gardens, bar, very comfortable. Highly recommended.
D **Apart Hotel Los Misiones**, C Luis Caballero, 1 block from church, T964 3021. Pleasant rooms around a courtyard, small pool, also has an apartment, good value.
E-G **Colonial**, Ñuflo de Chávez 7, ½ block from plaza, T964 3050. Good value, with hot shower, garden, hammocks on veranda, breakfast extra.
G **Residencial Westfalia**, C S Saucedo, 2 blocks from plaza, T964 3040. Cheaper without bath, German-owned, nice patio, good value.

San Ignacio de Velasco
A-B **La Misión**, Plaza 31 de Julio, T962 2333, www.hotel-lamision.com. Luxurious, colonial style with a/c, cable TV and pool, rooms of various standards and prices, includes buffet breakfast, tours arranged.
B **San Ignacio**, Plaza 31 de Julio, T962 2283, sanignacio@cotas.com.bo. In a restored former episiscopal mansion, non-profit (run by diocese, fubds support local indigenous communities), a/c, hot showers, breakfast.
F **Palace**, Comercio, off the plaza, T962 2063. With hot shower, includes breakfast, comfortable, good value. Other hotels (**D-G**) and places to eat near plaza.

San José de Chiquitos *p332*
E **Turubó**, on the plaza, T972 2037. With a/c, F with fan, cheaper with shared bath, variety of different rooms, good location, laundry service.
F **Hotel Denise**, Mons Géricke, 4 blocks east of plaza, T972 2230. With bath, a/c, cheaper with fan, nice patio, clean and comfortable, good value.

Parque Nacional Noel Kempff Mercado *p332*
There are 2 lodges in the park: 15 beds at a renovated ranch at **Flor de Oro**, with access to hikes in the pampas and forests, and river excursions to the Arco Iris and Federico Ahlfeld falls and to bays. At **Los Fierros** there are 30 beds at a more rustic facility, C pp including 3 meals. From here you can visit many different habitats and El Encanto falls. There are other lodging possibilities in small towns bordering the park and some camping is available. In all cases, contact *FAN* (Fundación Amigos de la Naturaleza – see above).

Puerto Suárez *p333*
A pp **Centro Ecológico El Tumbador**, T03- 762 8699, T7106 7712 (mob), eltumbador@yahoo.com. A non-profit- making organization working for sustainable development in the Bolivian Lowlands runs ½-day to 4-day river, trekking and 4WD tours from its research station and lodge on the lake; prices from US$82 per person all-inclusive.
D **Bamby**, Santa Cruz 31 y 6 de Agosto, T976 2015. A/c, E with fan, cheaper with shared bath, comfortable.
D-E **Sucre**, Bolívar 63 on main plaza, T976 2069. A/c, with bath, pleasant, good restaurant.

Quijarro *p333*
C-D **Bibosi**, Luis Salazar s/n, main street 3 blocks east of train station, T978 2113, htlbibosi@ hotmail.com. With a/c, E with fan, breakfast, pool, patio, restaurant, comfortable rooms with fridge, upscale for where it is.
E **Oasis**, Av Argentina 4, T978 2159. A/c, fridge, cheaper with shared bath and a/c, F with fan, OK.
E **Yoni**, Av Brasil opposite the station, T978 2109. A/c, fridge, F with shared bath and fan, OK, mosquito netting on windows.

Border with Brazil *p333*
AL **El Pantanal Resort**, Arroyo Concepción, T978 2020, www.elpantanalhotel.com. With all mod cons (poor internet connection), gateway to the Pantanal. They arrange cruises, tours and transport, expensive but worth it, discounts in dry season (very busy in Jan-Feb).

Eating

Chiquitano Jesuit Missions *p331*
† **Ganadero**, San Javier, in Asociación de Ganaderos on plaza. Best restaurant in town with excellent steaks. Others on plaza.

San José de Chiquitos *p332*
† **El Raffa**, between *la tranca* and petrol station on outskirts of town is highly recommended for *churrasco típico*.
† **El Solar**, on plaza. Hamburgers, milanesa, and salchipapa.

Brazil

Essentials	**340**
Rio de Janeiro	**348**
Sights	350
East of Rio	378
West of Rio	385
São Paulo	**391**
Sights	395
São Paulo coast	406
Minas Gerais and Espírito Santo	**411**
Belo Horizonte	411
East and south of Belo Horizonte	416
Espírito Santo	426
North of Belo Horizonte	430
Southern Brazil	**432**
Curitiba and around	432
Paranaguá and the coast	437
Santa Catarina	440
Rio Grande do Sul	448
Porto Alegre	448
Rio Grande do Sul state	453
Foz do Iguaçu	**458**
Salvador de Bahia	**463**
Sights	465
Inland from Salvador	478
South of Salvador	481
North of Salvador	488
Recife and the northeast coast	**490**
Recife	490
Around Recife	499
South of Recife	504
João Pessoa	507
Natal	509
Fortaleza and the north coast	**516**
Fortaleza	516

Coast east of Fortaleza	523
Coast west of Fortaleza	524
West of Fortaleza	530
The Amazon	**532**
Travel up the Amazon River	532
Belém and around	535
Belém to Manaus	542
Manaus	545
Amazon frontiers	**555**
Manaus to Colombia, Peru, Venezuela and Guyana	555
Southern Amazônia	559
Brasília and Goiás	**564**
Brasília	565
Goiás	571
Tocantins	576
The Pantanal	**577**
Ins and outs	577
Campo Grande and around	579
Corumbá	586
Cuiabá and around	588

Footprint features

Don't miss …	339
Touching down	341
Driving in Brazil	345
Carnival	372
Rodeo Romeos	410
O Aleijadinho	417
Carnival in Bahia	476
Paradise lost?	533

Introduction

Described as the sexiest nation on earth, Brazilians know how to flirt, flaunt and have fun. The Rio Carnival, with its intoxicating atmosphere and costumes to die for, is the most exuberant of a whole calendar of festivals. In this, the world's fifth largest country, football, looking good and dancing are the national passions. Everyone seems to be seduced by the sounds of samba ... and by the beach.

The coast of Brazil, all 7,408 km of it, has provided a suitable stretch of sand for every volleyball champion, surfer, dune-buggy driver and party animal. Just off shore there are many islands to sail to, from the huge Marajó with its water buffalo, to highly developed Santa Catarina, to the marine paradise of Abrolhos National Park.

But Brazilians also have a spiritual side to match their hedonistic streak. Many religions flourish, most obviously the African-based candomblé, which lives happily alongside Catholicism. In the 16th to 18th centuries, when Brazil was rich in gold and diamonds, the Portuguese colonists expressed their faith in some of the most beautiful baroque buildings created anywhere at that time.

For a change from cosmopolitan life, trek through the hills of the Chapada Diamantina, take the long road into the Pantanal wetlands and watch for hyacinth macaws and capybara, sling a hammock on a river boat up the mighty Amazon, or take a walk with the wildlife in the rainforest.

★ Don't miss ...

1 **Rio de Janeiro** One of the quintessential images of South America is Rio's setting of beaches, mountains and islands in the bay. Another is its carnival. And don't forget the football, or the nightlife ... where do you stop? page 348.

2 **Ouro Preto** In the heart of Minas Gerais is the capital of Brazilian baroque, built on the wealth of precious metals, and birthplace of the rebellion against colonial rule, page 417.

3 **Salvador de Bahia** The city of Salvador is Africa in Brazil, with a culture that has survived the slave trade in religion, music and cuisine. There's also a fine colonial heritage and some great beaches, page 463.

4 **Northeastern beaches** The states of Ceará and Rio Grande do Norte have beaches to die for: clear waters, golden sands and brightly coloured cliffs. There are dunes made for buggies, party towns and quiet hideaways, pages 510 and 516.

5 **The Amazon** Over half of Brazilian national territory is the Amazon Basin (which spreads beyond the country's borders). Travel between the few centres of population is by riverboat and the jungle provides fabulous wildlife viewing opportunities, page 532.

6 **Pantanal** This vast wetland is one the world's greatest wildlife preserves. Rivers criss-cross the plains where giant storks, giant guinea-pigs (*capybara*), giant fish and much else of a more regular size live alongside great herds of cattle, page 577.

Brazil

Essentials

Planning your trip

Where to go **Rio de Janeiro** was for a long time *the* image of Brazil, with its beautiful setting – the Sugar Loaf and Corcovado overlooking the bay and beaches, its world renowned carnival, the nightlife and its *favelas* (slums – which are now being incorporated into tourism). It is still a must on many itineraries, but Rio de Janeiro state has plenty of other beaches, national parks and colonial towns (especially **Paraty**) and the imperial city of Petrópolis. **São Paulo** is the country's industrial and financial powerhouse; with some fine museums and its cultural life and restaurants are very good. All the São Paulo coast is worth visiting and inland there are hill resorts and colonial towns. The **state of Minas Gerais** contains some of the best colonial architecture in South America in cities such as Ouro Preto, Mariana, São João del Rei and Diamantina. All are within easy reach of the state capital, Belo Horizonte. Other options in Minas include national parks with good hill scenery and birdwatching and hydrothermal resorts.

The atmosphere of the South is dominated by its German and Italian immigrants. The three states, Paraná, Santa Catarina and Rio Grande do Sul have their coastal resorts, especially near Florianópolis, capital of Santa Catarina. **Rio Grande do Sul** is the land of Brazil's *gaúchos* (cowboys) and of its vineyards, but the main focus of the region is the magnificent **Iguaçu Falls** in the far west of Paraná, on the borders of Argentina and Paraguay.

The Northeast is famous for beaches and colonial history. Combining both these elements, with the addition of Brazil's liveliest African culture, is **Salvador de Bahia**, one of the country's most famous cities and a premier tourist destination. Huge sums of money have been lavished on the restoration of its colonial centre and its carnival is something special. Inland, Bahia is mostly arid sertão, in which a popular town is **Lençóis**, a historical monument with a nearby national park. The highlight of the southern coast of Bahia is the beach and party zone around **Porto Seguro**, while in the north the beaches stretch up to the states of Sergipe and Alagoas and on into Pernambuco. **Recife**, capital of Pernambuco, and its neighbour, the colonial capital **Olinda**; also mix the sea, history and culture, while inland is the major handicraft centre of Caruaru. Travelling around to the north-facing coast, there are hundreds of beaches to choose from, some highly developed, others less so. You can swim, surf or ride the dunes in buggies. Last stop before the mouth of the Amazon is **São Luís**, in whose centre most of the old houses are covered in colonial tiles.

Through the North flows the **Amazon**, along which river boats ply between the cities of Belém, Santarém and Manaus. From **Manaus** particularly there are opportunities for exploring the jungle on adventurous expeditions or staying in lodges. North of Manaus is the overland route through Boa Vista to Venezuela. The forest stretches south to the central tableland which falls to the **Pantanal** in the far west. This seasonal wetland, the highlight of the Centre West, is one of the prime areas for seeing bird and animal life in the continent. At the eastern end of the Centre West is **Brasília**, built in the 1960s and now a World Heritage Site in recognition of its superb examples of modern architecture. Also in this region is one of the largest river islands in the world (Bananal – a mecca for fishing) and the delightful hill and river landscapes of **Bonito** in Mato Grosso do Sul.

When to go Brazil is a tropical country, but the further south you go the more temperate the winters become and there are places in the coastal mountains which have gained a reputation for their cool climate and low humidity. The heaviest rains fall at different times in different regions: November to March in the southeast, December to March in the centre west and April to August on the northeast coast around Pernambuco (irregular rainfall causes severe draughts). The rainy season in the north and Amazônia can begin in December and is heaviest March to May, but it is getting steadily shorter, possibly as a result of deforestation. It is only in rare cases that the rainfall can be described as either excessive or deficient. Few places get more than 2,000 mm: the coast north of Belém, some of the Amazon Basin, and a small area of the Serra do Mar between Santos and São Paulo, where the downpour has been harnessed to generate electricity.

May to September is usually referred to as winter, but this is not to suggest that this is a bad time to visit. On the contrary, April to June and August to October are recommended times to go to most parts of the country. One major consideration is that carnival falls within the hottest, wettest time of year (in February), so if you are incorporating carnival into a longer

⁝ Touching down

Airport tax The amount of tax depends on the class of airport. All airports charge US$36 for international departure tax. In some circumstances, this tax is collected when you buy your flight tickets (eg in the UK), but you must check if this is case. If it has not been collected you will have to pay on leaving Brazil. First-class airports charge R$9.50 domestic tax; second-class airports R$7; domestic rates are lower still in third- and fourth-class airports. Tax must be paid on checking in, in reais or US dollars. Tax is waived if you are in Brazil less than 24 hours.

Business hours Monday-Friday 0900-1800 for most businesses, which close for lunch some time between 1130 and 1400. **Shops**: open on Saturday till 1230 or 1300. **Government offices**: Monday-Friday 1100-1800. **Banks**: 1000-1600, but closed on Saturday.

In an emergency Ambulance T192. Directory enquiries T102. Police T190.

International phone code +55
Ringing: equal tones with long pauses.
Engaged: equal tones, equal pauses.

Official time Brazilian standard time is GMT -3; of the major cities, only the Amazon time zone, Manaus, Cuiabá, Campo Grande and Corumbá are different (GMT -4). The state of Acre is GMT -5. Clocks go forward one hour in summer for approximately five months (usually between October and February or March). (This does not apply to Acre.)

Tipping Tipping is usual, but less costly than in most other countries, except for porters. Restaurants, 10% of bill if no service charge but small tip if there is; taxi drivers, none; cloakroom attendants, small tip; cinema usherettes, none; hairdressers, 10-15%; porters, fixed charges but tips as well; airport porters, about US$0.65 per item.

VAT Rate varies from 7 to 25% at state and federal level; average 17-20%.

Voltage Generally 110 V 60 cycles AV, but in some areas 220 V 60 cycles. Sockets also vary, often combination sockets for twin flat and twin round pin.

Weights and measures Metric.

holiday, it may be wet wherever you go. Also bear in mind that mid-December to February is the national holiday season, which means that hotels, planes and buses may be full and many establishments away from the holiday areas may be shut.

The average annual temperature increases steadily from south to north, but even on the Equator, in the Amazon Basin, the average temperature is not more than 27°C. The highest recorded was 42°C, in the dry northeastern states. From the latitude of Recife south to Rio, the mean temperature is from 23° to 27°C along the coast, and from 18° to 21°C in the Highlands. From a few degrees south of Rio to the boundary with Uruguay the mean temperature is from 17° to 19°C. Humidity is relatively high in Brazil, particularly along the coast.

Finding out more Tourism is in the hands of the **Ministério do Turismo** ⓘ *Esplanada dos Ministérios, Bloco U, 2nd and 3rd floors, Brasília, www.turismo.gov.br or www.braziltour.com (in many languages)*. For information abroad, contact Brazil's representation overseas: France, T+33-1-5353 6962; Germany, T+49-69-9750 3251; Italy, T+39-2-8633 7791; Japan, T+81-8-5565 7591; Portugal, T+351-21-340 4668; Spain, T+34-91-503 0687; UK, T+44-207-7396 5551; USA, T+1-646-378 2126. Tourist information bureaux are not usually helpful with information on cheap hotels and it is difficult to get information on neighbouring states. Expensive hotels provide tourist information magazines for their guests. Telephone directories (not Rio) contain good street maps.

National parks are run by **Ibama**, the **Instituto Brasileiro do Meio Ambiente e dos Recursos Naturais Renováveis** (Brazilian Institute of Environmental Protection): ⓘ *SCEN Trecho 2, Av L-4 Norte, Edif Sede de Ibama, CEP 70818-900, Brasília, DF, www.ibama.gov.br*. For information, contact **Linha Verde** ⓘ *T0800-61-8080, linhaverde.sede@ibama.gov.br*. The Institute is underfunded, understaffed and visitors may find it difficult to get information. National parks are open to visitors, usually with a permit from Ibama. See also the Ministério do Meio Ambiente website, www.mma.gov.br. For further details, see individual parks.

Useful websites

See also the Tourist office sites under individual cities in the text.

www.ipanema.com Insider's guide to Rio in English.

www.copacabana.com On Copacabana in Portuguese.

www.maria-brazil.org A fun site with info, tips, recommendations, mostly about Rio, but other regions, too.

The following embassy sites have lots of information:

www.brasilemb.org (USA);

www.brazil.org.uk (UK).

www.brazilmax.com Bill Hinchberger's 'Hip Gringo's Guide' to Brazil with loads of news, cultural articles and travel information and a strong ecological angle.

www.brazilianmusic.com Introductions to musical styles and musicians, and more.

www.gringoes.com Information on all things Brazilian for visitors and ex-pats.

www.wwf.org.br The World Wide Fund for nature in Brazil.

www.socioambiental.org Accurate information on environmental and indigenous issues.

www.cartacapital.com.br Independent news magazine (Portuguese).

Maps and guides Editora Abril publishes *Quatro Rodas*, a motoring magazine, as well as excellent maps and guides in Portuguese and English from US$15. Its *Guia Brasil* is a type of Michelin Guide to hotels, restaurants (not the cheapest), sights, facilities and general information on hundreds of cities and towns in the country, including good street maps (we acknowledge here our debt to this publication). It also publishes an excellent guide to São Paulo, Sampa (in Portuguese), a guide to cheap travel, *Viajar Bem e Barato* and a *Guia das Praias*, with descriptions of all Brazil's beaches. All are available at news stands and bookshops all over the country. For information about the *Quatro Rodas* guides, see www.abril.com.br.

Visas and immigration Consular visas are not required for stays of up to 90 days by tourists from EU countries (except Cyprus, Estonia, Latvia, Lithuania, Malta and Romania), Israel, New Zealand, Norway, South Africa, Switzerland, South and Central American countries (except Mexico, Belize, El Salvador and Nicaragua) and some Caribbean, Asian and African countries. For them, only the following documents are required at the port of disembarkation: a passport valid for at least six months; and a return or onward ticket, or adequate proof that you can purchase your return fare, subject to no remuneration being received in Brazil and no legally binding or contractual documents being signed. Visas are required by US and Canadian citizens, Japanese, Australians and people of other nationalities, and those who cannot meet the requirements above, must get a visa before arrival, which may, if you ask, be granted for multiple entry. Visas are valid from date of issue. Visa fees vary from country to country, so apply to the Brazilian consulate, in the country of residence of the applicant. The consular fees range from US$20 to US$35 (for Australians), US$40 (Canadians) to US$100 for US citizens. Do not lose the emigration permit given to you when you enter Brazil. If you leave the country without it, you may have to pay a fine.

Foreign tourists may stay a maximum of 180 days in any one year. 90-day renewals are easily obtainable, but only at least 15 days before the expiry of your 90-day permit, from the Polícia Federal. You will have to fill out three copies of the tax form at the Polícia Federal, take them to a branch of Banco do Brasil, pay US$15 and bring two copies back. You will then be given the extension form to fill in and be asked for your passport to stamp in the extension. Regulations state that you should be able to show a return ticket, cash, cheques or a credit card, a personal reference and proof of an address of a person living in the same city as the office (in practice you simply write this in the space on the form). Some offices will only give you an extension within 10 days of the expiry of your permit. Some points of entry, such as the Colombian border, refuse entry for longer than 30 days, renewals are then for the same period, insist if you want 90 days. For longer stays you must leave the country and return (not the same day) to get a new 90-day permit. If your visa has expired, getting a new visa can be costly (US$35 for a consultation, US$30 for the visa) and may take up to 45 days. If you overstay your visa you will be fined US$7 per day, with no upper limit. After paying the fine to Polícia Federal, you will be issued with an exit visa and must leave within eight days. **Note** Officially, if you leave Brazil within the 90-day permission to stay and then re-enter the country, you should only be allowed to stay until the 90-day permit expires. If, however, you are given another 90-day permit, this may lead to charges of overstaying if you apply for an extension. For UK citizens a joint agreement allows visits for business or tourism of up to six months a year from the date of first entry.

Identification   You must always carry identification when in Brazil; it is a good idea to take a photocopy of the personal details in your passport, plus that with your Brazilian immigration stamp, and leave your passport in the hotel safe deposit. Always keep an independent record of your passport details. It is a good idea to register with your consulate to expedite document replacement if yours gets lost or stolen.

Brazilian embassies and consulates   Visit www.mre.gov.br/portugues/enderecos/embaixadas.asp for a full list of addresses.

Money   The unit of currency is the real, R = $ (plural reais). It floats freely against the dollar. Any amount of foreign currency and 'a reasonable sum' in reais can be taken in; residents may only take out the equivalent of US$4,000. Notes in circulation are: 100, 50, 10, 5 and 1 real; coins 1 real, 50, 25, 10, 5 and 1 centavo. Real **exchange rate** with US$: 1.91; with euro: 2.61 (July 2007). Banks open 1000-1600 (1630 Monday-Friday).

Credit cards   By far the best way to travel in Brazil is with a credit or debit card, preferably Visa, withdrawing money from ATMs. Machines are usually closed 2100-0400. For Visa the best are **Banco 24 Horas**, **Banco do Brasil** and **Bradesco**. Take another credit card stowed away for emergencies in case of robbery. For MasterCard, HSBC and the **Tecban** system have the best ATM network. Charges are around US$3 per withdrawal. Emergency phone numbers: MasterCard T0800-891 3294; Visa T000-811-342 0552.

Banks   In major cities banks will change cash and travellers' cheques. If you keep the exchange slips, you may convert back into foreign currency up to 50% of the amount you exchanged.

Take US dollars in cash, or euros, and perhaps a few travellers' cheques as a back-up. The commission on travellers' cheques can be as much as US$20 **per cheque**.

Cost of travelling   Owing to the strengthening of the real against other currencies since 2006, Brazil has become expensive for the traveller. It is hard to find a room costing less than US$15 per person, although dormitories are cheaper (US$10-15); in the cities and holiday centres hotels cost more, about US$25. Eating is relatively cheaper and *comida a kilo* (pay by weight) restaurants are good value. Bus prices are reasonable, but because of long distances, costs can mount up. Internal air prices, though, are high. Prices are highest in Rio and São Paulo.

Safety   Although Brazil's big cities suffer high rates of violent crime, this is mostly confined to the *favelas* (slums), which should be avoided unless accompanied by a tour leader, or NGO. If the worst does happen and you are threatened, try not to panic, but hand over your valuables. Do not resist, but report the crime to the local tourist police, who should be your first port of call in case of difficulty. The situation is much more secure in smaller towns and in the country. Also steer well clear of areas of drug cultivation and red light districts. In the latter drinks are often spiked with a drug called 'Goodnight Cinderella'. See the Safety section in Essentials at the beginning of the book for general advice.

Police   There are several types of police: **Polícia Federal**, civilian dressed, who handle all federal law duties, including immigration. A subdivision is the **Polícia Federal Rodoviária**, uniformed, who are the traffic police. **Polícia Militar** are the uniformed, street police force, under the control of the state governor, handling all state laws. They are not the same as the Armed Forces' internal police. **Polícia Civil**, also state-controlled, handle local laws; usually in civilian dress, unless in the traffic division. In cities, the Prefeitura controls the **Guarda Municipal**, who handle security. **Tourist police** operate in places with a strong tourist presence.

Getting around

Air   Because of the great distances, flying is often the most practical option. Internal air services are highly developed and the larger cities are linked several times a day. All national airlines offer excellent service on their internal flights. The largest airlines are **TAM** ① *T4002 5700, or 0800-570 5700, www.tam.com.br*, and **Varig** ① *T4003 7000 (or 0xx11-4003 7000), www.varig.com.br*.

The no-frills, ticketless airline **Gol** ① *To800-280 0465, English-speaking operators, To300-115 2121 (sales), or www.voegol.com.br (website in Portuguese)*, provides a good service. Book Gol flights at a travel agent and pay by credit card. Similar airlines are **Bra** ① *offices throughout Brazil, www.voebra.com.br*, **Ocean Air** ① *T4004 4040, or 0300-789 8916, www.oceanair.com.br*, and **Trip** ① *To300 789 8747, www.voetrip.com.br*. **Pantanal** *To800-602 5888, www.voepantanal.com.br*, with flights mainly between São Paulo and Mato Grosso do Sul. Internal flights often have many stops and are often quite slow. Most airports have left-luggage lockers (US$2 for 24 hours). Seats are often unallocated on internal flights; board in good time.

TAM offers a 21-day **air pass** covering all Brazil, costing US$560 for four coupons. Additional coupons, up to a maximum of nine, may be bought. All sectors must be booked before the start of the journey. Two flights forming one connection count as two coupons. **Varig** offers a 21-day air pass also, but as its routes are limited, the pass is poor value. It costs US$675 for up to 5 coupons, US$792 for six. Rerouting costs US$30, two flights forming one connection count as one coupon. Infants are charged 10%. Routes must be specified before arrival.

All airpasses must be purchased outside Brazil, no journey may be repeated and none may be used on the Rio-São Paulo shuttle. Remember domestic airport tax has to be paid at each departure. Passengers may arrive in Brazil on any carrier. Hotels in the Tropical and Othon chains, and others, offer discounts of 10% to Varig airpass travellers. Promotions on certain destinations offer a free flight, hotel room, etc; enquire when buying the airpass. Converting the voucher can take some hours, do not plan an onward flight immediately, check at terminals that the airpass is still registered, faulty cancellations have been reported. Cost and restrictions on the airpass are subject to change.

Small scheduled domestic airlines operate Brazilian-built Bandeirante 16-seater prop-jets into virtually every city and town with any semblance of an airstrip.

Bus There are three standards of **bus**: *comum* or *convencional*, which are quite slow, not very comfortable and fill up quickly; *executivo* (executive), which are a few reais more expensive, comfortable (many have reclining seats), but don't stop to pick up passengers en route and are therefore safer; *semi-leito* and *leito* (literally, bed), which run at night between the main centres, offering reclining seats with foot and leg rests, toilets, and sometimes refreshments, at double the normal fare. For journeys over 100 km, most buses have chemical toilets. A/c can make leito buses cold at night, so take a blanket or sweater (and plenty of toilet paper); on some services blankets are supplied. Some companies have hostess service. Ask for window seats (*janela*), or odd numbers if you want the view.

Buses stop frequently (every two to four hours) for snacks. The cleanliness of these *postos* is generally good, but standards of comfort on buses and in *postos* vary, which can be important on long journeys.

Bus stations for interstate services and other long-distance routes are called *rodoviárias*. They are normally outside the city centres and offer snack bars, lavatories, left-luggage stores (*guarda volume*), local bus services and information centres. Reliable bus information is hard to come by, other than from companies themselves (most take credit cards). Buses usually arrive and depart in very good time.

Taxi Taxi meters measure distance/cost in reais. At the outset, make sure the meter is cleared and shows tariff '1', except Sunday 2300-0600, and in December when '2' is permitted. Check the meter works, if not, fix price in advance. Radio taxi service costs about 50% more but cheating is less likely. Taxi services offered by smartly dressed individuals outside larger hotels usually cost twice as much as ordinary taxis. If you are seriously cheated, note the taxi number and insist on a signed bill, threatening to go to the police; it can work. **Note** Be wary of Moto Taxis. Many are unlicensed and a number of robberies have been reported.

Hitchhiking Hitchhiking (*carona* in Portuguese) is not a safe option and is difficult everywhere; drivers are reluctant to give lifts because passengers are their responsibility. Try at the highway-police check points on the main roads (but make sure your documents are in order) or at the service stations (*postos*).

Boat The main areas where boat travel is practical (and often necessary) are the Amazon region, along the São Francisco River and along the Atlantic coast. There are also some limited transport services through the Pantanal.

Driving in Brazil

Road Around 10% of roads are paved and several thousand more all-weather. The best highways are heavily concentrated in the southeast; those serving the interior are being improved to all-weather status and many are paved. Some main roads are narrow and therefore dangerous. Many are in poor condition.

Safety Try to never leave your car unattended except in a locked garage or guarded parking area.

Documents To drive in Brazil you need an international licence. A national driving licence is acceptable as long as your home country is a signatory to the Vienna and Geneva conventions. (See Motoring, Essentials.) There are agreements between Brazil and all South American countries (but check in the case of Bolivia) whereby a car can be taken into Brazil (or a Brazilian car out of Brazil) for a period of 90 days without any special documents. For cars registered in other countries, you need proof of ownership and/or registration in the home country and valid driving licence (as above). A 90-day permit is given by customs and procedure is very straightforward. Make sure you keep *all* the papers you are given when you enter, to produce when you leave.

Car hire Renting a car in Brazil is expensive: the cheapest rate for unlimited mileage for a small car is about US$65 per day. Minimum age for renting a car is 21 and it is essential to have a credit card. Companies operate under the terms *aluguel de automóveis* or *autolocadores*.

Fuel Fuel prices vary from week to week and region to region. *Gasolina comun* costs about US$1.35 per litre with *gasolina maxi* and *maxigold* a little more. *Alcool comun; alcool maxi* and diesel cost a little less. There is no unleaded fuel. Fuel is only 85 octane. It is virtually impossible to buy premium grades of petrol anywhere. With alcohol fuel you need about 50% more alcohol than regular gasoline. Larger cars have a small extra tank for 'gasolina' to get the engine started; remember to keep this topped up. Diesel fuel is cheap.

Train There are 30,379 km of railway track which are not combined into a unified system and most passenger services have been withdrawn. Brazil has two gauges and there is little transfer between them. Two more gauges exist for the isolated Amapá Railway and the tourist-only São João del Rei line. There are passenger services in the state of São Paulo.

Sleeping → *See page 58 for our hotel grade price guide.*

Hotels Usually hotel prices include breakfast; there is no reduction if you don't eat it. In the better hotels (category **B** and upwards) the breakfast is well worth eating: rolls, ham, eggs, cheese, cakes, fruit. Normally the apartamento is a room with bath; a quarto is a room without bath. *Pousadas* are the equivalent of bed-and-breakfast, often small and family run, although some are very sophisticated and correspondingly priced. The type known as *hotel familiar*, to be found in the interior – large meals, communal washing, hammocks for children – is much cheaper, but only for the enterprising. The service stations (*postos*) and hostels (*dormitórios*) along the main roads provide excellent value in room and food, akin to truck-driver type accommodation in Europe, for those on a tight budget. The star rating system for hotels (five-star hotels are not price-controlled) is not the standard used in North America or Europe. Business visitors are strongly recommended to book in advance, and this can be easily done for Rio or São Paulo hotels with representation abroad. If staying more than three nights in a place in low season, ask for a discount. In hotels ask if they have a backpackers' rate for double rooms; usually better value than doubles in hostels. Motels are specifically intended for very short-stay couples: there is no stigma attached and they usually offer good value (the rate for a full night is called the *pernoite*), though the decor can be a little unsettling.

Roteiros de Charme This is a private association of hotels and *pousadas* in the southeast and northeast, which aims to give a high standard of accommodation in establishments typical of the town they are in. If you are travelling in the appropriate budget range (our **AL** price range upwards), you can plan an itinerary which takes in these hotels, with a reputation for comfort and good food. Roteiros de Charme hotels are listed in the text and any one of them can provide information on the group, or visit www.roteirosdecharme.com.br.

Youth hostels For information about youth hostels contact **Federação Brasileira de Albergues da Juventude**① *R dos Andrades 1137, conj 214, Porto Alegre, Rio Grande do Sul, CEP 90020-007, Toxx51-3226 5380, www.albergues.com.br*. Its annual book and website provide a full list of good value accommodation. Another site for the Federação is www.hostel.org.br (Rio de Janeiro based, Toxx21-2286 0303). Also see the *Internet Guide to Hostelling*, which has list of Brazilian youth hostels: www.hostels.com/br.html. Low-budget travellers with student cards (photograph needed) can use the **Casa dos Estudantes** network.

Camping Members of the Camping Clube do Brasil or those with an international campers' card pay only half the rate of a non-member, which is US$10-15 per person. The Club has 37 sites around the country. For enquiries, **Camping Clube do Brasil** ① *R Senador Dantas 75, 29 andar, 20037-900 Centro, Rio de Janeiro, T021-3479 4200, www.campingclube.com.br*. In **São Paulo**① *R Minerva 156, 05007-030 – Perdizes, T011-3864 7133, F3871 9749*. In **Curitiba** ① *Al Dr Muricy 650, conj 161, CEP 80020-902, T/F041-3224 7869*. In **Belo Horizonte** ① *Av Amazonas 115, sala 1301, CEP 30180-000, T/F031-3201-6989*. In Salvador, *R Portugal 3, grupo 404/410, CEP 40015-000, T071-3243 0029*. It may be difficult to get into some Clube campsites during the high season (January to February). Private campsites charge about US$8 per person. For those on a very low budget and in isolated areas where there is no camp site, service stations can be used as camping sites (Shell stations recommended); they have shower facilities, watchmen and food; some have dormitories; truck drivers are a mine of information. There are also various municipal sites; both types are mentioned in the text. Campsites often tend to be some distance from public transport routes and are better suited to those with their own transport. Never camp at the side of a road; wild camping is generally not possible. Good camping equipment may be purchased in Brazil and there are several rental companies. Camping gas cartridges are easy to buy in sizeable towns in the south, eg in HM shops. *Quatro Rodas' Guia Brasil* lists main campsites, see page 342. Most sizeable towns have laundromats with self service. *Lavanderias* do the washing for you but are expensive.

Eating → *See page 58 for Eating price guide.*

The main meal is usually taken in the middle of the day; cheap restaurants tend not to be open in the evening. The most common dish is *bife (ou frango) com arroz e feijão*, steak (or chicken) with rice and the excellent Brazilian black beans. The most famous dish with beans is the *feijoada completa*: several meat ingredients (jerked beef, smoked sausage, smoked tongue, salt pork, along with spices, herbs and vegetables) are cooked with the beans. Manioc flour is sprinkled over it, and it is eaten with kale (*couve*) and slices of orange, and accompanied by glasses of aguardente (unmatured rum), usually known as *cachaça* (booze), though *pinga* (drop) is a more polite term. Almost all restaurants serve the *feijoada completa* for Saturday lunch (that means up to about 1630).

Throughout Brazil, a mixed grill, including steak, served with roasted manioc flour (*farofa*; raw manioc flour is known as *farinha* goes under the name of *churrasco* (originally from the cattlemen of Rio Grande do Sul), served in specialized restaurants known as churrascarias or *rodízios*; good places for large appetites Bahia has some excellent fish dishes (see note on page 489); some restaurants in most of the big cities specialize in them. *Vatapá* is a good dish in the north; it contains shrimp or fish sauce with palm oil, or coconut milk. *Empadinhas de camarão* are worth trying; they are shrimp patties, with olives and heart of palm.

Minas Gerais has two splendid special dishes involving pork, black beans, farofa and kale; they are *tutu á mineira* and *feijão tropeiro*. A white hard cheese (*queijo prata*) or a slightly softer one (*queijo Minas*) is often served for dessert with bananas, or guava or quince paste. *Comida mineira* is quite distinctive and very wholesome and you can often find restaurants serving this type of food in other parts of Brazil.

Meals are extremely large by European standards; portions are usually for two and come with two plates. Likewise beer is brought with two glasses. If you are on your own and in a position to do so tactfully, you may choose to offer what you can't eat to a person with no food. Alternatively you could ask for an *embalagem* (doggy bag) or get a take away called *a marmita* or *quentinha*, most restaurants have this service but it is not always on the menu. Many restaurants now serve *comida por kilo* where you serve yourself and pay for the weight of food on your plate. Unless you specify to the contrary many restaurants will lay a *coberto opcional*, olives, carrots, etc, costing US$0.65-1. **Warning** Avoid mussels, marsh crabs and other shellfish caught near large cities: they are likely to have lived in a highly polluted environment. In a restaurant, always ask the price of a dish before ordering.

For **vegetarians**, there is a growing network of restaurants in the main cities. In smaller places where food may be monotonous try vegetarian for greater variety. Most also serve fish. Alternatives in smaller towns are the Arab and Chinese restaurants.

If travelling on a tight **budget**, remember to ask in restaurants for the *prato feito* or *sortido*, a money-saving, excellent value table-d'hôte meal. The *prato comercial* is similar but rather better and a bit more expensive. *Lanchonetes* are cheap eating places where you generally pay before eating. *Salgados* (savoury pastries), *coxinha* (a pyramid of manioc filled with meat or fish and deep fried), *esfiha* (spicey hamburger inside an onion-bread envelope), *empadão* (a filling – eg chicken – in sauce in a pastry case), *empadas* and *empadinhas* (smaller fritters of the same type), are the usual fare. In Minas Gerais, *pão de queijo* is a hot roll made with cheese. A *bauru* is a toasted sandwich which, in Porto Alegre, is filled with steak, while further north it has tomato, ham and cheese filling. *Cocada* is a coconut and sugar biscuit.

Imported **drinks** are expensive, but there are some fair local wines. Chilean and Portuguese wines are sometimes available at little more than the cost of local wines. The Brahma, Cerpa and Antárctica beers are really excellent, of the lager type, and are cheaper by the bottle than on draught. Buying bottled drinks in supermarkets, you may be asked for empties in return. The local firewater, aguardente (known as cachaça or pinga), made from sugar-cane, is cheap and wholesome, but visitors should seek local advice on the best brands; São Francisco, Praianinha, Maria Fulô, '51' and Pitu are recommended makes. Mixed with fruit juices of various sorts, sugar and crushed ice, cachaça becomes the principal element in a *batida*, a delicious and powerful drink; the commonest is a lime batida or *batida de limão*; a variant of this is the *caipirinha*, a cachaça with several slices of lime in it, a *caipiroska* is made with vodka. Cachaça with Coca-Cola is a *cuba*, while rum with Coca-Cola is a *cuba libre*. Some genuine Scotch whisky brands are bottled in Brazil; they are very popular because of the high price of Scotch imported in bottle; Teacher's is the most highly regarded brand. Locally made gin, vermouth and campari are very good.

There are plenty of local soft drinks. Guaraná is a very popular carbonated fruit drink. There is an excellent range of non-alcoholic fruit juices, known as *sucos*: *caju* (cashew), *pitanga*, *goiaba* (guava), *genipapo*, *graviola* (chirimoya), *maracujá* (passion fruit), *sapoti* and *tamarindo* are recommended. Vitaminas are thick fruit or vegetable drinks with milk. *Caldo de cana* is sugar-cane juice, sometimes mixed with ice. Remember that *água mineral*, available in many varieties at bars and restaurants, is a cheap, safe thirst-quencher (cheaper still in supermarkets). Apart from the ubiquitous coffee, good tea is grown and sold. **Note** If you don't want sugar in your coffee or *suco*, you must ask when you order it. *Água de côco* or *côco verde* (coconut water from fresh green coconut) cannot be missed in the northeast.

Festivals and events → *See also Carnival section page 372.*

National holidays are 1 January (New Year); three days up to and including Ash Wednesday (Carnival); 21 April (Tiradentes); 1 May (Labour Day); Corpus Christi (June); 7 September (Independence Day); 12 October, Nossa Senhora Aparecida; 2 November (All Souls' Day); 15 November (Day of the Republic); and 25 December (Christmas). The local holidays in the main cities are given in the text. Four religious or traditional holidays (Good Friday must be one; other usual days: 1 November, All Saints' Day; 24 December, Christmas Eve) must be fixed by the municipalities. Other holidays are usually celebrated on the Monday prior to the date.

Telephones

Important telephone changes: All ordinary phone numbers in Brazil are changing from seven to eight figure numbers. The process was still under way as this guide went to press. Where confirmed, eight-digit numbers have been included in the text. Where numbers have changed an electronic message should redirect callers. If a seven-digit number included in the text doesn't work, try putting '3' as the first digit.

Rio de Janeiro → *Phone code: 0xx21. Colour map 4, grid C3.*

Brazilians say: God made the world in six days; the seventh he devoted to Rio (pronounced 'Heeoo' by locals). Rio has a glorious theatrical backdrop of tumbling wooded mountains, stark expanses of bare rock and a deep blue sea studded with rocky islands. From the statue of Christ on the hunchbacked peak of Corcovado, or from the conical Pão de Açúcar (Sugar Loaf), you can experience the beauty of a bird's-eye view over the city which sweeps 220 km along a narrow alluvial strip on the southwestern shore of the Baía de Guanabara. Although best known for the curving Copacabana beach, for Ipanema – home to the Girl and beautiful sunsets, and for its swirling, reverberating, joyous Carnival, Rio also has a fine artistic, architectural and cultural heritage from its time as capital of both imperial and republican Brazil. But this is first and foremost a city dedicated to leisure: sport and music rule and a day spent hang gliding or surfing is easily followed by an evening of jazz or samba.

Ins and outs

Getting there **Aeroporto Internacional** Antônio Carlos Jobim (Galeão) is on the Ilha do Governador. Left luggage only in Terminal 1. The air bridge from São Paulo ends at Santos Dumont airport in the town centre. Taxis from here are much cheaper than from the international airport. There are also frequent buses. International buses and those from other parts of Brazil arrive at the **Rodoviária Novo Rio** (main bus station) near the docks. ▶▶ *See also Transport, page 374.*

Getting around Because the city is a series of separate districts connected by urban highways and tunnels, you will need to take public transport. An underground railway, the **Metrô**, runs under some of the centre and the south and is being extended. Buses run to all parts, but should be treated with caution at night when taxis are a better bet.

Rio de Janeiro

Related maps
A Rio de Janeiro centre, page 351
B Glória, Santa Teresa, Catete, Flamengo, page 354
C Copacabana, page 356

| Sleeping |
| Ace Backpackers 4 | Chave do Rio de Janeiro 3 |
| Carioca Easy 1 | El Misti Hostel 2 |

Metrô lines / stations — Line 1 — Line 2

Climate Rio has one of the healthiest climates in the tropics. Trade winds cool the air. June, July and August are the coolest months with temperatures ranging from 22°C (18° in a cold spell) to 32°C on a sunny day at noon. December to March is hotter, from 32°C to 42°C. Humidity is high. It is important, especially for children, to guard against dehydration in summer by drinking as much liquid as possible. October to March is the rainy season. Annual rainfall is about 1,120 mm.

Tourist offices Riotur ① *R da Assembléia 10, 9th floor, T2217 7575, www.riodejaneiro-turismo.com.br/pt (also in English) and www.rio.rj.gov.br; also at Av Princesa Isabel 183, Copacabana, T2541 7522, Mon-Fri 0900-1800*, helpful with English, French and German spoken by some staff, has good city maps and a very useful free brochure *They*, in Portuguese and English. More information stands can be found at the **international airport** ① *0600-2400* and at **Rodoviária Novo Rio** ① *0800-2000*, both very friendly and helpful in finding accommodation. **Alô Rio** ① *T2542 8080/0800-707 1808, daily 0900-1800*, is an information service in English and Portuguese. **TurisRio** ① *R da Ajuda 5, 12th floor, T2215 0011, www.turisrio.rj.gov.br Mon-Fri 0900-1700, with stands at the bus station and Jobim airport*, has information on the state of Rio de Janeiro. *Trilhas do Rio*, by Pedro da Cunha e Meneses (Editora Salamandra, 2nd edition), US$22.50, describes walking trips around Rio. The guide *Restaurantes do Rio*, by Danusia Bárbara, published annually by Senac at around US$10 (in Portuguese only), is worth looking at for the latest ideas on where to eat in both the city and state of Rio. Many hotels provide guests with the weekly *Rio This Month*. ▸▸ *See also Tour operators, page 373.*

Safety The majority of visitors enjoy Rio's glamour and the rich variety of experience it has to offer without any problems. It is worth remembering that, despite its beach culture, carefree atmosphere and friendly people, Rio is one of the world's most densely populated cities. If you live in London, Paris, New York or Los Angeles and behave with the same caution in Rio that you do at home, you will be unlucky to encounter any crime. The **Tourist Police** ① *Av Afrânio de Melo Franco 159, Leblon (in front of the Casa Grande theatre), T3399 7170, 24 hrs*, publish a sensible advice leaflet (available from hotels and consulates: consulates also issue safety guidelines). Tourist police officers are helpful, efficient and multilingual. All the main tourist areas are patrolled. If you have any problems, contact the tourist police first.

Extra vigilance is needed on the beaches at night. Don't walk on the sand. Likewise in the backstreets between the Copacabana Palace and Rua Figueiredo de Magalhães. Santa Teresa is now far safer and better policed than before, but caution is needed walking between Santa Teresa and Lapa at night and around the small streets near the Largo das Neves. Never enter a *favela* on your own or without a person you know very well and trust. A tour with a reputable operator is worth taking (see Tour operators, page 373), but otherwise *favelas* remain extremely dangerous places.

Background

The Portuguese navigator, Gonçalo Coelho, arrived at what is now Rio de Janeiro on 1 January 1502. Thinking that the Baía de Guanabara (the name the local *indígenas* used) was the mouth of a great river, they called the place the January River. Although the bay was almost as large and as safe a harbour as the Baía de Todos Os Santos to the north, the Portuguese did not take of advantage of it. In fact, it was first settled by the French, who, under the Huguenot Admiral Nicholas Durand de Villegagnon, occupied Lage Island on 10 November 1555, but later transferred to Seregipe Island (now Villegagnon), where they built the fort of Coligny.

In early 1559-1560, Mem de Sá, third governor of Brazil, mounted an expedition from Salvador to attack the French. The Portuguese finally took control in 1567. Though constantly attacked by *indígenas*, the new city grew rapidly and when King Sebastião divided Brazil into two provinces, Rio was chosen capital of the southern captaincies. Salvador became sole capital again in 1576, but Rio again became the southern capital in 1608 and the seat of a bishopric.

Rio de Janeiro was by the 18th century becoming the leading city in Brazil. Not only was it the port out of which gold was shipped, but it was also the focus of the export/import trade of the surrounding agricultural lands. On 27 January 1763, it became the seat of the Viceroy. After independence, in 1834, it was declared capital of the Empire and remained so for 125 years.

Orientation

The city is usually divided into north and south zones, Zona Norte and Zona Sul, with the historical and business centre, O Centro, in between. The parts that most interest visitors are the centre itself and the Zona Sul, which has the famous districts of Flamengo, Botafogo, Urca, Copacabana, Ipanema, Leblon and then out to the newer suburb of Barra de Tijuca.

The city's main artery is the Avenida Presidente Vargas, 4½ km long and over 90 m wide. It starts at the waterfront, divides to embrace the famous Candelária church, then crosses the Avenida Rio Branco in a magnificent straight stretch past the Central do Brasil railway station, with its imposing clock tower, until finally it incorporates a palm-lined, canal-divided avenue. The second principal street in the centre is the Avenida Rio Branco, nearly 2 km long, on which only a few ornate buildings remain, by Cinelândia and the Biblioteca Nacional. Some of the finest modern architecture is to be found along the Avenida República do Chile, such as the Petrobrás, the Banco Nacional de Desenvolvimento Econômico and the former Banco Nacional de Habitação buildings and the new Cathedral.

City centre and Lapa

Around Praça 15 de Novembro

Praça 15 de Novembro (often called Praça XV) has always been one of the focal points in Rio. Today it has one of the greatest concentrations of historic buildings in the city. The last vestiges of the original harbour, at the seaward end of the Praça, have been restored. The steps no longer lead to the water, but a new open space leads from the Praça to the seafront, beneath the Avenida Pres Kubitschek flyover. This space now gives easy access to the ferry dock for Niterói. At weekends an antiques, crafts, stamp and coin fair is held from 0900-1900. Buses to Praça 15 de Novembro: No 119 from Glória, Flamengo or Botafogo; Nos 154, 413, 455, 474 from Copacabana, or No 415 passing from Leblon via Ipanema.

On Rua 1 de Março, across from Praça 15 de Novembro, there are three buildings related to the Carmelite order. The convent of the **Ordem Terceira do Monte do Carmo**, started in 1611, is now used as the Faculdade Cândido Mendes. The order's present church, the **Igreja da Ordem Terceira do Carmo** ① *R Primeiro de Março, Mon-Fri 0800-1400, Sat 0800-1200, is the other side of the old cathedral (see below) from the convent.* It was built in 1754, consecrated in 1770 and rebuilt between 1797 and 1826. It has strikingly beautiful portals by Mestre Valentim, the son of a Portuguese nobleman and a slave girl. He also created the main altar of fine moulded silver, the throne and its chair and much else.

Between the former convent and the Igreja da Ordem Terceira do Carmo is the old cathedral, the **Igreja de Nossa Senhora do Carmo da Antiga Sé**, separated from the Carmo Church by a passageway. It was the chapel of the Convento do Carmo from 1590 until 1754. A new church was built in 1761, which became the city's cathedral. In the crypt are the alleged remains of Pedro Alvares Cabral, the Portuguese explorer (though Santarém, Portugal, also claims to be his last resting place).

The **Paço Imperial** (former Royal Palace) ① *T2533 4407, Tue-Sun 1100-1830*, is on the southeast corner of the Praça 15 de Novembro. This beautiful colonial building was built in 1743 as the residence of the governor of the Capitania. It later became the Paço Real when the Portuguese court moved to Brazil. After Independence it became the Imperial Palace. It has an exhibition space and the Bistro and Atrium restaurants. Recommended.

Igreja de São José ① *R São José e Av Pres Antônio Carlos, Mon-Fri 0900-1200, 1400-1700, Sun 0900-1100*, is considerably altered since its 17th-century construction. The current building dates from 1824.

On the northwest side of Praça 15 de Novembro, you go through the Arco do Teles and the Travessa do Comércio to Rua do Ouvidor. The **Igreja Nossa Senhora da Lapa dos Mercadores** ① *R do Ouvidor 35, Mon-Fri 0800-1400*, was consecrated in 1750, remodelled 1869-1872 and has been fully restored. Across the street, with its entrance at Rua 1 de Março 36, is the church of **Santa Cruz dos Militares**, built 1780-1811. It is large, stately and beautiful and has been well renovated in a 'light' baroque style.

The Church of **Nossa Senhora da Candelária** (1775-1810) ① *on Praça Pio X (Dez), at the city end of Av Pres Vargas where it meets R 1 de Março, Mon-Fri 0730-1200, 1300-1630, Sat 0800-1200, Sun 0900-1300*, has beautiful ceiling decorations and romantic paintings.

The **Centro Cultural Banco do Brasil (CCBB)** ⓘ *entrances on Av Pres Vargas and R 1 de Março 66, T3808 2089, Tue-Sun 1230-1900*, is highly recommended for good exhibitions. It has a library, multimedia facilities, a cinema, concerts (US$6 at lunchtime) and a restaurant. Opposite is the **Espaço Cultural dos Correios** ⓘ *R Visconde de Itaboraí 20, T2503 8770, Tue-Sun 1300-1900*, which holds temporary exhibitions and a postage stamp fair on Saturdays. **Casa França-Brasil** ⓘ *R Viscone de Itaboraí 253 and Av Pres Vargas, T2253 5366, Tue-Sun 1200-2000*, dates from the first French Artistic Mission to Brazil and it was the first neoclassical building in Rio. **Espaço Cultural da Marinha** ⓘ *Av Alfredo Agache at Av Pres Kubitschek, T2104 6025, US$3.65 for museum and 1-hr boat trip*, this former naval establishment now contains museums of underwater archaeology and navigation and the Galeota, the boat used by the Portuguese royal family for sailing around the Baía de Guanabara. Moored outside is the warship, Bauru and boats give access to the beautiful **Ilha Fiscal** ⓘ *T3870 6879, Tue-Sun 1200-1700, boats to Ilha Fiscal, Fri, Sat, Sun, 1300, 1430, 1600.*

Rio de Janeiro centre

Eating 🍴		Bar Luiz 2	Rio Scenarium 6
Adega Flor de Coimbra 1		Cais do Oriente 3	Sabor Saúde 9
Albamar 7		Confeitaria Colombo 5	
Bar das Artes 4		Republique 8	

Just north of Candelária, on a promontory overlooking the bay, is the **Mosteiro** (monastery) **de São Bento** ① *daily 0800-1230, 1400-1730, shorts not allowed*. Every Sunday at 1000, mass is sung with Gregorian chant and music, which is free, but arrive an hour early to get a seat. On other days, mass is at 0715. It contains much of what is best in the 17th- and 18th-century art of Brazil. São Bento is reached either by a narrow road from Rua Dom Gerardo 68, or by a lift whose entrance is at Rua Dom Gerardo 40 (taxi from centre US$5). The main body of the church is adorned in gold and red. The carving and gilding is remarkable, much of it by Frei Domingos da Conceição. The paintings, too, should be seen. The Chapels of the Immaculate Conception (Nossa Senhora da Conceição) and of the Most Holy Sacrament (Santíssimo Sacramento) are masterpieces of colonial art. The organ, dating from the end of the 18th century, is very interesting.

Around Largo da Carioca

The second oldest convent in the city is the **Convento de Santo Antônio** ① *daily 0800-1800*, on a hill off the Largo da Carioca, built 1608-1615. Santo Antônio is a particular object of devotion for women looking for a husband and you will see them in the precincts. The church has a marvellous sacristy adorned with blue tiles and paintings illustrating the life of St Anthony. In the church itself, the baroque decoration is concentrated in the chancel, the main altar and the two lateral altars.

Separated from this church only by some iron railings is the charming church of the Ordem Terceira de **São Francisco da Penitência** ① *closed for renovation in 2007*. Its Baroque carving and gilding of walls and altar, much more than in its neighbour, is considered among the finest in Rio. There is also a Museu de Arte Sacra. Strongly recommended.

Across Ruas da Carioca and 7 de Setembro is the church of **São Francisco de Paula** ① *upper end of R do Ouvidor, Mon-Fri 0900-1300*. It contains some of Mestre Valentim's work. One long block behind the Largo da Carioca and São Francisco de Paula is the **Praça Tiradentes**, old and shady, with a statue to Dom Pedro I. At the northeast corner of the praça is the **Teatro João Caetano** ① *T2221 0305*. Shops nearby specialize in selling goods for umbanda, the Afro-Brazilian religion. South of the Largo da Carioca are the modern buildings on Avenida República do Chile including the new cathedral, the **Catedral Metropolitana** ① *www.catedral.com.br, 0600-1900*, dedicated in November 1976. It is a cone-shaped building with capacity of 5,000 seated, 20,000 standing. The most striking feature is four enormous 60-m-high stained-glass windows. It is still incomplete. Crossing Avendia República do Paraguai from the cathedral is the Petrobrás building and the station, with museum, for the tram to Santa Teresa (entrance on Rua Senador Dantas – see below).

Avenida Rio Branco

Facing Praça Marechal Floriano is the **Teatro Municipal** ① *T2299 1711, www.theatromunicipal.rj.gov.br, Mon-Fri 0900-1700, US$2, guided visits Mon-Fri 1300-1600, T2299 1667*. The box office is at the right hand side of the building; ticket prices start at about US$15. One of the most magnificent buildings in Brazil in the eclectic style, it was built in 1905-1909, in imitation of the Opéra in Paris. The decorative features inside and out represent many styles, all lavishly executed. Opera and orchestral performances are given here. To book a tour of the theatre, ask for extension – ramal – 935 in advance. The **Biblioteca Nacional** ① *Av Rio Branco 219, T2262 8255, Mon-Fri 0900, US$1*, also dates from the first decade of the 20th century. The monumental staircase leads to a hall, off which lead the fine internal staircases of Carrara marble. It houses over nine million volumes and documents. The **Museu Nacional de Belas Artes** ① *Av Rio Branco 199, T2240 0068, Tue-Fri 1000-1800, Sat, Sun and holidays 1400-1800, US$1*, was built between 1906 and 1908, in eclectic style. It has about 800 original paintings and sculptures and some thousand direct reproductions. One gallery, dedicated to works by Brazilian artists from the 17th century onwards, includes paintings by Frans Janszoon Post (Dutch 1612-1680), who painted Brazilian landscapes in classical Dutch style, and the Frenchmen Debret and Taunay. It has one of the best collections of Brazilian modernism in the country, with many important works by artists like Cândido Portinári and Emiliano Di Cavalcánti.

Praça Mahatma Gandhi, at the end of Avenida Rio Branco, is flanked on one side by the old cinema and amusement centre of the city, known as Cinelândia. Next to the praça is the **Passeio Público** ① *daily 0900-1700*, a garden planted in 1779-1783 by the artist Mestre Valentim, whose bust is near the old former gateway.

West of the Passeio and the Catedral Metropolitana is **Lapa**, an area slowly rediscovering its belle-époque, artistic past. After 40 years of neglect, streets with a reputation for extreme danger have revived; town houses have been renovated, antiques markets, cafés and music venues have opened and the area has become the heart of Bohemian Rio. You still need to be a bit vigilant here, but it's one of **the** places to go for a night out.

Praça Marechal Âncora/Praça Rui Barbosa
The **Museu Histórico Nacional** ⓘ *T2550 9224, Tue-Fri 1000-1730, Sat, Sun and holidays 1400-1800, US$2*, contains a collection of historical treasures, colonial sculpture and furniture, coins, maps, paintings, arms and armour, silver and porcelain. It also has a collection of beautiful colonial coaches, including one used by the emperor. **Museu da Imagem e do Som** ⓘ *also on Praça Rui Barbosa, T2262 0309, Mon-Fri 1300-1800*, has many photographs of Brazil and modern Brazilian paintings; also collections and recordings of Brazilian classical and popular music and a non-commercial cinema Friday-Sunday.

Zona Norte

West of the centre
About 3 km west of the public gardens of the Praça da República (beyond the Sambódromo – see box, Carnival, page 372) is the **Quinta da Boa Vista** ⓘ *daily 0700-1800*, formerly the Emperor's private park, from 1809 to 1889. If you are comfortable in crowds, perhaps the best time to visit is Saturday or Sunday afternoon. It is full of locals looking for fun and relaxation and therefore more police are on hand. **Note** Beware of thieves operating by the park entrance and in the park itself on weekdays.

In the entrance hall of the **Museu Nacional** ⓘ *Quinta da Boa Vista, Tue-Sun 1000-1600, US$2*, is the famous Bendegó meteorite, found in the State of Bahia in 1888; its original weight, before some of it was chipped, was 5,360 kg. The museum also has important collections which are poorly displayed. The building was the principal palace of the Emperors of Brazil, but only the unfurnished Throne Room and ambassadorial reception room on the second floor reflect past glories. The museum contains collections of Brazilian indigenous weapons, dresses, utensils, etc, of minerals and of historical documents. There are also collections of birds, beasts, fishes and butterflies. Despite the need for conservation work, the museum is still worth visiting. The safest way to reach the museum is by taking a taxi to the main door. Having said that, it can be reached by Metrô to São Cristóvão, then cross the railway line and walk five minutes to the park. This is safer than taking a bus. Also in the park is the **Jardim Zoológico** ⓘ *same opening hours, US$2*, with a captive breeding programme for some endangered animals, such as golden lion tamarins.

Maracanã Stadium ⓘ *T2568 9962, 0900-1700 (0800-1100 on match days), a guided tour of the stadium (in Portuguese) from Gate 16 costs US$6 and of the museum, US$0.50*. Highly recommended for football fans. This is one of the largest sports centres in the world, with a capacity of 200,000. Matches are worth going to if only for the spectators' samba bands. There are three types of ticket, but prices vary according to the game (expect to pay US$7.50-10). Agencies charge much more for tickets than at the gate. It is cheaper to buy tickets from club sites on the day before the match. Seats in the white section have good views. Maracanã is now used only for major games; Rio teams play most matches at their home grounds (still a memorable experience, about US$2 per ticket). Maracanã can be visited most safely during a game with www.bealocal.com, T9643 0366: all is organized including transport from hotel/hostel, tickets and a safe area from which to watch the game.

Santa Teresa → *see map, page 354.*

Known as the coolest part of Rio, and a haven for artists and intellectuals, this hilly inner suburb southwest of the centre, boasts many colonial and 19th-century buildings, set in narrow, curving, tree-lined streets. Today the old houses are lived in by artists, intellectuals and makers of handicrafts. As Rio's up-and-coming place to stay, it has hostels, hotels and homestays (including the upper floor of the former home of Ronnie Biggs, the British, 1960s great train robber). Most visitors in the daytime will arrive by tram. If you stay to the end of the line, Largo das Neves, you will be able to appreciate the small-town feel of the place. There are several bars here, including Goiabeira, simple and charming with a nice view of the praça. The essential stop is the Largo do Guimarães, which has some not to be missed eating places (see

Eating). **Chácara do Céu** ⓘ *R Murtinho Nobre 93, T2285 0891, Tue-Sun 1200-1700, US$1, take the Santa Teresa tram to Curvelo station, walk along R Dias de Barros, following the signposts to Parque das Ruínas*. Also called Fundação Raymundo Ottoni de Castro Maia, it has a wide range of art objects and modern painters, including Brazilian; exhibitions change through the year. The **Chalé Murtinho** ⓘ *R Murtinho 41, daily 1000-1700*, was in ruins until it was partially restored and turned into a cultural centre called **Parque das Ruínas** in 1998. There are exhibitions, a snack bar and superb views.

Santa Teresa is best visited on the traditional open-sided **tram** (US$0.40 one way), the *bondinho*. Take the Metrô to Carioca or Cinelândia, go to Rua Profesor Lélio Gama (look for Banco do Brasil on the corner). The station is up this street. Take the Paula Mattos line (a second line is Dois Irmãos) and enjoy the trip as it passes over the **Arcos**

Glória, Santa Teresa, Catete, Flamengo

Sleeping 🛏
Casa Áurea **1** *C2*
Catete Hostel **6** *C4*
Flórida **2** *D5*
Glória **3** *C5*

Imperial **4** *D4*
Inglês **5** *D5*
Novo Mundo **7** *D5*
Paysandu **8** *F5*
Riazor **9** *D4*

Rio Hostel **13** *B3*
Turístico **11** *C4*
Único **12** *E5*

0 metres 300
0 yards 300

Brazil Rio de Janeiro Santa Teresa

da Lapa aqueduct, winding its way up to the district's historic streets. At Largo das Neves, the tram turns round for the journey back to Rua Profesor L Gama. Normally a policeman rides each *bondinho*, but you are advised not to take valuables (see Safety, page 349). Buses Nos 206 and 214 run from Avenida Rio Branco in the centre to Santa Teresa. At night, only take a taxi, US$7.

Zona Sul → *see map, page 354*

The commercial district ends where Avenida Rio Branco meets the Avenida Beira Mar. This avenue, with its royal palms and handsome buildings, coasting the Botafogo and Flamengo beaches, makes a splendid drive, Avenida Infante Dom Henrique, along the beach over re-claimed land (the Aterro), leading to Botafogo and through two tunnels to Copacabana.

Glória, Catete and Flamengo
On the Glória and Flamengo waterfront, with a view of the Pão de Açúcar and Corcovado, is the **Parque do Flamengo**, designed by Burle Marx, opened in 1965 during the 400th anniversary of the city's founding and landscaped on 100 ha reclaimed from the bay. Security in the park is in the hands of vigilante policemen and it is a popular recreation area. (**Note** Beware armed robbery in Parque do Flamengo.) **Museu de Arte Moderna** ① *Av Infante Dom Henrique 85, city end of Parque Flamengo, T2240 4944, www.mamrio. com.br, Tue-Sun 1200-1700 (last entry 1630), US$2*. This spectacular building near the National War Memorial, suffered a disastrous fire in 1978. The collection is being rebuilt and several countries have donated works.

The **Monumento aos Mortos da Segunda Guerra Mundial/National War Memorial** ① *Av Infante Dom Henrique 75, opposite Praça Paris, crypt and museum open Tue-Sun 1000-1700, but beach clothes and rubber-thonged sandals are not permitted*, to Brazil's dead in the Second World War. The Memorial takes the form of two slender columns supporting a slightly curved slab, representing two palms uplifted to heaven. In the crypt are the remains of Brazilian soldiers killed in Italy in 1944-1945. The beautiful little church on the Glória Hill, overlooking the Parque do Flamengo, is **Nossa Senhora da Glória do Outeiro** ① *Sat-Sun 0800-1200, weekdays 1300-1700, is reached by bus 119 from the centre and 571 from Copacabana*. It was the favourite church of the imperial family; Dom Pedro II was baptized here. The building is polygonal, with a single tower. It contains some excellent examples of blue-faced Brazilian tiling. Its main altar, of wood, was carved by Mestre Valentim. The adjacent museum of religious art keeps the same hours, but is closed on Monday.

Parque do Catete is a charming small park with birds and monkeys between Praia do

Eating 🍴
Adega do Pimenta **1** *C2*
Alcaparra **2** *E5*
Alho e Óleo **3** *E5*
Aprazível **6** *D2*

Bar do Arnaudo **5** *C2*
Espírito Santa **9** *C2*
Estação República **4** *D4*
Lamas **10** *F4*
Sobrenatural **7** *C2*

Flamengo and the Palácio do Catete, which contains the **Museu da República** ⓘ *R do Catete 153, T2557 3150, Sun-Tue 1200-1700, Wed 1400-1700, US$2.50, free Wed, Sun. Signs in Portuguese only. Take bus 571 from Copacabana, or the Metrô to Catete station.* The palace was built in 1858-1866. In 1887 it was converted into the presidential seat, until the move to Brasília. The first floor is devoted to the history of the Brazilian republic. Highly recommended.

Museu do Folclore Edison Carneiro ⓘ *R do Catete 181, T2285 0441, Tue-Fri 1100-1800, Sat-Sun 1500-1800, free, signs in Portuguese, take bus 571 from Copacabana, or the Metrô to Catete station.* This museum's collection should not to be missed. There is an exhibit of small ceramic figures representing everyday life in Brazil, some very funny, some scenes animated by electric motors. There are fine Candomblé and Umbanda costumes, religious objects, ex-votos and sections on many of Brazil's festivals. It has a small, but excellent library, with helpful, friendly staff for finding books on Brazilian culture, history and anthropology.

The **Museu Carmen Miranda** ⓘ *Rui Barbosa 560, Parque do Flamengo (in front of the Morro da Viúva), T2299 5586. Tue-Fri 1100-1700, Sat-Sun 1400-1700, US$1,* houses over 3,000 items related to the famous Portuguese singer who emigrated to Brazil, then Hollywood, and is forever associated with Rio. These include her famous gowns, fruit-covered hats, jewellery and reviews, recordings and occasional showings of her films.

Botafogo

Museu Villa-Lobos ⓘ *R Sorocaba 200, T2266 3845, www.museuvillalobos.org.br, Mon-Fri 1000-1700, free.* Such was the fame and respect afforded to Latin America's most celebrated composer that Rio de Janeiro founded this museum only a year after his death in 1960. Inside the fine 19th-century building is the collection includes instruments, scores, books and recordings. The museum has occasional shows and concerts, and supports a number of classical music projects throughout Brazil. **Museu do Índio** ⓘ *R das Palmeiras 55, T2286 8899,*

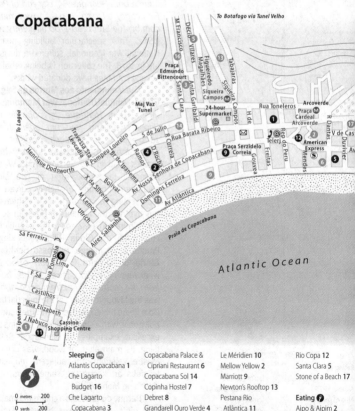

Copacabana

To Botafogo via Tunel Velho

Atlantic Ocean

Praia de Copacabana

Sleeping	Copacabana Palace &	Le Méridien 10	Rio Copa 12
Atlantis Copacabana 1	Cipriani Restaurant 6	Mellow Yellow 2	Santa Clara 5
Che Lagarto	Copacabana Sol 14	Marriott 9	Stone of a Beach 17
Budget 16	Copinha Hostel 7	Newton's Rooftop 13	
Che Lagarto	Debret 8	Pestana Rio	**Eating**
Copacabana 3	Grandarell Ouro Verde 4	Atlântica 11	Aipo & Aipim 2

0 metres 200
0 yards 200

www.museudoindio.org.br, Tue-Fri 0900-1700, Sat and Sun 1300-1700, US$1.50, Sun free. It's a 10-min walk from Botafogo Metrô; from Rodoviária, Bus 136 passes Rua São Clemente, also 172, 178, from Zona Sul 511, 512, 522 (to Botafogo Metrô). The museum houses 12,000 objects from many Brazilian indigenous groups. There is also a small, well-displayed handicraft shop.

Pão de Açúcar (Sugar Loaf mountain)

The Pão de Açúcar, or Sugar Loaf, is a massive granite cone at the entrance to Guanabara Bay that soars to 396 m. There is a restaurant (mixed reports on food, closes 1900) and a playground for children on the **Morro da Urca**, halfway up, where there are also shows at night (consult the cultural sections in the newspapers). You can get refreshments at the top. The sea level cable car station is in a military area, so it is safe to visit. At Praia Vermelha, the beach to the south of the rock, is the Círculo Militar da Praia Vermelha restaurant, which is open to the public (no sign). It has wonderful views, but is not so good for food or service; stop there for a drink anyway. From Praia Vermelha, the Pista Cláudio Coutinho runs around the foot of the rock. It is a paved path for walking, jogging and access to various climbing places. It is open 0700-1800, but you can stay on the path after that. Here you have mountain, forest and sea side-by-side, right in the heart of the city. You can also use the Pista Coutinho as a way of getting up the Pão de Açúcar more cheaply than the US$16 cable-car ride. About 350 m from the path entrance is a track to the left which leads though the forest to Morro de Urca, from where the cable car can be taken for US$10 (you can come down this way, too, but if you take the cable car from sea level you must pay full fare). You can save even more money, but use more energy, by climbing the Caminho da Costa, a path to the summit of the Pão de Açúcar. Only one stretch, of 10 m, requires climbing gear (some say it is not necessary), but if you wait at the bottom of the path for a group going up, they will let you tag along. This way you can descend to Morro de Urca by cable car for free and walk down from there. There are 35 rock routes up the mountain, with various degrees of difficulty. The best months for climbing are April to August. See Sport, page 372, for climbing clubs; there is also a book on climbing routes. ►► *For getting there, see Transport, page 376.*

To Botafogo

Tunel Novo

Villa Lobos Theatre

To Urca & Praia Vermelha

LEME

Gustavo Sampaio

a Lido end Fair

Av Atlântica

Praça Júlio de Noronha

Praia do Leme

MORRO DO LEME

Corcovado

Corcovado is a hunchbacked peak, 710 m high, surmounted by a 38-m-high statue of Christ the Redeemer, O Cristo Redentor, which was completed on 12 October 1931. There is a superb view from the top (sometimes obscured by mist), to which there are a cog railway and road; taxis, cooperative minivans and train put down their passengers behind the statue. Private cars are only allowed as far as Paineiras, from where you can catch train or cabs. The 3.8 km railway itself offers fine views. Average speed is 15 kph on the way up and 12 kph on the way down. There is an exhibition of the history of the railway. From the upper terminus there is a system of escalators, one with a panoramic view, to the top, near which there is a café (alternatively you can climb 220 steps up). To see the city by day and night ascend at 1500 or 1600 and descend on the last train, approximately 1815. Mass is held on Sunday in a small chapel in the statue pedestal. To reach the vast statue of Cristo Redentor at the summit of Corcovado, you have to go through Laranjeiras and Cosme Velho. The road through these districts heads west out of Catete. ►► *See Transport, page 376.*

A Marisquera 1
Armazém Carioca 10
Casarão 6
Cervantes 3
Churrascaria Palace 5
Mala e Cuia 4

Marakesh 9
Siri Mole & Cia 11
Traiteurs de France 12

The **Museu Internacional de Arte Naïf do Brasil** (MIAN) ① *R Cosme Velho 561, T2205 8612, www.museunaif.com.br, Tue-Fri 1000-1800, Sat, Sun and holidays 1200-1800; closed Mon, US$3.20; discounts for groups, students and senior citizens.* This is one of the most comprehensive museums of Naïve and folk paintings in the world. It is only 30 m uphill, on the same street as the station for Corcovado. There is a permanent collection of some 8,000 works by Naïve artists from about 130 countries. MIAN has a good shop at Avenida Atlântica 1998.

Those who want to see what Rio was like early in the 19th century should go to the **Largo do Boticário** ① *R Cosme Velho 822,* a charming small square in neo-colonial style. Much of the material used in creating the effect of the square came from old buildings demolished in the city centre. The square is close to the terminus for the Corcovado cog railway.

Copacabana → *Tourist police patrol Copacabana beach until 1700.*

Built on a narrow strip of land (only a little over 4 sq km) between mountain and sea, Copacabana has one of the highest population densities in the world: 62,000 per sq km, or 250,000 in all. Copacabana began to develop when the Túnel Velho (Old Tunnel) was built in 1891 and an electric tram service reached it. Weekend villas and bungalows sprang up; all have now gone. In the 1930s the Copacabana Palace Hotel was the only tall building; it is now one of the lowest on the beach. The opening of the Túnel Novo (New Tunnel) in the 1940s led to an explosion of population which shows no sign of having spent its force. Unspoilt art deco blocks towards the Leme (city) end of Copacabana are now under preservation order.

There is almost everything in this 'city within a city'. The shops, mostly in Avenida Nossa Senhora de Copacabana and the Rua Barata Ribeiro, are excellent. Even more stylish shops are to be found in Ipanema, Leblon and in the various large shopping centres in the city. The city's glamorous nightlife is beginning to move elsewhere and, after dark, Copacabana, has lost some of its former allure. A fort at the far end of the beach, Forte de Copacabana, was an important part of Rio's defences and prevents a seashore connection with the Ipanema and Leblon beaches. Parts of the military area are now being handed over to civilian use, the first being the Parque Garota de Ipanema at Arpoador, the fashionable Copacabana end of the Ipanema beach.

The world-famous beach is divided into numbered *postos*, where the lifeguards are based. Different sections attract different types of people, eg young people, artists and gays. The safest places are in front of the major hotels which have their own security, eg the Meridien on Copacabana beach or the Caesar Park on Ipanema. The Caesar Park also has 24-hour video surveillance during the summer season, which makes it probably the safest patch of sand in Rio. ▶▶ *See Transport page 376.*

Ipanema and Leblon → *see map, page 359.*

Beyond Copacabana are the seaside suburbs of Ipanema and Leblon. The two districts are divided by a canal from the Lagoa Rodrigo de Freitas to the sea, beside which is the Jardim de Alá. Ipanema and Leblon are a little less built-up than Copacabana and their beaches tend to be cleaner. Praia de Arpoadar at the Copacabana end of Ipanema is a peaceful spot to watch surfers, with the beautiful backdrop of Morro Dois Irmãos; excellent for photography, walk on the rocks. There is now night-time illumination of these beaches. The seaward lane of the road running beside the beach is closed to traffic until 1800 on Sundays and holidays; this makes it popular for rollerskating and cycling (bicycles can be hired).

Gávea, Lagoa and Jardim Botânico

Backing Ipanema and Leblon is the middle-class residential area of **Lagoa Rodrigo de Freitas**, by a saltwater lagoon on which Rio's rowing and small-boat sailing clubs are active. The lake is too polluted for bathing, but the road which runs around its shores has pleasant views. Avenida Epitácio Pessoa, on the eastern shore, leads to the Túnel Rebouças which runs beneath Corcovado and Cosme Velho.

Well worth a visit is the **Jardim Botânico** (Botanical Gardens) ① *T3874 1808, www.jbrj.gov.br, 0800-1700, US$2,* 8 km from the centre (see Transport, page 374). These were founded in 1808. The most striking features are the transverse avenues of 30 m high royal palms. Among the more than 7,000 varieties of plants from around the world are examples of the pau-brasil tree, now endangered, and many other threatened species. There is a herbarium, an aquarium and a library (some labels are unclear). A new pavilion contains sculptures by Mestre Valentim transferred from the centre. Many improvements were carried out before the 1992 Earth Summit, including a new Orquidário and an enlarged bookshop.

The **Planetário** ① *Padre Leonel Franco 240, Gávea, T2274 0096, www.rio.rj.gov.br/ planetario, observations on Tue-Thu 1830-2030, weekend shows for children; getting there: buses 125, 170, 523, 571, 750 and others*. Inaugurated in 1979, the planetarium has a sculpture of the Earth and Moon by Mario Agostinelli. There are occasional *chorinho* concerts on Thursday or Friday.

Southern suburbs

Leblon to Barra da Tijuca
The Pedra Dois Irmãos overlooks Leblon. On the slopes is Vidigal favela. From Leblon, two inland roads take traffic west to the outer seaside suburb of Barra da Tijuca: the Auto Estrada Lagoa-Barra, which tunnels under Dois Irmãos, and the Estrada da Gávea, which goes through Gávea. Beyond Leblon the coast is rocky. A third route to Barra da Tijuca is the Avenida Niemeyer, which skirts the cliffs on the journey past Vidigal, a small beach where the Sheraton is situated. Avenida Niemeyer carries on round the coast to São Conrado. On the slopes of the Pedra da Gávea, through which the Avenida Niemeyer has two tunnels, is the Rocinha favela.

The flat-topped **Pedra da Gávea** can be climbed or scrambled up for magnificent views, but beware of snakes. Behind the Pedra da Gávea is the Pedra Bonita. A road, the Estrada das Canoas, climbs up past these two rocks on its way to the Parque Nacional Tijuca. There is a spot on this road which is one of the chief hang-glider launch sites in the area (see page 371). See also Transport page 376.

Barra da Tijuca
This rapidly developing residential area is also one of the principal recreation areas of Rio, with its 20-km sandy beach and good waves for surfing. At the westernmost end is the small beach of Recreio dos Bandeirantes, where the ocean can be very rough. The channels behind the Barra are popular with jetskiers. It gets very busy on Sundays. There are innumerable bars and restaurants, clustered at both ends, campsites (see page 364), motels and hotels: budget accommodation tends to be self-catering. Although buses do run as far as Barra, getting to and around here is best by car. A cycle way links Barra da Tijuca with the centre of the city. A bit further out is the **Museu Casa do Pontal** ① *Estrada do Pontal 3295, Recreio dos Bandeirantes, Tue-Sun, 0900-1930,* a collection of Brazilian folk art. Recommended.

Ipanema & Leblon

Casa 6 **6**
Che Lagarto
Ipanema **7**
Crab Hostel **8**
Fasano Rio **12**
Harmonia **6**
Hostel Ipanema **6**
Ipanema Beach
House **5**
Ipanema Inn **2**

Lighthouse **6**
Marina All Suites &
Bar D'Hotel **9**
Marina Palace **4**
Mar Ipanema **3**
San Marco **10**

Eating ❼
Alessandro &
Frederico **6**

Amarelinho **17**
Arabe de Gávea **19**
Bistrô ZaZá **7**
Carlota **9**
Casa da Feijoada **13**
Celeiro **4**
Empório Saúde **18**
Fellini **1**
Forneria **3**
Gergelim **14**

Gero **10**
Guimas **8**
Manekineko **2**
Porção **5**
Roberta Sudbrack **16**
Satyricon **11**
Yemanjá **15**
Zuka **12**

Sleeping 🛏
Arpoador Inn **11**
Best Western Sol
Ipanema **1**

Parque Nacional Tijuca

ⓘ *National park information, T2492 5407. See also Transport page 377.*

The Pico da Tijuca (1,022 m) gives a good idea of the tropical vegetation of the interior and a fine view of the bay and its shipping. A two- to three-hour walk leads to the summit: on entering the park at Alto da Boa Vista (0600-2100), follow the signposts (maps are displayed) to Bom Retiro, a good picnic place (1½ hours' walk). At Bom Retiro the road ends and there is another hour's walk up a fair footpath to the summit (take the path from the right of the Bom Retiro drinking fountain; not the more obvious steps from the left). The last part consists of steps carved out of the solid rock; look after children at the summit as there are several sheer drops, invisible because of bushes. The route is shady for almost its entire length. The main path to Bom Retiro passes the Cascatinha Taunay (a 30-m waterfall) and the Mayrink Chapel (built 1860). Beyond the Chapel is the restaurant A Floresta. Other places of interest not passed on the walk to the peak are the Paulo e Virginia Grotto, the Vista do Almirante and the Mesa do Imperador (viewpoints). Allow at least five to six hours for the excursion. Maps of the park are available. If hiking in the national park other than on the main paths, a guide may be useful if you do not want to get lost: for walks organized by the **Ecotourism Sector** ⓘ *T2492 2252/2492 2253 – ext 217/212.*

Parque Estadual da Pedra Branca ⓘ *Núcleo Camorim, Camorim, Jacarepaguá, T3417 3642, www.ief.rj.gov.br,* the largest urban forest in the world, is also in Rio, though few Cariocas are aware of it. Pedra Branca is the city's best kept natural secret, protecting an astounding 12,500 ha of pristine rainforest, lakes and mountains, which are home to over 500 animal species. A number are threatened or critically endangered. There are many trails in the park, including one leading to the highest peak in Rio de Janeiro, the Pedra Branca (1,024 m).

Ilha de Paquetá

The island, the second largest in Guanabara Bay, is noted for its gigantic pebble shaped rocks, butterflies and orchids. At the southwest tip is the interesting Parque Darke de Mattos, with beautiful trees, lots of birds and a lookout on the Morro da Cruz. The island has several beaches, but ask about the state of the water before bathing. The only means of transport are bicycles and horse-drawn carriages (US$20 per hr, many have harnesses which cut into the horse's flesh). Neither is allowed into the Parque Darke de Mattos. A tour by trenzinho, a tractor pulling trailers, costs US$1.65, or just wander around on foot, quieter and free. Bicycles can be hired. The island is very crowded at weekends and on public holidays, but is usually quiet during the week. The prices of food and drink are reasonable. ▶ *See Transport page 377.*

● Sleeping

All hotels **AL-A** and above in the following list are a/c. A 10% service charge is usually added to the bill and tax of 5% or 10% may be added (if not already included). Note that not all higher-class hotels include breakfast in their room rates. The best and safest places to stay in Rio are Ipanema and southern Copacabana and there are a number of decent, new budget hostels in these areas. New backpacker hostels are opening all the time and hostelling sites (www.hostels.com, www.hostelworld.com) list latest options. With a few notable exceptions, Rio's other hotels in the higher and mid-range are a mix of anonymous business chain towers and fading leftovers from the 1970s, complete with period decor. Economy hotels are found mainly in the 3 districts of Rio: Flamengo/Botafogo (best), Lapa/Fátima and Saúde/Maúa: choose with care in those districts. The city is

noisy. An inside room is cheaper and much quieter. Always ask for the actual room price: it usually differs from that quoted. Also check if the quoted price is per room or per person. Prices rise considerably over New Year and Carnaval. Reserve well in advance, especially budget accommodation.

Santa Teresa *p353, map p354*
Santa Teresa is hilly and offers views out over Rio but is inconvenient for transport.
AL-E Cama e Café, R Progresso 67, next to Largo das Neves, T2224 5689, www.camaecafe.com.br. Many great deals and charming options for homestays with this company. They include Ronnie Biggs's former home and Mestre Valentim's castle-folly on their books. Excellent value and a good way to see Rio from an insider's point of view.

A-C **Casa Áurea**, R Áurea 80, Santa Teresa, T2242 5830, www.casaaurea.com.br. Small hotel in a converted colonial house. Rooms are bright and airy and service attentive. Breakfast is served in a little garden visited by marmosets in the mornings.
E pp **Rio Hostel**, R Joaquim Murtinho 361, T3852 0827, www.riohostel.com. Dormitories (B in double room), with breakfast, kitchen, bar, pool, internet, laundry service, hot water, airport pick-up US$17, relaxed, English spoken, events and trips organized. Owner loves English and Australians and has an inexplicable fixation with Jamie Oliver.

Glória, Catete and Flamengo *p355, map p354*
These are primarily residential areas between the centre and Copacabana. Catete, and Glória to the north and Flamengo to the south, lie next to a park landscaped by Burle Marx and a beautiful beach lapped by a filthy sea. They have good bus and Metrô connections, but are not as safe as Ipanema.
LL-L **Glória**, R do Russel 632, Glória, T2555 7572, www.hotelgloriario.com.br. Rio's other stylish and elegant 1920s hotel. Not as grand as the Copacabana Palace but with far more charm than any others in Copacabana or Ipanema. Rooms have mock Edwardian decoration. 2 pools, spa and in-house theatre. Highly recommended.
LL-AL **Novo Mundo**, Praia Flamengo 20, Catete, T2105 7000, www.hotelnovomundo-rio.com.br. Standard 4-star rooms, suites with balcony views of the Sugar Loaf. Recommended but noisy.
L-AL **Flórida**, Ferreira Viana, 71/81, Catete, T2195 6800, www.windsorhoteis.com. Business-orientated hotel, bars (for private hire), restaurant, and modestly decorated modern rooms.
A **Paysandu**, Paysandu, R Paissandu 23, Flamengo T2558 7270, www.paysanduhotel.com.br. Wonderful art deco tower next to the Palácio de República and Flamengo gardens, with spartan rooms but helpful staff, good location, organized tours available.

A-B **Turístico**, Ladeira da Glória 30, Glória, T2557 7698, F2558 5815. With breakfast, a/c, tourist information provided, mixed reports, some highly favourable.
B **Imperial**, R do Catete 186, T2556 5212, Catete, www.imperialhotel.com.br. One of the city's very first grand hotels (late 19th century). Rooms either in the grander, older main building, or the modern annexe (modern, US motel-style), better equipped but overlooking the parking lot.
B **Inglês**, R Silveira Martins 20, Glória, T2558 3052, www.hotelingles.com.br. Popular hotel next to the metro and in front of the Museu da República. The better rooms have been refurbished and have a/c.
C **Único**, Ferreira Viana 54, Catete, T2205 9932, F2205 8149. Plain rooms with TV, a/c and fridge. Recommended.
C-D **Riazor**, R do Catete 160, T2225 0121. Good budget option, a/c, TV, balcony, quiet, breakfast extra.
C-E pp **Catete Hostel**, R do Catete 92, casa 1, Catete, T3826 0522, www.catetehostel.com.br. Dorms and doubles, all with bath, a/c and fan, breakfast included.

Botafogo *p356*
Another quiet, middle-class neighbourhood with a great beach lapped by dirty water. Convenient for public transport and Mall shopping but care should be taken at night.
A **O Veleiro**, T2554 8980, Praia de Botafogo, www.oveleiro.com. Address given only with reservation. B&B with a great breakfast, Canadian/Carioca-owned, pick-up and drop-off from airport or bus station, Wi-Fi, tours, guiding, helpful staff. Recommended, but neighbourhood noisy at times.
D pp **Alpha Hostel**, R Praia de Botafogo 462, casa 3, Botafogo, T2286 7799, www.alpha hostel.com. Normal rate. B in double rooms. Breakfast included, laundry, kitchen, internet, tours, airport and bus terminal transfer available.

E pp **Chave do Rio de Janeiro**, R General Dionísio 63, Botafogo, T2286 0303, www.rio hostel.com.br. IYHA, cheaper for members, **B** in double rooms, laundry and cooking facilities, superb breakfast, noisy. Recommended.

E-F pp **Ace Backpackers**, R São Clemente 23, 1st floor, Botafogo, T2527 7452, www.ace hostels.com.br. Popular, lively, small but spotless dorms and rooms (**C** pp), kitchen, internet, tours, laundry. Other branches in Petrópolis and São Paulo.

E-F pp **El Misti Hostel**, R Praia de Botafogo 462, casa 9, T2226 0991, www.elmistihostel.com. Converted colonial house with 6 dorms, shared bath, doubles. **B-C**, kitchen, internet, capoeira classes, tour service. Convenient for public transport.

Pão de Açúcar: Urca *p357*

E pp **Carioca Easy**, R Marechal Cantuária 168, Urca, T2295 7805, www.cariocahostel.com.br. Bright little hostel in a colonial house in one of the safest and most spectacular neighbourhoods in Rio; at the base of Sugar Loaf. Pool, kitchen, bike rental, boat trips, dorms and doubles (**B**).

Copacabana *p358, map p356*

LL Copacabana Palace, Av Atlântica 1702, T2548 7070, www.copacabana palace.com.br. Justifiably world famous hotel with distinguished guest list, dripping in 1920's elegance. Go for cocktails and dinner if you can't afford to stay. Cipriani (**ᵮᵮᵮ**), is the best restaurant for formal evening dining in Rio with a chef from the Hotel Cipriani in Venice. Very good seafood and modern Italian fare.

LL Le Méridien, Av Atlântica 1020, T0800-111554, www.meridien-br.com. Air France hotel with pool, quite small rooms, breakfasts with a wonderful view, also good for business travellers.

LL Marriott, Av Atlantica 2600, T2545 6500, www.marriott.com. Rio's newest top end business hotel, specifically designed with a gamut of services for the business visitor.

L Pestana Rio Atlântica, Av Atlântica 2964, T2548 6332, www.pestana.com. Part of the Portuguese Pestana group, an excellent choice, spacious bright rooms and a rooftop pool and terrace with sweeping views, very high standards. Recommended.

AL Grandarell Ouro Verde, Av Atlântica 1456, T2542 1887, www.grandarrell.com.br. The best small hotel in Copacabana with spacious, well-decorated rooms and a decent restaurant. Good for families – the hotel has a Kid's club.

AL-A Copacabana Sol, R Santa Clara 141, T2549 4577, www.copacabanasolhotel.com.br. Safe, refurbished, helpful, quiet, with good breakfast, Wi-Fi and cable TV.

A Debret, Av Atlântica 3564, T2522 0132, www.debret.com. Bright, spacious seafront rooms, others are a little dark, modern. Good, helpful staff.

A Rio Copa, Av Princesa Isabel 370, T2275 6644, www.riocopa.com. Best Western, simple, well-maintained rooms 2 blocks back from beach. English-spoken. Recommended.

A Santa Clara, R Décio Vilares, 316, T2256 2650, www.hotel santaclara.com.br. Quiet, central location, a/c, TV, telephone, en suite bath, attentive service, breakfast included, tours arranged.

A-B Atlantis Copacabana, Av Bulhões de Carvalho 61, T2521 1142, atlantishotel@uol.com.br. Fading Arpoador hotel in a quiet, safe street very close to the beach. Small rooftop pool, sauna, very good value.

D-E pp Mellow Yellow, R General Barbosa Lima 51, T2547 1993, www.mellowyellow.com.br. **B** in double room. Nothing mellow about this enormous party hostel, but it is always packed, has its own bar, live music, tour services, internet facilities and free airport pick-up.

E pp Che Lagarto Copacabana, R Anita Garibaldi 87, T2256 2778, www.chelagarto.com. Discount for HI members. Includes breakfast and welcome drink. **B** in rooms with toilet and a/c. Also **E pp Che Lagarto Budget**, Santa Clara 304, T2257-3133, all dorm accommodation, some with a/c.

E pp Copinha Hostel, Felipe de Oliveira 11, T2275 8520, www.copinhahostel.com.br. Well-run little hostel with a range of dorms and doubles (**B**), with kitchen, cable TV and transport services.

E pp Stone of a Beach, R Barata Ribeiro 111, T3209 0348, www.stoneofabeach.com. Several dorms and doubles (**B**). Helpful, young party atmosphere, several languages spoken, organizes tours, includes breakfast, bar.

F pp Newton's Rooftop, R Siqueira Campos 182, T2545 7499, www.newtonsrooftop.com.br. Dorms and doubles (**C**), with breakfast, good atmosphere, with free *caipirinha* on Fri and *feijoada* on Sat, helpful, safe, internet, kitchen, tours.

Ipanema, Leblon and further west
p358, map p359

LL Fasano Rio, Av Vieira Souto 80, Ipanema, T3896 4000, www.fasano.com.br. Phillippe Starck-designed luxury hotel with rooftop terrace, fitness centre, etc, good bar and superior restaurant, **Fasano Al Mare**.

LL La Maison, R Sergio Porto 58, Gávea, T7812 5836, www.lamaisonrio.com. A boutique hidden away in a converted colonial townhouse on a quiet back street. Resolutely OTT decor, but the bedrooms are more understated and the views of the forest and Corcovado from the breakfast area are magnificent.

LL La Suite, R Jackson de Figueiredo 501, Joá, T2484 1962, fxdussol@hotmail.com. Versace meets Louis XIV in a riot of colour that Elton John would swoon over in this 7-room boutique between Leblon and Barra da Tijuca. Fabulous location – the pool sits eyrie-like over the exclusive beach at Joá with sweeping views out towards São Conrado. Every room has a terrace, view and a marble bathroom.

L Best Western Sol Ipanema, Av Vieira Souto 320, T2525 2020, www.bestwestern.com. Huge breakfast, good member of the US chain, popular.

L Marina Palace and Marina All Suites, Av Delfim Moreira 630 and 696, T2294 1794, www.hotelmarina.com.br. Two 1980s towers almost next door to each other. The former has smart, modern but standard rooms and a rooftop pool, the latter is a luxury boutique with 'designer' suites, with the excellent Bar D'Hotel (♜♜♜♜), light but very well-flavoured fish dishes served in cool surroundings. Also very good breakfasts and cocktails.

AL-A Arpoador Inn, Francisco Otaviano 177, T2523 0060, F2511 5094. Well-maintained, if undistinguished rooms, seafront restaurant, off-season special offers are a good deal.

AL-A Mar Ipanema, R Visconde de Pirajá 539, T3875 9190, www.maripanema.com. One block from the beach, simple, smart, modern rooms.

A Ipanema Inn, Maria Quitéria 27, behind Caesar Park, T2523 3092, F2511 5094. Good value and location.

B San Marco, R Visconde de Pirajá 524, T2540 5032, www.sanmarcohotel.net. Renovated 2-star 2 blocks from beach, with simple rooms and a free caipirinha for every internet booking, very helpful, internet US$2.70 per hr. Price includes breakfast. Recommended.

C-D Crab Hostel, R Prudente de Morais 903, T2267 7353, www.crabhostel.com.br. A block from the beach with a pool, sauna, cable TV and dorms with en suites.

C-E Casa 6, R Barão da Torre 175, casa 6, T2247 1384, www.casa6ipanema.com. Charming, colourful but simple French-owned B&B in a townhouse 3 blocks from the beach. Also has doubles (**A**), good long stay rates.

D pp Che Lagarto Ipanema, R Paul Redfern 48, T2512 8076, www.chelagarto.com. Bright red party hostel with young staff and a terrace with views of Corcovado, dorms and doubles (**B**), cheaper with HI card. See also Copacabana, above.

D pp Harmonia, R Barão da Torre 175, casa 18, T2523 4905, www.hostelharmonia.com. 3 blocks from beach, doubles or dormitories, cheaper without breakfast, kitchen facilities, English, Spanish, German and Swedish spoken, good internet. At casa 14 in the same building is **D-E pp Hostel Ipanema**, T2247 7269, www.hostelipanema.com, also doubles **B**.

D pp Ipanema Beach House, R Barão da Torre 485, T3202 2693, www.ipanemahouse.com. Dorms and doubles (**A**) all with shared baths. Great little hostel with rooms arranged around a garden and small pool. Small bar, kitchen, internet and tours, good service.

D-E pp The Lighthouse, R Barão da Torre 175, casa 20, T2522 1353, www.thelighthouse.com.br. One private room for up to 4 (**B**), and a dorm for 8, use of kitchen, internet, very helpful, New Zealand/Brazilian owners.

Camping

Camping Clube do Brasil, Av Sen Dantas 75, 29th floor, Centro, CEP 20037-900, T2210 3171, www.camping-club.com.br. Has 2 beach sites at Barra da Tijuca: Av Sernambetiba 3200, T2493

0628 (bus 233 from centre, 702 or 703 from the airport via Zona Sul, US$5 – a long way from the centre), sauna, pool, bar, café, US$12 (half price for members), during Jan and Feb this site is often full and sometimes restricted to members of the Camping Clube do Brasil; a simpler site at Estrada do Pontal 5900, T2437 8400, lighting, café, good surfing, US$6. Both have trailer plots.

If travelling by trailer, you can park at the **Marina Glória** car park, where there are showers and toilets, a small shop and snack bar. Pay the guards to look after your vehicle.

Self-catering apartments

A popular form of accommodation in Rio, available at all price levels: eg furnished apartments for short-term let, accommodating up to 6, cost US$300 per month in Flamengo. Copacabana, Ipanema and Leblon prices range from about US$25 a day for a simple studio, starting at US$500-600 a month up to US$2,000 a month for a luxurious residence sleeping 4-6. Heading south past Barra da Tijuca, virtually all the accommodation available is self-catering. Renting a small flat, or sharing a larger one, can be much better value than a hotel room. Blocks consisting entirely of short-let apartments can attract thieves, so check the (usually excellent) security arrangements; residential buildings are called *prédio familial*. Higher floors (*alto andar*) are considered quieter.

Apart-Hotels are listed in the Guia Quatro Rodas and Riotur's booklet. Agents and private owners advertise in *Balcão*, twice weekly, *O Globo* or *Jornal do Brasil* (daily); under 'Apartamentos – Temporada'; advertisements are classified by district and size of apartment: 'vagas e quartos' means shared accommodation; 'conjugado' (or 'conj') is a studio with limited cooking facilities; '3 Quartos' is a 3-bedroom flat. There should always be a written agreement when renting.

The following rent apartments in residential blocks:

Apartments Rio de Janeiro, www.rentinrio.com, with contact numbers in the USA and UK.

Copacabana Holiday, R Barata Ribeiro 90A, Copacabana, T2542 1525, www.copacabana holiday.com.br. Recommended, well-equipped small apartments from US$500 per month, minimum 30 days let.

Fantastic Rio, Av Atlântica 974, Suite 501, Copacabana, BR-22020-000, T/F2543 2667, hpcorr@hotmail.com. All types of furnished accommodation, owned by Peter Corr.

● For an explanation of the sleeping and eating price codes used in this guide, see page 58.
● Other relevant information is found in Essentials pages 345-347.

Rio Flat Rental, R Leopoldo Miguez 161, Copacabana, T9956 5147, www.rioflatrental.com. Fully furnished flats, 24-hr security. Free pick-up from the airport.

Youth hostel associations and B&Bs

ALBERJ (for Rio), R da Assembléia 10, l 61, T2531 2234, F2531 1943.
Federação Brasileira (Brazil), at Chave do Rio de Janeiro hostel. For web bookings see www.hostelworld.com.

🍴 Eating

The best of Rio's many restaurants are in Copacabana, Ipanema or Leblon. Expect to pay US$30+ per person in the better restaurants. You can eat well for an average US$5 per person, less if you choose the prato feito at lunchtime (US$2-7.50), or eat in a place that serves food by weight (starting at about US$10 per kg). Avoid mussels! Most restaurants are closed on 24 and 25 Dec.

Grill or barbecue houses (*churrascarias*) are relatively cheap, especially by European standards. There are many at São Conrado and Joá, on the road out to Barra da Tijuca. Look for the 'Churrascaria Rodízio', where you are served as much as you can eat. Galetos are lunch counters specializing in chicken and grilled meat, very reasonable. In the shopping centres there is usually a variety of restaurants and snack bars grouped around a central plaza where you can shop around for a good meal. Most less-expensive restaurants in Rio have basically the same type of food (based on steak, fried potatoes and rice) and serve large portions. Rio lacks that almost ubiquitous Brazilian institution, the corner bakery, and a decent breakfast can be hard to find. But there are plenty of stand-up juice bars serving fruit juices made from as many as 25 different fruits, all of which are wonderful.

City centre and Lapa *p350, map p351*
Many restaurants in the business district are open only for weekday lunch. Many lanchonetes in this area offer good, cheap meals. **R Miguel Couto** (opposite Santa Rita church) is called the **Beco das Sardinhas** because on Wed and Fri in particular is full of people eating sardines and drinking beer. There are several Arab restaurants on Av Senhor dos Passos, which are also open Sat and Sun. In addition to those listed there are plenty of cafes, including a few new chic options on R Lavradio in Lapa; where the lively Sat antiques market is held.

🍽🍽🍽 **Adega Flor de Coimbra**, R Teotônio Regadas 34, Lapa, T2224 4582. Founded 1938, Portuguese food and wines, speciality *bacalhau* (dried cod). Very good.

🍽🍽🍽 **Albamar**, Praça Marechal Âncora 184-6, T2240 8378. Populara, long-established fish and seafood, with lovely views of the bay. Open 1130-1600 Mon, 1130-2200 Tue-Sat.

🍽🍽🍽 **Cais do Oriente**, R Visc de Itaboraí 8, T2233 2531. Wonderful restaurant with several settings; the menu is a fusion of Mediterranean, Brazilian and oriental.

🍽🍽🍽 **Republique**, Praça da República 63 (2nd floor), T2532 9000. Refurbished and designed by the architect Chicô Gouveia. Chef Paulo Carvalho cooks a mix of Portuguese, Italian and French dishes.

🍽🍽 **Bar Luiz**, R da Crioca 39, T2262 6900. A little bar in a colonial house in the centre, famous as much for its clientèle as its tapas and *chope* in the evening, good for a quiet snack lunch, too.

🍽🍽 **Bar das Artes**, Praça 15 de Novembro 48 (Paço Imperial), T2215 5795. Salads, sandwiches and light meals in a neat, peaceful café in the former Imperial Palace.

🍽🍽 **Confeitaria Colombo**, R Gonçalves Dias 32, near Carioca Metrô station. Recommended for atmosphere and the only one of its kind in Rio. Over 100 years old, it has the original belle époque decor, open 0900-1800, no service charge so tip the excellent waiters. More modern but similar establishments in some of the main hotels.

¶ Sabor Saúde, R da Quitanda 21, T2252 6041. Breakfast and lunch only, vegetarian and wholefood dishes and sandwiches, also light meals (not always vegetarian).

Santa Teresa *p353, map p354*

¶¶¶ Aprazível, R Aprazível 62, T3852 4935. Decent but unspectacular Brazilian dishes and seafood with tables outdoors in a tropical garden overlooking Guanabara Bay. This is a good Sun lunch spot when they have Choro and Samba performed by Rio's equivalent of the Buena Vista Social Club.

¶¶ Adega do Pimenta, R Almte Alexandrino 296. Daily 1130-2200, Sun 1100-1800, closed Sat, Tue. A very small German restaurant in the Largo do Guimarães with excellent sausages, sauerkraut and cold beer.

¶¶ Bar do Arnaudo, Largo do Guimarães, R Almte Alexandrino 316, T2252 7246. A modest-looking restaurant decorated with handicrafts but serving generous portions of wonderful Northeast Brazilian cooking. Try the *carne do sol* (sun-dried beef, or jerky) with *feijão de corda* (brown beans and herbs), or the *queijo coalho* (a country cheese, grilled).

¶¶ Espírito Santa, R Almte Alexandrino 264, T2508 7095. Closed Mon, lunch only Tue, Wed, Sun. Upstairs is a chic Mediterranean restaurant with a wonderful sweeping view of the city, downstairs is a weekend basement club, good cocktails.

¶¶ Sobrenatural, R Almirante Alexandrino 432, T2224 1003. Open lunchtime and evening, closed Mon. A charming rustic restaurant serving fish caught daily on owner's boat. For a light lunch, order a mix of excellent appetizers. Recommended.

Glória, Catete and Flamengo *p355, map p354*

There are many cheap and mid-range eating places on R do Catete; including Amazônia No 234B, and Catelândia, No 204.

¶¶¶ Alcaparra, Praia do Flamengo 144, Flamengo, T2557 7236. Elegant traditional Italian popular with politicians and business people. Overlooking the sea.

¶¶¶-¶¶ Alho E Óleo, R Buarque de Macedo 13, Flamengo, T2557 8541. Fashionable Italian with a strong emphasis on pasta. Recommended.

¶¶ Lamas, Marquês de Abrantes 18A, Flamengo, T2556 0799. Steak, seafood and general Brazilian fare have been served here for over 130 years. Excellent value, great atmosphere, opens late, popular with Brazilian arts/media people. Recommended.

¶ Estação República, R do Catete 104, Catete, in the Palácio do Catete. More than 40 dishes in this per kilo restaurant, soups, sushi, salads and stews.

Botafogo *p356*

In Baixo Botafogo, those on a budget will find a number of enticing bars and restaurants on R Visconde de Caravelas.

¶¶¶ Carême Bistrô, R Visconde de Caravelas 113, Botafogo, T 2537 5431. An elegant and intimate little restaurant serving the best French food in Rio. Recommended.

¶¶ Raajmahal, R Gen Polidoro 29, Baixo Botafogo, T2542 6242. One of the few restaurants offering authentic Indian food.

¶¶ Yorubá, R Arnaldo Quintela 94, Botafogo, T2541 9387. Evenings only except weekends, closed Mon, Tue. Award-winning Bahian cooking.

¶ Aurora, R Visconde de Caravelas corner of R Capitão Salomão 43. Varied menu and good value simple fare.

¶ Botequim, R Visconde de Caravelas No 184. Also has a varied menu and is good value.

¶ Chez Michou and the ubiquitous chain restaurant **Habib's**, both in Rio Sul Shopping. Serve, respectively, crêpes and Arabic fast-food.

Copacabana, Ipanema and Leblon
p358, maps p356 and p359

¶¶¶ Alessandro & Frederico, R Garcia D'Ávila, 134 loja D, Ipanema, T2521 0828. Upmarket café with decent café latte and breakfasts. Great juice bar next door.

¶¶¶ Bistrô ZaZá, R Joana Angélica 40, Ipanema. Hippy-chic, pseudo Moroccan/ French restaurant, good fish dishes and cocktails and good fun. Evenings are best for intimate dining when the tables are lit by candles.

¶¶¶ Carlota, R Dias Ferreira 64, Leblon, T2540 6821. The best of many on a street lined with restaurants and bars. Great unpretentious Mediterranean food in an elegant dining room.

¶¶¶ Forneria, R Aníbal de Mendonça 112, Ipanema, T2540 8045. Serves superior bar snacks and supreme burgers in pizza dough to the elegant, after-beach crowd.

¶¶¶ Gero, R Aníbal de Mendonça 157, Ipanema, T2239 8158. Light Italian fare and excellent fish in a beautiful, minimalist space.

¶¶¶ Manekineko, R Dias Ferreira, 410, Leblon, T2540 7641, www.manekineko.com.br. Exquisite Japanese and Japanese fusion cooking served in an intimately designed modern dining room.

¶¶¶ Porção, Barão de Torre 218, Ipanema, T2522 0999 (also on Av NS de Copacabana). One of the city's best churrascarias, serving all manner of meat in unlimited quantities for a set price.

♥♥♥ Satyricon, R Barão da Torre 192, Ipanema, T2521 0627. The best seafood in Rio; especially the squid. Lively crowd in a large dining room. Avoid Sat when there is a seafood buffet.

♥♥♥ Zuka, R Dias Ferreira 233, Leblon, T3205 7154. One of the most fashionable restaurants in Rio with an exciting and eclectic fusion of everything – French and Japanese, American fast food and Italian.

♥♥ Casa da Feijoada, Prudente de Morais 10, Ipanema, T2523 4994. Serves an excellent feijoada all week. Generous portions.

♥♥ Celeiro, R Dias Ferreira 199, Leblon. Some of the best salads in the city, and light food by weight.

♥♥ Churrascaria Palace, R Rodolfo Dantas 16B, Copacabana. 20 different kinds of barbecued meat served on a spit at your table with buffet salads to accompany. Good value.

♥♥ Fellini, R General Urquiza 104, Leblon, T2511 3600, www.fellini.com.br. The best per kilo in the city with a range of delicious buffet options and plenty for vegetarians.

♥♥ Gergelim, R Vinícius de Moraes, 121, Ipanema T2523 7026. Vegetarian whole food in an a/c café atmosphere. Good puddings.

♥♥ Mala e Cuia, R Barata Ribeiro 638, Copacabana, T2545 7566. Comida mineira at one of the restaurants in this recommended chain (also in the centre).

♥♥ Rodizio Carretão, R Visconde de Pirajá 112, Ipanema, www.carretaochurrascaria.com.br. Good atmosphere, good food, reasonably priced (rises to ♥♥♥ at weekends).

♥♥ Siri Mole & Cia, R Francisco Otaviano 90, T2233 0107. Excellent Bahian seafood and Italian coffee in elegant a/c. At the upper end of this price bracket.

♥♥ Yemenjá, R Visconde de Pirajá 128, Ipanema, T2247 7004. Bahian cooking such as moqueca, vatapa cooked in dende palm or coconut oil.

♥ A Marisquera, Barata Ribeiro 232, Copacabana, T2547 3920. Reasonable seafood dishes and Brazilian standards – eg meat, rice, beans, chips.

♥ Aipo and Aipim, Av Nossa Senhora de Copacabana 391b and 599, Copacabana, and R Visconde de Pirajá 145, Ipanema, T2267 8313. Plentiful tasty food sold by weight at this popular chain.

♥ Amarelinho, R Farme de Amoedo 62, Ipanema. Great corner lanchonete with tables outside, fresh food, good value, friendly, open until 0300. Recommended.

♥ Armazém Carioca, corner of Princesa Isabel and Av NS Copacabana. A simple, friendly bar/restaurant with helpful waiters with tables on pavement. Comprehensive menu all in English includes delicious crab pancakes. Warmly recommended for eating as well as drinking, opens 0700.

♥ Casarão, Souza Lima 37A, Copacabana. Cheap but decent café food and breakfasts.

♥ Cervantes, Barata Ribeiro 07-B e Prado Júnior 335B, Copacabana. Stand-up bar or sit-down, a/c restaurant, open all night, queues after 2200. Said to serve the best sandwiches in town, a local institution.

♥ Empório Saúde, R Visconde de Pirajá, 414, Ipanema, T2522 1494. Closed Sun and evenings. A large variety of vegetarian cooking from quiches to stews.

♥ La Trattoria, Av Atlântica, opposite Hotel Excelsior. Italian, good food and service, very reasonable. Recommended.

♥ Marakesh, Av NS de Copacabana 599. Good value pay-by-weight food.

♥ Traiteurs de France, Av NS de Copacabana 386, Copacabana. Delicious tarts and pastries, not expensive.

There are stand-up bars selling snacks all around Copacabana and Ipanema.

Gávea, Jardim Botânico and Lagoa *p358*

Gávea is the grungy heartland of trendy 20-something Rio, while Jardim Botânico and Lagoa appear, at first sight, to offer no end of exciting upmarket dining opportunities. They're mostly all show and poor value. Here are a few exceptions:

♥♥♥ Olympe, R Custódio Serrão 62, Lagoa, T2539 4542. Elegant French restaurant servng a mixture of traditional cuisine and Franco-Brazilian fusions. Recommended.

♥♥♥ Roberta Sudbrack, Av Lineu de Paula Machado 916, Jardim Botânico, T3874 0139, www.robertasudbrack.com.br. Celebrated for her European-Brazilian fusion cooking, Roberta was the private chef for President Henrique Cardoso.

♥♥ Árabe da Gávea, Gávea shopping mall, R Marquês de São Vicente 52, T2294 2439. By far the best Arabic restaurant in Rio.

♥♥ Guimas, R José Roberto Macedo Soares, Baixo Gávea, T2259 7996. One of the places where the under 30s come to be seen, especially after 2200 towards the end of the week and on Mon, before moving down the street to the two tatty bars on the corner of the street and Praça Santos Dumont. The restaurant serves simple, traditional Portuguese food, at only a handful of tables.

♦ Bars and clubs

Rio nightlife is young and vivacious. The current hotspots are **Lapa** at weekends, with a string of clubs along Mem de Sá and Lavradio with dance steps from samba and forró to techno and hip hop. **Santa Teresa** is increasingly lively and is often used as a drinking spot before moving onto Lapa, or a night spot in its own. There is a cluster of bars around the Largo das Neves. Similarly busy, even on Sun and Mon is **Baixa Gávea**, where beautiful 20-somethings gather around Praça Santos Dumont. In **Ipanema/Leblon**, there is always activity on and around Av General San Martin and Rua Dias Ferreira. **Copacabana** nightlife is mostly seedy and tawdry. Discos like Help are sad places full of visiting males panting after the lowest common denominator. Exceptions to this rule are the clubs like Bunker, the only one to play European club music in Rio. The guidebook O Guia dos Botequins do Rio de Janeiro, describes Rio's best, most traditional bars and their history, US$20. You can find it in the Livraria da Travessa (see Shopping), together with similar books; some in English.

Bars Wherever you are, there's one near you. Beer costs around US$1.50 for a large bottle, but up to US$5 in the plusher bars; where you are often given an entrance card which includes 2 drinks and a token entrance fee. A cover charge of US$3-7 may be made for live music, or there might be a minimum consumption charge of around US$3, sometimes both. Snack food is always available. Copacabana, Ipanema and Leblon have many beach barracas, several open all night. The seafront bars on Av Atlântica are great for people-watching; though avoid those towards Leme as they tend to offer more than beer. The big hotels have good cocktail bars.

Clubs Clubs in Rio are either fake Europe (eg Melt and Bunker) and US (eg Nuth and 00), or samba halls undergoing a renaissance (eg Scenarium and Carioca da Gema).

Centre, Lapa and Santa Teresa
p350, map p351

Lapa is without doubt the centre of Rio nightlife and should not be missed if you are in Rio over a weekend. Ideally come early on Sat for the afternoon market and live street tango, eat and stay for a bar and club crawl. Always be wary of pickpockets around Lapa. See also Samba schools.
Bar do Mineiro, on the Largo dos Guimarães, R Pascoal Carlos Magno 99, T2221 9227. A very popular Santa Teresa bar.
Carioca da Gema, Av Mem de Sá 79, Centro, T2221 0043. Great samba club café, second only to Rio Scenarium, good food too.
Club Six, R das Marrecas 38, Lapa. Huge pounding European/NYC dance club with everything from hip hop to ambient house.
Dama da Noite, R Gomes Freire 773, Lapa. Samba, Chorinho and crepes in the pátio.
Espírito Santa, see Santa Teresa, Eating. The basement club has great Rio funk from DJ Zod on Sat from 2200, very popular.
Mercado, R do Mercado 32, Centro. A little bar with live Chorinho every Thu from 2030.
Rio Scenarium, R do Lavradio 20, Lapa,

T3852-5516, www.rioscenarium.com.br. Three-storey Samba club in a colonial house used as a movie prop warehouse. Overflowing with Brazilian exuberance and joie de vivre, with people dancing furiously, to the bizarre backdrop of a 19th-century apothecary's shop or a line of mannequins wearing 1920s outfits. This is Rio at its Bohemian best. Buzzes with beautiful people of all ages on Fri. Arrive after 2300.
Sacrilégio, Av Mem de Sá 81, next to Carioca da Gema, Lapa, T2507 3898. Samba, Chorinho, Pagode and occasional theatre. Close to many other bars.
Semente, R Joaquim Silva 138, T2242 5165. Popular for Samba, Choro and Salsa from 2200 Mon-Sat, US$2.50 cover; minimum consumption US$2. Book a table at weekends. Great atmosphere both inside and in the streets outside. Recommended.

Glória, Flamengo and Botafogo
p355, map p354

Look out for the frequent free live music performances at the Marina da Glória and along Flamengo beach during the summer.
Casa de Matriz, R Enrique de Novais 107, Botafogo. Great little grungey club with a bar, Atari room, small cinema and 2 dance floors. Full of Rio students.
Porão, under the Anglican church hall, R Real Grandeza 99, Botafogo. British ex-pats meet here on Fri night.

Copacabana and Ipanema
p358, maps p356 and p359

There is frequent live music on the beaches of Copacabana and Ipanema, and along the Av Atlântica throughout the summer; especially around New Year.
Académia da Cachaça, R Conde de Bernadotte 26-G, Leblon; with another branch at Av Armando Lombardi 800, Barra da Tijuca. The best cachaças, great caipirinhas and traditional Brazilian dishes. Good on Fri.
Barril 1800, Av Vieira Souto 110, Ipanema. Nice place to watch the sunset. Highly recommended.
Bip Bip, R Almirante Gonçalves 50, Copacabana. Botequim bar which attracts a crowd of jamming musicians every Tue, also Sun for great atmosphere.
Bom Bar, R General San Martin 1011, Leblon. A downstairs bar and an upstairs club, packed after 2300, especially Sat.
Bunker, R Raul Pompeira 94, Copacabana. European-style dance club where the likes of DJs Marky and Patife play. Busy from Wed-Sat, kicks off at about 0200. The queues have become a party in themselves – at the bar next door.

Devassa, Av General San Martin 1241, Leblon. A two-floor pub/restaurant/bar which is always heaving. Brews its own beer.

Empório, R Maria Quitéria 37, Ipanema. Street bar which attracts hordes. Mon is busiest.

A Garota de Ipanema, R Vinícius de Morais 49, Ipanema. Where the song *Girl from Ipanema* was written. Now packed with foreigners on the package Rio circuit listening to Bossa. For the real thing head up the street to Toca do Vinícius on Sun afternoon (see below).

Melt, R Rita Ludolf 47, T2249 9309. Downstairs bar and upstairs sweaty club. Occasional performances by the cream of Rio's new samba funk scene, usually on Sun. Always heaving on Thu.

Shenanigans, R Visconde de Pirajá 112, Ipanema. Obligatory mock-Irish bar with Guinness and Newcastle Brown. Not a place to meet the locals.

Vinícius, R Vinícius de Morais 39, Ipanema, 2nd floor. Mirror image of the Garota de Ipanema with slightly better acts and food.

Gávea, Jardim Botânico and Lagoa *p358*

00 (Zero Zero), Av Padre Leonel Franca 240, Gávea. Mock LA bar/restaurant/club with a small outdoor area. Currently the trendiest club in Rio for Brazil's equivalent of Sloanes or Valley Girls. Gay night on Sun.

Bar Lagoa, Av Epitácio Pessoa 1674, Lagoa. Attracts a slightly older, arty crowd on weekday evenings.

Caroline Café, R JJ Seabra 10, Jardim Botânico, T2540 0705, www.carolinecafe.com. Popular bar with Rio's young and good-looking middle classes. Kicks off after 2130. Food too.

Clan Café, R Cosme Velho 564 (in front of the Corcovado train station). Great little gem of a sit down Choro and Samba club with live music every night and decent bar food.

Cozumel, Av Lineu de Paula Machado 696, Jardim Botânico. The Rio equivalent of a foam disco, with free margaritas, tacky music and a crowd most of whom are looking not to go home alone.

Mistura Fina, Av Borges de Medeiros 3207, T2537 2844, www.misturafina.com.br. Downstairs restaurant, upstairs jazz and bossa nova club. One of the few places not oriented solely to the young.

Sítio Lounge, R Marques de São Vicente 10, Gávea. The nearest thing Rio has to a lounge bar, good for a chilled out Sat night.

El Turf (aka Jockey Club), opposite the Jardim Botânico, Praça Santos Dumont 31. Opens at 2200, gets going at 2300, you may have to wait to get in at the weekend if you arrive after midnight, no T-shirts allowed, very much a Rio rich kid singles and birthday party place; another branch in Rio Sul Shopping Centre.

Barra da Tijuca *p359*

Nuth, R Armando Lombardi 999, Barra da Tijuca, www.nuth.com.br. Barra's slickest club; very mock Miami with snacks. Mix of tacky Brazilian and Eurotrash music and some samba funk live acts. Expensive.

Pepe, at Posto 2, Barra da Tijuca beach. Very popular with surfers.

⏺ Entertainment

Rio de Janeiro *p348, maps p348 and p351*

Cinemas

There are cinemas serving subtitled Hollywood films and major Brazilian releases on the top floor of almost all the malls. The normal seat price is US$3, discounts on Wed and Thu (students pay half price any day of the week).

Centro Cultural do Banco do Brasil, see Sights, T2808 2020. One of Rio's better arts centres with the best art films and exhibitions from fine art to photography (Metro: Uruguaiana).

Cinemateca do MAM, Infante Dom Henrique 85, Aterro do Flamengo, T2210 2188. Cinema classics, art films and roving art exhibitions and a good café with live music. Views of Guanabara Bay from the balconies.

Estaçao Ipanema, R Visconde de Pirajá 605, Ipanema. European art cinema, less mainstream US and Brazilian releases.

Live music

Many young Cariocas congregate in Botafogo for live music. There are free concerts throughout the summer, along the Copacabana and Ipanema beaches, in Botafogo and at the parks: mostly samba, reggae, rock and MPB (Brazilian pop): there is no advance schedule, information is given in the local press (see below). Rio's famous jazz, in all its forms, is performed in lots of enjoyable venues, see the press. See www.samba-choro.com.br, for more information. Also see Clan Café, Melt, Nuth and Mistura Fina in Bars and clubs, above.

Canecão, R Venceslau Brás 215, Botafogo, T2295 3044. This big, inexpensive venue has live concerts most nights, see press for listings. For a taste of some purely local entertainment, make your way down here on Mon nights.

Centro Cultural Carioca, R do Teatro 37, T2252 6468 for advance information, www.centroculturalcarioca.com. An exciting venue that combines music (mostly samba) and dance, 1830-early morning. This restored old house with wrap-around balconies and exposed brick walls is a dance school and music venue that attracts a lovely mix of people. Professional dancers perform with musicians; after a few tunes the audience joins in. Thu is impossibly crowded; Sat is calmer. Bar food available. US$3 cover charge. Highly recommended.

Praia do Vermelha at Urca. Residents bring musical instruments and chairs onto beach for an informal night of samba from 2100-midnight, free. Bus No 511 from Copacabana.

Rhapsody, Av Epitácio Pessoa 1104, Lagoa, T2247 2104. Piano bar restaurant with mixture of Brazilian and Diana Krall-style crooning.

Toca do Vinícius, Vinícius de Moraes 129, Ipanema. Rio's leading Bossa Nova and Choro record shop with live concerts from some of the finest past performers every Sun lunchtime and 2000 Sun in summer.

🎉 Festivals and events

Rio de Janeiro *p348, maps p348 and p351*
Less hectic than Carnival, see box, page 372, but very atmospheric, is the festival of **Iemanjá** on the night of **31 Dec**, when devotees of the orixá of the sea dress in white and gather on Copacabana, Ipanema and Leblon beaches, singing and dancing around open fires and making offerings. The elected Queen of the Sea is rowed along the seashore. At midnight small boats are launched as offerings to Iemanjá. The religious event is dwarfed, however, by a massive New Year's Eve party, called **Reveillon** at Copacabana. The beach is packed as thousands of revellers enjoy free outdoor concerts by big-name pop stars, topped with a lavish midnight firework display. It is most crowded in front of Copacabana Palace Hotel. Another good place to see fireworks is in front of Le Meridien, famous for its fireworks waterfall at about 10 mins past midnight. **Note** Many followers of Iemanjá are now making their offerings on 29 or 30 Dec and at Barra da Tijuca or Recreio dos Bandeirantes to avoid the crowds and noise of Reveillon. The festival of **São Sebastião**, patron saint of Rio, is celebrated by an evening procession on **20 Jan**, leaving Capuchinhos Church, Tijuca, and arriving at the cathedral of São Sebastião. On the same evening, an **umbanda festival** is celebrated at the Caboclo Monument in Santa Teresa. **Carnival 2-5 Feb** 2008, **21-24 Feb 2009** (see page 372). Festas Juninas: Santo Antônio on **13 Jun**, whose main event is a mass, followed by celebrations at the Convento do Santo Antônio and the Largo da Carioca. Throughout the state of Rio, the festival of **São João** is a major event, marked by huge bonfires on the night of **23-24 Jun**. It is traditional to dance the quadrilha and drink quentão, cachaça and sugar, spiced with ginger and cinnamon, served hot. The Festas Juninas close with the festival of **São Pedro** on **29 Jun**. Being the patron saint of fishermen, his feast is

normally accompanied by processions of boats. **Oct** is the month of the feast of **Nossa Senhora da Penha**.

🛍 Shopping

Rio de Janeiro *p348, maps p348 and p351*
Bookshops **Argumento**, R Dias Ferreira 417, Leblon. Sells imported English books.
FNAC has a megastore at Barra Shopping, with French, English and other imported titles, CDs.
Livraria da Travessa, Travessa do Ouvidor 11-A, superb new branch at Av Rio Branco 44 and R Visconde de Pirajá 572, Ipanema. Excellent. Broad selection of novels, general books, magazines and guidebooks in English. Great café upstairs at the Ipanema branch for a coffee while you read.
Saraiva has a megastore at R do Ouvidor 98, T507 9500, also with a music and video shop and a café; other branches in Shopping Iguatemi and Shopping Tijuca. **Siciliano**, Av Rio Branco 156, loja 26. European books, also at Nossa Senhora de Copacabana 830 and branches; French books at No 298. **Da Vinci**, Av Rio Branco 185 lojas 2, 3 and 9. All types of foreign books.

Fashion Fashion is one of the best buys in Brazil; with a wealth of Brazilian designers selling clothes of the same quality as European or US famous names at a fraction of the price. Rio is the best place in the world for buying high-fashion bikinis. The best shops in Rio are on Garcia D'Ávila and R Nascimento Silva, which runs off it, in Ipanema. This is where some of the best Brazilian designers like Andrea Saletto and Rosana Bernardes, together with international big name stalwarts like Louis Vuitton and Cartier. Most of the international names, as well as all the big Brazilian names like Lenny (Brazil's best bikinis), Alberta, Salinas, Club Chocolate and so on are housed in the **Fashion Mall** in São Conrado.

Saara is a multitude of little shops along R Alfândega and R Senhor dos Passos (between city centre and Campo Santana), where clothing bargains can be found (especially jeans, kanga beach wraps and bikinis); it is known popularly as 'Shopping a Céu Aberto'. Little shops on Aires Saldanha, Copacabana (1 block back from the beach), are good for bikinis and cheaper than in shopping centres.
Jewellery Amsterdam Sauer, R Garcia D'Ávila 105, with10 shops in Rio and others throughout Brazil. They offer free taxi rides to their main shop.
Antônio Bernardo, R Garcia d'Ávila 121, Ipanema, T2512 7204, and in the Fashion Mall. Brazil's foremost jeweller who has been making beautifully understated jewellery with contemporary designs for nearly 30 years. Internationally well known, but available only in

Brazil. **H Stern**, next door to Amsterdam Sauer at R Visconde de Pirajá 490/R Garcia Dávila 113, Ipanema, has 10 outlets, plus branches in major hotels.

There are several good jewellery shops at the Leme end of Av NS de Copacabana. **Mineraux**, Av NS de Copacabana 195. For mineral specimens as against cut stones, Belgian owner.

Markets **Northeastern market** at Campo de São Cristóvão, with music and magic, on Sun 0800-2200 (bus 472 or 474 from Copacabana or centre). A recommended shop for north-eastern handicrafts is **Pé de Boi**, R Ipiranga 55, Laranjeiras, www.pedeboi.com.br. Sat antiques market on the waterfront near Praça 15 de Novembro, 1000-1700. Also in Praça 15 de Novembro is **Feirarte II**, Thu-Fri 0800-1800. **Feirarte I** is a Sun open-air handicrafts market (everyone calls it the Feira Hippy) at Praça Gen Osório, Ipanema, 0800-1800, items from all over Brazil. A **stamp, coin and postcard market** is held in the Passeio Público on Sun 0800-1300. Markets on Wed 0700-1300 on R Domingos Ferreira and on Thu, same hrs, on Praça do Lido, both Copacabana (Praça do Lido also has a Feirarte on Sat-Sun 0800-1800). **Sunday market** on R da Glória, colourful, cheap fruit, vegetables and flowers; **early-morning food market**, 0600-1100, R Min Viveiros de Castro, Ipanema. There is a **cheap market** for just about anything, especially electronic goods, outside Metro stop Uruguaiana. Excellent food and household-goods markets at various places in the city and suburbs (see newspapers for times and places).

Music **Modern Sound Música Equipamentos**, R Barata Ribeiro 502D, Copacabana. For a large selection of Brazilian music, jazz and classical. **Toca do Vinícius**, see Live music, above.

Shopping malls **Rio Sul**, at the Botafogo end of Túnel Novo, has almost everything the visitor may need. Some of the services in Rio Sul are: Telemar (phone office) for international calls at A10-A, Mon-Sat 1000-2200; next door is Belle Tours Câmbio, A10. There is a post office at G2. A good branch of **Livraria Sodiler** is at A03. For Eating and Entertainment, see above; live music at the **Terraço**; the **Ibeas Top Club** gym; and a cinema. A US$5 bus service runs as far as the Sheraton passing the main hotels, every 2 hrs between 1000 and 1800, then 2130.

Other shopping centres, which include a wide variety of services, include **Cassino** (Copacabana), **Norte Shopping** (Todos os Santos), **Plaza Shopping** (Niterói), **Barra** in Barra da Tijuca (see page 359) and **The Fashion Mall** in São Conrado, see above.

▲▲ Activities and tours

Rio de Janeiro *p348, maps p348 and p351*
There are hundreds of gyms and sports clubs; most will not grant temporary (less than 1 month) membership. Big hotels may allow use of their facilities for a small deposit.

Cycling **Rio Bikers**, R Domingos Ferreira 81, room 201, T2274 5872. Tours and bike hire.
Stop Bike, T2275 7345, Copacabana. Bike rental.
Diving **Squalo**, Av Armando Lombardi 949-D, Barra de Tijuca, T/F2493 3022, squalo1@hot mail.com. Offers courses at all levels, NAUI and PDIC training facilities, also snorkelling and equipment rental.
Football See under Maracanã stadium, page 353.
Hang-gliding **Delta Flight** and **Rio by Jeep**, T3322 5750/9693 8800 (mob), www.delta flight.com.br. Tandem flight tours above Rio from Pedra Bonita Mountain with instructors licensed by the Brazilian Hang-Gliding Association. Contact Ricardo Hamond. **HiltonFlyRio Hang Gliding Center**, T7840 6325/9964 2607 (mob), www.hiltonflyrio.com. DeHilton Carvalho is an ABVL certified instructor, very experienced.
Just Fly, T/F2268 0565, T9985 7540 (mob), www.justfly.com.br. Tandem flights with Paulo Celani (licensed by Brazilian Hang Gliding Association), pick-up and drop-off at hotel included, in-flight pictures US$15 extra, flights all year, best time of day 1000-1500 (5% discount for South American and Brazil Handbook readers on presentation of book at time of reservation).
Super-fly, T3322 2286, www.riosuperfly.com.br. A highly regarded, experienced hang-gliding operator from the Pedra Bonita. **Ultra Força Ltda**, Av Sernambetiba 8100, Barra da Tijuca, T3399 3114; 15 mins.
Helicopter rides **Helisight**, R Visconde de Pirajá 580, loja 107, Térreo, Ipanema, T2259 6995, www.helisight.com.br. Prices from US$100 pp for flights from Lagoa or Pão de Açucar over Sugar Loaf and Corcovado.
Horse racing and riding **Jockey Club Racecourse**, by Jardím Botânico and Gávea, meetings on Mon and Thu evenings and Sat and Sun 1400, entrance US$1-2, long trousers required. Take any bus marked 'via Jóquei'. **Sociedade Hípico Brasileiro**, Av Borges de Medeiros 2448, T527 8090, Jardim Botânico. For riding.
Parapenting **Barra Jumping**, Aeroporto de Jacarepaguá, Av Ayrton Senna 2541, T3151 3602, www.barrajumping.com.br. Tandem jumping (Vôo duplo). Several other people offer tandem jumping; check that they are accredited with the Associação Brasileira de Vôo Livre. Ask for the **Parapente Rio Clube** at São Conrado launch site.

Carnival

Carnival in Rio is spectacular. On the Friday before Shrove Tuesday, the mayor of Rio hands the keys of the city to Rei Momo, the Lord of Misrule, signifying the start of a five-day party. Imagination runs riot, social barriers are broken and the main avenues, full of people and children wearing fancy dress, are colourfully lit. Areas throughout the city such as the Terreirão de Samba in Praça Onze are used for shows, music and dancing. *Bandas* and *blocos* (organized carnival groups) seem to be everywhere, dancing, drumming and singing.

There are numerous samba schools in Rio divided into two leagues, both of which parade in the Sambódromo. The Carnival parades are the culmination of months of intense activity by community groups, mostly in the city's poorest districts. Every school presents 2,500-6,000 participants divided into *alas* (wings) each with a different costume and 5-9 *carros alegóricos*, beautifully designed floats. Each school chooses an *enredo* (theme) and composes a samba (song) that is a poetic, rhythmic and catchy expression of the theme. The *enredo* is further developed through the design of the floats and costumes. A *bateria* (percussion wing) maintains a reverberating beat that must keep the entire school, and the audience, dancing throughout the parade. Each procession follows a set order with the first to appear being the *comissão de frente*, a choreographed group that presents the school and the theme to the public. Next comes the *abre alas*, a magnificent float usually bearing the name or symbol of the school. Schools are given between 65 and 80 minutes and lose points for failing to keep within this time. Judges award points to each school for components of their procession, such as costume, music and design, and make deductions for lack of energy, enthusiasm or discipline.

The **Sambódromo** is a permanent site at R Marquês de Sapucaí, Cidade Nova, is 600 m long with seating for 4 3,000 people. Designed by Oscar Niemeyer and built in 1983-1984, it handles sporting events, conferences and concerts during the rest of the year.

Rio's ***bailes*** (fancy-dress balls) range from the sophisticated to the wild. The majority of clubs and hotels host at least one. The Copacabana Palace hotel's is elegant and expensive whilst the Scala club has licentious parties. It is not necessary to wear fancy dress; just join in, although you will feel more comfortable if you wear a minimum of clothing to the clubs. The most famous are the Red & Black Ball (Friday) and the Gay Ball (Tuesday) which are both televized.

Bandas and ***blocos*** can be found in all neighbourhoods and some of the most popular and entertaining are Cordão do Bola Preta (meets at 0900 on Saturday in Rua 13 de Maio 13, Centro), Simpatia é Quase Amor (meets at 1600 Sunday in Praça General Osório, Ipanema) and the transvestite Banda da Ipanema (meets at 1600 on Saturday and Tuesday in Praça General Osorio, Ipanema). It is necessary to join a bloco in advance to receive their distinctive T-shirts, but anyone can join in with the bandas.

The expensive hotels offer special Carnival breakfasts from 0530. Caesar Park is highly recommended for a wonderful meal and a top-floor view of the sunrise over the beach.

Tickets The Sambódromo parades start at 1900 and last about 12 hours. Gates (which are not clearly marked) open at 1800. There are *cadeiras* (seats) at ground level, *arquibancadas* (terraces) and *camarotes* (boxes). The best boxes are reserved for tourists and VIPs and are very expensive or by invitation only.

Rock climbing and hill walking Clube Excursionista Carioca, R Hilário Gouveia 71, room 206, T2255 1348. Recommended for enthusiasts, meets Wed and Fri. **ECA**, Av Erasmo Braga 217, room 305, T2242 6857. Personal guide US$100/ day. **Paulo Miranda**, R Campos Sales 64/801, RJ20270-210, T/F2264 4501. **Rio Hiking**, T2552 9204/ 9721 0594 (mob), www.riohiking.com.br. Hiking tours to the top of Rio's mountains.

Seats are closest to the parade, but you may have to fight your way to the front. Seats and boxes reserved for tourists have the best view, sectors 3, 5, 7, 9 and 11 all have good views (4, 7 and 11 house the judging points). 6 and 13 are at the end when dancers might be tired, but have more space. The terraces, while uncomfortable, house the most fervent fans, tightly packed; this is where to soak up the atmosphere but not take pictures (too crowded). Tickets are sold at travel agencies as well as the Maracanã Stadium box office; expect to pay in the hundreds of dollars. Tickets are usually sold out before Carnaval weekend but touts outside can generally sell you tickets at inflated prices. Samba schools have an allocation of tickets which members sometimes sell, if you are offered one of these check its date. Tickets for the champions' parade at 2100 on the Saturday following Carnival are much cheaper. Taxis to the Sambódromo are negotiable and will find your gate, the nearest metrô is Praça Onze and this can be an enjoyable ride in the company of costumed samba school members. You can follow the participants to the *concentração*, the assembly and formation on Avenida Presidente Vargas, and mingle with them while they queue to enter the Sambódromo.

Sleeping and security Reserve accommodation well in advance. Virtually all hotels raise their prices during Carnival, although it is usually possible to find a room. Your property should be safe inside the Sambódromo, but the crowds outside can attract pickpockets; as ever, don't brandish your camera, and only take the money you need for fares and food.

Taking part Most samba schools accept a number of foreigners and you will be charged upwards of US$125 (+ tax) for your costume (the money helps fund poorer members of the school). You should be in Rio for at least two weeks before carnival. Attend fittings and rehearsals on time and show respect for your section leaders – enter into the competitive spirit of the event.

Rehearsals *Ensaios* are held at the schools' *quadras* from October on and are well worth seeing. (Go by taxi, as most schools are based in poorer districts.) Tour agents sell tickets for glitzy samba shows, which are nothing like the real thing.

Samba Schools Acadêmicos de Salgueiro, R Silva Teles 104, Andaraí, T2268 0548, www.salgueiro.com.br. **Beija Flor de Nilópolis**, Pracinha Wallace Paes Leme 1025, Nilópolis, T2791 2866, www.beija-flor.com.br. **Imperatriz Leopoldinense**, R Prof. Lacê 235, Ramos, T2560 8037, www.imperatriz leopoldinense.com.br. **Mocidade Independente de Padre Miguel**, R Coronel Tamarindo 38, Padre Miguel, T3332 5823, www.mocidad eindependente.com.br. **Portela**, R Clara Nunes 81, Madureira, T2489 6440, www.gresportela.com.br. **Primeira Estação de Mangueira**, R Visconde de Niterói 1072, Mangueira, T3872 6786, www.mangueira.com.br. **Unidos da Viradouro**, Av do Contorno 16, Niterói, T2628 7840, www.unidosdoviradouro.com.br.

Useful information Freephone T0800-701 1250 (24 hrs, English, Spanish, Portuguese). **Riotur**'s guide booklet gives information on official and unofficial events (in English). The entertainment sections of newspapers and magazines such as *O Globo*, *Jornal do Brasil*, *Manchete* and *Veja Rio* are worth checking. *Liga Independente das Escolas de Samba do Rio de Janeiro*, T3213 5151, http://liesa.globo.com, for schools' addresses and rehearsal times and lots more information.

Tours
Most hotels offer tours but shop around if you have the time and want more choice. Organized trips to Samba shows cost US$50 including dinner, good, but it's cheaper to go independently.

4 Star Turismo do Brasil, R Senador Dantas 20, T1-800-746-4599 (USA), T3523 0379, www.4starBrazil.com. Custom and group tours in Brazil and throughout the region.

Atlantic Forest Jeep Tour, T2495 9827, T9974 0218 (mob). Jeep tours to the Parque Nacional Tijuca and trips to coffee fazendas in the Paraíba Valley, trips to Angra dos Reis and offshore islands and the Serra dos Órgãos.

Brazil Expedition, R Visconde Piraja 550 lj 201, Ipanema, T9998 2907 (mob), www.brazil expedition.com. Backpacker bus trips south to Paraty and Ilha Grande with stops along the Costa Verde. Day trips and Rio 'starter packs', accommodation advice. Recommended.

Favela Tour, Estr das Canoas 722, Bl 2, apt 125, São Conrado, T3322 2727, T9989 0074/9772 1133 (mob), www.favelatour.com.br. Guided tours of Rio's favelas, safe, different and interesting, 3 hrs. Also ask Marcelo Armstrong, the owner, about eco tours, river rafting and other excursions. He speaks English, French, Spanish, Italian and can provide guides in German and Swedish. For the best attention and price call Marcelo direct rather than through a hotel desk. Recommended.

Jeep Tour, T2108 5800, T9977 9610 (mob), www.jeeptour.com.br. Among their tours are escorted groups to favelas.

Metropol, R São José 46, T2533 5010, www.metropolturismo.com.br. Eco, adventure and culture tours to all parts of Brazil.

Rejane Reis Exotic Tours, T2179 6972/9222 6972 (mob), www.exotictours.com.br. Focuses on a tourism workshop in Rocinha favela. They also offer hang gliding, ultralights, paragliding, sailing, diving, voodoo, and daytime tours.

Rio G, R Teixeira de Melo, 25-A, Ipanema, T3813-0003, www.riogtravel.com. Very helpful, English spoken, specialists in the GLBT market.

Saveiros Tour, Av Infante Dom Henrique s/n, l 13/14, Marina da Glória, T2225 6064, www.saveiros.com.br. Offers tours in sailing schooners around the bay and down the coast, also 'Baía da Guanabara Histórica' historical tours.

Travel Café, R Cosme Velho 513, T2285 8302. City tours, rafting, sky diving, horse riding, night tours and packages along the Costa Verde, English spoken.

Turismo Clássico, Av NS de Copacabana 1059/805, T2523 3390, comercial@turismo classico.com.br. Warmly recommended.

www.bealocal.com. As well as guided tours to football matches, see under Maracanã stadium, page 353, also offer recommended visits to favelas.

Guides

Cultural Rio, R Santa Clara 110/904, Copacabana, T3322 4872, T9911 3829 (mob), www.culturalrio. com.br. Tours escorted personally by Professor Carlos Roquette, English/French spoken, almost 200 options available, entirely flexible to your interests.

Fábio Sombra, T9729 5455 (mob), fabiosombra@hotmail.com. Offers private

and tailor-made guided tours focusing on the cultural aspects of Rio and Brazil.

Luiz Amaral Tours, R Visc de Pirajá 550, office 215, Ipanema, T2259 5532, T9637 2522 (mob), www.travelrio.com/tours.htm. Good company offering personalized tours run by Luiz Felipe Amaral who speaks good English.

Transport

Rio de Janeiro *p348, maps p348 and p351*
Air
Rio has 2 airports: **Antônio Carlos Jobim International Airport** (T3398 4527), previously called Galeão, and the **Santos Dumont** airport on Guanabara Bay (T3814 7246), for domestic flights. **Jobim international airport** is situated on Governador Island some 16 km from the centre of Rio. It is in 2 sections: international and domestic. There is a **Pousada Galeão (AL)**, comfortable, good value, and **Luxor Aeroporto**, in Terminal 1, T3222 9700, www.luxorhoteis.com.br, if you need an early start, follow signs in airport.

There are a/c taxis; Cootramo and Transcopass have fixed rates (US$25 Copacabana). Buy a ticket at the counter near the arrivals gate before getting into the car. Fixed rate taxi fares from Terminal 2 are US$15 to Centro, US$20 to Copacabana/ Ipanema, US$25 to Barra da Tijuca. Credit cards accepted by some companies. The hire is for the taxi, irrespective of the number of passengers.

Make sure you keep the ticket, which carries the number to phone in case of difficulty. Ordinary taxis also operate with the normal meter reading (about US$16, but some may offer cheaper rates from Copacabana to the airport, US$9-10). Do not negotiate with a driver on arrival, unless you are a frequent visitor. Beware pirate taxis which are unlicensed. It is better to pay extra for an official vehicle than run the risk of robbery.

The a/c 'Real' bus runs frequently from the 1st floor of the airport to Recreio dos Bandeirantes via the municipal rodoviária and city centre, Santos Dumont Airport, Flamengo, Copacabana, Ipanema and Leblon. Fares are collected during the journey, to anywhere in Rio US$4.50. The driver will stop at requested points (the bus runs along the seafront from Leme to Leblon), so it's worth checking a map so that you can specify your required junction. The bus returns by the same route. Town buses M94 and M95, Bancários/Castelo, take a circular route passing through the centre and the interstate bus station. They leave from the 2nd floor of the airport.

There are câmbios in the airport departure hall. There is also a câmbio on the 1st floor of the international arrivals area, but it gives worse rates than the Banco do Brasil, 24-hr bank, 3rd floor, which has Visa ATMs (may not accept foreign cards) and will give cash advances against Visa. Duty-free shops are well stocked, but not especially cheap. Duty free is open to arrivals as well as departures. Only US dollars or credit cards are accepted on the air-side of the departure lounge. There is a wider choice of restaurants outside passport control.

The **Santos Dumont** airport on Guanabara Bay, right in the city, is used for Rio-São Paulo shuttle flights, other domestic routes, air taxis and private planes. The shuttle services operate every 30 mins from 0630 to 2230. Sit on the right-hand side for views to São Paulo, the other side coming back, book in advance for particular flights. The main airport, on Governador Island, some 16 km from the centre of Rio, is in 2 sections, international and domestic (including the jet shuttle from Rio to São Paulo).

Bus
Local There are good services, but buses are very crowded and not for the aged or infirm during rush hours; buses have turnstiles which are awkward if you are carrying luggage. Hang on tight, drivers live out Grand Prix fantasies. At busy times allow about 45 mins to get from Copacabana to the centre by bus. The fare on standard buses is US$0.55 and suburban bus fares are US$1. Bus stops are often not marked. The route is written on the side of the bus, which is hard to see until the bus has actually

pulled up at the stop. Private companies operate air-conditioned frescão buses which can be flagged down practically anywhere: **Real, Pegaso, Anatur**. They run from all points in Rio Sul to the city centre, Rodoviária and the airports. Fares are US$2 (US$2.40 to the international airport). City Rio is an a/c tourist bus service with security guards which runs between all the major parts of the city. Good maps show what sites of interest are close to each bus stop, marked by grey poles and found where there are concentrations of hotels. T0800 258060.

Long distance Rodoviária Novo Rio, Av Rodrigues Alves, corner with Av Francisco Bicalho, just past the docks, T2291 5151, www.novorio.com.br. Buses run from Rio to all parts of the country. It is advisable to book tickets in advance. The rodoviária has a **Riotur** information centre, which is very helpful, T2263 4857. Left luggage costs US$4. There are câmbios for cash only. The local bus terminal is just outside the rodoviária: turn right as you leave and run the gauntlet of taxi drivers – best ignored. The air conditioned Real bus (opposite the exit) goes along the beach to São Conrado and will secure luggage, US$1.30 to Copacabana. If you need a taxi collect a ticket, which ensures against overcharging, from the office inside the entrance (to Flamengo US$10). On no account give the ticket to the taxi driver. The main bus station is reached by buses M94 and M95, Bancários/Castelo, from the centre and the airport; 136, 172, Rodoviária/Glória/Flamengo/ Botafogo; 127, 128, 136, Rodoviária/Copacabana; 170, Rodoviária/Gávea/São Conrado; 128, 172, Rodoviária/Ipanema/Leblon.

Distances in km to some major cities with approximate journey time in brackets: Juiz de Fora, 184 (2¾ hrs); Belo Horizonte, 434 (7 hrs); São Paulo, 429 (6 hrs); Vitória, 521 (8 hrs); Curitiba, 852 (12 hrs); Brasília, 1,148 (20 hrs); Florianópolis, 1,144 (20 hrs); Foz do Iguaçu, 1,500 (21 hrs); Porto Alegre, 1,553 (26 hrs); Salvador, 1,649 (28 hrs); Recife, 2,338 (38 hrs); Fortaleza, 2,805 (48 hrs); São Luís, 3,015 (50 hrs); Belém, 3,250 (52 hrs).

International bus **Asunción**, 1,511 km via Foz do Iguaçu, 30 hrs (**Pluma**), US$70; **Buenos Aires (Pluma)**, via Porto Alegre and Santa Fe, 48 hrs, US$91 (book 2 days in advance).

Car
Service stations are closed in many places Sat and Sun. Road signs are notoriously misleading in Rio and you can easily end up in a favela. Take care if driving along the Estr da Gávea to São Conrado as it is possible to enter unwittingly Rocinha, Rio's biggest slum.

Metro

The Metrô provides good service, clean, a/c and fast. Line 1: between the inner suburb of Tijuca (station Saens Peña) and Siqueira Campos (Copacabana – being extended to Ipanema), via the railway station (Central), Glória and Botafogo. Line 2: from Pavuna, passing Engenho da Rainha and the Maracanã stadium, to Estácio. It operates 0500-2400 Mon-Sat, 0700-2300 Sun and holidays. The fare is US$0.65 single; multi-tickets and integrated bus/Metrô tickets are available. Changes in bus operations are taking place because of the extended Metrô system; buses connecting with the Metrô have a blue-and-white symbol in the windscreen.

Taxi

The fare between Copacabana and the centre is US$9.50. Between 2300 and 0600 and on Sun and holidays, 'tariff 2' is used. Official taxis are yellow with a blue stripe and have meters. Smaller ones (mostly Volkswagen) are marked TAXI on the windscreen or roof. Make sure meters are cleared and on tariff 1, except at those times mentioned above. Only use taxis with an official identification sticker on the windscreen. Don't hesitate to argue if the route is too long or the fare too much. Radio Taxis are safer but more expensive, eg **Cootramo**, T3976 9944 , **Coopertramo**, T2560 2022, **Central de Táxi**, T2593 2598, **Transcoopass**, T2590 6891. Luxury cabs are allowed to charge higher rates. Inácio de Oliveira, T2225 4110, is a reliable taxi driver for excursions, he only speaks Portuguese. Recommended. **Grimalde**, T2267 9812, has been recommended for talkative daytime and evening tours, English and Italian spoken, negotiate a price. Also **Eduardo**, T3361 1315 or 9708 8542, a/c taxi.

Pão de Açúcar *p357*

Bus Bus 107 (from the centre, Catete or Flamengo) and 511 from Copacabana (512 to return) take you to the cable-car station, Av Pasteur 520, at the foot.

Cable car Praia Vermelha to Morro da Urca: first car goes up at 0800, then every 30 mins (or when full), until the last comes down at 2200 (quietest before 1000). From Urca to Sugar Loaf, the first connecting cable car goes up at 0815 then every 30 mins (or when full), until the last leaves the summit at 2200; the return trip costs US$16 (US$10 to Morro da Urca, halfway up, or from Morro da Urca to the top). Termini are ample and efficient and the present Italian cable cars carry 75 passengers. Even on the most crowded days there is little queuing.

Corcovado *p357*

Bus Take a **Cosme Velho** bus to the cog railway station at R Cosme Velho 513: from the centre or Glória/Flamengo No 180; from Copacabana take No 583, 584, from Botafogo or Ipanema/Leblon No 583 or 584; from Santa Teresa Microônibus Santa Teresa.

Car If driving to Corcovado, the entrance fee is US$5 for the vehicle, plus US$5 pp. Coach trips tend to be rather brief and special taxis, which wait in front of the station, offer tours of Corcovado and Mirante Dona Marta for US$25.

Train Every 20-30 mins between 0830 and 1830, journey time 10 mins (cost: US$16 return; single tickets available). **Trem do Corcovado**, R Cosme Velho 513, T2558 1329, www.corcovado.com.br. Ignore touts for tours who say that the train is not running.

Taxis and minivans from Paineiras charge US$6.50 pp. Also, a 206 bus does the very attractive run from Praça Tiradentes (or a 407 from Largo do Machado) to Silvestre (the railway has no stop here now). An active walk of 9 km will take you to the top. For safety reasons go in company, or at weekends when more people are about.

Copacabana *p358, map p356*

Bus Many to and from the city centre, US$0.55. The buses to take are Nos 119, 154, 413, 415, 455, 474 from Av Nossa Senhora de Copacabana. If you are going to the centre from Copacabana, look for 'Castelo', 'Praça 15', 'E Ferro' or 'Praça Mauá' on the sign by the front door. 'Aterro' means the expressway between Botafogo and downtown Rio (closed Sun). From the centre to Copacabana is easier as all buses in that direction are marked. The 'Aterro' bus does the journey in 15 mins.

Jardim Botânico *p358*

Bus Take bus No 170 from the centre, or any bus to Leblon, Gávea or São Conrado marked 'via Jóquei'; from Glória, Flamengo or Botafogo take No 571, or 172 from Flamengo; from Copacabana, Ipanema or Leblon take No 572 (584 back to Copacabana).

Ipanema and Leblon *p358, map p359*

Bus From Botafogo Metrô terminal to Ipanema: some take integrated Metrô-Bus tickets; look for the blue signs on the windscreen. Many buses from Copacabana run to Ipanema and Leblon.

Barra da Tijuca *p359*

Bus From the city centre to Barra, 1 hr, are Nos 175, 176; from Botafogo, Glória or Flamengo take No 179; Nos 591 or 592 from Leme; and from Copacabana via Leblon No 523 (45 mins-1 hr). A taxi to Zona Sul costs US$25 (US$35 after 2400). A comfortable bus, Pegasus, goes along the coast from the Castelo bus terminal to Barra da Tijuca and continues to Campo Grande or Santa Cruz, or take the free 'Barra Shopping' bus. Bus 700 from Praça São Conrado (terminal of bus 553 from Copacabana) goes the full length of the beach to Recreio dos Bandeirantes.

Parque Nacional Tijuca *p360*
Bus Take bus No 221 from Praça 15 de Novembro, No 234 from the rodoviária or from Praça Sáens Pena, Tijuca (the city suburb, not Barra – reached by Metrô), for the park entrance, or No 454 from Copacabana to Alto da Boa Vista. Jeep tours are run by Atlantic Forest Jeep Tour, daily; T2495 9827, T9974 0218 (mob), or contact through travel agencies.

Ilha de Paquetá *p360*
Ferry Services that leave more or less every 2 hrs from Praça 15 de Novembro, where there is a general boat terminal; there are boats from 0515 (0710 on Sun and holidays) to 2300, T2533 7524, or hydrofoils between 1000 and 1600, Sat and Sun 0800-1630 hourly, T2533 4343 or Paquetá 3397 0656 (fare US$1 by boat, 1 hr, US$5 by hydrofoil, 20 mins' journey, which more than doubles its price Sat, Sun and holidays). Other boat trips: Several agencies offer trips to Paquetá. Some also offer a day cruise, including lunch, to Jaguanum Island (see under Itacuruçá) and a sundown cruise around Guanabara Bay.

⊙ Directory

Rio de Janeiro *p348, maps p348 and p351*
Airline offices Aerolíneas Argentinas, Av Rio Branco, 134, 7th floor, Centro, T2103 4200. Air France/KLM, Av Pres Antônio Carlos 58, 9th floor, T4003 9955, www.airfrance.com.br. American, Av Pres Wilson 165, 5th floor, T0300-789 7778, www.aa.com.br. Avianca, Av Almirante Barroso 52, 34th floor, T2240 4413, www.avianca.com.br. Bra, Av Rio Branco 85, 9th floor, Centro, T3213 3233, www.voebra.com.br. British Airways, T4004-4440 toll free. Continental, R da Assembléia 10, sala 3711, T0800-702 7500. Gol, T0800-701 2131, www.voegol.com.br. Iberia, Av Pres Antônio Carlos 51, 9th floor, T2282 1336. LAB, Av Calógeras 30A, T2220 9548, www.labairlines.com.br. LAN, R da Assembléia 92, office 1301, T2240 9388, www.lan.com.br. Ocean Air, Praça Senador Salgado Filho s/n, T0300-789 8160, www.oceanair.com.br. Offices in both airports. TAM, Av Rio Branco 245, T0800-570 5700, www.tam.com.br. TAP, Av Rio Branco 311 B, T2131 7771. United, Av Rio Branco 89, 17th floor, T0800-162323, www.united.com.br. Banks Citibank, R Assembléia 100, T2291 1232, changes large US$ TCs into smaller ones, no commission, advances cash on Eurocard/

MasterCard. ATM at branch on Av NS de Copacabana at Siqueira Campos. Banco do Brasil, there are only 2 branches in Rio which will change US$ TCs, Praia de Botafogo, 384A, 3rd floor (minimum US$200) and the central branch at R Sen Dantas 105, 4th floor (minimum US$500 – good rates). Banco do Brasil at the International Airport is open 0800-2200. The international airport is probably the only place to change TCs at weekends. Banco 24 horas ATMs around town and in airports. Good for Visa card withdrawal. Visa cash withdrawals also at Banco do Brasil (many ATMs at the R Sen Dantas branch, no queues) and Bradesco (personal service or machines). MasterCard and Cirrus cash machines at most HSBC branches in Centro, Copacabana, Ipanema and other locations. Some BBV branches have Visa and MasterCard ATMs. Also at Santos Dumont airport. Money changers: American Express, Av Atlântica 1702, loja 1, Mon-Fri 0900-1730, Av das Américas 500, Bloco 2, Loja 113, Barra da Tijuca, and at Jobim/Galeão airport, T4004 7797 (Sector C 1st floor), good rates (daily 0630-2230). Most large hotels and reputable travel agencies will change currency and TCs. Copacabana (where rates are generally worse than in the centre) abounds with câmbios and there are many also on Av Rio Branco. Câmbio Belle Tours, Rio Sul Shopping, ground floor, loja 101, parte A-10, Mon-Fri 1000-1800, Sat 1000-1700, changes cash. In the gallery at Largo do Machado 29 are Câmbio Nick at loja 22 and, next door but one, Casa Franca. Car hire For international car rental websites, see Car hire, Essentials, page 44. Interlocadora, international airport T3398 3181, domestic airport T2240 0754; Telecar, R Figueiredo Magalhães 701, Copacabana, T2548 6778, www.telecar.com.br. Many agencies on Av Princesa Isabel, Copacabana. A credit card is essential for hiring a car. Cultural centres Alliance Française, R Duvivier 43/103, Copacabana and Rua Garcia d'Avila 72, Ipanema, T2259 4489, www.rioaliancafrancesa.com.br. British Council, R Jardim Botânico, 518R, T2105 7500, www.britishcouncil.org.br. German Cultur-Institut (Goethe), R do Passeio 62, 2nd floor, T2533 4862, www.goethe.de/br/rio. Tue-Wed 1000-1200, Thu 1530-2000, Fri 1530-1800, Sat 0900-1300. See also Casa-França-Brasil, page 351. Embassies and consulates Argentina, Praia de Botafogo 228,T2553 1646, consacrio@openlink.com.br. Very helpful over visas, 1130-1600. Australia, Av Presidente Wilson 231, No 23, T3824 4624, honconau@terra.com.br. Mon-Fri 9000-1300, 1430-1800. Austria, Av Atlântica 3804, T2102 0020, rio-de-janeiro-gk@ bmaa.gv.at. Canada, Av Atlântica, 1130, 5th floor, T2543 3004, rio@international.gc.ca. France,

Av Pres Antônio Carlos 58, T3974 6699, consulatrio@rionet.com.br. **Germany**, R Pres Carlos de Campos 417, T2554 0004, gkrioalemao@terra.com.br (also serves Minas Gerais). **Ireland**, R 24 de Maio 347, Riachuelo, T2501 8455, rioconsulate@ ireland.com. **Japan**, Praia do Flemengo 200, 10th floor, T3461 9595, www.rio.br.emb-japan.go.jp. **Netherlands**, Praia de Botafogo 242, 10th floor, T2157 5400, rio@minbuza.nl. **Paraguay**, Praia de Botafogo 242, 2nd floor, T2553 2294, consulpar.rj.brasil@hotmail.com. **Sweden, Finland** and **Norway**, R Lauro Müller 116/2206, Rio Sul Shopping Center, Botafogo, T2541 7732, cg.riodejaneiro@mfa.no. **Switzerland**, R Cândido Mendes 157, 11th floor, T2221 1867, vertretung@rio.rep.admin.ch. **UK**, Praia do Flamengo 284, 2nd floor. T2555 9600, britishconsulaterio@terra.com.br, open Mon-Thu 0830-1645, Fri 08301630, Metrô Flamengo, or bus 170, issues a useful 'Guidance for Tourists' pamphlet. **Uruguay**, Praia de Botafogo 242, 6th floor,T2553 6030. **USA**, Av Pres Wilson 147, T3823 2000, www.consuladodoeua-rio.org.br. Mon-Fri 0830-1645. **Internet** Throughout the city. Several places in Rio Sul Shopping, Botafogo. Many on Av NS de Copacabana and others on R Visconde de Pirajá, Ipanema. **Language courses** Instituto Brasil-Estados Unidos, Av Copacabana 690, 5th floor, 8-week course, 3 classes a week, US$200, 5-week intensive course US$260. Good English library at same address. **IVM Português Prático**, R do Catete 310, sala 302, US$18 per hr for individual lessons, cheaper for groups. Helpful staff. Recommended. **Cursos da UNE** (União Nacional de Estudantes), R Catete 243, include cultural studies and Portuguese classes for foreigners. Private lessons with **Camila Queiraz**, T8828 3196/3339 3485, reasonable prices. **Medical services** Vaccinations at Saúde de Portos, Praça Mcal Âncora, T2240 8628/8678, Mon-Fri 1000-1100, 1500-1800 (international vaccination book and ID required). **Policlínica**,

Av Nilo Peçanha 38. Recommended for diagnosis and investigation. A good public hospital for minor injuries and ailments is **Hospital Municipal Rocha Maia**, R Gen Severiano 91, Botafogo, T2295 2295/2121, near Rio Sul Shopping Centre. Free, but there may be queues. **Hospital Miguel Couto**, Mário Ribeiro 117, Gávea, T2274 6050. Has a free casualty ward. **Health:** Dentist: English-speaking, **Amílcar Werneck de Carvalho Vianna**, Av Pres Wilson 165, suite 811. **Dr Mauro Suartz**, R Visconde de Pirajá 414, room 509, T2287 6745. Speaks English and Hebrew, helpful. **Post offices** The central Post Office is on R 1 de Março 64, at the corner of R do Rosário. Av NS de Copacabana 540 and many other locations. All handle international post. There is a post office at Galeão airport. Poste Restante: Correios, Av NS de Copacabana 540 and all large post offices (letters held for a month, recommended, US$0.10 per letter). **Federal Express**, Av Calógeras 23 (near Santa Luzia church) T2262 8565, is reliable. **Telephones** International calls can be made at Telemar offices: Av NS de Copacabana 540, 2nd floor; Jobim international airport (24 hrs); Novo Rio rodoviária; R Dias da Cruz 192, Méier-4, 24 hrs, 7 days a week; Praça Tiradentes 41, a few mins' walk from Metrô Carioca; R Visconde de Pirajá 111, Ipanema; R do Ouvidor 60, Centro. International telephone booths are blue. Larger Embratel offices have fax, as do many larger Correios. **Useful addresses** Immigration: Federal Police, Praça Mauá (passport section), entrance at Av Venezuela 2, T2291 2142. To renew a 90-day visa, US$12.50. **Ibama**, Praça 15 de Novembro 42, 8th floor, T2506 1734, edson.azeredo@ ibama.gov.br. **Student Travel Bureau**, Av Nilo Peçanha 50, sala 3103, Centro, T3526 7700, and R Visconde de Pirajá 550, lj 201, Ipanema, T2512 8577, www.stb.com.br (offices throughout the country) has details of travel, discounts and cultural exchanges for ISIC holders.

East of Rio

It is not only the state capital that is blessed with beautiful beaches, forests and mountains. There are chic resorts, surfing centres and emerald green coves, national parks in rainforest-clad hills and strange rocky mountains, and fine historical towns dating from both the colonial and imperial epochs. Within easy reach of Rio are the popular coastal resorts of Cabo Frio and Búzios and the imperial city of Petrópolis.

Niterói → *Phone code: 0xx21. Colour map 7, grid B5. Population: 459,451.*

This city is reached across Guanabara Bay by ferries which carry some 200,000 commuters a day. Founded in 1573, Niterói has various churches and forts, plus buildings associated with the city's period as state capital (until 1960). Many of these are grouped around the Praça da República. The **Capela da Boa Viagem** (1663) stands on a fortified island, attached by a causeway to the mainland. The most important historical monument is the **Fortaleza da Santa Cruz** ① *T2710 7840, daily 0900-1600, US$1.50, go with guide*. Dating from the 16th century and still a military establishment, it stands on a promontory which commands a fine view of the entrance to the bay. It is about 13 km from the centre of Niterói, on the Estrada Gen Eurico Gaspar Dutra, by Adão e Eva beach (taxi 30 minutes).

The **Museu de Arqueologia de Itaipu** ① *20 km from the city, T2709 4079, Wed-Sun 1300-1800*, is in the ruins of the 18th-century Santa Teresa Convent and also covers the archaeological site of Duna Grande on Itaipu beach. **Museu de Arte Contemporânea-Niterói** ① *Mirante da Praia da Boa Viagem, T2620 2400, www.macniterio.com, Tue-Sun 1000-1800, Sat 1300-1900, US$1, Wed free*, is an Oscar Niemeyer project and worth visiting. It is best seen at night, especially when the pond beneath the spaceship design is full of water. **Tourist office: Neltur** ① *Estrada Leopoldo Fróes 773, São Francisco, T2710 2727, 5 km from ferry dock, www.niteroiturismo.com.br*, has a useful map.

Local beaches Take buses No 33 and 49 from the dock, passing Icaraí and São Francisco, both with polluted water but good nightlife and plenty of eating places at the latter, to the fishing village of Jurujuba, with simple bars at the water's edge. About 2 km further along a narrow road are the twin beaches of Adão and Eva just before the Fortaleza da Santa Cruz (see above). To get to the ocean beaches, take a 38 or 52 bus from Praça Gen Gomes Carneiro to Piratininga, Camboinhas, Itaipu (see the archaeology museum, above) and Itacoatiara. These are fabulous stretches of sand, the best in the area, about 40 minutes' ride through picturesque countryside.

Lagos Fluminenses

To the east of Niterói lie a series of salt-water lagoons, the Lagos Fluminenses. The first major lakes, Maricá and Saquarema are muddy, but the waters are relatively unpolluted and wildlife abounds in the surrounding scrub and bush. An unmade road goes along the coast between Itacoatiara and Cabo Frio, giving access to the long, open beaches of Brazil's **Costa do Sol**.

In the holiday village of **Saquarema**, the little white church of Nossa Senhora de Nazaré (1675) is on a green promontory jutting into the ocean. Saquarema is a fishing town and one of the top spots for quality consistent pumping surf in Brazil.

The largest lake is **Araruama** (220 sq km), famous for its medicinal mud. The salinity is extremely high, the waters calm, and almost the entire lake is surrounded by sandy beaches, making it popular with families looking for safe, unpolluted bathing. The almost constant breeze makes the lake perfect for windsurfing and sailing. There are many hotels, youth hostels and campsites in the towns by the lakes and by the beaches. All around are saltpans and the wind pumps used to carry water into the pans. At the eastern end of the lake is **São Pedro de Aldeia**, which, despite intensive development, still retains some of its colonial charm.

Cabo Frio → *Phone code: 0xx22. Colour map 7, grid B5. Population: 140,000.*

Cabo Frio, 156 km from Rio, is a popular holiday and weekend haunt of Cariocas because of its cooler weather, white sand beaches, sailing and good underwater swimming. **Forte São Mateus**, 1616, is now a ruin at the mouth of the Canal de Itajurú, which connects the Lagoa Araruama and the ocean. A small headland at its mouth protects the nearest beach to the town, Praia do Forte, which stretches south for about 7½ km to Arraial do Cabo. The canal front, Av dos Pescadores, is pretty, lined with palm trees, restaurants and schooners tied up at the dock. It leads around to the bridge, which crosses to the Gamboa district. **Convento Nossa Senhora dos Anjos** (1696), Largo de Santo Antônio in the town centre, houses the **Museu de Arte Religiosa e Tradicional** ① *Wed-Fri 1400-2000, Sat-Sun 1600-2000*. Above the Largo de Santo Antônio is the **Morro da Guia**, which has a look-out and an 18th-century chapel (access on foot only). The beaches of **Peró** and **Conchas** ① *'São Cristovão' (with 'Peró' on its notice board) or 'Peró' bus, US$0.65, 15-20 mins, has lots of condos, but not many places to stay*, are lovely (a headland, Ponta do Vigia, separates the two and you can walk from one to the other). Peró. **Tourist office** ① *Av Américo Vespúcio s/n, Praia do Forte, at the junction of Av do Contorno and Av João Pessoa, T2647 6227/1689*. Kiosks in the centre sell maps.

Búzios → *Phone code: 0xx24. Colour map 7, grid B5. Population: 18,208. www.buzioschannel.com.br.*

Known as a lost paradise in the tropics, this village, 192 km from Rio, found fame in the 1964 when Brigite Bardot was photographed sauntering barefoot along the beach. The world's press descended on the sophisticated, yet informal resort, following the publicity. Originally a small fishing community, founded in 1740, Búzios remained virtually unknown until the 1950s when its natural beauty started to attract the Brazilian jet-set who turned the village into a fashionable summer resort. The city gets crowded at all main holidays, the price of food, accommodation and other services rises substantially and the traffic jams are long and stressful.

During the daytime, the best option is to head for one of the 25 beaches. The most visited are Geribá (many bars and restaurants; popular with surfers), Ferradura (blue sea and calm waters), Ossos (the most famous and close to the centre), Tartaruga and João Fernandes. Schooner trips of two to three hours pass many of the beaches: US$14-20. Escuna Queen Lory, T2623 1179. **Tourist office**: at Manguinhos, T0800-249999 (24 hours), on the western edge of the peninsula, and at Praça Santo Dumont, T2623 2099. See www.buziosonline.com.br.

Petrópolis → *Phone code: 0xx24. Post code: 25600. Colour map 7, grid B5. Population: 286,537.*

A steep scenic mountain road from Rio leads to this summer resort, 68 km north of Rio, known for its floral beauty and hill scenery, coupled with adventure sports. Until 1962 Petrópolis was the 'summer capital' of Brazil. Now it combines manufacturing industry (particularly textiles) and tourism. There are possibilities for whitewater rafting, hiking, climbing, riding and cycling in the vicinity. Petrópolis celebrates its foundation on 16 March. Patron saint's day, São Pedro de Alcântara, 29 June. **Tourist office**: **Petrotur** ① *Praça Liberdade, T0800-241516 or 2246 9377, www.petropolis.rj.gov.br/fctp, Mon-Tue 0900-1830, Wed-Sat 0900-2000, Sun 0900-1600.* Very helpful, good English. There are kiosks in the main sites of interest.

The **Museu Imperial** (Imperial Palace) ① *R da Imperatriz 220, T2237 8000, Tue-Sun 1100-1800, US$4*, is Brazil's most visited museum. It is an elegant building, neoclassical in style, fully furnished and equipped. It is so well kept you might think the imperial family had left the day before, rather than in 1889. It's worth a visit just to see the Crown Jewels of both Pedro I and Pedro II. In the palace gardens is a pretty French-style tearoom, the Petit Palais. The Gothic-style **Catedral de São Pedro de Alcântara** ① *Tue-Sun 0800-1200, 1400-1800, Mon 0800-1200*, completed in 1925, contains the tombs of the Emperor and Empress. The Imperial Chapel is to the right of the entrance. The summer home of air pioneer **Alberto Santos Dumont** ① *R do Encanto 22, T2247 3158, Tue-Sun 0930-1700, US$2.50*, is known as 'A Encantada' and is worth a visit. The interior of the **Casa de Petrópolis** ① *R Ipiranga 716, T2231 6197, Fri-Tue 1300-1830*, is completely original and over-the-top, but has been lovingly restored. It holds art exhibitions and classical concerts. A charming restaurant in the old stables is worth a stop for coffee, if not for lunch. **Orquidário Binot** ① *R Fernandes Vieira 390, T2248 5665, Mon-Fri 0800-1100, 1300-1600, Sat 0700-1100, take bus to Vila Isabel*, has a huge collection of orchids from all over Brazil (plants may be purchased).

Petrópolis

Sleeping
Casablanca Imperial **1**
Casablanca Palace **3**
Comércio **4**
Pousada da Alcobaça **6**

Solar do Império **7**
York **8**

Eating
Cantina Bom Giovanni **1**

Casa d'Ângelo **2**
Falconi **3**

Serra dos Órgãos

ⓘ *Tue-Sun 0800-1700, best months for trekking Apr-Sep, US$1, with an extra charge for the path to the top. For information from Ibama, Av Rotariana s/n, Alto Teresópolis, T2152 1100, www.ibama.gov.br.*

The Serra dos Órgãos, so called because their strange shapes are said to recall organ-pipes, is an 11,000-ha national park (created in 1939, the second oldest in the country). The main attraction is the precipitous Dedo de Deus ('God's Finger') Peak (1,692 m). The highest point is the 2,263 m Pedra do Sino ('Bell Rock'), up which winds a 14-km path, a climb of three to four hours. The west face of this mountain is one of the hardest climbing pitches in Brazil. Another well-known peak is the Pedra do Açu (2,245 m) and many others have names evocative of their shape. Near the Sub-Sede (off BR-116, just outside the park) is the **Von Martius natural history museum** *0800-1700*. By the headquarters (Sede) entrance is the Mirante do Soberbo, with views to the Baía de Guanabara. To climb the Pedra do Sino, you must sign a register (under 18 must be accompanied by an adult and have authorization from the park authorities).

Further information on the area from the **Teresópolis tourism office** ⓘ *R Prefeito Sebastião Teixeira 20, loja 211. Shopping New Fashion, T2742-7936, www.teresopolison.com, Mon-Fri 0900-1800, Sat 0900-1700, Sun 0900-1300.*

● Sleeping

Cabo Frio *p379*

A Othon Sítio do Portinho, R Cnel Ferreira 281, Portinho, T2644 9264, www.pousadasitiodo portinho.hpg.com.br. Cheaper in low season. Very nice rooms set in gardens in a residential suburb, a/c and all usual facilities, pool and bar.

B Pousada Água Marinha, R Rui Barbosa 996b, Centro, T2643 8447, p.aguamarinha@uol.com.br. **C** in low season, white rooms with comfortable beds, a/c, fan, TV, frigobar, breakfast, pool and parking. About 4 blocks from Praia do Forte.

B Pousada Suzy, Av Júlia Kubitschek 48, T2643 1742. 100 m from rodoviária, **C** in low season, with a/c, cheaper with fan. Shared rooms for 8, **D**. Plain rooms but not spartan, pool, sauna, garage.

C Pousada Velas ao Vento, Av Júlia Kubitschek 5, T2644 1235. Between rodoviária and centre. Cheaper in low season, comfortable, set back from the main road but still a bit of traffic noise. Hot water, a/c, helpful owner and staff.

D Marina dos Anjos, R Bernado Lens 145, Arraial do Cabo, T2622 4060, www.marinadosanjos.com.br. Superior HI hostel with spruce dorms and doubles, facilities including a games room, sun terrace and links to tour companies and dive shops.

Peró

AL La Plage, R das Badejos 40, T2647 1746, www.redebela.com.br. **B** in low season; fully equipped suites, those upstairs have sea view, excellent for families. Right on the beach, services include pool and bar, à la carte restaurant, hydromassage, sauna, 24-hr cyber café, garage.

B Pousada Espírito do Mar, R Anequim s/n, T2644 3077, www.espiritodomar.com.br. **C** in low season. Orange building with central swimming pool around which the rooms are built. Good, spacious but simple rooms, with extra bed available. A/c, frigobar, TV and fan. The bus to Cabo Frio passes outside.

D Peró Hostel, R Coutrin 13, T2647 7605, www.perohostel.com.br. Smart modern HI hostel with doubles and dorms, many with their own terraces, some with fridge, good services including tours and Tai Chi.

E pp Albergue Internacional da Juventude de Muxarabi, R Leonor Santa Rosa, 13, Jardim Flamboyant, T2643 0369.

Camping Clube do Brasil, Estrada dos Passageiros 700, 2 km from town, T2643 3124. **Camping da Estação**, on the same road, at No 370, T2643 1786.

Búzios *p379*

Prior reservations are needed in summer, at holidays such as Carnival and the New Year's Eve, and weekends. For cheaper options and better availability, try Cabo Frio.

The best rooms on the peninsula are not on the beaches, but on the Morro do Humaitá, superb views, 10 mins' walk from the town centre. Hire a beach buggy. Several private houses rent rooms, especially in summer and holidays. Look for the signs: 'Alugo Quartos'.

LL Boca do Ceu, Mirante de João Fernandes, R Hum s/n, T2623 4713, www.bocadoceu.com. Super luxurious, and very expensive, private home/mini pousada (owned by a famous Uruguayan interior designer) with the best views on the peninsula out across a carefully designed swimming pool and garden. All the fittings are by famous names.

● *For an explanation of the sleeping and eating price codes used in this guide, see page 58.*
● *Other relevant information is found in Essentials pages 345-347.*

LL **Hotel Pérola Búzios**, Av José Bento Ribeiro Dantas 222, Armação dos Búzios – Centro, 28950-000, T2620 8507, www.perolabuzios.com. Full facilities, accommodates up to 450 people. The only hotel in Búzios that can cater for such large numbers for meetings, etc.

LL-L **Casas Brancas**, Alto do Humaitá 8, T2623 1458, www.casasbrancas.com.br. Far and away the best hotel in Búzios; a series of rooms perched on the hill in mock-Mykonos buildings with separate terraces for the pool and spa areas, wonderfully romantic at night when all is lit by candlelight. If you can't afford to stay go for dinner.

LL-L **El Cazar**, Alto do Humaitá 6, T2623 1620. Next door to Casas Brancas and almost as luxurious; though a little darker inside. Beautiful artwork, tasteful and relaxing.

LL-L **Pousada Byblos**, Alto do Humaitá 14, T2623 1162, www.byblos.com.br. Wonderful views over the bay, bright, light rooms with tiled floors and balconies.

L **Pousada Pedra Da Laguna**, Rua 6, lote 6, Praia da Ferradura, T2623 1965, www.pedrada laguna.com.br. Spacious rooms, the best with a view 150m from the beach. Part of the Roteiros do Charme.

AL **Pousada Hibiscus Beach**, R 1 No 22, Quadra C, Praia de João Fernandes, T2623 6221, www.hibiscusbeach.com. A peaceful spot, 15 pleasant bungalows, garden, pool, light meals available, help with car/buggy rentals and local excursions. One of the best beach hotels.

AL-A **Brigitta's Guest House**, R das Pedras 131, T/F2623 6157, www.buziosonline.com. brigitta. Beautifully decorated little pousada where Bardot once stayed, just 4 rooms on the main street, delightful restaurant, bar and tea house overlooking the water are worth a visit.

A **Casa da Ruth**, R dos Gravatás, Geribá, T2623 2242, www.buziosturismo.com/casadaruth. Simple mock-Greek rooms in lilac overlooking the beach and pool.

C-E **Praia dos Amores**, Av José Bento Ribeiro Dantas 92, T2623 2422. IYHA, not far from the bus station, next to Praia da Tartaruga and just under 1 km from the centre. The best value in Búzios. Recommended.

C-E **Ville Blanche**, R Turibe de Farias 222, T2623 1840. New simple pousada, central, dorms for up to 10, and bright, tiled floor doubles with balconies.

E **Country Camping Park**, R Maria Joaquina Justiniano 895 (off Praça da Rasa), Praia Rasa, Km 12, T2629 1155, www.buzioscamping.com.br. Chalets and a well-run, shady campsite 1 km from the beach (directions on web site).

Petrópolis *p380, map p380*

LL **Solar do Império**, Av Koeler 276, T2103 3000, www.solardoimperio.com.br. Converted neo-classical colonial mansion set in gardens on Petrópolis's grandest street. Fittings evoke the imperial era but modern facilities include a pool, sauna and ofuro hot tub.

L **Pousada da Alcobaça**, R Agostinho Goulão 298, Correas, T2221 1240, www.pousadada alcobaca.com.br. Delightful, family-run country house in flower-filled gardens, pool and sauna. Worth stopping by for tea on the terrace, or dinner at the restaurant. Recommended.

AL-A **Casablanca Imperial**, R da Imperatriz 286, T2242 6662, www.casablancahotel.com.br. Most atmospheric of the 2 in this chain, cheaper rooms in modern extension, good restaurant, pool. Also **B Casablanca Palace**, R 16 de Março 123, T2231 0818.

B **York**, R do Imperador 78, T2243 2662, www.hotelyork.com.br. A short walk from the Rodoviária, convenient, helpful, the fruit and milk at breakfast come from the owners' own farm. Recommended.

C **Comércio**, R Dr Porciúncula 55, T2242 3500, opposite the Rodoviária. Some rooms with bath, simple, associated with **Trekking Petrópolis**, T2235 7607, www.rioserra.com.br/trekking, which offers trips in the surrounding mountains.

Serra dos Órgãos/Teresópolis *p381*

Ibama has some hostels, US$5 full board, or US$3 first night, US$2 thereafter, a bit rough. There is also the **Refugio do Parque**, 2 km from park entrance of Teresópolis side, T9687 4539 (mob), refugiodoparque@bol.com.br. Rooms with bath and dormitories with shower, breakfast and soup-and-bread supper included.

L Serra dos Tucanos, Caixa Postal 98125, Cachoeiras do Macacu, T2649 1557, www.serrados tucanos.com.br. British-run lodge in the Parque Estadual Três Picos near Teresópolis, with some of the very best birdwatching, guiding and facilities in the Atlantic coast forest. Cabins around a spring-water swimming pool. Airport transfers from Rio.

A Guapi Assu Bird Lodge, www.tropicalbirding. com/guapia/intro.html, c/o Regua (Reserva Ecologica de Guapi Assu), Nicholas Locke, Caixa Postal 98112, Cachoeiras de Macacu, T2745 3998, www.regua.co.uk. Private rainforest reserve with very comfortable accommodation in a spacious wooden house and guided walks through pristine forest, price is full board. Families of South America's largest and rarest primate, the woolly spider monkey live here, excellent birding.

D-E Recanto do Lord, R Luiza Pereira Soares 109, Teresópolis, T2742 5586, www.teresopolis hostel.com.br. Big, well-equipped HI hostel, dorms and doubles, wonderful mountain views and organized tours and 'adventure' trips in the Serra dos Órgãos.

Eating

Cabo Frio *p379*

There's a neat row of restaurants on Av dos Pescadores, most offering fish, local meats, or pastas. They have seating on the pavement under awnings, French-style. Upstairs are a number of bars and clubs.

ŸŸŸ-ŸŸ Picolino, R Mcal F Peixoto 319, T2643 2436. In a nice old building, very smart, mixed menu but mostly local fish and seafood, but also some international dishes.

ŸŸ Hippocampo, R Mcal F Peixoto 283, T2645 5757. Mostly seafood.

ŸŸ "In" Sônia, Av dos Pescadores 140 loja 04. Good service and tasty fish, many dishes for 2.

ŸŸ Populeti, Av dos Pescadores e Trav Maçonica, T2645 3876. Homemade pastas, a/c, entrance in Shopping Crystal Palace. **Galeto do Zé** (below it) for snacks. Also **Do Zé** on Av dos Pescadores, T2643 4277, serving Brazilian specialities.

ŸŸ Tonto, Av dos Pescadores next to "In" Sônia. Serves pizza and local dishes (T2645 1886 for delivery), has a bar too.

ŸŸ-Ÿ Kilo-Kura, Av Teixeira e Souza 121-A. Good self-service lunches, very popular.

Ÿ Bacalhauzinho, Praça Porto Rocha. Portuguese.

Ÿ Branca, Praça Porto Rocha. Lunches à kilo 1100-1700, also fast food, pizza after 1800, coffee, pastries and cakes, good, a big, popular place.

Ÿ Chico's, Av Teixeira e Souza 30, upstairs in Centro Comercial Víctor Nunes da Rocha, T2645 7454. Smart, does breakfast, self-service.

Búzios *p379*

There are many restaurants on and around R das Pedras and one of the charms of Búzios is browsing. The cheaper options tend to be off the main drag. There are plenty of beachside barracas all over the peninsula (closed out of season). A few places on Praça Santos Dumont off Rua das Pedras offer sandwiches and self-service food, including the homely La Prima on Av Manuel Turibo de Farias, which doubles as a bakery. There's a small supermarket a couple of doors away.

ŸŸŸ Acquerello, R das Pedras 130, T2623 6576. Smart a/c seafood and Italian restaurant with a reasonable wine list. The best on the street.

ŸŸŸ Satyricon, Av José Bento Ribeiro Dantas 500, Praia da Armação (in front of Morro da Humaitá), T2623 1595. Búzios's most illustrious restaurant specializing in Italian seafood. Decent wine list.

ŸŸ Moqueca Capixaba, R Manoel de Carvalho 116, Centro, T2623 1155. Bahian seafood with dishes cooked in coconut or dende oil.

Ÿ Banana Land, R Manoel Turíbio de Farias 50, T2623 0855. Cheap and cheerful per kilo buffet.

Ÿ Chez Michou, R das Pedras, 90, Centro, T2623 2169. An open-air bar with videos, music and dozens of choices of pancakes accompanied by ice cold beer. Always crowded.

Ÿ Fashion Cafe, R das Pedras 151, T2623 2697. Fast food and pizzas with a young crowd and a live band.

Petrópolis *p380, map p380*

ŸŸ Falconi, R do Imperador 757. Traditional Italian. Recommended.

Ÿ Cantina Bom Giovanni, R do Imperador 729 upstairs. Popular, Italian, lunch and dinner.

Ÿ Casa d'Ángelo, R do Imperador 700, by Praça Dom Pedro II. Traditional tea house with self service food that doubles as a bar at night.

Bars and clubs

Búzios *p379*

In season Búzios nightlife is young, beautiful and buzzing. Out of season it is non-existent. The bulk of the bars and the handful of clubs are on R das Pedras. These include **GuapoLoco**, a bizarrely shaped Mexican theme bar and restaurant with dancing. There are plenty of others including more upscale wine bar-style options like **Café Concerto**.

Privelege, Av José Bento Ribeiro Dantas 550, R Orla Bardot. One of Brazil's best European-style dance clubs with pumping techno, house and hip hop and 5 rooms including a cavernous dance floor, sushi bar and lounge.
Ta-ka-ta ka-ta, R das Pedras 256. Strewn with motorbike parts and covered with graffiti.

◎ Transport

Niterói *p378*
Bus No 996 Gávea-Jurujuba, 998 Galeão-Charitas, 740-D and 741 Copacabana-Charitas, 730-D Castelo Jurujba, US$1.
Car The toll on the Rio-Niterói bridge is US$1.
Ferry From the 'barcas' at Praça 15 de Novembro (ferry museum at the terminal), ferry boats and launches cross every 10 mins to Niterói (25-30 mins, US$0.65). There are also catamarans ('aerobarcas') every 10 mins Mon-Fri only (about 3 mins, US$3.25). They also go to Charitas, near São Francisco beach. Of the frequent ferry and catamaran services from Praça 15 de Novembro, Rio, the slow, cheaper ferry gives the best views.

Lagos Fluminenses: Saquarema *p379*
Bus Mil e Um (1001) Rio-Saquarema, every 2 hrs 0730-1800, 2 hrs, US$6.

Cabo Frio *p379*
Air A new airport has opened linking the area with **Belo Horizonte**, **Brasília**, **Rio de Janeiro** and **São Paulo**.
Bus Urban: Salineira and Montes Brancos run local services. US$1.50 to **Búzios, São Pedro da Aldeia, Saquarema, Araruama** and **Arraial do Cabo**. US$1 for closer destinations. The urban bus terminal is near Largo de Santo Antônio, opposite the BR petrol station.
Long distance: The rodoviária is well within the city, but a fair walk from centre and beaches. City buses stop nearby. To **Belo Horizonte** US$42 (a/c). To **Petrópolis** US$21. 1001 to **Rio de Janeiro**, Niterói US$8, to **São Paulo** US$45 at 2100.

Búzios *p379*
Bus Mil e Um from Novo Rio, T0xx21-2516 1001,US$15, 2½ hrs (be at the bus terminal 20 mins before departure). Departures every 2 hrs from 0700 to 1900 daily. You can also take any bus to **Cabo Frio** (many more during the day), from where it's 30 mins to Búzios. Buy the ticket in advance on major holidays. Búzios' rodoviária is a few blocks' walk from the centre. Some pousadas are within 10 mins on foot, eg La Coloniale, Brigitta's, while others need a local bus (US$1) or taxi. Buses from Cabo Frio run the length of the peninsula and pass several pousadas.
Car Via BR-106 takes about 2½ hrs from Rio.

Petrópolis *p380, map p380*
Bus From **Rio** every 15 mins throughout the day (US$6) with **Única Fácil**, Sun every hr, 1½ hrs, sit on the left hand side for best views. Return tickets are not available, so buy tickets for the return on arrival in Petrópolis. The ordinary buses leave from the rodoviária in Rio; a/c buses, hourly from 1100, from Av Nilo Peçanha, US$7.50. To **Teresópolis** for the Serra dos Órgãos, **Viação Teresópolis**, 8 a day, US$6. **Salutário** to **São Paulo**, daily at 2330.

Serra dos Órgãos *p381*
Bus Rio-Teresópolis: buses leave every 30 mins from the Novo Rio rodoviária. Book the return journey as soon as you arrive at Teresópolis; rodoviária at R 1 de Maio 100. Fare US$7.
Car The park has 2 dependencies, both accessible from the BR-116: the Sede (HQ, Av Rotariano, Alto Teresópolis, T/F0xx21-2642 1070) is closer to Teresópolis, the highest city in the state of Rio de Janeiro, while the Sub-Sede is just outside the park proper, off the BR-116.

◑ Directory

Cabo Frio *p379*
Internet Cyber Mar, CC V Nunes da Rocha, Av Teixeira e Souza 30. A/c, open 0800-2000 daily. **Cyber Tel**, Praça Porta Rocha 56, in gallery next to Banco do Brasil, T2649 7575. Only 3 machines, but good and fast.

Búzios *p379*
Internet buzios@internet, Av J B Ribeiro Dantas, 97, close to Shopping One.

Petrópolis *p380, map p380*
Banks Banco do Brasil, R Paulo Barbosa 81. A Banco 24 Horas ATM is at R Marechal Deodoro 98. Travel agencies with exchange: BKR, R Gen Osório 12, **Goldman**, R Barão de Amazonas 46, and **Vert Tur**, R 16 de Março 244, from 1000-1630. **Internet** Compuland, R do Imperador opposite Praça Dr Sá Earp. **Post offices** R do Imperador 350. **Telephone** Telerj, R Marechal Deodoro, just above Praça Dr Sá Earp.

West of Rio

One of the main attractions near the inland highway to São Paulo is the Itatiaia National Park, a good area for climbing, trekking and birdwatching. If you want a really beautiful route, though, take the Rio de Janeiro-Santos section of the BR101, which hugs the forested and hilly Costa Verde southwest of Rio.

Dutra Highway

The Dutra Highway, BR-116, heads west from Rio towards the border with São Paulo. It passes the steel town of **Volta Redonda** and some 30 km further west, the town of **Resende**. In this region, 175 km from Rio, is **Penedo** (five buses a day from Resende) which in the 1930s attracted Finnish settlers who brought the first saunas to Brazil. There is a Finnish museum, a cultural centre and Finnish dancing on Saturday. This popular weekend resort also provides horse riding, and swimming in the Portinho River. There are plenty of mid-range and cheap hotels in town. For tourist information, Toxx24-3351 1876.

Parque Nacional de Itatiaia

ⓘ *Entry per day is $10 per car. Information can be obtained from Ibama, Toxx24-3352 1461, for the local headquarters, or Toxx21-3224 6463 for the Rio de Janeiro state department. Avoid weekends and holidays if you want to see wildlife.*

This park, being so close to Rio and São Paulo, is a must for those with limited time who wish to see some of world's rarest birds and mammals in a whole range of different ecosystems. Trails from one hour to two days go through deep valleys shrouded in pristine rainforest, hiding icy waterfalls and clear-water rivers. The 30,000-ha mountainous park is Brazil's oldest, founded in 1937 to protect Atlantic Coast Rainforest in the Serra de Mantiqueira. Important species include jaguar, puma, brown capuchin and black-face titi monkeys. The park is particularly good for birds with a list of 350+, with scores of spectacular tanagers, humming, cotingas and manakins. The best trails head for Pedra de Taruga and Pedra de Maçã and the Poranga and Véu de Noiva waterfalls. The Pico das Agulhas Negras and the Serra das Prateleiras (up to 2,540 m) offer decent rock climbing. There is a **Museu de História Natural** ⓘ *Tue-Sun 1000-1600*, near the headquarters, with a depressing display of stuffed animals from the 1940s.

Information and maps can be obtained at the park office. The **Administração do Parque Nacional de Itatiaia** operates a refuge in the park, which acts as a starting point for climbs and treks. Although buses do run through the park calling at the hotels, hiring a car to visit Itatiaia is the best option.

Costa Verde (Emerald Coast)

The Rio de Janeiro-Santos section of the BR101 is one of the world's most beautiful highways, running along the aptly called Emerald Coast, which is littered with islands, beaches, colonial settlements and mountain fazendas. It is complete through to Bertioga (see page 407), which has good links with Santos and São Paulo. Buses run from Rio to Angra dos Reis, Paraty, Ubatuba, Caraguatatuba and São Sebastião, where it may be necessary to change for Santos or São Paulo.

Itacuruçá, 91 km from Rio, is a delightful place to visit. Separated from the town by a channel is the Ilha de Itacuruçá, the largest of a string of islands stretching into the bay. Further offshore is Ilha de Jaguanum, around which there are lovely walks. Saveiros (schooners) sail around the bay and to the islands from Itacuruça (Passamar, T9979 2429). Ilha de Itacuruçá can also be reached from **Muriqui**, a popular beach resort 9 km from Itacuruçá. There are hotels on the island. **Mangaratiba**, 22 km down the coast, is halfway from Rio to Angra dos Reis. Its beaches are muddy, but the surroundings are pleasant and better beaches can be found outside town.

Angra dos Reis → *Phone code: 0xx24. Post code: 23900. Colour map 7, grid B4. Pop: 119,247.*

Said to have been founded on 6 January 1502 (O Dia dos Reis – The Day of Kings), this is a small port, 151 km southwest of Rio, with an important fishing and shipbuilding industry. It has several small coves with good bathing within easy reach and is situated on an enormous bay full of islands. Of particular note are the church and convent of **Nossa Senhora do Carmo**, built in 1593 (Praça Gen Osório), the **Igreja Matriz de Nossa Senhora da Conceição** (1626) in the centre of town, and the church and convent of **São Bernardino de Sena** (1758-1763) on the

Morro do Santo Antônio. On the Largo da Lapa is the church of **Nossa Senhora da Lapa da Boa Morte** (1752), with a sacred art museum. On the Península de Angra, just west of the town, is the **Praia do Bonfim**, a popular beach, and a little way offshore the island of the same name, on which is the hermitage of Senhor do Bonfim (1780). **Tourist information** is opposite the bus station on the Largo da Lapa, very good, T3336 51175, ext 2186.

Ilha Grande → *Phone code: 0xx21. Colour map 7, grid B5.*

Ilha Grande is a mountain ridge covered in tropical forest sticking out of an emerald sea and fringed by some of the world's most beautiful beaches. As there are no cars and no roads either, just trails through the forest, the island is still relatively undeveloped. Much of it forms part of a State Park and **Biological Reserve**, and cannot even be visited. The island was a notorious pirate lair, then a landing port for slaves. By the 20th century it had become the site of an infamous prison for the country's most notorious criminals (closed in 1994 and now overgrown rubble). The weather is best from March to June and, like everywhere along the coast, the island is overrun during the Christmas, New Year and Carnaval period. **Convention and Visitors Bureau**① *at the ferry port on arrival, T021-2220 4323, Mon-Sat 0800-1800, Sun 0900-1300; all information at www.ilhagrande.com.br; also www.ilhagrande.org.*

The beach at **Vila do Abraão** may look beautiful to first arrivals but those further afield are far more spectacular. The two most famous are **Lopes Mendes**, two hours' walk from Abraão, and **Aventureiro**, six hours, but it can be reached via the Maria Isabel or Mestre Ernani boats (T3361 9895 or T9269 5877), which leave from the quay in front of the BR petrol station in Angra dos Reis. Good beaches closer to Abraão include the half moon bay at **Abraãoozinho** (15 minutes' walk) and **Grande das Palmas** which have a delightful tiny whitewashed chapel (one hour 20 minutes' walk), both east of town. Lagoa Azul, Freguesia de Santana and Saco do Céu are all boat trips. Good treks include over the mountains to Dois Rios, where the old jail was situated (13 km one way, about three hours), Pico do Papagaio (980 m) through forest, a stiff, three-hour climb (guide is essential) and Pico da Pedra d'Água (1,031 m).

Paraty → *Phone code: 0xx24. Post code: 23970. Colour map 7, grid B4. Population: 29,544.*

Paraty, 98 km from Angra dos Reis, is one of Brazil's prettiest colonial towns, whose centre has been declared a national historic monument in its entirety. It was the chief port for the export of gold in the 17th century and a coffee-exporting port in the 19th century. At the weekend Paraty buzzes with tourists who browse in the little boutiques and art galleries, or buy souvenirs from the indigenous Guaraní who sell their wares on the cobbles. Many of the numerous little bars and restaurants, like the pousadas, are owned by expat Europeans, who are determined to preserve Paraty's charm. During the week, especially off season, the town is quiet and intimate. Much of the accommodation available is in colonial buildings, some sumptuously decorated, with flourishing gardens or courtyards. The town centre is out of bounds for motor vehicles; heavy chains are strung across the entrance to the streets. In spring the roads are flooded, while the houses are above the water level. **Centro de Informações Turísticas** ① *Av Roberto Silveira, near the entrance to the historical centre, T3371 1266, daily 0900-1600.* More information is available at www.paraty.com.br (Portuguese, English, Spanish), www.pmparaty.rj.gov.br and www.paraty.tur.br (Portuguese).

There are four churches: **Santa Rita** (1722), built by the 'freed coloured men' in elegant Brazilian baroque, faces the bay and the port. It houses an interesting **Museum of Sacred Art** ① *Wed-Sun 0900-1200, 1300-1800, US$1.* **Nossa Senhora do Rosário e São Benedito** (1725, rebuilt 1757) ① *R do Comércio, Tue 0900-1200,* built by black slaves, is small and simple. **Nossa Senhora dos Remédios** (1787-1873)① *Mon, Wed, Fri, Sat 0900-1200, Sun 0900-1500,* is the town's parish church, the biggest in Paraty. **Capela de Nossa Senhora das Dores** (1800) ① *Thu 0900-1200,* is a small chapel facing the sea that was used mainly by the wealthy whites in the 19th century. There is a great deal of distinguished Portuguese colonial architecture in delightful settings. **Rua do Comércio** is the main street in the historical centre. The **Casa da Cadeia**, close to Santa Rita church, is the former jail and is now a public library and art gallery. On the northern headland is a small fort, **Forte do Defensor Perpétuo**, built in 1822.

The town's environs are as beautiful as Paraty itself. Just a few kilometres away lie the forests of the Ponta do Juatinga peninsula, fringed by wonderful beaches, washed by little waterfalls and still home to traditional fishing communities. At **Fazenda Murycana**, an old sugar estate and 17th-century cachaça distillery, you can taste and buy the different types of cachaça. It has an excellent restaurant. Mosquitoes can be a problem, take repellent and don't wear shorts. If short of time, the one must is to take a boat trip round the bay; some of its islands are home to rare animals. Boats also go to wonderful beaches like **Praia da Conçeicao, Praia Vermelha** and **Praia da Lula**, all of which have simple restaurants and are backed by forest and washed by gentle waves. Further south are **Saco da Velha**, protected by an island, and **Paraty Mirim** (17 km, also reached by bus, four a day, three on Sunday). The **Gold Trail**, *www.caminhodoouro.com.br*, hiking on a road dating from the 1800s, can be done on foot or horseback. Many other adventure sports are available (see Activities and tours, page 390).

Trindade

Trindade, 30 km south of Paraty, may not be as beautiful in its own right but its setting, sandwiched between rainforested slopes and emerald sea, is spectacular. It has a long, broad beach and has long been a favourite for surf hippies from São Paulo and Rio who come in droves over Christmas and New Year. It is gradually finding its place on the international backpacker circuit as the campsites, pousadas and restaurants are cheap and cheerful.

Note If travelling along the coast into São Paulo state as far as Guarujá, do not drive or go out alone after dark.

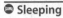 Sleeping

Parque Nacional de Itatiaia *p385*
Basic accommodation in cabins and dormitories is available in Itatiaia village, strung along the road leading to the park.
LL Simon, Km 13 on the road in the park, T3352 1122, www.hotelsimon.com.br. Price is for 3 days, full board. A 1970s concrete block at the top of the park, which marks the trailhead for the higher walks to Agulhas Negras and Três Picos. Wonderful views from fading rooms.
L-AL Hotel Donati, T3352 1110, www.hoteldonati.com.br. Delightful, mock Swiss chalets and rooms, set in tropical gardens visited by animals every night and early morning. A series of trails lead off from the main building and the hotel can organize professional birding guides. Decent restaurant and 2 pools. Highly recommended. Map on web site.
B Hotel Cabanas de Itatiaia, T3352 1252. Magical views from these comfortable but ridiculously Swiss chalets on a hillside. Pool and good restaurant too.
C pp Cabanas da Itatiaia, T3352 1152. Simple chalets in secondary forest in the lower reaches of the park. The sister hotel (Aldeia dos Pássaros) opposite has a pool. Both share facilities and are very helpful. Great breakfasts, good off season rates and a riverside sauna.
C Hotel Alsene, at 2,100 m, 2 km from the side entrance to the park, take a bus to São Lourenço and Caxambu, get off at Registro, walk or hitch from there (12 km). Very popular with climbing and trekking clubs, dormitory or camping, chalets available, hot showers, fireplace, evening meal after everyone returns, drinks but no snacks.
E-F Ipê Amarelo, R João Maurício Macedo Costa 352, Campo Alegre, T/F3352 1232. IYHA.
Camping Camping Clube do Brasil site is entered at Km 148 on the Via Dutra.

Costa Verde: Itacuruçá *p385*
A-B Resort Atlântico, Praia do Axixá, T/F2680 7168, www.divingbrasil.com. Dutch/Brazilian-owned pousada, helpful, good breakfast, English spoken, meals available, diving courses (PADI).

Angra dos Reis *p385*
B Caribe, R de Conceição 255, T3365 0033, F3365 3450. Central. Recommended.
C-E Angra Hostel, Praça da Matriz 152 (at the corner of Rua do Comércio), T3364 4759. Simple hostel (HI) with reasonable breakfast and internet. A block from the quays (just on the other side of the road from the post office) and convenient if you miss a boat.

Ilha Grande *p386*
There are many pousadas in Abraão and reservations are only necessary in peak season or on holiday weekends. Ignore dockside hotel touts who lie about hotel closures and flash pictures of their lodgings to unsuspecting tourists. Numerous eating places serve the usual fish/chicken, beans and rice options.

Abraão
B Ancoradouro, R da Praia 121, T3361 5153, www.ancoradouro.ilhagrande.com. Simple rooms with en suites in a beach front building, 10 mins' walk east of the jetty.
B Farol dos Borbas, Praia do Abraão, T3361 5866, www.ilhagrandetour.com.br. A minute from the jetty. Simple, well-maintained rooms with tiled floors, fan, breakfast tables and chairs. The best rooms have balconies, the worst have no windows. Boat trips organized.
C Estalagem Costa Verde, R Amâncio Felicio de Souza 239a, T3361 5808, www.estalagem costaverde.com.br. In the town ½ a block behind

the church. Bright hostel with light, well-decorated rooms, price rises in high season, rooms for 2, 3 and 4 people, great value.

C Porto Girassol, R do Praia 65, T3361 5277, portogirasol@ilhagrande.com. Simple rooms in a mock-colonial beachhouse 5 mins east of the jetty.

C-D Pousada Cachoeira, Rua do Bicão, T3361 9521, www.cachoeira.com. Lovely little pousada with a dining room palapa and living area, cabins and a terrace of rooms nestled in a forest garden next to a fast-flowing stream. Good breakfasts and boat tours. English and German spoken. **B** in high season.

C-E Aquário Hostel, Praia do Abraão, T3361 5405, www.aquario.ilhagrande.com. Beautifully located on a spit next to the beach and with scruffy rooms and dorms, spacious, airy public areas including a bar, huge sea-water swimming pool and wonderful ocean views.

E pp Albergue Holandés, R Assembléia de Deus, T3361 5034, www.holandeshostel.com.br. Dormitories and four little chalets (**D**) lost in the forest, great atmosphere, be sure to reserve, HI affiliated.

E pp Che Lagarto Ilha Grande, Canto da Praia s/n, Abraão, www.chelagarto.com. Includes breakfast and welcome drink. Basic dorms and doubles (**C**), some with private toilet, a/c and sea view, a loud bar, barbecue area and numerous tours and activities on offer.

Outside of town

LL-L Sítio do Lobo, T2227 4138, www.sitiodolobo.com.br. Access is only by boat. An architect commissioned house converted into a small boutique hotel, sitting on an isolated peninsula. The views are marvellous; the best room are the suites; others overlook the pool. The best food on the island.

AL-A Sankay, T3365 1090, Enseada do Bananal (1 hr by boat from Angra or Abraão), www.pousadasankay.com.br. Another beautiful little pousada perched on a peninsula with wonderful views. 5 rooms from 4 to 6 people, sauna and bar. Price includes boat transfers, breakfast, dinner and a boat trip.

Paraty *p386*
Over 300 hotels and pousadas; in mid-week look around and find a place that suits you best. Browse through www.paraty.com.br/frame.htm for yet more options.

LL Pousada Picinguaba, T12-3836 9105, www.picinguaba.com. Stylish French-owned hotel in a converted convent some 30 km from Paraty; with superior service, an excellent restaurant and simple, elegant (fan-cooled) rooms. Marvellous views out over a bay of islands. Booking ahead essential.

L Bromelias Pousada & Spa, Rodovia Rio-Santos, Km 562, Graúna, T/F3371 2791, www.pousadabromelias.com.br. Asian-inspired with its own aromatherapy products and massage treatments, tastefully decorated chalets in the Atlantic coastal forest. Pool, sauna and restaurant.

L Pousada do Ouro, R Dr Pereira (or da Praia) 145, T/F3371 1311, www.pousadaouro.com.br. Near Paraty's eastern waterfront, once a private home built from a gold fortune, suites in the main building, plainer rooms in an annexe, open-air poolside pavilion in a tropical garden. Has had many famous guests.

L Pousada do Sandi, Largo do Rosário 1, T3371 2100, www.pousadadosandi.com.br. 18th-century building with a grand lobby, comfortable, adjoining restaurant and pool.

L Pousada Pardieiro, R do Comércio 74, T3371 1370, www.pousadapardieiro.com.br. Quiet, with a calm, sophisticated atmosphere, a colonial building with lovely gardens, delightful rooms facing internal patios and a little swimming pool. Always full at weekends, no children under 15.

AL-A Hotel Coxixo, R do Comércio 362, T3371 1460, www.hotelcoxixo.com.br. Converted colonial building in the heart of the town, owned by movie-star Maria Della Costa. The best rooms in the hotel and in Paraty are the upper-floor colonial suites.

AL-A Pousada Mercado do Pouso, Largo de Santa Rita 43, T/F3371 1114, www.mercadode pouso.com.br. Historic building close to waterfront, good sea views, family atmosphere, no pool.

A Le Gite d'Indaitiba, Rodovia Rio-Santos (BR-101) Km 562, Graúna, T3371 7174, www.legitedindaiatiba.com.br. French-owned stylish chalets set in gardens on a hillside. Sweeping views of the bay, and French food to match the location.

A Morro do Forte, R Orlando Carpinelli, T/F3371 1211, www.pousadamorrodoforte.com.br. Out of the centre, lovely garden, good breakfast, pool, German owner Peter Kallert offers trips on his yacht. Recommended.

A Pousada Arte Colonial, R da Matriz 292, T3371 7231, www.paraty.com.br/artecolonial. **B** Sun-Thu, some rooms **AL** in high season. One of the best deals in Paraty: colonial building in the centre decorated with style and a genuine personal touch by its French owner. Helpful, breakfast included. Highly recommended.

B Pousada do Corsário, Beco do Lapeiro 26, T3371 1866, www.pousadadocorsario.com.br. New building with a pool and its own gardens; next to the river and 2 blocks from the centre, simple but stylish rooms, most with hammocks outside. Highly recommended.

B-C Marendaz, R Patitiba 9, T3371 1369, www.paraty.com.br/marendaz/index.asp. Family-run, simple, charming, a block from the historical centre, cheaper with fan, also has rooms for 3-5 people.

C Solar dos Gerânios, Praça da Matriz, T/F33711550, www.paraty.com.br/geranio. Beautiful colonial family house on main square in traditional rustic style, excellent value, English spoken. Warmly recommended.

D Pousada do Careca, Praça Macedo Soares, T3371 1291. Very simple rooms in the historic centre, those without street windows are musty.

D Pousada Miramar, Abel de Oliveira 19, T3371 2898. One room has its own kitchen, good value. Recommended.

D-E Che Lagarto Paraty, R Dr Derly Ellena 9, T3371 1369, www.chelagarto.com. Rates include breakfast and welcome drink. Rooms with private toilet and a/c.

E pp Casa do Rio, R Antônio Vidal 120, T3371 2223, www.paratyhostel.com. Peaceful little hostel with riverside courtyard and hammock, HI discount, kitchen, breakfast included. Offers jeep and horse riding trips. Recommended.

Camping Camping Beira-Rio, just across the bridge, before the road to the fort, T3371 1985.

Camping Club do Brasil, Av Orlando Carpinelli, Praia do Pontal, T3371 1050. Small, good, very crowded in Jan and Feb, US$8 pp. Also at Praia Jabaquara, T3371 7364.

Trindade p387

A-B Garni Cruzeiro do Sul, Rua Principal (first on the right as you enter the village), T3371 5102, www.hotelgarnicruzeirodosul.com.br. Smart little beachside pousada with duplex rooms, most of which have sea views, **AL** at Christmas.

D Pousada Marimbá, R Principal, T3371 5147. Simple colourful rooms and a little breakfast area.

D-F Ponta da Trindade Pousada & Camping, T3371 5113. Simple rooms with fan, sand-floored campsite with cold water showers and no power.

● Eating

Paraty p386

The best restaurants in Paraty are in the historic part of town and are almost as good as any you will find in Rio or São Paulo. Watch out for surreptitious cover charges for live music. The less expensive restaurants, those offering *comida a quilo* (pay by weight) and the fast-food outlets are outside the historical centre, mainly on Av Roberto Silveira. Paraty has some plates unique to the region, like peixe à Parati – local fish cooked with herbs, green bananas and served with *pirão*, a mixture of manioc flour and the sauce that the fish was cooked in.

₩₩₩ Bartolomeu, R Samuel Costa 176, T3371 3052. Argentinian steaks, delicious salads from a chef trained in Rio's Gourmet restaurant. Good atmosphere and cocktails.

₩₩₩ do Hiltinho, R Mcal Deodoro 233, T3371 1432. Decent seafood, including local dishes.

₩₩₩ Merlin O Mago, R do Comércio 376, T3371 2157, www.paraty.com.br/merlin.htm. Franco-Brazilian cooking in an intimate dining room/bar, by a German Cordon Bleu-trained chef and illustrious photojournalist. The best in town.

₩₩₩ Punto Di Vino, R Mcal Deodoro 129, T3371 1348. Wood-fired pizza and calzoni served with live music and a good selection of wine.

₩₩₩ Thai Brasil, R Dona Geralda 345, 3371 0127, www.thaibrasil.com.br. Beautiful restaurant ornamented with handicrafts and hand-painted furniture, the cooking loosely resembles Thai, without spices.

₩₩ Café Paraty, R da Lapa and Comércio. Sandwiches, appetizers, light meals, also bar with live music nightly (cover charge), a local landmark. Open 0900-2400.

₩₩ Dona Ondina, R do Comércio 2, by the river. Family restaurant with well-prepared simple food (closed on Mon, Mar and Nov), good value.

₩ Sabor da Terra, Av Roberto Silveira, next to Banco do Brasil. Reliable, if not bargain-priced, self service food, closes 2200.

🎵 Bars and clubs

Paraty *p386*

Bar Coupé, Praça Matriz. A popular hang-out with outside seating, good bar snacks and breakfast.
Bar Dinho, Praça da Matriz at R da Matriz. Good bar with live music at weekends, sometimes mid-week.
Grupo Contadores, The Puppet Show, R Dona Geralda 327, T3371 1575, ecparaty@ax.apc.org. Wed, Sat 2100, US$12: a silent puppet theatre for adults only which has toured throughout the USA and Europe. Not to be missed.
Umoya, R Comendador José Luiz. Video bar and café, live music at weekends.

⊛ Festivals and events

Paraty *p386*

Feb/Mar: Carnival, hundreds of people cover their bodies in black mud and run through the streets yelling like prehistoric creatures (anyone can join in). **Mar/Apr**: Semana Santa, with religious processions and folk songs. **Mid-Jul**: Semana de Santa Rita, traditional foods, shows, exhibitions and dances. **Aug**: Festival da Pinga, the cachaça fair at which local distilleries display their products and there are plenty of opportunities to over-indulge. **Sep** (around the 8th): Semana da Nossa Senhora dos Remédios, processions and religious events. **Sep/Oct**: Spring Festival of Music, concerts in front of Santa Rita church. The city is decorated with lights for Christmas. **31 Dec**: New ar's, a huge party with open-air concerts and fireworks (reserve accommodation in advance). As well as the Dança dos Velhos (see Music and dance, page 1514), another common dance in these parts is the ciranda, in which everyone, young and old, dances in a circle to songs accompanied by guitars.

The Festa Literária Internacional de Parati (FLIP, www.flip.org.br) occurs every northern summer and is one of the most important literary events in Latin America. It is always attended by big name writers.

🔺 Activities and tours

Parque Nacional de Itatiaia *p385*

Information on treks can be obtained from **Clube Excursionista Brasileira**, Av Almirante Barroso 2, 8th floor, Rio de Janeiro, T0xx21-2220 3695.
Wildlife guides Edson Endrigo, T3742 8374, www.avesfoto.com.br. Birding trips in Itatiaia and throughout Brazil. English spoken. Ralph Salgueiro, T3351 1823, www.ecoralph.com.

Angra dos Reis *p385*

Boat trips Trips around the bay are available, some with a stop for lunch on the island of Gipóia (5 hrs). Several boats run tours from the Cais de Santa Luzia and there are agencies for saveiros in town, boats depart between 1030-1130 daily, US$10-12 (during Jan and Feb best to reserve in advance).
Diving Aquamaster, Praia da Enseada, T3365 2416. US$60 for 2 dives with drinks and food, take a 'Retiro' bus from the port in Angra.

Ilha Grande *p386*

Boat trips US$13 without food or drinks, but include fruit. Ask about trips to good scuba diving sites around the coast.
Cycling Bikes can be hired and tours arranged; ask at pousadas.

Paraty *p386*

Antígona, Praça da Bandeira 2, Centro Histórico, T/F3371 2199. Daily schooner tours, 5 hrs, bar and lunch on board. Recommended.
Fausto Goyos, T9914 5506. Offers off-road tours in an ex-US military jeep to rainforest, waterfalls, historical sites, also photo safaris. He also has highly professional horse riding tours and offers lodging in youth-hostel style rooms, with or without meals.
Paraty Tours, Av Roberto Silveira 11, T/F3371 1327, www.paratytours.com.br. English and Spanish spoken.
Soberana da Costa, R Dona Geraldo 43, in Pousada Mercado do Pouso, T/F3371 1114. Also offers schooner trips in the bay. Recommended.

⊖ Transport

Parque Nacional de Itatiaia *p385*

Bus Itatiaia lies just off the main São Paulo-Rio motorway. There are connections to Itatiaia town or nearby Resende from both **Rio** and **São Paulo**. There is only 1 way into the park from Itatiaia town and 1 main road within it – which forks off to the various hotels, all of which are signposted. Four times a day (variable hours), a bus marked '504 Circular' leaves Itatiaia town for to the Park, calling at the hotels and stopping at the Simon. Coming from Resende this may be caught at the crossroads before Itatiaia. Through tickets to São Paulo are sold at a booth in the large bar in the middle of Itatiaia main street.

Costa Verde: Mangaratiba *p385*

Bus From Rio Rodoviária with **Costa Verde**, several daily, US$8.25.

Angra dos Reis *p385*

Bus To **Angra** at least hourly from Rio's rodoviária with **Costa Verde**, several direct, accepts credit cards, comfortable buses take the 'via litoral', sit on the left, US$12, 2½ hrs. From Angra to **São Paulo**, 5 buses daily (3 on Sat), US$24. To **Paraty**, many buses leave from bus station or just flag the bus down at bus stops on the highway, US$6.

Ilha Grande *p386*

Ferry Barcas SA, T21-4004 3113, www.barcas-sa.com.br: **Angra**-Abraão Mon-Fri 1530, Sat-Sun 1330. Abraão-Angra: daily 1000. **Magaratiba**-Abraão daily 0800 and Fri 2200; Abraão-Mangaratiba daily 1730. US$3 during the week, US$7.50 at weekends. **Barcas SA** boats leave Mon-Fri at 1530 from Angra for Abraão, US$3, 1330 at weekends, US$7.50, returning at 1000. 1 hr 20 mins to both destinations. Direct service to Rio with Eterno Beira Mar, T9955 9174/3361 9533, eternobeiramar@ zipmail.com.br, or ask for Alexandra (T8196 9895 mob) at the ferry dock on Ilha Grande at 0930. Eterno Beira Mar sails at 1000 to Mangaratiba, where a minivan or taxi will take you to Rio (hotel, bus station, airport, wherever); also does the journey in reverse, US$20. There are also frequent impromptu fishing boat trips on demand between Angra and Abraão, usually before lunchtime only and most frequently in summer months. Around US$6.50.

Paraty *p386*

Bus To **Fazenda Murycana** take a Penha/Ponte Branca bus from the rodoviária, 4 a day; alight where it crosses a small white bridge and then walk 10 mins along a signed, unpaved road.

Rodoviária at the corner of R Jango Padua and R da Floresta. 9 buses a day go to **Rio** (241 km), 4½ hrs, US$19, **Costa Verde** – see under Angra dos Reis for details; to Angra dos Reis (98 km, 1½ hrs, every 1 hr 40 mins, US$7.50, also **Colitur**). 3 a day to **Ubatuba** (75 km, just over 1 hr, Colitur, US$7.50). To **São Paulo**, 4 a day (304 km via São José dos Campos, 5½ hrs, US$15, **Reunidas**, booked up quickly, very busy at weekends). To **São Sebastião**, 2 a day with **Normandy** (who also go to Rio twice a day). On holidays and in high season, the frequency of bus services usually increases.

⊙ Directory

Ilha Grande *p386*

No **banks** or money changing on the island. **Internet** Several places in Abraão.

Paraty *p386*

Banks Banco do Brasil, Av Roberto Silveira, not too far from the bus station, exchange 1000-1500, long queues and commission. 2 ATMs in town for Visa and MasterCard, 0600-2200. **Internet** Many places but connection is not cheap. **Post offices** R Mcal Deodoro e Domingos Gonçalves de Abreu, 0800-1700, Sun 0800-1200. **Telephones** Telerj for international calls, Praça Macedo Soares, opposite the tourist office. Local and long distance calls can be made from public phones.

São Paulo → *Phone code: 0xx11. Colour map 7, grid B4.*

The city of São Paulo is vast and can feel intimidating at first. But this is a city of separate neighbourhoods, only a few of which are interesting for visitors and, once you have your base, it is easy to negotiate. Those who don't flinch from the city's size and who are prepared to spend money and time here, and who get to know Paulistanos, are seldom disappointed. (The inhabitants of the city are called Paulistanos, to differentiate them from the inhabitants of the state, who are called Paulistas.) Nowhere in Brazil is better for concerts, clubs, theatre, ballet, classical music, all round nightlife, restaurants and beautifully designed hotels.

Ins and outs

Getting there There are air services from all parts of Brazil, Europe, North and South America to the international **airport** at Guarulhos, also known as Cumbica, Avenida Monteiro Lobato 1985, T6445 2945 (30 km from the city). Varig has its own terminal for international flights, adjoining the old terminal which all other airlines use. The local airport of Congonhas, 14 km from the city centre on Avenida Washington Luiz, is used for the Rio-São Paulo shuttle, some flights to Belo Horizonte and Vitória and private flights only, T5090 9000. The **main rodoviária** is Tietê (T3235 0322), which is very convenient and has its own Metrô station. There are three other bus stations for inter-state bus services. ▶▶ *For more detailed information, see Transport, page 404.*

São Paulo

Related maps
A *São Paulo centre,*
page 394
B *Jardins & Avenida*
Paulista, page 397

Av Mq de São Vicente

Estação
Barra
Barra
Funda
Funda
Av Mario

Matarazzo

Cerro Cora

Av Pedroso de Morales

Av Sumaré

Vila
Madalena

VILA MADALENA

Sumaré

Av Paulo VI
Av Dr Arnaldo

Clínicas

Av das Nações

Fradique Coutinho

Luís Murat

Henrique Schaumann

Av Reboucas

JARDINS

Museu de Arte
Contemporâneo
(MAC)

Prof Melo Morales

Rio Pinheiros

Av das Nações Unidas

Av Frederico Herman Jr

Pedroso de Morais

Av das Nações

Museu de
Arqueologia
e Etnologia

Av da
Universidade

Casa do
Bandeirante

Av Marginal do Rio Pinheiros

PINHEIROS

dos Pinheiros

Av Reboucas

Av Brasil

CIDADE
UNIVERSITARIA

Av Afranio
Peixoto

Instituto
Butantan

Alvarenga

Av Vital Brasil

Av Brig Faria Lima

Av Eusabio
Matoso

Av Colombia

Groenlândia

Av 9 de Julho

Marques

SP-270

Av Francisco Morato

Av Lineu de P Machado

Av Magalhães de Castro

Av das Nações Unidas

Iguatemi
Shopping
Centre

Casa
Brasileira

Av Cidade Jardim

Butantã
Shopping
Centre

Jóquei
Clube

Av dos Tajuras

R Eng O Americano

MORUMBI

Gronchi

ITAIM

VILA

Giovanni

Palácio dos
Bandeirantes

Morumbi
Stadium

Alvorada

Cotavia

Museu da Fundaçao Maria
Luisa e Oscar Americano

Av Morumbi

Av Magalhães de Castro

Luis Carlos Bernini

NEW BUSINESS
DISTRICT

Ibirapuera
Shopping Centre

Av Jose Diniz

N

0 metres   500

0 yards   500

BROOKLIN

To Morumbi Cemetery
& Burle Marx Park

To Morumbi Shopping Centre

Getting around and orientation Much of the centre is pedestrianized, so walking is the only option if you wish to explore it. The best and cheapest way to get around São Paulo is on the Metrô system, which is clean, safe, cheap and efficient, though rather limited. Bus routes can be confusing and slow due to frequent traffic jams, but buses are safe, clean and only crowded at peak hours. All the rodoviárias (bus stations) are on the Metrô, but if travelling with luggage, take a taxi. The **Old Centre** (Praça da República, Sé, Santa Cecília) is a place to visit but not to stay. The central commercial district, containing banks, offices and shops, is known as the Triângulo, bounded by Ruas Direita, 15 (Quinze) de Novembro, São Bento and Praça Antônio Prado, but it is rapidly spreading towards the Praça da República. **Jardins**, the city's most affluent inner neighbourhood, is a good place to stay and to visit, especially if you want to shop and eat well. Elegant little streets hide hundreds of wonderful restaurants and accommodation ranges from the luxurious to the top end of the budget range. You are safe here at night. The northeastern section of Jardins, known as **Cerqueira César**, abuts one of São Paulo's grandest modern avenues, **Paulista**, lined with skyscrapers, shops and a few churches and museums including MASP (Museu de Arte de São Paulo). There are metro connections from here and a number of good hotels. **Ibirapuera Park and around**: the inner city's largest green space is home to a handful of museums, running tracks, a lake and frequent free live concerts on Sun. The adjoining neighbourhoods of Moema and Vila Mariana have a few hotels, but **Moema, Itaim** and **Vila Olimpia** are among the nightlife centres of São Paulo with a wealth of streetside bars, designer restaurants and European-style dance clubs. Hotels tend to be expensive as they are near the new business centre on Avenidas Brigadeiro Faria Lima and Luis Carlos Berrini. **Pinheiros and Vila Madalena** are less chic, but equally lively at night and with the funkiest shops.

São Paulo centre

Sleeping	Itamarati 7	Eating
Banri 1	Othon Palace 9	Boi na Brasa 2
Gran Corona 5	Plaza 2	Gombe 1

Beware of assaults and pickpocketing in São Paulo. Thieves often use the mustard-on-the-back trick to distract you while someone else robs you. The areas around Luz station, Praça da República and Centro are not safe at night, and do not enter favelas.

Tourist offices There are tourist information booths with English speaking staff in domestic and international arrivals (ground floor) at Guarulhos airport (Cumbica); and tourist booths in the Tietê bus station and in the following locations throughout the city: **Praça da República** ① *T3231 2922, daily 0900-1800*, very helpful; **Olido** ① *Av São João 473, daily 0900-1800*; **Avenida Paulista at Parque Trianon** ① *daily 0900-1800*; on **Avenida Brig Faria Lima** ① *opposite the Iguatemi Shopping Center, T3031 1277, closed temporarily 2007*; and in **Parque Ibirapuera** ① *gate 10, open weekends and holidays 0900-1800*. An excellent map is available free at all these offices, as well as free maps and pamphlets in English. Visit www.cidadedesaopaulo.com (Portuguese, English and Spanish), also www.guiasp.com.br for what's on and where to go. Editora Abril also publish maps and an excellent guide, *Sampa* (Portuguese).

National parks Ibama ① *Alameda Tietê 637, Jardim Cerqueira César, T3066 2633, analice.pereira@ibama.gov.br*.

Climate São Paulo sits on a plateau at around 800 m and the weather is temperamental. Rainfall is ample and temperatures fluctuate greatly: summer 20-30° C (occasionally peaking into the high 30s or 40s), winter 15-25° C (occasionally dropping to below 10° C). The winter months (April-October) are also the driest, with minimal precipitation in June/July. Christmas and New Year are wet. When there are thermal inversions, air pollution can be troublesome.

Background

Until the 1870s São Paulo was a sleepy, shabby little town known as 'a cidade de barro' (the mud city), as most of its buildings were made of clay and packed mud. The city was transformed at the end of the 19th century when wealthy landowners and the merchants of Santos began to invest. Between 1885 and the end of the century the boom in coffee and the arrival of large numbers of Europeans transformed the state out of all recognition. By the end of the 1930s São Paulo state had one million Italians, 500,000 each of Portuguese and immigrants from the rest of Brazil, nearly 400,000 Spaniards and nearly 200,000 Japanese. It is the world's largest Japanese community outside Japan. In the early 20th century, numbers of Syrian-Lebanese came to São Paulo. Nowadays, it covers more than 1,500 sq km – three times the size of Paris.

Old Centre

A focal point of the centre is the **Parque Anhangabaú**, an open space between the Triângulo and the streets which lead to Praça da República (Metrô Anhangabaú is at its southern end). Beneath Anhangabaú, north-south traffic is carried by a tunnel. Crossing it are two viaducts: **Viaduto do Chá**, which is open to traffic and links Rua Direita and Rua Barão de Itapetininga. Along

To Luz, Pinacoteca Museum & Tietê

São Bento

Largo São Bento
São Bento

Martinelli Building

Edifício Banespa

Praça António Prado

Parque Dom Pedro II

Pateo do Colégio & Museu Casa de Anchieta

Solar da Marquesa de Santos

Peixoto

José Bonifácio

V Bras

Praça da Sé

Teresa

Praça Clovis Bevilaqua

Sé

Catedral Metropolitana

Ordem Terceira do Carmo

Praça Dr João Mendes

R Tabatinguera

To Liberdade & ❶❶❸

Sushi Yassu **3**   Historic buildings walk - - ◆ - -
Terraço Italia **5**

its length sellers of potions, cures, fortunes and trinkets set up their booths. The **Viaduto Santa Ifigênia**, an iron bridge for pedestrians only, connects Largo de São Bento with Largo de Santa Ifigênia.

On **Largo de São Bento** is the **Igreja e Mosteiro de São Bento** ① *T3328 8799, www.mosteiro.org.br, which details services, including with Gregorian chant*, an early 20th-century building (1910-22) on the site of a 1598 chapel. Due south of São Bento is the **Martinelli building**① *on R Líbero Badaró at Av São João, closed*, the city's first skyscraper. On Praça Antônio Prado stands the **Edifício Banespa** ① *R João Brícola 24, T3249 7180, Mon-Fri 1000-1700, US$4*, with 360° views from the top, up to 40 km, smog permitting. The **Pateo do Collégio (Museu de Anchieta)** ① *Praça Pátio do Colégio, T3105 6899, www.pateodocollegio.com.br, Metrô Sé, with café, Tue-Sun 0900-1700, US$3*. The newly renovated building is an exact replica of the original Jesuit church and college but dates from 1950s. Most of the buildings are occupied by the Museu de Anchieta, named after the Jesuit captain who led the first mission. This houses, amongst other items a 17th-century font used to baptize indigenous people and a collection of Guaraní art and artefacts from the colonial era and a modernist painting of the priest, by Italian Albino Menghini.

A short distance southeast of the Pateo do Collégio is the **Solar da Marquesa de Santos**, an 18th-century residential building, which now contains the **Museu da Cidade** ① *R Roberto Simonsen 136, T3241 4238, Tue-Sun, 0900-1700*. The **Praça da Sé** is a huge open area south of the Pateo do Collégio, dominated by the **Catedral Metropolitana**① *T3107 6832, Mon-Sat 0800-1700, Sun 0800-1830*, a massive, peaceful space. The cathedral's foundations were laid over 40 years before its inauguration during the 1954 festivities commemorating the fourth centenary of the city. It was fully completed in 1970. This enormous building in neo-Gothic style has a capacity for 8,000 worshippers in its five naves. The interior is mostly unadorned, except for the two gilt mosaic pictures in the transepts: on the north side is the Virgin Mary and on the south Saint Paul.

West of the Praça da Sé, along Rua Benjamin Constant, is the Largo de São Francisco. Here is the **Igreja da Ordem Terceira de São Francisco** ① *T3105 6899, 0730-2000*. The convent was inaugurated in 1647 and reformed in 1744. To the right is the Igreja das Chagas do Seráphico Pai São Francisco (1787), painted like its neighbour in blue and gold. Across the Viaduto do Chá is the **Teatro Municipal** ① *T3223 3022*, one of the few distinguished early 20th-century survivors that São Paulo can boast. Viewing the interior may only be possible during a performance; as well as the full evening performances, look out for midday, string quartet and 'vesperais líricas' concerts.

Praça da República

In Praça da República the trees are tall and shady. There are also lots of police. Near the Praça is the city's tallest building, the **Edifício Itália**① *Av Ipiranga 344, T2189 2929, US$5*. There is a restaurant on top and a sightseeing balcony. If you walk up Avenida São Luís, which has many airline offices and travel agencies (especially in the Galeria Metrópole), you come to Praça Dom José Gaspar, in which is the **Biblioteca Municipal Mário de Andrade**, surrounded by a pleasant shady garden.

North of the centre

About 10 minutes' walk from the centre is the old **Mercado Municipal**① *R Cantareira 306, www.mercadomunicipal.com.br, Mon-Sat 0700-1800, Sun 0700-1300*, covering 27,000 sq m. **Parque da Luz** on Avenida Tiradentes (110,000 sq m) was formerly a botanical garden. It is next to the Luz railway station. There are two museums near the park: the **Museu de Arte Sacra** ① *Av Tiradentes 676, T3326 3336, http://artesacra.sarasa.com.br, Tue-Fri 1100-1800, Sat-Sun 1000-1900, US$2*, is modern and tasteful, housed in the serene **Igreja e Convento Nossa Senhora da Luz** (1774), still partially occupied. It has a priceless, beautifully presented collection including works by Aleijadinho, Benedito Calixto, Mestre Athayde and Francisco Xavier de Brito. The convent is one of the few colonial buildings left in São Paulo; the chapel dates from 1579. The **Pinacoteca do Estado** (State Art Collection)① *Av Tiradentes 141, T3229 9844, Tue-Sun 1000-1800, US$3* and its neighbouring sister gallery, the **Estação Pinacoteca** ① *Largo General Osório 66, T3337 0185, daily 1000-1730, US$2, Sat free*, preserve the best collection of modernist Brazilian art outside the Belas Artes in Rio, together with important works by Europeans like Picasso and Chagall. Both have good cafés, the Pinacoteca has a very good art bookshop.

Liberdade

Directly south of the Praça da Sé, and one stop on the Metrô, is Liberdade, the central Japanese district, now also home to large numbers of Koreans and Chinese. The Metrô station is in Praça da Liberdade, in which there is an oriental market every Sunday (see Shopping). The Praça is one of the best places in the city for Japanese food. **Museu da Imigração Japonesa** ① *R São Joaquim 381, 3rd floor, T3209 5465, www.nihonsite.com.br/muse, Tue-Sun 1330-1730, US$2.50*, is excellent, with a roof garden; ask at the desk for an English translation of exhibits.

West of the Old Centre

Jardins and Avenida Paulista

Either Metrô station Vergueiro or Paraíso is convenient for the southeastern end of Avenida Paulista, the highlight of which is **MASP**. This is the common name for The **Museu de Arte de São Paulo** ① *Av Paulista 1578 (above the 9 de Julho tunnel); T3251 5644, http://masp.uol.com.br, the nearest Metrô is Trianon-MASP; bus 805A from Praça da*

Jardins & Avenida Paulista

0 metres (approx)	500
0 yards (approx)	500

Sleeping
Brigadeiro **7** C3
Dona Ziláh **9** A2
Emiliano **1** B2
Fasano **2** B2
Formule 1 **3** C3
George V **4** B2
Golden Tulip Park Plaza **5** C3
Ibis São Paulo Paulista **6** A3
Landmark Residence **12** B2
Paulista Garden **8** C2
Pousada dos Franceses **10** C3
Renaissance **11** B3
Transamérica Ópera **13** B2
Unique **14** C2

Eating
A Mineira **1** C3
Baalbeck **2** B2
Café Antique **3** B2
Camelo **4** C2
Charlô Bistro **6** B2
Cheiro Verde **5** B2
DOM **7** B2
Figueira Rubaiyat **17** B1
Fran's Café **8** B2,C3
Gero **9** B2
Jun Sakamoto **10** A1
Kayomix **11** A2
La Tambouille **12** C1
Laurent **13** B2
MASP **16** B3
Massimo **14** B3
Nâmesa **15** A2
Sattva **18** A2
Sujinho **19** A3
Tâmara Café **20** B3

Bars & clubs
Apollinari **21** A2
Balcão **22** A2
Finnegan's Pub **23** A1

República goes by MASP, Mon 1400-1900, Tue and Thu 0900-2200, Wed, Fri, Sat, Sun 0900-1900, US$7.50, Mon free to 1800. The museum has the finest collection of European masters in the southern hemisphere with works by artists like Raphael, Bellini, Bosch, Rembrandt, Turner, Constable, Monet, Manet and Renoir. Also some interesting work by Brazilian artists, including Portinari. Temporary exhibitions are also held and when a popular show is on, it can take up to an hour to get in. There is a very good art shop.

Opposite MASP is **Parque Tenente Siqueira Campos** ① *daily 0700-1830*, which covers two blocks on either side of Alameda Santos; a bridge links the two parts of the park. It is a welcome green area in the busiest part of the city. The **Museu da Imagem e do Som** (MIS) ① *Av Europa 158, T3085 1498, www.mis.sp.gov.br, Tue-Sun 1000-1800*, has photographic exhibitions, archives of Brazilian cinema and music, and a nice café. Next to MIS is the **Museu Brasiliero da Escultura** (MuBE); free to temporary exhibitions and recitals in the afternoons. Av Europa continues to Av Brigadeiro Faria Lima, on which is the **Casa Brasileira** ① *Av Faria Lima 2705, T3032 3727, www.mcb.sp.gov.br, Tue-Sun 1000-1800, US$2*, a museum of Brazilian furniture. It also holds temporary exhibitions.

Cidade Universitária and Morumbi

The Cidade Universitária is on the west bank of the Rio Pinheiros, opposite the district of Pinheiros. The campus also contains the famous **Instituto Butantan** (Butantan Snake Farm and Museum) ① *Av Dr Vital Brasil 1500, T3726 7222, www.butantan.gov.br, Tue-Sun 0900-1630, US$2.50, getting there: from Praça da República take bus marked 'Butantan' or 'Cidade Universitária' (Nos 701U or 792U) along Av Paulista, and ask to be let out at Instituto Butantan*. The snakes are milked for their poison six times a day. It also deals with spider and scorpion venom, has a small hospital and is a biomedical research institute. Visitors see the museum of poisonous animals and public health, with explanations in Portuguese and English. The **Museu de Arte Contemporâneo** (MAC) ① *T3091 3538, www.mac.usp.br, Tue-Sun 1000-1900, free*, with an important collection of Brazilian and European modern art, is in the Prédio Novo da Reitoria. Also the **Museu de Arqueologia e Etnologia** (MAE) ① *R Reitoria 1466, T3091 4905*, with Amazonian and ancient Mediterranean collections. Not far from the Butantã Institute, just inside Cidade Universitária, is the **Casa do Bandeirante** ① *Praça Monteiro Lobato, T3031 0920*, the reconstructed home of a 17th-century pioneer.

On the west bank of the Rio Pinheiros, just southeast of the Cidade Universitária, is the palatial **Jóquei Clube/Jockey Club** ① *Av Lineu de Paula Machado 1263, T2161 8300, www.jockeysp.com.br*, racecourse in the Cidade Jardim area. Take Butantã bus from República. Race meetings are held Monday and Thursday at 1930 and weekends at 1430. It has a **Museu do Turfe** ① *Tue-Sun, closed Sat-Sun mornings*.

Morumbi is a smart residential district due south of the Cidade Universitária. In the area are the state government building, **Palácio dos Bandeirantes** ① *Av Morumbi 4500*, the small, simple **Capela de Morumbi** ① *Av Morumbi 5387*, and the Morumbi stadium of São Paulo Football Club, which holds 100,000 people. Motor racing fans might like to visit the Morumbi cemetery, last resting place of Ayrton Senna; take 6291 bus to Rua Profesor Benedito Montenegro.

Museu da Fundação Maria Luisa e Oscar Americano ① *Av Morumbi 3700, Morumbi, T3742 0077, Tue-Fri 1100-1700, Sat-Sun 1000-1700, US$4*, is a private collection of Brazilian and Portuguese art and furniture. The garden has fascinating paths, patios and plants. It is close to the Palácio dos Bandeirantes.

Burle Marx Park ① *Av Dona Helena Pereira de Moraes 200, Morumbi, daily 0700-1900*. Designed by famous landscape designer Burle Marx, it has trails leading through the Mata Atlântica (Atlantic rainforest).

South of the Old Centre

Ibirapuera

The **Parque do Ibirapuera** ① *entrance on Av Pedro Álvares Cabral, daily 0600-1730*, was designed by Oscar Niemeyer and landscape artist Roberto Burle Marx for the city's fourth centenary in 1954. Within its 1.6 million sq m is the **Assembléia Legislativa** and a **planetarium** ① *T5575 5206, shows Sat, Sun at 1500, Thu at 1930, US$5*. After many years of refurbishment it now has state-of-the-art fittings. Buy tickets 30 minutes before the show. Also in the park is the

Museu de Arte Moderna (MAM) ① T5085 1300, www.mam.org.br, Tue-Sun 1000-1800, US$2.75, students half price, free Sun, with art exhibitions and sculpture garden (see Nuno Ramos' Craca – Barnacle). It has a great café restaurant and art shop. **Museu Afro-Brasileiro** ① T5579 0593, Wed-Sun 1000-1800, free: temporary exhibitions, theatre, dance and cinema spaces, photographs and panels devoted to exploring African Brazil. **Pavilhão Japonês** ① T3573 6543, Sat, Sun 1000-1700, free except for exhibitions, exhibition space showing works from Japanese and Japanese-Brazilian artists, designed by Japanese and built exclusively with materials from Japan. It is set in Japanese gardens and has a traditional tea house upstairs. Bicycles can be hired in the par, US$3 per hour. Buses to Ibirapuera, 574R from Paraíso Metrô station; 6364 from Praça da Bandeira; to Cidade Universitária 702U or 7181 from Praça da República. Every even-numbered year the **Bienal Internacional de São Paulo** (São Paulo Biennial) at Ibirapuera has the most important show of modern art in Latin America, usually in September (next in 2008).

Parque da Independência

In the suburb of Ipiranga, 5½ km southeast of the city centre, the Parque da Independência contains the **Monumento à Independência**. Beneath the monument is the Imperial Chapel ① Tue-Sun 1300-1700, with the tomb of the first emperor, Dom Pedro I, and Empress Leopoldina **Casa do Grito** ① Tue-Sun 0930-1700, the little house in which Dom Pedro I spent the night before his famous cry of Ipiranga – 'Independence or Death' – is preserved in the park. The **Museu Paulista** ① T6165 8000, Tue-Sun 0900-1645, US$1, contains old maps, traditional furniture, collections of old coins and of religious art and rare documents, and a department of indígena ethnology. Behind the Museum is the **Horto Botânico/Ipiranga Botanical Garden** and the **Jardim Francês** ① Tue-Sun 0900-1700, getting there: take bus 478-P (Ipiranga-Pompéia for return) from Ana Rosa, or take bus 4612 from Praça da República.

Parque do Estado (Jardim Botânico)

This large park, a long way south of the centre, at **Água Funda** ① Av Miguel Estefano 3031-3687, T5573 6300, Wed-Sun 0900-1700, getting there: take Metrô to São Judas on the Jabaquara line, then take a bus, contains the Jardim Botânico, with lakes and trees and places for picnics, and a very fine orchid farm worth seeing during November-December (orchid exhibitions in April and November).

Excursions

In Tremembé, a little beyond Cantareira, 30 minutes north of downtown, is the **Horto Florestal** ① R do Horto 931, in Parque Estadual Alberto Löfgren, T6231 8555, www.hortoflorestal.com.br, daily 0600-1800, which contains examples of nearly every species of Brazilian woodland flora, 15 km of natural trails, a museum, a view of São Paulo from Pedra Grande on the right of the entrance to the park. **Embu** (M'Boy – Big Snake), 28 km from São Paulo, is a colonial town which has become a centre for artists and craftsmen. The town itself, on a hill, is surrounded by industry and modern developments and the colonial centre is quite small. Many of the old houses are painted in bright colours and most contain arts, furniture, souvenir or antiques shops. On Sunday afternoons there is a large and popular arts and crafts fair (0900-1800). On Monday almost everything is closed. In the Largo dos Jesuítas is the church of **Nossa Senhora do Rosário** (1690) and the **Museu de Arte Sacra** ① Tue-Fri 1300-1700, Sat-Sun 1000-1700.

◉ Sleeping

For both business and leisure, São Paulo has by far the best hotels in Brazil. The best area to stay is northeastern Jardins (also known as Cerqueria César), which is safe and well connected to the Metrô via Av Paulista. There are cheapies in the centre, but this is an undesirable area at night.

Old Centre p395, map p394
AL Othon Palace, R Líbero Badaró 190, T3291 5000, www.othon.com.br. The only business hotel of quality in the Triângulo; in a 1950s heritage building.
A Gran Corona, Basílio da Gama 101, T3214 0043, www.grancorona.com.br. In a small street. Comfortable, good services, good restaurant. Warmly recommended.

B-D Itamarati, Av Dr Vieira de Carvalho 150, T222 4133, www.hotelitamarati.com.br. Good location, safe, cheaper at weekends. Highly recommended and very popular.
D Plaza, Av São João 407, T3222 1355, reserva@plazahotel.tur.br. Budget option on this busy avenue, quieter rooms at back, breakfast included. Several other hotels on Av São João.

Liberdade *p397*
B Banri, R Galvão Bueno 209, T3207 8877. Good, Chinese owners, near the Metrô station. Recommended.

Jardins, Avenida Paulista and around
p397, map p397
LL Emiliano, R Oscar Freire 384, T3069 4369, www.emiliano.com.br. Bright and beautifully designed, attention to every detail and the best suites in the city. No pool but a relaxing small spa. Excellent Italian restaurant, location and service.
LL Fasano, R Vittorio Fasano 88, T3896 4077, www.fasano.com.br. One of the world's great hotels with decor like a modernist gentleman's club designed by Armani, a fabulous pool and the best formal haute cuisine restaurant in Brazil. Excellently positioned in Jardins.
LL Renaissance, Al Santos 2233 (at Haddock Lobo), T3069 2233, http://marriott.com/. The best business hotel off Av Paulista with standard business rooms, a good spa, gym, pool and 2 squash courts.
LL Unique, Av Brigadeiro Luis Antônio 4700, Jardim Paulista, T3055 4700, www.hotel unique.com. The most ostentatious hotel in the country, an enormous half moon on concrete uprights with curving floors, circular windows and beautiful use of space and light. The bar on the top floor is São Paulo's answer to the LA Sky Bar and is always filled with the rich and famous after 2130.
LL-AL George V, R José Maria Lisboa 1000, T3088 9822, www.george-v.com.br. Apartments with living rooms, fully equipped kitchens, huge bathrooms and comprehensive business services. Shared facilities include sauna, indoor pool and gym. Special deals through the web site.
AL Golden Tulip Park Plaza, Al Lorena 360, T3058 4055, www.parkplaza.com.br. Modern tower with apartments, spa and well-equipped modern gym. Good value.
AL Transamérica Ópera, Al Lorena 1748, T3062 2666, www.transamericaflats.com.br. Prices go up to L. Conservatively decorated but elegant and well-maintained modern flats between the heart of Jardins and Av Paulista.

A The Landmark Residence, Al Jaú 1607, T3082 8677, www.landmarkresidence.com.br. Spacious apartments, shared gym, gardens and modest business centre. Good location.
A-B Dona Ziláh, Av França 1621, Jardim Paulista, T3062 1444, www.zilah.com. Little pousada in a renovated colonial house, well maintained, decorated with a personal touch. Excellent location, bike rental and generous breakfast included.
A-B Ibis São Paulo Paulista, Av Paulista 2355, T3523 3000, www.accorhotels.com.br. Great value, modern business standard rooms with a/c, right on Paulista, cheaper at weekends.
B Formule 1, R Vergueiro 1571, T5085 5699, www.accorhotels.com.br. Another great value business-style hotel, apartments big enough for 3 make this an E option for those in a group. Right next to Paraíso Metro in a safe area, a/c.
B Paulista Garden, Al Lorena 21, T/F3885 8498, www.paulistagardenhotel.com.br. Small, simple rooms with a/c, cable TV and fridge, close to Ibirapuera Park.
C Pousada dos Franceses, R dos Franceses 100, Bela Vista, T3288 1592, www.pousadados franceses.com.br. Plain little pousada 10 mins' walk from Brigadeiro Metrô, with dorms, doubles and singles, free internet, TV room, breakfast included.
D Brigadeiro, Av Brig Luís Antonio 2564, T3288 3252, www.hotelbrigadeiro.com.br. Comfortable small rooms, TV, buffet breakfast, helpful.

South of the Old Centre *p398*
The area known as the New Centre, around **Av Brigadeiro Faria Lima** and **Av Luis Carlos Berrini**, has no sights of interest for the tourist, however it has the plushest, most expensive hotels.
LL Hyatt São Paulo, Av das Nações Unidas 13301, T6838 1234, http://Sãopaulo.hyatt.com. A superb business hotel, with spa, pool, state of the art business centre and marvellous views from the upper floor suites.
L-AL Blue Tree Towers, Av Brigadeiro Faria Lima 3989, Vila Olímpia, T3896 7544, www.bluetree.com.br. Modern business hotel with excellent service, ideally positioned for Faria Lima, Vila Olímpia and Itaim, pool, massage, gym, sauna and business centre.
C ACE Hostel, R Gastão da Cunha 253, Congonhas Airport, T2248 0534, www.bed andbreakfast.com.br. Pocket-sized hostel in a brightly painted house near Congonhas. Services include TV, DVD and movies, broadband, kitchen, laundry, book exchange and pick-up. Tours of São Paulo available.

● *For an explanation of the sleeping and eating price codes used in this guide, see page 58.*
● *Other relevant information is found in Essentials pages 345-347.*

D-E pp **Praça da Árvore**, R Pageú 266, Saúde, T5071 5148, www.spalbergue.com.br. Well-kept pousada in a quiet street, cheaper for HI members, helpful, 2 mins from Praça do Árvore metro, kitchen, laundry and internet service (overpriced). **Associação Paulista de Albergues da Juventude**, R 7 de Abril 386, Conj 22, T/F3258 0388, www.alberguesp.com.br.

Eating

Old Centre *p395, map p394*
Restaurants in the old centre tend to be lunchtime only; there are many per kg options and *padarias*.
Terraço Italia, Av Ipiranga 344, T3257 6566. Average and overpriced Italian food with the best restaurant views in the city – out over an infinity of skyscrapers. Come for a coffee.
Boi na Brasa, R Bento Freitas by Praça da República. Very good meat dishes and feijoada at a reasonable price.
Café da Pinacoteca, Pinacoteca Museum, Praça da Luz 2, T3326 0350. Portuguese-style café with marble floors and mahogany balconies. Great coffee, sandwiches and cakes.

Liberdade *p397*
Gombe, R Tomás Gonzaga 22, T3209 8499. Renowned for grilled tuna and noodle dishes.
Sushi Yassu, R Tomás Gonzaga 98, T3209 6622. The best of Liberedade's traditional Japanese restaurants. Excellent sushi/sashimi combinations.

Jardins *p397, map p397*
Those on a budget can eat to their stomach's content in per kg places or, cheaper still, bakeries (*padarias*) There's one on almost every corner and they serve sandwiches, delicious Brazilian burgers made from decent meat and served with ham, egg, cheese or salad. They always have good coffee, juices, cakes and set lunches (*almoços*) for a very economical price. Most have a designated sitting area – either at the *padaria* bar or in an adjacent room. Juices are made from mineral or filtered water.
Café Antique, R Haddock Lobo 1416, T3062 0882. French cooking by Erick Jacquin, a Maître Cuisinier de France, in an informal but traditional dining room atmosphere.
Charlô Bistro, R Barão de Capanema 440 (next to DOM), T3088 6790 (with another branch at the Jockey Club, Av Lineu de Paula Machado 1263, Cidade Jardim, T3034 3682). One of the premier VIP and old family haunts in the city run by a scion of one of the city's establishment families. Decked out in tribute to a Paris brasserie and with food to match.

DOM, R Barão de Capanema 549, T3088 0761. São Paulo's evening restaurant of the moment – Alex Attala has won the coveted Veja best chef of the year award twice. Contemporary food, fusing Brazilian ingredients with French and Italian styles and served in a large modernist dining room.
Fasano, in Hotel Fasano (see Sleeping), T3896 4077. Long regarded as the best restaurant for gourmets in São Paulo. A huge choice of modern Italian and French cooking from chef Salvatore Loi. Diners have their own lowly lit booths in a magnificent dining room, exemplary wine list, formal dress.
Figueira Rubaiyat, R Haddock Lobo 1738, T3063 3888. The most interesting of the Rubaiyat restaurant group, with Argentinian steaks prepared by Argentinian chef Francis Mallman. Very lively for Sun lunch, light and airy and under a huge tropical fig tree. The best meat is served at another restaurant in the chain, Baby Beef Rubaiyat, Av Brig Faria Lima 2954, T3078 9488.
Gero, R Haddock Lobo 1629, T3064 0005. Fasano's version of a French Bistrô à Côte, but serving pasta and light Italian. Ever so casual design; be prepared for a long wait at the bar alongside people who are there principally to be seen. Reservations are not accepted.
Jun Sakamoto, R Lisboa 55, T3088 6019. Japanese with a touch of French; superb fresh ingredients (some of it flown in especially from Asia and the USA).
La Tambouille, Av 9 de Julho 5925, Jardim Europa, T3079 6276. The favourite 'old money' Franco-Italian restaurant. Excellent wine list.
Laurent, Al Lorena 1899, Cerqueira César, T3062 1452. The best French cooking in the country, French style, Brazilian ingredients.
Massimo, Al Santos 1826, Cerqueira César, T3284 0311. One of São Paulo's longest established Italian restaurants serving Northern Italian food. Credit cards are not accepted, despite the costly price.
A Mineira, Al Joaquim Eugénio de Lima 697, T3283 2349. Self-service Minas food by the kilo. Lots of choice. Cachaça and pudding included.
Baalbeck, Al Lorena 1330, T3088 4820. Lebanese cooking vastly superior to its luncheonette setting. Great falafel.
Camelo, R Pamplona 1873, T3887 8764. More than 40 superior pizzas with a choice of dough as well as topping.
Fran's Café, Av Paulista 358, and throughout the city. Open 24 hrs, the Brazilian equivalent of Starbuck's but with proper coffee and light meals.
Kayomix, R da Consolação 3215, T3082 2769. Brazilian Oriental fusions like salmon taratare with shimeji and shitake.

Ⅶ Namesa, R da Consolação 2967, T3088 7498.
Great little gourmet snacky dishes, created by
the chef from DOM.

Ⅶ Restaurante do MASP, Av Paulista 1578, T3253
2829. In the basement of the museum, reasonably
priced standards like lasagna and stroganoff often
with a garnish of live music.

Ⅶ Sattva, R da Consolação 2904, T3083 6237.
Light vegetarian curries, stir fries, salads and pastas.

Ⅶ Sujinho, R da Consolação 2068, Consolação,
T3256 8026. South American beef in large
portions, other carnivorous options also available.

Ⅰ Cheiro Verde, R Peixoto Gomide 1413, T289
6853 (lunch only). Hearty veggie food, like
vegetable crumble in gorgonzola sauce and pasta
with buffalo mozarella and sun-dried tomato.

Ⅰ Tâmara Cafe, Al Santos 1518, T288 1248
(lunchtimes only). Arabic cooking with good
kibe, kofta and falafel.

South of the Old Centre *p398*
Vila Olímpia and Itaim

Restaurants here are ultra, ultra trendy; full of
the beautiful posing in beautiful surroundings.
We include only a handful of the best.

Ⅶ Boo, R Viradouro 132, T3078 7477. Opposite
Kosushi, with a carbon copy crowd, Luso-Asian
cooking and a beautiful garden setting.

Ⅶ Kosushi, R Viradouro 139, Itaim Bibi, T3167
7272. The first of São Paulo's chic Japanese
restaurants which began life in Liberdade and is
now housed in a beautifully designed Asian
modernist space. Great sushi combinations.

Ⅶ Parigi, R Amauri 275, Itaim, T3167 1575. One
of the city's premier evening places to be seen;
Franco-Italian dining in a beautiful dining room.

◑ Bars and clubs

The best places for nightlife are Itaim, Moema and
Vila Olímpia, and Vila Madalena/Pinheiros. Jardins'
best bars are in the top hotels. Vila Olímpia, Itaim
and Moema have a series of funky, smart bars
overflowing onto the street, filled with an eclectic
mix of after-workers, clubbers, singles and couples;
all united by being under 40 and having money.
These sit alongside imitation US and European
club/lounge bars playing techno, hip hop and the
like. The busiest streets for a bar wander are Rua
Atílio Inocenti near the junction of Av Juscelino
Kubitschek and Av Brigadeiro Faria Lima, Av Hélio
Pellegrino and Rua Araguari, which runs behind it.
Vila Madalena is younger still, more hippy-chic, but
is the best part of town to hear live, Brazilian music
and uniquely Brazilian close dances like Forró, as
opposed to international club sounds. The liveliest
streets are Aspicuelta and Girassol.

Jardins *p397, map p397*

Apollinari, R Oscar Freire 1206, T3061 9965. Smart
restaurant/bar frequented by the city's glitterati.

Bar Balcão, R Dr Melo Alves 150, T3063 6091.
After work meeting place, very popular with young
professionals and media types who gather on
either side of the long low wooden bar which
winds its way around the room like a giant snake.

Finnegan's Pub, R Cristiano Viana 358, Pinheiros.
One of São Paulo's various Irish bars, this one
actually run by an Irishman, popular with ex-pats.

West of the Old Centre *p397*
Vila Madalena/Pinheiros

AMP Galaxy, R Fradique Coutinho 352, T3085
7867, www.ampgalaxy.com.br. A fusion of retro
50s bar and café, clothing boutique and, after
2300, packed dance floor with alternate live
music and DJs. The crowd is 20-something
and bohemian.

A Marcenaria, R Fradique Coutinho 1378, T3032
9006, www.amarcenaria.com.br. The bar of choice
for the young and single who gather around 2130,
until the dance floor fills up around 2300.

Bourbon Street, R dos Chanés 127, Moema,
T5095 6100, www.bourbonstreet.com.br.
Great little club with emerging local acts and
international stars, too.

Grazie a Dio, R Girassol, 67, T3031 6568,
www.grazieadio.com.br. The best bar in Vila
Madalena for live music, different band every night,
samba on Sun. Great for dancing, always packed.

Mood, R Teodoro Sampaio 1109, T3060 9010.
European-style club with the latest sounds and DJs.

Posto 6, R Aspicuelta 644, Vila Madalena, T3812
7831. An imitation Rio de Janeiro Boteco with an
attractive crowd and a backdrop of Bossa Nova
and MPB. Busy from 2100 onwards.

Urbano, R Cardeal Arcoverde 614, Pinheiros,
T3085 1001, www.urbano.com.br. São Paulo's
premier dance club, modelled on a London club
with a lounge bar area, huge dance floor and a
combination of live bands and DJs. Popular with
musicians and creative industry people.

South of the Old Centre *p398*
Itaim, Moema and Vila Olímpia

Liquid Lounge, Av Hélio Pellegrino 801, Vila
Olímpia, T3849 5014, www.liquidlounge.com.br.
Pulsing European-style dance club with a smart
bar area. Always busy.

Lov.E Club & Lounge, R Pequetita 189, Vila
Olímpia, T 3044 1613. Trance, house, drum 'n'
bass; famous name DJs.

Na Mata Café, R da Mata 70, Itaim,
T3079 0300, www.namata.com.br. Popular
flirting and pick-up spot with a dark dance
room, varied Brazilian and European dance
tunes and select live bands.

🎭 Entertainment

São Paulo *p391, maps p394 and p397*
See the Guia da Folha section of Folha de São Paulo and Veja São Paulo of the weekly news magazine Veja for listings.

Cinema Entrance is usually half price on Wed; normal seat price is US$5 in the centre, US$7-8 in R Augusta, Av Paulista and Jardins. Cine clubs: **Cine SESC**, R Augusta 2075, and cinemas at: **Museu da Imagem e do Som**, **Centro Cultural Itaú** and **Centro Cultural São Paulo**.

Theatre The **Teatro Municipal** (see Sights) is used by visiting theatrical and operatic groups, as well as the City Ballet Company and the Municipal Symphony Orchestra who give regular performances. There are several other 1st-class theatres: **Aliança Francesa**, R Gen Jardim 182, Vila Buarque, T3017 5699, www.alianca francesa.com.br. **Paiol**, R Amaral Gurgel 164, Vila Buarque, T221 2462; among others. Free concerts at **Teatro Popular do Sesi**, Av Paulista 1313, T3284 9787, at midday, under MASP (Mon-Sat).

🎉 Festivals and events

São Paulo *p391, maps p394 and p397*
Foundation of the City 25 Jan. Carnival in **Feb** (most attractions are closed).This includes the parades of the escolas de samba in the Anhembi sambódromo – the São Paulo special group parades on the Fri and Sat and the Rio group on the Sun and Mon to maximize TV coverage. World's biggest **Gay Pride** march takes places in the Brazilian winter – usually **May** – on Av Paulista. In Jun there are the **Festas Juninas** and the **Festa de São Vito**, the patron saint of the Italian immigrants. **Festa da Primavera** in **Sep**. In Dec there are various Christmas and New Year festivities. Throughout the year, there are countless anniversaries, religious feasts, international fairs and exhibitions, look in the press or the monthly tourist magazines to see what is on while you are in town. See Sights for the São Paulo Biennial.

🛍 Shopping

São Paulo *p391, maps p392, p394 and p397*
Bookshops Duas Cidades, R Bento Freitas 158, near República. Good selection of Brazilian and Spanish American literature. **La Selva**, in various shopping malls, also at airports. Sells books in English. **Letraviva**, Av Rebouças 1986. Mon-Fri 0900-1830, Sat 0900-1400, specializes in books and music in Spanish. **Librairie Française**, R Barão de Itapetininga 275, ground floor. Wide selection, also at R Professor Atilio Innocenti 920, Jardins. **Livraria Cultura**, Av Paulista 2073, loja

153, also at Shopping Villa-Lobos, Avdas Nacões Unidas 4777, Jardim Universale. New books in English, including guidebooks. **Livraria Freebook**, R da Consolação 1924, ring bell for entry. Wide collection of art books and imported books in English. **Livraria Kosmos**, Av São Luís 258, loja 6. International stock. **Livrarias Saraíva**, in various shopping malls. Sells books in English. **Livraria Triângulo**, R Barão de Itapetininga 255, loja 23, Centro, sells books in English. **Sodiler**, Shopping Market Place, Av Nações Unidas 13947, Brooklin, loja 121A, floor T.

Handicrafts Casa dos Amazonas, Al Jurupis 460. For souvenirs. **Ceará Meu Amor**, R Pamplona 1551, loja 7. Good quality lace from the northeast. **Galeria Arte Brasileira**, Al Lorena 2163, galeria@dialdata.com.br. Good value. **Sutaco**, handicrafts shop at República Metrô station. This promotes items from the State of São Paulo, Tue-Fri 1000-1900, Sat 1000-1500; there is a showroom at R Augusta 435, 6th floor.

Jewellery There are many other shops selling Brazilian stones, including branches of **H Stern** and **Amsterdam Sauer**.

Maps Quatro Rodas, Mapograf, Cartoplam, and the map given out by the tourist kiosks; RGN Public Ltda produces a map which is given out free in various places and which is adapted to show its sponsors' locations. A variety of maps and timetables are sold in news stands. **Editorial Abril**, Av das Nações Unidas 7221, T3037 2087, www.abril.com.br. Map, magazine and guide book publisher. **Geo Mapas**, R Gen Jardim 645, 3rd floor, Consolação. Private map publisher (40% discount for volume purchases), excellent 1988 1:5,000,000 map of Brazil, town maps. **Mapolândia**, 7 de Abril 125, 1st floor.

Open-air markets Antiques market, below the Museu de Arte de São Paulo. Sun, 1000-1700. **Arts and handicrafts**, are also sold in Parque Tenente Siqueira Campos/Trianon on Sun from 0900-1700. **Flea markets**, in the main square of the Bixiga district (Praça Don Orione) and in Praça Benedito Calixto in Pinheiros. On Sun. **Ceasa flower market**, Av Doutor Gastão Vidigal 1946, Jaguaré. Tue and Fri 0700-1200, should not be missed. 'Hippy' market, on Praça da República. Sun, reopened after temporary closure, but with stricter licensing than in the old days. 'Oriental' fair, Praça de Liberdade. Sun 1000-1900, good for Japanese snacks, plants and some handicrafts, very picturesque, with remedies on sale, tightrope walking, gypsy fortune tellers, etc.

Shopping centres Typical of modern development are the huge **Iguatemi**, **Ibirapuera** and **Morumbi** shopping centres. They include luxurious cinemas, snack bars and most of the best shops in São Paulo. Other malls include **Paulista** and **Butantã**. On a humbler level are the big supermarkets of **El Dorado** (Av Pamplona 1704) and **Pão de Açúcar** (Praça Roosevelt, near the Hilton); the latter is open 24 hrs a day (except Sun). São Paulo is relatively cheap for clothes (especially shoes).

⊖ Transport

São Paulo *p391, maps p392, p394 and p397*

Air From the international airport Guarulhos (also known as Cumbica), T6445 2945, there are airport taxis which charge US$45-52 on a ticket system (the taxi offices are outside Customs, 300 m down on the left; go to get your ticket then take your bags right back to the end of the taxi queue). Fares from the city to the airport are US$45-52 and vary from cab to cab. **Emtu bus service** every 30 mins from Guarulhos to Praça da República 343 (northwest side, corner of R Arouche), US$8.50, 30-45 mins, very comfortable (in the airport buy ticket at the booth in Domestic Arrivals); the same company runs services from Guarulhos to the main bus terminal, Tietê (hourly), US$8, and to Congonhas airport, T5090 9000. Buses run to Bresser bus station from Guarulhos and there are other buses to Jabaquara bus terminal, without luggage space, usually crowded. Also **Airport Bus Service**, T6221 0244, www.airportbusservice.com.br. US$13.50. From Congonhas airport, there are about 400 flights a week to Rio.

Airport information Money exchanges, in the arrivals hall, Guarulhos, 0800-2200 daily. Post office on the 3rd floor of Asa A. The Infraero Sala VIP has been recommended for coffee, cable TV for US$5. Mon-Fri 0800 to 1800. See Ins and outs, page 391, for the tourist office.

Bus Maps of the local bus and metro system are available at depots, for example Anhangabaú. Some city bus routes are run by trolley buses. City bus fare is US$1.15. Take an SP-Pinheiros bus from Clínicas, which takes the main highway to **Embu**; 40 mins. Get out at Largo 21 de Abril in Embu. To return to São Paulo, walk up R da Matriz from Largo 21 de Abril, turn left down Av Júnior, then left again on R Solano Trindade to a junction where the buses stop.

The main rodoviária for long distance buses is Tietê, which handles buses to the interior of São Paulo state, all state capitals (but see also under Barra Funda and Bresser below) and international buses. The **left luggage** charges US$1 per day per item. You can sleep in the bus station after 2200 when the guards have gone; tepid showers cost US$2.65.

Buses from Tietê: To **Rio**, 6 hrs, every 30 mins, US$26 (leito, 37), special section for this route in the rodoviária, ask how to take the coastal route via Santos ('via litoral') unless you wish to go the direct route. To **Florianópolis**,

11 hrs, US$45 (leito 72). To **Porto Alegre**, 18 hrs, US$65. **Curitiba**, 6 hrs, US$21. **Salvador**, 30 hrs, US$102 (executive, 127). **Recife**, 40 hrs, US$120. **Cuiabá**, 24 hrs, US$84. **Porto Velho**, 60 hrs (or more), US$150. **Brasília**, 16 hrs, US$60 (leito, 120). **Foz do Iguaçu**, 16 hrs, US$44. **São Sebastião**, 4 hrs US$15 (say 'via Bertioga' if you want to go by the coast road, beautiful journey but few buses take this route).

International buses from Tietê: to **Montevideo**, via Porto Alegre, with TTL, departs Mon, Thu, Sat 2330, 31 hrs, US$134, cold a/c at night, plenty of meal stops, bus stops for border formalities, passengers disembark only to collect passport and tourist card on the Uruguayan side (also EGA, same price, US$90 to **Chuy**, Tue, Fri, Sun). To **Buenos Aires**, Pluma, 36 hrs. To **Santiago**, Pluma or Chilebus, 56 hrs, Chilebus, poor meals, but otherwise good, beware overbooking. To **Asunción** (1,044 km), 18 hrs with Pluma , Brújula or RYSA, all stop at Ciudad del Este. Cometa del Amambay runs to **Pedro Juan Caballero** and **Concepción**.

There are 3 other bus stations: Barra Funda, T3666 4682, with Metrô station, for buses from cities in southern São Paulo state, **Campo Grande**, 14 hrs, US$66, and many places in Paraná. Bresser, T6692 5191, on the Metrô, is for destinations in Minas Gerais. Buses from Santos arrive at **Jabaquara**, T5012 2256, at the southern end of the Metrô. To **Santos** and destinations on the southern coast of São Paulo state, use Jabaquara station. Buses from here for Santos leave every 15 mins, taking about 50 mins, last bus at 0100, US$7. Buses at Bresser, **Cometa** (6967 7255) or **Transul** (T6693 8061) go to Minas Gerais: **Belo Horizonte**, 10 hrs, US$30, 11 a day (leito 60); 9 a day with Gontijo. Translavras and Útil also operate out of this station. Prices are given under destinations.

Car The rodízio, which curbs traffic pollution by restricting car use according to number plate, may be extended beyond the winter months. Check.

Metrô Two lines intersect at Praça de Sé: north-south from Tucuruvi to Jabaquara; east-west from Corinthians Itaquera to Barra Funda (the interchange with Fepasa and RFFSA railways and site of the São Paulo and Paraná rodoviária); an extension east to Guaianases is under construction. A 3rd line runs from Vila Madalena in the west, along Av Paulista, to Imigrantes in the south, joining the Jabaquara line at Paraíso and Ana Rosa. A 4th line is being built from Vila Sônia to Luz. The system is clean, safe, cheap and efficient; the 2 main lines operate from 0500-2400, Ana Madalena to Ana Rosa 0600-2200. Fare US$1.15; backpacks are allowed. Combined bus and Metrô ticket are available, US$2, for example to Congonhas airport. Information T286 0111.

Taxi Taxis display cards of actual tariffs in the window (starting price US$4). There are ordinary taxis, which are hailed on the street, or at taxi stations such as Praça da República, radio taxis and deluxe taxis. For **Radio Taxis**, which are more expensive but involve fewer hassles, **Central Radio Táxi**, T6914 6630; **São Paulo Rádio Táxi**, T5583 2000; **Fácil**, T6258 5947; **Aero Táxi**, T6461 4090; or look in the phone book; calls are not accepted from public phones.

Train São Paulo has 4 stations: 1) **Estação da Luz** for commuter trains between the northwest and southeast of São Paulo state. There is also a Metrô stop here. A train runs from Luz 8 times a day to connect with the tourist train from Paranapiaçaba to Rio Grande da Serra, US$0.65. 2) **Barra Funda**, services go to São José do Rio Preto (overnight), Barretos, Londrina, Maringá, Sorocaba and Ponta Grossa. There is a Metrô station and a rodoviária at Barra Funda; 3) **Júlio Prestes station**, for commuter services to the west; T0800 550121 for these three. 4) **Roosevelt**, T6942 1199, for commuter trains to the east.

ⓘ Directory

São Paulo *p391, maps p394 and p397*
Airline offices Aerolíneas Argentinas, Araújo 216, 6th floor, T259 0319 (Guarulhos airport 6445 3806). **Alitalia**, Av São Luís 50, cj 291, T3257 1922 (6445 3791). **American Airlines**, Araújo 216, 9th floor, T0800 703 4000 or 3214 4000 (6445 3808). **Bra**, T6445 4310, sales offices all over the city, in shopping centres and at both airports, see www.voebra.com.br. **British Airways**, Av São Luís 50, 32nd floor, T3145 9700 (6445 2021). **Gol**, T0300-789 2121, www.voegol.com.br. **Iberia**, Araújo 216, 3rd floor, T2507 6711 (6445 2060). **JAL**, Av Paulista 542, 2nd floor, T251 5222 (6445 2040). **Lufthansa**, R Gomes de Carvalho 1356, 2nd floor, T3048 5868 (6445 2220). **OceanAir**, Av Washington Luis 7059, Av: Washington Luis 7059, Santo Amaro, T2176 1000, or 4004 4040. **Rio-Sul**, R Bráulio Gomes 151, T5561 2161. **TAM**, R da Consolação 247, 3rd floor, T0300-123 1000 (24 hrs), or 3155 6700 (6445 3474). **TAP**, Av São Luís 187, T255 5366 (6445 2400). **United**, Av Paulista 777, 9-10th floor, T3145 4200/ 0800-162323 (6445 3283). **Varig**, T4003 7000, Guarulhos 6445 3117, Congonhas 5091 2215.
Banks There are many national and international banks; most can be found either in the Triângulo, downtown, or on Av Paulista, or Av Brigadeiro Faria Lima. Hours 1000-1600; but some vary. All have different times for foreign exchange transactions (check at individual branches). Many **Banco 24 Horas** ATMs in the city. **Banco do Brasil** will change cash and TCs and will advance cash against Visa. All transactions are done in the

foreign exchange department of any main branch (eg Av São João 32, Centro), but queues are long. **Citibank**, Av Ipiranga 855, or Av Paulista 1111 (1100-1500), cash on MasterCard. **Banespa**, for example at R Duque de Caxias 200, Centro, or Praça da República 295, accepts Visa, TCs and cash. **MasterCard**, cash against card, R Campo Verde 61, 4th floor, Jardim Paulistano. MasterCard ATMs at branches of HSBC Bank. **American Express**, Al Santos 1437 (Hotel Mofarrej Sheraton) T251 3383, Av Maria Coelho Aguiar 215, Bloco F, 8th floor, T3741 8478 and Guarulhos international airport, terminal 1, 1st floor of Asa A, T6412 3515. **Western Union** at Banco Itamarati, T0800-119837. Money changers: there are many câmbios on or near Praça da República. There are none near the rodoviária or Tietê hotels. **Interpax**, Praça da República 177, loja 13, changes cash (many currencies) and TCs, 0930-1800, Sat 0930-1300. **Amoretur**, Praça da República 203, will change TCs. **Coraltur**, Praça da República 95. Most travel agents on Av São Luís change TCs and cash at good rates, but very few are open on Sat. **Avencatur**, Av Nações Unidas 1394, Morumbi, changes TCs, Deutschmarks, good rates.
Car hire See Car hire, Essentials for international car rental agencies, page 44. **Interlocadora**, several branches, São Luís T255 5604, Guarulhos T6445 3838, Congonhas T240 9287. **Cultural centres** Centro Brasileiro Britânico, R Ferriera de Araújo 741, Pinheiros, T3039 0567. **American Library**, União Cultural Brasil-Estados Unidos, R Col Oscar Porto 208. **Goethe-Instituto**, R Lisboa 974, T3088 4288 (Mon-Thu 1400-2030). **Centro Cultural Fiesp**, Av Paulista 1313, T3146 7405, 0900-1900 Tue-Sun, has foreign newspapers and magazines. See under Entertainment for Alliance Française Theatre. **Consulates** Argentina, Av Paulista 1106, T284 1355 (0900-1300, very easy to get a visa here). **Australia**, R Tenente Negrão 140, T3849 6281. **Bolivia**, R Oscar Freire 379, T3081 1618, www.embolivia.cjb.net. 0900-1700. **Canada**, Av Nações Unidas 12901, T5509 4343, spalo-immigration@dfait-maeci.gc.ca. 0800-1100, 1500-1600, Fri 0800-0930, 1200-1300. **Denmark**, R Oscar Freire 379, T3061 3625, 0900-1700, Fri until 1400 only. **France**, Av Paulista 1842, 14th floor, T3371 5400, www.ambafrance.org.br. 0830-1200. **Germany**, Av Brigadeiro Faria Lima 2092, T3814 6644, info.saopaulo@alemanha.org.br. 0800-1130 (also serves Paraná). **Italy**, Av Paulista 1963, T3549 5643, www.italconsul.org.br. **Israel**, Av Brig Faria Lima 1713, T3815 7788. **Japan**, Av Paulista 854, T287 0100, cgjsp@nethall.com.br. **Netherlands**, Av Brigadeiro Faria Lima 1779, T3811 3300, sao@minbuza.nl, 0900-1200. **New Zealand**, Av Campinas 579, 15th floor, T3148 0616, consuladonz@nzte.govt.nz, 0900-1300. **Norway and Sweden**, R Oscar Freire 379, 3rd floor, T883

3322 (Norway), 3061 1700 (Sweden) (Caixa Postal 51626), 0900-1300. **Paraguay**, R Bandeira Paulista 600, 15th floor, T3849 0455, 0830-1600. **Peru**, R Votuverava 350, T3819 1793, viceconsulperu@ originet.com.br. 0900-1300. **UK**, R Ferreira Araújo 741, 2nd floor, Pinheiros, T3094 2700, saopaulo@ gra-bretanha.org.br. **US**, R Henri Dunant 500, Chácara Santo Antônio, T5186 7000, www.consuladoamericanosp.org.br. 0800-1700. **Internet** at Av Paulista 1499, conj 1001 (Mêtro Trianon), 1100-2200, English spoken, secondhand books; **Saraíva Megastore**, Shopping El Dorado, US$3; **Kiosknet**, Shopping Light, 4th floor, R Cel Xavier de Toledo 23, opposite Teatro Municipal, T3151 3645, US$2.50 per hr; **Monkey Paulista**, Al Santos 1217 (Jardins, off Av Paulista behind Citibank). Superfast connection, US$0.70-1.15 per hr, more expensive at weekends. O Porão, R Tamandaré 1066, near Vergueiro metro station. **Language courses** Universidade de São Paulo (USP) in the Cidade Universitária has courses available to foreigners, including a popular Portuguese course, registry is through the **Comissão de Cooperação Internacional**, R do Anfiteatro 181, Bloco das Colméias 05508, Cidade Universitária. **Medical services** Hospital **Samaritano**, R Conselheiro Brotero 1486, Higienópolis, T824 0022. Recommended. **Emergency and ambulance** T192, no charge. **Fire**: T193. **Post offices** Correio Central, Praça do Correio, corner Av São João and Prestes Máia. Booth adjoining tourist office on Praça da República, weekdays only 1000-1200, 1300-1600, for letters and small packages only. **UPS**, Brasinco, Alameda Jaú 1, 1725, 01420 São Paulo. **Federal Express**, Av São Luís 187, Galeria Metropole, loja 45, is reliable, also at Av das Nações Unidas 17891; **DHL**, Av Vereador José Diniz 2421. **Telephone** Telefônica, R 7 de Abril 295, near Praça da República; many other offices. **Embratel**, Av São Luís 50, and Av Ipiranga 344. For the international operator dial 000111; for international collect calls dial 000107. Red phone boxes are for national calls, blue ones for international phone calls. **Useful addresses** Police: Deatur, special tourist police, Av São Luís 91, T3120 3984; Guarulhos airport T6445 2686; Congonhas airport T5090 9032. **Radio Patrol**, T190. **Federal Police**, Av Prestes Maia 700, 1000-1600 for visa extensions.

São Paulo coast

On the coast there are fine beaches, although pollution is sometimes a problem. The further northeast or southwest you go from the port of Santos, the more unspoilt the beaches become, with some areas of special natural interest.

Santos → *Phone code: 0xx13. Post code: 11000. Colour map 7, grid C4. Population: 417,983.*

Santos, on an island about 5 km from the open sea, is the most important Brazilian port. Over 40% by value of all Brazilian imports and about half the total exports pass through it. Santos is also a holiday resort with magnificent beaches and views. The scenery on the routes crossing the Serra do Mar is superb. The roadway includes many bridges and tunnels. From Rio the direct highway, the Linha Verde (see pages 385 and 407) is also wonderful for scenery. The port is approached by the winding Santos Channel; at its mouth is an old fort (1709). The centre of the city, on the north side of the island, is being renovated. Due south, on the Baía de Santos, is **Gonzaga**, where hotels and bars line the beachfront. Between these two areas, the eastern end of the island curves round within the Santos Channel. **Tourist offices** ① *at the rodoviária, T3219 2194, Ponta da Praia, T3236 9996, and Orquidário Municipal (limited opening); information by phone To800-173887.*

Sights The best way get around the centre of Santos is by the newly restored Victorian trams which leave on guided tours from in front of the Prefeitura Municipal on Praça Visconde de Mauá. The tram passes in front of most of the interesting sights, including the *azulejo*-covered houses on Rua do Comércio. The streets around **Praça Mauá** are very busy in the daytime. **Museu do Café** ① *R 15 de Novembro 95, T3219 5585, www.museudocafe.com.br, Tue-Sat 0900-1700, Sun 1000-1700*. The old Bolsa Oficial de Café was closed to all but rich men up until the mid-20th century, but is now a delightful museum, with large wall paintings by Benedito Calixto and a very impressive art deco stained-glass ceiling. Upstairs is a small but very well-presented collection of displays. The lobby café serves some of the best coffee in Brazil. Two churches in the centre are **Santo Antônio do Valongo** (17th century, but restored), which is by the railway station on Largo Monte Alegre, and the **Capela da Ordem Terceira de Nossa Senhora do Carmo** (1760, also later restored), Praça Barão do Rio Branco. **Fundação Pinacoteca** ① *Av Bartolomeu de Gusmão 15, T3288 2260, www.pinacoteca.unisanta.br, Tue-Sun 1400-1900, free*, a large collection of ecclesiastical paintings and landscapes by one of Brazil's most distinguished early 19th-century artists, is housed in one of Santos's few remaining coffee mansions.

At **Santos Football Stadium and Museum** ① *Princesa Isabel 77, Vila Belmiro, T3257 4000, www.santosfc.com.br*, the ground floor houses a collection of trophies and photographs chronicling the history of Pele's club, including several cabinets devoted to him and containing his shirts, boots and other memorabilia. **Monte Serrat**, just south of the city centre, has at its summit a semaphore station and look-out post which reports the arrival of all ships in Santos harbour. There is also a church, dedicated to Nossa Senhora da Monte Serrat. The top can be reached on foot or by **funicular** (every 30 minutes, US$8). **Museu do Mar** ① *R República do Equador 81*, is in the eastern part of the city; with a collection that includes several thousand shells. In the western district of José Menino is the **Orquidário Municipal** ① *daily 0800-1745, bird enclosure 0800-1100, 1400-1700, US$1*, the municipal orchid gardens, in the **Praça Washington**. The flowers bloom October to February; the orchid show is in November.

The **Ilha Porchat**, a small island reached by a bridge at the far end of Santos/São Vicente bay, has beautiful views of the high seas on one side and of the city and bay on the other. The lookout was designed by Oscar Niemeyer and, in summer, there is lively nightlife here.

Itatinga, 30 km from Santos in the Serra do Mar, has remnants of Atlantic forest, mangrove and sandbanks. The area is full of wildlife. There are trails graded according to difficulty. Visitors go with one of the travel agencies officially permitted to lead groups: contact the tourism office (see above). Access is either via the village of Itatinga by boat, three hours, then by street car. Or take the BR-101 (Santos-Rio) road, a three-minute crossing by boat and then 7½ km by street car.

São Sebastião → *Phone code: 0xx12. Post code: 11600. Colour map 7, grid B4. Population: 58,038.*

East of Santos, a vehicle ferry (free for pedestrians) crosses from Ponta da Praia to **Guarujá**, from where a road (SP-061) runs to **Bertioga**. The coastal road beyond Bertioga is paved, and the Rio-Santos highway, 1-2 km inland, provides a good link to São Sebastião. Beyond Praia Boracéia are a number of beaches, including **Camburi**, surrounded by the Mata Atlântica, into which you can walk on the Estrada do Piavu (bathing in the streams is permitted, but use of shampoo is forbidden). There are several good hotels and restaurants in Camburi and at Praia de Boracéia. The road carries on from Camburi, past clean beach **Maresias**, a fashionable place for surfers.

From Maresias it is 21 km to São Sebastião. In all there are 21 good beaches and an adequate, but not overdeveloped tourist infrastructure. The natural attractions of the area include many small islands offshore and a large portion of the **Parque Estadual da Serra do Mar** on the mainland, with other areas under protection for their different ecosystems. Trails can be walked through the forests. There are also old sugar plantations. In the colonial centre is a **Museu de Arte Sacra** ① *R Sebastião Neves 90*, in the 17th-century chapel of São Gonçalo. The town's parish church on Praça Major João Fernandes was built in the early 17th century and rebuilt in 1819. There is a **Museu do Naufrágio** near the church (free) exhibiting shipwrecks and natural history of the local area. **Tourist office** ① *Av Dr Altino Arantes 174, T4522 1808.*

The beaches within 2-3 km of São Sebastião harbour are polluted; others to the south and north are clean. Ilhabela is expensive in season, when it is cheaper to stay in São Sebastião.

Ilhabela → *Phone code: 0xx12. Pop: 20,836; rising to 100,000 in high season.*

The island of São Sebastião, known popularly as Ilhabela, is of volcanic origin, roughly 390 sq km in area. The four highest peaks are Morro de São Sebastião, 1,379 m, Morro do Papagaio, 1,309 m, Ramalho, 1,205 m, and Pico Baepi, 1,025 m. All are often obscured by mist. Rainfall on the island is heavy, about 3,000 mm a year. The slopes are densely wooded and 80% of the forest is protected by the Parque Estadual de Ilhabela. The only settled district lies on the coastal strip facing the mainland, the Atlantic side being practically uninhabited except by a few fisherfolk. The island abounds with tropical plants, flowers, and wild fruits, whose juice mixed with *cachaça* and sugar makes a delicious cocktail. The terraced **Cachoeira da Toca** ① *US$4, includes insect repellent*, waterfalls amid dense jungle close to the foot of the Baepi peak give cool freshwater bathing; lots of butterflies. You can walk on a signed path, or go by car; it's a few kilometres from the ferry dock. The locals claim there are over 300 waterfalls on the island, but only a few of them can be reached on foot. In all shady places, especially away from the sea, there thrives a species of midge known locally as *borrachudo*. A locally sold repellent (Autan) keeps them off for some time, but those allergic to insect bites should remain on the inhabited coastal strip. There is a small hospital (helpful) by the church in town. **Secretaria Municipal de Turismo** ① *R Bartolomeu de Gusmão 140, Pequeá, T3896 2440, www.ilhabela.com.br.*

No alterations are allowed to the frontage of the main township, **Ilhabela**. It is very popular during summer weekends, when it is difficult to find space for a car on the ferry. It is, however, a nice place to relax on the beach, with good food and some good value accommodation.

Visit the old **Feiticeira** plantation, with underground dungeons. The road is along the coast, sometimes high above the sea, towards the south of the island (11 km from the town). You can go by bus, taxi, or horse and buggy. A trail leads down from the fazenda to the beautiful beach of the same name. Another old fazenda is **Engenho d'Água**, which is nearer to the town, which gives its name to one of the busiest beaches (the fazenda is not open to the public).

Beaches and watersports On the mainland side the beaches 3-4 km either side of the town are polluted: look out for oil, sandflies and jellyfish on the sand and in the water. There are some three dozen beaches around Ilhabela, only about 12 of them away from the coast facing the mainland. **Praia dos Castelhanos**, reached by the rough road over the island to the Atlantic side (no buses), is recommended. Several of the ocean beaches can only be reached by boat. The island is considered the **Capital da Vela** (of sailing) because its 150 km of coastline offers all types of conditions. There is also plenty of adventure for divers.

Ubatuba → *Phone code: 0xx12. Post code: 11680. Colour map 7, grid B4. Population: 66,861.*
This is one of the most beautiful stretches of the São Paulo coast with a whole range of watersports on offer. In all, there are 72 beaches, some large, some small, some in coves, some on islands. They are spread out over a wide area, so if you are staying in Ubatuba town, you need to use the buses which go to most of them. The commercial centre of Ubatuba is at the northern end of the bay. Here are shops, banks, services, lots of restaurants (most serving pizza and fish), but few hotels. These are on the beaches north and south and can be reached from the Costamar bus terminal. **Comtur tourist office** ① *Av Iperoig opposite R Profesor Thomaz Galhardo, T0800-771 7400; www.ubatuba.com.br*, is very helpful.

Saco da Ribeira, 13 km south, is a natural harbour which has been made into a yacht marina. Schooners leave from here for excursions to **Ilha Anchieta** (or dos Porcos), a popular four-hour trip. On the island are beaches, trails and a prison, which was in commission from 1908-1952. Agencies run schooner trips to Ilha Anchieta and elsewhere. Trips leave Saco da Ribeira at 1000, returning 1500, four-hour journey, US$26 per person. A six-hour trip can be made from Praia Itaguá, but in winter there is a cold wind off the sea in the afternoon, same price. The Costamar bus from Ubatuba to Saco da Ribeira (every 20 minutes, 30 minutes, US$1.50) drops you at the turn-off by the Restaurante Pizzaria Malibu.

Straddling the border of São Paulo and Rio de Janeiro states is the **Parque Nacional Serra da Bocaina** ① *permission to visit must be obtained in advance from Ibama, Toxx12-3117 2183/88 in São José do Barreiro, the nearest town*. It rises from the coast to its highest point at Pico do Tira (or Chapéu) at 2,200 m, encompassing three strata of vegetation.

Southwest from Santos
Itanhaém (*Phone code: 0xx13*), 61 km from Santos, has a pretty colonial church of Sant'Ana (1761), Praça Narciso de Andrade, and the Convento da Nossa Senhora da Conceição (1699-1713), originally founded 1554), on a small hill. There are several good seafood restaurants along the beach, hotels and camping. There are more beaches 31 km south of Itanhaém at **Peruíbe**, where the climate is said to be unusually healthy owing to a high concentration of ozone in the air. Local rivers have water and black mud which has been proven to contain medicinal properties. There are plenty of places to stay and to eat in Peruíbe (none close to the bus station, some close out-of-season). Peruíbe marks the northernmost point of the **Estação Ecológico Juréia-Itatins** ① *contact the Instituto Florestal, R do Horto 931, CEP 02377-000, São Paulo, Toxx11-6997 5000, for permission to visit the ecological station*. The station was founded in 1986 and protects 820 sq km of Mata Atlântica, "as it was when the Portuguese arrived in Brazil". The four main ecosystems are restinga, mangrove, Mata Atlântica and the vegetation at 900 m on the Juréia mountain range.

Iguape → *Phone code: 0xx13. Colour map 7, grid C3. Population: 27,427.*
At the southern end of Juréia-Itatins is the town of Iguape founded in 1538. Typical of Portuguese architecture, the small **Museu Histórico e Arqueológico** ① *R das Neves 45, Tue-Sun 0900-1730*, is housed in the 17th-century Casa da Oficina Real de Fundição. There is also a **Museu de Arte Sacra** ① *Sat-Sun 0900-1200, 1330-1700*, in the former Igreja do Rosário, Praça Rotary. **Tourist office** ① *9 de Julho 63, T6841 3358*.

Opposite Iguape is the northern end of the **Ilha Comprida** with 86 km of beaches (some dirty and disappointing). This **Área de Proteção Ambiental** ① *the Ibama office of the Area de Proteção Ambiental Cananéia-Iguape-Peruíbe is at R da Saúde s/n, Canto do Morro, Iguape, T6841 2692/2388*, is not much higher than sea level and is divided from the mainland by the Canal do Mar Pequeno. The northern end is the busiest and on the island there are good restaurants, hotels, supermarkets – fresh fish is excellent. There is also accommodation.

Cananéia and Ilha do Cardoso → *Colour map 7, grid C3. Population: 12,298.*

At the southern end of Ilha Comprida, across the channel, is Cananéia, 270 km from São Paulo. The colonial centre, around Praça Martim Afonso de Souza and neighbouring streets, contains the 17th-century church of **São João Batista** and the **Museu Municipal**. To the south are a number of good beaches and the waterways are popular with fisherfolk. For guides, contact Manoel Barroso, Avenida Independencia 65, T013-3851 1273, Portuguese only. Recommended. Cananéia has several hotels, starting in price range **B**.

To reach the densely wooded Ilha do Cardoso, a Reserva Florestal e Biológica, take a ferry from the dock at Cananéia, four hours, three daily (T3851 1268). Alternatively, drive 70 km along an unpaved road, impassable when wet, to **Ariri**, from where the island is 10 mins by boat. The tiny village of Marujá, which has no electricity, has some rustic pousadas and restaurants. There are designated camping areas and lots of idyllic beaches; best for surfing is Moretinho.

◉ Sleeping

Santos *p406*
Many beachfront hotels on Av Pres Wilson, cheap hotels are near the Orquidário Municipal (Praça Washington), 1-2 blocks from the beach.
AL Atlântico, No 1, T3289 4500, www.atlantico-hotel.com.br. Good, a/c, sauna, restaurant, bar.
B Hotel Natal, Av Marechal Floriano Peixoto 104, T3284 2732, www.hotelnatal.com.br. Safe, comfortable, with cable TV, fridge, full breakfast.

Ilhabela *p407*
Several in the **L-AL** price range and some in the **A-B** range, mostly on the road to the left of the ferry.
AL Ilhabela, Av Pedro Paulo de Morais 151, T3896 1083, www.hotelilhabela.com.br. Family-oriented, gym, pool, good breakfast. Recommended.
A Pousada dos Hibiscos, Av Pedro Paulo de Morais 714, T3896 1375, www.pousadados hibiscos.com.br. Good atmosphere, swimming pool. Recommended.
A Vila das Pedras, R Antenor Custódio da Silva 46, Cocaia, T3896 2433, www.viladas pedras.com.br. 11 chalets in a forest garden, tastefully decorated, nice pool.
C Estância das Bromélias Pousada, Av Col José Vicente Faria Lima 1243, Perequê, T3896 3353, www.estanciadasbromelias.com.br. Welcoming, chalets for 5, great breakfast, garden, pool, horse riding and jeep excursions, very good.
Camping Pedras do Sino, at Perequê, near ferry dock, and at Praia Grande, 11 km south.

Ubatuba *p408*
At all holiday times it is expensive, with no hotel less than US$30. On many of the beaches there are hotels and pousadas, ranging from luxury resorts to more humble establishments.

AL Saveiros, R Lucian Strass 65, Praia do Lázaro, 14 km from town, T3842 0172, www.hotel saveiros.com.br. Pretty *pousada* with pool, restaurant, English spoken.
A São Charbel, Praça Nóbrega 280, T3832 1090, www.saocharbel.com.br. Helpful, comfortable, a/c, TV, restaurant, bar, swimming pool, etc.
A São Nicolau, R Conceição 213, T/F3832 5007. Good, TV, fridge, good breakfast.
A Xaréu, R Jordão Homem da Costa 413, T/F3832 1525. Pleasant, quiet. Recommended.
D Pousada Taiwan, R Felix Guisard Filho 60, T3832 6448. Fan or a/c, with breakfast, TV, fridge.
E-F J S Brandão, R Nestor Fonseca 173, Jardim Sumaré, CEP 11880-000, T3832 2337. 0700-2300, near the Tropic of Capricorn sign south of town.
E-F Cora Coralina, Rodovia Oswaldo Cruz, Km 89, T011-258 0388. 0800-2300, near Horto Florestal.
Camping There are about 10 sites in the vicinity, including 2 **Camping Clube do Brasil** sites at Lagoinha (25 km from town) and Praia Perequê-Açu, 2 km north.

Iguape *p408*
B-C Silvi, R Ana Cândida Sandoval Trigo 515, T6841 1421, silvihotel@virtualway.com.br. With bath and breakfast, simple but good.
Camping At Praia da Barra da Ribeira, 20 km north. Wild camping is possible at Praia de Juréia, the gateway to the ecological station.

▲ Activities and tours

Ubatuba *p408*
Companies offer trekking tours graded according to difficulty lasting from 2 hrs to 2 days. More details from the guide association, T9141 3692.

202, Cidade Jardim, T3296 3896, bus 2902 from Av Afonso Pena, in an old fazenda, is the last reminder of Belo Horizonte's predecessor, the village of **Arraial do Curral d'el Rey**. It has historical exhibits. **Jardim Botânico e Museu de História Natural** ① *Instituto Agronómico, R Gustavo da Silveira 1035, Cidade Nova, T3461 5805, Tue-Fri 0800-1130, 1330-1700, Sat-Sun 0900-1600 (take bus 8001)*, has geological, palaeontological and archaeological displays.

About 8 km northwest from the centre is the picturesque suburb of **Pampulha**, famous for its modern buildings and the artificial lake, created in the 1930s by Brasilia architect Oscar Niemeyer and landscaped by Roberto Burle Marx. The **Igreja São Francisco de Assis** ① *Av Otacílio Negrão de Lima Km 12, T3441 9325*, was inaugurated in 1943. The painter Cândido Portinari installed beautiful blue and white tiles depicting Saint Francis' life on the exterior. On the wall behind the altar is a powerful composition also by Portinari. On the opposite shore is the glass and marble **Museu de Arte de Pampulha** (MAP) ① *Av Octacílio Negrão de Lima 16585, T3443 4533, Tue-Sun 0900-1900, free*. It has a fine collection of modern art from Minas Gerais. The **Casa do Baile** ① *Av Octacílio Negrão de Lima 751, T3277 7433, TueoSun 0900-1900, free*, is a perfect example of Niemeyer's fascination with the curved line. Just south of the lake is the **Mineirão** football stadium, about 750 m away. This is the second largest stadium in Brazil after the Maracanã stadium in Rio. Seats cost between US$4 and US$9.

In the southern zone of the city, just 3 km from the central area, the **Parque de Mangabeiras** ① *Thu-Sun 0800-1800, is on the Serra do Curral at between 1,000 m and 1,400 m above sea level*. There are good views of the city, especially from the Mirante da Mata. Three forest trails have been laid out.

Belo Horizonte & Pampulha

Related map
A Belo Horizonte centre, page 413

| 0 km | 2 | | Sleeping ⊙ | Ouro Minas Palace **1** | Eating ❼ | Xapuri **2** |
| 0 miles | 2 | | Chalé Mineiro **3** | | Aurora **1** | |

◒ Sleeping

Belo Horizonte *p411, maps p412 and p413*
You may spend the night in the rodoviária only if you have an onward ticket (police check at 2400). There are cheaper options near the rodoviária and in R Curitiba, but many of these hotels are not used for sleeping in. You will have a more comfortable stay in one of the youth hostels.
LL Ouro Minas Palace, Av Cristiano Machado 4001, T3429 4001 (toll free 0800-314000), www.ourominas.com.br. The most luxurious hotel in the city with palatial suites, including several for women-only on the top floors, excellent service, pool, sauna, gym, excellent business facilities, not central but within easy reach of the centre and airports.
L Grandarrell Minas, R Espírito Santo 901, T3248 0000, www.grandarrell.com.br. One of the best

business hotels in the centre, full business facilities including fax and email modems in rooms, rooftop pool, not much English spoken.
L Liberty Palace, R Paraíba 1465, Savassi, T2121 0900, www.libertypalace.com.br. Business hotel in the Savassi restaurant district, standard rooms with spacious bathrooms, 24-hr room service, IDSL in all rooms and a well-appointed business centre.
L Othon Palace, Av Afonso Pena 1050, T3247 0000, www.hoteis-othon.com.br. 1980s hotel, glass-fronted, excellent, safe, good restaurant, pool, helpful staff, lower floors can be noisy.
AL Le Flamboyant, R Rio Grande do Norte 1007, Savassi, T3261 7370, www.clan.com.br. Well-maintained flats with separate sitting room, TV, kitchen, pool. Some flats have two bedrooms.

Belo Horizonte centre

Sleeping ◒	Othon Palace 8	Café Tina 13	Sushi Naka 5
Chalé Mineiro 1	Pousadinha Mineira 11	Chico Mineiro 1	Taste Vin 6
Continental 2	São Salvador 10	Dona Derna 2	Vecchio Sogno 7
Esplanada 3	Villa Emma 9	Dona Lucinha 3	
Grandarrell Minas 4		Flor de Líbano 4	**Bars & clubs** ♪
Le Flamboyant 5	**Eating** ♠	Kauhana 10	de James 14
Liberty Palace 6	A Cafeteria 8	La Traviata 11	de João 15
O Sorriso do Lagarto 7	Café da Travessa 9	Sushi Beer 12	Koyote 16

A Villa Emma, R Arturo Toscanini 41, Savassi, T32823388, www.clan.com.br. The cheapest option in Savassi, spacious flats in need of a lick of paint, with 2 bedrooms, separate living area and kitchen. Internet access in some rooms.

B Esplanada, Av Santos Dumont 304, T3273 5311. An upmarket cheapie with bright rooms with en-suites, soap and towels, generous breakfasts and triples available for little more than doubles. Prices are negotiable.

D Continental, Av Paraná 241, T3201 7944. Central, quieter interior rooms. Recommended.

D São Salvador, R Espírito Santo 227, T3222 7731. Small, the best rooms are the triples with en suites, reasonable breakfast. One of many similar cheapies in the area.

D-E pp Chalé Mineiro, R Santa Luzia 288, Santa Efigênia, T3467 1576, www.chalemineiro hostel.com.br. Attractive, HI affiliated, with a small pool, dorms, a shared kitchen, TV lounge and telephones. Towels and bed linen are extra.

F pp O Sorriso do Lagarto, R Padre Severino 285, Savassi, T3283 9325, www.osorrisodolagarto. com.br. Simple, small hostel in a converted town house with kitchen, internet, breakfast, lockers, washing machines and a living area with DVD player.

F pp Pousadinha Mineira, R Espírito Santo 604, Centro, T3273 8156, www.pousadinhamineira. com.br. Large central hostel with separate men's and women's wings, shared bath, breakfast extra, take your own bed linen, also has tow other branches for groups.

🍴 Eating

Belo Horizonte *p411, maps p412 and p413*
Mineiros love their food and drink and Belo Horizonte has a lively café dining and bar scene. Savassi overflows with street cafés, bars and restaurants and is the best place in the city for a food browse. There is a lively, cheap food market on R Tomé de Souza, between Pernambuco and Alagoas, in Savassi every night between 1900 and 2300. Pampulha has the best of the fine dining restaurants; which are well worth the taxi ride. And there are plenty of cheap per kilo restaurants and *padarias* near the budget hotels in the city centre.

♥♥♥ Aurora, R Expedicionário Mário Alves de Oliveira 421, São Luís, T3498 7567. One of the best restaurants in town, garden setting next to Lago da Pampulha. Imaginative menu fusing Mineira and Italian techniques and making use of unusual Brazilian fruits. Closed Mon-Tue.

♥♥♥ Taste Vin, R Curitiba 2105, Lourdes, T3292 5423. Excellent French, soufflés and provençale seafood. The wine list includes decent Brazilian options. Recommended.

♥♥♥ Vecchio Sogno, R Martim de Carvalho 75 and R Dias Adorno, Santo Agostinho, under the Assembléia Legislativo, T3292 5251. The best Italian in the city with an inventive menu fusing Italian and French cuisine with Brazilian ingredients, excellent fish. Lunch only on Sun.

♥♥♥-♥♥ Xapuri, R Mandacaru 260, Pampulha, T3496 6198. Great atmosphere, live music, very good food, a bit out of the way but recommended. Closed Mon.

♥♥ Chico Mineiro, R Alagoas 626, corner of Av Brasil, T3261 3237. Good local chicken specialities, lunchtime only except till 0100 at weekends.

♥♥ Dona Derna, R Tomé de Souza 1380, Savassi, T3223 6954. A range of restaurants in one. Upstairs is Italian fine dining with excellent dishes and a respectable wine list. Downstairs on weekdays is traditional Italian home cooking and by night a chic pizzeria called Memmo.

♥♥ Sushi Naka, R Gonçalves Dias 92, Funcionários, T3287 2714. Japanese, excellent sushi, sashimi and soups. Close to the centre.

♥♥-♥ La Traviata, Av Cristovão Colombo 282, Savassi, T3261 6392. A little moody Italian with terrace, strong on meat and fish, reasonable pasta and pizzas, good value house wine.

♥♥-♥ Sushi Beer, R Tomé de Souza, Savassi, T3221 1116. A large open air dining area overlooked by a long bar, superior per kilo Minas and Japanese food, plus meats and pizzas.

♥ Dona Lucinha, R Sergipe 811, Savassi, T3261 5930 and R Padre Odorico 38 (São Pedro), T3227 0562. Self service, decent meat dishes, generous portions. Lunch only on Sun. Recommended.

♥ Flor de Líbano, R Espírito Santo 234. Very cheap and good.

♥ Kauhana, R Tomé de Souza, Savassi, T3284 8714. Tasty wood-fire cooked pizzas both savoury and sweet, pleasant open-air dining area.

♥ Mala e Cuia, a chain of restaurants serving good comida mineira at R Gonçalves Dias 874, Savassi, T3261 3059, Av Antônio Carlos 8305, Pampulha, T3441 2993, Av Raja Gabaglia 1617, São Bento.

Cafés

A Cafeteria, Av Cristovão Colombo 152, Savassi, T3223 9901. Salads, great sandwiches in pitta bread and a range of mock-Italian standards served to a lively young crowd and accompanied by live music most nights. One of several such café bars on the corner of Colombo and Albuquerque.

🔴 *For an explanation of the sleeping and eating price codes used in this guide, see page 58.*
⚫ *Other relevant information is found in Essentials pages 345-347.*

Café da Travessa, Getúlio Vargas 1405 at Praça Savassi, T3223 8092. Great little café cum book and CD shop. Dishes range from rosti to Brazilian tapas, pasta and wraps, pizzas upstairs, great coffee. From breakfast until late.
Café Tina, Av Cristovão Colombo 336, Savassi, T3261 5068. Bohemian café serving soups, risottos and delicious puddings to an arty crowd. Closed Mon.

⊕ Bars and clubs

Belo Horizonte *p411, maps p412 and p413*
Rua Tomé de Souza in Savassi has umpteen lively bars, particularly between Paraíba and Sergipe. The beer and caipirinhas are cheap and plentiful. Try **Bar de João**, **Bar de James**, or **Bar Koyote**.
Alambique, Av Raja Gabáglia 3200, Chalé 1D, Estoril, T3296 7188. Specializes in cachaça, with mineira appetizers, designed like a country house.

⊕ Festivals and events

Belo Horizonte *p411, maps p412 and p413*
The city celebrates **Maundy Thursday**; Corpus Christi; **15 Aug**, **Assunção** (Assumption); **8 Dec**, Conceição (Immaculate Conception).

⊙ Shopping

Belo Horizonte *p411, maps p412 and p413*
Gemstones Manoel Bernardes, Av Contorno 5417, Savassi. Very reasonable.
Markets See above for the Sun handicraft fair on Av Afonso Pena. **Mercado Central**, Av Augusto de Lima 744. Large and clean, open every day.

▲ Activities and tours

Belo Horizonte *p411, maps p412 and p413*
For information on the cultural and adventure tourism possibilities on the **Estrada Real**, the colonial gold and diamond roads from Minas Gerais to Paraty and Rio de Janeiro, go to the head office at R Álvares Maciel 59, 11th floor, Santa Efigênia, T3241 7166.
Ametur, R Alvarengo Peixoto 295, loja 102, Lourdes, T/F3292 2139. Open 0900-1200, 1400-1900, has information on fazendas which welcome visitors and overnight guests.
Amo-Te, Associação Mineira dos Organizadores do Turismo Ecológico, R Monte Verde 125, Alípio de Melo, T3477 5430, oversees ecotourism in Minas Gerais. For companies which arrange trekking, riding, cycling, rafting, jeep tours, canyoning, visiting national parks, or fazendas, speak to Amo-Te in the first instance.

Master Turismo (Amex representative), R da Bahia 2140, T3330 3655, www.master turismo.com.br. At Sala VIP, Aeroporto de Confins, and Av Afonso Pena 1967, T3330 3603 (very helpful). Runs 10-day/9-night tours on the Estrada Real (see above).
Oasis Turismo, A de Lima 479/815, Centro, T3274 6422. Very helpful, manager Jacqueline.
Ouro Preto Turismo, Av Afonso Pena 4133, T3287 0505, www.ouropretotour.com.
Revetur, R Espírito Santo 1892, 1st floor, Lourdes, T3337 2500, www.revetour.com.br.
Tropa Serrana, Tullio Marques Lopes Filho, T3344 8986, http://troposerrana.zip.net. For recommended horse riding tours.

⊖ Transport

Belo Horizonte *p411, maps p412 and p413*
Air The international airport is near Lagoa Santa, at Confins, 39 km from Belo Horizonte, T3689 2700. Taxi to centre, US$54, cooperative taxis have fixed rates to different parts of the city. Airport bus, either *executivo* from the exit, US$14, or comfortable normal bus (Unir) from the far end of the car park hourly, US$2.65, both go to/from the rodoviária.
    Closer to the city is the national airport at Pampulha, which has shuttle services from several cities, including Rio and São Paulo, T3490 2001. Urban transportation to/from this airport is cheaper than from Confins. From Pampulha airport to town, take blue bus 1202, 25 mins, US$0.65, passing the rodoviária and the cheaper hotel district.
Bus The city has a good public transport system: red buses run on express routes and charge US$1; yellow buses have circular routes around the Contorno, US$0.65; blue buses run on diagonal routes charging US$0.85. There are also buses which integrate with the regional, overground Metrô.
    The rodoviária is by Praça Rio Branco at the northwest end of Av Afonso Pena, T3271 3000/8933. The bus station has toilets, post office, phones, left-luggage lockers (attended service 0700-2200), shops and is clean and well organized. Buses leave from the rather gloomy platforms beneath the ticket hall. Do not leave belongings unattended.
    To **Rio** with **Cometa** (T3201 5611) and **Útil** (T3201 7744), 6½ hrs, US$24 (ordinary), leito, US$51. To **Vitória** with São Geraldo (T3271 1911), US$32. To **Brasília** with Itapemirim (T3271 1019) and **Penha** (T3271 1027), 10 hrs, 6 a day including 2 leitos, only one leaves in daylight (0800), US$32.25-40. To **São Paulo** with **Cometa** and **Gontijo** (T3201 6130), 10 hrs, US$30. To **Foz do Iguaçu**, US$99, 22 hrs. To **Salvador** with Gontijo, US$78, 24 hrs, at 1900

Sights In the central **Praça Tiradentes** is a statue of the leader of the **Inconfidentes**, Joaquim José da Silva Xavier. Another Inconfidente, the poet Tomás Antônio Gonzaga lived at Rua Cláudio Manoel 61, close to São Francisco de Assis church. On the north side of the praça (at No 20) is a famous **Escola de Minas** (School of Mining), founded in 1876, in the fortress-like **Palácio dos Governadores** (1741-1748); it has the interesting **Museu de Mineralogia e das Pedras** ① *Tue-Fri 1200-1700, Sat-Sun 0900-1300, US$2*, with 23,000 stones from around the world. On the south side of the Praça, No 139, is the **Museu da Inconfidência** ① *T3551 1121, Mon-Fri 0800-1800, US$2*, a fine historical and art museum in the former **Casa de Câmara e Cadeia**, which has some drawings by Aleijadinho and the Sala Manoel da Costa Athayde, in an annex. In the Casa Capitular of NS do Carmo is **Museu do Oratório** ① *T3551 5369, daily 0930-1200, 1330-1730*, a collection of beautiful 18th- and 19th-century prayer icons and oratories including many made of egg and sea shell. **Casa dos Contos** ① *R São José 12, T3551 1444, Tue-Sat 1230-1730, Sun and holidays 0900-1500, US$0.65*. Built between 1782-1784, it is the Centro de Estudos do Ciclo de Ouro (Centre for Gold Cycle Studies) and a museum of money and finance. The **Casa Guignard** ① *R Conde de Bobadela 110, T3551 5155, Tue-Fri 1200-1800, Sat, Sun and holidays 0900-1500, free*, displays the paintings of Alberto da Veiga Guignard. The **Teatro Municipal** ① *in R Brigadeiro Musqueiro, daily 1230-1800*, is the oldest functioning theatre in Latin America. It was built in 1769.

São Francisco de Assis (1766-1796) ① *Largo de Coimbra, 0830-1145, 1330-1640, US$2.65*; the ticket also permits entry to NS da Conceição (keep your ticket for admission to the museum). This church is considered to be one of the masterpieces of Brazilian baroque. Aleijadinho worked on the general design and the sculpture of the façade, the pulpits and many other features. Mestre Athayde (1732-1827) was responsible for the painted ceiling. **Nossa Senhora da Conceição** (1722) ① *0830-1130, 1330-1700, Sun 1200-1700*, is heavily gilded and contains Aleijadinho's tomb. It has a museum devoted to him. **Nossa Senhora das Mercês e Perdões** (1740-1772) ① *R das Mercês, 1000-1400*, was rebuilt in the 19th century. Some sculpture by Aleijadinho can be seen in the main chapel. **Santa Efigênia** (1720-1785) ① *Ladeira Santa Efigênia e Padre Faria, 0800-1200*; Manuel Francisco Lisboa (Aleijadinho's father) oversaw the construction and much of the carving is by Francisco Xavier de Brito (Aleijadinho's mentor). It has wonderful panoramic views of the city. **Nossa Senhora do Carmo** (1766-1772) ① *R Brigadeiro Mosqueira, 1330-1700*, has a museum of sacred art with Aleijadinho sculptures. **Nossa Senhora do Pilar** (1733) ① *Praça Mons Castilho Barbosa, 1200-1700*, also contains a religious art museum. Entry is shared with São Francisco de Paula, Ladeira de São José (1804). **Nossa Senhora do Rosário** ① *Largo do Rosário*, dated from 1785, has a curved façade. The interior is much simpler than the exterior, but there are interesting side altars.

The **Mina do Chico Rei** ① *R Dom Silvério, 0800-1700, US$2*, is not as impressive as some other mines in the area, but is fun to crawl about in; restaurant attached. Near the Padre Faria Church (NS do Rosário dos Brancos) is another small mine, **Mina Bem Querer** ① *US$1.30*, with a swimming pool with crystal clear water that runs through the mine. Between Ouro Preto and Mariana is the **Minas de Passagem** ① *US$10, 0900-1730, last admissions at 1645*, gold mine, dating from 1719. A guided tour visits the old mine workings and underground lake (take bathing suit).

Mariana → *Phone code: 0xx31. Post code: 35420. Colour map 7, grid B5. Population: 46,710.*

Streets are lined with beautiful, two-storey 18th-century houses in this old mining city, which is much less hilly than Ouro Preto. Mariana's historical centre slopes gently uphill from the river and the Praça Tancredo Neves, where buses from Ouro Preto stop. **Tourist office**: Secretaria de Cultura e Turismo de Mariana ① *Praça Tancredo Neves, T3557 9044*. The tourist office will help with guides and tours and offer a map and a free monthly booklet, *Mariana Agenda Cultural*, packed with local information including accommodation and eating.

Sights The first street parallel with the Praça Tancredo Neves is Rua Direita, and is home to the 300-year-old houses. At No 54 is the **Casa do Barão de Pontal** ① *Tue 1400-1700*, whose balconies are carved from soapstone, unique in Minas Gerais. The ground floor of the building is a museum of furniture. At No 35 is the **Museu-Casa Afonso Guimarães** (or Alphonsus de Guimaraens) ① *free*, the former home of a symbolist poet: photographs and letters. At No 7 is the **Casa Setecentista**, which now belongs to the Patrimônio Histórico e Artístico Nacional.

Rua Direita leads to the Praça da Sé, on which stands the **Cathedral** ① *Basílica de Nossa Senhora da Assunção, organ concerts are given on Fri at 1100 and Sun at 1200, US$10*. The portal and the lavabo in the sacristy are by Aleijadinho. The painting in the beautiful interior and side altars is by Manoel Rabello de Sousa. Also in the cathedral is a wooden German organ (1701), a gift to the first diocese of the Capitania de Minas do Ouro in 1747. The **Museu Arquidiocesano** ① *R Frei Durão, Tue-Sun 0900-1200, 1300-1700, US$2*, has fine church furniture, a gold and silver collection, Aleijadinho statues and an ivory cross. Opposite is the **Casa da Intendência/Casa de Cultura** ① *R Frei Durão 84, 0800-1130, 1330-1700*, which holds exhibitions and has a museum of music. On the south side of Praça Gomes Freire is the **Palácio Arquiepiscopal**, while on the north side is the **Casa do Conde de Assumar**, who was governor of the Capitania from 1717 to 1720.

From Praça Gomes Freire, Travessa São Francisco leads to Praça Minas Gerais and one of the finest groups of colonial buildings in Brazil. In the middle of the Praça is the **Pelourinho**, the stone monument to Justice, at which slaves used to be beaten. On one side of the square is the fine **São Francisco church** (1762-1794) ① *daily 0800-1700*, with pulpits designed by Aleijadinho, paintings by Mestre Athayde, who is buried in tomb No 94, in a fine sacristy and one side-altar by Aleijadinho. At right angles to São Francisco is **Nossa Senhora do Carmo** (1784) *daily 1400-1700*, with steatite carvings, Athayde paintings, and chinoiserie panelling. Across Rua Dom Silvério is the **Casa da Câmara e Cadéia** (1768), at one time the Prefeitura Municipal. On Largo de São Pedro is **São Pedro dos Clérigos** (begun in 1753), one of the few elliptical churches in Minas Gerais. Restoration is under way.

Capela de Santo Antônio, on Rua Rosário Velho, is wonderfully simple and the oldest in town. It is some distance from the centre. Overlooking the city from the north, with a good viewpoint, is the church of **Nossa Senhora do Rosário**, Rua do Rosário (1752), with work by Athayde and showing Moorish influence.

Parque Nacional Caparaó

① *Contact R Vale Verde s/n, Alto do Caparaó, CEO 36836-000, Toxx32-3266 9090.*
This is one of the most popular parks in Minas (on the Espírito Santo border), with good walking through stands of Atlantic rainforest, páramo and to the summits of three of Brazil's highest peaks: Pico da Bandeira (2,890 m), Pico do Cruzeiro (2,861 m) and Pico do Cristal (2,798 m). The park, surrounded by coffee farms, features rare Atlantic rainforest in its lower altitudes and Brazilian alpine on top. Loss of forest and floral biodiversity has adversely affected wildlife, but there are nonetheless a number of Atlantic coast primates, like the brown capuchins, together with a recovering bird population. From the park entrance (where a small fee has to be paid) it is 6 km on a good unpaved road to the car park at the base of the waterfall. From the hotel (see page 423) jeeps (US$25 per jeep) run to the car park at 1,970 m (2½ hours' walk), then it's a three to four hour walk to the summit of the Pico da Bandeira, marked by yellow arrows; plenty of camping possibilities, the highest being at Terreirão (2,370 m). This is good walking country. It is best to visit during the dry season (April-October). It can be quite crowded in July and during Carnival. ▶ *See Transport, page 425, for how to get there.*

Congonhas → *Phone code: 0xx31. Post code: 36404. Colour map 7, grid B5. Population: 41,256.*

This hill town is connected by a paved 3½ km road with the Rio-Belo Horizonte highway. Most visitors spend little time in the town, but go straight to **O Santuário de Bom Jesus de Matosinhos** ① *Tue-Sun 0700-1900, there are public toilets on the Alameda das Palmeiras, the information desk at the bus station will guard luggage and you can visit the sanctuary between bus changes*, which dominates Congonhas. The great pilgrimage church was finished in 1771; below it are six linked chapels, or pasos (1802-1818), showing scenes with life-size Passion figures carved by Aleijadinho and his pupils in cedar wood. These lead up to a terrace and courtyard. On this terrace (designed in 1777) stand 12 prophets, sculpted by Aleijadinho between 1800 and 1805. Carved in soapstone with dramatic sense of movement, they constitute one of the finest works of art of their period in the world. Inside the church, there are paintings by Athayde and the heads of four sainted popes (Gregory, Jerome, Ambrose and Augustine) sculpted by Aleijadinho for the reliquaries on the high altar. To the left of the church, as you face it, the third door in the building alongside the church is the Room of Miracles, which contains photographs and thanks for miracles performed.

On the hill are souvenir shops, the Colonial Hotel and Cova do Daniel restaurant (both are good, hotel **E**). From the hotel the Alameda das Palmeiras sweeps round to the **Romarias**, which contains the Espaço Cultural, the headquarters of the local tourist office, workshops, the museums of mineralogy and religious art and the Memória da Cidade. To

Ouro Preto *p417*

Prices indicated here are for high season; many hotels offer, or will negotiate, lower prices outside holiday times or when things are quiet.

Ask at the tourist office for accommodation in *casas de família*, reasonably priced. Avoid touts who greet you off buses and charge higher prices than those advertised in hotels; it is difficult to get hotel rooms at weekends and holiday periods.

AL Pousada do Mondego, Largo de Coimbra 38, T3551 2040, www.mondego.com.br. Beautifully kept colonial house in a fine location by São Francisco church, room rates vary according to view, small restaurant, Scotch bar, popular with groups. Recommended (a Roteiro de Charme hotel, see page 346), the hotel runs a jardineira bus tour of the city, 2 hrs, minimum 10 passengers, US$10 for non-guests.

AL Pousada Solar de NS do Rosário, Av Getúlio Vargas 270, T3551 5200, www.hotelsolar dorosario.com.br. Fully restored historic building with a highly recommended restaurant, bar, sauna, pool; all facilities in rooms.

AL-B Pousada Mirante do Café, Fazenda Alto das Rubiáceas, Santo Antônio do Leite, 25 km west of Ouro Preto, T3335 8478, www.mirante docafe.com.br. Price varies with season and weekend. Coffee farm with full board available, visits allowed during coffee harvest, pool, trails, horse riding and other leisure activities.

A Luxor Pousada, R Dr Alfredo Baeta 16, Praça Antônio Dias, T3551 2244, www.luxor hoteis.com.br. Converted colonial mansion, no twin beds, comfortable but spartan, good views, restaurant good but service slow.

B Pousada Casa Grande, R Conselheiro Quintiliano, 96, T/F3551 4314, www.hotel pousadacasagrande.com.br. Including breakfast, safe, good views. Recommended.

B-C Pousada Nello Nuno, R Camilo de Brito 59, T3551 3375, http://pousadanellonuno.com. Cheaper rooms have no bath, friendly owner Annamélia speaks some French. Highly recommended.

C Colonial, Trav Padre Camilo Veloso 26, close to Praça Tiradentes, T3551 3133, www.hotelc olonial.com.br. With new rooms and refurbished older rooms, pleasant.

C Pousada Itacolomi, R Antônio Pereira 167, T3551 2891. Next door to the Museu da Inconfidência, small but well kept with good rates for the 3-room apartments.

C Pousada Tiradentes, Praça Tiradentes 70, T3551 2619. Spartan rooms, but well kept and moderately comfortable, TV, fridge, conveniently located.

C Pouso Chico Rey, R Brig Musqueira 90, T3551 1274. Fascinating old house with Portuguese colonial furnishings, very small and utterly delightful (but plumbing unreliable), book in advance.

C Solar das Lajes, R Conselheiro Quintiliano 604, T/F3551 3388, www.solardaslajes.com.br. A little way from centre but with an excellent view and a pool, well run.

D Pousada dos Bandeirantes, R das Mercês 167, T3551 1996. Behind the São Francisco de Assis church and offering beautiful views.

D Pousada São Francisco de Paula, Padre JM Pen 202, next to the São Francisco de Paula church, 100 m from rodoviária, T3551 3456, pousadas@hotmail.com. One of the best views of any in the city, from the rooms or from a hammock in the garden. Rooms with and without bath or breakfast, dormitory, use of a kitchen, multilingual staff, excursions. Snacks are available. Recommended (book in after 1200).

E Brumas, R. Pe José Marcos Pena 68, 150 m downhill from rodoviária, just below São Francisco de Paula church, T3551 2944, www.brumasonline.cjb.net. Hostel with dormitory, kitchen and laundry and superb views. Don't walk down from bus station after dark.

Camping Camping Clube do Brasil, Rodovia dos Inconfidentes Km 91, 2 km north, T3551 1799. Expensive but good.

Students may be able to stay, during holidays and weekends, at the self-governing student hostels, known as *repúblicas* (very welcoming, 'best if you like heavy metal music' and 'are prepared to enter into the spirit of the places'). The Prefeitura has a list of over 50 repúblicas with phone numbers, available at the Secretaria de Turismo. Many are closed between Christmas and Carnival.

Mariana *p418*

B Pousada do Chafariz, R Cônego Rego 149, T3557 1492, chafariz@veloxmail.com.br. Converted colonial building, TV, fridge, parking, breakfast included.

B Pousada Solar dos Corrêa, R Josefá Macedo 70 and R Direita, T/F3557 2080, www.pousadasolardoscorrea.com.br. Central, restored 18th-century town house with spacious a/c rooms, with breakfast, TV, fridge in room, internet, parking.

D-E Central, R Frei Durão 8, T/F3557 1630. A charming but run-down colonial building on the attractive Praça Gomes Freire. Recommended but avoid downstairs rooms.

D-E Providência, R Dom Silvério 233, T3557 1444, www.hotelprovidencia.com.br. Along the road that leads up to the Basílica; has use of the neighbouring school's pool when classes finish at noon, small rooms, quiet.

Parque Nacional Caparaó p419

A Caparaó Parque, T3747 2559, 2 km from the park entrance, 15 mins' walk from the town of Alto Caparaó, nice. Ask where camping is permitted.
C São Luiz, in **Manhumirim** (Population: 20,025), good value, but **Cids Bar**, next door, Travessa 16 do Março, has better food.

São João del Rei p420

A Beco do Bispo, Beco do Bispo 93, 2 mins west of São Francisco de Assis, T/3371 8844, www.becodobispo.com.br. The best in town, bright a/c rooms with firm mattresses, hot showers, cable TV, pool, convenient, very helpful English speaking staff. Organizes tours. Highly recommended.
B Lenheiros Palace, Av Pres Tancredo Neves 257, T/F3371 8155, www.hotellenheiros.com.brs. A modern hotel with good facilities, parking, Lenheiros Casa de Chá tea house, breakfast, no restaurant.
B Ponte Real, Av Eduardo Magalhães 254, T/F3371 7000, www.hotelpontereal.com.br. Also modern, comfortable, sizeable rooms, good restaurant.
B Pousada Casarão, opposite São Francisco church, in a converted mansion, Ribeiro Bastos 94, T3371 7447, www.pousadacasarao.com. In a delightful converted mansion house, firm beds, TV, fridge, swimming pool, games room.
C Aparecida, Praça Dr Antônio Viegas 13, T3371 2540. Central, by the bus and taxi stop, has a restaurant and lanchonete.
D Brasil, Av Presidente Tancredo Neves 395, T3371 2804. In an old house full of character and staircases, on the opposite side of the river from the railway station, cheap. Recommended but basic, no breakfast.
D Sinha Batista, R Manock Anselmo 22, T3371 5550. The best of the cheaper options, quite large rooms in a colonial building conveniently located by the central canal.

Tiradentes p420

L Solar da Ponte, Praça das Mercês (proprietors John and Anna Maria Parsons), T3355 1255, www.solardaponte.com.br. Has the atmosphere of a country house, the price includes breakfast and afternoon tea, only 12 rooms, fresh flowers in rooms, bar, sauna, lovely gardens, swimming pool, light meals for residents only, for larger meals, the hotel recommends 5 local restaurants (it is in the Roteiros de Charme group, see page 346). For horse-riding treks, contact John Parsons here. Recommended.
A Pousada Mãe D'Água, Largo das Forras 50, T3355 1206, www.pousadamaedagua.com.br. Including breakfast but not tax, very nice, outdoor pool in garden.

A Pousada Três Portas, R Direita 280A, T3355 1444, www.pousadatresportas.com.br. Charming, central, in restored town house, has sauna, thermal pool, hydromassage, heating.
A Pouso das Gerais, R dos Inconfidentes 109, T3355 1234, www.pousodasgerais. com.br. Fresh fan-cooled rooms, TV, marble basins, central, quiet, pool, breakfast included. Recommended.
B-C Pousada do Arco Iris, R Frederico Ozanan 340, T3355 1167, www.arcoiristiradentes mg.com.br. The best of a string of pousadas in houses on this stretch of road just out of town. Swimming pool, popular, family-run, 5 rooms only. Price includes breakfast. Book ahead.
C Pousada do Laurito, R Direita 187, T3355 1268. Central, good value, very popular with international backpackers.

São Tomé das Letras p421

Streets are hard to follow because their names seem to change almost from one block to the next; numbering is also chaotic. There are lots of pousadas and rooms to let all over town.
B Pousada Arco-Iris, R João Batista Neves 19, T/F3237 1212. Rooms and chalets, sauna, swimming pool.
C dos Sonhos II (do Gê), Trav Nhá Chica 8, T3237 1235. Very nice, restaurant, swimming pool, sauna. Recommended.
D pp Fundação Harmonia, Estrada para Sobradinho s/n, Bairro do Canta Galo, T3237 1280. 4 km from town, but shop on the main Praça. The community emphasizes several disciplines for a healthy lifestyle, for mind and body, 'new age', workshops, massage, excursions, vegetarian food, clean accommodation.
D-E pp Pousada Souza Reis, Praça do Rosário 540, T3237 1264. Next to Igreja de Pedra, with bath and breakfast, TV, good value, helpful.

Eating

Ouro Preto p417

Try the local liquor *de jaboticaba*.
Adega, R Teixeira Amaral 24, T3551 4171. Vegetarian smorgasbord, all you can eat, 1130-1530. Highly recommended.
Casa Grande and **Forno de Barro**, both on Praça Tiradentes (Nos 84 and 54 respectively). Decent Mineira cooking.
Ouro Grill, R Sen Rocha Lagoa 61. Self-service at lunchtime, US$5, good value after 1600.
Taverna do Chafariz, R São José 167, T3551 2828. Good local food. Recommended.
Beijinho Doce, R Direita 134A. Delicious pastries and cakes, try the truffles.
Café & Cia, R São José 187, T3551 0711. Closes 2300, very popular, comida por kilo at lunchtime, good salads, juices.

☦ **Deguste**, R São José next to Banco Itaú. Good value.

☦ **Pasteleria Lampião**, Praça Tiradentes. Good views at the back (best at lunchtime).

☦ **Vide Gula**, R Sen Rocha Lagoa 79a, T3551 4493. Food by weight, good, friendly atmosphere. Recommended.

Mariana p418

☦☦ **Engenho Nôvo**, Praça da Sé 26. Bar at night, English spoken by the owners and clients. Recommended.

☦☦ **Mangiare della Mamma**, D Viçoso 27. Italian. Recommended.

☦☦ **Tambaú**, R João Pinheiro 26. Regional food.

☦ **Panela de Pedra** in the Terminal Turístico serves food by weight at lunchtime.

São João del Rei p420

☦☦☦ **Churrascaria Ramón**, Praça Severiano de Resende 52. One of the town's better churrascarias with generous portions and plenty of side dishes.

☦☦☦ **Quinto do Ouro**, Praça Severiano de Rezende 04, T3371 7577. Tasty and well-prepared regional food. Said to be the best Mineira cooking in town.

☦☦ **Portal del Rey**, Praça Severiano de Rezende 134. Comida à kilo, Minas and Arabic food; good value.

☦ **Restaurant 611**, R Getúlio Vargas 145, T3371 8793. Very cheap but excellent Mineira cooking – eat as much as you like for less than US$2. Plenty of choice, very popular.

Tiradentes p420

There are many restaurants, snack bars and *lanchonetes* in town and it is a small enough place to wander around and see what takes your fancy.

☦☦☦ **Estalagem**, R Ministro G Passos 280. Excellent and generous traditional Mineira meat dishes.

☦☦☦ **Quartier Latin**, R São Francisco de Paula 46, Praça da Rodoviária, T3355 1552. French, cordon bleu chef, excellent.

☦☦☦ **Quinto de Ouro**, R Direita 159. Mineira and international dishes. Recommended.

☦☦☦ **Theatro da Vila**, R Padre Toledo 157, T3355 1275. Inventive and delicious Franco-Brazilian fusion cooking served in intimate rustic-chic dining room. Views out towards the Serra across the restaurant garden which has a little theatre with performances in summer.

☦☦☦ **Virados do Largo**, Largo do Ó. Good Mineira food and service.

☦ **Maria Luisa Casa de Chá**, Largo do Ó 1, diagonally opposite Aluarte, T3355 1502. Tea, cakes and sandwiches in an arty Bohemian atmosphere. Great for breakfast.

🍷 Bars and clubs

Tiradentes p420

Aluarte, Largo do Ó 1, is a bar with live music in the evening, nice atmosphere, US$4 cover charge, garden, sells handicrafts.

⊛ Festivals and events

Ouro Preto p417

Ouro Preto is famous for its **Holy Week** processions, which in fact begin on the Thu before Palm Sunday and continue (but not every day) until Easter Sunday. The most famous is that commemorating Christ's removal from the Cross, late on Good Friday. Many shops close during this holiday, and on winter weekends. Attracting many Brazilians, **Carnival** here is also memorable. In **Jun**, **Corpus Christi** and the **Festas Juninas** are celebrated. Every **Jul** the city holds the **Festival do Inverno da Universidade Federal de Minas Gerais** (UFMG), the Winter Festival, about 3 weeks of arts, courses, shows, concerts and exhibitions. Also in **Jul**, on the 8th, is the **anniversary of the city**. **15 Aug**: Nossa Senhora do Pilar, patron saint of Ouro Preto. **12-18 Nov**: Semana de Aleijadinho, a week-long arts festival.

Congonhas p419

Congonhas is famous for its **Holy Week** processions, which have as their focus the Bom Jesus church. The most celebrated ceremonies are the **meeting of Christ and the Virgin Mary** on the **Tue**, and the dramatized **Deposition from the Cross** late on **Good Friday**. The pilgrimage season, first half of **Sep**, draws thousands. **8 Dec**, Nossa Senhora da Conceição.

São João del Rei p420

Apr, Semana Santa; **15-21 Apr**, Semana da Inconfidência. **May or Jun**, Corpus Christi. **First 2 weeks of Aug**, Nossa Senhora da Boa Morte, with baroque music (novena barroca). Similarly, **12 Oct**, Nossa Senhora do Pilar, patron saint of the city. **8 Dec**, founding of the city. FUNREI, the university (R Padre José Maria Xavier), holds **Inverno Cultural** in **Jul**.

🛍 Shopping

Ouro Preto p417

Gems are not much cheaper from freelance sellers in Praça Tiradentes than from the shops, and in the shops, the same quality of stone is offered at the same price. If buying on the street, ask for the seller's credentials. Buy soapstone carvings at roadside stalls and bus stops rather than in cities; they are much cheaper. Many artisans sell carvings, jewellery and semi-precious stones in Largo de Coimbra in front of São Francisco de Assis church. Recommended are: **Gemas de Minas**, Conde de Bobadela 63; and **Manoel Bernardis**, Conde de Bobadela 48.

⊖ Transport

Sabará *p416*
Bus Viação Cisne No 1059 from R Catete, **Belo Horizonte**, US$1.50, 30 mins, circular route.

Parque Natural de Caraça *p417*
Turn off the BR-262 (towards Vitória) at Km 73 and go via Barão de Cocais to Caraça (120 km). There is no public transport to the seminary. **Buses** go as far as **Barão de Cocais**, from where you have to take a taxi, US$15 one way. You must book the **taxi** to return for you, or else **hitch** (which may not be easy). The park entrance is 10 km before the seminary. The alternatives are either to hire a **car**, or take a guide from Belo Horizonte, which will cost about US$100 (including guiding, transport and meals). It is possible to stay in **Santa Bárbara** (D Hotel **Karaibe**, D Santa Inés), 25 km away on the road to Mariana and hitchhike to Caraça. 11 buses a day from Belo Horizonte – Santa Bárbara (fewer on Sat and Sun).

Ouro Preto *p417*
Bus Don't walk from the rodoviária to town at night; robberies have occurred. The rodoviária is at R Padre Rolim 661, near São Francisco de Paula church, T3551 3252. A 'Circular' bus runs from the rodoviária to Praça Tiradentes, US$0.75. Taxi US$4.50. 11 buses a day from Belo Horizonte (2 hrs, **Pássaro Verde**), US$7. Day trips are run. Book your return journey to **Belo Horizonte** early if returning in the evening; buses get crowded. Bus to/from **Rio**, **Útil**, 3 a day, US$30, 12 hrs (book in advance). There are also Útil buses to **Congonhas** on the new Caminho de Ouro highway and services to **Conselheiro Lafaiete**, 3-4 a day via Itabirito and Ouro Branco (see below), US$7.50, 2¾ hrs. Other Útil services to Rio go via Belo Horizonte. Direct buses to **São Paulo**, 3 a day with Cristo Rei, 11 hrs, US$37. Gontijo go to Salvador via Belo Horizonte.

Mariana *p418*
Bus Mariana is only 12 km from Ouro Preto and can easily be visited as a side trip. Buses run between the Escola de Minas near Praça Tiradentes in Ouro Preto and the Secretaria de Cultura e Turismo de Mariana, Praça Tancredo Neves, every 30 mins.

Parque Nacional Caparaó *p419*
Bus The park is 49 km by paved road from Manhuaçu (about 190 km south of Governador Valadares) on the Belo Horizonte-Vitória road (BR-262). There are buses from **Belo Horizonte** (twice daily with **Pássaro Verde**), Ouro Preto or Vitória to **Manhumirim**, 15 km south of Manhuaçu. From Manhumirim, take a bus direct to Alto Caparaó, 8 a day, US$2. By **car** from the BR-262, go through Manhumirim, Alto Jaqutibá and Alto Caparaó village, then 1 km further to the Hotel Caparaó Parque.

Congonhas *p419*
Bus The Rodoviária is 1½ km outside town; bus to town centre US$0.75; for 'Basílica', see above. To/from **Belo Horizonte**, 1½ hrs, US$6, 8 times a day. To **São João del Rei**, 2 hrs, US$7, tickets are not sold until the bus comes in. Bus to **Ouro Preto**: direct on the new Caminho de Ouro highway, or go via Belo Horizon te or Conselheiro Lafaiete.

São João del Rei *p420*
Bus Rodoviária is 2 km west of the centre. Buses to **Rio**, 5 daily with **Paraibuna** (3 on Sat and Sun), 5 hrs, US$20. **Cristo Rei** to **São Paulo**, 8 hrs, 5 a day, and **Translavras**, 4 a day, US$24. **Belo Horizonte**, 3½ hrs, US$12.25. To **Tiradentes** with Meier, 8 a day, 7 on Sat, Sun and holidays, US$1.25.

Tiradentes *p420*
Bus Last bus back to **São João del Rei** is 1815, 2230 on Sun; fares are given above. **Taxi** To **São João del Rei** costs US$20. Around town there are pony-drawn taxis; ponies can be hired for US$10.

São Tomé das Letras *p421*
Bus There are 3 daily buses (2 on Sun) to São Tomé from **Tres Corações**, the birthplace of Pelé, the legendary football star (to whom there is a statue in Praça Col José Martins), US$3.15, 1½ hrs (paved road). Tres Corações has hotels and regular buses to **Belo Horizonte**, US$20, 5½ hrs, and **São Paulo**, US$15.

❶ Directory

Ouro Preto *p417*
Banks Banco do Brasil, R São José 189; high commission, changes TCs. **Bradesco**, corner of Senador Rocha Lagoa and Padre Rolim, opposite the Escola de Minas. **Banco 24 Horas**, Praça Alves de Brito, next to Correios. **Internet** Point Language School, Xavier da Veiga 501. **Post offices** Praça Alves de Brito.

● Sleeping

Vitória *p426*

A **Alice Vitória**, R Cnel Vicente Peixoto 95, Praça Getúlio Vargas, T3322 1144, and round the corner,
B **São José**, Av Princesa Isabel 300, T3223 7222, www.gruponeffa.com.br. In the busy lower city, good rooms with a/c, TV, comfy beds, typical business hotels, special offers. With ♥¶ Pizza **Gourmet** restaurant, which serves pizza, quick dishes and local specialities, open till 2300, modern cafeteria style, clean, clinical but OK.
C **Avenida**, Av Florentino Avidos 347, T3071 1031. With breakfast, cheaper without fridge, with TV, simple, thin mattresses, noisy avenue outside. Recommended.
C **Vitória**, R Cais de São Francisco 85, T3223 0222. Near Parque Moscoso. Comfortable rooms, some with round beds, a/c, TV, rambling building, good restaurant Mar e Sol. Quieter than Avenida.
D **Cidade Alta**, R Dionisio Rosendo 213, T3322 7188. Cheaper rooms without TV, with breakfast, hot water. Strange place on Cathedral praça, cavernous, basic, full of character.
D **Imperial**, 7 de Setembro, corner Praça Costa Pereira, T3233 5017. Noisy but cheap, cheaper without TV or bath, good value but tatty, hot water, fan, has its own à kilo restaurant (nearby are lots of other cheap eating places – see below).
  Adequate hotels can be found opposite the rodoviária. eg **Minas**, **Lírio**, **Spala**, **JS** and **Príncipe** nearby, which looks posher.

Camburi

A **Aruan**, Av Dante Michelini 1497, T3334 0777, www.grupohp.com.br. Good beachfront hotel with rooms with views, comfortable, free sauna, pool and internet, massage at R$15, restaurant serving wide variety of dishes, safes in rooms, helpful. In same group (same phones and www): **Porto do Sol**, Av Dante Michelini 3957, and A **Vitória Palace**, R José Teixeira 323, Praia do Canto, T3325 0999.
B **Alvetur**, Av Dante Michelini 877, T3225 3911, alvetur@matrix.com.br. All the usual facilities of a beachfront hotel, outside a bit faded and plain lobby, but rooms are well furnished if unfussy, big TV! In same group are **Mata da Praia**, Av Adalberto Simão Nader 133, T3227 9422, matadapraia@matrix.com.br, and **Aeroporto**, R Ary Ferreira Chagas 35, T3325 7888, haeroporto@ ebr.com.br (large rooms, well-furnished, good breakfast), both on way to airport from Camburi beach, and C **Camburi**, Av Dante Michelini 1007, T3334 0303 (rather tatty outside and in lobby).

Vila Velha

B **Itaparica Praia**, R Itapemirim 30, Coqueiral de Itaparica, Vila Velha, T3329 7385, www.hotelitaparica.com.br. More expensive in high season, rooms with sea view cost a bit more. Huge rooms with fridge and TV, pool, garage, quiet, safe and good. Next door is a good café serving breads cakes, Pão e Companhia (which has other branches).
C **Forte Príncipe**, R Aracruz 169, Coqueiral de Itaparica, in Vila Velha, 8 km from Vitória, T3339 1605, ask for Marcelo, www.forteprincipe.com.br. Cheaper without a/c and for HI members, all rooms with 2 floors, F pp in dorm, kitchen, TV, OK, no meals, garage. Convenient for Carone supermarket, beach and buses.
E-F **Jardim da Penha**, R Hugo Viola 135, Vitória, T3324 0738, F3325 6010, take 'Universitário' bus, get off at first University stop.

Inland from Vitória: Santa Teresa *p427*

A **Pierazzo**, Av Getúlio Vargas 115, T3259 1233, pierazzohotel@uol.com.br. Central, nice rooms with frigobar, TV, comfortable, helpful, small pool, sauna. Recommended.

Itaúnas and around: Conceição da Barra *p427*

B **Pousada Mirante**, Av Atlântica 566, T3762 1633. With a/c, completely renovated, spotless, English spoken.
B **Pousada Porto Márlin**, Praia Guaxindiba, T3762 1800, www.redemarlin.com.br. With a/c, TV, fridge, seaview, waterpark, restaurant and bar.
  For other places see www.portonet.com.br/cb/pousadas.asp).
Camping Camping Clube do Brasil, full facilities, Rodovia Adolfo Serra, Km 16, T3762 1346.

● Eating

Vitória *p426*

A local speciality is *Moqueca capixaba*, a seafood dish served in an earthenware pot. It is a variant of the moqueca which is typical of Bahia. Note that it's big enough for 2 people, but you can get half portions. It is served with rice and siri desfiado, crab and shrimp in a thick sauce, very tasty. Several places on R Joaquim Lírio, Praia do Canto, from breads to pastas to seafood. Lots of lanches, etc, on R G Neves at Praça Costa Pereira, in the city centre, and pizzas and others on R 7 de Setembro.
♥♥♥ **Pirão**, R Joaquim Lírio 753, Praia do Canto. Specializes in *moqueca*, also fish, seafood and a couple of meat dishes. Well-established and rightly highly regarded. Ask for a bib to keep your front clean. Closed in the evening.
♥ **Restaurante Expresso**, G Neves 22, T3223 1091. A better class of self-service for lunch, good choice and puddings, a/c, clean, popular.

Cafés/padarias

Cheiro Verde, R Prof Baltazar, next to Pão Gostoso. Churrascaria and comida caseira, self-service.

Expressa, as above, next door and open later in afternoon, on G Neves. For good breads, cakes, savouries and cold stuffs.

Pão Gostoso, R Prof Baltazar. Also selling breads, cakes, savouries and cold stuffs.

Inland from Vitória: Santa Teresa *p427*

† **Zitu's**, Av Getúlio Vargas 79. Self-service, good local food. There are many other eating places in the town.

Bars and clubs

Vitória *p426*

The junction of Joaquim Lírio and João da Cruz in Praia do Canto is known as O Triângulo (or Bermuda Triangle). 2 bars at the junction, **Bilac** and **Búfalo Branco** are very popular Fri and Sat with young crowd. Another bar is **Apertura**, J Lírio 811, quieter. All serve food. Many other places in the area, including The Point Plaza. From centre take any bus going to Camburi and get out opposite São José supermarket just before Ponte de Camburi.

Transport

Vitória *p426*

Air Eurico Salles airport is at Goiaberas, 11 km from the city. Several buses go there eg Nos 162, 163, 122, 212. Taxi from centre US$15.

Bus City buses are mostly green, US$0.75. No 212 is a good route, from rodoviária to airport, marked Aeroporto; make sure it says Via Av Beira Mar: it goes right along the waterfront, past the docks (ask to be let off for Av Princesa Isabel in centre), Shopping Vitória opposite the State Legislative Assembly, by the Third Bridge, MacDonald's near InJoy internet (look for inverted V arch on right side and immediately ring bell to get off – McDonald's is across the avenue), São José supermarket just before Ponte de Camburi, all along Camburi beach, then turns left to airport.

To Vila Velha: from Vitória take a yellow 500 bus marked 'Vilha Velha' from Praça Getúlio Vargas, or a 514 from Av Mal Mascarenhas de Moraes. No 508 connects Camburi and Vila Velha. Buses back to Vitória leave from the rodoviária, or a stop on Champagnat, almost opposite Carone supermarket, fare US$0.60. In Vila Velha, to get to Coqueiral de Itaparica (see Sleeping), go to the rodoviária and change to a blue bus, Linhas Alimentadores, No 605 or 606, marked

T Ibes (ask where to get off) – you shouldn't have to pay for this connection. For NS da Penha, ask to be let off the yellow bus into Vila Velha on Av Henrique Moscoso at or near R Antônio Ataíde, which you go down (right from direction of bus) to R Vasco Coutinho then turn right.

The rodoviária is a 15-min walk west of the centre; many buses go there and there is a city bus stop just outside. It has good lanches, sweet shops and toilets (R$0.70). **Rio**, 8 hrs, US$33. **Belo Horizonte**, see above. **Ouro Preto**, São Geraldo US$32, 6 hrs, poor road, also **Itapemirim**, which goes to other Minas Gerais destinations. Rio Doce to **Juiz da Fora** and **southern Minas Gerais**. **São Paulo**, US$57, 16 hrs. **Salvador**, 18 hrs, US$102, **Aguia Branca** at 1700; **Porto Seguro** direct 11 hrs with lots of stops **Aguia Branca**, 2 a day, US$52; alternatively, take a bus to Eunápolis, then change to buses which run every hour. **Alvorada** bus from Vitória to **Guarapari**, 1½ hrs, several daily, US$4.50.

Train Daily passenger service to **Belo Horizonte**, departs 0700, arrives Belo Horizonte at 1940, returns 0730, arrives 2100; US$25 executivo (very comfortable), US$16 econômico. T0800 992233, CAP Centro de atendimento de pasageiros. The station is called Pedro Nolasco, Km 1 BR-262: take a yellow bus saying 'Ferroviária', best is No 515 going to Campo Grande; to the city (cross the main road outside the station), Praia do Canto and Camburi, take a 'T Laranjeiras via Beira Mar' bus.

Inland from Vitória: Santa Teresa *p427*

Bus Several buses daily from **Vitória** rodoviária with **Lirio dos Vales**, US$6.25, most go via Fundão on the BR-101 going north, all paved. Fewer buses via Santa Leopoldina, not all paved, a beautiful journey.

Directory

Vitória *p426*

Airline offices TAM, R Eugênio Neto 111, T3325 1222. **Varig**, T4003 7000, Goiaberas airport T3327 0304 ext 220. **Banks** Banco do Brasil, Praça Pio XII, câmbio 1000-1600. ATM for Visa. Other banks close by. HSBC, Av Princesa Isabel 43, changes TCs, but very slow and 6% commission. **Car rental** Agencies at airport. **Internet** In Joy, Av Saturnino de Brito 169, Praia do Canto, T3225 2114, close behind McDonalds. Loads of machines, fast, US$0.55 per hr. Mon-Fri 1000-2200, Sat-Sun 1200-2200. **Telephones** Rios phone office (Telemar) on Praça Costa Pereira.

North of Belo Horizonte

Diamantina, the most remote of the colonial cities to the north of the State capital is reached from Belo Horizonte by taking the paved road to Brasília (BR-040). Turn northeast to **Curvelo**, beyond which the road passes through the impressive rocky country of the Serra do Espinhaço. Equally remote is the town of Serro, while in the Serra do Espinhaço itself is the Cipó national park, protecting high mountain grassland and rare species.

Diamantina → *Phone code: 0xx38. Post code: 39100. Colour map 7, grid A5. Population: 44,259.*
This centre of a once-active diamond industry Diamantina has excellent colonial buildings. Its churches are not as grand as those of Ouro Preto, but it is the least spoiled of all the colonial mining cities, with carved overhanging roofs and brackets. This very friendly, beautiful town is in the deep interior, amid barren mountains. It is lively at weekends. **President Juscelino Kubitschek**, the founder of Brasília, was born here. His **house** ① *R São Francisco 241, Tue-Sun 1000-1200, 1400-1800, US$2,* is now a museum. Festivals include Carnival, 12 September, which is O Dia das Serestas, the Day of the Serenades, for which the town is famous; this is also the anniversary of Kubitschek's birth. **Departamento de Turismo** ① *Casa de Cultura, Praça Antônio Eulálio 53, 3rd floor, T3531 1636*; pamphlets, reliable map, friendly and helpful, free tour of churches with guide (tip guide).

Sights The oldest church in Diamantina is **Nossa Senhora do Rosário** ① *Largo Dom Joaquim, Tue-Sat 0800-1200, 1400-1800, Sun 0800-1200,* built by slaves in 1728. **Nossa Senhora do Carmo** ① *R do Carmo, Tue-Sat 0800-1200, 1400-1800, Sun 0800-1200,* dates from 1760-1765 and was built for the Carmelite Third Order. It is the richest church in the town, with fine decorations and paintings and a pipe organ, covered in gold leaf, made locally.

São Francisco de Assis ① *R São Francisco, just off Praça JK, Sat 0800-1200, 1400-1800, Sun 0900-1200,* was built between 1766 and the turn of the 19th century. It is notable for its paintings and has been renovated (2006). Other colonial churches are the **Capela Imperial do Amparo** (1758-1776), **Nossa Senhora das Mercês** (1778-1784) and **Nossa Senhora da Luz** (early 19th century). The **Catedral Metropolitana de Santo Antônio**, on Praça Correia Rabelo, was built in the 1930s in neo-colonial style to replace the original cathedral.

After repeated thefts, the diamonds of the **Museu do Diamante** ① *R Direita 14, Tue-Sat 1200-1730, Sun 0900-1200, US$1,* are now kept in the Banco do Brasil. The museum houses an important collection of materials used in the diamond industry, plus oratories and iron collars used to shackle slaves. **Casa de Chica da Silva** ① *Praça Lobo Mesquita 266, Tue-Sat 1200-1730, Sun 0900-1200, free.* Chica da Silva was a slave in the house of the father of Padre Rolim (one of the Inconfidentes). She became the mistress of João Fernandes de Oliveira, a diamond contractor. Chica, who died 15 February 1796, has become a folk-heroine among Brazilian blacks.

Behind the 18th-century building which now houses the **Prefeitura Municipal** (originally the diamonds administration building, Praça Conselheiro Matta 11) is the **Mercado Municipal** or **Mercado dos Tropeiros** (muleteers) ① *Praça Barão de Guaicuí.* The **Casa da Glória** ① *R da Glória 297, Tue-Sun 1300-1700,* is two houses on either side of the street connected by an enclosed bridge. It contains the Instituto Eschwege de Geologia.

Walk along the **Caminho dos Escravos**, the old paved road built by slaves between the mining area on Rio Jequitinhonha and Diamantina. A guide is essential (ask at the Casa de Cultura), and beware of snakes and thunderstorms. Along the river bank it is 12 km on a dirt road to **Biribiri**, a pretty village with a well-preserved church and an abandoned textile factory. It also has a few bars and at weekends it is a popular, noisy place. About halfway, there are swimming pools in the river; opposite them, on a cliff face, are animal paintings in red. The age and origin are unknown. The plant life along the river is interesting and there are beautiful mountain views.

At **São Gonçalo do Rio das Pedras** and **Milo Verde** (35 and 42 km south of Diamantina on an unsealed road), there are trails for hiking and riding, waterfalls and some colonial buildings in the towns. Simple lodging is available.

The sleepy little town of **São Gonçalo do Rio Preto**, which sits next to a beautiful mountain river, is famous for its traditional festivals. It lies some 60 km from Diamantina on the edge of the **Parque Estadual de São Gonçalo do Rio Preto**, an area of pristine *cerrado* filled with flowering trees and particularly rich in birdlife. There are *pousadas* in São Gonçalo and cabins in the park (accessible by taxi). Guides are also available.

Serro → *Phone code: 0xx38. Post code: 39150. Colour map 7, grid B5. Population: 21,012.*

From Diamantina, 92 km by paved road and reached by bus from there or from Belo Horizonte, is this unspoiled colonial town on the Rio Jequitinhonha. It has six fine baroque churches, a museum and many beautiful squares. It makes queijo serrano, one of Brazil's best cheeses, being in the centre of a prosperous cattle region. The most conspicuous church is **Santa Rita** on a hill in the centre of town, reached by a long line of steps. On the main Praça João Pinheiro, by the bottom of the steps, is **Nossa Senhora do Carmo**, arcaded, with original paintings on the ceiling and in the choir. The town has two large mansions: those of the **Barão de Diamantina** ① *Praça Presidente Vargas*, now in ruins, and of the **Barão do Serro** ① *across the river on R da Fundição, Tue-Sat 1200-1700, Sun 0900-1200*, beautifully restored and used as the town hall and Casa de Cultura. The **Museu Regional Casa dos Ottoni** ① *Praça Cristiano Ottoni 72*, is an 18th-century house with furniture and objects from the region. There are hotels in town.

Parque Nacional da Serra do Cipó
① *Toxx31 3718 7228, www.guiaserradocipo.com.br/parquenacional.*
About 105 km northeast of Belo Horizonte, **Parque Nacional da Serra do Cipó**, 33,400 sq km of the Serra do Espinhaço, covers important cerrado and gallery forest habitats, which provide a home for rare bird species like the Cipó Canastero and Grey-backed Tachuri, as well as endangered mammals such as maned wolf and monkeys such as the masked titi and brown capuchin. There are a number of carnivorous plants. The predominant habitat is high mountain grassland, with rocky outcroppings. Take a guide because the trails are unmarked; ask locally.

● Sleeping

Diamantina *p430*
All are within 10 mins' walking distance of the centre unless otherwise stated.
AL Tijuco, R Macau do Melo 211, T3531 1022, www.hoteltijuco.com.br. A deliciously dated Niemeyer building with tastefully renovated plush wood interior and rooms which retain their 60s feel, great views.
A Relíquias do Tempo, R Macau de Baixo 104, T3531 1627, www.pousadareliquiasdotempo. com.br. Cosy rooms in a pretty 19th-century house just off Praça JK, decorated like a colonial family home, generous breakfasts.
A-B Pousada do Garimpo, Av da Saudade 265, T3531 1044, www.pousadadogarimpo.com.br. Plain, well-kept rooms in a smart hotel on the outskirts, pool, sauna, restaurant serving some of the city's best Minas cooking.
B-C Montanhas de Minas, R da Roman 264, T3531 3240, www.grupomontanhasde minas.com.br. Spacious rooms with stone floors, some with balconies, decent breakfasts.
C Pousada da Seresta, R Jogo da Bola 415, T3531 2368. Rambling colonial house, quiet, good views.
C-D Pousada dos Cristais, R Joga da Bola 53, T3531 3923, www.diamantinanet.com.br/ pousadadoscristais. A range of simple, large rooms in white on the edge of town, with views across the mountains.
C-D Pousada Ouro de Minas, R do Amparo 90A, T3531 2306, www.grupomontanhasde minas.com.br. Simple well-kept rooms with tiny bathrooms in a converted colonial house. In the same group is Pousada Acaiaca, R Acaiaca 65, T3531 8383.
C-D Santiago, Largo Dom João 133, T3431 3407, hotelsantiago@jk.net. Plain, small but spruce rooms, reasonable breakfast.
C-E Pousada Dona Daizinha, R Direita 131, T3531 1351. Simple wood-floor rooms in a colonial house; some with space for up to 5. Very good breakfast and friendly service.

Parque Nacional da Serra do Cipó *p431*
LL Toucan Cipó, exclusively through www.dehouche.com as part of a tour. Luxury *fazenda* in prisitine *cerrado* forest cut by clear-water streams. Very rich in bird and mammal life.
AL Cipó Veraneio, Rodovia MG-10, Km 95, Jaboticatubas, T3718 7000, www.cipo veraneiohotel.com.br. Comfortable a/c rooms with cable TV, fridge, in terraces of stone cabins, pool, sauna, very good tour operator and a *cachaça* distillery just up the road which produces some of Minas's finest.

● Eating

Diamantina *p430*
🍴 **Cantina do Marinho**, R Direita 113, T3531 1686. Formal, decorated with bottles of wine, black-tie waiters is celebrated for its *Salmão Provençale* and *Bacalhau*. Set lunch 🍴.

¶¶ **Caipirão**, R Campos Carvalho 15, T3531 1526.
Minas cooking with buffet lunch cooked over a
traditional wood-fired clay oven, evening à la carte.
¶¶ **Grupiara**, R Campos Carvalho 12, T3531 3887.
Decent regional cooking, convivial atmosphere,
good value per kilo options at lunch.
¶¶ **Recanto do Antônio**, Beco da Tecla 39,
T3531 1147. Minas food and decent steaks, chic
rustic dining room in a colonial house.
¶ **Sisisi**, Beco da Mota 89, T3531 3071. Pasta, Minas
cooking and good value *prato feito* at lunchtime.

🍷 Bars and clubs

Diamantina *p430*
Apocalipse Point, Praça Barão de Guaicuí 78,
T3531 9296. Sertaneja and Axe music. Lively.
Café a Baiuca, R da Quitanda. Coffee bar by day,
funky bar by night with music DVDs and a crowd
spilling out into the street.
Espaço B, R Beco da Tecla. A bookshop café
serving crêpes and draught beer until late.

🎉 Festivals and events

Diamantina *p430*
Vesperatas, musicians and singers serenade
from balconies along the colonial streets and
drum troupes and bands parade every other Sat.

🏔 Activities and tours

Diamantina *p430*
Diamantina Tour, Praça dos Garimpeiros 616,
T8801 1802. City tours, adventure activities
(rappel and trekking) and trips to nearby natural
attractions and Biri Biri. From US$8 pp per day.
Real Receptivo, R Campos Carvalho 19 loja 12,
T3531 1636, www.realreceptivo.com.br. City
tours and trips to nearby natural attractions.

⊙ Transport

Diamantina *p430*
Bus To **São Gonçalo do Rio Preto**, one bus
per day. 6 buses a day to **Belo Horizonte**, via
Curvelo, with **Pássaro Verde**: 2½ hrs to **Curvelo**,
US$4.50, to **Belo Horizonte**, US$30, 5 hrs. To
Bahia, 2 buses to **Araçuaí** per day (4 hrs); from
here combis and buses run to **Itaubim** from
where there are connections to Porto Seguro and
other destinations in Bahia. For **Brasília**: 1 bus a
day to **Montes Claros** for connections, also to
Parque Nacional Grande Sertão Veredas; or
connect in **Curvelo**, take any Belo Horizonte bus.

Parque Nacional da Serra do Cipó *p431*
Bus Take bus to Serro (2 daily) for Santa Ana do
Riacho and the Serra do Cipó.

Southern Brazil → *Population: 9.5 million.*

*Southern Brazil comprises three states: Paraná, Santa Catarina and Rio Grande do Sul.
Paraná has one of the premier tourist sites in South America, the Iguaçu Falls, described in its
own section (see page 458). The Paraná coastline, albeit short, has a large area of coastal
rainforest and little beach-fringed islands, like Ilha do Mel. Its main port, Paranaguá, is
connected with the capital, Curitiba, by one of the most impressive railways in South America.
It is the coast, however, from which Santa Catarina gains most of its reputation, with highly
regarded surfing beaches and a growing interest in whale watching. Inland, the state has a
distinctive European feel, including frosty and snowy winters in the highest parts. The culture
of the region has been heavily influenced by large immigrant communities from Japan,
Germany, Poland, Italy, Syria and the Ukraine. In Rio Grande do Sul this can be seen (and
tasted) in the Italian communities, well known for their wines. The southernmost state, as well
as having yet more beaches, has some beautiful national parks, the remnants of Jesuit
missions and the south's largest industrial centre, Porto Alegre. But above all, this is the land
of the gaúcho, the Brazilian cowboy.*

Curitiba and around → *Phone code: 0xx41. Post code: 80000. Colour map 7, grid C2.*

Situated in the Serra do Mar, Curitiba is regarded as one of Brazil's model cities for quality of
life. It has something of a European feel, with leafy squares and a street that is open 24 hours.
It makes a pleasant base for exploring the coast and the surrounding mountains, and is the
start of one of the world's most spectacular railway journeys.

Ins and outs

Tourist offices Setu ⓘ *R Deputado Mário de Barros 1290, Centro Cívico, T3313 3500, www.pr.gov.br/turismo.* **Disque Turismo** ⓘ *T3254 1516 (state), T3352 8000 (city)*; also booths at the airport and Rodoferroviária (T3320 3121, 0700-1300). **Kiosks** ⓘ *R 24 Horas, T3324 7036, 0800-2400, 2200 at weekends, Museu Oscar Niemeyer (address below), T3350 4466.* Annual *Guía Turística de Curitiba e Paraná,* US$4, on sale at kiosks; free weekly leaflet, *Bom Programa,* available in shops, cinemas, paper stands.

Sights

One of the cleanest cities in Latin America, the capital of Paraná state has extensive open spaces and some exceptionally attractive modern architecture. The commercial centre is the busy Rua 15 de Novembro, part of which is a pedestrian area called **Rua das Flores**. The **Boca Maldita** is a particularly lively part where local artists exhibit. On Praça Tiradentes is the **Cathedral** ⓘ *R Barão do Serro Azul 31, T3324 5136,* built in neo-Gothic style and inaugurated in 1893 (restored in 1993). Behind the cathedral, near Largo da Ordem, is a pedestrian area with a flower clock and old buildings, very beautiful in the evening when the old lamps are lit – nightlife is concentrated here. The oldest church in Curitiba is the **Igreja de Ordem Terceira da São Francisco das Chagas**, built in 1737 in Largo da Ordem. Its most recent renovation was in 1978-1980. In its annex is the **Museu de Arte Sacra** ⓘ *T3321 3265.* The **Igreja de Nossa Senhora do Rosário de São Benedito** was built in the Praça Garibáldi in 1737 by slaves and was the Igreja dos Pretos de São Benedito. It was demolished in 1931 and a new church was inaugurated in 1946. A mass for tourists, Missa do Turista, is held on Sunday at 0800. An art market is held in **Praça Garibáldi** on Sunday mornings. **Museu Paranaense** ⓘ *in the Palácio São Francisco, R Kellers 289, T3304 3300, www.pr.gov.br/museupr/, Tue-Fri 0930-1730, Sat-Sun 1100-1500, US$1,* holds permanent and temporary exhibitions, including documents, manuscripts, ethnological and historical material, stamps, works of art, photographs and archaeological pieces.

    Museu de Arte Contemporânea ⓘ *R Desembargador Westphalen 16, Praça Zacarias, T3222 5172, Tue-Fri 1000-1900, Sat-Sun 1000-1600,* displays Brazilian contemporary art in its many forms, with an emphasis on artists from Paraná. All that remains of the old **Palácio Avenida** ⓘ *Travessa Oliveira Belo 11, T3321 6249,* is the façade, which was retained during remodelling works in 1991. Nowadays it has offices, an auditorium for 250 people and cultural activities. A fine example of the use of steel and glass is **Rua 24 Horas**, where the whole street is protected by an arched roof. The street's shops, bars and restaurants never close. On Saturday mornings there is a small fish fair at **Praça Generosa Marques**.

    North of the centre, the **Solar do Barão** ⓘ *R Presidente Carlos Cavalcanti 53, T3321 3240,* built in 1880-1883, is used for concerts in the auditorium and exhibitions. The **Passeio Público**, in the heart of the city (closed Monday), inaugurated in 1886. It has three lakes, each with an island, and playground. The **Centro Cívico** is at the end of Avenida Dr Cândido de Abreu, 2 km from the centre: a monumental group of buildings dominated by the **Palácio Iguaçu**, headquarters of the state and municipal governments. In a patio behind it is a relief map to scale of Paraná. The **Bosque de João Paulo II** behind the Civic Centre on Rua Mateus Leme, was created in December 1980 after the Pope's visit to Curitiba. It also contains the **Memorial da Imigração Polonesa no Paraná** (Polish immigrants memorial). The **Museu Oscar Niemeyer** (MON) ⓘ *R Mal Hermes 999, T3350 4400, www.museuoscarniemeyer.org.br, Tue-Sun 1000-1800, US$2,* was designed by, and is devoted to the famous Brazilian modernist architect who designed Brasília and was a disciple of Le Corbusier, together with other Paranense artists. The stunning principal building is shaped like a giant eye. An underground passage, lined with exhibits and photographs, links it to a sculpture garden.

    About 4 km east of the rodoferroviário, the **Jardim Botânico Fanchette Rischbieter** has a fine glass house, inspired by Crystal Palace in London. The gardens are in the French style and there is also a **Museu Botánico** ⓘ *R Ostoja Roguski (Primeira Perimetral dos Bairros), T3362 1800 (museum), 0600-2000.* Take the orange Expreso buses from Praça Rui Barbosa.

Parque Nacional Vila Velha → *Colour map 7, grid C2.*

ⓘ *The park office (phone, toilets, lanchonete, tourist information) is 300 m from the highway and the park a further 1½ km (entrance US$3.50, 0800-1900). Allow all day if visiting all 3 sites (unless you hitch, or can time the buses well, it's a lot of walking).*
West of Curitiba on the road to Ponta Grossa is the **Museu Histórico do Mate** ⓘ *T3304 3300, free, BR 277 at Km 17,* an old water-driven mill where mate was prepared. On the same road is

Brazil Curitiba & around

Vila Velha, 91 km from Curitiba: the sandstone rocks have been weathered into most fantastic shapes. About 4 km away are the **Furnas**① *US$2*, three water holes, the deepest of which has a lift (US$1.30 – not always working) which descends almost to water level. Also in the park is the Lagoa Dourada (surrounded by forest) whose water level is the same as that in the Furnas.

● Sleeping → *See Telephone, page 347, for important phone changes.*

Curitiba *p432, map p434*

There are some good-value hotels in the A and B categories. Some of the cheaper central hotels are seedy. There are good hotels southeast of the centre in the vicinity of the Rodoferroviária, but the cheaper ones are close to the wholesale market, which operates noisily through the night.

L Bourbon Curitiba, R Cândido Lopes 102, T3221 4600, www.bourbon.com.br. Good modern hotel in the centre with a mock old-fashioned charm, rooms have jacuzzis, business centre.

L Grand Hotel Rayon, R Visconde de Nácar 1424, T2108 1100, www.rayon.com.br. Central, much the best option for business travellers with all the expected services, pool, saunas, well-equipped gym and travel agency.

A Del Rey, R Ermelino de Leão 18, T2106 0099, www.hoteldelrey.com.br. Central, upmarket yet relaxed, large rooms, good restaurant, gym, good value. Recommended.

B Bourbon Batel Express, Av Visconde de Guarapuava 4889, T3342 7990, www.bourbon.com.br. A/c, modern and comfortable, good breakfast, wireless internet in rooms US$3/day, attentive service, good value.

B-C Deville Express, R Amintas de Barros 73, T3322 8558, www.deville.com.br. Central hotel with a bar, small modest restaurant, a/c, with fridge.

C Estação Palace, R Des Westphalen 126, T3322 9840, www.hotel-curitiba.com.br/estacao. Excellent for price, 24-hr room service and internet, rather stark but immaculate. Recommended.

C Lumini, R Gen Carneiro 1094, T/F3264 5244, www.hotellumini.com.br. Good apartment hotel in a quiet street, all rooms a/c. Recommended.

Curitiba

Sleeping ●
Bourbon Curitiba 1
Bourbon Batel Express 13
Casa do Estudante Luterano Universitario 15
Cervantes 2

Curitiba Eco Hostel 7
Del Rey 5
Deville Express 3
Estação Palace 6
Grand Hotel Rayon 4
Hostel Roma 8

Lumini 9
Nova Lisboa 11
O'Hara 12

Eating ●
Baviera 1

C Nova Lisboa, Av 7 de Setembro 1948, T3264 1944. With breakfast, bargain for cheaper rates without breakfast. Recommended.

C O'Hara, R 15 de Novembro 770, T3232 6044, www.hotelohara.com.br. Good location, fan, excellent breakfast, parking.

D Cervantes, R Alfredo Bufrem 66, T3222 9593, www.cervanteshotel.cjb.net. Central, small but cosy.

E Casa do Estudante Luterano Universitario, R Pr Cavalcanti, T3324 3313. For those with ISIC student cards, good.

E pp Curitiba Eco Hostel, R Luiz Tramontin 1693, Campo Comprido, T3274 7979, www.curitibaeco hostel.com.br. Cheaper for HI members, **D** in double room, youth hostel association for Paraná is located in this suburb outside the centre – catch a bus from the Rodoviária to Praça Rui Barbosa, marked Expreso Centenário, then change to a Tramontina bus to the door.

F pp Hostel Roma, R Barão do Rio Branco 805, T3322 2838, www.hostelroma.com.br. Smart HI hostel with single-sex dorms, also family rooms, with bath, breakfast included, TV room, internet, members' kitchen.

Camping Camping Clube do Brasil, BR-116, Km 84, 16 km towards São Paulo, T358 6634.

Eating

Curitiba *p432, map p434*

Cheap food also near the old railway station and good meals in the bus station. Close to the Rodoferroviária is the market, where there are a couple of lanchonetes. Hot sweet wine sold on the streets in winter helps keep out the cold.

🍴🍴🍴 **Boulevard**, R Vol da Patria 539 (centre). The city's most celebrated restaurant serving a mix of French, Italian and Brazilian cooking. Closed Sun.

🍴🍴 **Baviera**, Al Augusto Stellfield, at Av Dr Murici (centre). A Curitiba institution, established over 30 years and serving pizza in an intimate beer cellar setting. Also deliver. Open 1830-0100.

🍴🍴 **Saccy**, R São Franscisco 350. Pizza, tapas and a popular bar with very good live music.

🍴🍴 **Salmão**, R Emiliano Perneta 924. In historic house, delicious fish and pizza, special promotions, live music every night, open until 0100. Short taxi ride from centre.

🍴 **Happy Rango**, Av Visconde de Nacar, 1350, near R 24 horas. Brightly lit, basic corner joint selling fast food and pizzas, open 24 hrs.

🍴 **Kisco**, 7 de Setembro near Tibagi. Good, huge *prato do dia*, friendly.

🍴 **Mister Sheik**, Av Vicente Machado, 534. Arabic fast food in pitta with salad, popular for deliveries. Recommended.

Bars and clubs

Curitiba *p432, map p434*

A cluster of bars at the Largo da Ordem have tables and chairs on the pavement, music, and bar food: **Fire Fox**, Av Jaime Reis 46, flanked by **Tuba's** and **The Farm**.

Entertainment

Curitiba *p432, map p434*

Cinema There are cinemas in several shopping centres, and other places showing international films. Tickets are usually US$4-5 Mon-Thu, and US$6-8 at weekends. Best to look in the newspaper for music and what's on in the bars, clubs and theatres; Gazeta do Povo has a what's on section called *Caderno G*.

Theatres Theatre festival in Mar. **Teatro Guaíra**, R 15 de Novembro, T3304 7999, www.tguaira.pr.gov.br. For plays and revues (also has free events – get tickets early in the day).

Boulevard 2
Happy Rango 5
Kisco 13
Mister Sheik 8
Saccy 10

Bars & clubs
Fire Fox 12
The Farm 17

O Shopping

Curitiba *p432, map p434*
Handicrafts Feira de Arte e Artesanato,
Praça Garibáldi, Sun 0900-1400.
Lojas de Artesanato, Casa de Artesanato
Centro, R Mateus Leme 22, T352 4021.
Lojas de Artesanato 'Feito Aquí', Dr Muricy
950, International Airport and Shopping Mueller.
Lojas Leve Curitiba, at several locations, R 24
Horas, Afonso Pena airport, Ópera de Arame,
Jardim Botánico, Memorial de Curitiba.

▲ Activities and tours

Curitiba *p432, map p434*
BMP Turismo, R Brigadeiro Franco, 1845, T3322
8566. American Express representative,
emergency cash available with Amex.
Scubasul, R 13 de Maio 894, Alto São Francisco,
T3232 0198, www.scubasul.com.br. Advice on
diving, courses arranged, reasonable prices.

⊖ Transport

Curitiba *p432, map p434*
Air Afonso Pena (21 km away) for international
and national flights, T3381 1515; good services:
ATMs, left luggage, hotel booking desk, and cafés.
Daily flights from Rio, São Paulo, Buenos Aires,
Asunción, and cities in the interior of Paraná state.
Two types of bus run from the Rodoferroviária to
the airport, making several stops along the way:
Aeroporto Executivo, 0500-2330 daily, 20 mins,
US$4.50; regular city bus, 40 mins, US$1.50.
Bus There are several route types on the
integrated transport system and you are advised
to pick up a map with details. **Express** are red
and connect the transfer terminals to the city
centre, pre-paid access, they use the silver 'tubo'
bus stops; **Feeder** orange conventional buses
connect the terminals to the surrounding
neighbourhoods; **Interdistrict** green buses run
on circular routes connecting transfer terminals
and city districts without passing through the
centre; **Direct or speedy** silver grey buses use
the 'tubo' stations to link the main districts and
connect the surrounding municipalities with
Curitiba; **Conventional** yellow buses operate
on the normal road network between the
surrounding municipalities, the Integration
Terminals and the city centre; **City circular** white
mini buses, **Linha Turismo**, circle the major
transport terminals and points of interest in the
traditional city centre area. US$5.75 (multi-ticket
booklets available), every 30 mins from
0900-1700, except on Mon. First leaves from
R das Flores, narrow street in front of McDonalds.
Three stops allowed.

Short-distance bus services within the
metropolitan region (up to 40 km) begin at
Terminal Guadalupe at R João Negrão s/n. The
Terminal Rodoviário/Estação Rodoferroviária
is on Av Afonso Camargo s/n, T3320 3000, for
other cities in Paraná and other states. Restaurants,
banks, bookshops, shops, phones, post office,
pharmacy, tourist agency, tourist office and
public services are all here. Frequent buses to
São Paulo (6 hrs, US$21) and **Rio** (12 hrs, US$50,
leito US$84). To **Foz do Iguaçu**, 10 a day, 10 hrs,
US$30. **Porto Alegre**, 10 hrs, US$40 (leito US$60).
Florianópolis, US$24, 4½ hrs; **Blumenau** 4 hrs,
US$12.50, 3 daily with **Penha**/Catarinense. Good
service to most destinations in Brazil. **Pluma** bus
to **Buenos Aires** (change buses at Foz de
Iguaçu) and to **Asunción**. TTL runs to
Montevideo, Wed, Fri, Sun 0510, 26 hrs, US$115.
Train Rodoferroviária, Av Afonso Camargo
s/n. There are two trains running on the line from
Curitiba to **Morretes** and **Paranaguá**: the
Litorina, a modern a/c railcar with on-board
service with bilingual staff, which stops at
Morretes, with a halt at Marumbi Park station;
hand luggage only; tickets can be bought two
days in advance; departs Sat, Sun and holidays
0915, returns 1500, US$59 one way, 3 hrs. Also
the **Trem Classe Convencional**, which runs daily
to Morretes, with a stop at Marumbi, and
continues to Paranaguá at weekends only, buy
tickets two days in advance, departs daily 0815,
returns 1500 (1400 from Paranaguá at
weekends), turístico, US$25, executivo US$39,
4 hrs to Paranaguá. Schedules change frequently;
check times in advance; delays are to be expected.
For information and reservations, **Serra Verde
Express**, T3323 4007, www.serraverde
express.com.br. Tickets sold at the Rodoferro
viária, Portão 8, 0700-1830 (till 1200 on Sun).
Sit on the left-hand side on journey from Curitiba.
On cloudy days there's little to see on the higher
parts. The train is usually crowded on Sat and
Sun. Serra Verde Express also gives information
about trips by car on the Estrada de Graciosa and
sells various packages to the coast.

Parque Nacional Vila Velha *p433*
Bus Take a bus from **Curitiba** to the park, not to
the town of Ponta Grossa 26 km away. **Princesa
dos Campos** bus from Curitiba 0745, 1415, 1715,
1½ hrs, US$8.50. One bus from Vila Velha between
1530-1600, US$1, 4½ hrs to turn-off to Furnas
(another 15 mins' walk) and Lagoa Dourada. Bus
Mon-Sat 1330 to **Furnas** – Ponta Grossa that
passes the car park at the top of the park. On Sun,
1200,1620,1800. It may be advisable to go to
Ponta Grossa and return to Curitiba from there
(114 km, many buses a day, US$10.50, **Princesa
dos Campos**, www.princesadoscampos.com.br.

⊕ Directory

Curitiba *p432, map p434*

Airline offices BRA, T3323 1073, airport T3381 1383. TAM, R Ermelino Leão 511, T3219 1200. Trip, at airport, T3381 1710. Varig, T4003 7000, at airport, T3381 1607. **Banks** Bradesco, R 15 de Novembro 155, Visa ATM. Plus or Cirrus associated credit cards can cash money at Citibank, R Marechal Deodoro 711 or at Buenos Aires 305 near Shopping Curitiba. Cotação, R Marechal Deodoro 500, 2nd floor, Centro. Also Galeria Suissa, R Marechal Deodoro 280, open Sat when many others are closed. Diplomata, R Presidente Faria 145 in the arcade. **Cultural centres** British Council, R Pres Faria 51, T3232 2912, curitiba@britishcouncil.org.br. Instituto Goethe, R Reinaldino S de Quadros 33, T3262 8422, www.goethe.de/ins/br/cur/deindex.htm. **Embassies and consulates** Austria, R Cândido Hartmann 570, Ed Champagnat, 28th floor, T3336 1166, Mon-Fri 1000-1300. Denmark, R Prof Francisco Ribeiro 683, T3641 1112, saio@novozymes.com. France, R Conselheiro Laurindo 490, 10th floor, T3320 5805, consuldefrance@softcall.com.br. Germany, R Emiliano Perneta 297, 2nd floor, T3222 6920, Mon-Fri 0800-1200. Netherlands, Av Candido de Abreu 469, conj 1606, T3353 2630, Holland@telecorp.com.br, open 1400-1700, except emergencies. UK, R Pres Faria 51, 2nd floor, T3322 1202, curitiba@gra-bretanha.org.br. Mon-Fri 0830-1200, 1400-1730. Uruguay, Av Carlos Cavalho 417, 32 floor, T3225 5550, conurucur@terra.com.br . **Internet** at Livraria Saraiva in Shopping Crystal, Livraria Curitiba, R das Flores (US$2 per hr), and Estação Plaza Shopping (four blocks from Rodoferroviária) after 1100. Also in R 24 Horas at Digitando o Futuro and Internet 24 Horas, in the bookshop, open 24 hrs, US$3 per hr. Get On, R Visc de Nacar 1388. Monkey, Av Vicente Machado 534, corner with R Brigadeiro. Cool, modern with lots of computers and internet games, open daily till 2400. **Medical services** Emergency: T190 for Police and T193 for ambulance or fire. The Cajuru Hospital is at Av São José 738, T3362 1121, and the Evangélico is at Al Augusto Stellfeld 1908, T3322 4141, both of which deal with emergencies. **Post offices** main post office is at Mal Deodoro 298; post offices also at R 15 de Novembro and R Pres Faria. **Telephones** Tele Centro-Sul, information, T102. Embratel, Galeria Minerva, R 15 de Novembro. **Useful addresses** Visa extensions: Federal police, Dr Muricy 814, 1000-1600.

Paranaguá and the coast

The railway to the coast winds its way around the slopes of the Marumbi mountain range, across rushing rivers and through the forest to the sea. There are pretty colonial towns en route. The coast itself only has a few beaches, but in compensation has some of the richest biodiversity in Brazil.

Curitiba to Paranaguá

Two roads and a railway run from Curitiba to Paranaguá. The railway journey is the most spectacular in Brazil. There are numerous tunnels with sudden views of deep gorges and high peaks and waterfalls as the train rumbles over dizzy bridges and viaducts. Near Banhado station (Km 66) is the waterfall of Véu da Noiva; from the station at Km 59, the mountain range of **Marumbi** can be reached. See page 436 for schedules and fares. Of the roads, the older, cobbled Estrada da Graçiosa, with numerous viewpoints and tourist kiosks along the way, is much more scenic than the paved BR277.

Parque Nacional Marumbi

Marumbi Park is a large area of preserved Atlantic rainforest and is a UNESCO World Heritage site and Biosphere Reserve. The forest in the 2,343-ha park is covered in banana trees, palmito and orchids. There are rivers and waterfalls and among the fauna are monkeys, snakes and toucans. A climbing trail reaches 625 m to Rochedinho (two hours). Hands need to be free to grasp trees, especially during the rainy season (December to March), when trails are muddy. The last five minutes of the trail is a dangerous walk along a narrow rock trail. At the park entrance, notify administration of your arrival and departure. There is a small museum, video, left luggage and the base for a search and rescue unit at weekends. Volunteer guides are available at weekends. Wooden houses can be rented for US$55 a night; take torch. Camping is free. To get there take the Paranaguá train from Curitiba at 0815, arriving Marumbi at 1020. Return at 1540 to Curitiba. If continuing the next day to Paranaguá your Curitiba-Marumbi ticket is valid for the onward journey.

Morretes → *Colour map 7, grid C3. www.morretes.com.br.*

Morretes, founded in 1721, is one of the prettiest colonial towns in southern Brazil. Whitewashed colonial buildings with painted window frames straddle the pebbly river and church spires stick up from a sea of red tiled roofs against the backdrop of forested hills. The Estrada da Graciosa road passes through Morretes and the train stops here too. Most of the numerous restaurants serve the local speciality, Barreado, a meat stew cooked in a clay pot – originally a day in advance of Carnaval in order to allow women to escape from their domestic chores and enjoy the party. There are a handful of pousadas too and a series of walks into the mountains. **Antonina**, 14 km from Morretes is as picturesque, less touristy, and sits on the Baía do Paranaguá. It can be reached by local bus from Morretes.

Paranaguá → *Phone code: 0xx41. Colour map 7, grid C3. Population: 128,000.*

The centre of Paranaguá is a pleasant place to stroll, especially around the waterfront. Colonial buildings decay in the heat and humidity; some are just façades encrusted with bromeliads. There is an interesting city **museum** ① *R General Carneiro 66, T3423 2511, www.proec.ufpr.br, temporarily closed 2007*, housed in a formidable 18th-century Jesuit convent. Other attractions are a 17th-century fountain, the church of **São Benedito**, and the shrine of **Nossa Senhora do Rocio**, 2 km from town. **Tourist information** ① *R General Carneiro 258, Setor Histórico, T3425 4542*. Boat schedules, toilet, and left-luggage available, www.helts.com.br/paranagua.

The Paranaguá region was an important centre of indigenous life. Colossal shell middens, called **Sambaquis**, some as high as a two-storey building, protecting regally adorned corpses, have been found on the surrounding estuaries. They date from between 7,000 and 2,000 years ago, built by the ancestors of the Tupinguin and Carijo people who encountered the first Europeans to arrive here. The Spanish and Portuguese disputed the bay and islands when gold was found in the late 16th century. More important is the area's claim to be one of Latin America's biodiversity hotspots and the best place on the Brazilian coast to see rare rainforest flora and fauna. Mangrove and lowland subtropical forests, islands, rivers and rivulets here form the largest stretch of Atlantic coast rainforest in the country and protect critically endangered species (see below). Most of the bay is protected by a series of national and state parks, but it is possible to visit on an organized tour from Paranaguá. The **Barcopar** cooperative ① *access from Praça 29 de Julho (Palco Tutóia), T3422 8159*, offers a range of excellent trips in large and small vessels ranging from two hours to two days, US$10 per person to US$100.

Ilha do Mel

Ilha do Mel sits in the mouth of the Baía de Paranaguá and was of strategic use in the 18th century. On this popular weekend escape and holiday island there are no roads, no vehicles and limited electricity. Outside of Carnaval and New Year it is a laid back little place. Bars pump out Bob Marley and Maranhão reggae; surfers lounge around in hammocks and barefooted couples dance forró on the wooden floors of simple beachside shacks. Much of the island is forested, its coastline is fringed with broad beaches, broken in the south by rocky headlands.

The rugged eastern half, where most of the facilities are to be found is fringed with curving beaches and capped with a lighthouse, Farol das Conchas, built in 1872 to guide shipping into the bay. The flat, scrub forest-covered western half is predominantly an ecological protection area, its northern side watched over by the Fortaleza Nossa Senhora dos Prazeres, built in 1767 on the orders of King José I of Portugal, to defend what was one of the principal ports in the country. The best surf beaches are Praia Grande and Praia de Fora. Both are about 20 minutes' walk from the Nova Brasilia jetty. Fortaleza and Ponta do Bicho on the north shore are more tranquil and are safe for swimming. They are about 45 minutes' walk from the jetty or five minutes by boat. Farol and Encantadas are the liveliest and have the bulk of the accommodation, restaurants and nightlife. A series of well-signposted trails, from 20 minutes to three hours, cover the island and its coast. It is also possible to take a long day walking around the entire island, but the stretch along the southern shore between Encantadas and Nova Brasilia has to be done by boat. **Information**: www.ilhadomel online.com, www.pousadasilhadomel.com.br.

Superagui National Park

The island of Superagui and its neighbour, Peças, the focus for the Guaraqueçaba Environmental Protection Area which is part of the Nature Conservancy's parks in peril programme (http://parks inperil.org). They also form a national park and UNESCO World Heritage Site. Access to the park and accommodation can be arranged through the village on Superagui beach, just north of Ilha do Mel. Many endangered endemic plants and animals live in the park, including hundreds of endemic orchids, Atlantic rainforest specific animals like brown howler monkeys and large colonies of red-tailed Amazons (a parrot on the red list of critically endangered species and which can be seen nowhere else). There are also jaguarundi, puma and jaguar. The *indígena* village is one of several Guarani villages in the area; other inhabitants are mostly of European descent, living off fishing. There is superb swimming from deserted beaches, but watch out for stinging jelly fish. Contact Ibama on the island, 2 km out of the village, for information.

⊜ Sleeping → *See Telephone, page 347, for important phone changes.*

Morretes *p438*

A-B Pousada Graciosa, Estrada da Graciosa Km 8 (Porto da Cima village), T3462 1807, www.morretes.com.br/pousadagraciosa. Much the best in the area; some 10 km north of Morretes with simple but comfortable wooden chalets set in rainforest. Promotes cycling tours.
B-C Pousada Cidreira, R Romulo Pereira 61, T3462 1604, loizetycidreira@uol.com.br. Central, plain tiled rooms, TV, most with balcony. Breakfast.
D Hotel Nhundiaquara, R General Carneiro 13, T3462 1228, F3462 1267. Smart, beautifully set on the river, but service, public areas and rooms do not match up to the exterior, with breakfast.

Paranaguá *p438*

AL Camboa, R João Estevão (Ponta do Caju), T3420 5200, www.hotelcamboa.com.br. Full- or half -board available. Family resort, tennis courts, large pool, saunas, trampolines, a restaurant and a/c rooms, out of town near the port. Book ahead.
AL San Rafael, R Julia Costa 185, T3423 2123, www.sanrafaelhotel.com.br. Business hotel with plain rooms, restaurants, pool and jacuzzis.
D Ponderosa, R Pricilenco Corea 68 at 15 Novembro, T3423 2464. A block east and north of the boat dock, some rooms with a view.
D Pousada Itiberê, R Princesa Isabel 24, T3423 2485. Very smart spartan rooms, some with sea views, helpful service from the elderly Portuguese owner, shared bath, 3 blocks east of the boat dock.
Camping Arco Iris, Praia de Leste, on the beach, 29 km south of Paranaguá, T458 2001.

Ilha do Mel *p438*

All rooms are fan cooled unless otherwise stated.
A-B Long Beach, Praia Grande, T9944 9204, www.lbeach.cjb.net. Best on the beach, chalets for up to 6, very popular with surfers. Book ahead.
B Caraguatá, Encantadas, T3426 9097, pousada caraguata@uol.com.br. A/c, fridge, close to jetty.
B Pôr do Sol, Nova Brasilia, T3426 8009, www.pousadapordosol.com.br. Simple, elegant rooms around a shady garden, large deck with cabins and hammocks by the beach. Breakfast.
C Enseada, Farol, T9978-1200, pousadaenseada@ uol.com.br. 4 rooms with en suites, TVs and fridges, charmingly decorated. Lots of rescued cats.

C Dona Quinota, Fortaleza, T3426 8171/9978 3495, http://donaquinota.zeta.8x.com.br. Little blue and cream cottages right on the beach, 3 km from Nova Brasilia. Includes breakfast and supper. Dona Clara next door is very similar.
C Recanto do Frances, Encantadas, T3426 9105, www.recantodofrances.com.br. Full of character, with each chalet built in a different style to represent a different French city. 5 mins from Prainha or Encantadas. Good crêpe restaurant.
D pp Aconchego, Nova Brasilia, T3426 8030, www.cwb.matrix.com.br/daconchego. Very clean, beachside deck with hammocks, TV and breakfast area, charming. Includes breakfast.
D D'Lua, Farol, T3426 8031, daluapousada_ ilhadomel@hotmail.com. Basic and hippy with a friendly new-age owner, Jô (closed low season).
D Farol da Ilha, Farol, T3426 8017/9136 2138. Dorms and double rooms in a garden, surf boards for rent. Price includes generous breakfast.
D Girassol, Farol, T3426 8006, heliodasilva@ onda.com.br. Wooden rooms in a little fruit tree and bougainvillea garden, close to jetty. Breakfast.
D Plâncton, Farol at Fora, T3426 8061. A range of wooden buildings in a hummingbird-filled garden, fresh atmosphere, Italian food in high season.
D Recanto da Fortaleza, Ponta do Bicho, T3426 8000, www.ilhadomelpousada.com.br. The best of the 2 next to the Fort, basic cabins, free pick-up by boat from Nova Brasilia (ring ahead), bike rental. Price includes breakfast and dinner.
D pp Recanto Tropical, Farol, opposite D'Lua, T3426 8054. Open out of season, good breakfast.
You can rent a fisherman's house on Encantadas, ask for Valentim's Bar, or for Luchiano. Behind the bar is Cabanas Dona Maria, shared showers, cold water; food available if you ask in advance. Many pousadas and houses with rooms to rent (shared kitchen and living room). Shop around, prices from US$10 double, low season, mid-week.
Camping There are mini campsites with facilities at Encantadas, Farol and Brasília. Camping is possible on the more deserted beaches (good for surfing). If camping, watch out for the bicho de pé which burrows into feet (remove with a needle and alcohol) and the borrachudos (discourage with Autan repellent).

⑦ Eating

Morretes *p438*

Ψ¶¶ Armazém Romanus R Visc Do Rio Branco 141. Family-run restaurant with the best menu and wine list in the region, dishes from home-grown ingredients, including barreado and desserts.

¶¶¶ Terra Nossa R 15 de Novembro 109. Barreado, pasta, pizzas and fish, generous portions.

¶ Madalozo R Alm Frederico de Oliveira 16, overlooking the river. Good barreado and generous salads.

Paranaguá *p438*

¶¶¶ Casa do Barreado R José Antônio da Cruz. Barreado buffet from a well established eatery.

¶¶¶ Danúbio Azul R 15 de Novembro 95. The best in town, fish and chicken dishes, pastas and pizzas; all in enormous quantities. 1 block back from the sea at the east end of town.

¶ Divina Gula R 15 de Novembro 165. Until 1400 only, sea food buffet and feijoada at weekends. 3 blocks east of the Ilha do Mel dock.

¶ Rosa R Praia 16. Decent seafood including good risotto. A block west of the Ilha do Mel boat dock.

Ilha do Mel *p438*

Many pousadas serve food, some only in season (Christmas-Carnaval). Many have live music or dancing (especially in high season) after 2200.

¶¶¶ Fim da trilha, Prainha (Fora de Encantadas), T3426 9017. Spanish seafood restaurant, one of the best on the island. Also has a *pousada*.

¶ Colmeia, Farol. Snacks, crêpes and good cakes and puddings.

¶ Mar e Sol, Farol. Huge portions of fish, chicken with chips and rice and a small selection of more adventurous dishes like bass in shrimp sauce.

¶ Toca do Abutre, Farol. Live music and the usual huge portions of fish or chicken with rice, beans and chips.

¶ Zorro, Encantadas. One of several cheap seafront restaurants, forró dancing in the evenings.

⊖ Transport

Ilha do Mel *p438*

Ferry By ferry from Paranaguá to Encantadas and Nova Brasilia, at 0930 and 1500, 1 hr 40 mins, US$7.50, boats leave from R Gen Carneiro (R da Praia) in front of the Tourist Information kiosk; by ferry from **Pontal do Paraná** (Pontal do Sul), daily from 0800 to 1800 (last boat from island to mainland) every hr at weekends, less frequently in the week. From **Paranaguá**, take the **bus** to Pontal do Sul (many daily, 1½ hrs, US$1), then wait for the ferry, US$4.75. There are handicraft stalls at the ferry point. The last bus back to Paranaguá leaves at 2200. Alternatively, go to the small harbour in Paranaguá and ask for a boat to Ilha do Mel, US$30 one-way (no shade). Make sure the ferry goes to your chosen destination (Nova Brasília or Encantadas are the most developed areas).

Superagui National Park *p438*

Ferry From Paranaguá Sat 1000 arriving 1400, return Sun 1530 (two stops en route), US$10 one way. Private boats from Praia da Fortaleza on Ilha do Mel run if the weather is good. Commercially organized tours are available through Ibama T252 0180, or Barcopar, T422 8159.

Santa Catarina

Famous for its beaches and popular with Argentine and Paraguayan holidaymakers in high summer, this is one of the best stretches of Brazilian coast for surfing, attracting 1½ million visitors to the 170 beaches just in the summer months of January and February. For the rest of the year they are pleasant and uncrowded. Immigrant communities, such as the German, give a unique personality to many towns and districts with the familiar European pattern of mixed farming. Rural tourism is important and the highlands, 100 km from the coast, are among the coldest in Brazil, giving winter landscapes reminiscent of Europe, or Brazil's southern neighbours.

Florianópolis → *Phone code: 0xx48. Colour map 5, grid B5. Population: 342,315.*

Halfway along the coast of Santa Catarina is the state capital and port of Florianópolis, founded in 1726 on the Ilha de Santa Catarina. The island is joined to the mainland by two bridges, one of which is Ponte Hercílio Luz, the longest steel suspension bridge in Brazil (closed for repairs). The newer Colombo Machado Salles bridge has a pedestrian and cycle way beneath the roadway. The natural beauty of the island, beaches and bays make Florianópolis a magnet for holidaymakers in summer. The southern beaches are usually good for swimming, the east for surfing, but be careful of the undertow. **Tourist office**: **Setur**, head office at ① *Portal Turístico de Florianópolis, mainland end of the bridge, Av Eng Max de Souza 236, Coqueiros, T3952 7000, open 0800-2000 (Sat-Sun 1800).* **Tourist information line** ① *T0800-644300.* Office in the **Largo da**

Alfândega ⓘ *Mon-Fri 0800-1830, Sat-Sun 0800-1800*. At Rodoviária, Avenida Paulo Fontes, *T3228 1095*, free maps; www.guiafloripa.com.br, and for the state www.sc.gov.br.

In the 1960s Florianópolis port was closed and the aspect of the city's southern shoreline was fundamentally changed, with land reclaimed from the bay. The two main remnants of the old port area are the late 19th-century **Alfândega** and **Mercado Público**, both on Rua Conselheiro Mafra, fully restored and painted ochre. In the Alfândega is a **handicraft market** ⓘ *Mon-Fri 0900-1900, Sat 0900-1200*. The market is divided into boxes, some are bars and restaurants, others **shops** ⓘ *T3224 0189, Mon-Fri 0600-1830, Sat 0600-1300*, a few fish stalls open on Sun. The **Cathedral** *on Praça 15 de Novembro*, was completed in 1773. **Forte Santana** (1763), beneath the Ponte Hercílio Luz, houses a **Museu de Armas Major Lara Ribas** ⓘ *Tue-Sun 0830-1200, 1400-1800 (Mon 1400-1800), free*, with a collection of guns and

Florianópolis

Sleeping 🛏
Central Sumaré 3 *D3*
Faial 4 *D2*
Farol da Ilha 7 *D2*
Florianópolis
Palace 6 *D4*
Ilha de Santa
Catarina 12 *D2*
Porto da Ilha 9 *C3*
Pousada Recanto
da Costa 10 *F4*
Valerim
Center 11 *D2*
Youth Hostel 13 *B1*

Eating 🍴
Café das Artes 1 *A3*
Kayskidum 12 *B4*
La Cucina 2 *C2*
Lindacap 3 *C1*
Macarronada
Italiana 10 *B4*
Mirantes 7 *D4*
O Mercador 4 *E3*
O Pirão 4 *E3*
Papparella 5 *A3*
Pizza da Piedra 11 *B4*
Toca da
Garoupa 14 *A4*
Trapiche 4 *E3*
Vida 6 *D4*

Bars & clubs 🍸
Box 32 13 *E3*
Café Cancun 8 *B2*
Ilhéu 9 *C3*

other items, mostly post Second World War. **Museu Histórico**ⓘ *in the 18th-century Palácio Cruz e Souza, Praça 15 de Novembre, Tue-Fri 0800-1900, Sat 1300-1900, Sun 1530-1900*, contains furniture, documents and objects belonging to governors of the state. **Museu de Antropologia** ⓘ *Trindade University Campus, Mon-Fri 0900-1200, 1300-1700*, has a collection of stone and other archaeological remains from the cultures of the coastal *indígenas*. **Museu do Homem Sambaqui**ⓘ *at the Colégio Catarinense, R Esteves Júnior 711, Mon-Fri 1330-1630*, exhibits pieces from the sambaqui culture and fossils. There is a look-out point at **Morro da Cruz**. To get there, take Empresa Trindadense bus, US$0.80, waits 15 minutes, or walk. **Boat trips** from US$12.50, can be made in the bay with **Scuna Sul**ⓘ *T3225 1806, www.scunasul.com.br*.

Ilha de Santa Catarina → *Colour map 7, grid C3.*

There are 42 beaches around the island. The most popular are the surfers' beaches such as Praia Moçambique; for peace and quiet try Campeche or the southern beaches; for sport, the Lagoa de Conceição has jet skis and windsurfing. You can walk in the forest reserves, hang glide or paraglide from the Morro da Lagoa, sandboard in the dunes of Joaquina. Surfing is prohibited 30 April-30 July because of the migration of the island's largest fish, the tainha.

Lagoa da Conceição has beaches, sand dunes, fishing, church of NS da Conceição (1730), market every Wednesday and Saturday, post office. From the Centro da Lagoa on the bridge there are daily boat trips to Costa da Lagoa which run until about 1830, check when you buy your ticket, US$5 return, the service is used mostly by the local people who live around the lake and have no other form of public transport.

Across the island at **Barra da Lagoa**ⓘ *getting there: 'Barra da Lagoa' bus, Transol No 403, every 15 mins from Terminal Urbano, 55 mins, US$1*, is a pleasant fishing village and beach, surfing, lively in the summer season, with plenty of good restaurants. The same bus goes to beaches at **Mole** (good for walking, soft sand beach, surfing) and at **Joaquina** (surfing championships in January).

There is a pleasant fishing village at **Ponta das Canas**, walk 1 km to Praia Brava for good surfing, and the beach at **Canasvieiras** is good. Also in the north of the island, is **Praia dos Ingleses** (bus 602). **Forte São José da Ponta Grossa** is beautifully restored with a small museum ⓘ *US$2*. To get there take a bus to Jureré and Daniela beaches go there, .

In the south of the island are **Praia do Campeche** ⓘ *getting there: 30 mins by bus (Pantano do Sul or Costa de Dentro) from Florianópolis*, **Praia da Armação** with, just inland, **Lagoa do Peri** (a protected area). Further south is **Pântano do Sul**, an unspoilt fishing village with a long, curved beach, lovely views, several pousadas, bars and restaurants, though not much nightlife. From here it's a good 4-km walk over rocks and a headland to beautiful **Lagoinha do Leste**. **Praia dos Naufragados**: take bus to Caieira da Barra do Sul and then a one hour walk through fine forests. **Forte Nossa Senhora da Conceição** is on a small island just offshore. It can be seen from the lighthouse near Praia dos Naufragados or take a boat trip with Scuna Sul from Florianópolis.

Porto Belo Beaches → *Phone code: 0xx47. Population: 10,704.*

On the coast north of Florianópolis there are many resorts. They include Porto Belo, a fishing village on the north side of a peninsula settled in 1750 by Azores islanders, with a calm beach and a number of hotels and restaurants. Around the peninsula are wilder beaches reached by rough roads: Bombas, Bombinhas, Quatro Ilhas (quieter, 15 minutes' walk from Bombinhas), Mariscal, and, on the southern side, Zimbros (or Cantinho). Many of the stunning beaches around **Bombinhas** are untouched, accessible only on foot or by boat. Its clear waters are marvellous for diving.

Camboriú → *Phone code: 0xx47. Colour map 7, grid C3. Population: 41,445.*

This is now the most concentrated development on Brazil's southern coast. From 15 December to end-February it is very crowded and expensive; the rest of the year it is easy to rent furnished apartments by the day or week. A few kilometres south, at Lojas Apple, there is Parque Cyro Gevaerd, a museum (archaeology, oceanography, fishing, arts and crafts) and aquarium; and Meia Praia, which is quieter and cleaner than Camboriú. A teleférico has been built to Praia Laraneiras, previously deserted; US$6.50 return from Barra Sul shopping centre to Laranjeiras via Mata Atlântica station. Between Camboriú and Itajaí is the beautiful, deserted (and rough) beach of Praia Brava.

Blumenau → *Phone code: 0xx47. Post code: 89100. Colour map 7, C3. Pop: 261,808.*

Some 47 km up the Rio Itajaí-Açu (61 km by paved road from Itajaí) is this prosperous city, where high-tech and electronics industries are replacing textiles as the economic mainstay. The surrounding district was settled mostly by Germans. It is clean and orderly with almost caricatured Germanic architecture. See the **Museu da Família Colonial** ① *Av Duque de Caxias 78, Mon-Fri 0800-1130, 1330-1730, Sat morning only, US$0.20*, German immigrant museum. Also worth a visit is the **German Evangelical Church**, and the houses, now **museums** *0800-1800*, of **Dr Bruno Otto Blumenau** and of **Fritz Müller** (a collaborator of Darwin), who bought the Blumenau estate in 1897 and founded the town. **Tourist office** ① *T3222 3176, www.blumenau.sc.gov.br.*

Oktoberfest, the second largest street party in Brazil, after Carnival is usually held in the first half of October. During the day the narrow streets are packed around the Molemann Centre, which contains a mixture of bars, live music and of course, Chopp beer. At 1900 the doors of the Oktoberfest pavilion open for different events, including drinking competitions, the 'sausage Olympics', traditional dress and cake making competitions. There is also a fun fair and folk dancing shows. Visitors report it is worth attending on weekday evenings but weekends are too crowded. It is repeated, but called a 'summer festival', in the three weeks preceding Carnival.

At **Pomerode**, 33 km west of Blumenau, the north German dialect of Plattdeutsch is still spoken and there are several folkloric groups keeping alive the music and dance of their ancestors. The **Museu Pomerano** ① *Rodovia SC 418, Km 3*, tells the story of the colonial family. **Museu Ervin Kurt Theichmann** ① *R 15 de Novembro 791*, has sculptures. The **Confeitaria Torten Paradies** ① *R 15 de Novembro 211*, serves excellent German cakes. *Festa do Pomerania* is in January. www.pomerode.sc.gov.br.

São Francisco do Sul

→ *Phone code: 0xx47. Colour map 7, grid C3. Population: 32300. www.saofranciscodosul.com.br.*

Some 80 km up the coast at the mouth of the Baia de Babitonga, São Francisco do Sul is the port for the town of Joinville, 45 km inland at the head of the Rio Cachoeira. There is an interesting **Museu Nacional do Mar** reflecting Brazil's seafaring history. The centre has over 150 historical sites and has been protected since 1987. The **cathedral** was built between 1699 and 1719 and still has its original walls made with sand, shells and whale oil. There are some excellent **beaches** nearby.

Joinville itself is the state's largest city. It lies 2 km from the main coastal highway, BR-101, by which Curitiba and Florianópolis are less than two hours away. The industry does not spoil the considerable charm of the city. The **Alameda Brustlein**, better known as the **Rua das Palmeiras**, is an impressive avenue of palm trees leading to the **Palácio dos Príncipes**. The trees have been protected since 1982. The **cathedral** ① *on Av Juscelino Kubitscheck with R do Príncipe*, is futuristic with spectacular windows recounting the story of man. The **Casa da Cultura** (Galeria Municipal de Artes 'Victor Kursansew') ① *R Dona Fransisca 800, Mon-Fri 0900-1800, Sat 0900-1300*, also contains the School of Art 'Fritz Alt', the School of Music 'Vila Lobos' and the School of Ballet. A number of museums and exhibition centres reflect the history of, and immigration to the area and the city's artistic achievements. In July, Joinville hosts the largest dance festival in the world, which attracts around 4,000 dancers who stay for 12 days and put on shows and displays ranging from jazz, folklore, classical ballet and other styles. There is also an annual beer festival, Fenachopp, in October. There are many good restaurants and good air and road links to other parts of Brazil. **Tourist office** ① *at the corner of Praça Nereu Ramos with R do Príncipe*. Promotur ① *R 15 de Novembro 4543, Glória, T3453 2663, or 0800-643 5015, www.promotur.com.br; also www.joinville.sc.gov.br.*

Southern Santa Catarina

At **Praia do Rosa**, 101 km south of Florianópolis, is the headquarters of the **Right Whale Institute** ① *Instituto Baleia Franca, www.praiadorosa.tur.br/baleias/institutobaleia.htm*, **Ibama** ① *Area de Proteção Ambiental da Baleia Franca, Av Mauro Ramos 1113, CCP660, 88020-301 Florianópolis, T3212 3300*, and one of Brazil's prime **whale-watching** sites. The right whales come to the bay to calve from May to November and trips can be arranged to see them. The institute's base is **Turismo Vida, Sol e Mar** ① *Praia do Rosa Imbituba, Santa Catarina, CEP 88780000, T3355 6111, www.vidasolemar.com.br*, which has nine years' experience in right whale watching and dolphin watching. There is also a **Pousada Vida, Sol e Mar** with cabins, pool, restaurant, tour operator (T3254 4199), horse riding and surf school. There are other lodgings at Praia do Rosa (eg **AL A Morada dos Bougainvilles**, T3355 6100, www.pousadabougainville.com.br, and **Pousada Caminho do Rei**, T3355 6062, www.caminhodorei.com.br) and other fine beaches in the area. The nearest major town is Imbituba.

Laguna → *Phone code: 0xx48. Colour map 7, grid C3. Population: 47,568.*

Some 15 km from Tubarão is the small fishing port of Laguna. The town, founded in 1676, was the capital of the Juliana Republic in 1839, a short-lived separatist movement led by Italian idealist Guiseppe Garibáldi. At Laguna is the **Anita Garibáldi Museum**, containing documents, furniture, and personal effects of Garibáldi's devoted lover.

About 16 km away (by ferry and road) are beaches and dunes at **Cavo de Santa Marta**. Also from Laguna, take a Lagunatur or Auto Viação São José bus to **Farol** (four buses a day Monday-Friday, one on Saturday, US$2, beautiful ride. You have to cross the mouth of the Lagoa Santo Antônio by ferry (10 minutes) to get to Farol; look out for fishermen aided by dolphins (botos). Here is a fishing village with a **lighthouse** (Farol de Santa Marta) ① *guided tours available, getting there: taxi, US$10, not including ferry toll*, built by the French in 1890 of stone, sand and whale oil. It is the largest lighthouse in South America and has the third largest view in the world. It may be possible to bargain with fishermen for a bed, or there are campsites at Santa Marta Pequena by the lighthouse, popular with surfers.

São Joaquim → *Colour map 7, grid C2. Population: 22,836. Altitude: 1,360 m.*

Buses from the coalfield town of Tubarão (27 km from Laguna) go inland to Lauro Müller, then over the Serra do Rio do Rastro (beautiful views of the coast in clear weather) to **Bom Jardim da Serra** which has an apple festival every April. The road continues to **São Joaquim**. The highest town in southern Brazil, it regularly has snowfalls in winter; a very pleasant town with an excellent climate. 11 km outside the town on the way to Bom Jardim da Serra is the **Parque Ecológico Vale da Neve** (Snow Valley). It is an easy hike and very beautiful, the entrance is on the main road, US$3, and there is a restaurant. The owner is American and an English speaking guide will take you for a 1½-hour walk through the forest. The **Parque Nacional de São Joaquim** in the Serra Geral (33,500 ha, on paper only, much of the land is still private) has canyons containing sub-tropical vegetation, and araucaria forest at higher levels. There is no bus (local Ibama office, T048-3278 4002, Secretaria de Turismo de São Joaquim, T049-3233 2790, www.serracatarinense.com).

⊙ Sleeping → *See Telephone, page 347, for important phone changes.*

Florianópolis *p440, map 441*

AL-A Porto da Ilha, R Dom Jaime Câmara 43, T3322 0007, hotel@portodailha.com.br. Central, comfortable, **A-B** at weekends. Recommended.

AL-A Valerim Plaza, R Felipe Schmidt 705, T0800-702 3000, www.hotelvalerim.com.br. Three-star, more modern than Valerim Center, buffet restaurant open till 2300.

A Faial, R Felipe Schmidt 603, T3225 2766, www.hotelfaial.com.br. Comfortable and traditional hotel with good restaurant. Also owns the **Farol da Ilha**, R Bento Gonçalves 163, T3225 3030, www.hotelfaroldailha.com.br, which is good too, convenient for the bus station.

A Florianópolis Palace, R Artista Bittencourt 14, T3224 9633, www.floph.com.br. Large a/c rooms, pool, sauna, 1970s hotel.

B Valerim Center, R Felipe Schmidt 554, T0800-702 3000. Large rooms, hot water, hard beds.
C Pousada Recanto da Costa, R 13 de Maio 41. With breakfast, hot water, laundry facilities, parking, 15 mins' walk from centre.
D Central Sumaré, R Felipe Schmidt 423, T222 5359. Breakfast, good value, rooms vary from **C** with bath, to **E**.
F pp **Ilha de Santa Catarina**, R Duarte Schutel 227, T3225 3781, alberguesfloripa@uol.com.br. HI, breakfast included, cooking facilities, clean, some traffic noise, very friendly, will store luggage. Prices rise in Dec-Feb; more expensive for non-members. Recommended.
Camping Camping Clube do Brasil, São João do Rio Vermelho, north of Lagoa da Conceição, 21 km out of town; also at Lagoa da Conceição, Praia da Armação, Praia dos Ingleses, Praia Canasvieiras. 'Wild' camping allowed at Ponta de Sambaqui and Praias Brava, Aranhas, Galheta, Mole, Campeche, Campanhas and Naufragados; 4 km south of Florianópolis, camping site with bar at Praia do Sonho on the mainland, beautiful, deserted beach with an island fort nearby. 'Camping Gaz' cartridges from Riachuelo Supermercado, on R Alvim and R São Jorge.

Ilha de Santa Catarina *p442*
Barra da Lagoa
C Pousada Floripaz, Servidão da Prainha 20 (across hanging bridge at bus station, take bus 403 from terminal municipal), T3232 3193, www.qlitoral.com.br/floripaz. Book in advance, safe, family run, helpful owners, will organize tours by boat and car on island. Highly recommended.
Apartments José Irineu e Terezinha, T0xx48-9981 6060, juliane.s.s@zipmail.com.br. Apartments to rent 200 m from beach, fully equipped, about US$110 a month.
Camping Marina da Barra, T3232 3199. Beautiful clean site, helpful owner.

Joaquina
A Joaquina Beach, R A Garibaldi Santiago, T3232 5059, reservas@joaquinabeach hotel.com.br. Pleasant hotel with a/c. safes, sea views more expensive, buffet breakfast.
D Pousada Dona Zilma, R Geral da Praia da Joaquina 279, T3232 5161. Quiet, safe. Recommended.

Ponta das Canas
A Moçambique, T/F3266 1172, www.mocambique.com.br. In centre of village, noisy at weekends. Also has beach hotel, Moçambique Praia.

Praia dos Ingleses
C Companhia Inglesa, R Dom João Becker 276, T3269 1350, www.hotelciainglesa.com.br. Little beach hotel with pool and helpful staff. Recommended for families.
C Marcos Barroso, T9983 4472. Good-value apartments.

Praia do Campeche
L-AL Pousada Natur Campeche, Servidão Família Nunes 59, T3237 4011, www.natur campeche.com.br. Also has a hotel at Av Pequeno Príncipe 2196, a little cheaper, both with gardens, quiet, pousada has a pool and is closer to the beach.
L-A Pousada Vila Tamarindo, Av Campeche 1836, T3237 3464, www.tamarindo.com.br. Tranquil setting with lovely views, gardens, helpful staff, good buffet breakfast.
AL Hotel São Sebastião da Praia, Av Campeche 1373, T/F3338 2020, www.hotel saosebastiao.com.br. Resort hotel on splendid beach, offers special monthly rate Apr to Oct, excellent value.

Near Pântano do Sul
B Pousada Sítio dos Tucanos, Estrada Geral da Costa de Dentro 2776, T3237 5084, www.pousadasitiodostucanos.com. **AL** in high season. English, French, Spanish spoken, spacious bungalows in garden setting, excellent organic food. Very highly recommended. Take bus to Pântano do Sul, walk 6 km or telephone and arrange to be picked up by German owner.
D Albergue do Pirata, R Rosalia P Ferreira 4973, Pântano do Sul, T9960 1344. Hostelling International. With breakfast, natural surroundings, lots of trails.

Blumenau *p443*
Reservations are essential during Oktoberfest.
A-B Glória, R 7 de Setembro 954, T3326 1988, hotelgloria@hotelgloria.com.br. German-run, excellent coffee shop, best deal is 'meal of soups', US$2.30 for salad bar, 4 soups, dessert and wine.
C Herrmann, Floriano Peixoto 213, T3322 4370. One of the oldest houses in Blumenau, rooms with or without bath, excellent big breakfast, German spoken. Many cheap hotels do not include breakfast.
F pp **Grün Garten Pousada**, R São Paulo 2457, T3339 6529, www.grungarten.com.br. Youth hostel with dorms, 15 mins' walk from rodoviária. **C** in double room.
Camping Municipal campsite, 3 km out on R Pastor Osvaldo Hesse; Paraíso dos Poneis, 9 km out on the Itajaí road, also Motel; Refúgio Gaspar Alto, 12 km out on R da Glória.

São Francisco do Sul *p443*
A Zibamba, R Fernandes Dias 27,
T/F3444 2077. Central, good restaurant.

Joinville *p443*
AL Tannenhof, Visconde de Taunay 340, T/F3433
8011, www.tannenhof.com.br. 4-star, pool, gym,
traffic noise, excellent breakfast, restaurant.
A-B Anthurium Parque, São José 226,
T/F4009 6299, anthurium@anthurium.com.br.
Colonial building, once home to a bishop, good
value, English spoken, pool, sauna.
C Mattes, 15 de Novembro 801, T3422 3582,
www.hotelmattes.com.br. Good facilities,
big breakfast, German spoken. Recommended.
D Novo Horizonte, R Paraíba 766, T3422 7269, at
bus station. Basic, clean.

Laguna *p444*
C Turismar, Av Rio Grande do Sul 207, Mar
Grosso, T3647 0024, F3647 0279. 2-star, view
over Mar Grosso beach, TV.
D Beiramar, R 3 de Maio 92, Mar Grosso, T3644
0260. No breakfast, TV, rooms with view over
lagoon.
D Recanto, Av Eng Machado Salles 108, T3644
0902. With breakfast, central, modern but basic.

São Joaquim *p444*
D Maristela, R Manoel Joaquim Pinto 220, T3233
0007. No heating so can be cold, helpful, good
breakfast; 5 mins' walk from rodoviária.
D Nevada, R Manoel Joaquim Pinto 190 (also
5 mins' walk from rodoviária), T3233 0259,
nevadahotel@brturbo.com.br. Expensive meals.

Bom Jardim da Serra
D Moretti, Rua Antão de Paula Velho, T3232
0106. Family atmosphere, owner very helpful.
Camping Clube do Brasil site.

🍴 Eating

Florianópolis *p440, map 441*
Take a walk along Rua Bocaiúva, east of R Almte
Lamego, to find the whole street filled with
Italian restaurants, barbecue places and an
exclusive fish restaurant, **Toca da Garoupa**
(turn on to R Alves de Brito 178). **Don Pepé
Forno a Lenha** is a great place to go for a quiet
romantic meal with a serenador (cover charge
added to bill for singer). Shrimp dishes are good
everywhere. A popular place to start a night out
(after 2100) is the **Nouvelle Vague**, more
commonly known as A Creperia, buzzing

every weekend, wide selection of sweet and
savoury pancakes.
Lindacap, R Felipe Schmidt 1132 (closed
Mon). Recommended, good views.
Macarronada Italiana, Av Beira Mar Norte
2458. Good Italian food.
O Mercador, Box 33/4 in the Mercado Público.
Self-service specializing in fish and seafood.
O Pirão overlooks the market square in the
Mercado Público. Elegant, self-service, open
1100-1430.
Papparella, Almte Lamego 1416. Excellent
giant pizzas.
Pizza da Piedra, next door to Macarronada
Italiana. Another good place for pizza.
Trapiche, Box 31 in the Mercado Público. Also
self-service fish and seafood (see also Bars, below).
Kayskidum, Av Beira Mar Norte 2566.
Lanchonete and crêperie, very popular.
La Cucina, R Padre Roma 291. Vegetarian buffet
lunch, Mon-Sat, pay by weight, good, vegetarian
choices. Recommended.
Mirantes, R Alvaro de Carvalho 246, Centro.
Self-service buffet, good value.
Vida, R Visc de Ouro Preto 298, next to Alliance
Française. Good vegetarian.
Café das Artes, R Esteves Junior 734 at north
end. Nice café with excellent cakes.
Cía Lanches, Ten Silveira e R Trajano, downstairs.
For a wide selection of juices and snacks.
Laranja Madura, **Sabor e Sucos** and
Lanchonete Dias Velho all in Edif Dias Velho at
R Felipe Schmidt 303. All have a good choice of
juices and snacks.

Ilha de Santa Catarina *p442*
Lagoa da Conceição
Bodeguita, Av das Rendeiras 1878.
Very good value and atmosphere.
Oliveira, R Henrique Veras. Excellent seafood.

Barra da Lagoa
Meu Cantinha, R Orlando Shaplin 89.
Excellent seafood.
Ponta das Caranhas, R Jornalista M de
Menezes 2377, T232 3076. Excellent seafood,
lovely location on the lake.

Blumenau *p443*
Cavalinho Branco, Av Rio Branco 165.
Good German food and huge meals.
Deutsches Eck, R 7 de Septembro 432.
Recommended, especially carne pizzaiola.
Frohsinn, Morro Aipim (panoramic view).
Good German food.

🫘 *For an explanation of the sleeping and eating price codes used in this guide, see page 58.*
● *Other relevant information is found in Essentials pages 345-347.*

Gruta Azul, Rodolfo Freygang 8. Good, popular.

Amigo, Peixoto 213. Huge cheap meals.

Internacional, Nereu Ramos 61. Chinese, very good, moderate prices.

Patisseria Bavaria, Av 7 Septembro y Zimmerman. Very good cakes and fruit juices, friendly and caring staff.

○ Bars and clubs

Florianópolis *p440, map 441*

Free open air concert every Sat morning at the market place near the bus terminal.

To find out about events and theme nights check the Beiramar centre for notices in shop windows, ask in surf shops or take a trip to the University of Santa Catarina in Trindade and check out the noticeboards. The news-paper Diário Catarinense gives details of bigger events, eg Oktoberfest. The Mercado Público in the centre, which is alive with fish sellers and stalls during the day, has a different atmosphere at night; the stall, **Box 32**, is good for seafood and becomes a bar specializing in cachaça for hard working locals to unwind.

Café Cancun, Av Beira Mar Norte, T225 1029. Wed-Sat from 2000, bars, restaurant, dancing, sophisticated.

Empórium, Bocaiúva 79. A shop by day and popular bar at night.

Ilhéu, Av Prof Gama d'Eça e R Jaime Câmara. Bar and club open until early hrs, tables spill outside, very popular with locals, fills up quickly, music a mixture of 1980s and 1990s hits but dance floor shamefully small.

Ilha de Santa Catarina *p442*

Throughout the summer the beaches open their bars day and night. The beach huts of Praia Mole invite people to party all night (bring a blanket). Any bars are worth visiting in the Lagoa area (around the Boulevard and Barra da Lagoa); the **Confraria das Artes** here is reckoned to be one of the coolest places in Brazil.

⊛ Festivals and events

Florianópolis *p440, map 441*

In **Dec** and **Jan** the whole island dances to the sound of the Boi-de-Mamão, a dance which incorporates the puppets of Bernúnça, Maricota (the Goddess of Love, a puppet with long arms to embrace everyone) and Tião, the monkey. The Portuguese brought the tradition of the bull, which has great significance in Brazilian celebrations. Around **Easter** is the Festival of the Bull, **Farra de Boi**. It is only in the south that, controversially nowadays, the bull is killed on Easter Sunday. The festival arouses fierce local pride and there is much celebration.

◉ Transport

Florianópolis *p440, map 441*

Air International and domestic flights arrive at Hercílio Luz airport, Av Deomício Freitas, 12 km from town. Take Ribeiroense bus 'Corredor Sudoeste' from Terminal Urbano.

Bus There are 3 bus stations for routes on the island, or close by on the mainland: Terminal de Ônibus Interurbano between Av Paulo Fontes and R Francisco Tolentino, west of the Mercado Público; Terminal Urbano between Av Paulo Fontes and R Antônio Luz, east of Praça Fernando Machado; a terminal at R Silva Jardim and R José da Costa. Yellow micro buses (Transporte Ejecutivo), starting from the south end of Praça 15 de Novembro and other stops, charge US$1-US$2 depending on destination. Similarly, normal bus fares vary according to destination, from US$0.85.

International and buses from other Brazilian cities arrive at the rodoviária Rita Maia on the island, at the (east) end of the Ponte Colombo Machado Salles.

Daily buses to **Porto Alegre** (US$30, 7 hrs), **São Paulo**, 9 hrs (US$45, leito US$72), **Rio**, 20 hrs (US$61 convencional, US$84 executive, US$108 leito); to **Foz do Iguaçu** (US$55), to **Curitiba** US$24. To **Blumenau** US$12, 3 hrs. To **São Joaquim** at 1145, 1830 with Reunidos, T3224 3727, 5 hrs, US$18; to **Laguna** US$7. **International buses Montevideo**, US$98, daily, by TTL. **Buenos Aires**, US$75, Pluma, buses very full in summer, book 1 week in advance.

Porto Belo Beaches *p442*

Bus **Florianópolis** to Porto Belo, several daily with **Rainha**, fewer at weekends, more frequent buses to **Tijuca**, **Itapema** and **Itajaí**, all on the BR-101 with connections. Buses from Porto Belo to the beaches on the peninsula.

Camboriú *p442*

Bus From **Florianópolis**, **Joinville** and **Blumenau**. TTL buses Montevideo-São Paulo stop here at about 1800, a good place to break the journey, US$101 to Montevideo.

Blumenau *p443*

Bus Rodoviária is 7 km from town (get off at the bridge over the river and walk 1 km to centre). Bus to the rodoviária from Av Presidente Castelo-Branco (Beira Rio). There are connections in all directions from Blumenau. To **Curitiba**, US$14, 4 hrs, 3 daily (Penha and Catarinense). To **Pomerode** Coletivos Volkmann (T387 1321) Blumenau-Pomerode daily US$1.50, 1 hr; check schedule at tourist offices.

São Francisco do Sul *p443.*
Bus Terminal is 1½ km from centre. Direct bus (Penha) daily to **Curitiba** at 0730, US$12, 3½ hrs.

Laguna *p444*
Bus To/from **Porto Alegre**, 5½ hrs, with **Santo Anjo Da Guarda**; same company goes to **Florianópolis**, 2 hrs, US$10, 6 daily.

São Joaquim *p444*
Bus To **Florianópolis** 0700 and 1700 via Bom Retiro (Reunidos) and 0800 via Tubarão (Nevatur), 5½ hrs, US$18. Florianópolis-Bom Jardim da Serra, US$1.

⊙ Directory

Florianópolis *p440, map 441*
Airline offices TAM, T0800 570 5700. Varig, T4003 7000, at airport, T3331 4154.

Banks Banco do Brasil, Praça 15 de Novembro, exchange upstairs, 1000-1 500, huge commission on cash or TCs. ATMs downstairs, some say Visa/Plus. Banco Estado de Santa Catarina (BESC), câmbio, R Felipe Schmidt e Jerônimo Coelho, also Praça 15 de Novembro 341, 1000-1600, no commission on TCs. Money changers on R Felipe Schmidt outside BESC.
Car hire Auto Locadora Veleiros, R Silva Jardim 1050, T3225 8207, hotel_veleiros@ uol.com.br. Locarauto, Silva Jardim 816, T3225 9000.
Internet Moncho, Tiradentes 181. Internet café on R Felipe Schmidt 705. And others.
Post offices Praça 15 de Novembro 5.
Telephones Praça Pereira Oliveira 20.

Blumenau *p443*
Banks Câmbios/travel agencies: Vale do Itajaí Turismo e Cambio, Av Beira Rio 167, very helpful, German spoken.

Brazil Santa Catarina Listings

Rio Grande do Sul → *Population: 10.2 million.*

Rio Grande do Sul is gaúcho country; it is also Brazil's chief wine producer. The capital, Porto Alegre, is the most industrialized city in the south, but in the surroundings are good beaches, interesting coastal national parks and the fine scenery of the Serra Gaúcha. On the border with Santa Catarina is the remarkable Aparados da Serra National Park. In the far west are the remains of Jesuit missions. Look out for local specialities such as comida campeira, te colonial and quentão. In southern Rio Grande do Sul there are great grasslands stretching as far as Uruguay to the south and Argentina to the west. In this distinctive land of the gaúcho, or cowboy (pronounced ga-oo-shoo in Brazil), people feel closer to Uruguay and Argentina than Brazil (except where football is concerned). The gaúcho culture has developed a sense of distance from the African-influenced society of further north. This separationist strain was most marked in the 1820s and 1830s when the Farroupilha movement, led by Bento Gonçalves, proclaimed the República Riograndense in 1835.

Porto Alegre → *Phone code: 0xx51. Colour map 7, inset. Population: 1,360,590.*

The capital of Rio Grande do Sul is where cowboy culture meets the bright lights. It lies at the confluence of five rivers (called Rio Guaíba, although it is not a river in its own right) and thence into the great freshwater lagoon, the Lagoa dos Patos, which runs into the sea. The freshwater port is one of the most up-to-date in the country and Porto Alegre is the biggest commercial centre south of São Paulo. It is also one of the richest and best educated parts of Brazil and held the first three World Social Forums (2001-2003), putting the city in a global spotlight. Standing on a series of hills and valleys on the banks of the Guaíba, it has a temperate climate through most of the year, though the temperature at the height of summer can often exceed 40°C and drop below 10°C in winter.

Ins and outs
Tourist offices To800-517686, www2.portoalegre.rs.gov.br/turismo. **Porto Alegre Turismo** ⓘ *Travessa do Carmo 84, Cidade Baixa, T3212 3464, daily 0830-1800; also at airport; Usina do Gasômetro, Tue-Sun 0900-2100; Mercado Público, Mon-Fri 0900-1900, Sat 0900-1800; Mercado do Bom Fim, Loja 12, T3333 1873, daily 0900-1830, the airport and various shopping centres.* For the state: **SETUR** ⓘ *Av Borges de Medeiros, 1501, 10th floor, T3288 5400, www.turismo.rs.gov.br.* The market area in Praça 15 de Novembro and the bus terminal are dangerous at night. Thefts have been reported in Voluntários da Pátria and Praça Parcão.

Camping Praia do Guarujá, 16 km out on Av Guaíba.

🍴 Eating

Porto Alegre *p448, map p450*
The Central Market along the Praça is lined with lancherias. Vegetarians might try some of the campeiro soups and casseroles.

🍴🍴🍴 **Al Dente**, R Mata Bacelar 210, Auxiliadora, T3342 8534. Expensive northern Italian cuisine. Closed Sun.

🍴🍴🍴 **Chopp Stübel**, R Quintino Bocaiúva 940, Moinhos de Vento, T3332 8895. Open 1800-0030, closed Sun, German food. Recommended.

🍴🍴🍴 **Wunderbar**, R Marquês do Herval 598, Moinhos de Vento, T3222 4967. German cooking, very busy 1830 till last diner leaves. Recommended, welcoming.

🍴🍴🍴-🍴🍴 **514 Lobby Bar and Restaurant**, Av Alberto Bins 514 (in Plaza São Rafael Hotel), T3220 7000. Daily lunch 1200-1430, dinner 1900-2300 (not Sun). Steaks, pasta and fish, good soups.

To Guaíba Bridge

🍴🍴 **Atelier de Massas**, R Riachuelo 1482, T3225 1125. Lunch and dinner, Italian, closed Sun, fantastic pastas and steaks, excellent value.

🍴🍴 **Coqueiros,** R João Alfredo 208, T3227 1833. 1130-1430, 1930-2400, closed Sun and Mon evening. Cheap and cheerful churrasco.

🍴🍴 **Gambrinus**, Central Market ground level, Praça 15 de Novembro. T3226 6914. Lunch and dinner, regional cooking, closed Sun.

🍴🍴 **Komka**, Av Bahia 1275, San Geraldo, T3222 1881. 1130-1430, 1900-2300, closed Sun, also do churrasco. Recommended.

🍴 **Chalé da Praça 15**, Praça 15 de Novembro. Average gaúcho food but recommended for early evening drinks and snacks.

🍴 **Ilha Natural**, R Gen Câmara 60, T3224 4738. Self-service vegetarian, lunch only Mon-Fri.

🍴 **Lancheria Primavera**, Av Farrapos 187. Good breakfasts (toasties and juice) if staying nearby. 0630-1930 closed Sun. Staff also run red metal shack round corner on R Dr Barros Cassal serving tasty German hotdogs and burgers.

🍴 **Nova Vida**, R Demétrio Ribeiro 1182, T3226 8876.1100-1500, closed Sun, vegetarian, good lasagne.

🍴 **Spaguetti Express**, Centro Comercial Nova Olária, Lima e Silva 776. Good Italian.

Cafés

Café Dos Cataventos, in Casa de Cultura Mário Quintana, R dos Andrades 736, in courtyard. Also **Restaurant Majestic** on roof, T3226 0153. Both serve good drinks, snacks and meals. Fantastic rooftop sunsets. 1200-2300.

The café in **Usina do Gasômetro** is very good for sandwiches and speciality coffee. Cheap.

🎵 Bars and clubs

Porto Alegre *p448, map p450*
Bars
On weekend nights, thousands spill out of the huge beer bars and clubs along Av Goethe between R Vasco de Gama and R Dona Laura in Rio Branco (a US$3 taxi ride from the centre).
Bar do Goethe, R 24 de Outubro 112, Moinhos de Vento, T3222 2043. Reunion each Tue, 2030, for foreign language speakers.
Bar do Nito, Av Cel Lucas de Oliveira 105, Moinhos de Vento. T3333 6221. Popular music bar.
Cía Sandwiches, Getúlio Vargas 1430, T3233 7414. 1800-0200, beer, sandwiches and music.
Sargeant Peppers, Dona Laura 329, T3331 3258. Live music Thu-Sat, closed Mon.

Clubs
Dr Jekyll, Travessa do Carmo 76, Cidade Baixa. T32269404. Mon-Sat from 2200.

Eating 🍴
514 **2**
Atelier de Massas **1**
Chopp Stübel **3**
Wunderbar **4**

451

Ossip, Av República 677 e João Afredo, T3224
2422. Pleasant wine bar.
Wanda Bar, R Comendador Coruja 169, Floresta.
T3224 4755. Gay club, open from 2030.

⊕ Entertainment

Porto Alegre *p448, map p450*
Art galleries Casa de Cultura Mário Quintana,
R dos Andradas 736, T3221 7147. A lively centre for
the arts, with exhibitions, theatre, pleasant bar, etc,
open 0900-2100, 1200-2100 Sat-Sun.
Theatre São Pedro, Praça Mal Deodoro, T3227
5100. Free noon and late afternoon concerts Sat,
Sun, art gallery, café.

⊛ Festivals and events

Porto Alegre *p448, map p450*
The main event is on **2 Feb** (a local holiday), with
the festival of **Nossa Senhora dos Navegantes**
(Iemanjá), whose image is taken by boat from the
central quai in the port to the industrial district of
Navegantes. **Semana Farroupilha** celebrates
gaúcho traditions with parades in traditional style,
its main day being on **20 Sep**. The Carnival parade
takes place in Av A do Carvalho, renamed Av
Carlos Alberto Barcelos (or Roxo) for these 3 days
only, after a famous carnival designer. **Feira do
Livro** in Praça da Alfândega, **Oct-Nov**.

⊙ Shopping

Porto Alegre *p448, map p450*
Bookshops Livraria Londres, Av Osvaldo
Aranha 1182. Used books in English, French and
Spanish and old Life magazines.
Markets There is a street market (leather
goods, basketware etc) in the streets around the
central Post Office. Good leather goods are sold
on the streets. Sun morning handicraft and
bric-a-brac market (plus sideshows) Av José
Bonifácio (next to Parque Farroupilha). There is
a very good food market.
Shopping centres The Praia de Belas
shopping centre, among the largest in Latin
America, is a US$2 taxi ride from town.

▲ Activities and tours

Porto Alegre *p448, map p450*
Two **boats trips** around islands in estuary:
Cisne Branco, from Cais do Porto, near Museu de
Arte de Rio Grande do Sul, T3224 5222,
www.barcocisnebranco.com.br. Several sailings on
Sun, fewer mid-week, 1 hr, US$7.50.
Noiva do Caí, from the Usina do Gasômetro,
T3211 7662. Several on Sun, fewer mid-week,
one hr, US$3 (check winter schedules).

452

⊙ Transport

Porto Alegre *p448, map p450*
Air The international airport is on Av dos
Estados, 8 km from the city, T3358 2000.
Bus 1st-class local minibuses (*Lotação*),
painted in a distinctive orange, blue and white
pattern, stop on request, fares about US$1. Safer
and more pleasant than normal buses (US$0.65).
There are regular buses to the rodoviária.
Torres, 9 a day, US$12.
    International and interstate buses arrive at the
rodoviária at Largo Vespasiano Júlio Veppo, on Av
Mauá with Garibáldi, T3210 0101, www.rodoviaria-
poa.com.br. Facilities include a post office and
long-distance telephone service until 2100. There
are 2 sections to the terminal; the ticket offices for
interstate and international destinations are
together in 1 block, beside the municipal tourist
office (very helpful). The intermunicipal (state)
ticket offices are in another block; for travel
information within the state, ask at the very
helpful booth on the station concourse.
    To **Rio**, US$90, 24 hrs with Itapemirim;
São Paulo, US$65-70, 18 hrs; **Florianópolis**,
US$30, 7 hrs with Santo Anjo (take an executivo
rather than a convencional, which is a much
slower service); **Curitiba**, from US$40
convencional to US$60 leito, coastal and Serra
routes, 11 hrs; **Rio Grande**, US$18, every
2 hrs from 0600, 4 hrs. **Foz do Iguaçu**, US$52-60,
13 hrs. To **Jaguarão** on Uruguayan border at
2400, 6 hrs, US$18. **Uruguaiana**, US$33,
8 hrs. Many other destinations.
International buses Note Take your
passport and tourist card when purchasing
international bus tickets. To **Montevideo**, with
TTL executivo daily 2030 US$70 (leito Fri only at
2100, www.ttl.com.br), or take an ordinary bus to
border town of Chuí, 7 hrs, US$45, then bus to
Montevideo (US$12). To **Asunción** with Unesul
at 1900, Tue, Fri, 18 hrs via **Foz do Iguaçu**. There
are bus services to **Buenos Aires**, 19 hrs with
Pluma, 1805 daily, route is Uruguaiana, Paso de
los Libres, Entre Ríos and Zárate. For **Misiones**
(Argentina), take 2100 bus (not Sat) to Porto
Xavier on the Río Uruguay, 11 hrs, US$30, get exit
stamp at police station, take a boat to San Javier,
US$2.50, go to Argentine immigration at the port,
then take a bus to Posadas (may have to change
in Leandro N Além).
Metrô Trensurb, to the Mercado Público, via
the rodoviária, US$0.75.
Road Good roads radiate from Porto Alegre,
and Highway BR-116 is paved to Curitiba (746
km). To the south it is paved (mostly in good
condition), to Chuí on the Uruguayan border,
512 km. In summer visibility can be very poor
at night owing to mist, unfenced cows are a

further hazard. The paved coastal road to Curitiba via Itajaí (BR-101), of which the first 100 km is the 4-lane Estrada General Osório highway, is much better than the BR-116 via Caxias and Lajes. The road to Uruguaiana is entirely paved but bumpy.

⊙ Directory

Porto Alegre *p448, map p450*
Banks Banco do Brasil, Av dos Estados 1515, T371 1955 (also has Visa/Plus ATM), and Av Assis Brasil 2487, T341 2466. 1000-1500, good rates for TCs. Branch at Uruguai 185 has Visa/Plus ATM. Many branches of **Bradesco** have Visa ATMs, also **Banco 24 Horas** for Visa ATMs. **Citibank**, R7 de Setembro 722, T3220 8619. MasterCard ATMs at any **HSBC** branch. **MasterCard**, cash against card, R 7 de Setembro 722, 8th floor, Centro. **Exprinter**, R Hilário Ribeiro 292 (best for cash). For other addresses consult tourist bureau brochure.
Cultural centres Instituto Goethe, 24 de Outubro 122, T3222 7832, www.goethe.de/br/poa/demail.htm. Mon-Fri, 0930-1230, 1430-2100, occasional concerts, bar recommended for German Apfelkuchen. **Embassies and consulates** Argentina, R Coronel Bordini 1033, Moinhos de Vento, T/F3321 1360, caleg@zaz.com.br. 1000-1600. **France**, R Ramiro Barcelos 1172, cj 217, T3222 6467, chfpoa@terra.com.br. **Germany**, R Prof Annes Dias 112, 11th floor, Centro, T3224 9592. 0830-1130. Italy, R José de Alencar 313, T3230 8200, www.consportoalegre.esteri.it. 0900-1200. Japan, Av João Obino 467, Alto Petrópolis, T3334 1299, cjpoa@terra.com.br. 0900-1130, 1400-1700. **Spain**, R Ildefonso Simões Lopes 85, Três Figueiras, T3338 1300, consuladoesp@terra.com.br. 0900-1430. **UK**, R Antenor Lemos 57 cj. 303, Menino Deus, T3232 1414, portoalegre@gra-bretanha.org.br. 0830-1230, 1330-1630.
Uruguay, Av Cristóvão Colombo 2999, Higienópolis, T3325 6200, conurugran@terra.com.br, 0900-1500. **Internet** Places in the centre, as well as **Livraria Saraiva Megastore**, Shopping Praia de Belas, Mon-Sat 1000-2200. **PC2**, Duque de Caxias 1464, T3227 6853. **Portonet**, R Mal Floriano 185, T3227 4696, 0900-2100. **Language courses** Portuguese and Spanish, **Matilde Dias**, R Pedro Chaves Barcelos 37, Apdo 104, T3331 8235, malilde@estadao.com.br. **Post offices** R Siqueira Campos 1100, Centro, Mon-Fri 0900-1800, Sat 0900-1230. **Telephones** R Borges de Medeiros 475, and upstairs at rodoviária.

Rio Grande do Sul state

Mountains, vineyards, cowboys, waterfowl and ruined Jesuit missions are all part of the mix that makes up Brazil's southernmost state.

Serra Gaúcha → *Population: Canela, 33,625; Gramado, 29,593.*
The Serra Gaúcha boasts stunningly beautiful scenery, some of the best being around the towns of Gramado and Canela, about 130 km north of Porto Alegre. There is a distinctly Swiss/Bavarian flavour to many of the buildings in both towns. It is difficult to get rooms in the summer/Christmas. In spring and summer the flowers are a delight, and in winter there are frequently snow showers. This is excellent walking and climbing country among hills, woods, lakes and waterfalls. For canoeists, the Rio Paranhana at Três Coroas is renowned, especially for slalom. Local crafts include knitted woollens, leather, wickerwork, and chocolate.

Gramado, at 850 m on the edge of a plateau with views, provides a summer escape from the 40° C heat of the plains. It lives almost entirely by tourism and the main street, Avenida Borges de Medeiros, is full of kitsch artisan shops and fashion boutiques. In the summer, thousands of hydrangeas (hortênsias) bloom. About 1.5 km along Avenida das Hortênsias towards Canela is the **Prawer Chocolate Factory** ⊙ *Av das Hortênsias 4100. T3286 1580, www.prawer.com.br, free tours of the truffle-making process and free tasting. 0830-1130, 1330-1700, closed weekends.* Opposite is the incongruous but good **Hollywood Dream Car Automobile Museum** ⊙ *Av das Hortênsias 4151, T3286 4515, 0900-1900, US$2.10,* with a collection of dating back to a 1929 Ford Model A and Harley Davidson motorbikes from 1926. For a good walk/bike ride into the valley, take the dirt road Turismo Rural 28, Um Mergulho no Vale (A Dive into the Valley), which starts at Avenida das Hortênsias immediately before Prawer. Each August, Gramado holds a festival of Latin American cinema. **Tourist office** ⊙ *Av das Hortênsias 2029, T3286 0200, www.gramadosite.com.br.* Internet at **Cyber** ⊙ *Av Borges de Medeiros 2016, 1300-2300, US$2.80 per hr.*

A few kilometres along the plateau rim, **Canela** is less tourism and shopping-oriented than its neighbour (frequent bus service from Gramado, 10 minutes). **Tourist office** ① *R Dona Carlinda 455, T3282 1510, www.canelaturismo.com.br.*

About 7 km away is the **Parque Estadual do Caracol** ① *T278 3035, 0830-1800, US$1.75*, with a spectacular 130-m high waterfall where the Rio Caracol tumbles out of thick forest. A 927-step metal staircase ("equivalent to a 45-storey building") leads to the plunge pool. There is an 18-km circular bike route continuing on to **Parque Ferradura**, where there is a good view into the canyon of the Rio Cai. From the Ferradura junction, take the right to continue to the **Floresta Nacional** ① *T282 2608, 0800-1700, free*, run by Ibama. From here, the dirt road continues round to Canela. Another good hike or bike option is the 4-km track southeast of Canela past Parque das Sequóias to **Morro Pelado**. At over 600 m, there are spectacular views from the rim edge.

Parque Nacional de Aparados da Serra → *Colour map 7, inset.*

① *Wed-Sat 0900-1700, US$2.10 plus US$1.75 for car, T251 1262. Further information from Porto Alegre tourist office or Ibama, R Miguel Teixeira 126, Cidade Baixa, Porto Alegre, CEP 90050-250, T3228 7290.*

The major attraction at the Parque Nacional de Aparados da Serra is a canyon, 7.8 km long and 720 m deep, known locally as the Itaimbezinho. Here, two waterfalls cascade 350 m into a stone circle at the bottom. For experienced hikers (and with a guide) there is a difficult path to the bottom of Itaimbezinho. One can then hike 20 km to Praia Grande in Santa Catarina state. As well as the canyon, the park, its neighbour, the **Parque Nacional da Serra Geral**, and the surrounding region have several bird specialities. The park is 80 km from São Francisco de Paula (18 km east of Canela, 117 km north of Porto Alegre).

Tourist excursions, mostly at weekends, from **São Francisco de Paula** (a few hotels and *pousadas*; tourist information at southern entrance to town, T3244 1602, www.saochico.com.br). At other times, take a bus to Cambará do Sul (0945, 1700, 1¼ hours, US$4): several pousadas and **D Pousada dos Pinheiros** ① *Estrada Morro Agudo, T3282 2503, pousadadospinheiros@via-rs.net, 12 km from Cambará, off road to Aparados da Serra and Praia Grande turn right (signposted) for 2 km*, rustic cabins, breakfast and dinner at isolated farm amid stunning scenery. Recommended. Also near Cambará is **Campofora** (T3278 1454, www.campofora.com.br) for riding expeditions in national park.

Caxias do Sul and around

→ *Phone code: 0xx54. Post code: 95000. Colour map 7, inset. Population: 360,419.*

This city's population is principally of Italian descent and it is an expanding and modern city, the centre of the Brazilian wine industry. Vines were first brought to the region in 1840 but not until the end of the century and Italian immigration did the industry develop. The church of **São Pelegrino** has paintings by Aldo Locatelli and 5 m-high bronze doors sculptured by Augusto Murer. There is a good **Museu Municipal** ① *R Visconde de Pelotas 586, T3221 2423, Tue-Sat 0830-1130, 1330-1700, Sun 1400-1700*, with displays of artefacts of the Italian immigration. Italian roots are again on display in the **Parque de Exposições Centenário**, 5 km out on Rua Ludovico Cavinato. January-February is the best time to visit. There is a tourist information kiosk in Praça Rui Barbosa. The **rodoviária** ① *R Ernesto Alves 1341, T3218 3000*, is a 15-minute walk from the main praça, but many buses pass through the centre. **Tourist office** ① *R Ludovico Cavinatto, 1431, T0800-541 1875, www.caxias.tur.br.*

Caxias do Sul's festival of grapes is held February to March. Many adegas accept visitors (but do not always give free tasting). Good tour and tasting (six wines) at Adega Granja União, R Os 18 de Forte 2346. Visit also the neighbouring towns and sample their wines: **Farroupilha** 20 km from Caxias do Sul. **Nova Milano**, 6 km away (bus to Farroupilha, then change – day trip). **Bento Gonçalves**, 40 km from Caxias do Sul, www.bentogoncalves.rs.gov.br. **Garibáldi**, which has a dry ski slope and toboggan slope – equipment hire, US$5 per hr. A restored steam train leaves Bento Gonçalves for a 2-hour trip to **Carlos Barbosa**; called 'a rota do vinho' (the wine run), it goes through vineyards in the hills. US$20-22.50, including wines, with live band; reserve in advance through **Giordani Turismo** ① *R 13 de Maio 581, Loja 109, Bento Gonçalves, T3455 2788, www.mfumaca.com.br.* Another worthwhile trip is to **Antônio Prado**, 1½ hours by Caxiense Bus. The town is now a World Heritage Site because of the large number of original buildings built by immigrants in the Italian style.

Jesuit Missions → *Colour map 7, grid C1. Colour map 8, grid A6.*

West of **Passo Fundo**, 'the most gaúcho city in Rio Grande do Sul', are the **Sete Povos das Missões Orientais**. The only considerable Jesuit remains in Brazilian territory (very dramatic) are at **São Miguel das Missões** (*www.saomiguel-rs.com.br/Turismo/*), some 50 km from **Santo Ângelo**. At São Miguel, now a World Heritage Site, there is a church, 1735-1745, and small **museum** *0900-1800*. A son et lumière show in Portuguese is held daily, in winter at 2000, and later in summer, although all times rather depend on how many people there are. The show ends too late to return to Santo Ângelo. Gaúcho festivals are held on some Sunday afternoons, in a field near the Mission.

Border with Argentina → *Colour map 8, grid A6.*

In the extreme west are **Uruguaiana**, a cattle centre 772 km from Porto Alegre, and its twin Argentine town of Paso de los Libres, also with a casino. A 1,400 m bridge over the Rio Uruguai links the cities. Brazilian immigration and customs are at the end of the bridge, five blocks from the main praça; exchange and information in the same building. Since 2003 this border crossing has not been recommended as Paso de los Libres was not safe. Should you cross here, there are hotels in each town. **Note** Exchange rates are better in the town than at the border.

South of Porto Alegre → *Colour map 7, inset.*

South of Quintão a track runs to the charming town of **Mostardas** (www.mostardas.rs.gov.br; **E** Hotel Mostardense ① *R Bento Conçalves 203, T3673 1368*, good), thence along the peninsula on the seaward side of the Lagoa dos Patos to São José do Norte, opposite Rio Grande (see below). Mostardas is a good base for visiting the national park **Lagoa do Peixe** ① *information: Praça Luís Martins 30, Mostardas, T3673 1464, free*, park has no infrastructure. This is one of South America's top spots for migrating birds: flamingos and albatross are among the visitors. The main lake (which has highest bird concentration) is about 20 km from Mostardas and the town of **Tavares**. The park is, however, under threat from invasive planting of trees.

São Lourenço do Sul About 40 km to the south (towards Rio Grande) begins the Costa Doce of the Lagoa dos Patos. São Lourenço (*Phone code 0xx53, Population 43,691, www.saolourenco.net*) is a good place to enjoy the lake, the beaches, fish restaurants and watersports. The town hosts a popular four-day festival in March. On the BR-116, **Pelotas** is the second largest city in the State of Rio Grande do Sul, 271 km south of Porto Alegre, on the Rio São Gonçalo which connects the shallow Lagoa dos Patos with the Lagoa Mirim. There are many good hotels and transport links to all of the state and the Uruguay border at Chuí.

South of Pelotas on the BR-471, is the **Taim** water reserve on the Lagoa Mirim. Many protected species, including black swans and the quero-quero (the Brazilian lapwing). Information T3503 3151, or from Ibama, esec-taim.rs@ibama.gov.br, or in Porto Alegre.

Rio Grande Some 59 km south of Pelotas, at the entrance to the Lagoa dos Patos, is the city Rio Grande (*Phone code: 0xx53, Population: 186,544, www.riogrande.rs.gov.br*). It is the distribution centre for the southern part of Rio Grande do Sul, with significant cattle and meat industries. During the latter half of the 19th century Rio Grande was an important centre, but today it is a rather poor town, notable for the charm of its old buildings. The **Catedral de São Pedro** dates from 1755-1775. **Museu Oceanográfico** ① *2 km from centre on Av Perimetral, T3232 9107, daily 0900-1100, 1400-1700, bus 59 or walk along waterfront*, has an interesting collection of 125,000 molluscs. The tourist kiosk is at junction of Rua Duque de Caxias and Rua General Becaleron.

Excursions To **Cassino**, a popular seaside town on the ocean, 24 km, over a good road. Travelling south, beaches are Querência (5 km), Stela Maris (9 km), Netuno (10 km), all with surf. The breakwater (the Barra), 5 km south of Cassino, no bus connection, through which all vessels entering and leaving Rio Grande must pass, is a tourist attraction. Barra-Rio Grande buses, from the east side of Praça Ferreira pass the Superporto. Across the inlet from Rio Grande is the little-visited settlement of **São José do Norte**, founded in 1725. There are ferries every half hour, 30 minutes, São José to Rio Grande; there are also three car ferries daily, T232 1500. **Tourist information** from Rua General Osório 127. Buses run north to Tavares and Mostardas.

Border with Uruguay: coastal route → *Colour map 7, inset. Population: 5,167.*

The Brazilian border town is **Chuí**. The BR-471 from Porto Alegre and Pelotas skirts the town and carries straight through to Uruguay, where it becomes Ruta 9. The main street crossing west to east, Avenida Internacional (Avenida Uruguaí on the Brazilian side, Avenida Brasil in Uruguay) is lined with clothes and household shops in Brazil, duty free shops and a casino in Uruguay. São Miguel fort, built by the Portuguese in 1737, now reconstructed with period artefacts, is worth a visit. A lighthouse 10 km west marks the Barro do Chuí inlet, which has uncrowded beaches and is visited by sea lions. Brazilian immigration is about 2½ km from the border, on BR-471, road to Pelotas. Buses stop at customs on both sides of the border, except those from Pelotas, on which you must ask the bus to stop for exit formalities. International buses make the crossing straightforward: the company holds passports; hand over your visitor's card on leaving Brazil and get a Uruguayan one on entry. Have luggage available for inspection. Make sure you get your stamp, or you will have trouble leaving Brazil.

Entering Brazil From Uruguay, on the Uruguayan side, the bus will stop if asked, and wait while you get your exit stamp (with bus conductor's help); on the Brazilian side, the appropriate form is completed by the rodoviária staff when you purchase your ticket into Brazil. The bus stops at Polícia Federal (BR-471) and the conductor completes formalities while you sit on the bus.

Border with Uruguay: inland routes → *Colour map 8, grid A6.*

At **Aceguá**, 60 km south of Bagé, there is a crossing to the Uruguayan town of Melo, and further east, **Jaguarão** with the Uruguayan town of **Rio Branco**, linked by the 1½ km long Mauá bridge across the Rio Jaguarão.

Entering Uruguay Before crossing into Uruguay, you must visit Brazilian Polícia Federal to get an exit stamp; if not, the Uruguayan authorities will send you back. The crossing furthest west is **Barra do Quaraí** to Bella Unión, via the Barra del Cuaraim bridge. This is near the confluence of the Rios Uruguai and Quaraí. Thirty kilometres east is another crossing from **Quaraí** to **Artigas** in a cattle raising and agricultural area.

The southern interior of the state is the region of the real gaúcho. Principal towns of this area include **Santana do Livramento**. Its twin Uruguayan city is Rivera. All one need do is cross the main street to Rivera, but by public transport this is not a straightforward border. The town has hotels and a youth hostel.

 Sleeping → *See Telephone, page 347, for important phone changes.*

Serra Gaúcha *p453*
Gramado
Plenty of hotels and places to eat (mostly expensive).
A Chalets do Vale, R Arthur Reinheimer 161 (off Av das Hortênsias at about 4700), T3286 4151, chaletsdovale@via-rs.net. 3 homely chalets in lovely setting, kitchen, TV, good deal for groups of 4/families.
E pp Albergue Internacional de Gramado, Av das Hortênsias 3880, T3295 1020, www.gramado hostel.com.br. Cosy and new, dormitory accommodation, also has double rooms, cheaper for HI members.

Canela
AL Serra Verde, Av Osvaldo Aranha 610, T3278 9700, www.serraverdehotel.com.br. With thermal pools, sauna, massage, TV and internet, parking, very good.

A Bela Vista, R Oswaldo Aranha 160, T/F3282 1327, hrabal@pdh.com.br, near rodoviária. Good breakfasts.
D pp Pousada do Viajante, R Ernesto Urbani 132, T3282 2017. Kitchen facilities, dormitories and double rooms.
Camping Camping Clube do Brasil, 1 km from waterfall in Parque do Caracol, 1 km off main road, signposted (8 km from Canela), T3282 4321. Sell excellent honey and chocolate. **Sesi**, camping or cabins, R Francisco Bertolucci 504, 2½ km outside Canela, T/F3282 1311. Clean, restaurant.

Caxias do Sul *p454*
Hotels fill up early in the afternoon.
C Grande, R Júlio de Castilhos 1064, Farroupilha, T3261 1025, grandehotel@zaz.com.br, 2 blocks from the church where the buses from Caxias do Sul stop, no breakfast, clean.

 For an explanation of the sleeping and eating price codes used in this guide, see page 58.
 Other relevant information is found in Essentials pages 345-347.

C **Pérola**, Marquês de Herval 237, T3223 6080. Good value.

C **Somensi**, R Siba Paes 367, Bento Gonçalves, T3453 3111, hotelsomensi@ibest.com.br, near the Pipa Pórtico and Cristo Rei church in the upper town. And others.

D **Pousada Casa Mia**, Trav Niterói 71, Bento Gonçalves, T3451 1215, www.pousada casamia.com.br. HI youth hostel with two branches (Av Osvaldo Aranha 381, T3454 4936).

Jesuit Missions *p455*
São Miguel
In the evening it is difficult to find a good place to eat, try one of the 2 snack bars for hamburgers.

B **Hotel Barichello**, Av Borges do Canto 1567, T3381 1272. Nice and quiet, restaurant with churrasco for lunch.

D **Pousada das Missões**, youth hostel, next to the ruins, T3381 1030, pousada.missoes@ terra.com.br. Very good.

Santo Ângelo
AL-B **Maerkli**, Av Brasil 1000, T/F3313 2127. Recommended.

D **Comércio**, Av Brasil 1178, T3312 2542. Good for the price, a bit run down.

D **Hotel Nova Esperança**, Trav Centenário 463, T3312 1173. Behind bus station, without breakfast.

South of Porto Alegre: Rio Grande *p455*
A **Atlântico Rio Grande**, R Duque de Caxias 55, T3231 3833. Recommended, good value.

C **Paris**, R Mal F Peixoto 112, T3231 3866. Old, charming and recommended.

Border with Uruguay: coastal route *p456*
Chuí
B **Bertelli Chuí**, BR-471, Km 648, 2 km from town, T3265 1266, www.bertellichuihotel.com.br. Comfortable, with pool.

D **Rivero**, Colômbia 163-A, T3265 1271. With bath, without breakfast.

D **San Francisco**, Av Colombia e R Chile. Shower, restaurant.

❶ Eating

Serra Gaúcha: Canela *p454*
¶¶ **Bifão e Cia**, Av Osvaldo Aranha 301. For meat, good local food and ambience.

South of Porto Alegre: Rio Grande *p455*
¶¶ **Blue Café**, R Luis Loréa 314. Expresso machine and good cake. 0830-1930 (2300 Fri when jazz/blues music).

¶¶ **Parrillada Don Lauro**, R Luís Loréa 369. Uruguayan steak in nice restaurant, fairly cheap.

¶ **Rio's**, R Val Porto 393. Vast but good churrascaria.

¶ **Tia Laura**, 29 km from town on BR-392 north to Pelotas. Excellent, specializes in home cooking and café colonial.

❷ Transport

Border with Argentina *p455*
Uruguaiana/Paso de los Libres
Taxi or **bus** across the bridge about US$5. Buses connect the bus stations and centres of each city every 30 mins; if you have to disembark for visa formalities, a following bus will pick you up without extra charge. There are buses to **Porto Alegre**. Planalto buses run from Uruguaiana via Barra do Quaraí/Bella Unión to **Salto** and **Paysandú** in Uruguay.

South of Porto Alegre *p455*
Lagoa do Peixe
Bus From Mostardas you can hop off the 1045 bus which passes through the northern end of the park on its way to the beach (basic hotels and restaurants). Three buses a week between Mostardas/Tavares and São José do Norte (130 km), via Bojuru.

São Lourenço do Sul
Bus From **Porto Alegre** US$12, 6 a day.

Rio Grande
Bus Frequent daily to and from **Pelotas** (56 km), 1 hr, US$3, **Bagé** (280 km), **Santa Vitória** (220 km), and **Porto Alegre** (5 a day, US$18, 4 hrs). All buses to these destinations go through Pelotas. Road to Uruguayan border at **Chuí** is paved, but the surface is poor (5 hrs by bus, at 0700 and 1430). Bus tickets to Punta del Este or Montevideo at 2330 from rodoviária.

Border with Uruguay: coastal route *p456*
Chuí
Bus Rodoviária on R Venezuela. Buses run from Chuí to **Pelotas** (6-7 daily, US$15, 4 hrs), **Rio Grande** (0700, 1400, 5 hrs, US$12) and **Porto Alegre** (1200, 2400, 7¾ hrs, US$45).

Border with Uruguay: inland route *p456*
Santana do Livramento
Bus Rodoviária is at Gen Salgado Filho e Gen Vasco Alves. Bus to **Porto Alegre**, 2 daily, 7 hrs, US$35; 3 daily to **Uruguaiana**, 4 hrs, US$18; services also to São Paulo and other destinations.

Foz do Iguaçu

The Iguaçu Falls are the most stunning waterfalls in South America. Their magnitude, and the volume of water that thunders over the edge, has to be seen to be believed. They are 32 km from the city of Foz do Iguaçu. For a description of the falls, maps and an account of road links between Argentina, Brazil and Paraguay, see the Argentina chapter.

Ins and outs

Tourist offices **Foz do Iguaçu:** Secretaria Municipal de Turismo ① *Praça Getúlio Vargas 69, T3521 1455, 0700-2300, www.fozdoiguacu.pr.gov.br.* Very helpful, English spoken. There is a 24-hour tourist help line number, T0800-451516. Very helpful. Airport tourist information is also good, open for all arriving flights, gives map and bus information, English spoken. Helpful office, free map, at the rodoviária, English spoken.

Parque Nacional Foz do Iguaçu → *Colour map 7, grid C1.*

① *US$10, payable in reais only, includes transport within the park. The park is open daily, 0900-1700 in winter, and to 1800 in summer (check if the park is closed until 1300 on Mon); www.cataratasdoiguacu.com.br.*

The Brazilian national park was founded in 1939 and the area was designated a World Heritage Site by UNESCO in 1986. Fauna most frequently encountered are little and red brocket deer,

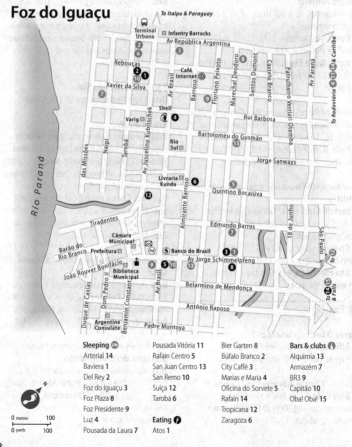

Foz do Iguaçu

Sleeping 😴	Pousada Vitória **11**	Bier Garten **8**	**Bars & clubs** 🍸
Arterial **14**	Rafain Centro **5**	Búfalo Branco **2**	Alquimia **13**
Baviera **1**	San Juan Centro **13**	City Caffé **3**	Armazém **7**
Del Rey **2**	San Remo **10**	Marias e Maria **4**	BR3 **9**
Foz do Iguaçu **3**	Suiça **12**	Oficina do Sorvete **5**	Capitão **10**
Foz Plaza **8**	Tarobá **6**	Rafain **14**	Oba! Oba! **15**
Foz Presidente **9**		Tropicana **12**	
Luz **4**	**Eating** 🍴	Zaragoza **6**	
Pousada da Laura **7**	Atos **1**		

0 metres 100
0 yards 100

South American coati, white-eared opossum, and a sub-species of the brown capuchin monkey. The endangered tegu lizard is common. Over 100 species of butterflies have been identified, among them the electric blue Morpho, the poisonous red and black heliconius and species of Papilionidae and Pieridae. The bird life is especially rewarding for birdwatchers. Five members of the toucan family can be seen.

Take a bus or taxi to the park's entrance, 17 km from Foz. There's a smart modern **visitors centre** here, with toilets, ATM, a small café, a large souvenir shop and a Banco do Brasil câmbio (0800-1900). An **Exposição Ecológica** has information about the natural history of the falls and surrounding park (included in entry fee). Nature lovers are advised to visit first thing in the morning, preferably in low season, as crowds can significantly detract from the experience of the falls and surrounding park (at peak times like Semana Santa up to 10,000 visitors a day arrive). From the entrance, shuttle buses leave every 10-15 minutes for the 8-km journey to the falls, stopping first at the start of the **Macuco Safari** (see page 461). From there it's another 10 minutes' drive to the Hotel Tropical das Cataratas and the start of a 1.2 km paved walk to the falls. This is an easy walk, taking you high above the Rio Iguaçu, giving splendid views of all the falls on the Argentine side from a series of galleries. At the end of the path, you can walk down to a viewing point right almost under the powerful Floriano Falls, a dramatic view, since you're in the middle of the river, though you will get completely soaked. A catwalk at the foot of the Floriano Falls goes almost to the middle of the river to give a good view of the Garganta del Diablo. From here, there are 150 steps up to the **Porto Canoas** complex (there is a lift for those who find stairs difficult); you can also return the way you came, and walk a little further along the road. The Porto Canoas complex consists of a big souvenir shop, toilets, a café, a fast food place (mixed reports) and smart **restaurant** ① *buffet lunch US$15, 1200-1600, good value*, all with good view of the river above the falls. Return to the visitor centre and entrance either by the free shuttle bus, by walking back along the forest path as far as Hotel das Cataratas (good lunch with a view of the falls) and take the bus from there. The whole visit will take around two hours, plus time for lunch. Never feed wild animals and keep your distance when taking photos; coatis have been known to attack visitors with food.

Foz do Iguaçu and around → *Phone code 0xx45. Population 301,400.*

A small, modern city, 28 km from the falls, with a wide range of accommodation and good communications by air and road with the main cities of southern Brazil and Asunción in Paraguay. The **Parque das Aves bird zoo** ① *Rodovia das Cataratas Km 16, 100 m before the entrance to the park, T/F3529 8282, www.parquedasaves.com.br, 0830-1700, US$10*, has received frequent good reports. It contains Brazilian and foreign birds, many species of parrot and beautiful toucans, in huge aviaries through which you can walk, with the birds flying and hopping around you. There are other birds in cages and a butterfly and hummingbird house.

The **Itaipu dam** ① *on the Río Paraná 12 km north, a short film is shown at the visitor centre 10 mins before each guided visit, all free, at 0800, 0900, 1000, 1400, 1500, 1530, Mon-Sat, check times with tourist office, and take passport, To800-645 4645, www.itaipu.gov.br*, is the site of the largest single power station in the world built jointly by Brazil and Paraguay. Construction of this massive scheme began in 1975 and it became operational in 1984. The main dam is 8 km long, creating a lake which covers 1,400 sq km. The 18 turbines have an installed capacity of 12,600,000 Kw and produce about 75 bn Kwh a year, providing 80% of Paraguay's electricity and 25% of Brazil's. The Paraguayan side may be visited from Ciudad del Este. There is also the **Ecomuseu de Itaipu** ① *Av Tancredo Neves, Km 11, T3520 5816, Sun 1400-1730, Tue-Sat 0830-1130, 1400-1730*, and **Iguaçu Environmental Education Centre** *free with guide*, are geared to educate about the preservation of the local culture and environment, or that part which isn't underwater. Recommended.

Border with Argentina

If entering Argentina only for the day, there is no need to obtain a Brazilan exit stamp but you must get Argentine stamps for any visit. The city bus between Foz do Iguaçu and Puerto Iguazú therefore only stops and waits at the Argentine border post, not the Brazilian one. If you are crossing from one country to the other for an extended period and need stamps from both, then you can ask the bus driver for a transfer, get off at the Brazilian border post and get on the next bus through without paying again. If entering Brazil only for the day, in principle a stamp is required, especially if you need a visa. In practice it is not asked for, but confirm this before corssing as practices change. Note that the bus will not wait for you at the Brazilian border post.

marked '400, Parque Nacional'. You can get on or off at any point on the route past the airport and Hotel das Cataratas, 40 mins, US$1 one way, payable in reais or pesos (the driver waits at the Park entrance while passengers purchase entry tickets, which are checked by a park guard on the bus). Taxi US$9.50, US$40 return including waiting (negotiate in advance).

Foz do Iguaçu p459, map p458

Air Iguaçu international airport, 18 km south of town near the falls. In Arrivals is Banco do Brasil and Caribe Tours e Câmbio, car rental offices, tourist office and an official taxi stand, US$15 to town centre. All buses marked Parque Nacional pass the airport in each direction, US$1, 0525-0040, does not permit large amounts of luggage but backpacks OK. Many hotels run minibus services for a small charge. Daily flights to **Rio, São Paulo, Curitiba** and other Brazilian cities.
Bus For transport to the falls see above under Parque Nacional Foz do Iguaçu. Long distance terminal (Rodoviária), Av Costa e Silva, 4 km from centre on road to Curitiba; bus to centre, any bus that says 'Rodoviária', US$1.25. Taxi US$7. Book departures as soon as possible. As well as the tourist office (see above), there is a Cetreme desk for tourists who have lost their documents, Guarda Municipal (police) and luggage store.
To **Curitiba**, Pluma, Sulamericana, 9-10 hrs, paved road, US$30. To **Guaíra** via Cascavel only, 5 hrs, US$18. To **Florianópolis**, Catariense and Reunidas, US$55, 14 hrs. Reunidas to **Porto Alegre**, US$52-60. To **São Paulo**, 16 hrs, Pluma US$44, executivo 6 a day, plus one leito. To **Rio** 22 hrs, several daily, US$75. To **Campo Grande**, US$53.

Foz do Iguaçu and around:
Itaipu dam p459

Bus Runs from outside the Terminal Urbano to the visitor centre, US$1, marked 'Usina Itaipu'. The Noelia company in Puerto Iguazú includes Itaipu in its tours of the Brazilian side of the falls, T422722.

Border with Argentina:
Foz do Iguaçu/Puerto Iguazú p459

Bus Marked 'Puerto Iguazú' run every 20 mins from the Terminal Urbano, crossing the border bridge; 30 mins' journey, 3 companies, US$2. See above for procedures regarding entry stamps. **Note** Be sure you know when the last bus departs from Puerto Iguazú for Foz (usually 1900); last bus from Foz 1950. If visiting the Brazilian side for a day, gt off the bus at the Hotel Bourbon, cross the road and catch the bus to the Falls, rather than going into Foz and out

again. Combined tickets to Puerto Iguazú and the falls cost more than paying separately. For buses to **Buenos Aires**, see Puerto Iguazú, Transport for the options. There is a Pluma bus direct from Foz and you can also go to Posadas via Paraguay.

Border with Paraguay:
Foz do Iguaçu/Ciudad del Este p460

Bus (Marked Cidade-Ponte) leave from the Terminal Urbana, Av Juscelino Kubitschek, for the Ponte de Amizade (Friendship Bridge), US$0.55. To **Asunción**, Pluma (0700), RYSA (direct at 1430, 1830), from Rodoviária, US$15 (cheaper if bought in Ciudad del Este).
Car If crossing by private vehicle and only intending to visit the national parks, this presents no problems. Another crossing to Paraguay is at **Guaíra**, at the northern end of the Itaipu lake. It is 5 hrs north of Iguaçu by road and can be reached by bus from Campo Grande and São Paulo. Ferries cross to Saltos del Guaira on the Paraguayan side.

❶ Directory

Foz do Iguaçu p459, map p458

Airline offices Gol, Rodovia das Cataratas, Km 16.5, T3521 4296. **TAM**, R Rio Branco 640, T3523 8500 (offers free transport to Ciudad del Este for its flights, all cross-border documentation dealt with).
Banks It is difficult to exchange on Sun but quite possible in Paraguay where US dollars can be obtained on credit cards. There are plenty of banks and travel agents on Av Brasil. Banco do Brasil, Av Brasil 1377. Has ATM, high commission for TCs. Bradesco, Av Brasil 1202. Cash advance on Visa. HSBC, Av Brasil 1151, for MasterCard ATM. Banco 24 Horas at Oklahoma petrol station. Câmbio at Vento Sul, Av Brasil 1162, no TCs, good rates for cash. Also Corimeira, Av Brasil 148. **Embassies and consulates** Argentina, Travessa Eduardo Bianchi 26, T3574 2969. Open Mon-Fri 1000-1500. France, R Francisco Fogaça do Nascimento 800, T3529 9366, royal.service@fnn.net, 0800-1200, 1430-1700. Paraguay, R Marechal Deodoro 901, T3523 2898, Mon-Thu 0830-1530, Fri 0830-1500. **Internet** Several including Cafe Internet, R Rebouças 950, 0900-2200, Sun 1600-2200, US$1.50 per hr. Zipfoz.com, R Barão do Rio Branco 412, corner with Av Juscelino Kubitschek. Smart, a/c, US$1.50 per hr. **Medical services** Free 24-hr clinic, Av Paraná 1525, opposite Lions Club, T3521 1850. Few buses: take taxi or walk (about 25 mins). **Post offices** Praça Getúlio Vargas 72. **Telephones** Several call centres.

Salvador de Bahia

→ *Phone code: 0xx71. Post code: 40000. Colour map 5, grid C5. Population: 3.2 million.*

Salvador, the third largest city in Brazil, is capital of the state of Bahia, dubbed 'Africa in exile' for its mixture of African and European which finds its most powerful expression in Carnival. Often referred to as Bahia, rather than Salvador, the city is home to a heady mix of colonial buildings, beautiful beaches, African culture and pulsating musical rhythms. It stands on the magnificent Bahia de Todos os Santos, a sparkling bay dotted with 38 islands. The bay is the largest on the Brazilian coast covering an area of 1,100 sq km. Rising above the bay on its eastern side is a cliff which dominates the landscape and, perched on top, 71 m above sea level, are the older districts with buildings dating back to the 17th and 18th centuries. Beyond the state capital are many fine beaches, particularly in the south around Porto Seguro, while inland is the harsh sertão, traversed by the Rio São Francisco.

Ins and outs

Getting there Luis Eduardo Magalhães airport is 32 km from city centre. The **Rodoviária** is 5 km from the city with regular bus services to the centre and Campo Grande; the journey can take up to one hour especially at peak periods. ▶▶ *For further information, see Transport, page 475.*

Getting around The broad peninsula on which the city of Salvador is built is at the mouth of the Bahia de Todos Os Santos. On the opposite side of the bay's entrance is the Ilha de Itaparica. The commercial district of the city and its port are on the sheltered, western side of the peninsula; residential districts and beaches are on the open Atlantic side. The point of the peninsula is called Barra, which is itself an important area. The centre of the city is divided into two levels, the Upper City (or Cidade Alta) where the Historical Centre lies, and the Lower City (Cidade Baixa) which is the commercial and docks district. The two levels are connected by a series of steep hills called *ladeiras*. The easiest way to go from one level to the other is by the 74-m-high **Lacerda** lift which connects Praça Cairu in the lower city with Praça Municipal in the upper (renovated 2003). There is also the Plano Inclinado Gonçalves, a funicular railway which leaves from behind the Cathedral going down to Comércio, the commercial district (closes 1300 on Saturday and all Sunday). Most visitors limit themselves to the Pelourinho and historical centre, Barra, the Atlantic suburbs and the Itapagipe peninsula, which is north of the centre. The roads and avenues between these areas are straightforward to follow and are well served by public transport. Other parts of the city are not as easy to get around, but have less of a tourist interest. If going to these areas a taxi may be advisable until you know your way around. ▶▶ *For more detailed information, see Transport, page 475.*

Climate Temperatures range from 25°C to 32°C, never falling below 19°C in winter. Humidity can be high, which may make the heat oppressive. It rains somewhat all the year but the main rainy season is between May and September. Nevertheless, the sun is never far away.

Tourist offices Bahiatursa ① *Av Simon Bolivar s/n, Centro de Convenções da Bahia, 1st floor, T3117 3000, www.bahiatursa.ba.gov.br*, has lists of hotels and accommodation in private homes. Other offices at: **Pelourinho** ① *R das Laranjeiras 12, T3321 2133, daily 0830-2100*, English and German spoken; **Instituto Mauá** ① *Praça Azevedo Fernandes 01, Porto da Barra, T3264 4671, Mon-Fri 0900-1800, Sat 1000-1500*; **Rodoviária** ① *T3450 3871, daily 0730-2100*, good, English spoken; **airport** ① *T3204 1244, daily 0730-2300*; in the **Mercado Modelo** ① *T3241 0242, Mon-Sat 0900-1800, Sun 0900-1330*; **Sac Shopping Barra** ① *Av Centenario 2992, T3264 4566, Mon-Fri 0900-1900, Sat 0900-1400*, and **Sac Shopping Iguatemi** ① *Av Tancredo Neves 148, Pituba, T480 5511, Mon-Fri 0900-2100, Sat 0900-1300*. Offices have noticeboards for messages and details of travel throughout the State of Bahia. See also www.bahia.com.br, www.cultura.ba.gov.br, the Secretaria de Cultura's website, and www.setur.ba.gov.br, the Secretaria de Turismo's site. **Maps:** from **Departamento de Geografia e Estadística** ① *Av Estados Unidos (opposite Banco do Brasil, Lower City*, and from newsstands or airport bookshop, US$1.50.

Security The authorities have made efforts to police the old part of the city and Barra, which are now well lit at night. The civil police are reported to be very sympathetic and helpful. Police are little in evidence after 2300, however, and at night you should leave valuables securely in your hotel. Also at night, the areas around and in the lifts and buses are unsafe. Do not walk down any of the links between the old and new city, especially the Ladeira de Misericórdia, which links the Belvedere, near the Lacerda Lifts, with the lower city. As in all large cities, use your common sense and be very careful of your possessions at all times and in all districts. There have been reports of armed muggings on the sand dunes surrounding Lagoa do Abaeté. Do not visit them alone. Should a local join you at your table for a chat, leave at once if drugs are mentioned.

Background

On 1 November 1501, All Saints' Day, the navigator Amérigo Vespucci sailed into the bay. As the first European to see it, he named it after the day of his arrival. The first Governor General, Tomé de Sousa, arrived on 23 March 1549 to build a fortified city to protect Portugal's interest from constant threats of Dutch and French invasion. Salvador was formally founded on 1 November 1549 and remained the capital of Brazil until 1763. By the 18th century, it was the most important city in the Portuguese Empire after Lisbon, ideally situated in a safe, sheltered harbour along the trade routes of the 'New World'.

The city's first wealth came from the cultivation of sugar cane and tobacco, the plantations' workforce coming from the West coast of Africa. For three centuries Salvador was the site of a thriving slave trade. Even today, Salvador is described as the most African city in the Western Hemisphere and the University of Bahia boasts the only chair in the Yoruba language in the Americas. The influence permeates the city: food sold on the street is the same as in Senegal and Nigeria, Bahian music is fused with pulsating African polyrhythms, men and women nonchalantly carry enormous loads on their heads, fishermen paddle

Salvador

Sleeping
Albergue do Porto 2
Bahia do Sol 3
Bella Barra 5
Catharina Paraguaçu 1
Ibis 6
Pestana Bahia 7
Pousade Ambar 8
Pousada Marcos 9
Tropical Hotel da Bahia 4
Villa Romana 8

dug-out canoes in the bay, the pace of life is a little slower than elsewhere. The pulse of the city is candomblé, an Afro-Brazilian religion in which the African deities of Nature, the Goddess of the sea and the God of creation are worshipped. These deities (or orixás) are worshipped in temples (terreiros) which can be elaborate, decorated halls, or simply someone's front room with tiny altars to the orixá. Candomblé ceremonies may be seen by tourists – but not photographed – on Sunday and religious holidays. Contact the tourist office, Bahiatursa, or see their twice monthly calendar of events. Salvador today is a city of 15 forts, 166 Catholic churches, 1,000 candomblé temples and a fascinating mixture of old and modern, rich and poor, African and European, religious and profane. It is still a major port exporting tropical fruit, cocoa, sisal, soya beans and petrochemical products. Its most important industry, though, is tourism. Local government has done much to improve the fortunes of this once rundown, poor and dirty city and most visitors feel that the richness of its culture is compensation enough for any problems they may encounter. The Bahianas – black women who dress in traditional 18th-century costumes – are street vendors who sit behind their trays of delicacies, savoury and seasoned, made from the great variety of local fish, vegetables and fruits. Their street food is one of the musts for visitors.

Sights

Centro Histórico
There is much more of interest in the Upper than in the Lower City. From Praça Municipal to the Carmo area 2 km north along the cliff is the Centro Histórico (Historical Centre), now a national monument and also protected by UNESCO. It was in this area that the Portuguese built their fortified city and where today stand some of the most important examples of colonial architecture in the Americas. This area is undergoing a massive restoration programme funded by the Bahian state government and UNESCO. Colonial houses have been painted in pastel colours. Many of the bars have live music which spills out onto the street on every corner. Patios have been created in the open areas behind the houses with open air cafés and bars. Artist ateliers, antique and handicraft stores have brought new artistic blood to what was once the bohemian part of the city. Many popular traditional restaurants and bars from other parts of Salvador have opened new branches here. Its transformation has also attracted many tourist shops and the area can get crowded.

Represa do Ipitanga
BA 337
Av Luiz Viana Filho
R Prof Pinto de Aguiar
Av Otávio Mangabeira
Parque Pituaçu
ITAPOÃ
PLACAFOR
PIATÃ
JAGUARIBE
CORSÁRIO
BOCA DO RIO
To Dorival, To Lagoa de Abaeté, Airport & Estrada do Coco to Arembepe & Praia do Forte
To Lagoa de Abaeté
Av Dorival Caymmi

Related map
A Salvador Centro Histórico, page 466

Eating
Solar Do Unhão 1

0 km 1
0 miles 1

N

Praça Municipal, Praça de Sé and Terreiro de Jesus
Dominating the Praça Municipal is the old Casa de Câmara e Cadeia or **Paço Municipal** (Council Chamber – 1660), while alongside is the **Palácio Rio Branco** (1918), once the Governor's Palace. Leaving it with its panoramic view of the bay, Rua Misericórdia goes north passing the **Santa Casa Misericórdia** ① *0800-1000, 1400-1700, T3322 7666* (1695 – see the high altar and painted tiles), to Praça da Sé. This praça with its mimosa and flamboyant trees leads into Terreiro de Jesus, a picturesque praça named after the church which dominates it. Built in 1692, the **church of the Jesuits** became the property of the Holy See in 1759 when the

Jesuits were expelled from all Portuguese territories. The façade is one of the earliest examples of baroque in Brazil, an architectural style which was to dominate the churches built in the 17th and 18th centuries. Inside, the vast vaulted ceiling and 12 side altars in baroque and rococo frame the main altar completely leafed in gold. The tiles in blue, white and yellow in a tapestry pattern are also from Portugal. It houses the tomb of Mem de Sá. The church is now the city Cathedral (**Catedral Basílica**) ① *0900-1100, 1400-1700*. On the eastern side of the square is the church of **São Pedro dos Clérigos** ① *Sun 0800-0930*, which is beautifully renovated, while close by, on the south-side, is the church of the **Ordem Terceira de São Domingos** (Dominican Third Order) ① *Mon-Fri 0800-1200, 1400-1700, US$0.30*, which has a beautiful painted wooden ceiling and fine tiles. Nearby is **Museu Afro-Brasileiro** ① *in the former Faculty of Medicine building, Terreiro de Jesus, Mon-Fri 0900-1800, Sat-Sun 1000-1700, US$1.65, students US$0.85*, compares African and Bahian Orixás (deities)

Salvador Centro Histórico

Bahíacafé.com **1**
Camafeu de Oxossi &
  Maria de São Pedro **10**
Coffee Shop **1**
Encontro dos Artistas **12**
Gramado **2**
Jardim das Delícias **3**
Mama Bahia **6**
Maria Mata Mouro **13**
O Nilo **8**
Pomerô **14**
Sorriso da Dadá **16**
Uauá **15**

Sleeping ⬤
Albergue das Laranjeiras **1**
Albergue do Passo **4**
Albergue do Pelô **4**
Albergue São Jorge **6**
Lucas Guesthouse **2**
O Convento do Carmo **5**
O Pagador de Promessas **7**
Pelourinho **8**
Pousada da Praça **3**
Quilombo do Pelô **9**

Eating 🍴
Axego **4**

Bars & clubs 🍸
Cantina de Lua **5**
Casa do Olodum **17**
do Reggae **9**
O Cravinho **11**

Quereres **7**

Churches ⛪
Carmo **13**
Conceição de Praia **1**
Igreja do Desterro **2**
Nossa Senhora
  da Ajuda **3**
Nossa Senhora do
  Rosário dos Pretos **4**
Ordem Terceira de São
  Domingos **5**
Ordem Terceira de
  São Francisco **6**
Palma **7**
Santa Casa Misericórdia **8**
Sant'Ana **9**
São Bento **12**
São Francisco **10**

São Pedro dos Clérigos **11**

Museums 🏛
Abelardo Rodrigues **1**
Afro-Brasileiro,
  Arqueológico e
  Etnográfico & Medicine **2**
Casa da Cultura
  Jorge Amado **4**
Casa do Benin **5**
Cidade **6**
Convento do Carmo **7**
Museu de Arte Sacra,
  Museu Costa Pinto,
  Museu de Arte de Bahia
  & Museu de Arte
  Moderno **8**

celebrations, beautiful murals and carvings, all in Portuguese. **Museu Arqueológico e Etnográfico** ① *in the basement of the same building, Mon-Fri 0900-1700, US$0.55*, houses archaeological discoveries from Bahia (stone tools, clay urns, etc), an exhibition on *indígenas* from the Alto Rio Xingu area (artefacts, tools, photos), recommended. There is a museum of medicine located in the same complex.

Facing Terreiro de Jesus is Praça Anchieta and the church of **São Francisco**. ① *0830-1700, entry to cloisters US$0.25, church free.* Its simple façade belies the treasure inside. The entrance leads to a sanctuary with a spectacular painting on the wooden ceiling, by local artist José Joaquim da Rocha (1777). The main body of the church is the most exuberant example of baroque in the country. The cedar wood carving and later gold leaf was completed after 28 years in 1748. The cloisters of the monastery are surrounded by a series of blue and white tiles from Portugal. Next door is the church of the **Ordem Terceira de São Francisco** (Franciscan Third Order – 1703) ① *daily 0800-1200, 1300-1700, US$1.30, students US$0.65.* It has a façade intricately carved in sandstone. Inside is a quite remarkable Chapter House with striking images of the Order's most celebrated saints.

Largo do Pelourinho

Leading off the Terreiro de Jesus is Rua Portas do Carmo (formerly Alfredo Brito), a charming, narrow cobbled street lined with fine colonial houses painted in different pastel shades. This street leads into the Largo do Pelourinho (Praça José Alencar), which was completely renovated in 1993. Considered the finest complex of colonial architecture in Latin America, it was once the site of a pillory where unscrupulous tradesmen were publicly punished and ridiculed. After the cleaning of the area, new galleries, boutiques and restaurants are opening, and at night the Largo is lively, especially on Tuesday (see Bars and clubs, page 472) . **Nosso Senhor Do Rosário Dos Pretos church** ① *small entry fee*, the so-called Slave Church, dominates the square. It was built by former slaves over a period of 100 years. The side altars honour black saints. The painted ceiling is very impressive, the overall effect being one of tranquillity in contrast to the complexity of the Cathedral and São Francisco.

At the corner of Portas do Carmo and Largo do Pelourinho is a small museum to the work of Jorge Amado, who died in 2002, **Casa da Cultura Jorge Amado** ① *Mon-Sat 0900-1900, free.* Information is in Portuguese only, but the café walls are covered with colourful copies of his book jackets. The Carmo Hill is at the top of the street leading out of Largo do Pelourinho. **Museu Abelardo Rodrigues** ① *Solar Ferrão, Pelourinho, R Gregório de Mattos 45, 1300-1900 except Mon, US$0.55*, is a religious art museum, with objects from the 17th, 18th and 19th centuries, mainly from Bahia, Pernambuco and Maranhão. **Museu da Cidade** ① *Largo do Pelourinho, Mon and Wed-Fri 0930-1800, Sat 1300-1700, Sun 0930-1300, free*, has exhibitions of arts and crafts and old photographs. From the higher floors of the museum you can get a good view of the Pelourinho. **Casa do Benin** ① *Mon-Fri 1000-1800, below NS do Rosario dos Pretos*, shows African crafts, photos, a video show on Benin and Angola.

The **Carmo church** (Carmelite Third Order, 1709) ① *Mon-Sat 0800-1130, 1400-1730, Sun 1000-1200, US$0.40*, houses one of the sacred art treasures of the city, a sculpture of Christ made in 1730 by a slave who had no formal training, Francisco Xavier das Chagas, known as O Cabra. One of the features of the piece is the blood made from whale oil, ox blood, banana resin and 2,000 rubies to represent the drops of blood. **Museu do Carmo** ① *in the Convento do Carmo, Mon-Sat 0800-1200, 1400-1800, Sun 0800-1200, US$0.15*, has a collection of icons and colonial furniture.

South of the Praça Municipal

Rua Chile leads to **Praça Castro Alves**, with its monument to Castro Alves, who started the campaign which finally led to the Abolition of Slavery in 1888. Two streets lead out of this square, Avenida 7 de Setembro, busy with shops and street vendors selling everything imaginable, and, parallel to it, Rua Carlos Gomes. **Museu de Arte Sacra** ① *R do Sodré 276 (off R Carlos Gomes), Mon-Fri 1130-1730, US$2*, is in the 17th-century convent and church of Santa Teresa, at the bottom of the steep Ladeira de Santa Teresa. Many of the 400 carvings are from Europe, but some are local. Among the reliquaries of silver and gold is one of gilded wood by Aleijadinho (see box, page 417). **São Bento church** ① *Av 7 de Setembro, Mon-Sat 0630-1230, 1600-1900, Sun 0700-1130, 1700-1900*, was rebuilt after 1624, but it has fine 17th-century furniture.

stylish, modern design in a rebuilt historic building. English-owned, 2 suites with terraces, spacious rooms, a/c, art gallery.

AL Pousada das Flores, R Direita de Santo Antônio 442, near Santo Antônio fort, T/F3243 1836, www.pflores.com.br. Brazilian/French owners, excellent breakfast, beautiful old house.

AL-A Pousada Santo Antônio, R Direita de Santo Antônio 130, T3326 1270, www.hotel-santoantonio.com. Bright and comfortable converted colonial house, best rooms with views over the bay, a/c, all rooms different, good service and breakfast.

B Pousada Villa Carmo, R do Carmo 58, T/F3241 3924, www.pousadavillacarmo.com.br. Italian/Brazilian owned, many European languages spoken, very comfortable, rooms with fan or a/c.

B-C Pousada Baluarte, R Baluarte, 13, T3327 0367, www.pousadabaluarte.com. Bohemian household, lovely owners, 5 rooms, cheaper without bath, the home made breakfasts are excellent.

C-D Pousada Hilmar, R Direita de Santo Antônio 136, T3243 4959, www.pousadahilmar.com.br. Several types of room with and without a/c and TV, with breakfast, a good option in a quiet street.

D pp Nalvas, R Direita de Santo Antônio 22. 4-bed rooms, fan, no towel, use of kitchen, related travel agency at No 22, good value.

Campo Grande/Vitória

Upmarket residential area, between Barra and city centre, convenient for museums.

L Tropical Hotel da Bahia, Av 7 de Setembro 1537, Campo Grande, T2105 2000, www.tropicalhotel.com.br. Well run, convenient for city centre, very much a business hotel.

A Bahia do Sol, Av 7 de Setembro 2009, T3338 8800, www.bahiadosol.com.br. Comfortable, safe and frigobar in room, family run, good breakfast and restaurant, bureau de change. Ask for a room onthe upper floors.

Barra p468

B-C Pousada Villa Verde, R da Palmeira 190, T3489 1978, www.pousadavillaverde.com. Reduced rates for longer stay, a/c studios with kitchen and double room with fan, garden, terrace, hammocks, internet, safe, very good. Recommended.

C Bella Barra, R Afonso Celso 439, T3264 3260, www.hotelbellabarra.com.br. Simple, a/c rooms, internet, plenty of services, safe, English spoken, tours, car hire arranged.

C Villa Romana, R Lemos Brito 14, T3264 6522, www.villaromana.com.br. 1960s hotel with basic a/c rooms and a pool, good location. Recommended.

C-D Pousada Ambar, R Afonso Celso 485, T3264 6956, www.ambarpousada.com.br. Also has albergue at **E-F**. Good service, breakfast, internet, convenient, French owner also speaks English.

C-D Pousada Santa Maria, Av 7 de Setembro 3835, T3264 4076, pousadasmaria@hotmail.com. Excellent breakfast, English and German spoken, TV, laundry service, internet, restaurant/bar, exchange, car rental.

E pp Albergue do Porto, R Barão de Sergy 197, T3264 6600, www.alberguedoporto.com.br. One block from beach, short bus ride or 20 mins on foot from historical centre. IYHA hostel in beautiful turn-of-the-century house, cheaper for members, breakfast, convenient, English spoken, double rooms with a/c and bath available (**B-C**, depending on season), kitchen, laundry facilities, safe, TV lounge, games room, internet, courtyard. Highly recommended.

E-F Pousada Marcos, Av Oceânica 281, T3264 5117, www.pousadamarcos.com.br. Youth hostel-style, great location near the lighthouse, very busy, notices in Hebrew for potential travelling companions, kitchen, efficient.

Private apartments Rooms to let in private apartments: Gorete, R 8 de Dezembro 522, Apt 002, Edif Ricardo das Neves, Graça, T3264 3016, gorete@cpunet.com.br. Convenient, use of kitchen, patio, internet, safe.

Atlantic beach suburbs p468

LL Pestana Bahia, R Fonte de Boi 216, Rio Vermelho, T/F2103 8000, www.pestana.com. One of the best in Salvador, all comfort and facilties including for the disabled.

A Sol Bahia Atlântico, R Manoel Antônio Galvão 1075, Patamares, 17 km from the city (next to one of the best beaches in Salvador), T3206 0500, www.solbahia.com.br. Modern family hotel set high on the hill with great views of the coastline with a pool, restaurant and sauna, private tram connects the higher and lower parts of the resort and there is free transport to the beach (around ½ km away).

A-B Catharina Paraguaçu, R João Gomes 128, Rio Vermelho, T3334 0089, www.hotel catharinaparaguacu.com.br. Charming, small, colonial-style, tastefully decorated.

B Ibis, R Fonte do Boi 215, T3330 8300, www.accorhotels.com.br. Large hotel in this budget business chain, safe, a/c and with sea views from the upper floors. Great value.

Itapoã

LL Sofitel, R Passargada s/n, T2106 8500, www.sofitel.com. Another superb hotel, in a park with 9-hole golf course, 5 mins from airport, shuttle bus to centre, all facilities.

AL **Catussaba**, R Alameida da Praia, 25 km from the city, T3374 8000, www.catussaba.com.br. Elegant resort hotel with a mock colonial interior and beautiful gardens which lead out to the beach. Beware of ocean currents when swimming. Convenient for the airport. Recommended.

A **Vila Farol**, R das 7 Casas, Praia do Pedra do Sal, T3374 2107. Small Swiss-run pousada, pool, homely, great restaurant Le Jardin, 1 block from beach. First class.

Camping Note that sea bathing is dangerous off shore near the campsites. **Camping Clube do Brasil**, R Visconde do Rosário 409, Rosário, T3242 0482. **Ecológica**, R Alameida da Praia, near the lighthouse at Itapoã, take bus from Praça da Sé direct to Itapoã, or to Campo Grande or Barra, change there for Itapoã, about 1 hr, then 30 mins' walk, T3374 3506. Bar, restaurant, hot showers. Highly recommended.

Pensionatos These are places to stay in shared rooms (up to 4 per room); part or full board available. **Pierre Marbacher**, R Carlos Coqueijo 68A, Itapoã, T3249 5754 (Caixa Postal 7458, 41600 Salvador). He is Swiss, owns a beach bar at Rua K, speaks English and rents houses or rooms.

At Carnival it's a good idea to rent a flat; the tourist office has a list of estate agents. They can also arrange rooms in private houses; however, caution is advised as not all householders are honest.

Itaparica p468
A **Pousada Arco Iris**, Estrada da Gamboa 102, Mar Grande, T3633 1316. Magnificent building and setting in mango orchard, expensive, good if slow restaurant, Manga Rosa. They have camping facilities next door, shady, not always clean.

A **Quinta Pitanga**, R da Alegria 10, in Itaparica town, T3631 1834. Beautifully decorated by the owner Jim Valkus, 3 suites and 2 singles, beachfront property, a retreat, excellent restaurant. Expensive but highly recommended, accepts day visitors and offers artists' residencies (www.sacatar.org).

C **Pousada Um Canto do Mar**, Av Beira Mar s/n, Praia de Aratuba, T3638 2244, www.pousadaumcantodomar.com.br. Bright, simple cabins overlooking what is a lively beach in summer, quiet the rest of the year, helpful staff, decent breakfast.

C **Sonho do Verão**, R São Bento 2, opposite Pousada Arco Iris, Mar Grande, T3633 1316, sonhodeverao@internet.com.br. Chalets and apartments, cooking facilities, French and English spoken. Like other pousadas they rent bicycles (US$3 per hr); they also rent horses (US$5 per hr).

C-D **Pousada Icaraí**, Praça da Piedade, Itaparica town, T3631 1110, hicarai@hotmail.com. Charming, good location.

C-D **Pousada Zimbo Tropical**, Estrada de Cacha Pregos, Km 3, Rua Yemanjá, Aratuba, T/F3638 1148. French/Brazilian-run, good breakfast, evening meals available. Recommended.

● Eating

Local specialities

The main dish is *moqueca*, seafood cooked in a sauce made from coconut milk, tomatoes, red and green peppers, fresh coriander and *dendê* (palm oil). It is traditionally cooked in a wok-like earthen-ware dish and served piping hot at the table. Served with moqueca is *farofa* (manioc flour) and a hot pepper sauce which you add at your discretion, it's usually extremely hot so try a few drops before venturing further. The dendê is somewhat heavy and those with delicate stomachs are advised to try the *ensopado*, a sauce with the same ingredients as the moqueca, but without the palm oil.

Nearly every street corner has a Bahiana selling a wide variety of local snacks, the most famous of which is the *acarajé*, a kidney bean dumpling fried in palm oil which has its origins in West Africa. To this the Bahiana adds *vatapá*, a dried shrimp and coconut milk pâté (also delicious on its own), fresh salad and hot sauce (*pimenta*). For those who prefer not to eat the palm oil, the *abará* is a good substitute. Abará is steamed, wrapped in banana leaves. Seek local advice on which are most hygienic stalls to eat from. Two good Bahianas are Chica, at Ondina beach (on the street to the left of Mar A Vista Hotel) and Dinha at Largo da Santana (very lively in the late afternoon), who serves acarajé until midnight, extremely popular. Bahians usually eat *acarajé* or *abará* with a chilled beer on the way home from work or on the beach at sunset. Another popular dish with African origins is *Xin-Xin de Galinha*, chicken on the bone cooked in dendê, with dried shrimp, garlic and squash.

Centro Histórico p465, map p466
♦♦♦ **Mama Bahia**, R Alfredo Brito 21, T3322 4397, Pelourinho, www.mamabahia.com.br. Steaks and northeastern meat dishes, good but modest South American wine list.

♦♦♦ **Maria Mata Mouro**, R da Ordem Terceira 8, Pelourinho, T3321 3929. International menu, excellent service, relaxing atmosphere, closed Sun night.

♦♦♦ **O Nilo**, R das Laranjeiras 44, T9159 0937. Superior Lebanese food in an intimate restaurant.

♦♦♦ **Sorriso da Dadá**, R Frei Vicente 5, T3321 9642, www.dada.com.br. Bahia's most famous chef has had many illustrious clients, excellent *moquecas* and *vatapas*.

⑪⑪⑪ Uauá, R Gregório de Matos 36, Pelourinho, T3321 3089. Elegant, colonial restaurant and bar, typical Bahian cuisine.

⑪⑪-⑪ Axego, R João de Deus1, T3242 7481. Celebrated for its seafood, also *feijoada* at Sun lunchtime.

⑪⑪-⑪ Encontro dos Artistas, R das Laranjeiras 15, T3321 1721. Very good seafood and *moquecas* served in a little street-side restaurant.

⑪⑪-⑪ Jardim das Delícias, R João de Deus 12, Pelourinho, T3321 1449. Elegant restaurant and antiques shop with tropical garden, very reasonable for its setting, classical or live music.

⑪ Quilombo do Pelô, R Portas do Carmo 13, see Sleeping. Rustic Jamaican restaurant, open daily from 1100, good food with relaxed, if erratic service, vegetarian options.

⑪ Senac, Praça José Alencar 13-15, Largo do Pelourinho, T3324 4557. State-run catering school, with typical Bahian cooking upstairs and per kilo lunches downstairs, both a/c. Upstairs is beter but lots of choice, including vegetarian, downstairs.

⑪⑪-⑪ Pomerô, R Portas do Carmo 33, Pelourinho, T3321 5556, www.pomero.com.br. Closed Mon. Good value, simple grilled meats, fish steaks, bar snacks, *moquecas*, popular.

⑪ Bahiacafé.com, Praça da Sé 20, T3322 1266. Smart, Belgian-run internet café, good breakfasts, excellent food, English spoken.

⑪ Coffee Shop, Praça da Sé 5, T3322 7817. Cuban-style café serving sandwiches; main attraction is excellent coffee, and tea served in china cups, doubles as cigar shop.

⑪ Gramado, Praça da Sé. One of few food-by-weight restaurants in area, basic, lunch only.

In and near Mercado Modelo

⑪⑪-⑪ Camafeu De Oxossi and **Maria De São Pedro**, at the bottom of the Lacerda Lift, at Praça Cairu, in the famous **Mercado Modelo**. On the upper floor of the market are 2 restaurants, both specializing in Bahian dishes, good view of the port, daily 1130-2000, Sat lunchtime is particularly busy, not very clean. Opposite the Mercado Modelo, the Paes Mendonça supermarket self-service counter (⑪) is good value, 1100-1500, 1st floor.

Between Historical Centre and Barra

⑪⑪⑪ Solar Do Unhão, on Av Contorno, in a beautiful 18th-century sugar estate on the edge of the bay, T3321 5559. Lunch and dinner (Bahian cuisine), expensive; also good for sunset drinks.Good *capoeira* can be seen here. It is best to go by taxi as bus connections are difficult.

Barra *p468*

⑪⑪⑪ Barravento, Av Oceânica 814, T3247 2577. Popular, upmarket beach bar restaurant, seafood, steaks, cocktails and *chope*.

⑪⑪⑪ Cantina Panzone, Av Oceânica 114, T3264 3644. Pizza and pasta, lively in season.

⑪⑪⑪ Oceánica, Pres Vargas 1, T3264 3561. Long-established, popular seafood restaurnat, open till late.

⑪⑪ Quatro Amicci, R Dom Marcos Teixeira 35. Excellent pizzas from wood-fired oven, bright, lively at weekends.

⑪ Caranguejo do Farol, Av Oceânica 235, above the road, T3264 7061. Specializing in crab, extremely busy, also a buzzing bar.

Many medium-priced a/c restuarnats in **Shopping Barra** and **Barra Center Shopping**.

Itparica *p468*

Philippe's Bar and Restaurant, Largo de São Bento, Mar Grande. French and local cuisine, information in English and French.

Restaurant Rafael in the main praça, Mar Grande. For pizzas and snacks.

There are many Bahianas selling *acarajé* in the late afternoon and early evening in the main praça by the pier at Mar Grande.

ⓞ Bars and clubs

Nightlife is concentrated on and around the Pelourinho where there is always a free live street band on Tue and at weekends. The Pelourinho area is also good for a bar browse; though be wary after 2300. There are many bars on the Largo de Quincas Berro d'Água, especially along R Portas do Carmo. R João de Deus and its environs are dotted with simple pavement bars with plastic tables. The most famous Salvador musicians are the *maracatú* drum orchestras like **Olodum** and **Ilê Aiyê** (see below). There is live music all year round but the best time to hear the most frenetic performers, particularly the *axê* stars, is during Carnaval.

Pelourinho *p467*

Bar do Reggae and **Praça do Reggae**, Ladeiro do Pelourinho, by Nossa Senhora dos Rosarios dos Pretos. Live reggae bands every Tue and more frequently closer to carnival.

Cantina da Lua, Praça 15 de Novembro 2, Terreiro de Jesus, T3322 4041. Daily, popular, good place to meet, outdoor seating, but the food isn't great.

Casa do Olodum, R Gregório de Mattos 22, T3321 5010, http://olodum.uol.com.br. Olodum's headquarters where they perform live every Tue and Sun at 1930 to packed crowds.

Ilê Aiyê, R do Curuzu 197, Liberdade, T3256 8800, www.ileaiye.com.br. Ilê Aiyê's headquarters. Details of live performances throughout Salvador are published here.

O Cravinho, Praça 15 de Novembro 3, T3322 6759. Dark little ba with occasional live music, cachaça made on the premises and bar food. Take care in this area after 2300.

Quereres, R Frei Vicente 7, T3321 1616. Lively little club in a colonial house playing Brazilian samba funk, hip hop and *axê*, busy Tue and Fri.

Barra *p468*

Most Barra nightlife happens at the Farol da Barra (lighthouse). R Marquês de Leão is very busy, with lots of bars with tables on the pavement. Like the Pelourinho, the whole area is good for a browse, but be wary of pickpockets.

Habeas Copos, R Marquês de Leão 172. Famous and traditional street side bar, very popular.

Atlantic suburbs *p468*

Once the bohemian section of town the nightlife in **Rio Vermelho** rivals Pelourinho. There are a number of lively bars around the Largo de Santana, a block west of the Hotel Catharina Paraguaçu.

Café Calypso, Trav Prudente Moraes 59, Rio Vermelho. Live Brazilian rock on Tue and Fri.

Havana Music Bar, R Cardeal da Silva 117, Rio Vermelho. Live bands Wed-Sat, best after 2230.

Pimentinha, Boca do Rio. One of the few clubs to be lively on Mon.

Teatro Sesi Rio Vermelho, R Borges dos Reis 9, Rio Vermelho, T334 0668. The best place in the city to see contemporary Salvador bands live.

⊕ Entertainment

Salvador de Bahia *p463, maps p464 and p466*
The **Fundação Cultural do Estado da Bahia**edits *Bahia Cultural*, a monthly brochure listing monthly cultural events. These can be found in most hotels and Bahiatursa information centres. Local newspapers *A Tarde* and *Correio da Bahia* have good cultural sections listing all events in the city.

Cinema The main shopping malls at Barra, Iguatemi, Itaigara and Brotas, and **Cineart** in Politeama (Centro), run more mainstream movies. The impressive Casa do Comércio building near Iguatemi houses the **Teatro do SESC** with a mixed programme of theatre, cinema and music Wed-Sun.

Music

During the winter (Jul-Sep) ring the blocos to confirm that free rehearsals will take place.

Ara Ketu, T3264 8800 www.araketu.com, hails from the sprawling Peripeti suburb in the Lower City. Once a purely percussion band Ara Ketu has travelled widely and borrowed on various musical forms (samba, candomblé, soukous, etc) to become a major carnival attraction and one of the most successful bands in Bahia. Rehearsals take place on Thu nights at 1930 on Trapiche Barnabé, Comércio. As these get very full, buy tickets in advance from Pida kiosks, the Central do Carnaval, Ticketmix and at the bloco's HQ, R Afonso Celso, 161, Barra.

Banda Olodum (address above) drumming troupe made famous by their innovative powerhouse percussion and involvement with Paul Simon, Michael Jackson and Branford Marsalis, their weekly rehearsals take place in front of packed crowds.

Didá Neguinho do Samba was the musical director of Olodum until he founded Didá, an all-woman drumming group based along similar lines to Olodum. They rehearse on Fri nights in the Praça Teresa Batista, Pelourinho. Starts 2000, US$10.

Filhos de Gandhi, the original African drumming group and the largest, was formed by striking stevedores during the 1949 carnival. The hypnotic shuffling cadence of Filhos de Gandhi's afoxé rhythm is one of the most emotive of Bahia's carnival.

Ilê Aiyê, address above. Established in Liberdade, the largest suburb of the city, Ilê Aiyê is a thriving cultural group dedicated to preserving African traditions which under the guidance of its president Vovô is deeply committed to the fight against racism. Rehearsals take place mid week at Boca do Rio and on Sat nights in front of their headquarters at Ladeira do Curuzu in Liberdade.

Timbalada, T3355 0680, www.timbalada.com. Carlinhos Brown is a local hero. He has become one of the most influential musical composers in Brazil today, mixing great lyrics, innovative rhythms and a powerful stage presence. He played percussion with many Bahian musicians, until he formed his own percussion group, Timbalada. He has invested heavily in his native Candeal neighbourhood: the Candy All Square, a centre for popular culture, is where the Timbalada rehearsals take place every Sun night. 1830, US$20 from Sep to Mar. Not to be missed.

Artists and bands using electronic instruments and who tend to play in the *trios eléctricos* draw heavily on the rich rhythms of the drumming groups creating a new musical genre known as **Axé**. The most popular of such acts are **Chiclete com Banana**, www.chicletecombanana.com.br, and **Ivete Sangalo**. Also look out for the internationally famous **Daniela Mercury**. **Gerónimo** was one of the first singer/songwriters to use the wealth of rhythms of the Candomblé in his music and his song *E d'Oxum* is something of an anthem for the city.

All the above have albums released and you can find their records easily in most record stores. See Shopping in the Pelourinho. Also try Flashpoint in Shopping Iguatemi.

Theatre

Castro Alves, at Campo Grande (Largo 2 de Julho), T3339 8000, www.tca.ba.gov.br, seats 1400 and is considered one of the best in Latin America. It also has its own repertory theatre, the **Sala de Coro**, for more experimental productions. The theatre's Concha Acústica is an open-air venue used frequently in the summer, attracting the big names in Brazilian music.
Theatro XVIII, R Frei Vicente, T 3332 0018, www.theatroxviii.com.br, an experimental theatre in the Pelourinho.
Teatro Gregório de Matos in Praça Castro Alves, T3322 2646, offers space to new productions and writers.
Vila Velha, Passéio Público, Gamboa da Cima, T3336 1384. A historically important venue where many of the *tropicalistas* first played. Nowadays it has an eclectic programme of modern dance, theatre and live music. **Grupo Teatro Olodum** often works here.

⦿ Festivals and events

Salvador de Bahia *p465, maps p464 and p466*
6 Jan (Epiphany); **Ash Wednesday** and **Maundy Thursday**, half-days; **2 Jul** (Independence of Bahia); **30 Oct**; **Christmas Eve**, half-day. An important local holiday is **Festa do Nosso Senhor do Bonfim**; it takes place on the 2nd Sun after Epiphany, but the washing or *lavagem* of the Bonfim church, with its colourful parade, takes place on the preceding Thu (usually mid-Jan). The **Festa da Ribeirav** is on the following Mon. Another colourful festival is that of the **fishermen of Rio Vermelho** on **2 Feb**; gifts for Yemanjá, Goddess of the Sea, are taken to sea in a procession of sailing boats to an accompaniment of candomblé instruments. The Holy Week processions among the old churches of the upper city are also interesting.
For **Carnival**, see box, page 476.

◯ Shopping

Pelourinho *p467*
Bookshops Graúna, Av 7 de Setembro 1448, and R Barão de Itapoã 175, Porto da Barra, many English titles. **Livraria Brandão**, R Ruy Barbosa 104, Centre. Secondhand English, French, Spanish and German books. **Livraria Planeta**, Carlos Gomes 42, loja 1, sells used English books.

Handicrafts Artesanato Santa Bárbara, R Portas do Carmo 7. Excellent hand-made lace products. **Atelier Portal da Cor**, Ladeira do Carmo 31. Run by a co-operative of local artists, Totonho, Calixto, Raimundo Santos, Jô, good prices. Recommended. **Instituto Mauá**, R Gregório de Matos 27. Open Tue-Sat 0900-1800, Sun 1000-1600, good-quality Bahian handicrafts at fair prices, better value and better quality for traditional crafts than the Mercado Modelo. **Loja de Artesanato do SESC**, Largo Pelourinho. Mon-Fri 0900-1800 (closed for lunch), Sat 0900-1300, similar store to Instituto Mauá. **Rosa do Prado**, R Inacio Aciolly, 5. Cigar shop packed with every kind of Brazilian 'charuto' imaginable.

Jewellery In the Pelourinho are: **Casa Moreira**, Ladeira da Praça, just south of Praça da Sé. Exquisite jewellery and antiques, most very expensive, but some affordable charms. **Scala**, Praça da Sé. Handmade jewellery using locally mined gems (eg. acquamarine, amethyst and emerald), workshop at back.

Markets Mercado Modelo, at Praça Cairu, lower city, offers many tourist items such as wood carvings, silver-plated fruit, leather goods, local musical instruments. Lace items for sale are often not handmade (despite labels), are heavily marked up, and are much better bought at their place of origin (for example Ilha de Maré, Pontal da Barra and Marechal Deodoro). Bands and dancing, especially Sat (but very much for money from tourists taking photographs), closed at 1200 Sun. The largest and most authentic market is the **Feira de São Joaquim**, 5 km from Mercado Modelo along the sea front: barkers, trucks, burros, horses, boats, people, mud, all very smelly, every day (Sun till 1200 only), busiest on Sat morning; interesting African-style pottery and basketwork; very cheap. (The car ferry terminal for Itaparica is nearby.) Every Wed from 1700-2100 there is a handicrafts fair in the 17th-century fort of Santa Maria at the opposite end of Porto da Barra beach.

Music in the Pelourinho The major carnival afro blocos have boutiques selling T-shirts, etc: **Boutique Olodum**, on Praça José Alencar, **Ilê Aiyê**, on R Francisco Muniz Barreto 16. **Cana Brava**, R João de Deus 22, T3321 0536. CD shop with knowledgeable American owner. **Oficina de Investigação Musical**, Portas do Carmo 24. Hand-made traditional percussion instruments (and percussion lessons, US$15 per hr), Mon-Fri 0800-1200 and 1300-1600.

Shopping centres Barra and Iguatemi are the largest and best stocked. They are the most comfortable places to shop – havens of a/c cool in the heat of summer.

⚲ Activities and tours

Salvador de Bahia *p465, maps p464 and p466*
Boat and bus tours Available from several companies. All-day boat trip on Bahia de Todos Os Santos last from 0800-1700 including a visit to Ilha dos Frades, lunch on Itaparica (not included), US$20 pp. City tours also cost US$20 pp
Capoeira A martial art, often said to have developed from the traditional foot-fighting technique introduced from Angola by African slaves, but latterly claimed to be have originated with the indigenous people of Brazil and then modified by slaves. The music is by drum, tambourine and berimbau; there are several different kinds of the sport. If you want to attempt Capoeira, the best school is **Mestre Bimba**, R das Laranjeiras, T3322 0639, open 0900-1200, 1500-2100, basic course in Capoeira regional, US$32 for 20 hours. Another Capoeira regional school is **Filhos de Bimba**, R Durval Fraga, 6, Nordeste, T3345 7329. Exhibitions take place in the Largo do Pelourinho every Friday evening around 2000, very authentic, in the upper city. You can also see capoeiristas in public spaces like the Pelourinho, outside the Mercado Modelo and at Campo Grande. Genuine capoeiristas do not expect a contribution, but if you wish to take pictures ask first. At the Casa da Cultura at Forte de Santo Antônio there is also free live music on Saturday night.

Tour operators and guides
Dieter Herzberg, T3334 1200. A recommended guide who speaks German,
Tatur Turismo, Av Tancredo Neves 274, Centro Empresarial Iguatemi, Sala 228, Bloco B, T3450 7216, www.tatur.com.br. Run by Irishman, Conor O'Sullivan. English spoken. Specializes in Bahia, arranges private guided tours and can make any necessary travel, hotel and accommodation arrangements. Highly recommended.

⊕ Transport

Salvador de Bahia *p465, maps p464 and p466*
Air An a/c bus service every 30-40 mins between the new Luis Eduardo Magalhães Airport and the centre, a distance of 32 km, costs US$4. It takes the coast road to the city, stopping at hotels en route. Service runs 0500-2200 (0600 at weekends) and 0630-2100 from the Praça da Sé to the airport. Also ordinary buses, US$0.90. 'Special' taxis to both Barra and centre (buy ticket at the airport desk next to tourist information booth), US$35; normal taxis (from outside airport), US$30. Allow plenty of time for travel to the airport and for check-in. ATMs are in a special area to the extreme right as you arrive, a good place to get money. **Banco do Brasil**

is to the extreme left, open Mon-Fri 0900-1500. **Jacarandá** exchange house is in front of international arrivals, open 24 hrs a day, but poor rates and only good for changing a small amount (count your money carefully). Tourist information booth open 24 hrs, English spoken, has list of hotels and useful map.
Daily flights to all the main cities.
Bus Local buses US$0.90, executivos, a/c, US$1.80, US$2 or US$4 depending on the route. On buses and at the ticket-sellers' booths, watch your change and beware pickpockets (one scam used by thieves is to descend from the bus while you are climbing aboard). To get from the old city to the ocean beaches, take a 'Barra' bus from Praça da Sé to the Barra point and walk to the nearer ones; the Aeroporto executivo leaves Praça da Sé, passing Barra, Ondina, Rio Vermelho, Amaralina, Pituba, Costa Azul, Armação, Boca do Rio, Jaguaripe, Patamares, Piatã and Itapoã, before turning inland to the airport. The glass-sided Jardineira bus goes to Flamengo beach (30 km from the city) following the coastal route; it passes all the best beaches; sit on the right hand side for best views. It leaves from the Praça da Sé daily 0730-1930, every 40 mins, US$2. For beaches beyond Itapoã, take the executivo to Stella Maris and Flamengo beaches. These follow the same route as the Jardineira.
Long distance buses leave from the Rodoviária, near Shopping Iguatemi. Bus RI or RII, 'Centro-Rodoviária-Circular'; in the centre, get on in the Lower City at the foot of the Lacerda lift; buses also go to Campo Grande (US$0.90). A quicker executive bus from Praça da Sé or Praça da Inglaterra (in front of McDonalds), Comércio, run to Iguatemi Shopping Centre, US$2, weekdays only, from where there is a walkway to the rodoviária (take care in the dark, or a taxi, US$15). To **Belém** US$112 comercial with **Itapemirim**. To **Recife**, US$42, 13 hrs, 2 a day and 1 leito, **Itapemerim**, T358 0037. To **Rio** (28 hrs, US$83, Itapemirim, good stops, clean toilets, recommended). **São Paulo** (30 hrs), US$102, leito US$127 (0815 with **Viação Nacional**, 2 in afternoon with São Geraldo). To **Fortaleza**, 19 hrs, US$77 at 0900 with Itapemerim. **Ilhéus**, 7 hrs, **Aguia Branca**, comercial US$27, several. To **Lençóis** 3 a day, 8 hrs, US$35 with **Real Expresso**. **Belo Horizonte**, Gontijo, T358 7448, at 1700, US$78, São Geraldo at 1800. There are daily bus services to **Brasília** along the fully paved BR-242, via Barreiras, 3 daily, 23 hrs, **Paraíso**, US$75. Frequent services to the majority of destinations; a large panel in the main hall lists destinations and the relevant ticket office.
Taxi Taxi meters start at US$0.75 for the 'flagdown' and US$0.15 per 100 m. They charge US$20 per hr within city limits, and 'agreed' rates

Carnival in Bahia

Carnival officially starts on Thursday night at 2000 when the keys of the city are given to the Carnival King 'Rei Momo'. The unofficial opening though is on Wednesday with the Lavagem do Porto da Barra, when throngs of people dance on the beach. Later on in the evening is the Baile dos Atrizes, starting at around 2300 and going on until dawn, very bohemian, good fun. Check with *Bahiatursa* for details, also http://home.centraldocarnaval.com.br/ and www.carnaval.salvador.ba.gov.br (see under Rio for carnival dates).

Carnival in Bahia is the largest in the world and it encourages active participation. It is said that there are 1½ million people dancing on the streets at any one time.

There are two distinct musical formats. The **Afro Blocos** are large drum-based troupes (some with up to 200 drummers) who play on the streets accompanied by singers atop mobile sound trucks. The first of these groups was the Filhos de Gandhi (founded in 1949), whose participation is one of the highlights of Carnival. Their 6,000 members dance through the streets on the Sunday and Tuesday of Carnival dressed in their traditional costumes, a river of white and blue in an ocean of multicoloured carnival revellers. The best known of the recent **Afro Blocos** are Ilê Aiye, Olodum, Muzenza and Malê Debalê. They all operate throughout the year in cultural, social and political areas. Not all of them are receptive to foreigners among their numbers for Carnival. The basis of the rhythm is the enormous surdo (deaf) drum with its bumbum bumbum bum anchorbeat, while the smaller repique, played with light twigs, provides a crack-like overlay. Ilê Aiye take to the streets around 2100 on Saturday night and their departure from their headquarters at Ladeira do Curuzu in the Liberdade district is not to be missed. The best way to get there is to take a taxi to Curuzu via Largo do Tanque thereby avoiding traffic jams. The ride is a little longer in distance but much quicker in time. A good landmark is the Paes outside. Taxi Barra-Centro US$5 daytime; US$6 at night. Watch the meter, especially at night; the night-time charge should be 30 higher than daytime charges.

Itaparica *p468*
Ferry The main passenger ferry leaves for Bom Despacho from São Joaquim (buses for Calçada, Ribeira stop across the road from the ferry terminal; the 'Sabino Silva – Ribeira' bus passes in front of the Shopping Barra). First ferry from Salvador at 0540 and, depending on demand, at intervals of 45 mins thereafter; last ferry from Salvador at 2230. Returning to Salvador the 1st ferry is at 0515 and the last at 2300. In summer ferries are much more frequent. Information from **COMAB/Ferry Fácil**, open 0700-2300 at terminal. A one way ticket for foot passengers Mon-Fri is US$1.30, Sat-Sun US$1.60. Catamarans depart for Bom Despacho twice daily, US$3 (US$3.75 at weekends). **Mar Grande** can be reached by a smaller ferry (**Lancha**) from the Terminal Marítimo in front of the Mercado Modelo in Salvador. The ferries leave every 45 mins and the crossing takes 50 mins, US$2.40 return.

❶ Directory

Salvador de Bahia *p465, maps p464 and p466*
Airline offices BRA, at airport, T3204 1027, www.voebra.com.br. **Gol**, T3204 1608. **Ocean Air**, T3204 1502. **TAM**, Praça Gago Coutinho, T0800-570 5700. **TAP**, Av Tancredo Neves 1632, salas 1206/7, T0800-707 7787. **Varig** T4003 7000, at airport T3204 1050, 0700-1800. **Banks** Banks are open 1000-1600. Selected branches of major banks have ATMs for Visa, eg **Bradesco**, also **Banco 24 Horas**. Don't change money on the street especially in the Upper City where higher rates are usually offered. Changing at banks can be bureaucratic and time-consuming. **Citibank**, R Miguel Calmon 555, Comércio, centre, changes TCs. Branch at R Almte Marquês de Leão 71, Barra, has ATM. MasterCard ATMs at branches of **HSBC**. Also at **Credicard**, 1st floor, Citibank building, R Miguel Calmon 555, Comércio. **Figueiredo**, opposite Grande Hotel da Barra on Ladeira da Barra will exchange cash at good rates. **Shopping Tour** in Barra Shopping centre changes dollars, as will other tour agencies. If stuck, all the big hotels will exchange, but at poor rates.

Mendonça supermarket on the corner of the street from where the bloco leaves. From there it's a short walk to the departure point.

The enormous **trios eléctricos** 12 m sound trucks, with powerful sound systems that defy most decibel counters, are the second format. These trucks, each with its own band of up to 10 musicians, play songs influenced by the **afro blocos** and move at a snail's pace through the streets, drawing huge crowds. Each **Afro Bloco** and **bloco de trio** has its own costume and its own security personnel who cordon off the area around the sound truck. The **bloco** members can thus dance in comfort and safety.

There are three official Carnival routes. The oldest is Osmar, from Campo Grande to Praça Castro Alves near the old town. The **blocos** go along Avenue 7 de Setembro and return to Campo Grande via the parallel R Carlos Gomes. The best night at Praça Castro Alves is Tuesday (the last night of Carnival) when the famous 'Encontro dos trios' (Meeting of the Trios) takes place. Trios jostle for position in the square and play in rotation until dawn (or later!) on Ash Wednesday. It is not uncommon for major stars from the Bahian (and Brazilian) music world to make surprise appearances.

The second route is Dodô, from Farol da Barra to Ondina. The **blocos alternativos** ply this route. These are nearly always **trios eléctricos** connected with the more traditional blocos who have expanded to this now popular district. The third and newest route is Batatinha, in the historic centre and the streets of Pelourinho. No trios eléctricos take part on this route, but marching bands, folkloric groups and fancy-dress parades.

Day tickets for these are available the week leading up to Carnival. Check with *Bahiatursa* for information on where the tickets are sold for the stands. There is little or no shade from the sun so bring a hat and lots of water. Best days are Sunday to Tuesday. For those wishing to go it alone, just find a barraca in the shade and watch the blocos go by.

Car hire If renting a car check whether credit card or cash is cheapest. See page 43, for multinational car rental agencies. **Embassies and consulates** France, Trav Francisco Gonçalves 1, sala 401, Comércio, T3241 0168, Mon, Tue, Thu morning only. Germany, R Jogo do Carneiro 49, Saúde, T3242 2670, Mon-Fri 0900-1200. Netherlands, R Largo do Carmo 04, Sl 101, Santo Antônio, T3241 3001, hleusen@ dannemann-sa.com.br, Mon-Fri 0900-1100. Spain, R Mcal Floriano 21, Canela, T3336 9055. Mon-Fri 0900-1400. Switzerland, Av Tancredo Neves 3343, 5th floor, sala 506b, T3341 5827. UK, R Caetano Moura 35, T3247 8216, lhanson@ uol.com.br, USA, Av Tancredo Neves 1632, Sala 1401, Salvador Trade Center – Torre Sul, Caminho das Árvores, T3113 2090, amcon@svn.com.br. Mon-Fri 1400-1600. **Internet** There are numerous internet cafés throughout the touristy parts of the city. **Language classes** Casa do Brasil, R Milton de Oliveira 231, Barra, www.casadobrazil.com.br. Diálogo, R Dr João

Pondé 240, Barra, T3264 0007, www.dialogo-brazilstudy.com. With optional dance, *capoeira* and cookery classes, accommodation with host families. **Medical services** Clinic: Barão de Loreto 21, Graça. Medical: yellow fever vaccinations free at Delegação Federal de Saúde, R Padre Feijó, Canela. **Post offices** Main post office and poste restante is in Praça Inglaterra, in the Lower City, Mon-Fri 0800-1700, Sat 0800-1200. Several other offices, including R Portas do Carmo 43, rodoviária, airport, Barra and Iguatemi Shopping Malls. **Useful addresses** Immigration: (for extensions of entry permits), Policia Federal, Av O Pontes 339, Aterro de Água de Meninos, Lower City, T3319 6082, open 1000-1600. Show an outward ticket or sufficient funds for your stay, visa extension US$17.50. Tourist Police: R Gregório de Matos 16, T3321 1092. Delegacia de Proteção ao Turista, Praça José de Anchieta 14, T3322 7155.

Inland from Salvador

There are strong historical associations inland from Salvador, seen in the colonial exploitation of sugar and diamonds. Lençóis, famous for the latter, also has some beautiful countryside, which is ideal for trekking. On the coast south of Salvador, there is a whole string of popular resorts. It was on this part of what is now Brazil that the Portuguese first made landfall. Bahia's north coast runs from the Coconut Highway onto the Green Line, just to give of an idea of how the shore looks – and don't forget the beaches there, too.

The Recôncavo
The area around Salvador, known as the Recôncavo Baiano, was one of the chief centres of sugar and tobacco cultivation in the 16th century. Some 73 km from Salvador is **Santo Amaro da Purificação**, an old sugar centre sadly decaying, noted for its churches (often closed because of robberies), municipal palace (1769), fine main praça, birthplace of the singers Caetano Veloso and his sister Maria Bethania and ruined mansions including Araújo Pinto, former residence of the Barão de Cotegipe. Other attractions include the splendid beaches of the bay, the falls of Vitória and the grotto of Bom Jesus dos Pobres. The festivals of **Santo Amaro**, 24 January-2 February, and **Nossa Senhora da Purificação** on 2 February itself are interesting. There is also the **Bembé do Mercado** festival on 13 May. Craftwork is sold on the town's main bridge. There are no good hotels or restaurants.

Cachoeira and São Félix
At 116 km from Salvador and only 4 km from the BR-101 coastal road are the towns of Cachoeira (Bahia's 'Ouro Preto', *Population: 30,416*) and São Félix (*Population 13,699*), on either side of the Rio Paraguaçu below the Cachoeira dam. Cachoeira was twice capital of Bahia: once in 1624-1625 during the Dutch invasion, and once in 1822-1823 while Salvador was still held by the Portuguese. There are beautiful views from above São Félix.

Cachoeira's main buildings are the **Casa da Câmara e Cadeia** (1698-1712), the **Santa Casa de Misericórdia** (1734 – the hospital, someone may let you see the church), the 16th-century **Ajuda** chapel (now containing a fine collection of vestments), and the Convent of the **Ordem Terceira do Carmo**, whose church has a heavily gilded interior. Other churches are the **Matriz** with 5-m-high azulejos, and **Nossa Senhora da Conceição do Monte**. There are beautiful lace cloths on the church altars. All churches are either restored or in the process of restoration. The **Museu Hansen Bahia** ① *R Ana Néri*, houses fine engravings by the German artist who made the Recôncavo his home in the 1950s. There is a great wood-carving tradition in Cachoeira. The artists can be seen at work in their studios. Best are Louco Filho, Fory, both in Rua Ana Néri, Doidão, in front of the Igreja Matriz and J Gonçalves on the main praça. A 300 m railway bridge built by the British in the 19th century spans the Rio Paraguaçu to São Felix where the Danneman cigar factory can be visited to see hand-rolling. **Tourist office** ① *Casa de Ana Néri, Cachoeira.*

Lençóis → *Phone code: 0xx75. Colour map 5, grid C4. Population: 8,910.*
This historical monument and colonial gem was founded in 1844 to exploit the diamonds in the region. While there are still some *garimpeiros* (gold prospectors), it is not precious metals that draw most visitors, but the climate, which is cooler than the coast, the relaxed atmosphere and the wonderful trekking and horse riding in the hills of the Chapada Diamantina. A few of the options are given below under Excursions, and pousadas and tour operators offer guiding services to point you in the right direction. This is also a good place for buying handicrafts. **Tourist office** ① *Av Sete de Setembro 10, T3334 1271.*

Parque Nacional da Chapada Diamantina → *Colour map 5, grid C4.*
Palmeiras, 50 km from Lençóis, is the headquarters of the Parque Nacional da Chapada Diamantina (founded 1985), which contains 1,500 sq km of mountainous country. There is an abundance of endemic plants, waterfalls, large caves (take care, and a strong torch, there are no signs and caves can be difficult to find without a guide), rivers with natural swimming pools and good walking tours. **Parque Nacional da Chapada Diamantina** Information, Ibama, ① *R Barão do Rio Branco 7, Palmeiras, Toxx75-3332 2420.*

Excursions near Lençóis and in the Chapada Diamantina ① *local guides can often arrange transport to the more remote excursions, certainly this is possible when groups are involved*. Near the town, visit the **Serrano** with its wonderful natural pools in the river bed, which give a great hydro massage. A little further away is the **Salão de Areia**, where the coloured sands for the bottle paintings come from. **Ribeirão do Meio** is a 45-minute walk from town; here locals slide down a long natural water chute into a big pool (it is best to be shown the way it is done and to take something to slide in). **Gruta do Lapão**, three hours from Lençóis, guide essential, is in quartz rock and therefore has no stalagmites. Some light rock climbing is required. **Cachoeira da Primavera**, two very pretty waterfalls close to town, recommended. **Cachoeira Sossego**, two hours from town, a 'picture postcard' waterfall, swimming pool, recommended. **Morro de Pai Inácio**, 30 km from Lençóis, has the best view of the Chapada, recommended at sunset (bus from Lençois at 0815, 30 minutes, US$1.50). In the park is the **Cachoeira da Fumaça** (Smoke Waterfall, also called **Glass**), 384 m, the second highest in Brazil. To see it, go by car to the village of **Capão** and walk 2½ hours. The view is astonishing; the updraft of the air currents often makes the water flow back up creating the 'smoke' effect. Olivia Taylor at the Pousada dos Duendes offers a three-day trek, the village of Capão and Capivara and Palmital falls from US$45.

⊜ Sleeping → *See Telephone, page 347, for important phone changes.*

Cachoeira *p478*

B Pousada do Convento de Cachoeira, Praça da Aclamação, T3425 1716. In a restored 16th-century convent, good restaurant.

C Pousada Labarca, R Inocêncio Boaventura 37, T3425 1070, cecilia.thomas@bol.com.br. Nice *pousada* with art gallery, paintings by Argentine owner, organizes local trips and to candomblé ceremonies.

D Santo Antônio, Praça Maciel 01, near the rodoviária, T3425 1402. Basic, safe, laundry facilities. Recommended.

Lençóis *p478*

LL-AL Canto das Águas, Av Senhor dos Passos, T/F3334 1154, www.lencois.com.br. Riverside hotel with a/c or fan, pool, efficient, best rooms are in the new wing. A Roteiro de Charme hotel.

L Portal de Lençóis, R Chacara Grota, at the top of the town, T3334 1233, www.portalhoteis.tur.br. 15 smart chalets in a mini-resort on the edge of the park, with pool, sauna, restaurant, bar and play area for kids. Activities and walks organized.

AL Hotel de Lençóis, R Altinha Alves 747, T3369 5000, www.hoteldelencois.com.br. Rooms organized in terraces set in a grassy garden on the edge of the park. Good breakfast, pool and restaurant.

C Águas Claras, R P Benjamin 27, T3334 1471 (100 m from the rodoviária). Simple, well-looked-after rooms; some with a fridge.

C Casa da Geleia, R Gen Viveiros 187, T3334 1151, casadageleia@hotmail.com. 6 smart chalets set in a huge garden at the entrance to the town, English spoken, good breakfast (Ze Carlos is a keen birdwatcher and an authority on the region, Lia makes excellent jams).

C O Casarão, Av 7 de Setembro 85, T3334 1198, lencois@ig.com.br. Modest *pousada* with a/c or fan, fridge. Recommended.

C-D Estalagem de Alcino, R Tomba Surrão 139, T3334 1171. An enchanting, beautifully restored house furnished with 19th-century antiques. Most have shared bathrooms. Superb breakfast served in hummingbird-filled garden. Highly recommended.

C-D Pousalegre, R Boa Vista 95, T3334 1916. Dormitories only with hot shared showers, tasty breakfast and good vegetarian restaurant.

D Casa de Hélia, R da Muritiba 3, T3334 1143, www.casadehelia.com.br. Attractive little guest-house, English and some Hebrew spoken, good facilities, legendary breakfast. Recommended.

D Tradição, R José Florêncio, T334 1137. Plain rooms with TV, breakfast, fridge, mosquito nets.

D-E Pousada dos Duendes, R do Pires, T/F3334 1229, www.pousadadosduendes.com. English-run *pousada*, shared hot showers, breakfast (vegetarians and vegans catered for), welcoming, comfortable. Their tour agency (**H2O Expeditions**) arranges tours and treks from 1 to 11 days and more, Olivia Taylor is very helpful.

Camping Alquimia, 2 km before Lençóis, T3334 1213, and **Camping Lumiar**, near Rosário church in centre, T3334 1241, with popular restaurant. Recommended.

House rental

Mostly very simple houses to rent: Juanita on R do Rosário rents rooms and offers washing and cooking facilities. Claudia and Isabel, R da Baderna 95, T3334 1229, rent houses all over town.

❼ Eating

Cachoeira and São Félix *p478*

♥♥ **Do Nair**, R 13 de Maio. Delicious food and sometimes Seresta music.

♥ **Cabana do Pai Thomaz**, 25 de Junho 12, excellent Bahian food, good value, also a hotel, **B** with private bath and breakfast.

♥ **Xang-hai**, São Félix. Good, cheap food. Warmly recommended. Try the local dish, *maniçoba* (meat, manioc and peppers).

Lençóis *p478*
♥♥ **Artistas da Massa**, R Miguel Calmon. Italian dishes, mainly pasta and pizza.
♥♥ **Picanha na Praça**, opposite the bandstand on the square above the main praça. Good steaks.
♥ **Goody**, R da Rodaviária s/n. Good simple cooking.

⊙ Bars and clubs

Lençóis *p478*
Bar Lençóis, on main praça. For drinks, good *cachaça* and *caipirinhas*.
Doce Bárbaros, R das Pedras 21. Lively bar almost any night of the week.

❀ Festivals and events

Cachoeira *p478*
São João (**24 Jun**), 'Carnival of the Interior' celebrations include dangerous games with fireworks. **Nossa Sehora da Boa Morte** (**early Aug**) is also a major festival. A famous candomblé ceremony at the Fonte de Santa Bárbara is held on **4 Dec**.

O Shopping

Lençóis *p478*
The Mon morning market is recommended. There is a local craft market just off the main praça every night.
Artesanato Areias Coloridas, R das Pedras, owned by Taurino, is the best place for local sand paintings made in bottles. These are inexpensive. They will make one as you wait.
Jota, the most original for ceramic work, whose workshop can be visited. Take the steps to the left of the school near the Pousada Lençóis.

▲ Activities and tours

Lençóis *p478*
Cirtur, R da Bandeira 41, T3334 1133, cirtur@neth.com.br.
Lentur, Av 7 de Setembro 16, T/F3334 1271. Speak to Paulo, who organizes day trips to nearby caves and to see the sunset at Morro do Pai Inácio.
Pé de Trilha Turismo Aventura, Praça 7 de Setembro, T3334 1124. Guiding, trekking, rent camping equipment, etc, can make reservations for most of the *pousadas* in the Chapada

Diamantina. Represented in Salvador by **Tatur Turismo**.
Venturas e Aventuras, Praça Horácio de Matos 20, T3334 1304. Excellent trekking expeditions, up to 6 days.

Guides
Each pousada generally has a guide attached to it to take residents on tours, about US$20-30. The following are recommended:
Edmilson (known locally as Mil), R Domingos B Souza 70, T3334 1319. Knows the region extremely well, knowledgeable and reliable.
Ereas, R José Florêncio 60, T3334 1155. The only specialist birding guide in the town.
Roy Funch, T/F3334 1305, royfunch@gd.com.br. The ex-director of the Chapada Diamantina National Park is an excellent guide and has written a visitors' guide to the park, which is available in English. (It is recommended as the best for information on the geography and trails of the Chapada.) Highly recommended. He can be booked through www.elabrasil.com from the USA or UK.
Índio, contact at **Pousada Diangela**, R dos Minheiros 60, Centro Histórico. Reliable, goes off the beaten track.
Luiz Krug, contact via Pousada de Lençóis, T3334 1102. An independent guide specializing in geology and caving. He speaks English.
Trajano, contact via **Casa da Hélia**, T3334 1143, Speaks English and some Hebrew and is a good-humoured guide for treks to the bottom of the Cachoeira da Fumaça.

⊖ Transport

Cachoeira *p478*
Bus From **Salvador** (Camurjipe) every hr or so from 0530; **Feira Santana**, 2 hrs, US$6.

Lençóis *p478*
Air Airport, Km 209, BR-242, 20 km from town T3625 8100.
Bus Real Expresso from **Salvador** 3 a day, US$28, *comercial*. Book in advance, especially at weekends and holidays. Buses also from **Recife**, **Ibotirama**, **Barreiras** or **Brasília**, 16 hrs, US$60 (take irregular bus to Seabra, then 2 a day to Brasília).

---

❶ Directory

Lençóis *p478*
Banks There are several banks with cashpoints and money changing facilities in town, including a Banco do Brasil and a Bradesco. **Post offices** main square, 0900-1700, Mon-Fri.

South of Salvador

On the coast south of Salvador, there is a whole string of popular resorts. It was on this part of what is now Brazil that the Portuguese first made landfall. Bahia's north coast runs from the Coconut Highway onto the Green Line, just to give of an idea of how the shore looks – and don't forget the beaches there, too.

Valença → *Phone code: 0xx71. Colour map 7, grid A6. Population: 77,509.*
In this small, attractive town, 271 km south of Salvador via a paved road, two old churches stand on rising ground; the views from Nossa Senhora do Amparo are recommended. It is at the mouth of the Rio Una, which enters an enormous region of mangrove swamps. The main attraction is the beaches on the mainland (Guabim, 14 km north) and on the island of Tinharé. **Secretaria de Turismo**, T3641 8610. Avoid touts at the rodoviária.

Tinharé and Morro de São Paulo → *Phone code: 0xx75.*
Tinharé is a large island (1½ hours south of Valença by boat) separated from the mainland by the estuary of the Rio Una and mangrove swamps, so that it is hard to tell which is land and which is water. The most popular beaches and pousadas are at Morro de São Paulo. Immediately south is the island of **Boipeba**, separated from Tinharé by the Rio do Inferno. Accommodation is split between the little town where the riverboat ferry arrives, the adjacent beach, Boca da Barra, which is more idyllic and the fishing village Moreré half an hour's boat ride south, US$20 (high tide only).

Morro de São Paulo is on the headland at the northernmost tip of Tinharé, lush with ferns, palms and birds of paradise. The village is dominated by the lighthouse and the ruins of a colonial fort (1630), built as a defence against European raiders. It has a landing place on the sheltered landward side, dominated by the old gateway of the fortress. From the lighthouse a path leads to a ruined look out with cannon, which has panoramic views. The fort is a good point to watch the sunset from. Dolphins can be seen in August. Fonte de Ceu waterfall is reached by walking along the beach to **Gamboa** then inland. Watch the tide; it's best to take a guide, or take a boat back to Morro (US$0.50-1). No motor vehicles are allowed on the island. On 7 September there's a big festival with live music on the beach. **Tourist office** ⓘ *Praça Aureliano Lima, T3652 1083, www.morrosp.com.br*, or visit *www.morrodesaopaulo.com.br*. **Note** There is a port tax of US$3.25 payable at the prefeitura on leaving the island.

Itacaré → *Phone code: 0xx73.*
This picturesque fishing village sits in the midst of remnant Atlantic Coast rainforest at the mouth of the Rio de Contas. Some of Bahia's best beaches stretch north and south. A few are calm and crystal clear, the majority are great for surfing. There are plenty of beaches within walking distance of town. Itacaré is rapidly becoming a sophisticated resort town for the São Paulo middle classes and is very busy with Brazilian tourists in high season. Much of the accommodation here is tasteful, blending in with the natural landscape and there are many excellent restaurants and lively if still low key nightlife. Pousadas are concentrated on and around Praia da Concha, the first beach south of the town centre. Besides surfing, operators are now offering trekking and mountain biking trips in the Mata Atlântica, off-roading, rafting, waterfall-climbing and other adrenalin activities. North of Itacaré is the **Peninsula de Maraú**, fringed with beautiful beaches to its tip at **Barra Grande**. To explore the area fully you will need a car. **Secretaria de Turismo de Itacaré** ⓘ *T3251 2134, prefietura 3251 2130, www.itacare.com.br.*

Ilhéus → *Phone code: 0xx73. Post code: 45650. Colour map 7, grid A6. Population: 222,127.*
At the mouth of the Rio Cachoeira, 462 km south of Salvador, the port serves a district which produces 65% of all Brazilian cocoa. A bridge links the north bank of the river with Pontal, where the airport is located. Ilhéus is the birthplace of Jorge Amado (1912-2002) and the setting of one of his most famous novels, *Gabriela, cravo e canela* (Gabriela, Clove and Cinnamon). The church of **São Jorge** (1556), the city's oldest, is on the Praça Rui Barbosa; it has a small museum. In Alto da Vitória is the 17th-century **Nossa Senhora da Vitória**, built to celebrate a victory over the Dutch. The **Secretaria de Turismo** is at ⓘ *R Santos Dumont s/n, anexo da Prefeitura, 5th floor, T2101-5500.*

North of Ilhéus, two good beaches are Marciano, with reefs offshore and good surfing, and Barra, 1 km further north at the mouth of the Rio Almada. South of the river, Pontal beaches can be reached by 'Barreira' bus; alight just after Hotel Jardim Atlântico. Between Ilhéus and **Olivença** are more fine beaches.

Porto Seguro and around
→ *Phone code: 0xx73. Post code: 45810. Colour map 7, grid A6. Population: 95,721.*

About 400 km south of Ilhéus on the coast is the old town of Porto Seguro. In 1500, Pedro Álvares Cabral sighted land at Monte Pascoal south of Porto Seguro. As the sea here was too open, he sailed north in search of a secure protected harbour, entering the mouth of the Rio Burnahém to find the harbour he later called Porto Seguro (safe port). Where the first mass was celebrated, a cross marks the spot on the road between Porto Seguro and Santa Cruz Cabrália. A rather uncoordinated tourist village, **Coroa Vermelha**, has sprouted at the site of Cabral's first landfall, 20 minutes by bus to the north of Porto Seguro.

Porto Seguro itself is Bahia's second most popular tourist destination, with charter flights from Rio and São Paulo and plenty of hustle and bustle. Contact the **Secretaria de Turismo de Porto Seguro** ① *Praça dos Pataxós, T3288 3708, turismo@portonet.com.br. Information desk at Praça Manoel Ribeiro Coelho 10.* A website for the entire coast is www.portonet.com.br.

To its historical quarter, **Cidade Histórica**, take a wide, steep, unmarked path uphill from the roundabout at the entrance to town. Three churches (Nossa Senhora da Misericórdia (1530), Nossa Senhora do Rosário (1534), and Nossa Senhora da Pena (1718), the former jail and the monument marking the landfall of Gonçalo Coelho comprise a small, peaceful place with lovely gardens and panoramic views.

Only 10 minutes north of Coroa Vermelha, **Santa Cruz Cabrália** is a delightful small town at the mouth of the Rio João de Tiba, with a splendid beach, river port, and a 450-year-old church with a fine view. A good trip from here is to Coroa Alta, a reef 50 minutes away by boat, passing along the tranquil river to the reef and its crystal waters and good snorkelling. Daily departure at 1000. A recommended boatman is Zezé on the square by the river's edge, helpful, knowledgeable. The trip costs around US$15 without lunch. A 15-minute river crossing by ferry to a new road on the opposite bank gives easy access to the deserted beaches of **Santo André** and **Santo Antônio**. Hourly buses from Santa Cruz to Porto Seguro (23 km).

Arraial da Ajuda → *Colour map 7, grid A6.*
Across the Rio Buranhém south from Porto Seguro is the village of Arraial da Ajuda, the gateway to the idyllic beaches of the south coast. Set high on a cliff, there are great views of the coastline from behind the church of Nossa Senhora da Ajuda in the main praça. Each August there is a pilgrimage to the shrine of Nossa Senhora da Ajuda. Ajuda has become very popular with younger tourists (especially Israelis) and there are many pousadas, from the very simple to the very sophisticated, restaurants, bars and small shops. The town has grown out of its former 'hippie' image, becoming more rave oriented. Parties are held almost every night, on the beach or in the main street, called the Broadway. At Brazilian holiday times it is very crowded.

The **beaches**, several protected by a coral reef, are splendid. The nearest is 15 minutes' walk away. During daylight hours those closest to town (take 'R da Praia' out of town to the south) are extremely busy; excellent barracas sell good seafood, drinks, and play music. The best beaches are Mucugê, Pitinga ('bronzeamento irrestrito' or nude sunbathing) and Taipé.

Trancoso → *Phone code 0xx73.*
Some 15 km from Ajuda, 25 km south of Porto Seguro by paved road, is Trancoso. This pretty, peaceful town, with its beautiful beaches (Praia dos Nativos is the most famous), has become very chic, with the rich and famous from home and abroad buying properties and shopping in the little boutiques. In summer it can get packed. Trancoso has an historic church, São João Batista (1656). From the end of Praça São João there is a fine coastal panorama. It is possible to walk along the beach to Ajuda via the village of Rio da Barra; allow three hours.

Caraíva → *Phone code 0xx73. www.caraiva.com.br.*
This atmospheric, peaceful fishing village on the banks of the Rio Caraíva, 65 km south of Porto Seguro, and near the Pataxó Indian Reserve has no wheeled vehicles, no electricity nor hot water, but has marvellous beaches and is a real escape from the more developed Trancoso and Porto Seguro. Despite the difficulty of getting there, it is becoming increasingly popular. Good walks are north to Praia do Satu (Sr Satu provides an endless supply of coconut milk), or 6 km south to a rather sad Pataxó Indian village (watch the tides). Horses can be hired from Pousada

Lagoa or Pizzaria Barra Velha. Boats can be hired for US$40 per day from Zé Pará to Caruípe beach, snorkelling at Pedra de Tatuaçu reef and Corombau (take your own mask and fins) or for diving (best December to February). Prainha river beach, about 30 minutes away, and mangrove swamps can also be visited by canoe or launch. The high season is December-February and July; the wettest months are April-June and November. Use flip-flops for walking the sand streets and take a torch. There are no medical facilities and only rudimentary policing.

Parque Nacional de Monte Pascoal → *Colour map 7, grid A6.*
South of Porto Seguro, reached by a 14 km paved access road at Km 796 of the BR-101, the Parque Nacional de Monte Pascoal set up in 1961 to preserve the flora, fauna and birdlife of the coastal area in which Europeans made landfall in Brazil (Caixa Postal 24, CEP 45836-000 Itamaraju, T0xx73-3294 1110). The Pataxó Indian reservation is located at Corombau village, on the ocean shore of the park. Corombau can be reached by schooner from Porto Seguro.

Caravelas and around → *Colour map 7, grid A6. Population: 20,103.*
Further south still, 107 km from Itamaruju (93 km south of Eunápolis), is this charming town, rapidly developing for tourism, but a major trading town in 17th and 18th centuries. Caravelas is in the mangroves; the beaches are about 10 km away at Barra de Caravelas (hourly buses), a fishing village. There are food shops, restaurants and bars.

The **Parque Nacional Marinho dos Abrolhos** is 70 km east of Caravelas. Abrolhos is an abbreviation of Abre os olhos: 'Open your eyes' from Amérigo Vespucci's exclamation when he first sighted the reef in 1503. Established in 1983, the park consists of five small islands (Redonda, Siriba, Guarita, Sueste, Santa Bárbara), which are volcanic in origin, and several coral reefs. The warm current and shallow waters (8-15 m deep) make for a rich undersea life (about 160 species of fish) and good snorkelling. The park is best visited in October-March. Humpback whales breed and give birth from July to December. Diving is best December to February. The archipelago is administered by Ibama and a navy detachment mans a lighthouse on Santa Bárbara, which is the only island that may be visited. Permission from **Parque Nacional Marinho dos Abrolhos** ① *Praia do Kitomgo s/n, Caravelas, Bahia 45900, T0xx73-3297 1111, or Ibama, Av Juracy Magalhães Junior 608, CEP 41940-060, Salvador, T/F0xx71-3240 7913, www.ibama.gov.br/ parna_abrolhos/.* Visitors can't stay on the islands, but may stay overnight on schooners.

● Sleeping → *See Telephone, page 347, for important phone changes.*

Valença *p481*
AL Portal Rio Una, R Maestro Barrinha, T/F3641 5050, www.portalhoteis.tur.br. Resort hotel by the riverside with a pool, tennis courts and organized activities.
B do Porto, Av Maçônica 50, T3641 5226, hdoporto@vca.mma.com.br. Helpful, safe, good breakfast, good restaurant.
B Guabim, Praça da Independência 74, T3641 4114, guaibimhotel@ig.com.br. Modest with bath and buffet breakfast, good **Akuarius** restaurant.
D Valença, R Dr H Guedes Melo 15, T3641 2383. Comfortable, good breakfast. Recommended.

Tinharé and Morro de São Paulo *p481*
Morro de São Paulo
There are many cheap pousadas and rooms to rent near the fountain (Fonte Grande) but this part of town is very hot at night. A number of beach hotels are at the bottom of the main street where you turn right on to Primeira Praia (first beach).
L-A Pousada Farol do Morro, Primeira Praia, T3652 1036, www.faroldomorro.com.br. Little huts running up the hill all with a sea view and served by a private funicular railway, pool.

AL-B Pousada Vista Bela, R da Biquinha 15, T3652 1001, www.vistabelapousada.com. Owner Petruska is extremely welcoming, good rooms, those to the front have good views and are cooler, all have fans, hammocks. Price depends on season and type of room.
B Pousada Colibri, R do Porto de Cima 5, T3652 1056, pousadacolibri@svn.com.br. 6 apartments up some steep steps. Cool, always a breeze blowing, excellent views, Helmut, the owner, speaks English and German.
C Pousada Gaúcho, R da Prainha 79, T3652 1243. On same street as the steps to Pousada Colibri. Huge breakfast, shared bath.
C Pousada Ilha do Sol, Primeira Praia, T3652 1576. Modest but scrupulously clean, good views.

Terceira Praia (3rd beach)
AL-A Pousada Fazenda Caeira, T3652 1042, www.fazendacaeira.com.br. Spacious, airy chalets in a coconut grove overlooking the sea, good breakfasts, library, games room.
AL-B Fazenda Vila Guaiamú, T3652 1035, www.vilaguaiamu.com.br. 7 tastefully decorated chalets set in tropical gardens visited by marmosets,

tanagers and rare cotingas, excellent food. The hotel has a spa and the Italian photographer-owner runs an ecotourism project protecting a rare species of crab which lives in the fazenda's river. Guided walks available. Highly recommended. **C Pousada Aradhia**, T3652 1239. Balconies with ocean view, very good facilities.

Boipeba
A Pousada Tassimirim, ½-hr walk south of town, T3653 6030, or 9981 2378 (R Com Madureira 40, 45400-000 Valença), www.ilhaboipeba.org.br/pousadas.html. Bungalows, bar, restaurant, including breakfast and dinner.
A-C Santa Clara, Boca da Barra, T3653 6085, www.santaclaraboipeba.com. Californian-owned, with the island's best restaurant, large, tasteful cabins and a good-value room for 4 at D pp. Therapeutic massages available. Recommended.
B-C Horizonte Azul, Boca da Barra, T3653 6080, www.ilhaboipeba.org.br/pousadas.html. Next to Santa Clara, a range of chalets in a hillside garden visited by hundreds of rare birds. Owners speak English and French. Lunch available. Recommended.
C Pousada Moreré, Moreré town, T9981 1303. Simple rooms with fan. Good restaurant and bar. The owner is the island's *prefeito*.

Itacaré *p481*
LL Txai Resort, Praia de Itacarezinho, T2101 5000, www.txai.com.br. The most self-consciously exclusive resort in Bahia; on a deserted beach with very tasteful bungalows overlooking a deep blue pool shaded by its own stand of palms. Excellent spa and a full range of activities including diving and horse riding.
LL-AL Villa de Ocaporan, between the town and Praia da Concha, T3251 2470, www.villadeocaporan.com.br. Brightly coloured, spacious chalets around a charming little pool, good Bahian restaurant.
A-B Art Jungle, T9975 1083, www.artjungle.org. 6 tree houses in a modern sculpture garden in the middle of forest, great views. A favourite with celebrities, but relatively unpretentious nonetheless.
A-B Pousada da Lua, Praia da Concha, T3251 2209, www.pousadadalua.com. A handful of little chalets in forest filled with marmosets and parakeets. Great breakfast.
B Pousada Litoral, R de Souza 81, 1 block from where buses stop, T3251 3046. The owner João Cravo speaks English and can organize tours to remote beaches and hire fishing boats. Recommended.
C-D Pousada Estrela, R Pedro Longo 34, T3251 2006, pousadaestrela@backpacker.com.br. Well-maintained, simple rooms, homemade breakfast with lots of choice, very helpful.

Ilhéus *p481*
Plenty of cheap hotels near the municipal rodoviária in centre and *pousadas* along the coast to Olivença.
A Ilhéus Praia, Praça Dom Eduardo (on beach), T3634 2533, www.ilheuspraia.com.br. Pool, helpful. Recommended.

Porto Seguro *p482*
Prices rise steeply Dec-Feb and Jul. Off-season rates can drop by 50%, for stays of more than 3 nights negotiate. Outside Dec-Feb rooms with bath and hot water can be rented for US$150 per month.
AL Alegrete Porto, Av Navegantes 567, T3288 1738, www.portonet.com.br/alegrete. All facilities, very helpful. Recommended.
AL Estalagem Porto Seguro, R Marechal Deodoro 66, T3288 2095, hotelestalagem@hotelestalagem.com.br. In an old colonial house, relaxing atmosphere, a/c, TV, pool, good breakfast. Highly recommended.
AL Pousada Casa Azul, 15 de Novembro 11, T/F3288 2180, p.casazul@uol.com.br. TV, a/c, good pool and garden, quiet part of town.
AL Vela Branca, R Dr Antonio Ricaldi (Cidade Alta), T3288 2318, www.velabranca.com.br. Luxury resort with a wonderful view out over the water. Beautiful pool, tennis courts, sauna and spacious a/c rooms.
B Pousada Jandaias, R das Jandaias 112, T3288 2611, www.jandaias.com.br. Fan, great breakfast.
B Pousada dos Navegantes, Av 22 de Abril 212, T3288 2390, www.portonet.com.br/navegantes. A/c, TV, pool, conveniently located. Recommended.
B-C Pousada Da Orla, Av Portugal 404, T/F3288 1131. Fan, good breakfast, great location. Highly recommended.
C-D Pousada Aquárius, R Pedro Álvares Cabral 174, T/F3288 2738. No breakfast, family-run, central.
Camping Camping Mundaí Praia, US$10 per night, T3679 2287. **Tabapiri Country**, BR-367, Km 61.5, next to the rodoviária on the road leading to the Cidade Histórica, T3288 2269.

Around Porto Seguro:
Santa Cruz Cabrália *p482*
B Victor Hugo, Villa de Santo Antônio, Km 3, T3671 4064, www.portonet.com.br/victorhugo. Smart, tasteful, right on the beach.
E pp Maracaia, Coroa Vermelha on road to Porto Seguro, Km 77.5, T3672 1155, www.maracaiahostel.com.br. Low season price, HI affiliated.

Arraial da Ajuda *p482*
At busy times, don't expect to find anything under US$15 pp in a shared room for a minimum stay of 5-7 days. Camping is best at these times.

L Pousada Pitinga, Praia Pitinga, T3575 1067, www.pousadapitinga.com.br. Bold architecture amid Atlantic forest, a hideaway, great food and pool, a Roteiros de Charme hotel.

AL Pousada Canto d'Alvorada, Esterada d' Ajuda 1993, T3575 1218. **B** out of season, Swiss run, 7 cabins, restaurant, laundry facilities.

A Pousada Erva Doce, Estrada do Mucugê 200, T3575 1113, www.ervadoce.com.br. Good restaurant, well-appointed chalets (**AL** in high season).

A Pousada do Roballo, T3575 1053, www.pousadadoroballo.com.br. Good grounds, welcoming, good pool.

B Pousada Flamboyant, Estrada do Mucugê 89, T3575 1025, www.flamboyant.tur.br. Pleasant courtyard, pool, good breakfast.

B Pousada Tubarão, R Bela Vista 74, beyond the church on the right, T3575 1086, tubarao@arraial.com.br. Good view of the coastline, cool, good restaurant.

C O Cantinho, Praça São Bras, T3575 1131, pousadacantinho@arraialnet.com.br. Terraces of smart rooms, a/c or fan, nice courtyard, excellent breakfast, discounts off season.

D-E pp Arraial d'Ajuda Hostel, R do Campo 94, T3575 1192, www.arraialdajudahostel.com.br. Backpacker hostel with HI discounts, more expensive in Jan, with breakfast, snack bar, pool, good location.

Camping Generally, Arraial da Ajuda is better for camping than Porto Seguro. **Chão do Arraial**, 5 mins from Mucugê beach, shady, good snack bar, also hire tents. Recommended. **Praia**, T3575 1020, on Mucugê Beach, good position and facilities.

Trancoso *p482*

There are many houses to rent, very good ones are rented by Clea who can be contacted at **Restaurant Abacaxi**. Also **Condominio dos Nativos**, condominiodosnativos@bol.com.br. Owned by Gustavo and Ana, excellent double-bedroom villas with kitchen and patio, 3 mins from beach, organize horse-riding, day trips, very welcoming.

L-A Mata N'ativa, Estrada Velha do Arraial (next to the river on the way to the beach), T3668 1830, www.matanativapousada.com.br. The best in town, a series of elegant cabins in a lovingly maintained garden by the riverside, cheaper in low season. Owners Daniel and Daniela are very hospitable. Good English, Spanish and Italian. Recommended.

A Caipim Santo, T3668 1122, to the left of the main praça, capimsanto@capimsanto.com.br . With breakfast, the best restaurant in Trancoso. Recommended.

There are other, cheaper *pousadas*. About 500 m inland away from main praça (known as the 'quadrado') lies the newer part of Trancoso (known as the 'invasão') with some good value *pousadas*.

Caraíva *p482*

A Pousada da Barra, T9985 4302, www.caraiva.com. **AL** in Dec-Jan. Rooms and bungalows between the river and sea, bar and restaurant in high season, boat trips. Horse riding and other excursions arranged.

A Pousada Lagoa, T3225 5845, or 9985 6862, www.lagoacaraiva.com.br. Chalets and bungalows under cashew trees, good restaurant, popular bar, own generator, internet. The owner, Hermínia, speaks English and is very helpful and can arrange local trips and excursions.

A-C Pousada da Terra, far end of village near Indian reserve, T9985 4417, www.caraiva.com.br/terra. With breakfast, bar, safe, also houses for rent. Recommended.

Caravelas *p483*

B Pousada Caravelense, Praça Teófilo Otoni 2, T3297 1182. TV, fridge, good breakfast, excellent restaurant. Recommended.

D Beco Shangri-lá, Sete de Setembro 219, T3297 1059. Simple rooms with bath, breakfast.

D Pousada Juquita, Praia do Grauçá, Barra de Caravelas, T3674 1038. Use of kitchen, big breakfast, bath, airy rooms, the owner is Secka who speaks English.

🍴 Eating

Tinharé and Morro de São Paulo *p481*

There are plenty of restaurants in Morro de São Paulo town and on the 2nd and 3rd beaches. Most are OK though somewhat overpriced. For cheap eats stay in a *pousada* which includes breakfast, stock up at the supermarket and buy seafood snacks at the *barracas* on the 2nd beach.

♯♯ Belladonna on the main street. Good Italian restaurant with great music, a good meeting point, owner Guido speaks Italian, English and French, open evenings only.

♯♯ Bianco e Nero, Morro town. Reasonably good pizza, pasta and grilled food.

♯♯ Chez Max, 3rd beach. Simple but decent seafood in a pretty restaurant overlooking the sea.

♯ Comida Natural, on the main street. Good breakfasts, *comida a kilo*, good juices.

Itacaré *p481*

There are plenty of restaurants in Itacaré, mostly on R Lodônio Almeida. Menus here are increasingly chic and often include a respectable wine list.

♯♯♯ Casa Sapucaia, R Lodônio Almeida, T251 3091. Sophisticated Bahian food with an international twist.

♯♯♯ Dedo de Moça, R Plínio Soares (next to the São Miguel Church), T251 3391. One of Bahia's best restaurants, with dishes which combine

Brazilian ingredients with French and Oriental techniques.

¶¶ **Boca de Forno**, R Lodônio Almeida 134, T251 2174. The busiest restaurant in Itacaré, serving good wood-fired pizzas in tastefully decorated surroundings.

¶ **O Restaurante**, Rua Pedro Longo 150, T251 2012. One of the few restaurants with a *prato feto*, and a mixed seafood menu.

Ilhéus *p481*

Try the local drink, *coquinho*, coconut filled with cachaça. Also try *suco de cacau* at juice stands.

¶¶¶ **Vesúvio**, Praça Dom Eduardo, next to the cathedral, made famous by Amado's novel (see above). Good but pricey.

¶¶ **Os Velhos Marinheiros**, Av 2 de Julho. A recommended eating place on the waterfront.

¶ **Nogar**, Av Bahia 377, near sea. Pizzas and pasta.

Porto Seguro *p482*

¶¶¶ **Cruz de Malta**, R Getúlio Vargas 358. Good seafood.

¶¶ **Anti-Caro**, R Assis Chateaubriand 26. Good. Recommended. Also antique shop, good atmosphere.

¶¶ **Les Agapornis**, Av dos Navegantes 180. Wide selection of crêpes and pizzas.

¶¶ **Tres Vintens**, Av Portugal 246. Good imaginative seafood dishes. Recommended.

¶¶ **Vida Verde**, R Dois de Julho 92, T2882766. Vegetarian food, open 1100-2100 except Sun.

¶ **da Japonêsa**, Praça Pataxós 38. Excellent value with varied menu, open 0800-2300. Recommended.

¶ **Pau Brasil**, Praça dos Pataxós. Good breakfast.

¶ **Ponto do Encontro**, Praça Pataxós 106. Good simple food, owners rent rooms, open 0800-2400.

¶ **Preto Velho**, on Praça da Bandeira. Good value à la carte or self-service.

Arraial da Ajuda *p482*

¶¶¶ **Don Fabrizio**, Estrada do Mucugê 402, T575 1123. The best Italian in town, in an upmarket open air restaurant with live music and reasonable wine.

¶¶¶ **Manguti**, Estrada do Mucugê, T575 2270, www.manguti.com.br. Reputed by some to be the best in town, meat, pasta, fish alongside other Brazilian dishes. Very popular and informal.

¶¶ **Nipo**, Estrada do Mucugê 250, T575 3033. Reasonably priced but decent Japanese with hotel delivery.

¶¶ **Pizzaria do Arraial**, Praça São Bras s/n. Basic pizzeria and pay by weight restaurant.

¶ **Mineirissima**, Estrada do Mucugê, T575 3790. Good value pay by weight with very filling Minas

Gerais food and moquecas. Opens until late but menu service only after 1800.

¶ **Paulinho Pescador**, Estrada do Mucugê. Open 1200-2200, excellent seafood, also chicken and meat, one price (US$5), English spoken, good service, popular, there are often queues for tables.

Recommended barracas are **Tem Q Dá** and **Agito** on Mucugê beach and **Barraca de Pitinga** and **Barraca do Genésio** on Pitinga.

Trancoso *p482*

Food in Trancoso is expensive. Those on a tight budget should shop at the supermarket between the main square and the new part of town. There are numerous fish restaurants in the *barracas* on the beach. None is cheap.

¶¶¶ **Cacao**, on the main square, T668 1266. One of the best in town with a varied international and Brazilian menu. Pleasant surrounds.

¶¶ **Laila**, in the new shopping area just before the main square. Elegant little restaurant serving good Moroccan and Lebanese food.

¶¶ **Silvana e Cia**, in the historical centre. Respectable Bahian food at a fair price.

¶ **Portinha**, on the main square. The only place serving food at a reasonable price. Excellent pay by weight options and good if overpriced juices.

Caraíva *p482*

There is forró dancing 0100-0600 at **Pelé** and **Ouriços** on alternate nights in season.

¶¶ **Bar do Pará**, by the river. Serves the best fish in the village, US$7-8 (try sashimi or moqueca). Also has simple lodging, **Pousada da Canoa**.

❶ Bars and clubs

Morro de São Paulo *p481*

There is always plenty going on in Morro. The liveliest bars are **87** and **Jamaica**, both on the 2nd beach. These tend to get going after 2300 when the restaurants in town empty.

Itacaré *p481*

There is frequent extemporaneous forró and other live music all over the city and most restaurants and bars have some kind of music between Oct and Apr.

Porto Seguro *p482*

Porto Seguro is famous for the lambada. There are lots of bars and street cafés on Av Portugal. **Pronto Socorro do Choppe, Doce Letal 50** and **Studio Video Bar** are all lively places.

Porto Prego on R Pedro Álvares Cabral. A good bar for live music, small cover charge.

Sotton Bar, Praça da Bandeira. Lively.

Arraial da Ajuda *p482*

The lambada is danced at the **Jatobar** bar (summer only), by the church on the main square (opens 2300 – pensão at the back is cheap, clean and friendly). **Limelight** has raves all year round. Many top Brazilian bands play at the beach clubs at Praia do Parracho during the summer, entry is about US$20. Entry to other beach parties is about US$10. There is also a capoeira institute; ask for directions.

⊛ Festivals and events

Ilhéus *p481*

Festa de São Sebastião, **17-20 Jan**, Carnival, Festa de São Jorge, **23 Apr**, Foundation day, **28 Jun**, and Festa do Cacau throughout **Oct**.

▲▲ Activities and tours

Porto Seguro *p482*

Diving Portomar Ltda, R Dois de Julho 178, T3288 2606. Arranges diving and snorkelling trips to the coral reefs offshore, professional instructors, equipment hire.

Tour operators
Several agencies at the airport.
Brazil travel, Av 22 de Abril 200, T/F3288 1824, braziltravel@braziltravel.tur.br. Dutch-run travel agency, all types of trips organized, English, German, Dutch, French and Spanish spoken.
Companhia do Mar, Praça dos Pataxós 15, T3288 2107. Daily trips by schooner to coral reefs. The most popular is to Recife de Fora, with good snorkelling; it leaves daily at 1000, returns 1630, pay extra for snorkelling gear.

⊖ Transport

Valença *p481*

Bus Long-distance buses from new rodoviária, Av Abel de Aguiar Queirós, Aguazinha, T3641 4805. Local buses from the old rodoviaria. Many buses a day to/from **Salvador**, 5 hrs, US$13, several companies including **Águia Branca**.
Ferry For the shortest route to Valença, take the ferry from São Joaquim to Bom Despacho on Itaparica island, from where it is 130 km to Valença via Nazaré das Farinhas. To/from **Bom Despacho** on Itaparica, **Camarujipe** and **Águia Branca**, 16 a day, 1 hr 45 mins, US$7.

Tinharé and Morro de São Paulo *p481*

Air Air taxi from Salvador airport US$75 1-way, 20 mins, **Addey** T3377 1993, www.addey.com.br.
Ferry From Salvador, several companies operate a catamaran (1 hr 30 mins) service from the Terminal Marítimo in front of the Mercado Modelo to Morro de São Paulo. Times vary according to the weather and season. **Catamara Gamboa do Morro**, T9975 6395. Part of the trip is on the open sea, which can be rough. Boats leave every day from **Valença** for Gamboa (1½ hrs) and Morro de São Paulo (1½ hrs) from the main bridge in Valença 5 times a day (signalled by a loud whistle). The fare is US$4.50. A *lancha rápida* taking 25 mins travels the route between Valença and Morro, US$12. Only buses between 0530-1100 from Salvador to Valença connect with ferries. If not stopping in Valença, get out of the bus by the main bridge in town, don't wait till you get to the rodoviária, which is a long way from the ferry. Private boat hire can be arranged if you miss the ferry schedule. A responsible local boatman is **Jario**. He also offers excursions to other islands, especially **Boipeba**. There is a regular boat from Valença to Boipeba on weekdays 1000-1230 depending on tide, return 1500-1700, 3-4 hrs.

Itacaré *p481*

Bus The rodoviária is a few mins' walk from town. Porters are on hand with barrows to help with luggage. Frequent buses 0700-1900 to **Ilhéus** (the nearest town with an airport), 45 mins, US$7 along the paved road. To **Salvador**, change at **Ubaitaba** (3 hrs, US$5), Ubaitaba-Salvador, 6 hrs, US$16, several daily.

Ilhéus *p481*

Bus Rodoviária is 4 km from the centre on Itabuna road. Several daily to **Salvador**, 7 hrs, US$27, **Expresso São Jorge**; 0620 bus goes via Itaparica, leaving passengers at Bom Despacho ferry station on the island – thence 50-mins ferry to Salvador. To **Eunápolis**, 5 hrs, US$10, this bus also leaves from the central bus terminal. Other destinations served; local buses leave from Praça Cairu. Insist that taxi drivers have meters and price charts.

Porto Seguro *p482*

Air Airport T3288 1880. Regular flights from **Rio**, **São Paulo**, **Salvador** and **Belo Horizonte**. Taxi airport-Porto Seguro, US$12. Also buses.
Bus From Porto Seguro: **Salvador** (Águia Branca), daily, 12 hrs, US$45. **Vitória**, daily, 11 hrs, US$52. **Ilhéus**, daily 0730, 5½ hrs, US$20. **Eunápolis**, 1 hr, US$4. For **Rio** direct buses (**São Geraldo**), leaving at 1745, US$70, 18 hrs, from Rio direct at 1600 (very cold a/c, take warm clothes), or take 1800 for Ilhéus and change at Eunápolis. To **Belo Horizonte** daily, direct, US$65 (São Geraldo). Other services via Eunápolis (those going north avoid Salvador) or Itabuna (5 hrs, US$18).

The rodoviária has reliable luggage store and lounge on the 3rd floor, on the road to

Brazil South of Salvador Listings

Eunápolis, 2 km from the centre, regular bus service (30 mins) through the city to the old rodoviária near the port. Local buses US$0.45. Taxis charge US$7 from the rodoviária to the town or ferry (negotiate at quiet times).

Arraial da Ajuda p482
Ferry Across the Rio Buranhém from Porto Seguro take 15 mins to the south bank, US$1 for foot passengers, US$6 for cars, every 30 mins day and night. It is then a further 5 km to Arraial da Ajuda, US$1 by bus; kombis charge US$1.50 pp; taxis US$10.

Trancoso p482
Bus Buses run regularly on the newly paved road between Porto Seguro, Ajuda and Trancoso, at least every hour in high season: US$4 Porto Seguro-Trancoso, US$2.40 Ajuda-Trancoso. Arriving from the south, change buses at Eunápolis from where the newly paved Linha Verde road runs.

Caraíva p482
Caraíva can only be reached by **canoe** across the river. Access roads are poor and almost impossible after heavy rain. There are services several times a day from Trancoso, which is the easiest point of access. **Aguia Azul** bus company takes this route from Porto Seguro at 1500. If arriving by bus from the south, change to **Aguia Azul** bus in Itabela, departs at 1500, or take a taxi, about 50 km. Heading south take the bus to Eunápolis at 0600, 3 hrs.

Parque Nacional de Monte Pascoal p483
From Caraíva there is a river crossing by **boats** which are always on hand. **Buses** run from **Itamaraju** 16 km to the south, at 0600 on Fri-Mon.

Caravelas p483
Bus To Teixeira de Freitas (4 a day), **Salvador**, **Nanuque** and **Prado**. **Flights** from **Belo Horizonte**, **São Paulo** and **Salvador** to Caravelas; otherwise fly to Porto Seguro.

Parque Nacional Marinho dos Abrolhos
The journey to the islands takes 1-6 hrs depending on the boat. Tours are available from Caravelas (about US$250 for a slow 2½ day tour by saveiro). 1-day tours can be made in a faster boat (US$130) from Abrolhos or the Marina Porto Abrolhos.

⊙ Directory

Porto Seguro p482
Banks Banco do Brasil, Av Beira Mar, open 1000-1500, changes TCs and US$ cash, also Visa ATM. Also at airport. **Bradesco**, Av Getúlio Vargas, Visa ATM. **Bicycle hire** Oficina de Bicicleta, Av Getúlio Vargas e R São Pedro, about US$13 for 24 hrs. Also at Praça de Bandeira and at 2 de Julho 242. **Car hire** Several companies at the airport. **Post offices** In the mini-shopping centre on the corner of R das Jandaias and Av dos Navegantes.

Arraial da Ajuda p482
Banks Mobile Banco do Brazil in the main square during high season. **Internet** Various places in town.

North of Salvador

The paved BA-099 coast road from near Salvador airport is known as the Estrada do Coco (Coconut Highway, because of the many plantations) and for 50 km passes some beautiful beaches. The best known from south to north are Ipitanga (with its reefs), Buraquinho, **Jauá** (with reefs, surfing, pools at low tide, clean water), Arembepe (with a Tamar turtle protection project, famous hippy village in 1960s), Guarajuba, Itacimirim, Castelo Garcia D'Ávila (with its 16th-century fort) and Forte. Regular buses serve most of these destinations.

Praia do Forte
The former fishing village, 80 km north of Salvador, takes its name from the castle built by a Portuguese settler, Garcia D'Ávila, in 1556 to warn the city to the south of enemy invasion. Praia do Forte is now a pleasant resort town with all but one of the streets of sand and lovely beaches. Inland from the coast is a restinga forest, which grows on sandy soil with a very delicate ecosystem. Near the village is a small *pantanal* (marshy area), which is host to a large number of birds, caymans and other animals. Birdwatching trips on the pantanal are rewarding. The **Tamar Project** ⓘ *Caixa Postal 2219, CEP 40223-970, Rio Vermelho, Salvador, Bahia, Toxx71-3676 1020, F3676 1067*, preserves the sea turtles which lay their eggs in the area. Praia do Forte is now the headquarters of the national turtle preservation programme and is funded by the Worldwide Fund for Nature.

The coast road north

The Linha Verde (the extension of the Estrada do Coco) runs for 142 km to the border of Sergipe, the next state north; the road is more scenic than the BR-101, especially near Conde. There are very few hotels or pousadas in the more remote villages. The most picturesque are **Imbassaí**, **Subaúma**, **Baixio** (very beautiful, where the Rio Inhambupe meets the sea) and **Conde**. Sítio do Conde on the coast, 6 km from Conde, has many pousadas, but the beaches are not very good. Sítio do Conde is an ideal base to explore other beaches at Barra do Itariri, 12 km south, at the mouth of a river (fine sunsets). The last stop on the Linha Verde is **Mangue Seco**. A steep hill rising behind the village to tall white sand dunes offers superb view of the coastline. There are plenty of small cheap places to stay along the seafront from the jetty, none with addresses or phone numbers (the village is tiny). There are simple restaurants around the main square next to the church. The beach has a handful of *barracas* serving cheap fish. Access from Sergipe is by boat on the Rio Real from Pontal (10-minute crossing). Buses run between Pontal and Estância twice a day. The ferry across the river usually leaves before 1000 in the morning. A private launch will cost US$10, but it usually possible to find someone to share the ride.

◉ Sleeping → *See Telephone, page 347, for important phone changes.*

North from Salvdor: Jauá *p488*
B Lagoa e Mar, Praia de Jauá, T/F3672 1573, www.hotellagoaemar.com.br. Very good breakfast, spacious bungalows, swimming pool, 350 m to beach, restaurant, helpful, transport to airport, 10% discount to Footprint owners.

Praia do Forte *p488*
Prices rise steeply in the summer season. It may be difficult to find cheap places to stay.
LL-AL Praia do Forte EcoResort, Av do Farol, T3676 4000, www.praiadoforte.com. Large scale family resort set in tropical gardens on the beach and with programmes to visit the nearby protected areas. Room are spacious, well appointed and comfortable. Service, which includes a spa and entertainment, is excellent. Beautiful pool.
AL Pousada Solar da Lagoa, R do Forte, T3676 1271, www.solardalagoa.com.br. Smart chalets with room enough for 4, a decent pool and excellent service. Price is for full board.
AL-A Sobrado da Vila, Av do Sol, T/F3676 1088, www.sobradodavila.com.br. Best in the village itself with a range of individually decorated rooms with balconies and a good-value restaurant, convenient for restaurants.
A Ogum Marinho, Av Alameda do Sol, T3676 1165, www.ogummarinho.com.br. A/c, cheaper with fan, nice little courtyard garden, good restaurant and service.
A-B Pousada Casa de Praia, Praça dos Artistas 08-09, T3676 1362, www.casadepraia.tur.br. Good value and location rooms, with and without a/c, popular.
B-C Pousada João Sol, R da Corvina, T3676 1054, www.pousadajoaosol.com.br. 6 well-appointed and newly refurbished chalets.

The owner speaks English, Spanish and German. Great breakfast.
C Pousada Tatuapara, Praça dos Artistas, T3676 1015, manfredweftrich@uol.com.br. Spacious and well maintained, fan, fridge, good breakfast.
D Tia Helena, just east of the Praça dos Artistas, T3676 1198. Helena, the motherly proprietor provides an excellent meal and enormous breakfast, simple rooms, well kept, reductions for 3-day stays.
E pp Albergue da Juventude, Praia do Forte, R da Aurora 3, T3676 1094, www.albergue.com.br. Smart youth hostel with decent shared rooms and rooms with en suites (**B-C**), a large breakfast, fan, kitchen and shop, cheaper for HI members.

◉ Eating

Praia do Forte *p488*
♢♢ Bar Da Souza, Av do Sol, on the right as you enter the village. Best seafood in town, open daily, live music at weekends. Recommended.
♢♢ O Europeu, Alameda do Sol, T3676 0232. English owned, with the most adventurous menu in town. The owner, William, is knowledgeable about the area. Good little arts and crafts shop upstairs.
♢ Cafe Tango, Praça das Artistas. Pleasant open-air tea and coffee bar with great pastries and cakes.
♢ La Crêperie, Alameda do Sol. Excellent crêpes, Tue to Sun, good music, popular, owner Klever very friendly.
♢ Pizzaria Le Gaston, Alameda do Sol. Good pizza and pasta, also good home-made ice creams, daily.

▲▲ Activities and tours

Praia do Forte *p488*
Praia do Forte is ideal for windsurfing and sailing owing to constant fresh Atlantic breezes.
Odara Turismo, in the EcoResort Hotel, T3676 1080. Imaginative tours to surrounding areas and outlying villages and beaches using 4WD vehicles. They are very friendly and informative. Recommended. The owners, Norbert and Papy, speak English and German.

⊖ Transport

Praia do Forte *p488*
Bus From **Salvador** (US$4): Santa Maria/Catuense 5 times daily from rodoviária, 1½ hrs.

Recife and the northeast coast

The eight states north of Bahia are historically and culturally rich, but generally poor economically. Steeped in history are, for instance, Recife, Olinda, or São Luís and cultural heritage abounds (eg 'Forró' and other musical styles, many good museums, lacework, ceramics). There is a multitude of beaches: if established resorts aren't your thing, you don't have to travel far for somewhere more peaceful, while off the beaten track are some which have hardly been discovered.

Pernambuco was the seat of Dutch Brazil in the 17th century. Its capital, Recife, and close neighbour, Olinda, have the most creative music scene in the northeast and their famous wild carnival draws thousands of visitors.

Recife → *Phone code: 0xx81. Post code: 50000. Colour map 5, grid B6. Population: 1.42 million.*

The capital of Pernambuco State, 285 km north of Maceió and 839 km north of Salvador, was founded on reclaimed land by the Dutch prince Maurice of Nassau in 1637 after his troops had burnt Olinda, the original capital. The city centre consists of three portions, always very busy by day; the crowds and the narrow streets, especially in the Santo Antônio district, can make it a confusing city to walk around. Recife has the main dock area, with commercial buildings associated with it. South of the centre is the residential and beach district of Boa Viagem, reached by bridge across the Bacia do Pina. Olinda, the old capital, is 7 km to the north (see page 499).

Ins and outs

Tourist offices **Empetur** (for the State of Pernambuco), **main office** ① *Complexo Viário Vice-Governador Barreto Guimarães s/n, Salgadinho, T3427 8000, between Recife and Olinda, www.empetur.com.br*. Branches at **airport** ① *T3341 6090, 24 hours*, helpful but few leaflets, English spoken, and **Praça of Boa Viagem** ① *T3463 3621*, English spoken, helpful. Maps are available, or can be bought at newspaper stands in city; also sketch maps in monthly guides Itinerário Pernambuco and Guia do Turista. For the **Secretaria de Turismo da Prefeitura do Recife** ① *T3224 7198*. Hours of opening of museums, art galleries, churches, etc are published in the *Diário de Pernambuco* and *Jornal do Comércio*. The former's website has lots of tourist information, www.dpnet.com.br/turismo/ or via www.pernambuco.com.

Opportunistic theft is unfortunately common in the streets of Recife and Olinda (especially on the streets up to Alto da Sé, Olinda). Prostitution is reportedly common in Boa Viagem – choose nightclubs with care.

Sights

The best sights are the churches of **Santo Antônio do Convento de São Francisco** (1606) *in the R do Imperador*, which has beautiful Portuguese tiles, and adjoining it the finest sight of all, the **Capela Dourada** (Golden Chapel, 1697) ① *Mon-Fri 0800-1130, 1400-1700, Sat morning only, US$1, no flash photography*; it is through the Museu Franciscano de Arte Sacra. **São Pedro dos Clérigos** (1782) ① *in São José district, daily 0800-1130, 1400-1600*, should be seen for its façade, its fine wood sculpture and a splendid trompe-l'oeil ceiling. **Nossa Senhora da Conceição dos Militares** (1771) ① *R Nova 309, Mon-Fri 0800-1700*, has

Recife orientation

Related maps
A Recife, page 492
B Boa Viagem, page 494

To Northern Beaches
Alto da Sé
Santa Teresa
OLINDA
J Nabuco
Av Presidente Kennedy
Rio Beberibe
Convention Centre & Empetur
Av Olinda
ENCRUZILHADA
Estrada de Belém
Av Norte
Gov A Magalhães
Av Cruz Cabugá
Rio Beberibe
RECIFE
Estrada Arraial
Casa Amarela, Sítio Trindade & Casa Forte complex
Cemitério Santo Amaro
P de Limoeiro
A Lisboa
Estr do Encanamento
Av Rota e Silva
Museu do Homen do Nordeste
Museu do Estado
Av João de Barros
Parque 13 de Maio
J Bonifácio
BOA VISTA
POÇO
Av Rui Barbosa
Rio Capibaribe
MADALENA
Gov A Magalhães
Av Caxangá
Dom Bosco
Central Metrô Station
Av San Martim
Joquei Clube
Estr dos Remédios
Joana Bezerra
Dantas Barreto
Bacia do Pina
Atlantic Ocean
M Gonçalves da Luz
R Imperial
Av Abdias de Carvalho
Afogados Ipiranga
A de Góis
H Bandeira
To the North & João Pessoa
Mangueira
R São Miguel
B
PINA
Santa Luzia
Rio Tijipo
Rio Jordão
Rio Pina
Av Domingos Ferreira
Av Boa Viagem
Edgar Werneck
Av Central
Barro
Dr J Rufino
Av Recife
IMBIRIBEIRA
Av Sul
Av Marechal Mascarenhas Morais
Gen MacArthur
Shopping Center Recife
Five Stations to Rodoviária
BOA VIAGEM
Canal Jordão
IBURA
Praça Boa Viagem
N
0 km   1
0 miles   1
To the South & Maceió
To Monte Guararapes & NS das Prazeres
To Piedade

a grand ceiling and a large 18th-century primitive mural of the battle of Guararapes (museum next door). Other important churches are **Santo Antônio** (1753-1791) ① *Praça da Independência, Mon-Fri 0800-1200, 1400-1800, Sun 1700-1900*, rebuilt in 1864. **Nossa Senhora do Carmo** (1663) ① *Praça do Carmo, Mon-Fri 0800-1200, 1400-1900, Sat-Sun 0700-1200*. **Madre de Deus** (1715) ① *in R Madre de Deus in the district of Recife, Tue-Fri 0800-1200, 1400-1600*, with a splendid high altar, and sacristy. The **Divino Espírito Santo** (1689) ① *Praça 17 in Santo Antônio district, Mon-Fri 0800-1630, Sat 0800-1400, Sun 1000-1200*, the original church of the Jesuits. There are many others.

Recife

Eating 🍴
Galo D'Ouro **1**
Gelattos **2**
Leite **3**

Churches ⛪
Capela Dourada **1**
Espírito Santo **2**
Madre de Deus **3**
Matriz de Boa Vista **4**
Nossa Senhora da
Conceição dos Militares **5**
Nossa Senhora
do Carmo **6**
Nossa Senhora
do Livramento **7**
Nossa Senhora do
Rosário dos Pretos **8**
Pilar **9**
Santo Antônio **10**
São José do Ribamar **11**
São Pedro dos Clérigos **12**
Santo Antônio do
Convento de São
Francisco **13**

Buses 🚌
To Itamaracá & Igarassu **1**
To Porto da Galinhas **2**
To Boa Viagem **3**

Sleeping 🛏
América **2**
Central **1**
Recife Plaza **4**

0 metres 200
0 yards 200

N

492

Forte do Brum ① *Tue-Fri 0900-1600, Sat-Sun 1400-1600* (built by the Dutch in 1629) is an army museum. **Forte das Cinco Pontas** (with **Museu da Cidade do Recife**) ① *Mon-Fri 0900-1800, Sat-Sun 1300-1700, US$0.50 donation advised*, with a cartographic history of the settlement of Recife, was built by the Dutch in 1630 and altered by the Portuguese in 1677. The two forts jointly controlled access to the port at the northern and southern entrances respectively. The first Brazilian printing press was installed in 1706 and Recife claims to publish the oldest daily newspaper in South America, Diário de Pernambuco, founded 1825 (but now accessible on www.dpnet.com.br/). The distinctive lilac building is on the Praça da Independência.

The artists' and intellectuals' quarter is based on the **Pátio de São Pedro**, the square round São Pedro dos Clérigos. Sporadic folk music and poetry shows are given in the square Wednesday to Sunday evenings (T3426 2728) and there are atmospheric bars and restaurants.

The square is an excellent shopping centre for typical northeastern craftware (clay figurines are cheapest in Recife). Not far away, off Avenida Guararapes, two blocks from central post office, is the **Praça do Sebo**, where the city's second-hand booksellers concentrate; this Mercado de Livros Usados is off the Rua da Roda, behind the Edifício Santo Albino, near the corner of Avenida Guararapes and Rua Dantas Barreto. You can also visit the city markets in the São José and Santa Rita sections.

The former municipal prison has now been made into the **Casa da Cultura** ① *T3284 2850 to check what's on in advance, Mon-Sat 0900-1900, Sun 0900-1400*. Many of the cells have been converted into art or souvenir shops and with areas for exhibitions and shows (also public conveniences). Local dances such as the ciranda, forró and bumba-meu-boi are held as tourist attractions. Among other cultural centres are Recife's three traditional **theatres**, **Santa Isabel** ① *Praça da República, open to visitors Mon-Fri 1300-1700*, built in 1850. **Parque** ① *R do Hospício 81, Boa Vista, 0800-1200, 1400-1800*, restored and beautiful. **Apolo** ① *R do Apolo 121, 0800-1200, 1400-1700*. The **Museu do Estado** ① *Av Rui Barbosa 960, Graças, Tue-Fri 0900-1700, Sat-Sun 1400-1700*, has excellent paintings by the 19th-century landscape painter, Teles Júnior. **Museu do Trem** ① *Praça Visconde de Mauá, Tue-Fri 0800-1200, 1400-1700, Sat 0900-1200, Sun 1400-1700*, small but interesting, especially the Henschel locomotive.

West of the centre is the **Museu do Homem do Nordeste** ① *Av 17 de Agosto 2223, Casa Forte, Tue-Fri 1100-1700, Sat-Sun 1300-1700, US$1*. It comprises the **Museu de Arte Popular**, containing ceramic figurines (including some by Mestre Alino and Zé Caboclo); the **Museu do Açúcar**, on the history and technology of sugar production, with models of colonial mills, collections of antique sugar bowls and much else; the **Museu de Antropologia**, the **Nabuco Museum** (No 1865) and the modern museum of popular remedies, **Farmacopéia Popular**. Either take the 'Dois Irmãos' bus (check that it's the correct one, with 'Rui Barbosa' posted in window, as there are two) from in front of the Banorte building near the post office on Guararapes, or, more easily, go by taxi.

Oficina Cerâmica Francisco Brennand ① *Av Caxangá, Várzea, T3271 2466, www.brennand.com.br*. A museum and 19th-century ceramics factory set in mock-Moorish gardens and filled with Brennand's extraordinary Gaudiesque ceramic sculptures and paintings. The artist, who is one of Brazil's most illustrious, can sometimes be seen walking here, cane in hand looking like an old Sigmund Freud. **Instituto Ricardo Brennand** ① *Alameda Antônio Brennand s/n, Várzea, T2121 0370, www.institutoricardobrennand.org.br, Tue-Sun 1300-1700, last admission 1630*. Another scion of the Brennand family has built this fantasy castle on the outskirts of the city to house his art collection. This is one of the most important in the country and includes the largest assemblage of New World Dutch paintings in the world (with many Franz Posts), Brazilian modern art, armoury and medieval maps.

Boa Viagem

Boa Viagem, the main residential and hotel quarter, is currently being developed at its northern end. The 8-km promenade commands a striking view of the Atlantic, but the beach is backed by a busy road, is crowded at weekends and not very clean. During the January breeding season, sharks come close to the shore. You can go fishing on jangadas at Boa Viagem with a fisherman at low tide. The main praça has a good market at weekends. Take any bus marked 'Boa Viagem'; from Nossa Senhora do Carmo, take buses marked 'Piedade', 'Candeias' or 'Aeroporto' – they go on Avenida Domingos Ferreira, two blocks parallel to the beach, all the way to Praça Boa Viagem (at Avenida Boa Viagem 500). Back to the centre take buses marked 'CDU' or 'Setubal' from Avenida Domingos Ferreira. About 14 km south of the

Boa Viagem

To Recife Centre

Boa Viagem detail

Atlantic Ocean

N

0 metres 200
0 yards 200

Sleeping
Aconchego **1**
Coqueiral **2**
Hostel Boa Viagem **9**
Maracatus do Recife **3**
Pousada da Julieta **5**
Pousada da Praia **6**
Recife Monte **7**
Uzi Praia **8**

Eating
Bargaço **1**
Chica Pitanga **2**
Churrascaria Porcão **3**
Ilha da Kosta **5**
La Capannina **6**
La Maison **7**
Parraxaxa **8**
Peng **9**
Realeza **10**
Romana **11**
Sushimi **4**
Tempero Verde **12**
Tio Dadá **13**

Bars & clubs
Baltazar **14**

Boa Viagem *p493, map p494*
Baltazar, R Baltazar Pereira 130, T3327 0475.
Live music nightly, bar snacks, large and popular.
Open 1600 to early hours.
Papillon Bar, Av Beira Mar 20, Piedade,
T3341 7298. Forró Wed-Sat.

⦿ Entertainment

Recife *p490, map p492*
Theatre Agenda Cultural details the cultural
events for the month, free booklet from tourist
offices. Shows in the **Recife/Olinda Convention
Center**, US$10, traditional dances in full costume.

⦿ Festivals and events

Recife *p490, maps p492 and 494*
1 Jan, Universal Brotherhood. **Carnival** in Recife
features a pre-carnavalesca week of shows,
processions and balls, before the Galo da
Madrugada, with up to a million participants
officially opens Carnaval on the Sat morning. The
festival continues until Tue with trios elétricos,
samba and the distinctive local maracatu and frevo
dances and rhythms. **12-15 Mar**, parades to mark
the city's foundation. **Mid-Apr**, Pro-Rock Festival,
a week-long celebration of rock, hip-hop and
manguebeat at Centro de Convenções, Complexo
de Salgadinho and other venues. Check Diário de
Pernambuco or Jornal do Comércio for details.
Jun, Festejos Juninos. The days of Santo Antônio
(13 Jun), São João (24 Jun), São Pedro and São
Paulo (29 Jun), form the nuclei of a month-long
celebration whose roots go back to the
Portuguese colony. Intermingled with the Catholic
tradition are Indian and African elements. The
annual cycle begins in fact on São José's day, **19
Mar**, historically the 1st day of planting maize; the
harvest in Jun then forms a central part of the
festejos juninos. During the festivals the forró is
danced. This dance, now popular throughout the
Northeast, is believed to have originated when the
British builders of the local railways held parties
that were 'for all'. **11-16 Jul**, Nossa Senhora do
Carmo, patron saint of the city. **Aug** is the Mes do
Folclore. **Oct**, Recifolia, a repetition of carnival
over a whole weekend; dates differ each year. **1-8
Dec** is the festival of Iemanjá, with typical foods
and drinks, celebrations and offerings to the
goddess; also **8 Dec**, Nossa Senhora da Conceição.

⦿ Shopping

Recife *p490, maps p494 and 492*
Bookshops Almanque Livros, Largo do
Varadouro 418, loja 58. Bohemian atmosphere,
sells food and drink. **Livraria Brandão**, R da
Matriz 22 (used English books and some French

and German), and bookstalls on the R do Infante
Dom Henrique. **Livraria Saraiva**, Rua 7 de
Setembro 280. The best selection of Brazilian
literature in the city. **Livro 7**, R do Riachuelo 267.
An emporium with an impressive stock.
Melquísidec Pastor de Nascimento, a local
character, has a second-hand stall at Praça do
Sebo. **Sodiler** at Guararapes airport has books in
English, newspapers, magazines; also in the
Shopping Center Recife.
Markets Afogados market. For herbal
remedies and spices. **Cais de alfandega**, Recife
Barrio, market of local work, 1st weekend of every
month. **Casa da Cultura**; the permanent craft
market. Prices for ceramic figurines are lower
than Caruaru. **Domingo na Rua**, Sun market in
Recife Barrio, with stalls of local artesanato and
performances. **Hippy fair** at Praça Boa Viagem,
on the sea front, wooden statues of saints,
weekend only. **Mercado São José** (1875) for local
products and handicrafts. **Sítio Trindade**, Casa
Amarela. Sat craft fair. On 23 Apr, here and in the
Pátio de São Pedro, you can see the *xangô* dance.
Shopping malls Shopping Center Recife
between Boa Viagem and the airport. **Shopping
Tacaruna**, Santo Amaro, buses to Olinda pass it.

▲ Activities and tours

Recife *p490, maps p492 and 494*
Diving Offshore are some 20 wrecks, including
the remains of Portuguese galleons, with diverse
marine life.
Mergulhe Coma, T3552 2355, T9102 6809 (mob),
atlanticdivingasr@hotmail.com. English speaking
instructors for PADI courses.
Seagate, T3426 1657/9972 9662, www.seaga
terecife.com.br. Daily departures and night dives.

⦿ Transport

Recife *p490, maps p492 and 494*
Air The Gilberto Freyre international airport, 12
km from the city in Boa Viagem, has been fully
refurbished and is now the best and most modern
in Brazil; with plenty of places for coffees and
magazines and boutiques of elegant little tourist
shops. T3322 4188. Internal flights to all major
cities. Bus to airport, No 52, US$0.60. Airport taxis
cost US$8 to the seafront. There is a bank desk
before customs which gives much the same rate
for dollars as the moneychangers in the lobby.
Bus City buses cost US$0.50-1; they are clearly
marked and run frequently until about 2300
weekdays, 0100 weekends. Many central bus
stops have boards showing routes. CID/SUB or
SUB/CID signs on the front tell you whether
buses are going to or from the suburbs from/to
the city centre (cidade). On buses, especially at

night, look out for landmarks as street names are written small and are hard to see. Integrated bus-**metrô** (see Train, below) routes and tickets (US$1.30) are available. Urban transport information, T158. See below for buses to Olinda and other destinations outside the city. Taxis are plentiful; fares double on Sun, after 2100 and on holidays; number shown on meter is the fare; don't take the taxi if a driver tells you it is km. **Porto de Galinhas** can be reached by bus from the southern end of Av Dantas Barreto, 8 a day, 7 on Sun, 0700-1700, US$2. Buses leave for **Igarassu** from Av Martins de Barros, in front of Grande Hotel, Recife, 45 mins, US$1.50.

The rodoviária, mainly for long-distance buses, is 12 km outside the city at São Lourenço da Mata (it is called Terminal Integrado dos Passageiros, or TIP, pronounced 'chippy'). T3452 1999. There is a 30-min metrô connection to the central railway station, entrance through Museu do Trem, opposite the Casa da Cultura, 2 lines leave the city, take train marked 'Rodoviária'. From Boa Viagem a taxi all the way costs US$26, or go to Central Metrô station and change there. Bus US$1.50, 1 hr, from the centre or from Boa Viagem. The train to the centre is much quicker than the bus. Bus tickets are sold at Cais de Santa Rita (opposite EMTU) and **Fruir Tur**, at Praça do Carmo, Olinda.

To **Salvador**, daily 1930, 12 hrs, US$43. To **Rio**, daily 2100, 44 hrs, US$100-150. To **São Paulo**, 1630 daily, 50 hrs, US$120-144. To **Foz do Iguaçu**, Fri and Sun 1030, 55 hrs, US$175. To **Brasília**, daily 2130, 39 hrs, US$125. To **Belo Horizonte**, daily 2115, 34 hrs, US$109. To **João Pessoa**, every 20-30 mins, 2 hrs, US$5. To **Caruaru**, see below. Buses to Olinda, see below; to beaches beyond Olinda from Av Dantas behind the post office. To **Cabo** (every 20 mins) and beaches south of Recife from Cais de Santa Rita. **Train** Commuter services, known as the **Metrô** (but not underground), leave from the central station; they serve the rodoviária (frequent trains, 0500-2300, US$0.60 single). To reach the airport, get off the Metrô at Central station (not Joana Bezerra, which is unsafe) and take a bus or taxi (US$15) to Boa Viagem.

❶ Directory

Recife p490, maps p492 and 494
Airline offices BRA, T3327 9911, or airport T3464 4655. **Gol**, T3464 4793. **TAM**, airport T3462 6799/0800-123100. **TAP**, Praça Min Salgado Filho, Imbiribeira, T3465 0300. **Trip**, at airport, T3464 4610. **Varig**, T4003 7000, at airport T3322 4809. **Banks** Banks open 1000-1600, hours for exchange vary 1000-1400, sometimes later. **Banco do Brasil**, Shopping Centre Boa Viagem (Visa), helpful. MasterCard, cash against card, Av Conselheiro Aguiar 3924, Boa Viagem. **Citibank**, Av Marques de

Olinda 126 and Av Cons Aguiar 2024, MasterCard with ATM. Also at branches of **HSBC**, eg Av Conde de Boa Vista 454 and Av Cons Aguiar 4452, Boa Viagem, and at **Banco 24 Horas**. Bradesco, at: Av Cons Aguiar 3236, Boa Viagem; Av Conde de Boa Vista; Rua da Concórdia 148; Getúlio Vargas 729; all have credit card facility, 24-hr ATMs but no exchange. **Exchange: Anacor**, Shopping Center Recife, loja 52, also at Shopping Tacaruna, loja 173. **Norte Câmbio Turismo**, Av Boa Viagem 5000, and at Shopping Guararapes, Av Barreto de Menezes. **Cultural centres British Council**, Domingos Ferreira 4150, Boa Viagem, T2101 7500, recife@britishcouncil.org.br. 0800-1500, reading room with current English newspapers, very helpful. **Alliance Française**, R Amaro Bezerra 466, Derby, T3222 0918, www.af.rec.br. **Embassies and consulates** Denmark, Av M de Olinda 85, Ed Alberto Fonseca 2°, T3224 0311, open 0800-1200, 1400-1800. **France**, Av Conselheiro Aguiar 2333, 6th floor, T3465 3290, consulfr@hotlink.com.br. **Germany**, R Antônio Lumack do Monte 128, 16th floor, Boa Viagem, T3463 5350, info.recife@ alemanha.org.br, Mon-Fri 0900-1200, serving the Northeast. **Italy**, Av Domingos Ferreira 2222, 2nd floor, T3466 4200, www.consrecife.esteri.it. Mon, Wed, Fri 0930-1200, serving the Northeast. **Japan**, R Padre Carapuceiro 733, 14th floor, Boa Viagem, T3327 7264. **Netherlands**, Av Conselheiro Aguiar 1472, Sala 142, T3465 6704, consuladoholandes. rec@uol.com.br. **Sweden**, R Ernesto de Paula Santos, Boa Viagem, T3465 2940. **Switzerland**, Av Conselheiro Aguiar 4880, loja 32, Boa Viagem, T3326 3144. **UK**, Av Cons Aguiar 2941, 3rd floor, Boa Viagem, T2127 0230, recife@british consulate.org.br. 0800-1130. **US**, Gonçalves Maia 163, Boa Vista, T3421 2441, F3231 1906. **Internet** Internet access in bookshop (signposted) in Shopping Centre Recife in Boa Viagem. Also, **Lidernet**, Shopping Boa Vista, city centre. **popul@r.net**, R Barão de Souza Leão, near junction with Av Boa Viagem. Daily 0900-2100. **Medical services** Unimed, Av Bernardo Vieira de Melo 1496, Guararapes, T3462 1955/3461 1530, general medical treatment. **Unicordis**, Av Conselheiro Aguiar 1980, Boa Viagem, T3326 5237, equipped for cardiac emergencies; also at Av Conselheiro Roas e Silva 258, Aflitos, T421 1000. **Note** Dengue fever has been resurgent in Recife. **Post offices** Including poste restante, Central Correios, 50001, Av Guararapes 250. In Boa Viagem, Av Cons Aguiar e R Col Sérgio Cardim. **Telephones** Embratel, Av Agamenon Magalhães, 1114, Parque Amorim district; also Praça da Independência. **International telephones: Telemar**, Av Conselheiro Aguiar, Av Herculano Bandeira 231, and Av Conde da Boa Vista, all open 0800-1800. **Useful addresses** Ibama, Av 17 de Agosto 1057, Casa Forte, T3441 6338, F3441 5033. **Tourist Police**, T3326 9603/3464 4088.

Around Recife

"Around Recife" is a bit of literary license because this section deals with not only fine colonial towns not far from the state capital, but also the Fernando de Noronha archipelago, way out in the Atlantic. Of the former, Olinda is one of the best examples in Brazil and only minutes from Recife. In the drier interior is Caruaru, a fascinating market town. Fernando de Noronha, best reached from Recife (hence its inclusion here), has a wonderful marine environment and is ideal for those who are seeking a remote destination.

Olinda → *Phone code: 0xx81. Post code: 53000. Colour map 5, grid B6. Population: 367,902.*

The old capital of Brazil founded in 1537 and named a World Heritage Site by UNESCO in 1982 is about 7 km north of Recife. A programme of restoration, partly financed by the Netherlands government, was initiated in order to comply with the recently conferred title of National Monument, but many of the buildings are still in desperate need of repair. The compact network of cobbled streets is steeped in history and invites wandering. This is a charming spot to spend a few relaxing days and a much more appealing base than Recife.

Many of the historic buildings have irregular opening hours, but can be viewed from the outside. The **Tourist office** ⓘ *Praça do Carmo, T3429 9279, daily 0900-2100*, provides a complete list of all historic sites with a useful map, Sítio Histórico. Guides with identification cards wait in Praça do Carmo. They are former street children and half the fee for a full tour of the city (about US$15) goes to a home for street children. If you take a guide you will be safe from mugging which, unfortunately, occurs.

Olinda

Sleeping
7 Colinas **1**
Albergue do Fortim **9**
Olinda Hostel **2**
Pousada Alquimia **3**
Pousada do Amparo **4**
Pousada d'Olinda **5**

Pousada D'Olinda no
  Varadouro **10**
Pousada dos Quatro
  Cantos **6**
Pousada Peter **7**
Pousada São Francisco **8**
São Pedro **11**

Eating
Goya **1**
Maison do Bonfim **2**
Mourisco **4**
Oficina do Sabor **5**

Bars & clubs
Farandola **6**
Marola **3**

The **Basílica e Mosterio de São Bento** ① *R São Bento, Mon-Fri 0830-1130, 1430-1700, mass Sat 0630 and 1800; Sun 1000*, with Gregorian chant. Monastery closed except with written permission. Founded 1582 by the Benedictine monks, burnt by the Dutch in 1631 and restored in 1761, this is the site of Brazil's first law school and the first abolition of slavery. The magnificent gold altar was on loan to New York's Guggenheim Museum at the time of writing. Despite its weathered exterior, the **Convento de São Francisco** (1585) ① *Ladeira de São Francisco, Tue-Fri 0700-1130, 1400-1700, Sat 0700-1200, US$0.40, mass Tue 1900, Sat 1700 and Sun 0800*, has splendid woodcarving and paintings, superb gilded stucco, and azulejos in the Capela de São Roque within the church of **Nossa Senhora das Neves** in the same building. Make the short, but very steep, climb up to the **Alto da Sé** for memorable views of the city and the coastline stretching all the way to Recife. Here, the simple **Igreja da Sé** (1537) ① *Mon-Fri 0800-1200, 1400-1700*, a cathedral since 1677, was the first church to be built in the city. Nearby, the **Igreja da Misericórdia**(1540) ① *R Bispo Coutinho, daily 1145-1230, 1800-1830*, has fine tiling and gold work. On a small hill overlooking Praça do Carmo, the **Igreja do Carmo** church (1581) has been closed for several years, with restoration planned.

There are some houses of the 17th century with latticed balconies, heavy doors and brightly painted stucco walls, including a house in Moorish style at **Praça João Alfredo 7**, housing the Mourisco restaurant and a handicrafts shop, Sobrado 7. The local colony of artists means excellent examples of regional art, mainly woodcarving and terracotta figurines, may be bought in the Alto da Sé, or in the handicraft shops at the **Mercado da Ribeira** ① *R Bernardo Vieira de Melo* (Vieira de Melo gave the first recorded call for independence from Portugal, in Olinda in 1710). Handicrafts are also sold at good prices in the Mercado Eufrásio Barbosa, by the junction of Av Segismundo Gonçalves and Santos Dumont, Varadouro. There is a **Museo de Arte Sacra** ① *R Bispo Coutínho, Tue-Fri 0900-1300*, in the former Palacío Episcopal (1696). At R 13 de Maio 157, in the 18th-century jail of the Inquisition, is the **Museu de Arte Contemporânea** ① *same hours as Museu Regional*. The **Museu Regional** ① *R do Amparo 128, Tue-Fri 0900-1700, Sat and Sun 1400-1700*, is excellent. **Museu do Mamulengo** ① *Amparo 59, 0900-1800, Sat-Sun 1100-1800*, has Pernambucan folk puppetry.

The **beaches** close to Olinda are reported to be seriously polluted. Those further north from Olinda, beyond Casa Caiada, are beautiful, usually deserted, palm-fringed; at **Janga**, and **Pau Amarelo**, the latter can be dirty at low tide (take either a 'Janga' or 'Pau Amarela' bus, Varodouro bus to return). At many simple cafés you can eat sururu (clam stew in coconut sauce), agulha frita (fried needle-fish), miúdo de galinha (chicken giblets in gravy) and casquinha de carangueijo (seasoned crabmeat and farinha de dendê served in crabshells). Visit the Dutch fort on Pau Amarelo beach; small craft fair here on Saturday nights.

Igarassu → *Colour map 5, grid B6, Population 82,277.*

Igarassu, 39 km north of Recife on the road to João Pessoa, has the first church ever built in Brazil (SS Cosme e Damião, built in 1535), the Livramento church nearby, and the convent of Santo Antônio with a small museum next door. The church of Sagrado Coração is said to have housed Brazil's first orphanage. Much of the town (founded in 1535) is a National Monument.

Caruaru → *Colour map 5, grid C6. Population: 253,634. Altitude: 554 m.*

The paved road from Recife passes through rolling hills, with sugar cane and large cattle fazendas, before climbing an escarpment. As the road gets higher, the countryside becomes drier, browner and rockier. Caruaru, 134 km west of Recife, is a busy, modern town, one of the most prosperous in the agreste in Pernambuco. It is also culturally very lively, with excellent local and theatre and folklore groups.

Caruaru is most famous for its markets. The Feira da Sulanca is basically a clothes market supplied mostly by local manufacture, but also on sale are jewellery, souvenirs, food, flowers and anything else that can go for a good price. The most important day is Monday. There is also the Feira Livre or do Troca-Troca (free, or barter market). On the same site, Parque 18 de Maio, is the Feira do Artesanato, leather goods, ceramics, hammocks and basketware, all the popular crafts of the region. It is tourist-oriented but it is on a grand scale and is open daily 0800-1800.

The little clay figures (figurinhas or bonecas de barro) originated by Mestre Vitalino (1909-1963), and very typical of the Nordeste, are the local speciality; most of the local potters live at **Alto da Moura**, 6 km away (a bumpy 30-minute bus ride, US$0.65), where a house once owned by Vitalino is open (the **Casa Museu Mestre Vitalino**), with personal objects and photographs, but no examples of his work.

Fernando de Noronha → *1 hr behind Brazilian Standard Time.*
This small archipelago 345 km off the northeast coast was declared a Marine National Park in 1988. There are many unspoilt beaches and interesting wildlife and excellent scuba-diving and snorkelling. Only one island is inhabited and is dominated by a 321 m peak. It is part of the state of Pernambuco administered from Recife. The islands were discovered in 1503 by Amérigo Vespucci and were for a time a pirate lair. In 1738 the Portuguese built the Forte dos Remédios (begun by the Dutch), later used as a prison in this century, and a church to strengthen their claim to the islands. Remains of the early fortifications still exist.

Vila dos Remédios, near the north coast, is where most people live and socialize. At Baía dos Golfinhos is a lookout point for watching the spinner dolphins in the bay. On the south side there are fewer beaches, higher cliffs and the coastline and islands are part of the marine park.

All development is rigorously controlled by Ibama, to prevent damage to the nature reserve. Many locals are dependent on tourism and most food is brought from the mainland; prices are about double. Entry to the island is limited to two plane-loads per day. There is a daily tax of US$30 for the first week of your stay. In the second week the tax increases each day. Take sufficient reais as dollars are heavily discounted. For information, contact the national park office, Al do Boldró s/n Fernando de Noronho, Toxx81-3619 1289. The rains are from February-July; the island turns green and the sea water becomes lovely and clear. The dry season is August-March, but the sun shines all year round. No repellent available for the many mosquitoes. Further information: www.fernandonoronha.com.br.

● Sleeping

Olinda *p499, map p499*
Prices at least triple during Carnival when 5-night packages are sold. Rooms at regular prices can often be found in Boa Viagem during this time. All of the following, and even most of the cheaper hotels outside the old city, have a pool.

Historic centre
If you can afford it, staying in one of the converted mansions (pousadas) is the ideal way to absorb Olinda's colonial charm.
AL 7 Colinas, Ladeira de São Francisco 307, T/F3439 6055, www.hotel7 colinas.com.br. Spacious, new hotel with all mod cons in private gated grounds with a large swimming pool.
AL Pousada do Amparo, R do Amparo 199, T3439 1749, www.pousadoamparo.com.br. Olinda's best hotel is a gorgeous, 18th-century house, full of antiques and atmosphere in the Roteiros do Charme group. Rooms have four poster beds and each is decorated differently. The public areas include a spacious, art-filled foyer, a pool and sauna area surrounded by a little garden and an excellent, delightfully romantic restaurant.
B-C Pousada dos Quatro Cantos, R Prudente de Morais 441, T3429 0220, www.pousada4 cantos.com.br. A large converted town house with a little walled garden and terraces, bright rooms and suites decorated with Pernambuco arts and crafts, furnished mostly with antiques, welcoming and full of character.
C Pousada São Francisco, R do Sol 127, T3429 2109, www.pousadasaofrancisco.com.br. Well-kept and airy a/c rooms with terraces and pokey bathrooms. Pool and bar in pleasant gardens visited by hummingbirds in the early

morning, restaurant, parking. Outside the historic centre but within walking distance.
C-D Pousada Peter, R do Amparo 215, T/F3439 2171, www.pousadapeter.com.br. Rather small a/c rooms in converted town house, spacious lobby decorated with Pernambuco arts and crafts and colourful art work by the cantankerous German owner. Breakfast is served on the terrace overlooking distant Recife and the modest pool.
C-E Olinda Hostel, R do Sol 233, T3429 1592, www.alberguedeolinda.com.br. HI hostel, 8-bed rooms with fan and shared bath, also doubles, tropical garden, TV room, hammocks, small pool.
C-E Pousada d'Olinda, P João Alfredo 178, T/F3494 2559, www.pousadadolinda.com.br. Basic but well-kept dorms and doubles around a pool, garden and communal breakfast area, good breakfast, lunchtime restaurant, 10% discount for owners of Footprint Handbooks in low season, English, French, German, Arabic and Spanish spoken.
C-E Pousada d'Olinda no Varadouro, R 15 de Novembro 98, T3439 1163, www.pousadadolinda varadouro.com.br. Little suites in a converted town house and cheaper communal rooms, best are on upper floors, spacious open air dining area/restaurant and a small pool.
D São Pedro, R 27 Janeiro 95, T3439 9546, www.pousadapedro.com. Quiet, walled garden, small shaded pool, delightful breakfast area and lobby decorated with art and antiques. Rustic rooms are tiny but tasteful, a/c, best are on the upper floor.
D-E Albergue do Fortim, R do Sol 151, T3429 1939, www.pousadadofortim.com.br. Simple but clean rooms with a/c at the cheapest rates in Olinda. Some are big enough for 4. Breakfast US$2 extra.

Outside the historic centre
Hotels on R do Sol and in Bairro Novo are below the old city and on the roads heading north.
C Cinco Sóis, Av Ministro Marcos Freire 633, Bairro Novo, T/F3429 1347. A/c, fridge, hot water, parking.
D Pousada Alquimia, R Prudente de Morais 292, T3429 1457. Simple, lovely house, good breakfast, caring owners whose son is a painter with a workshop at the front.
D Cheiro do Mar, Av Ministro Marcos Freire 95, T3429 0101. Very good small hostel with some doubles (room No 1 is noisy), cooking facilities, ask driver of 'Rio Doce/Piedade' or 'Bairra de Jangada/Casa Caiada' bus (see Transport, below) to drop you at Albergue de Juventude on the sea front.
Camping Olinda Camping, R Bom Sucesso 262, Amparo, T3429 1365. US$5 pp, space for 30 tents, 5 trailers, small huts for rent, quiet, well-shaded, on bus route, recommended.

Caruaru p500
Cheap hospedarias are around the central Praça Getúlio Vargas. Lots of cheap lunch restaurants.
A Grande Hotel São Vicente de Paulo, Av Ur Branco 365, T3721 5011, F3721 5290. Good, a/c, central, laundry, garage, bar, restaurant, pool, TV.
C Centenário, 7 de Setembro 84, T3722 4011, F3721 1033. Also suites, good breakfast, pool, central, can be noisy, otherwise recommended.
C Central, R Vigário Freire 71, T3721 5880. Suites or rooms, all with a/c, TV, good breakfast, in the centre. Recommended.

Fernando de Noronha p501
LL Pousada Maravilha, T3619 1290. One of the finest beach hotels in South America. Luxurious bungalows (and smaller annex rooms on a hill overlooking the Bahia do Sueste. Understated good taste in the public areas which overlook an infinity pool and the Atlantic. Excellent restaurant, gym, sauna, massage and help with tours and services on the island. Transfer from Rio, São Paulo or Recife can be arranged.
LL Pousada do Vale, T3619 1293, www.pousada dovale.com. Well-run pousada, comfortable rooms, best are the duplex wooden bungalows. 300 m from Vila dos Remedios town centre.
LL Zé Maria, R Eunice Cordeiro 1, T3619 1258, www.pousadazemaria.com.br. Spacious bungalows with generous beds, verandahs with hammocks and views to the Morro do Pico, small deep-blue half-moon pool.
L-AL Solar dos Ventos, T3619 1347, www.pousadasolardosventos.com.br. Next to the Maravilha, shares the same spectacular view, but not in the sameleague, well-appointed bungalows, no pool.
A Pousada dos Corais, Residencial Floresta Nova, Quadra "D" Casa 07, T3619 1147,

www.pousadacorais.com.br. 8 small, plain a/c rooms around a little pool. Good breakfast.
C Verde Livre, Vila Remédios, T3619 1312. With a/c, TV, fridge and breakfast, simple but good.

🍴 Eating

Olinda p499, map p499
Several lanchonetes and fast-food options along the seafront. The traditional Olinda drinks, **Pau do Índio** (contains 32 herbs) and **Retetel**, are both made on the R do Amparo. Also try tapioca, a local dish made of manioc with coconut or cheese.
🍴🍴🍴 **Goya**, R do Amparo, 157. Regional food, particularly seafood, beautifully presented.
🍴🍴🍴 **Oficina do Sabor**, R do Amparo, 355. Consistently wins awards, pleasant terrace overlooking city, food served in hollowed-out pumpkins and lots of vegetarian options.
🍴🍴 **Maison do Bomfim**, R do Bonfim, 115. Serene, fan-cooled, rustic-style restaurant, French cuisine, as well as Brazilian and Italian.
🍴🍴 **Samburá**, Av Min Marcos Freire 1551. With terrace, try caldeirada and pitu (crayfish), lobster in coconut sauce or daily fish dishes, very good.
🍴 **Mourisco**, Praça João Alfredo 7. Excellent, good value food by weight in lovely, part-covered, garden, delicious deserts. Warmly recommended.

Fernando de Noronha p501
🍴🍴🍴 **Ecologiku's**, Estr Velha do Sueste, T3619 1807. Opened sided restaurant with a little garden, great Bahian food, delicious *moqueca*. Good *caipirinhas*.
🍴🍴🍴 **Porto Marlin**, Porto de Santo Antônio, T3619 1452. Good Japanese food à la carte with an all you can eat buffet on Thu and Sat from 1800.
🍴 **Jacaré**, Praça Pres Eurico Dutra (next to the Banco Real), T3619 1947. Best value on the island with lunchtime seafood and general Brazilian buffet.
🍴 **Açai e Raizes**, BR363, Floresta Velha, T3619 0058. Roadside sandwich bar with good snacks, puddings and delicious cream of *cupuaçu* and *açai*.
🍴 **Cia da Lua**, Bosque dos Flamboyantes, T3619 1631. Decent coffee, snacks, sandwiches, internet access and car and buggy rental.

🎵 Bars and clubs

Olinda p499, map p499
Every Fri night bands of wandering musicians walk the streets serenading passers-by. Each Sun from 1 Jan to Carnival there is a mini Carnival in the streets.
Beginning at dusk, but best after 2100, the Alto da Sé becomes the scene of a street fair, with arts, crafts, makeshift bars and barbecue stands, and impromptu traditional music; even more animated at Carnival. Plenty of funky bars on R do Sol.
Cantinho da Sé, Ladeira da Sé 305. Lively, good view of Recife, food served.

Farandola, R Dom Pedro Roeser 190, behind Carmo church. Mellow bar with festival theme and 'big-top' style roof. Warmly recommended.
Marola, Trav. Dantas Barreto 66. Funky wooden barraca on rocky shoreline specializing in seafood, great caiprifrutas (frozen fruit drink with vodka – try the cashew), can get crowded. Recommended.
Pernambucanamente, Av Min Marcos Freire 734, Bairro Novo. Live, local music every night.

Fernando de Noronha *p501*
Vila dos Remédios town has several bars; including a pizzeria with lively weekend forró from 2200 on weekends, and a bar with live reggae nightly in high season.

⊛ Festivals and events

Olinda *p499, map p499*
At Olinda's **carnival** thousands of people dance through the narrow streets of the old city to the sound of the frevo, the brash energetic music which normally accompanies a lively dance performed with umbrellas. The local people decorate them with streamers and straw dolls, and form themselves into costumed groups to parade down the R do Amparo; **Pitombeira** and **Elefantes** are the best known of these groups. **Foundation Day** is celebrated with 3 days of music and dancing, **12-15 Mar**, night time only.

Caruaru *p500*
17 Dec-2 Jan, Festas Natalinas; Semana Santa, Holy Week, with lots of folklore and handicraft events; **18-22 May**, city's anniversary. **13 Jun** Santo Antônio and **24 Jun** São João, the latter a particularly huge forró festival, are part of Caruaru's Festas Juninas. **Sep**, Micaru, a street carnival; also in **Sep**, Vaquejada (a Brazilian cross between rodeo and bull fighting), biggest in the northeast.

⚑ Activities and tours

Olinda *p499, map p499*
Viagens Sob O Sol, Prudente de Moraes 424, T3429 3303, transport offered to all parts, any type of trip arranged, also car hire.
Victor Turismo, Av Santos Domont 20, Loja 06, T3494 1467. Day and night trips to Recife.

Fernando de Noronha *p501*
Boat trips and jeep tours are available; it is also possible to hire a beach buggy. **Locadora Ilha do Sol**, T3619 1132, or 9985 4051, for buggy rental and guided tours of the island. You can hitch everywhere as everyone stops. There are good hiking, horse riding and mountain biking possibilities, but you must either go with a guide or ranger in many parts.

Diving Diving is organized by **Atlantis Divers**, T0xx81-3619 1371, **Águas Claras**, T3619 1225, in the hotel grounds, and **Noronha Divers**, T3619 1112. Diving costs between US$65-100 and equipment rental from US$65. This is the diving mecca for Brazilian divers with a great variety of sites to explore and fish to see.
Surfing Iaponã, T3619 1947, or 9635 7176, iapadosurf@hotmail.com. Classes from one of the island's best; US$25 per class including equipment.

⊖ Transport

Olinda *p499, map p499*
Bus From **Recife** take any bus marked 'Rio Doce', No 981 which has a circular route around the city and beaches, or No 33 from Av Nossa Senhora do Carmo, US$0.80 or 'Jardim Atlântico' from the central post office at Siqueira Campos; from Boa Viagem, take bus marked 'Piedade/Rio Doce' or 'Bairra de Jangada/Casa Caiada' (US$0.80, 30 mins). Change to either of these buses from the airport to Olinda: take 'Aeroporto' bus to Av Domingos Ferreira, Boa Viagem, and ask to be let off; and from the Recife Rodoviária: take the metrô to Central station and then change. In all cases, alight in Praça do Carmo. Taxi drivers between Olinda and Recife try to put meters onto rate 2 at the Convention Centre (between the 2 cities), but should change it back to 1 when queried (taxi to Recife US$10.50, US$16 to Boa Viagem at night).

Caruaru *p500*
Bus The rodoviária is 4 km from the town; buses from Recife stop in the centre. Bus from centre, at the same place as Recife bus stop, to rodoviária, US$0.50. Many buses from TIP in **Recife**, 2 hrs, US$6.

Fernando de Noronha *p501*
Air Daily flights from **Recife** with **Trip** and **Varig** (T3619 1952, 0900-1600) and Trip, 1 hr 20 mins, US$400 return. From Natal **Trip**, 1 hr, US$300 return.

❶ Directory

Olinda *p499, map p499*
Banks There are no facilities to change TCs, or ATMs in the old city. **Banco do Brasil**, R Getúlio Vargas 1470. **Bradesco**, R Getúlio Vargas 729, Visa ATM. **Bandepe** on the same Av has MasterCard ATM. **Internet** Study Web, Praça do Carmo, US$1.20, 30 mins, a/c. Olind@.com, Av Beira Mar 15, US$1.50, 30 mins. **Post offices** Praça do Carmo, open 0900-1700. **Telephones** International calls can be made at **Telemar** office on Praça do Carmo, Mon-Sat 0900-1800.

South of Recife

Two small states, Alagoas and Sergipe, are wedged between Pernambuco and Bahia. For no good reason, most people pass through, but there are some good examples of colonial architecture and, like the entire northeast coast, some fine beaches.

Important telephone changes All ordinary phone numbers in Brazil are changing from seven to eight figure numbers, a process still under way as this guide went to press. Where confirmed, eight-digit numbers have been included in the text, but if a seven-digit number doesn't work, try putting '3' as the first digit.

South to Alagoas

There are many interesting stopping points along the coast between Recife and Maceió. The main highway, BR-101, heads a little inland from the coast, crossing the state border near Palmares. It then continues to Maceió. On the coast the Pernambuco-Alagoas border is by São José da Coroa Grande, after which a coastal road, unpaved in parts, runs to Barra do Camaragibe. Just after the mouth of the Rio Camaragibe is Praia do Morro, Pedra do Cebola and Carro Quebrado, where beach buggies can be hired for trips up the coast. Further south is **Barra de Santo Antônio**, a busy fishing village, with a palm fringed beach on a narrow peninsula, a canoe-ride away. The beaches nearby are beautiful: to the south, near the village of Santa Luzia, are Tabuba and Sonho Verde. Two unspoilt fishing villages, which have good places to stay and are pretty much close to paradise are **Japaratinga** ① *Pousada Doze Cabanas, Toxx82-3297 1338, www.dozecabanas.com.br* (has been recommended) and **Maragogi** *www.maragogionline.com.br*; try **Pousada Mariluz** *Toxx82-3296 1511, www.pousada mariluz.com.br*. The natural pools at the reef of As Galés are beautiful; trips can be arranged at the Frutos do Mar restaurant.

Maceió and around → *Phone code: 0xx82. Post code: 57000. Colour map 5, grid C6.*

The capital of Alagoas state (*Population 797,759*) is mainly a sugar port, but for tourism it's friendly, safe and good value. Two of its old buildings, the **Palácio do Governo**, which also houses the **Fundação Pierre Chalita** (Alagoan painting and religious art) and the church of **Bom Jesus dos Mártires** (1870, covered in tiles), are particularly interesting. Both are on the Praça dos Martírios (or Floriano Peixoto). The **cathedral**, Nossa Senhora dos Prazeres (1840), is on Praça Dom Pedro II. The helpful **tourist office** is at Setur ① *R Boa Vista 453, Centro, T3315 5700* (also at airport and rodoviária). The municipal tourist authority is Seturma ① *R Sá e Albuquerque 310, T3336 4409*; information post on Pajuçara beach, by Hotel Solara. Also visit www.turismomaceio.com.br.

Lagoa do Mundaú, a lagoon whose entrance is 2 km south at **Pontal da Barra**, limits the city to the south and west: excellent shrimp and fish are sold at its small restaurants and handicraft stalls; a nice place for a drink at sundown. Boats make excursions in the lagoon's channels. Beyond the city's main dock the beachfront districts begin; within the city, the beaches are smarter the further from the centre you go. The first, going north, is **Pajuçara** where there is a nightly craft market. At weekends there are wandering musicians and entertainers. Further out, **Jatiúca**, **Cruz das Almas** and **Jacarecica** (9 km from centre) are all good for surfing. The beaches, some of the finest and most popular in Brazil, have a protecting coral reef a kilometre or so out. Bathing is much better three days before and after full or new moon, because tides are higher and the water is more spectacular. Jangadas take passengers to a natural swimming pool 2 km off Pajuçara beach (**Piscina Natural de Pajuçara**), at low tide you can stand on the sand and rock reef (beware of sunburn). You must check the tides, there is no point going at high tide. Jangadas cost US$5 per person per day (or about US$20 to have a jangada to yourself). On Sunday or local holidays in the high season it is overcrowded (at weekends lots of jangadas anchor at the reef selling food and drink).

By bus (22 km south), past Praia do Francês, the attractive colonial town and former capital of Alagoas, **Marechal Deodoro**, overlooks the Lagoa Manguaba. The 17th-century **Convento de São Francisco**, Praça João XXIII, has a fine church (Santa Maria Magdalena) with a superb baroque wooden altarpiece, badly damaged by termites. You can climb the church's tower for views. Adjoining it is the **Museu de Arte Sacra** ① *Mon-Fri 0900-1300, US$0.40, guided tours available, payment at your discretion*. Also open to visitors is the

Igreja Matriz de Nossa Senhora da Conceição (1783). The town is the birthplace of Marechal Deodoro da Fonseca, founder of the Republic; the modest **house** ⓘ *Mon-Sat 0800-1700, Sun 0800-1200, free,* where he was born is on the Rua Marechal Deodoro, close to the waterfront. On a day's excursion, it is easy to visit the town, then spend some time at beautiful **Praia do Francês**. The northern half of the beach is protected by a reef, the southern half is open to the surf. Along the beach there are many barracas and bars selling drinks and seafood; also several pousadas.

Penedo → *Phone code: 0xx82. Post code: 57200. Colour map 5, grid C6. Population: 56,993.*

This charming town, some 35 km from the mouth of the Rio São Francisco, with a nice waterfront park, Praça 12 de Abril, was originally the site of the Dutch Fort Maurits (built 1637, razed to the ground by the Portuguese). The colonial town stands on a promontory above the river. Among the colonial architecture, modern buildings on Av Floriano Peixoto do not sit easily. On the Praça Barão de Penedo is the neoclassical **Igreja Matriz** (closed to visitors) and the 18th-century **Casa da Aposentadoria** (1782). East and a little below this square is the Praça Rui Barbosa, on which are the **Convento de São Francisco** (1783 and later) and the church of **Santa Maria dos Anjos** (1660). As you enter, the altar on the right depicts God's eyes on the world, surrounded by the three races, one Indian, two negroes and the whites at the bottom. The church has fine trompe-l'oeil ceilings (1784). The convent is still in use. Guided tours are free. The church of **Rosário dos Pretos** (1775-1816), on Praça Marechal Deodoro, is open to visitors. **Nossa Senhora da Corrente** (1764), on Praça 12 de Abril, and **São Gonçalo Garcia** (1758-1770) ⓘ *Av Floriano Peixoto, Mon-Fri 0800-1200, 1400-1700.* Also on Avenida Floriano Peixoto is the pink **Teatro 7 de Setembro** (No 81) of 1884. The **Casa de Penedo** ⓘ *R João Pessoa 126 (signs point the way up the hill from F Peixoto), Tue-Sun 0800-1800,* displays photographs and books on, or by, local figures. **Tourist information:** in the Casa da Aposentadoria.

An interesting crossing into Sergipe can be made by frequent ferry (car and foot passengers) from Penedo to **Neópolis**.

Aracaju → *Phone code: 0xx79. Post code: 49000. Colour map 5, grid C5. Population: 461,534.*

Capital of Sergipe founded 1855, it stands on the south bank of the Rio Sergipe, about 10 km from its mouth, 327 km north of Salvador. In the centre is a group of linked, beautiful parks: **Praça Olímpio Campos**, in which stands the cathedral, **Praça Almirante Barroso**, with the Palácio do Governo, and **Praças Fausto Cardoso** and **Camerino**. Across Av Rio Branco from these two is the river. There is a handicraft centre, the **Centro do Turismo** ⓘ *in the restored Escola Normal, on Praça Olímpio Campos, Rua 24 Horas, 0900-1300, 1400-1900;* the stalls are arranged by type (wood, leather, etc). The city's beaches are at **Atalaia**, 16-km by road, and the 30-km long **Nova Atalaia**, on Ilha de Santa Luzia across the river. It is easily reached by boat from the Hidroviária (ferry station), which is across Avenida Rio Branco from Praça Gen Valadão. For tourist information, try **Turismo Sergipe**, Travessa Baltazar Góes 86, Edifício Estado, T3179 1937, www.setur.se.gov.br.

São Cristóvão is the old state capital, 17 km southwest of Aracaju on the road to Salvador. It was founded in 1590 by Cristóvão de Barros. It is the fourth oldest town in Brazil. Built on top of a hill, its colonial centre is unspoiled: the **Museu de Arte Sacra e Histórico de Sergipe** contains religious and other objects from the 17th to the 19th centuries; it is in the **Convento de São Francisco** ⓘ *Tue-Fri 1000-1700, Sat-Sun 1300-1700.* Also worth visiting (and keeping the same hours) is the **Museu de Sergipe** in the former **Palácio do Governo** both are on Praça de São Francisco. Also on this square are the churches of **Misericórdia** (1627) and the **Orfanato Imaculada Conceição** (1646, permission to visit required from the Sisters), and the **Convento de São Francisco**. On Praça Senhor dos Passos are the churches **Senhor dos Passos** and **Terceira Ordem do Carmo** (both 1739), while on the Praça Getúlio Vargas (formerly Praça Matriz) is the 17th-century **Igreja Matriz Nossa Senhora da Vitória** ⓘ *Tue-Fri 1000-1700, Sat-Sun 1500-1700.*

Estância → *Colour map 5, grid C5*

On the BR-101, almost midway between Aracaju and the Sergipe-Bahia border, and 247 km north of Salvador, is Estância, one of the oldest towns in Brazil. Its colonial buildings are decorated with Portuguese tiles. The month-long festival of **São João** in June is a major event. There are pleasant hotels, but most buses stop at the Rodoviária, which is on the main road (four hours from Salvador).

505

😴 Sleeping → *See Telephone, page 347, for important phone changes.*

Maceió *p504*

It can be hard to find a room during the Dec-Mar holiday season, when prices go up. There are many hotels on Praia Pajuçara, mostly along Av Dr Antônio Gouveia and R Jangadeiros Alagoanos.

L Enseada, Av A Gouveia 171, T3214 3700, www.hotelenseada.com.br. 1980s business hotel on the waterfront with a pool and restaurant. Recommended.

AL Sete Coqueiros, Av A Gouveia 1335, T2126 7777, www.setecoqueiros.com.br. 3-star, a/c, TV, phone, good restaurant, pool.

A Velamar, Av A Gouveia 1359, T3327 5488, atendimento@hotelvelamar.com.br. A/c, TV, fridge, safes in rooms.

B Buongiorno, R Jangadeiros Alagoanos 1437, T3327 4447, vapini@ig.com.br. A/c, fridge, English-speaking owner, helpful.

B Casa Grande da Praia, R Jangadeiros Alagoanos 1528, T3231 3332, hcgpraia@matrix.com.br. A/c and TV, cheaper without. Recommended.

B Costa Verde, R Jangadeiros Alagoanos 429, T3231 4745. Bath, fan, good family atmosphere, English, German spoken.

B-D Pousada Cavalo Marinho, R da Praia 55, Riacho Doce (15 km from the centre), facing the sea, T3355 1247, www.pousadacavalo marinho.com. Use of bicycle, canoes and body boards including, hot showers, German and English spoken, tropical breakfasts, Swiss owner. Very highly recommended (nearby is **Lua Cheia**, good food and live music at night).

C Sol de Verão, R Eng Mário do Gusmão 153, Ponta Verde beach, T/F3231 6657. Small rooms without baths and some larger and more expensive a/c options with en suites.

Alagamar, R Prefeito Abdon Arroxelas 327, T3231 2246, alag@superig.com.br. Excellent hostel, good location and value. IH affiliated, requires reservations Dec-Feb, Jul and Aug.

Camping Camping Pajuçara, at Largo da Vitória 211, T3231 7561, clean, safe, food for sale.

Penedo *p505*

A São Francisco, Av Floriano Peixoto 237, T3551 2273, www.hotelsaofrancisco.tur.br. Standard rooms have no a/c, TV, fridge. Recommended except for poor restaurant.

B Pousada Colonial, Praça 12 de Abril 21, T3551 2355, F3551 3737. Luxo and suite have phone, TV and fridge, suites have a/c, spacious, good cheap restaurant, front rooms with view of Rio São Francisco.

C Pousada Estilo, Praça Jacome Calheiros 79, T3551 2465. Cheaper without TV, quiet, river views, very nice.

C Turista, R Siqueira Campos 143, T3551 2237. With bath, fan, hot water. Recommended.

Aracaju *p505*

A range of hotels in the centre, including:

A Grande, R Itabaianinha 371, T3211 1383, F3211 1388. A/c, TV, fridge, central, **Quartier Latin** restaurant.

B Brasília, R Laranjeiras 580, T3214 2964, F3214 1023. Good value, good breakfasts. Recommended.

🍴 Eating

Maceió *p504*

Local specialities include oysters, *pitu*, a crayfish (now becoming scarce), and *sururu*, a kind of cockle. Local ice cream, Shups, recommended. Many good bars and restaurants in Pajuçara, eg on Av Antônio Gouveia. The beaches for 5 km from the beginning of Pajuçara to Cruz das Almas in the north are lined with barracas (thatched bars), providing music, snacks and meals until 2400 (later at weekends). Vendors on the beach sell beer and food during the day: clean and safe. There are many other bars and barracas at Ponto da Barra, on the lagoon side of the city. Most hotels offer free transport to restaurants; ask at reception.

††† Spettus, Av Silvio Carlos Viana 1911, Ponta Verde. Excellent churrascaria, fine service and worth the expense.

†† Divina Gula, R Eng Paulo Brandão Nogueira 85, Jatiúca, T235 1016. Minas specialities, very good, huge helpings, also *cachaçaria*.

†† New Hakata, R Eng Paulo Brandão Nogueira 95, Jatiúca, T325 6160. Good Japanese with *rodizios* on Tue.

† Nativa, Osvaldo Sarmento 56. Vegetarian, good views.

† O Natural, R Libertadora Alagoana (R da Praia) 112. Vegetarian.

Aracaju *p505*

† Gonzaga, Rua Santo Amaro 181, T224 7278. Lunch only, good value, popular, excellent traditional dishes.

⊕ Festivals and events

Maceió *p504*

27 Aug: Nossa Senhora dos Prazeres; **16 Sep**: Freedom of Alagoas; **8 Dec**: Nossa Senhora da Conceição; **15 Dec**: Maceiofest, 'a great street party with trios elêctricos'; **Christmas Eve**; **New Year's Eve**, half-day.

⊙ Transport

Maceió *p504*

Air 20 km from centre, taxi about US$30. Buses to airport from near Hotel Beiriz, R João Pessoa 290 or in front of the Ferroviária, signed 'Rio Largo'; alight at Tabuleiro dos Martins, then 7-8 mins' walk to the airport, bus fare US$1.

Bus Frequent local buses, confusingly marked, serve all parts of the city. Bus stops are not marked: it is best to ask where people look as if they are waiting. The 'Ponte Verde/Jacintinho' bus runs via Pajuçara from the centre to the rodoviária, also take 'Circular' bus (25 mins Pajuçara to rodoviária); Taxis from town go to all the northern beaches, but buses run as far as Ipioca (23 km). The Jangadeiras bus marked 'Jacarecica-Center, via Praias' runs past all the beaches as far as Jacarecica. From there you can change to 'Riacho Doce-Trapiche', 'Ipioca' or 'Mirante' buses for Riacho Doce and Ipioca. To return take any of these options, or take a bus marked 'Shopping Center' and change there for 'Jardim Vaticana' bus, which goes through Pajuçara. Buses and kombis to Marechal Deodoro, Praia do Francês and Barra de São Miguel leave from R Zacarias Azevedo, near the ferroviária: bus US$1, kombi US$1.30 to Marechal Deodoro, 30 mins, calling at Praia do Francês in each direction. Last bus back from Praia do Francês to Maceió at 1800.

The rodoviária is 5 km from centre, on a hill with good views and cool breezes. Taxi, US$12 to Pajuçara. Bus to **Recife**, 10 a day, 3½ hrs express (more scenic coastal route, 5 hrs) US$12. **Maceió-Aracaju**, 5 hrs, US$12 with **Bonfim**. To **Salvador**, 10 hrs, 4 a day, US$40.

Penedo *p505*

Bus 451 km from **Salvador** (US$22, 6 hrs, daily bus 0600, book in advance), at same time for **Aracaju** (US$12). Buses south are more frequent from **Neópolis**, 6 a day (0630-1800) to Aracaju, 2 hrs, US$7. 115 km from **Maceió**, 5 buses a day in either direction, US$10.50, 3-4 hrs. **Rodoviária**: Av Duque de Caxias, behind Bompreço supermarket.

Aracaju *p505*

Bus Interstate rodoviária is 4 km from centre, linked by local buses from adjacent terminal (buy a ticket before going on the platform). To **Salvador**, 6-7 hrs, 11 a day with **Bonfim**, US$22.

João Pessoa → *Phone code: 0xx83. Post code: 58000. Colour map 5, grid B6. Pop: 597,934.*

It is a bus ride of two hours through sugar plantations over a good road from Recife (126 km) to João Pessoa, capital of the State of Paraíba on the Rio Paraíba. It's a pleasant, historical town with a rich cultural heritage. The beaches, beside the turquoise waters of the Atlantic, are wonderful. At Ponta do Seixas is the most easterly point in Brazil; near here the Transamazônica highway begins its immense, if not controversial, route west into the heart of the country. The city tourist office is **SETUR**, ⓘ *Praça Pedro Américo s/n, T3218-9852, www.joaopessoa.pb.gov.br/secretarias/setur/* and there is a **Centro Turístico** at ⓘ *Av Almte Tamandaré 100, Tambaú, T3214-8270*. The **Secretaria de Turismo** (Setde) is at Jaguaribe ⓘ *Av João da Mata s/n, Bloco 2, 1st floor, T3218 4400, www.setde.pb.gov.br*.

Sights

João Pessoa is a capital that retains a small town atmosphere. In the **Centro Histórico** is the São Francisco Cultural Centre (Praça São Francisco 221), one of the most important baroque structures in Brazil, with the beautiful church of **São Francisco** which houses the **Museu Sacro e de Arte Popular** ⓘ *Tue-Sat 0800-1100, Tue-Sun 1400-1700*. Other tourist points include the **Casa da Pólvora**, now the **Museu Fotográfico Walfredo Rodríguez** (Ladeira de São Francisco) ⓘ *Mon-Fri 0800-1200, 1330-1700*. Also the **Teatro Santa Roza** (1886) ⓘ *Praça Pedro Américo, Varadouro, Mon-Fri 1400-1800*. João Pessoa's parks include the 17-ha **Parque Arruda Câmara**, north of the centre, and **Parque Solon de Lucena** or **Lagoa**, a lake surrounded by impressive palms in the centre of town, the city's main avenues and bus lines go around it.

The beachfront stretches for some 30 km from Ponta do Seixas (south) to the port of **Cabedelo** (north), on a peninsula between the Rio Paraíba and the Atlantic Ocean. This is Km 0 of the Transamazônica highway. The ocean is turquoise green and there is a backdrop of lush coastal vegetation. About 7 km from the city centre, following Avenida Presidente Epitáceo Pessoa is the beach of **Tambaú** (take bus No 510 'Tambaú' from outside the rodoviária or the city centre, alight at Hotel Tropical Tambaú), which has many hotels and restaurants. Regional crafts, including lace-work, embroidery and ceramics are available at Mercado de Artesanato, Centro de Turismo, Almte Tamandaré 100. The town's main attractions are its beaches, where most tourists stay. About 14 km south of the centre is the Cabo Branco lighthouse at Ponta do Seixas, the most easterly point of continental Brazil and South America; there is a panoramic view from the cliff top. **Cabo Branco** is much better for swimming than **Tambaú**. Take bus 507 'Cabo Branco' from outside the rodoviária to the end of the line; hike up to the lighthouse.

The best known beach of the state is **Tambaba**, the only official nudist beach of the Northeast, 49 km south of João Pessoa in a lovely setting. Two coves make up this famous beach: in the first bathing-suits are optional, while the second one is only for nudists. Strict rules of conduct are enforced. Between Jacumã (many hotels, restaurants) and Tambaba are several nice beaches such as **Tabatinga** which has summer homes on the cliffs and **Coqueirinho,** surrounded by coconut palms, good for bathing, surfing and exploring caves.

Sleeping → *See Telephone, page 347, for important phone changes.*

João Pessoa *p507*
All those listed are at Tambaú, unless indicated otherwise:
L Tropical Tambaú, Av Alm Tamandaré 229, T2107 1900, www.tropicalhotel.com.br. An enormous round building on the seafront which looks like a military bunker and has motel-style rooms around its perimeter. Comfortable and with good service. Recommended.
L-AL Caiçara, Av Olinda 235, T/F2106 1000, www.hotelcaicara.com. A slick, business orientated place (Best Western) with a pleasant restaurant attached.
AL Xênius, Av Cabo Branco 1262, T3015 3519, www.xeniushotel.com.br. Popular standard 4-star with a pool, good restaurant and well kept but standard a/c rooms (low-season reductions).
A Royal Praia, Coração de Jesus, T2106 3000, www.royalhotel.com.br. Comfortable a/c rooms with fridges around a pool.
C-D Solar Filipéia, Av Incognito Coração de Jesus 153, T3247 3744, www.solarfilipeia.com.br. Brand new, very smart hotel with large, bright rooms with bathrooms in tile and black marble and excellent service. A real bargain.
C-D Tambía Praia, R Carlos Alverga 36, T3247 4101, www.tambiahotel.hpg.com.br. Centrally located and 1 block from the beach. Intimate, with balconies and sea view. Recommended.
C-D Villa Mare Apartment Hotel, Av Négo 707, T3226 2142, www.pbnet.com.br/openline/george. Comfortable apartments for 2 or 3 people with full amenities per night or from US$400-500 per month. Helpful staff. Recommended.
D Pousada Mar Azul, Av João Maurício 315, T3226 2660. Very clean large rooms, the best are on the upper level, right on the oceanfront road. Some have a/c and private bathrooms, others have fans. Well kept, safe and a real bargain.
D-E Hostel Manaíra, R Major Ciraulo 380, Manaíra, T3247 1962, www.manaira hostel.br2.net. Friendly, brand new hostel close to the beach, with a pool, internet, barbecue, cable TV and breakfast. A real bargain.

Eating

João Pessoa *p507*
There are few options in the centre, other than the stalls in Parque Solon de Lucena next to the lake, beside which are some simple restaurants. Every evening on the beachfront, stalls are set up selling all kinds of snacks and barbecued meats. At Cabo Branco there are many straw huts on the beach serving cheap eats and seafood.
¶¶¶ Adega do Alfredo, Coração de Jesus. Very popular traditional Portuguese restaurant in the heart of the club and bar area.
¶¶¶ Gulliver, Av Olinda 590, Tambaú. Fashionable French/Brazilian restaurant frequented by João Pessoa's upper middle classes.
¶¶ Mangaí, Av General Édson Ramalho 696, Manaíra. This is one of the best restaurants in the northeast to sample the region's cooking. There are almost 100 different hot dishes to choose from, sitting in copper tureens over a traditional wood-fired stove some 20 m long.
¶¶ Cheiro Verde, R Carlos Alverga 43. Self service, well established, regional food.
¶¶ Sapore d'Italia, Av Cabo Branco 1584, Standard Italian fare including pizza.

Bars and clubs

João Pessoa *p507*
There are many open bars on and across from the beach in Tambaú and Cabo Branco. The area known as Feirinha de Tambaú, on Av Tamandaré by the *Tambaú Hotel* and nearby streets, sees much movement even on weekend nights, with R Coração do Jesus being the centre. There are numerous little bars and *forró* places here.

Festivals and events

João Pessoa *p507*
Pre-carnival celebrations are renowned: the bloco Acorde Miramar opens the celebrations the Tue before Carnival and on Wed, known as **Quarta Feira de Fogo**, thousands join the Muriçocas de Miramar. Celebrations for the

patrones of the city, **Nossa Senhora das Neves**, take place for 10 days around **5 Aug**.

⚠ Activities and tours

João Pessoa *p507*
Half-day city tours (US$9), day trips to Tambaba (US$12) and Recife/Olinda (US$22).
Roger Turismo, Av Tamandaré 229, T3247 1856, www.rogerturismo.com.br. A range of tours, some English-speaking guides.

⊙ Transport

João Pessoa *p507*
Air Aeroporto Presidente Castro Pinto, Bayeux, 11 km from centre, T3232 1200; national flights. Taxi to centre costs US$19, to Tambaú US$31.
Bus Most city buses stop at the rodoviária and go by the Lagoa (Parque Solon de Lucena). Take No 510 for Tambaú, No 507 for Cabo Branco.

Rodoviária is at R Francisco Londres, Varadouro, 10 mins from the centre, T3221 9611; luggage store; PBTUR information booth is helpful. Taxi to the centre US$3, to Tambaú US$10. To **Recife** with Boa Vista or Bonfim, every 30 mins, US$5, 2 hrs. To **Natal** with Nordeste, every 2 hrs, US$13 convencional, US$15 executivo, 3 hrs. To **Fortaleza** with Nordeste, 2 daily, 10 hrs, US$45.

To **Salvador** with Progresso, 4 weekly, US$60, 14 hrs. To **Belém** with Guanabara, daily at 1000, US$90, 36-39 hrs.

⊙ Directory

João Pessoa *p507*
Airline offices BRA, R Corálio Soares de Oliveira 541, T3222 6222. **GOL**, at airport, T0300-789 2121. **TAM**, Av Senador Rui Carneiro 512, T3247 2400. **Banks** Banco do Brasil, Praça 1817, 3rd floor, Centro, helpful, or Isidro Gomes 14, Tambaú, behind Centro de Turismo, poor rates. MasterCard Cirrus and Amex cashpoints at **Banco 24 Horas**, kiosk in front of Centro de Turismo, Tambaú, and **HSBC**, R Peregrino de Carvalho 162, Centro. **PB Câmbio Turismo**, Visconde de Pelotas 54C, Centro, open Mon-Fri 1030-1630, cash and TCs. **Internet** Many cybercafés in Tambaú: at telephone office in Centro de Turismo, Almte Tamandaré 100. **Post offices** Main office is at Praça Pedro Américo, Varadouro; central office is at Parque Solon de Lucena 375; also by the beach at Av Rui Carneiro, behind the Centro de Turismo. **Telephones** Calling stations at: Centro de Turismo, Tambaú; Av Epitácio Pessoa 1487, Bairro dos Estados; rodoviária and airport. **Useful numbers** Polícia Federal, T194.

Natal → *Phone code: 084. Colour map 2, grid B6. Population: 713,000.*

Natal, capital of Rio Grande do Norte, located on a peninsula between the Rio Potengi and the Atlantic Ocean, is one of the most attractive cities of Brazil's northeast coast, as well as a popular destination for those seeking sun and good beaches. The air is said by NASA to be the second purest in the world, after Antarctica. The inventors of the beach-buggy must have had Rio Grande do Norte in mind as the dunes and strand that surround the city are ideal for daredevil stunts and whizzing along the open sands.

Ins and outs
Tourist offices Secretaria de Turismo do Estado (SETUR) ① *R Mossoró 359, Petrópolis, T232 2496, www.setur.rn.gov.br*. Information booths at **Centro de Turismo** ① *T211 6149 (see Shopping, page 514)*, **Avenida Pres Café Filho s/n** ① *Praia dos Artistas daily 0800-2100*, **Central do Cidadão** ① *Praia Shopping, T232 7234 (see Shopping, below, there is also a Policia Federal office here)*, **Cajueiro de Pirangi** ① *Parnamirim, T238 2347 (see Around Natal, below)*, **rodoviária** ① *T232 7310*, and **airport** ① *T643 1043*. For information T205 2428 (Disque Passagem), or, for the Policia Federal T204 5500, and for the Tourist Police T232 7404 (Delegacia do Turista).

Sights
The oldest part is the **Ribeira** along the riverfront where a process of renovation has been started. The **Cidade Alta**, or Centro, is the main commercial centre and Avenida Rio Branco its principal artery. The main square is made up by the adjoining **praças: João Maria, André de Albuquerque, João Tibúrcio** and **7 de Setembro**. At Praça André de Albuquerque is the old cathedral (inaugurated 1599, restored 1996). The small church of **Santo Antônio** ① *R Santo Antônio 683, Cidade Alta, Tue-Fri 0800-1700, Sat 0800-1400*, dates from 1766. It has a blue and white façade, a fine, carved wooden altar and a sacred art museum.

On a hill overlooking Ribeira is the **Centro do Turismo** ① *R Aderbal de Figueiredo 980, off R Gen Gustavo C Farias*, Petrópolis (see Bars and clubs, and Shopping, page 514). A converted prison with a wide variety of handicraft shops, art gallery, antique shop and tourist information booth, it offers good view of the Rio Potengi and the sea. At Praia do Forte, the tip of Natal's peninsula, is the **Forte dos Reis Magos** ① *T221 0342, 0800-1630 daily except Christmas Day, New Year and Carnaval, US$1*. The star-shaped fort was begun in 1598 and is now the city's main historical monument. Its blinding white walls contrast with the blue of sea and sky. You can wander round the interior rooms, mostly empty although the former military prison now houses a lanchonete, and there are guides. The easiest way to get there is by taxi or on a tour; no buses go to the entrance, from where you have to walk along a causeway to the fort. Between it and the city is a military installation.

The **Museu Câmara Cascudo** ① *Av Hermes de Fonseca 1440, Tirol, T211 8404, Tue-Fri 0800-1700, US$1*, has exhibits on archaeological digs, Umbanda rituals and the sugar, leather and petroleum industries. **Museu do Mar** ① *Av Dinarte Mariz (Via Costeira), Praia de Mãe Luiza, T215 4433, Mon-Fri 0800-1130, 1400-1700, free*. It has aquariums with regional sea life and exhibits with preserved specimens. At Mãe Luiza is a lighthouse with beautiful views of Natal and surrounding beaches (take a city bus marked 'Mãe Luiza'). It is only open on Sunday, until 1700; at other times T221 2631.

A large ecological zone, the **Parque das Dunas**, separates the commercial centre from Ponta Negra, 12.5 km away, the beach and nightlife spot where most visitors stay.

Beaches
Natal has excellent beaches, some of which are also the scene of the city's nightlife. East of the centre, from north to south are: **Praia do Forte, do Meio, dos Artistas, de Areia Preta** and **Mãe Luzia**. The first two have reefs offshore, therefore little surf, and are appropriate for windsurfing. The others are urban beaches and local enquiries regarding pollution are recommended before bathing. Mãe Luzia marks the start of the **Via Costeira**, which runs south along the ocean beneath the towering sand dunes of **Parque das Dunas** (access restricted to protect the 9 km of dunes), joining the city to the neighbourhood and popular beach of Ponta Negra. A cycle path parallels this road and provides great views of the coastline. Lining Mãe Luzia and Barreira d'Água (the beach across from Parque das Dunas) are the city's four and five-star hotels.

Furthest south is vibrant and pretty **Ponta Negra**, justifiably the most popular beach. The seafront, Avenida Erivan França, is a car-free promenade for much of its length; the remainder is the busiest part of town. It has many hotels, from albergues up to three- and four-star, restaurants and bars (see page 514). The northern end of the beach is good for surfing, while the southern end is calmer and suitable for swimming. At the south end of the beach is **Morro do Careca**, a 120-m high dune with a sand-skiing slope surrounded by vegetation. Although no longer used for sand-skiing, it remains one of the 'postcards' of the city.

Ponta Negra

Sleeping ⊜	Maria Bonita 2 **2**	Pousada América do Sol **10**
Ingá Praia **6**	Miramar **7**	Pousada Maravista **11**
Lua Cheia **12**	O Tempo e o Vento **4**	Pousada Porta do Sol **9**
Manary Praia **1**	Pousada Castanheira **3**	Verdes Mares **13**

Around Natal

The coast south of the city is referred to as **Litoral Sul**, to the north as **Litoral Norte**. Dune buggies are the only way to travel here. Tours are available through travel agencies (see page 514).

Pirangi do Norte, 25 km from Natal, has calm waters, is popular for watersports and offshore bathing (500 m out) when natural pools form between the reefs. In the town is the world's largest cashew-nut tree (cajueiro maior do mundo, entry US$0.75); branches springing from a single trunk cover an area of some 8,400 sq m, a whole city block. A guide on site offers a brief explanation and there is a look-out for seeing the tree from above. Outside are handicraft stalls, tourist information and musicians.

Beyond Barreta is the long, pristine beach of **Malembar**, access on foot or by a five-minute boat ride across the mouth of the **Lagoa Guaraíra** from Tibau do Sul at the south end. The ferries to/from Tibau do Sul costs US$7 return; buggy drivers should not add this fee to a day tour. Crossings are determined by the state of the tide (times are critical and you should follow the buggy driver's instructions regarding departure times). Around **Tibau do Sul** the lovely beaches circled by high cliffs, the lagoons, Atlantic forest and the dolphins are some of the attractions that make this one of the most visited stretches of the southern coast (it can get crowded during holiday periods and weekends). South of town there are fine, wide, white-sand beaches, separated by rocky headlands, set against high cliffs and coconut groves.

At Praia do Madeiro and neighbouring **Baía dos Golfinhos**, the ocean is calm and clear and dolphins can often be seen (ask locally for the best time). Between Praia do Madeiro and Pipa, on a 70-m high dune, is the **Santuário Ecológico de Pipa** ⓘ *0800-1600, US$4*. This 60-ha park was created in 1986 to conserve the mata atlântica forest; there are 17 trails and lookouts over the cliffs which afford an excellent view of the ocean and dolphins.

Praia da Pipa, 3 km further south (85 km from Natal), is popular with Brazilians and foreigners alike, for its beautiful beaches and charming restaurants. The town is expanding rapidly and its nightlife is the talk of the area.

The coast **north of Natal** is known for its many impressive, light-coloured sand dunes, some reaching a staggering 50 m in height. A 25-minute ferry crossing on the Rio Potengi takes you from Natal to **Redinha**, an urban beach, with ocean and river bathing, and buggies to hire.

The best-known beach in the state, **Genipabu** is 30 km north of the city. Its major attractions are very scenic dunes and the Lagoa de Genipabu, a lake surrounded by cashew trees and dunes where tables are set up on a shoal in the water and drinks served. There are also many bars and restaurants on the sea shore. The dunes are a protected **Parque Ecológico** ⓘ *T9974 8265*, and only authorized buggy drivers are allowed to enter. All buggy tours go through the dunes and make the most of the vehicles' manoeuvrability on the fantastic slopes and hollows: prepare yourself for 'emoção'. At the top of a dune overlooking the lake and coast are lots of colourful umbrellas and handicraft stalls. **Camel rides** ⓘ *dromedários, T225 2053, www.dromedunas.com.br, US$19 for 2 people, 12-14 mins*, start from here. Less exotic are **donkey rides** ⓘ *starting at a mere US$0.65 per person*.

North of Genipabu is **Jacumã**, 49 km from Natal. At Lagoa de Jacumã, a lake surrounded by dunes, you can aerobunda, sit in a sling and fly on a cable into the water. Really refreshing. To get back up to the top of the dune you take the fusca funicular, a 'cable car' made from a trolley on a rail, powered by a wheel-less VW Beetle. All this for only US$1.75. Lovely beaches continue along the state's coastline; as you get further away from Natal the beaches are more distant from the main highways and access is more difficult. At **Maracajaú**, 63 km from Natal, low tide reveals an extensive area of shallow water where you can snorkel (US$15 including equipment), or dive (US$30); contact **Maracajaú Diver** ⓘ *T261 6200, 9983 4264 (mob), www.maracajau diver.com.br*. It's 7 km out to sea and launches (15 minutes) or catamarans (30 minutes) take tourists out to rafts anchored on the reef. You must check tide times before going here.

◉ Sleeping → *See Telephone, page 347, for important phone changes.*

Natal *p509*
The **Via Costeira** is a strip of enormous, upmarket beachfront hotels, which are very isolated, with no restaurants or shops within easy walking distance. **Ponta Negra** is the ideal place to stay, with its attractive beach and concentration of restaurants. Economical hotels are easier to find in the city proper but there is otherwise not much reason to stay there (no nightlife and a long way from the action). Prices of beach hotels below are for the high season (Dec-Feb and Jul), unless otherwise stated.

In the centre

LL Maine, Av Salgado Filho 1791, Lagoa Nova, T4005 5774, www.hotelmaine.com.br. On the principal avenue leading from the centre to Ponta Negra. Full service in this 4-star hotel, including free internet service, restaurant with panoramic views.

B Natal Center, R Santo Antônio 665, T3221 2355, natalcenterhotel@samnet.com.br. Business hotel in the city centre, rooms with a/c, fridge and TV, restaurant and pool.

C Casa Grande, R Princesa Isabel 529, T211 0555. 'Big house' built around family home, popular with business visitors. A/c, cheaper without bath (also low season discounts), good breakfast, pleasant, excellent value. Recommended.

D Natal, Av Rio Branco 740, Centro, T3222 2792, www.hotelnatal.com. On a busy part of the main street, well-established, a/c, cheaper with fan, popular with local guests.

Near rodoviária

There are several in the area, but the only reason to stay here is if arriving very late or departing very early.

B Pousada Esperança, Av Capt Mor Gouveia 418, T205 1955. With bath, a/c, cheaper with fan or without bath.

Beaches *p510*
Praia do Meio, Praia dos Artistas and Praia de Areia Preta

The distinction between these 1st 2 beaches is often blurred. Most hotels here are on the beachfront Av Pres Café Filho, the numbering of which is illogical. Many pousadas open for just 1 season, then close for good.

A Bruma, Av Pres Café Filho 1176, Praia dos Artistas, T/F2202 4303, hotelbruma@zaz.com.br. Slick, intimate, beachfront balconies, also has more expensive suites, pool, terrace. Recommended.

D Pousada do Paxá, Av Pres Café Filho 11, T202 2848. Clean, beachfront, breakfast extra, real bargain, but also has more expensive rooms. Recommended.

Ponta Negra *p510, map p510*

Here, too, the street numbering is pretty chaotic.

LL-L Manary Praia, R Francisco Gurgel 9067, T/F3204 2900, www.manary.com.br. Price depends on view from room; phone in advance as prices vary greatly according to month. This is a very stylish hotel on a quiet corner, some rooms overlook the pool/terrace and beach, all are very comfortable, 'neocolonial' design using local materials, member of the Roteiro de Charme group, see page 346. Recommended.

AL Hotel e Pousada O Tempo e o Vento, R Elias Barros 66, T/F3219 2526, www.otempoeo vento.com.br. **C** in low season, a/c, fridge, safe in room, pool and wet bar, clean, luxo rooms are very comfortable, good breakfast. Recommended.

A Ingá Praia, Av Erivan França 17, T3219 3436, www.ingapraiahotel.com.br. **B** without sea view, **C** in low season (service tax not included). Very comfortable, clean and cosy, rooms have all the expected facilities. Recommended.

A Miramar, Av da Praia 3398, T3219 2131. Price reduced by half in low season. Quite high up with good views, family-run, very clean, internet for guests 0800-1800, restaurant, 2 pools, games room, English spoken.

A-B Pousada Castanheira, Rua da Praia 221, T3236 2918, www.pousadacastanheira.com.br. **C** in low season, English/Brazilian owners, comfortable spacious rooms with TV, fridge and safe, small pool, breakfast room with sea view, room service, parking, very helpful staff. Recommended.

B Maria Bonita 2, Estrela do Mar 2143, T3236 2941, www.mariabonita2.com.br. With a/c, **C** with fan, not as close to the beach as most, but near the Broadway and its nightlife.

C Pousada Maravista, R da Praia 223, T3236 4677, www.pousadamaravista.com. One of the cheaper options, next to Pousada Castanheira, high-ceilinged rooms, hot showers, TV, fan, good breakfast, simple, English spoken, Marilyn is very welcoming. Recommended.

C Pousada Porta do Sol, R Francisco Gurgel 9057, T3236 2555, www.pousadaportadosol.com.br. Clean and tidy, good seafront location, TV, fridge, a/c except in rooms with sea breeze, some fans, good mattresses, excellent breakfast, pool, good value, English and French spoken (ask for Patrick or Suerda). Recommended.

D pp Lua Cheia, R Dr Manoel Augusto Bezerra de Araújo 500, Ponta Negra, T3236 3696, www.luacheia.com.br. HI hostel in 'castle' with 'medieval' **Taverna Pub** in basement (see Bars and clubs below). Includes breakfast. Highly recommended.

D Pousada América do Sol, R Erivan França 35, T3219 2245, www.pousadaamerico sol.com.br. Price per person in albergue-style rooms with bath, hot water, lockers, cheaper without a/c, popular, simple, use of kitchen, breakfast included. Also has pousada rooms at **B** (half-price in low season), a/c, TV, frigobar, includes breakfast, parking.

E pp Verdes Mares, R das Algas 2166, Conj Algamar, Ponta Negra, T236 2872, www.hostelverdesmares.com.br. HI hostel, **C-D** in double room, includes breakfast, discount in low season, quiet, comfortable. Also recommended.

Around Natal: Praia da Pipa *p511*

In Pipa more than 30 pousadas and many private homes offer accommodation. See www.pipa.com.br for some listings.

AL Ponta do Madeiro, Rota do Sol, Km 3, Tibaú do Sul, T3246 4220, www.pontado madeiro.com.br. Beautifully set in Mata atlântica with access to Madeiro beach, between Pipa and Tibaú, 3 types of chalet in gardens, pool, restaurant, trips on land and sea.

AL Sombra e Água Fresca, Praia do Amor, Km 1, T3246 2258, www.sombraeaguafresca.com.br. **A** in low season. A/c, fridge, pools, restaurant with beautiful view especially at sunset.

AL Toca da Coruja, Av Baía dos Golfinhos, T3246 2226, www.tocadacoruja.com.br. Comfortable chalets and rooms (cheaper in low season), with all facilities including safe in room, in gardens with lots of trees, quiet, member of the Roteiros de Charme group, see page 346.

A Pousada da Bárbara, 1st right after church in centre, T3246 2351, pousadadabarbara@ yahoo.com.br. **B** in low season, 20 m from town beach, rooms with a/c TV, hot shower and veranda, swimming pool, very good.

A Pousada Bicho Preguiça, R Praia do Amor 15, T3246 2128, www.pipabicho preguica.com.br. A variety of rooms with cable TV, a/c, frigobar, internet for guests, 24-hr restaurant and bars.

B-C Pousada Pomar da Pipa, R da Mata, T3246 2256, www.pomardapipa.com. 150 m from praça, quiet, beautiful garden, very helpful, good value.

C-D Vera-My house,T9988 5154, veramyhouse @uol.com.br. With bath, **E** pp in dormitory, use of kitchen, no breakfast. Good value, friendly. Recommended.

🍴 Eating

Natal *p509*

Prawns feature heavily on menus here as Natal is the largest exporter in Brazil.

🍴🍴🍴 **Raro Sabor**, R Seridó 722, Petrópolis. Exclusive bistro serving international dishes, emphasis on French cuisine. Closed Mon.

🍴🍴 **Bella Napoli**, Av Hermes da Fonseca 960, Tirol. Good Italian food.

🍴🍴 **Camarões Express**, Av Sen Salgado Filho 2234, Natal Shopping. Express prawns in 15 styles. Open for lunch only at weekends.

🍴🍴 **Mangaí**, Av Amintos Barros 3300, Lagoa Nova. Very good regional food (carne do sol, tapioca and many other sertaneja dishes) in rustic atmosphere, open 0600-2200, closed Mon. Recommended.

🍴🍴 **Marenosso**, in the Centro do Turismo. Specializes in seafood and local dishes like carne do sol, sweets, expresso coffee.

🍴🍴 **Thin-San**, Av Hermes da Fonseca 890, Tirol. Good Chinese food, popular.

🍴 **China Palace**, Av Afonso Pena 554, Petrópolis. For cheap lunches, a mixture of Chinese and Brazilian dishes, self-service.

🍴 **Habib's**, also in Natal Shopping. A branch of the cheap Middle Eastern food chain.

🍴 **A Macrobiótica**, Princesa Isabel 524, vegetarian, shop, lunch only. Next door is **Neide**, at No 530, for coffee and sweets.

Beaches: Ponta Negra *p510*

🍴🍴🍴 **Sobre Ondas**, Av Erivan França 14. Seafood and international dishes, average food, underwater theme, has internet.

🍴🍴🍴 **Tereré**, Rota do Sol 2316. All-you-can-eat barbecue, including Argentinian beef, ribs, as well as fish and salad.

🍴🍴 **Barraca do Caranguejo**, Av Erivan França 1180. Live music nightly from 2100. 12 different types of prawn dish for US$6.75, rodízio style.

🍴🍴 **Beterraba**, Av Erivan França 108, Santa Fe Mall. Upstairs, overlooking street and sea, specializes in grills and salads, fruit salads and juices.

🍴🍴 **Camarões**, Av Eng Roberto Freire 2610. Also at Natal Shopping Centre. Touristy, but very good seafood.

🍴🍴 **Cipó Brasil**, Av Erivan França 3 and Rua Aristides Porpinho Filho 3111 (behind Lua Cheia youth hostel). Jungle theme, 4 levels, sand floors, lantern-lit, dishes and rinks well-presented. Serves pizzas and crêpes (house speciality), good for cocktails, live music nightly after 2100. In the same group is **Casa de Taipa**, R Dr Manoel E B de Araújo 130A, next to Taverna Pub (see below), serving tapioca, salads, juices and coffee.

🍴🍴 **Ponta Negra Grill**, Av Erivan França 22. Large, several terraces, popular for steaks, seafood and cocktails, lively.

🍴 **Grande Muralha**, Av Erivan França 12, Casa Branca Center. Upstairs, Chinese, Japanese and Brazilian food with executive meals at good prices.

Cafés

Dulce France, Av Afonso Pena 628, Vila Colonial Shopping, corner of R Mossoró. Café selling crêpes, salads and coffee.

The malls in Ponta Negra have a variety of cafés and bars:

Ponta Negra Mall, Av Erivan França 24. Smart stalls sell sandwiches and snacks, also shops and Fellini restaurant. It can be accessed from Av Roberto Freire.

Santa Fe Mall, Av Erivan França 108. With Beach Café, Blackout Beer (popular in early evening), *Beterraba* restaurant (see above) and Bistro de Suisse for pizzas, pastas, meats and drinks.

❶ Bars and clubs

Natal *p509*

Ponta Negra beach is lively at night and the venue for a full-moon party, when there is live music all night.

Aquamarina Praia, Av Roberto Freire 22a, Ponta Negra. Pavement beachfront bar, attached to restaurant/hotel, large TV screen, open 24 hrs. Also has internet.

Blackout B52, Rua Chile 25. 1940s theme, best night is 'Black Monday'.

Centro de Turismo (see Shopping, below) has Forró com Turista, a chance for visitors to learn this fun dance, Thu at 2200; many other enjoyable venues where visitors are encouraged to join in.

Downtown Pub, Rua Chile 11. Four bars, dancefloor, games area, cybercafé, live bands, open Thu-Sat. Both popular bar/nightclubs are in the Ribeira district, in restored historic buildings.

Taverna Pub, R Dr Maneol, A B de Araújo, 500, Ponta Negra. Medieval-style pub in youth hostel basement. Eclectic (rock, Brazilian pop, jazz, etc.) live music Tue-Sun from 2200, best night Wed. Recommended. This street and the one that joins it by Taverna/Lua Cheia is known as 'Broadway', with lots of bars and cafés.

Zás-Trás, Rua Apodi 500, Tirol. Daily shows, except Sun, with a variety of local dances and presentations and a comedy act. Also has handicraft shops and a restaurant.

✦ Festivals and events

Natal *p509*

In **Jan** is the **Festa de Nossa Senhora dos Navegantes** when numerous vessels go to sea from Praia da Redinha, north of town. **Mid-Dec** sees **Carnatal**, the Salvador-style out of season carnival, a lively 4-day music festival with dancing in the streets.

❶ Shopping

Natal *p509*

Handicrafts Centro Municipal de Artesanato, Av Pres Café Filho, Praia do Meio. Daily 1000-2200. Sand-in-bottle pictures are very common in Natal. **Centro de Turismo**, R Aderbal de Figueiredo, 980, off R Gen Gustavo C Farias, Petrópolis. A converted prison with a wide variety of handicraft shops, art gallery, antique shop, café, restaurant and tourist information booth, offers good view of the Rio Potengi and the sea, open daily 0900-1900, Thu at 2200 is Forró com Turista (see above).

Shopping centres Natal Shopping, Av Senador Salgado Filho 2234, Candelária,

between Ponta Negra and the centre. Large mall with restaurants, ATMs, cinemas and 140 shops. Free shuttle bus service to major hotels. **Praia Shopping**, Av Eng Roberto Freire 8790, Ponta Negra. Smart shops, including **AS Livros** book and coffee shop (lojas 505-506); food hall with lots of options and a **Habib's**. There are more restaurants outside, mostly fast food, on Rua Praia de Genipabu. It also has internet, exchange (see Directory, below) and the **Central do Cidadão**. This facility has a tourist office (see above), post office, federal police office and Banco do Brasil with ATM; open Tue-Fri 1000-2200, Sat 1000-1800.

▲▲ Activities and tours

Natal *p509*

Boat tours To natural swimming pools at Pirangi do Norte, 25 km south of Natal, and to the nearby beaches of the Litoral Sul are available from **Marina Badauê**, Pirangi do Norte. A 2-hr tour includes hotel pick-up, a snack (or breakfast if you take an early tour), and allows time for a swim, US$11.15 per person. The company has a restaurant and bar at the seashore. Boat trips to Barra do Cunhaú, 86 km south of Natal, go through mangroves, visit an island and a salt mine with **Passeio Ecológico Cunhaú**.

Diving Miami Dive, T202 4727, natalnautica @natal.digi.com.br. For groups of up to 10, beginners' courses, dives up to 20 m. Associated with Império do Sol chalets in Pipa, T3246 2381, www.imperiodosol.com.br. See also Maracajaú, page 511.

Tour operators

A city tour costs US$20; if it includes the northern beaches US$25-30, including southern beaches US$40-45. Buggy tours are by far the most popular, US$100 for a full day in high season, US$85 in low season (shorter options are available). If you book direct with the buggy owner, rather than through a hotel or agency, there will be a discount. The price should include all commissions and ferry crossings. Buggy drivers (bugueiros) have an association (APCBA, R Projetada 405, Praia de Genipabu, Extremoz, T225 2061, www.angelfire.com/ nt2/apcbarn/) and all members must be approved by Setur and Detran. Look for the sign 'Autorizado Setur' plus a number on the buggy.

Cariri Ecotours, T3086 3601/3234 4068, www.caririecotours.com.br. Mainly 4WD tours throughout Ceará, the Sertão, Paraíba and Pernambuco, to natural monuments and archaeological sites, with a strong ecological emphasis. Also works with **Aventura**

(www.aventuraturismo.com.br) for coastal Land Rover trips. Trustworthy, excellent guides.
Cascadura Turismo e Viagens Ecológicas, R Praia de Bessa 2089, sl 101, Ponta Negra, T3219 6334, www.cascadura.net. Land Rover tours to beaches and the interior, to historical and cultural sites, also packages to Fernando de Noronha.

⊖ Transport

Natal *p509*
Air Aeroporto Augusto Severo, Parnamirim, T3644 1041. The airport has a tourist office, VIP Câmbio, ATMs, car hire, restaurants and shops.
Bus Rodoviária, Av Capitão Mor Gouveia 1237, Cidade da Esperança. Regional tickets are sold on street level, interstate on the 2nd floor. To **Recife**, 5 daily, US$19 convencional, US$31 executivo, 4 hrs. With **Nordeste** to **Mossoró**, US$19 convencional, US$31 executivo, 4 hrs. To **Aracati**, US$24, 5½ hrs. To **Fortaleza**, US$35, US$75 leito, 7½ hrs. To **João Pessoa**, see page 509. With **São Geraldo** to **Maceió**, buses both direct and via Recife, US$45 convencional, 10 hrs. To **Salvador**, US$95 executivo, 20 hrs. With **Boa Esperança** to **Teresina**, US$95 executivo, 17-20 hrs. To **Belém**, US$125, 32 hrs.
Taxi Taxis are expensive compared to other cities; US$12 for 10-min journey.

Around Natal *p511*
Pirangi do Norte
Bus From Natal, new rodoviária, **Viação Campos**, many daily, US$1.25 to Pirangi, 1 hr.

Tibau do Sul and Pipa
Bus From Natal **Transul**, 6 a day to Tibau do Sul and on to Pipa, and **Oceano** buses, T3203 2440, www.expresso-oceano.com.br, from the new rodoviária, several daily, US$4.80. **Oceano** and VW combis go to **Goianinha** from where buses run south to João Pessoa.
Buggy tours Rivatur, Tibau do Sul, T9982 8331 (mob), ask for Rivaldo, rivatur@uol.com.br. Tours south and north of Natal and to the interior and Paraíba; US$100 for 5 hrs, US$175 for 8 hrs, US$24 to Natal, with sightseeing. Also arranges boat (US$13) and horse rides (US$15).

Redinha
Bus Regular **Oceano** (address above), from the old rodoviária to Redinha.
Ferry Frequent ferry service for Redinha from **Cais Tavares de Lira**, **Ribeira** (Natal), weekdays 0530-1900, weekend and holidays 0800-1830, US$1 per person, US$6 for car. If on a buggy tour, the fare is included in the cost.

Genipabu
Bus Guanabara from the old rodoviária every 30 mins from 0530, till 2030.

Jacumã
Bus Riograndense, from **Natal**, 1100 and 1800 to **Jacumã** (0730 and 1800, Sun).

⊕ Directory

Natal *p509*
Airline offices BRA, Av Prudente de Morais 507, Petrópolis, T3221 1155, at airport, T3643 2132. **TAM**, Av Afonso Pena 844, Tirol, T3201 2020, at airport, T3087 1458, freephone 0800-570 5700. **Trip**, Av Prudente de Morais 4283, sala2, T3643 1450. **Banks** Banco 24 horas, Natal Shopping, Cirrus, Visa, MasterCard and Plus. **Banco do Brasil**, Seafront ATM, Ponta Negra for Cirrus, Visa, MasterCard and Plus. Also, Av Rio Branco 510, Cidade Alta, US$ cash and TCs at poor rates, cash advances against Visa, Mon-Fri 1000-1600. **Dunas Câmbio**, Av Roberto Freire 1776, Loja B-11, Capim Macio (east of Parque das Dunas), cash and TCs, 0900-1700. **Natal Câmbio**, in Natal Shopping, open Mon-Sat 1000-2200. **Ponta Negra Câmbio**, Av Erivan França 91, cash and TCs, Mon-Fri 0900-2200, Sat 1000-2100, Sun 0900-2000. **Praia Câmbio** in Praia Shopping, open Mon-Sat 0900-2200, Sun 0900-1700. **Sunset Câmbio**, Av Hermes da Fonseca 628, Tirol, cash and TCs, 0900-1700. **Car hire** BR Rede Brasil, Av Eng Roberto Freire 9100, Ponta Negra, T3236 3344, www.redebrasil natal.com.br. **Dudu Locadora**, Av Rio Branco 420, Centro. There are many other rental agencies on Av Eng Roberto Freire for cars and buggies. Buggy rental about US$45 a day, price depends on make. **Internet** Café Arte and LM in Galeria Princesa Isabel, Av Princesa Isabel, Centro, Mon-Fri 0800-190, Sat 0900-1400. Both US$2.80 per hr, former serves coffee and lunches. **InterJato** in Praia Shopping, US$0.55 for 10 mins, then charges 10 centavos per min. **International Center Call**, Av Erivan França 91, Ponta Negra, internet, scanner, international, cellular and card phones, open 0900-2200, Sun 1000-2000. **Sobre Ondas**, Ponta Negra (also bar and restaurant, see above), open 0900-2400, 15 centavos 1 min.
Post offices R Princesa Isabel 711, Centro; Av Rio Branco 538, Centro, Av Engenheiro Hildegrando de Góis 22, Ribeira, Av Praia de Ponta Negra 8920, Ponta Negra. **Telephone** R Princesa Isabel 687 and R João Pessoa, Centro; Av Roberto Freire 3100, Ponta Negra, Shopping Cidade Jardim, Av Roberto Freire, Ponta Negra; and rodoviária.

Fortaleza and the north coast

→ *Phone code: 0xx88 outside metropolitan Fortaleza, but prefix numbers beginning with 3 with 0xx85.*

The state of Ceará has been dubbed A Terra da Luz, Land of Light. It has some of the finest beaches in Brazil, scenic dunes and almost constant sunshine. The sophisticated capital, Fortaleza, is still home to jangadas (traditional fishing boats), while its nightlife is famous throughout the country. As well as the mysterious Parque Nacional de Sete Cidades, Piauí shares with Maranhão the remarkable Parnaíba delta, which is beginning to be recognized as a major ecological site with great tourist potential. The Parque Nacional Lençóis Maranhenses, across the delta, is a landscape of fabulous sand dunes and crystal lakes. Maranhão's capital, São Luis is one of Brazil's UNESCO sites of worldwide cultural importance, because of its colonial centre.

Fortaleza → *Phone code: 0xx85. Post code: 60000. Colour map 5, grid B5. Population: 2.1 million.*

Fortaleza, the fifth largest city in Brazil, is a busy metropolis with many highrise buildings, an important clothes manufacturing industry, many hotels and restaurants and a lively nightlife. Fishermen's *jangadas* still dot the turquoise ocean across from the beach and transatlantic cruise ships call in for refuelling. The mid-day sun is oppressive, tempered somewhat by a constant breeze; evening temperatures can be more pleasant, especially by the sea. The wettest months are March to July, known locally as 'winter'.

Fortaleza

Sleeping
Abrolhos Praia 1
Agua Marinha 8
Albergue Praia
de Iracema 11
Alfa Residence 14

Backpackers 21
Beira Mar 19
Best Western Colonial Praia 5
Big 16
Caxambu 3
Ibis 15

Imperial Othon Palace 7
Ondas Verdes 9
Passeio 10
Ponta Mar 6
Pousada Atalaia 4
Pousada Beleza Tropical 2

N
0 metres   200
0 yards   200

Ins and outs

Tourist offices Setur, state tourism agency ① *Centro Administrativo Virgílio Távora, Cambeba, T3101 4639, www.setur.ce.gov.br*. Information booths at Centro de Turismo, has maps, information about beach tours (0700-1800, Sunday 0700-1200); rodoviária (0600-1800 daily), airport (24 hours) and Farol de Mucuripe (0700-1730). **Disque Turismo** ① *24-hour 0800-991516*. Posta Telefônica Beira Mar, on Beira Mar almost opposite Praiano Palace, information, sells Redenção tickets to Jericoacoara, good range of postcards and clothes, papers and magazines.

Safety In Fortaleza avoid the Serviluz favela between the old lighthouse (Avenida Vicente de Castro), the favela behind the railway station, the Passeio Público at night, Avenida Abolição at its eastern (Nossa Senhora da Saúde church) and western ends. Also be careful at Mucuripe and Praia do Futuro. Generally, though, the city is safe for visitors.

Sights

Praça do Ferreira, from which pedestrian walkways radiate, is the heart of the commercial centre. The whole area is dotted with shady squares. **Fortaleza Nossa Senhora da Assunção** ① *Av Alberto Nepomuceno, daily 0800-1100, 1400-1700*, originally built in 1649 by the Dutch, gave the city its name. Near the fort, on Rua Dr João Moreira, is the 19th-century **Passeio Público** or Praça dos Mártires, a park with old trees and statues of Greek deities. West of here, a neoclassical former prison (1866) houses the **Centro de Turismo do Estado** (Emcetur) ① *Av Senador Pompeu 350, near the waterfront, T0800-991516, closed Sun*, with museums, theatre and high-quality craft shops (bargaining expected). It houses the **Museu de Arte e Cultura Populares** and the **Museu de Minerais**. Further west along Rua Dr João Moreira, at **Praça Castro Carreira** (commonly known as Praça da Estação), is the nicely refurbished train station **Estação João Felipe** (1880).

Brazil Fortaleza

	Eating ⑦	Estoril **4**	Santa Clara Café
Pousada do Suíço **12**	Alma Gêmea **1**	Habib **3**	Orgânico **1**
Pousada Jardim **13**	Amici's **1**	Ideal **9**	Xadrez **7**
Praia de Iracema **17**	Blau d'Fame **2**	La Fiorentina **8**	
Praiano Palace **18**	Brazão **2**	La Habanera **10**	
Seara Praia **20**	Colher do Pau **5**	Le Sandras **6**	
Villamaris **1**			

The **Teatro José de Alencar** ① *on the praça of the same name, T229 1989, Mon-Fri 0800-1700, hourly tours, some English speaking guides, US$1, Wed free*, was inaugurated in 1910. This magnificent iron structure was imported from Scotland and is decorated in neo-classical and art nouveau styles. It also houses a library and art gallery. The new **cathedral**, completed in 1978, in gothic style but built in concrete, stands beside the new, semi-circular **Mercado Central** with beautiful stained glass windows. Both are on Praça da Sé, at Avenida Alberto Nepomuceno. The **Museu do Maracatu** ① *Rufino de Alencar 231, at Teatro São José*, houses costumes of this ritual dance of African origin.

The **Centro Dragão do Mar de Arte e Cultura** ① *R Dragão do Mar 81, Praia de Iracema*, hosts music concerts, dance, and art and photography exhibitions. It has various entrances, from Ruas Almirante Barroso, Boris and from junction of Monsenhor Tabosa, Dom Manuel and Castelo Branco. This last one leads directly to three museums: on street level, the **Memorial da Cultura Cearense**, with changing exhibitions; on the next floor down is an art and cultural exhibit; in the basement is an excellent audio-visual museum of **El Vaqueiro**. Also at street level is the Livraria Livro Técnico. There is a planetarium with a whispering gallery underneath. The centre also houses a contemporary art museum (**Museu de Arte Contemporânea do Ceará**) ① *T3488 8617, www.dragaodomar.org.br, Tue-Thu 1000-1730, Fri-Sun 1400-2130, US$0.75 for entry to each museum/gallery, free on Sun*. This area is very lively at night.

Fortaleza has 25 km of beaches, many of which are the scene of the city's nightlife; those between **Barra do Ceará** (west) and **Ponta do Mucuripe** (east) are polluted. **Praia de Iracema** is one of the older beach suburbs with some original turn-of-the-century houses. East of Iracema, the **Avenida Beira Mar** (Avenida Presidente Kennedy) connects **Praia do Meireles** with Volta da Jurema and **Praia do Mucuripe**, 5 km from the centre. Fortaleza's main fishing centre, jangadas, bring in the catch here. **Praia do Futuro**, 8 km southeast of the centre, is the most popular bathing beach, 8 km long, unpolluted, with strong waves, sand dunes and fresh-water showers, but no natural shade; there are many vendors and barracas serving local dishes. Thursday night, Saturday and Sunday are very busy. A city bus marked 'P Futuro' from Praça Castro Carreira, 'Praia Circular', does a circular route to Praia do Futuro; a bus marked 'Caça e Pesca' passes all southeast beaches on its route. Praia do Futuro has few hotels or buildings because the salt-spray corrosion is among the strongest in the world. About 29 km southeast of the centre is **Praia Porto das Dunas**, popular for watersports including surfing; the main attraction is **Beach Park** ① *US$25*, a water park.

Northwest of the centre is **Praia Barra do Ceará**, 8 km, where the Rio Ceará flows into the sea. Here are the ruins of the 1603 Forte de Nossa Senhora dos Prazeres, the first Portuguese settlement in the area. The beaches west of the Rio Ceará are cleaner, lined with palms and have strong waves. A new bridge across this river gives better access to this area, for example, **Praia de Icaraí**, 22 km, and **Tabuba**, 5 km further north. Beyond Tabuba, 37 km from Fortaleza, is **Cumbuco**, a lively beach, dirty in high season, chaotic bars, horse riding, dunes which you can sandboard down into a rainwater lake, palm trees.

● **Sleeping** → *See Telephone, page 347, for important phone changes.*

Fortaleza *p516, map p516*
Almost all hotels offer reduced prices in the low season. There are many pousadas in the Iracema/Meireles area, but they change frequently.

In the centre
C **Caxambu**, Gen Bezerril 22, T3226 6656. Reduction in low season. a/c, TV, fridge, room service, with breakfast, probably best bet in centre (opposite Cathedral), good value.
D **Passeio**, R Dr João Moreira 221, Centro, T3226 9640, F253 6165. Opposite Passeio Público (which is not so enticing when the prostitutes are about) and near Centro Turismo, homely, rooms with high ceilings, a/c or fan, gloomy passages, good value.

E pp **Backpackers**, R Dom Manuel 89, T3091 8997. Central, basic, shared bathrooms, no breakfast, helpful owner.
E **Big**, Gen Sampaio 485, on Praça da Estação in centre, T3212 2066. All rooms with fan, cheaper without TV, even cheaper without bath, simple breakfast, OK, but caution needed at night, right in thick of the central scrum.

By the beach
LL-L **Imperial Othon Palace**, Av Beira Mar 2500, Meireles, T3466 5500, www.othon.com.br. Beach front location, large hotel with all facilities common to this group, business and tourists catered for, pool, sauna, massage (recommended feijoada on Sat).

Caros Amigos, R Dragão do Mar, 22. Live music at 2030: Tue, Brazilian instrumental; Wed, jazz; Thu, samba; Sun, Beatles covers, $US1 (also shows music on the big screen).
Restaurant e Crêperie Café Crème, R Dragão do Mar 92, live music on Tue.

⊛ Festivals and events

Fortaleza p516, map p516
6 Jan, Epiphany; Ash Wednesday. **19 Mar**, São José; Christmas Eve; New Year's Eve, half-day. The **Festas Juninas** in Ceará are much livelier than carnival. A festival, the **Regata Dragão do Futuro**, takes place at Praia de Mucuripe on the last Sun in **Jul**, during which the traditional jangada (raft) races take place. Also during the last week of Jul, the out-of-season Salvador-style carnival, **Fortal**, takes place along Avs Almte Barroso, Raimundo Giro and Beira Mar. On **15 Aug**, the local Umbanda terreiros (churches) celebrate the **Festival of Iemanjá** on Praia do Futuro, taking over the entire beach from noon till dusk, when offerings are cast into the surf. Well worth attending (members of the public may 'pegar um passo' – enter into an inspired religious trance – at the hands of a pai-de-santo). For 4 days in **mid-Oct** Ceará Music, a festival of Brazilian music, rock and pop, is held Marina Park.

○ Shopping

Fortaleza p516, map p516
Bookshops Livraria Livro Técnico, see Dragão do Mar, above, has several branches, on Dom Luis, Praça Ferreira, Shopping Norte and at UFC university. **Livraria Nobel** bookstore and coffee shop in Del Paseo shopping centre in Aldeota. **Siciliano**, bookstore and coffee shop in new part of Iguatemi shopping mall, with just a bookstore in the old part.
Handicrafts Fortaleza has an excellent selection of locally manufactured textiles, which are among the cheapest in Brazil, and a wide selection of regional handicrafts. The local craft specialities are lace and embroidered textile goods; also hammocks (US$15 to over US$100), fine alto-relievo wood carvings of northeast scenes, basket ware, leatherwork and clay figures (*bonecas de barro*). Bargaining is OK at the **Mercado Central**, Av Alberto Nepomuceno (closed Sun), and the **Emcetur Centro de Turismo** in the old prison (see above). Crafts also available in shops near the market, while shops on R Dr João Moreira 400 block sell clothes. Every night (1800-2300) there are stalls along the beach at Praia Meireiles. Crafts also available in the commercial area along Av Monsenhor Tabosa.

Shopping centres The biggest is **Iguatemi**, south of Meireles on way to Centro de Convenções; it also has modern cinemas. Others are **Aldeota** and **Del Paseo** in Aldeota, near Praça Portugal.

⚠ Activities and tours

Fortaleza p516, map p516
Diving Projeto Netuno/Manta Diving Center, R Oswaldo Cruz 2453, Dionísio Torres, T3264 4114, www.pnetuno.com.br.
Surfing Surfing is popular on a number of Ceará beaches. Kite surfing also catching on.
Trekking The Fortaleza chapter of the Trekking Club do Brasil has walks once a month to different natural areas; visitors welcome, US$20 for transport and T-shirt, T212 2456.
Windsurfing A number of Ceará beaches are excellent for windsurfing. Equipment can be rented in some of the popular beaches such as Porto das Dunas and in the city. **Bio Board**, Av Beira Mar 914, T3242 1642, www.bio board.com.br. Looks after equipment for you, windsurf school, Açaizeiro Café with açaí, juices, sandwiches upstairs (opens 1000 till 2000, 1900 Sat, 1800 Sun), also travel agency. **Windclub**, Av Beira Mar 2120, Praia dos Diários, T9982 5449. Equipment rental, lessons also available.

Tour operators
Many operators offer city and beach tours. Others offer adventure trips further afield, most common being off-road trips along the beaches from Natal in the east to the Lençois Maranhenses in the west.
Ceará Saveiro, Av Beira Mar 4293, T263 1085. Saveiro and yacht trips, daily 1000-1200 and 1600-1800 from Praia de Mucuripe.
Dunnas Expedições, R Silva Paulet 1100, Aldeota, T3264 2514, www.dunnas.com.br. Off-road tours with a fleet of white Land Rover Defenders, experienced, environmentally and culturally aware, very helpful and professional staff. Recommended.
Martur, Av Beira Mar 4260, T263 1203. Sailing boat and schooner trips, from Mucuripe, same schedule as Ceará Saveiro.
Sunny Tour, Av Prof A Nunes Freire 4097, Dionísio Torres, T0xx85-9986 5689, also has a bus-cum-stand on Av Beira Mar near the craft fair. Offers beach tours (eg 3 in 1 day, 6 in 4 days, trips to Jericoacoara).

⊜ Transport

Fortaleza p516, map p516
Air Aeroporto Pinto Martins, Praça Eduardo Gomes, 6 km south of centre, T3477 1200. Airport has a tourist office, car hire, food hall upstairs, internet, Laselva bookstore and Banco do Brasil (changes cash, US$20 commission on TCs, open

1100-1500). Direct flights to major cities. Bus 404 from airport to Praça José de Alencar in the centre, US$0.80, also 066 Papicu to Parangaba and 027 Papicu to Siqueira, or luxury Guanabara service from Beira Mar via Iracema, a/c, US$1; taxis US$12 to centre, Av Beira Mar or Praia do Futuro, more at night depending on destination. Use Cooperativa Taxi Comum or Taxi Especial Credenciado.

Bus Rodoviária at Av Borges de Melo 1630, Fátima, 6 km south from centre. Many city buses (US$1) including 'Aguanambi' 1 or 2 which go from Av Gen Sampaio, 'Barra de Fátima-Rodoviária' from Praça Coração de Jesus, 'Circular' for Av Beira Mar and the beaches, and 'Siqueira Mucuripe' from Av Abolição. Taxi to Praia de Iracema, or Av Abolição US$10. There is a luggage store. Opposite the rodoviária is Hotel Amuarama, which has a bar and restaurant; there's also a lanchonete.

Nordeste: To **Mossoró**, 10 a day, US$15, **Natal**, 8 daily, US$35 executivo, US$75 leito, 7½ hrs. **João Pessoa**, 2 daily, US$45 semi-leito, 10 hrs. **Boa Esperança**, stops at Fortaleza on its Belém-Natal route only. **Itapemirim** to **Salvador**, US$77, 1900, 23 hrs. **Guanabara**, T256 0214, to **Recife**, 5 daily, US$59, 12 hrs, book early for weekend travel. **Guanabara** to **Teresina**, several daily, US$40, 10 hrs; to **Parnaíba** US$35; to **Belém**, 2 daily, US$80 executivo, 23 hrs. Piripiri, for **Parque Nacional de Sete Cidades**, US$30, 9 hrs, a good stop en route to Belém, also Guanabara, who go to **São Luís**, 3 daily, US$66, 18 hrs.

In **Ceará**: Guanabara to **Sobral** US$10, Ubajara 0800, 1800, return 0800, 1600, 6 hrs, US$15. Also Ipu Brasília to **Sobral** and to **Camocim** 1120, 1530. To **Majorlândia**, US$7.50.

○ Directory

Fortaleza *p516, map p516*
Airline offices BRA, T3261 1919, at airport T3477 1423. **TAM**, Av Santos Dumont 2849, Aldeota, T261 0916, T0800-570 5700. **Trip**, at airport T3477 1747 **Varig**, at airport, T3477 1720. **Banks** Banco do Nordeste, R Major Facundo 372, a/c, helpful, open 0900-1630. Recommended. TCs exchanged and cash with Visa at **Banco do Brasil**, R Barão do Rio Branco 1500, also on Av Abolição (high commission on TCs). **Banco Mercantil do Brasil**, Rua Major Facundo 484, Centro, Praca do Ferreira: cash against MasterCard. Cirrus/MasterCard ATM at international airport; others at **HSBC** and **Banco 24 Horas** throughout the city. ATM for Cirrus/MasterCard and Visa outside cinema at Centro Cultural Dragão do Mar. Also at Av Antonio Sales and Iguatemi Shopping. Exchange at **Tropical Viagens**, R Barão do Rio Branco 1233, **Libratur**,

Av Abolição 2194, open 0900-1800 Mon-Fri, 0800-1200 Sat; also has kiosk outside Othon hotel on Av Beira Mar which is open every day till 2300. Recommended. More câmbios on Av Mons Tabosa: eg **TourStar**, No 1587, **Sdoc**, No 1073.
Car hire Many car hire places on Av Monsenhor Taboso, and at its junction with Ildefonso Albano. **Brasil Rent a Car**, Av Abolição 2300, T0xx85-3242 0868. There are also many buggy rental shops. **Note** When driving outside the city, have a good map and be prepared to ask directions frequently as road signs are non-existent, or placed after junctions.
Embassies and consulates **Belgium**, R Eduardo Garcia 909, Aldeota, T3091 5185, consulbelce@ig.com.br. **France**, R João Cordeiro 831, Iracema, T3226 3470. **Germany**, R Dr Lourenço 2244, Meireles, T3246 2833, DghonkonsulBRD@aol.com. **Netherlands**, R Dom Luis 880, T3268 2700, consuladoholanda@tradetec.com.br. **Sweden** and **Norway**, R Leonardo Mota 501, Aldeota, T3242 0888, marcos@emitrade.com.br. **Switzerland**, R Dona Leopoldina 697, Centro, T3226 8057. **UK**, R Leonardo Mota, 501, Meireles, T3242 0888, annette@edsonqueiroz.com.br. **US**, Av Santos Dumont 2828, sala 708, T3486 1306.
Internet Many internet cafés around the city. **Beira Mar Internet Café**, Av Beira Mar 2120A, Meireles, open 0800-0200, US$2.60 per hr (discounts with receipt from Habib's), also international phones, coffee. Outside Avenida Shopping, Av Dom Luís 300, US$2.50 per hr. **Abrolhos Praia**, Av Abolição 2030, Meireles, part of hotel of same name, US$1.25 per hr, open daily0800-2000, closes 1400 Sat and all day Sun. **Cyber Net**, Av Beira Mar 3120 in small mall, smart, US$2.20 per hr. **Ligue.com**, Osvaldo Cruz in Beiramar Trade Center. **Cearápontocom**, Av Beira Mar e R dos Ararius, across from La Habanera. US$3 per hr, popular, cafés around it. **Internet Express**, R Barão de Aracati opposite Colonial Praia, opens 0800. Via Veneto Flat, Av Abolição 2324, has **C@fé Digital**, open to the public, US$2.25 per hr, open Sun evening. 2 doors from Pousada Casa Nossa is **Falô**, Av Abolição 2600 block, 0800-2000 daily, US$1.50 per hr, also phones. Others in Pôlo Comercial at Av Mons Tabosa e Ildefonso Albano. **Medical services** Instituto Dr José Frota (IJF), R Barão do Rio Branco 1618, T255 5000. Recommended public hospital. **Post offices** Main branch at R Senador Alencar 38, Centro; Av Monsenhor Tabosa 1109 and 1581, Iracema; at train station; opposite rodoviária. Parcels must be taken to Receita Federal office at Barão de Aracati 909, Aldeota (take 'Dom Luiz' bus). **Telephones** International calls from **Emcetur** hut on Iracema beach and from offices of **Telemar**; at rodoviária and airport.

Coast east of Fortaleza

Aquiraz, 31 km east of Fortaleza, first capital of Ceará which conserves several colonial buildings and has a religious art museum, is the access point for the following beaches: **Prainha**, 6 km east, a fishing village and 10 km long beach with dunes, clean and largely empty. You can see jangadas coming in daily in the late afternoon. The village is known for its lacework: you can see the women using the bilro and labirinto techniques at the **Centro de Rendeiras**. 18 km southeast of Aquiraz is **Praia Iguape**, another fishing and lacework village, 3 km south of which is **Praia Barro Preto**, wide, tranquil, with sand dunes, palms and lagoons. All these beaches have accommodation.

Cascavel, 62 km southeast of Fortaleza (Saturday crafts fair), is the access point for the beaches of **Caponga** and **Águas Belas**, where traditional fishing villages coexist with fancy weekend homes and hotels.

Some 4 km from **Beberibe**, 78 km from Fortaleza, is **Morro Branco**, with a spectacular beach, coloured craggy cliffs and beautiful views. Jangadas leave the beach at 0500, returning at 1400-1500, lobster is the main catch in this area. The coloured sands of the dunes are bottled into beautiful designs and sold along with other crafts such as lacework, embroidery and straw goods. Jangadas may be hired for sailing (one hr for up to six people US$30). Beach buggies (full day US$100) and taxis are also for hire. The beach can get very crowded at holiday times. There re pousadas, or you can rent fishermen's houses. Meals can also be arranged at beach-front bars. South of Morro Branco and 6 km from Beberibe is **Praia das Fontes**, which also has coloured cliffs with sweet-water springs; there is a fishing village and a lagoon. South of Praia das Fontes are several less developed beaches including **Praia Uruaú** or **Marambaia**. The beach is at the base of coloured dunes, there is a fishing village with some accommodation. Just inland is Lagoa do Uruaú, the largest in the state and a popular place for watersports. Buggy from Morro Branco US$45 for four.

Canoa Quebrada → *Colour map 5, grid B5. Visit www.canoa-quebrada.com.*

On the shores of the Rio Jaguaribe, **Aracati** is the access point to the southeastern-most beaches of Ceará; it is along the main BR-304. The city is best known for its Carnival and for its colonial architecture.

About 10 km from Aracati is Canoa Quebrada on a sand dune, famous for its labirinto lacework and coloured sand sculpture, for sand-skiing on the dunes, for the sunsets, and for the beaches. There are many bars, restaurants and forró establishments. Canoa Quebrada is beginning to suffer from unplanned development. To avoid biting insects (bicho do pé), wear shoes. There is nowhere to change money except Banco do Brasil in Aracati. In the second half of July the Canoarte Festival takes place, it includes a jangada regatta and music festival. South of Canoa Quebrada and 13 km from Aracati is **Majorlândia**, an attractive village, with many-coloured sand dunes and a wide beach with strong waves, good for surfing; the arrival of the fishing fleet in the evening is an important daily event; lobster is the main catch. It is a popular weekend destination with beach homes for rent and Carnaval here is lively.

Community tourism Some 120 km east of Fortaleza, in the district of Beberibe, is **Prainha do Canto Verde**, a small fishing village on the vast beach, which has an award-winning community tourism project. There are guesthouses (eg **E Dona Mirtes**, with breakfast, will negotiate other meals), houses for rent (**D Casa Cangulo**, or **Chalé Marésia**), restaurants (good food at Sol e Mar), a handicraft cooperative, jangada and catamaran cruises, fishing and walking trails. Each November there is a Regata Ecológica, with jangadas from up and down the coast competing. (For the regatta, Christmas and Semana Santa, add 30% to prices.) This is a simple place, which lives by artesanal fishing (ie no big boats or industrial techniques) and has built up its tourism infrastructure without any help from outside investors (they have been fighting the speculators since 1979). It's a very friendly place and foreigners are welcome to get to know how the fisher folk live; knowledge of Portuguese is essential. For information on Prainha do Canto Verde, see **www.prainhadocantoverde.com.br**. To get to Prainha do Canto Verde, take a São Benedito bus to Aracati or Canoa Quebrada, buy a ticket to Quatro Bocas and ask to be let off at Lagoa da Poeira, two hours from Fortaleza. If you haven't booked a transfer in advance, Márcio at the Pantanal restaurant at the bus stop will take you, US$4.

Ponta Grossa is near Icapuí, the last municipality before Rio Grande do Norte (access from Mossoró), from where you then head to Redonda. Ponta Grossa is down a sand road just before Redonda. Both Ponta Grossa and Redonda are very pretty places, nestled at the foot of the cliffs, but Ponta Grossa has its own community tourism development. One of the main attractions of Ponta Grossa is that, offshore, is one of the few places where manatees (*peixe boi marinho*) visit. You can try to spot them from the cliffs. Beach trips go from Canoa Quebrada to Ponta Grossa for lunch, but if you want to stay here, you need to speak Portuguese. Cabins for rent are under construction and there are restaurants/bars. The tourism coordinator is **Eliabe** ① *Toxx88-9964 5846*.

For further information on community tourism and the preservation of traditional ways of life in Ceará, contact **Instituto Terramar** ① *R Pinho Pessoa 86, Joaquim Távora, Fortaleza, Toxx85-3226 4154, www.terramar.org.br.*

● Sleeping → *See Telephone, page 347, for important phone changes.*

Canoa Quebrada *p523*
There are several pousadas in town. Villagers will let you sling your hammock or put you up cheaply (Verónica recommended, European books exchanged; Sr Miguel rents good clean houses for US$10 a day).

B Pousada Sete Mares, R Quatro Ventos 400, T3368 2247, www.pousada7mares hpg.com.br. A recommended pousada with a/c chalets, pool.

C Pousada California, R Nascer do Sol 136, T3421 7039, www.californiacanoa.com. Prices vary according to room and season, a/c, **E** pp in dorm, TV, pool, bar, internet, buggy tours, horse riding, kite surfing, book exchange, several languages spoken, use of kitchen.

C Pousada Lua Morena, R Principal, T3421 7030, www.canoaquebrada.com. A variety of chalets with direct access to beach, with a/c, fridge, TV, hot water, pool, good value, English, Dutch and German spoken.

C Pousada Quebramar, on the beach front, T416 1044. With breakfast, safe, hot water.

D-E Pousada Alternativa, R Francisco Caraço, T3421 7276, www.geocities.com/pousadaalternativa. Rooms with a/c and bath, cheaper with fan and without fridge, central, safe.

● Transport

Coast east of Fortaleza *p523*
Bus Daily bus service from Fortaleza rodoviária to **Prainha**, 11 daily, US$1.70; **Iguape**, hourly between 0600 and 1900, US$2. To **Caponga**: direct bus from Fortaleza rodoviária (4 a day, US$2.50) or take a bus from Fortaleza to Cascavel (80 mins) then a bus from Cascavel (20 mins). **São Benedito**, at Fortaleza rodoviária: to **Beberibe**, 10 a day, US$4; **Cascavel**, US$2.25; **Morro Branco**, 4 a day, US$4.50; **Canoa Quebrada**, 4 a day (5 on Sun), US$8; **Aracati**, 6 a day, US$7.750. **Natal**-Aracati bus via Mossoró, 6 hrs, US$15; from Mossoró (90 km) US$4.80, 2 hrs; **Fortaleza**-Aracati (142 km), besides São Benedito, Guanabara or Nordeste many daily, US$7.50, 2 hrs; Aracati-**Canoa Quebrada** from Gen Pompeu e João Paulo, US$1; taxi US$7.

Coast west of Fortaleza

Paracuru, a fishing port which has the most important Carnaval on the northwest coast, is two hours by bus from Fortaleza. West of Paracuru, about 120 km from Fortaleza and 12 km from the town of Paraipaba, is **Lagoinha**, a very scenic beach, with cliffs, dunes and palms by the shore; a fishing village is on one of the hills.

Some seven hours by bus and 230 km from Fortaleza is the sleepy fishing village of **Almofala**, home of the Tremembés Indians who live off the sea and some agriculture. There is electricity, but no hotels or restaurants, although locals rent hammock space and cook meals. Bathing is better elsewhere, but the area is surrounded by dunes and is excellent for hiking along the coast to explore beaches and lobster-fishing communities. In Almofala, the church with much of the town was covered by shifting sands and remained covered for 50 years, reappearing in the 1940s; it has since been restored. There is also a highly praised turtle project.

Jijoca de Jericoacoara (Gijoca) is near the south shore of scenic Lagoa Paraíso (or Lagoa Jijoca), the second largest in the state. There are pousadas on its shore. It is excellent for windsurfing as it has a 'comfortable' wind, very good for beginners and those gaining experience (Jericoacoara is for 'professionals'). There is also good for kite surfing. **Note** The low season, August to November, is the windy season.

Jijoca is one of the access points for **Jericoacoara**, or 'Jeri' (*Phone code*: oxx88). One of the most famous beaches of Ceará and all Brazil (if not the world), it has towering sand dunes, deserted beaches with little shade, cactus-covered cliffs rising from the sea and interesting rock formations. The most famous is the **Pedra Furada**, a rock arch by the sea. Its atmosphere has made it popular with Brazilian and international travellers, with crowds at weekends mid-December to mid-February, in July and during Brazilian holidays. Many places full in low season, too. Jericoacoara is part of an environmental protection area which includes a large coconut grove, lakes, dunes and hills covered in caatinga vegetation. The village east of Jeri, **Preá**, is much quieter, with simple fish restaurants (see Transport, page 529).

Parnaíba → *Phone code: 0xx86. Post code: 64200. Colour map 5, grid A4. Population: 132,282.*

Parnaíba is a relaxed, friendly place, with a regular connection here to Tutóia, for boats across the Parnaíba delta (see below). A tour in the delta costs US$25 per person. Porto das Barcas, a pleasant shopping and entertainment complex, has several good restaurants and a large open-air bar on the riverside. The tourist office, **Piemtur**, is at Rua Dr Oscar Clark 575 and at Porto das Barcas, T321 1532.

Parque Nacional Lençóis Maranhenses → *Colour map 5, grid A3.*

Crossing the Parnaíba delta, which separates Piauí from Maranhão, is possible by boat arriving in Tutóia: an interesting trip through swamps sheltering many birds. This truly amazing park has 155,000 ha of beaches, lakes and dunes, with very little vegetation and largely unstudied wildlife. It is a strange landscape of shifting white dunes, stretching about 140 km along the coast between **Tutóia** and Primeira Cruz, west of **Barreirinhas**. The best time to visit is during the rainy season (June-September), when the dune valleys fill with water. Reflections of the sky make the water appear vivid blue, a spectacular contrast against brilliant white sand. **Parque Nacional Lençóis Maranhenses** ① *national park office: Av Joaquim Soeiro de Carvalho 746, CEP 65590-000, Barreirinhas, Toxx98-349 1155*. Ribamar at **Ibama**, Avenida Jaime Tavares 25, São Luís, T231 3010, is helpful on walks and horse rides.

São Luís → *Phone code: 0xx98. Post code: 65000. Colour map 5, grid A3. Population: 870,028.*

The capital of Maranhão state, 1,070 km west of Fortaleza, founded in 1612 by the French and named after St Louis of France, is in a region of heavy tropical rains, but the surrounding deep forest has been cut down to be replaced by babaçu palms. It stands upon São Luís island between the bays of São Marcos and São José. The urban area extends to São Francisco island, connected with São Luís by three bridges. An old slaving port, the city has a large black population, and has retained much African culture. **São Luís** tourist office ① *Central de Informações Turísticas, Praça Benedito Leite, Centro, Mon-Fri 0800-1900, Sat-Sun 0900-1400*. **Setur** ① *R da Palma 83, Centro, www.saoluis.ma.gov.br/turismo/, Mon-Thu 1300-1900, Fri 0800-1400*. Also at the airport and rodoviária. See www.guiasaoluis.com.br and www.patrimonioslz.com.br.

The old part, on very hilly ground with many steep streets, is still almost pure colonial. The historical centre is being restored with UNESCO support and the splendid results (eg the part known as Reviver) rival the Pelourinho of Salvador. The damp climate stimulated the use of ceramic tiles for exterior walls, and São Luís shows a greater variety of such tiles than anywhere else in Brazil, in Portuguese, French and Dutch styles. The commercial quarter (R Portugal, also called Rua Trapiche) is still much as it was in the 17th century. One house on this street has been renovated as the **Casa do Maranhão** ① *Tue-Fri 0900-1900, Sat-Sun 0900-1800, free*, a showcase for the natural and cultural riches of the state, with displays of costumes and video presentations. The progress of the renewal of the historical centre can be seen in the 19th-century **Solar dos Vasconcelos** ① *R da Estrela, open from 0900 Mon-Fri, 1300 on Sat*.

The **Palácio dos Leões** (Governor's Palace) ① *Av Dom Pedro II, closed for refurbishment in 2007*, has beautiful floors of dark wood (jacarandá) and light (cerejeira), French furniture and china and great views from terrace. The restored **Fortaleza de Santo Antônio**, built originally by the French in 1614, is on the bank of the Rio Anil at Ponta d'Areia. The **Fábrica Canhamo** (CEPRAMA) ① *R São Pantaleão 1232, Madre de Deus, near Praia Grande, T3232*

2187, *Mon-Fri 0900-1900, Sat 0900-2000, Sun 0900-1300*, a restored factory, houses an arts and crafts centre. The **Centro da Creatividade Odylo Costa Filho** ① *R da Alfândego 200, Praia Grande, T231 4058, Mon-Fri 1300-1900*, is an arts centre with theatre, cinema, exhibitions, music, a bar and café; a good meeting place.

The best colonial churches are the **Cathedral** (1629), on Praça Dom Pedro II, and the churches of **Carmo** (1627), Praça João Lisboa, **São João Batista** (1665), Largo São João, **Nossa Senhora do Rosário** (1717), on Rua do Egito, and the 18th-century **Santana**, Rua de Santana. On Largo do Desterro is the church of **São José do Desterro**, finished in 1863, but with some much older parts.

The **Cafua das Mercês** ① *R Jacinto Maia 43, Mon-Fri 0900-1800*, is a museum housed in the old slave market, worth the effort to find: a building opposite the Quartel Militar. Also visit the Casa dos Negros, next door. **Museu de Artes Visuais** ① *Av Dom Pedro II, Tue-Fri 0900-1840, Sat-Sun 0900-1800, free*, has a collection of tiles, rare photographs, Marahnense artists and holds temporary exhibitions.

Alcântara → *Colour map 5, grid A3. Population: 21,291.*

Some 22 km away by boat is Alcântara the former state capital, on the mainland bay of São Marcos. Construction of the city began at the beginning of the 17th century and it is now a historical monument. There are many old churches, such as the ruined **Matriz de São Matias** – 1648, and colonial mansions (see the **Casa**, and **Segunda Casa, do Imperador**, also the old cotton barons' mansions with their blue, Portuguese tiled façades). In the Praça Gomes de Castro is the pillory, the **Pelourinho** (1648), also a small museum (0900-1300, US$0.25) and the **Forte de São Sebastião** (1663) now in ruins. See also the **Fonte de Mirititiua** (1747). Canoe trips go to **Ilha do Livramento**, good beaches, good walking around the coast (can be muddy after rain), mosquitoes after dark. A rocket-launching site has been built nearby.

São Luís historic centre

Sleeping → *See Telephone, page 347, for important phone changes.*

Coast west of Fortaleza *p524*
Jijoca de Jericoacoara
A-B Pousada do Paulo, Córrego do Urubu s/n, T0xx88-3669 1181, www.jericoacoara.tur.br/pousadadopaulo. Has a windsurf school, US$18.50 for beginner's course, US$20 equipment hire per hr, US$50 per day, longer rates negotiable. It's also a good place to stay (prices depends on season and cabin, lovely location with lake views, garden, beach, hammocks and various sizes of cabin, all very nice, some with TV and a/c; excellent restaurant, bar.

Jericoacoara
4-5-day packages for Reveillon are available, but prices rise steeply. Many places can be found on www.jericoacoara.tur.br. Ask around for families who take in guests.
LL-L Recanto do Barão, R do Forró 433, T3242 0685, www.recantodobarao.com. 21 rooms mostly for 3 to 5 (ie families, groups), nicely decorated with hibiscus theme, lots of hammocks, a/c, TV, fridge, hot shower, big rooms, upper balcony for sunset, pool, Land Rover tours. Good reputation.
A Casa do Turismo, R das Dunas, T669 2000, www.jericoacoara.com or www.casado turismo.com. Nice rooms, all a/c, hot shower, TV, some with upper floor with mattress. Information, tours, horse rental, Redenção bus tickets (only place selling them, 1030-1400 and 1730-2200), windsurf school, kite surf, sandboard rental, telephone calls, post office, exchange.
A-C Por do Sol, R das Dunas 50, T3669 2099, pordosoljeri@yahoo.com.br. Family atmosphere, lovely place to stay, with a/c or fan, buggy trips arranged. Recommended.
B Casa Nostra, R das Dunas, T3669 2035, www.jericoacoara.tur.br/casanostra/index.html. Nice rooms, good breakfast, money exchange, Italian spoken. Recommended.
B Isalana Praia, R Principal, T3660 1334, www.jericoacoara.tur.br/isalanapraiahotel/index.html. A/c, minibar, TV, very helpful, ask for Will Louzada.
B Pousada Papagaio, Beco do Forró, T3669 2142, www.jericoacoara.tur.br/pousadapapagaio/index.html. With bath, recommended, tours.
B Pousada Renata, T3669 2061, www.jericoacoara.tur.br/pousadadarenata. Owned by the sister of Fernanda at Pousada do Paulo at Jijoca. Patio with hammocks, breakfast, English, Italian and German spoken. Renata also has **Pousada do Serrote**, 100 m from Praia da Malhada, same phone, and 9961 5522 (mob), www.jericoacoara.tur. Br/pousadadoserrote.

B-C Pousada Azul, R das Dunas, T3669 2182, www.jericoacoara.tur.br/azulpousada. Under new ownership, redecorated, variety of rooms and suites.
C Calanda, R das Dunas (across from Casa do Turismo, by setting sun dune), T3669 2285, www.jericoacoara.tur.br/calanda. With solar energy, Swiss run, good rooms, good breakfast, restaurant with varied menu, good views, helpful, German, English and Spanish spoken, full moon party every month. Warmly recommended.
C Chalé dos Ventos, R São Francisco 50, T3669 2023, www.jericoacoara.tur.br/chaledosventos. Price depends on room, chalet on 2 floors, good views, great breakfast, nice atmosphere.
C Pousada do Véio, T3669 2015, www.jericoacoara.tur.br/pousadadoveio. All rooms with a/c, bath, hot water and fan, some have a/c and fridge.
D Pousada Tirol, R São Francisco 202, T669 2006. HI-affiliated, non-members pay more, also has double rooms at **B** (**C** in low season), with breakfast, hot water, safe, helpful, great fun. Recommended. Also has very busy cyber café, US$3 per hr – 10 mins free use for all guests.

Parnaíba *p525*
LL Cívico, Av Gov Chagas Rodrigues, T322 2470, www.hotelcivico.com.br. With a/c, good breakfast. Recommended.
AL Pousada dos Ventos, Av São Sebastião 2586, Universidade, T/F323 2555, www.pousada dosventos.com.br. Pool. Recommended.
C Pousada Chalé Suiço, Av Padre R J Vieira 448, Fátima, T321 3026, www.chalesuico.com.br. Cheaper without a/c or breakfast, bar, laundry, pool, tours arranged, wind-surfing, sandboarding, buggies and bikes.
D Pousada Rio Mar, Av São Sebastião 5013. Pleasant, quiet, TV, pool, good breakfast, helpful, many languages spoken. Other basic hotels in the centre.

Parque Nacional Lençóis Maranhenses *p525*
Tutóia
C Pousada Em-Bar-Cação, R Magalhães de Almeida 1064, T479 1219. On the beach, breakfast US$3. Recommended for good food and tiquira, a drink made of manioc.

Barreirinhas
C Pousada do Baiano, T0xx98-349 1130. Pousadas at Praia Cabure, 5 hrs by boat from Barreirinhas (or truck from Tutóia), friendly, fresh seafood daily.
C Pousada Igarape, R Coronel Godinho 320, Centro, T0xx98-3349 0641, igarape@backpacker.com.br. Clean, good.

C **Pousada Lins**, Av Joaquim Soeiro de Carvalho 550, T0xx98-3349 1494. Shared bath, good but shop around before taking their tours.

São Luís p525, map p526
Many cheap hotels can be found in R da Palma, very central (eg G **Pousada Ilha Bela**, safe), and R Formosa.
B **Pousada Colonial**, R Afonso Pena 112, T3232 2834, www.clickcolonial.com.br. In a beautiful restored, tiled house, a/c, comfortable. Recommended.
C **Lord**, R Nazaré 258, T/F3222 5544, facing Praça Benedito Leite, lord@elo.com.br. Comfortable, good breakfast. Recommended.
C **Pousada Solar dos Nobres**, R 13 de Maio 82, Centro, T3232 5705, www.pousadasolardosnobres.com.br. Bright, welcoming, superb breakfast, very good.
D **Hotel Casa Grande**, Rua Isaac Martins 94, Centro, T3232 2432. Basic, single, double, triple rooms, no a/c, big windows facing the bay. Recommended.
F pp **Solar das Pedras**, R da Palma 127, T/F3232 6694, www.ajsolardaspedras.com.br. Good breakfast, price is for dormitory, doubles are D, helpful, no a/c, lots of mosquitoes, but nice location.

Alcântara p526
Ask for hammock space or rooms in private houses, friendly but no great comfort; provide your own mineral water.
B **Pousada do Mordomo Régio**, R Grande 134, T3337 1197. TV, refrigerator, good restaurant.
C **Pelourinho**, Praça de Matriz 55, T3337 1126. Breakfast, good restaurant, shared bath. Recommended.

🍴 Eating

Coast west of Fortaleza: Jericoacoara p525
There are several restaurants serving vegetarian and fish dishes.
🍴 **Carcará**, R do Forró. Restaurant and bar, northeastern specialities, seafood and pastas, said to be "o mais fino" in town.
🍴 **Espaço Aberto**, R Principal. Meat dishes, delicious seafood, salads, pleasant atmosphere. Recommended.
🍴 **Naturalmente** On the beach. Nice atmosphere, wonderful crêpes. Recommended.
🍴 **Pizzaria Banana**, R Principal 26. Many choices of pizza, salads, sandwiches, good.
🍴 **Pizzaria Dellacasa**, R Principal, next to the phone office. Good variety of pizzas, pastas, salads, art gallery.
🍴 **Pizzaria Reggae**, R Principal. Another pizza place, with a Caribbean theme.

🍴 **Taverna**, R Principal. Cantina and restaurant, lovely pasta and pizza, crêpes, expresso coffee. Drinks.
🍴 **Tudo na Brasa**, R Principal. Recommended for the churrascaria.
🍴 **A Casa da Tia Angelita**, for tortas, tapiocas and other local fare.
🍴 **Tempero da Terra**, R São Francisco. Restaurant and lanchonete, comida caseira, meat and fish dishes, nothing fancy, but well cooked and tasty.

São Luís p525, map p526
R da Estrela has many eating places with good food and outdoor terraces (eg **Antigamente**, No 220, T3232 3964, and **Papagaio Amarela**, take in turns to open on Sun). R dos Afogados has many places for lunch. There is further choice in the São Francisco district, just across bridge. On Sun the old centre is largely closed and most people go to Praia Calhau to eat and relax.
🍴 **Cia Paulista**, R Portugal e R da Estrela. Good, simple food, cheap.
🍴 **Naturalista Alimentos**, R do Sol 517. Very good, natural foods shop and restaurant, open till 1900.

Alcântara p526
🍴🍴 **Bar do Lobato**, on the praça. Pleasant, with good, simple food, fried shrimps highly recommended.

🎵 Bars and clubs

Coast west of Fortaleza: Jericoacoara p525
Forró nightly in high season at R do Forró, Wed and Sat in low season, 2200. Action moves to bars when forró has stopped about 0200. There are also frequent parties to which visitors are welcome. Once a week in high season there is a folk dance show which includes capoeira. After forró, **Padaria Santo Antônio** opens, selling special breads, coconut, banana, cheese, 0230-0700.

☸ Festivals and events

São Luís p525, map p526
On **24 Jun** (São João) is the **Bumba-Meu-Boi**. For several days before the festival street bands parade, particularly in front of the São João and São Benedito churches. There are dances somewhere in the city almost every night in Jun. In **Aug**, São Benedito, at the Rosário church.

Alcântara p526
Principal festivals: Festa do Divino, at Pentecost (Whitsun); **29 Jun**, São Pedro; **early Aug**, São Benedito.

▲ Activities and tours

Coast west of Fortaleza:
Jericoacoara *p525*
Clube dos Ventos, R das Dunas, T3669 2288, www.clubedosventos.com. Same owner as Casa de Turismo, equipment hire US$18 per hr, US$44 per day for experienced, US$13 and US$31 for beginners, US$270 deposit (R$700). Basic course US$55.55, 3 hrs and up. Kite surfing at Preá and Lagoa Jijoca.
Jeri Off Road, T0xx88-3669 2022, 9961 4167 (Mob). João Gaúcho runs adventure trips in the area. Recommended, but popular. They also have a travel agency run by Paula Salles.
Buggy tours Cost US$44.45 for a buggy to all the sites. **Associação de Bugueiros**, ABJ, R Principal, barraca near Ibama. If seeking a bugueiro who speaks English, Spanish, Italian and French, ask for Alvaro, the school teacher, who is Uruguayan.

● Transport

Coast west of Fortaleza *p524*
Lagoinha
Bus from **Fortaleza**, 6 daily with **Brasileiro**, 3 hrs, US$3.50.

Almofala
Bus From **Fortaleza Redenção** to Almofala 0700, 1730, US$9.

Jijoca and Jericoacoara
Bus Redenção buses from Fortaleza to **Jijoca** and **Jericoacoara** from the rodoviária 1030, 1700 and the Av Beira Mar at the Posta Telefônica opposite Praiano Palace Hotel 30 mins later. The day bus goes via Jijoca and the night bus via Preá. The journey takes 6 hrs and costs US$18 one way. Always check times of the Redençao buses from Fortaleza as they change with the season. The night bus requires an overnight stop in Preá: make your own way to Jeri next day. A jardineira (open-sided 4WD truck) meets the Redenção bus from Fortaleza, at Jijoca (included in the Redenção price). Buses return from Jeri at 0730, 1400 (via Preá) and 2230 (via Jijoca); the jardineira leaves from Casa do Turismo (see above for ticket sale times). Hotels and tour operators run 2 or 3-day tours to Jeri from Fortaleza. If not on Redençao or a tour, 'guides' will besiege new arrivals in Jijoca with offers of buggies, or guiding cars through the tracks and dunes to Jeri for US$10. If you don't want to do this, ask if a pick-up is going: US$5 pp up front, 22 km, 30 mins. In a buggy it's US$25 per buggy.

If coming from Belém or other points north and west, go via Sobral (from Belém US$55, 20 hrs), where you change for Cruz, 40 km east of Jijoca, a small pleasant town with basic hotels (there is only one bus a day Sobral-Cruz, US$15, 3-4 hrs, but **Redenção** runs to **Cruz** from Fortaleza 4 times a day, US$14. Either continue to Jijoca the next day (Cruz-Jijoca, daily about 1400, US$2, meets jardineira for Jeri, Cruz-Jericoacoara, US$4) or take an horário pick-up Cruz-Jijoca.

An alternative from the west, especially if going through Parnaíba, is by buggy or jardineira from **Camocim** (a pleasant town at the mouth of the Rio Coreaú, facing the dunes on the eastern shore, which is 1½ hrs by road from Parnaíba. It has several hotels and eating places. You take a ferry across the river then the vehicle; they leave between 0900-1030. You can break the journey from Camocim to Jericoacoara at villages such as **Nova Tatajuba** (on the west margin of the outflow of Lagoa Grande; the beach is wide, dunes follow the shore, the ocean is clear and calm and there is a fishing village with a few basic pousadas), or **Guriú** where hammock space can be found. There is good bird watching here. Walk 4 hrs, or take a boat across the bay to Jericoacoara. The journey along the beach has beautiful scenery. In Jericoacoara ask around for buggy or jardineira rides to Camocim, about US$20 pp.

Parque Nacional Lençóis Maranhenses *p525*
Bus **Parnaíba-Tutóia**: bus, 4 hrs, US$13; river boat up the Parnaíba delta, 3 a week (ask at the port as departures depend on the tide), 8 hrs, US$13. Recommended. Private boat hire is also possible. **São Luis-Barreirinhas**: bus, 4 hrs on a new road, US$20. Ask at **Solar das Pedras** youth hostel about minivan trips, same price as bus. Private tour buses, US$30. 4WD trips into the park from Barreirinhas cost US$18. Plane (single propeller), 40 mins, US$70 pp. Recommended. A fabulous experience giving panoramic views of the dunes, pilots **Amirton**, or **Fénix** in Barreirinhas. Agencies arrange tours with flight.
Ferry Excursions from/to **Barreirinhas**: regular boat service between Barreirinhas and Atins (7 hrs return, US$10): boat along Rio Preguiça, 4 hrs then 1 hr walk to the dunes, US$24. The only forms of transport that can get across the dunes right into the park are a **jeep**

● *For an explanation of the sleeping and eating price codes used in this guide, see page 58.*
● *Other relevant information is found in Essentials pages 345-347.*

or a **horse**, both about US$30. It is a 2-3 hr walk from Barreirinhas to the park; you will need at least another 2 hrs in the dunes. At Mandacaru, a popular stop on tours of the area, the lighthouse gives a very impressive view.

Alcântara *p526*
Ferry
Ferries cross the bay daily, leaving São Luís dock or from São Francisco district at about 0700 and 0930, returning from Alcântara about 0830 and 1600: check time and buy the ticket at the hidroviária (west end of R Portugal, T3232 0692) the day before as departure depends on the tides. The journey takes 90 mins, return US$30, worth paying extra for 'panorámica' seat. The sea can be very rough between Sep and Dec. There are sometimes catamaran tours bookable through tour operators in São Luís, meals not included.

São Luís *p525, map p526*
Air Internal flights only, 15 km from centre, T3217 6133; buses ('São Cristovão') to city until midnight, US$1.
Bus Rodoviária is 12 km from the centre on the airport road, 'Rodoviária via Alemanha' bus to centre (Praça João Lisboa), US$1.
Bus to **Fortaleza**, US$66, 4 a day, 18 hrs. To **Belém**, 13 hrs, US$40, **Transbrasiliana**. Also to **Recife**, 25 hrs, and all other major cities and local towns.

⊙ Directory

São Luís *p525, map p526*
Banks TCs at Banco do Brasil, Praça Deodoro. HSBC, off Praça João Lisboa. Accepts Master Card/Maestro. **Agetur**, R do Sol 33-A, T231 2377.
Language courses Portuguese lessons: Sra Amin Castro, T227 1527. Recommended.
Medical services Clínica São Marcelo, R do Passeio 546, English speaking doctor.
Telephones Embratel, Av Dom Pedro II 190.

West of Fortaleza

Western Ceará
At 340 km from Fortaleza and at 840 m is **Ubajara** ⓘ *T634 1300 ext 231 for tourist information*, with an interesting Sunday morning market selling produce of the sertão. About 3 km from town is **Parque Nacional Ubajara** ⓘ *the Ibama office is at the park entrance, 5 km from the caves, Toxx85-634 1388, www.ibama.gov.br, there is bar by the entrance serving juices, snacks, refrigerantes, etc*, with 563 ha of native highland and caatinga brush. The park's main attraction is the Ubajara cave on the side of an escarpment. Fifteen chambers totalling 1,120 m have been mapped, of which 360 are open to visitors. Access is along a 6-km footpath and steps (2-3 hours, take water) or with a **cablecar** ⓘ *T634 1219, 0900-1430, last up at 1500, US$2, locals US$0.20 – they use it as a means of transport*, which descends the cliff to the cave entrance. Lighting has been installed in nine caverns of the complex. An Ibama guide leads visitors in the cave, which is completely dry and home to 14 types of bat. At one point the lights are turned out to appreciate total blackness. Several rock formations look like animals: horse's head, jacaré, snake. The views of the sertão from the upper cablecar platform are superb. In the national park there is a new easy walkway through the woods with stunning views at the end. Start either to the left of the Park entrance, or opposite the snack bar near the cable car platform. The locals' route, and another good trail through caatinga, is from Araticum, 8 km, which is 7 km by bus from Ubajara.

Teresina → *Phone code: 0xx86. Post code: 64000. Colour map 5, grid B3. Population: 715,360.*
About 435 km up the Rio Parnaíba is the state capital. The city is reputed to be the hottest after Manaus (temperatures rise to 42°C). The **Palácio de Karnak** (the old governor's palace) ⓘ *just west of Praça Frei Serafim, Mon-Fri 1530-1730*, contains lithographs of the Middle East in 1839 by David Roberts RA. Also see the **Museu do Piauí** ⓘ *Praça Marechal Deodoro, Tue-Fri 0800-1730, Sat-Sun 0800-1200, US$1*. There is an interesting **open market** by the Praça Marechal Deodoro and the river is picturesque, with washing laid out to dry along its banks. The market is a good place to buy hammocks, but bargain hard. Every morning along the river bank there is the **troca-troca** where people buy, sell and swap. An undercover complex (**Mercado Central do Artesanato**) ⓘ *Mon-Fri 0800-2200*, has been built at Rua Paissandu 1276 (Praça Dom Pedro II). Most of the year the river is low, leaving sandbanks known as coroas (crowns). There is a good, clean supermarket on Praça Marechal Deodoro 937 with

fresh food. Local handicrafts include leather and clothes. **Teresina: Piemtur** ① *R Acre s/n, Centro de Convenções, Cabral, T3221 7100, www.piemtur.pi.gov.br. Information office at Rua Magalhães Filho s/n (next to 55 N)*, English spoken; kiosks at rodoviária and airport.

Parque Nacional de Sete Cidades → *Colour map 5, grid B4.*
① *0800-1700, US$1.35 plus US$4.55 for compulsory guide.*

Unusual eroded rock formations decorated with mysterious inscriptions are to be found in the Parque Nacional de Sete Cidades, 12 km from Piracuruca, 190 km northeast of Teresina. The rock structures are just off the Fortaleza-Teresina road. From the ground it looks like a medley of weird monuments. The inscriptions on some of the rocks have never been deciphered; one theory suggests links with the Phoenicians, and the Argentine Professor Jacques de Mahieu considers them to be Nordic runes left by the Vikings. There is plenty of birdlife, and iguanas, descending from their trees in the afternoon. Ibama hostel in the park, **C**, T3223 3366, pleasant, good restaurant, natural pool nearby, camping (US$6.50). Local food is limited and monotonous: bring a few delicacies, and especially fruit. Piripiri is a cheap place to break the Belém-Fortaleza journey; several good hotels. **Parque Nacional de Sete Cidades:** For park information, contact **Ibama** ① *Rod Min Vicente Fialho, Piripiri, CEP 64260-000, T3343 1342.* Colourful brochures with good map.

⬤ Sleeping → *See Telephone, page 347, for important phone changes.*

Western Ceará: Ubajara *p530*
A Pousada da Neblina, Estrada do Teleférico, 2 km from town, near the park, T/F3634 1270. In beautiful cloud forest, swimming pool, with breakfast and private shower (**C** without breakfast) restaurant open 1100-2000. Meals recommended. Campground (US$15 per tent).
C Marina Camping, on Ibiapina road 4 km south from Ubajara town, T3634 1364. Restaurant, pool, sauna, good value.
D Paraíso, in the centre of Ubajara town, T3634 1728. Reckoned to be the best in town.
D Hotel Churrascaria Ubajara, R Juvêncio Luís Pereira 370, Ubajara town, T3634 1261. Small restaurant.
D Sítio do Alemão, take Estrada do Teleférico 2 km from town, after the Pousada da Neblina turn right, signposted, 1 km to Sítio Santana, in the coffee plantation of Herbert Klein, T0xx88-9961 4645, www.sitio-do-alemao.20fr.com. Here, down a path, there are 3 small chalets, with full facilities, and 2 older ones with shared bath, **E**, view from breakfast/hammock area to Sertão, excursions, bicycle hire offered, if chalets are full Mr Klein may accommodate visitors at the house (Caixa Postal 33, Ubajara, CE, CEP 62350-000). No meals other than breakfast but Casa das Delícias in Ubajara will send lasagne if necessary. Warmly recommended.
Note Camping is not allowed in the national park.

Teresina *p530*
Many cheap hotels and dormitórios around Praça Saraiva. Many other cheap ones in R São Pedro and in R Alvaro Mendes.
LL Rio Poty, Av Marechal Castelo Branco 555, Ilhota, T4009 4009, www.riopoty.com.br. 5-star. Recommended.

A-B Sambaíba, R Gabriel Ferreira 230-N, T3222 6712, hotelsambaiba@bol.com.br. 2-star, central, good.
C-D Fortaleza, Felix Pacheco 1101, Praça Saraiva, T3221 2984. Fan, basic. Recommended.
C-D Grande, R Alvaro Mendes 906, T3221 2713. Very friendly and clean.
C-D Teresinha, Av Getúlio Vargas 2885, opposite rodoviária, T3221 0919. With a/c, cheaper with fan.

⬤ Eating

Teresina *p530*
Many eating places for all pockets in Praça Dom Pedro II.
ⴶⴶ Camarão do Elias, Av Pedro Almeida 457, T232 5025. Good seafood.
ⴶⴶ Pesqueirinho, R Domingos Jorge Velho 6889, in Poty Velho district. For fish dishes.
ⴶ Sabores Rotisserie, R Simplício Mendes 78, Centro. By kg, good quality and variety.

⬤ Festivals and events

Teresina *p530*
Teresina is proud of its **Carnival**, which is then followed by **Micarina**, a local carnival in **Mar**. There is much music and dancing in **Jul** and **Aug**, when there is a **Bumba-meu-Boi**, the Teresina dance festival, **Festidanças**, and a convention of itinerant guitarists.

⬤ Transport

Western Ceará: Ubajara *p530*
Guanabara **bus** from **Fortaleza**, 0800, 1800, return 0800, 1600, 6 hrs, US$10.75.

Air Flights to **Fortaleza, Brasília, Rio, São Paulo, São Luís, Belém, Manaus**. Buses from outside the airport run straight into town and to the rodoviária.

Bus Rodoviária, T3218 1514. The bus trip from **Fortaleza** is scenic and takes 9 hrs (US$40). There are direct buses to **Belém** (13 hrs, US$45), **Recife** (16 hrs, US$54) and to **São Luís** (7 hrs, US$24).

Parque Nacional de Sete Cidades and Piripiri p531
Bus Free **Ibama** bus service leaves the Praça da Bandeira in Piripiri (26 km away, rodoviária T3276 2333), at 0700, passing *Hotel Fazenda Sete Cidades* at 0800 (**B**, at Km 63 on BR-222, T0xx86-3232 3030, camping US$4.50; also has a free pick-up to the

park), reaching the park 10 mins later. Return at 1630, or hitchhike (to walk takes all day, very hot, start early). Taxi from Piripiri, US$30, or from Piracuruca, US$42. Bus Teresina-Piripiri and return, throughout the day 2½ hrs, US$7.50. Bus São Luís-Piripiri, 3 a day, 10 hrs, US$30. Several daily buses Piripiri-**Fortaleza**, 9 hrs, US$30. Bus Piripiri-**Ubajara**, marked 'São Benedito', or 'Crateús', 2½ hrs; US$7.50, first at 0700 (a beautiful trip).

Directory

Banks There are ATMs for both Visa and MasterCard, eg **Banco 24 Horas – TecBan**, Av João XXIII 2220.

The Amazon

The area is drained by the mighty Amazon, which in size, volume of water – 12 times that of the Mississippi – and number of tributaries has no equal in the world. At the base of the Andes, far to the west, the Amazonian plain is 1,300 km wide, but east of the confluences of the Madeira and Negro rivers with the Amazon, the highlands close in upon it until there is no more than 80 km of floodplain between them. Towards the river's mouth – about 320 km wide – the plain widens once more and extends along the coast southeastwards into the state of Maranhão and northwards into the Guianas.

Brazilian Amazônia, much of it still covered with tropical forest, is 56% of the national area. Its jungle is the world's largest and densest rain forest, with more diverse plants and animals than any other jungle in the world. It has only 8% of Brazil's population, and most of this is concentrated around Belém (in Pará), and in Manaus, 1,600 km up the river. The population is sparse because other areas are easier to develop.

Northern Brazil consists of the states of Pará, Amazonas, Amapá and Roraima. The states of Rondônia and Acre are dealt with under Southern Amazônia, see page 559.

Ins and outs
Climate The rainfall is heavy, but varies throughout the region; close to the Andes, up to 4,000 mm annually, under 2,000 at Manaus. Rains occur throughout the year but the wettest season is between December and May, the driest month is October. The humidity can be extremely high and the temperature averages 26°C. There can be cold snaps in December in the western reaches of the Amazon basin. The soil, as in all tropical forest, is poor.

Travel up the Amazon River

Rivers are the arteries of Amazônia for the transport of both passengers and merchandise. The two great ports of the region are Belém, at the mouth of the Amazon, and Manaus at the confluence of the Rio Negro and Rio Solimões. Manaus is the hub of river transport, with regular shipping services east to Santarém and Belém along the lower Amazon, south to Porto Velho along the Rio Madeira, west to Tabatinga (the border with Colombia and Peru) along the Rio Solimões and northwest to São Gabriel da Cachoeira along the Rio Negro. There is also a regular service connecting Belém and Macapá, on the northern shore of the Amazon Delta, and Santarém and Macapá. The size and quality of vessels varies greatly, with the largest and most comfortable ships generally operating on the Manaus-Belém route. Hygiene, food and service are reasonable on most vessels but **overcrowding** is a common problem. Many of the larger

Food

Ample but monotonous, better food is sometimes available to cabin passengers. Meal times can be chaotic. Fresh fruit is a welcome addition; also take plain biscuits, tea bags, seasonings, sauces and jam. Fresh coffee is available; most boats have a bar of sorts. Plates and cutlery may not be provided. Bring your own plastic mug as drinks are served in plastic beakers which are jettisoned into the river. A strong fishing line and a variety of hooks can be an asset for supplementing one's diet; with some meat for bait, piranhas are the easiest fish to catch. Negotiate with the cook over cooking your fish. The sight of you fishing will bring a small crowd of new friends, assistants, and lots of advice – some of it useful.

In Amazônia Inevitably fish dishes are very common, including many fish with indengous names, eg matrinchã, jaraqui, pacu, tucunaré, and tambaqui, which are worth trying. Pirarucu is another delicacy of Amazonian cuisine, but because of overfishing it is in danger of becoming extinct. Also shrimp and crab dishes (more expensive). Specialities of Pará include duck, often served in a yellow soup made from the juice of the root of the manioc (tucupi) with a green vegetable (jambu); this dish is the famous pato no tucupi, highly recommended. Also tacaca (shrimps served in tucupi), vatapá (shrimps served in a thick sauce, highly filling, simpler than the variety found in Salvador), maniçoba (made with the poisonous leaves of the bitter cassava, simmered for eight days to render it safe – tasty). Caldeirada, a fish and vegetable soup, served with pirão (manioc puree) is a speciality of Amazonas. There is also an enormous variety of tropical and jungle fruits, many unique to the region. Try them fresh, or in ice creams or juices. Avoid food from street vendors.

Belém and around

From Belém, the great city near the mouth of the Amazon, to Parintins, site of a renowned annual festival, on the border with Amazonas state, it is 60 hours by boat. This section deals with the first few stops on the river, plus the route through Amapá state to the frontier with French Guiane.

Belém → *Phone code: 0xx91. Post code: 66000. Colour map 5, grid A1. Population: 1.3 million.*

Belém (do Pará) is the great port of the Amazon. It is hot (mean temperature, 26°C), but frequent showers freshen the streets. There are some fine squares and restored historic buildings set along broad avenues. Belém used to be called the 'City of Mango Trees' and there are many such trees remaining.

Tourist offices Belém Belemtur ① *Av José Malcher 592, T3242 0900, belemtur@ cinbesa.com.br; also at airport, T3211 6151.* **Paratur** ① *Praça Maestro Waldemar Henrique s/n, T3212 0575, www.paratur.pa.gov.br.* Helpful, many languages spoken; good map of Belém in many languages (but some references are incorrect). Town guidebook, US$3. **Ibama** ① *Av Conselheiro Furtado 1303, Batista Campos, CEP 66035-350, T3241 2621, F3223 1299.*

Belém has its share of crime and is prone to gang violence. Take sensible precautions especially at night. Police for reporting crimes, Rua Santo Antônio e Trav Frei Gil de Vila Nova.

Sights The largest square is the **Praça da República** where there are free afternoon concerts; the main business and shopping area is along the wide Av Presidente Vargas leading to the river and the narrow streets which parallel it. The neoclassical **Teatro da Paz** (1868-1874) ① *Tue-Fri 0900-1800, tours US$2,* is one of the largest theatres in the country. It stages performances by national and international stars and also gives free concert and theatre shows; worth visiting, recently restored. Visit the **Cathedral** (1748) ① *Mon 1500-1800, Tue-Fri 0800-1100, 1530-1800,* another neoclassical building which contains several remarkable paintings. It stands on Praça Frei Caetano Brandão, opposite the 18th-century **Santo Aleixandre** church, which is noted for its wood carving. The 17th-century **Mercês** church (1640), near the market, is the oldest church in Belém; it forms part of an architectural group known as the Mercedário, the rest of which was heavily damaged by fire in 1978 and is being restored.

The **Basílica of Nossa Senhora de Nazaré** (1909) ① *Praça Julho Chermont on Av Magalhães Barata, Mon-Sat 0500-1130, 1400-2000, Sun 0545-1130, 1430-2000,* built from rubber wealth in romanesque style, is an absolute must for its stained-glass windows and beautiful marble. A museum at the basilica describes the Círio de Nazaré religious festival. The **Palácio Lauro Sodré** or **Museu do Estado do Pará** ① *Praça Dom Pedro II, T3225 3853, Mon-Fri 0900-1800, Sat-Sun 1900-1200*, a gracious 18th-century Italianate building, contains Brazil's largest framed painting, 'The Conquest of Amazônia', by Domenico de Angelis. The **Palácio Antônio Lemos**, **Museu da Cidade** ① *Tue-Fri 0900-1200, 1400-1800, Sat-Sun 0900-1300*, which houses the **Museu de Arte de Belém** and is now the **Prefeitura**, was originally built as the Palácio Municipal between 1868 and 1883. In the downstairs rooms there are old views of Belém; upstairs the historic rooms, beautifully renovated, contain furniture, paintings etc, all well explained.

The Belém market, known as **'Ver-o-Peso'** was the Portuguese Posto Fiscal, where goods were weighed to gauge taxes due (hence the name: 'see the weight'). It now has lots of gift shops selling charms for the local African-derived religion, umbanda; the medicinal herb and natural perfume stalls are also interesting. It is one of the most varied and colourful markets in South America; you can see giant river fish being unloaded around 0530, with frenzied wholesale buying for the next hour; a new dock for the fishing boats was built just upriver from the market in 1997. The area around the market swarms with people, including many armed thieves and pickpockets.

In the old town, too, is the **Forte do Castelo** ① *Praça Frei Caetano Brandão 117, T3223 0041, daily 0800-2300*. The fort overlooks the confluence of the Rio Guamá and the Baía do Guajara and was where the Portuguese first set up their defences. It was rebuilt in 1878. The site also contains the Círculo Militar restaurant (entry US$1.30; drinks and salgadinhos served on the ramparts from 1800 to watch the sunset; the restaurant serves Belém's best Brazilian food). At the square on the waterfront below the fort the açaí berries are landed nightly at 2300, after picking in the jungle (açaí berries ground up with sugar and mixed with manioc a staple food in the region).

At the **Estação das Docas**, the abandoned warehouses of the port have been restored into a complex with an air-conditioned interior and restaurants outside. The Terminal Marítimo has an office of Valverde Tours, which offers sunset and nighttime boat trips. The Boulevard das Artes contains the Cervejaria Amazon brewery, with good beer and simple meals, an archaeological museum and arts and crafts shops. The Boulevard de Gastronomia has smart restaurants and the 5-star Cairu ice cream parlour (try açaí or the Pavê de Capuaçu). Also in the complex are ATMs, internet café, phones and good toilets.

Belém

Sleeping
Amazônia 2
Fortaleza 1
Grão Pará 11
Itaoca 3
Le Massilia 4
Machado's Plaza 10

Novo Avenida 5
Palácio 6
Palácio das Musas 6
Regente 7
Sete Sete 8
Unidos 9
Vila Rica 12

Eating
Açaí at Hilton Hotel 11
Boteco das Onze 5
Cantina Italiana 1
Churrascaria Rodeio 3
Churrascaria Tucuruvi 4

Doces
Bárbaros 8
Govinda 10
Lá em Casa 6
Mãe Natureza 9
Miako 7
Sabor Paraense 2

0 metres 300
0 yards 300

The **Bosque Rodrigues Alves** ① *Av Almte Barroso 2305, T3226 2308, 0900-1700, closed Mon*, is a 16-ha public garden (really a preserved area of original flora), with a small animal collection; yellow bus marked 'Souza' or 'Cidade Nova' – any number – 30 minutes from 'Ver-o-Peso' market, also bus from Cathedral. The **Museu Emílio Goeldi** ① *Av Magalhães Barata 376, Tue-Thu 0900-1200, 1400-1700, Fri 0900-1200, Sat-Sun 0900-1200, US$1.30, additional charges for specialist area*, takes up a city block and consists of the museum proper (with a fine collection of Marajó Indian pottery, an excellent exhibition of Mebengokre Indian lifestyle) and botanical exhibits including Victoria Régia lilies. Take a bus from the Cathedral.

A return trip on the ferry from Ver-o-Peso to **Icaoraci** provides a good view of the river. Several restaurants here serve excellent seafood; you can eat shrimp and drink coconut water and appreciate the breeze coming off the river. Icaoraci is 20 km east of the city and is well-known as a centre of ceramic production. The pottery is in Marajoara and Tapajonica style. Take the bus from Av Presidente Vargas to Icoaraci (one hr). Open all week but best on Tuesday to Friday. Artisans are friendly and helpful, will accept commissions and send purchases overseas.

The nearest beach is at **Outeiro** (35 km) on an island near Icoaraci, about an hour by bus and ferry (the bus may be caught near the Maloca, an *indígena*-style hut near the docks which serves as a nightclub). A bus from Icoaraci to Outeiro takes 30 minutes. Further north is the island of **Mosqueiro** (86 km) ① *buses Belém-Mosqueiro every hr from rodoviária, US$2, 80 mins*, accessible by an excellent highway. It has many beautiful sandy beaches and jungle inland. It is popular at weekends when traffic can be heavy (also July) and the beaches can get crowded and polluted. Many hotels and weekend villas are at the villages of Mosqueiro and Vila; recommended (may be full weekends and July). Camping is easy and there are plenty of good places to eat.

Ilha do Marajó → *Colour map 5, grid A1.*

At almost 50,000 sq km, the world's largest island formed by fluvial processes is flooded in rainy December to June and provides a suitable habitat for water buffalo, introduced from India in the late 19th century. They are now farmed in large numbers (try the cheese and milk). It is also home to many birds, crocodiles and other wildlife, and has several good beaches. It is crowded at weekends and in the July holiday season. The island was the site of the pre-Columbian Marajoaras culture.

Ponta de Pedras

Boats leave Belém (near Porto do Sal, seat US$4.35, cabin US$47 for two, five hours) most days for Ponta de Pedras (**D Hotel Ponta de Pedras**, good meals, buses for Soure or Salvaterra meet the boat). Bicycles for hire (US$1 per hour) to explore beaches and the interior of the island. Fishing boats make the eight-hour trip to Cachoeira do Arari (one pousada, **D**) where there is a Marajó museum. A 10-hour boat trip from Ponta de Pedras goes to the Arari lake where there are two villages, Jenipapo built on stilts, forró dancing at weekends, and Santa Cruz which is less primitive, but less interesting (a hammock and a mosquito net are essential). There is a direct boat service to Belém twice a week.

Soure → *Colour map 5, grid A1. Population: 20,000.*

The 'capital' of the island has fine beaches: Araruna (2 km – take supplies and supplement with coconuts and crabs, beautiful walks along the shore), do Pesqueiro (bus from Praça da Matriz, 1030, returns 1600, eat at Maloca, good, cheap, big, deserted beach, 13 km away) and Caju-Una (15 km). Small craft await passengers from the Enasa boats, for Salvaterra village (good beaches and bars: seafood), 10 minutes, or trips are bookable in Belém from Mururé, T3241 0891. There are also 17th-century Jesuit ruins at Joanes as well as a virgin beach. Changing money is only possible at very poor rates. Take plenty of insect repellent.

Macapá → *Phone code: 0xx96. Post code: 68900. Colour map 2, grid C6. Population: 283,308.*

The capital of Amapá State is situated on the northern channel of the Amazon Delta and is linked to Belém by boat and daily flights. Along with Porto Santana it was declared a Zona Franca in 1993 and visitors flock to buy cheap imported electrical and other goods. Each brick of the **Fortaleza de São José do Macapá**, built between 1764 and 1782, was brought from Portugal as ballast; 50 iron cannons remain. Today it is used for concerts, exhibits, and colourful festivities on the anniversary of the city's founding, 4 February. In the handicraft complex (**Casa do Artesão**) ① *Av Azárias Neto, Mon-Sat 0800-1900*, craftsmen produce their wares onsite. A feature is pottery decorated with local manganese ore, also woodcarvings, leatherwork and indigenous crafts. **São José Cathedral**, inaugurated by the Jesuits in 1761, is the city's oldest landmark.

The riverfront is a very pleasant place for an evening stroll. The **Complexo Beira-Rio** has food and drink kiosks, and a nice lively atmosphere. The pier (trapiche) has been rebuilt and is a lovely spot for savouring the cool of the evening breeze, or watching sunrise over the Amazon. There is a monument to the equator, **Marco Zero** (take Fazendinha bus). The equator also divides the nearby enormous football stadium in half, aptly named O Zerão. South of here, at Km 12 on Rodovia Juscelinho Kubitschek, are the **botanical gardens**. **Fazendinha** (16 km from the centre) is a popular local beach, very busy on Sunday. **Curiarú**, 8 km from Macapá, was founded by escaped slaves, and is popular at weekends for dancing and swimming.

Tourist offices: Detur ① *Av Raimundo Álvares da Costa 18, Centro, T3223 0627. Branch at airport. State website: www.amapa.net*. Ibama ① *R Hamilton Silva 1570, Santa Rita, CEP 68.906-440, Macapá, T/F214 1119*.

Border with Guyane → *Colour map 2, grid B6.*
The main road crosses the Rio Caciporé and continues to the border with Guyane at **Oiapoque** (*Population: 13,000*), on the river of the same name. It is 90 km inland from the Parque Nacional Cabo Orange, Brazil's northernmost point on the Atlantic coast. About 7 km to the west is Clevelândia do Norte, a military outpost and the end of the road in Brazil. Oiapoque is remote, with its share of contraband, illegal migration, and drug trafficking. It is also the gateway to gold fields in the interior of both Brazil and Guyane. Visitors should take care late at night; the town is popular with French Guiana weekenders, most of them single men in search of the town's numerous women of ill repute. Prices here are high, but lower than in neighbouring Guyane. The **Cachoeira Grande Roche** rapids can be visited, upstream along the Oiapoque River, where it is possible to swim, US$30 per motor boat. The road north to the Guyane border (BR-156) is unpaved from Tatarugalzinho and is difficult in parts, especially during the wet season (but open throughout the year). It is advisable to carry extra fuel, food and water from Macapá onwards. Immigration officers will stamp you out the day before if you want to make an early start to Guyane. A bridge linking Guyane and Amapá is under construction and the road is asphalted all the way to Cayenne. As combis to Cayenne leave before lunch it is best to get to St-Georges before 1000. There is already much deforestation along the Brazilian side of the road and many Brazilian *garimpeiros* and hunters are causing havoc in Guyane.

⊙ **Sleeping** → *See Telephone, page 347, for important phone changes.*

Belém *p535, map p536*
There are now a few decent mid-range hotels in the city and a few clean, well-kept bargains in the upper budget category. The cheapest rooms are still very scruffy in Belém: consider an upgrade, this is a place where US$3-4 can make an enormous difference.
L Machado's Plaza, R Henrique Gurjão 200, T4008 9800, www.machadosplazahotel.com.br. Bright, brand new hotel with smart and tastefully decorated a/c rooms, a small business centre, plunge pool and a pleasant a/c breakfast area. Good value.
AL Itaoca, Av Pres Vargas 132, T4009 2400, itaoca@canal13.com.br. Well kept, bright a/c rooms, the best are on the upper floors away from the street noise, and with river views. Decent breakfast.
AL Regente, Av Gov José Malcher 485, T3181 5000, www.hotelregente.com.br. Small, refurbished a/c rooms with standard 3 star fittings above a noisy street. Popular with US tour groups.

AL Vila Rica, Av Júlio César 1777, T3257 1522, www.hotelvilarica.com.br/hotel_belem.htm. 5 mins from airport, helpful with transfers, very good.
A Le Massilia, R Henrique Gurjão 236, T3224 2834, www.massilia.com.br. Intimate, French owned boutique hotel with chic little duplexes and more ordinary doubles. Excellent French restaurant (₸₸₸) and a tasty French breakfast.
B-C Grão Pará, Av Pres Vargas 718, T3224 9600. A/c rooms with contemporary fittings, smart, hot water, the best have superb river views, excellent breakfast, great value.
B-C Novo Avenida, Av Pres.Vargas 404, T3223 8893, www.hotelnovoavenida.com.br. Slightly frayed but spruce rooms with decent breakfast. Groups of can sleep in large rooms for **E** pp. Very good value.
C Sete Sete, Trav 1 de Março 673, T3222 7730. Refurbished, clean but still gloomy little rooms, good breakfast, convenient location, but be careful after dark.

538

C Unidos, Ó de Almeida 545, T3229 0600. Simple, spacious a/c rooms with cable TV and clean en suites.

D pp Amazônia, Av Gov José Malcher 592, Nazaré (between Quintino Bocaiúva and Rui Barbosa), T4008 4800, www.amazonia hostel.com.br. Good hostel.

D Palácio das Musas, Trav Frutuoso Guimarães 275, T3212 8422. Big rooms, shared bath.

D-E Fortaleza, Trav Frutuoso Guimarães 276, T3212 1055. Unkempt hotel with a range of basic wood-floor rooms and dorms around a communal sitting area. Popular with backpackers. Careful in this area after dark.

D-E Palácio, Trav Frutuoso Guimarães, T3212 8422. Opposite and almost identical to the *Fortaleza*, though with scruffier communal areas and slightly cleaner rooms, and a restaurant/snack bar.

Ilha do Marajó *p537*
Soure

B Ilha do Marajó, 2a Travessa 10, 15 mins' walk from centre, T/F3741 1315, himarajo@ interconect.com.br. A/c, bath, pool, popular with package tours.

B Marajó, Praça Inhangaíba 351, Centro, T3741 1396. A/c, bath, clean, helpful owner.

D Pousada Asa Branca, Rua 4, T3741 1414. A/c, **E** with fan, breakfast, dirty, poor food.

Salvaterra

A Pousada das Guarás, Av Beira Mar, Salvaterra, T/F4005 5656, www.pousadadosguaras.com.br. Well-equipped, tour programme, on beach.

Joanes

B Pousada Ventania do Rio-Mar, take bus, US$1.20 from Foz do Cámara, T3646 2067, 9992 5716 (mob), www.pousadaventania.com. Near the beach, with bath and breakfast, fan, hammocks, laundry service, arranges tours on horseback or canoe, Belgian and Brazilian owners. Ask about their social integration projects with locals.

Macapá *p537*

AL Ceta Ecotel, R do Matodouro 640, Fazendinha, T3227 3396, www.ecotel.com.br. 20 mins from town centre by taxi. All furniture made on site, a/c, sports facilities, gardens with sloths and monkeys, ecological trails. Highly recommended.

AL-A Atalanta, Av Coracy Nunes 1148, T3223 1612. 10 mins' walk from the river. The best business-style hotel in town with a rooftop pool and comfortable, modern a/c rooms, includes generous breakfast.

A Pousada Ekinox, R Jovino Dinoá 1693, T3223 0086, www.ekinox.com.br. Nice atmosphere, a/c, book and video library, excellent meals and service, riverboat tours available. Recommended.

C Glória, Leopoldo Machado 2085, T3222 0984. A/c, minibar, TV.

D-E Santo Antônio, Av Coriolano Jucá 485, T3222 0226, 1 block south and half a block east of Praça da Bandeira. Best rooms are on upper floors, cheaper with fan, good breakfast extra; **E** in dormitory.

Border with Guyane: Oiapoque *p538*
Plenty of cheap, poorly maintained hotels along the waterfront.

D Kayaman, Av Joaquim Caetano da Silva 760, T3521 1256. A/c and bath, **E** with fan, poor showers, lots of people hanging about, basic, international calls.

D Pousada Central, Av Coracy Nunes 209, one block from the river, T3521 1466. A/c, bath, **E** with fan and shared bath.

● Eating

Belém *p535, map p536*
All the major hotels have good restaurants.

♥♥♥ Açaí Hilton Hotel, Av Pres Vargas 882, T3242 6500. Recommended for regional dishes and others, Sun brunch or daily lunch and dinner.

♥♥♥ Boteco das Onze, Praça F C Brandão s/n, T3224 8599. About the best regional cooking in Belem with live music every night and a view over the river.

♥♥♥ Churrascaria Rodeio, Trav Pres Eutíquio 1308 and Rodovia Augusto Montenegro Km 4, T3248 2004. A choice of 20 cuts of meat and 30 buffet dishes for a set price. Well worth the short taxi ride to eat all you can.

♥♥♥ Churrascaria Tucuruvi, Trav Benjamin Constant 1843, Nazaré, T3235 0341. Good value.

♥♥♥ Lá em Casa, Av Governador José Malcher 247 (also in Estação das Docas). Try menu paraense, good cooking, fashionable.

♥♥ Cantina Italiana, Trav Benjamin Constant 1401. Very good Italian, also delivers.

♥♥ Mãe Natureza, Manoel Barata 889, T3212 8032. Vegetarian and wholefood dishes in a bright clean dining room. Lunch only.

♥♥ Miako, Trav 1 de Março 766, behind Praça de República. Very good Japanese, oriental and international food.

♥♥ Sabor Paraense, R Sen Manoel Barata 897, T3241 4391. A variety of fish and meat dishes served in a bright, light dining room.

● *For an explanation of the sleeping and eating price codes used in this guide, see page 58.*
● *Other relevant information is found in Essentials pages 345-347.*

Doces Bárbaros, Benjamin Constant 1658, T3224 0576. Cakes, snacks, sandwiches and decent coffee. Lunch only.

Govinda, Ó de Almeida 198. Basic but tasty vegetarian food. Lunch only.

Good snack bars serving *vatapá* (the Bahian dish), tapioca rolls, etc, are concentrated on Assis de Vasconcelos on the eastern side of the Praça da Republica.

Macapá *p537*

Chalé, Av Pres Vargas 499.
Nice atmosphere and good food.

Cantinho Baiano, Av Beira-Rio 1, Santa Inês. Good seafood. 10 mins' walk south of the fort. Many other restaurants along this stretch about 1½ km beyond the Cantino Baiano including the **Vista Amazônica**, see Sleeping, above.

Martinho's Peixaria, Av Beira-Rio 810. Another good fish restaurant.

Bom Paladar Kilo's, Av Pres Vargas 456. Good pay-by-weight buffet.

Sorveteria Macapá, R São José 1676, close to centre. Excellent ice cream made from local fruit.

⊙ Bars and clubs

Belém *p535, map p536*
Many venues around Av Doca de Souza Franco, often just called 'Doca', especially popular Thu. The Reduto district is also very popular at night.

African Bar, Praça Waldemar Henrique 2. Rock or Samba, weekends only.

Baixo Reduto, R Quintino Bocaiúva, Reduto. Blues on Wed; Brazilian pop, Thu; rock, Fri and jazz, Sat.

Bar Teatro Bora Bora, R Bernal do Couto 38, restaurant, bar and nightclub. MPB and Pagode open from 2100 until late Thu-Sun.

Cachaçaria Água Doce, R Diogo Móia 283 esq Wandenkolk. Specializes in fine cachaças, good appetizers, live music, informal atmosphere.

Colarinho Branco Chopperia, Av Visconde de Souza Franco 80, near the river. Open Tue-Sun 1800 to last customer, nightly performers of Brazilian popular music.

Escapóle, Rodovia Augusto Montenegro 400. Huge dance hall with various types of music, live and recorded, frequented by all age groups, open Wed-Sat from 2200 (take a radio taxi for safety), no a/c, dress informally.

Olê Olá, Av Tavares Bastos 1234. Disco, live music and dance floor. Thu-Sun, 2230 to last customer.

⊛ Festivals and events

Belém *p535, map p536*
Círio, the Festival of Candles in **Oct**, is based on the legend of the Nossa Senhora de Nazaré, whose image was found on the site of her Basílica around 1700. On the 2nd Sun in Oct, a procession carries a copy of the Virgin's image from the Basílica to the cathedral. On the Mon, 2 weeks later, the image is returned to its usual place. There is a Círio museum in the Basílica crypt, enter at the right side of the church; free. (Hotels are fully booked during Círio.)

Macapá *p537*
Marabaixo is the traditional music and dance of the state of Amapá; a festival held 40 days after Easter. The sambódromo, near Marco Zero, is used by Escolas de Samba during Carnaval and by Quadrilhas during the São João festivities.

⊙ Shopping

Belém *p535, map p536*
Belém is a good place to buy hammocks, look in the street parallel to the river, 1 block inland from Ver-o-Peso.

Arts and crafts market, Praça da República every weekend. Seed and bead jewellery, whicker, hammocks and raw cotton weave work, toys and other knic-knacs. Mostly predictable but the odd gem.

Complexo São Brás, Praça Lauro Sodré. Has a handicraft market and folkloric shows in a building dating from 1911.

Parfumaria Orion, Trav Frutuoso Guimarães 268. Sells a variety of perfumes from Amazonian plants, much cheaper than tourist shops.

⛰ Activities and tours

Belém *p535, map p536*
Most of the larger hotels organize city and one-day boat tours.

Amazon Star, R Henrique Gurjão 236, T/F3241 8624, amazonstar@amazonstar. com.br. City and river tours, Ilha de Marajó hotel bookings and tours, very professional, good guides, jungle tours, books flight tickets. Repeatedly recommended.

Amazônia Sport & Ação, Av 25 de Setembro, 2345, T3226 8442. Extreme sports, diving, rock-climbing.

Macapá *p537*
Awara, Av Presidente Vargas 2396-B, T/F222 0970. Recommended for city and river tours, English and French spoken.

Marco Zero, R São José 2048, T223 1922, F222 3086. Recommended for flights.

⊖ Transport

Belém *p535, map p536*

Air Bus 'Perpétuo Socorro-Telégrafo' or 'Icoaraci', every 15 mins from the Prefeitura, Praça Felipe Patroni, to the airport, 40 mins, US$0.65. Taxi to airport, US$15 (ordinary taxis are cheaper than Co-op taxis, buy ticket in advance in Departures side of airport). ATMs for credit cards in the terminal. Airport T3210 6272.

Daily flights south to **Brasília** and other Brazilian cities, and west to **Santarém** and **Manaus**. To **Paramaribo** and **Cayenne**, 2 a week with Surinam Airways. Travellers entering Brazil from Guyane may need a 60-day visa (takes 2 days) before airlines will confirm their tickets. Internal flights also offered by TAM.

Bus The rodoviária is at the end of Av Governador José Malcher 5 km from the centre (T3246 8178). Take Aeroclube, Cidade Novo, No 20 bus, or Arsenal or Canudos buses, US$1, or taxi, US$10 (day), US$12 (night) (at rodoviária you are given a ticket with the taxi's number on it, threaten to go to the authorities if the driver tries to overcharge). It has a good snack bar and showers (US$0.15) and 2 agencies with information and tickets for riverboats. Regular bus services to all major cities. To **Santarém**, via Marabá (on the Transamazônica) once a week (US$90, can take longer than boat, goes only in dry season). **Transbrasiliana** go direct to Marabá, 16 hrs, US$40. To **São Luís**, 2 a day, US$40, 13 hrs, interesting journey through marshlands. To **Fortaleza**, US$80 (24 hrs), several companies. To **Recife**, US$105, 34 hrs.

Ferry To **Santarém, Manaus**, and intermediate ports (see River Transport, Amazônia, page 534). All larger ships berth at Portobrás/Docas do Pará (the main commercial port) at Armazém (warehouse) No 10 (entrance on Av Marechal Hermes, corner of Av Visconde de Souza Franco). The guards will sometimes ask to see your ticket before letting you into the port area, but tell them you are going to speak with a ship's captain. Ignore the touts who approach you. **Macamazónia**, R Castilho Franca, sells tickets for most boats, open Sun. There are 2 desks selling tickets for private boats in the rodoviária; some hotels recommend agents for tickets. Purchase tickets from offices 2 days in advance. Smaller vessels (sometimes cheaper, usually not as clean, comfortable or safe) sail from small docks along Estrada Nova (not a safe part of town). Take a Cremação bus from Ver-o-Peso.

To **Macapá (Porto Santana)**, the quickest (12 hrs) are the catamaran Atlântico I or the launches Lívia Marília and Atlântico II (slightly slower), all leaving at 0700 on alternate days.

Other boats take 24 hrs: **Silja e Souza** (Wed) of Souzamar, Trav Dom Romualdo Seixas corner R Jerônimo Pimentel, T3222 0719, and **Almirante Solon** (Sat) of Sanave (Serviço Amapaense de Navegação, Castilho Franca 234, opposite Ver-o-Peso, T3222 7810), slightly cheaper, crowded, not as nice. Via Breves, ENAL, T3224 5210 (see River Transport in Amazônia, page 534). Smaller boats to Macapá also sail from Estrada Nova.

Ilha do Marajó *p537*

Ferry From Belém docks the Enasa ferry sails to Soure on Fri at 2000 (4 hrs, US$10). There are daily boats to Foz do Câmara at 0630, 0700 and 1300 (1½-3 hrs US$7.50). Then take a bus to Salvaterra and a ferry to Soure. Boats return from Foz do Câmara at 0800 and 1100. There is a 'taxi-plane' service to Soure leaving Belém at 0630 returning 1600, US$60.

Macapá *p537*

Air TAM (T223 2688), fly to Belém and other Brazilian cities. Gol fly to Belém (at night), Brasília and São Paulo.

Bus Rodoviária on BR-156, north of Macapá. To **Amapá**, **Calçoene** and **Oiapoque** (15-17 hrs, US$30), at least 2 daily. The road is from Amapá to the border is due to be paved; before then you may have to get out and walk up hills, bus has no a/c.

Ferry Ships dock at Porto Santana, 30 km from Macapá (frequent buses US$2.50, or share a taxi US$30). To **Belém**, Silja e Souza of Souzamar, Cláudio Lúcio Monteiro 1375, Santana, and Almirante Solon of Sanave, Av Mendonça Furtado 1766. See under Belém, River Services, for other boats. Purchase tickets from offices 2 days in advance. Also smaller and cheaper boats. The faster (12 hr) catamaran Atlântico I or launches leave for Belém most days. São Francisco de Paula I sails to **Santarém** and **Manaus**, not going via Belém.

Border with Guyane: Oiapoque *p538*

Air Flights to **Macapá** Mon-Fri with **Penta**, office on the waterfront, T/F3521 1117. While waiting for flights to Cayenne from St-Georges, it is much cheaper to stay on the Brazilian side.

Bus At least 2 a day for **Macapá**, 12-15 hrs (dry season), 14-24 hrs (wet season), US$30. Also shared jeeps, US$22.50 in the back, or US$55 in the cabin. You may be asked to show your Polícia Federal entry stamp and Yellow Fever vaccination certificate either when buying a ticket from the offices on the waterfront or at the bus station when boarding for Macapá.

Ferry Crossing to Guyane: motorized canoes cross to St-Georges de L'Oyapock, 10 mins down-stream, US$5 pp, bargain for return fare. A vehicle ferry will operate until the bridge is completed.

❶ Directory

Belém *p535, map p536*

Airline offices BRA, T3073 8800, at airport T3210 6227. **Penta**, Av Sen Lemos 4700, T3244 7777. **Rico**, Av Assis de Vasconcelos 207, Campinas, T3241 4433. **Surinam Airways**, R Gaspar Viana 488, T3212 7144, airport 211 6038, English spoken, helpful with information and documentation. **Banks** Banco do Brasil, Av Pres Vargas (near Hotel Central), good rates but US$20 commission and slow, Visa ATMs, and other Brazilian banks (open 0900-1630, but foreign exchange only until 1300). HSBC, Av Pres Vargas near Praça da República has MasterCard Cirrus and Amex ATMs. **Banco de Amazônia** (Basa), on Pres Vargas, gives good rates for TCs (Amex or Citicorp only), but does not change cash. Itaú, R Boaventura 580, good TCs and cash rates. Money can only be changed at banks during the week. At weekends hotels will only exchange for their guests, while restaurants may change money, but at poor rates. Exchange rates are generally the best in the north of the country. **Embassies and consulates** Denmark (Consul Arne Hvidbo), R Senador Barata 704, sala 1503, T3241 1588 (PO Box 826). Finland and Sweden, Av Senador Lemos 529, Umarizal, T3222 0148. Germany, R Tiradentes 67, sala 204, T3212 8366, hsteffen.bel@orm.com.br. UK, Av Governador Magalhães Barata 651, Sala 610, T4009 0050, chris.mayhew@wilsonsons.com.br. USA, Edifício Síntese 21, Av Conselheiro Furtado 2865, T3259 4566. Venezuela, opposite French Consulate, Av Pres Pernambuco 270, T3222 6396 (Venezuelan visa for those entering overland takes 3 hrs, costs US$30 for most nationalities, but we are told that it is better to get a visa at Manaus, Boa Vista or before you leave home. **Internet** Amazon, 2nd floor of Estação das Docas. In Shopping Iguatemi, US$1.90 per hr. **Medical services** Health: a yellow fever certificate or inoculation is mandatory. It is best to get a yellow fever vaccination at home (always have your certificate handy) and avoid the risk of recycled needles. Medications for malaria prophylaxis are not sold in Belém pharmacies.

Bring an adequate supply from home. **Clínica de Medicina Preventiva**, Av Bras de Aguiar 410 (T3222 1434), will give injections, English spoken, open 0730-1200, 1430-1900 (Sat 0800-1100). **Hospital Ordem Terceira**, Trav Frei Gil de Vila Nova 2, doctors speak some English, free consultation but it's a bit primitive. Surgery open Mon 1300-1900, Tue-Thu 0700-1100, 24 hrs for emergencies. The British consul has a list of English-speaking doctors. **Post offices** Av Pres Vargas 498, but international parcels are only accepted at the Post Office on the praça at the corner of Trav Frutuoso Guimarães e R 15 de Novembro, next door to NS das Mercês (hard to find). **Telephones** For phone calls: Telemar, Av Pres Vargas. Fax at the Post Office, Av Pres Vargas.

Macapá *p537*

Banks Banco do Brasil, R Independência 250, cash, Visa, ATM and TCs. Visa ATM also at Bradesco, Cândido Mendes 1316. MasterCard and Amex ATM at HSBC, Av Pres Vargas. **Casa Francesa**, Independência 232, changes euros (euros can be bought in Macapá and Belém). **Embassies and consulates** For the French honorary consul, ask at Pousada Ekinox, visas for Guyane have to be obtained from Brasília which can take a while. **Post offices** Av Coriolano Jucá. International calls can be made at São José 2050, 0730-1000.

Border with Guyane: Oiapoque *p538*

Banks Exchange: It is possible to exchange US$ and reais to euros, but dollar rates are low and TCs are not accepted anywhere. **Banco do Brasil**, Av Barão do Rio Branco, open 1000-1500, and **Bradesco**, have Visa facilities to withdraw reais which can be changed into euros. **Casa Francesa**, on the riverfront, and one câmbio in the market sell reais for US$ or euros. Rates are worse in St-Georges. Best to buy euros in Belém, or abroad. **Post offices** Av Barão do Rio Branco, open 0900-1200, 1400-1700. **Useful addresses** Immigration: Polícia Federal, for Brazilian exit and entry stamps, is on the road behind the church about 500 m from the river.

Belém to Manaus

A few hours up the broad river from Belém, the region of the thousand islands is entered. The passage through this maze of islets is known as 'The Narrows' and is perhaps the nicest part of the journey. The ship winds through 150 km of lanes of yellow flood with equatorial forest within 20 m or 30 m on both sides. On one of the curious flat-topped hills after the Narrows stands the little stucco town of **Monte Alegre**, an oasis in mid-forest (airport; some simple hotels, **D-E**). There are lagoon cruises to see lilies, birds, pink dolphins; also village visits (US$25-40 per day).

Santarém → *Phone code: 0xx93. Post code: 68000. Colour map 4, grid A5. Population: 262,538.*

The third largest city on the Brazilian Amazon is small enough to walk around. It was founded in 1661 as the Jesuit mission of Tapajós; the name was changed to Santarém in 1758. There was once a fort here and attractive colonial squares overlooking the waterfront remain. Standing at the confluence of the Rio Tapajós with the Amazon, on the southern bank, Santarém is halfway (two or three days by boat) between Belém and Manaus. Most visitors breeze in and out on a stopover by boat or air. **Tourist office:** SANTUR ① *Tv Inácio Corrêa 22, T/F3523 2434*, has good information available in English.

The yellow Amazon water swirls alongside the green-blue Tapajós; the **meeting of the waters**, in front of the market square, is nearly as impressive as that of the Negro and Solimões near Manaus. A small **Museu dos Tapajós** in the old city hall on the waterfront, now the **Centro Cultural João Fora** ① *closed Sat*, downriver from where the boats dock, has a collection of ancient Tapajós ceramics, as well as various 19th-century artefacts. The unloading of the fish catch between 0500 and 0700 on the waterfront is interesting. There are good beaches nearby on the Rio Tapajós.

Alter do Chão

Some 34 km west of Santarém is this friendly village on the Rio Tapajós, at the outlet of Lago Verde. Of particular interest is the **Centro do Preservação de Arte Indígena** ① *R Dom Macedo Costa, T527 1110, 0800-1200, 1300-1700*, which has a varied collection of artefacts from tribes of Amazônia and Mato Grosso. Good swimming in the Tapajós from the beautiful, clean beach.

Óbidos and around → *Phone code: 0xx93. Population: 46,500.*

At 110 km up-river from Santarém (five hours by boat), Óbidos is located at the narrowest and deepest point on the river. It is a picturesque and clean city with many beautiful, tiled buildings and some nice parks. Worth seeing are the **Prefeitura Municipal** ① *T547 1194*, the cuartel and the **Museu Integrado de Óbidus** ① *R Justo Chermont 607, Mon-Fri 0700-1100, 1330-1730*. There is also a **Museu Contextual**, a system of plaques with detailed explanations of historical buildings throughout town. The airport has flights to Manaus, Santarém and Parintins.

Just across the Pará-Amazonas border, between Santarém and Manaus, is **Parintins** (*Phone code: 0xx92. Post code: 69150-000*), 15 hours by boat upriver from Óbidos. Here, on the last three days of June each year, the **Festa do Boi** draws over 50,000 visitors. Since the town has only two small hotels, everyone sleeps in hammocks on the boats that bring them to the festival from Manaus and Santarém. The festival consists of lots of folkloric dancing, but its main element is the competition between two rival groups, the Caprichoso and the Garantido, in the bumbódromo, built in 1988 to hold 35,000 spectators.

● **Sleeping** → *See Telephone, page 347, for important phone changes.*

Santarém *p543*

AL Amazon Park I, Av Mendonça Furtado 4120, T3523 2800, amazon@netsan.com.br. Swimming pool, 4 km from centre, taxi US$4.

A-B Mirante, Trav Francisco Correa, 115, T3522 0275, www.mirantehotel.com. Homely, a/c, fridge, TV, some rooms with balcony, individual safes, internet, good value. Recommended.

B-C Brasil Grande Hotel, Trav 15 de Agosto 213, T3522 5660. Family-run, with restaurant.

B-C New City, Trav Francisco Correia 200, T3523 2351. A/c, frigobar, good, will collect from airport.

B-C Santarém Palace, Rui Barbosa 726, T3523 2820. A/c, TV, fridge, comfortable.

C Brasil, Trav dos Mártires 30, T3523 6665. Nice, family-run, includes good breakfast, communal bath, good food, good service.

C Horizonte, Trav Senador Lemos 737, T522 5437, horizontehotel@bol.com.br. With a/c, **F** with fan, modern.

C-D Rios, R Floriano Peixoto 720, T522 5701. Large rooms, comfortable, a/c, fridge and TV.

Alter do Chão *p543*

A Pousada Tupaiulândia, Pedro Teixeira 300, T0xx93-3527 1157. A/c, unimpressive but OK, very helpful, good breakfast for US$5, next to telephone office opposite bus stop.

D Pousada Villa Praia, first on the right as you enter the village, T3527 1130. Large rooms, a/c, very helpful staff, good value.

Óbidos *p543*

Several in our **C** price range.

C Braz Bello, R Corrêia Pinto, on top of the hill. Shared bath, full board available.

C Pousada Brasil, R Correia Pinto. Basic, with bath, cheaper without.

🍴 Eating

🍴 **Mascote**, Praça do Pescador 10.
Open 1000-2330, restaurant, bar and
ice cream parlour.
🍴 **Mascotinho**, Praça Manoel de Jesus
Moraes, on riverfront. Bar/pizzeria, popular,
outside seating, good view.
🍴 **Santa Antônio**, Av Tapajós 2061.
Churrasco and fish.
🍴 **Lucy**, Praça do Pescador. Good juices and
pastries. Recommended.

Alter do Chão p543
Lago Verde, Praça 7 de Setembro.
Good fresh fish, try caldeirada de tucunaré,
huge portions.

🎉 Festivals and events

Santarém p543
29 Jun, São Pedro, with processions of boats on
the river and boi-bumbá dance dramas.

Alter do Chão p543
2nd week in Sep, Festa do Çairé, religious
processions and folkloric events.

🚶 Activities and tours

Santarém p543
Amazon Jungle Tours, R Galdino Veloso 200,
T3529 0146, 9903 7320 (mob),
radarfinder@hotmail.com. Tours from
1 to 7 days by boat, English, French and
Spanish spoken.
Amazon Tours, Trav Turiano Meira 1084,
amazonriver@netsan.com.br,
www.amazonriver.com. The owner Steve
Alexander is a very friendly, helpful man
who can give you lots of hints on what to do.
He also organizes excursions for groups to
remote areas which are quite expensive.
Recommended.
Santarém Tur, in Amazon Park, and at R Adriano
Pimental 44, T3522 4847, www.santaremtur.com.br.
Owned by Perpétua and Jean-Pierre Schwarz
(speaks French), friendly, helpful, also group
tours (group of 5, US$65 per day pp).
Recommended.
Gil Serique, Av Adriano Pimentel 80, T522 5174,
9654 3702 (mob), www.youramazon.org.
English-speaking guide. Recommended.

🚌 Transport

Santarém p543
Air 15 km from town, T523 1021. Internal flights
only. Buses run to the centre or waterfront. From
the centre the bus leaves in front of the cinema in
Rui Barbosa every 80 mins from 0550 to 1910, or
taxis (US$15 to waterfront). The hotels Amazon
Park and New City have free buses for guests; you
may be able to take these.
Bus Rodoviária is on the outskirts, take
'Rodagem' bus from the waterfront near the
market, US$0.35. Santarém to **Marabá** on the
Rio Tocantins with Transbrasiliana. From
Marabá there are buses east and west on the
Transamazônica. Enquire at the rodoviária for
other destinations. Road travel during rainy
season is always difficult, often impossible.
Ferry To **Manaus**, **Belém**, **Macapá**, **Itaituba**,
and intermediate ports (see River transport, page
534). Boats to Belém and Manaus dock at the Cais
do Porto, 1 km west, take 'Floresta-Prainha',
'Circular' or 'Circular Externo' bus; taxi US$7.50.
Boats to other destinations, including Macapá,
dock by the waterfront by the centre of town.
Local service to **Óbidos**, US$18, 4 hrs, **Oriximiná**
US$20, **Alenquer**, and **Monte Alegre**
(US$18, 5-8 hrs).

Alter do Chão p543
Bus Tickets and information from the bus
company kiosk opposite Pousada Tupaiulândia.
From Santarém: bus stop on Av São Sebastião, in
front of Colégio Santa Clara, US$2, about 1 hr.

Óbidos and around: Parintins p543
Ferry Apart from boats that call on the
Belém-Manaus route, there are irregular sailings
from **Óbidos** (ask at the port). Journey times are
about 12-15 hrs from **Manaus** and 20 from
Santarém. There is also a small airport with
flights to **Manaus**, **Óbidos** and **Santarém**.

☎ Directory

Santarém p543
Airline offices Penta, Trav 15 de Novembro
183, T523 2532. **Banks** Cash withdrawals on Visa
at Banco do Brasil, Av Rui Barbosa 794. It is very
difficult to change dollars (impossible to change
TCs anywhere), try travel agencies. **Internet**
Tapajós On Line, Mendonça Furtado 2454,
US$3.50 per hr. **Post office** Praça da Bandeira
81. **Telephones** Posto Trin, R Siquiera Campos
511. 0700-1900 Mon-Sat, 0700-2100 Sun.

🔵 *For an explanation of the sleeping and eating price codes used in this guide, see page 58.*
🔵 *Other relevant information is found in Essentials pages 345-347.*

Manaus → *Phone code: 0xx92. Post code: 69000. Colour map 4, grid A3. Population 1.6 million.*

The next city upriver is Manaus, capital of Amazonas State – the largest in Brazil. Once an isolated urban island in the jungle, it now sprawls over a series of eroded and gently sloping hills divided by numerous creeks (igarapés). The city is growing fast and 20-storey modern buildings are rising above the traditional flat, red-tiled roofs. An initiative in 2001 saw the start of a restoration programme in which historic buildings have been given a new lease of life and theatres, cultural spaces and libraries created. Manaus is an excellent port of entry for visiting the Amazon. Less than a day away are river islands and tranquil waterways. The opportunities for trekking in the forest, canoeing and meeting local people should not be missed and, once you are out of reach of the urban influence, there are plenty of animals to see. There is superb swimming in the natural pools and under falls of clear water in the little streams which rush through the woods, but take locals' advice on swimming in the river (both for nature's animal hazards and man's pollution).

Ins and outs → *Manaus is 1 hr behind Brazilian standard time (2 hrs Oct-Feb, Brazil's summer time).*

Getting there Boats dock at different locations depending on where they have come from. The **docks** are quite central. The **airport** is 18 km from the centre, the **bus terminal** 9 km. Both are served by local buses and taxis.

Manaus

Sleeping			
10 de Julho **1**	Itália **8**		O Naturalista **4**
Ana Cassia Palace **2**	Krystal **9**	**Eating**	Pizzaria Scarola **6**
Best Western	Lider **13**	Alemã **1**	Senac **7**
Lord Manaus **3**	Manaós **10**	Búfalo **2**	Skina dos Sucos **8**
Brasil & Restaurant **7**	Mônaco **11**	Canto da Peixada **12**	Sorveteria Glacial **9**
Central **6**	Taj Mahal **4**	Fiorentina **3**	
Hostel Manaus **12**	Tropical &	Himawari **5**	
	Restaurant Tarumã **5**	La Barca **14**	

Getting around All city bus routes start below the cathedral in front of the port entrance; just ask someone for the destination you want. The city centre is easily explored on foot (although bear in mind an average temp of 27°C). ▸▸ *See Transport, page 553, for further details.*

Tourist office **AmazonasTur** (state tourism office) ① *R Saldanha Marinho 321, T2123 3800, www.amazonastur.am.gov.br, open 0800-1700. Offices at Avenida Eduardo Ribeiro 666, near Teatro Amazonas, T3231 1998, Mon-Fri 0800-1700, Sat 0800-1200.* Limited English and information. At the **airport** ① *daily 0700-2300, T3651 1120.* Also in **Amazonas Shopping Center** ① *T3648 1396,* in the new cruise ship terminal at the docks (open when a ship is in town). **ManausTur** ① *Av 7 de Setembro 157, T3622 4986, manaus@pmm.am.gov.br,* is a private tourism office. Weekend editions of A Crítica, newspaper, list local entertainments and events. See also www.manausonline.com.

Security Manaus is a friendly, if busy city and a good deal safer than the big cities of southern Brazil. As in any city, the usual precautions against opportunist crime should be taken, especially when arriving at night (see River transport in Amazônia on staying on boats in port). Bars and streets in the working heart of port area, south of Rua Quintino, are not places to hang around after dark. ▸▸ *See page 548 for advice on choosing a jungle tour.*

Sights

Dominating the centre is a **Cathedral** built in simple Jesuit style on a hillock; very plain inside or out. Nearby is the main shopping and business area, the tree-lined Avenida Eduardo Ribeiro; crossing it is Av 7 de Setembro, bordered by ficus trees. **Teatro Amazonas** ① *Praça São Sebastião, T3622 1880 for information on programmes, Mon-Sat 0900-1600, 20-min tour US$7. Recommended.* About same price for a concert. This opulent theatre was completed in 1896 during the great rubber boom following 15 years of construction. It has been restored four times and should not be missed. There are ballet, theatre and opera performances several times a week and free popular Brazilian music on Monday nights, June-December. **Igreja São Sebastião** (1888), on the same praça, has an unusual altar of two giant ivory hands holding a water lily of Brazil wood.

On the waterfront in the heart of the docks, the **Mercado Adolfo Lisboa**, Rua dos Barés 46, was built in 1902 as a miniature copy of the now demolished Parisian Les Halles. The wrought ironwork which forms much of the structure was imported from Europe and is said to have been designed by Eiffel. A short distance to the west the remarkable **Floating Harbour installations**, completed in 1902, were designed and built by a Scottish engineer to cope with the up to 14 m annual rise and fall of the Rio Negro. The large passenger ship floating dock is connected to street level by a 150 m-long floating ramp, at the end of which, on the harbour wall, can be seen the high water mark for each year since it was built. When the water is high, the roadway floats on a series of large iron tanks measuring 2½m in diameter. The large beige **Alfândega** (Customs House) ① *R Marquês de Santa Cruz, Mon-Fri 0800-1200, 1400-1600,* is at the entrance to the city if your boat arrives to dock at the Floating Harbour. It was entirely prefabricated in England, and the tower once acted as lighthouse.

The **Biblioteca Pública Estadual** (Public Library) ① *R Barroso 57, T234 0588, Mon-Fri 0730-1730,* inaugurated in 1871, features an ornate European cast iron staircase. It is well stocked with 19th-century newspapers, rare books and old photographs, and worth a visit. The **Centro Cultural Pálacio Rio Negro** ① *Av 7 de Setembro, T3232 4450, Tue-Fri 1000-1700, Sat-Sun 1600-2100,* was the residence of a German rubber merchant until 1917 and later the state government palace. It now holds various cultural events, including exhibitions, houses the Museu-Biblioteca da Imagem e do Som, shows and films; there is also a café.

There is a curious little church, **Igreja do Pobre Diabo** ① *at the corner of Av Borba and Av Ipixuna in the suburb of Cachoeirinha;* it is only 4 m wide by 5 m long, and was built by a tradesman, the 'poor devil' of the name. Take Circular 7 Cachoeirinha bus from the cathedral to Hospital Militar.

On Praça da Polícia is the very small **Museu Tiradentes** ① *closed 2006,* run by the military police and holds selected historical items and old photographs. A short distance away is **Museu do Homem do Norte** ① *Av 7 de Setembro 1385 (near Av J Nabuco), T3232 5373, Mon-Fri 0900-1200, 1300-1700, US$1,* which reviews the way of life of the Amazonian population; social, cultural and economic aspects are displayed with photographs, models and other pieces. **Instituto Geográfico e Histórico do Amazonas** ① *R Frei José dos Inocentes*

117 (near Prefeitura), T3232 7077, Mon-Fri 0900-1200, 1300-1600, US$1, located in a fascinating older district of central Manaus, houses a museum and library of over 10,000 books which thoroughly document Amazonian life through the ages, **Museu do Índio** ① R Duque de Caxias 296, T3635 1922, Mon-Fri 0800-1130, 1400-1630, Sat 0830-1130, US$4, kept by the Salesian missionaries: this interesting, if rather run down, museum's collection includes handicrafts, ceramics, clothing, utensils and ritual objects from the various indiegenous tribes of the upper Rio Negro; excellent craft shop.

Botanic Gardens, **Instituto Nacional de Pesquisas Amazonas** (INPA) ① Estrada do Aleixo, at Km 3, not far from the Museu de Ciências Naturais da Amazônia, T3643 3377, www.inpa.gov.br, Mon-Fri 0900-1100, 1400-1630, Sat-Sun 0900-1600, US$2, take any bus to Aleixo. At the centre for scientific research in the Amazon, labs (not open to the public) investigate farming, medicines and tropical diseases in the area. There is a small museum and restaurant, lots of birds, named trees and manatees (best seen Wednesday and Friday mornings when the water is changed), caimans and giant otters; worth a visit. **Museu de Ciências Naturais da Amazônia** ① Al Cosme Ferreira, Colonia Cachoeira Grande, 15 km from the city, T3644 2799, Mon-Sat 0900-1700, US$4, difficult to get to, take 'São José-Acoariquarape/Tropolis' bus 519 to Conjunto Petro, then 2 km walk. Best to combine with a visit to INPA, and take a taxi from there. The museum has a pavilion with insects and fish of the region. **Jardim Botânico 'Chico Mendes'** (Horto Municipal) ① Av André Araujo s/n, daily 0800-1200, 1400-1700, buses 'Aleixo', 'Coroado'. The botanical gardens contain a collection of plants from the Amazon region. The **zoo** ① Estrada Ponta Negra 750 (look for the life-size model jaguar), T3625 2044, Tue-Sun 0900-1630, US$0.65, plus US$1 for trail, getting there: take bus 120 or 207, 'Ponta Negra', from R Tamandaré, US$1. It is run by CIGS, the army jungle-survival unit. It has been expanded and improved and has a 800-m trail which leads into the zoo itself.

Excursions About 15 km from Manaus is the confluence of the yellow-brown Solimões (Amazon) and the blue-black Rio Negro, which is itself some 8 km wide, commonly known as the **'meeting of the waters'**. The two rivers run side by side for about 18 km (says one traveller) without their waters mingling. You can see this natural phenomenon in a range of ways depending on time and budget. Tourist agencies run boat trips to this spot (US$60-160) from town, or take you down to the Careiro ferry dock and make a trip from there. The simplest route is to take a taxi or No 713 'Vila Buriti' bus to the Careiro ferry dock, and take the car ferry across. The ferry (very basic, with no shelter on deck and no cabins) goes at 0700 returning 1000, and 1500 returning 1800 (approximately). Passenger ferries commute the crossing and you'll skim over the meeting of the waters for US$2 each way. Small private launches cross, 40 minutes' journey, US$15-20 per seat, ask for the engine to be shut off at the confluence, you should see dolphins especially in the early morning. Alternatively, hire a motorized canoe from near the market (US$15 approximately); allow three to four hours to experience the meeting properly). A 2-km walk along the Porto Velho road from the Careiro ferry terminal will lead to a point from which Victoria Regia water lilies can be seen in April/May-September in ponds, some way from the road. Agencies can arrange tours.

Arquipélago de Anavilhanas, the largest archipelago in a river in the world, is in the Rio Negro, some 100 km upstream from Manaus, near the town of Novo Airão. There are hundreds of islands, covered in thick vegetation. When the river is low, white sand beaches are revealed, as well as the roots and trunks of the trees. Tour companies arrange visits to the archipelago (see page 552).

Mamirauá ① 4-day, 3-night package US$360 all inclusive ("worth every penny"). Reservations through Toxx97-3343 4672, www.mamiraua.org.br. Can also be booked through their shop next to Teatro Amazonas on R 10 de Julho 495 (see Shopping). Book well in advance. All profits go to local projects and research. Daily flights Manaus-Tefé, then 1½ hours by boat to lodge. This sustainable development reserve, at the confluence of the Rios Solimões, Japurá and Auti-Paraná, is one of the best places to see the Amazon. It protects flooded forest (várzea) and is listed under the Ramsar Convention as an internationally important wetland. In the reserve Uakari is a floating lodge with 10 suites. Lots of mammals and birds to see, including cayman, dolphin and harpy eagles, also the endangered pirarucu fish. Visitors are accompanied by guides the whole time.

Tours from Manaus

There are two types of tours: those based at **jungle lodges** and **river boat trips**. Most tours, whether luxury or budget, combine river outings on motorized canoes with piranha fishing, caiman spotting, visiting local families and short treks in the jungle. Specialist tours include fishing trips and those aimed specifically at seeing how the people in the jungle, caboclos, live. Booking in advance on the internet is likely to secure you a good guide (who usually works for several companies and may get booked up). Be sure to ascertain in advance the exact itinerary of the tour, that the price includes everything (even drink and tips), that guides are knowledgeable and will accompany you themselves and that there will be no killing of anything rare. Ensure that others in your party share your expectations and are going for the same length of time. Choose a guide who speaks a language you can understand. A shorter tour may be better than a long, poor one. Packaged tours, booked overseas, are usually of the same price and quality as those negotiated locally.

Note There are many hustlers at the airport and on the street (particularly around the hotels and bars on Joaquim Nabuco and Miranda Leão), and even at the hotels. Don't go with the first friendly face you meet. Investigate a few operators, make enquiries and check for official and ABAV (Brazilian Association of Travel Agents) credentials personally. Secretaria de Estado da Cultura e Turismo is not allowed by law to recommend guides, but can provide you with a list of legally registered companies. Unfortunately, disreputable operations are rarely dealt with in any satisfactory manner and most continue to operate. When you are satisfied that you have found a reputable company, book direct with the company itself and ask for a detailed, written contract if you have any doubts.

Flights over the jungle give a spectacular impression of the extent of the forest (they were good value in 2006-2007). Bill Potter, resident in Manaus, writes: "opposite Manaus, near the junction of the Rio Negro and the Rio Solimões, lies the **Lago de Janauri**, a small nature reserve. This is where all the day or half-day trippers are taken, usually combined with a visit to the 'meeting of the waters'. Although many people express disappointment with this area because so little is seen and/or there are so many 'tourist-trash' shops, for those with only a short time it is worth a visit. You will see some birds and with luck dolphins. In the shops and bars there are often captive parrots and snakes. The area is set up to receive large numbers of tourists, which ecologists agree relieves pressure on other parts of the river. Boats for day trippers leave the harbour constantly throughout the day, but are best booked at one of the larger operators. Remember that in the dry season, one-day tours may not offer much to see if the river is low."

Those with more time can take the longer cruises and will see various ecological environments. To see virgin rainforest, a five-day trip by boat is needed. Most tour operators operate on both the Rio Solimões and the Rio Negro. The Rio Negro is considered easier to navigate, generally calmer and with fewer biting insects, but as it is a black water river with forest growing on poor soil and the tannin-filled waters are acidic, there are fewer frutiferous trees and fish and therefore fewer animals. The tributaries of the Solimões have higher concentrations of wildlife; including biting insects. Currently most Solimões tours go to the Rio Mamori area via the Port Velho highway and the Mamori river. There is plenty of deforestation along the initial stages of this river. The best lodges for wildlife are the furthest from Manaus but don't expect to see lots of animals. This is difficult anywhere in the Amazon, but you should see caiman, macaws, boa constrictors and river dolphins. It is the immensity of the forest and rivers and the seemingly limitless horizons, as well as a glimpse of the extraordinary way of life of the Amazon people, which make these tours exciting. For the best wildlife options in the Brazilian Amazon head for Alta Floresta, the Mamirauá reserve near Tefé (see above), or the little visited forests of northern Roraima.

Generally, between April and September excursions are only by boat; in the period October-March the Victoria Regia lilies virtually disappear. If using a camera, do remember to bring a fast film as light is dim.

Prices vary, but usually include lodging, guide, transport, meals and activities. The recommended companies charge within the following ranges (per person): one day, US$50-100; three days, eg to Anavilhanas Archipelago, US$195-285. Longer, specialized, or more luxurious excursions will cost significantly more. Most river trips incorporate the meeting of the waters on the first day, so there is no need to make a separate excursion. For Lodges, see under Sleeping, below.

What to take Leave luggage with your tour operator or hotel in Manaus and only take what is necessary for your trip. Long sleeves, long trousers, shoes and insect repellent are advisable for treks where insects are voracious. Take a mosquito net (and a hammock mosquito net if going on a cheaper tour) for trips in February-June. A hat offers protection from the sun on boat trips. Bottled water and other drinks are expensive in the jungle, so you may want to take your own supplies.

● Sleeping → See Telephone, page 347, for important phone changes.

Manaus p545, map p545

10% tax and service must be added to bills. Hotel booking service at airport (see Transport, below, on taxi drivers' ruses). The best option is the area around the Teatro Amazonas, where the Italianate colonial houses and cobbled squares have been refurbished. A less good alternative is the Zona Franca, which is convenient for shops, banks, restaurants and the port area, but is not very safe at night. Av Joaquim Nabuco and R dos Andradas have many cheap hotels (E), most of which charge by the hour and all of which are in an area which is undesirable after dark.

LL-L Taj Mahal Continental, Av Getúlio Vargas 741, T3627 3737, www.grupotajmahal.com.br. Large, impressive, one of best hotels in city, popular, tour agency for flights, revolving restaurant, massage and high level of service. Recommended.

LL-AL Tropical, Av Coronel Teixeira 1320, Ponta Negra, T2123 5000, www.tropicalhotel.com.br. A lavish, 5-star hotel 20 km outside the city (taxi to centre, US$25). All imaginable comforts and services, departure point for river cruises and agency which arranges them, churrascaria, pool, 24-hr coffee shop, open to well-dressed non-residents. Take minibus from R José Paranaguá in front of Petrobras building at the corner of Dr Moreira, US$6.50 return, 0830, 0930, 1130 to hotel, 1200, 1400, 1500, 1800 to town, or take Ponta Negra bus, US$1, then walk. It is rarely full, except in Jan-Feb. Companion hotel, **Tropical Business**, same price and web address, T2123 3000, is in a large tower block in the same grounds.

L-AL Best Western Lord Manaus, R Marcílio Dias 217, T3622 2844, bwmanaus@internext.com.br. Pleasant, spacious a/c lobby and standard, though well-presented rooms.

AL-A Lider, Av 7 de Setembro 827, T3621 9700, www.liderhotelmanaus.com.br. Small, modern a/c rooms with little breakfast tables. The best are at the front on the upper floors. Very well-kept.

A Ana Cassia Palace, R dos Andradas 14, T3303 3612, www.hotelanacassia.com.br. Gloriously faded, large rooms, some with great views of port, restaurant, pool.

A Manaós, Av Eduardo Ribeiro 881, T3633 5744, www.hotelmanaos.brasilcomercial.com. Recently renovated; smart a/c rooms with marble floors, decent breakfast, internet, next to Teatro Amazonas.

A-B Mônaco, R Silva Ramos 20, T2121 5026, www.hotelmonaco.tur.br. The furniture and fittings may be a bit old-fashioned and plastic, but wonderful views from the top floor rooms, restaurant and little pool, weekend rates **C**.

B Krystal, R Barroso 54, T3233 7535, www.kystallidermanaus-.com.br. A range of small though business-like, well-maintained modern a/c rooms.

B-C Brasil, Av Getúlio Vargas 657, T3233 7271, www.hotelbrasil.tur.br. Mid-market option close to centre, faded rooms and tiny bathrooms and balconies, small pool.

B-C Central, R Dr Moreira 202, T3622 2600, www.hotelcentralmanaus.com.br. A business hotel in the Zona Franca, check rooms thoroughly as many are very scruffy, but a few are good, excellent breakfast.

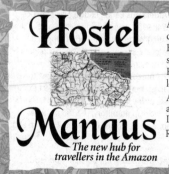

C-D 10 de Julho, R Dez de Julio 679, T3232 6280, www.hoteldezdejulho.com. Near opera house, a/c, much the best cheap option, very clean though simple rooms (some with a/c and hot water), efficient, but poor laundry, good tour operator (with different owner) and English-speaking staff.

D Itália, Rua Guilherme Moreira 325, T3234 7934. Very simple but well kept rooms in the heart of the Zona Franca, the best are on the upper floors. Generous breakfast.

E pp Hostel Manaus, Lauro Cavalcante 231, Centro, T3233 4545, www.hostelmanaus.com. **F** for HI members. Fine restored old house, with dormitory accommodation. Good location 1 block from Museu do Homem do Norte, reasonably central and quiet. Australian-run.

Camping There are no campsites near Manaus; it is difficult to find a good, safe place to camp wild.

Lodges near Manaus

There are several lodges within a few hrs boat or car journey from Manaus. Most emphasize comfort (although electricity and hot water is limited) rather than a real jungle experience and you are more likely to enjoy a nice buffet in pleasant company than come face to face with rare fauna. Nevertheless, the lodges are good if your time is limited and you want to have a brief taste of the Amazon rainforest. Agencies for reservations are also listed. Most of the lodges around Manaus apply the term 'ecotourism' very loosley. Very few of the lodges are locally owned and only a small percentage of labour is drawn from local communities. Only a handful of people have benefited from a boom which has seen the total number of beds rise from just 6 in 1979 to over 1000 today. See www.viverde.com.br for general information on lodges.

L Acajatuba Jungle Lodge, office at Conj Vila Municipal, Rua 07, no 87, Adrianópolis, T3642 0358, www.acajatuba.com.br. A 40-apartment lodge in a beautiful area on lake Acajatuba just below the Anavilhanas islands, 70 km from Manaus. Good piranha fishing, plenty of caiman and lots of várzea forest. It's close to Ariaú. Service can be patchy.

L Ariaú Amazon Towers, Rio Ariaú, 2 km from Archipélago de Anavilhanas, Manaus office at R Leonardo Malcher 699, T2121 5000, www.ariau towers.com.br. 60 km and 2 hrs by boat from Manaus on a side channel of the Rio Negro. Complex of towers connected by walkways, beach (Sep-Mar), trips to the Anavilhanas islands in groups of 10-20. Rates pp: US$280

for 2-days/1-night, US$400, 3 nights/ 4 days. Highly recommended.

L Amazon Ecopark Lodge, Igarapé do Tarumã, 20 km from Manaus, 15 mins by boat, jungle trails; 60 apartments with shower, bar, restaurant, T9146 0594, www.amazonecopark.com.br. Comfortable lodge with 60 apartments and a decent restaurant only 15 mins from Hotel Tropical and used by them for many of their day trips. Pleasant guided walks but poor for wildlife.

L Amazon Lodge, contact T3656 6030, naturesafaris@internext.com.br. A floating lodge on Lago do Juma, 80 km from Manaus, 30 mins by Careiro ferry, then 1½ hrs by bus, then 2 hrs by boat, 12 basic apartments with cold shower, restaurant, good excursions. Highly recommended as an excellent choice for wildlife.

L Boa Vida Jungle Resort, Rodovia 010, Km 53, on road to Itacoatiara, T3231 1661, www.boavida hotel.com.br. A small lodge with apartments and cabins with showers, fridge, bar and restaurant; good wildlife in the area.

L Juma Lodge, T3232 2707, www.juma hotel.com.br. Small lodge on the Rio Juma, idyllic location near the Rio Mamori, 2½ hrs south of Manaus by road and boat, all-inclusive packages. One of best options for wildlife and birdwatching.

L Pousada dos Guanavenas on Ilha de Silves, T3656 1500, www.guanavenas.com.br. 300 km from Manaus on the road to Itacoatiara then by boat along the Rio Urubu, views of Lago Canacari. Comfortable rooms with a/c and hot water and a good restaurant on a black water lake some 4-5 hrs from Manaus, but in an area with abundant wildlife.

AL Rainforest Lodge, contact MS Empreendimentos, T3233 9182, rflodge@ n3.com.br. On the banks of Lago Januacá, 4 hrs from Manaus, 14 bungalows with fans, pool, restaurant, snack bar.

AL Wild Cabanas, book through Brazilian Safaris (see Tour operators), www.wildcabana.com. Comfortable rooms and hammock space in a large maloca-like building on a caiman-filled lake close to the Rio Mamori. One of the best options for backpackers.

A Aldeia dos Lagos Lodge, Silves Project, T3248 9988, www.viverde.com.br/aldeia. Simple floating lodge on a lake, run in conjunction with the local community and WWF. Good for birds and caiman.

C-F Amazon Youth Hostel, near the town of Maués, southeast of Manaus. Contact Doña Nailê or Joe Maldonado, T9127 7941. US$75 per week in dormitory, US$150 per week in cabin, no electricity, take your own food and

---

For an explanation of the sleeping and eating price codes used in this guide, see page 58.
Other relevant information is found in Essentials pages 345-347.

hammock, kitchen, lounge, hiking, canoeing.
Rico Airlines, address on page 554, fly
Manaus-Maués US$75, 1 hr, or boat at 1600, arrive
1100 next day, US$25 (take own hammock).
In Maués go to Casa Quixada store and take a
water taxi to the hostel, US$30 per group.

ⓔ Eating

Manaus *p545, map p545*
Many restaurants close on Sun nights and
Mon. City authorities grade restaurants for
cleanliness: look for A and B.
ᵗᵗᵗ **La Barca**, R Recife 684, T642 3040. Wide
variety of fish dishes, very swanky, popular,
often has live music.
ᵗᵗᵗ **Himawari**, R 10 de Julho 618. Swish, sushi and
Japanese food, attentive service, opposite Teatro
Amazonas, open Sun night, when many
restaurants close. Recommended.
ᵗᵗᵗ-ᵗᵗ **Restaurant Tarumã** in Tropical Hotel
(see above). Dinner only.
ᵗᵗ **Búfalo**, churrascaria, Av Joaquim
Nabuco 628. Best in town, US$7, all-you-
can-eat Brazilian barbecue.
ᵗᵗ **Canto da Peixada**, R Emílio Moreira 1677 (Praça
14 de Janeiro). Superb fish dishes, lively atmosphere,
unpretentious, close to centre, take a taxi.
ᵗᵗ **Fiorentina**, R José Paranaguá 44, Praça da
Polícia. Fan-cooled, traditional Italian, including
vegetarian dishes, average food but one of best
options in centre, watch out for the mugs of
wine! Great feijoada on Sat, half-price on Sun.
ᵗᵗ **Pizzaria Scarola**, R 10 de Julho 739, corner
with Av Getúlio Vargas. Standard Brazilian menu,
pizza delivery, popular.
ᵗ **Alemã**, R José Paranaguá, Praça da Polícia.
Food by weight, great pastries, hamburgers,
juices, sandwiches.
ᵗ **Brasil**, Av Getúlio Vargas next to hotel of same
name. Food by weight, juice and sandwich kiosk
outside hotel.
ᵗ **O Naturalista**, R 7 de Setembro 752, 2nd floor.
Vegetarian pay-by-weight, lunch only, good.
ᵗ **Senac**, R Saldanha Marinho, 644. Cookery
school, self-service, open daily, lunch only.
Highly recommended.
ᵗ **Skina dos Sucos**, Eduardo Ribeiro e 24 de
Maio. Regional fruit juices and snacks.
ᵗ **Sorveteria Glacial**, Av Getúlio Vargas 161 and
other locations. Recommended for ice cream.

ⓕ Bars and clubs

Manaus *p545, map p545*
The city has very lively nightlife – especially live
forró and pagodé. **Mon Coração Blue**, Estrada
Ponta Negra, live forró and general dance in a
large club, US$2 entrance. **Tue Hollywood**

Rock, Estrada Ponta Negra, live pagodé, US$2
entrance. **Wed Antares**, Estrada Dom Pedro,
Kisia, live brega (a frenetic northern Brazilian
form of forró), US$2. **Thu Clube do Forró**,
Estrada do Aleixo, live forró, US$2. **Fri Simbola**,
Estrada Ponta Negra, big club with 3 floors
playing a mix of club music, forró and pagodé,
US$3.50. **Sat** numerous clubs especially **Simbola**
and **Taliãsm Forró** club in Cachoeirinha.
Sun Hollywoodand **Simbola**.
Bar do Armando, 10 de Julho e Tapajós, behind
the Teatro. Bohemian atmosphere, good place
for drinking outside.
DJ (Djalma) Oliveira, T9112 3942, specializes
in taking people out to sample Manaus club life,
is cheaper than taxis and speaks a little English.
He can be booked through Gero's Tours.
O Laranjinha, Ponta Negra, is lively any week
night and has a live Boi Bumba dance show on
Wed. Be wary of 'piranhas' of the female, human
kind after midnight.

ⓖ Entertainment

Manaus *p545, map p545*
Performing arts For Teatro Amazonas and
Centro Cultural Pálacio Rio Negro, see above.
Teatro da Instalação, R Frei José dos Inocentes,
T/F3622 2840. Performance space in recently
restored historic buildings with free music and
dance (everything from ballet to jazz), Mon-Fri
May-Dec at 1800. Charge for performances Sat
and Sun. Recommended.
Funfair In Praça da Saudade, R Ramos Ferreira,
there is a Sun funfair from 1700; try prawns and
calaloo dipped in tacaca sauce.

ⓗ Festivals and events

Manaus *p545, map p545*
6 Jan: Epiphany; **Ash Wednesday**, half-day;
Maundy Thursday; **24 Jun**: São João; **14 Jul**;
5 Sep; **30 Oct**; **1 Nov**, All Saints' Day, half-day;
Christmas Eve; New Year's Eve, half-day.
Feb: Carnival dates vary – 5 days of Carnival,
culminating in the parade of the Samba
Schools. 3rd week in **Apr**: Week of the Indians,
indigenous handicraft. In **Jun**: Festival do
Amazonas; a celebration of all the cultural
aspects of Amazonas life, indigenous,
Portuguese and from the northeast, especially
dancing; **29 Jun**: São Pedro, boat processions
on the Rio Negro. In **Sep**: Festival da Bondade,
last week, stalls from neighbouring states and
countries offering food, handicrafts, music and
dancing, SESI, Estrada do Aleixo Km 5. **Oct**:
Festival Universitário de Música – FUM, the
most traditional festival of music in Amazonas,
organized by the university students, on the

University Campus. **8 Dec: Processão de Nossa Senhora da Conceicão**, from the Igreja Matriz through the city centre and returning to Igreja Matriz for a solemn mass.

0155-1200). There is a good supermarket at the corner of Av Joaquin Nabuco and Av Sete de Setembro. **Shopping Amazonas**, outside the city, is a mall with cinema, supermarket, fast food.

O Shopping

Manaus *p545, map p545*
Since Manaus is a free port, the whole area a few blocks off the river front is full of electronics shops. All shops close at 1400 on Sat and all day Sun.
Bookshops Livraria Nacional, R 24 de Maio 415. Stocks some French books. **Paper Comunicação**, Av J Nabuco 2074-2. For maps. **Usados CDs e Livros**, Av Getúlio Vargas 766. Selection of used books, English, German, French and Spanish. **Valer**, R Ramos Ferreira 1195. A few English classics stocked, best bookshop in city.
Handicrafts There are many handicrafts shops in the area around the Teatro Amazonas, including **Ecoshop**, R 10 de Julho 509a, www.eco shop.com.br, with a good little a/c café and the **Mamirauá Shop**, R 10 de Julho 495, with a range of indigenous crafts and books and information on the Mamirauá Reserve. In the Praça do Congresso, Av E Ribeiro, there is a very good Sun craftmarket. The souvenir shop at the INPA has some interesting Amazonian products on sale. For hammocks go to R dos Andradas, many shops. **Central Artesanato**, R Recife s/n, near Detran. For local craft work. **Selva Amazônica**, Mercado Municipal. For wood carvings and bark fabric.
Markets and supermarkets Go to the Mercado Adolfo Lisboa (see above) early in the morning when it is full of good quality regional produce, food and handicrafts, look out for guaraná powder or sticks, scales of pirarucu fish (used for manicure), and its tongue used for rasping guaraná (open Mon-Sat 0500-1800, Sun and holidays

▲ Activities and tours

Manaus *p545, map p545*
Check agencies' licences from tourist office and ABAV. If in the least doubt, use only a registered company.
Swimming For swimming, go to Ponta Negra beach by Soltur bus, US$1, though the beach virtually disappears beneath the water in Apr-Aug; popular by day and at night with outdoor concerts and samba in the summer season. Every Sun, boats leave from the port in front of the market to beaches along Rio Negro, US$2.65, leaving when full and returning at end of the day. This is a real locals' day out, with loud music and food stalls on the sand. Good swimming at waterfalls on the Rio Tarumã, where lunch is available, shade, crowded at weekends. Take Tarumã bus from R Tamandaré or R Frei J dos Inocentes, 30 mins, US$1.10 (very few on weekdays), getting off at the police checkpoint on the road to Itacoatiara.

Tour operators
Amazon Clipper Cruises, R Sucupira 249, Conj Kissia, Planalto, www.amazonclipper.com.br. Informed guides, well-planned activities, comfortable cabins and good food.
Amazon Jungle Tours, R Dr Moreira 163, 1st floor, T3231 1067, www.arquipelagotours.com.br. A range of boat and trekking trips throughout the Rio Negro. Their Anavilhanas trips are very good.
Amazonatours, T3232 8271/9624 2419 or in Spain 34-61-521 9070, www.amazonatours.com. Spanish/Brazilian run agency offering trips further afield and to their small lodge in the Tupana Natural Reserve. Recommended.

Brazilian Safaris, R 10 de Julho 632, T8112 7154, www.braziliansafaris.com. Ground operator for many of the smaller agencies with their own lodge off the Rio Mamori and a range of good budget trips.

Gero's Tours, R 10 de Julho 679, T9983 6273, www.amazongerotours.com. Backpacker-oriented tours south of the Solimões and bookings made for lodges everywhere. Gero, the owner is very friendly and dedicated.

Heliconia, R Col Salgado 63, Aparecida, T3234 5915, www.heliconia-amazon.com. Run by French researcher Thérèse Aubreton.

Iguana Tour, R 10 de Julho 679, T3633 6507, or 9627 4151 (24 hrs), www.amazonbrasil.com.br. Short and long tours, plenty of activities, many languages spoken.

Jaguar Adventure Tours R Marciano Armond, Vila Operária 23A, Cachoeirinha, T3663 2998, 9156 7185 (mob), www.amazontoursbrazil.com. Carlos Jorge Damasceno, multilingual, deep jungle exploration with an ecological slant and visits to remote historical and indigenous settlements.

Jungle Experience, R dos Andradas 491, T3233 9423, antoniogomes5@hotmail.com. New agency working with **Hostel Manaus** (although based at **Hotel Ideal**). Can arrange usual trips, and have a quiet jungle camp about four hours out of town.

Swallows and Amazons, R Quintino Bocaiúva 189, Suite 13, T/F3622 1246, www.swallows andamazonstours.com. Mark and Tania Aitchison offer a wide range of riverboat tours and accommodation (up to 16 days); they have their own houseboat *Dona Tania*, river boat and 15-room private jungle lodge, The *Araras Lodge*, just before the Anavilhanas islands. They also offer fishing trips with **Yanna Ecofishing**. Very comprehensive service, with full assistance for travellers (reservations, email, transfers, medical, etc), English-, French- and Spanish-speaking guides. Prices start at US$65 per day.

Tucunaré Turismo, R Miranda Leão 194, T3234 5017, www.tucunareturismo.com.br. Branch at the airport and a few blocks east of the docks. Good for internal flights.

Guides

Guides are licensed to work only through tour agencies, so it is safest to book guides through approved agencies. Advance notice and a minimum of 3 people for all trips offered by these guides:

Samuel Basilio, T9616 3124, samuelbasilio@ hotmail.com. A guide from the upper Rio Negro specializing in long expeditions; has worked on many BBC documentaries as a location finder.

Moreno Ortelli, T9605 0519, morenojivaro@ hotmail.com. One of the few guides in Manaus who knows his birds. Excellent knowledge of indigenous culture and fascinating trips to explore this. Many languages.

Matthias Raymond, T8115 5716, raymathias@ hotmail.com. A Waipixana indigenous guide offering trips to further reaches of the forest including the Pico da Neblina (with notice). Many languages.

⊙ Transport

Manaus *p545, map p545*

Air Airport T3652 1212. **International flights**: Copa and TAM have flights to **Miami**. To the **Guyanas**, Meta (no office in town) flies from the small Eduardinho airport (by main airport) twice a week to **Georgetown** and **Paramaribo**, via Boa Vista. **Internal flights**: there are frequent internal flights with **Varig**, **Penta**, **TAM**, **Tavaj** and low cost airlines. You can usually get where you want to go, and if you can fly early, it can be quite cheap. **Rico Airlines** fly to Tefé, Tabatinga, Belém, Santarém, Porto Velho and other Amazon destinations. Domestic airport tax US$7. The taxi fare to or from the airport is US$16-19, with meter (check the driver uses it).

Bus to town leaves from stop outside terminal on the right. Bus No 306 'Aeroporto Internacional' (or from R Tamandaré near the cathedral), US$2. Buses are 24 hr, but less reliable in the night so get a taxi if time is critical. It is sometimes possible to use the more regular, faster service run by the Tropical Hotel; many tour agencies offer free transfers without obligation. Check all connections on arrival. Local flights leave from airport terminal 2: make sure in advance of your terminal. **Note** Check in time is 2 hrs in advance. Allow plenty of time at Manaus airport, formalities are very slow especially if you have purchased duty-free goods. The restaurant serves good à la carte and buffet food through the day. Many flights depart in the middle of the night and while there are many snack bars there is nowhere to rest.

Bus Manaus rodoviária is 9 km out of town at the intersection of Av Constantino Nery and R Recife, T3642 5805. Take a local bus from centre, US$0.70, marked 'Aeroporto Internacional' or 'Cidade Nova' (or taxi, US$6.50) and ask the driver to tell you where to get off. Local buses to Praça 14 or the airport leave from Praça Adalberto Vale (take airport bus and alight just after Antárctica factory) or take local bus to Ajuricaba. **Ferry** To **Santarém**, Belém, Porto Velho, Tefé, **Tabatinga** (for Colombia and Peru), **São Gabriel da Cachoeira**, and intermediate ports (see Boat services, page 534). Almost all passenger vessels now berth at the first (downstream) of the floating docks which is open to the public 24 hrs a day. Tickets are sold at booths at the boat terminal in front of the docks. A tourist office in a purpose-built shopping complex on the dockside will help travellers buy tickets (avoiding touts) and will translate for you as you look over the boats. The names and itineraries of departing vessels are displayed here as well as on the docked boats themselves. The port is relatively clean, well organized, and has a pleasant atmosphere.

ENASA (the state shipping company) sells tickets for private boats at its office in town (prices tend to be high here), R Mcal Deodoro 61, T3633 3280. Local boats and some cargo barges still berth by the concrete retaining wall between the market and Montecristi. Boats for São Gabriel da Cachoeira and Novo Airão go from São Raimundo, up river from the main port. Take bus 101 'São Raimundo', or 112 'Santo Antônio', 40 mins; there are 2 docking areas separated by a hill, the São Raimundo balsa, where the ferry to Novo Airão, on the Rio Negro, leaves every afternoon (US$13); and the Porto Beira Mar de São Raimundo, where the São Gabriel da Cachoeira boats dock (most departures Fri). **Note** Departures to the less important destinations are not always known at

the **Capitânia do Porto**, Av Santa Cruz 265, Manaus. Be careful of people who wander around boats after they've arrived at a port: they are almost certainly looking for something to steal.

Immigration For those arriving by boat who have not already had their passports stamped (eg from Leticia), the immigration office is on the first of the floating docks. Take the dock entrance opposite the cathedral, bear right, after 50 m left, pass through a warehouse to a group of buildings on a T section.

Road The Catire Highway (BR 319) from Manaus to Porto Velho (868 km), has been officially closed since 1990. Enquire locally if the road is passable for light vehicles; some bridges are flimsy. The alternative for drivers is to ship a car down river on a barge, others have to travel by boat.

O Directory

Manaus p545, map p545
Airline offices BRA, Av Santos Dumont s/n, Tarumã, T3631-0007. **LAB**, Av 7 de Setembro 993, T3633 4200. **Meta**, Av Santos Dumont 1350, T3652 1105. **Rico**, R 24 de Maio 60-B and at airport, T4009 8333, www.voerico.com.br. **TAM**, Av Joaquim Nabuco 1846 Sl-2, T3233 7744. **Trip**, Av Boulevard Álvaro Maia 2166, Adrianópolis, T3652 1243. **Varig**, T4003 7000, at airport T3652 1598. **Banks** Banco do Brasil, Guia Moreira, and airport changes US$ cash, 8% commission, both with ATMs for Visa/Plus, Cirrus/MasterCard. Most offices shut at 1500; foreign exchange operations 0900-1200 only, or even as early as 1100. **Bradesco**, Av 7 de Setembro 895/293, for Visa ATM. **HSBC**, R Dr Moreira, 226. ATM for Visa, Cirrus, MasterCard and Plus. **Credicard**, Av Getúlio Vargas 222 for Diner's cash advances. Cash at main hotels; **Câmbio Cortez**, 7 de Setembro 1199, converts TCs into US$ cash, good rates, no commission. Also in Amazonas Shopping Center, end of Av Djalma Batista. Do not change money on the streets. **Embassies and consulates** Austria, Rua 5, 4 Qde Jardim Primavera T3642 1939. **Belgium**, 13 qd D conj Murici, T3236 1452. **Colombia**, R 24 de Maio 220, Rio Negro Centre, T3622 6078, double check whether a Colombian tourist card can be obtained at the border. **Denmark**, R Timbiras 306, T3646 5330, also handles Norway. **Finland**, R Marcílio Dias 131, T3622 6276. **France**, Av Visc de Sepetiba 17, Flores, T3648 5959. **Germany**, Av 24 Maio 220, Ed Rio Negro Centre, sala 812, T3622 8800, 1000-1200. **Japan**, R Fortaleza 416, T3232 2000. **Netherlands**, R M Leão 41, T3622 1366, ilko@bemol.com.br. **Peru**, Rua H, 12, Morada do Sol, Aleixo, T3642 1203. **Portugal**, R Ferreira Pena 37, T3633 1235. **Spain**, Al Cosme

Ferreira 1225, Aleixo, T3644 3800. **Sweden**, R Rio Quixito 86, T3616 9043. **UK**, R Poraquê 240, Distrito Industrial, T3613 1819, vincent@internext.com.br. **US**, R Franco de Sá 310, Ed Atrium, São Francisco, T3611 3333; will supply letters of introduction for US citizens. **Venezuela**, R Rio Jataí 839, T3233 6006, 0800-1200. Some nationalities entering Venezuela overland need a visa (check in advance with a Venezuelan consulate); all need a yellow fever certificate. **Internet** Many around the Teatro including **Loginet**, R 10 de Julho 625. **Amazon Cyber Cafe**, Av Getúlio Vargas 626, corner with R 10 de Julho, US$1.50 per hr. Another at No 188, 0800-2300, US$2 per hr. **Discover Internet**, R Marcílio Dias 304, next to Praça da Polícia, cabins in back of shop with Internet phones and scanners, US$1.50 per hr. **Internext**, R 24 de Maio 220, US$3 per hr. **Medical services** Clínica São Lucas, R Alexandre Amorin 470, T3622 3678, reasonably priced, some English spoken, good service, take a taxi. **Hospital Tropical**, Av Pedro Teixeira (D Pedro I) 25, T3238 1711. Centre for tropical medicine, not for general complaints,

treatment free, some doctors speak a little English. Take buses 201 or 214 from Av Sete de Setembro in the city centre. **Pronto Soccoro 28 de Agosto**, R Recife 1581, T3642 4272, free for emergencies.

Post offices Main office including poste restante on Marechal Deodoro. On the 1st floor is the philatelic counter where stamps are sold, avoiding the long queues downstairs. Staff don't speak English but are used to dealing with tourists. For airfreight and shipping, Alfândega, Av Marquês Santa Cruz (corner of Marechal Deodoro), Sala 106. For airfreight and seamail, Correio Internacional, R Monsenhor Coutinho e Av Eduardo Ribeiro (bring your own packaging). **Telephone** International calls can be made from local call boxes with an international card. Also **Telemar**, Av Getúlio Vargas 950 e R Leo Malcher. **Useful addresses** Police: to extend or replace a Brazilian visa, take bus from Praça Adalberto Vale to Kissia Dom Pedro for Polícia Federal post, people in shorts not admitted, T3655 1517. **Ibama**: R Ministro João Gonçalves de Souza s/n, BR-319, Km 01, Distrito Industrial, Caixa Postal 185, CEP 69900-000, T3613 3277.

Amazon frontiers

To get to the border with Colombia and Peru, a river boat is the only alternative to flying and this, of course, is the true way to experience the Amazon. On the route to Venezuela, buses and trucks have almost entirely replaced river traffic to Boa Vista, from where roads go to Santa Elena de Uairén and Lethem in Guyana.

Rondônia and Acre, lands which mark not just the political boundaries between Brazil and Peru and Bolivia, but also developmental frontiers between the forest and colonization. Much of Rondônia has been deforested. Acre is still frontier country with great expanses of forest in danger of destruction.

Manaus to Colombia, Peru, Venezuela and Guyana

Benjamin Constant and around → *Phone code: 0xx97. Colour map 3, grid A5.*
Benjamin Constant is on the border with Peru, with Colombian territory on the opposite bank of the river. The **Ticuna Indian Museum** ① *Av Castelo Branco 396*, display photographs, costumes, traditional art and music. **Tabatinga** (*Phone code 0xx97*) is 4 km from Leticia (Colombia). The Port Captain in Tabatinga is reported as very helpful and speaks good English. The port area of Tabatinga is called **Marco**. A good hammock will cost US$20 in Tabatinga (try Esplanada Teocides) or Benjamin Constant. A mosquito net for a hammock is essential if sailing upstream from Tabatinga; much less so downstream. **Note** In this area, carry your passport at all times.

Border with Colombia and Peru
Check all requirements and procedures before arriving at this multiple border. Enquire carefully about embarkation/disembarkation points and where to go through immigration formalities. If waiting for transport, Tabatinga has convenient hotels for early morning departures, but Leticia has the best money changing facilities and more internet facilities (try the bookshop next to the church). **Note** When crossing these borders, check if there is a time difference (for example, Brazilian summer time, usually mid-October to mid-February). **Consulates** Brazilian ① *Cra 9, No 13-84, Leticia, T08-592 7530, brvcleticia@yahoo.com.br, 1000-1600, Mon-Fri, onward*

ticket and 2 black-and-white photos needed for visa (photographer nearby); allow 36 hrs, efficient, helpful. **Peruvian** ① *Cra 11, No 5-32, Leticia, T08-592 7204, 0900-1300; no entry or exit permits are given here.*

Brazilian immigration Entry and exit stamps are given at the Polícia Federal, 2 km from the Tabatinga docks, best to take a taxi, 24 hours. Proof of US$500 or an onward ticket may be asked for. There are no facilities in Benjamin Constant. One-week transit in Tabatinga is permitted. The Colombian consulate is at ① *R Gen Sampaio 623, T3412 2104, ctabatin@minrelext.gov.co, 0800-1600.* Tourist cards are issued on presentation of two passport photos. **Note** If coming from Peru, you must have a Peruvian exit stamp and a yellow fever certificate.

Colombian immigration DAS ① *C9, No 9-62, T59-24878, secamaadm@das.gov.co, Leticia, and at the airport.* Exit stamps to leave Colombia by air or overland are given by DAS no more than 1 day before you leave. If flying into Leticia prior to leaving for Brazil or Peru, get an exit stamp while at the airport. Check both offices for entry stamps before flying into Colombia. To enter Colombia you must have a tourist card to obtain an entry stamp, even if you are passing through Leticia en route between Brazil and Peru (the Colombian consul in Manaus may tell you otherwise; try to get a tourist card elsewhere). The Colombian Consular Office in Tabatinga issues tourist cards; 24-hour transit stamps can be obtained at the DAS office. If visiting Leticia without intending to go anywhere else in Colombia, you may be allowed to enter without immigration or customs formalities (but travellers' cheques cannot be changed without an entry stamp). Travel between Colombia and Brazil and Peru is given below. Travel from/into Colombia is given under Leticia. **Note** There are no customs formalities for everyday travel between Leticia and Tabatinga.

Peruvian immigration Entry/exit formalities take place at Santa Rosa. Every boat leaving and entering Peru stops here. There is also an immigration office in Iquitos (Mcal Cáceres 18th block, T235371), where procedures for leaving can be checked. There is no Brazilian consulate in Iquitos No exchange facilities in Santa Rosa; reais and dollars are accepted, but soles are not accepted in Leticia and only occasionally in Tabatinga.

Manaus to Venezuela and Guyana

The road which connects Manaus and Boa Vista (BR-174 to Novo Paraíso, then the Perimetral, BR-210, rejoining the BR174 after crossing the Rio Branco at Caracaraî) can get badly potholed. There are service stations with toilets, camping, etc, every 150-180 km, but all petrol is low octane. Drivers should take a tow cable and spares, and bus passengers should prepare for delays in the rainy season. At Km 100 is Presidente Figueiredo, with many waterfalls and a famous cave with bats, shops and a restaurant. About 100 km further on is a service station at the entrance to the **Uaimiri Atroari Indian Reserve**, which straddles the road for about 120 km. Private cars and trucks are not allowed to enter the Indian Reserve between sunset and sunrise, but buses are exempt from this regulation. Nobody is allowed to stop within the reserve at any time. At the northern entrance to the reserve there are toilets and a spot to hang your hammock (usually crowded with truckers overnight). At Km 327 is the village of Vila Colina with Restaurante Paulista, good food, clean, you can use the shower and hang your hammock. At Km 359 there is a monument to mark the equator. At Km 434 is the clean and pleasant Restaurant Goaio. Just south of Km 500 is Bar Restaurante D'Jonas, a clean, pleasant place to eat, you can also camp or sling a hammock. Beyond here, large tracts of forest have been destroyed for settlement, but already many homes have been abandoned.

At **Caracaraí**, a busy port with modern installations on the Rio Branco, a bridge crosses the river for traffic on the Manaus-Boa Vista road. It has hotels in our **D-E** range. Boa Vista has road connections with the Venezuelan frontier at Santa Elena de Uairén (237 km, paved, the only gasoline 110 km south of Santa Elena) and Bonfim for the Guyanese border at Lethem. Both roads are open all year.

Boa Vista → *Phone code: 0xx95. Post code: 69300. Colour map 2, grid B2. Population: 200,568.*
The capital of the extreme northern State of Roraima, 785 km north of Manaus, is a pleasant, clean, laid-back little town on the Rio Branco. Tourism is beginning here and there are a number interesting new destinations opening up, many offering a chance to explore far wilder and fauna-rich country than that around Manaus. The landscape is more diverse, too, with a mix of tropical forest, savannah and highlands dotted with waterfalls. The area immediately

around the city has been heavily deforested. It has an interesting modern cathedral; also a museum of local indigenous culture (poorly kept). There is swimming in the Rio Branco, 15 minutes from the town centre (too polluted in Boa Vista), reachable by bus only when the river is low. **Tourist office: Detur** ① *Av Capitão Julio Bezerra 193, T3623 2365, www.rr.gov.br.* Information is available at the rodoviária, T3623 1238; also in the **Prefeitura's tourist office** ① *R Floriano Peixoto, Centro, beside the Orla Tuamanan, Tue-Sun 1600-2200.*

Border with Venezuela

Border searches are thorough and frequent at this border crossing. If entering Brazil, ensure in advance that you have the right papers, including yellow fever certificate, before arriving at this border. Officials may give only two months' stay and car drivers may be asked to purchase an unnecessary permit. Ask to see the legal documentation. Everyone who crosses this border to Venezuela must also have a yellow fever certificate. Check requirements for visas beforehand (some nationalities need one, but not, for example, Western Europeans). See the Directory, below, for the Venezuelan consulate. There is another Venezuelan consulate in Manaus (see above). On the Brazilian side there is a basic hotel, Pacaraima Palace, a guest house, camping and a bank.

Border with Guyana → *Colour map 2, grid B3. Population: 9,326.*

The main border crossing between Brazil and Guyana is from **Bonfim**, 125 km (all paved) northeast of Boa Vista, to Lethem. The towns are separated by the Rio Tacutu, which is crossed by small boats for foot passengers, 5 minutes, US$2; vehicles cross by ferry on demand. The river crossing is 2.5 km from Bonfim, 1.6 km north of Lethem. A bridge is under construction. Formalities are strict on both sides of the border: it is essential to have a yellow fever vaccination both to leave Brazil and to enter Guyana The bus passes through Brazilian Immigration where you receive your exit stamp before stopping at the river. After the crossing, there are taxis to the Guyana Immigration office (US$3). You are given a visa for the exact amount of time you stipulate staying. The border is open 24 hours, but officials tend to leave immigration after 1800.

There is no Guayanese consul in Boa Vista, so if you need a visa for Guyana, you must get it in São Paulo or Brasília (see Guyana Documents in Essentials). Reais can be changed into Guyanese dollars in Boa Vista. There are no exchange facilities in Lethem, but reais are accepted in town.

⬤ **Sleeping** → *See Telephone, page 347, for important phone changes.*

Benjamin Constant and around *p555*
There are a number of very cheap, simple *pousadas* in town.
B Benjamin Constant, R Getulio Vargas 36, beside ferry, T3415 5638. A/c, some rooms with hot water and TV, good restaurant, arranges tours, postal address Apto Aéreo 219, Leticia, Colombia. Recommended.

Tabatinga
There are decent places to stay near the boat companies for Peru.
C Pousada do Sol, General Sampaio, T3412 3355. With sauna and pool, simple rooms, helpful.
D-E Travellers Jungle Home, R Marechal Rondón 86. Small hostel and tour operator with Brazilian and French owners.

Boa Vista *p556*
Accommodation is generally expensive. Economic hardship has caused an increase in crime, sometimes violent.
AL Aipana Plaza, Joaquim Nabuco 53, T3224

4116, aipana@technet.com.br. Best in town with plain rooms decorated with photos of Roraima, hot water, a/c, cable TV, attractive pool area with a shady little bar.
A Uiramutam Palace, Av Capt Ene Garcez 427, T3224 9757, uiramutam@technet.com.br. Business hotel with modest rooms, a/c, cable TV and large bathrooms. Decent pool.
B Barrudada, R Araújo Filho 228, T3623 1378. Simple a/c rooms in a modern tower block very close to the centre. The best on the upper floors have views out to the river. Breakfast and lunch included.
C Eusêbio's, R Cecília Brasil 1107, T3623 0300, F3623 9131. Spruce, modest rooms with a/c and en suites with c/w showers. The best are airy and on the upper floors. Pleasant pool and a laundry service. Has a good a/c restaurant (♈♈) serving fish, *feijoada* and meat dishes and a generous breakfast.

D Terraço, Av Cecília Brasil 1141. Without bath, noisy, friendly.

D-E Ideal, R Araújo Filho 481, T3224 6342. Simple but well-kept rooms, some have a/c, generous breakfast and convenient for the centre.
Camping Rio Caaumé, 3 km north of town (unofficial site, small bar, clean river, pleasant).

Border with Guyana: Bonfim *p557*
D Bonfim, owned by Mr Myers, who speaks English and is very helpful, fan, shower.

🍴 Eating

Benjamin Constant and around *p555*
In Benjamin Constant eat at **Pensão Cecília**, or **Bar-21 de Abril**, which is cheaper.
♥-♥ Canto do Peixado, on main street, Tabatinga. Excellent food. Highly recommended.
♥ Lanchonete e Sorveteria Mallet, Tabatinga, fresh juices, ice creams, burgers, popular.

Boa Vista *p556*
There are several restaurants serving snacks and juices on the riverside along R Floriano Peixoto.
♥♥ Peixada Tropical, R Pedro Rodrigues at Ajuricaba, T224 6040. A range of river fish dishes in various styles from Bahian sauces to Milanesa.
♥ 1000 Sabores, R Araújo Filho e Benjamin Constant. Pizzas, snacks and juices. Open early and closing late.
♥ Café com Leite Suíço, at Santa Cecilia, 15 mins by car on road to Bom Fim. Open 0630-1300 for regional food, US$4, good.
♥ Catequeiro, Araújo Filho e Benjamin Constant. Recommended *prato feito*.
♥ Frangão, R Homen de Melo e Cecília Brasil. Barbecued chicken, fish accompanied by salads, rice, beans, etc.
♥ La Góndola, Benjamin Constant e Av Amazonas. Good.

Border with Guyana: Bonfim *p557*
There is a café at the rodoviária, opposite the church, whose owner speaks English and gives information. **Restaurante Internacional**, opposite the rodoviária, on other side from church; another restaurant a bit further from the rodoviária serves good food. Local speciality, fried cashew nuts.

🍸 Bars and clubs

Boa Vista *p556*
R Floriano Peixoto is lively after dark at weekends when there is live music in and around the **Orla** Taumanan; a complex of little bars and restaurants.
Toca, Orla Taumanan, T9971 5454. River cruises and parties with live music and dancing.

⛷ Activities and tours

Benjamin Constant around around: Tabatinga *p555*
Travellers Jungle Home, R Marechal Rondon, 86. English and French owners, budget prices.

Boa Vista *p556*
Acqua, R Floriano Peixoto 505, T224 6576. Tours and boat trips on Rio Branco and surrounding waterways (jungle, beaches, Indian reservations). Guide Elieser Rufino is recommended.
Roraima Adventures, R Sebastião Diniz 787, T3624 9611, 9115 4171 (mob), www.roraima-brasil.com.br. A range of interesting trips to little known and little visited parts of Roraima including the spectacular Tepequem and Serra Grande mountains and the Rio Uraricoera, which is replete with wildlife. Pre-formed groups get the best prices, which are competitive with Manaus. Helpful with visas for Venezuela.

🚌 Transport

Border with Colombia and Peru *p555*
Brazil to Colombia
Air Local airlines provide flights in the region. From the airport at Tabatinga to town by minibus, US$1. See also under Leticia (Colombia). Regular minibus from airport to Leticia, US$0.90.
Ferry From Manaus to Benjamin Constant boats normally go on to Tabatinga, and start from there when going to Manaus. Boat services from Manaus to Benjamin Constant, 7 days, or more; to Manaus, 4 days, or more. They usually wait 1-2 days in both Tabatinga and Benjamin Constant before returning to Manaus; you can stay on board. It's quicker to get off the river boat in Benjamin Constant and take a fast ferry, US$3, 2 hrs, to Tabatinga, than stay on the river boat for the crossing from Benjamin Constant. Boats arrive in Benjamin Constant at 0600, so you can take the 0700 ferry and have a enough time in Tabatinga to get exit stamps and book the launch to Iquitos for the next day. For information on boats to/from Manaus, see Manaus Shipping and River Transport in Amazônia.
Taxi Travel between Tabatinga and Leticia is very informal; taxis between the 2 towns charge US$5 (more if you want to stop at immigration offices, exchange houses, etc; beware of taxi drivers who want to rush you expensively over the border before it 'closes'), or US$1 in a colectivo (more after 1800).

Brazil to Peru
Ferry Santa Rosa-Tabatinga or Leticia, US$2.50 (in reais, soles or pesos). Between Tabatinga and Iquitos in Peru there are 3 companies with 20-seater speedboats, US$60 one way, buy ticket 1 day in advance (**River Fox** not recommended,

unsafe). They take 11-12 hrs. Luggage limit is 15 kg. Departure from Tabatinga is 0530 (be there 0500). There are also cheaper, slower lanchas, which 2 days (US$15-17.50 hammock, US$25-30 cabin). Boat services are given under **Iquitos** in the Peru chapter. Passengers leaving and entering Peru must visit immigration at Santa Rosa when the boat stops there. For entry into Brazil, formalities are done in Tabatinga; for Colombia, in Leticia.

Boa Vista *p556*
Air Flights to **Manaus** with Meta, and to **Georgetown**. Also flights to São Paulo, Rio de Janeiro, Belém, etc. Book through **Aguia**, R Benjamin Constant 1683B, T3624 1516 (owner speaks some English). No left luggage, information or exchange facilities at the airport, which is 4 km from the centre. Bus 'Aeroporto' from the centre is US$0.50. Taxi to rodoviária, US$10, to centre US$13, 45 mins' walk.
Bus (See also Border Crossings, page 561.) Rodoviária is 3 km at the end of Av Ville Roy; taxi to centre, US$10, bus US$0.90, 10 mins (marked '13 de Setembro' or 'Joquey Clube' to centre). The local bus terminal is on Av Amazonas, by R Cecília Brasil, near central praça. It is difficult to get a taxi or bus to the rodoviária in time for early morning departures; as it's a 25-min walk, book a taxi the previous evening. To **Manaus**, US$55, several companies including **Eucatur**, 12 hrs, at least 6 daily, executivo service at 1800/1900 with meal stop. Advisable to book. Buses between Boa Vista and **Caracaraí** take 8 hrs.

Border with Venezuela *p557*
Bus One bus a day goes from Boa Vista rodoviária to **Santa Elena de Uairén**, stopping at all checkpoints, US$20, 4 hrs, take water. It is possible to share a taxi, US$10 pp. There are through buses to **Ciudad Guayana, Ciudad Bolívar** (eg Caribe), US$40.

Border with Guyana: Bonfim *p557*
Bus Boa Vista-Bonfim 6 a day US$10, 2½ hrs; colectivos charge US$25. **Ferry** To cross the river, take a canoe (see above), US$4 (no boats at night).

ⓘ Directory

Benjamin Constant around around: Tabatinga *p555*
Banks Banco do Brasil, Av da Amizade. Has a Visa cash point and changes TCs at poor rate. Best to change money in Leticia. Dollars are accepted everywhere; Colombian pesos are accepted in Tabatinga, Peruvian soles rarely accepted.
Internet Infocenter, Av da Amizade 1581.

Boa Vista *p556*
Airline offices Gol, Praça Santos Dumont 100, T3224 5824. Meta, Praça Santos Dumont 100, T3224 7490. **Banks** US$ and Guyanese notes can be changed in Boa Vista. TCs and cash in Banco do Brasil, Av Glaycon de Paiva 56, 1000-1300 (minimum US$200), has Visa/Plus ATM. There is no official exchange agency and the local rates for bolívares are low: the Banco do Brasil will not change bolívares. HSBC, Av Ville Roy 392, MasterCard ATM. Bradesco, Av Jaime Brasil 441, Visa ATM. Best rate for dollars, Casa Pedro José, R Araújo Filho 287, also changes TCs and bolívares; Timbo's (gold and jewellery shop), Av B Constant 170, will change money.
Embassies and consulates Guyana, R Benjamin Constant 1171, T9112 7017, open mornings only. Venezuela, Av Benjamin Constant 968, T623 9285, Mon-Fri 0830-1300. Visas available, relaxed service, allow 24-48 hrs.
Medical services Yellow fever inoculations are free at a clinic near the hospital.

Southern Amazônia

Porto Velho → *Phone code: 0xx69. Post code: 78900. Colour map 4, grid B1. Population: 450,000.*
This city stands on a high bluff overlooking a curve of the Rio Madeira. It prospered during the local gold and timber rush and although these activities have slowed, the city continues to grow. At the top of the hill, on Praça João Nicoletti, is the **Cathedral**, built in 1930, with beautiful stained glass windows; the **Prefeitura** is across the street. The principal commercial street is Avenida 7 de Setembro, which runs from the railway station and market hall to the upper level of the city, near the rodoviária. The centre is hot, noisy and sprawls from the river to the bus station (about 1½ km), but it is not without charm, and the port and old railway installations by the river are interesting. In the old railway yards known as Praça Madeira-Mamoré are the **Museus Ferroviário** and **Geológico** ⓘ *both 0800-1800*, the **Casa do Artesão** (see Shopping) and a promenade with bars by the river, a wonderful place to watch the sunset. A neoclassical **Casa do Governo** faces Praça Getúlio Vargas, while Praça

559

Marechal Rondon is spacious and modern. There are several viewpoints overlooking the river and railway yards: **Mirante I** (with restaurant) is at the end of Rua Carlos Gomes; **Mirante II** (with a bar and ice cream parlour), at the end of Rua Dom Pedro II, is the best place to watch the sunset over the river. There is a clean fruit and vegetable market at the corner of Rua Henrique Dias and Avenida Farquhar and a dry goods market three blocks to the south, near the port. **Tourist office**: Setur/Ro ① *Av Pdte Dutra 3004, Caiari, CEP 78900-550, T223 3496. See also www.guiarondonia.com.br and www.ronet.com.br/marrocos.*

About 5 km northeast of the city is the **Parque Nacional Municipal**, a small collection of flora in a preserved area of jungle and one of very few parks in the city. The **Cachoeira de Santo Antônio**, rapids on the Rio Madeira, 7 km upriver from Porto Velho, is a popular destination for a swim during the dry season; in the rainy season the rapids may be underwater and swimming is dangerous. Access is by boat, taking a tour from Porto Cai N'Água, one hour; or by city bus No 102, Triângulo, which runs every 50 minutes from the city bus terminus or from the bus stop on Rua Rogério Weber, across from Praça Marechal Rondon. Gold dredges may be seen working near Porto Velho, ask around. Malaria is common and the drinking water is contaminated with mercury (from gold panning).

The BR-364 → *Colour map 4, grid C2.*
The Marechal Rondon Highway, BR-364, is fully paved to Cuiabá, 1,550 km. A result of the paving of BR-364 is the development of farms and towns along it; least population density is in the south between Pimenta Bueno and Vilhena. From Porto Velho south, the towns include **Ariquemes** (202 km from Porto Velho). (*Phone code 0xx69*) , buses hourly from 0600, three to four hours, hotels, bank); **Ji Paraná** (*376 km, phone code: 0xx69*), on the shores of the Rio Machado, a pleasant town with a small riverside promenade, which has several bars, lively at night; several hotels. **Note** At the Mato Grosso state border, proof of yellow-fever inoculation is required: if no proof is presented, a new shot is given.

Parque Nacional Pacaás Novos → *765,800 ha.*
The Parque Nacional Pacaás Novos, lies west of the BR-364; it is a transitional zone between open plain and Amazonian forest. The majority of its surface is covered with cerrado vegetation and the fauna includes jaguar, brocket deer, puma, tapir and peccary. The average annual temperature is 23°C, but this can fall as low as 5°C when the cold front known as the friagem blows up from the South Pole. Details from **Ibama** ① *Av Tancredo Neves s/n, Campo Novo, T3239 2992, or Av Jorge Teixeira 3559, CEP 78.904-320, Toxx69-223 3597, Porto Velho.*

The Madeira-Mamoré Railway → *See www.efmm.net.*
Porto Velho was the terminus of the Madeira-Mamoré railway. It was supposed to go as far as Riberalta, on the Rio Beni, above that river's rapids, but stopped short at Guajará Mirim. Over 6,000 workers died during its construction (1872-1913). The BR-364 took over many of the railway bridges, leaving what remained of the track to enthusiasts to salvage what they could. The line no longer works, but the roundhouse, recently restored, has two antique locomotives, a collection of skulls and other items on display. Mr Johnson at the station speaks English.

Guajará Mirim → *Phone code: 0xx69. Colour map 4, grid B1. Population: 38,045.*
From Porto Velho, the paved BR-364 continues 220 km southwest to Abunã (hotels **E**), where the BR-425 branches south to Guajará Mirim. The BR-425 is a fair road, partly paved, which uses the former rail bridges (in poor condition). It is sometimes closed March-May. Across the Mamoré from Guajará Mirim is the Bolivian town of Guayaramerín, which is connected by road to Riberalta, from where there are air services to other Bolivian cities. Guajará Mirim is a charming town. The **Museu Municipal** ① *T541 3362, 0500-1200, 1400-1800,* is at the old Guajará Mirim railway station beside the ferry landing; interesting and diverse. Highly recommended. Banco do Brasil only changes money in the morning.

Border with Bolivia
Get Brazilian exit and entry stamps from **Polícia Federal** ① *Av Presidente Dutra 70, corner of Av Quintino Bocaiúva, T541 4021.* The Bolivian consulate is at Avenida Leopoldo de Matos 451, T541 8622, consuladodabolivia@gm-net.com, Guajará Mirim; visas are given here.

Rio Branco → *Post code: 69900. Phone code: 0xx68. Colour map 3, grid B6. Population: 253,059.*

The BR-364 runs west from Porto Velho to Abunã (239 km), then in excellent condition, 315 km to Rio Branco the capital of the State of Acre. This intriguing state, rich in natural beauty, history and the seringueiro culture, is still very much off the beaten track. During the rubber boom of the late 19th century, many Nordestinos migrated to the western frontier in search of fortune. As a result, the unpopulated Bolivian territory of Acre was gradually taken over by Brazil and formally annexed in the first decade of the 20th century. In compensation, Bolivia received the Madeira-Mamoré railroad, as described above. In 1913, Rio Branco became capital of the new Território Federal do Acre, which attained statehood in 1962. The chief industries remain rubber and castanho-de-pará (Brazil nut) extraction, but timber and ranching are becoming increasingly important and improved road access is putting the state's tropical forests at considerable risk. Despite improved air and road links, Rio Branco remains at the 'end of the line', a frontier outpost whose depressed economy, high unemployment and prevalent drug-running make the city unsafe at night.

The Rio Acre is navigable upstream as far as the Peru and Bolivia borders. It divides the city into two districts called Primeiro (west) and Segundo (east), on either side of the river. In the central, Primeiro district are **Praça Plácido de Castro**, the shady main square; the **Cathedral**, Nossa Senhora de Nazaré, along Avenida Brasil; the neo-classical **Palácio Rio Branco** on Rua Benjamin Constant, across from Praça Eurico Gaspar Dutra. There is a market off Rua Epaminondas Jácome. Two bridges link the districts. In the Segundo district is the **Calçadão da Gameleira**, a pleasant promenade along the shore, with plaques and an old tree marking the location of the original settlement. There are several large parks in the city; the **Horto Forestal**, popular with joggers, in Vila Ivonete (1° distrito), 3 km north of the centre ('Conjunto Procon' or 'Vila Ivonete' city-buses), has native Amazonian trees, a small lake, paths and picnic areas.

Museu da Borracha (Rubber Museum) ① *Av Ceará 1177, Mon-Sat 0730-1900*, in a lovely old house with a tiled façade, has information about the rubber boom, archaeological artefacts, a section about Acreano Indians, documents and memorabilia from the annexation and a display about the Santo Daime doctrine. Recommended. **Casa do Seringueiro** ① *Av Brasil 216, corner of Av Getúlio Vargas*, has a good exhibit on rubber tappers and on **Chico Mendes** in particular; the Sala Hélio Melo has a display of Melo's paintings, mainly on the theme of the forest. **Tourist office**: For Acre: **SEICT/AC** ① *R Mal Deodoro 219 fourth floor, Centro*, T223 1390, www.ac.gov.br/seict/. Rio Branco's municipal site: www.pmrb.ac.gov.br.

Note Rio Branco time is one hour behind Porto Velho and Manaus time; this means two hours behind Brazilian Standard Time.

Border with Bolivia and Peru

The BR-317 from Rio Branco heads south and later southwest, parallel to the Rio Acre; it is paved as far as **Xapuri** (the location of the Fundação Chico Mendes); one very basic lodging and two restaurants. The road continues to **Brasiléia** (four buses daily to/from Rio Branco, five hours in the wet, faster in the dry, US$10; three hotels, two basic lodgings, several restaurants – La Felicitá is good, Polícia Federal give entry/exit stamps), opposite the Bolivian town of Cobija on the Rio Acre. A striking, single-tower suspension bridge crosses the river. It is possible to stay in Epitaciolândia (**C Hotel Kanda**, five minutes' walk from the police post) and cross into Bolivia early in the morning. Ask the bus driver to let you off near Polícia Federal, open 0700-2200, to get passport stamped. Cobija is opposite. **Bolivian consulate** ① *R Hilário Meireles 236, T546 3851*. If going to Peru, a taxi from Polícia Federal to the Rodoviária costs US$2.

The road ends at Assis Brasil (120 km) where the Peruvian, Bolivian and Brazilian frontiers meet. Across the Rio Acre are Iñapari (Peru), border crossing difficult, even out of the wet season, and Bolpebra, Bolivia. A bus service operates only in the dry season beyond Brasiléia to Assis Brasil, 0700 and 1230, 2½ hours; access in the wet season is by 4WD vehicles. In **Assis Brasil**, there are three hotels, two restaurants (including a good churrascaria on the main street), some shops, a bank which does not change US dollars (the hotel owner may be persuaded to oblige). Cross to Iñapari from Assis Brasil (another distinctive suspension bridge is being built here), then take a shared taxi to Iberia or Puerto Maldonado. Immigration is open 0800-1830. **Note** There is no Polícia Federal in the village, get entry/exit stamps in Brasiléia. Take small denomination dollar bills or Peruvian soles as there is nowhere to change money on the Peruvian side.

● Sleeping → *See Telephone, page 347, for important phone changes.*

Porto Velho *p559*

The city is less safe than it used to be; do not walk around alone after dark nor during the day near the railway station and port. From the rodoviária, take bus No 301 'Presidente Roosevelt' (outside Hotel Pontes), which goes to railway station at riverside, then along Av 7 de Setembro as far as Av Marechal Deodoro. It passes several hotels.

AL Rondon Palace, Av Gov Jorge Teixeira 491, corner Jacy Paraná, away from the centre, T3224 3181. A/c, fridge, restaurant, pool, travel agency.

AL Vila Rica, Av Carlos Gomes 1616, T3224 3433, www.hotelvilarica.com.br. Tower block with restaurant, pool and sauna, about to be renovated as part of the **Ibis** group (2007).

A Central, Tenreiro Aranha 2472, T2181 2500, www.enter-net.com.br/hcentral. A/c, TV, fridge, reliable and remodelled. Recommended.

C Pousada da Sete, Av 7 de Setembro 894, T3221 8344. On No 301 bus route (see above). A/c, cheaper with fan, **E** with shared bath.

D Missionero, Av 7 de Setembro 1180, T3221 4080. On No 301 bus route (see above). Good, a/c, cheaper with fan, **E** with shared bath, fan. Recommended.

D Regina, R General Osório 255; T3224 3411. Best economic and clean option in town, central, one street back from the river, quiet.

D-E Tía Carmen, Av Campos Sales 2995, T3221 7910. Very good, honest, good cakes in lanche in front of hotel. Recommended.

Guajará Mirim *p560*

AL Pakaas Palafitas Lodge, Estrada do Palheta Km 18, T/F3541 3058, www.pakaas.com.br. 28 bungalows in a beautiful natural setting, price is per person per day.

C Jamaica, Av Leopoldo de Mato 755, T/F3541 3721. A/c, fridge, parking.

C Lima Palace, Av 15 de Novembro 1613, T3541 3421. A/c, fridge, parking.

D Fénix Palace, Av 15 de Novembro 459, T3541 2326. Recommended.

D Mamoré, R M Moraes, T3541 3753. Clean, friendly.

Centro Deportivo Afonso Rodrigues, Av 15 de Novembro, T541 3732. There's a basic dorm, **E**, opposite the rodoviária.

Rio Branco *p561*

Few economical hotels in the centre, but a reasonable selection by the rodoviária.

A Pinheiro Palace, Rui Barbosa 91, T3223 7191, pinheiro@mdnet.com.br. In 1° distrito (west bank), a/c, pool. Recommended.

B Rio Branco, R Rui Barbosa 193, T3224 1785, by Praça Plácido de Castro in 1° distrito. A/c, fridge, TV, nice but simple.

C Albemar, R Franco Ribeiro 99, T3224 1396. In 1° distrito (west bank), a/c, fridge, TV, good breakfast, good value. Recommended.

C Rodoviária, R Palmeiral 468, T3221 4434. In 2° distrito (east bank), in Cidade Nova by the rodoviária. A/c, fridge TV, **D** with shared bath, fan, good value.

C Triângulo, R Floriano Peixoto 893, T3224 9265. In 1° distrito (west bank), a/c, TV, fridge, restaurant.

D Chapuri, Nações Unidas 187, T3222 7268. In 1° distrito (west bank), shared bath, fan, basic, 15 mins' walk from the centre.

● Eating

Porto Velho *p559*

There are plenty of snack bars and *padarias* throughout the city. **Note** Avoid eating much fish because of mercury contamination.

♥♥♥ Caravela do Madeira, R José Camacho 104. The city's business lunch venue, a/c, international menu.

♥♥♥-♥♥ Barcaça Gourmet, Av Pinheiro Machado 3258, Centro, T3223 3334. Excellent menu with a variety of prices, a/c, singer most evenings.

♥♥ Almanara, R José de Alencar 3064. Good authentic Lebanese food, popular, not cheap. Recommended.

♥♥ Bella Italia, Joaquim Nabuco 2205. Italian, pizza and comida caseira.

♥♥ Emporium, Av P Machado e Av Dutra. Mid-range, nice atmosphere, good meats and salads, expensive drinks, open 1800-2400.

♥♥ Mirante II, at the end of R Dom Pedro II. Open all day for food and drink, live music at night, and the best place to watch the sunset.

♥ Churrascaria Natal, Av Carlos Gomes 2783. Good meat and chicken.

♥ Churrascaria Ponto Certo, Av Rio Madeira 45. Excellent meats, good view of the river, closed Mon.

Guajará Mirim *p560*

Oasis, Av 15 de Novembro 460. The best place to eat. Recommended (closed Mon).

Rio Branco *p561*

Local specialities *Tacacá*; a soup served piping hot in a gourd (*cuia*) combines manioc starch (*goma*), cooked jambu leaves which numb the mouth and tongue, shrimp, spices and hot pepper sauce; recommendation from Sra Diamor, Boulevar Augusto Monteiro 1046, Bairro 15 in the 2° distrito (bus Norte-Sul from the centre), other kiosks in town, ask around.

Brasília → *Phone code: 0xx61. Post code: 7000. Colour map 7, grid A3. Population: 2.1 million (2000).*

Ins and outs

Orientation   The Eixo Monumental divides the city into Asa Sul and Asa Norte (north and south wings) and the Eixo Rodoviário divides it east and west. Buildings are numbered according to their relation to them. For example, 116 Sul and 116 Norte are at the extreme opposite ends of the city. The 100s and 300s lie west of the Eixo and the 200s and 400s to the east; Quadras 302, 102, 202 and 402 are nearest the centre and 316, 116, 216 and 416 mark the end of the Plano Piloto. Residential areas are made up of six-storey apartment blocks, called 'Super-Quadras'. All Quadras are separated by feeder roads, along which are the local shops. There are also schools, parks and cinemas in the spaces between the Quadras (especially in Asa Sul). The main shopping areas, with more cinemas, restaurants, etc, are situated on either side of the city bus station (rodoviária). The private residential areas are west of the Super-Quadras, and on the other side of the lake. At right angles to these residential areas is the 'arrow', the 8-km-long, 250-m-wide **Eixo Monumental**. The main north-south road (Eixo Rodoviário), in which fast-moving traffic is segregated, follows the curve of the bow; the radial road is along the line of the arrow – intersections are avoided by means of underpasses and cloverleaves. Motor and pedestrian traffic is segregated in residential areas. A limited Metrô has been built to the southwestern suburbs. It is worth telephoning addresses away from the centre to ask how to get there. ▶▶ *See Transport, page 575, for more details.*

Climate   The climate is mild and the humidity refreshingly low, but overpowering in dry weather. The noonday sun beats hard, but summer brings heavy rains and the air is usually cool by night. Altitude: 1,171 m.

Tourist offices   Setur ① *Centro de Convenções, 3rd floor, T3429 7600, www.setur.df.gov.br*, helpful, English-speaking staff, good map of the city. There is a **branch** ① *at rodoferroviária, daily 0800-2000*, at the **TV Tower** ① *0900-1800*, and at the **airport** ① *T3033 9488, daily 0730-2230*; they will book hotels and have maps of the city, but have more limited information. The **Ministério do Turismo** is at Esplanada dos Ministérios, Bloco U, 2nd and 3rd floors, www.turismo.gov.br (in many languages). See also www.infobrasilia.com.br, www.dicasdebrasilia.com.br www.aboutbrasilia.com. **Maps** Detailed street maps of the city are impossible to find. Newsagents and the airport sell a map showing the *quadras*. Otherwise, see **Adetur**'s map.

Background

The purpose-built federal capital of Brazil succeeded Rio de Janeiro (as required by the Constitution) on 21 April 1960. The creation of an inland capital had been urged since the beginning of the 19th century, but it was finally brought into being after President Kubitschek came to power in 1956, when a competition for the best general plan was won by Professor Lúcio Costa, who laid out the city in the shape of a bent bow and arrow. (It is also described as a bird, or aeroplane in flight.) Only light industry is allowed in the city and its population was limited to 500,000; this has been exceeded and more people live in a number of shanty towns, with minimal services, located well away from the main city, which is now a UNESCO World Heritage Site. Brasília is on undulating ground in the unpopulated uplands of Goiás, in the heart of the undeveloped Sertão. The official name for central Brasília is the Plano Piloto.

Lago Do Paranoá

Palácio da Alvorada
Palácio do Jabaru
Palácio do Planalto
Praça dos Três Poderes
Avenida das Nações

N

0 metres 200
0 yards 200

Sights

At the tip of the arrow is the **Praça dos Três Poderes**, with the Congress buildings, the Palácio do Planalto (the President's office), the Supremo Tribunal Federal opposite it and the Ministério da Justiça and Palácio Itamaraty respectively below them. Nineteen tall Ministry buildings line the Esplanada dos Ministérios, west of the Praça, culminating in two towers linked by a walkway to form the letter H, representing Humanity. They are 28 storeys high: no taller buildings are allowed in B7rasília. Where the bow and arrow intersect is the city bus terminal (rodoviária), with the cultural and recreational centres and commercial and financial areas on either side. There is a sequence of zones westward along the shaft of the arrow; a hotel centre, a radio city, an area for fairs and circuses, a centre for sports, the **Praça Municipal** (with the municipal offices in the Palácio do Buriti) and, lastly (where the nock of the arrow would be), the combined bus and railway station (rodoferroviária) with the industrial area nearby. Other than the Santuário Dom Bosco and the JK bridge, the most impressive buildings are all by Oscar Niemeyer, Brazil's leading architect.

The **Palácio da Alvorada**, the President's official residence (not open to visitors), is on the lakeshore. The 80-km drive along the road round the lake to the dam is attractive. There are spectacular falls below the dam in the rainy season. Between the Praça dos Três Poderes and the lake are sites for various recreations, including golf, fishing and yacht clubs, and an acoustic shell for shows in the open air. The airport is at the eastern end of the lake. Some 395 ha between the lake and the northern residential area (Asa Norte) are reserved for the Universidade de Brasília, founded in 1961. South of the university area, the Av das Nações runs from the Palácio da Alvorada along the lake to join the road from the airport to the centre. Along it are found all the principal embassies. Also in this area is the attractive vice-presidential residence, the **Palácio do Jaburu** (not open to visitors). This area is very scenic.

A fine initial view of the city may be had from the **television tower** ① *West Eixo Monumental, Mon 1400-2000, Tue-Sun 0800-2000*, which has a free observation platform at 75 m up; also bar and souvenir shop. If the TV tower is closed, the nearby Alvorada hotel has a panoramic terrace on the 12th floor (lift to 11th only): ask at reception. A good and cheap way of seeing Brasília is by taking bus rides from the municipal rodoviária at the centre: the destinations are clearly marked. The circular bus routes 106, 108 and 131 go round the city's perimeter. If you go around the lake by bus, you must change at the Paranoá dam; to or from Paranoá Norte take bus 101, 'Rodoviária', and to and from Sul, bus 100, bypassing the airport. Tours from 1300-1700, start from the downtown hotel area and municipal rodoviária (US$12-20). Many hotels arrange city tours (see also Tour operators). Some buildings are open 1000-1400 Saturday-Sunday, with guided tours in English, well worth going.

Praça dos Três Poderes: **Congress** ① *Mon-Fri 0930-1200, 1430-1630 (take your passport), guides free of charge (in English 1400-1700)*. Visitors may attend debates when Congress is in session (Friday morning). Excellent city views from the 10th floor in Annex 3. The **Palácio do Planalto** ① *Sun 0930-1330, 30-min tours*, may also be visited. The guard is changed ceremonially at the Palácio do Planalto on Friday at 1730. The President attends if he is available. Opposite the Planalto is the Supreme Court building, **Supremo Tribunal Federal**. **Espaço Lúcio Costa** ① *Tue-Sun 0900-1800, free*, contains a model of Plano Piloto, sketches and autographs of the designer's concepts and gives the ideological background to the planning of Brasília. (Town clothes (not shorts or minis) should be worn when visiting all these buildings.) The **Museu Histórico de Brasília** ① *Tue-Sun and holidays 0900-1800*, is really a hollow monument, with tablets, photos and videos telling the story of the city. The sculpture 'Os Candangos' in front of the Planalto is a symbol of the city. By Bruno Giorgi, it pays homage to the candangos, or pioneer workers who built Brasília on empty ground. The marvellous building of the Ministry of Foreign Affairs, the **Itamarati** ① *guided visits Mon, Wed, Fri 1500-1700, free*, has modern paintings and furniture and beautiful water gardens. Opposite the Itamarati is the **Palácio da Justiça** ① *Mon-Fri 0900-1200, 1500-1700*, with artificial cascades between its concrete columns. The **Panteão Tancredo Neves** is a 'temple of freedom and democracy', built 1985-1986 by Niemeyer. It includes an impressive homage to Tiradentes, the precursor of Brazilian independence.

Niemeyer is well into his nineties but still working. His **Procuradaria Geral da República**, comprising two glass cylinders, one suspended from a concrete cog, opened in 2002. The **Museu Nacional de Brasília**, on the Conjunto Cultural da República (next to the cathedral), and the adjacent **Biblioteca Nacional** were due to open in 2007. They are the last grand projects Niemeyer designed for the capital. The former is particularly impressive, a huge dome of white concrete, blank but for a door halfway up, sitting in a shallow pool of water which reflects it like a mirror. This door is reached by a long sinuous ramp. Inside there will be a 700-seat auditorium and state-of-the-art galleries.

The **Catedral Metropolitana** ① *0800-1930, T3224 4073*, on the Esplanada dos Ministérios, is a spectacular circular building in the shape of the crown of thorns. Three aluminium angels, suspended from the airy, domed, stained-glass ceiling, are by the sculptor Alfredo Ceschiatti, who also made the five life-sized bronze apostles outside. The baptistery, a concrete representation of the Host beside the cathedral, is connected to the main building by a tunnel (open Sundays only). The outdoor carillon was a gift from the Spanish government: the bells are named after Columbus's ships.

South of the TV tower on Avenida W3 Sul, at Quadra 702, is the Sanctuary of **Dom Bosco** ① *T3223 6542, 0800-1800*. A modernist cube with tall gothic arches filled with stained glass which shades from light to dark blue and indigo as it ascends. It is particularly beautiful in the late afternoon when shafts of light penetrate the building.

The **Templo da Boa Vontade** ① *Setor Garagem Sul 915, lotes 75/76, T245 1070, 24 hrs, getting there: take bus 151 from outside the Centro do Convenções or on Eixo Sul to Centro Médico*. This is a seven-faced pyramid topped by one of the world's largest crystals, a peaceful place dedicated to all philosophies and religions.

A permanent memorial to Juscelino Kubitschek, the '**Memorial JK**' ① *daily 0900-1800, US$1.50*, contains his tomb and his car, together with a lecture hall and exhibits. It has toilets and a lanchonete. The **Monumental Parade Stand** has unique and mysterious acoustic characteristics (the complex is north of the Eixo Monumental, between the 'Memorial JK' and the rodoferroviária). There are remarkable stained glass panels, each representing a state of the Federation, on the ground floor of the Caixa Econômica Federal.

Some 15 km out along the Belo Horizonte road is the small wooden house, known as '**O Catetinho**', in which President Kubitschek stayed in the late 1950s during his visits to the city when it was under construction; it is open to visitors and most interesting. Northwest of Brasília, but only 15 minutes by car from the centre, is the **Parque Nacional de Brasília** (about 28,000 ha) ① *contact the park's Ibama office, BR 040 SMU, T3465 2016, US$1.35*. Founded in 1961 to conserve the flora and fauna of the Federal Capital, only a portion of the park is open to the public without a permit. There is a swimming pool fed by clear river water, a snack bar and a series of trails through gallery forest (popular with joggers in the early morning and at weekends). The rest of the park is grassland, gallery forest and cerrado vegetation. Large mammals include tapir, maned wolf and pampas deer; birdwatching is good.

◉ **Sleeping** → *See Telephone, page 347, for important phone changes.*

Brasília *p565*

The best area is the northern hotel zone which has shops and restaurants nearby. Prices usually include breakfast. Weekend discounts of 30% are often available but must be requested. Most cheap accommodation is around W3 703 and 704 in the Zona Sul where residential houses have been turned into cheap hostels. The quietest are north-west of the main Av W3 Sul. Beware of bus station touts. The tourist office has a list of *pensões*.

Asa Norte

Moderately priced hotels are mostly found in this sector only.

LL Blue Tree Park, Trecho 1, It1-B, Bl C (Lagoa Norte), T3424 7000, www.bluetree.com.br. The city's, newest, most luxurious business hotel, with rooms in a giant red horseshoe overlooking the lake, an enormous pool and excellent, comprehensive business facilities.

LL-L Kubitschek Plaza, Qd 2, bloco E, T3329 3333, www.kubitschek.com.br. Popular business hotel with modern rooms and excellent facilties; broadband in rooms, pool, sauna and gym. Sister hotel, the Manhattan Plaza (www.manhattan.com.br) next door is very similar.

AL-A Aristus, Qd 2 bloco O, T328 8675, www.aristushotel.com.br. Newly painted and delightfully dated seventies block with simple a/c rooms and breakfast.

A Casablanca, Qd 3 bloco A, T3328 8586, www.casablancabrasilia.com.br. Another 1970s delight; more intimate than most in the area, but some noisy rooms.

B El Pilar, Qd 3 bloco F, T328 5915, www.elpilar.com.br. Plain, freshly painted, with fan. Avoid rooms below street level as they collect car fumes.

C Mirage, Qd 2 bloco N, T/F3328 7150. Simple rooms with a fan but good value for the area.

Asa Sul

L Nacional, Qd 1 bloco A, T3321 7575,
www.hotelnacional.com.br. Cavernous, frayed
old-fashioned and a city landmark with many
tour agencies outside.

A Alvorada, Qd 4 bloco A, T2195 1122,
www.alvoradahotel.com.br. Another relic with
good view from roof terrace, look for special offers.

C-E Pousada dom Bosco, 703 Sul, bloco N, Casa
34, T3225 5021, with another branch at W3704,
M casa 9, T3213 1133. The best of the cheapies,
with simple but neat rooms some spacious and
airy, some small and windowless. Owner, Getúlio
Valente will pick up from airport or bus station
if you phone ahead and offers a range of other
rooms around the city as well as cheap city tours
(Portuguese only).

D Pousada da Nilza, W3 Sul 703, bloco A, T3225
5786. Pokey and a little musty but popular with
travellers. Various other similar *pousadas* next
door to this one.

D-E Pousada 47, 703 Sul, bloco A, casa 97, T3323
5718, www.pousada47.hpg.com.br. Simple dorms
and doubles with fan, best rooms at the front,
internet.

D-E Pousada do Sol, 703 Sul, bloco K, Casa 3,
T3224 9703/9969 6636. A range of simple rooms,
some without windows, some for as many as 5
people. Family run.

● Eating

Brasília *p565*
At weekends, few restaurants in central Brasília are
open. Plenty of choice of restaurants in all brackets
in the Pier 21 entertainment mall on the lake
shore. Other cheaper options along R 405/406.

Asa Norte

All of the large hotels in this area have upmarket
restaurants, most catering to business visitors.

₩₩ Alice, SHIN, Q 11, conjunto 9, casa 17, T3368
1099, www.restaurantealice.com.br. Frequent
award winner, serving French and
Brazilina-French fusion cooking.

₩₩ Trattoria da Rosario, SHIS QI 17, Bloco H,
Loja 215, Lago Sul, Fashion Park, T3248 1672,
closed Mon, lunch only on Sun. Northern Italian
food from chef Rosario Tessier. Excellent
Uruguayan lamb.

₩₩ Universal Diner, SCLS 210, Bloco B, loja 30,
T3443 2089 (lunch only on Sun), www.universal
diner.com.br. One of the city's best contemporary
restaurants with cooking strongly Asian influences
from New York trained chef Mara Alcamim.

₩ Boa Saúde, Av W3 Norte Quadra 702,
Edif Brasília Rádio Center. Sun-Fri 0800-2000.
Respectable vegetarian with a range of salads,
quiches and pies.

₩₩ Bom Demais, Av W3 Norte, Qd 706.
Comfortable, serving fish, beef and rice, etc,
live music at weekends (cover charge US$1).

₩ Conjunto Nacional, SDN, Cj A, enormous
mall and food court with 50 restaurants.

The municipal rodoviária provides the
best coffee and pasteis in town (bottom
departure level).

Asa Sul

There are many cheap places on Av W3 Sul,
eg at Blocos 502 and 506.

₩₩₩ La Chaumière, Av W3 Sul, Qd 408, bloco A,
loja 13, T3242 7599; lunch only Sun. The city's
favourite French cooking in classical
surroundings.

₩₩₩ Le Français, Av W3 Sul, Qd 404, bloco B, loja
27, T3225 4583. French food served in bistro
atmosphere, classic and modern dishes.

₩₩₩ Kosui, SCES, Trecho 4, lote 1B, Academia de
Tênis, T3316 6900. Best of the city's Japanese food,
from Tokyo born chef Ryozo Koniya. Great
Japanese banquet.

₩₩₩ O Convento, SHIS, QI 9, conjunto 9, casa 4,
T3248 1211, www.oconvento.com.br. The best
for regional and Brazilian cuisine in a mock
farmhouse dining room decorated with antiques
and arts and crafts.

₩₩₩ Piantella, SCLS 202, bloco A, loja 34, T3224
9408, www.piantella.com.br. A favourite of senior
politicians, vast menu combining *feijoada*, Italian
food, steaks and seafood, good wines, too.

₩₩ Porcão, Sector de Clubes Sul, Trecho 2, cj 35,
rest 3, T3223 2002, www.porcao.com.br.
Upmarket chain restaurant specializing in
churrasco, piano bar, large veranda.

₩₩ Oca da Tribo, SCES Trecho 2m opposite
Agenpol, T3226 9880, www.ocadatribo.com.br.
Wholefood restaurnat with vegetarian options
and others, good buffet lunch, Dutch chef.

₩₩ O Espanhol, Av W3 Sul, Qd 404, bloco C,
loja 07, T3224 2002. Open daily. Host to the
city's annual Spanish festival and serving
respectable seafood.

₩₩ Vercelli, SCLS 410, bloco D, loja 34,
T3443 0100. Lunch only. Pizzas, pastas
and a great deal more on a huge menu.

₩ Naturama, SCLS 102, bloco B, loja 9,
T3225 5125. Vegetarian and wholefood
dishes, lunchtime.

Places serving prato feito or comercial (cheap
set meals) can be found all over the city,
especially on Av W3 and in the Setor Comercial
Sul. Other good bets are the Conjunto Nacional
and the Conjunto Venâncio, 2 shopping/office
complexes on either side of the municipal
rodoviária. Tropical fruit flavour ice cream can be
found in various parlours, eg Av W3 Norte 302.
Freshly made fruit juices in all bars.

🔴 Bars and clubs

Brasília *p565*

Arena Café, CA 7, bloco F1, loja 33, T3468 1141. Popular gay bar with DJs from Thu to Sat.

Bar Brasília, SHC/S CR, quadra 506, bloco A, loja 15, parte A, T3443 4323. Little boteco with 1950s decor, draught beer and wooden tables. Lively after 1900, especially Fri.

Bier Fass, SHIS Q 5, bloco E, loja 52/53, T3248 1519. Cavernous bar/restaurant with live music Tue-Sun and 20/30s crowd. Happy hour from 1800.

Café Cancun, Shopping Liberty Mall, SCN, cuadra 3, bloco D, loja 52, T3327 1566. Tacky Mexican restaurant by day and teen and 20-something beautiful people club alter dark.

Clube de Choro, SDC, quadra 3, bloco G, T3327 0494, www.clubedechoro.com.br. Wed-Sat, one of the best clubs in the country devoted to the music which gave rise to samba. Top names from all over Brazil as well as the city itself. Great atmosphere. Tickets sold 9 days in advance.

Frei Caneca, Brasília Shopping, SCN, quadra 5, bloco A, lojas 82s/94s, T3327 0202. Similar to Café Cancun. Dreadful 'flashback' night on Thu, most interesting at weekends.

Gates Pub, Av W3 Sul 403, T3225 4576, www.gatespub.com.br. Great for forró dancing and live music with a young, middle class crowd.

UK Brasil Pub, SCLS 411, bloco B, loja 28, T3346 5214. Some of the best live bands in the city play here. Guinness, sandwiches, all ages.

🟣 Entertainment

Brasília *p565*

Information about entertainment, etc is available in 2 daily papers, *Jornal de Brasília* and *Correio Brasiliense*. Any student card (provided it has a photograph) will get you into the cinema/theatre/concert hall for half price.

Cinema **Pier 21**, SCSS, Trecho 2, Cj 32/33, is an enormous complex with 13 cinema screens, nightclubs, restaurants, video bars and children's theme park.

Theatre There are 3 auditoria of the **Teatro Nacional**, Setor Cultural Norte, Via N 2, next to the bus station, T3325 6239, foyer open 0900-2000, box office open at 1400; the building is in the shape of an Aztec pyramid. The Federal District authorities have 2 theatres, the **Galpão** and **Galpãozinho**, between Quadra 308 Sul and Av W3 Sul. There are several other concert halls.

🟢 Shopping

Brasília *p565*

Bookshops **Livraria Sodiler** in Conjunto Nacional and at the airport. English books (good selection).

Handicrafts **Artíndia**, SRTVS, Qd 702, also in the rodoviária and at the airport. For Amerindian handicrafts. **Feira hippy** at the base of the TV tower Sat, Sun and holidays. Leather goods, wood carvings, jewellery, bronzes. **Galeria dos Estados**, which runs underneath the eixo from Setor Comercial Sul to Setor Bancário Sul, 10 mins' walk from municipal rodoviária, south along Eixo Rodoviário Sul. For handicrafts from all the Brazilian states.

Shopping malls The best shopping centres are Shopping Brasília below the southern hotel zone and Patio Brasília below the northern. Both have a wide range of boutiques and fast food restaurants. There are many others.

🔺 Activities and tours

Brasília *p565*

Many tour operators have their offices in the shopping arcade of the Hotel Nacional.

City tours (3-4 hrs) with English commentary can also be booked at the airport by arriving air passengers – a convenient way of getting to your hotel if you have heavy baggage. Some tours have been criticized as too short, others that the guides speak poor English, and for night-time tours, the flood lighting is inadequate on many buildings.

Presmic Turismo, SIA trecho 03, lotes 625/695, Shopping SIA, sala 208C, T3225 0155, www.presmic.com.br. Full-, half-day and night-time city tours (0845, 1400 and 1930 respectively).

Toscano SCLS 413, Bloco D, loja 22/24, T242 9233. Recommended as cheap and good.

🟢 Transport

Brasília *p565*

Air Airport, 12 km from centre, T3364 9000. Frequent daily flights to **Rio** and **São Paulo** (1½ hrs in both cases) and to main cities. Bus 102 or 118 to airport, regular, US$1, 30 mins. Taxi is US$13 (meter rate 2 used to airport), worth it. Left luggage facilities at airport (tokens for lockers, US$0.65).

● *For an explanation of the sleeping and eating price codes used in this guide, see page 58.*
● *Other relevant information is found in Essentials pages 345-347.*

Bus The bus terminal (rodoferroviária, T3363 2281) beside the railway station, from which long-distance buses leave, has post office (0800-1700, Sat 0800-1200) and telephone facilities. Bus 131 between rodoviária, the municipal terminal, and rodoferroviária, US$1.65; taxi rodoferroviária to Setor Hoteleiro Norte, US$12. There are showers (US$0.65). Both bus stations have large luggage lockers. To **Rio:** 17 hrs, 6 comuns (US$63) and 3 leitos (about US$105) daily. To **São Paulo:** 16 hrs, 7 comuns (about US$60) and 2 leitos (about US$120) daily (**Rápido Federal** recommended). To **Belo Horizonte:** 12 hrs, US$32.25-40, also 2 leitos daily. To **Belém:** 36 hrs, 4 daily (US$74, **Trans Brasília**). To **Salvador:** 24 hrs, 3 daily (US$75). To **Cuiabá:** 17½ hrs (US$60) daily at 1200 with São Luis. For **Mato Grosso:** generally Goiânia seems to be the better place for buses. **Barra do Garças:** 0830 and 2000, takes 9 hrs with Araguarina, T3233 7598, US$24 return. All major destinations served. Bus tickets for major companies sold at the city rodoviária.

ⓘ Directory

Brasília p565
Airline offices BRA, at airport, T2105 0909. GOL, premium rate number, T0300-789 2121, airport 3364 9370. **TAM**, SHN Hotel Nacional, Gallery Store, 36/37, T3325 1300, or 4002 5700. **Varig**, Camara os Deputados/Anexo 4, Praça dos Três Poderes, T3216 9930; airport, T3364 9582, or 4003 7000. **Banks** Foreign currency (but not always Amex cheques) can be exchanged at branches of: **Banco Regional de Brasília**, SBS Q 1, Bl E, and **Banco do Brasil**, Setor Bancário Sul, latter also at airport (ATM, bank open weekends and holidays), charges US$20 commission for TCs. **MasterCard** office, SCRN 502, Bl B, loja 31-32, T225 5550, for cash against card; ATMs at Citibank, SCS Quadra 06, bloco A, loja 186, T215 8000, **HSBC**, SCRS 502, bloco A, lojas 7/12, and **Banco 24 Horas** at airport, and all over the city, including the Rodoferroviária. Good exchange rates at Hotel Nacional and hotels with 'exchange-turismo' sign. **Car hire** All large companies are represented at the airport and the Car Rental Sector. Multinational agencies and **Interlocadora**, airport, T0800-138000.**Unidas**, T2365 2266 at airport, Mon-Fri 0800-1800.
Cultural centres British Council, Ed Centro Empresarial Varig, SCN Q 04 bloco B, Torre Oeste Conjunto 202, T2106 7500, brasilia@british council.org.br. **Cultura Inglesa**, SCLRN 704 Bloco B/Loja Térrea 57, T3327 5400, gerente.asa.norte2@culturainglesa.net. **American Library**, Casa Thomas Jefferson, SEPS 706/906, Conj B, T3443 6588, www.thomas. org.br. **Aliança Francesa**, SEPS EQ 708/907 Lote A, T3242 7500, www.afbrasilia.org.br. **Instituto Cultural Goethe**, Av W5 Sul, SEPS-EQS 707/907, bloco F, salas 103-137, T3244 6776, www.goethe.de/brasilia. **Embassies and consulates** Australia, SES Av das Nações, Qd 801, conjunto K, lote 7, T3226 3111, www.brazil.embassy.gov.au. **Austria**: SES, Av das Nações 40, T3443 3111, emb.austria@ terra.com.br. **Canada**: SES, Av das Nações Q 803 lote 16, T3424 5400, www.dfait-maeci.gc.ca/ brazil. **Denmark**: Av das Nações Q 807, lote 26, T3445 3443, www.ambbrasilia.um.dk. **Finland**: SES, Av das Nações Q 807, lote 27, T3443 7151, brasilia@finlandia.org.br. **France**: SES, Av das Nações Q801, L04, T3312 9100, www.amba france.org.br. **Germany**: SES, Av das Nações Q807, L25, T3442 7000, www.brasilia.diplo.de/ pt/Startseite.htm. **Guyana**: SHIS QI 05, conj 19, casa 24, Lago Sul, T3248 0874, embguyana@ apis.com.br. **Israel**: SES, Av das Nações, Q 809, lote 38, T2105 0500, info@brasilia.mfa.gov.il. **Netherlands**: SES, Av das Nações Q 801, lote 5, T3961 3200, www.mfa.nl/brazilie. **New Zealand**: SHIS Q1 09, conj 16, casa 01, Lgo Sul, T3248 9900, zelandia@nwi.com.br. **South Africa**: SES, Av das Nações Q 801, lote 06, T3312 9500, www.africa dosul.org.br. **Sweden**: Av das Nações Q 807, lote 29, T3443 1444, swebra@opengate.com.br. **Switzerland**: SES, Av das Nações Q 811, lote 41, T3443 5500, www.eda.admin.ch/brasilia. **UK**: SES, Quadra 801, Conjunto K lote 8 (with British Commonwealth Chamber of Commerce), Av das Nações, T3329 2300, contato@reino unido.org.br. **US**: SES, Av das Nações Q801, L03, T3312 7000, www.embaixada-americana.org.br. **Venezuela**: SES, Av das Nações Q803, lote 13, T2101 1011, embven2@ rudah.com.br.
Internet Café.Com.Tato, CLS 505, bloco C, loja 17, Asa Sul, open daily. **Liverpool Coffee Shop**, CLS 108, R da Igreijinha. **Post offices** Poste restante, Central Correio, 70001; SBN-Cj 03, BL-A, Ed Sede da ECT, the central office is in the Setor Hoteleiro Sul, between Hotels Nacional and St Paul. Another post office is in Ed Brasília Rádio, Av 3 Norte.

Goiás

Goiânia → *Phone code: 062. Colour map 4, grid A1. Population: 1.1 million.*

The state capital is famous for its street cafés and is a good place to stop between Brasília and the rest of the Cent West. It is a spacious city, founded in 1933, with well-lit main avenues radiating out from the central **Praça Cívica**, on which stand the Government Palace and main Post office. Goiânia has more parks and gardens than any other of Brazil's large cities and many are filled with interesting forest and cerrado plants, as well as marmosets and remarkably large numbers of birds. **Tourist office**: Semtur ① *R 32 esq Rua 15, No 394, Setor Marista , T3524 1090, semtur@turismo.goiania.go.gov.br*, and the Prefietura's website: www.goiania.go.gov.br. **Agetur** (state tourism association) ① *R 30 corner of Rua 4, Centro de Convenções, T3201 8122, www.goiasbrasil.tur.br.* Tourist office at the Rodoviária, T3224 8466. Extensive information, maps and bus routes in Novo Guia Turístico de Goiás, available at news stands, US$2.25.

The **Museu Zoroastro Artiaga** ① *Praça Cívica 13, T201 4676*, has a small but interesting collection of indigenous and historical objects, fossils and religious items as well as cases depicting indigenous and early settler life in Goiás. **Museu Antropológico do UFG** ① *Praça Universitária, 1 km east of Praça Cívica, Mon-Fri 0900-1700*, houses wide-ranging ethnographic displays on the *indígenas* of the Centre West. The **Museu de Arte de Goiânia** ① *Rua 1 605, T524 1190, 0800-1700 Mon-Fri, 0800-1300 Sat, free*, in the Bosque dos Buritis gardens has a room showcasing the work of a number of local artists including Siron Franco, who is nationally renowned. The **Casa do Indio** is a centre for indigenous arts and craft production and an important meeting place for indigenous peoples like the Xavantes. The shop there sells a variety of handicrafts. The **Memorial do Cerrado Museum** ① *Av Bela Vista Km 2, Jd Olímpico, T562 4141, Mon-Sat 0800-2200, Sun 0800-1800, US$2.65*, just outside the city, provides an interesting introduction to Cerrado life, with reconstructions of indigenous villages, quilombos and colonial streets as well as planted cerrado vegetation.

Cidade de Goiás (Goiás Velho) → *Phone code: 062. Colour map 1, grid C5.*

This delightful town (*Population 30,000*) nestled amid cerrado-covered ridges is one of Central Brazil's hidden gems. Its cobbled streets lined with Portuguese whitewash and brilliant yellow and blue façades and elegantly simple baroque churches have been awarded UNESCO World heritage status. The town was founded in 1727 as Vila Boa and like its Minas counterparts became rich on gold, before becoming the capital of Goiás state, which it remained until just before the Second World War. The **tourist office** ① *T371 3047, daily 0900-1700*, is housed in the Quintal do Vinte, a beautiful 18th-century former barracks on Praça Brasil Caiado. No English is spoken. The Museu Casa de Cora Coralina is a better source of information. Churches are usually open in the mornings and closed on Monday.

The most interesting streets in the colonial part of town spread out from the two principal plazas, Praça Brasil Caiado and, immediately below it towards the river, Praça do Coreto. The former is dominated by a lavish baroque fountain which once supplied all the town's water. The oldest church, **São Francisco de Paula** (1763) ① *Praça Zacheu Alves de Castro*, sits on a platform overlooking the market and the Rio Vermelho. It has a beautiful 19th-century painted ceiling by André Antônio da Conceição, depicting the life of St Francis. **Nossa Senhora da Abadiá** ① *R Abadia s/n*, has a similarly understated but impressive painted ceiling, whilst the other 18th-century churches like **Nossa Senhora do Carmo** ① *R do Carmo – on the riverside*, and **Santa Bárbara** ① *R Passo da Pátria*, are even simpler. The latter sits on a hill a kilometre or so east of the town affords wonderful sunset views. The **Museu das Bandeiras** ① *Praça Brasil Caiado/Largo do Chafariz, T3371 1087, Tue-Fri 0900-1700, Sat 1200-1700, Sun 0900-1300, US$1.30*, was once the centre of local government. Its rooms, furnished with period pieces, sit over a small but forbidding dungeon. The old governor's palace, the **Palacio Conde dos Arcos** ① *Praça do Coreto, T3371 1200, Tue-Sat 0800-1700, Sun 0900-1300, US$1.30*, has a display of 19th-century furniture and plaques describing the town's life in colonial times. The **Museu de Artes Sacras** ① *Praça do Coreto, T3371 1200, Tue-Sat 0800-1700, Sun 0900-1300, US$1.30*, houses some 18th-century church silverware and a series of painted wooden statues by one of Brazil's most important religious sculptors, José Joaquim da Veiga Valle. A stroll from the Praça do Coreto, downhill and across the river will bring you to the **Museu Casa de Cora Coralina** ① *R do Cândido 20, T3371 1990, Tue-Sun 0900-1700, US$1.30*, the former home of Goiás's most respected writer, with a collection of her belongings and a restful walled riverside garden at the back. The staff here are extremely helpful and knowledgeable about the city, though they speak no English. The 18th-century **Mercado Municipal**, next to the old rodoviária, 500 m west of the central Praça do Coreto, is a wonderful spot for cheap lunches, breakfasts and photography. Little artisan shops are springing up all over the town.

Pirenópolis → *Colour map 1, grid C5. Phone Code: 062. Population: 23,000. Altitude: 770 m.*

This lovely colonial silver mining town, 165 km due west of Brasília, has a well-preserved centre. It's almost as pretty as Cidade de Goiás and is National Heritage Site. The city is the nation's unofficial silver capital and is a good place to stock up on presents. It's also a favourite weekend haunt for the capital's middle classes who congregate in the lively restaurants and bars which line the northern end of Rua do Rosário. One of Brazil's most unusual and vibrant festivals takes place here every May/June (see page 575) and at weekends the Praça Central fills with country folk in stetsons and spurs, blasting out Sertanejo music from their souped-up cars. **Tourist office**: Centro de Atendimento ao Turista ⓘ *R do Bonfim 14, Centro Histórico, T3331 2729, www.pirenopolis.tur.br.* Poor English.

The **Igreja Matriz Nossa Senhora do Rosário**, which has been restored after being gutted by a fire in 2002, is the oldest church in the state (1728). It is open to the public, but its lavish interior is sadly no more. **Nosso Senhor de Bonfim** (1750-1754), which houses an impressive lifesize crucifix from Bahia, was transported here on the backs of 260 slaves. **Nossa Senhora do Carmo** ⓘ *daily 1300-1700*, serves as a museum of religious art. **Museu Família Pompeu** ⓘ *R Nova 33, Tue-Fri 1300-1700, Sat 1300-1500, Sun 0900-1200*, displays the best collection of pictures and documents devoted to the history of the city (in Portuguese only). The tiny, private **Museu das Cavalhadas** ⓘ *R Direita 37, officially Fri and Sat 0800-1700, but sporadic, US$1.30*, has a collection of masks and costumes from the Festa do Divino. **Fazenda Babilônia** ⓘ *25 km southwest by paved road, Sat and Sun 0800-1700, US$2.65*, is a fine example of an 18th-century sugar fazenda, now a small museum, original mill, no public transport.

Chapada dos Veadeiros

These table top mountains, drained by countless fast-flowing rivers which rush through deep gorges and plummet over spectacular waterfalls are less famous, but much bigger than Diamantina or Guimarães. And unlike both those areas its forests have never been felled (it was designated a World Heritage Site by UNESCO in 2001). The Chapada is covered in cerrado forest – a habitat of such floral diversity that it has recently been declared a biological hotspot by Conservation International. Rare mammals including jaguar, maned wolf, puma, tapir, ocelot and giant anteater are abundant and although no one has yet compiled a serious bird list spectaculars and rarities include red shouldered macaw, coal crested finch, helmeted manakin and various key indicator species like rusty margined guan and bare face currasow. King vultures are abundant. At present trips within the park are limited to day visits only; but there are plans to change this as walks of as long as nine days can be easily organized at a good price. Entry to the park without a guide is not permitted and visits to the surrounding countryside without one not recommended – it is easy to get lost and guides are not expensive. The park is reached by paved state highway 118 to **Alto Paraíso de Goiás**, then a paved road around 40 km west to **São Jorge** (1 km from park entrance). Alto Paraíso is best for visits to the eastern sections of the Chapada, São Jorge for the park itself.

Parque Nacional Emas

ⓘ *Permission to visit from Ibama R 229 No 95, Setor Universitário, 74605-090 Goiânia, Toxx62-3901 1900. Day trips are not recommended, but 4-day, 3-night visits to the Park can be arranged through agencies (eg Focus Tours).*

In the far southwest of the state, covering the watershed of the Araguaia, Taquari and Formoso rivers, is the small **Parque Nacional Emas**, 98 km south of Mineiros just off the main BR-364 route between Brasília and Cuiabá (112 km beyond Jataí). Almost 132,868 ha of undulating grasslands and cerrado contain the **world's largest concentration of termite mounds**. Pampas deer, giant anteater, greater rhea, or 'ema' in Portuguese, and maned wolf are frequently seen roaming the grasses. The park holds the greatest concentration of blue-and-yellow macaws outside Amazônia, and blue-winged, red-shouldered and red-bellied macaws can also be seen. (There are many other animals and birds.) Along with the grasslands, the park supports a vast marsh on one side and rich gallery forests on the other. As many of the interesting mammals are nocturnal, a spotlight is a must.

Goiânia *p571*

The best hotels are 1 km from the centre in the Setor Oeste which has many restaurants and bars. Most hotels in the centre are frayed 1970s blocks.

L Castro's Park, Av República do Líbano 1520, Setor Oeste, T3096 2000, www.castrospark. com.br. 5-star tower a few blocks from the centre, gym, pool, best for business. Plenty of restaurants and bars nearby.

L Papillon, Av Republica do Libano 1824, T3219 1500, www.papillonhotel.com.br. Modern rooms and suites, pool, gym, sauna, business facilities, very popular, book ahead.

AL Address, Av República do Líbano 2526, T3257 1000, www.addresshotel.com.br. Well-equipped business hotel, the best, in the city, modern rooms with separate living areas, broadband access, gym, pool, restaurant, bar, good views from the upper floors.

A-B Rio Vermelho, R 4 No26, T3227 2500, www.hotelriovermelho.com.br. Simple, in a quiet street with lots of cheap restaurants, cheapest with fan, close to the centre.

B Oeste Plaza, 389 Rua 2, Setor Oeste, T3224 5012. Well-maintained, modern, small a/c rooms, those on higher floors have good views, small pool and gym.

C Karajás, Av Goiás and R 3 No 860, T3224 9666. Good value in a once luxury hotel now fallen somewhat from grace, convenient.

C-D Goiânia Palace, Av Anhangüera 5195, T3224 4874, Goiâniapalace@terra.com.br. Art deco building with a range of rooms from simple doubles with fan to suites, good breakfast, well located.

E Antoninho's, R 68 No 41, T3223 1815. Very basic but well looked after, only a few rooms have windows, safe, good breakfast.

E Paissandú, Av Goiás 1290 at R 55, T3224 4925. Very simple, fan or a/c, 8 blocks north of the centre.

Camping Itanhangá municipal site, Av Princesa Carolina, 13 km, T292 1145. Attractive wooded location, reasonable facilities.

Cidade de Goiás *p571*

AL-A Vila Boa, Av Dr Deusdete Ferreira de Moura, 1 km southeast of the centre on the Morro do Chapéu do Padre, T3371 1000. The best in town, though inconvenient for the centre, pool, bar, restaurant and good views.

A Casa da Ponte, R Moretti Foggia s/n, T3371 4467. An art deco building next to the bridge across the Rio Vermelho, a/c rooms, the best overlook the river.

C Pousada do Ipê, R Cel Guedes de Amorim 22, T3371 2065. Rooms around a courtyard

dominated by a huge mango tree. The annexe has a pool and bar.

C-D Pousada do Vovô Jura, R Sta Barbara 38, T3371 1746. Colonial house set in a little garden with views out over the river and Serra.

D Pousada do Sol, R Americano do Brasil, T3371 1717. Well maintained, fans, friendly and central.

D-E Pousada dos Sonhos, R 15 Novembro 22, T3372 1224. Simple and convenient, plain rooms with shared bath, good breakfast.

D-E Pousada Reis, R 15 Novembro 41, T3371 1565. A simple cheapie next to the Sonho offering similar rooms but shoddier service.

Camping Cachoeira Grande campground, 7 km along the BR-070 to Jussara (near the tiny airport). Attractive, well-run, with bathing place and snack bar. More basic site (**Chafariz da Carioca**) in town by the river.

Pirenópolis *p572*

At Festa do Divino (see page 575) it's essential to book ahead or visit from Brasília.

A Casa Grande, R Aurora 41, T3331 1758, www.casagrandepousada.com.br. Chalets in a tropical garden with a pool gathered around a large colonial house on the edge of town.

A Casarão, R Direita 79, T3331 2662, www.ocasarao.pirenopolis.tur.br. A converted colonial town house decorated with antiques, garden and small pool, a/c rooms with 4 poster beds, mosquito nets.

B-C Arvoredo, R Direita s/n, T3331 3479, www.arvoredo.tur.br. Peaceful, small pool, views over the town. Simple rooms with large beds and excellent special rates during the week.

C Pouso do Sô Vigario, R Nova 25, T3331 1206, www.pousadaspirenopolis.com.br. Small rooms but pleasant public areas, good location, decent breakfast in a little garden next to the pool.

D Rex, Praça da Matriz, T331 1121. Five rooms, all with fridge and TV, arranged around a courtyard. Good breakfast and location.

E-F Arco Iris, R dos Pireneus s/n, T3331 1686. Very simple but well-kept, fan, shared bath, no breakfast.

Camping Roots, R dos Pireneus 96, camproots@yahoo.com. In easy reach of the centre with power, hot water and some English-speaking staff.

Chapada dos Veadeiros *p572*
Alto Paraiso

AL-A Camelot, on the main road just north of town, T3446 1449, www.pousadacamelot. com.br. Delightfully kitsch mock-Arthurian

573

castle with proper hot showers and comfortable a/c rooms with satellite TV.

AL-A Portal da Chapada, 9km along the road to São Jorge, T3446 1820, www.portalda chapada.com.br. The best choice for birdwatchers, with cabins in the cerrado. Comfortable with a/c.

A Casa Rosa, R Gumersindo 233, T3446 1319, www.pousadacasarosa.com.br. Good a/c rooms, the best in chalets near the pool.

C-D Pousada do Sol, R Gumersindo 2911, T3446 1201. Small and simple, with a range of rooms, the best with balconies and fridges.

São Jorge

Prices often go up 30% at weekends.

AL Casa das Flores, T9976 0603, www.pousada casadasflores.com.br. Elegant, tastefully decorated rooms (candle-lit), sauna, pool and great breakfast.

AL-A Águas de Março, T3347 2082, www.chapadadosveadeiros.com.br. A range of simple rooms decorated by local artists' work, pleasant garden, saunas, good breakfast.

AL-A Trilha Violeta, T3455 1088, www.trilha violeta.com.br. Fan, rooms around a bougainvillea filled garden. Reasonable restaurant.

D Casa Grande, T9623 5515/446 1388, www.pousadacasagrande.com.br. Simple but well looked after, good breakfast.

Camping Tatoo, at the top of town, tattoo@ travessia.tur.br, or tattoosj@yahoo.com.br. Powered sites from only US$3. Pizzas from wood oven, small bar, English spoken, very helpful.

Parque Nacional Emas *p572*
Mineiros

B Pilões Palace, Praça Alves de Assis, T3661 1547. Restaurant, comfortable.

C 14 de Maio, R Onze 11, T3661 1532. No a/c, good churrasco restaurant attached.

Dorm accommodation at the park headquarters; kitchen and cook available but bring own food.

● Eating

Goiânia *p571*

Gioanian cooking is like that of neighbouring Minas – meat heavy, with huge portions of accompanying vegetable dishes and of course beans and rice. The city has a good range of restaurants and bars, especially around Praça Tamandaré and Av Rep de Líbano in the Setor Oeste. Other mid-range options exist on and around Av Anhaguera between Tocantins and Goiás. Street stands (pamonharías) sell pamonha snacks, tasty pastries made with green corn, sweet, savoury, or picante/spicy; all are served hot and have cheese in the middle, some include sausage.

Ψ Bella Luna, R 10 704 (Praça Tamandaré). Excellent pizza, pasta and northern Italian dishes.

ΨΨΨ Celson & Cia, R 15 539 at C 22. Very popular Goiás and Mineira meat restaurant with a good cold buffet. Evenings only except at weekends.

ΨΨΨ Chão Nativo, Av Rep Líbano 1809. The city's most famous Goiânian restaurant also serving local and Mineira food. Lively after 2000 and lunchtime on weekends.

ΨΨ China, R 7 623 (Praça Tamandaré). Chinese and Japanese food in a/c surroundings.

ΨΨ Floresta, R 2 at R 9. Lively corner bar with grilled steaks, Brazilian standards and snacks ($). Open until late.

ΨΨ Tribo do Açai, R 36 590. Buzzing little fruit juice bar with excellent buffet salads and health food.

ΨΨ Walmor, R 3 1062 at R 25-B. Large portions of some of Brazil's best steaks, attractive open-air dining area, best after 2000.

Ψ Buffalo's Grill, Praça Tamandaré. Pizzas, grilled meat, sandwiches and crêpes. Open 24 hrs.

Ψ Giraffa, Av Rep Líbano 1592. Fast food with some more sumptuous set plates.

Ψ Mineiro, R 4 No 53. Good Mineira per kilo buffet with lots of choice and some veggie options. One of several on this block.

Ψ Primo Patio, Av Rep Líbano (opposite Castro's Plaza). Pizza, pasta and grilled steak and chicken.

Cidade de Goiás *p571*

ΨΨ Dali, R 13 de Maio 26, T3372 1640. Riverside restaurant offering a broad range of international and local dishes.

ΨΨ Flor do Ipê, Praça da Boa Vista 32 (end of the road leading from the centre across the bridge, T3372 1133. The best Goiânian food, enormous variety, lovely garden setting. Highly recommended.

Ψ Degus't Fun Pizzaria, R Quinta Bocaiuva (next to Praça do Coreto), T3371 2800. Pizza, casseroles, soups and very friendly service from a mother and daughter team.

Pirenópolis *p572*

There are plenty of options along R do Rosário, serving a surprising range of international food including some vegetarian and Asian options. Many have live music at night (and an undisclosed cover charge – be sure to ask). There are cheaper options near the Igreja Bonfim in the upper part of town.

ΨΨ Caffe e Tarsia, R do Rosário 34, T3331 1274, www.caffetarsia.com.br. One of the best in town with rich Goiás cooking, a decent wine list and live music at the weekends.

Ψ Chiquinha, R do Rosário 19. Serves local cuisine (heavy on meat).

⊕ Bars and clubs

Goiânia p571
Goiânia is surprisingly lively, with some of the best nightlife in central Brazil. This is especially true around the various festivals and carnival. There is an active gay scene and plenty of choices of clubs and bars. Most locals tend to drink in the restaurants, many of which double up as bars (see above) before heading to a club at around 2300.

⊕ Festivals and events

Cidade de Goiás p571
Many festivals here and a very lively arts scene. The streets blaze with torches during the solemn Fogaréu processions of Holy Week, when hooded figures re-enact Christ's descent from the cross and burial. Carnaval is a good deal more joyous and still little known to outsiders. Plans are to make carnival a series of traditional masked balls, as it was at the turn of the 20th century.

Pirenópolis p572
Festa do Divino Espírito Santo, 45 days after Easter (Pentecost-**May/Jun**), is one of Brazil's most famous and extraordinary folkloric/religious celebrations. It lasts 3 days, with medieval costumes, tournaments, dances and mock battles between Moors and Christians, a tradition held annually since 1819. The city throbs with life over this period.

⊙ Shopping

Pirenópolis p572
Two of the best jewellers are **Cristiano**, who has travelled extensively in South America as is reflected in his designs, and **Rodrigo Edson Santos**, R do Rosário 3, T3331 3804.

▲ Activities and tours

Goiânia p571
Travel agents in town can arrange day tours. **Turisplan Turismo**, R 8 No 388, T3224 7076. Also sells regular bus tickets.

Cidade de Goiás p571
Frans and Susana Leeuweenberg (through Serra Dourada). Birding and wildlife trips in the surrounding area (or anywhere in Goiás – with advanced notice) from a husband and wife team of biologists who have been working hard to protect the cerrado for many years. English, French and Dutch spoken.
Serra Dourada Aventura, no fixed office, reachable on T3371 4277 or 9238 5195, through www.vilaboadegoias.com.br or orlei@ vilaboadegoias.com.br. Hiking in the Serra

Dourada and bespoke trips to the wilds of the Rio Araguaia (with notice). Very good value.

Pirenópolis p572
There are plenty of walks and adventure activities in the cerrado and hills, birding is good and there is a reasonably healthy population of maned wolf and the various South American cats, including jaguar. The landscape is rugged, with many waterfalls and canyons. Guides are essential as many of the attractions are well off the beaten track.
Drena, R do Carmo 11 (across the bridge and up the hill, on the left), T3331 3336. A range of walks and adventure activities, good value, well-run, d English spoken. They organize trips to **Santuário de Vida Silvestre Vagafogo**, T3335 8490, the private reserve of Evandro Engel Ayer: good birding (species list and library) and many interesting animals. Evandro is very knowledge-able and helpful, speaks good English and serves one of the best light lunches in Goiás. **Mosterio Buddhisto**, a simple Zen monastery near a series of beautiful cascades in the heart of pristine cerrado forest. Day visits with light walks or longer term retreats. Particularly magical at sunset.

Chapada dos Veadeiros p572
By far the easiest way to visit is with one of the tour operators in Alto Paraíso. Prices vary according to season and group number.
Alternativas, T3446 1000, www.alternativas. tur.br. Light adventure activities and treks, run by locals, excellent and really go out of the way to help. Sasa speaks good English. Recommended.
Chapada Ecotours, T3446 1345, www.transchapada.com.br. Light adventure and visits to the major sights.
EcoRotas, R dos Nascentes 129, T3446 1820, www.altoparaiso.com. Van-based tours to the principal sights. Suitable for all ages.
Travessia, T3446 1595, www.travessia.tur.br. Treks of several days to over a week and rappelling and canyoning from one of the country's most respected instructors, Ion David. Little English.

⊖ Transport

Goiânia p571
Air Santa Genoveva, 6 km northeast off Rua 57, T3265 1500. Flights to **Brasília**, **São Paulo** and other cities. Taxi from centre US$8.
Bus Rodoviária on Rua 44 No 399 in the Norte Ferroviário sector, about a 40-min walk to downtown (T3229 0070). Buses 'Rodoviária-Centro' (No 404) and 'Vila União-Centro' (No 163) leave from stop on city side of terminal, US$1; No 163 goes on to the Praça Tamandaré.

To **Brasília**, 207 km, at least 15 departures a day, 2½ hrs, US$10, and **São Paulo**, 900 km via

Barretos, US$48, 14½ hrs, leito services at night. To **Cidade de Goiás**, 136 km, hourly from 0500, 2½ hrs, US$10. **Pirenópolis** 0700 and 1700, 2 hrs, US$10. **Campo Grande**, 935 km, 4 services daily, 18 hrs, US$60. To **Cuiabá** (Mato Grosso), 916 km on BR-158/070 via Barra do Garças, or 928 km on BR-060/364 via Jataí (both routes paved, most buses use the latter route), 4 buses a day, US$38, 15-16 hrs, continuing to Porto Velho (Rondônia) and Rio Branco (Acre) – a very trying journey indeed.

Cidade de Goiás *p571*
Bus The rodoviária is 2 km out of town. Regular services to Goiânia (2½ hrs), Aruanã, Barra do Garças and Jussara. All buses stop at the old bus station (rodoviária velha) next to the Mercado Municipal. Ask to get out here.

Pirenópolis *p572*
Bus 2 a day to **Brasília** (2-4 hrs) and 2 per day to **Goiânia** (3 hrs).

Chapada dos Veadeiros *p572*
Bus At least 2 per day Brasília-Alto Paraíso (3-4 hrs) and on to São Jorge. One a day to **Palmas** in Tocantins.

Parque Nacional Emas *p572*
Bus Twice weekly from **Mineiros.Car** 6 hrs' drive from **Campo Grande**, 20 hrs from Goiânia, paved road poor. The road to the park is unpaved.

Tocantins

To the north of Goiás, and extracted from that state in 1988, is Tocantins, dominated by vast rivers, cerrado forests and, increasingly soya plantations. The state was formed largely at the whim of one powerful landowner, José Wilson Siqueira Campos; who for the first decade of its existence ran the state like a personal fiefdom. Although new to tourism Tocantins has some stunning scenery and is the only state in the country to have Amazonian forest, Pantanal, cerrado forest and sertão. The greatest draw is **Jalapão**, a region of sweeping yellow sand-dunes, vast plains cut by fast-flowing clear-water rivers and dotted with table top mountains eroded into bizarre shapes. The air is so clear that it is possible to see for hundreds of kilometres to every horizon; and the landscape so empty that cars can be heard from miles away. There is plentiful wildlife too – including maned wolf, puma and some of the world's rarest birds including Brazilian merganser and Spix's macaw.

The capital of Tocantins is **Palmas** (*Phone code oxx63. Colour map 5, grid C1, www.palmas.to.gov.br*), a modern planned city laid out in an incomprehensible mathematical plan and on the edge of the dammed and flooded Tocantins river. Brazil's newest city is an interesting detour on the highway between Belém (1,282 km away) and Brasília (973 km). There are waterfalls in the surrounding mountains and beaches on the River Tocantins, which make for a relaxing stop on an otherwise long drive. The BR-153 is close to the city and provides a good road connection, both north to Maranhão, Pará, and south to Goiás. Tourist offices at airport, T3219 3760, and Parque Cesamar (506 Sul, Av NS–04, LO 11, Área Verde), T3218 5570.

🔵 **Sleeping** → *See Telephone, page 347, for important phone changes.*

Tocantins *p576*
There are numerous hotels in Palmas.
A Pousada dos Girassóis, 103-C. cj 3, lt 44, T3219 4500, www.pousadadosgirassois.com.br. The best in town with standard 3 star rooms with fitted furniture and a/c and the best restaurant in town. Jalapão tours leave from here.
B Roma, Av L02-104 Norte, lote 23, T3215 3033, www.hotelroma-to.com.br. Pleasant, bright, airy rooms, internet access.
D-E Alfredo's, Av JK 103 Sul, Qd 101, lotes 23/24, T3215 3036. Simple rooms around a garden courtyard, with a/c or fan. Trips arranged.

🔺 **Activities and tours**

Tocantins *p576*
Korubo Expedicoes, T011-3667 5053, www.korubo.com.br. Excellent tours to Jalapão staying in their luxurious purpose-built safari camp, modelled on those in Botswana; whitewater rafting, trekking, jeep trips and wildlife tours included in the price.

🔵 **Transport**

Tocantins *p576*
Air Airport, Av NS 5, 2 km from centre, T3216 1237. Flights to Belém, Brasília, Goiânia and São Paulo.
Bus City buses are plentiful and cheap. Rodoviária, Acsuso 40, T3216 1603.

The Pantanal

This vast wetland, which covers a staggering 21,000 sq km (the size of Belgium, Portugal, Switzerland and Holland combined), between Cuiabá, Campo Grande and the Bolivian frontier, is one of the world's great wildlife preserves. Parts spill over into Bolivia, Paraguay and Argentina to form an area totalling some 100,000 sq km. Partly flooded in the rainy season (see below), the Pantanal is a mecca for wildlife tourism or fishing. Whether land or river-based, seasonal variations make a great difference to the practicalities of getting there and what you will experience. A road runs across Mato Grosso do Sul via Campo Grande to Porto Esperança and Corumbá, both on the Rio Paraguai; much of the road is across the wetland, offering many sights of birds and other wildlife.

Ins and outs

Wildlife → www.geocities.com/RainForest/1820/ (Portuguese and English).

The Pantanal plain slopes some 1 cm in every kilometre north to south and west to east to the basin of the Rio Paraguai and is rimmed by low mountains. One hundred and seventy five rivers flow from these into the Pantanal and after the heavy summer rains they burst their banks, as does the Paraguai itself; to create vast shallow lakes broken by patches of high ground and stands of *cerrado* forest. Plankton then swarm to form a biological soup that contains as many as 500 million microalgae per litre. Millions of amphibians and fish spawn or migrate to consume them. And these in turn are preyed upon by waterbirds and reptiles. Herbivorous mammals graze on the stands of water hyacinth, sedge and savanna grass and at the top of the food chain lie South America's great predators – the jaguar, ocelot, maned wolf and yellow anaconda. In June at the end of the wet when the sheets of water have reduced to small lakes or canals wildlife concentrates and then there is nowhere on earth where you will see such vast quantities of birds or such enormous numbers of crocodilians. Only the plains of Africa can compete for mammals and your chances of seeing a jaguar or one of Brazil's seven other species of wild cat are greater here than anywhere else on the continent. There are over 700 resident and migratory bird species in the Pantanal and birding along the Transpantaneira road in the north or in one of the fazendas in the south can yield as many as 100 species a day; especially between late June and early October. Many species overlap with the Amazon region, the Cerrado and Chaco and the area is particularly rich in waterbirds. Although the Pantanal is often described as an ecosystem in its own right, it is in reality made up of many distinct habitats which in turn have their own, often distinct biological communities. Botanically it is a mosaic, a mixture of elements from the Amazon region including *várzea* and gallery forests and tropical savanna, the *cerrado* of central Brazil and the dry *chaco* of Paraguay.

Only one area is officially a national park, the **Parque Nacional do Pantanal Matogrossense** in the municipality of Poconé, 135,000 ha of land and water, only accessible by air or river. Permission to visit the park needs to be obtained at **Ibama** ⓘ *R Rubens de Mendonça, Cuiabá, CEP 78008, T644 9100*. Hunting in any form is strictly forbidden throughout the Pantanal and is punishable by four years imprisonment. Fishing is allowed with a licence (enquire at travel agents for latest details); it is not permitted in the spawning season or piracema (1 October-1 February in Mato Grosso do Sul, 1 November-1 March in Mato Grosso). Like other wilderness areas, the Pantanal faces important threats to its integrity. Agro-chemicals and garimpo mercury washed down from the neighbouring planalto are a hazard to wildlife. Visitors must share the responsibility of protecting the Pantanal and you can make an important contribution by acting responsibly and choosing your guides accordingly: take out your rubbish, don't fish out of season, don't let guides kill or disturb fauna, don't buy products made from endangered species and report any violation of these norms to the authorities.

When to go

The Pantanal is good for seeing wildlife year-round. However, the dry season between July and October is the ideal time as animals and birds congregate at the few remaining areas of water.

During these months you are very likely to see jaguars. This is the nesting and breeding season, when birds form vast nesting areas, with thousands crowding the trees, creating an almost insupportable cacophony of sounds. The white sand river beaches are exposed, caiman bask in the sun, and capybaras frolic amid the grass. July sees lots of Brazilian visitors who tend to be noisy, decreasing the chances of sightings. From the end of November to the end of March (wettest in February), most of the area, which is crossed by many rivers, floods. At this time mosquitoes abound and cattle crowd on to the few islands remaining above water. In the southern part, many wild animals leave the area, but in the north, which is slightly higher, the animals do not leave.

What to take
Most tours arrange for you to leave your baggage in town, so you need only bring what is necessary for the duration of the tour with you. In winter (June-August), temperatures fall to 10° C, warm clothing and covers or sleeping bag are needed at night. It's very hot and humid during summer and a hat and sun protection, factor 30 or above, is vital. Wear long sleeves and long trousers and spray clothes as well as skin with insect repellent. Insects are less of a problem July-August. Take insect repellent from home as mosquitoes, especially in the North Pantanal, are becoming immune to local brands. Drinks are not included in the price of packages and tend to be over-priced, so if you are on a tight budget bring your own. Most importantly, make sure you take a pair of binoculars.

Getting there
There are three options for visiting the Pantanal: by tour, through a working ranch (*fazenda*) or by self-drive. Entry into the northern Pantanal comes either via the Transpantaneira road in the north, reached from the city of Cuiabá, which cuts through the wetland and is lined with fazendas, or the town of Barão do Melgaço which is surrounded by large lakes and rivers and is not as good for wildlife. In the south the access points are Campo Grande, Corumbá and Miranda, which offers access to many of the *fazendas*. *Fazendas* in the northern or southern Pantanal can also be booked directly; most now have websites and a tour of them can be taken with a hire car.

Types of tour
Tourist facilities in the Pantanal currently cater to four main categories of visitors. **Sport fishermen** usually stay at one of the numerous speciality lodges scattered throughout the region, which provide guides, boats, bait, ice and other related amenities. Bookings can be made locally or in any of Brazil's major cities. **All-inclusive tours** combining air and ground transportation, accommodation at the most elaborate fazendas, meals, guided river and land

tours, can be arranged from abroad or through Brazilian travel agencies. This is the most expensive option. **Moderately priced tours** using private guides, camping or staying at more modest fazendas can be arranged locally in Cuiabá (where guides await arrivals at the airport) or through the more reputable agencies in Corumbá. **The lowest priced tours** are offered by independent guides in Corumbá, some of whom are unreliable and travellers have reported at times serious problems here (see below). For those with the minimum of funds, a glimpse of the Pantanal and its wildlife can be had on the bus ride from Campo Grande to Corumbá, by lodging or camping near the ferry crossing over the Rio Paraguai (Porto Esperança), and by staying in Poconé and day-walking or hitching south along the Transpantaneira. **Note** Whatever your budget, take binoculars!

Choosing a tour

Most tours combine 'safari' jeep trips, river-boat trips, piranha fishing and horse riding with accommodation in lodges. Excursions often take place at sunset and sunrise as these are the best times for spotting bird and wildlife. A two-day trip, with a full day taken up with travel each way, allows you to experience most of what is on offer. Longer tours tend to have the same activities spread out over a longer period of time. The best way to enjoy a tour is not to have fixed expectations about what you will see, but to take in the whole experience that is the Pantanal.

Many budget travellers en route to or from Bolivia make Corumbá their base for visiting the Pantanal. Such tourists are often approached, in the streets and at the cheaper hotels, by salesmen who speak foreign languages and promise complete tours for low prices. They then hand their clients over to agencies and/or guides, who often speak only Portuguese, and may deliver something quite different. Some travellers have reported very unpleasant experiences and it is important to select a guide with great care anywhere. By far the best way is to speak with other travellers who have just returned from a Pantanal tour. Most guides also have a book containing comments from their former clients. Do not rush to sign up when first approached, always compare several available alternatives. Discuss the planned itinerary carefully and try to get it in writing (although this is seldom possible – threaten to go to someone else if necessary). Try to deal directly with agencies or guides, not salesmen (it can be difficult to tell who is who). Always get an itemized receipt. Bear in mind that a well-organized three-day tour can be more rewarding than four days with an ill-prepared guide. There is fierce competition between guides who provide similar services, but with very different styles. Although we list a few of the most reputable guides below, there are other good ones and most economy travellers enjoy a pleasant if spartan experience. Remember that travellers must shoulder part of the responsibility for the current chaotic guiding situation in Corumbá. Act responsibly and don't expect to get something for nothing.

It appears to be the case that once a guide is recommended by a guidebook, he ceases to guide and sets up his own business working in promoting and public relations, using other guides to work under his name. Guides at the airport give the impression that they will lead the tour, but they won't. Always ask who will lead the party and how big it will be. Less than four is not economically viable and he will make cuts in boats or guides.

Campo Grande and around

Campo Grande → *Phone code: 0xx67. Post code: 79000. Colour map 7, grid B1. Pop: 663,621.*
Capital of the State of Mato Grosso do Sul. It was founded in 1899. It is a pleasant, modern city. Because of the terra roxa (red earth), it is called the 'Cidade Morena'. In the centre is a shady park, the **Praça República**, commonly called the Praça do Rádio after the Rádio Clube on one of its corners. Three blocks west is **Praça Ari Coelho**. Linking the two squares, and running through the city east to west, is Av Afonso Pena; much of its central reservation is planted with yellow ypé trees. Their blossom covers the avenue, and much of the city besides, in spring. The municipal **Centro de Informação Turística e Cultural** ① *Av Noroeste 5140 corner Afonso Pena, T/F324 5830, Tue-Sat 0800-1900, Sun 0900-1200*, sells maps and books. Housed in Pensão Pimentel, a beautiful mansion built in 1913, it also has a database about services in the city and cultural information.

Some distance from the centre is the large **Parque dos Poderes**, which contains the Palácio do Governo and other secretariats, paths and lovely trees. Even larger is the 119-ha

Parque das Nações Indígenas. Despite its name this is almost completely covered with recreational grassy areas and ornamental trees. But it's a very pleasant place for a stroll or quiet read and has good birdlife and a couple of museums: **Museu de Arte Contemporânea** ① *R Antônio Maria Coelho 6000, Tue-Sun 1200-1800, US$2*. This preserves the largest collection of modern art in the state and one of the largest in the Centre West; permanent and temporary exhibitions. **Museu Dom Bosco (Indian Museum)** ① *Av Afonso Pena, Parque das Nações Indígenas, T312 6491, Tue-Fri 0800-1800, Sat 1300-1800, Sun 0800-1200, 1400-1700, US$1.50*, contains relics from the various tribes who were the recipients of the Salesians aggressive missionary tactics in the early and mid-20th century. The largest collections are from the Tukano and Bororo people from the Upper Rio Negro and Mato Grosso respectively, both of whose cultures the Salesians were responsible for almost completely wiping out. There is also a rather depressing display of stuffed endangered species (mostly from the Pantanal, though some are from other areas of Brazil or other countries), two-headed calves and seashells from around the world.

Bonito → *Phone code: 0xx67. Post code: 79290. Colour map 6, grid B6. Population: 17,000.*

The municipality of Bonito, 248 km from Campo Grande, is in the Serra do Bodoquena. It is surrounded by beautiful *cerrado* forest cut by clear-water rivers rich with fish and dotted with plunging waterfalls and deep caves. It has become Brazil's foremost ecotourism destination; which in Brazilian terms means that families come here to romp around in Nature: from light adventure activities like caving to gentle rafting and snorkelling, all with proper safety measures and great even for small children. Despite the heavy influx of visitors plenty of wildlife appears around the trails when it's quiet. The wet season is January to February; December to February is hottest, July to August coolest. **Tourist office Comtur** ① *Av Cel Pilad Rebuá 1250, T3255 2160 (no English spoken), www.bonito-ms.com.br*. Bonito is prohibitively expensive for those on a budget. All the attractions in the area can only be visited with prior booking through a travel agent. As taxis are exorbitant, it is best to book with one of the few agencies who offers tours and transport. Owners also enforce limits on the number of daily visitors so, at busy times, pre-booking is essential. Bonito is very popular, especially during December to January, Carnival, Easter, and July (at these times advance booking is essential).

Some 26 km from Bonito is **Lagoa Azul**. The cave is named after a lake 50 m long and 110 m wide, 75 m below ground level. The water, 20ºC, is a jewel-like blue as light from the opening is refracted through limestone and magnesium. Prehistoric animal bones have been

Campo Grande

Sleeping 🛏️
Advanced 1
Concord Inn 3
Cosmos 4
Iguaçu 6

Internacional 7
Jandaia 2
Nacional 8
Pousada LM 9
Youth Hostel 11

Eating 🍴
Cantina Romana 3
Comitiva Pantaneira 2
Gaúcho Gastão 1
Morada dos Bais 4

Not to scale

found in the lake. The light is at its best January-February, 0700-0900, but is fine at other times. A 25-ha park surrounds the cave. You must pay a municipal tax, US$10; if not using your own transport, a car for four costs US$20. Also open is **Nossa Senhora Aparecida cave**, which has superb stalactites and stalagmites; no tourism infrastructure.

The **Balneário Municipal** ① *7 km on road to Jardim, US$4*, on the Rio Formoso, with changing rooms, toilets, camping, swimming in clear water, plenty of fish to see (strenuous efforts are made to keep the water and shore clean). **Hormínio waterfalls** ① *13 km, US$1*, eight falls on the Rio Formoso, suitable for swimming; bar and camping. **Rafting** on the Rio Formoso: 2½ hours, minimum four people, US$15 per person, a mixture of floating peacefully downriver, swimming and shooting four waterfalls, lifejackets available; arranged by many agencies. The **Aquário Natural** ① *US$25*, is one of the springs of the Rio Formoso. To visit you must have authorization from the owners; you can swim and snorkel with five types of fish. Do not swim with suntan oil on. Other tours are: from the **springs of the Rio Sucuri** to its meeting with the Formoso (permission required to visit), about 2 km of crystal-clear water, with swimming or snorkelling, birdwatching, very peaceful; **Aquidaban**, a series of limestone/marble waterfalls in dense forest; **Rio da Prata** ① *US$24*, a spring with underground snorkelling for 2 km, stalactites, bats, very beautiful, also parrots and other animals can be seen on the trip, The **fishing** season is from 1 March-31 October. In late October, early November is the piracema (fish run), when the fish return to their spawning grounds. Hundreds can be seen jumping the falls. **Note** Bonito's attractions are nearly all on private land and must by visited with a guide. Owners also enforce limits on the number of daily visitors so, at busy times, pre-booking is essential.

Ponta Porã → *Post code: 79900. Phone code: 0xx67. Population: 67,000*

There is a paved road from Campo Grande to the Paraguayan border to Ponta Porã, separated from Pedro Juan Caballero in Paraguay only by a broad avenue. With paved streets, good public transport and smart shops, Ponta Porã is more prosperous than its neighbour, although Brazilians cross the border to play the casino and visit the cheaper shops. In addition to the free movement of people and goods, the blending of cultures here is impressive. There are many *Brasiguayos* with one parent of each nationality and *Portoñol* is the common tongue. There are many banks on Av Brasil (one block back from the border) with ATMs but no exchange facilities; many cambios on the Paraguayan side.

Border with Paraguay → *Colour map 7, grid B2.*

There are no border posts between the two towns. The **Brazilian Polícia Federal** ① *Av Pres Vargas 70, ½ block back from the border street, T3431 1428, Mon-Fri 0730-1130, 1330-1730*, is closed weekends but officers on duty might provide an entry stamp if you are on a bus that is passing through. The Paraguayan consulate in Ponta Porã (Av Pres Vargas 130, T3431 6312) does not issue visas, the nearest ones that do are in São Paulo, Curitiba and Foz do Iguaçu. **Check requirements carefully**, and ensure your documents are in order: without the proper stamps you will inevitably be sent back somewhere later on in your travels. Taking a taxi between offices can speed things up if pressed for time; drivers know border crossing requirements; US$10.

Campo Grande to Corumbá

BR-262 is paved from Campo Grande to Corumbá and the Bolivian border. The scenery is marvellous. Some 200 km west of Campo Grande is **Miranda**, where a road heads south to Bodoquena and Bonito. As a gateway to the Pantanal and Bonito, it is far closer to both than either Corumbá or Campo Grande. Many of the best of the southern Pantanal fazendas lie here, too. Every October Miranda throws the spectacular **Festa do Homen Pantaneiro**, four days of rodeos, lassoing and general revelry (dates vary each year). There is a tourist booth just outside the bus station, opposite the **Zero Hora** bakery and supermarket. Internet at **Star Informâtica**, Rua Francisco Rebúa 149. The town has both a **Bradesco** and a **Banco do Brasil**.

To the southern Pantanal

Many tours out of Campo Grande and Miranda take a dirt road running off the BR 262 Campo Grande-Corumbá highway called the **Estrada Parque**. It begins halfway between Miranda and Corumbá at a turn off called **Buraco da Piranha** (the Piranha hole), heads north into the Pantanal and then, after 51 km, turns west to Corumbá at a point called the **Curva do Leque**. This is the overland access point to **Nhecolândia**, a region particularly rich in wildlife.

Although there are excellent fazendas off the Estrada Parque road there are an increasing number opening up to tourism around Miranda.

⊙ Sleeping → *See Telephone, page 347, for important phone changes.*

Campo Grande *p579, map p580*

The better hotels are in the centre. There is a wide variety of cheaper hotels in the streets around the rodoviária so it is easy to leave bags in the *guarda volumes* and shop around. This area is not safe at night.

L Jandaia, R Barão do Rio Branco 1271, T3316 7700, www.jandaia.com.br. The city's best hotel, aimed at a business market. Modern well-appointed rooms (with IDSL) in a tower, pool, gym and some English spoken.

A Advanced, Av Calógeras 1909, T3321 5000, www.hoteladvanced.com.br. Spacious if spartan rooms with hot showers, in an 80s block, very small pool, cheaper with fan.

A Internacional, Allan Kardec 223, T3384 4677. Quiet street near rodoviária. Modern, comfortable with a/c or fan and some renovated suites, small pool, restaurant.

B Concord Inn, Av Calógeras 1624, T3321 2999. A standard town hotel with a small pool and recently renovated a/c rooms with modern fittings.

B Iguaçu, R Dom Aquino 761, T3322 4621, www.hoteliguacu.com.br. **D** with fan. Very popular well-kept hotel next to the rodoviária with smart, simple a/c rooms with cable TV. Good breakfast.

C-D Pousada LM, R 15 de Novembro 201, T3321 5207, www.lmhotel.com.br. Tiny, basic en suites around a courtyard, all with a TV, fridge and some with terraces. Cheaper with fan.

D Cosmos, R Dom Aquino 771, near the rodoviária, T3384 4270. Simple but bright and well-kept 1980s rooms with decent mattresses and en suites.

D Nacional, R Dom Aquino, 610, T3383 2561, hotelnacional@ig.com.br. Simple, quiet rooms with fans, some rooms with bath, proper mattresses in a well-kept hotel with a TV room and internet, good value.

D R Joaquim Nabuco 185, opposite rodoviária, T3321 0505, ajcampogrande@hotmail.com. Simple, musty little rooms with saggy foam mattresses and frayed bathrooms. Laundry, kitchen, internet; reception open 24 hrs.

Ecological Expeditions offer Pantanal trips from their office next door. Their other branch at R Barão Rio Branco 343, T3325 6874, has marginally better rooms for 10% more; but the mattresses are still hot and foamy.

Bonito *p580*

AL Pira Miuna, R Luis da Costa Leite 1792, T3255 1058, www.piramiunahotel.com.br. Ugly building with the most comfortable a/c rooms in the centre and a large pool area with jacuzzis and a bar.

AL Pousada Olho d'Água, Rod Três Morros, Km 1, T3255 1430, olhodagua@vip2000.net. Comfortable cabins with fan, set in a garden next to a small lake. Horse riding, bike rental, solar-powered hot water and great food from the vegetable garden. Recommended.

A Tapera, Estrada Ilha do Padre, Km 10, on hill above Shell station on road to Jardim, T3255 1700. Fine views, cool breezes, peaceful, a/c, very comfortable, own transport an advantage.

C Canaã, R Col Pilad Rebuá 1376, T3255 1282. A scruffy lobby leads to gloomy though well-maintained motel-style rooms with a/c and bath.

C-E Pousada São Jorge, Av Col Pilad Rebuá 1605, T3255 4046, www.pousadasaojorge.com.br. Clean dorms with bunks and en suites (the best with 2 bathrooms) and a pleasant public dining area with snack bar. Price per person for dorms.

D pp Pousada Muito Bonito, Pilad Rebuá 1448, T/F3255 1645. With bath, or rooms with bunkbeds, nice patio, excellent, helpful owners, including breakfast, also with tour company (Mario Doblack speaks English, French and Spanish). Warmly recommended.

D pp Pousada Rio do Peixe, R 29 de Maio 820, T3255 2212, pousadariodopeixe@viabonito.com.br. More expensive with TV, Italian-owned, very helpful, excellent breakfast, tours arranged.

E pp Albergue do Bonito, R Lúcio Borralho 716, T/F3255 1462, www.ajbonito.com.br. Price pp in dorm, HI affiliated hostel, cheaper for members, English spoken, pool, laundry facilities, use of kitchen, hot showers, secure parking, rents bicycles.

Camping At Ilha do Padre, 12 km north of Bonito, T/F255 1430. On island with natural pools, very pleasant, no regular transport. 4 rustic cabins with 4 bunk beds, or 2 bunks and a double, US$10 pp. Youth hostel with dorms, US$6 pp, same price for camping. Toilets, showers, clothes washing, meals, bar, electricity, lots of trees. You can swim anywhere, to enter the island for a day US$3. Camping also at **Poliana** on Rio Formosa, 100 m past Ilha do Padre, T255 1267. Very pleasant.

● *For an explanation of the sleeping and eating price codes used in this guide, see page 58.*
● *Other relevant information is found in Essentials pages 345-347.*

Ponta Porã *p581*

AL-A Barcelona, R Guia Lopes 45, T3431 3061, www.hotelbarcelonapp.com.br. Maze-like building, a/c, restaurant, indoor pool, parking.

A Pousada do Bosque, Av Pres Vargas 1151, T3431 1181, www.hotelpousadado bosque.com.br. 'Fazenda style' with lovely grounds and pool, sports fields, restaurant, parking, comfortable rooms with a/c and fridge.

A-B Interpark, Av Brasil 3684, T3431 1577, www.grupointerhoteis.com.br. Comfortable modern rooms with a/c and fridge, small pool, restaurant.

D Guarujá, R Guia Lopes 63, T3431 1619. With a/c and fridge, cheaper with fan, parking, faded but functional.

D Vila Velha, Av Marechal Floreano 2916, T3431 2760. Private bath, electric shower, fan, basic.

Campo Grande to Corumbá: Miranda *p581*

A-D Águas do Pantanal, Av Afonso Pena 367, T3242 1242, www.aguasdopantanal.com.br. Much the best in town, comfortable a/c rooms and cheaper backpacker accommodation, attractive pool surrounded by tropical flowers, helpful travel agency. Usually have a rep waiting at the rodoviária.

C Pantanal, Av Barão do Rio Branco 609, T3242 1068. Well-maintained a/c rooms with en suites along a gloomy corridor, pool.

D-E Diogo, Av Barão do Rio Branco s/n, T3242 1468. Very simple but well-kept doubles, triples and quadruples, some with a/c.

To the southern Pantanal *p581*

LL Refúgio Ecológico Caiman, 36 km from Miranda, T011-3706 1800 (São Paulo), www.caiman.com.br. The most comfortable, stylish accommodation in the Pantanal. Tours and guiding are excellent. A member of the Roteiros de Charme group (see page 346).

LL-L Fazenda Xaraés, Estrada Parque, www.xaraes.com.br. One of the most luxurious fazendas, with a pool, tennis court, sauna, air strip and surprisingly plain but well-appointed a/c rooms. The immediate environs have been extensively cleared, but there are some wild areas of savanna and *cerrado* nearby and there are giant otter in the neighbouring Rio Abodrai.

L-AL Fazenda Bela Vista, Estrada Parque, www.pousadabelavista.com.br. On the banks of the Rio Papagaio in the foothills of the Serra do Urucum hills in a transition zone between Pantanal and higher ground. Bird and primate life is very rich. Guiding is good, but express your interest in wildlife beforehand.

L-AL Fazenda Rio Negro, Estrada Parque, T3326 0002, www.fazendarionegro.com.br. A Conservation International project based at a 13,000-ha farm on the shores of the Rio Negro; the main aim is the protection of jaguars. One of the oldest fazendas in the Pantanal (1920s). Guiding is good, but express your interest in wildlife beforehand.

AL Cacimba de Pedra, Estr Agachi, T9982 4655, www.cacimbadepedra.com.br. A Jacaré caiman farm and pousada in beautiful dry deciduous forest with abundant wildlife. A/c rooms sit in front of an inviting pool.

AL Fazenda San Francisco, turn off BR 262 30km west of Miranda, T3242 3333, www.fazendasanfrancisco.tur.br. One of the best places in the Pantanal for wild cats, preserved through Roberto Coelho's pioneering Gadonça project (www.procarnivoros.org.br), a great success here. Birdwatching is also excellent. Accommodation simple in rustic a/c cabins around a pool in a garden filled with rheas. Food and guides are excellent.

AL Fazenda Santa Inés, Estr. La Lima Km 19, www.fazendasantaines.com.br. A very comfortable family-oriented fazenda overlooking an artificial lake. Tours are aimed firmly at the Campo Grande weekend market and although there is little wildlife here, food is excellent and there is a range of light adventure activities for kids.

AL Pousada Rio Vermelho, off Estrada Parque, T3321 4737, www.pousadariovermelho.com.br. A rustic fazenda in a wild area on the banks of a river famous for its population of jaguars. Simple, well-kept a/c rooms. Coordinate with other visitors through the fazenda in advance as the fazenda lies well off the Estrada Parque.

AL-A Fazenda Meia Lua, BR-262 Km 551, 10 mins from Miranda, T9988 2284, www.fazenda meialua.com.br. Charming newly opened fazenda with a pool, lovely garden filled with hummingbirds and accommodation in a/c cabins or simple a/c rooms, attentive owners.

AL-A Fazenda Baia Grande, Estr La Lima Km 19, T3382 4223, www.fazendabaiagrande.com.br. Very comfortable a/c rooms around a pool in a garden. The fazenda is surrounded by savanna and stands of cerrado. The owner, Alex is very eager to please and enthusiastic.

A Fazenda 23 de Março, T3321 4737, www.fazenda23demarco.com.br. Simple, rustic fazenda with 4 rooms and programmes oriented to budget travellers. Visitors can learn to lasso, ride a bronco and turn their hand to other Pantanal cowboy activities.

● Eating

Campo Grande *p579, map p580*
Local specialities *Caldo de piranha* (soup), *chipa* (Paraguayan cheese bread), sold on streets, delicious when hot, and local liqueur, *pequi com caju*, which contains *cachaça*. There are many cheap restaurants around the rodoviária and many other in a/c surrounds in the Shopping Campo Grande mall (R Afonso Pena 4909).
₮₮₮ Comitiva Pantaneira, R Dom Aquino 2221, T3383 8799. Hearty, tasty and very meaty regional dishes served by waiters in cowboy gear, or as a buffet, lunchtime only.
₮₮₮ Gaúcho Gastão, R 14 de Julho 775, T3384 4326. The best churrascaria in a town, famous for its beef, comfortable, a/c, lunch only.
₮₮ Cantina Romana, R da Paz, 237, T3324 9777. Over 20 years serving Italian dishes, salads and a lunchtime buffet, good atmosphere.
₮₮-₮ Sabor en Quilo, R Barão do Rio Branco 1118 and R Dom Aquino 1786, T3383 3911/3325 5102. Self-service per kilo restaurants with plenty of choice including sushi on Sat, lunchtime only.
₮ Morada dos Bais, Av Noroeste, 5140, corner with Afonso Pena, behind tourist office. Brazilian and Italian dishes, snacks and coffee served in a pretty courtyard, lunchtime only.

Bonito *p580*
₮₮₮-₮₮ Santa Esmeralda, R Cel Pilad Rebuá 1831. Respectable Italian food in one of the few a/c dining rooms.
₮₮ Cantinho do Peixe, R 31 de Março 1918, T3255 3381. A la carte Pantanal fish dishes including good *pintado na telha* (grilled surubim).
₮₮ Tapera, R Cel Pilad Rebuá 480, T3255 1110. Good, home-grown vegetables, breakfast, lunch, pizzas, meat and fish dishes, opens 1900 for evening meal.
₮ Da Vovó, R Sen F Muller 570, T3255 2723. A great per kilo serving Minas and local food all cooked in a traditional wood-burning aga. Plenty of vegetables and salads.
₮ Mercado da Praça, R 15 Novembro 376, T3255 2317. The cheapest in town, a snack bar in the local supermarket offering sandwiches, juices, etc, open 0600-0000.

Campo Grande to Corumbá: Miranda *p581*
₮₮ Cantina Dell'Amore, Av Barão do Rio Branco 515, T3242 2826. The best in town with fish, passable pasta and jacaré steak.
₮ Zero Jora, Av Barão do Rio Branco at the rodoviária, T3242 1330. 24 hour snack bar, provision shop and out the back, with its own private waterfall, a passable, good value per kilo restaurant.

● Shopping

Campo Grande *p579, map p580*
Arts and crafts There is a market (Feira Livre) on Wed and Sat. Local native crafts, including ceramics, tapestry and jewellery, are good quality. A local speciality is Os Bugres da Conceição, squat wooden statues covered in moulded wax. **Arte do Pantanal**, Av Afonso Pena 1743. **Barroarte**, Av Afonso Pena 4329. Very good selections. **Casa do Artesão**, Av Calógeras 2050, on corner with Av Afonso Pena. Housed in an historic building, Mon-Fri 0800-2000, Sat 0800-1200.
Shopping centre Shopping Campo Grande, Av Afonso Pena 4909, www.shoppingcampo grande.com.br, is the largest shopping mall in the city.

▲ Activities and tours

Campo Grande *p579, map p580*
City Tour, T3321 0800 or through larger hotels. Half day tours of the city's sights including the Museu Dom Bosco and the Parque das Nações Indígenas.
Ecological Expeditions, R Joaquim Nabuco 185, T3382 3505, www.pantanaltrekking.com and in Corumbá. Attached to the youth hostel at the bus station. Budget camping trips and lodge-based trips in Nhecolândia (sleeping bag needed) for 3, 4 or 5 days ending in Corumbá.
Impacto, R Padre João Crippa 686, T3325 1333, www.impactotour.com.br. Very helpful, Pantanal and Bonito tours. Prices vary according to standard of accommodation; a wide range is offered. 2-day packages for 2 people from US$190-600. English spoken.
Open Door, R Allan Kardec 87, Galeria Maria Auxiliadora, Sala 4, T3321 8303, www.opendoortur.com.br. Specialists in the Pantanal region and Amazon and booking agents for flights and buses.

Bonito *p580*
There is very little to choose between agencies in Bonito, who offer the same packages for the same price, so shop around to see which you like the feel of best. English speakers are hard to come by. We list only those who also offer transport or a specialist service such as cave diving.
Impacto, R Cel Pilad Rebuá 1515, T3255.1414, see above under Campo Grande. English speaking staff and the possibility of organized transport. These can be pre-booked through their efficient head office in Campo Grande or through Águas do Pantanal tours in Miranda.
Ygarapé, R Cel Pilad Rebuá 1956, T3255 1733, www.ygarape.com.br. One of the few to speak even basic English and to offer transport to the sights. Also PDSE accredited cave diving.

Campo Grande to Corumbá: Miranda *p581*
Both of the operators below can organize lodging
during the Festa do Homen Pantaneiro.
Águas do Pantanal Tours, Águas do Pantanal
hotel, Av Afonso Pena 367, T3242 1242,
www.aguasdopantanal.com.br. Well-organized
tours to the fazendas around Miranda, to those
on the Estrada Parque, to the sights around
Bonito. They also run exclusive 1 or 2-day trips on
the Rio Salobrinha to the Sanctuario Baía Negra, a
little-visited river which is great for snorkelling
and teeming with wildlife.
Marcello Yndio, lives in Bonito, contact him via
T9638-3520 (mob), yndian@hotmail.com,
marcelloyndio@gmail.com or marcelloyndio@
yahoo.com.br. Kadiweu indigenous guide with
many years experience. Very good English,
French, Spanish and Italian and decent Hebrew.
Great for small groups who want to get off the
beaten track. Prices are competitive with budget
operators in Campo Grande and Corumbá.

⊖ Transport

Campo Grande *p579, map p580*
Air Daily flights to most major cities. Airport
T3368 6000. City bus No 158, 'Popular' stops
outside airport. Taxi to airport, US$8. **Banco do
Brasil** at airport exchanges dollars; **Bradesco** just
outside has a Visa ATM. Airport also has tourist
information booths, car rental and airline offices.
It is safe to spend the night at the airport.
Bus Rodoviária is in the block bounded by Ruas
Barão do Rio Branco, Vasconcelos Fernandes, Dom
Aquino and Joaquim Nabuco, T3321 8797, all offices
on 2nd floor. At V Fernandes end are town buses,
at the J Nabuco end state and interstate buses. In
between are shops and lanchonetes, 1 km walk
from Praça República. Taxi to rodoviária, US$4.80.
   São Paulo, US$60, 14 hrs, 9 buses daily, 1st at
0800, last at 2400, leito US$65. **Cuiabá**, US$42, 10
hrs, 12 buses daily, leito at 2100 and 2200. To
Brasília, US$64, 23 hrs at 1000 and 2000. To
Goiânia, São Luís 1100, 2000, 15 hrs on 1900
service, US$60, others 24 hrs. **Corumbá**, with
Andorinha, 8 daily from 0600, 6 hrs, US$25.
Campo Grande-Corumbá buses connect with
those from Rio and São Paulo, similarly those from
Corumbá through to Rio and São Paulo. Twice
daily direct service to **Foz do Iguaçu** (17 hrs) with
Integración, US$53. To **Ponta Porã** for Paraguay,
see below.

Bonito *p580*
Bus Rodoviária is on the edge of town. From
Campo Grande, US$22, 5½-6 hrs, 1500, returns
at 0530. Bus uses MS-345, with a stop at
Autoposto Santa Cruz, Km 60, all types of fuel,
food and drinks available.

Ponta Porã *p581*
Bus The rodoviária is 3 km out on the Dourados
road (Brazilian city buses from the *ponto* in the
centre to Rodoviaria, **São Domingos** or **Sanga
Puitã**, 20 mins, US$1.50; taxi US$9. To/from
Campo Grande, Expresso Queiroz, 11 daily,
5 hrs, US$25; From Ponta Porã to **Bonito** or
Corumbá, change at **Jardim** (a friendly little
town with a good services, offering access to
various natural attractions similar to those of
Bonito at more modest prices): Ponta Porã-Jardim,
Cruzeiro do Sul (www.cruzeirodosulms.com.br)
at 0600 and 1530 Mon-Sat, 4 hrs, US$20; connect
the following day at 0500 from Jardim to Corumbá
(Corumbá to Jardim at 1400) via Bonito, 7 hrs,
US$26. Also Jardim to Miranda, 1430 daily, 4 hrs,
US$18. To **São Paulo**, Motta at 3 a day, 14 hrs,
US$91, US$120 *leito*.

Campo Grande to Corumbá: Miranda *p581*
Bus Campo Grande-Miranda, 12 a day, 2-3 hrs,
US$18.To **Corumbá**; 10 daily, 3-4 hrs, US$18. To
Bonito, 1 daily, 2-3 hrs, US$12 at 1630.

⊕ Directory

Campo Grande *p579, map p580*
Airline offices BRA, T382 1535,
www.voebra.com.br. Trip, T3368 6137. **TAM**, office
at airport, T0800-570 5700. **Banks** ATMs at
Banco do Brasil, 13 de Maio e Av Afonso Pena,
open 1000-1500, commission US$10 for cash,
US$20 for TCs, regardless of amount exchanged.
Visa ATM at Bradesco, 13 de Maio e Av Afonso
Pena. HSBC, R 13 de Maio 2837, ATM. **Banco 24
horas**, R Maracaju, on corner with 13 de Junho.
Also at R Dom Aquino e Joaquim Nabuco.
Overcash Câmbio, R Rui Barbosa 2750, open
Mon-Fri 1000-1600. **Car hire** Agencies on Av
Afonso Pena and at airport. **Embassies and
consulates** Bolivia, R 13 de Maio 2500, 4th
floor, s 403, T3025 4456, consulado_cgms04@
yahoo.com. **Internet** Cyber Café Iris, Av Alfonso
Pena 1975. Also in the youth hostel (see above)
and at Cyber Café, R Alan Kardec 374, T3384 5963,
near the Hotel Turis. **Medical services** Yellow
and Dengue fevers are both present in Mato
Grosso do Sul. Get your immunizations at home.
Post offices On corner of R Dom Aquino e
Calógeras 2309 and Barão do Rio Branco corner
Ernesto Geisel. **Telephones** Telems, R 13 de
Maio e R 15 de Novembro, daily 0600-2200.

Bonito *p580*
Banks Banco do Brasil, R Luiz da Costa Leite
2279, for Visa. Hoteliers and taxi drivers may
change money. **Post offices** R Col Pilad Rebuá.
Telephones Santana do Paraíso.

Corumbá→ *Phone code: 0xx67. Post code: 79300. Pop: 95,701.*

Situated on the south bank by a broad bend in the Rio Paraguai, 15 minutes from the Bolivian border, Corumbá offers beautiful views of the river, especially at sunset. It is hot and humid (70%); cooler in June to July, very hot from September to January. It has millions of mosquitoes in December to February. The municipal tourist office, **Sematur** ① *R América 969, T231 6996*, provides general information and city maps.

There is a spacious shady **Praça da Independência** and the port area is worth a visit. Av Gen Rondon between Frei Mariano and 7 de September has a pleasant palm lined promenade which comes to life in the evenings. The **Forte Junqueira**, the city's most historic building, which may be visited only through a travel agency, was built in 1772. In the Serra do Urucum to the south is the world's greatest reserve of manganese, now being worked. Corumbá has long been considered the best starting point for the southern part of the Pantanal and although many operators have shifted base to Campo Grande or Miranda, the town still offers various boat and jeep trips and access to the major hotel and farm accommodation. Almost all of the Campo Grande agencies have offices here and there are still a number of upmarket cruise companies along the water front.

Border with Bolivia

Over the border from Corumbá are Arroyo Concepción, Puerto Quijarro and Puerto Suárez. From Puerto Quijaro a 650-km railway runs to Santa Cruz de la Sierra. There is a road of sorts. There are flights into Bolivia from Puerto Suárez.

Brazilian immigration Formalities are constantly changing so check procedures in advance. Brazilian Polícia Federal stamp passports only at their office in the rodoviária ① *Mon-Fri 0800-1100, 1400-1600, Sat-Sun 1400-1700*, long queues for entry stamps but much quicker for exit. If leaving Brazil merely to obtain a new visa, remember that exit and entry must not be on the same day. Money changers at the border and in Quijarro offer the same rates as in Corumbá. **Bolivian consulate** ① *R Porto Carrero 288, 1st floor, Corumbá, T3231 5605, consuladobol@hotmail.com, Mon-Fri 0800-1600*. A fee is charged to citizens of those countries which require a visa. A yellow fever vaccination certificate is required; go to Rua 7 de Setembro, Corumbá, for an inoculation (preferably get one at home).

⊕ Sleeping → *See Telephone, page 347, for important phone changes.*

Corumbá *p586*
Although there are hostels around the bus station, this is a 10-min walk to the centre of town on the river bank where most of the hotels, restaurants and tour operators lie.
A-B Águas do Pantanal, R Dom Aquino Corrêa 1457, T3231 6582, www.aguasdopantanal hotel.com.br. The smartest in town together with the Nacional Palace, a/c rooms in a 1980s tower, pool and sauna.
A-B Nacional Palace, R América 936, T3234 6000, www.hnacional.com.br. Smart, modern a/c rooms, a decent pool and parking.
C-D Angola, R Antônio Maria 124, T3231 7727. Huge, scruffy, a/c and with fan. Internet via shared terminals. Safe as it is in front of the Polícia Federal.
C-E Salette, R Delamaré 893, T3231 6246. Cheap and cheerful with a range of rooms, the cheapest with fans and shared bathrooms. Recommended.
D Premier, R Antônio Maria Coelho 389, T3231 4937. Basic, small a/c rooms without windows. Prices are negotiable.

D Santa Rita, R Dom Aquino 860, T3231 5453. Modern, well-kept, a/c, all rooms TV and bath.
D-E Corumbá IYHA, R Colombo 1419, T3231 1005, www.corumbahostel.com.br. New, well-equipped modern hostel with helpful staff and a pool. Fan or a/c rooms and dorms.

⊘ Eating

Corumbá *p586*
Local specialities These include *peixadas corumbaenses*, a variety of fish dishes prepared with the catch of the day; as well as ice cream, liquor and sweets made of *bocaiúva*, a small yellow palm fruit, in season Sep-Feb. There are several good restaurants in R Frei Mariano. Lots of open-air bars on the river front.
♦♦♦-♦♦ Avalom, R Frei Mariano 499, T3231 4430. Chic little restaurant bar with streetside tables and decent pasta, pizza and fish. Especially busy after 2100 on Fri.

Almanara, R América 961. Arabic and Turkish food.

Laço de Ouro, R Frei Mariano 556, T3231 7371. Very popular fish restaurant with a lively atmosphere and tables spilling out onto the street.

Peixeria de Lulú, R Dom Aquino 700, T3232 2142. A local institution selling good river fishes for many years.

Panela Velha, R 15 de Novembro 156, T3232 5650. Popular lunchtime restaurant with a decent, cheap all you can eat buffet.

Verde Frutti, R Delamare 1164, T3231 3032. A snack bar with a wide variety of juices and great, ice-cold *acai na tigela*.

⊛ Festivals and events

Corumbá *p586*
2 Feb, Festa de Nossa Senhora da Candelária, Corumbá's patron saint, all offices and shops are closed. **24 Jun**, Festa do Arraial do Banho de São João, fireworks, parades, traditional food stands, processions and the main event, the bathing of the image of the saint in the Rio Paraguai. **21 Sep**, Corumbá's anniversary, includes a Pantanal fishing festival held on the eve. **Early-mid Oct**, Festival Pantanal das Águas, with street parades featuring giant puppets, dancing in the street and occasional water fights.

○ Shopping

Corumbá *p586*
Shops tend to open early and close by 1700.
Casa do Artesão, R Dom Aquino Correia 405. Open Mon-Fri 0800-1200, 1400-1800, Sat 0800-1200, good selection of handicrafts, small bookshop, friendly staff but high prices.
CorumbArte, Av Gen Rondon 1011. For good silk-screen T-shirts with Pantanal motifs.
Livraria Corumbaense, R Delamaré 1080. For state maps.
Supermarkets Frutal, R 13 de Junho 538, open 0800-2000. Ohara, Dom Aquino 621.

▲ Activities and tours

Corumbá *p586*
Ecological Expeditions, R Antônio Maria 78 (see under Campo Grande, above, for more details).
Green Track, R Antônio João, Corumbá, T3231 2258, with representatives in Campo Grande at their bus station office. One of the longest established budget operators offering camping and lodge based trips to Nhecolândia starting in Campo Grande or Corumbá, where they have a budget hostel. Basic, but good value tours.

Mutum Turismo, R Frei Mariano 17, T3231 1818, www.mutumturismo.com.br. Cruises and upmarket tours (mostly aimed at the Brazilian market) and help with airline, train and bus reservations.
Pantur, R América 969, T3231 2000, www.pantur.com.br. Packages to Bonito and the fazendas on the Estrada Parque, including some of the less visited like Bela Vista and Xaraes. Flights and bus tickets can be booked here too.

Fishing and river cruises
These all leave from Corumbá.
Pérola do Pantanal, in the Hotel Nacional (see above), T3231 1470, www.perolado pantanal.com.br. Fishing and 'eco' tours on their large river boat the *Kalypso* with options on additional jeep trips on the Estrada Parque.
O Pantaneiro, R Manoel Cavassa 225, quays, T3231 3372, www.opantaneirotur.com.br. Cruises on by far the most comfortable modern boat sailing out of Corumbá, with day excursions in small launches.

⊜ Transport

Corumbá *p586*
Air Airport, R Santos Dumont, 3 km. Daily flights to **Campo Grande**, **Cuiabá** and **São Paulo**. No public transport from airport to town, you have to take a taxi. Car hire at the airport.
Bus The rodoviária is on R Porto Carreiro at the south end of R Tiradentes, next to the railway station. City bus to rodoviária from Praça da República, US$1.50; taxis are extortionate but mototaxis charge US$1. **Andorinha** services to all points east. To **Campo Grande**, 7 hrs, US$25, 13 buses daily, between 0630 and midnight, interesting journey ('an excursion in itself') – take an early bus to see plentiful wildlife, connections from Campo Grande to all parts of Brazil.

Border with Bolivia: Corumbá/Arroyo Concepción *p586*
Bus Leaving Brazil, take Canarinho city bus marked Fronteira from the port end of R Antônio Maria Coelho to the Bolivian border (15 mins, US$0.90), walk over the bridge to Bolivian immigration, then take a colectivo to Quijarro or Puerto Suárez. Taxi from Corumbá rodoviaria to Bolivian border US$15, negotiable. Ask to be taken directly to Bolivian immigration, not to a Bolivian cab who will hold your luggage while your passport is stamped. Overcharging and sharp practices are common. Touts at the Corumbá rodoviária offer hotels, Pantanal tours and railway tickets to Santa Cruz. The latter cost double the actual fare and are not recommended.

When travelling from Quijarro, take a taxi or walk to the Bolivian border to go through formalities. Just past the bridge, on a small side street to the right, is the bus stop for Corumbá, take a bus to the rodoviária for Polícia Federal, US$0.90, don't believe taxi drivers who say there is no bus.

Train Timetables for trains from Puerto Quijarro to Santa Cruz change frequently, so check on arrival in Corumbá. It may be best to stay in Quijarro to get a good place in the queue for tickets.

⊕ Directory

Corumbá *p586*

Banks Banco do Brasil, R 13 de Junho 914, ATM. HSBC, R Delamare 1068, ATM. **Car hire** Unidas, R Frei Mariano 633, T/F231 3124. **Internet** Caffe.com, R Frei Mariano 635, T231 7730. PantanalNET, Rua América 403,Centro, US$2.50 per hr. **Post offices** main at R Delamaré 708; branch at R 15 de Novembro 229. **Telephones** R Dom Aquino 951, near Praça da Independência, open 0700-2200 daily. To phone Quijarro/Puerto Suárez, Bolivia, it costs slightly more than a local call, dial 214 + the Bolivian number.

Cuiabá and around

Cuiabá

➔ *Phone code: 0xx65. Post code: 78000. Colour map 7, grid A1. Pop: 483,346. Altitude: 176 m.*

The capital of Mato Grosso state on the Rio Cuiabá, an upper tributary of the Rio Paraguai, is in fact two cities: Cuiabá on the east bank of the river and Várzea Grande, where the airport is, on the west. It is very hot; coolest months for a visit are June, July and August, in the dry season.

Cuiabá has an imposing government palace and other fine buildings round the green **Praça da República**. On the square is the **Cathedral**, with a plain, imposing exterior, two clock-towers and, inside, coloured-glass mosaic windows and doors. Behind the altar is a huge mosaic of Christ in majesty, with smaller mosaics in side chapels. Beside the Cathedral is the leafy **Praça Alencastro**. On **Praça Ipiranga**, at the junction of Avs Isaac Póvoas and Tenente Col Duarte, a few blocks west of the central squares, there are market stalls and an iron bandstand from Huddersfield, UK. On a hill beyond the praça is the church of **Bom Despacho**, built in the style of Notre Dame de Paris (in poor condition, closed to visitors). In front of the Assembléia Legislativa, Praça Moreira Cabral, is a point marking the **Geogedesic Centre of South America** (see also under Chapada dos Guimarães). **Museus de Antropologia, História Natural e Cultura Popular** ⓘ *in the Fundação Cultural de Mato Grosso, Praça da República 151, Mon-Fri 0800-1730, US$0.50*, has historical photos, a contemporary art gallery, stuffed Pantanal fauna, indigenous, archaeological finds and pottery. At the entrance to Universidade de Mato Grosso, 10 minutes by bus from the centre (by swimming pool), is the small **Museu do Índio/Museu Rondon** ⓘ *T3615 8489, www.ufmt.br/icms/museurondon/museurondon, Tue-Sun 0800-*

Cuiabá

Sleeping 🛏
Amazon Plaza **6**
Best Western Mato Grosso Pálace **2**
Ipanema **5**
Mato Grosso **7**
Nacional **1**
Panorama **9**
Portal do Pantanal **3**
Pousada Ecoverde **8**

Eating 🍴
Choppão **2**
Getúlio **3**

1100, 1330-1700, US$1, with artefacts from tribes mostly from the state of Mato Grosso. Particularly beautiful are the Bororo and Rikbaktsa headdresses made from macaw and currasow feathers and the Kadiwéu pottery (from Mato Grosso do Sul). **Tourist information** at **Secretaria de Desenvolvimento do Turismo** ① *Sedtur, in the Centro Político Administrativo, T/F613 9300, www.sedtur.mt.gov.br, Mon-Fri 0700-1800.* Good maps, helpful, contact them if you have any problems with travel agencies; also book hotels and car hire, some English and Spanish spoken. Also at the airport, T682 2213, ext 2252. **Ramis Bucair** ① *R Pedro Celestino 280,* is good for detailed maps of the region. City maps also from **Hotel Best Western**.

Cuiabá to Pantanal → *Colour map 6, grid A6.*

A paved road turns south off the main Cuiabá-Cáceres road to **Poconé** (102 km from Cuiabá, hotels, 24-hour gas station – closed Sunday). From here, the Transpantaneira runs 146 km south to Porto Jofre (just a petrol station, petrol and diesel, but no alcohol available). The road is of earth, in poor condition, with ruts, holes and many bridges that need care in crossing. Easiest access is in the dry season (July-September), which is also the best time for seeing birds and, in September, the trees are in bloom. In the wet, especially January-February, there is no guarantee that the Transpantaneira will be passable. The wet season, however, is a good time to see many of the shyer animals because more fruit, new growth and other high calorie foods are available, and there are fewer people.

Campos de Jofre, about 20 km north of Porto Jofre, is said to be magnificent between August and October. In Poconé one can hitch to Porto Jofre, or hire a vehicle in Cuiabá. You will get more out of this part of the Pantanal by going with a guide; a lot can be seen from the Transpantaneira in a hired car, but guides can take you into fazendas some 7 km from the Transpantaneira and will point out wildlife. Recommended guides in Cuiabá are under Tour operators. Although there are gas stations in **Pixaim** (a bridge across the Rio Pixaim, two hotels and a tyre repair shop) and Porto Jofre, they are not always well stocked, best to carry extra fuel.

Barão de Melgaço → *Colour map 7, grid A1.*

On Rio Cuiabá, 130 km from Cuiabá (TUT bus at 0730 and 1500, US$8.50), Barão de Melgaço is reached by two roads: the shorter, via Santo Antônio de Leverger, unpaved from Santo Antônio to Barão (closed in the wet season), or via São Vicente, longer, but more pavement. The way to see the Pantanal from here is by boat down the Rio Cuiabá. Boat hire, for example from Restaurant Peixe Vivo on waterfront, up to US$100 for a full day; or enquire with travel agencies in Cuiabá. The best time of day would be sunset, but this may mean returning after dark. Initially the river banks are farms and small habitations, but they become more forested, with lovely combinations of flowering trees (best seen September-October). After a while, a small river to the left leads to Chacororé and Sia Mariana lakes, which join each other via an artificial canal which has led the larger of the two lakes to drain into the smaller and begin to dry out. Boats can continue beyond the lakes to the Rio Mutum, but a guide is essential because there are many dead ends. The area is rich in birdlife and the waterscapes are beautiful.

Cáceres → *Phone code: 065. Post code: 78200. Colour map 6, grid A6. Population: 85,857.*

On the banks of the Rio Paraguai, 200 km west of Cuiabá, Cáceres is very hot but clean and hospitable. It has a number of well preserved 19th-century buildings, painted in pastel colours.

The **Museu Histórico de Cáceres** ① *R Antônio Maria by Praça Major João Carlos,* is a small local history museum. The main square, Praça Barão de Rio Branco, has one of the original border markers from the Treaty of Tordesillas, which divided South America between Spain and Portugal; it is pleasant and shady during the day. In the evenings, between November and March, the trees are packed with thousands of chirping swallows (andorinhas). The praça is surrounded by bars, restaurants and ice cream parlours and comes to life at night. The city is known for its many bicycles as most people seem to get around on two wheels. Until 1960, Cáceres had regular boat traffic, today it is limited to a few tour boats and pleasure craft. The town is at the edge of the Pantanal. Vitória Regia lilies can be seen north of town, just across the bridge over the Rio Paraguai along the BR-174. Local festivals are the Piranha Festival, mid-March; International Fishing Festival in mid-September; annual cattle fair.

Border with Bolivia

An unpaved road runs from Cáceres to the Bolivian border at San Matías. Brazilian immigration is at Polícia Federal, Av Getúlio Vargas. Ask here for Fiscales Federales, which is the customs point for those entering or leaving by private vehicle. Leaving Bolivia, get your passport stamped at Bolivian immigration (1000-1200, 1500-1700), then get your passport stamped at Cáceres, nowhere in between, but there are luggage checks for drugs.

Chapada dos Guimarães

→ *Phone code: 065. Post code: 78195. Population 15,755. Colour map 7, grid A1.*

Some 68 km northeast of Cuiabá lies one of the oldest plateaux on earth. It is one of the most scenic areas of Brazil and visitors describe it as an energizing place. The pleasant town of Chapada dos Guimarães, the main centre, is a base for many beautiful excursions in this area; it has the oldest church in the Mato Grosso, **Nossa Senhora de Santana** (1779), a bizarre blending of Portuguese and French baroque styles, and a huge spring-water public swimming pool (on Rua Dr Pem Gomes, behind the town). Formerly the centre of an important diamond prospecting region, today Chapada is a very popular destination for Cuiabanos to escape the heat of the city at weekends and on holidays. It is a full day excursion from Cuiabá through lovely scenery with many birds, butterflies and flora. There is a post office at Rua Fernando Corrêa 848. The Festival de Inverno is held in last week of July, and Carnival is very busy. Accommodation is scarce and expensive at these times. The **Secretaria de Turismo e Meio Ambiente** office, Rua Quinco Caldas 100, near the praça, provides a useful map of the region and organizes tours. Weekdays 0800-1100, 1300-1800.

The Chapada is an immense geological formation rising to 700 m, with rich forests, curiously eroded rocks and many lovely grottoes, peaks and waterfalls. A **national park** has been established in the area just west of the town, where the **Salgadeira** tourist centre offers bathing, camping and a restaurant close to the Salgadeira waterfall.

The beautiful 85 m **Véu da Noiva** waterfall (Bridal Veil), 12 km before the town near Buriti (well-signposted, ask bus from Cuiabá to let you off), is reached by a short route, or a long route through forest. Other sights include the **Mutuca** beauty spot, **Rio Claro**, the viewpoint over the breathtaking 80 m-deep **Portão do Inferno** (Hell's Gate), and the falls of **Cachoeirinha** (small restaurant) and **Andorinhas**.

About 8 km east of town is the **Mirante do Ponto Geodésico**, a monument officially marking the Geodesic Centre of South America, which overlooks a great canyon with views of the surrounding plains, the Pantanal and Cuiabá's skyline on the horizon; to reach it take Rua Fernando Corrêa east. Continuing east, the road goes through agricultural land and later by interesting rock formations including a stone bridge and stone cross. Some 45 km from Chapada you reach the access for **Caverna do Francês** or Caverna Aroe Jari ('the dwelling of the souls' in the Bororo language), a sandstone cave over 1 km long, the second largest in Brazil; it is a 1-km walk to the cave, in it is Lagoa Azul, a lake with crystalline blue water. Take your own torch/flashlight (guides' lamps are sometimes weak). A guide is necessary to get through fazenda property to the cave, but not really needed thereafter.

Other excursions are to the **Cidade de Pedra** rock formations, 25 km from town along the road to the diamond prospecting town of Água Fria. Nearby is a 300 m wall formed by the Rio Claro and 60 km from town are the **Pingador** and **Bom Jardim** archaeological sites, caverns with petroglyphs dating back some 4,000 years.

● Sleeping → *See Telephone, page 347, for important phone changes.*

Cuiabá *p588, map p588*
L **Amazon Plaza**, Av Getúlio Vargas 600, T2121 2000, www.hotelamazon.com.br. By far the best in the centre with very smart modern rooms, good views over the city, shady pool area, excellent service includes broadband in all rooms.
AL **Best Western Mato Grosso Pálace**, Joaquim Murtinho 170, T3624 7747, www.hotelmatogrosso.com.br. Conveniently located behind the Praça República, standard 3-star rooms with cable TV, fridge, hot showers.

B-C **Mato Grosso**, R Comandante Costa 252, T3614 7777, www.hotelmatogrosso.com.br. The best value mid-range option in the centre with renovated a/c or fan-cooled rooms, the brightest of which are on the 2nd floor or above, good breakfast, very helpful. Recommended.
B-C **Panorama**, Praça Moreira Cabral 286, T3322 0072. Very simple, plain rooms, a/c or fan, some rooms with good views.
C **Pousada Ecoverde**, R Pedro Celestino 391, T3624 1386, www.ecoverdetours.com. The best

value, if idiosyncratic option, rooms with spacious bathrooms in a converted town house. Facilities include excellent tour agency, laundry service, internet and free airport/bus station pick-up (with 12 hrs notice).

By the rodoviária

B Nacional, Jules Rimet 22, T3621 3277. Right opposite the front of the bus station and convenient for those who don't need to go into town. Plain a/c rooms with renovated en suites..
C Ipanema, Jules Rimet 12, T3621 3069. Opposite the front of the bus station and with very well kept rooms, a/c or fan, cable TV, internet access, huge lobby TV for films or football. Many other options between here and the **Nacional**.
D pp Portal do Pantanal, Av Isaac Povoas 655, T/F3624 8999, www.portaldopantanal.com.br. HI hostel, with breakfast, cheaper with fan, internet access US$3 per hr, laundry, use of kitchen.

Cuiabá to Pantanal *p589*

L Fazenda Santa Teresa, Km 75. A working fazenda, rustic, a/c or fan, pool, hearty food. There are giant otters in the river adjacent to the farm which are fed daily for show; making sightings almost guaranteed.
L Pousada Rio Clarinho, Km 42, book through Fauna Tour. Charming budget option on the Rio Clarinho which makes up in wildlife what it lacks in infrastructure. The river has rare water birds, as well as river and giant otters and occasionally tapir.
L Pousada Rio Claro, Km 42, book through Natureco. Comfortable fazenda with a pool and simple a/c rooms on the banks of the Rio Claro which has a resident colony of giant otters.
L Pouso Alegre, Km 36 , T626 1545, www.pousoalegre.com.br. Rustic pousada, simple accommodation, a/c or fan. One of the largest fazendas and overflowing with wildlife and particularly good for birds (especially on the morning horseriding trail). Many species not yet seen elsewhere in the northern Pantanal have been catalogued here. Their remote oxbow lake is particularly good for water birds. Birding guides provided with advance notice. Best at weekends when the very knowledgeable owner Luís Vicente is there.
A Araras Lodge, Km 32, T3682 2800, www.araraslodge.com.br. Book direct or through Fauna Tour or Natureco. One of the most comfortable with 14 a/c rooms; pool, excellent tours and food, homemade *cachaça* and a walkway over a private patch of wetland filled with capybara and cayman. Very popular with small tour groups from Europe. Book ahead.
A Fazenda Piuval, Km 10, T3345 1338, www.pousadapiuval.com.br.The first fazenda

on the Transpantaneira and one of the most touristy, with scores of day visitors at weekends. Rustic farmhouse accommodation, pool, excellent horse and walking trails and boat trips on their vast lake.

Barão de Melgaço *p589*

L Pousada Passárgada, Sia Mariana, Barão de Melgaço, T3713 1128, in Barão de Melgaço on riverside, through **Nature Safaris**, Av Marechal Rondon, Barão de Melgaço, or agencies in Cuiabá. Much cheaper if booked direct with the owner, Maré Sigaud, Mato Grosso, CEP 786807, Pousada Passárgada, Barão de Melgaço. Programmes from 3 days up, full board, boat, Land Rover and trekking expeditions, transport from Barão de Melgaço either by boat or 4WD can be arranged with the owner who speaks English, French and German. Closed Dec-Feb.
C Barão Tour Hotel, in Barão de Melgaço town. Apartments with a/c, restaurant, boat trips and excursions (Cuiabá T322 1568). There are a handful of cheaper options near the waterfront.

Cáceres *p589*

A Caiçaras, R dos Operários 745, corner R Gen Osório, T3223 3187, F3223 2692. Modern, with a/c rooms and cheaper options without a fridge.
A-B Ipanema, R Gen Osório 540, T3223 1177, www.ipanemahotelmt.com.br. Simple town hotel with a/c rooms, a pool and a restaurant.
B-D Rio, Praça Major João Carlos 61, T3223 3387, F3223 3084. A range of rooms – the cheapest with no a/c and shared bathrooms.
C-D Charm, Col José Dulce 405, T/F3223 4949. A/c and fan-cooled rooms, with or without a shared bath.
D-E União, R 7 de Setembro 340. Near the rodoviária. Fan, cheaper with shared bath, basic but good value.

Chapada dos Guimarães *p590*

AL-A Solar do Inglês, R Cipriano Curvo 142, T3301 1389, www.chapadadosguimaraes.com.br. In an old converted house near town centre with 7 rooms each with bath, TV and frigobar. Garden, swimming pool and sauna. Breakfast and afternoon tea included.
A Estância San Francisco, at the entrance to town from Cuiabá (MT 251, Km 61), T3791 1102, F3791 1537. On a 42-ha farm with 2 lakes, said to have the best breakfast in town fresh from the farm. Good for birds.
B Turismo, R Fernando Corrêa 1065, a block from rodoviária, T3791 1176, F3791 1383. A/c rooms with a fridge, cheaper with fan, restaurant, breakfast and lunch excellent, very popular, German-run; Ralf Goebel, the owner, is very helpful in arranging excursions.

B-C **Rio's Hotel**, R Tiradentes 333, T3791 1126. A/c rooms with a fridge, cheaper with fan, cheaper with shared bath, good breakfast.
C **Pousada Bom Jardim**, Praça Bispo Dom Wunibaldo s/n, T3791 1244. Fan, comfortable, parking, good breakfast. Recommended.
D **São José**, R Vereador José de Souza 50, T3791 1152. Fan, cheaper with shared bath and no fan, hot showers, basic, no breakfast, good, owner Mário sometimes runs excursions.
Camping Aldeia Velha, in the Aldeia Velha neighbourhood at the entrance to town from Cuiabá, T322 7178 (Cuiabá). Fenced area with bath, hot shower, some shade, guard.

🍴 Eating

Cuiabá p588, map p588
City centre restaurants only open for lunch. On Av CPA are many restaurants and small snack bars. There are several cheap restaurants and lanchonetes on R Jules Rimet across from the rodoviária.
🍴🍴🍴 **Getúlio**, Av Getúlio Vargas 1147, T3264 9992. An a/c haven from the heat with black tie waiters, excellent food, with meat specialities, pizza, good buffet lunch on Sun. Live music upstairs on Fri and Sat from significant cult Brazilian acts.
🍴🍴-🍴 **Choppão**, Praça 8 de Abril, T3623 9101. A local institution, buzzing at any time of the day or night. Go for huge portions of delicious food or just for *chopp* served by fatherly waiters. The house dish of chicken soup promises to give diners drinking strength in the early hours and is a meal in itself. Warmly recommended.
🍴 **Panela de Barro**, R Cmdte Costa 543. Self-service, a/c lunchtime restaurant with a choice of tasty regional dishes.
🍴🍴-🍴 **Miranda's**, R Cmdte Costa 716. Decent self-service per kilo lunchtime restaurant with good value specials.
🍴 **Lanchonete da Marilda**, R Cmdte Costa 675. Simple snack bar with generous *prato feito*.

Cáceres p589
🍴 **Corimbá**, R 15 de Novembro s/n, on riverfront. Fish specialities, and general Brazilian food.
🍴 **Gulla's**, R Cel José Dulce 250. Buffet by kilo, good quality and variety. Recommended.
🍴 **Panela de Barro**, R Frei Ambrósio 34, near rodoviária. *Comida caseira* with the usual gamut of meat dishes with squash, rice, black beans and salads.

Chapada dos Guimarães p590
Pequi is a regional palm fruit with a spikey inside, used to season many foods; *arroz com pequi* is a rice and chicken dish.
🍴 **Nivios**, Praça Dom Wunibaldo 631. The best place for good regional food.
🍴 **O Mestrinho**, R Quinco Caldas 119. Meat, regional dishes, *rodízio* at weekends.
🍴 **Trapiche**, R Cipriano Curvo 580. Pizza, drinks, regional dishes.
🍴 **Choppada** (O Chopp da Chapada), R Cipriano Curvo near Praça. Drinks and meals, regional dishes, live music at weekends.
🍴 **Fogão da Roça**, Praça Dom Wunibaldo 488. Good *comida mineira* in generous portions. Recommended.

🍸 Bars and clubs

Cuiabá p588, map p588
Cuiabá is quite lively at night, bars with live music and dance on Av CPA. Av Mato Grosso also has many bars and restaurants. 4 cinemas in town.
Café Cancun, R Candido Mariano at São Sebastião. One of a chain of popular Brazilian club bars attracting a mid-20s to 40s crowd.
Rush, Isaac Povoas at Presidente Marquês. Teen and twenty something techno cub bar. **Tucano**, bar/restaurant, Av CPA. Beautiful view, specializes in pizza, open daily 1800-2300. Recommended.

🛍 Shopping

Cuiabá p588, map p588
Handicrafts in wood, straw, netting, leather, skins, Pequi liquor, crystallized caju fruit, compressed guaraná fruit (for making the drink), indigenous objects on sale at the airport, rodoviária, craft shops in centre, and daily market, Praça da República, interesting. Fish and vegetable market, picturesque, at the riverside.
Casa de Artesão, Praça do Expedicionário 315, T321 0603. Sells all types of local crafts in a restored building. Recommended.

Chapada dos Guimarães p590
Crafts, indigenous artefacts, sweets and locally made honey from **Casa de Artes e Artesanato Mato Grossense**, Praça Dom Wunibaldo. Regional sweets from **Doceria Olho de Sogra**, Praça Dom Wunibaldo 21. **João Eloy de Souza Neves** is a local artist, his paintings, music and history about Chapada (*Chapada dos Guimarães da descoberta aos dias atuais*) are on sale at **Pousada Bom Jardim**.

🔴 *For an explanation of the sleeping and eating price codes used in this guide, see page 58.*
⚫ *Other relevant information is found in Essentials pages 345-347.*

Essentials	**598**
Santiago and around	**605**
Around Santiago	623
Valparaíso and around	**625**
Valparaíso	625
Viña del Mar and around	633
North of Santiago	**637**
Ovalle to La Serena	637
North of La Serena	644
Far north	**648**
Antofagasta	648
North of Antofagasta	652
San Pedro de Atacama	656
Iquique and around	660
Arica and Lauca	665
Central Valley	**673**
Rancagua to Chillán	673
Concepción and around	678
Lake District	**684**
Temuco and around	684
Lagos Villarrica, Calafquén	
and Panguipulli	691
Valdivia and Osorno	701
Southern lakes	706
Puerto Montt and Chiloé	**713**
Puerto Montt	713
Chiloé	718
Carretera Austral	**726**
Puerto Montt to Chaitén	727
Chaitén to Coyhaique	729
Lago General Carrera and around	737

Far south	**742**
Punta Arenas and around	742
Puerto Natales and around	748
Parque Nacional Torres del Paine	753
Tierra del Fuego	758
Chilean Pacific Islands	**761**
Juan Fernández Islands	761
Rapa Nui/Easter Island	762

☃ Footprint features

Don't miss …	597
Touching down	600
Driving in Chile	603
The slow train to Uyuni	649
The cultural development of	
Easter Island	763

Introduction

Chile is a ribbon of land squashed between the Pacific and the Andes. Its landscape embraces glacial wilderness and moonscapes, lakes and volcanoes, beaches and salt flats. The north is characterized by the burnt colours of the driest desert in the world. Should rain fall in this barren land, flower seeds that have lain in wait seize the moment to bloom, bringing brilliant colours where no life seemed possible. Snow-capped volcanoes in the Lauca National Park seem close enough to touch in the rarefied air. In one day it is possible to scale a mountain with ice axe and crampons, soak off the exhaustion in a thermal bath and rest beneath the stars of the Southern Cross. Real stargazers will want to visit the astronomical observatories near La Serena, while lovers of mystery will head south for the folklore of Chiloé, Land of Seagulls. The Chilean Lake District is the homeland of the Mapuche, the people who resisted the Spaniards and who proudly maintain their culture and traditions. The lakes themselves are beautiful, set in farm land, overlooked by yet more snow-capped volcanoes. Before the road peters out, blocked by fjords and icefields, the Carretera Austral reveals ancient woodlands, hot springs beside the sea, mountains like castles and raging, emerald rivers – a paradise for fishing and cycling. To reach the ultimate goal of trekkers and birdwatchers, the fabulous granite towers and spires of the Torres del Paine National Park, you have to take a boat, or fly, or make the long haul through Argentina. There are seaports of every size, with their fishing boats, pelicans and sea lions. The most romantic is Valparaíso, described by one observer as 'a Venice waiting to be discovered', with its warren of streets and brightly painted houses, its singular lifts up to the clifftops and its old bars.

★ Don't miss ...

1 Valparaíso One of the great ports of the entire Pacific seaboard. Its hills are UNESCO World Heritage sites, up and down the coast are beach resorts and the seafood is out of this world, page 625.

2 Lauca National Park In the thin air of the altiplano, snow-capped volcanoes seem to be just arm's length away, waterfowl wade at the margins of lakes and shy vicuña graze the windswept grasses, page 668.

3 Lake District A string of lakes of all different shapes and sizes stretches along the western foothills of the Andes. In many are mirrored the perfect cones of volcanoes. Some buzz with holidaymakers, others are ideal for a spot of solitude, page 684.

4 Chiloé The fabled island of seagulls, full of legends, wooden churches and forests. Take a ferry from the mainland; watch out for dolphins in the surrounding waters; ride a horse along the beaches, page 718.

5 Carretera Austral Over 1,000 km of largely unpaved road runs through a spectacular landscape of ancient forests, tree-lined fjords, glaciers and dramatic volcanoes. This is one of the best places for mountain biking, with many lakes, hot springs and townships to explore, page 726.

6 Torres del Paine The Mecca for all long-distance hikers is one of the world's most stunning national parks: massive granite towers overlook white and turquoise lakes, wild-flower meadows and forests, page 753.

Chile

597

Essentials

Planning your trip

Where to go A great many of Chile's attractions are outdoors, in the national parks, adventure sports, etc, but the capital, **Santiago**, has a rich cultural life (museums, handicrafts shopping) and is a good base for visiting nearby areas. These include the vineyards of the Maipo Valley, the Andean foothills in the Cajón del Maipo and the ski resorts. The port of Valparaíso and the beach resorts to north and south, principally Viña del Mar, are only a couple of hours away.

North of Santiago is La Serena, a popular seaside resort, from which can be reached the Elqui Valley, where Chilean pisco is made, and three major astronomical observatories. Heading north, the land becomes more barren, but every few years after rain, usually September to October, the flowers that have lain dormant in the desert burst into bloom; if you are in the area, a sight not to be missed. Inland from Antofagasta, the next main city, a road goes to Calama, the huge copper mine at Chuquicamata and the isolated Andean town and popular tourist resort of San Pedro de Atacama. Its attractions are lunar landscapes, hot geysers, salt flats and the way of life at high altitude. Alternatively, from Antofagasta you can take the spectacular coast road to the **Far North** and the ports of Iquique, near which are several archaeological sites, thermal springs and abandoned nitrate mines, and Arica, the last main town before Peru. The road route into Bolivia from Arica passes through the magnificent Parque Nacional Lauca, with its wealth of Andean bird and animal life, high lakes and remote volcanoes.

South of Santiago, the longitudinal highway runs south through the Central Valley passing through or near a number of cities, such as Rancagua, Talca, Chillán and Concepción (the country's second city). There are national parks which deserve a visit in both the Andean foothills and the coastal range of mountains. You can visit vineyards, thermal springs, unspoilt beaches or simply enjoy real Chilean rural life.

The **Lake District** is home to the popular lakes of Villarrica and Llanquihue, but many others are far less developed. Protected areas of great beauty and first-class opportunities for adventure sports and fishing abound. Temuco, at the northern end of this region, is the centre of Mapuche culture and has a huge produce market. Wooded Valdivia, near the coast, is worth a detour for the trip to the rivermouth to see the ruined Spanish forts that protected this outpost of the empire. The southern gateway to the Lake District is Puerto Montt, the starting point for the long haul south. The city's fishing harbour, Angelmó, with its market and food stalls, is not to be missed. From Puerto Montt you can cross to Argentina by road and ferries on Lago Todos los Santos and neighbouring Lagos Frías and Nahuel Huapi on the way to Bariloche.

The island of **Chiloé**, a short bus and ferry ride from Puerto Montt, has a distinctive culture and a green landscape which is the result of its Pacific coastal climate. On the mainland, running south from Puerto Montt, the Carretera Austral has opened up an area of forests, lakes and rivers, linking small communities of settlers. The biggest town is Coyhaique and there are regular excursions by sea and air to the stunning glacier at the Laguna San Rafael. A four-day sea voyage from Puerto Montt takes you to Puerto Natales in **Chilean Patagonia**, near Chile's most dramatic national park, the Torres del Paine. Hiking around the vertical mountains with their forested slopes, past lakes and glaciers, in the presence of a multitude of southern Andean wildlife is an unforgettable experience (but do allow for the unpredictability of the weather). If you prefer not to venture this far south by ship, there are regular flights to the main city of Chilean Patagonia, Punta Arenas, and there is no problem crossing from Argentina by road or by ferry from **Tierra del Fuego**. The contrast between this southernmost part of the country with the dry, desert north could not be greater.

When to go The best times to visit vary according to geographical location. For the heartland, any time between October and April is good, but the most pleasant seasons are spring (September to November) and autumn (March-April). In Santiago itself, summers (December to February) are roasting hot and winters (June-August) polluted. The heat of the north is less intense from June to September. In the south December to March, summer, is the best time to visit. Along the Carretera Austral this is the only realistic time to travel because at other times ferry schedules are restricted and in mid-winter many transport services do not run at all. Further south, there is more leeway. The Torrres del Paine park is open year round, though snow, fewer hours of daylight and reduced accommodation mean that only day hikes are feasible in winter. Also bear in mind that January to February in the Lake District and further south are the busiest months, with raised prices, hotels and buses full, lots of backpackers on the road and advance booking often essential. In this holiday season business visitors may find making appointments difficult, but otherwise any time of year is good for working in Santiago.

Finding out more The national secretariat of tourism, **Sernatur** *www.sernatur.cl*, has offices throughout the country (addresses given in the text). City offices provide town maps and other information. A recommended book is Turistel, published annually in four parts, *Norte*, *Centro*, *Sur* and a camping guide with road map, with information and a wealth of maps covering the whole country and neighbouring tourist centres in Argentina (eg Mendoza, San Martín de los Andes, Bariloche), in Spanish only. Each volume costs between US$10-13, depending where you buy it, but buying the whole set is better value; they can be found in bookshops and news stands in most city centres. See www.turistel.cl (in Spanish). **CONAF** (the Corporacíon Nacional Forestal) ① *Presidente Bulnes 285, Santiago, T390 0125, www.conaf.cl*, publishes a number of leaflets (in Spanish and English) and has documents and maps about the national park system. **CODEFF** (Comité Nacional Pro-Defensa de la Fauna y Flora) ① *Luis Uribe 2620, Ñuñoa, Santiago, T274 7461, www.codeff.cl*, can also provide information on environmental questions.

Websites

www.chile.cl (Spanish and English), and **www.visitchile.org** (English, Spanish, French), both have information on Chile.

www.dibam.cl Official site for museums, libraries and galleries.

www.senderodechile.cl Information on the project to build a trekking/mountain biking path running the whole length of Chile.

www.turistel.cl/v2/secciones/mapas Excellent online maps, by Turistel.

www.trekkingchile.com Information site on hiking, trekking, mountaineering, culture and travelling in Chile.

www.chip.cl Chile Information Project, Av Santa María 227, of 12, Recoleta, Santiago, gives access to *The Santiago Times* English-language daily, travel information, hotels (with commission), history, wine and LOM books.

www.ancientforests.org/chile.htm Site of Ancient Forest International, Box 1850, Redway, CA 95560, T/F707-923 4475, USA. Information regarding Chilean forests.

www.chile-hotels.com Reservations for many hotels in Chile (particularly upmarket ones); prices may be cheaper booking direct.

www.backpackerschile.com and **www.backpackersbest.cl** Useful listings on good hostels and guesthouses, in English, German and Spanish.

Touching down

Airport taxes Airport tax is US$26 for international flights; US$8 for domestic flights. There is a surcharge on Transandean flights of US$10.

Business hours Banks: 0900-1400, closed on Saturday. **Government offices**: 1000-1230 (the public is admitted for a few hours only). **Other offices**: 0830-1230, 1400-1800 (Monday-Friday). **Shops (Santiago)**: 1030-1930, 0930-1330 Saturday.

In an emergency Emergency (Carabineros) T133. **Police** (Investigaciones) T134. **Policía Internacional**, head office Gral Borgoña 1052, Santiago, T02-737 2443/1292, handle immigration, lost tourist cards. **International phone code** +56.

Ringing: a double ring repeated regularly. Engaged: equal tones with equal pauses.

Official time GMT -4; -3 in summer. Clocks change from mid-September or October to early March.

Tipping In restaurants, if service is not included in the bill, tip 10%; tip a few pesos in bars and soda fountains. Porters: US$1 or US$0.15 a piece of luggage. Taxi-drivers are not tipped.

VAT/IVA 19%

Voltage 220 volts AC, 50 cycles. Sockets are 3 round pins in a line, which will accept 2-pin plugs.

Weights and measures The metric system is obligatory but the quintal of 46 (101.4 lbs) is used.

Maps The **Instituto Geográfico Militar** ① *Dieciocho 369, Santiago, T698 7278, www.igm.cl, Mar-Dec Mon-Fri 0900-1800, Jan-Feb Mon-Fri, 0800-1400*, publishes a *Guía Caminera*, with roads and city plans (available only at IGM offices, not 100% accurate). It also has detailed geophysical and topographical maps of the whole of Chile, useful for climbing; expensive (US$11) but the Biblioteca Nacional, Alameda 651 (T360 5200) will allow you to photocopy. **Matassi maps** (JLM Mapas) ① *F02-236 4808, jmatassi@ interactiva.cl, US$6-8*, usually with a red cover, are good value but often contain errors. The *Turistel Guides* (see above) are useful for roads and towns, but not all distances are exact. Good road maps are also published by Tur-Bus and Copec. Good trekking maps for Central Chile can be ordered from **www.trekkingchile.com**.

Visas and immigration Passport (valid for at least six months) and tourist card only are required for entry by all foreigners except citizens of Dominica, Kuwait, Egypt, Saudi Arabia and UAE, most African countries, Cuba and some former Eastern bloc countries, who require visas. It is imperative to check tourist card and visa requirements before travel. National identity cards are sufficient for entry by citizens of all South American countries. Tourist cards are valid for 90 days. For nationals of Greece and Indonesia validity is 60 days; Belize, Costa Rica, Malaysia and Singapore 30 days. Tourist cards can be obtained from immigration offices at major land borders and Chilean airports; you must surrender your tourist card on departure. If you wish to stay longer than 90 days (as a tourist), you must buy a 90-day extension from the Departamento de Extranjería (address under Santiago Useful addresses, page 622), or any local *gobernación* office. It costs US$100. To avoid the long queue and long-winded bureaucracy, make a day-trip to Argentina, Bolivia or Peru and return with a new tourist card (the authorities don't like it if you do this more than 3-4 times). An onward ticket is required. Tourist card holders may change their status to enable them to stay on in employment if they have a contract; they need to contact the Extranjería in whichever province they will be working. On arrival you will be asked where you are staying in Chile. **Note** On arrival by air, US citizens will be charged an administration fee of US$100, Canadians US$135, Australians US$34 and Mexicans US$15 (this is a reciprocal tax payable because Chileans have to pay the equivalent amount when applying for visas to enter these countries). This tax is not charged at land borders. The permission is valid for multiple entry and for the life of the passport. The tax should be paid in cash. For some nationalities a visa will be granted within 24 hours on production of an onward ticket, for others, authorization must be obtained from Chile. For other nationalities who need a visa, a charge is made. To travel overland to or from Tierra del Fuego a multiple entry visa is essential since the Argentine-Chilean border is crossed more than once (it is advisable to get a multiple entry visa before arriving, rather than trying to change a single entry visa once in Chile). A student card is useful for getting discounts on transport and access to various concessions and services. They can be obtained from Hernando de Aguirre 201, of 602, Providencia, T411 2000, and cost US$15, photo and proof of status required; www.isic.cl.

Chilean embassies and consulates Visit www.minrel.gov.cl for a complete list.

Money The unit of currency is the peso, its sign is $. Notes are for 1,000, 2,000, 5,000, 10,000 and 20,000 pesos and coins for 1, 5, 10, 50, 100 and 500 pesos. Small shops and bus drivers do not look kindly upon being presented with large notes, especially in the morning and in rural areas. **Exchange rate** (July 2007) US$1 = 541 pesos; €1 = 714.83 pesos. The best exchange rates offered are in Santiago. MasterCard emergency T1230-020-2012; Visa emergency call collect +44-20-7937 8091, F+44-17-3350 3670; Amex emergency call collect (USA) 336-393-1111.

Plastic/TCs/banks (ATMs) The easiest way to obtain cash is by using ATMs which operate under the sign Redbanc (www.redbanc.cl, for a full list); they take Cirrus (MasterCard), Maestro and Plus (Visa) and permit transactions up to US$500 per day. Instructions are available in English. Visa and MasterCard are common in Chile. American Express and Diner's Club are less useful. Travellers' cheques are most easily exchanged in Santiago, but you get better value for cash US dollars or euros. Even slightly damaged or marked foreign notes may be rejected for exchange. Exchange shops (casas de cambio) are open longer hours and often give slightly better rates than banks. It is always worth shopping around. Rates get worse as you go north from Santiago. Official rates are quoted in daily newspapers. Occasionally, prices may be quoted in US dollars; check if something seems cheap. Remember that in some hotels foreigners who pay with US dollars cash or travellers' cheques are not liable for VAT.

Cost of travelling The average cost for a traveller on an economical budget is about US$30-40 per day for food, accommodation and land transportation (more for flights, tours, car hire etc). Cheap accommodation costs US$9-18. Breakfast in hotels, if not included in the price, is about US$2.50 (instant coffee, roll with ham or cheese, and jam). Alojamiento in private houses and hostels (bed, breakfast and often use of kitchen) costs US$9-15 per person (bargaining may be possible). Internet costs US$0.60-1 per hour. Southern Chile is much more expensive between 15 December and 15 March. Santiago tends to be more expensive for food and accommodation than other parts of Chile.

Safety Chile is one of the safest countries in South America for the visitor. Like all major cities around the world, though, Santiago and Valparaíso do have crime problems. Law enforcement officers are *carabineros* (green military uniforms), who handle all tasks except immigration. *Investigaciones*, in civilian dress, are detective police who deal with everything except traffic.

Getting around

Air Most flights of **LAN** *www.lan.com*, and its subsidiary, **Lan Express**, between Santiago and major towns and cities, are given in the text. It has a very efficient electronic ticketing system. **Sky** *www.skyairline.cl*, whose network is not as extensive as LAN, and **Aerolíneas del Sur**, *www.aerolineasdelsur.cl*, with a smaller network still, are newer airlines. Try to sit on the left flying south, on the right flying north to get the best views of the Andes. LAN's 'South America Air Pass' can be used on all LAN routes within South America, including 16 Chilean cities and 31 other destinations throughout the continent. It must be purchased abroad in conjunction with an international ticket and reservations made well ahead since many flights are fully booked in advance. If bought with a LAN intercontinental flight the domestic single flights cost between US$85 and US$127 each, while international flights cost from US$85 to US$177. Flights to Easter Island cost US$257 each way. If you are using the airpass together with an intercontinental flight on another airline the coupons are about 20% more expensive. Air taxes must be paid on each flight. Reservations should be made well in advance since many flights are fully booked. Route changes and cancellations may be made prior to the flight date on payment of a penalty. Check with the airlines for student and other discounts. It is best to confirm domestic flights at least 24 hours before departure.

Chile Essentials

Bus Buses are frequent and on the whole good. Apart from holiday times, there is little problem getting a seat on a long-distance bus. Salón-cama services run between main cities on overnight services. **Tur-Bus** *www.turbus.com*, and **Pullman** *www.pullman.cl*, each covering the whole country, are among the best companies. Standards on routes vary. Tur-bus itineraries can be checked and tickets bought online. Prémium buses have six fully reclining seats. Salón-cama means 25 seats, semi-cama means 34 and Classico means 44. Stops are infrequent. Since there is lots of competition between bus companies, fares may be bargained lower with smaller operators, particularly just before departure. Prices are highest between December-March and during festivals such as Easter and the Independence celebrations in September. Students with ISIC cards may get discounts, amount varies, but not usually in high season. Most bus companies will carry bicycles, but may ask for payment.

Hitchhiking Hitchhiking is generally easy and safe throughout Chile, although you may find that in some regions traffic is sparse, so you are less likely to catch a lift (drivers will sometimes make hand signals if they are only going a short distance beyond – this is not a rude gesture!).

Taxis Taxis have meters, but agree beforehand on fares for long journeys out of city centres or special excursions. In some places a surcharge is applied late at night. Taxi drivers may not know the location of streets away from the centre. There is no need to tip unless some extra service, like the carrying of luggage, is given. Black colectivos (collective taxis) operate on fixed routes identified by numbers and destinations. They have fixed charges, often little more expensive than buses, which increase at night and which are usually advertised in the front windscreen. They are flagged down on the street corner (in some cities such as Puerto Montt there are signs). Take small change as the driver takes money and offers change while driving. Yellow colectivos also operate on some inter-urban routes, leaving from a set point when full.

Train There are 4,470 km of line, of which most are state owned. Passenger services in the south go from Santiago to Puerto Montt. Passenger services north of the Valparaíso area have ceased, though there are regional train lines in the Valparaíso and Concepción areas. Trains in Chile are moderately priced, and not as slow as in other Andean countries. See Santiago, Transport, page 621, rail company offices. See www.efe.cl, Chilean Railway Company, with useful information on timetables and fares.

Sleeping → *See page 58 for our hotel grade price guide.*
Chile is still relatively behind the times with accommodation, so the posher hotels are often uninspiring international chains, while the 'historic' hotels are often run down. Some characterful B&Bs are cropping up and in most parts of Chile accommodation is plentiful. Finding a room to suit your budget should be easy. In popular tourist destinations, especially in the south in high season, many families offer rooms: these are advertised by a sign in the window. People often meet buses to offer rooms, which vary greatly in quality and cleanliness; have a look before committing. In summer especially, single rooms can be hard to find.

On hotel bills IVA (VAT) is charged at 19%. Check on arrival whether hotel rates include IVA. In expensive hotels, if you pay in US$ cash or TCs, you may not have to pay IVA, but unless the establishment has an agreement with the government, hotels are not allowed to exclude IVA for dollar payments. When booking make certain whether meals are included in the price and don't rely on the list in the bedroom for prices.

Camping Camping is easy but not always cheap at official sites. A common practice is to charge US$12 for up to five people, with no reductions for any fewer. Copec run a network of 33 'Rutacentros' along Ruta 5 which have showers, cafeterias and offer free camping. Free camping is also available at many filling stations. If camping, trekking, cycling or skiing, consider taking all your own equipment because, although it may be available in Chile, it will be expensive. Also note that in the Lake District and Chiloé, between mid-December and mid-January, huge horseflies (*tábanos*) can be a real problem when camping, hiking and fishing: do not wear dark clothing.

Youth hostels There are youth hostels (*albergues*) throughout Chile; average cost about US$10-15 pp. Although some hostels are open only from January to the end of February, many operate all year round. The IH card is usually readily accepted, but YHA affiliated hostels are not

Driving in Chile

Road Most roads are in good condition and many are paved. The main road is the Panamericana (Ruta 5) from La Serena to Puerto Montt. A paved coastal route running much of the length of Chile is due to open 2007. Motorways tolls are very expensive, but the charge includes towing to the next city and free ambulance in case of accident.

Safety In the south (particularly on the Carretera Austral), and in the desert north, always top up your fuel tank and carry spare fuel (you may have to buy a can if renting a car). *Carabineros* (national police) are strict about speed limits (100-120 kph on motorways): Turistel maps mark police posts. Car drivers should have all their papers in order and to hand as there are occasional checks.

Documents For drivers of private vehicles entering Chile, customs type out a *título de importación temporal de vehículos* (temporary admission), valid for the length of stay granted by immigration. Your immigration entry/exit card is stamped *'entrada con vehículo'* so you must leave the country with your vehicle (so you cannot make an excursion to Bariloche, for example, without your car). Insurance is obligatory and can be bought at borders. A *carnet de passages* is not officially required for foreign-owned motorcycles: a temporary import paper is given at the border.

Organizations Automóvil Club de Chile, Av Andrés Bello 1863, Providencia, Santiago, T600-464 4040, www.automovil club.cl. Seven route maps of Chile, US$6 each or US$3 each if affiliated to motor organization. It has a car hire agency (with discounts for members or affiliates).

Car hire Shop around as there is a lot of competition. Reputable Chilean companies offer much better value than the well-known international ones, although rates may not always include insurance or 19% VAT. In northern Chile, where mountain roads are bad, check rental vehicles very carefully before setting out. Hire companies charge a large premium to collect the car from another city, so unless making a round-trip it makes economic sense to travel by public transport, then rent a car locally. If intending to leave the country in a hired car, you must obtain authorization from the hire company.

Fuel Gasoline costs US$0.80-0.90 a litre; it becomes more expensive the further north and further south you go. Unleaded fuel, 93, 95 and 97 octane, is available in all main cities. Diesel is widely available. Larger service stations usually accept credit cards, but check before filling up.

necessarily the best. In summer many are usually crowded and noisy, with only floor space available. Chilean YHA card costs US$6. A Hostelling International card costs US$30. These can be obtained from **Asociación Chilena de Albergues Turísticos Juveniles** ① *Hernando de Aguirre 201, of 602, Providencia, Santiago, T411 2050, www.hostelling.cl*, together with a useful guidebook of all hostels in Chile, *Guía Turística de los Albergues Juveniles*. In summer there are makeshift hostels in many Chilean towns, usually in the main schools; they charge up to US$6 per person.

Eating → *See page 58 for our restaurant price guide.*

Eating out Breakfast is poor: instant coffee or tea with bread and jam are common, although some hostels serve better fare. Lunch is from 1300 to 1530 and dinner between 2000 and 2230. *Onces* (Elevenses) is tea taken at 1700, often accompanied by a snack. Good, cheap meals can be found in *Casinos de Bomberos*, or around the market. Most restaurants offer a cheaper set meal at lunchtime; it is called *colación* or *el menú* and may not be included on the *menu la carta*.

Food A very typical Chilean dish is *cazuela de ave* (or *de vacuno*), a nutritious stew containing large pieces of chicken (or beef), pumpkin potatoes, rice, and maybe onions, and green peppers. *Valdiviano* is another stew, common in the south, consisting of beef, onion, sliced potatoes and eggs. *Empanadas de pino* are turnovers filled with meat, onions, raisins, olives and egg chopped up together. *Pastel de choclo* is a casserole of meat and onions with olives, topped with a maize-meal mash, baked in an earthenware bowl. *Humitas* are mashed sweetcorn mixed with butter and spices and baked in sweetcorn leaves. *Prieta* is a blood sausage stuffed with cabbage leaves. A normal *parrillada* or *asado* is a giant mixed grill served from a charcoal brazier. *Bife/lomo a lo pobre* (a poor man's steak) can be just the opposite: it is a steak topped by two fried eggs, chips and fried onions. The Valparaíso speciality is the *chorrillana*, chips topped with fried sliced steak, fried onions and scrambled eggs, while in Chiloé you can enjoy a *curanto*, a meat, shellfish and potato stew traditionally cooked in a hole in the ground.

What gives Chilean food its personality is the **seafood**. The delicious congrio fish is a national dish, and *caldillo de congrio* (a soup served with a massive piece of kingclip/ling, onions and potatoes) is excellent. A *paila* can take many forms (the paila is simply a kind of dish), but the commonest are made of eggs or seafood. *Paila Chonchi* is a kind of bouillabaisse, but has more flavour, more body, more ingredients. *Parrillada de mariscos* is a dish of grilled mixed seafood, brought to the table piping hot on a charcoal brazier. Other excellent local fish are the *cojinova*, the *albacora* (swordfish) and the *corvina* (bass). A range of mussels (*choritos/cholgas*) is available, as are abalone (*locos*), clams (*almejas*) and razor clams (*machas*). Some bivalve shellfish may be periodically banned because they carry the disease **marea roja** (which is fatal in humans). *Cochayuyo* is seaweed, bound into bundles, described as 'hard, leathery thongs'. The *erizo*, or sea-urchin, is also commonly eaten as are *picorocos* (sea barnacles) and the strong flavoured *piure*. *Luche* is dried seaweed, sold as a black cake, like 'flakey bread pudding' to be added to soups and stews. **Avocado** pears (*paltas*) are excellent, and play an important role in recipes. Make sure that vegetables are included in the price for the main dish; menus often don't make this clear. Local **fast food** is excellent. *Completos* are hot dogs with a huge variety of fillings. A *barros jarpa* is a grilled cheese and ham sandwich and a *barras luco* is a grilled cheese and beef sandwich. *Sopaipillas* are cakes made of a mixture including pumpkin, served in syrup. Ice cream is very good; try *lúcuma* and *chirimoya* (custard apple) flavours.

Drink Tap **water** is safe to drink in main cities but bottled water is safer for the north. The local **wines** are very good; the best are from the central areas. The bottled wines cost from US$2 upwards; the very best wines will cost about US$30 in a smart restaurant. The *Guía de vinos de Chile*, published every year in January (English edition available) has ratings and tasting notes for all Chilean wines on the market. **Beer** is quite good and cheap (about US$1.50 for a litre bottle, plus US$0.40 deposit in shops). Draught lager is known as Schop. Chilean brewed beers include Cristal and Royal Guard (light), Escudo (Amber), Austral (good in the far south) and Heineken. In Valdivia, Kunstmann brews three types of beer, good. Malta, a brown ale, is recommended for those wanting a British-type beer. There are good local breweries in Valparaíso and Llanquihue near Puerto Varas and several good microbreweries around the country.

Pisco, made from grapes, is the most famous spirit. It is best drunk as a 'Pisco Sour' with lime or lemon juice and sugar. Two popular drinks are **vaina**, a mixture of brandy, egg and sugar and **cola de mono**, a mixture of aguardiente, coffee, milk and vanilla served very cold at Christmas. **Chicha** is any form of alcoholic drink made from fruit, usually grapes. **Cider** (*chicha de manzana*) is popular in the south. **Mote con huesillo**, made from wheat hominy and dried peaches, is a soft drink, refreshing in summer. A *vitamina* is a 100% pure fruit juice drink.

Coffee is generally instant except in expresso bars such as **Café Haiti**, **Café Brasil** and **Tío Pepe**. Elsewhere specify *café-café*, *expresso* or *cortado*. Tea is widely available. If you order *café*, or *té*, *con leche*, it will come with lots of milk; if you want just a little milk, you must specify that. After a meal, try an *agüita* (infusion) – hot water in which herbs such as mint or aromatics suh as lemon peel, have been steeped. There is a wide variety, very refreshing.

Festivals and events

Public holidays 1 January, New Year's Day; Holy Week (Friday and Saturday); 1 May, Labour Day; 21 May, Navy Day; 15 August, Assumption; first Monday in September, Day of National Unity; 18, 19 September, Independence Days; 12 October, Columbus' arrival in America; 1 November, All Saints Day; 8 December, Immaculate Conception; 25 December.

Santiago and around

→ Phone code: 02. Colour map 8, grid B1. Population: 6 million. Altitude: 600 m.

Santiago, the political, economic and financial capital of Chile, is one of the most beautifully set of any South American city, standing in a wide plain with the magnificent chain of the Andes in full view – rain and pollution permitting. Nearly 40% of Chileans live in and around Santiago, which is now the sixth largest city in South America. It's a modern industrial capital, full of skyscrapers, bustle, noise and traffic, and smog is a problem especially between April and September. Santiago bursts with possibilities, with its parks, museums, shops and hectic nightlife, and is also within easy reach of vineyards, beaches and Andean ski resorts.

Ins and outs

Getting there The airport is 26 km northwest of the centre. **Tur-Bus**, US$3, and **Centropuerto**, US$2.50, run from airport to city centre. There are also shuttle services to/from hotels and private addresses (US$9-11) and taxis (US$20-25). The railway station, Estacíon Central, which only serves the south of the country, is on the Alameda, as are the four main bus terminals. All can be reached by buses, taxi or the Metro. The bus terminals are Alameda, for Pullman Bus and Tur-Bus services; next door is Terminal Santiago, for the south of the country, and some international destinations (metro Universidad de Santiago); San Borja, for regional and national destinations (metro Estación Central); Los Héroes (nearest the centre, metro Los Héroes) for some southern, northern and international routes; new terminal at Metro Pajaritos, for Valparaíso, Viña del Mar, the coast (airport buses stop here). ⏩ *See also Transport on page 619.*

Getting around The Metro (underground railway) has four lines: Line 1 runs west-east between Escuela Militar and San Pablo, under the Alameda. Line 2 runs north-south from Vespucio Norte to La Cisterna. Line 5 runs northwest-southeast from Quinta Normal to Vicente Valdés. The new Line 4 runs north-south from Tobalaba to Plaza de Puente Alto, with a branch from V Mackenna to La Cisterna. Fares cost US$0.60-0.90 depending on time of day. The east-west Line 1 follows the main axis, linking the bus and train stations, the centre, Providencia and beyond. Trains run daily from 0630 (Monday-Saturday), 0800 (Sunday and holidays) to about 2245. Metrobus services connect the metro with outlying districts. City buses: the old system of yellow *micros* is being replaced by *Transantiago* (2005-2010); details under Transport, below. You pay by *Bip* card (purchased in advance), about US$0.75 per journey. Taxis are abundant and not expensive. Colectivos (collective taxis) run on fixed routes to the suburbs.

Santiago orientation

Tourist offices Servicio Nacional de Turismo **Sernatur** ① *Av Providencia 1550, metro Manuel Montt, next to Providencia Municipal Library, T236 2420, info@sernatur.cl, Mon-Fri 0845-1830, Sat 0900-1400,* maps, brochures and posters. Good notice board. **Information office** also at the airport daily 0900-2100. **Municipal Tourist Board** ① *Casa Colorada, Merced 860, metro Plaza de Armas, T336700,* good free booklet: *Historical Heritage of Santiago: A Guide for visitors in English and Spanish,* on historic buildings, and walking tours on Wed, 1500. Almost all museums are closed on Monday and on 1 November.

> **Related maps**
> A *Santiago centre, page 607*
> B *West of centre, page 614*
> C *Bellavista & Lastarria, page 612*
> D *Providencia, page 608*

Chile Santiago & around

605

Orientation The centre of the old city lies between the Mapocho and the Avenida O'Higgins, which is usually known as the Alameda. From the Plaza Baquedano (usually called Plaza Italia), in the east of the city's central area, the Mapocho flows to the northwest and the Alameda runs to the southwest. From Plaza Italia the C Merced runs due west to the Plaza de Armas, the heart of the city, five blocks south of the Mapocho. A new urban motorway runs the length of Santiago from east to west under the course of the Río Mapocho.

Best time to visit There is rain during the winter, but the summers are dry. The rain increases to the south. On the coast at Viña del Mar it is 483 mm a year, but is less inland. Temperatures, on the other hand, are higher inland than on the coast. There is frost now and then, but very little snow falls. Temperatures can reach 33° C in January, but fall to 13° C (3° C at night) in July. Days are usually hot, the nights cool.

Security Like all large cities, Santiago has problems of theft. Pickpockets and bag-snatchers, who are often well-dressed, operate especially on the Metro and around the Plaza de Armas. Avoid the *poblaciones* (shanty towns), notably Pudahuel and parts of the north (such as Conchalí), especially if you are travelling alone or have only recently arrived.

Sights

Around the Plaza de Armas On the eastern and southern sides of the Plaza de Armas there are arcades with shops; on the northern side are the post office and the Municipalidad; and on the western side the Cathedral and the archbishop's palace. The **Cathedral**, much rebuilt, contains a recumbent statue in wood of San Francisco Javier, and the chandelier which lit the first meetings of Congress after independence; it also houses an interesting museum of religious art and historical pieces (0930-1230, 1530-1830, free). In the Palacio de la Real Audiencia on the Plaza de Armas is the **Museo Histórico Nacional** ① *No 951, T411 7000, www.dibam.cl/historico_nacional, Tue-Sun 1000-1730, US$1, free on Sun, signs in Spanish*, covering the period from the Conquest until 1925.

Just west of the Plaza is the **Museo Chileno de Arte Precolombino** ① *in the former Real Aduana, Bandera 361, www.pre colombino.cl, Tue-Sun 1000-1800, US$4, students and children free, displays in English*. Its collection of objects from the pre-Columbian cultures of Central America and the Andean region is highly recommended for the quality of the objects and their presentation. At Calle Merced 864, close to the Plaza de Armas, is the **Casa Colorada** (1769), home of the Governor in colonial days and then of Mateo de Toro, first president of Chile. It is now the **Museo de Santiago** ① *www.munistgo.cl/colorada, Tue-Sat 1000-1800, Sun and holidays, 1100-1400, US$2, students free*. It covers the history of Santiago from the Conquest to modern times, with excellent displays and models, some signs in English, guided tours. From the Plaza de Armas Paseo Ahumada, a pedestrianized street lined with cafés runs south to the Alameda four blocks away, crossing Huérfanos.

Four blocks north of the Plaza de Armas is the interesting **Mercado Central** ① *21 de Mayo y San Pablo*, the best place in Santiago for seafood. The building faces the Parque Venezuela, on which is the Cal y Canto metro station and, at its western end, the former **Mapocho Railway Station**, now a major cultural centre and concert venue. If you head east from Mapocho station, by the river, you pass through the Parque Forestal (see below), before coming back to Plaza Italia.

Along the Alameda The Alameda runs through the heart of the city for over 3 km. It is 100 m wide, and ornamented with gardens and statuary: the most notable are the equestrian statues of Generals O'Higgins and San Martín; the statue of the Chilean historian Benjamín Vicuña MacKenna who, as mayor of Santiago, beautified Cerro Santa Lucía (see below); and the great monument in honour of the battle of Concepción in 1879.

From the Plaza Italia, where there is a statue of Gen Baquedano and the Tomb of the Unknown Soldier, the Alameda skirts, on the right, Cerro Santa Lucía, and on the left, the Catholic University. Beyond the hill the Alameda passes the neoclassical **Biblioteca Nacional** ① *Moneda 650, Santa Lucia metro, www.dibam.cl/biblioteca_nacional, Mon-Fri 0900-1900, Sat 0910- 1400, free*, good concerts, temporary exhibitions. Beyond, on the left, between calles San Francisco and Londres, is the oldest church in Santiago: the red-walled church and monastery of **San Francisco** (1618). Inside is the small statue of the Virgin that Valdivia carried on his saddlebow when he rode from Peru to Chile. The **Museo Colonial San Francisco** ① *by Iglesia San Francisco, Londres 4, T639 8737, www.museosanfrancisco.cl,*

Tue-Sun 1000-1300, 1500-1800, US$1.50, houses religious art, including 54 paintings of the life of St Francis; in the cloisters is a room containing Gabriela Mistral's Nobel medal. South of San Francisco is the Barrio París-Londres, built 1923-1929, now restored. Two blocks north of the Alameda is **Teatro Municipal** ① *C Agustinas, www.municipal.cl, tours Tue 1300-1500, Sun 1100-1400, US$3*.

A little further west along the Alameda, is the Universidad de Chile; the Club de la Unión is almost opposite. Nearby, on Calle Nueva York is the **Bolsa de Comercio**; the public may view the trading; passport required. One block further west is Plaza de la Libertad. North of the plaza, hemmed in by the skyscrapers of the Centro Cívico, is the **Palacio de la Moneda** (1805), the Presidential Palace containing historic relics, paintings and sculpture, and the elaborate 'Salón Rojo' used for official receptions. Although the Moneda was damaged by air attacks during the military coup of 11 September 1973 it has been fully restored. Ceremonial changing of the guard every other day, 1000, never on Sunday. The courtyards, with sculptures and *carabineros* in dress uniform, are open to all – entry from the north. The large new **Centro Cívico Palacio La Moneda** ① *T355 6500, www.ccplm.cl, Tue-Sun 1000-2100, US$1.15, films US$2.30*, houses temporary exhibitions as well as an arts cinema and an interesting gallery of Chilean handicrafts.

Santiago centre

Sleeping 🛏
Fundador **12** *D2*
Galerías **3** *D3*
Majestic **6** *B1*
París **9** *D3*
Residencial Londres **10** *D3*

Eating 🍴
Bar Central **13** *A2*
Bar Nacional No 2 **15** *C2*

Café Caribe **3** *C2*
Café Colonia **12** *C3*
Café Haiti **2** *C2*
Café Ikabaru **4** *C3*
Círculo de Periodistas **16** *D1*
Congreso **14** *B1*
Da Carla **5** *B3*
El 27 de Nueva York **6** *D2*
El Naturista **7** *D3*
El Rápido **17** *C2*

Faisán d'Or **1** *B2*
La Caleta de Don Beno **8** *D2*
Las Tejas **9** *D2*
Lung Fung **10** *C3*
Masticón **11** *D2*
Salón de Té Cousiño **18** *C2*
San Marco **5** *B3*

West of the centre Barrio Brasil, with Plaza Brasil at its heart and the Basílica del Salvador two blocks from the plaza, is one of the earliest parts of the city. It has some fine old buildings, especially around Calle Concha y Toro, but now it's a more bohemian, studenty area with lots of places to stay as well as numerous bars, clubs, cafés and lively restaurants (Metro República). Five blocks south of the Alameda is the **Palacio Cousiño** ⓘ *C Dieciocho 438, www.palacio cousino.cl, Metro Toesca, Tue-Fri 0930-1330, 1430-1700, Sat-Sun 0930-1330, US$3, guided tour only (Spanish/English), cloth bootees provided to protect floors*. This large mansion in French rococo style has a superb Italian marble staircase and other opulent items. Recommended.

Parque O'Higgins ⓘ *10 blocks south of Alameda; take Metro Line 2 to Parque O'Higgins station, bus from Parque Baquedano via Avs MacKenna and Matta*. It has a small lake, tennis courts, swimming pool (open from 5 December), an open-air stage, a club, the racecourse of the Club Hípico and an amusement park, **Fantasilandia** ⓘ *daily in summer, winter weekends only till 2000, US$10, US$7.50 children, unlimited rides*. There are kite-flying contests on Sunday, good 'typical' restaurants, craft shops, an aquarium, an insect, reptile and shellfish museum and the **Museo del Huaso** ⓘ *T556 1927, Mon-Fri 1000-1700, Sun 1000-1400, free*, a collection of criollo clothing and tools. On 19 September there is a huge military parade in the park.

The Alameda continues west to the **Planetarium** ⓘ *Alameda 3349, US$6*. Opposite it on the southern side is the railway station (Estación Central or Alameda). On Avenida Matucana, running north from here, is the popular Parque Quinta Normal (at Avenida D Portales). It was founded as a botanical garden in 1830. Near the park is **Museo Artequín** ⓘ *Av Portales 3530, Tue-Fri 0900-1700, Sat-Sun 1100-1800, US$1.60*. Housed in the Chilean pavilion built for the 1889 Paris International Exhibition, it contains prints of famous paintings and activities and explanations of the techniques of the great masters. Recommended. The new Quinta Normal metro station has an underground cultural centre with theatres and a free art cinema (part of the Metro Arte project), which shows independent films. The government is building an enormous public library 200 m from the station, in front of which is **Centro Cultural Matucana**, with several exhibition halls and a theatre. (**Museo de la Solidaridad Salvador Allende** formerly by the park, is closed for possible relocation in 2007-08; T682 4954, www.mssa.cl, for information.)

Providencia

Sleeping	Santiago Hostel **3**	Café El Patio **4**
Atton **6**	Sheraton Santiago **5**	Coppellia **6**
Chilhotel **2**		El Giratorio **13**
Grand Hyatt Santiago **7**	**Eating**	El Huerto **7**
Orly **1**	A Pinch of Pancho **1**	Gatsby **8**

East of the centre **Cerro Santa Lucía** ① *closes at 2100*, bounded by Calle Merced to the north, Alameda to the south, Calles Santa Lucía and Subercaseaux, is a cone of rock rising steeply to a height of 70 m (reached by stairs and a lift from the Alameda). It can be climbed from the Caupolicán esplanade, on which stands a statue of that Mapuche leader, but the ascent from the northern side, with a statue of Diego de Almagro, is easier. A plaque to Darwin, who climbed the hill, has a quotation giving his impressions. There are striking views of the city from the top, where there is a fortress, the Batería Hidalgo (no public access). It is best to descend the eastern side, to see the small Plaza Pedro Valdivia with its waterfalls and statue of Valdivia.

Parque Forestal lies due north of Santa Lucía hill and immediately south of the Mapocho. **Museo Nacional de Bellas Artes** ① *www.mnba.cl (Spanish only), Tue-Sun 1000-1900, US$1.20, café*, is in an extraordinary example of neoclassical architecture. It has a large display of Chilean and foreign painting and sculpture; contemporary art exhibitions are held several times a year. In the west wing is the **Museo de Arte Contemporáneo** ① *www.mac. uchile.cl, US$1.20*. **Parque Balmaceda** (Parque Gran Bretaña), east of Plaza Italia, is perhaps the most beautiful in Santiago (the Museo de los Tajamares, which holds monthly exhibitions, is here).

Between the Parque Forestal, Plaza Italia and the Alameda is the **Lastarria** neighbourhood (Universidad Católica Metro). For those interested in antique furniture, objets d'art and old books, the area is worth a visit, especially the **Plaza Mulato Gil de Castro** ① *C José V Lastarria 305*. Occasional shows are put on in the square, which has a mural by Roberto Matta and a new visual arts museum. The **Museo Arqueológico de Santiago** ① *Plaza Mulato Gil de Castro, Lastarria 307, Tue-Sun 1030-1830, US$2, Sun free*, exhibits Chilean archaeology, anthropology and pre-Columbian art. Nearby, on Lastarria, is the Jardín Lastarria, a cul-de-sac of craft and antique shops.

The **Bellavista district**, on the north bank of the Mapocho from Plaza Italia at the foot of Cerro San Cristóbal (see below), is the main focus of nightlife in the old city. Around Calle Pío Nono are restaurants and cafés, theatres, galleries and craft shops (most selling lapis lazuli). **La Chascona** ① *F Márquez de la Plata 0192, Bellavista, T777 8741, www.fundacionneruda.org, Tue-Sun 1000-1300, 1500-1800, US$3 guided visits only (available in English)*. This was the house of the poet Pablo Neruda and now houses the Fundación Pablo Neruda (see page 634).

Providencia East of Plaza Italia, the main east-west axis of the city becomes **Avenida Providencia** which heads out towards the residential areas, such as **Las Condes**, at the eastern and upper levels of the city. It passes through the neighbourhood of Providencia, a modern area of shops, offices, bars and restaurants around Pedro de Valdivia and Los Leones metro stations (particularly Calle Suecia, which also contains the offices of Sernatur, the national tourist board. At Metro Tobalaba it becomes Avenida Apoquindo. Here, in **El Bosque Norte**, there are lots more good, mid-range and expensive restaurants.

Museo Ralli ① *Sotomayor 4110, Vitacura (further east still), Tue-Sun 1100-1700, closed in summer, free*, has an excellent collection of works by modern European and Latin American artists, including Dali, Chagall, Bacon and Miró.

The sharp, conical hill of **San Cristóbal**, to the northeast of the city, forms the **Parque Metropolitano** ① *open daily 0900-2100, there are 2 entrances: from Pío Nono in Bellavista and further east from Pedro de Valdivia Norte. Getting there: by funicular: every few minutes from Plaza Caupolicán at the northern end of C Pío Nono (it stops on its way at the Jardín Zoológico near the Bellavista entrance), US$3 return, 1000-2000 daily. By teleférico from Estación Oasis, Av Pedro de Valdivia Norte via*

Kimono **9**
Oriental **3**
Salvaje **15**

Bars & clubs 🎵
Brannigan Pub **2**
Louisiana River Pub **10**
Phone Box Pub **11**

Tupahue to San Cristóbal, the funicular's upper station, summer only, Mon 1430-1830, Tue-Fri 1030-1830, Sat-Sun 1030-1900, US$4 combined funicular/teleférico ticket. An open bus operated by the teleférico company runs to San Cristóbal and Tupahue from the Bellavista entrance with the same schedule as the teleférico itself. To get to Tupahue at other times you must take the funicular or a taxi (or walk to/from Pedro de Valdivia Metro station, about 1 km). By taxi either from the Bellavista entrance (much cheaper from inside the park as taxis entering the park have to pay entrance fee), or from Metro Pedro de Valdivia. Vehicles US$4. It is the largest and most interesting of the city's parks. On the summit (300 m) stands a colossal statue of the Virgin, which is floodlit at night; beside it is the astronomical observatory of the Catholic University which can be visited on application to the observatory's director. Further east in the Tupahue sector there are terraces, gardens, and paths; in one building there is a good, expensive restaurant Camino Real, T232 1758) with a splendid view from the terrace, and an Enoteca (exhibition of Chilean wines: you can taste one of the three 'wines of the day', US$3 per glass, and buy if you like, though prices are higher than in shops). Nearby is the Casa de la Cultura which has art exhibitions and free concerts at midday on Sunday. There are two good swimming pools (see Sports below). East of Tupahue are the Botanical Gardens, with a collection of Chilean native plants, guided tours available.

Southeast of the centre, in La Florida district, is the excellent **Museo Interactivo Mirador** (MIM) ① *Punta Arenas 6711, Mirador metro (Line 5), T280 7800, www.mim.cl, Mon 0930-1330, Tue-Sun 0930-1830, US$6, concessions US$4*, a fun, interactive science and technology museum, perfect for a family outing. There is also an aquarium in the grounds.

Cemeterio General ① *www.cemeteriogeneral.cl, to get there take any Recoleta bus from C Miraflores*. In the barrio of Recoleta, just north of the city centre, this cemetery contains the mausoleums of most of the great figures in Chilean history and the arts, including Violeta Parra, Víctor Jara and Salvador Allende. There is also an impressive monument to the victims, known as "*desaparecidos*" (disappeared) of the 1973-1990 military government.

● Sleeping

Santiago centre *p606, map p607*
Note Check if breakfast and 19% tax are included in the price quoted.
L Fundador, Paseo Serrano 34, T387 1200, www.hotelfundador.cl. Helpful, charming, good location, pool, spa, bar, restaurant, internet.
L Galerías, San Antonio 65, T470 7400, www.hotelgalerias.cl. Excellent, large rooms, generous breakfast, good location, welcoming.
A Majestic, Santo Domingo 1526, T695 8366, www.hotelmajestic.cl. With breakfast, excellent Indian restaurant open to non-residents, pool, English spoken, internet, cable TV, good value. Recommended.
C-D París, París 813, T664 0921. Great location, good meeting place, luggage store, breakfast and internet extra. Recommended, but can be noisy. Book in advance in summer.
D Res Londres, Londres 54, T/F638 2215, unico54@ctinternet.cl. Old mansion with original features in lovely area, perfect location near San Francisco church, without breakfast, cheaper without bath, pleasant common rooms, good, safe, laundry service, usually full, advance bookings in high season, arrive early. Recommended.

D-F Che Lagarto Santiago, Tucapel Jiménez 24, T699 1493, www.chelagarto.com. Metro Los Héroes. HI hostel, part of South American chain. Free breakfast and internet. Rooms with private toilet and fan, **D** pp in dorms. Comfortable common areas, kitchen facilities, satellite TV.
E pp **Hostelling Internacional Santiago**, Cienfuegos 151, T671 8532, www.hisantiago.cl (5 mins from Metro Los Héroes). **D** pp with bath. Modern, satellite TV, no cooking facilities, sterile, cafeteria, parking. Information from YHA, Hernando de Aguirre 201, of 602, Providencia, T233 3220, www.hostelling.cl. Supplies student cards (2 photos required and proof of student status, though tourist card accepted), US$30.

West of the centre *p608, map p614*
B Happy House Hostel, Catedral 2207, T688 4849, www.happyhousehostel.cl. Also dorms **D** pp. One of the best hostels in the city, in a restored mansion with all mod-cons, spacious kitchen and common areas, internet, pool table, bar, sauna, jacuzzi, roof terrace, breakfast, free tea and real coffee all day, book exchange, English and French spoken, lots of info. Highly recommended.

● *For an explanation of the sleeping and eating price codes used in this guide, see page 58.*
● *Other relevant information is found in Essentials pages 602-604.*

C Hostal Río Amazonas, Plaza Italia, Av Vicuña Mackenna 47, near to Argentine embassy, T635 1631, www.hostalrioamazonas.cl. In a restored mansion, with breakfast, private bathrooms, Wi-Fi internet, good value, near to metro, Charming host.

C La Casa Roja, Agustinas 2113, Barrio Brasil, T696 4241, www.lacasaroja.cl. Doubles with and without bath (**D**), **F** pp in dormitory, huge converted historic house, great location, kitchen facilities, meals extra, internet, swimming pool, camping, trips arranged, convenient for metro and lots of amenities, fun, but not if you want a quiet time.

D La Casa Amarilla, Santo Domingo 2433-2445, T696 4070, www.casaamarillasantiago.com. Close to metro Cumming, 2 houses in nice neighbourhood with rooms for overnight and long-stay lets, spacious, use of kitchen Wi-Fi, washing machine, large garden. Recommended.

Near bus terminals and Estación Central *map p614*

B Conde de Anzúrez, Av República 25, T696 0807, República metro. Convenient for airport bus, central station and bus terminals, helpful, safe, luggage stored.

B Tur Hotel Express, O'Higgins 3750, p 3, in the Turbus Terminal, T685 0100. Comfortable business standard with breakfast, cable TV, a/c, free internet. Particularly useful if you need to take an early flight as buses leave for the airport from here.

D Res Alemana, República 220 (no sign), T671 2388, ralemana@entelchile.net. República metro, **F** singles. Without bath, with breakfast, pleasant, good cheap meals available. Recommended.

D Res Mery, Pasaje República 36, off 0-100 block of República, T696 8883, m.mardones@ entelchile.net. Big green art deco building down an alley, most rooms without bath, quiet, helpful owners. Recommended.

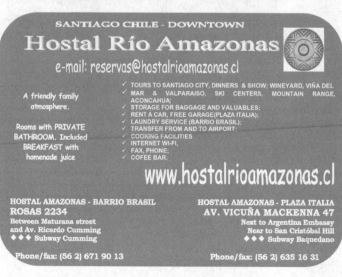

E SCS Habitat, Scott's Place, San Vicente 1798, T683 3732, scshabitat@yahoo.com. **F-G** in dorms, kitchen, laundry facilities, lots of interesting information, huge breakfast, popular (some mixed reports), English spoken, maps and camping equipment sold/rented, cycles for hire, safe bike parking. To get there take taxi from bus station.

East of the centre: Bellavista
p609, map p612

A-B Monte Carlo, Subercaseaux 209, T639 1569, montecarlo@manquehue.cl. At foot of Santa Lucía on a quiet street, modern, restaurant, heating, stores luggage, good.

C Hostal Casa Grande, Vicuña MacKenna 90, T222 7347, Baquedano metro, www.hostal casagrande.cl. **D** without bath, labyrinthine, old high-ceilinged building, quiet, good value.

C Hostal Forestal, Cnel Santiago Bueras 120, T638 1347, www.hostalforestal.cl. Doubles (some with bath) and dorms (**E-F** pp), with breakfast, on a quiet side street near the Plaza Italia. Comfy lounge with internet and big screen TV, barbeque area, kitchen facilities, good information, English spoken.

C Hostal Río Amazonas Plaza Italia, Vicuña Mackenna 47, T635 1631, www.hostalrio amazonas.cl. In a restored mansion, with breakfast, internet, good value, helpful, much cheaper to pay in dollars or euros than in pesos.

C-D Bellavista Hostel, Dardignac 0184, T732 8737, www.bellavistahostel.com. Breakfast included, European-style, **D** pp in dorms, sheets provided but make your own bed, kitchen facilities, free internet, good fun hostel in the heart of this lively area. Recommended.

C-D Casa Condell, Condell 114, T209 2343, www.casacondell.cl, Salvador metro. Also 4-bed dorms, **F** pp. Pleasant old house, central, quiet, nice roof-terrace, shared baths, no breakfast, kitchen facilities, free local phone calls, English spoken. Recommended.

Bellavista & Lastarria

Sleeping
Bellavista Hostel **1** B4
Casa Condell **6** C4
Eco Hostel Chile **9** C2
El Patio Suizo **7** C4
Hostal Casa
  Grande **5** C3
Hostal Forestal **3** C2

Hostal Río Amazonas
  Plaza Italia **4** C3
Marilu's B&B **8** C6
Monte Carlo **2** B1

Eating
Eladio **1** B4
El Kilómetro 11.680 **2** B4

El Otro Sitio **3** A3
El Tablao **4** B4
Gatopardo **6** C1
La Divina Comida **8** A3
La Tasca Mediterránea
  11 B3
Le Coq au Vin **5** B4
Les Assassins **10** B2

E pp **Eco Hostel Chile**, Gral Jofré 349B (Universidad Católica Metro), T222 6833, www.ecohostel.cl. Nice new hostel in a quiet district, shady courtyards, hammocks, hot shower, safe, kitchen, free internet, lockers, laundry facilities.

East of the centre: Providencia and Las Condes *p609, map p608*
L **Grand Hyatt Santiago**, Av Las Condes 4601, T950 1234, http://santiago.grand.hyatt.com. Superb, beautifully decorated, large outdoor pool, gym, Thai restaurant.
L **Sheraton Santiago**, Santa María 1742, T233 5000, www.sheraton.cl. One of the best, good restaurant, good buffet lunch, and all facilities.
A **Atton**, Alonso de Córdova 5199, Las Condes, T422 7979, www.atton.cl. Good value, comfortable, very helpful, internet in rooms, full disabled access. Recommended.
A **Orly**, Pedro de Valdivia 027, Metro Pedro de Valdivia, T231 8947, www.orly hotel.com. Small, comfortable, convenient, Cafetto café attached with good value meals. Recommended.
B **Chilhotel**, Cirujano Guzmán 103, T264 0643, metro Manuel Montt, www.chilhotel.cl. Small, comfortable, family-run, includes breakfast, luggage store, airport transfer US$19. Recommended.
B **El Patio Suizo**, Condell 847, T494 1214, www.patiosuizo.com. Metro Parque Bustamante. Comfortable Swiss-run B&B in a quiet residential part of Providencia, TV, patio, internet, English, German spoken; Spanish classes. Recommended.
B **Marilú's Bed and Breakfast**, Rafael Cañas 246 C, T235 5302, www.bedandbreakfast.cl. Comfortable, C with shared bath, no TCs or credit cards, good beds, English and French spoken, secure. Highly recommended.
E pp **Santiago Hostel**, Dr Barros Borgoño 199, T236 6091, www.santiagohostel.cl. Dorms only, European-style hostel, breakfast, kitchen facilities, garden, internet, excellent skiing information.

Longer stay accommodation
See the classified ads in *El Mercurio*; flats, homes and family pensiones are listed by district, or in *El Rastro* (weekly), or try the notice board at the tourist office. Estate agents handle apartments, but often charge ½ of the first month's rent as commission, while a month's rent in advance and 1 month's deposit are required. Recommended apartments are **Santa Magdalena**, Helvecia 244, Las Condes, T374 6875, www.santamagdalena.cl.

❻ Eating

Some of the best seafood restaurants are to be found in the Mercado Central (by Cal y Canto Metro, lunches only), or in the Vega Central market on the opposite bank of the Mapocho and on Av Cumming and C Reyes in Barrio Brasil. Visit *El Mercurio* online, www.emol.com, and go to "tiempo libre", to search for types of restaurants and areas of the city. It is difficult to eat cheaply in the evening apart from fast food, so if you're on a tight budget, make the lunchtime *almuerzo* your main meal.

Santiago centre *p606, map p607*
₸₸₸-₸₸ **Da Carla**, Maclver 577, T633 3739. Traditional Italian food, good.
₸₸₸-₸₸ **Opera Catedral**, Jose Miguel de la Barra 407, Bellas Artes metro, T664 5491. Very good, if expensive, French restaurant on the ground floor. Upstairs is a minimalist pub-restaurant, usually packed at night, serving fusion food at reasonable prices.
₸₸₸-₸₸ **San Marco**, Maclver, 2 doors from Da Carla. Even better than its neighbour, also Italian.
₸₸ **Congreso**, Catedral 1221. Good meat and wines, popular at lunchtime.

Statue of the Virgin
Cumbre Station (Teleférico)
Upper Station (Funicular)

Parque Metropolitano

Sofía Concha
Atz Casanova
M Concha

Bellavista

To Providencia & Las Condes

Av Andrés Bello
Salvador
Av Providencia
Av Salvador
Gral Salvo
Av José M Infante
Av Eleodoro Yáñez
To 8

⑤ ⑥

Libro Café Mediterráneo 11 *B3*
Michelle's 14 *B5*
Off the Record 18 *B4*
Opera Catedral 20 *B1*
Tragaluz 15 *B4*
Venezia 13 *B3*

Bars & clubs 🍷
Bogart 16 *B3*
Disco Salsa 17 *B4*
HBH 7 *A3*
La Casa en el Aire 12 *B4*
La Otra Puerta 19 *B3*
Restaurant/Pub
   Evelyn 9 *A3*

613

El 27 de Nueva York, Nueva York 27, T699 1555. Central, large, popular at lunchtime, good international menu, live music.
Faisán d'Or, Plaza de Armas. Good *pastel de choclo*, pleasant place to watch the world go by.
Lung Fung, Agustinas 715. Delicious oriental food, the oldest Chinese restaurant in Santiago, large cage in the centre with noisy parrots.
Bar Central, San Pablo 1063. Typical food. Recommended.
Bar Nacional No 2, Bandera 317. Popular, local specialities, big portions; also at Huérfanos 1151.
Círculo de Periodistas, Amunátegui 31, p 2. Unwelcoming entrance, good value lunches. Recommended.
El Naturista, Moneda 846. Excellent vegetarian, "healthy portions", wide-ranging menu, as well as juices, beer and wine, closes 2100.
El Rápido, next to Bar Nacional No 2. Specializes in *empanadas* and *completos*, good food, good fun, "happening locals' joint".

La Caleta de Don Beno, San Diego 397. Excellent *parrilladas*, also seafood, popular. Recommended.
Las Tejas, San Diego 234, south of the Alameda. For typical dishes, including *cazuelas*, and drinks, attracts a lively and rowdy crowd.
Masticón, San Diego 152, south of the Alameda. Good service, excellent value, popular, wide range of dishes.
Confitería Torres, Alameda 1570. Traditional bar/restaurant, good ambience, live music Fri-Sat.

Cafés

Café Caribe and **Café Haití**, both on Paseo Ahumada and elsewhere in centre and Providencia. Good coffee, institutions for the Santiago business community.
Café Colonia, MacIver 133. Splendid variety of cakes, pastries and pies, fashionable and pricey.
Café Ikabaru, Huérfanos 709. Good coffee, popular and intimate.

Santiago west of centre

Sleeping
Che Lagarto 1
Conde de Anzúrez 4
Happy House
  Hostel 3

Hostal Río Amazonas
Barrio Brasil 7
Hostelling Internacional
  Santiago 8
La Casa Amarilla 5

La Casa Roja 9
Residencial Alemana 6
Residencial Mery 11
SCS Habitat,
  Scotts Place 15

Café Manila, Ahumada 357. Central, quiet, very pleasant place for a snack or more.
Salón de Té Cousiño, Cousiño 107. Good coffee, snacks and *onces*, very popular, but not cheap.

West of centre *p608, map p614*
♥♥ **Las Vacas Gordas**, Cienfuegos 280, Barrio Brasil, T697 1066. Good value grilled steaks, nice wine selection, very popular so book in advance.
♥♥ **Los Chinos Ricos**, Brasil 373, on the Plaza, T696 3778. Good Chinese, popular with families on Sun lunchtime.
♥♥ **Ostras Azócar**, Gral Bulnes 37. Reasonable prices for oysters. Several other seafood restaurants in same street.

East of the centre: Bellavista and Lastarria *p609, map p608*
♥♥♥ **El Kilómetro 11.680**, Dardignac 0145, T777 0410. French restaurant with one of Chile's best wine lists.

Tur Hotel Express **2**

Eating ●
Confitería Torres **4**
Las Vacas Gordas **1**

Los Chinos Ricos **3**
Ostras Azócar **2**

♥♥ **El Otro Sitio**, López de Bello 53. Peruvian, excellent food, elegant, good service.
♥♥ **Eladio**, Pío Nono 251. Good steaks, Argentine cuisine, excellent value, also has bingo.
♥♥♥ **La Divina Comida**, Purísima 93. Italian with 3 rooms: Heaven, Hell and Purgatory, good seafood.
♥♥ **Le Coq au Vin**, López de Bello 0110. French, excellent, good value. Highly recommended.
♥♥ **Off the Record**, López de Bello 0155, T777 7710. Bar-restaurant, period design, nice atmosphere with live music on Fri-Sat nights, cheaper set lunch.
♥♥ **El Tablao**, Constitución 110, T737 8648. Traditional Spanish restaurant. The food is reasonable but the main attraction is the live flamenco show on Fri-Sat nights.
♥♥ **Gatopardo**, next door to El Rincón Español, T633 6420. Good value, Mediterranean and Bolivian cuisine, tasty lunch buffet. Highly recommended.
♥♥ **Michelle's**, Arzobispo 0615, T777 9919. Mediterranean bistro, excellent seafood and fish dishes. Recommended.
♥♥ **La Tasca Mediterránea**, Purísima 165. Good food, extensive menu including seafood. Recommended.
♥♥ **Les Assassins**, Merced 297, T638 4280. Good French cuisine in small, family-run bistro, with decent wine list; good-value set lunches.
♥♥ **Tragaluz**, Constitución 124. Good Chilean food, not cheap.
♥♥ **Venezia**, Pío Nono, corner of López de Bello. Huge servings of traditional Chilean home-cooked fare (allegedly one of Neruda's favourite haunts), good value.
♥ **Libro Café Mediterráneo**, Purísima, next door to La Tasca Mediterránea. Popular with students, lively, cheap.

East of the centre: Providencia *p609, map p608*
♥♥♥ **El Giratorio**, 11 de Septiembre 2250, p16, T232 1827. Revolving French restaurant offering great views and good food.
♥♥♥ **El Huerto**, Orrego Luco 054, Providencia, T233 2690. Vegetarian. Open daily, live music Fri and Sat evenings, varied menu, very good, popular. Recommended.
♥♥♥ **Oriental**, Manuel Montt 584. Excellent Chinese, one of the best in Santiago. Highly recommended.
♥♥♥ **Salvaje**, Av Providencia 1177. Good international menu, open-air seating, good value set lunches. Warmly recommended.
♥♥ **A Pinch of Pancho**, Gral del Canto 45, T235 1700. Very good fish and seafood.
♥♥ **Café El Patio**, Providencia 1652, next to Phone Box Pub. Tofu and pasta as well as fish dishes, tasty sandwiches, popular, good drinks, internet access. Very pleasant.

¶ Gatsby, Av Providencia 1984, T233 0732. American food, as-much-as-you-can-eat buffet and lunch/dinner, snack bar open till 2400, tables outside in warm weather, good (also has a good branch at the airport).
¶ Kimono, Av Providencia 1480. Vegetarian, tofu, miso soup, good snacks.

Cafés

For snacks and ice cream there are several good places on Av Providencia including **Coppellia**, No 2211, **Bravissimo**, No 1406, and **El Toldo Azul**, No 1936. Also **Salón de Té Tavelli**, drugstore precinct, Av Providencia 2124.

East of the centre: Las Condes *p609*

¶¶¶ Cuerovaca, El Mañío 1659, Vitacura, T246 8936. Serves fantastic steaks, Argentine and Chilean cuts.
¶¶¶ El Madroñal, Vitacura 2911, T233 6312. Spanish, excellent, booking essential.
¶¶¶ Sakura, Vitacura 4111. Good Japanese sushi.
¶¶¶-¶¶ Diego Pizza, El Bosque Norte y Don Carlos. Nice atmosphere, good cocktails, popular.
¶¶¶-¶¶ Mare Nostrum, La Concepción 281. Good for seafood.
¶¶ Le Fournil, Vitacura 3841, opposite Cuerovaca. Excellent French bakery and restaurant, popular a lunchtime.

⦿ Bars and clubs

For all entertainments, nightclubs, cinemas, theatres, restaurants, concerts, *El Mercurio* Online website has all listings and a good search feature, www.emol.com. Listings in weekend newspapers, particularly *El Mercurio* and *La Tercera*. Also *Santiago What's On*. Lively areas to head for are: **Bellavista**, good selection of varied restaurants, bars, clubs and salsotecas. Reasonable prices (Metro Baquedano). Avs Suecia and Gral Holley in **Providencia**, much of it pedestrianized. Lots of bars and some restaurants, clubs and salsotecas (Metro Los Leones). **El Bosque Norte**, chic bars and expensive restaurants for the Chilean jetset (Metro Tobalaba). **Barrio Brasil**, a number of bars and restaurants dotted around the Plaza Brasil and on Avs Brasil and Cumming. Popular with Chilean students (Metro República). **Plaza Ñuñoa**, a number of good bars dotted around the Plaza in the middle-class suburb of Ñuñoa.

East of the centre: Bellavista
p609, map p612

Bogart, Av López de Bello 34. Disco-rock bar.
Disco Salsa, Pío Nono 223. Good atmosphere, salsa and dance classes.
HBH Bars, Pío Nono 129 and Purísima y López de Bello, also at Irarrázaval 3176, near Plaza Ñuñoa,

and Gral Holley 124, Providencia. Bavarian-style beer brewed to traditional recipes in Temuco.
La Casa en el Aire, López de Bello 125. Pleasant atmosphere, live music. Recommended.
La Otra Puerta, Pío Nono 348. Lively salsoteca with live music.
Peña Nano Parra, San Isidro 57. Good folk club, cheap.
Restaurant/Pub Evelyn, Purísima 282. Austrian beers on tap, good atmosphere, not cheap.

East of the centre: Providencia
p609, map p608

Brannigan Pub, Av Suecia 35. Good beer, live jazz, one of many good bars on this avenue.
Flannery's Irish Geo Pub, Encomenderos 83. Beer, food, live music Wed and Fri, internet.
Golden Bell Inn, Hernando Aguirre 27. Popular with ex-pats.
Louisiana River Pub, Suecia y Gral Holly. Live music.
Phone Box Pub, Av Providencia 1652. Serves imported British and other European beers, popular with locals.

East of the centre: Las Condes *p609*
Country Village, Av Las Condes y Estoril. Mon-Sat from 2000, Sun lunchtime onwards, live music Fri and Sat.
Heaven, Recoleta 345. US$15 pp, Thu-Sat 2330-0500.
Ilé Habana, Bucaré, just off Suecia. Salsa bar, often live music, and a good dance floor.
Morena, Av Las Condes 10120. Good dance floor and sound system, techno, open till 0200, live music weekends.
Further east on Av Las Condes at Paseo San Damián are several popular bar-restaurants including **T'quila** (annex of Santa Fe, No 10690, a colourful, popular Mexican restaurant).

Ñuñoa
Club de Jazz de Santiago, José Pedro Alessandri 85, T274 2997, www.clubdejazz.cl. Regular live jazz in candle-lit bar, pleasant.

⦿ Entertainment

Santiago *p605, maps p607, p608, p613, p614*
There's a good guide to daily cinema in the free newspapers, *La Hora* and *tmg*, given out at metro stations on weekday mornings.
Cinemas 'Ciné Arte' (quality foreign films) is popular. Cinemas specializing in this type of film include: **El Biógrafo**, Lastarria 181, T633 4435. **Casa de Extensión UC**, Alameda 390, T635 1994. **Normandie**, Tarapacá 1181, T697 2979. **Tobalaba**, Av Providencia 2563, T231 6630. Try also Goethe-Institut (address below). Many

multiplex cinemas across the city show mainstream releases, nearly always in the original English with subtitles. Seats cost US$5-7 with reductions on Mon-Wed (elsewhere in the country the days vary).

Classical concerts Free concerts are sometimes given in San Francisco church in summer. Arrive early for a seat.

Theatres Teatro Municipal, Agustinas y San Antonio. Stages international opera, concerts by the Orquesta Filarmónica de Santiago, and the Ballet de Santiago, throughout the year. On Tue at 2100 there are free operatic concerts in the Salón Claudio Arrau; tickets range from US$10 for a very large choral group with a symphony orchestra, and US$12 for the cheapest seats at the ballet, to US$100 for the most expensive opera seats. Some cheap seats are often sold on the day of concerts. Teatro Universidad de Chile, Plaza Italia, http://teatro.uchile.cl/, is the home of the Orquesta y Coro Sinfónica de Chile and the Ballet Nacional de Chile. There are a great number of theatres which stage plays in Spanish, either in the original language or translations.

❂ Festivals and events

Santiago p605, maps p607, p608, p613, p614
During **Nov** there is a **free art fair** in the Parque Forestal on the banks of the Río Mapocho, lasting a fortnight. In **Oct** or **Nov** there are a sumptuous flower show and an annual agricultural and industrial show (known as **Fisa**) in Parque Cerrillos. Religious festivals and ceremonies continue throughout **Holy Week**, when a priest washes the feet of 12 men. The image of the Virgen del Carmen (patron of the Armed Forces) is carried through the streets by cadets on **16 Jul**.

O Shopping

Santiago p605, maps p607, p608, p613, p614
Antique stores in Plaza Mulato Gil de Castro and elsewhere on Lastarria (Merced end).

Bookshops Book prices are high compared with neighbouring countries and Europe. Apostrophes, Merced 324. Specializes in French books, book exchange, internet service. Books, Av Providencia 1652, Metro Pedro de Valdivia, T235 1205. Second-hand English books, exchange for best deal. Chile Ilustrado, next to Books at Av Providencia 1652, T235 8145, chileil@tnet.cl. Specializes in books relating to Chile, flora, fauna, history and anthropology (mostly in Spanish). Feria Chilena del Libro, Huérfanos 623, and in Drugstore precinct, Providencia 2124. Largest bookshop in Santiago, a few travel books and maps. LOM Ediciones, Estación Mapocho, Mon-Fri 1000-2000, Sat

1000-1400. Very good, large stock from its own publishing house (literature, history, sociology, art, politics), also bar and reading room with recent Chilean papers and magazines. Librería Albers, Vitacura 5648, Las Condes, T218 5371, F218 1458. Spanish, English and German, good selection, cheaper than most, helpful, also German and Swiss newspapers. Librairie Française, Estado 337. Books and newspapers. Librería Inglesa, Huérfanos 669, local 11, Pedro de Valdivia 47, Providencia 2653, Vitacura 5950, www.libreriainglesa.cl. Good selection of English books. Librería Universitaria, Alameda 1050, T695 1529, in unmistakable yellow building next to Universidad de Chile metro. Good selection of books in Spanish. South American Way, Apoquindo 6856, Las Condes, T211 8078. Sells books in English. The English Reader, Los Leones 116, T334 7388, www.englishreader.cl. Specializes in books in English.

For cheap English books, try the second-hand book kiosks on San Diego between Eleuterio Ramírez and Cóndor, 4 blocks south of Plaza Bulnes.

Camping equipment Camping gas cartridges (Italian substitute for Camping Gaz) can be bought at Fabri Gas, Bandera y Santo Domingo. Imported camping goods from Club Andino and Federación de Andinismo (see below). Casa Italiana, Tarapacá 1120. Repair of camping stoves. La Cumbre, Apoquindo 5258, Las Condes, T220 9907, la_cumbre@email.com. Dutch-owned, very helpful. Industria Yarur, Rosas 1289 y Teatinos, T672 3696 (metro Cal y Canto). Sells wide range of Doite products (Chilean, good value). Mountain Service, PO Box 233 Correo 35, Providencia, www.mountainservice.cl. English spoken, tents, stoves, clothing, equipment rental, recommended. Outdoors & Travel, Encomenderos 206, Las Condes, T/F335 7104. German/Chilean owned, clothing, equipment, maps. For second-hand equipment look for adverts in cheaper hotels or try Luz Emperatriz Sanhuela Quiroz, Portal Lyon, Loc 14, Providencia 2198 (Metro Los Leones), expensive for new equipment, as is Patagonia, Centro Comercial Alto Las Condes, where there are three other similar stores.

Handicrafts Chile Vivo, Dardignac 15, Bellavista, T735 0227, chilevivo@latinmail.com. Typical handicrafts, jewellery making, art gallery, internet café, owner Doris Berdichevsky is very helpful. Cooperativa Almacén Campesino, Purísima 303, Bellavista, T737 2127. A cooperative association in an attractive colonial building, selling handicrafts from all over Chile, including attractive Mapuche weavings, wood carvings, pottery and beautiful wrought copper and bronze. Highly recommended for variety, quality and value. Prices are similar to those in similar shops in Temuco. Ask about shipping. Los Graneros del

Alba, or **El Pueblo de Artesanos**, beside and behind the Iglesia de los Dominicos, on Av Apoquindo 9085. Open 1030-2100 in summer, 1000-1900 in winter. All types of ware on sale, classes given in some shops, interesting. To get there, take a No 326 or 327 bus from Av Providencia, marked 'Camino del Alba'; get out at the junction of Apoquindo y Camino del Alba and walk up to the church. **Plaza Artesanos de Manquehue**, Av Manquehue Sur, block 300-600, just off Apoquindo. Good range of modern Chilean crafts, from ceramics to textiles, at the biggest craft market in Chile. Take any bus east from Providencia or Escuela Militar which goes via Apoquindo. **Prisma de los Andes**, Santo Domingo 1690 T673 0540, Metro Santa Ana. Textiles, crafts, tapestries, rucksacks, bags, kids clothes etc.

Jewellery The gemstone lapis lazuli can be found in shops on C Bellavista between Pío Nono and Yáñez, but is cheaper in the arcades on south side of the Plaza de Armas and in the **Centro Artesanal Santa Lucía** (Santa Lucía Metro, south exit) which also has a wide variety of woollen goods, jewellery, some folk music and other miscellanea. **Amitié**, Ricardo León y Av Providencia (Metro Los Leones) and **Dauvin Artesanía Fina**, Providencia 2169, Local 69 (Metro Los Leones) have also been recommended.

Maps See Essentials, page 600, and Driving in Chile Box. **Librería Australis**, Av Providencia 1670, local 5. All sorts of local, regional and trekking maps.

Markets For food: **Mercado Central**, between Puente y 21 de Mayo by the Río Mapocho (Cal y Canto Metro) is excellent but quite expensive. There is a cheaper market, the **Vega Central**, on the opposite bank of the river. There are craft markets in an alleyway, 1 block south of the Alameda between A Prat and San Diego, on the 600 to 800 blocks of Santo Domingo (including pieces from neighbouring countries) and at Pío Nono y Santa María, Bellavista. The **Bío Bío** flea market on C Bío Bío, Metro Franklin (follow crowds), on Sat and Sun morning is huge; everything under the sun, lots of it having fallen off the back of a lorry.

Music Billboard, Providencia 2314 and at La Bolsa 75 (downtown). Good source for rock, jazz and alternative music. **Feria de Disco**, Paseo Ahumada and in numerous malls. The biggest chain, often sell tickets for rock concerts. **Musimundo**, Huérfanos 930 (with listening stations) and Providencia 2266, megastores.

Shopping malls Numerous; generally open daily 1000-2100. **Alto Las Condes**, Av Kennedy 9001; **Apumanque**, Manquehue y Apoquindo; **Mall del Centro**, Rosas 900 block, just north of the Plaza de Armas. The most central. **Parque Arauco**, Av Kennedy 5413, north of Metro Escuela Militar; **Plaza Vespucio** at terminus of Línea 5, Bellavista de La Florida.

Wine El Mundo del Vino, Isidora Goyenechea 2929, T244 8888. For all types of Chilean wines, good selection across the price range. **Vinopolis**, El Bosque Norte 038 and Pedro de Valdivia 036. Mon-Fri 0900-2300, Sat 1000-2300, Sun 1000-2200. Also at airport. Sells all types of Chilean wines, good selection across the price range. **The Wine House**, Vitacura 2904, Mall Parque Arauco, loc 333.

▲ Activities and tours

Santiago *p605, maps p607, p608, p613, p614*

Cricket Sat in summer at **Club Príncipe de Gales**, Las Arañas 1901 (bus from Tobalaba Metro), see www.cricketchile.cl for more information.

Cycling New models, parts and repairs at San Diego, 800 and 900 blocks, south of the Alameda.

Football Main teams including Colo Colo who play at the **Estadio Monumental**, T688 3244 (reached by any bus to Puente Alto; tickets from Av Monumental 5300, Macul, T294 7300), **Universidad de Chile**, Campo de Deportes, Ñuñoa, T239 2793 (Estadio Nacional, Grecia 2001, T238 8102) and **Universidad Católica** who play at San Carlos de Apoquindo, reached by bus from Metro Escuela Militar, tickets from Andrés Bello 2782, Providencia, T231 2777.

Horse racing Club Hípico, Blanco Encalada 2540, highly recommended, entry to main stand US$5, every Sun and every other Wed afternoon. **Hipódromo Chile** every Sat.

Skiing and climbing Club Alemán Andino, El Arrayán 2735, T232 4338, www.dav.cl. Open Tue and Fri, 1800-2000, May-Jun. **Club Andino de Chile**, Av Lib O'Higgins 108, T274 9252, www.skilagunillas.cl, ski club (open 1900-2100 on Mon and Fri). **Federación de Andinismo de Chile**, Almte Simpson 77A (T222 0888, www.feach.cl). Open daily (frequently closed Jan/Feb), has a small museum, library (weekdays except Wed 1930-2100), shop selling guides and equipment. Escuela Nacional de Montaña (ENAM), at same address, T222 0799, holds seminars and courses and has the addresses of all the mountaineering clubs in the country. It has a mountaineering school. **Skitotal**, Apoquindo 4900, of 40-42, T246 0156, for 1-day excursions and good value ski hire. Equipment hire is much cheaper in Santiago than in ski resorts. Sunglasses are essential. For ski resorts in the Santiago area see below.

Swimming Antilen, Cerro San Cristóbal. Open daily in summer except Mon 1000-1500 (check if they are open in winter, one usually is), US$10, fine views. In Parque O'Higgins, 1330-1830 summer only, US$4. Olympic pool in Parque Araucano (near Parque Arauco Shopping Centre, Metro Escuela Militar), open Nov-Mar Tue-Sat 0900-1900. **Tupahue**, Cerro San Cristóbal. Large pool with cafés, entry US$10 but worth it.

Tennis Municipal courts in Parque O'Higgins. Estadio Nacional, Av Grecia y Av Marathon, has a tennis club which offers classes.

Tours A number of agencies offer day trips from Santiago. Typical excursions are to the Wine Valleys, Isla Negra (Pablo Neruda's seaside villa), visits to nearby haciendas and adventure tours such as whitewater rafting, rock climbing or trekking in the Cajón del Maipo, southeast of the city. Many agencies advertise in the Sernatur tourist office (see above).

Asatej Student Flight Centre, H de Aguirre 201, Oficina 401, T335 0395, chile@asatej.com. For cheap flights and youth travel. Recommended.

Turismo Tajamar, Orrego Luco 023, Providencia, T336 8000, www.tajamar.cl. Good for flights.

Turismo Cocha, El Bosque Norte 0430, PO Box 191035, Providencia, Metro Tobalaba, T600-464 1000, www.cocha.com.

Adventure tours and trekking

Altue Expediciones, Encomenderos 83, p 2, Las Condes (above Geo Pub), T232 1103, altue@entelchile.net. For wilderness trips including tour of Patagonia. Recommended.

Antarctic Expeditions, Av Vitacura 2771, of 904, Las Condes, T236 5179, www.antarctic.cl. Expeditions to Patagonia and Antarctica from Punta Arenas on board their '*Antarctic Dream*'.

Azimut 360, General Salvo 159, Providencia, T235 1519, www.azimut.cl. Adventure and ecotourism including mountaineering all over Chile, low prices. Highly recommended.

Catamaranes del Sur, Pedro de Valdivia Norte 0210, Providencia, T231 1902, offers tours of Chilean Patagonia. In Puerto Chacabuco: José Miguel Carrera 50, T351112, www.catamaranesdelsur.cl.

Patagonia Connection SA, Fidel Oteíza 1921, of 1006, Providencia (Metro Pedro de Valdivia), T225 6489, www.patagonia-connection.com. For excursion by boat Puerto Montt-Coyhaique/Puerto Chacabuco-Laguna San Rafael.

Racies, Plaza Corregidor Zañartu 761, T/F638 2904. Cultural tours, including Robinson Crusoe Island and Antarctica.

Santiago Adventures, Coyancura 2270, of 801, Providencia, T415 0667, www.santiago adventures.com. US-run, offering adventure day tours, wine tours, city tours, skiing and Patagonia.

Sportstours, Moneda 970, p 18, T549 5200, www.sportstour.cl. German-run, 5-day trips to Antarctica (offices also at Hotels Carrera, and San Cristóbal), only for tours organized from abroad.

Turismo Cabo de Hornos, Agustinas 814, of 706, T664 3458, www.turismocabodehornos.cl. For DAP flights and Tierra del Fuego/Antarctica tours.

Valle Nevado, Av Vitacura 5250, No 304, Vitacura, T477 7000, www.vallenevado.com. Skiing, snowboarding, trekking and mountain biking.

⊖ Transport

Santiago *p605, maps p607, p608, p613, p614*

Air

International and domestic flights leave from **Arturo Merino Benítez Airport** at Pudahuel, 26 km northwest of Santiago, off Ruta 68, the motorway to Viña del Mar and Valparaíso. The terminal has most facilities, including Afex cambio, ATMs, Sernatur office which will book accommodation and a fast-food plaza. Left luggage US$8 per bag per day. Airport information T601 8758/690 1900, www.aeropuertosantiago.cl.

Airport taxi, about US$20 but bargain hard and agree fare beforehand: more expensive with meter. Taxi to airport is much cheaper, US$12-15, if flagged down in the street rather than booked by phone. Frequent bus services to/from city centre by 2 companies: **Tur-Bus**, from Terminal Alameda, US$3, every 30 mins; and **Centropuerto** (T601 9883, from Metro Los Héroes), US$2.50, first from centre 0600, last from airport 2230, every 15 mins. Buses leave from outside airport terminal and, in Santiago, call at Estación Central, Terminal Santiago, Metro Pajaritos and most other regular bus stops. **Delfos** (T601 1111), **Navett** (T695 6868), **Transfer** (T777 7707) and others run minibus services between the airport and hotels or other addresses: US$9 to/from city centre; US$11 to/from Las Condes. To go to the airport, book the previous day.

Bus

Local Yellow buses called *micros* are being replaced by Transantiago (www.transantiago.cl), new buses designed to reduce congestion and pollution. Bus lines will be main (green and white), for long journeys, and local and will integrate with the metro system. Payment will be by prepaid *Bip* card. *Micros* will be withdrawn by 2010. City buses display a number, the route and the fare (in early 2007 US$0.75). There are also *colectivos* (collective taxis) on fixed routes to the suburbs. Routes are displayed with route numbers. Taxis (black with yellow roofs) are abundant, and not expensive, with a minimum charge of US$0.40, plus US$0.15 per 200 m. Taxi drivers are permitted to charge more at night, but in the daytime check that the meter is set to day rates. At bus terminals, drivers will charge more – best to walk a block and flag down a cruising taxi. Avoid taxis with more than one person in them especially at night. For journeys outside the city arrange the charge beforehand. Various radio taxi services operate, but rates are above those of city taxis.

Long distance There are frequent, and good, interurban buses to all parts of Chile. Take a look at the buses before buying the tickets (there are big differences in quality among bus companies); ask about the on-board services, many companies offer drinks for sale, or free, and luxury buses have meals, videos, headphones. Reclining seats are standard and there are also salón cama sleeper buses. Fares from/to the capital are given in the text. On Fri evening, when night departures are getting ready to go, the terminals can be chaotic. There are 5 bus terminals: 1) **Terminal Alameda**, which has a modern extension called Mall Parque Estación (don't confuse with Mall Paseo Estación, see below) with left luggage (US$3.40 per day), ATMs and internet, O'Higgins 3712, Metro Universidad de Santiago, T270 1500. All **Pullman-Bus** and **Tur-Bus** services go from here, they serve almost every destination in Chile, good quality but prices a little higher than others. 2) **Terminal Santiago**, O'Higgins 3878, 1 block west of Terminal Alameda, T376 1755, Metro Universidad de Santiago. Services to all parts of southern Chile, including the only service to Punta Arenas (48 hrs). Also international departures. Has left luggage from 0700. 3) **Terminal San Borja**, O'Higgins y San Borja, 1 block west of Estación Central, 3 blocks east of Terminal Alameda, Metro Estación Central (entrance is, inconveniently, via a busy shopping centre, Mall Paseo Estación), T776 0645. Mainly departures to the Central Valley area, but also to northern Chile. Booking offices and departures organized according to destination. 4) **Terminal Los Héroes on Tucapel Jiménez**, just north of the Alameda, Metro Los Héroes, T420 0099. Left luggage 0630-2330. A smaller terminal with booking offices of 8 companies, to the north, the south and Lake District and some international services (Lima, Asunción, Montevideo, Buenos Aires, Bariloche, Mendoza). 5) **Metro Pajaritos**, to Valaparaíso, Viña del Mar and places on the central coast; efficient new terminal with café, toilets, public phones. Some long-distance buses call at Las Torres de Tajamar, Providencia 1108, which is more convenient if you are planning to stay in Providencia.

Note See the note under Taxis about not taking expensive taxis parked outside bus terminals, but note that official Tur-Bus taxis are good and reliable. Also check if student rates are available (even for non-students), or reductions for travelling same day as purchase of ticket; it is worth bargaining over prices, especially shortly before departure and out of summer season.

International buses Most services leave from Terminal Santiago, though there are also departures from Terminal Los Héroes. There are frequent services from Terminal Santiago through the Cristo Redentor tunnel to **Mendoza** in Argentina, 6-7 hrs, US$15, many companies, departures around 0800, 1200 and 2200, touts

approach you in Terminal Santiago. Many of these services continue to **Buenos Aires**, 24 hrs, US$50, and many companies in Terminal Santiago have connections to other Argentine cities (eg **Bahía Blanca**, **Córdoba**, **San Juan**, **Bariloche** and **Neuquén**). There are also minibuses to Mendoza from the Terminal Santiago, US$20, 6 hrs, shorter waiting time at customs. To **Lima**, **Ormeño** (Terminal Santiago), Tue and Fri 0900, 51 hrs, US$90, it is cheaper to take a bus to Arica, a colectivo to Tacna, then bus to Lima.

Car
Car hire Prices vary a lot so shop around first. Tax of 19% is charged, usually included in price quoted. If possible book a car in advance. Information boards full of flyers from companies at airport and tourist office. A credit card is usually asked for when renting a vehicle. Many companies will not hire a car to holders of drivers licences in left hand drive countries unless they have an international licence. Remember that in the capital driving is restricted according to licence plate numbers; look for notices in the street and newspapers. Main international agencies and others are available at the airport (see Essentials, page 44, for agency web addresses). **Automóvil Club de Chile** car rental from head office (see Maps), discount for members and members of associated motoring organizations. **Rosselot**, Francisco Bilbao 2032, Providencia, T381 3690, www.rosselot.cl. Also at airport, T690 1374. Reputable Chilean firm with national coverage. **Seelmann**, Monseñor Edwards 1279, La Reina, T277 9259. English and German spoken. **Verschae**, Manquehue Sur 660, T202 7266, www.verschae.com. Good value, branches throughout country.

Ferry operators
Navimag, Av El Bosque Norte 0440, p 11, Las Condes, T442 3120, www.navimag.com. For services from **Puerto Montt** to **Puerto Chacabuco**, **Puerto Natales** and **Laguna San Rafael**. M/n Skorpios: Augusto Leguía Norte 118, Las Condes, T477 1900, www.skorpios.cl. For luxury cruise out of Puerto Montt to **Laguna San Rafael** and adventure strips from Puerto Natales to Puerto Edén and the Campo Hielo del Sur.
Note Check schedules with ferry companies rather than Sernatur.

Metro
See www.metrosantiago.cl. Line 1 runs west-east between **San Pablo** and **Escuela Militar**, under the Alameda; Line 2 runs north-south from **Vesupcio Norte** to **La Cisterna**; the new Line 4 runs from **Tobalaba** on Line 1 south to **Plaza de Puente Alto**, with

a branch (4a) from **V Mackenna** to **La Cisterna**; Line 5 runs northwest-southeast from **Quinta Normal** via **Baquedano** to **Vicente Valdés** on Line 4. The trains are modern, fast, quiet, and very full. The first train is at 0630 (Mon-Sat), 0800 (Sun and holidays), the last about 2245. Fares vary according to time of journey; there are 2 charging periods: high 0715-0900, 1800-1930, US$1; economic, at all other times, US$0.70. The simplest solution is to buy a *tarjeta Bip*, US$3 (US$1 for subsequent top-ups), a charge card from which the appropriate fare is deducted.

Blue metrobus services connect with the metro at various stations for outlying districts, fare US$0.70.

Train

All trains leave from **Estación Central (Alameda)** at O'Higgins 3322. The line runs south to **Rancagua, Talca, Chillán, Concepción** and **Temuco**, with connections as far as **Puerto Montt**. There are several trains a day as far as Chillán and a day and a night train to Temuco. Fares to Temuco: US$19-26, *salón* class, or US$22-35 *preferente*. To continue to Puerto Montt change in Temuco to the Victoria-Puerto Montt line, twice a day. There is a connecting bus service from Temuco to Valdivia, Villarrica and Pucón. There are also frequent local Metrotren services to Rancagua and San Fernando. For reservations: T585 5000, open till 2230, www.efe.cl. **Booking offices** Alameda O'Higgins 3170, T585 5990, Mon-Sat 0700-2245; Sun 0800-2245; Universidad de Chile metro, loc 10, T688 3297, Mon-Fri 0900-2000, Sat 0900-1400. Left luggage office at Estación Central, open til 2300. **Note** Schedules change with the seasons, so check timetables in advance. Summer services are booked up a week in advance.

❶ Directory

Santiago *p605, maps p607, p608, p613, p614*
Airline offices Aerolíneas Argentinas, Roger de Flor 2921, Las Condes, T210 9300. **American Airlines**, Huérfanos 1199, T679 0000. **Continental**, Fidel Oteiza 1921, Suite 703, T200 2100. **Delta**, Isadora Goyenechea 2939, of 601, Las Condes, Tobalaba metro, T280 1600, www.delta.com. **Iberia**, Bandera 206, p 8, T870 1000. **KLM**, San Sebastián 2839, of 202, Las Condes, Tobalaba metro, T233 0011 (sales), 233 0991 (reservations), www.klm.com. **LAN**, Huérfanos 926, T600-526 2000, Universidad de Chile metro, and Av Providencia y Av Pedro de Valdivia, Mon-Fri 0900-1900, Sat 0900-1230 (to avoid queues, buy tickets at the office in the airport). **Lufthansa**, Av El Bosque Norte 500,

p 16, Las Condes, T630 1655, www.lufthansa.cl. **Sky Airline**, Fuenzalida 55, Providencia, and Huérfanos 815, T600-600 2828. **Banks** (Banks, open 0900-1400, closed on Sat. Exchange rates are published in El Mercurio.) For Cirrus/MasterCard and Visa ATMs go to any bank, pharmacy or Copec petrol station with Redbanc sign. **Banco de Chile**, Ahumada 251 and other branches, www.bancodechile.cl, minimum of formalities. **Citibank**, Av Providencia 2653, www.citibank.cl. **American Express**, Andrés Bello 2711, p 9, T350 6700, Tobalaba metro, also at Blanco Viajes, Gen Holley 148, T636 9100, blancoviajes@blancoviajes.cl. Some Amex services at branches of **Viajes Falabella** throughout the city. **Casas de Cambio** (exchange houses) in the centre are mainly situated on Paseo Ahumada and Huérfanos (metro Universidad de Chile or Plaza de Armas). Use them, not banks, for changing TCs. **Exprinter**, Bombero Ossa 1053, good rates, low commission. **Afex**, Moneda 1148, good rates for TCs. In Providencia several on Av Pedro de Valdivia. Some casas de cambio in the centre open Sat morning (but check first). Dollars can only be bought for Chilean pesos in casas de cambio. Most cambios charge 3% commission to change US$ TCs into US$ cash; check beforehand. Only residents can buy dollars against credit cards. Always avoid street money changers (particularly common on Ahumada and Agustinas): they pull any number of tricks, or will usually ask you to accompany them to somewhere obscure. The passing of forged notes and muggings are reported. **Cultural centres** **Centro Cultural Matucana**, Av Matucana 100 y Moneda, T682 4502, www.m100.cl. Art exhibitions, cheap films, sculpture workshop, café. **Instituto Chileno Británico de Cultura**, Santa Lucía 124, T413 2000, www.britanico.cl. 0930-1900, except 1330-1900 Mon, and 0930-1600 Fri, has British papers and library (also in Providencia, Darío Urzúa 1933, and Las Condes, Av Américo Vespucio Sur 631), runs language courses. **British Council**, Eliodoro Yáñez 832, near Providencia, T410 6900, www.britishcouncil.org/chile.htm. **Instituto Chileno Francés de Cultura**, Merced 298 (Francisco Noguera 176, Providencia, while being remodelled), T470 8060, www.icf.cl. In a beautiful house. **Instituto Chileno Alemán de Cultura**, Goethe-Institut, Esmeralda 650, T462 1800, www.goethe.de/ins/cl/sao/deindex.htm. **Instituto Chileno Norteamericano de Cultura**, Moneda 1467, T0800-200863, www.norte americano.cl. Good for US periodicals, cheap films on Fri. Also runs language courses and free Spanish/English language exchange hours (known as Happy Hours) which are a good way of meeting people. **Embassies and**

consulates Argentina, Miraflores 285, T582 2500, www.embargentina.cl/. Consulate Vicuña MacKenna 41, T582 2606. Australians need letter from their embassy to get visa here, open 0900-1400 (visa US$25, free for US citizens), if you need a visa for Argentina, get it here or in the consulates in Concepción, Puerto Montt or Punta Arenas, there are no facilities at the borders. **Australia**, Isidora Goyenechea 3621, T550 3500, www.chile.embassy.gov.au, 0900-1200. **Austria**, Barros Errázuriz 1968, p 3, T223 4774. **Belgium**, Av Providencia 2653, depto 1103, T232 1071. **Bolivia**, Santa María 2796, T232 8180 (Metro Los Leones). 0930-1400. **Canada**, Nueva Tajamar 481, p 12, T362 9660, www.dfait-maeci.gc.ca/latin-america/chile/embassy/embassy-en.asp (prints a good information book). **Denmark**, Jaques Cazotte 5531, T218 5949. **France**, Condell 65, T470 8000, www.france.cl. **Germany**, Las Hualtatas 5677, T463 2500. **Israel**, San Sebastián 2812, p 5, T750 0500. **Italy**, Clemente Fabres 1050, T470 8400. **Japan**, Av Ricardo Lyon 520, p 1, T232 1807. **Netherlands**, Av Apoquindo 3500, p 13, Las Condes, T756 9200. **New Zealand**, Av El Golf 99, of 703, Las Condes, T290 9800, embajada@ nzembassy.cl. **Norway**, San Sebastián 2839, T234 2888, www.noruega.cl/info/embassy.htm. **Peru**, Andrés Bello 1751, T235 2356 (Metro Pedro de Valdivia). **South Africa**, Av 11 de Septiembre 2353, p 17, T231 2862, www.embajada-sudafrica.cl. **Spain**, Av Andrés Bello 1895, Providencia, T235 2755. **Sweden**, 11 de Septiembre 2353, Torre San Ramón, p 4, Providencia, T940 1700, www.embajadasuecia.cl. **Switzerland**, Av Americo Vespucio Sur 100, p 14, T263 4211, F263 4094, metro Escuela Militar. Open 1000-1200. **United Kingdom**, El Bosque Norte 0125 (Metro Tobalaba), Casilla 72-D, T370 4100, www.britemb.cl. Will hold letters, consular section (F370 4170) open 0930-1230. **United States**, Andrés Bello 2800, T232 2600, www.embajadaeeuu.cl. **Hospitals** Emergency hospital at Marcoleta 377, T274 0093 (emergency), T633 2051 (general enquiries), charges for yellow fever vaccination and others (but not cholera). **Hospital del Salvador**, J M Infante 551, T225 6441, Mon-Thu 0800-1300, 1330-1645, Fri 0800-1300, 1330-1545. Also **Vaccinatoria Internacional**, Hospital Luis Calvo, MacKenna, Antonio Varas 360. **Clínica Central**, San Isidro 231-243, Santa Lucia metro, T463 1400, open 24 hrs, German spoken. **Note** If you need to get to a hospital, it is better to take a taxi than wait for an ambulance. **Internet** Internet cafés are everywhere; usual price US$0.60-1 per hr. **Language schools** Bellavista, Calle del Arzobispado 0609, Providencia, T732 3443, www.escuelabellavista.cl. Group and individual classes, lodging with families, free activities. **Escuela de Idiomas Violeta Parra**,

Ernesto Pinto Lagarrigue 362, Recoleta-Barrio Bellavista, T735 8211, www.tandemsantiago.cl. Courses aimed at budget travellers, information programme on social issues, arranges accommodation and visits to local organizations and national parks. **Instituto Chileno-Suizo de Idiomas y Cultura**, José Victorino Lastarria 93, p 2 (Metro Universidad Católica), T638 5414, www.chilenosuizo.cl. Coordinates stays in Chile for foreign-language students, courses in several languages, cyber café, meeting place, study area and art gallery. **Natalis Language Centre**, Vicuña Mackenna 6, p 7, T222 8721. www.natalislang.com. Many private teachers, including **Lucía Araya Arévalo**, T749 0706 (home), 731 8325 (office), 09-480 3727 (mob), lusara5@hotmail.com. Speaks German and English. **Carolina Carvajal**, Av El Bosque Sur 151, dpto Q, Las Condes, T734 7646, ccarvajal@interactiva.cl. Exchange library, internet access. Highly recommended. **Patricio Ríos**, Tobalaba 7505, La Reina, T226 6926. Speaks English. Recommended. **Patricia Vargas Vives**, JM Infante 100, of 308, T/F244 2283, www.escueladeespanol.cl. Qualified and experienced (US$12.50 per hr). Recommended. **Post offices** Plaza de Armas and Moneda between Morandé and Bandera. Also sub offices in Providencia at Av 11 de Septiembre 2092, Manuel Montt 1517, Pedro de Valdivia 1781, Providencia 1466, Luis Thayer Ojeda 0146 and in Estación Central shopping mall. These open Mon-Fri 0900-1800, Sat 0900-1230. Poste restante well organized (though only kept for 30 days), passport essential, list of letters and parcels received in the hall of central Post Office (one list for men, another for women, indicate Sr or Sra/Srta on envelope); Plaza de Armas office also has philatelic section, 0900-1630, and small stamp museum (ask to see it). If sending a parcel, the contents must first be checked at the Post Office. Paper, tape etc on sale. **Telephones** The cheapest call centres are on Calles Bandera, Catedral and Santo Domingo, all near the Plaza de Armas. International calls from here are half the price of main offices, eg **Entel**, Huérfanos 1133, Mon-Fri 0830-2200, Sat 0900-2030, Sun 0900-1400, calls cheaper 1400-2200. **Useful addresses** Immigration For extension of tourist visa, or any enquiries regarding legal status, go to **Departamento de Extranjería**, Agustinas 1235, p 2 (opposite Palacio de la Moneda), T674 4000, www.extranjeria.gob.cl. Mon-Fri 0900-1200. Take a numbered ticket from the machine and wait your turn. There are 3 options: Informaciones, Residencias/Visas, Estampados; if unsure which to choose, take tickets for all three while waiting for Informaciones. **Policia Internacional**: For lost tourist cards, see Touching down box, page 600.

Around Santiago

Pomaire
In this little town 65 km west of Santiago, pottery can be bought and the artists can sometimes be seen at work. The area is rich in clay and the town is famous for its *chicha de uva* and for its Chilean dishes, recommended.

Vineyards
Several vineyards in the Santiago area can be visited. **Cousiño Macul** ① *Av Quilin 7100, Peñalolén, east outskirts of the city, tours Mon-Fri at 1100, 1500, Sat at 1100, phone first T351 4175, www.cousinomacul.cl, US$9.50.* **Concha y Toro** ① *Pirque, near Puente Alto, 40 km south of Santiago, T476 5269, www.conchaytoro.cl, short tour (3 a day in Spanish, 3 in English), Mon-Sat, US$12, includes free wine glass and 2 tastings; book a day in advance, getting there: take Metro to Puente Alto (end of Línea 4), then blue Metrobus or taxi.* The **Undurraga vineyard** ① *Santa Ana, 34 km southwest of Santiago, T372 2850, www.und urraga.cl, 4 tours in English and Spanish Mon-Fri, 3 on Sat, Sun (reserve 2 days in advance), US$10, getting there: take a Melipilla bus (but not Rutabus 78) to the entrance.* **Viña Santa Rita** ① *Padre Hurtado 0695, Alto Jahuel, Buín, 45 km south, T362 2520 (362 2590 weekends), www.santarita.cl, good tour in English and Spanish, US$10 (free if you dine in the restaurant), reserve 2 days in advance, daily except Sun at specific times, getting there: take a bus from Terminal San Borja to Alto Jahuel.* Santiago tour operators (eg TourisTur) offer full-day tours to vineyards, US$40 for two.

Upper Maipo Valley
Southeast of Santiago is the rugged, green valley of the **Cajón del Maipo**. A road runs through the villages of San José de Maipo, Melocotón and San Alfonso, near which is the **Cascada de Animas** waterfall. At **El Volcán** (1,400 m), 21 km beyond San Alfonso, there are astounding views, but little else (the village was wiped away in a landslide). From El Volcán the road (very poor condition) runs 14 km east to the warm natural baths at **Baños Morales** ① *from Oct, US$4, brown water*; no mains electricity in the village. About 12 km further east up the mountain are **Baños Colina**, hot thermal springs. This area is popular at weekends and holiday times, but is otherwise deserted. There are horses for hire. If visiting this area or continuing further up the mountain, be prepared for military checks. There are no shops, so take food (local goat's cheese may be sold at the roadside, or at farmhouses).

Ski resorts
There are six main ski resorts near Santiago, four of them around the mountain village of **Farellones**. Farellones, on the slopes of Cerro Colorado at 2,470 m, only 32 km from the capital and reached by road in under 90 minutes, was the first ski resort built in Chile. Now it is more of a service centre for the three other resorts, but it provides accommodation, has a good beginners area with fairly basic equipment for hire and is connected by lift to El Colorado. Popular at weekends, it has several large restaurants. It offers beautiful views for 30 km across 10 Andean peaks and incredible sunsets. Daily ski-lift ticket, US$42, allows access to El Colorado; a combined ticket for all four resorts is also available, US$40-50 depending on season. One-day return shuttles are available from Santiago, US$10; enquire **Ski Club Chile** ① *Goyenechea Candelaria 4750, Vitacura (north of Los Leones Golf Club), T211 7341.*

El Colorado ① *www.elcolorado.cl*, is 8 km further up Cerro Colorado and has a large ski lodge at the base, offering all facilities, and a restaurant higher up. There are 16 lifts giving access to a large intermediate ski area with some steeper slopes. Daily lift ticket US$42 (including Farellones ski-lifts). **La Parva**, nearby at 2,816 m, is the upper class Santiago weekend resort with 30 pistes and 14 lifts, 0900-1730. Accommodation is in a chalet village and there are some good bars in high season. Good intermediate to advanced skiing, not suitable for beginners. Lift ticket, US$26; equipment rental, US$20-35 depending on quality.

Valle Nevado ① *T02-477 7000, www.vallenevado.com*, is 16 km from Farellones and owned by Spie Batignolles of France. It offers the most modern ski facilities in Chile with 34 runs, 40 km of slopes and 41 lifts. The runs are well prepared and are suitable for intermediate level and beginners. There is a ski school and heli-skiing. Lift ticket US$40 weekdays, US$52 weekends. In summer, this is a good walking area, but altitude sickness can be a problem.

Portillo ① *www.skiportillo.cl*, 2,855 m, is 145 km north of Santiago and 62 km east of Los Andes near the customs post on the route to Argentina. One of Chile's best-known resorts, Portillo is on the Laguna del Inca, 5½ km long and 1½ km wide; this lake, at an altitude of 2,835 m, has no outlet, is frozen over in winter, and its depth is not known. It is surrounded on three sides by accessible mountain slopes. The 23 runs are varied and well prepared, connected by 12 lifts, two of which open up the off-piste areas. This is an excellent family resort, with a highly regarded ski school. Cheap packages can be arranged at the beginning of and out of season. Lift ticket US$40, equipment hire US$30. There are boats for fishing in the lake (afternoon winds can make the homeward pull much longer than the outward pull). Out of season this is another good area for walking, but get detailed maps before setting out.

Lagunillas is 67 km southeast of Santiago in the Cajón del Maipo ① *www.skilagunillas.cl*. Accommodation is in the lodges of the **Club Andino de Chile** (see Skiing page 618). Lift ticket US$25; long T-bar and poma lifts, US$15; easy field, with 13 pistes and four ski-lifts. Being lower than the other resorts, its season is shorter, but it is also cheaper.

Santiago to Argentina

The route across the Andes via the Cristo Redentor tunnel is one of the major crossings to Argentina. Before travelling check on weather and road conditions beyond Los Andes. See International Buses, page 620. Some 77 km north of Santiago is the farming town of **Los Andes**. There is a monument to the Clark brothers, who built the Transandine Railway to Mendoza (now disused), and several workshops where hand-painted ceramics are made (the largest is Cala, Rancagua y Gen Freire). The town has several hotels and a tourist office on the main plaza, opposite the post office. The road to Argentina follows the Aconcagua valley for 34 km until it reaches the village of **Río Blanco** (1,370 m). East of Río Blanco the road climbs until Juncal where it zig-zags steeply through a series of 29 hairpin bends at the top of which is Portillo.

Border with Argentina Los Libertadores The old pass, with the statue of Christ the Redeemer (**Cristo Redentor**), is above the tunnel on the Argentine side. On the far side of the Andes the road descends 203 km to Mendoza. The 4 km long tunnel is open 24 hours September-May, 0700-2300 Chilean time June-August, toll US$5. Note that this pass is closed after heavy snowfall, when travellers may be trapped at the customs complex on either side of the border. The Chilean border post of Los Libertadores is at Portillo, 2 km from the tunnel. Bus and car passengers are dealt with separately. Bicycles must be taken through on a pick-up. There may be long delays during searches for fruit, meat and vegetables, which may not be imported into Chile. A Casa de Cambio is in the customs building in Portillo. Note that, entering Agentina, Chilean emigration, Argentine immigration and all customs formalities are done at the Argentine check point, while entering Chile you do everything on the Chilean side.

● Sleeping

Upper Maipo Valley *p623*

B pp **Refugio Alemán Lo Valdés**, 14 km east of El Volcán, just after Baños Morales, T220 7610 or T09-220 8525, www.refugiolovaldes.com. Stone-built chalets in a splendid region, full board, generator, good food, good for mountain excursions, open all year.

D **Pensión Díaz**, Río Maipo s/n, Manzana C, sitio 10, T861 1496. Basic, F for singles, good food.

E pp **Res El Tambo**, Baños Colina, full board, restaurant, also camping. No shops so take food.

F pp **Res Los Chicos Malos**, Baños Morales, T288 5380. Comfortable with breakfast, fresh bread, good meals, cabañas and a campsite.

Ski resorts *p623*

L **Hotel Portillo**, Portillio, reservations: Renato Sánchez 4270, Las Condes, T02-263 0606, www.skiportillo.cl. Lakefront suites, family apartments and bunk rooms without or with bath (from B up), on the shore of Laguna del Inca. Cinema, nightclub, swimming pool, sauna and medical service, parking charges even if you go for a meal, self-service lunch, open all year.

AL **Condominio Nueva Parva**, La Parva, reservations in Santiago at Av El Bosque Norte 0177, p 2, T02-339 8482, www.skilaparva.cl. Good hotel and restaurant.

AL **Posada Farellones**, Farellones, T02-201 3704, www.skifarellones.com. Price is for half-board. Cosy and warm, Swiss-style, decent restaurant, satellite tv and games room, transport to slopes.

C pp **Refugio Club Alemán Andino**, Los Cóndores 1451, T264 9899, www.refugio aleman.cl, see page 618. Hospitable, good food.

Hotel and apartment accommodation for weekly rental in El Colorado. Also several hotels (in our L bracket) and restaurants in Valle Nevado.

Santiago to Argentina *p624*

AL Baños El Corazón, at San Esteban, 2 km north of Los Andes, T034-482852, www.termaselcorazon.cl. Full board, swimming pool; thermal baths extra, take bus San Esteban/El Cariño (US$0.60).

⊖ Transport

Pomaire *p623*

Bus From Santiago take the Melipilla bus from outside the San Borja terminal, every few mins, US$1.50 each way, Rutabus 78 goes on the motorway, 1 hr, other buses via Talagante take 1 hr 25 mins (alight at side road to Pomaire, 2-3 km from town, colectivos every 10-15 mins – these buses are easier to take than the infrequent, direct buses).

Upper Maipo Valley *p623*

Bus From Santiago, Plaza Italia every 15 mins, or from metro station Bellavista La Florida on Metro Line 5 (follow signs to Transporte Intermodal) to San José de Maipo every 30 mins, 2 hrs, US$1.50; about every 2 hrs to El Volcán, 2½ hrs; to **Baños Morales**, 1200 daily from Plaza Italia, returns 1745, US$4.30, 3 hrs; buy return on arrival to ensure seat back. Otherwise hitch.

Ski resorts *p623*

Bus From Santiago leave from Av Apoquindo 4900 (Escuela Militar Metro), daily from 0730 in season, essential to book in advance, **Ski Total**, T246 6881, US$15 return. **Centro de Esqui El Colorado**, T02-246 3344, leaves from same place daily at 0800 in season to Farellones and El Colorado. Also **Manzur Expediciones**, Sótero del Rio 475, of 507, T777 4284. Wed, Sat and Sun 0830 from Baquedano metro in season to Farellones, Valle Nevado, El Colorado, Lagunillas and Portillo. It is easy to hitch from the junction of Av Las Condes/El Camino Farellones (YPF petrol station in the middle), reached by a Barnechea bus. Portillo is easily reached by any bus from Santiago or Los Andes to **Mendoza**; you may have to hitch back. Public transport goes up to San José de Maipo, 17 km west of the resort. Bus from Metro Parque O' Higgins, Av Norte-Sur, or west side of Plaza Ercilla, every 15 mins, US$1, 2 hrs.

Santiago to Argentina *p624*

Bus Terminal is 1 block from the plaza. To **Santiago** US$3. To **Mendoza** (Argentina); Mendoza buses drop at **Portillo** ski resort, US$10.

Valparaíso and around

Sprawling over a crescent of forty-two hills (cerros) that rear up from the sea, Valparaíso, the capital of V Región, is unlike any other Chilean city. The main residential areas obey little order in their layout and the cerros have a bohemian, slightly anarchic atmosphere. Here you will find mansions mingling with some of Chile's worst slums and many legends of ghosts and spirits. It is an important naval base and, with the new Congress building, it is also the seat of the Chilean parliament. Pacific beaches close to the capital include the international resort of Viña del Mar, Reñaca, Concón and several others. On the same stretch of coast is the port of San Antonio. This coastline enjoys a Mediterranean climate; the cold sea currents and coastal winds produce much more moderate temperatures than in Santiago and the central valley. Rainfall is moderate in winter and the summers are dry and sunny.

Valparaíso → *Phone code: 032. Colour map 8, grid B1. Population: 300,000.*

First settled in 1542 (but not officially 'founded' until the end of the 20th century), Valparaíso became a small port used for trade with Peru. It was raided by pirates, including Sir Francis Drake, at least seven times in the colonial period. The city prospered from independence more than any other Chilean town. It was used in the 19th century by commercial agents from Europe and the US as their trading base in the southern Pacific and became a major international banking centre as well as the key port for US shipping between the East Coast and California (especially during the gold rush) and European ships that had rounded Cape Horn. Its decline was the result of the development of steam ships which stopped instead at the coal mines around Concepción and the opening of the trans-continental railway in the United States and then the Panama Canal in 1914. It then declined further owing to the development of a container port in San Antonio, the shift of banks to Santiago and the move of the middle-classes to nearby Viña del Mar, but Valparaíso is now reviving. It is officially the Cultural Capital of Chile and much work is being done to renovate the historical centre and museums and to build new galleries.

Ins and outs

Getting there To Valparaíso from the international airport at Pudahuel: take a bus to Pajaritos, US$3, cross the platform and take a bus to Valparaíso. To return to the airport, catch any Santiago bus and ask to be let off at the 'paradero de taxis' before the Cruce de Pudahuel. Taxis wait here to go to the airport for US$6.65 (about 7 minutes' ride, compared with an hour if you go into Santiago). Taxis run 0700-2000 (2300 in summer). Only take a taxi with an official Airport Taxi sticker (pirates overcharge). The long distance bus terminal is on Pedro Montt 2800 block, corner of Rawson, 1 block from Av Argentina. ▶▶ See Transport, page 632, for full details.

Getting around Buses are frequent in El Plan, which is also served by a trolley bus (see below). Ascensores connect the lower and upper cities, as do taxis, colectivos and certain bus routes (fares and some routes are given under Transport, page 632).

Tourist offices Municipalidad ① *Condell 1490, Oficina 102, Mon-Fri 0830-1400, 1530-1730*. Also by Muelle Prat, the pier off Plaza Sotomayor ① *Nov-Mar, Mon-Fri 1030-1430, 1600-2000 (closed late 2006 for refurbishment)*; two kiosks meanwhile on Plaza Sotomayor and Plaza Italia. **Note** There are also two private kiosks at the bus terminal which give details on, and transport to, selected hotels. If you want impartial advice, go to one of the municipal offices.

Safety Robbery is an occasional problem in El Puerto and around the ascensores on Av Argentina. The upper outskirts of town, while offering amazing views, are not the safest places, particularly after dark. The poorer and rougher districts tend to be those furthest from the centre. Also, be aware that Calle Chacabuco (on which some hotels are located) is the pick-up point for local rent-boys, and between Plazas Echaurren and Aduana is the 'barrio chino' or red light district, both pretty seedy areas at night.

Sights

Little of the city's colonial past survived the pirates, tempests, fires and earthquakes of the period. Most of the principal buildings date from after the devastating earthquake of 1906 (further serious earthquakes occurred in July 1971 and in March 1985) though some impression of its 19th century glory can be gained from the banking area of the lower town which is known as **El Plan**. This is the business centre, with once fine office buildings on narrow streets strung along the edge of the bay. Above, covering the hills ('cerros'), is a fantastic, multicoloured agglomeration of fine mansions, tattered houses and shacks, scrambled in oriental confusion along the narrow back streets. Superb views over the bay are offered from most of the 'cerros'. The lower and upper cities are connected by steep winding roads, flights of steps and 15 ascensores or funicular railways dating from the period 1883-1914. The most unusual of these is **Ascensor Polanco** (entrance from Calle Simpson, off Avenida Argentina, a few blocks from the bus station), which is in two parts, the first of which is a 160 m horizontal tunnel through the rock, the second a vertical lift to the summit on which there is a *mirador*. Bag-snatching is not uncommon in El Puerto (the old port). One of the best ways to see the lower city is on the historic **trolley bus**, which takes a circular route from the Congress to the port (US$0.45). Some of the cars, imported from Switzerland and the US, date from the 1930s. Another good viewpoint is from top of Ascensor Barón, near the bus terminal.

The old heart of the city is the **Plaza Sotomayor**, dominated by the former Intendencia (Government House), now used as the seat of the admiralty. Opposite is a fine monument to the 'Heroes of Iquique' (see page 660). Bronze plaques on the Plaza illustrate the movement of the shoreline over the centuries and an opening, protected by a glass panel, shows parts of the original quay, uncovered when a car park was being excavated. The modern passenger quay is one block away (with poor quality, expensive handicraft shops) and nearby is the railway station for trains to Viña del Mar and Limache. The streets of El Puerto run on either side from Plaza Sotomayor. Serrano runs northwest for two blocks to the Plaza Echaurren, the oldest plaza in Valparaíso, once the height of elegance, today the home of sleeping drunks. Nearby stands the stucco church of **La Matriz**, built in 1842 on the site of the first church in the city. Remnants of the old colonial city can be found in the hollow known as El Puerto, grouped round La Matriz. **Museo del Mar Almirante Cochrane** ① *Merlet 195, Tue-Sun 1000-1800, free*, has temporary exhibitions and has good views over the port. Take Ascensor Cordillera from C Serrano, off Plaza Sotomayor, to Cerro Cordillera; at the top, on Plazuela Eleuterio Ramírez, take C Merlet to the left (a slightly dodgy area).

Viña del Mar and around

→ Phone code: 032. Colour map 8, grid B1. Population: 304,203.

Northeast of Valparaíso via Avenida España which runs along a narrow belt between the shore and precipitous cliffs is one of South America's leading seaside resorts, Viña del Mar. A mixture of fashionable seaside destinations and fishing communities lines the coast to the north, while south of Valparaíso are more popular resorts at the mouth of the Río Maipo. Pablo Neruda's famous seaside home at Isla Negra is also found here. For a change from the sea visit La Campana national park with its native woodlands, panoramic views and Darwinian associations. For **tourist information** in Viña del Mar try **Sernatur** ① *Valparaíso 507, of 305, T268 3355, infovalparaiso@sernatur.cl.* Municipal office on Plaza Vergara.

The older part of Viña del Mar is situated on the banks of a dried-up estuary, the Marga Marga, which is crossed by bridges. Around Plaza Vergara and the smaller Plaza Sucre to its south are the **Teatro Municipal** (1930) and the exclusive **Club de Viña**, built in 1910. The municipally owned Quinta Vergara, formerly the residence of the shipping entrepreneur Francisco Alvarez, lies two blocks south. The **Palacio Vergara**, in the gardens, houses the **Museo de Bellas Artes** and the **Academia de Bellas Artes** ① *T268 0618, museum Tue-Sun 1000-1400, 1500-1800, US$1.* Part of the grounds is a playground, and there is a modern outdoor auditorium where concerts are performed in the summer, and in February an international song festival, one of the premier music events is held. Tickets from the Municipal theatre, or Ticketmaster.

On a headland overlooking the sea is **Cerro Castillo**, the summer palace of the President of the Republic. Just north, on the other side of the lagoon is the Casino, built in the 1930s and set in beautiful gardens, US$5 (open all year). It now includes a five-star hotel, see Sleeping, below.

The main beaches, Acapulco and Mirasol are located to the north, but south of Cerro Castillo is Caleta Abarca, also popular. The coastal route north to Reñaca provides lovely views over the sea. East of the centre is the **Valparaíso Sporting Club** with a racecourse (meetings every Friday) and playing fields. North of here in the hills are the **Granadilla Golf Club** and a large artificial lake, the **Laguna Sausalito**. Nearby is the **Estadio Sausalito**, home to Everton football club ① *US$2.50, children under 11, US$1.75, getting there: take colectivo*

Viña del Mar

Sleeping	Girasoles de	Eating	Fellini 9
Agora 1	Agua Santa 11	Africa 1	La Flor de Chile 7
Andalué 2	Offenbacher Hof 6	Alster 2	Las Delicias del Mar 4
Cap Ducal 3	Residencia 555 10	Café Journal 3	Samoiedo 5
Del Mar 4	Residencial Blanchait 8	Club Giacomo 8	Shawarma Kabab 10
Gala 5	Residencial Capric 9	El Otro Estilo 6	
Genross 7	Vancouver Viña 12	Enjoy del Mar 12	

No 19 from C Viana. It has an excellent tourist and sports complex with swimming pools, boating, tennis courts, sandy beaches, water skiing, restaurants, etc.

Museo de la Cultura del Mar ① *in the Castillo Wolff, on the coast near Cerro Castillo, T262 5427, Tue-Sat 1000-1300, 1430-1800, Sun 1000-1400*, contains a collection on the life and work of the novelist and maritime historian, Salvador Reyes. **Palacio Rioja** ① *Quillota 214, Tue-Sun, visitors 1000-1400, 1500-1800, US$1.25*, was built in 1906 by a prominent local family and now used for official municipal receptions, ground floor preserved in its original state. Recommended. **Museo Sociedad Fonk** ① *C 4 Norte 784, Tue-Fri 1000-1800, Sat-Sun 1000-1400,US$2, children US$0.60*, is an archaeological and natural history museum, with objects from Easter Island and the Chilean mainland, including Mapuche silver. Recommended.

Jardín Botánico Nacional ① *8 km southeast of the city, US$2, getting there: take bus 20 from Plaza Vergara*. Formerly the estate of the nitrate baron Pascual Baburizza, this is now administered by CONAF. Covering 405 ha, it contains over 3,000 species from all over the world and a collection of Chilean cacti, but the species are not labelled. It's a good place for a picnic; there's also a canopy adventure trail, with ziplines linking trees within the park.

Resorts north of Viña del Mar

North of Viña del Mar the coast road runs through **Las Salinas**, a popular beach between two towering crags, **Reñaca** (long beach, upmarket, good restaurants) and **Cochoa**, where there is a sealion colony 100 m offshore, to **Concón** (18 km). Beware if cycling from Valparaíso, the road is very bad with lots of traffic. There is a much faster inland road, between Viña del Mar and Concón, on the southern shore of a bay at the mouth of the Río Aconcagua. It has six beaches and is famous for its seafood restaurants. Horses can be hired here. **Quintero** (*Population 16,000*) 23 km north of Concón, is a slightly dilapidated fishing town on a rocky peninsula with lots of small beaches (hotels and residenciales).

Horcón (also known locally as Horcones) is set back in a cove surrounded by cliffs, a pleasant small village, mainly of wooden houses. On the beach young travellers sell cheap and unusual jewellery and trinkets, while horses drag the small fishing boats out of the sea. Vegetation is tropical with many cacti on the cliff tops. Packed out in January-February, the rest of the year it is a charming place, populated by fishermen and artists. A new condominium by Playa Caucau has off-set some of the charm of the village. Further north is well-to-do **Maitencillo** (*Population 1,200*), with a wonderful long beach, heaving in high summer but a ghost town off season. Some 14 km beyond is **Zapallar** (*Population 2,200*) a fashionable resort with a lovely beach. A hint of its former glory is given by a number of fine mansions along Avenida Zapallar. At **Cachagua**, 3 km south, a colony of penguins on an offshore island may be viewed from the northern end of the beach; take binoculars. **Papudo** (*Phone code 033, Population 2,500*), 10 km further north, was the site of a naval battle in November 1865 in which the Chilean vessel Esmeralda captured the Spanish ship Covadonga. Following the arrival of the railway Papudo rivalled Viña del Mar as a fashionable resort in the 1920s but it has long since declined. With its lovely beach and fishing port, it is an idyllic spot.

Resorts south near the mouth of the Río Maipo

San Antonio is a commercial centre for this part of the coast. It is a container and fishing port and is the terminal for the export of copper brought by rail from El Teniente mine, near Rancagua. To the south are the resorts of Llolleo and Rocas de Santo Domingo. **Cartagena**, 8 km north of San Antonio, is the most popular resort on this part of the coast. The centre is around the hilltop Plaza de Armas. To the south is the picturesque Playa Chica, overlooked by many of the older hotels and restaurants; to the north is the Playa Larga. Between the two a promenade runs below the cliffs; high above hang old houses, some in disrepair but offering spectacular views. Cartagena is packed in summer, but out of season it is a good centre for visiting nearby resorts of Las Cruces, El Tabo and El Quisco. There are many hotels and bus connections are good. For more information on Cartagena, look at www.cartagena.cl

North of Cartagena in the village of **Isla Negra** is the beautifully-restored **Museo-Casa Pablo Neruda** ① *T035-461284, US$6, guided tour obligatory, in Spanish, French or English, summer Tue-Sun 1000-2000, rest of year Tue-Fri 1000-1400, 1500-1800*. Bought by Neruda in 1939, and constantly added to over time, this house, overlooking the sea, was his writing retreat in his later years. It contains artefacts gathered by Neruda from all over the world. Neruda and his last wife, Mathilde, are buried here; the touching gravestone is beside the house. The house has a good café specializing in Neruda's own recipes.

Parque Nacional La Campana

This 8,000-ha park ⓘ US$3, includes Cerro La Campana (1,828 m) which Darwin climbed in 1836 and Cerro El Roble (2,200 m). Some of the best views in Chile can be seen from the top. Near Ocoa there are areas of Chilean palms (*kankán* – which give edible, walnut-sized coconuts in March-April), now found in its natural state in only two locations in Chile. There are three entrances: at Granizos (from which the hill is climbed), reached by paved road from Limache, 4 km west, via Olmué; at Cajón Grande (with natural bathing pools), reached by unpaved road which turns off the Olmué-Granizos road; at Palmar de Ocoa to the north reached by unpaved road (10 km) leading off the Pan-American Highway at Km 100 between Hijuelas and Llaillay.

⊜ Sleeping

Viña del Mar *p633, map p633*
There are lots of small hotels in the Norte-Poniente quadrant, mostly **B**; discounts often possible in low season. There are also lots of cheaper places around Von Schroeders y Valparaíso, but this can be a rough area at night. Out of season agencies rent furnished apartments. In season it's cheaper to stay in Valparaíso.
L Hotel del Mar, Perú y Los Héroes, T250 0600, www.hoteldelmar.cl. Very expensive, luxurious hotel on the upper floors of the casino, panoramic views, suites, pool, spa, tours, several restaurants.
L-AL Gala, Arlegui 273, loc 10, T232 1500, www.gala hotel.cl. All mod-cons in excellent suites, and wide range of business facilities.
A Cap Ducal, Marina 51, T262 6655, www.cap ducal.cl. Old mansion charm – a ship-shaped building literally overhanging the ocean, with an elegant restaurant, serving good seafood.
B Agora, 5½ Poniente 253, T269 4669, www.hotel agora.cl. On a quiet side street, brightly coloured rooms, most with full-size bathtub. Wifi zones, English spoken, helpful staff (on 4 floors but no lift).
B Andalué, 6 Poniente 124, T268 4147, F268 4148. With breakfast, central. Recommended.
B Hostal Girasoles de Agua Santa, Pasaje Monterey 78, off Agua Santa, T248 2339, www.hostalgirasoles.cl. Upscale B&B in large wooden house on a quiet sidestreet, **D** pp with HI card, shared bath, pleasant, but not so convenient for the beach (25-min walk) and a bit overpriced. Also has a branch in Cerro Alegre, Valparaíso.
B-C Offenbacher Hof, Balmaceda 102, T262 1483, www.offenbacher-hof.cl. Large wooden house in a quiet residential street overlooking the city centre, peaceful, helpful. The best rooms are spacious with cable TV. Recommended.
B-C Residencia 555, 5 Norte 555, T273 9035, residencial@vtr.net. **D** for singles. Characterful wooden house with antique furniture. Rooms range widely in size and have cable TV, good value, though advance reservations difficult as deposit required and credit cards not accepted.
C Genross, Paseo Monterrey 18, T266 1711, genrosshotel@hotmail.com. Beautiful mansion, airy rooms, garden patio and sitting room, informative, English spoken.

C Vancouver Viña, 5 Norte 650, T248 2983, www.hotelvancouvervina.cl. Carpeted modest rooms with cable TV, good value, café downstairs.
D Res Blanchait, Valparaíso 82A, T297 4949, www.blanchait.cl. Breakfast extra, with hot water, good service.
D-E Res Capric, von Schroeders 39, T297 8295. Dark rooms, with breakfast, TV (special rates for HI card holders).

Resorts north of Viña del Mar *p634*
Concón
Several *cabañas*, including Los Romeros, T281 3671 and Río Mar, T281 4644, both **C**, and motels.

Horcón
Lots of cabañas in Horcón, generally **C-D** for 4 people, shop around.
D Arancibia, T279 6169. **E** without bath, pleasant gardens, good food.
D-E Juan Esteban, Pasaje Miramar, Casa 2, T279 6056, www.juanesteban.cl. English spoken, nice terrace with view, rooms and well equipped cabañas, **F** pp for 4-6. Recommended.

Papudo
C Carande, Chorrillos 89, T033-791105. Best in town (but many more), quiet.
C De Peppino, Concha 609, T033-791108. Cabins for 4-6 people.

Resorts south near the mouth of the Río Maipo *p634*
AL-A Rocas de Santo Domingo, La Ronda 130, San Antonio, T035-444356, F444494. Good, including decent breakfast, helpful staff, restaurant, 20 minutes to sea.
E Violeta, Condell 140, Cartagena, T035-450372. Swimming pool, good views.
F pp Hostal Casa Azul, Av Santa Luisa s/n, Isla Negra, T035-461154. Shared bath, hot showers, garden (camping available), kitchen and laundry, breakfast included, helpful. Highly recommended.
F pp Res Carmona, Playa Chica, Cartagena, T035-450485. Small rooms, basic but clean, good value.
F pp Res Paty's, Alacalde Cartagena 295, Cartagena, T035-450469. Nice spot, good value.

🍴 Eating

Viña del Mar p633, map p633
Many good bars and restaurants on and around
San Martín between 2 and 8 Norte; cuisine
ranging from Austrian to Mexican, and including
Argentine, Chinese and Italian. Cheap bars
and restaurants around Calle Valparaíso and
Von Schroeders. Not too safe at night.
₹₹₹ **Fellini**, 3 Norte 88, T297 5742. Wide range
of fresh pasta dishes in delicious sauces, good.
₹₹₹-₹₹ **El Otro Estilo**, 6 Norte 357, T288 3144.
Delightful tiny bistro, serving good value set lunch
and more adventurous à la carte dishes in the
evening. Simple décor but good food and service.
₹₹₹-₹₹ **Enjoy del Mar**, Av Perú s/n, T250 0785.
Modern restaurant serving everything from
gourmet dishes to barbecues and fast food,
all on an open terrace on the seafront.
₹₹₹-₹₹ **Las Delicias del Mar**, San Martín 459.
Award-winning Basque seafood restaurant,
"brilliant food, wine and service".
₹₹ **La Dieta de Nos**, 3 Norte y 5 Poniente, T246
0235. For people with special dietary needs: dishes
for diabetics, hypertensives and vegetarians.
₹ **Africa**, Valparaíso 324. Extraordinarily kitsch
façade, pasta and fast food.
₹ **Café Journal**, Alvarez near Von Schroeders.
Great set lunch, good beer, student favourite
at night. Recommended.
₹ **Club Giacomo**, Villanelo 131. A Viña institution,
traditional set lunches with a pool hall annex.
₹ **La Flor de Chile**, 8 Norte 607 y 1 Poniente.
Good, typical Chilean food.
₹ **Shawarma kabab**, Ecuador 255. Cheap,
authentic middle-eastern fare, including
kebabs and stuffed vine leaves.

Cafés

Alster, Valparaíso 225. Elegant but pricey.
Samoiedo, Valparaíso 637. Confitería,
old-time café.

🌙 Bars and clubs

Viña del Mar p633, map p633
Barlovento, 2 Norte y 5 Poniente. The designer
bar in Viña, on 3 floors with a lovely roof terrace,
serves great pizzas and good beer.

⛰ Activities and tours

Resorts north of Viña del Mar p634
Ritoque Expediciones, just north of Concón,
T032-281 6344/09-730 5212 , www.ritoque
expediciones.cl. Horse riding, full- or half-day
trips to lakes, sand dunes, scrubland, beaches,
you can help herd cows or just gallop, also full
moon rides, can collect from Valaparaíso
or Viña, English spoken. Highly recommended.

⊝ Transport

Viña del Mar p633, map p633
Bus 2 blocks east of Plaza Vergara at Av
Valparaíso y Quilpué. To **Santiago**, US$6, 1½ hrs,
frequent, same companies as for Valparaíso from
Pajaritos in Santiago, heavily booked in advance
for travel on Sun afternoons. Long distance
services: prices and itineraries similar to Valparaíso.
Note Beware pickpockets by shops and terminal.
Train Services on the Valparaíso Metropolitan
line (Merval) stop at Viña (details under Valparaíso).

Resorts north of Viña del Mar p634
Bus From Valparaíso and Viña del Mar: to
Concón several, eg bus 601, 602, US$0.75,
frequent; to **Quintero** and **Horcón**, **Sol del
Pacífico**, every 30 mins, US$2, 2 hrs; to **Zapallar**
and **Papudo**, **Sol del Pacífico**, 4 a day (2 before
0800, 2 after 1600), US$4. All of these from
Av Libertad in Viña, or Errázuriz in Valparaíso.

**Resorts south near the mouth of the Río
Maipo** p634
Bus From San Antonio: buses to **Valparaíso**,
Pullman Bus, every 30 mins until 2000, US$4;
to **Santiago**, Pullman Bus, every 30 mins in
summer, US$4. Regular bus services to **Isla Negra**
from Santiago (**Pullman Bus**) and Valparaíso
(**Pullman Lago Peñuelas**), 1½ hrs, US$4.

Parque Nacional La Campana p635
Euro Express micros from C Errázuriz in
Valparaíso and 1 Norte in Viña del Mar go to within
1 km of Granizos and Cajón Grande, US$1, 1½ hrs,
summer only, or take the train to Limache (1 hr),
and a "Granizo 45" micro or any colectivo marked
"Olmue" to Granizos. No public transport to Ocoa.
Get a bus to La Calera and bargain with a taxi or
colectivo driver. Expect to pay US$15-20.

🛈 Directory

Viña del Mar p633, map p633
Banks Many Redbanc ATMs on Libertad
near 7 y 8 Norte and on Arlegui; also on
C Valparaíso (but this is not a safe area at night).
Many casas de cambio on Arlegui; shop around
for best rates and avoid changing money on the
street, especially if alone. **Cultural centres**
Centro Cultural, Libertad 250 in the Palacio
Carrasco, holds regular exhibitions. **Internet**
Several the length of Calle Valparaíso,
prices range from US$0.60-0.80 per hr.
Telephones Several on C Valparaíso.

North of Santiago

Along the coast is a mixture of fishing villages, deserted beaches and popular resorts, while inland the scenery is wonderfully dramatic but little visited. The land becomes less fertile as you go further north. Ovalle is a good centre for trips to see petroglyphs and the coastal forests at the Parque Nacional Fray Jorge. The largest resort is La Serena, from where access can be made to the Elqui Valley, one of Chile's major pisco-producing regions and one of the world's major astronomical centres.

From the Río Aconcagua to the Río Elqui is a transitional zone between the fertile heartland and the northern deserts. The first stretch of the Pan-American Highway from Santiago is inland through green valleys with rich blue clover and wild artichokes. North of La Ligua, the Highway mainly follows the coastline, passing many beautiful coves, alternately rocky and sandy, with good surf, though the water is very cold. The valleys of the main rivers, the Choapa, Limarí and Elqui, are intensively farmed using irrigation to produce fruit and vegetables. There is a striking contrast between these lush valley floors and the arid mountains with their dry scrub and cactus. In some areas, condensation off the sea provides sufficient moisture for woods to grow. Rainfall is rare and occurs only in winter. On the coast the average temperature is 15°C in winter, 23°C in summer; the interior is dry, with temperatures reaching 33°C in summer, but it is cooler in winter and very cold at night.

Ovalle to La Serena

Ovalle and around → *Phone code: 053. Colour map 8, grid A1. Population: 53,000.*

This town lies inland, 412 km north of Santiago, in the valley of the Río Limarí, a fruit-growing and mining district. Market days are Monday, Wednesday, Friday and Saturday, till 1600; the market feria modelo) is off Benavente (east of the centre). The town is famous for its talabarterías (saddleries), products made of locally mined lapis lazuli, goats cheese and dried fruits. Wine is produced in the Limarí Valley and tours to *bodegas* such as Tamaya and Tabila are arranged under the Ruta del Vino heading. **Museo del Limarí**① *in the old railway station, Covarrubias y Antofagasta, Tue-Fri 0900-1300, 1500-1900, Sat-Sun 1000-1300, US$1, free on Sun,* has displays of petroglyphs and a good collection of Diaguita ceramics and other artefacts. Unofficial tourist information kiosk on the Plaza de Armas.

Monumento Nacional Valle del Encanto ① *about 22 km southwest of Ovalle, open all year, 0800-1800, US$2, getting there: no local bus service; you must take a southbound long distance bus and ask to be dropped off – 5 km walk to the valley; flag down a bus to return; alternatively, use a tour operator like Tres Valles, Libertad 496, T629650.* This is a most important archaeological site. Artefacts from hunting peoples from over 2,000 years ago have been found but the most visible remains date from the Molle culture (AD 700). There are over 30 petroglyphs as well as great boulders, distributed in six sites. There are camping facilities.

Termas de Socos ① *35 km southwest of Ovalle on the Pan-American Highway, bus US$2,* has a swimming pool and individual tubs fed by thermal springs, as well as sauna, jacuzzi and water massage (entrance US$9, very popular). It also boasts a reasonable hotel (see Sleeping, below) and a campsite (**G** per tent) nearby.

Monumento Natural Pichasca ① *47 km northeast of Ovalle, 0800-1800, US$4.30, getting there: daily buses from Ovalle to San Pedro pass the turn off about 42 km from the city, from here it is 3 km to the park and about 2 km more to sites of interest.* An unpaved and largely winding road leads to the park, which contains petrified tree trunks, archaeological remains, including a vast cave with vestiges of ancient roof paintings, and views of rock formations on the surrounding mountains.

Parque Nacional Fray Jorge① *90 km west of Ovalle and 110 km south of La Serena at the mouth of the Río Limarí, T620058, Sat, Sun and public holidays only, 0900-1600, last departure 1800, US$4.* Visits closely controlled owing to risk of fire. The Park is reached by a dirt road leading off the Pan-American Highway. It contains original forests which contrast with the otherwise barren surroundings. Receiving less than 113 mm of rain a year, the forests survive because of the almost constant covering of fog. Waterproof clothing is essential when you visit.

The good inland road between Ovalle and La Serena makes an interesting contrast to Ruta 5 (Panamericana), with a fine pass and occasional views of the Andes across cacti-covered plains and semi-desert mountain ranges. North of Ovalle 61 km a side road runs 44 km southeast (last 20 km very bad) to **Andacollo** (*Population 10,216, Altitude 1,050 m*). This old town, in an area of alluvial gold washing and manganese and copper mining, is one of the great pilgrimage sites in Chile. In the enormous **Basilica** (1893), 45 m high and with a capacity of 10,000, is the Virgen del Rosario de Andacollo. The **Fiesta Grande** from 23-27 December attracts 150,000 pilgrims. The ritual dances date from a pre-Spanish past. Colectivos run to the festival from Benavente, near Colocolo, in La Serena, but 'purists' walk (torch and good walking shoes essential). There is also a smaller festival, the Fiesta Chica on the first Sunday of October. The tourist office on the Plaza arranges tours to the Basilica and to mining operations.

Coquimbo → *Phone code: 051. Colour map 8, grid A1. Population: 106,000.*

On the same bay as La Serena, 84 km north of La Serena, is this important port, with one of the best harbours on the coast and major fish-processing plants. The city is strung along the north shore of a peninsula. On the south shore lies the suburb of Guayacán, with an iron-ore loading port, a steel church designed by Eiffel, an English cemetery and a 83-m high cross to mark the Millennium (US$2 to climb it). In 1981 heavy rain uncovered 39 ancient burials of humans and llamas which had been sacrificed; they are exhibited in a small **Museo del Sitio** ① *in the Plaza Gabriela Mistral, open Jan-Feb only, Mon-Sat 0930-2030, Sun 0930-1400, free, tourist information*. Tours of nearby islands with sealions go from beside the fish market, can be cold and rough but boats have blankets and life vests (US$2). Nearby is **La Herradura**, 2½ km from Coquimbo, slightly more upmarket and with the best beaches. Resorts further south, **Totoralillo** (12 km), **Guanaqueros** (37 km) and **Tongoy** (50 km), have good beaches and can be reached by rural buses or colectivos. A tourist kiosk in Plaza de Armas is open in the summer only.

La Serena → *Phone code: 051. Colour map 8, grid A1. Population: 120,000.*

La Serena, built on a hillside 2 km inland from Bahía de Coquimbo, is an attractive city and tourist centre, 11 km north of Coquimbo (473 km north of Santiago) and is the capital of IV Región (Coquimbo). The city was founded by Juan de Bohón, aide to Pedro de Valdivia, in 1544, destroyed by Diaguita Indians in 1546 and rebuilt by Francisco de Aguirre in 1549. The city was sacked by the English pirate Sharpe in 1680. In the colonial period the city was the main staging-post on the route north to Peru. In the 19th century the city grew prosperous from copper-mining. While retaining colonial architecture and churches, the present-day layout and style have their origins in the 'Plan Serena' drawn up in 1948 on the orders of Gabriel González Videla, a native of the city. Main **Sernatur** ① *Matta 461, of 108, in Edificio de Servicios Públicos (next to post office on the Plaza de Armas), T225199, infocoquimbo@ sernatur.cl, Mon-Fri 0845-1830 (2030 in summer), Sat-Sun 1000-1400 (1000-1400, 1600-2000 in summer). Kiosks at bus terminal (summer only) and Balmaceda y Prat, helpful, Mon-Sat 1100-1400, 1600-1900*. Also private kiosk at the bus terminal; do not confuse with Sernatur.

Around the attractive Plaza de Armas are most of the official buildings, including the Post Office, the **Cathedral** (built in 1844 and featuring a carillon which plays every hour) and the **Museo Histórico Regional** at the Casa González Videla ① *Tue-Sat 0900-1300, 1600-1900, Sun 1000-1300, US$1*, which includes several rooms on the man's life. Ticket are also valid for **Museo Arqueológico** ① *Cordovez y Cienfuegos, Tue-Sat 0900-1300, 1600-1900, Sun 1000-1300, US$1*. It has an outstanding collection of Diaguita and Molle Indian exhibits, especially of attractively decorated pottery, also Easter Island exhibits. There are 29 other churches, several of which have unusual towers. **La Recova**, the craft market, at Cienfuegos y Cantournet, includes a large display of handicrafts and, upstairs, several good restaurants. One block west of the Plaza de Armas is the **Parque Pedro de Valdivia** ① *daily 1000-2000, US$1.50*. One block south is the delightful **Parque Japonés**, "El Jardín del Corazón".

Avenida Francisco de Aguirre, a pleasant boulevard lined with statues and known as the Alameda, runs from the centre to the coast, terminating at the **Faro Monumental** *US$0.45*, a small, neo-colonial mock-castle and lighthouse, now a pub. A series of beaches stretch from here to Peñuelas, 6 km south, linked by the Av del Mar. Many apartment blocks, hotels, cabañas and restaurants have been built along this part of the bay. Most activity is around the middle of the beach, where swimming is safest. If you don't like crowds, head for the northern or southern extremes.

Elqui Valley

The valley of the Río Elqui is one of the most attractive oases in this part of northern Chile. There are orchards, orange groves, vineyards and mines set against the imposing, arid mountains. The Elqui Valley is the centre of pisco production with nine distilleries, the largest being Capel in Vicuña. Elqui is also well-known as a centre of mystical energy and is one of the main astronomical centres of the world, with three important observatories. Tour operators in La Serena and Coquimbo arrange tours to the smaller municipal observatory at Mamalluca near Vicuña.

At 2,200 m, 89 km southeast of La Serena in the Elqui Valley, 51 km south of Vicuña, **El Tololo** ① *www.ctio.noao.edu, visitors by permit only every Sat 0900-1200, 1300-1600; for permits (free) write to Casilla 603, La Serena, T051-205200, then pick your permit up before 1200 on the day before (the office is at Colina Los Pinos, on a hill behind the new University – personal applications can be made here for all three observatories), they will insist that you have private transport; you can hire a taxi, US$55 for the whole day, but you will require the registration number when you book* belongs to Aura, an association of US and Chilean universities. It possesses one of the largest telescopes in the southern hemisphere (4-m diameter), seven others and a radio telescope. At 2,240 m, 150 km northeast of La Serena **La Silla** ① *www.ls.eso.org, registration in advance in Santiago essential (Alonso de Córdoba 3107, Santiago, T02-463 3000) or write to Casilla 567, La Serena, T224527, every Sat, 1330-1700, except Jul-Aug* belongs to ESO (European Southern Observatory), and comprises 14 telescopes. From La Serena it is 114 km north along Route 5 to the turn-off, then another 36 km. At 2,510 m, 156 km northeast of La Serena, 30 km north of La Silla **Las Campanas** ① *T207301, or write to Casilla 601, La Serena, www.lco.cl, open with permission every Sat 1430-1730* belongs to the Carnegie Institute, has five

La Serena

Sleeping 🛏
Backpacker Lodging 1
Cabañas Bahía Drake 10
Casa Alejandro Muñoz 2
Casa de Huéspedes 3
Casa de María Pizarro 4
Celia Rivera 4
El Punto 5
Francisco de Aguirre 6

Gregoria Fernández 7
Hostal Croata 8
Hostal Pacífico 11
Hostal Villanueva
  de la Serena 16
La Serena Plaza 9
Residencial Carvajal 13
Residencial El Loa 12
Residencial Petit 14

Residencial Suiza 15

Eating 🍴
Bavaria 1
El Callejón 5
Daniela 2 3
Donde El Guatón 2
Govindas 6
La Mía Pizza 4

telescopes and is a smaller facility than the other two. To get there, follow Route 5 to the same junction as for La Silla, take the turning for La Silla and then turn north after 14 km. La Silla and Las Campanas can be reached without private transport by taking any bus towards Vallenar two hours, US$4, getting out at the junction (*desvío*) and hitch from there.

The road up the valley is paved as far as Pisco Elqui, 37 km beyond **Vicuña**, the valley's capital. This small, friendly town, 66 km east of La Serena, was founded in 1821. On the west side of the plaza are the municipal chambers, built in 1826 and topped in 1905 by a medieval-German-style tower, the Torre Bauer, imported by the German-born mayor of the time. The tourist office is on Plaza de Armas. There is an ATM. There are good views from Cerro La Virgen, north of town. The **Capel Pisco distillery** ① *1½ km east of Vicuña, to the right of the main road, guided tours (in Spanish) are offered Dec-Feb, daily 1000-1800, free, no booking required.* **Museo Gabriela Mistral** ① *Gabriela Mistral 759, www.dibam.cl/sdm_mgm_vicuna, Mon-Sat 1000-1900, Sun 1000-1800, US$1, students half price*, contains manuscripts, books, awards and many other details of the poet's life. Next door is the house where the poet was born. **Observatorio Astronómico Comunal de Vicuña** ① *Gabriela Mistral 260, Vicuña, T411352, www.mamalluca.org, on Cerro Mamalluca, 6 km north of Vicuña, 1500 m above sea level, offers tours to the public at 2030, 2230, 0030, 0230 in summer, 1830, 2030, 2230 in winter, price is US$6.65 for tour, including talk and viewing through telescope, plus US$2.85 for transport, guides in Spanish and English for groups of 5 or more, book in advance.*

From Vicuña a 46-km road runs south through the Andes to the village of **Río Hurtado**, a secluded, picturesque place in a spectacular valley. Beyond the village the old trading route from Argentina, known as the Inka Trail, leads to Vado Morrillas, 3 km west of Hurtado. Along the trail are rock paintings, old indigenous campsites and aqueducts.

From Vicuña the road runs through Paihuano (camping) to **Monte Grande**, where the schoolhouse where Gabriela Mistral lived and was educated by her sister is now a **museum** ① *C Principal s/n, T415015, Tue-Sun 1000-1300, 1500-1800 (till 1900 in Jan-Feb), US$0.80.* The poet's tomb is at the edge of town, opposite the Artesanos de Cochiguaz pisco distillery, which is open to the public. (Buses from the plaza in Vicuña.) Here the road forks, one branch leading to the Cochiguaz valley. There is no public transport. Along this road are several new age settlements; it is said that the valley is an important energy centre. There are several campsites. At night, there is no better place on earth to star gaze. When the moon is new, or below the horizon, the stars seem to be hanging in the air; spectacular shooting stars can be seen every couple of seconds, as can satellites crossing the night sky. Back on the main road, just south of Monte Grande, is the **Cavas del Valle** organic winery with free tastings and a sales room. The other branch road leads to **Pisco Elqui**, an attractive village with the newly restored church of Nuestra Señora del Rosario on a shady plaza. It's also famous for its night skies and beautiful scenery. Here there is the **Tres Erres** pisco plant, which is open to the public and gives guided tours in Spanish. There is a juice bar and pancake restaurant on the plaza and a well-stocked supermarket one block from the plaza. Horses can be hired, with or without guide, US$4 per hour with guide, worthwhile. Ask at the Hotel Elqui (Ramón Luis, T451168, is a recommended guide). Pisco Elqui is also a new age centre, where alternative therapies and massages are available.

Border Paso Agua Negra Paso Agua Negra (4,775 m) is reached by unpaved road from Guanta, 30 km past Rivadavia. Chilean immigration and customs at Juntas, 84 km west of the border, 88 km east of Vicuña. Border open 0800-1700; January-April only, check rest of year. No public transport beyond Rivadavia. Tell officials if you intend to camp between border posts.

● Sleeping

Ovalle and around *p637*
Accommodation is poor in Ovalle itself.
A **Termas de Socos**, Panamericana Norte Km 370, 35 km southwest of Ovalle, T053-198 2505, www.termasocos.cl. Reasonable hotel offering full board and access to thermal pools.
B **Turismo**, Victoria 295, T623258, Pleasant, comfortable, parking, modern.
C-D **Gran Hotel**, Vicuña Mackenna 210 (entrance through Galería Yagnam), T621084, yagnam@

terra.cl. Decent rooms, negotiate for a good price and a quiet room away from the main road.
E **Roxy**, Libertad 155, T620080. Constant hot water, big rooms, patio, welcoming. Recommended.
E **Venecia**, Libertad 261, T620968. Safe and welcoming, singles G. Recommended.

Parque Nacional Fray Jorge
Two campsites, one in the desert 3 km away at El Arrayancito and one at the admin area, both

with hot showers; also rooms available at
an old hacienda, **G** pp, and a cabaña, **B**.
Camping US$16 pp including park entry.

Coquimbo *p638*

Generally accommodation is much cheaper than
in La Serena. Several hotels in La Herradura.
D Iberia, Lastra 400, T312141, F326307. Cheaper
without bath, pleasant and recommended.
D Prat, Bilbao y Aldunate, T311845.
Comfortable, also pleasant, with breakfast.
E Vegamar, Las Heras 403, T311773.
With shared bath, basic.
Camping G Camping La Herradura, Av La
Marina 200, T263867, mac-food@ctinternet.cl.
Price for up to 5 people.

La Serena *p638, map p639*

Route 5 from La Serena to Coquimbo is lined with
cheap accommodation; Av del Mar, 500 m off the
highway, also hotels and other accommodation
(buses run along Route 5, not Av del Mar). The
tourist office in the bus terminal is helpful. Do not
be pressurized at the bus station into choosing
rooms. There is much more choice than touts
would have you believe. Similarly, do not be
pressurized to buy tours in hotels: established
agencies may give better service and deals.
A Francisco de Aguirre, Córdovez 210,
T222991, www.diegodealmagrohoteles.cl.
Recently refurbished, 4-star, with breakfast,
good rooms, pool, reasonable restaurant.
A La Serena Plaza, Francisco de Aguirre 0660,
T225665. Upmarket hotel by the beach with
spacious rooms, swimming pool, gym and
restaurant. Good value.
B Cabañas Bahia Drake, Av del Mar 1300,
T223367. Pleasant, fully-equipped *cabañas*
on the seafront, with swimming pool.
C-D El Punto, Andrés Bello 979, T228474,
www.punto.de. **F** pp without bath, with
breakfast, recently redecorated, tasteful,
comfortable, café, laundry, parking, book
exchange, English and German spoken, arranges
tours to Elqui Valley. Higwhly recommended.
D Casa Alejandro Muñoz, Brasil 720, T211619.
G for single. Rooms in family home in old part of
town, hot showers, good breakfast, garden,
English and French spoken, nice atmosphere.
D Gregoria Fernández, Andrés Bello 1067,
T224400, gregoria_fernandez@hotmail.com.
F-G for singles. Very helpful, good beds, some with
bath, close to terminal, excellent breakfast, garden,
good local information; if full she will divert you to
her mother's house, also good but less convenient
for the bus station. Highly recommended.
D Hostal Villanueva de La Serena, Colón 290,
T550260, www.hostalvillanueva.cl. Large rooms,
clean with hot water, TV and breakfast.

D Res Suiza, Cienfuegos 250, T216092,
residencial.suiza@terra.cl. With breakfast, good
beds, excellent value. Recommended.
D-E Casa de María Pizarro, Las Rojas 18,
T229282, www.hostalmariacasa.cl. Very
welcoming and helpful, near bus terminal,
laundry facilities, garden, camping, book in
advance, excellent value. Highly recommended.
D-E Hostal Croata, Cienfuegos 248, T/F224997,
hostalcroata@entelchile.net. **F** without bath,
with breakfast, kitchen and laundry facilities,
cable TV, patio, hospitable. Recommended.
E pp **Hostal Pacífico**, San Juan de Dios
Pení 339, T481018, www.residencialpacifico.cl,
cheaper in low season, internet, kitchen
and laundry, pleasant atmosphere,
charming hosts. With breakfast.
E pp **Amunátegui 315**. Kitchen facilities,
patio, good beds. Recommended.
E pp **Casa de Huéspedes**, El Santo 1410,
T213557. Convenient for bus terminal, including
breakfast, hot water, cable TV. Recommended.
E pp **Celia Rivera**, Las Rojas 21, T215838.
Near terminal, use of kitchen, nice place.
E Edith González, Los Carrera 889, T221941/
224978. **F** without bath, kitchen and laundry,
pick-up from bus terminal. Recommended.
E Hostal El Hibisco, Juan de Dios Peni 636,
T211407. Delightful hosts, welcome drink,
good breakfast included.
E pp **Hostal Gladys**, Pasaje Alberto Coddou 1360
(by Plaza de Armas), T551267, or 09-9540 3636
(mob). Breakfast available US$2.85, TV, hot water,
free internet, kitchen and laundry facilities,
bicycles for rent, helpful, Gladys works at tourist
information in bus terminal (15 mins away).
E pp **Res Carvajal**, Av El Santo 1056, T/F224059.
Family home, kitchen facilities, central camping.
E pp **Res El Loa**, O'Higgins 362, T210304.
Without bath, with breakfast, good
inexpensive home cooking, good value.
E pp **Res Lorena**, Cantournet 950, T223330,
hostal_lorena@msn.com. Quiet, pleasant.
E pp **Res Petit**, de la Barra 586, T212536. Hot water.
Camping Hipocampo, 4 km south on Av del
Mar (take bus for Coquimbo and get off at
Colegio Adventista, US$7.50 site by Playa
El Pescador), T214316. **Maki Payi**, 153 Vegas
Norte, about 5 km north of La Serena, near sea,
T213628. Self-contained cabins available.

Elqui Valley *p639*
Vicuña
A Halley, Gabriela Mistral 542, T412070, www.valle
deelqui.cl/hotelhalley.htm. Rooms around a
courtyard, Victorian-style, very good, breakfast.
B-C Hostería Vicuña, Sgto Aldea 101, T411301,
www.hosteriavicuna.cl. Swimming pool,
tennis court, restaurant.

C Sol del Valle, Gabriela Mistral 743, T411078. Including breakfast, swimming pool, vineyard, restaurant.

C-D Sundarie Hospedaje, C Principal 3, San Isidro (15 mins walk from Vicuña), T412072. Delightful bungalows, with breakfast, spotless, TV, internet, bicycles, pool in lovely gardens, yoga lessons.

D La Elquina, O' Higgins 65, T411317. Includes breakfast, **E** without bath, relaxed, quiet, lovely garden, laundry and kitchen facilities. Highly recommended.

D Valle Hermoso, Gabriela Mistral 706, T411206. Comfortable, parking. Recommended.

E Rita Klamt, Condell 443, T051-419611, rita_klamt@yahoo.es. **F** single. Impeccably kept bed and breakfast. Excellent breakfast, ample kitchen facilities, pleasant garden with pool, helpful, German and some English spoken. Highly recommended.

Camping Camping y Piscina Las Tinajas, east end of Chacabuco. Swimming pool, restaurant.

Río Hurtado

C Hacienda Los Andes, Vado Morrillos, T691822, www.haciendalosandes.com. German-Austrian management at this highly regarded colonial-style hacienda, all meals of local produce with organic fruit and vegetables, experts in horseback tours in unparalleled riding country (from US$93), plus trekking, biking and many other outdoor activities, from 1 to 8 days, English also spoken. All rooms with private bath; sauna and jacuzzi overlooking the river. Camping available, **G** pp, including hot showers. Access from Vicuña or Ovalle via Monumento Nacional Pichasca.

Pisco Elqui

Prices are much lower outside Jan-Feb; if you're heading for Argentina, there is basic, clean accommodation at Huanta (Guanta on many maps), 46 km from Vicuña.

A Los Misterios de Elqui, A Prat, T1982544, www.misteriosdeelqui.cl. Plush *cabañas*, sleep 2 or 4, swimming pool, good expensive restaurant.

B-C Los Dátiles, A Prat s/n, T451226, www.losdatileselqui.cl. *Cabañas* with kitchenette sleep 5, swimming pool, good restaurant serving Chilean country cooking.

B-C El Tesoro del Elqui, T051-451069, www.tesoro-elqui.cl. *Cabañas* for up to 4, dormitory for up to 4 with shared bath (**D**), café, pool, German spoken.

B Elqui, O'Higgins s/n by the plaza, T451130. Hot shower, central, swimming pool, good restaurant. Recommended.

G Hospedaje, Prat 17. Cheapest option, friendly, watch out for fleas.

Camping **G** Campsite behind Camping El Olivo (which is closed). Excellent facilities, cold water, lots of trees by river, helpful owner, laundry facilities, very nice.

❷ Eating

Ovalle *p637*

🍴 **Club Social Arabe**, Arauco 255. Spacious glass-domed premises, limited selection of Arab dishes.

🍴 **Casino La Bomba**, Aguirre 364. Run by fire brigade, good value almuerzos.

🍴 **El Quijote**, Arauco 294. Good seafood, intimate atmosphere, Ovalle's "Bohemian" hangout.

Coquimbo *p638*

Seafood tends to be better here than La Serena.

🍴🍴-🍴 **Sal y Pimienta del Capitán Denny**, Aldunate 769. Mainly fish cooked Chilean style, one of the best in town, pleasant, old fashioned.

🍴 **La Picada**, Costanera near statue of O'Higgins. Excellent, try the tasty *pebre*.

🍴 **La Bahía**, Pinto 1465. Good food and value.

🍴 **La Barca**, Ríos y Varela. Modest, but good food.

La Serena *p638, map p639*

Most restaurants close off season on Sun; generally more expensive here than in Coquimbo. For good fish lunches (mid-range/cheap) try the top floor of the Recova market, but the best place is the Sector de Pescadores (♈-♈) at **Peñuelas**, on the coast halfway between La Serena and Coquimbo. Take any bus to Coquimbo and get out at the junction with Los Pescadores; walk 300 m to the coast.

♈ **Bavaria**, E de la Barra 489. International menu, good service, chain restaurant.

♈ **Donde El Guatón**, Brasil 750. Parrillada, paradise for meat eaters, also good seafood.

♈ **La Mía Pizza**, O'Higgins 360, T215063. Italian, good value (also on Av del Mar, T212232).

♈-♈ **Diavoletto**, Prat 565 and O'Higgins 531. Fast food, popular.

♈-♈ **El Callejón**, O'Higgins 635. Student hangout serving cheap dishes. Popular bar at night.

♈ **Daniela 2**, F de Aguirre 460. Typical Chilean home cooking.

♈ **Govindas**, Lautaro 841, T224289. Hari Krishna centre serving very cheap vegetarian food, open Mon-Fri lunchtime only.

Café do Brasil, Balmaceda 461. Good coffee.

Café Morocco, Prat 566. Good coffee, fresh juices.

Colonial, Balmaceda 475 (next to Brasil). Real coffee, sandwiches, salads, good breakfast, good.

Tahiti, Córdovez 540, local 113. Real coffee, pastries. Recommended.

Elqui Valley: Vicuña *p639*

♈ **Club Social de Elqui**, Gabriela Mistral 435. Attractive patio, good value *almuerzo*, real coffee.

♈ **Halley**, Gabriela Mistral 404. Good meat, with local specialities, goat (huge portion) and rabbit.

♈ **Michel**, Gabriela Mistral 180. Popular, good value almuerzo.

♈ **Yo Y Soledad**, Gabriela Mistral 364. Inexpensive, hearty Chilean food, good value.

⊕ Bars and clubs

La Serena *p638, map p639*

Most of the clubs are on Av del Mar and in Peñuelas, but in town you could try the following:

Bar Real, Los Carrera y Cordovez, on the plaza. Nice bar with colonial-style interior.

Café del Patio, Prat 470. Café with bar, Tijuana Blues from 2100 with live music to the early hours. On Sat offers The Beatles Club from 2300.

⊕ Festivals and events

Coquimbo *p638*

Coquimbo hosts **La Pampilla**, by far the biggest independence day celebrations in Chile. Between 200-300,000 people come from all over the country for the fiesta, which lasts for a week from

14-21 Sep. It costs a nominal US$1.50 to enter the main dancing area peñas cost extra); plenty of typical Chilean food and drink.

▲ Activities and tours

La Serena *p638, map p639*

Valle del Elqui US$25, Parque Nacional Fray Jorge US$40, Tongoy US$35, Reserva Nacional Los Pingüinos and the Isla Damas US$42, Mamalluca observatory US$22, city tour US$15. Some also run tours to Valle del Encanto, Andacolla and Isla Chantaral. Responsible operators will not run tours to Mamalluca or Las Damas in bad weather.

Chile Safari, Matta 367, T250434, www.chilesafari.com.

Delfines, Matta 591, T223624, www.turismoaventuradelfines.cl.

Elqui Valley Tours, Los Carrera 515, T214846, www.elquivalleytour.cl. Good for local tours, enthusiastic guides.

Talinay Adventure Expeditions, Prat 470, in the courtyard, T218658, www.talinay chile.com. Offers a range of local tours including Valle del Elqui, Mamalluca, Reserva Nacional Pingüino de Humboldt, also trekking and climbing.

⊖ Transport

Ovalle and around *p637*

Bus Ovalle has 2 long-distance bus terminals, Terrapuerto Limarí, next to Feria Modelo, near Benavente 500 block, which all major companies use, and Terminal Media Luna, by the rodeo ring on Aritzía Oriente. Local buses leave from the terminal next to Terrapuerto Limarí. Buses to **Santiago**, several, 6½ hrs, US$9; to **Valparaíso**, 6 hrs, US$9; to **Antofagasta**, 14 hrs, US$20; to **La Serena**, 1½ hrs, US$3; to **Arica**, 24 hrs, US$28.

Parque Nacional Fray Jorge

Round trip in **taxi** from Ovalle, US$50, Abel Olivares Rivera, T Ovalle 620352.

Andacollo

Colectivo from Ovalle, US$3; **bus**, US$2.

Coquimbo *p638*

Bus Terminal at Varela y Garriga. To **La Serena**, US$0.75.

La Serena *p638, map p639*

Air Aeropuerto La Florida, 5 km east of the city, T271812. To **Santiago**, **LAN**; also to northern Chile. **Bus** City buses US$0.50. Bus terminal, El Santo y Amunátegui (about 8 blocks south of the centre). Tur-Bus office, Balmaceda entre Prat y Cordovez. Buses daily to **Santiago**, several companies, 7-8 hrs, US$10 classic, US$12 semi-cama-20 salón-cama. To **Valparaíso**, 7 hrs, US$18. To **Caldera**, 6 hrs, US$9. To **Calama**, US$28, 16 hrs. To **Antofagasta**, 12-13 hrs, several companies, US$25, and to **Iquique**, 17 hrs, and **Arica**, 20 hrs. To **Vicuña** and **Pisco Elqui**, see below. To **Coquimbo**, bus No 8 from Av Aguirre y Cienfuegos, US$0.75, every few mins. **Car hire** Daire, Balmaceda 3812, T226933, recommended, good service; Flota Verschae, Av Balmaceda 3856, T241685, good value, recommended; La Florida at airport, T271947. **Taxi** US$0.75 + US$0.20 per every 200 m. Colectivos with fixed rates, destination on roof; also to Coquimbo from Aguirre y Balmaceda, and Ovalle and Vicuña from Domeyko y Balmaceda.

Elqui Valley: Vicuña *p639*
Bus To **La Serena**, about 10 a day (more in summer), most by Via Elqui/Megal Bus, first 0800, last 1930, 1 hr, US$2, colectivo from Plaza de Armas US$3. To **Pisco Elqui**, 10 a day with Vía Elqui, 1 hr, US$3. Buses from Pisco Elqui to La Serena go via Vicuña, US$3.

● Directory

La Serena *p638, map p639*
Airline offices LAN, Prat y Balmaceda, T225981, also an office in the Mall Plaza. **Banks** ATMs at most banks, in the bus terminal and outside Las Brisas supermarket. Casas de cambio: Cambio Caracol, Balmaceda 460, in the basement, building closed 1400-1600. **Cambio Intercam**, De la Barra 435B. **La Portada**, Prat 515, open all day Sat. If heading north note that La Serena is the last place to change TCs before Antofagasta. **Cultural centres** Instituto Chileno Francés de Cultura, Cienfuegos 632, T224993. Library, films, etc. Centro Latino-Americano de Arte y Cultura, Balmaceda 824, T229344. Dance workshops, art gallery, artesanía. **Internet** Cybercafé at Ingservtur, Matta 611. **Cyber-Bazaar 2000**, Av F de Aguirre 343-A. **Net Café**, Cordovez 285, T212187, also bar. **Shalom**, Av F de Aguirre 343. **Telephones** Telefónica, Cordovez 446 and La Recova market. **Entel**, Prat 571.

North of La Serena

North of the Río Elqui, the transitional zone continues to the mining and agro-industrial centre of Copiapó. Thereafter begins the desert, which is of little interest, except after rain. Then it is covered with a succession of flowers, insects and frogs, in one of the world's most spectacular wildlife events. Rain, however, is rare: there is none in summer; in winter it is light and lasts only a short time. Annual precipitation at Copiapó is about 115 mm. Drivers must beware of high winds and blowing sand north of Copiapó.

The Huasco valley is an oasis of olive groves and vineyards. It is rugged and spectacular, dividing at Alto del Carmen, 30 km east of Vallenar, into the Carmen and Tránsito valleys. There are pisco distilleries at Alto del Carmen and San Félix. A sweet wine, Pajarete, is also produced.

Reserva Nacional Pingüino de Humboldt

Some 72 km north of La Serena, a road branches west off the Panamericana to **Punta de Choros**. This is the departure point for the Humboldt Penguin Natural Reserve, on Islas Chañaral, Choros and Damas. Besides penguins, there are seals, sea lions, a great variety of seabirds and, offshore, a colony of grey dolphin. Isla Damas has interesting flora, too. No public transport to Punta de Choros (42 km from Panamericana). Tours run from La Serena, 0830-1800. Permission to land on Isla Damas (US$3.50) from CONAF in Punta de Choros, T051-272798; toilet but no drinking water.

Vallenar → *Phone code: 051. Colour map 8, grid A1. Population: 47,000. Altitude: 380 m.*
This is the chief town of the Huasco valley, 194 km north of La Serena. It has a pleasant Plaza de Armas, with marble benches. About seven blocks southeast is the **Museo del Huasco** ① *Sgto Aldea 742, Tue-Fri 1500-1800, US$1.* It contains historic photos and artefacts from the valley. At the mouth of the river, 56 km west, is the pleasant port of Huasco (cheap seafood restaurants near the harbour). The staff at the Municipalidad on Plaza de Armas are helpful.

Copiapó → *Phone code: 052. Colour map 6, grid C2. Population: 127,000. Altitude: 400 m.*
The valley of the Río Copiapó, generally regarded as the southern limit of the Atacama desert, is an oasis of farms, vineyards and orchards about 150 km long. Copiapó is an important mining centre. Founded in 1744, Copiapó became a prosperous town after the discovery in 1832 of the third largest silver deposits in South America at Chañarcillo (the mine was closed in 1875). The

discoverer, Juan Godoy, a mule-driver, is commemorated at Matta y O'Higgins. Fiesta de la Candelaria, first Sunday in February. **Museo Mineralógico** ① *Colipí y Rodríguez, 1 block east from Plaza Prat, Mon-Fri 1000-1300, 1530-1900, Sat 1000-1300, US$1.* This is the best museum of its type in Chile, with a collection of weird and wonderful minerals and fossils from Chile and around the world. Many ores shown are found only in the Atacama desert. The Museo Ferroviario at the old railway station on Calle Ramírez opens irregularly, but the Norris Brothers steam locomotive and carriages used in the inaugural journey between Copiapó and Caldera in 1851 (the first railway in South America) can be seen at the Universidad de Atacama about 2 km north of the centre on Avenida R Freire. Helpful **tourist office** ① *Los Carrera 691, north side of Plaza Prat, T212838, infoatacama@sernatur.cl.*

Border with Argentina: Paso San Francisco

Paso San Francisco is reached either by poor unpaved road northeast from Copiapó, via the Salar de Maricunga and Laguna Verde or by an unpaved road southeast from El Salvador: the two roads join near the Salar de Maricunga, 96 km west of Paso San Francisco. On the Argentine side a paved road continues to Tinogasta; the border post is at Fiambalá, 210 km beyond the border, open 0700-1900, but there is also a police post at La Gruta, 24 km beyond the border. Chilean immigration and customs are near the Salar de Maricunga, 100 km west of the border, open 0900-1900; US$2 per vehicle charge for crossing Saturday, Sunday and holidays. This crossing is liable to closure after snow: T052-198 1009 for road reports. Always take spare fuel.

Caldera and around → *Phone code: 052. Colour map 6, grid C2. Population: 12,000.*

This is a port and terminal for the loading of iron ore, 73 km northwest of Copiapó. **Iglesia de San Vicente de Paul** (1862) on the Plaza de Armas was built by English carpenters working for the railway company. **Bahía Inglesa**, 6 km south of Caldera, 6 km west of the Highway, is popular for its beautiful white sandy beaches and unpolluted sea. It's rather expensive and can get crowded in summer and at weekends, but off season makes a perfect, deserted retreat. It was originally known as Puerto del Inglés after the visit in 1687 of the English 'corsario', Edward Davis. Tourist office (summer only, T316076) and cultural centre in revamped train station.

Chañaral → *Phone code: 052. Colour map 6, grid C2. Population: 12,000.*

The valley of the Río Salado, 130 km in length, less fertile or prosperous than the Copiapó or Huasco valleys, is the last oasis south of Antofagasta. Chañaral, a town with old wooden houses perched on the hillside at the mouth of the Salado, is 93 km north of Caldera. In its heyday it was the processing centre for ore from the nearby copper mines of El Salado and Las Animas. Now it is a base for visits to beaches and the Parque Nacional Pan de Azúcar. There's a tourist information kiosk on the Pan-American Highway at the south end of Chañaral (closed winter). If it is closed, go to the Municipalidad.

Parque Nacional Pan de Azúcar

① *US$6 (US$3 for Chileans). CONAF office in Caleta Pan de Azúcar, 0830-1800 daily (usually deserted at lunchtime), maps available. There are heavy fines for driving in 'restricted areas' of the park.*

The park, north of Chañaral, consists of the Isla Pan de Azúcar on which Humboldt penguins and other sea-birds live, and some 43,754 ha of coastal hills rising to 800 m. There are fine beaches (popular at weekends in summer). Fishermen near the CONAF office offer boat trips round Isla Pan de Azúcar to see the penguins, US$8.50 per person (minimum total US$85). Alternatively, a 2½-hr walk goes from the office to a mirador with extensive views over the south of the park. Vegetation is mainly cacti, of which there are 26 species, nourished by frequent sea mists (*camanchaca*). The park is home to 103 species of birds as well as guanaco and foxes. Pollution from nearby copper mining is a threat. There are two entrances: north by good secondary road from Chañaral, 28 km to Caleta Pan de Azúcar; from the Pan-American Highway 45 km north of Chañaral, along a side road 20 km (road in parts deep sand and very rough, 4WD essential).

Taltal → *Phone code: 055. Colour map 6, grid C2. Population: 9,000.*

This is the only town between Chañaral and Antofagasta, a distance of 420 km. Along Avenida Prat are several wooden buildings dating from the late 19th century, when Taltal prospered as a mineral port of 20,000 people. It is now a fishing port with a mineral processing plant. North 72 km is the Quebrada El Médano, a gorge with ancient rock-paintings along the upper valley walls.

● Sleeping

Reserva Nacional Pingüino de Humboldt: Punta de Choros *p644*

C Cabañas Los Delfines, Pilpilen s/n, sitio 33, T09-9639 6678 (mob). Cabins for up to 6. There are other sleeping and eating options in the area.

Vallenar *p644*

Listed hotels and restaurants all recommended.

B Hostería de Vallenar, Ercilla 848, T614379, hotval@ ctcinternet.cl. Excellent, pool, parking, good breakfast and restaurant, Hertz car hire office. Worth haggling over room rates.

B-C Cecil, Prat 1059, T614071. A good modern hotel with hot water and a swimming pool.

D Hostal Camino del Rey, Merced 943, T613184. Cheaper without bath, good value.

E Vall, Aconcagua 455, T613380, hostal_vall@ yahoo.es. With breakfast, parking, good value.

E Viña del Mar, Serrano 611, T611478. Nice rooms, clean *comedor*, a good choice.

Copiapó *p644*

There is often a shortage of rooms; book in advance.

A Diego de Almeida, O'Higgins 656, Plaza Prat, T/F212075, www.diegodealmagrohoteles.cl. Cable TV, fridge, good restaurant, spacious bar and pool.

B Hostería Las Pircas, Av Copayapu 095, T213220, hosteria.laspirca@chilnet.cl. Bungalows with nice rooms, pool, good breakfast, restaurant.

C San Francisco de la Selva, Los Carrera 525, T217013, hosanco@entelchile.net. Pleasant modern hotel, central, with TV, café-bar, garage.

C-D Montecatini, Infante 766, T211363, h.montecatini@terra.cl. Large rooms around a beautiful courtyard, or cheaper rooms without TV, foam mattresses, pool, helpful, good value.

D Palace, Atacama 741, T212852. Comfortable, central, pretty patio, parking. Good value.

E Res Rocío, Yerbas Buenas 581, T215360. Some rooms with bath and cable TV. **G** singles or without bath, good value, attractive patio.

E Res Nuevo Chañarcillo, Rodríguez 540, T212368. Without bath (more with), comfortable, nice lounge. Recommended.

F Res Torres, Atacama 230, T240727. Shared bath, **G** for singles, hot water, quiet, good value.

G Res Chacabuco, O'Higgins 921, T213428. Cheaper with shared bath, quiet, near bus terminal.

Caldera *p645*

Caldera is cheaper than Bahía Inglesa in summer.

B-C Hostería Puerta del Sol, Wheelwright 750, T315205. Includes tax, cabins with good beds, all mod cons, kitchen, swimming pool, view over bay.

B-C Portal del Inca, Carvallo 945, T315252. Cabins with kitchen, English spoken, restaurant not bad, order breakfast on previous night.

C Costanera, Wheelwright 543, T316007. Takes credit cards, simple rooms.

F pp Res Millaray, Cousiño 331, Plaza de Armas, T315528. Good value, basic.

Bahía Inglesa

B Cabañas Playa Paraíso, Av Costanera 6000, T09-8860 7666, www.cabanasparaiso.cl. Idyllic spot on the beach, 6 km south of town. Cosy cabins for up to 6, BBQs, kitchen, solar-powered, Reiki and massages available. Recommended.

B Los Jardines de Bahía Inglesa, Av Copiapó, T315359. Open all year, *cabañas*, good beds, comfortable.

C Camping Bahía Inglesa, Playa Las Machas, T315424. Fully equipped *cabañas* for up to 5 persons, **C** tent site.

C El Coral, Av El Morro, T315331. Restaurant overlooking sea, has some cabins, good seafood, groups welcome, open all year.

Chañaral *p645*

C Hostería Chañaral, Müller 268, T48050. Slightly dated, but spacious rooms and attentive service, except in the restaurant, although the food is good and beautiful dining room. With pool room and parking.

C Jiménez, Merino Jarpa 551, T480328. Clean rooms, **D** without bath, modern, patio with lots of birds, restaurant good value, convenient for Pullman Bus. Recommended.

C-D Nuria, Costanera 302, T480903. Good, if a little basic and overpriced (worth bargaining), with breakfast, parking.

E Sergio Molina, Pinto 583, T480075. Shared bath, kitchen and laundry facilities, nice family (owner runs good tours of the Pan de Azúcar park, see Activities and tours). Recommended.

Parque Nacional Pan de Azúcar *p645*

A-B CONAF cabañas, T213404 (book ahead). Perfectly placed *cabañas* on a deserted beach behind the *caleta*. Slightly rundown, poor beds and same price for 2 as for 6 people.

Some of the fishermen in the *caleta* let out rooms. They are quite basic and in the **G** pp range.

Camping E per site, showers, 20 litres of drinking water, take food; also 2 *cabañas*, T213404 (CONAF).

Taltal *p645*

D Hostal de Mar, Carrera 250, T611612. Comfortable, modern.

D Hostería Taltal, Esmeralda 671, T611173, btay@entelchile.net. Sea view, excellent restaurant, good value *almuerzo*.

E San Martín, Martínez 279, T611088. Without bath, good *almuerzo*.

🍴 Eating

Vallenar *p644*
Cheap eating places along south end of Av Brasil.
♯♯ **Bavaria**, Serrano 802. Chain restaurant, good.
♯♯ **Pizza Il Boccato**, Plaza O'Higgins y Prat. Good coffee, good food, popular.
♯ **La Pica**, Brasil y Faez. Good for cheap meals, seafood, cocktails.

Copiapó *p644*
♯♯ **Bavaria**, Chacabuco 487 (Plaza Prat) and on Los Carrera. Good variety, restaurant and cafe.
♯♯ **El Corsario**, Atacama 245. Good food, value and atmosphere.
♯ **Benbow**, Rodríguez 543. Good value *almuerzo*.
♯ **Chifa Hao Hwa**, Colipi 340 and Yerbas Buenas 334. Good Chinese, one of several in town.
♯ **Don Elias**, Los Carrera e Yerbas Buenas. Excellent seafood, popular.
♯ **La Pizza de Tito**, Infante y Chacabuco. Pizzas with good fillings, sandwiches and almuerzos.

Caldera *p645*
♯♯ **El Pirón de Oro**, Cousiño 218. Good but pricey.
♯ **Miramar**, Gana 090. At pier, good seafood.

Chañaral *p645*
♯♯-♯ **Restaurant Nuria**, Yungay 434, on the plaza, T489199. Good, fresh seafood, clean, friendly.
♯ **Rincón Porteño**, Merino Jarpa 567, T480070. Good and inexpensive sandwiches and snacks.

Taltal *p645*
♯♯ **Club Social Taltal**, Torreblanca 162. The former club of the British community (note the ballroom, billiard table and poker room), excellent, good value.
♯ **Caverna**, Martínez 247. Good seafood.

🏔 Activities and tours

Vallenar *p644*
If it rains (Sep-Oct), a tour of the desert in flower can be done with **Roberto Alegría**, T613865.
Agencia de Viajes Irazu, Prat 1121A, T/F619807. No excursions, but will organize flights.

Parque Nacional Pan de Azúcar *p645*
Subsole Atacama Adventure (Sergio Molina – see Sleeping), Merino Jarpa s/n, Chañaral, T09-9972 0077, kekomoli@123mail.cl. Offers tours in the park, US$28, enthusiastic and knowledgeable.

🚌 Transport

Vallenar *p644*
Bus Each company has its own terminal: **Tur-Bus**, Merced 561; **Pullman**, opposite (the most frequent buses going north); **Tas Choapa**, at Vallenar's main

terminal. To **La Serena**, 2 hrs, US$6. To **Copiapó**, 2 hrs, US$6. To **Valparaíso**, 10 hrs, US$15.

Copiapó *p644*
Air Desierto de Atacama Airport is 45 km northwest of Copiapó and 15 km east of Caldera. **LAN**, Colipi 484, T213512, airport T214360.
Bus Long-distance terminal 3 blocks from centre on Freire y Chacabuco. To **Santiago** US$15, 12 hrs. To **La Serena** US$8, 5 hrs. To **Caldera**, US$1-2, 1 hr, cheapest services on **Buses Recabarren** and **Casthere**.

Caldera *p645*
Bus Buses on the Panamericana do not go into Caldera, but stop at Cruce Caldera, outside town (**Restaurante Hospedaje Mastique**, Km 880, is a good place to eat and stay, D). Buses to **Copiapó** and **Santiago**, several daily. To **Antofagasta**, US$11, 7 hrs. To travel north, it may be better to take a bus to **Chañaral** (Inca-bus US$2), then change. Between Bahía Inglesa and Caldera colectivos charge US$1.50 all year; frequent bus service Jan-Feb US$0.50.

Chañaral *p645*
Bus There is no main terminal: **Pullman** at Los Baños y Costanera, **Tur-Bus** on the Panamericana, opposite Copec. Frequent services to **Antofagasta** US$12 semi cama, 5 hrs, and **Santiago**, US$21.

Parque Nacional Pan de Azúcar *p645*
A **taxi** costs US$25 from Chañaral, or hitch a lift from fishermen at sunrise.

Taltal *p645*
Bus To **Santiago**: 3 a day; to **Antofagasta**, Tur-Bus, US$7. Many buses bypass Taltal: to reach the Panamericana and pick up a bus from there, take a taxi, US$10.

☎ Directory

Copiapó *p644*
Banks Redbanc ATMs at central banks and in Plaza Real shopping mall, including **Cambio Fides**, office B123. **Bicycle repairs** Biman, Los Carrera 998A, T/F217391, excellent. **Cultural centres** Casa de la Cultura, O'Higgins 610, Plaza Prat. Wide range of arts, workshops, artesanía shops, good café El Bramador. **Internet** Several places in and around the centre, including **Zona Virtual**, Rodríguez y Colipi, T240308, average cost US$0.60 per hr. Terra, Chacabuco 380, US$1 per hr. **Post offices** Los Carrera y Colipi, Plaza Prat, Mon-Fri 1000-1400, 1600-2000. **Telephones** Several *centros de llamados* in town centre, including Telefónica, O'Higgins 531; Entel, Colipi 484.

Far north

Antofagasta, capital of the Second Region, is a major port for the export of copper from La Escondida and Chuquicamata. It is also a major commercial centre and home of two universities. The coast north of Antofagasta is much more picturesque than the aridity surrounding much of the Panamerican Highway. Two possible stops are the fishing port of Mejillones and Tocopilla, beneath towering cliffs. Despite this being the driest region, the climate is delightful. Temperature varies from 16°C in June and July to 24°C in January and February, never falling below 10° C at night.

From the mining service centre of Calama, the route heads up to the altiplano with its saltflats and lunar landscapes. In an oasis on the Río San Pedro is the historic town of San Pedro de Atacama. This has become a popular destination for visitors seeking high altitudes, clear skies, steaming geysers and volcanic horizons. It is also, increasingly, a staging post on the route between Bolivia's Salar de Uyuni and the Pacific Ocean. The Atacama Desert extends over most of the Far North to the Peruvian border. The main cities are Iquique and Arica; between them are old mineral workings and geoglyphs. Large areas of the Andean highland have been set aside as national parks; the most visited is Lauca with its volcanoes and lakes.

Antofagasta and around

→ *Phone code: 055. Colour map 6, grid C2. Population: 225,316.*

The largest city in Northern Chile, Antofagasta, 1,367 km north of Santiago, is not especially attractive in itself, but its setting beside the ocean and in view of tall mountains is dramatic. The **tourist office** ① *Prat 384, p 1, T451818, infoantofagasta@sernatur.cl, Mon-Fri 0930-1200, 1400-1700, Sat 1000-1400,* is very helpful. There is also a kiosk on Balmaceda ① *Mon-Fri 0930-1300, 1530-1930, Sat-Sun 0930-1300*; kiosk at airport (open summer only). CONAF, Argentina 2510, Antofagasta, T383332, antofaga@conaf.cl.

In the main square, Plaza Colón, is a clock tower donated by the British community in 1910 to commemorate 100 years of Chilean independence. It is a replica of Big Ben in London. Calle A Prat, which runs southeast from Plaza Colón, is the main shopping street. Two blocks north of Plaza Colón, at the old port, is the former Aduana, built as the Bolivian customs house in Mejillones and moved to its current site after the War of the Pacific. It houses the **Museo Histórico Regional** ① *Balmaceda 2786, www.dibam.cl/sdm_m_antofagasta, Tue-Fri 0900-1700, Sat, Sun, holidays 1100-1400, US$1, children half-price*, which has fascinating visual displays (explanations in Spanish only) on life on land and in the oceans, development of civilization in South America, minerals, human artefacts, recommended. Opposite are the former Capitanía del Puerto (now the administrative offices and library of the Museo Regional) and the former Resguardo Marítimo (now housing Digader, the regional coordinating centre for sport and recreation).

East of the port are the buildings of the Antofagasta and Bolivia Railway Company (FCAB) dating from the 1890s and beautifully restored, but still in use and difficult to visit. **Museo del Ferrocarril a Bolivia** ① *Bolívar 255, T206311, www.fcab.cl, make reservation 48 hrs in advance*, has an interesting museum of the history of the Antofagasta-Bolivia railway, with photographs, maps, instruments and furniture. **Museo Geológico** ① *Av Angamos 0610, inside the university campus, gchong@socompa.ucn, Mon-Fri, 0930-1300, 1530-1800, free, colectivo 114 or 333 from town centre*, is the mineral museum of the Universidad Católica del Norte. Tours of the port by boat leave from **La Cabaña de Mario** ① *C Aníbal Pinto s/n between the Museo Regional and the Terminal de Pescadores, 30 mins, US$5.*

The fantastic cliff formations and natural arch, which are used as the symbol of the **Second Region, at La Portada** are 16 km north, reached by any bus for Mejillones from the Terminal Centro (or ask at a travel agency). Taxis charge US$13 (for a small extra fee, taxis from the airport will drive past La Portada). Hitching is easy. From the main road it is 2 km to the beach which, though beautiful, is too dangerous for swimming; there is an excellent seafood restaurant La Portada) and café (open lunch-time only). A number of bathing beaches are also within easy reach.

The slow train to Uyuni

The line between Calama and Oruro in Bolivia is the only section of the old Antofagasta and Bolivia Railway still open to passenger trains. It is a long, slow journey but well worthwhile for the scenery. The journey is very cold, both during the day and at night (-15°C, no heating on board). From Calama the line climbs to reach its highest point at Ascotán (3,960 m); it then descends to 3,735 m at Cebollar, skirting the Salar de Ascotán.

Chilean customs are at Ollagüe and the train is searched at Bolivian customs at Avaroa, eight hours. From the border the line runs northeast to Uyuni, 204 km (eight hours), crossing the Salar de Chiguana and running at an almost uniform height of 3,660 m. Uyuni is the junction with the line south to the Argentine frontier at Villazón. Río Mulato is the junction for Potosí, but it is much quicker to travel by bus from Uyuni.

Juan López, 38 km north of Antofagasta, is a windsurfers' paradise. The sea is alive with birds, including Humboldt penguins, especially opposite Isla Santa María. For those with their own transport, follow the road out of Juan López to the beautiful cove at Conchilla. Keep on the track to the end at Bolsico. **Mejillones** (*Population 5,500*), a little fishing port 60 km north of Antofagasta, stands on a good natural harbour protected from westerly gales by high hills. Until 1948 it was a major terminal for the export of tin and other metals from Bolivia: remnants of that past include a number of fine wooden buildings: the Intendencia Municipal, the Casa Cultural (built in 1866) and the church (1906), as well as the Capitanía del Puerto. The town has been transformed in recent years by the building of what will be the largest port in South America. On completion, it will link Argentina, southern Brazil and Paraguay with the lucrative markets of the Asian Pacific Rim.

Sleeping

Antofagasta and around *p648, map p650*
B Plaza, Baquedano 461, T269046, hplaza@ chilesat.net. TV, salon de té, pool and sports, parking. Recommended, also has apartments.
C Colón, San Martín 2434, T261851. Comfortable, with breakfast, hot water, quiet, cash only, reasonable value
C Horizonte, Latorre 2450, T/F221886, www.hotel horizonte.cl. Cable TV, bar, bland building but friendly and pleasant, good value. Recommended.
C Marsal, Prat 867, T268063, www.marsal.cl. Modern, very comfortable, bright and spacious rooms, internet, Catalan owner. Recommended.
C Nadine, Baquedano 519, T227008, F265222. TV in rooms, parking, bar, cafetería serving real coffee, pastries and ice cream.
C Parina, Maipú 446, T223354, F266396. Modern, comfortable, restaurant, good value.
C San Martín, San Martín 2781, T263503, F268159. TV, parking, safe, convenient for Tur-Bus and Pullman, but very tatty.
D Ciudad de Avila, Condell 2840, T/F221 040. Spotless, good value, TV, basic restaurant. Recommended.
D Dakota, Latorre 2425, T251749. With breakfast and cable TV, popular, good value. Recommended.
D Hostal Frontera, Bolívar 558, T281219. Basic

but with good hot showers and decent beds, TV, convenient for Tur-Bus and Pullman.
D-E Res El Cobre, Prat 749, T225162. Some rooms with bath, set around a central courtyard, bright and clean, but tatty.
E Hostal del Norte, Latorre 3162, T251265, F267161. Some rooms with bath, comfortable, quiet, brighter annex at the back.
E Maykin, Condell 3130, T/F259400. Modern, helpful, good value. Recommended, but takes in short-stay guests.
E Valdivia, Ossa 2642, T265911. Recommended.
E-F Res La Riojanita, Baquedano 464, T381056. Basic, very helpful, noisy but recommended.
Camping To the south on the road to Coloso are: **Las Garumas**, Km 6, T247763 ext 42, **E** per site (ask for lower price out of season), **C** for cabins, cold showers and beach (reservations Av Angamos 601, casilla 606). Rucamóvil, Km 11, T223929 and 7 cabañas. Both open year-round, expensive, but bargain for lower price out of season.

Juan López
B Hotel La Rinconada, 10 km from Juan López, T261139. *Cabañas* and camping, prices for up to 5.
D Hostería Sandokan, Juan López, T223022. Standard facilities.

649

🍴 Eating

Antofagasta p648, map p650

Many bars and restaurants are closed on Sun.

🍴🍴🍴 Club de la Unión, Prat 474, p 2, T268371. Open to non-members, traditional atmosphere, excellent almuerzo and service.

🍴🍴 D'Alfredo, Condell 2539. Reasonable pizzas, good value, popular.

🍴🍴 El Arriero, Condell 2644, T264371. Good service, cheaper set lunch, popular, live music.

🍴🍴 Panda, Condell y Baquedano. Self-service, eat all you can for US$8.

🍴🍴 Pizzante, Carrera 1857, T223344. Good pasta, seafood and vegetarian options.

🍴🍴 Rincón Oriental, Washington 2432. Excellent Cantonese, `over the top' décor. Recommended.

🍴🍴 Tío Jacinto, Uribe 922. Friendly atmosphere, serves good seafood.

🍴 Chicken's House Center, Latorre 2660. Chicken, beef and daily specials, open till 2400.

🍴 El Curicano, Simón Bolívar 607. Good value, basic set menu lunches and dinners.

Above the market are several good places selling cheap seafood *almuerzos* and super-cheap set lunches, including **El Mariscal** and **Toledo**. Good fish restaurants in Terminal Pesquero Centro and at Caleta Coloso, 8 km south. Many restaurants and bars are closed on Sun.

Cafés

It is hard to find coffee or breakfast before 0900.
Café Bahía, Prat 474. Open at 0900 for for real coffee.

Antofagasta

To La Portada, Juan López, Tocopilla & Iquique via coast (Route 1)

Pacific Ocean

Fishing Port

Former Capitanía del Puerto

Yacht Club

Former Resguardo Marítimo

Former Aduana/ Museo Histórico Regional 🏛 9

Antofagasta & Bolivia Railway Co

Ramírez

Caracoles

Covadonga

Géminis

Riquelme

Serrano

To 🖲 🚉 north & Calama

Plaza Colón

Tur-Bus
Teatro Municipal

Pullman Bus

Bolívar

14

Aerolíneas del Sur

San Martín

2

A Prat

Cathedral

LAN

Sucre

7

3
8

Flota Barrios

To Pan-American Highway north & Calama

Washington

11

13

4

5

9

4

Baquedano

1

To 🖲, Universidad de Antofagasta, Huanchaca & Pan-American Highway south

Latorre

Maipú

Uribe

Condell

Orella

15

10

Matta

Ossa

Plaza del Mercado 🏛

12

16

8

14 de Febrero

Prat

CONAF

Av Argentina

To Argentina

N

0 metres 100
0 yards 100

Sleeping 🛏
Ciudad de Avila 3 B3
Colón 4 B2

Dakota 5 B2
Horizonte 15 C2
Hostal del Norte 6 A3
Hostal Frontera 7 B3
Marsal 8 C3
Maykin 17 A3
Nadine 9 B2
Parina 10 C2
Plaza 11 B2
Residencial El Cobre 12 C3

Residencial La Riojanita 13 B2
San Martín 14 B2
Valdivia 16 C3

Eating 🍴
Café Haiti 2 B2
Club de la Unión & Café Bahía 3 B2
D'Alfredo 4 B2

El Arriero 1 B2
El Curicano 8 B3
Panda 5 C2
Picadillo 6 C1
Pizzante 10 C2
Rincón Oriental 9 A2
Tío Jacinto 11 C2

Bars & clubs 🍸
Wally's Pub 7 C2

Café Haiti, in Galería at Prat 482. Real coffee.
Chez Niko's, Ossa 1951. Bakery, pasteleria, good pizzas, empanadas and bread.
Heladería Latorre, Baquedano y Latorre. Good for ice-cream.

🍸 Bars and clubs

Antofagasta *p648, map p650*
Thanks to Antofagasta's student population, the city's nightlife is buzzing. The most popular bars and clubs are 16 km south of the town in Balneario El Huascar. Take micro 2 from C Matta to get there.
Bar Picadillo, Av Grecia 1000. Lively atmosphere, also good food. Recommended.
Castillo Pub, Pasaje Carrera 884. Live music, good food with good value almuerzo, fun. Recommended.
Wally's Pub, Toro 982. British expat-style with darts, pool and beer, closed Sun.

🎭 Entertainment

Antofagasta *p648, map p650*
Teatro Municipal, Sucre y San Martín, T264919. Modern, state-of-the art theatre.
Teatro Pedro de la Barra, Condell 2495. Theatre run by University of Antofagasta, regular programme of plays, reviews, concerts etc, high standard, details in press.

✱ Festivals and events

Antofagasta *p648, map p650*
29 Jun, San Pedro, the image of the patron saint of the fishermen is taken out by launch to the breakwater to bless the first catch of the day. On the last weekend of **Oct**, the city's immigrant communities put on a joint festival on the seafront, with national foods, dancing and music.

⊙ Shopping

Antofagasta *p648, map p650*
Bookshops Librería Universitaria, Latorre 2515. Owner Germana Fernández knowledgeable on local history. **Multilibro**, opposite Librería Universitaria. Very good selection of Chilean, Latin American and English-language authors.
Food shops and supermarkets Las Brisas, Baquedano 750. **Korlaert**, on Ossa 2400-2500 block. **Líder** on road to La Portada. **Naturista**, Condell 2394. Health food specialist.
Markets Feria Modelo O'Higgins (next to fish market on Av Pinto). Excellent fruit and veg, also restaurants. The municipal market is at Matta y Uribe.

▲ Activities and tours

Antofagasta *p648, map p650*
Many tour companies offer packages to the Atacama, but it is generally better to book tours in San Pedro de Atacama.
Atacama Wustereiseseudienst, Apartado Postal 55, T243322. Alex Joseph Valenzuela Thompson guides German-speakers around the area.
Intitour, Baquedano 460, T266185, intitour@dtl.net. English speaking guides.
Tatio Travel, Washington 2513, T/F263532. English spoken, tours arranged for groups or individuals. Highly recommended.

⊖ Transport

Antofagasta and around *p648, map p650*
Air Cerro Moreno Airport, 22 km north. Taxi to airport US$10, but cheaper if ordered from hotel. Bus US$4 or less, Aerobus (T221047), Tur Bus and others. **LAN**, **Sky** and **Aerolíneas del Sur** fly daily to **Santiago**, **Arica**, **Iquique** and **Calama**; LAN also to **Copiapó** and **La Serena**.
Bus No main terminal; each company has its own office in town (some quite a distance from the centre). Buses for **Mejillones**, 1 hr, US$2, from Corsal terminal, Condell y Sucre; also minibuses Latorre y Sucre. To **Tocopilla**, 2½ hrs, US$5, many daily. Bus company offices: **Flota Barrios**, Condell 2682, T268559; **Géminis** and **Camus**, Latorre 3055, T251796; **Pullman Bus**, Latorre 2805, T262591; **Tur-Bus**, Latorre 2751, T264487. To **Santiago**, many companies: 18 hrs, US$35 semi cama, US$55 cama; book in advance in high season. If all seats to the capital are booked, catch a bus to **La Serena** (12 hrs, US$25, or US$35 cama service), or **Ovalle**, 14 hrs, US$20, and re-book. To **Valparaíso**, US$35 semi cama. To **Copiapó**, 7 hrs, US$18. Frequent buses to **Iquique**, US$15, 6 hrs. To **Arica**, US$20 semi cama, 11 hrs. To **Chuquicamata**, Tur-Bus, US$6, frequent, 3 hrs. To **Calama**, several companies, US$6, 3 hrs; to **San Pedro de Atacama**, Tur-Bus 7 daily, 5 hrs, US$8, or via Calama.
To **Salta, Argentina** Géminis, Wed, Sun 0700, via Calama, San Pedro de Atacama, Paso de Jama and Jujuy, US$38, 18 hrs. Tur-Bus, Wed and Sun 0615, US$42. Also check with **Pullman Bus**, who run services via San Pedro de Atacama and Jujuy. Book in advance and take food and as much warm clothing as possible for this journey; also small denomination US dollars, as nowhere to change Chilean pesos en route.

Juan López
Bus At weekends in summer only, also minibuses daily in summer from Latorre y Sucre, Antofagasta.

ⓘ Directory

Antofagasta p648, map p650
Airline offices Aerolíneas del Sur, Washington 2548, T228779. LAN, Paseo Prat, T265151, or 600-526 2000. **Sky**, Velásquez 890, T459090. **Banks** It's difficult to change TCs south of Antofagasta until you reach La Serena. ATMs at major banks around Plaza Colón, Hotel Antofagasta, and Las Brisas and Tricot supermarkets. **Casas de Cambio** are mainly on Baquedano, such as Ancla, No 524, Mon-Fri 0900-1400, 1600-1900 (at weekends try ice cream shop next door) and shopping centre at No 482-98. **Car hire** First, Bolívar 623, T225777. Iqsa, Latorre 3033, T264675. **Andrés Ljubetic Romo**, Atacama 2657, T268851, is a recommended mechanic. **Consulates** Argentina, Blanco Encalada 1933, T220440.

Bolivia, Washington 2675, p 13, T225010. France and Belgium, Baquedano 299, T268669. Germany, Pérez Zujovic 4940, T251691. Italy, Matta 1945, of 808, T227791. Netherlands, Washington 2679, of 902, T266252. Spain, Rendic 4946, T269596. **Cultural centres** Instituto Chileno Norteamericano, Carrera 1445, T263520. Instituto Chileno Alemán, Bolívar 769, T225946. Centro Cultural Nueva Acrópolis, Condell 2679, T222144, lots of activities, including tai chi and yoga, talks (Wed 2100), and discussions. **Internet** Cheapest is Intitour, see Activities and tours above, US$0.60 per hr. Cybercafé, Maipú y Latorre, US$1.30 per hr. Sucre 671, US$0.80 per hr. **Post offices** on Plaza Colón. 0830-1900, Sat 0900-1300. Also at Washington 2613. **Telephones** Telefónica, Condell 2529 and 2750 (the only office open Sun). Entel Chile, Condell 2451.

North of Antofagasta

Tocopilla → *Phone code: 055 Colour map 6, grid B2. Population: 24,600.*

Tocopilla is 187 km north of Antofagasta via the coastal road and 365 km via the Pan-American Highway. It has one of the most dramatic settings of any Chilean town, sheltering at the foot of 500-m high mountains that loom inland. A thermal power station and the port facilities used to unload coal and to export nitrates and iodine from María Elena and Pedro de Valdivia dominate the town. There are some interesting early 20th century buildings with wooden balustrades and façades, but generally it's a run-down place. There are two good beaches: Punta Blanca (12 km south) and Caleta Covadonga, 3 km south with a swimming pool.

East of Tocopilla a good paved road runs up the narrow valley 72 km to the Pan-American Highway. From here the paved road continues east to Chuquicamata. North of the crossroads 81 km is **Quillagua**, officially the driest place in the world (customs post, all southbound vehicles and buses are searched) and 111 km further is the first of three sections of the Reserva Nacional del Tamarugal. In this part are the **Geoglyphs of Cerro Pintados**, some 400 figures (humans, animals, geometric shapes) on the hillside (3 km west of the highway). The second part of Tamarugal is near La Tirana (see page 662), the third 60 km north of Pozo Almonte.

The coast road from Tocopilla north to Iquique is paved, 244 km, with fantastic views of the rugged coastline and tiny fishing communities. The customs post at **Chipana-Río Loa** (90 km north) searches all southbound vehicles for duty-free goods; 30 minutes delay. Basic accommodation is available at **San Marcos**, a fishing village, 131 km north. At **Chanaballita**, 184 km north there is a hotel, *cabañas*, camping, restaurant, shops. There are also campsites at **Guanillos**, Km 126, **Playa Peruana**, Km 129 and **Playa El Aguila**, Km 160.

Calama → *Phone code: 055. Colour map 6, grid B2. Population: 106,970. Altitude: 2,265 m.*

Calama lies in the oasis of the Río Loa, 202 km north of Antofagasta. Initially a staging post on the silver route between Potosí and Cobija, it is now an expensive, unprepossessing modern city, serving the nearby mines of Chuquicamata and Radomiro Tomic. Calama can be reached from the north by Route 24 via Chuquicamata, or, from the south, by a paved road leaving the Pan-American Highway 98 km north of Antofagasta at Carmen Alto (petrol, food). The road passes many abandoned nitrate mines, *oficinas*. **Tourist office** ⓘ *Latorre 1689, T345345, www.cala macultural.cl, Mon-Fri 0900-1300, 1430-1900.* Map, tours, helpful staff, English spoken.

Two kilometres from the centre on Avenida B O'Higgins is the **Parque El Loa** ⓘ *daily 1000-1800,* which contains a reconstruction of a typical colonial village built around a reduced-scale reproduction of Chiu Chiu church. Nearby in the park is the **Museo Arqueológico y Etnológico** ⓘ *Tue-Fri 1000-1300, 1400-1800, Sat-Sun 1400-1830, US$0.60,* with an exhibition of prehispanic cultural history. Also the **Museo de Historia Natural** ⓘ *Wed-Sun, 1000-1300, 1500-1830, US$0.90*, with an interesting collection on the oficinas and on the region's ecology and palaeontology.

Chuquicamata → *Phone code: 055. Colour map 6, grid B2. Altitude: 2,800 m.*

North of Calama 16 km is the site of the world's largest open-cast copper mine, employing 8,000 workers and operated by Codelco (the state copper corporation). The visual spectacle of the site makes for a memorable visit. Everything about Chuquicamata is huge: the pit from which the ore is extracted is four km long, two km wide and 730 m deep; the giant trucks, with wheels over 3½ m high, carry 310 ton loads and work 24 hours a day; in other parts of the plant 60,000 tons of ore are processed a day. Guided tours, by bus, in Spanish (although guides usually speak reasonable English) leave from the office of **Chuqui Ayuda** (a local children's charity) ⓘ *near the entrance at the top end of the plaza, Mon-Fri 1400, 1500 (less frequent in low season, tourist office in Calama has details), 1 hr, US$2 donation to the charity. Advance booking is needed for tours; either call the office in Chuquicamata (T327469) or from the tourist office in Calama; passport number essential.* In order to get on the tour, the tourist office in Calama recommends that you catch a colectivo from Calama at 0800, US$1 (ask them where it leaves from). From Calama: yellow colectivo taxis (marked 'Chuqui') from Abaroa entre Vargas y Ramírez, corner of the main plaza, US$1.75 to town centre, US$2 at night and to mine gates, 15 minutes. Wear covered shoes, long trousers and long sleeves; arrive 30 minutes early; filming is permitted in certain areas.

From Calama it is 273 km north to Ollagüe, on the Bolivian border. (There is no petrol between Calama and Uyuni in Bolivia. If really short try buying from the carabineros at Ollagüe or Ascotán, the military at Conchi or the mining camp at Buenaventura, 5 km from Ollagüe.) The road follows the Río Loa, passing Chiu Chiu (33 km), one of the earliest Spanish settlements in the area. Just beyond this oasis, a small turning branches off the main road to the hamlet of **Lasana**, 8 km north of Chiu Chiu. Petroglyphs are clearly visible on the right-hand side of the road. There are striking ruins of a pre-Inca pukará, a national monument; drinks are on sale. If arranged in advance, Línea 80 colectivos will continue to Lasana for an extra charge Pre-book the return trip, or walk back to Chiu Chiu. At **Conchi**, 25 km north of Lasana, the road crosses the Río Loa via a bridge dating from 1890 (it's a military zone, so no photographs of the view are allowed). Beyond Chiu Chiu the road deteriorates, with deep potholes, and, north of Ascotán carabinero checkpoint at 3,900 m), it becomes even worse (ask about the conditions on the Salares at Ascotán or Ollagüe before setting out, especially in December/January or August). The desert to the eastern side of the road by minefields. There are many llama flocks along this road and flamingoes on the salares.

Ollagüe → *Colour map 6, grid B2. Altitude: 3,690 m.*

This village, on the dry floor of the Salar de Ollagüe, is surrounded by a dozen volcanic peaks of over 5,000 m. The border with Bolivia is open 0800-2100; US$2 per vehicle charge for crossings 1300-1500, 1850-2100. A bad unmade road from Ollagüe runs into Bolivia and it is on the new Ruta Altiplanica, or "Inca Road" which runs from San Pedro de Atacama via El Tatio, Ascotán and Colchane to Visviri, with a planned continuation to Cuzco. The road improves north of Ascotán, as it crosses the Salares de Ascotán and de Carcote and Ollagüe; before setting out ask about the weather conditions at Ascotán or Ollagüe, especially in December and January, or August. There is a municipal hostel and the **Andean Project** ⓘ *T+44-20-8571 0737, John Barker, treasurer,* plans to build a hostel here. Food and drink is available in town. At this altitude the days are warm and sunny, nights cold (minimum -20° C). There are only 50 mm of rain a year, and water is very scarce. Ollagüe can be reached by taking the Calama-Uyuni train, but if you stop off, hitching is the only way out.

Between Chiu Chiu and El Tatio (see below), **Caspana** (*Population 400, Altitude 3,305 m*) is beautifully set among hills with a tiny church dating from 1641 and a **museum** ⓘ *Tue-Sun 1000-1300, 1500-1730,* with interesting displays on Atacameño culture. Basic accommodation is available (the nearest to El Tatio; see Lican Huasi). A poor road runs north and east through valleys of pampas grass with llama herds to **Toconce**, which has extensive prehispanic terraces set among interesting rock formations. There are archaeological sites nearby and the area is ideal for hiking. Further information from the tourist office in Calama, who may also help with arranging transport, or T321828, toconce@mixmail.com.

😴 Sleeping

Tocopilla *p652*

D Vucina, 21 de Mayo 2069, T/F813088. A busy, modern hotel, good rooms and a good restaurant.
E Hostal Central, A Pinto 1241. Huge, rambling place like something out of a Hitchcock film; very basic but friendly, vast rooms, no hot water.
F pp Casablanca, 21 de Mayo 2054, T813222. Helpful, good restaurant, good value.

Calama *p652*

AL Park, Camino Aeropuerto 1392, T319900, www.parkplaza.cl/calama. On the edge of town by the airport. First class, pool, bar and restaurant. Recommended.
A El Mirador, Sotomayor 2064, T340329, www.hotelmirador.cl. Price includes bath, internet, parking, TV and breakfast, good atmosphere and services, pleasant rooms, helpful.
A Hostería Calama, Latorre 1521, T341511, www.hotelcalama.co.cl. Comfortable heated rooms, good food, buffet breakfast and service; gym and small pool. Also owns **B Alfa**, Sotomayor 2016, T342496, hotelalfa@hotelalfa.cl. Central, comfortable, cable TV, but rooms could do with a revamp, breakfast included (neither juice nor fruit is fresh). Helpful staff, good cafetería, airport transfer from both hotels.
B Lican Antai, Ramírez 1937, T341621, hotellicanantai@terra.cl. With breakfast, central, good service and good restaurant, TV. Recommended.
C Res Alecris, Félix Hoyos 2143, T341616.
D without bath, single, double and triple rooms, well-maintained, very clean, family atmosphere, popular with miners, nice, safe (CCTV, near police station), no breakfast, modern, sunny courtyard. Chatty owner Alejandro.
D Cavour, Sotomayor 1841, T314718. Hot water, TV, no breakfast, rooms off an open-air corridor, simple, hospitable.
D San Sebastián, Pinto 1902, T343810. Meals available, family run, rooms with bath and TV in annex across the street.
D-E Hostal Res Splendid, Ramirez 1960, T341841. Good central place to stay, hot water, often full.
F pp Claris Loa, Granaderos 1631, T311939. Quiet, good value, central.
F pp Génesis, Granaderos 2148, T319075. Cheaper without bath, near Géminis bus terminal. Recommended.

🍴 Eating

Calama *p652*

On pedestrian part of C Eleuterio Ramírez, several cafés, juice bars, heladerías and fast food places.
♦♦ Bavaria, Sotomayor 2095. Good restaurant with cafetería downstairs, real coffee, open 0800, very popular, also cheaper café at Latorre 1935, upstairs.
♦♦ Los Braseros de Hanstur, Sotomayor 2030. Good ambience, good food.
♦♦ Mariscal JP, Félix Hoyos 2127. Best seafood in town, worth that bit extra (has another branch in the Mercado Central at Latorre 1974).
♦♦ Mexicano, Latorre 1986A. Genuine Mexican cuisine, live music at weekends.
♦♦-♦ Club Croata, on Abaroa, Plaza 23 de Marzo. Excellent value 4-course almuerzo, good service.
♦♦-♦ Nueva Chong Hua, Abaroa 2006. Best Chinese in Calama.

Cafés

Bon Apetit, Sotomayor 2131, open 0800-1530, 1900-2400. Set lunches, salón de té and café.
Panadería y Pastelería Alemana, Latorre 1998. Good, with OK *empanadas*.
Pastelería Delicius, Sotomayor 1950. *Panadería, pastelería*, also selling chocolates.
Tilomonte, Ramírez 1929. For breads and cakes.

🛍 Shopping

Calama *p652*

Craft stalls On Latorre 1600 block.
Market Feria Modelo on Antofagasta between Latorre and Vivar, selling fruit juices and crafts.
Supermarkets El Cobre, Vargas 2148. Económico, Grecia 2314.

🚶 Activities and tours

Calama *p652*

Several agencies run 1-day and longer tours to the Atacama region, including San Pedro; these are usually more expensive than tours from San Pedro and require a minimum number for the tour to go ahead. Be wary of agencies with poorly maintained vehicles and poor guides; standards here not generally very high. Operators with positive recommendations include: **Keps**, Sotomayor 1812-A, T318983, kepsturismo@terra.cl. Also **Azimut 360**, T/F333040, www.azimut.cl (see Santiago, Activities and tours), and operators listed under San Pedro de Atacama, below.

● *For an explanation of the sleeping and eating price codes used in this guide, see page 58.*
● *Other relevant information is found in Essentials pages 602-604.*

654

⊖ Transport

Tocopilla *p652*

Bus Bus companies' offices are on 21 de Mayo. Buses to **Antofagasta** many daily, US$5, 2½ hrs. To **Iquique**, along coastal road, 3 hrs, US$6, frequent. To **Chuquicamata** and **Calama**, 2 a day, 3 hrs, US$7.

Calama *p652*

Air Airport is modern and efficient with Redbanc ATM, restaurant upstairs, shop with internet. LAN (Latorre 1726, T600-526 2000), daily, to **Santiago**, via Antofagasta, **Sky** (Latorre 1497, T310190) 6 days a week. LAN also flies to **Iquique** and **Arica** twice a week. Taxi to town US$8 (courtesy vans from Hotels Calama, Alfa and Lican Antai – phone in advance). Also buses into town. Recommended service with **Alberto Molina**, T324834; he'll pick you up at your hotel.

Bus No main terminal, buses leave from company offices: **Flota Barrios**, Ramírez 2298; **Frontera**, Antofagasta 2041, T318543; **Géminis**, Antofagasta 2239, T341993; **Kenny Bus**, Vivar 1954; **Pullman**, Balmaceda y Sotomayor, T311410; **Tur-Bus**, Granaderos, about 12 blocks north of centre, tickets from Ramírez y Balmaceda. Beware of theft at bus stations. To **Santiago** 23 hrs, US$35, salon cama US$55, premium US$80. To **La Serena**, usually with delay in Antofagasta, 16 hrs, US$30. To **Antofagasta**, 3 hrs, several companies, US$6. To **Iquique**, 6 hrs, via Chuquicamata and Tocopilla, US$14, most overnight, but Tur-Bus have one early morning and one mid-afternoon service. To **Arica**, usually overnight, US$16, 9 hrs, or change in Antofagasta. To **Chuquicamata** (see above). To **San Pedro de Atacama**, Tur-Bus several daily, **Atacama**, Abaroa 2106, T364295, 1½ hrs, US$3, **Frontera**, Antofagasta 2041, T318543, several a day, US$3, 1½ hrs. To Toconao, see below. Buses **Manchego**, Alonso de Ercilla 2142, T316612, **Frontera** (Wed, Sun at 0700) and **Atacama** (Wed, Sun 2400) go to **Ollagüe**, US$6, 5 hrs. To **Salta**, Argentina, early morning on Tue, Fri and Sun, 15 hrs, **Géminis** US$38; **Pullman Bus**, US$45.

Local transport Public transport runs on a *colectivo* system, black cabs with a number on the roof. Just ask which number goes where you want to and flag it down. US$0.65 by day, US$0.75 after 2100. **Taxis**, basic fare US$3.80.

Car hire A hired car shared between several people is an economic alternative for visiting the Atacama region. A 4WD jeep (necessary for the desert) costs US$100 a day, a car US$70. Hire companies include **Alamo**, T364543, **Avis**, T319757, **Budget**, T341076, **Hertz**, T341380 and **IQSA**, T310281. All offices close Sat 1300 till Mon morning. Airport offices only open when flights arrive. If intending to drive in the border area, visit the police in San Pedro to get maps of which areas may have landmines. See Essentials for agency web addresses.

Train Station on Av Balmaceda opposite Sotomayor, T348900. To **Uyuni** (Bolivia), weekly service, Wed 2300, though often doesn't leave till early next morning. If on time the train arrives in **Ollagüe** at 0700, but can take up to 24 hrs. The Chilean engine returns to Calama and you have to wait up to 7 hrs for the Bolivian engine. You have to disembark at the border for customs and immigration. Interpol is in a modern building 400 m east of the station. Through fare to Uyuni is US$15. Book seats (passport essential) on Mon, Tue or Wed from the **Ferrocarril** office at the station (closed 1300-1500 for lunch), or a local travel agency. Catch the train as early as possible: although seats are assigned, the designated carriages may not arrive; passengers try to occupy several seats to sleep on, but will move if you show your ticket. Sleeping bag and/or blanket essential. Restaurant car operates to the border, cheap; food also available at Ollagüe. Money can be changed on the train once in Bolivia, but beware forged notes.

❶ Directory

Calama *p652*

Banks Exchange rates are generally poor especially for TCs. Many Redbanc ATMs on Latorre and Sotomayor. Several **cambios**, eg Marbumor, 2 branches on Sotomayor (at Latorre and Av Balmaceda), changes US$, TCs, Argentine pesos and bolivianos, **Moon Valley**, Vivar 1818, and **Parina**, Sotomayor 1984, US$ only. **Consulates** Bolivia, Latorre 1395, T341976, open (in theory) Mon-Fri 0900-1230, helpful. **Internet** Many places in the centre, usually about US$1 per hr. **Post office** Granaderos y V Mackenna. 0830-1300, 1530-1830, Sat 0900-1230, will not send parcels over 1 kg. **Telephones** Lots of phone offices. Entel, Sotomayor opposite Hotel Alfa, is good for phone, fax and internet.

San Pedro de Atacama → *Phone code: 055. Colour map 6, grid B2. Population: 2,824.*

San Pedro de Atacama (*Altitude 2,436 m*), 103 km southeast of Calama (paved, no fuel, food or water along the way) is a small town, more Spanish-Indian looking than is usual in Chile. Long before the arrival of the Spanish, the area was the centre of the Atacameño culture. There is a definite sense of history in the shady streets and the crumbling ancient walls, which drift away from the town into the fields, and then into the dust. Owing to the clear atmosphere and isolation, there are wonderful views of the night sky. Lunar landscapes, blistering geysers and salt flats are all close by. Now famous among visitors as the centre for excursions in this part of the Atacama, San Pedro can be overrun with visitors in summer. The **tourist office** on the plaza ⓘ *Toconao y Gustavo Le Paige, T851420, sanpedrodeatacama@sernatur.cl, open Mon-Wed and Fri 1000-1330, 1500-1930, Sat 1000-1400*. Helpful, has a useful suggestions book, with feedback from other visitors about agencies' tours. See also www.sanpedroatacama.com. **Note** The main tourist season October-end February is accompanied by high prices and pressure on resources.

The **Iglesia de San Pedro**, dating from the 17th century, is supposedly the second oldest church in the country. It has been heavily restored (the tower was added in 1964). The roof is made of cactus. Nearby, on the Plaza, is the **Casa Incaica**, the oldest building in San Pedro. **Museo Arqueológico** ⓘ *www.ucn.cl/museo, Mon-Fri, 0900-1200, 1400-1800 (Sat-Sun opens at 1000), US$4*. The collection of Padre Gustave Paige, a Belgian missionary who lived in San Pedro between 1955 and 1980, is now under the care of the Universidad Católica del Norte. It is a fascinating repository of artefacts, well organized to trace the development of prehispanic Atacameño society. Labels on displays (in Spanish) are good, and there is a comprehensive booklet in Spanish and English.

Around San Pedro de Atacama

The Valle de la Luna with fantastic landscapes caused by the erosion of salt mountains, is a nature reserve 12 km west of San Pedro. It is crossed by the old San Pedro-Calama road. Although buses on the new Calama-San Pedro road will stop to let you off where the old road

San Pedro de Atacama

Sleeping
Casa de Norma 1
El Tatio 2
Hostal Edén Atacameño 3
Hostal Martita 7
Hostal Takha-Takha 4
Hostal Vilacoya 5
Hostería San Pedro 6
Kimal 8
La Casa de Don Tomás 10

Mama Tierra 9
Red Lican Huasi 12
Residencial Chiloé 11
Residencial Licancábur 14
Residencial Puritama 19
Residencial Sonchek 15
Sumaj-Jallpa 13
Tambillo 16
Tulor 17

Eating
Adobe 1
Café El Viaje 2
Café Étnico 3
Café Export 4
Café Tierra
Todo Natural 5
Casa Piedra 1
La Casona 6
La Estaka 5

branches off 13 km northwest of San Pedro (signposted to Peine), it is far better to travel from San Pedro on the old road, either on foot (allow three hours there, three hours back; no lifts), by bicycle (only for the fit and difficult after sunset) or by car (a 20-km round trip is possible). The Valle is best seen at sunset (if the sky is clear), although this is also the most crowded time. Do not leave any rubbish behind on desert excursions – the dry climate preserves it perfectly. Take water, hat, camera and torch. Camping is forbidden.

The **Pukará de Quitor**, a pre-Inca fortress restored in 1981, is 3 km north of San Pedro along the river. The fortress, which stands on the west bank, was stormed by the Spanish under Pedro de Valdivia. A further 4 km up the river there are Inca ruins at Catarpe. At **Tulor**, 12 km southwest of San Pedro, there is an archaeological site where parts of a stone-age village (dated 800 BC-500 AD) have been excavated; can be visited on foot, or take a tour, US$8 pp. Nearby are the ruins of a 17th century village, abandoned in the 18th century because of lack of water.

El Tatio (*Altitude 4,500 m*), the site of geysers, is a popular attraction. From San Pedro it is reached by a maintained road which runs northeast past the thermal pools at **Puritama** (28 km, worth a visit). The geysers are at their best 0630-0830, though the spectacle varies: locals say the performance is best when weather conditions are stable. Warning: People have been killed or seriously injured by falling into the geysers, or through the thin crust of the mud. Do not stand too close as the geysers can erupt unexpectedly. A swimming pool has been built nearby (take costume and towel). There is no public transport and hitching is impossible. If going in a hired car, make sure the engine is suitable for very high altitudes and is protected with antifreeze. If driving in the dark it is almost impossible to find your way: the sign for El Tatio is north of the turn off (follow a tour bus). Tours arranged by agencies in San Pedro and Calama; nearest *hospedaje* in Caspana (see above).

Toconao (*Population 500*), 37 km south of San Pedro de Atacama, is on the eastern shore of the Salar de Atacama. All houses are built of bricks of white volcanic stone, *sillar*, which gives the village a very characteristic appearance totally different from San Pedro. The 18th-century church and bell tower are also built of volcanic stone. East of the village is a beautifully green gorge called the Quebrada de Jere, filled with fruit trees and grazing cattle (entry US$2). Worth visiting are the vineyards which produce a sweet wine. The quarry where the *sillar* is worked can be visited, about 1½ km east (the stones sound like bells when struck).

South of Toconao is one of the main entrances to the **Salar de Atacama** ① *entry is controlled by CONAF in Toconao, US$5*. This vast 300,000-ha salt lake (the third largest expanse of salt flats in the world) is home to flamingoes and other birds (though most of the flamingos have moved to lakes higher in the Andes and numbers depend on breeding times). The air is so dry that you can usually see right across the Salar. A huge lake half a metre below the surface contributes to a slight haze in the air. The area is also rich in minerals. Three areas of the Salar form part of the **Reserva Nacional de los Flamencos**, which is in seven sectors totalling 73,986 ha and administered by CONAF in San Pedro.

From Toconao the road heads south through scenic villages to the mine at Laco (one poor stretch below the mine), before proceeding to Laguna Sico (4,079 m), and Paso Sico to Argentina.

Border with Bolivia and Argentina
→ *Between Oct and Mar, Chilean time is 1 hr later than Bolivian.*

Hito Cajón for the border with Bolivia is reached by road 47 km east of San Pedro. The first 35 km are the paved road to Paso de Jama (see below), then it's unpaved to Hito Cajón. From the border it is 7 km north to Laguna Verde. Chilean immigration and customs are in San Pedro, open 0800-2300 (maybe closed lunchtimes). For the Bolivian consulate, see under Calama. Bolivian immigration only gives 1 month entry here.

The ride from San Pedro de Atacama to Salta on a fully paved road through the 4,400-m **Paso de Jama** is spectacular. It stays high on the puna, going by snow-capped peaks, lakes and salt pans, before reaching the Argentine border post, 160 km from San Pedro. There are no money changing facilities nor any other services here. Be prepared for cold. The road continues paved on the Argentine side to Susques and Jujuy. This is much more popular than the **Paso Sico** route, which is hardly used by any public or heavy traffic (paved to Socaire on the Chilean side, about 40% paved in Argentina to San Antonio de los Cobres, slow going on the unpaved parts). **Chilean immigration** and customs are in San Pedro. When crossing by private vehicle, check the road conditions before setting out as Paso de Jama can be closed by heavy rain in summer and blocked by snow in winter. **Note** At all border crossings, incoming vehicles and passengers are searched for fruit, vegetables and dairy produce, which may not be brought into Chile.

● Sleeping

San Pedro de Atacama p656, map p656
There is electricity, but take a torch (flashlight) for walking at night. Residenciales supply candles, but better to buy them in Calama beforehand. Rooms are scarce in Jan/Feb, and expensive all year round.
L Explora, Av Américo Vespucio Sur 80, p 5, Santiago, T206 6060, www.explora.com. Luxury full-board and excursion programme, advance booking only. Recommended.
AL Hostería San Pedro, Toconao 460, T851011, hsanpedro@chilesat.net. Pool (residents only), petrol station, tents for hire, cabins, hot water, has own generator, restaurant (good almuerzo), bar, takes Amex but no Tcs.
AL Tulor, Atienza, T/F851248, tulor@chilesat.net. Good service, pool, heating, laundry, excellent restaurant. Recommended.
A La Casa de Don Tomás, Tocopilla s/n, T851055, www.dontomas.cl. A bit of a walk from the centre, but pleasant, quiet, modern adobe style, pool, very helpful staff, no TV in rooms, hot water, good breakfast, snacks also served. Recommended, book in advance.
A Kimal, Atienza y Caracoles, T851159, kimal@entelchile.net. Comfortable, nice living room, excellent breakfast and restaurant, small pool with jacuzzi and spa. Recommended.
B El Tatio, Caracoles 219, T851092, eltatio@sanpedroatacama.com. Comfortable, small rooms, around courtyard, tiny pool, bargain off season, English spoken, very nice if a bit run down.
C Hostal Takha-Takha, Caracoles s/n, T851038. **F** pp for cheaper rooms, lovely garden, nice rooms, camping **G** pp, laundry. Recommended.
C Tambillo, Le Paige, T/F851078. Pretty, comfortable, 24-hr electricity and hot water, good value.
C Res Licancábur, Toconao, T851007, **D** off-season, cheaper rooms **F** pp, nicely furnished, with character.
C-E Mama Tierra, Pachamama 615, T851418. With and without bath, kitchen, hot showers, hammocks in garden, mini mart next door, peaceful, helpful, some English spoken, will pick up from bus stations. Recommended.
C-F Res Puritama, Caracoles 113, T851540. Simple but comfortable, large patio, kitchen facilities, good showers, camping possible, nice big dogs.
D Hostal Martita, Palpana 4. **G** singles. 5 mins' walk from centre, some rooms with bath, good beds, good value.

D Res Chiloé, Atienza, T851017. Hot water, sunny veranda, good beds and bathrooms, rooms with bath **B**, no singles, good meals, breakfast extra, laundry facilities, luggage store.
E Hostal Vilacoya, Tocopilla, T851006. Singles **G**. Set around courtyard, comfortable beds, hot water, helpful, well-equipped kitchen, luggage store, free internet access.
E La Quinta Adela, Toconao, T851272, qtadela@cvmail.cl. Hot water, no breakfast.
E pp Res Sonchek, Calama 370, T851112. Pleasant but strict, shared bath, also dormitory, no towels, laundry facilities, use of kitchen, garden, restaurant, French and English spoken, mixed reports.
E pp Casa de Norma, Tocopilla, T851114. Family accommodation, simple rooms, lovely patio. Recommended.
F pp Hostal Edén Atacameño, Toconao, T851154. Renovated, rooms with and without bath, hot water, laundry, parking, also camping with laundry and unkempt cooking facilities, **F**.
F pp Sumaj-Jallpa, Volcán El Tatio 703, on edge of town, T851416. Prices vary, some rooms more expensive, Swiss-Chilean owned, spacious, kitchen, pool table, new.
Camping See Swimming pools, in Activities and tours, below.
Rural tourism Red de Turismo Rural Lican Huasi, Caracoles 349, T851593, likanhuasi@gmail.com. A network of *casas de huéspedes* in San Pedro and villages in the II Region, such as Solor, Socaire, Ollagüe, Caspana and Chiu-Chiu, with good facilities.

Around San Pedro de Atacama:
Toconao p657
There are basic residenciales.
G pp, Residencial Valle de Toconao, on Láscar. Nice and quiet, also serving good, simple meals. And others.

● Eating

San Pedro de Atacama p656, map p656
Few places are open before 1000. Most places offer an evening special for under US$10. Drink bottled water as the local supply has a high mineral content, which not agree with those unaccustomed to it. A "pueblo turístico" has been built just east of town, with several late-night bars and clubs.

♥♥ **Adobe**, Caracoles. Open fire, internet, good atmosphere and meeting place, loud music. Described as "like Greenwich Village/ Islington in the Atacama".

♥♥ **Café Etnico**, Tocopilla 423, T851377, cafeetnico@ hotmail.com. Good food, juices and sandwiches, cosy, book exchange, internet (free for diners), also has a wine club.

♥♥ **Café Export**, Toconao y Caracoles. Nice decor, enormous *empanadas* (big enough to share), vegetarian options, real coffee, English spoken, loud music.

♥♥ **Casa Piedra**, Caracoles. Open fire, also has a cheap menu, many of the waiters are musicians who sometimes play live folk music, good food and cocktails. Recommended.

♥♥ **La Casona**, Caracoles. Good food, vegetarian options, cheap almuerzo, large portions. Interesting "Cubist-style" desert paintings. Popular and recommended.

♥♥ **La Estaka**, Caracoles 259, T851201. Wood fire, cane roof, jazz music, pizzería and other dishes, good food, bar and book exchange, lively after 2300, favoured spot of the local New Age crowd.

♥ **Café Kebab**, Toconao 544. Good for breakfast and coffee, good value.

♥ **Café Tierra Todo Natural**, Caracoles. Excellent fruit juices, "the best bread in the Atacama", real coffee, yoghurt, best for breakfast, opens earliest.

♥ **Café El Viaje**, Tocopilla in the Casa de la Arte. Nice patio, vegetarian food, travel information, internet access.

O Shopping

San Pedro de Atacama *p656, map p656*
Handicrafts Agrupación de Artesanos, beside the Biblioteca (opposite the school), is the place to go for local handicrafts. The **feria** which runs off the Plaza is mostly foreign goods, eg from Peru and Ecuador.
Supermarkets El Inca, Calama y Le Paige. For fruit and vegetables. El Oasis, Caracoles y Vilama.

▲ Activities and tours

San Pedro de Atacama *p656, map p656*
Mountain biking Bicycles for hire all over town, by the hour or full day: US$9 for 'professional' model, cheaper for 'amateur'. Tracks in the desert can be really rough, so check the bike's condition and carry a torch if riding after dark.
Horse hire US$11.
Swimming pools Piscina Oasis, at Pozo Tres, only 3 km southeast but walking there is tough and not recommended. Open all year daily (except Mon) 0500-1730, US$2 to swim, sometimes empty. Camping US$4,

good showers and picnic facilities, very popular at weekends.

Tour operators
Usual tour rates (may rise in high season): to Valle de la Luna, US$11, including US$3 entry fee. To the Salar de Atacama, Toconao and Altiplano lakes, 0700-1800, US$50, including US$10 entry fee. To El Tatio (begin at 0400) with trekking, US$30 (including US$4 entry; take swimming costume and warm clothing). El Tatio and villages, US$50. Beware of tours to Valle de la Luna leaving too late to catch sunset – leave before 1600. Before taking a tour, check that the agency has dependable vehicles, suitable equipment (eg oxygen for El Tatio), a guide who speaks English if so advertised, and that the company is well-established. Report any complaints to the municipality or Sernatur.
Atacama Connection, Caracoles y Toconao, T851548, www.atacamaconnection.com. For local tours, trekking, private tours.
Cactus Tours, Atienza 419, T851524, www.cactustour.cl. Good tours to local sites, good vehicles, most guides speak English. Recommended.
Cosmo Andino Expediciones, Caracoles s/n, T/F851069, cosmoandina@entelchile.net. Very professional and experienced, several languages spoken, owner Martin Beeris (Martín El Holandés). Recommended.
Desert Adventure, Caracoles s/n, T/F851067, www.desertadventure.cl. Good guides and range of trips, English spoken, modern fleet of vehicles, mostly good reports.
Rancho Cactus, Toconao, T851506, F851052. Offers horse riding with good guides to Valle de la Luna and other sites (Farolo and Valerie – speaks French and English), not for experienced riders.
Southern Cross Adventure, Toconao 544 (see under Santiago, Tour operators).
Space, Caracoles 166, T851935/09-817 8354 (mob), www.spaceobs.com. Run by French astronomer Alain, who speaks 3 languages and has set up a small observatory in the village of Solor, south of San Pedro; gives tours 2000-2330 to study the night sky, hot drink included but wear all your warmest clothes.
Turismo Colque, Caracoles, T851109, www.colquetours.com. Runs tours to Laguna Verde, Laguna Colorada, Uyuni and other sites in Bolivia. 3 days, changing vehicles at the border as the Bolivian authorities refuse permits for Chilean tour vehicles, basic accommodation, take food and especially water (1-day tour to Laguna Verde possible), entrance to Eduardo Avaroa Reserve in Bolivia is included. Passports are stamped en route (check if you need a visa for Bolivia in advance – consulate is in Calama).

Vulcano, Caracoles s/n, T851023, www.vulcano chile.cl. Mountain climbs, sandboarding and other adventure tours to infrequently-visited areas, mountain bike hire. Recommended.

⊙ Transport

San Pedro de Atacama *p656, map p656*
Bus To **Calama**: US$3, **Atacama**, **Frontera** (many daily), 1½ hrs, **Tur-Bus**, Licancábur 294, T851549, open 0700-2045, several including 1800 (continues to Antofagasta). Frequencies vary with more departures in Jan-Feb and some weekends. Book in advance to return from San Pedro on Sun afternoon. Tur-Bus to **Arica**, 2030, US$24. **Tur-Bus** to **Santiago**, 4 a day, 3 on Sun, US$45. **Frontera** to **Socaire**, Mon, Thu, Fri 1930, Sun 1230, 2200, US$4; to **Toconao**, 4 a day (3 on Sun), US$1.40. To **Argentina**: Géminis, on Toconao (changes bolivianos), Wed and Sun 1130, to **Salta**, US$45, 9 hrs, reserve in advance and book Salta hotel as bus arrives 0100-0200 (schedules change often). Pullman (Frontera office), Wed, Sun 1045, US$45.

Border with Bolivia
Tránsito público leaves San Pedro for **Hito Cajón** at 0800 or 0830 and costs US$5.70, return

about 1000 Chilean time. It is usually booked through an agency in town. Occasionally it runs in the afternoon. **Tránsito público** from the border to San Pedro takes passengers to their hotels after passing through immigration. There is no other public transport to Hito Cajón: do not be tempted to hitch to the border and beyond as you risk being stranded without water or shelter at sub-zero temperatures.

⊙ Directory

San Pedro de Atacama *p656, map p656*
Banks Redbanc ATM for Mastercard, Maestro and Cirrus on Le Paige, opposite the Museum. Also at Caracoles y Domingo Atienza. ATMs are unpredictable here; take pesos from Calama or elsewhere if possible. **Cambio Atacama** on Toconao, casi Caracoles, changes TCs, good rates for cash, 1030-1800 daily. Some places change euros; ask around. **Internet** Several places in town. **Post offices** in the Casa Parroquial on the Plaza, open 0900-1230, 1430-1800. **Telephones** Telefónica in Galería Peral at Caracoles 317, local 4, also has internet. Also at Caracoles y Vilama. Entel is on the corner of Plaza at Vilama, in the arcade.

Iquique and around

The Cordillera de la Costa slowly loses height north of Iquique, terminating at the Morro at Arica (see page 665): from Iquique north it drops directly to the sea and as a result there are few beaches along this coast. Inland, the central depression (pampa) 1,000-1,200 m is arid and punctuated by salt-flats south of Iquique. Between Iquique and Arica it is crossed from east to west by four gorges. East of this depression lies the sierra, the western branch of the Andes, beyond which is a high plateau, the altiplano (3,500-4,500 m) from which rise volcanic peaks. In the altiplano there are a number of lakes, the largest of which, Lago Chungará (see page 668), is one of the highest in the world. The coastal strip and the pampa are rainless; on the coast temperatures are moderated by the Pacific, but in the pampa variations of temperature between day and night are extreme, ranging from 30°C to 0°C. The altiplano is much colder.

Iquique → *Phone code: 057. Colour map 6, grid B2. Population: 145,139.*
Iquique is an attractive port and city with well-preserved historical buildings. Around it the desert pampa stretches north, south and to the mountains. Several oases also have strong historical associations, either in the form of geoglyphs, the last evidence of peoples long vanished, or the ghost towns of nitrate operations. Mamiña and Pica are thermal resorts within easy reach of Iquique; both are beautiful, tranquil places.

The name of the capital of I Región (Tarapacá) and one of the main northern ports, is derived from the Aymara word *ique-ique*, meaning place of 'rest and tranquillity'. The city, 492 km north of Antofagasta and 47 km west of the Pan-American Highway, is situated on a rocky peninsula at the foot of the high Atacama pampa, sheltered by the headlands of Punta Gruesa and Cavancha. The city, which was partly destroyed by earthquake in 1877, became the centre of the nitrate trade after its transfer from Peru to Chile at the end of the War of the Pacific. A short distance north of town along Amunátegui is the **Free Zone (Zofri)** ⓘ *Mon-Sat 0800-2100, limit on tax free purchases US$1,000 for foreigners, US$750 for Chileans, getting there: colectivo from the centre US$0.75*. It is worth visiting this giant shopping centre, which sells all manner of imported items, including electronic goods. It is much better value than its equivalent in Punta Arenas. **Tourist office** ⓘ *Sernatur, Anibal Pinto 436, T312238, infoiquique@sernatur.cl, Mon-Fri, 0830-1630*. Masses of information, very helpful.

In the centre of the old town is the **Plaza Prat**. On the northeast corner of the Plaza is the Centro Español, built in extravagant Moorish style by the local Spanish community in 1904; the ground floor is a restaurant, on the upper floors are paintings of scenes from Don Quijote and from Spanish history. Three blocks north of the Plaza is the old Aduana (customs house) built in 1871; in 1891 it was the scene of an important battle in the Civil War between supporters of President Balmaceda and congressional forces. Part of it is now the **Museo Naval** ⓘ *Esmeralda 250, Tue-Fri 1000-1300, 1600-1900, Sat 1000-1400, US$0.50*, focusing on the Battle of Iquique, 1879. Along Calle Baquedano, which runs south from Plaza Prat, are the attractive former mansions of the 'nitrate barons', dating from between 1880 and 1903. The finest of these is the **Palacio Astoreca** ⓘ *Baquedano y O'Higgins 350, Tue-Fri 1000-1300, 1400-1800, Sat 1000-1300, US$1*. Built in 1903, it was subsequently the Intendencia and now a museum of fine late 19th century furniture and shells. **Museo Regional** ⓘ *Baquedano 951, Mon-Fri 0800-1300, 1500-1850, Sat 1030-1300, Sun 1100-1600 (in summer 1000-1330)*, contains an archaeological section tracing the development of prehispanic civilizations in the region; an ethnographical collection of the Isluga culture of the Altiplano (AD 400), and of contemporary Aymara culture; also a section devoted to the nitrate era which includes a model of a nitrate office and the collection of the

Iquique

Pacific Ocean

To Zofri

Sleeping
Arturo Prat 1
Atenas 5

Barros Arana 2
Caiti 3
Cano 4
Hostal América 7
Hostal Cuneo 8
Hostal Li Ming 10
Inti-Llanka 11
Oregon 12
Residencial Nan-King 13

Eating
Bavaria 1
Bolivia 7
Boulevard 8
Brasileña 12
Café Estación Iquique 13
Casino Español 2
Cioccolata 3
Club de la Unión 4

Compañía Italiana
de Bomberos 9
El Barril del Fraile 5
El Tercero Ojito 15
La Picada Curicana 6
Nan King 14
Sciaraffia 10
Win Li 11

0 metres 200
0 yards 200

nitrate entrepreneur, Santiago Humberstone. Sea lions and pelicans can be seen from the harbour. There are **cruises** ① *US$4, 45 mins, minimum 10 people*, from the passenger pier.

The **beaches** at Cavancha just south of the town centre are good; those at Huaiquique are reasonable, November-March. There are restaurants at Cavancha. For surfers, etc, the better bet is the pounding surf of Playa Brava, further to the south. Piscina Godoy is a fresh water swimming pool on Av Costanera at Aníbal Pinto and Riquelme, open in the afternoon, US$1. Cerro Dragón, the large sand dune behind Iquique, is the place for sandboarding; great for views too. There are several hills where you can paraglide, good for beginners.

Around Iquique

Humberstone, a large nitrate town, is now abandoned. It is at the junction of the Pan-American Highway and the road to Iquique. Entry by 'donation', US$2, guided tours Saturday-Sunday, leaflets available, T751213. Colectivo from Iquique US$2; phone near site for booking return. Though closed since 1961, you can see the church, theatre, pulpería (company stores) and the swimming pool (built of metal plating from ships' hulls). Nearby are the ruins of other mining towns including Santa Laura. Local tour companies run trips to the area, including Humberstone, Santa Laura, Pisagua and **Pozo Almonte**, 52 km east (*Population c. 5,400*). This town was the chief service provider of the nitrate companies until their closure in 1960. The **Museo Histórico Salitrero** ① *on the tree-shaded plaza, Mon-Fri 0830-1300 and 1600-1900*, displays artefacts and photographs of the nitrate era.

To Cerro Pintados (see page 652) take any bus south, US$2.50, and walk from the Pan-American Highway then hitch back or flag down a bus. From Pozo Almonte 74 km (paved), **Mamiña** (*Population c. 600, Altitude 2,750 m*) has abundant thermal springs and a mud spring (**Baño Los Chinos** ① *0930-1300*). The therapeutic properties of the waters and mud are Mamiña's main claim to fame. Mineral water from the spring is sold throughout northern Chile. There are ruins of a prehispanic pukará (fortress) and a church, built in 1632, the only colonial Andean church in Chile with two towers. An Aymara cultural centre, Kaspi-kala, has an artesanía workshop and outlet.

La Tirana (*Population 550, Altitude 995 m*) is famous for a religious festival to the Virgen del Carmen, held from 10 to 16 July, which attracts some 150,000 pilgrims. Over 100 groups dance night and day, decked out in spectacular colourful masks, starting on 12 July. All the dances take place in the main plaza in front of the church; no alcohol is served. Accommodation is impossible to find, other than in organized camp sites (take tent) which have basic toilets and showers. It is 10 km east of the Pan-American Highway (70 km east of Iquique), turn-off 9 km south of Pozo Almonte. **Pica** (*Population 1,767, Altitude 1,325 m*), 42 km from La Tirana, was the most important centre of early Spanish settlement in the area. Most older buildings date from the nitrate period when it became a popular resort. The town is famous for its pleasant climate, citrus groves and two natural springs, the best of which is **Cocha Resbaladero** ① *0700-2000 all year, US$3, snack bar, changing rooms, beautiful pool, tourist office opposite*.

Many other sites around Iquique, including the Giant of the Atacama (see below) and places to see fossilised dinosaur footprints, are difficult to visit without a car; tours available though from Pica.

From Iquique to the Bolivian Border

At **Huara**, 33 km north of Pozo Almonte, a paved road turns off the Pan-American Highway to **Colchane**. At 13 km east of Huara are the huge geoglyphs of Cerro Unitas, with the giant humanoid figure of the Gigante del Atacama (86 m tall) and a sun with 24 rays, on the sides of two hills (best seen from a distance). Some buses from Iquique to La Paz and Oruro pass through, or La Paloma at 2300 from Esmeralda y Juan Martínez. 173 km northeast is the Bolivian border at Pisiga (open daily 0800-1300, 1500-2000). An unpaved road continues to Oruro, 233 km northeast.

Northwest of Colchane, the **Parque Nacional Volcán Isluga** ① *Park Administration at Enquelga, 10 km north of the entrance, but guardaparques are seldom there, Arica T58-250570 for details of hospedaje at the guardería*, covers 174,744 ha at altitudes above 2,100 m and is some of the best volcanic scenery in northern Chile. (**D** pp). The village of **Isluga**, near the park entrance, 6 km northwest of Colchane, has an 18th century Andean walled church and bell tower. Wildlife varies according to altitude but includes guanacos, vicuñas, llamas, alpacas, vizcachas, condors and flamingoes.

The Pan-American Highway runs across the Atacama desert at an altitude of around 1,000 m, with several steep hills which are best tackled in daylight (at night, sea mist, camanchaca, can reduce visibility). At **Zapiga**, 80 km north of Pozo Almonte, there is a crossroads: east through Camiña (*Population 500, Altitude: 2,400 m*), a picturesque village in an oasis, 67 km east of Zapiga along a poor road. Thence mountain roads lead across the Parque Nacional Volcán Isluga to Colchane. The westerly branch runs 41 km to **Pisagua** (*Population 200*), formerly an important nitrate port, now a fishing village. Several old wooden buildings are National Monuments. The fish restaurants make a pleasant stop for a meal. Mass graves dating from just after the 1973 military coup were discovered near here in 1990. At Km 57 north of Huara there is a British cemetery at Tiliviche dating from 1825. The Geoglyphs of Tiliviche representing a group of llamas (signposted, to left, and easily accessible), Km 127, can be seen from the highway.

● Sleeping

Iquique *p660, map p661*
Accommodation is scarce in the weeks before Christmas as many Chileans visit Iquique to shop in the Zofri. There's no campsite in Iquique but wild camping is possible on Playa la Brava. All hotels in the list are recommended.

A Arturo Prat, Aníbal Pinto 695, Plaza Prat, T427000, www.hotelarturoprat.cl. 4-star, attentive service, good value, pool, games room, health suite, expensive restaurant, tours arranged.

B Atenas, Los Rieles 738, Cavancha, T431100, atenashotel2000@yahoo.es. Pleasant, personal, good value, good service and food, pool.

B Barros Arana, Barros Arana 1302, T412840, www.hotelbarrosarana.cl. Modern (in 2 parts – newer section much nicer), internet, quiet area, pool, good value.

B Cano, Ramírez 996, T315580, www.iqq.cl/hotelcano. Big rooms, nice atmosphere, good value.

C Inti-Llanka, Obispo Labbé 825, T311104, www.inti-llanka.cl. Spacious rooms with good beds, helpful, good value.

D Caiti, Gorostiaga 483, T/F423038. Pleasant, with breakfast and all mod cons, rooms fairly basic and stuffy in the interior, ones with outside window are better .

D-E Hostal América, Rodríguez 550, near beach, T427524, transjaws81@hotmail.com. Shared bath, no breakfast, motorcycle parking, good value.

D-E Hostal Cuneo, Baquedano 1175, T428654, hostalcuneo@hotmail.com. Modern, nice rooms, shared bath, helpful, pleasant, piano in the living room, good value.

D-E Hostal Li Ming, Barros Arana 705, T421912, www.hostal.cl. Simple, good value, small rooms, cable TV.

D-E Res Nan-King, Thompson 752, T330961. Small but nice rooms, well-kept, cable TV, no breakfast.

E pp Oregon (also called Durana), San Martín 294, T410959. Central, hot water, breakfast included.

Around Iquique *p662*
Mamiña
There are several hotels and residenciales offering rooms with bath fed by the springs and full board.

AL pp Refugio del Salitre, Latorre 766, T319655, www.refugiodelsalitre.cl. Secluded, nice rooms and lovely views, helpful, pool, games room, pretty terrace. Recommended.

A pp Los Cardenales, Av Barrios Chinos s/n, T517000, slvezendy@yahoo.com. Beautifully designed, comfortable, superb food, English and German spoken, pool.

A Llama Inn, T419893, llamainn@vtr.net. Room only, good meals extra (including vegetarian on request), comfortable, pool, pool tables, casino table, massage, terrace. Highly Recommended.

C pp Termal La Coruña, T09-9543 0360. Good, Spanish cuisine, horse riding, nice views, games room, pool, children half price, very helpful. Highly Recommended.

Pica
Hotels fill up at weekends, holiday times and during La Tirana's festival 10-16 Jul: book ahead.

B Santa Rosa, Sector Comiño, Lote B, T741670, www.resortsantarosa.cl. Large rooms and stylish cabins (A) with kitchen and patio, lovely gardens, quiet, good restaurant, excellent value.

D Los Emilios, Cochrane 201, T741126. With breakfast, interesting old building with nice lounge and patio, small pool. Recommended.

D O'Higgins, Balmaceda 6, T721524. Modern, well furnished, F for singles.

E San Andrés, Balmaceda 197, T741319, gringa733@hotmail.com. F singles. . With breakfast, basic, good restaurant, serves cheap 4-course *almuerzos*.

● Eating

Iquique *p660, map p661*
The restaurants on the wharf on the opposite side of Av Costanera from the bus terminal are

poor value. Many chifas including **Win Li**,
San Martin 439, and many on Tarapacá 800/
900 blocks. There are several good, cheap
seafood restaurants on the 2nd floor of
the central market, Barros Arana y Latorre.
ⓎⓎ Bavaria, Pinto 926. Expensive German-
Chilean steakhouse chain restaurant,
reasonably priced café serving real coffee,
snacks and *almuerzo*.
ⓎⓎ Boulevard, Baquedano 790, T413695,
www.boulevard.cl. Good French and
Mediterranean cuisine, English and
French spoken.
ⓎⓎ Brasileña, Vivar 1143, T423236. Brazilian run,
serves seafood in the week, Brazilian food on Sat.
ⓎⓎ Casino Español, Plaza Prat, T423284. Good
meals well served in beautiful Moorish-style
1904 building.
ⓎⓎ Club de la Unión, Plaza Prat, T414236.
Roof terrace with panoramic views, open
lunchtimes only, good food.
ⓎⓎ Colonial, Plaza Prat. Fish and seafood,
popular, good value.
ⓎⓎ El Barril del Fraile, Ramírez 1181, T390334.
Good seafood, nice atmosphere.
ⓎⓎ Nan King, Amunátegui 533, T420434.
Large portions, good value, renowned
as best Chinese in town.
ⓎⓎ Sciaraffia, Sgto Aldea 803 (Mercado
Centenario). Open 24 hrs, good value,
large choice.
ⓎⓎ Ⓨ El Tercer Ojito, P Lynch 1420, T426517.
Peruvian specialities and a vegetarian menu.
Ⓨ Bolivia, Serrano 751. *Humitas* and
salteñas. Recommended.
Ⓨ Compañía Italiana de Bomberos,
Serrano 520. Authentic Italian cuisine,
excellent value *almuerzo*, otherwise more
expensive, but recommended.
Ⓨ La Picada Curicana, Pinto y Zegers.
Good hearty Central Chilean country
cooking (such as oven-roasted game,
served in clay pots), large portions,
good value *menú de la casa*.
Café Estación Iquique, P Lynch 787.
Cultural café with temporary exhibitions
and occasional live music.
Cioccolata, Pinto 487 (another branch in
the Zofri). Very good coffee and cakes.
Salon de Té Ricotta, Vivar y Latorre.
Very popular for *onces*, quite expensive.
Tropical, Baquedano y Thompson.
Recommended for juices and snacks.
Via Pontony, Baquedano y Zegers. Fruit
juices and *empanadas*, good.

Around Iquique: Pica *p662*
Try the local *alfajores*, delicious cakes filled
with cream and mango honey.

ⓎⓎ El Edén, Riquelme 12. 1st class local food
in delightful surroundings, fine ice cream,
best restaurant in town.
Ⓨ La Mía Pappa, Balmaceda, near plaza.
Good selection of meat and juices,
attractive location.
Ⓨ La Palmera, Balmaceda 115. Excellent
almuerzo, popular with locals, near plaza.
Ⓨ La Viña, Ibáñez 70, by Cocha de
Resbaladero. Good cheap *almuerzo*.

ⓞ Bars and clubs

Iquique *p660, map p661*
Most discos are out of town on the
road south to the airport.
Santa Fé, Mall Las Américas, locales 10-11-193.
Mexican, live music, great atmosphere, very
popular. Highly recommended.
Taberna Barracuda, Gorostiaga 601. For late
night food, drink, video entertainment, dancing,
nice decor, nice atmosphere.

▲ Activities and tours

Iquique *p660, map p661*
The tourist office maintains a full list of operators.
Parapenting Contact the Zone Norte branch
of the Chilean Hanggliding Association,
www.achvl.cl.
Altazor, Serrano 145, of 702, T431382,
www.altazorsky.com.
Avitours, Baquedano 997, T473775,
www.avitours.cl. Tour to Pintados, La Tirana,
Humberstone, Pica, etc, some bilingual guides,
day tours start at US$20.
Paraventura, T329041/09-9874 1334,
www.paraventura.cl. Frank Valenzuela, qualified
tandem pilot, professional and helpful, great
40-min flights. Recommended.

ⓞ Transport

Iquique *p660, map p661*
Air Diego Aracena international airport,
35 km south at Chucumata. Taxi US$11; airport
transfer, T310800, US$5 for 3 or more passengers,
unreliable. LAN, Aerolíneas del Sur and Sky fly
to **Arica**, **Antofagasta** and **Santiago**. LAN also
fly to **Calama**, **Copiapó** and **La Serena**. See
Getting there, Essentials, for international flights.
Bus Terminal at north end of Patricio Lynch (not
all buses leave from here); bus company offices
are near the market on Sgto Aldea and B Arana.
Tur-Bus, Esmeralda 594, T472987 (420634 at
terminal), with Redbanc ATM and luggage store.
Pullman, in terminal T426522. Southbound
buses are searched for duty-free goods, at
Quillagua on the Pan-American Highway and at

Chipana on the coastal Route 1. To **Arica**, buses and colectivos, US$7, 4½ hrs. To **Antofagasta**, US$14, 6 hrs. To **Calama**, 6 hrs, US$14. To **Tocopilla** along the coastal road, buses and minibuses, several companies, 3 hrs, US$8. To **La Serena**, 18 hrs, US$25. To **Santiago**, 25 hrs, several companies, US$36 (US$56 salón cama, US$72 for cama premium).

International buses To Bolivia Litoral, T423670, 2200 daily to Oruro, US$12, and **La Paz**, US$15. **Salvador** and others from Esmeralda near Juan Martínez around 2100-2300, same prices (passengers may have a cold wait for customs to open at 0800).

Car hire IQSA, Labbé 1089, T/F417068. Procar, Serrano 796, T/F413470 (airport T410920).

Around Iquique *p662*
Mamiña
Bus Transportes Tamarugal, Barros Arana 897, Iquique, daily 0800, 1600, return 1800, 0800, 2½ hrs, US$6, good service. Also with Turismo Mamiña, Latorre 779, daily, same prices and frequency.

Pica
Bus Minibus Iquique-Pica: San Andrés, Sgto Aldea y B Arana, Iquique, daily 0930, return 1800; Pullman Chacón, Barros Arana y Latorre, many daily; Santa Rosa, Barros Arana 777, daily 0830, 0930, return 1700, 1800. US$3.50 one-way, 2 hrs.

● Directory

Iquique *p660, map p661*
Airline offices LAB, Serrano 442, T407015. LAN, Tarapacá 465, T427600, and in Mall Las Américas. Sky, Tarapacá 530, T526200.
Banks Numerous Redbanc ATMs in the centre and the Zofri. Cambios: **Afex**, Serrano 396, for TCs. Money Exchange, Lynch 548, loc 1-2. Best rates for TCs and cash at casas de cambio in the Zofri, eg Wall Street (sells and cashes Amex TCs). **Consulates** Bolivia, Gorostiaga 215, Departamento E, T421777. Mon-Fri 0930-1200. Italy, Serrano 447, T421588. Netherlands, Tarapacá 123, T390900. Peru, Zegers 570, T411466. Spain, Manzana 2, Sitio 5 y 9, Zofri, T422330.
Internet Fassher Internet, Vivar 1497, p 2. About US$1 per hr. Same price is PC@NET Computación, Vivar 1373. More central is Obispo Labbé y Serrano, US$1.50 per hr.
Language schools Academia de Idiomas del Norte, Ramírez 1345, T411827, idiomas@chilesat.net. Swiss run, Spanish classes and accommodation for students.
Post offices Correo Central, Bolívar 485.
Telephones Telefónica, Serrano 620. Entel, Tarapacá 476. **Note** Correos and phone companies all have offices in the Plaza de Servicios in the Zofri.

Arica and Lauca

The Lauca national park, the most northerly in Chile, has some of the country's most stunning scenery: high lakes, snow-capped volcanoes, lava fields and varied bird life. Small Andean villages near the park retain their Aymara culture. Lauca is easily reached from Arica, Chile's northernmost city, which is the main outlet for Bolivian trade and is even closer to Peru. It's a busy place, dominated by the rocky headland of El Morro.

Arica → *Phone code: 058. Colour map 6, grid A1. Population: 174,064.*
Arica, 20 km south of the Peruvian border, is built at the foot of the Morro headland and is fringed by sand dunes. The Andes can be clearly seen from the anchorage. Arica used to be the principal route for travellers going overland to Bolivia, via the Parque Nacional Lauca. Now there is competition from the San Pedro de Atacama-Uyuni route, so new routes are being considered to link this part of the coast with San Pedro, via high altitude national parks. This is an important port and route-centre. The road route to La Paz via Tambo Colorado is now paved and Arica is a popular seaside destination for landlocked Bolivians, as well as Chileans. A 63-km railway runs north to Tacna in Peru. Regrettably, Arica is also becoming a key link in the international drugs trade. The **Sernatur tourist office** ① *San Marcos 101, T252054, in a kiosk next to the Casa de la Cultura, Mon-Fri 0830-1300, 1500-1830*, is very helpful, English spoken, good map, list of tour companies. Head office is at ① *Prat 305, p 2,T232101, infoarica@sernatur.cl.* Municipal kiosk also on San Marcos, opposite Sernatur, opens at 0830.

The **Morro**, with a good view from the park on top (10 minutes' walk by footpath from the southern end of Colón), was the scene of a great victory by Chile over Peru in the War of the Pacific on 7 June 1880. **Museo Histórico y de Armas** ① *summit of the Morro, daily 0830-2000 (2200 Jan-Feb), US$1.50,* contains weapons and uniforms from the War of the Pacific.

At the foot of the Morro is the **Plaza Colón** with the cathedral of San Marcos, built in iron by Eiffel. Though small it is beautifully proportioned and attractively painted. It was brought to

Arica from Ilo (Peru) in the 19th century, before Peru lost Arica to Chile, as an emergency measure after a tidal wave swept over Arica and destroyed all its churches. Eiffel also designed the nearby Aduana (customs house) which is now the **Casa de la Cultura** ① *Mon-Fri 0830-2000*. Just north of the Aduana is the La Paz railway station; outside is an old steam locomotive (made in Germany in 1924) once used on this line. In the station is a memorial to John Roberts Jones, builder of the Arica portion of the railway. The **Casa Bolognesi**, Colón y Yungay, is a fine old building painted blue and white. It holds temporary exhibitions.

Jach'a Kamaní, Arica Desert Gardens, in the Parque Centenario is a new project run by the Municipalidad, the UK's Eden Project and the Andean Project ① *T206391, www.munici palidaddearica.cl*, aimed at raising awareness of the biodiversity of the desert region, especially the plant life, and its culture. The Municipalidad has also set up a birdwatching site at the mouth (*desembocadura*) of the Río Lluta ① *same phone, dicma@municipalidaded arica.cl*, and has published leaflets and checklists.

Worthwhile sights outside Arica include the **Museo Arqueológico de San Miguel de Azapa** ① *at Km 13 on the road east to the Azapa valley, T205555, www.uta.cl/masma, daily Jan-Feb 0900-2000, Mar-Dec 1000-1800, US$2, getting there: take a yellow colectivo from P Lynch y Chacabuco and 600 block of P Lynch, US$1*. Built around an olive press, it contains a fine collection of pre-Columbian weaving, pottery, wood carving and basketwork from the coast and valleys, and also seven mummified humans from the Chinchorro culture (8000-2000 BC), the most ancient mummies yet discovered. Explanations in several languages are loaned free at the entrance. In the forecourt of the museum are several boulders with pre-Columbian petroglyphs. In San Miguel itself is an old cemetery and several typical restaurants. On the road between Arica and San Miguel there are several groups of geoglyphs of humans and llamas ('stone mosaics') south of the road (signed to Cerro Sagrado, Cerro Sombrero – an Azapa Archaeological Circuit is advertised). North of Arica along Route 11, between Km 14 and Km 16, is the **Lluta valley** where you can see along the hillsides four groups of geoglyphs, representing llamas, and eagle and human giants. The road continues through the Parque Nacional Lauca and on to Bolivia. Take a bus from Mackenna y Chacabuco.

By road to Bolivia

1) Via **Chungará** (Chile) and **Tambo Quemado** (Bolivia). This, the most widely used route, begins by heading north from Arica on the Pan-American Highway (Route 5) for 12 km before turning right (east towards the cordillera) on Route 11 towards Chungará via Putre and Parque Nacional Lauca. The road passes **Termas de Juasi** ① *just after Km 130, look for sign, US$2*, rustic thermal baths, with mud baths and a small swimming pool. This road is now paved to La Paz, estimated driving time six hours. 2) Via **Visviri** (Chile) and **Charaña** (Bolivia), following the La Paz-Arica railway line. This route should not be attempted in wet weather.

Border with Bolivia: Chungará Immigration is open 0800-2100; US$2 per vehicle crossing 1300-1500, 1850-2100 and Saturday, Sunday and holidays. For details of through buses between Arica and La Paz see below under Transport, Arica.

Border with Bolivia: Visviri Immigration is open 0800-2000. Chilean formalities at Visviri, 7 km west of the border, Bolivian formalities at Tambo Quemado, just over the border (local barter market every other Friday). When crossing with a private vehicle, US$2 per vehicle is charged between 1300-1500, 1850-2000 and Saturday, Sunday and holidays.

Border with Peru: Chacalluta-Tacna

→ *Between Oct-Mar Chilean time is 1 hr ahead of Peruvian, 2 hrs Oct-Mar.*

Immigration is open Sun-Thu 0800-2400, Fri-Sat 24 hrs; a fairly uncomplicated crossing. For Peruvian immigration. When crossing by private vehicle, US$2 per vehicle is charged between 1300-1500, 1850-2400 and on Saturday, Sunday, holidays. Drivers entering Chile are required to file a form, Relaciones de Pasajeros, giving details of passengers, obtained from a stationery store in Tacna, or at the border in a booth near Customs. You must also present the original registration document for your car from its country of registration. The first checkpoints outside Arica on the road to Santiago also require the Relaciones de Pasajeros form. If you can't buy the form, details on a piece of paper will suffice or you can get them at service stations. The form is not required for travel south of Antofagasta. There are informal exchange facilities at the border.

Arica

Arica centre

To Airport, Pan-American Highway (North) to Peru,
Parque Nacional Lauca & Bolivia

Raúl del Canto

Diego Portales

Buses &
Colectivos
to Tacna

Buses south
& to Bolivia

Río San José

JA Ríos

Av Santa María

Cemetery

To Playa Chinchorro

Parque Brasil

Parque General
C Ibáñez del Campo

Trains to
Tacna

La Paz
Station

Casa de la Cultura
(Former Aduana)

Plaza
Colón

Cathedral

7 de Junio

Harbour

Plaza Vicuña
Mackenna

Museo
Histórico y
de Armas

El Morro

To La Lisera, Playa
Brava & El Laucho Beaches

Bolivian
Consulate

Peruvian
Consulate

To Poblado Artesanal & Pan-American Highway (South) to Museo Arqueológico de San Miguel & Azapa Valley

Chile Arica & Lauca Listings

0 metres 200
0 yards 200

N

Sleeping
Almagro 2 *D2*
Arica 1 *E1*
D'Marie-Jeanne
y David 3 *C1*
El Paso 4 *C1*
Hostal Jardín del Sol 7 *D3*
Hostal Venecia 8 *D2*
Maison de France 9 *A1*
Plaza Colón 10 *Detail*
Residencial América 11 *D2*
Residencial
Blanquita 12 *Detail*

Residencial Nilda 14 *A2*
Savona 15 *E2*
Sotomayor 16 *Detail*
Sunny Days 18 *A1*
Tarapacá 19 *Detail*

Eating
Bavaria 1 *Detail*
Chin Huang Tao 2 *D2*
D'Aurelio 3 *Detail*
Don Floro 4 *C3*
El Andén 8 *D1*
El Rey del Marisco 5 *Detail*

Kau Chea 6 *D1*
La Bomba 7 *Detail*
Los Aleros del 21 9 *D3*
San Fernando 10 *Detail*
Yuri 12 *D2*

667

Parque Nacional Lauca

The Parque Nacional Lauca, stretching to the border with Bolivia, is one of the most spectacular national parks in Chile. It is 176 km east of Arica and access is easy as the main Arica-La Paz road runs through the park and is paved. On the way is a zone of giant candelabra cactus, between 2,300-2,800 m. At Km 90 there is a pre-Inca pukará (fortress) above the village of Copaquilla and, a few kilometres further, there is an Inca tambo (inn) at Zapahuira. Situated at elevations from 3,200 m to 6,340 m (beware of soroche unless you are coming from Bolivia), the park covers 137,883 ha and includes numerous snowy volcanoes including three peaks of over 6,000 m. At the foot of Volcán Parinacota and its twin, Pomerape (in Bolivia – they are known collectively as Payachatas), is a series of lakes among a jumble of rocks, called Cotacotani. Black lava flows can be seen above Cotacotani. **Lago Chungará** (4,517 m, 7 km by 3 km) is southeast of Payachatas, a must for its views of the Parinacota, Sajama and Guallatire volcanoes and for its varied wildlife. At the far end of the lake is the Chile/Bolivia border. The park contains over 140 species of bird, resident or migrant, as well as camelids, vizcacha and puma. A good base for exploring the park and for acclimatization is **Putre** (*Population 4,400, Altitude 3,500 m*), a scenic village, 15 km before the entrance with a church dating from 1670 and surrounded by terracing dating from pre-Inca times, now used for cultivating alfalfa and oregano. From here paths provide easy walking and great views. Festivals: Pacahayame, last Sunday in October, festival of the potato: religious celebration and traditional dancing. Feria de la Voz Andina, November (check dates and reserve room and transport in advance), with dancing, foods, handicrafts, very popular. **Tourist office** on main plaza, helpful, some English spoken, organizes tours.

At **Parinacota** (*Altitude 4,392 m*), at the foot of Payachatas, there is an interesting 17th century church – rebuilt 1789 – with 18th-century frescoes and the skulls of past priests (ask at the stalls outside the church for Señor Sipriani with the key, donations appreciated). Local residents knit alpaca sweaters, US$26 approximately; weavings of wildlife scenes also available. Weavings are sold from stalls outside the church. CONAF office, which administers the national park, is also here, open 0900-1200, 1230-1700. It's a walk of about one hour from the village to Cotacotani. From here an unpaved road runs north to the Bolivian border at Visviri (see above). You can climb Guane Guane, 5,097 m, in two to three hours, ask at the **CONAF refugio**. Lago Chungará is 20 km southeast of Parinacota.

During the rainy season (January-February), roads in the park may be impassable; check in advance with CONAF in Arica (see Useful addresses, Arica, below). It can be foggy as well as wet in January-March. A map of the park is available from Sernatur in Arica. Maps are also available from the Instituto Geográfico Militar. If driving off the main road, 4WD is necessary.

Reserva Nacional Las Vicuñas → *Altitude: 4,300-6,060 m*

South of Lauca is the beautiful Reserva Nacional Las Vicuñas, covering 209,131 ha of altiplano. Many of these beautiful creatures can be seen as well as, with luck, condors, rheas and other birds. Administration is at Guallatiri, reached by turning off the Arica-La Paz road onto the A147 2 km after Las Cuevas, where there is also a CONAF office. The same road leads into the Monumento Natural Salar de Surire, for which the same weather and road conditions apply. The Salar, also at 4,300 m, is a drying salt lake of 17,500 ha. It has a year-round population of 12,000-15,000 flamingos (Chilean, Andean and James). Administration is in **Surire**, 45 km south of Guallatiri and 129 km south of Putre. A normal car can reach Surire in the dry season, but a high clearance vehicle is essential for all other roads and, in the summer wet season (January to March, also August), 4WD vehicle: take extra fuel. In the wet, roads may be impassable. There is no public transport to these wildlife reserves, but tours can be arranged in Putre or Arica. Ask tour operators such as Latinorizons about routes through these parks from Arica to San Pedro de Atacama. Also check with CONAF in Arica about road conditions and whether the parks are closed at any time.

⬤ Sleeping

Arica *p665, map p667*
In Jan-Feb the municipality supplies cheap basic rooms, ask at the tourist office. Residenciales on Prat 500 block, Velázquez 700 block and P Lynch 600 block. Others opposite the bus terminal.

AL **Arica**, San Martín 599, about 2 km along shore (frequent micros and colectivos), T254540, www.panamericanahoteles.cl. 4-star, best, price depends on season, good value, good and decent restaurant, tennis court, pool, lava beach (not safe for swimming), American breakfast.

AL-A El Paso, Gral Velásquez 1109, T231965, www.hotelelpaso.cl. Bungalow style, nice suites, pleasant gardens, tennis courts, swimming pool, with breakfast, good restaurant Araksaya.

B Savona, Yungay 380, T231000, www.hotelsavona.cl. Comfortable, 3-star, quiet. Highly recommended.

C Almagro, Sotomayor 490, T224444, F221240. With breakfast, helpful, comfortable, parking, stores luggage. Recommended.

C Plaza Colón, San Marcos 261, T/F254424, www.hotelplazacolon.cl. With breakfast, comfortable, convenient location opposite the cathedral.

C Sotomayor, Sotomayor 367, T232970, www.hotelsotomayor.cl. Comfortable, helpful, restaurant, parking, cheaper if paying in dollars.

D Hotel D'Marie-Jeanne y David, Velásquez 792, T/F258231, hotelmariejeanneydavid@ hotmail.com. With breakfast, TV, laundry, parking, snacks in café, French spoken, quite comfy but some rooms by main road noisy.

D Hostal Jardín del Sol, Sotomayor 848, T232795, F231462. **E** singes, with breakfast, safe, kitchen facilities, large patio, laundry, very helpful staff. Often recommended.

D Sunny Days, Tomás Aravena 161 (a little over half way along P de Valdivia, 800 m from bus terminal, transport to hotel), T241038, sunnydaysarica@ hotmail.com. All-you-can-eat breakfast, hot water, kitchen, laundry facilities, videos, book exchange, bikes and body boards for rent, nice welcoming atmosphere, lots of information, New Zealand owner. Highly recommended.

D-E Maison de France, Aurelio Valdivieso 152, pob Chinchorro, T223463, atchumturist@ hotmail.com. Owned by Frenchman Cristian, breakfast US$2, good meals, kitchen facilities, information on tours and self-guided trips, convenient for beach and nightlife. Recommended.

E Hostal Venecia, Baquedano 741, T252877, hostalvenecia@gmail.com. Spotless, small rooms, hot water. Recommended.

E-F Res América, Sotomayor 430, T254148, www.residencialamerica.com. Hot water, some rooms with bath, hospitable, good value.

E Res Nilda, Raúl del Canto 947, T222743. Very nice *casa de familia*, kitchen facilities, laundry, near bus terminal and Playa Chinchorro.

E Tarapacá, Maipú 455, T252680, hoteltarapaca@ hotmail.com. With breakfast, helpful, laundry.

F pp Res Blanquita, Maipú 472, T232064, residencialblanquita@hotmail.com. Breakfast extra, pleasant, good value, laundry and kitchen facilities.

Parque Nacional Lauca *p668*
There are 2 CONAF refuges in the park (but check in advance with CONAF in Arica that they are open): at **Lago Chungará**, and **Las Cuevas** (emergencies only, no tourist facilities). Chungará has 8 beds, cooking facilities, hot showers, **F** pp, sleeping bag essential, take your own food, candles and matches. Advance booking recommended.

Putre
If arriving from Bolivia, remember that no fresh produce may be brought across the border into Chile, so plan accordingly if using a CONAF refugio.

A Hostería Las Vicuñas, T/F228564, www.chileanaltiplano.cl. Bungalow-style, half-board, helpful, heating, restaurant, does not accept US$, TCs or credit cards.

B Casa Barbarita, belonging to Alto Andino Nature Tours (see below), T300013, casa@birdingaltoandino.com. 2 bedroom house, heating, cooking facilities, naturalist library, information in English.

D Res La Paloma, O'Higgins 353, T09-9197 9319, lapalomahugopaco@hotmail.com. **E** with shared bath, hot showers after 0800 unless requested, no heating but lots of blankets, good food in large, warm restaurant, indoor parking; supermarket opposite.

E Hostal Cali, Baquedano 399, T885-66091, krlos_team@hotmail.com. **F** with shared bath or single, pleasant, no heating, hot water, good restaurant, supermarket.

F Hostal Chez Charlie, contact through *Latinorizons* (see Activities and tours, below). Comfortable, shared bath, hot water, good value, French and English spoken.

F Res Rosamel, Latorre y Carrera, on plaza, T300051. Hot water, pleasant, good restaurant.

Camping Sra Clementina Cáceres, blue door on C Lynch, allows camping in her garden and offers lunch.

Parinacota
Accommodation is available with various families, ask at the food and artesanía stands. You can camp behind the CONAF office for free, great site.

● For an explanation of the sleeping and eating price codes used in this guide, see page 58.
● Other relevant information is found in Essentials pages 602-604.

Reserva Nacional Las Vicuñas:
Salar de Surire *p668*
At Surire, 8 km beyond the borax mine,
there is a CONAF *refugio*, 15 beds, very
clean, heating and cooking facilities, prior
application to CONAF in Arica essential. There
is also a campsite at Polloquere, 16 km south
of Surire, no facilities, no water.

⊙ Eating

Arica *p665, map p667*
Many good places on 21 de Mayo and
offering meals, drinks, real coffee, juices
and outdoor seating.
⍩ **Los Aleros del 21**, 21 de Mayo 736, T254641.
One of the city's longest-established restaurants,
specializing in southern Chilean cuisine, large
portions, lots of pork dishes; recommended
also for seafood and service.
⍩ **D'Aurelio**, Baquedano 369, T231471. Italian
specialities, good pasta, seafood.
⍩ **Bavaria**, Colón 613, upstairs. Another
branch of the German-Chilean rotisserie chain.
Good restaurant, also coffee and cakes.
⍩ **Don Floro**, V MacKenna 847. Good seafood
and steaks, good service, popular little place.
Highly recommended.
⍩ **Chin Huang Tao**, Lynch 224. Excellent
Chinese, diners welcome to take away
'doggie bag'.
⍩ **El Rey del Marisco**, Colón 565, upstairs.
Excellent seafood, not always welcoming
and pricier than others similar.
⍩ ⍾ **El Andén**, in former La Paz railway station.
Good value, inventive menu, Mon-Fri, à la carte at
weekends. An old train carriage is one of the
dining areas.
⍩ ⍾ **Mata Rangi**, Muelle Turístico. Good food in
fishy environment, good value *menú de la casa*.
⍾ **La Bomba**, Colón 357, at fire station, T255626.
Good value *almuerzo*, friendly service.
⍾ **Kau Chea**, 18 de Septiembre y Prat.
Chinese, good value.
⍾ **San Fernando**, Baquedano y Maipú.
Simple breakfast, good value almuerzo.
There are many other cheap restaurants
on Baquedano 600/700 blocks.
⍾ **Yuri**, Maipú y Lynch. Good service, cheap
Chinese lunches. Recommended.

Parque Nacional Lauca: Putre *p668*
⍾ **Kuchamarka**, Baquedano between
La Paloma supermarket and Hostal Cali.
Popular, good value, specializes in local
dishes, including alpaca, as well as
vegetarian options.

⊙ Entertainment

Arica *p665, map p667*
Teatro Municipal de Arica, Baquedano 234.
Wide variety of theatrical and musical events,
exhibitions. Recommended.

⊛ Festivals and events

Arica *p665, map p667*
24-26 Jan, folk music and dance carnival.
Late Feb, Ginga Carnaval, annual Andean
music and dance competition, 3 nights. **June**,
Festival of Arica and the national *cueca* dance
championships. **29 Jun**, San Pedro, religious
service at fishing wharf and boat parades. First
weekend of **Oct**, Virgen de las Peñas, pilgrimage
to the site of the Virgin, 4-5 hrs inland.

⊙ Shopping

Arica *p665, map p667*
Many shopping galerías in the centre, also
pharmacies, electrical appliances and clothes
shops. Ferias for clothes on Velázquez.
Calle 21 de Mayo is pedestrianized, with
many shops, restaurants and internet cafés.
Crafts Poblado Artesanal, Plaza Las Gredas,
Hualles 2825 (take bus 2, 3 or 7). Expensive but
especially good for musical instruments, open
Tue-Sun 0930-1300, 1530-1930, *peña* Fri and Sat
2130; shop not always open out of season.
Markets Feria Turística Dominical, Sun
market, along Chacabuco between Valásquez
and Mackenna. Good prices for llama sweaters.
Mercado Central, Sotomayor y Sangra, between
Colón and Baquedano. Mostly fruit and
vegetables. Smaller fruit and veg market,
with food stalls, on Colón between 18 de
Septiembre and Maipú.

Parque Nacional Lauca: Putre *p668*
Putre has several stores, 2 bakeries and
several private houses selling fresh produce.
Cooperativo, on the plaza, is usually the
cheapest place for food. **Sra Daria Condori**
has a shop on C O'Higgins, selling locally made
artesanía and naturally-coloured alpaca wool.
Organic vegetables are available from **Freddy
Blanco**, opposite the Banco del Estado. Petrol is
more expensive than in Arica but available in
cans from the **Cali** and **Paloma** supermarkets and
from **ECA**, a government subsidized market on
the plaza (cheapest). Other than a small shop
with limited supplies in Parinacota, no food is
available outside Putre. Take drinking water with
you as water in the park is not safe.

Central Valley

One of the world's most fecund and beautiful landscapes, with snowclad peaks of the Andes to the east and the Cordillera de la Costa to the west, the Central Valley contains most of Chile's population. A region of small towns, farms and vineyards, it has several protected areas of natural beauty. Five major rivers cross the Central Valley, cutting through the Coastal Range to the Pacific: from north to south these are the Rapel, Mataquito, Maule, Itata and Biobío. Some of the river valleys provide ideal conditions for growing grapes and making wine and you can wander between vineyards. This is also Chilean cowboy country and at rural shows you can see displays of horsemanship.

Rancagua to Chillán

Rancagua → *Phone code: 072. Colour map 8, grid B1. Population: 167,000.*
The capital of VI Región (Libertador Gen Bernardo O'Higgins) lies on the Río Cachapoal, 82 km south of Santiago. Founded in 1743, it is a service and market centre. At the heart of the city is an attractive tree-lined plaza, the Plaza de los Héroes, and several streets of single-storey colonial-style houses. In the centre of the plaza is an equestrian statue of O'Higgins. The main commercial area lies along Avenida Independencia, which runs west from the plaza towards the bus and rail terminals. The National Rodeo Championships are held at the end of March, with plenty of opportunities for purchasing cowboy items. **Tourist office** ① *Germán Riesco 277, T230413, inforancagua@sernatur.cl.*

For information on the Cachapoal wine producing zone, with details on tours and vineyard visits, see the **Ruta del Vino** ① *Comercio 435, Rancagua, T553684, www.cachapoal wineroute.cl.* Around Santa Cruz and **San Fernando** (51 km south of Rancagua) is the Colchagua Valley, another wine-producing zone. For the Ruta del Vino here ① *Plaza de Armas 140, of 6, Santa Cruz, T072-823199, www.rutadelvino.cl.*

Los Lingües ① *Panamericana Sur, Km 124, 20 km northeast of San Fernando, www.loslingues.com,* is an hacienda where the beset horses in Chile are bred. Visits can be arranged to the 17th-century house, a gift of the King of Spain, and noe-day tours, including transport, rodeo and lunch, can be arranged. The hacienda is a member of the élite French Hotels et Relais et Chateaux, with accommodation starting at US$250.

Curicó → *Phone code: 075. Colour map 8, grid B1. Population: 103,919. Altitude: 200 m.*
Between the Ríos Lontué and Teno, 192 km from Santiago, Curicó is the only town of any size in the Mataquito Valley. It was founded in 1744. In mid-March is the Fiesta de la Vendimia with displays on traditional wine-making. In the Plaza de Armas there are fountains and a monument to the Mapuche warrior, Lautaro, carved from the trunk of an ancient beech tree. There is a steel bandstand, built in New Orleans in 1904, which is a national monument. The church of San Francisco (1732), also a national monument, partly ruined, contains the 17th century Virgen de Velilla, brought from Spain. Overlooking the city, the surrounding countryside and with views to the distant Andean peaks is Cerro Condell (100 m); it is an easy climb to the summit from where there are a number of walks. **Miguel Torres wine bodega** ① *5 km south of the city, T564100, daily 1000-1700 in autumn and winter, daily 1000-1700 in spring and summer; no organized tour, Spanish only, worthwhile. Getting there: take a bus for Molina from the local terminal or outside the railway station and get off at Km 195 on the Pan-American Highway.* For information on the vineyards of Curicó, see the **Ruta del Vino del Valle de Curicó** ① *Merced 331, p 2, Curicó, T328972, www.rvvc.cl.* The **tourist office** is at Gobernación Provincial ① *Plaza de Armas, Mon-Fri 0900-1330, 1600-1800,* helpful.

Area de Protección Radal Siete Tazas
① *Oct-Mar, administration is in Parque Inglés, entry US$3.*
The park is in two parts, one at Radal, 65 km east of Curicó, the other at Parque Inglés, 9 km further east. At Radal, the Río Claro flows through a series of seven rock cups (*siete tazas*) each with a pool emptying into the next by a waterfall. The river goes through a canyon, 15 m

deep but only 1½ m wide, ending abruptly in a cliff and a beautiful waterfall. There is excellent trekking in the park, through beautiful woods and scenery, similar to what can be found further south, but with a better climate.

Talca → *Phone code: 071. Colour map 8, grid B1. Population: 175,000.*

At 56 km south of Curicó (258 km from Santiago via dual carriageway) this is the most important city between Santiago and Concepción. It is a major manufacturing centre and the capital of VII Región (Maule). Founded in 1692, Talca was destroyed by earthquakes in 1742 and 1928. **Museo O'Higginiano** ① *just off the Plaza de Armas at 1 Norte y 2 Oriente, T210428, www.dibam.cl/subdirec_museos/moba_talca/home.asp, Tue-Fri 1030-1300, 1430-1845, Sat-Sun 1000-1300.* This museum is in a colonial mansion in which Bernardo O'Higgins lived as a child. The house was later the headquarters of O'Higgins' Patriot Government in 1813-14 (before his defeat at Rancagua). In 1818 O'Higgins signed the declaration of Chilean independence here: the room (Sala Independencia) is decorated and furnished in period style. The museum also has a collection of regional art. The **Maule valley** ① *information from the Villa Cultural Huilquilemu, 7 km southeast of Talca, T071-246460, www.valledelmaule.cl,* is another wine producing region, with vineyards that can be visited. The **tourist office** is at ① *1 Poniente 1281, T233669, infomaule@sernatur.cl, Mon-Fri 0830-1930 (1730 winter).*

Constitución and the coast

At the mouth of the Río Maule, 89 km from San Javier on the Pan-American Highway (south of Talca), **Constitución** is an important port and seaside resort. The coast, especially to the north, is beautiful, while south a paved road runs through thick forest to the small towns of Chanco, **Pelluhue** and Curanipe. There are black sand beaches and dunes in this little visited part of Chile.

Vilches

① *5 buses a day from Talca, US$2.60, 2 hrs.*

This is the starting point for the climb to the volcanoes **Quizapu** (3,050 m) and **Descabezado** (3,850 m). For walks on Descabezado Grande and Cerro Azul (ice axe and crampons needed) contact recommended guide Carlos Verdugo Bravo, Probación Brilla El Sol, Pasaje El Nickel 257, Talca (Spanish only), or contact **Casa Chueca** in Talca. The **Reserva Nacional Altos del Lircay** 2 km from Vilches ① *US$5.50,* , covers 12,163 ha and includes three peaks, several small lakes and the Piedras Tacitas, a stone construction supposedly made by the aboriginal inhabitants of the region. There are good hikes: Laguna del Alto, eight hours, and El Enladrillado, a high basalt plateau from where there are great views, 12 hours, and Mirador Valle El Venado; you can also hike between Radal and Vilches in three days. A visitors' centre and administration are near the entrance and the Talca municipal tourist office has maps.

To the border with Argentina: Paso Pehuenche

A road south of Talca, paved for the first 65 km, runs southeast from the Panamericana along **Lago Colbún** and up the broad valley of the Río Maule to reach the Argentine border at Paso Pehuenche. At the western end of the lake is the town of Colbún, from where a road goes to Linares on the Panamericana. Thermal springs 5 km south of Colbún at Panimávida, and 12 km, Quinamávida. Campsites on south shore. While in Panimávida, try the local *Bebida Panimávida*, made from spring water, sparkling or still, flavoured with lemon or raspberry. Paso Pehuenche (2,553 m) is reached by poor unpaved road southeast from Lago Colbún. Chilean customs is at La Mina, 106 km from Talca, 60 km from the border (Camping La Querencia, 4 km west of La Mina). On the Argentine side the road continues to Malargüe and San Rafael. The border is open December-March 0800-2100, April-November 0800-1900.

Chillán → *Phone code: 042. Colour map 8, grid B1. Population: 146,000. Altitude: 118 m.*

Chillán, 150 km south of Talca, is capital of Ñuble province and a service centre for this agricultural area. Following an earthquake in 1833, the site was moved slightly to the northwest, though the older site, Chillán Viejo, is still occupied. Further earthquakes in 1939 and 1960 ensured that few old buildings have survived. Chillán was the birthplace of Bernardo O'Higgins (Arturo Prat, Chile's naval hero, was born 50 km away at Ninhue). The Fiesta de la Vendimia is an annual wine festival held in the third week in March. **Tourist office** ① *18 de Septiembre 455, at the side of Gobernación, T042-223272, infochillan@sernatur.cl.* Street map of city, leaflets on skiing, Termas de Chillán, etc.

The centre of the city is **Plaza O'Higgins**, on which stands the modern **Cathedral** designed to resist earthquakes. Northwest of the Plaza O'Higgins, on the Plaza Héroes de Iquique, is the **Escuela México** ① *daily 1000-1300, 1500-1830*. It was donated to the city after the 1939 earthquake. In its library are murals by the great Mexican artists David Alvaro Siqueiros and Xavier Guerrero which present allegories of Chilean and Mexican history. The **Mercado y Feria Municipal** (covered and open markets at Riquelme y Maipón) sell regional arts and crafts and have many cheap, good restaurants, serving regional dishes; open daily, Sunday until 1300. Three blocks further south is the **Museo Naval El Chinchorro** ① *Collin y I Riquelme, Tue-Fri 0930-1200, 1500-1730*, containing naval artefacts and models of Chilean vessels. In Chillán Viejo (southwest of the centre) there is a monument and park at **O'Higgins' birthplace** ① *park 0830-2000*. It has a 60 m long mural depicting his life (an impressive, but sadly faded, mosaic of various native stones), and a Centro Histórico y Cultural, *0830-2000*, with a gallery of contemporary paintings by regional artists.

Chillán

Sleeping
Claris 2
Cordillera 3
Floresta 4
Gran Hotel
Isabel Riquelme 1
Hospedaje Sonia Segui 5

Libertador 6
Quinchamali 7

Eating
Arcoiris 1
Café París 3
Club Comercial 2

Jai Yang 5
La Casa Nostra 6
La Masc'a 7

Quinchamalí is 27 km southwest of Chillán, a little village famous for the originality of its craftsmen in textiles, basketwork, black ceramics, guitars and primitive paintings (all on sale in Chillán market). Handicraft fair, second week of February.

Termas de Chillán

East of Chillán 82 km by good road (paved for the first 50 km), 1,850 m up in the Cordillera, are thermal baths and, above, the largest ski resort in southern Chile. There are two open-air thermal pools (officially for hotel guests only) and a health spa with jacuzzis, sauna, mud baths etc. Suitable for families and beginners and cheaper than centres nearer Santiago, the ski resort has 28 runs (the longest is 13 km), 10 lifts, snowboarding and other activities. It also has two hotels (the five-star Gran Termas de Chillán Hotel, and the 3-star Pirigallo) and condominium apartments. Season: middle June to the end of September. Information and reservations from **Chillán Ski Centre** ⓘ *Barros Arana 261, T042-434200, www.termaschillan.cl, lift pass US$35 per day, US$27 per half-day, equipment hire about US$30 pp.*

⏺ Sleeping

Rancagua *p673*
A **Camino del Rey**, Estado 275, T232314, hotelcaminodelrey@terra.cl. 4-star, suites with full facilities, best in town.
B **Rancagua**, San Martín 85, T232663, www.hotelrancagua.galeon.com. Quiet, good accommodation, secure parking. Recommended.
C-D **España**, San Martín 85, T232663, noraberriosf@latinmail.com. Cheaper without bath, central, drab but clean, laundry service.

San Fernando
AL **Viña Casa Silva**, Angostura, San Fernando (Casilla 97), T072-716519, www.casasilva.cl. Turn off the Panamericana at Km 133. Elegant hacienda with homemade furniture and 7 luxury rooms, shared country-style living rooms, hot water, cable TV, delicious food and wine from their own vineyard. Recommended.

Curicó *p673*
B **Comercio**, Yungay 730, T310014, info@hotel comercio.cl. 3-star, clean. Recommended.
B **Prat**, Peña 427, T311069. Pleasant patio vines and figs, cheaper without bath, breakfast, hot water, laundry facilities.
E **Res Colonial**, Rodríguez 461, T314103, resi colonial@terra.cl. Good, basic, cable TV, cheaper without bath, helpful, use of kitchen, patio.

Area de Protección Radal Siete Tazas *p673*
D **Hostería La Flor de la Canela**, Parque Inglés, 3 km west of Siete Tazas, T491613. Breakfast extra, good food, good value. Highly recommended.
Campsite at Radal village, next to river and minimarket, US$2.50 pp. Several *hosterías* and campsites at Parque Inglés.

Talca *p674*
A **Cabañas Entre Ríos**, Panamericana Sur Km 250, 8 km north, T223336. Very good value, excellent breakfast, pool, very helpful

owner. Highly recommended.
B **Casa Chueca**, Camino Las Rastras, 4 km from Talca by the Río Lircay, Casilla 143, T197 0096, T09-9837 1440 (mob), casachueca@ hotmail.com (also www.trekkingchile.com). Phone hostal from bus terminal for directions on how to get there. G pp in shared rooms. With breakfast, very good vegetarian food (US$6), cheaper rooms with shared bath, Austrian and German owners, many languages spoken, lovely setting, swimming pool, mountain bikes, good tours (including climbing) arranged. Also Spanish classes. Enthusiastically recommended.
C **Cordillera**, 2 Sur 1360, T221817, www.cordillerahotel.cl. Decent standard, no frills, serves a good breakfast.
C **Hostal del Puente**, 1 Sur 407, T220930, hostaldelpuente@adsl.tie.cl. Large breakfast extra, cable TV, family-owned, parking in central courtyard, lovely gardens, English spoken. Recommended for atmosphere, price and surroundings.
C-D **Hostal del Río**, 1 Sur 411, T225448, www.amarillas.cl/hostaldelrio. Rival to Del Puente next door (run by owner's brother), a little cheaper, also good.
E pp **Hosp Santa Margarita**, at Pelarco, 18 km east, T09-9335 9051. Swiss run, with breakfast, other meals available, reservations advised (Casilla 1104, Talca). Open Dec-Mar only.

Constitución and the coast: Pelluhue *p674*
E pp **Res Hostería Las Palmeras**, Condell 837, T09-9579 2431. In an old, tatty house, great atmosphere, meals extra.

Vilches *p674*
D **Refugio del Tricahue**, in Maule Valley, south of Vilches (take Armerillo/La Mina bus from Talca, 1½ hrs, US$1.50), T09-9554 0800, www.refugio-tricahue.cl. Small hostel, French/Begian run, F in bunk room, G

camping, hot water, use of kitchen, hot springs, fishing gear, horses for rent, guides to private reserve, very pleasant.
Camping At Reserva Altos de Lircay, US$4.65, at 1,300 m, very cold, hot showers, light at each site, beautiful location.

To the border with Argentina:
Lago Colbún *p674*
D pp Ecological Reserve Posada Campesina, at Rabones on the road Linares/ Panimávida, T09-9752 0510, full board, estancia offering forest trails, trekking and horseback expeditions, English spoken, highly recommended.

Chillán *p674, map p675*
Lots of cheap hospedajes on Constitución 1-300.
A Gran Hotel Isabel Riquelme, Constitución 576, T213663, hotelir@termaschillan.cl. A bit overpriced, with cable TV, restaurant, laundry, parking.
B Quinchamalí, El Roble 634, T223381, hotelquinchamali@entelchile.net. Central, quiet, hot water and heated lounge.
B Cordillera, Arauco 619, on Plaza de Armas, T215211, hotelcordillera@entelchile.net. 3-star, small, all rooms with heating, good.
C-D Floresta, 18 de Septiembre 278, T222253. Quiet, old fashioned and welcoming.
D Claris, 18 de Septiembre 357, T221980. Welcoming, hot water, **F** pp without bath, clean, friendly, run down.
D Libertador, Libertad 85, T223255. Large rooms, without breakfast, parking, good, a few mins' walk from the railway station.
F pp Hosp Sonia Segui, Itata 288, T214879. Good, especially breakfast and the beds, huge almuerzo, helpful, but noisy and bathrooms dirty.

Termas de Chillán *p676*
At Las Trancas on the road to the Termas, Km 70-76 from Chillán are:
A Robledal, T214407, www.hotelrobledal.cl. Pleasant rooms, bar, restaurant, sauna and jacuzzi, tours offered.
AL Parador Jamón, Pan y Vino, Casilla 618, Chillán, T222682, www.nevadosdechillan.cl. Arranges horse riding expeditions. There are many other *cabañas* in the village, usually **B** for up to 6, and Galería de Arte de Luis Guzmán Molina, a painter from Chillán, Entrada por Los Pretiles Km 68.5. Camping available 2 km from the slopes.

🍴 Eating

Rancagua *p673*
There are eating places west of Plaza de los Héroes, eg on Independencia and Astorga.
⍾ La Cocina Artesanal, O'Carroll 60. Traditional meat and seafood dishes.

Curicó *p673*
⍾⍾-⍾⍾ Club de la Unión, Plaza de Armas. Good, innovative food in an elegant setting.
⍾⍾ Los Cisnes, Rodríguez 1186. *Parrilladas* and cheaper *almuerzos*.

Chillán *p674, map p675*
The Chillán area is well-known for its *pipeño* (very young) wine and *longanizas* (sausages).
⍾⍾ Arcoiris, El Roble 525. Vegetarian.
⍾⍾ Café París, Arauco 666. Fine restaurant upstairs, good bar.
⍾⍾ Los Adobes, in Chillán Viejo, on Parque O'Higgins. Good tasty food, good service, reasonable prices.
⍾ Club Comercial, Arauco 745. Popular for lunch, good value almuerzo, good bar at night.
⍾ Jai Yang, Libertad 250. Good value Chinese.
⍾ La Masc'a, 5 de Abril 544. Excellent cheap meals, *empanadas de queso*, drinks.

▲ Activities and tours

Constitución and the coast *p674*
For information, tours and lodging in this area, contact **Alejandro** of **Ruta Verde**, T744 8224, tours@rutaverde.cl. Speaks English, good fun. Recommended.

🚍 Transport

Rancagua *p673*
Bus The terminal for regional buses is at Doctor Salinas y Calvo, just north of the market. Frequent services to **Santiago** from **Tur-Bus** terminal at Calvo y O'Carroll, T241117, US$4, 1¼ hrs.
Train Train station on Av La Marina, T230361. Main line services between Santiago and Concepción and Chillán stop here. Also regular services to/from **Santiago** on Metrotren, 1¼ hrs, 10-19 a day, US$3.

Curicó *p673*
Bus Long distance terminal at Prat y Maipú. Local buses, including to coastal towns, as well as some long distance services, from Terminal Plaza, Prat y Maipú. Tur-Bus stop and office, M de Velasco, 1 block south. Pullman del Sur terminal, Henríquez y Carmen. Many southbound buses bypass Curicó, but can be caught by waiting outside town. To **Santiago** US$5, 2½ hrs, several companies, frequent. To **Talca** every 15 mins, US$3, 1 hr. To **Temuco**, Alsa and Tur-Bus, US$8.
Train Station is at the west end of Prat, 4 blocks west of Plaza de Armas, T310028. To/from **Santiago**, 6 a day, 2 hrs, US$10-20. To/from **Chillán**, 6 a day, 2¼ hrs, US$12-24.

Talca *p674*

Bus Terminal at 12 Oriente y 2 Sur. From Santiago, US$6.50. To **Chillán**, frequent, US$2. To **Temuco**, US$10, 6 hrs. To **Puerto Montt**, US$12, 10 hrs. Train: station at 2 Sur y 11 Oriente, T226254. To **Santiago**, 5 a day, US$11-22.

Chillán *p674, map p675*

Bus Two long-distance terminals: Central, Brasil y Constitución (Tur-Bus, Línea Azul, Tas Choapa, Alsa-LIT); Northern, Ecuador y O'Higgins for other companies. Local buses leave from Maipón y Sgto Aldea. To **Santiago**, 5½ hrs, US$9-11. To **Concepción**, every 30 mins, 1¼ hrs, US$4. To **Curicó** 2 a day, US$5. To **Temuco**, 4½ hrs, US$6. **Train** Station, 5 blocks west of Plaza de Armas on Brasil, T222424. To **Santiago**, 6 daily, 4½ hrs, salón US$17.50-26. **Note** No trains between Chillán and Temuco mid-2007 because of storm damage; no date set for resumption.

Area de Protección Radal Siete Tazas *p673*

Take a **minibus** from Terminal Plaza, Curicó, to **Molina**, 26 km south, US$0.75; from Molina bus at 1700 weekdays, 0800 Sun, to **Radal** village in summer, return 0730 (1800 Sun), 3 hrs, US$3. It's a further 6.5 km to Siete Tazas and 11 km to Parque Inglés. Access by car is best as the road through the park is paved.

Termas de Chillán *p676*

Ski **buses** run Jun-Sep from **Libertador** 1042 at 0800 and from Chillán Ski Centre, subject to demand, US$40 (includes lift pass). Summer bus service (Jan-mid-Mar), from **Anja**, 5 de Abril 594, Thu, Sat, Sun only, 0730, US$9 return, book in advance. **Taxi** US$40 one way, 1½ hrs. At busy periods hitching may be possible from Chillán Ski Centre.

⊙ Directory

Talca *p674*

Banks Edificio Caracol, Oficina 15, 1 Sur 898, for US$ cash. **Internet** 1 Poniente 1282 and 2 Sur 1661 (free, reserve in advance). **Post offices** 1 Oriente s/n. **Telephones** Telefónica, 1 Sur 1156 and 1 Sur 835.

Chillán *p674, map p675*

Banks Better rates than banks at **Casa de Cambio**, Constitución 550, or Café de París (ask for Enrique Schuler). ATMs at several banks on Plaza de Armas. **Internet** Gateway, Libertad 360. Planet, Arauco 683, p 2. **Post offices** Gobernación on Plaza de Armas. **Telephones** Entel, 18 de Septiembre 746. Telefónica, Arauco 625.

Concepción and around

→ *Phone code: 041. Colour map 8, grid B1. Population: almost 250,000.*

The third biggest city in Chile (516 km from Santiago) and the most important city in southern Chile, is also a major industrial centre. Capital of VIII Región (Biobío), Concepción is 15 km up the Biobío River. Founded in 1550, Concepción became a frontier stronghold in the war against the Mapuche after 1600. Destroyed by an earthquake in 1751, it was moved to its present site in 1764. The climate is very agreeable in summer, but from April to September the rains are heavy; the annual average rainfall, nearly all of which falls in those six months, is from 1,250 mm to 1,500 mm. **Tourist office:** Sernatur ① *Aníbal Pinto 460, corner of main plaza, T274 1337.*

Sights

In the attractive **Plaza de Armas** at the centre are the **Intendencia** and the **Cathedral**. It was here that Bernardo O'Higgins proclaimed the independence of Chile on 1 January 1818. **Cerro Caracol** can easily be reached on foot starting from the statue of Don Juan Martínez de Rozas in the Parque Ecuador, arriving at the Mirador Chileno after 15 minutes. From here it is another 20 minutes' climb to **Cerro Alemán**. The **Biobío** and its valley running down to the sea lie below. On the far side of the river you see lagoons, the largest of which, **San Pedro**, is a watersport centre.

The **Galería de la Historia** ① *Lincoyán y V Lamas by Parque Ecuador, Tue-Sun 1000-1330, 1500-1830, free*, is a depiction of the history of Concepción and the region; upstairs is a collection of Chilean painting. The **Casa del Arte** ① *Chacabuco y Paicaví, near Plaza Perú, T220 4290, Tue-Fri 1000-1800, Sat 1000-1600, Sun 1000-1300, free*, contains the University art collection; the entrance hall is dominated by La Presencia de América Latina, by the Mexican Jorge González Camerena (1965), a mural depicting Latin American history. Free explanations are given by University Art students.

The **Museo y Parque Hualpen** ① *16 km from Concepción, Tue-Sun 1000-1300, 1400-1900, free*, is a house built around 1885 (a national monument) and its gardens. It contains beautiful pieces from all over the world, two hour visit, recommended. The park also contains Playa Rocoto, at the mouth of the Río Biobío. Take a city bus to Hualpencillo from Freire, ask the driver to let you out then walk 40 minutes, or hitch. Go along Avenida Las Golondrinas to the Enap oil refinery, turn left, then right (it is signed).

Talcahuano → *Population: 244,000.*

At the neck of the Península de Tumbes, Talcahuano has the best harbour in Chile. It is Chile's main naval station and an important commercial and fishing port. Two good roads run from Concepción. The warship **Huáscar** ① *Tue-Sun 0900-1230, 1330-1730, US$1.50 (surrender*

Concepción

Sleeping
Alborada 1
Cecil 2
Concepción 3
El Dorado 4
Hostal Antuco 6

Hostal Bianca 7
Maquehue 5
Residencial Colo Colo 8
Silvia Uslar 10

Eating
Big Joe Saloon 1
El Rancho de Julio 4
Le Château 5
Piazza 7
Yiet-Xiu 8

N

0 metres 300
0 yards 300

679

passport at main gate), a relic of the War of the Pacific, is in the naval base and can be visited. On Península Tumbes is Parque Tumbes, owned by Codeff: paths lead along the coast, no services, no admission charge (details from Codeff office in Concepción, Caupolicán 346, T222 6649).

Costa del Carbón
South of the Biobío is the Costa del Carbón, until recently the main coal producing area of Chile, linked with Concepción by road and two bridges over the Biobío. **Lota** (*Population 52,000, 42 km south of Concepción*) was, until its closure in 1997, the site of the most important **coalmine** in Chile ① *T870682, guided tours by former miners, 1000-1700, US$7.* In the church on the main plaza you can see a virgin made of coal. The **Parque de Lota Isadora Cousiño** ① *daily 1000-1800, summer till 2000, US$3.50, no picnicking*, covers 14 ha on a promontory to the west of the town. It was the life's work of Isadora Cousiño, whose family owned the mine. Laid out by English landscape architects in the last century, it contains plants from all over the world, ornaments imported from Europe, romantic paths and shady nooks offering views over the sea, and peafowl and pheasants roaming freely. South of Lota the road runs past the seaside resort of **Laraquete** where there are miles of golden sand, very popular in summer.

Lebu → *Phone code: 041. Population: 20,000.*
Some 149 km south of Concepcíon, Lebu is a fishing port and coal washing centre. It lies at the mouth of the Río Lebu and is the capital of Arauco province. Enormous beaches to north and south are popular on summer weekends: 3 km north at Playa Millaneco are caves with steep hills offering good walks and majestic views.

Cañete → *Phone code: 041. Colour map 8, grid C1. Population: 15,642.*
A small town on the site of Fort Tucapel where Pedro de Valdivia and 52 of his men were killed by Mapuche warriors in 1553. **Museo Mapuche** ① *Juan Antonio Ríos, T261 1093, www.dibam.cl/subdirec_museos/mm_canete/home.asp, 1 km south on the road to Contulmo, 0930-1230, 1400-1830, daily in summer, closed Mon in winter, US$1.50*, is housed in a modern building inspired by the traditional Mapuche ruca; includes Mapuche ceramics and textiles. There is nowhere to change dollars in town.

Contulmo → *Population: 2,000.*
A road runs south from Cañete along the north side of **Lago Lanalhue** to Contulmo, a sleepy village at the foot of the Cordillera. It hosts a Semana Musical (music week) in January. The wooden Grollmus House and Mill are 3 km northwest along the south side of the lake. The house, dating from 1918, has a fine collection of every colour of copihue (the national flower) in a splendid garden. The mill, built in 1928, contains the original wooden machinery. From here the track runs a further 9 km north to the Posada Campesina Alemana, an old German-style hotel in a fantastic spot at the water's edge (open December-March, details from Millaray 135, Contulmo). The Monumento Natural Contulmo, 8 km south and administered by CONAF, covers 82 ha of native forest.

Los Angeles and around → *Phone code: 043. Colour map 8, grid C1. Population: 114,000.*
On the Pan-American Highway, Los Angeles is 110 km south of Chillán. It is the capital of Biobío province. Founded in 1739 as a fort, it was destroyed several times by the Mapuche. It has a large Plaza de Armas and a good daily market. The local **tourist office** in the Chamber of Commerce ① *Lautaro 267, T321700, www.ccla.cl/*, is a good source of information and arranges trips. See also www.tourbiobio.com (in Spanish). **CONAF**, Ercilla 936, T321086, hsoto@conaf.cl, 0900-1300. Some 25 km north of Los Angeles is the spectacular **Salto El Laja** where the Río Laja plunges 47 m over the rocks. Free entry out of season – swimming in some of the cool natural pools. It's quite commercialized with plenty of restaurants, accommodation and souvenir shops.

Parque Nacional Laguna de Laja → *Entry US$1.30.*
East of Los Angeles by 93 km via a road which runs past the impressive rapids of the Río Laja, this park is dominated by the Antuco volcano (2,985 m), which is still active, and the glacier-covered Sierra Velluda. The Laguna is surrounded by stark scenery of scrub and lava.

There are 46 species of birds including condors and the rare Andean gull. There are several trails. Nearby is the Club de Esquí de Los Angeles with two ski-lifts, giving a combined run of 4 km on the Antuco volcano (season, May-August).

Angol → *Phone code: 045. Colour map 8, grid C1. Population: 39,000.*

Capital of the Province of Malleco, Angol is reached by paved roads from Collipulli and Los Angeles. Founded by Valdivia in 1552, it was seven times destroyed by the *indígenas* and rebuilt. The church and convent of San Beneventura, northwest of the attractive Plaza de Armas, built in 1863, became the centre for missionary work among the Mapuche. El Vergel, founded in 1880 as an experimental fruit-growing nursery, now includes an attractive park and the **Museo Dillman Bullock** ① *Mon-Fri 0900-1900, Sat-Sun 1000-1900, US$1. 5 km from town, colectivo No 2,* with pre-Columbian indigenous artefacts. There is an excellent **Tourist Office** ① *O'Higgins s/n, T045-711255,* across bridge from the bus terminal. Ask here about lodging in Vegas Blancas for Nahuelbuta (see below). **CONAF**, Prat 191, p 2, T711870.

Parque Nacional Nahuelbuta

① *All year (snow Jun-Sep), US$4.50.*

Situated in the coastal mountain range at an altitude of 800-1,550 m, this beautiful park covers 6,832 ha of forest and offers views over both the sea and the Andes. Although the forest includes many species of trees, the monkey puzzle araucaria) is most striking; some are over 2,000 years old, 50 m high and 3 min diameter. There are also 16 species of orchids as well as pudu deer, Chiloé foxes, pumas, black woodpeckers and parrots. There is a **Visitors' Centre** ① *at Pehuenco, 5 km from the entrance, open spring and summer 0800-1300, 1400-2000, rough maps are available at the park entrance for US$0.25, camping is near the Visitors' Centre, US$9 – there are many free campsites along the road from El Cruce to the entrance, at Kms 20 and 21.*

🌑 Sleeping

Concepción *p678, map p679*
Good budget accommodation is hard to find.
A Alborada, Barros Arana 457, T911121, www.hotelalborada.cl. Good 4-star with all mod cons, disabled-friendly, tours offered.
A-B El Dorado, Barros Arana 348, T222 9400, www.hoteleldorado.co.cl. Comfortable, spacious rooms, central, bar, cafeteria, parking.
B-C Concepción, Serrano 512, T222 8851, hotel concepcion@entelchile.net. Central, comfortable, heating, English spoken. Recommended.
C Maquehue, Barros Arana 786, p 8, T291 1966, www.hotelmaquehue.cl. Good services, with restaurant, laundry. Highly recommended.
C-D Cecil, Barros Arana 9, T273 9981, near railway station. With breakfast, quiet. Highly recommended.
C-D Hostal Bianca, Salas 643-C, T225 2103, www.hostalbianca.cl. Some rooms with bath, with breakfast, food available, parking, student discounts.
D Hostal Antuco, Barros Arana 741, flats 31-33, T223 5485. Entry via Galería Martínez. Some rooms with bath. Simple and spartan, but clean and reasonable value.

D Res Colo Colo, Colo Colo 743, T222 7118. With breakfast, some single rooms have bath. Meals available.
D Silvia Uslar, Edmundo Larenas 202, T222 7449 (not signed). Excellent, good breakfast, quiet, comfortable.

Costa del Carbón: Lota *p680*
E Res Roma, Galvarino 233, T041-287 6257. Near main plaza in Lata Bajo, good rooms, with breakfast, patio, welcoming.

Lebu *p680*
D-E pp Central, Pérez 183, T/F251 1904.
F without bath, parking. Recommended.

Cañete *p680*
C-D Nahuelbuta, Villagrán 644, T261 1073, hotelnahuelbuta@lanalhueturismo.cl. Cheaper without bath, pleasant, parking.
D-E Derby, Mariñán y Condell, T261 1960. Without bath, basic, restaurant.
D-E Gajardo, 7° de la Línea 817 (1 block from plaza). Without bath, old fashioned, pleasant rooms.

● *For an explanation of the sleeping and eating price codes used in this guide, see page 58.*
● *Other relevant information is found in Essentials pages 602-604.*

Contulmo *p680*

E **Central**, Millaray 131, T261 8089, hotelcentral@lanalhueturismo.cl. Without bath, no sign, very hospitable.

E **Contulmo**, Millaray 116, T289 4903. G pp without bath, hospitable, an attractive retreat. Recommended.

Lago Lanalhue

B **Hostal Licahue**, 4 km north of Contulmo towards Cañete (Casilla 644, Correo Contulmo) T09-9870 2822 (mob). With breakfast, also full board, attractively set overlooking lake, pool. Highly recommended.

Camping Camping Huilquehue, 15 km south of Cañete on lakeside. **Elicura**, Contulmo. Clean, US$6. Recommended. **Playa Blanca**, Playa Blanca, 10 km north of Contulmo. Clean.

Los Angeles *p680*

A **Gran Hotel Müso**, Valdivia 222 (Plaza de Armas), T313183, www.hotelmuso.cl. 3-star business standard, good restaurant open to non-residents.

D-E Private house at Caupolicán 651. Large house offering good value rooms and large breakfast. Opposite, also No 651, basic, cheaper.

E pp **Res Angelina**, Colo Colo 335. Basic, good hot shower.

Outside town

B **Hostería Salto del Laja**, Salto El Laja, T321706, www.saltodellaja.cl. Good rooms, fine restaurant, 2 swimming pools, on an island overlooking the falls.

C **Complejo Turístico Los Manantiales**, Salto El Laja, T/F314275, with camping.

C pp **El Rincón**, Panamericana Sur Km 494 (20 km north of Los Angeles), exit El Olivo (Cruce La Mona) 2 km east, T09-9441 5019, www.Elrinconchile.cl. Beautiful property beside a small river, restful, South American and European cuisine, includes vegetarian, Spanish classes, horse riding and rafting tours arranged, English, French, German and Spanish spoken. Recommended.

Parque Nacional Laguna de Laja *p680*

C **Refugio Chacay**, 21 km from the lake, T043-222651. It offers food, drink and bed, closed in summer.

D **Hostería El Bosque**, in Abanico. Restaurant, also good campsite.

E 2 other refugíos: **Digeder**, 11 km from the park entrance, and **Universidad de Concepción**, both on slopes of Volcán Antuco, for both T041-229054, office O'Higgins 740.

E pp house with orange gates at park bus stop takes guests, food extra.

Angol *p681*

C **La Posada**, at El Vergel, T712103. Full board, nice hotel.

E **Millaray**, Prat, 2 blocks west of Plaza. Shared bath, good. Recommended.

F pp **Puren 539**. Basic *hospedaje* with shared hot shower.

❶ Eating

Concepción *p678, map p679*

♦♦♦ **Le Château** Colo Colo 340. French, seafood and meat, closed Sun.

♦♦ **Big Joe Saloon**, O'Higgins 808, just off plaza. Popular at lunchtime, open Sun evening, good breakfasts, vegetarian meals, snacks and pizzas.

♦♦ **Piazza**, Barros Arana 631, p 2r. Good pizzas.

♦♦ **El Rancho de Julio**, O'Higgins 36. Argentine *parrillada*.

♦ **Yiet-Xiu**, Angol 515. Good, cheap Oriental cuisine.

Cafés

Café El Dom, Caupolicán 415. One of several cafés near the Plaza de Armas, good, open Sun morning.

Café Haiti, Caupolicán 515. Open Sun morning, good coffee.

Fuente Alemana, Caupolicán 654, near Plaza de Armas. A recommended *fuente de soda*.

La Capilla, Vicuña MacKenna 769. Good ponches, popular.

Nuria, Barros Arana 736. Very good breakfasts and lunches, good value.

QuickBiss, O'Higgins between Tuscapel and Castellón. Salads, real coffee, good service, good lunches.

Saaya 1, Barros Arana 899. Excellent panadería/pastelería/rotisería.

Treinta y Tantos, Prat 356. Nice bar, good music, wide selection of empanadas, good breakfasts and lunches. Recommended.

Talcahuano *p679*

The market abounds with good quality but inexpensive seafood.

♦♦-♦ **Benotecas**, on the seafront, has a row of 4 restaurants sharing one window facing the harbour, superb fish and seafood in each one, reasonable prices, recommended.

♦♦-♦ **Domingo Lara**, Aníbal Pinto 450, seafood specialities, excellent.

Cañete *p680*

♦ **Café Nahuel**, just off the plaza. For real coffee.

♦ **Don Juanito**, Riquelme 151. A very good eating place recommended by the locals.

Los Angeles *p680*

♯♯ **El Arriero**, Colo Colo 235. Good parrillas and international dishes.

♯♯ **Di Leone**, Av Alemania 686. Good lasagne and other Italian dishes.

♯♯ **Rancho de Julio**, Colón 720. Excellent parrilla.

♯ **Julio's Pizzas**, Colón 542. Good pizzería.

O Shopping

Concepción *p678, map p679*
The main shopping area is north of the Plaza de Armas.

Handicrafts Feria Artesanal, Freire 757.

Malls and supermarkets Las Brisas, Freire y Lincoyán. Supermarket. Galería Internacional, Caupolicán y Barros Arana is worth a visit. Plaza del Trébol mall with multi-screen cinemas north of the city off the road to Talcahuano (near the airport). Take any bus for Talcahuano. Supermercado Unimarc, Chacabuco 70.

▲ Activities and tours

Concepción *p678, map p679*
Alta Luz, San Martín 586, p 2, T221 7727. Tours to national parks.

Chile Indomito Adventure, Serrano 551, of 3, T222 1618, Trekking in Reserva Nacional Ralco.

South Expeditions, O'Higgins 680, p 2, of 218D, T/F223 2290. Rafting, horseriding, fishing and trekking expeditions, 1 and 2-day programmes.

Los Angeles *p680*
Interbruna Turismo, Caupolicán 350, T313812, interbruna@hotmail.com. For local excursions, car rental or air tickets.

◉ Transport

Concepción *p678, map p679*
Air Airport north of the city, off the main road to Talcahuano. Taxi US$8. In summer flights daily to and from **Santiago** (LAN and Sky), fewer in winter; LAN less frequently to **Valdivia, Osorno** and **Puerto Montt**; both fly to **Temuco**.

Bus Main long distance terminal, known as Terminal Collao, is 2 km east, on Av Gral Bonilla, next to football and athletics stadium. (Several buses to city centre, US$0.60, taxi US$4.) Tur-Bus, Línea Azul and Buses Bío Bío services leave from Terminal Camilo Henríquez 2 km northeast of main terminal on J M García, reached by buses from Av Maipú in centre, via Terminal Collao. To **Santiago**, 6½ hrs, US$10. To **Valparaíso**, 8 hrs, US$12 (most via Santiago). To **Los Angeles**, US$3. To **Loncoche**, 5½ hrs US$7. To **Pucón**, direct in summer only, 7 hrs, US$10. To **Valdivia**, 7 hrs, US$10. To **Puerto Montt** several

companies, US$13, about 9 hrs (bus cama US$26). Best direct bus to **Chillán** is Línea Azul, 2 hrs, US$3. For a longer and more scenic route, take the Costa Azul bus which follows the old railway line, through Tomé, Coelemu and Ñipas on to Chillán (part dirt-track, takes 5½ hrs). Services to **Lota, Lebu, Cañete** and **Contulmo** are run by J Ewert (terminal at Carrera y Tucapel) and Los Alerces (terminal at Prat y Maipú). To **Talcahuano** frequent service from Plaza de Armas (bus marked 'Base Naval'), US$0.70, 1 hr, express US$1, 30 mins.

Train Station at Prat y Barros Arana, Efe ticket office, Av Padre Hurtado 570, T221 4648. Regular nightly service to/from **Santiago**, 10 hrs; clase preferente US$28, turista US$21 (or take bus/train combination via Chillán). Also suburban services from Talcahuano to Chiguayante.

Costa del Carbón: Lota *p680*
Bus Concepción-Lota, 1½ hrs, US$1. Many buses by-pass the centre: catch them from the main road.

Cañete *p680*
Bus Leave from 2 different terminals: J Ewert, Inter Sur and Thiele from Riquelme y 7° de la Línea, Jeldres, Erbuc and other companies from the Terminal Municipal, Serrano y Villagrán. To **Santiago**, Inter Sur, daily, 12 hrs. To **Concepción**, 3 hrs, US$4.50. To **Lebu** US$2. To **Angol** US$4.50.

Contulmo *p680*
Bus To **Concepción**, Thiele, US$6, 4 hrs; to **Temuco**, Thiele and Erbuc, US$7; to **Cañete**, frequent, US$1.50.

Los Angeles *p680*
Bus Long distance bus terminal on northeast outskirts of town, local terminal at Villagrán y Rengo in centre, by market. To **Salto de Laja**, every 30 mins with Bus Bío Bio, US$2 return. To **Santiago**, 6½ hrs, US$10, cama US$30. To **Viña del Mar** and **Valparaíso**, 8 hrs, US$14. Every 30 mins to **Concepción**, US$3, 2 hrs. To **Temuco**, US$6, hourly. To **Curacautín**, daily at 0945, 1600, 3 hrs, US$6 (otherwise change in Victoria).

Parque Nacional Laguna de Laja *p680*
Bus ERS Bus from Los Angeles (Villagrán 507, by market) to **Abanico**, 20 km past Antuco (6 a day, US$1.50), then 2 hrs/4 km walk to park entrance (hitching possible). Or bus to **Antuco**, 2 hrs, weekdays 5 daily, 2 on Sun and festivals, last return 1730, US$2, then hitch last 24 km. Details from CONAF in Los Angeles (see above).

Angol *p681*
Bus To **Santiago** US$10, **Los Angeles**, US$2.
To **Temuco**, Trans Bío-Bío, frequent, US$3.50.

Parque Nacional Nahuelbuta *p681*
Bus In Dec-Feb there is a direct bus from **Angol**, Sun 0800, return 1700. Otherwise, take the bus to **Vegas Blancas** (27 km west of Angol) 0700 and 1600 daily, return 0900 and 1600, 1½ hrs, US$2, get off at El Cruce, from where it is a steep 7 km walk to park entrance. Sometimes the bus goes to the park entrance, ask first.

---

① Directory

Concepción *p678, map p679*
Airline offices Aerolíneas del Sur, O'Higgins 659 of 602. LAN, Barros Arana 560, T224 8824. Sky, T221 8941 **Banks** ATMs at banks, most of which are on O'Higgins. Several cambios in Galería Internacional, entrances at Barros Arana

565 and Caupolicán 521. **Consulates** Argentina, O`Higgins 420, of 82, T223 0257, cconc@entelchile.net. **Cultural** centres Alliance Française, Colo Colo 1, T226 2703, www.alliancefrancaiseconce.cl. Library, concerts, films, cultural events. **Internet** Many in the centre, including at Barros Arana 541 and Caupolicán 567; English spoken. **Post offices** O'Higgins y Colo Colo. **Telephones** Telefónica, Colo Colo 487, Angol 483. Entel, Barros Arana 541, Caupolicán 567, p 2. **Useful addresses** Automóvil Club de Chile, O'Higgins 630, Of 303, T224 5884, for information and car hire (T222 2070). **Codeff** (Comité Nacional pro Defensa de la Fauna y Flora), Caupolicán 346, oficina E, p 4, T222 6649.

Los Angeles *p680*
Banks ATMs at banks and at supermarket at Av Alemania 686. **Agencia Interbruna**, Caupolicán 350, T313812, F325925, best rates.

Lake District

The Lake District, stretching southwards from Temuco to Puerto Montt, is one of Chile's most beautiful regions. There are some 12 great lakes of varying sizes, as well as imposing waterfalls and snowcapped volcanoes. There are a number of good bases for exploring. Out of season many facilities are closed, in season (from mid-December to mid-March), prices are higher and it is best to book well in advance, particularly for transport. About 20,000 Mapuches live in the area, particularly around Temuco. Although Mapudungun is becoming less prevalent, there are possibly 100,000 more of mixed descent who speak the native tongue, nearly all of them bilingual.

Temuco and around

→ *Phone code: 045. Colour map 8, grid C1. Population: 227,000. Altitude: 107 m.*

Although at first sight rather grey and imposing, Temuco is a lively university city and one of the fastest growing commercial centres in the south. Founded in 1881 after the final treaty with the Mapuches and the arrival of the railway, this city is the capital of IX Región (Araucanía), 677 km south of Santiago. Temuco is proud of its Mapuche heritage and it is this that gives it its distinctive character, especially around the outdoor market. The **Sernatur office** is at ① *Bulnes 586, on main plaza, T211969, infoaraucania@sernatur.cl. Daily in summer 0830-2030, Mon-Fri 0900-1900, 1500-1700 in winter.* It has good leaflets in English. Also in the municipal market. **CONAF** is at Bilbao 931, T234420, temuco@conaf.cl. Sernap for fishing permits, Miraflores 965. North and east of the city are five national parks and reserves, notably Conguillio with its araucaria forests, and flora and fauna found nowhere else. It is great for hiking, or touring by car or even mountain bike. There are also various skiing opportunities.

Sights

The centre is the Plaza Aníbal Pinto, around which are the main public buildings including the cathedral and the Municipalidad. Very little of the old city remains; practically every wooden building burned down following the 1960 earthquake. Temuco is the Mapuches' market town and you may see some, particularly women, in their typical costumes in the huge produce market, the **Feria** ① *Lautaro y Pinto*, one of the most fascinating markets in Chile. Mapuche textiles, pottery, woodcarving, jewellery etc are also sold inside and around the municipal market, Aldunate y Diego Portales (it also sells fish, meat and dairy produce), but these are increasingly touristy and poor quality. There is a handicraft fair every February in the main plaza. The **Casa de la Mujer Mapuche** ① *in the Gymnasium, between Corvalín and Almte Barroso, Padre las Casas suburb, T09-9169 4682, Mon-Fri 0930-1300, 1500-1830, getting*

The Lake District

To Concepción & Talca
To Termas de Tolhuaca (35 km) & Parque Nacional Tolhuaca
Victoria
Curacautín **10 ♦**
Lautaro
Lonquimay
To Paso Pino Hachado
Malalcahuello
Vilcún
V Llaima (3050m) ▲
Nehuentue
Carahue
Nueva Imperial
Cherquenco
Puerto Saavedra
Lago Budi
Puerto Domínguez
Temuco
1 ♦
Lago Icalma
Barros Arana
Melipeuco
Paso de Icalma
Teodoro Schmidt
Freire
Radal
Cunco
To Zapala
Toltén
Lago Colico
Lago Caburga **♦ 2**
Pacific Ocean
Trarilelfú
Quelhue
Caburga
♦ 8
Lago Villarrica
Pucón
Loncoche
Villarrica
Termas de Palguín
Mehuin
Lanco
Lican-Ray
V Villarrica (2840m) ▲ **3 ▲**
Lago Quillén
Curiñanco
Panguipulli
Lago Calafquén
V Quetrupillán
Coñaripe
Lago Tromén
Puesco
Paso Tromén
Niebla
Valdivia
Antilhue
Lago Panguipulli
Liquiñe
Lanín ▲
Corral
Lago Riñihue
Lake Neltume
Los Lagos
Riñihue
Choshuenco
Puerto Fuy
Lago Huechulafquen
8 ♦
Paillaco
V Choshuenco (2415m) **9 ♦**
Salto Huilo Huilo
Lago Pirehueico
Junín de los Andes
Futrono
Puerto Pirehueico
Lago Lolog
Paso Huahum
Puerto Nuevo
Llifén
Lago Ranco
Lago Lacar
San Martín de los Andes
Río Bueno
La Unión
Lago Maihue
Lago Hermoso
Trumao
Río Bueno
Riñinahue
Lago Ranco
Lago Huishué
Lago Falkner
Osorno
Lago Gris
Lago Traful
7 ♦
To Maicolpue & Pucatrihue
Río Negro
Entre Lagos
V Puyehue (2240m) ▲
Lago Puyehue
Río Golgol
Lago Constancia
Rupanco
Termas de Puyehue **♦ 4**
ARGENTINA
Lago Rupanco
Puerto Octay
Islote
Cerro Puntiagudo (2278m) ▲
Lago Nahuel Huapi
Nahuel Huapi
V Osorno (2680m) ▲
Paso Pérez Rosales
Frutillar
Lago Llanquihue
Lago Todos los Santos
Puerto Blest
Puerto Frías
Petrohué
Peulla
Puerto Varas
Ensenada
Río Petrohué
Cayutué
♦ 5
Tronador (3460m) ▲
Bariloche
La Poza
V Calbuco (2015m) ▲
Lago Fonck
Lago Gutiérrez
Río Maullín
Puerto Montt
Ralún
Lago Chapo
Cochamó
Lago Mascardi
To El Maitén & El Bolsón
Maullín
Isla Tengla
6 ♦
Lago Steffen
Calbuco
Isla Guar
Puelo
Pargua
La Arena
Chacao
Puelche
Isla Chiloé
Seno de Reloncaví
N

0 km 10
0 miles 10

National parks ♦
Alerce Andino **6**
Conguillio **1**
Huerquehue **2**
Lanín **8**
Mocho Choshuenco **9**
Nahuel Huapi **7**
Nalcas Malalcahuello **10**
Puyehue **4**
Vicente Pérez Rosales **5**
Villarrica **3**

there: take bus 8a or 10, colectivo 13a, sells many crafts, including textiles made by a Mapuche weavers' co-operative, all with traditional designs. A couple of km northwest of the centre is the **Museo de la Araucanía** ① *Alemania 84, Mon-Fri 0900-1700, Sat 1100-1700, Sun 1100-1300, US$1.50 (free Sun), getting there: take bus 1 from the centre.* It is devoted to the history and traditions of the Mapuche nation, with a section on German settlement. For information on visits to Mapuche settlements, eg Chol Chol, go to the Sernatur office in the Plaza. There are views of **Temuco from Cerro Ñielol** ① *US$1.50, 0830-2030.* This park has a fine collection of native plants in the natural state, including the national flower, the copihue rojo. This is a good site for a picnic and it has an excellent visitors' centre run by CONAF. A tree marks the spot where peace was made with the Mapuche. Bicycles are only allowed in before 1100. At the top of the hill there is a restaurant, which also has dancing (not always open).

Northeast of the centre, 2 km, is the **Museo Nacional Ferroviario Pablo Neruda** ① *Barros Arana 0565, T227613, www.temucochile.com, Tue-Sun 0900-1800, US$2, concessions US$0.75, take micro 1 Variante, 9 Directo, 4b, taxi from centre US$2.50,* the newly restored national railway museum. Exhibits include over 20 engines and carriages (including the former presidential carriage) dating from 1908 to 1953. The grounds contain rusting hulks and machinery. Temporary exhibitions in the annex.

Temuco

To Long Distance Bus Terminal, Mall Temuco Shopping Centre, Santiago & the North

Parque Nacional Cerro Ñielol

Visitor Centre

Cautin

Tucapel

Janequeo

Patzque

Av J Pinto

B Urrutia

Otella

To Railway Museum

Conaf

Bilbao

Rural

Av Balmaceda

JAC

Gra Mackenna

Cruz

Zenteno

Matta

Av Barros Arana

Maiква

Miraflores

Anglican

Av Caupolicán

Plaza Teodoro Schmidt

Produce

Av Prieto Norte

Lautaro

M Rodriguez

Municipal

D Portales

D Portales

EFE Railway Office

To 8

Av Alemania

M Montt

Cathedral

Museo de la Araucanía

Claro Solar

V Mackenna

Aldunate

To Pacific Coast & the South via Pan-American Highway

Thiers

Blanco

Carrera

A Varas

Plaza Aníbal Pinto

Freire

Las Heras

Lynch

Lagos

A Prat

Bello

M Bulnes

Av San Martín

Prieto Sur

O'Higgins

Quillas

Las

León Gallo

Río Cautín

Sleeping 🛏
Aitué **2**
Bayern **1**
Casa Blanca **4**
Chapelco **3**
Continental **5**
Don Eduardo **6**
Frontera **13**
Hospedaje 525 **4**
Hospedaje Aldunate **9**
Hospedaje Maggi Alvarado **8**
Hospedaje Millaray **10**
Hostal Montt **7**
La Casa de Juanita **12**
Oriente **14**
Terraverde **15**

Eating 🍴
El Ceache **1**
Kokaví **2**
La Parrilla de Miguel **3**
Otto **7**
Temedors **10**

N

0 metres 200
0 yards 200

Curacautín and around → *Population: 12,500. Altitude: 400 m.*

Curacautín is a small town 84 km northeast of Temuco (road paved) and 56 km southeast of Victoria by paved road. Deprived by new, stricter controls of its traditional forestry industry (there were several sawmills), Curacautín is trying to recreate itself as a centre for tourism. It is a useful base for visiting the nearby national parks and hot springs.

Termas de Manzanar, are indoor hot springs, 17 km east of Curacautín (US$8, open all year, sadly run down, overpriced) are reached by bus from Temuco and Victoria. The road passes the Salto del Indio , where there are 30-m high falls, US$1.30 (Km 71 from Victoria) and *cabañas*, and Salto de la Princesa, an even more impressive 50-m waterfall, 3 km beyond Manzanar hostería, with camping.

The beautiful pine-surrounded **Termas de Tolhuaca**① *all year, US$6, getting there: taxi from Curacautín US$21*, are 35 km to the northeast of Curacautín by unpaved road, or 82 km by rough, unpaved road from just north of Victoria (high clearance four-wheel drive vehicle essential). And 2 km north of the Termas is the **Parque Nacional Tolhuaca** ① *Dec-Apr, taxi from Curacautín US$17*, including waterfalls, two lakes, superb scenery and good views of volcanoes from Cerro Amarillo. Park administration is near Laguna Malleco, with a campsite nearby. Much of the park, together with the neighbouring Reserva Nacional Malleco, was severely damaged by forest fires in early 2002. It will take several decades fully to recover, but some half-day trails are open.

Reserva Nacional Nalcas Malalcahuello

Northeast of Curacautín, this 31,305 ha park is on the slopes of the **Lonquimay** volcano (2,865 m). It is much less crowded than nearby Parque Nacional Conguillio. The volcano began erupting on Christmas Day 1988; the new crater is called Navidad. To see it, access is made from Malalcahuello, 15 km south and half-way between Curacautín and Lonquimay town. In the park, which is one of the best areas for seeing unspoilt araucaria forest, CONAF has opened several marked trails, from one hour to two days in length. There is a municipal refugio at the foot of the volcano. The teacher at Malalcahuello school, José Córdoba, organizes tours and horse riding for groups. Sra Naomi Saavedra at Res Los Sauces arranges transport. From Malalcahuello it is a one-day hike to the Sierra Nevada mountain, or a two-day hike to Conguillio national park (with equipment and experience, otherwise use a guide). CONAF office on main road in Malalcahuello gives information, as does **La Suizandina**, which gives good access to treks and the ascent of the volcano, see Sleeping, below.

Los Arenales ski resort ① *T891071, www.arenalespark.cl, season Jun-Sep, taxi from Curacautín US$17, in winter access from Lonquimay town side only*, is at Las Raices Pass on the road from Malalcahuello to Lonquimay town. Four lifts go up to 2,500 m with great views, ski pass US$17, equipment hire US$15. It is a good, small resort with a nice restaurant. Also in winter, the main route from Malalcahuello to Lonquimay town, goes through the ex-railway tunnel of **Las Raices** ① *toll US$2*. At 4.8 km it was, until recently, the longest tunnel in South America. Now it's in poor condition, unlit and has constant filtration. There is talk of repair, but it's unwise to go through by bicycle.

Parque Nacional Conguillio

East of Temuco by 80 km, this is one of the most popular parks in Chile① *Dec-Mar, US$6*, but is deserted outside January/February and weekends. In the centre is the 3,125 m **Llaima volcano**, which is active. There are two large lakes, **Laguna Verde** and **Laguna Conguillio**, and two smaller ones, **Laguna Arco Iris** and **Laguna Captrén**. North of Laguna Conguillio rises the snow covered **Sierra Nevada**, the highest peak of which reaches 2,554 m. This is the best place in Chile to see araucaria forest, which used to cover an extensive area in this part of the country. Other trees include cypresses, lenga and winter's bark. Birdlife includes the condor and the black woodpecker and there are foxes and pumas.

Crampons and ice-axe are essential for climbing Llaima, as well as experience or a guide. Climb south from Guardería Captrén. Allow five hours to ascend, two hours to descend. Information on the climb is available from **Guardería Captrén**. There is a range of walking trails, from 1 km to 22 km in length. Details are available from park administration or CONAF in Temuco. Llaima ski resort, one of the prettiest in Chile, is reached by poor road from Cherquenco, 30 km west (high clearance vehicle essential).

There are three entrances: From Curacautín, north of the park: see Transport below; from Melipeuco, 13 km south of the southern entrance at Truful-Truful (open all year); and from

Cherquenco to the west entrance near the Llaima ski resort. It is then a two or three day hike around Volcán Llaima to Laguna Conguillio, which is dusty, but with beautiful views of Laguna Quepe, then on to the Laguna Captrén guardería. Information on all three roads into the park and administration by Lago Conguillio. There is a Visitors' Centre at Laguna Conguillio; free slide lectures and short, guided nature walks in summer.

Border with Argentina

Paso Pino Hachado (1,884 m) can be reached either by paved road, 73 km southeast from Lonquimay, or by unpaved road 129 east from Melipeuco. On the Argentine side this road continues to Zapala. Chilean immigration and customs are in Liucura, 22 km west of the border, open September-mid-May 0800-2000, winter 0800-1900. Very thorough searches and 2-3 hour delays reported, especially when entering Chile. Buses from Temuco to Zapala and Neuquén use this crossing: see under Temuco. **Paso de Icalma** (1,298 m) is reached by unpaved road, 53 km from Melipeuco, a good crossing for those with their own transport, although it maybe impassable in winter (phone Policía Internacional in Temuco, Prat 19, to check: T293890). On the Argentine side this road continues to Zapala. Chilean immigration is open mid-October to mid-March 0800-2000, winter 0800-1900.

● Sleeping

Temuco *p684, map p686*
Accommodation in private houses, category F minimum, can be arranged by tourist office.
AL Terraverde, Prat 0220, T239999, www.pan americanahoteles.cl. 5-star, the best hotel in town.
A Frontera, Bulnes 726, T200400, www.hotelfrontera.cl. With breakfast, good business standard, large conference room.
B Aitué, A Varas 1048, T212512, www.hotelaitue.cl. Business standard, central, bar, English spoken, comfortable.
B Don Eduardo, Bello 755, T214133, www.hoteldoneduardo.cl. Parking, suites with kitchen. Recommended.
B Holiday Inn Express, Av R Ortega 01800, T223300, www.holidayinnexpress.cl. A member of the Chileanized version of this chain, good value, with breakfast, a/c, heating, free internet, pool, out of town but worth considering if driving.
B-C Bayern, Prat 146, T276000, www.hotelbayern.cl. Standard 3-star. Small rooms, clean, helpful, buffet breakfast, parking, cheaper in dollars than pesos.
C Continental, Varas 708, T238973, www.turismochile.cl/continental. Popular with business travellers, old fashioned building, charming, large rooms with antique furniture, heating, with breakfast, good restaurant, popular bar, cheaper rooms without bath, parking. Neruda stayed here once. Recommended.
C Hostal Montt, M Montt 637, T910400, www.hostalmontt.cl. Comfortable if overpriced, some rooms with bath, parking, cable TV, breakfast included, gym.
C-D La Casa de Juanita, Carrera 735, T213203. Cheaper without bath, breakfast, hot water, laundry, heating, parking. Many others in this range on Bello, west of plaza.

D Blanco Encalada 1078, T234447. Use of kitchen, good breakfast.
D Chapelco, Cruz 401, T749393, www.hotelchapelco.cl. Airy, slightly run-down, cable TV, laundry, internet in lobby, comfortable, good service. Recommended.
D Hosp Aldunate, Aldunate 187, T270057. D-E singles, cooking facilities, some rooms with TV and bath.
D Oriente, M Rodríguez 1146, T/F233232, h-oriente@123mail.cl. Old but clean and friendly, good value rooms, cheaper without bath, heating, TV, parking, laundry, breakfast extra, some rooms with no windows. Recommended.
D-E Casa Blanca, Montt 1306 y Zenteno, T272667, www.hostalcasablanca.cl. **G** single with shared bath, slightly run down, but OK option, includes breakfast.
D-E Hospedaje 525, Zenteno 525, T233982. Without breakfast, new section has small rooms with bath, good value, older part has poor beds but also good value.
D-E Hosp Maggi Alvarado, Recreo 209, off Av Alemania, T409804. Small rooms (**F** singles), helpful, student place, nice atmosphere.
E Hosp Millaray, Claro Solar 471, T645720. Simple, basic, but unfriendly. Other private houses on this street, **F** pp.
G pp **Hospedaje**, unnamed but signed, at Aldunate 12. With hot shower and cable TV.

Curacautín and around *p687*
C-D Plaza, Yungay 157 (main plaza), T881256. Restaurant OK but pricey, accommodation overpriced.
C-D Hostal Las Espigas, Miraflores 315, T881138, rivaseugenia@hotmail.com.

Good rooms (**F** singles), kitchen, breakfast, dinner available on request.
E Turismo, Tarapacá 140, T881116. Good food, hot shower, comfortable, good value if old-fashioned (singles **G**).

Termas de Manzanar
AL-A Termas de Manzanar, T/F045-881200, termasmanzanar@indecom.cl. Overpriced, but also simple rooms with bath; includes access to thermal baths, full board available.
C-D Anden Rose, 5 km west of Manzanar, Casilla 123, Curacautín, T056-9-869 1700, www.andenrose.com. Cosy rooms, cheaper without bath, with breakfast, restaurant serving international and Bavarian food, bike, horse, kayak rental, jeep tours arranged, German/Chilean run.
E Hostería Abarzúa, Km 18, T045-870011. Simple, cheaper rooms without bath, full board available (good food), also campsite.

Termas de Tolhuaca
AL Termas de Tolhuaca, T045-881164, www.termasdetolhuaca.cl. With full board, including use of baths and horse riding, very good; jacuzzi and massage also available.
E Res Roja, **G** singles, food, camping near the river.
Campsite 10 km past the Termas, US$3.80 pp (US$15 with car), pleasant, cold water.

Lonquimay
B La Suizandina, Km 83 Carretera Internacional a Argentina, T045-1973725 or 09-884 9541, www.suizandina.com. Hostel 3 km before Malalcahuello Erbuc bus from Temuco 2½ hrs), with a range of rooms from private room with heating and large Swiss breakfast with home-baked bread, to shared rooms **E-F** pp, camping US$5, TCs accepted, laundry, book exchange, bike and ski rental, horse riding, travel and trekking information, German and English spoken, good meals available. "Like being in Switzerland". Recommended.
D pp **Centro de Ski Lonquimay**, 10 km from the bus stop. With breakfast, full board also available, open only in season.
D Res Los Sauces, in Malalcahuello, T09-9883 7880. Singles **F** with shared bath, some rooms with bath, use of kitchen extra, hot water, good value, breakfast extra, full board available.

Parque Nacional Conguillio *p687*
A La Baita, in the park, 3 km south of Laguna Verde, T416410, on-line bookings at www.labaita conguillio.cl/labaita. Cabins with electricity, hot water, kitchen and wood stoves, charming, lots of information, Italian/Chilean owned.

B cabañas Laguna Conguillio, summer only, sleep 6, no sheets or blankets, gas stove, and café/shop. Also campsite (US$15 per tent, hot water, showers, firewood), and a cheaper campsite *camping de mochileros* at Ñires, US$5.70 pp, with hot shower, US$2 for firewood).
D Adela y Helmut, Faja 16000, Km 5 Norte, Cunco (on the way to Melipeuco, 16 km from Cunco, website has directions, phone for pick-up from bus stop), T09-9724 4479, www.adelay helmut.com. Guesthouse and restaurant on a Mapuche/ German owned farm, room for families and for backpackers in 6-bed dorm, kitchens, hot showers, solar heating, mountain bike rental, 4WD tours, good reports. Ask about horse riding and rafting (www.esmeraldaraft.de) at neighbouring properties.
E Germania, Aguirre 399, Melipeuco. Basic, good food.
E Hospedaje Icalma, Aguirre Cerda 729, Melipeuco, T581108. **G** singles, spacious, basic rooms, with shower and breakfast. Recommended.
Camping Camping Los Pioneros, 2 km out of town on road to the park, T581005. Hot water. Various other sites dotted around the park, by Lakes Conguillio and Captrén, all administered by CONAF, T298213.

Eating

Temuco *p684, map p686*
Many good restaurants around Av Alemania and Mall Mirage, about 10 blocks west of centre. Make for the Mercado Municipal on Aldunate y Portales, or the rural bus terminal, where there are countless restaurants serving very cheap set meals at lunch.
La Parrilla de Miguel, Montt 1095, T275182. Good for meat, large portions, and wine; one of the better restaurants.
Otto, V MacKenna 530. German food, cakes, etc.
El Ceache, Cruz 231. Typical Chilean food, good value set lunch.
Kokavi, Rodríguez y Zenteno, T951625. Traditional Mapuche restaurant, popular at lunchtime.
Temedors, San Martín 827. Good value lunch.

Cafés
Il Gelato, Bulnes 420. Delicicious ice cream.
Marriet, Prat 451, loc 21. Excellent coffee.

Termas de Manzanar
La Rotonda del Cautín, T1971478. Good food, friendly.

Parque Nacional Conguillio *p687*
Buy supplies in Temuco, Curacautín or
Melipeuco: much cheaper than the shop in the
park. **Restaurant Los Troncos**, Aguirre 352.
Recommended. Also **Ruminot**, on same street.

O Shopping

Temuco *p684, map p686*
Camping equipment Eltit supermarket,
O'Higgins y Fresia. **Outdoors & Travel**,
Lincoyán 361, clothing, equipment, maps.
Crafts Best choice in the indoor municipal
market at Aldunate y Portales, and in the **Casa
de la Mujer Mapuche** (see Sights, above).
Fundación Chol-Chol, Sector Rengalil,
Camino Temuco–Nueva Imperial Km 16,
T614007, www.chol chol.org. Contact Johanna
Pérez (speaks English), or Esteban Bastias. A
non-profit organization which sells traditional
Mapuche textiles, naturally dyed and hand
woven by local women.
Market Temuco Feria, Lautaro y Aníbal
Pinto. This is one of the most fascinating
markets in Chile, with people bringing excellent
fruit and vegetables from the surrounding
countryside, including spices, fish, grains,
cheese and honey. Also many inexpensive
bars and restaurants nearby.
Supermarket Las Brisas, Caupolicán y
Montt, and Rodríguez 1100 block. There is a
modern shopping mall north of city; buses 2 or 7.
Frutería Las Vegas, Matta 274, dried fruit
(useful for climbing/trekking).

▲ Activities and tours

Temuco *p684, map p686*
Tours to Parque Nacional Conguillio
cost generally US$40 for 1 day; to Villarrica
volcano US$75.

⊕ Transport

Temuco *p684, map p686*
Air Manquehue Airport 6 km southwest of the
city. There is an airport transfer service to the city
and to hotels in Villarrica and Pucón, US$15 (may
not run out of season). Taxis charge US$8. There
is no public bus. LAN to **Santiago, Concepción,
Pucón, Osorno, Valdivia, Puerto Montt,
Balmaceda** and **Punta Arenas**. Sky to **Santiago,
Concepción, Pucón** and **Puerto Montt**.
Bus New long-distance bus terminal north of
city at Pérez Rosales y Caupolicán, city bus 2, 7
or 10; colectivo 11P; taxi US$2.50. JAC has its
own efficient terminal at Balmaceda y Aldunate,
7 blocks north of the Plaza, which also serves
neighbouring towns. NarBus and Igi-Llaima are

opposite. Buses to **Santiago**, many overnight,
8-9 hrs, US$11 salón-cama US$22). To
Concepción, Bío Bío (Lautaro entre Prat y
Bulnes), US$7, 4½ hrs. To **Chillán**, 4 hrs, US$6.
Cruz del Sur, 3 a day to **Castro**, 10 a day to
Puerto Montt (US$10, 5½ hrs). To **Valdivia**, JAC,
several daily, US$5, 2½ hrs. To **Osorno** US$5,
4 hrs. To **Villarrica** and **Pucón**, JAC, many
between 0705 and 2045, 1½ hrs, and 2 hrs,
US$4. Buses to neighbouring towns leave from
Terminal Rural, Pinto y Balmaceda. To **Coñaripe**,
3 hrs, and **Lican Ray**, 2 hrs. To **Panguipulli**,
Power and Pangui Sur 3 hrs, US$4. Pangui Sur to
Loncoche, US$2, **Los Lagos**, US$3, **Mehuin** in
summer only. To **Curacautín** via Lautaro, Erbuc,
US$3, 4 daily, 2½ hrs. To **Lonquimay**, Erbuc, 4
daily, 3½ hrs, US$4. To **Contulmo**, US$5, 2 hrs,
Cañete, US$5 and **Lebu**, Erbuc and Thiele.
Buses to Argentina: Igi Llaima and Narbus to
Junín de los Andes, early morning but not daily,
US$20, advance booking required. **Ruta Sur**
(Miraflores 1151) to **Zapala**, 10-12 hrs (US$25),
3 a week. To **Neuquén**, 7 companies, 16 hrs
(US$25), via Paso Pino Hachado. To **Bariloche**
you have to change bus in Osorno, Tas-
Choapa US$23.
Car hire Automóvil Club de Chile, Varas 687,
T248903 for car hire and at airport. **Christopher
Car**, Varas 522, T215988, recommended. **Euro**,
MacKenna 426, T210311, helpful, good value.
Full Famas, at airport and in centre T215420,
highly recommended.
Train No Station at Barros Arana y Lautaro
Navarro, T233416, www.efe.cl. There is another
ticket office at Bulnes 582, T233522, open
Mon-Fri 0900-1300, 1430-1800, Sun 0900-1300.
To **Santiago**: daily at 2200, 9 hrs: fares *salón*
US$19-28, *preferente* US$22-36, restaurant car
mid-price (or take your own food). To **Puerto
Montt** daily at 1235, US$6.50. **Note** No trains
between Chillán and Temuco mid-2007 because
of storm damage; no date set for resumption.

Curacautín *p687*
Bus Terminal on the main road, by the plaza.
Buses to/from **Temuco**, **Los Angeles** and
Santiago. **Taxi** from Temuco airport US$45.

Lonquimay
Bus Bus Erbuc from **Temuco** via Lautaro,
US$4 to **Malalcahuello**, 4 a day, 2½ hrs,
3½ to Lonquimay town, US$4. **Taxi**
Curacautín-Malalcahuello US$15.

Parque Nacional Conguillio *p687*
For touring, hire a 4WD vehicle in Temuco.
To the northern entrance: **taxi** from
Curacautín to Laguna Captrén, US$28 one way.
To **Melipeuco** (stops at Hospedaje Icalma),

Narbus from rural bus terminal, Temuco, 2½ hrs, US$3. Transport can be arranged from Melipeuco into the park (ask in grocery stores and hospedajes, US$26 one way). To the western entrance: Daily **buses** from Temuco to Cherquenco, from where there is no public transport to the park. Private transport is the best way to see the area.

● Directory

Temuco *p684, map p686*
Airline offices LAN, Bulnes 699 on Plaza, T526 2000. **Sky**, T747300, or 600-600 2828 for information. **Banks** Many ATMs at banks on Plaza Aníbal Pinto. Also at the JAC bus terminal (Visa). Many cambios around the plaza, all deal in dollars and Argentine pesos. Good rates at **Germaniotour**, M Montt 942, after 1100. **Bicycle repairs** on Balmaceda, **Don Cheyo**, No 1266, another at No 1294, **Monsalves**, No 1448, opposite rural bus terminal. Several others on Portales eg **Oxford, Bianchi. Consulates** Netherlands, España 494, Honorary Consul, Germán Nicklas, is friendly and helpful. **Internet** Many on Prat and Mackenna, south of the Plaza, up to US$1 per hr. **Hospitals** Manuel Montt 115. **Motor mechanic** ServiTren, Edgardo Schneider Reinike and Peter Fischer (peocito@yahoo.de), Matta 0545 y Ruta 5, T/F212775, for cars and motorcycles, German spoken. **Post offices** Portales 839.

Lagos Villarrica, Calafquén and Panguipulli

Wooded Lago Villarrica, 21 km long and about 7 km wide, is one of the most beautiful in the region, with the active, snow-capped Villarrica volcano (2,840 m) to the southeast. Villarrica and Pucón, resorts at the lake's southwest and southeast corners, are among the more expensive in the region, but are definitely worth a visit. South of Lago Villarrica, a necklace of six lakes with snowy peaks behind, form picture-postcard views. Calafquén and Panguipulli are the most visited, but there are also hot springs, national parks and interesting routes to Argentina.

Villarrica → *Phone code: 045. Colour map 8, grid C1. Population: 27,000. Altitude: 227 m.*

The quiet town of Villarrica, pleasantly set at the extreme southwest corner of the lake, can be reached by a 63-km paved road southeast from Freire (24 km south of Temuco on the Pan-American Highway), or from Loncoche, 54 km south of Freire, also paved. Founded in 1552, the town was besieged by the Mapuche in the uprising of 1599: after three years the surviving Spanish settlers, 11 men and 13 women, surrendered. The town was refounded in 1882. The **Muestra Cultural Mapuche** ① *Pedro de Valdivia y Zegers, open all summer*, features a Mapuche ruca and stalls selling good handicraft. There is a livestock market every Monday about 1400; riding equipment for sale. In January and February Villarrica has a summer programme with many cultural and sporting events (including the Semana de Chilenidad) and on 18-19 September the Gran Fiesta Campestre de Villarrica is held in the indoor riding arena of the Parque Natural Dos Ríos, with typical foods, music, dancing, competitions and shows. **Dos Ríos** is 13 km west of Villarrica between the Ríos Voipir and Toltén, a private nature park with bed-and-breakfast accommodation (**A, B** without breakfast, recommended), cafetería, lots of sports, especially riding, fishing, boating, birdwatching: T09-9419 8064, www.dosrios.de. **Tourist office** ① *Valdivia 1070, T411162, open daily in summer, Mon-Fri off season; information and maps.*

Pucón → *Phone code: 045. Colour map 8, grid C1. Population: 13,000. Altitude: 227 m.*

Pucón, on the southeastern shore of Lago Villarrica, 26 km east of Villarrica, is the major tourist centre on the lake. The black sand beach is very popular for swimming and watersports. Between New Year to end-February it is very crowded and expensive; off season it is very pleasant. Apart from the lake, other attractions nearby include whitewater rafting, winter sports (see Skiing below) and several **canopy** (see Ziplining under Activities and tours) sites. **Tourist office** in the municipal building ① *O'Higgins 483, T293002, www.pucon.com*, sells fishing licences (US$1 per month). Do not confuse with the Chamber of Tourism at the entrance to Pucón from Villarrica.

There is a pleasant *paseo*, the **Costanera Otto Gudenschwager**, which starts at the lake end of Ansorena (beside Gran Hotel Pucón, Holzapfel 190, T441001) and goes along the shore. Launch excursions from the landing stage at La Poza at the end of O'Higgins, twice daily at 1500 and 1900, summer only, US$7 for two hours.

Walk 2 km north along the beach to the mouth of the Río Trancura (also called Río Pucón), with views of the volcanoes Villarrica, Quetrupillán and Lanín. To cross the Río Pucón: head east out of Pucón along the main road, then turn north on an unmade road leading to a new bridge; from here there are pleasant walks along the north shore of the lake to Quelhue and Trarilelfú, or northeast towards Caburga, or up into the hills through farms and agricultural land, with views of three volcanoes and, higher up, of the lake. The journey to Caburga (see below) is a perfect mountain bike day trip.

Parque Nacional Villarrica

The park has three sectors: **Volcán Villarrica** ① US$6, **Volcán Quetrupillán** and the **Puesco sector** which includes the slopes of the Volcán Lanín on the Argentine border. Each sector has its own entrance and ranger station. A campsite with drinking water and toilets is below the refuge, 4 km inside the park. The Villarrica volcano, 2,840 m, 8 km south of Pucón, can be climbed up and down in seven to eight hours, good boots, ice axe and crampons, sunglasses, plenty of water, chocolate and sun block essential. Beware of sulphur fumes at the top – occasionally agencies provide gas masks, otherwise take a cloth mask moistened with lemon juice – but on good days you can see into the crater with lava bubbling at 1,250°. On the descent you toboggan down the snow rather than walk, good fun.

Entry to Volcán Villarrica is permitted only to groups with a guide and to individuals who can show proof of membership of a mountaineering club in their own country. Several agencies take excursions, US$70, including park entry, guide, transport to park entrance and hire of equipment (no reduction for those with their own equipment); at the park entrance equipment is checked – good boots, crampons and ice-axe essential. Entry is refused if the weather is poor. Reputable travel agencies will not start out if the weather is bad: establish in advance what terms apply in the event of cancellation and be prepared to wait a few days. Many guides, all with equipment; ask for recommendations at the tourist office. For US$10 you can take the ski lift for the first part of the ascent; this is recommended as it saves 400 m climbing on scree.

Skiing ① *Lift pass US$23-33 full day, depending on the season, to restaurant only US$10; ski season is Jul-Sep, occasionally longer. Equipment rental US$20 per day, US$110 per week. Information on snow and ski-lifts (and, perhaps, transport) from tourist office or Gran Hotel Pucón.* The Pucón resort, T441901, owned by the Gran Hotel Pucón, is on the eastern slopes of the volcano, reached by a track, 35 minutes. The centre offers equipment rental, ski instruction, first aid, restaurant and bar as well as wonderful views from the terrace. The centre is good for beginners; more advanced skiers can try the steeper areas. (Skiing trips to the summit are very tough going and only for the fit.)

Lagos Caburga and Colico

Lago Caburga (spelt locally Caburgua), a very pretty lake in a wild setting 25 km northeast of Pucón, is unusual for its beautiful white sand beach (it also has a black sand beach – other beaches in the area are of black volcanic sand) and has supposedly the warmest water of all the lakes here. The west and much of the shores of the lake are inaccessible to vehicles. The north shore can be reached by a road from Cunco via the north shore of Lago Colico, a more remote lake north of Lago Villarrica. The village of Caburga, at the southern end is reached by a turning off the main road 8 km east of Pucón. The southern end of the lake and around Caburga is lined with campsites. There is a supermarket in Caburga. Rowing boats may be hired US$3 per hour. Just off the road from Pucón, Km 15, are the Ojos de Caburga, beautiful pools fed from underground, particularly attractive after rain (entry US$0.60; ask bus driver to let you off). Alternatively, take a mountain bike from Pucón via the Puente Quelhue.

Parque Nacional Huerquehue

① *The park is open officially only Jan-Mar, but you can get in at other times, US$8 (students and teachers half-price), the warden is very helpful; parking 1½ km along the track, US$1.*
East of Lago Caburga, the park includes steep hills and at least 20 lakes, some of them very small. Entrance and administration are near Lago Tinguilco, the largest lake, on the western edge of the park. The park entrance is 7 km (3 km uphill, 3 km down, one along Lago Tinquilco) from Paillaco, which is reached by an all-weather road which turns off 3 km before Caburga. From the entrance there is a well-signed track north to three beautiful lakes, Lagos Verde, Chico and Toro. The track zig-zags up (sign says 5 km, but worth it) to Lago Chico, then splits left to Verde, right to Toro. From Toro you can continue to Lago Huerquehue and Laguna los

Patos (camping). People in the park rent horses and boats. There is a restaurant at Tinquilco. Otherwise take your own food.

South of the Huerquehue Park on a turning from the Pucón-Caburga road there are **Termas de Quimey-Co**, about 29 km from Pucón, campsite, two cabins and hotel **Termas de Quimey-Co** ① *T045-441607, www.termasquimeyco.com, US$8*, new, less ostentatious or expensive than **Termas de Huife Hostería** ① *T441222, www.termashuife.cl, Pucón, Km 33, US$13* high season (US$10 low), including use of pool, modern, pleasant (hotel offers daily shuttle from/to Pucón, or taxi from Pucón, US$23 return with taxi waiting, US$16 one way). Beyond Huife are the hot springs of **Los Pozones**, Km 35, set in natural rock pools, US$6, US$8 at night (a good time to go), basic but popular with travellers. The road there is rough.

Cañi Forest Sanctuary, south of Parque Nacional Huerquehue and covering 500 ha, was the first private forest reserve established in Chile, owned by the non-proft Fundación Lahuén ① *US$5*. It contains 17 small lakes and is covered by ancient native forests of coihue, lenga and some of the oldest araucaria trees in the country. From its highest peak, **El Mirador**, five volcanoes can be seen. There is a self-guided trail, US$8 plus transport; for tours with English-speaking guide, contact **the Cañi Guides Program** ① *Outdoor Experience in Pucón (see Activities and tours), or see www.ecole.cl.*

Route to Argentina

From Pucón a road runs southeast via Curarrehue to the Argentine border. At Km 18 there is a turning south to the **Termas de Palguín** ① *T441968, www.termasdepalguin.cl, US$8*. There are many beautiful waterfalls within hiking distance: for example, Salto China (entry US$1, restaurant, camping); Salto del Puma and Salto del León, both 800 m from the Termas (entry US$2 for both). From Pucón take Bus Regional Villarrica from Palguín y O'Higgins at 1100 to the junction (10 km from Termas); last bus from junction to the Termas at 1500, so you may have to hitch back. Taxi from Pucón, US$20.

Near Palguín is the entrance to the Quetrupillán section of the Parque Nacional Villarrica (high clearance vehicle necessary, horses best), free camping, wonderful views over Villarrica Volcano and six other peaks. Ask rangers for the route to the other entrance.

The road from Pucón to Argentina passes turnings north at Km 23 to **Termas de San Luis** and Km 35 to **Termas de Pangui** (15 km from main road, US$10), both with hotels, the latter with teepees (To45-411388 and 045-442039 respectively). It continues to Curarrehue, from where it turns south to Puesco and climbs via **Lago Quellelhue**, a tiny gem set between mountains at 1,196 m to reach the border at the **Mamuil Malal** or **Tromén Pass**. To the south of the pass rises the graceful cone of Lanín volcano. On the Argentine side the road runs south to Junín de los Andes, San Martín de los Andes and Bariloche.

Chilean immigration and customs at Puesco, open 0800-1900 (to 2100 Dec-Mar), US$2 per vehicle at other times. There are free CONAF campsites with no facilities at Puesco and 5 km from the border near Lago Tromén. Daily bus from Pucón, 1800, two hours, US$2. It's a hard road for cyclists, but not impossible.

Lago Calafquén → *Colour map 8, grid C1. Population: 1,700. Altitude: 207 m.*

Dotted with small islands, Lago Calafquén is a popular tourist destination. **Lican-Ray** 25 km south of Villarrica on a peninsula on the north shore, is the major resort on the lake. There are two fine beaches each side of the rocky peninsula. Boats can be hired (US$2 per hour) and there are catamaran trips (US$5 per hour; trips to islands US$18). Although very crowded in season, most facilities close by the end of March and, out of season, Lican-Ray feels like a ghost town. 6 km to the east is the river of lava formed when the Villarrica volcano erupted in 1971. The **tourist office**, on the plaza, is open daily in summer, Monday-Friday off season.

Coñaripe (*Population 1,253*), 21 km southeast of Lican-Ray at the eastern end of Lago Calafquén, is another popular tourist spot. Its setting, with a 3-km black sand beach surrounded by mountains, is very beautiful. From here a road (mostly ripio) around the lake's southern shore leads to Lago Panguipulli (see below) and offers superb views over Villarrica volcano, which can be climbed from here. Most services are on the Calle Principal. **Tourist office**, on the plaza, open 15 November-15 April daily, otherwise weekdays only.

Termas Vergara are 14 km northeast of Coñaripe by a steep ripio road which continues to Palguín. There are nice pools, a campsite and minimarket. **Termas Geometricas** ① *3 km beyond Termas Vergara, T214214, www.termasgeometricas.cl, US$18*. There are 17 good new pools, geometrically-shaped and linked by wooden walkways. There is a small café.

From Coñaripe a road runs southeast over the steep **Cuesta Los Añiques** offering views of tiny Lago Pellaifa. The **Termas de Coñaripe** are at Km 16 ① *T411407, www.termas conaripe.cl*. Further south at Km 32 are the **Termas de Liquiñe** ① *T317377, 8 different thermal centres, from US$6 to US$10 pp*. Opposite Liquiñe are the new Termas Río de Liquiñe, good heated cabañas, good food, personal spa bath, large outdoor thermal pool. From there you can walk up to the thermal source, US$0.40 to cross river by boat, one hour excursion. There is a road north to Pucón through Villarrica National Park, high-clearance and 4WD vehicle essential.

The border with Argentina, **Paso Carirriñe**, is reached by unpaved road from Termas de Liquiñe. It is open 15 October-31 August. On the Argentine side the road continues to San Martín de los Andes.

Lago Panguipulli and around
→ *Phone code: 063. Colour map 8, grid C1. Population: 8,000. Altitude: 136 m.*

The lake is reached by paved road from Lanco on the Pan-American Highway or unpaved roads from Lago Calafquén. A road leads along the beautiful north shore, wooded with sandy beaches and cliffs. Most of the south shore is inaccessible by road. **Panguipulli**, at the northwest corner of the lake in a beautiful setting, is the largest town in the area. The streets are planted with roses: it is claimed that there are over 14,000. The Iglesia San Sebastián is in Swiss style, with twin towers; its belltower contains three bells from Germany. Fishing excursions on the lake are recommended. Boat hire US$3. There are also good rafting opportunities on rivers in the area. In the last week of January is Semana de Rosas, with dancing and sports competitions. **Tourist office**, by the plaza, T310435, www.panguipulli.cl, open daily December-February, otherwise weekdays only.

Choshuenco (*Population 622*) lies 45 km east of Panguipulli at the eastern tip of the lake. To the south is the Reserva Nacional Mocho Choshuenco (7,536 ha) which includes two volcanoes: Choshuenco (2,415 m) and Mocho (2,422 m). On the slopes of Choshuenco the Club Andino de Valdivia has ski-slopes and three refugios. This can be reached by a turning from the road which goes south from Choshuenco to Enco at the east end of Lago Riñihue (the lake southwest of Lago Panguipulli). East of Choshuenco a road leads to Lago Pirehueico, via the impressive waterfalls of Huilo Huilo, where the river channels its way through volcanic rock before thundering down into a natural basin. The falls are three hours' walk from Choshuenco, or take the Puerto Fuy bus and get off at Alojamiento Huilo Huilo (see Sleeping, below), from where it is a five-minute walk to the falls.

East of Choshuenco is **Lago Pirehueico**, a long, narrow and deep lake, surrounded by virgin lingüe forest. It is totally unspoilt except for some logging activity. There are no roads along the shores of the lake, but two ports. **Puerto Fuy** (*Population: 300*) is at the north end 21 km from Choshuenco, 7 km from Neltume. **Puerto Pirehueico** is at the south end. A ferry runs between the two ports, then a road to the Argentine border crossing at Paso Huahum.

The border with Argentina, **Paso Huahum** (659 m), is a four-hour walk from Puerto Pirehueico (very hard for cyclists with steep climbs, no public transport to border). On the Argentine side the road, with buses, leads alongside Lago Lacar to San Martín de los Andes and Junín de los Andes. Chilean immigration is open summer 0800-2100, winter 0800-2000.

● Sleeping

Villarrica *p691*

Lodging in private homes in our **C-D** range can be found on blocks Muñoz 300 and 400, Koerner 300 and O'Higgins 700 and 800. More upmarket accommodation is on the lakefront.
L Villarrica Park Lake, Km 13 on the road to Pucón, T450000, www.villarricaparklakehotel.cl. 5-star, all rooms with balconies overlooking the lake, spa with pools, sauna, solarium, fishing trips.
A El Ciervo, Koerner 241, T411215, www.hotelelciervo.cl. German spoken, beautiful location, pool, German-style breakfast. Recommended.

A Araucarias, Caupolicán 243, T441286. Comfortable, indoor pool and spa, wifi area.
A-B Hotel y Cabañas El Parque, 3 km east on Pucón road, T411120, reservas@ hotelelparque.cl. Lakeside with beach, tennis courts, with breakfast, good restaurant set meals. Highly recommended.
A-B Hostería de la Colina, Las Colinas 115, overlooking town, T411503, www.hosteria delacolina.com. With breakfast, variety of rooms and cabins, large gardens, good service, internet, good restaurant, English spoken. Recommended.

B **Bungalowlandia**, Prat 749, T/F411635, www.bungalowlandia.cl. Cabañas for 2, dining room, good facilities, pool.

B **Hostería Bilbao**, Henríquez 43, T411186, bilbao@7lagos.com. Small rooms, pretty patio, good restaurant.

C **Hotel Yachting Kiel**, Koerner 153, T411631, www.chile-hotels.com/kielhost.htm. Cheaper off season, lakeside, good.

C **Kolping**, Riquelme 399, T/F411388. Good breakfast. Recommended.

C-D **La Torre Suiza**, Bilbao 969, T/F411213, www.torresuiza.com. Some rooms with bath (D), **F** pp in dorms, kitchen facilities, camping, cycle rental, book exchange, lots of info, good breakfast included, reserve in advance. "Very Swiss". Recommended.

D **Hostería Rayhuen**, Pedro Montt 668, T411571, guido-castillo@entelchile.net. Lovely garden. Recommended.

D-E **Chilepeppers**, Vicente Reyes 546, T414694, www.chilepeppers.cl. **F** pp in dorms, basic, cramped dorms, kitchen, internet, barbeque area, a fun place.

D-E **Hospedaje Nicolás**, Anfion Muñoz 477, T410232. **F** pp singles. Simple rooms with bathand cable TV. Breakfast included. Good value though walls are thin.

E **Vicente Reyes 854**, T414457. Good breakfast, good bathrooms but only one for 4-5 rooms, use of kitchen, camping in garden. Also E **Vicente Reyes 773**. Family of Elena Martínez, pleasant, cheaper without bath. Recommended.

F **Hosp y Restaurante Rayen**, Julio Zegers 950, T412056. Cosy, with TV, breakfast, good food including typical and vegetarian dishes.

F pp **Maravillas del Sur**, Bilbao 821, T411444. With bath and breakfast, good value, parking.

G pp **Res San Francisco**, Julio Zegers 646. Youth hostel, shared rooms.

Camping Many sites east of town on Pucón road, open in season only: nearest is E **Los Castaños**, T412330, up to 6 people.

Pucón *p691*

In summer (Dec-Feb) rooms may be hard to find. Plenty of alternatives (usually cheaper) in Villarrica. Prices below are Jan-Feb. Off-season rates are 20-40% lower and it is often possible to negotiate. Many families offer rooms, look for the signs or ask in bars/restaurants. Touts offer rooms to new arrivals; check that they are not way out of town.

L **Antumalal**, 2 km west, T441011, www.antumalal.com. Luxury class, very small, picturesque chalet-type, magnificent views of the lake (breakfast and lunch on terrace), gardens, with meals, open year round, pool, hot tob, sauna and private beaches.

AL Interlaken, Colombia y Caupolicán, T441276, www.hotelinterlaken.cl. Chalets, open Nov-Apr, water skiing, pool, TCs changed, no restaurant. Recommended.

A-B Gudenschwager, Pedro de Valdivia 12, T442326, hotelgudenschwager@yahoo.com. Classic Bavarian type, views over lake, volcano and mountains, attentive staff, comfortable, good restaurant (open in summer only), big-screen TV and Wi-Fi internet area. Good rates off season.

B La Posada Plaza-Pucón, Valdivia 191, T441088, laposada@unete.com. Pleasant rooms, cheaper without bath, full board available, also spacious cabins (**C**) low season), small breakfast, gardens and pool.

B-C Hostería ¡école!, Urrutia 592, T441675, www.ecole.cl. **F** pp dorms without breakfast, some rooms with bath, good vegetarian and fish restaurant, shop, forest treks (departure for Lahuen Foundation's Cani Forest Sanctuary), rafting and biking, information, language classes, massage. Recommended.

C Cabañas Ruca Malal, O'Higgins 770, T442297, www.rucamalal.cl. Lovely cabins in a pretty garden, spacious, well-equipped and decorated, various sizes, pool.

C Hostal Gerónimo, Alderete 665, T/F443762, www.geronimo.cl. Recently refurbished, rooms with cable TV, quiet, smart, bar, restaurant, open all year. Recommended.

C Kernayel, 1 km east at Camino Internacional 1395, T442164, www.kernayel.cl. Cabins and comfortable rooms, heating, hot water, good breakfast, pool.

C La Tetera, Urrutia 580, T/F441462, www.tetera.cl. 6 rooms, some with bath, with good breakfast, fresh coffee, German and English spoken, book swap, information centre, good Spanish classes, agency for Navimag ferries, book in advance. Recommended.

D Casa de Campo Kila-Leufu, about 20 km east on road to Curarrehue, T09-9711 8064, www.kilaleufu.cl. **E** pp in small dorms. Rooms on the Martínez family farm, contact Margot or Peter in advance, English spoken, price includes breakfast, home-grown food served, horse riding, boat tours, treks, camping facilities. Recommended.

D Hosp Víctor, Palguín 705, T443525, www.pucon.com/victor. **F** pp without bath, comfortable, kitchen use, TV, laundry, internet, information, a good choice.

D Res Lincoyán, Av Lincoyán 323, T441144, www.lincoyan.cl. Cheaper without bath, comfortable.

D-E Donde Germán, Brasil 640, T442444, www.dondegerman.cl. **F** pp in dorms. Fun, organizes tours, internet, book in advance.

D-E Hostal Backpackers, Palguín 695, T441373, www.backpackerspucon.tk. With or without bath, quiet, next to JAC buses, kitchen, internet, 10% discount on Politur activities, Navimag reservations, tourist information.

Camping There are many camping and cabin establishments. Those close to Pucón include: **G** pp **La Poza**, Costanera Geis 769, T441435, hot showers, good kitchen. Recommended. West along Lago Villarrica: **B-C Huimpalay-Tray**, Km 12, T450079 (Santiago 231 4248). Gorgeous location on lake, well-equipped. Recommended all round. **Saint John**, Km 7, T441165/92, Casilla 154, open Dec-Mar, also hostería. Several sites en route to volcano, including: **D** per site **L'Etoile**, Km 2, T442188, in attractive forest. **Mahuida**, Km 6. Cheaper sites en route to Caburga.

Private houses

F pp **Hosp Graciela**, Pasaje Rolando Matus 521 (off Av Brasil). Comfortable, good food.

F pp **Hosp Irma Torres**, Lincoyán 545. Cooking facilities.

F pp **Hosp Lucía**, Lincoyán 565, T441721, luciahostal@hotmail.com. Safe, quiet, cooking facilities.

F pp **Hosp Sonia**, Lincoyán 485, T441269, www.pucon.com/sonia. Use of kitchen, meals.
F pp **Tr@vel Pucón**, Blanco Encalada 190, T444093. Garden, tours, kitchen, Spanish classes, near Tur-Bus terminal.
F-G pp **Adriana Molina**, Lincoyán 312. With breakfast, helpful.
F-G pp **Familia Acuña**, Palguín 223 (ask at *peluquería* next door). Without breakfast, kitchen and laundry facilities.
G pp **Roberto y Alicia Abreque**, Perú 170. Basic, noisy, popular, kitchen and laundry facilities, information on excursions.

Lago Caburga *p692*
C **Landhaus San Sebastián**, east of Lago Caburga, F045-1972360, www.landhaus-chile.com. With bath and breakfast, good meals, laundry facilities, English and German spoken, Spanish classes, good base for nearby walks.
D **Hostería Los Robles**, near the lake shore, T236989. Views, restaurant, campsite, closed out of season.

Parque Nacional Huerquehue *p692*
C-E **Refugio Tinquilco**, 3½ km from park entrance, where forest trail leads to lakes Verde and Toro, T02-777 7673, T09-9822 7153 (mob), patriciolanfranco@entelchile.net. Most expensive rooms with bath, cheapest for bed and no sheets, meals extra, heating, hot water, 24-hr electricity, sauna, cooking facilities. Recommended.
D **Hospedaje Carlos Alfredo Richard**, southwest shore of the lake, 2 km from park entrance, parque_huerquehue@hotmail.com. Large rooms with bath, hot water, breakfast included, restaurant, rowing boats for hire (also at Arauco 171 in Pucón, shared rooms, use of kitchen, internet access).
D **Braatz** and **Soldans**, 2 German speaking families, offer accommodation, no electricity, food and camping (US$6); they also rent rowing boats on the lake. F pp Nidia Carrasco Godoy runs a hospedaje in the park, T09-9443 2725 (mob). With breakfast, hot water, camping.
Camping only at the park entrance, 2 sites, US$8. 1½ km before the park entrance.

Route to Argentina: Termas de Palguín *p693*
C **Rancho de Caballos** (Casilla 142, Pucón), T441575. Restaurant with vegetarian dishes, laundry and kitchen facilities; also, cabañas and camping, horse riding, self-guided trails, English and German spoken.

Lago Calafquén *P693*
Lican-Ray
D **Hostería Inaltulafquen**, on Playa Grande, Casilla 681, T431115, F410028. With breakfast, English spoken, comfortable.
D **Hosp Los Nietos**, Manquel 125, Playa Chica, T431078. Without breakfast.
E **Res Temuco**, G Mistral 515, Playa Chica, T431130. Without bath, with breakfast, good.
Camping Floresta, T211954, C for 6 people, 500 m east of town. 6 sites to west and many along north shore towards Coñaripe.

Coñaripe
D **Hospedaje Chumay**, on Plaza, T317287, turismochumay@hotmail.com. G singles. With restaurant, internet, tours, some English spoken, good.
Camping Sites on beach charge US$20, but if you walk ½-¾ km from town you can camp on the beach free. Cold municipal showers on beach, US$0.35. **Isla Llanchahue**, 5 km east, T317360. Campsite with *cabañas* on an island in Río Llanchahue.

Termas de Coñaripe
AL-A pp **Termas de Coñaripe**, T411407. Excellent hotel with four pools, good restaurant, cycles and horses for hire. Full board available.

Termas de Liquiñe
A pp **Termas de Liquiñe**, T063-317377. Full board, cabins, restaurant, hot pool, small native forest. E for accommodation in private houses.
F-G pp **Hosp La Casona**, Camino Internacional, T045-412085. Hot shower, good food, comfortable; tours from Lican-Ray in summer, US$20, 0830-1830 with lunch.

Panguipulli *p694*
B **Hostería Quetropillán**, Etchegaray 381, T311348. Comfortable.
D **Central**, Valdivia 115, T311331. Good breakfast, G singles. Recommended.
D Etchegaray 464. G singles, good breakfast. Reduced rates for longer stays.
D Hosp Familiar, Los Ultimos 62, T311483. G singles, English and German spoken, kitchen facilities, helpful, good breakfast.
F-G pp **Hostal Orillas del Lago**, M de Rosas 265, T311710 (or 312499 if no reply, friends have key). From plaza walk towards lake, last house on left, 8 blocks from terminal. Good views, kitchen, backpacker place.

● *For an explanation of the sleeping and eating price codes used in this guide, see page 58.*
● *Other relevant information is found in Essentials pages 602-604.*

Camping El Bosque, P Sigifredo 241, T311489, US$7.50 per site. Small, good, but not suitable for vehicle camping, hot water. Also 3 sites at Chauquén, 6 km southeast on lakeside.

Choshuenco
E Hostería Rayen Trai, María Alvarado y O'Higgins. Former yacht club with accommodation and good food, open all year.
E Restaurant Puerto Fuy, Puerto Fuy. Hot water, good food.
F pp Alojamiento Huilo Huilo, Km 9 east from Choshuenco (1 km before Neltume). Basic but comfortable and well situated for walks, good food.
F Hostal Kaykaen, Puerto Fuy. Meals, use of kitchen, bike rental. One of several private houses offering accommodation.
F-G pp Hostería Rucapillán, San Martín 85, T318220, rucapí@telsur.cl. Restaurant which lets out rooms, English spoken, tours.

Lago Pirehueico
G pp Restaurant San Giovani, Puerto Fuy. Family atmosphere, good rooms, breakfast and other meals. There is also accommodation in private houses.
Camping On the beach (take own food).

---

❶ Eating

Villarrica *p691*
¶¶¶ El Tabor, S Epulef 1187, T411901. Excellent but pricey.
¶¶¶ La Cava del Roble, Valentín Letelier 658, p 2, T416446. Excellent grill, specialises in exotic meat and game, extensive wine list. Recommended.
¶¶ Rapa Nui, V Reyes 678. Good, at cheaper end of the range, closed Sun.
¶¶ El Rey de Mariscos, Letelier 1030. Good seafood.
¶¶ The Travellers, Letelier 753. Varied menu including vegetarian, Asian food, good bar, English spoken.
¶ Alternativa, V Reyes 739. Good almuerzo.
¶ Café 2001, Henríquez 379. Coffee and ice cream, good.
¶ Casa Vieja, Letelier y Muñoz. Good value set lunch, family run.
¶ Pastelería Sweet, Prat 709. Excellent homemade cakes and pies, smoothies, nice deck overlooking lake.

Pucón *p691*
See Sleeping for other recommendations.
¶¶¶ La Maga, Fresia 125, T444277. Uruguayan grill, possibly the best steak you'll find in Chile, though pricey

¶¶¶ Puerto Pucón, Fresia 251. Spanish, long-established, stylish.
¶¶¶ ¶¶ Senzo, Fresia 284, T449005. Fresh pasta and risotto prepared by a Swiss chef.
¶¶ La Buonatesta, Fresia 243. Good pizzería, the first in Pucón, a little pricey.
¶¶ El Palet, Fresia 295. Genuine local food, good value. Recommended.
¶¶ El Refugio, Lincoyán 348. Some vegetarian dishes, expensive wine.
¶¶ Nafis Pucón, Fresia 477. Middle eastern cuisine, good value, helpful.
¶ Rap Hamburguesa, O'Higgins 625. Freshly made hamburgers, chips and Chilean fast food. Open late.

Cafés and bars
Several bars on O'Higgins.
Fresia Strasse, Fresia 161. Good coffee and cake.
Holzapfel Backerei, Holzapfel 524. German café. Recommended.
Patagonia Express, Fresia 223. Chocolates, icecreams, pancakes and snacks as well as coffee.

Lago Calafquén: Lican-Ray *p693*
¶¶-¶ Café Ñaños, Urrutia 105. Very good, reasonable prices, helpful owner.
¶¶-¶ Restaurant-Bar Guido's, Urrutia 405. Good value.

Panguipulli *p694*
¶¶-¶ Café Central, M de Rosas 750. Fixed menu, good and cheap at lunchtimes, expensive in evenings.
¶¶-¶ El Chapulín, M de Rosas 639. Good food and value. Several cheap restaurants in O'Higgins 700 block.

❍ Shopping

Pucón *p691*
Camping equipment Eltit supermarket, O'Higgins y Fresia. **Outdoors & Travel**, Lincoyán 361, clothing, equipment, maps.
Handicrafts market Just south of O'Higgins on Ansorena; local specialities are painted wooden flowers.

▲ Activities and tours

Villarrica *p691*
Fundo Huifquenco, just south of town (500 m) along Av Matta, T415040, www.fundohuif quenco.cl. A large working farm, trails, horseriding, carriage tours, bicycle hire, meals (book in advance). Prices from US$10.
Vuelatour, Camilo Henríquez 430, loc 1, T415766. General tour agency, trips to thermal springs etc, Navimag, LAN agent, airport transfer, car hire.

Pucón p691

Pucón and Villarrica are celebrated as centres for fishing on Lake Villarrica and in the beautiful Lincura, Trancura and Toltén rivers. In high season, sports shops open, especially for biking and watersports.

Fishing Local tourist office will supply details on licences and open seasons etc. Two fishing specialists are **Mario's Fishing Zone**, O'Higgins 580, T444259, www.pucon.com/fishing (expensive but good), and **Off Limits**, O'Higgins 560, T442681, www.offlimits.cl (English and Italian spoken).

Horse riding Rancho de Caballos (German run, see Termas de Palguín, above). Average hire costs about US$40 half day, US$70 full day. **Centro de Turismo Ecuestre Huepil Malal**, T09-9643 2673, www.huepil-malal.cl. Rodolfo Coombs and Carolina Pumpin, PO Box 16, Pucón, 40 mins from town. Highly recommended.

Hydrospeeding Several agencies including **Politur** and **Aventur**, US$30 for an afternoon.

Mountain biking Bike hire from US$2.50 per hr to US$20 per day from several travel agencies on O'Higgins.

Thermal springs There are dozens of thermal springs in the area, ranging from the upmarket to the natural. Transport is provided by tour operators.

Watersports Water-skiing, sailing, windsurfing at Playa Grande beach by Gran Hotel and La Poza beach end of O'Higgins (more expensive than Playa Grande, not recommended). Playa Grande: waterskiing US$15 for 15 mins, Laser sailing US$16 per hr, sailboards US$13 per hr, rowing boats US$6 per hr.

Whitewater rafting Very popular on the Río Trancura. Many agencies offer trips (see below), Trancura Bajo (grade 3) US$25; Trancura Alto (grades 3 and 4), US$35.

Ziplining Called **Canopy** (sliding from platform to platform along a metal cord). 6 agencies can arrange this, US$15-20 including transport. The best (and most safety conscious) are **Bosque Aventura**, O'Higgins 615, T09-9325 4795, www.canopypucon.cl.

Tour operators

Tour operators arrange trips to thermal baths, trekking to volcanoes, whitewater rafting, etc. For falls, lakes and termas it's cheaper, if in a group, to flag down a taxi and bargain. Many agencies, so shop around: prices vary at times, quality of guides and equipment variable. In high season, when lots of groups go together, individual attention may be lacking. Prices for climbing Villarrica are given below. Tours to Termas de Huife or Coñaripe, US$30 including entry.

Aguaventura, Palguín 336, T444246, www.aguaventura.com. French-run, in summer kayaking and rafting specialities, in winter "snowshop" for ski and snowboard rental, volcano climbing, trekking.

Outdoor Experience, Urrutia, next to Hostal école, T442809, www.outdoorexperience.org. Offers good tours of the area.

Politur, O'Higgins 635, T/F441373, www.politur.com. Well-established and responsible, good for volcano trek and rafting; a little pricier than others, but good.

Roncotrack, O'Higgins y Arauco, T449597, roncotrack@hotmail.com. Quadbike excursions and "ethnotourism"; also hires out good quality bicycles.

Southern Sky, Palguín 260, T443836, www.southern-sky-chile.cl. For treks on the volcanoes, Austrian/Chilean run, safety-conscious, good coffee.

Trancura, several offices on O'Higgins, T441189, www.trancura.com. The biggest and cheapest of the agencies. Recommended for trips to thermal springs (they have their own **termas**), but questionable safety standards for rafting and climbing.

Travel Aid, Ansorena 425, loc 4, T444040, www.travelaid.cl. Helpful general travel agency, sells terkking maps, guidebooks, lots of information, agents for **Navimag** and other boat trips, English and German spoken.

Several other reputable agencies including **Kayak Pucón**, **Aventur**, **Turismo Lafquén**, **Sur Expediciones**, **Sol y Nieve**.

Lago Calafquén: Coñaripe p693

Hiking to Villarrica Volcano (US$40-50) is organized by many guides, including Leo Barrios at Hospedaje Chumay, who also runs trips to various thermal springs, as does the tourist office in summer.

⊙ Transport

Villarrica p691

Bus Terminal at Pedro de Valdivia y Muñoz. JAC at Bilbao 610, T411447, and opposite for Pucón and Lican-Ray. Terminal Rural for other local services at Matta y Vicente Reyes. To **Santiago**, 10 hrs, US$20, several companies. To **Pucón**, with Vipu-Ray (main terminal) and JAC, in summer every 15 mins, 40 mins' journey, US$1; same companies to **Lican-Ray**, US$1.50. To **Valdivia**, JAC, US$5, 3 a day, 2½ hrs. To **Coñaripe** (US$2) and **Liquiñe** at 1600 Mon-Sat, 1000 Sun. To **Temuco**, JAC, US$4. To **Loncoche** (Ruta 5 junction for hitching), US$2. To **Panguipulli**, go via Lican-Ray, occasional direct buses. Buses to Argentina: buses from Temuco to **Junín de los**

Andes pass through Villarrica, fares are the same as from Temuco, T412733, book in advance. Note that if the Tromén pass is blocked by snow buses go via Panguipulli instead of Villarrica and Pucón.

Pucón p691
Air Airport 2 km on Caburga road. Lan Express and Sky fly to **Santiago** via Temuco in summer, 2-3 times a week each.
Bus No municipal terminal: each company has its own terminal: JAC, Uruguay y Palguín; Tur-Bus, O'Higgins, 910, east of town; Igi Llaima and Cóndor, Colo Colo y O'Higgins. JAC to **Villarrica** (very frequent, US$1), **Temuco** (frequent, US$4, 2 hrs, rápido US$5, 1¾ hr) and **Valdivia** (US$6, 3 hrs). Tur-Bus direct to **Valdivia**, **Osorno** and **Puerto Montt**, 6 hrs, US$9, daily. To **Santiago**, 10 hrs, US$12, many companies, early morning and late evening; salón cama service by Tur-Bus and JAC, US$33. Colectivos to **Villarrica** from O'Higgins y Palguín. Buses to Argentina: Buses from Temuco to **Junín** pass through Pucón, fares are the same as from Temuco.
Car hire Prices start at US$27 per day. Christopher Car, O'Higgins 335, T/F449013. Pucón Rent A Car, Camino Internacional 1395, T441922, kernayel@cepri.cl. **Sierra Nevada**, Palguín y O'Higgins, cars and 4WD reasonable.
Taxi Co-operative, T441009.

Lago Caburga p692
Taxi day trips from Pucón, US$30 return. JAC bus departs regularly for Caburga (US$1.50 single), and there are colectivos from Ansorena y Uruguay or you can try hitching. If walking or cycling, turn left 3 km east of Pucón (sign to Puente Quelhue) and follow the track (very rough) for 18 km through beautiful scenery. Recommended.

Parque Nacional Huerquehue p692
Bus Direct to park, take JAC from Pucón, 3 a day in summer, US$3, 1½ hrs. JAC from Pucón to Paillaco, 1½ hrs, US$3, Mon-Fri 0700, 1230, 1700, Sat-Sun 0700, 1600, returns immediately – last at 1800.

Lago Calafquén and around p693
Lican-Ray
Bus Leave from offices around plaza. To **Villarrica**, 1 hr, US$1.50, JAC frequent in summer. In summer, there are direct buses from **Santiago** (Tur-Bus US$14, 10 hrs, salón cama US$40) and **Temuco** (2½ hrs, US$6). To **Panguipulli**, Mon-Sat 0730.

Coñaripe
Bus To **Panguipulli**, 7 a day (4 off season), US$2 and 16 daily to **Villarrica**, US$2.

Nightly bus direct to **Santiago**, Tur-Bus and JAC, 11½ hrs, US$15, salón cama in summer, US$40.

Panguipulli p694
Bus Terminal at Gabriela Mistral y Portales. To **Santiago** daily, US$20. To **Valdivia**, frequent (Sun only 4), several companies, 2 hrs, US$5. To **Temuco** frequent, Power and Pangui Sur, US$5, 3 hrs. To **Puerto Montt**, US$8. To **Choshuenco**, Neltume and Puerto Fuy, 3 daily, 3 hrs, US$5. To **Coñaripe** (with connections for Lican-Ray and Villarrica), 7 daily, 4 off season, 1½ hrs, US$2.

Lago Pirehueico
Bus Daily Puerto Fuy to **Panguipulli**, 2 daily, 2 hrs, US$5.
Ferry The Hua Hum sails from Puerto Fuy to Puerto Pirehueico, 2-3 hrs, foot passengers US$2, cars US$20, bikes US$5. A beautiful crossing, comparable to the lakes crossing from Puerto Montt to Bariloche, but at a fraction the price (to take vehicles reserve in advance at the Hotel Quetropillán in Panguipulli, or ses www.panguipulli.cl/pasohuahum/index.html). Schedule: twice daily each way. In summer there is a daily bus service to **Argentina**.

⊙ Directory

Villarrica p691
Banks ATMs at banks on Pedro de Valdivia between Montt and Alderete. Carlos Huerta, A Muñoz 417, **Central de Repuestos**, A Muñoz 415 (good rates), **Turcamb**, Henríquez 576, and **Cristopher Exchange**, Valdivia 1061, all change TCs and cash. **Bicycle shops** Mora Bicicletas, G Korner 760, helpful. **Internet** At the Central de Llamadas, Henríquez 567, 2nd floor. Cybercafé Salmon, Letelier y Henríquez. **Post offices** A Muñoz 315. Open 0900-1300, 1430-1800 (Mon-Fri), 0900-1300 (Sat). **Telephones** Entel, Henríquez 440 and 575. Telefónica, Henríquez 544.

Pucón p691
Airline offices LanChile, Urrutia y Costanera, daily 1000-1400, 1800-2200.
Banks ATMs in Banco Santander, O'Higgins y Fresia, Eltit, supermarket, O'Higgins, Banco BCI, Fresia y Alderete, and in casino. Several casas de cambio on O'Higgins. Eltit, also changes TCs, but rates for TCs in Pucón are poor, better to change in Temuco. **Internet** Several sites on O'Higgins, US$2 per hr. **Post offices** Fresia 183. **Telephones** Telefónica, Gral Urrutia 472. Entel, Ansorena 299.

Valdivia and Osorno

Valdivia is a very pleasant city at the confluence of the Ríos Calle Calle and Cruces, which form the Río Valdivia. It is set in rich agricultural land receiving some 2,300 mm of rain a year. To the north of the city is a large island, Isla Teja, where the Universidad Austral de Chile is situated. The student population adds zest to the nightlife. At the mouth of the Rio Valdivia are a group of historic forts which make a good day's outing from the city. Osorno, further south, is not such a tourist city, but it is a base for visiting the attractive southern lakes.

Valdivia → *Phone code: 063. Colour map 8, grid C1. Population: 127,000. 839 km south of Santiago.*

Valdivia was one of the most important centres of Spanish colonial control over Chile. Founded in 1552 by Pedro de Valdivia, it was abandoned as a result of the Mapuche insurrection of 1599 and the area was briefly occupied by Dutch pirates. In 1645 it was refounded as a walled city, the only Spanish mainland settlement south of the Río Biobío. The coastal fortifications at the mouth of the river also date from the 17th century. They were greatly strengthened after 1760 owing to fears that Valdivia might be seized by the British, but were of little avail during the Wars of Independence: overnight on 2 February 1820 the Chilean naval squadron under Lord Cochrane seized San Carlos, Amargos and Corral and turned their guns on Niebla and Mancera, which surrendered the following morning. From independence until the 1880s Valdivia was an outpost of Chilean rule, reached only by sea or by a coastal route through Mapuche territory. From 1849 to 1875 Valdivia was a centre for German colonization of the Lake District. **Tourist offices** ① *Av Prat 555, by the dock, T342300, infovaldivia@sernatur.cl.* Good map of region and local rivers, list of hotel prices and examples of local crafts with artisans' addresses. Open daily in summer, weekdays only off season. **CONAF**, Ismael Váldez 431, T218822. **Automóvil Club de Chile**, García Reyes 49075, T250376, also for car hire.

Sights The city centre is the tree-lined, shady **Plaza de la República**. A pleasant walk is along **Avenida Prat** (or **Costanera**), which follows the bend in the river, from the bus station to the bridge to **Isla Teja**, the **Muelle Fluvial** (boat dock) and the riverside market. Boats can be hired

Valdivia

Sleeping		
Aires Buenos **5**	Hostal Centro Torreón **6**	**Eating**
A Muñoz 345 **2**	Hostal Prat **10**	Café Haussmann **1**
Camilo Henríquez 749,	Melillanca **7**	Cervecería Kunstmann **8**
Casa 6 **11**	Palace **8**	Entrelagos **3**
Hospedaje Internacional **3**	Puerta del Sur **9**	La Calesa **7**
Hostal Andwandter **1**	Residencial Germania **13**	Ritual **4**
Hostal Casagrande **4**		Sake **2**
		Volcán **5**

N

0 metres 100
0 yards 100

at the bend for US$3.50 per hour. Sealions lounge around the dock. On Isla Teja, near the library in the University, are a **botanic garden** and **arboretum** with trees from all over the world. West of the botanical gardens is the 30-ha **Parque Saval**, with areas of native forest, as well as the Lago de los Lotos (beautiful blooms in spring) ① *all open during daylight hours, US$0.50*. On boat trips round the island you can see lots of waterfowl. Also on Isla Teja is the **Museo Histórico y Antropológico** ① *daily, 1000-1300, 1400-1800, off season closed Mon, US$2*. Run by the University, it contains exhibits on archaeology, ethnography and the history of German settlement, beautifully housed in the former mansion of Carlos Andwanter, a prominent German immigrant. Next door is the **Museo de Arte Moderno** ① *open Jan-Feb, Tue-Fri 1000-1300, 1400-1800, Sat-Sun 1000-1300, 1500-1900, US$2*. Off season it is only open for occasional temporary exhibitions.

The surrounding district has lovely countryside of woods, beaches, lakes and rivers. The various rivers are navigable and there are pleasant journeys by rented motor boat on the **Ríos Futa** and **Tornagaleanes** around the **Isla del Rey**. Boat tours go to the **Santuario de la Naturaleza Carlos Andwandter**① *Boat Isla del Río, daily 1415, 6 hrs, US$22 pp*. The Refuge is an area on the Río Cruces which flooded as result of the 1960 earthquake; lots of bird species are visible. In summer there is a regular steam train service to **Antilhue** (20 km) ① *Ecuador 2000, T214978, every Sun Jan-Feb, other weekends and holidays throughout the year, phone to check. US$5 return, 1½-hr trip, return 2 hrs later*, where the train is met by locals selling all sorts of local culinary specialities. This is the only steam train in Chile (the engine dates from 1913), good; book in advance and ask about additional trips on public holidays.

Parque Oncol ① *27km northwest of Valdivia, park entry US$2, T96441439, www.parqueoncol.cl, buses Sat-Sun 1005, return 1700*, 754 ha of Valdivian native forest, with several trails and lookouts, zipline (*canopy*) site, picnic area and campsite.

Coastal resorts near Valdivia

At the mouth of the Río Valdivia there are attractive villages which can be visited by land or river boat. The two main centres are Niebla on the north bank and Corral opposite on the south bank. **Niebla**, 18 km from Valdivia, is a spread-out resort with seafood restaurants and accommodation (also plenty of cabañas and campsites on the road from Valdivia). To the west of the resort is the **Fuerte de la Pura y Limpia Concepción de Monfort de Lemus**① *daily in summer 1000-1900, closed Mon in winter, US$1.50, Sun free, tourist information and telephone office nearby*, on a promontory. Partially restored in 1992, it has an interesting museum on Chilean naval history.

Corral, quieter than Niebla, is a fishing port with several good restaurants 62 km from Valdivia by road (unsuitable for cars without four-wheel drive or high clearance). The dilapidated but atmospheric Castillo de San Sebastián, with 3 m wide walls, was defended by a battery of 21 guns. It has a museum and offers a view upriver. In summer there are re-enactments of the 1820 storming of the Spanish fort by the Chileans (daily, 1200 and 1800). ① *Entry US$5 Jan-Feb, US$1.50 off season*. North along the coast are the remains of Castillo San Luis de Alba de Amargos (3 km) Castillo de San Carlos, with pleasant beaches (4 km). The coastal walks west and south of Corral are splendid. The helpful tourist office on Corral's pier can provide some trekking tips.

In midstream, between Niebla and Corral is **Isla Mancera** a small island, fortified by the Castillo de San Pedro de Alcántara, which has the most standing buildings. The island is a pleasant place to stop, but it can get crowded when an excursion boat arrives.

Osorno and around → *Phone code: 064. Colour map 8, grid C1. Population: 132,000.*

Founded in 1553, abandoned in 1604 and refounded in 1796, Osorno later became one of the centres of German immigration. On the large Plaza de Armas stands the modern cathedral, while to the east of the plaza along MacKenna are a number of late 19th-century mansions built by German immigrants, now National Monuments. **Museo Histórico Municipal**① *Matta 809, entrance in Casa de Cultura, daily 1100-1900 in summer; winter Mon-Fri 0930-1730, Sat 1500-1800, US$1.50*, includes displays on natural history, Mapuche culture, refounding of the city and German colonization. The **Museo Interactivo de Osorno** (MIO) ① *in the former train station, 3 blocks southwest of the plaza, T212996, www.municipalidadosorno.cl/, Mon-Thu 0815-1300, 1445-1815, Fri closes 1715, Sat pm only*, is an interactive science museum designed for both children and adults. **Tourist offices: Sernatur** in provincial government office① *Plaza de Armas, O'Higgins 667, p 1, T234104, infosorno@ sernatur.cl*. Municipal office in the bus terminal and kiosk on the Plaza de Armas. Both open December-February. Contact **Skiing Club Andino**, see page 710, for advice on skiing.

About 47 km east of Osorno, **Lago Puyehue** (*Colour map 8, grid C1, Altitude 207 m*) is surrounded by relatively flat countryside. At the western end is **Entre Lagos** (*Population 4,000*) and the **Termas de Puyehue** ① *daily 0900-2000, US$5 outdoor pools, US$18 indoor pools*, is at the eastern end.

The **Parque Nacional Puyehue**, east of Lago Puyehue, stretches to the Argentine border. On the east side are several lakes and two volcanic peaks: **Volcán Puyehue** (2,240 m) in the north (access via private track US$14 belonging to **El Caulle** restaurant and hostal – **E** pp, www.elcaulle.com) and **Volcán Casablanca** (also called Antillanca, 1,900 m). Park administration is at Aguas Calientes, 4 km south of the Termas de Puyehue. There is a ranger station at Anticura. Leaflets on attractions are available.

At **Aguas Calientes** there is an **open-air pool** (dirty) ① *0830-1900, US$3, children US$1.50*, with very hot thermal water beside the Río Chanleufú, and a very hot **indoor pool** ① *Mon-Fri in season only, 0830-1230, 1400-1800, Sat, Sun and holidays year-round 0830-2030, US$8, children US$4*.

From Aguas Calientes the road continues 18 km southeast to Antillanca on the slopes of **Volcán Casablanca**, past three small lakes and through forests. This is particularly beautiful, especially at sunrise, with the snow-clad cones of Osorno, Puntiagudo and Puyehue forming a semicircle. The tree-line on Casablanca is one of the few in the world made up of deciduous trees (nothofagus or southern beech). From Antillanca it is possible to climb Casablanca for even better views of the surrounding volcanoes and lakes, no path, seven hours return journey, information from Club Andino in Osorno. Attached to the Hotel Antillanca is one of the smallest ski resorts in Chile; there are three lifts, ski instruction and first aid available. Skiing quality depends on the weather: though rain is common it often does not turn to snow. See under Osorno for buses. No public transport from Aguas Calientes to Antillanca; try hitching – always difficult, but it is not a hard walk.

Border with Argentina: Paso Puyehue
Chilean immigration Open the second Saturday in October to the second Saturday in March 0800-2100, otherwise 0800-1900. The Chilean border post is at Pajaritos, 4 km east of **Anticura**, which is 22 km west of the border. For vehicles entering Chile, formalities are quick (about 15 minutes), but includes the spraying of tyres, and shoes have to be wiped on a mat. This route is liable to closure after snow. Cyclists should know that there are no supplies between Entre Lagos and La Angostura (Argentina).

⊜ Sleeping

Valdivia *p701, map p701*
Accommodation is often scarce during Semana Valdiviana. In summer, rooms are widely available in private homes, usually **D**, or **G** singles.
AL-A Puerta del Sur, Los Lingües 950, Isla Teja T224500, www.hotelpuertadelsur.com. 5 star, all facilities and extensive grounds, the best.
A Melillanca, Alemania 675, T212509, www.melillanca.cl. 4-star, decent business standard, with restaurant, sauna, Wi-Fi areas. Recommended.
B Palace, Chacabuco y Henríquez, T213319, hotelpalace@surnet.cl. Good, comfortable, with breakfast, central.
C Hostal Centro Torreón, P Rosales 783, T212 622, hostorreon@telsur.cl. With breakfast, old German villa, nice atmosphere, cable TV, parking.
C-D Aires Buenos, Gral Lagos 1036, T206304, www.airesbuenos.cl. **F** pp in dorms. Some rooms with bath, refurbished 19th-century house, with breakfast, tours, English, French spoken, common areas, internet, HI affiliated. Recommended.

C-D Hostal Prat, Prat 595, T222020. TV, good breakfast, views to industrial zone over the river.
C-D Hosp Internacional, García Reyes 660, T212015. **D** pp singles. Some rooms with bath, with breakfast, helpful, English and German spoken, use of kitchen, barbecue area, book exchange, tours. Recommended.
D-E Camilo Henríquez 749, Casa 6, T222574, F204313. **G** pp singles. Charming tumbledown mansion, wildly sloping floors (after-effect of 1960 earthquake), large rooms, some with bath, kitchen, laundry, internet, some English spoken. Highly recommended.

Around the bus terminal
C Hostal Casagrande, Andtwandter 880, T202 035, hostalcasagrande@hotmail.com. Heated rooms in attractive old house, cable TV, internet, laundry, great views. Recommended.
D Hostal Andwandter, Anwandter 482, T218587. With bath, breakfast, TV, hot water.

D-E pp **Hosp Ana María**, José Martí 11, 3 mins from terminal, T222468. With breakfast, shared bath, use of kitchen, good value, also cabañas.
E pp **A Muñoz 580**, near terminal. Shared bath, use of kitchen, cable TV, OK.
E pp **Res Germania**, Picarte 873, T212405. With breakfast, poor beds, German spoken, HI reductions.
E-F pp **A Muñoz 345**, outside terminal. With breakfast.
Camping Camping Centenario, in Rowing Club on España. **F** per tent, overlooking river. Isla Teja, T213584, lovely views over river.

Coastal resorts near Valdivia *p702*
C Cabañas Fischer, Niebla, T282007. Cabins and 2 campsites. Worth bargaining out of season
D Hostería Mancera, Isla Mancera, T/F216296. Open Dec-Mar, depending on weather, no singles, phone first, water not drinkable.
D Hostería Los Alamos, Corral. A delightful hideout for those seeking a quiet life.
D pp **Villa Santa Clara**, Niebla, T282018 (Casilla 52, Valdivia). With breakfast, kitchen and laundry, also cabañas.
D Residencial Mariel, Tarapacá 36, Corral, T471290. Modern, good value.

Osorno *p702*
A Waeger, Cochrane 816, T233721, hotelwaeger@telsur.cl. 4-star, restaurant, comfortable. Recommended.
C Eduviges, Eduviges 856, T/F235023, www.hoteleduviges.cl. Spacious, quiet, attractive, gardens, also cabañas. Recommended.
C-D Res Riga, Amthauer 1058, T232945, resiriga@telsur.cl. Pleasant. Highly recommended but heavily booked in season.
D Res Hein's, Errázuriz 1757, T234116.
E without bath, **F** singles, old-fashioned, spacious, family atmosphere.
E There are plenty of cheap options near the bus terminal, for instance on Los Carrera.
Camping Municipal site off Ruta 5 near south entrance to city, open Jan-Feb only, poor facilities, US$9 per site, swimming pool.

Around Osorno *p703*
Lago Puyehue
L-AL Hotel Termas de Puyehue, at the Termas de Puyehue, T232157/371272. Cheaper May-mid-Dec. 2 thermal swimming pools (one indoors, very clean), well maintained, meals expensive, in beautiful scenery, heavily booked Jan-Feb, cheaper May to mid-Dec (postal address Casilla 27-0, Puyehue, or T Santiago 231 3417, F283 1010).
C Hosp Millarey, Ramírez 333, Entre Lagos, T371251. With breakfast, **E** singles, excellent.

C Hostal y Cabañas Miraflores, Ramírez 480, Entre Lagos, T371275, olivia.hostalmiraflores@gmail.com. Pleasant rooms and cabins.
E Ruta Gasthaus 215, Osvaldo Muñoz 148, Entre Lagos, T371357. **G** singles, with bath and good breakfast, German spoken, good value.
Camping Camping No Me Olvides, Km 56, on south shore of Lake Puyehue. US$15, also cabañas. Playa Los Copihues, Km 56.5, on south shore of Lake Puyehue. Hot showers, good.

Aguas Calientes and Antillanca
AL Chanleufú, Aguas Calientes, T236988. Good cabañas (cheaper in off season), also camping, US$4 pp with hot water, also has a poorly-stocked shop (better to take your own food), and an expensive café.
A Hotel Antillanca, T235114, www.skiantillanca.cl. More expensive with full board. Includes free mountain biking and parapenting, at foot of Volcán Casablanca, restaurant/café, with pool, sauna, friendly club-like atmosphere; also has a *refugio*.
Camping At Aguas Calientes, US$15 for one, US$19 for 2 or more, only one toilet block with hot water. CONAF refugio on Volcán Puyehue, but check with CONAF in Anticura whether it is open. Los Derrumbes, 1 km from Aguas Calientes, no electricity, US$25 per site.

❶ Eating

Valdivia *p701, map p701*
Several fish restaurants on the Costanera facing the boat dock serve cheap, tasty food and have nice atmosphere. There are others upstairs in the municipal market.
❶ La Calesa, Yungay 735, on the costanera. Peruvian and international food, plus music and art gallery. Highly recommended.
❶ La Cava del Buho, Av Alemania 660. Very good food, service and interesting decor.
❶ Cervecería Kunstmann, Ruta T350, No 950, T292969, www.cerveza-kunstmann.cl. On road to Niebla. Restaurant serving German/Chilean food, brewery with 5 types of beer, beautiful interior, museum. Recommended.
❶ Ritual, Prat 233. Trendy new bar/restaurant on the waterfront, varied menu, good value.
❶ Sake, Beauchef 629. Claims to be Japanese but really serves generic "oriental" food. Take-away service available.
❶ Volcán, Caupolicán y Chacabuco. *Pichangas*, *cazuelas*, great food at a good price.

Cafés
La Baguette, Libertad y Yungay. Panadería with French-style cakes, brown bread. Repeatedly recommended.

Café Haussmann, O'Higgins 394. A Valdivia institution. Good tea, cakes and *crudos*.
Café Moro, Independencia y Libertad. Airy café with a mezzanine art gallery. Popular bar at night.
Entrelagos, Pérez Rosales 622. Ice cream and chocolates.

Coastal resorts near Valdivia *p702*
♦♦ Las Delicias, Niebla, T213566. With restaurant with 'a view that would be worth the money even if the food wasn't good'. Also *cabañas* and camping.

Osorno *p702*
Good cheap restaurants in the municipal market.
♦♦♦ Atelier, Freire 468. Fresh pasta and other Italian delights, good.
♦♦ Dino's, Ramírez 898, on the plaza. Restaurant upstairs, bar/cafeteria downstairs, good.
♦♦ Peter's Kneipe, M Rodríguez 1039. Excellent German restaurant.
♦♦-♦ Club de Artesanos, MacKenna 634. Decent and hearty traditional Chilean fare.
♦ Café Central, on Plaza. Good food and coffee.
♦ Panadería, at Ramírez 977. Bakery with good wholemeal bread.
♦ Waldis, on Plaza de Armas. Real coffee.

Around Osorno: Lago Puyehue *p703*
♦♦ Chalet Suisse, Ruta 215, Km 55, on the south lakeshore (Casilla 910, Osorno, T Puyehue 647208, Osorno 064-234073). Hostería, restaurant with excellent food.
♦♦ Pub del Campo, Entre Lagos, T371220. Reasonable prices. Highly recommended.
♦♦ Restaurant Jardín del Turista, Entre Lagos. Very good.

❀ Festivals and events

Valdivia *p701, map p701*
Semana Valdiviana, in **mid-Feb**, culminates in Noche Valdiviana on the Sat with a procession of elaborately decorated boats which sail past the Muelle Fluvial. Accommodation is scarce during festival.

◎ Shopping

Valdivia *p701, map p701*
Bookshop/cultural centre Librería/Centro Cultural 787, Pérez Rosales 787. Old mansion, with hip café (La Ultima Frontera), books and art exhibitions.
Supermarket Hiper-Unico, Arauco 697 (4-screen cinema at Plaza Dos Ríos next door). There's a colourful riverside market with livestock, fish etc.

▲ Activities and tours

Valdivia *p701, map p701*
To Corral and Niebla and other boat trips along the river, many the kiosks along the Muelle Fluvial. Boats will only leave with a minimum of 10 passengers, so off-season organize in advance. Full list of operators in the tourist information office. Prices: city US$4 pp; Isla Teja US$7 pp; Corral-Mancera US$15-30. Several other options.

Sea kayaking.
Mi Pueblito Expediciones, San Carlos 190, T245055, www.pueblitoexpediciones.cl. Offer classes and trips in sea kayaks in the waters around Valdivia, US$20-30 for 4-5 hrs.

❂ Transport

Valdivia *p701, map p701*
Air LAN to/from **Santiago** every day via Temuco, or Concepción.
Bus Terminal at Muñoz y Prat, by the river. To **Santiago**: several companies, 10 hrs, most services overnight, US$15, salón cama US$30. Half-hourly buses to/from **Osorno**, 2 hrs, several companies, US$4. To **Panguipulli**, US$3, Empresa Pirehueico, about every 30 mins, US$4. Many daily to **Puerto Montt**, US$5, 3 hrs. To **Puerto Varas**, 2¾ hrs, US$5. To **Frutillar**, US$5, 2½ hrs. To **Villarrica**, by JAC, 6 a day, 2½ hrs, US$5, continuing to **Pucón**, US$6, 3 hrs. Frequent daily service to Riñihue via Paillaco and Los Lagos. To Argentina: to **Bariloche** via Osorno, 7 hrs, **Bus Norte**, US$19; to **Zapala**, Igi-Llaima, Mon, Thur, Sat, 2300, change in Temuco at 0200, arrive Zapala 1200-1500, depending on border crossing, US$40.

Coastal resorts near Valdivia *p702*
Ferry The tourist boats to **Isla Mancera** and **Corral** offer a guided half-day tour (US$15-30, some with meals) from the Muelle Fluvial, Valdivia (behind the tourist office on Av Prat 555). The river trip is beautiful, but you can also take a **bus** (orange No 20) to Niebla from outside bus station or along Calles Andwandter and Carampangue in Valdivia, regular service between 0730 and 2100, 30 mins, US$0.65 (bus continues to Los Molinos), then cross to Corral by boat, hourly, US$1.20, 30 mins. There are occasional buses from Valdivia to Corral.

Osorno *p702*
Air LAN, Matta 862, T314900, daily flights Osorno-**Santiago**, via Concepción and/or Temuco.
Bus Main terminal 4 blocks from Plaza de Armas at Errázuriz 1400. Left luggage open 0730-2030. Bus from centre, US$0.50. To **Santiago**, frequent,

US$155, salón cama US$35, 11 hrs. To **Concepción**, US$10. To **Temuco**, US$8. To **Pucón** and **Villarrica**, Tur-Bus, frequent, US$10. To **Frutillar**, US$2, **Llanquihue**, **Puerto Varas** and **Puerto Montt** (US$4) services every 30 mins. To **Puerto Octay**, US$2, hourly. Local buses to **Entre Lagos**, **Puyehue** and **Aguas Calientes** leave from the Mercado Municipal terminal, 1 block west of main terminal. **Train** 2 daily to **Puerto Montt**, US$1.85, 2 hrs.

Around Osorno: Lago Puyehue p703
Bus To **Entre Lagos** from Osorno, frequent services in summer, **Expreso Lago Puyehue** and **Buses Barria**, 1 hr, US$1.50, reduced service off-season. Some buses by both companies continue to **Aguas Calientes** (off-season according to demand) 2 hrs, US$3. Buses that continue to Aguas Calientes do not stop at the lake (unless you want to get off at Hotel Termas de Puyehue and clamber down).

Border with Argentinian: Anticura p703
Bus To Anticura, 2-3 buses daily from **Osorno**, 3 hrs, US$4.50. Several bus companies run daily services from **Puerto Montt** via Osorno to Bariloche along this route (see under Puerto Montt for details). Although less scenic than the

ferry journey across Lake Todos Los Santos and Laguna Verde (see page 707) this crossing is far cheaper, more reliable and still a beautiful trip (best views from the right hand side of the bus).

⊕ Directory

Valdivia p701, map p701
Airline offices LAN, Maipú 271, T5262000.
Banks Redbanc ATM at Supermercado Hiper-Unico (see above) and at several banks in the centre. Good rates for cash at **Banco Santander**, P Rosales 585, **Corp Banca** (Visa), Picarte 370, will change cash and TCs. **Banco Santiago**, Arauco e Independencia, MasterCard. Casa de Cambio at Carampangue 325, T213305. Turismo Austral, Arauco y Henríquez, Galería Arauco, accepts TCs. **Internet** Several in the centre, average charge US$0.80 per hr. **Post offices** O'Higgins y Maipú.

Osorno p702
Banks ATMs at Bancos BCI, MacKenna 801, and Santiago, MacKenna 787 (Visa). For good rates try Cambio Tur, MacKenna 1004, T234846. Turismo Frontera, Ramírez 949, local 11 (Galería Catedral). **Internet** Several places in the centre.

Southern lakes

This is one of the most beautiful areas in a part of Chile which already has plenty to boast about. Lago Llanquihue, with its views to volcanoes and German-influenced towns, adjoins the Parque Nacional Vicente Pérez Rosales. The oldest national park in the country, this contains another beautiful lake, Todos los Santos, three major volcanoes, waterfalls and a memorable lakes route to Argentina. The region ends at the Seno de Reloncaví, a peaceful glacial inlet, often shrouded in soft rain.

Lago Llanquihue
The lake, covering 56,000 ha, is the second largest in Chile. Across the great blue sheet of water can be seen two snowcapped volcanoes: the perfect cone of Osorno (2,680 m) and the shattered cone of Calbuco (2,015 m), and, when the air is clear, the distant Tronador (3,460 m). The largest towns, Puerto Varas, Llanquihue and Frutillar are on the western shore, linked by the Pan-American Highway. There are roads around the rest of the lake: that from Puerto Octay east to Ensenada is very beautiful, but is narrow with lots of blind corners, necessitating speeds of 20-30 kph at best in places (see below).

Puerto Octay → Phone code: 064. Colour map 8, grid C1. Population: 2,500.
A peaceful, picturesque small town at the north tip of the lake with a backdrop of rolling hills, Puerto Octay was founded by German settlers in 1852. The town enjoyed a boom in the late 19th century when it was the northern port for steamships on the lake. The church and the enormous German-style former convent survive from that period. **Museo el Colono**① *Independencia 591, Tue-Sun 1000-1300, 1500-1900, Dec-Feb only*, has displays on German colonization. Another part of the museum, housing agricultural implements and machinery for making chicha, is just outside town on the road to Centinela. 3 km south along an unpaved road is the Peninsula of Centinela, a beautiful spot with a launch dock and watersports. From the headland are fine views of the volcanoes and the Cordillera of the Andes; a very popular spot in good weather, good for picnics (taxi US$2.50 one way). Rowing boats and pedalos can be hired.

Frutillar Bajo → *Phone code: 065. Colour map 8, grid C1. Population: 9,000. Altitude: 70 m.*
About half-way along the west side of the lake, Frutillar is divided into Frutillar Alto, just off the main highway, and Frutillar Bajo beautifully situated on the lake, 4 km away. (Colectivos run between the two towns, five minutes, US$0.50.) Frutillar Bajo is possibly the most attractive – and expensive – town on the lake. At the north end of the town is the Reserva Forestal Edmundo Winckler, run by the Universidad de Chile, 33 ha, with a guided trail through native woods. **Museo Colonial Alemán** ① *daily 1000-1930 summer, Tue-Sun 1000-1330, 1500-1800 winter, US$3,* includes a watermill, replicas of two German colonial houses with furnishings and utensils of the period, a blacksmith's shop (personal engravings for US$8), a campanario (circular barn with agricultural machinery and carriages inside), gardens and handicraft shop. In late January to early February there is a highly regarded classical music festival and a new, state-of-the-art concert hall is being built for this on the lakefront (accommodation must be booked well in advance). Tourist office on lakeside opposite Club Alemán, T420198, summer only, helpful.

Puerto Varas and around → *Phone code: 065. Colour map 8, grid C1. Population: 22,000.*
This beauty spot was the southern port for shipping on the lake in the 19th century. It is a more popular centre for visiting the southern lakes than Puerto Montt, 20 km to the south. The Catholic church, built by German Jesuits in 1918, is a copy of the church in Marieenkirche in the Black Forest. North and east of the **Gran Hotel Puerto Varas** (1934) are German style mansions dating from the early 20th century. **Parque Philippi**, on top of the hill, is pleasant; walk up to Hotel Cabañas del Lago on Klenner, cross the railway and the gate is on the right. Puerto Varas is a good base for trips around the lake. On the south shore two of the best beaches are **Playa Hermosa** (Km 7) and **Playa Niklitschek** (Km 8, entry fee charged). **La Poza**, at Km 16, is a little lake to the south of Lago Llanquihue reached through narrow channels overhung with vegetation. **Isla Loreley**, an island on La Poza, is very beautiful (frequent boat trips); a concealed channel leads to yet another lake, the Laguna Encantada. The **tourist office** is in the Municipalidad ① *San Francisco 413, T321330, 0900-2100 in summer*, helpful, finds cheap accommodation, also has an art gallery. Beware of places offering "tourist information", eg on pier. They may be only giving information about their paying members' services. Many places close in the off-season.

Ensenada
East of Puerto Varas by 47 km, Ensenada is at the southeast corner of Lake Llanquihue, which is the town's main attraction. Minibuses run from Puerto Varas, frequent in summer (see below).

Volcán Osorno
North of Ensenada, Osorno volcano can be reached from Ensenada, or from a road branching off the Puerto Octay-Ensenada road at Puerto Klocker, 20 km southeast of Puerto Octay. Weather permitting, Aqua Motion (see Puerto Varas, Activities and tours) organize climbing expeditions with local guide, transport from Puerto Montt or Puerto Varas, food and equipment, US$150 pp payment in advance (minimum group of two, maximum of six with three guides) all year, setting out from the refugio at La Burbuja. They check weather conditions the day before and offer 50% refund if climb is abandoned because of bad weather. From La Burbuja it is six hours to the summit. CONAF, with whom everyone must register, do not allow climbing without a guide and insist on one guide to every two climbers. Only experienced climbers should attempt to climb right to the top, ice climbing equipment essential.

Parque Nacional Vicente Pérez Rosales
① *Free entry. The park is infested by horseflies in Dec and Jan: cover up as much as possible with light-coloured clothes which may help a bit.*
Lago Todos los Santos The most beautiful of all the lakes in southern Chile, this long, irregularly shaped sheet of emerald-green water has deeply wooded shores and several small islands rising from its surface. In the waters are reflected the slopes of Volcán Osorno. Beyond the hilly shores to the east are several graceful snow-capped mountains, with the mighty Tronador in the distance. To the north is the sharp point of Cerro Puntiagudo, and at the northeastern end Cerro Techado rises cliff-like out of the water. The ports of **Petrohué** at its western and **Peulla** at its eastern ends are connected by boat. Trout and salmon fishing are excellent in several parts including Petrohué. CONAF has an office in Petrohué with a visitors'

centre, small museum and 3D model of the park. There is a *guardaparque* office in Puella. Park offices have details of walks. There are no roads round the lake and the only scheduled vessel is the Andina del Sud service with connections to Bariloche (Argentina), but private launches can be hired for trips (tickets for two-hour lake tours are sold on the Petrohué-Puella ferry). Isla Margarita, the largest island on the lake, with a lagoon in the middle, can be visited (in summer only) from Petrohué, boats by Andina del Sud leave 1500, US$45. Walking to Laguna Margarita is difficult because of fallen trees.

Petrohué, 16 km northwest of Ensenada, is a good base for walking. The **Salto de Petrohué** *US$3*, is 6 km from Petrohué (unpaved, dusty, lots of traffic; bus US$1), 10 km (paved) from Ensenada. Near the falls is a snackbar; there are also two short trails, the Senderos de los Enamorados and Carileufú. **Peulla**, is a good starting point for hikes in the mountains. The Cascadas Los Novios, signposted above the Hotel Peulla, are stunning.

For crossing the border with Argentina, **Paso Pérez Rosales**. Chilean immigration is in Peulla, 30 km west of the border, open daily, summer 0800-2100, winter 0800-2000.

Seno de Reloncaví

The Reloncaví estuary, the northernmost of Chile's glacial inlets, is recommended for its local colour, its wildlife (including sealions and dolphins) and its peace. **Ralún**, a small village at the northern end of the estuary, is 31 km southeast from Ensenada by a poorly paved road along the wooded lower Petrohué valley. Roads continue, unpaved, along the east side of the estuary to Cochamó and Puelo and on the west side to Canutillar. In Ralún there is a village shop and post office. Just outside the village there are thermal springs with baths, US$2, reached by boat across Río Petrohué, US$2.50 pp.

Cochamó, 17 km south of Ralún on the east shore of the estuary, is a pretty village, with a fine wooden church similar to those on Chiloé, in a striking setting, with the estuary and volcano behind. **Puelo**, further south, on the south bank of the Río Puelo, is a most peaceful place. From here the road (very rough) continues to Puelche on the Carretera Austral.

● Sleeping

Puerto Octay *p706*
Camping wild and barbecues are forbidden on the lakeshore.
D Hosp Raquel Mardorf, Germán Wulf 712. **E** for single room. Comfortable, large breakfast. Owners have ♈ Restaurante La Cabaña at No 713.
D Pumalín Amarillo, 35 mins' walk north of town, T210787, www.zapatoamarillo.8k.com. **G** pp in dorms. Book in advance in high season, spotless kitchen, great breakfasts, homemade bread, meals, German/English spoken, mountain bikes, canoes, tours, house has a grass roof. Highly recommended.
F-G pp **Hosp La Naranja**, Independencia 361. Without bath, with breakfast, restaurant.
Camping El Molino, beside lake, US$5 pp. Recommended.

Centinela
AL-A Hotel Centinela, T 391326, www.hotel centinela.cl. Built in 1914 as a summer mansion, Edward VIII once stayed here. Newly restored, idyllic location with superb views, also has *cabañas*, excellent restaurant, bar, open all year.
E Hostería La Baja, Casilla 116, T391269. **F** singles. Beautifully situated at the neck of the peninsula, with breakfast and bath, good value.
Camping Municipal site on lakeside, T391326. US$18 per site. *Cabañas* on the peninsula.

East of Puerto Octay
E pp **Hostería Irma**, 2 km south of Las Cascadas. Very pleasant, good food; also farmhouse accommodation and camping.

Frutillar *p707*
Frutillar Bajo
A Ayacara, Av Philippi 1215, T421550. Beautiful rooms with lake view, welcoming, have a pisco sour in the library in the evening.
B Casona del 32, Caupolicán 28, T421369. With breakfast, comfortable old house, central heating, English and German spoken, excellent.
B Hostería El Arroyo, Av Philippi 989, T421560. With breakfast. Highly recommended.
B Residenz/Café am See, Av Philippi 539, T421 539. Good breakfast, café has German specialities.
B Winkler, Av Philippi 1155, T421388. Cabins. Recommended.
C Hosp Costa Azul, Av Philippi 1175, T421388. Mainly families, good breakfasts.
C Hosp Trayén, Av Philippi 963, T421346. With bath, nice rooms, good breakfast.
C Hosp Vivaldi, Av Philippi 851, T421382. Quiet, comfortable, excellent breakfast and lodging, also family accommodation. Recommended.
D Av Philippi 451, T421204. Clean, good breakfast.
D Pérez Rosales 590. Excellent breakfast.

North of Frutillar Bajo
A Salzburg, T421589 or Santiago 206 1419,
www.salzburg.cl. Excellent, restaurant, sauna,
mountain bikes, arranges tours and fishing.

Frutillar Alto
Several good-value places to stay along Carlos
Richter (main street). Cheap accommodation in
the school, sleeping bag required.
E Faralito, Winkler 245. Cooking facilities (owner
can be contacted at shop at Winkler 167, T421440).
Camping Los Ciruelillos, 2 km south,
T339123. Most services. **Playa Maqui**, 7 km
north of Frutillar, T339139. Fancy, expensive.
Sr Guido González, Casa 3, Población Vermont,
T421385. Recommended site.

Puerto Varas *p707*
L-A Cabañas del Lago, Klenner 195, T232291,
calago@entelchile.net. On Philippi hill overlooking
lake, recently rebuilt 4-star hotel, with good
breakfast, bar and restaurant. Also self-catering
cabins sleeping 5 (good value for groups), heating,
sauna, swimming pools and games room.
AL Colonos del Sur, Del Salvador 24, T235555,
www.colonosdelsur.cl. Good views, decent
rooms, good restaurant, tea room. Also an hotel
at Del Salvador 24, being refurbished (late 2006).
AL Bellavista, Pérez Rosales 60, T232011,
www.hotelbellavista.cl. 4-star hotel with king-size
beds; cheerful, restaurant and bar, overlooking
lake, sauna and parking.
AL-A Licarayén, San José 114, T232305, info@
hotelicarayen.cl. Overlooking lake, comfortable, with
gym and sauna, book in season. Recommended.
AL-A Los Alerces, Pérez Rosales 1281, T232060,
reservalosalerces@hotmail.com. 4-star hotel, with
breakfast, cabin complex (price depends on season
when rest of hotel is closed), attractive, helpful.
A-B Gran Reserva, Mirador 106, T346876,
www.granreserva.cl. Behind the Casino, good
boutique hotel with great views from breakfast
room, pleasant living room.
B Amancay, Walker Martínez 564, T232201,
cabamancay@chile.com. Cabañasfor 4, also has
rooms, **D** with bath, **E** without, includes breakfast,
good, German spoken. Recommended.
B El Greco, Mirador 104, T233388,
www.hotelelgreco.cl. Beautifully refurbished old
German mansion, wooden interior and full of
artworks, stylish boutique hotel with simple
rooms with cable TV. A good choice.
B-C Hostería Outsider, San Bernardo 318,
T/F232910, www.turout.com. With bath, some
rooms with internet, real coffee, meals, horse
riding, rafting, sea kayaking, climbing, German
and English spoken. Book ahead in season.
C-D Casa Azul, Manzanal 66 y Rosario, T232904,
www.casa azul.net. **F** pp in dorms. Lovely

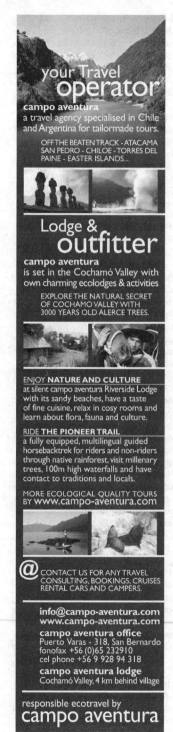

building, some rooms with bath, good buffet breakfast with home-made muesli (US$5), kitchen facilities, limited heating, garden, book exchange, German and English spoken. Reserve in advance in high season. Recommended.

C-D Compas del Sur, Klenner 467, T232044, www.compassdelsur.cl. **F** pp in shared rooms, Chilean-Swedish run, kitchen facilities, internet, small breakfast included (US$1 for extras), cable TV in comfy lounge, helpful, German, English, Swedish spoken. Highly recommended, but reserve in advance in high season (may be closed in low season).

C-D Hosp Ellenhaus, Martínez 239, T233577, www.ellenhaus.cl. More expensive with bath, **F** pp in dorms (cold showers), kitchen and laundry facilities, lounge, hospitable, German spoken. Recommended.

D Casa Margouya, Santa Rosa 318, T511648, www.margouya.com. **F** in shared rooms, with breakfast. Bright, colourful, kitchen facilities, lots of information, French run, English spoken.

D Hosp Carla Minte, Maipo 1010, T232880. **F** singles. Rooms with bath and breakfast in a family home, cable TV, very comfortable.

D Las Dalias, Santa Rosa 707, T233277. Quiet family home, cheaper with shared bath, central, good breakfast, parking, German spoken.

D Villa Germania, Nuestra Sra del Carmen 873, T233162. **F-G** singles. Old wooden mansion north of the centre, also *cabañas*.

F pp **Hosp Don Raúl**, Salvador 928, T310897, hospedajedonraul@hotmail.com. Laundry and cooking facilities, spotless, helpful, camping **G** pp. Recommended.

F pp **Patiperros**, Mirador 135, T235050, www.jardinsa.cl. Comfortable hostel, with breakfast.

Camping Wild camping and use of barbecues is not allowed on the lake shore. Sites on south shore of Lago Llanquihue east of Puerto Varas: **Campo Aventura**, San Bernardo 318, Puerto Varas, T/F232910, www.campo-aventura.com. 2 lodges with camping facilities, excellent horse riding, fishing, birdwatching, Spanish classes and vegetarian food.

Also: **CONAF**, Km 49, site at Puerto Oscuro, beneath road to volcano, very good. **Playa Hermosa**, Km 7, T252223, fancy, US$22 per site (negotiate in low season), take own supplies, recommended. **Playa Niklitschek**, Km 8, T338352. Full facilities. **Playa Venado**, Camping Municipal, Km 20. **Trauco**, Imperial 433.

Ensenada *p707*

AL-A Hotel Ensenada, Km 45, T212028, www.hotelensenada.cl. Olde-worlde, good food, good view of lake and Osorno Volcano, runs tours, hires mountain bikes (guests only). Also

hostal in the grounds, cooking facilities, cheaper. Closed in winter.

A-C Cabañas Brisas del Lago, T212012, www.brisasdellago.cl. Chalets for 6 on beach, good restaurant nearby, supermarket next door. Highly recommended for self-catering.

C-D Hosp Arena, Km 43, T212037. Some rooms with bath, breakfast. Recommended.

D Hosp Ensenada, T338278. Very clean, most rooms with bath, **F** singles, excellent breakfast.

Camping Montaña, central Ensenada. **F** per site. Fully equipped, nice beach sites. Also at Playa Larga, 1 km further east, US$15 per site, and at Puerto Oscuro, 2 km north, US$12. **Trauco**, 4 km west, T212033. Large site with shops, fully equipped, US$5-10 pp.

Volcán Osorno *p707*

The **Skiing Club Andino Osorno** (O'Higgins 1073, Osorno, T235114) has 3 refugios: north of the summit at La Picada (20 km east of Puerto Klocker) at 950 m; south of the summit: **La Burbuja**, 14 km north of Ensenada at 1,250 m; and, 15 km from Ensenada at 1,200 m **Refugio Teski Club**, **D** pp, bunk beds, restaurant and bar, sleeping bag useful, bleak site just below snow line; a good base for walking.

Parque Nacional Vicente Pérez Rosales *p707*

There is a small shop in Andino del Sud building but best to take your own food.

At Petrohué

L Fundo El Salto, near Salto de Petrohué, www.fly-fish-chile.com. Run by New Zealanders, an expensive fishing lodge, good home cooking, fishing trips arranged.

AL Hotel Petrohué, T065-212025, www.petrohue.com. Excellent views, **L** for half-board, also has cabins, pool, cosy, restaurant, log fires, sauna and heated swimming pool; organizes hiking, fishing and other activities. Albergue in the school in summer. CONAF office can help find cheaper family accommodation.

Peulla

AL Hotel Peulla, T02-196 4182, hpeullare servas@terra.cl. Including dinner and breakfast, cheaper out of season. Beautiful setting by the lake and mountains, restaurant and bar, expensive meals (lunch poor), cold in winter, often full of tour groups (tiny shop at back of hotel).

D pp **Res Palomita**, 50 m west of Hotel Peulla. Half board, family-run, simple, comfortable but small, shared rooms, separate shower, book ahead in season, lunches, expensive tours.

Camping Camping wild and picnicking in the national park is forbidden. At Petrohué on far side beside the lake, US$6 per site, no services, cold showers, locals around the site sell fresh bread (local fishermen will ferry you across, US$2). At Peulla, opposite CONAF office, US$4 per site. Good campsite 1½ hrs' walk east of Peulla, take food. A small shop in Peulla sells basic goods, including fruit and veg.

Seno de Reloncaví *p708*
Ralún
Lodging (**F** pp) is available with families and at restaurant **Navarrito** (**D-E**, basic) and **E** pp **Posada Campesino** (very friendly, clean and simple, without breakfast).

Cochamó
C Campo Aventura (San Bernadino 318, Puerto Varas) T/F065-232910, www.campo-aventura.com. 4 km south of Cochamó in Valle Río Cochamó, full board available (great breakfast), local food, and very fresh milk from their own cow, camping **F**. Kitchen, sauna, book exchange. Also a renovated mountain house at their other base in the valley of La Junta. They specialize in horseback and trekking between the Reloncaví Estuary and the Argentine border, 2-10 days.
D-E Cochamó, T216212. Basic but friendly and clean, often full with salmon farm workers, good meals. Next door is **D-E Mercado Particular Sabin**, one of several other *pensiones*.
E Edicar, on seafront by the dock/ramp. With breakfast, hot shower, good value. Recommended.
E Hosp Maura, JJ Molina 12. Beautiful location overlooking the estuary, excellent food, good for kids, highly recommended.
Also a large number of *cabañas*, a campsite and a few eating places.

Puelo
Basic lodging is available at the restaurant or with families – try Roberto and Olivia Telles, no bath/shower, meals on request, or Ema Hernández Maldona; 2 restaurants.

❶ Eating

Puerto Octay *p706*
El Rancho del Espanta-Pajaros, 6 km south on the road to Frutillar, T330049. In a converted barn with wonderful views over the lake, serves all kind of spit roasted meat. All-you-can-eat, with salad bar and drinks included, for US$12. Also arranges horse riding trips. Recommended.
Restaurante Baviera, Germán Wulf 582. Cheap and good, salmon and *cazuelas*.

Frutillar Bajo *p707*
Selva Negra, Varas 24 y Philippi. In a traditional German mill, with scores of toy witches hanging from the ceiling, open 1100-2300.

Casino de Bomberos, Philippi 1060. Upstairs bar/restaurant, memorable painting caricaturing the firemen in action (worth studying while awaiting your meal), good value.

Cafés
Many German-style cafés and tea-rooms on C Philippi (the lakefront) eg **Salón de Te Frutillar**, No 775, and **Guten Apetit**, No 1285. **Der Volkladen**, O'Higgins y Philippi. Natural products, chocolates and cakes, natural cosmetics.

Puerto Varas *p707*
Merlín, Imperial 0605, on road out of town. Most rate it as one of the best restaurants in the Lake District, though not to everyone's taste.
Di Carusso, San Bernardo 318. Italian trattoria, good fresh pasta dishes on Fri. Recommended.
La Olla, V Pérez Rosales 1071, on lakefront, 1 km east of town, T233540. Good, popular for seafood, fish and meat, traditional Chilean cuisine. Recommended.
Mediterráneo, Santa Rosa 068, T237268. On the lakefront, good international and local food, interesting varied menu.

Cafés
Café Danés, Del Salvador 441. Coffee and cakes.
Punto Café, Del Salvador 348. Cybercafé, bar and art gallery.

Ensenada *p707*
Most eating places close off season. There are a few pricey shops. Take your own provisions.
Latitude 42, Yan Kee Way resort, T212030. Expensive, excellent and varied cuisine, very good quality wine list. Lake views.
Canta Rana is recommended for bread and küchen.

❍ Shopping

Puerto Varas *p707*
Bookshop El Libro del Capitán, Martínez 417. Large selection of German and English books, also book swap.
Supermarkets Las Brisas, Salvador 495. Vyhmeister, Gramado 565. Good selection.

▲ Activities and tours

Puerto Varas *p707*
Cycling Thomas Held Expeditions, Martínez 239, T/F311889. Cycle hire US$20 per day. **Turismo Biker**, in Terranova Café, www.turismobiker.com. Touring and downhill as well as standard tours.

Fishing Licence US$2.50 a year, obtainable from Municipalidad. Expeditions organized by many operators.

Horse riding Cabañas Puerto Decher, Fundo Molino Viejo, 2 km north, T338033, guided tours, minimum 2 people, mixed reports. **Quinta del Lago**, Km 25 on road to Ensenada, T338275, www.quintadellago.com. All levels catered for, US$10 per hr, also trips in ox cart and cabañas. See also Campo Aventura, above.

Ziplining (*canopy*), offered by several operators.

Tours

Most tours operate in season only (1 Sep-15 Apr).
Al Sur, Del Salvador 100, T232300, www.alsurexpeditions.com. Rafting on Río Petrohué, good camping equipment, tours, trekking maps, English spoken, official tour operators to Parque Pumalín.

Andina del Sud, Del Salvador 72, T232511. Operate 'lakes' trip to Bariloche, Argentina via Lago Todos los Santos, Peulla, Cerro Tronador (see under Puerto Montt, To Argentina), plus other excursions.

Aqua Motion, San Francisco 328, T/F232747, www.aquamotion.cl. For trekking, rafting and climbing, German and English spoken, good equipment, several other activities.

Kokayak, San José 320, T346433, www.paddlechile.com. Kayaking and rafting trips, good equipment and after-trip lunch.

Tranco Expeditions, San Pedro 422, T311311. Trekking on volcano, rafting, fishing and more, Norwegian and English spoken, good equipment. Recommended.

Travel Art, Imperial 0661, T232198, www.travelart.cl. Biking and hiking tours, and general all-inclusive multi-day tours.

Seno de Reloncaví: Cochamó *p708*
Sebastián Contreras C Morales, T216220, is a recommended independent guide who offers tours on horseback and hires out horses.

⊖ Transport

Puerto Octay *p706*
Bus To **Osorno** hourly, US$2; to **Frutillar** (1 hr, US$1), **Puerto Varas** (2 hrs) and **Puerto Montt** (3 hrs, US$3) Thaebus, 5 a day. Around the east shore: to **Las Cascadas** (34 km), Mon-Fri 1730, returns next day 0700.

Frutillar Bajo *p707*
Bus Most leave from opposite the Copec station in Frutillar Alto. To **Puerto Varas** (US$1) and **Puerto Montt** (US$1.50), frequent, **Full Express**. To **Osorno**, Turismosur 1½ hrs, US$2.50. To **Puerto Octay**, Thaebus, 6 a day, US$1.

Puerto Varas *p707*
Bus To **Santiago**, normal US$24, semi cama US$36, cama US$48, Tur-Bus, 12 hrs. To **Puerto Montt**, 30 mins, Thaebus and Full Express every 15 mins, US$1.35, 30 mins. Same frequency to **Frutillar** (US$1, 30 mins) and **Osorno** (US$3, 1 hr). To **Valdivia** US$6, 3 hrs. To **Bariloche**, Andina del Sud, by lakes route, see above. Buses, eg Cruz del Sur, Tas Choapa, daily, 7 hrs, US$17. Minibuses to **Ensenada** leave from San Bernardo y Martínez, hourly. Taxi from Puerto Montt airport, US$16. **Train** The Puerto Montt-Frutillar-Osorno-Temuco trains pass through here twice a day. 20 mins to **Puerto Montt**, US$0.75; 1 hr 40 mins to **Osorno**, US$1.50; 6 hrs 20 mins to **Temuco**, US$6.50.

Parque Nacional Vicente Pérez Rosales *p707*
Minibuses Every 30 mins to Petrohué from Puerto Montt and Puerto Varas in summer (US$4, 1¼ hrs from Puerto Varas), much less frequent off season. Last bus to Ensenada at 1800.
Ferry The boat between Petrohué and Peulla costs US$22 one way (book in advance). It leaves Petrohué at 1030, Peulla at 1500 (not Sun, 2 hrs – most seating indoors, no cars carried, cycles free), commentaries in Spanish and English. This connects with the Andina del Sud tour bus between Puerto Montt and Bariloche (see under Puerto Montt). Local fishermen make the trip across the lake, charging less than the public service and their boats have no shelter if it rains.

Seno de Reloncaví *p708*
Bus From Puerto Montt to **Ralún**, **Cochamó** and **Puelo**, 5 a day via Puerto Varas and Ensenada, with **Bohle** and **Fierro**: US$3 to Ralún, US$5 to Cochamó (2½ hrs). **Boats** In summer boats sail up the Estuary from Angelmó. The **Sernatur** office in Puerto Montt has details of scheduled trips.

❶ Directory

Frutillar Bajo *p707*
Useful services Toilet, showers and changing cabins for beach on O'Higgins. **Banco Santander**, on the lakeside, has Redbanc ATM.

Puerto Varas *p707*
Banks Redbanc ATMs at several banks. **Turismo Los Lagos**, Del Salvador 257 (Galería Real, local 11). Daily 0830-1330, 1500-2100, Sun 0930-1330, accepts TCs, good rates. **Internet** Ciber Service, Salvador 264, loc 6-A. George's, San Ignacio 574. Av Gramado 560, p 2. San José 380, p 2. **Post offices** San José y San Pedro; Del Salvador y Santa Rosa. **Telephones** Several call centres in town.

Puerto Montt and Chiloé

→ *Phone code: 065. Colour map 8, grid C1. Population: 160,000.*

Just 20 minutes south of Puerto Varas, and 1,016 km south of Santiago, Puerto Montt is the gateway to the shipping lanes to the south, namely the island of Chiloé and the wilds of Patagonia. It's a rapidly growing, disordered modern city, developing in line with a boom in salmon fishing. Angelmó, a fishing port 2 km west, is most popular with visitors for its seafood restaurants and handicraft shops, but is not worth a visit of more than a day or two.

Puerto Montt

Ins and outs

Tourist offices Puerto Montt: Sernatur has two offices: in the Gobernación Provincial building on the Plaza de Armas. Daily in summer 0900-1300, 1500-1900, Monday to Friday in winter 0830-1300, 1400-1800. And, for regional information, in the Intendencia Regional, Avenida Décima Región 480 (p 2), T254580, infoloslagos@sernatur.cl, 0830-1300, 1330-1730 Monday to Friday. See www.puerto monttchile.cl for information on the web. For more information and town maps, go to the kiosk just southeast of the Plaza de Armas run by the municipality (open till 1800 on Saturday). **CONAF** is at Ochogavia 458, but cannot supply information on national parks. **Automóvil Club de Chile** ① *Esmeralda 70, T252968.*

Sights

The capital of X Región (Los Lagos) was founded in 1853 as part of the German colonization of the area. Good views over the city and bay are offered from outside the Intendencia Regional on Avenida X Region. The port is used by fishing boats and coastal vessels, and is the departure point for vessels to Puerto Chacabuco, Laguna San Rafael and for the long haul south to Puerto Natales. A paved road runs 55 km southwest to Pargua, where there is a ferry service to Chiloé.

The **Iglesia de los Jesuitas on Gallardo**, dating from 1872, has a fine blue-domed ceiling; behind it on a hill is the campanario (clock tower). **Museo Regional Juan Pablo II** ① *Portales 997 near the bus terminal, daily 1030-1800, US$1,* documents local history and has a fine collection of historic photos of the city; also memorabilia of the Pope John Paul II's visit in 1988. The fishing port of **Angelmó**, 2 km west, has become a tourist centre with seafood restaurants and handicraft shops (reached by Costanera bus along Portales and by colectivos Nos 2, 3, 20 from the centre, US$0.30).

The wooded **Isla Tenglo**, reached by launch from Angelmó (US$1 each way), is a favourite place for picnics. Magnificent view from the summit. The island is famous for its curantos, served by restaurants in summer. Boat trips round the island from Angelmó last 30 minutes, US$8. **Parque Provincial Lahuen Nadi** contains some ancient trees in swampland, more accessible than some of the remoter forests. Take the main road to the airport, which leads off Ruta 5. After 5 km, turn right (north) and follow the signs. West of Puerto Montt the Río Maullin, which drains Lago Llanquihue, has some attractive waterfalls and good fishing (salmon). At the mouth of the river is the little fishing village of **Maullin**, founded in 1602.

To Argentina via Lago Todos Los Santos

This popular but ever more expensive route to Bariloche, involving ferries across Lago Todos Los Santos, Lago Frías and Lago Nahuel Huapi is outstandingly beautiful whatever the season, though the mountains are often obscured by rain and heavy cloud. The route is via Puerto Varas, Ensenada and Petrohué falls (20 minutes stop) to Petrohué, where it connects with catamaran service across Lago Todos Los Santos to Peulla. Lunch stop in Peulla two hours (lunch not included in fare: Hotel Peulla is expensive, see page 710 for alternatives). Chilean customs in Peulla, followed by a 1½-hour bus ride through the Paso Pérez Rosales to Argentine customs in Puerto Frías, 20 minute boat trip across Lago Frías to Puerto Alegre and bus from Puerto Alegre to Puerto Blest. From Puerto Blest it is a beautiful one hour catamaran trip along Lago Nahuel Huapi to Puerto Pañuelo (Llao Llao), from where there is a 45-minute bus journey to Bariloche (bus drops passengers at hotels, camping sites or in town centre). From 1 May to 30 August this trip is done over two days with overnight stay in Peulla, add about US$90 to single fare for accommodation in Hotel Peulla. (Baggage is taken to Hotel Peulla automatically but for alternative accommodation see under Peulla.) Fares are given under Transport, below.

Sea routes south of Puerto Montt

To Puerto Natales The dramatic 1,460 km journey first goes through Seno Reloncaví and Canal Moraleda. From Bahía Anna Pink along the coast and then across the Golfo de Penas to Bahía Tarn it is a 12-17 hours sea crossing, usually rough. The journey continues through Canal Messier, Angostura Inglesa, Paso del Indio and Canal Kirke (one of the narrowest routes for large shipping). It takes just under 4 days. Navimag's vessel *Puerto Edén*, a functional but comfortable 114-metre-long freight and passenger roll-on roll-off ferry, makes the journey. It may call at Puerto Chacabuco en route south and north, and stops off Puerto Edén on Isla Wellington (one hour south of Angostura Inglesa). This is a fishing village with one hospedaje (20 beds), three shops, scant provisions, one off-licence, one café, but no camping, or running water. Population is 180, plus five carabineros and the few remaining Alacaluf Indians. It is the drop-off point for exploring Isla Wellington, which is largely untouched, with stunning mountains. If stopping, take food; maps (not very accurate) available in Santiago. Passengers on the *Puerto Edén* may disembark for an hour on Wednesday morning to walk around the village (on Saturday sailing north – hot wine is served after the visit). Between November and March, the *Puerto Edén* also visits the Pío XI, or Bruggen Glacier, the largest in South America, for an hour on the southward journey. Going north it stops at the Amalia or Brujo Glacier (depending on weather conditions) on Friday evening. The service is not very reliable so always check that it is running.

● Sleeping

Puerto Montt *p713, map p714*
Accommodation is expensive in season, much cheaper off season. Check with the tourist office.
L-AL Gran Hotel Don Vicente, Varas 447, T432900, www.granhoteldonvicente.cl. With

breakfast, business class, excellent restaurant, seafood. Recommended.
AL Club Presidente, Portales 664, T251666, www.presidente.cl. 4-star, with breakfast, very comfortable, also suites. Recommended.

Puerto Montt

To Pan-American Highway & Airport

Seno de Reloncaví

Sleeping ●
Alda González **2** *A4*
Casa Perla **6** *B1*
Club Presidente **7** *C4*
Colina **8** *C4*
Gran Hotel Don Luis **1** *B5*
Gran Hotel Don Vicente **25** *B4*

Hospedaje
Rocco **28** *C1*
Hostal Pacífico **14** *B2*
Hostal Suizo **13** *C1*
Le Mirage **15** *A5*
Millahue **16** *C6*
O'Grimm **18** *B4*

Residencial
El Turista **20** *C2*
Residencial Emita **23** *C1*
Vista al Mar **3** *B1*
Vista Hermosa **27** *C1*

N
0 metres 200
0 yards 200

AL-A Gran Hotel Don Luis, Quillota 146, T259001, www.hoteldonluis.cl. New 4-star, gym, sauna, business centre etc.

A-B O'Grimm, Gallardo 211, T252845, www.ogrimm.cl. With breakfast, cosy, pleasant rooms with lounge area, central, restaurant with occasional live music.

C Hostal Pacífico, J J Mira 1088, T256229. With breakfast, cable TV, parking, comfortable. Discounts for foreign visitors. Recommended.

C Le Mirage, Rancagua 350, T255125, F256302. Business-class hotel, with breakfast, small rooms.

C Millahue, Copiapó 64, T253829, www.hotelmillahue.cl. With breakfast, modern but slightly run down, good restaurant.

C-D Colina, Talca 81, T253502, hotcolina@ hotmail.com. Spacious, good restaurant, bar, car hire. Good value but can be noisy, otherwise recommended.

C-D Hostal Suizo, Independencia 231, T/F252640, rossyoelckers@yahoo.es. **F** pp in shared rooms, some rooms with bath. With small breakfast, painting and Spanish classes, German and Italian spoken, Spanish classes. The house is as quirky as the owner. Convenient for Navimag ferry.

D Alda González, Gallardo 552, T253334. **G** singles. With or without bath, with breakfast, cooking facilities, popular, German and English spoken, near the Plaza de Armas. Recommended.

D Res Emita, Miraflores 1281, T250725, hospedaje_emita@hotmail.com. **F** singles, some rooms with bath, includes breakfast with homemade bread, safe, near the bus terminal.

D-E Casa Perla, Trigal 312, T262104, www.casaperla.com. **G** pp in shared rooms. With breakfast, French, English spoken, helpful, meals, Spanish classes offered off season, laundry, internet, pleasant garden, good meeting place. Recommended.

D-E Hospedaje Rocco, Pudeto 233, T/F272897, hospedajerocco@hotmail.com. **F** in dorms. Renovated, with breakfast, real coffee, English spoken, laundry, quiet residential area, convenient for Navimag. Recommended.

D-E Res El Turista, Ancud 91, T263838. **F** singles. With and without bath, with breakfast, comfortable, small rooms, heating. Recommended.

D-E Vista al Mar, Vivar 1337, T255625, www.hospedajevistaalmar.unlugar.com. Helpful, welcoming, good breakfast, phone for a lift from bus station.

E Vista Hermosa, Miramar 1486, T268001, vistahermosa@mixmail.com. **G** singles without bath, with breakfast, very good, without bath, ask for front room for best views (10 mins' walk from terminal).

F pp **Mercedes Fuentes**, Aníbal Pinto 315, T273463. Bed and breakfast with shared bath, spacious rooms, helpful family, father is tour guide.

F-G pp **Hosp El Valle**, Chorrillos 1358, T258464. Hot showers, internet.
Several lodgings in **F-G** pp range on C Huasco, east of the Plaza de Armas.

Camping Camping Anderson, 11 km west, American-run, hot showers, private beach, home-grown fruit, vegetables and milk products. **Camping Metri**, 30 km southeast on Carretera Austral, T251235, Fierro bus, US$2 per tent. **Camping Municipal** at Chinquihue, 10 km west (bus service), open Oct-Apr, fully equipped with tables, seats, barbecue, toilets and showers. Small shop, no kerosene.

🍴 Eating

Puerto Montt *p713*, *map p714*
Local specialities include *picoroco al vapor*, a giant barnacle whose flesh looks and tastes like crab, and curanto. Cheap food in Puerto Montt bus terminal.

In Angelmó, there are several dozen small, seafood restaurants in the old fishing port, past the fish market, very popular, ask for *té blanco* (white wine) – they are not legally allowed to serve wine).

Other seafood restaurants in Chinquihue, west of Angelmó. In Pelluco (4 km east), many

Eating 🍴
Café Central **2** *B4*
Café Haussman **1** *B5*
Café Real **2** *B4*
Centro Español **3** *B5*
Club Alemán **4** *B5*
Club de Yates **5** *C5*
Dino **6** *B4*
Milton Plaza **7** *B5*

seafood restaurants, including **Pazos**, T252552. Best *curanto* in Puerto Montt. **Azurro**, good Italian restaurant and, around the corner, a great pub called **Taitao**, façade like a galleon.

ᵀᵀᵀ **Club Alemán**, Varas 264. Old fashioned, good food and wine.

ᵀᵀᵀ **Club de Yates**, Costanera east of centre. Excellent seafood.

ᵀᵀ **Café Haussman**, San Martín y Urmeneta. German cakes, beer and *crudos*. Recommended.

ᵀᵀ **Centro Español**, O'Higgins 233. Very good traditional Chilean and Spanish food.

ᵀ **Café Central**, Rancagua 117. Spartan décor, generous portions (sandwiches and *pichangas* - saavoury salad snack). Giant TV screen for football enthusiasts.

ᵀ **Café Real**, Rancagua 137. For *empanadas*, *pichangas*, *congrío frito*, and lunches.

ᵀ **Dino**, Varas 550. Restaurant upstairs, snacks downstairs (try the lemon juice), often has an all-you-can-eat buffet.

ᵀ **Milton Plaza**, Urmeneta y O´Higgins. Good seafood and snacks, doubles as a pool hall. Recommended.

Cafés

Asturias, Angelmó 2448. Often recommended.
Café Plaza, Urmeneta 326. Good location, pool table, nice atmosphere.

○ Shopping

Puerto Montt *p713, map p714*
Woollen goods and Mapuche-designed rugs can be bought at roadside stalls in Angelmó and on Portales opposite the bus terminal. Prices are much the same as on Chiloé, but quality is often lower.
Bookshop Libros, Portales 580. Small selection of English novels, also maps.
Supermarkets Fullfresh, opposite bus terminal, open 0900-2200 daily. Also in the Paseo del Mar shopping mall, Talca y A Varas, and in the old railway station. Santa Isabel, Varas y Chillán. A new mall, **Paseo Costanera**, is open on the seafront.

▲ Activities and tours

Puerto Montt *p713, map p714*
Rafting Alsur, Varas 445, T/F287628, www.alsurexpeditions.com. Rafting and other watersports, as well as trips to Pumalín Park.
Sailing 2 Yacht Clubs in Chinquihue:
Club de Deportes Náuticas, Reloncaví, Camino a Chinquihue Km 7, founded by British and Americans in 1940s, more oriented towards small boat sailing, windsurfing, watersports.
Marina del Sur (MDS), T/F251958. Modern, bar and restaurant, sailing courses, notice board for

crew tripulante) notices, MDS Charters office (also Santiago T/F231 8238) specializes in cruising the Patagonian channels. Charters US$3,200-10,000 per week depending on size of boat.

Tour operators

There are many tour operators. Some companies offer 2-day excursions along the Carretera Austral to Hornopirén, US$100 including food and accommodation. Most offer 1-day excursions to Chiloé (US$30) and to Puerto Varas, Isla Loreley, Laguna Verde, and the Petrohué falls: both these tours are much cheaper than bus company kiosks inside the bus terminal, eg Bohle, US$25 to Chiloé, US$20 to the lakes. We have received good reports about:

Andina del Sud, very close to central tourist kiosk, Varas 437-445, T257797/257686. A large agency selling tours to local sights, as well as skiing trips to the Osorno volcano. Its subsidiary **Cruce de Lagos** (www.crucedelagos.cl) runs the lake trips to Bariloche (see above, and Transport, below).

Petrel Tours, Benavente 327, T/F251780, petrel@telsur.net. Recommended.

Travellers, Casilla 854, Gral Bulnes 1009, T262099, www.travellers.cl. Open Mon-Fri 0900-1330, 1500-1830, Sat 0900-1400 for booking for Navimag ferry Puerto Edén to Puerto Natales, bespoke incoming tours, car hire, English-run.

⊖ Transport

Puerto Montt *p713, map p714*
Air El Tepual Airport is 13 km northwest of town. **ETM** bus from terminal (T294292) 1½ hrs before departure, US$3; also meets incoming flights. **ETM** minibus service to/from hotels, US$6. Taxi US$12. **LAN**, **Sky** and **Aerolíneas del Sur** have several flights daily to **Santiago**, from US$150 return (cheapest one-way fares with Aerolíneas del Sur). **LAN** also flies to **Concepción, Temuco, Valdivia, Balmaceda** (for Coihaique, from US$120 return) and **Punta Arenas** (from US$170 return), most daily. **Sky** also flies to Temuco, Balmaceda and Punta Arenas daily. In Jan, Feb and Mar you may well be told that flights are booked up, but cancellations may be available from the airport. To **Chaitén**, **Aerotaxi del Sur** and **Cielo Mar** daily, US$72.
Bus Terminal (very crowded, disorganized, beware hotel touts) on sea front at Portales y Lota, has telephone, restaurants, casa de cambio (left luggage, US$2 per item for 24 hrs). To **Puerto Varas** (US$1.35), **Llanquihue, Frutillar** (US$1.50), **Puerto Octay** (US$3) and **Osorno** (US$4) minibuses every few mins, **Expreso Puerto Varas, Thaebus** and **Full Express**. To **Ensenada** and **Petrohué**, Buses JM several

daily. To **Pucón**, US$10, 6 hrs. To **Temuco** US$9, to **Valdivia**, US$6, 3½ hrs. **Concepción**, US$11. To **Santiago**, *clásico* 12 hrs, US$20, *semi-cama* US$30, *salón-cama* US$40, several companies including **Tur-Bus**, very good, and **Tas Choapa Royal Class**. To **Punta Arenas**, **Pacheco** and **Queilen Bus**, 1-3 a week, about US$55 depending on company (bus goes through Argentina via Bariloche, take US$ cash for Argentina expenses en route), 32-38 hrs. Also take plenty of food for this "nightmare" trip. Book well in advance in Jan-Feb and check if you need a multiple-entry Chilean visa. Also book any return journey before setting out. For services to **Chiloé**, see page 718.

To Argentina via Lago Todos Los Santos
The route is operated only by **Andina del Sud** see under Tour operators. Bus from company offices daily at 0800; the fare is a hefty US$165 one way. Note that the trip may be cancelled if the weather is poor; difficulty in obtaining a refunds or assistance have been reported. Try both Puerto Montt and Puerto Varas offices if you want to take the trip in sections. If you take the boat from Petrohué to Peulla, you can cross to Argentina and carry on to Bariloche (but check on the availability of public transport, bus and boat, across the border). In high season you must book ahead.

Buses to Argentina via Osorno and the Puyehue pass Daily services to Bariloche on this route via Osorno, US$17, 7 hrs, are run by **Cruz del Sur**, **Río de la Plata**, **Tas Choapa** and **Bus Norte**. Out of season, services are reduced. Buy tickets for international buses from the bus terminal. Book well in advance in Jan and Feb; ask for a seat on the right hand side for the best views.

Car hire Automotric Angelmó, Talca 79. Cheap and helpful. Automóvil Club de Chile, Ensenada 70, T254776, and at airport. Autovald, Portales 1330, T256355. Cheap rates. Full Famas, Portales 506, T258060 and at airport, T263750. Helpful, good value, has vehicles that can be taken to Argentina. See Essentials for international agencies.

Ferry To **Puerto Natales**: The **Puerto Edén** sails to Puerto Natales throughout the year on Mon at 1600, taking 4 days and 3 nights, arriving in Puerto Natales Thu between 0800 and 1200. It returns on Fri 0600, arriving Puerto Montt Mon morning. Check-in in Puerto Montt must be done between 0900 and 1200 on day of departure. In Puerto Natales check-in is before 2100 on Thu for 0600 Fri sailing; dinner is not included. Confirm times and booking 48 hrs in advance. The fare, including meals, ranges from US$355 pp in C berth (sheets are extra, take your own or a sleeping bag), to US$1,750 double in cabin with a view (high season prices, Nov-Mar; US$300 and US$1,380 respectively Apr-Oct). First class is recommended,

but hardly luxurious. 10% discount on international student cards in cabin class only. Cars are carried for US$428, motorcycles for US$70, bicycles for US$37. Payment by credit card or foreign currency is accepted in all Navimag offices. The vessel is a mixed cargo/passenger ferry which includes live animals in the cargo. On board is a book exchange, video films are shown, there are guided talks and information sessions and you can play bingo. Food is good and plentiful and includes vegetarian options at lunch and dinner. Passengers tend to take their own food and alcohol. Standards of service and comfort vary, depending on the number of passengers and weather conditions. Take seasickness tablets, or buy them on board (you'll be advised when to take them!). **Booking** Tickets can be booked through many travel agencies, **Navimag** offices throughout the country, or direct from www.navimag.com. Book well in advance for departures between mid-Dec and mid-Mar especially for the voyage south (Puerto Natales to Puerto Montt is less heavily booked). It is well worth going to the port on the day of departure if you have no ticket. Departures are frequently delayed by weather conditions – or even advanced. For details and next season's fares see Navimag's website. **Note** It is cheaper to fly and quicker to go by bus via Argentina. The route does not pass Laguna San Rafael.

To **Puerto Chacabuco**: Navimag's ferry **Magallanes** sails every Wed to Puerto Chacabuco (80 km west of Coyhaique), returning Fri (check-in Thu night). The cruise to Puerto Chacabuco lasts about 24 hrs. The high-season fares are from US$71 for bunks, US$320 in most expensive double cabin, cars US$183, motorcycles US$46, bicycles US$37. There is a small canteen; long queues if the boat is full. Food is expensive so take your own. This same vessel goes to Laguna San Rafael from Puerto Montt, on specific dates depending on the time of year. It is a 5-day, 4-night trip, with activities, all meals and a boat trip to the glacier. Accommodation ranges from US$250 to US$1,040. You can also do the return trip from Puerto Chacabuco, or Puerto Montt-Laguna San Rafael-Puerto Chacabuco (www.navimag.com, for schedules and, if running, fares and dates).

To **Chaitén**: Naviera Austral operates the *Pincoya*, twice a week, and the *Alexandrina*, also twice a week, 10½ hrs, passengers US$25, reclining seats US$33, cars US$120, US$11 for a bicycle.

To **Laguna San Rafael**: The m/n *Skorpios 1* and *2* of **Skorpios Cruises** leave Puerto Montt (vessel *2*) or Puerto Chacabuco (*1*) for a luxury cruises with various itineraries. The fare varies according to season, type of cabin and number of occupants: double cabin from US$1,100 *Skorpios 2*. Generally service is excellent, the food superb, and at the glacier, you can chip ice off the face for your whisky. After the visit to San Rafael the ships visit Quitralco Fjord where there are thermal pools and boat trips on the fjord. From Puerto Montt it's a 6-day cruise. Skorpios' latest vessel *Skorpios 3* sails from Puerto Natales to Glaciar Pío XI in the Campo de Hielo Sur, 6 days/5 nights, fares from US$1,780. **Patagonia Connection SA**, Fidel Oteíza 1921, of 1006, Providencia, Santiago, T225 6489, www.patagonia-connection.com. Operates Patagonia Express, a catamaran which runs from Puerto Chacabuco to Laguna San Rafael via Termas de Puyuhuapi, see page 730. Tours lasting 4 to 6 days start from Puerto Montt and include the catamaran service, the hotel at Termas de Puyuhuapi and the day excursion to Laguna San Rafael. High season mid Nov-19 Mar, low season end Sep-mid Nov and 20 Mar-end Apr. High season fares for a 6-day tour from US$1430-2100, all inclusive, highly recommended. **Other routes**: See under Castro and Chaitén for details of sailings between Chiloé and the mainland.

Shipping offices in Puerto Montt: Cruce de Lagos, www.crucedelagos.cl, includes departures to **Puerto Varas** and **Bariloche**. Naviera Austral, Angelmó 2187, T270400, www.navieraustral.cl. **Navimag** (Naviera Magallanes SA), Terminal Transbordadores, Angelmó 2187, T253318, www.navimag.com. Skorpios Cruises, Angelmó 1660 y Miraflores, T252619, www.skorpios.cl.

Train Twice a day to **Temuco**, US$6.50, 6 hrs 40 mins, via **Puerto Varas**, US$0.75, **Frutillar**, US$1.15 and **Osorno**, US$1.85. The rail journey starts at Victoria, 1 hr north of Temuco.

❶ Directory

Puerto Montt *p713, map p714*
Airline offices Aerotaxis del Sur, A Varas 70, T731315. **Cielo Mar**, Quillota 245 loc 1, T264010. LAN, O'Higgins y Urmeneta, T526 2000. **Sky**, T437555, or 600-600 2828 for information.
Banks Many ATMS in the city. Commission charges vary widely. **Afex**, Portales 516. **Inter**, Talca 84. For cash, TCs, no commission on Amex. **Turismo Los Lagos**, Varas 595, local 13. **La Moneda de Oro** at the bus terminal exchanges some Latin American currencies (Mon-Sat 0930-1230, 1530-1800). Obtain Argentine pesos before leaving Chile. **Note** This is the last city on the mainland with Visa ATM before Coyhaique. **Consulates Argentina**, Pedro Montt 160, p 6, T253996, cpmon@entelchile.net, quick visa service. **Germany**, Varas y Gallardo, p 3, of 306. Tue-Wed 0930-1200. **Netherlands**, Chorillos 1582, T253003. **Spain**, Rancagua 113, T252557. **Cycle repairs** Kiefer, Pedro Montt 129, T253079. 3 shops on Urmeneta, none very well stocked. **Internet** In the city centre and on Av Angelmó. **Motorcycle repairs** Miguel Schmuch, Urmeneta 985, T/F258877. **Post offices** Rancagua 126. Open 0830-1830 (Mon-Fri), 0830-1300 (Sat). **Telephones** Pedro Montt 114 and Chillán 98. Entel, Urmeneta y Pedro Montt. **Telefónica del Sur**, A Varas entre Talca y Pedro Montt.

Chiloé → *Colour map 9, grid A1.*

The island of Chiloé is 250 km long, 50 km wide and covers 9,613 sq km. Thick forests cover most of its western side. The hillsides in summer are a patchwork quilt of wheat fields and dark green plots of potatoes. The population is 116,000 and most live on the sheltered eastern side. The west coast, exposed to strong Pacific winds, is wet for most of the year. The east coast and the offshore islands are drier, though frequently cloudy. The culture of Chiloé has been strongly influenced by isolation from Spanish colonial currents, the mixture of early Spanish settlers and native indians and a dependence on the sea. Religious and secular architecture, customs and crafts, combined with delightful landscapes, all contribute to Chiloé's uniqueness.

Ins and outs

Getting there Regular ferries cross the straits of Pargua between Pargua, 55 km southwest of Puerto Montt on the mainland, and Chacao on Chiloé. Seals, birds and occasionally dolphins can be seen. **Buses**: Puerto Montt to Pargua, frequent, US$2, one hour, though most buses go through to Ancud (3½-4 hours) and Castro. Transport to the island is dominated by **Cruz del Sur**, who also own Trans Chiloé and have their own ferries. Cruz del Sur run frequent services from Puerto Montt to Ancud and Castro, six a day to Chonchi and Quellón; their fares are highest but they are faster (their buses have priority over cars on Cruz del Sur ferries). **Fares from Puerto Montt**: to Ancud, Cruz del Sur US$4.50, Trans Chiloé US$4.50, **Queilén**

Bus (independent company), US$4; to Castro, Cruz del Sur US$7.50, Trans Chiloé US$6 and Queilén Bus; to Chonchi, US$7, Quellón, US$9. There are direct bus services from Santiago, Osorno, Valdivia, Temuco and Los Angeles to Chiloé. Buses drive on to the ferry (passengers may leave the bus). **Ferries** About 24 crossings daily, 30-minute crossing, operated by several companies including Transmarchilay and Cruz del Sur; all ferries carry buses, private vehicles (cars US$16 one way, motorcycles US$6, bicycles US$3, more expensive at night) and foot passengers (US$1). ▶ *For further information, see Transport, page 725.*

Background

The original inhabitants of Chiloé were the Chonos, who were pushed south by the Huilliches invading from the north. The first Spanish sighting was by Francisco de Ulloa in 1553 and in 1567 Martín Ruiz de Gamboa took possession of the islands on behalf of Spain. The small Spanish settler population divided the indigenous population and their lands between them. The rising of the Mapuche after 1598 which drove the Spanish out of the mainland south of the Río Bíobío left the Spanish community on Chiloé (some 200 settlers in 1600) isolated. During the 17th century, for instance, it was served by a single annual ship from Lima.

The islanders were the last supporters of the Spanish Crown in South America. When Chile rebelled the last of the Spanish Governors fled to the island and, in despair, offered it to Britain. Canning, the British Foreign Secretary, turned the offer down. The island finally surrendered in 1826.

The availability of wood and the lack of metals have left their mark on the island. Some of the earliest churches were built entirely of wood, using wooden pegs instead of nails. These early churches often displayed some German influence as a result of the missionary work of Bavarian Jesuits. Two features of local architecture often thought to be traditional are in fact late 19th century in origin. The replacement of thatch with thin tiles (*tejuelas*) made from alerce (larch) wood, which are nailed to the frame and roof in several distinctive patterns, and *palafitos* or wooden houses built on stilts over the water.

The island is also famous for its traditional handicrafts, notably woollens and basketware, which can be bought in the main towns and on some of the off-shore islands, as well as in Puerto Montt.

Although the traditional mainstays of the economy, fishing and agriculture, are still important, salmon farming has become a major source of employment. Seaweed is harvested for export to Japan. Tourism provides a seasonal income for a growing number of people. Nevertheless, the relatively high birth rate and the shortage of employment in Chiloé have led to regular emigration.

Ancud and around → *Phone code: 065. Colour map 9, grid A1. Population: 30,000.*

Ancud lies on the north coast of Chiloé 34 km west of the Straits of Chacao at the mouth of a great bay, the Golfo de Quetalmahue. Founded in 1767 to guard the shipping route around Cape Horn, it was defended by two fortresses, the Fuerte San Antonio and Fuerte Ahuí on the opposite side of the bay. The port is dominated by the **Fuerte San Antonio**, built in 1770, the site of the Spanish surrender of Chiloé to Chilean troops in 1826. Close to it are the ruins of the **Polvorín del Fuerte** (a couple of cannon and a few walls). A lovely 1 km walk north of the fort leads to the secluded beach, **Arena Gruesa**, where public concerts are held in summer. 2 km east is a **mirador** offering good views of the island and across to the mainland, even to the Andes on a clear day. Near the Plaza de Armas is the **Museo Regional** ① *Libertad 370, T622413, Tue-Fri 1000-1730, Sat-Sun 1000-1400, US$1, reductions for children and students.* As well as an interesting collection on the early history of Chiloé, it has good shops and café. **Tourist office: Sernatur** ① *Libertad 665, T622800, infochiloe@sernatur.cl. Mon-Fri 0830-2000, Sat-Sun (summer only) 0900-1800.* Ask here about the Agro Turismo programme, staying with farming families.

To **Faro Corona**, the lighthouse on Punta Corona, 34 km west, along the beach, offers good views with birdlife and dolphins (2-3 buses daily, though none is the right time for seeing birds). The best time of day to see birds is early morning or late afternoon/evening. The duty officer may give a tour, recommended. To **Pumillahue** ① *27 km southwest, 2-3 buses daily*, where nearby there is a penguin colony (the birds are seen early morning or late afternoon). Hire a fishing boat to see it, US$5.50 per person for a guided tour, or US$7 (in German/English) with the **Otway Foundation** ① *T95204121, www.fundacionotway.cl*, who look after the island.

Chepu (*Population 230*) on the coast southwest of Ancud (38 km) is famed for its sea-fishing and the drowned forest (Valley of Dead Trees, devastated by a tsunami in 1960) and environment of its river. There is a wide range of birdlife and good opportunites for horseriding and boat trips here. The **Mirador de Chepu** information centre, run by Fernando and Amory Uslar, gives views of the wetlands, information about the flora, fauna and tourist options, has a café and rents kayaks (US$3 per hour). Chepu is also the northern entry for the Parque Nacional Chiloé, see page 721.

Ancud to Castro

There are two routes: direct along Route 5, the Pan-American Highway, crossing rolling hills, forest and agricultural land, or via the east coast along unpaved roads passing through small farming and fishing communities. The two main towns along the coastal route, **Quemchi** (*Population 1,700, basic accommodation, small tourist office in the plaza*) and Dalcahue, can also be reached by roads branching off Route 5.

Dalcahue (*Population 5,000*), 74 km south of Ancud, is more easily reached from Castro, 30 km further south. It is one of the main ports for boats to the offshore islands, including Quinchao and Mechuque. The wooden church on the main plaza dates from the 19th century and, like all the Chilote churches, is a UNESCO World Heritage site. The market is on Sunday, from 0700 to 1300; good quality. Tourist kiosk in season. There are various basic hotels (**G** pp) and a restaurant. Buses to Castro, hourly, 40 minutes, US$1.50. Also colectivos to Castro and Achao, US$2.

Quinchao Island

The main settlement on this island is **Achao**, a quiet, pretty fishing village with a market. Its wooden church, built in 1730 and saved by a change of wind from a fire which destroyed much of the town in 1784, is a fine example of Chilote Jesuit architecture. The original construction was without use of nails. It now contains a small museum, US$1. The tourist office at Serrano y Progreso is open between December and March only. There are various hotels (**D-E** pp) and restaurants, and don't miss the oysters sold on the beach.

Castro → *Phone code: 065. Colour map 9, grid A1. Population: 29,000.*
The capital of Chiloé lies on a fjord on the east coast, 88 km south of Ancud. Founded in 1567, the centre is situated on a promontory, from which there is a steep drop to the port. On the Plaza de Armas is the large **Cathedral**, strikingly decorated in lilac and orange, with a splendid wood panelled interior, built by the Italian architect, Eduardo Provosoli in 1906. South of the Plaza on the waterfront is the **Feria**, or Mercado Municipal de Artesanía, where excellent local woollen articles (hats, sweaters, gloves) can be found (also imported goods). Palafitos can be seen on the northern side of town and by the bridge over the Río Gamboa. There are good views of the city from **Mirador La Virgen** on Millantuy hill above the cemetery. **Museo Regional** ① *on Esmeralda, summer Mon-Sat 0930-2000, Sun 1030-1300; winter Mon-Sat 0930-1300, 1500-1830, Sun 1030-1300*, contains history, folklore, handicrafts and mythology of Chiloé and photos of the 1960 earthquake. **Museo de Arte Moderno** ① *near the Río Gamboa, in the Parque Municipal, over 3 km northwest of the centre, T635454, www.mamchiloe.cl, 1000-1900*, is reached by following Calle Galvarino Riveros up the hill west of town, take bus marked 'Al Parque'. There are good views from the hill. **Tourist office**: Information kiosk run by hotels and agencies on the Plaza de Armas opposite Cathedral. It has a list of accommodation and prices. **CONAF**, Gamboa 424, T532501.

Chonchi → *Phone code: 065. Colour map 9, grid A1. Population: 4,500.*
Chonchi is a picturesque fishing village 25 km south of Castro. From the plaza Calle Centenario, with several attractive but sadly neglected wooden mansions, drops steeply to the harbour. Fishing boats bring in the early morning catch which is carried straight into the nearby market. The wooden church, on the plaza, was built in 1754, remodelled in neoclassical style in 1859 and 1897 (key from handicraft shop next door). Its steeple fell down in a storm in early 2002, but has been rebuilt. There is another 18th century church at Vilopulli, 5 km north. A tourist information kiosk is open in the main plaza in summer. Ask here about agrotourism options between Chonchi and Queilén, a fishing village on a peninsula, 46 km southeast. A good excursion is to the **Isla Lemuy** ① *free ferry 4 km south every 30 mins*; lovely walking, or hitching or buses to the villages.

Cucao

From Chonchi a road leads west to Cucao, 40 km, one of two settlements on the west coast of Chiloé. At Km 12 is **Huillinco** (road paved), a charming village on Lago Huillinco. Near Cucao there is an immense 15 km beach with thundering Pacific surf and dangerous undercurrents. It's about 30 minutes' walk: cross the river then continue to the park entrance then walk 10 minutes more.

Parque Nacional Chiloé

The park ① *US$3*, is divided into three sections. Much of its 43,057 ha is covered by evergreen forest. The northern sector, covering 7,800 ha, is reached by a path which runs south from **Chepu** (see page 720). The second section is a small island, **Metalqui**, off the coast of the north sector. The southern sector, 35,207 ha, is entered 1 km north of Cucao, where there is an administration centre (T09-99329193/ T532501, limited information), small museum and guest

Chiloé

Puerto Chacabuco ▼

bungalow for use by visiting scientists (applications to CONAF via your embassy). There is no access to the park by car, but there are decent camping facilities. Maps of the park are available (**Note** Refugios are inaccurately located.)

A path runs 3 km north from the administration centre to **Laguna Huelde** (many camp sites) and then north a further 12 km to Cole Cole refugio (US$10 pp, camping US$2, good site) offering great views, best done on horseback (return journey to/from Cucao nine hours by horse, five hours one way on foot). The next refugio is at **Anay** (US$10 pp), 5 km further north on the Río Anay. There are several other walks but signposting is limited. Many houses in Cucao rent horses at US$3.50 per hour, US$28 per day (check horses and equipment carefully). It usually costs about US$45 a day for the round trip on horseback to Rio Anay. **Miguelangelo Allende** has been recommended. If you hire a guide you pay for his horse too. Horseflies are bad in summer (wear light coloured clothing).

Quellón → *Phone code: 065. Colour map 9, grid A1. Population: 13,500. 92 km south of Castro.*
There are pleasant beaches nearby at Quellón Viejo (with an old wooden church), Punta de Lapa and Yaldad. The launch Puerto Bonito sails three times daily in summer from the pier, US$16 to tour the bay passing Punta de Lapa, Isla Laitec and Quellón Viejo. A trip can also be made to Chaiguao, 11 km east, where there is a small Sunday morning market. Horses can be hired US$3.50 per hour. Also kayaks with a guide, US$4 per hour. Camping US$4. **Museo de Nuestros Pasados** ① *Ladrilleros 255*, includes reconstructions of a traditional Chilote house and mill. **Tourist office**: kiosk on the Plaza de Armas, mid-December to mid-March. Ask about hospedajes not listed in their information leaflet. Amazing views of the mainland on a clear day.

From Quellón you can go to Chiloe's newest protected area, **Parque Tantauco**, still in its formative stages. It covers 120,000 ha of woods and wetlands at the southernmost part of the Island, with many endangered endemic species of mammal. It's a private park, with two camping areas and 12 walking trails. Access is by road or by a 5-hour boat trip from Quellón. Information from **Oficina Parque Tantauco** ① *Av La Paz 068, Quellón, T681064/680066*, or **Fundación Futuro** ① *Av Apoquindo 3000, p 19, Las Condes, Santiago, www.fundacionfuturo.cl.*

Sleeping

Ancud *p719*

AL-A **Hostería Ancud**, San Antonio 30, T622340, resancud@sumet.cl. Nice views of the bay, attractive, very comfortable, helpful, restaurant, tours offered, English spoken.
B-C **Hostería Ahui**, Costanera 906, T622415, hosteriaahui@terra.com. With breakfast, full of charm, good views.
B-C **Montserrat**, Baquedano 417, T/F622957, hotelmontserrat@hotmail.com. With breakfast, good views, modern, attractive.
C-D **Mundo Nuevo**, Costanera 748, T628383, www.newworld.cl. G pp in dorms. With breakfast, comfortable, one room has a boat-bed, great views over the bay, lots of info, heating, good showers, kitchen facilities, car and bicycle hire, English and German spoken. Highly recommended.
D **Hosp San José**, Las Américas 661, T622467, hostalsanjose6@hotmail.com. F singles. With breakfast, good family atmosphere, nice views from lounge, hot water, some rooms with bath, use of kitchen, internet, tours offered, bicycle hire. Recommended.
D **Hostal Lluhay**, Cochrane 458, T622656, hostallluhay@hotmail.com. Meals served. Attentive, nice lounge. Recommended.

D **Hosp Alto Bellavista**, Bellavista 449, T622384. Very helpful, good breakfast, some rooms with bath, G pp shared rooms.
D **Hosp Sra Marta**, Lautaro 988, T623748, martaalvarado@latinmail.com. F singles. With breakfast, TV, kitchen facilities, good beds. Recommended.
D **Hostal Vista al Mar**, Costanera 918, T622617, www.vistaalmar.cl. G pp in dorms, also self catering apartments C. Views over the bay, heating, internet, laundry, dinner served in barn in summer.
E **Hosp Ancud**, Los Carrera 821, T622296, macriser@latinmail.com. G singles. Nice house, welcoming, kitchen facilities.
E **Hosp Austral**, A Pinto 1318, T624847, hospedajeaustral@hotmail.com. Cosy wooden house, near bus station, with breakfast, shared bath, family of Mirta Ruiz, very welcoming, dinner extra, kitchen facilities (US$1). Frequently recommended.
E **Hosp O'Higgins 6**, O'Higgins 06, T622266. With breakfast, spacious, interesting objets d'art, near sea, nice views. Recommended
E **Hosp Su Casa**, Los Alerces 841, T623382. G singles. Excellent breakfast, hot shower, TV room, kitchen and laundry facilities.

G pp **Hosp Don Luis**, Av Almte Latorre 1225, T620325. With basic breakfast, private and shared rooms, good shared hot showers, friendly family, lots of information, use of kitchen.
G pp **San Bernardo**, Errázuriz 395, T622657. Good dormitory accommodation.

In summer the school on Calle Chacabuco is used as an albergue.

Camping Arena Gruesa, Av Costanera Norte 290, T623428, arenagruesa@yahoo.com. **Playa Gaviotas**, 5 km north, T09-9653 8096 (mob), also has *cabañas*. **Playa Larga Huicha**, 9 km north, **E** per site, bath, hot water, electricity.

Castro *p720*

Hotels on San Martín are convenient for the bus terminals. Several lodgings on Los Carrera 500-700 blocks, in our **E** pp range.
A Unicornio Azul, Pedro Montt 228, T632359, www.chiloeweb.com/pweb/unicornioazul. Good views over bay, comfortable, restaurant.
A-B Alerce Nativo, O'Higgins 808, T632267, hotelalerce@surnet.cl. Heating, helpful, breakfast, also has *cabañas* (4 km south of Castro) and restaurant.
A-B Hostería de Castro, Chacabuco 202, T632301, www.hosteriadecastro.cl. With breakfast, attractive building, wonderful views. Recommended.
A-B Cabañas Trayen, 5 km south of Castro, T633633, www.trayenchiloe.cl. Cheaper off season, lovely views, cabins for 4 to 6.
C Casa Blanca, Los Carrera 308, T632706, nelysald@surnet.cl. With breakfast, cheaper rooms with shared bath, modern, warm, also *cabañas*, sleep 6.
C Casita Española, Los Carrera 359, T635186. Heating, TV, parking, good if a little overpriced.
D Hosp Sotomayor, Sotomayor 452, T632464. **G** singles. With breakfast, TV, quiet, small beds.
D-E Hosp América, Chacabuco 215, T634364. **G** singles. With breakfast, shared bath, very good food, cable TV.
D-E Hosp Chiloé, San Martín 739. **G** singles. With breakfast. Recommended.
D-E Hosp El Molo, Barros Arana 140, T635026, elmolochiloe@gmail.com. Comfortable, safe, welcoming, internet, cooking facilities. Recommended.
D-E Hosp Jessie Toro, Las Delicias 287, off Esmeralda. **G** singles with good breakfast, helpful, spacious, good bathrooms, also *cabañas*. Recommended.
D-E Res Capullito, San Martín 709. **G** singles, a quiet, clean and friendly place to stay.

E Lidia Low, San Martín 890. Good breakfast, warm showers, use of kitchen, family home.
D Hosp El Mirador, Barros Arana 127, T633795, maboly@yahoo.com. With breakfast, some rooms with bath, **G** singles, cosy, relaxing, kitchen, broadband internet US$1.15. Warmly recommended.
Camping Camping Pudú, Ruta 5, 10 km north of Castro, T632476, cabins, showers with hot water, sites with light, water, kid's games. Several sites on road to Chonchi, including **Llicaldad**, Esmeralda 269, T635080, also has cabañas.

Chonchi *p720*

B Posada El Antiguo Chalet, Irrázavel s/n, T671221. **C** in winter, charming, beautiful location, very good.
C-D Cabañas Amankay, Centenario 421, T671367. Homely, kitchen facilities. Recommended.
D-E Esmeralda By The Sea, on waterfront 100 m south of market, T/F671328, esmeraldachonchi@hotmail.com. **G** pp in dorms. With breakfast, remodelled in 2006, shared bath, dinner available (cheap, good salmon), attractive, welcoming, English spoken, use of internet US$0.60, bunkhouse for 8, cooking facilities, book exchange, rents bicycles, boat trips offered, Landcruiser tours. Recommended.
E Hosp Mirador, Alvarez 198. With breakfast, **F-G** singles, with breakfast, good value. Recommended.
E Huildin, Centenario 102, T671388. Without bath, old fashioned, good beds, also cabañas **A**, garden with superb views, parking.
Camping Los Manzanos, Aguirre Cerda y Juan Guillermo, T671263. **E** per site.

Cucao *p721*

F pp **Chela**, close to beach and within walking distance of park. Helpful, use of kitchen, good breakfast extra, very nice. Recommended.
F pp **Posada Cucao**, T633040/09-9896 9855. With breakfast, meals available, hot water, pleasant.
F pp **Provisiones Pacifico**, with full board or demi-pension, friendly, good, home-made bread, candles provided, no hot water.
F pp **Parador Darwin**, after the bridge, Cucao sector, T633040. Breakfast, vegetarian and other meals, real coffee, fresh bread for sale. Camping also available. Recommended.
Camping Several campsites (check prices first), including **Lago Mar**, 2 km east of Cucao, T635552, US$15 per site.

● *For an explanation of the sleeping and eating price codes used in this guide, see page 58.*
● *Other relevant information is found in Essentials pages 602-604.*

Huillinco

F pp **Residencia**, good food, or stay at the post office

Quellón *p722*

C **Melimoyu**, P Montt 369, T681250. Good beds, parking.
D **El Chico Leo**, P Montt 325, T681567, elchicoleo@telsur.cl. Cheaper with shared bath, also has restaurant.
Other cheaper places in town.

O Eating

Ancud *p719*

Excellent cheap seafood restaurants in the market area.
†† **El Cangrejo**, Dieciocho 155. Seafood. Highly recommended.
†† **Hamburguería**, Av Prat. Much better than name suggests, good seafood.
†† **La Pincoya**, Prat 61, on waterfront. Good seafood, service and views.
†† † **Mar Pacífico**, Pudeto 346. Typical Chilote fare.
†† † **Sacho**, in the market. Renowned for its *curantos*, not fancy but huge portions and very reasonable.
† **El Pingüinito**, in an alley behind the market. Very cheap, decent lunches.

Cafés

La Candela, Pudeto y Libertad. Cosy, nice range of snacks, drinks and light meals.

Castro *p720*

Breakfast before 0900 is difficult to find. By the market many places offer set lunch, usually fish dishes. In the market, try *milcaos*, fried potato cakes with meat stuffing. Also *licor de oro*, like Galliano.
†† **Donde Eladio**, Lillo 97. Meat and seafood specialities.
†† **Don Octavio**, Pedro Montt 261. Good food and nice views over bay, specializes in seafood.
†† **La Playa**, Lillo 93. Good seafood.
† **Don Camilo**, Ramírez 566. Average food, also has pleasant accommodation.
† **Palafito** restaurants near the Feria Artesanía on the waterfront offer good food and good value, including **Rapa Nui**, **Brisas del Mar** and **La Amistad**.
† **Sacho**, Thompson 213. Good sea views, clean.

Cafés

Años Luz, San Martín on corner of Plaza. Good café/bar/restaurant, live music at weekends, great cocktails.

La Brújula del Cuerpo, Plaza de Armas. Fast food, good coffee, snacks.
Stop Inn Café, Martín Ruiz shopping centre, Gamboa. Good coffee.

Chonchi *p720*

†† **La Parada**, Centenario 133. Good selection of wines, very friendly but erratic opening hours. Recommended.
† **El Alerce**, Aguirre Cerda 106. Good seafood, excellent value.
† **El Trébol**, Irrazával 187. Good food and great harbour views.

Quellón *p722*

†† **Los Suizos**, Ladrilleros 399. Swiss cuisine, good, slow service, internet.
†† **Tierra del Fuego**, P Montt 445, T682079. For fish, seafood and other local dishes. In hotel of same name.
† **El Coral**, 22 de Mayo 215, T681472. Good, reasonably priced, superb views.

O Shopping

Castro *p720*

Bookshops Annay Libros, Serrano 357, El Tren, Thompson 229 and **Libros Chiloé**, Blanco Encalada 204. All for books on Chiloé. CDs of typical Chilote music are widely available.
Handicrafts Mercado Artesanal, Lillo on the wharf, good value woollens at reasonable prices.
Market The municipal market is on Yumbel, off Ulloa, uphill northwest of town: fish and vegetables.
Supermarket Beckna, O'Higgins y Aldea. Bakes good bread.

Chonchi *p720*

Handicrafts From Opdech (Oficina Promotora del Desarrollo Chilote), on the waterfront, and from the parroquia, next to the church (open Oct-Mar only).

▲ Activities and tours

Ancud *p719*

Aki Turismo, bus terminal, p 2, of 12, T545253, www.akiturismochiloe.cl. Good value trips to the penguin colony.
Austral Adventures, Cochrane 432, T/F625977, www.austral-adventures.com. Bespoke small group tours on land and sea. Good English speaking guides, lots of interesting choices. Ask director Britt Lewis about the return of blue whales to Chiloé's waters.
Paralelo 42, Latorre 558, T622458. Tours to Río Chepu area, including 2-day kayak trips, guide Carlos Oyarzún.

Patagón Chiloé, Bellavista 491, T622128, patagonchiloe@hotmail.com. Tours to the penguin colony and Chepu.

Castro *p720*
Tours to Parque Nacional Chiloé US$33, to Isla Mechuque (east of Dalcahue) US$45.
Turismo Pehuén, Blanco Encalada 299, T635254, pehuentr@entelchile.net. LAN agency, horse riding, trips to national park, penguin colony and islands.
Sergio Márquez, local guide, Felipe Moniel 565, T632617, very knowledgeable, has transport.
Turismo Isla Grande, Thompson 241, Navimag and Transmarchilay agents.
Turismo Quellén, Gamboa 502, T632776. Good tours to Chonchi and Chiloé National Park. Recommended.

⊖ Transport

Ancud *p719*
Bus Terminal on the east outskirts at Av Prat y Marcos Vera, reached by bus 1, or Pudeto colectivos. To **Castro**, US$3, frequent (see below), 1½ hrs. To **Puerto Montt**, frequent services by Cruz del Sur, **Trans Chiloé** and Queilén Bus, US$4.50. To **Quemchi** via the coast, 2 hrs, US$2.50.

Quinchao *p720*
Ferry From **Dalcahue**, frequent, free for pedestrians and cyclists. Arriagada **buses** from **Ancud**, 5 a day. Frequent to **Castro**, US$2, Achao Express.

Castro *p720*
Bus Frequent services to **Chonchi**, choose between buses **Cruz del Sur**, **Queilén Bus** and others, minibuses and colectivos (from Esmeralda y Chacabuco). **Arroyo** and **Ocean Bus** both run to **Cucao**, 6 a day in season, first 0930, last back 1600 1½ hrs, US$3 (1200 and 1600 off season, avoid Fri when school children are going home – much slower, lots of stops). To **Dalcahue** frequent services by **Gallardo** and **Arriagada**, also colectivos from San Martín 815. To **Achao** via Dalcahue and Curaco de Vélez, Arriagada, several daily, last return from Achao 1730, US$3. To **Puqueldón** on the island of Lemuy, Gallardo, 4 daily Mon-Sat, US$2. To **Quemchi**, daily with Queilén Bus, 1½ hrs, US$3. To **Quellón**, Regional Sur and Trans Chiloé, frequent. To **Queilén**, Queilén Bus and others, 6 a day, US$3.

Long distance buses leave from 2 terminals: **Cruz del Sur**, T632389, **Trans Chiloé** and Arriagada from Cruz del Sur terminal on San Martín 500 block behind the cathedral. Other services leave from the Municipal Terminal, San Martín, 600

block (2 blocks further north). Frequent services to **Ancud** and **Puerto Montt** by Cruz del Sur, Trans Chiloé and Queilén Bus. Cruz del Sur also run to **Osorno**, **Valdivia**, **Temuco**, **Concepción** and **Santiago**. Bus Norte to Ancud, Puerto Montt, Osorno and Santiago daily. To **Punta Arenas**, Queilén Bus, Mon, 36 hrs, US$70.
Ferry Naviera Austral's Pincoya sails Castro-**Chaitén** on Wed, Sat, Sun, US$30, US$23 without a seat.

Chonchi *p720*
Buses and **taxis** to **Castro**, frequent, US$1.15, from main plaza. Services to **Quellón** (US$1.90), Cucao (US$2.50) and **Queilén** from Castro and Puerto Montt also call here.

Cucao *p721*
Bus From Castro see above; in season as many as 4 buses a day, last departure 1600, reduced service off-season; hitching is very difficult. Taxi from Chonchi US$4.50.

Quellón *p722*
Bus To **Castro**, 2 hrs, frequent, Cruz del Sur, US$4; also to **Ancud** and **Puerto Montt**, US$8.
Ferry Naviera Austral's *Pincoya* sails Quellón-Chaitén on Fri and Alexandrina on Wed, 7 hrs, US$28, US$20 without seat. Off season services are irregular, perhaps one ferry per week.

❶ Directory

Ancud *p719*
Banks ATMs at BCI, off plaza. **Post offices** On corner of Plaza de Armas at Pudeto y Blanco Encalada. **Telephones** Plaza de Armas. Mon-Sat 0700-2200; ENTEL, Pudeto 219, with internet; Los Carrera 823.

Castro *p720*
Banks Many of the banks in the centre have ATMs for credit and bank cards (pesos only). Banco de Chile with ATM at Plaza de Armas, accepts TCs (at a poor rate). BCI, Plaza de Armas, MasterCard and Visa ATM. Better rates from **Julio Barrientos**, Chacabuco 286, cash and TCs. **Bicycle hire** San Martín 581. **Post offices** On west side of Plaza de Armas. **Telephones** Latorre 289. **Entel**: O'Higgins entre Gamboa y Sotomayor.

Quellón *p722*
Banks Banco del Estado, commission charged on TCs, no credit cards, no commission on US$ cash. **Shipping offices** Naviera Austral, (www.navieraustral.cl) and Navimag (www.navi mag.cl), Pedro Montt 457, Quellón, T682207.

Carretera Austral

A third of Chile lies to the south of Puerto Montt, but until recently its inaccessible land and rainy climate meant that it was only sparsely populated and unvisited by tourism. The Carretera Austral, or Southern Highway, has now been extended south from Puerto Montt to Villa O'Higgins, giving access to the spectacular virgin landscapes of this wet and wild region, with its mountains, fjords and islands, hitherto isolated communities, and picturesque ports. Ships were the only means of access and remain important for exporting the timber grown here, and for bringing visitors; see page 714. There is great hiking at Cerro Castillo, whitewater rafting at Futaleufú, and thermal springs at Chaitén and Puyuhuapi, as well as the unspoilt national parks of Hornopirén, Queulat and Parque Pumalín.

Puyuhuapi is the perfect place to break the journey, but the main town is Coyhaique, and from nearby Chacabuco, boats leave for the magnificent glacier of Parque Nacional Laguna San Rafael. Coyhaique is the only settlement of any size on the Carretera Austral. It's a good starting point for exploring the Carretera and for trekking and fishing expeditions, for instance on the Río Baker, an angler's paradise further south. Coyhaique is also a good place for booking San Rafael Glacier trips. The Carretera extends to Villa O'Higgins, beyond which the southern icefields and their glaciers bring the roadway to a halt.

The southernmost section of the Carretera Austral, 443 km, ends at Villa O'Higgins and is the wildest and most dramatic, with beautiful unspoilt landscapes around Lago General Carrera. The fairy tale peaks of Cerro Castillo offer challenging trekking, and there's world class fishing in the turquoise waters of Río Baker. A road runs off to Puerto Ibáñez for lake crossings to Chile Chico, a convenient border crossing to Argentina.

Ins and outs

Getting there and around This road can be divided into three major sections: **Puerto Montt-Chaitén**, **Chaitén-Coyhaique**, and **Coyhaique-Villa O'Higgins**. The road is paved only for about 150 km north and south of Coyhaique, from Puerto Chacabuco and Mañihuales to Villa Cerro Castillo. Currently, the rest is 'ripio' (loose stones) and many sections are extremely rough and difficult after rain. Cyclists can't expect to make fast progress and motorists need to carry sufficient fuel and spares, especially if intending to detour from the highway itself, and protect windscreens and headlamps from stones. Unleaded fuel is available all the way to Villa O'Higgins. There is now a road between Puerto El Vagabundo and Caleta Tortel, and the Carretera Austral is connected by a free ferry between Puerto Yungay and Río Bravo, where it continues to Villa O'Higgins. So far, there is little infrastructure for transport or accommodation among the tiny rural hamlets, so allow plenty of time for bus connections, and bring cash, as there are few banking facilities along the whole route. Having your own transport here is definitely preferable. Camping will give you more freedom for accommodation, and there are many beautiful sites, though note that food supplies are limited and tend to be expensive. ▸▸ *For further information, see Transport, pages 728, 736 and 741.*

Best time to visit The landscape throughout the region is lushly green because there is no real dry season. On the offshore islands and the western side of the Andes annual rainfall is over 2,000 mm, though inland on the steppe the climate is drier and colder. Westerly winds are strong, especially in summer, but there's plenty of sunshine too, especially around Lago General Carrera (described in the Southern Section), which has a warm microclimate. January and February are probably the best months for a trip to this region.

Information Portal for the Aisén region (in Spanish): www.patagoniachile.cl.

Puerto Montt to Chaitén

This section of the Carretera Austral, 242 km, includes two, sometimes three ferry crossings. Before setting out, it is imperative to check when the ferries are running and, if driving, make a reservation: do this in Puerto Montt (not Santiago), at the Naviera Austral office, Angelmó 2187, T065-270400, www.navieraustral.cl (Spanish only). The alternative to this section is by ferry (or catamaran) from Puerto Montt or Quellón to Chaitén.

The road (Ruta 7) heads east out of Puerto Montt, through Pelluco and after an initial rough stretch follows the shore of the beautiful Seno Reloncaví. It passes the southern entrance of the **Parque Nacional Alerce Andino** ① *US$8, no camping within park boundaries*, which contains one of the best surviving areas of alerce trees, some over 1,000 years old (the oldest is estimated at 4,200 years old). Wildlife includes pudú, pumas, vizcachas, condors and black woodpeckers. There are two entrances: 2½ km from Correntoso (35 km east of Puerto Montt) at the northern end of the park (with ranger station and campsite) and 7 km east of Lenca (40 km south of Puerto Montt) at the southern end. There are three other ranger posts, at Río Chaicas, Lago Chapo and Sargazo. Ranger posts have little information; map is available from CONAF in Puerto Montt.

At 46 km from Puerto Montt (allow one hour), is the first ferry at **La Arena**, across the Reloncaví Estuary to **Puelche**. See Transport, page 741, for Ferry details. **Río Negro** is now called **Hornopirén** after the volcano above it. From here you catch the second ferry, to Caleta Gonzalo, one of the centres for the Parque Pumalín (see below). At the mouth of the fjord is the small Isla Llancahué, with a hotel and thermal springs, good for hiking in the forests amid beautiful scenery. Boat to the island US$50 one-way shared between passengers, T6424857; look out for dolphins and fur seals en route.

Parque Pumalín

Caleta Gonzalo is the entry point for Parque Pumalín for visitors from the north (admission free). On the quay is a smart café serving excellent (and pricey) organic food, a visitor centre selling tasteful handicrafts, and cabañas for rent, tiny and perfectly designed, with lake views. The park, created by the US billionaire Douglas Tompkins, is a private reserve of 320,000 ha in two sections which has been given Nature Sanctuary status. Covering large areas of the western Andes, with virgin temperate rainforest, the park is spectacularly beautiful, and is seen by many as one of the most important conservation projects in the world. You can visit the model farm, a native tree nursery and an apiculture project, producing delicious honey, sold in the visitor centre. There are several self guided trails, showing examples of ancient alerce trees, rainforest and waterfalls (check which paths shown on maps are actually open). **Information centres** ① *Buin 356, Puerto Montt, T065-250079; Fiordo Reñihué, Caleta Gonzalo, T1712-196-4151 (not always open); O'Higgins 62, Chaitén, T065-731341. In USA T415-229-9339, www.parquepumalin.cl / www.pumalinpark.org (Spanish and English).*

South of Caleta Gonzalo the Carretera Austral winds through the park's beautiful unspoilt scenery, and there is a steep climb on the ripio road to two lakes, Lago Río Blanco and Lago Río Negro, with panoramic views. At Caleta Santa Bárbara, 12 km from Chaitén, there's a wonderful sweeping black sand beach fringed with woodland and with views of the mighty Morro Vilcum, good for swimming (cold!) and wild camping.

Chaitén → *Phone code: 065. Colour map 9, grid A1. Population: 3,258.*

The capital of Palena province, Chaitén is rather a bland town and a port for ferries to Puerto Montt and Quellón. Its charms lie in the splendour of its setting, against thickly forested vertical mountains, the dramatic peak of volcano Michimahuida, and the broad open bay of Corcovado. There's great hiking nearby and it's a base for exploring Parque Pumalín. It is becoming a popular centre for adventure tourism. Most facilities are along the coast road, Av Corcovado, with good views of the bay. There is excellent fishing nearby, especially to the south in the Ríos Yelcho and Futaleufú and in Lagos Espolón and Yelcho (see below). Fishing licences are sold at the Municipalidad on the plaza. Visits are possible to the offshore sealion colony at Isla Puduguapi. The rustic, open-air thermal pools, **Termas El Amarillo** ① *dawn to 2100, US$3 pp, highly recommended, several cabañas nearby,* in the middle of the beautiful forest, are 30 km south. **Tourist office** ① *Av B O'Higgins 284, Plaza de Armas, T731082, infopalena@ sernatur.cl.* Better information at Chaitur, see Activities and tours, page 728.

● Sleeping

Puerto Montt to Chaitén p727
Hornopirén
Electricity 1900-0100.

A Hotel Termas de Llancahué, Isla Llancahué. To get there, make arrangements by phoning T09-9642 4857. The hotel will send an open boat for you; the 1-hr crossing affords views of dolphins and fur seals. Price is for full board (excellent food), hot spring at the hotel.

C-D Hostería Catalina, Ingenieros Militares s/n, T217359, www.hosteriacatalina.cl. Comfortable rooms with breakfast and bath, a good place to stay.

D Hornopirén, Carrera Pinto 388, T217256. Rooms with shared bath, also *cabañas* and restaurant at the water's edge. Recommended.

E Holiday Country, O'Higgins 666, T217220. Hot shower, restaurant, also *cabañas*.

Parque Pumalín p727
Camping Sites, of which there are several, are exemplary, run on strict conservation lines, with well-designed picnic shelters and good washing facilities (but no hot water): US$8 per tent. Cabañas (**AL**), sleep up to 4; meals extra.

Chaitén p727
B Brisas del Mar, Av Corcovado 278, T731284, cababrisas@telsur.cl. Pleasant if a little cramped *cabañas* for 4 to 6 facing sea, but no view, Wi-Fi, best restaurant in town.

B Puma Verde, O'Higgins 54, T731184, reservasalsur@surnet.cl. Comfortable upscale hostel affiliated with Parque Pumalín, furnished with local products, English spoken.

C Mi Casa, Av Norte 206, up on hill at end of Diego Portales, T731285, hmicasa@telsur.cl. Small pleasant rooms, sauna, gym, and fine views from the restaurant which serves good fish and good value set meals. Recommended.

D Casa Hexagon, Blanco 36, T0-8286 2950. **F** singles. Extraordinary hexagonal building with tree trunk at its centre, very comfortable hostel, foam mattresses on beds, excellent kitchen facilities, owned – and built – by German origami master, ex-concert guitarist and fly-fishing expert. Highly recommended.

D-E Hosp Marisol, Pedro Aguirre Cerda 66, T731188, rumer@surnet.cl. **G** singles. With breakfast, family home, kitchen facilities, internet, cable TV, nice cabin in the garden (**B-C** for 5). Recommended.

D-E Hostería Llanos, Av Corcovdo 378, T731332. Small place facing the sea with kind owners and lovely rooms (no bath), basic breakfast, dinner in restaurant (US$5 for 2 courses). Recommended. Good mechanic next door.

E Casa Rita, Almte Riveros y A Prat, T731502. **G** singles. Warm, Rita runs a great place with comfy beds in whitewashed rooms, good atmosphere, use of kitchen, heating, no smoking. The best budget option, highly recommended.

E Hosp Anita, Pedro de Valdivia 129, T731413. **G** singles. With breakfast, typical family home with low ceilings, camping possible.

E pp Hosp Don Carlos, Almte Riveros 55. Shared hot shower, busy, lunch and dinner available.

Camping Los Arrayanes, Carretara Austral, 4 km north. Fabulous setting, right on the sea with great views of Volcán Corcovado, hot showers, and fire places.

● Eating

Chaitén p727
¶¶ El Refugio, Corcovado y Ercilla. Seafood, rustic furniture, better than some.

¶ Cocinerías Costumbristas, Portales 300 block. Several tiny restaurants serving local fare, large portions. Recommended.

¶ El Quijote, O'Higgins 42. More modest, bar snacks, also recommended.

¶ Flamengo, Corcovado 218. Family run, plain but good fish dishes, also serves meat. Others on Corcovado, eg **Marita Estrella**, good value, simple.

▲ Activities and tours

Chaitén p727
Chaitur, O'Higgins 67, T731429, another branch at Diego Portales 350, nchaitur@hotmail.com. This should be your first port of call in Chaitén. Run by Nicholas, a charming and helpful North American with information and booking for all buses and boats, and internet access. Excellent, personalized excursions to places far and near: Parque Pumalín (US$18.50 1100-1900), hiking at Ventisqueo Yelcho (astounding white glacier), Santa Bárbara beach, boat excursions, fishing, horses, trekking, mountain biking, very reasonable prices.

● Transport

Puerto Montt to Chaitén p727
Parque Nacional Alerce Andino
Bus To the north entrance: take a **Fierro** or **Río Pato** bus to **Correntoso** (or Lago Chapo bus which passes through Correntoso), several daily except Sun, then walk. To the south entrance: take any **Fierro** bus to **Chaicas, La Arena, Contau** and **Hornopirén**, US$1.50, getting off at Lenca sawmill, then walk (signposted).

La Arena to Puelche

Ferry Across the Reloncaví Estuary, 30 mins, every 1½ hrs, US$15 for a car, US$8 for motorcycle, US$4 for bicycle, US$1 for foot passengers, 0715-2000 daily. Arrive at least 30 mins early to guarantee a place; buses have priority. Roll-on roll-off type operating all year. See www.tmc.cl for more details.

Hornopirén

Bus Fierro (T253022) and Jordán (T254938) run Mon-Sat 0800 and 1330 (Sun 1500, 1730) from **Puerto Montt**, US$5.35; return 0530, 1330 Mon-Sat, 1245, 1500 Sun.

Ferry Hornopirén to **Caleta Gonzalo**, Naviera Austral, daily 1500, 5 hrs (may be much longer if the ferry cannot dock in rough weather). Going north the ferry leaves Caleta Gonzalo at 0900, daily. Fare for cars US$111 (capacity 21), motorbikes US$22, passengers US$18 (capacity 80), bicycles, US$11.50. Ferry operates Jan-Feb only and can be very busy; there can be a 2-day wait for vehicles to get on the ferry. See www.navieraustral.cl for more details.

Chaitén *p727*

Air Flights to **Puerto Montt** with Aerotaxi del Sur and Cielo Mar, daily, 35 mins, US$72.

Bus Several companies operate minibuses along the Carretera Austral to Coyhaique from next to Chaitur, O'Higgins 67: in Jan-Feb up to 6 a week, in winter 2 a week with overnight stop in La Junta or Puyuhuapi. Even in summer, prepare to wait extra days. All details from Chaitur, T731429. To

La Junta US$10, 4 hrs; to **Puyuhuapi** US$16.75, 5½ hrs; to **Coyhaique** US$30, 12 hrs. Buses travel full, so are unable to pick up passengers en route. To **Futaleufú**, US$12, 4-5 hrs, **Altamirano**, daily except Sun, **Chaitur**, daily 1530 except Sun; change here for buses to the Argentine border. To **Caleta Gonzalo**, Chaitur (see Activities and tours, above) daily Jan-Feb 0700 to connect with boats. Hitching the whole route is slow, even in summer.

Ferry Port about 1 km north of town.

To **Puerto Montt**, Naviera Austral, *Pincoya* Sun and Mon, *Alexandrina* Thu and Fri to **Puerto Montt**, and Thu (*Pincoya*) and Sat (*Alexandrina*) to **Quellón** and Wed, Fri, Sun to Castro (Chiloé). Catamaranes del Sur also run catamarans to Castro and Puerto Montt, about twice a week each in high season, but confirm if running in advance. **Navimag** office, Carrera Pinto 188, T731570, www.navimag.com. **Naviera Austral**, Av Corcovado 266, T731272. **Catamaranes del Sur**, Riveros y Cerda, T731199, www.catamaranesdelsur.cl. **Note** All boat services vary season to season: check with the local office. Reduced service in winter.

❶ Directory

Chaitén

Banks Banco del Estado, O'Higgins y Libertad, on plaza, changes dollars and Tcs in working hours. ATM for Maestro, Mastercard and Cirrus, not Visa. There is no other ATM between here and Coyhaique.

Chaitén to Coyhaique

This section of the Carretera Austral, runs 422 km though breathtaking and varied scenery, passing tiny villages, most notably the idyllic Puyuhuapi, where there are thermal pools, and good trekking in Parque Nacional Queulat. A road branches off east to the Argentine border, the picturesque Futaleufú, with excellent rafting, and west to Puerto Cisnes.

Puerto Cárdenas, 46 km south of Chaitén, is on the northern tip of **Lago Yelcho**, a beautiful lake on Río Futaleufú surrounded by hills, much loved by anglers for its salmon and trout. Further south at Km 60, a path leads to **Ventisquero Yelcho** (two hours' walk there), a dramatic glacier with high waterfalls. Note that the path passes a campsite whose administrator charges walkers to go to the glacier. Whether he is legally entitled to do this is a contentious issue.

At **Villa Santa Lucía**, an uninspiring modern settlement 87 km south of Chaitén, with basic food and accommodation, a road branches east to the Argentine border. There are two crossings: Futaleufú and Palena, both reached from **Puerto Ramírez** past the southern end of Lago Yelcho, 24 km east of Santa Lucia. Here the road divides: the north branch runs along the valley of the Río Futaleufú to Futaleufú and the southern one to Palena. The scenery is spectacular, but the road is hard going: single track ripio, climbing steeply in places (tough for bikes; allow plenty of time). Don't leave litter, take out all rubbish.

Futaleufú → *Phone code: 065.*

This once tranquil border town, 8 km west of the border, is growing into a hugely popular tourist centre. The rickety houses, neatly slatted with alerce wood, and spruce vegetable gardens, nestle in a bowl amid steep mountains on the Río Espolón. There is good hiking and some of the most challenging white water rafting in the world on the Río Futaleufú. **Lago Espolón**, west of Futaleufú, reached by a turning 41 km northeast of Villa Santa Lucía, is a beautiful lake in an area enjoying a warm microclimate: 30° C in the day in summer, 5° C at night, with excellent fishing at the lake's mouth. Several cabañas and campsites. The lake is even warm enough for a quick dip, but beware of the currents. Banco del Estado on the plaza has no ATM, but may change cash. **Tourist office** ① *on the plaza at O'Higgins and Prat, T721370/721241*, for accommodation and maps of walks.

Border with Argentina
Chilean immigration is at the border, 8 km east of Futaleufú. The border is just west of the bridge over the Río Grande: straightforward crossing, open summer 0800-1900; winter 0800-2000. For Argentinian immigration, see page 195. Change money in Futaleufú; nowhere to change at the border but you can pay the bus fare to Esquel (Argentina) in US dollars. Alternatively, cross into Argentina further south near **Palena**, which is 8 km west of the border and has a Chilean immigration office. **Note** If entering from Argentina, no fresh produce may be brought into Chile.

La Junta is a village 151 km south of Chaitén. It has a service station, where there's a minimarket (selling camping stove alcohol) and phone. From the village you can visit **Lago Rosselot**, surrounded by forest in the **Reserva Nacional Lago Rosselot**, 9 km east of La Junta. The same road continues east, 74 km, to Lago Verde and the Argentine border: open summer 0800-2200, winter 0800-2000. Another excursion, by new road and boat, leads northwest to the fishing village of **Puerto Raúl Marín Balmaceda**.

Puyuhuapi → *Phone code: 067. Population: 500.*
With the most idyllic setting along the whole Carretera Austral, Puyuhuapi lies in a tranquil bay at the northern end of the Puyuhuapi fjord, 45 km south of La Junta. The blissful thermal pools at Termas de Puyuhuapi are nearby. The village was founded by four German-speaking Sudeten families in 1935, and handwoven carpets are still made here by the Hopperditzel brothers, now world renowned. **Alfombras de Puyuhuapi** ① *T325131, www.puyuhuapi.com, daily in summer 0830-1930, closed lunch, English spoken*. This is the best stopping point between Chaitén and Coyhaique with phone, fuel, shops, but no banks: hotels may change dollars. **Tourist office** ① *by the Municipalidad, main street, Mon-Sat in season*, helpful.

South of Puyuguapi, 24 km, is the 154-ha **Parque Nacional Queulat** ① *CONAF, La Junta, T3141248, epinto@patagoniachile.cl, daily Dec-Mar 0830-2100, rest of year 0830-1830, US$3, camping US$15 per site, CONAF campsite with cold showers*. Luis Lepio, T325139, runs bus service to park daily if there's demand, Mon to Fri, 1030, also guide for fly fishing. It is most visited for the spectacular hanging glacier, **Ventisquero Colgante**. 2.5 km off the road passing the guardeparques' house, you'll find parking and camping areas. Three walks begin from here: a short stroll through the woodland to a viewpoint of the Ventisquero, or cross the river where the path begins to Laguna Tempanos, where boats cross the lake in summer. The third trail, 3.25 km, takes 2½ hours to climb to a panoramic viewpoint of the Ventisquero, where you can watch the ice fall into huge waterfalls like sifted sugar.

Puerto Cisnes
At 59 km south of Puyuhuapi, a winding road branches west and follows the Río Cisnes 35 km to Puerto Cisnes (*Population 1,784*), a quiet fishing village at the mouth of the river on Puyuhuapi fjord, set amongst steep mountains. The Río Cisnes, 160 km in length, is recommended for rafting or canoeing, with grand scenery and modest rapids except for the horrendous drop at Piedra del Gato. Good camping in the forest, and fuel is available in the village.

At 89 km south of Puyuhuapi is **Villa Amengual** and, at Km 92, a road branches east, 104 km to La Tapera and to the Argentine border. Chilean immigration is 12 km west of the border, open summer 0800-2200, winter 0800-2000. On the Argentine side the road continues to meet up with Ruta 40, a section with few services for fuel or food.

Coyhaique → *Phone code: 067. Colour map 9, grid A1. Population: 43,297.*
A growing centre for tourism, Coyhaique, 420 km south of Chaitén, is a busy small town perched on a hill between the Ríos Simpson and Coyhaique. It's a good idea to get cash here as there are no banks along the Carretera Austral. The **Museo Regional de la Patagonia Central** ① *Lillo 23, Tue-Sun winter 0830-1730, summer 0900-2000, US$1 is in the Casa de Cultura*. It traces local history through photos of the first pioneers, as well as sections on archaeology, mineralogy and

zoology. From the bridge over the Río Simpson look for the **Piedra del Indio**, a rock outcrop which looks like a face in profile. **Tourist offices**: In the bright green cabin in the plaza, helpful, with details on buses and accommodation. **Sernatur** office (very helpful, English spoken) ⓘ *Bulnes 35, T231752, infoaisen@sernatur.cl. Mon-Fri 0830-1700*. **CONAF**, Av Ogana 1060, T212109, aysen@conaf.cl.

Just outside the town, the **Reserva Nacional Coihaique** ⓘ *information from CONAF*, has some trails for walking or biking, with several picnic grounds and a campsite on the river bank. A satisfying walk is up to Cerro Cinchao, and great views from Sendero Los Leñeros to Laguna Verde. Walk to Laguna Verde and Laguna Venus particularly recommended. Follow Baquedano to the end, over bridge, and past the guardeparque's hut where all the trails begin. There are well-marked walks of between 20 minutes and five hours. Ski centre **El Fraile**, 29 km from Coyhaique, is 1599 m above sea level, with five pistes, powder snow, in the middle of ñire (Antarctic beech) and pine forests (1,000 people capacity).

Border with Argentina: Coyhaique Alto

A 43-km road runs east to this crossing. On the Argentine side the road leads through Río Mayo and Sarmiento to Comodoro Rivadavia. **Chilean immigration** is at Coyhaique Alto, 6 km west of the border, open May-August 0800-2100, September-April 0700-2300.

Puerto Aisén and Puerto Chacabuco

→ *Phone code: 067. Colour map 9, grid A1. Population: 13,050.*

The paved road between Coyhaique and Puerto Aisén passes through **Reserva Nacional Río Simpson**, with beautiful waterfalls, lovely views of the river and excellent fly-fishing. Administration/museum is at the entrance, no marked trails; campsite opposite turning to Santuario San Sebastián, US$7.

Coyhaique

Sleeping	Hospedaje Pochi 13	Casino de Bomberos 4
Albergue Las	Hostal Belisario Jara 8	Central 3
Salamandras 1	Hostal Bon 9	El Mastique 8
Cabañas Mirador 3	Hostal Las Quintas 7	Histórico Ricer &
Cabañas Río Simpson 10	Los Ñires 11	Café Ricer 2
Cabañas San Sebastián 6	San Sebastián 12	La Casona 5
El Reloj 4		Pizzería La Fiorentina 7
Hospedaje Baquedano 2	Eating	
Hospedaje María Ester 14	Café Oriente 1	Bars & clubs
Hospedaje Mondaca 5	Calor y Comida 9	Piel Roja 6

Puerto Aisén is 65 km west of Coyhaique at the meeting of the rivers Aisén and Palos. Formerly the region's major port, it has been replaced by Puerto Chacabuco, 15 km to the west, and though it remains an important centre for services, there's little of interest for the visitor. It's also very wet. In summer, the *Apulcheu* sails regularly down the northern shore of the Aisén Fjord to Termas de Chiconal, a spectacular one hour trip by boat, US$50 (take your own food) – book in the tourist office or **Turismo Rucaray**, on the plaza, rucaray@entelchile.net. **Tourist office** in the Municipalidad, Prat y Sgto Aldea, Dec-Feb only. www.portchacabuco.cl, gives information on shipping movements.

The Puente President Ibáñez, once the longest suspension bridge in Chile, and a paved road lead to **Puerto Chacabuco** 15km away; a regular bus service runs between the two. The harbour, rather a charmless place, is a short way from the town.

Balmaceda

From Coyhaique, the Carretera Austral heads south past huge bluffs, through deforested pasture and farmsteads edged with alamo (poplar) trees, before entering flatter plains and rolling hills. At around Km 41, a paved road runs east past the airport at Balmaceda to the Argentine border at Paso Huemules (no accommodation). **Chilean immigration** is open May-July 0800-2000, September-April 0800-2200.

Puerto Ibáñez

The Carretera Austral starts to climb again, past the entrance to the Reserva Nacional Cerro Castillo (see below). It winds up through the attractive narrow gorge of Río Horqueta, to a pass between Cerro Castillo and its neighbours, before dropping down a 6-km slalom into the breathtaking valley of Rio Ibáñez. (This is currently the most southerly paved section and the road is safe and wide here). Here the road forks east to Puerto Ibáñez, a further 31 km away, for the ferry crossing of vast Lago General Carrera.

Puerto Ibáñez (*Population 828*) is the principal port on the Chilean section of the lake, and as such you'll probably just pass through to reach the ferry. It is, however, a centre for distinctive pottery, leather production and vegetable growing (you can visit potters and buy salad from greenhouses). Local archaeology includes rock art and the largest Tehuelche cemetery in Patagonia. There are various hotels, but no other services. Fuel (sold in 5-litre containers) is available at Luis A Bolados 461 (house with five laburnum trees outside). Most shops and restaurants are closed Sunday. There are some fine waterfalls, including the Salto Río Ibáñez, 6 km north.

Villa Cerro Castillo

From the turning to Puerto Ibáñez the Carretera Austral goes through Villa Cerro Castillo (Km 8), a quiet village in a spectacular setting beneath the striking, jagged peaks of **Cerro Castillo**, overlooking the broad valley below. There's a petrol station, public phone, several food shops and a tiny tourist information kiosk by the road side (January-February only), with details of guides offering trekking to the Cerro, among them Jorge Aguilar and Francisco Calderón.

The village is a good place to stop for a few days with two appealing attractions. There's a truly spectacular four-day trek around the fairytale castle peaks of Cerro Castillo, in the **Reserva Nacional Cerro Castillo**, whose entrance is 64 km south of Coyhaique. The walk starts at Las Horquetas Grandes, a bend in the river Río Ibáñez, 8 km south of the park entrance, where any bus driver will let you off. It follows Río La Lima to the gorgeous Laguna Cerro Castillo, then animal trails around the peak itself, returning to the village (accommodation or bus back to Coyhaique). This is a challenging walk: attempt it only if fit, and ideally, take a guide, as trails are poorly marked (IGM map essential, purchase in advance in Coyhaique).The guardería is on the Senda Ibáñez, 50 m to the left of the main road (as you head south), opposite Laguna Chinguay to the right, with access to walks and campsite (camping US$5, November-March, take equipment – there are no refugios). The picnic ground is open summer 0830-2100, winter to 1830.

A few kilometres south of the village is the **Monumento Nacional Manos de Cerro Castillo** ⓘ *US$1 charged Dec-Apr*. In a shallow cave, a few handprints have been made on the side of vertical rocks high above the Río Ibáñez. There's no clue to their significance, but they're in a beautiful place with panoramic views. This makes a delightful two hours' walk. The site is accessible all year, signposted clearly from the road. There is also a small local museum, 2 km south of Villa Cerro Castillo ⓘ *open Dec-Mar 0900-1200*.

⊜ Sleeping

Chaitén to Coyhaique p729
Lago Yelcho
AL-B Cabañas Yelcho en la Patagonia, 7 km south of Puerto Cárdenas, T731337, www.yelcho.cl. A smart fishing lodge on banks of the lake with comfortable rooms and cabañas, tastefully decorated with views straight to the lake (booked solid Jan-Feb); also attractive campsite, cafetería, all facilities. Recommended.

Villa Santa Lucía
D pp Several places on main street: ask at **Nachito**, the café where the bus stops, which serves good breakfasts.

Futaleufú p729
L-AL El Barranco, O'Higgins 172, T721314, www.elbarrancochile.cl. Elegant rustic rooms, luxurious, pool, good restaurant, and expert fishing guides, horses and bikes for hire, half and full board available.
AL-A Río Grande, O'Higgins y Aldea, T721320. Also upmarket but not such good value, spacious attractive rooms, international restaurant, popular with rafting groups.
C pp **Antigua Casona**, Rodríguez y Cerda, T721311, pcoronadop@yahoo.es. Very attractive old house, owners speak English and have a delightful country house Posada Anchileufú, T721311. Has the best café and bar, cosy and stylish, serving delicious food and wines.
B Cabañas Río Espolón, Río Espolón, T721216, follow Cerda to the end. Cosy *cabañas* in secluded riverside setting, also recommended parrilla, bar. Popular with river-rafting groups, book ahead.
D Adolfo B&B, O'Higgins 302, T721256, hospedajeadolfo@hotmail.com. Best value in this range, very comfortable rooms in family home, shared hot showers, kitchen, with breakfast.
F pp **Continental**, Balmaceda 595, T721222.
G singles. Oldest in town, no breakfast, basic, but clean and welcoming.
Camping There are lots of campsites, many beautifully situated on river bank.

Border with Argentina: La Junta p730
A-B Espacio y Tiempo, T314141, www.espacioytiempo.cl. Spacious rooms, warm and cosy atmosphere, restaurant, attractive gardens, fishing expeditions. Recommended.
D Hostería Patagonia, Lynch 331, T314120. Good meals, small rooms, poor bathrooms.
D Res Copihue, Varas 611, T314184. **F** singles. With bath and breakfast, excellent value.
D Res Valdera, Varas s/n, T314105. **F** singles. With breakfast without bath, also excellent value.

Puyuhuapi p730
LL-L Puyuhuapi Lodge and Spa. Reservations: Patagonia Connection, Santiago, T225 6489, www.patagonia-connection.com, or directly at the hotel, T/F325103. Splendidly isolated on a nook in the sea fjord, the hotel owns the thermal baths: outdoors by the fjord so that you can dive in for a refreshing swim afterwards, or in the lovely indoor spa complex where there are jacuzzis of sea water, good for sufferers of arthritic and skin conditions, expert massage facilities. Good packages for de-stressing with all activities from riding, trekking, mountain biking, yoga and the thermals included. Price includes use of baths, boat transfer, full board US$50 extra, excellent restaurant. Guests met at Balmaceda airport, or arrive by boat from Puerto Chacabuco, taking in the San Rafael lake and glaciers (about US$1000 for 2 for 3 nights, all included, depending on season and room category). Highly recommended. Boats leave frequently from a 2 hrs' walk from town, US$5 each way, 10 mins' crossing.
L-AL El Pangue, 18 km north, Km 240 at end of Lago Risopatrón, Parque Nacional Quelát, T325128, cpangue@entelchile.net. Luxurious *cabañas* in splendid rural setting, with hot water and heating, horseriding, restaurant, trekking, mountain bikes, pool, great views, restful. Recommended.
C Hostería Alemana, Otto Uebel 450, T325118. A large traditional wooden house on the main road by the water, very comfortable, lovely lake views and garden. Warmly recommended.
C-D Casa Ludwig, Otto Uebel s/n, T/F325220, www.casaludwig.cl. Cheaper with shared bath. Open Nov-Mar; enquire in advance at other times. In a beautiful 4-storey house built by first German settlers, with wonderful views of bay, charming owner Luisa offers a range of rooms, including the snug attic with shared bath, good breakfast included, very comfortable; Luisa is knowledgeable about the area, speaks German and English. Highly recommended.
E Sra Leontina Fuentes, Llantureo y Circunvalación, T325106. Clean, hot water, good breakfast for US$2.

Puerto Cisnes p730
AL-C Cabañas Río Cisnes, Costanera 101, T346404. Cabins sleep 4 to 8. Owner, Juan Suazo, offers sea fishing trips in his boat.
E Res El Gaucho, Holmberg 140, T346514. With bath and breakfast, dinner available.
  Also various cabañas: **Brisas del Sur**, T346587, **Portal del Mar**, T346439, and **Cerro Gilberto**, T346440, all fine.

733

Villa Amengual

F pp **Res El Encanto**, Fca Castro 33-A, T188-2-1964517. With restaurant and café, one of several cheap options in town, including **Res Bienvenido** and **Villa Mañihuales** (T234803), both **E**, on Ibar.

Coyhaique *p730, map p731*

Plentiful accommodation is of a higher standard, and more expensive than elsewhere in southern Chile. The tourist office has a list.

AL Hostal Belisario Jara, Bilbao 662, T/F23 4150, www.belisariojara.itgo.com. Most distinctive and delightful, an elegant and welcoming small place, with TV and excellent breakfast. Recommended.

A El Reloj, Baquedano 828, T231108, htlelreloj@patagoniachile.cl. Tasteful, quiet place in a former sawmill, with a good restaurant, charming, comfortable wood panelled rooms, some with wonderful views, nice lounge. Highly recommended.

A-B Cabañas Mirador, Baquedano 848, T233191. Attractive, well-equipped *cabañas*, also rooms, in lovely gardens with panoramic views of the Reserva Forestal, and Río Coyhaique below, great value. Recommended.

A-B Cabañas Río Simpson, 3 km north on road to Pto Aisén, T/F232183, www.cabanas-rio-simpson.cl. Very reasonable for 4-9 people, fully equipped, horse hire, fishing and tours. Tame alpacas in grounds.

A-B Los Ñires, Baquedano 315, T232261, www.doncarlos.cl. Bland but pleasant place with comfortable small rooms, with breakfast, good restaurant, parking.

B San Sebastián, Baquedano 496, T/F233427. Modern, spacious rooms with great views over the Reserva, with breakfast, good value. Recommended. Also **Cabañas San Sebastián**, Freire 554, T231762, cabsebastian@hotmail.com. Central, very good.

C-D Hostal Las Quintas, Bilbao 1208, T231173. Spartan, but clean and very spacious rooms (some in very bizarre design) with bath and breakfast.

D Hospedaje Baquedano, Baquedano 20, T232520, Patricio y Gedra Guzmán. Welcoming, well-maintained, lovely place, simple cabañas, with splendid views over the Reserva Forestal, very helpful hosts who speak English, space for camping, access to river, great value. Recommended.

D Hospedaje María Ester, Lautaro 544, T233023. With breakfast (extra), some rooms with bath and TV, use of kitchen (extra charge), laundry facilities, also has *cabañas* (**D**) with bath, hot water and kitchenette, local information.

D Hosp Pochi, Freire 342, T256968. **F** singles. Rooms in a family home with bath and cable TV, breakfast included, very pleasant owners, good value. Recommended.

D Hostal Bon, Serrano 91, T231189, hostal_bon@hotmail.com. Simple but very welcoming place, with multilingual owner. They also have cabañas near Reserva Forestal 1km away.

D-E Hosp Mondaca, Av Simpson 571, T254676. **G** singles. Small (only 3 rooms) but spotless family home, hospitable, breakfast extra.

D-G Albergue Las Salamandras, Sector Los Pinos, 2 km south in attractive forest, T/F211865, www.salamandras.cl (excellent website). Double rooms, dorms (**F** pp) and camping, kitchen facilities, winter sports and trekking (Jun-Oct), cycling information. Highly recommended.

Many more hospedajes and private houses with rooms; ask tourist office for a list.

Camping Tourist office on plaza or Sernatur in Coyhaique have a full list of all sites in XI Región. There are many camping sites in Coyhaique and on the road between Coyhaique and Puerto Aisén, eg at Km 1, 2 (**Camping Alborada**, US$14 per site, T238868, hot shower), 24, 25, 35, 37, 41, 42 (**Camping Río Correntoso**, T232005, US$20 per site, showers, fishing, Automobile Club discount) and 43. Camping in Reserva Nacional Río Simpson, US$7.

Puerto Aisén and Puerto Chacabuco *p731*

Accommodation is hard to find, most is taken up by fishing companies in both ports. There are several places to eat along Tte Merino and Aldea in Puerto Aisén.

L Loberías del Sur, José Miguel Carrera 50, Puerto Chacabuco, T351112, www.loberiasdelsur.cl. Recently rebuilt 5-star hotel, the best around here and whose restaurant serves the best food in the area (handy for meal or a drink before boarding ferry – climb up steps direct from port). Same owner as Catamaranes del Sur (see Shipping, below), which also has a nearby nature reserve, Parque Aiken del Sur.

A-B Patagonia Green, 400m from bridge (on Pto Chacabuco side), T336796, www.patagoniagreen.cl. Nice cabins for up to 5, kitchen, heating, TV, gardens, arranges tours to Laguna San Rafael, fishing, mountain biking, riding, trekking etc, English spoken.

C Caicahues, Michimalonco 660, Puerto Aisén, T336633. The most recommended in this port, with heating and internet, book ahead.

D Hosp Mar Clara, Carrera 970, Puerto Aisén, T330945. **G** singles. More expensive with bath. Basic, clean, thin walls, looks nicer from outside than within.

Puerto Ibáñez *p732*

Various hotels in our **D-F** range, also a campsite.
C Cabañas Shehen Aike, Luis Risopatrón 55, T423284, www.shehenaike.cl. Swiss owned, large cabins, lots of ideas for trips, bike rental, organizes tours, fine food, welcoming, English host, best to phone in advance (poor email reception).
F Hospedaje Don Francisco, San Salvador y Lautaro. Very hospitable, good food round the clock. **F Vientos del Sur**, Bertrán Dixon 282, T423208. Good, nice family, dormitories, check the bill, cheap meals (restaurant open till late) but not as good as the lodging; also adventure activities.

Villa Cerro Castillo *p732*

E Hostería Villarrica, O'Higgins 59, next to Supermercado Villarrica, T419200. Welcoming, basic, hot showers, and meals too, kind owners can arrange trekking guides and horse riding.
E Hospedaje El Rodeo, Pedro Aguirre Cerda 281, T419200. Rosa Sandoval Múñoz is a great host, lots of information on nearby treks.
F pp La Querencia, Higgins 460, T411610. Comfortable rooms with shared bath, also serves cheap meals.

● Eating

Futaleufú *p729*

¶¶ **Futaleufú**, Cerda 407. Serves typical Chilean meat dishes and local foods.
¶¶ **Martín Pescador**, Balmaceda y Rodríguez, T721279. For fish and meat dishes, rustic.
¶¶ ¶ **Sur Andes**, Cerda 308, T721405. Café serving cakes, sweets, light meals and real coffee. Also sells handicrafts.

Puyuhuapi *p730*

¶¶ **Café Rossbach**, Costanera. Run by the descendants of the original German settlers, an attractive place by the water for delicious salmon, tea and *küchen*.
¶¶ **Lluvia Marina**, next to Casa Ludwig, veronet@entelchile.net. The best café, also selling handicrafts. Superb food in relaxed atmosphere, a great place to just hang out, owner Veronica is very helpful.

Coyhaique *p730, map p731*

¶¶¶ **Histórico Ricer**, Horn 48 y 40, p 2, T232920. Central, warm and cosy, serving breakfast to dinner, regional specialities, with good vegetarian options, historical exhibits. Also has **Café Ricer** at No 48, serving light food.
¶¶¶-¶¶ **Calor y Comida**, Baquedano 022, yelisa@patagoniachile.cl. Entrance through a private house to a restaurant with a fabulous view,

Patagonian/Mediterranean cuisine, large portions, good, wine by the glass.
¶¶ **La Casona**, Obispo Vielmo 77, T238894. Justly reputed as best in town, charming family restaurant serves excellent fish, congrio especially, but best known for grilled lamb.
¶¶-¶ **Casino de Bomberos** next to the fire station, Gral Parra 365, T231437. For great atmosphere and a filling lunch, can be slow when serving groups. Recommended.
¶¶ ¶ **Central**, Freire 319, T256885. Good set lunches, big screen TV (watch football here).
¶ **El Mastique**, Bilbao 141. Cheap but good pasta and Chilean food.
¶ **Pizzería La Fiorentina**, Prat 230. Tasty pizzas, good service. Recommended.

Cafés

Cafe Oriente, Condell 201. Coyhaique's oldest, was moved on rollers several blocks to its present position. Serves a good lunch and tasty cakes.

● Bars and clubs

Coyhaique *p730, map p731*

Piel Roja, Moraleda y Condell. Good music, drinking and dancing, laid back, popular with Europeans, open Wed, Fri, Sat 1000-0500 for dancing, pub other nights. Recommended, but not cheap.

● Shopping

Coyhaique *p730, map p731*

Camping equipment Condor Explorer, Dussen 357, T670349. Decent stock.
Handicrafts Artesanía Manos Azules, Riquelme 435. Sells fine handicrafts. **Feria de Artesanía** on the plaza.
Supermarkets Brautigam, Horn 47. Stocks fishing and camping gear. **Central**, Magallanes y Bilbao, open daily till 2230 and at Lautaro y Cochrane. **Multimas**, Lautaro 339, y Prat.

▲ Activities and tours

Futaleufú *p729*

Tour operators arrange whitewater rafting trips, prices starting from US$75 pp. Local fishing guides can also be found in the village.
Expediciones Chile, Mistral 296, T721386, www.exchile.com. Whitewater rafting, kayaking, etc. Offers the best multi-day trips, book in advance. Day trips can be booked at office.
Futaleufú Explore, O'Higgins 772, T721411, www.futaleufuexplore.com. A respected rafting company.
Rancho Las Ruedas, Pilota Carmona s/n, T721294. The best horseriding in the area.

Coyhaique *p730, map p731*

Tours only operate Dec to Mar.

Geo Turismo, E Lillo 315, T237456, www.geoturismopatagonia.cl. Impressive range of conventional tours and more specialized tours for photographers, fishing, kayaking, all equipment and expert guides included, horse riding and trekking, English spoken. San Rafael Glacier combined with other destinations, also goes to Caleta Tortel, taking boat from there to Steffens glacier, La Isla de los Muertos and Jorge Montt glacier. Fly drive holidays from Chaitén or Coyhaique, allowing you to leave the car at the other end.

Aysén Tour, Parra 97, T237070, www.aysentour.cl. Typical range of trips along the Carretera Austral, including glacier and cave tours.

Patagonia Adventure Expeditions, Riquelme 372, T/F219894, www.adventurepatagonia.com. Jonathan and Ian, both English speakers, organize professional adventure tourism, from half day trips to 22 day, multi-environment expeditions. Area of speciality is the Northern Patagonian ice cap, all extended adventures happen there. Also famed for rafting trips.

Turismo Prado, 21 de Mayo 417, T231271, www.turismoprado.cl. Good travel agent for flights and excursions, changes money and TCs without commission. Trips to Laguna San Rafael by charter flight, US$250pp, unforgettable 4-hr round trip.

⊖ Transport

Futaleufú *p729*

Bus To/from **Chaitén**: see above. Bus to **Puerto Montt** via Argentina, Mon 0630, 13 hrs, US$28, with **Transporte Patagonia Norte**.

Border with Argentina *p730*

Bus From west side of plaza in Futaleufú, a Jacobsen bus runs to the border, 3 times a week, and Mon-Fri in Jan-Feb, US$4, 30 mins, connecting with services to Trevelin and Esquel. From **Chaitén** to Palena, **Expreso Yelcho** bus twice weekly in summer, US$12, 5½ hrs.

La Junta

Bus To **Coyhaique**, with Daniela (T09-9512 3500), M&C (T242626), and **Lagunas**, 7 hrs, US$16. To **Chaitén**, 4 hrs, US$11. To **Puerto Cisnes**, with Empresa Entre Verde (T314275), US$8.

Puyuhuapi *p730*

Bus Daily to **Coyhaique**, US$13, 6 hrs, and north to **Chaitén**, plus 2 weekly to **Lago Verde**; also private minibuses to Coyhaique: ask at food shops and **Hosp Ventisquero** on O'Higgins.

736

Puerto Cisnes *p730*

Bus To **Coyhaique**, Transportes Terra Austral, T254335, Bus Alegría, T231350, run a daily (not Sun) service, US$14.

Coyhaique *p730, map p731*

Air Most flights from Balmaceda (see page 732), although Coyhaique has its own airport, Tte Vidal, about 5 km southwest of town. **Don Carlos** (www.doncarlos.cl), to **Chile Chico** (Mon-Sat, US$50), **Cochrane** (Mon, Thu, US$75) and **Villa O'Higgins** (Mon, Thu, US$111, recommended only for those who like flying, with strong stomachs, or in a hurry).

Bus Don Carlos, Subteniente Cruz 63, T231981, www.doncarlos.cl; Suray, A Prat 265, T238387; Inter Lagos, at bus terminal, T240840, www.turismointerlagos.cl; Valle Verde, at bus terminal, T255726. Full list of buses from tourist information. Terminal at Lautaro y Magallanes, but few buses use this. Most leave from their own bus company offices.

To **Puerto Aisén**, minibuses run every 45 mins, 1 hr **Valle Verde**, **Suray** and **Inter Lagos**, US$2. Suray continues to **Puerto Chacabuco**, 20 mins, US$0.75. To **Puerto Ibáñez** on Lago Gral Carrera, several minibus companies (connect with ferry to Chile Chico) pick up 0530-0600 from your hotel, 1½ hrs, book the day before (eg **Dario Figueroa Castro**, T08-977 9737, **Miguel Acuña**, Carrera y Moraleda, T251579, **Don Tito Segovia**, T250280), US$6.50.

Buses on the **Carretera Austral** vary according to demand, and they are always full so book early. Bikes can be taken by arrangement. North to **Chaitén**, Becker (Pdte Ibáñez 358, T232167), M&C Tours (Parra 329, T242626) and Daniela (at terminal, T09-9512 3500), between them 6 days a week, US$30, 12 hrs; in winter these stop overnight in La Junta, only northbound buses stop at Pto Aisén. To **Puerto Cisnes**, Terra Austral (T254335), Alegría (T231350), Mon-Sat, US$11. South to **Cochrane** daily in summer with either Don Carlos, or Inter Lagos, US$17-20. All buses stop at **Cerro Castillo** (US$6), **Bahía Murta** (US$10), **Puerto Tranquilo** (US$12) and **Puerto Bertrand** (US$15).

To Argentina: Giobbi, T232067, at Terminal Municipal, run buses **Comodoro Rivadavia**, US$35, via Sarmiento. Daily buses from Com Rivadavia to Bariloche. Other options are given under Balmaceda and Chile Chico.

Car hire If renting a car, a high 4WD vehicle is recommended for Carretera Austral. Buy fuel in Coyhaique, several stations. There are several rental agencies in town.

Ferry Navimag, Paseo Horn 47, T233306, www.navimag.com.

Taxi US$5 to Tte Vidal **airport** (US$1.65 if sharing). Fares in town US$2, 50% extra after 2100. Taxi colectivos (shared taxis) congregate at Prat y Bilbao, average fare US$0.70.

Puerto Aisén and Puerto Chacabuco *p731*
Bus See under **Coyhaique**, above.
Ferry Navimag's Puerto Edén sails each Fri from Puerto Chacabuco to Puerto Montt, taking about 24 hrs (fares given under Sea routes south of Puerto Montt, page 714). It diverts from its schedule in summer to run a 5-day trip from Puerto Montt to Laguna San Rafael, calling at Puerto Chacabuco. **Catamaranes del Sur** also have sailings to Laguna San Rafael, US$499 for a 1-day trip, US$990 for 3 days, all-inclusive. Shipping Offices: **Agemar**, Tte Merino 909, T332716, Puerto Aisén. **Catamaranes del Sur**, J M Carrera 50, T351115, www.catamaranesdelsur.cl. **Navimag**, Terminal de Transbordadores, Puerto Chacabuco, T351111, www.navimag.com. It is best to make reservations in these companies' offices in Puerto Montt, Coyhaique or Santiago. For trips to Laguna San Rafael, see page 717.

Balmaceda *p732*
Air Balmaceda airport is used for daily flights to **Santiago** (from US$130-250 return) with LAN, Sky and Aerolíneas del Sur, and to **Puerto Montt**, US$75-150 return. Minibuses to/from hotels, US$5, several companies. Taxi from airport to Coyhaique, 1 hr, US$10.
Bus Daily to **Coyhaique**, 0800, US$1.70.

Puerto Ibáñez *p732*
Bus Minibus to **Coyhaique**, 1½ hrs, US$6.50. There is a road to **Perito Moreno**, Argentina, but no public transport.
Ferry The car ferry, **Pilchero** sails from Puerto Ibáñez to **Chile Chico**, daily in summer, less often otherwise, US$4.90 per adult, US$1.50 for bikes, cars US$45, uncomfortable 2½ hr crossing, take food and warm clothing, as the ferries are completely open. Passports required, reservations essential: in Coyhaique, **Mar del**

Sur, Baquedano 146A, T231255; in Chile Chico T411864. At the quay, Café El Refugio has toilets and sells sandwiches and snacks. Minibuses meet the ferry in Puerto Ibáñez for Coyhaique, and buses meet the ferry in Chile Chico for Los Antigos, see page 741.

Villa Cerro Castillo *p732*
Bus 6 a week in summer to both **Coyhaique** and **Cochrane**, Don Carlos, Inter Lagos (T258203) and **Amin Ali** (T09-9313 1402).

⊙ Directory

Coyhaique *p730, map p731*
Airline offices Aerohein, Baquedano 500, T232772, aerohein@entelchile.net. **Don Carlos**, address under Bus, above. **LAN**, Moraleda 402, T231188 or 600-526 2000. **Sky**, Prat 203, T240827 or 600-600 2828. **Banks** Several Redbanc ATMs in centre. Casas de cambio: **Turismo Prado**, see Tour operators. **Emperador**, Bilbao 222, T233727.
Bicycle rental Figón, Simpson y Colón, T234616, check condition first, also sells spares.
Bicycle repairs Tomás Madrid Urrea, Pasaje Foitzich y Libertad, F252132. Recommended.
Internet Cyber Patagonia, 21 de Mayo 525. Cheap, good. Another branch at Prat 360, p 2. Others in centre. **Language schools** Baquedano International Language School, Baquedano 20, at Hospedaje of Sr Guzmán (see Sleeping), T232520, www.balasch.cl. US$400 per week course including lodging and all meals, 4 hrs a day one-to-one tuition, other activities organized at discount rates. **Post offices** Cochrane 202.
Telephones Entel, Prat 340, also has internet access, US$1.35 per hr.

Puerto Aisén *p731*
Banks Banco de Chile, Plaza de Armas, changes cash, not TCs. Redbanc ATM in Puerto Chacabuco.
Post offices south side of bridge. **Telephones** On south side of Plaza de Armas, next to Turismo Rucaray, which posts boat information and has internet. **Entel**, Libertad 408. Internet access.

Lago General Carrera and around

Southwest of Villa Cerro Castillo, the Carretera continues to afford stunning views, for instance minty-green Lago Verde and the meandering Río Manso, with swampy vegetation punctuated by the silver stumps of thousands of burnt trees, huge mountains behind. Lago General Carrera (Lago Buenos Aires in Argentina) straddles the border and, at 2,240 sq km, is the second largest lake in South America. It's an area of outstanding beauty. Sheltered from the icy west winds by the Campo de Hielo Norte, the region also has the best climate in Southern Chile, with little rain and some 300 days of sunshine. The lake crossing is by ferry between Chile Chico and Puerto Ibáñez (see above), but if you're not in a hurry, it's worth taking time to follow the Carretera Austral around the lake's western shores.

Bahía Murta (*Km 198, Population 586*), 5 km off the Camino, lies at the northern tip of the central 'arm' of the lake. There is a tiny tourist information hut, which opens summer 1000-1430, 1500-1930. Petrol is available from a house with a sign just before Puerto Murta. There's a public phone in the village.

Back on the Carretera Austral, **Puerto Río Tranquilo**, Km 223, is a slightly larger hamlet where the buses stop for lunch: fuel is available, with accommodation and meals in the house next door (see Sleeping, below). Capilla del Marmol, in fact a limestone cliff vaguely resembling sculpted caves, is reached by a wonderful boat ride (ask at petrol station, to hire a boat US$35 with guide).

El Maitén, Km 273 south of Coihaique, an idyllic spot at the southwest tip of Lago General Carrera, is where a road branches off east along the south shore of the lake towards Chile Chico, while the Carretera Austral continues south to Puerto Bertand.

South of El Maitén the Carretera Austral becomes steeper and more winding (in winter this stretch, all the way to Cochrane, is icy and dangerous). At Km 284, is the hamlet of **Puerto Bertrand**, lying by the dazzling turquoise waters of Río Baker. As this river is world renowned for fly fishing, good accommodation in Puerto Bertrand is either in one of the luxury cabañas that cater for wealthy anglers, or is a simple room above the village shop and phone box (Hostería Puerto Bertrand, see Sleeping, below).

At **Puerto Guadal**, 10 km east of El Maitén, there are shops, accommodation, restaurants, a post office, petrol and a lovely stretch of lakeside beach. Minibus to Chile Chico twice a week. Further east are the villages of Mallín Grande (Km 40) and Fachinal (locals will let you stay for free if you have a sleeping bag). Parts of this road were built into the rock face, giving superb views, but also dangerous, unprotected precipices.

Chile Chico → *Population: 3,757.*

This is a quiet town in a fruit-growing region, 122 km east of El Maitén. It has an annual fruit festival at end-January and a small museum (open summer only). There are fine views from Cerro de las Banderas. It's 9 km to Los Antiguos, Argentina, where food and accommodation are preferable. **Laguna Jeinimeni**, 52 km from Chile Chico, is a beautiful place with excellent fishing, where you can also see flamingos and black necked swans. The **tourist office** (helpful but usually closed) is in the Casa de la Cultura on O'Higgins. An unofficial purple tourist kiosk on the quay where the ferry arrives, sells bus tickets for Ruta 40 (Argentina), but has some accommodation information. Municipal website: www.chilechico.cl.

Border with Argentina

Chilean immigration 2 km east of Chile Chico. Open summer 0730-2200, winter 0800-2000. Argentine side closes for lunch 1300-1400. Remember that you can't take fresh food across in either direction, and you'll need ownership papers if crossing with a car.

Cochrane → *Population: 2,996.*

From Puerto Bertand heading south, the road climbs up to high moorland, passing the confluence of the Ríos Neff and Baker (there is a mirador – lookout – here), before winding into Cochrane, 343 km south of Coyhaique. The scenery is splendid all the way; the road is generally rough but not treacherous. Watch out for cattle on the road and take blind corners slowly. Sitting in a hollow on the Río Cochrane, Cochrane is a simple place, sunny in summer, good for walking and fishing. The **Reserva Nacional Lago Cochrane**, 12 km east, surrounds Lago Cochrane. Campsite at Playa Vidal. Boat hire on the lake costs US$15 per person. Northeast of Cochrane is the beautiful **Reserva Nacional Tamango** ① *Dec-Mar 0830-2100, Apr-Nov 0830-1830. Aask in the CONAF office about visiting because some access is through private land and tourist facilities are rudimentary, US$4, plus guided visits to see the huemules, Tue, Thu, Sat, US$80 for up to 6 people.* It has lenga forest, a few surviving huemul deer as well as guanaco, foxes and lots of birds including woodpeckers and hummingbirds. Access 9 km northeast of Cochrane, along Río Cochrane. There are marked paths for walks between 45 minutes and five hours, up to Cerro Tamango (1,722 m) and Cerro Temanguito (1,485 m). Take water and food, and windproof clothing if climbing the Cerros. The views from the reserve are superb, over the town, the nearby lakes and to the Campo de Hielo Norte to the west. It is inaccessible in the four winter months. **Tourist office** ① *Esmeralda y Dr Steffens, T522115, summer only, Mon-Sat 0900-1300, 1430-2000; in winter go to Municipalidad at Esmeralda 398.*

66 99 The glacier is very noisy; there are frequent cracking and banging sounds, resembling a mixture of gunshots and thunder ...

Caleta Tortel → *Population: 448.*

The Carretera Austral runs south of Cochrane and, after 105km, at the rather bleak looking Puerto Vagabundo, the road branches west to Caleta Tortel. This quiet village at the mouth of the river, was until very recently accessible only by water and has no streets, only walkways of cypress wood (slippery when wet). Surrounded by mountainous land with abundant vegetation, it has a cool, rainy climate, and its main trade is logging, though this is declining as the town looks towards tourism. Located between the Northern and Southern Ice Fields, Tortel is within reach of two glaciers: **Glaciar Steffens** is to the north, a three-hour boat journey and 2½-hour walk, crossing a glacial river in a rowing boat. A speedboat for nine people costs US$100 and a lancha US$120 for 12. **Glaciar Jorge Montt** is to the south, five hours by lancha through landscapes of pure ice and water, US$220 for 12 people, two hours by speedboat, US$170 for nine. Another boat trip is to the Isla de los Muertos, which has an interesting history. For all information and boat charters, contact the Municipality, T/F067-211876. There is a post office, open Monday-Friday 0830-1330. The phone office number is T234815.

Villa O'Higgins

The Carretera Austral runs to Puerto Yungay (122 km from Cochrane), then another 110 km to **Villa O'Higgins**. There is one free ferry crossing between Yungay (military base) and Río Bravo (several daily, 45 minutes, check timetable locally, capacity 4-5 cars). The road beyond Río Bravo is very beautiful, but often closed by bad weather (take food – no shops on the entire route, few people and few vehicles for hitching). Tourist information is available from the Municipalidad, Lago Christie 121, T/F067-211849, www.villaohiggins.cl. **CONAF**, Av Lago Cisnes s/n, T211849.

It is possible to go from Villa O'Higgins to El Chaltén, Argentina. The road continues 7 km south to Bahía Bahamóndez on Lago O'Higgins (bus US$3), from where a boat leaves twice a week in summer (once a week November, March, April), 3 hours, US$35, to Chilean immigration at Candelario Mancila ① *open Nov-Apr 0800-2200.* Then you have to trek or ride 14 km to the Argentine border (US$30 on horseback) and a further 5 km to Argentine immigration on Lago del Desierto. Then you take a boat across the lake, US$20, and finally a bus to El Chaltén, US$12. With this combination of bus, boat and horse this can be done in a day (depart Villa O'Higgins 0800, arrive El Chaltén 2130; full details on www.villaohiggins.cl). You can pay for each portion of the route separately. The route closes in late April. (Boats on Lago O'Higgins also make excursions to the O'Higgins and Chico glaciers.) With the opening of this route it is possible to do the Carretera Austral and go on to Argentina's Parque Nacional Los Glaciares and Chile's Torres del Paine without doubling back on yourself.

Parque Nacional Laguna San Rafael

① *US$6, at the glacier there is a small ranger station which gives information; a pier and 2 paths have been built, one of which leads to the glacier.*

Some 150 nautical miles south of Puerto Aisén is the **Laguna San Rafael**, into which flows a glacier, 30 m above sea level and 45 km in length. The glacier has a deep blue colour, shimmering and reflecting the light. It calves small icebergs, which seem an unreal, translucent blue, and which are carried out to sea by wind and tide. The glacier is very noisy; there are frequent cracking and banging sounds, resembling a mixture of gunshots and thunder. When a hunk of ice breaks loose, a huge swell is created and the icebergs start rocking in the water. The glacier is disintegrating and is predicted not to last beyond 2011. Some suggest that the wake from tour boats is contributing to the erosion.

The thick vegetation on the shores, with snowy peaks above, is typical of Aisén. The only access is by plane or by boat. The glacier is equally spectacular from the air or the sea. The glacier is one of a group of four that flow in all directions from Monte San Valentín. This icefield is part of the Parque Nacional Laguna San Rafael (1,740,000 ha), regulated by Conaf. In the national park are puma, pudú (miniature deer), foxes, dolphins, occasional sealions and sea otters, and many species of bird. Walking trails are limited (about 10 km in all) but a lookout platform has been constructed, with fine views of the glacier.

● Sleeping

Lago General Carrera *p737*
Bahía Murta
F Residencial Patagonia, Pje España 64, Bahía Murta, T419600. Comfortable, serves food. Free camping by lake at Bahía Murta.

Puerto Río Tranquilo
A Hostal el Puesto, Pedro Lagos 258, T1964555, www.elpuesto.cl. No doubt the most comfortable place in Río Tranquilo, also organizes tours.
C Campo Alacaluf, Km 44 on the Río Tranquilo-Bahía Exploradores side road, T419500. Wonderful guesthouse hidden away from civilization and run by very friendly German family. Recommended.
C-D Hostal Los Pinos, 2 Oriente 41, Puerto Río Tranquilo, T411576. Family run, well maintained, good mid-price meals. Recommended.
D Hostal Carretera Austral, 1 Sur 223, Río Tranquilo, T419500. Also serves mid-range/cheap meals.
F Cabañas Jacricalor, before the bridge, Puerto Río Tranquilo, T419500 (public phone).
G singles. Tent-sized *cabañas*, hot shower, good meals, good information for climbers.

El Maitén
AL Mallín Colorado Ecolodge, Carretera Austral Km 273, 2 km west of El Maitén, T(02) 234 1843, www.mallincolorado.cl. Comfortable *cabañas* in sweeping gardens, complete tranquillity, charming owners, 4-day packages available, including transfers from Balmaceda, horseriding, estancia trip, superb meals. Highly recommended.
B La Pasarela 2, just after the bright orange suspension bridge, El Maitén, T411425. Small comfortable rooms with bath, lakeside setting, welcoming staff, delicious food.
F pp Hospedaje (yellow house, unnamed), Mallín Grande, ask at the shop on the main road to Chile Chico. Basic, without breakfast, bathroom without shower, use of kitchen, very helpful owners.

Puerto Bertrand
A Patagonia Baker Lodge and Restaurant, Puerto Bertrand, towards the south side of the lake, T411903, www.pbl.cl. Stylish cabañas in

woodland, fishing lodge, fabulous views upriver towards rapids and the mountains beyond.
A Lodge Río Baker, Puerto Bertrand, T411499, riobaker@hotmail.com. Full board, warmly recommended fishing lodge, also all-inclusive fishing packages.
B-C Hostería Campo Baker, Puerto Bertrand, T411447, campobaker@entelchile.net. Family cabañas in a woodland setting, boats, horse riding, and of course, fishing.
D Hospedaje Doña Ester, Casa No 8, Puerto Bertrand, T09-9990 8541. Rooms in a pink house, **G** singles, good.
D Hostería Puerto Bertrand, Puerto Bertrand, T419900. **F** singles. With breakfast, other meals available, also *cabañas*, activities.
D Turismo Hospedaje Campo de Hielo Norte, Ventisquero Neff s/n. Owned by Anselmo Soto, open in tourist season only, very hospitable and helpful.

Puerto Guadal
AL Terra Luna Lodge, on lakeside, 2 km from Puerto Guadal, T431263, www.terra-luna.cl. Welcoming well-run place with lodge, bungalows and camping huts (**B**), also has restaurant, many activities offered.
B El Mirador Playa Guadal, 2 km from Puerto Guadal towards Chile Chico, T09-9234 9130, www.patagoniaplayaguadal.cl. Cabañas near beach, fishing, walks to nearby waterfalls. Recommended.
E Hostería Huemules, Las Magnolias 382, Puerto Guadal, T431212. Breakfast, good views.
Camping Site at east end of village.

Chile Chico *p738*
D Casa Quinta No me Olvides/Manor House Don't Forget Me, Sector Chacras, Camino Internacional s/n, T09-9833 8006. Hospedaje and camping, cooking facilities, shared bathrooms, hot showers, honey, eggs, fruit and vegetables for sale, tours arranged to Lago Jeinimeni and Cueva de las Manos. Recommended.
D Hostería de la Patagonia, Camino Internacional s/n, Casilla 91, T411337, F411414. **F** singles, also camping; full-board available. Good food, English, French and Italian spoken,

trekking, horse-riding and whitewater rafting. Recommended.
D Res Don Luis, Balmaceda 175, T411384.
G singles. Meals available, laundry, helpful.
E pp **Hospedaje** at Tel Sur phone centre, in the middle of O'Higgins. Use of kitchen, helpful owners also sell bus tickets for La Unión buses to Los Antiguos and Comodoro Rivadavia.
Camping Free site at Bahía Jara, 5 km west of Chile Chico, then turn north for 12 km.

Cochrane *p738*
In summer it is best to book rooms in advance.
B Cabañas Rogeri, Tte Merino 502, T522264. Cabañas for 4, with kitchen facilities, price includes breakfast.
B Wellmann, Las Golondrinas 36, T/F522171. Comfortable, warm, hot water, good meals. Recommended.
C Res Rubio, Tte Merino 4, T522173. Very nice, breakfast included, lunch and dinner extra.
D Res Cero a Cero, Lago Brown 464, T522158, ceroaco@ze.cl. With breakfast, welcoming. Recommended.
D Res Sur Austral, Prat 334, T522150. Breakfast included, hot water, also very nice.
E Res Cochrane, Dr Steffens 451, T522377. Also serves good meals, laundry, hot shower, breakfast. Recommended. Also camping.
E Res El Fogón, San Valentín 651, T522240. Its pub is the only eating place open in low season, it's the best restaurant at any time of year.

Caleta Tortel *p739*
There are several *hospedajes*. All prices are cheaper in the low season. For all T067-234815 (public phone).
E Hosp Casa Rural Sra Elisa Urrutia Iníquez, full board or bed and breakfast.
E Hosp Costanera, Sra Luisa Escobar Sanhueza. Cosy, warm, attractive, lovely garden, full board available, breakfast included (also open to non-guests).
Camping Free site near the beach, 15-mins' walk south of main plaza, cold showers, drinking water, long drop, fire places and cooking area.

Villa O'Higgins *p739*
There are various cabañas and private lodgings.
E Hospedaje Patagonia, Río Pascua 191 y Lago Christie, T234813. **G** singles, basic.
F Hospedaje y Residencial Apocalipsis 1:3, Pasaje Lago El Salto 345, T216927 or 234813.
G singles. Shared bathrooms, also serves food, good value.

Eating

Lago General Carrera *p737*
†††-† El Récor, Bahía Murta. Meals available here, US$4 for lunch.

Chile Chico *p738*
Café Refer, O'Higgins 416. Good, despite the exterior.
Cafetería Loly y Elizabeth, PA González 25, on Plaza serves coffee and delicious ice cream and cakes.
    Also try the supermarket on B O'Higgins for lunch.

Caleta Tortel *p739*
Café Celes Salom, bar/restaurant serving basic, cheap meals, disco on Sat, occasional live bands.

Activities and tours

Cochrane *p738*
Don Pedro Muñoz, Los Ñadis 110, T522244, F522245. Hires horses for excursions in the surrounding countryside. Recommended. There are other places for horse hire.
Samuel Smiol, T522487. Offers tours to the icefields and mountains, English spoken.

Transport

Chile Chico *p738*
Bus Seguel, T431214, Mon, Fri to **Puerto Guadal**, US$11. See above for ferry to Puerto Ibáñez and connecting minibus to Coyhaique.

Border with Argentina: Chile Chico-Los Antiguos *p738*
Bus In summer, minibuses run from Chile Chico ferry to Los Antiguos on the Argentine side, US$3.75 (in Chilean pesos), ½-1 hr including formalities: ask on quayside. **Trans Acuña**, T411553. Beware pirate vehicles which don't have the correct papers for crossing to Argentina.

Cochrane *p738*
Air Don Carlos to **Coyhaique**, Mon, Thu, US$75; also from **Balmaceda**.
Bus Company agencies: **Don Carlos**, Prat 344, T522150; **Los Ñadis**, Los Helechos 490, T522196. There are 6 buses a week between Coyhaique and Cochrane, check with companies for current timetables, US$20. To **Villa O'Higgins**, Los Ñadis, Mon 0930, via Vagabundo, return Tue 0930, US$12. To **Tortel**, **Acuario 13**, Río Baker 349,

● For an explanation of the sleeping and eating price codes used in this guide, see page 58.
● Other relevant information is found in Essentials pages 602-604.

741

T522143, daily US$10. Petrol is available, if it hasn't run out, at the **Empresa Comercial Agrícola** (ECA) and at the **Copec** station.

Caleta Tortel *p739*
Bus From **Cochrane**, see above.
Ferry Once a month there is a boat from Tortel to **Puerto Edén** (US$3, 24 hrs, rough, cold and uncomfortable, but very interesting). For the adventurous traveller who gets the timing right (ask the Municipalidad in Tortel in advance), you can catch the Navimag boat in Puerto Edén and continue to Puerto Natales. By going in stages from Puerto Montt to Tortel on the Carretera Austral, this works out cheaper than taking Navimag all the way.

Parque Nacional Laguna San Rafael *p739*
Air Taxi from Coyhaique (**Aerohein**), US$200 each if party of 5. Charters are also run by **Don Carlos**. The flights, which can be very rough, give a fine view before landing, after which there is a launch trip (5 hrs in all). Not all pilots will land on the airstrip.

Ferry Cruises are run by : **Skorpios** (see under Puerto Montt); **Catamaranes del Sur**, **Compañía Naviera Puerto Montt** and **Navimag**'s Puerto Edén. **Patagonia Express** runs catamaran trips from Puerto Chacabuco to Laguna San Rafael via Termas de Puyuhuapi, in tours lasting 4-6 days, from Puerto Montt via Coyhaique including the catamaran service, the hotel stay at Termas de Puyuhuapi and the day excursion to Laguna San Rafael (see page 718). Also **Iceberg Express**, Av Providencia 2331, of 602, Santiago, T02-335 0580, 12-hr luxury cruises. Other charters available. Private yachts can be chartered in Puerto Montt for 6-12.

● Directory

Chile Chico *p738*
Banks It's best to change money in Coyhaique. ATM in the middle of O'Higgins for Mastercard and Cirrus, not Visa. Dollars and Argentine pesos can be changed in small amounts in shops and cafés, including Loly y Elizabeth, at poor rates.
Hospital Lautaro s/n, T411334. **Post offices** On the plaza.

Far south

This wild and wind-blown area, covering the glacial regions of southern Patagonia and Chilean Tierra del Fuego, is beautiful and bleak, with stark mountains and open steppe. Little vegetation survives here and few people; though it represents 17.5% of Chile's total area, it is inhabited by under 1% of the population. The southernmost city of Punta Arenas and the attractive, quiet port of Puerto Natales are the two main centres, the latter being the gateway to the Torres del Paine and Balmaceda national parks. In summer it is a wonderful region for climbing, hiking, boat trips and the southernmost crossings to Argentina.

Summers are sunny and very variable, with highs of 15° C. In winter snow covers the country, except those parts near the sea, making many roads more or less impassable, except on horseback. Cold, piercing winds blow, particularly in spring, when they may exceed 100 kph. Despite chilly temperatures, protection against the sun's ultraviolet rays is essential here and in summer, too, windproof clothing is a must.

Punta Arenas and around

→ *Phone code: 061. Colour map 9, grid C2. Population: Punta Arenas 150,000, Puerto Natales 20,500.*

About 2,140 km south of Santiago, Punta Arenas lies on the eastern shore of the Brunswick Peninsula facing the Straits of Magellan at almost equal distance from the Pacific and Atlantic oceans. Founded in 1843, it has grand neoclassical buildings and an opulent cemetery, testimony to its wealthy past as a major port and centre for exporting wool. In the late 19th century, Salesian Missions were established to control the indigenous population so sheep farming could flourish. The city's fortunes slumped when the Panama Canal opened in 1914, but it remains a pleasant place, with attractive, painted wooden buildings away from the centre and superb fish restaurants. Good roads connect the city with Puerto Natales, 247 km north, and with Río Gallegos in Argentina.

Ins and outs

Tourist office Sernatur ⓘ *Magallanes 960, T225385, infomagallanes@sernatur.cl. 0830-1845 daily, closed Sat and Sun off season. See www.patagonia-chile.com.* Much more helpful is the tourist information **kiosk** in the plaza ⓘ *opposite Centro Español, T200610, Mon-Fri 0800-1900, Sat 0900-1900, Sun 0900-1300, informacionturistica @puntaarenas.cl.* Friendly staff, good town map with all hotels and internet places marked, English spoken. If coming from Argentina, note that Chile is twice as expensive. **CONAF** ⓘ *Av Bulnes 0309, p 4, T238554, magallan@conaf.cl.*

Punta Arenas

Sleeping 🛏
Aikén **1** *D2*
Backpackers'
  Paradise **2** *B3*
Cabo de Hornos **4** *C2*
Cóndor de Plata **25** *C2*
Ely House **5** *A3*
Finis Terrae **3** *C2*
Hospedaje
  Independencia **23** *D2*
Hospedaje
  Miramar **17** *D1*
Hostal Al Fin del
  Mundo **6** *C3*

Hostal de la Avenida **9** *B2*
Hostal del Sur **8** *B1*
Hostal Dinka's
  House **19** *A3*
Hostal Green
  House **10** *A3*
Hostal Hain **24** *D2*
Hostal La Estancia **11** *B3*
Hostal Paradiso **12** *A3*
Hostal Sonia
  Kuscevic **20** *A2*
José Nogueira (Palacio
  Sara Braun) **14** *C2*
Luna Hostal **15** *B3*

Monterrey **18** *B2*
Oro Fueguino **21** *C1*
Pink House **16** *A3*
Ritz **13** *C3*
Tierra del Fuego
  22 *C2*

Eating 🍴
Centro Español **1** *D2*
Damiana Elena **3** *B3*
Dino's Pizza **2** *B2*
El Quijote **4** *C3*
La Luna **5** *C3*
La Marmite **6** *B3*

Lomit's **9** *C2*
Remezón **7** *D2*
Santino **8** *C2*
Sotitos **12** *D3*
Turismo Punta
  Arenas **11** *D2*

Bars & clubs 🍸
La Taberna del Club
  de la Unión **13** *C2*
Pub Olijoe **14** *D3*

0 metres   200
0 yards   200

743

Sights

In the centre of the **Plaza Muñoz Gamero** is a striking statue of Magellan with a mermaid and two indigenous Fuegians at his feet. Around the plaza are a number of impressive neo-classical buildings, the former mansions of the great sheep ranching families of the late 19th century. **Palacio Sara Braun** (1895), now the Hotel José Nogueira, has several elegant rooms which are open to the public ⓘ *1000-1300, 1800-2030, US$2*. Around the corner, on Magallanes is the **Teatro Cervantes** (now a cinema with beautifully decorated interior). The fascinating **Museo de Historia Regional Braun Menéndez** ⓘ *Magallanes 949, T244216, www.dibam.cl, Mon-Sat 1030-1700, Sun 1030-1400 summer (1030-1300 daily in winter), US$2, guided tours in Spanish, information in English*, was once the mansion of Mauricio Braun, built in 1905. It has fabulously decorated rooms, with ornate furniture, paintings and marble and crystal imported from Europe. Highly recommended. Further north, is the impressive **Cemetery** ⓘ *Av Bulnes 929, daily, 0800-1800*, charting a history of European immigration and shipping disasters through the huge mausoleums, divided by avenues of huge trees.

The perfect compliment to this is **Museo Regional Salesiano Mayorino Borgatello** ⓘ *in the Colegio Salesiano, Av Bulnes 336 (entrance next to church), T241096, Tue-Sun 1000-1300, 1400-1800 (hours change frequently), US$4*. It covers the fascinating history of the indigenous peoples and their education by the Salesian missions, beside an array of stuffed birds and gas extraction machinery. The Italian priest, Alberto D'Agostini, who arrived in 1909 and presided over the missions, took wonderful photographs of the region and his 70-minute film can be seen on video (ask). Highly recommended. The **Instituto de la Patagonia** ⓘ *Av Bulnes Km 4 north (opposite the University), T244216, outdoor exhibits Mon-Fri 0830-1130, 1430-1830, Sat 0830-1230, US$2*, has an open-air museum with artefacts used by the early settlers, pioneer homes, library and botanical gardens.

Museo Naval y Marítimo ⓘ *Pedro Montt 981, T205479, Mon-Sat 0930-1230, 1400-1700, US$1.50*, has shipping instruments, maps, photos and relics from the Chilean navy and famous navigators. Recommended. West of the Plaza Muñoz Gamero on Calle Fagnano is the Mirador Cerro de La Cruz offering a view over the city and the Magellan Straits, complete with its various shipwrecks. The **Parque María Behety**, south of town along 21 de Mayo, features a scale model of Fuerte Bulnes and a campsite, popular for Sunday picnics; ice rink here in winter.

Around Punta Arenas

West of town (7 km) is the **Reserva Forestal Magallanes** ⓘ *US$5, taxi US$5*, with a self-guided nature trail and several places to visit, including a hill with beautiful views over town and the surroundings. Some 56 km south, **Fuerte Bulnes** is a replica of the wooden fort erected in 1843 by the crew of the Chilean vessel Ancud to secure Chile's southernmost territories after Independence. Little to see but an interesting story. Nearby is **Puerto de Hambre**, a beautiful, panoramic spot where there are ruins of the church built in 1584 by Sarmiento de Gamboa's colonists. Tours by several agencies, US$15. Some 104 km to the east on Ruta 255, towards Argentina, is **Parque Nacional Pali Aike** ⓘ *US$2, refugio for 4*, near Punta Delgada. One of the oldest archaeological sites in Patagonia (Pali Aike means 'desolate place of bad spirits' in Tehuelche). Evidence of aborigines from 10,000-12,000 years ago, in an extraordinary place with volcanic rock of different colours. Tour operators offer a full day trip, US$70; for more details, ask at CONAF, who manage the park.

Isla Magdalena, a small island 30 km northeast, is the location of the **Monumento Natural Los Pingüinos**, a spectacular colony of 60,000 pairs of Magellanic penguins, who come here to breed between November and January. Magdalena is one of a group of three islands (the others are Marta and Isabel), visited by Drake, whose men killed 3,000 penguins for food. Boat trips to the island are run by **Comapa** (see Activities and tours, below). Some 70 km north of Punta Arenas, **Otway Sound** ⓘ *Oct-mid Mar, US$5*, has a small colony of Magellanic penguins, viewed from walkways and bird hides, best seen in the morning. Rheas can also be seen.

⊕ Sleeping

Punta Arenas *p742, map p743*
Hotel prices are substantially lower during winter months (Apr-Sep). Most hotels include breakfast in the room price. For accommodation in private

houses, usually **E** pp, ask at the tourist office. No campsites in or near the city.
L Finis Terrae, Colón 766, T228200, www.hotelfinisterrae.com. Modern,

international style, comfortable, great views from rooftop café/bar, English spoken. Recommended.

L-AL Cabo de Hornos, Muñoz Gamero 1039, on the plaza, T715000, www.hotelesaustralis.com. 4-star (US$200 Sep-Apr, half that Apr-Sep), refurbished and comfy, bright and spacious rooms, with good views from 4th floor up.

L-AL José Nogueira, Plaza de Armas, Bories 959 y P Montt, in former Palacio Sara Braun, T248840, www.hotelnogueira.com. Best in town, stylish rooms, warm atmosphere, excellent service. Smart restaurant in the beautiful loggia. A few original rooms now a 'small museum', with a portrait of Sara Braun (1000-1300, 1800-2030, US$2).

AL Tierra del Fuego, Colón 716, T/F226200, www.patagoniahotels.com. Spacious, tasteful, TV, 2nd floor rooms have kitchenette. Popular Café 1900 downstairs, excellent restaurant open to non residents. Recommended.

A Cóndor de Plata, Av Colón 556, T247987, www.condordeplata.cl. Named after the aeroplane of German aviator and explorer Günther Plüschow, with relics, hot water, full-size bathtubs, TV, café, laundry service, internet.

B Hostal Sonia Kuscevic, Pasaje Darwin 175, T248543, www.hostalsk.50megs.com. One of the city's oldest guesthouses, with breakfast, kitchen facilities, hot water, heating, parking. Better value for longer than short stays, good discount with Hostelling International card.

B Oro Fueguino, Fagnano 356, T061-249401, www.orofueguino.cl. Well-appointed and decorated, TV and phone. Recommended. Often fills up with groups so book ahead.

C Hostal de la Avenida, Colón 534, T247532. Attractive rooms, TV, pretty courtyard, breakfasts.

C Hostal del Sur, Mejicana 151, T227249. Homely and impeccable old house with modern rooms in residential area, excellent breakfast, advance booking in summer. Recommended.

C Hostal La Estancia, O'Higgins 765, T249130. Simple but comfy rooms, some with bath, excellent breakfast, lots of information. Recommended.

C-D Hostal Al Fin del Mundo, O'Higgins 1026, T710185, alfindelmundo@123.cl. Lovely house 2 blocks from plaza, run by young Chilean couple, shared bath, with breakfast, welcoming and helpful, English spoken, laundry, internet. Highly recommended.

C-D Hostal Green House, Angamos 1146, T227939. Friendly hostel, with kitchen facilities, laundry, internet, German and a little English spoken. Recommended.

C-D Hostal Paredis0, Angamos 1073A, T224212. Lovely simple place, breakfast, parking, decent rooms with heating and cable TV, use of kitchen, great value, welcoming. Recommended.

C-D The Pink House, Caupolicán 99, T222436, pinkhouse@ctinternet.cl. **F** singles. Impeccable rooms with or without bath, breakfast included, internet. Pickup from bus station, English spoken. Recommended.

D Hostal Dinka's House, Caupolicán 169, T226056, www.dinkashouse.cl. With breakfast, use of kitchen, laundry, internet.

D Luna Hostal, O'Higgins 424, T221764, hostalluna@hotmail.com. Quiet house with delightful rooms, comfy beds with duvets, or **G** in dorms, use of kitchen, laundry facilities.

D Ritz, Pedro Montt 1102, T224422. **E** singles, all rooms with shared bath, breakfast extra, cosy old house, look for writer Bruce Chatwin's name in the guest book.

D-E Aikén, Errázuriz 612, T222629. **G** pp in dorms. Good beds, with duvet, some with view, large bathrooms, breakfast, internet, TV lounge, heating, kitchen facilities.

E Hosp Miramar, Almte Señoret 1190, T061-215446. Rooms and dorms (**G** pp), helpful staff, good breakfast, good views over the bay, though on the edge of the red-light district.

F Hospedaje Independencia, Independencia 374, T227572, independencia@chileaustral.com. **G** pp in shared rooms. Use of kitchen, laundry, bike rental, internet, good value. Highly recommended. Also good value cabañas away from the centre.

F Hostal Hain, José Nogueira 1600, remezona@hotmail.com. Convenient, secure, helpful, English spoken, kitchen facilities and internet, good.

E pp Monterrey, Bories 621, T220636, monterrey@turismoaventura.net. Tiny rooms with TV, clothes washing, use of kitchen, comfortable, charming people, great breakfast.

F pp Backpackers' Paradise, Carrera Pinto 1022, T240104, backpackersparadise@hotmail.com. Popular, limited bathroom facilities, only curtains dividing the large dorms, not exactly comfortable, cooking and laundry facilities, internet, luggage store, can book *refugios* in Torres del Paine.

F pp Ely House, Caupolicán 75, T226660. Lovely, with breakfast, comfortable, heating and hot water, kitchen, collect from airport.

For an explanation of the sleeping and eating price codes used in this guide, see page 58.
Other relevant information is found in Essentials pages 602-604.

🍴 Eating

Punta Arenas *p742, map p743*
Many eating places close Sun. Some of the main hotels have good value set lunches and dinners.
Note *Centolla* (king crab) is caught illegally by some fishermen using dolphin, porpoise and penguin as live bait. There are seasonal bans on *centolla* fishing to protect dwindling stocks, do not purchase *centolla* out of season. If there is an infestation of red tide (*marea roja*), a disease which is fatal to humans, bivalve shellfish must not be eaten. Mussels should not be picked along the shore because of pollution and the marea roja. Sernatur and the Centros de Salud have leaflets.
🍴 **Remezón**, 21 de Mayo 1469, T241029. Regional specialities such as krill. Very good, but should be, given sky-high prices.
🍴🍴 **Sotitos**, O'Higgins 1138. An institution, famous for seafood in elegant surroundings, excellent. Book ahead in season.
🍴 **Centro Español**, Plaza Muñoz Gamero 771, above Teatro Cervantes. Large helpings, limited selection, decent set lunch.
🍴 **Damiana Elena**, O'Higgins 694, T222818. Stylish restaurant serving Mediterranean food with a Patagonian touch, popular with locals, book ahead at weekends.
🍴 **La Luna**, O'Higgins 974, T228555. Fish, shellfish and local specialities, huge pisco sours, popular, reasonable.
🍴 **La Marmite**, Plaza Sampiao. Intimate, "mestizo" restaurant decorated in pastel shades, regional dishes with international twist, good value.
🍴 **Santino**, Colón 657, T220511. Good pizzas, large bar, good service.
🍴 **Dino's Pizza**, Bories 557. Good value pizza in a cheerful fast food atmosphere. Lots of choice.
🍴 **El Quijote**, Lautaro Navarro 1087, T241225. Good burgers, sandwiches and mid-range fish dinners, bright atmosphere. Recommended.
🍴 **Lomit's**, Menéndez 722. A fast-food institution, cheap snacks and drinks, open when the others are closed.
🍴 **Restaurant de Turismo Punta Arenas**, Chiloé 1280. Good, 26 varieties of sandwiches, open 24 hrs.

🍷 Bars and clubs

Punta Arenas *p742, map p743*
Kamikaze, Bories 655. Popular club with visitors. Recommended.
Pub Olijoe, Errázuriz 970. Like a traditional British pub, for beer in a lively atmosphere, plush leather interior. Recommended.
La Taberna del Club de la Unión, on the plaza in the basement of the Hotel Nogueira. Smoky but atmospheric bar, good for evening drinks.

🛍 Shopping

Punta Arenas *p742, map p743*
Punta Arenas has certain free-port facilities; but Zona Franca, 3½ km north of the centre, opposite Museo Instituto de la Patagonia, is not much cheaper than elsewhere. Closed 1230-1500 and Sun (bus E or A from Plaza Muñoz Gamero; many colectivos; taxi US$3).
Food and drink Cava de la Patagonia, Magallanes on the Plaza. For Chilean wines. **Chocolatta**, Bories 852. Tasty handmade chocolate (for which Punta Arenas is famous, several other places on Bories and at Carrera 663, **Chocolates Norweisser**).
Handicrafts Artesanías Ñandú, O'Higgins 1401, **Artesanía Ramas**, Independencia 799, **Chile Típico**, Carrera Pinto 1015, T225827, and outdoor stalls at the bottom of Independencia, by the port entrance.
Outdoor clothing and camping
The Wool House Patagonia, Fagnano 675. Good quality, reasonably priced clothes and wool goods. **Danilo Jordán**, O'Higgins 1120. For camping gas canisters.
Supermarkets Abu-Gosch, Bories 647, open daily 0900-2200. **Cofrima 2**, España 01375, 2 km from town. **Listo**, 21 de Mayo 1133. **Marisol**, Zenteno 0164. There is a new **Líder** supermarket out of town.

🏔 Activities and tours

Punta Arenas *p742, map p743*
Skiing Cerro Mirador, only 9 km west of Punta Arenas in the Reserva Nacional Magallanes, one of the few places in the world where you can ski with a sea view. **Transtur** buses 0900 and 1400 from in front of Hotel Cabo de Hornos, US$3, return, taxi US$7. Daily lift pass, US$11; equipment rental, US$9. Mid-way lodge with food, drink and equipment. Season Jun-Sep, weather permitting (scant snowfall and rising temperatures have all but eliminated skiing in recent years). In summer there is a good 2-hr walk on the hill, with labelled flora. Contact **Club Andino**, T241479, about cross-country skiing facilities. Also skiing at Tres Morros.

Tour operators
Most tour operators organize trips to Torres del Paine, Fuerte Bulnes, the pingüinera on Otway sound and Tierra del Fuego; shop around.
Arka Patagonia, Magallanes 345, T248167, www.arkaoperadora.com. All types of tours, rafting, fishing, etc.
Payne Turismo y Rent a car, Menéndez 631, T240852, www.payne.cl. Treks to San Isidro lighthouse, birdwatching, Pali Aike all-day trips, Estancia Punta Delgada, including lunch, car hire.

Turismo Aonikenk, Magallanes 619, T228332, www.aonikenk.com. Expensive but excellent tailor-made, multi adventure and trekking tours for all levels of fitness, top of the market, French, German, English spoken. Highly recommended.
Turismo Aventour, J Nogueira 1255, T241197, aventour@entelchile.net. Specialize in fishing trips, organize tours to Tierra del Fuego, helpful, English spoken.
Turismo Comapa, Magallanes 990, T200200, www.comapa.com. Tours to Torres del Paine (responsible, well-informed guides), Tierra del Fuego and to see the penguins at Isla Magdalena (3 times a week in summer, 2 hrs each way with 2 hrs on the island, US$30). Also sell tickets for sailings Puerto Montt to Puerto Natales. Agents for Cruceros Australis (see below).
Turismo Yamana, Errázuriz 932, T710567, www.yamana.cl. Conventional tours, trekking in Torres del Paine, kayaking in the Magellan straits, multilingual guides, camping equipment provided. Recommended.
Viento Sur, Fagnano 585, T710840, www.viento sur.com. Horse riding, kayaking in the Magellan straits, and hiking at Pale Aike, mountain biking up Mt Fenton, plus Torres del Paine, good tours.

☉ Transport

Punta Arenas *p742, map p743*
All transport is heavily booked from Christmas to Mar: advance booking strongly advised.
Air Carlos Ibáñez del Campo Airport, 20 km north of town. Bus service by Buses Transfer, Pedro Montt 966, T229613, scheduled to meet flights, US$3.75. Buses to Puerto Natales also stop. DAP have their own bus service to town, US$4. Taxi US$12. To Santiago, LAN and Aerolíneas del Sur daily, via Puerto Montt and Temuco, from US$200 return, cheapest one-way with Aerolíneas del Sur. When no tickets are available, go to the airport and get on the standby list. To Porvenir, Aerovías DAP twice daily Mon-Sat, 12 mins, US$26. To Puerto Williams, daily in summer, 1 hrs, US$70 one way. Also Antarctic trips including simple accommodation: Isla Rey Jorge 1 day, 2 days to 4 days, US$3,800. Services to Argentina: To Ushuaia, 1 hr, DAP twice a week, LAN 3 times a week in summer, US$140 (schedules change frequently). **Note** Take passport when booking tickets to Argentina.
Bus There's no central bus terminal; buses leave from company offices: Pingüino, T221812, Fernández, Sanhueza 745, T242313, www.buses fernandez.com. Pacheco, Colón 900, T225527; Central de Pasajeros, Colón y Magallanes, T245811, office for booking all tickets, including Sur, T244464. Bus Sur,

Menéndez 552, T614224. **Ghisoni**, Lautaro Navarro 971, T222078. Bus services: To **Puerto Natales**, 3½ hrs, **Fernández**, **Bus Sur**, and **Buses Transfer** several every day, last departure 2000, US$6, with pick-up at the airport, US$8, US$10.50 return. **Ghisoni** and **Austral** have services through Argentina to **Osorno**, **Puerto Montt** and **Castro**, US$60 (cheaper off season), 36 hrs.

To **Río Gallegos**, Argentina, via Punta Delgada, **Pingüino** daily; **Ghisoni**, Mon, Wed, Thu, Sat; **Pacheco**, Sun, Tue, Fri. Fares US$15, 5-8 hrs, depending on customs, 15 mins on Chilean side, up to 2 hrs on Argentine side, including 30 mins lunch at Km 160. To **Río Grande** and **Ushuaia** via **Punta Delgada** (none via Porvenir) **Pacheco** and **Austral**, 7-9 hrs, US$25, heavily booked. US$34 to Ushuaia, 12-14 hrs. Book well in advance in Jan-Feb.

To **Otway Sound**: Bus with **Fernández** 1530, return 1930, US$15. Tours by several agencies, US$19, entry US$4, taxi US$50 return. Useful tour goes on to **Puerto Natales**, daily with **Patagonia Adventure Leaders** (see below).
Car hire Payne, José Menéndez 631, T240852, www.payne.cl. **Internacional**, Waldo Seguel 443, T228323. **Note** You need a hire company's authorization to take a car into Argentina. This takes 24 hrs (not Sat or Sun) and involves mandatory international insurance at US$240.
Ferry Services to **Porvenir** (Tierra del Fuego), daily except Mon, 0900, Sun 0930. Same boat goes on to penguin colony at **Isla Magdalena** (until Mar). US$35, includes guide: Agencia Broom, Bulnes 5075 (Tres Puentes), through Comapa, see Tour operators, above.
Shipping offices: Navimag, in the same office as **Comapa** Compañía Marítima de Punta Arenas), Magallanes 990, T200200, www.navimag.com, www.comapa.com.
Shipping Services: For Navimag services Puerto Montt-Puerto Natales, see under Puerto Montt (confirmation of reservations is advised). Highly recommended is the cruise from Punta Arenas through the Magellan Straits and the 'avenue of glaciers' to Ushuaia, Puerto Williams and Cape Horn on Mare Australis. Lots of opportunities to disembark and see wildlife, very comfortable, unforgettable experience. 7-12 days, can just go as far as Ushuaia. Details from Comapa, and www.australis.com, US$1,600 in summer for 2 people. Advance booking (advisable) from **Cruceros Australis SA**, Santiago office, T02-442 3110, Buenos Aires office, T011-4325 8400.

To **Antarctica**: Most cruise ships leave from Ushuaia, but a few operators are based in Punta Arenas. Try **Antarctic Dream Shipping**, Roca 1016, T223676, www.antarctic.cl, or **Antarctic XXI**, Lautaro Navarro 987, p 2, T228783, www.antarcticaxxi.com. See under Santiago Tour Operators, page 619. Otherwise, another possibility is with the Chilean Navy. The Navy itself does not encourage passengers, so you must approach the captain direct. Spanish is essential. Two vessels, Galvarino and Lautaro, sail regularly (no schedule); usual rate US$80 pp per day, including 4 meals. isotop@mitierra.cl.

To **Monumento Natural Los Pingüinos**: The boat of Agencia Broom (see Ferries to Tierra del Fuego, below) booked through Comapa (see Activities and tours), sails on Tue, Thu and Sat at 1530 (Dec-Feb only), 2 hrs each way with 2 hrs on the island. It returns at 2100, US$30; take your own refreshments, as they are expensive on board. Highly recommended, but the trip may be cancelled if it's windy.

Taxi Ordinary taxis have yellow roofs. Colectivos (all black) run on fixed routes, US$0.60 for anywhere on route. Reliable service from **Radio Taxi Austral**, T247710/244409.

---

❶ Directory

Punta Arenas *p742, map p743*
Airline offices LAN, Bories 884, T600-526 2000. **Aerovías DAP**, O'Higgins

891, T223340, www.dap.cl. Open 0900-1230, 1430-1930. Helpful. **Sky**, Roca 933, T710645. **Banks** Most banks and some supermarkets have ATMs; many on the Plaza. Banks open Mon-Fri 0830-1400. **Casas de cambio** open Mon-Fri 0900-1230, 1500-1900, Sat 0900-1230. **Consulates** Argentina, 21 de Mayo 1878, T261912, open Mon-Fri 1000-1530, visas take 24 hrs. **Belgium**, Roca 817, Oficina 61, T241472. **Italy**, 21 de Mayo 1569, T221596. **Netherlands**, Magallanes 435, T248100. **Spain**, J Menéndez 910, T243566. **UK**, Cataratas de Nicaragua 01325, T211535. **Internet** All over the centre. **Medical services** Hospitals: Hospital Regional Lautaro Navarro, Angamos 180, T244040. Public hospital, for emergency room ask for La Posta. Has good dentists. **Clínica Magallanes**, Bulnes 01448, T211527. Private clinic, minimum charge US$45. **Hospital Naval**, Av Bulnes 200 esq Capitán Guillermos. Open 24 hrs, good, friendly staff. Recommended. **Post offices** Bories 911 y J Menéndez. Mon-Fri 0830-1930, Sat 0900-1400. **Telephones** There are several call centres in the centre of town but shop around as prices vary.

Puerto Natales and around

Beautifully situated on the calm waters of Canal Señoret fjord, an arm of the Ultima Esperanza Sound, edged with spectacular mountains, Puerto Natales, 247 km north of Punta Arenas, is a quiet town of brightly painted corrugated tin houses. It's the base for exploring the magnificent Balmaceda and Torres del Paine national parks, and although inundated with visitors in the summer, retains an unhurried feel, and is a place to relax for a few days.

Ins and outs

Tourist office Sernatur office on the waterfront, Avenida Pedro Montt 19, T412125, infonatales@sernatur.cl. No English spoken, but good leaflets on Puerto Natales and Torres del Paine in English, and bus and boat information in the park. Monday-Saturday 0900-1900. Also at Municipalidad, Bulnes 285, T411263. **CONAF**, O'Higgins 584, T411843.

Sights

Museo Histórico ① *Bulnes 285, T411263, Mon-Fri 0900-1300, 1500-2000, weekends afternoon only, free*, has displays and photos of early colonizers, as well as a small collection of archaeological and natural history exhibits. There are lovely walks along the waterfront or up to Cerro Dorotea which dominates the town, with superb views. Take any bus going east and alight at the road for summit (Km 9.5).

Monumento Natural Cueva Milodón ① *25 km north, US$6 to enter park, camping allowed, getting there: regular bus from Prat 517, T412540, leaves 0945 and 1500, returns 1200 and 1700. US$7; taxi US$24 return or check if you can get a ride with a tour; Adventur and Fernández tour buses to Torres del Paine stop at the cave*. In this cave (70 m wide, 45 m high and 270 m deep), formed by ice-age glacial lakes, remains were found of a prehistoric ground-sloth, together with evidence of occupation by early Patagonian humans some 11,000 years ago. There is a small, well-presented visitor centre, with restaurant and toilets.

Parque Nacional Bernardo O'Higgins

Usually referred to as the **Parque Nacional Monte Balmaceda** ① *US$5*, the park is at the north end of Ultima Esperanza Sound and can only be reached on boat trips from Puerto Natales (recommended). After a three-hour journey up the Sound, the boat passes the Balmaceda Glacier which drops steeply from the eastern slopes of Monte Balmaceda (2,035 m). The glacier is retreating; in 1986 its foot was at sea level. The boat docks one hour further north at Puerto Toro, from where it's a 1-km walk to the base of Serrano Glacier on the north slope of Monte Balmaceda. On the trip dolphins, sea-lions (in season), black-necked swans, flightless steamer ducks and cormorants can be seen. There's an optional three-hour boat trip by zodiac 35 km up the Río Serrano into PN Torres del Paine, which you can use to start trekking. Run by Onas (see Puerto Natales, Activities and tours) it takes about 4 hours, US$60, worth it for those with the budget and limited time (service starts on 1 November). Better going to the park than from the park (the view suddenly opens up and then just gets better and better).

Border with Argentina

There are three crossing points: **Villa Dorotea**, 16 km east of Puerto Natales. On the Argentine side the road continues to a junction, with alternatives south to Río Turbio and north to La Esperanza and Río Gallegos. Chilean immigration is open all year 0800-2400. **Paso Casas Viejas**, 16 km northeast of Puerto Natales. On the Argentine side this joins the Río Turbio-La Esperanza road. Chilean immigration is open 0800-2400 in summer, 0800-2200 in winter. **Cerro Castillo**, 65 km north of Puerto Natales on the road to Torres del Paine, open 0800-2400 in summer, 0800-2200 in winter. On the Argentine side, Paso Cancha Carrera (14 km), the road leads to La Esperanza and Río Gallegos. All buses from El Calafate go via Cerro Castillo, making it possible to transfer to a bus passing from Puerto Natales to Torres del Paine. Chilean immigration is open all year 0800-2200, and the small settlement has several hospedajes and cafeterías. Sheep shearing in December, and rodeo and rural festival third weekend in January. See also Argentina, page 219.

● Sleeping

Puerto Natales and around *p748, map p750*
In season cheaper accommodation fills up quickly after the arrival of the Magallanes ship from Puerto Montt. Hotels in the countryside open only in summer months: dates vary.
LL Costaustralis, Pedro Montt 262, T412000, www.hoteles-australis.com. Very comfortable, tranquil, lovely views (but not from inland-facing rooms), lift, English spoken, waterfront restaurant serves international and local seafood, half price cheaper off season (Apr-Sep).
L Indigo Patagonia, Ladrilleros 105, T413609, www.indigopatagonia.com. Relaxed atmosphere, on the water front, great views, recently refurbished and converted into a boutique hotel with roof-top spa (suite LL), breakfast included, café/restaurant serves good seafood and vegetarian dishes, internet access.
AL Hostería y Refugio Monte Balmaceda, T220174, aventour@entelchile.net or info@ aventouraventuras.com. Beautifully situated on Ultima Esperanza Sound, close to the Río Serrano. Comfortable rooms and refugio with well-lit, giant tents, beds and bathrooms, restaurant. Also organize tours and rent equipment. Handy for boat trip up Río Serrano. Recommended.
AL-A Cisne de Cuello Negro, T244506, T411498 (Av Colón 782, Punta Arenas). In a splendid

lakeside setting, about 5 km north of town at Km 275 near Puerto Bories. Comfortable, excellent cooking.
A Estancia 3 Pasos, 40 km north on the way to Torres del Paine, T221930, www.hotel3pasos.cl. Good value in this simple, beautiful place.
A Martín Gusinde, Bories 278, T412770. American buffet breakfast included, modern 3-star standard, smart, parking, expensive restaurant.
A-B Aquaterra, Bulnes 299, T412239, www.aquaterrapatagonia.cl. Good restaurant with vegetarian options, "resto-bar" downstairs, alternative therapy centre, nice decor, safe, warm and comfortable, very helpful staff.
A Hostal Lady Florence Dixie, Bulnes 655, T411158. Modern 3-star hotel, hospitable, variable room standards, superior are good value
A Weskar Patagonian Lodge, Ruta 9, Km 1, T414168, www.weskar.cl. Ecolodge (B in low season) with views of the fjord, onces and dinner served, internet, bicycles, boat trips, riding, birdwatching, fishing and other activities offered.
B Hostal Sir Francis Drake, Phillipi 383, T411553, www.hostalfrancisdrake.com. Calm and welcoming, tastefully decorated, smallish rooms with cable TV, filling breakfast, good views. Recommended.

B Hostel Natales, Ladrilleros 209, T411081. **E** pp in dorms, fully refurbished former hotel, now a luxury hostel, very comfy but pricey.

C-D Casa Cecilia, Tomás Rogers 60, T/F411797, redcecilia@entelchile.net. Welcoming, popular, with small simple rooms, some singles (**E**), other doubles **C** with bath, great breakfast. English, French and German spoken, rents camping equipment and bicycles, booking for tours and information for Torres del Paine, also shared rooms with bunk beds. Warmly recommended.

C-D Hostal Bulnes, Bulnes 407, T411307, www.hostalbulnes.com. With breakfast, cheaper with shared bath, simple but charming, comfortable, laundry facilities, stores luggage.

D Blanquita, Carrera Pinto 409, T411674. Looks like a giant portacabin from the outside but is quiet, simple rooms, singles **F**, heating, stores luggage. Recommended.

D Patagonia Adventure, Tomás Rogers 179, T411028, www.apatagonia.com. Lovely old house, bohemian feel, shared bath, **G** pp in dorms, good value, homemade bread for breakfast, luggage store, equipment hire, bike and kayak tours and tour arrangements for Torres del Paine (see Sendero Aventura, below). Recommended.

D-E pp **Niko's II**, Phillipi 528, ½ block from Plaza de Armas, T411500, residencialnicosii@ hotmail.com. Breakfast included, heating, English spoken, book exchange, dirty kitchen, internet for guests if staff not using it, information, tours to Paine and Perito Moreno glacier, tent rental.

E Casa Teresa, Esmeralda 463, T410472, freepatagonia@hotmail.com. Good value, warm and quiet, breakfast included, also cheap meals, tours to Torres del Paine arranged.

E Hosp Chila, Carrera Pinto 442, T412328. Use of kitchen, welcoming, laundry facilities, luggage store, bakes bread. Recommended.

E Hosp Nancy, Ramírez 540, T410022, www.nataleslodge.cl. Good breakfast, shared bath, warm and hospitable, use of kitchen, information, internet, laundry service, runs tours and hires camping equipment. Recommended.

E Los Inmigrantes, Carrera Pinto 480, T413482, losinmigrantes@hotmail.com. Good breakfast,

Puerto Natales

To Punta Arenas & Parque Nacional Torres del Paine

Seno Ultima Esperanza

Estero Natales

R Freire

Valdivia

Lagoper

Cootra

Plaza de Armas

M Bulnes

Municipalidad

Zaahj

Onas

JB & Fortaleza

Fernández

Esmeralda

Baquedano

Transfer

Pier for Balmaceda Glacier

Eberhard

Chiloé

Arturo Prat

Blanco Encalada

O'Higgins

Museo Municipal

Carrera Pinto

To El Favorito

Pier for Puerto Montt

Mendoza

Chorrillos

Bus Sur

E Ramírez

To Museo De Agostini

N

0 metres 100
0 yards 100

Sleeping
Aquaterra **17** *C2*
Blanquita **2** *C2*
Casa Cecilia **4** *B2*
Casa Teresa **22** *C2*
Costaustralis **6** *C1*
Hospedaje Chila **20** *C2*

Hospedaje Dos
  Lagunas **7** *B1*
Hospedaje Nancy **8** *C3*
Hostal Bulnes **3** *B2*
Hostal Lady
  Florence Dixie **9** *B3*
Hostal Sir Francis
  Drake **10** *A2*
Hostel Natales **1** *B1*
Indigo Patagonia **5** *B1*
Josmar 2 Camping **11** *C2*
Los Inmigrantes **23** *C2*
Martín Gusinde **13** *B2*

Mwono Lodge **14** *B1*
Niko's **15** *C3*
Niko's II **12** *A2*
Patagonia Adventure
  & Sendero Aventura **16** *B2*
Residencial Centro **25** *B2*
Residencial Dickson **18** *C2*
Residencial El Mundial **19** *B2*
Residencial Gabriela **24** *C2*

Eating
Andrés **10** *C1*
Angelica's **1** *B2*

El Asador
  Patagónico **2** *B2*
El Living **3** *B2*
El Marítimo **4** *B1*
La Caleta Económica **6** *B2*
La Mesita Grande **5** *B2*
Oveja Negra **11** *B2*
Parrilla Don Jorge **7** *B2*

Bars & clubs
El Bar de Ruperto **8** *B2*
Kaweshkar **9** *C1*

kitchen facilities, equipment rental, luggage store. Recommended.
E Res Centro, Magallanes 258, T411996. With bath and breakfast, **G** singles, use of kitchen, helpful family. Recommended.
E Res Dickson, Bulnes 307, T411871, lodgin@chileaustral.com. Good value, **G** singles, with good breakfasts, helpful, internet, cooking and laundry facilities.
E Res El Mundial, Bories 315, T412476, omar@fortalezapatagonia.cl. Large breakfast, good value meals, use of kitchen when owners do not need it, luggage stored.
E Res Gabriela, Bulnes 317, T411061. Good breakfast, owner Gabriela is very helpful, heating in rooms, luggage store. Recommended.
E-F pp Hosp Dos Lagunas, Barros Araña 104, T09-9642 2407, doslagunas@hotmail.com. Lovely hospitable place with good breakfast, dinner available, shared bath, use of kitchen, TV and reading room, excursions and buses booked, lots of information.
E-F Mwono Lodge, Eberhard 214, T411018, mwonopatagonia@ze.cl. Nice, brightly decorated place with comfy shared rooms, breakfast included. Recommended.
E-F Niko's, E Ramírez 669, T412810, nikores idencial@hotmail.com. Breakfast extra, hospitable, basic, family-run, warm kitchen to use, luggage store, helpful, good meals.
Camping Josmar 2, Esmeralda 517, in centre. Family run, convenient, hot showers, parking, barbecues, electricity, café, US$2.50 per site or **F** pp in double room.

Border with Argentina *p749*
A-B Hostería El Pionero, Cerro Castillo, 63 km north of Puerto Natales, T/F412911. Comfortable country house ambience, good service.
E pp Hospedaje Loreto Belén, Cerro Castillo, T413063, or 691932 (public phone, ask to speak to Loreto Belén). Rooms for 4, all with bath, breakfast included, also offers meals, good home cooking.

🍴 Eating

Puerto Natales *p748, map p750*
🍴🍴🍴-🍴🍴 **Angelicas**, Eberhard 532, T410365. Elegant Mediterranean style, well-prepared food with quality ingredients. Pricy but recommended.
🍴🍴🍴-🍴🍴 **El Asador Patagónico**, Prat 158 on the Plaza. Spit-roast lamb, salads, home-made puddings, attractive. Recommended.
🍴🍴🍴-🍴🍴 Parrilla Don Jorge, Bories 430, on Plaza, T410999. Also specializes in spit-roast lamb, but serves fish, too, good service.
🍴🍴 **El Marítimo**, on the waterfront. Excellent good value fish, friendly service, wonderful views. Recommended.

🍴🍴 **El Rincón de Don Chicho**, Luis Martínez 206, T414339. The best parrilla in town, all-you-can-eat, great fish too, veggie options by request, authentic atmosphere with the charismatic Don Chicho.
🍴🍴 **La Mesita Grande**, Prat 169 on the Plaza, T411571. Fresh pizzas from the wood-burning oven, also pasta and good desserts.
🍴🍴 **Oveja Negra**, Tomás Rogers 169, Plaza de Armas. Excellent local food, also book exchange.
🍴🍴-🍴 **La Caleta Económica**, Eberhard 261, T413969. Huge portions, fish, meat, good value.
🍴 **Andrés**, Ladrilleros 381. Recommended for fish, nice owner, good service.
🍴 **El Living**, Prat 156, Plaza de Armas, www.el-living.com. Just what you need: comfy sofas, good tea, magazines in all languages, book exchange, good music, delicious vegetarian food, British run.

Cafés
Café + Books, Blanco Encalada 224. Cosy café with a 2 for 1 book exchange.
Patagonia Dulce, Barros Arana 233. For the best hot chocolate in town.

🍸 Bars and clubs

Puerto Natales *p748, map p750*
El Bar de Ruperto, Bulnes 371, T414302. Lively place with DJs, live music, lots of drinks (try the vodka with chillies) and some food. Open 2100-0500.
Kaweshkar, Bulnes 43, T415821, kaweshkar@ yurhouse.com. Groovy laid-back bar, serving empanadas, hamburgers, vegetarian food. Try the parmesan molluscs tacos. Club at night with lounge music.

🛍 Shopping

Puerto Natales *p748, map p750*
Camping equipment Check all camping equipment and prices carefully. Average charges per day: whole set US$15, tent US$8, sleeping bag US$4-6, mat US$2, raincoat US$1, also cooking gear, US$2. (**Note** Deposits required: tent US$200, sleeping bag US$100.) Camping gas is widely available in hardware stores, eg at Baquedano y O'Higgins and at **Balfer**, Baquedano y Esmeralda. **Casa Cecilia**, Tomás Rogers 60, recommended. **Fortaleza**, Tomás Rogers y Bulnes. Good equipment at a fair price.
La Maddera, Prat 297. Outdoor clothing.
Patagonia Adventures, Tomás Rogers 179.
Supermarkets El Favorito, Bulnes 1085. Super Dos Bulnes y Balmaceda. Open 24 hrs, cheaper in Punta Arenas.

▲ Activities and tours

Puerto Natales *p748, map p750*
Many agencies along Eberhard. Reports of the reliability of agencies, especially for their trips to Parque Nacional Torres del Paine, are very mixed. It is better to book tours direct with operators in Puerto Natales than through agents in Punta Arenas or Santiago. Several agencies offer tours to the Perito Moreno glacier in Argentina, 1 day, US$60, 14-hr trip, 2 hrs at the glacier, without food or park entry fee. You can then leave the tour in Calafate to continue into Argentina. Recommended.

Bigfoot Expdeciones, Bories 206, T413247, www.bigfoot patagonia.com. Sea kayaking and ice-hiking (½-day from Refugio Grey, includes 3 hr trek, learning about various glacial features, followed by a climb up a sheer ice wall, reasonable level of fitness required), not cheap but worth it, professional. Recommended.

Estancia Travel, Casa 13-b, Puerto Bories, Puerto Natales, T412221, www.estanciatravel.com. Based at the Estancia Puerto Consuelo, 5 km north of Puerto Natales, offer horse riding trips from 1 to 10 days around southern Patagonia and Torres del Paine, with accommodation at traditional estancias. Also kayaking trips, British/Chilean run, bilingual, professional guides, at the top end of the price range. Recommended.

Onas, Eberhard 595, T414349, www.onaspatagonia.com. Tours of Torres del Paine, kayak trips. Onas offer boat trips to the Park by zodiac and from there on tour boats to Puerto Natales, US$90 pp all-inclusive.

Sendero Aventura, at Albergue Patagonia Adventure, Tomás Rogers 179, T411028, www.senderoaventura.com. Adventure tours, including trekking to Torres del Paine, boats in Balmaceda PN, camping equipment and bike hire. Recommended.

Skorpios, Prat 62, T412409, see also under Santiago, Ferry companies, www.skorpios.cl. Run Exploradores Kaweskar, and adventure tour from Puerto Natales to Puerto Edén, incorporating a sea journey on Skorpios 3 and expedition on the Campo Hielo del Sur.

Turismo Nunatak, Arturo Prat 353, turismonunatak@yahoo.com. Tours and camping equipment hire for Torres del Paine, etc. French owner, also speaks English and Spanish, very helpful. Recommended.

● Transport

Puerto Natales *p748, map p750*
Bus In summer book ahead. Buses leave from company offices: **Bus Fernández**, E Ramírez 399, T411111. **Pacheco**, Baquedano y O'Higgins. **Bus Sur**, Baquedano 668, T614220. **Transfer**, Baquedano 414, T421616. **Zaahj**, Prat 236, T412260.

To **Punta Arenas**, several daily, 3½ hrs, US$5.70, Fernández, Pacheco, Bus Sur and Transfer. To **Coyhaique**, Bus Sur Mon, US$45. To Argentina: to **Río Gallegos** direct, Bus Sur, **El Pingüino** and **Ghisoni**, 2-3 weekly each, US$18, 4-5 hrs. Hourly to **Río Turbio**, Lagoper, Baquedano y Valdivia, and other companies, US$5, 2 hrs (depending on Customs – change bus at border). To **El Calafate**, US$20, **Cootra** via Río Turbio, daily, 6 hrs; or Bus Sur (1 a week) and Zaahj (3 a week) both operating a more direct service via Cerro Castillo. Otherwise travel agencies run several times a week depending on demand, US$50 one way, US$57 for return, not including Perito Moreno glacier entry fee (12 hr trip), shop around, reserve 1 day ahead. Bus Sur also runs 3 buses a week to **Ushuaia** Oct-Apr, 15 hrs, US$38. **Note** See Torres del Paine section for buses from Puerto Natales into the park, page 757.

Car hire Bien al Sur, Bulnes 433, T414025. Motor Cars, Blanco Encalada 330, T415593. EMSA Avis, Bulnes 632, T410775. Hire agents can arrange permission to drive into Argentina, takes 24 hrs to arrange, extra insurance required.

Ferry See services from Puerto Montt. Comapa, Bulnes 533, T414300, www.comapa.com. Navimag, Manuel Bulnes 533, T414300, www.navimag.com.

To **Parque Nacional Bernardo O'Higgins**: Sailings to **Balmaceda Glacier** daily at 0815 in summer, returning 1630, Sun only in winter (minimum 10 passengers), US$60. Including Río Serrano, US$85. Bookings direct from **Turismo 21 de Mayo**, Eberhard 560, T411176, www.turismo21demayo.cl (also offers estancia accommodation). **Nueva Galicia**, Eberhard 169, T412352, or **Onas Turismo**, see Puerto Natales, Activities and tours. Expensive lunch extra, take picnic, drinks available on board. Heavily booked in high season. Take warm clothes, hat and gloves.

● Directory

Puerto Natales *p748, map p750*
Banks Rates for TCs, which can't be changed into US$ cash, are poor. **Banco Santiago**, ATM; several others. Casas de cambio on Blanco Encalada, eg 266 (**Enio América**). Others on Bulnes and Prat. **Bicycle repairs** El Rey de la Bicicleta, Ramírez 540, Arauco 779. Good, helpful. **Internet** Several, including Blanco Encalada 330. **Post offices** Eberhard 417, open Mon-Fri 0830-1230, 1430-1745, Sat 0900-1230. **Telephones** Telefónica, Blanco Encalada y Phillipi. Phones, internet, fax. Entel, Baquedano y Bulnes.

Parque Nacional Torres del Paine → Colour map 9, grid B1.

Nothing prepares you for the spectacular beauty of Parque Nacional Torres del Paine. World renowned for its challenging trekking, the park's 181,414 ha contain 15 peaks above 2,000 m. At its centre is the glacier-topped granite massif Macizo Paine, from which rise the vertical pink granite Torres (Towers) del Paine and, below them, the Cuernos (Horns) del Paine, swooping buttresses of lighter granite under caps of darker sedimentary rock. From the vast Campo de Hielo Sur icecap on its western edge, four main glaciers (ventisqueros), Grey, Dickson, Zapata and Tyndall, drop into vividly coloured lakes formed by their meltwater: turquoise, ultramarine and pistachio expanses, some filled with wind-sculpted royal blue icebergs. Wherever you explore, there are constantly changing views of dramatic peaks and ice fields. The park enjoys a micro-climate especially favourable to wildlife and plants: there are 105 species of birds including condors, ibis, flamingoes and austral parakeets, and 25 species of mammals including guanaco, hares, foxes, pumas and skunks. Allow 5-7 days to see it all properly.

Ins and outs

Information The park is administered by **CONAF**: the Administration Centre (T691931) is in the south of the park at the northwest end of Lago del Toro (open 0830-2000 in summer, 0830-1230, 1400-1830 off season). There are entrances at Laguna Amarga, Lago Sarmiento and Laguna Azul, and you are required to **register** and show your passport when entering the park, since rangers (*guardeparques*) keep a check on the whereabouts of all visitors. You must also register before setting off on any hike. Phone the administration centre for information (in Spanish) on weather conditions. It also has videos and exhibitions with summaries in English of flora and fauna, but no maps to take away. There are six ranger stations (*guarderías*) staffed by rangers, who give help and advice. They will also store luggage (except at Laguna Amarga where they have no room). *Guarderías* at Campamentos Las Torrres, Italiano and Paso are open October-April only. Entry for foreigners: US$28 (proceeds are shared between all Chilean national parks); climbing fees US$1,000. The national park received about 100,000 visitors in 2005. The impact of huge numbers of visitors to the park is often visible in litter around the refugios and camping areas. Take all your rubbish out of the park including toilet paper.

Getting around and accommodation The park is well set up for tourism, with frequent bus services running from Puerto Natales through the park, to pick up and drop off walkers at various hotels, to start treks, and to connect with boat trips. For details, see Transport below. Accommodation is available on three levels: there are hotels (expensive, over US$100 pp per night), *refugios*, six of which are privately-run, well-equipped, staffed, offering meals and free hot water for tea, soup etc (US$30-35 pp per night bed only, double this to include food), and 14 campsites. All options fill up quickly in peak summer months, Jan-Feb, so plan your trip and book hotels and refugios in advance. Pay in dollars to avoid IVA (tax). See Sleeping for more details. **Note** Mice have become a problem around camping sites and the free refugios; do not leave food in packs on the ground. ▸▸ *For further information, see Listings, page 756.*

Safety warning It is vital to be aware of the unpredictability of the weather (which can change in a few minutes, see Climate below) and the arduousness of some of the stretches on the long hikes. Rain and snowfall are heavier the further west you go and bad weather sweeps off the Campo de Hielo Sur without warning. The only means of rescue are on horseback or by boat; the nearest helicopter is in Punta Arenas and high winds usually prevent its operation in the park.

Forest fires are a serious hazard. Follow all instructions about lighting fires to the letter. An unauthorized campfire in 2005 led to the destruction of 10% of the northeast sector of the national park.

Equipment and maps A strong, streamlined, waterproof tent gives you more freedom than crowded refugios and is essential if doing the complete circuit. Also essential at all times of year are protective clothing against cold, wind and rain, strong waterproof footwear, a compass, a good sleeping bag, sleeping mat, camping stove and cooking equipment. Most refugios will hire camping equipment for a single night. Sun-screen and sunglasses are also necessary, and you'll want shorts in summer. At the entrance you are asked what equipment you have. Take your own food: the small shops at the Andescape refugios and at the Posada

Río Serrano are expensive and have a limited selection. Maps (US$7) are obtainable at **CONAF** offices in Punta Arenas or Puerto Natales. Other Torres del Paine maps are published by Mattassi and (more accurate) Cartografía Digital and Patagonia Interactiva; all three have a few mistakes, however.

Climate Do not underestimate the severity of the weather here. The Park is open all year round, although snow may prevent access in the winter. The warmest time is December to March, but also the most unstable; strong winds often blow off the glaciers, and rainfall can be heavy. It is most crowded in the summer holiday season, January to mid-February, less so in December or March. In winter there can be good, stable conditions and well-equipped hikers can do some good walking, but some treks may be closed and boats may not be running.

Hikes

There are about 250 km of well-marked trails, and walkers must keep to the paths: cross-country trekking is not permitted. The times indicated should be treated with caution: allow for personal fitness and weather conditions.

El Circuito (Allow at least seven days) The most popular hike is a circuit round the Torres and Cuernos del Paine: it is usually done anticlockwise starting from the Laguna Amarga *guardería*. From Laguna Amarga the route is north along the west side of the Río Paine to Lago Paine, before turning west to follow the Río Paine to the south end of Lago Dickson. From here the path runs along the wooded valley of the Río de los Perros before climbing steeply to Paso John Gardner (1,241 m, the highest point on the route), then dropping to follow the Grey Glacier southeast to Lago Grey, continuing to Lago Pehoé and the administration centre. There are superb views, particularly from the top of Paso John Gardner.

Camping gear must be carried. The circuit is often closed in winter because of snow. The longest lap is 30 km, between Refugio Laguna Amarga and Refugio Dickson (10 hours in good weather; one campsite, Serón), but the most difficult section is the very steep slippery slope between Paso John Gardner and Campamento Paso, a section exposed to strong westerly winds. The major rivers are crossed by footbridges, but these are occasionally washed away.

The W (Allow five days) A popular alternative to El Circuito, it can be completed without camping equipment by staying in refugios, and can be done in either direction. It combines several of the hikes described separately below. From Laguna Amarga the first stage runs west via Hostería Las Torres and up the valley of the Río Ascensio via Refugio Chileno to the base of the Torres del Paine (see below). From here return to the Hostería Las Torres and then walk along the northern shore of Lago Nordenskjold via Refugio Los Cuernos to Campamento Italiano. From here climb the Valley of the Río del Francés (see below) before continuing to Lodge Paine Grande. From here you can complete the third part of the 'W' by walking west along the northern shore of Lago Grey to Refugio Grey and Glaciar Grey before returning to Lodge Paine Grande.

The Valley of the Río del Francés (Allow five hours each way) From Lodge Paine Grande this route leads north across undulating country along the west edge of Lago Skottberg to Campamento Italiano and then follows the valley of the Río del Francés, which climbs between (to the west) Cerro Paine Grande and the Ventisquero del Francés, and (to the east) the Cuernos del Paine to Campamento Británico. Allow 2½ hours from Lodge Paine Grande to Campamento Italiano, 2½ hours further to Campamento Británico. The views from the mirador, 20 minutes above Campamento Británico, are superb.

Up the Río Pingo valley (Allow four hours each way) From Guardería Grey (18 km west by road from the Administration Centre) follow the Río Pingo, via Refugio Pingo and Refugio Zapata (four hours), with views south over Ventisquero Zapata (plenty of wildlife, icebergs in the lake). It is not possible to reach Lago Pingo as a bridge – marked on many maps – has been washed away. Ventisquero Pingo can be seen 3 km away over the lake.

To the base of the Torres del Paine (Allow four to five hours each way) From Laguna Amarga the route follows the road west to Hostería Las Torres before climbing along the west side of the Río Ascensio via Campamento Chileno to Campamento Las Torres, close to the base of the Torres and near a small lake. Allow 1½ hours to Hostería Las Torres, then two hours to

Campamento Chileno, two hours further to Campamento Torres where there is a lake: the path is well-marked, but the last 30 minutes is up the moraine; to see the towers lit by sunrise (spectacular, but you must have good weather), it's well worth humping camping gear up to Campamento Torres and spending the night (no *refugio*). One hour beyond Campamento Torres is the good site at Campamento Japonés.

To Laguna Verde (Allow four hours each way) From the administration centre follow the road north 2 km, before taking the path east over the Sierra del Toro and then along the south side of Laguna Verde to the Guardería Laguna Verde. This is one of the easiest walks in the park and may be a good first hike.

Parque Nacional Torres del Paine

Hostería Mirador
  del Payne **2**
Hostería Pehoé **5**
Posada Río Serrano **7**

Refugios ⌂
Chileno (Fantástico Sur) **1**
Lago Dickson
  (Andescape) **2**
Grey (Andescape) **3**
Las Torres
  (Fantástico Sur) **8**

Los Cuernos
  (Fantástico Sur) **9**
Lodge Paine Grande
  (Vértice) **10**

Camping ▲
Campamento Británico **1**
Campamento Chileno **3**
Campamento Italiano **4**
Campamento Japonés **5**
Campamento Las
  Guardas **6**

Campamento Las Torres **7**
Campamento Paso **8**
Serrano **9**
Laguna Azul **10**
Las Torres **11**
Los Perros **12**
Serón **13**
Lago Pehoé **14**

Ranger stations ⌂
  (*guarderías*)

Sleeping 🛏
Explora **1**
Hostería Lago Grey **3**
Hostería Las Torres **4**

0 km ——— 3
0 miles ——— 3
N

755

To Laguna Azul and Lago Paine (Allow 8½ hours each way) This route runs north from Laguna Amarga to the west tip of Laguna Azul (following the road for 7km), from where it continues across the sheltered Río Paine valley past Laguna Cebolla to the Refugio Lago Paine (now closed) at the west end of the lake.

● Sleeping

Parque Nacional Torres del Paine
p753, map p755
All the park's hotels are expensive, many feel overpriced. **Turismo Río Serrano**, Prat 258, Puerto Natales, T410684, and **www.Torresdelpaine.org**, T313 3389, hotelschile@terra.cl, offer accommodation, transfers and car hire, and **Experience Chile**, www.experiencechile.org offers hotels and tour itineraries. Discounted packages are sometimes available from **Ruta Chile**, T02-235 2384/951 5773, www.rutachile.cl.
LL Hotel Explora, T411247. The park's most expensive and exclusive is nestled into a nook at Salto Chico on edge of Lago Pehoé, spectacular views. Everything is included: pool, gym, horse riding, boat trips, tours, can arrange packages from Punta Arenas (reservations: Av Américo Vespucci 80, p 7, Santiago, T206-6060, www.explora.com).
LL-L Hostería Lago Grey, T410172, www.turismolagogrey.com. Great views over Lago Grey, but small rooms, glacier walks (reservations through Arka Patagonia in Punta Arenas). Accepts Visa.
LL-L Hostería Las Torres, head office Magallanes 960, Punta Arenas, T710050, www.lastorres.cl. Superb, comfortable rooms, beautiful lounge with wood fire and great views of the Cuernos, excellent restaurant with evening buffet, good service (but a bit of hard sell on the excursions etc), horse-riding, transport from Laguna Amarga ranger station, spa, disabled access. Accepts Visa. Recommended. Visitor centre and confitería open to non-residents for sandwiches, but prices double after 1900.
L Hostería Mirador del Payne, Estancia Lazo, lovely location on Laguna Verde on east edge of the park, 52 km from Sarmiento entrance, reservations from Fagnano 585, Punta Arenas, T061-228712, www.miradordelpayne.com. Comfortable, meals extra, but inconvenient for park itself, riding, hiking, birdwatching. Private transport essential, or hike there from the park.
L-AL Hostería Pehoé, T411390, www.pehoe.com, 5 km south of Pehoé ranger station, 11 km north of park administration. Beautifully situated on an island with spectacular view across Lago Pehoé, but rather run down.

Closed Apr-Oct, restaurant (reservations: Turismo Pehoé in Punta Arenas or Antonio Bellet 77, of 605, Santiago, T235 0252, F236 0917).
AL-A Posada Río Serrano, an old estancia, reservations through Baqueano Zamora, Baquedano 534, Puerto Natales, T061-613531, www.baqueanozamora.com. An old estancia, recently refurbished, some rooms with bath, some without, cable TV, near park administration, with expensive but good restaurant and a shop, may allow use of cooking facilities when quiet. Recommended.

Refugios
Three companies between them run half of the refugios in the park, providing dormitory space only (bring your own sleeping bag, or hire one for US$6.50). Prices are US$33.50-44 pp b&b, full board about US$62. Refugios have kitchen facilities, hot showers, and space for camping, US$6.50. All refugios hire tents for US$11.15 per night. Most refugios close in winter, although one or 2 may stay open, depending on the weather. Advance booking essential in high season; service can be poor. **Note** Contracts for running the refugios are due to change in 2007.
Andescape refugios (Eberhard 599, Puerto Natales, T412877, www.andes capetour.blogspot.com).
Refugio Grey, on the eastern shore of Lago Grey (has facilities for ice climbing).
Refugio Lago Dickson, on the northern part of the circuit.
Fantástico Sur refugios (book through Las Torres, T061-710050, albergue@lastorres.com).
Refugio Chileno, in the Valley of the Río Ascencio, at the foot of the Torres (very expensive meals).
Refugio Las Torres, next to the Hostería Las Torres (see above), good facilities.
Refugio Los Cuernos, on the northern shore of Lago Nordenskjold.
Vértice refugios. Book through Vértice Patagonia, T061-414300, www.verticepatagonia.cl.
Lodge Paine Grande, on the northwest tip of Lago Pehoé (expensive food, has internet).

● For an explanation of the sleeping and eating price codes used in this guide, see page 58.
● Other relevant information is found in Essentials pages 602-604.

Camping

Fires may only be lit at organized camping sites, not at campamentos. The guardaparques expect people to have a stove if camping. In addition to sites at the above refugios there are the following sites: **Camping Lago Pehoé** and **Camping Serrano**, both run by Turismo Río Serrano (address above), US$20 per site at former (maximum 6 persons, hot showers) and US$15 per site at latter (maximum 6 persons, cold showers, more basic). **Camping Laguna Azul**, hot showers, US$20 per site. **Camping Los Perros**, run by Andescape, US$6.50 pp (US$52 tent, mattress, 3 meals), shop and hot showers. **Camping Serón** and **Camping Las Torres** (at Hostería Las Torres, both run by Estancia Cerro Paine, US$4, hot showers. Free camping is permitted in 7 other locations in the park: these sites are known as campamentos. The wind tends to rise in the evening so pitch tent early. Beware mice, which eat through tents. Equipment hire in Puerto Natales (see above).

▲ Activities and tours

Parque Nacional Torres del Paine
p753, map p755
See under Puerto Natales, Activities and tours, page 752, for recommendations. There are increasingly mixed reports of tours. Before booking a tour, check carefully on details and get them in writing.
Boat trips From Refugio Lago Pehoé to Refugio Pudeto, US$19 one way with 1 backpack (US$8 for extra backpacks), from Pudeto 0930, 1200, 1800, from Pehoé 1000, 1300, 1900, 20 mins in high season, reserve in advance at the refugios at either end or at Catamarán Hielos Patagónicos, Los Arrieros 1517, Puerto Natales, T411380. Off-season, radio for the boat from Lodge Paine Grande. At all times check in advance that boats are running. See Parque Nacional Bernardo O'Higgins above for entry by 3-hr zodiac trip up the Río Serrano from Balmaceda glacier. Boat to face of glacier from **Hostería Grey**, twice daily, 3½ hrs, US$60 return. A one-way trip can be made via the glacier face to/from the Hostería to the **Refugio Grey** for US$50. Book direct or though **Turismo Runner** (T414141) in Puerto Natales.

⊖ Transport

Parque Nacional Torres del Paine
p753, map p755
Bus The park is 145 km northwest of Puerto Natales. Note that these timetables are likely

to change with the opening of the new road to the south side of the park in 2007, when complete it should cut the journey time from Puerto Natales to about 2 hrs. After mid-Mar there is little public transport and trucks are irregular. From early Nov-mid Apr, there are 3 companies running daily services into the park, leaving Puerto Natales between 0630 and 0800, and again at around 1430, 2½ hrs to Laguna Amarga, 3 hrs to the administration centre. To go to the Administration centre, all charge US$12 one way, US$22 open return (return tickets are not always interchangeable between different companies). Buses will stop anywhere en route, but all stop at Laguna Amarga entrance, Salto Grande del Paine and administration centre near Posada Serrano. **JB**, Prat 258, T412824. **Fortaleza**, Prat 258, T410595. **Bus Sur**, Baquedano 668, T614220. In high season the buses fill quickly so it is best to board at Administration for the return to Puerto Natales. All buses wait at Refugio Pudeto until the 1200 boat from Refugio Lago Pehoé arrives. Travel between two points within the park (eg Pudeto-Laguna Amarga) US$4. At other times services by travel agencies are dependent on demand: arrange return date with driver to coincide with other groups to keep costs down. **Luis Díaz** is reliable, about US$17 pp, minimum 3 people. Hostería Las Torres sometimes runs an employee bus back to Puerto Natales at 1700, US$5, ask at reception.

In season there are frequent minibus connections within the park: from Laguna Amarga to Hostería Las Torres, US$6.50, and from the administration centre to Hostería Lago Grey, US$17.65. Other than these routes getting around the park without your own transport is difficult and expensive. From Torres del Paine to **Calafate** (Argentina): take the direct bus run by **Chaltén Travel**, US$50, or take services from Puerto Natales (see above); alternatively take a bus from the park to Cerro Castillo (106 km south of administration centre) then catch a direct service to Calafate, on Bus Sur or Zaahj (see Puerto Natales Buses).
Car hire Hiring a pick-up in Punta Arenas is an economical proposition for a group (up to 9 people): US$400-420 for 4 days. If driving there yourself, the road from Puerto Natales is being improved and, in the park, the roads are narrow and winding with blind corners: use your horn a lot. It takes about 3 hrs from Puerto Natales to the administration centre. Petrol available at Río Serrano, but fill up in case.

Tierra del Fuego

The western side of this, the largest island off the extreme south of South America, belongs to Chile and the eastern to Argentina. Here the Andes cordillera runs from west to east, so that the north of the island is flat, covered with vast sheep farms, while the south has mountains, glaciers, lakes and forests. The major population centres, Ushuaia and Río Grande, are on the Argentine side, but Chile has the most southerly town in the world, Puerto Williams, on the island Isla Navarino below Tierra del Fuego. See Argentine Tierra del Fuego for Background.

Porvenir and around → *Phone code: 061. Colour map 9, grid C2. Population: 5,100.*

Porvenir is a quiet, pleasant place with many inhabitants of Croatian descent. Founded in 1894 in the gold boom, when many people came seeking fortunes from Croatia and Chiloé, it's a quiet, pleasant place with neat, painted tin houses and quaint, tall trees lining the main avenue. There is a small museum, the **Museo Fernando Cordero Rusque** *Samuel Valdivieso 402*, with archaeological and photographic displays on the Onas; good displays on natural history and the early gold diggers. There is a bank on the Plaza. **Tourist information** at the municipalidad ① *Zavattara 402, T580094*, and at tiny kiosk on the waterfront, helpful, sells fine handicrafts, kuanip@entelchile.net. Porvenir is the base for exploring the wonderfully wild virgin territory of Tierra del Fuego. Fly fishing, until recently the secret of Hollywood stars, is becoming world-renowned. The area is rich in brown trout, sea-run brook trout and steelheads, weighing 2-14 kg. Excursions are likely to involve camping and travel on horseback.

Driving east along **Bahía Inútil**, a wonderful windswept bay, there are views of distant hills and the snow-capped Darwin range along the horizon. At Caleta Josefina, 98 km east, you can visit a handsome ex-estancia built in 1833, where some old buildings remain. Highly recommended is horseriding to the forests of the **Darwin range**, wild and challenging. Other options are sailing from Porvenir to **Río Cóndor** across Bahía Inútil, south of Cameron, with trekking or riding from Cameron to **Seno Almirantazgo**, a beautiful, wild and treeless place, where mountains sink into blue fjords with icebergs. Also sailing to **Marinelli glacier**, where you can sail, kayak and dive. A recommended tour goes along the gold circuit, **Cordón Baquedano**, where you can see gold panning using the same techniques since mining began in 1881, a five-hour, 115-km round trip, good on horseback.

Border with Argentina → *Argentine time is 1 hr ahead of Chilean time, Mar-Oct.*

The only legal border crossing between the Chilean and Argentine parts of Tierra del Fuego is 142 km east of Porvenir at **San Sebastián**; open 0800-2200. On the Argentine side the road continues to Río Grande. **Note** There are two settlements called San Sebastián, on each side of the border but they are 14 km apart; taxis are not allowed to cross. No fruit, vegetables, dairy produce or meat permitted on entry to Chile. For entry to Argentina, see page 225.

Puerto Williams → *Phone code: 061. Colour map 9, grid C2. Population: 2,500.*

Puerto Williams is a Chilean naval base on **Isla Navarino**, south of the Beagle Channel. About 50 km south east of Ushuaia (Argentina) at 54° 55' 41" south, 67° 37' 58" west, it is small, friendly and remote. The island is totally unspoilt and beautiful, offering great geographical diversity, thanks to **Dientes de Navarín** range, with peaks over 1,000 m, covered with southern beech forest up to 500 m, and, south of that, great plains covered in peat bogs, with many lagoons and abundant in flora. The island was the centre of the indigenous Yaganes culture and there are 500 archaeological sites, the oldest from 3,000 years ago. **Museo Martín Gusinde** ① *Mon-Thu 1000-1300, 1500-1800, Sat-Sun1500-1800, Fri closed (subject to change), US$1*, is also known as the Museo del Fin del Mundo ('End of the World Museum'). It is full of information about vanished tribes, local wildlife, and voyages including Charles Darwin and Fitzroy of the Beagle, a must. The town has a bank, supermarkets and hospital. **Tourist information** ① *Municipalidad de Cabos de Hornos, Pres Ibáñez 130, T621011, isotop@mitierra.cl, closed in winter*. Ask for maps and details on hiking.

Around Puerto Williams

For superb views, climb **Cerro Bandera** (3-4 hours' round trip, steep, take warm clothes). **Villa Ukika**, 2 km east of town, is where the last descendants of the Yaganes people live, relocated from their original homes at Caleta Mejillones. There is excellent trekking around the **Dientes de Navarín**, the southernmost trail in the world, through impressive mountain landscapes, with superb views of Beagle Channel (challenging, 53 km in five days, December-March only, good level of fitness needed). Charter flights are available over Cape Horn and to **King George Island** on northern tip of Antarctic peninsula, where you can see the curvature of the earth on the horizon, with excursions to penguin and sea lion colonies. No equipment rental on island.

Cape Horn

It is possible to catch a boat south from Isla Navarino to Cape Horn (the most southerly piece of land on earth apart from Antarctica). There is one pebbly beach on the north side of the island; boats anchor in the bay and passengers are taken ashore by motorized dinghy. A rotting stairway climbs the cliff above the beach, up to the building where three marines run the naval post. A path leads from here to the impressive monument of an albatross overlooking the wild, churning waters of the Drake Passage below.

● Sleeping

Porvenir *p758*
B Los Flamencos, Tte Merino, T580049, www.hosterialosflamencos.com. Best place to stay with good food, a pleasant place for a drink, fine views of the bay. Recommended.
D Hostería y Turismo Yendegaia, Croacia 702, T581665, www.turismoyendegaia.com. Charming bright yellow building two blocks from plaza. Comfortable, airy rooms, with TV, good restaurant and helpful information from tourist agency. Recommended.
D Rosas, Phillippi 296, T580088. Heating, hot water, restaurant and bar, internet. Recommended.
E Hostal Kawi, Pedro Silva 144, T581638. Comfortable, rooms for 3, with bath, offers fly-fishing trips.
E Restaurant y Hotel El Chispa, Señoret 202, T580054. Simple, some rooms with bath, good restaurant for seafood and other Chilean dishes.
F pp España, Croacia 698, T580160. Some rooms with bath, breakfast extra. Good restaurant with fixed price lunch.

Punta Delgada (see Transport, below)
D Hostería Tehuelche, T061-694433 at Kamiri Aike, 17 km from the port, with restaurant.
F pp Hotel El Faro. In the town itself. There is also a cosy tea room Bahía Azul.

Border with Argentina: San Sebastián *p758*
C-F Hostería de la Frontera, T061-696004, frontera@entelchile.net. Where buses stop for meals and cakes, cosy, with bath (the annex is much more basic), good food.
E ACA motel, T02964-425542, 14 km east, across the border (open 24 hrs), in Argentine San Sebastián, basic; service station open 0700-2300.

Puerto Williams *p758*
D pp Pensión Temuco, Piloto Pardo 244, T621113. Full board (room only available),

comfortable, hospitable, good food, including breakfasts, hot showers. Recommended.
E pp Hostería Camblor, Vía 2 s/n, T621033, hosteriacamblor@terra.cl. Heavily booked up, rooms with bath, restaurant, good value.
F pp Hostal Yagan, Piloto Pardo 260, T621334, hostalyagan@hotmail.com. Comfortable, includes breakfast, dinner available, family run by Daniel and Berta Yevenes, Daniel offers tours.
F pp Res Onashaga, Uspashun 15, T621564. Run by Señor Ortiz – everyone knows him. Basic, but warm welcome, good meals, helpful, full board available. You can also stay at private houses.
Camping Near the Hostería.

Elsewhere in Chilean Tierra del Fuego
C-F Hostería Tunkelen, Arturo Prat Chacón 101, Cerro Sombrero, T061-212757, hosteria_tunkelen@hotmail.com. Also dorm **E** pp. Recommended.
　Cerro Sombrero, 46 km south of Primera Angostura, is a village built to administrate oil drilling in the area, there's a bank, fuel and several other hotels (**F-G**).
F Posada Las Flores, Km 127 on the road to San Sebastián, reservations via Hostal de la Patagonia in Punta Arenas.
G Refugio Lago Blanco, on Lago Blanco, T061-241197. The only accommodation on the lake.

● Eating

Porvenir *p758*
Ⅶ Club Croata next to the bus stop on the waterfront. A lively place where you can get a good lunch for US$5.
Ⅶ Restaurante Puerto Montt, Croacia 1169, for seafood. Recommended.
Many lobster fishing camps where fishermen will prepare lobster on the spot.

▲ Activities and tours

Porvenir *p758*

For adventure tourism and trekking activities contact tour operators in Punta Arenas (see Activities and tours above, page 746)

Turismo Cordillera de Darwin, Croacia 675, T09-9640 7204, www.explorepatagonia.cl. Organizes island tours, from 1 day to 1 week.

Hostería y Turismo Yendegaia, see address in Sleeping, above. Lots of conventional local tours and some fishing trips run too.

Puerto Williams *p758*

Boat trips Most recommended is the cruise around Cape Horn and on to Ushuaia, returning to Punta Arenas, run by **Cruceros Australis SA**, Santiago office T02-442 3110, www.australis.com. Book well in advance. **Victory Adventures**, Casilla 70, T061-621010, www.victory-cruises.com, Captain Ben Garrett offers recommended adventure sailing in his schooner *Victory* in Dec and Jan, around canals, glaciers and islands, and as far as Antarctica. You may get a lift on a yacht (unlikely); ask at the yacht club, 1 km west.

Tour operators

Karanka Expeditions, run by Maurice Van de Maele, T621127.

Sim Ltda, www.simltd.com. Sailing trips, trekking tours and many other adventure activities, including kayaking and wildlife spotting.

◑ Transport

Ferries to Tierra del Fuego

There are 2 crossings. The ferry company accepts no responsibility for damage to vehicles.

Punta Arenas to Porvenir The **Melinka**, sails from Tres Puentes (5 km north of Punta Arenas, bus A or E from Av Magallanes, or colectivo 15, US$0.40; taxi US$3) at 0900, and an afternoon sailing Tue, Wed, Thu, 0930 Sun, no service Mon in season; less frequent sailings off season. 2½-hr crossing (can be rough and cold, watch for dolphins), US$8 pp, US$15 per bike, US$50 per vehicle. Return from Porvenir varying times in afternoon between 1300 and 1800, daily except Mon. Timetable dependent on tides and subject to change; check in advance. Reservations essential especially in summer (at least 24 hrs in advance for cars), obtainable from **Transbordadora Austral Broom**, Punta Arenas, Bulnes 5075, T218100, www.tabsa.cl.

Punta Delgada to Punta Espora (Bahía Azul) This crossing is via the Primera Angostura (First Narrows), 170 km northeast of Punta Arenas (Punta Espora is 80 km north of Porvenir). Boats run every 40 mins, 0830-2215, for the 15-min crossing: foot passengers US$4, US$25 per car.

The ferry takes about 4 trucks and 20 cars; before 1000 most space is taken by trucks. There is no bus service to or from this crossing. If hitching, this route is preferable as there is more traffic.

Porvenir *p758*

Air From Punta Arenas – weather and bookings permitting, **Aerovías DAP**, Señoret s/n, T580089, Porvenir, www.dap.cl, twice daily Mon-Sat, 10-15 mins, US$50 one way. Heavily booked so make sure you have your return reservation confirmed.

Bus 2 a week between Porvenir and **Río Grande** (Argentina), Tue and Sat 1400, 5 hrs, **Transportes Gessell**, Duble Almeyda 257, T580488 (Río Grande 02964-425611), US$20, heavily booked, buy ticket in advance, or phone; Río Grande-Porvenir, Wed and Sun 0800.

Ferry Terminal at Bahía Chilota, 5 km west, see above for details. From bus terminal to ferry, taxi US$6, bus US$1.50.

Road All roads are gravel. Fuel is available in Porvenir, Cerro Sombrero and Cullen. Police may help with lifts on trucks to Río Grande; elsewhere is difficult as there is little traffic.

San Sebastián *p758*

Minibus From Porvenir to San Sebastián, US$14.

Puerto Williams *p758*

Air From Punta Arenas by air, **Aerovías DAP** (details under Punta Arenas) daily Mon-Sat, 1 hr, US$70 each way, in 7-seater Cessna, luggage allowance 10 kg. Book well in advance; long waiting lists (be persistent). The flight is beautiful (sit on right from Punta Arenas) with superb views of Tierra del Fuego, the Cordillera Darwin, the Beagle Channel, and the islands stretching south to Cape Horn. Also army flights available (they are cheaper), but the ticket has to be bought through DAP.

Ferry No regular sailings from Ushuaia (Argentina). Boats from Punta Arenas: **Ferry Patagonia** (Austral Broom), once a week, US$130 for reclining seat, US$170 for bunk, including food, 36 hrs. www.tabsa.cl. The Navarino leaves Punta Arenas in 3rd week of every month, 12 passengers, US$180 pp one way; contact the owner, **Carlos Aguilera**, 21 de Mayo 1460, Punta Arenas, T228066). The Beaulieu, a cargo boat carrying a few passengers, sails from Punta Arenas once a month, US$350 return, 6 days.

① Directory

Puerto Williams *p758*

Airline offices Aerovías DAP, Centro Comercial s/n, T621051, in town centre. **Post offices** Close 1900. **Telephones** Telefónica, Mon-Sat 0930-2230, 1000-1300, 1600-2200.

Chilean Pacific Islands

Chile has two national parks in the Pacific: Juan Fernández Islands, a little easier to reach (and leave) now than in Robinson Crusoe's time, and the remarkable Easter Island.

Juan Fernández Islands → *Phone code: 032. Population: 500.*

This group of small volcanic islands is a national park administered by CONAF and is situated 667 km west of Valparaíso. They were declared a UN World Biosphere Reserve in 1977. They enjoy a mild climate and the vegetation is rich and varied. Fauna includes wild goats, hummingbirds and seals. The best time to visit is October-March; take insect repellent. The islands are named after Juan Fernández, the first European to visit in 1574. There are three islands, Robinson Crusoe, the largest, which was the home (1704-1709) of Alexander Selkirk (the original of Defoe's Robinson Crusoe), Alejandro Selkirk and Santa Clara, the smallest. Selkirk's cave on the beach of Robinson Crusoe, about 4 km northwest of the village, can be visited on a boat trip. The only settlement is San Juan Bautista on Robinson Crusoe Island, a fishing village of wooden frame houses, located on Bahía Cumberland on the north coast of the island: it has a church, schools, post office, and radio station. The islands are famous for langosta de Juan Fernández (a pincerless lobster) which is sent to the mainland.

Robinson Crusoe Island The remains of the **Fuerte Santa Bárbara**, the largest of the Spanish fortresses, overlook San Juan Bautista. The island has long been the target for treasure-seekers who claim that looted gold from Inca times is buried there. In September 2005 600 barrels of coins, jewels and statuary were said to have been found. Near Santa Bárbara are the **Cuevas de los Patriotas**, home to the Chilean independence leaders, deported by the Spanish after the Battle of Rancagua. South of the village is the **Mirador de Selkirk**, the hill where Selkirk lit his signal fires. A plaque was set in the rock at the look-out point by British naval officers from HMS Topaze in 1868; nearby is a more recent plaque placed by his descendants. (Selkirk, a Scot, was put ashore from HMS Cinque Ports and was taken off four years and four months later by a privateer, the Duke.) The Mirador is the only easy pass between the north and south sides of the island. Further south is the anvil-shaped **El Yunque**, 915 m, the highest peak on the island, where Hugo Weber, a survivor from the Dresden, lived as a hermit for 12 years. (The Dresden was a German cruiser, cornered by two British destroyers in Bahía Cumberland in 1915; the scuttled Dresden still lies on the seabed and a monument on the shore commemorates the event.) The only sandy beach on Robinson Crusoe is **Playa Arenal**, in the extreme southwest corner, two hours by boat from San Juan Bautista.

Each February, the **yachting regatta** visits the islands; setting out from Algarrobo, south of Valparaíso, the yachts sail to Isla Robinson Crusoe, then to Talcahuano and Valparaíso. At this time Bahía Cumberland is full of colourful and impressive craft, and prices in restaurants and shops double for the duration. (Thomas G Lammers, Department of Botany, University of Miami.) There are no exchange facilities. Only pesos and US$ cash accepted. No credit cards, no traveller's cheques.

● Sleeping

Juan Fernández Islands *p761*
Lodging with villagers is difficult.
L-AL pp Hostería El Pangal, east of San Juan in Caleta Pangal, T02-273 1458. Half-board. Great views, pool, bar and restaurant, best on the island.
AL-A Aldea Daniel Defoe Hotel, Larraín Alcalde 449, T032-275 1233, ebeeche@terra.com. Half board, full board available, bar, laundry service, tours offered.

A Hostal Charpentier, Ignacio Carrera Pinto 256, T032-275 1020, hostalcharpentier@hotmail.com. Kitchen facilities, laundry, also has *cabañas*, half and full board available, tours offered.
B-C Hostería Martínez Green, El Castillo 116, T032-275 1039. Rooms with TV, full and half board available, views, tours.
D-E Hostería Villa Green, Larraín Alcalde 246, T032-275 1044. With breakfast and TV, restaurant, views, tours offered.

⊖ Transport

Juan Fernández Islands *p761*
Air Air taxi daily in summer (subject to demand) from **Santiago** (US$500-600 round trip), all leave from Tobalaba Aerodrome in La Reina (eastern outskirts of city). **Aerolíneas ATA**, 11 de Septiembre 2115 Torre B, of 1107, Providencia, Santiago, T234 3389, www.aerolineasata.cl. And **Lasa**, Av Larraín 7941, La Reina, Santiago, T273 4309, lassa@terra.cl. The plane lands on an airstrip in the west of the island; passengers are taken by boat to San Juan Bautista (1½ hrs, US$2 one way).

Ferry A boat service from **Valparaíso**, is operated by **Naviera del Sur**, Blanco Encalada 1623, of 602, Valparaíso, T259 4304, www.navieradelsur.cl. It is for cargo and passengers, modest accommodation, 36-hr passage, US$300 return, full board, leaving in first week of each month; preference is given to islanders, and passages are sometimes difficult to book. Also try **Agentur**, Esmeralda 940, Valparaíso, T032-250976. No fishing or cargo boats will take passengers.

Rapa Nui/Easter Island → *Phone code: 032. Always 2 hrs behind the Chilean mainland.*

Known as the navel of the world by the original inhabitants, this remote outpost is studded with giant carved statues that appear trance-like, their gaze fixed on a distant horizon on the Pacific. Isla de Pascua (Rapa Nui) is just south of the Tropic of Capricorn and 3,790 km west of Chile. Its nearest neighbour is Pitcairn Island.

Ins and outs

Information Tourist office Sernatur ① *Tu'u Maheke s/n esq Apina, T210 0255, ipascua@ sernatur.cl, Mon-Fri 0830-1300, 1400-1730.* **Websites** http://islandheritage.org (**Easter Island Foundation**, in English, very useful). Average monthly temperatures vary between 15-17°C in August and 24° C in February, the hottest month. Average annual rainfall is 1,100 mm. There is some rain throughout the year, but the rainy season is March to October (wettest in May). The tourist season is from September to April. Anyone wishing to spend time exploring the island would be well-advised to speak to **CONAF** first ① *Mataveri Otai s/n, T210 0236*; they also give good advice on special interests (biology, archaeology, handicrafts, etc).

Background

The island is triangular in shape, 24 km across, with an extinct volcano at each corner. It is now generally accepted that the islanders are of Polynesian origin. The late Thor Heyerdahl's theories, as expressed in *Aku-Aku, The Art of Easter Island* (New York: Doubleday, 1975), are less widely accepted than they used to be, and South American influence is now largely discounted (see below). European contact with the island began with the visit of the Dutch admiral, Jacob Roggeven, on Easter Sunday 1722, who was followed by the British James Cook in 1774 and the French Le Perouse in 1786. The island was annexed by Chile in 1888.

The original islanders called the island *Te Pito o te Henua*, the navel of the world. The population was stable at 4,000 until the 1850s, when Peruvian slavers, smallpox and emigration to Tahiti (encouraged by plantation-owners) reduced the numbers. Now it is about 2,800, of whom about 500 are from the mainland, mostly living in the village of **Hanga Roa**. About half the island, of low round hills with groves of eucalyptus, is used for horses and cattle, and nearly one-half constitutes a national park (entry US$11, payable at Orongo). The islanders have preserved their indigenous songs and dances, and are extremely hospitable.

Tourism has grown rapidly since the air service began in 1967. Paid work is now more common, but much carving is still done. The islanders have profited greatly from the visits of North Americans: a Canadian medical expedition left a mobile hospital on the island in 1966, and when a US missile-tracking station was abandoned in 1971, vehicles, mobile housing and an electricity generator were left behind.

Sights

The unique features of the island are the 600 (or so) *moai*, huge stone figures up to 9 m in height and broad in proportion. One of them, on **Anakena** beach, was restored to its (probably) original state with a plaque commemorating Thor Heyerdahl's visit in 1955. Other moai have since been re-erected.

The cultural development of Easter Island

Far from being the passive recipient of external influences, Easter Island shows the extent of unique development possible for a people left wholly in isolation. It is believed to have been colonized from Polynesia about AD 800: its older altars (*ahu*) are similar to those of (French) Polynesia, and its older statues (*moai*) similar to those of the Marquesas Island in the Pacific between 8°-10° S, 140° W.

The very precise stone fitting of some of the *ahu*, and the tall gaunt *moai* with elongated faces and ears for which Easter Island is best known were later developments whose local evolution can be traced through a comparison of the remains. Indigenous Polynesian society, for all its romantic idylls, was competitive, and it seems that the five clans which originally had their own lands demonstrated their strength by erecting these complex monuments.

The *moai* were sculpted at the Rano Raraku quarry and transported on wooden rollers over more or less flat paths to their final locations; their red topknots were sculpted at and brought from the inland quarry of Puna Pau; and the rounded pebbles laid out checkerboard fashion at the *ahu* all came from the same beach at Vinapu. The sculptors and engineers were paid out of the surplus food produced by the sponsoring family: Rano Raraku's unfinished *moai* mark the end of the families' ability to pay. Over several centuries form about AD 1400 this stone work slowed down and stopped, owing to the deforestation of the island caused by roller production, and damage to the soils through deforestation and heavy cropping. The birdman cult represented at Orongo is a later development after the islanders had lost their clan territoriality and were concentrated at Hanga Roa, but still needed a non-territorial way to simulate inter-clan rivalry.

The central feature of the birdman cult was an annual ceremony in which the heads of the lineages, or their representatives, raced to the islets to obtain the first egg of the sooty tern (known as the Manatara), a migratory seabird which nests on Motu Nui, Motu Iti and Motu Kao. The winning chief was named Bird Man, Tangato Manu, for the following year. It appears that the egg of the tern represented fertility to the cult, although it is less clear what the status of the Tangata Manu actually was. The petroglyphs at Orongo depict the half-man, half-bird Tangata Manu, the creator god Make Make the symbol of fertility, Komari.

A tour of the main part of the island can be done on foot. This would need at least two days, returning to Hanga Roa and setting out again the next day as camping is not permitted in the park. To see more, hire a horse or a vehicle. From Hanga Roa, take the road going southeast past the airport; at the oil tanks turn right to Vinapu, where there are two ahu and a wall whose stones are joined with Inca-like precision. Head back northeast along the south coast, past Vaihu (an *ahu* with eight broken moai; small harbour); Akahanga (ahu with toppled moai); Hanga Tetenga (one toppled moai, bones can be seen inside the ahu), Ahu Tongariki (once the largest platform, damaged by a tidal wave in 1960). Turn left to Rano Raraku (20 km), the volcano where the moai were carved. Many statues can be seen. In the crater is a small lake surrounded by reeds (swimming possible beyond reeds). Good views and a good place to watch the sunrise.

The road heads north past 'the trench of the long-ears' and an excursion can be made to **Poike** to see the open-mouthed statue that is particularly popular with local carvers (ask farmer for permission to cross his land). On Poike the earth is red; at the northeast end is the cave where the virgin was kept before marriage to the victor of ceremonies during the birdman cult. The road along the north coast passes Ahu Te Pito Kura, a round stone called the navel of the world and one of the largest moai ever brought to a platform. It continues to Ovahe, where there is a very attractive beach with pink sand, some rather recently carved faces and a cave.

From Ovahe, one can return direct to Hanga Roa or continue to Anakena, site of **King Hotu Matua's village** and Thor Heyerdahl's landing place. From Anakena, a coastal path of variable quality passes interesting remains and beautiful cliff scenery. At Hanga o Teo there appears to be a large village complex, with several round houses, and further on there is a burial place, built like a long ramp with several ditches containing bones. From Hanga o Teo the path goes west then south, inland from the coast, to meet the road north of Hanga Roa.

A six-hour walk from Hanga Roa on the west coast passes **Ahu Tahai** (a moai with eyes and topknot, cave house, just outside town). Two caves are reached, one inland appears to be a ceremonial centre, the other (nearer the sea) has two 'windows' (take a strong flashlight and be careful near the 'windows'). Further north is Ahu Tepeu (broken moai, ruined houses). Beyond here you can join the path mentioned above, or turn right to Te Pahu cave and the seven moai at Akhivi, which look straight into the setting sun. Either return to Hanga Roa, or go to Puna Pau crater (two hours), where the topknots were carved (good views from the three crosses at the top).

Rano Kau, south of Hanga Roa, is another important site to visit; one finds the curious Orongo ruins here. The route south out of Hanga Roa passes the two caves of Ana Kai Tangata, one of which has paintings. If on foot you can take a path from the Orongo road, just past the CONAF sign, which is a much shorter route to Rano Kau crater. 200 m below is a lake with many reed islands. On the seaward side is Orongo, where the birdman cult flourished, with many ruined buildings and petroglyphs. Out to sea are the 'bird islets', Motu Nui, Motu Iti and Motu Kao. It is very windy at the summit; good views at sunset, or under a full moon (it is easy to follow the road back to Hanga Roa in the dark).

In Hanga Roa is **Ahu Tautira**, next to a swimming area marked out with concrete walls and a breakwater (cold water). Music at the 0900 Sunday mass is 'enchanting'. **Museum** ① *near Tahai, US$6*, most objects are reproductions because the genuine articles were removed from the island, but it has good descriptions of island life. There is a cultural centre next to the football field, with an exhibition hall and souvenir stall.

● Sleeping

Rapa Nui/Easter Island *p762*
Unless it is a particularly busy season, there is no need to book in advance; mainland agencies make exorbitant booking charges. The accommodation list at the airport information desk only covers the more expensive places. Flights are met by large numbers of hotel and residencial representatives with whom you can negotiate, but it may be cheaper if you look around for yourself. Note that room rates, especially in residenciales can be much cheaper out of season and if you do not take full board.
L-AL Hanga Roa, Av Pont, T/F210 0299, www.hotelhangaroa.cl. Including all meals (120 beds), no credit cards.
L-AL Taha Tai, Api Na Nui s/n, T255 1192. Well kept bright hotel with cabins and sea view, small swimming pool, tours organized.
AL-A O'Tai, Te Pilo Te Henua s/n, T210 0250, otairapanui@entelchile.net. Great location 2 mins from sea, pool, lovely gardens, restaurants, better rooms with terrace, comfortable, family run. Recommended.
AL-A Taura'a, C Principal s/n, T210 0463, www.tauraahotel.cl. Upmarket b&b, very comfy, good beds, spacious bathrooms, good breakfast, nice garden, good service. Recommended.
Taura'a Tours is also recommended.

A-B Orongo, Atamu Tekena s/n, TF210 0572, www.hotelorongo.com. Half board available (excellent restaurant), good service, nice garden.
Private homes Many places offer accommodation and tours (rates ranging from US$25 to US$150 per person, includes meals):
A Martín and Anita's hotel, Simón Paoa s/n, opposite hospital in Hanga Roa, T210 0593, www.hostal.co.cl. With breakfast, **AL** with full or half board, hot water, TV, good food. Can arrange car, bike and horse hire, guides and tours.
A Mana Nui Inn, Tahai s/n, opp cemetery, T210 0811, www.rapanuiweb.com/mananui. Pleasant cabins on north edge of town, **C** singles, good breakfast with local specialities, tours run.
A Res Tadeo y Lili, Apina Ichi s/n, T210 0422, tadeolili@entelchile.net. Simple but clean, French-Rapa Nui run, all rooms with sea view and terrace, good breakfast, tours. Recommended.
AL Chez Cecilia, Policarpo Toro y Atamu Tekema, near Tahai Moai, T/F255 1965, www.rapanuichezcecilia.com. Cheaper for longer stays, packages with tours offered. With breakfast, excellent food, *cabañas*, quiet, internet, free airport transfer, also good-value camping.
B HI Kona Tau, Avareipua, T210 0321. HI-affiliated hostel, **E** pp in dorms, all rooms with bath, price includes bath and breakfast, kitchen facilities.

B Inaki Uki, C Principal s/n, opp Taura'a.
D singles. Simple but clean rooms, shared bath, kitchen facilities, no breakfast, but central, good budget option.

B Res Tahai, Calle-Rei-Miro, T210 0395, rapanui@entelchile.net. With breakfast, **A** full board, nice garden, good value.

C-E Mihinoa, Av Pont s/n, T255 1593, www.mihinoa.com. Campsite (**F**), which also hires out camping equipment, with a few rooms. Clean, breakfast extra, excellent fish barbecues (fishing trips also offered), kitchen facilities, hot showers, laundry, internet, welcoming, exceptional value. Recommended.

Camping Officially, camping is not allowed anywhere in the national park. Many people offer campsites in their gardens, US$8-12 pp, check availability of water first. Some families also provide food. Camping equipment can be hired from a shop on Av Policarpo Toro, US$50 per day for everything. **Note** Camping gas is expensive and poor quality.

🍴 Eating

Rapa Nui/Easter Island *p762*
Most residenciales offer full board. Vegetarians will have no problems on the island; locally produced fruit and vegetables are plentiful and cheaper than meat and other foodstuffs, which are imported from mainland. Locally caught fish is also good value. Coffee is always instant. Beware of extras such as US$3 charge for hot water.

♥♥♥ Jardín de Mau, Atanu Tekena s/n. Pasta/fusion using mostly local ingredients. Some of the pasta is freshly made, excellent tuna carpaccio. Friendly staff, better wine list than most, sea views.

♥♥♥ Taverne du Pecheur, Hanga Roa. French-run, boasts it's the best restaurant on the island and it probably is, especially for fish, lobster and other seafood. Expensive but worth it.

♥♥ Ka Tinita, Te Pito Te Henua s/n (closed Sun). Fish, prepared simply but well, large salads and side dishes, good value.

♥♥ Merahi'Ra, Te Pito Te Henua s/n (closed Thu). Well-known for fish.
Several places serve delicious *empanadas*.

🍸 Bars and clubs

Rapa Nui/Easter Island *p762*
There are 2 in Hanga Roa. Action begins after 0100. Drinks are expensive: pisco sour US$5, canned beer US$3. **Piriti**, near airport. Open Thu-Sat. **Toroko**, Caleta Hanga Roa, near harbour. Open daily.

✴ Festivals and events

Rapa Nui/Easter Island *p762*
Tapati, or **Semana Rapa Nui**, **end-Jan/ beginning-Feb**, lasts about 10 days. Dancing competitions, singing, sports (horse racing, swimming, modified decathlon), body-painting, typical foods (lots of small booths by the football field), necklace-making, etc. Everyone gets involved, many tourists too. Only essential activities continue outside the festival.

🛍 Shopping

Rapa Nui/Easter Island *p762*
All shops and rental offices close 1400-1700. On Av Policarpo Toro, the main street, there are lots of small shops and market stalls (which may close during rain) and a couple of supermarkets, cheapest **Kai Nene** or **Tumukai** (good *panadería* next door).

Handicrafts Wood carvings, stone moais, best bought from the craftsmen themselves, such as Antonio Tepano Tucki, Juan Acka, Hipolito Tucki and his son (who are knowledgeable about the old culture). The expensive municipal market, left of church, will give you a good view of what is available – no compunction to buy. The airport shop is expensive. Good pieces cost from US$30 to US$200. The cheapest handicrafts are available from the jail, behind the airport, where the prisoners earn money by carving and then selling semi-finished items to market stallholders. With a couple of days' notice you can ask for a design at modest prices. Souvenirs at several places on Policarpo Toro, including **Hotu Matuu's Favorite Shoppe**, good, quite expensive, designs own T-shirts, fixed prices; also sells music. There is a mercado artesanal next to the church and people sell handicrafts at Tahai, Vaihu, Rano Raraku and Anakena. Bargaining is only possible if you pay cash. Food, wine and beer are expensive because of freight charges, but local fish, vegetables, fruit and bread are cheap.

⛰ Activities and tours

Rapa Nui/Easter Island *p762*
Diving Mike Rapu Diving Center, Caleta Hanga Roa Otai s/n, T255 1055. Diving courses and expeditions and fishing trips. Orca, Caleta Hanga Roa, T255 0375, www.seemorca.cl, run by Michael García. Both at the harbour, all equipment provided, packages from US$45-US$80. After a check dive you will go to more interesting sights; ask for dives that suit your experience.
Hiking Allow at least a day to walk the length of the island, one way, taking in all the sites.

It is 5 easy hours from Hanga Roa to Rano Raraku (camp at ranger station); 5 hrs to Anakena (camp at ranger station, but ask first). You can hitch back to Hanga Roa, especially at weekends though there are few cars at other times.

Horse riding The best way to see the island, provided you are fit, is on horseback: horses, US$35 for a day, including guide. **Cabalgatas Pantu**, T210 0577, www.pantupikerauri.cl.

Tour operators

Many agencies, residenciales and locals arrange excursions around the island. The English of other tour guides is often poor. Maps are sold on Av Policarpo Toro for US$15-18, or at the ranger station at Orongo for US$10. A private tour of the island costs US$35 pp including guide.

Aku-Aku Tours, Tu'u Koihu s/n, T210 0770, akuakuturismo.cl. Wide range of tours.

Hanga Roa Travel, T210 0158, hfritsch@ entelchile.net. English, German, Italian and Spanish spoken, good value all-inclusive tours. Recommended.

⊜ Transport

Rapa Nui/Easter Island *p762*

Air The airport runway has been improved to provide emergency landing for US space shuttles! LAN fly daily a week in high season, less in low season, 5-5½ hrs. Most flights continue to Papeete, Tahiti. LAN office on Av Policarpo Toro y Av Pont, T210 0279, reconfirm flights here – imperative; do not fly to Easter Island unless you have a confirmed flight out (planes are more crowded to Tahiti than back to Santiago) and reconfirm your booking on arrival on the Island. For details of LAN's special sector fare to Easter Island and which must be purchased outside Chile, see Essentials. The cheapest return fare from Santiago in 2007, booked well in advance, was US$680, with occasional special deals available through travel agents. Students studying in Chile eligible for 30% discount. If flying to or from Tahiti, check if you can stay over till another flight or even if there is time for sightseeing before the flight continues. Airport tax: flying from Santiago to Easter Island incurs the domestic tax of US$16. Flying to Tahiti may incur international flight departure tax if not included in your ticket.

Car hire A high-clearance vehicle is better-suited to the roads than a normal vehicle. If you are hiring a car, do the sites from south to north since travel agencies tend to start their tours in the north. Jeep hire: at **Sonoco** service station, Vaihu, T100325 or 100239, on airport road. **Hertz**, opposite airport. Many other vehicle hire agencies on the main street. US$50 per day (US$100 with driver). Chilean or international driving licence essential. There is no insurance available, drive at your own risk (be careful at night, many vehicles drive without lights). Check oil and water before setting out. Motorbike hire: about US$40 a day including gasoline (Suzuki or Honda 250 recommended because of rough roads). Several car rental places on Av Policarpo Toro, shop around.

Taxi There are taxis and in summer a bus goes from Hanga Roa to Anakena on Sun at 0900, returning in the afternoon (unreliable). **Radiotaxi Vai Reva**, Sergio Cortés, Petero Atamu s/n, T210 0399, 24 hrs, reliable. For touring the island, it is cheaper to hire a car or take a tour.

⊙ Directory

Rapa Nui/Easter Island *p762*

Banks Changing money is best done in Santiago as local rates are poor. US dollars are widely accepted, again at poor rates. Prices are often quoted in dollars, but bills can be paid in pesos. There is one bank on Atamu Tekena s/n, with an ATM. Accepts MasterCard and Cirrus but not Visa. Cash can be exchanged in shops, hotels, etc, at about 5% less than Santiago. Poor rates on TCs at **Sonoco service station**. Credit cards are widely accepted for purchases, but all incur a 10% surcharge. **Bicycle hire** Some in poor condition, are available for rent for US$15 on main street or from *residenciales*. **Internet** Several cafés with broadband facilities, though expensive, have good connection. **Medical facilities** There is a 20-bed hospital as well as 3 resident doctors, a trained nurse and 1 dentist on the island. **Post offices** 0900-1300, 1430-1800, Sat 0900-1200; only sends packages up to 1 kg. **Telephones** Phone calls from the Chilean mainland are subsidized, at US$0.50 per min. Calls to Europe cost US$1 for 1 min. Phone numbers are being changed, with a prefix of 2 and, in some cases, the second 2 digits changing from 10 to 55. If 210-numbers don't work, try 255.

Colombia

Essentials	772
Bogotá	780
Sights	782
Around Bogotá	796
Bogotá to the Venezuelan border	799
Bogotá to Villa de Leiva	799
Tunja to Cocuy	804
To Bucaramanga and Cúcuta	806
Cartagena and the north coast	812
Cartagena	812
To Panama	823
Barranquilla	827
Santa Marta, Tayrona and Ciudad Perdida	828
To Venezuela	835
San Andrés and Providencia	838
Medellín and Chocó	842
Medellín	842
Around Medellín	848
Department of Chocó	849
La Zona Cafetera	852
Manizales and around	852
Pereira to Cartago	855
Cali and the Cauca Valley	859
Cali	859
Cauca and the coast	863
Popayán, Tierradentro and San Agustín	865
Popayán and Tierradentro	865
Popayán to San Agustín	869
Southern Colombia	876
South to Ecuador	876
Leticia and the Amazon	880

⁑ Footprint features

Don't miss …	771
Touching down	775
Driving in Colombia	777
The Gilded Man	800
The sacking of Cartagena	813

Introduction

The adventurous will love this land of sun and emeralds, with its excellent opportunities for climbing, trekking and diving. The gold museum in Bogotá, the Lost City of the Tayrona and San Agustín have superb examples of cultures long gone. Among several fine colonial cities, the jewel is Cartagena, whose history of slavery and pirates can be seen in the massive fortifications. Today, pelicans share the beach with holidaymakers. Colombia's Caribbean, which stretches to the Panamanian isthmus, is the inspiration for Gabriel García Márquez's world of magical realism and is the land of accordion-led vallenato music. Of the country's many snow-capped mountain ranges, the Sierra Nevada de Santa Marta with its secretive *indígenas*, is the most remarkable, rising straight out of the Caribbean. Also not to be missed is the cathedral inside a salt mine at Zipaquirá. There are mud volcanoes to bathe in, acres of flowers, coffee farms to visit and a CD library's worth of music festivals. In fact, dancing is practically a national pastime and having a good time is taken very seriously: as García Márquez once said, "five Colombians in a room invariably turns into a party." Despite the drug trade and the guerrilla violence which has scarred the minds and landscape of this beautiful country, Colombia is rebuilding its position on the tourist circuit.

★ Don't miss …

1. **Museo de Oro** One of the most significant museums in South America, with an awe-inspiring collection of pre-Columbian gold, page 786.

2. **Zipaquirá** Visit the cathedral carved out of a rock salt mine. This is truly one of the wonders of Colombia, page 796.

3. **Cartagena** A beautiful colonial city, with a fortified heart and fascinating history. Its other life is as a Caribbean beach resort, page 812.

4. **La Ciudad Perdida** Rising straight out of the Caribbean to over 5,000 m is the Sierra Nevada de Santa Marta. Hike through the forests of the Sierra's northern flank to the Lost City of the Tayrona civilization, page 831.

5. **La Zona Cafetera** Coffee has long been one of Colombia's top exports. Base yourself on a finca and enjoy the lovely countryside, page 852.

6. **San Agustín and Tierradentro** Mysterious statues carved out of stone look out over rolling green landscapes, while nearby the hills of Tierradentro are riddled with ancient burial chambers, page 866.

Essentials

Planning your trip

Where to go **Bogotá**, the capital, stands on a plateau in the eastern cordillera of the Andes. It epitomizes the juxtaposition of the historical and the modern, with many important colonial buildings and museums. Among its attractions are La Candelaria, the old centre of the city, and the magnificent Gold Museum, which houses a remarkable collection of prehispanic artefacts, one of the 'musts' of South America. Places to visit around Bogotá include the salt cathedral at Zipaquirá and the Chicaque Parque Natural, a fine preserved area of cloud forest.

Northeast from Bogotá, to Cúcuta on the Venezuelan border, the beautiful colonial town of **Villa de Leiva** is carefully preserved from the 18th century and well worth a visit. Further north, Santander department also has its attractions, including the most dramatic mountain scenery in Colombia in the **Parque Nacional Cocuy**. **Barichara** is one of the best kept colonial towns and nearby **San Gil** is an important adventure sports centre.

The obvious centre for exploring the north Caribbean coast and the tropical islands of San Andrés and Providencia is **Cartagena**. The city is a fashionable, modern beach resort and also the place where Colombia's colonial past can best be seen. Here are some of the greatest examples of Spanish architecture on the continent are to be found within the city's ramparts. **Santa Marta** to the northeast is a popular beach resort and the centre for the rocky coast to the east, including Taganga and **Parque Nacional Tayrona**. Treks to the **Ciudad Perdida** (Lost City), a major archaeological site, start in Santa Marta. Towards the Venezuelan border, **La Guajira**, a region of arid desert landscape and home to the indigenous group, the Wayúu, is becoming increasingly popular and accessible to visit. Northeast from Cartagena is the northern port of **Barranquilla**, where Carnival rivals some of those in Brazil. Inland from here, up the Río Magdalena, is the fascinating colonial town of **Mompós**.

In northwest Colombia, **Medellín** is a modern, vibrant city with many fine new buildings, old restored architecture and friendly, outgoing people. There are many fascinating places to visit in the surrounding department of Antioquia, including the colonial towns of **Rionegro** and **Santa Fé de Antioquia**. Further west is **Chocó**, one of the world's most biodiverse and wettest regions. Here, the Pacific coast is almost undeveloped for tourism, with pristine forests descending the mountain slopes to the ocean, but resorts such as Bahía Solano and Nuquí on the Atlantic, and Capurganá on the Caribbean coast, are beginning to open up. South of Medellín is the **Zona Cafetera**, with modern and colonial cities such as Manizales and Pereira and where coffee farms, in delightful countryside, welcome visitors.

Further south, in the Cauca Valley, is **Cali**, with its passion for salsa. Like Medellín it is shrugging off its notorious reputation from recent years. Off the Pacific coast, is **Gorgona**, an unspoilt, idyllic island offering excellent diving. From **Popayán**, a city with a strong colonial feel, are the difficult routes to the important archaeological sites of **Tierradentro** and **San Agustín**. South of Popayán is Pasto, a pleasant town in an attractive setting, Ipiales for the border with Ecuador and Tumaco, from where you can visit the coastal national parks.

In Colombia's far southeastern corner, towards the border with Brazil, lies **Leticia** from where jungle treks start.

When to go The best time to visit is December-February. These are generally the driest months, but many local people are on holiday. It gets busy and very crowded during Christmas and Easter, when many hotels put up their rates and transport can be overloaded. Climate is a matter of altitude: there are no real seasons, though some periods are wetter than others. Height in metres is given for all major towns. Generally, around 2,000 m is 'temperate'; anywhere higher will require warm clothing in the early mornings and evenings. There is heavy rain in many places in April-May and October-November though intermittent heavy rain can fall at any time almost anywhere.

Finding out more National tourism is handled by the Tourism Vice-Ministry, **Ditur** (Dirección de Turismo) ① offices at Calle 28, No 13A-15, p 18, Bogotá, T342 2626, part of the Ministry of Commerce, Industry and Tourism (www.mincomercio.gov.co gives access to Boletín Turístico, *Vive Colombia*, for tourism news), and by the **Fondo de Promoción Turística** ① Calle 69, No 11-66, T212 6315, www.turismocolombia.com. Departmental and city entities have their own offices responsible for tourist information: see the text for local details. These offices should be visited as early as possible not only for information on accommodation and transport, but also for details on areas that are dangerous to visit. Regional tourist offices are better sources of information on safety than the Dirección de Turismo in Bogotá or contact Colombia's representation overseas. See also Websites and Maps, below.

The National Parks service is the responsibility of the Unidad Administrativa Especial del Sistema de Parques Nacionales Naturales (UAESPNN) at the Ministerio del Medio Ambiente, Vivienda y Desarrollo Territorial (Ministry of the Environment) ① *Ecotourism office for information is in the Banco Agrario building (no obvious sign), Carrera 10, No 20-30, p 1, Bogotá, T341 3712/0676, www.minambiente.gov.co, open Mon-Fri 0800-1600*, referred to in this guide as **MA**. A small selection of books, handicrafts, souvenirs, good videos and useful CDs about the national parks is available. At the Ecotourism office, it is possible to get up-to-date information about the security situation and which parks are closed. Permits to visit the parks can be obtainable here and at the many MA offices near the parks themselves (see text). Permits, transport details and accommodation reservations for nationla parks can be easily obtained from offices of **Aviatur** travel agency, http://site.aviatur.com (addresses given in text). The national parks book, *Gran Libro de los Parques Nacionales de Colombia*, with superb photography and scientific information, costs US$50. Foreigners over 18 can participate on the voluntary park ranger programme. Details are available on the third floor of the UAESPNN offices in Bogotá (T343 1634/243 3095). You will have to provide photocopies of ID documents and Colombian entry stamp in your passport. A good level of Spanish is required. See also www.parquesnacionales.gov.co (which does not give the security situation at individual parks; enquire at the Ecotourism office). Other useful address: **Instituto Colombiano de Antropología e Historia** (ICANH) ① *C 12, No 2-41, T561 9600, Bogotá, icanh@mincultura.gov.co, Mon-Fri 0800-1700*, very helpful.

Websites

www.colombia.com Good Spanish portal, current affairs and entertainment news, information about national parks and festivals.

www.colombiajournal.org Interesting photo gallery and good selection of articles about Colombian current affairs, in Spanish and English.

www.conexcol.com Colombian search engine.

www.etniasdecolombia.org Useful introduction to Colombia's indigenous groups and black communities, in Spanish.

www.humboldt.org.co Instituto Von Humboldt. Colombia's ecosystems and ethnic communities in Spanish.

www.ideam.gov.co Weather forecasts and climate information, in Spanish.

www.natura.org.co Fundación Natura, excellent conservation information.

www.poorbuthappy.com/colombia Reliable information on travel, jobs and safety, in English.

www.posadasturisticas.com.co Gives information about places to stay in Colombia, including Chocó.

www.presidencia.gov.co The government website. You can also access:

www.gobiernoenlinea.gov.co, in Spanish and English.

www.quehubo.com Colombian Yellow Pages site.

Maps Maps of Colombia are obtainable at the **Instituto Geográfico Agustín Codazzi** ① *Carrera 30, Bogotá, No 48-51, T369 4000, www.igac.gov.co*, or from their offices in other large cities. They have a wide range of official, country-wide and departmental maps and atlases. The topographical details of the walking maps are generally accurate, but trails and minor roads less so. In Bogotá, they are open Monday-Friday 0800-1630, maps are mainly from US$2.50 to US$6 and you pay at the bank next door. There is a library open until 1630 and refreshments available at lunchtime. The best current maps of Colombia, *Mapa Vial de Colombia* by Rodríguez, scale 1:2,000,000, 1994, costs about US$4. An excellent guide with good, detailed road maps across the country is the annual *Guía de Rutas por Colombia* available at major bookstores and toll booths. Drivers' route maps are included in the *AutoGuía*, by Publicación Legis, US$8 (1997). Esso and other maps from some service stations, US$2 and a *Guía Vial de Colombia*, US$3, available at bookshops.

Visas and immigration Tourists are normally given 90 days permission to stay on entry, though this is not automatic. If you intend to stay more than 30 days, make sure you ask for longer. If not granted at the border, extension (*salvoconducto*) can be applied for at the DAS (security police) office in any major city. The *salvoconducto* is only issued once for a period of 30 days and is usually processed within 24 hours. Best to apply two to three days before your visa expires. Bring two recent photos and copies of your passport. If you overstay on any type of visa, you will be charged a fine, minimum US$55 up to US$800. The **DAS** office in Bogotá is ① *C 100, No 11B-27, T601 7200, www.das.gov.co* (see under Bogotá, Useful addresses). Arrive early in the morning, expect long queues and a painfully slow bureaucratic process. **Note** DAS does not accept cash payments; these are made at the appropriate bank with special payments slips. Alternatively, if you have good reason to stay longer (eg for medical treatment), apply at the embassy in your home country before leaving. If you wish to stay between seven to 10 days longer on a tourist visa, go to a DAS office with your onward ticket and they will usually grant you a free extension on the spot. An onward ticket may be asked for at land borders or Bogotá international airport. You may be asked to prove that you have sufficient funds for your stay.

To visit Colombia as a tourist, nationals of Republic of Ireland, countries of former Eastern Europe (except Romania) and the Middle East (except Israel), Asian countries (except Japan, South Korea, Malaysia, Phillipines, Indonesia and Singapore), Haiti, Nicaragua, and all African countries need a visa. At the time of writing, visa restrictions for nationals of the Republic of Ireland had been lifted, but in this and any other cases of doubt, check regulations before leaving your home country. Visas are issued only by Colombian consulates. When a visa is required you must present a valid passport, three photographs, the application form (in duplicate), £30 or equivalent (price varies according to nationality), onward tickets, and a photocopy of all the documents (allow two weeks maximum).

If you are going to take a Spanish course, you must have a student visa. You may not study on a tourist visa. A student visa can be obtained while in Colombia on a tourist visa. Proof of sufficient funds is necessary (US$400-600 for a six-month stay is usually deemed sufficient). You must be first enrolled in a course from a bona fide university to apply for a student visa. Various business and other temporary visas are needed for foreigners who have to reside in Colombia for a length of time. The **Ministerio de Relaciones Exteriores** (not DAS) ① *Cra 13, No 93-68, of 203, T640 0974/640 8576, Mon-Fri 0730-1200*, processes student and some work visas. In general, Colombian work visas can only be obtained outside Colombia at the appropriate consulate and or embassy. You must register work and student visas at a **DAS** office within 15 days of obtaining them, otherwise you will be liable to pay a hefty fine. Visas must be used within three months. Supporting documentary requirements for visas change frequently. Check with the appropriate consulate in good time before your trip.

When entering the country, you will be given the copy of your DIAN (Customs) luggage declaration. Keep it; you may be asked for it when you leave. If you receive an entry card when flying in and lose it while in Colombia, apply to any DAS office who should issue one and restamp your passport for free. Normally passports are scanned by a computer and no landing card is issued, but passports still must be stamped on entry. Note that to leave Colombia you must get an exit stamp from the DAS. They often do not have offices at the small border towns, so try to get your stamp in a main city.

Note It is highly recommended that you photocopy your passport details, including entry stamps which, for added insurance, you can have witnessed by a notary. Always carry a photocopy of your passport with you, as you may be asked for identification. This is a valid substitute for most purposes though not, for example, for cashing travellers' cheques or drawing cash across a bank counter. Generally acceptable for identification (eg to enter government buildings) is a driving licence, provided it is plastic, of credit card size and has a photograph. For more information, check with your consulate.

Colombian embassies and consulates Visit www.minrelext.gov.co for a full list of addresses.

Money The currency is the peso. There are coins of 50, 100, 200 and 500; there are notes of 1,000, 2,000, 5,000, 10,000, 20,000 and 50,000 pesos (the last can be difficult to change). Change is in short supply, especially in small towns, and in the morning. Watch out for forged notes. The 50,000-peso note should smudge colour if it is real, if not, refuse to accept it. Peso **exchange rate** with US$: 2,199 (March 2007); euro: 2,927. There is a limit of US$10,000 on the import of foreign exchange in cash, with export limited to the equivalent of the amount brought in.

Touching down

Airport and other taxes The airport departure tax for stays of over 60 days is US$51 (payable in US$, pesos; some airlines accept Visa). For stays of less than 60 days the tax is about US$26. You will need an exit tax exemption certificate from the *impuestos* desk (ground floor near check-in desks) to confirm you have been less than 60 days in the country. Travellers changing planes in Colombia and leaving the same day are exempt from this tax. When you arrive, ensure that all necessary documentation bears a stamp for your date of arrival; without it you will have to pay the full exit tax. There is also an airport tax on internal flights, US$2.30 (varies according to airport), usually included in the ticket price.

Business hours Offices Mon-Fri, 0800-1200 and 1400-1730 or 1800. Firms in the warmer towns such as Cali start at 0700 and finish earlier. **Government offices** generally follow the same hours as businesses, but prefer to do business with the public in the afternoon only. **Embassy** hours for the public are 0900-1200 and 1400-1700 (Mon-Fri). **Banks** Mon-Fri 0900-1500, except the last working day in the month when they close at 1200 or all day. Some banks are now open on Sat. Outside Bogotá banks open 0800-1130, 1400-1630. **Shops** Mon-Sat 0900-1230 and 1430-1830.

In an emergency Police T112; civil defence T144 (640 0090 in Bogotá); DAS security T153;

International phone code +57. Ringing: equal tones with long pauses. Engaged: short tones with short pauses.

Official time Five hours behind GMT.

Tipping Upmarket restaurants 10%, often included in the bill. Porters, cloakroom attendants and hairdressers US$0.05-0.25. Taxis are not tipped.

VAT 16% on most items; 10% on some services.

Voltage 120 volts AC. Transformer must be 110-150 volt AC, with twin flat-prong plugs (all of same size).

Weights and measures Generally metric, but US gallons for petrol.

Colombia Essentials

Plastic/TCs/banks Cash and travellers' cheques can in theory be exchanged in any bank, except the *Banco de la República*; go early to banks in smaller places to change these. In most sizeable towns there are *casas de cambio* (exchange shops), which are quicker to use than banks but sometimes charge higher commission. It's best to use euros and, even better, dollars. It can sometimes be difficult to buy and sell large amounts of sterling, even in Bogotá. Hotels may give very poor rates of exchange, especially if you are paying in dollars. It is dangerous to change money on the streets and you may well be given counterfeit pesos. Also in circulation are counterfeit US dollar bills. You must present your passport when changing money (a photocopy is not normally accepted). Take some US$ cash with you for emergencies.

Credit cards As it is unwise to carry large quantities of cash, credit cards are widely used, especially MasterCard and Visa; also Diners Club is also accepted. American Express is only accepted in expensive places in Bogotá. Many banks accept Visa (Visaplus and ATH logos) and Cirrus/MasterCard (Maestro and Multicolor logos) to advance pesos against the card, or through ATMs. There are ATMs for Visa and MasterCard everywhere but you may have to try several machines. All Carulla supermarkets have ATMs. **Credit card loss or theft**: Visa call collect to (44) 20-7937 8091 or fax (44) 17-3350 3670, MasterCard T0800-912 1303. **Note** ATMs do not retain cards. If your card is not given back immediately, do not proceed with the transaction and do not type in your pin number. There are reports of money being stolen from accounts when cards have been retained. When getting cash advances on a Visa card at **BanColombia** banks, you must show your passport and provide a photocopy. For cash advances on credit cards in banks, don't queue for cashiers, go directly to the customer services counter.

Note Only use ATMs in supermarkets, malls or where a security guard is present. Don't ask a taxi driver to wait while you use an ATM. Be vigilant in December as thieves are on the prowl.

Travellers' cheques When changing TCs, a photocopy of your passport may be required as well as the original, so take a supply of photocopies with you. The procedure is always slow, maybe involving finger printing and photographs. Take dollar TCs in small denominations; better still, take a credit card (see above). Sterling TCs are practically impossible to change. To change Amex TCs, use major banks. You may have to provide proof of purchase. Obtaining reimbursement for lost Amex TCs can be straightforward if you have the numbers recorded (preferably proof of purchase), a police certificate (*diligencia de queja*) covering the circumstances of loss, and apply to their offices at C 85, No 20-32, T593 4949, Mon-Fri 0800-1800, Sat 0900-1200 (see Bogotá, Banks). Banks may be unwilling to change TCs in remote areas, take local currency. TCs are not normally accepted in hotels, restaurants, shops etc.

Cost of travelling Prices are generally lower than Europe and North America for services and locally produced items, but more expensive for imported and luxury goods. For the traveller prices are among the lowest in South America. Modest, basic accommodation will cost about US$10-12 pp per night in Bogotá, Cartagena, Santa Marta and colonial cities like Villa de Leiva, Popayán or Santa Fé de Antioquia, but a few dollars less elsewhere. A *comida corriente* (set lunch) costs about US$1.50-2 and breakfast US$1-1.75. *A la carte* meals are usually good value and fierce competition for transport keeps prices low. Typical cost of internet is US$1-4 per hour.

Safety Travellers confirm that the vast majority of Colombians are polite, honest and will go out of their way to help visitors and make them feel welcome. In general, anti-gringo sentiments are rare. However, in addition to the general advice given in Essentials, see page 56, the following local conditions should be noted. Colombia is part of a major drug-smuggling route and still produces roughly 80% of the world's cocaine. Police and customs activities have greatly intensified and smugglers increasingly try to use innocent carriers. Do not carry packages for other people. Be very polite if approached by policemen in uniform, or if your hotel room is raided by police looking for drugs. Colombians who offer you drugs could be setting you up for the police, who are very active in Cali, on the north coast, San Andrés island and other tourist resorts.

There have been reports of travellers and Colombians being victims of *burundanga*, a drug obtained from a white flower, native to Colombia. At present, the use of this drug appears to be confined to major cities. It is very nasty, almost impossible to see or smell. It leaves the victim helpless and at the will of the culprit. Usually, the victim is taken to ATMs to draw out money. Be wary of accepting cigarettes, food and drink from strangers at sports events and in buses. In bars watch your drinks very carefully.

The internal armed conflict in Colombia is almost impossible to predict and the security situation changes from day to day. For this reason, it is essential to consult regularly with locals for up-to-date information. Taxi and bus drivers, local journalists, soldiers at checkpoints, hotel owners and Colombians who actually travel around their country are usually good sources of reliable information. Since 2002, incidents of kidnapping and homicide rates in major cities have been declining. Travelling overland between towns, especially during the holiday season and bank holiday weekends, has in general become much safer due to increased military and police presence along main roads. However, the government has launched a major offensive against the guerrilla (especially in the south) and in some areas fighting between the armed forces and guerrilla groups has intensified. The following areas are known as *zonas calientes* (hot zones) where there is active presence of guerrilla groups and/or paramilitaries: the rural areas down the eastern part of the country from Arauca and Casanare to Meta; Cáqueta and Putumayo; the Magdalena Medio and Norte de Santander; from Urabá near the border with Panamá into northwestern Antioquia and parts of Chocó; Sur de Bolívar and Carmen de Bolívar in the department of Bolívar; in and around La Macarena national park; the city of Buenaventura on the Pacific coast and Neiva in the department of Huila. Travellers wishing to go into rural areas in Cauca and Nariño in the southwest should also seek advice. As a loose rule, the conflict is often most intense in coca growing areas, oil producing regions and along Colombia's borders. Guerrilla activity usually increases in the run up to local and national elections. Incidents in cities, including Bogotá, may also occur. Do not travel between towns by road at night. Parts of the motorway in the above areas maybe randomly closed at night between 1800 -0600 for security reasons. If venturing into rural areas and hot zones ask first at your embassy. It is essential to follow this up with detailed enquiries at your chosen destination. If arriving overland, go to the nearest hotel favoured by travellers (these are given in the text) and make enquiries. Note that rural hot zones are often littered with land mines.

Driving in Colombia

Road Signposting is poor and roads may be in poor condition. There are toll stations every 60-100 km on major roads: toll is about US$2.50. Motorcycles don't have to pay.

Safety Lorry and bus drivers tend to be reckless, and stray animals are often encountered. Always check safety information for your route before setting out. Police and military checks are frequent in troubled areas, keep your documents handy. In town, only leave your car in an attended car park (*parqueadero*). Only park in the street if there is someone on guard, tip US$0.20.

Documents International driving licences are advised, especially if you have your own car. To bring a car into Colombia, you must also have documents proving ownership of the vehicle, and a tourist card/transit visa. These are normally valid for 90 days and must be applied for at the Colombian consulate in the country which you will be leaving for Colombia. A *carnet de passages* is recommended when entering with a European registered vehicle. Only third-party insurance issued by a Colombian company is valid (around US$70); there are agencies in all ports. You will frequently be asked for this document while driving. Carry driving documents with you at all times.

Car hire In addition to passport and driver's licence, a credit card may be asked for as additional proof of identity and to secure a returnable deposit to cover any liability not covered by the insurance. If renting a Colombian car, note that major cities have the *pico y placa* system which means cars are not allowed entry in the city during morning and afternoon rush hour depending on the day and car number plate (does not apply during the weekends and public holidays).

Fuel 'Premium 95' octane (only in large cities), about US$2 per US gallon; 'corriente' 84 octane, US$1.50 per US gallon. Diesel US$1.30. The cost of petrol is up to 70% cheaper near and on the Venezuelan border, eg in La Guajira and Cúcuta.

Amazonas, and to a lesser extent **Los Llanos**, have always been difficult to visit because of their remoteness, the lack of facilities and the huge distances involved (these factors also apply to La Guajira in the north). Our text is limited to Villavicencio, Florencia and the Leticia region all of which are comparatively safe. They should only be visited by air, except Leticia where river routes are safe.

Getting around

Air Avianca, www.avianca.com, is the main internal airline, T01-8000-123434 (free national call centre number). Other airlines are **Aires**, www.aires.com.co, **AeroRepública**, www.aerorepublica.com.co, and **Satena**, www.satena.com. *Avianca* offers a domestic air pass giving travel for 30 days, if arriving in Colombia by air from overseas. The pass must be bought outside Colombia in conjunction with an international air ticket and is also issued to passengers not travelling with Avianca from their original destination, for additional US$35-50. There are reductions for children and infants. The air pass allows three stops (US$169), four (US$222) or five (US$272). An extra US$70 is charged for travel to Cartagena and San Andrés. The Air Pass is non-refundable unless the whole has been unused. You may not pass through each city more than once (except for transfers), and a proposed itinerary (not firm) must be submitted when buying the ticket. Prices and conditions can change; enquire at an *Avianca* office. Sometimes there are good value reductions advertised in the press, eg weekend trips from Bogotá to the North coast and all-inclusive deals to San Andrés. Domestic airports vary in the services they offer and tourist facilities tend to close early on weekdays, and all Sunday. It is almost impossible to change money at small regional airports. There is a 16% sales tax on one way tickets and an 8% tax on returns. Local airport taxes are included in the price. Security checks can be thorough, watch your luggage. **Satena** fly to destinations in the south and remoter regions of Chocó, Los Llanos, Amazonas and Orinoquia and is generally slightly cheaper than Aires.

Bus Travel in Colombia is exciting. The scenery is generally worth seeing so travel by day: it is also safer and you can keep a better eye on your valuables. Almost all the main routes are paved, but the state of the roads varies considerably between departments. On main routes you usually have choice of company, and type of bus. The cheapest (*corriente*) are basically local buses, stopping frequently, uncomfortable and slow but offering plenty of local colour. Try to keep your luggage with you. *Pullman* (each company will have a different name for the service) are long distance buses usually with a/c, toilets, hostess service, videos (almost always violent films, Spanish/Mexican or dubbed English) and limited stop. Sit near the back with your walkman to avoid the video and the need to keep the blinds down. Luggage is normally carried in a locked compartment against receipt. *Colectivos*, also known as *vans* or *busetas*, run by **Velotax, Taxis Verdes**, etc are usually 12-20 seat vehicles, maybe with a/c, rather cramped but fast, saving several hours on long journeys (so not for the faint-hearted!). You can keep your eye on luggage in the back of the van. Fares shown in the text are middle of the range where there is a choice but are no more than a guide. Note that meal stops can be few and far between, and short; bring your own food. Be prepared for climatic changes on longer routes and for the vagaries of a/c on buses, sometimes fierce, sometimes none. **If you entrust your luggage to the bus companies' luggage rooms, remember to load it on to the bus yourself; it will not be done automatically.** There are few interdepartmental bus services on holidays. During holidays and high season, arrive at the bus terminal at least an hour before the departure time to guarantee a seat, even if you have bought a ticket in advance. If you are joining a bus at popular or holiday times, not at the starting point, you may be left behind even though you have a ticket and reservation. Always take your passport (or photocopy) with you: identity and luggage checks on buses are frequent and you may be body-searched at army roadblocks.

Cycling Cycling is a popular sport in Colombia. There are good shops for spares in all big cities, though the new standard 622/700 size touring wheel size is not very common. Take your own spare tyres. Around Calle13 with Cra 20 in front of La Sabana train station in Bogotá are several bicycle repair and accessory shops.

Hitchhiking Hitchhiking (*autostop*) is unadvisable and not common. In safe areas, try enlisting the co-operation of the highway police checkpoints outside each town and toll booths. Truck drivers are often very friendly, but be careful of private cars with more than one person inside. Travelling on your own is not recommended.

Taxi Whenever possible, take a taxi with a meter and ensure that it is switched on. If there is no meter, bargain and fix a price. All taxis are obliged to display the additional legal tariffs that may be charged after 2000, on Sunday and fiestas. Don't take a taxi which is old; look for 'Servicio Público' on the side. It is safest to call a radio taxi, particularly at night, rather than hailing one down in the street. Bars, hotels and restaurants will order taxis for customers. The dispatcher will give you the cab's number which should be noted in case of irregularities. The last two digits of the number from where the call was made is *el clave*, the security code. Remember it as taxi drivers will ask for the code before setting off. Never get into a taxi if there are already passengers in it. If the taxi 'breaks down', take your luggage and find another taxi immediately.

Sleeping → *See page 58 for our hotel grade price guide.*

Hotels The more expensive hotels charge about 10% VAT (IVA). Some hotels add a small insurance charge (about US$0.75 per night). From 15 December to 30 April, 15 June to 31 August and bank holidays (*puentes*), hotels in holiday centres may increase prices by at least 20-30%. Prices are normally displayed at reception, but in quiet periods it is always worth negotiating.

Camping Sites are given in the text but also check locally very carefully before deciding to camp. Local tourist offices have lists of official sites, but they are seldom signposted on main roads. Permission to camp with tent, camper van or car is usually granted by landowners in less populated areas. Many haciendas have armed guards protecting their property: this can add to your safety. Vehicles may camp at truck drivers' restaurants, *balnearios campestres* with armed guards, or ask if you may overnight beside police or army posts.

Youth Hostels **Federación Colombiana de Albergues Juveniles**, Cra 7, No 6-10, Bogotá, T91-280 3041, www.fcaj.org.co. The (FCA) is affiliated to Hostelling International.

Eating → *See page 58 for our Eating price guide.*

Eating out Colombia's food is regionally varied, but most major cities have restaurants with non-local Colombian food. Small towns do not cater for vegetarians. Restaurants in smaller towns often close on Sunday, and early on weekday evenings: if stuck, you will probably find something to eat near the bus station. If economising, ask for the excellent value *menú del día*, also known as *comida corriente* (daily set lunch). This consists of a filling three-course meal (juice, soup, meat or fish dish and dessert) for no more than US$2. If the menu states that 10% IVA is included in the price, this should not be added as an extra on the bill. Refuse to pay it.

Food A standard main course is *sancocho*, a filling combination of some root vegetable, including the tropical cassava and yam, with chopped fresh fish or any kind of meat. Colombia has its own variant of the inevitable *arroz con pollo* (chicken and rice) which is excellent. *Ajiaco de pollo* is a delicious chicken, maize, manioc, cabbage and potato stew served with cream and capers, and lumps of avocado; it is a Bogotá speciality; another Bogotá speciality is *sobrebarriga* (belly of beef). *Bandeja antioqueña* consists of meat grilled and served with rice, beans, potato, manioc and a green salad; *bandeja paisa* is a filling fry-up of minced beef with rice, beans, fried egg, chorizo, avocado; the simpler *carne asada* is cheaper. *Mazamorra*, boiled maize in milk, is a typical *antioqueño* sweet, and so is *salpicón*, a tropical fruit salad drink, also popular in Bogotá. (In Boyacá, however, *mazamorra* is a meat and vegetable soup.) *Lechona* (crispy sucking pig and herbs) is a speciality of Ibagué. Cartagena's rice is usually with coconut. In Nariño, guinea pig (*cuy*, *curí* or *conejillo de Indias*) is typical. *Tamales* are meat pies made by folding a maize dough round chopped pork mixed with potato, peas, onions, eggs and olives seasoned with garlic, cloves and paprika, and steaming the whole in banana leaves (which you don't eat); the best are from Tolima. From stalls in the capital and the countryside, try *mazorcas* (roast maize cobs), *arepas* (fried maize cakes), or *empanadas* (pies filled with meat and or cheese). On the Caribbean coast, eat an egg *arepa*, which consists of two layers of corn (maize) dough, fried with eggs in the middle. Also, try the popular *cazuela de mariscos*, a creamy, thick seafood casserole often served with grated cheese. Fried fish, including *mojarra* and *robalo* with rice and *patacones* (fried banana cakes) is the staple dish along the coast. *Huevos pericos*, eggs scrambled with onions/tomatoes, are popular for breakfast. *Pandebono*, best in Cali, is a delicious sour cheese-flavoured bread. Also from Cali, try the *pan de yuca*.

A good local sweet is the *canastas de coco*: pastry containing coconut custard flavoured with wine and surmounted by meringue. *Arequipe* is very similar to fudge, and popular (it is called *manjarblanco* in other parts of South America). *Brevas con arequipe*, figs filled with arequipe and covered in syrup, is a popular dessert from Cali. *Almojábanas*, a kind of sour-milk/cheese bread roll, are delicious if fresh. There is, indeed, quite an assortment of little fruit pasties and preserves. Then there are the usual fruits: bananas, oranges, mangoes, avocado pears, and (at least in the tropical zones) *chirimoyas*, *papayas*, and the delicious *pitahaya*, taken either as an appetizer or dessert. Colombia also has an abundance of other tropical fruits, all worth trying, eg the *guayaba* (guava), *guanábana* (soursop), *maracuyá* (passion fruit), *lulo* (*naranjilla*), *mora* (blackberry) and *curuba* (banana passion fruit). They make delicious juices, made with water, or with milk to make a *sorbete*, though *sorbetes* are best left alone unless you are satisfied the milk is fresh. There is also *feijoa*, a green fruit with white flesh, high in vitamin C. Fruit yoghurts are nourishing and cheap (try *Alpina* brand; *crema* style is best), or *kumis*, a kind of liquid yoghurt. Another drink you should try is *champús*, a corn base with lemon and other fruit.

Drink *Tinto*, the national small cup of black coffee, is taken at all hours and is usually sweetened. Colombian coffee is always mild. Coffee with milk is called *café perico*; *café con leche* is a mug of milk with coffee added. To make sure you get cold milk with your coffee, ask for it separately at an additional cost. *Agua de panela* is a common beverage (hot water with unrefined sugar), also made with limes, served with cheese. Many decent brands of beer are brewed,, including *Costeña*, *Aquila* and *Club Colombia*. Also popular is *Brava*. The local rum is good and cheap; ask for *ron* eg Santafe or Ron Viejo de Caldas. *Aguardiente* is a 'rougher' cane-based spirit served with or without aniseed (*aguardiente anisado*). Try *canelazo*, cold or hot *aguardiente* with water, sugar, lime and cinnamon, common in Bogotá. Local table wines include Isabella; none is very good. Wine is very expensive, US$15 in restaurants for an average Chilean or Argentine wine, more for European and other wines. If settling in at a bar or club for the night, order spirits by the bottle or half bottle, to cut down costs.

Festivals and events

Public Holidays: there are some 18 public holidays. The most important are: 1 January: Circumcision of our Lord; 6 January: Epiphany*; 19 March: St Joseph*; Maundy Thursday; Good Friday; 1 May: Labour Day; Ascension Day*; Corpus Christi*; Sacred Heart*; 29 June: SS Peter and Paul*; 20 July: Independence Day; 7 August: Battle of Boyacá; 15 August: Assumption*; 12 October: Columbus' arrival in America* (Día de la Raza); 1 November: All Saints' day*; 11 November: Independence of Cartagena*; 8 December: Immaculate Conception; 25 December: Christmas Day. When those marked with an asterisk (*) do not fall on a Monday, or when they fall on a Sunday, they will be moved to the following Monday. Public holidays are known as *puentes* (bridges).

Bogotá

→ *Phone code: 91. Colour map 1, grid B3. Population: 7.19 million (2005). Altitude: 2,650 m. Mean temperature: 14° C.*

Bogotá, the eighth-largest city in Latin America, is a vast sprawling metropolis where, despite its modernity, it is not uncommon to see the horse and cart still in use on the streets. It is the cultural centre of the country with cosmopolitan restaurants and a vibrant night life. Predictably, there are staggering extremes of wealth and poverty, with the city segregated between the rich north and the poorer south. The capital has advanced in leaps and bounds since the mid-1990s, winning awards for its environmental efforts, libraries, transport systems as well as improving quality of life. Since 2001, the TransMilenio, a rapid, efficient north-south bus route has helped to unclog Bogotá's gridlocked streets. On Sundays, the city's main streets are closed to traffic for the benefit of cyclists, joggers and rollerbladers. Emerald sellers do deals on street corners, but for a safer view of all that glitters, visit the Gold Museum, one of the most stunning collections of pre-Columbian treasures in the Americas. The old centre of La Candelaria has countless well-preserved colonial buildings and important museums that lie along cobbled streets with fine views over the city. A windy mountain road above the city leads to La Calera, offering panoramic views, a popular place for lunch and horse riding at weekends. As Bogotá is Latin America's third highest city, it gets chilly at night. Warm clothes are needed.

Ins and outs

Getting there El Dorado **airport** has two terminals, El Dorado and Puente Aéreo, 15 km west of the centre. A taxi to the city costs about US$8, more at night and early morning. Make sure you get a registered taxi, normally yellow, outside the main terminal or **Avianca** terminal. Near the exit from the baggage area, there is a taxi office where you can state your destination and receive a computer slip detailing the fare (if not available, ask the driver to quote the fare beforehand). There are *colectivos* (US$1 plus luggage pp) from airport to centre; also buses in the daytime, US$0.25 (not easy with bulky luggage and they may refuse to take you). Be vigilant with your belongings when coming out of the arrivals hall into the street. The long-distance **bus terminal**, Terminal de Transportes, is in the same direction as the airport, but not as far out. To get into town from the terminal take buses marked 'La Candelaria', 'Centro' or 'Germania'; ask the driver where to get off (the 'Germania' bus goes up to the centre and La Candelaria). Note there are two areas called La Candelaria, one in the north of the city and one in the south. Be sure to ask for La Candelaria in 'el centro histórico'. To get to North Bogotá from the terminal, take a bus heading in that direction on Cra 68. If taking a taxi, obtain a slip (as at the airport), to fix the fare: to the centre, about US$6. At airport and bus terminal, unofficial taxis are dangerous and must be avoided. ▶▶ *For more information, see Transport, page 793.*

Getting around Bus: Several types of bus cover urban routes. All stop when flagged down. There are also the red **TransMilenio** buses on dedicated lanes. **Taxi**: have meters which calculate units starting at 25. Total units for journey are converted into pesos using a table which must be displayed in the taxi. Taxis are relatively cheap and easy to come by (apart from when it's raining). If you are carrying valuables and especially at night, call for a radio taxi rather than taking one on the street. For reliable and safe radio taxi companies T311 1111 or 611 1111. **Street numbering**: The Calles (abbreviated 'C', or 'Cll') run at right angles across the Carreras ('Cra' or 'K'). It is easy enough to find a place once the address system, which is used throughout Colombia, is understood. The address Calle 13, No 12-45 would be the building on Calle 13 between Carreras 12 and 13 at 45 paces from Carrera 12; however transversals (Tra) and diagonals (Diag) can complicate the system. The Avenidas, are broad and important streets. One of the most important streets is Carrera 7, known as La Séptima, which runs from north to south of the city. Routes through the city are changing all the time, complicated by extensions of the TransMilenio. Potholes in both roads and pavements can be very deep: avoid them, especially when it is wet.

Orientation The mountains of the eastern cordillera always lie east, a useful landmark for getting your bearings. The city has three main interesting parts: La Candelaria, the well-preserved historic centre; Downtown Bogotá, known as 'El Centro', the old commercial centre with shops, high-rise offices and banks; and North Bogotá, where there has been great commercial expansion with the development of wealthy suburbs. **La Candelaria**, full of character, occupies the area bounded by Av Jiménez de Quesada, C 6, Cra 3 and Cra 10. There is some modern infill but many of the houses are well preserved in colonial style, of one or two storeys with tiled roofs, projecting eaves, wrought ironwork and carved balconies. The main colonial churches, palaces and museums are concentrated around and above the Plaza Bolívar. Some hotels are found in this part, more along the margins, eg Av Jiménez de Quesada. **Downtown Bogotá** runs in a band northeastwards along Cra 7 from Av Jiménez de Quesada to C26. It is a thorough mix of styles including modern towers and run-down colonial and later buildings, together with a few notable ones. The streets are full of life; they can be paralysed by traffic at busy times. The pavements can be congested too, particularly Cra 7 and Av 19. Many of the budget hotels and some of the better ones are found in this area. From C 50 to C 68 is **El Chapinero**, once the outskirts of the city and now a commercial district with a sprinkling of old, large, middle-class mansions. Next to the National Park, along La Séptima is **La Merced**, a cluster of English country-style houses. Beyond C 60, the main city continues north to a comparatively new district, **North Bogotá**. Most of the best hotels, restaurants and embassies are in this area which is regarded as the safest in Bogotá. **Maps** The best current maps of Bogotá are by *IGAC* (see Maps, in Essentials, Getting around), 1:30,000 published 2000, and *Cartur*, scale 1:25,000, 1994, about US$4 each. The **Instituto Distrital de Cultura y Turismo** (see below) gives out helpful street maps with attractions, of the city and La Candelaria.

Due to the **altitude**, go easy and be careful with food and alcoholic drinks for the first day or so. Using common sense and keeping vigilant, the majority of travellers experience no problems walking Bogotá's streets; unless heading to Downtown or North Bogotá, do not go beyond the bounds of La Candelaria. It is unsafe to walk around La Candelaria at night, use a taxi instead. Care should be exercised anywhere after dark particularly in downtown Bogotá. Also take care on and around Av Caracas from C 26 to the centre at night as these streets become a favourite spot for prostitutes and drug dealers. Away from the centre, the whole of the south and west of the city should be avoided unless there are specific reasons for a visit. As in any city of this size, take care not to tempt thieves by careless display of money or valuables. Also, anyone approaching you with questions, offering to sell you something or making demands, may well be a thief or a con-artist. The current favourite scam is a con-artist pretending to be a policeman demanding to see credit cards and money. Ignore them and walk on quickly.

Tourist offices Instituto Distrital de Cultura y Turismo ① *Cra 8, No 9-83, on corner of Plaza Bolivar, T327 4900, www.idct.gov.co, or www.bogotaturismo.gov.co, daily 0800-1800*. For information on Bogotá, including cultural events in La Candelaria; free maps, helpful and some English spoken. Also at the airport (both terminals) and bus terminal (helpful), operated by the city of Bogotá. Good local guide books and maps available. A useful website for information on Bogotá is www.terra.com.co/bogota (www.terra.com.co, also has pages on Cali and Medellín). The best monthly guide to what's on in the city, as well as lots of good info is *Plan B*, in bookshops, US$1.40, and *GO*, US$0.70, useful for trips outside Bogotá. **MA**, the National Parks Office, Cra 10, No 20-30, full details in Essentials, National Parks. Most museums are open and free on the last Sunday of the month. Many are free in August.

Sights

La Candelaria → *All museums are closed on Mon except where indicated.*

When the conquistadores first arrived in the 16th century, the area was inhabited by Chibcha Indians. The district, named after Nuestra Señora de la Candelaria, is where the conquistador Gonzalo Jiménez de Quesada founded Santafé (later renamed Bogotá) in 1538. Events in 1810 made La Candelaria synonymous with the Independence movement (see below), while the Franciscans and Jesuits founded schools and monasteries giving La Candelaria a reputation as a centre of learning. Among the oldest educational establishments is the **Colegio Nacional de San Bartolomé** ① *Calle 10, No 6-57*, across from the Chapel of **El Sagrario**, founded 1573, now a prestigious school. The **Colegio Mayor de Nuestra Señora del Rosario** ① *Calle 14, No 6-25* (1653), is a beautiful colonial building well worth a look (you can buy a good cheap lunch at the cafetería). The heart of the city and government is **Plaza Bolívar**, a good starting point for exploring the colonial district. It is claimed that here stands the first ever statue of South America's liberator, Simón Bolívar. Around the Plaza are the narrow cobbled streets and mansions of the Barrio La Candelaria. On the northern side of the Plaza is the **Corte Suprema de Justicia** (the supreme court) destroyed by fire in 1985 after the now extinct M-19 guerrilla group stormed in. The court was wrecked and the present building was completed in 1999. On the

Bogotá

To Facatativá

Sleeping 🛌	Embassy Suites **3**	La Fontana **6**
Capital (Forte Travelodge) **1**	Hacienda Royal **2**	Los Urapanes **7**
Casa Medina **14**	Hostal Moreno **4**	Nación **8**
Charleston **11**	La Casona del Patio Amarillo **5**	Richmond Suites **9**

Colombia Bogotá

west side of the plaza is the **Alcaldía Mayor de Bogotá** (the office of Bogotá's influential mayor and City Hall). On the south side is the **Capitolio Nacional** (congress), an imposing classical style structure with fine colonnades (1847-1925); to arrange a visit ① *T382 3000*.

East of Plaza Bolívar The **Catedral** was rebuilt 1807-1823 in classical style. It has a notable choir loft of carved walnut and wrought silver on the altar of the Chapel of El Topo. The banner brought by Jiménez de Quesada to Bogotá is now in the sacristy. There is a monument to Jiménez inside the Cathedral. Gregorio Vásquez de Arce y Ceballos (1638-1711), the most famous painter in colonial Colombia, is buried in one of the chapels and many of his paintings are in the Cathedral. Next door is the beautiful **Capilla del Sagrario** ① *Mon-Fri 0700-1200, 1300-1730, US$2.20*, built in the late 17th century, with several paintings by Vásquez de Arce.

At the southeastern corner of the plaza is the **Palacio Arzobispal**, with splendid bronze doors. See the **Casa del Florero** or **Museo 20 de Julio** ① *on the corner of Plaza Bolívar with Calle 11, Tue-Fri, 0900-1630, Sat-Sun 1000-1530, US$1.30 (reduction with ISIC)*. It was here that the first rumblings of independence began and houses the famous flower vase that featured in the 1810 revolution. Its ten rooms display the history of Colombia's independence campaigns and boasts portraits and personal belongings of heroes such as Simón Bolívar and Antonio Nariño. It still has original early 17th century Spanish-Moorish balconies.

In the block behind it is the colonial **Plazuela de Rufino Cuervo**. Here is the house of Manuela Sáenz, the mistress of Bolívar. Inside is the **Museo de Trajes Regionales** ① *Calle 10,*

Related map
A Bogotá centre, page 784

Rincón del Chicó **10**
Rosales Plaza **15**
Sofitel Victoria Regia **11**
Suamox **13**

Windsor House **12**

Eating 🍴
Danzashi **2**

Enoteca **3**
Harry Sasson **4**
La Fragata **1**

Trans Milenio
bus route - - -

No 6-20, Mon-Fri 0930-1630, Sat 1000-1600, US$0.90, less with ISIC, a small collection of traditional costumes from indigenous groups of Colombia. Beside it is the house in which Antonio Nariño printed in 1794 his translation of Thomas Paine's 'The Rights of Man' which had a profound influence on the movement for independence. You can read an extract of the text in Spanish on the wall of the building. Across from Plazuela de Rufino Cuervo is **San Ignacio**, a Jesuit church built in 1605 (being renovated in 2007). Emeralds from the Muzo mines in Boyacá were used in the monstrance and it has more paintings by Gregorio Vásquez de Arce. The **Museo de Arte Colonial** ① *Cra 6, No 9-77, Tue-Fri 0900-1700, Sat-Sun 1000-1600, US$0.90, less with ISIC*, is a fine colonial brick building. It belonged originally to the Society of Jesus, and was once the seat of the oldest University in Colombia and of the National Library. It has a splendid collection of colonial art and paintings by Gregorio Vásquez de Arce, all kinds of utensils, and two charming patios. Across Cra 6 is the **Palacio de San Carlos** ① *Calle 10, No 5-51, Mon-Fri 0900-1200, 1400-1700* , where Bolívar lived, which now houses the Foreign Ministry. Bolívar is said to have planted the huge walnut tree in the courtyard. On 25 September 1828, there was an attempt on his life. His mistress, Manuela, thrust him out of the window and he hid for two hours under the stone arches of the bridge across the Río San Agustín (now Calle 7). Santander, suspected of complicity, was arrested and banished.

South of the Palacio de San Carlos is the **Iglesia de María del Carmen** ① *Cra 5, No 8-36*, the most striking church building in Bogotá, in neo-Gothic style, with excellent stained glass and walls in bands of red and white. Almost opposite the Palacio de San Carlos is the **Teatro Colón** ① *Calle 10, No 5-32, T341 6141 tickets (average cost US$20), guided tours Tue-Sat 0930-1730, Sun 1300-1700, US$1.80, but the guard sometimes allows a quick look around for free*. It is considered the country's most prestigious theatre. Its opulent style is typical of late 19th-century Italian architecture. Opera, dance and ballet events are held here. One block northeast of here is the **Casa de la Moneda** (Mint) ① *Calle 11, No 4-93, Mon-Sat 0900-1900,*

Bogotá centre

Sleeping 😴
Ambala **2** *C3*
Aragón **1** *C3*
Avenida Jiménez **3** *C3*

Casa de La Botica **18** *B2*
Centro Plaza **4** *C3*
Dann Colonial **19** *C3*
Dorantes **6** *C3*
El Virrey **1**
Hostal Sue **5** *C4*
Internacional **8** *C3*
La Opera **9** *C2*
La Sabana **10** *B5*
Platypus **11** *C4*
Quiratama **13** *A4*

Regina **14** *C3*
San Sebastián **12** *C3*
Tequendama **16** *B5*
Youth Hostel **17** *B1*

Eating 🍴
Alina Pizza Gourmet **1** *C2*
Andante ma non Troppo **2** *C2*
Café Color Café **3** *C3*
Café L'Avenir **4** *C3*
Café Pasaje **5** *B3*

Casa Vieja **7** *B5, C3*
El Boliche **8** *B6*
El Rincón del Pacífico **11** *C3*
Fulanitos **13** *C2*
Lotus Azul **18** *C3*
Mi Viejo **19** *C2*
Moros y Cristianos **20** *B4*
Panadería Florida **21** *B4*
Pasaje La Macarena **22** *B4*
Pastelería Francesa **23** *C3*
Refugio Alpino **24** *B5*

Colombia Bogotá Sights

784

Sun and holidays, 1000-1700, closed Tue, free. The building dates back to 1620 when Felipe III of Spain ordered its construction, making this the first mint in the continent to produce gold coins. It houses Colombian and European art and sculptures and the machines used to produce gold and silver coins. The courtyard is worth seeing. Next door is the **Donación Botero Museum** ① *Calle 11, No 4-21/93, T343 1223, Mon-Sat 0900-1900, Sun 1000-1700, closed Tue, free.* This is a well-displayed, excellent collection of Botero's own donated sculptures and paintings, including his fine collection of modern and impressionist art including Picasso, Miró, Dalí and Monet. Well worth a visit. In the same street is the Banco de la República's modern **Biblioteca Luis Angel Arango** ① *No 4-41, library 0800-2000, closed Sun, free,* one of the best endowed and arranged in South America, with three reading rooms, research rooms, art galleries and a splendid concert hall. There are exhibitions and regular concerts. There is a good bookshop that also sells CDs on the ground floor and a good cafetería on the sixth floor. Opposite the library is a Juan Valdez coffee shop in a pleasant terrace.

The **Palacio de Nariño** (1906), the presidential palace and offices, occupies a large space due south of Plaza Bolívar. It has a spectacular interior and a fine collection of modern Colombian paintings. It is occasionally open to the public; enquire. The guard ceremonially changes Wednesday, Friday and Sunday, normally at 1730. To the south is the Church of **San Agustín**, strongly ornamented (1637). It, too, has fine paintings by Vásquez Arce and the Image of Jesus, which was proclaimed Generalísimo of the army in 1812. South again is the **Santa Bárbara** church (mid-16th century), one of the most interesting colonial churches, with paintings by Gregorio Vásquez Arce.

Up Calle 7 from the Palacio Nariño is the **Museo Arqueológico** ① *Cra 6, No 7-43, T243 0465, www.musarq.org.co, Tue-Fri 0830-1700, Sat 0930-1700, Sun 1000- 1600, US$1.30, ISIC discount,* a fine and extensive collection of Latin American, pre-Columbian pottery, in the restored mansion of the Marqués de San Jorge. The house itself is a beautiful example of 17th century Spanish colonial architecture. Below the Palacio Nariño is the **Museo del Siglo XIX** ① *Cra 8, No 7-93, Mon-Fri 0830-1730, Sat 0900-1300,* which has a fine collection of just about everything from the 19th century within a restored mansion. Nearby, the colonial **Santa Clara** church ① *Cra 8, No 8-91, Mon-Fri 0900-1700, Sat-Sun 1000-1600,* has a fine interior. It is now a religious museum and concert hall.

Several blocks west of Plaza Bolívar is **Parque Mártires** (Park of the Martyrs) ① *Cra 14 y C 10,* on the site of the plaza in which the Spanish shot and killed many patriots during the struggle for independence.

Up the hill, east of Plaza Bolivar is **Plaza de Chorro de Quevedo**, the spot where Jiménez de Quesada and his weary troops stopped to quench their thirst at the humble fountain that still adorns the plaza. The square is a good place for people-watching and there are plenty of student bars. Storytellers and street musicians gather here on Sunday afternoons.

Sociedad Económica **25** *B3*

Churches ⛪
Catedral **1** *B2*
Capilla del Sagrario &
Palacio Arzobispal **2** *B2*
La Tercera Orden **3** *B4*
La Veracruz **4** *B3*
Mária del Carmen **5** *C2*
San Augustín **6** *B2*

San Diego **7** *B5*
San Francisco **8** *B3*
San Ignacio **9** *B2*
Santa Bárbara **10** *B1*
Santa Clara **11** *B2*

Trans Milenio ------
bus route

Downtown Bogotá

Midway between Plaza Bolívar and Avenida Jiménez de Quesada, which marks the La Candelaria and Downtown boundary, is the **Palacio de Comunicaciones** (Post and Telegraph building) ① *Cra 7 y C 12A,* built on the site of the colonial church of Santo Domingo. Across the Avenida Jiménez de Quesada, in the commercial district, is

785

popular with Israelis, good, basic, hot water, colonial style, kosher restaurant, pool table, coin laundry service, adjacent internet café.

D Dorantes, C 13, No 5-07, T334 6640. Cheaper without bath, hot water, high ceilings, 1950s decor, most rooms with good view of Monserrate, reasonable, safe.

D Quiratama, C 17, No 12-44, T282 4515, F341 3246. Very nice rooms, good service.

D Regina, Cra 5, No 15-16, T334 5137. Safe, good value.

D San Sebastián, Av Jiménez No 3-97, T337 5031. Near La Candelaria, good value, comfortable large rooms, with hot water, good.

E Aragón, Cra 3, No 14-13, T342 5239/284 8325. Shared bath, favoured by travellers, safe, honest, hot water, will store luggage, parking facilities.

E Avenida Jiménez, Av Jiménez, No 4-71, T243 6685. Helpful, sauna, safe.

E-F Hostel Sue, C 16, No 2-55, T334 8894 (next door to Platypus). New traveller hostel in colonial house, welcoming, small dorms and private rooms, patio area, kitchen, free internet, laundry facilities. A good budget option.

E-F Internacional, Cra 5, No 14-45, T341 8731. Cheaper without bath, hot water, kitchen facilities, free coffee, popular with Israelis (specify the address, there are other hotels with similar names).

E-F Platypus, C 16, No 2-43, T/F341 2874/ 3104, www.platypusbogota.com. In La Candeleria, run by helpful German who is an excellent source of information about travelling in Colombia, kitchen facilities, hot water, free coffee, dorms and private rooms, book exchange, good all-round travellers' guest house. Highly recommended.

F pp Youth Hostel, Cra 7, No 6-10, 1 block beyond the Palacio de Nariño, T280 3041, F280 3460. The **Federación Colombiana de Albergues Juveniles**(FCA) is affiliated to the IYHA. Clean, well-run hostel with 90 beds, safe area, US$8 in dorm, separate dorms for men and women. Ask for full information about other hostels here.

North Bogotá *p787, map p782*
Most upmarket hotels are located in North Bogotá.

L Casa Medina, Cra 7, No 69A-22, T217 0288, www.hotelescharleston.com. Bogotá's most stylish hotel, housed within a handsome old mansion, with great antique-feel. First-class service and French restaurant.

L Charleston, Cra 13, No 85-46, T257 1100, www .hotelescharleston.com. Sister to **Casa Medina**, slightly less expensive but no less extravagant, with a fantastic restaurant, La Biblioteca.

L La Fontana, Av 127, No 21-10, T615 4400. Distinctive, very good (**Los Arcos** restaurant in hotel, superb, elegant).

AL Embassy Suites, C 70, No 6-22, T317 1313, F317 0464. Part of the Hilton group, good, safe location, all rooms comfortable, spacious mini-suites, restaurant and spa, business centre.

AL Hacienda Royal, C 114, No 6a-02, T657 8950, F657 8913. Next to Santa Bárbara shopping centre, safe, modern, comfortable rooms, business centre, spa, restaurant and bar.

AL Los Urapanes, Cra 13, No 83-19, T218 1188, www.hotellosurapanes.com.co. Very pleasant, smart, smaller hotel, includes breakfast.

AL Rosales Plaza, C 71A, No 5-47, T317 1100, www.hotelrosalesplaza.com. Spacious comfortable rooms, some with balcony, parking.

AL Sofitel Victoria Regia, Cra 13, No 85-80, T621 2666, www.sofitel.com. Rooms and suites, elegant, good location, pool, restaurant.

AL Windsor House, C 95, No 9-97, T616 6417, F617 0993. Large comfortable suites, elegant, restaurant, good service, safe, house taxis.

A Capital (Forte Travelodge), Av El Dorado, No 69A-51, T423 3000, F423 3003. Close to airport, modern, comfortable.

A Richmond Suites, C 93, No 18-81, T623 5623. Convenient, quiet, excellent rooms, spa.

B La Casona del Patio Amarillo, Cra 8, No 69-24, T212 8805, www.lacasonadelpatio.net. Various room sizes, negotiate price, some with bath, quiet, family atmosphere, pleasant patio, safe residential area. Recommended.

B Rincón del Chicó, C101, No 13-32, T214 7430. Hot water, safe, family atmosphere, TV, helpful, good restaurant, free pick-up from airport and bus terminal.

C Hostal Moreno, Transversal 33, No 95-28, T257 9127. Breakfast available, other meals on request, house taxi driver, near TransMilenio stop, safe for left luggage, quiet, comfortable, hot water.

C Nación, Cra 8, No 65-29/36, T249 5164, F347 5798. Just says hotel at the entrance, small rooms, safe, modern, good location.

C Suamox, C 38, No 16-07, T232 9800, suamox@empresario.com.co. Decent rooms, safe, fairly quiet area, restaurant.

☉ Eating

Many good value comedores on C 16 between Cras 4 y 5 and behind the National Museum where good set-lunches cost around US$2. Note that most restaurants that are open in the evenings in La Candelaria and Central Bogotá close around 2100. Many restaurants in La Candelaria are closed on Sundays.

La Candelaria *p782, map p784*
ͰͰͰ-ͰͰ Casa Vieja, Avenida Jiménez, No 3-57. Friendly service in olde-worlde setting, with great typical dishes including *ajiaco*, *fritanga* and *mazamorra chiquita*. Also opposite the Hotel Tequendama, Cra 10, No 26-60.

♈♈-♈♈ Mi Viejo, C 11, No 5-41. Good upmarket Argentinian steak house, busy lunchtime atmosphere, closed Sun.

♈♈ Alina Pizza Gourmet, C 9, No 2-81. Tasty pizzas in old colonial house setting.

♈♈ Fulanitos, Cra 3, No 8-61. Pretty antique decor with dishes from Cauca Valley and a nice terrace. Now a chain with branches in the north, eg C 85, No 11-11. Good lunches, normally closed evenings.

♈♈ Refugio Alpino, C 23, No 7-49, T284 6515. Good Swiss/French food.

♈♈ Sociedad Económica, C 11, No 6-42. Well-priced set lunches in a beautiful old mansión.

♈♈-♈ El Boliche, C 27, No 5-66. Good value pastas, arty decor.

♈♈-♈ Along Cr 4 up to C 19 are rows of local fish and seafood restaurants with Caribbean and Pacific flavours, popular at the weekend, eg **El Rincón del Pacífico**, Cra 4 No 13-57.

♈ Andante ma non Troppo, Cra 3, No 10-92, La Candeleria. Excellent fresh Italian pasta, good value, Mon-Sat 1200-1500. Recommended.

♈ Boulevar Sesame, Av Jiménez No 4-64. A popular vegetarian.

♈ Lotus Azul, Cra 5 y C 14. Good quality vegetarian and good value.

♈ Moros y Cristianos, C7, No 5-66. Converted tall-ceilinged house, with bright, fun decor and good Cuban cooking, open Sun lunch.

♈ Pasaje La Macarena, C 19, No 8-62. Rows of indoor food stalls, cheap Colombian dishes and set lunches, popular with local workers.

Café Color Café, Cra 2, No 13-06, Plaza de Chorro. Cosy coffee shop and bar, rustic, try canelazo.

Café L'Avenir, C 11, No 2-98. French style, *crêpes* a speciality, salads, pleasant atmosphere, useful noticeboard, 1000-2200. Recommended.

Café Pasaje, Cra 6, No 14-25, Plazoleta del Rosario. An institution for 75 years, cheap beers, good people-watching place. Gabriel García Márquez frequently visited this café as a young journalist.

Panadería Florida, Cra 7, No 21-46. Good pastries and is the place to try *chocolate santafereño*.

Pastelería Francesa, C 9, No 1-95. Charming bakery in colonial house with nice courtyard, good breakfasts, sandwiches and exquisite pastries.

Downtown Bogotá *p782, map p784*
Many good restaurants and cafes along Carrera 4 in Barrio La Macarena (behind the Bull Ring).

♈♈-♈♈ El Patio Liberty, Cra 4A, No 27-48. Good French/Mediterranean food, intimate, popular.

♈♈♈-♈♈ El Viejo, Cra 4a, No 27-10, T334 6805. Good Argentine steaks, live music and tango shows at weekends. Open Sun till 1800.

♈♈♈-♈♈ Restaurante 29, C 29, No 5-66, T232 3921. Excellent international gourmet cooking with Colombian twist, good service and cocktails. Recommended.

♈♈ El Patio, Cra 4, No 27-80. Popular trendy pizzería with terrace, good fresh pizza and calzone.

♈♈ Gaudi, Cra 4, No 26-4, La Macarena. Spanish food, good tortilla, vegetarian options and salads. Nice décor, intimate atmosphere. Closed Mon.

♈♈ La Orilla, Cra 5A, No 26-04. Mon-Sat 1200-1530, popular seafood restaurant, excellent *cazuela de mariscos* and fresh fish. Recommended.

♈♈ Los Cauchos, C 26, No 3A-20, T243 4059. Excellent typical, fresh Colombian food served in colonial house, serves daily lunch specials, fish dishes and soups. Recommended.

♈♈-♈ La Hamburguesería, Cra 4A, No 27-27. Popular, good hamburgers, good value, terrace.

♈ Al Wadi, Cr 27, No 4A-14. Good Arab food, falafel.

♈ Andante coffee shop, Torres del Parque (behind Torre A) Cra 5, No 26-57. Excellent cheap breakfasts and fresh pastries under US$1.50. Salads and pasta dishes too.

♈ Cositas Rápidas y Ricas. C 27, No 4-16. Good value and tasty *comida corriente*, popular with local office workers, nice decor, clean. Lunch only during the week. Recommended.

♈ La Casa de la Abuela C 27, No 4-75. Opposite and similar to the above place. Also recommended.

North Bogotá *p787, map p782*
For great dining and lively bars, head to the Zona T, the pedestrianized area close to the CC Andino, around C 82 and Cra 13. There's also a good selection around the main in plaza in Barrio Usaquén, close to CC Santa Barbara; take bus marked Usaquén on Cra 7.

♈♈♈ Amarti, C 119, No 6-24 on Usaquén plaza. Very popular fashionable Italian, excellent pasta, buffet and desserts.

♈♈♈ Balzac, C 83, No 12-19 on La Zona T. Excellent French cuisine, good steaks, seafood and oysters, slick service.

♈♈♈ Club Colombia, Av 82, No 9-11. Impressive decor in English country style mansion with log fire, trendy, stylish lounge bar serving excellent but pricey cocktails and outside terrace area serving typical Colombian food. Open late, closed Mon. Recommended.

♈♈♈ Di Lucca, Cra 13, No 85-32. Excellent fresh Italian food and cocktails, good service, pleasant courtyard, pricey but worth it. Open till late. Recommended.

♈♈♈ Harry Sasson, C 83, 12-49, Zona T. Busy celebrity chef restaurant, excellent fusion cooking, pricey but worth it. Excellent service, some English spoken. Open late, Sun until 1700.

♈♈♈ La Fragata, C 100, No 8A-55. 12th floor of World Center, revolving. Also in Hotel Radisson, C 114, No 9-65, at Cra 13, No 27-98 and **Fragata Fish Market**, Cra 9, No 77-19. Excellent fish.

♈♈♈ Miniburi, Cra 6, No 117-30, off main plaza in Usaquén, T620 9462. Elegant, excellent, fresh

789

authentic Thai food. Open Sun until 2100. Recommended.

ᵀᵀᵀ-ᵀᵀ Circa, C 69A, No 5-09 (opposite **La Barra**). Mediterrean fusion cooking, trendy, popular lounge bar upstairs, serves good cockails.

ᵀᵀᵀ-ᵀᵀ Enoteca, C 83, No 12-43, La Zona T. Delicious pizza and pasta, good service. Open Sun. Recommended.

ᵀᵀᵀ-ᵀᵀ Gaira, Cra 13, No 96-11. Excellent Colombian food from the Caribbean coast, good atmosphere, fashionable, owned by the singer Carlos Vives. Mon-Thurs 1200-1800, Fri-Sat 1100- 2400.

ᵀᵀᵀ-ᵀᵀ La Barra, C 69A, No 5-08, T321 0839. Authentic Spanish, good selection of tapas, bar and terrace area, almost a museum dedicated to bullfighting, closed Sun and holidays. Recommended.

ᵀᵀᵀ-ᵀᵀ Le Petit Bistrot, C 76, No 10-28, T249 4058. Excellent French cuisine.

ᵀᵀᵀ-ᵀᵀ Wok, C 93, No 12-28; Cra 13, No 82-74. Several branches of this highly-popular place serving oriental dishes.

ᵀᵀ Bagatelle, C 95, No 13-76, T256 1619. Great French-style food, pastries and several vegetarian options. Good breakfast and brunch place, terrace area, Wi-Fi internet connection.

ᵀᵀ Fridays, C 93A, No 11-27. US$10-12. Good value, US-style bar and restaurant, good service.

ᵀᵀ Houston's, Cra 17, No 93-17. Very popular, US-style, crowded Sun.

ᵀᵀ Marmara, C 93, No 12-73, on Parque 93. Nice terrace area, well-priced Mediterranean and Asian food. Good place for a pre-dinner cocktail. Daily happy hour until 1900.

ᵀᵀ Pizzería El Sol de Napolés, C 69, No 11-58, T345 3207. Small, cosy, excellent antipasto. Freshly made pasta, excellent cooking, open daily 1200-2400.

ᵀᵀ Tienda de Café, C 119, No 6-16. Arty restaurant, with happy hour. Also branch in Rosales, Cra 5, No 70A-07. Serves *ajiaco*, a Bogotá speciality.

ᵀᵀ Zhang, C 119, No 7-08. Trendy Chinese with terrace overlooking Usaquén plaza, good service, Wi-Fi internet connection.

ᵀ Golconda, C 118, No 6-73, on main plaza in Usaquén. Good bakery and tasty set lunches for under US$2.

ᵀ Crepes y Waffles, Cra 11, No 85-75. One of the best branches of this chain. Good fresh, cheap salad bar, excellent crêpes and ice-cream desserts, vegetarian options. In Bogotá and other main cities. Recommended.

ᵀ Sopas de Mamá y Postres de la Abuela, Trv 19A, No 116-09. The name says it all, with regional dishes, great value. Other branches in the city.

Café y Crepes, Diagonal 108, No 9A-11, T214 5312. Good food, good atmosphere, run by Mauricio Afanador, climbers meet here, also at Cra 16, No 82-17, T236 2688.

Café Juan Valdez, C 73, No 8-24 and C 11, No 4-15. Excellent 100% Colombian coffee but relatively expensive. Other branches in the city.

Café Oma, several locations, including Parque 93, Cra 15, No 82-58 and Av 19, No 118-78. Good food and coffee, nice atmosphere but relatively expensive, most are open late.

El Altillo del Sol, inside Santa Bárbara shopping centre, Plazoleta Zona B. Attractive, popular outside café serving snacks, good coffee and juices.

☉ Bars and clubs

Bogotá has good and varied nightlife, from classic salsa to heavy trance. Most clubs charge cover of US$6-9, check whether this includes a free drink. Partying starts on Wednesday night. There are many popular bars, discos etc in the Cra 11/15, C 79/85 region, known as the Zona Rosa which includes Zona T (a pedestarianized few blocks filled with street cafés, bars and restaurants), and on and around Parque 93. Others are on Cra 7, C 17/18, on Cra 5 with C 25, a relatively safe area, and around the plaza in Usaquén. For listings, see the *Plan B* events magazine.

In South Bogotá is an area known as Primero de Mayo, a working class neighbourhood with loads of lively bars and clubs popular at weekends. The atmosphere is less pretentious and prices are cheaper than in central Bogotá, but it is advised to go only with locals and use taxis there and back.

Downtown Bogotá *p782, map p784*

Cha Cha, Cra7, No 13-77, in former Hilton Hotel. The in place at the time of writing, fashionable crowd, trendy velvet decor, excellent views of the city at night, House, techno. Thu-Sat, cover US$8.

Enobra, Cra 4, No 26A-37, La Macarena, T284 0310. Popular lively bar, good food. Best nights Wed-Sat. Closed Mon. Minimalist urban décor.

Escobar y Rosas, Cra 4, No 15-01. One of the few good bars in La Candelaria. Converted old chemist, popular student hangout, packed Fri-Sat nights, trendy, DJs, acid jazz and funk. Wed-Sat 1730-0300.

QuiebraCanto, Cra 5, No 17-76. In colonial house, world music, funk and salsa, best nights Wed, Thu, friendly crowd.

North Bogotá *p787, map p782*

Bogotá Beer Company, Cra 11A, No 93-94 or C 82, No 12-10 in the Zona T. Decent British pints, very popular, European music, expensive bar food, happy hour 1600.

Café Village, Cra 8, No 64-29. Trendy and gay café.

Calles de San Francisco, Cra 13A, No 35-31. A popular gay bar.

Cameo, C 120A, No 4-90, Usaquén. Live house band, lively, friendly atmosphere.

Crab's Bar, Cra 13, No 73-23. One of the few bars offering live blues and jazz, best on Wed.
El Closet, Km 4.5 Vía La Calera (outside Bogota). Popular gay club.
El Salto del Angel, Cra 13, No 93A-45. Mexican restaurant and popular bar, attracts yuppie/embassy crowd, live music. Expect to queue to get in at the weekends. Cover US$7.
El Sitio, Cra 11A, No 93-52, just off Parque 93. Popular bar, good live house band at weekends, serves grills. Cover US$7
Galeria Café Libro, Cra 11a, No 93-42 (off Parque 93) and Cr 15A No 46-38. Excellent salsa bar for salsa aficionados and couples, international salsa bands play here. Recommended.
Guararé, C 38, No 13A-91. Lively salsa club, open after 0300.
In Vitro, C 59, No 6-38, right on corner, 2nd floor. Packed Wed nights (get there before 2230), quiet other nights, attracts model/media crowd, friendly, good atmosphere. Cover US$8.
Kathmandu, Cr 6A, No 117-28, Usaquén. Attractive Asian decor, intimate, decent cocktails. Mon-Sat.
Salsa Cámara, Cra 14, No 82-66. Good salsa bar with live salsa at weekends. Good atmosphere.
Son Salomé, Cra 7a, No 40 -31, 2nd floor. Good local salsa bar, intimate, cosy atmosphere, Thu-Sat. Recommended.
Teatrón, C 58, No 10-32. In old large theatre, gay and mixed crowd, attracts international DJs, good atmosphere. Be careful coming out of the club at night, use a taxi. Cover US$8.
The Pub, Cra 12, No 83-48. English-style pub, popular, friendly place with good beers.
The Red Lion, Cra 12, No 93-64, off Parque 93. Another popular English-style pub.

Entertainment

Bogotá *p782, maps p782 and 784*
Cinema Consult *El Espectador* or *El Tiempo*, *PlanB* magazine; there are frequent programme changes. **Cine Bar Lumiere**, Cra 14, No 85-59, T636 0485, US$5 weekends and holidays, cheaper mid-week, comfortable airplane-style seats, food and drink. **Cine Bar Paraíso**, Cra 6, No 119B-56, Usaquén, T215 5361, foreign art films. **Cinemania**, Cra14, No 93A-85, mainstream and foreign art films. **Museo de Arte Moderno** shows Colombian and foreign films every day, all day.

There are cinema complexes in the principal shopping centres (see below). The best are **Centro Comercial Andino**, **Unicentro**, and **Atlantis**. Most have discounted rates on Tue. For programme times call *CineColombia* T404 2463. Foreign films, old and new, are shown on weekend mornings in some commercial cinemas and there are many small screening rooms running features.

Admission, US$2-4. There is an international film festival in Oct (*Festival de Cine de Bogotá*) and a European film festival (*Eurocine*) in Apr/May.
Dance classes Galería Café Libro, Cra 11A, No 93-42, T218 3435. Weekly salsa classes, about US$7 pp. **Punta y Taco**, Salón de Baile, Cra 14, No 75-15, T481 9534. Tango and salsa classes Mon-Sat 0800-1900, free first class, flexible class times. Individual class US$11, for a couple US$15.
Theatre Many of the theatres are in the Candelaria area. Tickets usually from about US$5 up. For **Teatro Colón**, see details on page 784.

☺ Festivals and events

Bogotá *p782, maps p782 and 784*
There are many local religious festivals and parades at Easter and Christmas. One of the best is the **Jan Fiesta de Reyes Magos** (Three Kings) in the suburb of Egipto (up the hill to the east of Candelaria) with traditional processions.

In **Apr-May Feria Internacional del Libro** (book fair) is held in *Corferias*, Cra 40, No 22C-67, www.corferias.com. Bogotá hosts the biennial **Iberoamerican Theatre Festival** (next **2008**), www.festivaldeteatro.com.co. **Temporada de Opera y Zarzuela** held in the Teatro Colón in **May, Jun and Sep** with international artists. **Aug-Sep** is opera season. **Candelaria Festival** in **Sep** street theatre, music and dance events. In **Sep, Festival Internacional de Jazz**. In **Oct** there is **Rock al Parque**, the biggest annual rock festival in Latin America (www.rockal parque.gov.co). In **Dec** at Corferias is the **Expoartesanía** fair, an excellent selection of arts and crafts and regional food from across Colombia. Highly recommended.

☉ Shopping

Bogotá *p782, maps p782 and 784*
16% value-added tax on all purchases. Heavy duty plastic for covering rucksacks etc, is available at several shops around C 16 and Av Caracas; some have heat sealing machines to make bags to size. In Barrio Gaitán, Cr 30 y C 65, are rows of leather shops. This is an excellent area to buy made-to-measure leather jackets, good value; not safe at night, go during the day. Designer labels are cheaper in Colombia than in Europe.
Bookshops Ateneo, C 82, No 13-19, in the north of the city. Good selection of Colombian titles, knowledgeable staff. **Authors**, C 70, No 5-23, T217 7788, www.authors.com.co. Run by American owner, sells English books. **Exopotamia**, C 70, No 4-47. Good selection of books and Latin music, also branch in *Biblioteca Luis Angel Arango* in Candelaria. **Forum**, C 93, No 13A-49, just off Parque 93. Foreign magazines, CDs,

pleasant atmosphere. **Librería Central**, C 94, No 13-92. Some English and German books. **Librería Nacional** bookstores across town eg Unicentro and Santa Bárbara shopping centres. Good Colombian history and current affairs section and some foreign press. **Panamericana**, Cra 7, No 14-09. Disorganized, but has some guidebooks and maps. Other branches in the city. **Taschen**, C 26, No 10-18, next to *Hotel Tequendama*. Art books, small selection of English books and foreign magazines. Also at Museum of Modern Art. **Villegas Editores**, Av 82, No 11-50, int 3. Great coffee-table books on Colombia. **Tower Records** in Andino shopping centre, C 82, Cra 3, sells foreign press.

Camping equipment Monodedo, Cra 16, No 82-22, T616 3467. Good selection of camping and climbing equipment. Enquire here for information about climbing in Colombia.

Handicrafts Artesanías de Colombia, Claustro de Las Aguas, next to the Iglesia de las Aguas, Cra 3A, No 18-60; Cra 11 No 84-12 by CC Andino; and in Plaza de los Artesanos, Tr 48, No 63A-52. Beautiful but expensive designer crafts. **Galerías Cano**, Ed Bavaria, Cra 13, No 27-98 (Torre B, Int 1-19B), also at Unicentro, and Loc 218, Airport. Sell textiles, pottery, and gold and gold-plated replicas of some of the jewellery on display in the Gold Museum. **Mercado de Pulgas** (fleamarket) on Cra 7/C 24, in car park beside *Museo de Arte Moderno*, on Sun afternoons and holidays. A better fleamarket can be found at the Usaquén market around the plaza on Sun, also a good arts and crafts market at the top of the hill in Usaquén. **Pasaje Rivas**, C10 y Cra10. Persian-style bazaar. Hammocks, ceramics, cheap. A small arts and crafts market is open on most days opposite *Hotel Tequendama* in the centre.

Jewellery The pavements and cafés along Av Jiménez, below Cra 7, and on Plazoleta del Rosario are used on weekdays (especially Fri) by emerald dealers. Rows of jewellers and emerald shops also along C 12 with Cra 6. Great expertise is needed in buying: bargains, but synthetics and forgeries abound. **La Casa de la Esmeralda**, C 30, No 16-18. Wide range of stones. **Emerald Trade Centre**, Av Jiménez, No 5-43, p 1. German/English spoken. GMC **Galería Minas de Colombia**, C20, No 0-86, T281 6523, at foot of Monserrate diagonal from Quinta de Bolívar. Good selection of gold and emerald jewellery at reasonable prices.

Markets Paloquemao food market, Cra 27, entre C19 y 22. Bogotá's huge central market, good to visit just to see the sheer abundance of Colombia's tropical fruits and flowers. Cheap stalls serving *comida corriente*. Safe. **San Andresito**, Cra 38 y C12. Popular contraband market, cheap alcohol, designer sports labels, electrical goods, football shirts. Relatively safe.

Shopping centres Most have fast food malls, cinemas and *casas de cambio*. **Atlantis Plaza**, C 81, No 13-05. Upmarket centre with cafés, Hard Rock Café. **Centro Comercial Andino**, Cra 12, C 82/C 83. Upmarket shopping centre with cafes. **Hacienda Santa Bárbara**, Cra 7 y C 116. Charming converted colonial hacienda, Deprisa post office, Librería Nacional, internet café and Western Union agency. **Metrópolis**, Av 68, No 75A-50 (with Exito supermarket opposite). **Palatino**, Cr 7 No 139-07. Best in North Bogotá. **Unicentro**, Cra 15, No 123-30 (take 'Unicentro' bus from centre, going north on Cra 10). Huge complex with **Ley** supermarket. **Unilago**, Cra 15, No 78-33. For all electrical goods, often give discounts if paying in cash. Several large new shopping centres in the north of Bogota, eg SantaFe, autopista with C 200.

Supermarkets Carulla supermarket chain is good for its salad and bakery counters, eg C 63, No 7-09, open 24 hrs with chemist. **Exito** supermarket chain, good selection of fruits and fast food counter, cheap clothes and underwear, eg Cra 59A, No 79-30. **Ley**, Cra 7, No 22-36 and Plaza de Bolívar Cra 7 No 11-30. **Olímpico**, Avenida Jiménez No 4-74. **Pomona** supermarket chain for expensive imported foods, eg Cra 11, No 9B-80.

▲ Activities and tours

Bogotá *p782, maps p782 and 784*
Bullfighting On Sun during the season (Jan), and occasionally for the rest of the year, at the municipally-owned **Plaza de Toros de Santamaría**, Cra 6, No 26-50, T334 1482, near Parque Independencia. In season, the bulls weigh over 335 kg; out of season they are "comparatively small and unprofessional". (Local bullfight museum at bullring, door No 6.)

Cycling The *Ciclovía* is a set of streets leading from Cra 7 to the west, closed to motor traffic every Sun morning and bank holidays, 0700-1400 for cyclists, joggers, rollerskaters etc. There is also the extensive *Cicloruta* paths. For days out by bike, see the *Ciclopaseo* website, www.inssa.com.co.

Football Tickets for matches at El Campín stadium can be bought in advance at **Federación Colombiana de Futbol**, Av 32, No 16-22. It is not normally necessary to book in advance, except for the local Santa Fe-Millionarios derby, and of course, internationals. Take a cushion, matches Sun at 1545, Wed at 2000. Note that big matches can be rowdy and sometimes violent.

Horse riding Cabalgatas Carpasos, Km 7 Vía La Calera, T368 7242, about US$15 pp for 90 mins for groups of 4-5. Horse riding at night too. **Cabalgatas San Francisco**, C 51A, No 76A-15, T295 7715. Daily rides around coffee farms, in the mountains, by rivers and lakes, US$10 per hr.

Rafting and kayaking Natura Vive,
T311-809 4207, www.naturavive.com. Speciaists
in these sports in various locations.
Trekking Sal Si Puedes, hiking group arranges
walks every weekend and sometimes midweek
on trails in Cundinamarca, and further afield at
national holiday periods eg Semana Santa; very
friendly, welcomes visitors. Hikes are graded for
every ability, from 6 km to 4-day excursions of 70
km or more, camping overnight. The groups are
often big (30-60), but it is possible to stray from
the main group. Reservations should be made
and paid for a week or so in advance at Cra 7,
No 17-01, offices 640, T283 3765, open
0800-1200 and 1400-1800. You are advised to
check in advance if this service is operating as
it is sometimes temporarily suspended. There
are several other groups, good information on
Fri in *El Tiempo* newspaper, *Eskape* section and
in the monthly *Go Guía del Ocio* guide (has a
small section in English and French). A
recommended operator is **Caminar por
Colombia**, Cra 7, No 22-31, of 226 B, T286 7487,
caminarcolombia@hotmail.com, walks around
the capital every Sun, US$10 for small groups,
includes transport and guide.

Tour operators
Aviatur, Av 19, No 4-62, T234 7333,
http://site.aviatur.com. Good, efficient, lots of
branches across the country.
Bienvenidos, Cra 62, No 127-72, T/F271 4515,
www.bienvenidosturismocolombia.com.
Organizes cultural, trekking, beach and
adventure tours and can advise on diving.
Caters to tourists and business travellers,
English spoken, helpful.
Eco-Guías, Cra 3, No 55-10, of 501, T347 5736,
310-481 4090 (mob), www.ecoguias.com.
Colombian/English team specializes in tailor-
made trips, ecotourism, adventure sports,
trekking, riding and tourism on coffee fincas,
efficient, knowledgeable and well organized.
Highly recommended.
Edutravel Victoria Reps, C 140, No 16-04, T648
3327, F274 4887. Efficient, knowledgeable and
helpful, excellent English spoken by the owner,
Victoria. Books hotels in Chocó and stays on
coffee farms and in Los Llanos, open Sat morning.
Recommended.
Oficina de Sueños, T677 7163,
www.oficinadesuenos.org. Organizes good
walking city tours, including La Candeleria and
Zipaquirá, some with actors in period costume.
Some guides speak English.
Somos Aventureros, Cra 28, No 42-50, T605
7400, www.somosaventureros.com. Open
Mon-Fri 0830-1300, 1400-1800, Sat 0900-1300.
Arranges tours from Bogotá to Parque de los

Nevados during bank holiday weekends, rafting,
trekking, rock climbing
Viajes Chapinero, Cra 10, No 26-33, T 566 9270.
Helpful information, some English spoken, open
Sat 0900-1200.

Transport

Bogotá *p782, maps p782 and 784*
Air
There are 2 terminals on Av El Dorado, the Puente
Aéreo terminal being 1 km before the main
terminal (T425 1000 for flight information for
both terminals). All **Avianca** domestic flights and
some **Avianca** international flights use Puente
Aéreo, which is comfortable but there is not as
much duty-free shopping. **You must check
which terminal your flight will use**. (See
Ins and outs, page 780, for transport to the city.)
The departure areas with the usual duty-free
shops are of a high standard and comfortable.
Many snack bars and restaurants on 1st floor.
International calls can be made from **Telecom** on
1st floor open till 2100, credit cards accepted;
post office in main arrivals lounge. Exchange
rates are marginally lower in the city. Airport
bank changes travellers' cheques, but is not open
at holiday times. There is a *casa de cambio*, which
changes cash only. When closed, ask airport
police where to change money. Allow at least
2 hrs for checking in and security. Use only
uniformed porters. Baggage deposit in the main
terminal next to domestic arrivals exit (*llegadas
nacionales*). There are 2 tourist offices, in
international arrivals and in domestic arrivals,
open late. Both are near respective exits for taxis.
    For internal flights, which serve all parts of the
country, see page 777. Sometimes, flights are
overbooked, so check in well in advance. You
must reconfirm all flights about 48 hrs before
departure. For regional flights, it is sometimes
possible to reserve flights over the phone and
collect and pay for the ticket at the airport.

Bus
Local Fares start at US$0.40, depending on
length of route and time of day. Most buses have
day/night tariff advertised in the window.
Busetas (green) charge US$0.45, US$0.65 after
2000. There are some *ejecutivo* routes (red and
white) with plush seats, and *colectivos* (small
vans), cramped but faster than others, charge a
bit more. Fares are also higher on holidays. The
TransMilenio (www.transmilenio.gov.co), an
articulated bus system running on dedicated
lanes connects North, Central and South Bogotá
from C 170 (on the Autopista del Norte) to Portal
de Usme (where the road to Villavicencio leaves
the city). There is a spur to the west along C 80

and a link to Candelaria (Parque de Los Periodistas on Av Jiménez de Quesada with a stop at the Gold Museum). **Corriente** services stop at all principal road intersections, *expresos* limited stop only. The journey from the centre to the north takes less than 30 mins. More routes are planned. Journey cost US$0.50. Using the TransMilenio is a good, quick way of getting around the city but it tends to be crowded.

Long distance If going to towns in Boyacá or Cundinamarca for a long weekend, leave Bogotá before Fri 1200 as it can take 1½ hrs to get from Terminal to outskirts. Try to arrive back before 1300, or ask to be set down in North Bogota and take TransMilenio bus to centre.

The **Terminal de Transportes** is at C 33B, No 69-13, near Av Boyacá (Cra 72) between El Dorado (Av 26) and Av Centenario (C 13), T423 3600, www.terminaldetransporte.gov.co. There is also access from Cra 68. It is divided into modules serving the 4 points of the compass; each module has several bus companies serving similar destinations. If possible, buy tickets at the ticket office before travelling to avoid overcharging and to guarantee a seat, especially during bank holidays. Fares and journey times are given under destinations below. If you are travelling north, enquire if the bus company has a pick-up point on the Autopista del Norte around C 160. This saves considerable time, especially if already staying in North Bogotá. *Velotax busetas* are slightly quicker and more expensive than ordinary buses, as are colectivos, which go to several long-distance destinations. The terminal is well-organized and comfortable, but, as usual, watch out for thieves. Free self-service luggage trolleys are provided. There are shops and restaurants. There are showers at the terminal (between Nos 3 and 4), US$0.50, soap and towel provided. There are also several places to leave luggage. At the terminal's medical centre (modelo 4), it is possible to get yellow fever injections, Mon-Fri 0800-1700, Sat 0800-1400. To get there by bus, ask your hotel. Taxi around US$3.50.

International bus It is better not to buy a through ticket to Caracas with **Berlinas de Fonce** as this does not guarantee a seat and is only valid for 2 Venezuelan companies; moreover no refunds are given in Cúcuta. Ideally, if you have time, make the journey to Cúcuta in 2 stages to enjoy the scenery to the full. Bus connections from San Antonio de Táchira in Venezuela to Caracas are good. **Ormeño**, bus terminal modelo 2, T410 7522, www.grupo-ormeno.com/colombia.htm, has a twice-weekly Lima-Caracas service via Cúcuta (US$150 Lima-Cúcuta); there is also a Lima-Bogotá service weekly (US$130; Lima-Cali US$120). Bogotá-Caracas by this service US$60 on Thu. International tickets with Ormeño can only be bought only at

bus terminal. Reportedly more punctual than Ormeño are **Copetran**, Bogotá- Caracas, and **Bolivariano**, Bogotá-Ipiales-Quito, US$40.

Taxi
Taxis are relatively cheap, minimum fare US$1. Average fare from North Bogotá to the centre US$3.50. Check for additional charges above what the meter states eg: night charge and rides to the airport. At busy times, empty taxis flagged down on the street may refuse to take you to less popular destinations. If you are going to an address out of the city centre, it is helpful to know the neighbourhood (barrio) you are going to as well as the street address, eg Chicó, Chapinero (ask at your hotel). Radio taxis are recommended for safety and reliability; when you call the dispatcher gives you a cab number, confirm this when it arrives, eg **Taxis Libres**, T311 1111; **Teletaxi** T611 1111. (The latest scam is for the driver and an accomplice to force passengers to go from ATM to ATM emptying their deposit or credit card account – *paseos milionarios*. At night it is not recommended to travel by taxi along the Av Circunvalar.) Tipping is not customary, but is appreciated.

⊙ Directory

Bogotá *p782, maps p782 and 784*
Airline offices Domestic: Aviatur (T401 3434), **Avianca** and **Satena** (T423 8500), plus **Continental** and **Copa** (T01800-5507 700) are located next to the *Tequendama Hotel* in downtown Bogotá, and at the airport. Nearby is **AeroRepública**, Centro Internacional, Cra 10, No 27-51, T342 7221. **Aires**, El Dorado airport T413 9517. **International: Air Canada**, C 100, No. 8 A-49, Tr BP8, T296 5913; **Air Plus Comet** (budget airline to Madrid), C 76, No 11-17, p 5, T321 2036. **Air France and KLM**, Cra 9A, No 99-07, T01800-956 1111. **American**, Cra 7, No 26-20, T343 2424. **Delta**, Cra 7, Mp 99-11 loc 140, T01-800-9561 0352. **Iberia**, Cra 20, No 85-11, T616 6111. **Mexicana**, Carrera 15, No 112-36, T215 2626.
Banks Some head offices are grouped around the Avianca building and the San Francisco church, others are in North Bogotá on or near C 72. **Banistmo**, Cra 8, No 15-46/60, T334 5088, and 20 local agencies, will cash Thomas Cook and Amex TCs (0900-1300, with passport), will give advances against Visa, and will accept sterling, good rates. Most banks change TCs in the morning only. TCs can also be changed at the **Emerald Trade Centre**, Av Jiménez No 5-43. **BanColombia** banks will give advances against Visa. There are countless ATMs accepting Visa and MasterCard. **BBVA** is good for Visa, **Carulla** supermarkets for MasterCard. There is a daily limit

on how much money you can take out, usually US$170-260, depending on your bank account. Try **Davivienda** banks for a greater daily allowance. **Money changers: American Express:** for replacing lost Amex TCs, go to *American Express* (Expreso Viajes y Turismo), C 85, No 20-32, T593 4949 (has other branches), open 0800-1900, Sat 0900-1400, with full details, a police report of the loss and preferably proof of purchase. They first authorize cash advance on America Express cards and then direct you to the appropriate bank (**Banco Unión Colombia**). Also exchange at **Cambios Country**, Cra 11, No 71-40, Of 201, and at El Dorado airport, T413 8979. Several other city offices, good rates, speedy service. **Orotur**, Cra 10, No 26-05 (very small, below *Hotel Tequendama* in pedestrian subway) is quick and efficient, cash only, including sterling. **Cambios New York Money**, in CC Unicentro, Av 15, No 123-30, loc 1-118, accepts sterling, efficient. **Titan**, C 19, No 6-19, p 2, open afternoons (when all banks have ceased foreign transactions), many other branches. Other *cambios* on Av Jiménez de Quesada, between Cras 6 and 11, and in the north of the city. On Sun exchange is virtually impossible except at the airport. **CC Hacienda Santa Bárbara** has several *cambios* but buying sterling can be difficult.

Car hire See Essentials, Car hire, for agencies with continent-wide distribution. Car hire is expensive in Colombia, although one of the cheapest options is **Dollar**, at airport, T266 3835, and Av El Dorado, No 98-50, T413 5599.

Cultural centres British Council, Cra 9, No 76-49, p 5, T325 9090, www.britishcouncil.org/es/colombia. New modern centre, open Mon-Fri 0900-1700, good TEFL library, British newspapers. **Centro Colombo Americano**, C 19, No 2-49, T334 7640, www.colombobogota.edu.co. English and Spanish courses. Recommended. **Alianza Colombo- Francesa**, Cra 3, No 18-15, T341 3148 and Cra 7A, No 84-72, T256 3197, www.alianza francesa.org.co. Films in French, newspapers, library monthly bulletin etc. Other branches in major cities across Colombia. **Goethe Institut**, Cra 7, No 81-57, T254 7600, www.goethe.de/hn/bog/deindex.htm.

Embassies and consulates Opening times and rules for visas are changing continuously, phone before you go. Few embassies are open in the afternoon, best to go early morning. **Belgium**, Apt 3564, C 26, No 4A-45, p 7, T380 0380, bogota@ diplobel.org. **Brazil**, C 93, No 14-20, T218 0800, secom2@brasil.org.co. **Canada**, Cra 7, No 115-33, p 14, T657 9800, open 0800-1630, www.dfait-maeci .gc.ca. **Ecuador**, C 72, No 6-30, p 7, T212 6549, mecucol@cable.net.co. **France**, Cra 11, No 93-12, T638 1400, www.ambafrance.gov.co. **Germany**, Cra 69, No 43B-44, T423 2600. **Israel**, Edif Caxdac, C 35, No 7-25, p 14, T327 7500. **Italy**, C 93B, No

9-92, T218 7206, ambitbog@cable.net.co. **Japan**, Cra 7, No 71-21, Torre B p 11, T317 5001. **Netherlands**, Cra 13, No 93-40, p 5, T638 4200. **Panamanian Consulate**, C 92, No 7A-40, T257 4452. Mon-Fri, 0900-1300. **Spain**, C 92, No 12-68, T622 0090. **Switzerland**, Cra 9, No 74-08, oficina 101, T349 7230, open Mon-Thu 0900-1200, Fri 0900-1100. **UK**, Cra 9, No 76-49, p 9, T326 8300, www.britain.gov.co. **USA**, C 22D bis, No 47-51, T315 0811, consulate/ visas, T315 1566, http://bogota.usembassy.gov. **Venezuelan Consulate**, Av 13, No 103-16, T636 4011 (610 6622 visa information), 0830-1200. Visas can be collected the following day 1200-1630.

Internet There are plenty of internet centres all over the city, in commercial areas and in shopping centres. **Café del Cubo** in La Candelaria, Cr 4, No 13-57, Mon-Sat 0900-2200. **Foto and Internet Café**, Tequendama Hotel/Centro Internacional complex (2nd floor), loc 164, helpful, good service, Mon-Fri 0700-2000, Sat 0900-1600, US$0.90 per hr. Facilities also in hotels, eg *Hotel Platypus*. and *Centro Plaza*. Some fast and welcoming places in the North, include **Web Café**, Diag 27, No 6-81, Mon-Fri 0900-2000, Sat 1000-1800. **Coffeemail**, inside CC Santa Bárbara. Mon-Sat 1030-2000, Sun 1400-1800. Helpful staff. Prices per hr are US$1-2.

Language courses You need a student visa, not a tourist visa, to study. Some of the best Spanish courses are in the **Universidad Nacional** (see map, page 782), T316 5000, www.unal.edu.co, about US$180 for 2 months, 8 hrs per week, or **Universidad de los Andes**, T339 4949, www.uniandes.edu.co, US$300, 6 weeks, and **Pontificia Universidad Javeriana**, T320 8320 ext 4620, www.javeriana.edu.co. Good value Spanish courses at the **Universidad Pedagógica**, C 72, No 11-86, T594 1894. Good reports, around US$90 for 40 hrs, 2 hrs per day, one of the cheapest on offer. Enquire at Platypus hostel for more information. **Centro Latino Americano**, Departamento de Lenguas, Tr 4, No 42-00, p 4. Accommodation with local families can be arranged. Most other schools in Yellow Pages offer one-to-one private tuition at US$10-12 per hr.

Medical services 24-hr emergency health service, T125. **Cruz Roja Nacional**, Av 68, No 66-31, T428 0111. 0830-1800, consultations/ inoculations US$12.50. **Santa Fe de Bogotá**, C 119, No 9-33, T629 3066, and **El Bosque**, C 134, No 12-55, T274 0577, are both modern, private hospitals, with good service. **Farmacity**, is a chain of new, well-stocked chemists open 24 hrs across the city. For 24-hr home deliveries in Bogotá, T530-0000, C 93A, No-13-41, off Parque de la 93, Cra 13, No 63A-67, among others.

Post offices Main Avianca ticket office and Deprisa airmail office in basement of Ed Avianca, Cra 7, No 16-36, open 0730-1900 Mon to Fri,

0800-1500 Sat, closed Sun and holidays (*poste restante* 0730-1800, Mon-Sat, letters kept for only a month, US$1 per letter). Parcels by air are sent from here too. Also Cra 7 y C 26-27, near Planetarium; C 140 between Cra 19 y Autopista. Parcels by air, contact *Avianca*. **Adpostal**, Cra 7, No 27-54, handles international parcels.

Telephones International calls from several *Telecom* offices in central Bogotá (eg in the *Tequendama Hotel*/Centro Internacional complex); all close within 30 mins of 2000. Buying phone cards is recommended if you are using call boxes.

Useful addresses If you have problems with theft or other forms of crime, contact a **Centro de Atención Inmediata**, CAI, for assistance. Only at a CAI police office is it possible to report a theft and get the relevant paperwork, not at other police stations: downtown, C 60 y Cra 9, T217 7472, La Candelaria, Cra 7 y C6. There are many offices throughout the city, or T156. **Police**: T112 or 315 9188. **DAS**: Head office, Cra 28, No 17A-00, T208 6060, www.das.gov.co. Open 0730-1530, or T153. Cundinamarca office: C 58, No 10-55, T570 1077. **Dirección de Extranjería** (for extending entry permits): C 100, No 11B-27, T601 7200, open Mon-Thu 0730-1600, Fri 0730-1530. DAS will not authorize photocopies of passports; look in Yellow Pages for notaries, who will.

Useful numbers Ambulance: T125 or 132. Fire: T119. Red Cross: T132.

Around Bogotá

The basin on which Bogotá stands, with high ranges of the Cordillera to the east, is known as La Sabana de Bogotá and is the centre of Colombia's important cut-flower industry. Around La Sabana are many places of interest in nearby towns for weekend excursions out of the city.

Zipaquirá → *Phone code: 91. Colour map 1, grid B3. Population: 62,000. Altitude: 2,600 m.*

Twenty kilometres beyond Chía, on La Sabana with its flower greenhouses and dairy farms, is the famous rock salt mine, still producing salt after centuries. Within the mines, the **Salt Cathedral** ① *Mon-Fri 0930-1600, Sat, Sun and holidays 0900-1700, Sun mass at 1200, admission by ticket, US$4.50, half price on Wed, including 1½ hr guided tour, car park US$1,* is one of the major attractions of Colombia. The entrance is in hills about 20 minutes' walk west of the town from Parque Villaveces. At the site, there is an information centre and the **Museo de la Salmuera** ① *US$0.50*, which explains how salt is produced. The original underground cathedral was dedicated in 1954 to Nuestra Señora del Rosario (patron saint of miners). Continuing deterioration made the whole cave unsafe and it was closed. A remarkable, new salt cathedral, minimalist in style, was opened on 16 December 1995. Inside, near the entrance, are the 14 Stations of the Cross, each sculpted by a different artist. Other sections of the cathedral follow to the Nave, 180 m below the surface, with huge pillars "growing" out of the salt. All is discreetly illuminated and gives an austere impression.

Zipaquirá has a pleasant colonial plaza dominated by a brick cathedral. Tuesday is market day. In the town is the **Museo Quevedo Zornozo** ① *Calle 3, No 7-69, Tue-Fri 0930-1200, 1400-1600, Sat-Sun 0900-1700, US$1,* which displays musical instruments and paraphernalia including the piano of General Santander. The **Museo Arqueológico** ① *Calle 1, No 6-21, T852 3499, next to the Parque Villaveces entrance, Mon-Sun 0930-1800, US$1.30,* houses more than 1,500 pieces of pre-Columbian pottery. For eating and partying at weekends, a recommended place in **Chía** is **Andrés Carne de Res** (see Eating, below).

Around Zipaquirá

Nemocón, 15 km northeast of Zipaquirá, has salt mines (now closed) and a church with original 17th century frescos (currently under restoration). There is a small but interesting **Museo de Sal** ① *on the plaza, Tue-Sun 0800-1700, closed Tue after bank holiday, US$0.90,* which includes history of the salt industry in the time of the Chibcha Indians. ATM on main plaza. A side road connects with the Bogotá-Cúcuta highway. Some 8 km beyond Nemocón, with its own access to the main Tunja road, is **Suesca**, a centre of rock climbing on sandstone cliffs overlooking the Río Bogotá. ▶▶ *See Transport listings, page 799.*

Southwest of Bogotá

The Simón Bolívar Highway runs from Bogotá to Girardot; this 132 km stretch is extremely picturesque, running down the mountains. **Girardot**, the former main river port for Bogotá, is linked by road with the capital. Only small boats can go upriver from here. Girardot is a popular weekend and bank holiday haunt for Bogotanos looking for heat and sun. It's a relaxed place with a market on the main plaza. Cattle fairs are held on 5-10 June and 5-10

December. Across the bridge over the Río Magdalena towards Tolima is the small village of **Flandes**, known for its excellent local fish restaurants, eg **Club 60**, good river views, nice atmosphere, tasty fish platters, live music at weekends. Try the river fish *viuda de capaz*. From here launch rides on the river start from underneath the bridge; a one-hour trip to Isla del Sol is recommended (US$9). About 20 km along this road from the centre of Bogotá is Soacha, now the end of the built-up area of the city. A right fork here leads past the Indumil plant to the **Chicaque Parque Natural** ① *daily 0800-1600, US$9 for foreigners; take a bus to Soacha and ask for continuing transport to the park, T368 3114/3118, if driving, there is a better route via Mosquera on the Honda road, left towards La Mesa and in 11 km left again on the road to Soacha, the park sign is 6 km along this road*, a privately owned 300 ha park, principally cloud forest between 2,100 m and 2,700 m on the edge of the Sabana de Bogotá. It is a popular spot for walkers and riders at weekends with good facilities for day visitors and a Swiss-style *refugio*, about one hour down the trail from the entrance, which provides meals and accommodation for 70 or so costing US$20-25 per day including meals.

Northwest of Bogotá

The Sabana de Bogotá is dotted with white farms and groves of eucalyptus. The road passes through the small towns of Fontibón and Madrid, before reaching **Facatativá** (*Population: 67,000. Altitude: 1,800 m*) 40 km from Bogotá. Some 3 km from Facatativá, on the road to the west, is the park of Piedras de Tunja, a natural rock amphitheatre with enormous stones, numerous indigenous pictographs and an artificial lake. **Villeta**, 71 km from Facatativá (*Population: 13,000*) is a popular weekend resort. The road continues to Honda, half way to which is the interesting historical town of **Guaduas** (*Population: 23,000. Altitude: 1,000 m. Phone code: 91*). In the main plaza is a statue of the liberator Policarpa Salavarrieta, the cathedral and one of several museums in the town. Sunday market. Best local dish is *quesillos*. Bus to Honda, US$2.50, one hour. The surrounding countryside is beautiful, including waterfalls at Versalles (10 km). Transport for Facatativá, Villeta and Guaduas: take Bogotá-Honda buses.

Honda On the west bank of the river, Honda is 32 km upstream from La Dorada. It is a pleasant old town with many colonial houses, an interesting indoor market and three museums. The streets are narrow and picturesque, and the town is surrounded by hills. El Salto de Honda (the rapids which separate the Lower from the Upper Magdalena) are just below the town. Several bridges span the Ríos Magdalena and the Guali, at whose junction the town lies. In February the Magdalena rises and fishing is unusually good. People come from all over the region for the fishing and the festival of the Subienda, the fishing season. There is a row of good cheap restaurants across the Río Magdalena bridge in Puerto Bogotá.

Gateway to the Llanos

Through Colombia's impressive longest tunnel, Buenavista, and along a 110-km road running southeast from Bogotá lies **Villavicencio**, capital of Meta Department. The region is known as Los Llanos (the plains) and is at the foot of the eastern slopes of the Eastern Cordillera stretching more than 800 km east as far as Puerto Carreño, on the Orinoco in Venezuela. Los Llanos is cowboy country and the never ending expanse of fertile flat plains makes it ideal for cattle raising, the area's main industry. The area is also rich in oil and the flames from oil refineries based in Puerto Rico can be seen flickering on the distant horizon. Villavicencio, a modern town, is a good base for visiting the Llanos. The region is also known for its good meats and local delicacies. Try *chigüiro*. See Safety, page 777.

◉ **Sleeping**

Zipaquirá *p796*
C Hostería del Libertador, Vía Catedral de Sal, T852 6851. Restored colonial mansion, above the mine on top of the hill with nice views, good restaurant, includes breakfast. Negotiate prices in low season.
D Cacique Real, Cra 6, No 2-12, T851 0209, www.hotelcaciquereal.com. Near Parque Villaveces entrance, 18th-century colonial style,

rooms around pleasant patio, safe parking, helpful, with breakfast, good.

Around Zipaquirá: Suesca *p796*
C La Esperanza, Km 1 along railway from Suesca, T340 9062, www.hotellaesperanza .com.co. With breakfast, restaurant, conference centre, sauna, horse riding US$17 per hr, camping US$2.80.

Southwest of Bogotá: Girardot *p796*

A Tocarema, Cr 5a, No 19-41, T835 0808, www.ghlhoteles.com. Stylish, elegant, art-deco style, airy and bright, lovely large pool area with views, tennis courts, restaurant, a/c. Recommended.

B Bachué, Cra 8, No 18-04, T833 4790, F833 3830. Modern, large pool, a/c, restaurant, good.

E Río, Cra 10, No 16-31, T833 2805. Central near market, bit dirty, a/c, cheaper with fan, restaurant, laundry.

E Rosmar, C 16, No 9-37, T832 4437. A/c, cheaper with fan, central, TV, good.

E Bochica, Cra 9, No 18-39, T833 3867. Basic, safe location, a bit shabby but cheap, fan, restaurant.

Northwest of Bogotá *p797*
Guadas

E Hostería Colonial, on plaza, T846 6041. Great value, delightful restored mansion, TV, bath.

Honda

C Campestre El Guali, Vía Honda-Mariquita (entrada Colegio Pumarejo), Cra 32, No 12-293, T251 0000. Restaurant, pleasant pool area, parking, friendly staff.

E Calle Real , Cra 11, No 14-40, T251 7737. Central, safe, more expensive with fan, parking, restaurant, jacuzzi on rooftop. Recommended.

F Dorantes, C 14, No 12-57, T251 3423. With bath, TV, fan, basic.

Gateway to the Llanos: Villavicencio *p797*

B Villavicencio, Cra 30, No 35A-22, T662 6434. A bit old fashioned, a/c, central, hot water, restaurant, helpful, small roof pool.

C Galerón, C 38, No 31-45, T662 6379. A/c, with breakfast, internet access, parking.

E Centauros, C 38, No 31-05. Small rooms, reasonably clean and quiet.

E Hotel Restaurante Rosado, C 35, No 23-17, T662 6896. Decent budget option, with fan, bath, parking and TV.

Youth Hostel Granja los Girasoles, Barrio Chapinerito. 160 beds, 3 km from the bus station. Several eating places sell typical local food, also Chinese restaurants in the centre: others, some with swimming pools, on the road to Puerto López.

🍽 Eating

Zipaquirá *p796*

There are many restaurants on and around the main plaza.

🍽 Parque Restaurante Funzipa, C 1A, No 9-99. Colombian food served in a converted salt mill.

🍽 Asadero Colonial, C 5 y Cra 7. Good food, *arepas, bandejas*.

Chía

🍽 Andrés de Res, C 2, No 11-94. Open Thu-Sun. This arty, rustic restaurant and bar has become an institution with great typical food, highly original decor, 'performers' to liven things up and free arts and crafts workshops for children.

Southwest of Bogotá: Girardot *p796*

🍽 Al Passo Pizzería, Km 1 Vía Girardot-Bogotá, Ricaute. Good pizzas and grill in lovely patio.

Northwest of Bogotá: Guadas *p797*

🍽 Zaguán del Virrey, C 4, No 5-68. Good *comida corriente* in pleasant patio with art work.

🍸 Bars and clubs

Southwest of Bogotá: Girardot *p796*

Good nightlife on *puente* weekends (bank holidays).
Oasis Bar, inside Centro Comercial, Cra 10 y C 20. Popular rooftop bar, good atmosphere, small pool. Cover about US$5.

Gateway to the Llanos: Villavicencio *p797*

El Pentegrama Llanero, on Vía a Puerto López (in town). Good place to see *joropo* dancing and hear *llanero* music live on Fri and Sat nights.
Los Capachos, Vía Acacias (just out of town). The best, attracts young affluent crowd, popular, 2 floors, rustic setting. Cover charge US$7.

🎉 Festivals and events

Gateway to the Llanos: Villavicencio *p797*

International **Coleo** festival in mid **Oct**. Colourful event, rodeo style, cowboys attempt to make cattle fall down while on horseback. Bring hat and sunscreen. A string of festivals in **Dec**, with typical music (*joropo*) and beauty pageants.

🥾 Activities and tours

Around Zipaquirá: Suesca *p796*

Rock climbing For information call Hernán Wilke, T310-216 8119, or visit his climbing centre **Monodedo**, www.monodedo.com. In Suesca turn right at the entrance to Las Rocas, past *Rica Pizza* restaurant. He speaks English and German, experienced and knowledgeable. US$30 for half day climbing with guide, US$45 full day, open weekends and holidays 0830-2100. Also 5-day trips to Cocuy from US$70 pp per day. **Ricardo Cortés**, the owner of *Rica Pizza*, also arranges climbing trips and local accommodation.

⊖ Transport

Zipaquirá *p796*

Bus Many buses from **Bogotá**: Cra 30 (Av Ciudad de Quito), marked 'Zipa', **Flota Alianza**, or others from the C 170 terminus of the TransMilenio in North Bogotá opposite *Exito* supermarket, US$2 each way, 1¼ hrs. The Zipaquirá bus station is 15 mins walk from the mines and cathedral. Zipaquirá can also be reached from Tunja (see page 800), by taking a Bogotá-bound bus and getting off at La Caro for connection to Zipaquirá, US$2.40. Note when arriving via C170 terminus from Zipaquirá you need to buy a TransMilenio bus ticket to leave the station. To avoid this, ask the driver to drop you off before the bus station.

Train La Sabana station at C 13, No 18-24. A slow tourist steam train runs on Sat, Sun and holidays at 0830 calling at Usaquén in the north of Bogotá (see map), going north to Cájica and Zipaquirá (1200), back in Bogotá, La Sabana at 1700. (All times variable.) Cost: adult US$11, child up to 10, US$6. Tickets should be bought in advance here, at La Sabana station, T375 0558, or from travel agents, or Usaquén station, C100 y Cr 10, or from travel agents.

Southwest of Bogotá: Girardot *p796*

Bus Most buses bypass the town, so ask for a bus that actually stops in Girardot. To **Bogotá**, 132 km, US$7, 3½-4 hrs. To **Neiva**, US$6, 3½ hrs.

Northwest of Bogotá: Honda *p797*

From **Bogotá** by Velotax and Rápido Tolima, US$9, 4 hrs. **Manizales**, US$6. Rápido Tolima run ½-hourly buses to **La Dorada** (1 hr), and beyond, to **Puerto Boyacá** (3 hrs), US$4.50.

Gateway to the Llanos: Villavicencio *p797*

Air Aires and Satena to **Bogotá** daily. Satena flies to Saravena, Arauca and Tame in the Llanos; for other flights ask locally. Taxi to town, US$4.50, bus US$0.50.

Bus Station outside town, taxi US$1.50. La Macarena and Bolivariano run from **Bogotá** about every 30 mins, US$4, 4 hrs, or colectivos Velotax or Autollanos who run every hr, US$4.20. Be prepared to queue for tickets back to Bogotá.

Bogotá to the Venezuelan border

The main road route from Bogotá to Venezuela has some beautiful stretches and passes through, or near, several colonial towns. In Cundinamarca and Boyacá it gives access to the Laguna de Guatavita, perhaps the nearest place the Spaniards came to finding their El Dorado, historical battle sites and the Sierra Nevada del Cocuy, excellent climbing and hiking country. The principal towns, both with a strong colonial heritage, are Tunja and charming Villa de Leiva.

The highway crosses Santander and Norte de Santander Departments on its way to Cúcuta. That this was an important route for the Spaniards can be seen in the colonial villages, like Barichara, and the more important centres like Bucaramanga and Pamplona. There is also some grand scenery in the Chicamocha canyon and the eastern cordillera, with possibilities for adventure sports.

Bogotá to Villa de Leiva

Guatavita → *Phone code: 91. Colour map 1, grid B4. Population: 6,000. Altitude: 2,650 m.*

The modern town of Guatavita Nueva, 75 km from Bogotá, is a popular haunt for Bogotanos. It was rebuilt in replica colonial style when the old town of Guatavita was submerged by the reservoir. There is a small bullring, cathedral and two small museums, one devoted to the Muisca Indians and the other to relics of the old Guatavita church. The many artisan shops are good places to buy ruanas. Market day is Sunday. The tourist information booth can find accommodation for visitors. **Laguna de Guatavita** ① *US$4, with guide*, a sacred lake of the Muisca Indians, is where the legend of El Dorado originated. The lake is a quiet, beautiful place; you can walk right round it, 1½ hours, or climb to the rim of the crater. Opinions differ on whether the crater is volcanic or a meteorite impact, but from the rim at 3,100 m there are extensive views over the varied countryside. Just before the road reaches Boyacá Department, it passes the Sisca reservoir where there is fishing and windsurfing. At the *Refugio de Sisca* restaurant, try *empanadas de trucha* (cornmeal and trout snack), US$0.60, excellent.

The Gilded Man

The basis of the El Dorado (Gilded Man) story is established fact. It was the custom of the Chibcha king to be coated annually with resin, on which gold dust was stuck, and then to be taken out on the lake on a ceremonial raft. He then plunged into the lake and emerged with the resin and gold dust washed off. The lake was also the repository of precious objects thrown in as offerings; there have been several attempts to drain it (the first, by the Spaniards in colonial times, was the origin of the sharp cut in the crater rim) and many items have been recovered over the years. The factual basis of the El Dorado story was confirmed by the discovery of a miniature raft with ceremonial figures on it, made from gold wire, which is now one of the most prized treasures of the Museo del Oro in Bogotá. Part of the raft is missing; the story is that the gold from it ended up in one of the finder's teeth! (Read John Hemming's *The Search for El Dorado* on the subject.)

Tunja → *Phone code: 98. Colour map 1, grid B4. Population: 120,000. Altitude: 2,820 m.*

Tunja, capital of Boyacá Department and 137 km from Bogotá, has some of the finest, well-preserved colonial churches of Colombia. When the Spaniards arrived in what is now Boyacá, Tunja was already an indigenous city, the seat of the Zipa, one of the two Chibcha kings. It was refounded as a Spanish city by Gonzalo Suárez Rendón in 1539. The **Cathedral** and five other churches are all worth visiting, particularly for their colonial woodwork and lavish decoration. These include **Santo Domingo**, begun in 1594, **Santa Bárbara** and the **Santa Clara La Real** chapel (1580).

The **Casa del Fundador Suárez Rendón** ① *Plaza de Bolívar, daily 0800-1200, 1400-1600, US$0.70*, is one of Colombia's few mansions of a Spanish *conquistador* (1539-1543) and has a peaceful courtyard with fine views of the valley; see the unique series of plateresque paintings on the ceilings. The helpful **tourist office** is also here.

The market, near Plaza de Toros on the outskirts of town, is open every day (good for *ruanas* and blankets). Friday is main market day. During the week before Christmas, there is a lively festival with local music, traditional dancing and fireworks.

The battle of Boyacá was fought about 16 km south of Tunja, on the road to Bogotá. Overlooking the bridge at Boyacá is a large **monument to Bolívar** ① *daily 0800-1800, US$1.50 per car. There are several other monuments, an exhibition hall and restaurant at the site. Bus from Tunja, US$0.60, ask for "El Puente".* Bolívar took Tunja on 6 August 1819, and next day his troops, fortified by a British Legion, the only professional soldiers among them, fought the Spaniards on the banks of the swollen Río Boyacá. With the loss of only 13 killed and 53 wounded they captured 1,600 men and 39 officers. Only 50 men escaped, and when these told their tale in Bogotá the Viceroy Samao fled in such haste that he left behind him half a million pesos of the royal funds.

Villa de Leiva → *Phone code: 98. Colour map 1, grid B4. Population: 4,500. Altitude: 2,144 m.*

About 40 km west is the beautiful and unmissable colonial town of **Villa de Leiva** (also spelt Leyva) which has one of the largest plazas in the Americas. It is surrounded by cobbled streets, a charming, peaceful place. The town dates back to the early days of Spanish rule (1572), but unlike Tunja, it has been declared a national monument so will not be modernized. The first president of Nueva Granada, Andrés Días Venero de Leiva, lived in the town. Many of the **colonial houses** are now hotels, others are museums, such as the restored birthplace of the independence hero, **Casa de Antonio Ricaurte** ① *Cra 8 y C 15, Wed-Fri 0900-1200, 1400-1700, Sat, Sun and holidays 0900-1300, 1400-1800*. Ricaurte was born in Villa de Leiva and died in 1814 at San Mateo, Venezuela, fighting with Bolívar's army. The house has a nice courtyard and garden. **Casa de Nariño** ① *Cra 9, Mon-Sun 0900-1200, 1400-1700 (closed Wed)*, recently restored, displays documents from the Independence period. A **palaeontological museum** ① *15 mins' walk north of the town on Cra 9, Tue-Sat 0900-1200, 1400-1700, Sun 0900-1500, US$1.10*, is interesting and well displayed. The **Monasterio de las Carmelitas** ① *Calle 14 y Cra 10, Sat, Sun and holidays 1000-1300*, has one of the best museums of religious art in

Colombia. Part of the monastery is the **Iglesia del Carmen** and the **Convento**, all worth a visit. The shops in the plaza and adjoining streets have a great selection of Colombian handicrafts.

Some colonial houses close Monday to Friday out of season, but the trip is worthwhile for the views and for long, peaceful walks in the hills. Many places are closed Monday and Tuesday. Market day is Saturday, held in the Plaza de Mercado 0400-1300. During weekends and public holidays, the town is very crowded with Bogotanos. The **tourist office** ⓘ *Cra 9, No 13-04 just off the plaza, T732 0232, Tues-Fri 0800-1230, 1400-1800, Sat, 1000-1700, Sun and holidays 1000-1400*, has local maps, gives advice on cheaper accommodation and bus schedules and is most helpful.

The wide valley to the west of Villa de Leiva abounds in fossils. Some 5 km along the road to Santa Sofía is the fossil of a dinosaur (Kronosaurus) found in 1977, now with a museum built around it. A second fossil found in 2000 nearby has been put alongside. Look for road signs to **El Fósil** ⓘ *daily 0700-1800, US$1.20*. About 2 km from El Fósil along this road is the turning for (1 km) the archaeological site of **El Infiernito** ⓘ *Tue-Sun 0900-1200, 1400-1700, US$0.50*, where there are several carved stones believed to be giant phalli and a solar calendar. Some 6 km after the Infiernito turning is the **Monastery of Ecce-Homo** (founded 1620); note the fossils on the floor at the entrance. There are buses from Villa de Leiva (0800-1615) to Santa Sofía, US$1.20; it is 30 minutes to the crossing, then a 2-km walk to the monastery. Beyond Santa Sofía is La Cueva de Hayal, a cave set in beautiful scenery. A tour of most of these attractions leaves the plaza at 0930, Saturday/Sunday, US$5.

About 20 km north of Villa de Leiva is a right turn for the **Iguaque Flora and Fauna Sanctuary** (3 km) run by MA ⓘ *US$10 for foreigners, cars US$2.50; tourist centre with accommodation for 60; restaurant with good food US$1.80-2.20. Take a colectivo from Villa de Leiva-Arcabuco to the turn off to the park (1½ hrs' walk to ranger station); check for afternoon return times. (Camping is allowed, US$3 pp, safe.)* It contains oak woods, flora, fauna and lakes. There are guided paths and a marked trail to Lake Iguaque, a walk of 6½ hours. Best to arrive at the Sanctuary before 0900 to allow time to visit and return from the lake.

Villa de Leiva

To ⑨, Museo Paleontológico & Arcabuco

Av Circunvalar

C 16

C 15

Iglesia del Carmen

Plazuela de San Agustín

Monasterio de Las Carmelitas

C 14

Cra 9

Casa de Antonio Ricaurte

Museo Luis Alberto Acuña

Alcaldía ❸

Casa del Primer Congreso

Cra 10

Cra 11

❹

Plaza Mayor

C 12

Iglesia Parroquial

❷

Cra 7

Cra 8

❷

C 13

Cra 6

C 11

Parque Nariño ➓

Plaza de Mercado

Cra 5

C 10

Cra 4

Cra 3

To

To Santa Sofía, Ecce-Homo & El Fósil

❺

San Francisco

To ⑪ & Bogotá, via Tunja or Chiquinquirá

N

0 metres 100
0 yards 100

Sleeping		Eating
Colombian Highlands 9	Hostal El Mirador 5	Casa Blanca 2
El Molino la Mesopotamia 1	Plaza Mayor 8	Los Arcos 3
Hospedaje El Sol de la Villa 2	Posada La Villa de Alcalá 11	Sazón y Sabor 4
Hospedería Duruelo 3	Posada San Antonio 10	

Ráquira → *Market day Sun.*

At **Ráquira**, 25 km from Villa de Leiva, locals make mainly earthenware pottery in several workshops in and around the village. The small town has charming rows of pastel-coloured houses and a pleasant square. The ceramics, among the best known in Colombia, are sold in about 10 shops on the main street. There is also a good selection of hammocks and handicrafts. At weekends it is possible to eat at the Museo de Artes y Tradiciones Populares. Accommodation along the main street (**E**).

About 7 km along a very rough road, which winds up above Ráquira affording spectacular views, is the beautiful 17th-century **Convento de La Candelaria** ① *daily 0900-1200, 1300-1700, US$1 with a guided tour which includes a simple but interesting museum.* On the altar of the fine church is the painting of the Virgen de La Candelaria, dating from 1597, by Francisco del Pozo of Tunja. The painting's anniversary is celebrated each 1 February, in addition to 28 August, the saint's day of San Agustín. Next to the church is the cloister with anonymous 17th-century paintings of the life of San Agustín

Chiquinquirá → *Phone code: 98. Colour map 1, grid B3. Population: 38,000. Altitude: 2,550 m.*

On the west side of the valley of the Río Suárez, 134 km from Bogotá and 80 km from Tunja, this is a busy market town for this large coffee and cattle region. In December thousands of pilgrims honour a painting of the Virgin whose fading colours were restored by the prayers of a woman, María Ramos. The picture is housed in the imposing **Basílica**, but the miracle took place in what is now the **Iglesia de la Renovación** ① *Parque Julio Flores*. In 1816, when the town had enjoyed six years of independence and was besieged by the Royalists, this painting was carried through the streets by Dominican priests from the famous monastery, to rally the people. The town fell, all the same. There are special celebrations at Easter and on 26 December, the anniversary of the miracle. The town is known for making guitars.

● Sleeping

Tunja *p800*

The area around bus station is not safe at night.
C Hunza, C 21A, No 10-66, T742 4111. Best in town, modern, a bit bland, a/c, breakfast included, good restaurant, pool, sauna, parking.
D El Cid Plaza, Cra 10, No 20-78, T742 3458, F744 4417. Central, comfortable rooms, credit cards accepted.
D Dux, C 19, No 10-78, next to *Saboy*, T742 5736. On pedestrianized road, one block from main plaza. Good rooms, hot water, good value.
E Hostería San Carlos, Cra 11, No 20-12, T742 3716. Colonial style, interesting furniture, good restaurant for lunch. Highly recommended.
F Saboy, C 19, No 10-40, T742 3492. Nice covered patio, family-run.

Villa de Leiva *p800, map 801*

The town tends to be full of visitors at weekends and bank holidays when hotels increase their rates by around 10-30%. There many beautifully restored colonial houses, now hotels, to stay in. Booking is advisable (try bargaining Mon-Thu). It's essential to book in advance for the Festival of Light.
L Hospedería Duruelo, C 13, No 2-88, T732 0222. Large modern luxurious colonial style, beautiful views, nice gardens, also conference hotel, good food, 4 pools, gym, spa, tennis.

Rents horses and bikes. Good family hotel.
AL El Molino la Mesopotamia, C del Silencio (top of Cra 8), T732 0235. A beautifully restored colonial mill filled with antiques, 10% rebate for booking 10 days ahead, excellent home cooking, beautiful gardens, fresh water pool, memorable. Recommended.
B Plaza Mayor, Cra 10, No 12-31, T732 0425, hotelplazamayor@hotmail.com. On main square, beautifully restored colonial house, elegant rooms surround courtyard, restaurant.
C Posada San Antonio, Cra 8, No 11-80, T732 0538. Tastefully restored, nice patio, meals served.
D Hospedaje El Sol de la Villa, Cra 8, No 12-28. Safe, hot shower, good breakfast. Recommended.
D Hostal El Mirador, Tra 8, No 6-94, T732 0941. 5 blocks from main plaza, private bath, hot water.
D Posada La Villa de Alcalá, Cra 9, No 5-104, T/F732 0671. Family atmosphere, charming colonial patio with fountain, arranges horse riding.
D-E Colombian Highlands, 1 km from town (2 blocks from bus terminal), office in town at Cra 9, No 11-02, T732 1379/311 308 3739 (mob). Run by knowledgeable Colombian biologist Oscar Gilede, speaks English. Rooms with bath and one dorm, camping on grounds, US$3 with tent, US$4.50 without tent, BBQ area, hammocks, kitchen facilities, Oscar runs a variety of trips

● *For an explanation of the sleeping and eating price codes used in this guide, see page 58. Other*
● *relevant information is found in Essentials pages 778-779.*

(walking tours, horse rental and adventure sports). Recommended.

Camping Iguaque Campestre Camping Club, Km 1 Vía Hipódromo, T732 0889, US$19 pp includes breakfast and dinner. Restaurant, parking. No camping equipment for hire.

Ráquira *p802*
Several basic hotels on main plaza (D-E).

Chiquinquirá *p802*
C **El Gran**, C 16 No 6-97, T726 3700. Central, secure, comfortable, includes breakfast, good restaurant, laundry service, parking.
E **Sarabita**, C 16, 8-12, T726 2068. Business hotel, pool, sauna (when working), restaurant, building is a national monument.
F **Moyba**, Cra 9, No 17-53, T726 2649, facing plaza. Cheaper without bath, dingy.

🍴 Eating

Tunja *p800*
Fast food and pizza outlets in the pedestrianed streets near Plaza de Bolívar. Cafés on the plaza.
♥♥ **La Buona Vita**, Cra 9, No 23-45. Upmarket Italian, open late, nice decor.
♥♥-♥ **Bodegón de los Frailes**, Cra 10, No 18-41. Good for typical dishes.
♥♥-♥ **El Maizal**, Cra 9 y C 20, near Cathedral. Good typical food.

Villa de Leiva *p800, map 801*
Restaurants tend to close early in the evening, especially during the week.
♥♥ **Nueva Granada**, C 13, No 7-66. Good value, owner Jorge Rodríguez, plays classical guitar music if you ask.
♥♥-♥ **Casa Blanca**, C 13, No 7-02. Decent typical food, *comida corriente*.
♥ **La Misión**, Centro Verarte, Cra 9, No 13-09. Salads, light meals.
♥ **Los Arcos**, Plaza Mayor. Excellent *pizzería*.
♥ **Sazón & Sabor**, on main Plaza. Mexican food, also bar at night, helpful owner Mónica Pineda arranges tours around Villa de Leiva. Closed Mon.
♥ **Star de la Villa** C 13, No 8-85. Cheap breakfast, decent *comida corriente*.
Café y que Café, C 12, No 8-88. Excellent *tinto*.
La Galleta, C 13, No 7-17. Good desserts, pastries.
Panadería Francesa, Cra 10, No 11-82. Open 0800-1900, closed Wed, excellent.
Tienda de Teresa, Cra 10, 13-72. Good breakfasts.

Chiquinquirá *p802*
Plenty of reasonable places to eat around and near Parque Julio Flores.

⚙ Festivals and events

Villa de Leiva *p800, map 801*
Virgen del Carmen, **13-17 Jul** annually.
In **Aug** (check dates) an **international kite festival** is held in the Plaza Major and a popular **Festival of Light** is held every year in **mid-Dec**.

🛍 Shopping

Chiquinquirá *p802*
Many delightful toys are made locally. Along the south side of the Basilica are shops specializing in musical instruments.

🚌 Transport

Guatavita: Laguna de Guatavita *p799*
Bus Bogotá-Guatavita Nueva, **Flota Aguila**, at bus terminal, US$3, 2-3 hrs, several departures morning; last return bus at 1730. You can walk (2-3 hrs) or ride (US$7 per horse) from Guatavita Nueva to the lake. An easier approach is from a point on the Sesquilé-Guatavita Nueva road (the bus driver will let you off) where there is a sign 'via Lago Guatavita'. There is a good campsite and places to eat nearby. From the main road to the lakeside the road is paved as far as a school, about half way. Follow the signs. This road and subsequent track can be driven in a good car to within 300 m of the lake where there is a car park and good restaurant. Taxi tour from Bogotá US$60 full day.

Tunja *p800*
Bus Bus station is 400 m steeply down from city centre. From **Bogotá** Libertadores 2½-3 hrs, 4½-5 hrs weekends and holidays, US$5.50. To **Bucaramanga**, frequent services, 7 hrs, US$19.

Villa de Leiva *p800, map 801*
Bus Station in 8th block of Cra 9. Advisable to book the return journey on arrival at weekends. Buses to/from **Tunja**, 1 hr, US$2 with Cootax, minibuses 45 mins, US$2, every 20 mins. To **Bogotá** with Libertadores 0500, 1400, more on Sun (recommended, most direct and comfortable), good road takes 4-5 hrs (up to 6 on bank holiday weekends), US$6.50, several other companies, and via Zipaquirá and Chiquinquirá, US$6.70. If no direct bus services are available from Villa de Leiva to Bogotá, change at Tunja where there are more bus services. To **Ráquira** *busetas* 4 daily US$2, taxi, US$4. Bus at 1000 from Leiva to **Moniquirá** connects with bus to Bucaramanga.

Ráquira *p802*
From Villa de Leiva, take the continuation south of Cra 9 past the bus station out of town to Sáchira,

turn right to Sutamarchan and Tinjaca and left at
Tres Esquinas for Ráquira, a further 5 km. The road
from Tres Esquinas continues to Chiquinquirá.
Bus Ráquira is best reached from **Tunja**, 1 hr,
US$2, although there are direct buses from
Bogotá every 30 mins (**Rápido El Carmen**),
US$7, 5-6 hrs. Last bus to Tunja 1330. If stuck
after 1330, walk 5 km to Tres Esquinas, where
buses pass between 1530-1630, mostly going
east. There are *busetas* from **Villa de Leiva**.

Chiquinquirá *p802*
Bus To **Villa de Leiva** 1¾ hrs, US$5. To **Tunja**,
3 hrs, US$6. To **Zipaquirá**, US$6. To **Bogotá**, 2½
hrs, US$5.50.

⊙ Directory

Villa de Leiva *p800, map 801*
Banks 2 banks/ATMs in Plaza Mayor. **Post
offices** Opposite *Telecom* building, C 13, No 8-26.

Tunja to Cocuy

Paipa and around
Along the road 41 km northeast of Tunja is **Paipa**, noted for the **Aguas Termales** complex
ⓘ *3 km to the southeast, facilities daily 0600-2200, US$5, children US$3*. The baths and
the neighbouring **Lago Sochagota** (boat trips possible) are very popular with Colombians and
increasingly so with foreign tourists. From Paipa there is a minibus service, US$0.50, a taxi
costs US$1.50, or you can walk in 45 minutes. There are innumerable hotels (**D-F**) and
restaurants on the main street of Paipa and on the approach road to the Aguas Termales.
Paipa is a good place to buy carpets, hammocks and handicrafts.

Sogamoso → *Phone code: 98. Colour map 1, grid B4. Population: 70,000. Altitude: 2,569 m.*
At Duitama, a town 15 km beyond Paipa known for basket weaving, turn right and follow the
valley of the Río Chicamocha for **Sogamoso**, a large, mainly industrial town. This was an
important Chibcha settlement, and a **Parque Arqueológico** ⓘ *Tue-Sun 0900-1300, 1400-
1800, US$1.50, US$0.80 children*, has been set up on the original site. A comprehensive
museum, describes their arts of mummification, statuary, and crafts, including gold working.
Cafetería near the entrance. Camping possible in the grass car park opposite, with permission.

Lago de Tota and around
The main road south of Sogamoso climbs quite steeply to the continental divide at El Crucero at
3,100 m. At this point, the main road continues to Yopal. Turn right for **Lago de Tota** (3,015 m),
ringed by mountains. Virtually all round the lake, onions are grown near water level, and the
whole area has an intriguing 'atmosphere' of pine, eucalyptus and onion. **Aquitania** is the
principal town on the lake. There are plenty of food shops, and restaurants including *Luchos*,
Tunjo de Oro and *Pueblito Viejo* together on corner of plaza, and a bright, restored church with
modern stained glass windows. Above the town is a hill (El Cumbre) with beautiful views.

Monguí and around
Tópaga, 9 km northeast of Sogamoso, has a colonial church, unusual topiary in the plaza and
the bust of Bolívar to commemorate the battle of Peñón of 11 July 1819. Turn south before
Topagá to **Monguí**, which has earned the title of 'most beautiful village of Boyacá province'.
The upper side of the plaza is dominated by the beautiful basilica and convent. There are
interesting arts and crafts shops in all directions. Walk down Cra 3 to the Calycanto Bridge, or
up C 4, to the Plaza de Toros. The **tourist office** is in the Municipalidad on the plaza, helpful. A
recommended excursion is east to the **Páramo de Ocetá** with particularly fine *frailejones* and
giant wild lupins, a 3-hr walk from Monguí. Local craftwork includes leather and wool items.

Sierra Nevada del Cocuy → *Entrance fee, US$10 for foreigners.*
For information contact **MA** ⓘ *C 8 No, 4-74, Cocuy, T08-789 0359*, very helpful, provide maps.
    By the bridge over the Río Chicamocha at **Capitanejo** is the turning to the attractive **Sierra
Nevada del Cocuy** in the Eastern Cordillera, the best range in Colombia for mountaineering
and rock climbing. The Sierra consists of two parallel north-south ranges about 30 km long,
offering peaks of rare beauty, lakes and waterfalls. The flora is particularly interesting.
Everyone wears ruanas, rides horses and is friendly. The most beautiful peaks are Ritacuba
Negro (5,300 m), Ritacuba Blanco (5,330 m) and El Castillo (5,100 m). The main towns are to
the west of the Sierra.

The centre for climbing the main peaks is **Guicán**, about 50 km east of Capitanejo. From *Cabinas Kanwara* (see Sleeping below), it is a steep three hours' walk on a clear trail to the snowline on Ritacuba Blanco. Rope and crampons recommended for the final section above 4,800 m. The *Cabinas* is the best starting place for the four- to five-day walk round the north end of the Sierra, which is surrounded by snowcapped mountains. Guicán is 1-1½ hours' drive by jeep from the mountains, so it is recommended to stay higher up (jeep hire about US$17 from José Riaño or 'Profe' in Guicán). Also, to get to the *Cabinas* you can take the milk truck ('el lechero') which leaves Guicán around 0500 via Cocuy for La Cruz, one hour's walk below the cabins, arriving 1100, getting back to Guicán around 1230, a rough but interesting ride. Alternatively you can take the path leading steeply east from Guicán which leads to the *Cabinas* in about 9 km.

The other main town is **Cocuy**. Above Cocuy you can sleep at *Hacienda La Esperanza* (four hours from Guicán) US$5 pp per night, meals US$3 or you can camp and take your own food. Also camping and horses available at a nearby finca. La Esperanza is the base for climbing to the Laguna Grande de la Sierra (seven hours round trip), a large sheet of glacier-fed water surrounded by five snowcapped peaks, and also for the two-day walk to the Laguna de la Plaza on the east side of the Sierra, reached through awesome, rugged scenery. Between Cocuy and La Esperanza is Alto de la Cueva where you can stay at El Himat meteorological station for US$6, basic, including three meals. There is a fine walk from here to Lagunillas, a string of lakes near the south end of the range (five hours return). Permission to camp can be obtained. Sketch maps from the Cocuy tourist office. It takes six to eight days to trek from one end to the other through the gorge between the two ranges; crampons, ice axe and rope are necessary for climbing. Be prepared for unstable slopes and rockfalls, few flat campsites and treacherous weather. The perpendicular rock mountains overlooking the Llanos are for professionals only. The views east towards the Llanos are stupendous. The best weather is from December to April.

◉ Sleeping

Paipa *p804*
AL **Casona del Salitre**, Vía Toca, Km 3, T785 1508, www.casonadelsalitre.com. 5 mins' drive from town. A national monument and a memorable place to stay near the baths and lake in a well preserved hacienda where Simón Bolívar stayed before the Battle of Boyacá. Hot pools, spa, good restaurant, quiet, fireplace. Highly recommended.

Sogamoso *p804*
E **Bochica**, C 11, No 14-33, T770 7381. Good value, comfortable, hot water, TV, tourist info, restaurant.
E **Valparaíso**, C 11A, No 17-56, T771 6935, near bus station. With bath and TV.

Lago de Tota *p804*
B **Pozo Azul**, 3 km beyond Camino Real, in a secluded bay on the lake, T619 9524 (Bogotá), also cabins up to 6. With breakfast. Suitable for children, comfortable, watersport facilities, good food.
C **Camino Real**, Km 20 Vía Sogamoso a Aquitania, T770 0684, on the lake. Pleasant public rooms, colourful gardens, boat slipway, boats for hire, restaurant, sauna, tourist info.
E **Residencia Venecia**, C 8, No 144, Aquitania. Clean, basic, reasonable.
Camping Las Rocas Lindas campground, at Playa Blanca, southwest corner of lake. With bath and hot water, 2 cabins for 7, 1 for 8, boats for hire, dining room, bar, fireplaces. Recommended.

Monguí *p804*
C **El Portón de Ocetá**, near the plaza. Beautiful large converted colonial house.
D **Hostal Calycanto**, pink house next to the bridge. Lovely setting, restaurant, book in advance.
F **La Cabaña**, chalet on road beyond river (cross bridge, turn left). Basic, comfortable, food if advised.

Sierra Nevada del Cocuy *p804*
E **Cabinas Kanwara** at 3,920 m, 1,000 m above Guicán, 2 cabins for 15 people each, restaurant, open fires, electric showers, or camping F, horse rental and guide service. Highly recommended.
F **Posada Sierra Nevada**, Guicán, T098 8020601, T311-237 8619 (mob). Rooms with bath, can sleep up to 50, good, restaurant, organizes horse riding and nature walks, jeep hire.
Several hotels in Cocuy (E-F), eg F Hospedaje Cocuy (meals, laundry) and F Villa Real.

◉ Eating

Sogamoso *p804*
♥ **Susacá**, Cra 16, No 11-35, T770 2587. One of the best restaurants near the centre, specialities include trout, good *comida*, large portions.

◉ Transport

Sogamoso *p804*
Bus To **Bogotá**, 4-4½ hrs, US$7; to **Yopal**, US$5, 4 hrs, several daily.

Lago de Tota *p804*
Bus From **Sogamoso**, US$2.80, 1½ hr; from Bogotá (Flota Alianzana), via Tunja and Sogamoso, goes round the lake to Aquitania, passing Cuitiva, Tota and the Rocas Lindas.

Monguí *p804*
Bus Office on plaza. To **Bogotá**, Libertadores daily, US$8, 4½-6 hrs. To **Sogamoso**, every 30 mins by buseta, US$1, 45 mins.

Sierra Nevada del Cocuy *p804*
Bus To **Bogotá**, from both Guicán and Cocuy, 6 buses a day start 0400, about US$17, 10-11 hrs;

services by **Libertadores** (recommended) and others. From Cocuy to **Cúcuta**, one daily direct leaves in afternoon, 10-12 hrs. Between Cocuy and Guicán, several buses a day, US$1.50, 1 hr. To go north, change at Capitanejo from where buses go to **Bucaramanga** and to **Cúcuta**. Or change at **Pamplona** for more connections to Burcaramanga. From Capitanejo a picturesque road goes north to Málaga (35 km north of Capitanejo, several hotels), Pamplona (see below) and Cúcuta. To Bucaramanga is another spectacular trip through the mountains, but the road is not good and is very tortuous.

To Bucaramanga and Cúcuta

Socorro → *Phone code: 97. Colour map 1, grid B4. Population: 23,020. Altitude: 1,230 m.*
The main road goes northeast for 84 km to Socorro, with steep streets and single storey houses set among graceful palms. It has a singularly large stone cathedral. The **Casa de Cultura** museum (opening hours vary) covers the local history and the interesting part played by Socorro in the fight for Independence. It is well worth a visit. There is a daily market.

San Gil → *Phone code: 97. Colour map 1, grid B4. Population: 28,000. Altitude: 1,140 m.*
About 21 km beyond Socorro, northeast on the main road to Bucaramanga, is San Gil, an attractive colonial town with a good climate. It's a friendly, relaxed place and its main square is lively at night. San Gil is a centre for adventure sports (rafting, kayaking, parapenting, paragliding and caving) and is also a good place for biking, horse riding and walking. **El Gallineral** ① *daily 0800-1800, US$1.85*, a delightful riverside park with a freshwater swimming pool and beautiful trees covered with moss-like tillandsia (take insect repellent). The park has well-marked trials and is family friendly. Good view from La Gruta, the shrine overlooking the town (look for the cross). Visit Juan Curi waterfalls, 20 minutes drive from town.

Barichara → *Phone code: 97. Colour map 1, grid B4. Population: 10,000. Altitude: 1,300 m.*
From San Gil a paved road leads 22 km to Barichara, a beautiful, quiet colonial town founded in 1714 and designated as a national monument. Among Barichara's places of historical interest are the Cathedral and three churches, the cemetery and the house of the former president Aquiles Parra (the woman next door has the key). An interesting excursion is to **Guane**, 9 km away by road, or two hours' delightful walk by *camino real* (historic trail), where there are many colonial houses and an archaeological museum in the *casa parroquial*, collection of textiles, coins and a mummified woman (entry US$0.25). The valley abounds with fossils. There are morning and afternoon buses from Barichara. Another interesting trip is to the waterfall **Salto de Mica**, a 30-minute walk along a trail following the line of cliffs near Barichara. Between San Gil and Bucamaranga is the spectacular Río Chicamocha canyon, with the best views to the right of the road. There is a new visitors' centre with panoramic views, parking, snack bars and toilets. At the time of writing, a cable car is being built across the canyon, expected to open in 2009 (www.parquenacionaldelchicamocha.com).

Bucaramanga → *Phone code: 97. Colour map 1, grid B4. Population: 465,000. Altitude: 1,000 m.*
The capital of Santander, 420 km from Bogotá, was founded in 1622 but was little more than a village until the latter half of the 19th century. The city's great problem is space for expansion. Erosion in the lower, western side topples buildings over the edge after heavy rain. The fingers of erosion, deeply ravined between, are spectacular. The metropolitan area of this modern, commercial city, has grown rapidly because of the success of coffee, tobacco and staple crops. It is known as the 'city of parks' and is famous for its leather shoe industry.

The **Parque Santander** is the heart of the modern city, while the **Parque García Rovira** is the centre of the colonial area. On it stands the city's oldest church, Capilla de Los Dolores, a national monument. Just off Parque García Rovira is the **Casa de Cultura**. The **Casa de Bolívar**

ⓘ *Calle 37, No 12-15, Mon-Fri 0800-1200, 1400-1730, Sat 0800-1200, US$0.50,* where Bolívar stayed in 1828. It is interesting for its connections with Bolívar's campaign in 1813. On the way out of the city northeast (towards Pamplona) is the **Parque Morrorico**, well-maintained with a fine view. There is a sculptured Saviour overlooking the park, a point of pilgrimage on Good Friday. The **tourist office** ⓘ *(inside the mayor's office), C 30, No 26-117, T634 1132 (ext 123), Mon-Fri 0800-1200, 1400-1830,* is friendly and knowledgeable.

Around Bucaramanga

In **Floridablanca**, 8 km southwest, is the **Jardín Botánicao Eloy Valenzuela** ⓘ *Mon-Sat 0500-1700, free, take a* Floridablanca *bus and walk 1 km; taxi from centre, US$3.50,* belonging to the national tobacco agency. **Girón** a tobacco centre 9 km southwest of Bucaramanga on the Río de Oro, is a quiet and attractive colonial town. Its white buildings, beautiful church, bridges and cobbled streets are well preserved and the historic part of town unspoilt by modernization. Girón can be easily reached from Bucaramanga and makes a good day trip. By the river are *tejo* courts and open-air restaurants with *cumbia* and *salsa* bands. Bus from Cra 15 or 22 in Bucaramanga, US$1.25. **Piedecuesta** is 18 km southeast of Bucaramanga. Here you can see cigars being handmade, furniture carving and jute weaving. Cheap, hand-decorated *fique* rugs can be bought. There are frequent buses to all the surrounding towns; taxi costs US$6. Corpus Christi processions in these towns in June are interesting. Bus from Cra 22, US$0.45, 45 mins.

Bucaramanga to Pamplona

The road (paved but narrow) runs east to Berlín, and then northeast (a very scenic run over the Eastern Cordillera) to Pamplona, about 130 km from Bucaramanga. **Berlín** is an ideal place to appreciate the grandeur of the Eastern Cordillera and the hardiness of the people who live on the *páramo*. The village lies in a valley at 3,100 m, the peaks surrounding it rise to 4,350 m and the temperature is constantly around 10°C, although on the infrequent sunny days it may seem much warmer. There is a tourist complex with cabins and there are several basic eating places. Camping (challenging but rewarding) is possible with permission. At the highest point on the road between Bucaramanga and Berlín, 3,400 m, is a café where you can camp on the porch.

Pamplona → *Phone code: 975. Colour map 1, grid B4. Population: 43,700. Altitude: 2,200 m.*
Founded in the mountains in 1548, it became important as a mining town but is now better known for its university. It is renowned for its Easter celebrations. The climate is chilly. Pamplona is a good place to buy *ruanas* and has a good indoor market. The **Cathedral** in the spacious central plaza is the most attractive feature of this otherwise unprepossessing city. The earthquake of 1875 played havoc with the monasteries and some of the churches: there is now a hotel on the site of the former San Agustín monastery, but it is possible to visit the ex-monasteries of San Francisco and Santo Domingo. The **Iglesia del Humilladero**, adjoining the cemetery, is very picturesque and allows a fine view of the city. The **Casa Colonial** ⓘ *Calle 6, No 2-56, Mon-Fri 0800-1200, 1400-1800; Sat 0800-1200, US$0.50,* archaeological museum, is a little gem. **Casa Anzoátegui** ⓘ *Calle Real, No 7-48, Mon-Fri 0800-1200, 1400-1800,* houses a museum of the Independence period. One of Bolívar's generals, José Antonio Anzoátegui, died here in 1819, at the age of 30, after the battle of Boyacá. The state in northeast Venezuela is named after him. Tourist office ⓘ *Calle 5 y Cra 6, on main plaza.*

Cúcuta → *Phone code: 97. Colour map 1, grid B4. Population: 526,000. Altitude: 215 m.*
Some 72 km from Pamplona is the city of **Cúcuta**, capital of the Department of Norte de Santander, 16 km from the Venezuelan border. Founded in 1733, destroyed by earthquake 1875, and then rebuilt, its tree-lined streets offer welcome respite from the searing heat, as does the **cathedral**, on Avenida 5 between Calles 10 and 11. The international bridge between Colombia and Venezuela is southeast of the city. The modern, congested city is full of Venezuelan contraband and petrol and has some rough areas. See Warning, page 811. **Corporación Mixta de Promoción de Santander**, ⓘ *Calle 10, No 0-30, Edif Rosetal, T571 8981,* helpful. Tourist police at the bus station and airport.

    Just short of the border is the small town of **Villa Rosario**, where the Congress met which agreed the constitution of Gran Colombia in the autumn of 1821, one of the high points of the career of Simón Bolívar. The actual spot where the documents were signed is now a park beside which is the **Templo del Congreso**, in which the preliminary meetings took place. Also nearby is the **Casa de Santander**, where General Santander, to whom Bolívar entrusted the administration of the new Gran Colombia, was born and spent his childhood. The archaeological **museum** ① *Tue-Sat 0800-1200, 1400-1800, Sun 0900-1330*, is worth a visit. The **Casa de Cultura** (also known as Torre de Reloj) ① *Calle13 No 3-67*, has art exhibitions and the **Museo de la Ciudad** which covers the city's history and its part in the Independence Movement.

Border with Venezuela → *Phone code: 97*

Venezuela is one hour ahead of Colombia. If you do not obtain an exit stamp, you will be turned back by Venezuelan officials and the next time you enter Colombia, you will be fined.

Colombian immigration ① *DAS, Av 1, No 28-57, daily 0800-1130, 1400-1730*. Take a bus from the city centre to Barrio San Rafael, south towards the road to Pamplona. Shared taxi from border is US$6, then US$1 to bus station. Exit and entry formalities are also handled at the DAS office, the white building on the lefthand side of road just before the international border bridge. Another DAS office is at the airport and deals with land travellers. See page 1375 for Venezuelan immigration. There is no authorized charge at the border. For exchange, see Banks, page 811.

Venezuelan consulate ① *Av Camilo Daza, Zona Industrial, near airport and Copetran terminal, T579 1954/1956, Mon-Thu 0800-1100, 1300-1500, Fri 0800-1400, taxi US$1.50*. Nationals not requiring a visa are issued an automatic free tourist card by Venezuelan immigration officers at the border. Overland visitors requiring a visa to Venezuela can get one here, or at the Venezuelan Embassy in Bogotá, T640 1213, although they may send you to Cúcuta. As requirements change frequently, it is recommended that all overland visitors (whether requiring a visa or not) check first with a Venezuelan consulate in advance. Apply for visa at 0800 to get it by 1300. If you know when you will be arriving at the border, get your visa in your home country.

Leaving and entering Colombia by private vehicle Passports must be stamped with an exit stamp at the white DAS building before the border crossing. If not you will have to return later to complete formalities. Expect very long queues. Car papers must be stamped at the SENIAT office in Venezuela, see page 1375. With all the right papers, the border crossing is easy and traffic normally flows smoothly.

● Sleeping

Socorro *p806*
D Tamacara, C 14, No 14-15, T727 3515. Swimming pool, restaurant, good services.
E Colonial, Cra 15, No 12-45, T727 2842. Fan, TV, restaurant, parking.
E Nueva Venezia, C 13, No 14-37, T727 2350. Shower, dining room, nice old rooms, good value.

San Gil *p806*
Several budget options along Carrera 11 which overlooks the river.
B Bella Isla, south of town, Vía Javel San Pedro, T724 2971. Out of town, full services, great views, pool, beautiful gardens. Organizes adventure sports tours, helpful staff, secure parking.
D Faro del Fonce, Cra 10, No 1-44, T724 3298. Outside of town, family hotel, includes breakfast, good views, parking.
E Alcantuz, Cra 11, No 10-15, T724 3160. Near river, free coffee, fan, good location, a bit run-down, basic rooms.
E-F Macondo Guesthouse, C12, No 7-26, T724 4463, T311-828 2905 (mob), www.hosteltrail.com/macondo. Two blocks from main square, run by friendly Australian Shaun who also owns an adventure sports company. Good source of

information on trips and activities. Rooms and dorms in very pleasant colonial house, kitchen facilities, book exchange, patio, hammocks, washing machine, best to call in advance to reserve room, as hotel is not always fully staffed due to adventure activities. Guests are given a house key. Recommended.
F San Carlos, Cra 11, No 11-25, T724 2542. Cheaper without bath, upstairs rooms are preferable, basic.

Barichara *p806*
Ask at the *Casa de Cultura* about staying in rooms in private homes.
C Bahía Chalá, C 7, No 7-51, T726 7036. Colonial, rooms around patio, restaurant, price includes breakfast, helpful.
C Hostal Misión Santa Bárbara, C 5, No 9-12, T726 7163. Charming old colonial house, quiet, pool, suites, restaurant, parking, flowery patios, pool, hammock area, organizes local tours.
D Aposentos, C 6, No 6-40, T726 7294. On main plaza, with bath.
D Coratá, Cra 7, No 4-08, T726 7110. Colonial, with a charming courtyard, restaurant and lovely views of the cathedral. Recommended.

Daily **Avianca** flights to **Bogotá** (also AeroRepública and Satena), and to principal Colombian cities. **Satena** (C36, No 15-56, T670 7087) flies to Cúcuta, Quibdó, Medellín and Cali. **Bus** Local buses cost US$0.45.

The long distance terminal is on the Girón road, with cafés, shops and showers. Taxi to centre, US$2.30; bus US$0.45. To **Bogotá**, 9-12 hrs, US$25 (Pullman) with **Expreso Brasilia**. Same company to **Cartagena**, US$35, 12-13 hrs, 0830 and then frequent evening services 1900-2300. **Tunja**, 7-8 hrs, US$18. **Valledupar**, 8 hrs, US$23 at 1800. **Barranquilla**, 10-12 hrs, US$36. **Santa Marta**, 9-11 hrs, US$27, maybe more according to season, US$22 with **Expreso Brasilia**. To **Pamplona**, Expreso Brasilia, 4-5 hrs, night buses (0100-0600), US$9. To **Cúcuta**, Expreso Brasilia, 6-8 hrs, US$12.50 and colectivo US$17. The trip to Cúcuta is spectacular and passes through cloud forests and páramos. Best to start the journey early morning as thick fog usually covers the mountains by afternoon. **Barrancabermeja**, 3 hrs, US$7. To **El Banco** on the Río Magdalena, US$15, several companies, direct or change at Aguachica. Hourly buses to **San Gil**, with Expreso Brasilia, 2½ hrs, US$7. Other companies with local services to nearby villages on back roads, eg the folk-art buses of **Flota Cáchira** (C 32, Cra 33-34).
Taxi Most taxis have meters; beware of overcharging from bus terminals.

Pamplona p807
Bus To **Bogotá**, US$25, 13-16 hrs. To **Cúcuta**, US$4.20, 2½ hrs. To **Bucaramanga**, US$6.50, 5 hrs. To **Málaga** from main plaza, 5 a day from 0800, 6 hrs, US$6. To **Tunja**, US$22, 12 hrs (leaving at 0600). To **Berlín**, US$4. Buses leave from Cra 5 y C 4, minibuses to Cúcuta from Cra 5 y C 5.

Cúcuta p806, map p809
Air Do not buy airline 'tickets' from Cúcuta to Venezuelan destinations, all flights go from San Antonio: cross the border and fly from San Antonio airport (30 mins).

The airport is 5 km north of the town centre, 15 mins by taxi in normal traffic from the town and border, US$3. There are only domestic flights from Cúcuta airport. To **Bogotá** 3 daily and direct to other Colombian cities with **Avianca** and Satena. It is cheaper to buy tickets in Colombia for these flights than in advance in Venezuela.
Bus Bus station: Av 7 and C O (a really rough area). Taxi from bus station to town centre, US$1.50. **Berlinas de Fonce** and **Copetran** have their own terminals in the northwest of the city. Bus to **Bogotá**, hourly, 17-24 hrs, US$50, **Berlinas del Fonce** every 2 hrs from 0630 onwards, 2 stops, including 15 mins in **Bucaramanga**

(US$2.50 extra for *cochecama*), or **Bolivariano**, 20 hrs. There are frequent buses, even during the night (if the bus arrives in the dark, sit in the station café until light). To **Cartagena**, **Brasilia** 1330 and 1730, 18 hrs, US$45. To **Bucaramanga**, US$12.50, 6 hrs, with **Brasilia**, 5 departures daily.
Warning Cúcuta and the surrounding area is a large centre for smuggling and guerrilla activity. Be careful. Travellers have been reporting for years that the bus station is overrun with thieves and conmen, who have tried every trick in the book. This is still true. You must take great care, there is little or no police protection. On the 1st floor there is a tourist office for help and information and a café/snack bar where you can wait in comparative safety. Alternatively, go straight to a bus going in your direction, get on it, pay the driver and don't let your belongings out of your sight. For San Cristóbal, only pay the driver of the vehicle, not at the offices upstairs in the bus station. If you are told, even by officials, that it is dangerous to go to your destination, double check. Report any theft to the DAS office, who may be able to help. **Note** Exceptions to the above are the **Berlinas del Fonce** and Copetran terminals, which are much safer.

Border with Venezuela p808
Bus **San Cristóbal**, US$1.40 (Bolivariano), colectivo US$3; **San Antonio**, taxi US$8, bus and colectivo from C 7, Av 4/5, US$0.50 to DAS office, then US$0.40 to ONIDEX in San Antonio. From Cúcuta to **Mérida** or beyond, go to San Antonio or (better) San Cristóbal and change. On any form of transport which is crossing the border, make sure that the driver knows that you need to stop to obtain exit/entry stamps etc. You will have to alight and flag down a later colectivo.

🅾 Directory

Bucaramanga p806
Banks Bancolombia, by Parque Santander, will cash Thomas Cook and Amex TCs. Long queues (cheques and passports have to be photocopied). Other banks, many with ATMs. Cash (€ and US$) changed at Cambiamos SA, in *Vivero* supermarket, Viaducto La Flora, Mon-Sat 0900-1900, also MoneyGram agent, no TCs.

Pamplona p807
Banks Banco de Bogotá, main plaza, gives Visa cash advances. Cash machines nearby. **Post offices** Cra 6 y C 6, in pedestrian passage. **Telephones** C 7 y Cra 5A.

Cúcuta p806, map p809
Banks For the best exchange rates, it is recommended to change pesos to bolívares in

Cúcuta and not in Venezuela. Exchange rates fluctuate throughout the day. There is an ATM tucked away on the left side of the international bridge in Venezuela. Good rates of exchange at the airport, or on the border. It is difficult to change pesos beyond San Antonio in Venezuela. **Banco Ganadero/BBV** and **Banco de Los Andes** near the plaza will give cash against Visa cards. **Bancolombia** changes TCs. **Banco de Bogotá,** Parque Santander, advances on Visa. Money changers on the street all round the main plaza and many shops advertise bolívares exchange.

Casa de Cambio Cambiamos SA in *Vivero* supermarket, Av Demetrio Mendoza. **Cambios Exito** in *Ley* supermarket, C 12, No 6-65, T573 0339, Mon-Sat 0900-2000, Sun until 1800. Both supermarkets are located outside of town centre. Some *casas de cambio* have limited amounts of currency so if changing large amounts, you may have to go to several *casas*. **Internet** Centro Comercial, Gran Bulevar, across the street from Telecom, **Opinonet**, Internet Café oficina 606B. **Telephones** C 11 y Av 0.

Cartagena and the north coast

Caribbean Colombia is very different in spirit from the highlands: the coast stretches from the Darién Gap, through banana and palm plantations and swamps to the arid Guajira.

Cartagena → *Phone code: 95. Colour map 1, grid A2. Population: 746,000.*

Cartagena should not be missed. Besides being Colombia's top tourist destination and a World Heritage site, it is one of the most vibrant and beautiful cities in South America. It's an eclectic mix of Caribbean, African and Spanish tastes and sounds. The colonial heart of Cartagena lies within 12 km of ramparts. Within the walled city, El Centro, is a labyrinth of colourful squares, churches, mansions of former nobles and pastel houses along narrow cobbled streets. Most of the upmarket hotels and restaurants are found here. The San Diego quarter, once home to the middle classes, and Plaza Santo Domingo perhaps best capture the lure of Cartagena. Less touristy and developed is the poorer Getsemaní neighbourhood, where colonial buildings of former artisans are being rapidly restored. Here are most of the budget hotels. Immediately adjoining Getsemaní is the downtown sector known as La Matuna, where vendors and fruit juice sellers crowd the pavements and alleys between the modern commercial buildings and banks. Cartagena is also a popular beach resort and along Bocagrande and El Laguito are modern high-rise hotels on the seafront. During the high season the walled city becomes a playground for the rich and famous, while cruise liners dock at its port. Don't miss a drink at night in the cafés next to the city's oldest church, Santo Domingo, and in Plaza San Diego. Beyond Crespo on the road to Barranquilla is a fast-growing beach resort lined with luxury apartments. Trade winds during December-February provide relief from the heat.

Ins and outs

Getting there and around Rafael Núñez **airport** is 1½ km from the city in Crespo district, reached by local buses from Blas de Lezo, southwest corner of inner wall. Bus from one block from airport to Plaza San Francisco US$0.40. Taxi to Bocagrande US$4, to town US$3 (official prices). *Casa de cambio*, T656 4943, open, Mon-Fri 0830-2030, Sat 0830-1700, Sun 0830-2100, cashes Amex TCs but not *Bank of America*. Better rates in town. For information, ask at travel agents offices on upper level. Daily flights to all main cities and international destinations. **Bus terminal** is 30 mins from town on the road to Barranquilla, taxi US$7, or take city buses 'Terminal de Transportes', US$0.60. ▸▸ *For further information, see Transport, page 821.*

Information There is no official tourist office in Cartagena at present. Ask at hotels; **Santa Clara** and **Casa Viena** are helpful. The **Instituto de Patrimonio y Cultura de Cartagena** ① *C del Curato de Santo Toribio No 38-161, Edif Aquilar, p 1, T664 5361, may provide information. See also www.cartagenacaribe.com (in Spanish).* For maps, **Instituto Agustín Codazzi** ① *Calle 34, No 3-37, Edificio Inurbe.*

History

Cartagena de Indias was founded by Pedro de Heredia on 1 June 1533 and grew to be the most important port in the 'New World'. The core of the city was built on an island separated from the

Sleeping
Agua 10 *C2*
Casa de las Palmas 1 *F4*
Casa La Fe 3 *C3*
Casa Mara 2 *D5*
Casa Relax 4 *E4*
Casa Viena 5 *D4*
Centro 7 *D2*
Charleston/Santa Teresa 6 *D2*
Familiar 8 *E4*
Hostal Baluarte 9 *D5*
Hostal San Diego 11 *B4*
Hostal Santo Domingo 12 *D2*
Las Tres Banderas 13 *B3*
Marlin 18 *D5*
Montecarlo 14 *C4*
Monterrey 15 *E4*
Santa Clara 16 *B3*
Villa Colonial 17 *D5*

Eating
Bistro 1 *C2*
Café de la Plaza 2 *C2*
Donde Olano 3 *D2*
El Burlador de Sevilla 4 *C2*
El Mar de Juan 5 *B4*
Enoteca 6 *D2*
Girasoles 16 *C4*
Govinda 7 *D3*
La Casa de Socorro 8 *E3*
La Creperie 9 *D2*
La Vitrola 10 *D1*
Mar de Las Antillas 11 *E3*
Mesón Caribe 12 *C3*
Pacos 13 *C2*
Pazza Luna 14 *B3*
Pizza & Pasta 15 *C2*
Tienda Naturista 17 *C4*

1811. The monastery is now used by the Corporación Universitaria Rafael Núñez. Originally part of the Franciscan complex, the **Iglesia de la Tercera Orden** on the corner of Calle Larga is worth a visit.

Past the San Francisco complex is **Plaza de la Independencia**, with the landscaped **Parque del Centenario** beyond. At right angles to the Plaza runs the **Paseo de los Mártires**, flanked by the busts of nine patriots executed in the square on 24 February 1816 by the royalist Morillo when he retook the city. At its western end, the **Torre del Reloj** (clock tower) is one of Cartagena's most prominent landmarks. Through its arches (the main entrance to the inner walled city), slaves from Africa were brought to the **Plaza de los Coches**, which served as a slave market. Around almost all the plazas of Cartagena arcades offer refuge from the tropical sun. On the west side of this plaza is the **Portal de los Dulces**, a favourite meeting place, where sweets are still sold. At night, the area becomes a popular place for an evening drink.

The **Plaza de la Aduana**, which has a statue of Columbus, is flanked by the **Palacio Municipal** and the old Customs House. The **Museo de Arte Moderno** ⓘ *Mon-Fri 0900-1200, 1500-1800, Sat 1000-1300, US$1.30*, exhibits modern Colombian artists and has a shop. The **Art Gallery and Museum** ⓘ *Banco Ganadero, Plaza de la Aduana*, has contemporary Latin American paintings. Continue southwest to the **Church of San Pedro Claver and Monastery** ⓘ *Mon-Sat 0800-1730, Sun 0830-1700, US$2.20 (reduction with ISIC), guides US$3 in Spanish, a little more in English*. Built by Jesuits in 1603, it was later dedicated to San Pedro Claver, a monk in the monastery, who was canonized 235 years after his death in 1654. Known as the Slave of the Slaves (El Apóstol de los Negros), he used to beg from door to door for money to give to the black slaves brought to the city. His body is in a glass coffin on the high altar and his cell and the balcony from which he sighted slave ships are shown to visitors. The monastery has a pleasant courtyard filled with flowers and trees in which Pedro Claver baptised slaves.

The church and convent of **Santa Teresa** on the corner of C Ricaurte, was founded in 1609. It is now a hotel, renamed as the **Charleston Santa Teresa**; see page 818. Opposite is the **Museo Naval del Caribe** ⓘ *Tue-Sun 1000-1730, open Mon during high season, US$2.70, children half price*, displaying the naval history of Cartagena and the Caribbean.

● Sleeping

Cartagena: Historic centre *p813, map p814*
Hotel prices rise substantially, up to 50%, during high season: Jun-Jul and 1 Nov-31 Mar, especially 15 Dec-31 Jan (dates are not fixed and vary at each hotel). Bargain in low season. There are a growing number of attractive boutique hotels in Cartagena. Most budget hostels are on and around Calle Media Luna in Getsemaní. This area can be unsafe, but although it can be dirty and run down, it is still very popular with travellers. Muggings are reported here (2006-07), even during the day, so take care walking in and around Calle Media Luna and do not walk alone, especially at night.

L Agua, C de Ayos, No 4-29, T664 9479, www.agua bedandbreakfast.com. Exclusive, small boutique hotel, colonial, quiet, very pleasant patio.

L La Passion, C Estanco del Tabaco, No 35-81, T664 8605, www.lapassionhotel.com. New, Moroccan-style chic, helpful staff, colonial, patio, roof top pool, very pleasant.

L Santa Clara, Cra 8, No 39-29, T664 6070, www.hotelsantaclara.com. French Sofitel group, magnificently restored 16th-century convent, superb lunch buffet, lovely pool, garden with birds in cloisters, Aviatur office. A special place.

AL Charleston/Santa Teresa, Cra 3A, No 31-23, T664 9494, F664 9448. Formerly a convent, elegantly converted, stylish pool on roof with great views of the colonial district and sea.

A Casa La Fe, Parque Fernández de Madrid, Cra 7, No 36-125, T/F664 0306, www.casalafe.com. Discreet sign (pink building), run by English/ Colombian team. Very pleasant converted colonial house, quiet, jacuzzi on roof, includes breakfast served in patio. Recommended.

A Centro Hotel, C del Arzobispado, No 34-80, T664 0461. Central location, restored colonial building, a/c, spacious rooms, some with balcony overlooking street, safe.

A Monterrey, Paseo de los Mártires Cra 8 B, No 25-103, T664 8560, www.hmonterrey.com. Colonial style, nice terrace with jacuzzi, business centre, comfortable rooms, a/c.

B Casa Mara C Espíritu Santo 29-139, Getsemaní, T664 8724. Private house owned by friendly Italian lady, small pool.

B Hostal San Diego, C de las Bóvedas 39-120, T660 1433. Good location, safe, nice hotel decor and lobby but rooms don't match up.

B Las Tres Banderas, C Cochera de Hobo 38- 66, T660 0160. Off Plaza San Diego, popular, helpful owner, very pleasant, safe, quiet, good beds, spacious rooms, small patio.

C Casa Relax, Calle del Pozo No 25-105, Getsemaní. New, airy, bright hotel in colonial house, serves breakfast, rooms around pool, internet, a/c, pleasant, relaxed atmosphere, French and English spoken. Yacht available for rent.

C Hostal Santo Domingo, C Santo Domingo 33-46, T664 2268. Prime location, basic but clean rooms, safe, popular with Colombians.

D Casa de las Palmas, C Larga (Callejón de las Palmas 25-51), Getsemaní, T664 3530. Charming colonial house filled with antiques, nice patio, small pool, good restaurant. Recommended.

D Montecarlo, C 34, No 10-16, T673 5247. Modern, small rooms with a/c, safe, good location.

D Villa Colonial, C de las Maravillas 30-60, Getsemaní, T664 4996, hotelvillacolonial@ hotmail.com. Safe, well kept hostel run by friendly family, English spoken, a/c, cheaper with fan, TV, tours to Islas del Rosario.

E-F Marlin, C de La Media Luna, No 10-35, T664 3507/9193. Welcoming, laundry, safety deposit box, a/c, less with fan.

E-G Casa Viena, C San Andrés 30-53, T664 6242, www.casaviena.com. Popular traveller hostel, Austrian/Colombian run with very helpful staff. Owner, Hans, is an excellent source of information. Cooking facilities, washing machine, TV room, book exchange and internet, range of rooms, some with cable TV and private bath, cheaper in dormitory. Enquire here for information about boats to Panama.

F Hostal Baluarte, Calle Media Luna No 10-81, Getsemaní, T664 2208. Small basic rooms in colonial house, new rooms on 2nd floor, fan, TV, laundry service.

G Familiar, C El Guerrero No 29-66, Getsemaní, T664 2464. Very basic rooms and cooking facilities, some rooms with bath.

Beaches *p817*
Bocagrande

L Hilton, Av Almte Brion, El Laguito, T665 0666, F665 2211. Excellent, good bookshop with foreign press, ATM, family-oriented pool area, tennis courts, gym, spa, convention centre and restaurants. Overlooks the sea, own beach area.

AL Caribe, Cra 1, No 2-87, T665 0155, www.hotel caribe.com. The first hotel to be built in Cartagena, retaining some splendour of bygone years. Tropical gardens with exotic animals, large pool, beach bar, rooms with sea view.

AL Cartagena Millenium, Av San Martín No 7-135, T665 8499. Range of different suites and spacious rooms at various prices. New, chic and

● *For an explanation of the sleeping and eating price codes used in this guide, see page 58. Other relevant information is found in Essentials pages 778-779.*

trendy, minimalist decor, small pool, restaurant, good service.

A Charlotte, Av San Martín 7-126, T665 9201, www.hotelescharlotte.com. Colonial, Mediterranean-style decor, small pool, comfortable rooms, a/c, good.

B San Martín, Av San Martín No 8-164, T665 4631, www.hotelsanmartincartagena.com. Bright and airy, small rooms some with balcony, pool.

C Internacional, Av San Martín 4-110, T665 8968. Price includes breakfast, helpful staff, TV, family atmosphere, comfortable rooms. Recommended.

C Leonela, Cra 3, No 7-142, T665 8595, F665 8868. One of the best *residencias* on Cra 3. Helpful staff, nice atmosphere, restaurant.

C Toledo, Cra 2, No 6-40, T665 3294, hoteltoledo cartagena@yahoo.com. Prices include breakfast, a/c, cable TV, small pool, good restaurant.

F pp Mi Casa, Av 1 No 2-70, El Laguito, T665 8963, micasacartagena@hotmail.com. Entrance through restaurant, new hostel in a house, welcoming, homely, dorms only, good sea views, dipping pool, right on beach. A good budget option in Bocagrande.

Long stay El Conquistador, El Laguito, T665 0275/652 5015, opposite beach. Apartments for short and long term rent. Good services in building, internet, pool, cafeteria, laundry and phone centre but run down. Ask for Nidian Castro on the ground floor, local 4, who organizes rentals. Studio apartments from US$40 a night. Quality of apartments varies greatly. Best to see one first. Recommended for groups and long stays.

Marbella

There are several hotels and *pensiones* on the road to the airport, particularly at Marbella beach.

E Bellavista, Av Santander 46-50, T664 6411. Bohemian atmosphere, recently refurbished, peaceful patio areas, good restaurant, English and French spoken by owner Enrique. Recommended for longer stays.

Playa Blanca

L Baruchica, on private beach on Isla Barú, T312-670 3893, paulhiac56@hotmail.com. Eco-lodge owned and run by Olga Paulhiac, organic food, yoga available, evening cocktails, attentive service, delightful. Sleeps 8.

E-F Wittenburg, ask for Gilberto, 'el francés', T311-436 6215 (mob). Hammocks with mosquito nets, from US$2-3, dorms, rooms in a large beach bungalow, limited fresh water showers, food served, including vegetarian. Gilberto owns a boat and is often found at Casa Viena on Mon when transport to Playa Blanca can be arranged.

E-F Hugo's Place, T310-716 1021 (mob). Hammocks with mosquito nets, fish meals served, camping.

Islas del Rosario *p817*

AL Kokomo Islas del Rosario, Caño Ratón-Isla Grande, reservations with Yolanda Paz T310-741 8616 (mob) or through tour operators. All-inclusive private beach resort, pool and restaurant, transport to and from island.

🍴 Eating

There is a wide range of excellent, upmarket restaurants. All are busy during high season, reservations recommended.

Cartagena: Historic centre *p813, map p814*

♉♉♉ Donde Olano, C Santo Domingo y Inquisición, T664 7099, Tucked away, cosy, intimate atmosphere, great seafood with French influence.

♉♉♉ El Mar de Juan, Plaza San Diego. Seafood only, fine service and decor. Recommended.

♉♉♉ La Vitrola, C Baloco 2-01, El Centro, T660 0711. Attracts jet set crowd, great atmosphere, slick service, live Cuban band at weekends, good seafood and cocktails. Expensive but worth it, book ahead. Recommended.

♉♉♉-♉♉ Enoteca, C San Juan de Dios, No 3-39, T664 3806. The best thin, crispy pizza in town, attractive patio, delicatessen and bustling atmosphere. Recommended.

₮₮₮-₮₮ **La Casa de Socorro**, C Larga, No 8B -112, Getsemaní, T664 4658. Busy at lunchtime, excellent Caribbean food. Try shark starter and *cazuela de mariscos*. Highly recommended.

₮₮₮-₮₮ **Mar de Las Antillas**, C Larga, No 8B- 26, Getsemaní, T664 5710. Popular, good seafood.

₮₮₮-₮₮ **Pacos**, Plaza Santo Domingo. Well-established, good Spanish and seafood, try aubergine starter.

₮₮ **Bistro**, C de Ayos, No 4-27/46, T664 1799. German run, nice atmosphere, open all day, good bakery, breakfasts, seafood and steak. Closed Sun.

₮₮ **El Burlador de Sevilla**, C Santo Domingo 33-88, T660 0866. Spanish, open late, excellent paella, attentive service, good.

₮₮ **Pazza Luna**, Plaza San Diego, next to and same owners as **El Mar de Juan**. Good pizza.

₮₮ **San Pedro**, Plaza de San Pedro Claver. Elegant, lounge bar too, tables outside, a/c inside, Asian and fish specialities, sushi, good value. Open Sun, closed 1500-1900.

₮₮-₮ **Mesón Caribe**, C de La Tablada, No 7-62, San Diego, T660 2379. Popular with locals, good value lunches, nice atmosphere. Recommended.

₮₮-₮ **Pizza & Pasta**, C del Arzobispado y C del Coliseo, T664 8960. Decent set lunch, open late and on Sun.

₮ **Girasoles**, C de los Puntales, No 37-01, T664 5239. Small café, serves vegetarian food at lunch.

₮ **Govinda**, Plaza de los Coches 7-15. Vegetarian set lunch US$2. Recommended.

₮ **Tienda Naturista**, C Quero 9-09. Good, cheap vegetarian.

Café de la Plaza, Plaza Santo Domingo. Great atmosphere, open all day.

La Creperie, Plaza de Bolívar. Generous salads, fruit juices.

Outside the centre

₮₮₮ **Club de Pesca**, San Sebastián de Pastelillo fort, Manga island, T660 5863. Wonderful setting, excellent fish and seafood. Recommended.

Beaches: Bocagrande *p817*

₮₮₮-₮₮ **Arabe**, Cra 3A, No 8-83, T665 4365. Excellent large steaks and Arab food, belly dancer.

₮₮ **La Fonda Antioqueña**, Cra 2, No 6-161. Traditional Colombian.

₮₮-₮ **Riquismo**, Av 1, El Laguito, T665 6116. Ask for the good, cheap *almuerzos* (not on menu), clean, good juices, attentive service. Excellent toilets.

₮₮-₮ **Sandwich Qbano**, Av San Martín, No 9-124. Fast food chain, good sandwiches and salads.

₮ **Farah Express**, Cra 2 y C 9. Arab food, popular, also vegetarian dishes, open late, good value.

La Dulcería, Cra 2, No 6-53. Good Arab desserts, snacks, popular.

❶ Bars and clubs

Cartagena *p812, map 814*

Most night life is found in the historic district. Good bars and clubs along C del Arsenal, Getsemaní, and along Portal de los Dulces, opposite the clock tower. Most clubs charge cover, US$7-9.

Bar Comarca, C Santo Domingo, No 3-38. Interesting naval decor, charismatic owner, speaks English, live music at weekends, attracts middle-aged crowd.

Café del Mar, on ramparts at end of C Estribos. Lounge bar, live DJ, young trendy crowd. Excellent place for a drink at sunset, great views. Food served. Recommended.

Donde Fidel, Portal de los Dulces. Informal, one of the cheapest places for beers and classic salsa.

Joy Salvo, near **Café del Mar** on ramparts. Popular, dance music, open until 0600, cover US$10 (negotiate cover after 0300).

La Carbonera, C del Arsenal, Getsemaní. Salsa and Colombian classics, no shorts allowed.

Mister Babilla, C del Arsenal, Getsemaní. The best known spot in this area, fierce a/c, salsa and Colombian classics.

Quiebra Canto, Parque Independencia, next to *Hotel Monterrey*, 2nd floor. Good salsa, nice atmosphere, balconies with good views. Recommended.

Tu Candela, 2nd floor bar, Portal de los Dulces. Range of music and salsa. Beware, pretty and friendly girls may be prostitutes.

Vía Apia, C Santo Domingo, No 33-46. Small friendly bar, range of music. Popular with foreigners and Colombians. Tapas served.

❀ Festivals and events

Cartagena *p812, map 814*

La Candelaria, religious processions and horse parades (see La Popa). **Independence** celebrations, **2nd week of Nov**: masked people in fancy dress dance to the sound of *maracas* and drums. There are beauty contests, battles of flowers and general mayhem. This festival can be wild and dangerous. There is an **international film festival 2nd week of Mar**, www.festicine cartagena.com. The **Hay Literary Festival**, attracts international and Colombian writers.

❍ Shopping

Cartagena *p812, map 814*

Bookshops Forum Discos y Libros, Playa de la Artillería, No 33-12, T664 2457. **Librería Nacional**, Cra 7, No 36-27.

Handicrafts and jewellery In general shopping is better in Bogotá. Handicraft and emerald shops around Plaza de Bolivar and in the Plaza de las Bóvedas are good and have the best selection in Cartagena. In the Pierino Gallo building in Bocagrande are reputable jewellery shops. **El Centavo Menos**, C Román, No 5-08, Plaza de la Proclamación. Good selection of Colombian handicrafts.

Supermarket Supermarket Olympica, Cra 3, No 5-18, Bocagrande, open 24 hrs. Vivero, Av Venezuela y C del Boquete. A/c, with *cafetería*. Shopping malls with cinemas outside the city centre, eg Los Caracoles and Santa Lucía.

▲▲ Activities and tours

Cartagena *p812, map 814*
Bullfighting Bullfights take place in Jan in the new Plaza de Toros at the Villa Olímpica on Av Pedro de Heredia, away from the centre. The old, wooden Plaza de Toros (in San Diego, see map) is a fine structure, but is no longer used.
Diving Discounts are sometimes available if you book via the hotels, enquire. Recompression chamber at the naval hospital, Bocagrande.
Cultura del Mar, C del Pozo, No 25-95, Getsemaní, T664 9312, www.culturadelmar.com. Run by team of young, well-organized Colombians, diving and tours to Islas del Rosario, English spoken.
Diving Planet, Edif Alonso de Ojeda, 2-50, El Laguito, Bocagrande, T/F655 0154, also dive shop in Isla Grande (*Hotel Cocoliso*), www.divingplanet org. PADI open certificate course, 4 day, US$330, 2 dives including all equipment US$82, snorkelling trips, English spoken.
La Tortuga Dive Shop, Edif Marina del Rey, Av del Retorno 2-23, El Laguito, Bocagrande, T/F665 6994, www.tortugadive.com. 2 dives US$70. Fast boat, which allows trips to Isla Barú as well as Los Rosarios, same price at *Hotel Caribe Dive shop*, T665 3517, www.caribediveshop.com.
Windsurfing Rental in Bocagrande, US$8 per hr.
Tour operators There are many agencies along Av San Martín in Bocagrande.

☉ Transport

Cartagena *p812, map 814*
Air
Flights to major Colombian cities and twice a week to Miami with Avianca T01-8000-123434.To **San Andrés**, AeroRepública and Avianca. Flights can be overbooked Dec-Mar; even reconfirming and turning up 2 hrs early doesn't guarantee a seat; best not to book a seat on the last plane of the day. Flights to Panama.

Bus
Local Within the city large buses (with no glass in windows) cost US$0.30 (a/c buses US$0.50,

green and white Metrocar to all points recommended). From bus terminal to centre, 35 mins or more depending on traffic with Metrocar, US$0.50.
Long distance To **Santa Marta**, US$10-11 (with **Brasilia**, C 32, No 20D-55, ticket office in Bocagrande, Edif Antillas, opposite *Hotel Caribe*), 4-5 hrs. Few buses go direct to Santa Marta from Cartagena, most stop in Barranquilla. To **Barranquilla** US$6 with **Transportes Cartagena**, 2½-3 hrs. Pullman bus from Cartagena to **Medellín** 665 km, US$40 (**Brasilia**, or **Rápido Ochoa**, slightly cheaper, recommended). Several buses a day, but book early (2 days in advance at holiday times), takes 13-16 hrs. To/from **Bogotá** via Barranquilla and Bucaramanga with **Expreso Brasilia Pullman** (5 a day) or **Copetran**, US$45-50 (shop around), minimum 19 hrs (typically 21, but can take 28 hrs), depending on number of checkpoints. To **Magangué** on the Magdalena US$12, 4 hrs with **Brasilia**; to **Mompós**, **Unitransco**, 0730 daily, 12 hrs including ferry crossing from Magangué, US$15. To **Valledupar** with **Expreso Brasilia**, Pullman US$13 (with a 30-min stop in Barranquilla), for Sierra Nevada and Pueblo Bello. To **Riohacha**, US$12. Bus to **Maicao** on Venezuelan border US$18 (with **Expreso Auto Pullman**, **Expreso Brasilia** at 2000, or **Unitrasco**), 10-12 hrs; the road is in good condition.

Ferry
There are boats leaving most days for points south along the coast, for example to **Turbo** cargo boats take 24 hrs, about US$25 pp. Few travellers take this route. You can also go on up the Río Sinú to Montería, and up the Atrato as far as **Quibdó** (not recommended for safety reasons). For the trip to Quibdó see page 850. Enquire at **Club Náutico** for yachts to San Blas/ Panama, about US$250 one way. Note that during Jan and Feb strong winds can prevent sailing and it can be a very rough journey. There is good information at **Casa Viena** hotel. Get full independent advice before making direct arrangements with boat owners or captains. **Club Náutico**, Av Miramar, Isla Manga across the Puente Román, T660 4863, good for opportunities to crew or finding a lift to other parts of the Caribbean.

Hovercraft
New services to **Isla Barú**, leaves 0830, returns 1400 except Tue, US$60 pp includes lunch. Also expensive service to **Mompós**, leaves 0800. Book at any **Aviatur** office, eg at Hotel Santa Clara, airport, or at Av San Martín, No 7-109, Bocagrande, T665 1062.

Taxi
Within the old city and Bocagrande, minimum fare US$2, a bit more at night; from Bocagrande

to the centre US$2.20; for airport, see Ins and outs above. Set price before committing yourself and be prepared to bargain fares for long rides, few use meters. A horse-drawn carriage can be hired for US$17, opposite *Hotel El Dorado*, Av San Martín, in Bocagrande, to ride into town at night (short ride). Also, a trip around the walled city, up to 4 people, US$18, from Torre del Reloj.

Beaches: Playa Blanca *p817*

There are three ways of getting to Playa Blanca. The most common is to take a bus from the centre to **Pasacaballo**, US$0.60. From there take a 5-min ferry over the Río Magdalena, US$0.30. Then take a motortaxi or colectivo to **Santa Ana** (45 mins), US$3, and then another colectivo along a rough dirt road to Playa Blanca (45 mins). Do not give money or gifts to children dancing on the roadway. Alternatively, boats to Playa Blanca leave **Bazurto** market, near La Popa, from 0700-0930 daily, US$9 one way. Again, do not give money or gifts to dancing children. Be sure to pay the captain and not his 'helpers' and arrange a return pick-up time. There are also touristy, expensive boats from the tourist dock (**Muelle Turístico**) at 0830 which stop at Playa Blanca as part of a tour (but you'll have to pay for the whole tour).

Islas del Rosario *p817*

Travel agencies and hotels offer launch excursions from the Muelle Turístico, leaving 0700-0900 and returning 1600-1700, costing from US$10 to US$25, lunch included; smaller boats take 50 mins less. Overnight trips can be arranged through agencies but they are overpriced. Do not buy tours from touts. Note that there is an additional 'port tax' of US$2 payable at the entrance to the *Muelle* or on the boat, and MA park entrance fee, US$2. Check around for prices and book in advance. Recommended are **Excursiones Roberto Lemaitre**, C 6, Edif Granada, loc 22, opposite El Almirante Hotel, Bocagrande, T665 5622 (owner of *Club Isla del Pirata*). **Yates Alcatraz** are more economical; enquire at the quay. The *Santa Clara Hotel* runs day trips to Isla Majagua, US$40 including lunch. For 5 or more, try hiring your own boat for the day and bargain for around US$16 pp.

North of Cartagena: Volcán del Totumo *p817*

Bus from **Cartagena** bus terminal to Galerazamba in the morning, US$1.50, 2 hrs, ask to be dropped off at Lomito Arena and walk 2 km along the main road to a right turn signposted 'Volcán del Totumo', 1½ km along a poor road. Hitching possible. Many tour agencies, eg **Aviatur**, in the *Hotel Santa Clara*, organize trips to the volcano, including lunch and pickups from hotels; a good day trip.

Directory

Cartagena *p812, map 814*

Banks Banco Unión Colombiana, Av Venezuela (C 35), No 10-26, La Matuna, changes American Express and Thomas Cook TCs. **Bancolombia**, good rates for TCs. **Bancafé**, gives money on Visa cards, both on Av Venezuela. **Banco Sudameris**, opposite conference centre, for Visa cash advances. **Citibank**, Centro Plazoleta, Av Venezuela, for MasterCard ATM. Many other ATMs in La Matuna along Av Venezuela and Bocagrande including supermarkets, eg *Carulla* and in the *Hilton*. Also **A Toda Hora**, for Visa and MasterCard on Av Venezuela. **American Express** at branches of **Gema Tours**, eg Cabrera Cra 1, Av Santander, No 41-202, T660 2499; early morning only. There are **cambios** in the arcade at Torre del Reloj and adjoining streets which change Amex TCs. **Caja de Cambio América**, Av Venezuela, No 8-48, La Matuna. Daily 1000-1800, changes sterling, also at Av San Martín, No 2-52, Bocagrande. **Cambios Santo Domingo**, C de la Iglesia, Edif Ayos, Cra 4, No 35-14, T664 4803, changes Bank of America TCs and sterling. **Never change money on the street, you will be ripped off.** TCs can be changed Sat morning (arrive early) at **Joyería Mora**, Román 5-39, and at El Portal nearby, in the old city. Many casas de cambios are found along Av San Martín in Bocagrande, most closed on Sundays. **Cambios del Caribe**, Av San Martín, Hotel Playa Local No.3, T655 1243, changes sterling and cashes TCs. **Embassies and consulates** Panamanian Consulate, Centro Plaza San Pedro Claver, No 30-14, T664 1433. **Venezuela**, Cra 3, No 8-120, p 14, T665 0382/665 0353. Possible to get a visa the same day. **Language classes** Amaury Martelo, amartesi@yahoo.com. Good, professional teacher, polite, all levels catered for. **Internet** Café Punto com, El Laguito, Edif Belmar, loc 102, T665 5151. Good, also organizes apartment rentals. **Café Internet**, C Santo Domingo, No 35-40, broadband, US$0.90 per hr. Many others around town. **Post offices** in Avianca office near cathedral, open Mon-Fri 0800-1830, Sat 0800-1500.

Security Carry your passport, or a photocopy, at all times. Failure to present it on police request can result in imprisonment and fines. Generally, central areas are safe and friendly (although Getsemaní is less secure, especially at night), but should you require the police, there is a station in Matuna (Central Comercial La Plazoleta), another in Barrio Manga. Beware of drug pushers on the beaches, pickpockets in crowded areas and bag/camera snatchers on quiet Sun mornings. At the bus station, do not be pressurized into a hotel recommendation different from your own choice.

On the street, do not be tempted by offers of jobs or passages aboard ship: jobs should have full documentation from the Seamen's Union office. Passages should only be bought at a recognized shipping agency. **Telephones** Telecom, Av Urdaneta Arbeláez near corner of C 34; long distance phones behind this building; long distance also in Bocagrande. **Useful addresses** DAS: C 20B, No 29-18, T666 0438,

open 0730-1100, 1400-1600. **MA** (national parks office), C 4, No 3-204, Bocagrande, T665 5655, open 0800-1200, 1400-1800. **Volunteering:** If you are interested in working with local foundations/NGOs, contact cartagenitos@yahoo groups.com, www.cartagenitos.blogspot.com, who will find places for volunteers.

To Panama

Apart from the towns inland on the road to Medellín and the beaches around Tolú and Coveñas, this section is concerned with the troubled area of the Colombia/Panama border at Darién. Before going by road south of Cartagena, check the latest information on security.

South from Cartagena

The highway south towards Medellín goes through **Turbaco**, 24 km (**Botanical Garden** ① *1½ km before village on the left, Tue-Sun 0900-1600*), **Malagana**, 60 km, and **San Jacinto**, 90 km, known for its cumbia music using gaitas and local craft work (hand woven hammocks).

Magangué and Mompós

A road runs east from the highway to **Magangué** (*Phone code 952; Population: 65,000; Altitude: 30 m*), on the western loop of the Río Magdalena. It is the port for the savannas of Bolívar. From here boats go to the small town of **Mompós**, also spelt Mompox (*Phone code 952; Colour map 1, grid A3; Population: 33,000*), a UNESCO World Heritage site on the eastern arm of the river. Due to its relative isolation, little has changed in this sweltering, humid town since Alfonso de Heredia (brother of the founder of Cartagena) founded it in 1540. Simón Bolívar stayed here frequently and wrote, "If I owe my life to Caracas, I owe my glory to Mompós." Today, Mompós is one of Colombia's most beautiful colonial towns. Opposite the river are the mansions of Spanish merchants for whom this was an important stopping-off point on the Cartagena trade route. Rows of well-preserved, white one-storey buildings have served as a backdrop in many Colombian films. Its six churches, cemetery and plazas are well signed. Mompós is packed during Easter week when visitors flock to see its ornate traditional processions. It is also known for its handworked gold and silver jewellery and goldsmiths are still to be seen working. The town is safe and peaceful and, with improved security in the surrounding area and roads, tourism has increased significantly. But it is still recommended to check safety before setting off. Guided tours of the city on foot or motortaxi cost US$6 per hour. Boat trips along the Río Magdalena have received good reports. Ferocious mosquitoes and the odd bat are a nuisance after dusk; take insect repellent and wear long sleeves.

Sincelejo to Turbo

The capital of Sucre Department, **Sincelejo**, is a hot, dusty town and cattle centre. The dangerous *Fiestas de Las Corralejas*, 15-20 January, involves bulls and men chasing each other around a ring. At Easter is the '*Fiesta del Burro*' where people dress up donkeys and prizes go to the best and the funniest (a three-day party). There are various hotels (**C-F**) and restaurants.

On the coast, 35 km northwest of Sincelejo is **Tolú**, a fast developing holiday town popular for its mud volcanoes, offshore islands and diving. From Cartagena, the best approach is south from Malagana through San Onofre. This is also an easier and safer way for cyclists. For safety reasons, it is recommended not to travel this route at night. There are two mud volcanoes to visit. The nearer is in San Antero, 30 minutes' drive from Tolú, and farther is in San Bernardo del Viento, 1¼ hours. Both make good day trips. From Tolú, another good trip is by boat three hours to Múcura island in the **Islas de San Bernardo**, about US$15 (details on the mud volcanoes and Múcura from **Hostel Babilla** in Tolú, or in Cartagena). If camping, take your own supplies. Trips to the mangrove lagoons also recommended. A good agency is **Club Náutico Los Delfines** ① *Av 1A, No 11-08, T288 5202*, daily tours to San Bernardo Islands 0800, back 1600, including aquarium on Isla Palma, US$30 lunch and transport, US$15 just transport. There are three diving agencies in Tolú along Avenida de La Playa. There are better beaches at **Coveñas**, 20 km further southwest (several *cabañas* on the beach and hotels). This is the terminal of the oil pipeline from the oilfields in the Venezuelan border area. Buses and *colectivos* from Tolú.

The main road south from Sincelejo passes **Caucasia** (194 km from Sincelejo, *Altitude: 50 m*), a convenient stopping place between Cartagena and Medellín.

Montería the capital of Córdoba Department, on the east bank of the Río Sinú, can be reached from Cartagena by air, by boat, or from the main highway to Medellín. It is the centre of a cattle and agricultural area. It has one fine church, picturesque street life and friendly people.

On the Gulf of Urabá is the port of **Turbo** (*Phone code 94; Colour map 1, grid A2; Population: 127,000*), an important centre of banana cultivation. It is a rough border community so it's best to move on quickly. **Before going to Turbo, or contemplating crossing Darién by land, please see below**.

North of Turbo, on the road to Necoli, is a turning off for **Los Arboletes**. Here is a huge mud volcano surrounded by mangrove swamps, well worth visiting.

Border with Panama

There are various routes involving sea and land crossings around or through the **Darién Gap**, which still lacks a road connection linking the Panamanian Isthmus and South America. While maps of the region are available, there is no substitute for seeking informed local advice. In all cases, it is essential to be able to speak Spanish.

Latest information from Colombia is that armed groups, hostile to travellers including tourists, are active in the northwest corner of Colombia which includes the area on the Colombian and Panamanian sides of the border. If information has not improved before you set out to cross Darién by land either way, you are advised not to go. This warning includes visits to Los Katíos National Park (officially closed), the road south of Turbo to Dabeiba and the Río Atrato area up to Quibdó. The Río Atrato itself is widely used by both paramilitaries and guerrillas.

Colombian immigration DAS Office: see under Turbo directory below. If going from Colombia to Panama via Turbo you should get an exit stamp from the DAS office. You will also need a yellow fever certificate and an onward international ticket. There is also a DAS office in Capurganá (near *puesto de policia*, police booth), and a Panamanian consulate, but best not to leave it that late. If leaving Colombia, check the facts at any DAS office.

Entering Colombia Arriving from Panama, go to the DAS in Turbo for your entry stamp. Stamps from other DAS offices not accepted. A police stamp is no substitute, though can help.

Entering Panama Panamanian immigration at Puerto Obaldía will check all baggage for drugs and may ask for evidence of adequate funds for your stay: US$400, travellers' cheques or credit card. A ticket out of Panama is required, although a ticket from another Central American country may do. **Note** Colombian pesos are impossible to change at fair rates in Panama.

Crossing Darién: Caribbean side

On the Caribbean side, the starting point is Turbo from where you must cross the Gulf of Urabá to Acandí, Capurganá and Zapzurro (all in Colombia) and Puerto Obaldía (Panama). **Acandí** (*Phone code: 9816; Population: about 7,000*) has several *residencias*. Most have their own electricity generators. A little further north is **Capurganá**, with spectacular, unspoilt white sand beaches and bays, including Cabo Tiburón (which featured in a recent Colombian reality show). The weather is generally drier and less humid than the Pacific coast of Chocó. The area's main attraction is the large marine turtles that come from Mexico to lay their eggs on the beaches from April to mid-June. Take advice on whether it is safe to hike along this coast: otherwise, take boats between coastal towns.

Overland from Turbo The aim is to cross the central Gap to Paya, from where there is a recognised route to Yaviza: Paya-Púcuro, six hours on foot; Púcuro-Boca de Cupe, by dugout; Boca de Cupe-Pinogana, also by dugout, plus a walk, two hours in all; Pinogana-Yaviza, walk and ferries/dugouts. From Yaviza (one hotel, **F Tres Américas**, basic) buses can be caught to Panama City, road subject to wash-outs. Alternatively you may be able to get a boat from Paya to Boca del Cupe and on to El Real, which has an airstrip for flights to Panama.

Although there are two main routes to Paya, we hesitate to suggest either. The first is to take a boat from Turbo across the Gulf of Urabá into the Río Tarena to **Unguía**, which has a couple of *residenciales* and basic restaurants. From here it is three to four hours to the border, then three hours to the Río Paya. You then hike down the Río Paya through dense jungle to Paya itself (about 12 hours). Do not attempt the Unguía-Paya route without a guide. The other main route to Paya, by motorboat from Turbo across the Bahía de Colombia, through the Great Atrato Swamp and up the Río Atrato should not be attempted in the current political climate. It is too dangerous. It can be very difficult to get an entry stamp anywhere before Panama City on this route; try at every opportunity as hikers have been detained in the capital for not having an entry stamp. It may help to prove you have adequate funds for your stay.

Los Katíos National Park

① *Go first to the MA office in Turbo (see Turbo directory below) for information: at present (early 2007) the park is officially closed though hotels do arrange trips to the national park.* The park, extending in Colombia to the Panamanian border, contains several waterfalls: **Tilupo**, 125 m high; the water cascades down a series of rock staircases, surrounded by orchids and other fantastic plants, **Salto de La Tigra** and **Salto de La Tendal**. A full day's hike goes to Alto de Limón for a fine view of primary forest. Also in the park are the Alto de la Guillermina, a mountain behind which is a strange forest of palms called 'mil pesos', and the Ciénagas de Tumaradó, with red monkeys, waterfowl and alligators.

Crossing Darién: Pacific side

On the Pacific side, crossing into Panama involves travel by both boat and on foot, the quantity of each depending on the route chosen. Any routes through this part of Chocó are not advised because of violence, intense guerrilla and paramilitary activity and drug-running.

● Sleeping

Magangué *p823*
Several hotels and *residencias* (**C–F**). Few places to eat but very basic stalls along the riverfront serve decent cheap fish meals for breakfast and lunch.
D Avenida, Cra 3 y C 17, T687 7623. A/c, cheaper with fan, next to bus terminal.
E Julia, Cra 2A, No 12-37, T687 6160. Fan, more expensive with a/c.

Mompós *p823*
Malaria is endemic in the surrounding countryside. If staying overnight, mosquito nets and/or coils are a must. Essential to book in advance for Easter.
D Casa Hotel La Casona, Cra 2, No 18-58, T685 5307. Colonial style, a/c, much cheaper with fan.
D Hostal Doña Manuela, C Real del Medío (Cra 2), No 17-41, T685 5142, F685 6175. A converted colonial merchant's house, a/c, quiet and peaceful, restaurant is the best in town, pool also open to the public for the day US$2. Good service and knowledgeable managers. Recommended.
D-E San Andrés, Cra 2, No 18-23, T685 5886. Good, friendly owner, a/c or fan, TV, restaurant.

Sincelejo to Turbo *p823*
Tolú
C Alcira, Av La Playa 21-40, T288 5016, F288 5036. Includes breakfast, cheaper off season, a/c, TV, restaurant.
D Mar Adentro, Av La Playa 11-36, T288 5481. With bath, a/c, helpful, much cheaper with fan,

agency for trips to San Bernardo islands.
D-E Villa Babilla, C 20, No 3-40, Barrio el Cangrejo, T288 6124. www.villababillahostel.com. Run by Colombian/German team. 3 blocks from beach, well-organized, dorms, new rooms with bath, good restaurant, laundry service, good information on diving and island tours. Recommended travellers' hostel.
F El Turista, Av La Playa, No 11-68, T288 5145. With bath, TV, fan, basic, often full.

Caucasia
E Londres, C 19, No 2-27, T839 2879. A/c, laundry service, parking, restaurant, less with fan.

Montería
Many cheap dives around town.
AL Sinú, Cra 3, No 31-38, T782 3355, F782 3980. The best, a/c, swimming pool, spa, TV, internet, restaurant. Discounts possible.
D Alcázar, Cra 2, No 32-17, T782 4900. Comfortable, a/c, cheaper with fan.

Turbo *p824*
C Castilla de Oro, T827 2185. Best, a/c, safe, good restaurant, modern, reliable water and electricity.
D Playa Mar, Av de la Playa, T827 2205. Good, but somewhat run down, a/c, cheaper with fan, TV.
D Hotel 2000, C 101, No 11-203, T827 2333. Near bus terminal, TV, bath, less with fan.

Crossing Darién: Caribbean side p824

D **Hostal Marlin**, Capurganá, T824 3611. One of the cheapest options, a small comfortable wooden lodge, with hammocks overlooking the beach. US$95 pp for a 3-night, all-inclusive package. Arranges guides, walks and snorkelling trips. There are also several luxury resort hotels.

❼ Eating

Sincelejo to Turbo: Tolú p823
Aroma de Café, Av 1, No 11-46. Good value *comida*. Other places to eat nearby, eg **Cafetería** on corner of Plaza, good cakes.

❽ Transport

Magangué and Mompós p823
Air Flights to Montería from Mompós.
Bus and ferry Most *chalupas* (launches) and buses run in the morning. There is little public transport after 1400. From Magangué to Mompós: take a *chalupa* either direct to Mompós, 2 hrs, US$3.30, or to La Bodega, 30-45 mins, US$3, and then by taxi, frequent, 1½ hrs, US$3. The quickest and most comfortable route from Mompós to the coast is: taxi from Mompós to La Bodega, *chalupa* from La Bodega to Magangué, then taxi to **Barranquilla**, US$14, leave when full, 3-4 hrs direct to your destination in Barranquilla. **Brasilia** buses run from Magangué to Barranquilla. To **Cartagena** from Mompós with **Unitransco** at 0700, US$15, rough road in parts; also to Barranquilla.

To **Valledupar** and **Santa Marta**, either go from El Banco (further upriver), or cross the river at Talaigua (between Mompós and Magangué, *carritos* leave Mompós early morning) to **Santa Ana**. Buses leave Santa Ana 0700 for **Santa Marta** and **Valledupar**, first 2½ hrs unpaved, then paved; US$10 to Valledupar.

Sincelejo to Turbo p823
Tolú
Colectivo To **Cartagena**, 3hrs, US$9. Via Sincelejo, or direct from Cartagena. Several morning **buses**, 3-4 hrs, US$6. Also to **Medellín** with **Rápido Ochoa** and **Brasilia** 1100 and 1800, 10 hrs, US$32.

Caucasia
Bus From Caucasia to **Medellín** US$12, 6½-7 hrs, taxi US$18 (slightly quicker); to **Cartagena** US$20, 6-7 hrs.

Montería
Air Daily flights to **Bogotá**, **Barranquilla**, **Cartagena**, **Cúcuta** and **Medellín**.

Buses from **Cartagena**, US$13, 5 hrs, with Brasilia, has own terminal in Montería, or colectivo, US$11, 5 hrs.

Turbo p824
Air Small airport, few flights. More common to fly into Apartadó airport (30-min taxi ride, US$14, to Turbo, or microbus, US$1) where there are more flight options, including 3 daily flights to/from **Medellín**. Local services to Caribbean and Pacific resorts with **Satena**.
Buses From **Medellín**, buses every 1½ hrs to Turbo, US$20, 10-12 hrs. Fewer from **Cartagena** (if stuck get a bus from Cartagena to Montería, 5 hrs, US$13 and then to Turbo). Checkpoints and bad road in parts. Check safety carefully before travelling by road from Turbo to Santa Fé de Antioquia.
Ferries Available to Cartagena and up the Río Atrato to Quibdó, but services are unreliable, dangerous and therefore not advised.

To Panama p824
Air The simplest way is to fly from **Barranquilla**, **Bogotá**, **Cali**, **Cartagena**, **Medellín** or **San Andrés**.
Ferry Ask on the spot in Cartagena and in Colón if you wish to transport a vehicle between the two countries. Foot passengers may be able to travel on reputable cargo boats, but you must arrange with the captain the price and destination before departure. Small, irregular boats may well be contraband or arms runners and should not be used. See also under Cartagena, Ferry.

Crossing Darién: Caribbean side p824
Ferry From the small wharf, known as 'El Waffle', in Turbo take a daily launch direct to **Capurganá**. It leaves when it's full, any time between 0800-1000, US$18, 2-3 hrs. It is an uncomfortable and bumpy ride. There is a DAS office at the wharf but it keeps very irregular hours, apparently open in the morning only. From Puerto Obaldía (see above on immigration), boats go to Porvenir (San Blas Islands) or Colón, planes to Panama City (Mon-Sat).

❿ Directory

Turbo p824
Banks Banco Ganadero and others (ATMs available) but no banks are open for TC exchange Mon-Tue; try exchanging money in stores.
Note There is no ATM in Capurganá, if taking that route. **Useful addresses/services** DAS: Postadero Naval, north of town just before airport, take transport along Cra 13, open 0800-1630. **MA:** for information on Parque Nacional Los Katíos, office 1 km along the road to Medellín.

Barranquilla → *Phone code: 95. Colour map 1, grid A3. Population: 1,064,000.*

Barranquilla lies on the western bank of the Río Magdalena, about 18 km from its mouth, which, through deepening and the clearing of silted sandbars, makes it a seaport as well as a river port. During recent years, the city's commercial and industrial importance and its port have declined. Few colonial buildings remain. In the northwest of the city are pleasant leafy residential areas and parks. **Tourist office:** Fondo Mixto de Promoción del Atlántico ① *Vía 40, No 36-135, Edificio La Aduana, T351 0346.* Tourist information is also available at main hotels.

The main reason people visit Barranquilla is for its famous annual **Carnival**, held 40 days before Easter week, end-February/beginning of March. It's one of the oldest in Latin America and less commercial and touristy than the Rio Carnival. In 2003 UNESCO declared it a "masterpiece of the oral and intangible heritage of humanity". Pre-carnival parades and dances last through January until an edict that everyone **must** party is read out. Carnival itself lasts from Saturday, with the Batalla de las Flores, through the Gran Parada on Sunday, to the funeral of Joselito Carnaval on Tuesday. The same families going back generations participate, keeping the traditions of the costumes and dances intact. Prepare for three days of intense revelry and dancing with very friendly and enthusiastic crowds, spectacular float processions, parades and beauty queens. The main action takes place along, Calle 17, Carrera 44 and Vía 40. Tickets for the spectator stands are sold in major restaurants and bars, eg **Froggs Leggs** (see Bars and clubs). **La Casa de Carnaval** ① *Cra 54, No 49B-39, T379 6621, www.carnavaldebarranquilla.org,* is the official office and the best place to get information.

The church of **San Nicolás**, formerly the Cathedral, stands on Plaza San Nicolás, the central square, and before it is a small statue of Columbus. The new **Catedral Metropolitana** ① *Cra 45, No 53-120, opposite Plaza de la Paz,* has an impressive statue of Christ inside by the Colombian sculptor, Arenas Betancur. The commercial and shopping districts are round Paseo Bolívar, the main boulevard, a few blocks north of the old Cathedral, and in Avenida Murillo. The **Museo Romántico** ① *Cra 54, No 59-199,* covers the city's history with an interesting section on Carnival.

Barranquilla also attracts visitors because the most important national and international football matches are held here in Colombia's largest stadium, **Estadio Metropolitano** ① *Av Murillo, outside the city.* The atmosphere is considered the best in the country. Regular buses run from Paseo Bolívar and the church at Calle 33 y Carrera 41 to the attractive bathing resort of **Puerto Colombia**, 20 minutes. The **Pradomar Hotel** ① *Calle 2, No 22-61, T309 6011* (**B** good beach bar and restaurant), offers surfing lessons. South along the Magdalena, 5 km from the city, is **Soledad** (*Population: 16,000*); around the cathedral are narrow, colonial streets.

● Sleeping

Barranquilla *p827*
Hotel prices rise significantly during Carnival, essential to book well in advance.
L El Prado, Cra 54, No 70-10, T369 7777. Original 1920s building, a national monument, far from the centre. Nice pool, tennis, good restaurant.
A Country Norte, Cra 52, No 75-30, T368 0495. New, stylish hotel, with pool and business centre, spacious comfortable rooms, good service. Substantial weekend discounts.
A Las Brisas, C 61, No 46-41, T340 2455. TV, breakfast included, noisy but recommended.
D San Francisco, C43, No 43-128, T379 2927, F351 5532. Downtown, large rooms with fan,

cable TV, fridge, laundry service, parking, good restaurant, pleasant.
E Colonial Inn, C 42, No 43-131, T379 0241. With bath, TV, good cheap restaurant, fan.
E Olímpico, Cra 42, No 33-20, T351 8310. With fan, more with a/c, TV, restaurant. Recommended.
F El Diamante, C 41, No 38-65, T379 0157. With fan, more with a/c, TV room, laundry, parking.

● Eating

Barranquilla *p827*
Many places, for all tastes and budgets, on C 70 from **Hotel El Prado** towards Cra 42. At C 70 y

---

● *For an explanation of the sleeping and eating price codes used in this guide, see page 58. Other*
● *relevant information is found in Essentials pages 778-779.*

44B are several *estaderos*, bars with snacks and verandas. Many upmarket restaurants along Carrera 53. There are numerous good Arab restaurants, especially Lebanese, in Barranquilla due to waves of Arab immigration in the 20th century.

♥♥-♥♥ **Arabe Gourmet**, Cra 49C, No 76-181. More formal and expensive than others.

♥♥-♥♥ **La Cueva** C 59 y Cra 43. Formerly a high-class brothel and a favourite haunt of Gabriel García Márquez and his literati friends during the 1950s. Now its bohemian charm has gone, but it's still worth a visit for the interesting photos. Good typical food, live Cuban music at the weekends.

♥♥ **Arabe Internacional**, C 93, No 47-73, T378 2803. Good Arab cuisine in informal setting.

♥♥ **Crepes and Waffles**, Cra 51, No 76-47. Good fresh crêpes and salads as usual.

❶ Bars and clubs

Barranquilla *p827*
Froggs Leggs, C 93, No 43-122. Popular bar, good atmosphere.
Henry's Bar, C 80, No 53-18, CC Washington. Popular US-style bar, pizzería downstairs. Open daily from 1600.

❖ Shopping

Barranquilla *p827*
Bookshop Librería Nacional, in CC Buenavista (see below). Small selection of English books.
Market San Andrecito, or Tourist Market, Vía 40, is where smuggled goods are sold at very competitive prices; a good place to buy film. Picturesque and reasonably safe. Any taxi driver will take you there.
Shopping centres Centro Comercial Buenavista, Cra 53, C 98, has a good selection of shops, cinemas and fast food outlets.

❸ Transport

Barranquilla *p827*
Air Ernesto Cortissoz airport is 10 km from the city. Daily flights to **Bogotá**, **Cartagena** and **Medellín**, also to **Bucaramanga**, **Montería** and **Valledupar**. International flights to **Aruba**, **Curaçao**, **Miami** and **Panama City**. City bus from airport to town, US$0.35 (US$0.40 on Sun). Taxi to

town, US$7 (taxis do not have meters, fix fare in advance). To town, take only buses marked 'centro' from 200 m to right when leaving airport; the bus to the airport (marked Malambo) leaves from Cra 44 up C 32 to Cra 38, then up C 30 to Airport. Taxi to Cartagena, US$15 pp, leave when full. **Avianca**, C 72, No 57-79, T353 4691.

Bus The main bus terminal is south of the city near the Circunvalación. Some bus companies have offices around C 34 and Cra 45. Take a bus marked 'Terminal' along C 45. To **Santa Marta**, US$3.25, Pullman (less in non-a/c, **Coolibertador**), about 2 hrs, also direct to Santa Marta's Rodadero beach. To **Valledupar**, 5-6 hrs, US$10. To **Montería** direct, US$11, 7-8 hrs. To **Medellín** by Pullman, 16 hrs, US$40. To **Bucaramanga**, US$27 with **Copetran**, a/c, first class, departures at 1130 most days, 9 hrs. To **Bogotá**, 24 hrs, frequent, US$45 direct with Copetran. To **Caucasia**, US$17, 8-11 hrs. To **Maicao** US$14.50, 6 hrs (with **Brasilia**, every 30 mins from 0100-1500). To **Cartagena**, 3 grades of bus, 2½-3 hrs (US$4.50 with **Transportes Cartagena**, US$6 with **Expreso Brasilia**, by *Brasilia Van Tours* mini-bus, from their downtown offices as well as the bus terminals), 2 hrs by colectivo US$7.

Taxi Taxis within the town cost US$1.60 (eg downtown to northern suburbs).

❶ Directory

Barranquilla *p827*
Banks Bancolombia, Banco de Bogotá, etc, and many ATMs. *Casa de cambio* El Cairo, C 76, No 48-30, T360 6433, and at C 34, No 43-177, Paseo Bolívar, T379 9441. TCs, euros, dollars but not sterling, Mon-Fri and Sat 0900-1200.
Consulates Germany, C73, Vía 40-270, T353 2078. Netherlands, Cra 77B, No 57-141, of 806, T368 8387. USA, C 77B, No 57-141, of 511, T353 2001 (visas obtainable only in Bogotá). Venezuela, Edif Bancafé, Cra 52, No 69-96, p 3, T368 2228/2207, 0800-1500, visa issued same day, but you must be there by 0915 with photo and US$30 cash; onward ticket may be requested. **Post offices** Plaza Bolívar.
Useful addresses DAS: C 54, No 41-133, T371 7500. Tourist police:, Cra 43, No 47-53, T351 0415/340 9903.

Santa Marta, Tayrona and Ciudad Perdida

Santa Marta is a port with strong historical associations and popular beaches. Nearby are the Tayrona national park with pre-Columbian remains and the unspoilt Sierra Nevada de Santa Marta coastal range.

Santa Marta → *Phone code: 95. Colour map 1, grid A3. Population: 309,000.*

Santa Marta is Colombia's third largest Caribbean port and capital of Magdalena Department. It lies on a deep bay with high shelving cliffs to the north and south, at the mouth of the Río Manzanares. The snow-clad peaks of the Sierra Nevada, less than 50 km east, are occasionally visible. The main promenade (Carrera 1) along the sea front is lined with hotels, restaurants and bars and a beach reaching the port. Much more attractive beaches are to be found around Taganga and Parque Nacional Tayrona. Santa Marta is the base for treks to La Ciudad Perdida. For tourist information, go to **Turcol** ① *Cra 1C, No 20-15, T/F421 2256/433 3737*. It arranges trips to Ciudad Perdida, Parque Tayrona and Pueblito and provides guide services (details in text); recommended. Beware of jungle tours, or boat trips to the islands sold by street touts.

Santa Marta was the first town founded by the *conquistadores* in Colombia, in 1525 by Rodrigo de Bastidas. Most of the famous sea-dogs – the brothers Côte, Drake and Hawkins – sacked the city despite the forts on the mainland. It was here that Simón Bolívar, his dream of Gran Colombia shattered, came to die. Almost penniless, he stayed at San Pedro Alejandrino *hacienda*, see below. He died, aged 47, on 17 December 1830, apparently from tuberculosis, and was buried in the Cathedral, but his body was taken to the Pantheon at Caracas 12 years later.

In the city centre, well-preserved colonial buildings and early churches still remain and more are being restored. On **Plaza de la Catedral** is the impressive white cathedral, claimed to be Colombia's oldest church and one of the oldest in Latin America. **Casa de la Aduana/Museo del Oro Tairona** ① *Calle 14, No 2-07 on main plaza, Mon-Fri 0830-1200, 1400-1800, Sat 0900-1300, closed Sun and holidays (times change during the tourist season), free*, has an excellent archaeological collection, Tayrona culture exhibits and precolombian gold artefacts; visit recommended before going to Ciudad Perdida. **Museo Etnográfico de la Universidad del Magdalena** ① *Cra 1, C 22, 0800-1900, US$1*, is a new museum, tracing the history of Santa Marta, its port and the Tayrona culture, well-displayed.

Quinta de San Pedro Alejandrino ① *daily 0930-1630, US$3; take a bus or colectivo from the waterfront, Cra 1 C, in Santa Marta to Mamatoca and ask for the Quinta, US$0.25*, a 17th-century villa surrounded by gardens 5 km southeast of the city. Here is the simple room in which Simón Bolívar died, with a few of his belongings. Other paintings and memorabilia of the period are on display. This is an elegant memorial to Colombia's most revered man.

Sandy beaches and headlands stretch all along this coast, surrounded by hills, green meadows and shady trees. The largest sandy bay is that of Santa Marta, with Punta Betín, a rocky promontory protecting the harbour to the north and a headland to the south. The rugged Isla El Morro lies 3 km off Santa Marta, topped by a lighthouse. **Playa El Rodadero** is a crowded, tacky beach resort, 4 km south of the city (local bus service, taxi, US$3). Many of the buses coming from Barranquilla and Cartagena stop at Rodadero on the way to Santa Marta.

Santa Marta

Sleeping		Eating	Bars & clubs
Bahía Blanca **1**	Nueva Granada **10**	Café del Parque **1**	La Puerta **7**
Casa Vieja **4**	Panamerican **8**	El Jardín Paisa **6**	Valsao **5**
Costa Azul **5**	Park **9**	Merkabar/Welcome **2**	
Hospedaría Casa	Residencias El	Muelle 8 **3**	
Familiar **6**	Titanic **11**	San Valentín **4**	
Miramar **7**	Tayromar **12**		
	Turismar **2**		

0 metres 200
0 yards 200

Launches leave Rodadero beach every hour for the Aquarium, US$3 entry, last boat back 1600. From the Aquarium, it's a 10-minute walk to Playa Blanca where swimming is less crowded than elsewhere. Food is available at beach.

Around Santa Marta

The paved coast road to Santa Marta from Barranquilla passes salt pans and skirts the **Ciénaga de Santa Marta**, where all types of water birds, plants and animals may be seen. Cutting off the egress to the sea to build the coast road caused an ecological disaster, but a National Environment Programme is working to reopen the canals and restore the area. There are several villages built on stilts in the lake. On the east shore of the lagoon is **Ciénaga** (*Population: 75,000*), famous for *cumbia* music.

Aracataca, 60 km south of Ciénaga and 7 km before Fundación, is the birthplace of **Gabriel García Márquez**, fictionalized as Macondo in some of his stories (notably *100 Years of Solitude*). His home, now a modest museum, may be seen in the backyard of La Familia Iriarte Ahumada; it is 1½ blocks from the plaza, ask for directions (museum being renovated early 2007). There are *residencias* (under US$3) and a restaurant, but it is better to stay in **Fundación**. In 2007 a new train was inaugurated, El Tren Amarillo de Macondo, between Santa Marta and Aracataca. García Márquez himself, with a large entourage, joined the first run on 30 May 2007. Passenger services were scheduled to start in October 2007.

Along the Santa Marta-Riohacha road is **Quebra de Valencia** ① *US$1.20*, several natural swimming pools amid waterfalls, with good views. From the marked roadside entrance, it is a pleasant 20 minutes' walk along a clear path, or horse ride, to the waterfalls. It can get overcrowded during high season. Drinks and snacks available along the way.

Taganga

Close to Santa Marta is the popular fishing village and beach of Taganga, set in a little bay with good views. It is peaceful, laid back and Taganga's small community is very welcoming, which lures most visitors to stay far longer than planned. Swimming is good, especially on Playa Grande, 25 minutes' walk round coast or US$2-3 by boat, but watch out for thieving. Taganga is quiet during the week, but it is crowded on Sunday. Good fresh fish is served at places along the beach. Taganga is a popular place for diving and several well-established dive shops offer good value PADI courses. There is a good book exchange shop; no ATMs or broadband internet.

Parque Nacional Tayrona

① *0800-1700, US$9.50 foreigners, US$2.50 per car (more for larger vehicles), parking US$2.20 per day. During high season, the park is very crowded and sometimes temporarily closes because it is full. Best to arrive early. Park accommodation in Arrecifes and Cañaveral is managed by Aviatur, in Santa Marta, C15, No 3-20, T423 5745/421 3848 (just off Plaza Bolívar), or Bogotá, T243 1640.*

Stretching north of Taganga for some 85 km is the beautiful and mostly unspoilt coastline of Tayrona National Park, where, in its lush vegetation, you can see monkeys, iguanas and maybe snakes. The park entrance is at the east end of the park, at El Zaino, 35 km from Santa Marta. Tickets are sold here. It is a one hour walk into the park from the gate, or take a colectivo from the park entrance, US$0.50. The road goes to **Cañaveral**. 45 minutes west of Cañaveral on foot, or by horse, is **Arrecifes**, from where it is 45 minutes' walk to Cabo, then 1½ hours on a clear path up to the archaeological site of **Pueblito**. A guided tour around the site is free, every Saturday or as arranged with a park guard. Other Tayrona relics abound. At Pueblito there are indigenous people; do not photograph them. From Pueblito you can either return to Cañaveral, or continue for a pleasant two-hour walk up to Calabazo on the Santa Marta-Riohacha road. A circuit Santa Marta, Cañaveral, Arrecifes, Pueblito, Calabazo, Santa Marta in one day needs a 0700 start at least. It is easier (more downhill) to do the circuit in reverse, ask to be dropped at Calabazo. Tours can be arranged at **Turcol** and the *Hotel Miramar* in Santa Marta has a daily bus service leaving at 1000-1030 which takes you right into the Park, US$9 return (you do no have to stay there to go), returning 1600-1700. Recommended. Bathing near Cañaveral must take account of frequent heavy pounding surf and treacherous tides. Every year, people drown because they do not heed the warnings. Some 40 minutes' walk left along the beach is Arrecifes, but because of rocks and the dangerous surf, authorities do not recommend this route. Beyond Arrecifes, walk 30 minutes to La Piscina, a beautiful, safe natural swimming pool, excellent snorkelling.

Neguangue beach can be reached by colectivo from Santa Marta Market at 0700, return 1600, US$7. For good snorkelling, take a 10-minute boat ride from Neguangue beach to Playa Cristal/Playa Muerto. There are other beaches accessible by coastal path, or by boat. **Beyond Cañaveral**, east along the coast, is **Palomino**. Tours can be arranged from there to *indígena* villages taking up to six days, cost around US$35 per day. Enquire at *Turcol* in Santa Marta (see page 829), or *Hotel Miramar*, US$30-36.

It is advisable to inform park guards when walking in the park. Wear hiking boots and beware of bloodsucking insects. Take food and water, but no valuables as robbery is common. You may be able to hire donkeys for the Arrecifes-Pueblito stretch, US$5 each way, but watch them as these animals eat everything. Generally, the main trails and campsites are badly littered. The best information on the Park is in Santa Marta. See Transport, below, for how to get there.

Sierra Nevada de Santa Marta

The Sierra Nevada, covering a triangular area of 16,000 sq km, rises abruptly from the Caribbean to 5,800 m snow peaks in about 45 km, a gradient comparable with the south face of the Himalaya, and unequalled along the world's coasts. Pico Colón is the highest point in the country. The area is a drugs-growing, processing and transporting region. For this reason, the reluctance of some local *indígenas* to welcome visitors, plus the presence of guerrilla and paramilitary groups makes much of the Sierra Nevada de Santa Marta a no-go area. This is a tragedy since here can be found the most spectacular scenery and most interesting indigenous communities in the country. For the latest information check with *MA* in Santa Marta and Bogotá, *ICANH* in Bogotá (see page 773), and the **Fundación Pro-Sierra Nevada** ① *C 17, No 3-83, Santa Marta, T431 0551*, for guidance on what may be possible. It is extremely unwise and very dangerous to enter the area on your own. If you must, always travel with an experienced guide. Trekking tours into the fringes of the Nevada de Santa Marta can from time to time be arranged in the Santa Marta and Valledupar areas, check with the respective tourist offices.

Ciudad Perdida → *Colour map 1, grid A3.*

Ciudad Perdida was called Teyuna by the Tayrona, meaning mother nature. The city covers 400 ha and was built around 700 AD. It was the political and trading centre of the Tayrona. The circular and oval stone terraces were once the living quarters for some 1,400-3,000 people. The city was also an important religious and burial site. The Tayrona built sophisticated irrigation systems and walls to prevent erosion. By around 1600, the Tayrona were almost wiped out by the conquistadores and the few who survived were forced to flee. For the next four centuries, the city disappeared under the forest growth. In 1973, tomb looters searching for gold known to exist in burial urns and graves, rediscovered the city by chance. By 1975, the city was officially re-found, attracting local and international anthropologists and archeologists who started to excavate, leading to the first tourist groups in 1984. Today the area is a protected indigenous reserve, where three main indigenous groups, the Koguis, Arhuacos and Arsarios, continue to live.

The 20-km trek to the Lost City is, at times, gruelling and challenging. It is not a leisurely walk, but is well worth the effort for a rewarding and memorable experience. The trek is perhaps more spectacular than the archeological site itself. Along with lush tropical humid and dry forests, abundant flora and fauna, there are crystal clear rivers, waterfalls and natural swimming pools. Watch out for snakes. Along the way, you will pass friendly Kogui villages. There are some 1,200 steep slippery steps to climb to the summit of the city. Wrap clothes in plastic bags to keep them dry and take a sleeping bag as it gets cold at night. You may come across paramilitary groups along the way; do not take photos of them. Scores of tours leave Santa Marta every three to four days during the year, experiencing no problems.

⊜ Sleeping

Santa Marta *p829, map p829*
If you arrive by bus, beware taxi drivers who take you to a hotel of their choice. Calle 10C (near the port, 2 blocks from the beach) has many budget hotels interspersed with brothels and has become a popular small gringo ghetto. Be careful here, especially at night. There are plenty of budget hotels along Cra 2 as well. Around Rodadero beach

is considered unsafe. For groups of 4 or more, ask about apartments for short rent. Essential to book ahead during high season, when some hotels increase their prices by 50%.

In town
Av Rodrigo de Bastidas (Cra 1) has several high-rise hotels on the seafront while Cra 2 and

connecting streets have a good choice of budget *residencias*.

B Bahía Blanca, Cra 1A, No 11-13, T421 4439, F423 6411. Rooms around pleasant courtyard, helpful staff, a/c, less with fan. 30% cheaper in low season. Good.

C Panamerican, Cra 1, No 18-23, T421 1238, F421 4751. A/c or cheaper with fan, safe, cafetería, modern holiday hotel, accepts credit cards.

C Tayromar, C 20, No 1C-71, T421 7324, one block from beach. Helpful owners, well-organized, safety-deposit in rooms, modern, a/c (cheaper with fan), secure parking, good service. Recommended.

D Casa Vieja, C 12, No 1-58, T421 4852. A/c, less with fan, welcoming, good popular restaurant.

D Nueva Granada, C 12, No 3-17, T421 0685, www.hotelnuevagranada.com. Colonial building with rooms round a pleasant courtyard, quiet, cheaper with fan, safety-deposit in rooms, small pool, internet, includes breakfast. Accepts credit cards, 45% cheaper in low season. Good.

D Park, Cra 1, No 18-67, T421 1215, F421 1574. On seafront, modern holiday hotel, popular with families, pool, stores luggage, helpful.

D-E Costa Azul, C 17, No 2-09, T421 2236. A/c, cheaper with fan, windows into courtyard, simple.

E-F Turismar, Cra 1, No 11- 41, T421 2408. Basic rooms around courtyard, a/c, less with fan, restaurant.

F Hospedaría Casa Familiar, C 10 C, No 2-14, T421 1697, www.hospederiacasafamiliar .freeservers.com. **G** in dorms. Efficient, very helpful and welcoming, family-run, safe, motorbike parking. Recommended.

G Miramar, C 10C, No 1C-59, T423 3276, 2 blocks from beach. Under new joint ownership, Jairo is very knowledgeable and helpful. Guides to the Ciudad Perdida hang around here, sells tours at the official price, also good for tours to Tayrona and Taganga (where they have *Hotel Ramarim*). Tends to be crowded, basic dorms and some nicer more expensive private rooms, luggage store, motorbike parking, Wi-Fi internet, cheap restaurant. Often full. Reservations can be made via the internet (www.hosteltrail.com) and are held until 1500 on the day of arrival. Airline tickets also sold here.

G Residencias El Titanic, C 10C, No 1C-68, T421 1947. Fan, basic, safe, good value, motorbike parking, tours to Ciudad Perdida can also be bought here.

Playa El Rodadero

AL Irotama, Km 14, between airport and Rodadero Bay, T432 0600, www.irotama.com.

Resort in tropical gardens with own beach, full service, several restaurants, convention facilities, rooms, suites and bungalows.

AL Tamacá, Cra 2, No 11A-98, T422 7015. Direct access to beach, fair rooms with sea view, price includes 2 meals, good service, fine pool.

B Edmar, Cra 3, No 5-188, T422 7874, 2 blocks from beach. Price includes 2 meals, a/c, cafetería, welcoming, pool.

B La Guajira, Cra 4, No 23F-05, entrance to El Rodadero, T422 0918. Pleasant, modern, Wayúu manageress can advise about travel to La Guajira. Good breakfast, pool, safe parking, includes 2 meals.

C La Riviera, Cra 2, No 5-42, T422 7090. Small, safe, a/c, includes breakfast and TV.

D El Rodadero, C 11, No 1-29, T422 8295, Pool, helpful, restaurant, parking, some rooms with sea view, includes 2 meals.

E Tucuraca, Cra 2, No 12-53, T422 7493. Fan, will store luggage, helpful, TV.

E-G Hostería Tima Uraka, C 18, No 2-59, T422 8433. Shared rooms, nice garden, hammocks, laundry service.

Around Santa Marta *p830*

B Rancho Luna, T422 1722 (Santa Marta), 310-610 6614 (mob), azusaco@yahoo.com. Run by Colombian Azucena Samudio, who speaks English. About 48 km from Santa Marta on main road to Riohacha, just before Quebra de Valencia waterfalls, signpost on left side of the road. Comfortable eco-lodges with thatched roofs in secluded palm grooves overlooking tranquil beach, shared and private bath, price includes 2 meals and a snack, good Colombian home cooking. Well-run, relaxing, no electricity. Recommended, "a special place".

G pp Carpe Diem, 15 km from Santa Marta at 400 m. Ecological farm run by Belgians Mathias and Elsa, guests collected from **Miramar** (see above). Private rooms, dorm and hammocks, meals US$1.50-2 extra, horses riding, hiking, river bathing, tours to pre-Columbian sites, kitchen, book exchange, Dutch, French and English spoken. Recommended.

Fundación

E Caroli, Cra 8, No 5-30, T414 0273, is the best.
E Centro del Viajero, with a/c, good value. Also **Hotel Milán**, T414 0227.

Taganga *p830*

Travellers are increasingly staying here rather than in Santa Marta. Prices rise by around 30% during high season.

B La Ballena Azul, Cra 1, No 18-01, T421 9009. Attractive hotel with French riviera touch,

For an explanation of the sleeping and eating price codes used in this guide, see page 58. Other relevant information is found in Essentials pages 778-779.

832

comfortable, spacious rooms with sea views, also run boat tours to secluded beaches, horses for hire. Nice restaurant on the beach and good pancakes at the crêperie.

D Bahía Taganga, C 8, No 1-07, T421 9049/9151. Unmissable garish green sign on the cliff face. Overlooking bay, breakfast served on lovely terrace, hospitable, a/c, less with fan.

E Casa Blanca, near *La Ballena Azul*, T421 9232. On the beach, small rooms, some with good views, laundry.

E Techos Azules, look for the blue roofs at end of beach, T421 9141. Good sea views, hammock and terrace area, comfortable fully furnished studio apartments at US$10 pp.

E-F La Casa de Felipe, 3 blocks uphill from beach, follow the signs, T421 9101/9120. Cosy traveller place run by knowledgeable French team of Jean Phillipe and Sandra Gibelin. Good kitchen facilities, internet, laundry, hospitable, relaxing hammock and spacious garden area with sea views, studio apartments, dorms and rooms. Good information on trips to Tayrona (maps provided), English spoken. Highly recommended.

F pp Divanga, C 12, No 4-07, T421 9092, divangacolombia@yahoo.fr. French-owned hostel, includes breakfast, comfortable, 5-mins' walk from beach, nice views, attentive service, lovely atmsophere. Frequently recommended.

F Hostal Moramar, Cra 4, No- 178-83, T421 9202, www.hostalmoramar.com. New, 2 blocks uphill from beach opposite football pitch. Simple, quiet, rooms with bath and fan, bright, airy, patio area, laundry, attentive owners, welcoming.

F pp Pelikan Hostal, Cra 2, No 17-04, T421 9057. Another backpacker option of good report.

F-G Hotel Ramarim, C 12 entre Cra 3 y 4, T423 3276. Probably the cheapest option in Taganga. You get what you pay for. Basic rooms, camping is allowed in the patio but space is limited.

Parque Nacional Tayrona *p830*
Cañaveral
Comfortable up-market cabins with thatched roofs for 2-4 persons cost US$66 high season, US$45 low season, prices fixed by **Aviatur** (address above), offer privacy, great views over sea and jungle, decent elegant restaurant. Campsite US$4.50 pp in 5-person tent; hammocks US$6.50; has facilities, but only one restaurant with a tiny store, take all supplies; attractive site but plenty of mosquitoes. Beware of falling coconuts and omnivorous donkeys.

Arrecifes
Accommodation in Arrecifes is generally cheaper than in Cañaveral. Cabins fit 6 people, camping and hammock hire available. Campsites charge about US$3 to hire a hammock. **Rancho Bonito** and **El Paraíso** are the best, with facilities and food. At *El Paraíso* there are cabins and a restaurant. The other 2 sites are basic. 200 m along the main road east of the park entrance is a truck stop where cyclists may be able to stay the night (US$5). On the path to Pueblito there is a campsite at **Cabo** where the path turns inland, small restaurant and hammocks for hire; there are other camping and hammock places en route. There is nowhere to stay at Pueblito. You can continue along the coast to beaches, but the going is difficult.

❷ Eating

Santa Marta *p829, map p829*
In town
❚❚❚-❚❚ **Muelle 8**, Cra 1, No 10A-12, at the port terminal, second floor. Upmarket, excellent seafood and local dishes.

❚❚ **San Valentín**, C 19, No 2-17 (Parque de los Novios). Decent Italian overlooking square, nice atmosphere.

❚❚-❚ **Nuevo Toy San**, C22, No 3-78, T421 4702. Decent Chinese, generous portions. Open Sun.

❚ **El Jardín Paisa**, C 20, No 1C-20. Good value *comida corriente* and service, popular. Also rents out rooms (**D**).

❚ **Merkabar/Welcome**, C 10C, No 2-11. Family-run, pastas, good value seafood, vegetarian options, great pancakes, good juices, café frappé, good value, tourist advice, popular with travellers. Near **Hotel Miramar**. Che Luis in Taganga, on seafront, offers the same menu.

Café del Parque, Parque de Bolívar next to Casa de la Aduana. Juan Valdez coffee shop. Great shady place for coffee and snacks, try *café frappé* (with ice), closed Sun.

Taganga *p830*
Baguettes de María, up the hill from the beach on the same road to **Casa Felipe**. Great, good value generously filled sandwiches and fruit juices.

❸ Bars and clubs

Santa Marta *p829, map p829*
Barrio Sumario/a, C 17, , between Cra 3 and 4 (on same road as La Puerta). A popular bar playing local music in colonial setting and patio.

La Escollera, C 5, No 4-107, outside of town at El Lago. Huge club under open straw roof, concerts.

La Puerta, C 17, between Cra 3 and 4. Excellent bar and atmosphere in colonial house. Highly recommended.

Valsao, Cra 1, No, 19A-12, at the port terminal, second floor. Upmarket open air restaurant and bar with good sea views.

Taganga *p830*
El Garaje, C 8, No, 2-127. Good popular bar.
Mojito Net, C 14, No 1B-61 between beach and church, T421 9149. Good internet cafe, serves drinks, open till late.

▲ Activities and tours

Santa Marta *p829, map p829*
Tours Ask in hotels and tourist offices.

Taganga *p830*
Diving
There are several good, well-established dive shops in Taganga. Average prices: PADI course, 4 days, around US$200, 2 dives US$50. The standard of equipment varies, check everything carefully.
Calipso, C 12, No 1-40, T421 9146. Good reports.
Centro de Buceo Tayrona, C 18, No 1-39, T421 9195, T315-638 3307 (mob), www.cbtsyrona.com. 25 years' experience, well organized, daily dive trips 0900-1400, prices include equipment and light lunch. PADI course, 3-4 days. English, Dutch, German spoken. Friendly owner José. Recommended.
Nautilos, C 16, Cra 1 on beach front, T421 9007.
Poseidon, C 18, No 1-69, T421 9224, www.poseidon divecenter.com. Another good option, experienced, good reports. Ask for German owner, Max.

Ciudad Perdida *p831*
Tours
We strongly recommend that you buy tours directly from **Turcol** in Santa Marta or **Hotel Miramar**. Turcol is the only tour operator allowed into Ciudad Perdida. The rest who offer tours are all middlemen. Tours take 5, 6 or 7 days, depending on how easy you want to take it and how much time spent at the site. Usually, 3 days hike there, 1 day at site, 2 days back. A new cirucular trekking route around Ciudad Perdida is currently being offered which takes 7 days. Turcol recommended guides: Edwin Rey very knowledgeable, Wilson and Edilberto Montero, Walter Hinojoza and Eliezer Castro. All are well-organized, reliable and professional. No English speaking guides. Going on your own is almost impossible and very dangerous. For visiting Ciudad Perdida by helicopter, check with **Aviatur**, C15, No 3-20, Santa Marta, T421 3848, http://site.aviatur.com.

⊖ Transport

Santa Marta *p829, map p829*
Air Simón Bolívar, 20 km south of city; bus, US$0.35, taxi from Santa Marta, US$7, from Rodadero, US$4. Daily flights to **Bogotá** and **Medellín**; connections to other cities. During the

tourist season, get to the airport early and book well ahead (the same goes for bus reservations).
Bus Terminal southeast of the city, towards Rodadero, minibus US$0.30; taxi US$2.50 to centre, US$3.50 to Rodadero. To **Bogotá**, about US$45, 4-6 a day with **Brasilia**, T430 1569 (buses leaves from 1430-2030); if going direct, ask for **Vía La Dorada** buses which go by the new road, 15-18 hrs. With **Coopetran**, 3 a day US$30, usually slower than Brasilia. To **Medellín** at 1700 with **Coopetran**, US$35, with **Brasilia**, 4 daily US$45. To **Cali**, 3 daily, US$63. **Coopetran** and **Brasilia** to **Bucaramanga** about 8-9 hrs, US$31, frequent departures 0700-2200. Journey time is dependent on the number of police checks. Buses to **Barranquilla**, every 15 mins, 2-3hrs US$4.50. To **Cartagena**, 5 hrs US$10-11, Brasilia. To **Riohacha** US$8.50, 4 hrs. Frequent buses to **Maicao**, US$12 a/c, also cheaper non a/c, 4-5 hrs. Brasilia runs a through bus to **Maracaibo**, daily, US$28. To **Caracas**, usually stops at Marcaibo, US$60. Brasilia buses direct to **Rodadero Beach** from Barranquilla, taking 2 hrs and costing US$2.50.
Car (port) Without a *carnet de passages*, it can take up to 4 working days to get a car out of the port, but it is usually well guarded and it is unlikely that anything will be stolen.

Around Santa Marta: Aracataca and Fundación *p830*
Bus Ciénaga-Fundación, US$1; Fundación-Aracataca, US$0.20; **Santa Marta**-Aracataca, US$2.50, 90 mins; **Barranquilla**, goes via Ciénaga, US$2.50.

Taganga *p830*
Minibus from **Santa Marta** US$0.35 (frequent, 0600-2130), **taxi** US$2.70, 15-20 mins. Taxi from bus station, US$3.50.

Parque Nacional Tayrona *p830*
Bus To get to the park entrance in El Zaino, take a minibus from the market in Santa Marta, Cra 11 y C 11, about US$1.30, 45 mins, frequent service from 0700, last back about 2000 (check on the day with the bus driver). Tourist bus from **Hotel Miramar** in Santa Marta daily at 1100, US$4.50. This returns early afternoon; visitors normally stay overnight. Other hotels help in arranging tours, but there is no need to take guides (who charge US$20 or more pp for a day trip). Hire a boat in Taganga to Arrecifes, about 2 hrs along the scenic coast, US$110 for 8.

⊕ Directory

Santa Marta *p829, map p829*
Airline offices Avianca, Edif de los Bancos, Cra 2B y C 14, T214 4018, T432 0106 at airport.

Banks Most banks and ATMs in Plaza Bolívar. eg Banco Occidente (good rates for MasterCard). Plenty of cash machines. *Casas de cambio* in 3rd block of C 14. **Internet** Mundo Digital, C 15, No 2B-19, Edif Los Bancos, just off Plaza Bolívar, Mon-Sat 0700-2000, Sun 0900-1700. International calls too. Dialnet Café, C 13, No 3-13. **Useful addresses** MA office, C 22, No 2A-33, T423 0704. DAS Office, Cra 8, No 26A-15, T421 4917. Mon-Fri, 0730-1200, 1400-1800. Sr Chávez, DAS director at Santa Marta, runs a tight ship and is not flexible.

To Venezuela

Roads head for the insalubrious border town of Maicao, but on the way is plenty of interest: lagoons where flamingos feed, the pleasant city of Valledupar, which is home to Colombia's famous vallenato music, and the arid, empty Guajira Peninsula with its wildlife and special Wayúu culture.

Riohacha and around → *Phone code: 95. Colour map 1, grid A4. Population: 142,000.*

The port of Riohacha, 160 km east of Santa Marta and capital of Guajira Department, comes alive at the weekend, when it fills with party-goers and music (almost always vallenato) springs up all over the place. It was founded in 1545 by Nicolás Federmann, and in early years its pearling industry was large enough to tempt Drake to sack it (1596). Pearling almost ceased during the 18th century and the town was all but abandoned. Today, there is a pleasant stretch of beach with shady palms and a long wooden pier. A promenade along the beachfront (Calle 1) is lined with banks, hotels, restaurants and tour agencies. It is common to see Wayúus selling their wares and beautiful handmade *mochilas* (bags) along the seafront. Riohacha is a useful base for exploring the semi-desert landscape of La Guajira. Tourist office: **Dirección de Turismo de la Guajira** ① *Av La Marina, T727 1015*, little information, better to ask tour operators. Ask for the University of the Guajira, which has an excellent resource centre related to the region and the Wayuú culture (ID is necessary to get in).

Santuario Los Flamencos

① *Entry to the park is US$5.50. 95 km east of Santa Marta and 25 km short of Riohacha.*
There are several small and two large saline lagoons (Laguna Grande and Laguna de Navío Quebrado), separated from the Caribbean by sand bars. The latter is near Camarones (colectivo from Riohacha, new market) which is just off the main road. About 3 km beyond Camarones is 'La Playa', a popular beach to which some colectivos continue at weekends. Flamingoes normally visit the large lagoons between October and December, during the wet season, though some birds are there all year. They are believed to migrate to and from the Dutch Antilles, Venezuela and Florida. Across Laguna de Navío Quebrado is a warden's hut on the sand bar, ask to be ferried across by local fishermen or the park guards. **MA** has new, comfortable cabins (**E**) for up to eight, open all year. Showers available; meals at the tiendas by the entrance. There are several bars and two stores on the beach.

Valledupar → *Phone code: 955. Colour map 1, grid A4. Population: 260,000. Altitude: 110 m.*

South of Riohacha on an alternative road to Maicao and the Venezuelan border is **Cuestecita** (*Hotel Turismo*), where you can turn southwest to **Barrancas**, with one of the largest coal mines in the world, El Cerrejón (T350 5705 for information about pre-arranged visits to the mine). Continuing on this road, which takes you either round the Sierra Nevada to Barranquilla and Santa Marta via Fundación (see above) or south to Bucaramanga, you come to **Valledupar**, capital of César Department. Valledupar claims to be the home of the *vallenato* music. Each April (26-30), *La Festival de la Leyenda Vallenata* draws thousands of visitors. There are *casas de cambio* on Calle 16.

Guajira Peninsula

Beyond Riohacha to the east is the arid and sparsely inhabited Guajira Peninsula, the leading producer of natural gas in Colombia. The *indígenas* here collect dividivi (the curved pods of trees used in tanning and dyeing), tend goats, and fish. They are Wayúu (or Guajiros), and of special interest are the coloured robes worn by the women. There language is Wayuunaiki; beyond Cabo de Vela little Spanish is spoken. Sunsets in the Guajira are magnificent.

Note The Guajira peninsula is not a place to travel alone, parties of three or more are recommended. If going in your own transport, check on safety before setting out. Also remember it is hot, easy to get lost, and there is little cover and very little water. Locals, including police, are very helpful in giving lifts. Stock up with provisions and water in Riohacha or Maicao. Elsewhere, what little there is expensive.

To visit a part of the Peninsula take a bus from Riohacha (twice a day from the indigenous market) to Manaure, US$3, three uncomfortable hours through fields of cactus but offering fine views of flamingoes and other brightly coloured birds. **Manaure** is known for its salt flats southwest of the town. If you walk along the beach past the salt works, there are several lagoons where flamingoes congregate the year round (take binoculars). Local children hire out bicycles for US$3 per day to travel to the lagoons and salt flats. Take plenty of sunblock and water and a torch/flashlight for returning in the evening. 14 km from Manaure in this direction is **Musichi**, an important haunt of the flamingoes, sometimes out of the wet season. From Manaure there are *busetas* to **Uribia** (US$1), which has a Wayúu festival in May (no other reason to stop here), and thence to Maicao. You can get *busetas* from Uribia to Puerto Bolívar (from where coal from El Cerrejón is exported) and from there transport to **Cabo de Vela**, where the lagoons seasonally shelter vast flocks of flamingoes, herons and sandpipers. It costs about US$3 from Uribia to Cabo de Vela. There are fine beaches, but very strong currents offshore. Good walks through desert scrubland, eg to Pan de Azúcar hill (one hour from beach) and El Faro, with superb views of the coastline and desert. Tourism in Cabo de la Vela has boomed recently. To enjoy deserted beaches, avoid Christmas and Easter when the *cabañas* and beaches are crowded and full of cars. Jeep tours to Cabo de la Vela from Riohacha can be easily arranged.

Parque Nacional Macuira

① Entry free.

Towards the northeast tip of the Guajira peninsula is the Serranía de Macuira, a range of hills over 500 m which create an oasis of tropical forest in the semi-desert. Moisture comes mainly from clouds that form in the evening and disperse in the early morning. Its remoteness gives it interesting flora and fauna and indigenous settlements little affected by outsiders. To reach the area, you must travel northeast from Uribia either round the coast past Bahía Portete, or direct across the semi-desert, to Nazareth on the east side of the park. Macuira can be seen on two-day trips from **Nazareth**. There is no public transport, though trucks may take you from the Bahía Portete area to Nazareth, 6-8 hours (if you can find one). You may be able to arrange a trip in Cabo de Vela (see above – beautiful drive through fantastic desert scenery and past magnificent beaches), or Riohacha, try *Guajira Viva*. *Eco-Guías* (see Bogotá, Tour Operators) arrange trips here occasionally.

Maicao → *Phone code: 95. Colour map 1, grid A4. Population: 59,000. Altitude: 50 m.*

The paved Caribbean coastal highway runs direct from Santa Marta to Riohacha, then paved to Maicao. **Maicao**, 12 km from the Venezuelan border, is hot and dusty. It is full of Venezuelan contraband and petrol and is an important drug-running route. There is a strong Arab presence, with several mosques and restaurants selling Arabic food. The streets surrounding the main plaza are teeming with clothes stalls. Many of its streets are unsurfaced; most commercial premises close before 1600 and after 1700 the streets are unsafe. The market area is run-down and also unsafe at times. Plenty of *Telecom* offices and internet cafés.

Border with Venezuela

Colombian immigration is at the border. Entering Colombia by *por puesto* make sure the driver stops at the Colombian entry post. It is essential to have an exit stamp from Venezuela and make sure you get an entry stamp at DAS on the Colombian border. If not you will have to return later to complete formalities. With all the right papers, the border crossing is easy and there are few traffic delays. There are plenty of money changers hanging around at the border crossing.

There is no Venezuelan consul in Maicao. If you need a visa, get it in Barranquilla, Cartagena or Riohacha. Entering Venezuela, a transit visa will only do if you have a confirmed ticket to a third country within three days. See 'Entering Venezuela', page 1361.

⊜ Sleeping

Riohacha *p835*

A Arimaca, C 1, No 8-75, T727 3515. On beachfront, no obvious sign, some rooms with balcony, good sea views, helpful staff, a/c, comfortable rooms, pool, includes breakfast, good restaurant.

B Gimaura, Av La Marina, T727 0019. On seafront, past bridge, helpful staff, pool, parking, restaurant.

C Almirante Padilla, Cra 6, No 3-29, T727 2328. Much cheaper with fan, patio, laundry, restaurant with cheap *almuerzos*.

C El Castillo del Mar Suites, C 9A, No 15-352, T727 5043. Overlooking the beach, helpful German owner, TV, cheaper with fan.

E Colonial, C 7A, No 10-75, T727 3408. Central, near main plaza, basic small rooms with fan and bath, bit noisy. Water usually only available early morning or at night.

E Yalconia, Cra 7, No 11-26, T727 3487. Private bath, cheaper with fan, small rooms, safe, helpful, half way between beach and bus station.

F Internacional, Cra 7, No 13-37, T727 3483. Far from centre, difficult to find, no obvious sign, entrance through market shops. Small, basic rooms with fan and bath. Patio and parking.

Valledupar *p835*

B Vajamar, Cra 7, No 16A-30, T574 3939. With breakfast, pool, expensive food.

E Hotel/Restaurant Nutibara, C 19, No 9-19, T574 3225. A/c, with breakfast. Several others on C 19.

Guajira Peninsula *p835*
Manaure

D Palaaima, Cr 6, No 7-25, T717 8195, is the best in town. Comfortable, cool rooms with a/c or fan, helpful. There are always Wayúu locals hanging around the hotel who are eager to talk about their culture and traditions.

Uribia

Basic hotels and 1 *residencia* (no running water); most transport stops in Uribia.

Cabo de Vela

This area becomes very crowded during high season. Many huts along the beach to stay in, some have TV, a/c. There is a telecom centre. Most places have hammock space on the beach, US$4-6. Fish meals cost US$4-6, including a large breakfast.

Maicao *p836*

E El Dorado, Cra 10, No 12-45, T726 7242. Near central plaza, a/c, TV, good water supply, private bath, less with fan, helpful. Other hotels and residencias along C 13.

⊕ Eating

Riohacha *p835*

There are several juice bars at the south end of Av La Marina, opposite the beach.

₩ Malecón, C 1A, No 3-42, T727 6210. On seafront, thatched roof, popular, fast food. Recommended.

₩ Papillón, Cra 7, No 3-27, opposite Cámara de Comercio. Decent restaurant and bar.

₮ Glenppi, Av La Marina, No 8-17, T727 3356. Good value chicken and burger meals. Open late.

₮ La Mejor, on corner of Parque Almirante (main sqaure). OK bakery.

Maicao *p836*

₮ El Oriente, Cra 9, No 11-16. Near main plaza, good, cheap Arabic food, great falafel. Closes 2000.

⊙ Shopping

Riohacha *p835*

New market 2 km from town on Valledupar road; hammocks and bags woven by the Wayúu of the Guajira are sold. See also **Operadora Turística Wayúu**, in Activities and tours, below.

▲ Activities and tours

Guajira Peninsula *p835*

Trips to the Guajira Peninsula are best arranged in Riohacha. Tours to Cabo de la Vela, 1-2 days usually include Manaure (salt mines), Uribia, Pilón de Azucar and el Faro. Leave about 0600 and sometimes 0830-0900, return 1900-2000, US$30-35 pp (based on 4 people). All organise tours to Wayúu *rancherías* in the afternoon (includes typical goat lunch).

Guajira Total, stand in front of *Hotel Almirante Padilla* on sea front, T727 2328, T315-714 8057 (mob). Trips to Wayúu *rancherías*, Manaure and Cabo de Vela.

Guajira Viva, C 3, No 5-08, loc 1, T727 0607. 5-day tours to Alta Guajira, Cabo de la Vela, Santuario de Fauna y Flora los Flamencos. Recommended.

Lucho Freyle, T728 2885, T312-647 1434 (mob). Recommended Wayúu guide in Riohacha, jeep tours around La Guajira and Cabo de la Vela.

Operadora Turística Wayúu, C 1A, No 4-35, T311-400 7985 (mob). Wayúu-run, on seafront. Sells beautiful, colourful Wayúu *mochilas*. Organizes tours to *rancherías* and Cabo de la Vela.

Uribia

Kaishi, T311-429 6315/316-429 6315 (mob). Speak to Andrés Orozco, organizes jeep tours around La Guajira.

⊙ Transport

Riohacha *p835*

Bus Main terminal is on C 15 (El Progreso). (It is best to travel from Riohacha in a luxury bus, early morning as these buses are less likely to be stopped and searched for contraband.) **Coopcaribe Taxis** travel throughout the region and can be picked up almost anywhere in town, especially close to the old market area near the *Hotel Internacional*: daily to **Uribia**, US$7, 1½ hrs, **Manaure** US$8, 1¾ hrs. Leave when full (4 people), be prepared to pay slightly more if there are no travellers. Early morning best for travel, transport is scarce in the afternoon. No buses leave from Riohacha direct to Cabo de la Vela: travel to Uribia and wait for a jeep (leaves when full, irregular service) to Cabo de La Vela, long and uncomfortable. Take plenty of water with you. It is much easier and recommended to take a tour from Riohacha to Cabo de La Vela.

Valledupar *p835*

Air Aires Mon-Fri to Barranquilla.
Bus The bus and air terminals are 3 km southeast of the town, close to each other, taxi, US$2.50. From **Santa Marta**, 4 hrs, from **Cartagena**, US$13 (with **Expreso Brasilia**). To **Barranquilla**, 5-6 hrs, US$11. To **Bucaramanga**, 8 hrs US$30.

Maicao *p836*

Air Booking/changing flights, Flamingo Rosado, Cra 9, No 12026, T726 6619/0859, 725 0708.

Bus Buses to **Riohacha**, US$1.50, 1-1½ hr. **Santa Marta** (Expreso Occidente), US$9. **Barranquilla**, US$13-15. **Cartagena**, US$18. Trucks leave regularly for **Cabo de Vela**, 2½-3 hrs, US$6 (can be uncomfortably crowded). Take water. **Fleta** is the local name for the faster taxis. Colectivos, known as *por puestos* in Venezuela, Maicao-**Maracaibo**, US$6 pp, or microbus, US$3.50, very few buses to Venezuela after midday. Buses leave from the bus terminal where you can change money; buy bus tickets and food before journey. Taxis from Maicao to Maracaibo, US$5 (plus US$0.50 road toll) will stop at both immigration posts and take you to your hotel; safe, very easy transfer. Make sure you ask the taxi/bus driver to stop at DAS for a Colombian exit stamp.

⊙ Directory

Riohacha *p835*

Banks Most banks are on Parque Almirante. Banco de Bogotá, Cra 7, between C 2/3, for Visa. Mon-Fri, 0800-1600, Sat, 0900-1200. **Consulates** Venezuela, Cra 7, No 3-08, p7-B, T727 4076, F727 3967 (0900-1300, and closed from 1500 Fri to 0900 Mon). If you need a visa, you should check all requirements for your nationality before arriving at this consulate. Travellers report it is easier to get a Venezuelan visa in Barranquilla. **Internet and telephone** On Parque Almirante. **Post offices** C 2, Cra 6/7. **Useful addresses** DAS Office (immigration): C 5 y Cra 5, open 0800-1200, 1400-1800.

San Andrés and Providencia

Colombia's Caribbean islands of the San Andrés and Providencia archipelago are 480 km north of the South American coast, 400 km southwest of Jamaica, and 180 km east of Nicaragua. This proximity has led Nicaragua to claim them from Colombia in the past. In 2000, the Archipelago of San Andrés, Old Providence and Santa Catalina were declared a World Natural Heritage Site called the Seaflower Biosphere Reserve. San Andrés is larger and more developed than Providencia and has lost much of its colonial Caribbean feel. Both are very expensive by South American standards. Nevertheless, their surrounding islets and cays, good diving, white sand beaches and spectacular turquoise waters make them popular holiday resorts with Colombians and North Americans looking for sun during winter months. San Andrés is very crowded with Colombian shoppers looking for foreign-made, duty-free bargains. Alcoholic drinks are cheap, but international shoppers will find few bargains, and essentials and eating out are expensive. The original inhabitants, mostly descendants of Jamaican slaves, speak English, but the population has swollen with unrestricted immigration from Colombia. There are also Chinese and Middle Eastern communities. The islands are one of the few Colombian departments not affected by the internal armed conflict but drugs running abounds.

Ins and outs

Getting there Air A cheap way to visit San Andrés is by taking a charter flight from Bogotá or other major city, accommodation and food included. See supplements in the local Colombian press. The airport at San Andrés is 15 mins' walk to town centre; buses to centre and San Luis from across the road from the airport. Airline offices in town. Flights to most major Colombian cities with **Aero República**, Avianca and Satena and international flights to Panama and Canada. Sunday flights are always heavily booked, similarly Jul-Aug, Dec-Jan. If wait-listed, don't give up hope. Fares are changing all the time, so for best value, shop around.

Boat Cruise ships and tours go to San Andrés; there are no other official passenger services by sea. In Cartagena, you can enquire about possible sea crossings, ships leave from the Embarcadero San Andrés, opposite the Plaza de la Aduana. Check carefully any offers you may receive. ▸▸ *For further information, see Transport, page 842.*

San Andrés Tourist office ① *at airport and Circunvalar Av Newball, diagonal Club Náutica, Mon-Fri 0800-1200, 1400-1800,* helpful, English spoken, maps and hotel lists. On arrival in San Andrés, you must buy a tourist card, US$9. It is also valid for Providencia. Do not lose it. You must also have an onward or return ticket.

San Andrés → *Phone code: 98. Population: 80,000.*

The 11 km long San Andrés island is made of coral and rises at its highest to 104 m. The town, commercial centre, resort hotel sector and airport are at the northern end. A picturesque road circles the island. Places to see, besides the beautiful cays and beaches on the less developed southern side, include the Hoyo Soplador (South End), a geyser-like hole through which the sea spouts into the air when the wind is in the right direction. The west side is less spoilt, but there are no beaches. Instead there is The Cove, the islands deepest anchorage, and Morgan's Cave (Cueva de Morgan, reputed hiding place for the pirate's treasure) which is penetrated by the sea through an underwater passage. At The Cove, a road crosses up to the centre of the island and back to town over La Loma, on which is a Baptist Church, built in 1847.

San Andrés is famous in Colombia for its music, whose styles include the local form of calypso, soca, reggae and church music. Concerts are held at the **Old Coliseum** (every Saturday at 2100 in the high season).

Boats leave daily from San Andrés town to the Aquarium and Johnny Cay which has idyllic, white beaches with palm trees. Fish lunches served on the island, US$5; party atmosphere on Sunday (you can go in one boat and return in another; see Activities and tours, below). On San Andrés the beaches are in town and on the east coast. Best are at San Luis and Bahía Sonora/Sound Bay.

San Andrés town

Sleeping 🛏
Bahía Sardina 2
Cocoplum Beach 4
Decameron Aquarium 1

Decameron El Isleño 7
Decameron San Luis 5
Hernando Henry 10
Hill Side View 6

Mary May Inn 8
Residencia Restrepo 9
Verde Mar 11

Eating 🍴
Fisherman's Place 1
Margherita e
   Carbonara 2

Providencia → *Phone code: 98. Population: 5,500. 80 km north-northeast of San Andrés.*

Commonly called Old Providence, **Providencia** is mountainous, of volcanic origin. The barrier reef that surrounds it, the third largest in the world, is called Old Providence McBean Lagoon; it is easily visited. Providencia and its sister island **Santa Catalina** (an old pirate lair separated from Providencia by a channel cut to improve their defence) have an approximate surface of 22 square km. The official languages of its 5,000 inhabitants are Spanish and Caribbean English. Musical influences are the mento from the Antilles, calypso from Trinidad and reggae from Jamaica. The average temperature is 27°C; the rainiest months are October and November, while the driest are January to April. There are no high-rises, apartment blocks or shopping malls and its quieter atmosphere than San Andrés attracts more European visitors.

Superb views can be had by climbing from Casabaja/Bottom House or Aguamansa/ Smooth Water to the peak. There are relics of the fortifications built on the island during its disputed ownership. Horse riding is available, and boat trips can be made to Santa Catalina and, to the northeast, Cayo Cangrejo/Crab Cay (entrance US$1.50, good snorkelling - see Tours, below). Santa Catalina is joined to the main island by the wooden Lover's Bridge (Malecón de los Enamorados). Go left after crossing this bridge (right is a dead end) and walk for about 500 m. Climb stairs to the Virgin statue for excellent views of Providencia. If you continue past the Virgin and go down the flight of stairs you will arrive at a very small beach (nice snorkelling). On the west side is a rock formation called Morgan's Head; from the side it looks like a profile.

Of the three main beaches, Manzanillo is the best preserved and wildest. Not much space for lying out, but pleasant for walking. **Roland's Roots Bar** has excellent live, traditional island music on weekends. South West Bay/Suroeste has stunning beaches and is the best for hanging out. There is access at each end. Two Rasta bars, **Richard's** (the oldest) and **Olibert's Fuente**, are recommended. Agua Dulce is where most hotels and restaurants are. Between April-May, the island is awash with migrating black crabs.

● Sleeping

San Andrés *p839, map p839*

Hotels quote rates pp, but we list prices for double room. Prices include half board, but most hotels can be arranged without meals (saves US$8-10, but it costs more than that to eat in a restaurant). Most hotels raise their prices by 20-30% on 15 Dec. All this applies to Providencia, too.

L Decameron Aquarium, Av Colombia 1-19, T512 1090, www.decameron.com. Rooms and suites, large pool, marina, large balconies, excellent sea views, restaurant, bars. All hotels in this group allow guests to use their services; reservations made at central office in Cartagena, Cra 1, No 10-10, Bocagrande, T655 0123. Also **Decameron El Isleño**, Av Colombia 5-117, T512 4425. 2 blocks from airport, in palm grove, good sea views, all services.

A Bahía Sardina, Av Colombia No 5A-29, T512 3587. Beach across street, a/c, TV, fridge, good service, small pool, cheaper without sea view.

B Verde Mar, Av 20 de Julio No 2A-13, T512 5525. Quiet, a/c, modern, safety boxes.

C-D Hill Side View, La Loma, diagonal a la Primera Iglesia Bautista, T513 3149, T311-210 4949 (mob). Memorable views, restaurant, small pool, US$ accepted, English spoken.

D Mary May Inn, Av 20 de Julio, No 3-74, T512 5669. Perhaps the nicest hotel in the centre,

small, cosy, patio, bright, a/c. Recommended.

D-E Hernando Henry, Av Las Américas 4-84, T512 3416, F512 4009. Basic rooms, restaurant, fan, more with a/c, with balcony, often full, on road from airport.

F Residencia Restrepo, Cra 8, near airport. 'Gringo hotel', noisy ('share a room with a Boeing 727') till midnight, but you get what you pay for, dirty, unkempt, run-down, not recommended.

Out of town:

L Decameron San Luis, road to San Luis Km 15, Sound Bay, T513 0295. Comfortable cabins, 3 pools, a/c, good restaurants and service, popular with Canadians, hotel entertainers.

E Cocoplum Beach, Via San Luis No 43-49, T513 2646. Helpful, includes breakfast, restaurant.

Providencia *p840*

There are more hotels and cabañas than those listed below. The Asociación Ecológica y Turística de la Vieja Providencia y Santa Catalina, headed by Jennifer Archbold R of **Body Contact** travel agency, works hard to prevent the incursion of large, chain hotels and preserve the islands' character. Hotels in Agua Dulce are 10 mins by motor taxi (US$1) from centre or 1 hr walk. Suroeste is a 20-min walk from Agua Dulce.

● *For an explanation of the sleeping and eating price codes used in this guide, see page 58. Other* ● *relevant information is found in Essentials pages 778-779.*

A **Cabañas Miss Elma**, Agua Dulce, T514 8229. Small, a/c, comfortable spacious rooms, balcony overlooking the sea, light, TV, fridge, excellent service. Highly recommended.

A **Sirius**, Suroeste, T514 8213, F514 8808. Rooms and suites on the beach. A/c, TV, internet, dive centre, kayaks. Johnny the owner gives massages and speaks German, Italian and English. Also youth hostel for holders of *carnets*, D with breakfast.

A **Sol Caribe Providencia**, Agua Dulce, T514 8230, www.solarhoteles.com. Chain hotel, pool, sea views, a/c, TV, fridge, bright.

B **Miss Mary**, Suroeste, T514 8206, F514 8454. On the beach, a/c, fridge, TV, hot water.

B **Morgan**, Agua Dulce, T514 8232. Popular, a/c, TV, modern, nice views, supermarket, conference hall and a good restaurant.

D **Old Providence**, diagonal Alcaldía Municipal, Santa Isabel (centre), T514 8691, F514 8187. Modern, a/c, less with fan, some rooms with balcony, fridge, no meals. Often full.

◑ Eating

San Andrés *p839, map p839*
Good fish and seafood meals at San Luis beach.

Ⅲ **Donde Francesca**, San Luis, T513 0163. Excellent seafood, nice place to hang out, on beach.

Ⅲ-Ⅲ **Margherita e Carbonara**, Av Colombia, No 1-93. Good Italian and coffee.

Ⅲ **Fonda Antioqueña**, Av La Playa. Good value for fish, local specialities, on sea front.

Ⅲ **Punto Sur**, just past Hoyo Soplador. Good fish, on beach, nice place to hang out.

Ⅲ-Ⅰ **Fisherman's Place**, in fishing cooperative at north end of main beach, Av Colombia, No 13-34, T512 2774. On seafront, very good, simple, try the *rondón*. Mon-Sun, lunch only. Recommended.

Ⅲ-Ⅰ **Tabolara**, Av Providencia, No2-12, diagonal Policia Nacional. Good value typical food, fruit juice.

Ⅲ-Ⅰ **West View**, Circunvalar Km 11, No 10-987. Fish, local dishes.

Providencia *p840*
Typical dish is *rondón*, a mix of fish, conch, yucca and dumplings, cooked in coconut milk. Fish and crab are most common.

As well as hotels, good places include: **Arturo**, on Suroeste beach, next to Miss Mary. Ask for mix for two people, US$13.50 for 2 fish, snail, crab and crayfish with *patacón* fries. **Café Studio**, between Agua Dulce and Suroeste. Great pies and spaghetti. **Donde Martín**, Agua Dulce. Good food.

✹ Festivals and events

San Andrés *p839, map p839*
20 Jul: **independence** celebrations on San Andrés with various events. The **Green Moon**

Festival is held in **May**. There is a cultural centre at Punta Hansa in San Andrés town.

Providencia *p840*
The island holds its **carnival** in **Jun**.

◓ Shopping

Providencia *p840*
There are 3 supermarkets in Santa Isabel town.
Arts and Crafts Café, Agua Dulce, T514 8297. French owners Maria Blancard and Frenchy DelPlace sell local crafts and delicious homemade cookies and ice cream.

▲ Activities and tours

San Andrés *p839, map p839*
Diving Diving off San Andrés is good; depth varies from 3 to 30 m, visibility from10 to 30 m. There are 3 types of site: walls of seaweed and minor coral reefs, different types of coral, and underwater plateaux with much marine life. It is possible to dive in 70% of the insular platform. Diving trips to the reef:
Banda Dive Shop, *Hotel Lord Pierre*, L-102, T513 1080, www.bandadiveshop.com. PADI dive courses, including advanced certificate.

Good snorkelling at the Aquarium off Haynes Cay (20 mins), take a morning boat (US$5). Boats to Johnny Cay leave 0930-1000 daily, also stop off at the Aquarium (US$7 return). Use a mask and wear sandals as protection against sea-urchins; colourful fish. Snorkelling equipment can be hired on San Andrés for US$5, but it is better and cheaper on the shore than on the island.
Other watersports Windsurfing and sunfish sailing rental and lessons are available from Bar Boat, on the road to San Luis (opposite the naval base), 1000-1800 daily (also has floating bar, English and German spoken), and Windsurf Spot, *Hotel Isleño*; water-skiing at Water Spot, *Hotel Aquarium*, and Jet Sky. From Tominos Marina there are boat trips. 2-hr bay trips cost US$10, for 4 hrs US$19, including 3 free rum and cokes. *Cooperativa de Lancheros*, opposite *Hotel Abacoa* run fishing and boating trips. *TVG*, Av Duarte Blum, 20 de Julio, No 1A-100, T512 0169, also run fishing trips.

Providencia *p840*
Diving **Felipe Diving** in Agua Dulce, T514 8775 (next to *Cabañas El Recreo*) warmly recommended. Mini diving course for US$55, all included, 2½ hours. Scuba course for US$220, with 5 dives and certification. Advanced course for US$265, with 6 dives and a night dive. Also rents snorkel equipment.

Tours

A popular boat trip, by colectivo, passes Santa Catalina (no stops but a brief photo opportunity of Morgan's Head), on to Cayo Cangrejo (2 hrs), ending at Playa Suroeste for 2-hr lunch before heading back to Aguadulce, US$10. Or rent your own boat for the day, US$90, negotiable. Julius at **Pirata Morgan's** warmly recommended. Bring snorkelling equipment.

Body Contact, Agua Dulce, T098-514 8283. Excursions, fishing trips, money exchange, diving trips, hiking tours, etc, helpful. Recommended.

⊖ Transport

San Andrés *p839, map p839*

Air Flights to Montreal, Toronto. To **Bogotá** with **Avianca** and **Satena**.

Bus Local buses cover the eastern side of the island all day until 2030 (10 mins intervals), US$0.50.

Taxi To airport, US$4.50; in town, US$1.60; *colectivo* to airport, US$0.50 (does not enter airport, stops across the street).

Train A 'tourist train' (suitably converted tractor and carriages) tours the island in 3 hrs for US$5.50.

Providencia *p840*

Air Satena flies from San Andrés, US$60 one way, 20 mins, 3 times a day. Essential to confirm flights to guarantee a seat. Schedules change frequently. Taxi from airport to centre, US$6.50 (fixed).

Boat Cargo boat trips leave from San Andrés, taking 8 hrs, every Wed, Thurs, Fri.

Motorcycle hire No licence or deposit needed. Several places in Agua Dulce. Negotiate fee: US$25 per day, or US$5.50 per hr (less for longer rentals). Petrol station near airport, Mon-Sat 0700-2100, Sun 0700-1600, US$2.60/gallon.

⊙ Directory

San Andrés *p839, map p839*

Banks Banks close 1200-1400. **Banco de Bogotá** will advance pesos on a Visa card. **Banco Occidente** for MasterCard. ATMs available in town and at the airport (Davivenda, in the lobby at the foot of the stairs). Some shops and most hotels will change US$ cash; it is impossible to change TCs at weekends. **Titan** casa de cambio, inside CC Leda, Av de las Américas, open Mon-Fri, and Sat, 0830-1200, changes TCs, US$ and euros. **Internet** Cafés downtown, eg **Café Sol** (*Hotel Tiuna*), Av Duarte Blum, US$2 per hr. **Post offices** Depris at airport and Av Colón, Edif Salazar. **Vehicle rental** Bicycles are easy to hire, usually in poor condition, choose your own bike and check all parts thoroughly (US$2 per hr, US$7 per day). Motorbikes also easy to hire, US$22 a day. Cars can be hired for US$22 for 1 hr, US$65 a day. Usually just need a passport as a deposit.

Useful addresses DAS, right next to airport, T512 7182/5540.

Providencia *p840*

Banks Banco de Bogotá, Santa Isabel, Mon-Thu 0800-1130, 1400-1600, Fri 0800-1130, 1400-1630. An ATM is tucked away just before the Lover's Bridge, on the road to Santa Catalina. **Internet** In Santa Isabel. **Telephone** Telecom in Santa Isabel (centre), open Mon-Sat 0800-2200; Sun 0900-1230, 1400-1900. International long distance: 191. International phone enquiries: 198. **Useful numbers** Police: 2. Medical: 11. Ambulance: 514 8016 at hospital.

Colombia San Andrés & Providencia Listings

Medellín and Chocó

Medellín → *Phone code: 94. Colour map 1, grid B2. Population: 1,700,000. Altitude: 1,487 m.*

Antioquia is the largest of the western departments, full of diversity and an important agricultural and commercial region. With its roots in the Cordilleras, it still has 100 km of Caribbean coastline. The people of Antioquia, called 'paisas', are known for their efficiency, hospitality and astute business talents. Medellín, the capital of Antioquia, is Colombia's second city. It is an important textile centre and is considered the leader in Colombia's flourishing fashion industry. Sadly, the city will always be synonymous with its infamous drugs cartel, but since the death of Pablo Esocbar in 1993 and the break-up of his huge empire, Medellín has been shrugging off its notorious reputation. It is forward-looking, prosperous, with a vibrant arts scene. Though few colonial buildings remain, there are plenty of museums, interesting plazas, modern architecture and public artworks to enjoy. The efficient overland metro system makes it easy and safe to get around the city. On top of that, the city has an excellent climate; temperate, spring-like weather all year round.

Ins and outs

Getting there **International airport** José María Córdoba airport (also called Rionegro), 28 km from Medellín by new highway, and 9 km from the town of Rionegro; good shops and services, no left luggage, but tourist office may oblige. Taxi to town US$19 (fixed, more at night), or the recommended airport bus (green and white) to centre, 50 minutes, US$1.80, frequent service 0430-2100: sit on right going to town. The airport bus stops and leaves on Carrera 50 (behind Hotel Nutibara) a few blocks from Plaza Botero. There is a stop at the Intercontinental Hotel for passengers to El Poblado. To Rionegro, bus US$0.40, taxi US$7. The **city airport**, Enrique Olaya Herrera, has regional flights to all major destinations in Colombia. This is a good option if you wish to avoid the far longer journey to Rionegro.

The terminal for long-distance buses going north and east is **Terminal del Norte** at Cra 64 (Autopista del Norte) y Transversal 78, about 3 km north of the centre, with shops, ATMs, cafeterías, left luggage (US$0.50 per day) and other facilities. Quite safe, but check carefully before going by road anywhere in Antioquia outside Medellín. Bus service to city centre, US$0.30, buses to station from C 50, marked: 'Terminal de Transporte', or better, by Metro to Caribe. For buses going south, **Terminal del Sur**, Cra 65, C 10, alongside the Olaya Herrera airport. Take any bus marked 'Terminal del Sur' from C 49 along Cra 46, or the Metro to Poblado on Línea A, you will need a taxi for the 1½ km to the bus station. ▸▸ *For more detailed information see Transport, page 847.*

Getting around The centre of the city comprises **La Candelaria**, in which is Parque de Berrío, and the commercial centre of **Villanueva**, with Parque de Bolívar. In the south, **El Poblado** has become an upmarket residential area and many companies have moved their headquarters there from the centre. The best hotels and restaurants are in or near El Poblado, which is considered a relatively safe residential area. Around Cra 70 and C 44 are busy commercial and entertainment sectors with many hotels, shopping centres and the

Medellín

Sleeping 🛌
Arod **1**
Black Sheep **2**
Casa Jerusalem **3**

Casa Kiwi **7**
Hostal Medellín **9**
Intercontinental **4**
La Habana Vieja **8**

Lukas **5**
Palm Tree Hostal **6**

*Related map
A Medellín centre,
page 844*

Atanasio Girardot sports stadium nearby. The climate is generally warm and pleasant though it is often cloudy and rain can come at any time. For your first general view of the city, take the Metro. There are three lines: A from Niquía in the east to Itagüí in the south, B from San Javier to San Antonio, where they intersect, and K, which is the MetroCable, a cable car serving the neighbourhoods on the mountain slopes up to Santo Domingo Savio. Change at Acevedo on line A for cable car rides. A trip on the cable car is highly recommended and gives great views over the city, especially at dusk. **Taxi**: make sure meters are used; centre to El Poblado US$3-4.50. It is not recommended to visit the poorer districts, known as *las comunas*, which sprawl increasingly higher towards the mountain peaks.

Tourist offices Palacio de Exposiciones ① *Entrada 1, inside the centre, T285 1048 (closed Sun)*, for information on the city and trips around Medellín, helpful. Good map. There are tourist booths at both airports. **Turibus** ① *T285 1978, www.ceditrans.com*, runs a tour bus with stops at Medellín's major sites and plazas, US$5. Pick up the bus anywhere along its route, eg at Parque de los Pies Descalzos, Parque de Berrío. Last service at 1300.

In the centre → *Calle and Carrera have numbers for easy reference. Most streets also have names. See map.*
Plaza Botero ① *C 52 y Cra 52*, is dotted with 23 bronze sculptures of **Fernando Botero**, Colombia's leading contemporary artist, born in Medellín in 1932. One side of the plaza has **El Palacio de la Cultura Rafael Uribe**, formerly the governor's office which is now a cultural centre and art gallery (free entry). Across, is the **Museo de Antioquia** ① *Cra 52A, No 51A-29, US$3.50 adults, students US$2, children under 12 free, Mon-Sat 0930-1700, Sun and holidays 1000-1600*, well-displayed works of contemporary Colombian artists, including a large collection by Botero and pre-Columbian artefacts. It has a pleasant café too. More works of Botero can be seen in Parque San Antonio ① *between C 44/46 and Cra 46*. It includes the 'Torso Masculino' (which complements the female version in **Parque Berrío**), and the 'Bird of Peace' which was severely damaged by a guerrilla bomb in 1996. At Botero's request, it has been left unrepaired as a symbol of the futility of violence and a new one has been placed alongside to make the point yet more dramatically. **Parque de Bolívar** is dominated by the **Catedral Metropolitana**, built between 1875 and 1931, claimed to be the third largest brick building in the world. There are three early churches near the centre, **San Benito**, **La Veracruz** and **San José**, and three 18th century churches survive: **San Ignacio**, in Plaza San Ignacio, **San Juan de Dios**, and **San Antonio**. There is a fine sculpture, Monumento a la Vida next to the Edif Seguros Suramericana on Calle 50, by Rodrigo Arenas Betancur, where exhibitions of work by leading South American artists are held on the ground floor. There is a fine sculpture,

Medellín centre

Sleeping
Botero Plaza 1
Casa Dorada 3
Conquistadores 4

Linton 6
Nutibara 8

Eating
El Viejo Vapor 1
Govinda 2
Trigo y Miel 3

0 metres 200
0 yards 200

Monumento a la Vida ① *next to the Edif Seguros Suramericana on Calle 50*, by Rodrigo Arenas Betancur, where exhibitions of work by leading South American artists are held on the ground floor. **Museo Casa Gardeliana** ① *Cra 45 No 76-50, daily 0900-1700, US$0.90*, was the home of the legendary Argentine tango singer, Carlos Gardel, who in 1935 died in a plane accident in Medellín. His legacy can be seen in the popular tango bars in El Envigado.

Outside the centre

Museo de Arte Moderno ① *Cra 64B, No 51-54, Mon-Sat 1000-1300, 1400-1800, US$1.80, half price with ISIC*, has a small collection and shows foreign films daily (not Wednesdays, US$2.65, half price with ISIC). **Casa Museo Maestro Pedro Nel Gómez** ① *Cra 51B, No 85-24, T233 2633*, is the house of the painter and sculptor (1899-1984). **Joaquín Antonio Uribe gardens** ① *Cra 52, No 73-298, daily 0800-1730, US$1.80*, are near the University of Antioquia campus, with 600 species of plants, orchids and trees. There is a pleasant restaurant for lunches and snacks. Also here at the **Museo de la Universidad de Antioquia** ① *C 67, No 53-108 (metro Universidad), free*, are exhibitions of modern art, anthropology and the history of Antioquia. **Biblioteca Pública Piloto para América Latina** ① *Cra 64, No 50-32, T230 2422, Mon-Fri 0830-1900, Sat 0900-1800* is one of the best public libraries in the country, with art and photo exhibitions, readings and films. Two newer 'sights' are **Puntocero** ① *at the Calle 67 river bridge*, an elegant steel double arch with a pendulum marking the centre of the city (the idea of local university students) and **El Edificio Inteligente**, also known as the EPM building ① *Calle 43/Cra 58*, a highly energy-efficient building used jointly by Medellín's public services. **Parque de Los Pies Descalzos** (The Barefoot Park) ① *Cra 57, No 42-139, opposite the EPM building*, is a relaxing square with cafés, sand pits and fountains. It serves as a good example of how Medellín is reclaiming and renovating public space with thought-provoking modern architecture.

As you ride the Metro you will notice three prominent hills in the Aburrá valley: **Cerro Nutibara** ① *Calle 30A y Cra 55, T235 8370*, in the southwest with good views over the city, where there is a stage for open air concerts, sculpture park, miniature Antioquian village (known as Pueblito Paisa), souvenir shops and restaurants; **Cerro El Volador** (seen as the Metro turns between Universidad and Caribe stations), tree-covered and the site of an important indigenous burial ground; and **Morro El Salvador** (to the east of Alpujarra station) with a cross and statue on top, now mostly built over and not recommended for visits.

● Sleeping

Medellín: centre *p844, map 844*

B Nutibara, C 52A, No 50-46, T511 5111, www.hotelnutibara.com. Best in centre, opposite Plaza Botero, elegant, casino and pool, good internet café.

B-C Botero Plaza, Cra 50A, No 53-45, T511 2155, www.hotelboteroplaza.com. Central, excellent service, safe, stores luggage, some rooms with nice views of city. Bus to airport leaves on same road. Recommended.

E Casa Dorada, C 50, No 47-25, T512 5300. Carpeted rooms, TV, hot water, parking nearby.

E Conquistadores, Cra 54, No 49-31, T512 3232, http://webteam.com.co/hconquist. With fan, TV, safety boxes, laundry.

F Linton, Cra 45, No 47-74, T217 0847. Central, TV, hot water, safe parking nearby US$0.50 per night, central.

Medellín: outside the centre *p844, map p843*

AL Lukas, Cra 70 No 44A-28, T260 1761, F260 3765. Best hotel in this area.

D Arod, C 44, No 69-80, T260 1427. Small, secure, basement parking. Recommended.

E Hostal Medellín, Cra 65, No 48-144, T230 0505, www.hostalmedellin.com. Close to Metro Suramericana. **G** pp in dormitory, hot showers, café, big kitchen, internet, garden, helpful staff speak English and German.

F Palm Tree Hostal, Cra 67, No 48D-63, Barrio Suramericana, T260 2805, www.palmtree medellin.com. Good traveller hostel, shared bath, free coffee, use of kitchen, internet, laundry hot water, private rooms, and good noticeboard.

El Poblado and around

See also Getting around, page 843.

L Intercontinental, C 16, No 28-51, Variante Las Palmas, T319 4450, medellin@interconti.com. Huge complex, all services, excellent.

C La Habana Vieja, C 10 Sur, No 43A-7, T321 2557. Small, cosy, colonial style with antiques, nice atmosphere, with breakfast.

E-F Casa Kiwi, Cra 36, No 7-10, T268 2668, www.casakiwi.net. A good traveller hostal, internet, kitchen facilities, laundry, terrace, near Parque Lleras, cheaper without bath, welcoming, paragliding arranged. Recommended.

F Casa Jerusalem, C 10 Sur, No 45-08, T321 5230. As the name suggests, Israeli run and favoured by Israelis backpapers, dorms only, pool with nice terrace area, 24-hour cheap restaurant, parking, internet, laundry facilities, TV room. Recommended.

F The Black Sheep, Transversal 5a, No 45-133 (tell taxi drivers it's in Patio Bonito), T311 1589, T311-341 3048 (mob), www.blacksheep medellin.com (informative website about travelling in Colombia). Run by welcoming New Zealander, Kelvin, **D** in small private rooms, homely feel, well-organized, TV areas, good kitchen facilities, popular weekly BBQ, internet, washing machine, excellent service, salsa and Spanish lessons arranged. Information on paragliding. Warmly recommended.

⊘ Eating

Medellín: centre *p844, map 844*
Apart from the hotels, few of the better restaurants will be found here. Many good, cheap restaurants on Cra 49 (eg **La Estancia**, Ns 54-15).
††-† El Viejo Vapor, Cra 43, No 53-19. Café, bar, artist clientele, good meeting place, set lunch US$3.50.
† Govinda, C 51 No 52-17. Vegetarian, excellent for lunch.
† Trigo y Miel, C 53, No 43-54. Very good vegetarian, set lunch US$3.50. Recommended.

There are several cheap, round-the-clock cafés on Cra Junín between Maturín and Amador. There are also several upstairs bar/cafés in Pasaje Junín.
Balcones del Parque, in Pasaje Junín. Good for meals and refreshments while watching Medellín in action below.
Boulevard de Junín in Pasaje Junín. Similar to Balcones del Parque.
Crepes y Waffles, Cra 36, No 10-54. Good as usual, other branches around the city.
Salón de Té Astor, Cra 49, No 52-84. Excellent pastries at a delightful traditional tea house.

Medellín: outside the centre *p844, map p843*
Plenty of cheap restaurants and fast food outlets around Cra 70 and more upmarket restaurants on Parque Lleras.
††† San Carbón, Via Las Palmas x Transversal Inferior, C 14 No 30-10, T312 7512. Nice views, rustic setting with straw roof, good typical grills. Popular on Sun.
†††-†† Hatoviejo, Las Palmas, in front of Intercontinental Hotel. T268 5527. Good typical food in rustic setting, good service.
†† Asados La 80, Cra 81, No 30-7, T413 0539, and Cra 81, No 33A-7. Very good for typical food and meats, Colombian music, open daily, closes late Fri and Sat.

El Poblado and around

See Ins and outs, Getting around section.
†† El Ranchón, C 10, No 43E-64. Good typical food, try *bandeja paisa*.
†† Le Bon Café, Parque Lleras. French-style café, good salads and onion soup. Nice atmosphere, relaxing, magazines. Bar at night. Branch also at Parque de los Descalzos. Recommended.

Other recommended places on Parque Lleras are **Ay caramba!** for Mexican food, **Tarremezini** serves Italian food in intimate atmosphere.

⊙ Bars and clubs

Medellín *p844, maps p843 and 844*
Many popular clubs on C 50, between Cras 65 and 75, and Cra 70, between C 36 and C 44. Beyond Poblado, there are good nightspots in Envigado. Bars on Parque Lleras and Calle 10. Along Las Palmas are large clubs, often only couples are allowed in.
B Lounge, Cra 35, No 10-38. Small, trendy, lounge bar style, good atmosphere, cover US$7.
Bar Berlín, C 10, No 41-65. Good mix of low level music, snooker table, pub feel. Open every day.
Bar Blue Rock, C 10, No 40-20. Popular, especially Thu.
El Dec, Cr 40, No 10-34. Popular, techno music, sells food, Tues-Sun.
La Kasa, 5 km vía Las Palmas. Good club.
Mango's, Cra 42A, No 67A-15, CC Capicentro, Autopista Sur Itagüí. Perhaps Medellín's most famous club, good for people watching, beautiful people and dwarf waiters.
Melody Lounge, Cra 37, No 10-29. Lounge bar, relaxed atmosphere, techno music. Open daily.
Vinacure in Tablaza (Caldas). Cover US$5, free Thu, take transport from Itagüí Metro station or taxi (25 mins from El Poblado). Alternative club and art gallery with kitsch art, drag and magic shows at 2300 Thu-Sat, good atmosphere. Recommended.

⊙ Entertainment

Medellín *p844, maps p843 and 844*
Cinema Free foreign films daily at Universidad de Medellín or Universidad de Antioquia. **Centro Colombo Americano**, Cra 45, No 53-24, T513 4444. Shows foreign art films.
Live music Monthly concerts by the **Antioquia Symphony Orchestra**. Band concerts and other entertainments in the Parque Bolívar every Sun. Universidad de Medellín theatre has monthly tango shows.
Theatre Teatro Metropolitano, C 41, No 57-30, T232 8536, major artistic presentations. Many other theatres of all types, check press.

⊛ Festivals and events

Medellín *p844, maps p843 and 844*
International Orchid Fair (Exposicion
Internacional de Orquídeas) in **Mar** held at the
Botanical Garden. **International Jazz Festival** in
Jul. Flower fair (Feria de las Flores/Desfile de
Silleteros) is held annually in the **1st week of
Aug** with spectacular parades and music, one of
the finest shows in Colombia.

⦿ Shopping

Medellín *p844, maps p843 and 844*
Bookshops La Anticuaria, C 49, No 47-46, T511
4969. Antique and secondhand books, including in
English, helpful. **Centro Colombo Americano**, Cra
45, No 53-24, T513 4444. Good selection of books
in English (including Footprint Handbooks).
Handicrafts There are *artesanía* shops
on the top of Cerro Nutibara and a small
handicrafts market at C 52 near Cra 46 with
many stalls. **Aluzia Correas y Cinturones**,
Oviedo Shopping Center, Poblado, Unicentro
Medellín, also in Bogotá, for a wide selection of
belts, US$10-30. **Mercado San Alejo**, Parque
Bolívar, open on the first Sat of every month
except Jan, and before Christmas on Sat and
Sun (handicrafts on sale at good prices). Good
shopping generally around Parque de Bolívar.
Many textile mills have discount clothing with
good bargains; ask at your hotel.
Maps Instituto Geográfico Agustín Codazzi,
Fundación Ferrocarril building, Cra 52, No 43-42,
T381 0561, office in the basement. Local and
national maps.

▲ Activities and tours

Medellín *p844, maps p843 and 844*
Bullfights At the bullring of La Macarena, C 44
and Cra 63, in Jan and Feb; cheapest US$12,
usually fully booked.
Dance classes Academia Dance, Cra 46, No
7-9, T266 1522. Salsa classes. **Black Sheep**
residents get 10% discount. Individual lessons
US$6, good reports.
Sports complex Estadio Atanasio Girardot,
Cra 74, C 50, football, baseball, velodrome, next
to the *Estadio* Metro station.
Trekking Instituto de Deportes y Recreación
(Inder), T260 6611. Organize walking tours
around Medellín on Sundays.

⊖ Transport

Medellín *p844, maps p843 and 844*
Air Airport information, T562 2828. Frequent
services to **Bogotá**, **Cartagena**, and all major

Colombian cities. Municipal airport: **Olaya
Herrera**, national flights only, 10 mins by taxi
from the centre with flights to **Quibdó** (change
here for **Nuquí**), **Bahía Solano**, **Pereira** etc,
with **Satena** and **Aires**.
Bus From **Terminal del Norte**, T230 8514:
To/from **Bogotá**, 8-12 hrs, US$20-22, every 30
mins or so, with 5 companies. To **Cartagena**,
12-15 hrs, by **Pullman** bus, US$40 (take food with
you, the stops tend to be at expensive
restaurants). To **Barranquilla**, 13-15 hrs by
Pullman, US$36. To **Turbo**, US$22 with Gómez
(the best), 10-11 hrs. From **Terminal del Sur**,
T361 1499: Frequent buses for **Cali**, Flota
Magdalena US$16, 10-12 hrs. Frequent buses
to **Manizales**, 6 hrs US$8, by Empresa Arauca.
To **Pereira**, 6-8 hrs, US$12 by Flota Occidental
Pullman. To **Popayán**, US$22, 12 hrs, Flota
Magadalena. To **Ipiales**, US$29, 22 hrs,
Expreso Bolivariano (takes Visa). To **Quibdó**,
12-13 hrs, US$14. To **San Agustín**, Rápidos
Tolima, 0600, US$34.
Metro Operates 0430-2300 weekdays,
0500-2200 Sun and holidays (see map). One
journey (anywhere on the system) US$0.28, two
US$0.50, 10 US$2.25.
Taxi Minimum charge US$1. Radio taxis:
Aerotaxi for international airport, T235 7171.

⦿ Directory

Medellín *p844, maps p843 and 844*
Banks Most banks in the business zones have
ATMs. Many accept international cards.
Bancolombia, in El Poblada, cash against
MasterCard, Amex, good rates for TCs and cash.
Many banks open late and on Sat. Main hotels
will cash TCs for residents when banks are closed,
but at less favourable rates. Most **casas de
cambio** are found in the shopping malls, eg CC
El Tesoro. **Bicycle repairs** C 60, No 52-37,
T521 5801, bicycle repair workshop.
Consulates France, Cra 49, No 44-94, Local
258, T576 0780, open Tue and Thu only.
Germany, Cra 43F, No 17-419, T262 1756. UK, Cra
42, No 53-26, Autopista Sur - Itagüi, T377 9966,
open 0900-1230. **Cultural centres** Centro
Colombo Americano, Cra 45, No 53-24, T513
4444. English classes, library, bookshop, films and
exhibitions. Alianza Francesa, Cra 49, No 44-94,
T576 0780. **Internet** Plenty of internet cafés in
El Poblado, travellers' hostals and most shopping
centres. **Language classes** Eafit University,
Cra 49, No 7 Sur 50, Av Las Vegas, T261 9500.
US$265 for 2½ months, 2 hrs a day, popular,
well-organized Spanish courses, good reports.
Medical services Hospital San Vicente de
Paul, C 64/Cra 51D, T444 1333, one of the best.
Clínica Soma, C 51, No 45-93, T576 8400, good

on earth ('dry' season: December to March). In the northern part of the department, the mountain ranges rise directly from the ocean to reach a height of about 500 m. Transport is limited to water routes along the Pacific coast from Buenaventura in the south and up the rivers. Road access is via two unpaved routes across the Cordillera Occidental, one from Medellín via Bolívar, the other from Pereira to the southeast via La Virginia and Pueblo Rico (see page 855).

Chocó is home to a number of indigenous groups, including the Embera, whose communities are based on hunting, fishing, and subsistence farming. The coastline is also dotted with poor black fishing communities. The main small tourist resorts are concentrated in Nuquí, Bahía Solano on the Pacific coast and the more developed and expensive resort of Capurganá on the Caribbean (see page 824). The best time to go to Chocó is when humpback whales visit the area (end of July-October). Hotels usually offer all-inclusive packages for a three-night stay and arrange boat transport to and from the airport. Along the Río San Juan, in the south, there is gold prospecting around the towns of Tadó and Istmina. The construction of a road to the mouth of the Río Tribugá, where a deep sea port is planned as an alternative to Buenaventura, is raising fears of serious threat to Chocó's unique environment. Precautions against malaria, yellow fever, and dengue are recommended.

Warning The Department of Chocó, especially the lower Atrato, remains a very dangerous area (guerrillas, paramilitaries, kidnappings, drug running). Much caution and detailed advance enquiry are recommended. See also warning on page 824.

Quibdó → Phone code: 94. Colour map 1, grid B2. Population: 131,000. Altitude: 50 m.

Quibdó is on the eastern bank of the Río Atrato. Prices are higher here than in central Colombia (higher still in the coastal villages), so it is a good place to get supplies. There is an interesting mural in the cathedral. Hordes of birds fly in to roost at dusk and there are magnificent sunsets, which locals watch from the waterfront promenade, El Malecón. The San Pacho festival (20 September-4 October) has parades, partying and a San Francisco de Asís procession.

The road to Manizales and Pereira begins in a very poor state. Most is through jungle with colourful butterflies, waterfalls and few people. 60 km south is Las Animas where there is a turning east to cross the San Juan, reaching **Tadó** (8 km from Las Animas). **F Hotel Macondo**, very basic but restaurant OK; at least one other *residencia* and good places to eat. After crossing into Risaralda Department, the road improves before reaching the Cauca Valley (see page 855).

Pacific Coast

On the Gulf of Tribugá, surrounded by estuaries, mangroves and virgin beaches, **Nuquí** is gaining popularity among Colombian sports fishermen and vacationers. A number of luxury homes have been built nearby. Several small restaurants on road to airport serve mostly fish. Shops are well stocked with basic goods, prices somewhat higher than in Quibdó. To the south lies the wide curve of Playa Olímpica. To the north is the even smaller hamlet of Tribugá, a splendid beach and the proposed site of a deep sea port (see above). About 50 km north of Nuquí along the coast, **El Valle** has the best bathing and surfing beaches in the area. Between Nuquí and El Valle is **Parque Nacional Ensenada de Utría**, home to two varieties of whales, corals, needlefish, and many other aquatic species. The surrounding hillsides are covered with pristine rainforest and there are several magnificent white sand beaches. Most hotels organize day trips to the Park, or you can hire a boat with a group from El Valle, takes 1½ hours, or from Nuquí. Boat prices start at US$150 and vary considerably, depending on time and number of passengers. Ask at hotels for information. Insist on a life jacket.

Bahía Solano → Phone code: 9816.

The town lies on a large bay set against jungle covered hills. As a resort, it gets quite busy during holiday periods (the whale season and Easter) when prices rise. Good bathing beaches may be reached by launch or by walking about 1½ hours at low tide (for example Playa Mecana. Be sure to return before the tide rises or you will be stranded). There are no ATMs in the town.

● Sleeping

Quibdó *p850*
There are many places to stay along C los Robles de los Hoteles, Roma district.
B Los Farallones, C 28, No 1-70. A/c, restaurant,

some rooms with balcony.
C Los Robles, C 28, No 1-88, T671 3712.
Central, reliable, with a restaurant and laundry service. Recommended.

E Residencia Darién, Cra 4, No 26-68, T671 2997. Bath, fan, space to park motorcycle.

Pacific Coast: Nuquí *p850*
Along the beach at the north end of town, there are several tourist hotels usually fully booked during the holiday period, best to make arrangements through travel agents in Medellín or Bogotá. Many up-market hotels offer all-inclusive packages for 2-4 nights.

C pp Lodge Piedra Piedra, Nuqui, Choco, http://www.piedrapiedra.com/ Price includes breakfast; also a range of all-inclusive packages including meals (**AL**). Organizes local tours, wood and thatched lodges, dorms and private rooms, sleeps 17, meals provided, use of kitchen.

E Palmas del Pacífico, T683 6010. Fan, private bath, wooden cabin, helpful. For airport pick-up, phone in advance.

E Rosio del Mar, Cra 42, No 8-43, T683 6016. Cabins with bath.

F Doña Jesusita, T683 6094, south end of town in Barrio Pueblo Nuevo. Basic, fan, restaurant. It is possible to stay in Nuquí and Bahía Solano cheaply if you rent a basic room in a family house, around US$10 pp. Ask locals or look for rent signs on windows. Negotiate prices during low season.

Near Nuquí
Cabañas Pijiba, T574-474 5221 or Medellín 234 3502, www.pijibalodge.com. Award-winning ecotourism development with full board. Comfortable wooden lodges with thatched roofs. Arranges guided trips, diving, forest walks, airport pick-up (45-min boat ride to hotel), from US$445 (higher at Easter) double for 3 nights, longer packages available.

Ecolodge Nautilos, Guachalito, Nuquí, www.nautiloslodge.com. From US$265 for 3 nights pp, includes transport to lodge, 3 meals, and 2 guided tours. Pleasant eco-lodge on beach. Rents surfing equipment.

Bahía Solano *p850*
AL El Almejal, T230 6060 reservations in Medellín, www.almejal.com.co. Upmarket resort, comfortable wooden cabins, restaurant, hammocks. Full board packages for 3-5 nights. Arranges boat trips to Utria for US$22pp return.

C Balboa Palacio Cra 2, No 6-73, T682 7075. Large, central, modern, bland, pool, boat service to bathing beaches, decent restaurant.

C pp Playa de Oro Lodge, Playa Huina, T682 7481. Beach lodge organizes tours including whale watching, jungle walks and fishing. Offers fully inclusive packages with 3 meals a day, **B** pp.

D-E Mr Jerry, Playa Huina. Hammocks cheaper, basic, boat trips, snorkelling available, meals.

E Bahía, C 3, No 2-40, T682 7047, in same street as Satena office. With fan and private bath, central, good restaurant.

E Hostal del Mar, across the street from Bahía, T682 7415. One block from the sea. The owner, Rodrigo, is helpful and knowledgeable and arranges excursions, guides and snorkelling. Private basic wooden lodges with mosquito nets and bath, meals extra.

Eating

Quibdó *p850*
♥ **Ricuras del Mar**, Cra 4, No 27-36. Good for seafood and fish.

♥♥ **Jairo Parrilla**, Cra 7 in town centre. Good for meat grills.

Transport

Quibdó *p850*
Air Flights daily to **Medellín**, **Bogotá** and nearby towns with **Satena**.

Bus Flota Occidental to **Medellín** via Pereira, daily at 0600, 13 hrs, US$22. It is unsafe to take a night bus to Medellín. Check with locals first before setting off, even during the day. Buses daily to **Manizales** and Pereira via Tadó, and La Virginia. Local service to Santa Cecilia and Tadó.

Ferry From Buenaventura up the Río San Juan to **Istmina** and on by road; services infrequent. Irregular cargo service down the Río Atrato to **Turbo** and more regular weekly services to **Cartagena**, both usually takes passengers. Enquire at the wharves about safety and deal directly with boat captains.

Pacific Coast: Nuquí *p850*
Air Satena flies **Medellín**-Quibdó-Nuquí Mon, Wed, Fri only, US$100, one way.

As yet there is no **road** access for regular vehicles to Nuquí. A rough road runs 18 km from El Valle to Bahía Solano (passes by airport before town). Jeeps leave every morning, 1 hr ride, US$4.50, tickets can be purchased 1 day in advance. There are early morning **launches** south to **Arusi** (Mon, Wed, Fri), and north to **El Valle** (Tue, Thu, Sat), as well as occasional coastal vessels (small fuel barges) to **Buenaventura**. Sea taxis will take you to beaches along the coast.

Bahía Solano *p850*
Air There are 6 flights a week (not Sun) from Medellín to Bahía Solano with Satena.

Daily **jeep** service to **El Valle** and frequent trucks during the day, US$4.50, 1 hr (see above). A regular boat service runs south to **Buenaventura**, US$40, 6-7hrs, and occasional, uncomfortable, coastal cargo vessels, 24 hrs. Irregular service north to **Juradó** with a cargo vessel.

ⓘ Directory

Quibdó *p850*
Banks Several ATMs. **Banco de Bogotá**, cash against Visa, other banks do not change money.

A few shopkeepers sometimes change US$ cash, but rates are poor. It is best to buy pesos before arriving. **Useful addresses** DAS Office: C 25, No 6-08, T671 1501. No entry or exit stamps.

La Zona Cafetera

Modern and colonial cities line the fertile western slopes of the Cordillera Central which is the centre of Colombia's coffee production. The three departments of Caldas, Quindío and Risaralda are generally known as the 'Zona Cafetera'. Much of the land here is between the critical altitudes for coffee of 800 m-1,800 m, and has the right balance of rain and sunshine. The area has beautiful rolling countryside of coffee plantations, interspersed with bamboo, plantain and banana trees. The best way to enjoy the Zona Cafetera is to stay on a coffee farm, where you can tour the plantations and see how coffee is produced at harvest time (October-December). And off course, there is excellent, fresh, coffee all year round. In recent years, the Zona Cafetera has been building a reputation as an adventure sports destination, including rafting, kayaking and canopying (whizzing across ravines on steel cables).

Manizales and around

Rich in coffee and flowers, Manizales is one of the principal starting points for excursions to the Parque Nacional Los Nevados, which, as its name suggests, is dominated by snow-capped mountains. Earthquakes and volcanoes have been a feature of this volatile region.

Manizales → *Phone code: 96. Colour map 1, grid B2. Population: 335,000. Altitude: 2,153 m.*

Manizales, 309 km from Bogotá, is dominated by its enormous concrete Cathedral and the Nevado del Ruiz volcano, which erupted so catastrophically in November 1985. It sits on a mountain saddle, which falls away sharply from the centre into the adjacent valleys. The climate is humid (average temperature is 17°C, and the annual rainfall is 3,560 mm), encouraging prodigious growth in the flowers that line the highways to the suburbs north and south. Frequently the city is covered in cloud. The best months of the year are from mid-December through to early March. The city looks down on the small town of Villa María, "the village of flowers", now almost a suburb.

Several earthquakes and fires have destroyed parts of the city over the years, so the architecture is predominantly modern with high-rise office and apartment blocks. Traditional architectural styles are still seen in the suburbs and the older sections of the city. The departmental **Gobernación** building, opposite the Cathedral in the Parque de Bolívar, is an imposing example of neocolonial architecture and a national monument. Inside are a tourist office and a local arts and crafts shop. The **bullring**, on Avenida Centenario, is an impressive copy of the traditional Moorish style. Along Avenida 12 de Octubre to the suburb of Chipre is a recreational park, providing a great view to the west and paragliding opportunities (well visited on Sunday); El Tanque, on the Avenida, is a popular landmark and viewpoint.

Banco de la República ⓘ *Cra 23, No 23-06 (behind the cathedral), 0800-1130, free,* has a gold museum with classical music concerts in the afternoon. **Universidad de Caldas** ⓘ *Mon-Fri 0800-1200, 1400-1800 (take a 'Fátima' bus to the University),* has a natural history museum with a selection of butterflies, moths and birds. The **Centro de Museos** ⓘ *Cra 23, No 58-65, T885 1374, Mon-Fri, 0800-1200, 1400-1600,* also part of Caldas University, has an art gallery and exhibitions on geology and archaeology. **La Galería del Arte** ⓘ *Av Santander at C 55,* has exhibitions of work, which can be bought, by local artists. **Tourist office Fomento y Turismo** ⓘ *C 31, No 22-47, T884 6211. Open Mon-Fri 0730-1200, 1400-1830.* See also Gobernación, above.

Parque Nacional Los Nevados

This is a park with all the wild beauty of the high Cordillera, with mountains (snowcapped above 4,850 m), dormant volcanoes, hot springs and recent memories of tragic eruptions. The park comprises 58,000 ha and straddles the departments of Caldas, Quindío, Risaralda, and Tolima.

Visitors should come prepared for cold, damp weather, and remember to give themselves time to acclimatize to the altitude. See under Ibagué, page 857, for Nevado del Tolima.

Information Oficina del Parque de Los Nevados① *C 76B, No 18-14, Manizales, T/F886 4104*, for general information on visits and entrance fees. If you intend to do some serious mountain climbing and or mountain biking, you need to apply in writing to the above office, 5 days in advance. Book accommodation in the Park at the **Aviatur** office in Manizales① *C 56, No. 23-16, T886 6300*. The tourist office in Manizales can put you in touch with agencies who organize day trips to Nevado del Ruiz, usually only at weekends (US$35 for 1 day, for transport, guide, entrance fees, return via hot pools). Trips can be arranged with guides and extended to the Parque Nacional de los Nevados and Nevado del Tolima. **Mountain House**, a traveller hostel in Manizales, is an excellent source of information about trips to Los Nevados and provides maps. Maps are also available at the **Instituto Geográfico** in Manizales① *C 24, No 25-15, T884 5864*.

The recommended route to visit **Nevado del Ruiz** (5,400 m) with a vehicle is to take the Bogotá road from Manizales, to La Esperanza (22 km). Leave the main road here to the right for excursions towards the volcano. For an alternative, shorter route (4WD only), make for the Barrio La Anea (next to the airport) continuing on an unpaved, rough road for 22 km. This leads first to the hot pools of **Termales de Otoño**① *US$15*, then towards La Gruta, followed by the hot pools at **Termales del Ruiz** at 3,400 m. Both hot pools have hotels attached (T874 0280). 7 km further on, this road meets the road coming from La Esperanza. Turning right, and continuing 2 km brings you to Las Brisas (small restaurant 2 km beyond). You can walk from Las Brisas down to Manizales in 8 hours, start early and stop on the way at *Hotel Termales del Ruiz* (see Sleeping).

Past Las Brisas the road forks. To the left it continues over enormous landslides caused by the 1985 Nevado del Ruiz eruption, to the village of Ventanas (a very scenic drive) and on to Murillo in the department of Tolima. To the right it climbs steeply for 1 km to reach the **park entrance and visitors' centre**① *US$10, vehicle US$2, open 0700-1430*, at 4,050 m. In 4 km at 4,150 m is *Chalet Arenales* (see Sleeping). The turnoff (left) to Nevado del Ruiz is 10 km beyond the park entrance and you can drive to within 2 km of the snow line. On foot from 4,050 m to the summit takes six to seven hours if you are acclimatized. At 4,800 m, there is a basic hut, no water, no beds nor any facilities, but there may be refreshments during the day. Ask at the entrance if it is open. From here, it is about three hours to the summit. An authorized guide is obligatory if you wish to climb from the snowline to the crater (beware of fumaroles of toxic gas). Another climb nearby is La Olleta (4,850 m), the ash cone of an extinct volcano. You can go into the crater, but note your route well as fog can obliterate landmarks quickly. The road continues (south) below the Nevados del Cisne and de Santa Isabel (4,950m) between which you can visit the Laguna Verde. A guide to Santa Isabel costs US$53 for a day. Four-wheel drive vehicles are necessary beyond Nevado del Ruiz. 20 km further along the road and 39 km beyond the turnoff to Nevado del Ruiz is Laguna del Otún at the southern end of the park, trout fishing and camping with permission of *MA*. **Note** There are no kitchen facilities or meals at Laguna del Otún.

The main road from Manizales to Bogotá goes east to Honda (see page 797). It passes through **Mariquita** (21 km before Honda), in fruit-growing country. From Mariquita a road turns south to (32 km) **Armero**, which was devastated by the eruption of the Nevado del Ruiz volcano in November 1985. Over 25,000 people were killed as approximately 10% of the ice core melted, causing landslides and mudflows. (Armero can be reached by colectivo from Honda; nearest lodging at **Lérida**, 12 km south.)

⬤ **Sleeping**

Manizales *p852*
During the popular Feria de Manizales in Jan prices rise. **F-G** range hotels around C 18, Cra 22-23.
A Las Colinas, Cra 22, No 20-20, T884 2009, F884 1590. Just off Plaza Bolívar, modern, business centre, sauna, bars and restaurant.
B-C Escorial, C 21, No 21-11, T884 7696, F884 7722. Nicely decorated, central, restaurant.
C Camino Real, Cra 21, No 20-45, F884 6131, hotelesmanizales@yahoo.com. Central, helpful and pleasant.

D Tamá Internacional, C 23, No 22-43, T884 2124, next to Cathedral. With bath, popular lunchtime restaurant, good but noisy.
E Avenida, C 19, No 16-33, T884 2098. Opposite bus station, clean, cheaper without bath, TV.
E California, C 19, No 16-37, T884 7720. Opposite bus station, modern, small rooms, TV, laundry facilities, safe, car parking, helpful owner speaks English, internet café, help with trips to Los Nevados.

E Rokasol, C 21, No 19-16, T884 2084. Hot water, good restaurant, good reports.

F Mountain House, C 65, No 24-97, Avenida Lindzay, Barrio Guayacanes, T887 4736. Near Zona Rosa (bar district). Popular, homely travellers' hostel, includes breakfast, kitchen and laundry facilities, hammocks, TV room, book exchange, bike rental, hot showers, free coffee, restaurant. Dorms and 2 rooms with bath. Excellent information about trips to Los Nevados and coffee farms. Recommended.

Parque Nacional Los Nevados *p852*
Apart from the hotels at the Termas del Ruiz and Termas del Otoño (see above):

F pp El Cisne, run by MA, 22 km from Las Brisas, ask at Aviatur (see above). 1 cabin, US$10-12pp.

G Refugio Arenales, 4 km from the park entrance at 4,150 m. No rooms available, only camping facilities, US$1.30 pp, and toilets.

Camping available in the park **G**. Breakfast, lunch and dinner available, US$2-3. Advance reservations recommended.

🍴 Eating

Manizales *p852*
₹₹ El Balcón del Arriero, Cra 23, No 26-18. Good local dishes, reasonable prices.

₹₹ Las Brasas, Cra 23, No 75A-65. Good grill and *comida típica*.

₹₹ Fonda Paisa, Cra 23, No 72-130. Nice local dishes with local Andean music.

₹₹ Las Redes, Cra 23, No 75-97. Predominantly seafood, good but pricey.

₹ Caballo Loco, Cra 61, No 23-07. Good. Another with the same name at C 21, No 23-40 is mainly a bar but serves good pizzas.

🎭 Entertainment

Manizales *p852*
Cinema and theatre Centro Cultural y Convenciones los Fundadores has interesting wood-carved mural by Guillermo Botero, who also has murals in the *Club Manizales* and *Hotel Las Colinas*. Events held here and at other locations during Jazz and Theatre Festival in **Sep/Oct**. Free films at the *Universidad Nacional*, on Tue and Thu.

🎉 Festivals and events

Manizales *p852*
The **Feria de Manizales** held in early **Jan** includes a coffee festival, bullfights, beauty

parades and folk dancing as well as general partying.

▲ Activities and tours

Parque Nacional Los Nevados *p852*
Ecosistemas, Cra 21, No 23-21, Manizales, T880 8300. Charges US$35 for group of 4 to Los Nevados for a day. Trips normally arranged only at weekends. Longer trips to Los Nevados can be arranged.

Mountain House (see Sleeping, above) organizes a 1-day trip to Los Nevados for US$35pp. Includes transport, entrance to thermal baths and breakfast. Good reports. Trips leave most days from the hostel, minimum 6 people, non-hostel guests welcome.

🚍 Transport

Manizales *p852*
Air Avianca and Aires fly to **Bogotá**.
Bus Terminal with good restaurant, C 19 between Cras 15 and 17, T884 9183. Buses to **Medellín**: via Neira and Aguadas, 6 hrs, US$8; via Anserma, 10 hrs; 1st class US$8; colectivo to Medellín, US$10. Frequent buses to **Bogotá**, Pullman, Bolivariana, US$18, 7-9 hrs; *buseta*, US$13. To **Honda**, US$8. **Cali**, hourly, 6-7 hrs, US$13. **Pereira**, ¼-hourly, 1½ hrs, excellent road, beautiful scenery, US$3.50. **Armenia**, 3 hrs, US$7. To **Quibdó**, via Pereira, 14-17 hrs, US$18.

Parque Nacional Los Nevados *p852*
As the park entrance closes at 1430, it is advisable to start your journey to the park early in the morning. For those without transport, it is possible to catch a daily *chiva* which leaves opposite El Casino de Suboficiales del Batallón Ayacucho between 0430-0500, US$2.20. For further information contact **Mountain House Hostel** or Victor who runs the *chiva*, T880 9891, T311-380 0796 (mob). The **Rápido Tolima** bus daily, usually 1400, from the Terminal in Manizales to Murillo passes near the entrance to the Park, US$3, 2½ hrs. See under Pereira for access from there.

① Directory

Manizales *p852*
Banks Banks are along Cra 23. **Useful addresses** DAS Office: C 53, No 25A-35, T885 1616, Mon-Fri, 0730-1200, 1400-1400.

Pereira to Cartago

Still in the shadow of the Nevados, this is a region of modern cities (in several cases rebuilt after earthquakes), delightful scenery and a number of botanical parks and gardens. Coffee is still by far the most important agricultural product of the area, but there has been a good deal of diversification into other crops as varied as flowers, asparagus and even bamboo. Recently, coffee farms have been opening up to tourism, from day visits to overnight stays. No two fincas are the same; they range from beautiful historic country mansions to more modest accommodation options.

Pereira → *Phone code: 96. Colour map 1, grid B3. Population: 432,000. Altitude: 1,476 m.*

Capital of Risaralda Department and 56 km southwest of Manizales, Pereira stands within sight of the *Nevados* of the Cordillera Central. A severe earthquake on 5 February 1995 badly damaged several buildings and the city was also affected by the earthquake which devastated Armenia in 1999 (see below). Pereira is a pleasant modern city, founded in 1863. The central **Plaza de Bolívar**, is noted for the striking sculpture of a nude Bolívar on horseback, by Rodrigo Arenas Betancur. There are other fine works of his in the city. The **Cathedral** is unimpressive from the outside but has an elegant and interesting interior. The **Museo Quimbaya de Oro y La Cerámica** ① *in the Banco de la República building, Av 30 de Agosto/C 35*, is worth a short visit. The botanical garden, on the campus of Universidad Tecnológica de Pereria ① *T321 2523, US$4.50, Mon-Sat, 0700-1600, must book a visit in advance and use a guide*, is good for bird watching and has bamboo forests and 2-hour nature walks.

Tourist information: **Oficina de Fomento al Turismo** ① *Cra 7, No 18-55, 6th floor, T324 8030*. **Corporación Autónomo Regional de Risaralda** (Carder) ① *Avenida de las Américas, C 46, T314 1456*, has information but does not deal with park permits. Contact **Aviatur** ① *Av.30 de Agosto, No.34-38 L1/15, T3263630, http://site.aviatur.com*, for park permits. **Turiscafé** ① *C 19, No 5-48, office 901 (inside Novacentro shopping centre), T325 4157/58*, for good information on coffee farms in Risaralda.

Fifteen kilometres from Pereira is **Santa Rosa de Cabal**, from where several thermal pools can be reached, including Termales de Santa Rosa/Los Arbeláez ① *0800-2400, US$8*. An 9 km unpaved road from Santa Rosa leads to the hot baths (early morning *chiva* or taxi, US$9 to entrance). The Termales de Santa Rosa are surrounded by forests, with waterfalls and nature walks. It's packed at the weekend, quiet during the week. **Hotel Termales de Santa Rosa de Cabal** (attached to the hot baths, **A**), *T364 1322*, comfortable, chalet style, with restaurant. Further along this road, midway between Pereira and Manizales is **Chinchiná**, in the heart of the coffee zone. A coffee hacienda which takes day-visitors is **Finca Guayabal** ① *entry US$10, T06-840 1847, http://guayabal.tripod.com*, with a nature trail, full explanations of the coffee-growing process and lunch, US$12.

Northwest of Pereira, 30 km towards the Río Cauca, is **Marsella**, and the **Alexander von Humboldt Gardens**, a carefully maintained botanical display with cobbled paths and bamboo bridges. Just outside the town is the **AL Ecohotel Los Lagos** *T368 6529, www.ecohotelloslagos.com*, previously a gold mine, then a coffee *hacienda*, and now restored as a hotel and nature park with lakes.

Parque Ucumari

From Pereira it is possible to visit the beautiful **Parque Ucumari** ① *park office, T06-325 4781, open daily for good information. If you're just visiting for the day and not staying overnight, entrance is free*, one of the few places where the Andean spectacled bear survives. From Pereria, a *chiva* leaves daily (0900, 1500, more frequently during high season) with Transporte Florida from C12, No 9-40 to the village of El Cedral. From El Cedral it is a 2-2½ hour walk to *La Pastora*, the park visitors' centre and refuge. There is excellent camping, US$2.20 per person or US$6 at a refuge, meals extra. From La Pastora it is a steep, rocky 1-2 day hike to Laguna de Otún through beautiful scenery of changing vegetation (see page 853). The **Otún Quimbaya** flora and fauna sanctuary forms a biological corridor between Ucumari and Los Nevados; it protects the last remaining area of Andean tropical forest in Risaralda. There are marked paths as well as *cabaña* accommodation, camping and meals available.

Pereira to Armenia

A 44 km road runs through the heart of the *Zona Cafetera*. A turn off at the *Posada Alemana* goes east for 9 km to **Salento** *(Phone code 96; Population 3,500; Altitude 1,985 m)*, well into the foothills of the Cordillera. This small town is brightly painted with an attractive plaza. Up Carrera 6 (continuation of the north side of the plaza) is a 250-step climb, 14 stations of the cross to measure your progress, to an outstanding viewpoint, overlooking the upper reaches of the Quindío and Cárdenas rivers known as the Cocora valley, one of the finest views in Colombia. It is a popular weekend resort for Colombians for walking, riding and trekking but quiet during the week. There are several places to eat and to stay, ask around, but make arrangements early in the day. There are handicraft shops around the plaza. Fiesta is in the first week of January.

Valle de Cocora

The centre of the Cocora valley is 12 km up from Salento along a rough track, a picturesque 2-hour walk, or by jeep, 45 minutes, US$1.20, leave daily, 0730 from the main plaza, return 1700, more frequent services at weekends. Three restaurants (*Las Orillas, Las Palmas* and *Bosque de Cocora*) serve food at weekends, check in Salento during the week. Contact the **Plantation House** in Salento (see Sleeping) for details of day-treks in the valley. Some 5 km beyond Cocora at 2,770 m is the **Acaime Natural Reserve** with visitor centre, ponies for hire, beds for 20 and a small restaurant. There are humming birds, cloud forest and the most important area of wax palm (the national tree and one of the tallest trees of the world). In January is the Wax Palm Festival.

Armenia → *Phone code: 96. Colour map 1, grid B2. Population: 220,000. Altitude: 1,838 m.*

The capital of Quindío Department was founded in 1889. In January 1999, an earthquake flattened much of the city and parts of the surrounding department were also badly damaged. Impressive resurrection continues and Armenia is as busy as ever. The fine example of Rodrigo Arenas Betancur's work, the **Monumento al Esfuerzo**, in the Plaza de Bolívar poignantly portrays the spirit of the local people. The two main churches, the cathedral and San Francisco church were both badly damaged but have reopened to the public. The **Museo Quimbaya** ① *Avenida Bolivar, C 40 norte, US$ 0.45*, houses a well-displayed collection of ceramics and textiles of the Quimbaya indigenous group. There is also the **Museo del Oro Quimbaya** ① *Banco de República, Cra 23, No 23-14, Tues-Sat, 0900-1630, Sun and holidays, 1000- 1630*. **Parque de la Vida**, in the north of the city has bamboo structures, waterfalls and a lakeside theatre.

Near Calarca, 6 km from Armenia, is **Jardín Botánico y Mariposario** ① *T742 7254, Tues-Sun 0900-1600, US$3.50, children half price*, a huge covered butterfly house, with some 50 species of butterflies. There is also an insect zoo and forest walks.

Parque Nacional del Café

Some 12 km northwest of Armenia is **Montenegro**, near which is Pueblo Tapao (4 km) and the **Parque Nacional del Café** ① *T741 7417, in high season, daily 0900-1600, low season, Wed-Sun and public holidays, 0900-1600, general entrance, US$5.50, or US$12-21 for additional activities and rides, parking US$1; take a bus or colectivo (US$0.45) from Armenia to Montenegro and then a jeep marked 'Parque' (US$0.25) or taxi (US$2) to the entrance.* There are restaurants, a Juan Valdez coffee shop, a botanical garden, ecological walks, a Quimbaya Indian cemetery, a tower with a fine view and an interesting museum which covers all aspects of coffee. A cableway links to a children's theme park (roller coasters, water rides etc). Beyond Montenegro is **Quimbaya.** 7 km away is a large **Panaca**, an educational theme park ① *T758 2830, Tue-Sun 0900-1800, US$18*, with many varieties of horses (and a very good show/display), cattle and other animals. A good family outing.

Ibagué and around → *Phone code: 98. Colour map 1, grid B2. Population: 347,000.*

Quindío Pass, 3,350 m (known as *La Línea* after the power lines that cross the mountains) is on the Armenia to Ibagué road (105 km), across the Cordillera Central. On the east side of the Pass is **Cajamarca**, a friendly town in a beautiful setting at 1,900 m (**F** *Residencia Central*; *Nevado*, both on same street). *Bar El Globo*, on corner of the main plaza serves excellent coffee. Interesting market on Sunday.

Ibagué (*Altitude: 1,248 m*), capital of Tolima Department, lies at the foot of the Quindío mountains. Parts of the town are old: see the Colegio de San Simón and the market (good tamales). The Parque Centenario is pleasant and there is a famous Conservatory of Music. Try the local alcoholic drink called *mistela*.

Just outside, on the Armenia road, a dirt road leads up the Río Combeima to El Silencio and the slopes of the **Nevado del Tolima**, the southernmost '*nevado*' in the **Parque Nacional Los Nevados**. The climb to the summit (5,221 m) takes two to three days, camping at least one night over 4,000 m, ice equipment necessary. For safety reasons, it is recommended to visit the Nevado del Tolima only from Ibagué and not Manizales. A milk truck (*lechero*) leaves Ibagué marketplace for El Silencio between 0630 and 0730, US$2.50, two hours. A guide in Ibagué is: **Maklin Muñoz**, Cra 1, No 5-24, T261 5865, T300-675 6216 (mob).

Cartago → *Phone code: 92. Colour map 1, grid B2. Population: 130,000. Altitude: 920 m.*

From Pereira and Armenia roads run west to Cartago, at the northern end of the rich Cauca Valley, which stretches south for about 240 km but is little more than 30 km wide. The road, the Panamericana, goes south along this valley to Cali and Popayán, at the southern limit of the valley proper. There it mounts the high plateau between the Western and Central Cordilleras and goes through to Ecuador.

Founded in 1540, Cartago, 25 km southwest of Pereira, still has some colonial buildings, particularly the very fine **Casa del Virrey**, Calle 13, No 4-29, and the **cathedral**. Cartago is noted for its fine embroidered textiles.

⬤ Sleeping

Pereira *p855*

AL Hotel de Pereria, Cra 13, No 15-73, T335 0770, F335 0675. Best in town, comfortable, pool, sauna, conference centre, travel agency, all services.
B Gran, C 19, No 9-19, T335 9500, F335 7798. Including breakfast, older hotel, good restaurant, bar, travel agency, well managed. Recommended.
D Cataluña, C 19, No 8-61, T335 4527, F333 0791. 2 floors up, hot water, spacious.
D Marandúa, Cra 8, No 14-73, T335 7131, F333 4081. Central, restaurant. Recommended.
E Residencias Minerva, C 18, No 7-32, T333 4493. Central, safe, TV.

Coffee farms

There are dozens of coffee farms to stay at in the region. Coffee fincas range from huge traditional haciendas to smaller, more modern farms.
C pp El Bosque del Samán, Alcalá-Vereda La Cana, T336 5589, www.fincahotelelbosque.com. 26 km from Pereira, 27 km from Armenia. Claims to have the longest canopy run in Colombia (US$14 pp). Pool, hammocks, interactive farm, tour. Good.
D Finca Villa María, 12 km from Pereira, via Marsella, follow the signs, turning before La Bodega, unpaved 3-km road, T333 8977/3410, 315-530 1385 (mob). 25 mins taxi from Pereria, US$9. Charming typical coffee *hacienda* set in beautiful countryside. Large rooms, peaceful, full board. Pool, coffee plantations tours. Recommended.
D Villa Marta, from Pereria, via Marsella Km 9, Corregimiento Combia, via La Convención, T329 9261, 310-421 5920 (mob). Modern *finca* with bamboo decor, pool and lovely gardens. Comfortable rooms, excellent service, includes breakfast and dinner. Free pick-ups from airport/bus terminal in Pereria. Serves probably the best coffee in La Zona Cafetera.

Pereira to Armenia: Salento *p856*

C La Posada del Café, Cra 6, No 3-08, T759 3012. Breakfast, pleasant patio, helpful.
F pp Plantation House, C 7, No 1-04, T759 3403, www.hosteltrail.com/plantationhouse/index.shtm. Colombian owned hostel with typical rustic features in the heart of the coffee zone, with breakfast, free coffee, book exchange, laundry service, already building up a good reputation as "perfect for travellers", beautiful quiet rural setting, helpful with lots of information. Recommended.

Armenia *p856*

C Castillo Real, C 21, No 15-51, T744 5144. Central, with breakfast, small hotel, cafeteria.
D Maitamá, C 21 No 16-45, T741 0488. With breakfast, central. Recommended.
F Los Viajeros, Cra 18, No 17-22, T744 2039. With bath, laundry service, cooking facilities, restaurant.
F Moderno Aristi, C 18, No 19-67, T744 1286. Cheaper without bath, TV, cold water.

Parque Nacional del Café: Montenegro *p856*

C Hostal de la Vega, 200 m from Parque del Café, T741 5091, www.hostaldelavega.com.co. Bungalows for 2, includes breakfast, hot water.

Ibagué *p856*

B Ambala, C 11, No 2-60, T261 3888, F263 3490. With breakfast, TV, pool, sauna, parking, restaurant.
F Sandremo, C 16, No 2-88, T261 3339. Fan, TV.

Cartago *p857*

Many hotels in area around bus terminals (Cra 9) and railway station (Cra 9 y C 6).
C Don Gregorio, Cra 5, No 9-59, T211 5111. A/c, pool, sauna, cheaper with fan, includes breakfast.
F Río Pul, Diag 3, No 2-142, T211 0623. With fan and bath, TV. Recommended.

🍴 Eating

Pereira *p855*

Good restaurants on Av 30 de Agosto (the road west to the airport), and east on Av Circunvalar.

🍴 **El Mesón Español**, C 14, No 25-57. Spanish food.

🍴 **Mama Flor**, Barrio Los Alpes. Typical food, good.

🍴-🍴 **Pizza Piccolo**, Av Circunvalar going east C 5, La Terraza. Good Italian food and pizzas. Recommended. Other restaurants in same block.

🍴 **Mister Chuleta**, C 5 y Cra 17, Pinares. Decent, good value *comida corriente*, good service. Others on same block.

Pastelería Lucerna, C 19, No 6-49. Large coffee shop, fountain/garden, good cakes, snacks, ice cream, clean.

Salento *p856*

🍴🍴-🍴 **El Portal de Cocora**, 100m from Salento Vía Cocora, T759 3190. Memorable views, good food and atmosphere, try the trout. Recommended. Open Fri-Sun. Owners rent out 2 comfortable cabins opposite the restaurant, **A**.

🍴-🍴 **El Rincón de Lucía**, Calle Real. Popular, good.

🍴 **La Fonda de los Arrieros**, on Plaza, next to police station. Local dishes, good value, popular.

Armenia *p856*

🍴🍴🍴 **La Fogata**, Av Bolívar No 14N-39, T749 5980. International, expensive but good.

🍴🍴🍴-🍴 **Casa Verde**, Cra 14 No 11A-25, T746 6093. Seafood and meat dishes, good.

🍴🍴 **Asadero Sierra Dorada**, Cra 14 No 1-160. Good meat dishes.

🍴🍴-🍴 **Cafetería Barú**, Av Bolívar, No 22N-05. Light meals, salads, ice-cream.

Pastelería Lucerna, C 20, No 14-43. Light meals, good quality.

Ibagué *p856*

🍴🍴 **La Vieja Enramada**, Cra 8, No 15-03. Local and international dishes.

🍴🍴-🍴 **El Fogón Antioqueño**, Cra 6, No 26-03. Good local dishes.

❊ Festivals and events

Ibagué *p856*

National Folklore Festival, in **Jun**. The Departments of Tolima and Huila commemorate San Juan (**24 Jun**) and SS Pedro y Pablo (**29 Jun**) with bullfights, fireworks, and music. There are choral festivals biannually in **Dec**.

⛰ Activities and tours

Pereira *p855*

D'p@seo, Cra 13, No 14-60, local 109, T334 9883, www.dpaseo.com. Opposite **Hotel Pereira**.

Arranges weekend trips to Los Nevados, trips on Río la Vieja. Mon-Sat 0800-1200, 1400-1900.

Armenia *p856*

Territorio Aventura, Av Bolívar, No 14N-80, of 207, T749 9568, www.territorioaventura.com. Organize kayaking, rafting, fishing trips.

⊖ Transport

Pereira *p855*

Air Matecaña airport is 5 km to the south, bus, US$0.25. Daily flights to **Miami**, **Bogotá**, **Cali** and **Ibagué**; less frequent to other cities.

Bus Terminal is 1½ km south of city centre, stores luggage. Bus to **Armenia**, 1 hr, US$2, a beautiful trip. To **Cali**, US$8, 4½-5 hrs, colectivo by day, bus by night, same price. To **Medellín**, 6-8 hrs, US$10. To/from **Bogotá**, US$10-12, 7 hrs (route is via Girardot, Ibagué – both cities bypassed – and Armenia).

Pereira to Armenia: Salento *p856*

Bus To **Armenia** every 20 mins 0600-2000, US$1, 40 mins. To **Pereira**, 4 a day at weekends and public holidays, US$2.50, 1 hr. Jeep to **Cocora** valley US$8, or US$1.20 if you get a scheduled service.

Armenia *p856*

Air El Edén, 13 km from city. Daily flights to **Bogotá** and **Medellín** with Aires. Fog can delay flights.

Bus Terminal at C 35, No 20-68. To **Ibagué**, US$5.50, 2½ hrs. To **Bogotá**, hourly, 7-9 hrs, US$15. To **Neiva**, US$12, 8 hrs. **Cali**, US$7, 3 hrs, frequent.

Ibagué *p856*

Air Daily Aires flights to **Bogotá**, **Cali** and **Medellín**, also to **Pereira.**

Bus Terminal is between Cras 1-2 and C 19-20. Tourist police at terminal helpful. Frequent services to **Bogotá**, US$8, 4 hrs. To **Neiva**, US$8-9, 3 hrs, and many other places.

Cartago *p857*

Bus To **Cali**, US$7, 3½ hrs. To **Armenia**, US$2, 2½-3 hrs. To **Pereira**, US$1.50, 45 mins. To **Medellín**, US$12, 7 hrs.

❶ Directory

Pereira *p855*

Banks Banks around Plaza de Bolívar. Most have ATMs that take foreign cards. *Casas de cambio* change cash and some exchange TCs: several around Cra 9/C 18.

Salento *p856*

Banks One bank which gives cash advance against Visa card, no ATM, cash or TC exchange.

Cali and the Cauca Valley

The narrow Cauca valley has as its focus Cali, the country's southern industrial centre but at the same time one of Colombia's party hotspots. Cali calls itself the Salsa capital of the world, and few would dispute that claim. The region is served by the Pacific port of Buenaventura. 56 km off the coast is the high-security prison turned national park of Gorgona Island.

Cali → *Phone code: 92. Colour map 1, grid B2. Population: 1,780,000. Altitude: 1,030 m.*

Cali, Colombia's third city and capital of the Valle del Cauca Department, is the country's self-declared salsa capital. So if you're looking for *la rumba* and wanting to join swinging salsa couples on the dance floor, Cali should not to be missed. Sensuous, tropical rhythms are ubiquitous, seeming to seep from every part of the city's being. Cali's other more contentious claim is that it boasts the most beautiful girls in the country (though Medellín may beg to differ). The region is set in a rich agricultural area producing sugar, cotton, rice, coffee and cattle. Cali was founded in 1536, and until 1900 was a leisurely colonial town. Then the railway came, and Cali is now a rapidly expanding industrial complex serving the whole of southern Colombia.

Ins and outs
Getting there Palmaseca **airport** is 20 km from city. It has *casa de cambio*. **Bus Terminal** is at C 30N, No 2A-29, 25 minutes walk from the centre (leave terminal by the taxi stands, take first right, go under railway and follow river to centre). Hotel information available, left luggage US$0.60 per item, good food at terminal. Bus information, T668 3655. *Casa de cambio*, cash only. Showers on second level (US$0.40). Buses between the bus station and the centre, US$0.30. Taxi from centre to bus station, US$1.50. ➤ *For further information, see also Transport, page 862.*

Getting around Ensure that taxi meters are used. Prices, posted in the window, start at US$0.30. Extra charge on holidays, Sun and at night. Although the atmosphere in Cali is quite relaxed, carry your passport (or photocopy) at all times and be prepared for police checks. Cali has some rough parts, particularly east or south of Cra 10 and C 15, and caution is needed when walking around the city, especially at night.

Tourist offices Secretaría de Cultura y Turismo ① *Gobernación del Valle del Cauca building, p 2, T620 0063/64.* See also www.caliescali.com (news, chat, entertainment, music and tourist information on *La Guía* pages).

Sights
The city's centre is the **Plaza de Caicedo**, with a statue of one of the independence leaders, Joaquín Caicedo y Cuero. Facing the plaza is the elegant **Palacio Nacional** and the **Cathedral**, seat of the influential Archbishop of Cali. Nearby is the renovated church and 18th-century monastery of **San Francisco** with a splendidly proportioned domed belltower. Cali's oldest church, **La Merced** ① *Calle 7, between Cras 3 and 4,* has been restored by the Banco Popular. The adjoining convent houses two museums: **Museo de Arte Colonial** (closed but the nuns may let you in) and the **Museo Arqueológico** ① *Mon-Sat 0900-1300, 1400-1800, US$1,* with pre-Columbian pottery. Another church worth seeing is the Gothic-style **La Ermita**, on the river between Calles 12 and 13. **Museo del Oro** (also called Museo Calima) ① *Calle 7, No 4-69, Banco de la República building, Mon-Sat 0800-1800, free,* has pre-Columbian gold work and pottery.

The **Museo de Arte Moderno La Tertulia** ① *Av Colombia, No 5-105 Oeste, Tue-Sun 1000-1800, US$1.80, children half price,* exhibits South American, including local, modern art. To view the city, take a taxi to the **Monumento Las Tres Cruces**, northwest of the city, or to the **Monumento Cristo Rey**, 1,470 m, to the west of the city. The huge statue of Christ can be seen 50 km away across the Río Cauca. The neighbourhood of **San Antonio** (located behind the **Intercontinental Hotel**) is the city's oldest area, where Cali's colonial past can still be felt. The area has a relaxed, bohemian atmosphere, especially at weekends when it's livelier. There are good views of the city from the 18th century church of San Antonio.

● Sleeping

Cali *p859, map p860*

AL Intercontinental, Av Colombia, No 2-72, T882 3225, www.intercontinental.com. Modern, central, pleasant, includes breakfast, tennis courts, pool, restaurants, good buffets.

A-C Aparta Hotel Del Río, C 21N, No 2N-05, T660 2707, www.apartahoteldelrio.com. Comfortable, various suites and rooms with good facilities (gym, sauna, pool, laundry), safe, internet, good restaurant, parking.

B Aristi, Cra 9, No 10-04, T882 2521, www.hotel aristi.com.co. Weekend discounts and for stays over 5 days, cheaper with fan, art-deco style, turkish baths, rooftop pool, restaurant, central.

B Don Jaime, Av 6N, No 15N-25, T667 2828. Good location, modern, spacious rooms, with breakfast.

B Hostal Casa Republicana, C 7 No 6-74, T896 0949, F896 0840. Colonial house, nicely decorated, comfortable rooms, with breakfast, cable TV, restaurant, patio café. Recommended.

C Hostal San Fernando, C 3, No 27-87, T556 4820, near Parque del Perro (off map). Safe, pleasant, converted house, English spoken.

C Pensión Stein, Av 4N, No 3-33, T661 4927, www.hotelstein.com.co. Also houses the Swiss Embassy, run by very helpful Swiss consul, who speaks French, German and English. With breakfast, family-oriented, quiet, very safe, excellent food, small swimming pool, Alpine feel, parking. Recommended.

C Royal Plaza, Cra 4, No 11-69, T883 9243. On Plaza de Caicedo, good cheap rooftop restaurant with lovely views of the city, comfortable spacious rooms, nice atmosphere, credit cards accepted. Recommended.

D Astoria Real, C11, No 5-16, T883 0140, F880 5045. On corner of Plaza de Caicedo. Decent, bright, comfortable rooms, laundry.

D Plaza Cali, Cra 6, No 10-29, T882 2560. Modern, large rooms, can change money when manager is around, credit cards accepted, laundry, luggage stored, restaurant.

E-F Iguana, C 21N, No 9N-22, T661 3522. Dorms and other options, rooms with 2-3 beds, some with bath, nice patio area. Urs, the helpful Swiss manager, is a great source of local information. Laundry, internet, luggage store, kitchen facilities, motorcycle parking, excursions, language, paragliding and salsa classes arranged, good travellers' guesthouse, safe area. Recommended.

Cali

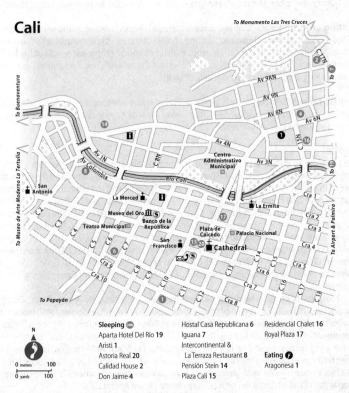

To Monumento Las Tres Cruces

To Buenaventura

To Museo de Arte Moderno La Tertulia

San Antonió

La Merced

Museo del Oro

Banco de la República

Teatro Municipal

San Francisco

Plaza de Caicedo

Palacio Nacional

Cathedral

La Ermita

Centro Administrativo Municipal

Av Colombia

Río Cali

Av 1N

Av 8N

Av 4N

Av 3N

Av 9AN

Av 9N

Av 8N

Av 6N

To Airport & Palmira

To Popayán

N

0 metres 100
0 yards 100

Sleeping ●
Aparta Hotel Del Río **19**
Aristi **1**
Astoria Real **20**
Calidad House **2**
Don Jaime **4**

Hostal Casa Republicana **6**
Iguana **7**
Intercontinental &
La Terraza Restaurant **8**
Pensión Stein **14**
Plaza Cali **15**

Residencial Chalet **16**
Royal Plaza **17**

Eating ●
Aragonesa **1**

F Calidad House, C 17N, No 9AN-39, T/F661 2338. Dorms and private rooms, recently renovated. Safe location, kitchen, laundry, will store luggage, pleasant, popular with travellers, internet, 2 big dogs, good.

G Residencial Chalet, Av 4N, No 15N-43, T661 0029. Safe, basic, quiet, small dark rooms.

Out of town

AL Radisson, Cra 100B, No 11A-99, T330 7777, F330 6477, in south of city, excellent service, pool, parking, restaurants, all Services.

B Hotel Aeropuerto, at the airport, T666 3229. Good, parking.

D Turístico La Luna, Autopista Sur, No 13-01, T558 2611, F558 6367. With breakfast, safe, large pool, restaurant, good parking.

E-F Casa Mochileros, C 13 Acopi, No 27A-25, T315-420 0315 (mob), http://hostelmochileros .googlepages.com/home. Take Autopista a Yumbo dirección Acopi, turn right at Callejón Harinera de Occidente, 7 mins drive from bus terminal. Traveller hostel, laundry service, kitchen facilities, organizes tours, dorms and camping too, surrounded by fruit trees.

● Eating

Cali *p859, map p860*
There are lots of sidewalk places to eat in the centre and along Av 6 in the north. Cafés and ice cream parlours abound near the university, across the river from the main part of town. Around Parque del Perro in San Fernando are upmarket restaurants and cafes. Good for an evening meal.

ŦŦŦ Los Girasoles, Av 6 N y C 35, T668 4646. Excellent Colombian menu, fish, ask for day's special. Recommended.

ŦŦŦ Las Dos Parrillas, Av 6N y C 35, T668 4646. Good steaks but expensive.

ŦŦŦ La Terraza, Av Colombia, No 2-72, T882 3225, in Intercontinental Hotel. Meat and international dishes, elegant, music and dance, nice atmosphere.

ŦŦ Cali Viejo, Cra 1, Parque El Bosque, T893 4927 (on south side of river near zoo). Colonial house, excellent local dishes.

ŦŦ Pizza al Paso, Cra 20 Este, No 2-55, El Peñón. Restaurant/bar with live music. Good reports.

ŦŦ Rancho Alegre, Av 15 Oeste, No 7-04, T893 4207. Colombian and international meat dishes.

ŦŦ San Mango, Cra 12, No 2-31, San Antonio. Modern decor in colonial house, good salads. Closed Mon.

ŦŦ-Ŧ Café Moro, C 6, No 8-11. Arab food and grills, nice decor, decent daily buffet US$2.50.

ŦŦ-Ŧ Clowns Deli, Av Colombia, No 5-105 (next to Museo de Arte La Tertulia). Fresh sandwiches and salads, nice terrace, good.

Ŧ Aragonesa, Av 6 N, No 13N-68. Good breakfasts, bakery.

Ŧ Comedor Vegetariano y Café, Cra 5 No 7-38. Clean, vegetarian food and desserts, lunch only, closed Sun.

Ŧ Tales & Tales, Cra 34, No 3A-03, Parque del Perro. Good value burgers.

Bread and pastry shops often have cafés or cafeterías eg **Punto Sabroso**, C 12, No 8-06; **Montecarlo**, Cra 5, No 14-22 in the centre.

● Bars and clubs

Cali *p859, map p860*
The nightlife along Av 6 N from C 16 upwards is safest and best known. There is a tour Fri-Sat on a *chiva* (open-sided bus) stopping off at various nightspots, US$14. Sometimes only couples are allowed into clubs.

Blues Brothers Bar, C 26N, No 5AN-51. Jazz and live rock bands. Good reports.

Costenita, Cra 15/C 15. Lots of local colour, Thu-Sun.

Kukaramakara, C 28N, No 2 Bis-97. The in place at the time of writing. Live bands, mix of music.

Lotus, C 15N, No 9N-27. Lounge, electronic music.

Praga, Vía Cali-Yumbo. Popular, mix of music.

Tin Tin Deo, C 5 y Cra 22. Good atmosphere, small, intimate, salsa at weekends. Recommended.

Tropicali, Av 6 N, No 15-66, T667 1006. Serves food, has a range of entertainments. Many others nearby.

Zaperoco, Av 5N, No 16-46. Salsa, recommended.

Barrio Juanchito has a range of salsa bars and discos, from thatched roofs to huge, hi-tech salsatecas (eg the popular **Don José**). It is worth visiting just to watch couples dancing salsa and to join in, if you dare! Go with locals and couples; groups of foreign male tourists might have a hard time getting in. Most advisable to take a registered radio taxi there and back; 15-min ride out of Cali, across the bridge over the Río Cauca.

● Entertainment

Cali *p859, map p860*
Cinema Alianza Colombo-Francesa, Av 6 N, No 21-34, T661 3431, and **Centro Colombo-Americano**, C 13N, No 8-45, T667 3539, both show films. Museo La Tertulia, Av Colombia, No 5-105 Oeste. Shows unusual films.

Theatre Teatro Experimental, C 7, No 8-63, T884 3820. Teatro Municipal, Cra 5, No 6-64,

● *For an explanation of the sleeping and eating price codes used in this guide, see page 58. Other*
● *relevant information is found in Essentials pages 778-779.*

T883 9107. Major cultural activities, including opera and concerts. **Teatro La Máscara**, Cra 10, No 3-40, San Antonio. Women's theatre group.

⊕ Festivals and events

Cali p859, map p860
Feria de Cali (Cali Fair) from **25-30 Dec**, biggest Salsa festival in Latin America, bullfights at the Canaveralejo bull-ring, carnival in streets, horse parades, masquerade balls, sporting contests and general heavy partying. Relatively safe.

⊙ Shopping

Cali p859, map p860
Best shopping districts are: Av 6N, from Río Cali to C 30 Norte and on Cra 5 in the south with several new shopping malls including: **Chipichape**, at the end of Av 6N. Vast, cinemas, **Librería Nacional** bookstore, good choice of restaurants and shops, supermarket.
Bookshops Bookstalls on the sidewalk on Cra 10 near C 10. **Librería Nacional**, on main plaza. Has a café, as do branches elsewhere in the city.
Handicrafts Artesanías de Colombia, C 12, No 1-20 and for larger purchases Av 6 N, No 23-45. **La Caleñita**, Cr 24, No 8-53. Good selection of typical handicrafts. **Parque Artesenal Loma de la Cruz**, C 5, Cras 15/16. Permanent handicraft market, nice setting and pleasant neighbourhood, safe, cafés around the park. Open 1130-2030. **Platería Ramírez**, C 1A, No 4B-44 Oeste, San Antonio. Good selection of jewellery, lessons offered in jewellery making.
Maps Instituto Geográfico Agustín Codazzi, Cra 6, No 13-56, T885 5611.

▲ Activities and tours

Cali p859, map p860
Diving Casco Antiguo Diving Centre, Cra 34, No 3-89 (Parque del Perro), cascoantiguo@ telesat.com.co. PADI certified. Organize all-inclusive expensive weekend diving tours to Gorgona Island, US$600pp and 8 day advanced diving tours to Isla Malpelo (36 hrs boat ride from Buenaventura US$2,500).
Paragliding Contact **Robin** through the Iguana Hostal, usually there on Tue.

Tours
Aviatur, Cra 5, No. 8-12, T889 3121, http://site.aviatur.com. For tours to Isla Gorgona, and other services. **Ecocolombia Tours**, Cra 37A, No 6-18, T514 0829, F557 1957. Trips to Gorgona,

Juanchaco, diving, tours in and around Cali. Recommended. **Panturismo**, C 18N, No 8-27, T668 2255, and other branches, including at airport, T666 3021. Organizes all inclusive trips to Gorgona. **Vela**, Cra 4, No 8-64, local 104, T889 0760. Student travel agency, cheap tickets. Recommended.

⊙ Transport

Cali p859, map p860
Air Frequent services to **Bogotá**, **Medellín**, **Cartagena**, **Ipiales** and other Colombian cities with Satena and **Avianca**. International flights to Miami, New York, and Panama. Minibus from airport, from far end of pick-up road outside arrivals, to bus terminal (2nd floor), every 10 mins from 0500 up to 2100, approximately 30 mins, US$1.50. Colectivo to city about US$1.20; taxi, US$11, 30 mins.
Bus Busetas (**Velotax** and others) charge 50% more than buses but save time; taxi-colectivos are about 2½ times bus prices and even quicker. To **Popayán**, US$5.50, 2½-3 hrs, also colectivos, US$9. To **Pasto**, US$11, 8-9 hrs. To **Ipiales** (direct), US$14, 12 hrs; to **San Agustín**, 9 hrs, US$14-16. To **Cartago**, 3½ hrs, US$4. To **Armenia**, US$7. To **Ibagué**, US$8, 6-7 hrs. To **Manizales**, US$13, 7 hrs. To **Medellín**, US$16, 8-10 hrs. To **Bogotá**, 10-15 hrs, by Magdalena, T668 7504 (recommended), US$25 (sit on left of the bus).

⊙ Directory

Cali p859, map p860
Banks BanColombia on Plaza de Caicedo, for Visa cash advances (take passport and a photocopy). Many other banks and *casas de cambio* on the Plaza, eg **Titan**. Changes Sterling and US TCs, open Mon-Fri, plus Sat 0830-1200.
Bicycle repairs Bike House, C 20N, No 6AN-49, T661 1733. Organizes free bike rides at weekends but you must have your own mountain bike. Cash discounts available. **Consulates** French, Av 3N, No 18N-24, Of 405, T883 5904. **German**, C 1B, No 66B-29, Barrio El Refugio, T323 8402. **Swiss**, Av 4N, No 3-33, T661 4927 (same building as *Pensión Stein*). **UK**, C 22N, No 6-42, Of 401, Edif Centro Granada, T667 7725, britishcali@uniweb.net.co.
Internet Many in the north, along Av 6A, and centre of the city eg **Internet Café**, Av 6N, No 13N-70, next to *Panadería Aragonesa*, open daily.
Post offices Adpostal for national service, C 10, No 6-25; **Depris** for international service, C 9, No 4-45. **Useful addresses** DAS office: Av 3AN, No 50-20 T664 3809. For national parks, **MA**, Av 3 GN, No 37-70, T654 3720 (see also **Aviatur**, above).

Cauca and the coast

To reach the Pacific you have to cross the western arm of the Andes, with a number of parks and recreational areas. There are plenty of beaches to the northwest of the port of Buenaventura while away to the south is the isolated national park islands of Gorgona and Mapelo.

Lago Calima

If you take the road from the colonial city of Buga (northeast of Cali, south of Cartago on the Panamericana), to Buenaventura you pass the **Laguna de Sonso** reserve, good for birdwatching, before crossing the Río Cauca. Beyond the river, near the crest of the Cordillera, is another park, **Reserva Natural Bosque de Yotoco**, noted for orchids. The road continues to the man-made **Lago Calima**. Many treasures of the Calima culture are said to have been flooded by the lake, when the dam was built. This is an important centre for watersports, riding and other activities. The northern route round the lake goes through **Darién** at 1,500 m with an **archaeological museum** ① *Tue-Fri 0800-1700, Sat-Sun 1000-1800*, with good displays of Calima and other cultures. There are hotels in the village, as well as cabins available at a Centro Náutico on the lakeside. Camping is possible near the village. Direct buses from Buga to Darién (one hour), and Cali (two hours).

From Cali to the coast

Both the toll and (unpaved) ordinary roads from Cali to Buenaventura give beautiful views of mountains and jungle, and from the old road you can reach the **Parque Nacional Farallones** ① *for information, ask at Aviatur in Cali*. At the time of writing the park is closed and is not safe to visit. The area around Pance, however, and the **Ecoparque del Río Pance**, 20 minutes from the centre of Cali, is a popular weekend haunt, with nature walks, swimming and camping all possible. To reach Pance, take a **Blanco y Negro** bus, Ruta 1, from Calle 5 or Avenida 6, US$0.60.

A popular excursion from Cali is to **San Cipriano**, 30 km on the road to Buenaventura. Get off the bus at Córdoba, from where rail cars, man-powered or motorbike-powered (US$5-7 return), go to the village in beautiful scenery. There are crystal-clear rivers and waterfalls and inner tubes can be rented for US$2 per day for floating downstream.

Buenaventura → *Phone code: 92. Colour map 1, grid B2. Population: 202,000. 145 km from Cali.*

Through a pass in the Western Cordillera is Buenaventura, Colombia's most important port handling some 80% of total exports, including coffee, sugar and frozen shrimp. It was founded in 1540, but not on its present site. It now stands on the island of Cascajal, on the Bay of Buenaventura, 20 km from the open Pacific. For excursions and beaches, see below. The commercial centre is now paved and has some impressive buildings, but the rest of the town is poor, with steep unpaved streets lined with shacks on stilts. The town beaches are not too clean and security has significantly detoriated in late 2006/early 2007. Check on the situation before going there. There is a festive atmosphere every night and the *Festival Folklórico del Litoral* is held in July. South of the town a swampy coast stretches as far as Tumaco (see page 877); to the north lies the deeply jungled Chocó Department. There are still problems with malaria. **Tourist information** Asturias travel agency, T242 4620 for information on trips around Buenaventura.

Beaches around Buenaventura

Beaches are plentiful northwest of Buenaventura along the coast. There is stunning scenery with virgin jungle, waterfalls and empty, black sand beaches. About 40 km from Buenaventura, near the mouth of the Río San Juan, is **Juanchaco**, a small fishing village, the location of spectacular **dolphin** and **humpback whale** sightings between August and October. By frequent launch from Buenaventura (*muelle turístico*) US$20 return by speedboat, one hour, slower boats available. Whale watching tours about US$15 for two hours. Beyond Juanchaco is **Ladrilleros**, a 30-minute walk, or take a jeep (5 minutes). One of the best and longest beaches, which turns into a football pitch at low tide to provide entertainment as you drink your beer or *cocoloco* (coconut milk and rum). Simple accommodation in Juanchaco (**E-F**) but better in Ladrilleros eg **D Palma Real**, good. Plenty of other small places around. Several small restaurants (good fish) and snack bars at the town end of the beach. Other beaches include La

Bocana and Pianguita, enquire for simple accommodation. Trips to beaches cost between US$12-40 for 10-person launch (rate per launch).

Gorgona Island → *Colour map 1, grid B1. 150 km down the coast from Buenaventura.*

ⓘ *Visits to the island are managed and run by Aviatur, Av 6 Norte, No 37B- 94 (opposite CC Chipichape), T664 5050 in Cali. All visitors must have a permit before arriving at the island, obtainable from Aviatur. It is recommended to book accommodation and boat tickets well in advance during high season. Entrance fee US$10 for foreigners, US$1-3 embarkation/disembarkation fee, US$5 diving permit per day, US$3.50 fishing permit per day.*

Until 1984 the island of **Gorgona** was Colombia's high security prison (a sort of Alcatraz). The prison is derelict but some parts can still be clearly seen. Convicts were dissuaded from escaping by the poisonous snakes on the island and the sharks patrolling the 30 km to the mainland (both snakes and sharks are still there). The national park boasts many unspoilt, deserted sandy beaches. From the paths you can see monkeys, iguanas, and a wealth of flora and fauna. (Rubber boots are provided and recommended.) There is an abundance of birds (pelicans, cormorants, geese, herons) that use the island as a migration stop-over. Snorkelling and diving is rewarding, equipment can be hired (but take your own if possible), exotic fish and turtles to be seen. Killer whales visit the area from July-September.

Isla Mapelo

Declared a UNESCO site in 2006, Isla Mapelo is located 506 km from Buenaventura in the Pacific and is an acclaimed birdwatching haven with great diving opportunities. The island is considered to be one of the world's best places to observe hammerhead sharks in great numbers. Boats leave from Buenaventura, a 36-hour bumpy voyage. There are no places to stay on the island and camping is not allowed. Contact MA office in Bogotá for more information, T243 2009. Diving permits for foreigners cost US$55 per person.

● Sleeping

Buenaventura *p863*

B Estación, C 2, No 1A-08, T243 4070, F243 4118. Best in town, charming, grand old white building on seafront, good restaurant, pool, helpful. Organizes trips to beaches.

C Gran, C 1, No 2A-71, T243 4527. Quieter rooms upstairs, a/c, restaurant, with breakfast.

E Felipe II, Cra 3A, No 2-44, T242 2820, F242 3493. A/c, restaurant serves Chinese food, helpful.

E Steven, Cra 4A, No 4-42, T241 3786. A/c, cheaper with fan, restaurant, Good breakfasts.

Gorgona Island *p864*

Dorm in cabins on the island, hold 16 people, US$21 pp in low season, and one private cabin (6 people). Try to book bunk beds in advance; if you can't, prepare for a scramble. There is a restaurant with a mainly fish menu. You can take your own food but all non-biodegradable items must be taken off the island. Apart from coconuts there is no other fruit on the island. Don't take alcohol, it will probably be confiscated. Do take drinking water, it is in short supply and expensive on the island.

❶ Eating

Buenaventura *p863*

Good seafood at Pueblo Nuevo market, but not very cheap. Pavement cafés in front of *Gran Hotel* are lively in the evening, a good place for a drink.

864

♈ Los Balcones, C 2 y Cra 3. Very good but pricey.

♈ Doña Cleo, C 5. A good seafood place.

♈ Rico Marisco. Excellent seafood and fish, large portions, open late. Recommended.

● Transport

Buenaventura *p863*

Air Flights to **Cali** and **Bogotá**, **Satena**.

Boat Ferries south to **Tumaco** and 3 times a week north to **Bahía Solano**.

Road There are plenty of buses to **Cali**, US$6.50, 3 hrs. Colectivos and taxis run at ½-hourly intervals to Cali, US$7-9 pp. The toll road to Cali is fully paved; the toll is about US$1.30 for cars and US$0.30 for motorcycles.

Gorgona Island *p864*

Organized tours It is recommended to book tours through **Aviatur**, they arrange permits, transport and accommodation. Aviatur offers a fast launch service to the island from the seaside town of **Guapi**, US$100 return, 2-3 hrs, leaves every Mon, Wed, Fri. Also **Panturismo**, see Cali, Activities and tours, offer tours to the island. To arrange on your own, find a boat at Buenaventura; they leave most days at 1600 from the El Piñal dock (Bodega Liscano) in Buenaventura. For further information, El Piñal dock, T244 6089. The trip, which costs US$90 return, takes around 9-12 hrs depending on conditions and can be an experience in itself. It is easier to take a tour. Alternatively, the island can be easily reached from Guapi, flights from Cali with Satena.

ⓘ Directory

Buenaventura *p863*
Banks Several banks will change cash and TCs.
Useful addresses DAS, Cra 19, No 4B-02, T241 2144, for those arriving or departing by boat from/to Panama.

Popayán, Tierradentro and San Agustín

The Pan-American Highway climbs out of the valley to Popayán, a historic city which gives access to the páramo of Puracé in the Cordillera Central and serves as a good base from which to visit some of Colombia's most exciting sights, including the burial caves of Tierradentro and, to the south, the remarkable archaeological site of San Agustín. The Cauca valley has strong indigenous cultures, notably the Páez Indians.

Popayán and Tierradentro

Popayán has retained its colonial character, even though it had to be fully restored after the March 1983 earthquake. The streets of two-storey buildings are in rococo Andalucian style, with beautiful old monasteries and cloisters of pure Spanish classic architecture. In contrast, the tombs of Tierradentro reveal much of the northern Andean world before the Spaniards arrived.

Warning Valle del Cauca and Cauca regions have had guerrilla problems recently. There have been violent clashes between indigenous groups and the police (late 2005). Enquire locally before travelling on minor roads.

Popayán → *Phone code: 92. Colour map 1, grid C2. Population: 223,000. Altitude: 1,760 m.*
Founded by Sebastián de Belalcázar, Francisco Pizarro's lieutenant, in 1536, Popayán became the regional seat of government, until 1717, to the Audiencia of Quito, and later to the Audiencia of Bogotá. It is now the capital of the Department of Cauca. The city lies in the Pubenza valley, a peaceful landscape of palm, bamboo, and the sharp-leaved agave. The early settlers, after setting up their sugar estates in the hot, damp Cauca valley, retreated to Popayán to live, for the city is high enough to give it a delightful climate. To the north, south, and east the broken green plain is bounded by mountains. The cone of the volcano Puracé (4,646 m) rises to the southeast.

Sights The Cathedral ① *Calle 5, Cra 6*, beautifully restored, has a fine marble madonna sculpture behind the altar by Buenaventura Malagón and the unusual statue of Christ kneeling on the globe. Other churches are **San Agustín** ① *Calle 7, Cra 6*, note the gilt altar piece; **Santo Domingo** ① *Calle 4, Cra 5*, used by the Universidad del Cauca; **La Ermita** ① *Calle 5, Cra 2*; **La Encarnación** ① *Calle 5, Cra 5*, also used for religious music festivals; **San Francisco** ① *Calle 4, Cra 9* (partly restored); and **El Carmen** ① *Calle 4, Cra 3*. Walk to **Belén** chapel ① *Calle 4 y Cra 0*, seeing the statues en route, and then continue to **El Cerro de las Tres Cruces** if you have the energy, and on to the equestrian statue of Belalcázar on the **Morro de Tulcán** which overlooks the city; this hill is the site of a pre-Columbian pyramid. It is said that Bolívar marched over the **Puente Chiquito** ① *Calle 2 y Cra 6*, built in 1713. **Museo Negret** ① *Calle 5, No 10-23, Mon-Fri 0900-1200, 1400-1800, US$0.60*, has works, photographs and furniture of Negret. **Museo Guillermo Valencia** ① *Cra 6 No 2-69*, is the birthplace of the poet. **Museo de Historia Natural** ① *Cra 2, No 1A-25, US$1*, has good displays of archaeological and geological items with sections on insects (particularly good on butterflies), reptiles, mammals and birds. During the week, the open markets are interesting – **Mercado Bolívar** ① *Calle 1N, Cra 5*, is best in the early morning – local foods such as *pipián, tamales* and *empanadas*.

The **tourist office** ① *Cra 5, No 4-68, T824 2251, Mon-Fri 0830-1230, 1400-1830*, helpful, has good maps of the city, prices of all lodgings, and bus schedules and prices. The Colegio Mayor de Cauca has details on art exhibitions and concerts. Try also the Casa de la Cultura ① *Calle 5, No 4-33*, for information on cultural events. **Note** Museums are closed on Monday.

Silvia → *Phone code: 92. Colour map 1, grid C2. Population: 5,000. Altitude: 2,520 m.*

Silvia, in a high valley 59 km northeast of Popayán, is best known for its Tuesday market when the friendly local Guambianos come into town in their typical blue and fuchsia costumes. The market, which is also full of Otavalo Indians from Ecuador and their goods more expensive than in Otavalo, is at its best between 0600 and 0830, is very colourful. A typical *indígena* settlement, La Campana, is one hour on the *lechero* or bus; two to three hours' walk downhill back to Silvia. Tourist information 1½ blocks up from plazuela on the right hand side (keeps irregular hours). *Banco Agrario* gives cash against Visa. For horse hire enquire at tourist office or hotels.

Tierradentro → *Colour map 1, grid C2*

East of Popayán is **Inzá** which is 67 km beyond **Totoró**. There are several stone statues in the new plaza. 9 km beyond Inzá is the Cruce de Pisimbalá (or Cruce de San Andrés or just El Cruce), where a road turns off to **San Andrés de Pisimbalá** (4 km). The village, at the far end of the Tierradentro Park, has a unique and beautiful colonial church with a thatched roof; for the key ask behind the church. 2 km or so before Pisimbalá is the **Tierradentro Museum** ① *0800-1100, 1300-1700,* of indigenous culture. It has very good local information. The second floor is dedicated to the work of the Páez Indians, not to be missed. The Páez Indians in the Tierradentro region can be seen on market days at Inzá (Saturday), and Belalcázar (Saturday); both start at 0600. The surroundings have spectacular natural beauty, with small indigenous villages in the mountains (get exact directions before setting out).

Parque Arqueológico Tierradentro ① *Park and Museum open 0800-1600, US$3, valid for 2 days. Walking between the sites, take a hat and plenty of water. It gets crowded at Easter-time.* At the archway directly opposite the museum or at Pisimbalá village you can hire

Popayán

Sleeping
Amalia 1 *C2*
Camino Real 4 *B2*
Casa Familiar Turística 6 *B2*
Catan 20 *C2*
Don Blas 8 *C2*
El Viajero 21 *C2*
Hostal Colonial 3 *B1*
Hostal Modelo 10 *A2*
La Casa del Virrey 12 *B2*

La Herrería 9 *B2*
La Plazuela 13 *B2*
Los Balcones 15 *B2*
Los Portales 7 *C2*
Monasterio 17 *B1*
Pakandé 18 *C2*
Residencias Líder 22 *A3*

Eating
Belalcázar 1 *C2*

Chung Wah 4 *C2*
La Brasa Roja 7 *B2*
La Cave 8 *B3*
La Fontana 9 *B2*
La Viña 11 *B2*
Los Quingos de Belén 12 *C3*
Mey Chow 13 *B3*
Peña Blanca 14 *C2*
Pizzería Don Sebastián 15 *B3*
Pizzería Italiana 16 *B2*

horses (US$2 per hour, make sure they are in good condition) or you can walk to the **Tierradentro** man-made burial caves painted with geometric patterns. There are four cave sites – Segovia, El Duende, Alto de San Andrés and El Aguacate. The main caves are now lighted, but a torch is advisable. At Segovia (15 minutes' walk up behind the museum across the river), the guards are very informative (Spanish only) and turn lights on in the main tombs. Segovia has about 30 tombs, five of which can be lit. 15 minutes up the hill beyond Segovia is El Duende (two of the four tombs are very good, faint paintings can be discerned but there are no lights, take torch/flashlight). From El Duende continue directly up to a rough road descending to Pisimbalá (40 minutes). El Tablón, with eight stone statues, is just off the road 20-30 minutes walk down. El Alto de San Andrés is 20 minutes from Pisimbalá. From the back of El Alto it is 1½ hours up and down hill, with a final long climb to El Aguacate. Only one tomb is maintained although there may be 30 more. The views from El Aguacate are superb. Guides are available. The whole area is good for birdwatching.

● Sleeping

Popayán *p865, map p866*
Prices can rise by 60% for Holy Week and festivals, eg 5-6 Jan, when it's essential to book in advance. It is not safe walking alone at night outside the central area and even in the historic centre it's quiet enough to warrant caution.
AL Monasterio, C 4, No 10-14, T824 2191, F824 3491. In what was the monastery of San Francisco, includes breakfast, lovely grounds, swimming pool, fully renovated, very good.
A Camino Real, C 5, No 5-59, T824 0685. Good service, includes breakfast, excellent restaurant, parking. Recommended.
B La Herrería, Cra 5, No 2-08, T839 2740. Converted large colonial house, family owned, good restaurant. Highly recommended.
B La Plazuela, C 5, No 8-13, T824 1084, F824 0912. Elegant colonial style, courtyard, comfortable rooms, nicely decorated, TV, good restaurant/café serving typical food.
C Los Balcones, C 3, No 6-80, T824 2030, F824 1814. Hot water, helpful. Below hotel is a Spanish-style restaurant for breakfast and lunch, good. Recommended.
C-D Los Portales, C 5, No 10-125, T821 0139, F821 0259. Colonial style, nicely decorated, restaurant, rooms around courtyard, good, helpful.
D La Casa del Virrey, C 4, No 5-78, T824 4237. Hot water in morning, big rooms, nice colonial house and atmosphere, helpful. Warmly recommended.
E Casa Familiar Turística, Cra 5, No 2-07, T824 4853. Hot water, family-run, rooms without bath, airy, bright, good traveller noticeboard, stores luggage, laundry service, central. Recommended.
E Don Blas, Cra 6 No 7-87, T824 0817. With bath, hot water, decent rooms, cable TV, modern. Recommended.
E Pakandé, Cra 6, No 7-75, T824 0846. Good beds but plain, hot shower, helpful, modern.

F Hostal Colonial, C 5, No 9-94, T831 7848. Modern, excellent value, hot water, cable TV. Recommended.

Around Mercado Bolívar
There are many budget hotels and *residencias* in this area on Cra 6 to the north of the river. Most are run down, very basic and have no hot water.
G Residencias Líder, Cra 6, No 4N-70, T823 0915. Very basic, friendly owner.

Near bus station
G Hostal Modelo, Cra 10, No 1N-34, T823 1723. Good value, pleasant, hot water, cable TV.

On and south of Calle 8
D Amalia, Cra 6, No 8-58, T824 1203. Hot water, cooking and laundry facilities, a bit run down.
F El Viajero, C 8, No 4-45, T824 3069. With bath, decent small rooms, watch your belongings, modern, luggage stored.
G Catan, Cra 5, No 8-27, T 824 0624. Probably cheapest option in town, a bit shabby rooms with private bath, but decent for the price.

Just outside town
C Campobello Bed & Breakfast (Myriam and Andre), C 33AN, No 14A-14, T823 5545, www.hostalcampobello.com. Off the Pan-American Highway, 300 m down road opposite *Torremolino* restaurant. Swiss/Colombian owners speak French, English and German, safe, family atmosphere, nicely decorated, terrace, breakfast included, laundry service. Near bus station. Recommended.
C La Posada del Rancho, 5 km on road to Cali, C 59AN, No 8-00, T832 6450. Chalet style, rural setting, pool, quiet. Suites and rooms, good restaurant.

● *For an explanation of the sleeping and eating price codes used in this guide, see page 58. Other*
● *relevant information is found in Essentials pages 778-779.*

buildings. Behind the school a 500 m-long path leads to Chorrera de las Monjas waterfalls on the Río Vinagre, which is notable for the milky white water due to concentrations of sulphur and other minerals.

At Km 22, look for the spectacular San Francisco waterfall on the opposite side of the valley. At Km 23 is the turning right to Puracé sulphur mines (6 km) which can be visited by applying to **Industrias Puracé SA** ① *Calle 4, No 7-32, Popayán*, best through the Popayán tourist office. About 1 km along this road is a turning left leading in 1½ km to **Pilimbalá** in the **Parque Nacional Puracé** at 3,350 m. Here there is a park office, and seven sulphur baths (cold, no bathing). At Pilimbalá, near the park entrance, there is a restaurant and three cabins (up to 12 per cabin), US$6.50 per person in high season. The national park contains Volcán Puracé (4,640 m) (for climbing see below), Pan de Azúcar (4,670 m) with its permanent snow summit, and the line of nine craters known as the Volcanes los Coconucos (a strenuous two-day hike can be made around the summits requiring high altitude camping and mountaineering equipment). The park also encompasses the sources of four of Colombia's greatest rivers: the Magdalena, Cauca, Caquetá and Patía. Virtually all the park is over 3,000 m. The Andean Condor is being reintroduced to the wild here from Californian zoos. There are many other birds to be seen and fauna includes the spectacled bear and mountain tapir. Pilimbalá is a good base from which to explore the northern end of the park.

Climbing Volcán Puracé On the hike to the summit, loose ash makes footholds difficult. Avoid getting down wind of the fumaroles, and do not climb down into the crater. Although the best weather is reported to be December-March and July-August, this massif makes its own climate, and high winds, rain and sub-zero temperatures can come in quickly at any time. A marked trail goes from behind the park office and eventually joins the road leading to a set of telecommunications antennae. **The area around these installations is mined, don't take shortcuts.** The summit is about one hour beyond the military buildings, total time from Pilimbalá at least four hours up and 2½ hours down. A guide is recommended.

Around Puracé

Continuing on the main road from Volcá Puracé to **La Plata** (whose central plaza has an enormous ceiba, planted in 1901) at Km 31 there is a viewpoint for Laguna Rafael, at Km 35 the **Cascada de Bedón** (also chemically charged water) and at Km 37 the entrance to the most northerly part of the Parque Nacional Puracé. Here there is a visitor centre, a **geology/ ethnology museum** ① *US$0.75*, and the very interesting **Termales de San Juan** ① *700 m from the road, US$0.40*, where 112 hot sulphur springs combine with icy mountain creeks to produce spectacular arrays of multi-coloured mosses, algae and lichens, a must if you are in the area (no bathing; accommodation available). The visitor centre has a *cafetería* (arrange meals beforehand through Popayán Tourist Office).

Southeast of La Plata is Pital where the road forks, southeast to **Garzón** *(phone code: 988; population: 44,000; altitude: 830 m)*, and south to near Altamira. Garzón is a pleasant cathedral town set in mountains, 54 km southeast of La Plata, 92 km south of Neiva (see below).

At Altamira, some 29 km further southwest, the main road heads to **Timaná** (basic accommodation, **G**) and continues paved on to San Agustín. Another road goes southeast to Florencia, capital of the Department of Caquetá. **Florencia**, was originally established in 1908. The plaza contains sculptures, fountains, a large forest tree (*saba*) and flower beds. The local saint's day is 16 July: candlelit procession in the evening.

Note At the time of writing, there is intense guerrilla activity in Florencia (guerrilla road blocks, electricity cuts, little transport and fighting between the armed forces and guerrilla groups). From Florencia the road runs northeast as far as San Vicente del Caguán, the centre of the demilitarized zone arranged between President Pastrana's government and the FARC guerrillas in November 1998. After the breakdown of peace negotiations in February 2002, government armed forces evicted the FARC guerrillas from the **'zona de despeje'**, which was centred on San Vicente and Cartagena del Chairá. The area should not be entered by tourists.

Pitalito *(Phone code 98; Population 63,000; Altitude 1,231 m)* has little to offer the tourist, save convenient access to the **Parque Nacional Cueva de los Guácharos** ① *US$3.20, cafetería, accommodation (when available) US$5 per night, pp*, which lies to the south. Between December and June swarms of oilbirds (*guácharos*) may be seen; they are nocturnal, with a unique radar-location system. The reserve also contains many of the unusual and spectacular cocks-of-the-rock and the limestone caves are among the most interesting in

Colombia. The rangers are particularly friendly, providing tours and basic accommodation; permission to visit the park must be obtained from the *MA* offices in Pitalito, Cra 4, No4-21, Neiva or Bogotá. Check with MA if the park is open.

Popayán to San Agustín direct

South of Puracé towards San Agustín is **Coconuco** (*Altitude*: 2,460 m). Coconuco's baths, **Agua Hirviendo** ① *1½ km beyond the Hotel de Turismo (see Sleeping), on a paved road (mostly), US$0.60*, have one major and many individual pools with an initial temperature of at least 80°C. There is one pool where you can boil an egg in five minutes. A track from town is quicker than the road. It gets crowded at weekends, but during the week it is a fine area for walking and relaxing in the waters. About 6 km beyond Coconuco, near the road, are Aguas Tibias, warm rather than hot, with similar facilities for visitors. South of Coconuco by 24 km is **Paletará** with high grassland on a grand scale with the Puracé/Pan de Azúcar volcanoes in the background. Below the village (roadside restaurant and MA post) flows the infant Río Cauca. 10 km south of Paletará, the road enters the Parque Nacional Puracé and there is a track northeast to Laguna del Buey. The road then enters a long stretch of virgin cloud forest. This section links Paletará with Isnos and San Agustín. Heavy rain has weakened this stretch, 25 km of which are impassable to light vehicles and very tedious for buses and trucks. No efforts are being made currently to improve this road. Some 62 km from Paletará at the end of the cloud forest is Isnos (see page 872) followed by a steep drop to a dramatic bridge over the Río Magdalena and shortly to the main road between Pitalito and San Agustín. **Warning** Avoid travelling by night between Popayán and San Agustín, the roads are dangerous. Cyclists should avoid taking the direct route. Reports of theft on the buses between these towns; do not trust 'helpfuls' and do not put bags on the luggage rack.

San Agustín → *Phone code: 98. Colour map 1, grid C2. Population: 6,000. Altitude: 1,700 m.*

The little town of San Agustín, near the source of the Río Magdalena, is a peaceful place with a few colonial houses and cobbled streets still intact. It is on every travellers' itinerary because of its proximity to the 'Valley of the Statues', where hundreds of large rough-hewn stone figures of men, animals and gods, dating from roughly 3300 BC to just before the Spanish conquest. Little is known of the culture which produced them or what exactly the stone sculptures represent. One theory suggests that this culture came from the Amazon region. The sculptures also display indigenous and Asian influences. No evidence of writing has been discovered, but traces of small circular bamboo straw-thatched houses have been found. The sites were burial and ceremonial sites where it is thought sacrifices, including of children, were made to the gods. Some sites were also residential areas. Various sculptures found here are exhibited in the National Museum at Bogotá. Only about 30% of the burial mounds in the area have been excavated and many of those that have been opened were previously ransacked by grave diggers, who had looted their precious statues. There are about 20 well-kept sites, described below. The area offers excellent opportunities for hiking, although some trails to remote sites are not well marked, and other adventure sports. The rainy season is April-June/July, but it rains almost all year, hence the beautiful green landscape; the driest months are November-March.

World Heritage Travel Office ① *C 3A, No 10-84, on corner, T/F837 3940*. This is a well-established travel agency providing useful maps and professional, helpful guides, which we recommend you to visit on arrival. For information see **www.turismosanagustin.com** (in Spanish and English). **Warning** Enquire about safety before walking to the more distant monuments. Beware of 'guides' and touts who approach you in the street. Have nothing to do with anyone offering drugs, pre-Columbian objects, gold, emeralds or other precious minerals for sale.

Sights near San Agustín

The whole area leaves an unforgettable impression, from the strength and strangeness of the statues, and the great beauty of the rolling green landscape. The nearest archaeological sites are in the **Parque Arqueológico** ① *0800-1600, US$2.70 including museum, Parque Arqueológico and Fuente de Lavapatas; if, at the end of the day, you wish to visit the following day for free, enquire first at the ticket office. It is recommended to hire a guide to gain a better understanding of the statues and what they represent. Luis Alfredo Salazar speaks English, French, Italian, US$15 for 3 hrs, recommended. Guidebook in Spanish/English US$3.75.* The park is 3 km from San Agustín.

The 130 statues and graves in the Parque are *in situ*, though those in the Bosque (a little wood) have been moved and rearranged, and linked by gravel footpaths. Originally, the statues were found lying down and covered in the graves. Those excavated have been placed upright next to the graves and fenced in. Beyond the central area are the carved rocks in and around the stream at the **Fuente de Lavapatas** in the park, where the water runs through carved channels. The **Alto de Lavapatas** ① *closes at 1600, expensive refreshment stands at 'Fuente' and on the way up to Lavapatas*, above the Fuente, has an extensive view. You can get a good idea of the Parque, the Bosque and the museum in the course of three hours' walking, or add in El Tablón and La Chaquira (see below) for a full day. The **Museo Arqueológico** ① *park entrance, 0900- 1700*, contains pottery and describes what is known about the San Agustín culture (Spanish only).

Around San Agustín

El Tablón is reached up Carrera 14, over the brow of the hill and 250 m to a marked track to the right. El Tablón (five sculptures brought together under a bamboo roof) is shortly down to the left. Continue down the path, muddy in wet weather, ford a stream and follow signs to the Río Magdalena canyon. **La Chaquira** (figures carved on rocks) is dramatically set half way down to the river. Walking time round trip from San Agustín, two hours. Plenty of houses offer refreshments as far as El Tablón.

At **La Pelota**, two painted statues were found in 1984 (three-hour return trip, six hours if you include El Tablón and La Chaquira, 15 km in all). Discoveries from 1984/86 include some unique polychromed sculptures at **El Purutal** near La Pelota and a series of at least 30 stones carved with animals and other designs in high relief. These are known as **Los Petroglifos** and can be found on the right bank of the Río Magdalena, near the **Estrecho** (narrows) to which jeeps run.

Alto de los Idolos ① *0800-1600, US$1.80*, is about 10 km by horse or on foot, a lovely (if strenuous) walk, steep in places, via **Puente de la Chaquira**. Here on a levelled hill overlooking San Agustín are 13 uncovered tombs and statues dating from 100BC-AD600. These statues, known as *vigilantes*, each guard a burial mound. One is an unusual rat totem; stone crocodiles are believed by some to have strong links with the Amazon region. The few excavated have disclosed large stone sarcophagi. It is not certain whether the vigilantes bear a sculpted resemblance of the inmate.

Alto de los Idolos can also be reached from **San José de Isnos** (5 km northeast) 27 km by road from San Agustín. The road passes the **Salto del Mortiño**, a 300 m fall 7 km before Isnos, 500 m off the road. The main plaza in Isnos has restaurants and cafés, eg **El Turista** (lunch, US$1.80) and a **Cootranshuila** bus office. Isnos' market day is Saturday (bus 0500, US$1.20, return 1100, 1300, otherwise bus from Cruce on Pitalito road, or hitch).

6 km north of Isnos is **Alto de las Piedras** ① *0800-1700*, which has seven interesting tombs and monoliths, including the famous 'Doble Yo' and the tombs of two children. There are still over 90 tombs waiting to be excavated. Only less remarkable than the statues are the orchids growing nearby. 8 km further is Bordones; turn left at end of the village and there is (500 m) parking for the **Salto de Bordones** falls ① *US$0.50*. Good for birdwatching.

Bogotá to San Agustin

① *Before travelling by road south to Neiva, check on safety.*

A lot of people travelling to Bogotá to San Agustín will pass through **Neiva**. The capital of Huila Department, Neiva is a pleasant, modern city on the east bank of the Río Magdalena, surrounded by rich coffee plantations. There is a large and colourful market every day. *Bancolombia*, near Parque Santander, will change US$ cash and travellers' cheques. South of Girardot, about 50 km before Neiva, is a small area (300 sq km) of scrub and arid eroded red soil known as the **Tatacoa** desert, with large cacti, isolated mesas and unusual wildlife. For information on visiting Tatacoa desert contact **Secretaría de Cultura y Turismo** in Villavieja ① *C 3No 4-53, T08-879 7744*, who can put you in touch with registered guides. Four- or five-hour walks through the desert cost US$10-12 per person per day. Daily bus from Neiva to Villavieja (Coomotor from Neiva bus terminal) 1-1½ hours, US$2.20. From Villavieja hire a taxi to Tatacoa desert, US$22 return. There is also a museum showing prehistoric finds in the area. You can cross the Magdalena by motorized canoe near Villavieja for US$1. Accommodation available in Villavieja.

● Sleeping

Puracé *p869*

G Residencias Cubina, safe, cold showers, secure parking.

Parque Nacional Puracé: Pilimbalá *p870*
Saloon cars will struggle up the last stretch to the centre, but it is an easy 2½ km walk from Km 23. Picnic shelters, restaurant, and a cheap *hospedaje* (cold) and 3 *cabañas* for up to 12, US$6.50 pp in high season. Firewood is provided. Camping costs US$3 pp. Sleeping bags or warm clothing recommended to supplement bedding provided.

Around Puracé *p870*
La Plata
E Berlín, C 4, No 4-76, T837 0229, by church on plaza, 3 blocks from the bus office. **F** without bath, unappealing toilets and bugs in the beds.
E Cambis, C 4, No 4-28, T837 1890. Modern, TV, helpful, near bus station. Recommended.
F El Portal de Valencia, C 6, No 3-58, T837 6394. With bath, TV, no hot water.
G Residencias Confort, C 6, No 2-57, T837 0121, Very basic, shared bath.
G Residencias Margarita, Cr 5, No 5-40, T837 0916. As above, but with bath.

Garzón
D Abeyma, Cra 10 y C 12, T833 2022. A state hotel, it is possible to camp in the grounds.
D Casablanca, Cra 9 y C 5, T833 0997. Restaurant, bar, parking, safe.
D Damasco, C 16, No 10-75, T833 2091. Colonial building, good meals, fan, fridge, a/c, near bus terminal. Recommended.
F Residencias Pigoanza, on main plaza. With bath. Recommended.

Florencia
The better hotels are round the plaza.
B Kamani, C 16, No 12-27, T835 4101. Breakfast.

Pitalito
C Calamó, Cra 5, No 5-41, T836 0832. Hot water, pool, cafetería, parking.
D Yoritania, C 7, No 3-51, T836 6044. Helpful, with bath, TV, laundry service, no hot water.
F Sevillana, Cra 5, No 3-52, T836 0305. Next to Taxis Verdes, no hot water, free coffee, bath, TV.

Popayán to San Agustín: Coconuco *p871*
C Hotel de Turismo/Confandi, 500 m out of town, 10 mins' drive to the baths, the best,

comfortable, hot water, price is full board, colonial style hotel run by Cali Tourist authority, restful atmosphere. There are several other modest hotels and restaurants in town.
At **Agua Hirviendo**, T827 7013/14/15, are 3 cabins at US$20 per day that will hold up to 6.

San Agustín *p871*
Some hotels increase prices during Easter and Christmas by around 10-20%.
E Colonial, C 3, No 11-25, T837 3159. Hot shower, pleasant, good restaurant, TV, central.
F Cambi, Cra 13, No 3-36, T837 3799. Colonial style, hot water, very basic, helpful, family atmosphere, motorcycle parking, laundry service. Also has restaurant in town, C3, No 10-66.
F Central, C 3, No 10-32, T837 3027, near bus offices. Cheaper without bath, or less still for a room just to dump your luggage in during day's visit, good meals, laundry facilities, secure motorcycle parking, will hire horses, cold water.
F Copacabana, Cra 14 Vía al Estrecho, No 3-42, T837 9222. Good meals and coffee, laundry service, kitchen facilities, parking, quiet, horse hire.
F La Casa de François, Vereda La Antigua, Cra 13, T837 3847, just outside town. Simple rooms, French-run, hot water, use of kitchen facilities at small extra cost.
F Mi Terruño, C 4, No 15-85. Some with bath, hot water, attractive garden, motorbike parking, good, owner Carlos Arturo Muñoz also has 3 cabins, **Los Andaqui** (**F**), C 5, No 23-71, restaurant.
F Posada Campesina, Cra 14, Camino al Estrecho (on the route to El Tablón), 1 km from town, T837 3956. A recommended farmhouse, owned by Doña Silviana Patiño, who makes good pizza and cheese bread, meals with family, simple working farm, shared bath, use of kitchen, camping possible, good walks nearby.
F Residencial Familiar, C 3, No 11-37, T837 3079. Hot water, laundry, book meals in advance or eat next door at the **Colonial**, horses for hire, but noisy disco nearby at weekends.
F Residencias El Jardín, Cra 11, No 4-10, T837 3455. Less without bath, colonial style, pleasant patio with parrots, hot water, quiet, cooking and laundry facilities, free coffee.
F Residencias Menezu, Cra 15, No 4-74, T837 3693. Shared bath, hot water, family atmosphere, safe, central. Recommended.
F Residencias Náñez, C 5, No 15-78, T837 3087. Hot water in shared bathrooms, good value. Recommended.

● *For an explanation of the sleeping and eating price codes used in this guide, see page 58. Other*
● *relevant information is found in Essentials pages 778-779.*

G **Casa de Nelly**, Vía la Estrella, 1½ km west along 2 Av, T837 3221. Attractive peaceful finca run by Nelly Haymann (French), hot water, good food nearby, free coffee. Recommended.

Camping Camping San Agustín, 1 km from town towards Parque Arqueológico, opposite clean public swimming pool, Las Moyas, T837 3804. US$3 pp with own tent, US$4.50 pp to hire tent, 1 large room with bath, US$3.50pp, clean, pleasant, toilets, lights, laundry service, horse hire (see below).

Private houses Accommodation in private houses is available for less than US$3 pp. The farm of **Constantino Ortiz** is recommended, 3½ km from town, first turn on left after the Parque Arqueológico, 4 rooms, best to take a sleeping bag, meals and horses available, peaceful, good cooking, free morning coffee, also has camping, reservations at C 5, No 11-13 in town.

Just outside San Agustín

D **Hacienda Anacaona**, Vía al Estrecho del Magdalena, 2 km from town, T837 9390, www.anacaona-colombia.com. Elegant colonial style, attractive, beautiful views and garden, hammocks, hot water, restaurant, quiet. Camping allowed on grounds. Good.

E-F **El Maco**, 1 km from town, 400 m past Piscina Las Moyas, T837 3437. Swiss owned, working organic farm, rustic, peaceful and quiet, cosy cabins, also dorms, welcoming, basic kitchen facilities, laundry service, good restaurant.

F **Finca El Paraíso**, 1 km from Parque Arqueológico, T837 3575, T312-360 8564, ask for Riecuarte Urbano. Working farm with great views, good beds, shared bath, meals, hot water, laundry service, horses for rent, peaceful, free pick up from town. Camping on grounds, US$4.50 pp.

Around San Agustín: Alto de los Idolos and around *p872*

Several basic, budget hotels (**E-F**) around main plaza in Isnos.

Bogotá to San Agustín: Neiva *p872*

B **Hostería Matamundo**, in old *hacienda* 3 km from centre, on road to Garzón and San Agustín, Cra 5, No 3S-51, T873 0217. A/c, pool, restaurant, disco.

B **Tumburagua**, C 5A, No 5-40, T871 2406. With breakfast, a/c, TV, restaurant, discounts possible, helpful. Recommended.

D **Casa Pablo**, C 5, No 12-45, T872 3100. Good service, parking, laundry, much more with a/c.

G **Residencia Magdalena**, C 1A Sur, No 8A-57, T873 3586. Close to new bus station, cold water.

874

🍴 Eating

Puracé *p869*
Two restaurants, one just above the church, meals around US$2.50.

Around Puracé: La Plata *p870*
Most eating places are closed by 2000. Good set meals opposite Banco Cafetero. Excellent bakery on main plaza.
🍴 **Asadero Los Vikingos**, C 4, near *Hotel Cambis*, pizzas and all meals.

San Agustín *p871*
Tap water in San Agustín is not safe to drink.
🍴🍴 **Donde Richard**, 1 km from town towards Parque Arqueológico. Good steaks. Recommended.
🍴-🍴 **Surabhi**, C 5, No 14-09. Vegetarian dishes or meat, pizzas, *menú*, juices, desserts. Recommended.
🍴-🍴 **Pizza Mania**, Cra 3, No 3-43. Decent pizzas, also sold by the slice, German run.
🍴 **Brahama**, C 5, No 15-11. *Comida* including soup and drink, good fruit salads, vegetarian meals, cheap. Recommended.
🍴 **El Fogón**, C 5 No 14-30. Family run, good *comida* and juices, fresh salads. Recommended.
🍴 **The Tea Rooms**, 20 m from *Casa de Nelly*. Good food, roasts on Sun (sometimes).

Bogotá to San Agustín: Neiva *p872*
🍴 **Avenida**, Av 26, opposite Red Cross. Decent *comida corriente*.
🍴 **Barbacoa**, Cra 4 between C10-9. Good *comida corriente*.

🍸 Bars and clubs

San Agustín *p871*
La Casa de Tarzan, C 2, No 8-04. Nice bamboo and wood interior, quiet.

🎉 Festivals and events

San Agustín *p871*
Santa María del Carmen in **mid-Jul** (date varies) in San Agustín. 2 festivals in **Jun** are San Juan (24th) with horse races and dances, and **San Pedro** (29th) with horse races, dances, fancy dress, and more. In the **1st week of Oct**, the Casa de Cultura celebrates **La Semana Cultural Integrada**, with folklore events from all parts of the country.

Bogotá to San Agustín: Neiva *p872*
A local festival is **18-28 Jun**, when the Bambuco Queen is elected: folklore, dances and feasting.

▲ Activities and tours

San Agustín *p871*
Guides Authorized and recommended guides from World Heritage Travel Office: **Fabio Burbano**, T311-867 5665, professional, reliable and knowledgeable. **Jorge Hurtado**, T311-292 4241 (speaks English). They charge US$15 for a half day, US$30 for a full day, up to 10 people per guide. Make sure you are charged the correct price based on the number of people in your group. World Heritage Travel organises 90-min white-water rafting trips on the Río Magdalena, US$50 with group of 6. You can make your own arrangements, and it may cost less, but we have received many reports of unsatisfactory experiences of unregistered guides. If you have any problems, ask at World Heritage Travel.

Lucio Marino Bravo M, C 5, No 17-300, Av Yalconia, T311-872 5497 (mob), takes walking, riding and minibus tours, authorized, professional, speaks English, French and Italian. Recommended. **Elvecio Silva Silva**, T311-442 7403 (mob), is helpful and knowledgeable.
Horse hire You are strongly advised to hire horses for trips around San Agustín through hotels or World Heritage Travel. Charges are about US$7 per half day, US$8 for a guide for the same time. If you require a guide, add the hire cost of his horse. There are fixed tariffs for 20 or so standard trips.
Rafting **Magdelana Rafting**, Km 2 Vía Parque Arqueológico, T311-271 5333 (mob), www.magdalenarafting.com. Run by the experienced Frenchman Amid Bouselahane, offers various rafting, kayaking and caving tours.
Vehicle tours Jeeps may be hired for between 4-6 people. Prices vary according to the number of sites to be visited, but the daily rate is about US$90. World Heritage Travel organizes a good leisurely day trip to the Salto de Bordones and Mortiño waterfalls, Alto de Las Piedras and Alto de Los Idoles for US$15 (not including entrance fees, guide and lunch). Jeeps direct to Tierradentro can be hired for about US$120 between 5-6 people. For those who like a good walk, most sites can be reached on foot, see above.

Bogotá to San Agustín: Neiva *p872*
Neivatur, C 7, No 6-07/13, T871 0229. **Aviatur** representative.

◉ Transport

Puracé *p869*
Bus There are several daily to Puracé from **Popayán**, the last returning around 1730. The bus stops 3½ km from Pilimbalá.

Around Puracé *p870*
La Plata
Bus To **Bogotá**, via Neiva, **Coomotor**, 9 hrs, in the evening, **Cootranshuila**, 5 a day, US$18. To **Garzón**, bus or jeep 1½ hrs, US$3. To **Popayán** 0500 and others, US$6, 5½ hrs. To **San Agustín**, direct US$9 or take a colectivo to Garzón or Pitalito and change. For **Tierradentro** take a bus towards Popayán (leaves 0600-0630) and alight at the Cruce US$6. Private jeep hire La Plata-Tierradentro US$40, cheaper if you pick up other passengers. To **Pitalito**, 3½ hrs, US$7.

Florencia
Air Aires flies daily to **Neiva** and **Bogotá** (also *Satena*, 6 a week) and most days to **Cali**.
Bus There are regular services from **Neiva** (US$11, 4-6 hrs), **Garzón** and **Altamira** (bus Altamira to Florencia, US$5). To **Bogotá** US$25.

Pitalito
Bus At the bus stations, both off and on buses, in Pitalito, Garzón and Neiva (see below), theft is common.

Plenty of buses and colectivos to **San Agustín**, US$2. Bus to **La Plata**, 3½ hrs, US$7. Buses in Pitalito go from the new bus station. **Taxis Verdes** from the main plaza (US$15 to Bogotá). Bus to **Mocoa** (in the Putumayo), US$10, 7-8 hrs, also jeeps from market square, 2 in morning. To **Parque Nacional Cueva de los Guácharos** take a bus/*chiva* to Palestina, US$2, 1 hr, and then a 40-min *chiva* to Mensura. From there it is an 8-km walk or horse ride to the Park visitors centre.

Parque Nacional Puracé *p870*
Bus All the places beyond Puracé village can be reached by bus from **Popayán** to La Plata or Garzón. The bus service can be erratic so check time of last daylight bus to Popayán and be prepared to spend a cold night at 3,000 m. The rangers will allow you to stay in the centre.

San Agustín *p871*
Bus To **Bogotá** by colectivo (**Taxis Verdes**, C 3, No 11-57) 4 daily, direct or change at Neiva, go early US$18, 9-11 hrs, or by bus (**Coomotor**, C 3, No 10-71), 1 a day, about US$18, 12-14 hrs. From **Bogotá**, Taxis Verdes will pick up at hotels (extra charge), T01-355 5555. Alternatively there are frequent services from Bogotá to **Neiva** as well as some to Pitalito (Taxis Verdes costs US$16). Most services going to Bogotá will stop at Garzón and Neiva. To **Tierradentro**, check first if any of the tourist offices is running a jeep (about US$120 for minimum 4 people), otherwise, **Taxis Verdes** or colectivos leave frequently to **Garzón** (US$3.50) or **Pitalito** (30 mins), then a colectivo jeep from Pitalito to **La Plata**, US$7, 3½ hrs. Usually you can

875

get a **chiva**, bus or colectivo, 2-3 hrs to Tierradentro (San Andrés de Pisimbalá) the same day. Daily buses to **Garzón**, US$4.50, 2½-3 hrs, from where more buses go to La Plata for Tierradentro. Do not take a night bus to Tierradentro. There are 3 daily buses from San Agustín to Popayán via Paletará and Coconuco with **Cootranshuila** (office on C 3, No 10-81), slow, bad unpaved road, 6 hrs, US$12; some continuing to Cali (US$16) and **Coomotor** on this route to Cali, 9 hrs. Do not travel between San Agustín and Popayán at night. The road is isolated and dangerous. It's best to book seats the day before. Ask at **World Heritage Travel** as services are sometimes cut and prices vary.

Bogotá to San Agustín: Neiva *p872*
Air La Marguita, 1½ km from city. Daily flights to/from **Bogotá** and principal cities, **Aires** and **Satena**. Taxi to bus terminal US$1.50.

Bus Station out of town; bus from the centre leaves from the old terminal (Cra 2, Cs 5 y 6). To **Bogotá**, 6 hrs, US$15. **Coomotor** to **San Agustín**, US$9, 6 hrs. To **Garzón**, US$4.50, 2 hrs with **Cootranshuila**. To **Pitalito**, US$7, 3 hrs. To **La Plata**, for Tierradentro, frequent services (especially early morning, 0400, 0500). To **Popayán**, US$13, 8-11 hrs, poor road in parts. To **Florencia**, US$11. To **Ibagué**, US$12.

❶ Directory

San Agustín *p871*
Banks Change TCs before arriving in San Agustín; the small shop opposite police station will exchange cash only, at a poor rate. **Banco Agrario** cash advances against Visa. One ATM, but do not rely on it to be working. **Internet** Galería Café, C 3, No 12-26, T837 9575, opposite mayor's office. Offers coffee and international calls.

Southern Colombia

This region includes the routes from Popayán to the border with Ecuador, Colombia's furthest stretch of Pacific coast and its toehold on the Amazon river. Pasto is the commercial outlet for the agricultural produce of the southern highlands and its history is tied up with the struggle for independence from Spain and the subsequent wrangling over Simón Bolívar's dream of Gran Colombia. The country's Amazonian port is Leticia, gateway to the jungle, Brazil and Peru.

South to Ecuador

From Popayán to Ecuador is scenic highland country, much of it open páramo intersected here and there by deep ravines. To the west is the long slope down to the Pacific including the mangrove swamps of much of the coast and the small port of Tumaco. To the east is the continental divide of the Cordillera Oriental and the beginning of the great Amazonian basin. The route rises still further to the border with Ecuador.

Pasto → *Phone code: 92. Population: 326,000. Altitude: 2,534 m.*
The Pan-American Highway continues south from Popayán to Pasto (285 km, five hours driving). The road drops to 700 m in the valley of the Río Patía before climbing to Pasto with big temperature changes. 38 km before Pasto is **Chachagüi**.

Pasto, 88 km from Ecuador, is overlooked from the west by Volcán Galeras (when not in cloud) and to the east by green hills not yet suburbanized by the city, and is in a very attractive setting. The city, capital of the Department of Nariño, stands upon a high plateau in the southwest and retains some of its colonial character. It was founded in the early days of the conquest. During the wars of independence, it was a stronghold of the Royalists and the last town to fall into the hands of the patriots after a bitter struggle. Then the people of Nariño Department wanted to join Ecuador when that country split off from Gran Colombia in 1830, but were prevented by Colombian troops. Today Pasto is a centre for agricultural and cattle industries. Pasto varnish (*barniz*) is mixed locally, to embellish the colourful local wooden bowls.

There are several churches worth visiting, the ornate churches of **San Juan Bautista** and **La Merced** ① *Calle 18A, No 25-11*, **Cristo Rey** ① *Calle 20, No 24-64* and **Santiago** ① *Cra 23 y Calle 13*, which has good views over the city to the mountains.

The **Museo de Oro del Banco de la República** ① *Calle 19, No 21-27, T721 5777, Mon-Fri 0800-1200, 1400-1800, Sat 0800-1300*, has a small well-displayed collection of pre-Columbian pieces from the cultures of southern Colombia, a library and auditorium **Museo Zambrano**

① *C 20, No 29-78*, houses indigenous and colonial period arts, especially *quiteño* (from Quito). The **tourist office** ① *just off the main plaza, C 18, No 25-25, T723 4962, Mon-Fri 0800-1200, 1400-1800*, is friendly and helpful.

Volcán Galeras and around

The volcano, Galeras (4,276 m), quiescent since 1934, began erupting again in 1989 and again in 2005. Check at the tourist office whether it is safe to climb on the mountain and whether you need a permit. A road climbs up the mountain to a ranger station and police post at 3,700 m. At the last report, you were not permitted beyond this point.

On the north side of the volcano lies the village of **Sandoná** ① *frequent buses and colectivos daily, US$2, 1½ hrs from Pasto,* where panama hats are made; they can be seen lying in the streets in the process of being finished. Sandoná market day is Saturday. There are good walks on the lower slopes through Catambuco and Jongovito (where bricks are made).

The 284 km road west from Pasto to Tumaco on the coast is paved, but is subject to landslides – check in Pasto. It leaves the Panamericana 40 km south of Pasto at El Pedregal, passing the brick factories of the high plains of the Cordillera Occidental. In **Túquerres** (*Altitude 3,050 m*) the market is on Thursday, good for ponchos. Ask in Túquerres about walking and climbing in the Laguna Verde/Volcán Azufral area.

About 90 km from Túquerres, at the village of **Chucunez**, a dirt road branches south to **Reserva Natural La Planada** ① *for further information contact the reserve T927-753396/7, fesplan@col2.telecom.com.co,* a private 3,200 ha nature reserve. This patch of dense cloud forest on a unique flat-topped mountain is home to a wide variety of flora and fauna, and believed to have one of the largest concentrations of native bird species in South America. Day visitors are welcome but camping is prohibited. There is accommodation, US$12.50 pp, including meals. Guides are available.

Tumaco → *Phone code: 92. Colour map 1, grid C2. Population: 115,000.*

Tumaco has two-storey wooden houses and a predominantly black population, and the roads, water and electricity supplies are not good. It is in one of the world's rainiest areas; the yearly average temperature is about 30°C. The northern part of the town is built on stilts out over the sea (safe to visit only in daylight). The town's beaches are polluted, but swimming is safe at El Morro beach, north of the town (watch out for poisonous rays). There are many discos specializing in Afro/South American rhythms. A few shops may buy dollars at a poor rate; change money in Cali or Pasto. The area around is noted for the archaeological finds associated with the Tumaco culture.

The coastal area around Tumaco is mangrove swamp, with many settlements on the rivers and inlets; negotiate with boatmen for a visit to the swamps or the beautiful island tourist resort of **Boca Grande**. The trip takes 30 minutes, US$8 return. There are several places to stay in the **G** category.

Border with Ecuador

It is possible to travel to Ecuador (San Lorenzo) by boat. Part of the trip is by river, which is very beautiful, and part on the open sea, which can be very rough; a plastic sheet to cover your belongings is essential. Take suncream. It is possible to go overland crossing the Río Mira to reach Ecuador, but there are no immigration offices so you cannot cross officially. Even if you could, it is not advisable to use this route (or the sea crossing) as guerrilla activity makes this a dangerous area.

Colombian immigration is at DAS, C 23, Manzana 10, Casa 16, Barrio Pradomar, T727 2010, Tumaco; obtain stamp for leaving Colombia here. Office open weekdays only. Visas for Ecuador (if required) should be obtained in Cali or Pasto. Entry stamps for Ecuador must be obtained in the coastal towns.

Entering Colombia through Tumaco: you will have to go to Ipiales to obtain the entry stamp. Apparently the 24/48 hours 'unofficial' entry is not a problem, but do not obtain any Colombian stamps in your passport before presentation to DAS in Ipiales.

The Putumayo

About 25 km east of Pasto, on the road to Mocoa is **Laguna La Cocha**, the largest lake in south Colombia (sometimes called Lago Guamuez). By the lake, 3 km from the main road, is the **C Chalet Guamuez**, T721 9306, with chalets, boat and jeep trips. Recommended. In the lake is the **Isla de La Corota** nature reserve with interesting trees (10 minutes by boat from the **C Hotel Sindanamoy,** camping possible). There are also cheap and friendly places to stay in and near El Encano (often marked El Encanto on maps) where there are also many restaurants serving trout.

Beyond El Encano there is a steep climb over the Sierra where a large statue of the Virgin marks the entry into the Putumayo. The road then descends steeply to Sibundoy, Mocoa and Puerto Asís. For many years this has been guerrilla territory and a drug growing and processing area. It is also the centre of the government-led coca eradication programme. Even if the authorities allow you to enter, you are strongly advised not to do so.

Ipiales → *Phone code: 92. Colour map 1, grid C2. Population: 72,000. Altitude: 2,898 m.*

Passing through deep valleys and a spectacular gorge, buses on the paved Pan-American Highway cover the 84 km from Pasto to Ipiales in 1½-2 hours. The road crosses the spectacular gorge of the Río Guáitara at 1,750 m, near El Pedregal, where *choclo* (corn) is cooked in many forms by the roadside. **Ipiales**, "the city of the three volcanoes", is famous for its colourful Friday morning indigenous market. The **Catedral Bodas de Plata** is worth visiting but the real attraction is the Sanctuary of the Virgin of **Las Lajas**, about 7 km east of Ipiales. Seen from the approach road, looking down into the canyon, the Sanctuary is a magnificent architectural conception, set on a bridge over the Río Guáitara: close up, it is very heavily ornamented in the gothic style. The altar is set into the rock face of the canyon, which forms one end of the sanctuary with the façade facing a wide plaza that completes the bridge over the canyon. There are walks to nearby shrines in dramatic scenery. It is a 10-15 minutes' walk down to the sanctuary from the village. There are great pilgrimages to it from Colombia and Ecuador (very crowded at Easter) and the Sanctuary must be second only to Lourdes in the number of miracles claimed for it. Colectivo taxis from Ipiales bus terminal go direct to Las Lajas (10 minutes), US$5.50 one way. Several basic hotels and a small number of restaurants at Las Lajas. You may also stay at the Casa Pastoral for about US$3 a night: amazing views of the Sanctuary.

Border with Ecuador

Ipiales is 2 km from the Rumichaca bridge across the Río Carchi into Ecuador. The border post stands on a concrete bridge, beside a natural bridge, where customs and passport examinations take place 0600-2200 (24 hours for pedestrians). All Colombian offices are in one complex: **DAS** (immigration, exit stamp given here), customs, **INTRA** (Dept of Transportation, car papers stamped here; if leaving Colombia you must show your vehicle entry permit) and **ICA** (Department of Agriculture for plant and animal quarantine). There is also a restaurant, Telecom, clean bathrooms (ask for key, US$0.10) and ample parking. See page 931 for the Ecuadorean side and see also Documents in Ecuador, Essentials, page 887. The **Ecuadorean consulate** ① *T773 2292, weekdays 0900-1230, 1430-1700*, is in the DAS complex. There are many money changers near the bridge on both sides. There are better rates on the Colombian side but check all calculations.

● Sleeping

Pasto *p876*

A Cuellar's, Cra 23, No 15-50, T723 2879, F723 8274. Roomy, well-furnished, restaurant, breakfast included. Recommended.

A Don Saul, C 17, No 23-52, T723 0618, F723 0622. One block from main plaza. Comfortable, good restaurant, with breakfast. Recommended.

B Galerías, Cra 26, No 18-71, p 3, T723 7390, F723 7069, above shopping mall. Comfortable, good restaurant, with breakfast, parking, central. Recommended.

C Casa Madrigal, C 26, No 15-37, T723 4592. Central, modern, with breakfast.

C El Dorado, C16A, No 23-42, T723 3260, With bath, quiet, TV.

D El Duque, Cra 20, No 17-17, T721 7390. Hot water, quiet, TV, good.

E Canchala, C 17, No 20A-38, T/F721 3965. Big, safe, hot water, TV, central.

E Koala Inn, C 18, No 22-37, T722 1101, koalainn@hotmail.com. Well-established, popular traveller hostal. Cheaper without bath, laundry facilities, speak to Luis Eduardo, very helpful, hot water, book exchange, restaurant serves breakfast. Recommended.

F Aica, C 17, No 20-75, T721 5311. Near Macro Económico supermarket. Safe, cheaper with shared bath, hot water, TV, but dirty.

F María Belén, C 13, No 19-15, Av de Las Américas, T723 0277. Central, safe, quiet, hot water.

Tumaco *p877*

Children meet arriving buses to offer accommodation; most cheap places are in C del Comercio, many houses and restaurants without signs take guests – most have mosquito nets. Be very careful of food and water because there are many parasites.

E El Dorado, C del Comercio, T727 2565, near water-front and *canoa* dock. Basic, TV, private and shared bath (half the price).

E Imperial, C Mosquera, No 11-23, T727 4746. A basic option.

Ipiales *p878*

C Mayasquer, 3 km on road to the border, T773 2643. Modern, nice restaurant, very good.

E Bachué, Cra 6, No 11-68, T773 2164. Central, safe, hot water, with bath, TV.

E Castillo Real, C 14, No 4-36, T773 4610. Central, with bath, TV, hot water.

F Belmonte, Cra 4, No 12-111, T773 2771 (near *Transportes Ipiales*). Hot water, parking opposite, good value but crowded. Recommended.

✴ Eating

Pasto *p876*

Local specialities include *arepas de choclo*, made with fresh ground sweet corn, sold at the kiosks beside the main road going north. *Cuy*, grilled guinea pig, is another typical dish.

¶¶ Asadero Inca Cuy, Cra 29, No 13-67, T723 8050. Good place to try *cuy*,

¶¶ Portón Veinte, C 20, No 35-05, T731 2940. Good typical food.

Tumaco *p877*

The main culinary attraction of the town is the fish, in the market and restaurants, fresh from the Pacific. A number of good restaurants on the main streets, C Mosquera and C del Comercio, though the best is probably **El Portón Marino** on C Sucre.

Ipiales *p878*

Plenty of cheap restaurants, better ones on Cra 7.
¶¶ Frimon, Cra 7, No 13-53, T773 4211. Good for typical dishes.

✴ Festivals and events

Pasto *p876*

During the new year's *fiesta* there is a **Día de los Negros** on **5 Jan** and a **Día de los Blancos** next day. On 'black day' people dump their hands in black grease and smear each others' faces. On 'white day' they throw talc or flour at each other. Local people wear their oldest clothes. On **28 Dec** and **5 Feb**, there is also a **Fiesta de las Aguas** when anything that moves gets drenched with water from balconies and even from fire engines' hoses. All towns in the region are involved in this legalized water war! In Pasto and Ipiales (see page 878), on **31 Dec**, is the **Concurso de Años Viejos**, when huge dolls are burnt; they represent the old year and sometimes lampoon local people.

○ Shopping

Pasto *p876*

Handicrafts Leather goods shops are on C 17 and C 18. Try the municipal market for handicrafts. **Artesanía-Mercado Bombona**, C 14 y Cra 27. **Artesanías Mopa-Mopa**, Cra 25, No 13-14, for *barniz*. **Artesanías Nariño**, C 26, No 18-91. **Casa del Barniz de Pasto**, C 13, No 24-9.

Markets and supermarkets Ley on C 18. **Supermercado Confamiliar de Nariño**, C 16B, No 30-53. Recommended.
On the main plaza (C 19 y Cra 25) is a shopping centre with many shops and restaurants.

Maps Maps of Colombia and cities from **Instituto Geográfico Agustín Codazzi**, C 18A, No 21A-18, limited selection.

▲ Activities and tours

Pasto *p876*

Every Sun paddle ball is played on the edge of the town (bus marked 'San Lorenzo') similar to the game played in Ibarra, Ecuador.

◉ Transport

Pasto *p876*

Air Daily with **Satena** to **Bogotá**, 3 a week to **Cali** and **Puerto Asís**. The airport is at Cano, 40 km from Pasto; by colectivo (beautiful drive), 45 mins, US$2.40 or US$13.50 by taxi. There are no currency exchange facilities, but the shop will change US$ bills at a poor rate.

Bus All interurban buses leave from the terminal at Cra 6, C 16, 4 km from centre, taxi, US$1. To **Bogotá**, 18-23 hrs, US$35 (Bolivariano Pullman most direct, recommended). To **Ipiales**, 2 hrs, US$3, sit on the left for the views. To **Popayán**, ordinary buses take 10-12 hrs, US$7; expresses take 5-8 hrs, cost US$11. To **Cali**, US$11, expresses, 8½ to 10 hrs. To **Tumaco**, 9 hrs by bus, 7 hrs by minibus, US$10.

● For an explanation of the sleeping and eating price codes used in this guide, see page 58. Other
● relevant information is found in Essentials pages 778-779.

Around Volcán Galeras: Túquerres *p877*
Bus To **Pasto** US$4.50, 2 hrs, Trans Ipiales; jeep to **Ipiales** from Carrera 14, C 20, US$2, 1½ hrs.

Tumaco *p877*
Air There are daily flights to and from **Cali**, 40 mins, and **Medellín** with Satena.
Bus To **Pasto**, 6-9 hrs, US$11, with Supertaxis del Sur or Trans Ipiales, 4 a day, interesting ride; minibus 7 hrs. From Ipiales go to El Espino (US$0.75, colectivo, US$1.15) and there change buses for Tumaco (US$4.80).

Border with Ecuador: Tumaco *p877*
Boat Daily service at 1200 (times change) to **San Lorenzo**, 7 hrs (but can take 14) tickets from C del Comercio (protective plastic sheeting provided). Ask around the water-front at 0600, or try at the fishing centre, El Coral del Pacífico for a cheaper passage, but seek advice on safety before taking a boat (robberies reported). Fares: motorized canoe US$25; launch US$56.

The Putumayo: Laguna La Cocha *p877*
Taxi To La Cocha from **Pasto**, US$9, or colectivo from C 20 y Cra 20. Or take a **bus** to **El Encano** and walk the remaining 5 km to the chalets of Chalet Guamuez, or 20 mins from bus stop direct to lake shore and take a *lancha* to the chalets for US$3.

Ipiales *p878*
Air San Luis airport is 6½ km out of town. Aires and Satena to **Medellín**, **Bogotá** and **Puerto Asís**. Taxi to Ipiales centre, US$4.
Bus Bus companies have individual departure points: *busetas/colectivos* mostly leave from main plaza. To **Popayán**, Expreso Bolivariano, US$12, 7½-8 hrs, hourly departures, 0800-2000; also colectivo taxis, US$14-16. Expreso Bolivariano to **Cali**, US$15, 10-12 hrs. To **Pasto** US$3.50, 2-3 hrs. Frequent buses to **Bogotá** every 2 hrs, 20-24 hrs, US$35 (check if you have to change buses in Cali). To **Medellín**, 2 daily, 20-22 hrs, US$33. To **Túquerres**, 2 hrs, US$4.50.

Border with Ecuador: Ipiales *p878*
Bus From Ipiales to **Tulcán**: *colectivo* from C 14 y Cra 11, US$0.60 to the border (buses to Ipiales arrive at the main plaza – they may take you closer to the colectivo point if you ask). Colectivo from border to **Tulcán** US$0.75, to Tulcán bus station, US$1. Ask the fare at border tourist office. To go to bus terminal, take blue bus from central plaza, US$0.05. Easiest to take a taxi in Ipiales to the border, US$3.
Car If entering Colombia by car, the vehicle is supposed to be fumigated against diseases that affect coffee trees, at the ICA office. The certificate must be presented in El Pedregal, 40 km beyond Ipiales on the road to Pasto. (This fumigation process is not always carried out.) You can buy insurance for your car in Colombia at Banco Agrario, in the plaza.

✪ Directory

Pasto *p876*
Banks For changing TCs, Bancolombia, C 19, No 24-52. Visa advances. Banco de Bogotá will change TCs 0930-1130. If going to Tumaco, this is the last place where TCs can be cashed. *Casas de cambio*, **Titan**, Cra 26, No 18-71, at Cra 25, No 18-97, and C 19, No 24-86, by the main plaza. **Post offices** Cra 23, 18-42.
Telephones Long distance calls, C 17 y Cra 23.
Useful addresses DAS: C 17, No 29-70, T731 3981/1500, will give exit stamps if you are going on to Ecuador.

Ipiales *p878*
Banks It is not possible to cash TCs, but cash against Visa is no problem at **Bancolombia**, C 14, No 5-32. *Casa de Cambio* on the plaza. Money changers on street, in plaza and at border, but they may take advantage if the banks are closed. Coming from Ecuador, peso rates compare well in Ipiales with elsewhere in Colombia.
Telephones International calls from Cra 6 y C 6/7.

Leticia and the Amazon

The extensive cattle lands from the Cordillera Central to the Orinoco are a good place to get away from it all in the dry season. Leticia, Colombia's port on the Amazon, is on the southern tip of a spur of territory which gives Colombia access to the great river, 3,200 km upstream from the Atlantic. There is a land border with Brazil a short distance to the east beyond which are Marco and Tabatinga. Directly south across the river is another important Brazilian port, Benjamin Constant, which is close to the border with Peru. On the north side of the Amazon, Colombia has a frontage on the river of 80 km to the land border with Peru.

Leticia → *Phone code: 98. Colour map 3, grid A5. Population: 23,000. Altitude: 82 m.*
Capital of Amazonas Department, the city is clean, modern, though run down near the river. Parque Santander y Orellana is pleasant and is a popular meeting place. It is rapidly merging

Ecuador

Essentials	886
Quito and around	893
Sights	896
Around Quito	916
Northern Ecuador	921
Quito to Otavalo	922
Otavalo and around	923
Otavalo to the Colombian border	928
Cotopaxi, Latacunga	
and Quilotoa	935
Cotopaxi and Latagunga	935
Quiltoa Circuit	940
Ambato	943
Baños and Riobamba	946
Baños and around	946
Riobamba and around	952
Cuenca and around	959
Cuenca to the Peruvian border	968
Vilcabamba to Peru	974
Guayaquil and south to Peru	976
Guayaquil	978
South to Peru	984
Pacific lowlands	987
Guayaquil to Puerto López	987
Manta and Bahía de Caráquez	993
Northern lowlands	999
The Oriente	1004
Northern Oriente	1005
Central and southern Oriente	1010
Galápagos Islands	1017
Background	1017
Ins and outs	1018
The islands	1020

⁑ Footprint features

Don't miss …	885
Touching down	888
Driving in Ecuador	891
Language schools in Quito	915
The railway from the coast to	
the Sierra	954
Galápagos tourist vessels	1024
Overseas agencies	1028

Introduction

Tucked in between Peru and Colombia, this country is small enough for you to have breakfast with scarlet macaws in the jungle, lunch in the lee of a snow-capped peak and, at tea time, be eyeballed by an iguana whose patch of Pacific beach you have just borrowed.

A multitude of national parks and conservation areas emphasise the incredible variety of Ecuador. They include mangroves; an avenue of volcanoes – many of them active – striding across the Equator; forests growing on the dry Pacific coast, in the clouds and under the Amazonian rains; not forgetting all the animals and birds which flourish in these habitats. In fact, as Ecuador is one of the richest places in the world for birds, with some of the planet's most beautiful species, the country is being promoted as a prime birdwatching destination.

The capital, Quito, has become one of the gringo centres of South America, bursting at the seams with language schools, travel agencies and restaurants. The last remaining segment of the line from Quito to the Pacific port of Guayaquil, with spectacular zig-zags and switchbacks, is a highpoint of railway engineering. The exotic wildlife of the Galápagos Islands will also keep you enthralled, whether it's sympathizing with Lonesome George, the last giant tortoise of his race, watching an albatross take off on its flight path, or admiring the sexual paraphernalia of the magnificent frigate bird. If the Galápagos are beyond your budget, the Isla de la Plata is a more accessible alternative for seeing marine life.

★ Don't miss ...

1 **Quito** The old centre is a World Heritage treasure trove of colonial art and architecture, while the new city is one of the places to which gringos gravitate to learn Spanish and get their bearings, page 893.

2 **Otavalo** This little town north of Quito is home to one of the largest and most colourful craft markets in South America, page 923.

3 **Nariz del Diablo** Although earthquakes and shortage of money have taken their toll on the famous railway from Quito to Guayaquil, one section is still run regularly. This, fortunately, is the part with the most amazing engineering and drama, page 954.

4 **Vilcabamba** In the far south of the Ecuadorean Andes is the fabled fountain of youth. Whether you'll live longer for going there or not, it's a great place to relax, or escape to the hills on foot or horseback, page 974.

5 **Northern jungles** Coca is the gateway to the northern Oriente, with some excellent lodges in the Yasuní National Park and the Cuyabeno Wildlife Reserve. Boating down a tributary of the Amazon to enter the rainforest is a great experience, page 1005.

6 **Galápagos Islands** Quite simply one of the world's most remarkable places, a sanctuary for wildlife that has evolved its own unique speciation and temperament. A visit here will surely be one of the highlights of a lifetime, page 1017.

Essentials

Planning your trip

Where to go The capital, **Quito**, boasts some of the best-preserved colonial architecture in South America in its 'Old Town', while the 'New City' is where you'll find most accommodation, restaurants, tour operators and language schools. From the capital many of the country's attractions are accessible by road in only a few hours. Day trips include nature reserves, hot springs, and, of course, the Equator. There is also good mountaineering and white-water rafting nearby. North of Quito is **Otavalo** with its outstanding handicrafts market, a regular one-day tour, but equally popular as a base for exploring nearby villages, more nature reserves and hiking or cycling routes. Carrying on towards the Colombian border is **Ibarra**, another good centre for visiting the north and the starting point for the journey to San Lorenzo on the Pacific.

In the Central Sierra, south of Quito is the national park surrounding **Cotopaxi**, one of Ecuador's most frequently climbed volcanoes. Further south is the **Quilotoa circuit**, a 200 km loop through small villages and beautiful landscapes, with lots of possibilities for trekking, cycling and riding. The starting point is Latacunga on the Pan-American Highway. On one of the main routes from the Sierra to the eastern jungle is **Baños**, a very popular spa town with climbing, hiking, riding and volcano watching opportunities close at hand. The heart of the central highlands is **Riobamba**, beneath Chimborazo volcano. This is another good base for climbing, biking and trekking, as well as the starting point for a very popular railway ride over La Nariz del Diablo (The Devil's Nose) – when the often-damaged line is open. The Inca ruin of **Ingapirca** is between Riobamba and **Cuenca**, a lovely colonial city in the Southern Sierra. Nearby is the Cajas National Park. En route from Cuenca towards Peru are the provincial capital of **Loja**, close to the Parque Nacional Podocarpus, and **Vilcabamba**, with a delightful climate and a favourite with backpackers. Several border crossings to Peru are accessible from Loja.

Ecuador's Pacific capital is **Guayaquil**, 45 minutes by air from Quito (eight hours by bus) and only four hours by bus south to the Peruvian border via Machala. Key areas of the city are being renewed, such as its historic riverfront. To the north stretch the **Pacific Lowlands** with beaches, pre-Columbian archaeological sites and peaceful little low-key resorts like Puerto López, Montañita, Canoa and Muisne, as well as a few highly developed ones like Bahía de Caráquez and Atacames. Near Puerto López the **Parque Nacional Machalilla** contains dry tropical forest, offshore islands and marine ecosystems. It is a good place for riding, diving, whale watching, birdwatching and relaxing on the beautiful Los Frailes beach.

The **Oriente** (eastern lowlands) offers good opportunities for nature tourism, with a number of specially designed jungle lodges, mainly in the north. A stay in one of these places is best booked in Quito or from home, but you can head for jungle towns like Coca, Lago Agrio, Tena, Puyo or Misahuallí to arrange a tour with a local agency or guide. The southern Oriente is less developed for tourism, but interest is growing, with Macas or Zamora as the places to aim for.

Ecuador is famous for its **hot springs** and, on either side of the Andes, there is great birdwatching in a wide variety of protected areas. Other special interest activities include diving, whitewater rafting and various volunteer programmes. The nature destination par excellence, though, is the **Galápagos Islands**, 970 km west of the mainland. Tours, which are best arranged in Quito, Guayaquil or from home, involve cruising from island to island to see new species with each landfall.

When to go Ecuador's climate is highly unpredictable. As a general rule, however, in the **Sierra**, there is little variation by day or by season in the temperature: this depends on altitude. The range of shade temperature is from 6°C to 10°C in the morning to 19°C to 23°C in the afternoon, though it can get considerably hotter in the lower basins. Rainfall patterns depend on whether a particular area is closer to the eastern or western slopes of the Andes. To the west, June to September are dry and October to May are wet (but there is sometimes a short dry spell in December or January). To the east, October to February are dry and March to September are wet. There is also variation in annual rainfall from north to south, with the southern highlands being drier. **Quito** is within 25 km of the Equator, but it stands high enough to make its climate much like that of spring in England, the days pleasantly warm and the nights cool. Rainy season is October to May with the heaviest rainfall in April. Rain usually falls in the afternoon. The day length (sunrise to sunset) is almost constant throughout the year.

Along the **Pacific coast**, rainfall also decreases from north to south, so that it can rain throughout the year in northern Esmeraldas and seldom at all near the Peruvian border. The coast, however, can be enjoyed year-round, although it may be a bit cool from June to November, when mornings are often grey with the *garúa* mists. January to May is the hottest and rainiest time of the year. Like the coast the **Galápagos** suffer from the *garúa* from May to December; from January to April the islands are hottest and brief but heavy showers can fall. In the **Oriente**, heavy rain can fall at any time, but it is usually wettest from March to September.

Ecuador's **high season** is from June to early September, which is also the best time for climbing and trekking. There is also a short tourist season in December and January. In resort areas at major fiestas, such as Carnival, Semana Santa and over New Year, accommodation can be hard to find. Hotels will be full in individual towns during their particular festivals, but Ecuador as a whole is not overcrowded at any time of the year.

Finding out more Ministerio de Turismo ⓘ *Eloy Alfaro N32-300 y Carlos Tobar, Quito, T250 7559, www.vivecuador.com*. Local offices are given in the text. Outside Ecuador, tourist information can be obtained from Ecuadorean Embassies. National parks, of which Ecuador has an outstanding array, are controlled by the **Ministerio del Ambiente** ⓘ *Ministerio de Agricultura y Ganadería building, p 8, Amazonas y Eloy Alfaro, Quito, T02-250 6337*. The ministry has less information than the park offices in the cities nearest the parks themselves.

Websites

www.ecuadorexplorer.com;www.ecuador-tra vel-guide.org; and **www.ecuaworld.com** are all travel guides.

www.saexplorers.org South American Explorers has information about how to become a member, the club's services and volunteering. See page 894 for address.

www.explored.com.ec General information about Ecuador in Spanish, including a guide to national parks.

www.quitogay.net Gay information.
www.thebestofecuador.com/volunt.htm Vo lunteering ideas page on a comprehensive guide to the country.

Maps and guide books Instituto Geográfico Militar (IGM) ⓘ *Senierges y Telmo Paz y Miño, on top of the hill to the east of Parque El Ejido. From Av 12 de Octubre, opposite the Casa de la Cultura, take Jiménez (a small street) up the hill. After crossing Av Colombia continue uphill on Paz y Miño behind the Military Hospital and then turn right to the guarded main entrance. You have to deposit your passport or identification card. T02-254 5090, www.igm.gov.ec. Map sales room open Mon-Thu 0800-1600, Mon-Fri 0800-1300*. They sell country maps and topographic maps, covering most areas of Ecuador, in various scales, US$2 each. Maps of border areas and the seacoast are 'reservado' (classified) and not available for sale without a military permit (requires extra time). Buy your maps here, they are rarely available outside Quito. If one is sold out you may order a photocopy. Map and geographic reference libraries are located next to the sales room. The *IGM* is on top of the hill to the east of El Ejido park. From 12 de Octubre, opposite the *Casa de la Cultura*, take Jiménez (a small street) up the hill. After crossing Av Colombia continue uphill on Paz y Miño behind the Military Hospital and then turn right to the guarded main entrance; you have to deposit your passport or identification card. There is a beautiful view from the grounds. A good series of road maps, pocket maps and city guides by Nélson Gómez, published by **Ediguías** in Quito, are available in book shops throughout the country.

Visas and immigration All visitors to Ecuador must have a passport valid for at least six months and an onward or return ticket. The latter is seldom asked for, but can be grounds for refusal of entry. Citizens of the following countries do not require a visa to visit Ecuador as tourists: EU countries, North and South American countries (except Guyana, Suriname and Mexico), Australia, Israel, South Africa and Switzerland; contact your embassy for further details. New Zealanders apparently do need a visa, even though the Ministry of Foreign Relations website says they do not; check with an Ecuadorean consulate before arrival. Note that members of the Sikh faith, irrespective of nationality, may need a visa and should check with an Ecuadorean consulate before travelling. Upon entry all visitors must complete an international embarkation/disembarkation card, which is stamped along with your passport.

Touching down

Keep this card with your passport, losing it can cause all manner of grief when leaving the country.

Warning: you are required by Ecuadorean law to carry your passport at all times. Failure to do so can result in imprisonment and/or deportation. An ordinary photocopy of your passport is not an acceptable substitute and you will generally not be permitted to return to your hotel to fetch the original document. A photocopy certified by your embassy or the immigration police may be acceptable, but you should also have your original passport close at hand. Tourists are not permitted to work under any circumstances.

Length of stay Tourists are entitled to visit Ecuador for up to 90 days during any 12 month period. This may be extended up to 180 days at the discretion of the **Policía Nacional de Migración**. In practice, those travelling by land from Peru or Colombia are seldom granted more than 30 days on arrival, but this can usually be extended. When arriving at Quito or Guayaquil airport you will be asked how long you plan to stay. If you have no idea, ask for 90 days.

Extensions *Prórrogas* (extensions) for stays of up to 90 days may be requested at any *jefatura provincial* (provincial headquarters) of the Policía Nacional de Migración (www.migracion.gov.ec). Most are located in provincial capitals and addresses are given under each town, but smaller offices are not always familiar with the procedure. Quito, Guayaquil and Cuenca, which are the only offices at which to request extensions beyond 90 days, are your best bet. In Quito you may go to either the **Jefatura Provincial de Migración de Pichincha** ⓘ *Isla Seymour 44-174 y Río Coca, T/F02-224 7510*, or the **Dirección Nacional de Migración** ⓘ *Amazonas 171 y República, T245 4122*. Immigration offices are open Monday to Friday 0800- 1200 and 1500-1800. Obtaining an extension can take less than an hour, but do not leave it to the last minute. If you overstay your visa, you will be fined US$200. Regulations are subject to change. Polite conduct and a neat appearance are important.

Tourists attending a course at a language school do **not** need a student visa (unless staying more than 180 days). There are many options for foreigners who wish to stay in Ecuador longer than six months, but if you enter as a tourist you cannot change your status while in the country.

Note In addition to your passport, all international travellers must carry an **international vaccination certificate**, although it is seldom asked for. An **International Student Identity Card (ISIC)** may help you obtain discounts when travelling. ISIC cards are sold in Quito by **Grupo Idiomas** ⓘ *Roca 130 y 12 de Octubre, p 2, T250 0264, www.idiomas.com.ec*. They need proof of full-time enrolment in Ecuador or abroad (minimum enrollment 20 hours/week), 2 photos and US$12.

Ecuadorean embassies and consulates For a complete list, visit www.mmrree.gov.ec.

Money The **US dollar** is the only official currency of Ecuador. Only US$ bills circulate. US coins are used alongside the equivalent size and value Ecuadorean coins. Ecuadorean coins have no value outside the country. Many establishments are reluctant to accept bills larger than US$20 because of counterfeit notes or lack of change. Counterfeit US$1 and Ecuadorean 50 cents coins also circulate, so check any bills and coins they receive as change. There is no substitute for cash-in-hand when travelling in Ecuador. Euros are slowly gaining acceptance, but **US$ cash** in small denominations is by far the simplest and the only universally accepted option. All other currencies are very difficult to exchange and fetch a very poor rate.

Plastic/traveller's cheques/banks (ATMs) The most commonly accepted credit cards are Visa, MasterCard, Diners and American Express. Cash advances on credit cards can be obtained through many ATMs, but daily limits apply. Larger advances on Visa and MasterCard are available in the offices of **Pacificard**, as well as branches of **Banco del Pacifico**, **Banco del Austro** and **Banco Bolivariano**. Paying by credit card at most upscale establishments may incur a surcharge (at least 10%). Although less popular than in the past, US traveller's cheques remain useful in Ecuador. They can be exchanged for cash in many cities. **American Express** is the most widely accepted brand. The best places to change TCs are **Produbanco**, **Vazcorp** (in Quito, Otavalo and Cuenca) and **Banco del Pacífico**; some *casas de cambio* charge exorbitant commissions. A passport is always required to exchange TCs and, less frequently, the original purchase receipt for the cheques. Internationally linked **ATMs** are common, although they cannot always be relied on. The affiliations of banks to the Plus and Cirrus systems change often, so ask around. Debit cards are less easy to use. American Express has offices in Quito and Guayaquil; they sell TCs against an Amex card (or a cardholder's personal cheque) and replace lost or stolen TCs, but they do not give cash for TCs, nor TCs for cash. Their service is very efficient; a police report is required if TCs are stolen.

Funds may be rapidly wired to Ecuador by *Western Union*, but high fees and taxes apply. International bank transfers, however, are not recommended.

Cost of living/travelling Despite dollarization, prices remain modest by international standards and Ecuador is still affordable for even the budget traveller. A very basic daily travel budget in 2007 was US$15-20 per person based on two travelling together. For US$50 a day you can enjoy a good deal of comfort. Internet use is about US$0.60-2 per hour.

Safety Urban street crime, bag snatching and slashing, and robbery along the country's highways are the most significant hazards. In an effort to fight crime, army and police patrols operate in some cities and along some highways. Don't be taken aback to see these troops on duty. Secure your belongings, be wary of con tricks, avoid crowds and travel only during the daytime. The countryside and small towns are generally safest, but theft and robbery have been reported from several places where tourists gather. It is the big cities, Guayaquil, Quito, and to a lesser extent Cuenca, which call for the greatest care. The coast is more prone to violence than the highlands, and the northern border with Colombia, including the provinces of Esmeraldas, Carchi, and especially Sucumbíos, call for additional precautions. Armed conflict in Colombia has caused an influx of refugees, and parts of these provinces have come under the influence of insurgents. Enquire locally before travelling to and in any northern border areas.

Occasional social unrest is part of life in Ecuador and you should not overreact. Strikes and protests are usually announced days or weeks in advance, and their most significant impact on tourists is the restriction of travel. **Drugs use or purchase in Ecuador is punishable by up to 16 years' imprisonment**.

Ecuador's active volcanoes are spectacular, but have occasionally threatened nearby communities. The following have shown visible activity in recent years: Reventador northeast of Quito, Tungurahua near Baños, and Sangay southeast of Riobamba. Cotopaxi is also active. The **National Geophysics Institute** provides updates at **www.igepn.edu.ec**.

Getting around

Air TAME① *reservations: Quito T290 9900, Guayaquil T231 0305, www.tame.com.ec*, is the main internal airline, flying to all major airports and the Galápagos. Enquire locally for up-to-date routes and timetables as they change constantly. TAME offices are listed under each relevant town or city. Smaller airlines include **Aerogal,** ① *www.aerogal.com.ec*, which serves Quito, Guayaquil, Cuenca, Manta and the Galápagos; and **Icaro** ① *T1-800-883567, www.icaro.com.ec*, which flies from Quito to Guayaquil, Cuenca, Bahía de Caráquez, Esmeraldas, Loja, Manta and Coca. **VIP** ① *T1-800-847847, www.vipec.com*. Serves Coca, Guayaquil, Lago Agrio, Quito, Salinas and Tena. Confirm and reconfirm all flight reservations frequently.

Bus Bus travel is generally more convenient and regular than in other Andean countries. Several companies use comfortable air-conditioned buses on their longer routes; some companies have their own stations, away from the main bus terminals, exclusively for these better buses. **Note** Throughout Ecuador, travel by bus is safest during the daytime.

Hitchhiking Public transport in Ecuador is so abundant that there is seldom any need to hitchhike along the major highways. On small out-of-the-way country roads however, the situation can be quite the opposite, and giving passers-by a ride is common practice and safe, especially in the back of a pickup or truck. A small fee is usually charged, check in advance.

Train Sadly, the spectacular Ecuadorean railway system has all but ceased operations. In 2006, only a few tourist rides were still being offered: over the Devil's Nose from **Riobamba to Sibambe** and back, and the lowland route **Huigra to Bucay** is operating at weekends and holidays (work continues on the Alausí to Huigra link and was expected to be operational for the 2007 high season). A weekend excursion runs from **Tambillo, south of Quito to the El Boliche station** near Parque Nacional Cotopaxi.

Sleeping → *See page 58 for our hotel grade price guide.*
Hotels Outside the provincial capitals and a few resorts, there are few higher-class hotels. Service of 10% or of 12% are added to better hotel and restaurant bills. Some cheaper hotels apply the 12% tax, but check if it is included. Larger towns and tourist centres often have more hotels than we can list. This is especially true of Quito. The hotels that are included are

Driving in Ecuador

Roads A good network of paved roads runs throughout the coast and highlands. Maintenance of major highways is franchised to private firms, who charge tolls of US$0.50-1. In the Oriente, most roads are dirt or gravel; some that appear paved are in fact crude oil sprayed onto compacted earth.

Safety Unexpected potholes and other obstructions, the lack of road signs, and local drivers' tendency to use the middle of the road make driving 'an experience'. Beware the bus drivers, who often drive very fast and rather recklessly. Driving at night is not recommended.

Documents Obtaining temporary admission to Ecuador for a car or motorcycle can be complex and time-consuming, as is shipping in a vehicle, especially through Guayaquil. A *carnet de passages* is the preferred document for bringing in a private vehicle, but this rule is not consistently applied. Some drivers without it have been allowed to stay in the country, others have had to pass through to the Peruvian or Colombian border in three days. A valid driver's licence from your home country is generally sufficient to drive in Ecuador and rent a car, but an international driving licence is helpful. All documents must be originals, accompanied by a Spanish translation.

Car hire To rent a car you must be 21 and have an international credit card. Surcharges may apply to clients aged 21-25. You may pay cash, which is cheaper and may allow you to bargain, but they want a credit card for security. You may be asked to sign two blank credit card vouchers, one for the rental fee itself and the other as a security deposit, and authorization for a charge of as much as US$5,000 may be requested against your credit card account. The uncashed vouchers will be returned to you when you return the vehicle. Make sure the car is parked securely at night. A small car suitable for city driving costs around US$450 per week including tax and insurance. A 4WD (recommended for the Oriente and unpaved roads) costs about US$725 a week.

Fuel There are two grades of petrol, 'Extra' (82 octane, US$1.48 per US gallon) and 'Super' (92 Octane, US$1.98). Both are unleaded. Extra is available everywhere, while Super may not be available in more remote areas. Diesel fuel (US$1.03) is notoriously dirty and available everywhere.

among the best in each category, selected to provide a variety of locations and styles. Many hotel rooms have very low wattage bulbs, keen readers are advised to take a head torch.

Camping Camping in protected natural areas can be one of the most satisfying experiences during a visit to Ecuador. Organized campsites, car or trailer camping on the other hand are virtually unheard-of. Because of the abundance of cheap hotels you should never *have to* camp in Ecuador, except for cyclists who may be stuck between towns. In this case the best strategy is to ask permission to camp on someone's private land, preferably within sight of their home for safety. It is not safe to pitch your tent at random near villages and even less so on beaches. *Bluet Camping Gas* is easily obtainable, but white gas, like US Coleman fuel, is hard to find. Unleaded petrol (gasoline) is available everywhere and may be an alternative for some stoves.

Eating → *See page 58 for our Eating price guide.*

Eating out Upmarket restaurants add 22% to the bill, 12% tax plus 10% service. All other places add the 12% tax, which is also charged on non-essential items in food shops. The cuisine varies with region. The following are some typical dishes.

In the highlands *Locro de papas* (potato and cheese soup), *mote* (corn burst with alkali, a staple in the region around Cuenca, but used in a variety of dishes in the Sierra), *caldo de patas* (cowheel soup with *mote*), *llapingachos* (fried potato and cheese patties), *empanadas de morocho* (fried snacks: a ground corn shell filled with meat), *sancocho de yuca* (vegetable soup with manioc root), roast *cuy* (guinea pig), *fritada* (fried pork), *hornado* (roast pork), *humitas* (tender ground corn steamed in corn leaves), and *quimbolitos* (similar to *humitas* but prepared with corn flour and steamed in *achira* lily leaves). *Humitas* and *quimbolitos* come in both sweet and savoury varieties.

On the coast *Empanadas de verde* (fried snacks: a ground plantain shell filled with cheese, meat or shrimp), *sopa de bola de verde* (plantain dumpling soup), *ceviche* (marinaded fish or seafood, popular everywhere, see below), *encocadas* (dishes prepared with coconut milk, may be shrimp, fish, etc, very popular in the province of Esmeraldas), *cocadas* (sweets made with coconut), *viche* (fish or seafood soup made with ground peanuts), and *patacones* (thick fried plantain chips served as a side dish).

In Oriente Dishes prepared with yuca (manioc or cassava root) and river fish.

Throughout the country If economizing ask for the set meal in restaurants, *almuerzo* at lunch time, *merienda* in the evening – very cheap and wholesome; it costs US$1.50-3. *Fanesca*, a fish soup with beans, many grains, ground peanuts and more, sold in Easter Week, is very filling (it is so popular that in Quito and main tourist spots it is sold throughout Lent). *Ceviche*, marinated fish or seafood which is usually served with popcorn and roasted maize (*tostado*), is very popular throughout Ecuador. Only *ceviche de pescado* (fish) and *ceviche de concha* (clams) which are marinated raw, potentially pose a health hazard. The other varieties of *ceviche* such as *camarón* (shrimp/prawn) and *langostino* (jumbo shrimp/king prawn) all of which are cooked before being marinated, are generally safe (check the cleanliness of the establishment). *Langosta* (lobster) is an increasingly endangered species but continues to be illegally fished; please be conscientious. Ecuadorean food is not particularly spicy. However, in most homes and restaurants, the meal is accompanied by a small bowl of *ají* (hot pepper sauce) which may vary in potency. *Colada* is a generic name which can refer to cream soups or sweet beverages. In addition to the prepared foods mentioned above, Ecuador offers a large variety of delicious fruits, some of which are unique to South America.

Drink The best fruit drinks are *naranjilla*, *maracuyá* (passion fruit), *tomate de árbol*, *piña* (pineapple), *taxo* (another variety of passion fruit) and *mora* (blackberry), but note that fruit juices are sometimes made with unboiled water. Main beers available are *Pilsener*, *Club*, *Biela*, *Brahma* and *Clausen*. Argentine and Chilean wines are available in the larger cities. Good *aguardiente* (unmatured rum, *Cristal* is recommended), also known as *puntas*, *trago de caña*, or just *trago*. The usual soft drinks, known as *colas*, are available. Instant coffee or liquid concentrate is common, so ask for *café pasado* if you want real coffee. In tourist centres and many upscale hotels and restaurants, good cappuccino and espresso can be found.

Festivals and events

1 January: New Year's Day; 6 January: Reyes Magos y Día de los Inocentes, a time for pranks, which closes the Christmas-New Year holiday season. 27 February: Día del Civismo, celebrating the victory over Peru at Tarqui in 1829. Carnival: Monday and Tuesday before Lent, celebrated everywhere in the Andes, except Ambato, by throwing water at passers-by: be prepared to participate. Easter: Holy Thursday, Good Friday, Holy Saturday. 1 May: Labour Day. 24 May: Battle of Pichincha, Independence. Early June: Corpus Christi. 10 August: first attempt to gain the Independence of Quito. 9 October: Independence of Guayaquil. 2 November: All Souls' Day. 3 November: Independence of Cuenca. 1-6 December: Foundation of Quito. 25 December: Christmas Day.

Quito and around

→ *Phone code: 02. Colour map 11, grid A4. Population: 1,399,378. Altitude: 2,850 m.*

Few cities have a setting to match that of Quito, the second highest capital in Latin America after La Paz. The city is set in a hollow at the foot of the volcano Pichincha (4,794 m). The city's charm lies in its colonial centre – the Old City as it's known – a UNESCO World Heritage Site, where cobbled streets are steep and narrow, dipping to deep ravines. From the top of Cerro Panecillo, 183 m above the city level, there is a fine view of the city below and the encircling cones of volcanoes and other mountains.

North of the Old City is Modern Quito – or New City – with broad avenues lined with contemporary office buildings, fine private residences, parks, embassies and villas. Here you'll find Quito's main tourist and business area in the district known as Mariscal Sucre (or La Mariscal), bordered by Avenidas Amazonas, Patria, 12 de Octubre and Orellana.

Ins and outs

Getting there **Mariscal Sucre airport** is about 5 km north of the main hotel district. It is served by city buses, the trolley bus ('El Trole' – not designed for heavy luggage) and taxis (US$5 to the New City, US$6 to the Old City, recommended as the safest option). Most long-distance bus services arrive at the Terminal Terrestre at the junction of Maldonado and Cumandá, south of the Old City. It is safest to arrive and leave the terminal by taxi (US$4 to the New City), although the Cumandá stop of El Trole is nearby. A new Terminal Terrestre was under construction in 2007 in Quitumbe, at the south end of the city. Once opened, city transport will change accordingly and new hotels near the terminal should open. Some luxury bus services run to their own offices in the New City. ►► *For more detailed information, see Transport, page 912.*

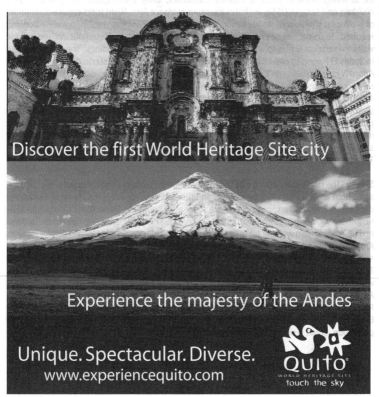
Ecuador Quito & around

Sights

Old City

Quito's revitalized colonial district is a pleasant place to stroll and admire the architecture, monuments and art. At night, the illuminated plazas and churches are very beautiful. The heart of the Old City is **Plaza de la Independencia** or **Plaza Grande**, dominated by a somewhat grim **Cathedral** ① *Mon-Sat, 1000-1600, Sun 1000-1400, US$2*, built 1550-1562, with grey stone porticos and green tile cupolas. On its outer walls are plaques listing the names of the founding fathers of Quito, and inside are the tomb of Sucre and a famous Descent from the Cross by the *indígena* painter Caspicara. There are many other 17th and 18th century paintings; the interior decoration shows Moorish influence. Facing the Cathedral is the **Palacio Arzobispal**, part of which now houses shops. Next to it, in the northwest corner, is the **Hotel Grand Plaza** (1930), with an eclectic façade, the first building in the old city with more than two storeys. On the northeast side is the concrete **Municipio**, which fits in quite well. The low colonial **Palacio de Gobierno** or **Palacio de Carondelet**, silhouetted against the flank of Pichincha, is on the northwest side of the Plaza. On the first floor is a gigantic mosaic mural of Orellana navigating the Amazon. The ironwork on the balconies looking over the main plaza is from the Tuilleries in Paris. Ask at the gate and you may be allowed in as far as the foyer.

From Plaza de la Independencia two main streets, Venezuela and García Moreno, lead straight towards the Panecillo. Parallel with Venezuela is Calle Guayaquil, the main shopping street. These streets all run south from the main plaza to meet Calle Morales, or Calle La Ronda (after the district it's in), worth seeing for its cobbles and wrought-iron balconies. La Ronda has been refurbished, with new shops, coffee houses and restaurants. On García Moreno is the beautiful **El Sagrario** ① *Mon-Sat, 0800-1800, Sun 0800-1330, free*, church with a gilded door. The **Centro Cultural Metropolitano** is at the corner of Espejo, housing temporary exhibits and the **Museo Alberto Mena Caamaño** ① *T295 0272, www.centrocultural-quito.com, Tue-Sun 0900-1700, US$1.50*. This wax museum depicts scenes of Ecuadorean colonial history. The scene of the execution of the revolutionaries of 1809 in the original cell is particularly vivid. The fine Jesuit church of **La Compañía** ① *García Moreno by the corner of Sucre, Mon-Fri 0930-1100, 1300-1800, Sat 1000-1600, Sun 1200-1600, US$2*, has the most ornate and richly sculptured façade and interior. Many of its most valuable treasures are in vaults at the Banco Central. Opposite is the **Casa Museo María Augusta Urrutia** ① *García Moreno N2-60 y Sucre, T258 0103, Tue-Fri 1000-1800, Sat-Sun 0930-1730, US$2.50*, the home of a Quiteña who devoted her life to charity, showing the lifestyle of 20th century aristocracy. Housed in the fine restored, 16th Century Hospital San Juan de Dios, is the **Museo de la Ciudad** ① *T228 3882, www.museociudadquito.gov.ec, Tue-Sun 0930-1730, US$2, students US$1.50, guide service US$6*. It takes you through Quito's history from prehispanic times to the 19th century, with imaginative displays.

On **Cerro Panecillo** ① *0900-1800, US$2 to enter; also see Safety page 894*, there is a statue to the Virgen de Quito and a good view from the observation platform. In the museum of the monastery of **San Diego** (by the cemetery of the same name, just west of Panecillo) ① *Calicuchima 117 y Farfán, entrance to the right of the church, T295 2516, 0930-1300, 1430-1730 daily, US$2*, guided tours (Spanish only) take you around four colonial patios where sculpture and painting are shown. Of special interest are the gilded pulpit by Juan Bautista Menacho and the Last Supper painting in the refectory, in which a *cuy* and *humitas* have taken the place of the paschal lamb.

Plaza de San Francisco (or Bolívar) is west of Plaza de la Independencia; here are the great church and monastery of the patron saint of Quito, **San Francisco** ① *Mon-Fri 0900-1300, 1400-1700, Sat-Sun 0900-1200*. The church was constructed by the Spanish in 1553 and is rich in art treasures. A modest statue of the founder, Fray Jodoco Ricke, the Flemish Franciscan who sowed the first wheat in Ecuador, stands at the foot of the stairs to the church portal. See the fine wood-carvings in the choir, a high altar of gold and an exquisite carved ceiling. There are some paintings in the aisles by Miguel de Santiago, the colonial *mestizo* painter. The **Museo Franciscano Fray Pedro Gocial** ① *Plaza de San Francisco, T295 2911, www.museofranciscanoquito.com, Mon-Fri 0900-1300, 1400-1700, Sat 0900-1800, Sun 0900-1200, US$2*, has a collection of religious art. Adjoining San Francisco is the **Cantuña Chapel** ① *0800-1200, 1500-1800*, with sculptures. Not far away to the north along Calle Cuenca is the church of **La Merced** ① *0630-1200, 1200-1800*. In the monastery of La Merced is

Quito's oldest clock, built in 1817 in London. Fine cloisters are entered through a door to the left of the altar. La Merced contains many splendidly elaborate styles; note the statue of Neptune on the main patio fountain.

At **Plaza de Santo Domingo** (or Sucre), southeast of Plaza de la Independencia, is the church and monastery of **Santo Domingo**, with its rich wood-carvings and a remarkable Chapel of the Rosary to the right of the main altar. In the monastery is the **Museo Dominicano Fray Pedro Bedón** ① *T228 0518, Mon-Sat 0900-1630, Sun 0900-1300, US$2*, another fine

Quito Old City

To New City

To Train Station

Ecuador Quito & around Sights

N			
0 metres 100			
0 yards 100			

E Ecovía
M Metrobus
T Trole

Sleeping
Catedral Internacional 6
Huasi Continental 1
Margarita 13
Marsella 14
Patio Andaluz 10
Plaza del Teatro 5
Plaza Grande 8
Posada Colonial 7
Real Audiencia 2
Relicario del Carmen 9
Secret Garden 11
Sucre 3
The Guest House 12
Viena International 4

Eating
Café del Fraile 5
Café del Museo 1
Café del Teatro 4
Criollo 9
Cucurucho de Santa
Clara 8
El Portal 5
Govinda 3
Hasta La Vuelta Señor 5
La Cueva del Oso 2
La Fuente del
Conquistador 10
Mea Culpa 5
Theatrum 6
Tianguez 7
Vista Hermosa 11

897

Quito New City

To ⑭ & Mall El Jardín

To ⑳ To ⑨ ② ⑬

To ⑭ To ③ ②⑦

TAME

Alonso de Mercadillo

Novaclínica

Fray Antonio de Marchena

Santa Clara

Santa Clara (North)

Ramírez Dávalos

Santa Clara (South)

Carrión

San Gregorio

Mariscal (North)

Bolivia

Reina del Camino

Mariscal (South)

18 de Septiembre

Flota Imbabura

Portoviejo

Supertaxis Los Lagos to Otavalo

Asunción

Flor del Valle to Mindo

Santiago

Ejido (South)

Caracas

Bogotá

Río de Janeiros

Buenos Aires

José Riofrío

Feliciano Checa

Arenas

La Alameda (South)

La Alameda (North)

Luis Cordero

Biking Dutchman

Mega Cambios

Libri Mundi

Aerogal

Euromoney

VazCorp

Zenith Travel

Ecuadorean Tours

Produbanco

Metropolitan Touring

Transportes Ecuador

Mercado Artesanal La Mariscal

South American Explorers

Galo Plaza

Casa de la Cultura

Parque El Ejido

Ejido (North)

Parque El Ejido

Parque El Arbolito

US Embassy

Casa de la Cultura & Museums

Universidad Católica Museums

Av Patria

Diego Ladrón de Guevara

Queseras del Medio

Hospital Militar

Congress

Instituto Geográfico Militar & Planetario

El Belén

Parque Alameda

To Parque Itchimbía

Baquerizo Moreno

Juan Rodríguez

Lizardo García

Joaquín Pinto

Manuela Cañizares

Presidente Wilson

Veintimilla

N

0 metres 50
0 yards 50

Ecuador Quito & around Sights

Sleeping 🛏
Adventure 6 *A2*
Amazonas Inn 8 *A2*
Backpackers Inn 5 *A3*
Café Cultura 1 *C2*
Casa Helbling 2 *B3*
Casa Paxee 14 *A1*
Cayman 15 *A3*
Chalet Suisse & Restaurant 3 *A3*
Crossroads 19 *A3*
El Arupo 24 *A3*
El Cafecito 4 *A3*
El Taxo 7 *A2*
Hostal de la Rábida 9 *A3*
Hostelling International 10 *A3*
Hothello 11 *C2*
Iguana Lodge 26 *A3*
Kinara 12 *D1*

La Cartuja 16 *C3*
La Casa de Eliza 35 *B3*
La Casa Sol 33 *A3*
La Casona de Mario 36 *B3*
La Galería 38 *A3*
La Pradera 31 *A3*
L'Auberge Inn 13 *E2*
Mansión del Angel 29 *A2*
Posada del Maple 17 *A3*
Queen's Hostel 18 *B3*
Quito 37 *C3*
Rincón Escandinavo 32 *A3*
Río Amazonas 20 *A3*
Sebastián 21 *A3*
Sierra Madre 22 *B3*
Sol de Quito 27 *A1*
Titisee 28 *A3*
Villa Nancy 30 *B3*
Villantigua 38 *C3*

Eating 🍴
Adam's Rib 1 *A3*
Baalbeck 19 *B3*
Café Colibrí 6 *A2*
Café Trovero 7 *A3*
Chandani Tandoori 10 *A3*
Chez Alain 16 *B2*
Crêpes & Waffles 2 *A3*
El Cebiche 29 *A3*
El Maple 4 *A3*
Happy Panda 5 *B3*
Kallari 23 *A2*
La Canoa Manabita 11 *A3*
La Casa de Mi Abuela 13 *A3*
La Chacha 7 *A3*
La Choza 3 *A3*
Magic Bean 8 *A3*
Mama Clorinda 20 *A3*
Mango Tree 28 *A3*
Paléo 22 *A3*

Pavarotti 3 *A3*
Raclette 24 *A2*
Rincón de Francia 26 *B2*
Shorton Grill 9 *A3*
Sushi 21 *A3*
Tex Mex 12 *B3*
Yu Su 27 *A3*

Bars & clubs 🍸
Ghoz 14 *A3*
No Bar 15 *A3*
Patatu's 25 *A2*
Reina Victoria Pub 17 *B2*

Ecovía stop ᴱ
Trole stop 🚏

collection of religious art. In the centre of the plaza is a statue of Sucre, pointing to the slopes of Pichincha where he won his battle against the Royalists. Nearby is the **Museo Histórico Casa de Sucre** ⓘ *Venezuela y Sucre, T295 2860, Tue-Fri 0800-1600, Sat-Sun 1000-1630, US$1*, the beautiful house of Sucre.

Museo de Santa Catalina ⓘ *Espejo y Flores, T295 8465, Mon-Sat 0800-1600, US$2*, said to have been built on the ruins of the Inca House of the Virgins, depicts the history of cloistered life. Many of the heroes of Ecuador's struggle for independence are buried in the monastery of **San Agustín** (Flores y Chile), which has beautiful cloisters on three sides where the first act of independence from Spain was signed on 10 August 1809. Here is the **Museo de San Agustín** ⓘ *Chile y Guayaquil, T258 0263, Mon-Sat 0900-1200, 1500-1730 (not Sat), US$2*, with religious art.

The **Basílica** ⓘ *on Plaza de la Basílica, 7 blocks northeast of Plaza de la Independencia, 0930-1730, US$2*, is very large, has many gargoyles, stained glass windows and fine, bas relief bronze doors (begun in 1926; some final details remain unfinished due to lack of funding). A coffee shop in the clock tower gives good views over the city. To the west of the city, the **Museo del Agua**, called Yaku ⓘ *El Placer Oe11-271, T257 0359, Thu-Sun 0900-1700, US$2*, overlooks the Carcel García Moreno and has great views of the city. Its main themes are water and nature, society and heritage. The best there way is take a taxi or walk up Calle Chile, go under the tunnels road then left to El Placer. To the east of the colonial city is **Parque Itchimbía**, a natural lookout over the city with walking and cycle trails and a cultural centre housed in a 19th century "crystal palace" which came from Frankfurt, once one of the city's markets. For spectacular views ride the **Teleférico** ⓘ *Av Occidental above La Gasca, T1800-835333, www.teleferiqo.com, Mon 1400-2200, Tue-Thu 0900-2200, Fri-Sat 0800-0000, Sun 0800-2000, US$4 regular or US$7 for express line, bus service from luxury hotels and Quicentro Shopping US$1 each way, busy at weekends*. The cable car is part of a complex with an amusement park, shops and food courts. It climbs to 4,050 m on the flanks of Pichincha, where there are walking trails.

New City

Parque Alameda has the oldest **astronomical observatory** in South America ⓘ *Mon-Fri 0900-1200, 1430-1730, US$0.50, ring bell; T257 0765 for details of observations on clear nights, 1900, US$1*. There is also a splendid monument to Simón Bolívar, lakes, and in the northwest corner a spiral lookout tower with a good view. A short distance north of Parque Alameda, opposite Parque El Ejido, at the junction 6 de Diciembre and Patria, there is a large cultural and museum complex housing the **Casa de la Cultura** ⓘ *T222 3392, ext 320, Tue-Fri 0900-1700, Sat 0900-1400, US$2, good toilets*, and the Museo Nacional del Banco Central del Ecuador (see below). Museums belonging to the Casa de la Cultura are: **Museo de Arte Moderno**, paintings and sculpture since 1830; **Museo de Traje Indígena**, traditional dress and adornments of indigenous groups; **Museo de Instrumentos Musicales**, an impressive collection of musical instruments, said to be the second in importance in the world; **Museo del Libro**, with the first book printed here and works by Ecuador's early explorers.

If you have time to visit only one museum in Quito, it should be the **Museo Nacional del Banco Central del Ecuador** ⓘ *entrance on Patria, T222 3259, Tue-Fri 0900-1700, Sat-Sun 1000-1600, US$2, students with ISIC or national student card, US$1, guided tours in English, French or German by appointment*, also housed in the Casa de la Cultura. It has three floors, with five different sections. The **Sala de Arqueología** is particularly impressive with beautiful pre-Columbian ceramics. The **Sala de Oro** has a nice collection of prehispanic gold objects. The remaining three sections house art collections: the **Sala de Arte Colonial** (rich in paintings and sculptures especially of religious themes), the **Sala de Arte Republicano** and the **Sala de Arte Contemporáneo**. There are also temporary exhibits, videos on Ecuadorean culture, a bookshop and cafetería. Highly recommended. Near the Casa de la Cultura, in the Catholic University library building, is the **Museo Jijón y Caamaño** ⓘ *12 de Octubre y Roca, T299 1700 ext 1242, Mon-Fri 0800-1300, 1400-1600, US$2*, with a private collection of archaeological objects, historical documents, art, portraits, uniforms, etc, very well displayed.

The **Santuario de Guápulo** ⓘ *Mon-Sat 0900-1200, 1500-1730* (1693, built by Indian slaves), perched on the edge of a ravine east of the city, is well worth seeing for its many paintings, gilded altars, stone carvings and the marvellously carved pulpit. The **Museo Fray Antonio Rodríguez** ⓘ *Av de los Conquistadores, T256 5652, Mon-Fri 0900-1200, 1500-1730*, has religious art and furniture, from the 16th to the 20th centuries. Guided tours

(Spanish only) include a visit to the beautiful Santuario. Take bus 'Hospital del Sur-Guápulo' from Calle Venezuela by Plaza de la Independencia, 'Guápulo-Dos Puentes' eastbound along Av Patria, or walk down the steep stairway behind *Hotel Quito*. **Cima de la Libertad** ① *T228 8733, Tue-Thu 0830-1630, Fri-Sat 0900-1300, US$1, children and seniors US$0.25*, the museum at the site of the 1822 Battle of Pichincha, has great views. Take a taxi there as the suburbs are dangerous, or the trolley to El Recreo and a taxi from there.

Museo Guayasamín ① *Bosmediano 543, Bellavista, northeast of La Mariscal, T245 2938, Mon-Fri 1000-1700, US$3*, is highly recommended. As well as the eponymous artist's works there is a pre-Columbian and colonial collection. Works of art may be purchased (ask to see the whole collection) and also modern jewellery. It's easiest to take a taxi there. Also presenting Guayasamín's work and 5 blocks from the museum is **La Capilla del Hombre** ① *Mariano Calvache y Lorenzo Chávez, Bellavista, T244 8492, Tue-Sun 1000-1700, US$3, students and seniors US$2 (US$1 discount if visiting both sites)*, a collection of murals depicting the fate of Latin America from pre-Columbian to modern times.

In the eastern suburb of San Rafael is **La Casa de Kingman Museo** ① *Portoviejo y Dávila, 1 block from San Rafael park, Valle de los Chillos, T286 1065, www.fundacionkingman.com, Thu-Fri 1000-1600, Sat-Sun 1000-1700, US$4, students US$3, children under 7 free*. This is a collection of the renowned artist's work and other colonial, republican and 20th-century art. Take a taxi or a Sangolquí bus from La Marín as far as San Rafael park.

● Sleeping

There are few good places to stay near the bus station and even fewer by the airport. Taxis are cheap so plan ahead about what type of lodgings and what part of town best suit you, and take a cab to your first choice. Large international chain hotels are represented in the city and meet their international standards. For more information see: www.sheraton.com, www.radisson.com, www.swissotel.com, www.hilton.com, www.hotelesdann.com/html/dann_carlton_quito.html, www.hojo.com (Howard Johnson), http://marriott.com/default.mi, www.mercure.com, www.bestwestern.com, Compass (www.hotelquito.com.ec).

Old City *p896, map p897*
LL Plaza Grande, García Moreno N5-16, Plaza de la Indpendencia, T251 0777, www.plazagrande quito.com. Exclusive luxury hotel with an exceptional location. The former Hotel Majestic now in a new, top-of-the-line version, re-inaugurated in Dec 2006. 15 suites, 3 restaurants including La Belle Epoque, gourmet French cuisine and a wine cellar, jacuzzi in all rooms, climate control, mini-spa, Wi-Fi internet.
AL Patio Andaluz, García Moreno N6-52 y Mejía, T228 0830, www.hotelpatioandaluz.com. 5-star 'boutique hotel', beautifully reconstructed colonial mansion, very nice place to stay, restaurant.
AL Relicario del Carmen, Venezuela 1041 y Olmedo, T228 9120, www.hotelrelicario delcarmen.com. Beautifully refurbished colonial house, includes breakfast, cafeteria, good rooms and service, no smoking.
C Posada Colonial, García Moreno 1160 y Mejía, T228 0282, posadacolonial@yahoo.com. Nicely

refurbished colonial building, a bit pricey but includes breakfast, restaurant serves economical set meals, electric shower .
C Real Audiencia, Bolívar Oe3-18 y Guayaquil at Plaza de Santo Domingo Trole stop, T295 0590. Includes breakfast, restaurant/bar

on top floor, spacious, well furnished rooms, baggage stored, safety deposit box, great views. Highly recommended.

D Viena Internacional, Flores 600 y Chile, T295 9611. English spoken, good value, phone, good meals, secure.

D Catedral Internacional, Mejía Oe6-36 y Cuenca, T295 5438. In a colonial house, hot water, good rooms, inexpensive restaurant.

E Plaza del Teatro, Guayaquil N8-75 y Esmeraldas, T295 9462. Restaurant, parking, carpeted rooms, stylish, good service.

E-F Huasi Continental, Flores N3-08 y Sucre, T295 7327. Colonial house, restaurant, cheaper with shared bath, hot water, good value.

G Sucre, Bolívar 615 and Cuenca, Plaza San Francisco, T295 4025. Shared bath, laundry facilities, terrace with great views over the Old City, restaurant, bit noisy, often full.

Apartments

A Apart-Hotel Amaranta, Leonidas Plaza N20-32 y Washington, T254 3619. Comfortable, well-equipped suites, from US$850 a month, good restaurant.

A Apart-Hotel Antinea, Rodríguez 175 y Almagro, T250 6839, www.hotelantinea.com. Suites and apartments, from US$800 per month, lovely rooms.

C Apartamentos Modernos, Amazonas N31-75 y Mariana de Jesús, T/F223 3766 ext 800, modernos@uio.satnet.net. From US$550 per month, good location near La Carolina park and Mall El Jardín, English spoken, spotlessly clean.

In between the new and old cities

D The Guest House, Julio Castro 379 y Valparaíso, T252 5834, marcoatm@hoy.net. Rooms for long stays in a nicely restored house, laundry and cooking facilities, nice views, helpful, US$130/month.

E Kinara, Bogotá 534 y Av América, T/F222 8524, kinara@andinanet.net. Includes breakfast, cooking and laundry facilities, safe deposit boxes, library, English/ French spoken, free tea and coffee, spotless. Highly recommended.

E L'Auberge Inn, Av Colombia 1138 y Yaguachi, T255 2912, www.auberge-inn-hostal.com. Restaurant, cheaper without bath, parking, duvets on beds, internet café, cheap international calls for guests, garden, lovely terrace and communal area, helpful, good atmosphere.

E Marsella, Los Ríos 2035 y Espinoza, T295 5884. Cheaper without bath, parking, good rooftop terrace with views over Parque La Alameda, top floor rooms best but noisy, luggage stored, often full by 1700, safe deposit, notice board, good value but not a safe area

E Secret Garden, Antepara E4-60 y Los Ríos, T295 6704, www.secretgardenquito.com. Australian-Ecuadorean run hostel, very popular, cheaper in dorm, terrace for dinner (also for non-residents, tasty meals, vegetarian choices), 2 dachshunds, double-check bookings, can be noisy.

F Margarita, Los Ríos N12-118 y Espinoza, T295 0441. Breakfast, parking, good beds, sheets changed daily, great value. Highly recommended.

New City *p899, map p898*

AL Mansión del Angel, Wilson E5-29 y JL Mera, T255 7721, mansion@mansiondelangel.com.ec. Includes breakfast, refurbished old building, very elegant, lovely atmosphere.

B Villa Nancy, Muros 146 y 12 de Octubre, T256 2483, www.villanancy.com. In a quiet residential, homely, comfortable, helpful multilingual staff, includes breakfast, internet, airport transfers, lobby bar.

A Café Cultura, Robles E6-62 y Reina Victoria, T/F250 4078, www.cafecultura.com. Beautiful garden, welcoming staff, restaurant with good food, safe deposit and luggage store (extra).

A Hostal de la Rábida, La Rábida 227 y Santa María, T222 1720, www.hotelrabida.com. Good restaurant, Italian-run, bright, comfortable. Highly recommended.

A Río Amazonas, Cordero E4-375 y Amazonas, T255 6667, www.hotelrioamazonas.com. Buffet breakfast, restaurant, internet, pleasant, safe, all facilities.

A Sebastián, Almagro N24-416 y Cordero, T222 2400, www.hotelsebastian.com. Restaurant, internet, comfortable, safe, Wi-Fi, garage, very good.

B La Cartuja, Plaza 170 y 18 de Septiembre, T252 3577, www.hotelcartuja.com. Includes breakfast, restaurant, beautifully decorated, spacious comfortable rooms, safety deposit boxes, garden, very helpful and hospitable. Highly recommended.

B La Casa Sol, Calama 127 y 6 de Diciembre, T223 0798, www.lacasasol.com. Includes breakfast, small with courtyard, 24-hr cafeteria, very helpful, hot water, English and French spoken, suites available. Recommended.

B La Pradera, San Salvador 222 y Pasaje Martín Carrión, La Carolina, T222 6833, www.hostallapradera.com. Includes breakfast, restaurant, comfortable, quiet, residential area.

B Sierra Madre, Veintimilla 464 y Luis Tamayo, T250 5687, www.hotelsierramadre.com. Hotel and restaurant, fully renovated old-style villa, comfortable, sun roof.

B Sol de Quito, Alemania N30-170 y Vancouver, T254 1773, www.soldequito.com. Includes breakfast, lovely converted house, restaurant, helpful. Recommended.

B Villantigua, Washington E9-48 y Tamayo, T252 8564, alariv@uio.satnet.net. Furnished with antiques, suites with fireplace more expensive, quiet, multilingual staff.

C Cayman, Rodríguez E7-29 y Reina Victoria, T256 7616, www.hotelcaymanquito.com. Includes breakfast, good hotel with smallish rooms, bright breakfast room, sitting room with fireplace, garden, parking.

C Chalet Suisse, Reina Victoria N24-191 y Calama, T256 2700. Includes breakfast, excellent restaurant, convenient location, rooms facing street noisy.

C Hothello, Amazonas N20-20 y 18 de Septiembre, T/F256 5835, www.hotelothello.com. Includes breakfast, restaurant, modern, heating, safety deposit, helpful, multilingual staff.

C Posada del Maple, Rodríguez E8-49 y 6 de Diciembre, T254 4507, www.posadadelmaple.com. Includes full breakfast, restaurant, laundry and cooking facilities, cheaper with shared bath or

in dorm, warm atmosphere, free tea and coffee.

D El Arupo, Juan Rodríguez E7-22 y Reina Victoria, T255 7543. Includes breakfast, laundry and cooking facilities, comfortable dorms for 4, hot water, luggage store, good, English and French spoken.

D Rincón Escandinavo, Leonidas Plaza N24-306 y Baquerizo Moreno, T/F222 5965, www.hotelescandinavo.com. Restaurant, small, modern, well- furnished, convenient location, English spoken.

D Villa Nancy, Carrión 335 y 6 de Diciembre, T256 3084, www.villa-nancy.com. Swiss-Ecuadorean owned, pleasant, includes breakfast, some rooms with shared bath, airport pickup, cooking facilities, travel info.

D-E Casa Helbling, Veintimilla E8-166 y 6 de Diciembre, T222 6013, www.casa helbling.de. Cooking and laundry facilities, cheaper with shared bath, helpful, German spoken, family atmosphere, good information, tours arranged.

D-E Crossroads, Foch E5-23 y JL Mera, T223 4735, www.crossroadshostal.com. Cheaper with shared bath, excellent hot showers, good restaurant for breakfast and snacks, videos.

E Adventure, Pinto E2-24 y Amazonas, T222 6340, rfcedeno@interactive.net.ec. Cheaper with shared bath, cooking facilities, simple, terrace, helpful.

E Amazonas Inn, Pinto E4-324 y Amazonas, T222 5723, amazonasinn@yahoo.com. Carpeted rooms, some sunny, 1st floor best, café, very nice.

E Backpackers Inn, Rodríguez E7-48 y Reina Victoria, T250 9669, gertschi17@yahoo.de. Popular hostel, breakfast available, cheaper with shared bath, hot water, laundry and cooking facilities, adequate dorms.

E Casa Paxee, Pasaje Navarro 326 y La Gasca, T250 0441, gusojeda1@hotmail.com. Price includes breakfast, cooking and laundry facilities, discounts for longer stays.

E El Cafecito, Luis Cordero 1124 y Reina Victoria, T223 4862, www.cafecito.net. Cheaper in dorm, Canadian-owned, relaxed atmosphere, superb food in café including vegetarian, good information.

E Hostelling International, Pinto 325 y Reina Victoria, T254 3995, www.hostelling-ecuador.org. Pricey modern hostel with capacity for 75. Double room with bath, cheaper in dormitory with lockers. Discounts for IYHF members and ISIC holders, restaurant, laundry service, coin-operated washing machines, hot water, safe deposit, luggage store, closed circuit TV security system.

🔴 *For an explanation of the sleeping and eating price codes used in this guide, see page 58. Other*
⚫ *relevant information is found in Essentials pages 890-892.*

E Iguana Lodge, Calama E4-45 y JL Mera, T256 9784, iguanalodge@yahoo.com. Breakfast available, cheaper with shared bath, hot water, large common room makes for a very sociable atmosphere, hosts speak English and French.

E La Casa de Eliza, Isabel La Católica N24-679 (La Floresta), T222 6602, manteca@ uio.satnet.net. Kitchen and laundry facilities, shared rooms, safety deposit, very popular and homely, no smoking.

E La Casona de Mario, Andalucía 213 y Galicia (La Floresta), T/F223 0129, www.casonademario.com. Laundry and storage facilities, near Universidad Católica, sitting room, big garden, book exchange, several languages spoken, small kitchen with scant equipment, very helpful, popular.

E La Galería, Calama 233 y Almagro, T250 0307, hostallagaleria@hotmail.com. Nice family run hostel, breakfast available, hot water, free internet, cooking facilities, carpeted rooms, sitting room, patio with tables, English spoken.

E Queen's Hostel/Hostal De La Reina, Reina Victoria 836 y Wilson, T255 1844, vicent1@interactive.net.ec. Cooking and laundry facilities, nice, small, popular, fireplace, café.

E Titisee, Foch E7-60 y Reina Victoria, T252 9063, www.hostaltitisee.com. Nice place, helpful owner, cheaper with shared bath, large rooms, cooking facilities, lounge.

F El Taxo, Foch 909 y Cordero, T222 5593. Constant hot water, internet, cooking facilities, hostel-type, large family house, helpful, open fire, good meeting place.

🍴 Eating

Eating out in Quito, especially in the New City, is excellent, varied, and increasingly cosmopolitan. In the Old City there are a number of elegant, upmarket places serving Ecuadorean and international food, plus many small, cheap places serving set meals; most of these close by early evening. All those listed here are recommended. Be very careful with seafood restaurants; some are not hygienic. Also note that many restaurants close on Sun.

Old City *p896, map p897*

♥♥♥ Cucurucho de Santa Clara, Rocafuerte y Benalcázar, T228 5866, Tue-Sat 1230-2300, Sun 1230-1600. A slight variation on traditional Ecuadorean cuisine, in a converted 19th-century market, Sun buffet, parking.

♥♥♥ La Cueva del Oso, Chile Oe3-66 y Venezuela, across from the Plaza de la Independencia, T257 2786. Mon-Sat 1200-2400, Sun 1200-1600. Ecuadorean specialties in an elegant covered courtyard, art deco interior, great atmosphere.

♥♥♥ Mea Culpa, Plaza Independencia, upstairs in public part of Archbishop's Palace, T295 1190. Formal and elegant, excellent international and Mediterranean food, reservations required.

♥♥♥ Theatrum, Plaza del Teatro, Teatro Sucre p 2, T228 9669. Mon-Fri 1230-1600, 1930-2330, Sat 1930-2330, Sun 1230-1600. Excellent creative gourmet cuisine in the city's most important theatre.

♥♥ Café del Teatro, Plaza del Teatro opposite Teatro Sucre, Mon-Wed 1100-2100, Thu-Sat 11-2100. Ecuadorean and international dishes, nice location and atmosphere, live music Thu-Sat from 2000.

♥♥ Hasta la Vuelta Señor, Pasaje Arzobispal, p 3. Mon-Sat 1200-2300, Sun 1200-1600. A *Fonda Quiteña* perched on an indoor balcony with Ecuadorean *comida típica* and snacks.

♥♥ La Fuente del Conquistador, Benalcázar N7-44 y Olmedo, Sat and Mon-Wed 0800-1700, Thu-Fri 0800-2200. Economical set lunches, grill, local and international food à la carte.

♥♥ Tianguez, Plaza de San Francisco under the portico of the church, Wed-Sat 0830-0000, Sun 0830-2200. International and local dishes, good coffee, snacks, sandwiches, popular, also craft shop, run by Fundación Sinchi Sacha.

♥ Criollo, Flores N7-31 y Olmedo, Mon-Sat 0800-2130, Sun 0800-1700. Economical set meals (a bit pricier at weekends), tasty chicken dishes and Ecuadorean food à la carte.

♥ Govinda, Esmeraldas y Oe3-115 y Venezuela. Mon-Sat 0800-1600. Vegetarian dishes and set meals, also breakfasts.

Cafés

Café del Fraile, Pasaje Arzobispal, p 2, Mon-Sat 1000-2400, Sun 1200-1930. On a balcony above one of the patios of the Palacio Arzobispal.

Café del Museo, García Moreno 572 at the Museo de la Ciudad. Tue-Sun 0930-1700. Snacks and soups, coffee, elegant decor.

El Portal, Pasaje Arzobispal, ground floor, enter from C Venezuela. Daily 1000-2100. Snacks, 20 varieties of coffee, drinks, modern decor.

Vista Hermosa, Mejía 453 y García Moreno. Mon-Sat 1400-0000, Sun 1200-2100. Drinks, pizza, light meals, live music on weekends, lovely terrace-top views of the Old City.

New City *p899, map p898*

♥♥♥ Chalet Suisse, Reina Victoria N24-191 y Calama, T256 2700. Daily 1100-1500, 1900-2300. Steaks and some Swiss dishes, good service.

♥♥♥ El Cebiche, JL Mera 1236 y Calama, and Amazonas 2428 y Moreno Bellido, T252 6380. Tue-Sun 1000-1600. Great ceviche.

♥♥♥ El Galpón, Colón E10-53, behind Folklore

Olga Fisch, T254 0209, Sun-Fri 1200-2000. Very good Ecuadorean cooking, decorated with antiques, a pleasant place for relaxed dining.

Il Risotto, Eloy Alfaro N34-447 y Portugal, T224 6850. Very popular, very good, closed Sun evening.

La Choza, 12 de Octubre N24-551 y Cordero, T223 0839. Mon-Fri 1200-1600, 1900-2230, Sat-Sun 1200-1630. Traditional cuisine, good music and special decor.

La Jaiba, Coruña y San Ignacio, T254 3887. Mon 1100-1530, Tue-Sat 1100-1600, 1900-2100, Sun 1100-1630. Varied seafood menu, an old favourite at new premises.

La Paella Valenciana, República y Almagro. Tue-Sat 1200-1500, 1900-2300, Sun 1200-1600. Superb fish and paella, an institution.

Los Troncos, Los Shyris 1280 y Portugal, T243 7377, Mon-Sat 1000-2200, Sun 1000-1600. Argentine, excellent for meats, fish, pasta, salads, busy on Sun.

Pavarotti, 12 de Octubre N24-551 y Cordero, T256 6668, Mon-Fri 1200-1530,1900-2300, Sat 1900-2300. Creative Italian cuisine, good service.

Rincón de Francia, Roca 779 y 9 de Octubre, T255 4668, www.rincondefrancia.com. Mon-Fri 1200-1600, 2000-2300, Sat 1200-1530, 2000-2200. Excellent French cuisine but very expensive, reservation essential, slow service.

Rincón de La Ronda, Belo Horizonte 406 y Almagro, T254 0459. Daily 1200-2300. Nice atmosphere, huge Sun buffet, local and international, Sun evening folklore show.

Sake, Paul Rivet N30-166 y Whymper, T252 4818. Mon-Sat 1200-1530, 1900-2300, Sun 1230-1600. Sushi bar and other Japanese dishes, very trendy, great food.

Shorton Grill, Calama E7-73 y Almagro, and Urrutia N14-233 y Eloy Alfaro, T252 3645. Meat and seafood, salad bar, large portions, smart decor.

Raclette, Mall El Jardín, Amazonas y Mariana de Jesús, p 3. Mon-Sat 1130-2200, Sun 1200-1600. Swiss specialities including raclette and fondue with a great variety of ingredients to add, simple, modern decor.

Adam's Rib, Calama E6-16 y Reina Victoria. Closed Sat. For steak, ribs and pecan pie. Happy hour 1730-2100.

Baalbeck, 6 de Diciembre y Wilson. Good Arabic food.

Capuletto, Eloy Alfaro N32-544 y Los Shyris, 0900-2400 (2200 on Sun). Excellent fresh pasta and desserts, Italian deli, lovely outdoor patio.

Crêpes & Waffles, La Rábida 461 y Orellana, opens 1200. Succulent savoury crêpes and salads and delicious desserts.

Happy Panda, Isabel la Católica N24-464 y Cordero. Daily 1230-2300. Hunan specialties.

Hong Tai, La Niña 234 y Yanez Pinzón. Tue-Sat 1300-1500, 1900-2300, Sun 1300-1600. Authentic Chinese cuisine.

La Casa de mi Abuela, JL Mera 1649 y la Niña. Mon-Sat 1100-1430, 1900-2200, Sun 1100-1430. Steak and other dishes, salads.

La Guarida del Coyote, Japón 542 y Naciones Unidas, also at Portugal 572 y 6 de Diciembre. Tue-Sun 1230-2230. Good Mexican food.

Las Ensaladas/Mi Frutería, Quicentro Shopping. daily 1000-2200. Gorgeous fresh fruit salads and coastal Ecuadorean food.

The Magic Bean, Foch 681 y JL Mera, T256 6181. Mon- Sat 1200-1530, 1900-2200, Sun 1200-1530. Specializes in fine coffees and natural foods, more than 20 varieties of pancakes, good salads, large portions, outdoor seating (also has popular lodging, **D-E**).

Mama Clorinda, Reina Victoria 1144 y Calama, Sun-Mon 1200-1700, Tue-Sat 1200-2100. A la carte and set meals, filling, good value.

Mango Tree Café, Foch 721 y JL Mera, Mon-Fri 0800-2100, Sun 0900-1700. Salads, Mexican and Caribbean dishes, fruit juices, coffee, homemade bread and bagels, nice patio.

Paléo, Cordero E5-48 y JL Mera, Mon-Sat 1230-1530, 1830-2100. Authentic Swiss specialties such as rösti and raclette. Also serves a good economical set lunch. Recommended.

Pekín, Whimper 300 y Orellana, Mon-Sat 1200-1500, 1900-2230, Sun 1200-2030. Excellent Chinese, very nice atmosphere.

Puerto Camarón, Av 6 de Diciembre y Granaderos, Centro Comercial Olímpico. Sun-Thu 0900-1600, Fri-Sat 0900-1700. Seafood menu.

Sushi, Calama E5-104 y JL Mera. Mon-Sat 1200-2300, Sun 1200-1600. Sushi bar, pleasant atmosphere with nice balcony, good value happy hour 1700-1900.

Tex Mex, Reina Victoria 847 y Wilson. 1300-2200, closed Sun. The Tex Mex Mixta especially recommended, lively.

Café Colibrí, Pinto 619 y Cordero. Daily 0800-1830. Large choice of breakfasts and German specialties, pleasant garden setting.

Chandani Tandoori, JL Mera N24-277 y Cordero. Mon-Sat 1100-2200. Simple little place with good authentic Indian cuisine.

Chez Alain, Baquedano 409 y JL Mera. Mon-Fri 1200-1600, 1830-2200. Choice of good 4-course set meals at lunch, à la carte in the evening, pleasant relaxed atmosphere.

El Maple, Foch E8-15 y Almagro.Daily 0730-2330. Strictly vegetarian, menu, good meals and fruit juices, covered patio. Recommended.

La Canoa Manabita, Calama y Reina Victoria. Daily 1200-2100. Great seafood, very clean.

La Chacha, Foch y J L Mera. Mon-Fri. Small open air restaurant with heating, very good, cheap Italian fare.

Las Palmeras, Japón N36-87 y Naciones Unidas, opposite Parque la Carolina. Daily 0800-1800. Good *comida esmeraldeña*, outdoor tables, good value.

Rincón Ecuatoriano Chileno, 6 de Diciembre N28-30 y Bello Horizonte. Daily 1200-1600. Delicious, good value, busy at weekends.

Yu Su, Ed Torres de Almagro, Almagro y Colón. Korean-run sushi bar, takeaway service, closed Sat evening and Sun.

Cafés

Café Trovero, JL Mera y Pinto. Mon-Fri 1230-2200, Sat 1330-2200. Espresso and sandwich bar, pastries, pleasant atmosphere, nicely decorated with plants.

Kallari, Wilson E4-266 y JL Mera, T223 6009, www.kallari.com. Fair trade and organic coffee, chocolate, breakfasts and lunches, handicrafts, all associated with a community project in Napo province, "great atmosphere and sound aims". Frequently recommended.

Mirador de Guápulo, Rafael León Larrea, behind Hotel Quito, daily 1000-0000. Snacks such as empanadas, crêpes, sandwiches, drinks, great views, portable heaters for outdoor seating at night.

🟠 Bars and clubs

New City *p899, map p898*

El Pobre Diablo, Isabel La Católica y Galavis, 1 block north of Madrid, T222 4982, Mon-Sat 1600-0200. Relaxed atmosphere, jazz, sandwiches, Ecuadorean snacks and some meals, a good place to hang out and chill. Nice.

Ghoz, La Niña 425 y Reina Victoria, T223 9826, from 1800. Swiss-owned, excellent Swiss food, pool, darts, videos, games, music, German book exchange.

Happy Bar, Cordero E4-303 y Amazonas, T223 5892. Mon-Sat 1200-0200. Free entry, pool, karaoke, dancing, friendly crowd and owners, wide selection of drinks, good value.

Kilkenny Irish Pub, Lizardo García 559 y Reina Victoria, T290 1467, Wed-Sun 1700-0200. Typical of the genre, retro sounds, micro-brewery.

Kings Cross, Reina Victoria 1781 y La Niña, T252 3597. Classic rock, good BBQ, best hamburgers, wings, popular with all ages. Recommended.

Mario's, Roca 668 y Amazonas, T222 4033. Tue-Sat 1400-0100. Relax and enjoy classical music and tropical drinks with fellow oldies.

Matrioshka, Pinto 376 y JL Mera, T255 2668, Wed-Sat from 1900. Gay and lesbian bar. Only gets started around 2200.

No Bar, Calama y JL Mera. Open till 0200, closed on Sun. Good mix of Latin and Euro dance music always packed on weekends, entry US$4 on weekends.

Papillon, Pinzón y Colón. Mon-Sat 2000-0200. Very popular with locals and tourists, no cover, happy hour 2000-2200.

Patatu's, Wilson y JL Mera. Mon-Sat 2030-0200. Good drinks, pool table, happy hour all night Mon, music, dancing, owner speaks English and German.

Reina Victoria Pub, Reina Victoria 530 y Roca, T222 6369. Open Mon-Sat from 1700. Darts, relaxed atmosphere, English style with microbrews and Irish and Scotch whisk(e)ys, happy hour 1800-2000, moderately priced bar meals, meeting point for British and US expats.

Santurrón, Calama E4-21 y Amazonas, T252 3090. Classy place to hang out, live music (Thu-Sat) and dance, no cover, happy hour 1400-2000, snacks.

Seseribó, Veintimilla y 12 de Octubre, T256 3598, Thu-Sat 2100-0100. Caribbean music and salsa, a must for *salseros*, very popular, especially Thu and Fri. Recommended.

Turtle´s Head, La Niña 626 y JL Mera, T256 5544. Mon-Sat 1700-0200, Sun 1200-0200. Amazing microbrews, great fish and chips and curry, also serves Sun lunch, pool table, darts.

Varadero, Reina Victoria 1721 y La Pinta. Mon-Fri 1200-2400, Sat 1800-0300. Bar-restaurant, live Cuban music Wed-Sat, meals and snacks, good cocktails, older crowd and couples.

Vruma Room, Isabel La Católica y Cordero, T255 5022. 1900-0200. Live piano music on Fri-Sat, owner is a well-known local pianist and composer, Dr Nelson Maldonado, DJ Wed-Thu.

🟠 Entertainment

Quito *p893, map p897 and 898*
There are always many cultural events taking place in Quito, usually free of charge. Consult the monthly municipal booklet *Quito Cultura* or www.quitocultura.com. Films are listed daily in *El Comercio*, www.elcomercio.com.

Cinema

Casa de la Cultura, Patria y 6 de Diciembre, T290 2272, http://cce.org.ec. Shows foreign films, often has documentaries, film festivals.

Ocho y Media, Valladolid y Guipuzcoa, La Floresta. Good for art films and specials, also has a café, programme available at *Libri Mundi* and elsewhere. There are several multiplexes, eg **Cinemark 7**, www.cinemark.com.ec, and **Multicines**, www.multicines.com.ec.

Dance schools

One-to-one or group lessons are offered for US$4-6 per hr.

Son Latino, Reina Victoria 1225 y García, T223 4340. Specializes in several varieties of salsa.

Tropical Dancing School, Foch E4-256
y Amazonas, T222 4713.
Universal Salsa, Amazonas 884 y Wilson, T255
6516. Salsa, capoeira and other dances.

Music

Local folk music is popular in *peñas*.
Most places do not come alive until 2230.
La Casa de la Peña, García Moreno
1713 y Galápagos, by the Basílica,
T228 4179, Thu-Sun from 2130. Show of Quito
legends, Sat at 2200. Busy Fri and Sat.
Ñucanchi, Av Universitaria Oe5-188
y Armero. Tue-Sat 2000-0200.
Concerts by the **Orquesta Sinfónica Nacional**,
at Teatro Politécnico, Queseras del Medio,
opposite Coliseo Rumiñahui, La Floresta, T256
5733, at **Teatro Sucre** (see below), or in one of the
colonial churches. **Casa de la Música**, Valderrama
s/n y Mariana de Jesús, T226 7093,
www.casadelamusicaonline.com for schedule.
Many concerts, good accoustics. **Jacchigua**, the
Ecuadorean folk ballet, performs at Teatro
Demetrio Aguilera Malta, at Casa de la Cultura, 6
de Diciembre y Patria, T295 2025, Wed at 1930.
Entertaining, colourful and touristy, reserve ahead,
US$25. **Ballet Andino Humanizarte** performs at
Teatro Humanizarte, Leonidas Plaza N24-226 y
Baquerizo Moreno, T222 6116. Ecuadorean folk
ballet every Wed at 1930, US$10. Plays and
comedies are also often in their repertoire,
restaurant on the premises.

Theatre

Agora, open-air theatre of Casa de la Cultura, 12
de Octubre y Patria. Stages many concerts.
Centro Cultural Afro-Ecuatoriano (CCA),
Tamayo 985 y Lizardo García, T252 2318.
Sometimes has cultural events and published
material, useful contact for those interested in
the black community.
La Casa de al Lado, Valladolid N24-438 y
Cordero, T222 6398, www.lacasadealado.org.
Hosts many cultural events, has art gallery, library
with Wi-Fi and bar/restaurant.
Teatro Bolívar, Flores 421 y Junín, T258 2486,
www.teatrobolivar.org. Despite restoration work
there are still tours, presentations and festivals.
Teatro Sucre, Plaza del Teatro, Manabí y
Guayaquil, T228 1644, www.teatrosucre.com.
Beautifully restored 19th century building.

⊛ Festivals and events

Quito *p893, map p897 and 898*
New Year, Años Viejos: life-size puppets satirize
politicians and others. At midnight on 31 Dec a will
is read, the legacy of the outgoing year, and the
puppets are burnt; good along Amazonas

between Patria and Colón, very entertaining and
good humoured. On New Year's day everything is
shut. The solemn **Good Friday** processions are
most impressive. **24 May** is Independence,
commemorating the Battle of Pichincha in 1822
with early morning cannonfire and parades,
everything closes. **Aug**: Agosto Arte y Cultura,
organized by the municipality, cultural events,
dance and music in different places throughout
the city. The city's main festival, **Día de Quito**,
celebrated **1-6 Dec**, commemorates the
foundation of the city with elaborate parades,
bullfights, performances and music in the streets,
very lively. Hotels charge extra, everything except a
few restaurants shuts on 6 Dec. Foremost among
Christmas celebrations is the **Misa del Gallo**,
midnight mass. Over Christmas, Quito is crowded,
hotels are full and the streets are packed with
vendors and shoppers.

⊙ Shopping

Quito *p893, map p897 and 898*
Shops open generally 0900-1900 on weekdays,
some close at midday and most shut Sat pm and
Sun. Shopping centres are open at weekends.
The main shopping districts are along Av
Amazonas in the north and C Guayaquil in the
Old City. In the New City much of the shopping
is done in huge malls (see list under Foodstuffs).
For maps see Essentials, page 887.

Bookshops

Abya-Yala, 12 de Octubre 14-30 y Wilson.
Good for books about indigenous cultures
and anthropology, also has excellent library
and museum.
Confederate Books, Calama 410 y JL Mera.
Open 1000-1900, excellent selection of
second-hand books, including travel guides,
mainly English but also German and French.
Libri Mundi, JL Mera N23-83 y Veintimilla, and at
Quicentro Shopping. Excellent selection of
Spanish, English, French, German, and some
Italian books, sells Footprint *Ecuador, South
American Handbook* and other titles,
knowledgeable and helpful staff, noticeboard of
what's on in Quito, open Mon-Sat 0800-1800
(also Sun at Quicentro). Very highly
recommended.
Libro Express, Amazonas 816 y Veintimilla, also
at Quicentro Shopping and El Bosque. Has a
good stock of maps, guides and international
magazines.
Mr Books, El Jardín Mall, 3rd floor. Good stock,
many in English including Footprint travel guides,
open daily. Recommended.

Camping

Camping gas is available many of the shops listed below, white gas (*combustible para lámpara Coleman, gasolina blanca*) at times from **Kywi**, Centro Comercial Olímpico, 6 de Diciembre, 2 blocks north of the stadium, and other locations.
Los Alpes, Reina Victoria N23-45 y Baquedano. Local and imported equipment, also rentals.
Altamontaña, Jorge Washington 425 y 6 de Diciembre. Imported climbing equipment for sale, rentals, good advice.
Antisana, Centro Comercial El Bosque, ground floor. Sales only.
Aventura Sport, Quicentro Shopping, top floor. Tents, good selection of glacier sunglasses, upmarket.
Camping Sports, Colón E6-39 y Reina Victoria. Sales only.
Equipos Cotopaxi, 6 de Diciembre N20-50 y Patria. Ecuadorean and imported gear for sale, no rentals, lockable pack covers, made to measure.
Tatoo, JL Mera 820 y Wilson. Quality backpacks and outdoor clothing.
The Altar, J L Mera N22-93 y Veitimilla. Imported and local gear for sale, good prices for rentals.
The Explorer, Reina Victoria E6-32 y Pinto. Sales and rentals, very helpful, will buy US or European equipment.

Foodstuffs

Mi Comisariato, another well-stocked supermarket and department store, at Quicentro Shopping (Naciones Unidas y Shyris) and García Moreno y Mejía in the Old City.
Santa María, Av Iñaquito y Pereira, Bolívar 334, entre Venezuela y García Moreno and Versalles y Carrión. A growing chain of supermarkets, good value and no membership, so you don't pay a surcharge if you don't have a card.
Supermaxi at Mall El Jardín, CCI, El Bosque, Centro Comercial Plaza Aeropuerto (Av de la Prensa y Homero Salas), Multicentro, Megamaxi (6 de Diciembre y Julio Moreno), and El Recreo. Very well stocked supermarket and department store, local and imported goods, not cheap.

Handicrafts

A wide selection can be found at the **Mercado Artesanal La Mariscal**, on Jorge Washington, between Reina Victoria and JL Mera. This interesting and worthwhile market, built by the municipality to house street vendors, is open daily 1000-1800. There are also souvenir shops on García Moreno in front of the Palacio Presidencial in the colonial city. **El Indio**, Roca E4-35 y Amazonas, T255 5227, daily 0900-1900. A craft market with stalls selling a variety of products, also has a coffee shop. **Museo de Artesanía**, 12 de Octubre 1738 y Madrid, Mon-Fri 0900-1900, Sat 0900-1700. Another craft market with many vendors and products. There is an exhibition and sale of paintings in **Parque El Ejido**, opposite *Hotel Hilton Colón*, on Sat and Sun mornings.

Local garments (for natives rather than tourists) can be seen and bought on the north end of the Plaza de Santo Domingo and along the nearest stretch of C Flores.

Recommended shops with a wide selection are:
La Bodega, JL Mera 614 y Carrión. Recommended for antiques and handicrafts
Camari, Marchena 260 y Versalles. Direct sale shop run by an artisan organization. Member of the Fair Trade organization.
Folklore, Colón E10-53 y Caamaño, the store of the late Olga Fisch. Attractive selection of handicrafts and rugs, expensive as designer has international reputation; also at *Hotel Hilton Colón* and *Hotel Patio Andaluz*.
Galería Latina, JL Mera 823 y Veintimilla. Fine selection of alpaca and other handicrafts from Ecuador, Peru and Bolivia, visiting artists sometimes demonstrate their work.
Hilana, 6 de Diciembre 1921 y Baquerizo Moreno. Beautiful unique 100% wool blankets with Ecuadorean motifs, excellent quality, purchase by metre possible, inexpensive.
Marcel Creations, Roca 766, entre Amazonas y 9 de Octubre. Panama hats.
Homero Ortega, Isabel La Católica N24-100. Outlet for one of the Panama hat manufacturers in Cuenca.
Productos Andinos, Urbina 111 y Cordero. Artisan's co-op, good selection, including Panama hats.
Saucisa, Amazonas 2487 y Pinto, and a couple other locations in La Mariscal. Very good place to buy Andean music CDs and Andean musical instruments.
The Ethnic Collection, Amazonas N21-63 y Robles, T250 0155, www.ethniccollection.com. Wide variety of clothing, leather, bags, jewellery, balsa wood and ceramic items from across Ecuador.

Jewellery

Alquimia, Juan Rodríguez 139. High quality silversmith.
Argentum, JL Mera 614. Excellent selection, reasonably priced.
Hamilton, 12 de Octubre 1942 y Cordero. Fine silver and gold crafts and jewellery, native designs.
Jeritsa, Mall El Jardín, local 234. Good selection, prices and service.

Markets

Main produce markets, all accessible by Trole:

Mercado Central, Av Pichincha y Olmedo (also on the Ecovía), Mercado Santa Clara, Versalles y Ramírez Dávalos and Mercado Iñaquito, Iñaquito y Villalengua. Mercado Ipiales, on Chile uphill from Imbabura, where clothing, appliances and stolen goods are sold (a particularly unsafe area).

▲ Activities and tours

Quito *p893, map p897 and 898*
Climbing and trekking
Climbs and trekking tours can be arranged in Quito and several other cities; the following Quito operators have been recommended (see also Tour operators below for contact information):
Agama Expediciones, J Washington 425 y 6 de Diciembre, p 2, T290 3164, www.cotopaxi-carasur.com. Run by experienced climbing guide Eduardo Agama, also own Albergue Cara Sur on Cotopaxi.
Campo Base, Jacinto de Evia N60-121 (north of the airport), T259 9737, www.campobase turismo.com. Climbing, trekking and cycling tours, run by Manuel and Diego Jácome, very experienced climbing guides, they also have a mountain lodge 15 km south of Sangolquí, near Sincholagua, good for acclimatization at 3050 m.
Compañía de Guías, Jorge Washington 425 y 6 de Diciembre, T/F250 4773, www.companiadeguias.com. Climbing and trekking specialists, but sell other tours, English, German, French and Italian spoken.
Pamir Travel and Adventures, chief guide Hugo Torres is very experienced and speaks English.
Safari Tours, 2 climbers per guide, trekking tours, has own transport and equipment, large and small groups, several languages spoken, very knowledgeable, well organized and planned. Also runs a high altitude glacier school, with courses of 2-3 days with bilingual guides.

Sierra Nevada, chief guide Freddy Ramírez is fluent in French, English and German, has his own equipment, and takes mostly large groups.
Surtrek arranges guided climbs of most peaks, also rents and sells equipment, 2 climbers per guide, large and small group.
Independent guides do not normally provide transport or full service, ie food, equipment, insurance and, without a permit from the **Ministerio de Ambiente**, they might be refused entry to national parks. Local climbing clubs welcome new members, but they do not provide free guiding service. It is not really worth joining if you are in Ecuador for only a few weeks.
The following all have climbing clubs: **Colegio San Gabriel, Universidad Católica, Nuevos Horizontes** (Colón 2038 y 10 de Agosto, T255 2154) and **Club Sadday** (Alonso de Angulo y Galo Molina).
If planning to go to Cotopaxi with a Quito tour operator or guide, you must ensure that they have the requisite permits (*patentes*). A cheap tour may leave you stranded at the national park gates if your guide or transport does not have the correct papers.

Cycling and mountain biking
Quito has a couple of bike paths, **Ciclopaseos**, one around the perimeter of Parque La Carolina and a second one in the south, along Quebrada Ortega in the Quitumbe neighbourhood. The city organizes a ciclopaseo every fortnight. Key avenues are closed to vehicular traffic and thousands of cyclists cross the city in 24 km from north to south.
Aries, Wilson 578 y Reina Victoria, T/F290 6052, after hours T09-981 6603 (Mob), www.ariesbikecompany.com. 1-3 day mountain bike tours, all equipment provided.
Bike Tech, 6 de Diciembre N39-59 y El Telégrafo, T226 3421. A meeting place for long distance

bikers. Owner Santiago Lara has informal 'meets' almost every weekend, anyone is welcome, no charge, they ride 20 or more routes around Quito, they also have a good repair shop and cheap parts.

Biking Dutchman, Foch 714 y JL Mera, T254 2806, after hours T09-4205 349 (mob), www.biking-dutchman.com. One and several-day tours, great fun, good food, very well organized, English, German and Dutch spoken, pioneers in mountain biking in Ecuador.

Ciclo Vivas 6 de Diciembre y Louvre, Centro Comercial Junior, No 5. Stocks Jamis, Shimano and Wheeler.

See also **Safari** below.

Jogging

Hash House Harriers, enquire at *Reina Victoria Pub*, T222 6369. Club for runners and walkers,

Paragliding

Escuela Pichincha de Vuelo Libre, Carlos Endara Oe3-60 y Amazonas, T02-225 6592 (office hours) T09-947 8349 (Mob), parapent@uio.satnet.net, is a good point of contact. Offers complete courses for US$350-500 and tandem flights for US$40-60.

Rugby

Friendly games are played when there are

enough people, see noticeboard at the **Reina Victoria Pub**.

Swimming

There are a number of good, clean, heated public pools in the city. Swimming cap, towel and soap are compulsory for admission. One is in Miraflores, at the upper end of Av Universitaria, a 10-min walk from Amazonas. Open Tue-Sun 0900-1600. Another is at Batán Alto, on Cochapata y Abascal, off Gaspar de Villaroel. The pool and sauna at Colegio Benalcázar are also open to the public, 6 de Diciembre y Portugal, Benalcázar stop on the Ecovía.

Tour operators

National park fees are rarely included in prices.

Advantage Travel, El Telégafo E10-63 y Juan de Alcántara, T246 2871, www.advantagecuador.com. Tours to Machalilla and Isla de la Plata. Also 4-5 day tours on a floating hotel on Río Napo.

Anaconda Travel, Foch 635 y Reina Victoria, p 1, T/F222 4913, anacondaec@andinanet.net. Runs Anaconda lodge in the upper Napo, jungle trips, sell tours to Galápagos and other destinations.

Andando Tours - Angermeyer Cruises, Mariana de Jesús E7-113 (326) y Pradera, T323 7186, www.andandotours.com.

Andes Explorer, Reina Victoria 927 (entre Pinto

Ecuador Quito & around Listings

y Wilson), Quito, T290 1493, www.andes-explorer.com. Experienced tour operator specializing in the Galápagos, representing over 60 cruise ships from economy to luxury.

Campus Trekking, Joaquina Vargas 99 y Ab Caldero, Conocoto, Valle de los Chillos, T234 0601, www.campustrekking.com. Good value trekking tours run by experienced agency.

Canodros, Portugal 448 y Catalina Aldaz, T225 6759, www.canodros.com. Run luxury Galápagos cruises and jungle tours in the Kapawi Ecological Reserve, also have office in Guayaquil.

EcoAndes, Baquedano E5-27 y JL Mera, T222 0892, www.ecoandestravel.com. For classic tours, adventure travel, Galápagos and Amazon. Also have 2 hotels, **Fuente de Piedra I** and **II**, in La Mariscal district, and **Coraza** in Otavalo, www.ecuahotel.com.

Eco Tours, Magnolias N51 y Cristantemos, La Primavera, Cumbaya, T/F289 7316, www.ecotoursecuador.com. Exclusive booking agent for the Napo Wildlife Center (www.NapoWildlifeCenter.com).

Ecuador Amazing, Pinto 521 y Amazonas, p6, T254 7257, www.ecuadoramazing.com. Full service tour operator and owner of a group of tour services. See advert for tours offered.

Ecuadorian Tours, Amazonas 329 y Washington, several other locations, T256 0488, www.ecuador iantours.com. (Also Amex representative.) Airline tickets and tours in all regions.

Enchanted Expeditions, de las Alondras N45-102 y de los Lirios, T334 0525, www.enchantedexpeditions.com. Operate Galápagos cruises in various categories, jungle and trekking tours.

Galacruises Expeditions, 9 de Octubre N22-118 y Veintimilla, T/F252 3324, www.galacruises.com. Yachts and catamarans, cruises and expeditions.

Galasam, Cordero 1354 y Amazonas, T290 3909, www.galasam.com. Full range of day and multi-day tours in highlands, jungle trips to their own lodge on the Río Aguarico, Galápagos trips.

Galextur, Portugal 600 (E10-271) y 6 de Diciembre, T226 9626, www.galextur.com. Run Galápagos tours (see also page 1026).

Geo Reisen, Yugoeslavia 265 y Azuay, T292 0583, www.georeisentours.com. Specializing in cultural, adventure and nature tours adapted for individuals, groups or families.

Green Planet, JL Mera N23-84 y Wilson, T252 0570, greenpla@interactive.net.ec. Ecologically sensitive jungle trips, lodge on Río Aguarico, good food.

Kapok Expeditions, Pinto E4-225, T/F255 6348. Jungle tours to Cuyabeno and Yasuní, trekking, Machalilla, hacienda tours (participate in daily farm activities).

Kempery Tours, Ramírez Dávilos 117 y Amazonas, Ed Turismundial, p 2, T250 5599, www.kempery.com. German, English and Dutch spoken, all kinds of tours, including Galápagos and jungle, good value.

Klein Tours, Eloy Alfaro N34-151 y Catalina Aldaz, also Shyris N34-280 y Holanda, T226 7000, www.kleintours.com. Galápagos cruises and mainland tours, tailor-made, English, French and German spoken.

Metropolitan Touring, Av Las Palmeras N35-74 y Las Orquídeas, T298 8200/8380, www.metro politan-touring.com. Galápagos tours, arranges climbing, trekking expeditions led by world-known climbers, as well as tours of Quito, Parque Nacional Machalilla, rail journeys, jungle camps.

Palmar Voyages, Alemania 575 y Av Mariana de Jesús, T256 9809, www.palmarvoyages.com. Small specialist company, custom-made itineraries to all areas of Ecuador or Peru, good rates.

Pamir Travel and Adventures, JL Mera 721 y Veintimilla, T254 2605, F254 7576. Galápagos cruises, climbing and jungle tours.

Pluma Verde Tours, contact Rudy Gelis, T255 0797, www.plumaverdetours.com. For birdwatching and wildlife tours.

Positiv Turismo, Voz Andes N41-81, T244 0604, www.positivturismo.com. Swiss-Austrian-run company offers trips to Galápagos, cultural trips, trekking and special interest tours.

Rolf Wittmer Turismo Galapagos, Foch e 7-81 y Diego de Almagro, La Mariscal, Quito, T252 6938, www.rwittmer.com. Tailor-made tours throughout Ecuador and the Galápagos.

Quasar Náutica, Brasil 293, Edif IACA p 2, T244 6996, T1-800 247 2925 (USA), www.quasarex.com. Highly recommeded 7-10 day naturalist and diving Galápagos cruises on 8-16 berth luxury and power yachts.

Rainforestur, Amazonas 420 entre Roca y Robles, T223 9822, www.rainforestur.com.ec. Also have an office in Baños. Offers climbing and jungle trips to Cuyabeno and the Puyo area.

Safari, Foch E5-39 y JL Mera, T255 2505, www.safari.com.ec. Run by Jean Brown, expat Brit, very knowledgeable and informative. Excellent adventure travel, personalized itineraries, mountain climbing, cycling, rafting, trekking and cultural tours. They also book Galápagos tours, sell jungle trips and run a high-altitude glacier school. An excellent source of travel information. Open daily 0930-1830. Highly recommended.

Sangay Touring, Amazonas N24-196 y Cordero, T250 8922. Operate a variety of custom designed tours and sell Galápagos trips, efficient service.

Sierra Nevada, Pinto 637 y Cordero, T255 3658, snevada@accessinter.net. Climbing, rafting, jungle expeditions, experienced multi-lingual guides.

Surtrek, Amazonas 897 y Wilson, T256 1129, www.surtrek.com. Climbing, trekking expeditions, jungle and Galápagos tours, also flights.

Tierra de Fuego, Amazonas N2323 y Veintimilla, T250 1418, www.ecuadortierradefuego.com. Travel agency and tour operator with a small fleet of vehicles to provide land services and tours throughout the country.

Tours Unlimited, Julio Castro 379 y Valparaíso, T222 2564, www.tours-unlimited.com. Custom-made itineraries in all regions, specializing in trips for honeymooners.

Tropic Ecological Adventures, República E7-320 y Diego de Almagro, Edif Taurus, dpto 1-A, T222 5907, www.tropiceco.com. Run by Andy Drumm and Sofía Darquea, naturalist guides with many years experience in Galápagos, who work closely with conservation groups. Winners of awards for responsible tourism in 1997 and 2000. Their ecologically responsible and educational tours are recommended for anyone seriously interested in the environment. Part of each fee is given to indigenous communities and ecological projects. Also sell Galápagos and highland trips.

TrueColorsTravel, Guayaquil N9-59 y Oriente, of 304, T/F295 5345. Offers general high-end tours, Galápagos, exclusive haciendas, etc.

Zenith Travel, JL Mera 453 y Roca, T252 9993, www.zenithecuador.com. Economical Galápagos cruises as well as various land tours in Ecuador and Peru. All-gay Galápagos cruises available. English and French spoken, knowledgeable helpful staff, good value.

Whitewater rafting
Sierra Nevada (see Tour operators above), excellent trips from 1 to 3 days, chief guide Edison Ramírez (fluent English/French) is certified by *French Association*.
Yacu Amu/Ríos Ecuador, Foch 746 y JL Mera, T290 4054, www.yacuamu.com. Australian-owned (Steve Nomchong), guide Gynner Coronel, very professional, rafting trips of 1-6 days, also kayak courses, good equipment. Highly recommended.
   All these outfits charge US$50-70 per day.

⊖ Transport

Quito *p893, map p897 and 898*
Air
Mariscal Sucre Airport, T294 4900. The safest and easiest way to travel between town and the airport is to take a **taxi**. You can catch one from the rank right outside arrivals, having bought a ticket first at the booth. The fixed fare from the airport to the New City is about US$5; to the Old City or to a first-class hotel US$6 (more at night, but beware of overcharging). Alternatively, you can use the **Trans-Rabbit** van service, whcih are good value for groups of four or more. Individuals who buy a ticket for a van must either pay more or wait until they get enough passengers. **Public buses** are not recommended unless you have virtually no luggage or are desperately low on funds. Buses and trolley alike are too crowded to enter with even a small backpack so the risk of theft is very high. The bus stop is 1 block west of terminal, in front of Centro Comercial Aeropuerto. For the New City take a southbound bus marked 'Carcelén-Congreso' along Av Amazonas, fare US$0.25. For the Old City take a green *alimentador* (feeder bus line) from the same location as above to the northern terminus of the trolley line, combined fare US$0.25. There is no bus or trolley service late at night when most flights from North America arrive. Left luggage facilities are just outside international arrivals. **Moneyzone** cambio in International Arrivals and Departures, poor rates for various currencies, 4% commission for TCs, office at Departures daily 0430-2100. There are duty-free shops in the international departure lounge. Details of internal services are given in the respective destinations.

Bus
Local Quito has 3 parallel bus lines running from north to south on exclusive lanes, covering almost the length of the city. The fare is US$0.25. **Trole** (T266 5016, Mon-Fri 0500-2345, weekends and holidays 0600-2145) is system of trolley buses, with feeder bus lines (*alimentadores*, painted turquoise) from the suburbs. It runs along Av 10 de Agosto in the north of the city, C Guayaquil (southbound) and C Flores (northbound) in the Old City, and mainly along Av Pedro Vicente Maldonado in the south. The northern terminus is north of 'La Y', the junction of 10 de Agosto, Av América and Av de la Prensa; at El Recreo, on Av Maldonado is an important transfer station, known as Terminal Sur, and the southern terminus, Morán Valverde, is in Ciudadela Quitumbe in the far south. Trolleys have a special entrance for wheelchairs. **Ecovía** (T243 0726, Mon-Sat 0500-2130, Sun and holidays 0600-2100) is a line of articulated buses running along Av 6 de Diciembre, from La Marín near the Old City to the Estación Río Coca, at C Río Coca east of 6 de Diciembre, in the north. Ecovía feeder buses are dark red. **Metrobus** (T346 5149, Mon-Fri 0530-2230, weekends and holidays 0600-2100) also runs articulated buses along Av América and Av de la Prensa from La Marín to the neighbourhood of Carcelén, in the north. This line will be extended from La Marín to the south. There are also 3 types of **city buses**: *selectivos* are red, take mostly sitting passengers and a limited number standing, US$0.25. *Bus Tipo* are royal blue, take sitting and standing passengers, US$0.25. There are few *populares* left, these are light blue, US$0.18, can get very crowded. Many bus lines go through La Marín at the north end of the Old City. Extra caution is advised here: it is a rough area, pickpockets abound and it is best avoided at night.

   Short distance Outer suburbs are served by *Interparroquial* buses painted green. Those running east to the valleys of Cumbayá, Tumbaco and beyond leave from the Estación Río Coca (see Ecovía above). Buses southeast to Valle de los Chillos leave from La Marín. Buses going northwest leave from San Blas, those north from C Larrea and Asunción and those going south from Villaflora.
Long distance Until the new terminal in Quitumbe is complete, the Terminal Terrestre, at Maldonado y Cumandá (south of Plaza Santo Domingo), handles most long-distance bus services and is really the only place to get information on schedules, 24-hr luggage store US$1.75 per day. US$0.20 to enter platforms. It is unsafe at all hours, worst at night. To or from the Terminal Terrestre, take a taxi (highly recommended), or the trolley bus (unsafe with luggage). There are company booking offices but staff shout destinations of buses leaving; you can get on board and pay

later (but confirm fare in advance). For buses out of Quito it is sometimes advisable to reserve the day before (eg on holiday weekends). See under destinations for fares and schedules.

Several companies run better quality coaches on the longer routes, those with terminals in the New City are: **Flota Imbabura**, Manuel Larrea 1211 y Portoviejo, T223 6940, for **Cuenca** and **Guayaquil**; Transportes Ecuador, JL Mera 330 y Jorge Washington, T250 3642, to **Guayaquil**; **Transportes Esmeraldas**, Santa María 870 y Amazonas, T250 5099, for Esmeraldas; **Reina del Camino**, Larrea y 18 de Septiembre, T258 5697, for **Portoviejo**, **Bahía** and **Manta**; **Panamericana Internacional**, Colón 852 y Reina Victoria, T250 1585, for **Huaquillas**, **Machala**, **Cuenca**, **Loja**, **Guayaquil**, **Manta** and **Esmeraldas**. They also run an international service: daily to **Bogotá**, changing buses in Tulcán and Ipiales, US$70, 28 hrs; **Caracas**, US$100; to **Lima**, changing buses in Aguas Verdes and Túmbes, US$70, 38 hrs. **Ormeño Internacional**, from Perú, Shyris N34-432 y Portugal, T246 0027, twice a week to **Lima** (US$70, 36 hrs), **La Paz**, US$150, **Santiago** (US$165, 4 days) and **Buenos Aires** (US$200, 1 week). Another international service is run by **Rutas de América**, Selva Alegre Oe1-72 y 10 de Agosto, T250 3611. To **Lima**, Sat at 2200, US$52, 31 hrs; to **Caracas**, Wed and Sun 2200, US$132, 58 hrs. They do not enter any Colombian cities but passengers can be let off at the roadside (eg by **Popayán**, US$32). It is quicker and cheaper to take a bus to the border and change. The route to **Peru** via Loja and Macará takes much longer than the Huaquillas route, but is more relaxed. Do not buy Peruvian (or any other country's) bus tickets here, they are much cheaper outside Ecuador.

Taxi
Taxis are a safe, cheap and efficient way to get around the city. Be reasonable and remember that the majority of taxi drivers are honest and helpful. For airport taxis, see above. From the Terminal Terrestre to the New City is US$4; and journeys around the New City cost from US$1. Expect to pay US$1-2 more at night. All taxis must have working meters by law, but make sure the meter is running (if it isn't, fix the fare before). Also insist that the taxi drops you precisely where you want to go. All legally registered taxis have the number of their co-operative and the individual operator's number prominently painted on the side of the vehicle and on a sticker on the windshield. They are safer and cheaper than unauthorized taxis. Note the registration and the licence plate numbers if you feel you have been seriously overcharged or mistreated. You may then complain to the transit police or tourist office.

At night it is safer to use a radio taxi, there are several companies including: **Taxi Amigo**, T222 2222; **City Taxi**, T263 3333; and **Central de Radio Taxis**, T250 0600. Make sure they give you the taxi number so that you get the correct taxi and can trace anything you may leave behind. To hire a taxi by the hour costs from US$8. For trips outside Quito, agree the fare beforehand: US$70-85 a day. Outside the luxury hotels co-operative taxi drivers have a list of agreed excursion prices and most drivers are knowledgeable. For taxi tours with a guide, try **Hugo Herrera**, T226 7891. He speaks English and is recommended.

Train
Regular passenger service has been discontinued throughout the country. A tourist train runs from to the **Cotopaxi** station in Area Nacional de Recreación El Boliche. Trains normally depart from Quito railway station, 2 km south of the Old City, along the continuation of C Maldonado (Chimbacalle trolley stop if northbound, Jefferson Pérez stop if southbound, then walk uphill along Maldonado). Sat and Sun 0800, returns 1430. US$4.60 return, children under 12 and seniors US$2.30. At the end of 2006, the track was closed south of the city because of road construction. Until it reopens, a bus takes passengers at 0800 from the Chimbacalle (Quito) station to the Tambillo station. Best purchase tickets in advance either at the train station, T265 6142, daily 0800-1630 or at Bolívar 443 y García Moreno in the Old City, T258 2930, Mon-Fri 0800-1630; you need a passport number for all the tickets you purchase and the person's age. Last minute sales at Tambillo are for box cars only, same price. If you wish to return by bus, it is a 2 km walk from the Cotopaxi station to the Pan-American highway. **Metropolitan Touring**, see above, offers various tours involving train travel.

⚫ Directory

Quito p893, map p897 and 898
Airline offices National: Aerogal, Amazonas 607 y Carrión and Av Amazonas 7797, opposite the airport, T225 7202, 1-800-237 6425, www.aerogal.com.ec. Icaro, JL Mera N26-221 y Orellana, Shyris N34-108 y Holanda, T299 7400, T1-800-883567. Saéreo, Indanza 121 y Amazonas, T330 2280, 1-800-SAERO. TAME, Amazonas N24-260 y Colón, 6 de Diciembre N26-112, several others, T290 9900. VIP, Foch 265 y 6 de Diciembre, T254 6600, T1-800-847847. International: Air France/KLM, 12 de Octubre N26-27 y Lincoln, T298 6828. American, Amazonas 4545 y Pereira, T299 5000. Avianca, Coruña 1311 y San Ignacio, T1-800-003434.

Continental, 12 de Octubre 1830 y Cordero, World Trade Center, p 11, T225 0905. Copa, República de El Salvador 361 y Moscú, edif Aseguradora del Sur, T227 3082. Delta, Los Syris y Suecia, edif Renazzo Plaza, T1-800-101080. Iberia, Eloy Alfaro 939 y Amazonas, edif Finandes, p 5, T256 6009. LAN, Orellana 557 y Coruña and Quicentro Shopping, T299 2300, 1-800-101075. Santa Bárbara, Portugal 794 y República de El Salvador, T225 3972 TACA, República de El Salvador N36-139 y Suecia, T292 3170.

Banks Banco del Austro, Amazonas y Santa María, Benalcázar N3-21 y Sucre and others. Banco Bolivariano, Naciones Unidas E6-99 y Shyris, Amazonas 752 y Veintimilla. Banco del Pacífico, Naciones Unidas y Los Shyris, Amazonas y Roca, Mall El Jardín and CC El Bosque. Pacificard, Naciones Unidas E7-97 y y Shyris, p2. Produbanco, Amazonas N35-211 y Japón (opposite CCI), Amazonas 366 y Robles (also open Sat 0900-1300), Espejo y Guayaquil. The American Express representative is Ecuadorian Tours, see above, sells and replaces Amex TCs, does not change TCs or give cash advances.

Casas de cambio: All open Mon-Fri 0900-1800, Sat 0900-1300. Euromoney, Amazonas N21-229 y Roca, T252 6907. Change cash euros, sterling, soles, pesos colombianos and other currencies. Mega Cambios, Amazonas N24-01 y Wilson, T255 5849. 3% commission for US$ TCs, change cash euros, sterling, Canadian dollars. Vazcorp, Amazonas N21-147 y Roca, T252 9212. Good rates and many services, recommended.

Car hire All the main car rental companies are at the airport. For multinational rental agencies, see Essentials, page 43. City offices of local companies: Bombuscaro, Amazonas N51-21, T330 3304. Expo, Av América N21-66 y Bolívia, T222 8688. Good value. Trans-Rabbit, at the international arrivals section of the Airport, rent vans for up to 10 passengers, with driver, for trips in Quito and out of town, T330 1496; also Achupallas Tours, T330 1493, vanrent@andinanet.net. **Cultural** centres Alliance Française, at Eloy Alfaro N32-468, T245 2017, www.afquito.org.ec. French courses, films and cultural events. Casa Humboldt, Vancouver E5-54 y Polonia, T254 8480, www.asociacion-humboldt.org. German centre, Goethe Institute, films, talks, exhibitions. **Embassies and consulates** Austria, Gaspar de Villaroel E9-53 y Los Shyris, p 3, T244 3272, przibra@interactive.net.ec, 1000-1200. Belgium, República de El Salvador 1082 y Naciones Unidas, p 10, T227 6145, www.diplomatie.be/quitoes. Mon-Thu 0830-1230. Canada, 6 de Diciembre 2816 y Paul Rivet, edif Josueth González p 4, T223 2114, www.quito.gc.ca, 0900-1200. Colombia

(consulate), Atahualpa 955 y República, edif Digicom p 3, T245 8012, consuladoenquito@andinanet.net. 0900-1300 1400-1600. Finland, Whimper N30-91 y Coruña, T290 1501. France, L Plaza 107 y Patria, T294 3800, www.ambafrance-ec.org. Mon-Thu 0900-1300. 1430-1730, Fri 0830-1330. Germany, Naciones Unidas E10-44 y República de El Salvador, edif City Plaza, T297 0820, www.embajada-quito.de. 0830-1130. Ireland, Ulloa 2651 y Rumipamba, T245 1577, 0900-1300. Israel, 12 de Octubre y Salazar, Edif Plaza 2000, p 9, T223 7474. 1000-1300. Italy, La Isla 111 y H Albornoz, T256 1077, www.ambitalquito.org. 0830-1230. Japan, JL Mera N19-36 y Patria, T256 1899, embapon@ uio.satnet.net. 0930-1200, 1400-1700. Netherlands, 12 de Octubre 1942 y Cordero, World Trade Center, p 1, T222 9229, www.embajadadeholanda.com, 0830-1300, 1400-1730. Norway, Pasaje Alfonso Jerves 134 y Orellana, T250 9514, 0900-1200. Peru, República de El Salvador 1942 y Cordero, edif World Trade Center p 9, T223 1990, embapar@uio.telconet.net, 0830-1330. Spain, La Pinta 455 y Amazonas, T256 4373. 0900-1200. Sweden, República de El Salvador N39-399 e Irlanda, T227 8188. Switzerland, Juan Pablo Sanz 3617 y Amazonas, edif Xerox p 2, T243 4949, www.eda.admin.ch/quito. 0900-1200. United Kingdom, Naciones Unidas y República de El Salvador, edif Citiplaza, p 14, T297 0800, www.britembquito.org.ec. Mon-Thu 0800-1230, 1330-1600, Fri 0830-1230. USA, 12 de Octubre y Patria, T256 2890, www.usembassy.org.ec. 0800-1230, 1330-1700. **Internet** Quito has very many cyber cafés, particularly in the Mariscal tourist district. Rates start at about US$0.60 per hr, but US$1 is more typical. **Language schools** The following schools have received favourable reports. In the New City: Academia Latinoamericana de Espanol, Noruega 126 y 6 de Diciembre T225 0946, www.latinoschools.com. Amazonas, Washington 718 y Amazonas, edif Rocafuerte, p3, T252 7509, www.eduamazonas.com. Beraca, Amazonas N24-66 y Pinto, p2, T290 6642, www.beraca.net. Bipo & Toni's Academia de Español, Carrión E8-183 y L Plaza, T250 0732, www.bipo.net. Colón, Colón 2088 y Versalles, T250 6508, www.colonspanish school.com. Equinoccial, Reina Victoria 1325 y García, T/F256 4488, www.ecuadorspanish.com. Small school. La Lengua, Colón 1001 y JL Mera, p 8, T/F250 1271, www.la-lengua.com. Swiss/Ecuadorean run. Also has a school at Puerto López, on the Pacific coast. Mitad del Mundo, Patria 640 y 9 de Octubre, Edif Patria 1204, T254 6827, www.mitadmundo.com.ec. Repeatedly recommended. San Francisco, Amazonas 2262 y

Language schools in Quito

Quito is one of the most important centres for Spanish language study in Latin America with over 80 schools operating. There is a great variety to choose from. Identify your budget and goals for the course: rigorous grammatical and technical training, fluent conversation skills, getting to know Ecuadoreans or just enough basic Spanish to get you through your trip.

Visit a few places to get a feel for what they charge and offer. Prices vary greatly, from US$4 to US$10 per hour, but you do not always get what you pay for. There is also tremendous variation in teacher qualifications, infrastructure and resource materials. Schools usually offer courses of four or seven hours tuition per day. Many correspondents suggest that four is enough. Some schools offer packages which combine teaching in the morning and touring in the afternoon. A great deal of emphasis has traditionally been placed on one-to-one teaching, but remember that a well-structured small classroom setting can also be very good.

The quality of homestays likewise varies, the cost including meals runs from US$12 to US$25 per day. Try to book just one week at first to see how a place suits you, don't be pressed into signing a long term contract right at the start. For language courses as well as homestays, deal directly with the people who will provide services to you, and avoid intermediaries. Always get a detailed receipt whenever you make a payment.

If you are short on time then it can be a good idea to make your arrangements from home, either directly with one of the schools or through an agency, who can offer you a wide variety of options. If you have more time and less money, then it may be more economical to organize your own studies after you arrive. *South American Explorers* provides a free list of recommended schools and these may give club members discounts.

We list schools for which we have received positive recommendations each year. This does not imply that schools not mentioned are not recommended.

Ramírez Dávalos, T252 1306, www.sanfranciscospanish.com. **Simón Bolívar**, Foch E9-20 y 6 de Diciembre, T223 4708, www.simon-bolivar.com. Have their own travel agency. **Sintaxis**, 10 de Agosto 15-55 y Bolivia, edif Andrade, p 5, T252 0006, www.sintaxis.net. Consistently recommended. **South American Language Center**, Amazonas N26-59 y Santa María, T/F254 2715, www.southamerican.edu.ec. **Superior**, Darquea Terán 1650 y 10 de Agosto, T222 3242, www.instituto-superior.net. They also have a school in Otavalo (Sucre 1110 y Morales, p 2, T06-292 2414), in Galápagos (advanced booking required) and can arrange voluntary work. **Universidad Católica**, 12 de Octubre y Roca, Sección de Español, T299 1700 ext 1388, lbvillagomez@puce.edu.ec. **Medical services** Most embassies have the telephone numbers of doctors and dentists who speak non-Spanish languages. **Hospitals: Hospital Voz Andes** Villalengua Oe 2-37 y Av 10 de Agosto, T226 2142 (reached by Trole, la Y stop). Emergency room, quick and efficient, fee based on ability to pay, run by Christian HCJB organization, has out-patient dept, T243 9343. **Hospital Metropolitano**, Mariana de Jesús y Occidental, just east of the western city bypass, T226 1520, ambulance T226 5020, catch a Quito Sur-San Gabriel bus along América, or the Trole (Mariana de Jesús stop) and walk up, or take a taxi. Very professional and recommended, but expensive. **Clínica Pichincha**, Veintimilla E3-30 y Páez, T256 2296, ambulance T250 1565. Another very good, expensive hospital. **Clínica Pasteur**, Eloy Alfaro 552 y 9 de Octubre, T223 4004. Also good and cheaper than the above. **Novaclínica Santa Cecilia**, Veintimilla 1394 y 10 de Agosto, T254 5390, emergency T254 5000. Reasonable prices, good. **Med Center Travel Clinic** (Dr John Rosenberg), Foch 476 y Almagro, T252 1104, 09-973 9734. General and travel medicine with a full range of vaccines, speaks English and German, very helpful GP. **Fybeca** is a reliable chain of 33 pharmacies throughout the city. Their 24-hr branches are at Amazonas y Tomás de Berlanga near the Plaza de Toros, and at Centro Comercial El Recreo in the south. **Post offices** All branches open Mon-Fri 0800-1800,

Sat 0800-1200. In principle all branches provide all services, but your best chances are at Colón y Almagro in the Mariscal district, and at the main sorting centre on Japón near Naciones Unidas, behind the CCI shopping centre. The branch on Eloy Alfaro 354 y 9 de Octubre frequently loses mail; best avoided. There is also a branch in the Old City, on Espejo entre Guayaquil y Venezuela, and between the old and New Cities at Ulloa and Ramírez Dávalos, behind the Mercado Santa Clara. This is the centre for parcel post, and you may still be directed there to send large packages. *Poste Restante* at the post offices at Espejo and at Eloy Alfaro (less efficient). All *poste restante* letters are sent to Espejo unless marked 'Correo Central, Eloy Alfaro', but you are advised to check both *postes restantes*, whichever address you use. Letters can be sent care of American Express, Apdo 17-01-0265, Quito. *South American Explorers* hold mail for members. **Telephones** There are cabins (*cabinas*) all over the city for national and international calls. There are also debit card cell phones throughout the city. **Useful addresses** Emergencies: T911 for all types of emergency in Quito. **Immigration Offices**: see Essentials. **Police**: T101. **Servicio de Seguridad Turística, Policía de Turismo**, Reina Victoria y Roca, T254 3983. Report robberies here. Also at **Fiscalía de Turismo, Ministerio de Turismo**, Eloy Alfaro N32-300 y Tobar, T250 7559 (ext 1014), Public Prosecutors Office, Mon-Fri 0800-1200, 1400-1800.

Around Quito

Mitad del Mundo and around

The location of the equatorial line here (23 km N of Quito, nearest town San Antonio de Pichincha) was determined by Charles-Marie de la Condamine and his French expedition in 1736, and agrees to within 150 m with modern GPS measurements. The monument forms the focal point of a park and leisure area built as a typical colonial town, with restaurants, gift shops, Post Office with philatelic sales, travel agency, and has a very interesting **ethnographic museum** inside ① *Mon-Thu 0900-1800, Fri-Sun 0900-1900 (very crowded on Sun), US$2, children US$1, includes entrance to the pavilions; entry to the ethnographic museum US$3 (includes guided tour of museum in Spanish or English).* In the museum; a lift takes you to the top, then you walk down with the museum laid out all around with different indigenous cultures every few steps. There is a **Planetarium** ① *US$1.50, group of 15 minimum*, with hourly 30-minute shows and an attractive and interesting model of old Quito, about 10 m square, with artificial day and night, which took seven years to build. **Museo Inti-Ñan** ① *200 m north of the monument, T239 5122, 0930-1730 daily, US$3*, shows the exact location of the equator, with certificates for visitors, eclectic and very interesting. Two minutes' walk before the Monument is the restaurant *Equinoccio*, about US$10 a meal, live music on Sunday, open 1000-1600 daily, T239 4091. Available at the restaurant or at stalls outside are 'certificates' recording your visit to the Equator (free with a meal).

Pululahua

① *US$5.* A few kilometres beyond the Monument, off the paved road to Calacalí, is the Pululahua crater which can be seen from a lookout on the rim. It is a geobotanical reserve. Try to go in the morning, there is often cloud later. There is a rough track down from the rim to the crater. To get to the park and experience the rich vegetation and warm micro-climate inside, continuing past the village in the crater, turn left and follow an unimproved road up to the rim and back to the main road, a 15-20 km round trip.

Papallacta

At the **Termas de Papallacta** ① *64 km east from Quito, 1 km from the road to Baeza, 0600-2100, T02-256 8989, www.papallacta.com.ec* there are ten thermal pools, three large enough for swimming, and four cold plunge pools, the best developed hot springs in the country. There are two public complexes of springs: the regular pools ① *US$7 pp*, and the spa centre ① *US$17 (massages and other special treatments extra).* For accommodation, the hotel (**A**) has heated rooms with private bath (one with private jacuzzi) surrounding small private pools (access only to guests). A set of cabins for families or groups of up to six people (**AL**), surround more private pools. Guests are provided with identification and can enter any part of the pools; massages and other treatments at the spa centre have 50% discount. Meals are extra. For weekends book a room at least a week in advance; holiday weekends a month or more in advance. The complex is tastefully done and recommended. The view, on a clear day, of Antisana while enjoying the thermal waters is superb. There are several excellent self-guided routes in the reserve behind the pools ① *Fundación Ecológica Rumicocha, T02-321 4833 for details, www.rumicocha.org.ec, US$3 for trails, US$5 for camping.* Access to the road to Oyacachi, 45 km, is beside the information centre. It is advisable to obtain permission before trying to go through; call the Ministerio del Medio Ambiente in Cayambe, T211 0370. Likewise call the same office to use the guest cabin in the Cayambe-Coca reserve and fish in several of the lakes.

Refugio de Vida Silvestre Pasochoa
① *Foreigners US$10, very busy at weekends, 45 mins southeast of Quito by car.*
This natural park set in humid Andean forest is run by the **Fundación Natura** ① *Elia Liut N45-10 y El Telégrafo, T227 2863 ext 328, www.fnatura.org.* The reserve has more than 120 species of birds (unfortunately some of the fauna has been frightened away by the noise of the visitors) and 50 species of trees, situated between 2,700 m and 4,200 m. There are walks of 30 minutes to eight hours. Camping is permitted in the park (US$3 per person). Take food and water as there are no shops and take your rubbish away with you. There is also a refuge (US$6-10 per person per night, with shower, has cooking facilities, camping US$4), but you will need a sleeping bag.

Western slopes of Pichincha → *Altitude: 1,200-2,800 m.*
Despite their proximity to the capital (two hours from Quito), the western slopes of **Pichincha** and its surroundings are surprisingly wild, with fine opportunities for walking and especially birdwatching. This scenic area has lovely cloud forests and many nature reserves. The main tourist town in this area is Mindo. To the west of Mindo is a warm subtropical area of clear rivers and waterfalls, where a growing number of tourist developments are springing up. Northwest of Quito two roads drop into the western lowlands: the old, rough route through Nono and Mindo, newly dubbed the **Ecoruta**, or **Paseo del Quinde** (Route of the Hummingbird, see www.comunidadandina.org/turismo/maximo/quinde.htm) begins towards the northern end off Avenida Occidental, Quito's western ring road, at the intersection with C Machala. A newer, paved route starts by the Mitad del Mundo monument, goes through Calacalí, Nanegalito, San Miguel de los Bancos, Pedro Vicente Maldonado and Puerto Quito, before joining the Santo Domingo–Esmeraldas road at La Independencia. There are several connecting roads between these two routes.

On the Paseo del Quinde With increased awareness of the need to conserve the cloud forests of the northwest slopes of Pichincha and of their potential for tourism, the number of reserves here is steadily growing. Keen birdwatchers are no longer the only visitors, and the region has much to offer all nature lovers. Infrastructure at reserves varies considerably. Some have comfortable upmarket lodges offering accommodation, meals, guides and transport. Others may require taking your own camping gear, food, and obtaining a permit. There are too many reserves and lodges to mention here; see *Footprint Ecuador* for more details.

At Km 62 on the old road to Mindo via Tandayapa is **Bellavista**, with excellent birdwatching and botany at the *Hostería Bellavista*. For Bellavista and Maquipucuna (see next paragraph) take a bus to Nanegalito then hire a pick-up (US$15-20), or arrange everything with the lodges (see Sleeping, below) or in Quito.

The cloud forest in the 18,500-ha **Maquipucuna Biological Reserve** contains a tremendous diversity of flora and fauna, including over 325 species of birds. The reserve has trails of varying length, from 15 minutes to full day (US$5 per person). Full board accommodation available (**AL**), for transport see next paragraph. For reservations: **Fundación Maquipucuna** ① *www.maqui.org*, supports the conservation of biodiversity and sustainable use of natural resources.

Next to Maquipucuna is **Santa Lucía** ① *T215 7242, www.santaluciaecuador.com.* Access to this reserve is 30 minutes by car from Nanegal. Day tours combining Pululahua, Yunguilla and Santa Lucía are available. Bosque Nublado Santa Lucía is a community-based conservation and eco-tourism project protecting a beautiful 650-ha tract of cloud forest. The area is very rich in birds (there is a Cock-of-the-rock lek) and other wildlife. There are waterfalls and walking trails, including the ancient Camino de los Yumbos. There is a lodge, **A** for full board and guiding.

Yunguilla ① T09-114 4610, www.yunguilla.org, 5 km north of the Calacalí-La Independencia road, is a community-run eco-tourism project located at the upper elevation border of Maquipucuna Reserve. It has a cabin (**B**) with shared bath, and full board. Also organizes lodging with families (same price) and camping. Access by pick-up from Calacalí US$4, guiding US$20 per day

Bosque Protector Mindo-Nambillo → *Colour map 10, grid A3*

Mindo, a small town surrounded by dairy farms and lush cloud forest climbing the western slopes of Pichincha, is the main access for the 19,500-ha Bosque Protector Mindo-Nambillo. The town gets very crowded with Quiteños at weekends and holidays. The reserve, which ranges in altitude from 1,400 to 4,780 m, features beautiful flora (many orchids and bromeliads), fauna (butterflies, birds including the cock of the rock, golden-headed quetzal and toucan-barbet) and spectacular cloud forest and waterfalls. A controversial oil pipeline built right through the heart of the reserve in 2002 has not diminished the area's many attractions. **Amigos de la Naturaleza de Mindo** ① *1½ blocks from the Parque Central, T390 0423, US$1*, runs the **Centro de Educación Ambiental** (CEA), 4 km from town, within the 17 ha buffer zone, capacity for 25-30 people. Guide service, lodging and food are available. Lodging **E** per person, full board including excursion **B** per person. Take food if you wish to prepare your own (nice kitchen facilities US$1.50). Arrangements have to be made in advance. During the rainy season, access to the reserve can be rough. Vinicio Pérez (T390 0412, vinicioperez@andinanet.net) is an excellent birding guide, a little English spoken, recommended. Mindo also has orchid gardens and a butterfly farm 3 km from town. Activities include rappelling in the La Isla waterfalls, and 'tubing' regattas in the rivers.

West of Mindo

The road continues beyond the turn-off to Mindo, descending to the subtropical zone north of Santo Domingo de los Colorados. It goes via San Miguel de los Bancos and Pedro Vicente (PV) Maldonado to La Independencia on the Santo Domingo-Esmeraldas road. There are many new hostales and places to visit along the route, of particular interest to birdwatchers. There are tours from Quito. See Sleeping, below, for resorts.

On the shores of the lovely Río Caoni is **Puerto Quito**, a small town which was once intended to be the capital's port. The main road bypasses the centre of town to the south. Along the Caoni and other rivers in the region are several reserves and resorts. This is a good area for birdwatching, swimming in rivers and natural pools, walking, kayaking, or simply relaxing in pleasant natural surroundings.

● Sleeping

Mitad del Mundo and around *p916*
C **Hostería Alemana**, Av Manuel Córdoba Galarza, 700 m south of the complex, in San Antonio de Pichincha, T239 4243. Very good restaurant, recommended.

Papallacta *p916*
D **Antisana**, up the hill close to the Termas, T06-232 0626. Cheaper with shared bath and cold water, simple, some new rooms.
D **La Choza de Don Wilson**, junction of main road with road to Termas, T06-232 0627. Hot water, good restaurant, pool, spa, good service. Several simple places to eat, trout is a speciality.
E **Coturpa**, next to public baths in Papallacta town, T06-232 0640. Includes breakfast, thermal pool, sauna, good value.
E **Res El Viajero**, in Papallacta town, T232 0580. Basic, shared bath, hot water, good value, restaurant with reasonable meals.

East of Papallacta
L **Guango Lodge**, reservations needed, Quito T254 7403, www.ecuadorexplorer.com/sanisidro. Including 3 good meals. Situated in temperate forest, grey-breasted mountain toucans are regularly seen here along with many other birds.

Western slopes of Pichincha *p917*
L **Tandayapa Lodge**, T224 1038 (Quito), www.tandayapa.com. Includes full board, 12 very comfortable rooms with private bath and hot water, some rooms have a canopy platform for observation, large common area for socializing, packages available including guide and transport from Quito.
AL **Bellavista Cloud Forest Reserve**, Bellavista, T211 6232 (Bellavista), in Quito at Washington E7-23 y 6 de Diciembre, T290 3165/6, www.bellavistacloudforest.com. Full board (vegetarian on request), hot showers; **A** in dormitory with shared bath. Camping US$7 per

person. Package tours can be arranged including transport from Quito and guide, best booking in advance. A dramatic dome-shaped lodge perched in beautiful cloud forest. Recommended.

A San Jorge, Km 4 via antigua Quito-Nono, to the west of Av Occidental, T249 4002, www.hostsanjorge.com.ec. A traditional hacienda on a 80 ha private reserve on the slopes of Pichincha, heated rooms, includes breakfast, full board available, good pricey restaurant, pool, sauna and Turkish bath. Nature reserve (part of a group of reserves) has *páramo* and one of the few remnants of native forest near Quito, horse riding and birdwatching. Recommended.

Mindo *p918*
L El Monte, 2 km from Mindo on road to CEA, T255 8881, www.ecuadorcloudforest.com. Includes 3 meals and some excursions, birdwatching, tubing, walking, swimming.
AL El Carmelo de Mindo, 1 km west of town, T390 0409, www.mindo.com.ec. Includes 3 meals, restaurant, pool, rooms, cabins and treehouses, camping US$5, fishing, horse rental, excursions, midweek discounts.
AL Mindo Gardens, 3 km from Mindo on road to CEA, T225 2488 ext102 (Quito). Full board, very good food, expensive restaurant, snack bar, comfortable, tastefully decorated cabins, beautiful setting, good birdwatching.
A Séptimo Paraíso, 2 km from Calacalí-La Independencia road along Mindo access road, then 500 m right on a small side road, well signed, T09-368 4417, www.septimoparaiso.com. All wood lodge in a 420-ha reserve, includes breakfast, expensive restaurant, pool and jaccuzi, comfortable, lovely grounds, walking trails open to non-guests for US$5.
C El Descanso, 300 m from main street, 1st right

after bridge, T390 0443, www.eldescanso.net. Comfortable, cheaper in loft with shared bath, includes breakfast, parking. Recommended.
C Hacienda San Vicente, 'Yellow House', 500 m south of the plaza, T390 0424. Including breakfast and dinner, family-run, nice rooms, good walking trails nearby, great value. Recommended.
D-E Jardín de las Orquídeas. 2 blocks from church, T390 0431, www.orchids-birding.com. In beautiful orchid garden, includes breakfast, meals on request, vegetarian available, cheaper in room with shared bath, nice atmosphere.
E El Bijao, Av Quito near entrance to town, T390 0430. Includes breakfast, restaurant, cheaper with shared bath, hot water, simple but nice, family run, under new management.
E Jardín de los Pájaros, 2 blocks from the main street on side street past the bridge, T390 0459. Family run, hot water, small pool, parking, large covered terrace, good value. Recommended.
F El Toucanet, Barrio El Progreso, behind stadium, T390 0411. Pleasant family run hostel, breakfast available, shared bath, electric shower, good value.
F Flor del Valle, on lane beside church, T390 0469. Shared bath, hot water, good value, basic.

West of Mindo *p918*
LL Arasha, 4 km west of PV Maldonado, at Km 141, T390 0007, 244 9881 (Quito) for reservations, www.arasharesort.com. Resort and spa with pools, waterfalls and hiking trails, price includes all meals (world class chef), transport from Quito, use of the facilities and tours, elegant and very upmarket.
A Reserva Río Guaycuyacu, accessed from PV Maldonado, www.ecuadorexplorer.com. Exotic fruit farm with 400 varieties, and birdwatching. Includes 3 hearty vegetarian meals a day, maximum 8 guests. Booking ahead by e-mail essential. One-month agricultural apprenticeships

Ecuador Around Quito Listings

can be arranged.

D Mirador del Río Blanco, San Miguel de Los Bancos, T277 0307. Includes breakfast, restaurant, parking, rooms a bit small, terrace with lovely views overlooking the river.

Puerto Quito *p918*

B Itapoa, 2 km north of the main road, turn-off at Km 142, west of Puerto Quito, T09-478 4992, itapoa_25@hotmail.com. A small lodge within 12- ha reserve, botanical gardens, tropical fruit farm and native forest. Full board and guided tours included, shared bath, owner is a biologist.

B-C Selva Virgen, Km 132 on the main road, east of town, T390 1317. Nice *hostería* set in a 100 ha property owned by the Universidad Técnica Equinoccial (UTE), staffed by students. Includes breakfast, restaurant, spacious comfortable cabins with a/c, fridge, jacuzzi, cheaper in rooms with ceiling fan. Pool, lovely grounds with trails, facilities also open to patrons of the restaurant.

C Cabañas Don Gaucho, 22 km from Puerto Quito, T/F233 0315 (Quito), www.ecuador-sommergarten.com. Comfortable, well furnished rooms with bath and hot water, fan, balcony, includes breakfast, restaurant specializing in Argentinian *parrilladas*, nice grounds on the shores of the Río Salazar. Tours to tropical forest, fruit plantations, Colorado Indians.

E Grand Hotel Puerto Quito, along the highway bypass, T215 6363. Pleasant hotel, restaurant, hot water, fan, pool and sauna, parking, good value.

● Eating

Pululahua *p916*

El Cráter, on the rim of the crater, signed access before (east) the road to the mirador, T223 9399, daily 1230-1700. Popular upscale restaurant with excellent views.

▲ Activities and tours

Mitad del Mundo *p916*

Calimatours, Manzana de los Correos, Oficina 11, Mitad del Mundo, T239 4796, calima@ andinanet.net. Tours to all the sites in the vicinity, US$8 per person for 2 hrs. Offers beautiful certificates to record your visit. Recommended.

Pululahua *p916*

Horse riding The Green Horse Ranch, Astrid Muller, T02-237 4847, www.horseranch.de.

● Transport

Mitad del Mundo and around *p916*

Bus A paved road runs from Quito to the

Monument; take a 'Mitad del Mundo' *interparroquial* bus from the Av del Maestro stop on the Santa Prisca-La Ofelia line. An excursion by **taxi** to Mitad del Mundo (with 1 hr wait) and Pululahua is US$30 per taxi. Just a ride from the New City costs about US$12.

Pululahua *p916*

Bus For the rim, from Mitad del Mundo you can take a **Calacalí** bound bus and alight at the turnoff (infrequent). There is plenty of traffic at weekends for hitching a lift. There is no public transport to the reserve.

Papallacta *p916*

Bus From **Quito**, Terminal Terrestre, 2 hrs, US$2: ask to be let off at the road to the springs; it's a steep 30-min walk up to the baths.

Refugio de Vida Silvestre Pasochoa *p917*

Bus From Quito buses run from La Marín to Amaguaña US$0.40 (ask the driver to let you off at the 'Ejido de Amaguaña'); from there follow the signs. It's about 8-km walk, with not much traffic except at weekends, or book a pick-up from Amaguaña, about US$6 for up to 3 people. There is a **Movistar** public phone at the information centre (take a debit card) to call **Cooperativa Pacheco Jr** in Amaguaña, T287 7047.

Mindo *p918*

Bus From **Quito**, Cooperativa Flor del Valle (Cayambe), M Larrea N10-44 y Asunción, T252 7495. Mon-Sat at 0800 and 1530, Sat also at 0720, 0900, Sun at 0720, 0800, 0900, 1345, 1645; US$2.50, 2½ hrs. To Quito, Mon-Fri 0530, 1400, Sat-Sun 0630, 1400, 1500, 1600 (Sun only), 1700. Weekend buses fill quickly, buy ahead. **Cooperativa Kennedy** to/from **Santo Domingo** 5-6 a day, US$4, 3½ hrs. If buses to Quito are booked, try taking a Santo Domingo-bound bus to the main highway or to **San Miguel de los Bancos** and transfer there. The most direct route is along the Calcalí-La Concordia road; at Km 79 to the south is the turn-off to Mindo. Taxis wait here till 1930 for the 7 km ride to town.

West of Mindo *p918*

Several companies leave from the Terminal Terrestre in **Quito** for San Miguel de los Bancos, US$3, 2½ hrs, continuing on to Pedro Vicente Maldonado and Puerto Quito; **Trans Esmeraldas** also go from their own station in the New City, Santa María 870. Once in Los Bancos there are buses to **Mindo**, 6 daily (service from Santo Domingo), US$1, 30 mins; and **Santo Domingo**, frequent along the main road, US$3, 3 hrs. Quito to **Puerto Quito**, US$3.75, 3 hrs.

rooms with fireplace and frigo-bar.
D Cabañas de Nápoles, Panamericana Norte Km 1, T236 0366. Good restaurant, parking, OK cabins near highway.
D Shungu Huasi, Camino a Granobles, 1 km northwest of town, T236 1847, www.plentagos.com. Excellent Italian restaurant, comfortable, internet, nice setting, offers horse riding excursions. Recommended.
E La Gran Colombia, Panamericana y Calderón, T236 1238. Modern multi-storey building, restaurant, hot water, parking.
E-F Mitad del Mundo, Panamericana a little south of town, T236 0226. Restaurant, cheaper with shared bath, pool (open weekends), laundry facilities, parking.

🍴 Eating

Cayambe *p922*
🍴🍴🍴 **Casa de Fernando**, Panamericana Norte Km 1.5. Varied menu, good international food.
🍴 **Aroma**, Bolívar 404 y Ascázubi. Large choice of set lunches and à la carte, variety of desserts, very good, open until 2100, Sun until 1800, closed Wed.

🚌 Transport

Cayambe *p922*
Bus Flor del Valle, leaves from M Larrea y Asunción in Quito, every 10 mins, 0400-1900, US$1.25, 1½ hrs. Their Cayambe station is at Montalvo y Junín. To **Otavalo**, from traffic circle at Bolívar y Av N Jarrín, every 15 mins, US$0.60, 40 mins.

Volcán Cayambe *p922*
Road Most vehicles can go as far as the **Hacienda Piemonte El Hato** (at about 3,500 m) from where it is a 3-4 hr walk, sometimes longer if heavily laden, or if it is windy, but it is a beautiful walk. Regular pick-ups can often make it to 'la Z', a sharp curve on the road 30-mins' walk to the refugio. 4WDs can often make it to the refugio. Pick-ups can be hired by the market in Cayambe, Junín y Ascázubi, US$30, 1½-2 hrs. It is difficult to get transport back to Cayambe. A milk truck runs from Cayambe's hospital to the hacienda at 0600, returning between 1700-1900.

Otavalo and around

→ *Phone code: 06. Colour map 11, grid A4. Population: 56,000. Altitude: 2,530 m.*

Otavalo, only a short distance from the capital, is a must on any tourist itinerary in Ecuador. The main paved road from Cayambe crosses the *páramo* and suddenly descends into the land of the *Otavaleños*, a thriving, prosperous group, famous for their prodigious production of woollens. The town itself, consisting of rather functional modern buildings, is one of South America's most important centres of ethno-tourism and its enormous Saturday market, featuring a dazzling array of textiles and crafts, is second to none and not to be missed. Men here wear their hair long and plaited under a broad-brimmed hat; they wear white, calf-length trousers and blue ponchos. The women's colourful costumes consist of embroidered blouses, shoulder wraps and many coloured beads. Native families speak Quichua at home, although it is losing some ground to Spanish with the younger generation. Otavalo is set in beautiful countryside, with mountains, lakes and small villages nearby. The area is worth exploring for three or four days.

Ins and outs
Tourist offices iTur ⓘ *Bolívar 8-38 y Calderón, T292 1313, sdt@andinanet.net, Mon-Fri 0800-1230, 1400-1730, some Sat 0900-1600*, local and regional information. **Cámara de Turismo** ⓘ *Sucre y García Moreno, T292 1994, www.otavaloturismo.com, Mon-Fri 0830-1230, 1400-1800*, has information and pamphlets.

Otavalo
The **Saturday market** comprises four different markets in various parts of the town with the central streets filled with vendors. The *artesanías* market is held 0700-1800, based around the Plaza de Ponchos (Plaza Centenario). The livestock section begins at 0500 until 1000: large livestock is sold outside town in the Viejo Colegio Agrícola; go west on Colón from the town centre. The small animal market is held on Collahuazo by the bus terminal. The produce market lasts from 0700 till 1400, in Plaza 24 de Mayo. The *artesanías* industry is so big that the Plaza de Ponchos is filled with vendors every day of the week. The selection is better on Saturday but prices are a little higher than other days when the atmosphere is more

relaxed. Polite bargaining is appropriate in the market and shops. Otavaleños not only sell goods they weave and sew themselves, but they bring crafts from throughout Ecuador and from Peru and Bolivia. Indigenous people in the market respond better to photography if you buy something first, then ask politely. The **Instituto Otavaleño de Antropología** ① *Av de los Sarances y Pendoneros, 1 block west of the Panamericana Norte, T292 0321, Mon-Thu 0830-1200, 1430-1800, Fri 0830-1200, 1430-1700, free,* has a library, an archaeological museum with artefacts from the northern highlands, a collection of musical instruments, and an ethnographic display of regional costumes and traditional activities. **Museo de Tejidos El Obraje** ① *Sucre 608 y Olmedo, T292 0261, US$2, Mon-Sat 0800-1200, 1500-1800,* shows the process of traditional Otavalo weaving from shearing to final products. Traditional weaving lessons are available.

Around Otavalo

Otavalo weavers come from dozens of communities. The easiest to visit are Ilumán (visit the Conterón-de la Torre family of *Artesanías Inti Chumbi*, on the northeast corner of the plaza; there are also many felt hatmakers in town and *yachacs*, or shamen, mostly north of the plaza - look for signs); Agato (the Andrango-Chiza family of *Tahuantinsuyo Weaving Workshop*, gives weaving demonstrations and sells textiles); Carabuela (many homes sell crafts including wool sweaters); Peguche (the Cotacachi-Pichamba family, off the main plaza behind the church, sells beautiful tapestries). These villages are only 15-30 minutes away and all have a good bus service; buses leave from the Terminal and stop at Plaza Copacabana (Atahualpa y Montalvo). You can also take a taxi. Allow 1-1½ hours each way.

To reach the lovely **Cascada de Peguche**, from Peguche's plaza, facing the church, head right and continue straight until the road forks. Take the lower fork to the right, but not the road that heads downhill. From the top of the falls (left side, excellent views) you can continue the walk to Lago de San Pablo. The *Pawkar Raimi* festival is held in Peguche during carnival. At the falls there is a small information centre (contributions are appreciated).

Lago de San Pablo

There is a network of old roads and trails between Otavalo and Lago de San Pablo, none of which takes more than two hours to explore. It is worth walking either to or back from the lake for the views (if you take the main road, beware traffic fumes and litter). From **San Pablo del Lago** it is possible to climb **Imbabura** volcano (4,630 m, frequently under cloud), allow at least six hours to reach the summit and four hours for the descent. An alternative access is from La Esperanza (see below). Easier, and no less impressive, is the nearby Cerro Huarmi Imbabura, 3,845 m. Take a good map, food and warm clothing.

🌙 Sleeping

Otavalo *p923, map p925*
In town
Hotels may be full on Fri night before market.
B Ali Shungu, Quito y Miguel Egas, T292 0750, www.alishungu.com. Good restaurant with live music at weekends, nice rooms, lovely garden, no smoking, safe deposit boxes, can arrange transport from Quito, reliable. US-run, credit cards only accepted over the internet using Paypal, surcharge for TCs. Recommended. Also has
AL-A Ali Shungu Mountaintop Lodge, 5 km west of Otavalo by the village of Yambiro, T292 0750, www.ranchoalishungu.com. Comfortable country inn on a 16 ha private reserve.
B El Indio Inn, Bolívar 904 y Calderón, T292 2922, hindioinn@andinanet.net. Restaurant, includes breakfast, also suites, spotless, attractive.
C Coraza, Calderón y Sucre, T/F292 1225, www.ecuahotel.com. Good restaurant, modern, quiet and comfortable. Recommended.

C Doña Esther, Montalvo 4-44 y Bolívar, T292 0739, www.otavalohotel.com. Nicely restored colonial house, good pizzeria downstairs, simple rooms, colourful decor.

B Hotel Otavalo, Roca 504 y J Montalvo, T292 3712, www.hotelotavalo.com.ec. Good breakfast, expensive restaurant, refurbished colonial house, large rooms, patio, good service, helpful.
D Riviera Sucre, García Moreno 380 y Roca, T292 0241, www.rivierasucre.com. Good breakfasts, café, cheaper without bath, book exchange, garden, secure, good meeting place.
D-E Acoma, Salinas 07-57 y 31 de Octubre, T292 6570. A lovely modern hotel built in colonial style, includes breakfast, cafeteria, cheaper with shared bath, parking, comfortable rooms, one suite with kitchenette **B**, good value.
D-E El Indio, Sucre 1214 y Salinas, near Plaza de Ponchos, T292 0060. In multi-storey building,

restaurant, cheaper with shared bath, helpful.

E Los Andes, Sucre y Quiroga by Plaza de Ponchos, T292 1057. Restaurant, cheaper without bath, simple, modern, good value.

E Rincón del Viajero, Roca 11-07 y Quiroga, T292 1741, www.rincondelviajero.org. Includes good breakfast, cheaper without bath, pleasant hostel and meeting place, rooftop hammocks, sitting room with fireplace, US/Ecuadorean-run. Recommended.

E Samay Inn, Sucre 1009 y Colón, T292 1826. Nice modern hotel, small but comfortable rooms, hot water, second location at Sucre 14-14 y Quito with bright rooms and ample parking.

E Valle del Amanecer, Roca y Quiroga, T292 0990. Includes breakfast, good restaurant, small rooms around courtyard, popular, bike hire.

E-F Rocío, Morales y Egas, T292 0584.

Hot showers, cheaper without bath, helpful, good value. Also has **E Cabañas El Rocío**, Barrio San Juan west of Panamericana, near stadium, T292 0584, attractive.

F El Geranio, Ricaurte y Colón, T292 0185, hgeranio@hotmail.com. Breakfast available, cheaper without bath, cooking and laundry facilities, quiet, family-run, helpful, popular, good value, runs trips. Recommended.

F María, Jaramillo y Colón, T/F292 0672. Modern, convenient, cafeteria, good value. Recommended.

F San Luis, Abdón Calderón 6-02 y 31 de Octubre, T292 0614. Cheaper with shared bath, hot water, basic, family run.

Out of town
L Casa Mojanda, Vía Mojanda Km 3.5, T292 2986, www.casamojanda.com. Includes breakfast and

Otavalo

Sleeping
Acoma 2
Ali Shungu 1
Coraza 4
Doña Esther 10
El Geranio 5
El Indio 17
El Indio Inn 6
Los Andes 3
María 8
Otavalo 9
Rincón del Viajero 11
Riviera Sucre 12
Rocío 13
Samay Inn 7
San Luis 15
Valle del Amanecer 16

Eating
Ali Allpa 1
Café Mundi 2
Deli 3
Delicias del Mar 10
Empanadas Argentinas 6
Fontana di Trevi 7
La Herradura 8

Mi Otavalito 5
Oraibi & Diceny Viajes 11
Quino 17
Shanandoa Pie Shop 9
SISA 4

Bars & clubs
Casa de Arte Da Pinto 15
Peña Amauta 14
Peña La Jampa 16

one other meal, beautiful setting in a forested gorge, organic garden, comfortable, quiet, spa and traditional hot tub with great views, horse riding. Highly recommended.

AL Hacienda Pinsaquí, Panamericana N Km 5, T294 6116, www.haciendapinsaqui.com. With breakfast, restaurant, 300 m north of the turn-off for Cotacachi. Beautiful antiques, lovely dining room, lounge with fireplace, colonial ambience, gardens, horse riding.

A Vista del Mundo, Panamericana at Pinsaquí toll, halfway between Otavalo and Ibarra, T294 6333, www.thegoldenspa.com. Unusual luxury hotel spa, built around the theme of world peace. Includes breakfast, dinner and use of heated pool, expensive restaurant serves good food.

B Las Palmeras, outside Quichinche, 15 mins by bus from Otavalo, T292 2607, www.laspalmeras inn.com. With breakfast, restaurant, cheaper without bath, tranquil rural setting, nice grounds.

C La Casa de Hacienda, entrance at Panamericana Norte Km 3, then 300 m east, T269 0245, www.casadehacienda.com. Includes breakfast, restaurant, tasteful cabins with fireplace, advance reservations required for horse riding.

E-F La Luna de Mojanda, on a side-road going south off the Mojanda road at Km 4, T09-973 7415, www.hostallaluna.com. Pleasant country hostel, restaurant, cheaper in dorm, parking, some rooms with fireplace and private bath, terrace with hammocks, pleasant dining room-lounge, camping possible, taxi from Otavalo US$3, bus information on hostel's web site, excursions arranged, popular. Recommended.

Around Otavalo: Peguche p924

B Casa Andina (Casa Sol), near the Cascada de Peguche, 3 km from Otavalo, T269 0500, www.lacasasol.com. Hacienda-style modern hotel perched on a hillside. Rooms and suites with balcony, some with fireplace, lovely attention to detail, includes breakfast and dinner, restaurant.

D Aya Huma, on the railway line, T269 0333, www.ayahuma.com. Restaurant, cooking facilities, quiet, pleasant atmosphere, Dutch-run, live folk music on Sat. Highly recommended.

D-E Peguche Tío, near centre of the village, T269 0179, peguchetio@mail.com. With breakfast, restaurant, internet, nice lounge with fireplace, decorated with works of art, interesting museum, sports fields, caters for groups.

Lago de San Pablo p924

AL Cusín, in a converted 17th-century *hacienda* on the east side of the lake, San Pablo del Lago, T291 8013, www.haciendacusin.com. With fireplace, including breakfast, fine expensive restaurant, sports facilities (horses, mountain bikes, squash court, pool, games room), library, lovely grounds, book in advance, British-run, German spoken. Recommended.

A Puerto Lago, Panamericana Sur, Km 6, on the west side of the lake, T292 0920, www.puertolago.com. Modern, lovely setting, good expensive restaurant, rooms and suites with fireplaces, very hospitable, includes the use of row-boats, pedalos and kayaks, other water sports extra.

B Jatun Cocha, 5½ km from the Panamericana on the east side of the lake, T/F291 8191, ecuador@ranfturismo.com. Rooms with fireplaces, breakfast included, restaurant, kayaks, windsurfing, bicycles.

🍴 Eating

Otavalo p923, map p925

🍴 **Fontana di Trevi**, Sucre 12-05 y Salinas, p 2, 1130-2200. Good pizza and pasta, nice juices, friendly service.

🍴 **Quino**, Roca 740 y Juan Montalvo, Tue-Sun 1030-2300, Mon1730-2300. Traditional coastal cooking and some meat dishes, pleasant seating around a patio.

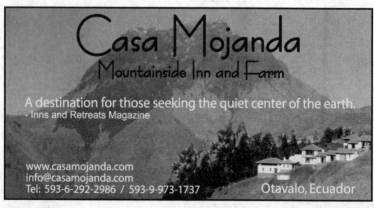

♥-♥ **Deli**, Quiroga y Bolívar, Sun-Thu 1100-2000, Fri 1100-220, Sat 0800-2200. Small cramped place serving good Mexican food, also pizza.

♥-♥ **Delicias del Mar**, Quito y 31 de Octubre, daily 0800-1530. Fish and seafood restaurant, popular with locals.

♥-♥ **SISA**, Calderón 409 y Sucre, open 1200-2200. Cultural centre, restaurant on second floor serves excellent set meals and à la carte, coffee shop with cappuccino, slow service, also bookstore.

♥ **Ali Allpa**, Salinas 509 at Plaza de Ponchos. Good value set meals and à la carte, trout, vegetarian, meat. Recommended.

♥ **Café Mundi**, Quiroga 608 y Jaramillo, Plaza de Ponchos, daily 0700-2200. Good food and value, nice atmosphere, vegetarian available.

♥ **La Herradura**, Bolívar 10-05. Good set meals and à la carte, outdoor tables.

♥ **Mi Otavalito**, Sucre y Morales. Good for lunch also international food à la carte.

♥ **Oraibi**, Colón y Sucre. Good choice of meals, many vegetarian dishes, salads, quiche, snacks, pleasant courtyard, live music Fri and Sat evenings.

Cafés
Empanadas Argentinas, Morales 502 y Sucre. Good savoury and sweet *empanadas*.
Shanandoa Pie Shop, Salinas y Jaramillo. Good pies, milk shakes and ice cream, expensive, good meeting place, recommended for breakfast, book exchange, daily movies at 1700 and 1900.

🟊 Bars and clubs

Otavalo *p923, map p925*
Otavalo is generally safe but avoid deserted areas at night. Peñas are open Fri-Sat from 2000, entrance US$2.
Casa de Arte Da Pinto, Colón 4-10 y Bolívar Colourfully decorated, live Latin music on weekends, drinks, pizza and snacks.
Peña Amauta, Morales 5-11 y Jaramillo. Good local bands, welcoming, mainly foreigners.
Peña la Jampa, Jaramillo 5-69 y Quiroga, Fri-Sat 1930-0300. Andean and dancing music, popular with Ecuadoreans and foreigners.

⊛ Festivals and events

Otavalo *p923, map p925*
The **end of Jun** combines the **Inti Raymi** celebrations of the summer solstice (**21 Jun**), with the **Fiesta de San Juan** (**24 Jun**) and the **Fiesta de San Pedro y San Pablo** (**29 Jun**). These combined festivities are known as **Los San Juanes**. The celebration begins with a ritual bath in the Peguche waterfall (a personal spiritual activity, best carried out without

visitors and certainly without cameras). Most of the action takes place in the smaller communities surrounding Otavalo. There are bullfights in the plaza and regattas on Lago San Pablo. In Otavalo, indigenous families have costume parties, which at times spill over onto the streets. In the San Juan neighbourhood, near the Yanayacu baths, there is a week-long celebration with food, drink and music. **Fiesta del Yamor** and **Colla Raimi 1st 2 weeks of Sep**, local dishes are cooked, amusement parks are set up, bands in the plaza and there are sporting events including bullfights. **Mojandas Arriba** is an annual 2-day hike from Quito over Mojanda to reach Otavalo for the **31 Oct** foundation celebrations.

▲ Activities and tours

Otavalo *p923, map p925*
Mountain bikes Several tour operators rent bikes and offer cycling tours for US$35-60 a day trip. **Hostal Valle del Amanecer** (see Sleeping), US$8 per day. **La Tierra** craft shop, Salinas 503 y Sucre, Plaza de Ponchos, good equipment. **Taller Ciclo Primaxi**, Atahualpa 2-49 y García Moreno and at the entrance to Peguche, good bikes, US$1 per hr.
Horse riding Several operators offer riding tours. Half-day trips to nearby attractions cost US$20-25. Full day trips such as Cuicocha or Mojanda run US$35-40.

Tour operators
Most common tours are to native communities, Cuicocha and Mojanda, US$20-30 pp. Independent travel to the Lagunas de Mojanda is not recommended because of armed robbery and public safety problems. Only go with a tour.
All about EQ, Colón 412 y Sucre, T292 3633, www.all-about-ecuador.com (in the same office as Chachimbiro Tours). Interesting itineraries, trekking and horse riding tours, climbing, cycling, trips to Intag, Piñán, Cayambe, Oyacachi, rafting and kayaking on the Río Intag. English and French spoken, guides carry radios. Recommended.
Chachimbiro Tours, Colón 412 y Sucre, T06-292 3633, www.chachimbiro.com. Trips to the Complejo Ecoturístico Chachimbiro 1 hr northwest of Otavalo.
Diceny Viajes, Sucre 10-11 y Colón, T292 1217, zulayviajes@hotmail.com. Run by Zulay Sarabino, an indigenous Otavaleña, knowledgeable native guides. Recommended.
Ecored Sierra Norte, Jaramillo y Morales, p 2, T292 6814, ecored_sierranorte@yahoo.es. Represents five different community tourism projects in northern Ecuador. Information and bookings.
Leyton's Tours, Quito y Jaramillo, T292 2388.

Horseback and bike tours.
Runa Tupari, Sucre y Quiroga, Plaza de Ponchos T/F292 5985, www.runatupari.com. Arranges indigenous homestays in the Cotacachi area, also the usual tours, trekking, horse riding and cycling trips.
Zulaytur, Sucre y Colón, p 2, T292 1176, F292 2969. Run by Rodrigo Mora, English spoken, information, map of town, slide show, horse riding. Recommended.

⊙ Transport

Otavalo *p923, map p925*
Note: Never leave anything in your car or taxi, even if it is being watched for you.
Bus Terminal at Atahualpa y Ordóñez (see map). To **Quito** 2½ hrs, US$2, every 10 mins; all depart from the Terminal Terrestre in Quito, **Coop Otavalo** and **Coop Los Lagos** go into Otavalo, buses bound for Ibarra drop you off at the highway, this is not safe at night. From **Quito** by taxi takes 1½ hrs, US$40; shared taxis with **Supertaxis Los Lagos** (in Quito, Asunción y Versalles T256 5992; in Otavalo, Roca 8-04, T292 3203) who run a hotel (in the New City only) to hotel service and will divert to resorts just off the highway; hourly Mon-Fri 0700-1900, Sat 0700-1600, Sun 0800-1800, 2 hrs, US$7.50 pp, buy ticket the day before. They continue to **Ibarra**, every 15 mins, US$0.50, 45 mins. To **Peguche**, city bus on Av Atahualpa, every 10 mins, bus stops in front of the terminal and at Plaza Copacabana, US$0.20. To the **Intag region**, 5 daily.

Lago de San Pablo *p924*
Bus From **Otavalo**-San Pablo del Lago every 25 mins, more often on Sat, US$0.25, 30 mins; taxi US$4.

⊙ Directory

Otavalo *p923, map p925*
Banks Banco del Austro, Sucre y Quiroga. Banco del Pacífico, Bolívar 614 y García Moreno. **Fax Cambios**, Salinas y Sucre, T292 0501, Mon-Sat 0745-1900, poor rates for cash, 3% commission on TCs. **Vaz Corp**, Jaramillo y Saona, Plaza de Ponchos, T292 2926, Tue- Sat 0830-1700. **Internet** Prices about US$1 per hr. Many in town, specially on C Sucre. **Language schools** Instituto Superior de Español, Sucre 11-10 y Morales, p 3, T299 2414, www.instituto-superior.net. **Mundo Andino Internacional**, Salinas 404 y Bolívar, T292 1864, www.mandinospanishschool.com. Salsa and cooking classes included. **Otavalo Spanish Institute**, 31 de Octubre 47-64 y Salinas, p 3, T292 1404, also offers Quichua lessons. **Post offices** Corner of Plaza de Ponchos, entrance on Sucre, 1st floor, Mon-Fri 0700-1500, Sat 0800-1200.

Otavalo to the Colombian border

The route passes the Cotacachi-Cayapas reserve and then divides into two roads beyond the city of Ibarra. A detour heads down the mountains into the lush Chota valley and beyond, into the tropical lowlands and the coastal city of San Lorenzo. The Panamericana reaches the border at the busy town Tulcán, with its fantastic topiary.

Cotacachi

West of the road between Otavalo and Ibarra is Cotacachi, where leather goods are made and sold. There is access along a cobbled road from Otavalo through Quiroga. The **Casa de las Culturas** ⓘ *Bolívar y 9 de Octubre*, a beautifully refurbished 19th century building is a monument to peace. It houses a library, internet café, the tourist information office, iTur ⓘ *T291 5140, www.cota cachi.gov.ec*, temporary exhibits and shows. The **Museo de las Culturas** ⓘ *García Moreno 13-41 y Bolívar, T291 5945, Mon-Fri 0900-1200, 1400-1700, Sat 1400-1700, Sun 1000-1300, US$1*, has good displays about early Ecuadorean history, regional crafts and traditions (some English explanations). Local festivals include *Inti Raymi/San Juan* in June and *Jora* during the September equinox.

Laguna Cuicocha → *Altitude: 3,070 m.*
ⓘ *15 km from Cotacachi. US$1 to visit the lake and visitor centre, which has good natural history and cultural displays. US$5 park fee must be paid if going on longer hikes into the national park.*
The area is part of the **Reserva Ecológica Cotacachi-Cayapas**, which extends from Cotacachi volcano to the tropical lowlands on the Río Cayapas in Esmeraldas. This is a crater lake with

two islands, although these are closed to the public for biological studies. There is a well-marked, 8-km path around the lake, which takes 4-5 hours and provides spectacular views of the Cotacachi, Imbabura and, occasionally, Cayambe peaks. The best views are in the morning, when condors can sometimes be seen. There is lookout at 3 km, two hours from the start. It's best to go anticlockwise; take water and a waterproof jacket. Motor boat rides around the islands, US$1.80 per person for minimum eight persons.

Warnings There have been reports of armed robberies around the lake: don't take valuables and always enquire locally before heading out. Do not eat the berries which grow near the lake, as some are poisonous. The path around the lake is not for vertigo sufferers.

To the northwest of Otavalo lies the lush subtropical region of **Intag**, reached along a road that follows the southern edge of Cuicocha and continues to the town of **Apuela**. (See **Defensa y Conservación Ecológica de Intag** (Decoin), www.decoin.org, for conservation through community projects.) The **Asociación Agroartesanal de Café Río Intag** (AACRI) ① *on the main street opposite the health centre, T06-264 8489, aacri@andinanet.net,* a fair trade organic coffee grower's association, offers tours of coffee, sisal and sugar cane plantations and processing plants, also lodging and volunteer opportunities. Beyond, are pleasant thermal baths at **Nangulví**. The area is rich in cloudforest and has several nature reserves. On the southwest boundary of the Cotacachi-Cayapas reserve is **Los Cedros Research Station**, 6,400 ha of pristine cloudforest, with abundant orchids and bird life. Full board in **B** range. Contact ① *T08-460 0274, www.reservaloscedros.org,* for reservations.

Ibarra and around → *Phone code: 06. Colour map 11, grid A4. Pop: 137,000. Altitude: 2,225 m.*

Once a pleasant colonial town (founded in 1606), Ibarra has grown to become the main commercial centre of the northern highlands. The city has an interesting ethnic mix, with blacks from the Chota valley and Esmeraldas alongside Otavaleños and other highland *indígenas*, mestizos and Colombian immigrants. **Ministerio de Turismo** ① *García Moreno 376 y Rocafuerte, T295 8547, www.imbabura.gov.ec, Mon-Fri 0830-1300, 1400-1700,* is very helpful; free city map and tourist leaflets, English spoken. **Cámara Provincial de Turismo de Imbabura** ① *Oviedo y Bolívar, of 102, T/F264 2531, Mon-Fri 0800-1300, 1500-1800,* is also very helpful but in Spanish only.

On **Parque Pedro Moncayo** stand the Cathedral, the Municipio and Gobernación. One block away is the smaller Parque 9 de Octubre, at Flores y Olmedo, more commonly called **Parque de la Merced** after its church. A walk down Pérez Guerrero leads to the large covered **Mercado Amazonas** ① *on Cifuentes, by the railway station, daily, busiest Sat and Sun.* The **Museo Regional Sierra Norte** ① *Sucre 7-21 y Oviedo, T260 2093, Mon-Fri, 0830-1700, Sat 1000-1300, 1400-1600, US$1,* run by the Banco Central, has interesting displays about cultures from northern Ecuador. Virgen del Carmen festival is on 16 July and Fiesta de los Lagos is in the last weekend of September, Thursday-Sunday.

Off the main road between Otavalo and Ibarra is **San Antonio de Ibarra**, well known for its wood carvings. Bargaining is difficult; it's worth seeing the range of styles and techniques and shopping around in the galleries and workshops. Buses leave from Ibarra, 13 km, 10 minutes, US$0.20. About 8 km from Ibarra on the road to Olmedo is **La Esperanza**, a pretty village in beautiful surroundings. Ask in town for makers of fine clothes and embroidery. Further west, along a road that starts at Avenida Atahualpa, and also 8 km from Ibarra, is the community of **San Clemente**, which has a very good grassroots tourism project, **Pukyu Pamba**, which offers simple lodging opportunities with indigenous families. You can climb **Cubilche** volcano in three hours from La Esperanza (2½ hours from San Clemente) for beautiful views. From the top you can walk down to Lago de San Pablo (see page 924), another three hours.

Ibarra to the coast The spectacular train ride from Ibarra to San Lorenzo on the Pacific coast (see page 1001) no longer operates. See Transport, page 934, for alternatives.

Some 24 km north of Ibarra is the turn-off west for Salinas and the very scenic paved road down to San Lorenzo on the Pacific coast; 15 minutes beyond Salinas is **Tulquizán**, further ahead is **Guallupe** and **El Limonal** (see Sleeping, below). There is an immense variety of wildlife in the surrounding tropical forest. In **Lita**, 20 km from Guallupe, there is the adequate *Residencial Villalobos* (**G**) and several restaurants about 1 km uphill from the train station. The remaining 93 km through a scenic area are prone to landslides during the rainy season.

Northwest of Ibarra Along a secondary road to the northwest of Ibarra is the pretty town of

Urcuquí with a basic hotel. Urcuquí is the starting point for walking to the **Piñán lakes**, a beautiful, remote, high *páramo* region, part of the Reserva Ecológica Cotacachi-Cayapas. The local community of Piñán has a tourism programme, native guides and muleteers. Otavalo agencies and Chachimbiro hotels also offer trekking tours to Piñán. Beyond Urcuquí, almost two hours' drive from Ibarra, 8 km from the village of Tumbabiro, along a side road is the **Complejo Ecoturístico Chachimbiro** ⓘ *entry to recreational pools US$3, to medicinal pools and spa US$6, www.chachimbiro.com*. Clean hot mineral pools, simple cabins (**C** with full board, access to pools) and restaurants; weekends can be crowded. Tours and reservations through Chachimbiro Tours in Otavalo (see above).The Tumbabiro region is just opening to tourism, with great potential for linking the local communities to the wildlife reserves that surround it. Apart from Cotacachi-Cayapas, other cloudforests, the Afro-Ecuadorean zone of the Chota Valley and opportunites for trekking, riding and biking are all within reach.

North to Colombia

The Pan-American highway goes past Laguna Yahuarcocha (with a few hotels and restaurants) and then descends to the hot dry Chota valley, a centre of Afro-Ecuadorean culture. Beyond the turn-off for Salinas and San Lorenzo, 30 km from Ibarra, is a police checkpoint at **Mascarilla**: have your documents at hand. Here ceramic masks are made (hostal run by the women's craft group, **El Patio de mi Casa**, **D** full-board). After Mascarilla the highway divides. One branch follows an older route through Mira and El Angel to Tulcán on the Colombian border. This road is paved and in good condition as far as El Angel, but deteriorates thereafter. It is passable with 4WD and is a great mountain bike route. In the dry season cars with high clearance can get through to Tulcán.

Along the old Panamericana is **El Angel** (3,000 m), with a Monday market. The main plaza retains a few trees sculpted by José Franco (see Tulcán Cemetery, below). The **Reserva Ecológica El Angel** ⓘ *T/F297 7597, US$10 for foreigners, office in El Angel at the Municipio, information available*, nearby protects 15,715 ha of *páramo* ranging in altitude from 3,400 to 4,768 m. The reserve contains large stands of the velvet-leaved *frailejón* plant, also found in the Andes of Colombia and Venezuela. Also of interest are the spiny *achupallas* with giant compound flowers. The fauna includes *curiquingues* (birds of prey), deer, foxes, and a few condors. There are several small lakes scattered throughout the reserve. It can be very muddy during the rainy season and the best time to visit is May to August.

From El Angel follow the poor road north towards Tulcán for 16 km to **El Voladero** ranger station, where a self-guided trail climbs over a low ridge (30 mins' walk) to two crystal-clear lakes. Camping is possible here, but you must be self-sufficient and take great care not to damage the fragile surroundings. Pickups or taxis can be hired in the main plaza of El Angel for a day trip to El Voladero, US$20 return with one-hour wait. A longer route follows an equally poor road to Cerro Socabones, beginning in the town of **La Libertad**, 3½ km north of El Angel. This route climbs gradually to reach the high *páramo* at the centre of the reserve and, in 40 minutes, the **El Salado** ranger station. Another 40 minutes ahead is **Socabones**, from where the road descends to the village of **Morán** (the local guides Hugo Quintanchala or Carlos Castro can take you further through the valley). There are many paths criss-crossing the *páramo* and it is easy to get lost. Transport from El Angel to Cerro Socabones, US$30 return, a helpful driver is **Sr Calderón**, T09-128 4022. A third access to the reserve, from the north along the Tufiño-Maldonado road, is not recommended (see Tulcán Safety, below).

Eastern route to the border

The second branch (the modern Pan-American Highway), in good repair but with many heavy lorries, runs east through the warm Chota valley to El Juncal, before turning north to reach Tulcán via Bolívar and San Gabriel. A good paved road runs between Bolívar and El Angel, connecting the two branches.

Bolívar is a neat little town where the houses and the interior of its church are painted in lively pastel colours. There is a Friday market. Five kilometres north of Bolívar is the turn-off east for the town of **La Paz**, from which a steep but good cobbled road descends for 5 km to the **Gruta de La Paz**. The area is a religious shrine, receiving large numbers of pilgrims during Holy Week, Christmas, and especially around 8 July, feast day of the Virgin of La Paz. There are thermal baths nearby.

Some 10 km north of La Paz is **San Gabriel**, an important commercial centre. The spectacular 60-m high **Paluz** waterfall is 4 km north San Gabriel, beyond a smaller waterfall.

Follow C Bolívar out of the main plaza and turn right after the bridge, or take a taxi (US$6,25).

East of San Gabriel by 20 km is the tiny community of **Mariscal Sucre**, also known as Colonia Huaquenia, the gateway to the **Guandera Reserve and Biological Station** ① *the reserve is part of the Fundación Jatun Sacha. Reservations should be made at Pasaje Eugenio de Santillán N34-248 y Maurián, Quito, T02-331 7163, www.jatunsacha.org.* You can see bromeliads, orchids, toucans and other wildlife in temperate forest and *frailejón páramo*. There is a lodge (**C**), take warm clothes as it gets very cold. From San Gabriel, take a taxi to Mariscal Sucre, one hour, then walk 30 minutes to the reserve, or make arrangements with Jatun Sacha.

Tulcán → *Phone code: 06. Colour map 11, grid A4. Population: 63,000. Altitude: 2,960 m.*

The chilly town of Tulcán is the busy capital of the province of Carchi. There is a great deal of informal trade here with Colombia, a textile and dry goods fair takes place on Thursday and Sunday. The old and new branches of the Panamericana join at Las Juntas, 2 km south of the city. In the cemetery, two blocks from Parque Ayora, the art of topiary is taken to beautiful extremes. Cypress bushes are trimmed into archways, fantastic figures and geometric shapes in *haut* and *bas* relief. To see the stages of this art form, go to the back of the cemetery where young bushes are being pruned. The artistry, started in 1936, is that of the late Sr José Franco, born in El Angel (see above), now buried among the splendour he created. The tradition is carried on by his sons.

Safety Don't wander about at night. The area around the bus terminal is unsafe. Tulcán and the traditionally tranquil border province of Carchi have seen an increase in tension due to the guerrilla conflict in Colombia. Do not travel outside town (except along the Panamericana) without advance local inquiry. The **tourist office, Unidad de Turismo** ① *entrance to the cemetery, T298 5760, Mon-Fri 0800-1300, 1500-1800,* is helpful, some English spoken.

Border with Colombia

The border at Rumichaca is open 0600-2200 for vehicles, 24-hours for pedestrians. It is well organized. There is an *Andinatel* office for phone calls, an **iTur** tourist office ① *in the restored customs house, T06-298 3077, Mon-Fri 0900-1700,* and a snack bar. Try to ask for 90 days on entering Ecuador if you need them, although you will most likely only be given 30. See page 877 for Colombian immigration.

⬤ Sleeping

Cotacachi *p928*

B Mesón de las Flores, García Moreno 1376 y Sucre, T291 6009. Refurbished colonial house in the heart of town, includes breakfast, restaurant in lovely patio, carpeted rooms, live music at lunch Sat-Sun. Recommended.

D Sumac Huasi, Montalvo 11-09 y Moncayo, T291 5873. Includes breakfast, large well-furnished rooms, nice rooftop terrace.

E Munaylla, 10 de Agosto y Sucre, T291 6169. Modern, hot water, comfortable, good value.

E-F Tierra Mía, Bolívar 12-26 y 10 de Agosto, 3rd floor, T291 5327. Refurbished, hot water, indoor parking, basic but adequate rooms, family run. Recommended.

The municipality has set up a system of homestays in nearby villages. Visitors experience life with a native family by taking part in daily activities. The comfortable rooms have space for 3, fireplace, bathroom and hot shower, and cost US$23 per person including breakfast, dinner and transport from Otavalo. Arrange with *Runa Tupari*, www.runatupari.com, or other Otavalo tour operators.

Laguna Cuicocha *p928*

B Los Pinos de Cuicocha, Hacienda Sta Rosa, Km 4 Via a Intag, T09-900 1516, jorge@lospinos decuicocha.com. Comfortable heated rooms in a working farm, includes breakfast and horse riding, restaurant (♥♥), parking, nice grounds (no views of the lake from rooms), English and German spoken.

C Hostería Cuicocha, by the pier on the lakeshore, T264 8040, www.cuicocha.org. Modern comfortable rooms overlooking the lake, includes half board, restaurant with lake views (♥♥).

E Cabañas Mirador, on a lookout above the pier, follow the trail, T08-682 1699, miradordecuicocha@yahoo.com. Simple rooms in a great location, some with fireplace, good cheap restaurant, trout is their specialty, parking, transport provided to Quiroga (US$4) or Otavalo (US$10), owner Ernesto Cevillano is knowledgeable about the area and arranges trips to the Piñan Lakes or to climb Cotacachi.

Ibarra *p929*

The better class hotels tend to be fully booked during holidays and at weekends.

A Ajaví, Av Mariano Acosta 16-38 y Circunvalación, T295 5221, h-ajavi@imbanet.net. Comfortable, restaurant, pool, on main road to town from south.

C El Prado, Barrio El Olivo, off the Panamericana at Km 1.5, T/F295 9570. Includes breakfast, restaurant, pool, spa, set in fruit orchards.

C Nueva Estancia, García Moreno 7-58 y Sánchez y Cifuentes, Parque La Merced, T95 1444, nuevaestancia@andinanet.net. Modern, central, includes breakfast, restaurant, small rooms.

D Montecarlo, Av Jaime Rivadeneira 5-61 y Oviedo, T295 8266. Restaurant, heated pool open weekends only, a better class hotel near the obelisk.

D Royal Ruiz, Olmedo 9-40 y P Moncayo, T264 1999, royalruiz@hotmail.com. Modern, includes breakfast, *Gourmet de Luc* restaurant, solar heated water, parking, comfortable.

E El Ejecutivo, Bolívar 9-69 y Colón, T295 6575, mchaconf@yahoo.com. Hot water, internet, family-run, good meeting place.

E El Retorno, Pasaje Pedro Moncayo 4-32 entre Sucre y Rocafuerte, T295 7722. Restaurant, cheaper without bath, nice views from terrace. Recommended.

E Hostal Madrid, Olmedo 8-69 y Moncayo, T264 4918, rubenmoncayo@hotmail.com. Parking, modern and comfortable. Recommended.

E Las Garzas, Flores 3-13 y Salinas, T295 0985, paulpita@yahoo.com. Simple, comfortable, hot water, sitting room doubles as café/bar with a pleasant atmosphere.

F Colón, Chica Narváez 8-62 y Velasco, T295 8695. Basic, cheaper with shared bath, electric shower, laundry facilities, patio.

Around Ibarra

Along the Pan-American Highway south towards Otavalo are several country inns, some in converted haciendas. From south to north are:

B Chorlaví, Panamericana S Km 4, T293 2222, www.haciendachorlavi.com. In an old hacienda, with breakfast, pool, expensive restaurant, excellent parillada, popular, folk music and crafts on Sun.

C Natabuela, Panamericana Sur Km 8, T293 2032, hosterianatabuela@andinanet.net. Restaurant, covered pool, jacuzzi, comfortable rooms.

E Casa Aída, La Esperanza, T266 0221. Simple rooms, good beds, shared bath, hot water, breakfast extra, restaurant, Aída speaks some English.

Ibarra to the coast: El Limonal *p929*

D-E Bospas Farm, in El Limonal, about 600 m uphill from the main square, T264 8692, www.bospas.org. Family-run organic fruit farm in a lovely setting; 3 private rooms with terrace and a dorm (cheaper), great views of the valley, includes good breakfast with delicious home-made bread, tasty meals available, small pool, camping by the river, treks and horse-riding trips, salsa lessons, excursions to El Angel and to the coast for mangroves, volunteer opportunities. Belgian-Ecuadorean run, knowledgeable. Recommended.

Northwest of Ibarra *p929*

B Hostería Pantaví, 7 km from Salinas, at the entrance to Tumbabiro, T(02) 234 7476, www.hosteriapantavi.com. Stylish inn in a tastefully restored and decorated old hacienda. Very comfortable rooms, includes breakfast, good restaurant, pool, gardens, games room, excursions to Piñán lakes, good value.

C Hostería San Francisco, at Hacienda San Francisco, 8 km past Tumbabiro, by turn-off to the complex, T293 4161, www.hosteriasanfrancisco.com. Nicely restored rooms, includes breakfast, restaurant, small pool, horse stables, excursions to Piñán.

North to Colombia: El Angel *p930*

AL Polylepis Lodge, abutting the reserve, 14 km

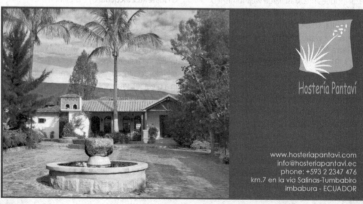

from El Angel along the road to Socabones, T295 4009, www.polylepislodge.com. Rustic cabins with fireplace by a nice 12-ha polylepis forest, price includes 3 meals (vegetarian on request) and 3 guided walks, jacuzzi.
C Hostería El Angel, at entrance to village, T/F297 7584, www.ecuador-sommergarten.com. Includes breakfast, meals available on request, caters for groups, reservations required, contact Quito T/F233 0315. Offers trips into El Angel reserve and also has **C Cotinga Lodge** in the Río Morán valley, a good place for birdwatching.
F Paisajes Andinos, Riofrío y 3a Transversal, T297 7557. Adequate hostel, in better new part rooms with bath, older part has shared, electric shower.

North to Colombia: San Gabriel *p930*
E Gabrielita, Mejía y Los Andes, above the agricultural supply shop , T229 1832. Modern hostel, includes breakfast, best in town.

Tulcán *p931*
Many hotels on C Sucre.
C Sara Espíndola, Sucre y Ayacucho, on plaza, T298 6209. Comfortable rooms, best hotel with nicest restaurant in town, spa, helpful.
D Machado, Bolívar y Ayacucho, T298 4221. Includes breakfast, comfy, parking.
E Lumar, Sucre y Rocafuerte, T298 0402. Modern, hot water, comfortable.
E Sáenz Internacional, Sucre y Rocafuerte, T298 1916. Very nice, modern, hot water, good value. Recommended.
E Torres de Oro, Sucre y Rocafuerte, T298 0296. Hot water, restaurant, parking, modern, nice.
F Los Alpes, JR Arellano next to bus station, T298 2235. Restaurant, hot water, OK, good value.
F-G Florida, Sucre y 10 de Agosto, T298 3849. Cheaper without bath, hot water, modern section at back, good value.

Eating

Cotacachi *p928*
A local specialty is *carne colorada* (spiced pork). There is an excellent traditional food plaza at the bus terminal, spotless, well-organized and cheap.
♯♯ Asadero La Tola, Rocafuerte 0-18 y 9 de Octubre. Grill, in an old courtyard.
♯♯ El Leñador, Sucre 10-12 y Montalvo. Varied menu, mid-range prices.
♯♯-♯ La Marqueza, 10 de Agosto y Bolívar, daily 0730-2130. 4-course set lunches and à la carte.
♯ El Viejo Molino, 10 de Agosto 10-65 y Moncayo. Set meals and à la carte, good value and quality.

Ibarra *p929*
♯♯ Café Floralp, Av Teodoro Gómez 7-49 y

Atahualpa. Crêpes, fondue, good breakfast, bread, yoghurt, cold cuts, excellent coffee, good selection of Chilean wines, the 'in place' to meet and eat, Swiss-owned. Warmly recommended.
♯♯ El Argentino, Sucre y P Moncayo, at Plazoleta Francisco Calderón, Tue-Sun. Good mixed grill and salads, small, pleasant, outdoor seating.
♯♯ Pizza El Horno, Rocafuerte 6-38 y Flores. Good Italian dishes, live music Sat night, closed Mon.
♯ Aroma Gourmet, Sánchez y Cifuentes 8-80 y Oviedo. Popular for a good set lunch.
♯ Casa Blanca, Bolívar 7-83. Family run, in colonial house with seating around a central patio with fountain, great food, closed Sun. Recommended.
♯ El Chagra, Olmedo 7-48 y Flores. *Platos típicos*, good trout. Recommended.
♯ Inti Raymi, Av Pérez Guerrero 6-39 y Bolívar. Good simple vegetarian lunches.

Cafés and heladerías
Antojitos de Mi Tierra, Sucre y P Moncayo, at Plazoleta Francisco Calderón, afternoons. Outdoor seating, local drinks and snacks.
Café Arte, Salinas 5-43 y Oviedo, daily 1700 until late. Café-bar serving drinks, Mexican snacks, sandwiches and some à la carte dishes.
Irish Coffee, García Moreno 4-36 y Sucre. Pleasant quiet café, breakfast, good capuccino, snacks, fondue.
Heladería Rosalía Suárez, Oviedo y Olmedo. Excellent homemade *helados de paila* (fruit sherbets made in large copper basins), an Ibarra tradition since 1896. Highly recommended.

Tulcán *p931*
♯ Café Tulcán, Sucre 52-029 y Ayacucho. Café, snacks, desserts, juices.
♯ El Patio, Bolívar 50-050 y 10 de Agosto. For Colombian specialities.
♯ Los Leños, Olmedo y Ayacucho. Set meals and à la carte.
♯ Mama Rosita, Sucre entre Boyacá y Atahualpa. Typical Ecuadorean dishes.
♯ Tequila, Sucre entre Junín y Boyacá. Varied à la carte menu.

Bars and clubs

Ibarra *p929*
Bar Buda, Sucre y Pedro Moncayo, at Plazoleta Francisco Calderón. Outdoor seating, a good place for an afternoon drink.
El Encuentro, Olmedo 9-59. Piano bar, interesting drinks, very popular, pleasant, unusual decor.
Farra Ibarra Flores 530 y Sucre, bar and club, the inn place among young Ibarreños.

⛰ Activities and tours

Ibarra *p929*
A unique form of paddle ball is played at weekends near the railway station and other places; ask around for details. Players have huge studded paddles for striking the 1 kg ball.

Paragliding
Fly Ecuador, Oviedo 9-13 y Sánchez Cifuentes, T0295 3297, www.flyecuador.com.ec.

Tour operators
EcuaHorizons, Bolívar 4-67 y García Moreno,T295 9904, ecuahorizons@andinanet.net. Bilingual guides for regional tours.
Intipungo, Rocafuerte 6-08 y Flores, T295 7766. Regional tours.
Metropolitan Touring, Flores 5-76 y Sucre, see Quito.

⊖ Transport

Cotacachi *p928*
Bus Terminal at 10 de Agosto y Salinas by the market. Frequent service from the Otavalo terminal, US$0.25, 25 mins; service alternates between the Panamericana and the Quiroga roads. To **Ibarra**, every 15 mins, US$0.45, 45 mins.

Laguna Cuicocha *p928*
Pick-ups From **Otavalo** US$10. From **Cotacachi** market, US$5 one way, US$10 return with short wait. From **Quiroga** US$4. Return service from the lake available from **Cabañas El Mirador**, same rates.

Los Cedros Research Station
Bus Access by daily 1300 bus from Otavalo to Chontal, which is north of Pacto and west of García Moreno, then a 4 hr **walk**.

Ibarra *p929*
Bus Terminal is at Av Teodoro Gómez y Av Eugenio Espejo, to the south of the centre, T264 4676. At the terminal there are small shops, two food courts and a telephone office. All inter-city transport runs from here. City buses go from the terminal to the centre or you can walk in 15 mins. To/from **Quito**, frequent service, US$3, 3 hrs. Shared taxis with **Supertaxis Los Lagos** (Quito address and schedules under Otavalo above, in Ibarra at Flores 924 y Sánchez Cifuentes, Parque La Merced, T295 5150), buy ticket at their office the day before travelling, US$7.50 pp, 2½ hrs. To **Tulcán**, hourly, US$2, 3 hrs. To **Otavalo**, frequent service, US$0.50, 30 mins. To **Cotacachi**, US$0.45, 45 mins, some continue to **Quiroga**. To **the coast**

several companies leave from the Terminal Terrestre, some go all the way to **San Lorenzo** US$4, 3 hrs, others only as far as **Lita**, US$3.50, 2 hrs. To **Ambato**, CITA goes via El Quinche and bypasses Quito, 8 daily, US$5, 5 hrs. To **Lago Agrio**, **Valle de Chota**, daily mid-morning, US$9, via La Bonita. To **La Esperanza** Bus from Parque Germán Grijalva (east of the Terminal Terrestre, follow C Sánchez y Cifuentes, south from the centre), every 30 mins, US$0.25, 30 mins.
Train Autoferro to **Primer Paso**, 45 km out of Ibarra to Primer Paso, just beyond Tulquizán (see above), US$3.80 one way, leaves Mon-Fri 0700, returning 1400, Sat-Sun 0800, returning 1600, minimum 12 passengers, T295 5050. You can continue by bus to San Lorenzo from Tulquizán.

North to Colombia: El Angel *p930*
Bus From **Ibarra** Terminal Terrestre to **Mira**, every 30 minutes, US$0.90, 1 hr; to **El Angel**, hourly, US$1.30, 1½ hrs. From **El Angel** to **Mira**, every 30 min, US$.50, 20 minutes. From El Angel to **Tulcán**, US$1.30, 1½ hrs. From El Angel to **Quito**, US$4, 4 hrs.

Eastern route to the border *p930*
San Gabriel
Bus From **San Gabriel** to **Tulcán**, vans and jeeps US$0.60, shared taxis US$0.85, 30 mins, all from the main plaza. From San Gabriel to **Ibarra**, buses, US$1.65, 2 hrs. From San Gabriel to **Quito**, buses, US$3.50, 3½ hrs. For **La Paz**, public transport from Tulcán and San Gabriel on weekends only; you must hire a taxi at other times.

Tulcán *p931*
Air TAME (Sucre y Ayacucho, T298 0675) flies Mon, Wed and Fri to **Quito** (US$42) and to **Cali** in Colombia (US$91).
Bus The bus terminal is 1½ km uphill from centre; best to take a taxi, US$1. To **Quito**, US$4, 5 hrs, every 15 mins. To **Ibarra**, 3 hrs, US$2. **Otavalo**, US$3, 3 hrs (make sure the bus is going to Otavalo; if not get out on the Highway at the turnoff), or transfer in Ibarra. To **Guayaquil**, 20 a day, 13 hrs, US$13. To **Lago Agrio**, 3 a day with **Putumayo**, US$7, 7 hrs, spectacular, but it does go close to the Colombian border.

Border with Colombia: Tulcán-Ipiales
p931
Bus Minivans and shared taxis Tulcán-border leave when full from Parque Ayora (near the cemetery) US$0.75 pp, private taxi US$3.
Note These vehicles cross the international bridge and drop you off on the Colombian side, where Colombian transport waits. Remember to cross back over the bridge for Ecuadorean immigration.

Directory

Ibarra p929
Banks Banco del Pacífico, Moncayo y Olmedo. Banco del Austro, Colón 7-51. **Internet** Several places in town centre; US$0.75 per hr. **Language courses** Centro Ecuatoriano Canadiense de Idomas (CECI), Pérez Guerrero 6-12 y Bolívar, T295 1911, US$3.50 per hr. **Medical services** Clínica Médica del Norte, Oviedo 8-24, T295 5099, 24 hrs. **Post offices** Flores opposite Parque Pedro Moncayo, 2nd floor.

Tulcán p931
Banks Banco del Austro, Bolívar y Ayacucho. Few places accept credit cards. Nowhere in Tulcán to change TCs. Pesos Colombianos can easily be changed on Plaza de la Independencia.
Consulates Colombia: Bolívar 386 y Junín, T298 7302, visas require up to 20 days, Mon-Fri 0800-1300, 1430-1530. **Internet** Prices US$1 per hr, many places in town. **Post offices** Bolívar 53-27.

Cotopaxi, Latacunga and Quilotoa

An impressive roll call of towering peaks lines the route south of Quito, appropriately called the Avenue of the Volcanoes. This area obviously attracts its fair share of trekkers and climbers, while the less active tourist can browse through the many colourful indígena markets and colonial towns that nestle among the high volcanic cones. The Panamericana heads south from Quito towards the central highlands' hub of Ambato. The perfect cone of Cotopaxi volcano is ever-present and is one of the country's main tourist attractions. Machachi and Lasso are good places to acclimatize, while Latacunga is a good base for the region, and for the impossibly beautiful Quilotoa circuit of small villages and vast expanses of open countryside.

Cotopaxi and Latacunga

Machachi → *Phone code: 02. Colour map 11, grid A3. Population: 25,000. Altitude: 2,900 m.*
In a valley between the summits of Pasochoa, Rumiñahui and Corazón, lies the town of **Machachi**, famous for its mineral water springs and cold, crystal clear swimming pool (open 0800-1530 daily). The water, 'Agua Güitig' or 'Tesalia', is bottled in a plant 4 km from the town and sold throughout the country. Annual highland 'rodeo', El Chagra, third week in July.

Reserva Ecológica Los Ilinizas
Machachi is a good starting point for a visit to the northern section of the **Reserva Ecológica Los Ilinizas** *US$5*. There is a *refugio*, a shelter below the saddle between the two peaks, at 4,750 m, with beds for 12 and cooking facilities, take a mat and sleeping bag, US$10 per night (check at the **Hostal Llovizna** on the way out of Chaupi, if Vladimir or his assistant is not at the hut, then they key is at the Hostal). Iliniza Norte (5,126 m) can be climbed without technical equipment in the dry season but a few exposed, rocky sections require utmost caution, allow 2-4 hours for the ascent from the refuge, take a compass, it's easy to mistake the descent. Iliniza Sur (5,245 m) has some ice climbing, but the glacier is disappearing fast: full climbing gear and experience are absolutely necessary. Access to the reserve is through a turnoff west of the Panamericana 6 km south of Machachi, then it's 7 km to the village of El Chaupi. A dirt road continues from here 9 km to 'La Virgen' (statue). Nearby are woods where you can camp.

> ✱ *Robberies of lone walkers have been reported, best go in a group. Take a stick to fend off dogs.*

Parque Nacional Cotopaxi → *Colour map 11, grid B4.*
① *Visitors to the park must register at the entrance. Entrance fee: US$10. Park gates are open 0700-1500, although you can stay until 1800. The park administration, a small museum (0800-1200, 1300-1700), the Paja Blanca restaurant and a simple shelter (US$12.50 pp with breakfast, T02-231 4234 or 09-851 3133), are 10 km from the park gates, just before Limpio Pungo. (See also Transport section below.) The museum has a 3D model of the park and stuffed animals.*

Cotopaxi volcano (5,897 m) is at the heart of a much-visited national park. This scenic snow-covered perfect cone is the second highest peak in Ecuador and a very popular climbing destination. Cotopaxi is an active volcano, one of the highest in the world, and its most recent eruption took place in 1904. Volcanic material from former eruptions can be seen strewn about the páramo surrounding Cotopaxi; there is a high plateau with a small lake (Laguna Limpio Pungo), a lovely area for walking and admiring the delicate flora, and fauna including wild horses and native bird species such as the Andean Lapwing and the Chimborazo Hillstar hummingbird. The lower slopes are clad in planted pine forests, where llamas may be seen.

The **main entrance** to the Parque Nacional Cotopaxi is approached from Chasqui, 25 km south of Machachi, 6 km north of Lasso, and is marked by a Parque Nacional Cotopaxi sign. Once through the national park gates, go past Laguna Limpio Pungo to a fork, where the right branch climbs steeply to a parking lot (4,600 m). From here it is 30 minutes to one hour on foot to the José Ribas refuge, at 4,800 m; beware of altitude sickness. Walking from the highway to the refuge takes an entire day or more. At the national park gate the main route is joined by the **El Boliche access**, starting 16 km south of Machachi. This begins near a sign for the Clirsen satellite tracking station, which has a museum for visitors. This route goes past Clirsen then via **Area Nacional de Recreación El Boliche** (shared entry with Cotopaxi, pay only once) for over 30 km along a signposted dirt road. This road skirts the western flanks of Rumiñahui volcano; it starts higher and stays higher making it a longer but easier approach, especially for cyclists. **A third entrance**, from the northwest, goes from Machachi via Santa Ana del Pedregal (21 km from the Panamericana), 35 km in total to the car park. There are infrequent buses to Pedregal (2 a day) then the hike in is shorter but still a couple of hours. For more details, and equipment, ask Quito tour operators who run tours here, or *South American Explorers* in Quito. The **Ticatilín access** approaches Cotopaxi from the south. From the Panamericana, 1 km north of Lasso, at 'Aglomerados Cotopaxi' (the northern access to Saquisilí) a road goes to the village of San Ramón and on to Ticatilín where a contribution is expected to open the chain at the access point (US$1-2 per vehicle). If coming from the south, San Ramón is accessed from Mulaló. It leads to a less impacted páramo and the private Albergue Cotopaxi Cara Sur. Walking 4 hours from here you reach Campo Alto, a tent camp used by climbers. There are other access points from the north, east and south, which go through private land and combine with the Cotopaxi circuit trek.

Climbing Cotopaxi The ascent from the refuge takes 5-8 hours, start climbing at 0100 as the snow deteriorates in the sun. A full moon is both practical and a magical experience. Check out snow conditions with the guardian of the refuge before climbing. Equipment and experience are required. Take a guide if you're inexperienced on ice and snow. The best season is December-April. There are strong winds and clouds in August-December but the ascent is still possible for experienced mountaineers. Climbing guides can be hired through operators in Quito, Latacunga, Riobamba and Baños. Just north of Cotopaxi are the peaks of Sincholahua (4,893 m), Rumiñahui (4,712 m) and Pasochoa (4,225 m). To the southeast is Quilindaña (4,878 m). The southwest flank has not received as much impact as the north side. There is good walking, and you can climb Morurco (4,881 m) as an acclimatization hike. Condors may sometimes be seen. To climb to the summit in one day you have to stay at Campo Alto (see above, and Sleeping below). The route is reported easier and safer than the north face, but a little longer. The last hour goes around the rim of the crater with impressive views.

Lasso → *Phone code: 03. Colour map 11, grid B3. Altitude: 3,000 m.*
The railway and the Pan-American Highway cross one another at Lasso, a small town, 33 km south of Alóag. In the surrounding countryside are several *hosterías*, converted country estates, offering accommodation and meals. There are roadside restaurants along the Panamericana.

Latacunga → *Phone code: 03. Colour map 11, grid B3. Population: 92,000. Altitude: 2,800 m.*
The capital of Cotopaxi Province is a place where the abundance of light grey pumice has been artfully employed. Volcán Cotopaxi is much in evidence, though it is 29 km away. Provided they are not hidden by clouds, which unfortunately is all too often, as many as nine volcanic cones can be seen from Latacunga; try early in the morning. The colonial character of the town has been well preserved. The central plaza, **Parque Vicente León**, is a beautifully maintained garden (locked at night). There are several other gardens in the town including **Parque San**

Francisco and **Lago Flores**. **Casa de los Marqueses de Miraflores** ⓘ *Sánchez de Orellana y Abel Echeverría, T280 1410, Mon-Fri 0800-1200, 1400-1800, free,* in a restored colonial mansion has a modest museum, with exhibits on Mama Negra (see Festivals and events, below), colonial art, archaeology, numismatics and a library (free).

Casa de la Cultura ⓘ *Antonia Vela 3-49 y Padre Salcedo T281 3247, Tue-Fri 0800-1200, 1400-1800, Sat 0800-1500, US$1,* built around the remains of a Jesuit Monastery and the old Monserrat watermill, houses an excellent museum with pre-Columbian ceramics, weavings, costumes and models of festival masks; also art gallery, library and theatre. It has week-long festivals with exhibits and concerts for all the local festivities. There is a Saturday **market** on the Plaza de San Sebastián (at Juan Abel Echeverría). Goods for sale include *shigras* (fine stitched, colourful straw bags) and homespun wool and cotton yarn. The produce market, Plaza El Salto has daily trading and larger fairs on Tuesday and Saturday.

Tourist offices: Cámara de Turismo de Cotopaxi ⓘ *Sánchez de Orellana y Guayaquil, at Plaza de Santo Domingo, T281 4968, Mon-Fri 0800-1200, 1400-1700,* local and regional information, Spanish only. **Oficina de Turismo**, at the Terminal Terrestre, second floor ⓘ *Mon-Fri 0900-1200, 1330-1800, Sat 0900-1600, Sun 0900-1400,* staffed by high school students, local and some regional information.

⊜ Sleeping

Machachi *p935*

C-D La Estación de Machachi, 3 km west of the Panamericana, by Aloasí, T230 9246. Beautiful old house, family-run, fireplaces, access to Volcán Corazón, reserve in advance.

D Chiguac, Los Caras y Colón, 4 blocks from the main park, T231 0396, germanimor@punto.net.ec. Small family run hostel, comfortable, includes breakfast, restaurant, shared bath.

E Estancia Real, Luis Cordero y Panzaleo, 3 blocks east of park, T231 5760. Hot water, parking, good.

E-F Papa Gayo, in Hacienda Bolívia, 500 m W of the Panamericana, T231 0002, h_eran@ yahoo.com. Chilly old farmhouse, nice communal area with fireplace and library. Restaurant, cheaper with shared bath, parking, homely atmosphere, excursions arranged, popular.

Reserva Ecológica Los Ilinizas *p935*

D Hacienda San José del Chaupi, 3 km southwest of El Chaupi, T09-4671692 (mob), haciendasanjosedelchaupi@yahoo.com. Converted farm house and cabins, including breakfast, shared bath, hot water, meals available if requested in advance, horse riding.

E La Llovizna, 100 m behind church, on the way to the mountain, T09-969 9068. Pleasant hostel, sitting room with fireplace, includes breakfast, restaurant, some rooms with bath,

Latacunga

Sleeping ⊜	Makroz 6	Tilipulo 9	Chifa China 2
Amazonas 2	Rodelú 7		Los Copihues 4
Cotopaxi 1	Rosim & Pizzería Los	Eating ⑦	Pingüino 7
Estambul 3	Sabores de Italia 8	Café-Libro Volcán 3	Pizzería Buon
Los Nevados 5	Santiago 4	Cafetería El Pasaje 1	Giorno 5

hot water, call ahead to check it's open, owned by guardian of the Iliniza refuge, horse rental.

F-G Nina Rumy, at the entrance to the plaza, Chaupi, T286 4688. Shared bath, electric shower, basic and friendly.

Parque Nacional Cotopaxi *p935*

All these inns are good for acclimatization at altitudes between 3,100 and 3,800 m. There are 2 very basic *cabañas* and a couple of campsites below Limpio Pungo (US$2 per tent, no facilities). The **José Ribas refuge** (entry US$1) has a kitchen, water, and 60 bunks with mattresses; US$17 pp per night, bring sleeping bag and mat, also padlock for your excess luggage when you climb, or use the lockable luggage deposit, US$2.50. **E Albergue Cotopaxi Cara Sur** at the southwestern end of the park, at the end of the Ticatilín access road, T02-290 3164 (Agama Expediciones, Quito), www.cotopaxi-carasur.com. Mountain shelter at 4,000 m. Total capacity 40, meals available with advance notice, use of kitchen, hot shower, bunk beds and blankets, transport from Quito and climbing tours available. Campo Alto tent camp US$5 pp, 4 hrs walk from the shelter, horse to take gear to camp US$12.

Outside the park

LL Hacienda San Agustín de Callo, entrance from the Panamericana 1.6 km north of the southern park access, marked by a painted stone, 10 min ride from the highway, T03-271 9160, www.incahacienda.com. Some rooms in ancient Inca structure, with fireplaces, bathtub, breakfast and dinner included, horse and bicycle hire. To the southeast of the park lies an area of rugged *páramos* and mountains dropping down to the jungle. The area has several large *haciendas* which form the Fundación Páramo, a private reserve with restricted access.

LL Hacienda Yanahurco, reservations: Quito, T02-224 1593, www.ecuador-yanahurco.com. Ranch style rooms with fireplace or heater, includes meals, 2-4 day programs, all-inclusive.

B Hacienda El Porvenir, between El Pedregal and the northern access to the park, T09-972 7934, T02-223 1806 (Quito), www.tierra delvolcan.com. Lodge in a working hacienda at the foot of Rumiñahui. Sitting-room with fireplaces, 3 types of rooms, includes breakfast, set meals available, horses and mountain bikes for hire. Camping **F** pp. Package including full board and transport from Quito available.

C-D Cuello de Luna, 2 km northwest of the park's main access on a dirt road, T09-970 0330, www.cuellodeluna.com. Comfortable rooms with fireplaces, includes breakfast, meals available, parking, cheaper in dorm (a very low loft). Can arrange transport to Cotopaxi, horse riding and

mountain biking.

C Tambopaxi, within the park at 3,750 m, 3 km south of the northern entrance (1 hr drive from Machachi) or 4 km north (left) of the turnoff for the climbing shelter, Quito T02-222 0242, www.tambopaxi.com. 3 double rooms and several dorms, duvets, good restaurant serving set meals and Swiss specialties, shared bath with hot shower, camping **G** pp, horse riding and llama trekking with advance notice.

Lasso *p936*

AL-A Hostería La Ciénega, 2 km south of Lasso, west of the Panamericana, T271 9052, www.geocities.com/haciendaec/. An historic *hacienda* with nice gardens, an avenue of massive eucalyptus trees, nice rooms with heater, good expensive restaurant.

A Hacienda Hato Verde, Panamericana Sur Km 78, by entry to Mulaló, southeast of Lasso, T271 9348, www.haciendahatoverde.com. Lovely old hacienda on the south flank of Cotopaxi, tastefully restored. 6 rooms with wood-burning stoves, includes breakfast.

A San Mateo, 4 km south of Lasso west of the Panamericana, T/F271 9471, www.hosteria sanmateo.com. Bright rooms, pricey restaurant, horse riding included, small but nice, adjoining working *hacienda* can be visited.

E Cabañas Los Volcanes, at the south end of Lasso, T271 9524, maexpediciones@yahoo.com. Small roadside hostel, nice rooms, cheaper with shared bath, hot water, laundry facilities, discounts for HI members. Runs trips to Cotopaxi.

Latacunga *p936, map p937*

D Makroz, Valencia 8-56 y Quito, T280 0907. Economical restaurant (closed Sun), parking, modern, comfortable.

D Rodelú, Quito 16-31, T280 0956, rodelu@ uio.telconet.net. Includes breakfast, excellent restaurant (closed Sun), parking, comfortable.

D-E Estambul, Belisario Quevedo 6-46 y Padre Salcedo, T280 0354. Simple quiet hostel, cheaper with shared bath, long popular with travellers, provide transport service to Quilotoa and Cotopaxi (also tours), internet in building. Recommended.

E Cotopaxi, Padre Salcedo 5-61 on Parque Vicente León, T280 1310. Cafetería, hot water after 0700, rooms with view over plaza are noisy at weekends.

E Rosim, Quito 16-49 y Padre Salcedo, T280 2172, hotelrosim@hotmail.com. Carpeted rooms, quiet, comfortable, discounts for IYHF members and in low season.

E Tilipulo, Guayaquil y Belisario Quevedo, T281 0611. Comfortable, helpful, parking, cafetería, noisy at weekends. Recommended.

F Los Nevados, Av 5 de Junio 53-19 y Eloy Alfaro, near bus terminal, T280 0407. Restaurant, parking, modern, spacious rooms, good value but unpleasant area.

F Santiago, 2 de Mayo 7-16 y Guayaquil, T280 0899. Pleasant hotel, cheaper with bath outside the room (not shared), small but comfortable rooms, good value.

G Amazonas, Valencia 47-36 y Amazonas on Plaza El Salto, T281 2673. Simple, overlooking the market, cheaper with shared bath, electric shower, adequate rooms, gets noisy early in the morning.

🍴 Eating

Machachi *p935*
🍴🍴-🍴 **Café de la Vaca**, 4 km south of town on the Panamericana. Very good meals using produce from own farm, open daily for breakfast and lunch until 1600, very popular.
🍴 **El Chagra**, take the road that passes in front of the church, on the right-hand side, about 5 km from church. Good typical food, reasonably priced.
🍴 **El Mesón del Valle**, near the Parque Central. Good food, helpful owner.

Lasso *p936*
🍴 **Parador Chalupas**, 5 km south of Lasso at La Avelina. Popular cafetería, busy at weekends.
🍴 **Parador La Avelina**, 5 km south of Lasso, opposite Chalupas. Known for its cheese and ice cream, a traditional stopping place.
🍴 **Parador de la Estación**, north of the railway line. Serves good Ecuadorean meals.

Latacunga *p936, map p937*
Few places are open on Sun.
🍴🍴-🍴 **Los Copihues**, Quito 14-25 y Tarqui. International menu, 4-course set lunch, good generous portions, Mon-Sat 1000-2200. Recommended.
🍴 **Chifa China**, Antonia Vela 6-85 y 5 de Junio. Chinese, large portions, open daily to 2200.
🍴 **Pizzería Buon Giorno**, Sánchez de Orellana y Gral Maldonado. Great pizzas and lasagne, huge selection, 1300-2300, closed Sun.
🍴 **Pizzería Los Sabores de Italia**, Quito 16-57 next to Hotel Rosim. Good pizza and Italian dishes, open daily 1200-2200.

Cafés
Café-Libro Volcán, Belisario Quevedo 5-56 y Padre Salcedo, Mon-Fri 1400-2200, Sat 1400-2000. Snacks, tacos, drinks, board games, a place to hang around.
Cafetería El Pasaje, Padre Salcedo 43-16, p 2, on pedestrian mall, Mon-Sat 0830-2030. Snacks, burgers, coffee and other drinks.

Pingüino, Quito 73-106, 1 block from Parque Vicente León. Good milk shakes and coffe.

🍸 Bars and clubs

Latacunga *p936, map p937*
Beer Center, Sánchez de Orellana 74-20. Good atmosphere, bar and disco.
Kahlúa Bongo Bar, Padre Salcedo 4-56, on pedestrian mall. Bar, open Wed-Sat 1900-0100.

🎉 Festivals and events

Latacunga *p936, map p937*
The Fiesta de la Mama Negra is held on **23-25 Sep**, in homage to *the Virgen de las Mercedes* and the *Santísima Tragedia*. It celebrates the black slaves brought by the Spanish to work on the plantations with dancing in the streets and colourful costumes. The civic festival of **Mama Negra** is on the **weekend before 11 Nov**.

🛍 Shopping

Latacunga *p936, map p937*
Azul, Padre Salcedo 4-20, on pedestrian mall. Ceramics, bronze and wooden items.
La Mama Negra, Padre Salcedo 4-43, on pedestrian mall. A variety of crafts.

⛰ Activities and tours

Latacunga *p936, map p937*
All operators and some hotels offer day trips to **Cotopaxi** and **Quilotoa** (US$35 pp, includes lunch and a visit to a market town if on Thu or Sat); prices for 3 or more people. Climbing trips to Cotopaxi are US$120-130 pp for 2 days (includes equipment, park entrance fee, meals, refuge fees), minimum 2 people. **Note** Many agencies require passport as deposit when renting equipment. Trekking trips to Cotopaxi, Ilinizas, etc US$30-40 pp, per day.
Metropolitan Touring, Guayaquil y Quito, T280 2985. See Quito Tour operators. Makes airline reservations.
Neiges, Guayaquil 5-19 y Quito, T/F281 1199, neigestours@hotmail.com. Day trips and climbing.
Ruta de los Volcanes, Padre Salcedo 4-55 y Quito, T281 2452. Tour to Cotopaxi follows a secondary road through interesting country, instead of the Panamericana.
Selvanieve, Padre Salcedo 4-38, T281 2895, selvanieve1@hotmail.com. Various tours, climbing, also has an agency in Baños, runs tours throughout Ecuador.
Tovar Expediciones, Guayaquil 5-38 y Quito,

T281 1333. Climbing and trekking, Fernando Tovar is an experienced mountain guide.

⊖ Transport

Machachi *p935*
Bus To **Quito**, 1 hr, US$0.55 from Av Amazonas 1 block south of the park – *especiales* go to the Terminal Terrestre, *populares* to El Recreo, 2-3 blocks before the Trole station of that name, US$0.75. To **Latacunga**, from the obelisk at the Panamericana, US$0.55, 1 hr.

Reserva Ecológica Los Ilinizas *p935*
Bus There is a frequent bus service from Av Amazonas opposite the market in Machachi to **El Chaupi** (30 min, US$0.30), from where you can walk to the *refugio* in 7-8 hrs. Horses can be hired at *Hacienda San José* or ask around the village (see also **Hostal Llovizna**, above). A pick-up from Machachi to 'La Virgen' takes about 45 mins (US$25), where it takes 3 hrs to walk with a full pack to the *refugio*.

Parque Nacional Cotopaxi *p935*
To the **Main park entrance and Refugio Ribas**, take a Latacunga bus from Quito and get off at the main access point. Do not take an express bus as you can't get off before Latacunga. At the turnoff to the park there are usually vehicles from **Cooperativa Zona Verde** which go up to the park. US$25 to the parking lot before the refuge for up to 5 passengers. From **Machachi**, pick-ups go via the cobbled road to El Pedregal on to the Limpio Pungo and the refugio parking lot, US$35. From **Lasso**, pick-up US$25 one-way to the refugio parking lot, 1½ hrs, US$60 return with 1 hr wait.
To **Cara Sur** from Quito, Agama

Expediciones offer transport to the **Albergue Cara Sur**, US$60 per vehicle up to 5 passengers. Alternatively take a Latacunga bound bus and get off at **Aglomerados Cotopaxi** and take a pick-up from there, US$15 per vehicle for up to 5 passengers.

Latacunga *p936, map p937*
Bus Buses leave from the terminal on the Panamericana just south of 5 de Junio, except **Coop Santa**, which has its own terminal at Eloy Alfaro 28-57 y Vargas Torres, 3 blocks north of the Terminal Terrestre along the Panamericana, T281 1659, serving **Cuenca**, **Loja**, and **Guayaquil** via Riobamba and Pallatanga. To **Quito**, every 15 mins, 2 hrs, US$2. To/from **Ambato**, 1 hr, US$1. To **Guayaquil**, US$7, 7 hrs. To **Saquisilí**, every 20 mins (see below). Through buses do not stop at Latacunga Terminal but go along a bypass road called Av Eloy Alfaro, to the west of the Panamericana. To try to get on one of these buses during daytime (0600-1700) you have to ask for the Puente de San Felipe, 4 blocks from the terminal. Buses on the Zumbahua, Quilotoa, Chugchilán, Sigchos circuit are given below.
Note On Thu most buses to nearby communities leave from Saquisilí market instead of Latacunga.

⊙ Directory

Latacunga *p936, map p937*
Banks Banco de Guayaquil, Maldonado y Sánchez de Orellana. For Visa and MasterCard. Banco del Austro, Quito y Guayaquil. **Internet** Prices around US$1 per hr. **Medical** services Hospital: at southern end of Amazonas y Hnos Páez, T281 2505, good service. **Post offices and telephones** Both at Belisario Quevedo y Maldonado.

Quilotoa Circuit

The popular and recommended round trip from Latacunga to Pujilí, Zumbahua, Quilotoa crater, Chugchilán, Sigchos, Isinliví, Toacazo, Saquisilí, and back to Latacunga can be done in two to three days by bus (times given below are approximate; buses are often late owing to the rough roads or requests for photo stops). It is 200 km in total. It is also a great route for biking and only a few sections of the loop are cobbled or rough. The best access is from Lasso or Latacunga.

Latacunga to Zumbahua

A fine paved road leads west to **Pujilí** ① *15 km, bus US$0.25*, which has a beautiful church. Good market on Sunday, and a smaller one on Wednesday. Colourful Corpus Christi celebrations. Beyond Pujilí, many interesting crafts are practised by the *indígenas* in the **Tigua** valley: paintings on leather, hand-carved wooden masks and baskets. **Chimbachuco**, also known as Tigua, is home to the Toaquiza family, most famous of the Tigua artists. The road goes on over the Western Cordillera to Zumbahua, La Maná and Quevedo. This is a great downhill bike route. It carries very little traffic and is extremely twisty in parts but is one of the most beautiful routes connecting the highlands with the coast. Beyond Zumbahua are the pretty towns of **Pilaló** (two restaurants and petrol pumps), **Esperanza de El Tingo** (two restaurants and lodging at *Carmita's*, T03-281 4657) and **La Maná**.

Zumbahua

Zumbahua lies ½ km from the main road, 65 km from Pujilí. It has an interesting Saturday market (starts at 0600) for local produce, and some tourist items. You can find a cheap meal in the market. Just below the plaza is a shop selling dairy products and cold drinks. Friday nights involve dancing and drinking. Take a fleece, as it can be windy, cold and dusty. There is a good hospital in town, Italian-funded and run. The Saturday trip to Zumbahua market and the Quilotoa crater is one of the best excursions in Ecuador.

Quilotoa

Zumbahua is the point to turn off for a visit to Quilotoa, a volcanic crater filled by a beautiful emerald lake, to which there is a steep path from the rim. From the rim of the crater, 3,850 m, several snowcapped volcanoes can be seen in the distance. The crater is reached by a paved road which runs north from Zumbahua (about 12 km, 3-5 hours' walk). There's a 300-m drop down from the crater rim to the water (US$1 to visit lake). The hike down takes about 30 minutes (an hour or more to climb back up). The trail starts to the left of the parking area down a steep, canyon-like cut; if unsure, take a guide. You can hire a mule to ride up from the bottom of the crater, but arrange it before heading down. Take a stick to fend off dogs. Everyone at the crater tries to sell the famous naïve Tigua pictures and carved wooden masks, so expect to be besieged (also by begging children). Be prepared, too, for sudden changes in the weather, it gets very cold at night.

Chugchilán, Sigchos and Isinliví → *Phone code: 03.*

Chugchilán, a poor village in one of the most scenic areas of Ecuador, is 22 km by road from the Quilotoa crater. It is a six-hour walk; or walk around part of the crater rim, then down to Guayama, and across the canyon (Río Sigüí) to Chugchilán, 11 km, 5-6 hours.

Continuing from Chugchilán the road runs through Sigchos, the starting point for the Toachi Valley walk, via Asache to San Francisco de las Pampas (0900 bus daily to Latacunga). Southeast of Sigchos is Isinliví, on the old route to Toacazo and Latacunga. It has a fine woodcarving shop and a pre-Inca pucará. Trek to the village of Guantualó, which has a fascinating market on Monday. You can hike to or from Chugchilán (5 hours), or from Quilotoa to Isinliví in 7-9 hours.

The road east to Toacazo (**C La Quinta Colorada**, T271 6122, price includes breakfast and dinner, very nice) is cobbled and from there to Saquisilí it is paved (there are petrol stations at Toacazo and Yalo, below Sigchos).

Saquisilí → *Phone code: 03.*

Some 16 km southwest of Lasso, and 6 km west of the Panamericana is the small but very important market town of Saquisilí. Its Thursday market (0500-1400) is famous throughout Ecuador for the way in which its seven plazas and some of its streets become jam-packed with people, the great majority of them local *indígenas* with red ponchos and narrow-brimmed felt hats. The best time to visit the market is between 0900 and 1200 (before 0800 for the animal market). Be sure to bargain, as there is a lot of competition. Saquisilí has colourful Corpus Christi processions.

⊜ Sleeping

Latacunga to Zumbahua *p940*
Pujilí
F **Res Pujilí**, Rocafuerte ½ block from highway, T272 3648. Simple, with bath, restaurant.

Tigua-Chimbacucho
C **Posada de Tigua**, 3 km east of Tigua-

Chimbacucho, 400 m north of the road, T281 3682, laposadadetigua@latinmail.com. Refurbished hacienda, part of a working dairy ranch, 5 rooms, wood-burning stove, includes tasty home-cooked breakfast and dinner, pleasant family atmosphere, horses for riding, trails, nice views.

Zumbahua *p941*
There are only a few phone lines in town, which are shared among several people. Expect delays when calling to book a room.

E Quilotoa, at the north side (bottom) of the plaza, next to the abattoir. Fancy fixtures but a bit run down, private bath, hot water, not too clean.

F Cóndor Matzi, overlooking the market area, T281 4611 (at the hospital). Basic but adequate, serves Fri supper (extra cost), other meals on request, shared bath, hot water, one of the better choices, reserve ahead.

F Hostal Richard, opposite the market on the road in to town, T281 4605 (at Oro Verde). Modern but still missing some finishing touches, some rooms with toilet, hot water in shared shower, laundry and cooking facilities, parking, family run, owners can provide transport to Quilotoa.

F Res Oro Verde, first place on the left as you enter town, T281 4605. Shared bath, hot water, has small store, Fri and Sat meals, others on request.

Quilotoa *p941*
B Quilotoa Crater Lake Lodge, on the main road facing the access to Quilotoa, T09-717 5780, 02-223 8665 (Quito), www.quilotoalodge.com. Hacienda-style lodge, includes breakfast, restaurant with fireplace and great views, electric blankets, homely atmosphere, the most upscale place in Quilotoa. Recommended.

E Cabañas Quilotoa, on the left side of the access road, T09-212 5962. Includes breakfast and dinner, cheaper with shared bath, hot water, wood-burning stoves. Owned by Humberto Latacunga who will organize treks, he is also a good painter.

E Hostal Pachamama, at the top of the hill by the rim of the crater, T09-785 5914. Includes breakfast and dinner, shared bath, electric shower.

E Princesa Toa, at the top of the hill by the rim of the crater. A community run hostel with accommodation in a large room with a fireplace and several beds, price includes breakfast and dinner, also runs a basic hostel in the crater.

Chugchilán *p941*
A-B The Black Sheep Inn, a few mins below the village, T281 4587, www.blacksheepinn.com. Run by Andy Hammerman and Michelle Kirby. A lovely eco-friendly resort which received several awards in 2005/6. Nice private rooms with fireplace, includes excellent vegetarian dinner and breakfast. Composting toilets, book exchange, organic garden, sauna, hot tub, gym and water-slide. Cheaper with shared bath, **D** pp in dorm. Discounts for ISIC, seniors, SAE members and cyclists. Highly recommended, reservations advised.

C-D Hostal Mama Hilda, 100 m from centre of Chugchilán towards Sigchos, T281 4814. A pleasant family-run hostel, warm atmosphere, large rooms some with fireplace, includes good dinner and breakfast, cheaper with shared bath, **F** pp in dorm, parking, arrange horse-riding and walking trips, good value. Highly recommended.

E Hostal Cloud Florest, at the entrance to town, 150 m from the centre, T281 4808, josecloudforest@gmail.com. Simple but nice family-run hostel, includes dinner (good local fare or vegetarian) and breakfast, cheaper with shared bath, hot water, parking, very helpful owners.

Sigchos *p941*
F Res Sigchos, Carlos Hugo Páez y Rodrigo Iturralde, T271 4107. Basic but clean, large rooms, shared bath, hot water.

G La Posada, Los Ilinizas y Galo Arteaga, T271 4224. A modern, simple hotel, restaurant downstairs, private bath, hot water.

Isinliví *p941*
E Llullu Llama, T281 4790, www.llullullama.com. Nicely refurbished house, cosy sitting room with wood-burning stove, tastefully decorated rooms, private, semi-private

and dorm (**G** pp), good hearty meals available, shared composting toilet with great views, abundant hot water, organic herb garden, warm and relaxing atmosphere, a lovely spot. Recommended.

Saquisilí *p941*

D Gilocarmelo, by the cemetery, 800 m from town on the road north to Guaytacama, T09-966 9734, 02-340 0924 (Quito), carlosrlopezc@yahoo.com. Restored hacienda house in a 4 ha property. Rooms with fireplace, includes breakfast, restaurant, heated pool, sauna, jacuzzi, opened in 2006.
F San Carlos, Bolívar opposite the Parque Central. A multi-storey building overlooking the main square, private bath, electric shower, parking, good value, but watch your valuables.
G Pensión Chavela, Bolívar by main park, T272 1114. Shared bath, cold water, very basic.

⦿ Transport

Zumbahua *p941*

Bus Many daily on the Latacunga-Quevedo road (0500-1900, US$1.25, 1½ hrs). Buses on Sat are packed full; ride on roof for best views, get your ticket the day before. A pick-up truck can be hired from Zumbahua to **Quilotoa** for US$5-10 depending on number of passengers; also to **Chugchilán** for around US$30. On Sat mornings there are many trucks leaving the Zumbahua market for Chugchilán which pass Quilotoa.
Taxi Day-trip by taxi to Zumbahua, Quilotoa, return to **Latacunga** is US$40.

Quilotoa *p941*

Bus From the terminal terrestre in Latacunga Trans Vivero daily at 1100, 1200, 1300 and 1400, US$2, 2 hrs. Note that this leaves from Latacunga, not Saquisilí market, even on Thu. Return bus to Latacunga around 0300 and 0500. Buses returning around 1300-1600 go only as far as Zumbahua, from where you can catch a Latacunga bound bus at the highway. Also, buses going through Zumbahua bound for Chugchilán will drop you at the turnoff, 5 mins from the crater, where you can also pick them up on their way to Zumbahua and Latacunga.

Chugchilán *p941*

Bus From **Latacunga**, daily at 1130 (except Thu) via Sigchos, at 1200 via Zumbahua; on Thu from **Saquisilí market** via Sigchos around 1130, US$2.50, 3½-4 hrs. Buses return to Latacunga daily at 0300 via Sigchos, at 0400 via Zumbahua. On Sun there are 2 extra buses to Latacunga leaving 0900-1000. There are extra buses going as far as Zumbahua Wed 0500, Fri 0600 and Sun between 0900-1000; these continue towards the coast. Milk truck to Sigchos around 0900-1000. On Sat also pick-ups going to/from market in Zumbahua and Latacunga. Taxi from Latacunga US$60. From **Sigchos**, through buses as indicated above, US$0.60, 1-1½ hrs. Pick-up hire to Sigchos US$25, up to 5 people, US$5 additional person. Pick-up to **Quilotoa** US$25, up to 5 people, US$5 additional person.

Sigchos *p941*

Bus From **Latacunga** frequent daily service US$1.50, 2-2½ hrs. From/to **Quito** direct service on Fri and Sun, US$3, 3 hrs. To **La Maná** on the road to Quevedo, via Chugchilán, Quilotoa and Zumbahua, Fri at 0500 and Sun at 0830, US$3.50, 6 hrs (returns Sat at 0730 and Sun at 1530). To **Las Pampas**, at 0330 and 1400, US$2.50, 3 hrs. From Las Pampas to **Santo Domingo**, at 0300 and 0600, US$2.50, 3 hrs.

Isinliví *p941*

From **Latacunga** daily (except Thu) at 1245 (14 de Octubre) via Sigchos and 1245 (Trans Vivero, on Sat at 1030) direct, on Thu both leave from Saquisilí market around 1030, US$1.80, 2 hrs. Both buses return to Latacunga at 0330, except Sun 0700 via Sigchos, 1200 direct, Mon one at 1430, Wed one at 0700. Connections to Chugchilán, Quilotoa and Zumbahua can be made in Sigchos. Bus schedules are posted on www.llullullama.com.

Saquisilí *p941*

Bus Frequent service between **Latacunga** and Saquisilí, US$0.30, 20 mins; many buses daily to/from **Quito**, depart from the bus terminal, 0530-1300, US$2, 2hrs. Buses and trucks to many outlying villages leave from 1000 onwards. Bus tours from Quito cost US$45 pp, taxis charge US$60, with 2 hrs wait at market.

Ambato → *Phone code: 03. Colour map 11, grid B3. Population: 184,000. Altitude 2,700 m.*

Almost completely destroyed in the great 1949 earthquake, Ambato lacks the colonial charm of other Andean cities, though its location in the heart of fertile orchard-country has earned it the nickname of 'the city of fruits and flowers' (see annual festival below). It is also the principal supply town of the central highlands and a major centre for the leather industry.

Tourist office: Ministerio de Turismo ① *Guayaquil y Rocafuerte, T282 1800. Open Mon-Fri 0830-1300, 1430-1800,* helpful.

The modern cathedral faces the pleasant **Parque Montalvo**, where there is a statue of the writer Juan Montalvo (1832-1889) who is embalmed in a memorial in a neighbouring street. His **house** ① *Bolívar y Montalvo, T282 4248, US$1,* is open to the public and has a good restaurant, **El Quijote**. In the **Colegio Nacional Bolívar** is the **Museo de Ciencias Naturales Héctor Vásquez** ① *Sucre entre Lalama y Martínez, T282 7395, Mon-Fri 0800-1200, 1400-1730, closed for school holidays, US$1,* with stuffed birds and animals and items of local historical interest, recommended. The **Quinta de Mera** ① *Wed-Sun 0830-1600, US$1, take bus from Espejo y 12 de Noviembre,* an old mansion in beautiful gardens, is in Atocha suburb. The main **market**, one of the largest in Ecuador, is held on Monday, with smaller markets on Wednesday and Friday. They are interesting, but have few items for the tourist.

Ambato to Baños

To the east of Ambato, an important road leads to **Salasaca**, where the *indígenas* sell their weavings; they wear distinctive black ponchos with white trousers and broad white hats. Further east, 5 km, is **Pelileo**, the blue jean manufacturing capital of Ecuador with good views of Tungurahua. From Pelileo, the road descends to Las Juntas, where the Patate and Chambo rivers meet to form the Río Pastaza. About 1 km east of Las Juntas bridge, the junction with the closed road to Riobamba is marked by a large sculpture of a macaw and a toucan (locally known as Los Pájaros – the lower bird is buried by volcanic debris). It is a favourite volcano watching site. The road to Baños then continues along the lower slopes of the volcano.

Eight kilometres northeast of Pelileo on a paved side-road is **Patate**, centre of the warm, fruit growing Patate valley. There are excellent views of Volcán Tungurahua from town and its surroundings. *Arepas*, sweets made of squash (unrelated to the Colombian or Venezuelan variety), are the local delicacy; sold around the park. The fiesta of Nuestro Señor del Terremoto is held on the weekend leading to **4 February**, featuring a parade with floats made with fruit and flowers.

Ambato to Guaranda

To the west of Ambato, a paved road climbs through tilled fields, past the páramos of Carihuairazo and Chimborazo to the great Arenal (a high desert at the base of the mountain), and down through the Chimbo valley to Guaranda (see page 953). This spectacular journey on the highest paved road in Ecuador takes about three hours. It reaches a height of 4,380 m and vicuñas can be seen.

Ambato to Riobamba

After Ambato, the Pan-American Highway runs south to Riobamba (see page 952). About half way is **Mocha**, where guinea pigs (*cuy*) are bred for the table. You can sample roast *cuy* and other typical dishes at stalls and restaurants by the roadside, *Mariadiocelina* is recommended. The highway climbs steeply south of Mocha and at the pass at **Urbina** (one hostal) there are fine views in the dry season of Chimborazo and Carihuairazo.

◉ Sleeping

Ambato *p943*
There are a lot of cheap residenciales, hotels and restaurants around Parque 12 de Noviembre, the area is not safe at night. The suburb of Miraflores is a pleasant walk from the centre, or bus to Av Miraflores.
A Miraflores, Av Miraflores 15-27, T284 3224, www.hmiraflores.com.ec. Includes breakfast, nice modern facilities, good restaurant, heating, suites with jacuzzi.
B Ambato, Guayaquil 01-08 y Rocafuerte, T242 1791, www.hotelambato.com. Includes breakfast, modern, Wi-Fi, good restaurant, casino, squash court, best in city centre. Recommended.

B Florida, Av Miraflores 1131, T242 2007. Includes breakfast, restaurant with good set meals, pleasant setting.
D Cevallos, Montalvo y Cevallos, T282 4877. Includes breakfast, restaurant, parking, good.
D Colony, 12 de Noviembre 124 y Av El Rey, near the bus terminal, T282 5789. Modern, large rooms, includes breakfast, parking.
D Pirámide Inn, Cevallos y Mariano Egüez, T242 1920. Includes breakfast, parking, comfortable, English and Italian spoken.
E Nürenberg, 12 de Noviembre 09-25 y L A Martínez, T282 8455. Hot water, simple, good value, opened in 2006.

E Royal, Cevallos 05-60 y Vargas Torres, T282
3528. A small modern hotel, rooms are small,
comfortable and clean, good value.
E-F Madrid, Juan Cajas y Cumandá, T282 8679.
Adequate hostel convenient to the bus terminal,
restaurant, cheaper with shared bath, hot
water, disco.

Ambato to Baños: Salasaca and Pelileo
p944
D Runa Huasi, 1 km north off main highway,
look for signs and ask around, T09-984 0125,
alonsopilla@hotmail.com. Simple hostel, includes
breakfast, other meals on request, cooking
facilities, nice views, guided walks.
F Hostal Pelileo, Eloy Alfaro 641, T287 1390.
Shared bath, hot water, simple.

Ambato to Baños: Patate *p944*
A Hacienda Leito, on de road to El Triunfo, T285
9329, www.haciendaleito.com.
Farm accommodation, includes breakfast and
dinner, classy, facing Tungurahua, good.
B Hacienda Los Manteles, in the Leito valley on
the road to El Triunfo, T09-604 1818, 02-223 3484
(Quito), www.haciendamanteles.com. Nice
converted hacienda with restaurant, great views of
Tungurahua and Chimborazo, includes breakfast,
fruit, hot drinks, walk to waterfalls, hiking and
horse riding. Reserve ahead.
B Hostería Viña del Río, 3 km from town on the
old road to Baños, T/F03-287 0314. Cabins on a
22 ha ranch, restaurant, pool, spa, horse riding
and mini golf.
E Jardín del Valle, M Soria y A Calderón, 1 block
from the main park, T287 0209. Nicely furnished,
good breakfast available, good value.
Recommended.

Ambato to Riobamba: Urbina *p944*
E Posada de la Estación, in the solitary old
railway station at 3,619 m, Urbina (signed), 2 km
west of the highway, T/F03-294 2215,
aventurag@ch.pro.ec. Meals available, shared
bath, hot water, magnificent views, clean and
comfortable but very cold at night. This is a
good place for acclimatization, friendly and
helpful, horses, trips and equipment arranged.
Recommended.

🍴 Eating

Ambato *p943*
¥¥ El Alamo Chalet, Cevallos 1719 y Montalvo,
open 0800-2300 (2200 Sun). Ecuadorean and
international food. Set meals and à la carte,
Swiss-owned, good quality.
¥¥ Farid, Bolívar 705 y JL Mera, daily 1100-2300.

Grilled meat served in middle eastern sauces.
¥¥ La Buena Mesa, Quito 924 y Bolívar.
French, elegant, closed Sun. Recommended.
¥¥ Miramar, Quito y Rocafuerte. Good seafood.
¥¥ ¥ Mama Miche, 13 de Abril y JL Mera, Centro
Comercial Ambato, daily 1000-0600. Grill, a
variety of meats.
El Quijote, at Casa de Montalvo, Montalvo y
Bolívar, Mon-Sat 0930-1900. Spanish and
Ecuadorean cuisine, à la carte and very good 4
course set meals, nice décor and pleasant
atmosphere.
Govinda's, JB Vela 8-24 y Montalvo, Mon-Sat
0800-2030, Sun 0800-1600. Vegetarian set meals
and à la carte.
¥ La Fornace, Cevallos 1728 y Montalvo.
Wood oven pizza. Opposite is **Heladería La
Fornace**, Cevallos y Castillo. The best coffee in
town, snacks, sandwiches, ice-cream, very
popular.
¥ Nueva Hong Kong, Bolívar 768 y Martínez.
Good cheap *chifa*.

Cafés
Café Marcelo´s, Rocafuerte y Castillo, daily
0900-2100. Good cafeteria serves hamburgers
and other snacks, also ice cream.
Pastelería Quito, JL Mera y Cevallos. Coffee and
pastries, good for breakfast.

🎉 Festivals and events

Ambato *p943*
Ambato has a famous festival in **Feb** or **Mar**, the
Fiesta de frutas y flores, during carnival when
there are 4 days of bullfights, festivities and
parades (best Sun morning and Mon night).
It is impossible to get a hotel room unless
you book ahead.

🛍 Shopping

Ambato *p943*
Leather Many stores for leather shoes along
Bolívar. Leather jackets, bags, belts on Vela
between Lalama and Montalvo. Take a local bus
up to the leather town of Quisapincha for the
best deals, everyday, but big market on Sat.

🏔 Activities and tours

Ambato *p943*
Metropolitan Touring, Centro Comercial
Caracol, Local 59-62, T282 0211, www.metro
politan-touring.com. A branch of the large Quito
operator, also sells airline tickets.

independent centres and massage therapists. These offer a combination of sauna, steam bath (Turkish or box), jacuzzi, clay and other types of baths, a variety of massage techniques (Shiatsu, Reiki, Scandinavian) and more.

Around Baños

There are many interesting **walks** in the Baños area. The **San Martín shrine** is a 45-minute easy walk from town and overlooks a deep rocky canyon with the Río Pastaza thundering below. Beyond the shrine, crossing to the north side of the Pastaza, is the **Ecozoológico San Martín** ① *T274 0552, 0800-1700, US$1.50*, with the **Serpentario San Martín** ① *daily 0900-1800, US$1* opposite. 50 m beyond is a path to the **Inés María waterfall**, cascading down, but polluted. You can also cross the Pastaza by the new **Puente San Francisco** road bridge, behind the kiosks across the main road from the bus station (a larger vehicular bridge has been built here). From here a series of trails fans out into the surrounding hills, offering excellent views of Tungurahua from the ridge-tops in clear weather. A total of six bridges span the Pastaza near Baños, so you can make a round trip.

On the hillside behind Baños, it is a 45-minute hike to the **statue of the Virgin** (good views). Go to the south end of Calle JL Mera, before the street ends, take the last street to the right, at the end of which are stairs leading to the trail. A steep path continues along the ridge, past the statue. Another trail begins at the south end of JL Mera and leads to the *Hotel Luna Runtún*, continuing on to the village of Runtún (five- to six-hour round-trip). Along the same hillside, to the **Bellavista cross**, it is a steep climb from the south end of Calle Maldonado, 50 minutes. There are two cafés at the cross. You can continue from the cross to Runtún.

On the Puyo road the first town you reach beyond the Agoyán generating station is Río Blanco. Beyond is the hamlet of La Merced with a lookout and a trail with a swingbridge over the Pastaza going to the base of the lovely **Manto de La Novia** waterfall, on the Río Chinchín Chico. A new cable car goes right over the falls. About 1 km beyond is the *tarabita* (cable car) crossing the Pastaza to the village of San Pedro; it is powered by an old lorry engine, US$1. From the cable car you have nice views of the Pastaza and the **San Pedro falls** on the river of the same name. Several other *tarabitas* are being installed along this road.

About 3 km beyond and 17 km from Baños is the town of **Río Verde**, at the junction of the Verde and Pastaza rivers. The Río Verde has crystalline green water with several waterfalls on its course. The most spectacular are **El Pailón del Diablo** (the Devil's Cauldron). In Río Verde, cross the river and take the path to the right after the church, then follow the trail down towards the suspension bridge for about 20 minutes. Just before the bridge take a side trail to the right (signposted) which leads you to **Paradero del Pailón**, a kiosk selling drinks and snacks with viewing platforms above the falls (US$1). Five minutes' walk along a different trail are the smaller **San Miguel falls**; in town cross the bridge and take the first path to the right. It is also possible to hire bikes for the day from Baños and cycle downhill, passing El Pailón del Diablo and numerous other waterfalls on the way. Then take a bus back to Baños; several snack bars and restaurants in Río Verde let you leave the bike while you visit the falls. Do not take valuables when cycling this route and enquire about safety before setting out.

⊙ Sleeping

Baños *p947, map p947*
Baños has plenty of accommodation but can fill during holiday weekends.
AL Luna Runtún, Caserío Runtún Km 6, T274 0882, www.lunaruntun.com. Includes dinner and breakfast, restaurant, internet, beautiful setting overlooking Baños, very comfortable rooms with balconies, gardens. Excellent service, English, French and German spoken. Hiking, horse riding and biking tours, nanny facilities. Highly recommended.
A-C Sangay Spa, Plazoleta Ayora 100, opposite the waterfall and thermal baths, T274 0490, www.sangayspahotel.com. Includes breakfast,

good restaurant, pool and spa open to non-residents 1600-2000 (US$5), tennis and squash courts, attentive service, 3 categories of rooms. Recommended.
B Monte Selva, Halflants y Montalvo, T274 0566, www.ecoparquemonteselva.com. Includes breakfast, restaurant, warm pool, cabins overlooking town, bar, spa, excellent service.
B Volcano, Rafael Vieira y Montalvo, T274 2140, www.volcano.com.ec. Nice spacious modern hotel, large rooms with fridge, some with views of the waterfall, includes buffet breakfast, restaurant, heated pool, massage, nice garden.
B-C Palace, Montalvo 20-03, T274 0470,

hotelpalace@hotmail.com. Includes breakfast, restaurant, nice garden and pool, free internet, nicely old-fashioned, front rooms with balcony. Pools and spa open to public, US$5.

C La Floresta, Halflants y Montalvo, T274 1824, www.lafloresta.banios.com. Excellent breakfast, good restaurant, parking, comfortable rooms, nice garden. Recommended.

C Posada del Arte, Pasaje Velasco Ibarra y Montalvo, T274 0083, www.posadadelarte.com. Cosy, includes breakfast, good restaurant (⓫), sitting room and pricier rooms with fireplace.

C-D Isla de Baños, Halflants 1-31 y Montalvo, T/F274 0609, islabanos@andinanet.net. Nicely decorated and comfortable hotel, includes European breakfast and steam bath, internet US$1 per hr, spa open when there are enough people, pleasant garden.

D Flor de Oriente, Ambato y Maldonado on Parque Central, T274 0418, www.floridesoriente. banios.com. Includes breakfast, very good but can be noisy at weekends, cafeteria, parking.

D-E Le Petit Auberge, 16 de Diciembre y Montalvo, T274 0936, reservation_banos@ hotmail.com. Includes breakfast, good restaurant, parking, French-run, rooms with fireplace, patio, quiet.

E Buena Vista, Martínez y Pastaza, T274 0263. Hot water, quiet, simple, good value, discounts in low season.

E Carolina, 16 de Diciembre y Martínez, T274 0592. Hot water, cooking facilities, terrace, restaurant, good value. Recommended.

E El Edén, 12 de Noviembre y Montalvo, T274 0616, hostaleleden@andinanet.net. Pleasant wheelchair-accessible hotel with a patio. Includes breakfast, restaurant, parking, rooms with balconies.

E El Oro, Ambato y JL Mera, T274 0736. Includes breakfast, cooking and laundry facilities, good value. Recommended.

E Huilla Cuna, 12 de Noviembre y Montalvo, T274 2909, yojairatour@yahoo.com. Nice hostel decorated with paintings and antiques. Bright modern rooms, hot water, patio with fireplace and games. Its gallery of modern art also sells paintings and coffee-table books.

E Jireh, Ambato y León, T274 0321. Pleasant, large rooms, hot water, laundry and cooking facilities, parking, good.

E Llanovientos, Martínez 1126 y Sebastián Baño, T274 0682, www.llanovientos.banios.com. A modern breezy hostel with wonderful views, comfortable, cafeteria, hot water, cooking facilities, parking, nice garden. Recommended.

E Posada El Marqués, Pasaje Velasco Ibarra y Montalvo, T274 0053, posada_marques@ yahoo.com. Spacious, good beds, garden, cooking facilities, quiet area. Recommended.

E Rincón Alemán, C de los Motilones, 10 min walk from the terminal, follow C Oriente to the east, right at the coliseum, then first left, T274 3193. Relatively new hostel in a quiet location, breakfast available, cheaper with shared bath, hot water, owner speaks German.

E Transilvania, 16 de Diciembre y Oriente, T274 2281, www.hostal-transilvania.com. Simple rooms, includes breakfast, Middle Eastern restaurant, hot water, free internet, nice views from balconies, large TV and many movies in sitting room, pool table, luggage storage, popular, good value. Recommended.

E Verde Vida, Maldonado y Oriente, T274 2947. Nice modern hostel, hot water, small terrace with views, good value.

E-F Plantas y Blanco, 12 de Noviembre y Martínez, T/F274 0044, option3@hotmail.com. Pleasant popular hostel decorated with plants, a variety of rooms and prices, cheaper with shared bath and in dorm, hot water, free internet, excellent breakfast, fruit salads and self service drinks in rooftop cafeteria, steam bath, classic films, bakery, French run, good value. Repeatedly recommended.

E-F Santa Cruz, 16 de Diciembre y Martínez, T274 0648, santacruzhostal@yahoo.com. Comfortable, breakfast available, hot water, free internet, cooking facilities, sitting room with fireplace, games, book exchange, good value. Recommended.

E-F Timara, Maldonado 381 y Martínez, T274 0599, arte_con_natura@hotmail.com. Small, simple family-run hostel, shared bath, internet, laundry and cooking facilities, nice garden.

E-F Villa Santa Clara, 12 de Noviembre y Velasco Ibarra, T274 0349, www.hotelvilla santaclara.com. Simple rooms in older section and nice cabins in quiet location, cheaper with shared bath, hot water, laundry facilities, garden.

F Dinastía, Oriente y Alfaro, T274 0933. Hot water, nice, quiet, very helpful, good value.

F El Belén, Reyes y Ambato, T03-2741024, www.hotel-elbelen.com. Nice hostel, hot water, cooking facilities, parking, helpful staff.

F Princesa María, Rocafuerte y Mera, T274 1035. Hot water, laundry and cooking facilities, popular meeting place, bicycle hire, good value. Frequently recommended.

Around Baños p948

B Pequeño Paraíso, 1½ km east of Río Verde, west of Machay, T08-461 4867, www.pequenoparaiso.com. Comfortable cabins in lovely surroundings, abundant hot water, includes breakfast and dinner, tasty vegetarian meals, small pool, camping possible, climbing wall, Swiss-run. Recommended.

🍽 Eating

Baños *p947, map p947*
🍴🍴🍴 **Le Petit Restaurant**, 16 de Diciembre y
Montalvo. Closed Wed. Parisian owner, excellent
food, including vegetarian, great atmosphere.
🍴🍴 **Mariane**, Halflants y Rocafuerte. Provençal
cuisine, large portions, daily 1600-2300.
Recommended.
🍴🍴-🍴 **Buon Giorno**, Ambato y Pasaje Ermita de la
Vírgen west of the market, and at Rocafuerte y 16
de Diciembre, Tue-Sun 1130-2230. Good,
authentic Italian dishes.
🍴🍴-🍴 **El Jardín**, 16 de Diciembre y Rocafuerte.
International and some vegetarian food, juices,
also bar, good atmosphere and nice garden.
🍴🍴-🍴 **Pancho Villa**, Halflants y Martínez, Mon-Sat
1230-2130. Very good quality Mexican food,
good service. Recommended.
🍴🍴-🍴 **Pizzería El Napolitano**, 12 de Noviembre y
Martínez. Good pizza and pasta, pleasant
atmosphere, pool table.
🍴 **Ambateñito**, Ambato y Eloy Alfaro. Good set
meals and BBQ chicken.
🍴 **Café Hood**, Maldonado y Ambato, at Parque
Central, closed Tue. Mainly vegetarian food, fruit
juices, also meats, excellent food, nice atmosphere,
English spoken, always busy. Also rents rooms.
🍴 **Casa Hood**, Martínez between Halflants and
Alfaro, closed Wed. Varied vegetarian menu
including Indonesian and Thai dishes, some meat
dishes, juices, good desserts, travel books and
maps sold, book rental and exchange, repertory
cinema. Recommended.
🍴 **Chifa Shan He**, Oriente y Alfaro. Large portions.
🍴 **El Paisano**, Rafael Vieira y Martínez. Variety
of vegetarian meals and herbal teas.
🍴 **La Puerta de Alcalá**, Av Amazonas (main
highway), ½ block downhill from bus terminal.
Good value set meal.
🍴 **C Ambato**, has many restaurants serving
economical set meals and local fare, the
picanterías on the outside of the market serve
local delicacies such as *cuy* and *fritada*.

Cafés
Ali Cumba, Maldonado opposite Parque Central,
daily 0700-1800. Excellent breakfasts, fruit salads,
coffee, espresso, muffins, large sandwiches.
Pricey but good, Danish-Ecuadorean run.
Café Blah Blah, Halflants 620 y Ambato, Tue-Sun
0700-1900. Good coffee, snacks, small, cosy,
sidewalk seating, popular meeting place.
Pancho's, Rocafuerte y Maldonado, at Parque
Central. Snacks, hamburgers, coffee.
Rico Pan, Ambato y Maldonado. Good
breakfasts, hot bread, good fruit salads,
pizzas and meals.

Rincón de Suiza, Martínez y Halflants, Tue-
Sun 0900-0000. Snacks, drinks, good coffee,
cappuccino, good cakes and pastries. Pleasant
atmosphere, books, games, pool table, ping-
pong. Swiss-Ecuadorean run. Recommended.

🍸 Bars and clubs

Baños *p947, map p947*
Eloy Alfaro, between Ambato and Oriente
has many bars including:
Bamboos Bar, Pablo A Suárez y Oriente, at the
east end of town. Popular for salsa, live music at
weekends.
Buena Vista, Alfaro y Oriente. A good place
for salsa and other Latin music.
Jack Rock Café, Alfaro y Ambato. A favourite
travellers' hangout, fantastic *piña colada*
and juices.
Kasbah, Alfaro y Oriente, open 1900-0200. Latin
music, pool table, snacks and pizza.
Mocambo´s Bar, Ambato y Halflants. Large
screen TV, loud, modern music.

🎭 Entertainment

Baños *p947, map p947*
Córdova Tours has a *Chiva Mocambo*, an
open-sided bus, cruises town playing music, it
will take you to different night spots.
Peña Ananitay, 16 de Diciembre y Espejo.
Good live music and dancing.

✷ Festivals

Baños *p947, map p947*
During Carnival and Holy Week hotels are
full and prices rise.
Oct: Nuestra Señora de Agua Santa with daily
processions, bands, fireworks, sporting events
and partying through the month. Week-long
celebrations ending **16 Dec**: the town's
anniversary, parades, fairs, sports, cultural events.
The night of **15 Dec** is the **Verbenas**, when each
barrio hires a band and there are many parties.

⚙ Shopping

Baños *p947, map p947*
Look out for jaw-aching toffee (*melcocha*) made in
ropes in shop doorways, or the less sticky
alfeñique.
Camping equipment Varoxi, Maldonado 651
y Oriente. Quality packs, repairs luggage.
Handicrafts Crafts stalls at Pasaje Ermita de la
Vírgen, off C Ambato, by the market. Tagua
(vegetable ivory made from palm nuts) crafts on
Maldonado entre Oriente y Espejo. Leather shops
on Rocafuerte entre Halflants y 16 de Diciembre.

Latino Shop, Ambato y Alfaro and 2 other locations. For T-shirts.

Las Orquídeas, Ambato Y Maldonado by the Parque Central and at *Hostal El Floresta*. Excellent selection of crafts, some guides and coffee-table books.

Recuerdos, on the road to Ambato. For painted balsa-wood birds. You can see crafts-people at work here.

Tucán Silver, Ambato esq Halflants. For jewellery.

▲ Activities and tours

Baños *p947, map p947*
A number of potentially hazardous activities are popular in Baños, including mountaineering, white water rafting, canyoning, canopying and bridge jumps. Safety standards vary greatly. There is seldom any recourse in the event of a mishap so you undertake these activities entirely at your own risk.

Canyoning Many agencies offer this sport, rates US$25-35.

Climbing and trekking There are countless possibilities for walking and nature observation near Baños and east towards Oriente. Baños operators offer climbing and trekking tours to several destinations. Remember that Tungurahua has been officially closed to climbers since 1999. There is nobody to stop you from entering the area, but the dangers of being hit by flying volcanic bombs are very real. Unless volcanic activity has completely ceased, do not be talked into climbing to the crater or summit.

Cycling Many places rent bikes, quality varies, rates from US$4 per day; check brakes and tyres, find out who has to pay for repairs, and insist on a helmet, puncture repair kit and pump. The following have good equipment:

Carrillo Hermanos, 16 de Diciembre y Martínez. Rents mountain bikes and motorcycles (reliable machines with helmets, US10 per hr).

Hotel Isla de Baños runs cycling tours.

Horse riding There are several places, but check their horses as not all are well cared for. Rates average US$5 per hr. The following have been recommended:

Angel Aldaz, Montalvo y JL Mera (on the road to the statue of the Virgin).

José and Two Dogs, Maldonado y Martínez, T274 0746. Flexible hours.

Hotel Isla de Baños, see above. Horses for rent; 3½ hrs with a guide and jeep transport costs US$25 per person, English and German spoken.

José & Two Dogs, Maldonado y Martínez, T274 0746. Flexible hours.

Ringo Horses, 12 de Noviembre y Martínez

(*Pizzeria Napolitano*). Nice horses, offers rides outside Baños.

"Puenting" Many operators offer this bungee-jumping-like activity from the bridges around Baños, US$10-15 per jump, heights and styles vary.

River rafting Fatal accidents have occurred, but not with the agencies listed here. The Chambo, Patate and Pastaza rivers are all heavily polluted.

Geotours, see below. Half-day US$25-30, US$50 for full day (rapids and calm water in the jungle).

Tour operators

There are many tour agencies in town, some with several offices, as well as 'independent' guides who seek out tourists on the street (the latter are generally not recommended). Quality varies considerably; to obtain a qualified guide and avoid unscrupulous operators, it is best to seek advice from other travellers who have recently returned from a tour. We have received some critical reports of tours out of Baños, but there are also highly respected and qualified operators here. In all cases, insist on a written contract. Most agencies and guides offer trips to the jungle (US$30-50 per day pp) and 2 day climbing trips to Cotopaxi (approximately US$130 pp) or Chimborazo (approximately US$140 pp). There are also volcano-watching, trekking and horse tours, in addition to the day-trips and sports mentioned above. The following agencies and guides have received positive recommendations but the list is not exhaustive and there are certainly others.

Córdova Tours, Maldonado y Espejo, T274 0923, www.cordovatours.banios.com. Tours on board their *chiva mocambo*, an open-sided bus to the waterfalls, Puyo, and night tours with music and volcano watching.

Deep Forest Adventure, no storefront, T09-837 4530 (mob), deepforestadventure@hotmail.com. Eloy Torres, speaks German, English and French, off-the-beaten-track destinations.

Expediciones Amazónicas, Oriente 11-68 y Halflants, T274 0506, www.amazonicas. banios.com. Run by Hernán and Dosto Varela, the latter is a recommended mountain guide.

Explorsierra, Halflants y Oriente, T274 0628, explorsierra1@hotmail.com. Guido Sánchez. Tours and equipment rental.

Geotours, Ambato y Halflants, next to Banco del Pichincha, T274 1344, www.geotoursecuador. com. Geovanny Romo offers various tours, and rafting.

Marberktour, Rocafuerte y Halflants, T274 1695, info_marberktour@yahoo.es. Arturo Ribera, speaks English and Dutch.

Rainforestur, Ambato 800 y Maldonado, T/F274 0743, www.rainforestur.com.ec. Run by Santiago

Herrera, guides are knowledgeable and environmentally conscious.

⊖ Transport

Baños *p947, map p947*
Bus City buses run throughout the day from Alfaro y Martínez east to Agoyán and from Rocafuerte by the market, west to El Salado and the zoo. To **Rio Verde** take any Puyo bus from Maldonado y Amazonas, opposite Baños bus station, 20 mins, US$0.50.

The long distance bus station is on the Ambato-Puyo road (Av Amazonas) a short way from the centre, and is the scene of vigorous volleyball games most afternoons. To/from **Quito**, via Ambato, US$3, 4 hrs, frequent service; going to Quito sit on the right for views of Cotopaxi, buy tickets early for weekends and holidays. To **Ambato**, 1 hr, US$1. To **Riobamba**, landslides caused by Tungurahua's volcanic activity damaged the direct Baños-Riobamba road, buses go via Ambato, 2 hrs, US$2. To **Latacunga**, 2 hrs, US$2. To **Puyo**, 1½ hrs, US$2; pack your luggage in plastic as all goes on top of the bus which drives through waterfalls; delays possible because of construction work. Sit on the right. You can cycle to Puyo and take the bus back

(passport check on the way). To **Tena**, 4 hrs, US$4. To **Misahuallí**, change at Tena, or at the Río Napo crossing, and **Macas**, 6 hrs, US$6 (sit on right).

⊕ Directory

Baños *p947, map p947*
Banks Banco del Austro, Halflants y Rocafuerte. Cooperativa de Ahorros de Ambato, Maldonado y Espejo. TCs, 2% commission. Mon-Fri 0900-1700. Don Pedro, Halflants y Martínez, hardware store, open weekends, 3% commission on TCs. Also exchanges Euros and other currencies. **Internet** Plenty of cyber cafés in town, prices US$2 per hr. **Language schools** Spanish lessons cost US$5 per hr. Baños Spanish Center, Oriente 820 y Julio Cañar, T274 0632, elizbasc@uio.satnet.net. Elizabeth Barrionuevo, English and German-speaking, flexible, salsa lessons, recommended. Instituto de Español Alternativo IDEA, Montalvo y Alfaro, T/F274 1315. International Spanish School, 16 de Diciembre y Espejo, T/F274 0612, Martha Vaca F. **Mayra's**, Montalvo y 16 de Diciembre T274 2850, www.mayraschool.com. Raíces, 16 de Diciembre y Pablo A Suárez, T274 0090, racefor@hotmail.com. **Post offices** Halflants y Ambato, across from Parque Central.

Riobamba and around

Guaranda and Riobamba are good bases for exploring the Sierra. Riobamba is the bigger of the two and is the starting point for what remains of the famous railway which used to go to Guayaquil. Because of their central location Riobamba and the surrounding province are known as 'Corazón de la Patria' – the heartland of Ecuador – and the city boasts the nickname 'La Sultana de Los Andes' in honour of lofty Mount Chimborazo.

Riobamba → *Phone code: 03. Colour map 11, grid B3. Population: 160,700. Altitude: 2,754 m.*
The capital of Chimborazo Province is built in the wide **Tapi Valley** and has broad streets and many ageing but impressive buildings. **Tourist office:** iTur ① *Av Daniel León Borja y Brasil, T294 7389, Mon-Fri 0800-1230, 1430-1800, Spanish only,* municipal information office. The **Ministerio de Turismo** ① *3 doors from iTur, in the Centro de Arte y Cultura, T/F294 1213, Mon-Fri 0800-1300, 1400-1700,* is very helpful and knowledgeable, English spoken.

The main plaza is **Parque Maldonado** around which are the **Santa Bárbara Cathedral**, the **Municipality** and several colonial buildings with arcades. The Cathedral has a beautiful colonial stone façade and an incongruously modern interior. Four blocks northeast of the railway station is the **Parque 21 de Abril**, named after the Batalla de Tapi, 21 April 1822, the city's independence from Spain. The park, better known as **La Loma de Quito**, affords an unobstructed view of Riobamba and Chimborazo, Carihuairazo, Tugurahua, El Altar and occasionally Sangay. It also has a colourful tile tableau of the history of Ecuador. The **Convento de la Concepción** ① *Orozco y España, entrance at Argentinos y J Larrea, T296 5212, Tue-Sat 0900-1200, 1500-1800, US$2, the guides are friendly and knowledgeable (tip expected),* is now a religious art museum. The priceless gold monstrance, Custodia de Riobamba Antigua, is the museum's greatest treasure, one of the richest of its kind in South America. **Museo del Banco Central** ① *Veloz y Montalvo, T296 5501, Mon-Fri 0900-1700, Sat 1000-1600, US$1,* has well displayed exhibits of archaeology and colonial art. **Museo de la Ciudad** ① *Primera Constituyente y Espejo, at Parque Maldonado, T295 1906, Mon-Fri*

0800-1230, 1430-1800, Sat 0900-1600, free, in a beautifully restored colonial building, has displays on regional national parks, temporary exhibits, and Friday evening concerts.

Riobamba is an important **market** centre where indigenous people from many communities congregate. Saturday is the main market day when the city fills with colourfully dressed *indígenas* from many different parts of the province of Chimborazo, each wearing their distinctive costume; trading overflows the markets and buying and selling go on all over town. Wednesday is a smaller market day. The 'tourist' market is in the small **Plaza de la Concepción or Plaza Roja** ① *Orozco y Colón, Sat and Wed only, 0800-1500*, south of the Convento de la Concepción (see above). It is a good place to buy local handicrafts and authentic Indian clothing. The main produce markets are **San Alfonso**, Argentinos y 5 de Junio, which on Saturday spills over into the nearby streets and also sells clothing, ceramics, baskets and hats, and **La Condamine** ① *Carabobo y Colombia, daily*, largest market on Fridays. Other markets in the colonial centre are **San Francisco** and **La Merced**, near the churches of the same name.

Guano is a carpet-weaving, sisal and leather working town 8 km north of Riobamba. Many shops sell rugs and you can arrange to have these woven to your own design. Buses leave from the Mercado Dávalos, García Moreno y New York, every 20 minutes, US$0.25, last bus returns to Riobamba at 1800. Taxi US$4.

Guaranda → *Phone code: 03. Colour map 11, grid B3. Population: 48,500. Altitude: 2,650 m.*

This quaint town, capital of Bolívar province, proudly calls itself 'the Rome of Ecuador' because it is built on seven hills. There are fine views of the mountains all around. Locals traditionally take an evening stroll in the palm-fringed main plaza, **Parque Libertador Simón Bolívar**, around which are the Municipal buildings and a large stone **Cathedral**. Although not on the tourist trail, there are many sights worth visiting in the province, for which Guaranda is the ideal base. Of particular interest is the highland town of **Salinas**, with its community development project (good cheeses), as well as the *subtrópico* region, the lowlands stretching west towards the coast. Towering over the city, on one of the hills, is an impressive statue of **El Indio Guaranga**, a local Indian leader after whom the city may have been named; museum (free), art gallery and auditorium. Take a taxi (US$1); or take a 'Guanujo' bus to the stadium, walk past the stadium to Av La Prensa and follow it till you reach the first turning on the right (10 minutes' walk).

Market days are Friday (till 1200) and Saturday (larger), when many indigenous people in typical dress trade at the market complex at the east end of Calle Azuay, by Plaza 15 de Mayo (9 de Abril y Maldonado), and at Plaza Roja (Avenida Gen Enríquez). Carnival in Guaranda is among the best known in the country. **Tourist office**: Oficina Municipal de Información Turística ① *García Moreno entre 7 de Mayo y Convención de 1884, Mon-Fri 0800-1200, 1400-1800*. Information, maps, guided tours, horse riding and camping, Spanish only.

Reserva Faunística Chimborazo → *See also Riobamba Tour operators.*

① *US$10 entrance fee*. The most outstanding features of this reserve, created to protect the camelids (vicuñas, alpacas and llamas) which were re-introduced here, are the beautiful snow-capped volcano of **Chimborazo** and its neighbour **Carihuairazo**. Chimborazo, inactive, is the highest peak in Ecuador (6,310 m), while Carihuairazo, 5,020 m, is dwarfed by its neighbour. Day visitors can enjoy lovely views, a glimpse of the handsome vicuñas and the rarefied air above 4,800 m. There are great opportunities for trekking on the eastern slopes and of course climbing Ecuador's highest peak. Horse riding tours are offered along the Mocha Valley between the two peaks and downhill cycling from Chimborazo is popular. Many agencies run tours here.

To the west of the reserve runs the Vía del Arenal which joins San Juan, along the Riobamba-Guaranda road, with Cruce del Arenal on the Ambato-Guaranda road. A turn-off from this road leads to the main park entrance and beyond to the **Refugio Hermanos Carrel**, a shelter at 4,800 m. The access from Riobamba (51 km, paved to the park entrance) is very beautiful. Along the Vía del Arenal past San Juan are a couple of small native communities which grow a few crops and raise llamas and alpacas. The *arenal* is a large sandy plateau at about 4,400 m, to the west of Chimborazo, just below the main park entrance. It can be a harsh, windy place, but it is also very beautiful; take the time to admire the tiny flowers which grow here. This is the best place to see vicuñas, which hang around either in family groups, one male and its harem, or lone males which have been expelled from the group.

The railway from the coast to the Sierra

The spectacular 464-km railway line (1.067 m gauge), which was opened in 1908, passes through 87 km of delta lands and then, in 80 km, climbs to 3,238 m. At Urbina on the summit, it reaches 3,609 m, then falls and rises before reaching the Quito plateau at 2,857 m.

Unfortunately, in 1997/98 El Niño damaged the lowland section between Durán and Bucay; it is unlikely this will be reopened. Trains do run on the Bucay-Huigra section and connection with the line's greatest achievements, the Alausí loop and the Devil's Nose double zigzag (including two V switchbacks), was expected in 2007. Alausí and the Devil's Nose are on the part of the line most regularly open to trains, Sibambe to Riobamba. **Sibambe**, the current turning point of the train, has no hotels or bus service, so you must return by train to Alausí. Shortly after leaving Sibambe the train starts climbing the famous **Nariz del Diablo** (Devil's Nose), a perpendicular ridge rising in the gorge of the Chanchán to a height of 305 m. This almost insurmountable engineering obstacle was finally conquered when a series of switchbacks was built on a 5½% grade.

Next comes **Alausí**. After crossing the 120 m long Shucos bridge, the train pulls into **Palmira**, on the crest of the first range of the Andes crossed by the railway. One by one the great snow-capped volcanoes begin to appear: Chimborazo, Carihuairazo, Altar and the burning heads of Tungurahua and Sangay, all seeming very close because of the clear air.

Climbing Chimborazo At 6,310 m, this is a difficult climb owing to the altitude. No-one without mountaineering experience should attempt the climb, and rope, ice-axe and crampons must be used. It is essential to have at least one week's acclimatization above 3,000 m. The best seasons are December and June-September. Ice pinnacles, *penitentes*, sometimes prevent climbers reaching the main, Whymper summit.

The Devil's Nose Train

Train service is very limited, but the most spectacular part of the trip – the **Devil's Nose** and **Alausí Loop** – can still be experienced. The train usually leaves **Riobamba** three days a week (see Transport, below) and goes via **Alausí** to **Sibambe** before returning to Alausí. Riding on the roof is fun, but hang on tight and remember that it's very chilly early in the morning. It's also a good idea to sit in the middle on the roof to avoid getting covered in oil from the exhaust. The train service is subject to frequent disruptions and timetables are always changing, best enquire locally about current schedules. Also lock all luggage, even side pockets, as theft is common. The train is popular, especially at weekends and public holidays, so you'll have to queue early. The railway administration office is on Espejo, next to the Post Office, where information is available during office hours, T296 0115, or at the station itself T296 1909. On the days when the train is not running, you can still experience the Devil's Nose and the scenery, by walking along the tracks down from Alausí; a pleasant day trip. Horse rides in the area are also offered.

Alausí → *Phone code: 03. Colour map 11, grid B3. Population: 9,400. Altitude: 2,350 m.*

This is the station where many passengers join the train for the amazing descent over *La Nariz de Diablo* to Sibambe. There is a Sunday market, in the plaza by the church, just up the hill from the station; and a *Fiesta de San Pedro* on 29 June.

Sangay National Park

Riobamba provides access to the central highland region of **Parque Nacional Sangay** *US$10*, a beautiful wilderness area with excellent opportunities for trekking and climbing. A controversial new road runs from **Guamote**, a quiet, mainly indigenous town, which comes to life during its colourful Thursday market, to Macas in the Oriente, cutting through Parque Nacional Sangay.

Now complete, it makes a spectacular ride, with five-hour bus services Riobamba-Macas. Deforestation and colonization of the area have begun. Sangay is an active volcano; **South American Explorers** has information on organizing a trip; equipment, helmet, etc, and guide essential. This seven-day trek is tough: expect long, hard days of walking and severe weather. Protection against falling stones is vital. With a little coaching a *mecánica* can make shields, arm loops welded to an oil drum top. December/January is a good time to climb Sangay. Porters can be hired in the access towns of Alao (the *hacienda* here accepts guests and rents horses) and Guargualla. Guargualla also has a community tourism project with accommodation and native guides. For information go to the **Ministry of the Environment,** Avenida 9 de Octubre y Quinta Macají, at the western edge of Riobamba, north of the roundabout at the end of Avenida Isabel de Godin, T296 3779; the office is only open Monday-Friday 0800-1300, 1400-1700. From town take city bus San Gerardo-El Batán.

Also in Sangay National Park is the beautiful **El Altar** volcano, whose crater is surrounded by nine summits. The most popular route begins beyond Candelaria at Hacienda Releche.

● Sleeping

Riobamba *p952, map p956*
Many of the upmarket hotels are out of town.
B Abraspungu, Km 3 on the road to Guano, T294 0820, abraspungo@andinanet.net. Beautiful house in country setting, comfortable, good service, excellent restaurant.
B El Troje, 4½ km on the road to Chambo, T296 0826, www.eltroje.com. Good restaurant, pool and sauna, internet, nice rooms, good views.
B La Andaluza, 16 km north of Riobamba along the Panamericana, T294 9370. Includes breakfast, good restaurant, nice rooms in old hacienda, with heaters and roaring fireplaces, lovely views, good walking.
B Zeus, Av Daniel L Borja 41-29, T296 8036, www.hotelzeus.com.ec. Restaurant, jacuzzi, gym, bathtubs with views of Chimborazo, parking. Recommended.
C Montecarlo, Av 10 de Agosto 25-41 entre García Moreno y España, T296 0557. Includes breakfast, nice house in colonial style, restaurant, parking, central.
C Rincón Alemán, Remigio Romero y Alfredo Pareja, Ciudadela Arupos del Norte, T260 3540, www.rincon-aleman.com. Family-run hotel in a quiet residential area. Includes breakfast, laundry and cooking facilities, parking, garden, sauna, fitness room, fireplace, German spoken. Recommended.
D La Estación, Unidad Nacional 29-15 y Carabobo, T295 5226. A nicely refurbished building, convenient for the train station, good beds, sitting rooms, terrace with hammocks and good views, restaurant, good value.
E El Libertador, Av Daniel L Borja 29-22 y Carabobo, across from the train station, T294 7393. Modern hotel with comfortable, ample rooms, hot water, opened in 2006.
E Oasis, Veloz 15-32 y Almagro, T296 1210. Small, pleasant, family-run, quiet location, laundry facilities, some rooms with kitchen and fridge, parking, nice garden, pick-up service from the Terminal. Recommended.

E Tren Dorado, Carabobo 22-35 y 10 de Agosto, T/F296 4890, htrendorado@hotmail.com. Convenient for the train station, early breakfast available, restaurant serves good vegetarian lunch, reliable hot water, modern, nice large rooms, very good value. Recommended.
E Whymper, Av Miguel Angel León 23-10 y Primera Constituyente, T296 4575. Hot water, parking, spacious rooms, a bit rundown.
E-F Los Shyris, Rocafuerte 21-60 y 10 de Agosto, T/F296 0323, hshyris@yahoo.com. Cheaper without bath, hot water 0600-1000 and 1800-2200, internet, laundry facilities, good rooms, service, and value. Rooms at the back are quieter.

Guaranda *p953*
C La Colina, Av Guayaquil 117, on road to Ambato, T/F298 0666. Bright, attractive rooms, lovely views, restful, includes breakfast, best in town but restaurant mediocre and expensive (good for Sun lunch though), covered pool.
D Bolívar, Sucre 704 y Rocafuerte, T298 0547. Simple but pleasant, small courtyard, good restaurant (closed Sun) serving good value set meals, breakfast, has a nice display of Andean musical instruments, parking.
D-E Cochabamba, García Moreno y 7 de Mayo, T298 1958, vviteriv@gu.pro.ec. A bit faded but good service, best restaurant in town, parking.
E Hostal de Las Flores, Pichincha 402 y Rocafurete, T298 4396. Renovated colonial house with covered courtyard, well-decorated rooms, hot water.
E Márquez, 10 de Agosto y Eloy Alfaro, T298 1306, F298 1101. Pleasant, family atmosphere, parking, a bit old fashioned but good value.
E-G Acapulco, 10 de Agosto y 9 de Abril, T298 1953. Basic, small rooms, restaurant, cheaper with shared bath.

Alausí p954

A **Posada de las Nubes**, 11 km from Alausí, on
the north side of the Río Chanchán, pick-up taxi
from Alausí US$7, T09-701 4613, 03-293 0535
(Alausí). A converted hacienda house at 2,600 m,
7 rooms, some with bath, full board, arranges
tours, cloud forest nearby. Reservations required.

E **San Pedro**, 5 de junio y 9 de Octubre, T293
0086, hostalsanpedro@hotmail.com. Modern
hotel with comfortable rooms, cheaper in older
section, electric shower, parking, best value in
town. Restaurant downstairs serves decent set
meals.

E-F **Europa**, 5 de Julio y Orozco, T293 0200.
Rooms vary from functional to comfortable, ,
cheaper with shared bath, hot water, restaurant,
ample parking.

E-F **Panamericano**, 5 de Junio y 9 de Octubre,
near the bus stop, T293 0278. Cheap restaurant,
rooms cheaper without bath, hot showers, quiet
at the back.

F **Tequendama**, 5 de Junio 152, T293 0123.
Shared bath, electric shower, basic but clean and
welcoming.

Sangay National Park p954

D **Hostal Capac Urcu**, at Hacienda Releche, just
outside the village, T294 9761, 296 0848
(Riobamba). Pleasant and relaxing small working
hacienda. Use of kitchen (US$6) or good meals
prepared on request, rents horses for the trek to
Collanes, US$8 per horse each way, plus US$8 per
muleteer. Also runs the E per person refugio at
Collanes, by the crater of El Altar: thatched-roof

rustic shelters, use of kitchen with gas stove and all
utensils US$6. No hot water or blankets, take a
warm sleeping bag. Recommended.

D-E **Inti Sisa**, Vargas Torres y García Moreno,
Guamote, T03-291 6529, www.intisisa.org. A nice
hostel, part of a community development
project, run by Belgian and Dutch volunteers,
meals available, most rooms with bath, cheaper
in dorm, dining room and communal area with
fireplace, horse riding and cycling tours to
highland villages, reservations necessary.

🍴 Eating

Riobamba p952, map p956

Most places closed after 2100 and on Sun.

🍴🍴🍴 **El Delirio**, Primera Constituyente 2816 y
Rocafuerte (Bolívar stayed in this house). Tue-Sun
1200-2130. Ecuadorean and international dishes,
popular with tour groups and overpriced.

🍴🍴 **Bonny**, Villarroel 1558 y Almagro. Daily
1000-2000. Cheap set meals and very good
seafood (mid-range, à la carte), very popular.

🍴🍴 **Cabaña Montecarlo**, García Moreno 21-40 y 10
de Agosto, Tue-Sat 1200-2100, Sun-Mon
1200-1500. Good value set lunch, pricier à la carte,
good service, large portions, 'old Riobamba'
atmosphere, popular with locals.

🍴🍴 **Cafetería Montecarlo**, 10 de Agosto 25-45 y
García Moreno. 0700-1200, 1600-2200 (0500
breakfast can be arranged before train ride).
Ecuadorean and international, good breakfasts,
snacks and complete meals, nice atmosphere.

🍴🍴 **La Gran Havana**, Daniel León Borja 42-52

Riobamba

Sleeping 😴
El Libertador 8
La Estación 7
Los Shyris 4
Montecarlo 5

Oasis 11
Tren Dorado 8
Whymper 9
Zeus 10

Eating 🍴
Bonny 3
Cabaña
  Montecarlo 2
Café VIP 11

Cafetería
  Montecarlo 2
El Delirio 4
La Fogata 6
La Gran Havana 1

0 metres 100
0 yards 100

y Duchicela, daily 1100-1600. Economical set lunch, very good Cuban and international food à la carte.

Mónaco Pizzería, Diego Ibarra y Duchicela, Mon-Tue 1530-2200, Wed-Fri 1400-2200, Sat-Sun 1200-2300. Delicious pizza and pasta, nice salads, very good food, service and value.

Parrillada de Fausto, Uruguay 2038 y Av Daniel L Borja. Good meat and fish, nice atmosphere (closed 1500-1800).

Sierra Nevada, Primera Constituyente y Rocafuerte, Mon-Sat 0800-2200, Sun 1130-1600. Excellent value set lunch, vegetarian on request. Nice atmosphere. Recommended.

Café VIP, Rocafuerte entre 10 de Agosto y Primera Constituyente, Mon-Fri 1200-1500, 1800-2200, Thu until 0100. Economical vegetarian set lunch, café in the evening, live music on Thu.

La Fogata, Av Daniel León Borja y Carabobo, opposite the train station, daily 0700-2200. Good economical Ecuadorean food, set meals and breakfast.

Natural Food, Tarqui entre Veloz y Primera Constituyente, Mon-Sat 1200-1430. Set meals only, vegetarian available.

Cafés and bakeries

Helados de Paila, Espejo y 10 de Agosto. Homemade ice cream, café, sweets, popular.
La Abuela Rosa, Brasil y Esmeraldas, Tue-Sat 1600-2100. Cafetería in grandmother's house serving typical Ecuadorean snacks. Nice atmosphere and good service.

La Vienesa, Larrea 2116 y Guayaquil and Av Daniel León Borja y Brasil. A Riobamba tradition, try their fresh *palanquetas* (buns).
Pan Van, 10 de Agosto y España, also Daniel Borja y Epiclachima. Excellent quality and variety.
Puro Café, Pichincha 21-37 y 10 de Agosto, Mon-Sat 0900-1330, 1530-2130. Very nice small European-style coffee shop, good coffee and sandwiches, a good place to hang out.

Guaranda p953

See also Sleeping. Most places closed on Sun.
La Bohemia, Convención de 1884 y 10 de Agosto, Mon-Sat 0800-2100. Very good Ecuadorean set meals and international à la carte, nice décor, very popular. Recommended.
Pizza Buon Giorno, Sucre at Parque Bolívar, Tue-Sun 1200-2200. Pizza and salads.
La Estancia, García Moreno y Sucre. Good quality and value set meals and à la carte, nicely decorated, pleasant atmosphere.
Mentuccia, Cándido Rada y Gen Enríquez, near Plaza Roja, Mon-Sat 1100-2130. Small simple Italian restaurant.

Cafés

Cafetería 7 Santos, Convención de 1884 y Olmedo, Mon-Sat 0900-2200. Pleasant café and bar with an open courtyard. Good coffee and snacks, fair prices, nicely decorated, fireplace, live music at weekends, popular meeting place.
Juad's, Convención de 1884 y Azuay, closed 1300-1500 and Sun. Very good, popular, cappuccino, hot chocolate, sandwiches, fruit salad, pastries, go early. Recommended.

Bars and clubs

Riobamba p952, map p956

Gens-Chop Bar Av Daniel L Borja 42-17 y Duchicela. Bar, good music and sport videos, open daily, popular. Recommended.
Romeo Bar, Vargas Torres y Av Daniel León Borja, US$2 cover. Popular, nice bar and club, from Latin to Rythym and Blues, pleasant sitting area on the second floor.
San Valentín, Av D L Borja y Vargas Torres. Good Mexican dishes, pizza, hamburgers and other snacks, bar and disco with a dance floor large enough for 2-3 couples. Very popular.
Vieja Guardia Av Flor 40-43 y Av Zambrano. Bar and open air disco, US$1 cover.

Entertainment

Riobamba p952, map p956

Casa de la Cultura, 10 de Agosto y Rocafuerte, T296 0219. Sometimes has a good *peña* on Thu-Sat evenings.

Mónaco Pizzería **7**
Natural Food **5**
Parrillada de Fausto **8**
Puro Café **10**
Sierra Nevada **9**

❀ Festivals and events

Riobamba *p952, map p956*
Fiesta del Niño Rey de Reyes, with street parades, music and dancing, starts in Dec and culminates on **6 Jan**. Around **21 Apr** there are independence celebrations lasting several days, hotel prices rise. **29 Jun Fiestas Patronales** in honour of San Pedro. **11 Nov** is the festival to celebrate the first attempt at independence from Spain.

○ Shopping

Riobamba *p952, map p956*
Camping gear Some of the tour operators hire camping and climbing gear. **Hobby Sport**, 10 de Agosto y Rocafuerte. Sleeping bags, tents, fishing supplies. **Protección Industrial**, Rocafuerte 24-51 y Orozco, T296 3017. For waterproof ponchos and suits, fishing supplies, ropes.

Handicrafts Crafts are sold at the Plaza Roja on Wed and Sat (see above). Nice tagua carvings and other crafts are on sale at *Alta Montaña* (see Tour operators below). **Almacén Cacha**, Orozco next to the Plaza Roja. A co-operative of native people from the Cacha area, sells woven bags, wool sweaters, other crafts and honey, good value (closed Sun-Mon). **Artesanías Ecuador**, Carabobo y 10 de Agosto. Good selection of crafts, ceramics, wood, tagua.

Supermarkets Camari, Av Daniel León Borja y Lavalle. Small crafts section, woollens. **La Ibérica**, Av Daniel L Borja 37-62.

▲▲ Activities and tours

Riobamba and around *p952*
Mountain biking Pro Bici, at Primera Constituyente 23-40 or 23-51 y Larrea, T295 1759, www.probici.com. Run by guide and mechanic, Galo Brito. Bike trips and rental, guided tours with support vehicle, equipment, US$35 pp per day, excluding meals and overnight stays. Also **Alta Montaña** and **Julio Verne** (see Tour operators), rental US$10 per day; tours including transport, guide, meals, US$35 per day.

Tour operators
Most companies offer climbing trips (from US$150 per person for 2 days) and trekking (from US$50 per person per day). **Note** Many hotels offer tours, not all are run by qualified guides. **Alta Montaña**, Av Daniel L Borja 35-17 y Diego Ibarra, T294 2215, www.bikingspirit.com. Trekking, climbing, cycling, birdwatching, photography and horse riding tours in mountains and jungle,

transport, equipment rental, English spoken. Recommended.
Andes Trek, Colón 22-25 y 10 de Agosto, T294 0964, www.andes-trek.com. Climbing, trekking and mountain biking tours, transport, equipment rental.
Expediciones Andinas, Vía a Guano, Km 3, across from *Hotel Abraspungo*, T296 4915, www.expediciones-andinas.com. Climbing expeditions, operate Chimborazo Base Camp on south flank of mountain. Cater for groups, contact well in advance, German spoken, run by Marco Cruz, a certified guide of the *German Alpine Club*. Recommended.
Julio Verne, El Espectador 22-25 y Daniel L Borja, 2 blocks from the train station, T296 3436, www.julioverne-travel.com. Climbing, trekking, cycling, jungle and Galápagos trips, transport to mountains, equipment rental, Ecuadorean-Dutch-run, uses official guides. Recommended.
Metropolitan Touring, Lavalle y Veloz, T296 9600, www.metropolitan-touring.com. Rail tours, air tickets, DHL and Western Union rep.
Veloz Coronado, Chile 33-21 y Francia, T296 0916 (call after 1900). Enrique Veloz Coronado, a recognized climber, is very helpful, his sons are also guides and work with him.

⊖ Transport

Riobamba *p952, map p956*
Bus Terminal Terrestre on Epiclachima y Av Daniel L Borja for buses to Quito, Guayaquil, Ambato, etc. Buses from Baños and the Oriente arrive at the Terminal Oriental, Espejo y Córdovez. Taxi from one terminal to another, US$1. **Quito**, US$4, 4 hrs, about every 30 mins. To **Guaranda**, US$2, 2 hrs; the road is paved to San Juan, from where there are 2 scenic routes: via Gallo Rumi, unpaved, or via the Arenal, partly paved (some *Flota Bolívar* buses take this route), sit on the right for the beautiful views on either route. To **Ambato**, US$1, 1 hr, sit on the right. To **Alausí**, see below. To **Cuenca**, 6 a day via Alausí, 6 hrs, US$6. This road is paved but landslides are a constant hazard and the road is often under repair. To **Guayaquil**, frequent service, US$5, 5 hrs, the trip is really spectacular for the first 2 hrs. To **Baños**, see above. To **Puyo**, also via Ambato, US$4, 4 hrs direct. To **Macas** 5 hrs, US$5.

Guaranda *p953*
Bus Terminal at Eliza Mariño Carvajal, on road to Riobamba and Babahoyo; if you are staying in town get off closer to the centre. Many daily buses to: **Ambato**, US$2, 2 hrs. **Riobamba**, see above. **Babahoyo**, US$3, 3 hrs, beautiful ride. **Guayaquil**, US$4, 5 hrs. **Quito**, 3 companies run almost 20 daily services, US$5, 5 hrs.

Reserva Faunística Chimborazo *p953*
There are no buses that will take you to the shelters. You can arrange transport with a tour operator or taxi from Riobamba (about US$25 one way). You can also take a bus travelling between Riobamba and **Guaranda** which goes on the Vía del Arenal (**Flota Bolívar** 8 daily, 0700-1800, check that it is taking this route; from Riobamba US$0.90, 1 hr), alight at the turn-off for the refuges and walk the remaining steep 5 km to the first shelter. To the eastern slopes, there are trekking tours, arrange transport from an agency or take a bus between Riobamba and **Ambato**, get off at the turnoff for Posada La Estación and Urbina.

The Devil's Nose Train *p954*
The train usually leaves **Riobamba** on Wed, Fri and Sun at 0700, arrives in **Alausí** around 1100, reaches **Sibambe** about 1130-1200, and returns to Alausí by 1330-1400. From Riobamba to Sibambe and back to Alausí costs US$11; Alausí-Sibambe-Alausí US$7.80; Alausí back to Riobamba US$3.40. Tickets go on sale the day before departure from 1500-1600 on, or the same morning at 0600, seats are not numbered, best arrive early. In **Alausí** tickets go on sale around 0930. To check if it's running, T293 0126. At times when the tracks are in poor shape due to rain, a motorized rail-car (*autoferro*) runs as a replacement for the longer train. (See box, page 954.) **Metropolitan Touring** operates a private *autoferro* on the Riobamba-Sibambe route. They require a minimum number of passengers but will run any day and time convenient to the group. Approximately US$120 pp.

The continuation of the line from Alausí to **Huigra** was expected to be running with the *autoferro* in high season, 2007, and the line from Huigra to **Bucay** has a tourist service on Sat, Sun and holidays.

Alausí *p954*
Bus From **Riobamba**, 1½ hrs, US$1.50, 84 km. To **Quito**, from 0600 onwards, about 8 a day, 5 hrs, US$5; often have to change in Riobamba. To **Cuenca**, 4 hrs, US$5. To **Ambato** hourly, 3 hrs, US$3. To **Guayaquil**, 4 a day, 4 hrs, US$5. **Coop Patria**. Colombia y Orozco, 3 blocks up from the main street; **Trans Alausí**, 5 de Junio y Loza. Many through buses don't go into town, but have to be caught on the highway.

Sangay National Park *p954*
The most common access point for climbing Volcán Sangay is the town of **Alao**. Buses leave Riobamba for Alao from Parque La Dolorosa, Puruhá y Primera Constituyente, Mon-Sat 0530, 0630 and hourly 1145-1845, Sun 0630, US$1, 1½ hrs. All departure times approximate, be there at least 1 hr beforehand and wait. From the Terminal Oriental in Riobamba, to **Candelaria**, Mon-Sat 0630, 1215 and 1700, Sun 0630; get there early, sometimes they leave ahead of schedule, US$1, 1½ hrs.

⊙ Directory

Riobamba *p952, map p956*
Banks Banco del Pacífico, Av D L Borja y Zambrano. **Produbacno**, Veloz y Gracía Moreno. **Internet** Many places, rates about US$1 per hr. **Post offices** 10 de Agosto y Espejo. **Useful addresses** Immigration, Av Leopoldo Freire (Av de la Policía) by the Police station, Barrio Pucará, T296 4697.

Guaranda *p953*
Banks Banco del Pichincha, Azuay y 7 de Mayo, ATM only. **Internet** Compumás, 10 de Agosto y 7 de Mayo. **Tortilla Net**, 10 de Agostoy Sucre, pleasant cafetería. Price US$1. **Post offices** Azuay y Pichincha. **Useful addresses** Immigration, Guayaquil y Manabí 231, T298 0108.

Cuenca and around

→ *Phone code: 07. Colour map 11, grid C3. Pop: 340,000. Altitude 2,530 m.*
Founded in 1557 on the site of the Inca settlement of Tomebamba, much of Cuenca's colonial air has been preserved, with many of its old buildings recently renovated. Its cobblestone streets, flowering plazas and whitewashed buildings with old wooden doors and ironwork balconies make it a pleasure to explore. The climate is spring-like, but the nights are chilly. In 1999 Cuenca was designated a UNESCO World Heritage Site.

Ins and outs
Getting there The **Terminal Terrestre** is on Avenida España, 20 minutes' walk northeast of the centre, T282 7061. The **airport** is five minutes' walk from the Terminal Terrestre, T286 2203. Both can be reached by city bus. The **terminal for local buses** in the province is at the

Feria Libre on Avenida Las Américas. Many city buses pass here. ▸▸ *For more detailed information see Transport, page 967.*

Getting around The city is bounded by the Río Machángara to the north and the Ríos Yanuncay and Tarqui to the south. The Río Tomebamba separates the colonial heart from the newer districts to the south. Avenida Las Américas is a ring road around the city and the new multi-lane highway bypasses the city to the south.

Tourist offices Ministerio de Turismo ① *Sucre y Benigno Malo, on Parque Calderón next to the municipio, T282 2058, helpful. Mon-Fri, 0830-1700.* Cámara de Turismo ① *the Terminal Terrestre, T286 8482. Mon-Sat 0830-1200, 1230-1800.*

Safety Though safer than Quito or Guayaquil, routine precautions are advised. The city centre is deserted and unsafe after 2300. The areas around El Puente Roto (south end of Vargas Machuca), Cruz del Vado (south end of Juan Montalvo), around the Terminal Terrestre and the market areas, especially Mercado 9 de Octubre, call for caution after dark.

Sights

On the main plaza, **Parque Abdón Calderón**, are the Old Cathedral, **El Sagrario**, begun in 1557, and the immense 'New' **Catedral de la Inmaculada**, started in 1885. It contains a famous crowned image of the Virgin, a beautiful altar and an exceptional play of light and shade through modern stained glass. Other churches which deserve a visit are **San Blas**, **San Francisco** and **Santo Domingo**. Many churches are open at irregular hours only and for services. The church of **El Carmen de la Asunción**, close to the southwest corner of La Inmaculada, has a flower market in the tiny **Plazoleta El Carmen** in front. There is a colourful daily market in **Plaza Rotary** where pottery, clothes, guinea pigs and local produce, especially baskets, are sold. Thursday is the busiest.

Museo del Monasterio de las Conceptas ① *Hermano Miguel 6-33 entre Pdte Córdova y Juan Jaramillo, T283 0625. Mon-Fri 0900-1730, Sat and holidays 1000-1300, US$2.50,* in a cloistered convent founded in 1599, houses a well displayed collection of religious and folk art, in addition to an extensive collection of lithographs by Guayasamín.

The **Banco Central 'Pumapungo'** ① *C Larga y Huayna Capac, entrance is on the far left of the building, T283 1255, Mon-Fri 0900-1800, Sat 0900-1300, US$3,* is a museum complex on the edge of the colonial city at the actual site of Tomebamba excavations. It has a **Parque Arqueológico Pumapungo**. The **Museo Arqueológico** section contains all the Cañari and Inca remains and artifacts found at this site. Other halls in the premises house the **Museo Etnográfico**, with information on different Ecuadorean cultures, including a special collection of *tsantsas* (shrunken heads from Oriente), the **Museo de Arte Religioso**, the **Museo Numismático** and temporary exhibits. There are also book and music libraries, free cultural videos and music events. **Museo de las Culturas Aborígenes** ① *Larga 5-24 y Hermano Miguel, T283 9181, Mon-Fri 0830-1800, Sat 0900-1400, US$2; guided tours in English, Spanish and French,* has a good private collection of pre-Columbian archaeology. It is the private collection of Dr J Cordero López. The **Museo Remigio Crespo Toral** ① *C Larga 7-07 y Borrero,* has various collections housed in a restored mansion, nice café in basement.

On Plaza San Sebastián is **Museo Municipal de Arte Moderno** ① *Sucre 1527 y Talbot, T282 0638, mcmartem@etapanet.net, Mon-Fri 0830-1300, 1500-1830, Sat-Sun 0900-1300, free,* has a permanent contemporary art collection and art library. It holds a biennial international painting competition and other cultural activities. Across the river from the Museo del Banco Central, the **Museo de Artes de Fuego** ① *Las Herrerías y 10 de Agosto, Mon-Fri, except for lunchtime, and Sat morning.* has a display of wrought iron work and pottery. It is housed in a beautifully restored old building. Also south of city, on Avenida Fray Vicente Solano, beyond the football stadium, is **Turi church, orphanage and mirador**. It's a two-hour walk or take a taxi; a tiled panorama explains the magnificent views.

There are sulphur baths at **Baños**, with a domed, blue church in a delightful landscape, 5 km southwest of Cuenca. These are the hottest commercial baths in Ecuador. Above *Hostería Durán* (see Sleeping) are three separate complexes of warm baths, *Merchan, Rodas* and *Durán* ① *dawn till 2100 or 2200, US$3.50.* The latter is by far the largest and best maintained, there are numerous hot pools and tubs and steam baths.

Ingapirca → *Colour map 1a, grid B3.*
① *Daily 0800-1800, US$6, including museum and guided tour in Spanish; bags can be stored. A small café serves cheap set lunches.*

Ecuador's most important Inca ruin, at 3,160 m, lies 8½ km east of the colonial town of **Cañar** (hostales in **E-F** range, www.imcanar.gov.ec). Access is from Cañar or **El Tambo**. The Inca Huayna Capac took over the site from the conquered Cañaris when his empire expanded North into Ecuador in the third quarter of the 15th century. Ingapirca was strategically placed on the Royal Highway that ran from Cuzco to Quito and soldiers may have been stationed there. The site shows typical imperial Cuzco-style architecture, such as tightly fitting stonework and trapezoidal doorways. The central structure may have been a solar observatory. Nearby is a throne cut into the rock, the **Sillón del Inga** (Inca's Chair) and the **Ingachugana**, a large rock with carved channels. A 10 minute walk away from the site is the **Cara del Inca**, or 'face of the Inca', an immense natural formation in the rock looking over the landscape. On Friday there is an interesting indigenous market at Ingapirca village. There is a good co-operative craft shop next to the church. There is a beautiful four-hour, 16-km walk from Ingapirca to Cañar. The start of the road is clearly signposted, along the main street; take water.

Inca Trail to Ingapirca

The three-day hike to Ingapirca starts at **Achupallas**, 25 km from Alausí. The walk is covered by three 1:50,000 *IGM* sheets, Alausí, Juncal and Cañar. The Juncal sheet is most important, the name Ingapirca does not appear on the latter, you may have to ask directions near the end. Also take a compass. Good camping equipment is essential. Take all food and drink with you as there is nothing along the way. A shop in Achupallas sells basic foodstuffs. There are persistent beggars the length of the hike, especially children. Tour operators in Riobamba and Cuenca offer this trek for about US$200-250 per person, three days, everything included.

Northeast of Cuenca

Northeast of Cuenca, on the new road to Méndez in the Oriente, is **Paute**, with a pleasant park and modern church. **Gualaceo** is a thriving, modern town set in beautiful landscape, with a charming plaza and Sunday market. There is a small **Museo Artesanal** at the entrance to the Parador Turístico ①*Tue-Sun 0800-1800, free,* with good displays about Panama hats and *macanas,* Ikat-dyed shawls. The **iTur** ① *at the Municipio, Gran Colombia y 3 de Noviembre, Parque Central, T225 5131, Mon-Fri 0800-1300, 1400-1700* is very helpful, Spanish only.

South of Gualaceo is **Chordeleg**, a touristy village famous for its crafts in wood, silver and gold filigree, pottery and panama hats. At the Municipio is the **Centro de Interpretación** ① *C 23 de Enero, Mon-Fri 0800-1300, 1400-1700,* an exhibition hall with fascinating local textiles, ceramics and straw work, some of which are on sale at reasonable prices. Watch out for fake jewellery: *Joyería Dorita* and *Joyería Puerto del Sol,* on Juan B Cobos y Eloy Alfaro have been recommended. It's a good uphill walk from Gualaceo to Chordeleg, and a pleasant hour downhill in the other direction. South of Gualaceo, 83 km from Cuenca, **Sígsig**, an authentic highland town where women can be seen weaving hats 'on the move'. It has a fine Sunday market and two *residenciales.*

Parque Nacional Cajas

① *Park office at Presidente Córdova y Luis Cordero, Edif Morejón, p 2, T282 9853, www.etapa.com.ec, Mon-Fri 0800-1300, 1500-1800. Park entry is US$10, payable at the entrance gates at Laguna Toreadora, Laguna Llaviuco or Soldados.*

Northwest of Cuenca, Cajas is a 29,000 ha national park with over 230 lakes. Near the entrance is an altar and pilgrim area where a teenager saw 'Our Lady of the Faith' in 1988. The *páramo* vegetation, such as chuquiragua and lupin, is beautiful and contains interesting wildlife. Cajas is very rich in birdlife; 125 species have been identified, including the condor and many varieties of hummingbird (the violet-tailed metaltail is endemic to this area). On the lakes are andean gulls, speckled teal and yellow-billed pintails. On a clear morning the views are superb, even to Chimborazo, some 300 km away.

There are two access roads. The paved road from Cuenca to Guayaquil via Molleturo goes through the northern section and is the main route for Laguna Toreadora, the visitors' centre and Laguna Llaviuco. Skirting the southern edge of the park is a poor secondary road, which goes from Cuenca via San Joaquín to the Soldados entrance and the community of Angas beyond. (See Transport, page 967.) There is nowhere to stay after the *refugio* at Laguna Toreadora (see Sleeping, below) until you reach the lowlands between Naranjal and La Troncal.

The park offers ideal but strenuous walking, at 3,150 m-4,450 m altitude, and the climate is rough. There have been deaths from exposure. The best time to visit is August-January, when you may expect clear days, strong winds, night-time temperatures to -8ºC and occasional mist. From February-July temperatures are higher but there is much more fog, rain and snow. It is best to arrive in the early morning since it can get very cloudy, wet and cool after about 1300. Local maps are not always exact. It is better to get the *IGM* maps in Quito (Chaucha, Cuenca, San Felipe de Molleturo, or Chiquintad 1:50,000) and take a compass. It is easy to get lost as signs are of little help.

Cuenca

Sleeping		
Carvallo **1** *B3*	El Príncipe **13** *C3*	Pichincha **14** *B2*
Casa Naranja **3** *A2*	El Quijote **10** *B4*	Posada del Angel **24** *B2*
Casa del Barranco **18** *D3*	Gran Hotel **11** *B2*	Posada Todos
Chordeleg **4** *B2*	Inca Real **16** *B2*	Santos **23** *D4*
Colonial **9** *B3*	Italia **17** *B5*	Presidente **15** *B4*
El Cafecito **6** *C3*	La Orquídea **19** *B3*	Santa Fe **25** *C3*
El Conquistador &	Macondo **5** *A2*	Santa Lucia **22** *C3*
Las Tres Caravelas **7** *B3*	Mansion Alcázar **20** *B2*	Verde Limón **26** *C4*
El Dorado **8** *B3*	Milán **12** *C3*	Victoria & El Jardín
	Pachamama **21** *D4*	Restaurant **2** *D3*

		Eating
		Angelus **6** *B3*
		Austria **1** *C3*
		Balcón Quiteño **2** *B4*
		Cacao y Chocolate **8** *C3*
		El Jordán **7** *D3*
		Eucalyptus **3** *B3*
		Grecia **3** *B3*
		Heladería Holanda **14** *B3*
		La Fornace **5** *C3*

Ecuador Cuenca & around

0 metres 200
0 yards 200

N

To Turi

⊜ Sleeping

Cuenca and around *p959, map p962*

AL Mansión Alcázar, Bolívar 12-55 y Tarqui, T282 3918, www.mansionalcazar.com. Boutique hotel in a converted 19th/20th century mansion, fine decorations, central, with breakfast, restaurant, garden. Best y to book ahead.

AL Oro Verde, Ordóñez Lazo, T283 1200, www.oroverdehotels.com. On the road to Cajas, on a lagoon in the outskirts of town. Good restaurant, small pool, internet.

⑤　　　　　⑥

Pedregal Azteca **12** *B2*　　Wunderbar **11** *D3*
Raymipampa **9** *B3*
Tutto Freddo **10** *B3*
Villa Rosa **13** *B2*

Bars & clubs ⊙
Café del Tranquilo **12** *C3*
La Mesa Salsoteca **16** *B4*
Pop Art **17** *E2*
San Angel **4** *C4*

AL Santa Lucía, Borrero 8-44 y Sucre, T282 8000, www.santaluciahotel.com. An elegantly renovated colonial house, comfortable and very nice, excellent Italian restaurant in the patio.

A Carvallo, Gran Colombia 9-52, entre Padre Aguirre y Benigno Malo, T283 2063. Combination of an elegant colonial-style hotel and art/antique gallery, includes breakfast, restaurant, comfortable rooms, all have bath tubs, very nice.

A El Conquistador, Gran Colombia 665, T283 1788, www.hotelconquistador.com.ec. Buffet breakfast, good restaurant, internet, disco, avoid back rooms Fri and Sat, good value.

A El Dorado, Gran Colombia 787 y Luis Cordero, T283 1390, www.eldoradohotel.com.ec. Elegant modern hotel, includes buffet breakfast, cafeteria open 0530-2300, until 0400 Thu-Sat, parking, sauna, gym. A meeting place among Cuencanos.

B Victoria, Larga 6-93 y Borrero, T283 1120, santaana@etapaonline.net.ec. Elegant refurbished hotel overlooking the river, includes breakfast, excellent expensive restaurant, *El Jardín*, comfortable modern rooms, nice views.

C Apartamentos Otorongo, Av 12 de Abril y Guayas, T281 8205, pmontezu@az.pro.ec. 10-15 mins walk from centre. Furnished apartments with kitchenette, TV, phone, cleaning service included, friendly owners, US$380-480/month.

C El Príncipe, J Jaramillo 7-82 y Luis Cordero, T284 7287, htprince@etapaonline.net.ec. A refurbished colonial house, central, comfortable, nice patio with plants, includes breakfast, restaurant serves lunch.

C El Quijote, Hermano Miguel 9-58 y Gran Colombia, T284 3197, www.hotelquijote.com. Nicely restored old building with patio, includes breakfast, restaurant, carpeted rooms.

C Inca Real, G Torres 8-40 entre Sucre y Bolívar, T282 3636, incareal@cue.satnet.net. Refurbished colonial house with rooms around patios, includes breakfast, restaurant, parking, comfortable.

C Italia, Av España y Huayna-Cápac, by Terminal Terrestre, T284 0060, hitalia@cue.satnet.net. Modern hotel, includes buffet breakfast, restaurant, parking, comfortable and nice.

C Posada del Angel, Bolívar 14-11 y Estévez de Toral, T284 0695, www.hostalposadadel angel.com. Nicely restored colonial house, includes breakfast, parking, comfortable rooms, sitting area in patio, helpful staff. Recommended.

C Presidente, Gran Colombia 659 y Hermano Miguel, T283 1341. Comfortable, convenient, includes breakfast, good restaurant, parking, good value.

D Chordeleg, Gran Colombia 11-15 y Gral Torres, T282 2536, hostalfm@etapaonline.net.ec.

*(vertical margin text)* Ecuador Cuenca & around Listings

Charming colonial house with courtyard and fountain, includes breakfast, cafeteria, carpeted rooms.

D Colonial, Gran Colombia 10-13 y Padre Aguirre, T/F284 1644. Refurbished colonial house with beautiful patio, includes breakfast, restaurant for lunch, carpeted rooms, some to the street, others interior.

D La Orquídea, Borrero 9-31 y Bolívar, T282 4511, www.hostalorquidea.com. Nicely refurbished colonial house. Bright rooms, restaurant serves economical set meals, fridge, discounts in low season, good value.

D Macondo, Tarqui 11-64 y Lamar, T284 0697, www.hostalmacondo.com. Nice restored colonial house, includes breakfast, cheaper with shared bath, laundry and cooking facilities, pleasant patio with plants, garden, very popular, US run. Highly recommended.

D-E Casa Naranja, Lamar 10-38 y Padre Aguirre, T282 5415, www.casanaranja.galeon.com. Restored colonial house, cheaper with shared bath or in dorm, cooking facilities, motorcycle parking, storage room, long stay discounts.

E Casa del Barranco, Calle Larga 8-41 entre Benigno Malo y Luis Cordero, T283 9763, grupobar@etapaonline.net.ec. Nicely refurbished colonial house, some rooms have river views, breakfast available, cafeteria, cheaper with shared bath, hot water, parking.

E Gran Hotel, Gral Torres 9-70 y Bolívar, T283 1934. Includes breakfast, restaurant, hot water, some rooms dark but nice patio, popular.

E Milán, Pres Córdova 989 y Padre Aguirre, T283 1104, hotmilan@etapaonline.net.ec. Includes breakfast, restaurant, cheaper with shared bath, hot water, laundry facilities, view over market, rooms variable and some are noisy, but clean, popular and good value.

E Pachamama, Calle Larga 2-38 y Manuel Vega, T282 9465. Central, hot water, helpful, family atmosphere, a good choice.

E Posada Todos Santos, C Larga 3-42 y Tomás Ordóñez, T282 4247. Nice, tranquil hostel, includes breakfast, very good, attentive service.

E Verde Limón, J Jaramillo 4-89 y Mariano Cueva, T282 0300, www.verdelimonhostal.com. Rooms for 1 to 4 people, includes basic breakfast, cafeteria-bar in open patio, shared bath, hot water, cooking facilities, sitting room with games and DVDs.

E-F El Cafecito, Honorato Vásquez 7-36 y Luis Cordero, T283 2337, www.cafecito.net. Colonial house, small dorms, good restaurant and bar in nice patio, cheaper in dorm, hot water, popular with travellers.

E-F Santa Fé, Borrero 5-57 y Juan Jaramillo, T282 2025, hostalsantafe2005@yahoo.com. In a refurbished old house, private bath, cheaper in dorm, hot water, family run.

F Pichincha, Gral Torres 8-82 y Bolívar, T282 3868, hpichincha@etapanet.net. Shared bath, hot water, cooking facilities, spacious rooms but a little noisy on the street side. Helpful and recommended.

Baños
B Hostería Durán, Km 8 Vía Baños, T289 2485, www.hosteriaduran.com. With a restaurant, its own well-maintained, very clean pools, US$4 for non-residents, steam bath, camping is allowed. There are also a couple of cheap *residencias*.

Ingapirca *p961*
B Posada Ingapirca, 500 m above ruins (follow dirt road from parking lot up the hill, no signs), T221 5116, or T283 0064 (Cuenca). Converted hacienda, comfortable rooms, heating, including typical breakfast, excellent restaurant, good service. Recommended.

E Inti Huasi, in the village of Ingapirca, T221 5171. Nice rooms, simple, hot water, restaurant serves cheap meals.

El Tambo
This is the nearest town to Ingapirca. It also provides access to the ruins.

D Cuna del Sol, 1 km south of El Tambo, T223 3633. Rustic cabins in a tourist complex, deserted during the week, includes breakfast, restaurant open weekends and with advance notice, pool at weekends. Mediocre and overpriced.

E-F Chaski Huasi, on main street 3 blocks north of centre, T09-854 7845. Simple rooms with shared bath. Second location, 1 block north of plaza, near Banco del Austro due open in 2007.

E-F Sunshine, Panamericana y Ramón Bravo, at north end of town, T09-829 5070. Simple, family run, not always staffed, cheaper with shared bath, electric shower.

Inca Trail to Ingapirca: Achupallas *p961*
F Ingañán, T293 0652. Basic, with bath, hot water, meals on request, camping possible.

Northeast of Cuenca *p961*
Paute
A Hostería Uzhupud, 10 km from Paute, T225 0329, www.uzhupud.com. Set in the beautiful Paute valley, deluxe, relaxing, rooms at the back have best views, swimming pool and sauna (US$5 for non-residents), sports fields, gardens, lots of orchids. Recommended.

E-F Cutilcay, Abdón Calderón, by the river, T225 0133. An older hostel, basic, cheaper with shared bath and cold water.

Gualaceo

E Pachacamac, Sector Bulcay El Carmen on the main road to Cuenca, T220 3620. Modern hotel in one of the weaving communities. Functional rooms, hot water, good value.

E-F Residencial Gualaceo, Gran Colombia 302 y FA Piedra, T225 5006. Older hotel with clean basic rooms, cheaper with shared bath, hot water, parking, good value.

Parque Nacional Cajas *p961*

There is a *refugio* at **Laguna Toreadora**, cold, cooking facilities, and camping at **Laguna Llaviuco**. Other shelters in the park are primitive.

B Hostería Dos Chorreras, Km 14½ vía al Cajas, sector Sayausí, T285 3154, doschorreras@etapaonline.net.ec. Hacienda style inn outside the park. Heating, includes breakfast, restaurant serves excellent fresh trout, reservations recommended, horse rentals with advanced notice.

❶ Eating

Cuenca *p959, map p962*

Most places are closed on Sun evening. There are cheap *comedores* on the 2nd floor of Mercado Modelo, on 10 de Agosto y 18 de Noviembre.

♈♈♈ Balcón Quiteño, Sangurima 6-49 y Borrero, and Av Ordóñez Lazo 311 y los Pinos. Ecuadorean, good. Popular with the locals after a night's hard partying.

♈♈♈ El Jordán, C Larga 6-111, T285 0517. International and some Middle Eastern dishes, economical set lunch. Belly dancing show at weekends. Popular.

♈♈♈ Molinos del Batán, 12 de Abril y Puente El Vado, T281 1531. Excellent *comida típica Cuencana* in a nice setting by the river.

♈♈♈ Rancho Chileno, Av España 13-17, next to airport and a couple other locations, T286 4112. A Cuenca tradition. Serves good steak, seafood and *empanadas chilenas*, slow service.

♈♈♈ Villa Rosa, Gran Colombia 12-22 y Tarqui, T284 2443. Very elegant, excellent international food.

♈♈ Café Eucalyptus, Gran Colombia 9-41 y Benigno Malo, Mon-Fri variable hours. A pleasant restaurant, café and bar, elegant. Large menu with dishes from all over the world. British-American run and recommended.

♈♈ La Fornace, Borrero 8-29 y Sucre, Remigio Crespo 5-13 e Imbabura, and other locations. Good pizza and other Italian food, attentive service.

♈♈ Las Tres Caravelas, Gran Colombia 6-65 in hotel *El Conquistador*. Good value, Ecuadorean and international fare. Live music at weekends.

♈♈ Pedregal Azteca, Gran Colombia 10-29 y Padre Aguirre. Good Mexican food in a colonial building, live music Fri evening, closed Sun.

♈♈ Raymipampa, Benigno Malo 8-59, T283 4159, on Parque Calderón. Very good international food, central. Fast service, popular, at times it is hard to get a table.

♈♈-♈ Café Austria, Benigno Malo 5-99 y J Jaramillo, daily 0900-0000. A traditional Cuenca café, also serves international food. Pastries are still very good here.

♈♈-♈ Casa Vieja, Pres Borrero 5-80 y Juan Jaramillo, Mon-Fri 0930-0000, Sat from 1700. Restaurant and bar serving economical set lunches, snacks and drinks in the evening. Live music Fri and Sat nights.

♈ El Festín, Remigio Crespo 5-05, Mon-Sat 1130-2000, Sun 1100-1700. All you can eat Ecuadorean buffet for US$4.

♈ Good Afinity, Av Ordóñez Lasso y Av Américas, Mon-Sat 1100-1500. Very good vegetarian food, economical set lunch, nice garden seating.

♈ Grecia, Gran Colombia y Padre Aguirre, Mon-Sat 1200-1500. Good quality and value set lunch.

Cafés

Angelus, Benigno Malo y Bolívar. Good ice-cream, crèpes, sandwiches and sweets. Reasonable prices. .

Cacao y Chocolate, Juan Jaramillo y Borrero. Chocolate in every imaginable form. Pleasant atmosphere at night.

Heladería Holanda, Benigno Malo 9-51. Open 0930, yoghurt for breakfast, good ice-cream, fruit salads, cream cakes. Recommended.

Monte Bianco, Bolívar 2-80 y Ordóñez, and a couple of other locations. Good cakes, ice-cream, open Sun.

Panesa, Benigno Malo entre Gran Colombia y Sucre. Bakery with good bread and sweets.

Tutto Freddo, Benigno Malo 9-40 y Bolívar. Ice-cream, pizza and sandwiches.

❶ Bars and clubs

Cuenca *p959, map p962*

Café del Tranquilo, Borrero 7-47 y Presidente Córdova. Pleasant popular bar, live music US$3.

La Mesa Salsoteca, Gran Colombia 3-36 entre Vargas Machuca y Tomás Ordóñez (no sign). Latin music, salsa, popular among travellers and locals.

Pop Art, Remigio Crespo y Solano. Modern music, young crowd.

San Angel, Hermano Miguel 6-88 y Presidente Córdova. Popular bar and dance spot, live music, for a mixed-age crowd.

Tapitas y Canciones, Remigio Crespo y

Galápagos. Small quaint *peña*.

Wunderbar, entrance from stairs on Hermano Miguel y Calle Larga, T283 1274. A café-bar-restaurant, drinks, good coffee and food including some vegetarian dishes. Nice atmosphere, popular with travellers, German magazines, book exchange, German-run.

☻ Entertainment

Cuenca *p959, map p962*

Cinemas Casa de la Cultura, Luis Cordero y Sucre. Films are shown in the evening. **Multicines**, Av José Peralta, complex of 5 theatres and food court, also at Mall del Río.

Dance Classes Cachumbambe, Remigio Crespo 7-79 y Guayas, above *Restaurante Charito*, T288 2023. Salsa, merengue and a variety of other rhythms.

☻ Festivals and events

Cuenca *p959, map p962*

On **24 Dec** there is an outstanding parade: **Pase del Niño Viajero**, probably the largest and finest Christmas parade in all Ecuador. Children and adults from all the *barrios* and surrounding villages decorate donkeys, horses, cars and trucks with symbols of abundance. Little children in colourful indigenous costumes or dressed up as Biblical figures ride through the streets accompanied by musicians. The parade starts at about 1000 at San Sebastián, proceeds along C Simón Bolívar and ends at San Blas about 5 hrs later. In the days up to, and just after Christmas, there are many smaller parades. **12 Apr** is the Foundation of Cuenca. On **Good Friday** there is a fine procession through the town to the Mirador Turi. **May-Jun** Septenario, the religious festival of Corpus Christi, lasts a week. On **3 Nov** is **Independence of Cuenca**, with street theatre, art exhibitions and night-time dances all over the city. Cuenca hosts an internationally famous art competition every 2 years, which begins in **Apr** or **May**. The next *bienal* is due in 2009. Information from Bolívar 13-89, T283 1778.

○ Shopping

Cuenca *p959, map p962*

Camping equipment Bermeo Hnos, Borrero 8-35 y Sucre, T283 1522. **Explorador Andino**, Borrero 7-52 y Sucre, T284 7320. **Tatoo**, Av Solano 4-31 y Florencia Astudillo, T288 4809, www.tatoo.ws. Good camping, hiking and climbing gear, locally made.

Handicrafts Good souvenirs are carvings, leather, basketwork, painted wood, onyx, ceramics, woven stuffs, embroidered shirts,

jewellery. There are many craftware shops along Gran Colombia, Benigno Malo and Juan Jaramillo alongside Las Conceptas. There are several good leather shops in the arcade off Bolívar between Benigno Malo and Luis Cordero.

Arte Artesanías y Antigüedades, Borrero y Córdova. Textiles, jewellery and antiques. **Artesa**, L Cordero 10-31 y Gran Colombia, several branches. Modern Ecuadorean ceramics at good prices. **Centro Artesanal Municipal 'Casa de la Mujer'**, Gral Torres 7-33, T284 5854. Crafts market with a great variety of handicrafts. **Colecciones Jorge Moscoso**, Juan Jaramillo 6-80 y Borrero, T282 2114. Weaving exhibitions, ethnographic museum, antiques and handicrafts. **El Barranco**, Hermano Miguel 3-23 y Av 3 de Noviembre. Artisans' cooperative selling a wide variety of crafts. **El Tucán**, Borrero 7-35. Ecuadorean *artesanía*. Recommended. **Galápagos**, Borrero 6-75. Excellent selection of crafts. **Torres**, between Sucre y Córdova, or **Tarqui**, between Córdova and the river, for *polleras*, traditional Indian skirts.

Jewellery Galería Claudio Maldonado, Bolívar 7-75, has unique pre-Columbian designs in silver and precious stones. **Unicornio**, Gran Colombia y Luis Cordero. Good jewellery, ceramics and candelabras.

Panama hats Kurt Dorfzaun, Gil Ramírez Dávalos 4-34, T280 7563, www.kdorfzaun.com. Good prices and display of the complete hat making process.

Exportadora Cuenca, Mcal Lamar 3-80. Jaime Ortega Ramírez and his wife, Tania, will make to order and won't apply bleach if so asked. Highly recommended. **Homero Ortega P e Hijos**, Av Gil Ramírez Dávalos 3-86, T280 1288, www.homeroortega.com. Highest quality. He will show you his factory opposite bus station, open 0900-1200, 1500-1800 for visits.

Supermarkets and markets Feria Libre, Av de las Américas y Av Remigio Crespo, west of the centre. The largest market, also has dry goods and clothing, busiest Wed and Sat. **Mercado 9 de Octubre**, Sangurima y Mariano Cueva, busiest on Thu. Nearby at **Plaza Rotary**, Sangurima y Vargas Machuca, crafts are sold, best selection on Thu. **Mercado 10 de Agosto**, C Larga y Gral Torres. Daily produce market with a prepared foods and drinks section on the second floor

▲ Activities and tours

Cuenca *p959, map p962*

Day tours to Ingapirca US$35-45 pp. Trekking in Cajas about US$35 pp per day.

Apullacta, Gran Colombia 11-02 y Gral Torres,

T283 7815, www.apullacta.com. Offers the usual tours and also hires tents, sleeping bags and other camping equipment.

Ecotrek, Paseo 3 de Noviembre entre Jacarandá y Cedros, 3 blocks from Hotel Oro Verde, T283 4677, ecotrek@cue.sat.net. Manager Juan Gabriel Carrasco specializes in shaman trips and climbing tours in addition to the standard trips.

Metropolitan Touring, C Larga 6-96, T283 7000, www.metropolitan-touring.com. A branch of the Quito operator, also sells airline tickets.

The Travel Center, Hermano Miguel 5-42 entre Honorato Vázquez y Juan Jaramillo, T282 3782, www.terradiversa.com. Several tour operators under one roof with lots of useful information, helpful staff, a pleasant sitting area, small library and bulletin boards. Recommended. The tour operators are: **Biking Adventures**, all types of cycling tours, US$43 pp per day; **Montaruna Tours**, horse-riding day-trips and longer excursions; US$50 pp per day; **Terra Diversa**, Ingapirca, Cajas, community tourism in Saraguro, and other options, US$35-80 pp per day. The more common destinations have fixed departures. Also sell jungle trips, Galápagos tours and flight tickets.

⊖ Transport

Cuenca *p959, map p962*
Air Airport is 5 mins walk beyond the terminal. No ticket reservations at the airport. To **Quito**, US$68, and **Guayaquil**, US$49, with **Aerogal**, **TAME** and **Icaro**. **Icaro** inaugurated commercial flights to **Piura** in Peru in early 2007. Schedules change often so ask. Arrive at least 1 hr before departure.
Bus Terminal for local services is at the Feria Libre on Av Las Américas. Many city buses pass here. City buses US$0.25. Buses for **Baños** go from Cuenca and back every 5-10 mins,

0600-2330, US$0.25; buses pass the front of the Terminal Terrestre, cross the city on Vega Muñoz and Cueva, then down Todos los Santos to the river, along 12 de Abril and onto Av Loja.

The long distance Terminal Terrestre is on Av España, northeast of centre, 20 mins walk, or take a minibus or taxi. Take daytime buses to enjoy scenic routes. To **Riobamba**, 6 hrs, US$6. To **Ambato**, 7 hrs, US$8. To **Quito**, 10 hrs, US$11. To **Loja**, 5 hrs, US$6. To **Machala**, 4 hrs, US$5, sit on the left, wonderful scenery. To **Guayaquil**, via Cajas and Molleturo, 4 hrs, or via Zhud, 5 hrs, both US$5. To **Cajas National Park**, see below. To **Macas** via Guarumales or Limón, 10 hrs, US$9; spectacular scenery but prone to landslides, check in advance if roads are open. To **Huaquillas**, 5 hrs, US$6. To **Saraguro**, US$5, 3 hrs. To **Gualaquiza**, in the southern Oriente, there are 2 routes, via Gualaceo and Plan de Milagro and via Sígsig, 6 hrs, US$6.25. To **Alausí**, 4 hrs, US$5; all Quito-bound buses pass through.
Taxi US$1 for short journey; US$2 to airport, US$1.50 to the bus station.
To **Baños** costs US$5.

Ingapirca *p961*
Bus Transportes Cañar has 2 direct buses daily from **Cuenca** to Ingapirca, at 0900 and 1300, returning 1300 and 1600, US$2.50, 2 hrs. From **Cañar**, corner of 24 de Mayo and Borrero, local buses leave every 15 mins for Ingapirca, 0600-1800, US$0.50, 30 mins; last bus returns at 1700. The same buses from Cañar go through **El Tambo**, US$0.40, 20 mins. If coming from the north, transfer in El Tambo. From **Alausí to Achupallas**, for the Inca Trail to Ingapirca, bus daily around 1400, US$1, 1hr, a nice ride; also a truck around 1200 daily. Alternatively, take any bus along the Panamericana to **La Moya**, south of Alausí, at the turn-off for Achupallas, and a pick-up

from there (best on Thu and Sun). To hire a pick-up from Alausí costs US$15, from La Moya US$10.

Northeast of Cuenca p961

Bus To Gualaceo: from Terminal Terrestre in Cuenca, US$0.55, 50 mins. To **Chordeleg**: frequently from Gualaceo market, every 15 mins, US$0.20; direct bus from Cuenca, 1 hr, US$0.80. To **Sigsig**: Bus from Cuenca 1½ hrs, US$1.25, via Gualaceo and Chordeleg, every 30 min.

Parque Nacional Cajas p961

Bus From Cuenca's Terminal Terrestre take any **Guayaquil** bus that goes via Molleturo (not Zhud), US$1-1.50, 30 mins to turn-off for Llaviuco, 45 mins to Toreado. **Coop Occidental** (to Molleturo) leaves from its own station in Cuenca, at Lamar y M Heredia, west of the centre. For the Soldados entrance, catch a bus from Puente del Vado in Cuenca, daily at 0600, US$1.25, 1½ hrs; the return bus passes the Soldados gate at about 1600.

● Directory

Cuenca p959, map p962
Airline offices Aerogal, Aurelio Aguilar y Solano, T286 1041. Icaro, Av España 1114, T280 2700. TAME, Florencia Astudillo 2-22, T288 9581.
Banks Banco del Austro, Sucre y Borrero. Visa ATM. **Pacificard** office at Bolívar y T Ordóñez, T284 5666. **Produbanco**, Padre Aguirre 9-72 y Gran Colombia. **Vazcorp**, Gran Colombia 7-98 y

Cordero, T283 3434. Mon-Fri 0830-1300, 1430-1745, Sat 0900-1230. TCs with commission, also change Euros, Peruvian Soles and other currencies, efficient. **Car rental** Bombuscaro, España y Elia Liut, by the airport, T286 6541. Localiza, at the airport, T280 3198, www.localiza.com.ec. **Internet** Rates US$0.60-1 per hr. Many to choose from. **Language courses** Rates US$6-10 per hr. Centro Abraham Lincoln, Borrero 5-18 y Honorato Vásquez, T282 3898. Small Spanish language section. Estudio Internacional Sampere, Hermano Miguel 3-43 y C Larga, T284 1986, samperec@samperecen.com.ec. At the high end of the price range. Fundación Centro de Estudios Interamericanos, Tarquí 13-45 y Pío Bravo, T283 9003, www.cedei.org. Spanish and Quichua, accommodation, Hostal Macondo attached. Recommended. Sí Centro de Español e Inglés, Padre Aguirre 9-43 y Gran Colombia, T282 0429, www.sicentrospanishschool.com. Good teachers, competitive prices, helpful and enthusiastic, tourist information available. Recommended. **Medical services** Clinics: Clínica Santa Ana, Av Manuel J Calle 1-104, T281 4068. Hospital Santa Inés, Av Toral 2-113, T281 7888. Dr Jaime Moreno Aguilar speaks English. Farmacia Botica Internacional, Gran Colombia 7-20 y Borrero. Experienced staff, wide selection. **Post offices** Gran Colombia y Borrero, helpful. **Useful addresses** Immigration: Av Ordóñez Lazo y Los Cipreces, Edif Astudillo, T283 1020. For tourist visa extensions, Mon-Fri 0800-1230, 1500-1830.

Cuenca to the Peruvian border

From Cuenca various routes go to the Peruvian border, fanning out from the pleasant city of Loja, due south of which is Vilcabamba, famous for its invigorating climate, lovely countryside and, nowadays, its excellent services for tourists.

South to Loja

From Cuenca, the Pan-American Highway runs south to La Y, about 20 km away. Here the road divides: one continues the Pan-American to Loja, the other runs west through sugar cane fields to Pasaje and Machala. Most buses between Cuenca and the Peruvian border at Huaquillas (see page 985) go northwest to La Troncal, then south down the coast. The road between Cuenca and Loja is paved but often deteriorates after heavy rains. It undulates through several passes and is one of the most beautiful and breathtaking in Ecuador.

Saraguro → Phone code: 07. Colour map 11, grid C3. Population: 7,500. Altitude: 2,500m.

On the road to Loja is this old city, where the local people, the most southerly Andean group in Ecuador, dress all in black. The men are notable for their black shorts, sometimes covered by a whitish sort of divided apron, and a particular kind of saddle bag, the *alforja*, and the women for their pleated black skirts, necklaces of coloured beads and silver *topos*, ornate pins fastening their shawls. The town has a picturesque Sunday market and interesting Mass. Saraguro is developing community tourism, with a craft fair planned for every second Sunday, and home-stay opportunities including meals and activities with native families. Contact **Fundación Kawsay** ① *18 de Noviembre y Av Loja, T220 0331, www.kawsay.org*, or the **Oficina Municipal de Turismo** ① *C José María Vivar on the main plaza, T220 0100 ext 18, turismosaraguro@yahoo.es, Mon-Fri 0800-1200, 1400-1800. See also www.saraguros.com and wwwsaraguro.org.* There is also good birdwatching in the area.

Loja → *Phone code: 07. Colour map 11, grid C3. Population: 165,000. Altitude: 2,060 m.*

This friendly, pleasant highland city, encircled by hills, is a traditional gateway between the highlands and southern Amazonia. It was founded on its present site in 1548, having been moved from La Toma, and was rebuilt twice after earthquakes, the last of which occurred in the 1880s. The city has two universities, with a well-known law school. The Universidad Nacional has good murals on some of its buildings. There are crude paintings on the patio walls of many of the old houses. Loja has won international awards for its beautiful parks and its recycling programme. **Tourist offices: iTur** ① *José Antonio Eguiguren y Bolívar, Parque Central, T258 1251 ext 220, www.municipiodeloja.gov.ec, Mon-Fri 0800- 1300, 1500-1800, Sat 0900-1200.* Local and regional information and map, helpful, some English spoken. Also has offices at the Terminal Terrestre and the airport. **Ministerio de Turismo** ① *Bolívar 12-39 entre Mercadillo y Lourdes, p 3, at Parque San Sebastián, T257 2964, fronterasur@turismo.gov.ec, Mon-Fri 0830-1330, 1430-1700.* Information for all of Ecuador, Spanish only.

The **Cathedral** and **Santo Domingo church**, Bolívar y Rocafuerte, have painted interiors. **El Valle** church, on the south edge of the city is colonial, with a lovely interior. Housed in a beautifully restored house on the main park is the **Centro Cultural Loja** home of the **Museo del Banco Central** ① *10 de Agosto 13-30 y Bolívar, T257 3004, Mon-Fri 0900-1300, 1400-1700, US$0.40,* with well displayed archaeology, ethnography, art, and history halls. There are also temporary exhibits, a library and an auditorium. Loja is famed for its musicians and has one of the few musical academies in the country and two symphonic orchestras. Musical evenings and concerts are often held around the town. The **Museo de Música** ① *Valdivieso 09-42 y Rocafuerte, T256 1342. Mon-Fri 0900-1300, 1500-1900, free,* housed in the restored Colegio Bernardo Valdivieso, honours ten Lojano composers. It also has rotating exhibits, not necessarily about music, and a café. **Mercado Centro Comercial Loja** (Mercado Modelo) ① *10 de Agosto y 18 de Noviembre, Mon-Sat (the main market day) 0600-1630, Sun 0600-1330,* is worth a visit. It is efficient and the cleanest in Ecuador. At Puente Bolívar, by the northern entrance to town, is a fortress-like monument and a lookout over the city, known as **La Puerta de la Ciudad** ① *Mon-Fri 0830-2130, Sat-Sun 0900-2130.* It has art exhibits at ground level and a small café upstairs, a good place to take pictures. Also in the north of the city, a couple of blocks east of the Terminal is the **Parque Recreacional Jipiro**, a well maintained, clean park, good to walk and relax in. It is popular at weekends. Take the city bus marked 'Jipiro', a five-minute ride from the centre.

Parque Universitario Francisco Vivar Castro (Parque La Argelia) ① *Tue-Sun 0800-1700, US$1, city bus marked 'Capulí-Dos Puentes' to the park or 'Argelia' to the Universidad Nacional and walk from there,* is superb, with trails through the forest to the *páramo*. It is 500 m before the police checkpoint on road south to Vilcabamba. Across the road and 100 m south is the **Jardín Botánico Reynaldo Espinosa** ① *Mon-Fri 0800-1600, Sat-Sun 0900-1730, US$1,* which is nicely laid out.

Parque Nacional Podocarpus

① *Park entry is US$10, valid for 5 days at all entrances. Information from Ministerio del Ambiente in Loja, Sucre entre Quito e Imbabura, T/F257 9595, podocam@easynet.net.ec. In Zamora contact the Ministerio at T/F260 6606. Their general map of the park is not adequate for navigation.*

Podocarpus (950 to 3,700 m) is one of the most diverse protected areas in the world. It is particularly rich in birdlife, including many rarities and some newly discovered species, and includes one of the last major habitats for the spectacled bear. The park protects stands of *romerillo* or podocarpus, a native, slow-growing conifer. The park is divided into two areas, an upper premontane section with spectacular walking country, lush tropical cloud forest and excellent birdwatching, and a lower subtropical section, with remote areas of virgin rainforest and unmatched quantities of flora and fauna. Both zones are quite wet, making hiking or rubber boots essential. There are sometimes periods of dry weather October to January. The upper section is also very cold, so warm clothing and waterproofs are indispensable year-round. **Cajanuma** is the trailhead for the eight-hour hike to **Lagunas del Compadre**, 12 lakes set amid rock cliffs, camping is possible there. At **San Francisco**, the *guardianía* (ranger's station), operated by Fundación Arcoiris, offers nice accommodation (see below). This section of the park is a transition cloud forest area at around 2,160 m, very rich in birdlife. This is the best place to see the podocarpus trees: a trail (four hours return) goes from the *guardianía* to the podocarpus.

Entrances to the upper section: at Cajanuma, about 8 km south of Loja on the Vilcabamba road. From the turn-off it is 8 km uphill to the guard station. At San Francisco, 24 km from Loja along the road to Zamora. The southwestern section of the park can be reached by trails from Vilcabamba, Yangana and Valladolid. Entrances to the lower section: Bombuscara can be reached from Zamora; the other entrance is at Romerillos, two hours south of Zamora. Conservation groups working in and around the park include: Arcoiris, Segundo Cueva Celi 03-15 y Clodoveo Carrión, T/F07-257 7499, www.arcoiris.org.ec; Naturaleza y Cultura Internacional, Avenida Pío Jaramillo y Venezuela, T257 3691, www.natureandculture.org.

Zamora → *Population: 12,500.*

The road to the Oriente crosses a low pass and descends rapidly to Zamora, an old mission settlement about 65 km away at the confluence of the Ríos Zamora and Bombuscaro. The road is beautiful as it wanders from *páramo* down to high jungle, crossing mountain ranges of spectacular cloud forest, weaving high above narrow gorges as it runs alongside the Río Zamora. The town itself is hilly, with a pleasant climate. As well as being the gateway to the lowland portion of Parque Nacional Podocarpus, it also gives access to Alto Nangaritza (see page 1012). There are two *orquidearios*, **Tzanka** ⓘ *José Luis Tamayo y Jorge Mosquera, T260 5692, US$2* and **Pafinia** ⓘ *Av del Ejército Km 2, T260 5911.* For information about the town: **iTur** ⓘ *Sevilla de Oro by the Terminal Terrestre, T260 5016, Mon-Fri 0800-1200, 1400-1700;* about the province: **Departamento de Turismo** ⓘ *Concejo Provincial, Jorge Mosquera y Orellana, T260 5132 ext 138, Mon-Fri 0800-1200, 1400-1800.*

Loja to the Peruvian border

Of all the crossings from Ecuador to Peru, by far the most efficient and relaxed is the scenic route from Loja to Piura via Macará. Other routes are from Vilcabamba to La Balsa (see page 975), Huaquillas (see page 985) and along the Río Napo in the Oriente (see page 1006).

Leaving Loja on the main paved highway going west, the airport at **La Toma** (1,200 m) is reached after 35 km. La Toma is also called **Catamayo** ⓘ *taxi to airport US$1, or 20 mins walk*, where there is basic lodging. At Catamayo, where you can catch the Loja-Macará-Piura bus, the Pan-American Highway divides: one branch runs west, the other south.

On the paved western road, at San Pedro de La Bendita, a secondary road climbs to the much-venerated pilgrimage site of **El Cisne**, dominated by its large incongruous French-style Gothic church. There is a small museum, a basic *pensión* and places to eat. Vendors and beggars fill the town and await visitors (see Festivals and events, below). Continuing on the western route, **Catacocha** is spectacularly placed, a town built on a rock. There are pre-Inca ruins around the town. From Catacocha, the paved road runs south to the border at Macará.

The south route from Catamayo to Macará is via Cariamanga, fully paved. The road goes to **Cariamanga**, via **Gonzanamá**, a pleasant, sleepy little town (basic *hostales*), famed for the weaving of beautiful *alforjas* (multi-purpose saddlebags). It's 27 km to Cariamanga (six hotels, banks), then the road twists along a ridge westwards to **Colaisaca**, before descending steeply through forests to **Utuana** and Sozoranga (one hotel), then down to the rice paddies of **Macará**, on the border. There is a choice of accommodation here and good road connections to Sullana and Piura in Peru.

Border with Peru Ecuadorean immigration is open 24 hours. Formalities last about 30 minutes. It is a much easier crossing than at Huaquillas. During the day there are money changers dealing in soles at the international bridge and in Macará at the park where taxis leave for the border. The international bridge over the Río Macará is 2½ km from town. There is taxi and pick-up service (US$0.25 shared, US$1 private). On the Peruvian side, minivans and cars run La Tina-Sullana (try to avoid arriving in Sullana after dark).

Alternative border crossing

From Cariamanga (see above), a rough, unpaved road runs two hours south to **Amaluza**, a pleasant town, with a nice plaza and a nice, well-attended church. There are two hotels (best is **E Guambo Real**, Av Chigua y Manuel Enrique Rojas, below the plaza, T265 3061, comfortable rooms with small bath, cold water), and several well stocked shops. *Unión Cariamanga* buses from Loja to Amaluza, US$4.75, 5 hours. There are six *rancheras* a day from the plaza at Amaluza to **Jimbura**, US$1, 1 hour. Jimbura is a nice quiet town, with one basic residencial and comedor. It is a 5-km walk to the international bridge and a further 2 km to the Peruvian village of Espíndola (taxi US$7). Ecuadorean immigration is just outside Jimbura, open 24 hours. Peruvian immigration in Espíndola is also open 24 hours, but you may have ask for the officer. There are no services at all at the border bridge, but shopkeepers in Jimbura change soles at poor rates. To Ayabaca (Peru), a pickup leaves Espíndola about 0500 daily; if staying in Jimbura, go to Espíndola and let the driver know, he will pick you up in the morning. There is no fixed schedule during the day, patience is required on this route.

● Sleeping

Saraguro *p968*

D-E Achik Huasi, on a hillside above town, contact Fundación Kawsay, T220 0331, www.kawsay.org. Community-run *hostería*, somewhat improvised but adequate, nice views, parking.

F Saraguro, Loja No 03-2 y A Castro, T220 0286. Cheaper with shared bath, nice courtyard, electric shower, family-run, basic, good value.

Loja *p969*

There are a few basic *residenciales* in our **F** range on Rocafuerte, also some along Sucre with mostly short stay customers.

A La Casa Lojana, París 00-08 y Zoilo Rodríguez, T258 5984, casalojanahotel @utpl.edu.ec. Refurbished in elaborate colonial style, but plain rooms, includes breakfast, elegant dinning room, lovely grounds and views. Staffed by students of the Universidad Particular de Loja.

B Andes del Prado, Mariana de Jesús entre 10 de Agosto y Rocafuerte, T258 8271, andesdelprado@speedtelecom.net.ec. Refurbished modern home overlooking the city, bright comfortable rooms, includes breakfast, parking.

B Bombuscaro, 10 de Agosto y Av Universitaria, T257 7021, www.bombuscaro.com.ec. Comfortable rooms and suites, includes buffet breakfast, restaurant, airport transfers, car rental, good service. Recommended.

B Libertador, Colón 14-30 y Bolívar, T257 0344, hlibloja@impsat.net.ec. Comfortable, central, includes buffet breakfast, good restaurant, pool and spa, parking, suites available, very good.

C Aguilera Internacional, Sucre 01-08 y Emiliano Ortega, T257 2894. North of centre, comfortable rooms, includes breakfast, restaurant, parking.

C Hostal Del Bus, Av 8 de Diciembre y Flores, T257 5100, hdelbus@easynet.net.ec. Opposite the terminal, nice rooms, includes breakfast,

good restaurant, parking.

C Vilcabamba Internacional, Iberoamérica y Pasaje la FEUE, T257 3393. Includes breakfast, pleasant, restaurant, discount for *Handbook* users.

D Acapulco, Sucre 7-61 y 10 de Agosto, T257 0651, acapulcohotel@yahoo.com. Pleasant, central, nicely furnished small rooms, basic breakfast, cafetería, first floor rooms are quieter.

E Chandelier, Imbabura 14-82 y Sucre, T256 3061, chandelierhotel@hotmail.com. Cheaper with shared bath, electric shower, parking, hospitable, OK.

E San Luis, Sucre 04-62 y Quito, T257 0370. Large rooms, hot water, parking, simple but clean.

E Internacional, 10 de Agosto 15-30 entre Sucre y 18 de Noviembre, T257 8486. Cheaper with shared bath, electric shower, older place but refurbished and OK.

F Londres, Sucre 07-51 y 10 de Agosto, T256 1936. Well-maintained old house, shared bath, hot water, basic, good value.

Parque Nacional Podocarpus *p969*

At **Cajanuma**, there are cabins with beds and mattresses, US$3 pp per night, bring warm sleeping bag, stove and food. At **San Francisco**, the *guardianía* (ranger's station), operated by **Fundación Arcoiris** offers nice accommodation with shared bath, hot water and kitchen facilities, US$8 pp if you bring a sleeping bag, US$10 if they provide sheets. At **Bombuscara** there is a cabin with kitchen facilities, US$3 pp.

Zamora *p970*

B-D Copalinga, Km 3 on the road to the Bombuscara entrance of Podocarpus national park, T260 5043 or T09-347 7013, www.copalinga.com. Comfortable cabins (some with bath) in a lovely setting, meals available if

971

arranged in advance, excellent birdwatching, English and French spoken, Belgian run, helpful. Recommended.

E Betania, Francisco de Orellana entre Diego de Vaca y Amazonas, T260 7030, hotelbetaniaz@hotmail.com. Includes breakfast, hot water, parking, modern.

E Chonta Dorada, Pío Jaramillo y Diego de Vaca, T260 6384. Hot water, parking for small vehicles, OK, good value.

E Orillas del Zamora, Diego de Vaca y Alonso de Mercadillo, T260 5754. Modern, hot water, comfortable, good value, away from centre. Recommended.

G Seyma, 24 de Mayo y Amazonas, T260 5583. Shared bath, cold water, basic.

Loja to the Peruvian border *p970*
Catamayo
D Los Almendros, on main road west of town, T267 7293. Best in town but reported run-down, includes breakfast, restaurant and bar on weekends, 2 pools, parking.

E-F Rossana, Isidro Ayora y 24 de Mayo, T267 7006. Cheaper with shared bath, cold water, also cheaper annexe next door.

Macará
E El Conquistador, Bolívar y Calderón, T269 4057. Includes breakfast, hot water, fan, parking, modern and comfortable.

E Karina, 10 de Agosto y Antonio Ante, T269 4764, kari_20_08@hotmail.com. Small rooms, some with hot water, a/c, cheaper with fan.

E Santigyn, Bolívar y Rengel, T269 5035. Hot water, fan, some rooms with fridge, modern, comfortable.

E Terra Verde, Lázaro Vaca s/n, near the Hospital Civil, T269 4540, patricioluzuriaga@hotmail.com. Quiet location 2 blocks from the Coop Loja bus station. Includes breakfast, a/c, rooftop terrace, helpful.

F Colina, Olmedo y Loja, T269 4871. Some rooms have electric showers, fan, nice, modern and good value.

F-G Bekalus, Valdivieso entre 10 de Agosto y Rengel, T269 4043. Cheaper with shared bath, cold water, simple, good value.

🍴 Eating

Saraguro *p968*
Several restaurants around the main plaza serve economical meals.

Loja *p969*
🍴🍴 **Parrilladas Uruguayas**, Juan de Salinas y Av Universitaria, Tue-Sun 1200-0100, Mon 1800-0100. Good grilled meat, helpful owner.

🍴🍴 **200 Millas**, Juan José Peña y 10 de Agosto. Good fish and seafood, open 0900-1600.

🍴🍴 **José Antonio's**, Eguiguren 12-94 y Bernardo Valdivieso, Mon-Sat 1000-2200. The French cooking is very good when the owner/chef is in. Economical set lunches are OK.

🍴🍴 **Parrilladas El Fogón**, 8 de Diciembre y Flores, opposite bus station. Good grill and salad bar.

🍴🍴 **Mar y Cuba**, Rocafuerte 09-00 y 24 de Mayo, Tue-Sun 1000-1600, 1900-2200. Seafood and Cuban specialties, friendly service.

🍴🍴 **Mi Tierra**, 10 de Agosto 11-14 y Juan José Peña. Cheap set lunches, international à la carte.

🍴🍴 **Pizzería Forno di Fango**, Bolívar 10-98 y Azuay, Tue-Sun 1200-2230. Excellent wood-oven pizza. Recommended.

🍴 **Casa Sol**, 24 de Mayo 07-04 y José Antonio Eguiguren, daily 0900-0000. Economical set meals and à la carte. Pleasant seating on a balcony overlooking Parque Cristóbal Ojeda.

🍴 **Diego's**, Colón 14-88 y Sucre, 2nd floor. Very good cheap set lunch and mid-range à la carte, very popular, Mon-Sat 0800-2130, Sun 0800-1530, popular with locals.

🍴 **El Paraíso**, Quito 14-50 y Bolívar, daily 0700-2100. Good vegetarian food, set meals and some à la carte dishes.

🍴 **Tamal Lojano**, 18 de Noviembre y Imbabura. Mon-Sat 0830-2030. Economical set lunches, good tamales and other local snacks in the evening.

Cafés
Café del Museo, Bernardo Valdivieso 09-42 y Rocafuerte, at the Museo de Música, Mon-Sat 1000-1300, 1500-1900. Local snacks such as *tamales* and *quesadillas*, fruit salads, coffee and other drinks.

El Jugo Natural, J Eguiguren 14-18 y Bolívar. Very good fresh juices and breakfast. Closed Sun.

El Sendereo, Bolívar 13-13 y Mercadillo, Tue-Sat 1530-2200. Fruit juices and snacks, nice balcony overlooking Plaza San Sebastián.

Zamora *p970*
🍴 **Chifa Zhang's**, Diego de Vaca across from the market, daily to 2200. Good Chinese food.

🍴 **King Ice**, Diego de Vaca y José Luis Tamayo, by the plaza, daily 0900-0000. Snacks and a few à la carte dishes.

Spiga Pan, 24 de Mayo, ½ block downhill from the plaza. Great bakery with a variety of hot breads, cream cakes and fresh fruit yoghurt. Best choice in town.

⊛ Festivals and events

Loja *p969*
15 Aug Fiesta de la Virgen del Cisne, the statue

of the Virgin spends a month each year travelling around the province; the most important peregrination is the 3-day 70 km walk from El Cisne to Loja cathedral, beginning **16 Aug**. End-May, the last 2 weeks of Aug and the 1st week of Sep are crowded.

▲ Activities and tours

Loja *p969*
Aratinga Aventuras, Lourdes 14-84 y Sucre, T/F258 2434, aratinga@loja.telconet.net. Specializes in birdwatching tours, overnight trips to cloud forest. Pablo Andrade is a knowledgeable guide.
Biotours, 24 de Mayo 08-28 y 10 de Agosto, T257 9387, biotours_ec@yahoo.es. City, regional, cycling and jungle tours, flight tickets.

Zamora *p970*
Wellington Valdiviezo, T09-380 2211, manacus_manacus@yahoo.es. Organizes visits to shamans and tours to the Alto Nangaritza. Contact him in advance.

⊖ Transport

Saraguro *p968*
Bus To and from **Cuenca** throughout the day, US$5, 3 hrs; to **Loja**, US$1.75, 2 hrs. Check if your bus is leaving from the plaza or the Panamericana.

Loja *p969*
Air The airport is at La Toma (Catamayo), 35 km west, shared taxi US$4 pp (see Loja to the Peruvian border above). There are TAME (24 de Mayo y E Ortega, T257 0248) and **Icaro** (24 de Mayo y 10 de Agosto, T258 5955) flights to Quito direct (US$70). Flights are often cancelled due to strong winds or fog.
Bus All buses leave from the Terminal Terestre at Av Gran Colombia e Isidro Ayora, at the north of town, some companies also have ticket offices in the centre. From terminal buses every 2 mins to/from centre, 10 mins journey; left luggage, information desk, shops, US$0.15 terminal tax. Taxi from centre, US$1. To **Cuenca**, 5 hrs, US$6. **Machala**, 10 a day, 6 hrs, US$6 (3 routes, via Piñas, for **Zaruma**, unpaved and rough but very scenic; via Balsas, fully paved and also scenic; and via Alamor, for **Puyango petrified forest**, military checkpoints on route). **Quito**, US$14, 13 hrs. **Guayaquil**, 8 hrs, US$10. To **Huaquillas**, US$5, 6 hrs direct. To **Macará**, see below. To **Piura (Peru)**, luxury coach service with

Loja Internacional, via Macará, at 0700, 1300, 2230 and 2300 daily, US$8, 8 hrs including border formalities; buy ticket 24 hrs in advance. Also **Unión Cariamanga** at 0000 and 0600.

Parque Nacional Podocarpus *p969*
For **Cajanuma**, take a Vilcabamba bound van or *taxiruta*, get off at the turnoff, US$1-1.20, it is a 8-km walk from there. Direct transport by taxi to the park gate, about US$10 (may not be feasible in the rainy season) or with a tour from Loja. You can arrange a pick up later from the guard station. To the **lower section**: there are 2 possible entrances. Bombuscaro can be reached from **Zamora**: take a taxi US$6 to the entrance, then walk 1 km to the refuge. The other entrance is at **Romerillos**, 2 hrs south by bus. Bus departs Zamora 0630 and 1415, return to Zamora at 0815 and 1600. A 3-5 day hike is possible into this part of the park, contact the **Ministerio del Ambiente** in Zamora (see above) or **Fundación Maquipucuna** in Quito, Baquerizo Moreno E9-153 y Tamayo, T02-250 7200, www.maqui.org.

Zamora *p970*
Bus Leave from Terminal Terrestre. To **Loja**, frequent, 1½ hrs, US$2.40; to **Gualaquiza**, US$3.50, 5 hrs, where you can change buses for Macas.

Loja to the Peruvian border *p970*
Macará
Bus Coop Loja and Cariamanga have frequent buses, daily from Macará to **Loja**; 6 hrs, US$6. Transportes Loja buses, which have 4 direct buses daily Loja-**Piura**, can also be boarded in Macará, US$4 to Piura, 3 hrs. Likewise **Unión Cariamanga** buses on the Loja-Piura route. *Coop Loja* also has service to **Quito**, US$15, 15 hrs, and **Guayaquil**, US$11, 8 hrs.

⊙ Directory

Loja *p969*
Banks Banco del Austro, Eguiguren 14-12 y Bolívar. Produbanco, Bernardo Valdivieso y José Antonio Eguiguren, on the plaza. Comercial, José Antonio Eguiguren 15-61 y 18 de Noviembre, T256 0579, Mon-Fri 0900-1300, 1500-1800, Sat 0900-1200. Small informal place, changes cash euros and Peruvian soles at poor rates. **Embassies and consulates** Peru, Zoilo Rodríguez 03-05, T07-2587330, Mon-Fri 0900-1300, 1500-1700. **Internet** US$1 per hr. **Post offices** Colón y Sucre; no good for sending parcels.

Vilcabamba to Peru

Vilcabamba → *Phone code: 07. Colour map 11, grid C3. Population 4,300. Altitude: 1,520 m.*

Once an isolated village, Vilcabamba has become increasingly popular with foreign travellers, an established stop along the gringo trail between Ecuador and Peru. The whole area is beautiful and tranquil, with an agreeable climate (17°C minimum, 26°C maximum, the rainy season is November to April; July and August can be very ddry and windy). There are many places to stay and several good restaurants. There are many great day-walks and longer treks throughout the area, as well as ample opportunities for horse riding. A number of lovely private nature reserves are situated east of Vilcabamba, towards Parque Nacional Podocarpus. Trekkers can continue on foot through orchid-clad cloud forests to the high cold *páramos* of Podocarpus. **Tourist office:** iTur ① *Diego Vaca de Vega y Bolívar, on the corner of the main plaza, T264 0090, daily 0800-1300, 1500-1800*, has various pamphlets, helpful. See www.vilcabamba.org.

Rumi Wilco ① *10-min walk northeast of town, take C Agua de Hierro towards C La Paz and turn left, following the signs, US$2 valid for the duration of your stay in Vilcabamba.* This 40-hectare private nature reserve has several signed trails. Many of the trees and shrubs are labelled with their scientific and common names. There are great views of town from the higher trails, and it is a very good place to go for a walk. Over 100 species of birds have been identified here. Volunteers are welcome.

Climbing **Mandango**, 'the sleeping woman' mountain (US$1.50, includes a small bottle

Vilcabamba

Sleeping
Don Germán 1
Izhcayluma 14
Jardín Escondido
  & Restaurant 2
Las Margaritas 5
Le Rendez-Vous 15

Madre Tierra 6
Mandango 7
Paraíso 3
Pinar del Río 4
Ruinas de Quinara 11
Rumi Wilco 12
Valle Sagrado 13

Eating
El Punto 4
La Terraza 4
Layseca's Bakery 1
Natural Yogurt 5
Shanta's 6
Vegetariano 7

of mineral water and a small bag of panela, local raw sugar), is a popular and scenic half-day walk. The signed access is along the highway, 250 m south of the bus terminal. Be careful on the higher sections when it is windy and enquire about safety before going as hold-ups took place in 2006-07.

Vilcabamba to Peru

Many daily buses run from Loja or Vilcabamba to **Zumba** (see Loja, Transport), 112 km south of Vilcabamba. It is a 1½ -hour rough ride by *ranchera* (open-sided bus, 0800, 1430, US$1.75) from Zumba to **La Balsa**, where there is an immigration post (supposedly open 24 hours). Passports may also be checked at Pucapamba, north of La Balsa. A new vehicle bridge has been built over the river to the Peruvian border post (open 0800-1300, 1500-2000); entering Peru, visit immigration and the PNP office. On the Peruvian side a minibus service runs to **Namballe**, 15 minutes away, and cars run to Namballe and **San Ignacio** (Peru) when full, two hours, from where there is transport to **Jaén**. This opens a faster, more direct route between **Vilcabamba and Chachapoyas**, which can now be done, with luck, in two days, but it's a very rough ride.

● Sleeping

Vilcabamba *p974, map p974*
Note You may be approached by people touting for hotels. For its size, Vilcabamba has one of the best selections of accommodation in all Ecuador, so you are better off choosing on your own.
B **Madre Tierra**, 2 Km north on road to Loja, follow signs, T264 0269, www.madretierra1.com. A variety of rooms from ample to small and simple, eclectic colourful decor. Includes breakfast and dinner, vegetarian available, nice grounds, pool, spa (massages and other treatments from US$18), videos, ping-pong. English spoken, US-run.
D-E **Izhcayluma**, 2 km south on highway, T264 0095, www.izhcayluma.com. Comfortable cabins with terrace and hammocks, cheaper with shared bath, F in dorm, includes very good breakfast available all day, excellent restaurant with European specialties, nice grounds, pool, dining area with wonderful views, pleasant bar, games, includes use of bikes to get to town. English and German spoken, helpful. Highly recommended.
D-E **Jardín Escondido**, Sucre y Diego Vaca de Vega, T/F264 0281, www.vilcabamba.org. Nicely refurbished old house around a lovely patio. Brightly decorated comfortable rooms, includes very good and generous breakfast, excellent restaurant, small pool, Jacuzzi extra, parking for a small vehicle. English spoken.
D-E **Las Ruinas de Quinara**, Diego Vaca de Vega east of centre, T264 0301, www.lasruinasde quinara.com. More expensive rooms include breakfast and dinner, restaurant, cheaper in dorm, pool and sauna, laundry facilities, parking, hammocks, videos, sports facilities. Looks OK but persistent attention at bus station.
D-E **Rumi Wilco Ecolodge**, 10-min walk northeast of town, take C Agua de Hierro towards C La Paz and turn left, www.rumiwilco.com. Nice adobe cabins and a wooden one on stilts (the 'Pole House') located in the Rumi Wilco reserve. Lovely setting on the shores of the river, very

tranquil, cheaper with shared bath, laundry facilities, fully furnished kitchens, discounts for long stays, Argentine owners Orlando and Alicia. English spoken, recommended.
E **Cabañas Río Yambala**, Yamburara Alto, 4 km east of town, T09-106 2762, www.vilcabamba.cwc.net. Cabins in a beautiful tranquil setting on the shores of the Río Yambala. Meals available on request, cheaper with shared bath, hot water, cooking facilities, access to Las Palmas private nature reserve, good birdwatching. English spoken. Recommended.
E **Las Margaritas**, Sucre y Clodoveo Jaramillo, T264 0051, www.vilcabamba.org. Small family-run hotel with very comfortable rooms, includes good breakfast, small pool, parking, solar-heated water, nice garden. Good value.
E **Le Rendez-Vous**, Diego Vaca de Vega 06-43 y La Paz, T09-219 1180, www.rendezvousecuador.com. Very comfortable rooms with terrace and hammocks around a lovely garden. Includes good breakfast, hot water, pleasant atmosphere, French run by Isabelle and Serge, English also spoken. Good value and recommended.
E **Paraíso**, Av Eterna Juventud (the main highway) 500 m north of the centre, T264 0266. Cabins on nice grounds, a bit faded but adequate, includes breakfast, restaurant, hot water, pool and spa, parking, massage available in an 'energized' metal pyramid.
E **Pinar del Río**, La Paz y Agua de Hierro, T09-385 6638. Small family-run hostel, meals on request, hot water, patio with hammocks, pool table, good value.
E-F **Valle Sagrado**, Luis Fernando de Vega y Av de la Eterna Juventud, T264 0386, www.vilcabamba.org. Ample grounds, basic rooms, cheaper with shared bath, electric shower, laundry and cooking facilities, parking.
F **Don Germán**, Bolívar y Clodoveo Jaramillo (no

sign), T264 0130. Shared bath, electric shower, laundry and cooking facilities, simple, family run, friendly owner: Sra Libia Toledo.

F Mandango, Huilcopamba y Juan Montalvo behind the market, T264 0058. Cheaper with shared bath, electric shower, lovely views from the balconies on the top floors.

Vilcabamba to Peru *p975*
E-F El Emperador, Colón y Orellana, Zumba, T230 8063. Newest in town, cheaper with shared bath, cold water, opened in 2006.
F San Luis, 12 de Febrero y Brasil, Zumba, T230 8017. Basic, shared bath, cold water.

❷ Eating

Vilcabamba *p974, map p974*
¶¶-¶ Shanta's, 800 m from town on the road to Yamburara, daily 1200-0000. Restaurant and bar, good international food with specialties such as trout and frogs' legs, tasty pizza, nicely decorated rustic setting, pleasant atmosphere.
¶¶-¶ La Terraza, D Vaca de Vega y Bolívar, daily 1000-2100. Popular, sidewalk seating, right on the main plaza. A variety of international dishes.
¶ Vegetariano, Valle Sagrado y Diego Vaca de Vega, daily 0830-2030. Small vegetarian restaurant in a nice garden. Very good 3 course set meals and a few à la carte dishes, also breakfasts. Recommended.

Cafés
El Punto, Sucre y Luis Fernando de Vega, 0800-2100, closed Tue. Sidewalk café on the main plaza, breakfast, snacks, good pizza, sandwiches on home-made bread, sweets, coffee and drinks.
Layseca's Bakery, Bolívar y Clodoveo Jaramillo. Home-made Belgian chocolate, bread and sweets.
Natural Yogurt, Bolívar, at the main plaza, daily 0800-2200. Home-made yoghurt, savoury and sweet crêpes, pasta dishes.

▲ Activities and tours

Vilcabamba *p974, map p974*
See under Sleeping, above, for more options.
Horse riding Short trips US$5 per hour, half day US$16, full day with lunch US$25. Overnight

trips cost US$25-35 per day, including accommodation and meals.
Caballos Gavilán, Sucre y Diego Vaca de Vega, T08-632 3285, gavilanhorse@yahoo.com. Run by New Zealander Gavin Moore, lots of experience, good horseman.
Centro Ecuestre, Diego Vaca de Vega y Bolívar. A group of local guides, helpful.
La Tasca, Diego Vaca de Vega y Sucre, T09-184 1287. Riding tours with experienced guide, René León.
Monta Viejo Luis, Luis Fernando de la Vega y Valle Sagrado, T264 0176. Riding with Lucho Bejarano.

❺ Transport

Vilcabamba *p974, map p974*
Loja to Vilcabamba, a spectacular 1½-hour bus ride; from Loja's Terminal Terrestre,
Vilcabambaturis vans and mini-buses, every 15 min, 0545-2045, US$1, 1 hr; or *taxirutas* (shared taxis) from Av Pío Jaramillo y Maximiliano Ortega, 0600-2015, US$1.20, 45 min. To **Loja**, vans and shared taxis leave from the small terminal behind the market.

To **Zumba** via Vilcabamba, with 4 companies, several daily (1st at 0530), 6-7 hrs, US$7.50, shop around. First from Vilcabamba 0630, US$6.50, 5-6 hrs.

❶ Directory

Vilcabamba *p974, map p974*
Banks There are no banks, only one stand-alone ATM (often out of order) at Diego Vaca de Vega y Bolívar, next to iTur. Best to bring cash but if stuck you can try the **San Pablo grocery store** on Clodoveo Jaramillo across from the bus station; they may help with cash euros and soles, TCs, Visa and MC cash advances, but only when the owner is in. **Internet** US$1-1.25 per hr, **Mandango**, at the hostel, 0900-2100. A couple of others near the park. **Massage** Beauty Care, Bolívar y Diego Vaca de Vega, T09-326 1944, daily 1000-1800. Karina Zumba, facials, waxing, Reiki, 1 hr US$10. **Shanta's** (see Eating, above), T08-562 7802, Lola Encalada is a physiotherapist, 1¼ hr therapeutic massage US$11, waxing.

Guayaquil and south to Peru

→ *Phone code: 04. Colour map 11, grid B2. Population: 2,300,000. Altitude: sea level.*
Guayaquil is hotter, faster and brasher than the capital. It is Ecuador's largest city and the country's chief seaport; an industrial and commercial centre, some 56 km from the Río

Guayas' outflow into the Gulf of Guayaquil. The Puerto Marítimo handles three-quarters of the country's imports and almost half of its exports. Industrial expansion continually fuels the city's growth. Founded in 1535 by Sebastián de Benalcázar, then again in 1537 by Francisco Orellana, the city has always been an intense political rival to Quito. Guayaquileños are certainly more lively, colourful and open than their Quito counterparts. Since 2000, Guayaquil has cleaned-up and 'renewed' some of its most frequented downtown areas, there is a new airport terminal, a new transit system, the Metrovía, and the bus station is being rebuilt. The city as a whole is becoming more attractive and the authorities are trying hard to encourage tourism.

Thriving and ever increasing banana plantations, with shrimp farms among the mangroves, are the economic mainstay of the coastal area bordering the east flank of the Gulf of Guayaquil. Rice, sugar, coffee and cacao are also produced. The Guayas lowlands are subject to flooding, humidity is high and biting insects are fierce. Mangroves characterize the coast leading south to Huaquillas, the main border crossing to Peru.

Ins and outs

Getting there José Joaquín de Olmedo International **airport** is 10 minutes north of the city centre by taxi (recommended for safety, US$4). Neither the Metrovía nor buses to the centre (eg Línea 130 'Full 2') are safe or practical with luggage. For groups, **Trans Rabbit** (T216 9228) has van service (US$12 downtown). If going straight on to another city, get a cab directly to the **Terminal Terrestre** (bus station), which is close by; US$3. The northern terminus of the Metrovía is opposite the Terminal Terrestre and many city buses go from the bus station to the city centre, (eg Línea 84 to Plaza Centenario) but these are not safe with luggage; take a taxi (US$3-4). ▸▸ *For more detailed information see Transport, page 983.*

Getting around Not surprisingly for a city of this size, you will need to get around by public transport. A number of hotels are centrally located in the downtown core. The Metrovía crosses the city from north to south with articulated busses. There are also city buses and *furgonetas* (minibuses), all cost US$0.25 and get overcrowded at rush hour, watch out for pickpockets. Taxis are the safest and most comfortable option. Meters are not used, so always agree on the fare in advance. The rates are slightly lower for taxis taken in the street, outside the airport or bus terminal. Short trips costs US$2.50, the fares from the centre to Urdesa, Policentro or Alborada are around US$3-4.

Orientation The centre is on the west bank of the Río Guayas. **Barrio Centenario** to the south of the centre is the original residential sector, now a peaceful, tree-shaded haven. Newer residential areas are **Urdesa**, northwest of the centre, in between two branches of the Estero Salado (about 15 minutes from downtown, traffic permitting); five minutes by taxi from the international airport and bus terminal are the districts of **La Garzota**, **Sauces** and **Alborada**. They are cleaner, less congested and safer than the centre, but with all services, 10-15 minutes by taxi. A road tunnel under Cerro Santa Ana links the northern suburbs to downtown. The city is divided into four quadrants separated by a north-south axis and an east-west axis. All north-south streets are called *avenidas* and the east-west streets are *calles*. Each has an alpha-numeric designation such as Avenida 12 south-east. The airport and bus terminal are in the northeastern quadrant, the commercial heartland in the southeastern quadrant. Although this system is officially in place, the old street names persist and the population uses only the old nomenclature.

Tourist offices Centro de Información Turística del Municipio ① *Clemente Ballén y Pichincha, Plaza de la Administración, T232 4182 ext 19, Wed-Sat 1000-1700, English spoken*, has pamphlets and city maps. There is also an information booth on a railway car in Malecón 2000, next to La Rotonda monument. **Ministerio de Turismo** ① *P Ycaza 203 y Pichincha, p 5, T256 8764, Mon-Fri 0830-1700*. Information about the coastal provinces of Ecuador, Spanish only. In 2006, the municipality published bilingual pocket guides to Guayaquil's attractions, restaurants and bars, available in bookstores; see www.guayaquilguides.com. Websites with information about Guayaquil and the coast include www.visitaguayaquil.com, www.guayaquil.gov.ec, and www.turismoguayas.com.

Climate From May-December it is dry with often overcast days but pleasantly cool nights, whereas the hot rainy season from January-April can be oppressively humid.

Safety Despite an ongoing public safety campaign by the municipal authorities, residential neighbourhoods hide behind bars and protect themselves with armed guards. Criminal gangs are an important security issue. The Malecón, parts of Avenida 9 de Octubre and the Las Peñas neighbourhood are heavily patrolled and reported safe. The area around Plaza Centenario is not safe, day or night. The rest of the city carries all the usual risks of a large seaport and metropolis, so it is best not to walk anywhere with valuables and always take taxis at night.

Guayaquil

Sights

A wide, tree-lined waterfront avenue, the Malecón Simón Bolívar runs alongside the Río Guayas from the **Mercado Sur**, past the exclusive **Club de la Unión**, the Moorish clock tower, by the imposing **Palacio Municipal** and **Gobernación** and the old Yacht Club to Las Peñas. The riverfront along this avenue is an attractive promenade, known as **Malecón 2000**, where visitors and locals can enjoy the fresh river breeze and take in the views. There are gardens, fountains, monuments and walkways. You can dine at upmarket restaurants, cafés and food courts. Towards the south end are souvenir shops, a shopping mall and the old **Mercado Sur** (prefabricated by Eiffel 1905-1907), now known as **Palacio de Cristal**, used as a gallery housing temporary exhibits.

Guayaquil orientation

Ecuador Guayaquil & south to Peru

At the north end of the Malecón is the **Museo Antropológico y de Arte Contemporaneo** (MAAC) ⓘ *T230 9400, Wed-Sat 1000-1730, US$1,50; Sun and holidays 1000-1600, free*, with excellent collections of ceramics and gold objects from coastal cultures and an extensive modern art collection.

At the north end is the old district of **Las Peñas**, the last picturesque vestige of colonial Guayaquil with its brightly painted wooden houses and narrow, cobbled main street (Numa Pompilio Llona). Recently gentrified, it is now an attractive place for a walk to **Cerro Santa Ana**, which offers great views of the city and the mighty Guayas. The area is heavily guarded and safe. It has a bohemian feel, with bars and restaurants. A large open-air exhibition of paintings and sculpture is held here during the *fiestas julianas* (24-25 July). **Santo Domingo**, the city's first church founded in 1548, stands just by Las Peñas. Other churches of note are **San Francisco**, with its restored colonial interior, off 9 de Octubre and P Carbo, and the beautiful **Basílica La Merced**.

In the pleasant, shady **Parque Bolívar** stands the **Cathedral**, in Gothic style, inaugurated in the 1950s. In the park are many iguanas and the park is popularly referred to as Parque de las Iguanas. The nearby **Museo Municipal** ⓘ *in the Biblioteca Municipal, Sucre y Chile, Tue-Sat 0900-1700, free*, has paintings, gold and archaeological collections, shrunken heads, a section on the history of Guayaquil and a good newspaper library.

Between the Parque Bolívar and the Malecón is the **Museo Nahim Isaías** ⓘ *Pichincha y Clemente Ballén, T04-2324283, Wed-Sat 1000-1700, Sun 1100-1500, US$1.50, free on Sun*, a colonial art museum with a permanent religious art collection and temporary exhibits.

Halfway up 9 Octubre is the main plaza, **Parque Centenario** with a towering monument to the liberation of the city erected in 1920. Overlooking the park is the museum of the **Casa de la Cultura** ⓘ *9 de Octubre 1200 y P Moncayo, T230 0500 Tue-Fri 1000-1800, Sat 0900-1500. US$0.50. English-speaking guides available* which houses an impressive collection of prehistoric gold items in its archaeological museum. Also here is the **Pinacoteca Manuel Rendón Seminario**, a photo collection of old Guayaquil.

North of Parque Centenario, below Cerro El Carmen, the huge, spreading **Cemetery** with its dazzling, high-rise tombs and the ostentatious mausoleums of the rich is worth a visit. A flower market over the road sells the best selection of blooms in the city. Go on a Sunday when there are plenty of people about.

Sights outside the city

Parque Histórico Guayaquil ⓘ *Vía Samborondón, near Entreríos, T283 3807, www.parquehistorico.com, Tue-Sun 0900-1630, US$4.50, children and seniors US$1.50, CISA buses to Samborondón leave from the Terminal Terrestre every 20 mins, US$0.25.* The park recreates Guayaquil and its rural surroundings at the end of the 19th century. There is a natural area with native flora and fauna, a traditions section where you can learn about rural life and how crafts are made, an urban section with wooden architecture and an educational farm. A pleasant place for a stroll. The **Botanical Gardens** are northwest ⓘ *Av Francisco de Orellana, in Ciudadela Las Orquídeas, T289 9689, daily 0800-1600, US$3, guiding service US$5. bus line 63 or furgoneta Orquídeas.* Good views and a long but pleasant walk. There are over 3,000 plants, including 150 species of Ecuadorean and foreign orchids. The **Malecón Estero Salado**, west of the centre, is a pleasant waterfront promenade along a brackish estuary. It has various monuments, eateries specializing in seafood, and rowboats and pedal-boats for hire.

Bosque Protector Cerro Blanco ⓘ *US$4, additional guiding fee US$7-12 depending on trails visited, camping US$7 pp, lodge available.* The reserve, run by **Fundación Pro-Bosque**, is set in tropical dry forest with an impressive variety of birds (over 200 species) and with sightings of howler monkeys, ocelot, puma, jaguar and peccaries, among others. Reservations required during weekdays and for groups larger than 8 at weekends, and for birders wishing to arrive before or stay after normal opening hours (0800-1530). Vía a la Costa, Km 16, entrance beyond the Club Rocafuerte, T287 4947, www.bosquecerroblanco.com. Taxi from Guayaquil US$10-20. The yellow and green 'Chongonera' buses leave every 30 mins from Parque Victoria and pass the park entrance on the way to Puerto Hondo. On the other side of the road is **Puerto Hondo**. Canoe trips through the mangroves can be arranged on the spot at weekends from the *Fundación Pro-Bosque* kiosk for US$7 per person with guides, or during the week with the Cerro Blanco office (see above).

Heading east then south from Guayaquil, 22 km beyond the main crossroads at Km 50 on the road to Naranjal, lies the **Ecological Reserve of Manglares Churute** ① *US$10; a boat trip costs an extra US$40 (up to 15 people)*. Arrange several days ahead through the Ministerio del Ambiente office in Guayaquil, Av Quito 402 y Padre Solano, p 10, T229 3131; or Biólogo Fernando Cedeño, T09-961 9815 (Mob). Buses leave the terminal every 30 minutes going to Naranjal or Machala. Ask to be let off at Churute information centre.Canoe trips into the mangroves with guides can see waterbirds, monkeys, dolphins and lots of other wildlife. There is a trail through the dry tropical forest (1½ hours' walk) and you can also walk (one hour) to Laguna Canclón or Churute, a large lake where ducks nest.

● Sleeping

Guayaquil *p978, map p981.*
Guayaquil has some of the best top-class accommodation in Ecuador. Major class hotels include: **LL Hilton Colón**, Av Francisco de Orellana in Kennedy Norte (outside downtown), T268 9000, www.hilton.com (superb), **L Oro Verde**, 9 de Octubre y Gracía Moreno, T232 7999, www.ororverdehotels.com, and **A Ramada**, Malecón 606 e Imbabura, T256 5555, www.hotelramada.com (excellent location right on the Malecón). Decent economy hotels are few and far between. They are mostly downtown and concentrated around Parque Centenario, an unsafe area at all hours.

L Hampton Inn Boulevard, 9 de Octubre 432 y Baquerizo Moreno, T256 6700, www.hampton.com.ec. Buffet breakfast, restaurant, internet, central, very good facilities.
AL Continental, Chile y 10 de Agosto, T232 9270, www.hotelcontinental.com.ec. Includes breakfast, 24 hr restaurant, a *KLM Golden Tulip* hotel, 5-star, good coffee shop, central location.
AL Palace, Chile 214 y Luque, T232 1080, www.hotelpalaceguayaquil.com.ec. Includes breakfast, 24-hr cafeteria, excellent, good value for business travellers, modern, traffic noise on Av Chile side, travel agency. Recommended.
A Grand Hotel Guayaquil, Boyacá 1600 y 10 de Agosto, T232 9690, www.grandhotel guayaquil.com. Includes buffet breakfast, good restaurants, a/c, pool (US$6 for non-residents), gym and sauna.
A-D Casa Alianza, Av Segunda 318 y C 12, Los Ceibos, T235 1261, www.casaalianza.com. Good hostel, far from the centre, a variety of rooms and prices, cafeteria, a/c, cheaper with shared bath and fan, **E** pp in dorm with a/c, run by Norwegian NGO.
B Hostal Quil, Pres L Cordero Crespo y Sufragio Libre, Ciudadela Naval Norte, Mz 6, solar 10, 5 mins from airport, T239 1294, hostalquil@yahoo.es. With breakfast, a/c, cable TV, café, owned by *Creter Tours*, www.cretertours.com.
B La Fontana, P Ycaza y Córdova, T230 3967. Nice hotel in an excellent location, bright ample rooms, suites with balconies, includes breakfast, restaurant, bar with live music, a/c, discounts at weekends, reserve ahead.

B Las Peñas, Escobedo 1215 y Vélez, T232 3355, www.hlpgye.com. Includes breakfast, cafeteria, a/c, good location in refurbished part of town.
B Sol de Oriente, Aguirre 603 y Escobedo, T232 5500, hsolorie@gye.satnet.net. Includes breakfast, restaurant, minibar, gym, excellent value.
B-C Iguanazú, Ciudadela La Cogra, Manzana 1, Villa 2, off Av Carlos Julio Arosemena Km 3½, T220 1143, www.iguanazuhostel.com. Lovely suburban guesthouse, includes breakfast, **E** pp in dorm, pool and jacuzzi, cooking facilities, parking, terrace with hammocks and views of the city, French spoken.
C Hostal de La Alborada, Alborada IX, Manzana 935, Villa 8, near airport but hard to find, T223 7251. Clean hostel with simple but comfortable rooms, includes breakfast, a/c.
C La Torre, Chile 303 y Luque, p 13-15, T253 1316, www.latorrehotel.com.ec. Popular hotel in a downtown office building, includes breakfast, cafeteria, a/c, nice views, reasonably quiet for where it is, busy, advance booking advised.
C Malecón Inn, Sucre 203 y Pichincha, p7, 1 block from the Malecón, T251 1290, www.maleconinn.com. Occupying a couple of floors in a multi-storey building. Rooms and suites, some with jacuzzi, includes breakfast, restaurant, a/c, gym, parking.
C Tangara Guest House, Manuela Sáenz y O'Leary, Manzana F, Villa 1, Ciudadela Bolivariana (a residential area between the airport and downtown), T228 4445. Includes breakfast, a/c, fridge, nice. Recommended.
D-E Europa, Pres Jaime Roldós 4 NE, primer paseo 14A-NE, T228 4751, imporras@uio.telconet.net. A/c, cheaper with fan, better rooms have fridge, convenient location for the airport and bus terminal, but the traffic and aircraft noise are deafening.
D-E Savoy II, Junín 607 y Boyacá, T231 0206. Modern hotel in a central location, a/c, good value, opened in 2006.
E-F Vélez, Vélez 1021 y Quito, T253 0356. Large budget hotel by Plaza Centenario, very popular and often full, does not take bookings. Cafeteria, private bath, cold water, a/c, cheaper with fan, very good value but do not leave valuables in rooms.

🍴 Eating

Guayaquil *p978, map p981*
Main areas for restaurants are the centre with many in the larger hotels, around Urdesa and the residential and commercial neighbourhoods to the north.

🍴 **El Manantial**, Estrada y Las Monjas, Urdesa, T238 2983, Mon-Sat 0900-1200. Seafood and meat specialties, good.

🍴 **La Trattoria da Enrico**, Bálsamos 504 y las Monjas, Urdesa, T238 7079, Mon-Sat 1230-1530, 1930-1130, Sun 1230-2230. The best in food and surroundings, very exclusive, good antipasto.

🍴 **Lo Nuestro**, Estrada 9-03 e Higueras, Urdesa, T238 6398, daily 1100-1530, 1900-2330. Colonial decor, great seafood platters.

🍴 **La Parilla del Ñato**, Estrada 1219 y Laureles in Urdesa; Av Francisco de Orellana opposite the Hilton Colón; Luque y Pichincha downtown; and several other locations, daily 1200-0000. Large variety, salad bar. Good quality grill, generous portions.

🍴 **Tasca Vasca**, C Ballén 422 y Chimborazo, T253 4597, Mon-Fri 1000-0000, Sat 1000-2200, Sun 1000-1500. Specialties are paella and 'corvina a la vasca'.

🍴 **Tsuji**, VE Estrada 813 y Guayacanes, Urdesa, T288 1183, Tue-Sun 1200-1500, 1900-2300. Wonderful authentic dishes, a Guayaquil tradition.

🍴🍴 **Riviera**, Estrada y Ficus, Urdesa and Mall del Sol. Good pasta, antipasto, salads, bright surroundings, good service.

🍴 **La Canoa** in *Hotel Continental*, and in *Mall del Sol*, cheaper. Open 24 hrs, for traditional dishes

Guayaquil

To Airport & Bus Station
To Cemetery

Rio Guayas

N
0 metres 100
0 yards 100
Ⓜ Metrovía

Sleeping
Continental 3
Grand Guayaquil 4
Hampton Inn Boulevard 5
La Fontana 1
Las Peñas 12
La Torre 2

Malecón Inn 9
Oro Verde 6
Palace 7
Ramada 8
Savoy II 14
Sol de Oriente 10
Vélez 11

Eating
Asia 2
La Parrilla del Ñato 3
Los Tres Canastos 4
Tasca Vasca 1

rarely found these days, with different specials during the week.

¶¶¶ La Vaca Gaucha, Av Principal y Av Las Aguas, Urbanor, Tue-Fri 1800-2300, Sat 1200-2000, Sun 1200-1700. Excellent quality, all you can eat for US$10.

¶¶-¶ Cantonés, Av G Pareja y C 43, La Garzota. Huge emporium with authentic dishesvery good, closes 2200.

¶ Asia, Sucre 321 y Chile. Good food, vegetarian dishes on request.

¶ Ollantay, Tungurahua 508 y 9 de Octubre, west of downtown. The best choice for vegetarian food.

¶ Rey del Pescado Frito, Boyacá y Junín, Malecón 2000, and Av Pareja, Alborada. Open daily, all day. Good quality fish and seafood.

Crab houses are almost an institution and great fun. Prices are quite uniform: a stuffed crab, *carapacho relleno* (delicious), costs about US$10, an *arroz con cangrejo* US$4-5.

¶¶¶ Manny's, Av Miraflores y Segunda, T220 2754, daily 1000-2200. *Arroz con cangrejo* is the specialty, good quality and value.

¶¶¶ Red Crab, Estrada y Laureles, Urdesa, T238 0512, daily 1100-0000. Wide variety of excellent seafood, interesting décor.

¶¶¶ Sandunga's, Av Plaza Dañín frente al Asilo de Ancianos, Tue-Fri 1200-1600, 1800-2330, Sat-Sun 1200-2330. Delicious seafood.

¶¶¶-¶¶ El Cangrejo Criollo, Av Rolando Pareja, Villa 9, La Garzota, daily 0900-0100. Excellent, varied seafood menu.

Cafés

Aroma Café, Malecón 2000 by Tomás Martínez, daily 1200-0000. Café, also serves regional food, nice garden setting.

Bopán, VE Estrada y Las Monjas, Urdesa, Mon-Sat 0800-0000; P Icaza y Malecón, downtown, Mon-Fri 0830-2200. Excellent sandwiches and local snacks, salads, coffee, breakfast.

California Gourmet, Escobedo 1215 y Vélez, below Hotel Las Peñas, Mon-Sat 0700-2000, Sun 0700-1400. Breakfast, snacks, drinks, sweets.

Fruta Bar, Malecón e Imbabura, downtown; VE Estrada 608 y Monjas, Urdesa. Excellent fruit juices and snacks, unusual African decor, good music.

Los Tres Canastos, Chile 126-128 y Vélez and several other locations. Breakfast, snacks, safe fruit juices and smoothies.

Pasteles & Compañía, Luque y Pichincha and Policentro. A variety of sandwiches and baked goods. Mid-range prices. Open 0900-2000.

● Entertainment

Guayaquil *p978, map p981*
Guayaquil nightlife is not cheap. Most discos charge a cover of around US$5-10 on weekdays, US$10-15 at weekends, and drinks are expensive. There are clubs, bars and casinos in most of the major hotels, as well as in the northern suburbs, especially at the **Kennedy Mall**. Also in vogue are the **Las Peñas/Cerro Santa Ana** area the **Zona Rosa**, between the Malecón Simón Bolívar and Rocafuerte, and between C Loja and C Roca. Both these areas are considered reasonably safe. **Cinemas** are at the main shopping centres and cost around US$3-4. The **IMAX Cinema**, on the Malecón 2000, projects impressive films on its oversize screen.

Boat parties The **Capitan Morgan**, US$5, a tour and party boat, sails from the Malecón every evening. It offers pricey drinks, snacks, music and dancing, with nice views of the city.

Resaca, Malecón 2000, at the level of Junín, daily 1130-0000, Lovely setting overlooking the river, live tropical music Fri-Sat night. Also serves economical set lunches on weekdays (go early), regional dishes at mid to expensive prices (Mon-Wed, all you can eat crabs and beer US$13) and pricey drinks.

● Festivals and events

Guayaquil *p978, map p981*
The foundation of Guayaquil is celebrated on **24-25 Jul**, and the city's independence on **9-12 Oct**. Both holidays are lively and there are many public events; cultural happenings are prolonged throughout Oct.

● Shopping

Guayaquil *p978, map p981*
There are lots of shopping malls – ideal for cooling off on hot days.

Bookshops El Librero, in the Ríocentro. Has English books. **Mr Books**, at Mall del Sol. Good selection including some English books and travel guides. **Nuevos Horizontes**, 6 de Marzo 924. For book exchange. **Sagitario**, Mall del Sol. Excellent bookstore, has English books. **Selecciones**, Av 9 de Octubre 830 and in Albán Borja Mall has a choice of pricey novels and lots of magazines in English.

Camping equipment Casa Maspons, Ballén 517 y Boyacá. For camping gas.

Handicrafts Mercado Artesanal del Malecón 2000, at the south end of the Malecón, has many small kiosks selling varied crafts.

Mercado Artesanal, Baquerizo Moreno between Loja and J Montalvo. Greatest variety, almost a whole block of permanent stalls with good prices. El Telar in Albán Borja Mall. Good variety of *artesanías*. Ramayana, in Albán Borja Mall. Good ceramics.

Malls Centro Comercial Malecón 2000 is at the south end of the Malecón. Centro Comercial San Marino, Av Francisco de Orellana y L Plaza Dañín. Huge, one of the largest in South America. Mall del Sol is near the airport on Av Constitución y Juan Tanca Marengo. It has craft shops. Las Bahías, is a huge bazaar area on either side of Olmedo from Villamil to Chile, by the south end of the Malecón. It was traditionally where contraband was sold from boats which put into the bay and is one of the city's oldest marketplaces. It's still very popular for electrical appliances, clothing and shoes. It has been cleaned up a bit in recent years but you must watch your valuables and be prepared to bargain.

▲ Activities and tours

Guayaquil *p978, map p981*
Details about agencies operating Galápagos cruises page 1020. A 3-hr city tour costs about US$14 pp in a group.
Canodros, Urb Santa Leonor, Mz 5, local 10, T228 5711, www.galapagosexplorer.com. Runs luxury Galápagos cruises and also operates the Kapawi Ecological Reserve in the southern Oriente.
Centro Viajero, Baquerizo Moreno 1119 y 9 de Octubre, No 805, T256 2565, centrovi@ telconet.net. Custom-designed tours to all regions, travel information and bookings, car and driver service, well informed about good value options for Galápagos, English spoken. Highly recommended.
Cruceros Discovery, Muelle Malecón y Tomás Martínez, T230 4824, www.crucerosdiscovery. com. Runs boat trips to Isla Santay, a Ramsar site wetland with walking trails (Tue-Sun 1100-1600, 2½ hrs, US$7), and various other river cruises.
Ecoventura, Av Francisco de Orellana 222, Mz 12, Solar 22, Kennedy Norte, T228 3182, www.ecoventura.com. Excellent high-end Galápagos tours, the "first CarbonNeutral travel company in the Galápagos and South America".
Ecuadorian Tours, Esmeraldas 816 y 9 de Octubre, p 2, T228 6900, www.ecuadoriantours gye.com.ec. Land tours in all regions and Galápagos cruises. Amex representative.
Galasam, Edificio Gran Pasaje, 9 Octubre 424, ground floor, T230 4488, www.galapagos-islands.com. Has boats, mostly for charter, for Galápagos cruises, city tours, tours to reserves near Guayaquil, diving trips, also run highland and jungle tours.
Kleintours, Av Alcívar, Mz 410, Solar 11, Kennedy Norte, T268 1700, www.kleintours.com. Land and Galápagos tours.
La Moneda, Av de las Américas 809 y C 2, and P Icaza 115 y Pichincha, T269 0900, www.lamoneda.com.ec. City and coastal tours, whale watching, tours in other areas of Ecuador.
Macchiavello Tours, Antepara 802-A y 9 Octubre, T228 1056. Very good whale and dolphin watching tours.
Metropolitan Touring, Antepara 915 y 9 de Octubre and at *Hotel Hilton Colón*, T232 0300, www.metropolitan-touring.com. High-end land tours and Galápagos cruises.

⊙ Transport

Guayaquil *p978, map p981*
Air The information booth outside international arrivals (T216 9000, open 24 hrs) has hotel and transport information. On the ground floor are a Banco de Guayaquil (Mon-Fri 0830-1800, ATM, changes euros at poor rates, no TCs), post office, luggage storage (0800-2200, US$5 for 24 hours) and car hire agencies. There is also a food court, several ATMs, phone office and internet. For transport, see Ins and outs, above. Many flights daily to **Quito**. Sit on the right side for the best views. Also to **Cuenca** and **Loja**. Daily to **Galápagos** (see page 1018).
Bus Metrovía (T269 1611, US$0.25) is an integrated transport system of articulated buses running on exclusive lanes and *alimentadores* (feeder buses) serving suburbs from the northern and southern terminuses. It runs from the Terminal Río Daule, opposite the Terminal Terrestre, in the north to the Terminal El Guasmo in the south. In the city centre it runs along Boyacá southbound and Pedro Carbo northbound.

City buses and *furgonetas* (vans) are only permitted on a few streets in the centre; northbound buses go along Rumichaca, southbound along Lorenzo de Garaicoa or García Avilés, US$0.25.
Long distance The Terminal Terrestre, just north of the airport, is off the road to the Guayas bridge. In early 2007, this terminal was closed for reconstruction and it was expected to reopen by the end of the year. A temporary terminal was operating nearby. Several companies to/from **Quito**, 8 hrs, US$9; also non-stop, a/c services, eg **Transportes Ecuador**, Av de las Américas y Hermano Miguel, opposite the new airport terminal, T229 4788. To **Cuenca**, 4 hrs via Molleturo/Cajas, 5 hrs via Zhud, both US$5. **Riobamba**, 5 hrs, US$5. To **Santo Domingo de los Colorados**, 5 hrs, US$5. **Manta**, 4 hrs, US$4.

Esmeraldas, 8 hrs, US$8. To Bahía de
Caráquez, 6 hrs, US$5. To Ambato, 6 hrs, US$6.
Regular and frequent buses to Playas, 2 hrs,
US$2; and to Salinas, 2½ hrs, US$3. For the
Peruvian border, to/from Huaquillas direct, 4½
hrs, US$6; to/from Machala, 3 hrs, US$5. Direct
bus to Tumbes 10 daily, US$6, 5½ hrs, and to
Piura, 4 a day, 10 hrs, US$10-12 with CIFA, T214
0379.

⊕ Directory

Guayaquil *p978, map p981*
Airline offices Aerogal, Junín 440 y Cordova,
T04-310346. American Airlines, Gral Córdova y
Av 9 de Octubre, Edificio San Francisco, p 20,
T259 8800. Continental, Av 9 de Octubre 100 y
Malecón, T1-800-222333. Iberia, Av 9 de Octubre
101 y Malecón, T232 9558. Icaro, Av Francisco de
Orellana, edif World Trade Centre, T263 0620.
KLM, at the airport, T216 9070. TAME, 9 de
Octubre 424, edif Gran Pasaje, T231 0305.
Banks Banco del Austro, 9 de Octubre y
Boyacá and VE Estrada y Dátiles, Urdesa. Banco
del Pacífico, P Icaza 200, p 4. Cambiosa, 9 de
Octubre y Pichincha. Pacificard, VM Rendón 415
y Córdova, T04-2511500. Produbanco, Pedro
Carbo 604 y Luque , Garaycoa 817 y 9 de Octubre
and VE Estrada 206 y Bálsamos, Urdesa.
American Express, *Ecuadorian Tours*, 9 de
Octubre 1900 y Esmeraldas. Replaces lost Amex
TCs and sells TCs to Amex card holders, but does
not exchange TCs or sell them for cash. Open
Mon-Fri 0900-1300, 1400-1800. **Car hire** All the
main car rental agents are at the airport.
Embassies and consulates Austria, 9 de
Octubre 1312 y Quito, No 1, T228 2303. Belgium,
Lizardo García 301 y Vélez, T236 4429. Canada,
Córdova 808 y VM Rendón, Edif Torre de la
Merced, p 21, T256 3580. Colombia, 9 de Octubre
y Córdova, edif San Francisco, p 2, T256 8753.

Denmark, Gen Córdova 604 y Mendiburo, p 3,
T230 8020. France, José Mascote 909 y Hurtado,
T229 4334. Germany, Av Carlos Julio Arosemena
Km 2, Edif Berlín, T220 0500. Italy, Baquerizo
Moreno 1120, T231 2523. Netherlands, Quisquis
1502 y Tulcán, p 1, T228 0156. Peru, Av Francisco
de Orellana y Alberto Borges, Edif Porta, p 14,
Kennedy Norte, T228 0135. Spain, Urdesa C
Circunvalación, Solar 118 y C Unica, T288 1691.
Sweden, Km 6.5 vía a Daule, T225 4111.
Switzerland, 9 de Octubre 2105, T245 3607. UK,
Gen Córdova 623 y Padre Solano, T256 0400.
USA, 9 de Octubre 1571 y García Moreno, T232
3570. **Internet** There are many cyber cafés in
the centre and suburbs alike, the greatest
number are concentrated in shopping malls.
Prices around US$1 per hr. **Medical
services** For doctors and dentists, contact your
consulate for recommendations. Hospitals: the
main hospital used by the foreign community is
the Clínica Kennedy, Av San Jorge y la 9na, T228
9666. Also has a branch in Ciudadela La Alborada
XIII, Mz-1227. It contains the consulting rooms of
almost every kind of specialist doctor and
diagnostic laboratory (Dr Roberto Morla speaks
German); very competent emergency
department. Also reliable are: Clínica Alcívar,
Coronel 2301 y Azuay, T258 0030; Clínica
Guayaquil, Padre Aguirre 401 y General Córdova,
T256 3555 (Dr Roberto Gilbert speaks
English and German). **Post offices and
telephones** Pacifictel and the central Post
office are in the same block at Pedro Carbo y
Aguirre. DHL, Malecón 2000, Galería B or 9 de
Octubre y P Carbo, edif San Francisco 300,
T1-800-989898. Recommended for international
service. Servientrega, offices throughout the city,
for deliveries within Ecuador. **Useful
addresses** Immigration: Av Río Daule, near
the bus terminal, T214 0002, for visa extensions.

South to Peru

Machala → *Phone code: 07. Colour map 11, grid C2. Population: 204,580.*
The capital of the province of El Oro is a booming agricultural town in a major banana producing
and exporting region with an annual banana fair in September. It is not particularly attractive,
somewhat dirty, oppressively hot and unsafe. For the tourist, the only reasons for stopping here
are to go to the beautiful tranquil uplands of El Oro, and to catch a through CIFA bus to Peru (if
not caught in Guayaquil) for the beaches around Máncora. **Tourist office** ⊕ *9 de Mayo y 9 de
Mayo, Municipio p 2, T292 0400, Spanish only, open Mon-Fri 0800-1230,1500-1800.*
  Puerto Bolívar, on the Estero Jambelí among mangroves, is a major export outlet for over
two million tonnes of bananas annually. From the old pier canoes cross to the beaches of
Jambelí (US$2.40) on the far side of the mangrove islands which shelter Puerto Bolívar from
the Pacific. The beaches are crowded at weekends, deserted during the week and not very
clean. Boats can be rented for excursions to the **Archipiélago de Jambelí**, a maze of islands
and channels just offshore, stretching south between Puerto Bolívar and the Peruvian border.

These mangrove islands are rich in birdlife (and insects for them to feed on, take repellent), the water is very clear and you may also see fish and reefs.

Zaruma → *Phone code: 07. Colour map 11, Grid C3. Population: 8,900. Altitude: 1,300 m.*

Southeast from Machala is the lovely old gold-mining town of Zaruma (118 km). It is reached from Machala by paved road via Piñas, by a scenic dirt road off the main Loja-Machala road, or via Pasaje and Paccha on another scenic dirt road off the Machala-Cuenca road.

Founded in 1549 on orders of Felipe II to try to control the gold extraction, Zaruma is a delightful town perched on a hilltop, with steep, twisting streets and painted wooden buildings. The **Oficina de Turismo** ① *in the Municipio, at the plaza, T07-297 3533, www.vivezaruma.org, Mon-Fri 0800-1200, 1300-1700, Sat 0900-1600, Sun 0830-1230* is very friendly and helpful. They can arrange for guides and accommodation with local families. Next door is the small **Museo Municipal** ① *free, ask for the key at the tourist office if closed.* It has a collection of local historical artefacts. The Zaruma area has a number of pre-Hispanic archaeological sites and petroglyphs are also found in the region. On top of the small hill beyond the market is a public swimming pool (US$1), from where there are amazing views over the hot, dry valleys. For even grander views, walk up **Cerro del Calvario** (follow Calle San Francisco); go early in the morning as it gets very hot. The area has virtually no tourists and is well worth a visit.

Piñas, 19 km west of Zaruma, along the road to Machala is a pleasant town which conserves just a few of its older wooden buildings. There are buses along scenic secondary roads to **Paccha**, up in the hills to the north, and to **Ayapamba** and many other old gold mining villages. Northwest of Piñas, 20 minutes along the road to Saracay and Machala, is **Buenaventura**, to the north of which lies an important area for bird conservation. Many rare birds have been found in the few remaining tracts of forest, with over 310 bird species recorded in the area, which is also rich in orchids. The Jocotoco Foundation (www.fjocotoco.org) protects a 1,500-ha forest in this region, entry US$15, L category lodge, advance booking required.

Puyango

① *110 km south of Machala, US$5 includes tour, camping US$5 pp.*

At Puyango a great number of petrified trees, ferns, fruits and molluscs, 65 to 120 million years old, have been found. Over 120 species of birds can be seen. No accommodation in the village, but ask around for floor space or try at the on-site information centre. If not, accommodation is available in **Alamor**, 20 km south (three hotels, best is **E SICA** *T07-268 0230*). Campsites are also provided. For further information, contact the Dirección Provincial de Turismo, Machala, T293 2106.

Huaquillas → *Phone code: 07. Colour map 11, grid C2. Population: 50,000.*

The stiflingly hot Ecuadorean border town of Huaquillas is something of a shopping arcade for Peruvians. The border runs along the Río Zarumilla and is crossed by the international bridge at the western end of Avenida La República. It is a shortish walk from the bus terminals which are mostly on Avenida Teniente Cordovez.

Border with Peru

The border is open 24 hours; if closed for transit permits on Sunday, they will let you cross if you prefer to sleep in Ecuador. Passports are stamped 3 km north of Huaquillas along the road to Machala. No urban transport to immigration; inter-city buses US$0.18 from Huaquillas, taxis US$1. Allow an hour to complete formalities. Then walk along the main street and across the international bridge into Peru. The main Peruvian immigration and customs complex is outside Zarumilla, 3 km south of the international bridge. The **Huaquillas-Tumbes** crossing can be harrowing, made worse by the crowds and heat. You must always watch your belongings carefully. In addition to cheating by money changers and cab drivers, this border is known for its thefts and con tricks on travellers. Those on the direct **CIFA** bus Guayaquil-Tumbes or Piura should have fewer hassles, otherwise it is best to cross in a group. Women are advised not to cross alone. Those seeking a more relaxed crossing to or from Peru should consider Macará (see page 970) or the new crossings which have opened following the peace treaty between Ecuador and Peru.

● Sleeping

Machala p984
L Oro Verde, Circunvalación Norte, Urb Unioro, T293 3140, www.oroverdehotels.com. Luxury, beautiful gardens, nice pool (US$6 for non-residents), tennis courts, 2 restaurants, casino. Best in town.

C Centro Hotel, Sucre y Guayas, T293 1640. Includes breakfast, cafeteria, a/c, parking, modern and comfortable, free internet.

C Oro, Sucre y Juan Montalvo, T293 0032, orohotel@oro.satnet.net. A/c, includes breakfast, good, helpful, expensive restaurant but good, cheaper café downstairs. Recommended.

D Ejecutivo, Sucre y 9 de Mayo, T292 3162. Cafeteria, a/c, parking, modern and good.

E San Miguel, 9 de Mayo y Sucre, T293 5488. Hot water, a/c, cheaper with fan, fridge, good quality and value.

Zaruma p985
C Hostería El Jardín, Barrio Limoncito, 10 min walk from centre (taxi US$1), T297 2706. Lovely palm garden and terrace with views, includes breakfast, comfortable rooms, small zoo, family-run. Recommended.

C-D Roland, at entrance to town on road from Portovelo, T297 2800. Restaurant with lovely views, pool, comfortable rooms and 5 cabins.

D Cerro de Oro, Sucre 40, T/F297 2505. Modern. Recommended.

D Finca Gálvez, Santa Marianita, vía a Paccha Km 3 (enquire at Bazar María Alejandra, Sucre 005), T296 4063. Includes breakfast, meals on request, nice tree house on a coffee plantation, orchid garden, family run, quiet. Recommended.

E Romería, on main plaza facing the church, T297 2173. Old wooden house with balcony, with bath, floors creak a bit but friendly. Recommended.

Huaquillas p985
E Hernancor, 1 de Mayo y Hualtaco, T299 5467. Cafeteria, a/c, best in town.

E Vanessa, 1 de Mayo y Hualtaco, T/F299 6263. A/c, fridge, parking, OK.
There are several other basic hotels in town.

● Eating

Machala p984
The best food is found in the better hotels.

†† Mesón Hispano, Av Las Palmeras y Sucre. Very good grill, attentive service.

† Chifa Central, Tarqui y 9 de Octubre. Good Chinese.

† Chifa Gran Oriental, 9 de Octubre entre Guayas y Ayacucho. Good food and service.

Zaruma p985
†† Mesón de Joselito, At the entrance to town from Portovelo. Good seafood.

† Cafetería Central, on the plaza. Very good local specialties.

● Transport

Machala p984
Bus There is no Terminal Terrestre. Do not take night buses into or out of Machala as they are prone to hold-ups. To **Quito**, with Occidental (Buenavista entre Sucre y Olmedo), 10 hrs, US$10, 8 daily, and Panamericana (Colón y Bolívar), 7 daily, also luxury service. To **Guayaquil**, see above, hourly with Ecuatoriano Pullman (Colón y 9 de Octubre), CIFA and Rutas Orenses (both 9 de Octubre y Tarqui). There are 3 different routes to **Loja**, each with bus service. They are, from north to south: via **Piñas** and **Zaruma**, partly paved and rough but very scenic; via **Balsas**, fully paved and also scenic; and via **Arenillas** and **Alamor**, for Puyango petrified forest. Fare to **Loja**, 6 hrs, US$6. To **Cuenca**, half-hourly with Trans Azuay (Sucre y Junín), 4 hrs, US$5. To **Huaquillas**, with CIFA (Bolívar y Guayas) and Ecuatoriano Pullman, direct, 1½ hr, US$2, every 30 mins. To **Piura**, in Peru, with CIFA, 4 a day, US$6, 6 hrs; also to **Tumbes**, 8 daily, US$2, 3 hrs.

Zaruma p985
Bus To/from Machala with Trans Piñas or TAC, half-hourly, US$3, 3 hrs. To **Piñas**, take a Machala bound bus, US$1, 1 hr. Also daily service to **Guayaquil**, US$6.50, 6½ hrs, **Quito**, US$10, 12 hrs, **Cuenca**, US$7, 6 hrs and **Loja**, US$5, 5 hrs (may have to change at Portovelo).

Puyango p985
Puyango is west of the highway: alight from bus at turn-off at the bridge over the Río Puyango, where there is a military control. Hourly *rancheras* run between Arenillas and Alamor. Buses from **Machala** (Trans Loja 0930, 1315 and 2130, return buses pass the bridge about 1100, 1330 and 1700, their final destination may not be Machala, so ask), US$3, 3½ hrs. From **Loja** (*Trans Loja* 0900, 1430 and 1930), US$5, 5 hrs. From **Huaquillas** (*Trans Loja* 0730, to Huaquillas at 1000), US$2, 1½ hrs.

Huaquillas p985
Bus There is no Terminal Terrestre, each bus company has its own office, many on Teniente Cordovez. If you are in a hurry, it can be quicker to change buses in Machala or Guayaquil. There are

checkpoints along the road north from Huaquillas, keep your passport to hand. To **Machala**, with CIFA (Santa Rosa y Machala) and Ecuatoriano Pullman, direct, 1 hr, US$2, every hour between 0400 and 2000; via Arenillas and Santa Rosa, 2 hrs, every 10 mins. To **Quito**, with Occidental, every 2 hrs, 12 hrs, US$10; with Panamericana, luxury service, 11½ hrs, 3 daily via Santo Domingo; 2 daily via **Riobamba** and **Ambato**, 12 hrs. To **Guayaquil**, frequent service with CIFA and Ecuatoriano Pullman, fares above. To **Cuenca**, 8 daily, 5 hrs, US$6. To **Loja**, 6 daily, 6 hrs, US$5.

● Directory

Machala p984
Banks For Visa: Banco del Pacifico, Rocafuerte y Junín. **Embassies and consulates** Peruvian Consulate, Urb Unioro, Mz 14, V 11,

near Hotel Oro Verde, T293 0680, Mon-Fri 0900-1800. **Internet** Prices around US$1 per hr. **Post offices** Bolívar y Montalvo.

Huaquillas p985
Banks Many street changers, recognized by their black briefcases, deal in soles and US$ cash. Check the rate beforehand on the internet or with travellers leaving Peru, as there are many tricks and travellers are often cheated. Do not change more US$ than you need to get to Tumbes, where there are reliable cambios, but get rid of all your soles here as they are difficult to exchange further inside Ecuador. Do your own arithmetic - there have been reports of 'doctored' calculators, count your change carefully and watch out for counterfeit bills. Especially avoid those changers who chase after you. **Internet** Several on Av La República, US$1.50 per hr.

Pacific lowlands

This vast tract of Ecuador covers everything west of the Andes and north of the Guayas delta. Though popular with Quiteños and Guayaquileños, who come here for weekends and holidays, the Pacific Lowlands receive relatively few foreign visitors, which is surprising given the natural beauty, diversity and rich cultural heritage of the coast. Here you can surf, watch whales, visit archaeological sites, or just relax and enjoy the best food this country has to offer. The Parque Nacional Machalilla protects an important area of primary tropical dry forest, pre-Columbian ruins, coral reef and a wide variety of wildlife. Further north, in the province of Esmeraldas, there are not only well-known party beaches, but also opportunities to visit the remaining mangroves and experience two unique lifestyles: Afro-Ecuadorean on the coast and native Cayapa further inland. Coastal resorts are busy and more expensive from December to April, the temporada de playa.

Guayaquil to Puerto López

Southwest of Guayaquil is the beach resort of Playas and, west of it, the Santa Elena Peninsula, with Salinas at its tip. North of Santa Elena, the coastal road stretches for 737 km to Mataje on the Colombian border; along the way are countless beaches and fishing villages, and a few cities. The coastal strip is known as 'Ruta del Sol'. Puerto López is the perfect base from which to explore the beautiful Parque Nacional Machalilla.

Playas and Salinas → *Phone code: 04. Colour map 11, grid B1. Population: 37,000 and 36,000 respectively.*
The beach resorts of Playas and Salinas remain as popular as ever with vacationing Guayaquileños. Both can be reached along a paved toll highway from Guayaquil. The road divides after 63 km at El Progreso (Gómez Rendón). One branch leads to General Villamil, normally known as **Playas**, the nearest seaside resort to Guayaquil. Look out for the bottle-shaped ceibo (kapok) trees between Guayaquil and Playas as the landscape becomes drier, turning into tropical thorn scrub. Fishing is still important in Playas and a few single-sailed balsa rafts can still be seen among the motor launches returning laden with fish. These rafts are unique, highly ingenious and very simple. The same rafts without sails are used to spread nets close offshore, then two gangs of men take 2-3 hours to haul them in. In high season, December to April, and at weekends, Playas is prone to severe crowding, although the authorities are trying to keep the packed beaches clean and safe (thieving is

rampant during busy times). Out of season or midweek, the beaches are almost empty especially north towards Punta Pelado (5 km). Playas has six good surf breaks. There are showers, toilets and changing rooms along the beach, with fresh water, for a fee. Many hotels in our **B-F** ranges. Excellent seafood and typical dishes from over 50 beach cafés (all numbered and named). Many are closed out of season. **Tourist office** ① *on the Malecón, Tue-Fri 0800-1200, 1400-1800, Sat-Sun 0900-1600.*

Salinas, surrounded by miles of salt flats, is Ecuador's answer to Miami Beach. **Turismo Municipal** ① *Eloy Alfaro y Mercedes de Jesús Molina, Chipipe, T277 3931, Tue-Fri 0800-1700, Sat 0800-1400.* There is safe swimming in the bay and high-rise blocks of holiday flats and hotels line the seafront. More appealing is the (still urban) beach of Chipipe, south of the well equipped and very exclusive Salinas Yacht Club. During *temporada* (December-April) it is overcrowded, with traffic jams and rubbish-strewn beaches, and its services are stretched to the limit. During off season it is quieter, but still not for 'getting away from it all'. On the south shore of the Santa Elena peninsula, 8 km south of La Libertad, is **Punta Carnero**, with a magnificent 15-km beach with wild surf and heavy undertow, virtually empty during the week. In July, August and September there is great whale watching.

North to Puerto López

The '**Ruta del Sol**' north to Puerto López in the province of Manabí parallels the coastline and crosses the Chongón-Colonche coastal range. Most of the numerous small fishing villages along the way have good beaches and are slowly being developed for tourism. Beware of rip currents and undertow.

Valdivia

San Pedro and Valdivia are two unattractive villages which merge together. There are many fish stalls. This is the site of the 5,000 year-old Valdivia culture. Many houses offer 'genuine' artefacts (it is illegal to export pre-Columbian artefacts from Ecuador) and one resident at the north end of the village will show you the skeletons and burial urns dug up in his back garden. Ask for Juan Orrala, who makes excellent copies, and lives up the hill from the **Ecomuseo Valdivia** ① *daily, US$1,* which has displays of original artefacts from Valdivia and other coastal cultures. There is also a handicraft section, where artisans may be seen at work, and lots of local information. At the museum is a restaurant and 5 rooms with bath to let. Most of the genuine artefacts discovered at the site are in museums in Quito and Guayaquil.

Manglaralto → *Phone code: 04. Colour map 11, grid B2.*

Located 180 km north of Guayaquil, this is the main centre of the region north of Santa Elena. A tagua nursery has been started; ask to see examples of worked 'vegetable ivory' nuts. It is a nice place, with a quiet, clean beach, good surf but little shade. *Pro-pueblo* is an organization working with local communities, to foster family run orchards and cottage craft industry, using tagua nuts, paja toquilla (the stuff Panama hats are made from), and other local products. They have a craft shop in town (opposite the park), an office in San Antonio south of Manglaralto, T278 0230, and headquarters in Guayaquil, T268 3569, www.propueblo.com. *Proyecto de Desarrollo Ecoturístico Comunitario* ① *T252 9968, coorcpr@interactive.net.ec, or contact Paquita Jara* T09-174 0143 has a network of simple lodgings with local families (US$9 per person), many interesting routes into the Cordillera Chongón Colonche and whale watching and island tours.

Montañita, Baja Montañita and Olón

About 3 km north of Manglaralto, **Montañita** (*Population: 23,425*) has mushroomed over the past few years into a major surf resort, packed with hotels, restaurants, surf-board rentals, tattoo parlours and craft/jewellery vendors. There are periodic police drug raids in Montañita and several foreigners are serving long sentences in jail. At the north end of the bay, 1 km away, is another hotel area with more elbow-room, **Baja Montañita** (or Montañita Punta, Surf Point). Between the two is a lovely beach where you'll find some of the best surfing in Ecuador. Various competitions are held during the year and at weekends, in season, the town is full of Guayaquileños. A few minutes north of Montañita is **Olón**, with a spectacular long beach.

Ayampe to Salango

North of Montañita, by **La Entrada**, the road winds up and inland through lush forest before continuing to the small, poor village of **Ayampe** (many popular places to stay at south end of the beach). North of Ayampe are the villages of **Las Tunas**, **Puerto Rico** and **Río Chico**. There are places to stay all along this stretch of coast. Just north of Río Chico is **Salango**, worth visiting for the excellent **Presley Norton archaeological museum** ① *daily 0900-1200, 1300-1700, US$1*. Artefacts from the excavations in town are housed in a beautiful museum on the plaza. It also has a craft shop.

Puerto López → *Phone code: 05. Colour map 11, grid B2. Population: 9,900.*

This pleasant little fishing town is beautifully set in a horseshoe bay. The beach is cleanest at the far north and south ends, away from the fleet of small fishing boats moored offshore. The town is becoming increasingly visited by foreign tourists for whale watching, approximately mid-June to September, Parque Nacional Machalilla and Isla de la Plata. Several internet places charge US$1.20-1.50 per hour; there are no ATMs or exchange services.

Parque Nacional Machalilla

① *US$12 for mainland portions, US$15 for Isla de la Plata, US$20 if visiting both areas (ask for 5-6 days), payable at the park office in Puerto López (C Eloy Alfaro y García Moreno), daily 0800-1200, 1400-1600, or directly to the park rangers (insist on a receipt).*

The Park extends over 55,000 ha, including Isla de la Plata, Isla Salango, and the magnificent beach of **Los Frailes** and preserves marine ecosystems as well as the dry tropical forest and archaeological sites on shore. At the north end of the beach is a trail through the forest leading to a lookout with great views and on to Machalilla. The land-based part of the park is divided into three sections which are separated by private land, including the town of Machalilla. Recommended for birdwatching, especially in the cloud forest of Cerro San Sebastián; also several species of mammals and reptiles.

About 5 km north of Puerto López, at Buena Vista, a dirt road to the east leads to **Agua Blanca** (park kiosk at entry). Here, 5 km from the main road, in the national park, amid hot, arid scrub, is a small village and a fine, small **archaeological museum** ① *0800-1800, US$3 for a 2-3 hr guided tour of the museum, ruins (a 45-min walk), funerary urns and sulphur lake, horses can be hired for the visit, camping is possible and there's a cabin and 1 very basic room for rent above the museum for US$5 per person*, containing some fascinating ceramics from the Manteño civilization. **San Sebastián**, 9 km from Agua Blanca, is in tropical moist forest at 800 m; orchids and birds can be seen and possibly howler monkeys. Although part of the national park, this area is administered by the Comuna of Agua Blanca, which charges its own fees in addition to the park entrance. It's 5 hrs on foot or by horse. A tour to the forest costs US$30-35 per day for the guide (fixed rate). You can camp (minimum 2 days), otherwise lodging is with a family at extra cost. Horses are also extra and you have to pay to get to Agua Blanca to start the excursion.

About 24 km offshore is **Isla de la Plata**. Trips have become popular because of the similarities with the Galápagos. Wildlife includes nesting colonies of waved albatross, frigates and three different booby species. Whales can be seen from June to September, as well as sea lions. It is also a pre-Columbian site with substantial pottery finds, and there is good diving and snorkelling, as well as walks. Take a change of clothes, water, precautions against sun and seasickness (most agencies provide snorkelling equipment. Staying overnight is not permitted.

Puerto López to Manta

North of Machalilla, the road forks at **Puerto Cayo**, where whale-watching tours may be organized June-August. One road follows the coast, partly through forested hills, passing Cabo San Lorenzo with its lighthouse. The other route heads inland through **Jipijapa**, a dusty, unattractive trading centre for cotton, cocoa, coffee and kapok. At **La Pila**, due north of Jipijapa, the main industry is fake pre-Columbian pottery, with a thriving sideline in erotic ceramics. A few kilometres further northwest is **Montecristi**, below an imposing hill, high enough to be watered by low cloud which gives the region its only source of drinking water. The town is renowned as the centre of the panama hat industry. Also produced are varied straw- and basketware, and wooden barrels which are strapped to donkeys for carrying water. Ask for José Chávez Franco, Rocafuerte 203, where you can see panama hats being made; wholesale and retail.

● Sleeping

Salinas *p987*

A Calypsso, Malecón, near Capitanía de Puerto, T277 2435, www.hotelcalypsso.com. A/c, pool, gym, restaurant, all facilities, good whale-watching tours.

A El Carruaje, Malecón 517, T/F277 4282. Includes breakfast, good restaurant, a/c, fridge, comfortable rooms, some with ocean view.

C Francisco 1, Enríquez Gallo y Rumiñahui, T277 4106. A/c, hot water, comfortable, pool, restaurant. **Francisco 2**, Malecón y Las Palmeras, T277 3471, is **B**, also good.

C Las Olas, C 17 y Av Quinta, T277 2526, pachecobolivar@hotmail.com. A/c, cheaper with fan and shared bath, very clean and good value.

D Grey, 12 de Octubre y Tomalá, T277 1787, hotelgrey@hotmail.com. Modern, comfortable.

E Yulee, downhill from church, near the beach, T277 2028. Restaurant, a/c, cheaper with fan and shared bath, older place but well maintained. Several different types of rooms, the cheaper ones are simple and good value.

Valdivia *p988*

C Valdivia Ecolodge, at Km 40, just south of San Pedro, T291 6128. Screened cabins without walls in a nice location above the ocean, fresh and interesting. Includes breakfast, restaurant, pool and access to nice bathing beach.

Manglaralto *p988*

See also *Proyecto de Desarollo Ecoturístico Comunitario*, page 988.

C-D Marakaya, 2 blocks south of the main plaza, 1 block from the beach, T290 1294. With hot water, safe, a/c, mosquito net.

E Manglaralto, half a block north of the plaza, T290 1369. Pleasant hotel, fan, restaurant.

|E Manglaralto Sunset, 1 block from the Plaza, T290 1405, manglaralto_beach@yahoo.com. Nice modern place, comfortable rooms, hammocks, cafeteria bar, electric shower, parking.

Montañita *p988*

There are many places to stay in town; the quieter ones are on the outskirts of the village.

B Baja Montañita, Baja Montañita, T09-189 8542, www.bajamontanita.com. A small resort on its own, includes breakfast, restaurant, a/c, pool, comfortable rooms, internet.

C La Barranca, on the road to the Santuario, T283 2095. Nice setting with lovely views. Spacious rooms, terrace with hammocks, includes breakfast, restaurant, a/c, jacuzzi.

C-E La Casa del Sol, Baja Montañita, T09-129 3222, www.casasol.com. Restaurant, a/c, cheaper with fan and shared bath, surfing packages.

D-E Rosa Mística, in Montañita Punta, T09-798 8383, www.hostalrosamistica.com. Small, nice cabins, quiet, restaurant, cheaper with shared bath, lovely garden.

E Charo's, Malecón, in town by the beach, T09-319 2222, www.charoshostal.com. Very nice, ample rooms, restaurant, hot water, garden, English spoken, very good value, opened in 2006.

E Paradise South, just north of town across bridge, T09-787 8925, paradise_south@ hotmail.com. Restaurant, cheaper with shared bath, pool, pleasant grounds, quiet, good value.

E Ricky, in town, T09-413 9036, loboricky@ hotmail.com. Simple, cheaper with shared bath, **F** in tents with beds, electric shower, cooking facilities, mosquito net, balcony with hammocks, relaxed, good meeting place, free surfing lessons.

E Sumpa Pro, across the bridge, near the highway, T09-749 3222, chesurf20@hotmail.com. Three lovely cabins in a quiet location, spacious.

E Tabuba, away from centre at south end of town, T09-748 6215, 04-223 8603 (Guayaquil). Modern, large rooms, restaurant, hot water, parking, quiet, very good value in low season.

E-F Tierra Prometida, in town, T09-944 6363, www.thepromisedlandmontanita.com. Cheaper with shared bath, fan, colourful and popular.

Olón *p988*

E Hostería N & J, on the beach, T239 0643, j27261@yahoo.com. Ocean views, basic but ample rooms with bath, 2 rooms have hot water, fan, parking, terrace.

E Quimbita, 100 m from the beach, T278 0204. Hotel and art gallery, owner is a known painter. Simple rooms in an older building, restaurant, with electric shower.

Ayampe to Salango *p989*

L-AL Atamari, on the headland south of Ayampe, a 15-min walk from the highway, T04-278 0430, 02-222 8470 (Quito), www.resortatamari.com. Beautiful cabins with rooms and suites in spectacular surroundings on cliffs above the sea, restaurant with wonderful food, pool, packages including half board available May-Oct.

B-D Hostería Alandaluz, T04-278 0690, T02-2248604 (Quito), www.alandaluz.com. Just south of Puerto Rico, ask to get off bus at Puerto Rico, though the centre is easily seen from the road. Cheaper with shared bath, cabins range from bamboo with thatched roofs and compost toilets to more luxurious with flush toilets, all with bath. Good homegrown organic food, vegetarian or seafood, bar, all at extra cost. Very peaceful, clean beach, stunning organic vegetable and flower gardens in the middle of the desert. 10% student discount with ISIC, camping with own tent **G** pp. Tours to *Cantalapiedra Cabins*, in a lovely forested setting by the Río Ayampe and other locations; not cheap. Often busy, advance bookings required. Highly recommended.

C Hostería La Barquita, by Las Tunas, 4 km south of Ayampe and 1 km south of Alandaluz, T04-278 0683, www.labarquita-ec.com. Restaurant and bar are in a boat on the beach with good ocean views, rooms with fan and mosquito nets, tours, games, Swiss run; French, English and German spoken.

C Piqueros Patas Azules, 10-min drive from Río Chico toward the beach, T04-278 0279. Cabins overlooking the beach, restaurant, fan, price includes entry to the local museum.

E Cabañas de la Iguana, Ayampe, T04-278 0605, www.ayampeiguana.com. Cabins for 4, mosquito nets, quiet, meals with advance notice, cooking facilities US$2, Swiss-Ecuadorean run, family atmosphere, helpful and knowledgeable, organizes excursions. Recommended.

E Finca Punta Ayampe, south of other Ayampe hotels, T04-278 0616, info@fincapuntaayampe.com. Bamboo structure high on a hill with great ocean views, restaurant, bath, hot water, mosquito nets, helpful staff.

F Cabaña Mar, Salango, on the Malecón, T05-278 0722. Bamboo cabin, shared bath, hot water, simple, helpful, good value. Offers snorkelling tours to Isla Salango, US$10 pp, minimum 4 people.

Puerto López *p989*

A Mantaraya Lodge, 3 km south of town, T09-404 4050, www.mantarayalodge.com. Restaurant and bar, pool, comfortable rooms, nice view, colourful decor, horse riding, fishing and diving trips organized.

C Mandala, Malecón at north end of the beach, T230 0181, www.hosteriamandala.info. Nice cabins decorated with art, lovely garden, excellent restaurant, fan, mosquito nets, games, music room, Swiss-Italian run, English spoken, knowledgeable owners. Recommended.

C-E Pacífico, Malecón y González Suárez, T230 0147, hpacific@manta.ecua.net.ec. Includes breakfast, restaurant, a/c, friendly, comfortable, cheaper in old wing with fan and shared bath, nice grounds, pool, boat tours. Recommended.

D La Terraza, on hill north behind the clinic, T230 0235. Great views over the bay, gardens, hot water, spacious, good breakfast, evening meals on request, run by German Peter Bernhard, free car service to/from town if called in advance. Highly recommended.

E Spondylus, towards the north end of the Malecón, T09-324 8168. Modern, quiet, opposite the beach, good rooms with bath.

E Villa Colombia, García Moreno behind market, T230 0105. Hostel, with hot water, fan, cooking facilities, mosquito nets, garden with hammocks.

E-F Los Islotes, Malecón 532 y Gen Córdova, T230 0108, hostallosislotes@hotmail.com. Fan, modern, good value, cheaper in dorm. Recommended.

E-F Máxima, González Suárez y Machalilla, T09-953 4282, www.hotelmaxima.net. Restaurant and bar, cheaper with shared bath, laundry and cooking facilities, parking, modern, comfortable, English spoken, good value.

E-F Sol Inn, Montalvo entre Eloy Alfaro y Lascano, T230 0248, hostal_solinn@hotmail.com. Cheaper with shared bath, hot water, fan, laundry and cooking facilities, parking, garden, pool table. Popular, nice atmosphere, English and French spoken, good value.

F Monte Líbano, southern extreme of Malecón, T230 0231. Breakfast available, cheaper with shared bath, hot water, cooking facilities terrace with views, popular.

Puerto López to Manta *p989*

There are other places to stay; many close out of season.

D Puerto Cayo, south end of beach, Puerto Cayo, T261 6019, T09-752 1538 (mob). Good restaurant, fan, comfortable rooms with hammocks and terrace overlooking the sea.

E Luz de Luna, 5 km north of Puerto Cayo on the coastal road, T261 6031, T02-240 0562 (Quito), www.hosterialuzdeluna.com. On a clean beach, comfortable spacious rooms with balcony, full board **C**, restaurant, cold water in cabins, shared hot showers available, fan and mosquito net, pool, disco, quieter in low season when discounts are available.

🍴 Eating

Salinas *p987*

A couple of blocks inland from the Malecón are food stalls serving good *ceviches* (US$4-5) and freshly cooked seafood: **Cevichelandia**, María González y Las Palmeras; **La Lojanita**, Enríquez Gallo y Leonardo Avilés, recommended; others are around the Libertad Peninsular bus station at María González y León Avilés.

ᵀᵀ La Bella Italia, Malecón y C 17, near *Hotel El Carruaje*. Pizza and international food, good.

ᵀᵀᵀ-ᵀᵀ Mar y Tierra, Malecón y Valverde. Excellent seafood and some meat dishes.

ᵀᵀ Oyster Catcher, Enríquez Gallo entre C 47 y C 50, closed in low season. Restaurant and bar, friendly place, safe oysters.

ᵀ El Mayquito, , Av 2 y C 12. Simple place with very good food and friendly service.

♯♯ **La Ostra Nostra**, Eloy Alfaro y Los Almendros. Good set meals.
♯ **Nuevo Flipper**, Malecón y 24 de Mayo. Simple, clean and friendly.

Manglaralto *p988*
♯♯ **La Calderada**, on the Plaza, closed Tue. Very good seafood, try their *calderada* (fish soup).

Montañita *p988*
♯♯ **Marea Pizzería Bar**, Opposite Hotel Montañita. Great pizzas. Recommended.
♯♯ **Zoociedad**, in town. Rustic, Italian and international, very popular.
♯ **Café del Mar**, in the centre. Vegetarian food, cakes, good coffee.
♯ **Desde Montañita con Amor (DMCA)**, Guido Chiriboga opposite *Hostal La Casa Blanca*. Vegetarian, very fresh food, delicious.

Olón *p988*
Several cheap, simple places to eat, eg **Flor de Olón** and **María Verónica**.

Ayampe to Salango *p989*
♯♯ **El Delfín Mágico**, in Salango. Order meal before visiting museum because all food is cooked from scratch (very fresh and safe), try the *spondilus* (spiny oyster) in fresh coriander and peanut sauce with garlic coated *patacones*.
♯ **El Pelícano**, behind the church. Excellent seafood, also caters for vegetarians.

Puerto López *p989*
♯♯ **Bellitalia**, Montalvo y Abdón Calderón, 1 block back from the Malecón. Italian-run, excellent food, nice setting, opens 1800. Highly recommended.
♯ **Flipper**, Gen Córdova next to *Banco del Pichincha*. Good set meals. Recommended.
♯ **Patacón Pisao**, Gen Córdova ½ block from the Malecón. Colombian food, giant *patacones*, *arepas*, sandwiches. Recommended.
♯ **The Whale Café**, towards the south end of the Malecón. Good pizza, sandwiches and meals, good cakes and pies, nice breakfasts. US-run, owners Diana and Kevin are very helpful and provide travel information. Recommended. The *panadería* behind the church serves good banana bread and other sweets.

🎵 Bars and clubs

Puerto López *p989*
La Resaca, on the beach opposite *Whale Café*, in a converted old fishing boat.

▲ Activities and tours

Salinas *p987*
Avista Travel, T277 0331. Whale watching tours in season.
Calypsso, see under Sleeping, above.
Centro Informativo Natural Peninsular, T277 7335, T09-372 2486 (mob), bhaase@ecua.net.ec. Naturalist guide Ben Haase runs birdwatching tours to the Ecuasal salt ponds, US$20 per group of up to 10 people. He is also knowledgeable about whales. He can be contacted at *Oyster-catcher* restaurant/bar, see above.

Puerto López *p989*
Whale watching Puerto López has become a major centre for trips from Jun to Sep/Oct, with many more agencies than we can list. **Note** Whales can also be seen further north. There is a good fleet of small boats (16-20 passengers) running excursions, all have life jackets and a toilet. All agencies offer the same tours for the same price. In high season: US$30 pp for whale watching, Isla de la Plata and snorkelling, including a snack and drinks, US$25 for whale watching only. In low season tours to Isla de la Plata and snorkelling cost US$25 pp, US$20 for whale watching only. These rates don't include the National Park fee. Trips depart around 0800 and return around 1700. Agencies also offer tours to the mainland sites of the national park. A day tour combining Agua Blanca and Los Frailes costs US$25 pp.
Bosque Marino, Malecón y Sucre, T260 4106,T09-337 6505 (mob). Experienced guides, some speak English.
Ecuador Amazing, Gen Córdova, T230 0011. Tours to Isla de la Plata and whale watching. Also transport from airport or Quito.
Excursiones Pacífico, Malecón at *Hotel Pacífico*, T/F230 0133. Good boat and service.
Exploramar Diving, Malecón y Gral Córdova, T230 0123, www.explora diving.com. French-run, Quito-based. Two 8-12 person boats and compressor to fill dive tanks, PADI divemaster, advance notice required for US$85 pp all-inclusive diving day tour (2 tanks). Also offer diving lessons. Recommended.
Machalilla Tours, Malecón y Eloy Alfaro and Gral Córdova y Machalilla, T230 0234, machalillatours@yahoo.com. Surfing US$25 pp.
Manta Raya, on Malecón Norte, T230 0233. They have a comfortable and spacious boat. They also have diving equipment and charge US$130 pp, all inclusive.
Orcados Aventura, Gral Córdova y Montalvo, T230 0106, bosmartag@hotmail.com. Run a very good boat for excursions.

Sercapez, at the Centro Comercial on the highway, T230 0173. All- inclusive trips to San Sebastián, with camping, local guide and food, US$30 pp per day. Also offer trips further north with **Guacamayo Bahía** in Bahía de Caráquez.

⊖ Transport

Playas *p987*
Bus **Transportes Posorja** and **Transportes Villamil** leave from stations along Av Menéndez Gílbert, a couple of blocks back from the beach. To **Guayaquil**, frequent, 2 hrs, US$2; taxi US$25.

Salinas *p987*
Bus For Ruta del Sol, **Puerto López** and points north, transfer at La Libertad or Santa Elena. Buses may say 'Salinas', but the terminal is in La Libertad. To **Guayaquil**, take **Coop Libertad Peninsular**, María González y León Avilés, every 10 mins, US$3, 2½ hrs.

Manglaralto *p988*
Bus **La Libertad**, US$1. **Puerto López**, 1 hr, US$1.50.

Montañita *p988*
Bus To **Puerto López**, US$1.50, 45 mins. CLP have daily direct buses starting in Olón going to **Guayaquil**, at 0500, 1300, 1630 and 1500 at weekends (same schedule from Guayaquil), US$5, 3½ hrs.

Puerto López *p989*
Bus To **Santa Elena** or **La Libertad**, every 30 mins, US$2.50, 2½ hrs. To **Montañita** and **Manglaralto**, US$1.50, 1 hr. There are pick-ups for hire to nearby sites are by the market, east of the highway. To/from **Manta**, direct, every 2 hrs, US$3, 3 hrs. To **Quito**, 2 a day, 10 hrs, US$12.

Parque Nacional Machalilla *p989*
Bus To Los Frailes: take a bus towards Jipijapa (US$0.25), or a pick-up (US$5), and alight at the turn-off just south of the town of Machalilla, then walk for 30 mins. Show your national park ticket on arrival. No transport back to Puerto López after 2000 (but check in advance). To **Agua Blanca**: take tour, a pick-up (US$5) or a bus bound for Jipijapa (US$0.20); it is a hot walk of more than 1 hr from the turning to the village. To **Isla de la Plata**: the island can only be visited on a day trip. Many agencies offer tours, see Puerto López above.

Puerto López to Manta: Jipijapa *p989*
Bus From Jipijapa to **Manglaralto** (2 hrs, US$2), **Puerto López** (1 hr, US1), **Manta** (1 hr, US$1), **Quito** (10 hrs, US$9). Buses leave from the terminal on the outskirts.

❻ Directory

Salinas *p987*
Banks Banco de Guayaquil, Malecón y 24 de Mayo. Banco del Pichincha, Malecón y Armando Barreto. **Internet** Several places, US$1.50 per hr.

Ecuador Manta & Bahía de Caráquez

Manta and Bahía de Caráquez

Two quite different seaside towns: Manta is the quintessential maritime city, growing fast and prospering on fishing and trade. Bahía de Caráquez is a relaxed town and a pleasant place to spend a few days. It is proud of its 'eco' credentials. Just beyond Bahía, on the other side of the Río Chone estuary, is the village of Canoa, boasting some of the finest beaches in Ecuador.

Manta and around → *Phone code: 05. Colour map 11, grid B2. Population: 235,000.*
Ecuador's second port after Guayaquil is a busy town that sweeps round a bay filled with all sorts of boats. A constant sea breeze tempers the intense sun and makes the city's *malecones* pleasant places to stroll. The Malecón Escénico, at the gentrified west end of town has a cluster of bars and seafood restaurants. It is a lively place especially at weekends, when there is good music, free beach aerobics and lots of action. Playa Murciélago is a popular beach with wild surf (flags indicate whether it is safe to bathe), with good surfing from December to April. The **Museo del Banco Central** ① *Av 8 y C 7, Tue-Sat 1000-1700, US$1, Sun 1100-1500, free,* has a small but excellent collection of archaeological pieces from seven different civilizations which flourished on the coast of Manabí between 3500 BC and AD 1530. Two bridges join the main town with its seedy neighbour, **Tarqui. Tourist offices**: Ministerio de Turismo ① *Paseo José María Egas 1034 (Av 3) y C 11, T262 2944, Mon-Fri 0900-1230, 1400-1700*; and **Cámara de Turismo** ① *Centro Comercial Cocco Manta, Malecón y C 23, T262 0478. Mon-Fri 0900-1300, 1500-1800,* are both helpful and speak some English.

Portoviejo → *Phone code: 05. Colour map 11, grid B2. Population: 211,000.*

Inland from Manta and capital of Manabí province, Portoviejo is a sweltering commercial city, so hot in fact that visitors will be reduced to the same level of activity as the sloths in the trees in Parque Eloy Alfaro. Kapok mattresses and pillows are made here from the fluffy fibre of the seed capsule of the *ceibo* tree.

Crucita → *Phone code: 05. Colour map 11, grid B2. Population: 13,000.*

A rapidly growing resort, 45 minutes by road from Portoviejo, Crucita is busy at weekends and holidays when people flock here to enjoy ideal conditions for paragliding, hang-gliding and kite-surfing. The best season for flights is July to December. There is also an abundance of sea birds in the area. There are many simple restaurants and kiosks serving mainly fish and seafood along the seafront. **Alas Delta 1 and 2** serve good seafood, try their *conchas asadas*.

North to Bahía

About 60 km north of Portoviejo (30 km south of Bahía de Caráquez) are **San Clemente** and, 3 km south, **San Jacinto**. The ocean is magnificent but be wary of the strong undertow. Both get crowded during the holiday season and have a selection of *cabañas* and hotels. Don't go barefoot; parasites can be a problem.

Bahía de Caráquez and around → *Phone code: 05. Colour map 11, grid B2. Population: 26,800.*

Set on the southern shore at the seaward end of the Chone estuary, Bahía has an attractive riverfront laid out with parks on the Malecón Alberto Santos. The beaches in town are nothing special, but there excellent beaches nearby between San Vicente and Canoa and at Punta Bellaca (the town is busiest July-August). Bahía has declared itself an 'eco-city', where recycling projects, organic gardens and ecoclubs are common. Tricycle rickshaws called 'eco-taxis' are a popular form of local transport. The city is also a centre of the less than ecologically friendly shrimp farming industry, which has boosted the local economy but also destroyed much of the estuary's precious mangroves. With awareness of the damage done, Bahía now boasts the first certified organic shrimp farm in the world. Information about the eco-city concept can be obtained from the **Planet Drum Foundation** ① *www.planetdrum.org*. **Tourist office:** Bolívar y Circunvalación, Spanish only. The **Museo Bahía de Caráquez** ① *Malecón Alberto Santos y Aguilera, Tue-Fri 1000-1700, Sat-Sun 1100-1500, US$1*, of the Banco Central, has an interesting collection of archaeological artefacts from prehispanic coastal cultures, a life-size balsa raft and modern sculpture.

The Río Chone estuary has several islands with mangrove forest. The area is rich in birdlife, dolphins may also be seen, and conditions are ideal for photographers because you can get really close, even under the mangrove trees where birds nest. The male frigate birds can be seen displaying their inflated red sacks as part of the mating ritual; best from August to January. At **Isla Corazón** where a boardwalk has been built through an area of protected mangrove forest. At the end of the island are some bird colonies which can only be accessed by boat. Agencies run tours to the estuary, islands and the village of Puerto Portovelo, which runs an ecotourism project (US$6). The **Chirije** archaeological site is a 45-minute ride south. It was a seaport of the Bahía culture (500 BC to AD 500), which traded from Mexico to Chile (museum on site). It is surrounded by dry tropical forest and beaches. There are **C** cabins with ocean views and a restaurant; walking and birdwatching in the area. Tours from Bahía take an open-sided *chiva* along the beach (US$30 per person, includes lunch). **Saiananda** ① *T239 8331, owner Alfredo Harmsen, reached by taxi or any bus heading out of town, US$2*, is a private park with extensive areas of reforestation and a large collection of mainly domestic fowl and animals, but also native animals. It has a cactus garden and spiritual centre. Vegetarian meals are served in an exquisite dining area over the water.

San Vicente and Canoa

On the north side of the Río Chone, San Vicente is reached by ferry from Bahía or by road west from Chone. The **Santa Rosa church**, 100 m to the left of the wharf, contains excellent mosaic and glass work by **José María Peli Romeratigui** (better known as Peli). There is a good airport at San Vicente but no commercial flights were operating in 2006.

Canoa is a quiet fishing and tourist town, with a 200-m wide, clean and relatively isolated beach, one of the nicest in Ecuador. The choice of accommodation is very good and this, along with the lovely setting, has made it especially popular with travellers. The beautiful 17-km beach between San Vicente and Canoa is a good walk, horse or bike ride. Horses and bicycles can be hired through several hotels. Surfing is good, particularly during the wet season, December to April. In the dry season there is good wind for windsurfing. Canoa is also a good place for hang-gliding and paragliding; flights can be arranged through the **Hotel Sol y Luna**, see below. Tents for shade and chairs are rented at the beach for US$3 a day.

Pedernales → *Colour map 10, grid A2. Population: 15,365.*
The coastal road cuts across Cabo Pasado to Jama (1½ hours; cabins and several *hostales*), then runs parallel to the beach past coconut groves and shrimp hatcheries, inland across some low hills and across the Equator to Pedernales, a market town and crossroads with nice undeveloped beaches to the north. In town, where beaches are less attractive, they are trying to capture the *quiteño* holiday market. A mosaic mural on the church overlooking the plaza is one of the best pieces of work by Peli (see above); exquisite examples of his stained glass can be seen inside the church. A poor unpaved road goes north along the shore to Cojimíes. The main coastal road, fully paved, goes south to San Vicente and north to Chamanga, El Salto, Muisne and Esmeraldas. Another important road goes inland to El Carmen and on to Santo Domingo de los Colorados: this is the most direct route to Quito.

Santo Domingo de los Colorados → *Phone code: 02. Colour map 11, grid A3. Population: 345,000.*
In the hills above the western lowlands, Santo Domingo, 129 km from Quito, became Ecuador's main transport hub in the mid-1960s when the road from Quito through Alóag was completed. Since then it has experienced very rapid growth and become an important commercial centre for surrounding palm oil and banana producing areas. The city itself is noisy and streets are prone to flooding after heavy rains. Santo Domingo is not safe late at night, caution is recommended at all times in the market areas, including the pedestrian walkway along 3 de Julio and in peripheral neighbourhoods. Sunday is market day, shops and banks are closed Monday instead. The name 'de los Colorados' is a reference to the traditional red hair dye, made with achiote (annatto), worn by the native Tsáchila men. Today the Tsáchila only wear their native dress on special occasions and they can no longer be seen in traditional garb in the city. There are less than 2,000 Tsáchilas left, living in eight communities off the roads leading from Santo Domingo to Quevedo, Chone and Quinindé. Their lands make up a reserve of some 8,000 ha. Visitors interested in their culture are welcome at the *Complejo Turístico Huapilú*, in the Comunidad Chigüilpe, where there is a small but interesting museum (contributions expected). Access is via the turn-off east at Km 7 on the road to Quevedo, from where it is 4 km. Tours are run by travel agencies in town.

● Sleeping

Manta and around *p993*
All streets have numbers; those above 100 are in Tarqui (those above 100 are not safe).
AL Oro Verde, Malecon y C 23, on the beach front, T262 9200, www.oroverdehotels.com. With all luxuries, best in town.
A Vistalmar, C M1 y Av 24B, at Playa Murciélago, T262 1671, www.vistalmarecuador.com. Exclusive hotel overlooking the ocean. Ample cabins and suites tastefully decorated with art, a/c, pool, cooking facilities, gardens by the sea.
A-B Costa del Sol, Malecón y Av 25, T262 0025. Includes breakfast, a/c, pool, parking, modern, comfortable, ocean- side rooms with balconies are very nice.
B-C Barbasquillo, at Playa Barbasquillo, T262 0718. Includes breakfast, variety of rooms, comfortable, a/c, restaurant, pool and gym, fridge, parking.
D Yara María, Av 11 y C 20, T261 3219, yaramariahostal@hotmail.com. Nice hostel in a

residential area, a/c, jacuzzi, parking, rooms on the top floor are better, terrace, garden, quiet.
E Centenario, C 11 No 602 y Av 5, T262 9245, josesanmartin@hotmail.com. In refurbished house, central, shared bath, some rooms with a/c, cooking facilities, nice views, quiet.

Tarqui
D Chavez Inn, Av 106 y C 106, T262 1019. Nice modern hotel with lovely rooms, includes breakfast, restaurant, a/c, very good value.
D-E Panorama Inn, C 103 y Av 105, T262 2996, panoramainn@paginas amarillasec.com. Has 2 sections, a new block with nice modern rooms and an older cheaper section with fair rooms, includes breakfast, restaurant, cold water, a/c, cheaper with fan, pool, helpful.

Portoviejo *p994*
A-B Ejecutivo, 18 de Octubre y Pedro Gual, T263 0840, www.hotelejecutivoportoviejo.com. Nice

hotel with various types of room, includes breakfast, restaurant, a/c, fridge, parking, discounts at weekends

D-E New York, Francisco de Moreira y Olmedo, T263 2395. In a quiet area, restaurant, a/c and fridge, cheaper with fan, good.

E Conquistador, 18 de Octubre y 10 de Agosto, T263 3259. A/c, cheaper with fan, friendly.

Crucita p994

D-E Casa Grande, Malecón, near the church, T234 0133. Very nice fully-equipped cabins for up to 6, older cabins are cheaper, restaurant, cold water, fan, 2 pools, parking.

E Cruzita, at the south end of the beach, T234 0068, flyraul2005@hotmail.com. Beautiful hostel with great views right on the beach, restaurant, cold water, fan, pool, parking, good value. Owner Raul Tobar offers paragliding flights and lessons.

E Hostal Voladores, away from town, T234 0200, hvoladores@hotmail.com. Restaurant, cheaper with shared bath, small pool, simple but nice place, sea kayaks available. Owner Luis Tobar is very helpful, organizes tandem parapent flights and lessons.

E Russia, C 9 y 25 de Mayo, at the south end, T234 0291. Nice carpeted rooms, restaurant, electric shower, garden with pool, parking.

North to Bahía p994
San Clemente and San Jacinto

C Chediak, between San Clemente and San Jacinto, T261 5499. Restaurant, fan, mosquito net, parking, comfortable, nicely furnished, great views from upper floor balconies.

E Cabañas Rocío, in San Jacinto, T261 5476. Cold water, fan, fridge, small but nice cabins with well-equipped kitchen.

E Cabañas Tío Gerard, between San Clemente and San Jacinto, T261 5517. Cold water, fan, small, simple rooms.

Bahía de Caráquez p994

B La Piedra, Circunvalación near Bolívar, T269 0156, piedraturi@easynet.net.ec. Pool, good restaurant but expensive, laundry, modern, good service, beach access, lovely views, rents bikes.

C-E La Herradura, Bolívar e Hidalgo, T269 0446. A/c, cheaper with fan and cold water, comfortable, restaurant, good value.

D El Bucanero, Cecilia Intriago y Padre Laennen, T269 0016. Refurbished hotel in a quiet location, large rooms, restaurant, a/c, disco on weekends.

D-E Italia, Bolívar y Checa, T/F269 1137. A/c, cheaper with fan, hot water, comfortable, restaurant.

E Bahía, Malecón y Vinueza, T269 0509. Rooms at the back are nicer, fan, TV, good value, helpful.

E Bahía Bed & Breakfast Inn, Ascázubi 322 y

Morales, T269 0146. With breakfast, fan, cheaper without bath, restaurant, basic, cold water, discount for Canadians.

E El Viajero, Bolívar 910 y Riofrío, T269 0792. Nicely decorated old house, large rooms, cold water, fan, pleasant.

F Los Paraguayos, Ante 112 y Montúfar, T269 1581. Cheaper without bath, cold water, basic.

San Vicente p994

D Cabañas Alcatraz, on the road to Canoa, T267 4566. Cold water, a/c, cheaper with fan, clean pool, older place but still nice.

E Hostal del Mar, Malecón y Juan Montalvo, across from San Vicente park, T267 4778. Well furnished modern rooms, café, good value.

E Vacaciones, Malecón, close to the dock, T267 4116. Older hotel but maintained, restaurant and disco, a/c, cheaper with fan, pool, runs local tours.

Canoa p994

B Hostería Canoa, 1 km south of town, T261 6380, ecocanoa@mnb.satnet.net. Cabins and rooms, with breakfast, pool, sauna, whirlpool, good restaurant and bar.

D-E País Libre, Filomeno Hernández y San Andrés de Canoa, T261 6387. Spacious rooms, upper floors have pleasant breeze and good views, restaurant, disco in high season, cheaper with shared bath, pool, surf board rentals. Recommended.

E La Vista, on the beach, towards the south end of town, T09-419 6000. All rooms have balconies to the sea, cold water, bar, Norwegian-Ecuadorean run, good value, opened in 2006.

E Paraíso Canoa, 200 m from the beach, near the main street, T09-973 4033, www.hotel paraisocanoa.com. Small hotel with nice rooms, hot water, also rents flats for 2-10 people.

E Posada de Daniel, at back of the village, a couple of blocks from the beach, T261 6373. Attractive, nice grounds, cabins with good views, fan, pool, internet, surf boards and bicycles for rent, can organize tours. Discounts for long stays.

E Sol y Luna, 2 km south of town, T261 6363. Good hostel, large comfortable rooms, restaurant, hot water, fan, pool.

E-F Bambú, on the beach by town, T261 6370. Pleasant location and atmosphere. A variety of rooms and prices, good restaurant including vegetarian options, cheaper with shared bath and in dorm, camping possible, hot water, fan, surfing classes and board rentals. Dutch-Ecuadorean run, very popular. Highly recommended.

E-F Coco Loco, on the beach, towards the south end of town, T09-397 2884. Pleasant breezy hotel with nice views, café serves breakfast with home-made bread, also snacks, cheaper with

shared bath, **G** pp in dorm, hot showers, cooking facilities, Dutch-Belgian run, opened in 2006.
E-F Shelmar, 1 block from the beach, T09-8644892, shelmar66@hotmail.com. Basic clean hostel, restaurant, cheaper with shared bath, hot water, bike rentals, English and French spoken.

Pedernales *p995*
B-D Punta Prieta Guest House, by Punta Prieta, 14 km north of Jama and 40 km south of Pedernales, T09-983 7056, T02-286 2986 (Quito), meche14@accessinter.net. Gorgeous setting on headland high above the ocean with access to pristine beaches. Meals available, comfortable cabins with fridge, suites and rooms with shared bath by the beach, balcony with hammocks. Perfect place to get away from it all.
C Catedral del Mar, Pereira y Malecón, T268 1136. Spacious rooms, hot water, a/c, fridge, restaurant, parking, near the beach.
C Cocosolo, on a secluded beach 20 km north of Pedernales, T09-921 5078, T268 1156 (Pedernales). A lovely hideaway set among palm trees. Restaurant, cheaper with shared bath, cabins and rooms, camping possible, horses for hire. French and English spoken.
E Mr John, Plaza Acosta y Malecón, 1 block from beach, T268 1107. Nice rooms and views, cold water, balcony, fan, parking, modern, good value.
E-G Playas, Juan Pereira y Manabí, near airport, T268 1125. Fans, mosquito nets, comfortable.

Santo Domingo de los Colorados *p995*
Many hotels are along Av 29 de Mayo, a noisy street, so request a room away from the road. Plenty of new hotels close to the bus terminal, clean and cheap; choose room not overlooking the terminal or the approach road.
B Grand Hotel Santo Domingo, Río Toachi y Galápagos, T276 7947, www.grandhotelsed.com. Includes breakfast, restaurant, a/c, pool and spa, parking, comfortable rooms.
C-D Hotel del Pacífico, 29 de Mayo 510 e Ibarra, T275 2806. Central, comfortable rooms, includes breakfast, restaurant, a/c, cheaper with fan.
E Diana Real, 29 de Mayo y Loja, T275 1380, dianreal@ecnet.ec. Modern spacious rooms, hot water at night, fan, good restaurant.
D-E Puerta del Sol, 29 de Mayo y Cuenca, T/F275 0370, hotelpsol@ecnet.ec. Small upscale restaurant, fan, nice rooms, good value.
E Safiro Internacional, 29 de Mayo 800 y Loja, T276 0706. Comfortable modern hotel, cafeteria, hot water, a/c, good value, new in 2006.
E-F Royal Class, Cadmo Zambrano y César López, near the bus station, T274 3348. Multi-storey modern hotel, hot water, parking, the best choice near the bus station, reasonably

quiet location, very good value.

Out of town
AL Tinalandia, 16 km from Santo Domingo, on the road to Alluriquín, poorly signposted, look for a large rock painted white; T09-946 7741 (mob), in Quito T244 9028, www.tinalandia.com. Includes full board, nice chalets in cloud forest reserve, great food, spring-fed pool, good birdwatching, entry US$10 for non-residents.
B Zaracay, Av Quito 1639, T275 0316, 1½ km from the centre on the road to Quito. Includes breakfast, restaurant, gardens and swimming pool, parking, good rooms and service. Advance booking advised, especially at weekend.
C Hotel del Toachi Km 1, just west of Zaracay, T/F275 4688. Spacious rooms, good showers, swimming pool, parking.

● Eating

Manta *p993*
Restaurants on Malecón Escénico serve local seafood.
⊞ Club Ejecutivo, Av 2 y C 12, top of Banco del Pichincha building. First class food and service, great view.
⊞ El Marino, Malecón y C 110, Tarqui. Classic fish and seafood restaurant, for ceviches, sopa marinera and other delicacies, open for lunch only. Recommended.
⊞-⊞ Beachcomber, C 20 y Av Flavio Reyes. Cheap set lunch and mid-range grill in the evening.
⊞ Café Trovador, Av 3 y C 11, Paseo José María Egas, closes 2100. Very good coffee, snacks, sandwiches and economical set lunches.
⊞ Paraná, C 17 y Malecón, near the port. Local seafood and grill. Highly recommended.

Portoviejo *p994*
⊞ El Tomate, on the road to Crucita and Bahía. Excellent traditional Manabí food.
⊞ El Galpón, C Quito. Good food and prices, local music at night, very popular.
⊞ La Carreta, C Olmedo y Alajuela and at Andrés Vera near the terminal. Good food and service, especially at the Andrés Vera location.

Bahía de Caráquez *p994*
⊞ ⊞ Muelle Uno, by the pier where boats leave for San Vicente. Good grill and seafood in a lovely setting over the water.
⊞ Arena Bar Pizerría, Av Bolívar y Arenas. Great pizza, snacks, drinks, music. Recommended.
⊞ Brisas del Mar, Hidalgo y Circunvalación. Good ceviches and fish.
⊞ Columbiu's, Av Bolívar y Ante. Good à la carte and set meals (seriously cheap), good service and value. Recommended.

¶ Doña Luca, Cecilio Intriago y Sergio Plaza, towards the tip of the peninsula. Excellent *ceviches*, *desayuno manabita* (a wholesome breakfast), lunches.

¶ La Chozita, On the Malecón south of the pier where canoes leave for San Vicente. BBQ and cheap set lunch.

Canoa *p994*

¶ Café Flor, 100 m behind **Hotel La Vista**, around the corner from the petrol station. Café-restaurant, best breakfast in town, pizza, crêpes, vegetarian dishes, drinks.

¶ Comedor Jixsy, on main street near the beach. Set meals, fish dishes.

¶ El Torbellino, 4 blocks from the beach along the main street (Javier Santos). Good for typical dishes, large servings.

¶ Shamrock, at the beach in town. Restaurant-bar with international food, snacks, desserts, cocktails.

Pedernales *p995*

Many good, simple *comedores* in town (check where locals are eating), as well as bamboo huts at the beach selling drinks and playing music, plus several good soda bars on Eloy Alfaro.

Santo Domingo de los Colorados *p995*

¶¶ Parrilladas Che Luis, on the road to Quito. One of the best grills in town.

¶¶¶-¶¶ D'Marco, Río Baba y Mulaute. Very good steaks and international food.

¶¶-¶ La Cocina de Consuelo, Av Quito y Chimbo, 0700-2230, Sun and Mon to 1700. Very good à la carte dishes and 4-course set meals.

▲ Activities and tours

Manta *p993*

Delgado Travel, Av 6 y C 13, T262 2813, vtdelgad@hotmail.com. City and regional tours, whale watching trips, Parque Nacional Machalilla, run *Hostería San Antonio* at El Aromo, some 15 km south of Manta.

Metropolitan Touring, Av 4 y C 13, T262 3090. Local, regional and nationwide tours.

Bahía de Caráquez *p994*

Ceibos Tours, Av Bolívar 200 y Checa, T269 0801, www.ceibostours.com. Runs tours to Isla Corazón and Cerro Seco.

Guacamayo Bahía Tours, Av Bolívar y Arenas, T269 1412, www.riomuchacho.com. Runs tours, rents bikes, sells crafts and is involved in environmental work in Río Muchacho. Part of tour fees go to community environmental programmes. Discounts for Kiwis and SAE members. Also has a small office at La Posada de

998

Daniel in Canoa, where you can be picked up for trips to Río Muchacho.

Santo Domingo de los Colorados *p995*

Turismo Zaracay, 29 de Mayo y Cocaniguas, T275 0546, zaratur@andinanet.net. Runs tours to Tsáchila commune, minimum 5 persons; rafting, fishing trips, bird/butterfly watching tours, English spoken.

⊙ Transport

Manta *p993*

Air Eloy Alfaro airport. **Aerogal** (T261 2588), **TAME** (T262 2006) and **Icaro** (T262 7484) to **Quito** daily, US$50-70.

Bus All buses leave from the terminal on C 7 y Av 8 in the centre. A couple of companies have their own private terminals nearby and run services to their own terminals in Quito. To **Quito**, 10 hrs, US$10. **Guayaquil**, 4 hrs, US$4, hourly. **Esmeraldas**, 3 daily, 10 hrs, US$8. **Santo Domingo**, 7 hrs, US$6. **Portoviejo**, 45 mins, US$0.75, every 10 mins. **Jipijapa**, 1 hr, US$1, every 20 mins. **Bahía de Caráquez**, 3 hrs, US$3, hourly.

Portoviejo *p994*

Bus To **Quito**, US$9, 8 hrs; routes are either east via Quevedo (147 km), or, at Calderón, branch northeast for Calceta, Chone and on to **Santo Domingo de los Colorados**. Services also to **Guayaquil**, US$3, 3 hrs. To/from **Bahía de Caráquez** 2 hrs, US$2, and **Canoa** 3 hrs. Bus station is 1 km south of the centre, across the Río Portoviejo, taxi US$1.

Crucita *p994*

Bus Run along the Malecón. There is frequent service to **Portoviejo**, US$0.80, 1 hr and **Manta**, US$1.20, 1½ hrs.

North to Bahía: San Clemente *p994*

Bus To **Portoviejo**, every 15 mins, US$1.25, 1¼ hrs. To **Bahía de Caráquez**, US$0.50, 30 mins, a few start in San Clemente in the morning or you can wait for a through bus at the highway.

Bahía de Caráquez *p994*

Bus Buses leave from new bus terminal on main road out of town, near **Hostal La Querencia**. To **Quito**, 9 hrs, US$7, also more expensive *ejecutivo* service. **Santo Domingo de los Colorados** regular, 6 hrs, US$5, *ejecutivo*, US$7.50. **Esmeraldas**, at 1515, 9 hrs, US$8. **Portoviejo**, see above. **Puerto López** or **Manta**, go to Portoviejo or Jipijapa and change. To **Guayaquil**, *ejecutivo*, or regular hourly US$5, 6 hrs.

Ferry *Pangas* or *lanchas* cross to/from **Bahía**

0615-1800 (fewer till 2300), 10 mins, US$0.30; car ferry every 20 mins or so, 0630-2000, US$2, free for foot passengers, very steep ramps so difficult for low clearance cars.

Taxis Eco bicycle taxis into town US$0.50.

San Vicente and Canoa *p994*
Bus All companies leave from a new bus terminal at the market on the San Isidro road. **Portoviejo**, US$2.50, 2½ hrs. To **Guayaquil**, US$7, 7 hrs. To **Quito**, with *Reina del Camino*, US$8, 8½ hrs, more services from Bahía, or take a bus to **Pedernales** from the plaza beneath the church on the paved road (US$3, 2½ hrs) and change. For **Esmeraldas** and northern beaches, take a bus to **Chamanga**, at 0810, 1430 or 1700, US$4.50, 3¼ hrs, and transfer there. Buses San Vicente-**Canoa**, every 30 mins, 0700-1730, US$0.50, 30 mins; taxi US$5.

Pedernales *p995*
Bus To **Santo Domingo**, via El Carmen, every 15 mins, 3½ hrs, US$4, transfer to Quito. To **Quito** direct 5½ hrs, US$6.25. To **Chamanga**, 1½ hrs, US$1.60, continuing to **El Salto**, where you can make a connection for **Muisne**, or continue to **Esmeraldas**, US$2.50, 2 hrs from Chamanga.

Santo Domingo de los Colorados *p995*
Bus The bus terminal is on Av Abraham Calazacón, at the north end of town, along the city's bypass. Long distance buses do not enter the city. Taxi downtown, US$1, bus US$0.25. As it is a very important transportation centre, you can get buses going everywhere in the country. To **Quito** via Alóag US$3, 3 hrs; via San Miguel de los Bancos, 5 hrs. Also **Sudamericana Taxis**, on Cocaniguas, p 2, near central plaza, T02-275 2567, for shared taxis, which will call at hotels en route. To **Ambato** US$4, 4 hrs. To **Loja** US$13, 11 hrs. To **Guayaquil** US$5, 5 hrs. To **Huaquillas** US$10, 10 hrs, via Guayaquil. To **Esmeraldas** US$3, 3 hrs. To **Manta** US$6, 7 hrs. To **Bahía de Caráquez** US$5, 6 hrs. To **Pedernales** US$3.20, 2½ hrs.

ⓓ Directory

Manta *p993*
Banks Banco del Pacífico, Av 2 y C 13. Produbanco, Malecón y C17. **Internet** Service runs about US$1.20.

Bahía de Caráquez *p994*
Banks Banco de Guayaquil, Av Bolívar y Riofrío. ATM. **Internet** US$1.20-1.50 per hr.

Santo Domingo de los Colorados *p995*
Banks Produbanco, Av Quito 1246 y Chorrera de Napa. **Internet** Many in the centre, US$0.50-0.80 per hr.

Northern lowlands

A mixture of beaches, mangroves (where not destroyed for fruit and shrimp production), tropical forests and Cayapa Indian communities characterize this part of Ecuador's Pacific lowlands as they stretch to the Colombian border.

North to Atacames
North of Pedernales the coastal highway veers northeast, going slightly inland, then crosses into the province of Esmeraldas near **Chamanga** (*San José de Chamanga, population 4,300*), a thriving little hub with houses built on stilts on the freshwater estuary. This is a good spot from which to explore the nearby mangroves, there is one basic *pensión* and frequent buses north and south. Town is 1 km from the highway. Inland, and spanning the provincial border is the **Reserva Ecológica Mache-Chindul**, administered by the **Jatun Sacha Foundation** (www.jatunsacha.org). North of Chamanga is **Portete**, with nice estuary and beach, and, 7 km from the main road along a poor side road, **Mompiche**, one of Ecuador's best surfing spots. The road continues through El Salto, the crossroads for coastal town of Muisne.

A few hours north of El Salto, between the villages of **Punta Galera** and **Tonchigüe** is the turn-off for **Playa Escondida** (see Sleeping below). Further north, and a 15-minute bus ride south of Atacames, is **Súa** a quiet and friendly little beach resort, set in a beautiful bay. Just down the road is Playa de **Same**, with a long grey sandy beach lined with palms and, mostly, high-rise apartment blocks for wealthy Quiteños. Safe swimming; good birdwatching in the lagoon behind the beach.

Atacames → *Phone code: 06. Colour map 11, grid A2. Population: 12,800.*

One of the main resorts on the Ecuadorean coast, Atacames, 25 km south of Esmeraldas, is a real 24-hour party town during the high season (July-September), at weekends and national holidays. Those who prefer some peace and quiet should head instead for Súa or Playa Escondida (see above). Most hotels are on a peninsula between the Río Atacames and the ocean. The main park, most services and the bus stops are to the south of the river. Information from **Oficina Municipal de Turismo** ① *Av Principal, T273 1912, Mon-Fri 0800-1230, 1330-1600, municipioatacamesturismo@andinanet.net*.

Camping on the beach is unsafe and along the beach from Atacames to Súa there is a high risk of mugging. Also the sea can be very dangerous, there is a powerful undertow and many people have been drowned. The sale of black coral jewellery has led to the destruction of much of the offshore reef. Consider the environmental implications before buying.

Esmeraldas → *Phone code: 06. Colour map 11, grid A2. Population: 95,000.*

This eopnymous provincial capital has little to offer and suffers from water shortages. Despite its wealth in natural resources (gold mining, tobacco, cacao, cattle ranching), Esmeraldas is among the poorest provinces in the country. Shrimp farm development has destroyed much mangrove and timber exports are decimating Ecuador's last Pacific rainforest. Baskets made by the Cayapa people are sold in the market across from the Post Office, behind the vegetables. Tolita artefacts are nearby. **Tourist office**: Ministerio de Turismo ① *Cañizares entre Bolívar y Sucre, T271 1370. Mon-Fri 0830-1215, 1430-1730*. Mosquitoes and malaria are a serious problem throughout Esmeraldas province, especially in the rainy season (June-December is the dry season). Most *residencias* provide mosquito nets (*toldos* or *mosquiteros*), or buy one in the market near the bus station. Take care in town, especially on arrival at bus terminal.

La Tola to Limones

La Tola is 122 km from Esmeraldas (San Mateo bridge) and is where you catch the boat for Limones and on to San Lorenzo. The road passes Camarones, Río Verde, Rocafuerte and **Las Peñas**, which is being transformed from a sleepy seaside village with a nice wide beach into a holiday resort. The completion of a paved highway from Ibarra has made Las Peñas the closest beach to any highland capital (only 4 hours by bus) and rapid haphazard development is taking place. Ibarreños pack the place at weekends and holidays.

The shoreline changes from sandy beaches to mangrove swamp. The wildlife is varied and spectacular, especially the birds. Avoid staying overnight in La Tola; women especially are harassed. East of town is **El Majagual** *US$3*, forest with the tallest mangrove tree in the world (63.7 m). There is a walkway, good birdwatching and many mosquitos, take repellent. In **Olmedo**, just northwest of La Tola, the *Women's Union of Olmedo* runs an ecotourism project; they have accommodation: see Sleeping, below. To the northeast of La Tola and on an island on the northern shore of the Río Cayapas is **La Tolita**, a small, poor village, where the culture of the same name thrived between 300 BC and AD 700. Many remains have been found here, several burial mounds remain to be explored and looters continue to take out artefacts to sell.

Limones (also known as Valdez) is the focus of traffic downriver from much of northern Esmeraldas Province, where bananas from the Río Santiago are sent to Esmeraldas for export. The Cayapa Indians live up the Río Cayapas and can sometimes be seen in Limones, especially during the crowded weekend market, but they are more frequently seen at Borbón (see below). Two good shops in Limones sell the very attractive Cayapa basketry. There has been a great deal of migration from neighbouring Colombia to the Limones, Borbón and San Lorenzo areas. Smuggling, including drugs, is big business and there are occasional searches by the authorities. There are two hotels, both barely habitable; best to stay at San Lorenzo.

Inland from Limones

On the Río Cayapas past mangrove swamps, **Borbón** is dirty, unattractive, busy and dangerous, with the highest incidence of malaria in the country. It is developing as a centre of the timber industry. Ask for Papá Roncón, the King of Marimba, who, for a beer or two, will put on a one-man show. Upriver from Borbón are Cayapa or Chachi Indian villages and Afro-Ecuadorean communities, you will see the Chachis passing in their canoes and in their open long-houses on the shore. To visit these villages, arrangements can be made through

Hostal Brisas del Río. Alternatively, around 0700, canoes arrive at the malecón in Borbón and return to their homes around 1000. You can arrange to go with them. For any independent travel in this area take a mosquito net, some food and means of water purification. Upriver along the Río Cayapas are the villages of **Pichiyacu** and **Santa María**, above the confluence with the Río Onzole (2 hours, US$3.50), **Zapallo Grande**, a friendly village with many gardens (3½ hours, US$6) and **San Miguel**, beautifully situated on a hill at the confluence of the San Miguel and Cayapas rivers (4 hours, US$8). Along this river are a couple of lodges, the ride is none to comfortable but it is an interesting trip. San Miguel is the access point to **Reserva Ecológica Cotacachi-Cayapas**, about 30 minutes upriver. The community also runs its own 1,200 ha forest reserve, abutting on the national reserve, and has an ecotourism project with accommodation and guiding service.

San Lorenzo → *Phone code: 06. Colour map 1a, grid A3. Population: 14,600.*

The hot, humid town of San Lorenzo stands on the Bahía del Pailón, which is characterized by a maze of canals. The area around San Lorenzo is rich in timber and other plants, but unrestricted logging is putting the forests under threat. At the seaward end of the bay is a sandy beach at San Pedro, with fishing huts but no facilities. At weekends canoes go to the beaches around 0700-0800 and 1400-1500, US$3 for the 1-2 hour ride. Marimba can be seen during the local fiesta on 6-10 August. Groups practise Thursday-Saturday; ask around. From San Lorenzo you can visit the mangroves of the **Reserva Ecológica Cayapas-Mataje** (REMACAM), which protects most of the islands in the estuary northwest of town. Also the **Reserva Playa de Oro**, 10,406 hectares along the Río Santiago, a good place for birdwatching. Contact Mauro Caicedo ① *T06-278 0962, www.touchthejungle.org*. Access is from **Selva Alegre** (a couple of basic *residenciales*). Trips can also be made upriver from Selva Alegre, or sometimes Playa de Oro into unspoiled rainforest where you can see howler and spider monkeys and jaguar prints; an unforgettable experience. Contact Risa Jordan to make arrangements for a visit, rosaj@look.ca, or contact Jean Brown at **Safari Tours** in Quito (see page 911).

Border with Colombia

The Río Mataje is the border with Colombia. From San Lorenzo, Colombia can be reached by boat, arriving eventually at the port of Tumaco in Colombia, or inland along the coastal road which ends on the Ecuadorean side at the village of Mataje. There are no facilities to get immigration entry or exit stamps at either of these locations. Given the poor public safety situation and the armed conflict in Colombia, travel in this area is not recommended.

● Sleeping

North to Atacames *p999*
Mompiche
D **Iruña**, east along the beach, access only at low tide or by launch, T09-947 2458, www.playa-ecuador.com. A lovely secluded hideaway with 4 nice cabins. Large terraces and hammocks, restaurant, fan, nice gardens, Spanish run.
E **Gabeal**, 300 m east of town, T09-969 6543. Nice quiet place, lovely ocean views, balconies, small rooms and cabins, good restaurant. The owner can arrange visits to his private forest reserve, good for birdwatching.

Punta Galera/Tonchigüe
D **Playa Escondida**, 10 km west of Tonchigüe, 6 km east of Punta Galera, T273 3106, www.intergate.ca/playaescondida.
A charming beach hideaway, set in 100 ha stretching back to dry tropical forest. Run by Canadian Judith Barett on an ecologically sound basis. Volunteers are welcome for reforestation.

Excellent but pricey restaurant, nice rustic cabins overlooking a lovely little bay, rooms cheaper with shared bath, cold water, camping possible. Good swimming and walking along the beach at low tide. Isolated, wonderfully relaxing.

Súa
D **Buganvillas**, ½ block from the Malecón, T273 1008. Very nice, room 10 has the best views, pool.
E **Chagra Ramos**, on the beach, T273 1006. Good restaurant, fan, nice views, good value.
E **Los Jardines**, 150 m from the beach, T273 1181. Cold water, fan, parking, nice, good value.
F **Súa**, on the beach, T09-535 3825. Simple hostel with 4 rooms, cold water, fan, reasonably comfortable.

Same
B **El Acantilado**, on the hill by the sea, south of Same, T273 3466, T02-245 3606 (Quito). Rooms

and cabins (minimum 4 people), pool, whale watching tours in season.

B El Rampiral, at south end of the beach, T273 3299, T02-226 4134 (Quito), www.rampiral.com. Comfortable seaside cabins for 4-5, restaurant, fan, pool, fridge, parking, popular with Ecuadorean families, reservations required, may close out of season.

D Seaflower, on the beach, T273 3369. Simple rooms, excellent expensive restaurant, fan, mosquito net, can get very noisy in high season, German-Chilean run, English spoken.

D-E La Terraza, on the beach, T273 3320. Cabins and rooms, pleasant, hammocks, with breakfast, cheaper with fan, Spanish owners, good pizzería.

Atacames p1000

Prices quoted are for the high season; discounts are available in the low season. Hotels are generally expensive for Ecuador. It's best to bring a mosquito net as few hotels supply them.

AL-A Juan Sebastián, towards the east end of the beach, T273 1049, www.hoteljuansebastian. com. A/c, TV, restaurant, spa, pool, parking, luxurious.

A Marbella, on the beach, T273 1129. Pleasant rooms for 4-5, fan, pool, **D** in low season when it is good value.

B Cielo Azul, on the beach near the stadium, T273 1813, www.hotelcieloazul.com. Rooms with balconies and hammocks, fan, pool, fridge, comfortable and very good.

B Lé Castell, on the beach, T273 1476. Includes breakfast, pool, garage, restaurant, comfy.

C Marimba, T273 1321. Includes breakfast, restaurant, a/c, pool, parking, quiet and comfortable, nice gardens.

C Rogers, west end of the beach, T275 1041. Quiet, constant water supply, restaurant, bar, good value. Recommended.

C-D Tahiti, on the beach, T276 1355, 02-244 4584. Good restaurant, some rooms with a/c others with fan, pool, parking, mosquito nets provided.

D Der Alte Fritz, on the Malecón, T273 1610, www.deraltefritz-ecuador.com. Good breakfast, restaurant serving German and international food, German and English spoken, discounts for longer stays, owner organizes whale-watching and fishing trips.

D Los Bohíos, 1 block from the beach by the footbridge, T273 1089. Bungalows with fresh water showers, comfortable, good value.

E Charito, 2 blocks from the bus station, T276 7678. Small hostel in a quiet location except for the buses, with bath and fan, parking, hospitable.

E La Casa del Manglar, 150 m from the beach beside the footbridge, T273 1464. Cheaper without bath, fan, laundry, small dark rooms.

E Las Guadúas, Malecón del Río, 2 blocks from the beach, T276 0091, lasguaduas1@on.net.ec. Quiet hotel on the riverside, cold water, good value, new in 2006.

Esmeraldas p1000

Hotels in the centre are poor; instead stay in the outskirts.

B-C Apart Hotel Esmeraldas, Libertad 407 y Ramón Tello, T272 8700, aparthotelesmeraldas@ andinanet.net. Includes breakfast, good restaurant, casino, a/c, fridge, parking, excellent.

D Hotel del Mar, at the far end of Av Kennedy in Las Palmas, T272 3707. A decent breezy hotel in Esmeraldas' beach area, restaurant, patio cafetería, cold water, a/c, parking, good service. Recommended.

E El Galeón, Piedrahita 330 y Olmedo, T272 3820. With a/c, cold water, cheaper with fan, reasonable.

D Zulema 2, Malecón y Rocafuerte, T272 6757. Modern, with TV, cold water, fan, large rooms, parking.

La Tola to Limones p1000
Olmedo

D Casa del Manglar, a 20-min walk or short boat ride from La Tola, T278 6126 (Catalina Montes or her son Edwin). A wood cabin with porch by the shore. Dormitory for 15 people, meals available, shared bath, mosquito nets, quiet and pleasant. Take drinking water or means of purification. Organizes tours to mangroves, La Tolita and other sights.

Inland from Limones p1000
Borbón

E Brisas del Río Santiago, Malecón y 23 de Noviembre, T278 6211. Basic concrete hostel with good air circulation, shared bath, cold water, fan, meeting point for travellers going upriver. Owner Sr Betancourt can arrange canoes for excursions.

E Castillo, 5 de Agosto, near Trans Esmeraldas bus office, T278 6613. With bath, cold water, fan, parking, clean, friendly.

San Miguel

A Eco-Lodge San Miguel, above the village of San Miguel, contact Fundación Verde Milenio, Quito, T02-290 6192, www.verdemilenio.org. Community run lodge with lovely views, shared bath, more luxurious cabins are planned in 2007. Price includes transport from Borbón, 3 meals and excursion to the forest, the community also runs the basic ranger's house next door with bunk beds, **F** pp (food and guiding extra). Advance booking advised.

San Lorenzo p1001

Expect to be mobbed by children wanting a tip to show you to a hotel or restaurant. Also take insect repellent.

A Playa de Oro, on the Río Santiago, upriver from Borbón, contact Mauro Caicedo, T06-2780962, www.touchthejungle.org. Basic cabins with shared bath, includes 3 meals and guided excursion.

E Carondelet, on the plaza, T278 1119. Breakfast available, some rooms with bath, fan, mosquito net, some rooms are small, helpful, discos nearby, noisy on Fri and Sat night.

E Pampa de Oro, C 26 de Agosto y Tácito Ortiz, T278 0214. Adequate family run hotel, cold water, fan, mosquito net.

E-F San Carlos, C Imbabura near the train station, T278 0284. Simple concrete hotel, cheaper with shared bath, cold water, fan, mosquito nets.

🍴 Eating

North to Atacames: Súa p999

🍴 **El Caracol**, on the Malecón. Good seafood, friendly.

🍴 **Kikes**, On the Malecón. Very good set meals and great variety of seafood.

🍴 **La Margarita**, across from the police station. Pizza and French cuisine, French run.

Atacames p1000

The beach is packed with bars and restaurants offering seafood. The best and cheapest *ceviche* is found at the stands at the west end of the beach and at the market, but avoid *concha*.

Esmeraldas p1000

Typical restaurants and bars by the beach sell *ceviches*, fried fish and *patacones*.

🍴🍴 **Chifa Asiático**, Cañizares y Bolívar. Chinese and seafood, a/c, excellent.

🍴🍴-🍴 **El Manglar**, Quito y Olmedo. Good *comida esmeraldeña* such as *encocado* and *tapado*, efficient service.

🍴 **Las Redes**, main plaza. Good fish, set meals and à la carte.

🍴 **Tapao.con**, 6 de Diciembre 1717 y Piedrahita. A popular place for typical dishes such as *tapado*, *encocado* and *ceviche*.

San Lorenzo p1001

🍴 **El Ave Tururú**, 10 de Agosto. Good European and local dishes.

🍴 **El Chocó**, Imbabura. Good fish and local specialties. Also economical set lunches and the best *batido de borojó* (milkshake) in town.

🍸 Bars and clubs

Esmeraldas p1000

Expresiones, Sucre y Manabí, opposite the cathedral. Bar and gallery displaying paintings by local artists. By the beach in Las Palmas there are a great variety of bars blasting salsa, merengue and regaetón.

🚌 Transport

North to Atacames p999

Bus **Mompiche** to **Esmeraldas**, 5 a day, US$3, 3½ hrs. To **Playa Escondida**: take a ranchera or bus from Esmeraldas for Punta Galera, 5 a day, US$2, 2 hrs. A taxi from Atacames costs US$12 and a pick-up from Tonchigüe US$5. To **Súa** and **Same**: Buses every 30 mins to and from **Atacames**, 15 mins, 18 km, US$0.35. Make sure it drops you at Same and not at Club Casablanca.

Atacames p1000

Bus To/from **Esmeraldas**, every 15 mins, US$0.80, 40 mins; to **Guayaquil**, US$8, 8 hrs. To **Quito**, about 10 daily, US$8, 6½ hrs.

Esmeraldas p1000

Air Gen Rivadeneira Airport is near the town of Tachina, on the east shore of the Río Esmeraldas. A taxi to the city centre (30 km) costs US$6, buses to the Terminal Terrestre from the road outside the airport pass about every 30 mins. Daily flights except Sat to **Quito** with TAME (Bolívar y 9 de Octubre, T272 6863), 30 mins, US$40. Check in early, planes may leave 30 mins before scheduled time.

Bus To **Quito** and **Guayaquil** there is *servicio directo* or *ejecutivo*, a better choice as they are faster buses and don't stop for passengers. To **Quito**, US$7, 6 hrs, via Santo Domingo, frequent service on a good paved road, with Trans-Esmeraldas (10 de Agosto at Parque Central, recommended), **Panamericana** (Colón y Salinas), slow but luxurious, and others. To **Ibarra**, 9 hrs, US$10, via Borbón and San Lorenzo. To **Santo Domingo**, US$3, 3 hrs. To **Ambato**, 6 a day, US$8, 8 hrs. To **Guayaquil**, hourly, US$8, *directo*, 8 hrs. To **Bahía de Caráquez**, via Santo Domingo de los Colorados, US$8, 9 hrs. To **Manta**, US$8, 10 hrs. La Costeñita and El Pacífico, both on Malecón, to/ from **La Tola** 8 daily US$3.75, 3 hrs. To **Borbón**, frequent service, US$3.50, 3 hrs. To **San Lorenzo**, 8 daily, US$4.50, 4 hrs. To **Súa**, **Same** and **Atacames**, every 15 mins from 0630-2030, to Atacames US$0.80, 1 hr.

Limones p1000

Ferry There are launches between **La Tola** and Limones, US$3, 1 hr, and 3 daily Limones-**San**

Lorenzo, 2 hrs US$3. You can also hire a launch to **Borbón**, a fascinating trip through mangrove islands, passing hunting pelicans, approximately US$10 per hr.

Inland from Limones: Borbón *p1000*
Bus To/from **Esmeraldas**: frequent service, US$3.50, 3 hrs.
Ferry 4 motor launches a day run to different communities upriver, leaving 1030-1100. Check how far each one is going as only one goes as far as **San Miguel**, US$8, 4 hours, it is run by the community and runs daily.

San Lorenzo *p1001*
Bus To **Ibarra**, 10 daily, 4 hrs, US$4. They leave

from the train station or environs. To **Esmeraldas**, via Borbón, 8 daily, US$4.50, 3 hrs.
Ferry Two companies that offer launch service are **Coopseturi**, T/F278 0161; and **Costeñita**, both near the pier. All services are subject to change and cancellation. To **Limones**, 3 daily, 2 hrs, US$3. To **La Tola**, US$6, 4 hrs. To **Palma Real**, for beaches, 2 daily, US$3, 3 hrs.

ⓘ Directory

Esmeraldas *p1000*
Banks Banco del Austro, Bolívar 310 y Cañizares. **Produbanco**, Bolívar 415 y Cañizares.
Internet Many in town.

The Oriente

East of the Andes the hills fall away to tropical lowlands. Some of this beautiful wilderness remains unspoiled and sparsely populated, with indigenous settlements along the tributaries of the Amazon. Large tracts of jungle are under threat, however: colonists are clearing many areas for agriculture, while others are laid waste by petroleum exploration or gold mining. The Ecuadorean jungle, especially the Northern Oriente, has the advantage of being relatively accessible and tourist infrastructure here is well developed. The eastern foothills of the Andes, where the jungle begins, offer the easiest access and a good introduction to the rainforest for those with limited time or money. Further east lie the remaining large tracts of primary rainforest, teeming with life, which can be visited from several excellent (and generally expensive) jungle lodges. Southern Oriente is as yet less developed, for tourism as well as other activities. Precisely for this reason, it offers unique opportunities and demands extraordinary respect.

Ins and outs

Getting there There are scheduled commercial flights from Quito to Lago Agrio, Coca and Macas. From Quito, Macas and Shell, light aircraft can be chartered to any jungle village with a landing strip. Much of western Oriente is also accessible by roads which wind their way down from the highlands. Quito to Lago Agrio via Baeza, Baños to Puyo, and Loja to Zamora are fully paved. Otherwise roads are narrow and tortuous and subject to landslides in the rainy season, but all have regular, if poor bus services and all can be attempted in a jeep or in an ordinary car with good ground clearance. Deeper into the rainforest, motorized canoes provide the only alternative to air travel. Finally, a road runs from Tulcán to Lago Agrio, a short trip but very close to the Colombian border and therefore unsafe.

Jungle tours These fall into four basic types: **lodges**; **guided tours**, **indigenous ecotourism** and **river cruises**. When staying at a jungle lodge (normally a *cabaña* complex located in a natural setting), you will need to take a torch, insect repellent, protection against the sun and a rain poncho that will keep you dry when walking and when sitting in a canoe. Rubber boots can be hired. See also Jungle lodges on the Lower Napo, below. **Guided tours** of varying length are offered by tour operators and independent guides. These should be licensed by the Ecuadorean **Ministerio de Turismo**. Tour operators and guides are mainly concentrated in Quito, Baños, Puyo, Tena, Misahuallí, Coca, and, to a lesser extent, Macas and Zamora. A number of indigenous communities and families offer **ecotourism** programmes in their territories. These are either community-controlled and operated, or organized as joint ventures between the indigenous community or family and a non-indigenous partner. These programmes usually involve guides who are licensed as *guías nativos* with the right to guide within their communities. You should be prepared to be more self-sufficient on such a trip than on a visit to a jungle lodge or a tour with a high-end operator.

office for exit stamps and boats can be hired for the 2-hour trip down river to the Peruvian border town of **Pantoja**, US$60 per boat, try to share the ride. Peruvian entry stamps are given in Pantoja and, although there is no hotel, you can arrange to stay with a family for a small charge. In addition to immigration, you may have to register with the navy on either side of the border so have your passport at hand. Onward boat services from Pantoja to Iquitos will be found in the Peru chapter, under Iquitos, Transport. The second option is to take a tour with a Coca agency, taking-in various attractions on route, and continuing to Iquitos or closer Peruvian ports from which you can catch onward public river transport. We have received complaints about some of these tours (not with the agencies we list), so ask around carefully, confirm all details in advance. Thirdly, and the most expensive, is to see if any of the river cruise boats listed below is going all the way to Iquitos.

● Sleeping

Baeza p1005
E Bambús, Av de los Quijos, at the east end of the new town, T232 0615. Hot water, parking, pleasant and friendly.
E La Casa de Rodrigo, in the old town, T232 0467, rodrigobaeza@andinanet.net. Modern and comfortable, hot water, owner organizes rafting trips.
E-F Samay, Av de los Quijos, in the new town, T232 0170. Cheaper with shared bath, electric shower, older place but welcoming and OK.
F La Casa de Gina, Jumandy y Batallón Chimborazo, just off the highway in the old town, T232 0471. Hot water, nicely furnished, good value.

Around Baeza
LL Cabañas San Isidro, in the Cosanga Valley, 19 km south of Baeza, reservations necessary: T02-254 7403, www.ecuadorexplorer.com. Price includes 3 excellent meals. This is a 1,200-ha private reserve with rich bird life, comfortable accommodation, hot water and warm hospitality, reservation required. Recommended.
C The Magic Roundabout, 12 km south of Baeza, T09-934 5264, www.themagicround about.info. Phone reservations advised. Cabins with shared bath and droms (cheaper) on a hillside. Great views, cosy social area, hiking trails to waterfalls. Includes good breakfast, other meals available including vegetarian options. British run, "the best English pub for miles". Recommended.
E Hostería El Reventador, on main highway next to bridge over the Río Reventador, T06-281 8221, 09-3577143 (mob), turismovolcanreventador@yahoo.com. Meals on request, hot water, pool, simple rooms, busy at weekends, well located for visits to San Rafael Falls and Volcán Reventador.

Lago Agrio p1006
Virtually everything can be found on the main street, Av Quito.
B Arazá, Quito 610 y Narváez, T283 0223. Quiet

location away from centre. Includes breakfast, restaurant, a/c, pool (US$5 for non-residents), fridge, parking, comfortable, best in town. Recommended.
C El Cofán, 12 de Febrero 2-12 y Av Quito, T283 0526. Includes breakfast, restaurant, a/c, fridge, parking, well cared-for.
C Gran Hotel de Lago, Km 1½ Vía Quito, T283 2415. Includes breakfast, restaurant, pool, internet, cabins, nice gardens, quiet. Recommended.
C La Cascada, Quito y Amazonas, T283 0124, aliarcos@yahoo.com. A/c, cheaper with fan and cold water, variety of different rooms, some with fridge, small but nice.
D D'Mario, Quito 171, T283 0172. Restaurant, cheaper with cold water, a/c, small pool, some rooms have fridge, good, helpful owner. Recommended.
D Gran Colombia, Quito y Pasaje Gonzanamá, T283 1032. Good restaurant, a/c, cheaper with fan and cold water, central, many different types of rooms, modern and adequate.
E Lago Imperial, Colombia y Quito, T283 0453. A/c cheaper with fan, cold water, convenient, good value.
E Machala 2, Colombia y Añazco, T283 0673. Good restaurant, cold water, fan, parking, safe.
F Americano, Quito 118 y Colombia, T283 0555. With bath, cold water, fan, small rooms but good value.
F Casa Blanca, Quito y Colombia, T283 0181. With bath, hot water, fan, nice bright rooms, good value.

Coca p1006
Many hotels and *residencias* are populated by oil workers and range from basic to barely habitable.
B-D El Auca, Napo y García Moreno, T288 0600, helauca@ecuanex.net.ec. A/c, cheaper with fan, hot water, comfortable, big garden with hammocks, manager speaks English, good place to make up a tour party, restaurant and disco.
B-D La Misión, by riverfront, T288 0261, www.hotelamision.com. A/c, English spoken,

internet, pool, restaurant and disco, arranges tours. Recommended.

C Puerto Orellana, Av Alejandro Labaka, at the entrance to town from Lago Agrio, T288 0129, jesseniabrito@andinanet.net. Electric shower, a/c, parking, out of the way but modern and very nice. Popular, best book in advance.

D Amazonas, 12 de Febrero y Espejo, T288 0444. Nice relaxed setting by the river, away from centre, restaurant, a/c, cheaper with fan, parking, quiet, good.

D-E San Fermín, Bolívar y Quito, T288 0802. A/c, cheaper with fan and cold water, parking, modern and comfortable, good value.

E Oasis, between the bridge and La Misión, T288 0206. Electric shower, a/c, cheaper with fan, parking, quiet, simple but adequate.

E Payamino, Rocafuerte y Quito, T288 0097. With bath, cold water, a/c, cheaper with fan, simple but adequate.

Lodges on the lower Río Napo *p1006*

All Napo area lodges count travel days as part of their package, which means that often a '3-day tour' spends only one day actually in the forest. Also, the return trip must start before dawn if it is to connect with that day's Coca-Quito flight; if it starts later it will be necessary to spend the night in Coca. Most lodges have fixed departure days from Coca (eg Mon and Fri) and it is very expensive to get a special departure on another day.

Bataburo, Quito office: **Kempery Tours**, see Quito Tour operators, page 910. A lodge in Huaorani territory near Parque Nacional Yasuní, on the Río Tiguino, a 3-6 hr canoe ride from the end of the Vía Auca out of Coca. Some cabins have private baths and there are shared showers. Guides are mostly local. The birds here have been little studied but macaws and other large species are present. The mammal population also appears to be quite good. US$275 for 4 days.

Napo Wildlife Center, in Quito, L García y J L Mera, T02-290 9090, www.ecoecuador.org. Operated by and for the local Añangu community, 2½ hrs downstream from Coca. Winners of a 2006 responsible tourism award. This area of hilly forest is rather different from the low flat forest of some other sites, and the diversity is slightly higher. There are big caimans and mammals, including giant otters, and the birdwatching is excellent with two parrot clay-licks and a 35 m canopy tower. The local guide, Giovanny Rivadeneyra, is one of the most knowledgeable birders in the Oriente. US$650 for 4 days. Recommended.

La Selva, Quito office: Mariana de Jesús E7-211 y La Pradera, T02-255 0995, www.laselva junglelodge.com. An upmarket lodge, 2½ hrs downstream from Coca on a picturesque lake. Surrounded by excellent forest, especially on the far side of Mandicocha. Bird and animal life is exceptionally diverse. Many species of monkey are seen regularly. A total of 580 bird species have been found, one of the highest totals in the world for a single elevation. Comfortable cabins and excellent meals. High standards, most guides are biologists. 45 m canopy tower. US$697 for 4 days.

Sacha, Quito office, Julio Zaldumbide 397 y Valladolid, T02-2566090, www.sachalodge.com. An upmarket lodge 2½ hrs downstream from Coca. Very comfortable cabins, excellent meals. The bird list is outstanding; local bird expert, Oscar Tapuy (Coca T06-2881486), can be requested in advance. Canopy tower and 275m canopy walkway. Several species of monkey are commonly seen. Nearby river islands provide access to a distinct habitat. US$645 for 4 days.

Sani, Quito office: Roca 736 y Amazonas, Pasaje Chantilly, T02-255 8881, www.sanilodge.com. All proceeds go to the Sani Isla community, who run the lodge with the help of outside experts. It is located on a remote lagoon which has 4-5 m long black caiman. This area is rich in wildlife and birds, including many species such as the scarlet macaw which have disappeared from most other Napo area lodges. There is good accommodation and a 30 m canopy tower. An effort has been made to make the lodge accessible to people who have difficulty walking; the lodge can be reached by canoe (total 3½ hrs from Coca) without a walk. US$450 for 4 days. Good value, recommended.

Yuturi, 5 hrs downstream from Coca, Quito office: Amazonas N24-240 y Colón, T/F02-250 4037, www.yuturilodge.com. Birdwatching is excellent and wildlife is good. The guides are usually locals accompanied by translators. 4 days cost US$280, exclusive of airfare. Visits can be combined with **Yarina**, the closest lodge to Coca, about 1 hr down the Napo. Thatched roof cabins and a 40-ft canopy tower (US$75 per night).

🍽 Eating

Baeza *p1005*

🍴 **El Viejo**, east end of Av de los Quijos, the road to Tena in the new town, daily 0700-2100. Good set meals and à la carte.

🍴 **Gina**, Batallón Chimborazo, just off the highway in the old town, daily 0730-2200. Trout is the speciality, friendly and popular.

Lago Agrio *p1006*

There are good restaurants at the larger hotels (see above); also many cheap *comedores*.

Coca *p1006*

🍴🍴 **Parrilladas Argentinas**, Cuenca e Inés Arango. Argentine-style grill.

🍴🍴-🍴 **Pizza Choza**, Rocafuerte y Napo. Good pizza,

friendly service, English spoken. Daily 1800-2200.
♥ **Media Noche**, Napo, in front of *Hotel El Auca*.
Chicken dishes, open 1800-0000.
♥ **Ocaso**, Eloy Alfaro between Napo and
Amazonas. Good set meals and à la carte.

▲ Activities and tours

Cuyabeno Wildlife Reserve *p1006*
To visit Cuyabeno it is best to shop around in
Quito, as few operators have offices in Lago Agrio
(see Quito Tour operators, page 909). Some
agencies can be found on C Quito in Lago Agrio.
The following have been recommended for
jungle trips to Cuyabeno:
Ecuador Verde País, Calama E6-19 y Reina
Victoria, T02-222 0614, www.cabanasjamu.com.
Run *Jamu Lodge* in Cuyabeno, good service, 4
days/3 nights US$160-200 pp, plus transport and
park fees, starting in the village of Cuyabeno.
Green Planet, see page 910.
Kapok Expeditions, see page 910.
Neotropic Turis, Av Amazonas N24-03 y Wilson,
Quito, T02-252 1212, www.neotropicturis.com.
Operate the *Cuyabeno Lodge*; pioneer lodge with
cabins by the Laguna Grande, in the heart of this
fauna-rich reserve. US$295 pp for 4 days and 3
nights (including meals, guides – who speak
English – but not transport to and from Lago
Agrio and park fee).

Coca *p1006*
Jungle tours from Coca *See also p909*
Ecu-Astonishing, Malecón next to Hotel Oasis,
288 0251, juliojarrin@andinanet.net. Julio Jarrín
offers tours to his cabins near Pañacocha.
Emerald Forest Expeditions, Quito y Espejo,
T288 2309. Luis García offers tours to Pañacocha,
Parque Nacional Yasuní and Iquitos, Peru.
Wymper Torres, T288 0336. He specializes in the
Río Shiripuno and Pañacocha areas, also trips to
Iquitos, Spanish only.

River cruises on the lower Río Napo
Flotel La Misión, Quito T02-256 4675,
www.hotellamision.com. Sails between Coca and
Pañacocha. US$570 for 4 days.
Jungle Discovery, Quito office: **Kempery Tours**,
Ramirez Dávalos 117 y Amazonas, Oficina 101,
T02-250 5599, www.kempery.com. This
30-passenger vessel sails between Coca and
Nuevo Rocafuerte. US$600 for 4 days.
Manatee, Quito office: **Advantage Travel**,
T02-246 2871, www.advantageecuador.com. This
30-passenger vessel sails between Coca and
Pañacocha. US$461 for 4 days. First-class guides,
excellent food, en suite cabins.

⊖ Transport

Baeza *p1005*
Bus Buses to and from **Tena** pass right through
town. If arriving on a **Lago Agrio** bus, get off at
La "Y" and walk or take a *camioneta* for
US$0.25.

Lago Agrio *p1006*
Air Airport is 5 km southeast of the centre.
TAME to **Quito**, daily except Sun, US$52. Book
1-2 days in advance and reconfirm. If there is no
space available to **Lago Agrio**, fly to **Coca**, from
where it is 3 hrs by bus on a good road.
Bus *Terminal terrestre* is north of town,
but buses for Coca leave from the market area on
Orellana, 3 blocks south of Av Quito. To **Quito** (2
routes: through El Dorado de Cascales, and,
slightly longer through, Coca and Loreto), US$8, 7
hrs. **Baeza**, US$8.70, 5 hrs. **Coca**, US$3, 3 hrs. To
Tena, US$7, 8 hrs.

Coca *p1006*
Air Flights to **Quito** with Icaro (office in *Hotel
La Misión*, T288 0546), TAME (T288 1078) and
VIP, US$60, several daily, reserve as far in advance
as possible and always reconfirm.
Bus Long distance buses depart from company
offices in town; local destinations, including Lago
Agrio, are served from the terminal, a 20-min
walk north from *Hotel Auca* (ask to be let off in
town). To **Quito**, 10 hrs, US$10, several daily
1030-2200, **Trans Baños**, **Trans Esmeraldas** and
Zaracay depart from their offices near junction of
Napo y Cuenca. To **Lago Agrio**, see above. To
Tena, 6 hrs, US$7. To **Baeza**, US$7.50,
8 hrs. To **Baños**, US$11, 9 hrs.
River Down the Río Napo to **Nuevo
Rocafuerte** on the Peruvian border: most
reliable is **Cooperativa de Transporte Fluvial
Orellana**, at the dock, T288 0087, motorized
canoes Mon and Thu at 0800, 10 hrs, US$10;
returning Wed and Sun at 0530, 12 hrs. Buy
tickets a day in advance, be at the dock early, take
food, water, hat, sun-screen, etc. Another canoe
leaves Coca Fri early morning, returning Tue. An
18-passenger Peruvian canoe may be chartered
for touring and transport to **Pantoja** (Peru) and
beyond, contact Sra. Lilly Valles, T08-630 1047.
Departure dates of boats from **Pantoja** to
Iquitos are irregular. Four *lanchas* operate the
route, but they only come upriver as far as
Pantoja when they have sufficient cargo, so
several weeks can go by without any boat calling
on the town. Try calling Iquitos in advance, to
inquire when the next boat will sail from Pantoja:
T+51-65-242082 for the **Victor** and the **Camila**,
or T+51-65-266159, 51-65-961 3049 (mob) for

the Jeisawell and the **Siempre Adelante**. They have no berths, only deck space to hang your hammock and are very unsanitary by the end of the trip. The 5-7 day trip from Pantoja all the way to Iquitos costs US$30 including very basic food, but it may be possible to pick up faster transport at **Santa Clotilde**, about half way to Iquitos, or **Mazán**. Take a hammock, cup, bowl, cutlery, extra food and snacks, drinking water or purification, insect repellent, toilet paper, soap, towel, etc. Cash dollars and soles in small notes are indispensable, but soles cannot be purchased in Coca.

① Directory

Lago Agrio *p1006*
Banks Banco de Guayquil, Quito y 12 de

Febrero; **Banco de Pichincha**, 12 de Febrero y Añasco; both for ATM only. **Casa de Cambio**, Quito y Colombia, for Colombian *pesos*. These can also be changed in shops.

Coca *p1006*
Banks Banco de Pichincha, Bolívar y 9 de Octubre, ATM only. **Cambiaria Ramírez**, Napo y García Moreno, T288 1229, Mon-Sat 0800-2000, 4% commission on TCs (Amex only). Does not change Peruvian *soles* or other currencies.
Immigration Rocafuerte y Napo, Edif Amazonas, p 3, T288 1594, Mon-Sat 0800-1200, 1500-1800, Sun 0800-1200. For travel to or from Peru by river, passports are normally stamped at Nuevo Rocafuerte, not Coca, but you can confirm details here before sailing. **Internet** Prices around US$1.20 per hr.

Central and southern Oriente

Quito and Baños are the starting points for the cental Oriente. To the south, in addition to the roads from Cuenca and Zamora, there are new routes leading down from the Sierra, from Riobamba and Azogues (near Cuenca). There are many different options for visiting the jungle here.

Archidona → *Phone code: 06. Colour map 11, grid B4. Population: 10,000.*

Roads from both Baeza and Coca go south to Archidona, 65 km from Baeza. It has a striking, small painted church and not much else but there are some excellent trips in the surrounding area. The road leaving Archidona's plaza to the east goes to the village of San Pablo, and beyond to the Río Hollín. Along this road, 7 km from Archidona, is the **Reserva Ecológica Monteverde** ① *entry for day visits US$2*, a 25 ha reserve with primary and secondary forest, and medicinal plants. There are walking trails, river bathing and medicinal plants. Reservations necessary, contact **Residencial Regina** ① *in Archidona T288 9144, or Quito T02-289 1041, taxi from Archidona US$6*. Along the same road, 15 km from Archidona, is **Reserva El Para**, an 500 ha forest reserve with many rare birds. It is owned by *Orchid Paradise* (see Archidona hotels below), who runs tours to the reserve. Groups pay US$30 for a guide plus US$40 for transport. Tours can be arranged to the **Izu Mangallpa Urcu (IMU) Foundation** ① *3 km east of Archidona off a side turning down the road to San Pablo, contact Elias Mamallacta in Archidona, T288 9383, www.izu-mangallpa-urcu.freehomepage.com*, set up by the Mamallacta family to protect territory on Galeras mountain. They charge US$35 per day for accommodation and day trips, minimum two people; tough going but the forest is wonderful. Just outside Archidona, to the south, a small turning leads to the river. About 200 m along there is a large rock with many **petroglyphs** carved on its surface, the easiest to find of several within a 30 km radius.

Tena and around → *Phone code: 06. Colour map 11, grid B4. Population: 31,000.*

Some 10 km further south, **Tena** is the capital of Napo Province. Like Archidona, it was founded in 1560 and both were important colonial missionary and trading posts. It is now a commercial centre with an attractive plaza overlooking the confluence of the Ríos Tena and Pano. Tena is quite spread out. There is a pedestrian bridge and a vehicle bridge which link the two halves of the town. There are several cyber cafés in town. The Tena area, which lacks the pristine jungle found deeper in the Oriente, has instead developed interesting opportunities for ethno-tourism and has become the rafting and kayaking mecca of Ecuador. **Tourist office** ① *García Moreno entre Calderón y JL Mera, near the river, T288 6536, Mon-Fri 0800-1230, 1330-1700.*

Comunidad Capirona is one hour by bus from Tena, then a further hour on foot. Visits can be arranged here or to nine other communities in the area. This is part of a highly regarded project which combines eco/ethnotourism and community development. There are also opportunities for volunteers. Contact the **Red Indigena de las Comunidades del Alto Napo para la Convivencia Intercultural y El Ecoturismo (Ricancie)** ① *Jumandí y Radio Tena, T288 8479, http://ricancie.nativeweb.org.*

Misahuallí → *Phone code: 06. Colour map 11, grid B4. Population: 4,900.*

This small port, at the junction of the Napo and Misahuallí rivers, is perhaps the best place in Ecuador from which to visit the 'near Oriente', but your expectations should be realistic. The area has been colonized for many years and there is no extensive virgin forest nearby (except at *Jatun Sacha*, see below. Access is very easy however, prices are reasonable, and while you will not encounter large animals in the wild, you can still see birds, butterflies and exuberant vegetation – enough to get a taste for the jungle. There is a fine, sandy beach on the Río Misahuallí, but don't camp on it as the river can rise unexpectedly. A narrow suspension bridge crosses the Río Napo at Misahuallí and joins the road along the south shore. There is an interesting *mariposario* (butterfly farm) ① *US$1.50*, two blocks from the main square in Misahuallí. Several colourful species can be observed and photographed close up. Make arrangements through *Ecoselva*. (See Activities and tours, below.

Jungle tours from Misahuallí There are many guides available to take parties into the jungle for trips of one to 10 days, all involving canoeing and varying amounts of hiking. Travellers should ask to see a guide's licence as there are frequent reports of unlicensed guides cheating tourists. The going rate is between US$25 and US$50 per person per day, depending on the season, size of group and length of trip. This should include food and rubber boots, which are absolutely essential. Quality varies, so try to get a personal recommendation from travellers who have just returned from a trip. For Tour operators based in Quito, see page 909).

Jatun Sacha Biological Station

Eight kilometres downriver from Misahuallí, reached by road or river, is the **Jatun Sacha Biological Station** ('big forest' in Quichua) *www.jatunsacha.org*. The biological station conserves 1,300 ha of tropical wet forest. So far, 507 bird, 2,500 plant and 765 butterfly species have been identified. Activities include environmental education, field research, ecotourism and excursions with good views and a well-developed trail system. US$28 per night, guiding extra. It's 25 minutes by boat, US$3.20; or by road on the south bank of the Río Napo, 25 km from the bridge in Puerto Napo.

Puyo → *Phone code: 03. Colour map 11, grid B4. Population: 35,000.*

The capital of the province of Pastaza and the largest centre in the whole Oriente. It feels more like a small lowland city anywhere rather than a typical jungle town. Visits can nonetheless be made to nearby forest reserves and tours deeper into the jungle can also be arranged from Puyo. It is the junction for road travel into the northern and southern Oriente, and for traffic heading to or from Ambato via Baños. The Sangay and Altar volcanoes can occasionally be seen from town. The **Museo Etno-Arqueológico** ① *Atahualpa y General Villamil, p 3*, has displays of the traditional dwellings of various cultures of the province of Pastaza. **Tourist offices: Ministerio de Turismo** ① *Francisco de Orellana y General Villamil, Mon-Fri 0830-1230, 1330-1700*. Also **Consejo Provincial** ① *Orellana 145 y 27 de Febrero, ground floor.*

Omaere ① *T288 7656, daily 0800-1700, US$3, www.omaere.net*, is a 15.6 ha ethnobotanical reserve 2 km north of Puyo on the road to Tena. Huts show Shuar, Achuar and Huaorani lifestyles and there is a garden. There are other small private reserves of varying quality in the Puyo area and visits are arranged by local tour operators (see below). You cannot however expect to see large tracts of undisturbed primary jungle here. Sites include: **Criadero de Vida Silvestre Fátima** ① *9 km north on the road to Tena, US$2*, which attempts to 'rehabilitate' captive jungle animals; **Jardín Botánico Las Orquídeas** ① *3 km south on the road to Macas, US$5*, orchids and other tropical plants; **Fundación Ecológica Hola Vida**, 27 km from Puyo near **Porvenir**, rustic accommodation in the forest and a canoe trip.

Shell

Shell is 13 km west of Puyo, 50 km from Baños, 1 hour. It has an airfield and at Mera, 15 km further northwest, on the road to Baños, is an army checkpoint where foreigners may be asked to register (passport required).

Macas → *Phone code: 07. Colour map 10, grid B4. Population 17,000, Altitude 1,000 m.*

Capital of Morona-Santiago province, Macas is situated high above the broad Río Upano valley, and developing rapidly thanks to nearby oil deposits and beef production. Sangay volcano can be seen on clear mornings from the plaza, creating an amazing backdrop to the tropical jungle surrounding the town. The modern cathedral, with beautiful stained-glass windows, houses the much-venerated image of La Purísima de Macas. Five blocks north of the cathedral, in the Parque Recreacional, which also affords great views of the Upano Valley, is a small orchid collection. The **Fundación Chankuap** ① *Soasti y Bolívar, T270 1176, www.chankuap.com*, sells a nice variety of locally produced crafts and food products. **Tourist office**: **Cámara de Turismo** ① *Domingo Comín y Soasti, T07-2701606, Mon-Fri 0800-1200, 1400-1700, Sat 0800-1200*. In clear weather, the surrounding hills give excellent views of the volcano **Sangay**, 5,230 m, within the **Parque Nacional Sangay** ① *US$10, information from Ministry of the Environment in Macas, Juan de la Cruz y 29 de Mayo*. The lowland area of the park has interesting walking with many rivers and waterfalls. See also Sangay (page 954) for notes on the new road to Guamote.

Sucúa → *Phone code: 07. Colour map 11, grid B4. Population: 12,000.*

Sucúa, 23 km from Macas, is of particular interest as the centre of a branch of the ex-head-hunting Shuar (Jívaro) Indians. Their crafts can be seen and bought but it is tactless to ask them about head-hunting and shrinking (a practice designed to punish those who bewitched others and to deter anyone wishing to cause sickness or disaster in future). You can try to contact the **Shuar Federation** at Domingo Comín 17-38, T/F274 0108, about visiting traditional villages, but the federation does not encourage tourists. Nearby is the Río Upano, a 1½ hour walk, with plenty of Morpho butterflies. Also close by is the Río Tutanangoza, a 15-minute walk, with rapids and good swimming, but be careful of the current after rain.

Sucúa to Zamora → *For Zamora see page 970.*

From Sucúa, the road heads south for 23 km to Logroño and then, another 29 km south to (Santiago de) **Méndez**, a nice town with a modern church. Market day Sunday. A road descends from the Sierra, from Azogues via Paute, to Méndez. Some 35 km south of Méndez is **Limón**, official name General Leónidas Plaza Gutiérrez, a mission town founded in 1935, now a busy place surrounded by high jungle. Buses, all from Calle Quito, go to Cuenca, Macas and Gualaquiza. Continuing south from Limón the road passes **Indanza** before reaching **Gualaquiza**, a pioneer town off the tourist track. It is surrounded by densely forested mountains, in which are interesting side trips. From Limón the road to Cuenca (132 km) passes through Gualaceo. From Limón the road rises steeply with many breathtaking turns and the vegetation changes frequently, partly through cloud forest and then, at 4,000 m, through the *páramo*, before dropping very fast down to the valley of Gualaceo. There is nowhere to stay along the Limón-Gualaceo road.

The road south from Gualaquiza passes El Pangui and Yantzaza (55 km), 8 km south of which is **Zumbi** (basic hotel near the plaza), where a bridge crosses the Río Zamora. At Zumbi, a sideroad goes southeast to Guayzimi and the beautiful **Alto Nangaritza** region. The upper Río Nangaritza flows through Shuar territory and a magnificent jungle-covered gorge with 200-m-high walls. There are also oilbird caves and other natural attractions. There is bus service to the area from Zamora, and tours can be arranged by Biotours (see Loja, Activities and tours, page 973). South of Zumbi along the paved road to Zamora (35 km), the broad valley of the Río Zamora becomes progressively narrower, with forested mountains and lovely views on either side.

● Sleeping

Archidona *p1010*

Water supply in most cheaper hotels is poor.
B Orchid Paradise, 2 km north of town, T288 9232. Cabins in nice secondary forest with lots of birds. Includes breakfast, other meals available, tours arranged.
C Hakuna Matata, Vía Chaupi Shungu Km 3.9, off the road between Tena and

Archidona, T288 9167 (to leave message), www.hakunamat.com. Includes all meals, comfortable cabins in a spectacular setting by the Río Inchillaqui. Belgian hosts, good food, horse riding. Recommended.
E Palmar del Río, Av Napo y Transversal 13, 4 blocks south of the plaza, T288 9274. Private bath, cold water, parking, simple but adequate.

Small restaurant serves breakfast and lunch.
E Res Regina, Rocafuerte 446, T288 9144. Private bath, cold water, ample parking, pleasant, family-run. Recommended.

Tena *p1010*

C Christian's Palace, JL Mera y Sucre, T288 6047. Includes breakfast, restaurant, a/c, cheaper with fan, pool and small spa, modern and comfortable.
C Los Yutzos, Augusto Rueda 190 y 15 de Noviembre, T288 6717, www.uchutican.com. Comfortable rooms and beautiful grounds overlooking the Río Pano, quiet and family-run. A/c, cheaper with fan, parking, simple annex next door is cheaper. Recommended.
D Hostería Los Helechos, 2 km from town on the road to Archidona, T288 8351. Breakfast available, electric shower, pool, parking, comfortable rooms and nice ample grounds.
D Villa Belén, on Baeza road (Av Jumandy), T288 6228. Excellent rooms, quiet, fan, laundry and cooking facilities. Recommended.
D-F Traveler's Lodging, 15 de Noviembre 438 y 9 de Octubre, T288 8204. Many different rooms and prices, front ones noisy, look around and choose for yourself. **Cositas Ricas** restaurant and **Amarongachi Tours** agency on the premises.
E Austria, Tarqui y Diaz de Pineda, T288 7205. Includes breakfast, electric shower, fan, parking, spacious rooms, quiet, good value, popular. Recommended.
E Canela, Amazonas y Abdón Calderón, T288 6081, canelahostal@yahoo.com. With bath and hot water, fan, modern, nice.
E Establo de Tomás, in Muyuna, via a San Antonio 5 km, T288 6318, T09-877 8709, paorivade@ hotmail.com. Meals on request, swimming in river, cabins in a pleasant setting, solar hot water, gets busy at weekends.
E Vista Hermosa, 15 de Noviembre 622, T288 6521. Restaurant, hot water, fan, parking, nice rooftop terrace with views over river.
E A Welcome Break, Augusto Rueda 331 y 12 de Febrero, T288 6301, a_welcome_break@ yahoo.com. Restaurant, shared bath, hot water, cooking facilities, parking, small terrace with hammocks, basic rooms, good value.
E-F Limoncocha, Sangay 533, Sector Corazón de Jesús, 4 blocks from terminal, T288 7583, limoncocha@andinanet.net. Shared bath, hot water, terrace with hammocks, internet, laundry and cooking facilities, German-Ecuadorean run, organize good tours, cafeteria. Pleasant atmosphere, enthusiastic owners, but in a humble neighbourhood.
F Jumandy, Amazonas y Abdón Calderón, T288 6419. Shared bath, cold water, with balcony, the Cerda family also arrange jungle tours.

Misahuallí *p1011*

AL Jardín Alemán, on the Río Misahuallí, 3 km from town, T289 0122, www.eljardin aleman.com. Includes 3 meals and river tour, restaurant and bar, comfortable rooms and cabins with ceiling fans and balconies, parking. On a 120-ha reserve, ample grounds with captive animals.
C France Amazonia, on road to Tena across from the high school, T289 0009, www.france-amazonia.com. Includes breakfast, pool, parking, grounds with river views, cozy rooms, French run, helpful. Recommended.
C Hostería Misahuallí, across the river from town, T289 0063, www.misahuallijungle.com. Meals on request, fan, pool and tennis court, cabins for up to 6, nice setting, lovely sunsets.
E Centro de Recreación Ecológica, on Santander at entrance to town, T289 0061. Electric shower, fan, ample rooms and grounds.
E El Albergue Español, on Arteaga, T289 0127, www.albergueespanol.com. Screened rooms, adequate but could be better maintained, restaurant, private bath, hot water, fan, can arrange tours to its own reserve.
E El Paisano, Rivadeneyra y Tandalia, T289 0027. Hot water, simple rooms, pleasant atmosphere, good value, restaurant.
F Shaw, Santander on the plaza, T289 0019, www.ecoselva-jungletours.com. Includes breakfast, with bath, hot water, fan, simple, operate their own tours, English spoken, very knowledgeable, good value. Recommended. Downstairs is **Ecocafé**, for good breakfast, meat and vegetarian dishes, set meals and à la carte.

Lodges on the upper Río Napo *p1011*

Casa del Suizo, Quito office: Julio Zaldumbide 397 y Valladolid, T02-256 6090, www.casadel suizo.com. On north shore at Ahuano, resort with capacity for 200, comfortable rooms, well-tended grounds, pool, gift shop, great river views. Swiss-Ecuadorean owned. US$79 per night.
Cotococha, Amazonas N24-03 and Wilson, CJ Building, p 2, Quito, T02-223 4336, www.coto cocha.com. Comfortable well-screened cabins with road access. Offers jungle walks, tubing, community visits and waterfalls. US$103 for 3 days.
Gareno, contact Michael Saur, T02-234 4350, or Roeland Van Lede, T02-224 9225 (both in Quito), www.guaponi.com. Located in Huarorani territory, accessible by road. Sightings of nesting Harpy Eagles have been reported, and the area is of special interest to birdwatchers. US$55 per night plus a one-time US$20 contribution to the Huaorani community. Recommended.
Liana Lodge, on the Río Arajuno near its confluence with the Napo, accessible by road, T09-980 0463, 06-288 7304 (Tena), www.amazoonico.org. 6 cabins with terraces and

river views. German spoken. *Centro de rescate* has captive animals on site. US$153 for 4 days.
Yachana Lodge, Quito T02-252 3777, www.yachana.com. Located in the village of Mondaña, 2 hrs downstream from Misahuallí. Proceeds go toward supporting community development projects. The comfortable lodge has 14 double rooms and 4 family cabins, all with solar power. US$405 for 4 days. Recommended.

Puyo *p1011*
B Hostería Safari, outside town at Km 5 on the road to Tena, T288 5465, www.hosteriasafari.com. Includes breakfast and dinner, ample grounds, peaceful.
C Turingia, Ceslao Marín 294, T288 5180, www.hosteriaturingia.com. Restaurant, fan, small pool, parking, comfortable, nice garden.
D Casablanca, 20 de Julio y Bolívar, T288 8169. Comfortable rooms, some with balcony, includes breakfast, good restaurant. Recommended.
E Colibrí, C Manabí entre Bolívar y Galápagos, T288 4768, cascadayanarumi@ yahoo.es. Away from centre, hot water, parking, simple but nice, good value. Recommended.
E Las Palmas, 20 de Julio y 4 de Enero, 5 blocks from centre, T288 4832, www.laspalmas.pastaza.net. Includes breakfast, hot water, comfortable multi-storey hotel.
E Libertad, Francisco de Orellana y Villamil, opposite the Coliseo Municipal, T288 3282. Restaurant, electric shower, basic but good value.
E Majestic Inn, Ceslao Marín y Vallamil, T288 5417. With bath, hot water, fan, clean and simple.

Shell *p1011*
E Germany Hostal, down a side street, ½ block from the main road, T279 5134. Simple cabins in a nice setting, restaurant, with bath, hot water.
E Wakany, Ernesto Quiñónez y Zulay, T279 5158. Private bath, hot water, parking, modern, larger rooms are at the back.

Jungle lodge on the Río Pastaza
Kapawi Ecolodge and Reserve. Operated by Canodros, Guayaquil, T04-228 5711, www.kapawi.com. A top-of-the-line lodge located on the Río Capahuari near its confluence with the Pastaza, in the heart of Achuar territory not far from the Peruvian border. Accessible only by small aircraft and motor canoe, visitors are usually flown in through Shell. The lodge was built in partnership with the Achuar indigenous organization and is due to be turned over to them in 2008. The biodiversity is good, but more emphasis is placed on ethno-tourism here than at other upmarket jungle lodges. US$676 for 4 days, plus US$224 for the return flight from Quito. Recommended.

Macas *p1012*
A Cabañas Ecológicas Yuquipa, on the Río Yuquipa, 1½ hrs walk from Km 12 on the road to Puyo, enquire in advance at Panadería Pancesa, Soasti y 10 de Agosto, T270 0071. Includes accommodation, 3 meals, guide and transport.
D Casa Blanca, Soasti 14-29 y Sucre, T270 0195. Includes breakfast, modern and comfortable, very helpful, good value. Often full, book in advance. Recommended.
E Esmeralda, Cuenca 6-12 y Soasti, T270 0130. With hot water, family run, adequate and friendly but some rooms are small.
E La Orquídea, 9 de Octubre 13-05 y Sucre, T270 0970. Cheaper with cold water, older place with clean ample rooms.
E Plaza, 10 de Agosto y Amazonas, T270 1683, lilipo29_64@hotmail.com. Nice rooms, helpful staff, good value. Recommended.
E Sol de Oriente, Tarqui y Soasti, T270 2911. Modern hotel in a multi-storey building, hot water, parking, spacious rooms.
E-F Esplendit (Splendid), Soasti 15-18 y Domingo Comin, T270 0120. With hot water, parking, cheaper in older basic rooms with shared bath and cold water, new section is also simple but a little better.

Sucúa *p1012*
E Arutam, Vía a Macas Km 1, north of town, T274 0851. Restaurant, pool and spa, modern and comfortable, very nice.
E Athenas, Domingo Comín y Serafín Solís, T274 0216. Parking, modern big rooms.
E Romanza, Carlos Olson y Edmundo Carvajal, T274 1141. Includes breakfast, nice rooms, attentive service.

Sucúa to Zamora *p1012*
Méndez
E Interoceanico, C Quito on the plaza, T276 0245. Modern, good value, best in town, parking.
E-F Hostal Los Ceibos, C Cuenca 1 block west of the plaza, T276 0133. Cheaper with shared bath, modern, small rooms.

Limón
F pp Dream House, Quito y Bolívar, T277 0166. New, with shared bathrooms.

Gualaquiza
E Internacional, C Cuenca y García Moreno, T278 0637. Restaurant, cheaper with cold water, most rooms have fan, best in town.
E-F Guadalupe, Gonzalo Pesántez 8-16 y García Moreno, T278 0113. Cheaper with shared bath, cold water, simple, popular, good value.
E-F Wakis, Orellana 08-52 y Domingo Comín, T278 0138. *Aroma Café* downstairs, cheaper

with shared bath, cold water, small rooms, enthusiastic owner Antonio Quezada speaks English and organizes tours.

Alto Nangaritza *p1012*
E **Cabañas Yankuam**, at the end of the road, 3 km south of Las Orquídeas, reservations required, Zamora T07-260 6147, www.lindoecuadortours.com. Rustic cabins in a lovely setting , includes breakfast, other tasty meals on request. Cheaper with shared bath, cold water, no electricity, good walking in surrounding hills, organizes trips up the Río Nangaritza. Family-run, English and Swedish spoken. Recommended.

🍴 Eating

Archidona *p1010*
There are several simple *comedores*, eg **Mama Chavica**, near **Residencial Regina**.

Tena *p1010*
There are several *chifas* and various cheap *comedores* in town.
🍽 **Chuquitos**, García Moreno by Plaza, Mon-Sat 0730-2130, Sun 1100-2130. Popular, good food, à la carte only, on a balcony overlooking the river.
🍴 **Pizzería La Massilia**, inside **Hotel Los Yutzos** annex, Mon-Sat 1700-2100. Good pizza, nice location by the river.

Misahuallí *p1011*
🍴 **Doña Gloria**, Arteaga y Rivadeneyra by corner of plaza. Open 0730-2030 daily. Good set meals.
🍴 **La Posada**, at the Plaza. Varied à la carte menu, good food, nice porch setting, slow service.

Puyo *p1011*
🍽 **El Alcázar**, 10 de Agosto 936 y Sucre, Mon-Sat 0900-2300, Sun 0900-1600. Very good, Spanish-European flavour in the Ecuadorean Amazon. Good value set meals and varied à la carte. Recommended.
🍽 **El Jardín**, on the Paseo Turístico in Barrio Obrero. Tue-Sun 1200-2200. Pleasant setting and atmosphere, international food.
🍽 🍴 **Pizzería Buon Giorno**, Orellana entre Villamil y 27 de Febrero, Mon-Sat 1200-2300. Good pizza and salads, very popular.
🍴 **La Posada de Gurmiek**, Ceslao Marín y 27 de Febrero, daily 0730-2200. Nice place, good value set lunch.
🍴 **Panadería Susanita**, Ceslao Marín y Villamil. Bakery, also serves breakfast and set lunch.
🍴 **Sal y Pimienta**, Atahualpa y 27 de Febrero. Grilled meats, popular, opens 0700.

Shell *p1011*
Several cheap *comedores* on the main street.

Macas *p1012*
🍽 **Chifa Pagoda China**, Amazonas y Domingo Comín. Very good, open 1030-2300.
🍽 **La Italiana**, Bolívar 6-07 y Soasti, daily 1000-0000. Pizza and pasta.
🍽 🍴 **La Napolitana**, Amazonas y Tarqui, daily 0700-2300. Open-air seating, breakfast and varied à la carte menu.
🍴 **Chaplin**, 24 de Mayo 14-55 y Sucre. Good economical set meals, popular.

Sucúa *p1012*
There are several cheap and basic places in town.
🍴 **Gyna**, Domingo Comín ½ block south of the park. Set meals and à la carte.
🍴 **La Orquídea**, 8 de Diciembre y Domingo Comín. Cheap set meals, good.

🔺 Activities and tours

Tena *p1010*
Amarongachi Tours, address as for **Traveller's Lodging**, above.
Ríos Ecuador-Yacu Amu, Tarqui 230 y Díaz de Pineda, Tena, T288 6346, www.riosecuador.com. Highly recommended white-water rafting and kayak trips and a 4-day kayak school. Has the best safety records and standards.
River People, 15 de Noviembre y 9 de Octubre, T288 8384, www.riverpeoplerafting ecuador.com. Whitewater rafting and kayaking.
Runa Ñambi, JL Mera 628 y Abdón Calderón, T288 6318, runanambi@yahoo.com.

Misahuallí *p1011*
Ecoselva, Santander on the plaza, T289 0019, www.ecoselva-jungletours.com. Recommended guide Pepe Tapia González speaks English and has a biology background. Well organized and reliable.
Selva Verde, Santander on the plaza, T06-2890165. Guide Luis Zapata speaks English and offers a variety of tours.
Quindi Tour, Napo opposite the plaza (in *La Posada*), T289 0031. Run by Carlos Santander and his brothers. Friendly, good food.

Puyo *p1011*
All of the following offer jungle tours of varying lengths; prices from US$25-50 pp per day.
Amazonía Touring, Atahualpa y 9 de Octubre, T288 3064.
Coka Tours, 27 de Febrero y Ceslao Marín, T288 6108.
Nave de Santos, at the Terminal Terrestre, T288 3974. Owner, Marco Naveda.

Papangu Tours, 27 de Febrero y Sucre, T288 7684, papangu@andinanet.net. Operated by the Organización de Pueblos Indígenas de Pastaza (OPIP), visits to local reserves and longer trips.

Macas *p1012*
Tour opportunies include the Las Tolitas archaeologic site, rafting on the Río Upano, visits to lowland portions of Parque Nacional Sangay, to local native communities as well as deeper into the jungles of the Cordillera de Cutucú.
Insondu, Bolívar y Soasti, T270 2533, www.insondumundoshuar.com.ec.
Planeta Tours, Domingo Comín 7-35 y Soasti, T270 1328, tours run by Taylor Rodríguez.

⊖ Transport

Tena *p1010*
Air One flight a week to **Quito** with VIP (T1-800-847847), Thu, US$60. Check locally for charters.
Bus To **Quito**, US$6, 5 hrs. To **Ambato**, via Baños, US$5, 5 hrs. To **Baños**, 4 hrs, US$4. To **Riobamba**, via Puyo and Baños, 6 hrs, US$6. To **Archidona** every 20 mins, US$0.25, 15 mins. To **Misahuallí**, hourly, US$1, 45 mins, buses leave from the local bus station not the long distance terminal. To **Coca** and **Lago Agrio**, fares given above. To **Puyo**, US$3, 3 hrs on a rough road.

Misahuallí *p1011*
Bus Local buses run from the plaza to **Tena** every 45 mins 0700-1800, fare above. Make all long distance connections in Tena, or get off at Puerto Napo to catch southbound buses. To **Quito**, 1 bus a day at 0830, US$6, 6 hrs.
Ferry With the increase in roads, river traffic is diminishing along the upper Napo. Scheduled passenger services from Misahuallí have been discontinued. Motorized canoes wait at the beach and can be hired for touring (but better to go with a guide) or transport to the location of your choice: to **Coca**, 5-7 hrs, US$200 for 8-10 people.

Puyo *p1011*
Bus Leave from the new Terminal Terrestre on the outskirts of town on the Shell/Baños road, 15-min wlak or taxi US$1. To **Baños**, US$2, 1½ hrs. To **Ambato**, US$3, 3 hrs. To **Quito**, US$5, 5 hrs via Ambato (9 hrs via Baeza). To **Riobamba**, US$4, 4 hrs. To **Tena**, see above. To **Macas**, US$5, 5 hrs. The first leg of the Puyo-Macas bus journey

goes as far as the Río Pastaza (70 km, in poor shape in 2007). An impressive modern bridge crosses the Pastaza and a newly paved road continues 60 km south to Macas.

Macas *p1012*
Air Flight to **Quito**, daily except Sat with TAME (T270 1162) or **Saereo**, (T270 1236), US$50-60. To **Cuenca**, Mon, Wed, Fri, with **Saereo**, US$50. Sit on left to Quito for best views of Volcán Sangay.
Bus Terminal Terrestre near the market. To **Puyo**, see above. To **Quito**, via Puyo, Baños and Ambato, US$10, 9 hrs. To **Cuenca**, US$9, via Méndez and Paute, 8-9 hrs; via Limón and Gualceo, 10 hrs. Both routes are subject to landslides after heavy rain. There are now buses on the new road to Riobamba. To **Gualaquiza**, US$8, 9 hrs, where you can get a bus to Zamora, US$3.50, 5 hrs, and to Loja, US$6, 7 hrs. To **Sucúa**, every 30 min, US$0.80, 1 hr.

Macas: Parque Nacional Sangay *p1012*
The park may be reached by **bus** 1½ hrs to village of 9 de Octubre, US$1.50, 1½ hrs, then walk. Local residents may be able to guide you from there to attractions in the park.

Sucúa *p1012*
Bus To **Macas**, see above. *Rancheros* leave for **Yantzaza** in the morning, from where a bus reaches **Zamora** before dark (see page 970).

⊕ Directory

Tena *p1010*
Banks Banco del Austro, 15 de Noviembre y Diaz de Pineda. **Amazon Money**, 15 de Noviembre 422 y 9 de Octubre, p 2, T288 8766, Mon-Fri 0900-1300, 1400-1830, Sat 0900-1200, 5% commission for TCs, poor rates for cash euros.
Hostal Limoncocha (see Sleeping), 3% commission for TCs.

Puyo *p1011*
Banks Cambios Puyo, 9 de Octubre y Atahualpa, T288 3064, Commission on TCs. Helpful.

Macas *p1012*
Banks Nowhere to change TCs. Banco del Austro, 24 de Mayo y 10 de Agosto. Visa.
Internet US$1 per hr. **Post offices** 9 de Octubre y Domingo Comín, next to the park.

Galápagos Islands → Colour map 11.

A trip to the Galápagos Islands is an unforgettable experience. The islands are world-renowned for their fearless wildlife but no amount of hype can prepare the visitor for such a close encounter with nature. Here you can snorkel with penguins and sea-lions, and encounter the odd hammerhead shark, watch giant 200 kg tortoises lumbering through cactus forest and enjoy the courtship display of the blue-footed booby and magnificent frigate bird, all in startling close-up.

Lying on the Equator, 970 km west of the Ecuadorean coast, the Galápagos consist of six main islands (San Cristóbal, Santa Cruz, Isabela, Floreana, Santiago and Fernandina – the last two uninhabited), 12 smaller islands (Baltra and the uninhabited islands of Santa Fe, Pinzón, Española, Rábida, Daphne, Seymour, Genovesa, Marchena, Pinta, Darwin and Wolf) and over 40 islets. The islands have an estimated population of 28,000, but this does not include temporary inhabitants. The largest island, Isabela (formerly Albemarle), is 120 km long and forms half the total land area of the archipelago. Its notorious convict colony was closed in 1958; some 2,400 people live there now, mostly in and around Puerto Villamil, on the south coast. San Cristóbal (Chatham) has a population of 7,000 with the capital of the archipelago, Puerto Baquerizo Moreno. Santa Cruz (Indefatigable) has 18,400, with Puerto Ayora the main tourist centre; and Floreana (Charles) about 100.

Background

The Galápagos have never been connected with the continent. Gradually, over many hundreds of thousands of years, animals and plants from over the sea somehow migrated there and as time went by they adapted themselves to Galápagos conditions and came to differ more and more from their continental ancestors. Unique marine and terrestrial environments, due to the continuing volcanic formation of the islands in the west of the archipelago and its location at the nexus of several major marine currents, has created laboratory-type conditions where only certain species have been allowed access. The formidable barriers which prevent many species from travelling within the islands, has led to a very high level of endemism. A quarter of the species of shore fish, half of the plants and almost all the reptiles are found nowhere else. In many cases different forms have evolved on the different islands. Charles Darwin recognized this speciation within the archipelago when he visited the Galápagos on the *Beagle* in 1835 and his observations played a substantial part in his formulation of the theory of evolution.

This natural experiment has been under threat ever since the arrival of the first whaling ships and even more so since the first permanent human settlement. New species were introduced and spread very rapidly, placing the endemic species at risk. Quarantine programmes have since been implemented in an attempt to prevent the introduction and spread of even more species, but the rules are not easy to enforce. There have also been campaigns to eradicate some of the introduced species on some islands, but this is inevitably a very slow, expensive and difficult process.

One extraordinary feature of the islands is the tameness of the animals. The islands were uninhabited when they were discovered in 1535 and the animals still have little instinctive fear of man.

Plant and animal species are grouped into three categories. **Endemic species** are those which occur only in the Galápagos and nowhere else on the planet. Examples are the **marine** and **land iguana**, **Galápagos fur seal**, **flightless cormorant** and the **'daisy tree'** (*Scalesia pedunculata*). **Native species** make their homes in the Galápagos as well as other parts of the world. Examples include all three species of **boobies**, **frigate birds** and the various types of **mangroves**. Although not unique to the islands, these native species have been an integral part of the Galápagos ecosystems for a very long time. **Introduced species** on the other hand are very recent arrivals, brought by man, and inevitably the cause of much damage. They include **cattle**, **goats**, **donkeys**, **pigs**, **dogs**, **cats**, **rats** and over 500 species of plants such as **elephant grass** (for grazing cattle), and fruit trees. The unchecked expansion of these introduced species has upset the natural balance of the archipelago.

Ins and outs

Getting there

Air There are two airports which receive flights from mainland Ecuador, but no international flights to Galápagos. The most frequently used airport is at **Baltra**, across a narrow strait from Santa Cruz, the other at **Puerto Baquerizo Moreno**, on San Cristóbal. The two islands are 96 km apart and on most days there are local flights in light aircraft between them, as well as to **Puerto Villamil** on Isabela. There is also boat service between Puerto Ayora, Puerto Baquerizo Moreno, Puerto Villamil and occasionally Floreana. All flights to Galápagos originate in Quito and stop on route in Guayaquil. **TAME** has two daily flights to Baltra and operates Wed and Fri to San Cristóbal. **AeroGal** also flies twice daily to Baltra, and on Mon, Thu, Sat and Sun to San Cristóbal. The return fare in high season (1 November-30 April and 15 June-14 September) is US$395 from Quito, US$346 from Guayaquil. The low season fare is US$339 from Quito, and US$301 from Guayaquil. The same prices apply regardless of whether you fly to San Cristóbal or Baltra; you can arrive at one and return from the other. You can also depart from Quito and return to Guayaquil or vice versa.

The above prices are subject to change without notice. Discount fares for Ecuadorean nationals and residents of Galápagos are not available to foreigners and these rules are strictly enforced. A 15% discount off the high season fare on TAME or Aerogal is available to students with an ISIC card.

Airport transfer Two buses meet flights from the mainland at Baltra: one runs to the port or *muelle* (10 mins, no charge) where the cruise boats wait; the other goes to Canal de Itabaca, the narrow channel which separates Baltra from Santa Cruz. It is 15 minutes to the Canal, free, then you cross on a small ferry for US$1, another bus waits on the Santa Cruz side to take you to Puerto Ayora in 45 minutes, U$1.80. If you arrive at Baltra on one of the local inter-island flights (see below) then you have to wait until the next flight from the mainland for bus service, or hire two pick-up trucks and a motorboat at the canal (total US$25). For the return trip to the airport, 2 buses per flight leave Puerto Ayora from the station on Av Baltra, 2 km from the pier. Purchase tickets from the CITTEG office near the pier, T252 6232, enquire in advance for current schedules. Pick-up truck from town to bus station, US$1. The airport at Puerto Baquerizo Moreno is within walking distance of town, but those on prearranged tours will be met by transport. Pick-ups can be hired if you are on your own and have lots of gear (US$1). ▶ *For more information, see Transport, page 1032.*

Getting around

Emetebe Avionetas ① *in Guayaquil T04-229 2492, emetebe@ecua.net.ec, see Directory for local offices,* offers inter-island flights in two light twin-engine aircraft. Two daily flights operate between **Puerto Baquerizo Moreno** (San Cristóbal), **Baltra** and **Puerto Villamil** (Isabela), most days except Sun, but this varies with passenger demand. Baggage allowance 20 lbs, strictly enforced. All fares US$158 one way, including taxes.

INGALA ① *for ticket sales in Puerto Baquerizo Moreno inquire by the Muelle Turístico, T252 0133; in Puerto Ayora upstairs from post office, T252 6151,* boat service from Puerto Baquerizo Moreno to Puerto Ayora, Mon and Thu 0700, returning Tue and Fri 1200, US$30, 4 hrs, but frequently suspended. Also once a month to Floreana. *Fibras* (fiberglass motor launches) daily between Puerto Ayora and Puerto Baquerizo Moreno, 2½ hrs, and between Puerto Ayora and Puerto Villamil, 3 hrs, all charge US$30 one way. They leave Puerto Baquerizo Moreno and Puerto Villamil early each morning and return from Puerto Ayora in the afternoon. Tickets are sold by several agencies in Puerto Baquerizo Moreno, at the pier in Puerto Ayora, and by the plaza in Puerto Villamil. This can be a wild wet ride and life vests are not always carried. Take sun protection, your own drinking water, and avoid single-engine boats.

Information and advice

Tourist offices Santa Cruz (Puerto Ayora): **Ministerio de Turismo** ① *Av Charles Darwin y Tomás de Berlanga, T252 6174, mturgal@gpsinter.net, Mon-Fri 0800-1230, 1400-1730.*

The **Dirección Municipal de Turismo** ① *kiosk next to post office (daily 1000-1700) and another at Baltra airport,* www.santacruz.gov.ec, has information about Puerto Ayora and Santa Cruz Island. **CAPTURGAL** ① *Galápagos Chamber of Tourism, Av Charles Darwin y Charles Binford, T252 6206,* www.galapagostour.org, *Mon-Fri 0730- 1200, 1400-1730,* English spoken. This is the place to present any serious complaints about cruise vessels, agencies or other tourist services. **San Cristóbal** (Puerto Baquerizo Moreno): **CAPTURSAN** ① *Malecón Charles Darwin y Española, T252 0592,* ctcsancrist@easynet.net.ec. *Mon-Fri 0730-1200, 1400-1700,* the San Cristóbal Chamber of Tourism. The **Municipal Tourist Office** ① *at the Municipio, Malecón Charles Darwin y 12 de Febrero, T252 1166,* www.sancristobalgalapagos.com. *Mon-Fri 0730-1230, 1400-1700,* has local information.

Every foreign visitor has to pay a **national park tax of US$100** on arrival, cash only. Be sure to have your passport to hand. Do not lose your park tax receipt; boat captains need to record it.

Basic rules: Do not touch any of the animals, birds or plants. Do not transfer sand, seeds or soil from one island to another. Do not leave litter anywhere; nor take food on to the islands. Uninhabited islands are no-smoking zones.

What to take A remedy for seasickness is recommended; the waters south of Santa Cruz are particularly choppy. A good supply of sun block and skin cream to prevent windburn and chapped lips is essential, as are a hat and sunglasses. You should be prepared for dry and wet landings, the latter involving wading ashore. Take plenty of film or memory cards with you; the animals are so tame that you will use far more than you expected; a telephoto lens is not essential, but if you have one, bring it. Also take filters suitable for strong sunlight. Snorkelling equipment is particularly useful as much of the sea-life is only visible under water. Most of the cheaper boats do not provide equipment and those that do may not have good snorkelling gear. If in doubt, bring your own, rent in Puerto Ayora, or buy it in Quito. Always bring some US$ cash to Galápagos. There is only one bank and ATM system, which may not work with all cards.

Tipping A ship's crew and guides are usually tipped separately. The amount is a very personal matter; you may be guided by suggestions made onboard or in the agency's brochures, but the key factors should always be the quality of service received and your own resources.

If you have problems Raise any issues first with your guide or ship's captain. Additional complaints may be made to CAPTURGAL in Puerto Ayora, see above.

Best time to visit The Galápagos climate can be divided into a hot season (December-May), when there is a possibility of heavy showers, and the cool or garúa (mist) season (June-November), when the days generally are more cloudy and there is often rain or drizzle. July and August can be windy, force 4 or 5. Daytime clothing should be lightweight. (Clothing generally, even on 'luxury cruises', should be casual and comfortable.) At night, however, particularly at sea and at higher altitudes, temperatures fall below 15°C and warm clothing is required. Boots and shoes soon wear out on the lava terrain. The sea is cold July-October; underwater visibility is best January-March. Ocean temperatures are usually higher to the east and lower at the western end of the archipelago. The islands climate and hence its wildlife are also influenced by the El Niño phenomenon. Despite all these variations, conditions are generally favourable for visiting Galápagos throughout the year.

The authorities At least five different authorities have a say in running theGalápagos islands and surrounding marine reserve. 1) **Instituto Nacional Galápagos** (INGALA), under control of the president of Ecuador, which issues residency permits; 2) the **National Park Service**, under the authority of the Ministerio del Ambiente, which regulates tourism and manages the 97% of the archipelago which is parkland; 3) the **Charles Darwin Research Station** (www.darwinfoundation.org), part of an international non-profit organization which supporting scientific research, advises other authorities regarding conservation, and channels funds for this purpose; 4) the **Ecuadorean Navy**, which patrols the waters of the archipelago and attempts to enforce regulations regarding both tourism and fishing; 5) local **elected authorities** including municipalities, the provincial council, and a member of the national Congress. There are also various other **international NGOs** working in Galápagos, each with its own agenda.

Choosing a tour

There are two ways to travel around the islands: a cruise (*tour navegable*), where you sleep on the boat, or shore-based tours on which you take day trips to the islands. On the former you travel at night, arriving at a new landing site each day, with more time ashore. On a land-based tour you spend less time ashore, cover less ground and cannot visit the more distant islands. Itineraries are controlled by the National Park to distribute tourism evenly throughout the islands. Boats are expected to be on certain islands on certain days. They can cut landings, but have to get special permission to add to a planned itinerary. A third option is independent travel on the populated islands. Although neither cheap nor a substitute for either of the above, it can be done and allows those with plenty of time to explore a small part of the archipelago at their leisure. All tours begin with a morning flight from the mainland on the first day and end on the last day with a midday flight back to the mainland.

The less expensive boats are normally smaller and less powerful so you see less and spend more time travelling; also the guiding may be mostly in Spanish. The more expensive boats will probably have air conditioning, hot water and private baths. All boats have to conform to certain minimum safety standards; more expensive boats are better equipped. A water maker can be a great asset. Note that boats with over 18 passengers take quite a time to disembark and re-embark people, while the smaller boats have a more lively motion, which is important if you are prone to seasickness. Note also that there may be limitations for vegetarians on the cheaper boats, enquire in advance. The least expensive boats (called economy class) cost US$110-135 per day. For around US$150-245 per day (tourist and tourist superior class) you will also be on a faster small boat, leaving more time to spend ashore. US$250-600 per day is the first class and luxury brackets, with far more comfortable and spacious cabins, as well as a superior level of service and cuisine. No boat may sail without a park-trained guide.

Booking a tour in advance You can book a Galápagos cruise in several different ways: 1) over the internet; 2) from either a travel agency or directly though a Galápagos wholesaler in your home country; 3) from one of the very many agencies found throughout Ecuador, especially in Quito but also in Guayaquil; or 4) from agencies in Puerto Ayora but not Puerto Baquerizo Moreno. The trade-off is always between time and money: booking from home is most efficient and expensive, Puerto Ayora cheapest and most time-consuming, while Quito and Guayaquil are intermediate. Prices for a given category of boat do not vary all that much however, and it is not possible to obtain discounts or make last-minute arrangements in high season, when boats are busiest, or low season, when boats are usually in dry dock.

To arrange last-minute tours, a highly recommended contact is Jenny Divine at **Moonrise** travel agency (see page 1030). Especially on cheaper boats, check carefully about what is and is not included (eg drinking water, snorkelling equipment, etc).

The islands

Santa Cruz: Puerto Ayora → *Phone code: 05. Population: 16,000.*

Santa Cruz is the most central of the Galápagos islands and the main town is Puerto Ayora. About 1½ km from Puerto Ayora is the **Charles Darwin Research Station** ① *at Academy Bay, office Mon-Fri 0700-1600, visitor areas 0600-1800 daily*. A visit to the station is a good introduction to the islands as it provides a lot of information. Collections of several of the rare sub-species of giant tortoise are maintained on the station as breeding nuclei, together with tortoise-rearing pens for the young. See their website for more information, page 1019.

One of the most beautiful beaches in the Galápagos Islands is at **Tortuga Bay**, 45 minutes easy walk (2.5 km each way) west from Puerto Ayora on an excellent cobbled path through cactus forest. Start at the west end of Calle Charles Binford; further on there is a gate where you must register, open 0600-1800 daily. Take sun screen, drinking water, and beware of the very strong undertow. Also, do not walk on the dunes above the beach, which are a marine tortoise nesting area. Ten minutes' walk to the west end of Tortuga Bay is a trail to a lovely mangrove-fringed lagoon, with calmer and warmer water and shade under the mangroves.

Las Grietas is a beautiful gorge with a pool at the bottom which is splendid for bathing. Take a water taxi from the port to the dock at Punta Estrada (5 minutes, US$0.50). It is a 5-minute walk from here to the *Finch Bay* hotel and 15 minutes further over rough lava boulders to Las Grietas – well worth the trip. The highest point on Santa Cruz Island is **Cerro Crocker** at 864 m. You can hike here and to two other nearby 'peaks' called **Media Luna** and **Puntudo**. The trail starts at Bellavista (7 km from Puerto Ayora) where a rough trail map is painted as a mural on the wall of the school! The round trip from Bellavista takes six to eight hours. A permit and guide are not required, but a guide may be helpful. Always take food, water and a compass or GPS.

There are a number of sites worth visiting in the interior, including **Los Gemelos**, a pair of twin sinkholes, formed by a collapse of the ground above a fault. The sinkholes straddle the road to Baltra, beyond Santa Rosa. You can take a *camioneta* all the way, otherwise take a bus to Santa Rosa (see below), then walk. It's a good place to see the Galápagos hawk and barn owl.

There are several **lava tubes** (natural tunnels) on the island. Some are at **El Mirador**, 3 km from Puerto Ayora on the road to Bellavista. Barn owls can be seen here. Two more lava tubes are 1 km from Bellavista. They are on private land, it costs US$1.50 to enter the tunnels (bring a torch) and it takes about 30 minutes to walk through the tunnels. Tours to the lava tubes can be arranged in Puerto Ayora.

Another worthwhile trip is to the **El Chato Tortoise Reserve**, where giant tortoises can be seen in the wild during the dry season. The trail starts at Santa Rosa, 22 km from Puerto Ayora. Past the school in Santa Rosa, a Parque Nacional Galápagos sign warns that tourists have been lost along the trail. Turn left here and follow a badly overgrown path south between 2 barbed wire fences. After 3 km you reach a wooden memorial to an Israeli tourist and a better trail running east-west. Turn right and follow the trail west for 20 minutes to a sign, "Entrada Al Chato". There are many confusing trails in the reserve itself; take food, water and a compass or GPS. The round trip on foot takes a full day, or horses can sometimes be hired at Santa Rosa. Best take a guide if you have no hiking experience; tours can also be arranged in Puerto Ayora.

Near the reserve is the **Butterfly Ranch** (Hacienda Mariposa) ① *US$2, camping possible for $10-15 pp*, where you can see giant tortoises in the pastures, but only in the dry season. In the wet season the tortoises are breeding down in the arid zone. The ranch is beyond Bellavista on the road to Santa Rosa (the bus passes the turn-off, walk 1 km from there).

San Cristóbal: Puerto Baquerizo Moreno → *Phone code: 05. Pop: 6,600.*

Puerto Baquerizo Moreno, on San Cristóbal island to the east, is the capital of the archipelago. It is a pleasant place to spend a few days, with interesting excursions in the area.

In town, the **cathedral** ① *on Av Northía, 2 blocks up from the post office, 0900-1200, 1600-1800*, has interesting mixed-media relief pictures on the walls and altar. To the north of town, opposite Playa Mann, is the Galápagos National Park visitors' centre or **Centro de Interpretación** ① *T252 0138, ext 102, 0700-1700, free*. It has an excellent display of the natural and human history of the islands.

A good trail goes from the Centro de Interpretación to the northeast through scrub forest to **Cerro Tijeretas**, a hill overlooking town and the ocean, 30 minutes away (take water). Side trails branch off to some lookouts on cliffs over the sea. Frigate birds nest in this area and can be observed gliding about, there are sea lions on the beaches below. To go back, if you take the trail which follows the coast, you will end up at **Playa Punta Carola,** a popular surfing beach, too rough for swimming. Closer to town is the small **Playa Mann** (follow Avenida Northía to the north), more suited for swimming and in town is **Playa de Oro**, where some hotels are located. Right in the centre of town, along the sand by the tidal pool, sea lions can be seen, be careful with the male who 'owns' the beach. To the south of town, 20 minutes' walk past the airport, is **La Lobería,** a rocky bay with shore birds, sea lions and marine iguanas.

Around San Cristóbal There are five buses a day inland from Puerto Baquerizo Moreno to **El Progreso** ① *6 km, 15 mins, US$0.20*, then it's a 2½ hour walk to El Junco lake, the largest body of fresh water in Galápagos. There are also frequent pick-up trucks to El Progreso ① *US$2*, or you can hire a pick-up in Puerto Baquerizo Moreno for touring: US$18 to El Junco, US$30 continuing to the beaches at Puerto Chino on the other side of the island, past a man-made tortoise reserve (the road is poor). Prices are return and include waiting. At El Junco there is a path to walk around the lake in 20 minutes. The views are lovely in clear weather but it is cool and wet in the *garúa* season, so take adequate clothing. Various small roads fan out from El Progreso and make for pleasant walking.

It's a three-hour hike from the landing site at **Caleta Tortuga**, on the northwest shore of the island, to **La Galapaguera Natural** where you can see tortoises in the wild. **Isla Lobos** is an islet with a large sea and nesting site for sea birds northeast of Puerto Baquerizo Moreno. It is also a dive site.

Boats go to **Puerto Ochoa**, 15 minutes, for the beach; to **Punta Pitt** in the far north where you can see all three species of booby (US$65 for tour). Off the northwest coast is **Kicker Rock** (León Dormido), the basalt remains of a crater; many seabirds, including Nazca and blue-footed boobies, can be seen around its cliffs (five hour trip, including snorkelling, recommended, US$35).

Note: Always take food, plenty of water and a compass or GPS when hiking on your own on San Cristóbal. There are many crisscrossing animal trails and it is easy to get lost. Also watch out for the large-spined opuntia cactus and the poisonwood tree (*manzanillo*), which is a relative of poison ivy and can cause severe skin reactions.

Isabela Island

This is the largest island in the archipelago, formed by the extensive lava flows from six volcanoes. Five of the volcanoes are active and each has (or had) its own separate sub-species of giant tortoise. Isabela is developing for land-based tourism. If you have a few days to spare and are looking for tranquillity, in a South-Pacific-island setting this may be just the place. Most residents live in **Puerto Villamil**. In the highlands, there is a cluster of farms at Santo Tomás. There are several lovely beaches right by town, but mind the strong undertow and ask locally about the best spots for swimming. It is 2½ hours walk west to **Muro de las Lágrimas**, a gruesome place built by convict labour under hideous conditions. Along the same road 30 minutes from town is the **Centro de Crianza**, a breeding centre for giant tortoises surrounded by lagoons with flamingos and other birds. In the opposite direction, 30 minutes east toward the *embarcadero* (fishing pier) is **Concha Perla Lagoon**, with a nice access trail through mangroves and a little dock from which you can go swimming with sea lions and other creatures. Fishermen can take you to **Las Grietas**, a set of small islets in the harbour where white-tipped reef sharks may be seen in the still crystalline water (US$20 per person for a three-hour tour). **Sierra Negra Volcano** has the largest basaltic caldera in the world, 9 x 10 km. It is 19 km (1 hour) by pickup truck to the park entrance (take passport and National Park entry receipt), where you switch to horses for the 1½ hr beautiful ride to the crater rim at 1,000m. It is a further 1½ hrs walk along bare brittle lava rock to **Volcán Chico**, with several fumaroles and more stunning views. You can camp on the crater rim but must take all supplies, including water, and obtain a permit the day before from the National Park office in Puerto Villamil. A half-day tour including transport, horses and lunch costs US$30 per person.

A visit to **Punta Moreno**, on the southwest part, starts with a dinghy ride along the beautiful rocky shores where penguins and shore birds are usually seen. After a dry landing there is a hike through sharp lava rocks. **Elizabeth Bay**, on the west coast, is home to a small colony of penguins living on a series of small rocky islets and visited by dinghy. **Tagus Cove**, on the west coast across the narrow channel from Fernandina island, is an anchorage that has been used by visiting ships going back to the 1800s, and the ships' names can still be seen painted on the cliffs. A trail leads inland from Tagus Cove past Laguna Darwin, a large saltwater lake, and then further uphill to a ridge with lovely views.

Floreana Island

Floreana, the island with the richest human history has 100 inhabitants, most in Puerto Velasco Ibarra, the rest in the highlands. Unless you visit with one of the few boats which land at Black Beach for a few hours, it is difficult to get onto and off the inhabited part of the island. Services are limited; you should be very flexible about travel times and self-sufficient, unless staying with the Wittmers (delightful, see below). The pace of life is gentle and locally produced food is good, but you will not be entertained. Margret Wittmer died in 2000, however you can meet her daughter and granddaughter. The climate in the highlands is fresh and comfortable, good for birdwatching. Places to visit include the **Devil's Crown** snorkelling site, **Punta Cormorant**, a green beach near which is a lake normally inhabited by flamingos and **Post Office Bay**, on the north side. There is a custom for visitors to Post Office Bay since 1793 to place unstamped letters and cards in a barrel, and deliver, free of charge, any addressed to their own destinations.

Unpopulated islands

Bartolomé is a small island in Sullivan Bay off the eastern shore of Santiago. It is probably the most visited and most photographed of all the islands with its distinctive **Pinnacle Rock** (a trail leads to the summit). A second visitor site has a lovely beach from which you can snorkel or swim and see the penguins. **Daphne**, west of Baltra (see page 1018), has very rich bird-life, in particular the nesting boobies, but visits are limited to one a month. **Española** is the southernmost island of the Galápagos and, following a successful programme to remove all the feral species, is now the most pristine of the islands. Gardner Bay, on the northeastern coast, is a beautiful white sand beach with excellent swimming and snorkelling. Punta Suárez, on the western tip of the island, has a trail through a rookery. As well as a wide range of seabirds (including blue-footed and masked boobies) there are sea lions, the largest and most colourful marine iguanas of the Galápagos and the original home of the waved albatrosses. **Fernadina** is the youngest of the islands, about 700,000 years old, and the most volcanically active. At Punta Espinosa, on the northeast coast, a trail goes up through a sandy nesting site for huge colonies of marine iguanas. You can also see flightless cormorants and go snorkelling in the bay.

Genovesa, at the northeast part of the archipelago, is an outpost for many sea birds. It is an eight to ten hour all-night sail from Puerto Ayora. Like Fernandina, Genovesa is best visited on longer cruises or ships with larger range. One of the most famous sites is Prince Phillip's Steps, an amazing walk through a seabird rookery that is full of life. You will see tropic birds, all three boobies, frigates, petrels, swallow-tailed and lava gulls, and many others. There is also good snorkelling at the foot of the steps, with lots of marine iguanas. The entrance to Darwin Bay, on the eastern side of the island, is very narrow and shallow and the anchorage in the lagoon is surrounded by mangroves, home to a large breeding colony of frigates and other seabirds.

One of the closest islands to Puerto Ayora is **Plaza Sur**. It has a combination of both dry and coastal vegetation. Walking along the sea cliffs is a pleasant experience as the swallowtail gull, shearwaters and red billed tropic birds nest here. There are also lots of blue-footed boobies and a large population of land iguanas on the island. **Rábida**, just south of Santiago, has a salt water lagoon, occasionally home to flamingos. There is an area of mangroves near the lagoon where brown pelicans nest. You can snorkel and swim from the beach. On **Santa Fe**, between Santa Cruz and San Cristóbal, the lagoon is home to a large colony of sea lions who are happy to join you for a swim. This little island has its own sub-species of land iguana.

Santiago, a large island, also known as James, is east of Isla Isabela. It has a volcanic landscape full of cliffs and pinnacles, and is home to several species of marine birds. James Bay, on the western side of the island, has a wet landing on the dark sands of Puerto Egas. Fur seals are seen nearby. Espumilla Beach is another visitor site with a walk through a mangrove forest to a lake usually inhabited by flamingos, pintail ducks and stilts. Sea turtles dig their nests at the edge of the mangroves. Buccaneer Cove, in the northwest, was a haven for pirates during the 1600s and 1700s. Sullivan Bay, on the eastern coast opposite Bartolomé (see

Ecuador Galápagos Islands The Islands

Galápagos tourist vessels

The following table lists various categories of tourist vessels operating in Galápagos with their respective descriptions, capacities and websites. Note that all sailers also have motors, and many frequently operate under engine power.
The categories and prices shown are approximate and subject to change.

The names, owners, operators, agents or websites of boats may likewise change. Remember also that captains, crews and guides regularly change on all boats. These factors, as well as the sea, weather and your fellow passengers will all influence the quality of your experience.

Name	Description	Capacity	Website
Luxury and first class (over US$250 per person per day)			
Galap Explorer II	cruise ship	100	www.canodros.com
Galap Legend	cruise ship	100	www.kleintours.com
Xpedsition	cruise ship	98	www.galapagosxpedition.co.uk
Santa Cruz	cruise ship	90	www.galapagosvoyage.com
Polaris	cruise ship	80	www.expeditions.com
Eclipse	cruise ship	48	various
Islander	cruise ship	48	www.expeditions.com
Isabela II	cruise ship	40	www.galapagosvoyage.com
Coral I	motor yacht	36	www.kleintours.com
Evolution	cruise ship	32	www.quasarnautica.com
Coral II	motor yacht	20	www.kleintours.com
Eric	motor yacht	20	www.ecoventura.com
Flamingo I	motor yacht	20	www.ecoventura.com
Letty	motor yacht	20	www.ecoventura.com
Lammer Law	2-mast trimaran	18	www.quasarnautica.com
Alta	3-mast ketch	16	www.quasarnautica.com
Anahi	motor catamaran	16	www.galapagoscatamarans.com
Beluga	motor yacht	16	www.enchantedexpeditions.com
Cachalote	2-mast schooner	16	www.enchantedexpeditions.com
Cormorant II	motor catamaran	16	www.galapagoscatamarans.com
Cruz Del Sur	motor yacht	16	www.galasam.com
Edén	motor yacht	16	www.galapagostours.net
Estrella de Mar I	motor yacht	16	www.galasam.com
Galap Adventure	motor yacht	16	various
Galap Adventure II	motor yacht	16	various
Integrity	motor yacht	16	various
Estrella de Mar I	motor yacht	16	various
Parranda	motor yacht	16	www.quasarnautica.com

Queen of Galapagos	motor catamaran	16	www.galasam.com
Reina Silvia	motor yacht	16	www.reinasilvia.com
Sagitta	3-mast sailing ship	16	www.angermeyercruises.com
The Beagle	2-mast schooner	16	www.angermeyercruises.com
Tip Top III	motor yacht	16	www.rwittmer.com
Samba	motor yacht	14	www.angermeyercruises.com
Diamante	2-mast sailer	12	www.angermeyercruises.com
Mistral II	motor yacht	12	www.quasarnautica.com
Nemo I and II	1-mast catamarans	12	www.galapagos-tours.com
Sea Cloud	2-mast sailer	8	www.angermeyercruises.com

Tourist superior and tourist class (US$150-245 per person per day)

Aida Maria	motor yacht	16	www.galapagostours.net
Angelique	2-mast sailer	16	www.galapagos-angelique.com
Angelito I	motor yacht	16	www.enchantedexpeditions.com
Daphne	motor yacht	16	various
Floreana	motor yacht	16	various
Friendship	motor vessel	16	various
Guantanamera	motor yacht	16	various
Lobo de Mar III	motor yacht	16	www.unigalapagos.com
Pelikano	motor yacht	16	www.galapagos-tours.com
Rumba	motor yacht	16	www.galapagostours.net
Sea Man	motor yacht	16	www.galacruises.com
Sulidae	2-mast ketch	16	www.hotelsilberstein.com
Tip Top II	motor yacht	16	www.rwittmer.com
Golondrina I	motor vessel	10	various
Vision	1-mast catamaran	8	various
Merak	1-mast sailer	8	various

Economy class (from US$110 per person per day)

Darwin	motor vessel	16	various
Flamingo	motor vessel	12	various
Yolita	motor vessel	12	various
Poseidon	motor vessel	10	various

Live-aboard diving cruises

Deep Blue	motor yacht	16	various
Sky Dancer	motor yacht	16	www.ecoventura.com
Jesús del Gran Poder	motor yacht	14	various
Encantada	2-mast schooner	12	www.scubagalapagos.com

above) has a trail across an impressive lunar landscape of lava fields. Just off the southeastern tip is Sombrero Chino island, noted for its volcanic landscape. On **Seymour Norte,** just north of Baltra, the tourist trail leads through mangroves in one of the main nesting sites for blue-footed boobies and frigates in this part of the archipelago.

⊜ Sleeping

Puerto Ayora *p1020*
Hotel space at the upper end of the market is limited. Reservations essential in high season.
LL Royal Palm, Km 18, Vía Baltra, T252 7409, www.royalpalmgalapagos.com. Includes breakfast, villas and suites with all luxuries, jacuzzi in rooms, private lounge at airport, part of Millennium international chain. Most expensive hotel in Ecuador.
LL-AL Red Mangrove Inn, Darwin y las Fragatas, on the way to the research station, T252 7011, www.redmangrove.com. Full of character, restaurant, jacuzzi, deck bar. Owner Polo Navaro offers day tours and diving. Recommended.
L Sol y Mar, Darwin y Binford, T252 6281. Nice location overlooking the bay, completely rebuilt in 2006, includes breakfast.
AL Finch Bay, on a small bay south of Puerto Ayora, accessible only by boat, T252 6297, www.finch bayhotel.com. Luxury hotel on a beautiful beach, restaurant, pool, lovely beach, bar, good service, comfortable rooms. Book through **Metropolitan Touring** in Quito.
AL Silberstein, Darwin y Piqueros, T252 6277, www.hotelsilberstein.com. Modern, comfortable, lovely grounds, small pool, buffet breakfast, restaurant, bar, some rooms with a/c, others with fan, spacious. Recommended.
AL-A Angemeyer Waterfront Inn, by the dock at Punta Estrada, T09-472 4955, tangermeyer@yahoo.com. Gorgeous location overlooking the bay. Very comfortable modern rooms and apartments, opened in 2006.
A Lobo de Mar, 12 de Febrero y Darwin, T252 6188, www.lobodemar.com.ec. Modern, balconies and rooftop terrace, great views over the harbour, includes breakfast, a/c, small pool, comfortable, attentive service. Recommended.
B Castro, Los Colonos y Malecón, T252 6113. Pleasant, older but well maintained, quiet, includes breakfast, restaurant, a/c, rooftop terrace.
B Palmeras, Berlanga y Naveda, T252 6139, hotelpalmeras@hotmail.com. Includes breakfast, restaurant, a/c, cheaper with fan, pool, their better rooms are modern and comfortable.
C Estrella de Mar, by the water on a lane off 12 de Febrero, T252 6427. Nice quiet location with views over the bay. Includes breakfast, a/c, fan, spacious rooms, sitting area.
C-D Lirio del Mar, Naveda y Berlanga, T252 6212. Multi-story building with terrace, electric

shower, a/c, cheaper with ceiling fan, good value.
D Peregrino, Darwin e Indefatigable, T252 6323. Away from the centre of town, includes breakfast, electric shower, a/c, nice rooms, small garden, family run, homely atmosphere.
D Salinas, Naveda y Berlanga, T252 6107. Cheaper with cold water, fan, pleasant and simple.
D Santa Fe Suites, Charles Binford entre Juan Montalvo y Las Ninfas, T252 6419, santafeii@islasantacruz.com. Rooms with small kitchenettes in a quiet area, fan, pool, convenient for long stays.
D-E Flamingo, Berlanga y Naveda, T/F252 6556. Fan, courtyard, older rooms are basic, adequate overall.
D-E Gardner, Berlanga y Naveda, T/F252 6108, pensiongardner@yahoo.com. Pleasant and quiet, older rooms are cheaper, cold water, fan, spacious rooms, small sitting area with hammocks and outdoor cooking facilities, popular and good value. Recommended.
E Darwin, Herrera y Binford, T252 6193. OK, cold water, small and basic.
E Los Amigos, Darwin y 12 de Febrero, T252 6265. Small place with 4-bed rooms, with bath, cold water, laundry facilities, basic but good value.

Puerto Baquerizo Moreno *p1021*
AL Miconia, Darwin y Melville, T252 0608, www.miconia.com. Includes breakfast, restaurant, a/c, small pool, large well-equipped gym, modern.
B Hostal Galápagos, at Playa de Oro, T252 0157, www.galahost.com. Quiet location, a/c, fridge, rooms refurbished in 2006.
B-E Alojamiento en Hogares. An association of community B&Bs offering accommodation in private homes. Well suited for long stays. Prices vary. For information and bookings contact Jaqueline Vázquez at Hotel Casablanca (below).
C Casablanca, Mellville y Darwin, T252 0392, jacquivaz@yahoo.com. Large white house with lovely terrace and views of harbour. Breakfast available, each room is individually decorated by the owner who has an art studio on the premises.
C-D Chatham, Northía y Av de la Armada Nacional, on the road to the airport, T252 0137, chathamhotel@hotmail.com. Patio with hammocks, meals on request, electric shower,

rooms in newer section have a/c and fridge, older rooms with fan are cheaper, well maintained and nice.

D **Los Cactus**, Juan José Flores y Av Quito, T252 0078. Includes breakfast, electric shower, fan, away from the centre, family run and nice.

D **Mar Azul**, Northía y Esmeraldas, T252 0139. Newer annex across the street has large modern rooms, electric shower, some with a/c and fridge, cheaper with fan, good value. Recommended.

D **Northía**, Northía y 12 de Febrero, T/F252 0041, hotelnorthia@gmail.com. Small balconies, a/c and ceiling fan, ageing but adequate.

E **Doña Pilo**, Northía y Quito, T252 0098. With electric shower, fan, family run, simple but adequate.

E **San Francisco**, Malecón Charles Darwin y Villamil, T252 0304. Cold water, fan, rooms in front are nicer, simple, good value.

Isabela Island *p1022*

AL-A **La Casa de Marita**, east end of village, T252 9238, www.galapagosisabela.com.

Definitely upscale, even chic. Includes breakfast, other meals on request, a/c and fridge, Jacuzzi, very comfortable, each room is a bit different and some have balconies. A little gem. Recommended.

B **The Wooden House**, 500m from town along the road to the fishing pier, T252 9484, www.thewoodenhouse.com. True to its name, a wooden house with small garden and pool, includes breakfast, other meals on request, a/c, includes use of kayaks.

B-D **Ballena Azul and Isabela del Mar**, Conocarpus y Opuntia, T252 9030, www.hosteriaisabela.com.ec. An older wooden building next to modern cabins, both are very nice. Solar hot water, fan, large balcony, pleasant, Swiss run, helpful. Recommended.

D-E **Cormorant Beach House**, Antonio Gil y Los Flamencos, T252 9192, albemarle20@ hotmail.com. Nice location on the beach. Electric shower, one room with a/c, cooking facilities, small terrace with hammock, very pleasant.

D-E **San Vicente**, Cormoranes y Pinzón

UK

Galapagos Classic Cruises, 6 Keyes Rd, London NW2 3XA, T020-8933 0613, www.galapagoscruises.co.uk. Specialists in tailor-made cruises and diving holidays to the islands with additional land tours to Ecuador and Peru on request.

Select Latin America, incorporating Galápagos Adventure Tours, 79 Maltings Pl, 169 Tower Bridge Rd, London SE1 3LJ, T020-7407 1478, www.selectlatinamerica.com. David Horwell arranges quality tailor-made tours to Ecuador and the Galápagos islands.

USA and Canada

Galápagos Holidays, 14 Prince Arthur Av, Suite 109, Toronto, Ontario M5R 1A9, T416-413 9090, T1-800-661 2512, www.galapagos holidays.com.

Galápagos Network, 5805 Blue Lagoon Dr, Suite 160, Miami, FL 33126, T305-2626264, T800-6337972 (toll free), www.ecoventura.com.

Inca Floats (Bill Robertson), 1311 63rd St, Emeryville, CA 94608, T510-420 1550, www.inca1.com.

International Expeditions, 1 Environs Park, Helena, Alabama, 35080, T205-428 1700, T1-800-633 4734, www.internationalexpeditions.com.

Sol International, PO Box 370, Cosby, TN 37722, T931-536 4893, T1-800-7655657, www.solintl.com.

Wilderness Travel, 1102 Ninth Street, Berkeley, CA 94710, T510-558 2488, T1-800-368 2794, www.wildernesstravel.com.

Artesano, T252 9140. Very popular, offers tours and kayak rentals, cold water, a/c, cheaper with fan, cooking facilities and fridge, meals on request, rooms a bit small but nice, camping possible, family run, good value. Recommended.

There are a couple of other basic places to stay in town.

Floreana *p1023*
AL Pensión Wittmer, right on Black Beach, T252 9506. Includes 3 delicious meals, fan (when there is electricity), simple and comfortable, a very special place, reservations required.

❶ Eating

Puerto Ayora *p1020*
††††† Angermeyer Point, at the end of Barranco, access by watertaxi, T252 7007, Tue-Sat 1800-2200, Sun brunch 1100-1600. In the old home of the Angermeyer family, Gorgeous setting over the water, excellent, innovative and varied menu, reservations advised. Highly recommended.

††††† Dolce Italia, Charles Darwin entre Naveda y 12 de Febrero, second location called **Trattoria de Pippo** at Charles Darwin entre Indefatigable y Isla Floreana, daily 1100-1500, 1800-2200. Italian and seafood, wine list, a/c, pleasant atmosphere, attentive owner.

†††-†† La Garrapata, Charles Darwin entre 12 de Febrero y Tomás de Berlanga, Mon-Sat 0830-2200, Sun 1700-2200. Good food, attractive setting and good music, juice bar and sandwiches during the day, set meals at lunch, and la carte at night.

†† Chocolate Galápagos, Charles Darwin entre Tomas de Berlanga y Charles Binford, daily 0700-2200. Breakfast, snacks, meals, and desserts, outdoor seating, popular.

†† Hernán, Av Baltra y Opuntia, 0730-2230 daily. Restaurant and bar, international menu, includes pizza, burgers, capuccino.

†† New Island, Charles Darwin y Charles Binford, Mon-Sat 0900-2100. Breakfast, fruit juices, seafood, ceviches.

††-† Media Luna, Charles Darwin y Los Piqueros, 1500-2200, closed Tue. Good pizza and pasta, also sandwiches, excellent brownies.

† El Descanso del Guía, Charles Darwin y Los Colonos, near bus company offices, no sign. Good value set meals, popular with locals.

† Kiosks along Charles Binford between Padre Herrera and Rodríguez Lara sell traditional food, including good economical seafood: **Servi-Sabrosón** cooks well, as does **William**. All have simple outdoor seating and a lively atmosphere, popular with locals and busy at night.

† Talia, Naveda y Berlanga, no sign. Economical set lunch, grilled fish or meat in the evening, small friendly place, good value.

La Casa del Lago, Moisés Brito y Juan Montavo, in Barrio Las Ninfas, a quiet area away from the

main drag, T09-851 4015,
www.galapagoscultural.com, Mon-Sat
0700-2200. Drinks, snacks and ice cream, live
music, art and cultural activities. Friendly owners
Enrique and Helena also rent two apartments
nearby.

Puerto Baquerizo Moreno *p1021*
♥♥ **La Playa**, Av de la Armada Nacional, by the
navy base. Nice location, varied menu, popular.
♥♥ **Miconia**, Darwin e Isabela. Varied menu, good
food, lovely terrace seating overlooking the
harbour.
♥♥-♥ **Cevichería El Langostino**, Melville y
Hernandez, daily from 0600. Simple place,
ceviches only, reported good.
♥♥-♥ **Rosita** Ignacio de Hernández y
General Villamil, closed Sun. Set meals and varied
à la carte menu, old-time yachtie hangout.
♥ **Deep Blue**, Darwin y Española. Ceviches in
morning, good set lunch, closed evenings.
Mockingbird Café, Española y Hernandez. Fruit
juices, brownies, snacks, internet.
Panadería Fragata, Northía y Rocafuerte.
Excellent bread and pastries, good selection.

Isabela Island *p1022*
♥♥-♥ **El Encanto de la Pepa**, Antonio Gil on the
Plaza. Set meals and à la carte, lots of character,
good food, pleasant outdoor seating.
♥♥-♥ **La Choza**, Antonio Gil y Las Fragatas. Varied
menu, a bit pricey, pizza must be ordered the
morning before.
♥ **Tropical**, Las Fragatas ½ block from Plaza, open
daily. Good quality and value set meals, popular
with locals.

◐ Bars and clubs

Puerto Ayora *p1020*
La Panga, Av Charles Darwin y Berlanga and **Bar
Bongo**, upstairs, are both popular.

Limón y Café , Charles Darwin y 12 de Febrero.
Snacks and drinks, lots of music, pool table.
Also see **La Casa del Lago** above.

Puerto Baquerizo Moreno *p1021*
Calypso, Darwin y Manuel J. Cobos, daily
1800-0000. Snacks and drinks, pleasant outdoor
seating.
Iguana Rock, Quito y Juan José Flores, some live
music, pool table, popular.

Isabela Island *p1022*
Beto's Beach Bar, Antonio Gil y Los Flamencos
along the beach. Pleasant location, irregular
hours, very relaxed. Has one room to rent.

◐ Shopping

Do not buy items made of black coral as it is an
endangered species.

Puerto Ayora *p1020*
Most basic foodstuffs generally can be purchased
on the islands, but cost more than on the
mainland. There is an attractive little **Mercado
Artesanal** (craft market) at Charles Darwin y
Tomás de Berlanga. **Proinsular**, opposite the pier,
is the largest and best stocked supermarket. The
small **mercado municipal** is on Padre J Herrera,
beyond the telephone office, on the way out of
town to Santa Rosa.
 There are various T-shirt, souvenir, and
highbrow jewellery shops along the length of Av
Charles Darwin, all touristy and expensive.

Puerto Baquerizo Moreno *p1021*
A good little supermarket is **Dos Hermanos**,
Quito y Juan José Flores; a small produce market
is located a block away at Juan José Flores y 12
de Febrero. There are a few souvenir shops along
the Malecón selling T-shirts and crafts.

Ecuador Galápagos Islands Listings

▲ Activities and tours

Puerto Ayora p1020

Cycling Mountain bikes can be hired from travel agencies in town. Prices and quality vary, so shop around.

Diving The National Park rules prohibit collecting samples or souvenirs, spear-fishing, touching animals, or other environmental disruptions. Guides apply the rules and they can stop your participation if you do not cooperate. The experienced dive guides can help visitors have the most spectacular opportunities to enjoy the wildlife. There are several diving agencies in Puerto Ayora offering courses, equipment rental, dives within Academy Bay (2 dives for US$90), and other central islands (2 dives, US$140), daily tours for 1 week in the central islands and several day live-aboard tours. There is a hyperbaric chamber in Puerto Ayora to treat divers in case of decompression sickness (US$1,500 per hr, 50% discount if your dive operator is affiliated): 12 de Noviembre y Rodríguez Lara, T252 6911, www.sssnetwork.com. Confirm in advance whether your diving insurance is accepted and make sure you have adequate coverage. To avoid the risk of decompression sickness, divers are advised to stay an extra day on the islands after their last dive before flying to the mainland, especially to Quito at 2,840 m above sea level.

Galápagos Sub-Aqua, Av Charles Darwin e Isla Floreana, T252 6633, www.galapagos-sub-aqua.com (Guayaquil: Orellana 211 y Panamá, No 702, T04-230 5514). Open Mon-Sat 0800-1230, 1430-1830. Instructor Fernando Zambrano offers full certificate courses up to PADI divemaster level. Repeatedly recommended.

Nautidiving, Av Charles Darwin, T252 7004, www.nautidiving.com. Offers 8-day, 7-night trips.

Scuba Iguana, Charles Darwin near the research station, T252 6497, www.scubaiguana.com. Matías Espinoza runs this long-time reliable and recommended dive operator. Courses up to PADI divemaster.

Horse riding For riding at ranches in the highlands, enquire at Moonrise Travel.

Snorkelling: masks, snorkels and fins can be rented from travel agencies and dive shops, US$6 a day, deposit required. Closest place to snorkel is by beaches near Darwin Station.

Surfing There is surfing at Tortuga Bay (see Excursions) and at other more distant beaches accessed by boat. **Note** There is better surfing near Puerto Baquerizo Moreno on San Cristóbal. The **Lonesome George** agency (see below) rents surfboards for US$10-$15 per half-day.

Tour operators

Avoid touts who approach you at the airport or in the street offering cheap tours . Also be wary of agencies who specialize in cut-rate cruises. For Tour operators in Quito offering cruises, see page 909.

Lonesome George, Av Baltra y Enrique Fuentes, T252 6245, lonesomegrg@yahoo.com. Run by Víctor Vaca. Sells tours and offers a variety of gear rentals: bicycles, surfboards, snorkelling equipment and motorcycles.

Moonrise Travel, Av Charles Darwin y Charles Binford, opposite Banco del Pacífico, T252 6348, www.galapagosmoonrise.com. Last-minute cruise bookings, day-tours to different islands, bay tours, highland tours, airline reservations. Owner Jenny Devine speaks English, she is very knowledgeable, helpful and reliable. Highly recommended.

Puerto Baquerizo Moreno p1021

Cycling Bikes can be hired from travel agencies.

Diving There are several dive sites around San Cristóbal, most popular being Kicker Rock, Roca Ballena and Punta Pitt (at the northeastern side). See Tour operators (below) who offer dives. The nearest hyperbaric chamber is in Puerto Ayora.

Ecuador Galapagos Islands Listings

1031

Surfing There is good surfing in San Cristóbal, the best season is Dec-Mar. **Punta Carola** near town is the closest surfing beach; popular among locals. There is a championship during the local *fiesta*, the 2nd week of Feb.

Tour operators
Chalo Tours, Española y Hernandez, T252 0953, www.chalotours.com. Bay tours to Kicker Rock and Isla de los Lobos, boat tours to the north end of the island, highland tours, diving tours, bike rentals, snorkelling gear, book exchange.
Galakiwi, Española y Darwin, T252 1562, galakiwi@yahoo.com.au. Owned by New-Zealander Tim Cooney. Highland and diving tours, kayaks and other gear rentals.

Isabela Island *p1022*
Hotels can arrange visits to local attractions, mostly operated by Antonio Gil at **Hotel San Vicente**, reliable.
Carapachudo Tours, Escalecias y Tero Real, T08-596 7179, info@carapachudotours.com. Mountain biking tours, downhill from Sierra Negra and to other attractions, US$42 for a full day including lunch.

⊖ Transport

Puerto Ayora *p1020*
Pick-ups may be hired for transport throughout town, US$1-2, agree fare in advance. Up to the highlands, they leave throughout the day from in front of the Tropidurus store, Padre Herrera corner Jaime Roldos, 2 blocks past the market: to **Bellavista** US$0.25, 10 min; to **Santa Rosa** US$1, 20 min; to **Playa Garrapatero** US$30 for the vehicle round trip including wait. **Water taxis** (*taxis marítimos*) from the pier to anchored boats and Punta Estrada, US$0.25 pp.

---

❶ Directory

Puerto Ayora *p1020*
Airline offices Aerogal, Padre J Herrera y 10 Mayo, T252 6798, Mon-Fri 0800-1200, 1400-1700, Sat 0900-1300. TAME, Av Charles Darwin y 12 de Febrero, T252 6527. Mon-Fri 0800-1200, 1400-1700, Sat 0900-1200. Emetebe, Av Charles Darwin near port, 2nd floor of Ferroinsular

hardware store next to Proinsular supermarket, T252 6177. **Banks** Banco del Pacífico, Av Charles Darwin y Charles Binford. Mon-Fri 0800-1530, Sat 0930-1230. US$5 commission for TCs, maximum US$500 per transaction. ATM works with Cirrus, Plus and MC but not Visa; cash advances from tellers on Visa and MC.
Embassies and consulates British Consul, David Balfour, T252 6159. **Medical services** Hospitals: there is a hospital on Av Baltra for first aid and basic care. For anything serious, locals usually fly to the mainland. See also under Diving, above. **Internet** There are several cybercafés throughout town, US$2/hr. **Post offices** By the port. Post Office often runs out of stamps (never leave money and letters). DHL courier and Western Union, across the street from Hotel Silberstein. **Useful addresses** Immigration: at the police station on 12 de Febrero. They are usually able to extend tourist visas up to 90 days, but always check well before your time expires.

Puerto Baquerizo Moreno *p1021*
Airline offices Aerogal, at the airport, T252 1118. TAME, Charles Darwin y Manuel J Cobos, T252 1351, Mon-Fri 0830-1230, 1400-1700, Sat 0830-1230. Airport counter T252 1089.Emetebe, at the airport terminal, T252 0615. **Banks** Banco del Pacífico, Charles Darwin entre Española y Melville. Same hours and services as in Puerto Ayora. **Internet** US$2 per hr.
Laundry Lavandería Limpio y Seco, Av Northía y 12 de Febrero. Wash and dry US$2. Open daily 0900-2100. **Medical services** There is a hospital providing only basic medical services. **Dr David Basantes**, opposite Hotel Mar Azul, T252 0126, is a helpful GP. Farmacia San Cristóbal, Villamil y Hernández. **Post offices** Malecón Charles Darwin y 12 de Febrero. **Useful services** Immigration and Police: at Police Station, Malecón Charles Darwin y Española, T/F252 0129.

Isabela Island *p1022*
Airline offices Emetebe, Antonio Gil y Las Fragatas, T252 9155, Mon-Fri 0730-1230, 1400-1600, Sat 0700-1230. **Banks** There are no banks on Isabela, no ATMs, and nowhere to use credit cards or change TCs. You must bring US$ cash. **Internet** There are a couple of slow cybercafés in town, US$1.50-$2.50/hr.

Paraguay

Essentials	1036
Asunción	1039
Sights	1040
East of Asunción	1050
South of Asunción	1056
North of Asunción	1061
The Chaco	1063

❊ Footprint features

Don't miss …	1035
Touching down	1037
Driving in Paraguay	1039

Introduction

An air of mystery hangs over this under-explored pocket of South America, a country of farmland, forest and folklore. From the hot, wild impenetrable Chaco in the north to the lush tropical south, there is great birdlife, rivers to navigate and opportunities for rural tourism. Land-locked Paraguay has had a strange history of charismatic leaders, steadfastness and isolation. Its music, too, marks it apart from its neighbours, sentimental songs and European dances accompanied by virtuoso harp players and guitarists. Now, though, the country is part of the Mercosur economic union, with trade routes to Argentina and Brazil well established. Moreover, the road to Bolivia is gradually becoming easier – in the dry season, at least: the Trans-Chaco is one of the great road adventures in South America.

The remains of the Mission settlements built by Jesuits near the banks of the Río Paraná are testimony to one of the major social experiments on the continent. It is also renowned for a vigorous line in contraband and a dedication to the consumption of *mate* second to none. The indigenous language, Guaraní, is officially recognized, but all those odd-looking names cannot hide the warmth of Paraguayan hospitality.

★ Don't miss ...

1. **Plaza de los Héroes, Asunción** Central Asunción has several squares, parks and historic buildings, but none more loaded with memory than that commemorating all those who died in the tragic wars that have punctuated Paraguay's independent history, page 1041.

2. **Itaipú** This huge hydroelectric scheme is shared with Brazil. You can visit the facilities on either side of the border and the Iguaçu Falls are within easy reach, page 1053.

3. **Jesuit missions** Near Encarnación on the Río Paraná are the remains of the Jesuit *reducciones* which flourished in the 18th century. At Trinidad and Jesús are vestiges of the beautiful craftsmanship of the Guaraní people who were the Jesuits' flock, page 1057.

4. **The Chaco** Inhabited only by a few Mennonite communities, groups of indigenous peoples and scattered military outposts, Paraguay's western half is the best place to see wildlife. Its marshes give way to a thorny wilderness, where it is not advisable to venture alone (if at all), page 1063.

Plastic/TCs/banks Asunción is a good place for obtaining US$ cash on MasterCard or Visa especially if heading for Brazil. ATMs for Visa and MasterCard are common in Asunción and offer good rates of exchange. Many banks in Asunción (see page 1048) give US$ cash, but charge up to 5½% commission. Rates for all foreign currencies, except bolivianos, are reasonable. Casas de cambio may want to see customers' records of purchase before accepting TCs. Visitors are advised to check on the situation on changing travellers' cheques in advance. Visa and MasterCard cash advances are possible in Asunción, Caacupé, Ciudad del Este and Encarnación. Street dealers operate from early morning until late at night, even on public holidays.

Cost of travelling Allow US$25-30 per person per day to cover all expenses, less if staying in the cheapest hotels and not moving around much. The average cost of internet in urban areas is US$0.75-1.25 per hour.

Safety Paraguay is generally safe and visitors are treated courteously. As a sign of increased freedom of political expression, there are demonstrations in both the capital and the countryside. Beware police seeking bribes, especially at Asunción bus station and at border crossings. See **www.policia.gov.py** for all matters related to the police and **www.mspbs.gov.py** for current health risks in Paraguay.

Getting around

Air There are scheduled services to most parts of the country by Líneas Aéreas de Transporte Nacional (LATN), Ladesa, and Transportes Aéreos del Mercosur (TAM), www.tam.com.py. Domestic fares are subject to 2.5% tax.

Buses Along main roads buses stop anywhere for anyone, so all timings are approximate.

Train The 441-km rail network has been closed since Feb 2001, but a tourist steam train runs from Asunción to Aregua each Sunday (see page 1048). Visit www.ferrocarriles.com.py.

Sleeping → *See page 58 for our hotel grade price guide.*

There are a few hotels in our **G** range and many good ones in our **D-F** ranges, with private shower and toilet. Most hotels have two rates – one for a room with a/c, the other without. Almost all include breakfast.

Eating → *See page 58 for our restaurant price guide.*

Eating out Lunch is served early in most restaurants, 1130-1300. Evening meals are hard to find in small towns.

Food Typical local foods include *chipas*, cheese breads which come in a number of varieties: *almidón*, made with yuca flour; *maíz*, made with corn flour; *guazú*, made with fresh corn; *maní*, made with peanuts (better warm than cold). *Chipa soo* is maize bread with meat filling. *Sopa paraguaya* is a kind of sponge of ground maize and cheese. *Soyo* is a delicious soup of different meats and vegetables; *albóndiga* a soup of meat balls; *bori bori* another type of soup with diced meat, vegetables, and small balls of maize mixed with cheese. *Palmitos* (palm hearts) should not be missed. The beef is excellent in the better restaurants (best cuts are *lomo* and *lomito*). Paraguayan *chorizo* (sausage) is good. *Parrillada completa* is recommended and there are many *churrascarías* serving huge quantities of meat, with salad, vegetables and pasta. *Surubí*, a Paraná river fish, prepared in many different ways, is delicious. Although vegetarian restaurants are scarce, there are lots of fruits, salads and vegetables. Try *empanadas de choclo*, *palmito* or *cuatro quesos*. Sugar-cane juice, greatly beloved, is known as *mosto*. The fruit is also magnificent.

Drink The Paraguayan national drink is *tereré* (cold mate with digestive herbs) for warm days and hot mate to warm you up on cold days. *Baviera*, a local lager beer is very good. *Cerveza de invierno* is Brazilian black beer. The cane-sugar spirit, *caña* is good (the best is 'Aristocrata'; ask for 'Ari'). *Guaraná* is a local soft drink (originally from Brazil).

Festivals and events

1 January; 3 February; 1 March (anniversary of the death of former president Francisco Solano López); Maundy Thursday; Good Friday; 1, 14, 15 May; Corpus Christi, 12, 23 June; 15 August (Day of the Child, in honour of the boys who died at the Battle of Acosta Ñu – see page 1041), 25 August; 29 September; 12 October; 1 November; 8 and 25 December.

⁞ Driving in Paraguay

Road Around 10% of roads are paved. Roads serving the main centres are in good condition and are continually being upgraded. A highway links Asunción with Iguazú Falls (six hours). Potholes are a hazard, especially in Asunción. Unsurfaced roads may not be passable in bad weather, especially November-April. There are regular police checks; it's advisable to lock doors.

Safety Beware of stray cattle on the road at night. Driving at night is not advisable.

Documents Neither a *carnet de passages* nor *libreta de pasos por aduana* is required for a car or motorcycle, but the carnet may make entry easier. Temporary admission for a private vehicle is usually 30 days.

Organizations Touring y Automóvil Club Paraguayo (TACP), 25 de Mayo y Brasíl, p 2, Asunción, T021-210550, www.tacpy.com.py, produces a road map and provides information about weather and roads. TACP is also in charge of **Rural Tourism**. Information also from the office of the traffic police in Asunción, T021-493390.

Car hire Weekly and free-km rates available. Rates are from US$45 per day to US$150 for 4WD.

Fuel Unleaded only (some has sugar-cane alcohol added). Most vehicles are diesel-powered. 95 octane US$0.74 per litre; 97 octane US$0.86 per litre; diesel US$0.70 per litre. Motor fuel and oil are sold by the litre. There are few service stations in the Chaco.

Asunción → *Phone code: 021. Colour map 6, grid C6. Population: over 1.2 million.*

Looking out over a bay on the eastern bank of the Río Paraguay, almost opposite its confluence with the Río Pilcomayo, Asunción's centre is a testament to 19th-century ideals, with names reflecting its heroes and battles. Tree-lined avenues, parks and squares break up the rigid grid system. In July and August the city is drenched in colour with the prolific pink bloom of the lapacho trees, which grow everywhere. Behind the 21st-century consumerism, there are quaint corners, top-class restaurants and the nostalgia of harp and guitar music.

Ins and outs

Getting there The international **airport** is 15 km northeast of the city, to which taxis, buses and an airport-to-hotel minibus service run. It takes from 30-45 minutes from the airport to town. The **bus terminal** is south of the centre, also 30-45 minutes away. You can go by taxi or by city bus (see page 1047 for the correct one). Both the airport and bus terminal have tourist information desks. ▶▶ *For more detailed information see Transport, page 1047.*

Getting around Most of the historical sights of interest are in a relatively small area by the river, so walking between them is not a problem. Similarly, there are many central hotels which can safely be reached on foot. Places outside this zone are easily reached by taxi or bus. The bus system is extensive and runs 0600-2400; buses stop at signs before every street corner. Asunción is very spread out and transport so slow that you need to allow 1½ hours to get beyond its limits.

Tourist offices **Secretaría Nacional de Turismo** ① *Palma 468, T494110/441530, Mon-Fri 0800-1300 (phone Mon-Sat 0800-1900 for information).* Good free map (ask for it), information on all parts of Paraguay, but you may need to be persistent. Another map is sold in bookshops. Information on Asunción at www.asu-cvb.org.py (Spanish and English).

Addresses Plaza de la Independencia is often referred to as Plaza Constitución or Plaza Juan de Salazar. Plaza de los Héroes is made up of four separate squares with different names but these are very rarely used; it is sometimes referred to as Plaza Independencia.

Sights

Historic centre

At the bottom of Avenida Colón, just before it joins El Paraguayo Independiente, are the colonial façades of **La Recova**, shops selling local arts and crafts. **La Aduana** (Customs) is at this same junction. Continue along El Paraguayo to a small plaza on your left with a statue of the former dictator, Alfredo Strossener. After his deposition, the statue was crushed and placed inside a block of concrete, only his hands and face protruding. Next to this is the **Palacio Gobierno**, built in the style of Versailles by Alan Taylor as a palace for Francisco Solano López (1860-1869). During the later years Taylor was forced to use child labour as all adult men were enlisted to fight in the Triple Alliance War. It now houses government departments. Down the side of the palace towards the river is a platform for viewing the back of the building. Directly opposite the Palace is the **Manzana de la Rivera** ① *Ayolas 129 y El Paraguayo Independiente, Mon-Sat 0700-2000, library Mon-Fri 0700-1900, Sat 0800-1200*, nine restored buildings dating from 1700s including **Casa Viola** with Museo Memoria de la Ciudad with historical photos and city information, **Casa Clari**, with exhibition halls and a bar, and **Casa Vertua**, the municipal library.

Next to the Palace is the new **Congreso Nacional**, built in steel and glass representing a huge ship moored on the river bank and incorporating part of the old congress building. On **Plaza de la Independencia** there is a small memorial to those who died in the struggle for democracy (also look out for statues of the frog and the dog). On the Plaza are the **Antiguo Colegio Militar** (1588) originally a Jesuit College, now home to government ministries, the **Cabildo** ① *Mon-Fri 0900-1900, Sat 0800-1200, free*, now the **Centro Cultural de la República**, with temporary exhibitions, indigenous and religious art, museum of music, film and video on the top floor, and the **Catedral Metropolitana** (mid-17th century, rebuilt in the mid-19th century) ① *not always open, possible to view the interior before, after or during mass, usually*

Asunción

Sleeping 🛏
Adelia **1** *C6*
Amalfi **2** *C4*
Aspen Apart Hotel **5** *C1*
Asunción Palace **3** *B1*
Bavaria **6** *B6*
Cardel **7** *C6*
Cecilia **8** *B6*
Chaco **9** *B4*
City **10** *C3*

El Lapacho **11** *A6*
Excelsior **13** *C3*
Granados Park **14** *B2*
Gran Armele **15** *B1*
La Española **12** *C4*
Los Alpes Apart Hotel **22** *A6*
Miami **17** *B5*
Paramanta **18** *A6*
Plaza **20** *A5*
Portal del Sol **19** *A6*

Residencial Itapúa **21** *C6*
Sabe Center **16** *B4*
Westfalenhaus **23** *A6*
Yasy **24** *C6*
Yessika **25** *C6*

Eating 🍴
Bistro **2** *B2*
Bolsi **3** *B3*
Café Literario **4** *B4*

around 1100 daily. The altar, decorated with Jesuit and Franciscan silver, is very beautiful. Between the river and the historical buildings is **La Chacarita**, a shanty town which is home to many poor families who have moved from the countryside in search of work. From the Plaza turn right onto Alberdi and to your right is the **post office**, a colonial building with a lovely planted courtyard; it also has public toilets and a small museum. At Alberdi and Pdte Franco is the **Teatro Municipal**, fully restored to its former colonial glory and re-opened for performances in 2007. The **Estación San Roque** ⓘ *Ayala y México, left of Plaza Uruguaya, T447848,* was built in 1856 with British and European help. Paraguay had the first passenger carrying railway in South America. No trains now run from the station but it has a small **museum** ⓘ *0700-1200, free,* featuring the old ticket office, machinery from Wolverhampton and Battersea and the first steam engine in Paraguay, the **Sapucai** (1861). **Plaza Uruguaya** with its prostitutes, shady trees and fountain is another spot to stop and rest. From here take Mcal Estigarribia towards Plaza de Los Héroes. The **Museo Nacional de Bellas Artes** ⓘ *Estigarribia e Iturbe, T447716, Tue-Fri 0700-1900, Sat-0700-1200, closed Sun-Mon,* has some interesting Paraguayan art and a good small collection of European paintings including works by Tintoretto and Murrillo.

Estigarribia becomes Palma at the intersection with Independencia Nacional (the names of all streets running east to west change at this point). On **Plaza de los Héroes** is the **Panteón Nacional de los Héroes** ⓘ *Palma y Chile, open daily,* which is based on Les Invalides in Paris, begun during the Triple Alliance War and finished in 1937. It contains the tombs of Carlos Antonio López, Mariscal Francisco Solano López, Mariscal Estigarribia, the victor of the Chaco War, an unknown child-soldier, and other national heroes. The child-soldiers honoured in the Panteón were boys aged 12-16 who fought at the battle of Acosta Ñu in the War of the Triple Alliance, 15 August 1869. Most of the boys died and nine out of 10 adult Paraguayan men were killed during the war. On the Plaza at Chile y Oliva (Plaza Libertad) there are **covered market stalls** selling traditional Paraguayan arts and crafts in wood, cotton and leather. Along Palma Maca Indian women sell colourful woven bags, beads and baskets. You may be approached by Maca men selling whistles, bows and arrows or feather headdresses. A few blocks further along Palma is the **tourist information office**; it has craft stalls for those not wishing to buy on the street. On Saturday morning, till 1200, Palma becomes a pedestrian area, with stalls selling arts, crafts, clothes and during the summer there is entertainment outside the tourist office. On Sunday there are stalls selling second-hand or antique items around Plaza de los Héroes. From Palma turn right at 14 de Mayo to the **Casa de la Independencia** ⓘ *14 de Mayo y Pres Franco, Mon-Fri 0700-1830, Sat 0800-1200, free* (1772), with a historical collection; the 1811 anti-colonial revolution was plotted here. The **Iglesia de Encarnación** ⓘ *14 de Mayo y Víctor Haedo* is a tranquil place to end your tour.

Heading out of the centre along Avenida Mariscal López

The **Museo Histórico Militar** ⓘ *in the Ministry of National Defence, Mcal López y 22 de Septiembre (surrender passport on entry),* has articles from both the Triple Alliance and the Chaco Wars. These include blood-stained flags from the Triple Alliance as well as clothes and personal possessions of Franciso Solano López and his Irish mistress, Eliza Lynch. The national cemetery, **Cementerio Recoleta** ⓘ *Av Mcal López y Chóferes del Chaco,* resembles a miniature city with tombs in various architectural styles. It contains the tomb of

To Parque Caballero, Jardín Botánico, Puerto Falcón, Argentina & Chaco

To ⑪ ⑬ ⑱ ⑲ ㉒ ㉓, Airport & Luque

Río Monday

Av España

Ⅲ Museo Dr Andrés Barbero

Bogado (Rutas 1 & 2)

San Roque ⑧

Estación an Roque ⑰

Eligio Ayala

Plaza ruguaya

Mcal Estigarribia

25 de Mayo

⑲

Cerro Corá

To ⑥ Av Mcal López, Airport & Luque

⑧ ⑫

Av Estados Unidos

To ② ㉒ & Bus Terminal

To ① ⑦ ⑩ ⑳

⑤

Paraguarí Antequera Tacuary

To Itá Enramada

⑥

㉑

Da Vinci **6** B2
Estrella **7** B2
La Flor de la Canela **8** B5
La Vida Verde **1** B2
Le Saint Tropez **10** B4
Lido **11** B3
Metropol **12** B6
Mirasol **5** B4
Oliver's (Hotel Presidente) **14** C3

San Roque **17** B5
Taberna Española **18** C1

Bars & clubs 🎵
Britannia Pub **19** B5

Paraguay Asunción Sights

1041

Madame Lynch (ask guide to show you the location), and, separately, the tomb of her baby daughter Corrine (Entrada 3 opposite Gran Unión supermarket). Eliza Lynch's home at the corner of Yegros and Mcal Estigarribia was, until 1999, the Facultad de Derecho.

The **National Universidad de Agronomía** ① *campus of the Universidad Nacional, Mon-Fri 0800-1530, closed Jan, free*, has natural history collections. Ask guard at gate for directions

On the outskirts of Asunción is **San Lorenzo** (Km 12). Reached via Ruta 2 (Mariscal Estigarribia Highway) or take buses 12, 56, 26 and get off at central plaza with blue, 18th-century neo-Gothic church. The **Museo Guido Boggiani** ① *Bogado 888, 1½ blocks from plaza, small sign, daily until 1900, ring the bell if door is shut*, is staffed by a very helpful lady who explains the exhibits and history. It has a well-displayed collection of tribal items from the northern Chaco from the turn of the 20th century. The shop across the road sells crafts at good prices. There's also a small Museo Arqueológico near the church and a daily market.

Heading out of the centre along Avenida España

Museo Etnográfico Dr Andrés Barbero ① *España y Mompox, T441696, Mon-Fri 0700-1100, Mon, Wed, Fri 1500-1700, free*, is anthropological with a good collection of tools and weapons of the various Guaraní cultures. The Centro de Artes Visuales includes the **Museo del Barro** and the **Museo de Arte Indígena** ① *Grabadores del Cabichuí entre Cañada y Emeterio Miranda, T607996, www.museodelbarro.org.py, daily, except Sun and holidays, 1600-2030, take bus 30 or 44A from the centre past Shopping del Sol, ask driver for Cañada*. Contains both contemporary and indigenous art, café. Highly recommended.

Luque (take bus 30), founded 1636, has an attractive central plaza with some well-preserved colonial buildings and a pedestrianized area with outdoor cafes. It is famous for the making of Paraguayan harps and guitars (**Guitarras Sanabria** ① *Km 13, T021-2291*, is one of the best-known firms), and for fine filigree jewellery in silver and gold at very good prices, many shops on the main street (ask for Alberto Núñez). Tourist information at Plaza Gral Aquino. There are some fine musical instrument shops on the road to Luque along Av Aviadores del Chaco.

Other Sights

The best of several parks is **Parque Carlos Antonio López**, set high to the west along Colón and, if you can find a gap in the trees, with a grand view. Good views are also offered from **Cerro de Lambaré**, 7 km south (buses 9 and 29 from Gral Díaz).

The **Jardín Botánico** (250 ha) 6 km east, on Av Artigas y Primer Presidente, lies along the Río Paraguay, on the former estate of the López family. The gardens are well-maintained, with signed walks, a rose garden and an 18-hole golf course. In the gardens are the former residences of Carlos Antonio López, a one-storey typical Paraguayan country house with verandas, which now houses a **Museo de Historia Natural** and library, and of Solano López, a two-storey European-inspired mansion which is now the **Museo Indigenista** ① *Both museums are free, Mon-Sat 0730-1130, 1300-1730, Sun 0900-1300. Getting there: by bus (Nos 2, 6, 23, and 40, US$0.15, 35 mins from Luis A Herrera, or Nos 24, 35 or 44B from Oliva or Cerro Corá)*. Neither is in good condition. The church of **Santísima Trinidad** (on Santísimo Sacramento, parallel to Avenida Artigas), where Carlos Antonio López was originally buried, dating from 1854 with frescoes on the inside walls, is well worth a visit. Nearby is the wreck of the **Ycuá Bolaños supermarket** ① *Santísima Trinidad y Estigarribia*, which was destroyed by fire in August 2004, killing over 400 people when the doors were locked to prevent looting. It is now a memorial with a donation box for the families of the dead. The **Maca Indian reservation** ① *US$0.30, guide US$0.50, getting there: take bus 42 or 44*, is north of the Botanical Gardens. The *indígenas*, who live in very poor conditions, expect you to photograph them (US$0.15).

Around Asunción

Many villages close to Asunción can be visited on a day trip, Aregua and San Bernadino on Lago Ypacari (see page 1050), Altos, great views over the lake, Itauguá. Alternatively take a tour from any travel agent (see Activities and tours, page 1046) of the **Circuito de Oro**: destinations vary but tend to include, Itá, Yaguarón, Paraguarí, Piribebuy, Caacupé, San Bernardino, Aregua, Itauguá, 200 km on paved roads, seven hours. The route goes through the hills, no more than 650 m high, which is beautiful, with hidden waterfalls and a number of spas. Chololó, Piraretá (near Piribebuy) and Pinamar (between Piribebuy and Paraguarí) are the most developed. The **Camino Franciscano** is similar, including the historical towns of Ypané, Altos, Itá, Atyra, Yaguarón, Piribebuy, Tobatí, Caacupé, Valenzuela, Villarrica, Caazapá and San Juan Neopomuceno.

Sleeping

The hotel bill does not usually include a service charge. Look out for special offers.

Asunción *p1040, map p1040*

LL-L Hotel Casino Yacht y Golf Club Paraguayo, 14 km from town, at Lambaré, on its own beach on the Río Paraguay, T906117/121, www.hotelyacht.com.py. 7 restaurants and cafés, super luxury, with pool, gym, golf, tennis, airport transfers, etc; many extras free and special deals.

L-AL Sabe Center, 25 de Mayo y México, T450093, www.sabecenterhotel.com.py. Luxury hotel in modern tower, with all facilities, discounts available.

AL Excelsior, Chile 980, T495632, www.excelsior.com.py. Luxurious, stylish, gym, pool, tennis, internet, cell phone rental, bar and restaurant.

AL Granados Park, Estrella y 15 de Agosto, T497921, www.granadospark.com.py. Luxury, top quality hotel, with breakfast, all facilities, good restaurant *Il Mondo*.

AL-A Westfalenhaus, Sgto 1 M Benítez 1577 y Stma Trinidad, T292374, www.paraguay-hotel.com. Comfortable, German-run, service and facilities of international quality (certificate ISO 9001-2000), with pool, internet (wireless LAN), safe deposit box, a/c, international restaurant, *Piroschka*, gym, massage and spa, English, German and Spanish spoken. Also has travel information and a travel agency: www.paraguay-travel.de.

A Aspen Apart Hotel, Ayolas y Gral Díaz, T493097, www.aspen.com.py. With breakfast, pool, sauna, gym, internet, lower price for longer stays.

A Cecilia, Estados Unidos 341 y Estigarribia, T210365, www.hotelcecilia.com.py. Comfortable, internet, good restaurant, *La Preferida* (♟♟♟), but pool may be dirty.

A Paramanta, Av Aviadores del Chaco 3198, T607053, www.paraguay-hotel.de. 4-star, mid-way between airport and centre, buses stop outside, with bath, TV, internet access, bar, restaurant, pool, gym, gardens, and many other services. English and German spoken.

A-B Chaco, Caballero 285 y Estigarribia, T492066, www.hotelchaco.com.py. With breakfast, parking nearby, rooftop swimming pool, bar, good restaurant (♟♟♟)

B Bavaria, Chóferes del Chaco 1010, T600966, www.bavaria.f2s.com. Comfortable, beautiful garden, pool, a/c, good value, German spoken.

B El Lapacho, República Dominicana 543, casi Av España, T210662. Family-run, welcoming, comfortable, a bit run down, rooms available at lower prices. Convenient for local services, 10 mins from centre by bus, pool, 24-hr internet access.

B Portal del Sol, Av Denis Roa y Santa Teresa, T609395, www.hotelportaldelsol.com. Comfortable hotel with breakfast, free airport pick-up and internet, pool.

C Amalfi, Caballero 877, T494154, www.hotel amalfi.com.py. Modern, comfortable, spacious rooms, breakfast included, internet and restaurant. Recommended.

C Asunción Palace, Colón 415 y Estrella, T/F492151, www.geocities.com/aphotel. With breakfast, very helpful, elegant, colonial style, laundry, internet, older rooms may be available at backpacker rates.

C Gran Armele, Palma y Colón, T444455, www.hotelarmele.com.py. With breakfast, a/c, gym, sauna, restaurant, pool, used by tour groups.

D City Hotel, Humaitá 209, T491497, www.city hotel.com.py. A/c, good, with breakfast in City Cafetería in lobby.

D Plaza, Eligio Ayala 609, T444772, www.plaza hotel.com.py. Discounts available, a/c, basic, luggage stored, with breakfast, restaurant.

E La Española, Herrera y Yegros, T449280. Central, comfortable, a/c, parking. Highly recommended.

E Miami, México 449 y 25 de Mayo, T444950. With breakfast, a/c, cheaper rooms fan only, basic.

F **Cardel**, Ygurey 1145 and Av Dr. Eusebio Alaya, T/F213622, cardel@highway.com.py. Halfway between bus station and centre of town, breakfast included.
F **Residencial Itapúa**, Fulgencio R Moreno 943, T445121. Breakfast available at small cost, a/c, cheaper with fan, kitchen for drinks and snacks, no cooking, quiet, comfortable.

Near bus terminal
F **Adelia**, Av F de la Mora y Lapacho, T553083. With breakfast, modern, TV a/c.
F **Yasy**, Av F de la Mora 2390, T551623. A/c and TV, cheaper with fan; both are overpriced. Many more behind these in C Dolores.
G pp **Yessika**, Lapacho y Encarnación, 10 mins' walk from terminal. With bath, basic and quiet.

Out of the city: San Lorenzo
Estancia Oñondivemi, Tourism farm, Km 27.5 on Ruta 1 just past the turn off to Ruta 2 at San Lorenzo, 30 mins from Asunción, T0295-20344, onondivemi@yahoo.com. A pleasant escape from the city. Serves all meals, food organically grown on site. Horse riding, fishing, swimming, nature walks (they have a nearby property with a waterfall, lovely for swimming), attractive accommodation with a/c. Contact for prices (includes meals).
Camping If camping, take plenty of insect repellent. The pleasant site at the Jardín Botánico charges US$1.50 pp plus tent, cars also permitted, cold showers and 220v electricity, busy at weekends.

You can camp at rear of **Restaurant Westfalia**, Av Perón y Av F Bogado, T331772, hotelrestaurantwestfalia@hotmail.com. Owner speaks English, French, German, very knowledgeable, US$1 per night for car, showers, laundry, noisy, animals. Take Av General Santos, towards Lambaré. Rest Westfalia is 5 km from Asunción (bus 19, 23 or 40).

❼ Eating

Asunción *p1040, map p1040*
Many restaurants are outside the scope of the map. A few restaurants close at weekends, but may open at night. A good meal in the food halls at the shopping malls, which you pay for by weight, as you do in some of the city centre restaurants, is about US$2.50. Average price of a good meal in quality restaurants: US$15. The following are open most days of the week, day and night.
₸₸₸ **Acuarela**, Mcal López casi San Martín, T609217. Very good churrascaría.

₸₸₸ **Bistro**, 15 de Agosto y Estrella. Excellent, US$25.
₸₸₸ **Bolsi**, Estrella 399, T491841. Wide choice of wines, good for breakfast, excellent food (Sun 1200-1430). Has great diner next door, lower prices, popular.
₸₸₸ **Churrasquería Sajón**, Av Carlos A López, bus 26 from centre. Good Paraguayan harp/guitar group; restaurant serving meat.
₸₸₸ **Fabio Rolandi's**, Mcal López y Infante Rivarola, T610447. Delicious pasta, steak and fish. Recommended.
₸₸₸ **Fina Estampa**, Senador Long 789 y Tte Vera, T601686. Peruvian food. Good Sun lunch buffet.
₸₸₸ **La Pergola Jardín**, Perú 240, T214014. Under same ownership as Bolsi, excellent.
₸₸₸ **Le Saint Tropez**, México entre Cerro Corrá y 25 de Mayo, T441141. Bar and restaurant, pizzería, open for lunch and dinner.
₸₸₸ **Mburicao**, González Rioboó 767, T660048. Mediterranean food. Highly recommended.
₸₸₸ **Oliver's**, Hotel Presidente, Azara e Independencia Nacional. Very good, pricey, live music.
₸₸₸ **Shangrilá**, Aviadores del Chaco y San Martín, T661618. Very good food at upmarket Chinese.
₸₸₸ **Taberna Española**, Ayolas 631, T441743. Spanish food, very good.
₸₸ **Da Vinci**, Estrella 695. Good Italian (and other) food, nice terrace. Recommended.
₸₸ **Hacienda Las Palomas**, Guido Spano y Senador Long, T605111. Mexican food, popular.
₸₸ **Hiroshima**, Chóferes del Chaco y Av Moreno. Authentic Japanese.
₸₸ **Il Sik**, Perú 1091 y Colombia. Very good, open every day 1000-2300.
₸₸ **Lido Bar**, Plaza de los Héroes, Palma y Chile, T446171. An institution in Asunción, loads of character. Good for breakfast, empanadas and watching the world go by. Good quality and variety, famous for fish soup, delicious. Open daily 0700-2300, very popular. Recommended.
₸₸ **San Roque**, Eligio Ayala y Tacuary, T446015. Traditional, relatively inexpensive.
₸₸ **Sukiyaki**, in Hotel Uchiyamada, Constitución 763. Good Japanese, about US$10 pp.
₸₸-₸ **Paulista Grill**, San Martín casi Mcal López, T662185. Another good churrascaría, good value, cheaper in the week, popular.
₸ **El Cheff y sus Tradiciones Peruanas**, Gral Garay y Del Maestro. Good quality, cheap Peruvian food.
₸ **La Vida Verde**, Palma 634, T446611. Vegetarian, Chinese influenced, with buffet lunch, open till 1700, closed Sun.

⬤ For an explanation of the sleeping and eating price codes used in this guide, see page 58.
⬤ Other relevant information is found in Essentials page 1038.

Mirasol, 25 de Mayo, entre Yegros e Iturbe. Vegetarian and Chinese, open till 1600 for buffet lunch, closed Sun.

Tembi'u he, Dr Francisco Fernández y Av Stma Trinidad, T293324. Paraguayan food. Unnamed Chinese restaurant on Haedo between O'Leary and 15 de Agosto serves stylish vegetarian by weight. Recommended.

Cafés and snacks

Most cheap lunch places close around 1600.
Café Literario, Palma casi México. Mon-Fri from 1600, cosy café/bar, books and good atmosphere.
El Molino, España 382 near Brasil. Good value, downstairs for sandwiches and homemade pastries, upstairs for full meals in a nice setting, good service and food (particularly steaks) but pricey. Recommended.
Estrella, Estrella y 15 de Agosto. Pizza, empanadas.
Heladería París, Brasilia y Siria, San Martín casi Pacheco and NS de Asunción y Quinta Avenida. Heladería/café/bar. Very popular.
La Flor de la Canela, Tacuary 167 con Eligio Ayala. Cheap lunches.
Metropol, Estados Unidos 341 y 25 de Mayo. Café and shop with European food, sandwiches, cheese and meats.
Michael Bock, Pres Franco 828. Excellent bread and sweet shop.
Quattro D (4d), San Martín y Dr Andrade. Heladería offering great range of ice cream, also weekday lunches from US$1.40.
Sugar's, several branches including most Shopping Centres and Brasilia 662.

🅝 Bars and clubs

Asunción *p1040, map p1040*
Bars
Austria Pub, Austria 1783 y Viena, T604662, and in Mall Excelsior. German run, brews own beer, popular. Recommended.
Britannia Pub, Cerro Corá 851. Evenings only, closed Mon-Tue, good variety of drinks, German spoken, popular expat hangout, book exchange.
Café Bohemia Senador Long 848 casi España, T662191. Original decor and atmosphere, Mon and Tues live blues/jazz.
Déjà Vu, Galería Colonial, Av España casi San Rafael, T615098. Popular.
El Bar, Paseo Carmelitas, Av Espana y Malutin. Another popular bar.
Oshun Lounge, Galería Colonial, Av España casi San Rafael. Yet another popular bar.

Clubs

Av Brasilia has a collection of clubs such as **Arena Café**, **Face's** and **Mouse Cantina** (No 803).

Asunción Rock, Mcal Estigarribia 991 casi Estados Unidos, T442034. Wed-Sat, 2200 till late. 2 dance floors, rock and alternative music.
Coyote Night & Fun, Sucre casi Av San Martín. Fri, Sat. Recommended.
El Sitio, Av Rep Argentina 1035 casi McMahon, T612822. Latin and retro.
Glam, Av San Martín entre Lillo y Bertoni. Open Thu, Fri and Sat. Same owners as **Caracol Club**, Av Perón y Concepción Yegros, T332848 (temporarily closed in 2007).
Pirata Bar, Benjamín Constant y Ayolas, T452953. Fri-Sat.
Trauma, 25 de Mayo y Antequera y Tacuary. Gay/transvestite/mixed, Fri, Sat, 2300.

🎭 Entertainment

Asunción *p1040, map p1040*
Cinema Cinema programmes are given in the press; latest releases, admission US$3.40 (Wed and matinées half price). Modern cinemas at: **Shopping del Sol**, 6 screens, **Shopping Villa Mora** 6 screens, and **Mall Excelsior**, **Hiperseis** (see Supermarkets and shopping centres, below). **Centro Cultural de la Ciudad**, Haedo 347, T442448, for quality foreign films, US$1.50.
Theatre See newspapers for performances of concerts, plays, ballets. Various Cultural centres also put on theatrical productions. **Teatro Municipal**, Alberdi y Pdte Franco, T445169. Restored 2007. Ticket sales Mon-Sat 0800-2200. **Banco Central**, T6192243, the Paraguay Philharmonic gives monthly recitals May-Dec. **Teatro de las Américas**, J Bergés 297, concerts are given here.

🎊 Festivals and events

Asunción *p1040, map p1040*
Two weeks in **Jul**, **Expo**, an annual trade show at Mariano Roque Alonso, Km 14.5 on the Trans Chaco Highway, www.expo.com.py. The biggest fair in the country with local and international exhibitors. Bus from centre takes 30 mins.

🅞 Shopping

Asunción *p1040, map p1040*
Bookshops 'Books', at Shopping del Sol and Mcal López 3971, also opposite Villa Morra shopping centre, very good for English books, new titles and classics. **El Lector** at Plaza Uruguaya y 25 de Mayo, T491966, also at San Martín y Austria, T614256 (has café and internet connection), www.ellector. com.py. Has a selection of foreign material and a range of its own titles on Paraguay, including the beautiful *Paraguay Porã* album. **Librería Alemana**, Av Luis

A de Herrera 292, warmly recommended for German books. **Librería Internacional**, Oliva 386, Estrella 723 and Palma 595. Good for maps.

Camping Safari Sport, Montevideo 258, Camping 44, Pres Franco casi Ayolas, **Gauchito Deportes**, Av Fernando de la Mora 2477 casi Cedro, T555953, or **Unicentro**, Palma y 15 de Agosto.

Crafts Check the quality of all handicrafts carefully, lower prices usually mean lower quality. Many leading tourist shops offer up to 15% discount for cash. For leather goods there are several places on Colón and on Montevideo including: **Boutique Irene**, No 463; **Boutique del Cuero**, No 329; **La Casa Del Portafolio**, No 302, and **Galería Colón 185** (recommended). **Artes de Madera** at Ayolas 222. Wooden articles and carvings. **Casa Overall 1**, Mcal Estigarribia y Caballero, good selection. Also **No 2** at 25 de Mayo y Caballero, T447891. **Casa Vera**, Estigarribia 470, for Paraguayan leatherwork, cheap and very good. **Doña Miky**, O'Leary 215 y Pres Franco, recommended. **Folklore**, Mcal Estigarribia e Iturbe, T/F494360, good for music, woodcarvings and other items. **Victoria**, **Arte Artesanía**, Iturbe y Ayala, interesting selection of wood carvings, ceramics etc. Recommended.

Electronic goods Cheap electronic goods in the Korean-run shops.

Markets Mercado Cuatro on Pettirossi, a huge daily market selling food, clothing, electrical items, DVDs, CDs, jewellery, toys, is a great place to visit. Good, cheap Chinese restaurants nearby. There is a daily market on Av Dr Francia, best visited during the week. See also under Historic centre, Sights. **Shopping Mariscal López** (see below) has a fruit and vegetable market, Tue, in the car park, and a small plant/flower market, including orchids, Wed, at the entrance.

Shopping centres Asunción has a number of modern Shopping Malls with shops, ATMs, cafés, supermarkets, cinemas and *patio de comidas* all under one a/c roof. **Shopping Villa Morra** (Av Mcal López y San Roque González). **Shopping Mariscal López** (Quesada 5050 y Charles de Gaulle, behind Shopping Villa Morra). **Shopping del Sol** (Av Aviadores de Chaco esq D F de González, www.delsol.com.py). **Mall Excelsior** (Chile y Manduvirá).

Supermarkets Hiperseis at Boggiani y Mcal López; Stock at Shopping del Sol and Mall Excelsior. **Superseis** at Shopping Villa Morra; Casa Rica, Av San Martín y Aviadores de Chaco, good for speciality foods and some European imports. **Real**, Boggiani y Av Argentina, has an imported food aisle, mainly USA.

▲ Activities and tours

Asunción *p1040, map p1040*

Football Asunción is the permanent home of the **South American Football Confederation**, on the Autopista heading towards the airport, opposite Ñu Guazú Park. At the moment this imposing building with its striking 'football' fountain houses only offices and a small football library but a new museum at the site is due for completion in 2007. T645781 in advance for visits. **Estadio Defensores del Chaco**, Mayor Martínez y Alejo García, T480409, is the national stadium, hosting international, cup and major club matches

Horse riding Club Hípico Paraguayo, Av Gral Andrés Rodríguez y Cleto Romero, Barrio Mariano Roque Alonso, T756148. Members club open to the public. US$50 per month but daily rates available. Friendly and helpful.

Rural tourism *Turismo rural* has become one of the most enjoyable ways to visit the country and get a feel for a Paraguayan way of life that revolves around agriculture and ranching. The **Touring y Automóvil Club Paraguayo** (25 de Mayo y Brasil, p 2, T210550, www.tacpy.com.py) is officially in charge of rural tourism, through the **Paraguayan Rural Tourism Association** (APATUR) T210550-3, int 126-7, or www.turismorural.org.py, and its own travel agency, **Touring Viajes**. They organize visits to ranches and farms all over Paraguay. One-day tour prices start at about US$50 pp including accommodation, food and drink (not alcohol); tours of three or more days for groups of 2-12, US$30-100. All the ranches listed under APATUR have good facilities. Transport to and from these ranches from Asunción is sometimes included in the package. Visitors experience living and working on a ranch, can participate in a variety of activities, and enjoy typical food, horse riding, photo safaris and nature watching. Another agency for visiting *estancias* is **Emitur**, T0782-20286, T021-222081 or T0975-626780, and see www.senatur.gov.py/estancias.htm for a list of these and other ranches.

Tennis Academia de Tenis at Parque Seminario, 25 de Mayo y Kubicheck, T206379 to reserve a court. Price US$4 per hr daytime and US$5 per hr evening. Coaching available.

Tours

Many agencies offer day tours of the Circuito de Oro or Camino Franciscano (from US$50). Trips to local estancias, Encarnación and the Jesuit Missions, Itaipú and Iguazú or the Chaco region are all offered as 1 or 2-day tours. Prices from US$100. Most agencies will also provide personalized itineraries on request. City tours also available. For more information contact **Dirección General de**

Turismo or the **Paraguayan Association of Travel Agencies and Tourism** (ASATUR), Juan O'Leary 650, p 1, T491755/491728.

Alda Saguier, Yegros 941, p 2, T446492. English and German spoken.

Aries Travel, Rodríguez de Francia 140 e Yegros, T442334, ariestravel@emociones.org.py.

Canadá Viajes, Rep de Colombia 1061, T2211192, canada.viajes@quanta.com.py. Good Chaco tours.

Inter Tours, Perú 436 y España, T211747, www.intertours.com.py. Tours to Chaco, Iguazú and Jesuit missions. Recommended.

Itra Travel, Venezuela 663 y España, T450722, itra@itra.com.py. Also offer ecotourism.

Menno Travel, Rep de Colombia 1042 y Brasil, T493504, mennotravel@gmx.net. German spoken.

Paraguay Natural, Barka Viajes, Gral Santos y 18 de Julio, T302027, www.paraguaynatural.com.py. Specialists in nature tourism throughout the country and to Brazilian Pantanal. See the website for details.

Siboney, 25 de Mayo 2140 y 22 de Septiembre, T214018, www.siboney.com.py.

Time Tours, 15 Agosto y Gral Díaz, T449737, Villa Morra T601780, timetour@conexion.com.py. Fluent English, runs Camino Franciscano tours. Recommended.

Vips Tour, México 782, T/F441199, vipstours@telesurf.com.py.

⊝ Transport

Asunción p1040, map p1040

Air Silvio Pettirossi Airport, T645600. Several agencies have desks where you can book a taxi to your hotel, US$15-20. Bus 30 goes every 15 mins between the red bus stop outside the airport and Plaza de los Héroes, US$0.25, difficult with luggage. Minibus service from your hotel to airport run by **Tropical**, T424486, book in advance, US$8 (minimum 2 passengers, or pay for 2). The terminal has a tourist office (free city map and hotel information), bank (turn right as you leave customs – better rates in town), post office (0800-1800), handicraft shop, restaurant and several travel agencies who arrange hotel bookings and change money (very poor rates). Left luggage US$3 per day per item.

Bus City buses: Journeys within greater Asunción US$0.25. Buses are busy at rush hours. Turnstiles are awkward for large backpacks. Keep your ticket for inspection until you leave bus.

Long-distance: The Terminal de Omnibus is south of the centre at República Argentina y Fernando de la Mora (T552154/551737). Local bus No 8 is the only direct one from Oliva, which goes via Cerro Corá and Av Brasil from the centre, and stops outside the terminal, US$0.25. From the terminal to the centre it goes via Av Estados Unidos, Luis A

Herrera, Antequera and E Ayala; get off at Chile y Díaz. Other buses Nos 10, 25, 31, 38 and 80, follow very circuitous routes. Taxi to/from centre, recommended if you have luggage, US$3.25, journey time depends on the amount of traffic, about 20 mins. The terminal has a bus information desk, free city/country map, restaurant (quite good), café, casa de cambio (poor rates), post office, phone booths and shops. There are many touts for bus companies at the terminal. Allow yourself time to choose the company you want and don't be bullied, or tricked, into buying the wrong ticket. Main companies: **Nuestra Señora de la Asunción**, T551667, www.nsa.com.py, has booking office at main terminal and at Mcal Estigarribia y Antequera, off Plaza Uruguaya. RYSA, T444244, rysa1@supernet.com.py. Bus company offices on the top floor are in 3 sections: short-distance, medium and long. Local departures, including for Yaguarón and Paraguarí from the basement. Hotels nearby: turn left from front of terminal, 2 mins' walk. Bus times and fares within Paraguay are given under destinations.

To Uruguay EGA (Eligio Ayala 693, T492473, www.egakeguay.com) runs to **Montevideo** 3 times a week 20 hrs, US$52, as does **Brújula/Cynsa** (Pres Franco 995, T441720). The route is Encarnación, Posadas, Paso de los Libres, Uruguaiana, Bella Unión, Salto, Paysandú; the only customs formalities are at Bella Unión; passport checks here and at Encarnación.

To Argentina There is a road north from Asunción (passing the Jardín Botánico on Primer Presidente) to a concrete arch span bridge (Puente Remanso – US$1 toll, pedestrian walkway on upstream side, 20 mins to cross) which leads to the border at Puerto Falcón (about 40 km) and then to **Clorinda** in Argentina. The border is open 24 hrs; local services are run by **Empresa Falcón** to Puerto Falcón (US$0.50, every hr, last bus from Falcón to the centre of Asunción 1830; from Falcón to Clorinda costs US$0.25), but it is cheaper to book direct from Asunción to Argentina. Buses don't wait for you to go through formalities: wait for the same company's next bus, or buy a new ticket.

Buses to **Buenos Aires** (18 hrs) daily, many companies, via Rosario and Santa Fe (average fare US$53 luxury, US$33-40 diferencial, US$27-30 común). To **Formosa**, 4 a day, Brújula/La Internacional (T551662, US$5.40, plus US$0.50 luggage) many drug searches on this road; to **Posadas**, Singer, 3 a week at midnight. To **Salta**, take Brújula at 0600 to **Resistencia**, 8 hrs, then change to La Veloz del Norte, 1800.

To Brazil Many Paraguayan buses advertise that they go to destinations in Brazil, when, in fact you have to change buses and book again at the frontier. Note also that through services to **Campo Grande** (US$18) and **Corumbá** via Pedro Juan

Caballero and Ponta Porã do not stop for immigration formalities. Check all details carefully. **Crucero del Este**, **Nuestra Señora** and **Rysa**, and the Brazilian companies **Pluma** (T445024) and **Unesul**, have services to Ciudad del Este, continuing to **Foz do Iguaçu** (Brazil), US$8, 5-7 hrs, 6 direct buses a day in all. Seat reservations recommended. To **Curitiba**, with Pluma, buses daily, 15½ hrs. To **São Paulo**, Rápido Yguazú, **Pluma** and **Brújula**, 20 hrs, Sun-Thu, US$27-29 (leito, US$61). **Pluma** to **Rio de Janeiro**, US$50; to **Porto Alegre**, Unesul, 4 a week, US$24; **Nacional Expresso** (Santa Rosa 1116, T669966, F557369) to **Brasília** 3 a week. Services also to **Blumenau** (Catarinense, T551738, Tue, Thu and Sat, 17 hrs, US$19) and **Florianópolis**, US$22, 20 hrs, daily (Pluma and Catarinense).

To Bolivia Via the Chaco, to Santa Cruz, **Yacyretá**, T551725, most reliable, Mon, Wed, Fri, and Sat at 2030. **Stel Turismo**, T558196, daily at 2000, **Pycazú**, Thu and Sat at 2100, but you cannot get on in Mariscal Estigarribia. All fares US$47. All buses normally travel via Mariscal Estigarribia, for Paraguayan immigration where foreigners must get an exit stamp; La Patria, where the pavement ends (Feb 2006); Infante Rivarola at the border; Ibibobo, for Bolivian immigration; and Villamontes, where the pavement starts again, to Santa Cruz de la Sierra. Advertised as 24 hrs, the trip can take 7 days if the bus breaks down or if it rains. Some food provided but take your own, plus extra water just in case; also take toilet paper. The buses can be very crowded. In summer the route can be very hot and dusty, but in winter, it can be cold at night. Alternative route to Bolivia via Salta, Argentina (see above).

Buses to Bolivia do not go through Filadelfia or the other Mennonite colonies, so take a local services from Asunción (see page 1068). After visiting the Chaco, you can usually get on a Bolivia-bound bus in Mariscal Estigarribia, where the bus companies have agents (see page 1066), but enquire in advance with their offices in Asunción.

River boat To escape the city take a short trip across the river to the **Mbiguá Club** to sunbathe and relax. Ask at Aduanas for information. A small launch leaves every 20 mins from the pier at the bottom of Montevideo to **Chaco-i**, a strip of land between the Ríos Paraguay and Pilcomayo, US$0.50 each way. The Argentine town of Clorinda is just the other side of the Pilcomayo. Ferry to **Puerto Pilcomayo** (Argentina) about every 30 mins, US$0.50 (Argentine immigration closed at weekends for tourists).

Boats for **Concepción** leave from the bottom of Montevideo. Offices for information/prices El Paraguayo Independiente 813 y Ayolas (not always staffed). Sailings weekly (Wed), 27-30 hrs, US$20 1st class, US$13 2nd, US$7 deck space. Sleeping space

is sometimes available. Take food, water, toilet paper, warm clothes, sleeping bag and mosquito repellent. If you want more luxury take a 5-star cruise on the **Crucero Paraguayo**, Nuestra Sra de la Asunción 1102 e Ibáñez del Campo (Jejuí), T447710, www.cruceroparaguay.info. Offers 4-10 day cruises, visits historical and ecological sites along the river, on-board entertainment, international menu, swimming pool and cinema. Reservations also available through larger tour operators.

Taxi Minimum fare in Asunción : US$0.35, and US$0.05 per 100 m. The average journey costs about US$1.50. Minimum fare is about 30-50% more at night. Hire by the hr: minimum US$5, outside the city US$2 per km. There are many taxi ranks throughout the city. **Radiotaxi** recommended, T550116/311080.

Train A tourist steam train runs from Estación Botánico, outside the Jardín Botánico, to Aregua, Sun 1030, return 1630, US$20 for foreigners, US$5 for Paraguayans, price includes soft drink, *empanadas* and on-board entertainment (actors presenting 19th-century scenes); 4 hrs in Aregua for lunch and sightseeing. Highly recommended. You can buy tickets on the day or in advance from Estación San Roque, Ayala y Plaza Uruguaya. See page 1056 for the locomotive workshops at Sapucay.

⊙ Directory

Asunción p1040, map p1040
Airline offices Aerolíneas Argentinas, España 2220, T450577, arasugsa@sap.com.py. **AeroSur**, Senador Long 856 y España, T614743, www.aerosur.com. **Gol**, contact via webpage: www.voegol.com.br. **Iberia**, Mcal López 995, T214246, asuuu@iberia.es. **LAB**, 14 de Mayo 563, ground floor, T441586, susklb@rieder.net.py. **Lan**, 15 de Agosto 588, T491784, www.lan.com. **Lufthansa**, N S de la Asunción 208, T447962, lhasu@cmm.com.py, admin and cargo only, ticket information from travel agents. **TAM/Arpa**, Oliva 761 y Ayolas, T491040, www.tam.com.py. **United Airlines**, Mcal López 310, T213019, viase@supernet.com.py. **Banks** Be careful to count money received from street money changers (Palma and surrounding area – their rates are poor when banks and cambios are closed). See Currency section in Essentials. Lots of ATMs, accepting credit and debit cards, give dollars and guaraníes. **Lloyds TSB Bank**, Palma y O'Leary, T419700, Av Mscal López y Av San Martín (and several other agencies in Greater Asunción). Accepts Visa. **Citibank**, Estrella y Chile. Will change Citibank TCs into US$ cash, and gives US$ cash on MasterCard. **ABN AMRO**, Estrella y Alberdi, T490001, and at Shopping Mscal López accepting several cards. **Interbanco**, Oliva 349

Thousands of people from Paraguay, Brazil and Argentina flock to the shrine, especially for the **Feast of the Immaculate Conception** on 8 December. Besides fireworks and candlelit processions, pilgrims watch the agile gyrations of Paraguayan bottle-dancers; they weave in intricate measures whilst balancing bottles pyramided on their heads. The top bottle carries a spray of flowers and the more expert dancers never let drop a single petal.

Tobati, a town north of Caacupé, specializes in woodwork. A *villa artesenal* is a short walk from the bus stop outside the house of Zenon Páez, a world famous sculptor. There are some amazing rock formations on the way to Tobati. To get there, take a bus from the corner below the park on the main Asunción road in Caacupé; ask the driver to let you off at Páez' house.

Piribebuy

At Km 64 beyond Caacupé a paved road runs 13 km southeast to the small town of Piribebuy, founded in 1640 and noted for its strong local drink, *caña*. In the central plaza is the church (1640), with fine sculptures, high altar and pulpit. The town was the site of a major battle in the War of the Triple Alliance (1869), commemorated by the **Museo Histórico Pedro Juan Caballero** ① *free*, which contains artefacts from the Chaco War. Buses from Asunción by Transportes Piribebuy. Near the town are the attractive falls of Pirareta. The road continues via Chololó, 13 km south, and reaches Ruta 1 at Paraguarí, 28 km from Piribebuy (see page 1056). Between Pirbebuy and Paraguarí is an outdoor pursuits centre, **Eco-reserva Mbatoví**. There is a visitors centre ① *US$3, for reservations and information visit www.mbatovi.com.py*, an outdoor pursuits course① *US$35*, or a guided walk① *US$10*, taking in early settlements, local folklore and beautiful scenery.

Vapor Cué National Park

A turn-off from Eusebio Ayala (Km 72) goes 23 km to Caraguatay, 5 km from which is the Vapor Cué National Park, where boats from the War of the Triple Alliance are preserved. Although officially a national park, it is more of an open-air museum. Next to the (indoor) museum is a pleasant hotel, called **Hotel Nacional de Vapor Cué** (**E**, T0517-222395). Frequent buses run from Asunción to Caraguatay.

Coronel Oviedo and around → *Phone code: 0521. Colour map 6, grid C6. Population: 21,80.0*

An important route centre, although not worth a stop, 3 km south of the junction of west-east highway and the major north-south Ruta 8; buses drop passengers at the junction (El Cruce). Ruta 8 runs north to **Mbutuy**, continuing as Ruta 3 to Yby Yaú, where it meets Ruta 5 (Concepción-Pedro Juan Caballero). At Mbutuy (Km 56, parador, restaurant, petrol station) Ruta 10 branches off northeast to the Brazilian frontier at Salto del Guaíra.

Salto del Guaíra (*Phone code 046*) is named after the waterfalls now under the Itaipú lake. There is a 900-ha wildlife reserve, Refugio Biológico Mbaracayú. Salto del Guaíra, a free port, can also be reached by a paved road which runs north from Hernandarias, via Itaquyry to meet Ruta 10 at Cruce Carambey. **Note** There is nowhere to change travellers' cheques here.

Mbaracayú Forest Reserve ① *To visit you must book and pay in advance, and sign a disclaimer at the Moisés Bertoni Foundation in Asunción (see National Parks, page 1036); entry US$5, lodging US$15 pp, camping US$10 per tent, take your own food, cook available US$8 per day plus US$3 per day for gas, transport US$0.28 per km. You must hire a guide for US$20 per day. There is public transport to Villa Igatimi from where they pick you up, 20 km to the park. Pay ahead for transport you will require within the park. Buses from Asunción to Curuguaty: La Coruguateña and Santa Ana, 0900 and 1430, 6 hrs, US$5. From Curuguaty to Iguatimi local buses take 1 hr.* One of the finest national parks (not to be confused with Refugio Biológico further east), the reserve boasts 64,406 ha of protected rainforest and is the largest area of representative ecosystems in good conservation status in Paraguay. It contains 48% of all mammal species and 63% of all bird species (over 400) found in eastern Paraguay. There are trails, waterfalls and spectacular view points. There are also two groups of indigenous community, the Aché and Guaraní. There is a visitor centre and small museum at Igatimi.

At Santa Rosa, 143 km north of Mbutuy, there is petrol, pensión and restaurants. A dirt road runs southwest for 27 km to **Nueva Germania** founded in 1866 by Bernhard Förster and Elisabeth Nietzsche (the philosopher's sister) to establish a pure Aryan colony. This road goes on to San Pedro and Puerto Antequera on the Río Paraguay (88 km). A further 23 km north of Santa Rosa, a dirt road runs northeast through jungle to the interesting **Capitán Badó** (120 km), which forms the frontier with Brazil. From here a road follows the frontier north to Pedro Juan Caballero (100 km). About 50 km north of the turn off to Capitán Badó is Yby Yaú, see page 1061.

Villarrica → *Phone code: 0541. Colour map 6, grid C6. Population: 21,210.*

Villarrica, 42 km south of Coronel Oviedo, is delightfully set on a hill rich with orange trees. A very pleasant, friendly place, it has a fine cathedral, built in traditional style with veranda, and various pleasant parks. The museum (closed weekends) behind the church has a foreign coin collection; please contribute. Products of the region are tobacco, cotton, sugar, yerba mate, hides, meat and wine produced by German settlers. There is a large student population.

German colonies near Villarrica

Some 7 km north is an unsigned turn off to the east, then 20 km to tiny **Colonia Independencia**, which has some beautiful beaches on the river (popular in summer). German-speaking travellers can also visit the German co-operative farms. A great mate and wine producing area and, at harvest time, there is a wine festival. They also have beer festival in October.

East from Coronel Oviedo

The paved Ruta 7 runs 195 km through cultivated areas and woods and across the Caaguazú hills. Ruta 7 continues from here to the spectacular 500-m single span 'Friendship Bridge' across the Paraná (to Brazil) at Ciudad del Este.

Ciudad del Este → *Phone code: 061. Colour map 7, grid C1. Population: 133,900.*

Originally founded as Ciudad Presidente Stroessner in 1957, this was the fastest growing city in the country until the completion of the Itaipú hydroelectric project, for which it is the centre of operations. Ciudad del Este has been described as the biggest shopping centre in Latin America, attracting Brazilian and Argentine visitors who find bargain prices for electrical goods, watches and perfumes. Don't buy perfume on the street and , it's only coloured water. And make sure that shops pack what you actually bought. The main shopping street is Avenida San Blas, lined with shopping malls and market stalls, selling a huge variety of goods, both original and imitations – usually the latter. Watch the exchange rates if you're a short-term visitor. Parts are of the city are dirty and frantic during business hours, but away from the shopping arcades people are friendly and more relaxed. The leather market is well worth a visit, be sure to bargain. **Tourist office** ① *Coronel Rafael Franco entre Pampliega y Curupayty, Edificio Líbano p 1 of 104, T866264 (mob), senaturcde@senatur.gov.py.*

Around Ciudad del Este The **Monday falls** ① *0700-1700, US$0.35, taxi US$20 return*, where the Río Monday drops into the Paraná Gorge, are worth seeing. Nearby is the popular beach resort and biological refuge **Tatí Yupí.** There are two biological reserves bordering the Itaipú dam, **Itabó** and, further north, **Limoy.** Take the unpaved road north from Ciudad del Este towards Salto del Guaíra. Itabó is at the first turn off to Dorila, and Limoy the turnoff at Colonia San Lorenzo.

Ciudad del Este

To Itaipú
To Foz do Iguaçu (Brazil)
To Asunción

Cap Miranda
Emiliano Fernández
Mongelos
Camilo Recalde
Cnel Toledo
Av San Blas
Ruta 7 Internacional
Av Mñor Rodríguez
Nanawa
Av Adrián Jara
@ $
Boquerón
Abay
Av Carlos López
Rgto Piribebuy
Rgto Itá Ybaté
García
Av Paí Pérez
Av Domingo Robledo
Av Nicanor Pampliega
Francisco Cedzich
Pampliega
Curupayty
Av Mñor
A Matiauda
Av Bernardina Caballero
Av Alejo García
Av Vicente
Pampliega
Carlos López
Oscar Ribas Ortellado

To Monday Falls

N
0 metres 100
0 yards 100

Sleeping
Austria **1**
California **2**
Caribe **3**
Convair **4**
Executive **5**

Munich **7**
New Cosmos
Apart-Hotel **8**
Panorama Inn **9**
Tía Nancy **11**

Border with Brazil

The border crossing over the Friendship Bridge to Foz do Iguaçu is very informal. No passport stamps are required to visit Ciudad del Este for the day. The Friendship Bridge is jammed with vehicles and pedestrians all day long. Motorcycle taxis (helmet provided, hang on tight) are a good option if you have no luggage. Otherwise, to enter Paraguay here, hire a taxi and go very early in the morning, or take your gear to the Paraguayan bus terminal (left luggage facilities) by city bus, then shuttle back and forth on foot to get passport stamped; long and tiring. (Do not fail to get a Paraguayan entry stamp; without it you will be fined. If you do get fined, get a receipt.) Paraguay and Brazilian immigration formalities are dealt with on opposite sides of the bridge. There is a friendly tourist office in the customs building on the Paraguayan side. Note that Adjust your watch to local time (Brazil is one hour ahead). The **Brazilian consulate** ① *Ciudad del Este, Pampliega 205, T500984/510636, F500985, Mon-Fri 0700*, issues visas. The Argentine Consulate is at ① *Av Adrián Jara y Boquerón, Edificio Oriental, T500638/500945*.

Itaipú and around

① *www.itaipu.gov.py. Mon-Fri 0730-1200, 1330-1700, Sat, Sun and holidays 0800-1100. Bus tours Mon-Fri 0800, 0930, 1400, 1500, Sat 0800, 0930, 1030, 1400, 1500 (morning only Sun and holidays). Free tours of the project with film show (several languages – ask). Take passport. Buses going to Hernandarias will drop you at the visitor centre.*

The Itaipú project (a huge hydroelectric project covering an area of 1,350 sq km) is close to Ciudad del Este, and well worth a visit.

On the way to Itaipú is **Flora y Fauna Itaipú Binacional** ① *0730-1130, 1400-1700*, zoo and museum containing animals and plants; it is about 2 km from the visitor's centre on the road back to Ciudad del Este. At the Centro Ambiental de Itaipú is the new **Museo de la Tierra Guaraní** ① *T061-599 8040, Tue-Sat 0800-1130, 1430-1700 (Mon afternoon only, Sun morning only)*, which offers a view of the science and culture of the Guaraníes via natural history displays and interactive screens.

Hernandarias, north of Ciudad del Este grew rapidly with the building of Itaipú. A paved road runs north to Cruce Carambey, where it meets Ruta 10 (see above, page 1051). From Hernandarias, boat trips on Lago Itaipú go to Puerto Guaraní where there is a museum.

● Sleeping

San Bernardino p1050

There are plenty of hotels other than those listed, many with good restaurants (eg de Sol and Los Alpes, US$3.30 for buffet lunch and use of pool). Wander around and see what takes your fancy.

L Sol de San Ber, E A Garay y Decond, Opposite Del Lago, T233138, pueblo@telesurf.com.py. New, super luxury.

B-C San Bernardino Pueblo, Paseo del Pueblo y Mbocayá, T232195, pueblohotel@hotmail.com. Swimming pool, a/c, by the lake. Weekend packages, 2 nights for US$55 pp.

D Del Lago, near lake in town, T232201. With breakfast, attractive 19th-century building but run down, pool, lovely gardens.

D Los Alpes, Ruta Gral Morínigo Km 46.5, 3 km from town, T232083 or 0981-552066. A/c, cable TV, lovely gardens, 2 pools, excellent self-service restaurant, children's playground, beach 1 km away, frequent buses to centre.

Camping At Km 43 is **Casa Grande Camping Club** with all facilities. For info, Corfín Paraguaya, Ayolas 437 y Estrella, T492360/1, Asunción. **San Vicente**, 1km off Ruta 2, excursions, horse riding and birdwatching, T232274.

Caacupé p1050

Cheaper than Lago Ypacaraí. Prices increase during the Feast of the Immaculate Conception.

D Virgen Serrana, plaza, T42366. A/c, **D** with fan.

E El Mirador, T42652, on plaza. With bath.

E Katy María, Eligio Ayala y Dr Pino, T42860/42441, beside Basílica. Well-kept, welcoming.

Camping **Club de Camping Melli**, 1 km east of town, all facilities, T42313. West of Tobati is **Atyrá** (15km from Caacupé), 2 camp grounds: **Chorro Carumbey** and **Balneario Atyrá**.

Tourism farm

AL Estancia Aventura, Km 61.5, Ruta 2, T0981-441804, www.estancia-aventura.com. 225 acres of countryside, worth spending a few days. Good, horse riding, tennis swimming, can arrange airport pickup from Asunción.

Piribebuy p1051

C pp La Quinta, 10 km from Piribebuy, 19 km from Paraguarí, 82.5 km from Asunción (take bus to Piribebuy then bus to Chololó, bus passes in front of hotel), T971-117444, www.laquinta. com.py. Price based on 4 sharing in cabins, also

suites, also open for day visits, has its own stream
and is close to falls at Piraretá and Chololó.
G Pensión Santa Rosa. Basic.
G Rincón Viejo, T0515-212251. Reasonable.

Coronel Oviedo and around *p1051*
Salto del Guaíra
D-E Peralta, Av Paraguay y Capitán Capii Pery,
T242235. Pleasant, with breakfast and bath,
F without.

Villarrica *p1052*
C Villarrica Palace Hotel, Ruta 8 Blas Garay,
turn right on road entering Villarrica, T43048,
vph@telesurf.com.py. New hotel, restaurant,
parking, pool, sauna.
D Ybytyruzú, C A López y Dr Bottrell, T42390.
Best in town, breakfast, more with a/c,
restaurant.
F La Guairana, Mcal López y Talavera,
T42369. With bath and a/c, cheaper with
fan, friendly.
F-G Central Comuneros y Pa'í Anasagasti,
by Plaza Ybaroty at entrance to town. With bath,
a/c, electric shower, family run.

German colonies near Villarica *p1052*
Colonia Independencia
C-E Hotel Restaurant Panorama, set on
top of a hill on the road 12 km from Colonia
Independencia. German chalet-style
accommodation, also a good restaurant.
D-E Hotel Tilinski, out of town, T0548-265240,
F0548-265340. Peaceful, German spoken,
swimming pool (filled with river water),
meals for residents.
Camping There is camping nearby
at Melgarejo.

Between Coronel Oviedo and
Ciudad del Este *p1052*
B pp Estancia Golondrina, José Domingo
Ocampo, Km 235. Contact manager Gustavo
Helman (no English, but helpful) at T0527-20122
or 0971-410200 (mob), haraslapaz@ges
golondrina.com.py, or Asunción office T/F026-
2238/2893/2894 (weekdays only), acsilvero@
gesgolondrina.com.py, or through APATUR (see
Rural tourism, page 1046). Take the unpaved
road to the right, 17km to the ranch. A good
place for combining rural and ecotourism. The
ranch has extensive agricultural land as well as
12,000 ha of protected virgin forest and
abundant wildlife. There are trails for walking or
horse riding, boat trips on the river, and
picturesque accommodation (a/c, private
bathroom, very comfortable) overlooking the
river. Price includes all meals and transportation
from the main road.

Ciudad del Este *p1052, map p1052*
B Convair, Adrián Jara y García, T508555,
convairhotel@compacom.com.py. A/c,
comfortable, cheaper rooms without bath.
B Executive, Adrián Jara y Curupayty, T500942/3,
executive@fnn.net. Including a/c, breakfast –
restaurant recommended.
C Panorama Inn Pampliega y Eusebio Alaya,
T500110, HpanoRin@cde.reider.net.py. Modern,
corporate atmosphere, breakfast.
D California, C A López 642, T/F500350, hotelcal@
hotmail.com. Including breakfast, TV, a/c, several
blocks from commercial area, large, modern with
swimming pool, attractive gardens, restaurant.
D New Cosmos Apart-Hotel, Edif Cosmopolitan
1, Paí Pérez y Pampliega, T511030, F511090.
Apartment style with kitchenette and living room.
E Austria (also known as Viena), Fernández 165,
T504213/214, austriahotel@hotmail.com. Above
restaurant, good breakfast, a/c, Austrian family,
good views from upper floors. Warmly
recommended.
E Munich, Fernández y Miranda, T500347. With
breakfast, a/c, garage. Recommended.
F Caribe, Miranda y Fernández, opposite Hotel
Austria, T62450. A/c, hot water, nice, garden,
helpful owner. Recommended.
F Tía Nancy, Arturo Garcete y Cruz del Chaco,
by terminal, T502974. With electric shower, clean
and convenient for bus station.

🍴 Eating

Villarrica *p1052*
Many eating places on CA López and Gral Díaz.
Good restaurants are **La Tranquera** (good value,
more expensive at weekends), **Asunción**, **Casa
Vieja** and **La Cocina de Mamá**. At night on the
plaza with the Municipalidad stands sell tasty,
cheap steaks. Good nightclubs are **Monasterio**
(the most popular) and **La Tirana**, great
atmosphere.

German colonies near Villarica *p1052*
Colonia Independencia
Che Valle Mi, Sr Jacob Esslinger, Correo
Melgarejo. Recommended.
Ulli y Klaus, restaurant next door. Recommended.

Ciudad del Este *p1052, map p1052*
Cheaper restaurants along García and the market.
Hotel Austria (see above). Good-value
Austrian fare.
Mi Ranchero, Adrián Jara. Good food and prices.
New Tokyo, Arco Iris supermarket, Bernandino
Caballero. Good, authentic Japanese.
Osaka, Adrián Jara. Good, authentic Japanese.
Patussi Grill, Monseñor Francisco Cedzich casi
Av Alejo García. Good churrasquería.

Pub Cosmopolitan, same building as Cosmos Hotel. Local food.

⊖ Transport

Itauguá *p1050*
Bus Frequent from **Asunción**, 1 hr, US$0.30.

Aregua *p1050*
Bus From **Asunción**, Transportes Ypacaraínse, every 30 mins, but do not leave from the terminal; alternatively take local bus to Capiatá and change.

San Bernardino *p1050*
Bus From **Asunción**, 3 companies: Altos, Loma Grande and Ciudad de San Bernadino, every 10 mins, 45 km, 1-2 hrs, US$0.50.

Caacupé *p1050*
Bus From **Asunción**, US$0.50, get off at Basilica rather than Caacupé station.

Coronel Oviedo and around *p1051*
Salto del Guaíra
Bus To **Asunción**, US$9, 5 daily; to **Ciudad del Este**, US$7. **To Brazil** Regular launches cross the lake to Guaíra, 20 mins, US$1. Also an hourly bus service, 30 mins, US$1. Buses run north of the lake to Mondo Novo, where they connect with Brazilian services. Brazilian Consulate is at Destacamento de Caballería y Defensores del Chaco, T2333.

Villarrica *p1052*
Bus To **Coronel Oviedo**, US$1.50. To **Asunción**, frequent, US$3, 3½ hrs (Empresa Guaireña). Also direct service to **Ciudad del Este**, 4 daily, US$3.50, 4 hrs.

Colonia Independencia *p1052*
Bus Direct to **Asunción**, 3 daily (US$1.50, 4 hrs), as well as to **Villarrica**.

Ciudad del Este *p1052, map p1052*
Air Full jet airport, Aeropuerto Guaraní. To **Asunción**, TAM daily en route from São Paulo. TAM, Curupayty 195 y Eusebio Alaya, T506030-35.
Bus Terminal is on the southern outskirts, T510421 (No 4 bus from centre, US$0.40, taxi US$2.50, recommended). Many buses to and from **Asunción**, US$7.80 rápido, 4½ hrs, at night only; US$5.40 común, 5 hrs. **Nuestra Señora** recommended (they also have an office in Shopping Mirage, Pampliega y Adrián Jara), **Rysa** (T501201) and others. To **Villarrica**, 10 a day,

last 1620, 4 hrs, US$2.80 (**Guaireña**). To **Pedro Juan Caballero**, 7 hrs, overnight US$7.80. To **Concepción**, **García**, 11 hrs, 1 per day. To **Encarnación** (for Posadas and Argentina), paved road, frequent, 4 hrs, US$5 (this is probably cheaper than via Foz do Iguaçu).

Border with Brazil *p1052*
Bus The international bus goes from outside the Ciudad del Este terminal to the Rodoviária in Foz. There are also local buses from the terminal and along Av Adrián Jara, every 15 mins, 0600-2000, US$0.50, which go to the city terminal (terminal urbana) in Foz. Most buses will not wait at immigration, so disembark to get your exit stamp, walk across the bridge (10 mins) and obtain your entry stamp; keep your ticket and continue to Foz on the next bus free. Paraguayan taxis cross freely to Brazil (US$18), although they are not keen to, and it is cheaper and easier to walk across the bridge and then take a taxi, bargain hard. You can pay in either currency (and often in Argentine pesos). Obtain all necessary exit and entry stamps.
To Argentina Direct buses to **Puerto Iguazú**, leave frequently from outside the terminal, US$1. You need to get Argentine and Paraguayan stamps (not Brazilian), bus does not wait so keep ticket.

Itaipu and around: Hernandarias *p1053*
Bus Frequent from **Ciudad del Este**, US$0.40.

---

❶ Directory

Ciudad del Este *p1052, map p1052*
Banks Local banks (open Mon-Fri 0730-1100). Citibank, Adrián Jara y Curupayty. ATM, changes TCs, 0830-1200. **Amex**, Curupayty casi Adrián Jara, T502259. Dollars and guaraníes can be changed into reais in town. Several Casas de Cambio: **Cambio Guaraní**, Av Monseñor Rodríguez, changes TCs for US$0.50, branch on Friendship Bridge has good rates for many currencies including dollars and reais. **Cambios Alberdi**, Adrián Jara by Hotel Puerta del Sol, good rates. Casa de cambio rates are better than street rates. Money changers (not recommended) operate at the bus terminal but not at the Brazilian end of the Friendship Bridge.
Internet Setik Technology, Av 29 de Setiembre, T509009. Cyber Café, Shopping Mirage, Pampliega y Adrián Jara. **Telephones** Copaco, Alejo García y Pai Pérez, near centre on road to bus terminal, for international calls.

South of Asunción

Ruta 1 runs south from Asuncion to Encarnacion and the Argentine border. This is an attractive area of fertile landscapes, sleepy towns and the historically important Jesuits settlements, some of which have been extensivly restored.

Itá (Km 37) is famous for rustic pottery, but also sells wood, leather and textile items including hammocks. You can visit the workshop of **Rosa Brítez**, a local ceramics artist recognized by UNESCO. Its church, San Blas, was built in 1585 and the town has a lagoon which is reputed never to dry up.

Yaguarón
Founded in 1539, Yaguarón, Km 48, was the centre of the Franciscan missions in colonial times. At the centre of the town, marooned on an island of green, mown grass, stands the church of **San Buenaventura**, with its external bell-tower① *daily 0700-1100, 1330-1630, on Sun morning only.* The simplicity and symmetry of the exterior is matched by the ornate carvings and paintings of the interior. The tints, made by the *indígenas* from local plants, are still bright on the woodcarvings and the angels have Guaraní faces. Built in Hispano-Guaraní Baroque style by the Franciscan order between 1755 and 1772, it was reconstructed in 1885 and renovated in the late 20th century. Stations of the Cross behind the village lead to a good view of the surroundings.

Museo Del Doctor Francia ① *leaving the church, 500 m down the road to your left, Tue-Sun 0730-1130, free guided tour in Spanish*, with artefacts from the life of Paraguay's first dictator, 'El Supremo', plus paintings and artefacts from the 18th century. The 18th-century single-storey adobe building with bamboo ceilings and tiled roof belonged to Francia's father. Fiesta patronal is in mid-July. There are a few basic hotels (**G**).

Paraguarí and around → *Colour map 6, grid C6. Population: 5,725.*
Founded 1775 (Km 63), the north entrance to the mission area, at the foot of a range of hills. Its restored church has two bell towers, separate from the main structure. Buses between Asunción and Encarnación stop here. There is an interesting Artillery Museum inside the nearby military base with cannons and artefacts from the Chaco War. You can stroll to the top of Cerro Perõ for views from the cross on top. More challenging is a one-hour climb through dense forest to the summit of Cerro Jhu, ask for directions in Barrio San Miguel behind the abandoned train station.

Supucay, 25 km east of Paraguarí, is the location of the **workshops** ① *Mon-Fri, take a bus from Asunción at 0700, 1200, 88 km, 3 hrs, US$1*, for the wood-burning steam locomotives. There are cheap *hospedajes*.

Northeast from Paraguarí 15 km is **Chololó** ① *bus US$0.45*, with a small but attractive series of waterfalls and rapids with bathing facilities and walkways, mainly visited in the summer.

Parque Nacional Ybycuí
At **Carapeguá**, Km 84 (*hospedaje* on main street, basic, friendly; blankets and hammocks to rent along the main road, or buy your own, made locally and cheaper than elsewhere), a road turns off to Acahay, Ybycuí and the **Parque Nacional Ybycuí** ① *0800-1700, for camping get a permit from the Environmental Department, Madame Lynch 3500, in Asunción (see National parks, page 1036),* 67 km southeast, one of the most accessible National Parks, if you have a car and one of the few remaining areas of rainforest in eastern Paraguay. Founded in 1973, the 5,000 ha park includes one of the few remaining areas of rainforest in eastern Paraguay. Good walks, a beautiful campsite and lots of waterfalls. At the entrance is a well set out park and museum, plus the reconstructed remains of the country's first iron foundry (La Rosada). Crowded on Sunday but deserted the rest of the week. Guides available. The only shops (apart from a small one at the entrance selling drinks, eggs, etc, and a good T-shirt stall which helps support the park) are at **Ybycuí**, 30 km northwest.

Ruta 1 continues through **Villa Florida**, 162 km from Asunción, on the banks of the Río Tebicuary. Its a popular spot in January-February for its sandy beaches and the fishing is first-rate. The **Hotel Nacional de Villa Florida** (**E**), one of three such places run by Senatur (see also Vapor Cué, page 1051 and Ayolas, below, www.senatur.gov.py/hoteles.htm) would make a convenient place to stop when travelling on this route.

The next colony is **Obligado**; it has an ATM in the centre of town. About 5 km further north is **Bella Vista** (Km 42, ATM), where it is possible to visit various yerba mate plantations. The most geared for visitors is **Pajarito** ① *T0767-240240, www.pajarito.com.py. For those interested in mate see www.yerba-mate.info.*

⬤ Sleeping

Paraguarí and around *p1056*
G Hospedaje Bonanza, Gral Caballero ½ block from highway, T531-32320. Shared bath, fan, nice patio, basic. Owner Juan Aliendre is a composer, he plays and teaches the harp.

Ybycuí *p1056*
E Hotel Pytu'u Renda, Av General Caballero 509 y Quyquyho, T534-226364. Good food, cooking facilities.
Pensión Santa Rosa and **San Juan**, both **F**, latter has no sign but is nice.
Tourism farm B Estancia Santa Clara, Km 141, Ruta 1, Caapucú, T021-605729, www.estanciasantaclara.com.py. Rural activites in a beautiful setting between Paraguarí and San Ignacio Guazú, full board or visit for the day (does have a minizoo).

San Ignacio Guazú and around *p1057*
C Parador Piringó, Ruta 1, Km 223, T082-232913. Modern, on outskirts, with a/c, **E** pp without, recommended, restaurant open 24 hrs.
E La Casa de Loly, Mcal López casi Calle Última, San Ignacio, T082-232362, lacasadeloly@yahoo.com, on outskirts. Nice atmosphere, pool, a/c, with breakfast, other meals on request.
F pp Unión, San Ignacio, T082-232544. With bath, a/c and breakfast.
Camping is possible outside the town.

Ayolas, Santiago and San Cosme *p1057*
E Hotel Nacional de Ayolas, Av Costanera, T072-222273. Overlooking the river, popular with fishing groups. More info from Asunción tourist office, www.senatur.gov.py/hoteles.htm.

Encarnación *p1057, map p1058*
A-B Encarnación Resort Hotel, Villa Quiteria on outskirts Ruta 1, Km 2, T207250, www.encarnacionresorthotel.com.py. First class, comfortable, very well run. Highly recommended.
D Paraná, Estigarribia 1414, T204440. Good breakfast, helpful. Recommended.
E Cristal, Mcal Estigarribia 1157, T/F202371, cristalh@telesurf.com.py. Pool, restaurant, TV and a/c, helpful staff.
E Viena, PJ Caballero 568, T203486, beside Copaco. With breakfast, German-run, good food, garage.

F Acuario, J L Mallorquín 1550 casi 25 de Mayo, T/F202676, acuaris@telesurf.com.py. Pool, a/c, with breakfast.
F Central, Mcal López 542, Zona Baja, T203454. With breakfast, nice patio, German spoken.
F Germano, Cabañas y C A López, opposite bus terminal, T203346. **G** without bath or a/c, German and Japanese spoken, small, very accommodating. Highly recommended.
F Itapúa, C A López y Cabanas, T200239, SF205045, opposite bus station. Dark rooms, modern.
F Liz, Av Independencia 1746, T202609. Comfortable, restaurant, recommended.

Santísima Trinidad del Paraná and Jesús de Tavarangüe *p1058*
B Hotel Tirol, Ruta 6 at Km 18.5, by Capitán Miranda, T071-202388, www.hoteltirol.com.py. Has chalets, cheaper without pool view, swimming pools filled freezing cold spring water, restaurant with plain cuisine, and beautiful views.
G pp León, a good hotel and restaurant next to the entrance to the hilltop site of the Jesuit reducción at Trinidad.
Centro Social, Trinidad. Food and shower available, take sleeping gear.
Camping is permitted behind the souvenir stall at Trinidad. No facilities and beware theft.

German colonies on the road to Ciudad del Este *p1058*
B Biorevital Hotel and Spa, Av Mcal López 275, Obligado, T0717-20073, www.spa-kur.com.py. German run, includes all meals, all organic food, swimming pools with mineral water, yoga, internet, homeopathic treatments.
C Papillón, Ruta 6, Km 44, Bella Vista, T0767-240235, www.papillon.com.py. A/c, internet, pool, gardens, very pleasant, German, French, English, Flemish spoken, excellent and popular restaurant, full and half-board available. Highly recommended. Organizes excursions in the area including in a light aircraft.
E Plaza, Samaniego 1415, Bella Vista, T0757-240236.

🍴 Eating

Paraguarí and around *p1056*
La Frutería, about 2½ km before the town. Wide selection of fruit, outdoor seating and a restaurant serving *empanadas*, hamburgers, beer, fruit salad.

Encarnación *p1057, map p1058*
🍴 **American Grill**, Av Irrazábal just before International Bridge. Good *churrasquería*.
🍴 **Parrillada las Delicias**, Estigarribia 1694. Good steaks, comfortable, Chilean wines.
🍴 **Provenza**, Dr Mallorquín, just past the rail tracks. International cuisine.
🍴 **Tokio**, Mcal Estigarribia 472. Good Japanese, real coffee.
🍴-🍴 **Cuarajhy**, Estigarribia y Pereira. Terrace seating, good food, open 24 hrs.
🍴-🍴 **Hiroshima**, 25 de Mayo y L Valentinas (no sign), T206288. Excellent Japanese, wide variety, fresh sushi, Tue-Sun 1130-1400, 1900-2330.
🍴 **Rubi**, Mcal Estigarribia 519. Chinese, good.

⊖ Transport

Yaguarón *p1056*
Bus Every 15 mins from **Asunción**, US$0.50.

Paraguarí and around *p1056*
Bus City buses leave from lower level of the Asunción terminal every 15 mins throughout the day, but much faster to take an Encarnación-bound bus from the upper level, same fare US$0.80.

Parque Nacional Ybycuí *p1056*
Bus There are 2 per day, 1000 and 1600 from **Ybycuí**, US$0.50, take bus going to the Mbocaya Pucú colony that stops in front of the park entrance. Hitching is easy. From Asunción take a bus to Acahay, **Transportes Emilio Cabrera**, 8 daily and change, or bus to Ybycuí, 0630, US$1.30.

San Ignacio Guazú *p1057*
Bus Regular services to/from **Asunción**, US$4 común, US$6.50 rápido; to **Encarnación**, frequent, US$5 común, US$7.50 rápido.

Santa María
Bus From **San Ignacio** from the Esso station, 6 a day from 0500, 45 mins.

San Cosme y Damián
Bus From **Encarnación**, La Cosmeña and Perla del Sur, US$2.50, 2½ hrs.

Encarnación *p1057, map p1058*
Bus The bus terminal is at Estigarribia y Memmel. Good cheap snacks. To/from **Asunción**, Alborada, Encarnaceña (recommended, T203448), **Flecha de Oro, Rysa, Nuestra Señora de la Asunción**, all except latter at least 4 a day, 6 hrs, US$12. Stopping (común) buses are cheaper, but much slower (6-7 hrs). To **Ciudad del Este**, US$5, several daily, 4 hrs.

Border with Argentina *p1057*
Bus Take any 'Posadas/Argentina' bus from opposite bus terminal over the bridge, US$0.60, 30 mins. Bus passengers should keep all luggage with them and should retain bus ticket; buses do not wait. After formalities (queues common), use ticket on next bus. **Taxi** costs US$5. **Cycles** are not allowed to use the bridge, but officials may give cyclists a lift. **Ferry** costs US$1: immigration formalities must be undertaken at the main offices.

Santísima Trinidad del Paraná and Jesús de Tavarangue *p1058*
Bus Many go from **Encarnación** to and through Trinidad, take any bus from the terminal marked Hohenau or Ciudad del Este, US$1 (beware overcharging). A **taxi** tour from Encarnación costs about US$20. Bus direct **Encarnación-Jesús** 0800; buses run **Jesús-Trinidad** every hr (30 mins, US$0.40), from where it is easy to get back to Encarnación, so do Jesús first. Last bus Jesús-Trinidad 1700; also collective taxis, return Trinidad-Jesús US$3.50. No buses on Sun. Enquire locally as taxis try to overcharge.

🛈 Directory

Encarnación *p1057, map p1058*
Banks Most banks now in the upper town, eg **Banco Continental**, Mcal Estigarribia 1418, Visa accepted. **Lloyds TSB Bank**, Mcal Estigarribia y Av G Caballero, Visa ATM, Mon-Fri 0845-1215. **Citibank**, Mcal Estigarribia y Villarrica, ATM. Casas de cambio for cash on Mcal Estagarribia (eg **Cambios Financiero** at No 307, **Cambio Iguazú** at No 211). **Cambio Chaco** Irrazábal casi Memmel, inside Superseis supermarket. Money changers at the Paraguayan side of the bridge but best to change money in town.
Consulates Argentina, Artigas 960, T201066, Mon-Fri 0800-1300. Brazil, Memmel 452, T206335. Germany, Memmel 631, T204041, F202682. **Telephones** Copaco, Capitán PJ Caballero y Mcal López, 0700-2200, only Spanish spoken.

North of Asunción

The winding Río Paraguay is 400 m wide and is the main trade route for the products of northern Paraguay. Boats carry cattle, hides, yerba mate, tobacco, timber and quebracho, a tree that provides the purest form of tannin. On the river, a boat trip to Concepción is one of the most interesting ways to see the country. East of the river, towards Brazil, is the historically significant Cerro Corá national park.

Asunción to Concepción

North from Asunción by river, you pass Villa Hayes where the bridge marks the beginning of the Trans-Chaco Highway. Further upstream is Puerto Antequera and 100 km beyond is Concepción. **By road there are two alternative routes**. One is via the Trans-Chaco Highway and Pozo Colorado. The Pozo Colorado-Concepción road, 146 km, is now completely paved. This route offers spectacular views of birdlife. Via Ruta 2 to Coronel Oviedo, Ruta 3 to Yby Yaú (paved) and thence west along Ruta 5 (paved). North of Coronel Oviedo, at Tacuara (Km 225), a road heads west to Rosario, from where you can visit the Mennonite community of **Colonia Volendam**, nine hours by bus from Asunción (two a day, San Jorge, US$3). German and Spanish are spoken here.

Concepción → *Phone code: 031. Colour map 6, grid B6. Population: 35,000.*

A free port for Brazil, Concepción, 312 km north of Asunción, stands on the east bank of the Río Paraguay. To appreciate the colonial aspect of the city, walk away from the main commercial streets. At Plaza La Libertad are the Catedral and Municipalidad (undergoing restoration in 2006). Sunsets from the port are beautiful. The town is the trade centre of the north, doing a considerable business with Brazil. The **Brazilian Consulate** ① *Pdte Franco 972, T42655, vcconcep@telesurf.com.py*, issues visas Monday-Friday 0800-1400. The market, a good place to try local food, is east of the main street, Agustín Pinedo (which is a kind of open-air museum). From here Avenida Pdte Franco runs west to the port. Along Avenida Agustín Pineda is a large statue of María Auxiliadora with Christ child. There are stairs to balconies at the base of the monument which offer good views of the city. The **Museo Municipal** ① *Mcal López y Cerro Corá, Mon-Fri 0700-1200*, contains a collection of guns, religious art and other objects. Plaza Agustín Fernando de Pinedo has a permanent craft market. About 9 km south is a bridge across the Río Paraguay, which makes for an interesting walk across the shallows and islands to the west bank, about an hour return trip, taxi US$6. The island in the Río Paraguay facing Concepción is Isla Chaco'I, where you can stroll through the fields. Row boats take passengers to the island from the shore next to the port, US$0.20 per person.

East of Concepción

There is a 215-km road (Ruta 5 – fully paved) from Concepción, eastwards to the Brazilian border. This road goes through Horqueta, Km 50, a cattle and lumber town of 10,000 people. Further on the road is very scenic. From **Yby Yaú** (junction with Ruta 8 south to Coronel Oviedo) the road continues to Pedro Juan Caballero.

Six kilometres east of Yby Yaú a road branches off to the very pleasant, uncrowded **Parque Nacional Cerro Corá** (22,000 ha), which is the site of Mariscal Francisco Solano López' death and the final defeat of Paraguay in the War of the Triple Alliance. There is a monument to him and other national heroes; the site is constantly guarded. It has hills and cliffs (some with pre-Columbian caves and petroglyphs), camping facilities, swimming and hiking trails. The rocky outcrops are spectacular and the warden, Carmelo Rodríguez, is helpful and will provide free guides. When you have walked up the road and seen the line of leaders' heads, turn right and go up the track passing a dirty-looking shack (straight on leads to a military base). Administration office is at Km 180 on Ruta 5, 5 km east of the main entrance.

Pedro Juan Caballero → *Phone code: 036. Colour map 7, grid B1. Population: 65,000.*

Pedro Juan Caballero This border town is separated from the Brazilian town of Ponta Porã, by a road (Dr Francia on the Paraguayan side, on the Brazilian side either Rua Marechal Floreano or Avenida Internacional): anyone can cross as they please (see below for immigration formalities). Ponta Porã is the more modern and prosperous of the two. In addition to liquor and electronics, everything costs less on the Paraguayan side. **Shopping China** is a vast emporium on the eastern outskirts of town and **Maxi** is a large well stocked supermarket in the centre. You can pay in guaraníes, reais or US$, at good exchange rates. **Arte Paraguaya**, Mariscal López y Alberdi, has a good selection of crafts from all over the country.

Border with Brazil

This is a more relaxed crossing than Ciudad del Este. For day crossings you do not need a stamp, but passports must be stamped if travelling beyond the border towns. Paraguayan **migraciones** ① *T36-72195, Mon-Fri 0700-2100, Sat 0800-2100, Sun 1900-2100, take bus line 2 on the Parguside, or any Brazilian city bus that goes to the Rodoviaria, taxi US$4*, is in the customs building on the eastern outskirts of town near *Shopping China*. Then report to Brazilian federal police in Ponta Porã (closed Sat-Sun). The **Brazilian consulate** ① *Mcal Estigarribia, casi Carlos Antonio López, T/F36-72218, Mon-Fri 0800-1300*, issues visas, fees payable only in guaraníes, take passport and a photo, go early to get visa the same day. There is another crossing to Brazil at Bella Vista on the Río Apá, northwest of PJ Caballero; buses run from the Brazilian border town of Bela Vista to Jardim and on to Campo Grande. There is Paraguayan **migraciones** at Bella Vista there but no Brazilian Policia Federal in Bela Vista. To cross here, get Paraguayan exit stamp then report to the local Brazilian police who may give a temporary stamp, but you must later go to the Policia Federal in either Ponta Porã or Corumbá.

⊜ Sleeping

Asunción to Concepción *p1061*
B pp **Estancia Jejui**, set on the Río Jejui, 65 km north of Tacuara on Ruta 3, address in Asunción, Telmo Aquino 4068, T021-600227, www.coinco. com.py/jejui. All rooms with a/c, bathroom and hot water, fishing, horse riding, tennis, boat rides extra, US$60 pp including all meals.
F pp **Hotel Waldbrunner**, Colonia Volendam, T0451-20175. Bath, G without a/c, good restaurant.

Concepción *p1061*
C **Francés**, Franco y C A López, T42383. With a/c, D with fan, breakfast, rooms are aging, nice grounds with pool (US$1.50 non-guests), restaurant, parking.
C **Victoria**, Franco y Caballero, T42256. Nice rooms, a/c, fridge, D with fan (basic), restaurant, parking.
D **Concepción**, Don Bosco y Cabral near market, T42360. With simple breakfast, a/c, E with fan, family run, good value.

Pedro Juan Caballero *p1061*
A **Hotel Casino Amambay**, Av Dr Francia 1 at the west end of town, T72200, hcassino@uol.com.br. A posh establishment centred around its casino, simple rooms compared to its surroundings, include buffet breakfast, a/c, fridge, balcony, lovely grounds with large pool.
B-C **La Siesta**, Alberdi 30 y Dr Francia, T73021. With breakfast, a/c, fridge, balcony, restaurant, pool, aging but still OK, rooms in upper floor have been refurbished and are nicer.

C **Eiruzú**, Mcal López y Mcal Estigarribia, T72435. With breakfast, a/c, fridge and pool, starting to show its age but still good.
E **La Victoria**, Teniente Herrero y Alberdi, near bus station, T72733. With breakfast, electric shower and a/c, cheaper with fan, family run, simple.

⊘ Eating

Concepción *p1061*
♥ **Hotel Francés**, good value buffet lunch, à la carte in the evening.
♥ **Hotel Victoria**, set lunches and à la carte, grill in *quincho* across the street.
♥ **Pollería El Bigote**, Pdnte Franco y E A Garay. Simple, good chicken, sidewalk seating.
♥ **Ysapy**, Yegros y Mcal Estigarribia at Plaza Pineda. Pizza and ice-cream, terrace or sidewalk seating, very popular, daily 1630-0200.

Pedro Juan Caballero *p1061*
♥ **Mr Grill** at *Maxi* supermarket, Mcal López y J Estigarribia. Good quality buffet by the kilo.
♥ **Pepes**, Dr Francia y Alberdi. Buffet, à la carte.
♥ **Pizza House**, Mcal López y José de J Martínez.

⊖ Transport

Concepción *p1061*
Bus The terminal is on the outskirts, 8 blocks north along Gral Garay, but buses also stop in the centre, Av Pinedo, look for signs Parada Omnibus. A shuttle bus (Línea 1) runs between the terminal and the port. Taxi from terminal or port to centre, US$1.75; terminal to port U$2.50. To **Asunción**, 7 a day with **Nasa/Golondrina**, 2 with

Santaniana, plus other companies, US$10, 5½ hrs via Pozo Colorado, 9 hrs via Coronel Oviedo. To **Pedro Juan Caballero**, frequent service, several companies, **Amambay** is best, US$4.50, 4-5 hrs. To **Horqueta**, 1 hr, US$1. To **Filadelfia**, Nasa/Golondrina direct at 0730 daily, US$10, 5 hrs, otherwise change at Pozo Colorado. To **Ciudad del Este**, García direct at 1230 daily, US$12, 9 hrs, otherwise change at Coronel Oviedo.

Boat To **Asunción**, the Cacique sails Sun 0700 (in theory), 22 hrs, tickets sold on board in advance of departure (fares and other services on p 1048). To **Fuerte Olimpo**, **Bahía Negra**, and intermediate points along the upper Río Paraguay, the **Río Aquidabán** sails Tue 1100, arriving Bahía Negra on Fri morning and returning immediately to arrive back in Concepción on Sun, US$15 to Bahía Negra plus US$8.50 for a berth if you want one. Take food and water. Tickets sold in office just outside the port, T42435, Mon-Sat 0700-1200. There is no regular boat service beyond Bahía Negra for Bolivia or Brazil. *Desplizadores* (motor launches) may be hired but beware overcharging and seek advice from the Prefecura Naval. **Note** Since there is no immigration office in Concepción nor further upriver, the last place to get an exit stamp is Asunción, although they may refuse and send you to a land border instead. In all, a time consuming, adventurous and expensive journey.

Pedro Juan Caballero *p1061*
Air TAM, Curupayty y Mariscal López, T74501, to **Asunción**, Mon-Fri, US$55. Airport is 30 km from town on road to Yby Yaú, TAM has free shuttle bus before flights, taxi US$17.
Bus To **Concepción**, frequent, 4-5 hrs, US$4.50. To **Asunción**, 5-6 hrs via 25 de Diciembre, 7½ hours via Coronel Oviedo. **Santaniana** has nicest

buses, *bus cama* US$12; *semicama* US$10. **Amambay** 0700 via Oviedo US$10, twice via 25 de Diciembre, US$11. **Nasa** 2 a day US$10. To **Bella Vista**, Perpetuo Socorro 3 a day, US$4.20, 4 hrs. To **Campo Grande** **Amambay** 3 a day, US$13, 5 hrs, they stop at Policia Federal in Ponta Porã for entry stamp. **Nacional Expresso** to **Brasília** via Campo Grande and Goiânia, US$55, 22 hrs.

❶ Directory

Concepción *p1061*
Banks Nowhere to change TCs. **Norte Cambios**, Pres Franco y 14 de Mayo, Mon-Fri 0830-1700, Sat 0830-1100, fair rates for US$ and euros, cash only. **Financiera Familiar**, Pres Franco y Gral Garay, US$ cash only.
Internet Cybercom Internet Café, Pres Franco casi 14 de Mayo, open until 2230. **Post office** Presidente Franco. **Telephone** Copaco and other cabinas on Pres Franco.

Pedro Juan Caballero *p1061*
Banks Many *cambios* on the Paraguayan side, especially on Curupayty between Dr Francia and Mcal López. Good rates for buying guaraníes or reais with US$ or euros cash, better than inside Brazil, but TCs are difficult to change and there is only one ATM. Banks on Brazilian side do not change cash or TCs but have a variety of ATMs. **BBVA**, Dr Francia y Mcal Estigarribia. Mon-Fri 0845-1300, changes US$ cash to guaraníes only, and Cirrus ATM. **Norte Cambios**, Curupayty entre Dr Francia y Mcal López, Mon-Fri 0830-1630, Sat 0830-1100, fair rates for cash, 3% commission for TCs. **Internet** Several places including Maxi supermarket, spacious, quiet, a/c, US$0.80 per hr. **Telephones** Copaco, behind the bus station, plus many *cabinas*.

The Chaco

West of the Río Paraguay is the Chaco, a remarkable area of marshes and farmland, with a substantial population of indigenous peoples. Birdlife is spectacular and common. Apart from the large cattle estancias, agriculture in the Chaco has been developed by German-speaking Mennonites. Through this partly tamed land the Trans-Chaco Highway runs to Bolivia. Most of the region is pristine, perfect for those who want to escape into the wilderness with minimal human contact and experience nature at its finest.

Ins and outs
Getting there The Paraguayan Chaco covers 24 million ha, but once away from the vicinity of Asunción, the average density is less than one person to the sq km. A single major highway, the Ruta Trans-Chaco, runs in a straight line northwest towards the Bolivian border. It is paved and in excellent condition as far as La Patria, 125 km beyond Mariscal Estigarribia (Paraguayan immigration post). Paving continues between La Patria and Infante Rivarola on the Bolivian frontier. Until paving is completed, those travelling by bus are advised to take their own food

and water for a few days as buses may get stuck for a week or more. They depart regardless of road conditions and simply go until they get bogged, then wait for a tractor to pull them out. When completed (no firm date) the Trans-Chaco will be part of a *corredor bi-oceánico*, connecting ports on the Pacific and Atlantic oceans. The elevation rises very gradually from 50 m opposite Asunción to 450 m on the Bolivian border.▶▶ *For further information, see Transport, page 1068.*

Getting around Most bus companies have some a/c buses on their Chaco routes (a great asset December-March), enquire in advance. There is very little local public transport between the three main Mennonite towns, you must use the buses headed to/from Asunción to travel between them as well as Mariscal Estigarribia. No private expedition should leave the Trans-Chaco without plentiful supplies of water, food and fuel. No one should venture onto the dirt roads alone. (And since this is a major smuggling route from Bolivia, it is unwise to stop for anyone at night.) In the Middle and Low Chaco, there are service stations at regular intervals along the highway; beyond Mariscal Estigarribia there is one stop for diesel. Winter temperatures are warm by day, cooler by night, but summer heat and mosquitoes can make it very unpleasant (pyrethrum coils – *espirales* – are available throughout the region).

Information Consejo Regional de Turismo Chaco Central (CONRETUR) coordinates tourism development of the three cooperatives and the private sector. Contact **Hans Fast** ① *T492-52422, Loma Plata, fast@telesurf.com.py.* The **Fundación para el Desarrollo Sustentable del Chaco** ① *in Loma Plata, T492-52235, www.desdelchaco.org.py*, operates conservation projects in the area and has useful information but does not offer tours. ▶▶ *For tour operators, see page 1067. See also under individual towns for local tourist offices.*

Background
The Low Chaco (the most highly populated part of the Chaco) is just west of Asunción across the Río Paraguay. It is a picturesque area of palm savanna, much of which is seasonally inundated because of the impenetrable clay beneath the surface, although there are 'islands' of high ground. Cattle ranching on gigantic estancias is the prevailing economic activity; some units lie several hundred kilometres down tracks off the highway. Remote estancias have their own airfields, and all are equipped with two-way radios.

In the **Middle Chaco**, the natural vegetation is scrub forest, with a mixture of hardwoods, and cactus in the north. The palo borracho (bottle-tree) with its pear-shaped, water-conserving, trunk, the palo santo, with its green wood and beautiful scent, and the tannin-rich *quebracho* (axe-breaker) are the most important native species. This is the best area in Paraguay to see large mammals, especially once away from the central Chaco Mennonite colonies.

The **High Chaco** is characterized by low dense thorn forest which has created an impenetrable barricade of spikes and spiny branches resistant to fire, heat and drought, very tough on tyres. Towards Bolivia cactus becomes more prevalent as rainfall decreases. There are a few estancias towards the south, where the brush is bulldozed into hedges and the trees left for shade. Summer temperatures often exceed 45°C.

Reserva de la Biósfera del Chaco
This 7.4-million-ha biosphere reserve in the Chaco and Pantanal eco-systems includes six national parks, monuments and indigenous reserves: Defensores del Chaco, Médanos del Chaco, Teniente Enciso, Cerro Cabrera-Timane, Cerro Chovoreca, and Río Negro. All are north of the Trans-Chaco and most are along the Bolivian border. Teniente Enciso is the smallest park and the only one accessible by public transport, although not easily, see below. The others can only be visited with a private 4WD vehicle or on expensive tours from Loma Plata and Asunción. Most of the country's remaining jaguars are found here. Puma, tapir and peccary also inhabit the area, as well as taguá (an endemic peccary) and a short-haired guanaco, possibly a new sub-species (discovered in Médanos del Chaco in 2003). The best time to see them is, with great patience, around water holes at nightfall. Cerro León (highest peak 600 m), the only hilly area of the Chaco, is located in the park. This road from Filadelfia is very rough, 4WD vehicles only.

Parque Nacional Defensores del Chaco, some 220 km from Filadelfia, has three visitors sites with accommodation, a/c, kitchen, shared bath. Distances are long between sites, visitors may be able to travel with rangers, but cannot count on this. **Parque Nacional**

Teniente Enciso, 20 km from La Patria, has a nice visitor's site with free accommodation, one room with bath, others shared, a/c, take sleeping bag and all food. **Nasa** minibus from Filadelfia to Teniente Enciso via Mariscal Estigarribia and La Patria, see Transport, page 1068.

The Trans-Chaco Route

To reach the Ruta Trans-Chaco, you leave As unción by the route across the Río Paraguay to Villa Hayes. Birdlife is abundant and visible in the palm savannah, but other wild animals are usually only seen at night, and otherwise occur mostly as road kills. The first service station after Asunción is at Km 130. **Pirahú**, Km 252, has a service station and is a good place to stop for a meal; it has a/c, good empanadas and fruit salad. The owner of the parador owns an old-fashioned carbon manufacturing site 2 km before Pirahú. Ask for him if you are interested in visiting the site. At Km 271 is **Pozo Colorado**, the turning for Concepción (see page 1061). There are two restaurants, a basic hotel (**F** pp with fan, cheaper without), supermarket, hospital, a service station and a military post; for hitching, try truck drivers at the truck stop. The Touring y Automóvil Club Paraguayo provides a breakdown and recovery service from Pozo Colorado (To93-516). At this point, the tidy Mennonite homesteads, surrounded by flower gardens and citrus orchards, begin to appear. At Km 282 is one of the most pleasant places to stay or eat, Rancho Buffalo Bill, 14 km northwest of Pozo Colorado, To21-298381.The restaurant, set beside a small lake, is in a picturesque thatched roof log cabin. Excellent homemade food, a/c. The estancia has 10,000 ha, limited but good accommodation (**D**), ask at restaurant. Horse riding, ecological walks and camping possible. At Km 320 is **Río Verde**, with fuel, police station and restaurant. The next acceptable place to stay or eat on the Trans-Chaco is **Cruce de los Pioneros**, at Km 415, a weekend excursion from Asunción where accommodation (**D** Los Pioneros, T491-32170, hot shower, a/c), limited supermarket, vehicle repair shop, and fuel are available. A new paved road is being built from Cruce Boquerón, northwest of Cruce de los Pioneros, to Loma Plata.

The Mennonite communities

The Middle Chaco near Filadelfia has been settled by Mennonites, Anabaptists of German extraction who began arriving in the late 1920s. There are three administratively distinct but adjacent colonies: Menno (from Russia via Canada); Fernheim (directly from Russia) and Neuland (the last group to arrive, also from Russia, after the Second World War). Among themselves, the Mennonites speak 'plattdeutsch' ('Low German'), but they readily speak and understand 'hochdeutsch' ('High German'), which is the language of instruction in their schools. Increasingly, younger Mennonites speak Spanish, while English is not unknown. The people are friendly and willing to talk about their history and culture. Altogether there are 150 villages with a population of about 15,000 Mennonites and 20,000 *indígenas*. Increasing numbers of Paraguayans are migrating to the area in search of economic opportunities while indigenous people (eight distinct groups) occupy the lowest rung on the socioeconomic ladder.

The Mennonites have created a remarkable oasis of regimented prosperity in this harsh hinterland. Their hotels and restaurants are impeccably clean, services are very efficient, large modern supermarkets are well stocked with excellent dairy products and all other goods, local and imported. Each colony has its own interesting museum. All services, except for hotels, a few restaurants and one gas station in Filadelfia, close on Saturday afternoon and Sunday. The main towns are all very spread out and have no public transport except for a few expensive taxis in Filadelfia, most residents use their private vehicles. Walking around in the heat and dust can be tiring. Transport between the three main towns is also limited, see Transport, page 1068.

Filadelfia → *Phone code: 0491. Colour map 6, grid B5. Population: 4,100.*

Filadelfia (Fernheim Colony), 466 km from Asunción, the largest town of the region, feels least like a Mennonite colony and is increasingly mainstream Paraguayan. The **Unger Museum** ① *US$1 including video*, provides a glimpse of pioneer life in the Chaco, as well as exhibiting artefacts of the aboriginal peoples of the region. The Manager of the Hotel Florida will open the museum upon request, when things are not too busy. Next to the museum is **Plaza de los Recuerdos**, a good place to see the *samu'u* or *palo borracho* (bottle tree). A craft shop, Librería El Mensajero, next to Hotel Florida, is run by Sra Penner, very helpful and informative.

The Fernheim community does not encourage tourism hence there is no tourist office in Filadelfia. General information may be obtained from the co-op office.

Loma Plata → *Phone code: 0492. Population: 3,364.*

The centre of the largest of the colonies, Menno, Loma Plata is 25 km east of Filadelfia. Although slightly smaller than Filadelfia, it has more to offer the visitor. Good museum **Museo de la Colonia Menno** ① *Mon-Fri 0700-1130, 1400-1800; Sat 0700-1300, free, but a fee of US$1.50 may be introduced.* **Balneario Oasis swimming complex** ① *Nord Grenze, 700 m past airport north of Loma Plata, T52704, US$1.50, Sep-Apr 1500-2100, except Sun and holidays, 1100-2100.* Three pools with slides and snack bar. A welcome break from the summer heat. **Tourist office** (contact Walter Ratzlaff) ① *next to the Chortitzer Komitee Co-op, T492-52301, turismo@chortitzer.com.py, Mon-Fri 0700-1130, 1400-1800, Sat 0700-1300,* very helpful. For general information about the colony, not tourism, www.chortitzer.com.py.

Wetlands around Loma Plata To the southeast of Loma Plata is the Riacho Yacaré Chico watershed, with many salt water lagoons, generally referred to as Laguna Salada. This is a wonderful place to see bird life such as Chilean flamingos, swans, spoonbills and migratory shorebirds from the Arctic. There are extensive walks though the eerily beautiful landscape. **Laguna Capitán**, a 22-ha recreation reserve, 30 km from town, has several small lagoons, a swimming lake, basic bunk bed accommodation (**F** per person, shared bath), kitchen facilities, meals on request, camping US$1 per person. Reserve directly at T0991-650101 or through the Cooperative information office in Loma Plata. There is no public transport. Taxi US$20 one way; full-day tour combining Laguna Capitán with visit to the Cooperative's installations and museum, US$60 per group plus transport. **Chaco Lodge**, a 2,500-ha-private reserve, 70 km from town, is a Ramsar wetland site (no accommodation despite the name). The lovely Laguna Flamenco is the main body of water surrounded by dry forest. Large numbers of Chilean flamingos and other water birds may be seen here. **Campo María**, a 4,500-ha reserve within the co-operative's land 90 km from town, also has a large lake and can be visited on a tour.

Indigenous Foundation for Agricultural and Livestock Development (FIDA) ① *30 km from Neuland, Filadelfia and Loma Plata, T0491-32116.* Located within Yalve Sanga, the first Indigenous version of the Mennonite cooperative colonies, this provides an interesting insight into the lives of the indigenous communities. Limited handicrafts available in the Yalva Sanga supermarket (better selection in Neuland).

Neuland → *Phone code: 0493. Population: approx 1,700.*

Neuland, also known as Neu-Halbstadt is 33 km south of Filadelfia, the centre of Neuland Colony. There is a small museum containing historical objects brought by the first Mennonites from Russia, set in the building of the first primary school of the area. **Neuland Beach Park** ① *US$1.40, swimming pool, in the centre of town, snack bar with a/c.* **Parque la Amistad**, 500 m past swimming pool, is 35 ha of natural vegetation where paths have been cleared for nature walks. Most spectacular are the wild orchids (September-October), cacti and bird life. Enrique (Heinz) Weibe is the official guide of the Neuland colony; also ask for Harry Epp ① *contact through Neuland Co-op office, T493-240201, chaco@neuland.com.py, Mon-Fri 0700-1130, 1400-1800, Sat 0700-1130*, who is very knowledgeable about the flora and fauna and is an informative and entertaining guide. He also gives tours of Neuland in a horse drawn buggy. Phone booths and post office are in centre of town next to the supermarket.

Around Neuland **Fortín Boquerón**, 27 km from Neuland, is the site of the decisive battle of Chaco War (September 1932) and includes a memorial, a small, well-presented museum and walks around the remainder of the trenches. **Campamento Aurora Chaqueña** is a park 15 km from town on the way to Fortín Boquerón, there is simple accommodation with fan (**G** per person, take your own food and water). **Parque Valle Natural**, 10 km from Neuland on the way to Filadelfia, is a *partillar*, a dry riverbed with natural brush around it and a few larger trees. Camping possible although there is only a small covered area.

Mariscal Estigarribia and on to Bolivia → *Colour map 6, grid B5.*

Around 525 Km from Asunción, Mariscal is a former garrison town with aspirations of becoming a transport hub once paving of the Trans-Chaco is completed. The few services are spread out over four km along the highway: three gas stations – the last reliable fuel supply on the Trans-Chaco, a couple of small expensive supermarkets, two mediocre hotels, and one remarkably excellent restaurant (see listings below). Better services are found in Filadelfia, Loma Plata and Neuland. The immigration office (24 hours) is at the southeast end of town near the Shell station. Customs is next door. All buses stop at the terminal (**Parador Aramí**), at the northwest end of town, where travellers entering from Bolivia are subject to thorough searches for drugs. The people are friendly and helpful. There is good birdwatching nearby along the dirt road called Picada 500, as well as some indigenous communities nearby where crafts are made.

There are no reliable services of any kind beyond Mariscal Estigarribia. In February 2006, the pavement ended at **La Patria**, 125 km northwest, where there is a petrol station selling only diesel fuel, and one small expensive shop. At La Patria the road divides: 128 km west to Infante Rivarola (being paved, in very poor condition while work progresses) continuing to Villamontes, Bolivia, with Bolivian immigration at Ibibobo; 128 km northwest to General Eugenio A Garay continuing to Boyuibe, Bolivia (unused except by smugglers; shifting sand makes it treacherous).

In Bolivia, from Villamontes or Boyuibe, a paved road runs north to Santa Cruz and south to Yacuiba on the Argentine border, see page 328. Take small denomination dollar notes as it is impossible to buy bolivianos before reaching Bolivia (if entering from Bolivia street changers in Santa Cruz sell guaraníes at good rates).

⬤ Sleeping

Filadelfia *p1065*
Accommodation in Filadelfia and elsewhere in the Chaco is heavily booked in Sep.
D Florida, Av Hindenburg 165-S opposite park, T32151/5, hotelflorida@telesurf.com.py. Breakfast, a/c, fridge, **F** in basic annex with shared bath, fan and without breakfast. Pool (US$1.40/hr for non-guests), restaurant (†) for buffet and à la carte.
D-E Golindrina, Av Hindenburg 635-S at entrance to town, T/F32643, www.hotelgolondrina.com. Modern, with breakfast, a/c and fridge, 4 types of room (cheapest with fan, shared bath and no breakfast), restaurant.

Loma Plata *p1066*
D-E Loma Plata Inn, Eligio Ayala y Dr Manuel Gondra, T53235. With buffet breakfast, large rooms, a/c, fridge, new in 2005.
D-E Palace, Av Fred Engen, T52180, hpalace@telesurf.com.py. With breakfast, TV, a/c, mini bar, decent restaurant in out-of-the-ordinary setting around indoor pool (free for diners), friendly staff, best facilities in town.
E Mora, Sandstrasse 803, T52255. With breakfast, a/c, new wing has spacious rooms with fridge, nice grounds, family run, good value, good breakfast, basic meals available on request. Recommended.
E Pensión Loma Plata, J B Reimer 1805, T52829. A/c, breakfast, comfortable rooms, homely atmosphere, very helpful, good value. Includes breakfast, other meals on request. Recommended.

Neuland *p1066*
D-E Hotel Boquerón, Av 1 de Febrero opposite the Cooperative, T0493-240311. With breakfast, a/c, cheaper in older wing without TV, restaurant.
F Parador HR, Av 1 de Febrero y C Talleres, T0493-240567. With breakfast, a/c, **G** with fan and shared bath, restaurant.

Mariscal Estigarribia *p1066*
D-E Parador Arami, northwest end of town and far from everything, also known as *la terminal*, T0494-247230. Functional rooms, a/c, meals on request, agents for Stel Turismo and Nasa bus lines.
F La Laguna, next to the Municipio. With bath, a/c, cheaper with fan, very small rooms, mosquitoes, nice garden but otherwise neglected.

⊘ Eating

Filadelfia *p1065*
† **El Girasol**, Unruh 126-E y Hindenburg. Good buffet and *rodizio*, cheaper without the meat. Mon-Sat 1100-1400, 1800-2300, Sun 1100-1400.

Loma Plata *p1066*
† **Chaco's Grill**, Av Dr Manuel Gondra, T52166. Open daily for buffet and *rodizio* plus à la carte, very good, patio, live music at weekends.
† **Norteño**, almost opposite supermarket. Good, simple, lunch till 1400 then open for dinner.
† **Pizzería San Marino**, Av Central y Dr Gondra. Pizza and German dishes, daily 1800-2300.

Mariscal Estigarribia *p1066*
† **Italiano**, at the southwest end of town behind the Shell station, T0494-247231. Excellent cooking with a European touch, top quality meat, large portions, an unexpected treat in the outback. Italian owner Mauricio is friendly and helpful, open daily for lunch and dinner.

▲▲ Activities and tours

Many agencies in Asunción offer Chaco tours. Note that some are just a visit to Rancho Buffalo Bill and do not provide a good overview of the natural or cultural attractions. Hans Fast and Harry Epp also run tours to national parks. In Loma Plata ask around for bicycle hire to explore nearby villages.

⊖ Transport

Filadelfia *p1065*

Bus From **Asunción**, Nasa/Golondrina, 5 daily; Stel Turismo, 1 overnight; **Ovetense** 2 daily; all 6-7 hrs, US$11. To **Loma Plata**, Nasa/Golondrina 0800 going to Asunción, 0600 and 1900 coming from Asunción, 1 hr, US$1.75. To **Neuland**, local service Mon-Fri 1130 and 1800, 1 hr, US$1.75. Also **Stel Turismo** at 1900 and Nasa/Golondrina at 2115, both coming from Asunción. To **Mariscal Estigarribia**, Ovetense at 1800 coming from Asunción, 1½ hrs, US$2. Also **Nasa** at 0500 Mon and Fri, continuing to La Patria and Parque Nacional Teniente Enciso (see page 1065), 5-6 hrs, US$8.50, returns around 1300 same day (new service in 2006, confirm all details in advance).

Loma Plata *p1066*

Bus **Asunción**, Nasa/Golondrina, 3 daily, 7-8 hrs, US$11. To **Filadelfia**, Mon-Fri 1300, Sat 1100, Sun 1200, daily 2130, all continuing to Asunción, 1 hr, US$1.75.

Neuland *p1066*

Bus To **Asunción**, Nasa/Golondrina 1t 1945, and **Stel Turismo** at 1800, via Filadelfia, 7-8 hrs, US$11. Local service to Filadelfia, Mon-Fri 0500, 1230, 1 hr, US$1.75.

Mariscal Estigarribia *p1066*

Bus From **Filadelfia** Nasa/Golondrina 1100 daily, **Ovetense** 1200 and 2000 daily; **Asunción** Nasa/Golondrina, Sun-Fri 2 daily, Sat one bus; Ovetense 2 daily, 7-8 hrs, US$11.0700. Buses from Asunción pass through town around 0300-0400 en route to Bolivia: **Yaciretá** on Tue, Thu, Sat, Sun (agent at Barcos y Rodados petrol

station, T0494-247320); **Stel Turismo** daily (agent at Parador Arami, T0494-247230). You can book and purchase seats in advance but beware overcharging, the fare from Mariscal Estigarribia should be about US$10 less than from Asunción.

ⓘ Directory

Filadelfia *p1065*

Banks There are no ATMS in the Chaco, neither in the Mennonite colonies nor in Mariscal Estigarribia. **Fernheim Cooperative Bank**, Hindenburg opposite the Cooperative building, changes US$ and euro cash, no commission for US$ TCs. **Internet** At Shopping Portal del Chaco and opposite **Radio ZP30**. **Telephone** Copaco on Hindenburg, opposite supermarket, Mon-Sat 0700-2100, Sun 0700-1200, 1500-2000.

Loma Plata *p1066*

Banks Chortitzer Komitee Co-op, Av Central, Mon-Fri 0700-1730, Sat 0700-1100, good rates for US$ and euros, US$1 commission per TC. **Internet Microtec**, Fred Engen 1229, Mon-Sat 0800-1130, 1400-2200, US$0.80 per hr. **Telephone** Copaco, Av Central across from supermarket, Mon-Sat 0700-2000, Sun 0700-1200, 1500-2000.

Neuland *p1066*

Banks Neuland Cooperative changes US$ cash and TCs, Mon-Fri 0700-1130, 1400-1800, Sat 0700-1130.

Mariscal Estigarribia *p1066*

Banks No banks or cambios. Shell station has best rates for US$, cash only, small bills preferred. **Telephones** Copaco, one street back from highway, ask for directions.

Peru

ssentials	**1070**
ima	**1079**
Sights	1081
uaraz and the Cordilleras	**1107**
Huaraz	1107
Cordillera Blanca	1115
Cordillera Huayhuash	1123
orth coast	**1124**
Trujillo and around	1127
Chiclayo and around	1137
Piura and around	1143
North to Ecuador	1146
orthern Highlands	**1151**
Trujillo to Cajamarca	1152
Chachapoyas Region	1158
Chachapoyas to the Amazon	1163
Chachapoyas to Ecuador	
and the coast	1166
outh coast	**1167**
South from Lima	1167
Nazca and around	1172
requipa and the	
far south	**1178**
Arequipa	1178
Colca Canyon	1188
Cotahuasi Canyon	1192
South to Chile	1193
ake Titicaca	**1196**
The islands	1203
To Cuzco	1204
Border with Bolivia	1206

Cuzco	**1208**
Southeast from Cuzco	1232
Sacred Valley of the Incas	**1234**
Machu Picchu	1240
Inca trails	1243
Vitcos and Vilcabamba	1246
West from Cuzco	1247
Central Highlands	**1248**
Lima to Huancayo	1248
Huancayo and around	1250
Huancavelica	1254
Ayacucho	1256
Ayacucho to Cuzco	1260
East and north of La Oroya	1262
Amazon Basin	**1266**
North from Huánuco	
to Pucallpa	1266
Yurimaguas and	
Pacaya-Samiria	1269
Iquitos and around	1271
Southeastern jungle	1277

🌡 Footprint features

Don't miss...	1069
Touching down	1073
Driving in Peru	1077
Inca society	1211

Introduction

Cuzco, capital of the Inca world, is now South America's main gringo hangout, with its access to Machu Picchu, the Sacred Urubamba Valley and a buzzing nightlife. On the border with Bolivia is Lake Titicaca, blessed with a magical light and fascinating islands. But in Peru, the Egypt of the Americas, this is just the tip of the pyramid.

The coastal desert may sound uninhabitable, yet pre-Inca cultures thrived there. They left their monuments in sculptures etched into the surface of the desert, most famously at Nasca. Civilization builders welcomed gods from the sea and irrigated the soil to feed great cities of adobe bricks. After the Incas came the Spanish *conquistadores*, who left some of their own finest monuments. You can trek for ever amid high peaks and blue lakes, cycle down remote mountainsides, look into canyons deeper than any others on earth, or surf the Pacific rollers. There are enough festivals to brighten almost every day of the year, while the spiritual explorer can be led down mystical paths by a shaman.

East of the Andes the jungles stretch towards the heart of the continent with some of the richest biodiversity on earth. And, should you tire of nature, there is always Lima, loud, brash, covered in fog, but with some of the best museums and liveliest nightlife in the country.

trekking and climbing elsewhere in the country. At this time the days are generally clear and sunny, though nights can be very cold at high altitude. The highlands can be visited at other times of the year, though during the wettest months November-April some roads become impassable and hiking trails can be very muddy.

The **jungle**: April-October, dry season, temperatures up to 35°C. This is the best time to visit the jungle. In the jungle areas of the south, a cold front can pass through at night. November-April, wet season, heavy rainfall at any time, humid and hot. During the wet season, it only rains for a few hours at a time, which is not enough to spoil your trip, but enough to make some roads virtually impassable.

Finding out more Tourism promotion and information is handled by **PromPerú** ① *Edif Mincetur, C Uno Oeste 50, p 13, urb Córpac, San Isidro, T01-224 3131, www.peru.info.* PromPerú runs an information and assistance service, **i perú** ① *T01-574 8000 (24 hrs). The main office in Lima is at Jorge Basadre 610, San Isidro, T421 1627, iperulima@ promperu.gob.pe, Mon-Fri 0830-1830. There is a 24-hr office at Jorge Chávez airport; there are offices around the country, addresses of which are given in the text.*

There are offices in most towns, either run by the municipality, or independently, which provide tourist information. Outside Peru, information can be obtained from Peruvian embassies and consulates. **Indecopi** ① *in Lima T224 7888, rest of Peru 0800-42579 (not available from payphones), www.indecopi.gob.pe,* is the government-run consumer protection and tourist complaint bureau. They are friendly, professional and helpful. An excellent source of information is **South American Explorers**, in Lima (see page 1080) and Cuzco. See also Essentials, page 32. They have information on travellers held in prison, some for up to one year without sentencing, and details on visiting regulations. A visit will be really appreciated!

Websites

www.**conam.gob.pe** National Environmental Commission (Spanish).

www.**perucultural.org.pe** Information on cultural activities, museums textiles (Spanish).

www.**yachay.com.pe** Red Científica Peruana, click 'Turismo' to get to travel page.

www.**adonde.com** and
www.**perulinks.com** are portals.

www.**terra.com.pe** Click 'Turismo' to get to travel page (in Spanish).

http://**travel.peru.com/travel/english** Peru.Com's travel page (English).

www.**traficoperu.com** Online travel agent with lots of information (Spanish and English).

www.**livinginperu.com** Informative guide in English for people living in Peru.

www.**perurail.com** Peru Rail.

www.**geocities.com/perutraveller/** (English)

www.**aboutcusco.com**,

www.**cuscoonline.com**, .
www.**cuscoperu.com**, and
www.**cusco.net** websites about Cuzco.

www.**machu-picchu.info** On Machu Picchu

www.**isidore-of-seville.com/machu** Lots of links to sites about Machu Picchu.

www.**yachay.com.pe/especiales/nasca** Nazca lines (in Spanish).

www.**arequipa-tourism.com** On Arequipa.

www.**andeanexplorer.com** and
http://**huaylas.com** For Huaraz and the Callejón de Huaylas, both in English.

www.**perunorte.com** Northern Peru (La Libertad, Cajamarca and Lambayeque), in Spanish, English and German.

www.**xanga.com/TrujilloPeru** Mainly for the north of the country, packed full of links.

www.**caretas.com.pe** The most widely-read weekly magazine, *Caretas*.

Maps The **Instituto Geográfico Nacional** in Lima sells a selection of maps, see page 1098. Lima 2000's *Mapa Vial del Perú* (1:2,200,000) is probably the most correct road map available. Maps can be obtained from the **South American Explorers**, who will give good advice on road conditions. The **Touring y Automóvil Club del Perú** ① *Av César Vallejo 699, Lince, Lima, T221 2432, www.touringperu.com.pe,* with offices in most provincial cities, gives news about the roads and hotels (for the most up-to-date information also try bus and colectivo offices). It sells a very good road map at US$5 (Mapa Vial del Perú, 1:3,000,000, Ed 1980) and route maps covering most of Peru. The *Guía Toyota* (Spanish), which is published annually, is one of the best guides for venturing off the beaten track. Other maps can be bought from street vendors in Colmena and Plaza San Martín, Lima. 'Westermanns Monatshefte; folio Ecuador, Peru, Bolivien' has excellent maps of Peru, especially the archaeological sites.

A good tourist map of the Callejón de Huaylas and Cordillera Huayhuash, by Felipe

Díaz, is available in many shops in Huaraz, including Casa de Guías. **Alpenvereinskarte Cordillera Blanca Nord 0/3a** and **Alpenvereinskarte Cordillera Blanca Süd 0/3b** at 1:100,000 are the best maps of that region, US$12, available in Huaraz and Lima, but best bought outside Peru. **Cordillera Huayhuash map,** 1:50,000 (The Alpine Mapping Guild, 2nd ed, 2004) is recommended, available in Huaraz at Café Andino, US$15.

Visas and immigration   Tourist cards: no visa is necessary for citizens of countries in the EU, Asia, North and South America, and the Caribbean, or for citizens of Andorra, Iceland, Liechtenstein, Norway, Switzerland, Australia, New Zealand and South Africa. A Tourist Card is free on flights arriving in Peru, or at border crossings for visits up to 90 days. Insist on getting the full 90 days. The form is in duplicate, the original given up on arrival and the copy on departure, and may be renewed (see below). A new tourist card must be obtained for each re-entry or when an extension is given. If your tourist card is stolen or lost, get a new one at **Inmigraciones** ① *Av España 700 y Av Huaraz, Breña, Lima, Mon-Fri 0900-1330.*

Tourist visas For citizens of countries not listed above (including Turkey), cost about US$38 or equivalent, for which you require a valid passport, a departure ticket from Peru (or a letter of guarantee from a travel agency), two colour passport photos, one application form and proof of economic solvency. Keep identification, preferably a passport, on you at all times. You must present your passport when reserving tickets for internal, as well as, international travel. An alternative is to photocopy the important pages of your passport – including the immigration stamp, and have it legalized by a 'Notario público' (US$1.50). This way you can avoid showing your passport. We have received no reports of travellers being asked for an onward ticket at the borders at Tacna, Aguas Verdes, La Tina, Yunguyo or Desaguadero. Travellers arriving by air are not asked for an onward flight ticket at Lima airport, but it is possible that you will not be allowed to board a plane in your home country without showing an onward ticket.

Renewals and extensions To extend a tourist card at Immigration in Lima (address above), go to the third floor and enter the long narrow hall with many 'teller' windows. Go to window number 5 and present your passport and tourist card. The official will give you a receipt for US$20 (the cost of a one-month extension) which you will pay at the Banco de la Nación on the same floor. Then go down to the first floor and buy form F007 for S/24 (US$6.75). Fill out the form and return to window 5 on the third floor. Give the official the paid receipt, the filled-out form, your passport and tourist card. Next, you will wait two minutes for your passport to be stamped and signed. **Note** Three extensions like this are permitted, although it's unlikely that you will be allowed to buy more than one month at a time. Peruvian law states that a tourist can remain in the country for a maximum of six months, after which time you must leave. Crossing the border out of Peru and returning immediately is acceptable. You will then receive another 90 days and the process begins all over again.

If you let your tourist visa expire you can be subject to a fine of US$20 per day, but this is up to the discretion of the immigration official. You can extend your visa in Lima, Cuzco, Puno, Puerto Maldonado, and Iquitos, but in the provinces it can take more time.

Business visas If a visitor is going to receive money from Peruvian sources, he/she must have a business visa: requirements are a valid passport, two colour passport photos, return ticket and a letter from an employer or Chamber of Commerce stating the nature of business, length of stay and guarantee that any Peruvian taxes will be paid. The visa costs £21.60 (or equivalent) and allows the holder to stay 90 days in the country. On arrival business visitors must register with the *Dirección General de Contribuciones* for tax purposes.

Student visas To obtain a one year student visa you must have: proof of adequate funds, affiliation to a Peruvian body, a letter of recommendation from your own and a Peruvian Consul, a letter of moral and economic guarantee from a Peruvian citizen and four photographs (frontal and profile). You must also have a health check certificate which takes four weeks to get and costs US$10. Also, to obtain a student visa, if applying within Peru, you have to leave the country and collect it in La Paz, Arica or Guayaquil from Peruvian immigration (it costs US$20).

Peruvian embassies and consulates Visit www.rree.gob.pe, the Ministry of Foreign Affairs website for details of Peruvian embassies and consulates.

Money
Currency The new sol (s/) is divided into 100 céntimos. Notes in circulation are: S/200, S/100, S/50, S/20 and S/10. Coins: S/5, S/2, S/1, S/0.50, S/0.20, S/0.10 and S/0.05 (being

‣ Touching down

Airport taxes US$30 on international flight departures, payable in dollars or soles; US$4.50 on internal flights (when making a domestic connection in Lima, you don't have to pay airport tax; contact airline personnel at baggage claim to be escorted you to your departure gate). 19% state tax is charged on air tickets; it is included in the price of the ticket.

Business hours Shops: 0900 or 1000-1230 and 1500 or 1600-2000. In the main cities, supermarkets do not close for lunch and Lima has some that are open 24 hours. Some are closed on Sat and most are closed on Sun. **Banks:** most banks around the country are open 0930-1200 and 1500-1800. Banks in Lima and Cuzco are open 0900/0945-1700/1800. Many banks in Lima and Cuzco have Sat morning hours from 0900-1200 or 1300. **Offices:** Continuous hours 0900-1700 and most close on Sat. **Government offices:** Mon-Fri 0830-1130, Jan-Mar. The rest of year Mon-Fri 0900-1230, 1500-1700, but this changes frequently.

In an emergency Tourist Police Administrative office at Jr Moore 268,

Magdalena at the 38th block of Av Brasil, Lima, T460 1060, daily 24 hrs; for public enquiries etc, Jr Pachitea at the corner of Belén, Lima, T424 2053. You should come here if you have had property stolen. They are friendly, helpful and speak English and some German.

International phone code +51.

Time GMT -5.

Tipping Restaurants: service is included in the bill, but tips can be given for exceptional service. Give the tip to the right person. Taxi drivers, none (bargain the price down, then pay extra for good service). Cloakroom attendants and hairdressers (very high class only), US$0.50-1. Airport or railway porters, US$0.50. Car wash boys, US$0.30, car 'watch' boys, US$0.20. If going on a trek or tour, it is customary to tip the guide as well as the cook and porters.

VAT/IVA 19%.

Voltage 220 volts AC, 60 cycles throughout the country, except Arequipa (50 cycles). Most four- and five-star hotels have 110 volts AC. Plugs are either American flat-pin or twin flat and round pin combined.

Weights and measures Metric.

phased out). Some prices are quoted in dollars in more expensive establishments, to avoid changes in the value of the sol. You can pay in soles, however. Try to break down large notes whenever you can. Sol **exchange rate** with US$: 3.25; with euro: 4.24 (July 2007).

Warning A large number of forged US dollar notes (especially US$20 and larger bills) are in circulation. Soles notes and coins are also forged. Always check your money when you change it, even in a bank (including ATMs). Hold notes up to the light to inspect the watermark and that the colours change according to the light. The line down the side of the bill spelling out the bill's amount should appear green, blue and pink. Fake bills are only pink and have no hologram properties. There should also be tiny pieces of thread in the paper (not glued on). In parts of the country, forged one-, two- and five-sol coins are in circulation. The fakes are slightly off-colour, the surface copper can be scratched off and they tend to bear a recent date. Posters in public places explain what to look for in forged soles. There is a shortage of change in museums, post offices, railway stations and even shops, while taxi drivers are notorious in this regard – one is simply told 'no change'. Do not accept this excuse.

Credit cards, traveller's cheques (TCs), Banks and ATMs Visa (by far the most widely-accepted card in Peru), MasterCard, American Express and Diners Club are all valid. There is often an 8-12% commission for all credit card charges. Most banks are affiliated with Visa/Plus system; those that you will find in almost every town and city are **BCP** and **BBVA Continental**. **Interbank** ATMs accept Visa, Plus, MasterCard, Maestro, Cirrus and American Express. Scotiabank (ex-**Banco Wiese Sudameris**) ATMs accept Visa, Plus, MasterCard, Maestro and Cirrus. There are also **Red Unicard** ATMs which accept Visa, Plus, MasterCard, Maestro and

harge the wait for trial in
ed by the narcotics police
a witness. **Drug use or
number of foreigners in**

lude slipping a packet of
or somewhere involving a
caine. In all cases, a plain
ey, at your feet in the taxi,
em, minus a large part of
ot to be intimidated. Being
cularly vulnerable. Beware
anting to search for drugs;

a free drink. The drinks are
ur drink being made and
k system doesn't appear to
disco, even if their tourist
ightclubs and bars in Lima
skin colour and assumed

em to be a thing of the past,
pletely non-functional. It is
, but in 2006-07 it was safe
gle areas east of Ayacucho

Touching down Box, your
Explorers, who issue the
o 245484, or in Quito). You
tails above in **Finding out**
g complaints, they will help

equipa, Cajamarca, Chiclayo,
oto, Trujillo and Tumbes) are
om. For destinations such as
d Tacna flights are offered by
re.com.pe. Lan www.lan.com
a service on the Lima-Cuzco
ally cost US$66-99 one-way
oliday times (Semana Santa,
elections. During these times
light schedules and departure
ancellations occur. Flights into
orts of bad weather. Flights to
een national and international
ixed in US dollars (but can be
be better early morning than
cm x 37 cm) to avoid the risk of
e leaving from at least 24 hours
minutes before departure, the
f those who haven't turned up.

inland to Huancayo, Ayacucho
ses to major centres (different
ices, eg Imperial, Ideal, Royal).
) service and the difference is
seats (bus cama). **Cruz del Sur**

Peruvian cuisine The best **coastal** dishes are seafood based, the most popular being *ceviche*. This is a dish of raw white fish marinated in lemon juice, onion and hot peppers. Traditionally, *ceviche* is served with corn-on-the-cob, *cancha* (toasted corn), yucca and sweet potatoes. *Tiradito* is *ceviche* without onions made with plaice. Another mouth-watering fish dish is *escabeche* – fish with onions, hot green pepper, red peppers, prawns (*langostinos*), cumin, hard-boiled eggs, olives, and sprinkled with cheese (it can also be made with chicken). For fish on its own, don't miss the excellent *corvina*, or white sea bass. You should also try *chupe de camarones*, which is a shrimp stew made with varying ingredients. Other fish dishes include *parihuela*, a popular bouillabaisse which includes *yuyo de mar*, a tangy seaweed, and *aguadito*, a thick rice and fish soup said to have rejuvenating powers. A favourite northern coastal dish is *seco de cabrito*, roasted kid (baby goat) served with the ubiquitous beans and rice, or *seco de cordero* which uses lamb instead. Also good is *aji de gallina*, a rich and spicy creamed chicken, and duck is excellent. *Humitas* are small, stuffed dumplings made with maize. The *criollo* cooking of the coast has a strong tradition and can be found throughout the country. Two popular examples are *cau cau*, made with tripe, potatoes, peppers, and parsley and served with rice, and *anticuchos*, which are shish kebabs of beef heart with garlic, peppers, cumin seeds and vinegar.

The staples of **highland** cooking, corn and potatoes, come in a variety of shapes, sizes and colours. *Causa* is a dish of yellow potatoes, lemons, pepper, hard-boiled eggs, olives, lettuce, sweet cooked corn, sweet cooked potato and fresh cheese, served with onion sauce (it can be made with tuna, avocado or prawns). Another potato dish is *papa a la huancaína*, which is topped with a spicy sauce made with milk and cheese. *Ocopa* is a similar dish in which slices of potato are served with a sauce made from milk, herbs and pecan nuts. *Papa rellena* is a deep-fried mashed potato ball stuffed with vegetables, egg and meat. The most commonly eaten corn dishes are *choclo con queso*, corn on the cob with cheese, and *tamales*, boiled corn dumplings filled with meat and wrapped in a banana leaf.

The main ingredient in jungle cuisine is fish, especially the succulent, dolphin-sized *paiche*, which comes with the delicious *palmito*, or palm-hearts, and yucca and fried bananas. *Juanes* are a jungle version of tamales, stuffed with chicken and rice.

A dish almost guaranteed to appear on every restaurant menu is *lomo saltado*, a kind of stir-fried beef with onions, vinegar, ginger, chilli, tomatoes and fried potatoes, served with rice. *Rocoto relleno* is spicy bell pepper stuffed with beef and vegetables, *palta rellena* is avocado filled with chicken salad, Russian salad or prawns. *Estofado de carne* is a stew which often contains wine and *carne en adobo* is a cut and seasoned steak. Others include *fritos*, fried pork, usually eaten in the morning, *chicharrones*, deep fried chunks of pork ribs and chicken or fish, and *lechón*, suckling pig. A delicacy in the highlands is *cuy*, guinea pig. Filling and good value are the many kinds of soup, such as *yacu-chupe*, a green soup made from potato, with cheese, garlic, coriander, parsley, peppers, eggs, onions, and mint, *and sopa a la criolla* containing thin noodles, beef heart, egg, vegetables and pleasantly spiced.

The various Peruvian fruits are of good quality: they include bananas, the citrus fruits, pineapples, dates, avocados (*paltas*), eggfruit (*lúcuma*), the custard apple (*chirimoya*) which can be as big as your head, quince, papaya, mango, guava, the passion-fruit (*maracuyá*) and the soursop (*guanábana*).

Drink The most famous local drink is *pisco*, a clear brandy which, with egg whites and lime juice, makes the famous pisco sour. The most renowned brands come from the Ica valley. The best wines are from Ica, Tacama and Ocucaje. Tacama blancs de blancs and brut champagne have been recommended, also Gran Tinto Reserva Especial. Viña Santo Tomás, from Chincha, is reasonable and cheap. Casapalca is not recommended. Beer is best in lager and porter types, especially the *Cusqueña* and *Arequipeña* brands (lager) and *Trujillo Malta* (porter). In Lima only *Cristal* and *Pilsener* (not related to true Pilsen) are readily available, others have to be sought out. Look out for the sweetish 'maltina' brown ale, which makes a change from the ubiquitous pilsner-type beers. *Chicha de jora* is a maize beer, usually homemade and not easy to come by, refreshing but strong, and *chicha morada* is a soft drink made with purple maize. The local rival to Coca Cola, the fluorescent yellow *Inca Cola*, is made from lemongrass. Peruvian coffee is good, but the best is exported and many cafés only serve coffee in liquid form or Nescafé. There are many different kinds of herb tea: the commonest are *manzanilla* (camomile) and *hierbaluisa* (lemon grass). *Mate de coca* is frequently served in the highlands to stave off the discomforts of altitude sickness.

1078

d their use is widespread. The
ur card has to be pretty obscure
reases outside Cuzco and other
inesses displaying credit card
s. For credit card loss: **American**
res, Lima, To1-690 0900,
35, San Isidro, To1-221 2050;
800-307 7309; **Visa** ① *Travel*
(por cobrar) to 410-902 8022

uld be brought into Peru from
oreign exchange. Banks are the
. Some charge commission from
to branch, month to month. The
anging money at a bank always
or *casas de cambio* (exchange
ier. Street changers give the best
ding paperwork and queuing, but
, check their calculators, etc, and
es think about taking a taxi after
ngregate near an office where the
g better rates than on the street.
Lima airport, and you can change
he various borders. **Note** No one,
in any way damaged or torn.
olders only, but will not exchange
e Lima branch only. They are also
eport is needed. Most of the main
, Interbank and BSCH accept Visa
anches handle Citicorp cheques.
cheques in the jungle area, even
ues in blue or black ink or ballpen.

-35 per person a day for living
ow budget travel. Your budget will
ow many flights you take between
per person for the most basic
Cuzco. For meal prices, see Eating,
ow those in Lima, although Cuzco is
ce of using the internet is generally
tes vary from US$1.50 to US$4.

international students' card, except
wner's photograph. An ISIC card can
ranco, T247 3230; Portal de Panes
Santo Domingo 123, of 307, p 3,
-226789, Chiclayo; Calle Real 151,
592; www.intej.org.

hide the fact that most Peruvians are
, please see the Security, Essentials,
. Always use licensed taxis: anyone
but "pseudo taxis" are not safe. The
Arequipa and Puno, has been greatly
crease in aggressive assaults in Lima
Puno and in particular Cuzco have, at
utside the July-August peak holiday
iendliness. A friendly attitude on your
, can help you out of trouble.
le, anyone carrying any is almost

Festivals and events

Two of the major festival dates are **Carnaval**, which is held over the weekend before Ash Wednesday, and **Semana Santa** (Holy Week), which ends on Easter Sunday. Carnival is celebrated in most of the Andes and Semana Santa throughout Peru. Another important festival is **Fiesta de la Cruz**, held on the first of May in much of the central and southern highlands and on the coast. In Cuzco, the entire month of June is one huge *fiesta*, culminating in **Inti Raymi**, on 24 June, one of Peru's prime tourist attractions. Another national festival is **Todos los Santos** (All Saints) on 1 November, and on 8 December is **Festividad de la Inmaculada Concepción**. A full list of local festivals is listed under each town. Apart from the festivals listed above, the main holidays are: 1 January, New Year; 6 January, **Bajada de Reyes**; 1 May, Labour Day; 28-29 July, Independence (Fiestas Patrias); 7 October, Battle of Angamos; 24-25 December, Christmas.

Note Most businesses such as banks, airline offices and tourist agencies close for the official holidays while supermarkets and street markets may be open. Sometimes holidays that fall during mid-week will be moved to the following Monday. The high season for foreign tourism in Peru is June to September while national tourism peaks at Christmas, Semana Santa and Fiestas Patrias. Prices rise and accommodation and bus tickets are harder to come by.

Lima → Phone code: 01. Colour map 3, grid C2. Population: 8.2 million (metropolitan area).

Lima's colonial centre and suburbs, shrouded in fog which lasts eight months of the year, are fringed by the pueblos jóvenes *which sprawl over the dusty hills overlooking the flat city. It has a great many historic buildings, some of the finest museums in the country and its food, drink and nightlife are second to none. Although not the most relaxing of South America's capitals, it is a good place to start before exploring the rest of the country.*

Ins and outs

Getting there All international flights land at Jorge Chávez **airport**, 16 km northwest of the Plaza de Armas. Transport into town by taxi or bus is easy. If arriving in the city by **bus**, most of the recommended companies have their terminals just south of the centre, many on Av Carlos Zavala. This is not a safe area and you should take a taxi to and from there. ▶▶ *For more detailed information including getting away from the airport, see Transport, page 1101.*

Getting around Downtown Lima can be explored on foot by day; at night a taxi is safest. Miraflores is 15 km south of the centre. Many of the better hotels and restaurants are here and in neighbouring San Isidro. Transport between the centre and the suburbs is not a problem. Three types of bus provide an extensive public transport system; all vehicles stop when flagged down. The route of the bus is posted on a coloured sticker on the windscreen; ignore destinations written on the side. **Taxis** do not use meters. Agree the price of the journey beforehand and insist on being taken to the destination of your choice. On both buses and taxis be ready to pay the exact fare. At night, on Sunday and holidays expect a surcharge of 35-50% is made in taxis.

Addresses Several blocks, with their own names, make up a long street, a jirón (often abbreviated to Jr). Street corner signs bear both names, of the jirón and of the block. New and old names of streets are used interchangeably: Colmena is also Nicolás de Piérola, Wilson is Inca Garcilaso de la Vega, and Carabaya is also Augusto N Wiese. The city's urban motorway is often called 'El Zanjón' (the ditch) or Vía Expresa.

Climate Only 12° south of the equator, one would expect a tropical climate, but Lima has two distinct seasons. The winter is May-November, when a *garúa* (Scotch mist) hangs over the city, making everything look grey. It is damp and cold, 8-15°C. The sun breaks through around November and temperatures rise to as high as 30°C. Note that the temperature in the coastal suburbs is lower than the centre because of the sea's influence. Protect against the sun's rays when visiting the beaches around Lima, or elsewhere in Peru.

Tourist information i perú has offices at Jorge Chávez international airport ① *T574 8000, open 24 hrs*; Casa Basadre ① *Av Jorge Basadre 610, San Isidro, T421 1627, Mon-Fri*

0830-1830; and Larcomar shopping centre ① *Módulo 14, Plaza Gourmet, Miraflores, T445 9400, 1200-2000.* **Info Perú** ① *Jr de la Unión (Belén) 1066, of 102, T424 7963, infoperu@ qnet.com.pe, Mon-Fri 0930-1800, Sat 0930-1400,* is helpful with lots of advice, English, French spoken. Ask for the free, *Peru Guide* published in English by Lima Editora, T444 0815, available at travel agencies. **Fertur Peru,** has lots of information, see under Tour operators. **South American Explorers** ① *Piura 135, (Casilla 3714), Miraflores, T445 3306 (dial 011-51-1 from USA) www.saexplorers.org.* See also Essentials, page 32.

Background

Lima, capital of Peru, is built on both sides of the Río Rímac, at the foot of Cerro San Cristóbal. It was originally named *La Ciudad de Los Reyes*, in honour of the Magi, at its founding by Spanish conquistador Francisco Pizarro in 1535. From then until the independence of the South American republics in the early 19th century, it was the chief city of Spanish South America. The name Lima, a corruption of the Quechua name *Rimac* (speaker), was not adopted until the end of the 16th century.

The Universidad de San Marcos was founded in 1551, and a printing press in 1595, both among the earliest of their kind in South America. Lima's first theatre opened in 1563, and the Inquisition was introduced in 1569 (it was not abolished until 1820). For some time the Viceroyalty of Peru embraced Colombia, Ecuador, Bolivia, Chile and Argentina. There were few cities in the Old World that could rival Lima's power, wealth and luxury, which was at its height during the 17th and early 18th centuries. The city's wealth attracted many freebooters and in 1670 a protecting wall 11 km long was built round it, then destroyed in 1869. The earthquake of 1746 destroyed all but 20 houses, killed 4,000 inhabitants and ended its pre-eminence. It was only comparatively recently, with the coming of industry, that Lima began to change into what it is today.

Lima

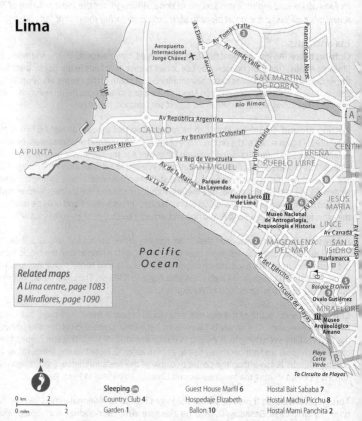

Related maps
A *Lima centre, page 1083*
B *Miraflores, page 1090*

Pacific Ocean

Sleeping	Guest House Marfil **6**	Hostal Bait Sababa **7**
Country Club **4**	Hospedaje Elizabeth	Hostal Machu Picchu **8**
Garden **1**	Ballon **10**	Hostal Mami Panchita **2**

Modern Lima is seriously affected by smog for much of the year, and is surrounded by 'Pueblos Jóvenes', or settlements of squatters who have migrated from the Sierra. Villa El Salvador, a few kilometres southeast of Lima, may be the world's biggest 'squatters' camp' with 350,000 people building up an award-winning self-governing community since 1971.

Over the years the city has changed out of recognition. Many of the hotels and larger business houses have relocated to the fashionable suburbs of Miraflores and San Isidro, thus moving the commercial heart of the city away from the Plaza de Armas.

Half of the town-dwellers of Peru now live in Lima. The metropolitan area contains eight million people, nearly one-third of the country's total population, and two-thirds of its industries. Callao, Peru's major port, runs into Lima; it is a city in its own right, with over one million inhabitants. Within its boundaries is the Jorge Chávez airport. The docks handle 75% of the nation's imports and some 25% of its exports. Callao has a serious theft problem, avoid being there in the evening.

Sights

The traditional heart of the city, at least in plan, is still what it was in colonial days. Although parts of it are run down, much of the old centre is undergoing restoration and many colonial buildings have been cleaned. It is worth visiting the colonial centre to see the architecture and works of art. Most of the tourist attractions are in this area. Churches open between 1830 and 2100 unless otherwise stated. Many are closed to visitors on Sunday. Some museums are only open 0900-1300 from January-March, and some are closed in January.

Plaza de Armas

One block south of the Río Rímac lies the Plaza de Armas (also called Plaza Mayor since 1998),

Cerro San Cristóbal ▲

RIMAC

IMA

Cerro El Agustino ▲ MONTERRICO

Av 28 de Julio

Av Chosica

LA CTORIA

Av Nicolas Arriola

SAN BORJA

Museo de la Nación 🏛

URQUILLO Av Javier Prado Este

Via de Evitamiento

Hipódromo de Monterrico

Instituto Geográfico Militar

Av Aviación

Av Angamos

Av Panamericana Sur

avides

BARRANCO | To Chorrillos

Hostal Residencial Victor **3** Sonesta El Olivar **5**
Libertador **4**
Sofitel Royal Park **9**

which has been declared a World Heritage Site by UNESCO. Running along two sides are arcades with shops: Portal de Escribanos and Portal de Botoneros. In the centre of the plaza is a bronze fountain dating from 1650. The **Palacio de Gobierno**, on the north side of the Plaza, stands on the site of the original palace built by Pizarro. The changing of the guard is at 1200. To take a tour register a day in advance (T01-311 3908), or at the office of public relations, Edificio Palacio 269, oficina 201 (ask guard for directions); the free, 45-minute tours are in Spanish and English Monday-Friday, in the morning. The **Cathedral** ① *T427 9647, Mon-Sat 0900-1630, US$1.50,* was reduced to rubble in the earthquake of 1746. The reconstruction, on the lines of the original, was completed 1755. Note the splendidly carved stalls (mid-17th century), the silver-covered altars surrounded by fine woodwork, mosaic-covered walls bearing the coats of arms of Lima and Pizarro and an allegory of Pizarro's commanders, the 'Thirteen Men of Isla del Gallo'. The supposed remains of Franscisco Pizarro lie in a small chapel, the first on the right of the entrance, in a glass coffin, though later research indicates that they reside in the crypt. Museo de Arte Religioso in the cathedral, free guided tours (English available, give tip), ask to see the picture restoration room. Next to the cathedral is the **Archbishop's Palace**, rebuilt in 1924, with a superb wooden balcony.

Just off the plaza is the **Philatelic Museum** ⓘ *at the Central Post Office, Mon-Sun 0815-1300, 1400-1800, free*. Incomplete collection of Peruvian stamps and information on the Inca postal system. There is a stamp exchange in front of the museum every Saturday and Sunday, 0900-1300. Commemorative issues can be bought here. Nearby is the **Casa Aliaga** ⓘ *Unión 224. Lima Tours has exclusive rights to include the house in its tours (T424 5110)*. It is still occupied by the Aliaga family but has been opened to the public. The house contains what is said to be the oldest ceiling in Lima and is furnished entirely in the colonial style.

The baroque church of **San Francisco** ⓘ *on the 1st block of Jr Lampa, corner of Ancash, a few blocks from the Plaza de Armas, T427 1381, daily 0930- 1730, church and monastery US$1.50, US$0.50 children, only with guide, Spanish and English (recommended)*, was finished in 1674 and withstood the 1746 earthquake. The nave and aisles are lavishly decorated in Mudéjar style. The monastery is famous for the Sevillian tilework and panelled ceiling in the cloisters (1620). The Catacombs under the church and part of the monastery are well worth seeing. The late 16th-century **Casa de Jarava** or **Pilatos** ⓘ *Jr Ancash 390*, is opposite San Francisco church. Close by, **Casa de las Trece Monedas** ⓘ *Jr Ancash 536*, still has the original doors and window grills.

The **Palacio Torre Tagle** (1735) ⓘ *Jr Ucayali 363, Mon-Fri during working hours,* is the city's best surviving example of secular colonial architecture. Today, it is used by the Foreign Ministry, but visitors are allowed to enter courtyards to inspect the fine, Moorish-influenced wood-carving in balconies and wrought iron work. **Casa de la Rada,** or **Goyoneche** ⓘ *Jr Ucayali 358*, opposite, is a fine mid- 18th-century French-style town house which now belongs to a bank. The patio and first reception room are open occasionally to the public. **Museo Banco Central de Reserva** ⓘ *Jr Ucayali at Jr Lampa, T01-613 2000 ext 2655, http://museobcr.perucultural. org.pe/, Mon-Fri 1000-1630, Sat-Sun 1000-1300, free, photography prohibited*. This is a large collection of pottery from the Vicus or Piura culture (AD 500-600) and gold objects from Lambayeque, as well as 19th and 20th-century paintings: both sections highly recommended. **San Pedro** ⓘ *3rd block of Jirón Ucayali, Mon-Sat 0930-1145, 1700-1800*, finished by Jesuits in 1638, has marvellous altars with Moorish-style balconies, rich gilded wood carvings in choir and vestry, and tiled throughout. Several Viceroys are buried here; the bell called La Abuelita, first rung in 1590, sounded the Declaration of Independence in 1821.

Between Avenida Abancay and Jr Ayacucho is **Plaza Bolívar**, where General José de San Martín proclaimed Peru's independence. The plaza is dominated by the equestrian statue of the Liberator. Behind lies the Congress building which occupies the former site of the Universidad de San Marcos; visit recommended. Behind the Congress is Barrio Chino, with many *chifas* and small shops selling oriental items. **Museo del Tribunal de la Santa Inquisición** ⓘ *Plaza Bolívar, C Junín 548, near the corner of Av Abancay, Mon-Sun 0900-1700, free, students offer to show you round for a tip; good explanations in English*. The main hall, with a splendidly carved mahogany ceiling, remains untouched. The Court of Inquisition was held here from 1584; 1829-1938 it was used by the Senate. In the basement there is a recreation *in situ* of the gruesome tortures. A description in English is available at the desk.

The 16th-century **Santo Domingo church and monastery** ⓘ *T427 6793, monastery and tombs open Mon-Sat 0900-1230, 1500-1800; Sun and holidays morning only, US$0.75*, is on the first block of Jr Camaná. The Cloister, one of the most attractive, dates from 1603. The second Cloister is less elaborate. Beneath the sacristy are the tombs of San Martín de Porres, one of Peru's most revered saints, and Santa Rosa de Lima (see below). In 1669, Pope Clement presented the alabaster statue of Santa Rosa in front of the altar. Behind Santo Domingo is **Alameda Chabuca Granda**, named after one of Peru's greatest singers. In the evening there are free art and music shows and you can sample foods from all over Peru. A few blocks away, **Casa de Oquendo** or **Osambela** ⓘ *Conde de Superunda 298, 0900-1300*, stages art exhibitions. A few blocks west is **Santuario de Santa Rosa** ⓘ *Av Tacna, 1st block, T425 1279, daily 0930-1300, 1500-1800, free to the grounds*, a small but graceful church. A pilgrimage centre; here are preserved the hermitage built by Santa Rosa herself, the house in which she was born, a section of the house in which she attended to the sick, her well, and other relics. Nearby, **Casa La Riva** ⓘ *Jr Ica 426*, has an 18th-century porch and balconies, a small gallery with 20th-century paintings.

San Agustín ⓘ *Jr Ica 251, T427 7548, daily 0830-1130, 1630-1900, ring for entry*, is west of the Plaza de Armas: its façade (1720) is a splendid example of churrigueresque architecture. There are carved choir stalls and effigies, and a sculpture of Death, said to have frightened its maker into an early grave. The church has been restored after the last earthquake, but the sculpture of Death is in storage. **Las Nazarenas Church** ① *Av Tacna, 4th block, T423 5718, daily 0700-1200, 1600-2000,* is built around an image of Christ Crucified painted by a

Lima centre

Sleeping	Kamana **11**	L'Eau Vive **8**
Familia Rodríguez **3**	Maury **14**	Machu Picchu **9**
Hostal Belén **6**	Pensión Ibarra **15**	Manhatten **10**
Hostal de las Artes **8**		Natur **11**
Hostal España **7**	**Eating**	Neydi **6**
Hostal Iquique **9**	Antaño **8**	Salon Capon **12**
Hostal La Posada	Azato **1**	San Martín **13**
del Parque **12**	Cordano **3**	Wa Lok **14**
Hostal Roma	El Maurito **4**	
& Café Carrara **10**	Govinda **5**	
Hostal San Francisco **2**	La Choza Náutica **7**	

0 metres 200
0 yards 200

liberated slave in 1655. This, the most venerated image in Lima, and an oil copy of El Señor de los Milagros (Lord of Miracles), encased in a gold frame, are carried on a silver litter the whole weighing nearly a ton through the streets on 18, 19, and 28 October and again on 1 November (All Saints' Day). *El Comercio* newspaper and local pamphlets give details of times and routes.

Northeast of Plaza de Armas

From the Plaza, passing the Palacio de Gobierno on the left, straight ahead is the **Desamparados** ① *free*, railway station, which now houses fascinating exhibitions on Peruvian themes. **The Puente de Piedra**, behind the Palacio de Gobierno, is a Roman-style stone bridge built in 1610, crossing the Río Rímac to the district of that name. On Jr Hualgayoc is the bullring in the **Plaza de Acho**, inaugurated on 20 January 1766, with the **Museo Taurino** ① *Hualgayoc 332, T482 3360, Mon-Sat 0800-1600, US$1, students US$0.50, photography US$2*. Apart from matador's relics, the museum contains good collections of paintings and engravings, some of the latter by Goya. There are two bullfight seasons: October to first week in December and during July. They are held in the afternoons on Sunday and holidays. The **Convento de Los Descalzos** ① *on the Alameda de Los Descalzos in Rímac, T481 0441, daily 1000-1300, 1500-1800, except Tue, US$1, guided tour only, 45 mins in Spanish (worth it)*, was founded in 1592. It contains over 300 paintings of the Cuzco, Quito and Lima schools which line the four main cloisters and two ornate chapels. The chapel of El Carmen was constructed in 1730 and is notable for its baroque gold leaf altar. The museum shows the life of the Franciscan friars during colonial and early republican periods. The cellar, infirmary, pharmacy and a typical cell have been restored.

   Cerro San Cristóbal dominates downtown Lima and can be visited in a one-hour tour, run by *Ofistur*, departing from in front of Santo Domingo, Jr Camaná ① *Sat and Sun 1000-2100; departures every 15 mins, US$1.50*. It includes a look at the run-down Rímac district, passes the Convento de los Descalzos (see above), ascends the hill through one of the city's oldest shanties with its brightly painted houses and spends about 20 minutes at the summit, where there is a small museum and café. Excellent views on a clear day.

South of Plaza de Armas

The Jr de La Unión, the main shopping street, runs to the Plaza de Armas. It has been converted into a pedestrian precinct which teems with life in the evening. In the two blocks south of Jr Unión, known as C Belén, several shops sell souvenirs and curios. **La Merced** ① *Unión y Miró Quesada, T427 8199, 0800-1245, 1600-2000 (Sun 0700-1300, 1600-2000); monastery daily 0800-1200 and 1500-1730*, is in Plazuela de la Merced. The first mass in Lima was said here on the site of the first church to be built. The restored façade is a fine example of colonial Baroque. Inside are some magnificent altars and the tilework on some of the walls is noteworthy. A door from the right of the nave leads into the Monastery. The cloister dates from 1546. Jr de la Unión leads to **Plaza San Martín**, which has a statue of San Martín in the centre. The plaza has been restored and is now a nice place to sit and relax.

   Museo de Arte ① *9 de Diciembre 125, T423 4732, http://museoarte.perucultural.org.pe/, Thu-Tue 1000-1700, US$3.65, free guide, signs in English*, is in the Palacio de la Exposición, built in 1868 in Parque de la Exposición (designed by Gustave Eiffel). There are more than 7,000 exhibits, giving a chronological history of Peruvian cultures and art from the Paracas civilization up to today. It includes excellent examples of 17th- and 18th-century Cuzco paintings, a beautiful display of carved furniture, heavy silver and jewelled stirrups and also pre-Columbian pottery. The Filmoteca (movie club) is on the premises and shows films just about every night. See the local paper for details, or look in the museum itself. The **Gran Parque Cultural de Lima** ① *0800-2030*, is in the grounds. Inaugurated in January 2000, this large park has an amphitheatre, Japanese garden, food court and children's activities. Relaxing strolls through this green, peaceful and safe oasis in the centre of Lima are recommended.

   Museo de Arte Italiano ① *Paseo de la República 250, T423 9932, Tue-Fri 0900-1900, Sat-Sun 1100-1700, US$1*, is in a wonderful neo-classical building, given by the Italian colony to Peru on the centenary of its independence. Note the remarkable mosaic murals on the outside. It consists of a large collection of Italian and other European works of art and houses the Instituto de Arte Contemporáneo, which has many exhibitions.

San Borja

Museo de la Nación ① *Javier Prado Este 2465, T476 9933, Tue-Sun 0900-1800, closed major public holidays, US$1.80. 50% discount with ISIC card,* in the huge *Banco de la Nación* building, is the museum for the exhibition and study of the art and history of the aboriginal races of Peru. It contains the **Museo Peruano de Ciencias de la Salud** ① *from Av Garcilaso de la Vega in downtown Lima take a combi with a "Javier Prado/Aviación" window sticker. Get off at the 21st block of Javier Prado at Av Aviación. From Miraflores take a bus down Av Arequipa to Av Javier Prado (27th block), then take a bus with a "Todo Javier Prado" or "Aviación" window sticker. Taxi from downtown Lima or Miraflores US$2,* which has a collection of ceramics and mummies, plus an explanation of pre-Columbian lifestyle. There are good explanations in Spanish and English on Peruvian history, with ceramics, textiles and displays of almost every ruin in Peru. Guided tours in English/Spanish. It is arranged so that you can follow the development of Peruvian precolonial history through to the time of the Incas. A visit is recommended before you go to see the archaeological sites themselves. There are displays of the tomb of the Señor de Sipán, artefacts from Batán Grande near Chiclayo (Sicán culture), reconstructions of the friezes found at Huaca La Luna and Huaca El Brujo, near Trujillo, and of Sechín and other sites. Temporary exhibitions are held in the basement, where there is also an Instituto Nacional de Cultura bookshop. The museum has a cafetería.

Pueblo Libre

The original museum of anthropology and archaeology is **Museo Nacional de Antropología, Arqueología e Historia** ① *Plaza Bolívar in Pueblo Libre, not to be confused with Plaza Bolívar in the centre, T463 5070, http://museonacional.perucultural.org.pe/, Tue-Sun 0930-1700, US$3.35, students US$1, guides available for groups.* On display are ceramics of the Chimú, Nazca, Mochica and Pachacámac cultures, various Inca curiosities and works of art, and interesting textiles. **Museo Nacional de Historia** ① *T463 2009,* in a mansion occupied by San Martín (1821-1822) and Bolívar (1823-1826) is next door. It exhibits colonial and early republican paintings, manuscripts and uniforms. Take any public transport on Avenida Brasil with a window sticker saying "Todo Brasil." Get off at the 21st block called Avenida Vivanco. Walk about five blocks down Vivanco. The museum will be on your left. From Miraflores take bus SM 18 Carabayllo-Chorrillos, marked "Bolívar, Arequipa, Larcomar", get out at block 8 of Bolívar by the Hospital Santa Rosa, and walk down Av San Martín five blocks until you see the 'blue line'; turn left. The 'blue line' marked on the pavement, very faded, links the Museo Nacional de Antropología, Arqueología e Historia to the Museo Larco (see below), 10 minutes' walk. Taxi from downtown US$2; from Miraflores US$2

    Museo Larco de Lima ① *Av Bolívar 1515, T461 1312, www.museolarco.org, 0900-1800; texts in Spanish, English and French, US$7.55 (half price for students), disabled access, photography not permitted.* Located in an 18th-century mansion, itself built on a seventh-century pre-Columbian pyramid, this museum has a collection which gives an excellent overview on the development of Peruvian cultures through their pottery. It has the world's largest collection of Moche, Sicán and Chimú pieces. There is a Gold and Silver of Ancient Peru exhibition, a magnificent textile collection and a fascinating erotica section. Don't miss the storeroom with its vast array of pottery, unlike anything you'll see elsewhere. It is surrounded by beautiful gardens.Take any bus to the 15th block of Avenida Brasil. Then take a bus down Avendia Bolívar. From Miraflores, take the SM 18 Carabayllo-Chorrillos, see above, to block 15 of Bolívar. Taxi from downtown, Miraflores or San Isidro, 15 minutes, US$2.50. Follow the 'blue line' marked on the pavement to the Museo Nacional de Antropología, Arqueología e Historia (see above), 10 minutes' walk.

San Isidro

To the east of Avenida La República, down Calle Pancho Fierro, is **El Olivar**, an olive grove planted by the first Spaniards which has been turned into a park. Between San Isidro and Miraflores, is **the Pan de Azúcar**, or **Huallamarca** ① *C Nicolás de Rivera 201 and Av Rosario, 0900-1700, closed Mon, US$1.75. Take bus 1 from Av Tacna, or minibus 13 or 73 to Choquechaca, then walk.* An adobe pyramid of the Maranga culture, it dates from about AD 100-500. There is a small site museum. There are many good hotels and restaurants in San Isidro; see Sleeping, page 1088 and Eating, page 1093.

    South of San Isidro is the rundown seaside resort of **Magdalena del Mar**, inland from

D Hostal Roma, Jr Ica 326, T/F427 7576, www.hostalroma.8m.com. With bath, **E** without bath, hot water all day, safe to leave luggage, basic but clean, often full, internet extra but good, motorcycle parking (**Roma Tours**, helpful for trips, reservations, flight confirmations, Errol Branca speaks English). Highly recommended.

E-F Hostal de las Artes, Jr Chota 1460, Breña, T433 0031, http://arteswelcome.tripod.com/. **F** without bath (no singles with bath), **G** pp in dormitory, Dutch owned, English spoken, safes in rooms and safe luggage store, nice colonial building, solar hot water system, book exchange, airport transfer US$12.

E-F Hostal Iquique, Jr Iquique 758, Breña (discount for SAE members), T433 4724, www.barrioperu.terra.com.pe/hiquique. **F** without bath, noisy and draughty, otherwise good, use of kitchen, warm water, storage facilities, rooms on the top floor are best.

F Hostal San Francisco, Jr Azángaro 127, T426 2735, hostalsf@lanpro.com.pe. Dormitories with and without bathrooms, new, safe, Italian/Peruvian owners, good service, internet and cafeteria.

G pp Familia Rodríguez, Av Nicolás de Piérola 730, p 2, T423 6465, jotajot@ terra.com.pe. With breakfast, popular, some rooms noisy, will store luggage, also has dormitory accommodation with only one bathroom (same price), transport to airport US$10 pp for 2 people, US$4 pp for 3 or more, good information, secure.

F Hostal Belén, Belén 1049, just off San Martín, T427 8995. Discount for groups of 3 or more but give prior notice, Italian spoken, basic breakfast extra, hot water, basic, noisy.

G Hostal España, Jr Azángaro 105, T427 9196, www.hotelespanaperu.com. **F** with bath (3 rooms), **G** pp in dormitory, fine old building, hot showers, English spoken, internet service, motorcycle parking, luggage store (free) and lockers, laundry service, don't leave valuables in rooms, roof garden, good café, can be very busy.

G Pensión Ibarra, Av Tacna 359, p 14-16, T/F427 8603 (no sign), pensionibarra@ekno.com. Breakfast US$2, discount for longer stay, use of kitchen, balcony with views of the city, very helpful owner, hot water, full board available (good small café next door).

G pp Hostal Machu Picchu, Av Juan Pablo Fernandini 1015 (block 10 of Av Brasil), Breña, T9794 4257. Family run, shared bath, hot water, kitchen facilities, cable TV, laundry service, excellent value.

Pueblo Libre *p1085*

F pp Guest House Marfil, Parque Ayacucho 126, at the 3rd block of Bolívar, T261 1206, cosycoyllor@ yahoo.com. English spoken, breakfast, kitchen facilities and laundry free of charge, internet, Spanish classes arranged, family atmosphere.

G Hostal Bait Sababa, Av San Martín 743, near the hospital, T01-261 4990, baitsababa@ hotmail.com. The home of a Jewish family who also speak Spanish and English, very helpful, Fri evening meal provided, restaurants, laundry, internet and phone nearby.

San Isidro *p1085*

LL Country Club, Los Eucaliptos 590, T611 9000, www.hotelcountry.com. Excellent, fine service, luxurious rooms, safes in rooms, cable TV, free internet for guests, good bar and restaurant, classically stylish.

LL Sonesta El Olivar, Pancho Fierro 194, T712 6060, www.sonestaperu.com. Also excellent, one of the top 5-star hotels in Lima, modern, many eating options, bar, garden, swimming pool, quiet, popular.

L Libertador Hotels Peru, Los Eucaliptos 550, T421 6666, www.libertador.com.pe (reservations: Las Begonias 441, office 240, T442 1995/444 3720). Golden Tulip hotel, overlooking the golf course, full facilities for the business traveller, comfortable rooms, fine service, good restaurant. A rich collection of true hospitality and Peruvian culture with hotels in Arequipa, Cuzco, Huaraz, Máncora, Puno, Tambopata, Trujillo, Valle del Colca, Urubamba and Valle Sagrado.

L-AL Sofitel Royal Park, Av Camino Real 1050, T215 1616, www.sofitel.com. Excellent rooms, charming, part of the French group, prices can be negotiated.

A Garden, Rivera Navarrete 450, T442 1771, reservas@gardenhotel.com.pe. Includes breakfast, good beds, small restaurant, ideal for business visitors, convenient, free internet, good value.

E Hospedaje Elizabeth Ballon, Av del Parque Norte 265, San Isidro, T980 07557, hospedajeebr@ yahoo.fr. Family house in residential area 7 mins' walk from Cruz del Sur bus station. Shared or private bathrooms, TV room, laundry, luggage storage, breakfast included, airport transfers US$13.

San Miguel *p1080*

C Hostal Mami Panchita, Av Federico Gallessi 198, T263 7203, www.mamipanchita.com. Dutch-Peruvian owned, English, French, Dutch, Spanish and German spoken, includes breakfast and welcome drink, comfortable rooms with

● *For an explanation of the sleeping and eating price codes used in this guide, see page 58. Other*
● *relevant information is found in Essentials pages 1076-1078.*

bath, hot water, living room and bar, patio, email service, book exchange, Raymi Travel agency (good service), 15 mins from airport, 15 mins from Miraflores, 20 mins from historical centre. Frequently recommended.

Miraflores *p1086, map p1090*
LL Miraflores Park, Av Malecón de la Reserva 1035, T242 3000, www.mira-park.com. An Orient Express hotel, excellent service and facilities, beautiful views over the ocean, top class.
AL La Hacienda, 28 de Julio 511 y Av Larco, T213 1000, www.bwlahacienda.com. English spoken, excellent service, breakfast included, has casino.
AL-A Sonesta Posadas del Inca, Alcanfores 329, T241 7688, www.sonestaperu.com. Part of renowned chain of hotels, convenient location, cable TV, a/c, restaurant.
A Casa Andina, Av 28 de Julio 1088, T241 4050, www.casa-andina.com. One of a recommended chain, all with similar facilities and decor (others in the Cuzco area, Puno, Arequipa and Nazca). Very neat, with many useful touches, comfortable beds, 10 mins free internet, a/c, fridge, safe, laundry service, buffet breakfast, other meals available.
A José Antonio, 28 de Julio 398 y C Colón, T445 7743, www.hotelesjoseantonio.com. Good in all respects, including the restaurant, huge rooms, jacuzzis, internet, swimming pool, business facilities, helpful staff speak some English.
B Alemán, Arequipa 4704, T445 6999, www.hotelaleman.com.pe. No sign, comfortable, quiet, garden, excellent breakfast included, enquire about laundry service, smiling staff, free internet.
B Colonial Inn, Comandante Espinar 310, T01-241 7471, coloinn@terra.com.pe. Includes breakfast. A colonial style hotel with excellent service, but it can be noisy from traffic, parking.
B Hostal Esperanza, Esperanza 350, T444 2411, http://barrioperu.terra.com.pe/ htlesperanza. Modern, convenient, good hot water, very helpful

staff and manager, café, bar, secure, good value.
B Hostal La Castellana, Grimaldo del Solar 222, T444 4662, lacastellan@terra.com.pe. Pleasant, good value, nice garden, safe, expensive restaurant, laundry, English spoken, special price for South American Explorers (SAE) members.
B Hostal Lucerna, Las Dalias 276 (parallel with 12th block of Larco), T445 7321, hostallucerna@ terra.com.pe. Safe, quiet, cosy, excellent value, but drinks and restaurant are expensive.
B San Antonio Abad, Ramón Ribeyro 301, T447 6766, www.hotelsanantonioabad.com. Secure, quiet, helpful, tasty breakfasts, 1 free airport transfer with reservation, justifiably popular.
B-C Hostal El Patio, Diez Canseco 341, T444 2107, www.hostalelpatio.net. Includes breakfast, reductions for long stays, very nice suites and rooms, comfortable, English and French spoken, convenient, *comedor*, gay-friendly.
C El Carmelo, Bolognesi 749, T446 0575, carmelo@amauta.rcp.net.pe. With TV, great location a couple of blocks from the Parque del Amor, small restaurant downstairs serving *criolla* food and *ceviche*, price includes breakfast, good value, comfortable.
C Hostal Señorial, José González 567, T445 9724, senorial@viabcp.com. Includes breakfast, comfortable, nice garden.
C Sipán, Paseo de la República 6171, T447 0884, www.hotelsipan.com.pe. Breakfast and tax included, very pleasant, in a residential area, TV, fridge, security box, internet access. Free airport transfers available.
D Casa de Baraybar, Toribio Pacheco 216, T441 2160, www.casadebaraybar.com. One block from the ocean, extra long beds, breakfast included, TV, 24-hr room service, laundry, airport transfers free for stays of 3 nights. Bilingual staff, internet. Recommended.
D-E Home Peru, Av Arequipa 4501 (no sign), T241 9898, www.homeperu.com. In a 1920s mansion with huge rooms, with breakfast, E-F pp with shared bath, group discounts, very welcoming and

Peru Lima Listings

helpful, use of kitchen, luggage store, English spoken, laundry service, internet, safe, near Plaza Vea hypermarket. Can help with bus and plane tickets, connected to other *hostales* in Peru.

D-E Hospedaje Atahualpa, Atahualpa 646c, T447 6601. Cheaper without bath, including breakfast, long-stay rates available, parking, hot water, cooking and laundry facilities, luggage stored, taxi service.

Miraflores

	Hostal Lucerna **15** *D1*	Café Tarata **29** *C2*
	Hostal Señorial **16** *D1*	Café Voltaire **7** *B3*
	Inka Lodge **22** *A2*	Café Zeta **33** *B2*
	José Antonio **18** *C1*	C'est si Bon **8** *A2*
0 metres 50	La Hacienda **19** *C1*	Chef's Café **1** *C2*
0 yards 50	Lex Luthor's	Coco de Mer **41** *B1*
	House **21** *C1*	Cuarto y Mitad **10** *A2*
Sleeping	Lion Backpackers **31** *C3*	Dalmacia **38** *D1*
Adventures House **13** *A2*	Loki Backpackers **32** *B3*	Dino's Pizza **12** *A2*
Albergue Verde **10** *D2*	Miraflores Park **23** *D1*	Dove Vai **14** *B2*
Albergue Turístico	Pakacuna Backpackers	El Beduino **39** *D2*
Juvenil Internacional **1** *D3*	**33** *D3*	El Kapallaq **11** *B3*
Alemán **2** *A3*	Residencial El Castillo	El Parquetito **15** *B2*
Casa Andina **4** *D2*	Inn **24** *C3*	El Rincón Gaucho **16** *D1*
Casa de Baraybar **17** *A2*	San Antonio Abad **25** *D3*	El Señorío de Sulco **3** *A2*
Colonial Inn **5** *A2*	Sipán **26** *D2*	Haiti **17** *B3*
El Carmelo **3** *B1*	Sonesta Posadas	Heladería 4D **18** *A3*
Eurobackpackers **20** *C1*	del Inca **27** *C2*	Il Postino **19** *C3*
Explorer's House **6** *A1*	Stop and Drop **30** *B2*	La Gloria **20** *B3*
Flying Dog	Wayruro's	La Palachinke **21** *B2*
Backpackers **7** *C2*	Backpackers **29** *A2*	Las Brujas de Cachiche **4** *B1*
Friend's House **8** *C1*		Las Tejas **25** *C2*
Home Perú **28** *A3*	**Eating**	La Tiendecita Blanca **22** *B3*
Hospedaje Atahualpa **9** *A3*	Astrid y Gaston **2** *C3*	La Tranquera **23** *B2*
Hostal El Patio **11** *C2*	Bohemia **40** *A2*	La Trattoria **24** *C3*
Hostal Esperanza **12** *C3*	Café Café **5** *B2*	Madre Natura **26** *A3*
Hostal La Castellana **14** *C2*	Café de la Paz **6** *B2*	Pardo's Chicken **27** *D2*

Pizza Street **28** *B2*	
Ricota **29** *C2*	
San Antonio **31** *A3*	
Sandwich.com **14** *B2*	
Sí Señor **34** *B1*	
Super Rueda **32** *B2*	
Tapas Bar **13** *B3*	
Vivaldi **35** *B3*	
Zugatti **36** *C2*	
Bars & clubs	
Media Naranja **37** *B2*	
Murphys **42** *C3*	
The Old Pub **30** *B2*	
Voluntarios Pub **9** *B2*	

D-E Lion Backpackers, Grimaldo del Solar 139, T447 1827, www.lionbackpackers.com. 3 blocks from Parque Kennedy, double and dorms, good atmosphere, safe, breakfast, very helpful.

E pp Inka Lodge, Elias Aguirre 278, T242 6989, www.inkalodge.com. Also with dorms (**F pp**), convenient, excellent breakfast included, internet, laundry, very helpful.

E pp Residencial El Castillo Inn, Diez Canseco 580, T446 9501. All rooms with bath and hot water, family home, use of lounge, negotiate for longer stay.

E-F pp Eurobackpackers, Manco Cápac 471 (no sign, look for the cat with the world on his stick), T791 2945, www.eurobackpackers.com. Dormitory, also doubles, breakfast included, family atmosphere, comfortable, safe, internet. Good reputation although rooms downstairs are not as airy as those on first floor.

F pp Albergue Verde, Grimaldo del Solar 459, T445 3816, www.albergueverde.com. Nice small hostal, comfortable beds, **C pp** in double, friendly owner, Arturo Palmer, breakfast included, airport transfers US$15.

F pp Explorer's House, Av Alfredo León 158, by 10th block of Av José Pardo, T241 5002, explorers_house@yahoo.es. No sign, but plenty of indications of the house number, with breakfast, dormitory with shared bath, or double rooms with bath, hot water, use of kitchen, laundry service, Spanish classes, English spoken, very welcoming.

F pp Flying Dog Backpackers, Diez Canseco 117, T445 6745, www.flyingdog.esmartweb.com. Dormitories or private rooms, shared bath (**D-E** in en suite room), very popular so reserve through the web, central, comfortable, hot water, secure, free internet and local calls, book exchange, kitchen facilities. Full transport information and tickets can be arranged.

F Friend's House, Jr Manco Cápac 368, T446 6248, friendshouse_peru@yahoo.com.mx. Dormitory accommodation with hot water, cable TV, use of kitchen, includes breakfast, very popular with backpackers, near Larcomar shopping centre, plenty of good information and help. Highly recommended. They have another branch at José Gonzales 427, T446 3521. **E pp** with bath, same facilities, except private rooms only and more like a family home. Neither branch is signed.

F pp Adventures House, Jr Cesareo Chacaltana 162, T241 5693, www.adventureshouse.com. Rooms for up to 4, with bath and hot water, free internet, national calls, pleasant, quiet, a short walk from all main facilities, airport transfer, use of kitchen, bike rental US$15/day. Associated with **Fly Adventures**, see Paragliding, below.

F pp Loki Backpackers (formerly Incahaus), Av Larco 189, T242 4350, www.lokihostel.com. Restored 1920s house with period details and modern facilities. The capital's sister to the party hostel of the same name in Cuzco, **D** in double room, good showers, with breakfast (cooked breakfast extra), Fri barbecues, use of kitchen, free internet, lockers, airport transfer extra.

F pp Pakacuna Backpackers, Juan de la Fuente 647, T445 3205, www.pakacuna.com. Rooms with or without bath, price includes breakfast, internet, kitchen, cable TV and movies, garden.

F pp Stop and Drop, Berlín 168, p2, T243 3101, www.stopandrop.com. **D** double rooms with private bath. Backpacker hotel and guesthouse, also surf and Spanish school. Bar, kitchen facilities, luggage store, laundry, TV, movies, internet, games, comfy beds, safe, hot showers 24 hrs, adventure sports (including diving, horse riding) and volunteer jobs. Airport pick up US$15.

F Wayruro's Backpackers, Enrique Palacios 900, T444 1564, www.wayruros.com. B&B, comfortable dorms, kitchen facilities, free tea and coffee, cheap bar, 24-hr hot water, laundry service, luggage storage, internet, TV, airport pick-up.

G pp Lex Luthor's House, Porta 550 (look for the green lights), T242 7059, luthorshouse@hotmail.com. Breakfast included, pleasant house, small and basic but clean, use of kitchen, good value.

Barranco *p1086*

C Domeyer, C Domeyer 296, T247 1413, domeyerhostel@peru.com. Hot water 24 hrs, laundry service, secure, welcomes gay and lesbian travellers.

C Hostal Gémina, Av Grau 620 in Galerías Gémina, T477 0712, hostalgemina @yahoo.com. In a modern building, comfortable rooms, decorations include old radios and sewing machines, with breakfast, hot water, TV, café.

C pp Suites California, or Villa Barranquina, Martínez Pinillos 129, corner with San Martín, T477 0772, hcalifor@viabcp.com. If you are looking for a flat, this would be a good choice, fully-equipped flatlets in a fascinating 1906 mansion, kitchen, lounge with sofa beds, bathroom, good bedrooms. Also has restaurant and laundry services.

D-E La Quinta de Alison, Av 28 de Julio 281, T247 1515. Breakfast extra, modern, lovely rooms with TV and bath, hot water, some rooms with jacuzzi (extra), excellent value, parking.

E Safe in Lima, Alfredo Silva 150, T252 7330, www.safeinlima.com. Quiet, Belgian-run hostal with family atmosphere in new premises, with breakfast, very helpful, airport pick-up US$14, good value, reserve in advance, lots of information for travellers.

F pp Barranco's Backpackers Inn, Malecón Castilla 260, T247 1326, www.barrancobackpackers.com. All rooms shared, with lockers, hot water in bathrooms, breakfast included. D for double room, kitchen, laundry service, internet access, modern.

F pp Mochileros Hostal, Av Pedro de Osma 135, 1 block from main plaza, T447 4506, backpackers@backpackersperu.com. Beautiful house, completely redecorated, English-speaking owner, huge shared rooms with lockers, gay friendly, use of kitchen, good pub on the premises, a stone's throw from Barranco nightlife.

F pp The Point, Malecón Junín 300, T247 7997, www.thepointhostels.com. Rooms range from doubles to large dormitories, all with shared bath, very popular with backpackers (book in advance at weekends), breakfast included, internet, cable TV, laundry, kitchen facilities, gay-friendly, party atmosphere most of the time, *The Pointless Pub* opens 2000 till whenever, weekly barbecues, therapeutic massage next door, can arrange bungee jumping, flight tickets and volunteering. Also has hostels in Arequipa and Cuzco.

Youth hostels *map p1080*

F Albergue Juvenil Malka, Los Lirios 165 (near 4th block of Av Javier Prado Este), San Isidro, T442 0162, hostelmalka@terra.com.pe. Youth hostel, 20% discount with ISIC card, dormitory style, 4-8 beds per room, English spoken, cable TV, laundry, kitchen, climbing wall, nice café.

F pp Albergue Turístico Juvenil Internacional, Av Casimiro Ulloa 328, San Antonio, T446 5488, www.limahostell.com.pe. Dormitory accommodation, D in a double private room, basic cafeteria, travel information, cooking (minimal) and laundry facilities, swimming pool often empty, extra charge for kitchen facilities, safe, situated in a nice villa; 20 mins walk from the beach. Bus No 2 or colectivos pass Av Benavides to the centre; taxi to centre, US$2.50.

🍴 Eating

19% state tax and 10% service will be added to your bill in middle and upper class restaurants. Chinese is often the cheapest at around US$5 including a drink.

Central Lima *p1081, map p1083*

♨ **Antaño**, Ucayali 332, opposite the Torre Tagle Palace, T426 2372. Good, typical Peruvian food, nice patio. Recommended.

♨ **L'Eau Vive**, Ucayali 370, also opposite the

Torre Tagle Palace, T427 5612. Run by nuns, open Mon-Sat, 1230-1500 and 1930- 2130, fixed-price lunch menu, Peruvian-style in interior dining room, or à la carte in either of dining rooms that open onto patio, excellent, profits go to the poor, Ave Maria is sung nightly at 2100.

† Manhatten, Jr Miró Quesada 259. Open Mon-Fri 0700-1900, low end executive-type restaurant, local and international food from US$5-10, good.

†† El Maurito, Jr Ucayali 212, T426 2538. Peruvian/international, good pisco sours.

†† San Martín, Av Nicolás de Piérola 890, off Plaza San Martín. Typical Peruvian food from both coast and highlands, good value, reasonably cheap.

† Centro de Medicina Natural, Jr Chota 1462, next door to Hostal de las Artes. Very good vegetarian.

† Cordano, Jr Ancash 202. Typical old Lima restaurant/watering hole, slow service and a bit grimy but full of character. Definitely worth the time it takes to drink a few beers.

† Govinda, Av Garcilaso de la Vega 1670, opposite Gran Parque de Lima. Vegetarian, also sells natural products, good.

† Machu Picchu, near Hostal Europa at Jr Ancash 312. Huge portions, grimy bathrooms (to say the least), yet very popular, closed for breakfast.

† Natur, Moquegua 132, 1 block from Jr de la Unión, T427 8281. Vegetarian, the owner, Humberto Valdivia, is also president of the South American Explorers' board of directors, good for food and casual conversation.

† Neydi, Puno 367. Good, cheap seafood, open daily 1100-2000, popular.

Cafés

Café Carrara, Jr Ica 330, attached to Hostal Roma. Open daily until 2200, multiple breakfast combinations, pancakes, sandwiches, nice ambience, good.

Chinatown map p1083

There are many highly recommended chifas in the district of Barrios Altos. For example:

††† Wa Lok, Jr Paruro 864, T427 2656. Owner Liliana Com speaks fluent English, very friendly. Has another branch at Av Angamos Oeste 703, T447 1280, good food in a tasteful, modern setting, †††-††.

† Kin Ten, Ucayali y Paruro. Excellent vegetarian options.

† Salon Capon, Jr Paruro 819. Very good. Has another branch in Larcomar shopping centre, Miraflores, which is †††, elegant.

Breña map p1083

†† La Choza Náutica, Jr Breña 204 behind Plaza

Bolognesi. Good ceviche and friendly service.

† Azato, Av Arica 298, 3 blocks from Plaza Bolognesi, T423 4369. Excellent and cheap Peruvian dishes.

A variety of Lima's better-known restaurants and cafés have branches on Avenida Primavera: eg Antica Pizzería (No 275, T372 2698) and Delicass (No 654, T372 5203), both also in San Isidro, a branch of the San Antonio Café chain (see Miraflores, Cafés, below), and the main branch of T'Anta (No 692, T372 3528, chacarilla@tanta.com.pe), a coffee shop-cum-restaurant which specializes in the Novo Andino cuisine of Gastón Acurio (of Café del Museo and Astrid & Gastón, see below); also in Miraflores, San Isidro and central Lima.

Pueblo Libre p1085

†† Café del Museo at the Museo Larco, Av Bolívar 1515, Pueblo Libre, T461 1312, www.cafedelmuseo.com. Daily 0900-1800, seating inside and on the terrace. Specially designed interior, offers a selection of salads, fine Peruvian dishes, pastas and seafood, a tapas bar of traditional Peruvian foods, as well as snacks, desserts and cocktails. Highly regarded.

†† Antigua Taberna Quierolo, Av San Martín 1090, 1 block from Plaza Bolívar. Atmospheric old bar with glass-fronted shelves of bottles, marble bar and old photos, owns bodega next door. Serves simple lunches, sandwiches and snacks, good for wine, does not serve dinner.

San Isidro p1085

†††† Alfresco, Santa Lucía 295 (no sign), T422 8915. Best known for its tempting seafood and ceviche, also pastas and rice dishes, expensive wines.

†††† Antica Pizzería, Av Dos de Mayo 728, T222 8437. Very popular, great ambience, excellent food, Italian owner. Also Antica Trattoria in Barranco at Alfonso Ugarte 242, and an excellent bar, Antica Taberna, with a limited range of food at Conquistadores 605, San Isidro, very good value, fashionable, get there early for a seat.

†††† Asia de Cuba, Conquistadores 780, T222 4940. Popular, serving a mix of Asian, Cuban and Peruvian dishes. It also has a reputation for its bar and nightclub; try the martinis.

†††† Matsuei, C Manuel Bañon 260, T422 4323. Sushi bar and Japanese dishes, very popular, among the best Japanese in Lima.

†††† Valentino, Manuel Bañon 215, T441 6174. One of Lima's best international restaurants, formal, look for the tiny brass sign.

††† Chez Philippe, Av 2 de Mayo 748, T222-4953. Pizza, pasta and crêpes, wood oven, rustic decor (same owners as Pizza B&B in Huaraz).

Chilis, Ovalo Gutiérrez. A branch of the American chain with a Peruvian twist, popular, like most of the places on the Ovalo.

Delicass, Miguel Dasso 131. Great deli with imported meats and cheeses, good coffee, open late, slow service.

Segundo Muelle, Av Conquistadores 490, T421 1206, and Av Canaval y Moreyra (aka Corpac) 605. Excellent *ceviche* and other very good seafood dishes, popular with the younger crowd.

MiniMarket Kasher, Av Pexet 1472. Kosher products, excellent, cheap *chala* bread every Fri.

Cafés
Café Olé, Pancho Fierro 115 (1 block from *Hotel El Olívar*). Huge selection of entrées and desserts, very smart with prices to match.

Café Positano/Café Luna, Miguel Dasso 147. Popular with politicians, café and bistro.

News Café, Av Santa Luisa 110. Great salads and desserts, popular and expensive.

Miraflores *p1086, map p1090*
Calle San Ramón, known as 'Pizza Street' (across from Parque Kennedy), is a pedestrian walkway lined with outdoor restaurants/bars/discos open until the wee small hours. It's very popular, with good-natured touts trying to entice diners and drinkers with free offers.

Astrid y Gaston, Cantuarias 175, T444 1496. Exceptional local/Novo Andino and international cuisine, one of the best in Lima, owners are Gastón Acurio and his wife Astrid. Also has a bar.

Las Brujas de Cachiche, Av Bolognesi 460, T447 1883. An old mansion converted into bars and dining rooms, traditional food (menu in Spanish and English), best Lomo Saltado in town, live *criollo* music.

Café Voltaire, Av Dos de Mayo 220. International cuisine with emphasis on French dishes, beautifully-cooked food, pleasant ambience, good service, closed Sun.

Coco de Mer, Av Grau 400, T243 0278, www.cocodemerlima.com. Run by Englishwoman Lucy Ralph, popular, Mediterranean and Peruvian dishes, cocktails, events, open daily 1200 till whenever.

Cuarto y Mitad, Av Espinar 798, T446 2988. Popular Grill, also serves seafood.

La Gloria, Atahualpa 201, T446 6504. Very smart, excellent food and service.

El Kapallaq, Av Petit Thouars 4844, T444 4149. Prize-winning Peruvian restaurant specializing in seafood and fish, excellent *ceviches*. Open Mon-Fri 1200-1700 only.

El Rincón Gaucho, Av Armendáriz 580, T447 4778. Good grill, renowned for its steaks.

Rosa Náutica, T445 0149, www.larosa nautica.com. Built on old British-style pier (Espigón No 4), in Lima Bay. Delightful opulence, finest fish cuisine, experience the atmosphere by buying an expensive beer in the bar at sunset, open 1230-0200 daily.

El Señorío de Sulco, Malecón Cisneros 1470, T441 0183, http://senoriodesulco.com. Overlooking a clifftop park, with ocean views from upstairs. Forget the Footprint grading, this is a 'five-fork' restaurant which some believe is the best in Lima, all Peruvian food, à la carte and buffet, piscos, wines, piano music at night.

Las Tejas, Diez Canseco 340. Open 1100-2300 daily, good, typical Peruvian food, recommended for ceviche.

La Tranquera, Av Pardo 285. Argentine-owned steak house, very good.

La Trattoria, Manuel Bonilla 106, 1 block from Parque Kennedy. Italian cuisine, popular, good cheesecake.

Sí Señor, Bolognesi 706, T445 3789, www.sisenor.org. Mexican food, cheerful, interesting décor, huge portions.

El Beduino, Av 28 de Julio 1301, T242 6642. Good, authentic Arabic food.

Bohemia, Av Santa Cruz 805, Ovalo Gutiérrez. Large menu of international food, great salads and sandwiches. Also at Av El Polo 706, p 2, and at Pasaje Nicolás de Rivera 142, opposite the main post office near the Plaza de Armas, Lima centre, T427 5537.

Café Tarata, Pasaje Tarata 260. Good atmosphere, family-run, good varied menu.

Dalmacia, San Fernando 401. Spanish- owned, casual gourmet restaurant, excellent.

La Palachinke, Av Schell 120 at the bottom of Parque Kennedy. Recommended for pancakes.

Il Postino, Colina 401, T446 8381. Great Italian food.

Ricota, Pasaje Tarata 248. Charming café on a pedestrian walkway, huge menu, big portions.

Dino's Pizza, Av Cdte Espinar 374 and many other branches. Great pizza at a good price, delivery service.

Madre Natura, Chiclayo 815. Natural foods shop and eating place, very good, closes 2100.

Pardo's Chicken, Av Benavides 730. Chicken and chips, very good and popular (branches throughout Lima).

El Parquetito, Diez Canseco 150. Good cheap menu, serves breakfast, eat inside or out.

Sandwich.com, Av Diagonal 234. Good, cheap sandwiches with interesting combinations of fillings.

Super Rueda, Porta 133, also Av Pardo 1224. Mexican food a-la Peru, fast-food style.

Cafés

Café Café, Martin Olaya 250, near the Parque Kennedy roundabout. Very popular, good atmosphere, over 100 different blends of coffee, good salads and sandwiches, very popular with 'well-to-do' Limeños. Also in Larcomar.

Café de la Paz, Lima 351, middle of Parque Kennedy. Good outdoor café right on the park, expensive, great cocktails.

Café Zeta, Mcal Oscar R Benavides 598 y José Gálvez. American owned, excellent Peruvian coffee, teas, hot chocolate, and the best homemade cakes away from home, cheap too.

C'est si bon, Av Cdte Espinar 663. Excellent cakes by the slice or whole, best in Lima.

Chef's Café, Av Larco 763. Nice place for a sandwich or coffee. Also has a little cart in Parque Kennedy until 2200 with good hot coffee to go.

Dove Vai, Diagonal 228. A bright *heladería* in this block of eating places; try the *encanto* with lumps of chocolate brownie.

Haiti, Av Diagonal 160, Parque Kennedy. Open almost round the clock daily, great for people watching, good ice cream.

Heladería 4D, Angamos Oeste 408. Open 1000-0100 daily, Italian ice cream, at other locations throughout Lima.

La Tiendecita Blanca, Av Larco 111 on Parque Kennedy. One of Miraflores' oldest, expensive, good people-watching, very good cakes, European-style food and delicatessen.

San Antonio, Av Angamos Oeste 1494, also Vasco Núñez de Balboa 770, Rocca de Vergallo 201, Magdalena del Mar and Av Primavera 373, San Borja. Fashionable *pastelería* chain, good, not too expensive.

Tapas Bar, Manuel Bonilla 103, T242 7922. Expensive but very good tapas bar behind huge wooden doors, the tapas are a meal in themselves, extensive wine list, reserve a table at weekends.

Vivaldi, Av Ricardo Palma 260, 1 block from Parque Kennedy. Good, expensive, reminiscent of a gentlemen's club. Also **Vivaldi Gourmet**, Conquistadores 212, San Isidro, an international restaurant.

Zugatti, Av Larco 361, across from Parque Kennedy. Good Italian gelato.

Barranco *p1086*

♥♥♥ **La Costa Verde**, on Barranquito beach, T441 3086. Excellent fish and wine, expensive but recommended as the best by Limeños, open 1200-2400 daily, Sun buffet.

♥♥♥ **Manos Morenas**, Av Pedro de Osma 409, T467 0421. Open 1230-1630, 1900-2300, creole cuisine with shows some evenings (cover charge for shows).

♥♥♥ **Ñaylamp**, Av 2 de Mayo 239, T467 5011.

Good seafood and ceviche, fashionable.

♥♥ **Festín**, Av Grau 323, T247 7218. Huge menu, typical and international food.

♥♥ **El Hornito**, Av Grau 209, on corner of the main plaza, T477 2465. Pizzería and creole food.

♥♥ **Las Mesitas**, Av Grau 341, open 1200-0200. Traditional tea rooms-cum-restaurant, serving creole food and traditional desserts which you won't find anywhere else.

♥ Bars and clubs

Central Lima *p1081, map p1083*
The centre of town, specifically Jr de la Unión, has many discos. It's best to avoid the nightspots around the intersection of Av Tacna, Av Piérola and Av de la Vega. These places are rough and foreigners will receive much unwanted attention.

For latest recommendations for gay and lesbian places, check out www.deambiente.com, www.gayperu.com and http://lima.queercity.info/index.html.

Estadio Futbol Sports Bar, Av Nicolás de Piérola 926 on the Plaza San Martín, T428 8866. Beautiful bar with a disco on the bottom floor, international football theme, good international and creole food.

La Jarrita, Camaná 949, www.lajarrita.com. Gay restaurant/video-pub in the centre. Its quieter partner is **Lima de Noche**, Av Garcilaso de la Vega 718, p 2. Best to take a taxi at night.

Piano Bar Munich, Jr de la Unión 1044 (basement). Small and fun.

Queirolo Bar, Jr Camaná 900 at Jr Quilca. Excellent for local colour. Opposite is the Centre's version of **La Noche** (see above).

El Rincón Cervecero, Jr de la Unión (Belén) 1045. German pub without the beer, fun.

San Isidro *p1085*
Palos de Moguer, Av Emilio Cavenecia 129, T221 8363. Brews 4 different kinds of beer, typical bar food.

Punto G, Av Conquistadores 512. Very popular, really small.

Miraflores *p1086, map p1090*
Barcelona, in Larcomar, T445 4823. One of the best pubs in the city.

Barra Brava, Av Grau 192. Lots of fun, sports bar(ish).

The Clash, Psje Tello 269, Miraflores, T444 3376. Pub and gallery, excellent drinks, friendly staff, great decor, exclusively gay.

Cocodrilo Verde, Francisco de Paula 226 near corner with Bellavista, Miraflores. Relaxed, stylish bar, slightly pricey but worth it for the Wed night jazz, and live music at weekends, occasionally charges cover for music at weekends.

Dionygreeks Pub, Av Dos de Mayo 385.
Nice pub with Greek decor.
Media Naranja, Schell 130, at the bottom of
Parque Kennedy. Brazilian bar with typical drinks
and food.
Murphys, C Schell 627. Great Irish pub,
"a must", also doing food such as fish'n'chips.
The Old Pub, San Ramón 295 (Pizza Street).
Cosy, with live music most days.
La Sede, Av 28 de Julio 441,
www.publasede.com. Very popular, great music,
fun crowd, gay friendly.
Satchmo, Av La Paz 538, T442 8425.
Live jazz, creole and blues shows.
Teatriz, Larcomar shopping center,
T242 3084. Modern, expensive, very popular.
Voluntarios Pub, Independencia 131, T445
3939, www.voluntariospub.org. All staff are
volunteers from non-profit organizations which
benefit by receiving 90% of the profits made by
the pub. Good atmosphere, music and drinks,
nice to know that while you are partying other
people are benefiting.

Barranco *p1086*

Barranco is the capital of Lima nightlife. The
following is a short list of some of the better bars
and clubs. Pasaje Sánchez Carrión, right off the
main plaza, used to be the heart of it all. Watering
holes and discos line both sides of this pedestrian
walkway, but crowds and noise are driving
people elsewhere. Av Grau, just across the street
from the plaza, is also lined with bars, eg El
Ekeko, Av Grau 266, and Las Terrazas, Av Grau
290. Many of the bars in this area turn into clubs
as the night goes on.
Bosa Nova, Bolognesi 660. Chilled student-style
bar with good music.
El Dragón, N de Piérola 168, T797 1033,
dragoncultural@hotmail.com. Popular bar and
venue for music, theatre and painting.
El Grill de Costa Verde, part of the *Costa Verde*
restaurant on Barranco beach. Young crowd,
packed at weekends.
Juanitos, Av Grau, opposite the park. Barranco's
oldest bar, and perfect to start the evening.
La Noche, Bolognesi 307, at Pasaje Sánchez
Carrión. A Lima institution and high standard, live
music, Mon is jazz night, kicks off around 2200
(also in Central Lima).
La Posada del Angel, three branches on Pedro
de Osma between 164 and 222. These are
popular bars serving snacks and meals.
La Posada del Mirador, near the Puente de los
Suspiros (Bridge of Sighs). Beautiful view of the
ocean, but you pay for the privilege.
Sargento Pimienta, Bolognesi 755. Live music,
always a favourite with Limeños. Opposite is the
relaxed **Trinidad**.

🎧 Entertainment

Lima *p1081, maps p1083 and p1090*
Cinemas
The newspaper *El Comercio* lists cinema
information in the section called *Luces*. Most
charge US$2 in the centre and around US$4-5 in
Miraflores; two tickets for the price of one often
offered on Tue. The cultural institutions (see
below) usually show films once a week. Most films
are in English with Spanish subtitles. The best
cinema chains in the city are **Cinemark**,
Cineplanet and **UVK Multicines**. Also good is
Multicine Starvision El Pacífico, on the Ovalo by
Parque Kennedy, Miraflores, T445 6990. Some *Cine
Clubs* are **Cine Club Miraflores**, Av Larco 770, in
the Miraflores Cultural Centre building, T446 2649.
Filmoteca de Lima, Av 9 de Diciembre 125 (better
known as Colón), T331 0126.

Peñas
Las Brisas de Titicaca, Pasaje Walkuski 168, at
1st block of Av Brasil near Plaza Bolognesi, T332
1881, www.brisasdeltiticaca.comS. A Lima
institution.
De Cajón, C Merino 2nd block, near 6th block of
Av Del Ejército, Miraflores. Good *música negra*.
La Candelaria, Av Bolognesi 292, Barranco,
T247 1314. A good Barranco *peña*, open
Fri-Sat 2130 onwards.
Del Carajo, San Ambrosio 328, Barranco, T241
7977. All types of traditional music.
La Estación de Barranco, at Pedro de Osma
112, T477 5030. Good, family atmosphere,
varied shows.
Peña Poggi, Av Luna Pizarro 578, Barranco,
T247 5790/885 7619. Over 30 years old.

Theatre
Most professional plays are staged at **Teatro
Segura**, Jr Huancavelica 265, T427 9491. There are
many other theatres in the city, some of which are
related to Cultural centres (see below). The press
gives details of performances. Theatre and concert
tickets booked through Teleticket, T01-610 8888,
Mon-Fri 0900-1900, www.e-teleticket.com.

🎉 Festivals and events

Lima *p1081, maps p1083 and p1090*
18 Jan: Founding of Lima. Semana Santa,
or Holy Week, is a colourful spectacle with
processions. **28-29 Jul**: is Independence, with
music and fireworks in the Plaza de Armas on the
evening before. **30 Aug**: Santa Rosa de Lima.
Oct: is the month of Our Lord of the Miracles;
see Las Nazarenas church, above page 1083.

O Shopping

Lima *p1081, maps p1083 and p1090*

Bookshops

Crisol, Ovalo Gutiérrez, Av Santa Cruz 816, San Isidro, T221 1010, Below *Cine Planet*. Large bookshop with café, titles in English, French and Spanish. Also in Jockey Plaza Shopping Center, Av Javier Prado Este 4200, Surco, T436 004.
La Familia, Av Diagonal 382, T01-447 8353, and Schell 279, T01-444 3993, Miraflores. Has a good selection of books on a wide variety of topics, helpful staff. Other branches at *La Tertulia*, CCPUCP, Av Camino Real 1075, San Isidro, and in the Jockey Plaza and El Polo commercial centres in Surco.
Ibero Librerías, Av Diagonal 500, T01-242 2798, Larco 199, T01-445 5520, and in Larcomar, Miraflores. Stocks Footprint Handbooks as well as a wide range of other titles.
Special Book Services, Av Angamos Oeste 301, Miraflores, T01-241 8490, www.sbs.com.pe. Holds stock of international books in several languages. Has branches in San Isidro and Surquillo.
Virrey chain has a great selection, but few in English: Larcomar Shopping Center (local 210), Miraflores, Pasaje Nicolás de Rivera, Lima centre behind the Municipalidad, T427 5080, and Miguel Dasso 141, San Isidro (next door is **Librería Sur**, No 143).

For magazines, whether in downtown Lima or Miraflores, almost all street kiosks sell magazines in English. For the most recently published magazines and newspapers, try **Mallcco's** on Av Larco 175, on the Parque Kennedy roundabout, open daily 0800-2100. In front of Café Haiti by Parque Kennedy, men sell newspapers taken from arriving international flights; bargain hard.

Camping equipment

It's better to bring all camping and hiking gear from home. Camping gas (in small blue bottles) is available from any large hardware store or bigger supermarket, about US$3.
Alpamayo, Av Larco 345, Miraflores at Parque Kennedy, T445 1671. Sleeping mats, boots, rock shoes, climbing gear, water filters, tents, backpacks etc, very expensive but top quality equipment. Owner speaks fluent English and offers good information.
Camping Center, Av Benavides 1620, Miraflores, T242 1779. Selection of tents, back-packs, stoves, camping and climbing gear.
Huantzan, Jr Tarapacá 384, Magdalena, T460 6101. Equipment sales and rentals, MSR stoves, backpacks, boots.
Mountain Worker, Centro Comercial Camino Real, level A, store 17, San Isidro, T813 8367. Quality camping gear for all types of weather, made to order products as well.
El Mundo de las Maletas, Preciados 308, Higuereta-Surco, T449 7850. 0900-2200 daily for suitcase repairs.
Outdoor Peru, Centro Comercial Chacarilla, store 211, on Av Caminos del Inca 257, Surco, T372 0428. Decent selection.
Todo Camping, Av Angamos Oeste 350, Miraflores, near Av Arequipa, T447 6279. Sells 100% deet, bluet gas canisters, lots of accessories, tents, crampons and backpacks.

Handicrafts

Since so many artisans have come to Lima, it is possible to find any kind of handicraft in the capital. Miraflores is a good place for high quality, expensive handicrafts; there are many shops on and around Av La Paz.
Agua y Tierra, Diez Canseco 298 y Alcanfores, Miraflores, T444 6980. Fine crafts and indigenous art.
Artesanía Santo Domingo, Plaza Santo Domingo, by the church of that name, in Lima centre, T428 9860. Good Peruvian crafts.
La Casa de la Mujer Artesana, Juan Pablo Ferandini 1550 (Av Brasil cuadra 15), Pueblo Libre, T423 8840, www.casadelamujer artesana.com. A cooperative run by the Movimiento Manuela Ramos, excellent quality work mostly from *pueblos jóvenes*, open Mon-Fri 0900-1300, 1400-1700.
Centro Comercial El Alamo, corner of La Paz y Diez Canseco, Miraflores. *Artesanía* shops with good choice.
Kuntur Wasi, Ocharan 182, Miraflores, T444 0557. English-speaking owner very knowledgeable about Peruvian textiles, often has exhibitions of fine folk art and crafts.
Las Pallas, Cajamarca 212, 5th block of Av Grau, Barranco, T477 4629, Mon-Sat 0900- 1900. Very high quality handicrafts, English, French and German spoken.
Luz Hecho a Mano, Berlín 399, Miraflores, T446 7098, www.luzhechoamano.com. Lovely hand made handbags, wallets and other leather goods including clothing which last for years and can be custom made.
There are bargains in high quality Pima cotton.
Shops selling **alpaca** items include:
Alpaca 111, Av Larco 671, Miraflores, T447 1623, www.alpaca111.com. High quality alpaca, baby alpaca and vicuña items.
Alpaca 859, Av Larco 859, Miraflores. Good quality alpaca and baby alpaca products.
Alpaka Studio, Av Larco 1144, Store 9, Miraflores. Fashionable alpaca garments.
Da Capo, Aramburú 920, dpto 402, San Isidro, T441 0714. Beautiful alpaca scarves and shawls in new designs.

La Casa de la Alpaca, Av La Paz 665, Miraflores, T447 6271. Open Mon-Fri 0930-2030.
Orígenes Andinos, Larcomar, Miraflores, T241 8472, www.origenesandinos.com. T-shirts and polo shirts made from Peruvian cotton with designs from the Nazca, Chimú, Moche, Mochica, Inca and other cultures.
Silvania Prints, Diéz Canseco 337A, Miraflores. Modern silk-screen prints on Pima cotton with pre-Columbian designs.
Dédalo, Paseo Sáenz Peña 295, Barranco, T477 0562. A labyrinthine shop selling furniture, jewellery and other items, as good as a gallery. It also has a nice coffee shop and has cinema shows.
Jewellery Ilaria, Av 2 de Mayo 308, San Isidro, T221 8575. Jewellery and silverware with interesting designs. There are other branches in Lima, Cuzco and Arequipa. Recommended. On C La Esperanza, Miraflores, dozens of shops offer gold and silverware at reasonable prices.

Maps

Instituto Geográfico Nacional, Av Aramburú 1190, Surquillo, T475 3030, ext 119, www.ign peru.gob.pe. Open Mon-Fri 0800-1730. It has topographical maps of the whole country, mostly at 1:100,000, political and physical maps of all departments and satellite and aerial photographs. They also have a new series of tourist maps for trekking, eg of the Cordillera Blanca, the Cuzco area, at 1:250,000.
Instituto Geológico Minero Y Metalúrgico (Ingemmet), Av Canadá 1470, San Borja, T225 3128, www.ingemmet.gob.pe. Open Mon-Fri 0800-1300, 1400-1600. Sells a huge selection of geographic maps ranging from US$12 to US$112. Also satellite, aeromagnetic, geochemical and departmental mining maps. Enquire about new digital products.
Lima 2000, Av Arequipa 2625, Lince (near the intersection with Av Javier Prado), T440 3486, www.lima2000.com.pe. Open Mon-Fri 0900-1300 and 1400-1800. Has an excellent street map of Lima (the only one worth buying), US$10, or US$14 in booklet form. Provincial maps and a country road map as well. Good for road conditions and distances, perfect for driving or cycling.
Ministerio de Transporte, Av 28 de Julio 800, Lima centre, T433 7800, www.mtc.gob.pe. Open Mon-Fri 0800-1230, 1400-1600. Maps and plans of land communication routes, but very bureaucratic.
Servicio Aerofotográfico Nacional, Av Las Palmas s/n, Barranco, T477 3682, informes@ sanperu.com. Open Mon-Fri 0800-1400. Aerial photographs available from mid-1950's aerial survey, but they are expensive. Expect a waiting period as short as 1 day or as long as 2 weeks.

Markets

All are open 7 days a week until late.
Av Petit Thouars, in Miraflores. At blocks 51-54 (near Parque Kennedy, parallel to Av Arequipa). An unnamed crafts market area with a large courtyard and lots of small flags. This is the largest crafts arcade in Miraflores. From here to Calle Ricardo Palma the street is lined with crafts markets.
Feria Artesanal, Av La Marina y Av Sucre, in Pueblo Libre. Smaller than it used to be but is cheaper than Av Petit Thouars. It is no longer regarded as a safe area.
Parque Kennedy, the main park of Miraflores, hosts a daily crafts market from 1700-2300.
Polvos Azules, on García Naranjo, La Victoria, just off Av Grau in the centre of town. The 'official' black market, sells just about anything; it is generally cheap and very interesting; beware pickpockets.
La Portada del Sol, on cuadra 54 of Petit Thouars, has a small café with reasonable prices and good coffee.

Supermarkets

Lima's supermarkets are well stocked and carry a decent supply of imported goods. **Santa Isabel**, on Av Pardo in Miraflores is open 24 hrs.

▲▲ Activities and tours

Lima *p1081, maps p1083 and p1090*
Cycling
Best Internacional, Av Cdte Espinar 320, Miraflores, T446 4044. Open Mon-Sat 1000-1400, 1600-2000. Sells leisure and racing bikes, also repairs, parts and accessories.
Biclas, Av Conquistadores 641, San Isidro, T440 0890. Open Mon-Fri 1000-1300, 1600-2000, Sat 1000-1300. Knowledgeable staff, tours possible, good selection of bikes, repairs and accessories, cheap airline boxes for sale.
BikeMavil, Av Aviación 4023, Surco, T449 8435. Open Mon-Sat 0930-2100. Rental service, repairs, tours, selection of mountain and racing bikes.
Casa Okuyama, Manco Cápac 590, La Victoria, T330 9131. Open Mon-Fri 0900-1300, 1415-1800, Sat 0900-1300. Repairs, parts, try here for 28-in tyres, excellent service.
Neuquén, Jr Paruro 875, El Cercado, T427 2379. For Shimano parts.
Perú Bike, Parque Nueva Castilla, Calle A, D-7, Surco, T449 5234, www.perubike.com. Experienced agency leading tours, professional guiding, mountain bike school and workshop.
Willy Pro (Williams Arce), Av Javier Prado Este 3339, San Borja, T346 4082. Open Mon-Sat 0800-2000. Selection of specialized bikes, helpful staff.

Peru Expeditions, Av Arequipa 5241 - 504, Lima 18, T447 2057, www.peru-expeditions.com. Specializing in expeditions in 4WD vehicles and Andes crossings.

Peru For Less, ASTA Travel Agent, US office: T1-877-269 0309; UK office: T020-3002 0571; Peru (Lima) office: T272 0542, www.peruforless.com. Will meet or beat any published rates on the internet from outside Peru.

Peru Travel Bureau, Sebastián Tellería 45, San Isidro, T222 1909, www.ptb.com.pe. Recommended.

Roma Tours, Jr Ica 330, next to Hostal Roma, T/F427 7572, dantereyes@hotmail.com. Good and reliable. Administrator Dante Reyes is very friendly and speaks English.

Rutas del Peru SAC, Av Enrique Palacios 1110, Miraflores, T444 5405, www.rutasdelperu.com. Bespoke trips and overland expeditions in trucks.

Victor's Travel Service, Jr de la Unión (Belén) 1068, T431 4195, 24-hr line 867 6341, victortravel@terra.com.pe, Hotel reservations (no commission, free pick-up), free maps of Lima and Peru, Mon-Sat 0900-1800, very helpful.

Viracocha, Av Vasco Núñez de Balboa 191, Miraflores, T445 3986, peruviantours@viracocha.com.pe. Very helpful, especially with flights, adventure, cultural, mystical and birdwatching tours.

Private guides The MITINCI (Ministry of Industry Tourism, Integration and International Business) certifies guides and can provide a list. Most are members of **AGOTUR** (Asociación de Guías Oficiales de Turismo), La Venturosa 177, Surco, T448 5167, agoturlima@ yahoo.com. Book in advance. Most guides speak a language other than Spanish.

Escorted Economic Overland Peru, T/F567 5107, victormelgar777@yahoo.com. Run by experienced tour guide Víctor Melgar (of **Hostal Víctor** – see Sleeping), who escorts individuals, families and groups throughout Peru and Bolivia, safely and economically.

⊖ Transport

Lima *p1081, maps p1083 and p1090*
Air
Arrivals or departures flight information T511 6055, www.lap.com.pe. **Jorge Chávez Airport**, 16 km from the centre of Lima. At the customs area, explain that you are a tourist and that your

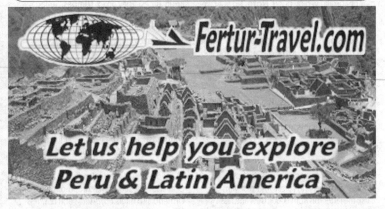

personal effects will not be sold in Peru; items such as laptops, cameras, bicycles, climbing equipment are exempt from taxes if they are not to be sold in Peru.

Information desks can be found in the national and international foyers. There is also a helpful desk in the international arrivals hall. It can make hotel and transport reservations. The Perú Perú shops sell gifts and books, including some English-language guidebooks.

Global Net ATM (accepting American Express, Visa, MasterCard and the Plus, Maestro and Cirrus systems), a **Casa de Cambio** (money changing desk) and a bank can be found at the same end as the stairs up to national departures. There are also exchange facilities for cash in the international arrivals hall, but rates are poorer than outside. There are **public telephones** around the airport and a Telefónica del Peru *locutorio*, open 0700-2300 daily. Internet facilities are more expensive than in the city. There are postal services.

Transport from the airport *Remise* taxi (Mitsui or CMV) from desks outside International Arrivals and National Arrivals, US$11.75 to centre, US$14.50 to San Isidro and Miraflores, US$17.50 to Barranco. There are many taxi drivers offering their services outside Arrivals with similar or higher prices (more at night). Taxi Green have been recommended as reliable and economical. See below for other taxi fares. There is a service called **Urbanito**, from the airport to the centre, Breña and San Miguel US$3, Pueblo Libre, San Isidro and Miraflores US$5 (slow, as it calls at all hotels), T424 3650, 9957 3238 (mob), urbanito@terra.com.pe. Local buses (US$0.35) and colectivos run between the airport perimeter and the city centre and suburbs, their routes are given on the front window (eg 'Miraflores' for Miraflores). Outside the pedestrian exit are the bus, colectivo and taxi stops. At busy times (ie anytime other than late at night or early in the morning), luggage may not be allowed on buses. **Note** Do not take the cheapest, stopping buses to the centre along Av Faucett. They are frequently robbed. Pay more for a non-stop bus. If you are feeling confident and not too jet-lagged, go to the car park exit and find a taxi outside the perimeter, by the roundabout. They charge US$3-6 to the city centre. The security guards may help you find a taxi.

Internal air services There are daily flights to most destinations (most options are given in the text) but flights may be cancelled in the rainy season.

Bus

Local The bus routes are shared by buses, combis (mid-size) and colectivos (mini-vans or cars); the latter run from 0600-0100, and less frequently through the night, they are quicker and stop wherever requested. Buses and combis charge US$0.35, colectivos a little more. On public holidays, Sun and from 2400 to 0500 every night, a small charge is added to the fare.

Buses to **Miraflores**: Av Arequipa runs 52 blocks between the downtown Lima area and Parque Kennedy in Miraflores. Public transport has "Todo Arequipa" on the windscreen. When heading towards downtown from Miraflores the window sticker should say "Wilson/Tacna". To get to Parque Kennedy from downtown look on the windshield for "Larco/Schell/Miraflores," "Chorrillos/ Huaylas" or "Barranco/ Ayacucho". On Vía Expresa, buses can be caught at Avs Tacna, Garcilaso de la Vega, Bolivia and Ugarte (faster than Av Arequipa, but watch for pickpockets). The main stop for Miraflores is Ricardo Palma, 4 blocks from Parque Kennedy.

Long distance There are many different bus companies, but the larger ones are better organized, leave on time and do not wait until the bus is full. For approximate prices, frequency and duration of trip, see destinations. **Note** In the weeks either side of 28/29 Jul (Independence), and of the Christmas/ New Year holiday, it is practically impossible to get bus tickets out of Lima, unless you book in advance. Bus prices double at these times.

Cruz del Sur, Jr Quilca 531, Lima centre, T431 5125, www.cruzdelsur.com.pe. This terminal has routes to many destinations in Peru with *Ideal* service, quite comfortable buses and periodic stops for food and bathroom breaks, a cheap option with a quality company. They go to: **Ica, Arequipa, Cuzco, Puno, Chiclayo, Trujillo, Chincha, Camaná, Ilo, Moquegua, Pisco** and **Juliaca**. The other terminal is at Av Javier Prado Este 1109, San Isidro, T225 6163. This terminal offers the *Imperial* service (luxury buses), more expensive and direct, with no chance of passengers in the aisle, and *Cruzero* service (super luxury buses). They go to: **Tumbes, Sullana, Huancayo, Piura, Chiclayo, Trujillo, Huaraz, Jauja, Camaná, Arequipa, Moquegua, Ilo, Tacna, Cuzco** and **La Paz** (change buses in Arequipa). *Imperial* buses stop at the central terminal when going north and *Ideal* buses stop at the Javier Prado terminal when going south.

The following buses are all owned and operated by Ormeño: *Expreso Ancash* (routes to the **Huaraz area**), *Expreso Continental* (routes to **the north**), *Expreso San Cristóbal* (to **the southeast**), and *Expreso Chinchano* (to the **south coast** and **Arequipa**). These depart from and arrive to: Av Carlos Zavala 177, Lima centre, T427 5679; also Av Javier Prado Este 1059, Santa Catalina, T472 5000, www.grupo-ormeno.com. Ormeño also offers *Royal Class* and *Business* cheques with Amex card only. Or branches of *Viajes Falabella*, eg Jr Belén 630, T428 9779, or Av Larco 747-753, Miraflores, T444 4239, lgutierrez@viajesfalabella.com.pe. **MasterCard**, Porta 111, p 6, Miraflores, T311 6000. **Moneygram**, Ocharan 260, Miraflores, T447 4044. Safe and reliable agency for sending and receiving money. Locations throughout Lima and the provinces. Exchanges most world currencies and TCs. **Western Union** Main branch: Av Petit Thouars 3595, San Isidro, T422 0036. Av Larco 826, Miraflores, T241 1220 (also *TNT* office). Jr Carabaya 693, Lima centre, T428 7624. **Car rental** Most ompanies have an office at the airport, where you can arrange everything and pick up and leave the car. It is recommended to test-drive before signing the contract as quality varies. It can be much cheaper to rent a car in a town in the Sierra for a few days than to drive from Lima; also companies don't have a collection service. See page 43 for international rental agencies. Cars can be hired from: **Paz Rent A Car**, Av Diez Canseco 319, of 15, Miraflores, T446 4395, 9993 9853 (mob), pazrent@latinmail.com. Prices range from US$40 to US$60 depending on type of car. Make sure that your car is in a locked garage at night. **Cultural centres** Alianza Francesa, Av Arequipa 4595, Miraflores, T446 5524, www.alianzafrances alima.edu.pe. Various cultural activities, library. **British Council**, Torre Parque Mar, p 22, Av José Larco 1301, T617 3060, www.britishcouncil.org/ peru.htm. **CCPUCP** (cultural centre of the Universidad Católica), Camino Real 1075, San Isidro, T616 1616, http://cultural.pucp.edu.pe. Excellent theatre (tickets US$7.15), European art films (US$1.45 Mon- Wed), galleries, good café and a bookshop selling art and literature titles. Recommended. **Centro Cultural Peruano Japonés**, Av Gregorio Escobedo 803, Jesús María, T463 0606, postmast@ apjp.org.pe. Has a concert hall, cinema, galleries, museum of Japanese immigration, cheap and excellent restaurant, lots of activities. Recommended. **Goethe Institute**, Jr Nazca 722, Jesús María, T433 3180, www.goethe.de. Mon-Fri 0800- 2000, library, German papers. **Instituto Cultural Peruano- Norteamericano**, Jr Cusco 446, Lima Centre, T428 3530, with library. Central office at Av Angamos Oeste 120, Miraflores, T242 6300, www.icpna. edu.pe. Theatre productions, modern dance performances etc. Also Spanish lessons; see Language schools, below. **Embassies and consulates** Note During the summer, most embassies only open in the morning. **Australia**, Av Víctor Andrés Belaúnde 147, Vía Principal 155, Ed Real 3, of 1301, San Isidro, Lima 27, T222 8281, info.peru@ austrade.gov.au. **Austria**, Av Central 643, p 5, San Isidro, T442 0503. **Belgian Consulate**, Angamos Oeste 392, Miraflores, T422 8231.

Bolivian Consulate, Los Castaños 235, San Isidro, T442 3836, postmast@emboli.org.pe (0900-1330), 24 hrs for visas (except those requiring clearance from La Paz). **Brazilian Consulate**, José Pardo 850, Miraflores, T421 5650, Mon-Fri 0930-1300. **Canada**, Libertad 130, Casilla 18-1126, Lima, T444 4015, lima@ dfait-maeci.gc.ca. **Chilean Consulate**, Javier Prado Oeste 790, San Isidro, T611 2211, embchile@mail.cosapidata.com.pe. Open 0900-1300, need appointment. **Ecuadorean Consulate**, Las Palmeras 356, San Isidro (6th block of Av Javier Prado Oeste), T440 9991, embjecua@ amauta.rcp.net.pe. **French Embassy**, Arequipa 3415, San Isidro, T215 8400, france.embajada@ computextos.com.pe. **Germany**, Av Arequipa 4202, Miraflores, T212 5016, emergency number 9927 8338. **Ísrael**, Natalio Sánchez 125, p 6, Santa Beatriz, T433 4431. **Italy**, Av G Escobedo 298, Jesús María, T463 2727. **Japan**, Av San Felipe 356, Jesús María, T463 0000. **Netherlands Consulate**, Torre Parque Mar, Av José Larco 1301, p 13, Miraflores, T01-213 9800, info@nlgovlim.com, open Mon-Fri 0900-1200. **New Zealand Consulate**, Av Camino Real 390, Torre Central, p 17 (Casilla 3553), San Isidro, T221 2833, reya@nzlatam.com. Open Mon-Fri 0830-1300, 1400-1700. **Spain**, Jorge Basadre 498, San Isidro, T212 5155, open 0900-1300. **Sweden**, C La Santa María 130, San Isidro, T442 8905, konslima@terra.com.pe. **Switzerland**, Av Salaverry 3240, Magdalena, Lima 17, T264 0305, embsuiza@correo.tnet com.pe. **UK**, Torre Parque Mar, p 22, T617 3000, www.britishembassy.gov.uk/ peru. Open 1300-2130 (Dec-Apr to 1830 Mon and Fri, and Apr-Nov to 1830 Fri), good for security information and newspapers. **USA**, Av Encalada block 17, Surco, T434 3000, for emergencies after hrs T434 3032, http://lima.usembassy.gov. The Consulate is in the same building. **Internet** Lima is completely inundated with internet cafés, so you will have absolutely no problem finding one regardless of where you are. An hour will cost you S/2-3 (US$0.60-0.90). **Language schools** Conexus, Av Paseo de la República 3195, of 1002, San Isidro, T421 5642, www.conexusinstitute.com. Reasonably priced and effective. **Instituto Cultural Peruano-Norteamericano**, see Cultural centres, above. Classes are on Mon-Fri from 0900 to 1100, US$80 per month, no private classes offered. **Instituto de Idiomas (Pontífica Universidad Católica del Perú)**, Av Camino Real 1037, San Isidro, T442 8761. Classes Mon-Fri 1100-1300, private lessons possible. Recommended. **El Sol School of Languages**, Grimaldo del Solar 469, Miraflores, T242 7763, www.elsol.idiomasperu. com. US$15 per hr for private tuition, also small groups US$11 per hr. Family homestays and volunteer programmes available. **Independent teachers** (enquire about rates): Sra Lourdes

1105

Gálvez, T435 3910. Highly recommended, also Quechua. **Sra Georgelina Sadastizágal**, T275 6460. Recommended. Also Sr Mariano Herrera and Sr Dante Herrera: all these 4 can be contacted through peruidiomas@ LatinMail.com. **Srta Susy Arteaga**, T534 9289, T9989 7271 (mob), susyarteaga@ hotmail.com, or susyarteaga@ yahoo.com. Recommended. **Srta Patty Félix**, T521 2559, patty_fel24@yahoo.com. **Luis Villanueva**, T247 7054, www.acspanishclasses.com. Flexible, reliable, helpful. **Medical services** (It's also worth contacting your consulate for recommendations.) Hospitals: **Clínica Anglo Americano**, Av Salazar 3rd block, San Isidro, a few blocks from Ovalo Gutiérrez, T221 3656. Stocks Yellow Fever for US$18 and Tetanus. Dr Luis Manuel Valdez recommended. **Clínica Internacional**, Jr Washington 1471 y Paseo Colón (9 de Diciembre), downtown Lima, T433 4306. Good, clean and professional, consultations up to US$35, no inoculations. **Instituto Médico Lince**, León Velarde 221, near 17th and 18th blocks of Av Arenales, Lince, T471 2238. Dr Alejandro Bussalleu Rivera speaks English, good for stomach problems, about US$28 for initial consultation. Repeatedly recommended. Recommended Gynaecologists are **Dra Alicia García** and **Dr Ladislao Prasak**. **Instituto de Medicina Tropical**, Av Honorio Delgado near the Pan American Highway in the Cayetano Heredia Hospital, San Martín de Porres, T482 3903. Good for check-ups after jungle travel. Recommended. **Clínica del Niño**, Av Brasil 600 at 1st block of Av 28 de Julio, Breña, T330 0066, www.isn.gob.pe. **Centro Anti-Rabia de Lima**, Jr Austria 1300, Breña, T425 6313. Open Mon-Sat 0830-1830. Consultation is about US$2.50. **Clínica Padre Luis Tezza**, Av El Polo 570, Monterrico, T610 5050, www.clinicatezza.com.pe. Clinic specializing in a wide variety of illnesses/disorders etc, expensive; for stomach or intestinal problems, ask for Dr Raúl Morales (speaks some English, US$28 for first consultation). **Clínica Ricardo Palma**, Av Javier Prado Este 1066, San Isidro, T01-224 2224, www.crp.com.pe. For general medical consultations, English spoken. **Dr José Luis Calderón**, general practitioner recommended. **Backpackers Medical Care**, T9735 2668, backpackersmc@yahoo.com. The 'backpackers' medic', Dr Jorge Bazán, has been recommended as professional and good value, about US$13 per consultation. **International Health Department**, at Jorge Chávez airport, T517 1845. Open 24 hrs a day for vaccinations. **Pharmacy**: Pharmacy chains are modern, well-stocked, safe and very professional. They can be found throughout the city, often in or next to supermarkets. Some offer 24-hr delivery service. **Boticas Fasa**, T619 0000 for delivery, www.boticasfasa.com.pe; **Superfarma**, T267 9000 for delivery, servicioalcliente@superfarma.com.pe. **Pharmax**, Av Salaverry 3100, San Isidro, Centro Comercial El Polo, Monterrico (near the US embassy). Pharmacy/hypermarket, with imported goods (Jewish food products sometimes available at Av Salaverry branch, which is open 24 hrs). **Farmacia Deza**, Av Conquistadores 1144, San Isidro. Open 24 hrs. **Post offices** The central post office is on Jr Camaná 195 in the centre of Lima near the Plaza de Armas. Mon-Fri 0730-1900 and Sat 0730-1600. Poste Restante is in the same building but is considered unreliable. In Miraflores the main post office is on Av Petit Thouars 5201 (same hours). There are many small branches around Lima, but they are less reliable. For express service: **DHL**, Los Castaños 225, San Isidro, T215-7500. **UPS**, Av del Ejército 2107, San Isidro, T264 0105. **Federal Express**, Av Jorge Chávez 475, T242 2280, Miraflores, C José Olaya 260, Miraflores. **EMS**, next to central post office in downtown Lima, T533 2020. When receiving parcels from other countries that weigh in over 1 kg, they will be automatically sent to one of Lima's 2 customs post offices. Take your passport and a lot of patience as the process can (but not always) take a long time: Teodoro Cárdenas 267, Santa Beatriz (12th block of Av Arequipa); and Av Tomás Valle, Los Olivos (near the Panamerican Highway). **Note** Long trousers must be worn when going to these offices.

Telephones Easiest to use are the many independent phone offices, *locutorios*, all over the city. They take phone cards, which can be bought in *locutorios*, or in the street nearby. There are payphones all over the city. Some accept coins, some only phone cards and some both. **Useful addresses** Tourist Police, Jr Moore 268, Magdalena at the 38th block of Av Brasil, T460 1060, open daily 24 hrs. For public enquiries, Jr Pachitea at the corner of Belén (Jr de la Unión), Lima, T424 2053. They are friendly and very helpful, English spoken. It is recommended to visit when you have had property stolen. **Immigration:** Av España 700 y Jr Huaraz, Breña, open 0900-1330. Procedure for extensions is described on page 1072. Provides new entry stamps if passport is lost or stolen. **Intej**, Av San Martín 240, Barranco, T477 2846. They can extend student cards, change flight itineraries bought with student cards. **National library**, Av Abancay 4th block, with Jr Miró Quesada, T428 7690. Open Mon-Sat 0800-2000, Sun 0830-1330.

Huaraz and the Cordilleras

The spectacular Cordillera Blanca is an area of jewelled lakes and snowy mountain peaks attracting mountaineers and hikers in their thousands. Huaraz is the natural place to head for. It has the best infrastructure and the mountains, lakes and trails are within easy reach. This region, though, also has some sites of great archaeological significance, the most notable of which must be Chavín de Huantar, one of Peru's most important pre-Inca sites.

Ins and outs

North from Lima the Pan-American Highway parallels the coast. A series of roads climb up to Huaraz, in the Callejón de Huaylas, gateway to Parque Nacional Huascarán. Probably the easiest route to Huaraz is the paved road which branches east off the Pan-American Highway north of Pativilca, 203 km from Lima. The road climbs increasingly steeply to the chilly pass at 4,080 m (Km 120). Shortly after, Laguna **Conococha** comes into view, where the Río Santa rises. A dirt road branches off from Conococha to **Chiquián** (see page 1123) and the **Cordilleras Huayhuash** and **Raura** to the southeast. After crossing a high plateau the main road descends gradually for 47 km until **Catac**, where another road branches east to Chavín and on to the **Callejón de Conchucos** (the eastern side of the Cordillera Blanca). Huaraz is 36 km further on and the road then continues north between the towering Cordillera Negra, snowless and rising to 4,600 m, and the snow-covered Cordillera Blanca. The alternative routes to the Callejón de Huaylas are via the Callán pass from Casma to Huaraz (see page 1127), and from Chimbote to Caraz via the Cañon del Pato (page 1125).

Huaraz → *Phone code: 043. Colour map 3, grid B2. Population: 80,000. Altitude: 3,091 m.*

The main town in the Cordillera Blanca, 420 km from Lima, Huaraz is expanding rapidly as a major tourist centre, but it is also a busy commercial hub, especially on market days. It is a prime destination for hikers and a Mecca for international climbers.

Ins and outs

Tourist office iPerú ① *Luzuriaga on Plaza de Armas, T428812, iperuhuaraz@promperu. gob.pe, Mon-Fri 0800-1830, Sat-Sun 0800-1300.* **Policía de Turismo** ① *on second floor of same building, T421341 ext 315, Mon-Fri 0900-1300, 1600-1900, Sat 0900-1300*, is the place to report all crimes and mistreatment by tour operators, hotels, etc. Huaraz has its share of crime, especially since the arrival of mining in the area and during the high tourist season. On no account should women go to surrounding districts and sites alone.

Sights

Huaraz, capital of Ancash department, was almost completely destroyed in the earthquake of May 1970. The Plaza de Armas has been rebuilt, with a towering, white statue of Christ. A new **Cathedral** is still being built. The setting, at the foot of the Cordillera Blanca, is spectacular. The main thoroughfare, Avenida Luzuriaga, is bursting at the seams with travel agencies, climbing equipment hire shops, restaurants, cafés and bars. A good district for those seeking peace and quiet is La Soledad, 6 blocks uphill from the Plaza de Armas on Avenida Sucre. Here, along Sucre as well as Jr Amadeo Figueroa, every second house seems to rent rooms, most without signs. **Museo Arqueológico de Ancash** ① *Instituto Nacional de Cultura, Plaza de Armas, 0800-2000, US$1.80*, contains stone monoliths and *huacos* from the Recuay culture, well labelled. The **Sala de Cultura SUNARP** ① *Av Centenario 530, Independencia, T421301, Mon-Fri 1700-2000, Sat 0900-1300, free*, often has interesting art and photography exhibitions by local artists.

About 8 km to the northeast is **Willkawain** ① *US$1.50, take a combi from 13 de Diciembre and Comercio, US$0.55 direct to Willkawain.* The ruins (AD 700-1000, Huari Empire) consist of one large three-storey structure with intact stone roof slabs and several small structures. About 500 m past Willkawain is Ichiwillkawain with several similar but smaller structures. Take a torch if it's late. If walking, go past the Hotel Huascarán. After crossing a small bridge take a second right marked by a blue sign, it is about two hours' uphill walk; ask directions as there are many criss-crossing paths used regularly by local people. North of Huaraz, 6 km along the road to Caraz, are the thermal baths at **Monterrey** (at 2,780 m). ① *The lower pool is US$0.85; the upper pool, which is nicer (closed Mon for cleaning), US$1.35; also individual and family tubs US$1.35 per person for 20 mins; crowded at weekends and holidays.* There are restaurants and hotels (B-C). City buses along Av Luzuriaga go as far as Monterrey (US$0.22), until 1900; taxi US$2-3. There is also an alternative road from Willkawain to Monterrey.

● Sleeping

Huaraz *p1107, maps p1109 and p1111*
Hotels fill up rapidly during high season (May-Sep), especially during public holidays and special events when prices rise (beware overcharging). Unless otherwise stated, all hotels listed are recommended.

AL Andino Club, Pedro Cochachín 357, some way southeast from the centre (take a taxi after dark), T421662, www.hotelandino.com. Good international standard hotel with restaurant, free internet, safe parking, Swiss run, upper floors have views of Huascarán. New section has suites with sauna, among other details (more expensive). Recommended.

A Hostal Colomba, Francisco de Zela 278, just off Centenario across the river, T421501, www.huarazhotelcolomba.com. Lovely old hacienda, family-run, garden, safe parking, gym and well-equipped rooms with cable TV, comfortable beds, internet connection.

A-C The Lazy Dog Inn, 30 mins' drive from Huaraz (US$8-10 by taxi), close to the boundary of Huascarán National Park, 3.1 km past the town of Marian, close to the Quebrada Cojup, T978 9330, www.thelazydoginn.com. Eco-tourism lodge actively involved in community projects, water recycling systems and composting toilets. Beautifully designed in warm colours, great location gives access to several mountain valleys. Owners Wayne and Diana can organize horse-riding and hiking trips, excellent home cooking on request.

B El Patio, Av Monterrey, 250 m downhill from the Monterrey baths, T424965, www.elpatio.com.pe. Very colonial-style with lovely gardens, comfortable rooms, some with balconies. Meals on request, bar. Recommended.

B San Sebastián, Jr Italia 1124, T426960, www.hotelhuaraz.com. Elegant, modern hotel, comfortable beds with duvets, parking available, internet, helpful, buffet breakfast included, good views. Recommended.

C Steel Guest House, Alejandro Maguiña 1467 (a fair walk from the centre – take taxi late at night), T429709, www.steelguest.com. Comfortable, excellent view of the major peaks from the roof terrace, small but comfortable rooms with TV, sauna, kitchen for guests, internet access, good value.

D Albergue Churup, Jr Figueroa 1257, T422584, www.churup.com. Price includes breakfast, **F** in dormitory without breakfast, hot water, fire in sitting room on 4th floor, internet (including wireless) access, cafeteria, use of kitchen, sauna and massage room, roof terrace, lots of information, luggage store, laundry, book exchange, English spoken, Spanish classes, extremely helpful. Recommended.

D Apu Wasi, Jr Federico Sal y Rosas 820, T426035, h_apuwasi@yahoo.com. Modern but simple, with TV, very comfortable beds, includes a basic breakfast. Discounts for longer stays.

D Hostal Montañero, Plaza Ginebra 30-B, T426386, www.trekkingperu.com. Includes breakfast, hot water, comfortable, good contact point for quality mountain and trekking guides, climbing equipment rental and sales.

D Olaza Guesthouse, J Argüedas 1242, T422529, www.andeanexplorer.com. Recently upgraded, comfortable beds, run by Tito Olaza. Safe, stylish, luggage stored, nice terrace with views, breakfast included. Pick up from bus station with room reservation. Downstairs there's an office for **Mountain Bike Adventures** (see below), run by Julio Olaza. They have a second office closer to the centre at Jr Lúcar y Torre 530.

D The Way Inn Lodge, www.thewayinn.com. Excellent lodge located at 3,712 m, close to the border of Huascarán National Park. Dorm rooms and camping **F** and **G** respectively; accommodation includes an excellent breakfast. 60% of vegetables are grown on site and the lodge is aiming to be as self-sustaining as possible. Many activities available, from paragliding to yoga classes and mountain biking. Good place to chill and base yourself.

E Alojamiento Soledad, Jr Amadeo Figueroa 1267, T421196, ghsoledad@hotmail.com. Price

Peru Huaraz

includes breakfast, some hard beds, hot water, kitchen, use of internet, family-run, secure, trekking information given. More expensive (**D**) in high season.

E Angeles Inn, Av Gamarra 815, T422205, solandperu@yahoo.com. No sign, look for *Sol Andino* travel agency in same building (www.solandino.com), kitchen and laundry

Huaraz

Related map
A Huaraz centre, page 1111

N

| 0 metres | 100 |
| 0 yards | 100 |

Sleeping
Albergue Churup **1** C3
Alojamiento El Jacal **2** C3
Alojamiento Marilla **4** C3
Alojamiento Nemy's **5** C3
Alojamiento Norma **6** D2
Alojamiento Soledad **7** C3
Andino Club **9** D3
Angeles Inn **10** D2
Apu Wasi **8** D3
Backpackers **11** B1
Casa de Jaimes **12** C1
Casa Jansy's **13** C2

Edward's Inn **15** B1
El Patio **14** B3
Hatun Wasi **16** A1
Hostal Colomba **18** A2
Hostal Continental **19** C1
Hostal Estoico **20** C1
Hostal Quintana **26** C1
Jo's Place **29** A2
La Cabaña **30** C3
La Casa de Zarela **31** C3
La Estancia **3** A1
Lazy Dog Inn **17** B3
Lodging Casa Sucre **32** D3
Lodging House
 Ezama **21** A3
Olaza Guesthouse **33** D3
Steel Guest House **22** D3
Way Inn Hostel **23** C3
Way Inn Lodge **24** B3

Eating
Bistro de los Andes **2** C2
Café California **6** C1
Café El Centro **3** C1
Cafetería y Jugería **25** C2
Fuente de Salud **4** B1
Huaraz Querido **5** D2
Las Puyas **7** B1
Pachamama **9** C1
Panadería La Alameda **26** B1
Panadería Montserrat **27** D1
Pepe's Place **10** B1
Pizza Bruno **11** D1
Siam de Los Andes **12** C2

Bars & clubs
Chacraraju/Chill-Out **28** C2
Extreme **14** D1
La Cascada **29** D1

Transport
Chavín Express **1** C1
Combis to Caraz **2** A1, A2
Combis to Wilcawain **3** A2
Terminal Terrestre
 Transportistas
 Zona Sur **7** C1
Trans Rodríguez **8** C1
Trans Huandoy **4** A2

1109

facilities, garden, hot water, owners Max and Saul Angeles are official guides, helpful with trekking and climbing, rent equipment.

E Edward's Inn, Bolognesi 121, T/F422692, www.edwardsinn.com. Cheaper without bath, nice garden, laundry, breakfast extra, insist on proper rates in low season, popular. Edward speaks English and has 30 years' experience trekking, climbing and guiding in the area. He also rents gear. Highly recommended.

E La Casa de Zarela, J Arguedas 1263, T421694, www.lacasadezarela.com. Hot water, use of kitchen, laundry facilities, popular with climbers and trekkers, owner Zarela who speaks English organizes groups and is very knowledgeable.

E-F Hatun Wasi, Jr.Daniel Villayzán 268, T425055, www.hatunwasi.net. New family-run hotel next to *Jo's Place*. Spacious rooms, with hot water, pleasant roof terrace, ideal for breakfasts, with great views of the Cordillera.

E-F The Way Inn Hostel, Jr Buenaventura Mendoza 821, near Parque Fap, T428714, www.thewayinn.com. Dorms and private rooms, run by Alex and Bruni, all mattresses are orthopaedic, kitchen (including oven and fridge), huge video library, laundry facilities, camping equipment for hire, free information on treks, places to eat, hanging out, etc, sauna and steam room. Good place to meet other travellers. Also see *The Way Inn Lodge* (above).

F Alojamiento Marilla, Sucre 1123, T428160, alojamaril@latinmail.com. Good views, modern, rooms with and without bath (**G**), also dormitory, hot water, breakfast available, kitchen facilities, luggage store, knowledgeable owners.

F Alojamiento Nemy's, Jr Figueroa 1135, T422949. Secure, hot shower, breakfast US$2.40, good for climbers, luggage store. Recommended.

F Alojamiento Norma, Pasaje Valenzuela 837, near Plaza Belén, T421831, www.residencialng. com. Includes breakfast, cheaper without bathroom, hot water. Recommended.

F Familia Meza, Lúcar y Torre 538, T426367, familiameza_lodging@hotmail.com. Shared bath, hot water, use of kitchen, laundry facilities, popular with trekkers, mountaineers and bikers.

F Hostal Estoico, San Martín 635, T422371. Cheaper without bath, safe, hot water, laundry facilities, good value.

F Hostal Gyula, Parque Ginebra 632, opposite the Casa de Guías, T421567, hostal_gyula_inn@yahoo.com. Hot water, helpful but noisy at weekends, has good information on local tours, stores luggage.

F Hostal Quintana, Mcal Cáceres 411, T426060, www.geocities.com/hostal_quintana/. Cheaper without bath, hot shower, laundry facilities, basic, stores luggage, popular with trekkers.

F Hostal Tany, Lúcar y Torre 468A, T422534. Cheaper without bath, hot water at night, spotless, money exchange, tours, café/restaurant.

F Jo's Place, Jr Daniel Villayzan 276, T425505, www.josplacehuaraz.com. Safe, hot water at night, nice mountain views, garden, terrace, kitchen facilities, English owner, warm atmosphere, popular. Recommended.

F La Cabaña, Jr Sucre 1224, T423428, www.huaraz.org/lacabana. Shared and double rooms, hot showers, laundry, kitchen, computer, DVD, popular, safe for parking, bikes and luggage, english and French spoken, good value.

F Lodging Caroline, Urb Avitentel Mz D-Lt 1, T422588, 20 min walk from centre. Price includes breakfast, free pick-up from bus station (phone in advance), hot water, kitchen facilities, tourist information and guides, laundry, very helpful. Frequently recommended.

F Lodging Casa Sucre, Sucre 1240, T422264, filibertor@terra.com.pe. Private house, kitchen, laundry facilities, hot water, English, German and French spoken, mountaineering guide, Filiberto Rurush, can be contacted here.

F Oscar's Hostal, La Mar 624, T/F422720, cvmonical@hotmail.com. Hot water, cheap breakfast next door, good beds, cheaper in low season, helpful.

F-G Alojamiento El Jacal, Jr Sucre 1044, T424612, reservaseljacal@yahoo.es. With or without shower, hot water, helpful family, garden, use of kitchen, laundry facilities, luggage store, internet café.

F-G Casa Jansy's, Jr Sucre 948. Hot water, meals, laundry, owner Jesús Rivera Lúcar is a mountain guide. Recommended.

F-G pp Cayesh Guesthouse, Jr Julián de Morales 867, T428821, www.cayesh.net. Comfortable new hostel with good location, solar hot water system, kitchen, TV lounge with over 250 DVDs. Owner is an enthusiastic climber and happy to provide advice.

G pp Backpackers, Av Raimondi 510, T429101, http://huaraz.com/backpackers. Without breakfast, spacious, hot showers, good views, a real bargain.

G Casa de Jaimes, Alberto Gridilla 267, T422281, 2 blocks from the main plaza, www.casajaimes.com. Dormitory with hot showers, laundry facilities, has maps and books of the region, use of kitchen, 1 hr free internet use per day. Noisy but recommended.

G Hostal Continental, 28 de Julio 586 near Plaza de Armas, T424171. Hot water, cafeteria serving good breakfasts. Recommended but avoid rooms on street as there are 2 noisy *peñas* nearby.

G La Estancia, Jr Huaylas 162, Centenario, T423183. With shared shower, luggage store,

Morales and Sucre, Bolívar cuadra 6, and elsewhere. **Andean Expressions**, Jr J Arguedas 1246, near La Soledad church, T422951, olaza@ qnet.com.pe. Open 0800-2200, run by Lucho, Mauro and Beto Olaza, recommended for hand-printed clothing and gifts.

Markets The central market offers a wide variety of canned and dry goods, as well as fresh fruit and vegetables. Beware pickpockets in this area.

Supermarkets Ortiz, Luzuriaga 401 corner Raymondi (good selection).

▲▲ Activities and tours

Huaraz *p1107, maps p1109 and p1111*
Try to get a recommendation from someone who has recently returned from a tour, climb or trek. All agencies run conventional tours to Llanganuco, Pastoruri (both US$10 per person, both very long days, acclimatization needed for the latter) and Chavín (8-10 hrs, US$6-10 per person), entry tickets not included. Many hire equipment.

Horseriding
Sr Robinson Ayala Gride, T423813. Contact him well in advance for half-day trips (enquire at **El Cortijo** restaurant, on Huaraz-Caraz road, Km 6.5). He is a master paso rider.
Posada de Yungar, at Yungar (about 20 km on the Carhuaz road), T421267, 967 9836 (mob). Swiss run. Ask for José Flores or Gustavo Soto. US$4.50 per hr on nice horses; good 4-hr trip in the Cordillera Negra.

Mountain biking
Mountain Bike Adventures, Lúcar y Torre 530, T424259, julio.olaza@terra.com.pe, or www.chakinaniperu.com. Contact Julio Olaza. US$20 for 5 hrs, various routes, excellent standard of equipment. Julio speaks excellent English and also runs a book exchange, sells topo maps and climbing books. Recommended.

River rafting and canoeing
Ario Ferri, T961 3058/963 5920 (mob, between 1800-2000), www.yurakyaku.com, or contact through Café Andino. Multilingual rafting guide and certified kayak instructor. Also a well regarded climbing and hiking guide.

Trekking and climbing
Trekking tours cost US$40-70 pp per day, climbing US$90-140 pp per day.
Active Peru, Av Gamarra 699, T423339, www.activeperu.com. Offers the classic treks, climbing, plus the standard tours to Chavín, Pastoruri and Llanganuco, among others.

Andean Kingdom, Luzuriaga 522, www.andeankingdom.com. Free information, maps, climbing wall, rock and ice climbing, including multi-day courses, treks, equipment rental, English and some Hebrew spoken, can be very busy. The company is building a lodge near the rock climbing site of Hatun Machay and should be moving to a new office in 2007: Jr San Martín 613, p 2, T425555.
Andean Sport Tours, Luzuriaga 571, T421612. Have a basic practice wall behind the office. Also organize mountain bike tours, ski instruction and river rafting.
Andeno Viaggio, Av Luzuriaga 627, T428047, www.andenoviaggio.com. Offers the usual range of day tours (Llanganuco, Pastoruri, Chavin) plus trekking and climbing, reputable.
Andescamp, Malecón Sur 310 (Río Quillkay), T428214, www.andescamp.com. Popular, especially with budget travellers, qualified climbing guides, a great variety of treks on offer, plus rafting, paragliding and more.
Chacraraju Expeditions, Jr.José de Sucre 959, T426172, www.chacrarajuexpedition.com. Tours and equipment for hire, plus a small climbing wall and the Chill-out Bar next door.
Cordillera Blanca Adventures, run by the Mejía Romero family, T424352. Experienced, quality climbing and trekking trips, good guides and equipment.
Explorandes, Av Centenario 489, T421960, postmast@exploran.com.pe.
Galaxia Expeditions, Jr Mariscal Cáceres 428, T425691, galaxia_expeditions@hotmail.com. Reputable agency with the usual range of tours, equipment rental, etc.
Huascarán, Jr Figueroa 1257 (below Albergue Churup), T424504, peruhuascaran@yahoo.com. Contact Pablo Tinoco Depaz, one of the brothers who run the company. 4-day Santa Cruz trip recommended. Good food and equipment, professional service, free loan of waterproofs and pisco sour on last evening. Recommended.
Kallpa, José de la Mar y Luzuriaga, p 2, T427868, www.peruviantrek.com. Organizes treks, rents gear, arranges arrieros and mules, very helpful.
Montañero, Parque Ginebra 30-B, T426386, www.trekkingperu.com. Run by veteran mountain guide Selio Villón, German, French and English spoken.
Monttrek, Luzuriaga 646, upstairs, T421124, F426976. Good trekking and climbing information, advice and maps, run ice and rock climbing courses (at Monterrey), tours to Laguna Churup and the 'spectacular' Luna Llena tour; they also hire out mountain bikes, run ski instruction and trips, and river rafting. Helpful, conscientious guides. Next door in the Pizzería is a climbing wall, good maps, videos and slide

shows. For new routes and maps contact Porfirio Cacha Macedo, 'Pocho', at Monttrek or at Jr Corongo 307, T423930.

Peruvian Andes Adventures, José Olaya 532, T421864, www.peruvianandes.com, www.perutrekkingclimbing.com. Run by Hisao and Eli Morales, professional, registered mountain and trekking guides. All equipment and services for treks of 3-15 days, climbing technical and non-technical peaks, or just day walks. Vegetarians catered for.

Guides

Some guides speak English and are friendly but lack technical expertise; others have expertise but lack communicative ability. You pays your money and takes your choice.

Casa de Guías, Plaza Ginebra 28-g in Huaraz, T421811, casa_de_guias@hotmail.com. Mon-Sat 0900-1300, 1600-1800. This is the climbers' and hikers' meeting place. Has a full list of all members of the Asociación de Guías de Montaña del Perú (AGMP) throughout the country. It is useful with information, books, maps, arrangements for guides, *arrieros*, mules, etc. Notice board, postcards and posters for sale.

Ted Alexander, Skyline Adventures, Jr José de San Martín 637, T427097, www.sladventureschool.com. US outward bound instructor, very knowledgeable.

Koky Castañeda, T421694, or through *La Casa de Zarela* or *Café Andino*. Speaks English and French, AGMP certified.

Aritza Monasterio, through *Casa de Guías*. Speaks English, Spanish and Euskerra.

Augusto Ortega, Jr San Martín 1004, T424888, is the only Peruvian to have climbed Everest.

Filiberto Rurush Paucar, Sucre 1240, T422264 (*Lodging Casa Sucre*), speaks English, Spanish and Quechua.

Hugo Sifuentes Maguiña and his brother César (speaks English and a little French), at Siex (Sifuentes Expeditions), Av Centenario 687, T426529, www.siex.org.

Max and Saul Angeles, T422205 (*Sol Andino* agency), speak some English, know Huayhuash well.

Christopher Benway, La Cima Logistics, T421203, cafeandino@hotmail.com. American, leads treks in the Huayhuash.

Vladimiro and Máximo Hinostrosa, Mountain Shop Chacraraju, T969 2395. Trekking guides with knowledge of the entire region.

Tjen Verheye, Jr Carlos Valenzuela 911, T422569, is Belgian and speaks Dutch, French, German, and reasonable English, runs trekking and conventional tours and is knowledgeable about the Chavín culture.

Genaro Yanac Olivera, T422825, speaks good English and some German, also a climbing guide.

Prices: The Dirección de Turismo issues qualified guides and *arrieros* (muleteers) with a photo ID. Always check for this when making arrangements; note down the name and card number in case you should have any complaints. Prices for specific services are set so enquire before hiring someone. Prices: *arriero*, US$10 per day; donkey or mule, US$4-5 per day; trekking guides US$40-50 per day (more for foreign guides); climbing guides US$70-120 per day (more for foreign guides), depending on the difficulty of the peak; cooks US$25-30 per day. You are required to provide or pay for food and shelter for all *arrieros*, porters, cooks and guides.

Camping gear The following agencies are recommended for hiring gear: Anden Sport Tours, Galaxia Expeditions, Monttrek, Kallpa and Montañero. Also Skyline, Alpandes, Luzuriaga 557, T424646, and MountClimb, Jr Mcal Cáceres 421, T426060, mountclimb@ yahoo.com. Tatoo, on Parque Ginebra, T422966, www.tatoo.ws, is good for climbing and outdoor clothes and gear, locally produced and international brands. Casa de Guías rents equipment and sells dried food. Check all camping and climbing equipment very carefully before taking it. Gear is of variable quality and mostly second hand, left behind by others. Also note that some items may not be available, so it's best to bring your own. All prices are standard, but not cheap, throughout town. All require payment in advance, passport or air ticket as deposit and will only give 50% of your money back if you return gear early. Many trekking agencies sell camping gaz cartridges. White gas is available from *ferreterías* on Raymondi below Luzuriaga and by Parque Ginebra. Campers have complained that campsites are dirty, toilet pits foul and that rubbish is not taken away by groups.

Tour operators

Chavín Tours, Luzuriaga 502, T421578, F724801. All local tours, long-standing agency.

Pablo Tours, Luzuriaga 501, T421142/ 421145. For all local tours, also with many years of operation.

Transport

Huaraz p1107, maps p1109 and p1111

Bus To/from **Lima**: 7-8 hrs, US$6-14. There is a large selection of ordinary service and luxury coaches throughout the day. Many of the companies have their offices along Av Raymondi and on Jr Lúcar y Torre. Some recommended companies are: Cruz del Sur, Bolívar y José de la Mar, T423969; Transportes Rodríguez, Tarapacá

622, T421353; **Civa**, Morales opposite Lúcar y Torre; **Móvil**, Bolívar 452, T422555 (2 standard and 2 cama services a day); **Empresa 14**, Fitzcarrald 216, T421282, terminal at Bolívar 407.

Other long distance buses: To **Casma** via the Callán pass and Pariacoto (150 km) 7 hrs, US$6, the lower section of the road is very poor, landslides and closures are common (sit on the left for best views): **Transportes Huandoy**, Fitzcarrald 261, T427507 (terminal at Caraz 820), daily at 0800, 1000 and 1300. **Yungay Express**, Raymondi 744, T424377, 3 a day. They continue to Chimbote, 185 km. To Chimbote via Caraz and the Cañon del Pato (sit on the right for the most exciting views) *Yungay Express*, daily, US$7, 10 hrs. Other companies go to **Chimbote** via Pativilca; US$6, 7 hrs (to **Pativilca**, 160 km, 4 hrs, US$3.50). Most continue to **Trujillo**, all buses go at night, 8-9 hrs, US$8.60: **Chinchaysuyo** (J de Morales 650, T426417), **Línea** (Simón Bolívar 450, T426666), **Móvil** and **Empresa 14**, addresses above.

Within the Cordillera Blanca: Several buses and frequent minivans run daily, 0500- 2000, between Huaraz and **Caraz**, 1¼ hrs, US$1.35, from the parking area under the bridge on Fitzcarrald and from the open space beside the bridge on the other side of the river (beware of thieves here). To **Chavín**, 110 km, 2 hrs (sit on left side for best views), US$3: **Chavín Express**, Mcal Cáceres 338, T424652, 3 a day; **Trans Río Mosna**, Tarapacá 576, T726632, 0700 and 1300. Both companies have buses that go on to Huari, 6 hrs, US$5. **Renzo**, Raymondi 821, T424915, runs to Chacas and San Luis (0615 Mon-Sat, 0645 Sun), Yanama, Piscobamba and Pomabamba (0630, best service). **Los Andes**, same office as Yungay Express, T427362, goes daily at 0630 to Yungay, US$0.75, Lagunas de Llanganuco, US$3.45, Yanama, US$3.45, Piscobamba US$5.20 and Pomabamba, US$6 (8 hrs). Also to **Pomabamba** via Yungay, Lakes Llanganuco and Yanama, **Transvir**, Caraz y Comercio, and **La Perla de Alta Mayo**, 0630, 8 hrs,

US$6. To **Sihuas**, **Chavín Express**, twice a week, and **Perú Andino**, once a week, 8 hrs, US$7. Colectivos to **Recuay**, US$0.45, and **Catac**, US$0.55, leave daily at 0500-2100, from Gridilla, just off Tarapacá (Terminal de Transportistas Zona Sur). To **Chiquián** for the Cordillera Huayhuash (see below). To **Huallanca** (Huánuco), the route now taken is the paved road through Conococha, Chiquián, Aquia to Huansala, then by dirt road to Huallanca and La Unión. Departs Huaraz 0800, 1300, 1500, 6 hrs, with **Trans El Rápido**, Bolognesi 216, T043-422887. There are regular colectivos from Huallanca to La Unión from the corner of Comercio y 28 de Julio, 1 hr, US$0.75.

Taxi Standard fare in town is about US$0.60, US$0.70 at night; radio taxis T421482 or 422512.

❶ Directory

Huaraz *p1107, maps p1109 and p1111*
Banks BCP, on Plaza de Armas, closed 1300-1630, changes cash, 3.25% commission on TCs into soles, good rates, into cash dollars 5% commission, cash advance on Visa, Visa ATMs. **Interbank**, on Plaza de Armas, no commission on TCs into soles, Mastercard ATM. **Scotiabank**, Sucre 766, changes cash and TCs. **Casa de Cambio: Oh Na Nay**, opposite *Interbank*, cash only, good rates. Street changers and *casas de cambio* on Luzuriaga (be careful). **Internet** There are internet places everywhere, US$0.30 per hr on average. **Sayuri**, Bolívar 683. As well as internet, has digital photo services and international phone calls. Cafés usually offer videophones, scanning, CD burning and printing services. **Post offices** Serpost, Luzuriaga 702, open 0800-2000 daily. **Telephones** Telefónica, Sucre y Bolívar, Plaza de Armas, national and international phone and fax, open 0700-2300 daily. Many calling centres on Luzuriaga.

Cordillera Blanca

Apart from the range of Andes running along the Chile-Argentina border, the highest mountains in South America lie along the Cordillera Blanca and are perfectly visible from many spots. From Huaraz alone, you can see more than 23 peaks of over 5,000 m, of which the most notable is Huascarán (6,768 m), the highest mountain in Peru. Although the snowline is receding, the Cordillera Blanca still contains the largest concentration of glaciers found in the world's tropical zone and the turquoise-coloured lakes, which form in the terminal moraines, are the jewels of the Andes. Here also is one of Peru's most important pre-Inca sites, at Chavín de Huantar.

Parque Nacional Huascarán

Established in July 1975, the park includes the entire Cordillera Blanca above 4,000 m, with an area of 3,400 sq km. It is a UNESCO World Biosphere Reserve and part of the World Heritage Trust. The park's objectives are to protect the flora, fauna, geology, archaeological sites and scenic beauty of the Cordillera. Take all your rubbish away with you when camping. The park office charges visitors US$1.25 for a day visit. For visits of up to seven days (ie for trekking and climbing trips) a permit costing US$20 (65 soles) must be bought. If you stay longer than seven days, you will need another permit. Fees for visiting the national park are collected at rangers posts at Llanganuco and Huascarán (for the Llanganuco to Santa Cruz trek), and at Collón on the way up the Quebrada Ishinca. The park office is at Jr Federico Sal y Rosas 555, by Plazuela Belén, T422086; open Monday-Friday 0830-1300, 1430-1700. It is principally administrative.

In September 2006 INRENA (www.inrena.gob.pe) announced new regulations governing the Huascarán national park. Similar to rules governing the Inca Trails at Machu Picchu, local guides will be mandatory for everywhere except designated 'Recreation Zones' (areas accessible by car) and climbers attempting difficult routes will have to have a local climbing guide to accompany them. At the time of writing these regulations had not been instituted, nor the cost of permits announced, but anyone wishing to trek or climb independently should make enquiries before setting out.

Trekking and climbing in the Cordillera Blanca
The Cordillera Blanca offers popular backpacking and trekking, with a network of trails used by the local people and some less well-defined mountaineers' routes. Most circuits can be hiked in five days. Although the trails are easily followed, they are rugged with high passes, between 4,000 and 5,000 m, so backpackers should be fit and acclimatized to the altitude, and carry all equipment. Essential items are a tent, warm sleeping bag, stove, and protection against wind and rain (the weather is unreliable and you cannot rule out rain and hail storms even in the dry season). Less stamina is required if you hire mules to carry equipment. The season is from May to September, although conditions vary from year to year. The rainy season in Huaraz is December-March.

Advice to climbers The height of the Cordillera Blanca and the Callejón de Huaylas ranges and their location in the tropics create conditions different from the Alps or even the Himalayas. Fierce sun makes the mountain snow porous and glaciers move more rapidly. Deglaciation is rapidly changing the face of the Cordillera. Older maps do not provide a reliable indication of the extent of glaciers and snow fields (according to some studies 15% of the range's glaciers have disappeared since the 1970s), so local experience is important. If the new INRENA rules preventing independent treks or climbs have not been instigated (see above), move in groups of four or more, reporting to the Casa de Guías (see also above) or the office of the guide before departing, giving the date at which a search should begin, and leaving your embassy's telephone number, with money for the call. International recommendations are for a 300m per day maximum altitude gain. Be wary of agencies wanting to sell you trips with very fast ascents (but ask around if this is what you want). The **Policía Nacional de Perú** ① T043-393333, usam@ pnp.gob.pe, has a 35-member rescue team in Yungay, with 24-hour phone service and vhf/uhf radio dispatch. They have two helicopters and trained search-and- rescue dogs. At present, they will rescue anyone – climbers, trekkers, tourists – without asking for cash up front. PNP rescues are currently free for uninsured climbers. They will bill insured climbers, but do not ask for any cash up front. Since this policy may change, and because they will only take the injured person as far as Huaraz hospital (from where additional costly medical evacuation may be required), it remains imperative that all climbers carry adequate insurance (it cannot be purchased locally). Be well prepared before setting out on a climb. Wait or cancel your trip when the weather is bad. Every year climbers are killed through failing to take weather conditions seriously. Climb only when and where you have sufficient experience.

Note Before heading out on any route, always enquire locally about public safety. The Cordillera Blanca is generally safe, but muggings have taken place on the way to Laguna Churup, to the Mirador Rataquena above Huaraz, the Mirador above Monterrey, and at Wilkawain. On all treks in this area, respect the locals' property, leave no rubbish behind, do not give sweets or money to children who beg and remember your cooking utensils and tent would be very expensive for a *campesino*, so be sensitive and responsible.

Huaraz to Chavín → *For Guides and prices, see Listings, page 1113.*
South of Huaraz is **Olleros** (Altitude 3,450 m). The spectacular and relatively easy three to four-day hike to Chavín, along a pre-Columbian trail, starts from Olleros. Some basic meals and food supplies available. At 38 km via the main road from Huaraz is **Catac** (two basic hotels

short walk to the plants. Return transport leaves between 1230 and 1300. If you miss the bus, you can walk back to Pueblo Libre in four hours, to Caraz in 6-8 hours, but it is easy to get lost and there are not many people to ask directions along the way.

Laguna Parón From Caraz a narrow, rough road goes east 32 km to Laguna Parón, in a cirque surrounded by several, massive snow-capped peaks, including Huandoy, Pirámide Garcilazo and Caraz. The water level has been lowered to protect Caraz, and the water from the lake is used for the Cañón del Pato hydroelectric scheme. The gorge leading to it is spectacular. It is a long day's trek for acclimatized hikers (25 km) up to the lake at 4,150 m, or a 4-5 hour walk from the village of Parón, which can be reached by combi. Camping is possible next to the Duke Energy refuge.

Santa Cruz Valley One of the finest treks in the area is the 4-5 days route over the path from the Santa Cruz valley, by Mount Huascarán to the Lagunas de Llanganuco (described below). The most popular way to do this famous hike starts at Cashapampa in the Santa Cruz valley (see Transport below). It takes four to five days over the pass of Punta Unión, 4,750 m, to Vaquería or the Llanganuco lakes. Many recommend this 'anticlockwise' route as the climb is gentler, giving more time to acclimatize, and the pass is easier to find. You can hire an *arriero* and mule in Cashapampa, prices given in Listings, Activities and tours, below. Campsites are at Llamacorral and Taullipampa before Punta Unión, and Quenoapampa (or Cachina Pampa) after the pass. You can end the hike at Vaquería on the Yanama-Yungay road, or, a day later with a night at the Paccha Pampa campsite, at the Llanganuco lakes, from where cars go back to Yungay.

Yungay → *Colour map 3, grid B2.*
The main road goes on 12 km south of Caraz to Yungay which was completely buried during the 1970 earthquake by a massive mudslide; a hideous tragedy in which 20,000 people lost their lives. The earthquake and its aftermath are remembered by many residents of the Callejón de Huaylas. The original site of Yungay, known as Yungay Viejo, desolate and haunting, has been consecrated as a *camposanto* (cemetery). The new settlement is on a hillside just north of the old town, and is growing gradually. It has a pleasant plaza and a concrete market, good on Wednesday and Sunday. October 17 is the *Virgen del Rosario* fiesta and October 28 is the anniversary of the founding of the town. The tourist office is on the corner of the Plaza de Armas.

Lagunas de Llanganuco
The Lagunas de Llanganuco are two lakes nestling 1,000 m below the snowline beneath Huascarán and Huandoy. The first you come to is Laguna Chinancocha (3,850 m), the second Laguna Orconcocha (3,863 m). The park office is situated below the lakes at 3,200 m, 19 km from Yungay. Accommodation is provided for trekkers who want to start the Llanganuco- Santa Cruz trek from here, US$2 per person. From the park office to the lakes takes about five hours (a steep climb). For the last 1½ hours, a nature trail, Sendero María Josefa (sign on the road), takes 1½ hours to walk to the western end of Chinancocha where there is a control post, descriptive trail and boat trips on the lake. Walk along the road beside the lake to its far end for peace and quiet among the quenoal trees, which provide shelter for 75% of the birdlife found in the park

Carhuaz → *Colour map 3, grid B2.*
After Yungay, the main road goes to **Mancos** (8 km south, 30 minutes) at the foot of Huascarán. There is a dormitory at *La Casita de mi Abuela*, some basic shops and restaurants. From Mancos it is 14 km to Carhuaz, a friendly, quiet mountain town with a pleasant plaza. There is very good walking in the neighbourhood (eg to thermal baths; up the Ulta valley). Market days are Wednesday and Sunday (the latter is much larger). The local fiesta of *Virgen de las Mercedes*, 14 -24 September, is rated as among the best in the region.

Peru Cordillera Blanca Listings

🛏 Sleeping

Olleros *p1116*
D **Altas Montañas**, at edge of village, T722569, altasmont@yahoo.es. Small 3-star lodge, Belgian-run, with hot showers, good breakfast included, dinner available, bar, birdwatching, guided treks, information,

laundry, recommended for start or end of trek, phone 24 hrs in advance, preferably at 2000, to arrange free pick-up from Huaraz.

Chavín *p1117*
E **La Casona**, Wiracocha 130, Plaza de Armas,

T454048, lacasonachavin@peru.com. In a renovated house with attractive courtyard, cheaper without bath, insufficient hot water, 1 double room, motorcycle parking.

D Ri'kay, on 17 de Enero 172N, T454027, 01-9657 4013 (mob). Set around 2 patios, modern, best in town, TV, hot water, restaurant does Italian food in the evening. Recommended.

F Hostal Chavín, Jr San Martín 141-151, half a block from the plaza, T/F454055. Pleasant courtyard, hot water, will provide breakfast for groups, best of the more basic hotels but beds are poor.

F Inca, Wiracocha 160, T454021. In a renovated house, cheaper without bath, good beds, hot water on request, nice garden.

Camping Inside park gates at archaeological site for vehicles, ask for permission.

Caraz *p1118*

B-C O'Pal Inn, Pativilca/Caraz Km 265.5, T043-391015, www.opalsierraresort.com. Scenic, bungalows and rooms, swimming pool. Recommended.

D Chamanna, Av Nueva Victoria 185, 25 mins walk from centre, T978 4841/953 5279 (mob), www.chamanna.com. Cabañas in beautiful garden, hot water, secure, excellent French and international cuisine in expensive restaurant, German run. Recommended.

D-F Los Pinos, Parque San Martín 103, 5 blocks west of plaza, T391130, lospinos@ apuaventura.com. Rooms with and without bath, hot water, comfortable and airy, garden open to all travellers, camping US$2.50, use of internet US$0.50 per hr, use of kitchen US$3, laundry service, safe, book exchange, information and travel agency Apu-Aventura. Breakfast and dinner are available, bar with movies every night. Recommended.

E La Alameda, Av Noé Bazán Peralta 262, T391177, jtorres@viabcp. com.pe. Comfortable rooms, hot water, breakfast, parking, gardens. Recommended.

E Caraz Dulzura, Sáenz Peña 212, about 10 blocks from the city centre, T391523, hostalcarazdulzura@hotrmail.com. Modern building in an old street, hot water, cheaper without bath and TV, comfortable, great service, airy rooms, breakfast extra. Recommended.

E La Perla de los Andes, Plaza de Armas 179, T/F392007. Comfortable rooms, hot water, TV, helpful, average restaurant, has a large new annex 1 block up San Martín.

F Chavín, San Martín 1135 just off the plaza, T391171, hostalchavin66@hotmail.com. Warm water, good service but a bit grubby, breakfast extra, guiding service, tourist info.

F Regina, Los Olivos s/n y Gálvez, at the south end

of town, 1 block west of road to Yungay, T391520. Modern, hot water, good value.

F Restaurant Oasis, Raymondi 425. Small, hot water, welcoming, good value, TV.

G Alojamiento Caballero, D Villar 485, T391637, or ask at *Pony's Expeditions* on the plaza. Shared bath, hot water, laundry facilities, stores luggage, basic, family run.

G Hostal La Casona, Raymondi 319, 1 block east from the plaza, T391334. Cheaper without bath, hot water, lovely little patio.

Yungay *p1119*

F pp Complejo Turístico Yungay (COMTURY), Prolongación 2 de Mayo 1019, 2.5 km south of the new town, 700 m east of main road in Aura, the only neighbourhood of old Yungay that survived, T969 1698 (mob). Nice bungalows, pleasant country setting, hot water, fireplace, restaurant with regional specialities, camping possible.

F Hostal Gledel, Av Arias Graziani, north past plaza, T393048, rugamboa@viabcp.com. Owned by Sra Gamboa, who is hospitable and a good cook, shared bath, hottish water, no towels or soap, cheap meals prepared on request, nice courtyard.

F Hostal Sol de Oro, Santo Domingo 07, T393116. With bath, hot water, comfortable, good value, best in town.

G Hostal Mery, 28 de julio s/n. Hot water, simple but OK, rooms at front noisy.

Carhuaz *p1119*

B-C El Abuelo, Jr 9 de Diciembre y Tumbes, T394149, www.elabuelohostal.com. Modern, comfortable but overpriced, café, parking, ask at *Heladería El Abuelo* on main plaza.

C pp Casa de Pocha, 1 km out of town towards Hualcán, at foot of Nevado Hualcán, ask directions in town, T961 3058 (mob, 1800-2000), lacasadepocha@hotmail.com. Including breakfast and dinner, country setting, entirely solar and wind energy powered, hot water, sauna and pool, home-produced food (vegetarian available), horses for hire, camping possible, many languages spoken. Recommended. Book in advance.

F Hostal Señor de Luren, Buin 549, 30 m from Plaza de Armas. Hot water, TV, safe motorcycle parking, very hospitable. F four family run *hospedajes* have been built as part of a community development project. All have private bath and hot water. The better 2 are: **Hospedaje Robri**, Jr Comercio 935, T394505. Modern. **Alojamiento Las Torresitas**, Jr Amazonas 603, T394213.

G Hostal La Merced, Ucayali 724, T394241 (Lima 442 3201). Hot water (usually), "like going back to the 1950s", luggage store.

🍴 Eating

Chavín *p1117*

🍴🍴 **Chavín Turístico**, middle of 17 de Enero. The best in town, good *menú* and à la carte, delicious apple pie, nice courtyard, internet.

🍴🍴 **La Portada**, towards south end of 17 de Enero. In an old house with tables set around a pleasant garden. Recommended.

🍴 **La Ramada**, towards north end of main street, 17 de Enero. Regional dishes, also trout and set lunch.

Caraz *p1118*

🍴🍴 **La Punta Grande**, D Villar 595, 10 mins' walk from centre. Best place for local dishes, closes 1700.

🍴 **Esmeralda**, Av Alfonso Ugarte 404. Good set meal, breakfast. Recommended.

🍴 **Heladería Caraz Dulzura**, D Villar on the plaza. Excellent home made ice cream, good value meals, pastries.

🍴 **Jeny**, Daniel Villar on the plaza. Good food at reasonable prices.

Cafés

Café de Rat, Sucre 1266, above *Pony's Expeditions*. Serves breakfast, vegetarian dishes, pizzas, drinks and snacks, darts, travel books, nice atmosphere. Recommended.

El Turista, San Martín 1117. Open in morning and evening only. Small, popular for breakfast, ham omelettes and ham sandwiches are specialities.

Panificadora La Alameda, D Villar y San Martín. Very good bread and pastries, ice cream, popular with locals. Also **Establo La Alameda**, D Villar 420. Excellent *manjar blanco* (they let you try it first), cakes and sweets.

Yungay *p1119*

🍴 **Alpamayo**, Av Arias Graziani s/n. At north entrance to town, good for local dishes, lunchtime only.

🍴 **Café Pilar**, on the main plaza. Good for juices, cakes and snacks.

Carhuaz *p1119*

🍴🍴 **El Abuelo**, Plaza de Armas. International and local food, produce from own garden including all natural ice cream.

🍴🍴 **La Bicharra**, just north of Carhuaz on main road, T978 0893 (mob). Innovative North African/Peruvian cooking, lunch only, busy at weekends, call ahead to check if they are open on weekdays.

🍸 Bars and clubs

Caraz *p1118*

Taberna Disco Huandy, Mcal Cáceres 119. Good atmosphere.

🛍 Shopping

Caraz *p1118*

Camping supplies Fresh food in the market. Some dried camping food is available from **Pony's Expeditions**, who also sell camping gaz canisters and white gas.

🏔 Activities and tours

Caraz *p1118*

Agencies in Caraz arrange treks in the Cordillera Huayhuash, as well as more local destinations.

Apu-Aventura, D Villar 215, T392159, www.apuaventura.com. Offer all sorts of adventure sports and equipment rental.

Pony's Expeditions, Sucre 1266, near the Plaza de Armas, T/F391642, www.ponyexpeditions.com. Mon-Sat 0800-2200, English, French and Quechua spoken, reliable information about the area. Owners Alberto and Aidé Cafferata are knowledgeable about treks and climbs. Local tours and trekking with guides are arranged, maps and books for sale, also equipment for hire, mountain bike rental (US$15 for a full day). Highly recommended.

Mariano Araya, ask at the municipality. He is a trekking guide who is also keen on photography and archaeology.

🚌 Transport

Chavín *p1117*

Bus It is much easier to get to Chavín (even walking!) than to leave the place by bus. All buses to **Huaraz** originate in Huari or beyond. They pass through Chavín at irregular hours and may not have seats available. Buying a ticket at an agency in Chavín does not guarantee you will get a seat or even a bus. For buses from **Huaraz**, see under Huaraz. **Chavín Express** passes through around 1200, 1600 and 1700 daily; **Río Mosna** around 0430, 1600, 1800, 2000, and 2200 daily. Bus to Huaraz takes 2 hrs, US$3. To **Lima**: 438 km, 12 hrs, US$9, with **Trans El Solitario** and **Perú Andino** daily. Most locals prefer to travel first to Huaraz and then take one of the better companies from there.

To other destinations in the Callejón de Conchucos, either use buses coming from Huaraz or Lima, or hop on and off combis which run between each town. To **San Marcos**, 8 km, and **Huari**, 38 km, take one of the combis which leave regularly from the main plaza in Chavín, 20 mins and 30 mins respectively. There are buses during the day from Lima and Huaraz which go on to **Huari**, with some going on to **San Luis**, a further 61 km, 3 hrs; **Piscobamba**, a further 62 km, 3 hrs; and **Pomabamba**, a further 22 km, 1 hr; such as **El Solitario** which passes through Chavín at 1800. Gasoline is available at north end of Chavín.

Huari *p1117*
Bus Companies have their offices around Parque Vigil. To **Huaraz**, 5-6 hrs, US$3.75, departures through the day. Services also to **San Luis** and **Lima**.

Yanama *p1118*
Bus Daily between **Yungay** and Yanama over the 4,767 m Portachuelo de Llanganuco (3 hrs, US$4.50), continuing to Pomabamba.

Pomabamba *p1118*
To **Piscobamba**, combis depart hourly, 1 hr, US$1.20. There are no combis from Piscobamba to San Luis. To **Lima**, 18 hrs, US$11, via San Luis (4 hrs, US$3), Huari (6 hrs, US$4.50) and Chavín (9 hrs, US$6) with **El Solitario** Sun, Mon and Thu at 0800; via **Yungay** and **Huaraz** with La Perla del Alto Mayo, Wed, Thu, Sat, Sun, 16 hrs, US$11.

Sihuas *p1118*
Bus To **Pomabamba**, combis at 0700 and 1100, 4 hrs, US$3. To **Huaraz**, via Huallanca, with Transvir, daily at 0830, 8 hrs, US$7; **Trans Chavín Express**, Wed and Sat, and **Perú Andino** on Tue, 1100, 8 hrs, US$7. To **Tayabamba**, for the Marañón route north to Huamachuco and Cajamarca: **Andía** passes through from Lima on Mon, Wed and Sat at 0100-0200, **La Perla del Alta Mayo** passes through Wed and Sat 0000-0200; also twice a week with **Garrincha** and once a week with **San Antonio de Padua**; all 7-8 hrs, US$6, the beginning of a long wild ride. To **Huacrachuco**, Trans Andina, daily at 1000. To **Chimbote**, La Perla de Alta Mayo on Tue, Thu and Sun, 10 hrs, US$9. To **Lima** (17 hrs, US$9) via Chimbote, Andía daily around 0200-0500; confirm all times locally.

Caraz *p1118*
Bus From Caraz to **Lima**, 470 km, 5 companies on D Villar and Jr Córdova, daily, US$7 (**El Huaralino, Expreso Ancash**, T791509, **Móvil, Rodríguez**, T391184), 10-11 hrs. All go via Huaraz and Pativilca. To **Chimbote**, Yungay Express (D Villar 318), via Huallanca and Cañon del Pato 0830 every day, US$6.60, 8 hrs. Sit on right for best views. To **Trujillo**, via Huaraz and Pativilca, Chinchaysuyo (Córdova 830, T391930), 1845

1122

daily, US$9.10, 11-12 hrs, stops in Casma (US$7.60) and Chimbote (US$7.60). To **Huaraz**, combis leave 0400-2000, 1¼ hrs, US$1.35. They leave from a terminal on the way out of town, where the south end of C Sucre meets the highway. To **Yungay**, 12 km, 15 mins, US$0.30. To **Huallanca** (for the Cañon del Pato), combis and cars leave from Córdova y La Mar, 0700-1730, US$1.50.

Treks from Caraz *p1119*
Laguna Parón
To the village of **Parón** pickups from Santa Cruz y Grau by the market, Mon to Sat 0400 and 1300, Sun 0300 and 1300, 1 hr, US$1.30. They return from Parón at 0600 and 1400. From **Caraz**, colectivos go to the lake if there are enough passengers and only in the dry season, US$3-4 pp. **Pony's Expeditions** have a pool of well-trained drivers who make daily departures to Laguna Parón at 0800, US$25 for 4, including 1-hr visit to the lake and 1-hr walk downhill to the bridge, where diver will pick up the group (extra hours at US$3). Also, you can hire a bike (US$15 per day), take a car up (US$6 with 4 passengers) and ride back down.

Santa Cruz Valley
To **Cashapampa** (Quebrada Santa Cruz) buses from Santa Cruz y Grau, Caraz, hourly from 0830 to 1530, 2 hrs, US$1.50. Yanama to Yungay combis can be caught at Vaquería between 0800-1400, US$3, 3 hrs.

Yungay *p1119*
Buses and colectivos run the whole day to **Caraz**, 12 km, US$0.30, and **Huaraz**, 54 km, 1½ hrs, US$1. To lakes **Llanganuco**, combis leave when full, especially 0700- 0900, from Av 28 de Julio 1 block from the plaza, 1 hr, US$1.50. To **Yanama**, via the Portachuelo de Llanganuco Pass, 4,767m, 58 km, 3½ hrs, US$3; stopping at María Huayta (for the Llanganuco-Santa Cruz trek), after 2 hrs, US$2. To **Pomabamba**, via Piscobamba, **Trans Los Andes**, daily at 0800, the only company with a ticket office in Yungay; **Transvir** and **La Perla de Alta Mayo** buses coming from Huaraz, 0730, stop if they have room, 6-7 hrs, US$6. After passing the Llanganuco lakes and crossing the Portachuelo the buses descend to Puente Llacma, where it is possible to pick up buses and combis heading south to San Luis, Chacas and Huari.

Carhuaz *p1119*
All transport leaves from the main Plaza. To **Huaraz**, *colectivos* and buses leave 0500-2000, US$0.75, 40 mins. To **Caraz**, 0500-2000, US$0.75, 1 hr. There are **trucks** (only

1 or 2 a day) and 1 minivan (0800) going up the Ulta valley to **Chacas** (see page 1118), 87 km, 4-5 hrs, US$4.50. The road works its way up the Ulta valley to the pass at Punta Olímpica from where there are excellent views. The dirt road is not in a very good condition owing to landslides every year (in the wet season it can be closed). Trucks continue to **San Luis** (see page 1118), a further 10 km, 1½ hrs. Each Thu, a **bus** (Transportes Huandoy) does the trip from Carhuaz to Chacas and returns, US$6 one way, 5 hrs.

⊙ Directory

Chavín *p1117*
Internet Librería Aquariu's, 17 de Enero y Túpac Yupanqui, US$1 per hr. **Post offices** 17 de Enero 365N; open 0630-2200.
Telephones Payphones all over town.

Huari *p1117*
Post offices Luzuriaga 324 by Parque Vigil.
Telephones Libertad 940, open 0700-2200 daily.

Caraz *p1118*
Banks No ATM in town. BCP, D Villar 217, cash and TCs at good rates, no commission, cash withdrawals on credit card. **Importaciones América**, Sucre 721, T391479, good rates and service, open weekends and evenings.
Internet Many places around the Plaza and throughout town, US$0.30. **Post offices** San Martín 909.
Telephones National and international phone and fax at Raymondi y Sucre. Also several others, eg at Sucre y Santa Cruz, and on Plaza de Armas next to *Jeny*. No collect calls can be made except from private lines. Very few of the coin boxes take phone cards.

Cordillera Huayhuash

The Cordillera Huayhuash, lying south of the Cordillera Blanca, has azure trout-filled lakes interwoven with deep quebradas and high pastures around the hem of the range and is perhaps the most spectacular cordillera for its massive ice faces that seem to rise sheer out of the Puna's contrasting green. You may see tropical parakeets in the bottom of the gorges and condors circling the peaks. The complete circuit is very tough; allow 10-12 days. Trekkers have to pay in total US$30-35 per person to the different communities in charge of security (*rondadores*) along the whole loop; this has greatly improved security. The trail head is at **Cuartel Huain**, between Matacancha and the **Punta Cacanan** pass (the continental divide at 4,700 m). There are up to eight passes over 4,600 m, depending on the route. A half-circuit is also possible, but there are many other options. Both ranges are approached from Chiquián in the north, **Oyón**, with links to Cerro de Pasco to the southeast, **Churín** in the south or Cajatambo to the southwest. The area offers fantastic scenery and insights into rural life.

   Chiquián is a town of narrow streets and overhanging eaves. *Semana Turística*: first week of July. Buy all your food and supplies in Huaraz as there are only basic supplies in Chiquián and almost nothing in the hamlets along the route. **Mule hire** It may take a day to bring the mules to your starting point from Llamac or Pocpa where they are kept. (Very basic supplies only can be bought in either village.) Ask for mules (US$4-5 per day) or horses (US$7 per day) at the hotels or restaurants in Chiquián. A guide for the Huayhuash is **Sr Delao Callupe**, ask for him in Chiquián.

   Cajatambo is the southern approach to the Cordillera Huayhuash, a small market town with a beautiful 18th-century church and a lovely plaza. There are various hotels (**G**) and some good restaurants around the plaza. Note that the road out of Cajatambo is not for the fainthearted. For the first 3-4 hours it is no more than a bus-width, clinging to the cliff edge.

⊜ Sleeping

Cordillera Huayhuash *p1123*
E Gran Hotel Huayhuash, 28 de Julio 400, Chiquián, T447049, www.hotelhuayhuash.com. Private bathroom, hot water, TV, restaurant, laundry, parking, modern, great views, information and tours.
F Hostal San Miguel, Jr Comercio 233, Chiquián, T447001. Nice courtyard and garden, clean, many rooms, popular.
G pp Los Nogales de Chiquián, Jr Comercio 1301, T447121 (in Lima T460 8037), www.andestop-peru.com/site/nogalesing.htm. Cheaper without bath, hot water, cable TV, cafeteria, parking. Recommended.

🍴 Eating

Cordillera Huayhuash *p1123*

¶ **Panificadora Santa Rosa**, Comercio 900, on the plaza, Chiquián, for good bread and sweets, has coin-operated phones and fax.

¶ **El Refugio de Bolognesi** and **Yerupajá**, on Tarapacá, both offer basic set meals.

🚍 Transport

Cordillera Huayhuash *p1123*

Coming from Huaraz, the road is now paved beyond Chiquián to Huansala, on the road to Huallanca (Huánuco). Two bus companies run from **Huaraz to Chiquián**, 120 km, 3½ hrs: **El Rápido**, at Bolognesi 216, T422887, at 1345, and

Chiquián Tours, on Tarapacá behind the market. From Chiquián to Huaraz: buses leave the plaza at 0500 daily, US$1.75, except **El Rápido**, Jr Figueredo 216, T447049, at 0500 and 1330, US$3.65. Also colectivo Chiquián-Huaraz 1500, 3 hrs, US$2.45 pp. There is also a connection from Chiquián to Huallanca (Huánuco) with buses coming up from Lima in the early morning and combis during the day, which leave when full, 3 hrs, US$2.50. From Huallanca there are regular combis on to La Unión, 1 hr, US$0.75, and from there transport to Huánuco. From Cajatambo buses depart for **Lima** at 0600, US$8.80, daily with **Empresa Andina** (office on plaza next to Hostal Cajatambo), **Tour Bello**, 1 block off the Plaza, and **Turismo Cajatambo**, Jr Grau 120 (in Lima, Av Carlos Zavala 124 corner of Miguel Aljovin 449, T426 7238).

North coast

The north of Peru has been described as the Egypt of South America, as it is home to many ruined pre-Inca treasures. Many tourists pass through without stopping on their way to or from Ecuador, missing out on one of the most fascinating parts of the country. Along a seemingly endless stretch of desert coast lie many of the country's most important pre-Inca sites: Chan-Chán, the Moche pyramids, Túcume, Sipán, Batán Grande and El Brujo. The main city is Trujillo, while Chiclayo is more down-to-earth, with one of the country's largest witchdoctors' market. The coast is also famous for its deep-sea fishing, surfing, and the unique reed fishing boats at Huanchaco and Pimentel. Inland lies colonial Cajamarca, scene of Atahualpa's last stand. Further east, where the Andes meet the jungle, countless unexplored ancient ruins await the more adventurous traveller.

North of Lima

The Pan-American Highway is four-lane (several tolls, about US$2) to Km 101, at **Huacho**, 19 km east of **Puerto Huacho** (several hotels in Huacho, but none at the port). The beaches south of the town are clean and deserted. The journey inland from Huacho, up the Huaura valley, is splendid. Beyond Sayán the road follows the Huaura valley which narrows almost to a gorge before climbing steeply to **Churín**, with hot, sulphurous springs which are used to cure a number of ailments, and various hotels and restaurants. The climate is dry with temperatures ranging from 10° to 32°C. The area is famous for cheese, yoghurt and other natural products. Other hot springs nearby are **Huancahuasi**, **Picoy** (both good) and **Chiuchín** (neglected).

Caral and Paramonga → *Phone code: 01.*

A few kilometres before Barranca (158 km from Lima) a turning to the right (east) leads to **Caral** ⓘ *Proyecto Especial Caral, Unión 1040, Lima 1, T332 5380, www.caralperu. gob.pe, 0900-1700, US$3, US$1 with student card; US$6 per group with guide, all visitors must report to the tourist post in the car park*. This ancient city, 20 km from the coast, dates from about 2,600 BC. Many of the accepted theories of Peruvian archaeology have been overturned by Caral's age and monumental construction. It appears to be easily the oldest city in South America. The dry, desert site lies on the southern fringes of the Supe valley, along whose flanks there are many more unexcavated ruins. Caral covers 66 ha and contains eight significant pyramidal structures. To date seven have been excavated by archaeologists from the University of San Marcos, Lima. They are undertaking careful renovation on the existing foundations to re-establish the pyramidal tiers. It is possible to walk around and, in some cases, up on to the pyramids. A viewpoint provides a panorama across the whole site. Detailed, illustrated, bilingual (Spanish/ English) information panels are located around the site. The site is well organized, criss-crossed by marked paths which must be adhered to. Allow at least two hours to visit the site. See Listings for tours and transport

Some 4 km beyond the turn-off to Huaraz, beside the Highway, are the well preserved ruins of the Chimú temple of **Paramonga** ① *US$1.20; caretaker may act as guide.* Set on high ground with a view of the ocean, the fortress-like mound is reinforced by eight quadrangular walls rising in tiers to the top of the hill.

Casma and Sechín → *Phone code: 043. Colour map 3, grid B2. Population: 22,600*

Casma has a pleasant Plaza de Armas, several parks and two markets including a good food market. It is a base from where to explore **Sechín** ① *www.xanga.com/sechin, the site is open daily 0800-1800, photography best around midday, US$1.50 (children and students half price); ticket also valid for the Max Uhle Museum by the ruins and Pañamarca, an archaeological site in the Nepeña Valley, north of Casma.* Frequent colectivos leave from in front of the market in Casma, US$0.30 pp, or motorcycle taxi US$1, one of the most important ruins 5 km away on the Peruvian coast. It consists of a large square temple completely faced with about 500 carved stone monoliths narrating, it is thought, a gruesome battle in graphic detail. The style is unique in Peru for its naturalistic vigour. The complex as a whole is associated with the pre-Chavín Sechín culture, dating from about 1600 BC. Three sides of the large stone temple have been excavated and restored, but you cannot see the earlier adobe buildings inside the stone walls because they were covered up and used as a base for a second storey, which has been completely destroyed.

Chimbote → *Phone code: 043. Colour map 3, grid B2. Population: 313,500.*

The port of Chimbote serves the national fishing industry and the smell of the fishmeal plants is overpowering. As well as being unpleasant it is also unsafe. Take extensive precautions, always use taxis from the bus station to your hotel and don't venture far from the hotel. **Note** The main street, Avenida Víctor Raul Haya de la Torre, is also known by its old name, José Pardo. At weekends two-hour boat trips go around the bay to visit the cliffs and islands to see the marine birdlife and rock formations.

Chimbote to Callejón de Huaylas

Just north of Chimbote, a road branches northeast off the Pan-American Highway and goes up the Santa valley following the route of the old Santa Corporation Railway which used to run as far as **Huallanca** (Ancash – not to be confused with the town southeast of Huaraz), 140 km up the valley. At Chuquicara, three hours from Chimbote (paved – very rough thereafter), is Restaurante Rosales, a good place to stop for a meal (US$1-1.30; you can sleep here, too, but it's very basic). At Huallanca there are also places to stay and eat. Fuel is available. At the top of the valley by the hydroelectric centre, the road goes through the very narrow and spectacular **Cañon del Pato**. You pass under tremendous walls of bare rock and through 35 tunnels, but the flow of the river has been greatly reduced by the hydroelectric scheme. After this point the road is paved to the Callejón de Huaylas and the road south to Caraz and Huaraz.

An alternative road for cyclists (and vehicles with a permit) is the 50-km private road known as the 'Brasileños', used by the Brazilian company Odebrecht which has built a water channel for the Chavimochic irrigation scheme from the Río Santa to the coast. The turn-off is 35 km north of the Santa turning, 15 km south of the bridge in Chao, on the Pan-American Highway at Km 482. It is a good all-weather road via Tanguche. Permits are obtainable from the Chavimochic HQ at San José de Virú, US$6.50, or from the guard at the gate on Sunday.

● Sleeping

Casma and Sechín *p1125*
D **Hostal El Farol**, Túpac Amaru 450, T711064, hostalfaro@yahoo.com. Very nice, cheaper in low season, hot water, swimming pool, pleasant garden, good restaurant, parking, information.
F **Gregori**, Luis Ormeño 530, T711073. Cheaper

without bath, café downstairs.
F **Hostal Celene** Ormeño 595, T711065. Large pleasant rooms.
F **Monte Carlo**, Nepeña 370, T711421. TV, internet, laundry, good value.
F **Rebeca**, Huarmey 377, T711258. Modern, hot

water only at night, good.

G Las Dunas, Luis Ormeño 505, T/F711057. An upgraded and enlarged family home, friendly.

Chimbote *p1125*

Plenty of hotels, so try to negotiate a lower rate.

B Cantón, Bolognesi 498, T344388. The most modern, luxury hotel in the city, has a good but pricey chifa restaurant.

C Ivansino Inn, Haya de la Torre 738, T321811, ivansino@hotmail.com. Including breakfast, comfortable, modern.

D D'Carlo, Villavicencio 376, on the plaza, T/F321047. Friendly, TV, mini-bar, restaurant.

D San Felipe, Haya de la Torre 514, T323401. Hot water, comfortable, restaurant.

E Felic, Haya de la Torre 552, T325901. **F** without bath, quiet. Recommended.

E Hostal Karol Inn, Manuel Ruiz 277, T/F321216. Hot water, good, family run, laundry, cafetería.

E Residencial El Parque, E Palacios 309, on plaza, T323963. Converted old home, hot water, nice, secure.

F Hostal El Ensueño, Sáenz Peña 268, 2 blocks from Plaza Central, T328662. **G** without bath, very good, safe, welcoming.

F Tany, Palacios 553, T/F323411. Includes breakfast, TV, good value.

⊘ Eating

Casma and Sechín *p1125*

Cheap restaurants on Huarmey. The local ice-cream, *Caribe*, is available at Ormeño 545.

♯ Tío Sam, Huarmey 138. Specializes in fresh fish.

♯ Venecia, Huarmey 204. Local dishes, popular.

Chimbote *p1125*

♯ Aquarius, Haya de la Torre 360. Vegetarian.

♯ Chifa Jin Lon, adjoining *Hostal Karol Inn*. Well-prepared Chinese food, popular.

♯ Delca, Haya de la Torre 568. Excellent bakery.

♯ Las Flores, Jr Enrique Palacios, 2 blocks west of the Plaza. Open 24 hrs, good breakfasts.

♯ Recutecu, L Prado 556. Good set lunch with a wide choice, popular with locals.

▲ Activities and tours

Casma and Sechín *p1125*

Sechín Tours, in Hostal Monte Carlo, Casma, T711421. Organizes tours in the local area. The guide, Renato, only speaks Spanish but has knowledge of local ruins and can be contacted on T712528, renatotours@yahoo.com. US$3 per hr, including use of mototaxi.

⊖ Transport

Huara Valley *p1124*

Bus Litsa to **Huacho** from **Lima** 2½ hrs, US$2, or **Comité 18**, daily colectivos, US$2.50. To **Churín** Estrella Polar, Espadín and Beteta have several times a day from **Lima**, 4-5 hrs, US$5.

Caral and Paramonga *p1124*

Bus To **Barranca** stops opposite the service station (*el grifo*) at the end of town. From **Lima** to Barranca, 3½ hrs, US$3. As bus companies have their offices in Barranca, buses will stop there rather than at Pativilca or Paramonga. Bus from Barranca to **Casma** 155 km, several daily, 2½ hrs, US$3. From Barranca to **Huaraz**, 4 hrs, US$6, daily buses or trucks. The good, paved road to Huaraz turns off the Panamericana just past Pativilca. **Caral** is best visited from Barranca or Supe. Colectivos leave from Av Lima, 2 blocks from the market, in Barranca for the village of Caral from 0700, 1½ hrs, US$1.50. The ruins are 25 km along a rough road which runs up the Supe valley. A path leads from the road across the valley to the ruins, though the river may be impassable Dec-Mar, 30 mins. Colectivos can also be picked up in Supe or at the signposted turn-off to the ruins on the Panamericana at Km 185, if they have room. A taxi in Barranca or Supe costs US$20, including a 2-hr wait. Another approach is from the south along a rough road, 28 km, through the Granja Toshi chicken farm: no regular transport but taxis wait at the Km 160 turn-off on the Panamericana, 2 hrs, US$20, including a 2-hr wait. This route is unsigned but may be the only way in the rainy season.

Buses run only to Paramonga port (3 km off the Highway, 4 km from the Paramonga ruins, about 15 mins from Barranca). **Taxi** From Paramonga to the ruins and return after waiting, US$4.50, otherwise take a Barranca-Paramonga port bus, then a 3 km walk.

Casma and Sechín *p1125*

Bus Half hourly from **Lima** to **Chimbote** which can drop you off in Casma, 370 km, 6 hrs, US$5. If going to **Lima** many of the buses from Trujillo and Chimbote stop briefly opposite the petrol station, block 1 of Ormeño or, if they have small offices, along blocks 1-5 of Av Ormeño. To **Chimbote**, 55 km, it is easiest to take a Los Casmeños colectivo, huge old Dodge cars, which depart when full from in front of the petrol station, block 1 of Ormeño, or from Plaza Poncianos, 45 mins, US$1.20. To **Trujillo** it is best to go first to Chimbote bus station and then take an **América Express** bus. To **Huaraz** (150km), via Pariacoto, buses come from Chimbote, 6-7 hrs, US$6. **Transportes Huandoy**, Ormeño 166, T712336, departs at 0700, 1100 and 1400, while **Yungay**

Express, Ormeño 158, departs at 0600, 0800 and 1400. This difficult but beautiful trip is worth taking in daylight. From Casma the first 30 km are paved, a good dirt road follows for 30 km to **Pariacoto** (basic lodging). From here to the **Callán pass** (4,224 m) the road is rough (landslides in rainy season), but once the Cordillera Negra has been crossed, the wide, gravel road is better with lovely views of the Cordillera Blanca (150 km to Huaraz). Most Huaraz buses go via Pativilca, which is further but the road is much better, 6 hrs, US$6, **Móvil Tours** and **Trans Chinchaysuyo**, all run at night.

Chimbote p1125
Warning Under no circumstances should you walk to the centre: minibus costs US$0.30, taxi US$1.30. There are no hotels near the terminal; some companies have ticket offices in the centre.
Bus The station is 4 km south on Av Meiggs. From **Lima**, to Chimbote, 420 km, 6 hrs, US$7-9, several buses daily, **Trans Isla Blanca** has the most frequent service. To **Trujillo**, 130 km, 2 hrs, US$1.50, **América Express** buses every 20 mins. To **Huaraz** most companies, with the best buses, go the 'long way round', ie down the Panamericana to Pativilca, then up the paved highway, 7 hrs, US$6. The main companies start in Trujillo and continue to **Caraz**. To Huaraz via Pariacoto, 7 hrs, US$6, **Trans Huandoy** (Etseturh),

T354024, at 0600, 1000 and 1300, 7 hrs, US$5.50, and **Yungay Express** at 0500, 0700 and 1300. To **Caraz** via Cañón del Pato, 7-8 hrs, US$7.60, **Yungay Express** at 0830 (for a description of this route see above). Sit on the left-hand-side for the best views. If arriving from Caraz via the Cañón del Pato there is usually time to make a connection to Casma or Trujillo/Huanchaco and avoid overnighting in Chimbote. If travelling to Caraz, however, overnighting in Chimbote is almost unavoidable. Casma is near enough to stay in but you will need to buy your Caraz ticket the day before; the bus station is on the Casma side of Chimbote.

① Directory

Casma and Sechín p1125
Banks Good rates for cash and TCs, no commission, at BCP, Bolívar 181. **Internet** Café on west side of Plaza, 0900-2100. **Post offices** Fernando Loparte, ½ block from Plaza de Armas.

Chimbote p1125
Banks BCP and Interbank, both on Bolognesi and M Ruiz, for TCs and cash. **Casa Arroyo**, M Ruiz 292, cash only. There are other *casas* and street changers along M Ruiz between Bolognesi and VR Haya de la Torre. **Internet** At Palacios 518, Aguirre 278 and J Pardo 660.

Trujillo and around → Phone code: 044. Colour map 3, grid B2. Population: 850,000.

The capital of La Libertad Department, 548 km from Lima, disputes the title of second city of Peru with Arequipa. The compact colonial centre, though, has a small-town feel. The greenness surrounding the city is a delight against the backcloth of brown Andean foothills and peaks. Founded by Diego de Almagro in 1534 as an express assignment ordered by Francisco Pizarro, it was named after the latter's native town in Spain. Nearby are some of Peru's most important Moche and Chimú archaeological sites and a stretch of the country's best surfing beaches.

Ins and outs
Getting there The **airport** is west of the city; the entry to town is along Avenida Mansiche. There is no central bus terminal. **Bus stations** are spread out on three sides the city beyond the inner ring road, Avenida España. Many companies have premises north and south along the Panamericana. There are few hotels around them, but plenty of taxis and colectivos. Insist on being taken to your hotel of choice. ▶ *For more detailed information, see Transport, page 1150.*

Getting around Trujillo is best explored on foot. Taxis in town charge US$0.55-70; always use official taxis, which are mainly yellow. The major sites outside the city, Chan Chán, the Moche pyramids and Huanchaco beach are easily reached by public transport, but take care when walking around. A number of recommended guides run tours to these and other places.
Note The city is generally safe but be careful at bus stations when arriving or leaving. Also take care beyond the inner ring road, Avenida España, as well as obvious places around bus stops and terminals, and at ATMs.

Tourist offices i perú ① *Municipalidad building, Pizarro 402, p 2, Plaza Mayor, T294561,* iperutrujillo@promperu.gob.pe, Mon-Sat 0800-1900, Sun 0800-1400. Useful websites: www.xanga.com/TrujilloPeru and www.laindustria.com/industria. **Tourist Police** have an office at Independencia 630, Casa Ganoza Chopitea, T291705, policia_turismo_tru@hotmail.com, open Mon-Sat 0800-2000, they provide useful information. **Indecopi** ① *Jr Bolivia 251, Urb El Recreo, T295733*, for tourist complaints. Maps available from **Touring and Automobile Club** ① *Argentina 258, Urb El Recreo, T290736, trujillo@touringperu.com.pe.*

Sights

The focal point is the pleasant and spacious **Plaza Mayor**. The prominent sculpture represents agriculture, commerce, education, art, slavery, action and liberation, crowned by a young man holding a torch depicting liberty. Fronting it is the **Cathedral**, dating from 1666, with its museum of religious paintings and sculptures next door. Also on the Plaza are the *Hotel Libertador,* the colonial style Sociedad de Beneficencia Pública de Trujillo and the Municipalidad. The **Universidad de La Libertad**, second only to that of San Marcos at Lima, was founded in 1824. Two beautiful colonial mansions on the plaza have been taken over. The Banco Central de Reserva is in the Colonial-style **Casa Urquiaga (or Calonge)** ① *Pizarro 446, Mon-Fri 0900- 1500, Sat-Sun 1000-1330, free 30-min guided tour, take passport,* which contains valuable pre-Columbian ceramics. The other is **Casa Bracamonte (or Lizarzaburu)** ① *Independencia 441*, with occasional exhibits. Opposite the Cathedral on Independencia, is the **Casa Garci Olguín** *(Caja Nor Perú)*, recently restored but boasting the oldest façade in the city and Moorish-style murals. The buildings that surround the Plaza, and many others in the vicinity, are painted in bright pastel colours. Near the Plaza de Armas is the spacious 18th- century **Palacio Iturregui**, now occupied by the **Club Central** ① *Jr Pizarro 688, Mon-Sat 1100- 1800, free entry to patio, US$1.45 to see the ceramics.* An exclusive and social centre of Trujillo, it houses a private collection of ceramics.

Other mansions, still in private hands, include **Casa del Mayorazgo de Facalá** ① *Pizarro 314,* now Scotiabank (ex-Banco Wiese). **Casa de la Emancipación** ① *Jr Pizarro 610 (Banco Continental), Mon-Sat, 0915-1230, 1600-1830,* is where independence from Spain was planned and was the first seat of government and congress in Peru. The **Casa del Mariscal de Orbegoso** ① *Orbegoso 553, open daily from 0930, free, take passport or photocopy,* is the Museo de la República owned by the *BCP* bank. **Casa Ganoza Chopitea** ① *Independencia 630,* architecturally the most representative house in the city.

One of the best of the many churches is the 17th-century **La Merced** ① *at Pizarro 550, 0800-1200, 1600-2000, free,* with picturesque moulded figures below the dome. **El Carmen** ① *at Colón y Bolívar, Mon-Sat 0900-1300, US$0.85, church is open for mass Sun 0700-0730,* church and monastery, has been described as the 'most valuable jewel of colonial art in Trujillo'. Next door is the Pinacoteca Carmelita. **La Compañía** ① *near Plaza de Armas,* is now an auditorium for cultural events.

Museo de Arqueología ① *Junín 682 y Ayacucho, Casa Risco, T249322, www.uni tru.edu.pe/cultural/arq, Mon 0900-1445, Tue-Fri 0900- 1300, 1500-1900, Sat and Sun 0930-1600. US$1.50,* houses a large and interesting collection of thematic exhibits. The basement of the **Cassinelli garage** ① *on the fork of the Pan-American and Huanchaco roads, 0900-1300, 1500-1900, US$1.50,* contains a superb private collection of Mochica and Chimú pottery, recommended. Demonstrations of the whistling *huacos* are given. The **Museo del Juguete** ① *Independencia 705 y Junín, Mon-Sat 1000-1800, US$0.85, children US$0.30, café open 0900-2300,* is a toy museum containing examples from prehistoric times to 1950, collected by painter Gerardo Chávez. Downstairs is the Espacio Cultural Angelmira with a café bar; in a restored *casona,* worth a visit. **Museo de Zoología de Juan Ormea** ① *Jr San Martín 368, Mon-Fri 0800-1900, Sat 0800-1300, US$0.60,* has interesting displays of Peruvian animals.

Huacas del Sol and de la Luna

① *0830-1600 (last entry, but site open till sunset), US$3.50 with guide, some of whom speak European languages (students half price, children US$0.40), booklet in English or Spanish US$2.85. See Proyecto Huaca de la Luna, Jr Junín 682, Trujillo, T297430, www.huacadelaluna.org.pe; also www.huacas.com. The visitors' centre (T834901) has a café showing videos and a souvenir shop and good toilets.*

A few kilometres south of Trujillo are the huge and fascinating Moche pyramids, the Huaca del Sol and the Huaca de la Luna. Until the Spaniards destroyed a third of it in a vain search for treasure, Huaca del Sol was the largest man-made structure in the western hemisphere, at 45 m high. It consisted of seven levels , with possibly six remodellings over the first six centuries AD. Today, about two-thirds of the pyramid have been lost and it is closed to the public. Huaca de la Luna, 500 m away, received scant attention until extensive polychrome moulded decorations were found throughout the 1990s. The colours on these remarkable geometric patterns and deities have faded little and it is now possible to view impressive friezes of the upper four levels on the northern exterior wall of the huaca. The highest mural is a 'serpent' which runs the length of the wall, beneath it there are repeated motifs of 'felines' holding decapitated heads of warriors, then repeated motifs of 'fishermen' holding fish against a bright blue background and, next, huge 'spider/crab' motifs. The bottom two levels show dancers or officials grimly holding hands and, below them, victorious warriors following naked prisoners past scenes of combat and two complex scenes, similar to those at Huaca Cao Viejo at El Brujo (see below). Combined with intricate, brightly painted two- dimensional motifs in the sacrificial area atop the huaca, and with new discoveries in almost every excavation, Huaca de la Luna is now a truly significant site well worth visiting. In an outside patio craftsmen reproduce ceramics in designs from northern Peru. Also good toilets.

Chan Chán

ⓘ *5 km from Trujillo. 0830-1700, last entry 1600. Site may be covered up if rain is expected. Tickets cost US$3.50 (discount with ISIC card), include entrance fees for Chan Chán, site museum, Huaca El Dragón and Huaca La Esmeralda (for 2 days). A guide costs US$5.80 per hr – worth it; map and leaflet in English US$0.75. See note about safety, page 1136*

These vast, unusually decorated crumbling ruins of the imperial city of the Chimú domains are the largest adobe city in the world. The ruins consist of nine great compounds built by Chimú kings. The 9-m high perimeter walls surrounded sacred enclosures with usually only one narrow entrance. Inside, rows of storerooms contained the agricultural wealth of the kingdom, which stretched 1,000 km along the coast from near Guayaquil to the Carabayllo Valley, north of Lima.

Most of the compounds contain a huge walk-in well which tapped the ground water, raised to a high level by irrigation further up the valley. Each compound also included a platform mound which was the burial place of the king, with his women and his treasure, presumably maintained as a memorial. The Incas almost certainly copied this system and transported it to Cuzco where the last Incas continued building huge enclosures. The Chimú surrendered to the Incas around 1471 after 11 years of siege and threats to cut the irrigation canals.

The dilapidated city walls enclose an area of 28 sq km containing the remains of palaces, temples, workshops, streets, houses, gardens and a canal. What is left of the adobe walls bears well-preserved decorations of fish and other animals, and painted designs have been found on pottery unearthed from the debris of a city ravaged by floods, earthquakes, and *huaqueros* (grave looters). Owing to the damage, many of the interesting mouldings are closed to visitors. The **Ciudadela of Tschudi** has been restored (20 mins walk from the road).

The **site museum** ⓘ *0830-1600*, on the main road, 100 m before the turn-off, has a son et lumière display of the growth of Chan Chán as well as objects found in the area.

The partly-restored temple, **Huaca El Dragón** ⓘ *0900-1630 (in theory), on the west side of the Pan-American Highway in the district of La Esperanza; combis from Huayna Cápac y Los Incas, or Av España y Manuel Vera marked 'Arco Iris/La Esperanza', taxi costs US$2,* dating from Huari to Chimú times (AD 1000-1470), is also known as **Huaca Arco Iris** (rainbow), after the shape of friezes which decorate it.

The poorly preserved **Huaca La Esmeralda** is at Mansiche, between Trujillo and Chan Chán, behind the church (not a safe area). Buses to Chan Chán and Huanchaco pass the church at Mansiche.

El Brujo

ⓘ *US$3.50. See www.xanga.com/ElBrujoPeru.*

A complex collectively known as **El Brujo**, 60 km north of Trujillo, is considered one of the most important archaeological sites on the north coast. Covering 2 sq km, it was a ceremonial centre for up to 10 cultures, including the Moche. Huaca Cortada (or El Brujo) has a wall decorated with high relief stylized figures. Huaca Prieta is, in effect, a giant rubbish tip dating back 5,000 years, which once housed the very first settlers. Huaca Cao Viejo has extensive friezes, polychrome reliefs up to 90 m long, 4 m high and on five different levels. The mummy of a tattooed woman, dating from 450 AD, has also been found (see *National Geographic*, June 2006). In front of

Trujillo

To Emtrafesa Buse

Sleeping
- Casa de Clara **18** *F6*
- Chan Chán Inn **1** *A5*
- Colonial **3** *C4*
- Continental **3** *D4*
- El Gran Marqués **4** *F2*
- Gran Bolívar **6** *B5*
- Hostal Americano **8** *C4*
- Hostal Malibú **7** *F2*
- Hostería El Sol **5** *A1*
- Libertador **12** *D3*
- Los Conquistadores **13** *E3*
- Primavera **14** *A1*
- Residencial Vanini **9** *F2*
- Saint Germain **15** *C4*
- San Martín **16** *B3*

Eating
- ABC **1** *C3*
- Asturias **16** *C4*
- Café Amaretto **3** *C3*
- Café Oviedo **16** *C4*
- Café Santo Domingo **24** *E3*
- Demarco **16** *C4*
- Dulcería Doña
  Carmen **25** *B4*
- El Chileno **6** *E4*
- El Mochica **7** *E4*
- El Sol **8** *C4*
- Juguería San Agustín **9** *D4*
- La Casona **26** *B3*

- Turismo **10** *D5*

- Milenium **10** *C3*
- Panadería José
  Antonio **11** *D4*
- Panadería Sandoval **12** *E5*
- Parnasillo **4** *C3*
- Pizzería Pizzanino **13** *E1*
- Rincón de Vallejo **15** *C3*
- Romano **16** *C4*
- Romano-Rincón
  Criollo **17** *F3*
- Sal y Pimienta **18** *B3*

Bars & clubs
- Canana **19** *B3*
- El Estubo **23** *B4*
- Juguete **21** *C4*

0 metres 100
0 yards 100

Peru Trujillo & around

Cao Viejo are the remains of one of the oldest Spanish churches in the region. It was common practice for the Spaniards to build their churches near these ancient sites in order to counteract their religious importance. Excavations will continue for many years. Trujillo travel agencies run tours. There are exhibitions at the Chan Chán site museum, Banco Wiese (Scotiabank) and Museo de la Nación in Lima.

Huanchaco and around

An alternative to Trujillo is this fishing and surfing village, full of hotels, guest houses and restaurants (but little nightlife). It is famous for its narrow pointed fishing rafts, known as *caballitos* (little horses) *de totora*, made of totora reeds and depicted on Mochica, Chimú and other cultures' pottery. Unlike those used on Lake Titicaca, they are flat, not hollow, and ride the breakers rather like surfboards (fishermen offer trips on their *caballitos* for US$1.50, be prepared to get wet; groups should contact Luis Gordillo, El Mambo, T461092). You can see fishermen returning in their reed rafts at about 0800 and 1400 when they stack the boats upright to dry in the fierce sun. Overlooking Huanchaco is a huge church from the belfry of which are extensive views. Post Office at Grau y Manco Capac, open Mon-Sat 1300-1800.

Puerto Malabrigo (**Chicama**), is known by surfers as the best surf beach in Peru, claiming that it has the longest left-hand point-break in the world. It is 70 km north of Trujillo. There are several basic places to stay and eat.

🛏 Sleeping

Trujillo *p1127, map p1130*
Trujillo has confusing double street names: the smaller printed name is that generally shown on maps, in guide books and in general use.
AL Libertador, Independencia 485, Plaza de Armas, T232741, trujillo@libertador.com.pe. Including tax, pool (can be used by non-guests if they buy a drink), cafetería and restaurant, breakfast US$5, excellent buffet lunch on Sun. Recommended.
A Los Conquistadores, Diego de Almagro 586, T203350, losconquistadores@ viabcp.com. Includes American breakfast, internet, bar, restaurant, very comfortable.
A El Gran Marqués, Díaz de Cienfuegos 145-147, Urb La Merced, T/F249366, www.elgran marques.com. Price includes

Stradivarius **22** *B4*
Taverna Chelsea **20** *B5*

Transport 🚌
Buses to Huaca del Sol y de la Luna **3** *D6*
Chinchaysuyo **5** *B2*
Combi A to Huanchaco, Chan Chán **4** *E2, E5*
Combis A & B & Micros B, H & H Corazón to Chan Chán & Huanchaco **13** *B1*
Combi A & Micro H to Chan Chán & Huanchaco **1** *E1*

Combi B & Micro B to Chan Chán & Huanchaco **14** *A5, B3*
El Dorado **6** *B1*
Ittsa **8** *B2, C2*
Turismo Díaz **9** *B1*
Oltursa & Flores **10** *A5*
Ormeño **11** *A5*

breakfast, modern, free internet connection in rooms, pool, sauna, jacuzzi, restaurant. Recommended.

B Gran Bolívar, Bolívar 957, T222090, www.granbolivarhotel.net. Includes breakfast, airport transfer and welcome drink, in converted 18th-century house, internet, café, bar, parking.

B-D Hostal Malibú, Av Larco 1471, Urb La Merced, T284811, www.hostalmalibu.com. Variety of rooms, restaurant, room service, mini-bar, laundry, massage, currency exchange. Also sister hotel of same name at Av Larco 1000, Huanchaco.

C Saint Germain, Junín 585, T208102, www.perunorte.com/saintgermain. Price includes breakfast, hot water, TV, internet, laundry, safe, parking.

D Continental, Gamarra 663, T241607, F249881. Opposite market, good breakfast, helpful, safe.

D-E Colonial, Independencia 618, T258261, hostalcolonialtruji@hotmail.com. Attractive but small rooms, hot showers, basic breakfast, good restaurant, especially for set lunch. Recommended.

E Almagro, Jr Almagro 748, T044-223845. New hotel with cable TV, hot water, cafetería (breakfast extra), good.

E San Martín, San Martín 749, T/F252311, www.deperu.com/sanmartin. Good value, attractive, TV, small restaurant, good for breakfast, noisy, otherwise recommended.

E Turismo, Gamarra 747, T244181. Includes continental breakfast, central, good services TV, restaurant, parking, travel agency.

F Hostal Americano, Pizarro 764, T241361. Vast, rambling building, most rooms without window, can be noisy, cold water, rundown, mixed reports.

F Hostería El Sol, Brillantes 224, Urb Santa Inés, T044-231933, near bus terminals on Av Nicolás de Piérola. With hot shower, restaurant, all meals available for US$2.60.

F Primavera, Av N de Piérola 872, Urb Primavera, T231915, F257399. Hot water, restaurant, bar, pool.

F Residencia Vanini, Av Larco 237, outside Av España, T200878, enriqueva@hotmail.com. Youth hostel in a converted private house, a good option but not in the centre, some rooms with bath, others with shared shower.

G pp Casa de Clara, Cahuide 495, T243347, www.xanga.com/TrujilloPeru. Cheaper without bath. Meals on request, very helpful, lots of information, many languages spoken (see Guides, below). Restaurants and fast internet nearby. Recommended.

G pp Chan Chán Inn, Av Ejército 307, T/F294281, mocheperu@hotmail.com. Close to several bus terminals so noisy, includes breakfast (cheaper without), popular with backpackers, luggage store, café, laundry, internet, money exchange, information.

Huanchaco *p1131*

C Las Palmeras, Av Larco 1150, sector Los Tumbos, T461199, www.lasplamerasdehuan chaco.com. One of the best, rooms with terrace, bath, TV, hot water, dining room, pool and gardens.

D Caballito de Totora, Av La Rivera 219, T/F461154, www.caballitodetotora.com. Includes taxes, **E** in low season (when restaurant is closed), surfers' room **G**, pool, English spoken, nice garden, restaurant with good food and coffee, off site parking, good value, noisy. Recommended.

D Hospedaje Huankarute, La Rivera 233, T044-461705, www.huanchaco.com/huankarute. On the sea-front, with small pool, bar, sun terrace, friendly; some rooms larger, more luxurious and more pricey. Recommended.

D Hostal Bracamonte, Los Olivos 503, T461162, www.hostalbracamonte.com. Comfortable chalets with bath **C**, pool, own water supply, emergency generator, rents bicycles, secure, good restaurant, English spoken. Camping. Highly recommended.

D Hostal Huanchaco, Larco 287 on Plaza, T461272, www.huanchacohostal.com. With breakfast, TV, hot water, good but expensive cafetería, video, pool table. Recommended.

D Hostal Sol y Mar, La Rivera 400, T461120, www.ctsolymar.cjb.net. With pool, restaurant and garden. Recommended.

D-E El Malecón, Av La Rivera 225, T461275. Overlooking the sea, some rooms with terrace, clean, hot water, TV, café, helpful staff.

E Hostal Los Esteros, Av Larco 618, T461300, huanchacoesteros@yahoo.com. Hot water, restaurant, safe motorcycle parking, can arrange surfing and *caballitos de totora* trips.

E Huanchaco Inn, Los Pinos 528, T461158, www.huanchacoinn.com. Rooms with and without bath, new and still expanding, hot water, cable TV, internet cabins, use of kitchen, laundry service, small pool.

E Las Brisas, Raymondi 146, T461186, lasbrisas@hotmail.com. Hot water, café, cable TV, comfortable.

F Naylamp, Prolongación Víctor Larco 3, northern end of seafront in El Boquerón, T461022, www.hostalnaylamp.com. Rooms set around a courtyard, dorms **G** pp, hammocks, garden, good beds, hot water, camping US$2.45, US$3 to hire tent, laundry, safe, many languages spoken, Italian food, good breakfasts. Recommended.

G Casa Hospedaje Los Ficus, Los Ficus 516, T461719, www.huanchaco.net/losficus. Breakfast and laundry extra. Family run, hot water, use of kitchen. Recommended.

G pp Cherry's, Los Pinos 448, T461837, juancarlos160@yahoo.es. Owner Juan Carlos speaks English, cheaper without bath, hot water, use of kitchen, shop, bar, internet with good machines, even a small swimming pool.

G pp Golden Club, Av La Rivera 217, T461306.

Gym, pool, restaurant, use of kitchen, popular with surfers, laid back, excellent value.

G pp Hospedaje El Boquerón, R Palma 330, T461968, maznaran@hotmail.com. 1 block from beach, modern, shared bathrooms, hot water, fully equipped kitchen, laundry, internet, French spoken.

G Hospedaje My Friend, Los Pinos 533, T461080, magowave@hotmail.com. Popular new place with surfers and foreigners, good for meeting others and for a meal in the restaurant (closed 1500-1900), with hot water, TV room, information. Tours arranged.

G Hostal Ilablo, La Orquídeas 339, T9579753. Hot water, roof terrace, popular with backpackers.

G Hostal Solange, Los Ficus 484, 1 block from the beach, T461410, hsolange@yahoo.es. Hot showers, good food, laundry facilities, limited use of kitchen, popular meeting point. Highly recommended.

G pp Huanchaco's Garden, Av Circunvalación Mz 'U', lote 3, T461194, www.huanchacogarden.com. Family-run, bungalows, cable TV, also camping, hot water, use of kitchen, free luggage store, helpful, garden with two pools (one for children), internet US$0.65, parking, laundry. Frequently recommended.

G pp Sra Mabel Díaz de Aguilar, Túpac Amaru 248, T461232, mabel_minerva@ hotmail.com. Near football ground, shared bath, hot water, English spoken.

🍴 Eating

Trujillo *p1127, map p1130*
A speciality is *shambar*, a thick minestrone made with gammon, served on Mon. There are five cheap seafood restaurants at Plazuela El Recreo, at the end of Pizarro. For really cheap meals try the central market at Grau y Ayacucho.

ᵀᵀ Demarco, Pizarro 725. Good food, excellent desserts, one of a cluster of eateries in the centre.

ᵀᵀ El Mochica, Bolívar 462. Good typical food and occasional live music.

ᵀᵀ Pizzería Pizzanino, Av Juan Pablo II 183, Urb San Andrés, opposite University. Recommended for pizzas, pastas, meats, desserts, evening only.

ᵀᵀ Romano, Pizarro 747. International food, good *menú*, poor salads, breakfasts, coffee, excellent milkshakes, cakes, slow service.

ᵀᵀ Romano-Rincón Criollo, Estados Unidos 162, Urb El Recreo, 10-min walk from centre, T244207. Northern Peruvian cuisine, *menú* for US$2, smart.

ᵀ Asturias, Pizarro 741. Nice café with excellent meals, good juices and snacks.

ᵀ Café Oviedo, Pizarro 737. With vegetarian options, good salads and cakes, helpful.

ᵀ Café Santo Domingo, Larco 268. Popular with locals in the morning.

ᵀ El Sol, Pizarro 660. The original and best vegetarian, but not exclusively, cheap set meals, also serves other dishes.

ᵀ Juguería San Agustín, Bolívar 526. Good juices, good *menú*, popular, excellent value.

ᵀ La Casona, San Martín 677. Their set lunch menu is popular with locals.

ᵀ Milenium, Gamarra 316. Vegetarian, good.

ᵀ Parnasillo, Gamarra 353, T/F234715, Mon-Sat 1300-1530. Restaurant and hotel school, good *menú* US$1.70-2.25, small portions.

ᵀ Rincón de Vallejo, Orbegoso 303. Good *menú*, typical dishes, very crowded at peak times.

ᵀ Sal y Pimienta, Colón 201. Very popular for lunch, US$1 and US$1.85, close to buses for Huanchaco and Chan Chán.

Cafés

Café Amaretto, Gamarra 368. Smart, good selection of real coffees, "brilliant" cakes, sweets, snacks and drinks.

Dulcería Doña Carmen, San Martín 814. Serves local specialities such as *alfajores*, *budin*, *king kong*, etc.

El Chileno, Ayacucho 408. Café and ice cream parlour, popular.

Fitopán, Bolívar 406. Good selection of breads, also serves lunches.

Panadería José Antonio, Ayacucho 561-65, in the Mercado Central. Good selection of breads.

Huanchaco *p1131*
There are about 30 restaurants on the beachfront. Many close in the low season.

ᵀᵀᵀ Big Ben, Víctor Larco 836, near A Sánchez, T461869. Seafood and international, very good. Open 1130-1730.

ᵀᵀᵀ Club Colonial, La Rivera 171, on the beachfront, T461015. A smart restaurant and bar, open in the evenings, Belgian owner.

ᵀᵀᵀEl Mochica, Av Larco 552, T293441. Same owners and quality as this restaurant in Trujillo, very nice dining area and panorama.

ᵀᵀᵀ El Mococho, Bolognesi 535. One of the best seafood restaurants, expensive, caters for groups.

ᵀᵀ El Caribe, just around the corner from Pisagua at Atahualpa 291. Another good seafood and fish place.

ᵀᵀ Estrella Marina, Av Víctor Larco, next door to Lucho del Mar. Great value for fish.

ᵀᵀ La Barca, Raimondi 111, T461855. Very good seafood, well-run, popular, but loud music or TV usually playing.

ᵀᵀ Los Herrajes, Av Larco 712. Excellent seafood and nice sea-view terrace. In low season only open at weekends and on holidays.

Lucho del Mar, Av Víctor Larco. On seafront road, serves excellent sea food.

Sabes?, V Larco 920, T461555, ysabes@yahoo.com. Pub with food, internet café, popular, owned by an American tour guide.

Otra Cosa, Av Larco 921, T461346, www.otracosa. info. A vegetarian restaurant overlooking the sea (fairtrade and organic produce), with Dutch owners, also has a volunteering agency, internet, massage, Spanish lessons, book exchange, movies, tourist information and surfing services. Open Wed-Sun 0900-2000. Recommended.

Casa Tere, Víctor Larco 280, Plaza de Armas. For best pizzas in town, also pastas, burgers and breakfasts.

Chelita, Deán Saavedra 270. Good value menú, fish dishes are best, very popular.

La Charapita, Huáscar 162. Modest but very popular restaurant serving large portions.

Piccolo, Los Abetos 142, 5 blocks from the plaza. Cheap, friendly, live folk music weekends, excellent, surf and art shop.

❶ Bars and clubs

Trujillo *p1127, map p1130*
Bar/Café Juguete, Junín y Independencia. An old style café serving good coffee. Open to midnight.

Bar/Café Stradivarius, Colón 327. An attractive café with sofas, open in the evenings only.

Canana, San Martín 788. Bars and restaurant, disco, live music at weekends (US$1.50-3), video screens (also has travel agency). Recommended, but take care on leaving.

El Estubo, San Martin 380. A new club playing a wide genre of sounds and attracting a mixed crowd.

Taverna Chelsea, Estete 675, T257032. Bar, restaurant, live Salsa at weekends (US$4 entry), exclusive and lively. Highly recommended.

❸ Festivals and events

Trujillo *p1127, map p1130*
The 2 most important festivals are the **National Marinera Contest** (end of **Jan**) and the **Festival Internacional de La Primavera** (last week of **Sep**), with cultural events, parades, beauty pageants and Trujillo's famous **Caballos de Paso**.

Huanchaco *p1131*
In the 1st week of **May** is the **Festival del Mar**, a celebration of the disembarkation of Taycanamo, the leader of the Chimú period. A procession is made in Totora boats. **30 Jun**, **San Pedro**, patron saint of fishermen: his statue is taken out to sea on a huge totora-reed boat. Also the

annual **Olímpiadas Playeral** and **El Festival Internacional de la Primavera** (see Trujillo above). There are also surf competitions. Carnival and New Year are also popular celebrations.

⊙ Shopping

Trujillo *p1127, map p1130*
Bookshops Librería Adriatica, Jr Junín 565, T291569, libreria@adriaticaperu.com. A very good bookshop, stocks Footprint. **Librería Peruana**, Pizarro 505, just off the Plaza. Best selection in town, ask for Sra Inés Guerra de Guijón.

Handicrafts APIAT, craft market, Av España near Zela. The largest craft market in the city, good for ceramics, totora boats, woodwork and leather, competitive prices.

Markets Mercado Central, on Gamarra, Ayacucho and Pasaje San Agustín. **Mercado Mayorista**, between Sinchi Roca and Av Los Incas (not a safe zone). **Merpisa**, Pizarro y Junín and Av Larco y Los Angeles. The best supermarket.

Huanchaco *p1131*
Artesanía del Norte, Los Olivos 504, www.artesaniadelnorte.com. Sells items mostly to the owner, Mary Cortijo's, design using traditional techniques.

▲ Activities and tours

Trujillo *p1127, map p1130*
Tour operators
Prices vary and competition is fierce so shop around for the best deal. Few agencies run tours on Sun and often only at fixed times on other days. To Chan Chán, **El Dragón** and **Huanchaco**, 3 hrs for US$8.50 pp. To **Huacas del Sol** and **de la Luna**, 2 hrs for US$7 pp. To **El Brujo**, US$17 pp. **City tours** cost US$5.65 pp (min of 2 people; discounts for 4 or more). Prices do not include entrance fees.
Chacón Tours, Av España 106-112, T255212. Sat afternoon and Sun morning. Recommended.
Guía Tours, Independencia 580, T234856, guitour@amauta.rcp.net.pe. Also Western Union agent. Recommended.
Tesores del Perú, Pizarro 575, of 03, T044-582381, oscarcampos10@hotmail.com. Oscar Campos Santa María organizes custom-made tours to archaeological sites, as far as Lambayeque.
Trujillo Tours, San Martín y Almagro 301, T257518, ttours@pol.com.pe. Works with *Lima Tours*.

Guides
Many hotels work on a commission basis with taxi drivers and travel agencies. If you decide on a guide, make your own direct approach and always agree what is included in the price. The Tourist Police (see Directory) has a list of guides; average

cost US$7 per hr. Beware of cowboy outfits herding up tourists around the plazas and bus terminals for rapid, poorly-translated tours. Also beware scammers offering surfing or salsa lessons and party invitations. **Clara Bravo**, Cahuide 495, T243347, www.xanga.com/TrujilloPeru. An experienced tourist guide who speaks Spanish, English, German and understands Italian. She takes tourists on extended circuits of the region (archaeological tour US$16 for 6 hrs, city tour US$7 pp, US$53 per car to El Brujo, with extension to Sipán, Brüning Museum and Túcume possible - tours in Lambayeque involve public transport, not inlcuded in cost). Clara works with English chartered accountant **Michael White** (same address, microbewhite@ yahoo.com, also speaks German, French and Italian), who provides transport. He is very knowledgeable about tourist sites. They run tours any day of the week; 24-hr attention, accommodate small groups. **Laura Durán**, T281590, lauraduran@ yahoo.com. Speaks English, German and some Hebrew, lots of information, very accommodating. **Zaby Miranda Acosta**, Camelias 315, Huanchaco, T01-996 66421, zabymiranda@hotmail.com. Speaks German, Italian, US$10 per day. **Oscar and Gustavo Prada Marga**, Miguel Grau 169, Villa del Mar, or at Chan Chán. Both are experienced guides. **Jannet Rojas Sánchez**, Alto Mochica Mz Q 19, Trujillo, T934 4844, jannarojas@hotmail.com. Speaks English, enthusiastic, works independently and for *Guía Tours*. **Celio Eduardo Roldán**, celioroldan@hotmail.com. Helpful and informative taxi driver. **José Soto Ríos**, Atahualpa 514, dpto 3, T251489. He speaks English and French.

Huanchaco *p1131*
Surfing
Un Lugar, Bolognesi 457, T957 7170, unlugarsurfingschool@hotmail.com. Ask for English-speaking Juan Carlos.
Picolo, Los Abetos 142. For rental and instruction, wet suits and boards, owner is a local champion.
The Wave, Av Larco 525. With small Mexican restaurant, staff speak English.
Yenth Ccora, Av Larco 468, T940 3871, ycc_mar@hotmail.com. Surfing equipment manufacture, repair, rental and surfing school.

⊙ **Transport**

Trujillo *p1127, map p1130*
Air To **Lima**, 1 hr, daily flights with **Lan Star Perú** (also to **Chiclayo**) and **WayraPerú** (also to **Talara** and **Tumbes**). Taxi to airport, US$4; or take bus or colectivo to Huanchaco and get out

at airport turn-off (US$0.25) and walk 2 km.
Bus Micros (small buses with 25 or more seats) and combis (up to 15 passengers), on all routes, cost US$0.15-0.30; *colectivos* (cars carrying 6 passengers), US$0.25, tend to run on main avenues starting from Av España. None is allowed inside an area bounded by Av Los Incas in the east to Ovalo Mansiche in the west and the north and south perimeters of Av España.

To and from **Lima**, 561 km, 8 hrs in the better class buses, average fare US$14.30- 18.50, 10 hrs in the cheaper buses, US$7.15-11.50. There are many bus companies doing this route, among those recommended are: **Ormeño**, Av Ejército 233, T259782, 3 levels of service, 5 daily (also runs north as far as Tumbes); **Cruz del Sur**, Amazonas 437 near Av Ejército, T261801; **Turismo Díaz**, Nicolás de Piérola 1079 on Panamericana Norte, T201237, leaves at 2230; **Línea** (recommended), Av América Sur 2857, T297000, ticket office at Orbegoso 300, T255181, 3 levels of service, also to **Chimbote** hourly, **Huaraz** 2100, 9 hrs, US$8.65, **Cajamarca** 5 a day, US$4.25-10, **Chiclayo**, hourly, US$3.35 (from Carrión by Av Mansiche, T235847, on the hour), and **Piura**, 2300, US$7. Also **Flores** (Av Ejército 350, T208250), **Ittsa** (Av Mansiche 145, T251415; No 431 for northern destinations – good service, T222541), **Móvil**, Av América Sur 3959, T286538. **Oltursa**, Av Ejército 342, T263055, *bus cama* service to Lima, 2200.

Small **Pakatnamú** buses leave when full, 0400-2100, from Av N de Piérola 1092, T206564, to **Pacasmayo**, 102 km, 1¼ hrs, US$2. To **Chiclayo**, 3 hrs from Trujillo, US$3.35, several companies. Among the best are **Emtrafesa**, Av Túpac Amaru 285, T471521, on the half-hour every hour; to **Piura**, 6 hrs, US$7; and **Tumbes**, US$8.50, 8 hrs. Other companies include: **Transportes El Dorado**, Av América Norte opposite Díaz, T291778, leave at 1245, 2220 to **Piura** and **Sullana**, US$4.30/5.75.

Direct buses to **Huaraz**, 319 km, via Chimbote and Casma (169 km), with **Línea** and **Móvil**, 8 hrs, US$8.60 special. Also **Chinchaysuyo**, Av Mansiche 391, at 2030, 10 hrs. There are several buses and colectivos to **Chimbote**, with **América Express** from Lloque 162, 135 km, 2 hrs, US$2.20, departures every 30 mins from 0530 (ticket sales from 0500); then change at Chimbote (see above – leave Trujillo before 0600 to make a connection from 0800). Ask Clara Bravo and Michael White (see Guides, above) about transport to Caraz avoiding Chimbote (a very worthwhile trip via the Brasileños road and Cañon del Pato).

To **Cajamarca**, 300 km, 7-8 hrs, US$4.55-10: with **Línea**, **Emtrafesa**, see above, at 2200, and **Tur Díaz** 4 a day. To **Huamachuco**, 170 km, 6 hrs, US$4.55-5.50, **Trans Gran Turismo**, Prol Vallejo

1368, T425391, 4 a day; **Trans Horna**, Av N de Piérola 1279, T294880, 4 a day; **Turismo Negreiros**, Prol Vallejo block 13, 0900, 1300, recommended. To **Chachapoyas**, *Móvil*'s Lima-Chiclayo- Chachapoyas service passes through Trujillo at 1600 and Chiclayo at 2000 (US$11.50).

To **Tarapoto**, via Moyobamba, **Turismo Tarapoto**, Av N de Piérola 1239, T470318, at 2230, US$14.30, and **Ejetur** Av N de Piérola 1238, T222228, at 1100, 1315, US$15, also to Yurimaguas at 0900, US$20, and to Jaén at 1600, US$7.50.
Taxi Town trip, US$0.55 within Av España and US$0.70 within Av América. To airport US$4. Beware of overcharging, check fares with locals. Taxi from in front of Hotel Libertador, US$7 per hr, about the same rate as a tour with an independent guide or travel agent for 1-2 people.

Huaca del Sol and Huaca de la Luna *p1128*
Combis (blue and yellow) every 15 mins from Ovalo Grau; less safe stops at Huayna Cápac blocks 5 and 6, southeast of Av Los Incas, and Suárez y Los Incas. On the return go to Ovalo Grau for onward connections, or you can get out at Huayna Cápac y Los Incas. US$0.30. Taxis about US$2; plenty at site for return, or US$9.50 return with 1 hr wait.

Chan Chán *p1129*
Take any transport between Trujillo and Huanchaco (see below) and ask to get out at the turn-off to Chan Chán, US$0.25. A taxi is US$3 from Trujillo to the ruins, US$0.85 from museum to ruins, US$1.85 to Huanchaco. **Note**: It is not safe to walk on the dirt track from turn-off to site, unless in a group, 20 mins. There have been reports of robbery even within the site itself. On no account walk the 4 km to, or on, Buenos Aires beach near Chan Chán as there is serious danger of robbery and of being attacked by dogs.

El Brujo *p1129*
The complex can be reached by taking one of the regular buses from Trujillo to Chocope, US$0.55, and then a colectivo (every 30 minutes) to Magdalena de Cao, US$0.45, then a taxi to the site, including wait, US$4.50, or a 5 km walk to the site.

Huanchaco *p1131*
Two combi routes run between Trujillo and Huanchaco, A and B. Three micros run between Trujillo and Huanchaco: B (also known as Mercado Mayorista), H (UPAO) and H-Corazón (with red heart, Mercado Hermelinda). Combis run 0500-2030, micros 0630-2030, every 5-10 mins. Fare is US$0.35 for the 20-min journey. The easiest place to pick up any of these combis or micros is Ovalo Mansiche, 3 blocks northwest of Av España

in front of the Cassinelli museum. In Trujillo, combi A takes a route on the south side of Av España, before heading up Av Los Incas. Combi B takes the northerly side of Av España. From Huanchaco to the **Línea**, **Móvil Tours** and southern bus terminals, take micro H. It also goes to Ovalo Grau where you can catch buses to the Huacas del Sol and de la Luna. For **Cruz del Sur**, **Ormeño**, **Flores**, **Oltursa**, etc, take combi or micro B from Huanchaco. Colectivos and taxis minimum US$3, more likely US$4-5.

Puerto Malabrigo/Puerto Chicama *p1131*
Combis and colectivos from the Santa Cruz terminal at Av Santa Cruz y Av América Sur.

ⓘ Directory

Trujillo *p1127, map p1130*
Airline offices Lan, Pizarro 340-42, T221469. Star Perú, Almagro 539, of 102, T293392, 0900-1930. WayraPerú, Jr Alfonso Ugarte 310, T200434. **Banks** BCP, Gamarra 562. No commission on cash into soles, but US$12 fee on TCs or changing into dollars, cash advance on Visa card, ATM (Visa). Interbank, Pizarro y Gamarra. Good rates for cash, no commission on Amex TCs into soles, reasonable rate, Visa cash advance, quick service, also has Visa, Mastercard and Maestro ATMs (doesn't close for lunch). Scotiabank, Pizarro 314, *Casa de Mayorazgo de Facalá*. Changes Amex TCs, with commission into soles or dollars, ATM for Visa/Plus. BBV Continental, Pizarro 620. Amex TCs and Visa card accepted, US$10 commission up to US$500. Note that banks close 1300-1615. There is little difference between the rates for cash dollars given by banks and street changers, *casas de cambio* and travel agencies. There are many *casas de cambio* and street changers on the plazoleta opposite the Casa de Condes de Aranda and all along the 600 block of Bolívar. **Western Union**, Almagro 581, España y Huayna Cápac, see also *Guía Tours*, above. **Cultural centres** Alianza Francesa, San Martín 858-62, T231232, www.ucv.edu.pe/alianzafrancesa-trujillo. Instituto de Cultura Peruano Norteamericano, Av Venezuela 125, Urb El Recreo, T232512, www.elcultural.com.pe. **Consulates** UK, Honorary Consul, Mr Winston Barber, Jesús de Nazareth 312, T235548, winstonbarber@ terra.com.pe. Mon-Fri 0900-1700. **Internet** There are internet offices all over the centre, mostly on Pizarro blocks 1 and 6, and Av España blocks 1 and 8. **Medical services** Hospital: Hospital Belén, Bolívar 350, T245281. Clínica Peruano Americana, Av Mansiche 702, T231261, English spoken, good. **Pharmacies** Several pharmacy chains in the

centre (on Pizarro and Gamarra) and others on either side of Belén hospital on Bolognesi. **Post offices** Independencia 286 y Bolognesi. 0800-2000, stamps only on special request. DHL, Almagro 579. **Telephones** Telefónica, headquarters at Bolívar 658. Private call centres at Pizarro 561, Ayacucho 625, Gamarra 450, on 5th block of Orbegoso and Av España 1530. **Useful**

addresses Immigration: Av Larco 1220, Urb Los Pinos. Open Mon-Fri 0815-1230, 1500-1630. Gives 30-day visa extensions, US$20 (proof of funds and onward ticket required), plus US$1 for *formulario* in Banco de la Nación (fixers on the street will charge more).

Chiclayo and around

Lambayeque department, sandwiched between the Pacific and the Andes, is a major agricultural zone, especially for rice and sugar cane. The boasts a distinctive cuisine and musical tradition, and an unparalleled ethnographic and archaeological heritage. Chiclayo's witchcraft market is famous and excavations at nearby adobe pyramid cities are uncovering fabulous treasures.

Chiclayo → *Phone code: 074. Colour map 3, grid B1. Population: 411,536.*
Since it was founded in 1560 by Spanish priests, Chiclayo has grown to become a major commercial hub. The city has an atmosphere all of its own and a distinctive musical tradition featuring Afro-indian rhythms, but is best known for the spectacular cache of archaeological treasures that lie at its doorstep. **Tourist offices**: Centro de Información Turística (CIT) ① *Sáenz Peña 838, T238112*. For complaints and tourist protection, Indecopi ① *Av Balta 506, T209021, ctejada@indecopi.gob.pe, Mon- Fri 0800-1300, 1630-1930*. The **tourist police** ① *Av Sáenz Peña 830, T236700, ext 311, 24 hours a day*, are very helpful and may store luggage and take you to the sites themselves. There are tourist kiosks on the Plaza and on Balta.

In the city itself, on the Plaza de Armas, is the 19th-century neoclassical **Cathedral**, designed by the English architect Andrew Townsend. The **Palacio Municipal** is at the junction of Avenida Balta, the main street and the Plaza. The private **Club de la Unión** is on the Plaza at the corner of Calle San José. Continue five blocks north on Balta to the **Mercado Modelo**, one of northern Peru's liveliest and largest daily markets. Don't miss the handicrafts stalls (see *Monsefú*) and the well-organized section (off C Arica on the south side) of ritual paraphernalia used by traditional curers and diviners (*curanderos*): herbal medicines, folk charms, curing potions, and exotic objects including dried llama foetuses to cure all manner of real and imagined illnesses. At *Paseo de Artesanías*, 18 de Abril near Balta, stalls sell handicrafts in a quiet, custom-built open-air arcade.

Monsefú and the coast
The traditional town of **Monsefú**, southwest, is known for its music and handicrafts; good market, four blocks from the plaza. Handicraft stalls open when potential customers arrive (see also Festivals above). Beyond Monsefú are three ports serving the Chiclayo area. **Pimentel**, 8 km from Chiclayo, is a beach resort which gets very crowded on Sunday. You can walk along the decaying pier for US$0.25. There are several seafood restaurants. The surfing between Pimentel and the Bayovar Peninsula is excellent, reached from Chiclayo (14½ km) by road branching off from the Pan-American Highway. Sea-going reed boats (*caballitos de totora*) are used by fishermen and may be seen returning in the late afternoon. Nearby **Santa Rosa** has little to recommend it and it is not safe to walk there from Pimentel. The most southerly is **Puerto Eten**, a quaint port with some nice wooden buildings on the plaza, 24 km by road from Chiclayo. Its old railway station has been declared a national heritage. In the adjacent roadstead, Villa de Eten, panama hats are the local industry, but it is not as picturesque.

The ruined Spanish town of **Zaña**, 51 km south of Chiclayo, was destroyed by floods in 1726, and sacked by English pirates on more than one occasion. There are ruins of five colonial churches and the convents of San Agustín, La Merced and San Francisco.

Lambayeque
About 12 km northwest from Chiclayo is Lambayeque, its narrow streets lined by colonial and republican houses, many retaining their distinctive wooden balconies and wrought iron grill-work over the windows. For example, on 8 de Octubre are **Casona Iturregui Aguilarte**, No

410, and, at No 328, **Casona Cúneo** with the only decorated façade in the town; opposite is **Casona Descalzi**, perhaps the best preserved. On Calle 2 de Mayo see especially **Casa de la Logia o Montjoy**, whose 64 m long balcony is said to be the longest in the colonial Americas. Also of interest is the 16th-century **Complejo Religioso Monumental de San Pedro** and the baroque church of the same name which stands on the **Plaza de Armas 27 de Diciembre**. There are hotels in town, should you prefer not to stay in Chiclayo, and good value restaurants, including opposite Museo Brüning.

The reason most people visit is to see the town's two museums. The older of the two is the **Brüning Archaeological Museum** ① *0900-1700, US$3.50, a guided tour costs an extra US$2.85*, in a modern building, specializing in Mochica, Lambayeque/Sicán and Chimú cultures. Three blocks east is the more recent **Museo de las Tumbas Reales de Sipán** ① *Tue-Sat 0900-1700, US$9, http://sipan.peru cultural.org.pe*, shaped like a pyramid. The magnificent treasure from the tomb of 'The Old Lord of Sipán' (see below), and a replica of the Lord of Sipán's tomb are displayed here. A ramp from the main entrance takes visitors to the third floor, from where you descend, mirroring the sequence of the archaeologists' discoveries.

Mórrope, on the Pan-American Highway 20 km north of Lambayeqye still produces pottery using prehispanic techniques. The beautifully restored 16th-century **Capilla de la Ramada Las Animas** is on the plaza.

Sipán
① *Daily 0800-1600 and the museum is open 0800-1700, entrance for tombs and museum is US$2; guide at site US$2.85 (may not speak English). To visit the site takes about 3-4 hrs.*

At this imposing complex a short distance east of Chiclayo (turn-off well-signed in the centre of Pomalca), excavations since 1987 in one of three crumbling pyramids have brought to light a cache of funerary objects considered to rank among the finest examples of pre-Columbian art. Peruvian archaeologist Walter Alva, leader of the dig, continues to probe the immense mound that has revealed no less than 12 royal tombs filled with 1,800-year-old offerings worked in precious metals, stone, pottery and textiles of the Moche culture (circa AD 1-750). In the most extravagant Moche tomb discovered, El Señor de Sipán, a priest was found clad in gold (ear ornaments, breast plate, etc), with turquoise and other valuables. A site museum features photos and maps of excavations, technical displays and replicas of some finds.

In another tomb were found the remnants of what is thought to have been a priest, sacrificed llama and a dog, together with copper decorations. In 1989 another richly appointed, unlooted tomb contained even older metal and ceramic artefacts associated with what was probably a high-ranking shaman or spiritual leader, called 'The Old Lord of Sipán'. Three tombs are on display, containing replicas of the original finds. You can wander around the previously excavated areas to get an idea of the construction of the burial mound and adjacent pyramids. For a good view, climb the large pyramid across from the Sipán excavation.

East from Pomalca is Chongoyape, just before which is the turning to the **Chaparrí** private ecological reserve, 34,000 ha, set up and run by the Comunidad Muchik Santa Catalina de Chongoyape, 75 km from Chiclayo. Visitors can go for the day or stay at the Chaparrí EcoLodge ① *US$3 for a day visit. US$10 entry if intending to stay overnight, www.chaparri.org*. All staff and guides are locals; for every 10 people you have to have a local guide (this provides work and helps to prevent rubbish). There are no dogs or goats in the area so the forest is recuperating; it contains many bird and mammal species of the dry forest, including White-winged Guan and Spectacled Bear. The Tinajones reservoir is good for birdwatching.

Túcume
① *Daily 0800-1600 (the site stays open till 1700), US$2; guides charge US$2.85.*

About 35 km north of Chiclayo, beside the old Panamericana to Piura, lie the ruins of this vast city built over 1,000 years ago. A short climb to the two *miradores* on **Cerro La Raya** (or **El Purgatorio**) offers the visitor an unparalleled panoramic vista of 26 major pyramids, platform mounds, walled citadels and residential compounds flanking a ceremonial centre and ancient cemeteries. One of the pyramids, Huaca Larga, where excavations were undertaken from 1987-1992, is the longest adobe structure in the world, measuring 700 m long, 280 m wide and over 30 m high. There is no evidence of occupation of Túcume previous to the Sicán, or Lambayeque people who developed the site AD 1000-1375 until the Chimú conquered the region, establishing a short reign until the arrival of the Incas around 1470. The Incas built on top of the existing structure of **Huaca Larga** using stone from Cerro La Raya. Among the other pyramids which make up this huge complex are: **Huaca El Mirador** (90 m by 65 m, 30 m high), **Huaca Las Estacas**, **Huaca Pintada** and **Huaca de las Balsas** which is thought to have housed people of elevated status such as priests. (Do not climb the fragile adobe structures.)

Excavations at the site, which were once led by the late Norwegian explorer-archaeologist Thor Heyerdahl of *Kon-Tiki* fame, challenged many conventional views of ancient Peruvian culture. Some suspect that it will prove to be a civilization centre greater than Chan Chán. **A site museum** (same entrance as site), contains architectural reconstructions, photographs and drawings. No excavations are visible at the site, where there is little shade. There is a good, new hostel, **F**, built of traditional materials, next to the huacas.

The town of Túcume is a 10-15 minute walk from the site. On the plaza is the interesting **San Pedro Church**. The surrounding countryside is pleasant for walks and swimming in the river. *Fiesta de la Purísima Concepción*, the festival of the town's patron saint, is eight days prior to Carnival in February, and also in September.

Chiclayo

To Combis to Túcume (2 blocks)
To Combis to Batán Grande (1 block)

Peru Chiclayo & around

Sleeping
Adriático 1 *B3*
América 2 *B2*
Costa del Sol 3 *C3*
El Sol 4 *B1*
Europa 5 *B2*
Garza 6 *C3*
Gran Hotel Chiclayo 7 *B1*
Hospedaje San
  Eduardo 16 *C3*
Hostal San José 8 *A2*

Hostal Santa Victoria 9 *C3*
Hostal Sicán 10 *C2*
Inca 11 *B2*
Kalu 12 *A3*
Mochicas 13 *C2*
Paracas 14 *A3*
Paraíso 15 *A3*
Pirámide Real 19 *C3*
Santa Rosa 17 *B2*
Sol Radiante 18 *C2*

Eating
Boulevar 1 *B2*
Café Astoria 2 *C2*
D'Onofrio 3 *C3*

El Huaralino 4 *C1*
Fiesta 6 *B1*
Govinda 7 *B3*
Hebrón 8 *C3*
Kaprichos 9 *A3*
La Panadería 10 *B2*
La Parra 11 *C3*
La Plazuela 12 *B1*
Las Américas 13 *B3*
Mi Tía 14 *B2*
Roma 15 *C3*
Romana 16 *C3*
Tradiciones 17 *C3*

Transport
Brüning Express to
  Lambayeque 1 *B1*
Civa 2 *C3*
Colectivos to Lambayeque 3 *A2*
Colectivos to Monsefú 4 *A3*
Colectivos to Puerto Etén 5 *A3*
Combis to Pimental 6 *A2, B1*
Cruz del Sur 7 *C3*
Emtrafesa 8 *C3*
Flores/Cial 9 *C3*
Línea 10 *C2*
Oltursa 11 *B1*
Tepsa 12 *C2*
Transportes Chiclayo 13 *B1*

Ferreñafe and Sicán

The colonial town of **Ferreñafe**, 20 km northeast of Chiclayo, is worth a visit, especially for the **Museo Nacional Sicán** ① *T286469, Tue-Sun 0900-1700, US$2.40, students US$1, http://sican.perucultural.org.pe*. This excellent new museum on the outskirts of town houses objects of the Sicán (Lambayeque) culture from near Batán Grande. **Tourist office**: helpful **Mincetur** office on the Plaza de Armas ① *T282843, citesipan@mincetur.gob.pe*.

The entrance to **El Santuario Histórico Bosque de Pómac** ① *free, visitors' centre, T9807 2291, dalemandelama@gmail.com, 0900-1700, a guide (Spanish only) can be hired with transport, US$3, horses for hire US$6*, which includes the ruins of **Sicán**, lies 20 km beyond Ferreñafe along the road to Batán Grande (there is another entrance from the Panamericana near Túcume). Visiting the sanctuary is not easy because of the arid conditions and distances involved: it is 10 km to the nearest huaca (pyramid). At the visitors' centre food and drinks are available and camping is permitted. The guide covers a two-hour tour of the area which includes at least two huacas, some of the most ancient carob trees and a mirador (viewpoint), which affords a beautiful view across the emerald green tops of the forest with the enormous pyramids dramatically breaking through. Sicán has revealed several sumptuous tombs dating to AD 900-1100. The ruins comprise some 12 large adobe pyramids, arranged around a huge plaza, measuring 500 by 250 m, with 40 archaeological sites in total. The city, of the Sicán (or Lambayeque culture) was probably moved to Túcume (see above), 6 km west, following 30 years of severe drought and then a devastating El Niño related flood in AD 1050-1100. These events appear to have provoked a rebellion in which many of the remaining temples on top of the pyramids were burnt and destroyed. The forest itself has good birdwatching possibilities.

Two hours beyond Pómac is **Laquipampa Wildlife Refuge** ① *contact zr_laquipampa@inrena.gob.pe, www.inrena.gob.pe*, 8,329 ha, in a green and fertile high Andean valley. The dry forest here, from 500-2,500 m, is the habitat of many birds endemic to the Tumbesian zone, also the spectacled bear and rare flora. Take a passing bus for Incahuasi.

North of Chiclayo

On the old Pan-American Highway 885 km from Lima, **Olmos** is a tranquil place (several hotels and *Festival de Limón* last week in June). A paved road runs east from Olmos over the Porculla Pass, branching north to Jaén and east to Bagua Grande (see page 1166). The old Pan-American Highway continues from Olmos to Cruz de Caña and Piura. At Lambayeque the new Pan-American Highway, which is in good condition, branches off the old road and drives 190 km straight across the Sechura Desert to Piura. There is also a coast road, narrow and scenic, between Lambayeque and Sechura via Bayovar.

Olmos is the best base for observing the critically endangered White-winged Guan, a bird thought extinct for 100 years until its rediscovery in 1977. On the outskirts is the White-winged Guan captive breeding centre, **Zoocriadero Bárbara d'Achille** ① *Km 103, Olmos*, which also has an aviary of rescued birds, and the **Asociación Cracidae Perú** (director Fernando Angulo Pratolongo) ① *Torres Paz 708, Chiclayo, T074-238748, cracidae@llampayec.rcp.net.pe*. Captive breeding started in 1979 and the first reintroduction into the wild was made in 2001 at Chaparrí (see p 1138). One place where the guans can be seen in the wild is Quebrada Limón (or Frejolillo), where guides from the local community check on the guans' whereabouts in order to take visitors to see them in the early morning. Ask at the breeding centre for how to get there.

The Sechura Desert is a large area of shifting sands separating the oases of Chiclayo and Piura. Water for irrigation comes from the Chira and Piura rivers, and from the Olmos and Tinajones irrigation projects which bring water from the Amazon watershed by means of tunnels (one over 16 km long) through the Andes to the Pacific coast. **Note** Solo cyclists should not cross the desert as muggings have occurred. Take the safer, inland route. In the desert, there is no water, no fuel and no accommodation. Do not attempt this alone.

⊙ **Sleeping**

Chiclayo *p1137, map p1139*

A Gran Hotel Chiclayo, Villareal 115, T234911, www.granhotelchiclayo.com.pe. With breakfast, a/c, pool, safe car park, changes dollars, jacuzzi,

entertainments, restaurant. Recommended.

A-B Garza, Bolognesi 756, T228172, www.garza hotel.com. A/c, excellent bar/restaurant, pool, car park, tourist office in lobby provides maps, information in English, car hire, close to bus stations so there is activity at all hours. Recommended.

B Costa del Sol, Balta 399, T227272, www.costadelsolperu.com. Smart, TV, non-smoking rooms, small pool, sauna, jacuzzi. *Páprika* restaurant, good value Sunday buffets US$7.50, vegetarian options.

C Inca, Av L González 622, T235931, www.incahotel.com. A/c, restaurant, garage, comfortable, helpful.

D América, Av L González 946, T229305, americahotel@latinmail.com. Comfortable, restaurant, good value but laundry and breakfast expensive. Recommended.

D Hostal Santa Victoria, La Florida 586, Urb Santa Victoria, T/F225074. Hot water, good, restaurant, free parking, exchange cash dollars, 15-20 mins' walk from the centre.

D-E El Sol, Elías Aguirre 119, T232120, hotelvicus@hotmail.com. Hot water, big rooms, restaurant, pool by car park, TV lounge, comfortable, good value.

E Europa, Elías Aguirre 466, T237919, hotele uropachiclayo@terra.com.pe. Hot water **G** without bath (single rooms small), restaurant, good value.

E Kalu, Pedro Ruíz 1038, near the Mercado Modelo, T/F228767, hotelkalu@hotmail.com. Comfortable, TV, laundry, safe, good.

E Mochicas, Torres Paz 429, T237217, mochcas1@hotmail.com. Fan, TV, helpful, good service.

E Paracas, Pedro Ruíz 1046, near Mercado Modelo, T221611. TV, good value. Recommended.

E Paraíso, Pedro Ruíz 1064, near the Mercado Modelo, T/F222070, hparaiso@terramail. com.pe. Also comfortable and well- appointed, but can be noisy. Recommended.

E Pirámide Real, MM Izaga 726, T224036. Compact but spotless, good value, very central.

E Santa Rosa, L González 927, T224411. Hot water, fan, laundry, international phone service, breakfast downstairs in snack bar, good value.

F Hospedaje San Eduardo, 7 de Enero 235, Urb San Eduardo, T209423. A 10-min walk from the centre; no sign other than a little notice in the window. Family run, large rooms, quiet, safe, cable TV, hot water.

F Hostal Sicán, MM Izaga 356, T237618. With breakfast, hot water, TV, comfortable, welcoming and trustworthy.

F Sol Radiante, Izaga 392, T237858, robertoiza@mixmail.com. Cold water, comfortable, TV, pleasant.

G There are plenty of hotels in this price bracket on Av Balta and around the Mercado Modelo. Most are basic and fairly grim.

Chaparrí *p 1138*

A-C EcoLodge Chaparrí, T074-960 4635 or 084-249718, www.chaparrilodge.com. A delightful oasis in the dry forest, 6 beautifully decorated cabins, built of stone and mud, nice and cool, solar power. Price is for all-inclusive package (except horse hire). Complimentary cup of wine on arrival, first-class food. Sechuran foxes in the gardens; hummingbirds bathe at the pool about 0600 every day. Recommended.

Olmos *p 1140*

D El Remanso, San Francisco 100, T427158, elremansolmos@yahoo.com. Like an hacienda with courtyards, small pool, whitewashed rooms, colourful bedding, flowers and bottled water in room, hot water (supposedly). Price is full board, good restaurant. Charming owner.

① Eating

Chiclayo *p1137, map p1139*

For delicious, cheap ceviche, go to the Nativo stall in the Mercado Central, a local favourite.

⑪⑪⑪ Fiesta, Av Salaverry 1820 in 3 de Octubre suburb, T201970. Local specialities, first class.

⑪⑪⑪ El Huaralino, La Libertad 155, Santa Victoria. Wide variety, international and creole.

⑪⑪ Hebrón, Balta 605. For more upmarket than average chicken, but also local food and *parrilla*, good salads. Also does an excellent breakfast and a good buffet at weekends.

⑪⑪ Kaprichos, Pedro Ruíz 1059, T232721. Chinese, delicious, huge portions.

⑪⑪ Las Américas, Aguirre 824. Open 0700-0200, good service. Recommended.

⑪⑪ Roma, Izaga 706. Wide choice, also has a bar.

⑪⑪ Romana, Balta 512,T223598. First-class food, usually good breakfast, popular with locals.

⑪⑪ Tradiciones, 7 de Enero Sur 105, T221192. Open 0900-1700 daily. Good variety of local dishes, including ceviche, and drinks, nice atmosphere and garden, good service.

⑪ Boulevar, Colón entre Izaga y Aguirre. Good, friendly, *menú* and à la carte.

⑪ Café Astoria, Bolognesi 627. Open 0800-1200, 1530-2100. Breakfast, good value *menú*.

⑪ Govinda, Balta 1029. Good vegetarian, open daily 0800-2000.

⑪ Mi Tía, Aguirre 650, just off the plaza. Large portions, very popular at lunchtime, but not good for breakfast.

⑪ La Parra, Izaga 746. Chinese and creole, *parrillada*, very good, large portions.

⑪ La Plazuela, San José 299, Plaza Elías Aguirre. Good food, seats outside.

Greycy, Elias Aguirre y Lapoint. Good ice cream.

D'Onofrio, Balta y Torres Paz. Great ice cream.

La Panadería, Lapoint 847. Good choice of breads, including *integral*, snacks and soft drinks.

⊛ Festivals and events

Chiclayo *p1137, map p1139*

6 Jan: Reyes Magos in Mórrope, Illimo and other towns, a recreation of a medieval pageant in which pre-Columbian deities become the Wise Men. On **4 Feb**: Túcume devil dances (see below). Holy Week, traditional Easter celebrations and processions in many villages. **2-7 Jun**: Divine Child of the Miracle, Villa de Eten. **27-31 Jul**: Fexticum in Monsefú, traditional foods, drink, handicrafts, music and dance. **5 Aug**: pilgrimage from the mountain shrine of **Chalpón** to Motupe, 90 km north of Chiclayo; the cross is brought down from a cave and carried in procession through the village. At **Christmas** and **New Year**, processions and children dancers (*pastorcitos* and *seranitas*) can be seen in many villages, eg **Ferreñafe**, **Mochumi**, **Mórrope**.

⚑ Activities and tours

Chiclayo *p1137, map p1139*

The Lambayeque's museums, Sipán and Túcume (see Around Chiclayo) can easily be visited by public transport. Expect to pay US$18-25 pp for a 3-hr tour to Sipán; US$25-35 pp for Túcume and Lambayeque (5 hrs); Sicán is US$45-55 pp for a full-day tour including Ferreñafe and Pómac; to Zaña and coastal towns, US$35-55 pp. These prices are based on 2 people; discount for larger groups.
Indiana Tours, Colón 556, T222991, www.indianatoursperu.com. Daily tours to nearby archaeological sites and museums and a variety of other daily and extended excursions with 4WD vehicles; English and Italian spoken, Handbook users welcome, reservations for national flights and hotels.
InkaNatura, in Gran Hotel Chiclayo (address above), T209948, www.inkanatura.net. Run historical and nature tours throughout northern Peru. Good service.
Peruvian Treasures Explorer, Balta 398, T233435. Archeological tours, helpful.

Horse riding

Rancho Santana, in Pacora, T074-971 2145 (mob), rancho_santana_peru@yahoo.com. Relaxing tours on horseback in Santuario Histórico Bosque de Pómac, Swiss run (Andrea Martin), good horses, free camping possile at the ranch, or lodging in **G** range.

⊙ Transport

Chiclayo *p1137, map p1139*

Air José Abelardo Quiñones González airport 1 km from town, T233192; taxi from centre US$1.

Daily flights to/from **Lima** and **Piura** with Lan (MM Izaga 770) and **Star Perú** (not Sun; Av Bolognesi 316, T271173).
Bus No terminal terrestre; most buses stop outside their offices on Bolognesi. To **Lima**, 770 km, US$12 and US$22 for *bus cama*: Civa, Av Bolognesi 714, T223434; **Cruz del Sur**, Bolognesi 888, T225508; **Ormeño**, Haya de la Torre 242, 2 blocks south of Bolognesi, T234206; **Línea**, Bolognesi 638, T222221, *especial* and *bus cama* service; **Móvil**, Av Bolognesi 195, T271940 (goes as far as Tarapoto); **Oltursa**, ticket office at Balta e Izaga, T237789, terminal at Vicente de la Vega 101, T225611; **Tepsa**, Bolognesi 504-36 y Colón, T236981; **Transportes Chiclayo**, Av L Ortiz 010, T237984, www.transportes chiclayo.com. Most companies leave from 1900 onwards. To **Trujillo**, 209 km, with **Emtrafesa**, Av Balta 110, T234291, almost hourly from 0530-2015, US$3.35, and *Línea*, as above. To **Piura**, US$3.65, **Línea** and **Transportes Chiclayo** leave hourly throughout the day; also **Emtrafesa** and buses from the **Cial/Flores** terminal, Bolognesi 751, T239579. To **Sullana**, US$4.35. To **Tumbes**, US$5.75, 9-10 hrs; with **Cial**, or **Transportes Chiclayo**; **Oltursa** overnight service at 2015, arrives 0530 (good for crossing to Ecuador the next day), seats can be reserved, unlike other companies which tend to arrive full from Lima late at night. Many buses go on to the **Ecuadorean border** at **Aguas Verdes**. Go to the *Salida* on Elías Aguirre, mototaxi drivers know where it is, be there by 1900. All buses stop here after leaving their terminals to try and fill empty seats, so discounts may be possible. To **Cajamarca**, 260 km, US$4.55-9, eg **Línea**, normal and *bus cama*; many others from Tepsa terminal, Bolognesi y Colón, eg **Días**, T224448. To **Chachapoyas**, US$9-12: **Civa** 1730 daily, 10-11 hrs; **Turismo Kuélap**, in Tepsa station, 1830 daily, **Móvil**, address above, at 2000. To **Jaén**, US$4.35-7.50: eg **Móvil**, **Civa**, and **Transcade**. To **Tarapoto**, 18 hrs, US$18.20, with **Móvil**, also **Turismo Tarapoto**, Bolognesi 751, T636231.
Taxi Mototaxis are a cheap way to get around; US$0.50 anywhere in city, but they are not allowed in the very centre.

Monsefú and the coast *p1137*

Combis to **Monsefú** cost US$0.45 from Amazonas y 7 de Enero, beyond the Mercado Modelo; colectivos from 7 de Enero y Arica. The **ports** may be visited on a half-day trip. Combis leave from Vicente de la Vega entre Angamos y Av L Ortiz, Chiclayo, to Pimentel; others leave from González y L Prado, 20 mins, US$0.25. Colectivos to Eten from 7 de Enero y Arica.

Lambayeque *p1137*
Colectivos from **Chiclayo** US$0.45, 25 mins, from Pedro Ruíz at the junction with Av Ugarte. Also **Brüning Express** combis from Vicente de la Vega entre Angamos y Av L Ortiz, every 15 mins, US$0.20.

Sipán *p1138*
Buses to Sipán leave from Terminal Este Sur-Nor Este on C Nicolás de Piérola, east of the city (take a taxi, US$1; area can dangerous), US$0.45, 1 hr.

Chaparrí *p1138*
Take a public bus from Leoncio Prado y Sáenz Peña, Chiclayo, to **Chongoyape** (1¼ hrs, US$1.10), then a mototaxi to **Chaparrí**, US$7.50.

Túcume *p1138*
Combis from **Chiclayo**, Angamos y Manuel Pardo, US$0.70, 45 mins; a combi from Túcume to the village of **Come** passes the ruins, hourly. Combi Túcume-**Lambayeque**, US$0.35, 25 mins.

Ferreñafe and Sicán *p1140*
Colectivos from Chiclayo to the centre of Ferreñafe leave every few mins from 8 de Octubre y Sáenz Peña, 15 mins, U$0.30, take a mototaxi to the museum, 5 mins, US$0.50. Alternatively, combis for Batán Grande depart from the Terminal Nor-Este, Av N de Piérola in Chiclayo, and pass the museum every 15-20 mins, 20 mins, US$0.50.

❶ Directory

Chiclayo *p1137, map p1139*
Banks Beware of counterfeit bills, especially among street changers on 6th block of Balta, on Plaza de Armas and 7th block of MM Izaga. **BCP**, Balta 630, no commission on TCs for US$100 or more (US$12 commission if less), cash on Visa, Visa ATM. **Scotiabank**, Balta 625, changes Amex TCs, cash advance on Visa card, ATM for Visa/Plus. **Interbank**, on Plaza de Armas, no commission on TCs, OK rate, good rates for cash, Mastercard ATM. All open Sat morning. **Cultural centres** Alianza Francesa, Cuglievan 644, T237571, www.universidadperu.com/ alianza-francesa-de-chiclayo.php. Instituto de Cultura Peruano-Norteamericana, Av Izaga 807, T231241, icpnachi@mail.udep.edu.pe. Instituto Nacional de la Cultura, Av L González 375, T237261, occasional poetry readings, information on local archaeological sites, lectures, etc. **Internet** Lots of places, particularly on San José and Elías Aguirre, average price US$0.60 per hr. **Medical services** Ambulance: Max Salud, 7 de Enero 185, T234032, maxsalud@ telematic.edu.com. **Post offices** On 1 block of Aguirre, 6 blocks from Plaza. **Telephones** Telefónica, headquarters at Aguirre 919; bank of phone booths on 7th block of 7 de Enero behind Cathedral for international and collect calls. Phone card sellers hang around here.

Piura and around → *Phone code: 073. Colour map 3, grid A1. Population: 324,500.*

A proud and historic city, Piura was founded in 1532, three years before Lima, by the conquistadores left behind by Pizarro. The city has two well-kept parks, Cortés and Pizarro (with a statue of the *conquistador*, also called Plaza de las Tres Culturas), and public gardens. Old buildings are kept in repair and new buildings blend with the Spanish style of the old city. Three bridges cross the Río Piura to Castilla, the oldest from Calle Huancavelica, for pedestrians (Puente San Miguel), another from Calle Sánchez Cerro, and the newest from Avenida Panamericana Norte, at west end of town. The winter climate, May-September, is very pleasant although nights can be cold and the wind piercing; December to March is very hot.

Tourist offices Information at the tourist office ⓘ *Ayacucho 377, T310772. Open 0900-1900. See www.munipiura.gob.pe/turismo/ in Spanish for lots of information and links.*. **Dirección Regional de Turismo** ⓘ *Av Fortunato Chirichigno, Urb San Eduardo, T308229*, at the north end of town, helpful when there are problems, open 0900-1300, 1600-1800. *Indecopi* is also here, T304045.

Sights

Standing on the **Plaza de Armas** is the **cathedral**, with gold covered altar and paintings by Ignacio Merino. A few blocks away is **San Francisco** (under reconstruction), where the city's independence from Spain was declared on 4 January 1821, nearly eight months before Lima. **María Auxiliadora** stands on a small plaza on Libertad, near Avenida Sánchez Cerro. Across the plaza is the **Museo de Arte Religioso**. The birthplace of Admiral Miguel Grau, hero of the War of the Pacific with Chile, is **Casa Museo Grau** ⓘ *Jr Tacna 662, opposite the Centro Cívico, 0800-1300, 1600-1900, free*. It is a museum and contains a model of the *Huáscar*, the largest Peruvian warship in the War of the Pacific, which was built in Britain. It also contains interesting old photographs. Interesting local craftwork is sold at the **Mercado Modelo**. The small but interesting **Museo Municipal Vicús** ⓘ *Sullana, near Huánuco, Mon-Sat 0800-2200, Sun 0800-1200*, includes 60 gold artefacts from the local Vicús culture. It also has an art section.

Catacaos, 12 km to the southwest of Piura, is famous for its *chicha* (quality not always reliable), *picanterías* (local restaurants, some with music, *La Chayo*, San Francisco 493, recommended), tooled leather, gold and silver filigree jewellery, wooden articles, straw hats (expensive) and splendid celebrations in Holy Week. About 2 km south of Catacaos is the **Narihualá** archaeological site.

The port for the area, 50 km from Piura, **Paita** exports cotton, cotton seed, wool and flax. Built on a small beach, flanked on three sides by a towering, sandy bluff, it is connected with Piura and Sullana by paved highways. It is a fishing port with a long history. Several colonial buildings survive, but in poor condition. Bolívar's mistress, Manuela Sáenz, lived the last 24 years of her life in Paita, after being exiled from Quito. She supported herself until her death in

Piura

Sleeping 🛏
California 2
Continental 3
El Almirante 4
El Sol 5
Esmeralda 6
Hospedaje Aruba 7
Hostal Los Jardines 8
Hostal Moon Night 9
La Capullana 10

Los Portales 11
Oriental 12
Perú 13
San Jorge 14
San Miguel 15

Eating 🍴
Alex Chopp's 1
Brosti Chopp 2
Carburmer 3

Chalán de la Avenida 4
Chalán del Norte 5
D'Pauli 7
Ganímedes 9
Italia 11
La Carreta 14
Las Tradiciones Piuranas
  & Piura Tours 12
Picantería Los Santitos 3
Romano 13

1856 by weaving, embroidering and making candy, after refusing the fortune left her by her husband. Her house is on the road into town, adjoining a petrol station. On a bluff looming over Paita is a small colonial fortress built to repel pirates. Paita was a port of call for Spanish shipping en route from Lima to Panama and Mexico. It was a frequent target for attack, from Drake (1579) to Anson (1741).

● Sleeping

Piura *p1143, map p1144*

A Los Portales, Libertad 875, Plaza de Armas, T321161, www.hoteleslosportales.com. Includes breakfast and welcome cocktail, attractively refurbished, the city's social centre, elegant, a/c, hot water, pleasant terrace and patio, nice pool.
D Esmeralda, Loreto 235, T/F331205, www.hotelesmeralda.com.pe. Hot water, fan (**C** with a/c), comfortable, good, restaurant.
D San Miguel, Lima 1007, Plaza Pizarro, T305122. Modern, comfortable, TV, café.
E El Almirante, Ica 860, T/F335239. With fan, modern, owner is knowledgeable about the Ayabaca area.
E Perú, Arequipa 476, T333919. With fan, safe, laundry service, cold water, modern small rooms, all meals in restaurant are extra.
E San Jorge, Jr Loreto 960, T327514. With fan, cheaper without cable TV, hot water.
E El Sol, Sánchez Cerro 411, T324461. Hot water, small pool, snack bar, parking, accepts dollars cash or TCs but won't change them. Recommended.
F La Capullana, Junín 925, T321239. Some cheap single rooms, welcoming.
F Continental, Jr Junín 924, T334531. Some rooms with bath, comfortable, no breakfast.
F Hostal Los Jardines, Av Los Cocos 436, T326590. Hot water, TV, laundry, parking, good value.
F Hostal Moon Night, Junín 899, T336174. Comfortable, modern, spacious, **G** without bath or TV, cold water, good value.
G pp California, Jr Junín 835, upstairs, T328789. Shared bath, own water-tank, mosquito netting on windows, roof terrace, brightly decorated. Recommended (some short stay, though).
G Hospedaje Aruba, Junín 851, T303067. Small rooms but comfortable, shared bath, fan on request. Recommended.
G Oriental, Callao 446, T304011. Cheaper without bath and fan, good value but very noisy, TV in reception. Convenient for buses

● Eating

Piura *p1143, map p1144*

† † † Carbumer, Libertad 1014, T332380. Very good lunches and dinners, also pizza.
† † † Picantería Los Santitos, in the same precinct is Carbumer. Lunch only, wide range of

traditional dishes in a renovated colonial house.
† † Alex Chopp's, Huancavelica 538, T322568. A la carte dishes, seafood, fish, chicken and meats, beer, popular at lunchtime.
† † Brosti Chopp, Arequipa 780, T303753. Similar, but with lunch *menú* for US$1.45.
† † La Carreta, Huancavelica 726, T304231. Popular for roast chicken.
† † Romano, Ayacucho 580. Popular with locals, extensive menu, excellent set meal for US$1.55. Recommended.
† † Las Tradiciones Piuranas, Ayacucho 579, T803084. Regional specialities, nice atmosphere, art gallery.
† Ganímedes, Lima 440, T329176. A good vegetarian restaurant, very popular set lunch, à la carte is slow but well worth it, try the excellent yoghurt and fruit.
† Italia, Grau 172. For breakfasts, snacks, desserts and juices.

Cafés

Chalán del Norte several branches for sweets, cakes and ice cream, Tacna 520 on Plaza de Armas, Grau 173 and 450 (*Chalán de la Avenida*).
D'Pauli, Lima 541. Sweets, cakes and ice-cream.

▲ Activities and tours

Piura *p1143, map p1144*
Piura Tours, C Ayacucho 585, T326778, piuratours@cpi.udep.edu.pe. The manager Mario speaks very good English.

● Transport

Piura *p1143, map p1144*
Air Capitán Guillermo Concha airport is in Castilla, 10 mins from the centre by taxi (US$1). It has gift shops and two car rental agencies (see below). 2 daily flights with **Lan** (Av Grau 140) to **Lima** via **Chiclayo**. Icaro inaugurated flights between Piura and **Cuenca** (Ecuador) in January 2007.
Bus Most companies are on Av Sánchez Cerro, blocks 11, 12 and 13 (see www.munipiura.gob.pe/turismo/transporte.shtml). To **Lima**, 1,038 km, 14-16 hrs, from US$7 (eg *Tepsa*), on the Panamericana Norte. Most buses stop at the major cities on route; Ittsa, Sánchez Cerro 1142, T308645 (US$17.15 on top floor, US$21.50 on lower floor);

Línea, Sánchez Cerro 1215, T327821; Tepsa, Loreto 1198, T323721. To **Chiclayo**, 190 km, 3 hrs, US$3.65, several buses daily. Also several daily buses to **Trujillo**, 7 hrs, 487 km, US$7, to travel by day change in Chiclayo. To **Tumbes**, 282 km, 4½ hrs, US$4.80, several buses daily, eg **Cruz del Sur** (Av Circunvalación 160, T337094, also to Lima), **Cial** (Bolognesi 817, T304250) and **Emtrafesa** (Los Naranjos 255, T337093, also to Chiclayo and Trujillo); also colectivos, US$5.75. To **Talara**, US$2, 2 hrs, with **Eppo**, T304543. To **Paita**, Trans Dora, Sánchez Cerro 1391, every 20 mins, 1 hr, US$0.75; also from Paita terminal on Av Gullman, just off Sánchez Cerro. To **Máncora**, US$3.15, 3 hrs, with **Eppo**.

To Ecuador: To **Machala** and **Guayaquil**, the fastest route if you are heading directly to Quito, **CIFA**, Los Naranjos y Sánchez Cerro (cuadra 11-12) opposite Emtrafesa, T305925, 5 a day, Machala US$6, 6 hrs, Guayaquil US$10, 9 hrs. Otherwise, go to Tumbes and travel on from there for the Aguas Verdes crossing. To **Loja**, the best option if you want to visit the southern or central highlands of Ecuador, **Transportes Loja**, Sánchez Cerro 1480, T309407, 4 daily, US$8, 8 hrs, to **Macará** US$4. Or **Unión Cariamanga**, Sánchez Cerro (cuadra 18) y Av Vice, Urbanización Santa Ana, T990 0135 (mob), at 1330 and 2000. Alternatively take a bus to **Sullana**, 38 km, 30 mins (US$0.45), **Eppo**, Sullana Express and Turismo del Norte, all on 1100 block of Sánchez Cerro; also colectivos (US$1). To **La Tina** on the Ecuadorean frontier, is a further 128 km, 1¾ hrs, US$2.85. It's best to take an early bus to Sullana (start at 0430, leave when full), then a colectivo (see under Sullana).

Catacaos *p1144*
Combis From **Piura** to Catacaos leave when full from bus terminal at block 12 of Av Sánchez Cerro, US$0.25, 20 mins.

❶ Directory

Piura p1143, map p1144
Banks BCP, Grau y Tacna. Cash and Visa and Amex TCs (US$12 commission), cheques changed in the mornings only, has ATM. BBV Continental, Plaza de Armas. Changes Amex TCs with US$10 commission. Interbank, Grau 170, changes Visa TCs, ATM for Visa, Mastercard and AmEx. *Casas de cambio* are at Arequipa 600 block and 722, and Ica 366, 456 and 460. Street changers can be found on Grau outside *BCP*.
Car hire Vicús, T342051, www.vicusr entacar.com; Servitours, T342008, www.servi tourspiura.com. Both at airport, US$50 per day for a small vehicle; they also provide transfers to Punta Sal US$80. **Consulates** Honorary British Consul, c/o American Airlines, Hancavelica 223, T305990, F333300. Honorary German Consul, Jutta Moritz de Irazola, Las Amapolas K6, Urb Miraflores, Casilla 76, T332920, F320310.
Internet Several in the centre. 10 machines in the Biblioteca Municipal, Urb Grau, US$0.60 per hr. **Post offices** Libertad y Ayacucho on Plaza de Armas. **Telephones** Loreto 259, national and international phone and fax. Also at Ovalo Grau 483.

North to Ecuador

Sullana, built on a bluff over the fertile Chira valley, is a busy, modern place 38 km north of Piura. Here the Pan-American Highway forks. To the east it crosses the Peru-Ecuador border at La Tina and continues via Macará to Loja and Cuenca. The excellent paved road is very scenic. The more frequently used route to the border is the coastal road which goes from Sullana northwest towards the Talara oilfields, and then follows the coastline to Máncora and Tumbes.

Border at La Tina-Macará The border crossing is problem-free; **Peruvian immigration** is open 24 hours and officials are helpful. Go to Peruvian immigration at the end of the bridge, get a stamp, walk across and then go to Ecuadorean immigration. There are no customs searches (vehicles, including colectivos, are subject to full searches, though). There are banks at each side for changing cash only, Monday-Friday; rates are a little better in Macará. There is one *hospedaje* and several eating places on the road down to the bridge.

New border crossing beyond Ayabaca East from Piura or Sullana is Ayabaca (225 km northeast of Piura; several *hostales*), home of El Señor Cautivo de Ayabaca whose shrine is the most famous in northern Peru. From Ayabaca a rough road with great views goes via Samanguilla 64 km to **Espíndola**, a tiny frontier village with a satellite phone, a simple comedor and no other services. A very poor road continues 2 km to Peruvian immigration at the small international bridge over the Río Espíndola, open 24 hours. An equally poor road

30 km from Tumbes, T/F072-544222, casagrillo@hotmail.com. Take colectivo from Tumbes market to Los Pinos, or get off bus on Pan-American Highway at Km 1236.5, Youth Hostel, excellent restaurant including vegetarian, great place to relax, 6 rooms for up to 4, made of local materials, shared bath, hot water, laundry, surfing, scuba diving, fishing, cycling, trekking, horse riding, camping available. Recommended.

Tumbes *p1147, map p1149*
Av Tumbes is still sometimes referred to by its old name of Teniente Vásquez. At holiday times it can be very difficult to find a room.
B Costa del Sol, San Martín 275, Plazuela Bolognesi, T523991, ventastumbes@costadel solperu.com. Best in town (but avoid noisy front rooms), hot water, minibar, fan, restaurant, good food and service, parking extra, nice garden with pool, helpful manager.
E Lourdes, Mayor Bodero 118, 3 blocks from main plaza, T522966. Fan, roof restaurant, slow service. Recommended.
E Roma, Bolognesi 425 Plaza de Armas, T524137. With fan, pleasant, convenient.
F Amazonas, Av Tumbes 317, T525266. With fan, noisy, water unreliable morning.
F Elica, Tacna 319, T523870. With fan, quiet.
F El Estoril, Huáscar 317, 2 blocks from main plaza, T521360. With cold water, good, welcoming, discount for long stay.

F Hostal Tumbes, Grau 614, T522203. With cold water, fan, good value. Recommended.
F Toloa 1, Av Tumbes 430, T523771. With fan, safe, helpful.
F Toloa 2, Bolívar 458, T524135. With fan, OK.
G Sudamericano, San Martín 130, Paseo de la Concordia. Shared bath, basic but good value. Many other cheap hotels by the market.

Border with Ecuador *p1148*
Zarumilla/Aguas Verdes
If stuck overnight in the border area there is a hotel in Aguas Verdes **F Hostal Francis**, Av República de Perú 220, T561177, OK. Aguas Verdes also has phone booths and airline ticket offices. There are 4 hotels in Zarumilla, at Km 1290 on the Pan- American Highway, 5 km south of Aguas Verdes.

🍴 Eating

Máncora and Punta Sal *p1147*
Máncora
🍴 **Laguna Camp**, T9401 5628, www.vivamancora.com/lagunacamp. 100 m from the sea near new breakwater, thatched roofs, hammocks, delicious food, breakfast, lunch and dinner, pizza and barbeque nights, cabins sleeping up to 6 people, helpful. Recommended.
🍴 **Café La Bajadita**, is the best place in the evening to hang out, eat chocolate cake or

Tumbes

To Airport & Aguas Verdes (Ecuador Border)

C Francisco Navarrete
C Abad Puell
Av Teniente Vásquez (formerly Av Teniente Vásquez)
C Bolívar
Plazuela Bolognesi
C Fco Feijoó
C Mariscal Castilla
A. Araujo
Diego de Almagro
C Fco Ibáñes
C Tarapacá
C Arica
Colectivos to Aguas Verdes
Paseo Los Libertadores (formerly San Martín)
Paseo de la Concordia (formerly San Martín)
Alipio Rosales
Buses & Combis to Aguas Verdes
C Piura
C Piura
Bolognesi
C Huáscar
C Alfonso Ugarte
Av Tacna
Av Tumbes
Bodero
C Grau
Colonial Public Library
Old Houses
Old Houses
Plazuela Alipio Rosales
Cathedral
Ecuadorean Consulate
Plaza de Armas
Centro Cívico
Los Andes
7 de Enero
General Vivanco
7 de Enero
Plazuela de los Héroes
Río Tumbes
Malecón Benavides

To Sullana, Piura & Lima

N
0 metres 100
0 yards 100

Sleeping 🛏
Amazonas **1**
Costa del Sol **2**
El Estoril **4**
Elica **3**

Hostal Tumbes **5**
Lourdes **6**
Roma **7**
Sudamericano **8**
Toloa 1 **9**

Toloa 2 **10**

Eating 🍴
Chifa Wakay **1**
Classic **2**

Latino **3**
Los Gustitos **3**
Si Señor **4**

1149

manjarblanco and listen to rock and reggae.

¶ **Stephanies**, adjoining *Sol y Mar* hotel, overlooking beach. Serves *fuentes*, huge plates big enough for 2.

Also good are **La Espada** and **Don Pedro** on the highway. Several internet cafés on the highway.

Tumbes *p1147, map p1149*
There are cheap restaurants on the Plaza de Armas, Paseo de la Concordia and near the markets.
¶¶-¶ **Chifa Wakay**, Huáscar 413. Smart, good.
¶¶-¶ **Classic**, Tumbes 185. Popular for local food. Recommended.
¶¶-¶ **Los Gustitos**, Bolívar 148. Excellent menús and à la carte.
¶¶-¶ **Latino**, Bolívar 163, on Plaza de Armas. Good set meals (à la carte expensive), *peña* most evenings.
¶ **Heladería La Suprema**, Paseo Libertadores 298. Good ice cream, sweets and cold drinks.
¶ **Pizzería Studio**, on the plaza. Good pizza and desserts.
¶ **Sí Señor**, Bolívar 119 on the plaza. Good for snacks.

▲ Activities and tours

Tumbes *p1147, map p1149*
Most companies offer day tours of the local area for US$20 pp, minimum 2, and US$35-50 pp to the hinterland.
Preference Tours, Grau 427, T525518. Knowledgeable and friendly.
Rosillo Tours, Tumbes 293, T/F523892. Information, tickets, Western Union agents.

⊖ Transport

Sullana *p1146*
Bus Several bus companies including Ormeño use a new Terminal Terrestre. To **Tumbes**, 244 km, 4-5 hrs US$5, several buses daily. To **Chiclayo** and **Trujillo** see under Piura. To **Lima**, 1,076 km, 14-16 hrs, US$9-18, several buses daily, most coming from Tumbes or Talara, luxury overnight via Trujillo with Ittsa (T503705) US$18, also with Cruz del Sur and Ormeño. To **Talara**, Eppo and Emtrafesa, Comercio, 1 block from Lama block 3, hourly, Eppo are faster but more expensive, US$1.25. To **Máncora**, Eppo, 5 a day, 2½ hrs, US$3.

Border with Ecuador:
La Tina-Macará *p1146*
Buses leave frequently from Ecuadorean side for Loja, so if you are not taking the through bus (see under Piura), you can go from Sullana to Loja in a day. From the border to Sullana, cars may leave before they are full, but won't charge extra.
Combis Leave from Sullana to the international
1150

bridge from Terminal Terrestre La Capullana, off Av Buenos Aires, several blocks beyond the canal. They leave when full, US$2.85 per person, 1¾ hrs. It's best to take a taxi or mototaxi to and from the terminal. From the border to Macará is 4 km: walk over the bridge and take one of the pick-ups which run from the border (10 mins, US$0.30, or US$1.25 for whole car).

Border with Ecuador: Ayabaca *p1146*
To **Ayabaca** from Piura, **Trans Vegas**, Av Panamericana frente al cementerio, Urb San Ramón, T308729 (best), daily 0830 and 1500, plus Sat 0800, Sun 2300, 6 hrs, US$7. **Poderoso Cautivo**, Av Sullana Norte next to Iglesia Cristo Rey, T309888, daily 0900 and 1500, Sun also 2300. To **Piura**, both companies are on Cáceres at Plaza de Armas. **Vegas**, T471080, Tue-Sun 0830 and 1500, Mon 0800, 0900 and 1500. **Poderoso Cautivo**, T471247, daily 0830 and 1500, Fri also 1530 and 1630. From Ayabaca to **Espíndola**, station wagons and pickups leave when full from Leoncio Prado y Bolognesi, near the market, only 1 or 2 a day, so go early, US$3 pp, US$18 for the vehicle, 3½ hrs. Arrange for driver to take you to the international bridge and preferably on to Jimbura. To Ayabaca, a pickup leaves Espíndola about 0500 daily; if staying in Jimbura, go to Espíndola and let the driver know, he will pick you up in the morning. There is no fixed schedule, patience is required.

Talara *p1147*
Bus To **Tumbes**, 171 km, 3 hrs, US$3.50, most coming from Piura and stopping at major towns going north; several daily. To **Piura**, 2 hrs, US$1.75.

Máncora and Punta Sal *p1147*
Bus Talara to **El Alto** (Cabo Blanco), 32 km, 30 mins, US$0.75, continuing to Máncora, 28 km, 30 mins, US$0.75. To **Talara/Sullana/ Piura** with Eppo, 5 a day, US$3; to **Tumbes** (and points in between), combis leave when full, US$1.50, 2 hrs.

Tumbes *p1147, map p1149*
Air Daily flights to and from **Lima** (Wayra Perú, Av Tumbes Norte 270, T525020).
Bus Daily to and from **Lima**, 1,320 km, 18-20 hrs, depending on stopovers, US$12 (normal service), US$25 (*Cruz del Sur*), US$34 (*Cruz del Sur VIP* service). Several buses daily, all on Av Tumbes: Civa, No 518, T525120; Ormeño, Av Tumbes s/n, T522228; Cruz del Sur, No 319, T896163; Trans Chiclayo, No 466, T525260. Cheaper buses usually leave 1600-2100, more expensive ones 1200-1400. Except for luxury service, most buses to Lima stop at major cities en route. Tickets to anywhere between Tumbes

and Lima sell quickly, so if arriving from Ecuador you may have to stay overnight. Piura is a good place for connections in the daytime. To **Sullana**, 244 km, 3-4 hrs, US$4.50, several buses daily. To **Piura**, 4-5 hrs, 282 km, US$4.80 with **Trans Chiclayo**, Cruz del Sur, El Dorado (Piura 459, T523480) 6 a day; Comité Tumbes/Piura (Tumbes N 308, T525977), US$7 pp, fast cars, leave when full, 3½ hrs. To **Chiclayo**, 552 km, 6 hrs, US$5.75, several each day with *Cruz del Sur, El Dorado*, and others. To **Trujillo**, 769 km, 10-11 hrs, US$7.15-14.35, *Ormeño, Cruz del Sur, El Dorado, Emtrafesa*. Transport to the Border with Ecuador, see below.

To **Ecuador**: CIFA to **Machala** and **Guayaquil**, 6 a day, luxury bus at 1000, US$6, 5 hrs to Guayaquil, recommended for crossing the border.

Santuario Nacional los Manglares de Tumbes *p1147*
Combis From Tumbes market to **Zarumilla**, 20 mins, US$0.50. In Zarumilla hire a mototaxi for the 7 km run (20 mins, US$1.50) to the Centre. A 2½-hr guided visit costs US$12, for up to 6 people.

Border with Ecuador *p1148*
Zarumilla/Aguas Verdes
Between Tumbes and the border Colectivos leave from block 3 of Av Tumbes, US$1 pp or US$6 to hire car, and wait at the immigration office before continuing to the border, 30-40 mins. Colectivos can cross the bridge, taxis cannot (so don't hire a Peruvian taxi to take you into Ecuador). **Note** Make sure the driver takes you all the way to the border and not just as far as the complex 4 km south of the bridge. Returning from the border, some colectivos leave from near the bridge, but charge more than others which leave 2 blocks down along main street by a small plaza opposite the church. Combis leave from the market area along Mcal Castilla across from Calle Alipio Rosales, US$0.50, luggage on roof. They leave passengers at the immigration office. Old, slow city buses ply the same route as combis, US$0.40. Combis and

buses return to Tumbes from an esplanade 3 blocks east of the colectivo stop, but don't wait at immigration. All vehicles only leave when full. From the border to Zarumilla by mototaxi costs US$0.50 pp. Taxi to Tumbes, including wait at immigration, US$6.

Entering Peru It is easier to take a colectivo to Tumbes and then a bus south, rather than trying to get on a bus from the border to a southern destination. When driving into Peru, vehicle fumigation is not required, but there is one outfit who will attempt to fumigate your vehicle with water and charge US$10. Beware of officials claiming that you need a *carnet* to obtain your 90-day transit permit; this is not so, cite Decreto Supremo 015-87-ICTI/TUR. Frequent road tolls between Tumbes and Lima, approximately US$2 each.

❶ Directory

Sullana *p1146*
Banks BCP, San Martín 685, will change cash and TCs. *Casas de cambio* and street changers on San Martín by Tarapacá. **Internet** Several in the centre, on San Martín and Av Lama. **Post offices** San Martín 778, Mon-Sat 0800-1930, Sun 0800-1300. **Telephones** Telephone and fax at Miró Quesada 213. **Useful addresses** Immigration: Grau 939.

Tumbes *p1147, map p1149*
Banks BBV Continental, Bolívar 121, cash and Amex TCs only, US$5 commission. **Cambios Internacionales**, Av Bolívar 161, cash only, good rates. Money changers on the street (on Bolívar, left of the Cathedral), some of whom are unscrupulous, give a much better rate than banks or *cambios*, but don't accept the first offer you are given. None changes TCs. **Consulates** Ecuadorean Consulate, Bolívar 129, Plaza de Armas, T521739, consultum@speedy.com.pe. **Internet** Widely available in many cheap cafés and major hotels. **Post offices** San Martín 208. **Telephones** San Martín 210.

Northern Highlands

Leaving the Pacific coast behind, you climb in a relatively short time up to the Sierra. It was here, at Cajamarca, that the defeat of the Incas by the Spaniards began, bringing about cataclysmic change to this part of the world. But, unlike this well-documented event, the history of the Incas' contemporaries and predecessors has to be teased out of the stones of their temples and fortresses, which are shrouded in cloud in the 'Eyebrow of the Jungle'.

Trujillo to Cajamarca

To the northeast of Trujillo is Cajamarca, an attractive colonial town surrounded by lovely countryside and the commercial centre of the northern mountain area. It can be reached by the old road via Huamachuco and Cajabamba, or by paved road via Pacasmayo. The former road is being improved, but, for cyclists especially, is lonely, taking a couple of days by bus (as opposed to 7-8 hours via Pacasmayo, see below), but it is more interesting, passing over the bare puna before dropping to the Huamachuco valley.

Huamachuco → *Colour map 3, grid B2. Altitude: 3,180 m.*

This colonial town formerly on the royal Inca Road, 181 km from Trujillo, has the largest main plaza in Peru, with fine topiary, and a controversial modern **cathedral**. There is a colourful **Sunday market**, with dancing in the plaza, and the Founding of Huamachuco festival, second week in August, with spectacular fireworks and the amazing, aggressive male dancers, called *turcos*. **Museo Municipal Wamachuko** ① *Sucre 195, Mon-Sat 0900-1300, 1500-1900, Sun 0900-1200, free*, displays artefacts found at nearby Cerro Amaru (a hill-top system of wells and water worship) and **Marca Huamachuco**: access is via a poor vehicle road or a mule track (preferable for walking), off the road to Sanagorán, there is an archway at the turnoff, 5 km from Huamachuco, mototaxi to turnoff US$2; combis to Sanagorán in the morning. These hilltop pre-Inca fortifications rank in the top 10 archaeological sites in Peru. They are 3 km long, dating back to at least 300 BC though many structures were added later. Its most impressive features are: El Castillo, a remarkable circular structure with walls up to 8 m high located at the highest point of the site, and El Convento complex, five circular structures of varying sizes towards the northern end of the hill. The largest one has been partially reconstructed. The extensive Huari ruins of **Wiracochapampa** are 3 km north of town, 45 minutes' walk. Although much of the site is overgrown the Waman Raymi festival is held here on the second Sunday in August (a northern version of Cuzco's Inti Raymi).

Cajabamba is a small market town and a useful stop-over point between Cajamarca and Huamachuco.

Pacasmayo → *Colour map 3, grid A2. Population: 12,300.*

Pacasmayo, 102 km north of Trujillo and port for the next oasis north, is the main road connection from the coast to Cajamarca. The paved 180 km road branches off the Pan-American Highway soon after it crosses the Río Jequetepeque (bus Pacasmayo-Cajamarca US$4.30, five hours; to Chiclayo US$1.70, two hours). The river valley has terraced rice fields and mimosas may often be seen in bloom, brightening the otherwise dusty landscape. A few kilometres northwest on the other side of Río Jequetepeque are the ruins of **Pacatnamú** comparable in size to Chan Chán pyramids, cemetery and living quarters of nobles and fishermen, possibly built in the Chavín or Moche periods. Taxi bus to Guadalupe, 10 km from ruins, then another taxi, US$20 to the site. Micros run in summer. Where the Pan-American Highway crosses the Jequetepeque are the well-signed ruins of **Farfán** (separate from those of Pacatnamú, but probably of the same period; no explanations at the site).

Cajamarca → *Phone code: 076. Colour map 3, grid B2. Population: 117,500. Altitude: 2,750 m.*

At Cajamarca Pizarro ambushed and captured Atahualpa, the Inca emperor. This was the first showdown between the Spanish and the Incas and, despite their huge numerical inferiority, the Spanish emerged victorious, executing Atahualpa in the process. The nearby **Yanacocha gold mine** ① *www.yanacocha.com.pe*, has brought new wealth to the town (and major ecological concerns and social problems) and Cajamarca is the hub of tourism development for the whole of the northwest via the *Circuito Turístico Nororiental* (Chiclayo-Cajamarca-Chachapoyas). **Tourist offices**: Dirección Regional de Turismo and Instituto Nacional de Cultura ① *in the Conjunto Monumental de Belén, Belén 631, T362997, cajamarca@mincetur.gob.pe, www.inccajamarca.org, Mon-Fri 0730-1300, 1430- 1800.* **Cámara Regional de Turismo (Caretur)** ① *José Gálvez 771, T831579, caretur cajamarca@regionalcaj.zzn.com.* The University tourist school has an office at Del Batán 289, T361546, offering free advice and leaflets, open Mon-Fri 0830-1300, 1500-2200. The **Indecopi** office is at Tarapacá 815, p 2, T363315, inguzman@indecopi.gob.pe. All museums are closed on Tuesday but open at weekends.

Complejo Belén ① *0900-1300, 1500-1730, Sat-Sun 0900-1230, US$1.20, valid for more than 1 day, a ticket is also valid for the Cuarto de Rescate, a guide for all the sites costs US$2.85 (US$5.75-8.50 for guides in other languages).* The complex comprises the tourist office and Institute of Culture, a beautifully ornate church, considered the city's finest. See the inside of the dome, where eight giant cherubs support an intricate flowering centrepiece. In the same courtyard is the **Museo Médico Belén**, which has a collection of medical instruments. Across the street is a maternity hospital from the colonial era, now the **Archaeological and Ethnological Museum,** Junín y Belén. It has a range of ceramics from all regions and civilizations of Peru. The **Cuarto de Rescate** ① *entrance at Amalia Puga 750,* is not the actual ransom chamber but in fact the room where Atahualpa was held prisoner. A red line on the wall is said to indicate where Atahualpa reached up and drew a mark, agreeing to have his subjects fill the room to the line with treasure. The chamber is roped off but can be viewed from the outside. Pollution and weather have had a detrimental effect on the stone.

You can also visit the plaza where Atahualpa was ambushed and the stone altar set high on **Santa Apolonia hill** ① *US$0.60, take bus marked Santa Apolonia/Fonavi, or micro A,* where he is said to have reviewed his subjects. There is a road to the top, or you can walk up from Calle 2 de Mayo, using the steep stairway. The view is worth the effort, especially at sunrise (but go in a group).

The **Plaza de Armas**, where Atahualpa was executed, has a 350-year-old fountain, topiary and gardens. The **Cathedral**, opened in 1776, is still missing its belfry, but the façade has beautiful baroque carving in stone. On the opposite side of the plaza is the 17th century **San Francisco Church**, older than the Cathedral and with more interior stone carving and elaborate altars. The attached **Museo de Arte Colonial** ① *Mon-Sat 1430-1800, US$0.85, entrance is unmarked on far left corner of church,* is filled with colonial paintings and icons. The guided tour of the museum includes entry to the church's spooky catacombs.

The city has many old colonial houses with garden patios, and 104 elaborately carved doorways: see the **Bishop's Palace**, across the street from the Cathedral; the **palace of the Condes de Uceda**, at Jr Apurímac 719 (now occupied by BCP bank); and the **Casa Silva Santiesteban** (Junín y 2 de Mayo).

Museo Arqueológico Horacio H Urteaga ① *Del Batán 289, Mon-Fri 0700-1445, free, donations accepted,* of the Universidad Nacional de Cajamarca, has objects of the pre-Inca Cajamarca and other cultures. The university maintains an experimental arboretum and agricultural station, the **Museo Silvo-agropecuario** ① *Km 2.5 on the road to Baños del Inca,* with a lovely mural at the entrance.

Excursions About 6 km away are the sulphurous thermal springs of **Los Baños del Inca** ① *0500-1945, T348385, www.inkatermas.com.pe, US$0.60, combis marked Baños del Inca cost US$0.20, 15 mins, taxis US$1.80.* The water temperature is 78° C. Atahualpa tried the effect of these waters on a festering war wound and his bath is still there. The complex is renewed regularly, with gardens and various levels of accommodation (see Sleeping, below). The main baths are divided into five categories, with prices ranging from US$1 to US$1.50, all with private tubs and no pool. Sauna US$3, massage US$6-9 (take your own towel; soaps are sold outside). Only spend 20 minutes maximum in the water; obey instructions; many of the facilities allow bathers in shifts, divided by time and/or sex.

Other excursions include **Llacanora**, a typical Andean village in beautiful scenery (13 km southeast; nice walk downhill from Baños del Inca, two hours). **Ventanillas de Otusco** ① *0800-1800, US$1, combi US$0.15,* part of an old pre-Inca cemetery, has a gallery of secondary burial niches. There are good day walks in this area; local sketch maps available.

A road goes to **Ventanillas de Combayo** ① *occasional combis on weekdays; more transport on Sun when a market is held nearby, 1 hr,* some 20 km past the burial niches of Otusco. These are more numerous and spectacular, being located in an isolated, mountainous area, and distributed over the face of a steep 200 m high hillside.

Cumbe Mayo, a *pampa* on a mountain range, is 20 km southwest of Cajamarca. It is famous for its extraordinary, well-engineered pre-Inca channels, running for 9 km across the mountain tops. It is said to be the oldest man-made construction in South America. The sheer scale of the scene is impressive and the huge rock formations of Los Frailones ('big monks') and others with fanciful names are strange indeed. On the way to Cumbe Mayo is the Layzón ceremonial centre. There is no bus service; guided tours run from 0900-1300 (recommended in order to see all the pre-Inca sites); taxi US$15. To walk up takes 3-4 hours (take a guide, or a tour, best weather May-September). The trail starts from the hill of Santa Apolonia (Silla del Inca), and goes to Cumbe Mayo straight through the village and up the hill; at the top of the mountain, leave the trail and take the road to the right to the canal. The walk is not difficult and you do not need hiking boots. Take a good torch. The locals use the trail to bring their goods to market.

The **Porcón** rural cooperative, with its evangelical faith expressed on billboards, is a popular excursion, 30 km northwest of Cajamarca. It is tightly organized, with carpentry, bakery, cheese and yoghurt-making, zoo and vicuñas. A good guide helps to explain everything. If not taking a tour, contact **Cooperativa Agraria Atahualpa Jerusalén** ① *Chanchamayo 1355, Fonavi 1, T/F825631, granjaporcon@yahoo.com.*

Some 103 km east of Pacasmayo is the mining town of Chilete, 21 km north of which on the road to San Pablo is **Kuntur Wasi**. The site was devoted to a feline cult and consists of a pyramid and stone monoliths. Extensive excavations are under way and significant new discoveries are being made (excellent site museum). There are two basic *hostales* in Chilete; very limited facilities.

● Sleeping

Huamachuco *p1152*

C-E Real, Bolívar 250, T441402, www.hotelrealperu.com. New, TV, sauna, internet, many of the fittings are of wood. Recommended.

D-F Hostal Santa Fe, San Martín 297, T441019, hs_turistico_santafe@hotmail.com. New, TV, hot water. Recommended.

E Hospedaje Colonial Plaza, Castilla 208, on the plaza, T441760. An old colonial house with beautiful patios, some rooms retain original furniture, hot water, laundry facilities. Can arrange horse-riding.

E Hostal Gran Colonial, Castilla 537, T511101, grancolonialhostal@hotmail.com. An attractive old colonial house, with hot water, TV, restaurant is good value. Recommended.

F Hostal Noche Buena, San Román 401 on the main plaza, T441435. Clean with hot showers, TV, laundry, overlooking the plaza.

F Huamachuco, Castilla 354, on the plaza, T441393. With hot showers (**G** without), good value, has parking.

Cajabamba *p1152*

F Hostal La Casona, Jr Alfonso Ugarte 586, Plaza de Armas, T848385. Small rooms, electric shower, with restaurant.

F Jhoel, Jr Grau 633, T551653. With electric shower, patio, pleasant, good value.

Pacasmayo *p1152*

G Panamericano, Leoncio Prado 18, T522521. With private cold shower, basic, small, safe, reasonable restaurant downstairs.

G San Francisco, Leoncio Prado 21, T522021. Opposite and cleaner than the *Panamericano*, still basic, OK.

Cajamarca *p1152, map p1155*

AL Posada del Puruay, 5 km north of the city,
T367928, postmast@p-puruay.com.pe. A 17th-century *hacienda* converted into a 'hotel museum', high standards and beautiful colonial furnishings. Recommended.

A Costa del Sol, Cruz de la Piedra 707, T343434, ventascajamarca@costadelsolperu.com. New hotel on the Plaza de Armas, part of a Peruvian chain, with breakfast, airport transfer, welcome drink; restaurant, café and bars, pool.

B-C El Ingenio, Av Vía de Evitamiento 1611-1709, T367121, www.elingenio.com. 1½ blocks from new El Quinde shopping mall. With solar-powered hot water, spacious, very relaxed, helpful. Highly recommended.

C Casa Blanca, Dos de Mayo 446 on Plaza de Armas, T/F822141. Safe, nice old building with garden, good restaurant.

C El Cumbe Inn, Pasaje Atahualpa 345, T366858, www.elcumbeinn.com. Includes breakfast and tax, comfortable, bright rooms, hot water, internet, small gym, will arrange taxis. Recommended.

C El Portal del Marqués, Del Comercio 644, T/F368464, portalmarques@terra.com.pe. Attractive converted colonial house, TV, internet, laundry, safe, parking, restaurant *El Mesón*. Recommended.

D Los Balcones de la Recoleta, Amalia Puga 1050, T363302, luchi9200@yahoo.com.pe. Beautifully restored 19th-century house, central courtyard full of flowers, some rooms with period furniture, internet, breakfast extra. Recommended.

D El Cabildo, Junín 1062, T367025, cabildoh@latinmail.com. Includes breakfast, in historic monument with patio and modern fountain, full of character, elegant local decorations, comfortable, breakfast served, gym. Recommended.

D Hostal Cajamarca, colonial house at Dos de Mayo 311, T362532, hostalcajamarca@hotmail.com. Sizeable rooms, hot water, food excellent in *Los Faroles* restaurant. Recommended.

D Hostal Los Pinos, Jr La Mar 521, T/F365992, pinoshostal@yahoo.com. Includes breakfast, lovely colonial house with a new extension, decorated in old style, comfortable, other meals on request, very nice.

D Portada del Sol, Pisagua 731, T363395, PortadadelSol@terra.com.pe. Good rooms, tastefully decorated, hot water, comfortable beds. Also has *Portada del Sol Hacienda* at Km 6 on road to Cumbe Mayo (**C**).

E Colonial Inn, Av Los Héroes 350, T313551, www.colonialprado.com. Hot water, cheaper with shared bath, English spoken, meals extra, convenient for buses.

E Hospedaje Los Jazmines, Amazonas 775, T361812, hospedajelosjasmines@yahoo.com. In converted colonial house with courtyard and café, 10 rooms with bath, 2 without, all profits go to disabled children (some staff are disabled), guests can visit the project's school and help. Recommended.

E Hostal Becerra, Del Batán 195, T367867. With hot water and TV, modern, pleasant, will store luggage until late buses depart.

F Hostal Atahualpa, Pasaje Atahualpa 686, T342629. Hot water 0600-1100 (usually), a bit run-down but clean, meals extra, restaurant 0800-2200.

F Hostal Dos de Mayo, Dos de Mayo 585, T362527. Shared bath, hot water, simple, quite dark, good value *menú* in the restaurant.

F pp Casa Pensión, Dos de Mayo 712, T369888. full board, shared rooms, some with bath.

Baños del Inca
L-AL Laguna Seca, Av Manco Cápac 1098, T594600, www.lagunaseca.com.pe. In pleasant surroundings with thermal streams (atmospheric misty mornings), private hot thermal baths in rooms, swimming pool with thermal water, good restaurant, bar, health spa with a variety of treatments (US$10-48), disco, horses for hire. Recommended.

B Hostal Fundo Campero San Antonio, 2 km off the Baños road (turn off at Km 5), T/F348237, jc_luna@viabcp.com. An old *hacienda*, wonderfully restored, with open fireplaces and gardens, 15 mins walk along the river to Baños del Inca, includes breakfast, riding on *caballos de paso*, own dairy produce, fruit and vegetables,

Cajamarca

Sleeping
Casa Blanca **1**
Casa Pensión **2**
Colonial Inn **3**
Costa del Sol **12**

El Cabildo **4**
El Cumbe Inn **5**
El Ingenio **6**
El Portal del Marqués **7**
Hospedaje Los
  Jazmines **14**
Hostal Atahualpa **8**
Hostal Becerra **9**
Hostal Cajamarca **10**
Hostal Dos de Mayo **11**
Hostal Los Pinos **15**

Los Balcones
  de La Recoleta **17**
Portada del Sol **18**

Eating
Akaesh **2**
Casa Club **12**
Cascanuez **3**
Don Paco **1**
El Batán Gran
  Bufet de Arte **4**

El Cajamarqués **5**
El Capulí **10**
El Pez Loco **6**
El Zarco **7**
Heladería Holanda **8**
Om-Gri **9**
Pizzería El Marengo **11**
Querubino **13**
Salas **14**
Sanguchón.com **15**

catch your own trout for supper; try the *licor de sauco*. Recommended.

🍴 Eating

Huamachuco *p1152*

🍴 **La Casona**, Sánchez Carrión 294. Open daily 0700-0900, 1200-1430, 1900-2030. Serves good value and quality set meals and local dishes, popular. Also places on the Plaza de Armas.

🍴 **Bar Michi Wasi**, San Román 461 on the plaza. Attractive bar and good place to meet locals who know the area.

Cajabamba *p1152*

🍴 **Don Lucho**, Jr Leoncio Prado 227. Good local trout and other à la carte dishes.

🍴 **Quengococha** at Bolognesi 790. Tasty local dishes.

Cajamarca *p1152, map p1155*

🍴🍴🍴 **El Batán Gran Bufet de Arte**, Del Batán 369, T366025. International dishes and nouvelle cuisine, good wine list and wide choice of drinks, local dishes on non-tourist menu, live music at the weekend, art gallery on the 2nd floor.

🍴🍴🍴 **Querubino**, Amalia Puga 589. Mediterranean-style decoration with American and French influence in the cooking, specializes in fish, breakfasts, cocktails, coffees, expensive wines.

🍴🍴 **Casa Club**, Amalia Puga 458-A, T340198. Open 0800-2300. Menú, including vegetarian, and extensive selection à la carte, family atmosphere, slow but attentive service.

🍴🍴 **El Cajamarqués**, Amazonas 770, T362128. Has good value *menú* available after 1300, elegant colonial building with garden full of exotic birds.

🍴🍴 **Don Paco**, Amalia Puga 390, T362655. Opposite San Francisco. Typical, including novo andino, and international dishes, tasty food, desserts, drinks.

🍴🍴 **Om-Gri**, San Martín 360, near the Plaza de Armas. Good Italian dishes, small, friendly, French spoken, opens 1300 (1830 Sun).

🍴🍴 **El Pez Loco**, San Martín 333. Good for fish.

🍴🍴 **Pizzería El Marengo**, Junín 1201. Good pizzas and warm atmosphere, T368045 for delivery.

🍴🍴 **Salas**, Amalia Puga 637, on the main plaza, T362867. A Cajamarca tradition, open 0700-2200. Fast service, excellent local food (try their *cuy frito*), best *tamales* in town; also has a branch in Baños del Inca (1100-1600, Fri-Sun and holidays).

🍴🍴-🍴 **El Zarco**, Jr Del Batán 170, T363421. Open Sun-Fri 0700-2300. Very popular, also has short *chifa* menu, good vegetarian dishes, excellent fish, popular for breakfast; also *El Zarco Campestre*, off road to airport, use own produce, recommended for pork.

🍴 **Natur's Center**, Amalia Puga 409. New vegetarian place with a good selection of dishes.

Cafés

Akaesh, 2 de Mayo 334, 368108. Café with couches, also has a bar, live music Fri night, closed Sun.

El Capulí, Jr Junín, in the Complejo Belén. Open 0900-1300, 1500-2000 (2400 Fri-Sat). Coffee, drinks, sandwiches and snacks. Lovely atmosphere for a quiet coffee.

Cascanuez, Amalia Puga 554. Great cakes, extensive menu including *humitas*, breakfasts, ice creams and coffees.

Heladería Holanda, Amalia Puga 657 on the Plaza de Armas, T340113. Dutch-owned, easily the best ice-creams in Cajamarca, 50 flavours (but not all on at the same time), try *poro poro*, *lúcuma* or *sauco*, also serves coffee. Also has a branch in Baños del Inca.

Sanguchón.com, Junín 1137. Best burgers in town, sandwiches, also popular bar.

⚙ Festivals and events

Cajamarca *p1152, map p1155*

The pre-Lent Carnival is very spectacular and regarded as one of the best in the country; it is also one of the most raucous. In Porcón, 16 km to the northwest, Palm Sunday processions are worth seeing. On **24 Jun**: is San Juan in Cajamarca, Chota, Llacanora, San Juan and Cutervo. An agricultural fair is held in **Jul** at Baños del Inca; on the first Sun in **Oct** is the Festival Folklórico in Cajamarca.

🛍 Shopping

Cajamarca *p1152, map p1155*

Handicrafts Cheap, but bargain hard. Specialities including gilded mirrors and cotton and wool saddlebags (*alforjas*). Items can be made to order. The market on Amazonas is good for *artesanía*; also daily handicraft market on block 7 of Belén. There are several shops on 300 block of Dos de Mayo.

Supermarkets

El Quinde, Av Hoyos Rubio, blocks 6 and 7, Fonavi. New shopping centre (end-2006) on road to airport, with well-stocked supermarket.

⛰ Activities and tours

Cajamarca *p1152, map p1155*

Agencies around the Plaza de Armas offer trips to local sites and further (eg Kuntur Wasi, Kuélap), trekking on Inca trails, riding *caballos de paso* and handicraft tours. Average prices: Kuntur Wasi

US$30, Cumbe Mayo, US$7.55, Ventanillas de Otusco US$6, Porcón US$6.

Asociación Civil para el Rescate del Ecosistema de Cajamarca, Aprec, Av Manco Cápac 1098, Baños del Inca, T894600, www.aprec.org. The association, sponsored by Pro Aves Perú, Hotel Laguna Seca and Yanacocha mines, aims to "restore the ecological health" of the Cajamarca region, including the preservation of the endangered Grey-bellied Comet hummingbird (*cometa ventigris*); four Inca trail loops for hikers.

Atahualpa Inca Tours, La Mar 435, T367014 (in Hostal El Mirador), www.nunura.com/elmirador.

Cajamarca Tours, Dos de Mayo 323, T362813 (also DHL, Western Union and flight reconfirmations).

Clarín Tours, Del Batán 161, T/F366829, www.clarintours.com.

Cumbemayo Tours, Amalia Puga 635 on the plaza, T362938, cumbemayotours@ usa.net. Guides in English and French.

Inca Baths Tours, Amalia Puga 667, T364310, incablaz@hotmail.com.

Socio Adventures, Ben Eastwood, Pje Chota 123, Dpto 1A, Urb Ramón Castilla, Cajamarca, T341118, or contact via www.socioadventures.com. They offer a Stove Trek Tour, where you donate materials and help a local family build a cooking stove while taking a 5-day, 5-night guided tour of the area. You stay at their lodge called the *Blur Poncho* near Chota, excellent food and accommodation.

⊖ Transport

Huamachuco *p1152*
Bus From **Trujillo**, 170 km, 6 hrs, US$4.55-5.50: **Horna** (San Martín 875, T441070) 4 a day, **Mercedes** (Av 10 de Julio 766, T441582), **Tunesa/Negreiros** (Balta y Suárez), 0900, 1300. To **Cajabamba**, Trans Los Andes, Psje Hospital 109, 3 combis a day, 3 hrs, US$2.50.

Cajabamba *p1152*
Bus To/from **Cajamarca**, US$3, 4 hrs, several companies; combis 3 hrs, US$3.50.

Cajamarca *p1152, map p1155*
Air To/from **Lima**: **Aerocóndor** (Dos de Mayo 323, T365674) daily, and **LC Busre** (Comercio 1024, T076-361098), daily except Sat. Airport 3 km from town; taxi US$1.50, mototaxi US$0.75.
Bus Buses in town charge US$0.15. To **Lima**, 856 km, 12-14 hrs, *económico* US$9-12, to

US$21-24.25 on **Civa**'s double-deckers, to US$27-33 for **Cruz del Sur**'s luxury service (includes taxi to your lodging in Lima), several buses daily. The road is paved. To **Pacasmayo**, 189 km, 5-6 hrs, US$7, several buses and hourly colectivos. To **Trujillo**, 296 km, 6½ hrs, US$4.55-10, regular buses daily 0900-2230 most continue to Lima. To **Chiclayo**, 260 km, 6 hrs, US$4.55-9, several buses daily; you have to change buses to go on to Piura and Tumbes. To **Celendín**, 112 km, 4 hrs, US$3, at 0700 and 1300 (**Atahualpa**), 0900 (**Royal Palace's**, poor minibuses). The route follows a fairly good dirt road through beautiful countryside. Among the bus companies are: **Atahualpa**, Atahualpa 299, T363060 (Lima, Celendín, Cajabamba); **Civa**, Ayacucho 753, T361460 (Lima); **Cruz del Sur**, Atahualpa 600, T361737 (Lima). **Emtrafesa**, Atahualpa 299, T369663 (to Trujillo); **Línea**, Atahualpa 318, T363956 (Lima, Trujillo, Chiclayo). **Rojas**, Atahualpa 405, T360548 (to Cajabamba, buses not coming from Lima); **Royal Palace's**, Atahualpa 339, T365855 (Lima, Trujillo, Celendín); **Tepsa**, Sucre 594, T076-363306 (Lima); **Turismo Días**, Sucre 422, T368289 (to Lima, Chimbote, Trujillo, Chiclayo).
Taxi US$0.60 within city limits. Mototaxis US$0.30.

❶ Directory

Cajamarca *p1152, map p1155*
Banks BCP, Apurímac 719. Changes Amex TCs without commission, cash advance on Visa, Mascercard and Amex, 0.5% commission, Visa and Mastercard ATM. Scotiabank, Amazonas 750. Accepts Amex Tcs with commission, cash advance and ATM for Visa and Mastercard. Interbank, 2 de Mayo 546, on Plaza. Accepts Visa TCs without commission if paid in soles, US$5 if in dollars, Visa, Mastercard, Amex ATM. Telebanco 24 Horas ATM (Visa) at the gas station next to Cial buses on Av Atahualpa. Dollars can be changed in most banks and travel agencies on east side of Plaza, but euros hard to change. Casa de cambio in Casa del Artefacto musical and electrical store at Amazonas 537. Good rates, cash only. Casas de cambio also at Jr del Comercio y Apurímac and at Amalia Puga 673. Street changers on Jr Del Batán by the Plaza de Armas and at Del Batán y Amazonas.
Internet There are cabins everywhere, US$0.35 per hr. **Post offices** Serpost, Amalia Puga 778. Open 0800-2045. **Telephones** Public phone offices can be found all over the centre.

Chachapoyas Region

Cajamarca is a convenient starting point for the trip east to the province of Amazonas, which contains the archaeological riches of the Chachapoyans, also known as Sachupoyans. Here lie the great pre-Inca cities of Vilaya (not yet developed for tourism), Cerro Olán and the immense fortress of Kuélap, among many others. The road is in terrible condition to Chachapoyas, and barely passable in the rainy season because of landslides. It follows a winding course through the north Andes, crossing the wide and deep canyon of the Río Marañón at Balsas. The road climbs steeply with superb views of the mountains and the valleys below. The fauna and flora are spectacular as the journey alternates between high mountains and low rainforest.

Celendín → *Phone code: 076. Colour map 3, grid B2.*
East from Cajamarca, this is the first town of note, with a pleasant plaza and cathedral. Festival 16 July (Virgen del Carmen). There is also an interesting local market on Sunday where you can buy cheap sandals and saddlebags. The **Museo Cultural Huauco** in the nearby village of Sucre ① *Bolívar 211, T552096*, is interesting for local history (friendly curator).

Leymebamba and around
There are plenty of ruins around this pleasant town, many of them covered in vegetation. The *Comité Turístico* on the plaza is the place to go for all information on how to reach sites, including Laguna de los Cóndores (see below), for guides and horse hire. See www.leymebamba.org.

La Congona, a Chachapoyan site, is well worth the effort, with stupendous views. It consists of three hills: on the easterly, conical hill, the ruins are clustered in a small area, impossible to see until you are right above them. The other hills have been levelled. La Congona is the best preserved of three sites, with 30 round stone houses (some with evidence of three storeys) and a watch tower. The two other sites, El Molinete and Pumahuanyuna, are nearby. It is a brisk three hours' walk from Leymebamba along a clearly marked trail which starts at the end of the street with the hotels. All three sites can be visited in a day but a guide is advisable; ask in the Comité Turístico.

At **Laguna de los Cóndores**, in 1996, a spectacular site consisting of six burial *chullpas*, containing 219 mummies and vast quantities of ceramics, textiles, woodwork, *quipus* and everyday utensils from the late Inca period, was discovered near a beautiful lake in a jungle setting. The trip to Laguna de los Cóndores takes 10-12 hrs on foot and horseback from Leymebamba, nine hours return. All the material was moved to a new **museum** at San Miguel ① *Tue-Sun 0930-1630, US$4.35, http://centromallqui.org.pe for information*, 3 km south of Leymebamba: 30-40 minutes' walk, take the footpath and ask directions constantly, the road is much longer. It is beautifully laid-out, very informative and has a café.

The road to Chachapoyas (being paved) crosses the Utcubamba River, passes through **Palmira** and heads north. Before Puente Santo Tomás there is a turn-off which heads east beyond **Duraznopampa** to the small town of **Montevideo** (basic *hospedaje*). Another Chachapoyan site is **Cerro Olán**, reached by colectivo to San Pedro de Utac, a small village beyond Montevideo, then a 30 minute walk. From the Plaza a clear trail rises directly into the hills east of town to the ruins, which can be seen from the village. Here are the remains of towers which some archaeologists claim had roofs like mediaeval European castles.

Further north are the towns of **Yerbabuena** and **Puente Santo Tomás**, which is at the turn-off for the burial *chullpas* of **Revash**, of the Revash culture (AD 1250).

The attractive town of **Jalca Grande** (or La Jalca as it is known locally), at 2,800 m, lies between Montevideo and Tingo, up on the east side of the main valley. In the town itself, one block west of the Plaza de Armas, is the interesting and well-preserved Chachapoyan habitation of **Choza Redonda**, which was inhabited until 1964. There is one very basic *hostal*, otherwise ask the mayor. Take a torch.

Tingo → *Phone code: 041. Colour map 3, grid B2. Altitude: 1,800 m.*
Situated in the Utcubamba valley, 25 km from Leymebamba, 37 km south of Chachapoyas by road, much of this village was washed away in the floods of 1993. About 3½ km above Tingo in the hills is **Tingo Nuevo**. There is a petrol station here, the only one between Celendín and Chachapoyas.

Kuélap → *Altitude: 3,000 m.*

ⓘ *0800-1700, US$3 (50% discount for students with identification).*

Kuélap is a spectacular pre-Inca walled city which was re-discovered in 1843. It was built over a period of 200 years, from AD 900 to 1100 and contained three times more stone than the Great Pyramid at Giza in Egypt. The site lies along the summit of a mountain crest, more than 1 km in length. The massive stone walls, 585 m long by 110 m wide at their widest, are as formidable as those of any pre-Columbian city. Some reconstruction has taken place, mostly of small houses and walls, but the majority of the main walls on both levels are original, as is the inverted, cone-shaped dungeon. The structures have been left in their cloud forest setting, the trees covered in bromeliads and moss, the flowers visited by hummingbirds. Guides are available; pay them what you think appropriate. In 2005-2006 a huge restoration programme was undertaken at Kuélap, with furhter funding destined for other Chachapoyan sites. A small Centro de Interpretaciones is open 0800-1630; it has a good model of the site. There is also a toilet block. The ruins are locked; the guardian, Gabriel Portocarrero, has the keys and accompanies visitors, and is very informative.

Chachapoyas → *Phone code: 041. Colour map 3, grid B2. Population: 25,000. Altitude: 2,234 m.*

The capital of the Department of Amazonas, founded in 1538, was an important crossroads between coast and jungle until the 1940s. Archaeological and ecological tourism in the 1990s is slowly bringing in new economic benefits. The modern cathedral stands on the spacious Plaza de Armas. **INC Museum** ⓘ *Ayacucho 904, Mon-Fri 0800-1300, 1400-1645, free*, contains a small collection of artefacts and mummies in display cases, with explanations in Spanish. **Tourist offices:** i perú ⓘ *Jr Ortiz 588, Plaza de Armas, Chachapoyas, T477292, iperuchachapoyas@promperu.gob.pe, Mon-Sat 0800-1300, 1500-1900.* **Dirección Regional de Turismo** ⓘ *Grau 640, T041-478355, www.chachapoyasonline.com, www.regionamazonas.gob.pe.* Another useful site is *http://camayocperu.com/lerche.htm* of the German ethnologist, Doctor Peter Lerche.

Huancas ⓘ *colectivos leave from Jr Ortiz Arrieta y Libertad; 20 min, US$0.60 (0700-1800),* which produces rustic pottery, can be reached by a two-hour walk on the airport road. Walk uphill from Huancas for a magnificent view into the deep canyon of the Río Sonche.

Levanto was built by the Spaniards and was their first capital of the area, directly on top of the previous Chachapoyan structures. The church dates from 1538. Although the capital was moved to Chachapoyas a few years later, Levanto retained its importance for a while, but is now an unspoilt colonial village overlooking the massive canyon of the Utcubamba River. Kuélap can, on a clear day, be seen on the other side of the rift. There are two small bar-bodegas in the village. A 30-minute walk from Levanto are the partly cleared ruins of **Yalape**, which seems to have been a massive residential complex, extending over many hectares. The local people will guide you to the ruins. It is due to be restored, as is the trekking route on prehispanic roads to Kuélap.

East of Chachapoyas

On the road to Mendoza via Pipus and Cheto are the pre-Inca ruins of **Monte Peruvia** (known locally as Purunllacta), hundreds of white stone houses with staircases, temples and palaces. The ruins have been cleared by local farmers and some houses have been destroyed. The ruins are two-hour walk from Cheto. A guide is useful as there are few locals of whom to ask directions. If you get stuck in Pipus, ask to sleep at restaurant *Huaracina* or the police station next door. There are no hotels in Cheto but a house high up on the hill above the town with a balcony has cheap bed and board. The same family also has a house on the Plaza.

The road east from Chachapoyas continues on to **Mendoza**, the starting point of an ethnologically interesting area in the Guayabamba Valley, where there is a high incidence of fair-skinned people.

Northwest of Chachapoyas

On a turn-off on the road 37 km from Chachapoyas to Pedro Ruíz, is **Lamud**, which is a convenient base for several interesting sites, such as San Antonio and Pueblo de los Muertos. About 20 minutes' drive south of Lamud, on the same road, is the village of **Luya**. From here, more sites can be reached: **Chipuric** and **Karajía**, where remarkable, 2½-m high sarcophagi set into an impressive cliff face overlook the valley (entry at Karajía US$1; mototaxi to sarcophagi US$1.65 round trip). In a lush canyon, 1½ hours' walk from the road to Luya is

Wanglic, a funeral site with large circular structures built under a ledge. Nearby is a beautiful waterfall, a worthwhile excursion. Ask for directions in Luya. Best to take a local guide (US$3.50-5 a day). Buses and combis to Lamud and Luya are listed under Chachapoyas, Transport. The road is unpaved but in reasonable condition.

● Sleeping

Celendín *p1158*

F Hostal Celendín, Unión 305, Plaza de Armas, T555041. Hot water, TV, pleasant, good restaurant.

F Loyer's, José Gálvez 410, T555210. Cheaper without bath, patio, nice.

F Naranja Mecánica (Orange), Jr Unió 217, T555640, Celendín, www.celendinperu.com. New Dutch-Peruvian owned hostal in the centre, small, bed and breakfast, shared bath, also with a café with a set-price menu (open Wed-Sun 1500-2100, vegetarians catered for), book exchange.

G Maxmar, Dos de Mayo 349. Cheaper without bath, hot shower extra, basic, clean, parking, good value, owner Francisco is very helpful.

G Raymi Wasi, Jr José Gálvez, beside La Reserve, T555374. With bath, hot water, TV, large rooms, has patio, quiet, clean, parking, good value.

Leymebamba *p1158*

D Hostal La Casona, Jr Amazonas 223, Leymebamba, T830106, www.lacasonadeleymebamba.com. With bath, hot water, breakfast available on request.

E Hostal La Petaca, Jr Amazonas 461, opposite the church, T770288. With bath, hot water.

E Laguna de los Cóndores, Jr Amazonas, half a block from plaza, T770208, www.chachapoyasperu.com.pe/hostallagunadeloscondores.htm. Cheaper without bath, warm water, a good choice.

Tingo *p1158*

F pp Albergue León, Jr Saenz Peña s/n, no sign, walk 50 m from police checkpoint to corner and turn left, it's the third house on left (right-hand door), T999390. Basic, run by Lucho León, who is very knowledgeable.

Kuélap *p1159*

Walking up from Tingo, the last house to the right of the track (**El Bebedero**) offers very basic rooms with bed, breakfast and evening meal from US$6, friendly, helpful). The **Instituto Nacional de Cultura** (INC) hostel is 100 m below the ruins, with a dorm for 12, US$1.75 pp, no running water, lovely setting, simple meals. Free camping.

Choctámal

C Marvelous Spatuletail Lodge, 3 km outside village, T041-478078 (in USA 1-866-396-9582), www.marvelousspatuletail.com. Check beforehand at Chachapoyas Tours, address below. Heated rooms, hot showers, hot tub, telescope for nighttime star-gazing. All meals extra, US$4-8. Treks to ruins can be arranged, good chance to see the endangered Marvelous Spatuletail hummingbird.

Chachapoyas *p1159, map p1161*

C Gran Vilaya, Ayacucho 755, T477664, vilaya@wayna.rcp.net.pe. The best in town, comfortable rooms with firm beds, parking, English spoken, all services.

D Casa Vieja, Chincha Alta 569, T477353, www.casaviejaperu.com. In a converted old house, very nicely decorated, family atmosphere, hot water, cable TV, *comedor*, continental breakfast, internet and library. Recommended.

D Casona Monsante, Jr Amazonas 746, T477702, www.casonamonsante.com. Converted elegant colonial house with patio, cable TV, cafeteria, breakfast US$1.50.

E Belén, Jr Ortiz Arrieta 540, T477830, www.hostalbelen.com.pe. On the plaza, modern, hot water, nicely furnished.

E Kuélap, Amazonas 1057, T477136, www.hotelkuelap.com. Hot water, cheaper without TV, cheaper still with shared bath and cold water, basic breakfast, parking.

E Puma Urcu, Jr Amazonas 833, T477871, hotelpumaurcu@peru.com. Modern, carpeted rooms, hot water, cable TV, *Café Café* next door, both hotel and café receive good reports.

E Revash, Grau 517, Plaza de Armas, T477391. Hot showers, patio, helpful, laundry, sells local items, good local information, restaurant, local tours sold. Recommended.

F El Dorado, Ayacucho 1062, T477047. Hot water, helpful.

F Tourist Complex Chacha, Grau 534, Plaza de Armas, T477654. On 1st floor, same entrance as restaurant, electric shower, laundry, OK.

G Hostal El Danubio, Tres Esquinas 193 y Junín 584, Plazuela Belén, some distance from centre, T477337. Hot water, cheaper with shared bath and cold water, meals can be ordered in advance.

G Hostal Johumaji, Ayacucho 711, T477279, olvacha@ddm.com.pe. Hot water, cell-like, basic, cheaper without TV, meals extra.

G Laguna de los Cóndores, Salamanca 941, T477492. Very basic, shared bath, cold water.

Levanto *p1159*

F pp **Levanto Lodge**, kuelap@msn.com. **G** pp
with own sleeping bag; hot shower, lounge with
fireplace and kitchen, meals US$1.

Northwest of Chachapoyas *p1159*

D **Hostal Kuélap**, Garcilaso de la Vega 452, on
the plaza, Lamud. Cheaper without bath or hot
water, basic. A few doors down is **Restaurant
María**, cheap, excellent value, popular, the
owner's son is a good local guide and charges
around US$10 per day.

🍴 Eating

Celendín *p1158*

🍴-🍴 **La Reserve**, José Gálvez 313.
Good quality and value.
🍴 **Bella Aurora**, Gran 485. Good food.
🍴 **Jalisco**, Jr Unión, on plaza. Good value breakfasts
and other meals, but beware of overcharging.

Leymebamba *p1158*

🍴 **Cely Pizza's**, Jr La Verdad 530, 2 blocks from
Plaza de Armas, opposite the health centre.
Good value, 2-course set meals for US$2.50,
regional food, pizzas take 20 mins unless you
book in advance, vegetarian meals at 24 hrs
notice, great for breakfast.
🍴 **El Sabor Tropical**, 16 de Julio. Good
chicken and chips, friendly.

Tingo *p1158*

Restaurant Kuélap, at the junction of the
main road with the road on the south bank
of the Río Tingo. Two other eating places.

Chachapoyas *p1159, map p1161*

🍴-🍴 **Chacha**, Grau 534, Plaza de Armas. Good
quality, nice atmosphere.
🍴 **Chifa Chuy Xien**, Amazonas 848. Authentic
Chinese, daily specials and à la carte.
🍴 **El Edén**, Grau y Ayacucho. Vegetarian, good,
large helpings, open by 0830, closed Sat pm.
🍴 **Kuélap**, Ayacucho 832. Good food.
🍴 **Mari Pizza**, Ayacucho 912. Serves good pizza.
🍴 **Matalache**, Amazonas y Grau. Good and
very popular, huge portions.

Chachapoyas

To Capilla de la Virgen Asunta (500m)
To Airport
To Pozo de Yanayacu (500m)
Jr Santa Ana
Quebrada Santa Lucía
Jr Libertad
To Mirador Guayamil (300m)
Santa Domingo
Chincha Alta
BCP
Palacio Municipal
Plaza de Armas
INC
Banco de la Nación
Cathedral
Jr Ortiz Arrieta
Jr Grau
Jr 2 de Mayo
Jr Triunfo
Jr La Merced
Jr Amazonas
Jr Unión
Jr Ayacucho
Jr Recreo
Jr Salamanca
Jr Junín
To

N
0 metres 200
0 yards 200

Sleeping
Belén **1** *A1*
Casa Vieja **2** *A1*
Casona Monsante **12** *B2*
El Dorado **3** *A1*
Gran Vilaya **5** *B2*
Hostal El Danubio **7** *B1*
Johumaji **8** *B2*

Kuélap **9** *B1*
Laguna de los
 Cóndores **10** *A2*
Puma Urcu &
 Café Café **13** *B2*
Revash **11** *B2*
Tourist Complex
 Chacha **4** *B2*

Eating 🍴
Chacha **1** *B2*
Chifa Chuy Xien **3** *B2*
Dulcería Santa Helena **11** *B2*

El Edén **5** *A2*
Kuélap **4** *B2*
Las Rocas **6** *A2*
La Tushpa **2** *B1*
Mari Pizza **10** *A2*
Mass Burguer **7** *B1*
Matalache **8** *B2*
Panadería San José **9** *B2*

Transport 🚌
Cars to Bagua Grande **7** *A2*
Cars to Pedro Ruiz **2** *A2*
Colectivos to Huancas **1** *A2*

Combis to Leymebamba **4** *B2*
Comité Interprovincial
 Santo Tomás & Trans
 Rollers combis **6** *A2*
San Juan de Luya
 Combis **8** *A2*
Trans Zelada **9** *A2*
Turismo Kuélap **10** *A1*
Virgen del Carmen **11** *A3*

Panadería San José, Ayacucho 816. Good breakfasts and other meals, good regional snacks.
Las Rocas, Ayacucho 932 on Plaza. Popular, local dishes, open Sun evening.
Tinkuy Wasi, Prolongación Jr Kuélap, Barrio Santa Rosa, above El Mirador del Colorado. Very good regional food, in a country setting above town, lovely views.
La Tushpa, Jr Ortiz Arrieta 753. Open for lunch and dinner. The best in town, international food, good meats, *platos criollos*, wine list, spotless kitchen. Recommended.
Dulcería Santa Helena, Amazonas 800. Very good for desserts.
Mass Burguer, Ortiz Arrieta, Plaza de Armas. Excellent juices, cakes, fruit salads.

▲ Activities and tours

Chachapoyas *p1159, map p1161*
Tours in the surrounding area include: city tour, Levanto, Yalape (0800-1530, US$8.65), Kuélap (see page 1159), Karajía, La Jalca, Leymebamba (all full day, US$12-20, depending on distance and number of passengers, including guide and food), Revash (by vehicle to Santo Tomás, then 2-hr hike), Gran Vilaya or Laguna de los Cóndores (4-5 days each, depending on size of group), Mendoza (groups of 6 to 8).
Andes Tours, address as **Hostal Revash**. Daily trips to Kuélap, other conventional tours to ruins and caves in the area and trekking to Gran Vilaya, Laguna de los Cóndores, etc, combining travel by car, on horseback and walking.
Chachapoyas Tours, Grau 534, Plaza Armas, p 2 (Tourist Complex Chacha), T478078, www.kuelapperu.com, or in the USA T1-866-396-9582, Int T001-407-583 6786. Reliable, with 20 years' experience, benefitting local communities, multilingual staff and guides, good service. Recommended.
Vilaya Tours, c/o Gran Hotel Vilaya, Jr Grau 624, T477506, www.vilayatours.com. All-inclusive area treks throughout northern Peru catering to international clientele, mostly booked from abroad.
Guides: Robert Dover is British, contact him through **Vilaya Tours**. Vilaya Tours has a regular newsletter and also work in conjunction with community projects. Recommended. **Martín Chumbi**, contact through Chachapoyas Tours.

◎ Transport

Celendín *p1158*
Bus To **Cajamarca**, 107 km, 4-5 hrs: with **Atahualpa**, 2 de Mayo 707, Plaza de Armas, T555256, at 0700 and 1300 daily, US$3; **Royal Palace's**, Jr Unión 333, Plaza de

Armas, at 0645 and 1300 daily, poor minibuses, US$3. To **Chachapoyas** via Balsas and Leymebamba, 12-15 hrs (may be much longer in the rainy season, take warm clothing, food and water): **Virgen del Carmen**, Cáceres 117, on Sun and Thu at 1100, US$11. Other local transport leaves from the market area.

Leymebamba *p1158*
Bus From **Chachapoyas** to **Celendín** pass Leymebamba about 3½ hrs after departure; no guarantee of a seat. There are also combis, minibuses and trucks.

Jalca Grande *p1158*
Combis from **Chachapoyas** at about 1300 daily (except Sat); 3½ hrs, US$3.65; return from La Jalca at 0500 daily.

Tingo *p1158*
For transport from **Chachapoyas** to Tingo, see Chachapoyas, Transport. Several combis (from 0500) daily to Chachapoyas. Tingo to **Leymebamba** takes 2 hrs, US$1.75.

Kuélap *p1159*
There are 4 options: 1) Take a tour from Chachapoyas. 2) Hire a vehicle with driver in Chachapoyas, US$35 per vehicle. 3) Take a combi from Chachapoyas to María or Quisongo, or to Choctámal, the mid-point on the 36 km tortuous road from Tingo to Kuélap (see under Chachapoyas for details). You can stay in Choctámal with a family or at the lodge (see above), then walk 19 km (4-5 hrs) along the road to the site. In María there are several hospedajes, **G** pp with hot water. Alternatively, go early from Chachapoyas to Tingo, hike up to Kuélap then walk down to María (2-3 hrs) and spend the night there. 4) Take a combi from Chachapoyas to Tingo, spend the night, then take the 3½-4 hrs' strenuous walk uphill from Tingo; take waterproof, food and drink, and start early as it gets very hot. Only the fit should try to ascend and descend in one day on foot. In the rainy season it is advisable to wear boots; at other times it is hot and dry (take all your water with you as there is nothing on the way up).

Chachapoyas *p1159, map p1161*
Air It is hoped that flights to Chachapoyas will resume in 2007, after improvements to the airport's radar.
Bus To **Chiclayo** (10 hrs), **Trujillo** and **Lima** (22 hrs), the best option is **Móvil**, Libertad 464, T478545, to Lima 1230 daily, US$24; to Trujillo 2000 daily, US$12, to Chiclayo US$10.60, on either schedule. **Zelada**, Jr Ortiz Arrieta 310, to Lima, 1100 daily, US$20. **Civa**, San Juan de la Libertad

956, T478048, to Lima at 1230, US$17-27; to Chiclayo, 1800 daily, US$9-10.60. **Turismo Kuélap**, Ortiz Arrieta 412, T478128, to Chiclayo, at 1700 daily, US$9. To **Celendín**, Virgen del Carmen, Av Salamanca 650, on Tue and Fri at 0600, 12-15 hrs (or more), US$11. To **Pedro Ruíz**, for connections to Chiclayo or Tarapoto, combis (US$2.15, 2 hrs, 0800-1800) and cars (US$3, 1¾ hrs) leave from Grau y Salamanca and also from Ortiz Arrieta and Libertad. To **Bagua Grande**, 0430-1800, cars US$6, 3 hrs, from Grau 355 y Libertad. To **Mendoza** (86 km), **Trans Zelada**, 1600 daily, US$3.65, 3½ hrs; cars 0400-2000, from Ortiz Arrieta, cuadra 3 (uphill from Zelada), US$4.55, 3 hrs. For **Kuélap**, Roller's, Grau 302, combis or cars, at 0400 and 1430, from Kuélap to Chacha at 1200 and 1700. **Kuélap** US$3.65, 3 hrs; **Choctámal**, US$2.50; **Yumal** US$3.65, 3 hrs; **María** US$3, 2½ hrs; **Lónguita** US$2.42, 2 hrs; **Tingo** US$1.50, 1½ hrs. Combis to **Tingo** from Grau y Salamanca, US$2.25, 1½ hrs. To **Santo Tomás**: Comité Interprovincial Santo Tomás, Grau, by the cul-de-sac between Salamanca and Libertad, 0800-1600, Santo Tomás, US$2.75, 3 hrs; Cruce de Revash US$2.75, 2½ hrs; Tingo US$2.25, 1½ hrs. To **Leymebamba**, combis and small buses from 2 de Mayo y Libertad, 1200, 1600 (also from cuadra 8 of Libertad), US$3, 2½ hrs. To **Jalca Grande**, Comité Interprovincial Santo Tomás, departures about 1300 onwards (few if any on Sat), US$3.65 (return in morning). To **Luya** and **Lamud**, from **San Juan de Luya**, Ortiz Arrieta 364, cars 0400-2000, US$2.25, 1 hr to Lamud, same price to Luya. Taxis may be hired from the Plaza for any local destination.

Levanto *p1159*
Levanto is 2 hrs by truck or 6 hrs walk from **Chachapoyas** (3-4 hrs back). Trucks leave from the market in Chachapoyas most days at 0600, US$1; trucks and combis from outside Bodega El Amigo on Jr Hermosura at 1400. The nicest way to get there is by the Inca Road, 4-5 hrs. Take the road out of Chachapoyas for 40 mins, then take the stone path on the left. It is in pretty good shape, with one 15-m long stone stairway in excellent condition. A taxi from Chachapoyas to Levanto and back, including driver waiting while you look around, is US$14.50.

Monte Peruvia/Purunllacta *p1159*
There is no direct transport from Chachapoyas. Take a combi at 0930 and 1500 from Jr Salamanca, 4th block down from market, to Pipus, at the turn-off to Cheto; 1½ hrs, US$1.35. A camioneta leaves Pipus for Cheto early morning, US$0.90; or a 2 hr walk on a rough road.

❶ Directory

Chachapoyas *p1159, map p1161*
Banks BCP, Ortiz Arrieta 576, on plaza, gives cash on Visa card, changes cash and TCs, Visa ATM. No Mastercard ATM or agent. There are two well-signed places on Ayacucho, Plaza de Armas, which change cash. **Internet** Many places around the plaza and elsewhere, US$0.45 per hr. **Post offices** Grau on Plaza de Armas. **Telephones** Ayacucho 926, Plaza de Armas, and Grau 608.

Chachapoyas to the Amazon

From Chachapoyas the road heads north through the beautiful river canyon for 2-3 hours to a crossroads, **Pedro Ruíz** (three hotels; basic restaurants), where you return to the coast or continue to Yurimaguas, making the spectacular descent from high Andes to high jungle. The road, which goes through **Rioja** (198 km, with basic hotels) is paved as far as Tarapoto. In the rainy season, the road may be subject to landslides. Near Pedro Ruíz is the **Gocta**, or Amazon Slopes Waterfall (771 m), third highest in the world (or 5th, or 14th, according to various ratings). It's about 2 hours' walk away, set in beautiful cloud forest with many monkeys and other wildlife. Local tour operators offer tours, but beware overcharging.

Moyobamba → *Phone code: 042. Colour map 3, grid B2. Population: 14,000. Altitude: 915 m.*
Moyobamba, capital of San Martín department, is a pleasant town, in the attractive Río Mayo valley. The area is renowned for its orchids and there is a Festival de la Orquídea over three days around 1 November. Among several places to see orchids is **Orquideario Wakanki** ① *0900- 1700, US$0.60*, where the plants have been placed in trees. Just beyond are **Baños Termales San Mateo**, ① *5 km southeast, 0500-2200, US$0.30*, which are worth a visit. There are **sulphur baths** ① *6.5 km west, 0500-1800, US$0.30*, at Oromina. **Puerto Tahuishco** is the town's harbour, a pleasant walk seven blocks north of the centre, where boat trips can be taken. **Morro de Calzada** ① *free, signed 15 km by mototaxi*, is an isolated outcrop in white sand forest, good for birdwatching. Turn right at town of Calzada on the

Moyobamba-Rioja road and ask for the track. A path leads to the top and a look out; you can go over top and down other side.

Tourist offices: Dircetur ① *Jr San Martín 301, on the plaza, T562043, www.turismo sanmartin.com*. Helpful, some leaflets and a map. **Oficina Municipal de Información** ① *Jr Pedro Canga 262, T562191, www.munimoyobamba.gob.pe, Tue-Sun 0900-1300, 1600-2000*, very helpful. Information on excursions and hikes is available from the **Instituto Nacional de Cultura** ① *Jr Benavides 352, Mon-Fri 0800-1300, 1400-1700*, which also has a small departmental museum.

Tarapoto → *Phone code: 042. Colour map 3, grid B2. Altitude: 500 m.*

Tarapoto is a very friendly place, eager to embrace tourism and agricultural development with a good local market 1½ blocks from Plaza de Armas on Av Raimondi. **Información turística** office at the Municipalidad ① *Jr Gregorio Delgado 260, open 0730-1330, 1500-1800* and Dircetur ① *Jr Angel Delgado Morey, cuadra 1, T522567, tarapoto@mincetur.gob.pe*. The 109 km from Moyobamba to Tarapoto is heavily used by trucks, with fuel and meals available. At 35 km from Tarapoto towards Moyobamba a road leads off to **Lamas** where there is a small **museum** ① *US$0.60, custodian will show you round*, with exhibits on local indigenous community (Lamistas). In the town, **Rolly's** ① *San Martín 925, just off the plaza*, serves good food, Rolly is friendly. Take a colectivo from Tarapoto, 30 minutes, US$0.85, from Paradero Lamas on road to Moyobamba (take mototaxi from centre, US$0.45).

About 15 km from Tarapoto on the spectacular road to Yurimaguas are the 50-m falls of **Ahuashiyacu** ① *US$0.65, toilets US$0.15, can be visited by tour from Tarapoto (US$4.50 by mototaxi)*. This is a popular place at lunchtimes and weekends. There are many other waterfalls in the area.

On the road to Yurimaguas, 20 minutes after Ahuashiyacu, there is a tunnel (stop at the police control for birdwatching, mototaxi US$6), after which you descend through beautiful forest perched on rocky cliffs to Pongo de Caynarachi (several basic *comedores*), where the flats start and the road widens and improves. Note that the route is prone to hold-ups and travellers should only during daylight hours.

● Sleeping

Moyobamba *p1163*

B Puerto Mirador, Jr Sucre, 1 km from centre, T/F562050, www.barrioperu.terra.com.pe. Includes breakfast, nice location, lovely grounds and river views, pool, good restaurant.
C-D Marcoantonio, Jr Pedro Canga 488, T/F562045, www.altomayoperu.com. Smartest in town centre, includes breakfast, hot water, TV, restaurant.
D La Casona, Alonso de Alvarado 682, T563858. Nicely refurbished old home, lovely courtyard with orchids, comfortable rooms, includes breakfast. Recommended.
E Hostal Atlanta, Alonso De Alvarado 865, T562063. Hot water (**F** without), TV, fan, good but noisy, no breakfast.
F Hostal Cobos, Jr Pedro Canga 404, T562153. With bath, cold water, simple but good.
F Hostal Country Club, Manuel del Aguila 667, T562110. Hot water, comfortable, garden, has travel agency. Recommended.
F Hostal Royal, Alonso de Alvarado 784, T562662, F562564. Hot water, TV, laundry, café.

Tarapoto *p1164*

A Puerto Palmeras, Carretera F Belaúnde Terry Km 614, T524100, www.puertopalmeras.com.

Some distance from town on Juanjui road, nice grounds, with horses, lake has a monkey island, pet parrots, poolside bar. Good restaurant, nice rooms with TV, hot water, helpful staff, favours birdwatching. Resorts in the same group at Pomacochas and Yuirmaguas.
B Nilas, Jr Moyobamba 173, T527331, http://inka web.tripod.com/nilas.html. Modern, breakfast, hot water, a/c, TV, fridge, internet access, pool, jacuzzi, gym, airport transfer, very well appointed.
B Río Shilcayo, Pasaje Las Flores 224, 1 km east of town in La Banda de Shilcayo, T522225 (in Lima T447 9359). Excellent meals, non-residents can use the swimming pool for a fee.
C Lily, Jiménez Pimentel 405-407, T523154, F522394. Hot water, a/c, TV, includes breakfast and tax, laundry, sauna, restaurant.
D La Posada Inn, San Martín 146, T522234, laposada@terra.com.pe. Central, comfortable, hot water, fridge, TV, some rooms with a/c, nice atmosphere, breakfast and lunch.
E El Mirador, Jr San Pablo de la Cruz 517, T522177. 5 blocks uphill from the plaza, cold water, fan, TV, very welcoming, laundry facilities, breakfast (US$2) and hammocks on roof terrace with good views, also offers tours. Recommended.

F Edinson, Av Raimondi y Maynas, 10 m from Plaza Mayor, T523997, T/F524010. Cheaper without bath and a/c, cold water, breakfast, comfortable, karaoke bars and disco.
G Hostal San Antonio, Jr Jiménez Pimentel 126, T522226. With TV, fan, courtyard, no breakfast. Noisy but recommended.
G pp Alojamiento Santa Juanita, Av Salaverry 602, Morales (20 mins from centre). Good beds, fan, family run, English spoken, safe.

⊙ Eating

Moyobamba *p1163*
♥♥ La Olla de Barro, Pedro Canga y S Filomeno. Typical food, the most expensive but still good value. Open for breakfast. Also owns ♥♥ **La Tullpa de Mamá**, at Punta de Tahuishco.
♥ La Buena Salud, off Jr Callao, block 8. Opposite the market, vegetarian set meals and à la carte.
♥ Edén, down the stairs at the end of Jr San Martín, 1 block from the Plaza de Armas. Vegetarian.
♥ Rocky's, Pedro Canga 402. Typical food, good, has cheap *menú*. Open for breakfast.

Tarapoto *p1164*
♥♥ Real Grill, on Moyobamba on the Plaza. One of the best in town, but expensive.
♥ Helados Regionales La Muyuna, Jr Ramón Castilla 271. Good natural ice cream and drinks made with jungle fruits, 0900-2300 except closed Fri from 1800 and Sat until 1815.
♥ El Maguaré, Jr Moyobamba corner Manco Cápac. Choice of set meals and à la carte, good food and service.

⊙ Transport

Chachapoyas to the Amazon *p1163*
Pedro Ruíz to Moyobamba Many buses to and from **Chiclayo**, **Tarapoto** (9-10 hrs) and **Chachapoyas** all pass through town. There is no way to reserve a seat and buses are usually full. Better to take combis (US$1.75) and cars (US$2.75) to **Bagua Grande**, 1½ hrs; to **Moyobamba** US$6, 4 hrs. Combis (US$2.15) and cars (US$3) also go to Chachapoyas, 2 hrs. Pedro Ruíz to **Nueva Cajamarca**, US$4.55 (combi), 2 hrs, then a further 20 mins, US$0.90 to **Rioja**. There are regular combis from Rioja to **Moyobamba** (21 km, US$0.90, 20 mins).

Moyobamba *p1163*
Bus Terminal Terrestre, about a dozen blocks from the centre on Av Grau, which leads out of town (mototaxi to the centre US$0.30). To **Tarapoto** (many companies including Tarapoto Tours, T563539, **Móvil**), US$3.60, 2 hrs. Buses en route from Tarapoto to Pedro Ruíz and Chiclayo

(US$7.60-15, 12 hrs) arrive at about 1030, but they will not sell you a ticket the day before if you are going to an intermediate destination such as Pedro Ruiz (US$6-7.60, 3½-4 hrs), they do take you if they have room when the bus arrives. **Combis** Transportes y Turismo **Selva**, Jr Callao entre Benavides y Varacadillo: to **Tarapoto** US$3, 2½ hrs. **Colectivos** Transportes y Turismo Cajamarca, Serafín Filomeno y Benavides, and **Empresa San Martín**, Benavides 276; to **Tarapoto**, US$6, 2 hrs, to **Rioja** US$0.90, 20 mins, to **Nueva Cajamarca**, US$1.50, 40 mins. There is no service direct to Pedro Ruiz or Yurimaguas unless you have enough people to fill a car.

Tarapoto *p1164*
Air US$3 per taxi airport to town, US$1.50 mototaxi (no bus service, but no problem to walk). To **Lima**, 1 hr, with **Lan**, Ramírez Hurtado, at the Plaza Mayor, daily, and **Star Perú** (San Pablo de la Cruz 100, T528765). **Wayra Perú** (Plaza Mayor 195, T531991) flies to Lima and Iquitos daily.
Bus To the west leave from Av Salaverry, Morales, 10 mins by mototaxi from the Plaza. Many companies to **Moyobamba**, 116 km, US$3.65, 2 hrs, **Pedro Ruíz**, US$7.20 (US$8.65 Tarapoto Tours and Paredes Estrella) 6 hrs, **Chiclayo**, 690 km, 12 hrs, US$18.20, **Trujillo**, 15 hrs, US$21.20, and **Lima**, 24 hrs, US$27.30-32 (all fares **Móvil**, Salaverry 858, other companies less). Combis to Moyobamba leave from **Turismo La Selva**, Av Salaverry. Cars to Moyobamba, US$6. Buses to **Yurimaguas** leave from the eastern side of Tarapoto, US$3.65, 7-8 hrs, several companies (same price by combi, 5 hrs); pick-ups, daily, US$4.55 in front, US$2.50 in the back; cars US$7.50.

⊙ Directory

Moyobamba *p1163*
Banks BCP, Alonso de Alvarado 903 y San Martín. ATM for Visa/Plus. **BBV Continental**, San Martín 494. **Novedades D'Valeria**, San Martín 481, good rates for cash.

Tarapoto *p1164*
Banks Scotiabank, Ramírez Hurtado y Grau, corner of Plaza. ATM for Plus/Visa and MasterCard/Maestro/Cirrus. **BBV Continental**, Ramírez Hurtado, Plaza Mayor, with Visa/Plus ATM. **Interbank**, Grau 119, near the Plaza, for MasterCard. Charges no commission on changing TCs for soles. La Inmaculada supermarket, Compagñón, just off Plaza, has *Global Net* ATM. **Internet** Several places in the centre.

Chachapoyas to Ecuador and the coast

The road from Pedro Ruiz (see page 1163) goes west to Bagua Grande and then follows the Río Chamaya. It climbs to the Abra de Porculla (2,150 m) before descending to join the old Pan-American Highway at Olmos (see page 1140). From Olmos you can go southwest to Chiclayo, or northwest to Piura. **Bagua Grande** is the first town of note heading west and a busy, dusty place with many hotels and restaurants on the main street.

To Ecuador

Some 50 km west of Bagua Grande, a road branches northwest at Chamaya to **Jaén** (*Phone code: 076. Colour map 3, grid B2. Population: 25,000*), a convenient stopover en route to the jungle. It is a modern city and a centre for growing rice. Festival, *Nuestro Señor de Huamantanga*, 14 September.

A road runs north to **San Ignacio** (109 km, being paved), near the border with Ecuador (*fiesta* 30 July, Semana Turística, third week in September). San Ignacio is a pleasant town with steep streets and a modern plaza in the centre of a coffee growing area. The nearby hills offer excursions to waterfalls, lakes, petroglyphs and ancient ruins. From San Ignacio the narrow, unpaved road runs 45 km through green hills to **Namballe**. Just to the north a dirt road goes west to the **Santuario Tabaconas-Namballe** ① *reserve office at San Martín 332, Jaén, T846166, snntabaconasnamballe@yahoo.es*, a 29,500-ha reserve, at 1,200-3,800 m protecting several Andean eco systems. The border is 15 minutes from town at **La Balsa**, a handful of houses on either side of the international bridge. A few shops sell drinks and basic items and there are money changers. To leave Perú head directly to immigration, open 0800-1300, 1500-2000. (When entering Peru you have to stop at the PNP after immigration.) Ecuadorean immigration is supposedly open 24 hours, knock on the door or ask for the officer if not in sight. From the frontier transport goes to Zumba and then to Vilcabamba and Loja. See Transport, page 1167.

● Sleeping

To Ecuador *p1166*
Jaén
C **El Bosque**, Av Mesones Muro 632, T431184, hoteleraelbosque@speedy.com.pe. On main road by bus terminals, just below roundabout for turn to San Ignacio, quiet rooms at the back in gardens, nice pool, good restaurant.
D **Hostal Valle Verde**, Mcal Castilla 203 on Plaza de Armas, T432201, hostalvalleverde@hotmail.com. Modern, large comfortable rooms and beds, a/c, E with fan, hot water, frigobar, parking, includes breakfast. Recommended.
D **Prim's**, Diego Palomino 1341, T431039. Comfortable, a/c, hot water, pool. Recommended.
E **Cancún**, Diego Palomino 1413, T433511. Pleasant, hot water, fan, restaurant, pool. Recommended.
E **César**, Mesones Muro 168, T431277, F431491. Spacious rooms, comfortable, fan, TV (cheaper without), parking.
F **Hostal Diego**, Diego Palomino 1267, T803125. With bath, fan, TV, views over the river, good value.
G **Hostal Santa Elena**, Sánchez Carrión 142, T803020. With bath, cold water, fan, good value.

North of Jaen
E **Sol de la Frontera**, 1½ km north of Namballe,
5 km from La Balsa , isabelayub@yahoo.es. Being built by a British woman, Isabel Wood. Some rooms open, bath tubs with plugs, gas water heaters, continental breakfast included, rural setting in 2.5 ha of countryside.
F **El Olivar**, Av San Ignacio 145, San Ignacio, T076-8446052. G with shared bath, cold water, basic, restaurant.
F **La Posada**, Jr Porvenir 218, San Ignacio, T/F 076-8846180. Best in town, some rooms with hot water, G with shared bath, simple, pleasant, helpful, decent restaurant.
G **Hostal Maldonado**, near the Plaza, Namballe, T076-330011 (community phone). Shared bath, cold water, basic.

● Eating

To Ecuador *p1166*
Jaén
Ⓨ **Claudy Chicken**, Diego Palomino 1284. Selection of set meals (*comida criolla*) at midday, Chinese in the evening, *pollo a la brasa*.
Ⓨ **Lactobac**, Bolívar 1382 at Plaza de Armas. Variety of à la carte dishes, snacks, desserts, very popular, also open for breakfast. Recommended.

⊖ Transport

Chachapoyas to Ecuador & the coast *p1166*
Cars (US$2.75) and combis (US$1.75) depart
from Jr B Alcedo at the east end of Bagua
Grande when full to **Pedro Ruíz**, 1 hr.

To Ecuador *p1166*

Jaén

Bus Arrange bus transport at Mesones Muro, block
4; enquire where the bus leaves from as some
companies also have ticket offices in the centre. To
Chiclayo, 6 hrs: **Móvil**, bus cama at 1700, US$7.60,
5½ hrs; regular service at 2330, US$6.65. **Civa** at
1330 and 2230, US$4.55. **Transcade** at 1000 and
2100, US$4.55. In front of the bus terminal at
Mesones Muro are cars, to Chiclayo US$9, 5 hrs. To
Lima: **Móvil** bus cama at 1700, US$21.20, 15½ hrs;
regular service at 2330, US$18.20. **Civa** at 1700,
US$18.20, 16 hrs. Service to Lima also goes through
Trujillo. To **Piura**, 8 hrs, US$7.60: **Tarapoto Tours** at
2200; **Sol Peruano**, at 2230. To **Pedro Ruiz**,
US$4.55, 3hrs, **Moyobamba**, US$5.45, 7 hrs, and
Tarapoto, US$ 7.60, 9 hrs: **Jaén Express** at 1730,
Tarapoto Tours at 1930, **Sol Peruano** at 2030. To
Bagua Grande: cars US$1.80, 1hr; combis US$1.50,
1¼ hrs. To **San Ignacio**, combis from Av Pinillos
638, 0400-1900, US$3.65, 3 hrs.

North of Jaén

Bus From San Ignacio to **Chiclayo**, daily with
Turismo Adriazén, Av San Ignacio 406, and

Ramírez Tours, Cajamarca 179. To **Jaén**, combis
from Av Mariano Melgar, block 3, US$3.65, 3 hrs.
To **Namballe** and **La Balsa** (border with
Ecuador), cars from Jr Santa Rosa corner
Progreso: Namballe US$2.45 1¾ hrs; La Balsa
US$3, 2 hrs. Ranchera from La Balsa to **Zumba** at
1230 and 1730, US$1.75. There are no pickups, no
carreras to Zumba. If it has not been raining and
the road is passable, there is one bus
(Transportes Nambija) which goes from La Balsa
directly to Loja at 2030, US$7.50, 8-9 hrs. There
are military controls at Pucapamba, 20 min north
of La Balsa and just north of Zumba, keep
passport to hand.

ⓘ Directory

To Ecuador *p1166*

Jaén

Banks BCP, Bolívar y V Pinillos. Cash only;
ATM (Visa/Plus - no MasterCard ATM). **BBV
Continental**, Ramón Castilla y San Martín. Cash,
US$5 commission for TCs. **Cambios Coronel**, V
Pinillos 360 (*Coronel* across the street at 339).
Cash only, good rates. Others on plaza, next to
public phones. Cash only. **Internet** Fotocenter
Erick, Pardo Miguel 425. US$1.15 per hr.

North of Jaén

Banks Centro Comercial Unión, Av San Ignacio
393, San Ignacio, for exchange. **Internet** Places
in both San Ignacio and Namballe.

South coast

*The Pan-American Highway runs all the way south from Lima to the Chilean border. This
part of Peru's desert coast has its own distinctive attractions. The most famous, and
perhaps the strangest, are the mysterious Nazca Lines, whose origin and function continue
to puzzle scientists the world over. But Nazca is not the sole archaeological resource here:
remains of other pre-Columbian civilizations include outposts of the Inca empire itself.
Pisco and Ica are the main centres before Nazca. The former, which is near the famous
Paracas marine reserve, is named after the latter's main product, the pisco grape brandy
and a number of places are well-known for their bodegas.*

South from Lima

Beyond the beaches which are popular with Limeños the road passes near several towns
worth a stop: eg Chincha with its Afro-Peruvian culture. The Paracas peninsula, near Pisco,
is one of the world's great marine bird reserves and was home to one of Peru's most
important ancient civilizations. Further south, the Ica valley, with its wonderful climate, is
home to that equally wonderful grape brandy, pisco. Most beaches have very strong
currents and can be dangerous for swimming; if unsure, ask locals.

Cañete valley

A paved road runs inland from Cañete, mostly beside the Río Cañete, to **Lunahuaná** (40 km). It
is 8 km beyond the Inca ruins of **Incawasi**, which dominated the valley. You can taste the

wines of the *bodegas* (wine cellars) in the valley. *Fiesta de la Vendimia*, grape harvest, first weekend in March. At the end of September/beginning October is the *Fiesta del Níspero* (medlar festival). Several places offer rafting and kayaking: from November-April rafting is at levels 4-5. May-October is low water, levels 1-2 only. Excellent kayaking is 2½ hours upriver. A festival of adventure sports is held every February. There are several hotels, ranging from **B** to **F**, and restaurants in Lunahuaná and surrounding districts.

Beyond Lunahuaná the road ascending the Cañete valley leaves the narrow flood-plain and runs through a series of gorges to the market town of **Yauyos** (basic accommodation, 5 km off the road). After the attractive village of **Huancaya**, the valley is transformed into one of the most beautiful upper valleys in all Peru, on a par with Colca. Above Huancaya the high Andean terrain lies within the **Nor-Yauyos National Reserve** and the river descends through a series of absolutely clear, turquoise pools and lakes, interrupted by cascades and white-water rapids. Culturally, the valley is fascinating for its dying indigenous languages and perhaps the best pre-Columbian terracing anywhere in Peru. Further upstream **Llapay** is a good base because it is in the middle of the valley (**G** *Hostal Llapay*, basic but very friendly, will open at any hour, restaurant). Places to visit include the village of Laraos and the pre-Inca ruins of Huamanmarca (two-hour walk from village of Carania, which is a one-hour drive from Llapay). 17 July Fiesta Nor-Yauyina in Llapay, large and popular. Beyond Llapay, the Cañete valley narrows to an exceptionally tight canyon, with a road squeezed between nothing but rock and rushing water for the steep climb to the 4,600-m pass. Beyond, the road drops to Huancayo (see page 1250).

Pisco and around → *Phone code: 056. Colour map 3, grid C3. Population: 82,250.*

The largest port between Callao and Matarani is a short distance to the west of the Pan-American Highway and 237 km south of Lima. The two parts of town, Pisco Pueblo with its colonial-style homes, and Pisco Puerto, which, apart from fisheries, has been replaced as a port by the deep-water Puerto General San Martín, have expanded into one.

In Pisco Pueblo, half a block west of the quiet Plaza de Armas at Avenida San Martín 132, with its equestrian statue of San Martín, is the **Club Social Pisco**, the headquarters of San Martín after he had landed at Paracas Bay. There is an old Jesuit church on San Francisco, one block from the plaza, separated from the Municipalidad by a narrow park. The newer **Cathedral** is on the main plaza. Avenida San Martín runs from the Plaza de Armas to the sea.

Chincha Alta, 35 km north of Pisco, is a fast-growing town where the negro/criollo culture thrives. The famous festival, *Verano Negro*, is at the end of February while, in November, the *Festival de las Danzas Negras* is held in El Carmen, 10 km south. Chincha is a good place to sample locally produced wine and pisco and local *bodegas* have guided tours.

A 317 km paved road goes to Ayacucho in the sierra, with a branch to Huancavelica. At Castrovirreyna it reaches 4,600 m. The scenery on this journey is superb. **Tambo Colorado** ① *US$1.50,* one of the best-preserved Inca ruins in coastal Peru, is 48 km from Pisco, up the Pisco valley. It includes buildings where the Inca and his retinue would have stayed. Many of the walls retain their original colours. On the other side of the road is the public plaza and the garrison and messengers' quarters. The caretaker will act as a guide, he has a small collection of items found on the site. Tours with Pisco agencies US$10-15 with guide, minimum 2 people.

Paracas National Reserve

① *US$1.65 pp, www.inrena.gob.pe/ianp/web_rnp/rnp.swf.*

Down the coast 15 km from Pisco Puerto is the bay of **Paracas**, sheltered by the Paracas peninsula. The name means 'sandstorm' (these can last for three days, especially in August; the wind gets up every afternoon, peaking at around 1500.) Paracas can be reached by the coast road from San Andrés, passing the fishing port and a large proportion of Peru's fishmeal industry. Alternatively, go down the Pan-American Highway to 14.5 km past the Pisco turning and take the road to Paracas across the desert. After 11 km turn left along the coast road and one km further on fork right to Paracas village. The peninsula, a large area of coast to the south and the Ballestas Islands is a National Reserve, and one of the best marine reserves, with the highest concentration of marine birds in the world. It's advisable to see the peninsula as part of a tour it is not safe to walk alone and it is easy to get lost.

Return to the main road for the entrance to the Reserve (ask for a map here). There's the **Julio Tello site museum** ① *daily 0900-1700, US$2, a shop (guide books, film, drinks), a visitors' centre and a natural history museum. A mirador* offers views of flamingoes feeding in

Paracas bay, but you need binoculars (boat trips do not go to see flamingoes; in January-March the flamingoes go to the Sierra). The tiny fishing village of **Lagunilla** is 5 km from the museum across the neck of the peninsula; its beaches are free from sting rays but not very clean. The eating places tend to be overpriced. A network of firm dirt roads, reasonably well signed, crosses the peninsula (details from Park Office or ask for 'Hoja 28-K' map at Instituto Geográfico Militar in Lima). Other sights on the peninsula include **Mirador de los Lobos** at Punta El Arquillo, 6 km from Lagunilla, with view of sea lions; and a rock formation in the cliffs called **La Catedral**, 6 km from Lagunilla in the opposite direction. About 14 km from the museum is the pre-Columbian Candelabra (**Candelabro** in Spanish) traced in the hillside, at least 50 m long, best seen from the sea.

Ballestas Islands

Trips to the **Islas Ballestas** leave from the jetty at El Chaco, the beach and fishing port by Paracas village. The islands are spectacular, eroded into numerous arches and caves (*ballesta* means bow, as in archery), which provide shelter for thousands of seabirds, some of which are very rare, and hundreds of sea lions. The book *Las Aves del Departamento de Lima* by Maria Koepcke is useful (see also www.avesdelima.com/playas.htm).

Few tours include **Isla San Gallán**, where there are thousands of sea lions. You will see, close up, thousands of inquisitive sea lions, guano birds, pelicans, penguins and, if you're lucky, dolphins swimming in the bay. Most boats are speedboats with life jackets, some are very crowded; wear warm clothing and protect against the sun. The boats pass Puerto San Martín and the Candelabra en route to the islands.

Ica and Huacachina → *Phone code: 056. Colour map 3, grid C3. Population: 161,400.*

Ica, 70 km southeast of Pisco, is Peru's chief wine centre and is famous for its *tejas*, a local sweet of *manjarblanco*. The **Museo Regional** ① *southwest of the centre, Mon-Sat 0800-1900, Sun 0900-1800, US$3.75, reduction for students, US$1.25 to take photos, take bus 17 from the Plaza de Armas (US$0.50),* has mummies, ceramics, textiles and trepanned skulls from the Paracas, Nazca and Inca cultures; a good, well-displayed collection of Inca counting strings (*quipus*) and clothes made of feathers. Behind the building is a scale model of the Nazca lines with an observation tower; a useful orientation before visiting the lines. The kiosk outside sells copies of motifs from the ceramics and textiles. **Dircetur** is at ① *Av Grau 148, T238710, ica@mincetur.gob.pe.* Some tourist information is available at travel agencies. Also try **Touring y Automóvil Club del Perú** ① *C Fermín Tangüis 102, Urb San Miguel, T219393, ica@touringperu.com.pe.*

Wine bodegas that you can visit are: **La Caravedo**, Panamericana Sur 298, T01-446 0478, with organic production and sophisticated presentation; **El Carmen**, on the right-hand side when arriving from Lima (has an ancient grape press made from a huge tree trunk); **El Catador** ① *José Carrasco González, T403295, 1000-1800, US$1.50, 10 km outside Ica, in the district of Subtanjalla, combi from the 2nd block of Moquegua, every 20 mins, US$0.40, taxi takes 10 mins, good tours in Spanish,* has a shop selling home-made wines and pisco, and traditional handicrafts associated with winemaking. In the evening it is a restaurant-bar with dancing and music, best visited during harvest, late February to early April, wine and pisco tasting usually possible. Near El Catador is **Bodega Alvarez**, whose owner, Umberto Alvarez, is very hospitable and won the gold medal for the best pisco in Peru in 1995. Ask about *pisco de mosto verde* and the rarer, more expensive *pisco de limón*. The *Ocucaje* winery, 30 km south of Ica, makes wines and *pisco*. There is a hotel at the winery, which also has a collection of fossilized whale and other sea creatures' bones in the garden. The winery's restaurant has a limited menu but serves good food.

About 5 km from Ica, round a palm-fringed lake and amid amazing sand dunes, is the oasis and summer resort of **Huacachina** ① *take a taxi from Ica for under US$1,* an increasingly popular gringo spot to warm up after the Andes. Its green sulphur waters are said to be curative and thousands of visitors come to swim here. There are lots of eating places and bars with music around the lake. Sometimes the water and shore get dirty and polluted. **Sandboarding** on the dunes is a major pastime here; board hire US$1.50 per hour. **Note** For the inexperienced, sandboarding can be dangerous on the big dunes. **Dune buggies** also do white-knuckle, rollercoaster tours for US$12, or you can hire a buggy and scare yourself for US$6 per person for three to four hours.

● Sleeping

Pisco and around *p1168*

C Hostal Villa Manuelita, San Fransisco 227, T/F535218, hostalvillamanuelita@ hotmail.com. Elegantly decorated colonial mansion converted into hotel with cafeteria and restaurant, cable TV, fan, helpful, tranquil.

D Regidor, Arequipa 201, T/F535220, regidor@mail.cosapidata.com.pe. With TV, fan, jacuzzi, café and restaurant, sauna, very good, price negotiable at quiet times.

E Hostal San Isidro, San Clemente 103, T/F536471, www.hostalsanisidro.com. **F** without bath, hot water, safe, laundry facilities, use of kitchen, English spoken, pool, parking, arranges dune buggies. Recommended.

E Posada Hispana Hostal, Bolognesi 236, T536363, www.posadahispana.com. Rooms with loft and bath, also rooms with shared bath (**G** pp), hot water, can accommodate groups, comfortable, breakfast extra, information service, English, French, Italian and Catalan spoken. Recommended.

E Hostal Los Inkas Inn, Prol Barrio Nuevo Mz M Lt 14, Urb San Isidro, T536634, los_inkas_ inn@hotmail.com. 5 blocks from the Plaza de Armas, comfortable and straightforward, private rooms or dorms with shared bath, pool (not always full), internet, cafetería, sauna, laundry service, garage. Tours can be arranged.

F El Condado, Arequipa 136, Plazuela Belén, T533623, hostalcondado@hotmail.com. Hot water, cable TV, laundry, good if a bit noisy, expensive breakfast, tours to Ballestas arranged.

F Hostal Belén, Arequipa 128, Plazuela Belén, T533046. Basic, a bit outdated, but safe, hot water. Better rooms in new annex.

F Hostal La Portada, Alipio Ponce 250, T532098, hostallaportada@terra.com. Free coffee, hot water, TV, laundry service. Recommended.

G pp **Hostal Pisco Playa** (Youth Hostel), Jr José Balta 639, Pisco Playa, T532492. Kitchen and laundry facilities, quite nice, breakfast US$1.50.

Chincha Alta **B Hacienda San José**, 17th-century ranch-house, 9 km south of town in El Carmen district, T056-221458, hsanjose@ terra.com.pe. Full board (cheaper Mon-Thu), beautiful buildings, but overpriced, pool, garden, small church, colonial crafts, the tunnels believed to link up with other ranches and the catacombs, where many slaves were interred, can be visited, US$3 pp, very busy at weekends.

Paracas National Reserve *p1168*

AL-A Paracas, bungalows on beach, T545100, hparacas@terra.com.pe. Good food, not cheap, good buffet lunch on Sun US$25, fine grounds facing the bay, it is a good centre for excursions to the Peninsula and flights over Nazca, tennis

courts, open-air pool (US$2 for non-residents), also houses the Masson ceramics collection which is worth seeing. 2-hr dune-buggy trips can be arranged for US$25 pp.

B-C El Mirador, at the turn-off to El Chaco, T545086, www.elmiradorhotel.com. Hot water, good service, boat trips arranged, meals available, sometimes full board only.

F Hostal Los Frayles, Av Paracas Mz D, Lote 5, P2, T545141. Good value, nice terrace, no TV.

Ica and Huacachina *p1169*

Hotels are fully booked during the harvest festival and prices rise. If taking a taxi, insist on going to the hotel of your choice.

A Hacienda Ocucaje, Carretera Panamericana Sur Km 334, Ocucaje (30 km south), T837049, www.hotelocucaje.com. A lovely ex-hacienda, with good rooms, cheaper mid-week, restaurant and bar, pool, sauna, sandboarding, visits to fossils at Cerro Blanco, to bodegas, flights over Nazca Lines can be arranged.

A Las Dunas, Av La Angostura 400, T256224, www.lasdunashotel.com. Lima offices: Malecón Armendáriz 193, Miraflores, Lima, T241 8000. Prices do not include service, about 20% cheaper on weekdays. Highly recommended, in a complete resort with restaurant, swimming pool, horse riding and other activities, it has its own airstrip for flights over Nazca, 50 mins.

C Sol de Ica, Lima 265, T236168, 1 block from Plaza de Armas, www.hotelsoldeica.com. Quite comfortable, breakfast extra, swimming pool, tour agency.

D-E Hostal Siesta I, Independencia 160, T233249. Hot water, hospitable owner, noisy. Siesta II, T234633, similar.

E Princess, Urb Santa María D-103, T215421, www.geocities.com/hotel_princess. Taxi ride from the main plaza, small rooms, hot water, TV, pool, tourist information, helpful, peaceful, very good.

E-F Arameli, Tacna 239, T239107. A good choice, cable TV, 1 block from Plaza, clean.

G Hostal Paraíso, Bolívar 418, T227582. Clean, quiet but thin walls, basic.

Huacachina **B Mossone** is at the east end of the lake, T213660, reserva@derrama.org.pe. Elegant, hacienda-style, full board available, lovely patio, pool, bicycles and sandboards for guests' use. Recommended.

C Hostería Suiza, Malecón 264, T238762, hostesuiza@terra.com.pe. Overlooking lake, lovely grounds, quiet, includes breakfast, safe parking. Recommended.

F Casita de Arena, T215274, casadearena@hotmail.com. Basic rooms,

G without bath, bar, small pool, laundry facilities, board hire, popular with backpackers, check your bill and change carefully, don't leave valuables unattended.

F **Hostal Rocha**, T222256. Hot water, G without bath, family run, kitchen and laundry facilities, board hire, small pool, popular with backpackers, but a bit run-down.

G **Hostal del Barco**, Balneario de Huacachina 180. A very relaxed place with hammocks on the front terrace, basic rooms, bar, use of kitchen, can arrange tours.

G **Hostal Salvatierra**, T232352. A grand old place being renovated, not on waterfront, charming, pool, relaxing courtyard, rents sandboards, good value.

G **Hostal Titanic**, T229003. Small rooms, pool and café, clothes washing, board hire, good value for lodging and set meals.

🍴 Eating

Pisco and around *p1168*
There are seafood restaurants along the shore between Pisco and San Andrés and in San Andrés itself.

ⓘ-ⓘ **As de Oro**, San Martín 472. Good food, decent prices, closed Mon, disco and karaoke on Sat.

ⓘ-ⓘ **El Bossa Nova**, Av San Martín 176, p 2. Stylish café/bar for an espresso or your favourite trago, good night and day.

ⓘ-ⓘ **La Casona**, San Martín. Good value, new, specializing in grilled meats, large portions.

ⓘ **El Dorado**, main plaza opposite Cathedral. Good value local dishes.

Panadería/Café San Fransisco, next to Zarcillos Tours on the main Plaza. Good empanadas and baked goods, with a restaurant next door, cheap.

Ica and Huacachina *p1169*
ⓘ-ⓘ **Las Brujas de Cachiche**, Cajamarca 118. Serves local dishes.

ⓘ-ⓘ **Chifa Karaoke Central**, Urb Los Viñedos de Santa María E-25, T221294. Excellent Chinese.

ⓘ-ⓘ **El Otro Peñoncito**, Bolívar 255. Set lunch (US$6) in a pleasant atmosphere, good toilets.

ⓘ-ⓘ **Pizzería Venecia**, Lima 252. Best pizzas.

Café Mogambo, Tacna 125. Good for breakfast.

Tejas Helena, Cajamarca 137. The best *tejas* in town are sold here.

🎉 Festivals and events

Ica and Huacachina *p1169*
Wine harvest festival in early **Mar**. The image of El Señor de Luren, in a fine church in Parque Luren, draws pilgrims from all Peru to the twice-yearly festivals in **Mar** and **Oct (15-21)**, when there are all-night processions.

⛰ Activities and tours

Ballestas Islands *p1169*
A full day tour of the islands and Paracas Peninsula costs US$20 pp; a half-day boat tour to the islands US$10 pp, usually starting at 0730, returning 1100 to avoid rougher seas in the afternoon; out of season tours are a lot cheaper. The main hotels in Pisco and Paracas will arrange tours (eg *Hotel Paracas*, US$18 in their own speedboat, 0900-1700). Often, agencies will put clients together in one boat. Don't book tours on the street. Recommended operators for trips to Islas Ballestas:

Amigos Adventure Travel Agency, Jr Progreso 167, p 2, T311984, amigos_adventures@ hotmail.com. Island tours, Reserve tours, sandboarding, many languages spoken.

Ballestas Travel Service, San Francisco 251, Pisco, T535564.

Blue Sea Tours, Chosica 320, San Andrés, Pisco, also at El Chaco. Guides Jorge Espejo and Hubert Van Lomoen (speaks Dutch) are frequently recommended, no time limit on tours.

The Zarcillo Connection, Callao 137, suite B-21, Pisco, T536543, www.zarcilloconnections.net. For Paracas National Reserve, Tambo Colorado, trekking and tours to Ica, Chincha and Nazca. Also has its own hotel, **Zarcillo Paradise II**, on Paracas Bay.

Ica and Huacachina *p1169*
Ica Desert Trip, icadeserttrip@yahoo.es. Roberto Penny Cabrera (speaks Spanish and English) offers 1, 2 and 3-day trips off-road into the desert, archaeology, geology, etc. US$50 pp per day, 4 people maximum, contact by email in advance. Take toilet paper, something warm for the evening, a long-sleeved loose cotton shirt for daytime and long trousers. Recommended, but "not for the faint-hearted".

La Ruta del Pisco, Lima travel agencies arrange 3-day, 2-night tours from Lima including transport, accommodation and visits to bodegas, from US$70-100.

🚌 Transport

Cañete valley *p1167*
The road from Cañete to Huancayo is being improved, so buses may become more frequent. ETAS run from **Cañete** (in front of AEDO petrol station, T01-287 8831 or 01-9771 1254) to **Huancayo** (Loreto 744, T215424). Information about ETAS buses on posters in the villages. Daily bus from **Lunahuaná** between 1900-2200 to **Yauyos** stops at a shop on the road on request. Bus from Yauyos to **Llapay** between 0100-0230,

their adoration not only in the desert, but also on their ceramics and on the engraved stones of the Paracas culture. Isla and Reindel believe that the Palpa lines predate those at Nazca and that the lines and drawings themselves are scaled up versions of the Paracas drawings. In addition, objects in the shape of drops of water, whales and chilis, found in the grave of El Señor de Palpa, are repeated in the desert. This new research proposes that the Nazca culture succumbed not to drought, but to heavy rainfall, probably during an El Niño event.

Other excursions

The Nazca area is dotted with over 100 cemeteries and the dry, humidity-free climate has perfectly preserved invaluable tapestries, cloth and mummies. At **Chauchilla** ① *30 km south of Nazca, last 12 km a sandy track*, grave robbing *huaqueros* ransacked the tombs and left bones, skulls, mummies and pottery shards littering the desert. A tour takes about two hours and should cost about US$7 per person with a minimum of three people. Gold mining is one of the main local industries and a tour usually includes a visit to a small family processing shop where the techniques used are still very old-fashioned. Some tours also include a visit to a local potter's studio. That of Sr Andrés Calle Benavides, who makes Nazca reproductions, is particularly recommended.

To the Paredones ruins and aqueduct: the ruins, also called Cacsamarca, are Inca on a pre-Inca base. They are not well preserved. The underground aqueducts, built 300 BC-AD 700, are still in working order and worth seeing. By taxi it is about US$10 round trip, or go with a tour.

Cantalloc is a 30 minutes to one hour walk through Buena Fe, to see markings in the valley floor. These consist of a triangle pointing to a hill and a *tela* (cloth) with a spiral depicting the threads. Climb the mountain to see better examples.

Cahuachi, to the west of the Nazca Lines, comprises several pyramids and a site called **El Estaquería** ① *to visit the ruins of Cahuachi costs US$10, minimum 2 people. See also the Museo Antonini, above.* The latter is thought to have been a series of astronomical sighting posts, but more recent research suggests the wooden pillars were used to dry dead bodies and therefore it may have been a place of mummification.

The road from Nazca towards Cuzco

Two hours out of Nazca on the newly paved road to Abancay and Cuzco is the **Reserva Nacional Pampas Galeras** at 4,100 m, which has a vicuña reserve. There is an interesting Museo del Sitio, also a military base and park guard here. It's best to go early as entry is free. At Km 155 is **Puquio**, then it's another 185 km to **Chalhuanca**. Fuel is available in both towns. There are wonderful views on this stretch, with lots of small villages, valleys and alpacas.

South of Nazca

Chala (*Phone code 054*), 173 km from Nazca, is a fishing village with beaches. There are dozens of restaurants. There are several hotels (**D-G**), all in Chala Sur, 10 minutes' walk south from where the buses stop in Chala Norte. No banks or ATMs, but several internet places. Colectivos from Nazca cost US$3.50. Lima-Arequipa buses pass Chala about 0600.

About 10 km north of Chala are the large pre-Columbian ruins of **Puerto Inca** on the coast. This was the port for Cuzco. The site is in excellent condition: the drying and store houses can be seen as holes in the ground (be careful where you walk). On the right side of the bay is a cemetery, on the hill a temple of reincarnation, and the Inca road from the coast to Cuzco is clearly visible. The road was 240 km long, with a staging post every 7 km so that, with a change of runner at every post, messages could be sent in 24 hours. The site is best appreciated when there is no *garúa* (ie when the sun is shining).

● Sleeping

Nazca *p1172, map p1175*
If arriving by bus beware of touts who tell you that the hotel of your choice (notably *Alegría*) is closed, or full, and no longer runs tours. If you phone or email the hotel they will pick you up at the bus station free of charge day or night.
AL-A Maison Suisse, opposite airport, T/F522434, www.aeroica.net. Comfortable, safe car park,

expensive restaurant, pool, suites with jacuzzi, accepts Amex, good giftshop, shows video of Nazca Lines. Also has camping facilities. Ask for packages including flights over Nazca Lines.
A Casa Andina, Jr Bolognesi 367, T523563, www.casa-andina.com. One of this chain of hotels, which all offer standardized services in distinctive style. Bright, modern decor, a/c, pool,

TV, internet, restaurant open all day.

A Nazca Lines, Jr Bolognesi, T522293, reservanasca@derramajae.org.pe. With a/c, comfortable, rooms with private patio, hot water, peaceful, American breakfast included, restaurant, good but expensive meals, safe car park, pool (US$4.50 for non-guests, or free if having lunch), they can arrange package tours which include 2-3 nights at the hotel plus a flight over the lines and a desert trip. Recommended.

B Majoro, Panamericana Sur Km 452, T522490, www.hotelmajoro.com. A charming old hacienda about 5 km from town past the airstrip, beautiful gardens, pool, restaurant, quiet and homely, attentive service, serene surroundings, good arrangements for flights and tours.

B Nido del Cóndor, opposite the airport, Panamericana Sur Km 447, T522424, contanas@terra.com.pe. Large rooms, hot water, good restaurant, bar, shop, swimming pool, camping US$3, parking, English, Italian German spoken, free pick-up from town, reservation advised.

C-D pp Hotel Alegría, Jr Lima 168, T/F522702, www.nazcaperu.com. Rooms with bath, a/c, continental breakfast, bungalows with hot shower, rooms with shared bath **G pp**, hot water, café, garden, pool, English, Italian, German and Hebrew spoken, laundry facilities, safe luggage deposit, book exchange, email facilities for US$2 per hr, netphone also US$2, free video on the Lines at 2100, very popular. Recommended. Efraín Alegría also runs a tour agency and guests are encouraged to buy tours (see Activities and tours), flights and bus tickets arranged.

D Paredones Inn, Jr Arica 115, T522181, paredoneshotel@terra.com. 1 block from the Plaza de Armas, ample rooms with cable TV, modern, great views from roof terrace, laundry service, bar, suites with jacuzzi, helpful staff.

E Hostal Las Líneas, Jr Arica 299, T522488. Spacious, cheaper without bath, restaurant. Recommended.

E Internacional, Av Maria Reiche, T522744, hostalinternacional@hotmail.com. Hot water, garage, café and nice bungalows.

E Mirador, Tacna 436, T523121, F523714. On main plaza, comfortable, cheaper with shared bath, TV, new, modern.

E Nasca, C Lima 438, T/F522085. Hot water, cheaper without bath, clothes washing facilities, luggage store, new annexe at the back, nice garden, safe motorcycle parking.

F pp Hostal Alegría, Av Los Incas 117, opposite *Ormeño* bus terminal, T522497. Basic, hot water, hammocks, nice garden, camping, restaurant.

F The WalkOn* Inn, JM Mejía 108, 3 blocks from Plaza de Armas, T/F056-522566, www.walkoninn.com. Formerly Vía Morburg, rooms with bathroom, hot water, family feel, small swimming pool, TV room, excellent and cheap restaurant on top floor for breakfast and salads, very helpful staff, internet, luggage store, works with **Nasca Trails** for flights and tours, information given. Recommended.

F Posada Guadalupe, San Martín 225, T522249. Family run, lovely courtyard and garden, **G** without bath, hot water, good breakfast, relaxing (touts who try to sell tours are nothing to do with hotel).

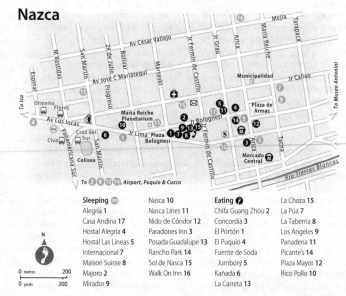

Nazca

Sleeping
Alegría 1
Casa Andina 17
Hostal Alegría 4
Hostal Las Líneas 5
Internacional 7
Maison Suisse 8
Majoro 2
Mirador 9
Nasca 10
Nasca Lines 11
Nido de Cóndor 12
Paredones Inn 3
Posada Guadalupe 13
Rancho Park 14
Sol de Nasca 15
Walk On Inn 16

Eating
Chifa Guang Zhou 2
Concordia 3
El Portón 1
El Puquio 4
Fuente de Soda Jumbory 5
Kañada 6
La Carreta 13
La Choza 15
La Púa 7
La Taberna 8
Los Angeles 9
Panadería 11
Picante's 14
Plaza Mayor 12
Rico Pollo 10

0 metres 200
0 yards 200

F Rancho Park, on Panamericana 1 km from town towards the airport, T521153. On farmland, 2 swimming pools (1 for children), entry to pools US$1, popular at weekends, good restaurant.
F Sol de Nasca, Callao 586, T522730. Rooms with and without hot showers, TV, restaurant, pleasant, don't leave valuables in luggage store.

The road from Nazca to Cuzco *p1174*
F Hostal Jousef, Ayacucho 246, Puquio, T066-407415. New, hot water, TV, clothes washing possible. Recommended.
F Hostal Los Andes, 9 de Diciembre 286, Puquio, T066-452323. The best alternative, in an older house, hot water.

South of Nazca *p1174*
B Puerto Inka, 2 km along a side road from Km 610 Panamericana Sur (for reservations T054-551055), www.puertoinka.com.pe. Bungalows on the beautiful beach, hammocks outside, great place to relax, boat hire, diving equipment rental, camping US$3, low season discounts, used by tour groups, busy in summer.

● Eating

Nazca *p1172, map p1175*
♥-♥ La Carreta, Bolognesi, next door to Los Angeles. Nuevo Andino dishes using traditional ingredients, rustic, lively atmosphere, live music.
♥-♥ La Choza, Bolognesi 290. Nice atmosphere with woven chairs and thatched roof, all types of food, live music at night.
♥-♥ Concordia, Lima 594. Good, also rents bikes at US$1 an hour.
♥-♥ Plaza Mayor, on the Plaza. Specializes in barbecue of all types, roasted chicken, steaks, anticuchos and great salads. Recommended.
♥-♥ El Portón, Moresky 120, in front of Hotel Nazca Lines. Popular with tours, specializes in Peruvian food of all types, indoor/outdoor setting. Recommended.
♥-♥ El Puquio, Bolognesi 50 m from plaza. Good food, especially pastas, pleasant atmosphere, good for drinks, popular.
♥-♥ La Taberna, Jr Lima 321, T521411. Excellent food, live music, popular with gringos, it's worth a look just for the graffiti on the walls.
♥ Los Angeles, Bolognesi 266. Good, cheap, try *sopa criolla*, and chocolate cake.
♥ Chifa Guang Zhou, Bolognesi 297, T522036. Very good.
♥ Kañada, Lima 160, nazcanada@ yahoo.com. Cheap, good *menú*, excellent pisco sours, nice wines, popular, display of local artists' work, email service, English spoken, helpful. Recommended.
♥ La Púa, Jr Lima, next to *La Taberna*. Good espresso, also pizzas, pastas and sandwiches.

♥ Rico Pollo opposite *Hostal Alegría*. Good local restaurant, cheap.
Fuente de Soda Jumbory, near the cinema. Good *almuerzo*.
Panadería, Bolognesi 387.
Picante's, Av Bolognesi 464. Delicious real coffee, good cakes. The owner, Percy Pizzaro is very knowledgeable about the Lines.

▲ Activities and tours

Nazca *p1172, map p1175*
All guides must be approved by the Ministry of Tourism and should have an official identity card. As more and more touts (*jaladores*) operate at popular hotels and the bus terminals, they are using false ID cards and fake hotel and tour brochures. They are all rip-off merchants who overcharge and mislead those who arrive by bus. Only conduct business with agencies at their office, or phone or email the company you want to deal with in advance. Some hotels are not above pressurising guests to purchase tours at inflated prices. Taxi drivers usually act as guides, but most speak only Spanish. Do not take just any taxi on the plaza for a tour, always ask your hotel for a reputable driver.
Air Nasca Travel, Jr Lima 185, T521027, guide Susi recommended. Very helpful and competitive prices. Can do all types of tours around Nazca, Ica, Paracas and Pisco. Recommended.
Algería Tours, Lima 186, T522444, www.naz caperu.com. Offers inclusive tours which have been repeatedly recommended. Guides with radio contact and maps can be provided for hikes to nearby sites. Guides speak English, German, French and Italian. Tours go as far as Ica, Paracas and the Ballestas Islands. *Alegría* run a bus from Nazca to Pisco every day at 1000 (returns at 1000 from Pisco's Plaza de Armas), via Ica, Huacachina and *bodegas*.
Andean Tempo, Ignacio Moresky 126, Parque Bolognesi, T522379, 969 9255 (mob), andeantempo@hotmail.com. Run by Enrique Levano Alarcón, adventure tours, many off the beaten track. Recommended.
Jesús Erazo Buitrón, Juan Matta 1110, T523005. Very knowledgeable, he speaks a little English but his Spanish is easy to follow.
Fernández family, who run the *Hotel Nasca*, also run local tours. Ask for the hotel owners and speak to them direct.
Nanasca Tours, Jr Lima 160, T/F522917, T962 2054 (mob), nanascatours@yahoo.com. Very helpful.
Nasca Trails, Juan Tohalino Vera, Bolognesi 550, T522858, nascatrails@terra.com.pe. English, French, German and Italian spoken. Recommended.
Félix Quispe Sarmiento, 'El Nativo de Nazca', Fedeyogin5@hotmail.com. He has his own museum, Hantun Nazca, at Panamericana Sur

447 and works with the Instituto Nacional de Cultura, tours off the beaten track, can arrange flights, knowledgeable, ask for him at Kañada restaurant. Recommended.

Tours of the Nazca Lines
On land Taxi-guides to the mirador, 0800-1200, cost US$4-6 pp, or you can hitch, but there is not always much traffic. Travellers suggest the view from the hill 500 m back to Nazca is better. Go early as the site gets very hot. Or take a taxi and arrive at 0745 before the buses.
By air Small planes take 3-5 passengers to see the Nazca Lines. Flights last 30-35 mins and are controlled by air traffic personnel at the airport to avoid congestion. The price for a flight is US$50 pp. You also have to pay US$3 airport tax. It is best to organize a flight with the airlines themselves at the airport. Flights are bumpy with many tight turns – many people get airsick so it's wise not to eat or drink just before a flight. Best times to fly are 0800-1000 and 1500-1630 when there is less turbulence and better light (assuming there is no fog). Make sure you clarify everything before getting on the plane and ask for a receipt. Also let them know in advance if you have any special requests. Taxi to airport, US$1.35, bus, US$0.10. These companies are recommended; there are others.
Aerocóndor, Panamericana Sur Km 447, Hostal Nido del Cóndor, T521168, or their office at Av Angostura 400, Hotel Las Dunas in Ica, T256230 – see also Lima listings, www.aero condor.com.pe. From Lima, they offer flights over the lines in a 1-day tour (lunch in Nazca), or flights from Ica.
Aero Ica in Jr Lima and at the airport. In Lima, T446 3026, www.aeroica.net. Offers full-day packages from Ica and Lima with lunch at Maison Suisse, plus flight over the lines, but book 48 hrs in advance. Make sure you clarify everything before getting on the plane and ask for a receipt.
Alas Peruanas, T522444, www.alasperuanas.com. Flights can also be booked at Hotel Alegría. Experienced pilots. They also offer 1-hr flights over the Palpa and Llipata areas, where you can see more designs and other rare patterns (US$75 pp, minimum 3). They can also organize flights from Pisco (US$140) and Ica (US$130). All *Alas Peruanas* flights include the BBC film of Nazca.

☉ Transport

Nazca *p1172, map p1175*
Bus It is worth paying the extra for a good bus – reports of robbery on the cheaper services.

Over-booking is common.
To **Lima**, 446 km, 6 hrs, several buses and colectivos daily. **Ormeño**, T522058, *Royal Class* at 0530 and 1330 US$21.50 from Hotel Nazca Lines, normal service from Av Los Incas, 6 a day, US$12.50; **Civa**, Av Guardia Civil, T523019, normal service at 2300, US$6; **Cruz del Sur**, Av Guardia Civil 290, T523713, 4 daily, US$6. Ormeño's *Royal Class* arrives in Santa Catalina, a much safer area of Lima. **Ormeño** to **Ica**, 2 hrs, US$1.50, 4 a day. For **Pisco** (210 km), 3 hrs, buses stop 5 km outside town (see under Pisco, Transport), so change in Ica for direct transport into Pisco. To **Arequipa**, 565 km, 9 hrs: **Ormeño** 1530, 2000, 2400, from Av Los Incas, US$10, with *Royal Class* at 2130, US$20, 8 hrs. **Cruz del Sur** has 4 buses daily between 1900 and 2400, US$10-27. **Civa**, US$20, 8 hrs. **Flores** has 9 buses daily, US$15, but trip takes 15-16 hrs. Delays are possible out of Nazca because of drifting sand across the road or because of mudslides in the rainy season. Travel in daylight if possible. Book your ticket on previous day.

Buses to **Cuzco**, 659 km, via **Chalhuanca** and **Abancay** (13 hrs). On the **Lima-Nazca-Abancay-Cuzco** route **Expreso Wari** have 6 services a day, normal US$17, and *Imperial* service US$20. Their offices are at the exit from Nazca on the road to Puquío. The highway from Nazca to Cuzco is paved and is safe for bus travellers, drivers of private vehicles and motorcyclists. Also buses to Cuzco with **Ormeño**, US$27, and **Cruz del Sur**, 2015, 2100, US$27, but via Arequipa.

Puerto Inca *p1174*
Taxi from **Chala** US$5, or take a colectivo to Nazca as far as the turnoff for Puerto Inca, Km 610, if it has space, about US$1 pp, beware overcharging.

ⓘ Directory

Nazca *p1172, map p1175*
Banks BCP, Lima y Grau, changes cash and Visa TCs, cash advance on Visa, decent rates, Visa ATM. Some street changers will change TCs for 8% commission. **Internet** Many places on Jr Bolognesi. Facilities at *Hotel Alegría* and *Casa Andina*. **Post offices** At Fermín de Castillo 379, T522016. **Telephones** Telefónica for international calls with coins on Plaza Bolognesi; also on Plaza de Armas and at Lima 359. **Useful addresses** Police: at Av Los Incas, T522105, or T105 for emergencies.

Arequipa and the far south

The colonial city of Arequipa, with its guardian volcano, El Misti, is the ideal place to start exploring southern Peru. It is the gateway to two of the world's deepest canyons, Colca and Cotahuasi, whose villages and terraces hold onto a traditional way of life and whose skies are home to the magnificent condor. From Arequipa there are routes to Lake Titicaca and to the border with Chile.

Arequipa → *Phone code: 054. Colour map 6, grid A1. Population: 1 million. Altitude: 2,380 m.*

The city of Arequipa, 1,011 km from Lima, stands in a beautiful valley at the foot of El Misti volcano, a snow-capped, perfect cone, 5,822 m high, guarded on either side by the mountains Chachani (6,057 m), and Pichu-Pichu (5,669 m). The city has fine Spanish buildings and many old and interesting churches built of sillar, a pearly white volcanic material almost exclusively used in the construction of Arequipa. The city was re-founded on 15 August 1540 by an emissary of Pizarro, but it had previously been occupied by Aymara Indians and the Incas. It is the main commercial centre for the south, and its people resent the general tendency to believe that everything is run from Lima. It has been declared a World Cultural Heritage site by UNESCO.

Ins and outs
Getting there Transport to and from the **airport** (7 km west) is described below under Transport. It takes about half an hour to town. The main **bus terminal** is south of the centre, 15 minutes from the centre by colectivo, 10 minutes by taxi. ▶▶ *For more detailed information, see Transport, page 1195.*

Getting around The main places of interest and the hotels are within walking distance of the Plaza de Armas. If you are going to the suburbs, take a bus or taxi. A cheap tour of the city can be made in a *Vallecito* bus, 1½ hours for US$0.30. It is a circular tour which goes down Calles Jerusalén and San Juan de Dios.

Climate The climate is delightful, with a mean temperature before sundown of 23ºC, and after sundown of 14½ºC. The sun shines on 360 days of the year. Annual rainfall is less than 150 mm.

Security In 2006 there were many reports of taxi drivers in collusion with criminals to rob both tourists and locals. Theft can be a problem in the market area ans the park at Selva Alegre. Be very cautious walking south of the Plaza de Armas area at night. The police are conspicuous, friendly, courteous and efficient, but their resources are limited.

Tourist office i perú ① *Casona Santa Catalina, C Santa Catalina 210, T221227. i perú also has an office in the airport, 2nd floor, T444564, daily 0630-1730.* **Municipal tourist office** is in the Municipalidad ① *on the south side of the Plaza de Armas, No 112, T211021.* See www.arequipa-tourism.com. **Indecopi**, the tourist protection bureau, has two offices: ① *Moral 316, T212054, mcornejo@indecopi.gob.pe* and ① *Quezada 104, Yanahuara, T270181. Or T0800-42579, 24 hours, toll-free.* **Tourist Police** ① *Jerusalén 315, T201258,* very helpful with complaints or giving directions.

Sights
The elegant **Plaza de Armas** is faced on three sides by arcaded buildings with many restaurants, and on the fourth by the massive **Cathedral**, founded in 1612 and largely rebuilt in the 19th century. It is remarkable for having its façade along the whole length of the church (entrance on Santa Catalina and San Francisco). Inside are the fine Belgian organ and elaborately carved wooden pulpit. In the June 2001 earthquake which devastated much of southern Peru, one of the cathedral's twin towers famously collapsed. It has been rebuilt. Behind the Cathedral there is an alley with handicraft shops and places to eat.
  Santa Catalina Convent ① *Santa Catalina 301, T229798, www.santacatalina. org.pe, 0900-1600, US$7.25.* This is by far the most remarkable sight, opened in 1970 after four

centuries of mystery. The convent has been beautifully refurbished, with period furniture, pictures of the Arequipa and Cuzco schools and fully equipped kitchens. It is a complete miniature walled colonial town of over 2 ha in the middle of the city at Santa Catalina 301, where about 450 nuns lived in total seclusion, except for their women servants. The few remaining nuns have retreated to one section of the convent, allowing visitors to see a maze of cobbled streets and plazas bright with geraniums and other flowers, cloisters and buttressed houses. These have been painted in traditional white, orange, deep red and blue. There is a good café, which sells cakes made by the nuns and a special blend of tea. There are tours of 1½ hrs, no set price, many of the guides speak English or German (a tip of US$2.85 is expected); also night tours.

Museo Santuarios Andinos ① *La Merced 110, T200345, www.ucsm.edu.pe/ santury, Mon-Sat 0900-1800, Sun 0900-1500, US$5 includes a 20-min video of the discovery in English followed by a guided tour in English, French, German, Italian or Spanish (tip the guide), discount with student card, tour lasts 1 hr.* It contains the frozen Inca mummies found on Mount Ampato; the mummy known as 'Juanita' is fascinating as it is so well preserved. From January to April, Juanita is often jetting round the world, and is replaced by other child sacrifices unearthed in the mountains.

Arequipa is said to have the best preserved colonial architecture in Peru, apart from Cuzco. As well as the many fine churches, there are several fine seignorial houses with large carved tympanums over the entrances. Built as single-storey structures, they have mostly withstood earthquakes. They have small patios with no galleries, flat roofs and small windows, disguised by superimposed lintels or heavy grilles. Good examples are the 18th-century **Casa Tristán del Pozo**, or **Gibbs-Ricketts house** ① *San Francisco 108, 0915-1245, 1600-1800,* with its fine portal and puma-head waterspouts (now *Banco Continental*). **Casa del Moral** ① *Moral 318 y Bolívar, Mon-Sat 0900-1700, Sun 0900-1300, US$1.80, US$1 for students,* also known as Williams house. It is now the *Banco Industrial* and has a museum. **Casa Goyeneche** ① *La Merced 201 y Palacio Viejo,* now an office of the *Banco Central de la Reserva,* ask the guards to let you view the courtyard and fine period rooms. The oldest district is **San Lázaro,** a collection of tiny climbing streets and houses quite close to the **Hotel Libertador,** where you can find the ancient **Capilla de San Lázaro.**

Among the many fine churches is **La Compañía** ① *General Morán y Alvarez Thomas,* the main façade (1698) and side portal (1654) are striking examples of the florid Andean *mestizo* style. To the left of the sanctuary is the **Capilla Real** (Royal Chapel) ① *Mon-Fri 0900-1130, 1500-1730, US$0.65.* Its San Ignacio chapel has a beautiful polychrome cupola. Also well worth seeing is the church of **San Francisco** ① *Zela 103,* opposite which is the interesting **Museo Histórico Municipal** ① *Plaza San Francisco 407, Mon-Fri 0900-1700, US$0.50,* with much war memorabilia. **La Recoleta** ① *Jr Recoleta 117, T270966, Mon-Sat 0900-1200, 1500-1700, US$1.50,* a Franciscan monastery built in 1647, stands on the other side of the river, on Recoleta. It contains several cloisters, a religious art museum, a pre-Columbian museum, an Amazon museum and a library with many rarities

The central **San Camilo market,** between Perú, San Camilo, Piérola and Alto de la Luna, is worth visiting, as is the Siglo XX market, to the east of the rail station. **Museo de Arte Contemporaneo** ① *Tacna y Arica 201, T221068, Tue-Fri 1000-1700, Sat-Sun 1000-1400, US$1,* in the old railway station, is a new museum dedicated to painting and photography from 1900 onwards. The building is surrounded by gardens and has a Sunday market. The **archaeological museum** ① *Av Independencia entre La Salle y Santa Rosa, apply to Dr E Linares, the director, T229719, Mon-Fri 0800-1300, US$1,* the Universidad de San Agustín, has a collection of ceramics and mummies.

Excursions near Arequipa

At **Yanahuara,** 2 km northwest, is a 1750 *mestizo*-style church, with a magnificent churrigueresque façade, all in *sillar* (opens 1500). On the same plaza is a *mirador,* through whose arches there is a fine view of El Misti with the city at its feet, a popular spot in the late afternoon. To get there, cross the Puente Grau, turn right up Av Bolognesi. In the hillside suburb of **Cayma** is the delightful 18th-century church ① *open until 1700.* There are many old buildings associated with Bolívar and Garcilaso de la Vega. Many local buses go to Cayma.

Tingo ① *bus 7, US$0.20,* which has a very small lake and three swimming pools, should be visited on Sunday for local food. Some 3 km past Tingo, beside the Río Sabandía on the Huasacanche road, is **La Mansión del Fundador** ① *0900-1700, US$2.50.* Originally owned by the founder of Arequipa, Don Garcí Manuel de Carbajal, it has been restored as a museum with original furnishings and paintings. also has cafetería and bar.

About 8 km southeast of Arequipa is the **Molino de Sabandía** ① *US$1.50, ring bell for admission; round trip by taxi US$4*. This is the first stone mill in the area, built in 1621. It has been fully restored and the guardian diverts water to run the grinding stones when visitors arrive. Adjoining Sabandía is **Yumina** ① *tourist fee of US$6 payable, which may be asked for on the bus to Chivay*, with many Inca terraces which are still in use and between Sabandía and Arequipa is Paucarpata, with an old church and views of terraces, El Misti and Chachani.

Climbing El Misti and Chachani At 5,822 m, El Misti volcano offers a relatively straight-forward opportunity to scale a high peak. Start from the hydroelectric plant, after first registering with the police there, then you need one day to the Monte Blanco shelter, at 4,800 m. Start early for the four to six hours to the top, to get there by 1100 before the mists obscure the view. If you start back at 1200 you will reach the hydroelectric plant by 1800. Alternatively, take a jeep at 3,300 m to the end of the rough road, then four to five hours hike to the campground at 4,600 m. Only space for three tents. Buses leave Arequipa for Baños Jesús, then on to Chiguata, from where you can walk to the base of El Misti. Guides may be available at Cachamarca. Be sure to take plenty of food, water and protection against the weather; it takes two days to reach the crater.

In recent years climbing Chachani (6,057 m), northwest of El Misti, has also become popular. This peak retains it's icy covering longer than El Misti, though this is fast disappearing. Remember that both summits are at a very high altitude and that this, combined with climbing on scree, makes it hard going for the untrained. Recent reports of hold-ups of climbers make it inadvisable for you to go alone. Join a group or take a guide. Further information is available from travel agencies and professional guides (see page 1185, Activities and tours).

● Sleeping

Arequipa *p1178, maps p1181 and p1184*
When arriving by bus, do not believe taxi drivers who say the hotel of your choice is closed or full. This applies to *El Indio Dormido*, *La Reyna* and *Tambo Viejo*. Ring the door bell and check for yourself.

L-AL Libertador Ciudad Blanca, Plaza Simón Bolívar, Selva Alegre, T215110, www.libertador.com.pe. Safe, large comfortable rooms, good service, swimming pool (cold), gardens, good meals, pub-style bar, cocktail lounge, squash court.

A Sonesta Posadas del Inca, Portal de Flores 116, T215530, www.sonestaperu.com. On the Plaza de Armas, all the services associated with this chain, Inkafé café and bar with good views, restaurant, tiny outdoor pool, business centre with internet.

A-B Casa Andina, C Jerusalén 603, T202070, www.casa-andina.com. Part of the attractive Casa Andina chain, with breakfast, comfortable and colourful, central, modern, good restaurant, safe, cable TV, phones, car parking.

C Casa de Mi Abuela, Jerusalén 606, T241206, www.lacasademiabuela.com. Safe, hot water, laundry, cable TV, internet, swimming pool, rooms at the back are quieter and overlook the garden, **E** without bath, self-catering if desired, English spoken, parking, internet access

US$3 per hr, tours and transport organized in own agency (*Giardino*, T221345, www.giardinotours.com), which has good information (expensive), small library of European books, breakfast or evening snacks on patio or in beautiful garden.

C De La Fuente, Urb La Campiña Paisajista D-14A, San Lázaro, T203996, delafuente_hostal@hotmail.com. With breakfast, family-style, welcoming, cable TV, free internet, safe.

C Hostal Solar, Ayacucho 108, T/F241793, solar@star.com.pe. Nice colonial building, TV, bath, hot water, includes good breakfast served in nice patio, sun lunge on roof, very secure, quiet.

C-D Posada el Castillo, Pasaje Campos 105, Vallecito, T201828, www.posadaelcastillo.com. Newly built Dutch-owned hotel in colonial style 15 mins walk south of Plaza de Armas. Variety of rooms and suites, some with balcony and view of El Misti, free internet, TV, pool, wonderful breakfast, laundry. Recommended.

D Buena Vista Hostal, C Ugarte 623, Yanahuara, T(01) 9720 5646, www.buenavistahostal.com. Singles, doubles, twins and triples with bath and hot water, breakfast included, free airport transfer, Wi-Fi, cable TV, English 24 hrs.

D Los Balcones de Moral y Santa Catalina, Moral 217, T201291, losbalcones@ hotmail.com.

Convenient, 1 block from Plaza de Armas and close to Santa Catalina, large rooms, comfy beds, hot water, laundry, café, tourist information.

D **La Casa de Avila**, San Martín 116, T213177, www.casadeavila.com. All rooms with bathroom and hot water, price includes good breakfast, spacious, courtyard, guests' kitchen, internet, can arrange airport/bus station pick-up, Spanish courses (which are recommended) and other activities.

D **Casa de Melgar**, Melgar 108, T/F222459, www.lacasademelgar.com. 18th-century building, excellent rooms with bath, hot water (solar panel), safe, courtyard, good breakfast in café (open am and 1730-2100). Good taxi driver (Angel). Recommended.

D **La Casa de Margott**, Jerusalén 304, T229517, lacasademargotthostal@hotmail.com. Bright with a massive palm tree in patio, spacious, convenient, small bar/café, cable TV, phone,

Arequipa

Related map
A Arequipa centre, page 1184

Peru Arequipa Listings

N

0 metres 100
0 yards 100

To 4, Bus Station & the South

To 11 15

To Siglo XX Market

Sleeping		Eating
Casa Andina 1	Hostal Rivero 7	Libertador Ciudad
Casa de Mi Abuela 2	Hostal Tumi de Oro 8	Blanca 10
El Indio Dormido 4	La Casa de Avila 16	Miamaka 12
Home Sweet Home 5	La Casa de Tintin 11	Point Arequipa 14
Hostal Núñez 6	La Estación 3	Posada El Castillo 15
	Las Torres de Ugarte 9	Tambo Viejo 13

Eating
La Quinta 2
Nómadas 1

security box. Recommended.

D La Casa de Tintin, Urbanización San Isidro F1, Vallecito, T284700, www.hoteltintin.com. 15 mins' walk, 5 mins by taxi from the Plaza de Armas, Belgian/Peruvian owned, hot water, cable TV, garden, terrace, sauna, laundry service, restaurant, café and bar and internet, mountain bike rental, very pleasant and comfortable, breakfast included. Recommended.

D Miamaka, San Juan de Dios 402, T241496, hotel_miamaka@terra.com.pe. Excellent service, helpful, cable TV, English spoken.

D-E Casablanca Hostal, Puente Bolognesi 104, a few m from the Plaza de Armas, T221327, www.casablancahostal.com. Super stylish hostal, lovely minimalist rooms in a colonial building. Ambient lighting, most rooms with bath (hot water) and balcony.

D-G Tambo Viejo, Av Malecón Socabaya 107, IV Centenario, T288195, www.tamboviejo.com. 5 blocks south of the plaza near the rail station. 15 rooms ranging from double with bath to dormitory, quiet, English and Dutch spoken, walled garden, hot water, choice of 8 fresh breakfasts (extra), vegetarian restaurant, laundry service, cable TV, safe deposit, coffee shop, bar, book exchange (2 for 1), money changed, tourist information for guests, internet, phone for international calls, bike rental, popular with young travellers, luggage store extra, tours and volcano climbs arranged. For a small fee, you can use the facilities if passing through. Free pick-up from bus terminal (call when arriving), US$5 for airport pick-up.

E La Estación, Loreto 419, Umacollo, T273852, www.backpackerperu.com. Unusual dormitory accommodation in 2 train carriages, includes breakfast, hot water, restaurant next door. 10 mins' walk from Plaza, ask directions for 'el Ovalo del Vallecito', English spoken.

E Home Sweet Home, Rivero 509A, T405982, www.homesweethome-peru.com. Run by María and daughter Cathy, who runs a travel agency and speaks Spanish, English, Italian, French, very helpful, warm and inviting atmosphere, substantial fresh breakfast included. Private or shared bath, hot water all day, simple rooms.

E Hospedaje El Caminante Class, Santa Catalina 207-A, 2nd floor, T203444. Cheaper without bath, hot water, comfortable, laundry service and facilities, sun terrace, very helpful owners. Recommended.

E Hostal Núñez, Jerusalén 528, T233268, hostal_nunez@terra.com.pe. Hot water, TV, laundry, safe, small rooms, breakfast on roof terrace overlooking the city.

E Hostal Regis, Ugarte 202, T226111. Colonial house, French-style interior, hot water all day, cooking and laundry facilities, sun terrace with good views, safe deposit, luggage store, video rental, tours arranged, but poor breakfast.

E Hostal Tumi de Oro, San Agustín 311A, 2½ blocks from the Plaza de Armas, T/F281319. French and English spoken, hot water, roof terrace, book exchange, tea/coffee facilities, safe.

E Lluvia de Oro, Jerusalén 308, T214252, lluvia_de_oro@hotmail.com. Cheaper without bath, English-spoken, breakfast US$2, laundry service, good views.

E La Posada del Cacique, Puente Grau 219, T202170, posadadelcacique@yahoo.es. Old house with tall ceilings, teeny patio, sun terrace, hot water, English spoken, family atmosphere, **F** without bath, also dorm accommodation, safe storage facilities, breakfast available, laundry service, will pick up from terminal. Recommended.

E Las Torres de Ugarte, Ugarte 401, T/F283532, hostaltorresdeugarte@star.com.pe. Next to Santa Catalina convent, occasional hot water, cable TV, laundry service, roof terrace, parking, safe, luggage store, price includes breakfast.

F Casa Itzhak, Av Parra 97, T204596, T994 6643 (mob). With and without bath, includes breakfast, cable TV, laundry service, restaurant, free transport to bus station, very helpful.

F Colonial House Inn, Puente Grau 114, T/F223533, colonial houseinn@hotmail.com. Hot water, quieter rooms at the back, laundry facilities and service, kitchen facilities, roof terrace, good choice of breakfasts, owners speak English.

F Hostal La Reyna, Zela 209, T286578, hostalreyna@yahoo.com. With or without bath, two more expensive rooms at the top of the house, hot water, the daughter speaks English, laundry, breakfast for US$1.15, rooftop seating, will store luggage, ask about rips to the Colca Canyon and volcanoes.

F Hostal Posada Santa Catalina, Santa Catalina 500, T054-243705. Comfortable rooms arranged around a courtyard, roof terrace with great views, charming and helpful staff. Can arrange trips and accommodation in other cities.

F Hostal Rivero, Rivero 420, T229266. Cheaper with shared bath, hot water, cable TV extra, medical assistance, laundry facilities, very helpful, good value.

F Piccola Daniela, Bolivar 400, T054-405727, piccoladanielaaqp@hotmail.com. Includes breakfast, **F** without bath, good value, cable TV, hot water, tiny patio, no English.

F pp The Point Arequipa, Av Lima 515, Vallecito, T286920, www.thepointhostels.com. In a relaxed suburb, free airport/bus station pick-up. Nice building with big garden, great place to meet other travellers, lots of services (free internet, laundry, DVDs etc) and a big party pad.

G La Casita de Ugarte, Ugarte 212, T204363. English/Peruvian run, large basic rooms in a colonial building, new, good value.

G La Fiorentina, Puente Grau 110, T202571. Cheaper without bath, hot water, comfortable, family atmosphere, tours arranged, laundry facilities, use of kitchen extra.

G pp El Indio Dormido, Av Andrés Avelino Cáceres B-9, T427401, the_sleeping_indian@yahoo.com. Close to bus terminal, free transport to centre, some rooms with bath, TV, very helpful.

G La Posada del Virrey, Puente Grau 103, T224050, laposadadelvirrey@yahoo.es. Spacious rooms, shared bath, hot water, kitchen and laundry facilities, helpful.

Eating

Arequipa *p1178, maps p1181 and p1184*

¶¶¶ La Quinta, Jerusalén 522. Excellent food, large portions of local food but limited menu, some vegetarian dishes, attentive service, quiet garden, aimed primarily at the tourist market. Also has a *peña*, weekends mainly, US$1.50 cover.

¶¶¶ Tradición Arequipeña, Av Dolores 111, Paucarpata, T246467. Restaurant serving excellent food, popular with tourists and locals alike, also dance hall. There are many other restaurants and discos on this avenue.

¶¶ Ary Quepay, Jerusalén 502. Excellent local meat and vegetarian dishes, open 1000-2400, very touristy but fun.

¶¶ Café-Restaurante Bóveda San Agustín, Portal San Agustín 127-129. Attractive, good value breakfasts and lunches, evening specials, opens at 0700.

¶¶ La Casita de José Antonio, Plaza San Francisco 401 y Zela. *Cevichería*, fish and seafood, lunchtime only.

¶¶ Nómadas, Melgar 306. Swiss and South American owned, breakfasts, wide menu including vegetarian, sandwiches.

¶¶ Pizzería Los Leños, Jerusalén 407. Excellent, good atmosphere, evenings only, popular, especially with tourists.

¶¶ Sonccollay, Portal de San Agustin 149. Serving 'Inca and Pre-Inca' dishes, stone-cooked alpaca steaks and meats are a speciality,

---

● *For an explanation of the sleeping and eating price codes used in this guide, see page 58. Other*
● *relevant information is found in Essentials pages 1076-1078.*

entertaining owner, copious *chicha*.

Zig Zag, Zela 210. In a colonial house, European (including Swiss) and local dishes, meats include ostrich and alpaca, delicious. They also have a **crêperie** at Santa Catalina 208.

Café El Buho, in Casona Chávez de la Rosa (UNSA), San Agustín. Evenings only. Recommended.

El Turko, San Francisco 216. Kebabs, coffee, breakfasts recommended, good sandwiches, open 0700-2200. Also **El Turko II** at San Francisco 315, also very good.

Fez, San Francisco 229. Delicious falafel and Middle-Eastern fast food. Good coffee, pleasant courtyard. Same company as **El Turko**.

Lakshmivan, Jerusalén 402. Vegetarian, set lunch for US$1.25, pleasant courtyard, good value and healthy, but slow service.

Mandala, Jerusalén 207. Good-value vegetarian, breakfast, 3 set menus for lunch, buffet, dinner, friendly staff. Recommended.

Tacos y Tequila, Ugarte 112. All the Mexican regulars, tacos, burritos, enchiladas, quesadillas, as vegetarian or carnivorous as you like, good value.

Cafés

Café Capriccio, Mercaderes 121. Not that cheap, but excellent coffee, cakes, etc.

Café Manolo, Mercaderes 107 and 113. Great cakes and coffee, also cheap lunches.

Café Valenzuela, Morán 114. Fantastic coffee, locals' favourite.

La Canasta, Jerusalén 115. Excellent baguettes twice daily, also serves breakfast and delicious apple and brazil nut pastries, courtyard seating.

Cioccolata, Mercaderes 120. Among the best for cakes, nicely decorated.

Pushkin, Ugarte 121B. Good for set breakfasts, crêpes, burgers, very friendly and pleasant.

Salchichería Alemana, San Francisco 137. Wide choice of sausages, plus very good empanadas and sandwiches. Good value and popular.

Zun Zun, San Francisco 304, T054-283086. Best bagels in town, pastries, burritos and excellent coffee. Fresh fruit juices and smoothies, very friendly owner and staff. Free internet for customers.

Typical Arequipeño food is available at the San Camilo market. Try the *queso helado* – frozen fresh milk mixed with sugar and a sprinkling of cinnamon. The local chocolate is excellent: **La Ibérica**, in Patio del Ekeko, Mercaderes 141 (see Shopping), is top quality, but expensive.

🎵 Bars and clubs

Arequipa *p1178, maps p1181 and p1184*
There are many good clubs on Av Ejército in

1184

Yanahuara, but most ravers head to Av Dolores, a short taxi ride away (US$1).

Blue Margarita, Melgar 119. Large club with several areas, good mix of music.

Le Café Art Montreal, Ugarte 210. Canadian-run jazz/blues restaurant/ bar with live music Wed and Sat, good atmosphere.

Déjà Vu, San Francisco 319-B. Café/restaurant and bar, good food, DJ evenings, shows movies, popular, 2000-2400.

Farren's Irish Bar, Pasaje Catedral. Good meeting place, pool table, great music.

Arequipa centre

Sleeping
Casa de Melgar **1** A2
Casablanca Hostal **6** B1
Colonial House Inn **2** A1
Hospedaje El
  Caminante Class **3** B1
Hostal La Reyna **5** A1
Hostal Posada Santa
  Catalina **14** A1
Hostal Regis **7** A1
Hostal Solar **9** A2
La Casa de Margott **4** A2
La Casita de Ugarte **8** A1
La Fiorentina **10** A2
La Posada del
  Cacique **13** A2
La Posada del Virrey **16** A2
Lluvia de Oro **11** A2
Los Balcones de Moral
  y Santa Catalina **12** B1
Sonesta Posadas
  del Inca **15** B1

Eating 🍴
Ary Quepay **2** A2

Bóveda San Agustín **4** B1
Café Capriccio **5** B2
Café Manolo **7** B2
Café Valenzuela **1** B2
Cioccolata **6** B2
El Turko **13** A2
El Turco II **9** A1
Fez **3** B1
La Canasta **16** B2
La Casita de
  José Antonio **17** A1
Lakshmivan **19** A2
Mandala **20** A2
Pizzería Los Leños **21** A2
Pushkin **23** A2
Salchichería Alemana **8** B1
Soncollay **29** B1
Tacos y Tequila **10** A2
Zig Zag **24** A1
Zig Zag Crêperie **22** A1
Zun Zun **12** A2

Bars & clubs 🎵
Blue Margarita **26** A2
Déjà Vu **25** B1
Farren's **27** B1
Forum **25** A1
Las Quenas **11** A1

Forum, San Francisco 317. Rock café, live music Thu-Sat 1800-0400, disco, pool tables, US$5 cover if band is playing, includes 1 drink, drinks US$1.50, popular.
Las Quenas, Santa Catalina 302. For *peña* music, Mon-Fri 2100.

🎇 Festivals and events

Arequipa *p1178, maps p1181 and p1184*
A full list of the department's many festivals is available locally.
10 Jan: Sor Ana de Los Angeles y Monteagudo, festival for the patron saint of Santa Catalina monastery. **Mar-Apr**: Semana Santa celebrations involve huge processions every night, culminating in the burning of an effigy of Judas on Easter Sunday in the main plazas of Cayma and Yanahuara, and the reading of his will, containing criticisms of the city authorities. **27 Apr**: the celebration of the apostle Santiago. **May** is known as the *Mes de Las Cruces*, with ceremonies on hilltops throughout the city. **3 Aug**: a procession through the city bearing the images of Santo Domingo and San Francisco. **6-31 Aug**: Fiesta Artesanal del Fundo El Fierro is a sale and exhibition of *artesanía* from all parts of Peru, taking place near Plaza San Francisco. **6-17 Aug**: celebration of the city's anniversary (the 15th, many events including a mass ascent of El Misti). **2 Nov**: Day of the Dead celebrations in cemeteries.

🛍 Shopping

Arequipa *p1178, maps p1181 and p1184*
Bookshops
For international magazines, look along C San Francisco, between Mercaderes and San José.
Librería El Lector, San Francisco 211. Wide selection, including of Peruvian authors, book exchange in various languages (2 for 1), stocks Footprint.
Librerías San Francisco has branches at Portal de Flores 138, San Francisco 102-106 and 133-135. Books on Arequipa and Peru, some in English.
SBS Book Service, San Francisco 125. Has a good selection of travel books etc.

Handicrafts
Alpaca 21, Jerusalén 115, of 125, T213425. Recommended.
Colca Trading Company, Santa Catalina 300B, T242088, colcatradingperu@yahoo.com. Sells a wide variety of naturally coloured cotton and alpaca clothing for adults and children.
Michell y Cia, Juan de la Torre 101, T202525, www.michell.com.pe. Factory outlet, excellent

place for alpaca yarn in huge variety of colours, also a clearance room for baby and adult alpaca yarn is sold. They also sell other types of wool. Alpaca garments also for sale. 1920s machinery on display. Michell has opened a new outlet, Sol Alpaca, Santa Catalina 210, T221454, with branches in Lima and Cuzco, for their latest lines in alpaca and pima cotton clothing.
Millma's, Pasaje Catedral 117 and 112 opposite, millmas@hotmail.com. 100% baby alpaca goods, run by Peruvian family, high quality, beautiful designs, good prices.

Markets
The covered market opposite the Teatro Municipal in C Mercaderes is recommended for knitted goods, bags, etc.
Fundo del Fierro, the large handicraft market behind the old prison on Plaza San Francisco, is also worth a visit. Shop 14 sells alpaca-wool handicrafts from Callalli in the Colca canyon.

Shopping centres
Patio del Ekeko, Mercaderes 141, www.patiodelekeko.com. A commercial centre with upmarket handicrafts, *Alpaca 111* (recommended for high-quality alpaca and vicuña products), *Ilaria* for fine jewellery, *La Ibérica* chocolate shop, café, internet, cinema and Museo de Arte Textil upstairs (Mon-Sat 1000-2030, Sun 1000-1530).

⛰ Activities and tours

Arequipa *p1178, maps p1181 and p1184*
Climbing, cycling, rafting and trekking
International recommendations are for a 300 m per day maximum altitude gain. Be wary of agencies wanting to sell you trips with very fast ascents.
Julver Castro, who has an agency called *Mountrekk*, T601833, julver_mountrekk@hotmail.com. A climbing guide recommended as experienced and "full of energy".
Colca Trek, Jerusalén 401 B, T206217, www.trekinperu.com. Run by the knowledgeable and English-speaking Vlado Soto, recommended for climbing, trekking and mountain biking in the Colca Canyon. Vlado is one of the best guides for the Cotahuasi Canyon. He also rents equipment and has topographical maps.
Cusipata, Jerusalén 408, T203966, www.cusipata.com. Recommended as the best local rafting operator, run 6-day trips on the Río Colca. May-Dec, Río Chili 1-day kayak courses, also trekking and mountain bike tours.
Naturaleza Activa, Santa Catalina 211, T204182, naturactiva@yahoo.com. Experienced guides, knowledgeable, climbing and trekking.

Peru Adventures Tours, Jerusalén 410, T221658, www.peruadventurestours.com. Downhill mountain biking with 4WD support, 3-hr trip into Misti and Chachani mountains, stopping along the way for sightseeing. Cycle ride starts at Azufrero, 5,000 m, finishing in Arequipa at 1600, all equipment, oxygen and snack provided, English-speaking guide. Also other adventure sports, in southern Peru.

Sacred Tours, Jerusalén 400, T330408, sacred_road@hotmail.com. Arranges hiking and rock climbing in Colca Canyon and elsewhere, experienced guides, equipment available.

Selern Services, Urb Puerta Verde F13, José LB y Rivero, Arequipa, T348685, www.selernexpediciones.com. Trekking, adventure tourism, mountain climbing.

Volcanyon Travel, C Villalba 414, T205078, mario-ortiz@terra.com.pe. Trekking and some mountain bike tours in the Colca Canyon, also volcano climbing.

Carlos Zárate Aventuras, Santa Catalina 204, of 3, T202461, www.zarateadvenures.com. Run by Carlos Zárate of the Mountaineering Club of Peru. Good family run business that always works with qualified mountain guides. A specialist in mountaineering and exploring, with a great deal of information and advice and some equipment rental. Carlos also runs trips to the source of the Amazon, Nevado Mismi, as well as trekking in the Cotahuasi canyon and climbing tougher peaks such as Coropuna.

Tour operators

Many agencies on Jerusalén, Santa Catalina and around Plaza de Armas sell air, train and bus tickets and offer tours of Colca, Cotahuasi, Toro Muerto and city. Prices vary greatly so shop around. As a general rule, you get what you pay for, so check carefully what is included in the cheapest of tours. Always settle the details before starting the tour and check that there are enough people for the tour to run. Travel agents frequently work together to fill buses (even the more expensive agencies may not have their own transport) and there are lots of touts. Many tourists prefer to contract tours through their hotel. If a travel agency puts you in touch with a guide, make sure he/she is official. The following have been recommended as helpful and reliable.

A.I. Travel Tours, Santa Catalina 203, Office 1, T425957, www.aitraveltours.com. Peruvian-Dutch tour operator offering cultural and adventure tours for groups or individuals, volunteer work and Spanish courses, large book exchange.

Eco Tours, Jerusalén 409, T202562, ecotours@terra.com.pe. Regular and adventure tours, recommended for Colca tours, Spanish lessons, accommodation arranged.

Holley's Unusual Excursions, T/F258459 (home) any day 1700-0700, or all day Sat and Sun, or Mon-Fri 0800-1600 T222525 and leave a message, angocho@terra.com.pe. Expat Englishman Anthony Holley runs trips in his Land Rover to El Misti, Toro Muerto, the desert and coast.

Pablo Tour, Jerusalén 400-AB-1, T203737, www.pablotour.com. Family-run agency, owns several hostals in Cabanaconde and know area well, 3-day mixed tours in the Colca Canyon with mountain biking, trekking and rafting, free tourist information, maps for sale, bus and hotel reservation service. Son Edwin Junco Cabrera can usually be found in the office, T961 1241 (mob), he speaks fluent French and English.

Santa Catalina Tours, Santa Catalina 219-223, T216994. Offer unique tours of Collagua communities in the Colca Canyon, open daily 0800-1900.

Servicios Aéreos AQP SA, head office in Lima, Los Castaños 347, San Isidro, T01-222 3312, tours@saaqp.com.pe. Offers tours to Arequipa, Colca and to all parts of the country.

Transcontinental Arequipa, Puente Bolognesi 132, of 5, T213843, transcontinental-aqp@ terra.com.pe. Cultural and wildlife tours in the Colca Canyon.

⊖ Transport

Arequipa *p1178, maps p1181 and p1184*
Air
Rodríguez Ballón airport is 7 km from town, T443464. To and from **Lima**, 1 hr 10 mins, several daily with **Lan**, **Aero Cúndor**, **Star Perú**, **Taca** and **WayraPerú**. Lan also serves **Juliaca**, 30 mins, and **Cuzco**, 40 mins.
A reliable means of transport to and from the airport to the hotel of your choice is with **King Tours**, T243357/283037, US$1.30 pp; give 24 hrs notice for return pick-up from your hotel; journey takes 30-40 mins depending on traffic. Transport to the airport may be arranged when buying a ticket at a travel agency, US$1 pp, but not always reliable. Local buses go to about ½ km from the airport.

Bus
There are 2 terminals at Av Andrés A Cáceres s/n, Parque Industrial, south of the centre, 15 mins by colectivo US$0.30, or taxi US$1. The older Terminal Terrestre contains a tourist office, shops and places to eat. The newer Terrapuerto, across the carpark, has a tourist office (which makes hotel reservations) and its own hostal (**E** without breakfast), T421375. Terminal tax US$0.30. Buses may not depart from the terminal where you bought your ticket. All the bus companies have

offices in Terminal Terrestre and several also have offices in Terrapuerto.

Note Theft is a serious problem in the bus station area. Take a taxi to and from the bus station and do not wander around with your belongings. No one is allowed to enter the terminal 2100-0500, so new arrivals cannot be met by hoteliers between those hours; best not to arrive at night.

To **Lima**, 1,011 km, 16-18 hrs, 'normal' service US$8.70, 'imperial' US$17.40, 'crucero' US$23-29 several daily; **Enlaces** (T430333, office only in Terrapuerto), **Tepsa** (T054-424135), **Ormeño** (T424187) and **Cruz del Sur** (T217728) are recommended (prices quoted are of Cruz del Sur). The road is paved but drifting sand and breakdowns may prolong the trip.

To **Nazca**, 566 km, 9 hrs, US$7.25-10 (US$30 on luxury services), several buses daily, mostly at night and most buses continue to Lima. Also US$7.25 to **Chala**, 8 hrs. Some bus companies charge the same fare to Nazca as to Lima. To **Moquegua**, 213 km, 3 hrs, US$3-5.85, several buses and colectivos daily. To **Tacna**, 320 km, 6-7 hrs, US$7-11, several buses daily, most with *Flores*.

To **Cuzco**, all buses go via Juliaca or Puno, US$15-23, 10 hrs. Most companies use double-decker buses (toilet, TV, hostess, etc), eg **Enlaces, Cruz del Sur, Cial** and **Ormeño**, running one morning and, some companies, one afternoon bus. There is a new, quick paved road to **Juliaca**, US$3 via Yura and Santa Lucía, 4 hrs, and **Puno**, 6 hrs, US$4.50-6. Most buses and colectivos continue to Puno. **Flores, Sur Oriente** and **Julsa** recommended.

Taxi

US$4-5 airport to city (can be shared). US$0.70-0.85 around town. **Nova Taxi**, T252511; **Taxi 21**, T212121; **Telemóvil**, T221515; **Taxitur**, T422323.

Train

The railway system goes from **Arequipa** to **Juliaca**, where it divides, 1 line going north to **Cuzco**, the other south to **Puno**. With the opening of the new Arequipa-Juliaca highway, passenger services no longer run to Juliaca.

⊙ Directory

Arequipa *p1178, maps p1181 and p1184*
Airline offices Lan, Santa Catalina 118-C, T201100. **Star Perú**, Santa Catalina 105A, T221896. **Taca**, Av Cayma 636 y Av Ejército, p 1, T0800 18222. **WayraPerú**, Portal de San Agustín 113, T222627. Most tour agencies sell air tickets.
Banks ATM Globalnet cash machines

everywhere, eg on the Plaza, at **i perú** offices. Many give cash in soles or US$ and they accept a wide range of cards: Visa, Plus, Diners Club, Amex, Maestro, Cirrus and many Peruvian cards. **Interbank**, Mercaderes 217. Mastercard representative and ATM. **BCP**, San Juan de Dios 125, accepts Visa Card and gives good rates, no commission, Visa ATM. **BBV Continental**, San Francisco 108. Visa ATM. **BSCH**, C Jerusalén, close to Post Office, will change TCs, low rates, Visa and Mastercard ATM. Also *cambios* on Jerusalén and San Juan de Dios, and several travel agencies. **Sergio A del Carpio D**, Jerusalén 126, T242987, good rates for dollars. **Via Tours**, Santo Domingo 114, good rates. **Casa de Cambio**, San Juan de Dios 109, T282528, good rates. It is almost impossible to change TCs on Sat afternoon or Sun; try to find a sympathetic street changer. Better rates for cash dollars in banks and *casas de cambio*. **Consulates** Bolivia, Rivero 408, of 6, T213391. Mon-Fri 0900-1400, 24 hrs for visa (except those needing clearance from La Paz), go early. Chile, Mercaderes 212, p 4, Of 400-402, Galerías Gameza, T219429, entrance to lift 30m down passageway down Mercaderes on left. Mon-Fri 0900-1300, present passport 0900-1100 if you need a visa. Italy, La Salle D-5, T221444, 1130-1300; in the afternoon T254686 (home). Netherlands, Gonzales Prada 122 esq Juana Espinoza, Umacollo, T252649. Mon-Fri 0900-1300, 1630-1830. Spain, Ugarte 218, p 2, T214977. Mon-Fri 1100-1300, Sat 0900-1300. Sweden, Av. Villa Hermoza 803, Cerro Colorado, T/F252499. Switzerland, Av Miguel Forga 348, Parque Industrial, T229998. UK, Mr Roberts, Tacna y Arica 145, T241340, gerencia@ gruporoberts.com. Mon-Fri 0830-1230, 1500-1830, reported as very friendly and helpful. **Cultural centres** Alianza Francesa, Santa Catalina 208, T215579, www.afarequipa. org.pe. **Instituto Cultural Peruano-Norte Americano**, Casa de los Mendiburo, Melgar 109, T891020, www.ccpna.edu.pe, has an English Library. **Instituto Cultural Peruano Alemán**, Ugarte 207, T218567, icpa@terra. com.pe. **Instituto Nacional de Cultura**, Alameda San Lázaro 120, T213171. **Internet** Many places throughout the centre, about US$0.50 per hr. **Language courses** Centro de Intercambio Cultural Arequipa (CEICA), Urb Universitaria G-9, T/F231759, www.ceica-peru.com. Individual classes at US$6 per hr, US$4.50 for groups, accommodation with families arranged, with board (US$70 per week) or without (US$30), also excursions. Recommended. **Escuela de Español Ari Quipay (EDEAQ)**, T257358, 999 2995 (mob), www.edeaq.com. Peruvian-Swiss run, experienced, multilingual staff, recognized by Peruvian Ministry of Education, in a colonial house near the Plaza de Armas, one-to-one and group classes, home stay available. **Silvana Cornejo**, 7 de Junio 118, Cerrito Los Alvarez, Cerro Colorado, T254985, silvanacornejo@ yahoo.com. US$6 per hr, negotiable for group, she speaks German fluently and is recommended. Her sister Roxanna charges US$3 per hr. **Liz and Edwin Pérez**, T264068, edwinett@mixmail.com. US$5 per hr one-to-one tuition, will go to the hotel you are staying at. Classes are also available at the Instituto Peruano-Norte Americano and Instituto Cultural Peruano Alemán (see Cultural Centres), the latter is US$4 per hr, compared with US$10 at the former, good. **Cecilia Pinto Oppe**, Jerusalén 406 and Zela 209, T996 1638, www.cepes maidiomasceci.com. Good value lessons, held in a café which helps orphaned children. **Carlos Rojas Núñez**, Filtro 405, T285061, carlrojas@ mixmail.com. Private or group lessons to students of all levels, encourages conversation, knowledgeable on culture and politics. Recommended. **Medical services** Only use reputable hospitals or clinics, not practitioners who advertise independent services. Hospitals: **Regional Honorio Delgado**, Av A Carrión s/n, T238465/231818 (inoculations). **Central del Sur**,

Filtro y Peral s/n, T214430 in emergency. Clinics: **Clínica Arequipa SA**, esq Puente Grau y Av Bolognesi, T253424, fast and efficient with English-speaking doctors and all hospital facilities, consultation costs US$18, plus US$4 for sample analysis and around US$7 for a course of antibiotics. **Paz Holandesa**, Av Jorge Chávez 527, T/F206720, www.pazholandesa.com. Dutch foundation dedicated to helping the impoverished, which also has a travel clinic for tourists. Dutch and English spoken, 24-hour service. Highly recommended (see their website if you are interested in volunteering). Emergencies: Ambulance T289800; also **San Miguel**, T283330 (24 hrs). Pharmacy: **Farmacia Libertad**, Piérola 108, owner speaks English.

Post offices The central office is at Moral 118, opposite *Hotel Crismar*. Letters can only be posted at the Post Office during opening hours: Mon-Sat, 0800-2000, Sun 0800-1400. DHL, Santa Catalina 115, T234288 for sending documents and money, also Western Union rep.

Telephones Alvarez Thomas y Palacio Viejo. Many **locutorios** and internet cafés offer cheap international calls, from around US$0.25 per minute.

Colca Canyon → *Tourist tax US$10, payable to park rangers at various points in the Canyon.*

The Colca Canyon is deep: twice as deep as the Grand Canyon. The Río Colca descends from 3,500 m above sea level at Chivay to 2,200 m at Cabanaconde. In the background looms the grey, smoking mass of Sabancaya, one of the most active volcanoes in the Americas, and its more docile neighbour, Ampato (6,288 m). Unspoiled Andean villages lie on both sides of the canyon, inhabited by the Cabana and Collagua peoples, and some of the extensive pre-Columbian terraced fields are still in use. High on anyone's list for visiting the canyon is an early-morning trip to the Cruz del Cóndor, to see these majestic birds at close quarters. From January to April is the rainy season, but this makes the area green, with lots of flowers. This is not the best time to see condors. May to December is the dry, cold season when there is more chance of seeing the birds. Conditions vary annually, though.

From Arequipa there are two routes to **Chivay**, the first village on the edge of the Canyon: the old route, via Cayma, and the new route, through Yura, following the railway, longer but quicker. It can be cold in the morning, reaching 4,825 m in the Pata Pampa pass, but the views are worth it. Cyclists should use the Yura road; better condition and less of a climb at the start. The main road from Arequipa to Chivay has been paved. The old dirt route runs north from Arequipa, over the altiplano. About an hour out of Arequipa is the **Aguada Blanca National Vicuña Reserve**. If you're lucky, you can see herds of these rare animals near the road. This route affords fine views of the volcanoes Misti, Chachani, Ampato and Sabancaya.

Chivay is the chief linking point between the two sides of the canyon; there is a road bridge over the river here (others at Yanque and Lari). The road continues northeast to **Tuti** (small handicrafts shop), and **Sibayo** (*pensión* and grocery store). A long circuit back to Arequipa heads south from Sibayo, passing through **Puente Callalli**, **Chullo** and **Sumbay**. This is a little-travelled road, but the views, with vicuña, llamas, alpacas and Andean duck are superb. Crossing the river at Chivay going west to follow the canyon on the far side, you pass the villages of **Coporaque**, **Ichupampa** (a footbridge crosses the river between the two villages and foot and road bridges connect the road between Coporaque and Ichupampa with Yanque), **Lari**, **Madrigal** (footbridge to Maca) and **Tapay** (connected to Cabanaconde by a footbridge).

Chivay to Cabanaconde

Chivay (3,600 m) is the gateway to the canyon. The **Maria Reiche Planetarium and Observatory** ① *in the grounds of the Casa Andina hotel, 6 blocks west of the Plaza between Huayna Capac and Garcilazo (www.casa-andina.com), US$6, discounts for students*, makes the most of the Colca's clear Southern Hemisphere skies with a powerful telescope and two 55-minute presentations per day at 1830 (Spanish) and 1930 (English). There is a very helpful **tourist office** in the Municipalidad on the west side of the plaza. The tourist police, also on the plaza, can give advice about locally trained guides.

The hot springs of **La Calera** ① *US$3, regular colectivos (US$0.25) or a 1 hr walk from town,* are 4 km away and are highly recommended after a hard day's trekking.

From Chivay, the main road goes west along the Colca Canyon. The first village encountered is **Yanque** (8 km, excellent views), with an interesting church and a bridge to the villages on the other side of the canyon. A large thermal swimming pool is 20 minutes walk from the plaza, beside the renovated Inca bridge on the Yanque-Ichupampa road, US$0.75. The road continues to **Achoma** and **Maca**, which barely survived an earthquake in November 1991. New housing has been built. Then comes the tiny village of **Pinchollo**, with a basic *hostal* on the plaza (a room full of beds and one shared bathroom). The Mirador, or **Cruz del Cóndor** ① *rangers collect the tourist tax here,* is at the deepest point of the canyon. The view is wonderful and condors can be seen rising on the morning thermals (0900, arrive by 0800 to get a good spot) and sometimes in the late afternoon (1600-1800). Camping here is officially forbidden, but if you ask the tourist police in Chivay they may help. The 0500 bus from Chivay to Cabanaconde will stop here briefly at 0630 (if not, ask), US$0.75. Take the return bus from Cabanaconde (0730) and ask to be dropped off at the Mirador.

From the Mirador it is a 20-minute ride (or three-hour walk) to **Cabanaconde** (3,287 m), a friendly, typical village, but very basic (it does have 24-hour electricity). It is the last village in the Colca Canyon. The views are superb and condors can be seen from the hill just west of the village, a 15-minute walk from the plaza, which also gives views of the agrcultural terraces, arguably the most attractive in the valley, to the south of the village. Cabanaconde is an excellent base for visiting the region, with interesting trekking and climbing. Local guides are beginning to see new opportunities for biking and horse riding and many are keen to encourage respectful tourism in the area.

There's a friendly tourist information office, T280212, willing to give plenty of advice, if not maps. It's a good place to find trekking guides and muleteers (mule hire US$30 a day including guide).

Two hours below Cabanaconde is **Sangalle**, an 'oasis' of palm trees and swimming areas and three campsites with basic bungalows and toilets (three-4½ hours back up, ask for the best route in both directions, horses can be hired to carry your bag up, US$5.85), a beautiful spot, recommended. A popular hike involves walking east on the Chivay road to the Mirador de Tapay (before Cruz del Cóndor), then descending to the river on a steep track (four hours, take care). Cross the bridge to the north bank. At the village of San Juan de Chuccho you can stay and eat at a basic family hostel, of which there are several. Hostal Roy and Casa de Rebelino (**G**) are both good. US$2 will buy you a good meal. From here pass **Tapay** (also possible to camp here) and the small villages of Malata and Cosnirhua, all the time heading west along the north side of the Río Colca (take a guide or ask local directions - there are many trails). After about three hours walking, cross another bridge to the south bank of the Río Colca, follow signs to Sangalle, spend the night and return to Cabanconde on the third day. This route is offered by many Arequipa and local agencies.

● Sleeping

Colca Canyon *p1188*

Families in the Colca Canyon offer meals for about US$1 and lodging at US$2.

A **Colca Lodge**, between Coporaque and Ichupampa, T054-202587, www.colca-lodge.com. Very pleasant and relaxing, with beautiful hot springs beside the river, spend at least a day to make the most of the activities on offer. Recommended.

Chivay to Cabanconde *p1189*
Chivay

AL **Estancio Pozo del Cielo**, over the Puente Inca from Chivay amid pre-Inca terraces, T531041, www.pozodelcielo.com.pe. Very comfortable, warm rooms, good views, good service and restaurant. Recommended.

A **Casa Andina**, Huayna Cápac s/n, T531020, www.casa-andina.com. Attractive cabins with hot showers and a cosy bar/dining area, another member of this recommended hotel chain, heating, internet, parking.

C Colca Inn, Salaverry 307, T531111, www.hotelcolcainn.com. A good mid-range option, modern, spick and span, hot water, with a decent restaurant.

D Hostal Posada Chivay, Salaverry 325, T531032, posadachivay@hotmail.com. Central, good rooms, hot water, breakfast included.

D Wasi Kolping, 10 blocks south of town opposite Plaza de Toros, T521076. Comfortable cabins with hot shower, quiet, good views.

E La Casa de Lucila, M Grau 131, T607086. Comfortable, coffee, guides available.

E La Pascana, C Siglo XX 106, T531190, hrlapascana@hotmail.com. Northwest corner of the Plaza. Excellent value with spacious en-suite rooms, hot water, most rooms overlook a pleasant garden. Includes breakfast, parking, a good restaurant.

E-F Hospedaje Restaurant Los Portales, Arequipa 603, T521101. Good value, though beds have rather 'floppy' mattresses, breakfast included. Restaurant downstairs.

F Hostal Anita, north side of plaza, T531114. Rooms with bath look onto a small garden. Recommended.

G Hospedaje Jessy, Zarumilla 218, 1 block from market. Simple, clean, excellent showers, cheaper without bath, helpful, parking.

G pp Rumi Wasi, Sucre 714, 6 blocks from plaza (3 mins' walk), T531114. Good rooms, breakfast included, hot water, helpful, mountain bike rental (in poor condition).

Between Chivay and Yanque

AL Parador del Colca, T054-288440, www.peruorientexpress.com.pe. 3½ km from Yanque, 10 km from Chivay, owned by Orient Express. Built of local materials, with solar power, on an old estate, lots of activities; comfortable cabin-like suites, typical food and home-grown vegetables, meals extra. Rustic but comfortable and very welcoming. Recommended. Closed for refurbishment till Jan 2008.

Yanque

D Tradición Colca, on main road. In Arequipa contact C Argentina 108, Urb Fecia JL Bustamante y Rivero, T054-424926, 935 7117 (mob) for reservations, www.tradicion colca.com. Price is per unit, **E** in low season, includes breakfast, with gardens, restaurant, bar, games room, also has backpackers' rooms and a travel agency. Recommended.

E La Casa de la Bella Flor, Cuzco 303, T280454. Charming small lodge run by Sra Hilde Checca, flower-filled garden, tasteful rooms, good meals

(also open to non-residents), Hilde's uncle, Gregorio, guides visitors to pre-Columbian sites.

Cabanaconde

B Kuntur Wassi, C Cruz Blanca s/n, on the hill above the plaza, T812166, kunturwassi@ terra.com.pe, or waltertinta@hotmail.com. Excellent, 3-star, breakfast included, fine traditional meals on request. Creative design with rooms spaced between rock gardens and waterfalls. Viewing 'tower' and conference centre above. Owners Walter and María very welcoming. Recommended.

C Posada del Conde, C San Pedro, T440197, pdelconde@yahoo.com. Cheaper in low season, with hot shower, excellent value, very good restaurant.

E-F Hostal Valle del Fuego, 1 and 2 blocks from the plaza on C Grau, T830032, www.pablotour. com. 2 places, both with restaurants serving meals for around US$3. Good rooms with comfortable beds, all with bath and hot water, laundry facilities. The Junco family have a wealth of information, with a small family 'empire', including the Arequipa agency **Pablo Tour**, the **Oasis Paradise** in Sangalle (discounts for clients of Valle del Fuego) and a new bar, the **Casa de Pablo Club** at the end of the street. They usually meet the incoming buses. Good value.

G Virgen del Carmen, 5 blocks up from the plaza. Hot showers, may even offer you a welcoming glass of chicha. Recommended.

⊙ Eating

Chivay p1189

♥-♥ **Fonda del Cazador**, north side of plaza. Good food including alpaca.

♥-♥ **Lobos Pizzería**, on the plaza. Has good pizzas and pastas, fast service and good bar, popular.

♥-♥ **Los Sismos**, by the petrol station. Great alpaca steaks, often has live folklore shows.

♥-♥ **Witete**, Siglo XX 328. Good international food and some local dishes.

♥-♥ **McElroys's Irish Pub**, on the plaza. Bar run by a Peruvian and an Irishman, warm, good selection of drinks (sometimes including expensive Guinness), sandwiches, pizza, pasta and music. Mountain bikes for hire. Accepts Visa.

♥ **La Pascana**, near the Plaza de Armas. Another place serving local food; also has lodging (**E**).

Cabanaconde p1189

Both hotels **Posada del Conde** and **Kuntur Wasi** offer excellent food (♥♥ – might need some notice). There are several basic restaurants around the plaza (all ♥).

♥-♥ **Casa de Pablo Club**, Calle Grau. Excellent

fresh juices and pisco sour, cable TV (football!), small book exchange and some equipment hire.

♦ **Don Piero**, signposted just off main plaza. Excellent choice and good information.

♦ **Limeño**, just to the north of the Plaza. Excellent value breakfasts, friendly service.

♦ **Rancho del Colca**, on the plaza. Serves mainly vegetarian food.

⊛ Festivals and events

Colca Canyon *p1188*
Many in the Colca region: **2-3 Feb**: Virgen de la Candelaria, Chivay, Cabanaconde, Maca, Tapay. **Feb**: Carnaval, Chivay. Semana Santa. **3 May**: Cruz de la Piedra, Tuti. **13 Jun**: San Antonio, Yanque, Maca. **14 Jun**: San Juan, Sibayo, Ichupampa. **21 Jun**: anniversary of Chivay. **29 Jun**: San Pedro y San Pablo, Sibayo. **14-17 Jul**: La Virgen del Carmen, Cabanaconde. **25 Jul**: Santiago Apóstol, Coporaque. **26 Jul-2 Aug**: Virgen Santa Ana, Maca. **15 Aug**: Virgen de la Asunta, Chivay. **8 Dec**: Immaculada Concepción, Yanque, Chivay. **25 Dec**: Sagrada Familia, Yanque. Many of these festivals last several days and involve traditional dances and customs.

⛰ Activities and tours

Colca Canyon *p1188*
Trekking
There are many hiking possibilities in the area, with *hostales* or camping for longer treks. Make sure to take enough water, or purification, as it gets very hot and there is not a lot of water available. Moreover, sun protection is a must. Some treks are impossible if it rains heavily in the wet season, but this is very rare. Check beforehand. Ask locals for directions as there are hundreds of confusing paths going into the canyon. Buy food for longer hikes in Arequipa. Topographical maps are available at the *Instituto Geográfico Militar* in Lima (IGM 1:100,000 Huambo and Chivay sheets give the best coverage), and at Colca Trek or Pablo Tour in Arequipa, and good information from *South American Explorers*. From Chivay you can hike to Coporaque and Ichupampa, cross the river by the footbridge and climb up to Yanque, a 1-day hike. It is a 2-hr walk from the Mirador to Cabanaconde (or the other way round - horses can be hired) by a short cut, following the canyon instead of the road, which takes 3 hrs. It takes

2-3 days to walk from Chivay to Cabanaconde (70 km), you can camp along the route, then take a bus back. See above for the main trek from Cabanaconde.

Tours
Travel agencies in Arequipa arrange a 'one-day' tour to the Mirador at Cruz del Cóndor for US$20-25: depart Arequipa at 0400, arrive at the Cruz del Cóndor at 0800-0900, expensive lunch stop at Chivay and back to Arequipa by 2100. For many, especially for those with altitude problems, this is too much to fit into one day (the only advantage is that you don't have to sleep at high altitude). Two-day tours are about US$25-30 pp with an overnight stop in Chivay; more expensive tours range from US$45 to US$90 with accommodation at the top of the range. Allow at least 2-3 days to appreciate the Colca Canyon fully, more if planning to do some trekking.

Chivay *p1189*
Ampato Adventure Sports, Plaza de Armas (close to **Lobos Pizzería**), Chivay, T531073, www.ampatocolca.com. Offer information and rent good mountain bikes.
Colca-Turismo, Av Salaverry 321, Chivay, T503368, and guide **Zacarías Ocsa Osca**, zacariasocsa@hotmail.com, seem to offer a professional service.

⊙ Transport

Colca Canyon *p1188*
Bus Trans Milagros, La Reyna (recommended) and **Andalucia** have 7 departures daily from Arequipa to **Chivay**, continuing to **Cabanaconde**; a further 75 km, 2 hrs, US$1. **La Reyna** has the quickest service, about 6 hrs, US$3.85, others US$3. Buses return to Arequipa from new bus station in Chivay, three blocks from the main plaza, next to the stadium. Combis and colectivos leave from the new terminal to any village in the area. Ask the drivers.
Chivay-Cabanaconde Bus at 0500. Buses run infrequently in each direction, fewer on Sun. Buses leave Cabanaconde for Arequipa 0730 to 1500 from the Plaza de Armas, US$4.50. It is difficult to go to Cuzco from Chivay: you can take a colectivo to Puente Callalli, but the police there are unwilling to let passengers wait for a passing Cuzco-bound bus, which may not stop anyway. Best to go back to Arequipa.

Cotahuasi Canyon

Toro Muerto

ⓘ *US$2; entrance 10 mins' drive from the petroglyphs.*
West of Arequipa, a dirt road branches off the Pan-American to Corire, Aplao and the Río Majes valley. The **world's largest field of petroglyphs** at Toro Muerto is near Corire, where there are several hotels and restaurants near the plaza. For Toro Muerto, turn off on the right heading back out of Corire; one hour walk; ask directions. The higher you go, the more interesting the petroglyphs, though many have been ruined by graffiti. The designs range from simple llamas to elaborate human figures and animals. The sheer scale of the site is awe-inspiring and the view is wonderful (UNESCO World Heritage Site). Take plenty of water, sunglasses and sun cream.

Cotahuasi Canyon

Beyond Aplao the road heads north through **Chuquibamba** (festivals 20 January; 2-3 February; 15 May) traversing the western slopes of Nevado Coropuna (6,425 m), before winding down into **Cotahuasi** (*Phone code 054, Population 3,200, Altitude 2,600 m*). The peaceful colonial town nestles in a sheltered hanging valley beneath Cerro Huinao. Its streets are narrow, the houses whitewashed. Local festival is 4 May.

Several kilometres away a canyon has been cut by the Río Cotahuasi, which flows into the Pacific as the Río Ocuña. At its deepest, at Ninochaca (just below the village of Quechualla), the canyon is 3,354 m deep, 163 m deeper than the Colca Canyon and the deepest in the world. From this point the only way down the canyon is by kayak and it is through kayakers' reports since 1994 that the area has come to the notice of tourists (it was declared a Zona de Reserva Turística in 1988). There is little agriculture apart from some citrus groves, but in Inca times the road linking Puerto Inca and Cuzco ran along much of the canyon's course. Note that the area is not on the tourist route and information is hard to come by.

Following the Río Cotahuasi to the northeast up the valley, you come to **Tomepampa** (10 km), a neat hamlet at 2,700 m, with painted houses and a handsome chapel. The hotsprings of **Luicho** ⓘ *18 km from Cotahuasi, 24 hrs, US$1.50*, are a short walk from the road, across a bridge. Beyond is **Alca** (20 km, one hostal), above which are the small ruins of Kallak, Tiknay and a 'stone library' of rock formations. All these places are connected by buses and combis from Cotahuasi. Buses leave Alca for Arequipa around 1400, combis when full. **Puica** ⓘ *connected to Alca by combi (2 hrs, US$1.50*, is the last village of any significance in the valley, hanging on a hillside at nearly 3,700 m. Nearby attractions include: Churca and a vast prairie of Puya Raimondi cacti; the Ocoruro geysers; and the ruins of Maucallacta. Horses can be hired for US$3 a day, and locals can act as guides. Puica's fiesta is on 28 July.

One of the main treks in the region follows the Inca trade road from Cotahuasi to Quechualla. From the football pitch the path goes through Piro, the gateway to the canyon, and Sipia (three hours, two suspension bridges to cross), near which are the powerful, 150 m high Cataratas de Sipia (take care near the falls if it is windy). Combis from Cotahuasi go to within an hour's walk of the Cataratas; they leave 0600 and 1930, return 0900 and 1400. It's best to visit at midday. A road is being built from this point to the falls, and may be complete by the time you read this. The next three-hour stretch to Chaupo is not for vertigo sufferers as the path is barely etched into the canyon wall, 400 m above the river in places. At Chaupo ask permission to camp; water is available. Next is Velinga, then the dilapidated but extensive ruin of Huña, then **Quechualla**, a charming village and administrative capital of the district. Ask Sr Carmelo Velásquez Gálvez for permission to sleep in the schoolhouse.

● Sleeping

Cotahuasi *p1192*
F Hostal Alcalá II, Arequipa 116, T581090. Very good, hot showers, excellent beds, doubles and triples. Recommended. Run by same family as
F-G Hostal Alcalá, Alca, T280224. One of the best hostales in the valley, 2 rooms with shower, others shared, hot water, restaurant, good food. Prices vary according to season and demand.

G Alojamiento Chávez, Jr Cabildo 125, T581029. Basic rooms around a flower-filled courtyard, Sr José Chávez is helpful on places to visit.
G Hostal Fany Luz, Independencia 117, T581002. Basic but amenable, shared hot showers, double room with cold water only.
G Hostal Villa, Independencia 118, off the plaza, T581018. Basic, bathroom away from the rooms.

ⓘ Eating

Cotahuasi *p1192*

Three small restaurants/bars on Jr Arequipa offer basic fare, best is **BuenSabor**, opposite Hostal Alcalá II. There are many well-stocked tiendas, particularly with fruit, vegetables and local wine.
♥ **El Pionero**, Jr Centenario. Clean, good menú.
♥ **Las Quenas** and **Las Delicias**, both on main square, have decent menus.

ⓘ Transport

Toro Muerto *p1192*

Empresa Del Carpio buses to **Corire** leave from **Arequipa** main terminal hourly from 0500, 3-4 hrs, US$3. Ask to be let out at the beginning of the track to Toro Muerto, or from the plaza in Corire take a taxi, US$6-10 including 2-hr wait.

Cotahuasi *p1192*

Buses daily from **Arequipa** bus terminal, 11-12 hrs, US$9: **Alex** at 1530; **Reyna** at 1600; all return from the plaza in Cotahuasi at the same times. They stop for refreshments in Chuquibamba, about halfway. Both companies continue to Alca.

ⓘ Directory

Cotahuasi *p1192*

Useful services No money exchange. PNP, on plaza; advisable to register with them on arrival and before leaving. **Maps:** some survey maps in Municipalidad and PNP; they may let you make photocopies (shop on the corner of the plaza and Arequipa). Sr Chávez has photocopies of the sheets covering Cotahuasi and surroundings.

South to Chile

Moquegua → *Phone code: 053. Colour map 6, grid A1. Population: 110,000. Altitude: 1,412 m.*
This town 213 km from Arequipa in the narrow valley of the Moquegua River enjoys a sub-tropical climate. The old centre, a few blocks above the Pan-American Highway, has winding, cobbled streets and 19th-century buildings. The Plaza de Armas, with its mix of ruined and well-maintained churches, colonial and republican façades and fine trees, is one of the most interesting small-town plazas in the country. **Museo Contisuyo** ⓘ *on the Plaza de Armas, within the ruins of the Iglesia Matriz, T461844, http://bruceowen.com/contisuyo/Museo E.html, Mon-Sun 0800-1300, 1430-1730, Tue 0800-1200, 1600-2000, US$0.45,* covers the cultures which thrived in the Moquegua and Ilo valleys, including the Huari, Tiahuanaco, Chiribaya and Estuquiña, who were conquered by the Incas. Artefacts are well-displayed explained in Spanish and English. Día de Santa Catalina, 25 November, is the anniversary of the founding of the colonial city. There are several email offices on or near the Plaza de Armas. Municipal **tourist office** on the plaza ⓘ *Ayacucho y Ancash, Mon-Fri 0800-1600.*

A highly recommended excursion is to **Cerro Baúl** ⓘ *30 mins by colectivo, US$1.70,* 2,590 m, a tabletop mountain with marvellous views and many legends, which can be combined with the pleasant town of Torata, 24 km northeast.

The Carretera Binacional, from the port of Ilo to La Paz, has a breathtaking stretch from Moquegua to Desaguadero at the southeastern end of Lake Titicaca. It skirts Cerro Baúl and climbs through zones of ancient terraces to its highest point at 4,755 m. On the altiplano there are herds of llamas and alpacas, lakes with waterfowl, strange mountain formations and snow-covered peaks. At Mazo Cruz there is a PNP checkpoint where all documents and bags are checked. Approaching Desaguadero the Cordillera Real of Bolivia comes into view. The road is fully paved and should be taken in daylight.

Tacna → *Phone code: 052. Colour map 6, grid A1. Population: 174,366. Altitude: 550 m.*
Only 36 km from the Chilean border and 56 km from the international port of Arica, Tacna has free-trade status. It is an important commercial centre and Chileans come for cheap medical and dental treatment. Around the city the desert is gradually being irrigated. The local economy includes olive groves, vineyards and fishing. Tacna was in Chilean hands from 1880 to 1929, when its people voted by plebiscite to return to Peru. Above the city (8 km away, just off the Panamericana Norte), on the heights, is the **Campo de la Alianza**, scene of a battle between Peru and Chile in 1880. The cathedral, designed by Eiffel, faces the Plaza de Armas, which contains huge bronze statues of Admiral Grau and Colonel Bolognesi. They stand at either end of the Arca de los Héroes, the triumphal arch which is the symbol of the city. The bronze fountain in the Plaza is said to be a duplicate of the one in the Place de la Concorde (Paris) and was also designed by Eiffel. The **Parque de la Locomotora** ⓘ *daily 0700-1700,*

US$0.30; knock at the gate under the clock tower on Jr 2 de Mayo for entry, near the city centre, has a British-built locomotive, which was used in the War of the Pacific. There is a very good railway museum at the station. The house of **Francisco Zela** ① *Zela 542, Mon-Sat 0830-1230, 1530-1900*, who gave the Cry of Independence on 20 July 1811, is a museum.

Tourist office, **Dircetur** ① *Blondell 50, p3-4, T422784, tacna@mincetur.gob.pe, Mon-Fri 0730-1515*. Also by the Centro Cultural Miculla ① *Blondell y Francisco Lazo, Mon-Fri 0800-1300, Spanish only*, has city map and regional information, at the Terminal Terrestre Nacional ① *T427007, 0600-2200*; and at the Terminal Internacional ① *Mon-Fri 0800-1500, Sat 0800-1200*, city map, helpful, list of official taxi rates; www.mincetur.gob.pe/regiones/tacna. **Tourist police** ① *Jr Callao 121, T414141, ext 245.* **Touring y Automóvil Club del Perú** ① *Av 2 de Mayo 67, T744237, tacna@touringperu.com.pe.*

Border with Chile

There is a checkpoint before the border, which is open 0800-2300 (24 hours Friday and Saturday). You need to obtain a Peruvian exit stamp and a Chilean entrance stamp; formalities are straightforward (see below). If you need a Chilean visa, you have to get it in Tacna (address below). Peruvian time is 1 hour earlier than Chilean time March-October; 2 hours earlier September/October to February/March (varies annually). No fruit or vegetables are allowed into Chile or Tacna.

Crossing by private vehicle For those leaving Peru by car buy *relaciones de pasajeros* (official forms, US$0.45) from the kiosk at the border or from a bookshop; you will need four copies. Next, return your tourist card, visit the PNP office, return the vehicle permit and finally depart through the checkpoints.

Exchange See under Banks, below. Changers can also be found at counters in the international bus terminal; rates are much the same as in town.

◉ Sleeping

Moquegua *p1193*
Most hotels do not serve breakfast.
D **Alameda**, Junín 322, T463971. Includes breakfast, large comfortable rooms, welcoming.
E **Arequipa**, Jr Arequipa 360, T461338, javierhotelareqiupa@hotmail.com. Clean and pleasant, hot water sometimes.
E **Hostal Adrianella**, Miguel Grau 239, T/F463469. Hot water, TV, safe, helpful, tourist information, close to market and buses, bit faded.
E **Hostal Plaza**, Ayacucho 675, T461612. Modern and comfortable, good value.
F **Hostal Carrera**, Jr Lima 320 (no sign), T462113. Hot water (F shared bath, solar-powered hot water, best in afternoon), laundry facilities on roof, good value. Recommended.
G pp **Hospedaje Cornejo**, Tarapacá 281-A, T507681. Shared bath, electric showers, basic but clean.

Tacna *p1193, map p1195*
B **Gran Hotel Tacna**, Av Bolognesi 300, T424193, www.derrama.org.pe. Includes breakfast, internet access in rooms US$1/hr, pool open to non-guests with minimum US$8 purchase in restaurant or bar, best in town, gardens, safe car park, English spoken.
C **Dorado**, Arias Araguez 145, T415741, www.doradohotel.com. Includes breakfast, restaurant, modern and comfortable.
D **El Mesón**, Unánue 175, T425841,

www.mesonhotel.com, . With breakfast, TV, central, modern, comfortable, safe, wireless internet in rooms. Recommended.
D **Maximo's**, Arias Araguez 281, T242604, www.maximoshotel.com. With breakfast, modern rooms with frigo-bar, Wi-Fi, sauna.
E **Copacabana**, Arias Araguez 281 y 2 de Mayo, T421721, www.copahotel.com. With breakfast, good rooms.
E **Hostal Anturio**, 28 de Julio 194 y Zela, T244258, www.anturiohostaltacna.com. Cafetería downstairs, breakfast extra, clean, modern and good value.
F **Hostal Bon Ami**, 2 de Mayo 445, T244847. Cheaper without bath, hot water best in afternoon, simple, secure.
F **Hostal HC**, Zela 734, T242042. Hot water, TV, family run, good value, discounts available, laundry service. Recommended.
F **Lido**, San Martín 876-A, near Plaza de Armas, T577001. With hot showers, no breakfast, simple but adequate.

◉ Eating

Moquegua *p1193*
♀♀ **Pizzería Casa Vieja**, Moquegua 326. Mon-Sat 1830-2300, pizza and pasta.
♀ **Moraly**, Lima y Libertad. The best place for meals. Breakfast, good lunches, *menú* US$1.75, open Mon-Sat 1000-2200, Sun 1000-1600.

Tacna *p1193, map p1195*

🍴 **DaVinci**, San Martín 596 y Arias Araguez. Mon-Sat 1100-2300, pizza and other dishes, nice atmosphere, bar upstairs Tue-Sat 2000-0200.

🍴 **Il Pomodoro**, Bolívar 524 y Apurimac. Closed Sun evening and Mon midday, upscale Italian serving set lunch on weekdays, pricey à la carte in the evening, attentive service.

🍴 **Cusqueñita**, Zela 747, 1100-1600, excellent 4-course lunch, large portions, good value, variety of choices. Recommended.

🍴 **El Sabor Criollo**, Ayacucho 86-C. A popular lunch-time restaurant.

🍴 **Fu-Lin**, Arias Araguez 396 y 2 de Mayo, Mon-Sat 0930-1600, vegetarian Chinese.

🍴 **Koyuki**, Bolívar 718. Generous set lunch daily, sea food and other à la carte in the evening, closed Sun evening. Several other popular lunch places on the same block.

La Espiga, San Martín 431. Good bakery and pastry shop. Verdi, Pasaje Vigil 57. Café serving excellent *empanadas* and sweets, also set lunch.

⊖ Transport

Moquegua *p1193*

Bus All bus companies are on Av Ejército, 2 blocks north of the market at Jr Grau, except **Ormeño**, Av La Paz casi Balta. From **Lima**, US$15-30, 15 hrs, many companies with executive and regular services. To **Tacna**, 159 km, 2 hrs, US$3, hourly buses with **Flores**, Av del Ejército y Andrés Aurelio Cáceres. To **Arequipa**, 3½ hrs, US$5.50, several buses daily. Colectivos for these two destinations leave when full from Av del Ejército y Andrés Aurelio Cáceres, almost double the bus fare - negotiate. To **Desaguadero** and **Puno**, San Martín-Nobleza, 4 a day, 6 hrs, US$7.50; the 2130 bus continues to Cuzco; to **Cuzco** direct at 1100, 13 hrs, US$13.50. **Mily Tours**, Av del Ejército 32-B, T464000, colectivos to Desaguadero, 4 hrs, US$15.

Tacna *p1193, map p1195*

Air The airport (T314503) is at Km 5 on the Panamericana Sur, on the way to the border. To go from the airport directly to Arica, call the bus terminal (T427007) and ask a colectivo to pick you up on its way to the border, US$4. Taxi from airport to Tacna centre US$2-3. To **Lima**, 1½ hrs; daily flights with **Lan** (Av San Martín 259, T428346) and **WayraPerú** (28 de Julio 102, T426642). **Aerocóndor** (Arias Araguez 135,

Tacna

Sleeping
Copacabana 1
Dorado 5
El Mesón 2
Gran Tacna 6
Hostal Anturio 8
Hostal Bon Ami 3

Hostal HC 4
Maximo's 9

Eating
Cusqueñita 1
Da Vinci 3
El Sabor Criollo 2

Fu Lin 4
Il Pomodoro 5
Koyuki 6
La Espiga 7
Verdi 8

T248187) to Lima via **Arequipa** on Tue, Thu, Sat, direct on other days.

Bus Two bus stations on Hipólito Unánue, T427007, 1 km from the plaza (colectivo US$0.25, taxi US$0.60 minimum). One terminal is for international services (ie Arica), the other for domestic, both are well-organized, local tax US$0.30, baggage store, easy to make connections to the border, Arequipa or Lima. To **Moquegua** (prices above) hourly buses with **Flores** (Av Saucini behind the Terminal Nacional, T426691). To **Arequipa**, 6 hrs, US$6.50-9.50, several buses daily, most with **Flores**. To **Nazca**, 793 km, 12 hrs, several buses daily, en route for Lima (fares about US$3 less than to Lima). Several companies daily to **Lima**, 1,239 km, 21-26 hrs, US$15-20 regular, US$30-40 *bus-cama*, eg **Flores**, **Cruz del Sur** and **Ormeño** (on Arias Araguez by the petrol station), recommended. Buses to **Desaguadero, Puno** and **Cuzco** leave from Terminal Collasuyo (T312538), Av Internacional in Barrio Altos de la Alianza neighbourhood; taxi to centre US$0.75. **San Martín-Nobleza** (T952 4252) is recommended, 4 a day to **Desaguadero** and **Puno**, US$10, 8-10 hrs; 1900 bus continues to **Juliaca** and **Cuzco**; to Cuzco direct at 0830, US$15, 15 hrs, or change in Moquegua.

At **Tomasiri**, 35 km north of Tacna, passengers' luggage is checked, whether you have been out of the country or not. Do not carry anything on the bus for anyone else, just your own belongings. Passports may be checked at Camiara, a police checkpoint some 60 km from Tacna.

To **La Paz**, Bolivia, the quickest and cheapest route is via Moquegua and Desaguadero; it also involves one less border crossing than via Arica and Tambo Colorado.

Border with Chile: Tacna *p1193*

Road 56 km, 1-2 hrs, depending on waiting time at the border. Buses to Arica charge US$1.80 and colectivo taxis US$4-5 pp. All leave from the international terminal in Tacna throughout the day. Colectivos which carry 5 passengers only leave when full. As you approach the terminal you will be grabbed by a driver or his agent and told that the car is "just about to leave". This is hard to verify as you may not see the colectivo

until you have filled in the paperwork. Once you have chosen a driver/agent, you will be rushed to his company's office where your passport will be taken from you and the details filled out on a Chilean entry form. You can change your remaining soles at the bus terminal. It is 30 mins to the Peruvian border post at Santa Rosa, where all exit formalities are carried out. The driver will hustle you through all the procedures. A short distance beyond is the Chilean post at Chacalluta, where again the driver will show you what to do. All formalities take about 30 mins. It's a further 15 mins to Arica's bus terminal. A Chilean driver is more likely to take you to any address in Arica.

Train Station is at Av Albaracín y 2 de Mayo. *Autoferro* to Arica, Mon-Sat 0545 and 1600 (from Arica at 0900 and 1800 Peruvian time), US$1.50, 1½ hrs, customs and immigration at railway stations. Ticket office 0800-0900 and 1430-1600, for the morning train best buy the morning before as it sells out.

❶ Directory

Moquegua *p1193*
Banks **BCP**, Moquegua y Tarapacá. Changes TCs, advances money on Visa, Visa ATM. Street changers at Mercado Central. **Internet** Many places all over town, US$0.35 per hr.

Tacna *p1193, map p1195*
Banks **BCP**, San Martín 574, no commission for TCs (Amex, Citicorp) into soles. **Scotiabank**, San Martín 476. ATM for Visa/Plus, MasterCard/Maestro. **Interbank**, San Martín 646, has ATM for Visa/Plus, Mastercard/Cirrus and Amex. Several *casas de cambio* at San Martín y Arias Araguez, all offering good rates for dollars cash, also change euros, pesos chilenos and bolivianos. Street changers stand outside the Municipalidad. **Consulates** Bolivia, Av Bolognesi 1751 y Piura, T245121, Mon-Fri 0900-1500. **Chile**, Presbítero Andía block 1, TT423063. Open Mon-Fri 0800-1300. **Internet** Many on San Martín, several open 24 hrs. Others around the centre. Average price US$0.35 per hr. **Post offices** Av Bolognesi 361. Open Mon-Sat 0800-2000. **Telephones** Public *locutorios* everywhere; shop around for best prices.

Lake Titicaca

Straddling Peru's southern border with Bolivia are the sapphire-blue waters of mystical Lake Titicaca, a huge inland sea which is the highest navigable lake in the world. Its shores and islands are home to the Aymara and Quechua, who are among Peru's oldest peoples. Here you can wander through traditional villages where Spanish is a second language and where ancient myths and beliefs still hold true. Newly paved roads climb from the coastal deserts and oases to the high plateau in which sits Lake Titicaca (Arequipa-Yura-Santa Lucía-Juliaca-Puno; Moquegua- Desaguadero-Puno). The steep ascents lead to wide open views of pampas with agricultural communities, desolate mountains, small lakes and salt flats. It is a rapid change of altitude, so be prepared for some discomfort and breathlessness.

Puno and around

→ *Phone code: 051. Colour map 6, grid A2. Population: 100,170. Altitude: 3,855 m.*

On the northwest shore of Lake Titicaca, Puno is capital of its department and Peru's folklore centre with a vast array of handicrafts, festivals and costumes and a rich tradition of music and dance.

Ins and outs

Tourist offices: i perú ① *Jr Lima y Deústua, near Plaza de Armas, T365088*. They are friendly and helpful with general information and maps. **Dircetur** ① *Ayacucho 682, T364976, puno@mincetur.gob.pe*. **Indecopi**, the tourist protection bureau, has an office at ① *Lima y Fermín Arbulú, p 2, T/F366138, odipun@indecopi.gob.pe*. **Tourist police** ① *Jr Deústua 538, T364806. Report any scams, such as unscrupulous price changes, and beware touts (see page 1201)*. www.punored.com is a portal for the Puno area. Puno gets bitterly cold at night: from June to August the temperature at night can fall to -25°C, but generally not below -5°C.

Sights

The **Cathedral**, completed in 1657, has an impressive baroque exterior, but an austere interior. Beside the Cathedral is the **Balcony of the Conde de Lemos** ① *Deústua esquina Conde de Lemos*, where Peru's Viceroy stayed when he first arrived in the city. The **Museo Municipal Dreyer** ① *Conde de Lemos 289, Mon-Fri 0730-1330, US$1*, has been combined with the private collection of Sr Carlos Dreyer. A short walk up Independencia leads to the **Arco Deústua**, a monument honouring those killed in the battles of Junín and Ayacucho. Nearby, is a mirador giving fine views over the town, the port and the lake beyond. The walk from Jr Cornejo following the Stations of the Cross up a nearby hill, with fine views of Lake Titicaca, has been recommended, but be careful and don't go alone (the same applies to any of the hills around Puno, eg Huajsapata).

The *Yavari*, the **oldest ship on Lake Titicaca** ① *0800-1715, free but donations of US$6 welcome to help with maintenance costs*, is berthed near the entrance to the Sonesta Posada del Inca hotel and is now open as a museum (the hotel runs a Happy Hour till 2230). The ship was built in England in 1862 and was shipped in kit form to Arica, then by rail to Tacna and by mule to Lake Titicaca. The journey took six years. The *Yavari* was launched on Christmas Day 1870. Visitors are very welcome on board. Project addresses: England: 61 Mexfield Rd, London SW15 2RG, T/F44- 20-8874 0583, info@yavari.org. Peru/Lima: Giselle Guldentops, T01-9998 5071, Yavari. gulden@dwp.net; in Puno: Asociación Yavari, c/o Capitán Carlos Saavedra, T051-369329, carlosalberto@yavari.org. For general information, volunteering, donations, etc, visit www.yavari.org. In the harbour is Hull (UK)-built MS *Ollanta*, which sailed the lake from 1926 to the 1970s. **PerúRail** has restored the vessel. A new Malecón Bahía de los Incas, near the port, is a pleasant place for a stroll with views of the lake. The bay by Puno is, however, noticeably polluted. There is also a small museum ① *US$0.15*, at the jetty, displaying stuffed birds and fish from the lake.

Around Puno

Anybody interested in religious architecture should visit the villages along the western shore of Lake Titicaca. An Inca sundial can be seen near the village of **Chucuíto** (19 km), which has an interesting church, La Asunción, and houses with carved stone doorways. Visits to Chucuíto usually include the Templo de la Fertilidad, **Inca Uyo**, which boasts many phalli and other fertility symbols. The authenticity and original location of these objects is the subject of debate.

Juli, 80 km, has some fine examples of religious architecture. **San Pedro** on the plaza, designated as the Cathedral, has been extensively restored. It contains a series of paintings of saints, with the Via Crucis scenes in the same frame, and gilt side altars above which some of the arches have baroque designs. No opening hours are displayed. **San Juan Letrán**

① *mornings only, US$1.15,* has two sets of 17th-century paintings of the lives of St John the Baptist and of St Teresa, contained in sumptuous gilded frames. San Juan is a museum. It also has intricate *mestizo* carving in pink stone. **Santa Cruz** is closed to visitors, but there is a view of the lake from the plaza in front. The fourth church, **La Asunción** ① *US$0.85,* is also a museum. The nave is empty, but its walls are lined with colonial paintings with no labels. The original painting on the walls of the transept is fading. Its fine bell tower was damaged by earthquake or lightning. Outside is an archway and atrium which date from the early 17th century. Needlework, other weavings, handicrafts and antiques are offered for sale in town. Near Juli is a small colony of flamingoes. Many other birds can be seen from the road. Colectivo Puno-Juli US$0.75; return from Juli outside market at Ilave 349.

A further 20 km along the lake is **Pomata** ① *daily 0700-1200, 1330-1600, free, but give a donation, getting there: US$0.30 from Juli,* whose church of Santiago Apóstol is built of red sandstone. It has a beautiful interior, with superb carving and paintings. At **Zepita**, near Desaguadero, the 18th-century Dominican church is also worth a visit.

Near Puno are the *chullpas* (pre-Columbian funeral towers) of **Sillustani** ① *32 km from Puno on an excellent road, US$1.65, take an organized tour; about 3-4 hrs, leave 1430, US$6.30, tours usually stop at a Colla house on the way, to see local products,* in a beautiful setting on a peninsula in Lake Umayo. John Hemming writes: "Most of the towers date from the period of Inca occupation in the 15th century, but they are burial towers of the Aymara-speaking Colla tribe. The engineering involved in their construction is more complex than anything the Incas built – it is defeating archaeologists' attempts to rebuild the tallest 'lizard' *chullpa.*" There is a museum and handicraft sellers wait at the exit. Photography is best in the afternoon light, though this is when the wind is strongest. The scenery is barren, but impressive. There is a small community at the foot of the promontory.

Llachón → *Population: 1,300.*

At the eastern end of the Península de Capachica, which encloses the northern side of the Bahía de Puno, is Llachón, a farming village which has introduced community-based tourism. It has electricity and one phone (To51-832323). On Capachica there are currently six community tourism organizations, each with a dozen or more families and links to different tour operators in Puno, Cuzco or abroad. The scenery is very pretty, with sandy beaches, pre-Inca terracing, trees and flowers. The view of the sunset from the Auki Carus hill is reckoned to be better even than from Taquile. Visitors share in local activities and 70% of all produce served is from the residents' farms. Throughout the peninsula the dress of the local women is very colourful, with 4-cornered hats called *monteros*, matching vests and colourful *polleras*. The peninsula is good for hiking, mountain biking and sailing; boats can be hired.

● Sleeping

Puno *p1197, map p1200*
Puno sometimes has power and water shortages. Check if breakfast is included in the hotel price.
AL Libertador Isla Esteves, on an island linked by a causeway 5 km northeast of Puno (taxi US$3), T367780, www.libertador.com.pe. Built on a Tiahuanaco-period site, spacious, good views, phone, bar, good restaurant, disco, good service, electricity and hot water all day, parking.
AL-A Sonesta Posadas del Inca, Av Sesquicentenario 610, Huaje, 5 km from Puno on the lakeshore, T364111, www.sonestaperu.com. 62 rooms with heating, facilities for the disabled, friendly, local textile decorations, good views, *Inkafé* restaurant has an Andean menu, folklore shows.
AL Casa Andina Private Collection Puno, Av Sesquicentenario 1970, T363992. New addition to this recommended chain, on the lakeshore. The group also has **A Casa Andina Plaza**, Jr Grau 270, 1 block from plaza, T367520, includes

breakfast, TV, heating, non-smoking rooms, safe, central. Business centre with internet, parking; and **A Casa Andina Tikarani**, Independencia 185, T367803, similar to the **Plaza**, but further from the centre. Visit www.casa-andina.com.
A-B Plaza Mayor, Deústua 342, T/F366089, www.plazamayorhostal.com. Comfortable, well-appointed, good big beds, buffet breakfast included, hot water, laundry. Recommended.
B Balsa Inn, Cajamarca 555, T363144, www.hotelbalsainn.com. With breakfast, hot water, TV, comfortable, safe, heating, very helpful.
B El Buho, Lambayeque 142, T/F366122, www.peruhotelsguide.com/hotelbuho. Hot water, nice rooms with heaters, TV, restaurant, safe, discount for Footprint book owners, travel agency for trips and flights. Recommended.
B Colón Inn, Tacna 290, T351432, www.titicaca-peru.com. Colonial style, good rooms with hot shower, price includes tax and

buffet breakfast, good service, safe, restaurant *Sol Naciente* and pizzería *Europa*, the Belgian manager Christian Nonis is well known, especially for his work on behalf of the people on Taquile island. Recommended.

B Hostal Hacienda, Jr Deústua 297, T/F356109, haciendahostal@hotmail.com. Refurbished colonial house, hot water, TV, includes breakfast, café, comfortable. Recommended.

B Sillustani, Jr Lambayeque 195, T351881, www.sillustani.com. Price includes breakfast and taxes, hot water, cable TV, safety deposit, heaters, internet, very good.

C Hostal Italia, Teodoro Valcarcel 122, T352521, www.hotelitaliaperu.com. 2 blocks from the station. With breakfast, cheaper in low season, good, safe, hot water, good food, small rooms, staff helpful.

C Hostal Pukara, Jr Libertad 328, T/F368448, pukara@terra.com.pe. Excellent, English spoken, central, quiet, free coca in evening, breakfast.

D Hostal Imperial, Teodoro Valcarcel 145, T352386, imperial_hostal_puno@yahoo.com. **D-E** low season, basic but big rooms, good hot showers, safe, helpful, stores luggage, comfortable.

D Hostal Monterrey, Lima 441, T351691, monterreytours@hotmail.com. **F** without bath, better rooms with good showers, hot water, breakfast and TV included, secure for luggage, motorcycle parking US$0.50.

D Posada Don Giorgio, Tarapacá 238, T363648, dongiorgio@titicacalake.com. Breakfast, hot water, large rooms, nicely decorated, TV, comfortable.

D-E Hospedaje Don Julio, Av Tacna 336, T363358, hostaldonjulio@hotmail.com. Hot water, breakfast, homely, some English spoken.

D-E Hostal Rubi 'Los Portales', Jr Cajamarca 152-154, T/F353384, www.mancocapacinn.com. Safe, breakfast US$2, hot water, TV, good, tours arranged. Recommended.

E-F Hostal Los Pinos, Tarapacá 182, T/F367398, hostalpinos@hotmail.com. Family run, hot showers, safe, luggage store, laundry facilities, helpful, cheap tours organized. Recommended.

E Los Uros, Teodoro Valcarcel 135, T352141, huros@speedy.com.pe. Cheaper without bath, hot water, breakfast available, quiet at back, good value, small charge to leave luggage, laundry, often full, changes TCs a reasonable rate. Recommended.

E Hospedaje Residencial Margarita, Jr Tarapacá 130, T352820, hostalmargarita@hotmail.com. Large building, family atmosphere, hot water most of the day, stores luggage, tours can be arranged. Recommended.

E-F Hostal Arequipa, Arequipa 153, T352071, hotelarequipa@speedy.com.pe. Hot water, will change TCs at good rates, stores luggage, secure, arranges tours to the islands, OK.

E-F Hostal Nesther, Deústua 268, T363308. Also has triples, hot water. Recommended.

E-F Hostal Q'oñiwasi, Av La Torre 135, opposite train station, T365784, qoniwasi@mundomail.net. **E** without bath and in low season, heating extra, hot water, laundry facilities and service, luggage store, breakfast extra, lunch available, safe, helpful.

F Hostal Europa, Alfonso Ugarte 112, near train station, T353026, hostaleuropa@ hotmail.com. Very popular, cheaper without bath, luggage may be stored (don't leave valuables in your room), hot water sometimes, garage space for motorcycles.

F Hostal Illampu, Av La Torre 137-interior, T353284, www.illampu.3a2.com. Warm water, breakfast and TV extra, café, laundry, safe box (do not leave valuables in room), exchange money, arranges excursions (ask for Santiago).

G pp Albergue Juvenil Virgen de Copacabana, Ilave 228, T363766, hostelling_virgen_copacabana@yahoo.com. Hot water, good location, quiet, unhelpful, staff tend to move guests without notice. Entrance is down a passageway.

Around Puno p1197

E pp Albergue Juvenil Las Cabañas, Chucuíto, T351276, www.chucuito.com. Great wee cottages, meals, will collect you from Puno if you phone in advance. Highly recommended.

Llachón p1198

Families offer accommodation on a rotational basis (**F** per bed). Contact **Don Valentín Quispe**, T051-982 1392 (mob), llachon@ yahoo.com or visit www.titicaca-peru.com/capachicae.htm. Meals are served in his house: breakfast US$1.20, other meals US$2. Other families offering lodging are Tomás Cahui Coila, **Centro Turístico Santa María Llachón**, T992 3595 (mob).

F Primo Flores, near church and bus stop in Llachón, T051-968 0040 (mob), primopuno@yahoo.es. Rustic family accommodation, includes breakfast, other meals on request US$2.50, knowledgeable and friendly (Sr Flores is the head of one of the community tourism groups.) All hosts can arrange boat transport to Amantaní.

Eating

Puno *p1197, map p1200*

¶ **IncAbar**, Lima 356-A. Open for breakfast, lunch and dinner, interesting dishes in creative sauces, fish, pastas, curries, café and couch bar, nice decor.

¶ **Internacional**, Moquegua 201. Very popular, excellent trout, good pizzas, service variable.

¶ **La Plaza**, Puno 425, Plaza de Armas. Good food, including fish.

¶ **Mojsa**, Lima 635 p 2, Plaza de Armas. Good international and *novo andino* dishes, also has an arts and crafts shop. Recommended.

¶-¶ **Apu Salkantay**, Lima 357 and in 400 block.

Wide menu of meats, fish (more expensive), pastas, sandwiches, pizza, coffee, popular.

♥♥-♥ **La Caywa Andean Cuisine Bar**, Jr Arequipa 410. Open 1000-2200. Typical and international. Recommended.

♥♥-♥ **Lago de Flores**, Lima 357. Local dishes and pizza, very good food, open fire in the shape of a pizza oven keeps diners warm.

♥♥-♥ **Don Piero**, Lima 360. Huge meals, live music, try their 'pollo coca-cola' (chicken in a sweet and sour sauce), slow service, popular, tax extra.

♥♥-♥ **Pizzería El Buho**, Lima 349 and at Jr Libertad 386. Excellent pizza, lively atmosphere, open 1800 onwards, pizzas US$2.35-3.

♥ **Chifa Fon Seng**, Arequipa 552. Good food, service and value, Chinese, popular.

♥ **Chifa Nan Hua**, Arequipa 167, 1 block from Plaza de Armas. Tasty Chinese, big portions.

♥ **Govinda**, Deústua 312. Cheap vegetarian lunch menus, closes at 2000.

♥ **Remembranzas**, Jr Moquegua 200. Pizzas as well as local food. Open 0630-2200.

♥ **Vida Natural**, Libertad 449. Open for breakfast, salads, fruits, yoghourt.

Cafés

Cafetería Mercedes, Jr Arequipa 351. Good menú US$1.50, bread, cakes, snacks, juices.

Casa del Corregidor, Deústua 576, aptdo 2, T051-355694. In restored 17th-century building, sandwiches, good snacks, coffee, good music, great atmosphere, nice surroundings with patio.

Panadería Una, Lima 317 and Arequipa 144. For croissants, fresh bread and cakes.

Ricos Pan, Jr Lima 424. Café and bakery, great cakes, excellent coffees, juices and pastries, breakfasts and other dishes, Mon-Sat 0600-2300. Branches at Av Titicaca 155 and Moquegua 330.

Bars and clubs

Puno *p1197, map p1200*

Café Concert, Lima 723. Open daily 2000-2300.

Dómino, Libertad 443. "Megadisco", happy hour

Puno

El Buho **4** *Puno centre*
Hospedaje Don Julio **5** *Puno centre*
Hospedaje Residencial Margarita **6** *B2*
Hostal Arequipa **7** *B2*
Hostal Europa **8** *Puno centre*
Hostal Hacienda **9** *Puno centre*
Hostal Illampu **15** *B3*
Hostal Imperial **20** *B3*
Hostal Italia **10** *B2*
Hostal Los Pinos **11** *B2*

Hostal Monterrey **12** *Puno centre*
Hostal Nesther **13** *Puno centre*
Hostal Pukara **14** *Puno centre*
Hostal Q'oñiwasi **15** *B3*
Hostal Rubi 'Los Portales' **16** *C3*
Libertador Isla Esteves **19** *A4*
Los Uros **20** *B3*
Plaza Mayor **22** *Puno centre*
Posada Don Giorgio **23** *B2*

Sillustani **24** *Puno centre*
Sonesta Posadas del Inca **25** *A4*

Eating
Apu Salkantay **1** *Puno centre*
Café Concert **11** *C2*
Cafetería Mercedes **3** *Puno centre*
Casa del Corregidor **4** *C2*
Chifa Fon Seng **5** *Puno centre*
Chifa Nan Hua **7** *B2*

Sleeping
Albergue Juvenil Virgen de Copacabana **1** *B1*
Balsa Inn **2** *C2*
Casa Andina Plaza **17** *B2*
Casa Andina Private Collection Puno **27** *A4*
Casa Andina Tikarani **26** *B2*
Colón Inn **3** *Puno centre*

2000-2130 Mon-Thu, good.
Peña Hostería, Lima 501. Good music, also restaurant. Recommended.
Pub Ekeko's, Lima 355. Live music every night, happy hour 2000-2200.

⊛ Festivals and events

Puno *p1197, map p1200*
Feb: at the **Fiesta de la Virgen de la Candelaria**, 1st 2 weeks in **Feb**, bands and dancers from all the local towns compete in a *Diablada*, or Devil Dance. The festivities are better at night on the streets than the official functions in the stadium. Check the dates in advance as Candelaria may be moved if pre-Lentern carnival coincides with it. A candlelight procession through darkened streets takes place on **Good Friday**. **3 May**: **Invención de la Cruz**, an exhibition of local art. **29 Jun**: colourful festival of **San Pedro**, with a procession at Zepita (see page 1198); also **20 Jul**. **4-5 Nov**: pageant dedicated to the founding of Puno and the emergence of Manco Cápac and Mama Ocllo from the waters of Lake Titicaca.

⊙ Shopping

Puno *p1197, map p1200*
Markets Beware pickpockets in the market. You will be hassled on the street and outside restaurants to buy woollen goods, so take care.

In the covered part of the market mostly foodstuffs are sold (good cheeses), but there are also model reed boats, attractive carved stone amulets and Ekekos (household gods). This central market covers a large area and on Saturday it expands down to the stadium (mostly fruit and vegetables) and along Av Bolívar (potatoes and grains). The markets between Av Los Incas and Arbulu (*Ccori Wasi*) and on the railway between Av Libertad and Av El Puerto are 2 of the best places in Peru for llama and alpaca wool articles, but bargain for a fair price, especially in the afternoon. **Ichuña**, Libertad 113, www.ichunia.org. A cooperative selling weavings from a village 90 km from Puno.

⛰ Activities and tours

Puno *p1197, map p1200*
Watch out for unofficial tour sellers, *jalagringos*, who offer hotels and tours at varying rates, depending on how wealthy you look. They are everywhere: train station, bus offices, airport and hotels. Ask to see their guide's ID card. Only use agencies with named premises, compare prices and only hand over money at the office, never on the street or in a hotel.

Agencies organize trips to the Uros floating islands (see page 1203) and the islands of Taquile and Amantaní, as well as to Sillustani, and other places. Make sure that you settle all details before embarking on the tour. We have received good reports on the following:
All Ways Travel, Tacna 234, T/F355552, www.titicacaperu.com. Very helpful, kind and reliable, speak German, French, English and Italian. They offer a unique cultural tour to the islands of Anapia and Yuspique in Lake Wiñaymarka, beyond the straits of Tiquina, "The Treasure of Wiñaymarka", departures Thu and Sun.
Arcobaleno, Jr Lambayeque 175, T/F351052, www.titicacalake.com. Local tours, Western Union representative.
Ecoturismo Aventura, Jr Lima 458, T355785. Very helpful.
Edgar Adventures, Jr Lima 328, T/F353444, www.edgaradventures.com. English, German and French spoken, very helpful.
Käfer Viajes, Arequipa 179, T354742, www.kafer-titicaca.com. Efficient and helpful.
Kontiki Tours, Jr Melgar 188. T355887,

Puno centre

Don Piero **6** *Puno centre*
Govinda **9** *Puno centre*
IncAbar **10** *Puno centre*
Internacional **20**
  Puno Centre
La Caywa Andean
  Cuisine Bar **8** *Puno centre*
Lago de Flores **1** *Puno centre*
La Plaza **13** *C2*
Mojsa **14** *C2*
Pizzería El Buho **15**
  Puno centre
Remembranzas **2**
  Puno Centre

Ricos Pan **16**
  Puno centre
Vida Natural **18**
  Puno centre

Bars & clubs 🍸
Pub Ekeko's **12**
  Puno Centre

Peru Puno & around Listings

www.kontikiperu.com. Receptive tour agency specializing in special interest excursions.
Nayra Travel, Jr Lima 419, of 105. T337934, www.nayratravel.com. Small but very helpful staff, offering local tours.
Pirámide Tours, Jr Rosendo Huirse 130, T366107, www.titikakalake.com. Out of the ordinary and classic tours, flexible, personalized service, modern fast launches, very helpful, works only via internet, overseas clients.
Titikaka Explorers, Av La Torre 339-4, T355219, peru-titikaka@hotmail.com. Good service, helpful.

⊜ Transport

Puno *p1197, map p1200*

Bus All long-distance buses, except some Cuzco services and buses to La Paz (see below), leave from the Terminal Terrestre, which is between Av Simón Bolívar and the lake, southeast of the centre. It has a tourist office, snack bars and toilets. Platform tax US$0.30. Small buses and colectivos for Juliaca, Ilave and towns on the lake shore between Puno and Desaguadero, including Yunguyo, leave from Av Bolívar between Jrs Carabaya and Palma. Daily buses to **Arequipa**, 6 hrs via Juliaca, 297 km, most buses take this route, US$4.50-6 (**Cruz del Sur**, **Best Way**, **Destinos**, **Julsa**, **Señor de Milagros**, or **Sur Oriente**, most have a morning and evening bus – better quality buses go at night). To **Moquegua**, US$4.50-6, and **Tacna**, US$10. To **Lima**, 1,011 km, 22 hrs, US$21-25, *bus cama* US$30, all buses go through **Arequipa**, sometimes with a change of bus. See Arequipa, page 1195. To **Juliaca**, 44 km, 45 mins, US$0.85.

Note If you wish to travel by bus and cannot get on a direct bus, it is no problem to take separate buses to Juliaca, then to Sicuani, then to Cuzco.

To **Cuzco**, 388 km, 5-7 hrs, **Tour Perú**, at Terminal, T352991, tourperu@mixmail.com, 0830, 2000, US$4.50-6 (less in low season); **Libertad**, at Terminal, T363694, 4 a day, **Cisnes**, at Terminal, T368674, 2 a day, and others. **First Class** (Jr Tacna 280, T365192, firstclass@terra.com.pe) and **Inka Express** (Jr Tacna 314-B, T365654), both at 0830 arriving 1800, US$20, 10 hrs, daily. This service leaves a little later than the train and is comfortable, with a good lunch stop and visits to Pukará, La Raya, Raqchi and Andahuaylillas en route. **Note** We have received many reports of robbery on night buses on the Juliaca- Puno-Cuzco route; travel by day, or by train.

Boats on Lake Titicaca Boats to the islands leave from the terminal in the harbour (see map); *trici-taxi* from centre, US$1.

Taxi 3-wheel 'Trici-Taxis', cost about US$0.20 per km and are the best way to get around.

Trains The railway runs from Puno to Juliaca (44 km), where it divides, to Cuzco (381 km) and Arequipa (279 km; no passenger service). To **Cuzco** on Mon, Wed and Sat at 0800, arriving in Juliaca at 0910 and in Cuzco at about 1800 (try to sit on the right hand side for the views). The train stops at La Raya. In the high season (Jun especially), tickets sell well in advance. In the wet season services may be cancelled for short periods. Always check. **Fares**: Puno-Cuzco, *turismo*, US$19; *1st class*, US$130 including meal. The ticket office is open from 0630-1030, Mon-Sun. Tickets can be bought in advance, or 1 hr before departure if there are any left. The station is well guarded by police and sealed off to those without tickets.

Llachón *p1198*

Boats Only 1 weekly public boat from Llachón to Puno, Fri 0900, returning to Llachón Sat 1000. The daily 0800 boat to Amantantí may drop you off at Colata (at the tip of the peninsula), a 1 hr walk from Llachón, confirm details in advance. Returning to Puno, you can try to flag down the boat from Amantaní which passes Colata between 0830 and 0930. All fares US$3 one way. **Combis** run daily from Bellavista market in Puno to **Capachica**, from 0700 to1200, 1½ hrs, US$1, where you get another *combi* or bus to **Llachón**, leave when full, 30 mins, US$0.80.

⊕ Directory

Puno *p1197, map p1200*

Banks BCP, Lima 510. Changes TCs before 1300 without commission, cash advance on Visa and Visa ATM. **Banco Continental**, Lima 411. Visa ATM. **Interbank**, Lima 444, changes TCs morning and afternoon, 0.5% commission, Visa ATM. **Scotiabank**, Lima y Deústua, MasterCard and Visa ATM. For cash go to the *cambios*, the travel agencies or the better hotels. Best rates with money changers on Jr Lima, many on 400 block, and on Tacna near the market, eg Arbulu y Tacna. Check your Peruvian soles carefully. Rates for bolivianos are sometimes better in Puno than in Yunguyo; check with other travellers.
Consulates Bolivia, Jr Arequipa 136, T351251, consular visa on the spot, US$10, Mon-Fri 0830-1400. **Internet** There are offices everywhere in the centre, upstairs and down. Average price US$0.45 per hr; many have overnights. **Post offices** Jr Moquegua 267. **Telephones** Telefónica at Puno y Moquegua for local and international calls. Another phone office at Lima 489. **Useful addresses** Immigration: Ayacucho 280, T357103, for renewing entry stamps, etc. The process is very slow and you must fill in 2 application forms at a bank, but there's nothing else to pay.

The islands

The Uros
ⓘ *US$0.60 entry.*
The people of Uros or the 'floating islands' in Puno Bay fish, hunt birds and live off the lake plants, most important of which are the reeds they use for their boats, houses and the very foundations of their islands. Visitors to the floating islands encounter more women than men. These women wait every day for the tour boats to sell their handicrafts. The few men one does see might be building or repairing boats or fixing their nets. The rest are out on the lake, hunting and fishing. The Uros cannot live from tourism alone, and the extra income they glean from tourists merely supplements their more traditional activities. They appreciate gifts of pens, paper, etc for their two schools. Many tourists find that, though the people are friendly, they are very poor and a few subject visitors to a hard-sell approach for handicrafts and the replacement of "invalid" entry tickets. The islands visited by tour boats are little more than 'floating souvenir stalls'. All the same, this form of tourism on the Uros Islands is now well-established and, whether it has done irreparable harm or will ultimately prove beneficial, it takes place in superb surroundings. Take drinking water as there is none on the islands.

Taquile
ⓘ *US$0.60 to land.*
Isla Taquile, 45 km from Puno, on which there are numerous pre-Inca and Inca ruins, and Inca terracing, is only about 1 km wide, but 6-7 km long. Ask for the (unmarked) **museum of traditional costumes**, which is on the plaza, and also where you can see and photograph local weaving. There is a co-operative shop on the plaza that sells exceptional woollen goods, which are not cheap, but of very fine quality. Shops on the plaza sell film, postcards, water and dry goods. You are advised to take some food, particularly fruit, bread and vegetables, water, plenty of small-value notes, candles and a torch. Take precautions against sunburn. Easter, from 2-7 June, the *Fiesta de Santiago* over two weeks in mid-July, and 1 and 2 August are the principal festival days, with many dances in between.

Amantaní
ⓘ *US$0.60 to land.*
Another island worth visiting, is Amantaní, very beautiful and peaceful. There are six villages and ruins on both of the island's peaks, **Pacha Tata** and **Pacha Mama**, from which there are excellent views. There are also temples and on the shore there is a throne carved out of stone, the **Inkatiana**. On both hills, a fiesta is celebrated on 15 January (or thereabouts). The festivities are very colourful, musical and hard-drinking. There is also a festival the first Sunday in March with brass bands and colourful dancers. The residents make beautiful textiles and sell them quite cheaply at the Artesanía Cooperativa. They also make basketwork and stoneware. The people are Quechua speakers, but understand Spanish. Islanders arrange dances for tour groups (independent travellers can join in), visitors dress up in local clothes and join the dances. Small shops sell water and snacks, but more expensive than Puno.

Anapia and Yuspique
In the Peruvian part of the Lago Menor are the islands of **Anapia**, a friendly, Aymara-speaking community, and **Yuspique**, on which are ruins and vicuñas. The community has organized committees for tourism, motor boats, sailing boats and accommodation with families (All Ways Travel, see page 1201, arranges tours). To visit Anapia independently, take a colectivo from Yunguyo to Tinicachi and alight at Punta Hermosa, just after Unacachi. Boats to Anapia leave Punta Hermosa on Sunday and Thursday at 1300 (they leave Anapia for Yunguyo market on the same days at 0630); bus from Puno Sunday, Tuesday, Thursday, US$3. It's two hours each way by boat. On the island ask for José Flores, who is very knowledgeable about Anapia's history, flora and fauna. He sometimes acts as a guide.

● Sleeping

Taquile *p1203*

Average rate for a bed is US$3 pp, plus US$1.50 for breakfast. Other meals cost extra. Several families now have sizeable *alojamientos* (eg Pedro Huille, on the track up from the north entry, with showers, proper loos). Instead of staying in the busy part around the main square, the Huayllano community is hosting visitors. This is on the south side of the island. Contact **Alipio Huata Cruz**, T952 4650 (mob, you can leave a voicemail that he will retrieve from Puno as there is no reception on the island) or you can arrange a visit with **All Ways Travel**.

Amantaní *p1203*

There are no hotels, you stay with local families. Ask your boat owner where you can stay. Accommodation, including 3 meals, is US$6 pp. Some families have mainland addresses for booking, eg **Hospedaje Jorge Wasi**, basic, but nice family, great view of lake from room, or j.manani.cari@eudoramail.com; or **Familia Victoriano Calsin Quispe**, Casilla 312, Isla Amantaní, T051-360220 or 363320.

● Eating

Taquile *p1203*

There are many small restaurants around the plaza and on the track to the Puerto Principal (eg Gerardo Hualta's **La Flor de Cantuta**, on the steps; **El Inca** on the main plaza). Meals are generally fish (the island has a trout farm), rice and chips, tortilla and *fiambre*, a local stew. Meat is rarely available and drinks often run out. Breakfast consists of pancakes and bread.

Amantaní *p1203*

There is 1 restaurant, **Samariy**. Food at the family lodgings is frequently reported to be dreadful (a reflection of the artificially low price), so take your own supplies, especially bread and fruit.

● Transport

The Uros *p1203*

Boat Motorboats from the dock charge about US$3 pp for a 2-hr excursion. Boats go about every 30 mins from about 0630-1000, or whenever there are 10 or more people to fill the boat. The earlier you go the better, to beat the crowds of tourists. Almost any agency going to the other islands in the lake will stop first at Los Uros.

Taquile *p1203*

Boats Leave Puno daily at 0700 and 0800; 3 hrs, return 1430 and 1500, US$3 one way. This doesn't leave enough time to appreciate the island fully (if you buy a return ticket, don't get charged again for the return leg). Organized tours can be arranged for about US$10-16 pp, but only give you about 2 hrs on the island. Tour boats usually call at Uros on the outward or return journey.

Amantaní *p1203*

Boats Leave from the harbour in Puno at 0800 daily, return 0800, arriving in Puno around 1200, US$4.50 one way. The journey takes 4-5 hrs, take water and seasickness pills. A 1-day trip is not possible. Several tour operators in Puno offer 2-3 day excursions to Amantaní, Taquile and a visit to the floating islands, starting at US$12 pp (price depends on the season and size of group); including meals, 1 night on Amantaní and 3-4 hrs on Taquile. Despite what touts may tell you, it is possible to visit the islands independently and at your own pace. In this way the islands reap most of the reward from visitors, but that doesn't make it any cheaper. The majority of tour companies are owned in Puno. To visit both Taquile and Amantaní, it is better to go to Amantaní first; from there a boat goes to Taquile around 0800 when full, US$2.50 pp.

To Cuzco

Juliaca → *Phone code: 051. Colour map 6, grid A2. Population: 134,700. Altitude: 3,825 m.*

Freezing cold at night, Juliaca, 289 km northeast of Arequipa, is not particularly attractive. As the commercial focus of an area bounded by Puno, Arequipa and the jungle, it has grown very fast into a chaotic place with a large impermanent population, lots of contraband and more *tricitaxis* than cars. Monday, market day, is the most disorganized of all. A Sunday woollens market, La Dominical, is held near the exit to Cuzco. The handicrafts gallery, *Las Calceteras*, is on Plaza Bolognesi. Túpac Amaru market, on Moquegua seven blocks east of railway line, is a cheap market. There are several internet places in the centre. **Tourist office**, Dircetur ① *Jr Noriega 191, p 3, T321839.*

The unspoiled little colonial town of **Lampa**, 31 km northwest of Juliaca is known as the 'Pink City'. It has a splendid church, La Inmaculada, containing a copy of Michelangelo's 'Pietà'. Also of interest is the Museo Kampac, Ugarte 462, a museum with sculptures and ceramics from the Lampa and Juli areas; the owner lives next door. It also has a good Sunday market. Buses and trucks daily, one hour, US$0.70, from Plaza de Armas in Juliaca.

Puno to Cuzco

The road Puno-Juliaca-Cuzco is now fully paved and in good condition. Bus services are consequently an acceptable alternative to the train, at an average altitude of 3,500 m. There is much to see on the way, but neither the daytime buses nor the trains make frequent stops. You would have to be using your own transport, or taking buses from town to town to sample what the places en route have to offer, eg pottery bulls at Pucará (rooms available at the station); knitted alpaca ponchos and pullovers and miniature llamas at Santa Rosa (rooms available). There are also hotels in **Ayaviri**.

The road and railway crosses the altiplano, climbing to **La Raya**, the highest pass on the line; 210 km from Puno, at 4,321 m. Up on the heights breathing may be a little difficult, but the descent along the Río Vilcanota is rapid. To the right of **Aguas Calientes**, the next station, 10 km from La Raya, are steaming pools of hot water in the middle of the green grass; a startling sight *US$0.15*. The temperature of the springs is 40° C, and they show beautiful deposits of red ferro-oxide. Communal bathing pools and a block of changing rooms have been opened. At **Marangani**, the river is wider and the fields greener, with groves of eucalyptus trees.

At 38 km beyond La Raya pass is **Sicuani** (*Phone code 084, Altitude 3,690 m*), an important agricultural centre. Excellent items of llama and alpaca wool and skins are sold on the railway station and at the Sunday morning market. Around Plaza Libertad there are several hat shops. (For more information about places between Sicuani and Cuzco, see page 1232.)

◉ Sleeping

Juliaca *p1204*
There are water problems in town, especially in the dry season. Many cheap hotels near the corner of Nuñez and Cuzco.
A Suites Don Carlos, Jr M Prado 335, on the outskirts of town, T321571, www.hotelesdon carlos.com. Good facilities, continental breakfast US$6.50, lunch or dinner US$13.
B-C Royal Inn, San Román 158, T321561, www.royalinnhoteles.com. Decent place with hot water, heaters, TV, safe, laundry, good restaurant La Fonda del Royal (♚♚). Recommended.
C Hostal Don Carlos, Jr 9 de Diciembre 114, Plaza Bolognesi, T323600, www.hotelesdon carlos.com. Comfortable, modern facilities, hot water, TV, heater, good service, breakfast, restaurant and room service. Recommended.
D Karlo's Hostal, Unión 317, T321817, lanzap@ hotmail.com. Comfortable if overpriced, firm beds, hot water, TV, laundry, restaurant attached.
E Hostal Luquini, San Brasesco 409, Plaza Bolognesi, T321510. Comfortable, patio, helpful, reliable hot water in morning only, good value, motorcycle parking. Recommended.
G Hostal La Casona, on the Plaza in the village of Lampa, T360228, mariaelenafd@hotmail.com. In newly refurbished old house, very nice.

Sicuani *p1205*
The bus terminal is in the newer part of town, which is separated from the older part and the

Plaza by a pedestrian walkway and bridge. At the 'new' end of the bridge, but also close to the centre of town, are several *hostales* advertising hot water and private bathrooms.
F Obada, Tacna 104, T351214. Large, hot showers, has seen better days.
F Samariy, Av Centenario 138, T352518. West side of old pedestrian bridge. Good value.
G José's, Av Arequipa 143, T351254. With bath, good.

◉ Eating

Juliaca *p1204*
♚♚ **Trujillo**, San Román 163. Extensive menu, daily specials, US$3-5.50 for main dishes, US$7.50 for fish.
♚ **Asador**, Unión 119. Chicken, grill and pizza, pleasant atmosphere.
Ricos Pan, San Román. Bakery with café, popular. Recommended.

Sicuani *p1205*
♚ **El Fogón**, C Zevallos. Good chicken and chips, smart.
♚ **Pizzería Bon Vino**, 2 de Mayo 129, p 2. Good Italian.
♚ **Mijuna Wasi**, Jr Tacna 146. Closed Sun. Serves local dishes in a dilapidated, atmospheric courtyard.

⊖ Transport

Juliaca *p1204*

Air Airport is small but well organized, airport tax US$3. To/from **Lima**, 2¼ hrs via **Arequipa** (30 mins) or **Cuzco**, twice daily with **Lan** (T322228 or airport T324448). **StarPerú** also daily via Arequipa (San Román 175, T327478). Minibuses 1-B, 6 and 14 to airport from 2 de Mayo at either Núñez or San Román, US$0.15; from airport to town they take you to your hotel. Beware overcharging for transport from Juliaca airport. If you have little luggage, combis stop just outside the airport parking area. Taxi from Plaza Bolognesi, US$1.75. Tourist buses run direct from Puno to the airport and vice versa; US$3.50 pp, 1 hr. You can book ahead with **Rossy Tours**, T366709. Also taxis, US$11.75. If taking a public colectivo from Puno to Juliaca for a flight, allow plenty of time as they drive around Puno looking for passengers to fill the vehicle first.

Bus Terminal Terrestre is at Jr Mantaro y San Agustín: go down San Martín 10 blocks and cross Av Circunvalación. Lots of companies serve **Desaguadero**, **Moquegua**, **Arequipa** (US$3), **Lima** (US$17- 43) and **Cuzco** (US$3-4). To **Cuzco**, 344 km, 5-6 hrs, with **Tour Perú** (tourperu@ mixmail.com), day and night buses, prices as from Puno. **First Class** and **Inka Express** (inkaex@ yahoo.com) have pullman tourist buses which stop for sightseeing and lunch, with guide, see under Puno. The road is paved and in good condition. To **Puno**, 44 km, 1 hr, US$0.60; small buses leave from Piérola y 18 de Noviembre, 2 companies. **Note** We have received many reports of robbery on night buses on the Juliaca-Puno-Cuzco route; travel by day, or by train. Combis to Puno leave from Terminal Terrestre on Plaza Bolognesi, also US$0.60. See below for how to get to the Bolivian border and page 1207 for transport.

Train See information under Puno or Cuzco. The station at Juliaca is the junction for services between **Arequipa** (no passenger services), **Puno** and **Cuzco**. Prices to Cuzco are the same as from Puno. There is no ticket office. You can get on the train in Juliaca, but you must buy the ticket in Puno or Cuzco.

Sicuani *p1205*

Bus To **Cuzco**, 137 km, US$1.25.

Border with Bolivia → *Peruvian time is one hour behind Bolivian time.*

There are three different routes across the border:

Puno-La Paz via Yunguyo and Copacabana **Peruvian immigration** is five minutes' drive from **Yunguyo** and 500 m from the Bolivian post; open 24 hours a day (but Bolivian immigration is only open 0830-1930). Ninety days are normally given when entering Peru. Be aware of corruption at customs and look out for official or unofficial people trying to charge you a fee, on either side of the border (say that you know it is illegal and ask why only gringos are approached to pay the 'embarkation tax').

Bolivian consulate is at Jr Grau 339, T856032, near the main plaza in Yunguyo, open Monday-Friday 0830-1500, for those who need a visa; some nationalities have to pay. Note that US citizens now need a visa for Bolivia; check for 2007 rates. For **Bolivian immigration**, see page 266. Rates of exchange can be poor unless you negotiate for current rates; find out what they are before you arrive. For those entering Peru cash can be changed in the main plaza in Yunguyo. Traveller's cheques can be exchanged in the *cambio* here, poor rates. See also Puno, Banks.

Puno-Desaguadero Desaguadero is an unscrupulous place, with poor restaurants and dubious accommodation. Tuesday and Friday are *feria* days, busy with locals and their contraband. There is no need to stop in Desaguadero as all roads to it are paved and if you leave La Paz, Moquegua or Puno early enough you should be at your destination before nightfall. Combis and minibuses Puno-Desaguadero hourly 0600-1900, 2½ hrs, US$1.80. Taxi US$33. **Border offices** are open 0830-1230 and 1400-2000. It is easy to change money on the Peruvian side. This particular border crossing allows you to stop at Tiahuanaco en route.

Along the east side of Lake Titicaca This is the most remote route, via **Huancané** and **Moho** (several *hostales*, **F-G**). Some walking may be involved as there is little traffic between Moho and **Puerto Acosta**, Bolivia. Make sure you get an exit stamp in Puno, post-dated by a couple of days. From Juliaca there are buses to Huancané, Moho and Tilali, the last village in Peru with basic lodgings (see Transport, above). The road is paved to Huancané, then poor (improvement supposed to be due), but the views are wonderful. From Tilali it is 2-km walk to the **Peruvian**

customs post and a further 2-km steep climb to the international frontier at Cerro Janko Janko (see page 266). Puerto Acosta in Bolivia is a further 10 km. You must get a preliminary entry stamp at the police station on the plaza, then the definitive entry stamp at Migración in La Paz.

😴 Sleeping

Yunguyo *p1206*
A few places to stay in **G** range.
G Hostal Isabel, San Francisco 110, near Plaza de Armas, T856019, shared bath, hot water, modern, good value, will change money and arrange transport.

North shore of Lake Titicaca
LL Hotel Isla Suasi, T051-962 2709, a Casa Andina Private Collection hotel, www.casa-andina.com. The hotel is the only house on this tiny, tranquil island. There are beautiful terraced gardens, best Jan-Mar. The non-native eucalyptus trees are being replaced by native varieties. You can take a canoe around the island to see birds and the island has six vicuñas, a small herd of alpacas and one vizcacha. The sunsets from the highest point are beautiful. Facilities are spacious, comfortable and solar-powered, rooms with bath, hot water, hot water bottles. Price includes full board, national drinks, entrance to island, land transfers, services and taxes. For boat transport, contact Casa Andina. Massage room and sauna, internet US$20 per hr. Private boats from Puno are expensive and take 4-6 hrs (2½ hrs by fast boat, US$450 up to 15 passengers), but you can call at the islands or Llachón en route. A car for 4 people will cost US$75. Otherwise take public transport from Juliaca to Tilali (see below) or Conima bus (Mon 1300, Thu 1300, Sun 0800, 2½-3 hrs, US$1.80) and alight in Cambría, about 20 min past Moho. Walk down to the shore and take a rowing boat to Suasi, 10 mins, US$1.50 pp.

🚌 Transport

Border with Bolivia: Yunguyo *p1206*
Bus The road is paved from Puno to Yunguyo and the scenery is interesting. In Puno 3 companies sell bus tickets for the direct route from Puno to La Paz, taking 6-8 hrs (fare does not include the Tiquina ferry crossing, US$0.25): **Colectur**, Tacna 221, T352302, 0730, US$6.50, combines with *Galería* in Bolivia; **Panamericano**, Tacna 245, T354001, 0700, US$7.35, combines with *Diana Tours*; **Tour Perú** (address under Puno Transport), 0700 from your hotel, US$8.75, combines with *Combi Tour* (fares rise at holiday times) They stop at the borders and 1 hr for lunch in Copacabana, arriving in La Paz at about 1700. You only need to change money into Bolivianos for lunch on this route. Bus

fare Puno-Copacabana US$4.40-5.80. To Yunguyo, from the Terminal Zonal in Puno, combis and mini buses hourly 0600-1900, 2½ hrs, US$1.80. From Yunguyo to the border (Kasani), colectivos charge US$0.25 pp. From the border it is a 20-min drive to Copacabana; colectivos and minibuses leave from just outside Bolivian immigration, US$0.50 pp. Taxi from Yunguyo to Copacabana costs about US$1.50 pp. **Note** Don't take a taxi Yunguyo-Puno without checking its reliability first, driver may pick up an accomplice to rob passengers.

To La Paz by hydrofoil or catamaran
There are luxury services from Puno/Juli to La Paz by **Crillon Tours** hydrofoil, with connections to tours, from La Paz, to Cuzco and Machu Picchu. In Puno their office is at **Arcobaleno Tours** (see Activities and tours), or contact head office in La Paz, see page 258 for details. The itinerary is: Puno- Copacabana by bus; Copacabana-Isla del Sol-Huatajata (Bolivia) by hydrofoil; Huatajata-La Paz by bus; 13 hrs. Similar services, by catamaran, are run by **Transturin**, whose dock is at Chúa, Bolivia; bookings through **Transturin** in La Paz.

Along the east side of Lake Titicaca *p1206*
Combis to from Juliaca to **Huancané**, 51 km, from Grifo San Juan del Oro, Sucre y Ballón, US$0.45, 1 hr. From Hunacané, combis leave for Julica when full throughout the day. Buses to **Moho** (40 km from Huancané), from Moquegua y Ballón, past Túpac Amaru market, 4 daily, 2-2½ hrs, US$1.50. From Moho to Juliaca, buses leave at 0130, 0800 and 1300 daily. Buses to **Tilali**, Transportes Lucero, 1 or 2 daily in early morning, **Aguila del Sur**, 1 daily in morning, both from Circunvalación y Lambayeque, 4 hrs, US$2.50 (schedules change daily; ask in advance). Daily buses from Tilali to Juliaca, around 0100, plus a morning bus, 0800-1000 on Sun, Tue and Fri. On market days trucks go to Puerto Acosta and La Paz. Try hitching to catch bus from Puerto Acosta to La Paz (daily) about 1400 (note Bolivian time is 1 hour ahead of Peru), more frequent service on Sun, 5 hrs, US$3.75. If you are in a hurry and miss the bus, ask the truck to drop you off 25 km further in Escoma, from where there are frequent minivans to La Paz. Buses leave La Paz for Puerto Acosta at 0600 daily. Transport from Puerto Acosta to border only operates on market days, mostly cargo trucks.

Cuzco → *Phone code: 084. Colour map 3, grid C4. Altitude: 3,310 m.*

The ancient Inca capital is said to have been founded around AD 1100, and since then has developed into a major commercial and tourism centre of 275,000 inhabitants, most of whom are Quechua. The city council has designated Qosqo (Cuzco in Quechua) as the official spelling. Today, colonial churches, monasteries and convents and extensive pre-Columbian ruins are interspersed with countless hotels, bars and restaurants that cater for the hundreds of thousands of visitors. Almost every central street has remains of Inca walls, arches and doorways; the perfect Inca stonework now serves as the foundations for more modern dwellings. This stonework is tapered upwards (battered); every wall has a perfect line of inclination towards the centre, from bottom to top. The curved stonework of the Temple of the Sun, for example, is probably unequalled in the world.

Ins and outs

Getting there The **airport** is to the southeast of the city and the road into the centre goes close to Wanchac station, at which **trains** from Juliaca and Puno arrive. The **bus terminal** is near the Pachacútec statue in Ttio district. Transport to your hotel is not a problem from any of these places by taxi or in transport arranged by hotel representatives. ▸▸ *For more detailed information, see Transport, page 1229.*

Getting around The centre of Cuzco is quite small and possible to explore on foot. Taxis in Cuzco are cheap and recommended when arriving by air, train or bus and especially when returning to your hotel at night. Cuzco is only slightly lower than Puno, so respect the altitude: two or three hours rest after arriving makes a great difference; avoid meat and smoking, eat lots of carbohydrates and drink plenty of clear, non-alcoholic liquid; remember to walk slowly. To see Cuzco and the surrounding area properly (including Pisac, Ollantaytambo, Chinchero and Machu Picchu) you need five days to a week, allowing for slowing down because of altitude.

Tourist information Official tourist information ① *Portal Mantas 117-A, next to La Merced church, T263176, open 0800-2000.* There is also an **i perú** tourist information desk at the airport ① *T237364, open daily 0600-1300,* and another at ① *Av Sol 103, of 102, Galerías Turísticas, T234498, daily 0830-1930.* **Dircetur** ① *Av de la Cultura 734, p 3, T223701, open Mon-Fri 0800-1300,* gives out good map. Other information sources include **South American Explorers** ① *Choquechaca 188, apto 4 (2 blocks behind the Cathedral), T245 484, www.saexplorers.org, Mon-Fri 0930-1700, Sat 0930-1300.* Sells good city map, members get many local discounts, has comprehensive recycling centre. As with SAE's other clubhouses, this is the place to go for specialized information, member-written trip reports and maps. For full details on South American Explorers, see page 32. Many churches close to visitors on Sunday; 'official' opening times are unreliable. No photographs are allowed in any museums. **Automóvil Club del Perú** ① *Av Sol 349, nivel 2, T/F224561, cusco@ touringperu.com.pe,* has some

A WONDERFUL EXPERIENCE IS WAITING FOR YOU...

PERU
AN EXOTIC COUNTRY

Discover it with **DOMIRUTH**. The leading tour operator in Peru and South America provides you with wide range of tour programs e.g. historical, cultural, ecological, gastronomic, adventure, and private. **DOMIRUTH** holds the prestigious **ISO 9001 : 2000** certificate.

Benefits of using **DOMIRUTH** as your tour operator:

- ☑ 22 Years of Experience
- ☑ Guaranteed Departures
- ☑ Confirmation in 24 Hours
- ☑ Travels tailored to suit your needs
- ☑ Call Center Assistance: (511) 0801-00-600
- ☑ Travel Insurance
- ☑ Network Throughout the Country
- ☑ Auto Pullman

CONTACT US:
Main Office: Av. Petit Thouars 4305 Miraflores, Lima - Perú
Phone: (511) 610-6000 **Opc.** 8 / (511) 215-6000 / **Ext.** 2221 / 2403 / 2401
Fax: (511) 222-5145
Emergency Phones (24/7): (511) 9997-2264 / (511) 9803-7606 / (511) 9803-3553
E-mail: mharbaum@domiruth.com.pe / mharbaum33@hotmail.com
Websites: www.domiruth.com.pe / www.turisticalperu.com

Travel Service
Tour Operator & Travel Agency

ISO 9001:2000

1209

Peru Cuzco

maps. Motorists beware; many streets end in flights of steps. There are very few good maps of Cuzco available. **Maps and guidebooks**: maps of the city, the Inca Trail and the Urubamba Valley are available at tour companies. There are information booklets on Machu Picchu and the other ruins at the bookshops.

Visitors' tickets A combined entry ticket, called *Boleto Turístico General* (BTG), is available to most of the sites of main historical and cultural interest in and around the city, and costs as follows: 70 soles (US$21) for all the sites and valid for 10 days; or 40 soles (US$12) for either the churches and museums in the city, or Sacsayhuaman, Qenqo, Puka Pukara and Tambo Machay, or Pisac, Ollantaytambo, Chinchero, Tipón and Piquillacta; these 40 soles ticket is valid for one day. Tickets can be bought at the **OFEC office** ⓘ *Casa Garcilaso, Plaza Regocijo, esquina Calle Garcilaso, T226919, Mon-Sat 0800-1600, Sun 0800-1200; Av Sol 103, T227037, Mon-Fri 0800-1800, Sat 0830- 1230*, or at any of the sites included in the ticket. There is a 50% discount for students with a green ISIC card, which is only available at the OFEC office (Casa Garcilaso) upon presentation of the ISIC card. Take your ISIC card when visiting the sites, as some may ask to see it. Photography is not allowed in the churches, and museums.

Entrance tickets for the Santo Domingo/Qoricancha, the Inka Museum (El Palacio del Almirante) and La Merced are sold separately, while the Cathedral and churches of El Triunfo, La Sagrada Familia, La Compañia and San Blas and the Museo de Arte Religioso del Arzobispado are included on a new religious buildings ticket which costs 36 soles (US$10) and is valid for 10 days. Machu Picchu ruins and Inca trail entrance tickets are sold at the **Instituto Nacional de Cultura** (INC) ⓘ *San Bernardo s/n entre Mantas y Almagro, T236061, Mon-Fri 0900-1300, 1600-1800, Sat 0900-1100*.

Security Police patrol the streets, trains and stations, but one should still be vigilant. On no account walk back to your hotel after dark from a bar or club, strangle muggings and rape are frequent. For safety's sake, pay the US$1 taxi fare, but not just any taxi. Ask the club's doorman to get a taxi for you and make sure the taxi is licensed. Other areas in which to take care include Santa Ana market (otherwise recommended), the San Cristóbal area, and at out-of-the-way ruins. Also take special care during Inti Raymi. The **Tourist Police**, C Saphi 510, T249665/221961, or Ovalo de Pachacútec, T249654. If you need a *denuncia* (a report for insurance purposes), which is available from the Banco de la Nación, they will type it out. Always go to the police when robbed, even though it will cost you a bit of time. The Tourist Protection Bureau (**Indecopi**) is at Portal Carrizos, Plaza de Armas. Toll free 0800-42579 (24-hour hotline, not available from payphones).

Sights

The heart of the city in Inca days was *Huacaypata* (the place of tears) and *Cusipata* (the place of happiness), divided by a channel of the Saphi River. Today, Cusipata is Plaza Regocijo and Huacaypata is the Plaza de Armas, around which are colonial arcades and four churches. To the northeast is the early 17th-century baroque **Cathedral** ⓘ *until 1000 for genuine worshippers –*

the first Christian church in Cuzco, built on the site of the Inca Roundhouse (the *Suntur Huasi*). It has a statue of the Virgin of the Descent, reputed to have helped the Spaniards repel Manco Inca when he besieged the city in 1536.

On the southeast side of the plaza is the beautiful **La Compañía de Jesús**, built on the site of the Palace of the Serpents (*Amarucancha*, residence of Inca Huayna Capac) in the late 17th century. Its twin-towered exterior is extremely graceful, and the interior rich in fine murals, paintings and carved altars. Nearby is the **Santa Catalina** church ① *Arequipa at Santa Catalina Angosta, daily 0900-1200, 1300- 1700, except Fri 0900-1200, 1300-1600*, convent and museum. There are guided tours by English-speaking students; tip expected.

La Merced ① *on Calle Márquez, church 0830-1200, 1530-1730; monastery and museum 1430-1700, except Sun, US$0.85*. The church was first built 1534 and rebuilt in the late 17th century. Attached is a very fine monastery with an exquisite cloister. Inside the church are buried Gonzalo Pizarro, half-brother of Francisco, and the two Almagros, father and son. The church is most famous for its jewelled monstrance, which is on view in the monastery's museum during visiting hours.

Much **Inca stonework** can be seen in the streets and most particularly in the Callejón Loreto, running southeast past La Compañía de Jesús from the main plaza. The walls of the *Acllahuasi* (House of the Chosen Women) are on one side, and of the *Amarucancha* on the other. There are also Inca remains in Calle San Agustín, to the east of the plaza. The stone of 12 angles is in Calle Hatun Rumiyoc halfway along its second block, on the right-hand side going away from the Plaza. The **Palacio Arzobispal** stands on Hatun Rumiyoc y Herrajes, two blocks northeast of Plaza de Armas. It was built on the site of the palace occupied in 1400. It contains the **Museo de Arte Religioso** ① *Mon-Sat, 0830-1130, 1500-1730*, a collection of colonial paintings and furniture. The collection includes the paintings by the indigenous master, Diego Quispe Tito, of a 17th-century Corpus Christi procession that used to hang in the church of Santa Ana.

The **Palacio del Almirante**, just north of the Plaza de Armas on Ataud, is impressive. It houses the **Museo Inka** ① *Mon-Sat 0800-1730, US$2.40*, which is run by the Universidad San Antonio de Abad, the museum exhibits the development of culture in the region from pre-Inca, through Inca times to the present day: textiles, ceramics, metalwork, jewellery, architecture, technology. See the collection of miniature turquoise figures and other offerings to the gods. Weaving demonstrations are given in the courtyard. On the northwest side of the Plaza de las Nazarenas is **Museo de Arte Precolombino** ① *daily 0900-2200, US$6, US$3 with student card, shops, MAP Café (see Eating, below),*

Related map
A Around Plaza de Armas, page 1218

Chihuampata

Recoleta

Collacalle

Tullumayo

Buses to Pisac

Store of Weavers

Plazoleta Limacpampa

Av de la Cultura

To Piquillacta, Puno & Bolivia

Ahuacpinta

Panti Pata

Tullumayo

Huáscar

Av Garcilaso

Manco Cápac

Manco Inca

Centro Qosco de Arte Nativo

Av Sol

Av Pardo

Pachacutec

Wanchac Station

Mercado Artesanal

To Airport

To Bus Terminal

Manu Nature Tours

⑤ ② ⑥

Eating 🍴
A Mi Manera 1 *B3*
Baco 4 *B4*
Café Cultural Ritual 12 *B4*
Café Manu & Manu Nature Tours 2 *E6*
Chocolate 14 *B4*
El Encuentro 23 *B4*
Granja Heidi 3 *B4*
Inkafe 19 *B4*
Inkanato 5 *C4*
Jack's Café 15 *B4*
La Bodega 6 *A4*
Los Toldos 7 *D3*
Macondo 8 *A4*

Moni 20 *C4*
Mundo Hemp 22 *A4*
Pachapapa 9 *B4*
Panadería El Buen Pastor 10 *A4*
The Muse 17 *A4*
Witches Garden 13 *B4*

Bars & clubs 🍸
Bar 7 16 *A3*
Km 0 (Arte y Tapas) 18 *A4*
Mandela's 11 *B3*
Siete Angelitos 21 *A4*

Peru Cuzco

housed in the **Casa Cabrera**. This beautiful museum is set around a spacious courtyard and contains many superb examples of pottery, metalwork (largely in gold and silver), wood carvings and shells from the Moche, Chimú, Paracas, Nazca and Inca cultures. There are some vividly-rendered animistic designs, giving an insight into the way Peru's ancient people's viewed their world and the creatures that inhabited it. Every exhibit carries explanations in English and Spanish. Highly recommended. The **Convento de las Nazarenas**, also on Plaza de las Nazarenas, is now an annex of Orient Express' *Monasterio* hotel. You can see the Inca-colonial doorway with a mermaid motif, but ask permission to view the lovely 18th-century frescos inside. In the San Blas district, now firmly on the tourist map, the small church of **San Blas** ① *Carmen Bajo, 0800-1130 (except Thu), 1400-1730* has a beautiful carved *mestizo* cedar pulpit, which is well worth seeing. See Shopping Local crafts, below.

Santo Domingo, southeast of the main Plaza, was built in the 17th century on the walls of the **Qoricancha, Temple of the Sun** ① *Mon-Sat 0800-1700, Sun 1400-1600 (closed holidays), US$1.50, English-speaking guides, tip of US$2-3 expected,* and from its stones. Excavation has revealed more of the five chambers of the Temple of the Sun, which shows the best Inca stonework to be seen in Cuzco. The Temple of the Sun was awarded to Juan Pizarro, the younger brother of Francisco, who willed it to the Dominicans after he had been fatally wounded in the Sacsayhuaman siege. The baroque cloister has been gutted to reveal four of the original chambers of the great Inca temple – two on the west have been partly reconstructed in a good imitation of Inca masonry. The finest stonework is in the celebrated curved wall beneath the west end of Santo Domingo. This was rebuilt after the 1950 earthquake, at which time a niche that once contained a shrine was found at the inner top of the wall. Below the curved wall was a garden of gold and silver replicas of animals, maize and other plants. Excavations have revealed Inca baths below here, and more Inca retaining walls. The other superb stretch of late Inca stonework is in C Ahuacpinta outside the temple, to the east or left as you enter.

Museo de Sitio Qorikancha (formerly Museo Arqueológico) ① *Av Sol, Mon-Sat 0900-1200, 1300-1700, Sun 0800-1400,* is under the garden below Santo Domingo. It contains a limited collection of pre-Columbian items, Spanish paintings of imitation Inca royalty dating from the 18th century, and photos of the excavation of Qoricancha. Between the centre and the airport on Alameda Pachacútec, the continuation of Avenida Sol, 20 minutes walk from the Plaza de Armas, there is a **statue of the Inca Pachacútec** ① *1000-2000, small galleries and coffee shop,* placed on top of a lookout tower, from which there are excellent views of Cuzco. The palace called **Casa de los Cuatro Bustos**, whose colonial doorway is at San Agustín 400, is now the **Hotel Libertador**. The general public can enter the Hotel from Plazoleta Santo Domingo, opposite the Temple of the Sun/Qoricancha.

Museo de Historia Regional ① *in the Casa Garcilaso, Jr Garcilaso y Heladeros, 0730-1700,* tries to show the evolution of the Cuzqueño school of painting. It also contains Inca agricultural implements, colonial furniture and paintings. **San Francisco** ① *on Plaza San Francisco, 3 blocks southwest of the Plaza de Armas, 0600-0800, 1800-2000,* is an austere church reflecting many indigenous influences. Its monastery is being rebuilt and may be closed. **San Pedro** ① *in front of the Santa Ana market, Mon-Sat 1000-1200, 1400-1700,* was built in 1688. Its two towers were made from stones brought from an Inca ruin.

Above Cuzco, on the road up to Sacsayhuamán, is **San Cristóbal**, built to his patron saint by Cristóbal Paullu Inca. The church's atrium has been restored and there is a sidewalk access to the Sacsayhuamán Archaeological Park. North of San Cristóbal, you can see the 11 doorway-sized niches of the great Inca wall of the **Palacio de Colcampata**, which was the residence of Manco Inca before he rebelled against the Spanish and fled to Vilcabamba.

Sacsayhuaman

① *Daily 0700-1730; free student guides, give them a tip.*

There are some magnificent Inca walls in this ruined ceremonial centre, on a hill in the northern outskirts. The Incaic stones are hugely impressive. The massive rocks weighing up to 130 tons are fitted together with absolute perfection. Three walls run parallel for over 360 m and there are 21 bastions. Sacsayhuaman was thought for centuries to be a fortress, but the layout and architecture suggest a great sanctuary and temple to the Sun, which rises exactly opposite the place previously believed to be the Inca's throne – which was probably an altar, carved out of the solid rock. Broad steps lead to the altar from either side. The hieratic, rather than the military, hypothesis was supported by the discovery in 1982 of the graves of priests, who would have been unlikely to be buried in a fortress. The precise functions of the site, however, will probably continue to be a matter of dispute as very few clues remain, owing to its steady destruction. The site is about a 30-minute walk up Pumacurco from Plaza de las Nazarenas.

Along the road from Sacsayhuaman to Pisac, past a radio station, is the temple and amphitheatre of **Qenqo** with some of the finest examples of Inca stone carving *in situ*, especially inside the large hollowed-out stone that houses an altar. On the same road are **Puka Pukara** (Red Fort, but more likely to have been a *tambo*, or post-house), wonderful views; and the spring shrine of **Tambo Machay**, which is in excellent condition. Water still flows by a hidden channel out of the masonry wall, straight into a little rock pool traditionally known as the Inca's bath. Take a guide to the sites and visit in the morning for the best photographs. Carry your multi-site ticket, there are roving ticket inspectors. You can visit the sites on foot, a pleasant walk of at least half a day through the countryside; take water, sun protection, and watch out for dogs. Alternatively, take the Pisac bus up to Tambo Machay (US$0.35) and walk back, or arrange a horseback tour with an agency.

● Sleeping

Cuzco *p1208, maps p1212 and p1218*
In Jun and other busy times, double-booking occurs so double-check reservations. Book more expensive hotels well in advance, particularly for the week or so around Inti Raymi, when prices are greatly increased. Prices given are for the high season in Jun-Aug. When there are fewer tourists hotels may drop their prices by as much as half. Always check for discounts. Train passengers are approached by unlicensed hotel agents for medium-priced hotels who are often misleading about details; their local nickname is *jalagringos* (gringo pullers), or *piratas*. Taxis and tourist minibuses meet the train and (should) take you to the hotel of your choice for US$0.75-1, but be insistent. Since it is cold here and many hotels have no heating, ask for an *estufa*, a heater which some places will provide for an extra charge.

LL El Monasterio, C Palacios 136, Plazoleta Nazarenas, T241777, www.monasterio.orient-express.com. 5-star, beautifully restored Seminary of San Antonio Abad (a Peruvian National Historical Landmark), including the Baroque chapel, spacious comfortable rooms with all facilities (some rooms offer an oxygen-enriched atmosphere to help clients acclimatize, US$25 extra), very helpful staff, price includes buffet breakfast (US$19 to non-residents, will fill you up for the rest of the day), good restaurants, lunch and dinner à la carte, business centre with email for guests (US$3 per hr).

LL Libertador Palacio del Inka, Plazoleta Santo Domingo 259, T231961, www.libertador.com.pe. 5-star, price includes buffet breakfast, good, especially the service, warm and bright, *Inti Raymi* restaurant, excellent, folk music in the evening.

LL Novotel, San Agustín 239, T881030, www.novotel.cuzco.com.pe. 4-star, cheaper in modern section; price includes buffet breakfast, converted from colonial house with beautiful glass-roofed courtyard, spacious rooms, cable TV, central heating, 2 restaurants and a French chef.

AL Casas Andina Private Collection Cusco, Plazoleta de Limacpampa Chico 473, T232610, www.casa-andina.com. Upmarket chain hotel in 16th-century mansion, very high standards, gourmet restaurant, good *piscos*.

AL Sonesta Posadas del Inca, Portal Espinar 108, T227061, www.sonestaperu.com. Includes buffet breakfast, warmly decorated rooms with heating and cable TV, safe, some rooms on 3rd floor with view of Plaza, very helpful, English spoken, restaurant with Andean food, excellent service.

A Casa Andina Plaza, Portal Espinar 142, T231733, www.casa-andina.com. 40 rooms, new hotel near plaza, cable TV, private bathroom, internet access, ATM and safe deposit box. Equally recommendable are **Casa Andina Koricancha**, San Agustín 371, T252633, **Casa Andina Catedral**, Santa Catalina Angosta 149, T233661, and the

A Casa Andina San Blas, Chihuampata 278, San Blas, T263964, all of which are in the same vein.

A Casa San Blas, Tocuyeros 566, just off Cuesta San Blas, T237900, www.casasanblas.com. New boutique hotel, bright and airy rooms with traditional textiles, breakfast and internet included, attentive service.

A Cuzco Plaza 2, Saphi 486, T263000, www.cuscoplazahotels.com. Same management as **A-B Cuzco Plaza 1** (Plaza Nazarenas 181, T246161). Nicely-decorated rooms set around 3 charming covered patios, includes American breakfast, cable TV and heating.

A El Arqueólogo, Pumacurco 408, T232569, www.hotelarqueologo.com. Includes breakfast, hot water, heating extra, helpful, French and

---

● *For an explanation of the sleeping and eating price codes used in this guide, see page 58. Other*
● *relevant information is found in Essentials pages 1076-1078.*

English spoken, will store luggage, garden, cafeteria and kitchen.

A Los Apus Hotel and Mirador, Atocsaycuchi 515 y Choquechaca, San Blas, T264243, www.losapushotel.com. Includes breakfast and airport transfer, full of character, very smart, central heating, good views, disabled facilities.

A Royal Inka I, Plaza Regocijo 299, T231067, royalin@speedy.com.pe (also *Royal Inka II* on Santa Teresa, a little pricier). Price includes taxes and breakfast, bar, dining room, good service. These hotels run a bus to Pisac at 1000 daily, returns 1800, free for guests.

A-C Marqueses, Garcilaso 256, T264249, marqueses@sastravelperu.com. Recently restored in Spanish colonial style, with 16/17th-century style religious paintings and 2 lovely courtyards. Rooms have heavy curtains and some are a little dark; luxury rooms have bath. Buffet breakfast.

B Hostal Casa de Campo, Tandapata 296-B (at the end of the street), T/F244404, info@ hotelcasadecampo.com. Some of the highest rooms have a *lot* of steps up to them, hot water, includes Continental breakfast and airport/ rail transfer with reservations, discount for longer stays, 10% discount for Footprint book owners, safe deposit box, sun terrace, quiet and relaxing,

all rooms have great views, Dutch and English spoken, take a taxi there after dark.

B Hostal El Balcón, Tambo de Montero 222, T236738, balcon1@terra.com.pe. With breakfast, homely atmosphere, very welcoming, quiet, laundry, sauna, bar, meals on request, English spoken, wonderful views, beautiful garden.

B Hostal Rumi Punku, Choquechaca 339, T221102, www.rumipunku.com. 3-star hotel with a genuine Inca doorway leading to a sunny courtyard, comfortable rooms, helpful staff, safe. Highly recommended.

B-C Casona Pleiades, Tandapata 116, T506430, www.lacasonapleiades.com. Small guesthouse in renovated colonial house, cosy and warm, generous hosts, hot water, cable TV, Wi-Fi, roof terrace, video lounge and book exchange, café, free ariport pickup with reservation, lots of info.

C Hostal Cahuide, Saphi 845, T222771, F248262. Discount for long stay, hot water, good rooms, quiet, good laundry service, storage facilities, helpful, good value breakfasts.

C Hostal San Isidro Labrador, Saphi 440, T226241, labrador@qnet.com.pe. Pleasant, elegant but simple decor, colonial arches lead to breakfast area (continental breakfast included) and 2 lovely patios, hot water, heating.

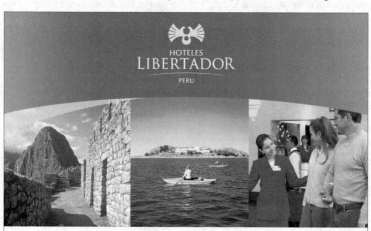

C **Niños Hotel**, Meloc 442, T/F231424, www.ninos hotel.com. Hot water, excellent breakfast extra, restaurant, laundry service, luggage store, Dutch, English, German and French spoken, run as part of the Dutch foundation *Niños Unidos Peruanos* and all profits are invested in projects to help street children. Also has *Niños 2*, on C Fierro, with all the same features.

C **Pensión Alemana**, Tandapata 260, San Blas, T/F226861. Swiss owned, welcoming, price includes American breakfast, comfortable, discount in low season.

C **Pensión Loreto**, Pasaje Loreto 115, Plaza de Armas, T/F226352, www.hloreto.com. Rooms with Inca walls and electric heaters, a bit dark, cheap laundry service, comfortable and secure, taxis and other travel can be arranged, Lucio here is a good guide, safe luggage deposit.

D **Casa Elena**, Choquechaca 162, T/F241202, www.geocities.com/casa_elena. French/Peruvian hostel, very comfortable, good choice, breakfast.

D **El Grial**, Atocsaycuchi 594, T223012, San Blas, www.cusco-peru.de. With continental breakfast, hot water, cable TV, charming, traditional style, spacious, books in English, German and French, videos, tours arranged.

D **Hostal Amaru**, Cuesta San Blas 541, T/F225933, www.cusco.net/amaru. Cheaper without bath, hot water, laundry, nice views, rooms in first courtyard are best (also has E **Hostal Anita**, safe, quiet, good American breakfast).

D **Hostal Kuntur Wasi**, Tandapata 352-A, San Blas, T227570. Great views, F without bath, use of kitchen US$0.60, laundry service, owner speaks a bit of English and is very helpful and welcoming, a pleasant place to stay.

D **Hostal María Esther**, Pumacurco 516, T224382. Very comfortable, helpful, includes breakfast, garden.

D **Hostal Q'Awarina**, Suecia 575, T228130. Includes breakfast, group rates available, great views and great value.

D **Marani**, Carmen Alto 194, San Blas, T/F249462, www.hostalmarani.com. Full of character, set around a courtyard, breakfast available, Dutch-owned hostel associated with the Hope Foundation (www.stichtinghope.org), which builds schools, helps teachers and hospitals, good value.

E **El Balcón Colonial**, Choquechaca 350, T238129, balconcolonial@hotmail.com.

Accommodation for 11 people in 6 rooms, hot showers, breakfast, kitchen and laundry facilities all extra, comfortable, safe, generous hosts.
E Hostal Familiar, Saphi 661, T239353.
E without bath, hot water, good beds, popular.
E (F pp) Hostel Loki, Cuesta Santa Ana 601, T243705, info@lokihostel.com. Huge, funky new

hostel in a restored viceroy's residence on the steep Cuesta Santa Ana, dorms and rooms set around a beautiful courtyard, comfortable beds, hot water, free internet. A great meeting place.
E Hostal Pakcha Real, Tandapata 300, San Blas, T237484, pakcharealhostal@ hotmail.com. Family run, hot water, relaxed. Breakfast, cooking and

Around Plaza de Armas

Plateros detail

Sleeping
Casa Andina Catedral **16** *B3*
Casa Andina Plaza **15** *C2*

El Procurador del Cusco **1** *A2*
Hostal Q'Awarina **6** *A2*
Hostal Resbalosa **7** *A3*
Hostal Royal
  Frankenstein **8** *B1*
Marqueses **2** *B1*
Pensión Loreto **9** *C2*
Royal Inka I **12** *B1*
Royal Inka II **13** *A1*
Sonesta Posadas
  del Inca **3** *B2*
The Point **4** *C1*

Eating
Al Grano **1** *C3*
Amaru **2** *Plateros detail*
Blueberry Lounge **3** *B3*
Bohemia **18** *B3*
Café Ayllu **4** *B3*
Café Halliy **6** *Plateros detail*
Chez Maggy Clave
  de Do **7** *A2*
Chez Maggy El Corsario **8** *B2*

Chez Maggy La
  Antigua **9** *A2*
Cicciolina **44** *C3*
Dolce Vita **10** *C3*
El Encuentro **12** *C3*
El Truco & Taberna
  del Truco **13** *B1*
Fallen Angel **14** *B3*
Inka Grill **15** *B2*
Kintaro **16** *B1*
Kusikuy **17** *B3*
La Retama **19** *B2*
Incanto & Greens
  Organic **21** *C3*
MAP Café **47** *B3*
Mia Pizza **24** *A2*
Pachacútec Grill
  & Bar **25** *B2*
Paititi **26** *C3*
Pomodoro **46** *C2*
Pucará **28** *Plateros detail*
The Real McCoy **11**
  Plateros detail

Trotamundos **31** *B2*
Tupananchis **5** *C1*
Tunupa & Cross
  Keys Pub **32** *B2*
Varayoc **33** *B2*
Victor Victoria **34** *A2*
Yaku Mama **35** *A2*

Bars & clubs
Big Blue Martini **30** *A2*
Corruption **20** *A2*
El Garabato Video Music
  Club **42** *B2*
Extreme **27** *B3*
Kamikaze **36** *B2*
Los Perros **37** *A2*
Mama Africa **45** *B2*
Norton Rat's Tavern **39** *C2*
Paddy Flaherty's **40** *C3*
Rosie O'Grady's **41** *C3*
Ukuku's **43** *Plateros detail*
Uptown **38** *C3*

laundry facilities extra. Airport/train/bus pick-up, but call ahead if arriving late.

E Hostal Rickch'airy, Tambo de Montero 219, T236606. **G** with shared bath, hot water in the morning, laundry service, free luggage store, breakfast available, nice garden with good views, will collect guests from train station, tourist information, mixed reports.

E Hostal Royal Frankenstein, San Juan de Dios 260, 2 blocks from the Plaza de Armas, T236999, ludwig_roth@hotmail.com. Eccentric place, hot water, safe, cooking and laundry facilities (US$0.30/day), German-owned, German and English spoken.

E Qorichaska, Nueva Alta 458, some distance from centre, T228974, qorichaska77@yahoo.com. Hot water, includes breakfast, use of kitchen, will store luggage, safe, great value.

E Hostal Resbalosa, Resbalosa 494, T224839. Cheaper without bath, hot water in the mornings and evenings, ask for a room with a view, luggage stored, laundry facilities, full breakfast for US$1.45.

E Suecia II, Tecseccocha 465, T239757. **G** without bath, good security, breakfast US$1.40 from 0500, beautiful building, good meeting place, water not always hot or bathrooms clean, best to book in advance (if full, they'll find alternative accommodation, which may not be as good).

E-F Hostal Familiar Mirador del Inka, Tandapata 160, off Plaza San Blas, T261384, miradordelinka@latinmail.com. Cheaper without bath, hot water, laundry, son Edwin rents trekking equipment.

E-F Hospedaje Plaza de San Blas, Plazoleta San Blas 630, T235358, psanblas@cori huasi.com. Welcoming, good location, breakfast included, has a 4-bed family room.

F Albergue Casa Campesina, Av Tullumayo 274, T233466, ccamp@apu.cbc.org.pe. Includes breakfast, shared bath, lovely place, funds support the Casa Campesina organization (www.cbc.org.pe/casacamp/), which is linked to local campesina communities (see also Store of the Weavers under Shopping, below). 23% discount for SAE members.

F Estrellita, Av Tullumayo 445, parte Alta, T234134. Includes breakfast, basic kitchen for guests, most rooms with shared bath, 2 with private bath, basic but excellent value, safe parking available for bikes.

F Hostal Familiar Carmen Alto, Carmen Alto 197, T224367, 1st on the right down steps (there is no sign), 3 blocks from central plaza. If there's no answer at the bell, go to the shop next door. Tranquil and full of character, family run, use of kitchen and washing machine, breakfast US$2, shared bath.

F Hostal Luzerna, Av Baja 205, near San Pedro train station (take a taxi at night), T232762. Hot water, safe to leave luggage, good beds, nice family, with breakfast, use of kitchen.

F pp The Point, Mesón de la Estrella 172, T252266, www.thepointhostels.com. Latest addition to the Point's stables. Dormitory accommodation, also has doubles **E**, includes breakfast, free internet, hot showers, good atmosphere.

G Hospedaje El Artesano de San Blas, Suytucato 790, San Blas, T263968, manosandinas@yahoo.com. Many bright and airy rooms, taxis leave you at Plaza San Blas, then it's a steep walk uphill for 5-10 mins.

G pp Hospedaje Inka, Suytuccato 848, T231995. Also steep walk up from Plaza San Blas, or phone the hostal. Includes breakfast, wonderful views, spacious rooms, owner Américo is very helpful.

G Hospedaje Familiar Inti Quilla, Atocsaycuchi 281, T252659. Shared rooms around a pleasant little courtyard, hot water 24 hrs, no breakfast or kitchen.

G pp The Blue House, Kiskapata 291 (parallel and above Tandapata), T242407. Cosy hostal, good value. Reductions for longer stays, includes breakfast, DVDs, shared kitchen, great views.

Youth hostels

E Maison de la Jeunesse (affiliated to HI), Av Sol, Cuadra 5, Pasaje Grace, Edif San Jorge (down a small side street opposite Qoricancha) T235617, www.hostellingcusco.com. French/Peruvian run, dormitories and private rooms, TV and video room, cooking facilities and very hot water, includes breakfast.

E-F El Procurador del Cusco, Coricalle 440, Prolongación Procuradores, T243559. Price includes use of the basic kitchen (no fridge) and laundry area, basic rooms, but upstairs is better, helpful, good value. Recommended.

F Albergue Municipal, Quiscapata 240, San Cristóbal, T252506, albergue@municusco. gob.pe. Dormitories and double rooms, helpful staff, luggage store, great views, bar, cafeteria, laundry, safe deposit, discount for members.

❶ Eating

Cuzco *p1208, maps p1212 and p1218*
There are many good cheap restaurants on Procuradores, Plateros and Tecseccocha.

₸₸₸ Cicciolina , Triunfo 393, 2nd floor, T239510. Sophisticated cooking focusing largely on Italian/Mediterranean cuisine, impressive wine list. Good atmosphere, great for a special occasion.

₸₸₸ Fallen Angel, Plazoleta Nazarenas 221, T258184, www.fallenangelincusco.com. International and Novo Andino gourmet cuisine, great steaks, genuinely innovative interior design, worth checking out their events. Open daily, Sun from 1500.

₸₸₸ Incanto, Santa Catalina Angosta 135, T254753. Under same ownership as Inka Grill and with the same standards, restaurant has Inca stone work and serves pastas, grilled meats, pizzas, desserts, accompanied by an extensive wine list. Open daily 1100-2400. Also Peruvian delicatessen. Upstairs is **Greens Organic** with exclusively organic ingredients in fusion cuisine and a fresh daily buffet.

₸₸₸ Inka Grill, Portal de Panes 115, Plaza de Armas, T262992. According to many the best food in town, specializing in Novo Andino cuisine (the use of native ingredients and 'rescued' recipes), also homemade pastas, wide vegetarian selection, live music, excellent coffee and homemade pastries 'to go'.

₸₸₸ MAP Café, in Museo de Arte Precolombino, Plaza de las Nazarenas 231. Café by day (1000-1830), from 1830 to 2200 serves top-class international and Peruvian- Andean cuisine, innovative children's menu

₸₸₸ Pachacútec Grill and Bar, Portal de Panes 105, Plaza de Armas. International cuisine, seafood and Italian specialities, folk music nightly.

₸₸₸ Paititi, Portal Carrizos 270, Plaza de Armas.

Live music, good atmosphere, Inca masonry, excellent pizzas.

₸₸₸ La Retama, Portal de Panes 123, 2nd floor. Good food (also Novo Andino) and service, live music and dance, art exhibitions.

₸₸₸ El Truco, Plaza Regocijo 261. Excellent local and international dishes, buffet lunch 1200-1500, nightly folk music at 2045, next door is **Taberna del Truco**, open 0900-0100.

₸₸₸ Pomodoro, Loreto 125, T221397. Best Italian food in Cuzco, bastion of 'slow food', with all pasta and pizza handmade on the spot. Superb.

₸₸₸ Tunupa, Portal Confiturias 233, p 2, Plaza de Armas (same entrance as *Cross Keys*). Large restaurant, small balcony overlooking Plaza, international, Peruvian and Novo Andino cuisine, good buffet US$15, nicely decorated, cocktail lounge, live music and dance at 2030.

₸₸₸ Tupananchis, Portal Mantas 180, T976 4494. Tasty Novo Andino and Fusion cuisine in a sophisticated atmosphere. Recommended.

₸₸₸ ₸₸ Bohemia, Portal de Carnes 254, T222642. Wide selection of international food and drinks, nice ambience, attentive service, English spoken.

₸₸ A Mi Manera (Culturas Peru), Triunfo 393, T222 219, www.culturasperu.com. Remodelled in 2006, imaginative Novoandina cuisine with open kitchen. Great hospitality and atmosphere.

₸₸ Al Grano, Santa Catalina Ancha 398, T228032. Authentic Asian dishes, menu changes daily, excellent food, best coffee in town, vegetarian choices, open 1000-2100, closed on Sun.

₸₸ Baco, Ruinas 465, T242808. Wine bar and bistro-style restaurant, same owner as *Cicciolina*. Specializes in BBQ and grilled meats, also veggie dishes, pizzas and good wines. Unpretentious and comfy, groups welcome.

₸₸ Blueberry Lounge, Portal de Carnes 236, Plaza de Armas, T221397. In a beautifully restored colonial house, open fires in the evening, cosy place to read, listen to music, watch TV or videos, menu specializes in Asian dishes, with touches of the Novo Andino, good for breakfast, vegetarian options.

₸₸ Inkanato, San Agustín 280, T222926. Good food, staff dressed in Inca outfits and dishes made only with ingredients known in Inca times, calls itself a "living museum".

₸₸ Jack's Café, Choquechaca y San Blas. Excellent varied menu, generous portions, relaxed atmosphere, can get very busy at lunchtime.

₸₸ Kintaro, Heladeros 149. Japanese and vegetarian, homemade and low fat food, good for high altitude, Japanese owner, closed Sun.

₸₸ Kusikuy, Suecia 339, T292870. Open 0800-2300 Mon-Sat, local, national and international dishes, good service, set lunch unbeatable value at only US$2.

₸₸ La Bodega, Carmen Alto 146, San Blas. Snug Dutch and Peruvian-owned café/restaurant, good food, salads, drinks.

Los Toldos, Almagro 171 and San Andrés 219. Grilled chicken, fries and salad bar, also *trattoria* with homemade pasta and pizza, delivery T229829.

Macondo, Cuesta San Blas 571, T229415. Interesting restaurant with an imaginative menu, good food, well-furnished, gay friendly.

Pachapapa, Plazoleta San Blas 120, opposite church of San Blas, T241318. A beautiful patio restaurant in a colonial house, good Cusqueña dishes, at night diners can sit in their own, private colonial dining room. Recommended.

Pucará, Plateros 309. Mon-Sat 1230-2200. Peruvian and international food, nice atmosphere.

The Real McCoy, Plateros 326, 2nd floor, T261111. A retreat for homesick Brits and Aussies, good value breakfast buffet (US$2), English classics for dinner, puddings too.

Varayoc, Espaderos 142, T232404. Swiss restaurant, including Peruvian ingredients (cheese fondue US$10-13); also has a variety of pastas, good desserts, literary atmosphere.

Witches Garden, Carmen Bajo 169, T244077. Good Novo Andino and international food and desserts, warmly decorated, videos for patrons to choose.

Mundo Hemp, Qanchipata 560, www.mundohemp.com. Foccacia bread, interesting savoury pancakes, quiche, healthy desserts and good fresh juices. Nice atmosphere with a beautiful sunny courtyard. Also has a shop with a range of hemp products, man.

Café Cultural Ritual, Choquechaca 140. Good value and tasty vegetarian food, including some good Indian dishes, US$ 2.20.

Chez Maggy, 3 branches: **La Antigua** (the original) at Procuradores 365, **El Corsario** No 344 and **Clave de Do** No 374 (open at 0700 for buffet breakfast).

El Encuentro, Santa Catalina Ancha 384 and Choquechaca 136. One of the best value eateries in Cuzco, 3 courses of good healthy vegan food and a drink for US$1.35, very busy at lunchtime.

Inkafe, Choquechaca 131-A. Great food and value in a nice setting, English spoken.

Mia Pizza, Procuradores 379. Good range of economical menus, including one with a reasonable curry.

Víctor Victoria, Tecseccocha 466, T252854. Israeli and local dishes, first-class breakfasts, good value (not to be confused with similar sounding place on Tigre).

Cafés

Amaru, Plateros 325, 2nd floor. Limitless coffee and tea, great bread and juices, even on 'non-buffet' breakfasts (US$1.15 for simple), colonial balcony. Also has bar.

Café Ayllu, Portal de Carnes 208. Classical/folk music, good atmosphere, superb range of milk products, wonderful apple pastries, good selection for breakfast, great juices, quick service.

Café Halliy, Plateros 363. Popular meeting place, especially for breakfast, good for comments on guides, has good snacks and 'copa Halliy' (fruit, muesli, yoghurt, honey and chocolate cake), also good vegetarian *menú* and set lunch.

Café Manu, Av Pardo 1046. Good coffee and good food too.

Chocolate, Choquechaca 162. Good for coffee and cakes, but the highlights are the gourmet chocolates.

Granja Heidi, Cuesta San Blas 525. Delicious yoghurt, granola, ricotta cheese and honey and other great breakfast options, vegetarian dishes.

Dolce Vita, Santa Catalina Ancha 366. Delicious Italian ice cream, open 1000-2100.

Moni, San Agustín 311, T231029. Peruvian/English-owned, good fresh food and breakfast, British music, magazines, bright and comfortable.

The Muse, Tandapata 682, Plazoleta San Blas. Funky little café with fresh local coffee, good food, including vegetarian lasagne and carrot

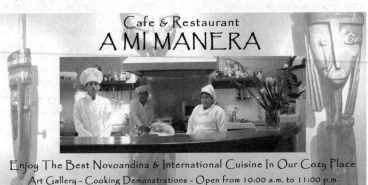

cake, smoothies, often has live music, helpful English owner. Will refill water bottles for a small charge in an attempt to minimize plastic waste.
Trotamundos, Portal Comercio 177, 2nd floor. Balcony overlooking the plaza, nice atmosphere, especially at night with open fire, good coffees and cakes, safe salads, internet service, open Mon-Sat 0800-2400.
Yaku Mama, Procuradores 397. Good for breakfast, unlimited fruit and coffee.

Panaderías
Panadería El Buen Pastor, Cuesta San Blas 579. Very good bread and pastries, proceeds go to a charity for orphans and street children.

ⓝ Bars and clubs

Cuzco *p1208, maps p1212 and p1218*
Bars
Bar 7, Tandapata 690, San Blas, T506472. Good food and drinks in a trendy bar which specializes in local ingredients.
Big Blue Martini, Tecseccocha 148, T248839. Sophisticated, split-level sofa bar with funky lighting, very good cocktails, food and a lively music scene, jazz sessions on Thu, and on Sat a guest DJ.
Cross Keys Pub, Plaza de Armas, Portal Confiturías 233 (upstairs). Open 1100-0130, run by Barry Walker of **Manu Expeditions**, a Mancunian and ornithologist, darts, cable sports, pool, bar meals, plus daily half price specials Sun-Wed, great pisco sours, very popular, great atmosphere.
Km 0 (Arte y Tapas), Tandapata 100, San Blas. Mediterranean themed bar tucked in behind San Blas, good snacks and tapas, with live music every night (around 2200 - lots of acoustic guitar etc).
Los Perros Bar, Tecseccocha 436. Open 1100-0100. Great place to chill out on comfy couches, excellent music, welcoming, good coffee, tasty meals available (including vegetarian), book exchange, English and other magazines, board games.
Mandela's Bar, Palacio 121, p 3, T222424. Bar/restaurant with African theme, good atmosphere and lots of space to relax. Serves breakfast, lunch and drinks in the evening, also Sun BBQs and special events through the year. Great views from the roof.
Norton Rat's Tavern, Loreto 115, p 2, same entrance as Hostal Loreto, T246204. Also serves meals, cable TV, popular, English spoken, fine balcony, pool, darts, motorcycle theme with information for motorcyclists from owner, Jeffrey Powers.
Rosie O'Grady's, Santa Catalina Ancha 360, T247935. Good music, tasty food, English and

Russian spoken, good value, open 1100 till late (food served till 2400).
Paddy Flaherty's, Triunfo 124 on the corner of the plaza. Irish theme pub, deservedly popular, open 1300-0100, good grub.

Clubs
Corruption, Calle Tecseccocha, just below **Los Perros** on the same side of the street. Wide range of music, very en vogue with Israeli backpackers.
Extreme, Suecia, next to Magtas's. Movies in the late afternoon and early evening, but after midnight this place really gets going with an eclectic range of music, from 60's and 70's rock and pop to techno and trance.
El Garabato Video Music Club, Espaderos 132, p 3. Open daily 1600-0300, dance area, lounge for chilling, bar, live shows 2300-0030 (all sorts of styles) and large screen showing music videos.
Kamikaze, Plaza Regocijo 274, T233865. *Peña* at 2200, good old traditional rock music, candle-lit cavern atmosphere, entry US$2.50.
Mama Africa, Portal de Harinas, 2nd floor. Cool music and clubber's spot, good food with varied menu, happy hour till 2300, good value.
Siete Angelitos, Siete Angelitos 638. Tiny club, just a couple of rooms, but spectacular cocktails, a friendly owner by the name of Walter and an awesome atmosphere when things get going.
Ukuku's, Plateros 316. US$1.35 entry, very popular, good atmosphere, good mix of music including live shows nightly.
Uptown, Portal Belén 115, 2nd floor. Has a dancefloor and a large video screen. The music is middle of the road, from local music through 70's classics to the latest releases.

ⓔ Entertainment

Cuzco *p1208, maps p1212 and p1218*
Folklore Regular nightly folklore show at **Centro Qosqo de Arte nativo**, Av Sol 604, T227901. Show from 1900 to 2030, entrance on BTG ticket. **Teatro Inti Raymi**, Saphi 605, nightly at 1845, US$4.50, well worth it. **Teatro Municipal**, C Mesón de la Estrella 149 (T227321 for information 0900- 1300 and 1500-1900). Plays, dancing and shows, mostly Thu-Sun. They also run classes in music and dancing from Jan to Mar which are great value.

ⓕ Festivals and events

Cuzco *p1208, maps p1212 and p1218*
Carnival in Cuzco is a messy affair with flour, water, cacti, bad fruit and animal manure being thrown about in the streets. **Easter Monday**: procession of **El Señor de los Temblores** (Lord of the Earthquakes), starting at 1600 outside the Cathedral. A large crucifix is paraded through the

streets, returning to the Plaza de Armas around 2000 to bless the tens of thousands of people who have assembled there. **2-3 May**: Vigil of the Cross takes place at all mountaintops with crosses on them, a boisterous affair. **Jun**: Q'Olloriti, the Snow Star Festival, is held at a 4,700 m glacier north of Ocongate (Ausangate) 150 km southeast of Cuzco. Several agencies offer tours. (The date is moveable.) On **Corpus Christi** day, the Thu after Trinity Sunday, all the statues of the Virgin and of saints from Cuzco's churches are paraded through the streets to the Cathedral. The Plaza de Armas is surrounded by tables with women selling *cuy* (guinea pig) and a mixed grill called *chiriuchu* (*cuy*, chicken, *tortillas*, fish eggs, water-weeds, maize, cheese and sausage) and lots of Cusqueña beer. **24 Jun**: the pageant of **Inti Raymi**, the Inca festival of the winter solstice, is enacted in Quechua at 1000 at the Qoricancha, moving on to Sacsayhuaman at 1300. Tickets for the stands can be bought a week in advance from the Emufec office, Santa Catalina Ancha 325, US$35. Standing places on the ruins are free but get there at about 1030 to defend your space. Travel agents can arrange the whole day for you, with meeting points, transport, reserved seats and packed lunch. Those who try to persuade you to buy a ticket for the right to film or take photos are being dishonest. On the night before Inti Raymi, the Plaza de Armas is crowded with processions and food stalls. Try to arrive in Cuzco 15 days before Inti Raymi for the Cusqueña beer festival (US$6 entry) and other festivals, parades etc. **28 Jul**: Peruvian Independence Day. Prices shoot up during these celebrations. **Aug**: on the last Sun is the **Huarachicoy** festival at Sacsayhuaman, a spectacular re-enactment of the Inca manhood rite, performed in dazzling costumes by boys of a local school. **8 Sep**: Day of the Virgin is a colourful procession of masked dancers from the church of Almudena, at the southwest edge of Cuzco, near Belén, to the Plaza de San Francisco. There is also a splendid fair at Almudena, and a free bull fight on the following day. **1 Nov**: All Saints Day, celebrated everywhere with bread dolls and traditional cooking. **8 Dec**: Cuzco: when churches and museums close at 1200. **24 Dec**: Santuranticuy, 'the buying of saints', with a big crafts market in the plaza, very noisy until early hours of the 25th.

O Shopping

Cuzco *p1208, maps p1212 and p1218*
Arts and crafts
In the Plaza San Blas and the surrounding area, authentic Cuzco crafts still survive. A market is held on Sat. Many leading artisans welcome

visitors. Among fine objects made are Biblical figures from plaster, wheatflour and potatoes, reproductions of pre-Columbian ceramics and colonial sculptures, pious paintings, earthenware figurines, festive dolls and wood carvings.

Cuzco is the weaving centre of Peru and excellent textiles can be found at good value. Be very careful of buying gold and silver objects and jewellery in and around Cuzco.
Agua y Tierra, Plazoleta Nazarenas 167, and also at Cuesta San Blas 595, T226951. Excellent quality crafts from rainforest communities.
Apacheta, Santa Catalina 313, T238210, www.apachetaperu.com. Replicas of Pre-Inca and Inca textiles, ceramics, alpaca goods, contermporary art gallery, books on Andean culture.
Inkantations, Choquechaca 200. Radical baskets made from natural materials in all sorts of weird and wonderful shapes. Also ceramics and Andean weavings. Interesting and original.
La Mamita, Portal de Carnes 244, Plaza de Armas, sells the ceramics of Pablo Seminario (see under Urubamba, page 1235), plus cotton, basketry, jewellery, etc.
Mercado Artesanal, Av Sol, block 4, is good for cheap crafts.
Pedazo de Arte, Plateros 334B. A tasteful collection of Andean handicrafts, many designed by Japanese owner Miki Suzuki.
La Pérez, Urb Mateo Pumachua 598, Huanchac, T232186. A big co-operative with a good selection; they will arrange a free pick-up from your hotel.

Bookshops
Centro de Estudios Regionales Andinos Bartolomé de las Casas, Av Tullumayo 465, T233472, www.cbc.org.pe. Good books on Peruvian history, archaeology, etc, Mon-Sat 1100-1400, 1600-1900.
Jerusalem, Heladeros 143, T235408. English books, guidebooks, music, postcards, book exchange (3 for 1).
Book exchange, 1 for 1, at **The Sun**, Plazoleta Limacpampa Chico 471, café/restaurant, run by an Aussie.

Camping equipment
For renting equipment, there are several places around the Plaza area. Check the equipment carefully as it is common for parts to be missing. An example of prices per day: tent US$3-5, sleeping bag US$2 (down), US$1.50 (synthetic), stove US$1. A deposit of US$100 is asked, plus credit card, passport or plane ticket. White gas (*bencina*), US$1.50 per litre, can be bought at hardware stores, but check the purity. Stove spirit (*alcoól para quemar*) is available at pharmacies; blue gas

canisters, costing US$5, can be found at hardware stores and camping shops. You can also rent equipment through travel agencies.
Edson Zuñiga Huillca, Mercado Rosaspata, Jr Abel Landeo P-1, T802831, 993 7243 (mob). Three mins from Plaza de Armas, for repair of camping equipment and footwear, also equipment rental, open 24 hrs a day, 7 days a week, English and Italian spoken.
Soqllaq'asa Camping Service, owned by English-speaking Sra Luzmila Bellota Miranda, at Plateros 365 No 2F, T252560, is recommended for equipment hire, also buy and sell camping gear and make alpaca jackets, open Mon-Sat 0900-1300, 1600-2030, Sun 1800-2030.

Fabrics and alpaca clothing
Alpaca 3, Ruinas 472 (English spoken). For quality items.
Alpaca 111, Plaza Regocijo 202, T243233. High quality alpaca clothing with outlets also in hotels *El Monasterio*, *Libertador* and *Machu Picchu Sanctuary Lodge*.
Arte Vivo del Cusco al Mundo, beside Capilla San Ignacio, Plaza de Armas. Open 1030-1300, 1530-2100. Outlet for 2 weaving co-ops.
The Center for Traditional Textiles of Cuzco, Av Sol 603, T228117, www.textilescusco.org. A non-profit organization that seeks to promote, refine and rediscover the weaving traditions of the Cuzco area. Tours of workshops, weaving classes, you can watch weavers at work. Over 50% of the price goes direct to the weaver. Recommended.
Josefina Olivera, Portal Comercio 173, Plaza de Armas. Sells old textiles and weavings, expensive but worth it to save pieces being cut up to make other items, open daily 1100-2100.
Store of Weavers (Asociación Central de Artesanos y Artesanas del Sur Andino Inkakunaq Ruwaynin), Av Tullumayo 274, T233466, www.cbc.org.pe/tejidosandinos. Store run by 6 local weaving communities, some of whose residents you can see working on site. All profits go to the weavers themselves.

Food
Casa Ecológica Cusco, Triunfo 393, www.casaecologicacusco.com. Organic foods, wild honey, coffee, granola. Casa Ecológica also offers natural medicines, indigenous art and weavings.
La Cholita, Portal Espinar 142-B and at airport. Special chocolates made with local ingredients.

Jewellery
Calas, Siete Angelitos 619-B, San Blas. Handmade silver jewellery in interesting designs and alpaca goods from the community of Pitumarca.
Carlos Chaquiras, Triunfo 375 y Portal Comercio, T227470, www.carlos chaquiras.com. Very upmarket, with lots of Inca figures, among other designs.
Ilaria, Portal Carrizos 258, T246253. Branches in hotels *Monasterio*, *Libertador* and at the airport. For recommended jewellery and silver.
Mullu, Triunfo 120, T229831. Contemporary silver jewellery with semi-precious stones and cotton clothing with interesting designs, open Mon-Sat 1000-2100.
Spondylus, Cuesta San Blas 505 and Plazoleta San Blas 617, T226929. A good selection of interesting gold and silver jewellery and fashion tops with Inca and pre-Inca designs.

Music
Taki Museo de Música de los Andes, Hatunrumiyoq 487-5. Shop and workshop selling and displaying musical instruments, knowledgeable owner, who is an ethnomusicologist. Recommended for anyone interested in Andean music.

Markets
Wanchac, Av Garcilaso (southeast of centre) and **Santa Ana Market**, opposite Estación San Pedro, sell a variety of goods.

Supermarkets
La Canasta, Av La Cultura 2000 block. Very well-stocked, takes credit cards, ATM outside.
D'Dinos Market, Av La Cultura 2003, T252656 for home delivery. Open 24-hrs, well-supplied, takes credit cards.
Gato's Market, Portal Belén 115.
Mega, Matará 271, and Av Garcilaso at Plaza Túpac Amaru, US-style.

▲ Activities and tours

Cuzco *p1208, maps p1212 and p1218*
For a list of recommended Tour operators for Manu, see page 1283.

There are many travel agencies in Cuzco. The sheer number and variety of tours on offer is bewildering and prices for the same tour can vary dramatically. Always remember that you get what you pay for and that, in a crowded market, organization can sometimes be a weak point. In general you should only deal directly with the agencies themselves. You can do this when in town, or you can raise whatever questions you may have in advance (or even in Cuzco), and get replies in writing, by email. Other sources of advice are visitors returning from trips, who can give the latest information, and the trip reports for members of the South America Explorers. Students will normally receive a discount on production of an ISIC card. Do not deal with guides who claim to be employed by agencies listed below without verifying their credentials. City tours cost about US$6 for 4 hrs; check what sites are included and that the guide is experienced.

Only a restricted number of agencies are licensed to operate **Inca Trail** trips. INRENA, Av José Gabriel Cosio 308, Urb Magisterial, 1 etapa, T229297, will verify operating permits, and all relevant information (agencies and guides with permits, regulations, reservations, etc) can be found on the INC website, www.inc-cusco.gob.pe: go to "Sistema de Reservas RCI" (see Visitors' tickets, above, for INC office). Unlicensed agencies will sell Inca Trail trips, but pass clients on to the operating agency. This can cause confusion and booking problems at busy times. There is a quota for agencies and groups to use the Trail, but modifications to the procedures encouraged some agencies to make block bookings way in advance of departure dates. This made it much harder for agencies to guarantee their clients places on the Trail. Current advice is to book your preferred dates as early as possible, between 2 months and a year in advance, depending on the season when you want to go, then confirm nearer the time. There have been many instances of disappointed trekkers whose bookings did not materialise. Don't wait to the last minute and check your operator's cancellation fees. **Note** See page 1244, under The Inca Trail, for regulations governing the Trail.

Inca Trail and general tours
Amazing Peru, Av Tullumayo 213, T262720 (9 Alma Rd, Manchester M19 2FG, T0808 2346805), www.amazingperu.com. Highly recommended, professional and well-organized, "perfect tour", knowledgeable guides.
Andina Travel, Plazoleta Santa Catalina 219, T251892, www.andinatravel.com. Specializes in trekking and biking, notably the Lares Valley, working with traditional weaving communities. Recommended.
Big Foot, Triunfo 392 (oficina 213), T238568, www.bigfootcusco.com. Tailor-made hiking trips, especially in the remote corners of the Vilcabamba and Vilcanota mountains; also the Inca Trail.
Ch'aska, Plateros 325, 2nd floor, T240424, www.chaskatours.com. Dutch-Peruvian company offering cultural, adventure, nature and esoteric tours. They specialize in the Inca Trail, but also llama treks to Lares, treks to Choquequirao.
Cóndor Travel, C Saphi 848-A, T225961, www.condortravel.com.pe (for flights diviajes@condortravel.com.pe). A high- quality, exclusive agency that will organize trips throughout Peru and the rest of the world. Also

adventure travel and international flight tickets.
Culturas Peru, Tandapata 354, T263859, www.culturasperu.com. Swiss-Peruvian company offering adventure, cultural, ecological and spiritual tours. Also specialize in alternative Inca trails.
Destinos Turísticos, Portal de Panes 123, oficina 101-102, Plaza de Armas, T228168, www.destinosturisticosperu.com. The owner speaks Spanish, English, Dutch and Portuguese and specializes in package tours from economic to 5-star budgets. Advice on booking jungle trips and renting mountain bikes. Very helpful.
Ecotrek Peru, Totorapaccha 769, T247286, T972 7237 (mob), www.ecotrekperu.com. Run by Scot and long-time Cuzco resident Fiona Cameron, environmentally friendly, wide range of adventures bookable through website, specializing in little visited areas such as the Pongo de Mainique and Espíritu Pampa/Vilcabamba Vieja. Fiona's partner, David Ugarte, is a mountain biking specialist and speaks English, T084-974 4810 (mob).
Enigma Adventure, Jirón Clorinda Matto de Turner 100, Magisterio 1a Etapa, Cuzco, T222155, www.enigmaperu.com. Run by Spaniard Silvia Rico Coll. Well-organized, innovative trekking expeditions, Inca Trail and a variety of challenging alternatives. Also cultural tours to weaving communities, Ayahuasca Therapy, climbing and biking itineraries on demand.
Explorandes, Av Garcilaso 316-A (not to be confused with C Garcilaso in the centre), T238380, www.explorandes.com. Experienced high-end adventure company. Arrange a wide variety of mountain treks; trips available in Peru and Ecuador, book through website. Also arranges tours across Peru for lovers of orchids, ceramics or textiles. Award-winning environmental practices.
Flamenco Travels, Portal de Confiturias 265, oficina 3, info@ponyexpeditions.com. Associated with **Pony 's Expeditions** of Caraz, Classic Inka Trail pooled trek with daily departures (average of 8-10 people). Also the 5-day Salkantay trek.
Gatur Cusco, Puluchapata 140 (a small street off Av Sol 3rd block), T223496, www.gaturcusco.com. Esoteric, ecotourism, and general tours. Owner Dr José (Pepe) Altamirano is knowledgeable in Andean folk traditions. Excellent conventional tours, bilingual guides and transportation. Guides speak English, French, Spanish and German. They can also book internal flights.
Hiking Peru, Portal de Panes 109, office 6, T247962/965 1414 (mob), www.hikingperu.com. 8-day treks to Espíritu Pampa; 7 days/6 nights around Ausangate; 4-day/3-night Lares Valley Trek.
Inca Explorers, Ruinas 427, T241070, www.inca explorers.com. Specialist trekking agency for small

group expeditions in socially and environmentally responsible manner. Also 2-week hike in the Cordillera Vilcanota (passing Nevado Ausangate), and Choquequirao to Espíritu Pampa.

Liz's Explorer, Medio 114B, T246619, www.lizexplorer.com. 4-day/ 3-night Inca Trail trek (minimum group size 10, maximum 16), other lengths of trips available. Reports of good trips but haphazard organization.

Machete Tours, Tecseccocha 161, T224829, T963 1662 (mob), info@machetetours.com. Many innovative trekking trips: eg 9-day traverse of the Cordillera Vilcabamba, expeditions to Espíritu Pampa, Ausangate and the Inca Trail. Also have rainforest lodge on Río Blanco, south of the Manu Biosphere Reserve. Not all guides speak English.

Peru Planet, Suecia 318, T221181, www.peru-planet.net. Peruvian/Belgian owned agency offering tours of Inca Trail, other treks around Cuzco and packages within Peru, also Bolivia and Patagonia.

Peruvian Andean Treks, Av Pardo 705, T225701, www.andeantreks.com. Manager Tom Hendrickson has 5-day/4-night Inca Trail for US$500 using high-quality equipment and satellite phones. His 7-day/6-night Vilcanota Llama Trek to Ausangate includes a collapsible pressure chamber for altitude sickness. Also organizes interesting extended trekking itineraries.

Peru Treks and Adventure, C Garcilaso 265, Office 11, 2 blocks from main square, T505863, www.perutreks.com. Trekking agency set up by Englishman Mike Weston and his wife Koqui González. They pride themselves on good treatment of porters and support staff and have been consistently recommended for professionalism and customer care, a portion of profits go to community projects. Treks offered include Salkantay, the Lares Valley and Vilcabamba Vieja. Mike also runs the **Andean Travel Web**, www.andeantravelweb.com.

Q'ente, Garcilaso 210, int 210b, T222535, www.qente.com. Their Inca Trail service is recommended. Also private treks to Salkantay, Ausangate, Choquequirao, Vilcabamba and Q'eros. Horse riding to local ruins costs US$35 for 4-5 hrs. Very good, especially with children.

Sky Travel, Santa Catalina Ancha 366, interior 3-C (down alleyway next to Rosie O'Grady's pub),

T261818, www.skyperu.com. English spoken. General tours around city and Sacred Valley. Inca Trail with good-sized double tents and a dinner tent (the group is asked what it would like on the menu 2 days before departure). Other trips include Vilcabamba and Ausangate (trekking).

SAS Travel, Portal de Panes 143, T237292 (staff in a 2nd office at Medio 137, mainly deal with jungle information and only speak Spanish), www.sas travel.com. Discount for SAE members and students. Inca Trail includes the bus down from Machu Picchu to Aguas Calientes and lunch on the last day. SAS have their own hostel in Aguas Calientes. Offer alternatives to the classic Inca Trail, including Salkantay and Santa Teresa. Also mountain bike, horse riding and jungle tours. All guides speak some English. They can book internal flights at cheaper rates than from overseas. Solid reputation but recent reports mixed.

Tambo Tours, 4405 Spring Cypress Rd, Suite 210, Spring, TX 77388, USA, T1-888-2-GO-PERU (246-7378), T001-281 528 9448, www.2GOPERU.com. Long established adventure and tour specialist with offices in Peru and the US. Customized trips to the Amazon and archaelogical sites of Peru and Ecuador.

Trekperu, Ricaldo Palma N-9, Santa Mónica, T252899, www.trekperu.com. Experienced trek operator as well as other adventure sports and mountain biking. Offers 'culturally sensitive' tours. Cusco Biking Adventure includes support vehicle and good camping gear (but providing your own sleeping bag).

Tucan Travel, T241123, cuzco@tucantravel.com. Offer adventure tours and overland expeditions.

United Mice, Plateros 351y Triunfo 392, T221139, www.unitedmice.com. Inca Trail and alternative trail via Salkantay and Santa Teresa, including entrance to Machu Picchu. Good English-speaking guides; Salustio speaks Italian and Portuguese. Discount with student card, good food and equipment. City and Sacred Valley tours and treks to Choquequirao. Cheaper than most.

Wayki Trek, Procuradores 3512nd floor, T224092, www.waykitrek.net. Budget travel agency, recommended for their Inca Trail service. Owner Leo knows the area very well. Treks to several almost unknown Inca sites and interesting variations on the 'classic' Inca Trail with visits to porters' communities. Also treks to Ausangate, Salkantay and Choquequirao.

Rafting, mountain biking and trekking

When looking for an operator please consider more than just the price of your tour. Competition between companies in Cuzco is intense and price wars can lead to compromises in safety. Consider the quality of safety equipment (lifejackets, etc) and the number and experience of rescue kayakers and support staff. On a large and potentially dangerous river like the Apurímac (where fatalities have occurred), this can make all the difference.

Amazonas Explorers, Av Collasuyo 910, Miravalle, PO Box 722, Cuzco, T252846 or 976 5448 (mob). Experts in rafting, hiking and biking; used by BBC. English owner Paul Cripps has great experience, but takes most bookings from overseas (in England, T01437-891743). However, he may be able to arrange a trip for travellers in Cuzco. Rafting includes Río Apurímac and Río Tambopata including Lake Titicaca and Cuzco, with all transfers from Lima. Also 5-day/4-night Inca Trail, 14-day expedition to the Río Tuichi in Bolivia, and an excellent variation of the Ausangate Circuit. Multiactivity and family trips are a speciality. All options are at the higher end of the market and are highly recommended.

Apumayo, Av Garcilaso 316, Wanchaq, T084-246018, www.apumayo.com. Mon-Sat 0900-1300, 1600-2000. Urubamba rafting (from 0800-1530 every day); 3- to 4-day Apurímac trips. Also mountain biking to Maras and Moray in Sacred Valley, or from Cuzco to the jungle town of Quillabamba. This company also offers tours for disabled people, including rafting.

Atoq, C Saphi 704, T084-253902, www.atoq offroad.com. Specialists in innovative biking trips, from novice level to hardcore suicidal! Road and single-track tours range from day-trips to multi-week expeditions; prices depend on number of clients and the level of service/support required. Professional guides and excellent equipment.

Eric Adventures, Plateros 324, T234764, www.ericadventures.com. Specialize in adventure activities. They clearly explain what equipment is included in their prices and what you will need to bring. Rafting; mountain biking to Maras and Moray; Inca Trail to Machu Picchu, rent motorcross bikes for US$45 (guide is extra). Prices are more expensive if you book by email. A popular company.

Land of the Inkas, with **Instinct**, Av de la Cultura 1318, Wanchaq, T233451, www.landoftheinkas. com. Run by the very experienced Juan and Benjamín Muñiz, largely operates through web-based bookings, arranging multi-week expeditions and shorter adventures for those already in the Cuzco area. **Instinct** offers activities as diverse as surf safaris on Peru's north coast to multi-day horse riding tours in the Sacred Valley.

MAYUC Ecological Tourism Adventure Travel, Portal Confiturías 211, Plaza de Armas, T232666, www.mayuc.com. One of the longest-running river rafting companies. Departures are on the 1st and 3rd Sun of every month May-Nov. **Mayuc** now have a permanent lodge, **Casa Cusi**, on the upper Urubamba, which forms the basis of 2-day, Class III-IV trips in the area. Other tours include Inca Trail and alternative routes into Machu Picchu.

Medina Brothers, contact Christian or Alain Medina on T225163 or 965 3485/969 1670(mob). Family-run rafting company with good equipment and plenty of experience. They usually focus on day rafting trips in the Sacred Valley, but services are tailored to the needs of the client.

Swissraft-Peru, Plateros 369, T264124, www.swissraft-peru.com. This company has professionally-run tours on the Apurímac and Urubamba rivers, with the focus above all on safety. Equipment is new and of good quality.

Terra Explorer Peru, T237352, www.terraexplorerperu.com. Offers a wide range of trips from high-end rafting in the Sacred Valley and expeditions to the Colca and Cotahuasi canyons, trekking the Inca Trail and others, mountain biking, kayaking (including on Lake Titicaca) and jungle trips. All guides are bilingual.

Conservation

The Condor Lodge, Nueva Alta 432-A, T221287, www.thecondorlodge.com. Multidisciplinary organization dedicated to the preservation of the condor and other species. Offers 2 and 3-day tours to the Apurímac canyon to look for condors, with riding, trekking, fishing, visits to ruins and hot springs. Recommended.

Cultural tours

Milla Tourism, Av Pardo 689 and Portal Comercio 195 on the plaza, T231710, www.millaturismo.com. Mon-Fri 0800-1300, 1500-1900, Sat 0800-1300. Mystical tours to Cuzco's Inca ceremonial sites such as Pumamarca and The Temple of the Moon. Guide speaks only basic English. They also arrange cultural and environmental lectures and courses.

Mystic Inca Trail, Unidad Vecinal de Santiago, bloque 9, dpto 301, T221358, ivanndp@ terra.com.pe. Specialize in tours of sacred Inca sites and study of Andean spirituality. This takes 10 days but it is possible to have shorter 'experiences'.

Shamans and drug experiences

San Pedro and Ayahuasca have been used since before Inca times, mostly as a sacred healing experience. If you choose to experience these incredible healing/teaching plants, only do so under the guidance of a reputable agency or

shaman and always have a friend with you who is not partaking. If the medicine is not prepared correctly, it can be highly toxic and, in rare cases, severely dangerous. Never buy from someone who is not recommended, never buy off the streets and never try to prepare the plants yourself. **Another Planet**, Triunfo 120, T084-229379, www.anotherplanetperu.net. Run by Lesley Myburgh (who also runs **Casa de La Gringa**, Pasñapacana y Tandapata 148, San Blas, T241168, 965 2006 (mob), sleeping in E range), who operates all kinds of adventure tours and conventional tours in and around Cuzco, but specializes in jungle trips anywhere in Peru. Lesley is an expert in San Pedro cactus preparation and she arranges San Pedro journeys for healing at physical, emotional and spiritual levels in beautiful remote areas. The journeys are thoroughly organized and a safe, beautiful, unforgettable experience.
Eleana Molina, T975 1791 (mob), misticanativa@ yahoo.com. For Ayahuasca ceremonies.

Paragliding and ballooning
Richard Pethigal, T993 7333 (mob), www.cloudwalkerparagliding.com. For a condor's-eye view of the Sacred Valley, from May-Sep Richard runs half-day tandem paraglider flights, very experienced, high-quality equipment. Magnificent scenery, soaring close to snowcapped mountains makes this an awesome experience. He is licensed and charges US$70, but if weather conditions are good, for US$120 he can fly you all the way back to Cuzco, touching down in the ruins of Sacsayhuaman above the city.
Globos de los Andes, Av de la Cultura 220, suite 36, T232352, www.globosperu.com. Hot-air ballooning in the Sacred Valley and expeditions with balloons and 4WD lasting several days.

Private guides
As most of the sights do not have any information or signs in English, a good guide can really improve your visit. Either arrange this before you set out or contract one at the sight you are visiting. A tip is expected at the end of the tour. Set prices: City tour US$15-20 per day; Urubamba/Sacred Valley US$25-30, Machu Picchu and other ruins US$40-50 per day.

⊖ Transport

Cuzco p1208, maps p1212 and p1218
Air
The airport is at Quispiquilla, near the bus terminal, 1.6 km from centre, airport information T222611/ 601. **Note** Check in 2 hrs before flight. Reconfirm 48 hrs before your flight. Cuzco-Lima, flights may be delayed or cancelled during the wet season.

Planes may leave early if the weather is bad. To **Lima**, 55 mins, daily flights with **Taca**, **Star Perú** and **Lan**. Flights are heavily booked in school holidays (May, Jul, Oct and Dec-Mar) and national holidays. To **Arequipa**, 30 mins daily with **Lan**. To **Puerto Maldonado**, 30 mins, with **Lan**. To/from **La Paz**, **LAB** but not daily. Taxi to and from the airport costs US$2 (US$3.50 by radio taxi). Colectivos cost US$0.20 from Plaza San Francisco or outside the airport car park. Many representatives of hotels and travel agencies operate at the airport, with transport to the hotel with which they are associated. Take your time to choose your hotel,
at the price you can afford.

Bus
Long distance Terminal on Av Vallejo Santoni, block 2 (Prolongación Pachacútec), colectivo from centre US$0.20, taxi US$0.60. Platform tax US$0.30. All direct buses to **Lima** (20-24 hrs) go via **Abancay**, 195 km, 5 hrs (longer in the rainy season), and **Nazca**, on the Panamerican Highway. This route is paved but floods in the wet season often damage large sections of the highway. If prone to travel sickness, be prepared on the road to Abancay, there are many, many curves, but the scenery is magnificent. At Abancay, the road forks, the other branch going to **Andahuaylas**, a further 138 km, 10-11 hrs from Cuzco, and **Ayacucho**, another 261 km, 20 hrs from Cuzco. On both routes at night, take a blanket or sleeping bag to ward off the cold. All buses leave daily from the Terminal Terrestre. **Molina**, who also have an office on Av Pachacútec, just past the railway station, have buses on both routes. They run 3 services a day to Lima via Abancay and Nazca, and one, at 1900, to Abancay and Andahuaylas; **Expreso Wari** has 4 buses a day to Abancay, Nazca and Lima. **Cruz del Sur**'s *Ideal* service to Lima via Abancay leaves at 0730 and 1400, while their more comfortable *Imperial* service departs at 1500 and 1600. **San Jerónimo** and **Los Chankas** have buses to Abancay, Andahuaylas and Ayacucho at 1830. **Turismo Ampay** and **Turismo Abancay** go 3 times a day to Abancay, and **Expreso Huamanga** once. **Bredde** has 5 buses a day to Abancay. Fares: Abancay US$3.65, Andahuaylas US$6, Ayacucho US$12, Nazca US$17-20, Lima US$20 (*Cruz del Sur*, *Ideal* Class) to US$32 (*Cruz del Sur*, *Imperial* Class). In Cuzco you may be told that there are no buses in the day from Abancay to Andahuaylas; this is not so as **Señor de Huanca** does so. If you leave Cuzco before 0800, with luck you'll make the connection at 1300 – worth it for the scenery.

To Lake Titicaca and Bolivia: To **Juliaca**, 344 km, 5-6 hrs, US$3-4. The road is fully paved, but after heavy rain buses may not run. To **Puno**, 44 km from Juliaca, US$4.50-6; there is a good service with **Ormeño** at 0900, US$10, 6 hrs. **First Class**, Av Sol 930, have a bus at 0800, calling at Andahuaylillas church, Raqchi and Pucará, US$25, lunch but not entrance tickets included. Other services are run by **Tour Perú** and **Libertad** (both at night), 6½-8 hrs. **Note** We have received many reports of robbery on night buses on the Juliaca- Puno-Cuzco route; travel by day, or by train.

To **Arequipa**, 521 km, **Cruz del Sur** use the direct paved route via Juliaca and have 3 *Ideal* services leaving daily, 10½ hrs, US$7, and 1 *Imperial* service at 2000, 10 hrs, US$23. Ormeno's fare is US$18. Other buses join the new Juliaca-Arequipa road at Imata, 10-12 hrs, US$7.75 (eg **Carhuamayo**, 3 a day).

To the **Sacred Valley**: To **Pisac**, 32 km, 1 hr, US$0.85, from C Puputi on the outskirts of the city, near the Clorindo Matto de Turner school and Av de la Cultura. Colectivos, minibuses and buses leave whenever they are full, between 0600 and 1600. Buses returning from Pisac are often full. The last one back leaves around 2000. An organized tour can be fixed up with a travel agent for US$5pp. Taxis charge about US$20 for the round trip. To Pisac, **Calca** (18 km beyond Pisac) and **Urubamba** a further 22 km, buses leave from Av Tullumayo 800 block, Wanchac, US$1. Combis and colectivos leave from 300 block of Av Grau, 1 block before crossing the bridge, for **Chinchero**, 23 km, 45 mins, US$0.45; and for **Urubamba** a further 25 km, 45 mins, US$0.45 (or US$1 Cuzco- Urubamba direct, US$1.15 for a seat in a colectivo taxi). To **Ollantaytambo** from Av Grau, 0745, 1945, US$2.85, or catch a bus to Urubamba. Tours can be arranged to Chinchero, Urubamba and Ollantaytambo with a Cuzco travel agency. To Chinchero, US$6 pp; a taxi costs US$25 round-trip. Usually only day tours are organized for visits to the valley, US$20-25. Using public transport and staying overnight in Urubamba, Ollantaytambo or Pisac allows more time to see the ruins and markets.

Taxi

In Cuzco they are cheap and recommended when arriving by air, train or bus. They have fixed prices: in the centre US$0.60 (after 2200 US$0.90); to the suburbs US$0.85-1.55. In town it is safest to take taxis which are registered; these have a sticker with a number in the window and a chequerboard pattern on the sides. Taxis on call are reliable but more expensive, in the centre US$1.25: **Ocarina** T247080, **Aló Cuzco** T222222. Trips to **Sacsayhuaman** US$10; ruins of **Tambo Machay** US$15-20 (3-4 people); day trip US$40-70.

Recommended taxi drivers: **Manuel Calanche**, T227368, T969 5402 (mob), enthusiastic, attentive (Spanish only). **Carlos Hinojosa**, T251160. **Angel Marcavillaca Palomino**, Av Regional 877,

T251822, amarcavillaca@yahoo.com. Helpful, patient, reasonable prices. **Movilidad Inmediata**, Juan Carlos Herrera Johnson, T962 3821 (mob), local tours with English-speaking guide. **Ferdinand Pinares Cuadros**, Yuracpunco 155, Tahuantinsuyo, T225914, T968 1519 (mob), English and French spoken, reasonable prices. **Angel Salazar**, Marcavalle 1-4 Huanchac, T224679, English speaking, helpful, arranges good tours. **Milton Velásquez**, T222638, T968 0730 (mob), an anthropologist and tour guide who speaks English.

Train

There are 2 stations in Cuzco. To Juliaca and Puno, **Perú Rail** trains leave from the Av Sol station, Estación Wanchac, T238722. When arriving in Cuzco, a tourist bus meets the train to take visitors to hotels whose touts offer rooms. Machu Picchu trains leave from Estación San Pedro, opposite the Santa Ana market.

The train to **Juliaca/Puno** leaves at 0800, Mon, Wed and Sat, arriving at Puno at 1800, sit on the left for views. The train makes a stop to view the scenery at La Raya. Always check whether the train is running, especially in the rainy season, when services may be cancelled. Fares are given under Puno, Transport. Ticket office is open Mon-Fri 0800-1700, Sat 0900-1200 (take you passport or a copy when buying tickets, and be patient). You can buy tickets on www.perurail.com, or through a travel agent. Meals are served on the train. To **Ollantaytambo** and **Machu Picchu**, see page 1242.

⊙ Directory

Cuzco *p1208, maps p1212 and p1218*
Airline offices Aerocóndor, at airport, T252774. **LAB**, Santa Catalina Angosta 160, T222990, airport 229220. **Lan**, Av Sol 627-B, T225552. **Star Perú**, Av Sol 679, of 1, T234060. **Taca**, Av Sol 602, T249921. **Banks** Most of the banks are on Av Sol, and all have ATMs from which you can withdraw dollars or soles. **BCP**, Av Sol 189, cash advances on Visa, changes TCs to soles with commission, 3% to dollars; Visa ATM. **Interbank**, Av Sol y Puluchapata, no commission on TCs, Mastercard and Visa ATM. Next door **Banco Continental**, Av Sol ATM, US$4 commission on TCs. **BSCH**, Av Sol 459, Amex TCs, reasonable rates, ATM for Visa and MasterCard. **Scotiabank**, Maruri entre Pampa del Castillo y Pomeritos, gives cash advances on Mastercard and Visa in dollars. There are ATMs around the Plaza de Armas and on Av La Cultura. Many travel agencies and *casas de cambio* (eg on Portal de Comercio, Plaza de Armas, and Av Sol) change dollars; some of them change TCs as well, but charge 4-5% commission. **LAC Dollar**, Av Sol 150, T257762, Mon-Sat 0900-2000, with

delivery service to central hotels, cash and TCs. The street changers hang around Av Sol, blocks 2-3, every day; they will also change TCs. In banks and on the street check the notes. Dollars are accepted at many restaurants and at the airport. **Western Union**, Santa Catalina Ancha 165, T233727, money transfers in 10 mins; also at *DHL*, see below. **Consulates** Belgium, Av Sol 954, T221098. **France**, Jorge Escobar, C Michaela Bastidas 101, p4, T233610. **Germany**, Sra Maria-Sophia Júrgens de Hermoza, San Agustín 307, T235459, Casilla Postal 1128, Correo Central, open Mon-Fri, 1000-1200, appointments may be made by phone, also book exchange. **Ireland**, Charlie Donovan, Santa Catalina Ancha 360 (Rosie O'Grady's), T243514. **Italy**, Sr Fedos Rubatto, Av Garcilaso 700, T224398. Mon-Fri 0900-1200, 1500-1700. **Netherlands**, Sra Marcela Alarco, Av Pardo 854, T224322, marcela_alarco@yahoo. com, Mon-Fri 0900-1500. **Spain**, Sra Juana María Lambarri, T965 0106 (mob). **UK**, Barry Walker, Av Pardo 895, T239974, bwalker@amauta.rcp.net.pe. **US Agent**, Dra Olga Villagarcía, Apdo 949, Cuzco, T222183, F233541 or at the Binational Center (ICPNA), Av Tullumayo 125, Wanchac. **Internet** You can't walk for 5 mins in Cuzco without running into an internet café, and new places are opening all the time. Most have similar rates, around US$0.60 per hr, although if you look hard enough you can find cheaper places. The main difference between cafés is the speed of internet connection and the facilities on offer. The better places have scanners, webcams and CD burners, among other gadgets, and staff in these establishments can be very knowledgeable. **Language schools** **Academia Latinoamericana de Español**, Av Sol 580, T243364, www.latino schools.com. The same company also has schools in Ecuador (Quito) and in Bolivia (Sucre). They can arrange courses that include any combination of these locations using identical teaching methods and materials. Professionally run with experienced staff. Many activities per week, including dance lessons and excursions to sites of historical and cultural interest. Good homestays. Private classes US$170 for 20 hrs, groups, with a maximum of 4 students US$125, again for 20 hrs. **Acupari**, the German-Peruvian Cultural Association, San Agustín 307, T242970, www.acupari.com. Spanish classes are run here. **Amauta Spanish School**, Suecia 480, T241422, PO Box 1164, www.amautaspanish.com. Spanish classes, one-to-one or in small groups, also Quechua classes and workshops in Peruvian cuisine, dance and music, US$10.50 per hr one-to-one, but cheaper and possibly better value for group tuition (2-6 people), US$98 for 20 hrs. They have pleasant accommodation on site, as well as a free internet café for students, and can arrange excursions and can help find voluntary work. They also have a school in Urubamba and can arrange courses in the Manu rainforest, in conjunction with Pantiacolla Tours SRL. **Amigos Spanish School**, Zaguán del Cielo B-23, T/F242292, www.spanishcusco.com. Certified, experienced teachers, friendly atmosphere. All profits support a foundation for disadvantaged children. Private lessons for US$8 per hr, US$108 for 20 hrs of classes in a small group. Comfortable homestays and free activities available, including a 'real city tour' through Cuzco's poor areas. **Cusco Spanish School**, Garcilaso 265, of 6 , p 2, T226928, www.cuscos panishschool.com. US$175 for 20 hrs private classes, cheaper in groups. School offers homestays, optional activities including dance and music classes, cookery courses, ceramics, Quechua, hiking and volunteer programmes. They also offer courses on an *hacienda* at Cusipata in the Vilcanota valley, east of Cuzco. **Excel**, Cruz Verde 336, T235298, www.excel-spanishlanguage programs-peru.org. Very professional, US$7 per hr for private one-to-one lessons. US$229 for 20 hrs with 2 people, or US$277 with homestay, one-on-one for 20 hrs. **La Casona de la Esquina**, Purgatorio 395, corner with Huaynapata, T235830, www.spanish lessons.com.pe. US$5 per hr for one-to-one classes. Recommended. **Mundo Verde**, C Nueva Alta 432-A, T221287, www.mundoverdespanish.com. Spanish lessons with the option to study in the rainforest and the possibility of working on environmental and social projects while studying. Some of your money goes towards developing sustainable farming practices in the area. US$250 for 20 hours tuition with homestay. **San Blas Spanish School**, Tandapata 688, T247898, www.spanish schoolperu.com. Groups, with 4 clients maximum, US$90 for 20 hrs tuition (US$130 one-to-one). **Massage and therapies** Casa de la serenidad, Pumacurco 636, T233670, www.shamanspirit.net. A shamanic therapy centre run by a Swiss-American healer and Reiki Master who uses medicinal 'power' plants. It also has bed and breakfast and has received very good reports. Healing Hands, based at *Loki Hostel*, faeryamanita@hotmail.com. Angela is a Reiki, Shiatsu and CranioSacral Therapist. Very relaxing and recommended. **Medical services** Clinics: Hospital Regional, Av de la Cultura, T227661, emergencies 223691. **Clínica Pardo**, Av de la Cultura 710, T240387, www.clinicapardo.com. 24 hrs daily, trained bilingual personnel, complete medical assistance coverage with international insurance companies, highly regarded. **Clínica Paredes**, Lechugal 405, T225265. Director: Dr Milagros Paredes, whose speciality is gynaecology. **Motorcycle hire** Perú Mototours, Saphi 578, alc@ perumototours.com. Helpful, good prices and machines. **Post offices** Av Sol, block 5, Mon-Sat 0730-2000; Sun and holidays 0800-1400. Stamps and postcards available. *Poste restante* is free and helpful. DHL, Av Sol 627, T244167. **Telephones** Phone offices around town. Telefónica, Av Sol 386, for telephone and fax, open Mon-Sat 0700-2300, Sun and holidays 0700-1800. International calls by pay phone or go through the operator (long wait possible), deposit required. **Useful addresses** Migraciones, Av Sol s/n, block 6 close to post office, T222740, Mon-Fri 0800-1300 (for extending stay in Peru.) ISIC-Intej office, Portal de Panes 123, of 107 (CC Los Ruiseñores), T256367. Issues international student cards.

Southeast from Cuzco

There are many interesting villages and ruins on this road. **Tipón** ruins ① *US$1.80, or BTG ticket*, between the villages of Saylla and Oropesa, are extensive and include baths, terraces, irrigation systems, possibly an agricultural laboratory and a temple complex, accessible from a path leading from just above the last terrace (5 km climb from village; take a combi from Cuzco to Oropesa, then a taxi, or taxi from Cuzco US$6). **Oropesa**, whose church contains a fine ornately carved pulpit, is the national 'Capital of Bread'.

At **Huambutío**, north of the village of Huacarpay, the road divides; northwest to Pisac and north to **Paucartambo**, on the eastern slope of Andes. This remote town, 80 km east of Cuzco, has become a popular tourist destination. The *Fiesta de la Virgen del Carmen* is a major attraction, with masked dancers enacting rituals and folk tales: 15-17 July. (There is basic accommodation in town.) From Paucartambo, in the dry season, you can go 44 km to **Tres Cruces**, along the Pilcopata road, turning left after 25 km. Tres Cruces gives a wonderful view of the sunrise in June and July: peculiar climactic conditions make it appear that three suns are rising. Tour agencies in Cuzco can arrange transport and lodging.

Further on from Huacarpay are the Huari (pre-Inca) ruins of **Piquillacta** ① *daily 0700-1730*,

US$1.80 or BTG ticket a large site, with some reconstruction in progress. Buses to Urcos from Avenida Huáscar in Cuzco will drop you at the entrance on the north side of the complex, though this is not the official entry. The Piquillacta Archaeological Park also contains the Laguna de Huacarpay (known as Muyna in ancient times) and the ruins that surround it: Kañarakay, Urpicancha and the huge gateway of Rumicolca. It's good to hike or cycle and birdwatch around the lake.

Andahuaylillas is a village 32 km southeast from Cuzco, with a fine early 17th-century church (the 'Andean Sistine Chapel'), with beautiful frescoes, a splendid doorway and a gilded main altar. Taxis go there, as does the *Oropesa* bus (from Avenida Huáscar in Cuzco) via Tipón, Piquillacta and Rumicolca. The next village, **Huaro**, also has a church whose interior is entirely covered with colourful frescoes.

Beyond Andahuaylillas is **Urcos**. There are three very basic hostales. A spectacular road from Urcos crosses the Eastern Cordillera to Puerto Maldonado in the jungle (see page 1278). Some 47 km after passing the snow line Hualla-Hualla pass, at 4,820 m, the super-hot thermal baths of **Marcapata** ① *173 km from Urcos, US$0.10,* provide a relaxing break.

Some 82 km from Urcos, at the base of **Nevado Ausangate** (6,384 m), is the town of **Ocongate**, which has two hotels on the Plaza de Armas. Beyond Ocongate is **Tinqui**, the starting point for hikes around Ausangate and in the Cordillera Vilcanota. On the flanks of the Nevado Ausangate is Q'Olloriti, where a church has been built close to the snout of a glacier. This place has become a place of pilgrimage (see Cuzco, Local festivals, page 1223).

Hiking around Ausangate The hike around the mountain of Ausangate takes six days: spectacular, but quite hard, with three passes over 5,000 m, so you need to be acclimatized. Temperatures in high season (April-October) can drop well below zero at night. It is recommended to take a guide or *arriero*. *Arrieros* and mules can be hired in Tinqui for US$7 per day for an *arriero*, US$6 for a mule, but more for a saddle horse. *Arrieros* also expect food. Make sure you sign a contract with full details. Buy all food supplies in Cuzco. Maps are available at the **IGM** in Lima or **South American Explorers**, who also have latest information.

From Urcos to Sicuani (see page 1205), the road passes **Cusipata** (with an Inca gate and wall), **Checacupe** (with a lovely church) and **Tinta**, 23 km from Sicuani (church with brilliant gilded interior and an interesting choir vault). There are frequent buses and trucks to Cuzco, or take the train from Cuzco. Continuing to Sicuani, **Raqchi** is the scene of the region's great folklore festival starting on 24 June, *Wiracocha*, when dancers come from all over Peru. Raqchi is also the site of the **Viracocha Temple** ① *US$1.75, take a bus or truck from Cuzco towards Sicuani, US$1.50.* John Hemming wrote: "What remains is the central wall, which is adobe above and Inca masonry below. This was probably the largest roofed building ever built by the Incas. On either side of the high wall, great sloping roofs were supported by rows of unusual round pillars, also of masonry topped by adobe. Nearby is a complex of barracks-like buildings and round storehouses. This was the most holy shrine to the creator god Viracocha, being the site of a miracle in which he set fire to the land – hence the lava flow nearby. There are also small Inca baths in the corner of a field beyond the temple and a straight row of ruined houses by a square. The landscape is extraordinary, blighted by huge piles of black volcanic rocks."

● Sleeping

Ausangate *p1233*
G **Ausangate**, Tinqui. Very basic, but warm, friendly atmosphere. Sr Crispin (or Cayetano), the owner, is knowledgeable and can arrange guides, mules, etc. He and his brothers can be contacted in Cuzco on F227768. All have been recommended as reliable sources of trekking and climbing information, for arranging trips.
G **Hostal Tinqui Guide**, on the right-hand side as you enter Tinqui. Meals available, the owner can arrange guides and horses.

● Transport

Paucartambo *p1232*
Bus A minibus leaves for Paucartambo from Av Huáscar in **Cuzco**, every other day, US$4.50, 3-4 hrs; alternate days Paucartambo-Cuzco. Trucks and a private bus leave from the Coliseo, behind Hospital Segura in Cuzco, 5 hrs, US$2.50. Agencies in Cuzco can arrange round trip on 15-17 Jul, US$30.

Ausangate *p1233*
Bus from Cuzco, to **Tinqui** Mon-Sat 1000 from C Tomasatito Condemayta, near Coliseo Cerrado; 172 km, 6-7 hrs, US$3.50.

Sacred Valley of the Incas

The name conjures up images of ancient rulers and their god-like status, with the landscape itself as their temple. And so it was, but the Incas also built their own tribute to this dramatic land in monuments such as Machu Picchu, Ollantaytambo, Pisac and countless others. For the tourist, the famous sights are now within easy reach of Cuzco, but the demand for adventure, to see lost cities in a less 21st-century context, means that there is ample scope for exploring. But if archaeology is not your thing, there are markets to enjoy, birds to watch, trails for mountain-biking and a whole range of hotels to relax in. The best time to visit is April to May or October to November. The high season is June-September, but the rainy season, from December to March, is cheaper and pleasant enough.

Pisac → *Phone code 084. Colour map 3, grid C4.*

Pisac, 30 km north of Cuzco, has a traditional Sunday morning **market**, at which local people sell their produce in exchange for essential goods. It is also a major draw for tourists who arrive after 0800 until 1700. Pisac has other, somewhat less crowded but more commercial markets on Tuesday and Thursday morning. Each Sunday at 1100 there is a Quechua mass. On the plaza are the church and a small interesting **Museo Folklórico**. There are many souvenir shops on Bolognesi. Local fiesta: 15 July.

High above the town on the mountainside is a superb **Inca fortress** ① *0700-1730, guides charge about US$5, if you do not show your BTG multi-site ticket on the way up, you will be asked to do so by the warden.* The walk up to the ruins begins from the plaza (but see below), past the Centro de Salud and a new control post. The path goes through working terraces, giving the ruins a context. The first group of buildings is Pisaqa, with a fine curving wall. Climb then to the central part of the ruins, the Intihuatana group of temples and rock outcrops in the most magnificent Inca masonry. Here are the Reloj Solar ('Hitching Post of the Sun') – now closed because thieves stole a piece from it, palaces of the moon and stars, solstice markers, baths and water channels. From Intihuatana, a path leads around the hillside through a tunnel to Q'Allaqasa, the military area. Across the valley at this point, a large area of Inca tombs in holes in the hillside can be seen. The end of the site is

The Sacred Valley

Kanchiracay, where the agricultural workers were housed. Road transport approaches from this end. The descent takes 30 minutes. At dusk you will hear, if not see, the *pisaca* (partridges), after which the place is named. Even if going by car, do not rush as there is a lot to see and a lot of walking to do. Road transport approaches from the Kanchiracay end. The drive up from town takes about 20 minutes. Walking up, although tiring, is recommended for the views and location. It's at least one hour uphill all the way. The descent takes 30 minutes on foot. Horses are available for US$3 per person. Combis charge US$0.60 per person and taxis US$3 one way up to the ruins from near the bridge. Then you can walk back down (if you want the taxi to take you back down negotiate a fare). Overnight parking allowed in the parking lot.

Pisac to Urubamba

Calca, 2,900 m, is 18 km beyond Pisac. The plaza is divided in two: Urubamba buses stop on one side; and Cuzco and Pisac buses on the other side of the dividing strip. *Fiesta de la Vírgen Asunta* 15-16 August. There are basic hotels and eating places in town.

The **Valle de Lares** is beautiful for walking and cycling, with its magnificent mountains, lakes and small villages. You start near an old hacienda in Huarán (2,830 m), cross two passes over 4,000 m and end at the hot springs near Lares. From this village, transport runs back to Calca. Alternatively, you can add an extra day and continue to Ollantaytambo. Several agencies in Cuzco offer trekking and biking tours to the region and some offer this trek as an alternative Inca Trail.

About 3 km east of Urubamba, **Yucay** has two grassy plazas divided by the restored colonial church of Santiago Apóstol, with its oil paintings and fine altars. On the opposite side from Plaza Manco II is the adobe palace built for Sayri Túpac (Manco's son) when he emerged from Vilcabamba in 1558. In Yucay monks sell fresh milk, ham, eggs and other dairy produce from their farm on the hillside.

Urubamba → *Phone code 084. Altitude: 2,863 m.*

Like many places along the valley, Urubamba is in a fine setting with snow-capped peaks in view. Calle Berriózabal, on the west edge of town, is lined with pisonay trees. The large market square is one block west of the main plaza. The main road skirts the town and the bridge for the road to Chinchero is just to the east of town. Visit **Seminario-Bejar Ceramic Studio** ① *Berriózabal 111, T201002, kupa@ terra.com.pe*, in the beautiful grounds of the former Urpihuasi hostal. They investigate and use pre-Columbian techniques and designs, highly recommended. ATM on the main road not far from the bridge; internet at **Connections** *Av M Castilla y Av La Convención*. For local festivals, May and June are the harvest months, with many processions following ancient schedules. Urubamba's main festival, *El Señor de Torrechayoc*, occupies the first week of June.

About 6 km west of Urubamba is **Tarabamba**, where a bridge crosses the Río Urubamba. Turn right after the bridge to **Pichingoto**, a tumbled-down village built under an overhanging cliff. Also, just over the bridge and before the town to the left of a small, walled cemetery is a salt stream. Follow the footpath beside the stream to Salineras, a small village below which are a mass of terraced Inca salt pans which are still in operation (entry US$1.80); there are over 5,000. The walk to the salt pans takes about 30 minutes. Take water as this side of the valley can be very hot and dry.

Chinchero and Moray

Chinchero (3,762 m) ① *site 0700-1730, on the BTG combined entrance ticket (see page 1210)*, is just off a direct road to Urubamba. It has an attractive church built on an Inca temple. The church has been restored to reveal in all their glory the interior paintings. The ceiling, beams and walls are covered in beautiful floral and religious designs. The church is open on Sunday for mass and at festivals; ask in the tourist office in Cuzco for other times. Recent excavations there have revealed many Inca walls and terraces. The food market and the handicraft market are separate. The former is held every day, on your left as you come into town. The latter, on Sunday only, is up by the church, small, but attractive. On any day but Sunday there are few tourists. Fiesta, day of the Virgin, on 8 September.

At Moray, there are three 'colosseums', used by the Incas, according to some theories, as a sort of open-air crop nursery, known locally as the laboratory of the Incas. The great depressions contain no ruined buildings, but are lined with fine terracing. Each level is said to have its own microclimate. It is a very atmospheric place which, many claim, has mystical power, and the scenery is absolutely stunning (entry US$1.80). The most interesting way to get to Moray is from Urubamba via the Pichingoto bridge over the Río Urubamba. The climb up from the bridge is fairly steep but easy. The path passes by the spectacular **salt pans**, still in production after thousands of years, taking 1½-2 hours to the top. The village of Maras is about 45 minutes further on, then it's 9 km by road or 5 km through the fields to Moray. Tour companies in Cuzco offer cycle trips to Moray. There are no hotels at all in the area, so take care not to be stranded. (See Transport, below, for further details on how to get there.)

Ollantaytambo → *Phone code 084. Colour map 3, grid C4. Altitude: 2,800 m.*

① *Inca ruins open 0700-1730. If possible arrive very early, 0700, before the tourists. Admission is by BTG visitor's ticket, which can be bought at the site (otherwise US$6.50).*
The Inca town, or *Llacta*, on which the present-day town is based is clearly seen in the fine example of Inca *canchas* (blocks), which are almost entirely intact and still occupied behind the main plaza. Entering Ollantaytambo from Pisac, the road is built along the long wall of 100 niches. Note the inclination of the wall: it leans towards the road. Since it was the Inca's practice to build with the walls leaning towards the interiors of the buildings, it has been deduced that the road, much narrower then, was built inside a succession of buildings. The road out of the plaza leads across a bridge, down to the colonial church with its enclosed *recinto*. Beyond is a plaza (and car park) with entrances to the archaeological site.

The so-called **Baño de la Ñusta** (bath of the princess) is of grey granite, and is in a small area between the town and the temple fortress. Some 200 m behind the Baño de la Ñusta along the face of the mountain are some small ruins known as Inca Misanca, believed to have been a small temple or observatory. A series of steps, seats and niches have been carved out of the cliff. There is a complete irrigation system, including a canal at shoulder level, some 6 ins deep, cut out of the sheer rock face (under renovation). The flights of terraces leading up above the town are superb, and so are the curving terraces following the contours of the rocks overlooking the Urubamba. These terraces were successfully defended by Manco Incas warriors against Hernando Pizarro in 1536. Manco Inca built the wall above the site and another wall closing the Yucay valley against attack from Cuzco. These are visible on either side of the valley.

The temple itself was started by Pachacútec, using Colla Indians from Lake Titicaca - hence the similarities of the monoliths facing the central platform with the Tiahuanaco remains. The massive, highly finished granite blocks at the top are worth the climb to see. The Colla are said to have deserted half-way through the work, which explains the many and you shouldn't leave the path. The climb takes up to 90 minutes but the steps are dangerous after bad weather. The path is open 0700-1300, with the latest return time being 1500; and you must register at a hut at the beginning of the trail (400 visitors maximum per day). The other trail to Huayna Picchu, down near the Urubamba, is via the Temple of the Moon, in two caves, one above the other, with superb Inca niches inside. For the trail to the Temple of the Moon: from the path to Huayna Picchu, take the marked trail to the left. It is in good shape, although it descends further than you think it should. After the Temple you may proceed to Huayna Picchu, but this path is overgrown, slippery in the wet and has a crooked ladder on an exposed part about 10 minutes before reaching the top (not for the faint-hearted). It is safer to return to the main trail to Huayna Picchu, although this adds about 30 minutes to the climb. The round trip takes about four hours. Before doing any trekking around Machu Picchu, check with an official which paths may be used, or which are one-way.

The famous Inca bridge is about 45 minutes along a well-marked trail south of the Royal Sector. The bridge (on which you cannot walk) is spectacularly sited, carved into a vertiginous cliff-face. East of the Royal Sector is the path leading up to **Intipunku** on the Inca Trail (45 minutes, fine views).

Aguas Calientes

Those with more time should spend the night at Aguas Calientes and visit the ruins early in the morning, when no one's around. Most hotels and restaurants are near the railway station, on the plaza, or on Avenida Pachacútec, which leads from the plaza to the **thermal baths** ① *0500-2030, US$3.15, 10 mins walk from the town* (a communal pool, smelling of sulphur) good bar for cocktails in the pool. You can rent towels and bathing costumes (US$0.65) at several places on the road to the baths; basic toilets and changing facilities and showers for washing *before* entering the baths; take soap and shampoo, and keep an eye on valuables.

● Sleeping

Machu Picchu *p1240*
L **Machu Picchu Sanctuary Lodge**, reservations as for the *Monasterio Hotel* in Cuzco, which is under the same management (Peru Orient Express Hotels), T211039, www.sanctuary lodge.net. Comfortable, good service, helpful staff, food well-cooked and presented. Electricity and water 24 hrs a day, will accept American Express travellers' cheques at the official rate, restaurant for residents only in the evening, but the buffet lunch is open to all. Usually fully booked well in advance, try Sun more as other tourists find Pisac market a greater attraction.

Aguas Calientes *p1241*
L **Inkaterra Machu Picchu**, T211122, Km 110, 5 mins walk along the railway from the town. For reservations: Jr Andalucía 174, Miraflores, Lima, T01-610 0404; in Cuzco at Plaza las Nazarenas 167 p2, T245314, www.inkaterra.com. Beautiful colonial-style bungalows in village compound surrounded by cloud forest, lovely gardens, pool, expensive restaurant, also campsite with hot showers at good rates, offer tours to Machu Picchu, several guided walks on and off the property, great buffet breakfasts included in price. Also has the Café Inkaterra by the railway line. Recommended, but there are a lot of steps between the public areas and rooms. Guests can also stay in one of the guest suites in a separate villa (min 2 nights), with its own private gardens

and plunge pool. The hotel is involved in a project to rehabilitate spectacled bears, and re-release them into the wild.
B **Presidente**, at the old station, T211034 (Cuzco T/F244598), presidente@terra.com.pe. Adjoining Hostal Machu Picchu, see below, more upmarket but little difference, rooms without river view cheaper, price includes breakfast.
C **Hostal Pachakúteq**, up the hill beyond *Hostal La Cabaña*, T/F211061. Hot water, good breakfast, quiet, family-run. Recommended.
C **La Cabaña**, Av Pachacútec M20-3, T/F211048. With breakfast, hot water, café, laundry service, helpful, popular with groups.
C **Gringo Bill's** (**Hostal Q'oñi Unu**), Colla Raymi 104, T/F211046, gringobills@yahoo.com. With breakfast, hot water, laundry, money exchange, luggage stored, good beds, lot of traffic so watch belongings, staff not too friendly, good but expensive meals in *Villa Margarita* restaurant, breakfast from 0530, US$4 packed lunch.
D **Hostal Machu Picchu**, at the old station, T211212. Functional, quiet, Wilber, the owner's son, has travel information, hot water, nice balcony over the Urubamba, grocery store, price includes breakfast and taxes. Recommended.
D **Rupa Wasi**, Huanacaure 180, T211101, http://perucuzco.com/rupawasi/lodge_english.h tm. Charming 'eco-lodge' up a small alley off Collasuyo, laid back, comfortable, great views from the balconies, purified water available,

organic garden under development, good breakfasts US$3.

D-E Jardín Real, Wiracocha 7, T/F211234, jardinrealhotel@hotmail.com. Modern, hot water, good value, price negotiable (same owner as the *Pizzería Los Jardines* on Pachacútec).

E Hospedaje Quilla, Av Pachacútec between Wiracocha and Tupac Inka Yupanki, T/F211009. Price includes breakfast, hot water, rents bathing gear for the hot springs.

E Hostal Wiracocha Inn, C Wiracocha, T211088. Hot water, breakfast included, small garden, helpful, popular with groups.

E Las Orquídeas, Urb Las Orquideas A-8, T211171. From Av Pachacútec, cross the bridge over the river to the football pitch, find a small dirt path on the right. With bath, hot water, quiet, pleasant.

E-F Hospedaje Inca Tambo, Huanacaure s/n, T211135, hostalinkatambo@latinmail.com. Basic but clean, just below *Rupa Wasi* (see above); negotiate for a good price.

E-F pp Las Bromelias, Colla Raymi, T211145, just off Plaza before Gringo Bill's. Cheaper without bath, small, hot water.

E Hostal Samana Wasi, C Tupac Inka Yupanki, T211170, quillavane@hotmail.com. Hot water 24 hrs, cheaper without bath, pleasant place.

Camping The only official campsite is in a field by the river, just below Puente Ruinas station. Do not leave your tent and belongings unattended.

🍴 Eating

Aguas Calientes p1241
The old station and Av Pachútec are lined with eating places. At the station are, among others: **Aiko**, recommended; **La Chosa Pizzería**, good value; **Las Quenas**, café and baggage store (US$0.30 per locker); and 2 branches of **Pizza Samana Wasi**.

♨♨♨ Café Inkaterra, on the railway, just below the Machu Picchu Pueblo Hotel. US$15 for a great lunch buffet with scenic views of the river.

♨♨ Indio Feliz, C Lloque Yupanqui, T/F211090. Great French cuisine, excellent value and service, set 3-course meal for US$10, good pisco sours. Highly recommended.

♨♨ Inka's Pizza Pub, on the plaza. Good pizzas, changes money and accepts traveller's cheques. Next door is **Illary**, which is popular.

♨♨ Inca Wasi, Av Pachacútec. Very good choice.

♨♨ Pueblo Viejo, Av Pachacútec (near plaza). Good food in a spacious but warm environment. Price includes use of the salad bar.

♨♨ Toto's House, Av Imperio de los Incas, on the railway line. Same owners as Pueblo Viejo. Good value and quality *menú*.

♨ Clave de Sol, Av Pachacútec 156. Same owner

1242

as Chez Maggy in Cuzco, serving Italian food for about US$4, changes money, also has a vegetarian menu, 1200-1500, 1800-whenever.

♨ Govinda, Av Pachacútec y Túpac Inka Yupanki. Vegetarian restaurant with a cheap set lunch. Recommended.

🎵 Bars and clubs

Aguas Calientes p1241
Waisicha Pub, C Lloque Yupanqui. For good music and atmosphere.

🚌 Transport

Machu Picchu p1240
Bus Buses leave **Aguas Calientes** for Machu Picchu every 30 mins from 0600 until 1300, 25 mins; they return 1200-1730. US$12 return, US$6 single, valid 48 hrs. The walk up from Aguas Calientes takes about 2½ hrs, following the Inca path.

Train PerúRail trains to Machu Picchu run from San Pedro station in Cuzco. They pass through Poroy and Ollantaytambo to Aguas Calientes (the official name of this station is 'Machu Picchu'). The station for the tourist trains at Aguas Calientes is on the outskirts of town, 200 m from the Pueblo Hotel and 50 m from where buses leave for Machu Picchu ruins. The ticket office is open Mon-Fri 0700-1700, Sat, Sun and holidays 0700-1200; there is a guard on the gate. There is a paved road in poor condition between Aguas Calientes and the start of the road up to the ruins. **Note** Train schedules may be affected by mudslides in the rainy season. Delays occur.

There are 3 classes of tourist train: **Vistadome** (US$113 return, US$66 one-way); **Backpacker** (US$73 return, or US$46 one-way); and the luxurious Hiram Bingham service (US$547 return). These trains depart from Cuzco; Hiram Bingham departs from Poroy and, on the other two services you can disembark at Poroy for a quicker bus ride into Cuzco on the return. There are further Vistadomes and Backpackers from **Urubamba** and **Ollantaytambo** to Machu Picchu, at US$77 and US$57 return, respectively.

The **Vistadome** leaves **Cuzco** daily at 0600 and 0700, stopping at Ollantaytambo some 2hrs after Cuzco, and Machu Picchu at 0940 or 1100. It returns from Machu Picchu at 1530 and 1700, passing Ollantaytambo at 1700 and 1830, reaching Cuzco at 1920 and 2125. The Backpacker leaves Cuzco at 0615, passing Ollantaytambo at 0840 and Machu Picchu at 1015. It returns at 1555, passing Ollantaytambo at 1740, getting to Cuzco at 2020.

The Ollantaytambo Vistadomes leave at 1030 and 1455, arriving at 1145 and 1615, returning from Machu Picchu at 0835 and 1320, reaching

Ollantaytambo at 1005 and 1440. The Ollantaytambo Backpacker leaves at 0905, arriving at 1100, returning from Machu Picchu at 1620, reaching Ollantaytambo at 1800. The Vistadome from Urubamba leaves at 0610, passing Ollantaytambo at 0705, reaching Machu Picchu at 0820. It returns at 1645, passing Ollantaytambo at 1805 and reaching Urubamba at 1915 (Urubamba trains must be booked at least 10 days in advance). Seats can be reserved even if you're not returning the same day. The Vistadome tickets include food in the price. These trains have toilets, video, snacks and drinks for sale. Tickets for all trains should be bought at Wanchac station in Cuzco, on Av Pachacútec. You must have your original passport to travel on the trains to Machu Picchu. Several Urubamba and Yucay hotels offer free transport to and from the Urubamba station, which is in the grounds of the **Libertador Tambo del Inka** hotel. Tickets can be bought through PerúRail's website, www.perurail.com and from travel agents. Services other than those listed above are entirely at the discretion of PerúRail. Note that the timetable and prices are subject to frequent change.

The **Hiram Bingham** service departs Poroy at 0900 Mon-Sat, brunch is served on board, and arrives at Machu Picchu 1215 (the timing is good because you can enter the site at a time when most visitors are leaving for their journey back to Cuzco). The return journey is at 1800 (pre-dinner cocktails in bar accompanied by live entertainment, and then a 4-course dinner) reaching Poroy at 2125 with bus service to Cuzco hotels.

There is a cheap way to travel by train to Machu Picchu, but it is not advertised on Peru Rail's website. A Backpacker Noche train leaves Ollantaytambo at 2000, arriving Aguas Calientes 2120. It returns from Aguas at 0545, arriving Ollantaytambo at 0740. Tickets cost US$44 return, 30 one-way, they can be bought at the Wanchac station in Cuzco or in Ollantaytambo. If you use this service you have to stay two nights in Aguas Calientes if you want to see Machu Picchu.

Tourists may not travel on the local train to Machu Picchu, but there is a way to avoid the train altogether: Take a bus from Cuzco towards Quillabamba at 1900, US$6 (other buses in the day may not connect with onward transport). Get out at **Santa María** (about 7 hrs) where minibuses wait to go to **Santa Teresa**, 2 hrs, US$2.10. Your reach Santa Teresa by sunrise in time to buy breakfast. From Santa Teresa you have to cross the Río Urubamba. A controversial bridge is being built (we think); until complete you have to use a metal basket on a cable. Walk 6 km to the Central Hidroeléctrica, a nice, flat road, or hitch a ride on workers' truck, US$1.25. From the Hidroeléctrica train station it's 40 mins on the local train to Aguas Calientes at 1520, US$8 for tourists, or you can walk along the railway in 2-3 hrs (at Km 114.5 is **G Hospedaje Mandor**, about 2 km from bridge to Machu Picchu). To return, at 0600 walk from Aguas Calientes to Santa Teresa to catch a bus at 1000 to Santa María, arrive at 1200. At 1300 take a bus back to Cuzco, arriving between 1900-2000. Or take the local train from Aguas Calientes to Santa Teresa at 1210, stay in a hostal, then take the 1000 bus to Santa María. If using this route, don't forget to buy your ticket for Machu Picchu in Cuzco, unless you want to buy it in Aguas Calientes

⊙ Directory

Aguas Calientes p1241
Banks Several ATMs in town. **Internet** Many interent shops, average price US$1 per hr; slow connection. **Post offices** Serpost agencies: just off the plaza, between the Centro Cultural Machu Picchu and Galería de Arte Tunupa.
Telephones Office is on C Collasuyo and there are plenty of phone booths around town.

Inca trails

The most impressive way to reach Machu Picchu is via the centuries-old Inca Trail that winds its way from the Sacred Valley near Ollantaytambo, taking three to five days. The spectacular hike runs from Km 88, Qorihuayrachina (2,299 m), a point immediately after the first tunnel 22 km beyond Ollantaytambo station. A sturdy suspension bridge has now been built over the Río Urubamba. Guided tours often start at Km 82, Piscacucho, reached by road. New rules for hiking the trail are detailed below. What makes this hike so special is the stunning combination of Inca ruins, unforgettable views, magnificent mountains, exotic vegetation and extraordinary ecological variety.

Ins and outs
Equipment The Inca Trail is rugged and steep (beware of landslides), but the magnificent views compensate for any weariness which may be felt. It is cold at night, however, and

weather conditions change rapidly, so it is important to take not only strong footwear, rain gear and warm clothing but also food, water, water purification for when you fill bottles from streams, insect repellent, a supply of plastic bags, coverings, a good sleeping bag, a torch/flashlight and a stove for preparing hot food and drink to ward off the cold at night. A stove using paraffin (kerosene) is preferable, as fuel can be bought in small quantities in markets. A tent is essential, but if you're hiring one in Cuzco, check carefully for leaks. Walkers who have not taken adequate equipment have died of exposure. Caves marked on some maps are little better than overhangs, and are not sufficient shelter to sleep in.

All the necessary equipment can be rented; see page 1223 under Camping equipment and Activities and tours. Good maps of the Trail and area can be bought from **South American Explorers** in Lima or Cuzco. If you have any doubts about carrying your own pack, reasonably priced porters/guides are available. Carry a day-pack for your water, snacks etc in case you walk faster than the porters and you have to wait for them to catch you up.

Tours Travel Agencies in Cuzco arrange transport to the start, equipment, food, etc, for an all-in price for all treks that lead to the Machu Picchu Historical Sanctuary. Prices vary from about US$200 to US$300 per person for a four day/three night trek on the Classic Inca Trail. If the price is under US$180, you should be concerned as the company will be cutting corners and may not be paying the environment the respect the new rules were designed to instil. All are subject to strict rules introduced in 2001 and must be licensed. Tour operators taking clients on any of the Inca Trails leading to the Machu Picchu Historical Sanctuary have to pay an annual fee. Groups of up to seven independent travellers who do not wish to use a tour operator will be allowed to hike the trails if they contact an independent, licensed guide to accompany them, as long as they do not contact any other persons such as porters or cooks. There is a maximum of 500 visitors per day allowed on the Classic Inca Trail. Operators pay US$12.15 for each porter and other trail staff; porters are not be permitted to carry more than 25 kg. Littering is banned, as is carrying plastic water bottles (canteens only may be carried). Pets and pack animals are prohibited, but llamas are allowed as far as the first pass. Groups have to use approved campsites only.

Trail tickets On all hiking trails (Km 82 or Km 88 to Machu Picchu, Salkantay to Machu Picchu, and Km 82 or Km 88 to Machu Picchu via Km 104) adults must pay US$60, students and children under 15 US$30. On the Camino Real de los Inkas from Km 104 to Wiñay-Wayna and Machu Picchu the fee is US$30 per adult, US$15 for students and children and Salkantay to Huayllabamba and Km 88, US$30. The Salkantay trek is subject to a charge of US$36. It is likely that the Instituto Nacional de Cultura will introduce charges on more trails in 2007, further eroding the scope for independent trekking in this region. All tickets must be bought at the INC office on Calle San Bernardo in Cuzco; none is sold without evidence that you are going with a licensed tour operator. None is sold at the entrance to any of the routes. See page 1225 on the need to reserve your place on the Trail in advance. You can save a bit of money by arranging your own transport back to Ollantaytambo in advance, either for the last day of your tour, or by staying an extra night in Aguas Calientes and taking the early morning train, then take a bus back to Cuzco. If you take your own tent and sleeping gear, some agencies give a discount. Make sure your return train ticket to Cuzco has your name on it for the tourist train, otherwise you have to pay for any changes.

The Annual Inca Trail Clean-up takes place usually in September. Many agencies and organizations are involved and volunteers should contact South American Explorers in Cuzco for full details of ways to help. **The Trail is closed each February for cleaning and repair.**

Advice Four days would make a comfortable trip (though much depends on the weather). Allow a further day to see Machu Picchu when you have recovered from the hike. You are not allowed to walk back along the trail, though you can pay US$6 at Intipunku to be allowed to walk back as far as Wiñay-Wayna. You cannot take backpacks into Machu Picchu; leave them at ticket office, US$0.50. The first two days of the Trail involve the stiffest climbing, so do not attempt it if you're feeling unwell. Leave all your valuables in Cuzco and keep everything inside your tent, even your shoes. Security has, however, improved in recent years. Avoid the July-August high season and check the conditions in the rainy season from November to April (note that this can vary). In the wet it is cloudy and the paths are very muddy and difficult. Also watch out for coral snakes in this area (black, red, yellow bands).

The trail

The trek to the sacred site begins either at Km 82, **Piscacucho**, or at Km 88, **Qorihuayrachina**, at 2,600 m. In order to reach Km 82 hikers are transported by their tour operator in a minibus on the road that goes to Quillabamba. From Piri onward the road follows the riverbank and ends at Km 82, where there is a bridge. You can depart as early as you like and arrive at Km 82 faster than going by train. The Inca Trail equipment, food, fuel and field personnel reach Km 82 (depending on the tour operator's logistics) for the Inrena staff to weigh each bundle before the group arrives. When several groups are leaving on the same day, it is more convenient to arrive early. Km 88 can only be reached by train, subject to schedule and baggage limitations. The train goes slower than a bus, but you start your walk nearer to Llaqtapata and Huayllabamba. Note that the route from Km 82 goes via **Cusichaca**, rather than Llaqtapata. (See below for details of variations in starting points for the Inca Trail.)

The walk to **Huayllabamba**, following the Cusichaca River, needs about three hours and isn't too arduous. Beyond Huayllabamba, a popular camping spot for tour groups, there is a camping place about an hour ahead, at **Llulluchayoc** (3,200 m). A punishing 1½ hour climb further is **Llulluchapampa**, an ideal meadow for camping. If you have the energy to reach this point, it will make the second day easier because the next stage, the ascent to the first pass, **Warmiwañuska** (Dead Woman's Pass) at 4,200 m, is tough; 2½ hours.

Afterwards take the steep path downhill to the Pacamayo valley. Beware of slipping on the Inca steps after rain. You could camp by a stream at the bottom (1½ hours from the first pass). It is no longer permitted to camp at **Runkuracay**, on the way up to the second pass (a much easier climb, 3,850 m). Magnificent views near the summit in clear weather. A good overnight place is about 30 minutes past the Inca ruins at **Sayacmarca** (3,500 m), about an hour on after the top of the second pass.

A gentle two-hour climb on a fine stone highway leads through an Inca tunnel to the third pass. Near the top there's a spectacular view of the entire Vilcabamba range. You descend to Inca ruins at **Phuyopatamarca** (3,650 m), well worth a long visit, even camping overnight. There is a 'tourist bathroom' here where water can be collected (but purify it before drinking).

From there steps go downhill to the impressive ruins of **Wiñay-Wayna** (2,700 m), with views of the recently cleared terraces of Intipata. Access is possible, but the trail is not easily visible. There is a basic hostel with bunk beds, **F** per person, showers and a small restaurant. There is a small campsite in front of the hostel. After Wiñay-Wayna there is no water and no camping till Machu Picchu. The path from this point goes more or less level through jungle until the steep staircase up to the **Intipunku** (two hours), where there's a magnificent view of Machu Picchu, especially at dawn, with the sun alternately in and out, clouds sometimes obscuring the ruins, sometimes leaving them clear.

Get to Machu Picchu as early as possible, preferably before 0830 for best views but in any case before the tourist train arrives at 1030. **Note** Camping is not allowed at Intipunku; guards may confiscate your tent. You may only camp in the field by the river below Puente Ruinas station.

Alternative Inca Trails

The **Camino Real de los Inkas** starts at Km 104, where a footbridge gives access to the ruins of Chachabamba and the trail which ascends, passing above the ruins of Choquesuysuy to connect with the main trail at Wiñay-Wayna. This first part is a steady, continuous ascent of three hours (take water) and the trail is narrow and exposed in parts. Many people recommend this short Inca Trail. Good hiking trails from Aguas Calientes (see page 1241) have been opened along the left bank of the Urubamba, for day hikes crossing the bridge of the hydroelectric plant to Choquesuysuy. A three-night trek goes from Km 82 to Km 88, then along the Río Urubamba to Pacamayo Bajo and Km 104, from where you take the Camino Real de los Inkas.

Two treks involve routes from **Salkantay**: one, known as the **High Inca Trail** joins the classic Trail at Huayllabamba, then proceeds as before on the main Trail through Wiñay Wayna to Machu Picchu. To get to Salkantay, you have to start the trek in Mollepata, northwest of Cuzco in the Apurímac valley. *Ampay* buses run from Arcopata on the Chinchero road, or you can take private transport to Mollepata (three hours from Cuzco). Salkantay to Machu Picchu this way takes three nights. The second Salkantay route, known as the **Santa Teresa Trek**, takes four days and crosses the 4,500-m Huamantay Pass to reach the Santa Teresa valley, which you follow to its confluence with the Urubamba. The goal is the town of Santa Teresa from where you can go to La Hidroeléctrica station for the local train to Aguas Calientes (see page 1243).

There are other routes which approach the Inca Trails to Machu Picchu, such as Km 77, Chillca, up the Sillque ravine in the Qente valley, which is commonly called the Lago Ancascocha route. A common starting point for this trek is the community of Huarocondo. You can end this trek either at Huayllabamba, where you join the Classic Inca Trail (for further walking), or at the railway line at Km 82 (for transport to the Sacred Valley) or Km 88 (for the train to Aguas Calientes). Then there is another access through the Millpo Valley in the Salkantay area. From the Vilcabamba mountain range, one can reach Machu Picchu by hiking down from Huancacalle to Chaulla by road, getting to Santa Teresa and walking to La Hidroeléctrica station. Tour operators which specialize in trekking can advise on these routes.

Vitcos and Vilcabamba

The Incas' last stronghold is reached from **Chaullay**, a village on the road between Ollantaytambo and Quillabamba. The road passes through Peña, a beautiful place with snowy peaks on either side of the valley, then the climb to the pass begins in earnest – on the right is a huge glacier. Soon on the left, Verónica begins to appear in all its huge and snowy majesty. After endless zig-zags and breathtaking views, you reach the Abra Málaga pass (road is paved to here). The descent to the valley shows hillsides covered in lichen and Spanish moss. At Chaullay, the road crosses the river on the historic Choquechaca bridge.

From Chaullay you can drive, or take a daily bus or truck (4-7 hours) to the village of **Huancacalle**, the best base for exploring the nearby Inca ruins of **Vitcos**, with the palace of the last four Inca rulers from 1536 to 1572, and **Yurac Rumi** (or **Chuquipalta**), the impressive sacred white rock of the Incas. There are a few restaurants, shops and basic places to stay at Huancacalle. There is a hostal, F-G Sixpac Manco (managed by the Cobos family). Alternatively villagers will let you stay on their floor, or you can camp near the river below the cemetery. Allow time for hiking to, and visiting Vitcos. It takes one hour to walk from Huancacalle to Vitcos, 45 minutes Vitcos-Chuquipalta, 45 minutes Chuquipalta-Huancacalle. Horses can be hired.

The road from Chaullay continues to **Vilcabamba La Nueva**. You can also hike from Huancacalle; a three-hour walk through beautiful countryside with Inca ruins dotted around. There is a missionary building run by Italians, with electricity and running water, where you may be able to spend the night.

Vilcabamba Vieja

Travellers with ample time can hike from Huancacalle to **Espíritu Pampa**, the site of the **Vilcabamba Vieja** ruins, a vast pre-Inca ruin with a neo-Inca overlay set in deep jungle at 1,000 m. The site is reached on foot or horseback from Pampaconas. From Chaullay, take a truck to Yupanca, Lucma or Pucyura: there rent horses or mules and travel through breathtaking countryside to Espíritu Pampa. From Huancacalle a trip will take 3-4 days on foot, with a further day to get to Chaquiri and transport back to Quillabamba. It is advisable to take local guides and mules. Maps are available from the South American Explorers in Cuzco and Lima. Ask around in Huancacalle for guides. The Sixpac Manco hostal has various guides and other people in the village will offer their services. Distances are considerable and the going is difficult. *Sixpac Manco*, by Vincent R Lee (available in Cuzco), has accurate maps of all archaeological sites in this area, and describes two expeditions into the region by the author and his party, following in the footsteps of Gene Savoy, who first identified the site in the 1960s. His book, *Antisuyo*, is also recommended reading. The best time of year is May to November, possibly December. Outside this period it is very dangerous as the trails are very narrow and can be thick with mud and very slippery. Insect repellent is essential, also pain-killers and other basic medicines.

⊙ Transport

Huancacalle *p1246*
Bus Four companies leave Cuzco's bus terminal for **Quillabamba**, taking 8-14 hrs for the 233 km, depending on season, US$4.75 (**Ampay** is best company). Then take a **combi** from Quillabamba, 0900 and 1200, US$3.30 to Huancacalle, 4-7 hrs. On Fri they go all the way to Vilcabamba.

West from Cuzco

Beyond Anta on the Abancay road, 2 km before Limatambo at the ruins of **Tarahuasi**, a few hundred metres from the road, is a very well-preserved **Inca temple platform**, with 28 tall niches, and a long stretch of fine polygonal masonry. The ruins are impressive, enhanced by the orange lichen which give the walls a honey colour.

Along the Abancay road 100 km from Cuzco, is the exciting descent into the Apurímac canyon, near the former Inca suspension bridge that inspired Thornton Wilders' *The Bridge of San Luis Rey*.

Choquequirao
① *Entry US$3.35.*

Choquequirao is another 'lost city of the Incas', built on a ridge spur almost 1,600 m above the Apurímac. Although only 30% has been uncovered, it is reckoned to be a larger site than Machu Picchu, but with fewer buildings. The main features of Choquequirao are the **Lower Plaza**, considered by most experts to be the focal point of the city. The **Upper Plaza**, reached by a huge set of steps or terraces, has what are possibly ritual baths. A beautiful set of slightly curved agricultural terraces run for over 300 m east-northeast of the Lower Plaza.

Usnu is a levelled hilltop platform, ringed with stones and giving awesome 360-degree views. The **Ridge Group**, still shrouded in vegetation, is a large collection of unrestored buildings some 50-100 m below the Usnu. The **Outlier Building**, isolated and surrounded on three sides by sheer drops of over 1½ km into the Apurímac Canyon, possesses some of the finest stonework within Choquequirao. **Capuliyoc**, nearly 500 m below the Lower Plaza, is a great set of agricultural terraces, visible on the approach from the far side of the valley.

There are three ways in to Choquequirao. None is a gentle stroll. The shortest way is from **Cachora**, a village on the south side of the Apurímac, reached by a side road from the Cuzco-Abancay highway, shortly after Saywite. It is four hours by bus from Cuzco to the turn-off, then a two-hour descent from the road to Cachora (from 3,695 m to 2,875 m). Guides (Celestino Peña is the official guide) and mules are available in Cachora. From the village you need a day to descend to the Río Apurímac then seven hours to climb up to Choquequirao. Allow 1-2 days at the site then return the way you came. The second and third routes take a minimum of eight days and require thorough preparation. You can start either at Huancacalle, or at Santa Teresa, between Machu Picchu and Chaullay. Both routes involve an incredible number of strenuous ascents and descents. You should be acclimatised for altitudes ranging from 2,400 m to between 4,600 and 5,000 m and be prepared for extremes of temperature. In each case you end the trail at Cachora. It is possible to start either of these long hikes at Cachora, continuing even from Choquequirao to Espíritu Pampa. Cuzco tour companies are now offering this adventure.

Saywite → *3 km from the main road at Km 49 from Abancay, 153 km from Cuzco, US$3. Altitude 3,500 m.*
Beyond the town of Curahuasi, 126 km from Cuzco, is the large carved rock of Saywite. It is a UNESCO World Heritage site. The principal monolith is said to represent the three regions of jungle, sierra and coast, with the associated animals and Inca sites of each. It is fenced in, but ask the guardian for a closer look. It was defaced, allegedly, when a cast was taken of it, breaking off many of the animals' heads. Six further archaeological areas fall away from the stone and its neighbouring group of buildings. The site is more easily reached from Abancay than Cuzco.

● Sleeping

Choquequirao *p1247*
G pp La Casona de Ocampo, Jr San Martín 122, Cachora, T084-237514, lacasonade ocampo@yahoo.es. Hot shower, free camping, owner Carlos Robles organizes treks to Choquequirao. 2 other places in the village.

● Transport

Choquequirao *p1247*
Buses run from Abancay (Jr Prado Alto entre Huancavelica y Núñez) to **Cachora** at 0500 and 1400, return 0630 and 1100, 2 hrs, US$1.50. Cars run from the Curahuasi terminal on Av Arenas, Abancay, US$10 for whole vehicle. Trek from Cachora to Choquequirao.

Central Highlands

The Central Andes are remote mountain areas with small, typical villages. The vegetation is low, but most valleys are cultivated. Roads, all dirt, are in poor condition, sometimes impassable in the rainy season; the countryside is beautiful with spectacular views and the people are friendly. The road into the central Andes has been improved and is paved throughout, offering fine views. Huancayo lies in a valley which produces many crafts; the festivals are very popular and not to be missed.

Lima to Huancayo

The Central Highway more or less parallels the course of the railway between Lima and Huancayo (335 km). With the paving of roads from Pisco to Ayacucho and Nazca to Abancay, there are now more options for getting to the Sierra and the views on whichever ascent you choose are beyond compare. You can also reach the Central Highlands from Cuzco (via Abancay and Andahuaylas) and from Huaraz (via La Unión and Huánuco), so Lima is not the sole point of access overland.

Chosica and Marcahuasi
Chosica (860 m) is the real starting place for the mountains, 40 km from Lima. It's warm and friendly and a great place to escape Lima's grey cloud. Beyond the town looms a precipitous range of hills almost overhanging the streets. There are four basic *hostales*, all with water problems. Up the Santa Eulalia valley 40 km beyond Chosica, is **Marcahuasi**, a table mountain (US$3) about 3 km by 3 km at 4,200 m, near the village of **San Pedro de Casta**. There are three lakes, a 40-m high 'monumento a la humanidad', and other mysterious lines, gigantic figures, sculptures, astrological signs and megaliths, which late Daniel Ruzo describes in his book, *La Culture Masma*, Extrait de l'Ethnographie, Paris, 1956. Others say that the formations are the result of wind erosion. The trail starts behind the village of San Pedro, and bends to the left. It's three hours to the *meseta*; guides cost about US$3 a day and are advisable in misty weather. Mules for carrying bags cost US$4 to hire, horses US$4.45. Tourist information at the municipality on the plaza sells a map of the plateau for US$1.50. At a shop on the plaza in San Pedro you can buy everything for the trip, including bottled water. Tours can be arranged with travel agencies in Lima.

Lima to Huancayo

Chosica to Huancayo
For a while, beyond Chosica, each successive valley looks greener and lusher, with a greater variety of trees and flowers. Between Río Blanco and **Chicla** (Km 127, 3,733 m), Inca contour-terraces can be seen quite clearly. After climbing up from **Casapalca** (Km 139, 4,154 m), there are glorious views of the highest peaks, and more mines, at the foot of a deep gorge. The road ascends to the Ticlio Pass, before the descent to **Morococha** and **La Oroya**. A large metal flag of Peru can be seen at the top of Mount Meiggs, not by any means the highest in the area, but through it runs Galera Tunnel, 1,175 m long, in which the Central Railway reaches its greatest altitude, 4,782 m. The railway itself is a magnificent feat of engineering, with 68 bridges and 71 tunnels, passing beautiful landscapes. It is definitely worth the ride on the new tourist service (see Transport, below). **La Oroya** (3,755 m) is the main smelting centre for the region's mining industry. It stands at the fork of the Yauli and Mantaro rivers. Any traveller, but asthmatics in particular, beware, the pollution from the heavy industry causes severe irritation. (For places to the east and north of La Oroya, see page 1262.)

The old town of **Jauja** (*Phone code 064, Population 105,000, Altitude 3,330 m*), 80 km southeast of La Oroya, was Pizarro's provisional capital until the founding of Lima. It has a very colourful Wednesday and Sunday market. There is an **archaeological museum**, which is recommended for the Huari culture. The **Cristo Pobre** church is claimed to have been modelled after Notre Dame and is something of a curiosity. On a hill above Jauja there is a fine line of Inca storehouses, and on hills nearby the ruins of hundreds of circular stone buildings from the Huanca culture (John Hemming). There are also ruins near the **Paca lake**, 3½ km away. The western shore is lined with restaurants, many of which offer boat trips at weekends, US$0.75 (combi from Avenida Pizarro US$0.30).

On the road to Huancayo 18 km to the south, is **Concepción** (*Altitude 3,251 m*), with a market on Sunday. From Concepción a branch road (6 km) leads to the **Convent of Santa Rosa de Ocopa** ① *0900-1200 and 1500-1800, closed Tue, 45-min tours start on the hour, US$1.10, colectivos from the market in Concepción, 15 mins, US$0.25*, a Franciscan monastery set in beautiful surroundings. It was established in 1725 for training missionaries for the jungle. It contains a fine library with over 20,000 volumes, a biological museum and a large collection of paintings.

● Sleeping

Chosica *p1248*
G **Hospedaje Chosica**, Av 28 de Julio 134, T01-361 0841. Rooms with and without bath. Recommended.
G **La Posada**, Jr Trujillo y Salaverry, just off main road. Comfortable, hot water.

San Pedro de Casta *p1248*
Locals in town will put you up for US$0.60 pp; ask at tourist information at the municipality on the plaza, T01-571 2087. Take all necessary camping equipment for Marcahuasi trek.
F **Marcahuasi**, just off the plaza. G pp without bath, the best hotel in San Pedro; it also has a restaurant. There are 2 other restaurants.

La Oroya *p1248*
F **Hostal Chavín**, Tarma 281; and G **Hostal Inti**, Arequipa 117, T391098. Both basic.

Jauja *p1248*
F pp **Hostal Manco Cápac**, Jr Manco Cápac 575, T361620, niegemannilse@hotmail.com. Central, good rooms, good breakfast and coffee, German run. Recommended (reserve at weekends).
F **Hostal María Nieves**, Jr Gálvez 491, 1 block from the Plaza de Armas, T362543. Safe, helpful, price includes large breakfast, hot water all day. Recommended.
G **Hostal Los Algarrobos**, Huancayo 264, T362633. Shared bath, hot water in the morning, good value.

● Eating

La Oroya *p1248*
♔ **El Tambo**, 2 km outside town on the road to Lima. Good trout and frogs, recommended as the best in and around town.

Jauja *p1248*
♔ **Centro Naturista**, Huarancayo 138. Fruit salad, yoghurt, granola, etc.
♔ **Ganso de Oro**, R Palma 249. Good restaurant in hotel of same name, US$2-4 per meal, the best in town.
♔ **Marychris**, Jr Bolívar 1166, T362386. Lunch

only, excellent.
♔ **La Rotunda**, Tarapacá 415. Good lunch menú and pizzas in the evening.

● Transport

Chosica *p1248*
Colectivos for Chosica leave from Av Grau, **Lima**, when full, between 0600 and 2100, US$0.60. Most **buses** on the Lima-La Oroya route are full; colectivo taxi to La Oroya US$3.60, 3 hrs, very scenic, passing the highest railway in the world.

San Pedro de Casta/Marcahuasi *p1248*
Bus To San Pedro de Casta leave **Chosica** from Parque Echenique, opposite market, 0900 and 1500, 4 hrs, US$2; return 0700 and 1400.

La Oroya *p1248*
Bus To **Lima**, 4½ hrs, US$5.20. To **Jauja**, 80 km, 1½ hrs, US$1. To **Tarma**, 1½ hrs, US$1.35. To **Cerro de Pasco**, 131 km, 3 hrs, US$2.20. To **Huánuco**, 236 km, 6 hr, US$4.35. Buses leave from Zeballos, adjacent to the train station. Colectivos also run on all routes.

Jauja *p1248*
Bus To **Lima**: with Cruz del Sur, Pizarro 220, direct, 5 hrs, US$8. Most companies have their offices on the Plaza de Armas, but their buses leave from Av Pizarro. To **Huancayo**, 44 km, takes 1 hr and costs US$1.25. To **Cerro de Pasco**, Oriental leave from 28 de Julio 156, and **Turismo Central** from 28 de Julio 150, 5 hrs, US$3.55. Oriental and Turismo Central also go to **Huánuco**, 7 hrs, US$5.35. To **Tarma**, US$2, hourly with Trans Muruhuay and ET San Juan from Jr Tarma; the latter continues to **Chanchamayo**, US$4.50.

● Directory

Jauja *p1248*
Banks Dollar Exchange Huarancayo, on Jr Huarancayo, gives a much better rate than BCP (no TCs). **Internet** All along Junín blocks 9 to 12. **Post offices** Jr Bolívar. **Telephones** Ricardo Palma, opposite *Hotel Ganso de Oro*.

Huancayo and around

→ *Phone code: 064. Colour map 3, grid C3. Population: over 500,000. Altitude: 3,271 m.*

The city is in the beautiful Mantaro Valley. It is the capital of Junín Department and the main commercial centre for inland Peru. All the villages in the valley produce their own original crafts and celebrate festivals all year round. At the important festivals in Huancayo, people flock in from far and wide with an incredible range of food, crafts, dancing and music. The Sunday market gives a little taste of this every week (it gets going after 0900), but it is better to go to the villages for local handicrafts. Jr Huancavelica, 3 km long and four stalls wide, still sells clothes, fruit, vegetables, hardware, handicrafts and traditional medicines and goods for witchcraft. There is also an impressive daily market behind the railway station and a large handicrafts market between Ancash and Real, block 7, offering a wide selection.

Tourist offices Huancayo: Dirección Regional de Turismo, Dircetur, Av Libertad 204, T433007. Has information about the area and is helpful; 0800-1300, 1400-1700 Monday-Friday. **Touring y Automóvil Club del Perú**, Jr Lima 355, T231204, huancayo@touringperu.com.pe.

The **museum** ⓘ *at the Salesian school, Mon-Fri 0800-1200, 1500-1800, Sun 1000-1200, US$1.35,* has over 5,000 pieces, including a large collection of jungle birds, animals and butterflies, insects, reptiles and fossils. Recommended. The **Parque de Identidad Wanka** ⓘ *on Jr San Jorge in the Barrio San Carlos northeast of the city, entry free, but contributions are appreciated,* is a fascinating mixture of surrealistic construction interwoven with indigenous plants and trees and the cultural history of the Mantaro Valley.

Mantaro Valley

The whole Mantaro valley is rich in culture. On the outskirts of town is **Torre-Torre**, impressive, eroded sandstone towers on the hillside. Take a bus to Cerrito de la Libertad and walk up. The ruins of **Warivilca** (15 km) ⓘ *1000-1200, 1500-1700 (museum mornings only), US$0.15, take a micro for Chilca from C Real* are near **Huari**, with the remains of a pre-Inca temple of the Huanca tribe. Museum in the plaza, with deformed skulls, and modelled and painted pottery of successive Huanca and Inca occupations of the shrine. Between Pilcomayo and Huayo (15 km) is the **Geophysical Institute of Huayo**, on the 'Magnetic Equator' 12½° south of the geographical equator (best to visit in the morning, or when the sun is shining). Take bus from Jr Giráldez to Chupaca, but get out by bridge before Chupaca, where the road splits, then take a colectivo.

East of the Mantaro River The villages of **Cochas Chico** and **Cochas Grande**, 11 km away, are where the famous *mate burilado*, or gourd carving, is done. You can buy them cheaply direct from the manufacturers, but ask around. Beautiful views of the Valle de Mantaro and Huancayo. *Micros* leave from the corner of Amazonas and Giráldez, US$0.25.

Hualahoyo (11 km) has a little chapel with 21 colonial canvases. **San Agustín de Cajas** (8 km) makes fine hats, and **San Pedro** (10 km) makes wooden chairs; **Hualhuas** (12 km) fine alpaca weavings which you can watch being made. The weavers take special orders; small items can be finished in a day. Negotiate a price.

The town of **San Jerónimo** is renowned for the making of silver filigree jewellery; Wednesday market. Fiesta on the third Saturday in August. There are ruins 2-3 hours' walk above San Jerónimo, but seek advice before hiking to them.

Between Huancayo and Huancavelica, **Izcuchaca** is the site of a bridge over the Río Mantaro. On the edge of town is a fascinating pottery workshop whose machinery is driven by a water turbine (plus a small shop). A nice hike is to the chapel on a hill overlooking the valley; about one to 1½ hours each way.

⬤ Sleeping

Huancayo *p1250, map p1251*
Prices may be raised in Holy Week. **Note**: The Plaza de Armas is called Plaza Constitución.
C El Marquez, Puno 294, T219026, www.elmarquezhuancayo.com. With TV and free internet access, good value, efficient, popular with

local business travellers, safe parking.
C Presidente, C Real 1138, T231735, same email as *Turismo*. Helpful, safe, serves breakfast. Recommended.
C Turismo, Ancash 729, T231072, hotelhyo@correo.dnet.com.pe. Old building, some rooms

small, quiet, good meals for US$3.50.
D Retama Inn, Ancash 1079, T219193,
retamainn73@hotmail.com. All amenities,
comfortable beds, TV, café/bar, helpful, internet
US$1.50 per hr, breakfast US$2.
D Santa Felicita, Giráldez 145, Plaza
Constitución, T235285. Hot water, good.
**E pp Casa Alojamiento de Aldo y Soledad
Bonilla**, Huánuco 332, ½ block from Mcal
Cáceres bus station, T232103. Cheaper without

full board, colonial house, owners speak English,
laundry, secure, relaxing, nice courtyard, can
arrange tours, best to book ahead.
E Hospedaje César Ada, Pasaje Santa Teresa
294, El Tambo-3 Esquinas, 5 km from centre,
T253646 for pick-up, wadaycesar@hotmail.com.
Quiet, shared bath, garden, meals available, use
of kitchen, breakfast included.
E La Casa de la Abuela, Av Giráldez 691,
T223303. Hot shower, breakfast included, some

Huancayo

0 metres 100
0 yards 100

Sleeping 🛌
Casa Alojamiento de
 Aldo y Soledad Bonilla **1** C2
Casa Hospedaje **2** B2
Confort **3** A2
El Marquez **5** A2
Hostal Baldeón **6** B3
Hostal Santo Domingo **8** B1
La Casa de La Abuela **9** B3
Peru Andino **10** A3
Presidente **11** C2
Pussy Cat **12** B3
Retama Inn **15** C2
Santa Felicita **13** B2
Turismo **14** B2

Eating 🍴
Berisso **1** B2
Café El Parque **2** B2
Chanchamayo **6** B2
Chez Viena **3** B3
Chifa El Centro **4** B2
El Paraíso **7** C2
El Pino **8** B2
ImaginArte **5** A2
La Cabaña **9** B3
Panadería Koky **11** B2
Pizzería Antojitos **12** B2

1251

rooms with antique beds, dormitory **G**, laundry facilities, meals available, internet, sociable staff, good meeting place, free pickup from bus station if requested in advance.

F Confort, Ancash 231, 1 block from the main Plaza, T233601. Rooms with hot water are nicer, but more expensive than those with cold water, all rooms good value, safe for bicycles, car parking US$1.

F Pussy Cat, Giráldez 359, T231565. **F** without bath, hot water, safe, luggage stored, good beds.

G pp Casa hospedaje, Huamanmarca 125, T219980. Central, small, comfortable, hot water, shared showers, family run, nice atmosphere.

G pp Hostal Baldeón, Amazonas 543, T231634. Kitchen and laundry facilities, nice patio, hot shower on request, basic rooms, safe, good value.

G Hostal Santo Domingo, Ica 655, T235461. Set around 2 pleasant patios, basic, good value.

G pp Peru Andino, Pasaje San Antonio 113-115, on Av Centenario go 3 blocks from 2 de Mayo to San José, then 3 blocks left (north), 10-15 mins walk from the centre (if taking a taxi, stress that it's *Pasaje* San Antonio), T223956, www.geocities.com/ peruandino_1. Including breakfast, hot showers, several rooms with bath, safe area, cosy atmosphere, run by Sra Juana, daughter speaks some English, owner Luis runs trekking and mountain bike tours, cooking and laundry facilities, Spanish classes. Highly recommended.

Mantaro Valley *p1250*
Izcuchaca has 1 hotel on the plaza, no bathroom, use the public bath by the river; the other is just off the plaza, a yellow 3-storey house, **G**, no shower, toilet suitable for men only, chamber pot supplied, only blankets on bed, cold.

❶ Eating

Huancayo *p1250, map p1251*
Breakfast is served in Mercado Modelo from 0700. Better class, more expensive restaurants, serving typical dishes for about US$4-5, plus 18% tax, drinks can be expensive. Lots of cheap restaurants along Av Giráldez.

♥♥ La Cabaña, Av Giráldez 652. Pizzas, ice cream, *calentitos*, and other dishes, folk music at weekends.

♥♥ Pizzería Antojitos, Puno 599. Attractive, atmospheric pizzeria with live music some nights.

♥ Chifa El Centro, Giráldez 238. Chinese food, good service and atmosphere.

♥ El Pino, Real 539. Typical dishes for about US$2-3 and fixed price *menú*.

Cafés
Berisso, Giráldez 258. Good for cakes and quiche, friendly.

Café El Parque, Giráldez y Ancash, on the main plaza. Smart place to take coffee and cake.

Chanchamayo, Puno 209. Good little family café, cheap, good for breakfast.

Chez Viena, Puno 125. Another smart place serving good coffee and cakes.

ImaginArte, Jr.Ancash 260. Principally an art gallery, often displaying work based on ethnic Peruvian culture. Good coffee and cakes.

Panadería Koky, Ancash y Puno. Good for breakfasts and pastries during the day.

El Paraíso, Arequipa 429. Good vegetarian food and service, great value.

Mantaro Valley *p1250*
♥ Restaurant El Parque on plaza, Izcuchaca. Opens 0700, delicious food.

❶ Bars and clubs

Huancayo *p1250, map p1251*
Clubs Most open around 2000 and close at 0200. Some charge an entrance fee of US$3-4. **Peñas** All the *peñas* have folklore shows with dancing, open normally Fri, Sat and Sun from 1300 to 2200. Entrance fee is about US$2 pp. Eg **Ollantaytambo**, Puno, block 2, and **Taki Wasi**, Huancavelica y 13 de Noviembre.

❸ Festivals and events

Huancayo *p1250, map p1251*
There are so many festivals in the Mantaro Valley that it is impossible to list them all. Nearly every day of the year there is some sort of celebration in one of the villages.

Jan: 1-6, New Year celebrations; 20, **San Sebastián y San Fabián** (recommended in Jauja). **Feb**: there are carnival celebrations for the whole month, with highlights on 2, **Virgen de la Candelaria**, and 17-19 **Concurso de Carnaval**. **Mar-Apr**: Semana Santa, with impressive Good Friday processions. **May**: Fiesta de las Cruces throughout the whole month. **Jun**: 15 Virgen de las Mercedes; 24, San Juan Bautista; 29, Fiesta Patronal. **Jul**: 16, Virgen del Carmen; 24-25, Santiago. **Aug**: 4, San Juan de Dios; 16, San Roque; 30, Santa Rosa de Lima. **Sep**: 8, Virgen de Cocharcas; 15, Virgen de la Natividad; 23-24, Virgen de las Mercedes; 29, San Miguel Arcángel. **Oct**: 4, San Francisco de Asís; 18, San Lucas; 28-30 culmination of month-long celebrations for El Señor de los Milagros. **Nov**: 1, Día de Todos los Santos. **Dec**: 3-13, Virgen de Guadalupe; 8, Inmaculada Concepción; 25, Navidad (Christmas).

O Shopping

Huancayo *p1250, map p1251*
Thieves in the market hand out rolled up paper and pick your pocket while you unravel them.
Crafts All crafts are made outside Huancayo in the many villages of the Mantaro Valley, or in Huancavelica. The villages are worth a visit to learn how the items are made.
Casa de Artesano, on the corner of Real and Paseo La Breña, at Plaza Constitución. Has a wide selection of good quality crafts.

▲ Activities and tours

Huancayo *p1250, map p1251*
Tour operators
American Travel & Service, Plaza Constitución 122, of 2 (next to the Cathedral), T211181, 932 5767 (mob), www.traveltourshuancayo.com. Wide range of classical and more adventurous tours in the Mantaro Valley and in the Central Jungle. Transport and equipment rental possible. Most group based day tours start at US$8-10 pp.
Andina Tours, C Real 455, of 2, T253434, 999 8168 (mob), andinatours_hyo@hotmail.com. Professional organizer of tours.
Incas del Perú, Av Giráldez 652, T223303, www.incasdelperu.org. Associated with the **La Cabaña/Otra Lado** restaurants and **La Casa de la Abuela**. Run jungle, biking and riding trips throughout the region, as well as language and volunteer programs. Very popular with travellers in the region.
Peruvian Tours, Plaza Constitución 122, p 2, of 1, T213069, 966 1044 (mob). Next to the Cathedral and American Travel & Service. Classic tours of the Mantaro valley, plus day trips up to the Huaytapallana Nevados above Huancayo, plus long, 16-hr excursions to Cerro de Pasco and Tarma.

Guides
Marco Jurado Ames, andinismo_peru@ yahoo.es. Organizes long-distance treks on the `hidden paths of Peru'. Many of these include Huancayo, such as a two-week trip from Lima to Machu Picchu via Huancayo, the Amazon lowlands and Vilcabamba.

⊖ Transport

Huancayo *p1250, map p1251*
Bus A new bus terminal for all buses to all destinations is planned 3 km north of the centre. There are regular buses to **Lima**, 6-7 hrs on a good paved road, US$10-13. Travelling by day is recommended for the fantastic views and, of course, for safety. If you must travel by night, take warm clothing. Recommended companies: **Ormeño**, Av Mcal Castilla 1379, El Tambo; **Cruz del Sur**, Ayacucho 281, T235650, **Turismo Central**, Jr Ayacucho 274, T223128 (double-decker *bus cama*), and **Transportes Rogger**, Lima 561, T212687, *cama* and *semi-cama* at 1300 and 2330, comercial at 2230.

To **Ayacucho**, 319 km, 9-10 hrs, US$6.65-7.55. **Molina**, C Angaráes 334, T224501, 3 a day, recommended. The road is paved for the first 70 km, then in poor condition and is very difficult in the wet. Take warm clothing. (**Note** If driving to Ayacucho and beyond, roads are "amazingly rough". Don't go alone. Count kilometres diligently to keep a record of where you are: road signs are poor.) After Izcuchaca, on the railway to Huancavelica, there is a good road to the Quichuas hydroelectric scheme, but thereafter it is narrow with hair-raising bends and spectacular bridges. The scenery is staggering.

To **Huancavelica**, 147 km, 5 hrs, US$2.85. Many buses daily, including **Transportes Yuri**, Ancash 1220, 3 a day. The road is in poor condition and takes much longer in the wet. The scenery is spectacular.

To **Cerro de Pasco**, 255 km, 5 hrs, US$4. Several departures. Alternatively, take a bus to La Oroya, about every 20 mins, from Av Real about 10 blocks north of the main plaza. From La Oroya there are regular buses and colectivos to Cerro. The road to La Oroya and on to Cerro is in good condition. To **Huánuco**, 7 hrs, **Turismo Central** at 2115, US$6, good service.

To **Chanchamayo**: Empresa San Juan, Ferrocarril 161 and Plaza Amazonas, and **Tans Muruhuay** each have an hourly service via Jauja to Tarma, 3 hrs, US$2.50, some of which continue on to La Merced, 5 hrs, US$4.

To **Cañete**, 289 km, 10 hrs, US$4, **ETAS/Angoma**, Loreto 744, T215424. It is a poor road, with beautiful mountain landscapes before dropping to the valley of Cañete.

To **Jauja**, 44 km, 1 hr. Colectivos and combis leave every few mins from Huamanmarca y Amazonas, and Plaza Amazonas, US$1.50. Ones via San Jerónimo and Concepción have 'Izquierda' on the front. Most buses to the Mantaro Valley leave from several places around the market area. Buses to **Hualhuas** and **Cajas** leave from block 3 of Pachitea. Buses to **Cochas** leave from Amazonas y Giráldez.
Train There are 2 unconnected railway stations. The Central station serves **Lima**, via La Oroya: Service on this railway with trains at weekends run by **Ferrocarril Centro Andino**, T01-361 2828, ext 222, www.ferroviasperu.com. The fare is US$48 return. The train leaves Lima

Fri 0700, arrives Huancayo 1800, returns Sun 1800, arrives Lima 0500. Coaches have reclining seats, heating, restaurant, tourist information, toilets, and nurse with first aid and oxygen. Information on forthcoming departures can be obtained from Incas del Perú, see Activities and tours, above.

From the small station in Chilca suburb (15 mins by taxi, US$1), trains run to **Huancavelica**, on a narrow gauge (3 ft). There are 2 trains: the *autovagón* (*expreso*) at 1300 daily, US$4, has 1st class and Buffet carriages. This "classic" Andean train journey takes 7 hrs and has fine views, passing through typical mountain villages where vendors sell food and crafts. There are 38 tunnels and the line reaches 3,676 m. The local train leaves at 0630 daily and takes 5 hrs. There are 1st, US$2.55, 2nd, US$2.20, and Buffet, US$4, classes. Services are often suspended, especially in the rainy season.

Mantaro Valley *p1250*
Train From **Huancavelica** arrive in Izcuchaca at 0800 and 1400-1430, then continue to **Huancayo**; US$1.70. Trains from Huancayo pass

at around 0900 and 1600. They tend to be very crowded. Daily **colectivo** to Ayacucho at 1000-1100, 8 hrs.

❶ Directory

Huancayo *p1250, map p1251*
Banks BCP, Real 1039, changes TCs with no commission, cash advance on Visa. Scotiabank, Real casi Ica. Interbank and Banco Continental are on block 6 of Real. There are several *casas de cambio* on Ancash; street changers hang out on Giráldez, 100 block. **Internet** Numerous places round Plaza Constitución on Giráldez, Paseo La Breña; average price under US$0.75 per hr.
Language classes Incas del Perú (see Activities and tours, above) organizes Spanish courses for beginners for US$100 per week, including accommodation at Hostal La Casa de La Abuela, Av Giráldez 691, and all meals, also homestays and weaving, playing traditional music, Peruvian cooking and lots of other things. Katia Cerna is a recommended teacher, T225332, katiacerna@hotmail.com. She can arrange home stays; her sister works in adventure tourism.

Huancavelica → *Phone code: 064. Colour map 3, grid C3. Population: 37,500. Altitude: 3,660 m.*

Huancavelica is a friendly and attractive town, surrounded by huge, rocky mountains. It was founded in the 16th century by the Spanish to exploit rich deposits of mercury and silver. It is predominantly an indigenous town, and people still wear traditional costume. There are beautiful mountain walks in the neighbourhood. The Cathedral, located on the Plaza de Armas, has an altar considered to be one of the finest examples of colonial art in Peru. Also very impressive are the five other churches in town. The church of San Francisco, for example, has no less than 11 altars. Sadly, though, most of the churches are closed to visitors. **Tourist office:** Dircetur ① *Jr Victoria Garma 444, T452938, dircetur_hcv@hotmail.com.* Very helpful.

Bisecting the town is the Río Huancavelica. South of the river is the main commercial centre. North of the river, on the hillside, are the **thermal baths** ① *0600-1500, US$0.15 for private rooms, water not very hot, US$0.10 for the hot public pool, also hot showers, take a lock for the doors.* The handicraft sellers congregate in front of the Municipalidad on M Muñoz and the Biblioteca on the Plaza de Armas (V Toledo). Most handicrafts are transported directly to Lima, but you can still visit craftsmen in neighbouring villages. The Potaqchiz hill, just outside the town, gives a fine view, about one hour walk up from San Cristóbal. *Instituto Nacional de la Cultura* ① *Plazoleta San Juan de Dios, T453420, inc_huancavelica@yahoo.es,* is a good source of information on festivals, archaeological sites, history, etc. Gives courses on music and dancing, and lectures some evenings. There is also an interesting but small **Museo Regional** ① *Arica y Raimondi, Mon-Sat 1000-1300, 1500-1900.*

Huancavelica to Ayacucho

The direct route from Huancavelica to Ayacucho (247 km) goes via **Santa Inés** (4,650 m), 78 km. Out of Huancavelica the road climbs steeply with switchbacks between herds of llamas and alpacas grazing on rocky perches. Around Pucapampa (Km 43) is one of the highest habitable *altiplanos* (4,500 m), where the rare and highly prized ash-grey alpaca can be seen. Snow-covered mountains are passed as the road climbs to 4,853 m at the Abra Chonta pass, 23 km before Santa Inés. By taking the turnoff to Huachocolpa at Abra Chonta and continuing for 3 km you'll reach the highest drivable pass in the world, at 5,059 m. Nearby are two lakes (Laguna Choclacocha) which can be visited in 2½ hours. 52 km beyond Santa Inés at the Abra de Apacheta (4,750 m), 98 km from Ayacucho, the rocks are all the colours of the rainbow, and running through this fabulous scenery is a violet river. See Transport, below, for road services and lodging options on this route.

There is another route to Ayacucho from Huancayo, little used by buses, but which involves not so much climbing for cyclists. Cross the pass into the Mantaro valley on the road to **Quichuas** . Then to **Anco** and **Mayocc** (lodging). From here the road crosses a bridge after 10 km and in another 20 km reaches **Huanta** (see page 1258). Then it's a paved road to Ayacucho.

🛌 Sleeping

Huancavelica *p1254*
D **Presidente**, Plaza de Armas, T452760. Cheaper without bath, lovely colonial building, overpriced.
F **Camacho**, Jr Carabaya 481, T753298. Best of the cheap hotels, cheaper without bath, hot shower morning only, good value, safe.
F **San José**, Jr Huancayo, at top of Barranca (past Santo Domingo), T752958. Hot water 1700-1900, G without bath, nice beds, helpful.
G **Santo Domingo**, Av Barranca 366, T953086. Very basic, shared bath, cold water.

Huancavelica to Ayacucho *p1254*
G **Alojamiento Andino**, in Santa Inés, a very friendly restaurant, **El Favorito**, where you can sleep, and several others.
G **Hostal Recreo Sol y Sombra**, in Quichuas. Charming, small courtyard, helpful, basic.
G **Hostal Gabi**, in Anco. Appalling, but better than anything else.

🍴 Eating

Huancavelica *p1254*
♯♯ **Mochica Sachún**, Av Virrey Toledo 303. Great *menú* US$1.50, otherwise expensive.
♯ **Cami**, Barranca y Toledo. No sign, small, lively, good set menus and juices.
♯ **La Casona**, Jr Virrey Toledo 230. Cheap and good *menú*, also a *peña*.

🎉 Festivals and events

Huancavelica *p1254*
The whole area is rich in culture. **Fiesta de los Reyes Magos y los Pastores**, **4-8 Jan**. **Fiesta del Niño Perdido** is held on **2nd Sun in Jan**. **Pukllaylay Carnavales**, celebration of the first fruits from the ground (harvest), **20 Jan-mid Mar**. **Semana Santa**, Holy Week. **Toro Pukllay** festival **last week of May, 1st week of Jun**. **Fiesta de Santiago** is held in **May and Aug** in all communities. **Los Laygas** or **Galas** (scissors dance), **22-28 Dec**.

🚌 Transport

Huancavelica *p1254*
Bus All bus companies have their offices on, and leave from the east end of town, around Parque M

Castilla, on Muñoz, Iquitos, Tumbes and O'Donovan. To **Huancayo**, 147 km, 5 hrs, US$2.85, rough road, **Transportes Yuri** and **Transportes Ticllas** (O'Donovan 500). To **Lima** via Huancayo, 445 km, 13 hrs minimum, US$5.70. Most buses to Huancayo go on to Lima, there are several a day. The other route is to **Pisco**, 269 km, 12 hrs, US$7 and **Ica**, US$8, 1730 daily, with **Oropesa**, O'Donovon 599. Buy your ticket 1 day in advance. The road is poor until it joins the Ayacucho-Pisco road, where it improves. Most of the journey is done at night. Be prepared for sub-zero temperatures in the early morning as the bus passes snowfields, then for temperatures of 25-30°C as the bus descends to the coast.
Train See under Huancayo; the *autovagón* leaves for Huancayo daily at 0630, the local train at 1300, daily.

Huancavelica to Ayacucho *p1254*
There is no direct transport from Huancavelica to Ayacucho, other than 0430 on Sat with **San Juan Bautista** (Plazoleta Túpac Amaru 107, T803062), US$5.70. Otherwise you have to go to **Rumichaca** just beyond Santa Inés on the paved Pisco-Ayacucho road, also **San Juan Bautista** 0430, 4 hrs, then wait for a passing bus to Ayacucho at 1500, US$2, or try to catch a truck. Rumichaca has only a couple of foodstalls and some filthy toilets. This route is the highest continuous road in the world. The journey is a cold one but spectacular as the road rarely drops below 4,000 m for 150 km.
The best alternative is to take a colectivo Huancavelica-**Lircay**, a small village with F unnamed hostal at Sucre y La Unión, with bath and hot water, much better than Hostal El Paraíso, opposite, also with bath, G without (Transportes 5 de Mayo, Av Sebastián Barranca y Cercado, US$4.55, 2½ hrs, leave when full). The same company runs from Lircay Terminal Terrestre hourly from 0430 to Julcamarca (colonial church, **Hostal Villa Julcamarca**, near plaza, no tap water, really basic), 2½ hrs, US$3, then take a minibus from Julcamarca plaza to Ayacucho, US$2, 2 hrs; beautiful scenery all the way. Another option is to take the train to Izcuchaca, stay the night and take the colectivo (see above).

Banks BCP, Virrey Toledo 300 block. There is a *Multired* ATM on M Muñoz in front of the Municipalidad. **Internet** Despite what they say, internet places open around 0900 till 2100-2200. There are places on V Toledo and M Muñoz. **Librería Municipal**, Plaza de Armas, US$0.60 per hr. **Post offices** Ferrua Jos, at block 8 of M Muñoz. **Telephones** Carabaya y Virrey Toledo.

Ayacucho → *Phone code: 066. Colour map 3, grid C3. Population: 105,918. Altitude: 2,748 m.*

A week can easily be spent enjoying Ayacucho and its hinterland. The climate is lovely, with warm, sunny days and pleasant balmy evenings, and the people are very hospitable. Semana Santa celebrations are famous throughout South America. Ayacucho was founded on 9 January 1539. On the Pampa de Quinua, on 9 December 1824, the decisive Battle of Ayacucho was fought, bringing Spanish rule in Peru to an end. In the middle of the festivities, the Liberator Simón Bolívar decreed that the city be named Ayacucho, 'City of Blood', instead of its original name, Huamanga.

The city is built round the Plaza Mayor, the main plaza, with the Cathedral, Municipalidad, Universidad Nacional de San Cristóbal de Huamanga (UNSCH) and various colonial mansions facing on to it. It is famous for its Semana Santa celebrations, its splendid market and its 33 churches. **Tourist offices: i perú** ① *Portal Municipal 48, on the Plaza, T318305, iperuayacucho@promperu.gob.pe, daily 0830-1930, Sun 0830-1430.* Very helpful. **Dirección Regional de Industria y Turismo** (Dircetur) ① *Asamblea 481, T312548. Mon-Fri 0800-1300,* friendly and helpful. **Tourist Police** ① *Arequipa cuadra 1, T312055.*

Sights

The **Cathedral** ① *daily 1700-1900, Sun 0900-1700,* built in 1612, has superb gold leaf altars. It is beautifully lit at night. On the north side of the Plaza Mayor, on the corner of Portal de la Unión and Asamblea, are the **Casonas de los Marqueses de Mozobamba y del Pozo**, also called Velarde-Alvarez. The **Museo de Arte Popular Joaquín López Antay** ① *Portal de la Unión 28, in the BCP building, museo@ unsch.edu.pe, Tue-Fri 1030-1700, Sat 1030-1230,* displays local craft work. North of the Plaza is **Santo Domingo** (1548) ① *9 de Diciembre, block 2, Mass daily 0700-0800.* Its fine façade has triple Roman arches and Byzantine towers.

Jr 28 de Julio is pedestrianized for two blocks. A stroll down here leads to the prominent **Arco del Triunfo** (1910), which commemorates victory over the Spaniards. Through the arch is the church of **San Francisco de Asís** (1552) ① *28 de Julio , block 3, daily for morning mass and 1730-1830.* It has an elaborate gilt main altar and several others. Across 28 de Julio from San Fancisco is the **Mercado de Abastos Carlos F Vivanco**, the packed central market. As well as all the household items and local produce, look for the cheese sellers, the breads and the section dedicated to fruit juices.

Santa Clara de Asís ① *Jr Grau, block 3, open for Mass,* is renowned for its beautifully delicate coffered ceiling. It is open for the sale of sweets and cakes made by the nuns (go to the door at Nazarenas 184, it's usually open). On the 5th block of 28 de Julio is the late 16th-century **Casona Vivanco**, which houses the **Museo Andrés A Cáceres** ① *Jr 28 de Julio 508, T066-812360, Mon-Sat 0900-1300, 1400-1800. US$1.25.* The museum has baroque painting, colonial furniture, republican and contemporary art, and exhibits on Mariscal Cáceres' battles in the War of the Pacific. Further south still, on a pretty plazuela, is **Santa Teresa** (1683) ① *28 de Julio, block 6, daily Mass, usually 1600,* with its monastery. The nuns here sell sweets and crystallized fruits and a *mermelada de ají*, made to recipe given to them by God; apparently it is not picante. **San Cristóbal** ① *Jr 28 de Julio, block 6, rarely open,* was the first church to be founded in the city (1540), and is one of the oldest in South America. With its single tower, it is tiny compared with Santa Teresa, which is opposite.

The 16th-century church of **La Merced** ① *2 de Mayo, block , open for Mass,* is the second oldest in the city. The high choir is a good example of the simplicity of the churches of the early period of the Viceroyalty. **Casa Jáuregui**, opposite, is also called **Ruiz de Ochoa** after its original owner. Its outstanding feature is its doorway, which has a blue balcony supported by two fierce beasts with erect penises.

Ayacucho

To Museo Anfasep
To 10
To Pisco & Lima

Mercado Artesanal Shosake Nagase 🅜
To Museo Anfasep

Quinua
6 🚌
ℹ️

Manco Capac
Libertad
Garcilaso de la Vega
9 de Diciembre
Asamblea
Pasaje Cáceres
Los Andes
Miller

To Combis for Huari, Quinua & Huanta

5 🚌
7 🚽
11 🚽
🚽 4
🚽 8
2 🚌

Av Mariscal Cáceres

✉️ 1
Santo Domingo
Bellido
5
🚽 9
Tres Máscaras
Sol
Cuzco
4

Museo de Arte Popular Joaquín López Antay
Callao
15
2 1
🏛️
Casonas de los Marqueses de Mozobamba y del Pozo
Municipalidad
12
Cuzco

Prefectura
Lima
9
12
Casas de Cambio
Plaza Mayor
✝️ Cathedral
ℹ️
Arequipa

La Compañía de Jesús
Centro Turístico Cultural San Cristóbal
San Martín
4 7
Casa Jaúregui
✝️ La Merced
8

Libertad
Grau
28 de Julio
13
Nazareno
Carlos F Vivanco
Arco del Triunfo
Av Ramón Castilla
🚌 10
To Airport & Cuzco

Huancasolar
3 🚌
✝️ Santa Clara
Mercado de Abastos Carlos F Vivanco
San Francisco de Asís
Londres
14
13

S J de Dios
5

Mercado 12 de Abril 🅜
Raymondi
C Chorro
2 de Mayo

Museo Andrés A Cáceres (Casona Vivanco) 🏛️
10

Río Alameda

Santa Teresa
San Cristóbal
To Barrio Santa Ana
To 16
San Cristóbal

N
0 metres 100
0 yards 100

Sleeping 🛏️
Ayacucho Hotel Plaza 1
El Marqués de Valdelirios 16
Florida 4
Grau 5
Hospedaje El Centro 7
Hostal 3 Máscaras 8
Hostal San Blas 13
La Crillonesa 13
La Posada de Santa Inés 10
Marcos 2
San Francisco 15
Santa Rosa 12

Eating 🍴
Brasa Roja 12
Cabo Blanco 10
Café Dorado 11
Chifa Hua Lin 1
La Casona 3
La Miel 9
Las Flores 13
Mía Pizza 4
Nino 5
Portal 1 8

Tradición 7
Urpicha 14

Transport 🚌
Colectivos to Julcamarca 2
Combis to Vilcashuaman 10
Cruz del Sur 5
Libertadores 9
Molina 6

Ormeño 3
Reybus 4
Turismo Los Chankas 8
Wari 1

Museo de Anfasep (Asociación Nacional de Familiares de Secuestrados Detenidos y Desaparecidos del Perú) ⓘ *Prol Libertad 1226, 15 mins' walk fro Mercado Artesanal Shosake Nagase, or mototaxi, entry free but give a donation*, provides an insight into the recent history of this region during the violence surrounding the Sendero Luminoso campaign and the government's attempts to counter it.

For a fascinating insight into Inca and pre-Inca art and culture, a visit to **Barrio Santa Ana** is a must. The district is full of *artesanía* shops, galleries and workshops (eg **Galería de Arte Latina** ⓘ *Plazuela de Santa Ana 105, T528315, wari39@ hotmail.com*, and **Wari Art Gallery** ⓘ *Jr Mcal Cáceres 302, T312529*). Galleries are closed on Sunday.

Excursions

The Inca ruins of **Vilcashuamán** are 120 km the south, beyond Cangallo. Vilcashuamán was an important provincial capital, the crossroads where the road from Cuzco to the Pacific met the empire's north-south highway. Tours can be arranged with Travel Agencies in Ayacucho, US$13 per person, only with eight passengers, full day tour (0500-1800), including **Intihuatana** (Inca baths about one hour uphill from the village of Vischongo, one hour from Vilcashuamán, five from Ayacucho, also Puya Raimondi plants); alternatively stay overnight (three hotels, **G**, basic but clean). Market day is Wednesday. Buses and colectivos run from Avenida M Castilla, daily 0400-1500, four hours, US$3.

A good road going north from Ayacucho leads to **Huari** ⓘ *22 km from Ayacucho, 0800-1700, US$0.90*, dating from the 'Middle Horizon' (AD 600-1000), when the Huari culture spread across most of Peru. This was the first urban walled centre in the Andes. The huge irregular stone walls are up to 3-4 m high and rectangular houses and streets can be made out. The most important activity here was artistic: ceramics, gold, silver, metal and alloys such as bronze, which was used for weapons and for decorative objects. The ruins now lie in an extensive *tuna* cactus forest (don't pick the fruit). There is a museum at the site.

Quinua village, 37 km northeast of Ayacucho, has a charming cobbled main plaza and many of the buildings have been restored. There is a small market on Sunday. Nearby, on the Pampa de Quinua, a 44 m-high obelisk commemorates the battle of Ayacucho. The village's handicrafts are recommended, especially ceramics. Most of the houses have miniature ceramic churches on the roof. San Pedro Ceramics, at the foot of the hill leading to the monument, and Mamerto Sánchez, Jr Sucre, should be visited, but there are many others. *Fiesta de la Virgen de Cocharcas*, around 8 September. Trips can be arranged to Huari, La Quinua village and the battlefield; US$7.55 per person, minimum four people. Combis leave from Paradero a Huari Quinua, corner of Jr Ciro Alegría and Jr Salvador Cavero, when full from 0700; 40 minutes to Huari, US$0.75, then on to Quinua, 25 minutes, US$0.50 (US$1 from Ayacucho – ask the driver to go all the way to the Obelisco for an extra US$0.50).

The Huanta valley is a picturesque region, 48 km northeast of Ayacucho. The town of Huanta is one hour from Ayacucho, on the road to Huancayo (US$0.90 by combi). From Huanta, several lakes can be visited (difficult in rainy season), also the valley of Luricocha, 5 km away, with its warm climate. Huanta celebrates the *Fiesta de las Cruces* during the first week of May. Its Sunday market is large and interesting. There are places to stay and eat around the Plaza.

On the road to Huanta 24 km from Ayacucho, is the site of perhaps the oldest known culture in South America, 20,000 years old, evidence of which was found in the cave of **Pikimachay**. The remains are now in Lima's museums.

⊜ Sleeping

Ayacucho *p1256, map p1257*

B Ayacucho Hotel Plaza, 9 de Diciembre 184, T312202, hplaza@derrama.org.pe. Beautiful colonial building but the rooms don't match up, comfortable, TV, some rooms overlook the plaza.
D Marcos, 9 de Diciembre 143, T316867. Comfortable, modern, in a cul-de-sac ½ block from the Plaza, quiet, hot water, TV, price includes breakfast in the cafetería.
D Santa Rosa, Jr Lima 166, T314614,

www.hotel-santarosa.com. Lovely colonial courtyard in building with historical associations, roof terrace, warm rooms, hot water, attentive staff, car park, good restaurant with good value menú. Recommended.
E Hostal 3 Máscaras, Jr 3 Máscaras 194, T314107, hoteltresmascaras@yahoo.com. New rooms with bath better, but with less character, than the old ones without, nice colonial building with patio, hot water, breakfast extra, car park.

E El Marqués de Valdelirios, Alameda Bolognesi 720, T318944. Lovely colonial-style mansion, beautifully-furnished, pick-up from the airport for US$3, includes breakfast, hot water, bar, reserve at least 24 hrs in advance. Recommended.

E San Francisco, Jr Callao 290, T312353, www.sanfranciscohotel.cjb.net. Breakfast extra (none on Sun), hot water, comfortable, a bit like a museum with a nice patio, popular choice. Recommended.

E-F Florida, Jr Cuzco 310, T312565, F316029. Small, pleasant, quiet, patio with flowers, TV, hot water from electric showers.

F Grau, Jr San Juan de Dios 192, T312695. Rooms on 3rd floor by the markets, **G** without bath, hot water, laundry facilities, good value, safe but noisy, breakfast extra. Recommended.

F Hospedaje El Centro, Av Cáceres 1048, T313556. Rooms without bath and TV are **G**, large rooms, hot water, good value, on a busy avenue.

G Hostal San Blas, Jr Chorro 167, T312712. Hot water, cheaper with shared bath, laundry facilities, nice rooms, cheap meals available, discount for longer stay, kitchen facilities, laundry service, bicycles to lend. Recommended.

G La Crillonesa, El Nazareno 165, T312350, hotelcrillonesa@hotmail.com. Special price for tourists, very good value, hot water, kitchen and laundry facilities, 1 hr free internet, discount for longer stay, great views from roof terrace, loads of information, very helpful, Carlos will act as a local tour guide and knows everyone. Recommended.

G La Posada de Santa Inés, Jr Chorro 139, T319544, posada_staines@hotmail.com. Hot water morning and evening, TV, terrace with small swimming pool (ask in advance for it to be cleaned), good value.

🍴 Eating

Ayacucho *p1256, map p1257*
Those wishing to try *cuy* should do so in Ayacucho as it's a lot cheaper than Cuzco. For a cheap, healthy breakfast, try *maca*, a drink of maca tuber, apple and quinoa, sold outside the market opposite Santa Clara, 0600-0800.

♥♥ Las Flores, Jr José Olaya 106, Plaza Conchopata, east of city. Specializes in *cuy*, open 0900-1900 daily. taxi US$1 from centre.

♥♥ Tradición, San Martín 406. Also specializes in local food; has a good cheap *menú*.

♥♥ Urpicha, Jr Londres 272, T813905. Recommended for typical food.

♥♥-♥ La Casona, Jr Bellido 463. Open 1200-2200. Dining under the arches and in dining room, regional specialities, try their *puca picante* and *cuy*, and a wide menu. Recommended.

♥♥-♥ Nino, Jr 9 de Diciembre 205, on small plaza opposite Santo Domingo church, T814537. Open daily, pleasant decor, terrace and garden (look for the owls in the trees); chicken, pastas, pizzas, including take-away.

♥ Brasa Roja, Jr Cuzco block 1. More upmarket chicken place with food cooked *a la leña*, salads, very good.

♥ Cabo Blanco, Av Maravillas 198, T818740, close to Shosaku Nagase market (see Shopping) .Cebiches, seafood and fish dishes, small place with personal service.

♥ Café Dorado, Jr Asamblea 310. Excellent value set menu and chicken dishes in a long, cavernous dining room, has a wood oven.

♥ Chifa Hua Lin, Asamblea 257. Very popular Chinese, said to be the best in town.

♥ Mía Pizza, San Martín 420-424. Open 1800-2400, for pizzas, pastas and karaoke (also has a bar to get you in the mood for singing).

Cafés
Centro Turístico Cultural San Cristóbal, 28 de Julio 178, some expensive cafés (eg **Lalo's**, No 115, open 0900-2100, **New York**, No 114) as well as other restaurants; all have tables in the pleasant courtyard.

La Miel, Portal Constitución 11-12, 2 locations. Good coffee, hot drinks, juices, shakes, cakes and snacks, also ice cream.

Portal 1, Portal Constitución 1. A good café on the corner of the plaza serving snacks, light meals and ice cream.

✹ Festivals and events

Ayacucho *p1256, map p1257*
The area is well-known for its festivals throughout the year. Almost every day there is a celebration in one of the surrounding villages. Check with the tourist office. **Carnival in Feb** is reported as a wild affair. **Semana Santa** begins on the Fri before Holy Week. There follows one of the world's finest Holy Week celebrations, with candle-lit nightly processions, floral 'paintings' on the streets, daily fairs (the biggest on Easter Saturday), horse races and contests among peoples from all central Peru. All accommodation is fully booked for months in advance. Many people offer beds in their homes during the week. Look out for notices on the doors, especially on Jr Libertad. **25 Apr**: anniversary of the founding of Huamanga province.

◎ Shopping

Ayacucho *p1256, map p1257*
Handicrafts Ayacucho is a good place to buy

local crafts including filigree silver, which often uses *mudéjar* patterns. Also look out for little painted altars which show the manger scene, carvings in local alabaster, harps, or the pre-Inca tradition of carving dried gourds. The most famous goods are carpets and *retablos*. In both weaving and *retablos*, scenes of recent political strife have been added to more traditional motifs. For carpets, go to Barrio Santa Ana, see under Sights above. **Familia Pizarro**, Jr San Cristóbal 215, Barrio Belén. Works in textiles and *piedra huamanga* (local alabaster), good quality. **Mercado 12 de Abril**, Chorro y San Juan de Dios. For fruit and vegetables **Shosaku Nagase**, on Jr Quinua. A large new handicraft market.

▲ Activities and tours

Ayacucho *p1256, map p1257*
Urpillay Tours, Portal Independencia 62, T315074, urpillaytours@terra.com. All local tours and flight tickets. **Wari Tours**, Portal Independencia 70, T311415. Recommended for local tours. Also handles Ormeño bus tickets and Western Union. **Warpa Picchu**, Portal Independencia 66, T315191. All the regular tours, but with an ecotourism angle. **Willy Tours**, Jr 9 de Diciembre 107, T314075. Personal guides, also handles flight and bus tickets.

Guides
Adán Castilla Rivera, T315789, 970 1746 (mob), castilla68@hotmail.com. An archaeologist who guides tours to local sites and the city, very knowledgeable.

⊕ Transport

Ayacucho *p1256, map p1257*
Air From/to **Lima**, 55 mins, with **Aerocóndor** (9 de Diciembre 123, T313060), 3 times a week, via

Andahuaylas, 30 mins. **LC Busre** (Jr Lima 178, T316012) flies from/to Lima daily.
Bus To **Lima**, 9-10 hrs on a good paved road, via Ica (7 hrs). For **Pisco**, 332 km, 6 hrs, take a Ica/Lima bus and get out at San Clemente, 10 mins from Pisco, and take a bus or combi (same fare to San Clemente as for Ica). Companies include: **Wari**, Pasaje Cáceres (opposite ReyBus), T326323, US$5.15 at 1800; and **Reybus**, Pasaje Cáceres 166, US$5.80. More expensive are **Cruz del Sur**, Av Mcal Cáceres 1264, T812813, US$15.15, **Libertadores**, Tres Máscaras 493, T313614, and **Ormeño**, Jr Libertad 257, T312485, US$7.55 and US$12.

To **Huancayo**, 319 km, 9-10 hrs, US$6.65- 7.55. Daily with **Molina**, Jr 9 de Diciembre 458, T312984, 3 a day. The road is paved but poor as far as Huanta, thereafter it is rough, especially in the wet season, except for the last 70 km (paved). The views are breathtaking.

For **Huancavelica**, take an Ormeño 0730 bus as far as **Rumichaca**, US$2, where combis wait at 1030 for Huancavelica, 4 hrs. Otherwise take a Huancayo bus as far as **Izcuchaca**, then take another bus, a longer route.

⊙ Directory

Ayacucho *p1256, map p1257*
Banks BCP, Portal Unión 28. No commission on TCs, cash advance on Visa, Visa ATM. Interbank, Jr 9 de Diciembre 183. ATM for Visa, Mastercard/Cirrus and AmEx. Opening hours 0915-1315, 1630-1830, Sat 0930-1230. Many street changers and *casas de cambio* at Portal Constitución on Plaza, good rate for cash.
Internet All over the centre. Connections and machines are good, average price is US$0.60 per hr, some charge US$0.90 at night. All 0800-2300 daily. **Post office** Asamblea 293. **Telephones** Many phone offices in the centre.

Ayacucho to Cuzco

Beyond Ayacucho are two highland towns, Andahuaylas and Abancay, which are possible stopping, or bus-changing places on the road to Cuzco. The road towards Cuzco climbs out of Ayacucho and crosses a wide stretch of high, treeless páramo before descending through Ocros to the Río Pampas (6 hours from Ayacucho). It then climbs up to **Chincheros**, 158 km from Ayacucho, and Uripa (good Sunday market).

Andahuaylas is about 80 km further on, in a fertile valley. It offers few exotic crafts, but beautiful scenery, great hospitality and a good market on Sunday. On the north side is the Municipalidad, with a small **Museo Arqueológico**, which has a good collection of pre-Columbian objects, including mummies. A good nearby excursion is to the **Laguna de Pacucha** ⓘ *colectivo from Av Los Chankas y Av Andahuaylas, at the back of the market, US$0.75, 40 mins*. On the shore is the town of Pacucha and various places to eat. A road follows the north shore of the lake and a turn-off climbs to **Sóndor** ⓘ *US$0.60 (beware overcharging by the guardian)*, an Inca archaeological site at 3,300 m. Various buildings and small plazas lead up to a conical hill with concentic stone terracing and, at the summit, a large rock or *intihuatana*. Each 18-19 June Sóndor Raymi is celebrated. Taxi from Andahuaylas, US$10; walk from Pachuca 8-10 km, or take a colectivo to Argama (also behind Andahuaylas market), which passes the entrance. With any form of public transport you will have to walk back to Pacucha, unless very lucky. **Tourist office: Dircetur** ① *Av Túpac Amaru 374, T421627.*

Nestled between mountains in the upper reaches of a glacial valley, the friendly town of **Abancay** (*Phone code: 084, Altitude 2,378 m*) is first glimpsed when you are many kilometres away. The town is growing in importance now that the paved Lima-Nazca-Cuzco road passes through. **Tourist office** ① *Lima 206, T321664, 0800-1430,* or **Dircetur,** Av Arenas 121, p 1, T321664. **Santuario Nacional de Ampay** ① *US$1.50,* north of town, has lagoons called Angasccocha (3,200 m) and Uspaccocha (3,820 m), a glacier on Ampay mountain at 5,235 m and flora and fauna typical of these altitudes. By public transport, take a colectivo to Tamburco and ask the driver where to get off. To get to the glacier you need two days trekking, with overnight camping. See page 1247 for sites of interest between Abancay and Cuzco.

● Sleeping

Andahuaylas *p1260*

D **El Encanto de Oro**, Av Pedro Casafranca 424, T723066, www.encantodeoro.4t.com. Modern, comfy, good facilities, breakfast included, TV, hot water, laundry service, restaurant, organizes trips on request. Reserve in advance.

E **Sol de Oro**, Jr Juan A Trelles 164, T721152, soldeorohotel@hotmail.com. Includes breakfast, hot water, TV, laundry service, garage, tourist information, restaurant alongside, near buses.

F **El Encanto de Apurímac**, Jr Ramos 401 (near Los Chankas and other buses), T723527. With bath, hot water, TV, very helpful.

G **Las Américas**, Jr Ramos 410, T721646. Also near buses, a bit gloomy in public areas, but rooms are fine if basic, cheaper without bath, hot water, helpful.

G **Hostal Waliman**, Av Andahuaylas 266. Basic, cold water in shared bathrooms, helpful.

Abancay *p1261*

C-D **Turistas**, Av Díaz Barcenas 500, T321017, hotursa@terra.com.pe. The original building is in colonial style, rooms (D) a bit gloomy, breakfast not included. Newer rooms on top floor (best) and in new block (C), including breakfast. Good restaurant (�♈), wood panelled bar, internet (US$0.60 per hour), parking.

E **Imperial**, Díaz Barcenas 517, T321538. Great beds and hot water, spotless, very helpful, parking, good value, rooms also available without bath or breakfast.

F **Hostal Arenas**, Av Arenas 192, T322107. Brand new hotel almost finished beside the old one, well-appointed rooms, good beds, hot showers, TV, internet, helpful service, restaurant.

G **Apurímac Tours**, Jr Cuzco 421, T321446. New building, rooms with bath have tiny bathrooms, hot water, breakfast and lunch extra in *comedor* in courtyard, good value, helpful.

● Eating

Andahuaylas *p1260*

♈ **El Dragón**, Jr Juan A Trellas 279. A recommended chifa serving huge portions, excellent value (same owner as Hotel El Encanto de Apurímac).

♈ **Il Gatto**, Jr G Cáceres 334. A warm pizzería, with wooden furniture, pizzas cooked in a wood-burning oven.

♈ **Nuevo Horizonte**, Jr Constitución 426. Vegetarian and health food restaurant, open for breakfast.

Abancay *p1261*

♈ **Focarela Pizzería**, Díaz Bárcenas 521, T083-322036. Simple but pleasant décor, pizza from a wood-burning oven, fresh, generous toppings, popular (ask for vino de la casa!).

♈ **Pizzería Napolitana**, Diaz Barcenas 208. Wood-fired clay oven, wide choice of toppings.

▲ Activities and tours

Abancay *p1261*

Apurimak Tours, at Hotel Turistas, see Sleeping. Run local tours and 1 and 2-day trips to Santuario Nacional de Ampay: one-day, 7 hours, US$40 per person for 1-2 people (cheaper for more people). Also a 3-day trip to Choquequirao including transport, guide, horses, tents and food, just bring your sleeping-bag, US$60 pp.

Carlos Valer, guide in Abancay - ask for him at Hotel Turistas, very knowledgeable and kind.

● Transport

Ayacucho to Cuzco *p1260*

Ayacucho to Andahuaylas, 261 km, takes 10-11 hrs (more in the rainy season), the road is unpaved but in good condition when dry, but landslides occur in the wet. The scenery is stunning. Daytime buses stop for lunch at Chumbes (4½ hrs), which has a few restaurants, a shop selling fruit, bread and refrescos, and some grim toilets. **Wari** at 0400; **Los Chankas**, Pasaje Cáceres 144, T312391, at 0630 (good) and 1900, all US$7.55. Only Los Chankas' 1900 service is direct to **Cuzco**, US$12, but you still have to change buses in Andahuaylas. There are no other direct buses to Abancay or Cuzco.

Andahuaylas to Ayacucho: Wari, Av José María Arguedas opposite El Piloto petrol station, at 0800; **Los Chankas**, Av José María Arguedas y Jr Trelles, T722441, 0600 and 1800 or 1840, one coming from Cuzco. To **Abancay**, **Señor de Huanca**, Av Martinelli 170, T721218, 3 a day, 5 hrs, US$3.40; **Los Chankas** at 0630, US$4. To **Cuzco**, San Jerónimo, Av José María Arguedas 425, T801767, via Abancay, 1800 or 1830, also 1900 Sun, US$6, and **Los Chankas**. To **Lima**, buses go via Ayacucho or Pampachiri and Puquio: **Wari** take the latter route, 3 a day, US$15.15. On all night buses, take a blanket.

In **Abancay**, 138 km from Andahuaylas, 5 hrs, the new Terminal Terrestre is on Av Pachacútec, on the west side of town. Taxi to centre US$0.60, otherwise it's a steep walk up to the centre. Several companies have offices on or near the El Olivo roundabout at Av Díaz Bárcenas y Gamarra, others on Av Arenas. Buses go to **Cuzco**, **Andahuaylas**, and **Nazca** (464 km, via Chalhuanca and Puquio), continuing to **Lima**. To **Cuzco**, 195 km, takes 4½ hrs, US$3.65. The scenery en route is dramatic, especially as it descends into the Apurímac valley and climbs out again.

Bus companies, all leave from Terminal Terrestre; office addresses are given: Bredde, Gamarra 423,T321643, 5 a day to Cuzco. **Cruz del Sur**, Díaz Bárcenas 1151, T323028. **Los Chankas**, Díaz Bárcenas 1011, El Olivo, T321485. **Molina**, Gamarra 422, T322646. 3 a day to Cuzco, to Andahuaylas at 2330. **San Jerónimo**, to Cuzco at 2130 and Andahuaylas at 2130. **Señor de Huanca**, Av Arenas 198, T322377, 3 a day to Andahuaylas. **Wari**, Av Arenas 200 block, 6 a day to Lima, also to Andahuaylas. Several others to Lima and Cuzco.

❶ Directory

Ayacucho to Cuzco *p1260*
Andahuaylas and **Abancay** have ATMs, **casas de cambio** and plenty of internet cabins.

East and north of La Oroya

A paved road heads north from La Oroya towards Cerro de Pasco and Huánuco. Just 25 km north of La Oroya a branch turns east towards Tarma, then descends to the relatively little-visited jungles of the Selva Central. This is a really beautiful run. North of La Oroya the road crosses the great heights of the Junín pampa and the mining zone of Cerro de Pasco, before losing altitude on its way to the Huallaga Valley. On this route you can connect by road to the Cordillera Blanca via La Unión.

Tarma and around → *Phone code: 064. Colour map 3, grid C3. Population: 105,200. Altitude: 3,050 m.*
Founded in 1538, Tarma, 60 km from La Oroya, is a growing city but still has a lot of charm. The **Semana Santa celebrations** are spectacular, with a very colourful Easter Sunday morning procession in the main plaza. Accommodation is hard to find at this time, but you can apply to the Municipalidad for rooms with local families. The town is also notable for its locally made fine flower-carpets. Good, friendly market around C Amazonas and Ucayali. The surrounding countryside is beautiful. **Tourist office** ① *2 de Mayo 775 on the Plaza, T321010, turistarma@hotmail.com, very helpful. Mon-Fri 0800-1300, 1600-1800*. Around 8 km from Tarma, the small town of **Acobamba** has *tapices* made in San Pedro de Cajas which depict the Crucifixion. There are festivities during May. About 2 km up beyond the town is the **Santuario de Muruhuay**, with a venerated picture painted on the rock behind the altar.

Beyond Tarma the road is steep and crooked but there are few places where cars cannot pass one another. In the 80 km between Tarma and La Merced the road, passing by great overhanging cliffs, drops 2,450 m and the vegetation changes dramatically from temperate to tropical. The towns of San Ramón and La Merced are collectively known as **Chanchamayo** (*Population 7,000*). **San Ramón** is 11 km before La Merced and has several hotels (**C-G**) and restaurants. There are regular combis and colectivos between the two towns. **La Merced** (*Population 15,000*), lies in the fertile Chanchamayo valley. Campa Indians can usually be found around the central plaza selling bows, arrows, necklaces and trinkets. There is a festival in the last week of September. There are several hotels (**C-F**) and restaurants.

About 22 km north from La Merced is **San Luis de Shuaro**, from where the road has been extended over an intervening mountain range. A turn-off east leads to **Puerto Bermúdez**. This is a great base for exploring further into the San Matías/San Carlos national reserve in the Selva Central Peruana, with trips upriver to the Asháninca communities. Tours arranged by **Albergue Humboldt** cost US$18-28 a day, depending on group size. Boat passages possible from passing traders. To go further downriver to Pucallpa, there is transport via Puerto Palcazu, US$10.

North of La Oroya

A paved road runs 130 km north from La Oroya to Cerro de Pasco. It runs up the Mantaro valley through canyons to the wet and mournful Junín pampa at over 4,250 m, one of the world's largest high-altitude plains. An obelisk marks the battlefield where the Peruvians under Bolívar defeated the Spaniards in 1824. Blue peaks line the pampa in a distant wall. This windswept sheet of yellow grass is bitterly cold and the only signs of life are the youthful herders with their sheep and llamas. The road follows the east shores of the Lago de Junín. The town of **Junín** lies some distance south of the lake and has the somewhat desolate feel of a high puna town, bisected by the railway.

The **Lago Junín National Reserve** ⓘ *US$5, ticket from Inrena in Junín*, protects one of the best bird-watching sites in the central Andes where the giant coot and even flamingos may be spotted. It is easiest to visit from the village of Huayre, 5 km south of Carhuamayo, from which it is a 20-minute walk down to the lake. Fishermen are usually around to take visitors out on the lake. Carhuamayo is the best place to stay: *Gianmarco*, Maravillas 454, and *Patricia*, Tarapacá 862, are the best of several basic *hostales*. There are numerous restaurants along the main road.

Cerro de Pasco → *Phone code: 063. Population: 29,810. Altitude: 4,330 m.*

This long-established mining centre, 130 km from La Oroya, is not attractive, but is nevertheless very friendly. Copper, zinc, lead, gold and silver are mined here, and coal comes from the deep canyon of Goyllarisquisga, the 'place where a star fell', the highest coal mine in the world, 42 km north of Cerro de Pasco. The town is sited between Lago Patarcocha and the huge abyss of the mine above which its buildings and streets cling precariously. Nights are bitterly cold. *BCP* is on Jr Bolognesi. Money changers can be found on Jr Bolognesi between the market and the Cathedral.

Southwest of Cerro de Pasco by 40 km is **Huayllay**, near which is the **Santuario Bosque de Piedras** ⓘ *US$1, payable only if the guides, Ernesto and Christian, are there, camping is permitted within the Sanctuary*. These unique weathered limestone formations are in the shape of a tortoise, elephant, alpaca, etc. At the Sanctuary (4,100-4,600 m), four tourist circuits through the spectacular rock formations have been laid out. The village of Huallay is 30 minutes beyond the sanctuary entrance. The Central Highway from Cerro de Pasco continues northeast another 528 km to Pucallpa, the limit of navigation for large Amazon river boats. The western part of this road (Cerro de Pasco-Huánuco) has been rebuilt into an all-weather highway. The sharp descent along the nascent **Río Huallaga** is a tonic to travellers suffering from *soroche*. The road drops 2,436 m in the 100 km from Cerro de Pasco to Huánuco, and most of it is in the first 32 km. From the bleak high ranges the road plunges below the tree line offering great views. The only town of any size before Huánuco is **Ambo**.

Huánuco → *Phone code: 062. Colour map 3, grid B3. Population: 118,814. Altitude: 1,894 m.*

This is an attractive Andean town on the Upper Huallaga with an interesting market. **Tourist office** ⓘ *Gen Prado 716, on the Plaza de Armas, T512980.* A website giving local information is www.webhuanuco.com. About 5 km away on the road west to La Unión is *Kótosh* (*Altitude 1,912 m*) ⓘ *US$0.75, including a guide around a marked circuit which also passes through a small botanical garden of desert plants, taxi US$5 from the centre, with 30 mins' wait.* At this archaeological site, the Temple of Crossed Hands, the earliest evidence of a complex society and of pottery in Peru, dates from 2000 BC. From Huánuco, a spectacular but very poor dirt road leads to **La Unión**, capital of Dos de Mayo district. It's a friendly, fast developing town with a couple of hotels (**E** to **G**) and restaurants, but electricity can be a problem and it gets very cold at night. On the pampa above La Unión are the Inca ruins of **Huánuco Viejo** ⓘ *US$1.50, allow 2 hrs*, a 2½ hour walk from the town, a great temple-fortress with residential quarters. It has impressive Inca stonework and a fine section of Inca road running south. The route to the Callejón de Huaylas goes through **Huallanca (Huánuco)**, an attractive town, with mining projects nearby. Check local political conditions before taking this route. See Transport, below.

😴 Sleeping

Tarma *p1262*

B Los Portales, Av Castilla 512, T321411, www.hoteleslosportales.com. Out of town, hot water, heating, quiet, includes breakfast, good restaurant.

C Hacienda La Florida, 6 km from Tarma, T341041, www.haciendalaflorida.com. 18th-century, working hacienda, with hot water, includes breakfast, other meals extra, owned by German-Peruvian couple Inge and Pepe who arrange excursions. Recommended. Also camping for US$3.

C Hacienda Santa María, 2 km out of town at Sacsamarca 1249, T321232, www.haciendasantamaria.com. A beautiful (non-working) 17th-century hacienda, beautiful gardens and antique furniture. Includes breakfast and light evening meal. Excellent guides for local day trips. Recommended.

E Hostal Campestre Auberge Normandie, beside the Santuario de Muruhuay, Acobamba, T064-349 5440, www.normandie.com.pe. 16 cabins with hot water, TV, bar, restaurant.

D-E El Caporal, Lima 616, T323636, hostalelcaporal@yahoo.es. Includes breakfast, good location, hot water, cable TV. Recommended.

F La Colmena, Jauja 618, T321157. Old building, convenient for Huancayo buses.

F Hostal Central, Huánuco 614, T310149. Shared bath, hot water, laundry facilities, bit rundown but popular, has observatory (opens Fri 2000).

F Hostal El Márquez, Huaraz 389, T321060. Old building with character, shared showers, hot water.

G Hostal El Dorado, Huánuco 488, T321598. Hot water, cheaper without bath, rooms set round a patio, first floor rooms better, reasonable.

Puerto Bermúdez *p1263*

G pp Albergue Cultural Humboldt, by the Río Pachitea at La Rampa, T063-830020, www.geocities.com. US$5 extra for 3 meals a day. The owner, Basque writer Jesús, has created a real haven for backpackers, with maps, library and book exchange. Recommended. Jesús will arrange tours, from day trips to camping and trekking in the primary forest. Ask him about volunteering at a local Asháninka school.

Cerro de Pasco *p1263*

D Señorial, in the district of San Juan, 5 mins north of Cerro by taxi, T721026, hotelsenorial@hotmail.com. The most comfortable in town, hot water, TV, and a fine view back across the mine pit.

E Wong, Carrión 99, T721515. Hot water 24 hrs, TV, run-down and noisy but friendly, motorcycle parking.

F Hostal Arenales, Jr Arenales 162, near the bus station, T723088. Modern, TV, hot water in the morning.

F Welcome, Av La Plata 125, opposite the entrance to the bus station, T721883. Some rooms without window, hot water 24 hrs.

Huánuco *p1263*

B Grand Hotel Huánuco, Jr D Beraun 775, T514222, www.grandhotelhuanuco.com. Includes breakfast, internet, restaurant, pool, sauna, gym, parking. Recommended.

D Hostal Caribe, Huánuco 546, T513645, and adjoining it **D Hostal Mariño**. Two large modern hotels with big rooms, TV.

E Hostal Miraflores, Valdizan 564, T512848, www.granhostalmiraflores.com. Hot water and cable TV, quiet, safe, laundry service.

F Imperial, Huánuco 581, T518737. With cold shower (intermittent water), reasonable value, clean and quiet.

F Las Vegas, 28 de Julio 936, on Plaza de Armas, T/F512315. Small rooms, hot water, TV. Restaurant next door. Good.

G El Roble, Constitución 629, T512515. Without bath, clean, good value.

Huallanca *p1263*

E Hotel Milán, 28 de Julio 107. Modern, TV and hot water, best in town, good restaurant.

G Hostal Yesica, L Prado 507. Hot water, shared bathroom, the best of the basic ones.

🍴 Eating

Tarma *p1262*

♥ Chifa Roberto Siu, Lima 557. A good option for Chinese food, popular with locals.

♥ Comedor Vegetariano, Arequipa 695. Open 0700-2100, vegetarian, small and cheap, sells great bread.

♥ Lo Mejorcito de Tarma, Arequipa 501. Open 0700-2300. Good set menú US$1.50, local specialities, also has tourist information.

♥ Señorial/Pollería Braserita, Huánuco 138. Good *menú*, extensive choice, open late.

Cerro de Pasco *p1263*

♥ Los Angeles, Jr Libertad, near the market. Excellent *menú* for US$1.50. Recommended.

♥ San Fernando, bakery in the plaza. Opens at 0700, great hot chocolate, bread and pastries.

Huánuco *p1263*

♥ Chifa Men Ji, 28 de Julio, block 8. Good prices, nice Chinese food.

♥ Govinda, 2 de Mayo 1044. Reckoned to be the best vegetarian restaurant.

¶ **La Olla de Barro**, Gral Prado 852, close to main plaza. Serves typical food, good value.
¶ **Pizzería Don Sancho**, Prado 645. Best pizzas in town.

⊛ Festivals and events

Huánuco *p1263*
20-25 Jan: is Carnaval Huanuqueño. **3 May**: La Cruz de Mayo. **16 Jul**: Fiesta de la Virgen del Carmen. **12-18 Aug**: Tourist Week in Huánuco. **28-29 Oct**: Fiesta del Rey y del Señor de Burgos, the patron of Huánuco.
25 Dec: Fiesta de los Negritos.

⊖ Transport

Tarma *p1262*
Bus To **Lima**, 231 km (paved), 6 hrs, US$5.50. Transportes Chanchamayo, Callao 1002, T321882, recommended, 3 a day, en route from Chanchamayo; Transportes Junín, Amazonas 667, 3 a day, with *bus cama* night bus. Trans La Merced, Vienrich 420, 3 a day. Trans Muruhuay, Huaraz y Amazonas, (several daily) start in Tarma. To **Jauja** and **Huancayo**, Transportes San Juan, from the stadium hourly on the half hour, buses coming from Chanchamayo; Trans Muruhuay leave when full, 0500-1800, to Jauja 2 hrs, US$2. All buses continue to Huancayo, 3 hrs, US$3. Colectivos depart when full from Callao y Jauja, 2 hrs, US$4, and 3 hrs, US$6, respectively. To **Cerro de Pasco**, Empresa Junín, Amazonas 450, 4 a day, 3 hrs, US$2.50. Also colectivos when full, 2 hrs, US$4. Buses to **La Oroya** leave from opposite the petrol station on Av Castilla block 5, 1 hr, US$1.25, while colectivos leave from the petrol station itself, 45 mins, US$2. To **Chanchamayo**, Transportes San Juan from the stadium every hour on the half hour, 1½ hrs, US$1.50 to San Ramón, and 2 hrs, US$1.75 to La Merced. Also, colectivos, 1-1¼ hrs, US$3 and US$3.50 respectively.
   Colectivos and Canary **buses** to **Acobamba** and up to **Muruhuay** every 10 mins, US$0.35.

San Ramón *p1262*
Air Flights leave from San Ramón. There is a small airstrip where **Aero Montaña**, T064-339191, rfmamsa@hotmail.com, has air taxis that can be chartered (*viaje especial*) to the jungle towns, with a maximum of 3 people, but you have to pay for the pilot's return to base. Flights cost US$250 per hr. **Puerto Bermúdez** takes 33 mins. You can also just go to the air base, across the river, on the east side of town.

La Merced *p1262*
Bus Many buses go here from **Lima**: Expreso

Satipo, Trans Lobato, Junín, La Merced and Chanchamayo (recommended) each have several buses during the day, 8 hrs, US$6.50. To **Tarma** Transportes San Juan, hourly, 2½ hrs, US$1.75, or Selva Tours colectivos, just over 1 hr, US$3.50. To **Puerto Bermúdez** Empresa Transdife, Villarrica and Servicio Especial all have 4WD pick-ups or minibuses and go at 0330 and 0430 (or when full). You can buy your tickets in advance at the bus terminal, US$8.80; standing in the back of pick-up US$7; seat in pick-up cabin, US$10. This is not a paved road and takes around 8 hrs in the dry season.

Huayllay *p1263*
Minibuses to Huallay from Cerro de Pasco's terminal leave throughout the day, about 1 hr, US$1. They return until 1800-1900.

Cerro de Pasco *p1263*
Bus There is a large bus station. To **Lima** several companies including Carhuamayo and Transportes Apóstol San Pedro, hourly 0800-1200, plus 4 departures 2030-2130, 8 hrs, US$4-5. If there are no convenient daytime buses, you could change buses in La Oroya. To **Carhuamayo, Junín** and **La Oroya**: buses leave when full, about every 20-30 mins, to Carhuamayo 1 hr, US$1; to Junín 1½ hrs, US$1; to La Oroya, 2½ hrs, US$2. Colectivos also depart with a similar frequency, 1½ hrs, US$2.50, to La Oroya.
   To **Tarma**, Empresa Junín, 0600, 1500, 3 hrs, $2.50. Colectivos also depart hourly, 1½ hrs, US$4. To **Huancayo**, various companies leave throughout the day, 5 hrs, US$4. To **Huánuco**, buses and cars leave when full, about half hourly, 2½ hrs and 1½ hrs, US$2 and US$4 respectively.

Huánuco *p1263*
Air Airport T513066. From **Lima**, LCBusre (2 de Mayo 1355, T518113), daily, 55 mins.
Bus To **Lima**, US$9, 8 hrs. León de Huánuco, Malecón Alomía Robles 821, 3 a day. Also Bahía Continental, Valdizan 718, recommended, Transportes El Rey, 28 de Julio 1215 (28 de Julio 1192, La Victoria, Lima). The majority of buses of all companies leave 2030-2200, most also offer a bus at 0900-1000. A colectivo to Lima, costing US$20, leaves at 0400, arriving at 1400; book the night before at Gen Prado 607, 1 block from the plaza. Recommended. To **Cerro de Pasco**, 3 hrs, US$2, colectivos under 2 hrs, US$4. All leave when full from the Ovalo Carhuayna on the north side of the city, 3 km from the centre. To **Huancayo**, 7 hrs, US$6: Turismo Central, Tarapacá 530, at 2100. Colectivos run to **Tingo María**, from block 1 of Prado close to Puente Calicanto, 2½ hrs, US$5. Also Etnasa, 3-4 hrs, US2.

For **Pucallpa**, take a colectivo to Tingo María, then a bus from there. This route has many checkpoints and robberies can occur. Travel by day and check on the current situation regarding safety. To **La Unión**, Transportes El Niño, Aguilar 530, colectivos, depart when full, 5 hrs, US$7.15. This is a rough road operated by old buses of which **Transportes Santa Peregrina**, Tarapacá 448, and **Transportes Rosario**, Tarapacá 400 block, 0730, 6 hrs, US$5.70, are the most reliable.

La Unión *p1263*
Bus To **Huánuco**: *El Niño* colectivos, Jr Comercio 12, T062-515952, 5 hrs, US$7.15; bus companies leave at 0630 (no afternoon/evening departures), 5-6 hrs, US$4.

To **Huallanca (Huánuco)**, combis leave from the market, about half hourly, when full and follow the attractive Vizcarra valley, 1 hr, US$0.75. Then take an *El Rápido* bus to Huaraz. Combis leave when full about half hourly, from the corner of Comercio y 28 de Julio in Huallanca for La Unión.

🛈 Directory

Tarma *p1262*
Banks BCP, Lima 407, changes Amex TCs, ATM.
Internet Internet offices all along Av Lima and Malecón José Gálvez. **Telephones** On the Plaza de Armas.

Huánuco *p1263*
Banks BCP, at Dos de Mayo 1005, Visa ATM.
Internet Several in the centre. **Post offices** 2 de Mayo on the Plaza. Open 0800-2000 Mon-Sat, 0800-1400 Sun. **Telephones** 28 de Julio 1170.

Amazon Basin

Cooled by winds sweeping down from the Andes but warmed by its jungle blanket, this region contains important tropical flora and fauna. In the north of the region, Iquitos, on the Amazon itself, is the centre of jungle exploration. It is a very varied landscape, with grasslands and tablelands of scrub-like vegetation, inaccessible swamps, and forests up to 2,000 m above sea level. The principal means of communication in the jungle is by its many rivers, the most important being the Amazon, which rises high up in the Andes as the Marañón, then joins the Ucayali to become the longest river in the world. The northern tourist area is based on the River Amazon itself with, at its centre, a sizeable city, Iquitos. Although it has lost its rubber-boom dynamism, Iquitos is still at the heart of life on the river. There are jungle lodges upstream and down, each with its own speciality and level of comfort, but none more than half a day away by fast boat. To get right into the wilds, head for Peru's largest national reserve, Pacaya-Samiria, accessed by boat from Iquitos or the little town of Lagunas.

North from Huánuco to Pucallpa

Huánuco to Tingo María
The journey to Tingo María from Huánuco, 135 km, is very dusty but gives a good view of the jungle. Some 25 km beyond Huánuco the road begins a sharp climb to the heights of Carpish (3,023 m). A descent of 58 km brings it to the Huallaga River again; it then continues along the river to Tingo María. The road is paved from Huánuco to Tingo María, including a tunnel through the Carpish hills. Landslides along this section are frequent and construction work causes delays. Although this route is reported to be relatively free from terrorism, robberies do occur and it is advisable to travel only by day.

Situated on the middle Huallaga, in the Ceja de Montaña, on the edge (literally 'eyebrow') of the mountains, **Tingo María** *(Phone code 062, Population 20,560, Altitude 655 m, Annual rainfall 2,642 mm)* is isolated for days in the rainy season. The altitude prevents the climate from being oppressive. The Cordillera Azul, the front range of the Andes, covered with jungle-like vegetation to its top, separates it from the jungle lowlands to the east. The mountain which can be seen from all over the town is called La Bella Durmiente, the Sleeping Beauty. The meeting here of highlands and jungle makes the landscape extremely striking. Bananas, sugar cane, cocoa, rubber, tea and coffee are grown. The main crop of the area, though, is coca, grown on the *chacras* (smallholdings) in the countryside, and sold legitimately and otherwise in Tingo María. A small university outside the town, beyond the *Hotel Madera Verde*, has a little

museum-cum-zoo ① *free but a small tip would help to keep things in order*; it also maintains botanical gardens in the town. About 6½ km from Tingo, on a rough road, is a fascinating cave, the **Cueva de las Lechuzas** ① *US$0.90 for the cave, take a torch, and do not wear open shoes, getting there: take a motorcycle-taxi from town, US$1.75; cross the Río Monzón by new bridge.* There are many oilbirds in the cave and many small parakeets near the entrance. **Tourist office** ① *Av Ericson 162, T562310, cataperu10@hotmail.com*. Note that Tingo María is a main narco-trafficking centre and although the town is generally safe, it is not safe to leave it at night. Always keep to the main routes.

Tingo María to Pucallpa

From Tingo María to the end of the road at Pucallpa is 255 km, with a climb over the watershed - the Cordillera Azul – between the Huallaga and Ucayali rivers. The road is in poor shape for most of the journey, but some paving is in progress. Travel by day: it is safer the views are tremendous as you go from the high jungle to the Amazon Basin. Sit on the righthand side of the bus. When the road was being surveyed it was thought that the lowest pass over the Cordillera Azul was over 3,650 m high, but an old document stating that a Father Abad had found a pass through these mountains in 1757 was rediscovered, and the road now goes through the pass of Father Abad, a gigantic gap 4 km long and 2,000 m deep. At the top of the pass is a Peruvian Customs house; the jungle land to the east is a free zone. Coming down from the pass the road bed is along the floor of a magnificent canyon, the Boquerón Abad. It is a beautiful trip through luxuriant jungle, ferns and sheer walls of bare rock, punctuated by occasional waterfalls plunging into the roaring torrent below. East of the foot of the pass the all-weather road goes over the flat pampa, with few bends, to the village of **Aguaytía** (narcotics police outpost, gasoline, accommodation in the **F Hostal San Antonio**, clean, and two restaurants). From Aguaytía the road continues for 160 km to Pucallpa - five hours by bus. There is a service station three hours before Pucallpa.

Pucallpa → *Phone code: 061. Colour map 3, grid B3. Population: 400, 000.*

Pucallpa is a rapidly expanding jungle town on the Río Ucayali, navigable by vessels of 3,000 tons from Iquitos, 533 nautical miles away. The town's newer sections have paved streets, sewers and lights, but much of the frontier atmosphere still exists. The floating ports of La Hoyada and Puerto Italia are about 5 km away and worth a visit to see the canoe traffic and open-air markets. (When river levels are low, boats leave from a different port, Pucallpillo.) The economy of the area includes sawmills, plywood factories, a paper mill, oil refinery, fishing and boat building. Large discoveries of oil and gas are being explored, and gold mining is underway nearby. Local festivals are *Carnival* in February, *San Juan* on 24 June, and the Ucayali regional fair in October. The town is hot and dusty between June and November and muddy from December to May. **Note** There is narcotics activity in the area. The city itself is safe enough to visit, but don't travel at night. **Museo Regional** ① *Jr Inmaculada 999, 0800-1200, 1600-1800,US$0.90,* has some good examples of Shibipo ceramics, as well as some delightful pickled snakes and other reptiles. **Tourist office** Dirección Regional de Turismo ① *Jr 2 de Mayo 111, T571303, ucayali@mincetur.gob.pe, Mon-Fri 0730-1300, 1330-1515.* Information also at **CTAR-Ucayali**, Raimondi block 220, T575018, oppto-ucayali@pres.gob.pe.

Around Pucallpa The Hospital Amazónico Albert Schweitzer, which serves the local *indigena*, is on picturesque Lake **Yarinacocha** ① *20 mins by colectivo or bus from the market in Pucallpa, US$0.30, or 15 mins by taxi, US$2,* the main tourist attraction near Pucallpa. River dolphins can be seen in the lake. There are many restaurants on the waterfront and near the plaza. A good place to swim is at **San José**; take the road out behind the power station.

San Francisco and **Santa Clara** can be visited at the far end of the lake on its western arm. Both are Shibipo villages still practising traditional ceramic and textile crafts. In San Francisco a nice place to spend the night is in the house of Alberto Sánchez Ríos (Casa Artesanal Shibipo), which is very friendly and warmly recommended. To reach these villages take one of the motorized canoes, *peke-pekes,* which leave from Puerto Callao when full, US$0.90.

The beautifully located reserve, **Jardín Botánico Chullachaqui** *free,* can be reached by boat from Puerto Callao, the port on Lake Yarinacocha, to Pueblo Nueva Luz de Fátima, 45 minutes, then one hour's walk to the garden. For information about traditional medicine contact Mateo Arevalomayna, San Francisco de Yarinacocha (president of the group Ametra; T573152, or ask at Moroti-Shobo).

😴 Sleeping

See also Activities and tours below for more information on lodges. Hotels are often ful,.

Tingo María *p1266*

C Madera Verde, Av Universitaria s/n, out of town on the road to Huánuco, near the University, T/F561800, maverde@terra.com.pe. Chalets in beautiful surroundings, with and without bath, restaurant, swimming pool.

E Hospedaje Agroturístico Villa Jennifer, Km 3.4 Carretera a Castillo Grande, 10 mins from Tingo María, T960 3509, www.villajennifer.es.vg. Danish-Peruvian owned, includes breakfast, weekend packages and tours to local sites, birdwatching, restaurant, laundry service. Rooms are surrounded by local flora, with lots of birdlife.

F Hostal Marco Antonio, Jr Monzón 364, T562201. Quiet, restaurant of the same name next door.

F Nueva York, Av Alameda Perú 553, T562406. Cheaper without bath and TV, laundry, good value, restaurant.

Pucallpa *p1267*

A Sol del Oriente, Av San Martín 552, T/F575154, hsoliriente@qnet.com.pe. Price includes breakfast, pool, minizoo, good restaurant.

E Arequipa, Jr Progreso 573, T571348. Good but no a/c, comfortable, safe, TV, restaurant.

E Mercedes, Raimondi 601, T575120. Good, but noisy with good bar and restaurant attached, swimming pool.

F Barbtur, Raimondi 670, T572532. **F** without bath, central, good beds.

F Komby, Ucayali 360, T571184. Comfortable, swimming pool, excellent value.

F Sun, Ucayali 380. Cheaper without bath, good value, next to *Komby*.

Yarinacocha *p1267*

C La Cabaña Lodge, T616679. Full board, including transport to and from Yarinacocha harbour, run by Ruth and Leroy from USA, great food, jungle trips US$50 per day including boat, guide and food.

C-D pp La Perla, next door to La Cabaña Lodge. Price includes all meals, German-Peruvian owned, English and German spoken, no electricity after 2100, jungle tours organized.

D Jana Shobo Amazonian Lodge, Lake Yarinacocha, T596943, www.janashobo.tk. Small lodge is set in 10 ha of forest on the lakeshore. Price includes meals and airport transfer, packages and tours available. Camping possible,

living room, reading room and kitchen.

E-F Los Delfines, T571129. With bath, fan, fridge, some with TV.

G El Pescador, in Puerto Callao, cheapest in town, restaurant.

🍴 Eating

Tingo María *p1266*

♥ El Antojito 2, Jr Chiclayo 458. Local food.

♥ Girasol, Av Raimondi 253, T562065. Chicken, burgers, cakes and fruit juices.

Pucallpa *p1267*

♥♥ El Alamo, Carretera Yarinacocha 2650, T571510. Good typical food.

🍸 Bars and clubs

Pucallpa *p1267*

Billy's Place, on Arica, on the street east of Jr Mcal Cáceres. A decent bar run by an American called Rick (Billy is his pet jaguar). He only sells beer, has TV and pinball. All the locals know it; the area is very dark late at night.

🛍 Shopping

Pucallpa *p1267*

Many Shibipo women carry and sell their products around Pucallpa and Yarinacocha. **Agustín Rivas**, at Jr Tarapacá 861, above a small restaurant whose entrance is at No 863 (ask for it). For local wood carvings visit the workshop of this sculptor, whose work is made from huge tree roots. **Artesanías La Selva**, Jr Tarapacá 868, has a reasonable selection of indigenous craftwork.

⛰ Activities and tours

Tingo María *p1266*

Tingo María Travel Tours, Av Raimondi 460, T562501. For local excursions.

Pucallpa *p1267*

If organizing a group tour with the boatmen on the waterfront, expect to pay around US$30 per day pp. Only use accredited guides. **Laser Viajes y Turismo**, Raimondi 470, T571120. Helpful, recommended for planning a jungle trip.

🚌 Transport

Tingo María *p1266*

Bus To **Huánuco**, 119 km, 3-4 hrs, US$2 with Etnasa (not recommended - theft and drug-trafficking); take a micro, US$2, or colectivo, US$5, 2 hrs, several daily. Direct buses continue to Lima, 12 hrs, with **Trans Rey**, US$15 *bus cama*, **León de Huánuco** and **Bahía** (T01-424 1539), US$11. To **Pucallpa**, 255 km, 12 hrs, US$4.30-8.50. **Ucayali Express** colectivos leave from Raimondi y Callao. There are other colectivos and taxis, which all leave in the early morning in convoy.

Pucallpa *p1267*
Air To **Lima**, 1 hr, daily flights with **WayraPerú** (Jr Coronel Portillo 522, T592715) and **Star Perú** (7 de Junio 865, T590585). Airport to town, bus US$0.25; taxi US$1; taxi US$2-3.
Bus There are regular bus services to **Lima**, 812 km, 18-20 hrs (longer in the rainy season, Nov-Mar), US$11. To **Tingo María**, 255 km, 7-9 hrs, US$4.30-8.50, combis leave at 0600, 0700 and 0800 with **Ucayali Express**, 7 de Junio y San Martín. All buses have police guard and go in convoy. Take blankets as the crossing of the Cordillera at night is bitterly cold.
Ferry To **Iquitos** the trip takes 3-5 days, and costs US$20 pp for hammock space, or US$30 for a bed in a cabin.
 You must ask around for the large boats to Iquitos; they can be docked at Puerto La Hoyada, Puerto Italia or Pucallpillo. A mototaxi to any of the ports costs US$0.75 from the Plaza de Armas, taxis charge US$3. The Capitanía on the waterfront may give you information about sailings, but this is seldom reliable. Departure times are marked on chalk boards on the deck. Schedules seem to change almost hourly. Do not

pay for your trip before you board the vessel, and only pay the captain. Some boat captains may allow you to live on board a couple of days before sailing. Bottled drinking water can be bought in Pucallpa, but not cheaply. See General hints for river travel, page 1275.

ⓘ Directory

Tingo María *p1266*
Internet Several places on Raimondi and near Plaza de Armas, fast and cheap but strange hours.

Pucallpa *p1267*
Banks It is easy to change dollars cash at the banks, travel agencies, the better hotels and bigger stores. There are also lots of street changers (watch them carefully). BCP, Raimondi y Tarapacá, is the only place to change Tcs, cash on Visa. Also at Interbank. **Cultural centres** Art school: Usko Ayar Amazonian School of Painting, in the house of artist Pablo Amaringo, a former *vegetalista* (healer), Jr LM Sánchez, Cerro 465-467, www.egallery.com/coll/amazon.php. The school provides art classes for local people, and is dependent upon selling their art. The internationally renowned school welcomes overseas visitors for short or long stays to study painting and learn Spanish and/or teach English with Peruvian students. **Police** Policia Nacional, Jr Independencia 3rd block, T575211.

Yurimaguas and Pacaya-Samiria

Yurimaguas
The Río Huallaga winds northwards for 930 km. The Upper Huallaga is a torrent, dropping 15.8 m per km between its source and Tingo María. The Lower Huallaga moves through an enervation of flatness, with its main port, Yurimaguas, below the last rapids and only 150 m above the Atlantic Ocean, yet distant from that ocean by over a month's voyage. Between the Upper and Lower lies the Middle Huallaga: the third of the river which is downstream from Tingo María and upstream from Yurimaguas.
 Downriver of Tingo María, beyond Bellavista, the orientation is towards **Yurimaguas** (*Phone code 065, Population 25,700*), which is connected by road with the Pacific coast, via Tarapoto and Moyobamba (see page 1164). It's a very relaxed jungle town and, as the roadhead on the lower Río Huallaga, is an ideal starting point for river travel in the Peruvian Amazon. It has a fine church of the Passionist Fathers, based on the Cathedral of Burgos, in Spain. A colourful market is held from 0600-0800, full of fruit and animals. Excursions in the area include the gorge of Shanusi and the lakes of Mushuyacu and Sanango. Tourist information is available from the Consejo Regional building (which also has a small archaeological museum) on the main plaza, T352676.

Pacaya-Samiria
All river traffic to Iquitos stops at **Lagunas**, 12 hours from Yurimaguas. From here there are good jungle trips from Lagunas to the **Pacaya-Samiria Reserve** ⓘ *Reserve office in Iquitos,*

Ricardo Palma 113, p 4, T232980, Mon-Fri 0800-1300, 1500-1800, has general information and an updated list of tour operators authorized to enter the reserve. You must go here to obtain proof of payment for the park entry fee (US$33), payment itself must be made at Banco de la Nación. Pacaya-Samiria Reserve, at 2,080,000 ha, is the country's largest protected area. It is bounded by the rivers Marañón and Ucuyali, narrowing to their confluence near the town of Nauta. The reserve's waterways and wetlands provide habitat for manatee, tapir, river dolphins, giant otters, black cayman, boas, 193 species of fish and some 330 bird species. Many of the animals found here are in danger of extinction. Trips are mostly on the river, sleeping in hammocks, and include fishing. The main part of the reserve is off-limits to tourists, who may only be taken to forest surrounding the reserve. Iquitos operators enter through Nauta to Yarina where there is a shelter, also through Requena. Another entry point is the village of **Leoncio Prado** (with a couple of *hospedajes*), on the Marañón, opposite the outflow of the Río Samiria.

🛏 Sleeping

Yurimaguas *p1269*
B **Puerto Pericos**, Malecón Paranapura, T352009, www.puertopalmeras.com.pe. Same group as **Puerto Palmeras** in Tarapoto, includes breakfast, with hot water, restaurant, gardens.
D **Hostal Residencial El Naranjo**, Arica 318, T351560, hotel_elnaranjo@hotmail.com. Best in town, a/c (E with fan), hot water, comfortable, small pool, with good restaurant.
E **Luis Antonio**, Av Jáuregui 407, T352061, antonio@vibcp.com. With fan C with a/c), cold water, balconies overlooking small pool, very helpful. Recommended.
F **Hostal El Caballito**, Av Jáuregui 403, T352427. Cold water, fan, pleasant, good value.
F **Leo's Palace**, Sgto Lores 106, Plaza de Armas, T351499. Good, reasonable value (D) with a/c, restaurant.

Lagunas *p1269*
G **Hostal Isabel**, Miraflores 1 block from plaza. Shared bath, cold water, basic, meals available. Several other basic places in town.
G **Hostal La Sombra**, Jr Vásquez 1121. Shared bath, basic, good food.

🥾 Activities and tours

Yurimaguas *p1269*
Manguares Expeditions, Sargento Lores 126, near Plaza de Armas.
Nilo Hidalgo, Jr Elena Pardo 115, T352832, www.nilotour.cjb.net. US$70-100 per person per day.

Pacaya-Samiria *p1269*
There are 5 registered operators in Lagunas. These include **Manuel Rojas**, T401116, and **Gamaniel Valles**, T401007. Guides charge US$15 per day. **Klever Oliver**, Saldana Vargas, Fitzcarrald W325, T401009, very good tours and service, professional guides to Pacaya-Samiria. Trips to Pacaya-Samiria can also be arranged in

Iquitos. Expeditions must be booked in advance, all equipment and food is provided. **Asiendes** (Asociación Indígena en Defensa de la Ecología Samiria), asiendesperu@hotmail.com, or contact through **Yellow Rose of Texas** restaurant in Iquitos. A local association which runs trips into Pacaya-Samiria, promoting the jungle and benefiting the community, from 4 to 7 days, US$50 per day, all inclusive except boat passage from Iquitos and price of entry to the park. You stay at rangers' stations or can camp, very good experience, respectful of wildlife, knowledgeable and accommodating guides. Recommended.

🚌 Transport

Yurimaguas *p1269*
Bus There are plans to pave the road to Tarapoto, which would considerably shorten the journey. **Paredes Estrella**, office on 5th block of Mariscal Cáceres, 0700 daily to **Tarapoto** (8 hrs, US$3.65), **Moyobamba** (10 hrs, US7.50), **Pedro Ruiz** (for Chachapoyas, 16 hrs, US$10.50), **Chiclayo** (24 hrs, US$15), **Trujillo** (28 hrs, US$18), and **Lima** (34 hrs, US$24). Also **Huamanga** and **Sol Peruano**, offices on same street. If travelling only as far as Tarapoto, faster alternatives to the bus are colectivos (cars, 4 hrs, US$7.50), pickups (5 hrs, US$4.55 in cab, US$2.50 in the back), and combis (5 hrs, US$3.65).
Ferry To **Iquitos**, 2 days and 2 nights, **Eduardo** company is best, Elena Pardo 114, T351270 (see under Iquitos, Transport).

🏛 Directory

Yurimaguas *p1269*
Banks Interbank or travel agents charge poor rates. **Negocios Zerimar**, Jáuregui ½ block from plaza, changes US$ cash, Mon-Sat 0700-2100, Sun 0700-1500. **Internet** Café on Plaza de Armas, US$1.70 per hr.

Iquitos and around → *Phone code: 065. Colour map 3, grid A4. Population: 600,000.*

Iquitos stands on the west bank of the Amazon and is a chief town of Peru's jungle region. Some 800 km downstream from Pucallpa and 3,646 km from the mouth of the Amazon, the city is completely isolated except by air and river. Its first wealth came from the rubber boom (late 19th century to second decade of 20th century). The main economic activities are logging, commerce and petroleum and it is the main starting point for tourists wishing to explore Peru's northern jungle. **Tourist offices: i perú** ① *Napo 232, on the Plaza de Armas, in the Municipal building, T236144, iperuiquitos@promperu.gov.pe, 0830-1930 daily,* also at the airport, 0800-1300, 1600-2000 daily. Both offices are helpful. If arriving by air, go first to this desk. They will give you a list of clean hotels, a map, tell you about the touts outside the airport etc. **Dircetur** ① *Ricardo Palma 113, p 5, T234609, loreto@mincetur.gob.pe.* The local paper is **La Región**, www.diariolaregion.com. **Indecopi**, the tourism protection service, is at ① *Huallaga 325, T243490, ameza@indecopi.gob.pe.* The incongruous **Iron House/Casa de Fierro** stands on the Plaza de Armas, designed by Eiffel for the Paris exhibition of 1889. It is said that the house was transported from Paris by a local rubber baron and is constructed entirely of iron trusses and sheets, bolted together and painted silver. It now houses a restaurant and snack bar.

Iquitos

Sleeping 🛏
Acosta *7*
Amazonas *1*
El Dorado *3*
El Dorado Plaza *4*
El Sitio *5*
Europa *6*
Hostal Alfert *11*
Hostal Ambassador *8*

Hostal Colibrí *16*
Internacional *12*
Isabel *13*
Jhuliana *14*
La Casa de Samantha *9*
Marañón *10*
Royal Inn *2*
Victoria Regia *15*

Eating 🍴
Ari's Burger *1*
Chifa Long Fung *2*
El Nuevo Mesón *3*
Fitzcarrald *4*
Hausaí *11*
Heladería *13*
La Gran Maloca *5*
La Vida es Salud *6*

Montecarlo *7*
Paulina *8*
Pollón *1*
Yellow Rose of Texas *12*

Bars & clubs 🍸
Snack Bar Arandú *9*
Teatro Café Amauta *10*

0 metres 200
0 yards 200

Peru Yurimaguas & Pacaya-Samiria

1271

Belén, the picturesque, lively waterfront district, is worth visiting, but is not safe at night. Most of its huts are built on rafts to cope with the river's 10 m change of level during floods (January-July); now they're built on stilts. On Pasaje Paquito are bars serving local sugar cane rum. The main plaza has a bandstand made by Eiffel. In the high season canoes can be hired on the waterfront for a tour of Belén, US$3 per hour. The market at the end of the Malecón is well worth visiting, though you should get there before 0900 to see it in full swing.

Of special interest are the older buildings, faced with *azulejos* (glazed tiles). They date from the rubber boom of 1890 to 1912, when the rubber barons imported the tiles from Portugal and Italy and ironwork from England to embellish their homes. Werner Herzog's film *Fitzcarraldo* is a *cause célèbre* in the town and Fitzcarrald's house, the **Casa de Barro**, still stands on the Plaza de Armas. **Museo Amazónico**, in the renovated Prefectura, Malecón Tarapacá y Morona, has displays of native art. Next door to the tourist office on the Plaza is a **City Museum** ① *free*, with stuffed animals and wood carvings of local native peoples.

Excursions

There is a beach at **Bellavista**, which is safe for swimming and popular at weekends in summer. Boats can be hired from here to see the meeting of the Nanay and Amazon rivers, and to visit villages en route. There are lots of food stalls selling typical local dishes. Take a bus from Jr Próspero to 'Bellavista Nanay', 15 minutes, US$0.40.

Allpahuayo-Mishana Reserve ① *Iquitos office at Instituto de Investigaciones de la Amazonía Peruana (IIAP), Av Quiñones on the way to the airport, T265515.* Some 25 km south of Iquitos by road or 2-3 hours by boat from Bellavista, this reserve protects the largest concentration of white sand jungle (*varillales*) in Peru. Part of the Napo ecoregion, biodiversity here is among the highest in the Amazon basin. It has several endangered species including two primates, several endemic species; the area is rich in birds (500 species have been recorded). The beautiful **Lake Quistococha** in lush jungle is 4 km south of the city, with a fish hatchery at the lakeside. There's a good two-hour walk through the surrounding jungle on a clearly marked trail. See particularly the *paiche*, a huge Amazonian fish whose steaks (*paiche a la loretana*) you can eat in Iquitos' restaurants. There are also bars and restaurants on the lakeside and a small beach. Boats are for hire on the lake and swimming is safe but the sandflies are vicious, so take insect repellent. A map and information is available from zoo's ticket office . The **zoo** ① *US$1.30 0900-1700*, itself is squalid. **Pilpintuhuasi Butterfly Farm** ① *near the village of Padre Cocha, T232665, www.amazon animalorphanage.org, Tue-Sun 0900-1600, US$5*, as well as butterflies, has a small well-kept zoo, Austrian-Peruvian run. It is a 20-minute walk from Padre Cocha to the butterfly farm.

Border with Brazil

Details on exit and entry formalities seem to change frequently, so when leaving Peru, check in Iquitos first at Immigration or with the Capitanía at the port. Boats stop in Santa Rosa for Peruvian exit formalities. All details are given in the Brazil chapter.

● Sleeping

Iquitos *p1271, map p1271*
Hotels are generally more expensive than the rest of the country, but discounts can be negotiated in the low season (Jan-Apr). Around Peruvian Independence Day (27 and 28 Jul) and Easter, Iquitos can get crowded and prices rise at this time.
AL El Dorado Plaza, Napo 258 on main plaza, T222555, www.eldoradoplazahotel.com. 5 star, very good accommodation and restaurant, excellent service, bar, internet access, prices include service, breakfast, welcome drink and transfer to/from airport. Recommended.
A El Dorado, Napo 362, T232574, dorado@eldoradoplazahotel.com.

Same ownership, pool (open to restaurant users), cable TV, bar and restaurant, prices include service and airport transfer. Recommended.
A Victoria Regia, Ricardo Palma 252, T231983, www.victoriaregiahotel.com. A/c, fridge, cable TV, free map of city, safe deposit boxes in rooms, good restaurant and pool. Recommended.
C Acosta, Calvo de Araujo y Huallaga, T235974, www.hotelacosta.com. Includes breakfast and airport transfer, a/c, TV, safety deposit boxes, good restaurant.
C Amazonas, Plaza de Armas, Arica 108, T242431. Modern, a/c, phone, fridge bar, TV.
C Europa, Próspero 494, T231123,

rcpowerv@terra.com.pe. A/c, cable TV, phone and fridge in every room, pleasant café/bar, good views from 5th floor.

C Jhuliana, Putumayo 521, T/F233154. Includes breakfast, nice pool, restaurant. Recommended.

C La Posada de Lobo, Pantoja 417 y Yavari, T236140. A/c, hot water, TV, fridge, swimming pool, jacuzzi, gym, laundry, email service, price includes breakfast, relaxed atmosphere, pleasant, good value.

D Hostal Ambassador, Pevas 260, T233110, www.paseosamazonicos.com. Includes breakfast, a/c, transport to and from airport, member of Peruvian Youth Hostel Association, cafeteria, owns Sinchicuy Lodge (see page 1275). Recommended.

D Internacional, Próspero 835, T/F234684. A/c, TV, fridge, phone, secure, medium-priced restaurant, good value. Recommended.

D Marañón, Nauta 285, T242673, hotelmaranon@terra.com.pe. Includes breakfast, airport transfer, small pool, a/c, hot water, comfortable. Recommended.

D Royal Inn, Aguirre 793, T224244, royalinn_casinohotel@terra.com. Includes breakfast, a/c, frigobar, hot water, bidet, modern and comfortable.

F Hospedaje Mi Selvita, Av Quiñónez Km 3.5, Pasaje Roma No 14, T260165, raxafe@operamail.com. A charming small *hostal* in lovely gardens, run by Aydee Ríos Cárdenas, who is a travel agent (she speaks some English). Near the airport, simple rooms with cool shower, fan, TV, meals.

F El Sitio, Ricardo Palma 541, T234932. Fan, cafeteria, spotless. Highly recommended.

F Hostal Alfert, García Sanz 01, T234105. Hard beds, good views of river, safe, but in market area, arranges jungle trips but not an authorized operator.

E Hostal Colibrí, Nauta 172, T241737. One block from Plaza and 50 m from the river, new building, TV, fan, hot water, secure, good value, helpful staff, a/c rooms more expensive.

G La Casa de Samantha, Nauta 787, T231005. Shared bath, cold water, small place, family-run, helpful.

G Isabel, Brasil 156, T234901. Good, but plug the holes in the walls, secure, often full.

❷ Eating

Iquitos *p1271, map p1271*
Local specialities Try palm heart salad (*chonta*), or *a la Loretana* dish on menus; also try *inchicapi* (chicken, corn and peanut soup), *cecina* (fried dried pork), *tacacho* (fried green banana and pork, mashed into balls and eaten for

breakfast or tea), *juanes* (chicken, rice, olive and egg, seasoned and wrapped in bijao leaves and sold in restaurants) and the *camu-camu*, an acquired taste, said to have one of the highest vitamin C concentrations in the world. Try the local drink *chuchuhuasi*, made from the bark of a tree, which is supposed to have aphrodisiac properties (for sale at Arica 1046), and *jugo de cocona*, and the alcoholic *cola de mono* and *siete raices* (aguardiente mixed with the bark of 7 trees and wild honey), sold at Exquisita Amazónica, Abtao 590.

Many private homes offer set lunch, look for the board outside.

♥♥♥ Fitzcarrald, Malecón Maldonado 103 y Napo. Smart, best pizza in town, also good pastas and salads.

♥♥♥ La Gran Maloca, Sargento Lores 170, opposite Banco Continental. A/c, high class.

♥♥♥ Montecarlo, Napo 140. Next to the casino, said to be the best in town.

♥♥ Ari's Burger, Plaza de Armas, Próspero 127. Medium-priced fast food, good breakfasts, popular with tourists.

♥♥ Chifa Long Fung, San Martín at Plaza 28 de Julio. Good Chinese if a little expensive, a/c, 1200-1500, 1900-000 daily.

♥♥ El Nuevo Mesón, Malecón Maldonado 153. Local specialities include wild boar, alligator, turtle, tapir and other endangered species, has lots of regular dishes, too.

♥♥ Pollón, next door to *Ari's Burger*. Chicken and chips, open in the daytime.

♥♥ The Regal, in the *Casa de Hierro*, Plaza de Armas, Próspero y Putumayo, 2nd floor. Nice location, good set lunch US$2.30, other meals more expensive.

♥♥ Yellow Rose of Texas, Putumayo 180. Run by the ex-director of the tourist office, Gerald W Mayeaux, very helpful. Varied food including local dishes, Texan atmosphere. Open 24 hrs so you can wait here if arriving late at night, good breakfasts, lots of information, also has a bar, Sky TV and Texan saddle seats.

♥ Huasaí, Napo 326. Varied and innovative *menú*, popular and recommended, 0730-1600 daily.

♥ Paulina, Tacna 591. Good set lunch, popular but noisy.

♥ La Vida es Salud, Aguirre 759 on Plaza 28 de Julio. Vegetarian, simple little place, good value, open daily.

Cafés
Heladería, Próspero 415. Good ice-cream (try local flavour *aguaje*). **Juguería Paladar**, Próspero 245. Excellent juices.

🎵 Bars and clubs

Iquitos *p1271, map p1271*
Noa Noa, Pevas y Fitzcarrald. Popular disco, varied music, open Tue-Sat.
La Ribereña, Raymondi 453. With terraced seats on a newly-built plaza.
Snack Bar Arandú, Malecón Maldonado. Good views of the Amazon river.
Teatro Café Amauta, Nauta 248. Live music, open 2200-2400, good atmosphere, popular, small exhibition hall.
Tuspa, Raimondi block 2. Light rock, lively, good place to listen to music.

⚜ Festivals and events

Iquitos *p1271, map p1271*
5 Jan: founding of Iquitos. **Feb-Mar**: Carnival.
3rd week in Jun: tourist week.
24 Jun: San Juan. **28-30 Aug**: Santa Rosa de Lima. **8 Dec**: Immaculate Conception, celebrated in Punchana, near the docks.

🛒 Shopping

Iquitos *p1271, map p1271*
Hammocks in Iquitos cost about US$6. **Amazon Arts & Crafts**, Napo block 100. **Artesanías de la Selva**, R Palma 190. **Mad Mick's Trading Post**, next to the Iron House, hires out rubber boots for those going to the jungle. **Mercado Artesanal de Productores**, 4 km from the centre in the San Juan district, on the road to the airport, take a colectivo. Cheapest in town with more choice than elsewhere.

⛰ Activities and tours

Iquitos *p1271, map p1271*
Jungle tours from Iquitos All agencies are under the control of the local office of the Ministry of Tourism. They arrange one day or longer trips to places of interest with guides speaking some English. Package tours booked in your home country, over the internet or in Lima are much more expensive than those booked locally. Take your time before making a decision and don't be bullied by the hustlers at the airport (they get paid a hefty commission). You must make sure your tour operator or guide has a proper licence (the Municipalidad has a full list). Do not go with a company which does not have legal authorization; there are many unscrupulous people about. Find out all the details of the trip and food arrangements before paying (a minimum of US$45 per day). Speed boats for river trips can be hired by the hour or day at the

Embarcadero Turístico, at the intersection of Av de la Marina and Samánez Ocampo in Punchana. Prices vary greatly, usually US$10-20 per hr, and are negotiable. In fact, all prices are negotiable, except **Muyuna**, who do not take commissions.
General information and advice Take a long-sleeved shirt, waterproof coat and shoes or light boots on jungle trips and a good torch, as well as espirales to ward off the mosquitoes at night – they can be bought from pharmacies in Iquitos. Premier is the most effective local insect repellent. The dry season is from Jul-Sep (Sep is the best month to see flowers and butterflies).
Amazon Isula Retreat, Pasaje Los Quipus Mz OIB Lte 3 Residencial Los Girasoles, Chosica, T01-358-2193. About 3 hrs from Iquitos, by boat and road via Mazán, on the Suni Mirano lake, bungalow accommodation, traditional meals, many activities, including cultural, adventure, academic and spiritual. Recommended.
Amazon Wilderness Expeditions, Jr Putumayo 163, altos 202, T234565. Good tours to Emerald Forest Camp, on Río Yanayacu, 185 km from Iquitos, US$65 per day. Comfortable, simple accommodation (no shower – wash in river), good food. Ask for guide Juan Carlos Palomino Berndt, T993 5472 (mob).
Blue Morpho Tours, Moore 144, T231168, www.bluemorphotours.com.
A rustic camp on the Río Aucayacu, a tributary of the Ucayali 300 km south of Iquitos. Centre for shamanic studies and workshops, tours US$80 pp per day, all inclusive except for bar and snacks.
Cumaceba Lodge and Expeditions, Putumayo 184 in the Iron House, T/F232229, www.cumaceba.com. Tours of 2-8 days to their lodges on the Amazon and Yarapa rivers, good birdwatching guides, 3 days/2 nights. Very good all round.
Explorama Tours, by the riverside docks on Av La Marina 340, PO Box 446, T252530, www.explorama.com, are highly recommended as the most efficient and, with over 40 years in existence, certainly the biggest and most established. Their sites are: **Ceiba Tops**, 40 km (1½ hrs) from Iquitos, is a resort providing 'an adventure in luxury', 75 a/c rooms with electricity, hot showers, pool with hydromassage and beautiful gardens. The food is good and, as in all Explorama's properties, is served communally. There are attractive walks and other excursions, a recommended jungle experience for those who want their creature comforts, US$200 pp for 1 night/2 days, US$98 for each additional night (1-2 people). **Explorama Lodge** at Yanamono, 80 km from Iquitos, 2½ hrs from Iquitos, has palm-thatched accommodation with separate bathroom and shower facilities connected by covered walkways, cold water, no

electricity, good food and service. US$285 for 3 days/2 nights and US$85 for each additional day (1-2 people). **Explornapo Lodge** at Llachapa on the Sucusai creek (a tributary of the Napo), is in the same style as Explorama Lodge, but is further away from Iquitos, 160 km (4 hrs), and is set in 105,000 ha of primary rainforest, so is better for seeing wildlife, US$820 for 5 days/4 nights. Nearby is the impressive canopy walkway 35 m above the forest floor and 500 m long, 'a magnificent experience and not to be missed'. It is associated with the **Amazon Center for Tropical Studies (ACTS)**, a scientific station, only 10 mins from the canopy walkway. **Explor Tambos**, 2 hrs from Explornapo, offer more primitive accommodation, 8 shelters for 16 campers, bathing in the river, offers the best chance to see rare fauna. Close to Explornapo is the ReNuPeRu medicinal plant garden, run by a curandero. Members of South American Explorers are offered 15% discount.
Heliconia Lodge, Ricardo Palma 242, T231959, www.amazonriverexpeditions.com. On the Río Amazonas, 1½ hrs from Iquitos, the lodge has hot water, electricity for 3 hrs a day, good guiding and staff; rustic yet comfortable, 3 days/2 nights US$180. Under same management as Zungarococha, see below, and in same group as Hotels Victoria Regia and Acosta, see above. They organize trips to Allpahuayo-Mishana, to Pacaya-Samiria with Amazon Tours and Cruises, see above, and to the ACTS canopy walkway. Jacamar Amazon Jungle Lodge, 5079 Mariana Lane, Tega Cay, SC 29708, USA, T1-803-548 6738, www.jacamarlodge.com. In the Reserva Comunal de Tamshiyacu-Tahuayo. Do as much or as little to do as you please, plemty of activities, remote, great food and attentive staff. Fully screened rooms, no electricity, flushing toilets, capacity for 24 guests. Recommended.
Muyuna Amazon Lodge, Putumayo 163, T242858, 993 4424 (mob), www.muyuna.com. 140 km from Iquitos, also on the Yanayacu, before San Juan village. Packages from 1 to 5 nights available, 2 nights/3 days US$300, but users of this Handbook should make reservations in person for discounted price (similarly SAE members, 10%). Everything is included in the price. Good guides, accommodation, food and service, very well organized and professional, flexible, radio contact, will collect passengers from airport if requested in advance. They offer a 7-day birdwatching trip, combining several areas including Allpahuayo-Mishana Reserve; also have a new underwater microphone for listening to dolphins. Highly recommended.
Paseos Amazónicos Ambassador, Pevas 246, T/F231618, operates the **Amazonas Sinchicuy Lodge**, US$70 per person per night. The lodge is

1½ hrs from Iquitos on the Sinchicuy river, 25 mins by boat from the Amazon river. The lodge consists of several wooden buildings with thatched roofs on stilts, cabins with bathroom, no electricity but paraffin lamps are provided, good food, and plenty activities, including visits to local villages. Recommended. They also have Tambo Yanayacu and Tambo Amazónico lodges, organize visits to Pacaya Samiria and local tours.
Tahuayo Lodge, Amazonia Expeditions, 10305 Riverburn Drive, Tampa, FL 33647, toll free T800-262 9669, www.perujungle.com. Near the Reserva Comunal de Tamshiyacu- Tahuayo on the Río Tahuayo, 145 km upriver from Iquitos, comfortable cabins with cold shower, buffet meals, good food, laundry service, wide range of excursions, excellent staff. A 7-day programme costs US$1,295, all inclusive, extra days US$100. Recommended. The lodge is associated with the Rainforest Conservation Fund, see www.rain forestconservation.org.

⊖ Transport

Iquitos *p1271, map p1271*
Air Francisco Secada Vigneta airport, T260147. Taxi to the airport costs US$2.85; *motocarro* (motorcycle with 2 seats), US$2. A bus from the airport, US$0.20, goes from the main road; most go through the centre of town. To **Lima**, daily; **Lan**, **Star Perú** and **WayraPerú**. **Grupo 42** flies once a week to **Lagunas** for Pacaya Samiria (US$50), **Yurimaguas** (US$55), **Tarapoto** (US$80) and **Pucallpa** (US$60). Iquitos flights are frequently delayed; be sure to reconfirm your flight in Iquitos, as they are often overbooked, especially over Christmas; check times in advance as itineraries frequently change.
  Airline offices Grupo 42, Sgto Lores 127, T233224. **Lan**, Napo 374, T232421. **Star Perú**, Próspero 428, T236208. **WayraPerú**, Napo 374, T221047.
Ferry General hints for river travel: large passenger and cargo vessels are called *lanchas*, smaller faster craft are called *rápidos* or *deslizadores* (speedboats). You can find information on boats and tickets at **Bellavista**, Malecón Tarapacá 596; or in the Puerto Masusa district of Puchana, at Av La Marina with Masusa (take a bus from the centre, 10 mins).
  All *lanchas* leave from Masusa, 2 km north of the centre, a dangerous area at night. All sailings around 1800-2000, the first night's meal is not included. Always deal directly with boat owners or managers, avoid touts and middle-men. All fares are negotiable. You can buy either a ticket to sling your hammock on deck, or for a berth in a cabin sleeping four people.
  A hammock is essential. A double, of material

(not string), provides one person with a blanket. Board the boat many hours in advance to guarantee hammock space. If going on the top deck, try to be first down the front; take rope for hanging your hammock, plus string and sarongs for privacy. On all boats, hang your hammock away from lightbulbs (they aren't switched off at night and attract all sorts of strange insects) and away from the engines, which usually emit noxious fumes. Guard your belongings from the moment you board. It's safer to club together and pay for a cabin in which to lock your belongings, even if you sleep outside in a hammock. There is very little privacy; women travellers can expect a lot of attention. There are adequate washing and toilet facilities, but the food is rice, meat and beans (and whatever can be picked up en route) cooked in river water. Stock up on drinking water, fruit and tinned food. Vegetarians must take their own supplies. There is a good cheap bar on board. Take plenty of prophylactic enteritis tablets; many contract dysentery on the trip. Also take insect repellent and a mosquito net. If arriving in Iquitos on a regular, slow boat, take extreme care when disembarking. Things get very chaotic at this time and theft and pickpocketing is rife.

Lanchas serve all of the following destinations: **Pucallpa**, 3-5 days up river along the Amazon and Ucayali, hammock US$22, berth US$35. To **Yurimaguas**, 3-4 days up river along the Amazon, Marañón and Huallaga, 2nd class hammock space US$18, 1st class hammock space US$25, berth US$35. **Eduardo** company is recommended, **Eduardo IV and V** are their newest vessels. **Islandia** for **Leticia** (Colombia) and **Tabatinga** (Brazil), 2-3 days down river on the Amazon, hammock space US$15, berth US$22. **Gran Diego** is a nice vessel. Passengers disembark in Peru for immigration formalities (no exchange facilities), then take another US$1 boat to **Marco**, the port for **Tabatinga**. Most boats for **Manaus** depart from Marco.

To **Pantoja** (for Ecuador), 5-7 days up river on the Napo, hammock space US$30, no berths. There are 4 basic boats: **Victor** and **Camila** (same owner, T242082) and **Jeisawell** and **Siempre Adelante** (same owner, T266159, T961 3049, mob). Each sails twice a month, but will not go all the way to Pantoja unless there is cargo. To reduce the voyage by a day, take a small boat to **Indiana** and cross to **Mazán** to catch the lancha on the Napo, but there may not be much space left onboard. Alternatively, you can take a rápido from Mazán to **Santa Clotilde** (5 hrs, US$24, less than half-way to Pantoja, one *hospedaje*, **G**) and wait for the *lancha*, or try to find a smaller boat going to Pantoja.

Rápidos for **Tabatinga** (Brazil) leave from El Embarcadero Turístico, at 0600 daily except Mon, 11 hrs, US$60. There are no boats direct to Manaus. Boats go to **Santa Rosa** on the border, opposite **Tabatinga**. Be at the port at 0445 for customs check. They go to Santa Rosa for immigration formalities then take passengers across to Tabatinga, US$2. Purchase tickets in advance from company offices: **Brastur**, Arica 46, **Trans Turismo Amazonas**, Av La Marina 135, or **River Fox**, Raymondi 344, T243404 (not recommended). All include a small breakfast of a sandwich and coffee, a passable lunch and mineral water (ask for it). All carry life jackets and have clean bathrooms. Luggage limit is 15 kg. Most travel agencies sell tickets. Hotels have details of sailings; ask around which boats are reliable.

Lake Quistococha *p1272*
Combis leave every hour until 1500 from Plaza 28 de Julio, Iquitos; the last one back leaves at 1700. Alternatively take a **motocarro** there and back with a 1 hr wait, which costs US$6. Perhaps the best option is to hire a **motorbike** and spend the day there. The road can be difficult after rain.

⊙ Directory

Iquitos *p1271, map p1271*
Banks BCP, Plaza de Armas. For Visa, also cash and TCs at good rates, Visa ATM around the corner on Próspero. **BBV Continental**, Sgto Lores 171. For Visa, 1% commission on TCs. **Banco de la Nación**, Condamine 478. Good rates. **Casa de cambio** at Tienda Wing Kong, Próspero 312, Mon-Sat 0800-1300, 1500-2000, Sun 0900-1200. Western Union, Napo 359, T235182. Don't change money on the streets. **Consulates** : Colombia, Calvo de Araujo 431, T231461. UK, Casa de Hierro (Iron House), Putumayo 182A, T222732, Mon-Fri 1100-1200. **Note** There are no Brazilian or Ecuadorean consulates. If you need a visa, you must get it in Lima or in your home country. **Internet** There are places everywhere, US$0.80 per hr. **Medical services** Clínica Loreto, Morona 471, T233752, 24-hr attention, recommended, Spanish only. **Motorcycle** hire Park Motors, Tacna 579, T/F231688. Addresses of others from tourist office, see above. **Post offices** On the corner of C Arica with Morona, near Plaza de Armas, daily 0700-1700. **Telephones** Arica 276. Cheap private cabins at Próspero 523, national and international calls, helpful staff. **Useful addresses** Immigration: Mcal Cáceres 18th block, T235371. **Tourist police**: Sargento Lores 834, T231851, helpful with complaints. In emergency T241000 or 241001.

Southeastern jungle

The southern selva is in Madre de Dios department, which contains the Manu National Park (2.05 million ha), the Tambopata National Reserve (254,358 ha) and the Bahauja- Sonene National Park (1.1 million ha). The forest of this lowland region (Altitude 260 m) is technically called Sub-tropical Moist Forest, which means that it receives less rainfall than tropical forest and is dominated by the floodplains of its meandering rivers. The most striking features are the former river channels that have become isolated as ox-bow lakes. These are home to black caiman and giant otter. Other rare species living in the forest are jaguar, puma, ocelot and tapir. There are also howler monkeys, macaws, guans, currasows and the giant harpy eagle. As well as containing some of the most important flora and fauna on Earth, the region also harbours gold-diggers, loggers, hunters, drug smugglers and oil-men, whose activities have endangered the unique rainforest. Various conservation groups are working to protect it.

Ins and outs

Access to Manu The multiple use zone of Manu Biosphere Reserve is accessible to anyone and several lodges exist in the area (see Lodges in Manu below). The reserved zone is accessible by permit only. Entry is strictly controlled and visitors must visit the area under the auspices of an authorized operator with an authorized guide. Permits are limited and reservations should be made well in advance. In the reserved zone the only accommodation is in the comfortable Manu Lodge or in the comfortable but rustic Casa Machiguenga in the Cocha Salvador area. Several companies have tented safari camp infrastructures, some with shower and dining facilities, but all visitors sleep in tents. The entrance fee to the Reserved Zone is 150 soles pp (about US$40) and is included in package tour prices.

Useful addresses In Lima Asociación Peruana para la Conservación de la Naturaleza (APECO) ① *Parque José Acosta 187, p 2, Magdalena del Mar, T01-264 0094, www.ape co.org.pe.* **Pronaturaleza** ① *Av Alberto de Campo 417, Lima 17, T01-264 2736, and in Puerto Maldonado, Jr Cajamarca cuadra 1 s/n, T082-571585, www.pronaturaleza.org.* **In Cuzco Perú Verde** ① *Ricardo Palma J-1, Santa Mónica, T084-226392, www.peruverde.org.* This is a local NGO that can help with information and has free video shows about Manu National Park and Tambopata National Reserve. Friendly and helpful and with information on research in the jungle area of Madre de Dios. Further information can be obtained from the **Manu National Park Office** ① *Av Micaela Bastidas 310, Cuzco, T084-240898, pqnmanu@terra.com.pe, open 0800-1400.* They issue a permit for the Reserved Zone which costs about US$40.

Climate The climate is warm and humid, with a rainy season from Novemer to March and a dry season from April to October. Cold fronts from the South Atlantic, called *friajes*, are characteristic of the dry season, when temperatures drop to 15-16° C during the day, and 13° C at night. Always bring a sweater at this time. The best time to visit is during the dry season when there are fewer mosquitoes and the rivers are low, exposing the beaches. This is also a good time to see nesting and to view animals at close range, as they stay close to the rivers and are easily seen. Note that this is also the hottest time. A pair of binoculars is essential and insect repellent is a must.

Manu Biosphere Reserve

No other reserve can compare with Manu for the diversity of life forms; it holds over 1,000 species of birds and covers an altitudinal range from 200 to 4,100 m above sea-level. Giant otters, jaguars, ocelots and 13 species of primates abound in this pristine tropical wilderness, and uncontacted indigenous tribes are present in the more remote areas, as are indigenous groups with limited access.

The reserve is one of the largest conservation units on Earth, encompassing the complete drainage of the Manu River. It is divided into the **Manu National Park** (1,692,137 ha), where only government sponsored biologists and anthropologists may visit with permits from the Ministry of Agriculture in Lima; the **Reserved Zone** (257,000 ha) within the Manu National Park, set aside for applied scientific research and ecotourism; and the **Cultural Zone** (92,000 ha), which contains acculturated native groups and colonists, where the locals still employ their traditional way of life. Among the ethnic groups in the Cultural Zone are the Harakmbut, Machiguenga and Yine in the Amarakaeri Reserved Zone, on the east bank of the Alto Madre de Dios. They have set up their own ecotourism activities. Associated with Manu are other areas protected by conservation groups, or local people (for example the Blanquillo reserved zone) and some cloud forest parcels along the road. The **Nahua-Kugapakori Reserved Zone**, set aside for these two nomadic native groups, is the area between the headwaters of the Río Manu and headwaters of the Río Urubamba, to the north of the alto Madre de Dios.

Cuzco to Puerto Maldonado via Mazuko

This route is Cuzco-Urcos-Quincemil-Mazuko-Puerto Maldonado. Bus and truck details are given under Transport, below. It's a painfully slow journey on an appalling road; trucks frequently get stuck or break down. **Quincemil**, 240 km from Urcos on the road to Mazuko, is a centre for alluvial gold-mining with many banks. Accommodation is available in **F Hotel Toni**, friendly, clean, cold shower, good meals. Quincemil marks the half-way point and the start of the all-weather road. Gasoline is scarce in Quincemil because most road vehicles continue on 70 km to Mazuko, which is another mining centre, where they fill up with the cheaper gasoline of the jungle region. The changing scenery is magnificent and worth the hardship and discomfort.

To Puerto Maldonado via Pilcopata and Itahuania

The arduous 255 km trip over the Andes from Cuzco to Pilcopata takes about 16-18 hours by bus or truck (20-40 hours in the wet season). On this route, too, the scenery is magnificent. From Cuzco you climb up to the pass before Paucartambo (very cold at night), before dropping down to this mountain village at the border between the departments of Cuzco and Madre de Dios. The road then ascends to the second pass (also cold at night), after which it goes down to the cloud forest and then the rainforest, reaching **Pilcopata** at 650 m.

Pilcopata to Itahuania After Pilcopata, the route is hair-raising and breathtaking, passing through **Atalaya**, the first village on the Alto Madre de Dios River and tourist port for hiring boats to Boca Manu (basic accommodation). The route continues to Salvación, where a Park Office and Park Entrance are situated. There are basic hostals and restaurants. Basic restaurants can be found in Pilcopata and Atalaya.

The road, which bypasses the previous port of **Shintuya**, continues to **Itahuania**, the starting point for river transport. It won't be long before the port moves down river as the road through Nuevo Eden, 11 km away, and Diamante is under construction. It is planned to drive the road through to Boca Colorado one day. **Note** It is not possible to arrange trips to the Reserved Zone of the National Park from Itahuania, owing to park regulations. All arrangements, including permits, must be made in Cuzco.

Itahuania to Puerto Maldonado Cargo boats leave for the gold mining centre of Boca Colorado on the Río Madre de Dios, via Boca Manu, but only when the boat is fully laden (see Transport below). Very basic accommodation can be found here, but it is not recommended for lone women travellers. From Colorado you can take a colectivo taxi to Puerto Carlos, cross the river, then take another colectivo to Puerto Maldonado; 4½ hours in all.

Boca Manu is the connecting point between the rivers Alto Madre de Dios, Manu and Madre de Dios. It has a few houses, an air strip and some food supplies. It is also the entrance to the Manu Reserve and to go further you must be part of an organized group. The park ranger station is located in Limonal. You need to show your permit here. Camping is allowed if you have a permit. There are no regular flights from Cuzco to Boca Manu. These are arranged the day before, if there are enough passengers. Check at Cuzco airport; or with the tour operators in Cuzco.

To the Reserved Zone Upstream on the Río Manu you pass the *Manu Lodge* (see Sleeping, below), on the Cocha Juárez, 3-4 hours by boat. You can continue to Cocha Otorongo, 2½ hours and Cocha Salvador, 30 minutes, the biggest lake with plenty of wildlife. From here it is 2-3 hours to Pakitza, the entrance to the National Park Zone. This is only for biologists with a special permit.

Between Boca Manu and Colorado is **Blanquillo**, a private reserve (10,000 ha). Bring a good tent with you and all food if you want to camp and do it yourself, or alternatively accommodation is available at the *Tambo Blanquillo* (full board or accommodation only). Wildlife is abundant, especially macaws and parrots at the macaw lick near *Manu Wildlife Centre*. There are occasional boats to Blanquillo from Shintuya; 6-8 hours.

Puerto Maldonado → *Phone code: 082. Colour map 3, grid C5. Pop: 40,000. Altitude: 250 m.*

Puerto Maldonado is an important starting point for visiting the south eastern jungles of the Tambopata Reserve or departing for Bolivia or Brazil. It overlooks the confluence of the rivers

Tambopata and Madre de Dios and its isolation makes it relatively expensive and because of the gold mining and timber industries, the immediate surrounding jungle is now cultivated. There is a **Dircetur tourist office** ① *Urb Fonavi, F20, Pasaje 12 de Septiembre, T571164, 970 3987 (mob), carloagpe@yahoo.com*. There is also an office at the airport.

The beautiful and tranquil **Lago Sandoval** is a one-hour boat ride along the Río Madre de Dios, and then a 5-km walk into the jungle (parts of the first 3 km are a raised wooden walkway; boots are advisable). Entry to the lake coasts US$9.50. You must go with a guide; this can be arranged by the boat driver. Boats can be hired at the Madre de Dios port for about US$25 a day, minimum two people (plus petrol) to go to Lago Sandoval (don't pay the full cost in advance).

Jungle tours from Puerto Maldonado

Trips can be made to **Lago Valencia**, 60 km away near the Bolivian border, four hours there, eight hours back. It is an ox-bow lake with lots of wildlife. Many excellent beaches and islands are located within an hour's boat ride. Mosquitoes are voracious. If camping, take food and water.

It is quite easy to arrange a boat and guide from Puerto Maldonado (see Tour operators below) to the **Tambopata National Reserve** (TNR) ① *Inrena, Av 28 de Julio s/n, block 8, Puerto Maldonado, T573278, US$9.50 to enter the TNR, US$20 if going beyond the Malinowski/ Tambopata confluence, this is included in lodge packages*, between the rivers Madre de Dios, Tambopata and Heath. Some superb ox-bow lakes can be visited and the birdwatching is wonderful.

The **Bahuaja-Sonene National Park**, declared in 1996, stretches from the Heath River across the Tambopata, incorporating the Río Heath National Sanctuary. It is closed to visitors.

Río Las Piedras

Lying to the northeast of, and running roughly parallel to the Río Manu, this drainage runs some 700 km from rainforest headwaters in the Alto Purús region. The lower, more easily accessible section of the river, closer to Puerto Maldonado and outside state protection, runs through rich tropical forests, very similar to those in the Manu and Tambopata areas. Close to 600 species of birds, at least eight primate species and some of the Amazon's larger mammals, giant otter, jaguar, puma, tapir and giant anteater, are all present. Hunting pressure has resulted in wildlife being somewhat shier and more secretive than in Manu or Tambopata, but this remains an excellent wildlife destination.

To Iberia and Iñapari

Daily public transport runs on the improved dirt road which begins across the Río Madre de Dios and runs to **Iberia** and **Iñapari** on the border with Brazil. In the wet season the road may only be passable with difficulty, especially between Iberia and Iñapari. In the dry, though, it is a fast road and dangerous for motorcyclists because of passing traffic. Along the road there remains no primary forest, only secondary growth and small *chacras* (farms). There are also picturesque *caseríos* (settlements) that serve as processing centres for the brazil nut. Approximately 70% of the inhabitants in the Madre de Dios are involved in the collection of this prized nut.

Iberia, Km 168, has two hotels, the best is **G Hostal Aquino**, basic, cold shower. Just outside the town the local rubber tappers association has set up an interesting Reserve and Information Centre.

Iñapari, at the end of the road, Km 235, has two basic hotels and a restaurant, but **Assis Brasil** across the border is much more attractive and has a much nicer basic hotel (**G**) on the main plaza. A suspension bridge now links the two countries.

There is a road from Assis Brasil into Brazil and connections to Cobija in Bolivia from Brasiléia. There are no exchange facilities en route and poor exchange rates for Brazilian currency at Iñapari. Crossing between Peru and Bolivia on this route is not easy.

Crossing to Brazil

Take one of the car colectivos that leave for Iñapari from Puerto Maldonado between 0700-0800, 4 hours, US$10 (three companies). The cars stop near **immigration in Iñapari**. Exit stamps can be obtained at immigration, open 0800-1830. In Assis Brasil, there is no Policía Federal office. You have to travel on to Brasiléia to obtain your Brazil entry stamp at Policía Federal in the Rodoviária (bus station). You must have a yellow fever certificate to enter Brazil.

● Sleeping

Manu Biosphere Reserve *p1277*
Lodges in Manu
Amazonia Lodge, on the Río Alto Madre de Dios just across the river from Atalaya. In Cuzco at Matará 334, T/F084-231370, amazonia1@correo.dnet.com.pe. An old tea hacienda run by the Yabar family, famous for its bird diversity and fine hospitality, a great place to relax, contact Santiago in advance and he'll arrange a pick-up.
Casa Machiguenga, near Cocha Salvador, upriver from Manu Lodge. Contact **Manu Expeditions** or **Apeco** NGO, T084-225595. Machiguenga-style cabins run by local communities with NGO help.
Cock of the Rock Lodge, on the road from Paucartambo to Atalaya at 1,500 m, next to a Cock of the Rock *lek*, 8 double rooms and some private cabins, run by the **Perú Verde** group (see Ins and outs, above).
Erika Lodge, on the Alto Madre de Dios, 25 mins from Atalaya, offers basic accommodation and is cheaper than the other, more luxurious lodges. Contact **Manu Ecological Adventures** (see below).
Manu Cloud Forest Lodge, at Unión, at 1,800 m on the road from Paucartambo to Atalaya, owned by **Manu Nature Tours**, 6 rooms with 4 beds.
Manu Lodge, on the Manu river, 3 hrs upriver from Boca Manu towards Cocha Salvador, run by **Manu Nature Tours** and only bookable as part of a full package deal with transport.
Manu Wildlife Centre, 2 hrs down the Río Madre de Dios from Boca Manu, near the Blanquillo macaw lick. Book through **Manu Expeditions** or **InkaNatura**. 22 double cabins, with private bathroom and hot water. Also canopy towers for birdwatching and a Tapir lick.
Pantiacolla Lodge, 30 mins down-river from Shintuya. Owned by the Moscoso family. Book through **Pantiacolla Tours** (see page 1283).
Yanayaco Lodge, Procuradores 46, Cuzco, T084-248122, 084-9606368 (mob), www.yanayacolodge.com. About 1 hr by boat above Diamante village on the southern bank of the Madre de Dios, close to a small parrot *collpa* (mineral lick). Using local river transport to arrive at the lodge rates are very reasonable, US$35 including food and board in double room. The lodge also offers several different itineraries in Manu.

To Puerto Maldonado via Pilcopata and Itahuania *p1278*
Turismo Indigena Wanamei, T084-254033, 965 2520 (mob), or Av 26 de Diciembre 276, Puerto Maldonado, T082- 572539, www.ecoturismowanamei.com. New initiative by the people of the Amarakaeri Communal Reserve,

located between Manu and Tambopata. They offer 4-9 day trips starting and ending in Cuzco. Accommodation includes lodges, communities and camping. The trips aim not only to offer excellent wildlife viewing opportunities but also an insight in to the daily life of indigenous peoples. It's advised that you speak Spanish. The 5 day/4 nights trip costs US$200 and includes all transport, meals, lodging and a guide.
D Boca Manu Lodge, book through **Emperadores Tours**, Procuradores 190, Cuzco, T084-239987. Run by Juan de Dios Carpio, who owns a general store in Boca, reasonably priced.
G Hospedaje Manu, Boca Colorado, on street beside football field. Cell-like rooms, open windows and ceilings but comfy mattresses and mosquito netting.
G Sra Rubella in Pilcopata. Very basic but friendly.
Yine Lodge, next to Boca Manu airport. A cooperative project between **Pantiacolla Tours** and the Yine community of Diamante. Also **G** pp **Hostal** in Boca Manu run by the community. Basic accommodation.

Puerto Maldonado *p1278*
B Wasai Lodge & Expeditions, Billinghurst opposite the Capitanía; reservations: Las Higueras 257, Residencial Monterrico, La Molina, Lima 12, T/F572290, www.wasai.com. In a beautiful location overlooking the Madre de Dios River, with forest surrounding cabin-style rooms, a/c, TV, shower, small pool with waterfall, good restaurant (local fish a speciality). Recommended. They can organize local tours and also have a lodge on the Río Tambopata (see page 1282).
C Cabañaquinta, Cuzco 535, T571045, www.hotelcabanquinta.com. With breakfast, a/c (cheaper rooms without a/c and hot water), free drinking water, interent, good restaurant, lovely garden, very comfortable, airport transfer. Recommended.
D Don Carlos, Av León Velarde 1271, T571029. Nice view over the Río Tambopata, a/c, restaurant, TV, phone, good.
E Amarumayo, Libertad 433, 10 mins from the centre, T573860, residenciamarumayo@hotmail.com. Comfortable, with breakfast, with pool and garden, good restaurant. Recommended.
E Hospedaje Español, González Prada 670, T572381. Comfortable, set back from the road, in a quiet part of town.
E Hospedaje La Bahía, 2 de Mayo 710, T572127. Cheaper without bath or TV, new, large rooms, a good choice.
E Royal Inn, 2 de Mayo 333, T571048.

Modern and clean, rooms at back are less noisy. **F Hostal El Astro**, Velarde 617, T572128. Clean, safe, family run.

Tambopata p1279
Some of the lodges along the Tambopata river offer guiding and research placements to biology and environmental science graduates. For more details send an SAE to **TReeS**: UK - J Forrest, PO Box 33153, London, NW3 4DR, www.geocities.com/treesperu

Lodges on the Río Madre de Dios
C Casa de Hospedaje Mejía, to book T571428, visit **Ceiba Tours**, L Velarde 420, T573567, turismomejia@hotmail.com. Attractive rustic lodge close to Lago Sandoval, full board can be arranged, canoes are available. 3 days/2 nights cost US$70.

El Corto Maltés, Billinghurst 229, Puerto Maldonado, T/F573831, cortomaltes@ terra.com.pe. On the Madre de Dios, halfway to Sandoval which is the focus of most visits. Hot water, huge dining-room, well run. 3 days/2 nights cost US$180.

Eco Amazonia Lodge, on the Madre de Dios, 1 hr down-river from Puerto Maldonado. In Lima: Av Larco 1083, of 408, Miraflores, T01-242 2708, in Cuzco T084-225068, www.ecoamazonia. com.pe. Basic bungalows and dormitories, good for birdwatching, has its own Monkey Island with animals taken from the forest, US$150 for 3 days/2 nights.

Estancia Bello Horizonte, 20 km northwest of Puerto Maldonado, Loreto 258, Puerto Maldonado, T572748 (in Heladería Gustitos del Cura), www.estanciabellohorizonte.com. In a nice stretch of forest overlooking the Madre de Dios, a small lodge with bungalows for 25 people, with private bath, hammock and pool. 3 days/2 nights US$95-140, depending on the package. It is part of the scheme to train and employ young people. Suitable for those wanting to avoid a river trip.

Inkaterra Reserva Amazónica, 45 mins by boat down the Madre de Dios. To book: **Inkaterra**, Andalucía 174, Lima 18, T01-610 0400; Cuzco T084-245314; Puerto Maldonado T082- 572283, www.inkaterra.com. Tastefully redecorated hotel in the jungle with suites and bungalows, solar power, good food in huge dining room supported by a big tree. Jungle tours in its own 10,000 ha plus their new canopy walk; also tours to Lago Sandoval. US$345 pp for 3 days/2 nights package, up to US$1381 for 5 days/4 nights. The lodge has Isla Rolín for the recovery of primates, which are readapted to their natural environment.

Sandoval Lake Lodge, 1 km beyond *Mejía* on Lago Sandoval, book through **InkaNatura**, address under Manu, Tour operators. Usual access is by canoe after a 3-km walk or rickshaw ride, huge bar and dining area, electricity, hot water. US$215 pp for 3 days/2 nights.

Lodges on the Tambopata
Lodges on the Tambopata are reached by vehicle to Bahuaja port, 15 km up river from Puerto Maldonado by the community of Infierno, then by boat.

Casas de Hospedaje Baltimore, several families in the community of Baltimore on the banks of the Río Tambopata, 60 km upriver, www.baltimoreperu.com. They are developing accommodation for visitors (with EU funding), 4-12 tourists per home. They offer the opportunity to experience the forest close-up and an insight into daily life in the forest at a more economical price. Prices vary depending on method of access: about US$120, 3 days/2 nights. Guiding in Spanish, English speaking guide can be arranged. Researchers and volunteers also welcomed by arrangement.

Casa de hospedaje Picaflor, Casilla 105, Puerto Maldonado, picaflor_rc@yahoo.com. A small (4 rooms), family-run guest house with solar lighting, a good library, great cakes and fresh bread baked daily. Just downriver from Libertador Tambopata Lodge, guiding in English/ Spanish, good trail system, visits also made to Lake Condenados. Suited to backpackers and birders, US$20pp per night plus TNR fee and transport. Special arrangements also for researchers and volunteers wanting to stay 4 or more weeks.

Explorers Inn, book through Peruvian Safaris, Alcanfores 459, Miraflores, Lima, T01-447 8888, or Plateros 365, T084-235342, Cuzco, or Fonavi H15, Puerto Maldonado, T/F082-572078, www.peruviansafaris.com. Just before the La Torre control post, adjoining the TNR, in the part where most research work has been done, 58 km from Puerto Maldonado. 2½ hrs up the Río Tambopata (1½ hrs return), one of the best places in Peru for seeing jungle birds (580 plus species have been recorded), butterflies (1,230 plus species), also giant river otters, but you probably need more than a 2-day tour to benefit fully from the location. Offers tours through the adjoining community of La Torre. The guides are biologists and naturalists undertaking research in the reserve. They provide interesting wildlife-treks, including to the macaw lick (*collpa*). US$450 for 5 days/4 nights.

Libertador Tambopata Lodge, on the Río Tambopata, to make reservations Suecia 343, Cuzco, T084-245695, www.tambopatalodge.com. Rooms with solar- heated water, good guides, excellent food. Trips go to Lake Condenado, some to Lake Sachavacayoc, and to the Collpa de

Chuncho, guiding mainly in English and Spanish, package US$200 pp for 3 days/2 nights, naturalists programme provided.

Posada Amazonas Lodge, on the Tambopata river, 1½ hrs by vehicle and boat upriver from Puerto Maldonado. Book through **Rainforest Expeditions**, Aramburú 166, of 4B, Miraflores, Lima 18, T01-421 8347, or Portal de Carnes 236, Cuzco, T084-246243, www.peru nature.com. A collaboration between the tour agency and the local native community of Infierno. Attractive rooms with cold showers, visits to Lake Tres Chimbadas, with good birdwatching including the Tambopata Collpa. Offers trips to a nearby indigenous primary health care project where a native healer gives guided tours of the medicinal plant garden. Service and guiding is very good. Recommended. Prices start at US$190 for a 3 day/2 night package, or US$690 for 5 days/4 nights including the **Tambopata Research Centre**, the company's more intimate, but comfortable lodge, about 6 hrs further upriver. Rooms are smaller than Posada Amazonas, shared showers, cold water. The lodge is next to the famous Tambopata macaw clay lick. 2 hrs from Posada Amazonas, Rainforest Expeditions also has the **Refugio Amazonas**, close to Lago Condenados. It is the usual stopover for those visiting the collpa. 3 bungalows accommodate 70 people in en-suite rooms, large, kerosene lit, open bedrooms with mosquito nets, well-designed and run, atmospheric. Prices are for Posada Amazonas.

Wasai Lodge and Expeditions, Río Tambopata, 120 km (4½ hrs) upriver from Puerto Maldonado, T082-572290, owned by Hotel Wasai, www.wasai.com. 20 km of trails around the lodge, guides in English and Spanish. The Collpa de Chuncho is only 1 hr up river; 3 day/2 night trips US$300, 5 day/4 nights US$400, including 1 night in Puerto Maldonado.

Río Las Piedras

Amazon Rainforest Conservation Centre, contact Pepe Moscoso, Jr Los Cedros B - 17, Los Castaños, Puerto Maldonado, T082-573655, www.laspiedrasamazon.com. Roughly 8 hrs up Río Las Piedras, overlooking a beautiful oxbow lake, Lago Soledad, which has a family of giant otters. Comfortable bungalows, with bath and hot water. Activities include a viewing platform 35 m up an ironwood tree, a hide overlooking a macaw lick, and walks on the extensive trail network. Most trips break the river journey half way at Tipishca Camp, overlooking an oxbow lake with a family of otters. 6-days/5-nights with 5-7 people costs US$985.

Las Piedras Biodiversity Station, T/F082-573922, www.rainforestresearch.netfirms. com. A small lodge in a 4,000-ha concession of 'primary' rainforest 90 km up the Río Las Piedras. Visitors camp en route to the lodge. 20 beds in 10 rooms, central dining-room, shared bath, no electricity, library, guiding in English/ Spanish. Minimum package is for 4 days/3 nights, US$470 pp based on a group of 4.

Eating

Puerto Maldonado *p1278*

♯♯-♯ **Carne Brava**, on the Plaza de Armas. One of the smart new joints for a steak and chips. Similar, also on the Plaza, is **Vaka Loca**.

♯♯-♯ **El Califa**, Piura 266. Some regional specialities. Recommended.

♯♯-♯ **El Hornito/Chez Maggy**, on the plaza. Cosy, good pizzas, busy at weekends.

♯ **El Buen Paladar**, González Prada 365. Good value lunch menu.

♯ **La Casa Nostra**, Velarde 515. Sells huge fruit juices for US$0.50, as well as *tamales, papas rellenas* and enormous fancy cakes.

♯ **La Estrella**, Velarde 474, the smartest and best

of the *pollos a la brasa* places.

Gustitos del Cura, Loreto 258, Plaza de Armas. An ice-cream parlour run by a project for homeless teenagers, offering delicious and unusual flavours such as lúcuma and brazil-nut, only US$0.30 for a large cone!

Tu Dulce Espera, Av L.Velarde 475. Good for evening juices and snacks.

⊕ Bars and clubs

Puerto Maldonado *p1278*

Coconut, east side of the plaza. Disco.

El Witite, Av León Velarde 153. A popular, good disco, latin music, open Fri and Sat.

Le Boulevard, behind **El Hornito**. Live music, popular. There is a billiard hall at **Puno 520**.

T-Saica, Loreto 335. An atmospheric bar with live music at weekends.

▲ Activities and tours

Manu Biosphere Reserve *p1277*

Warning Beware of pirate operators on the streets of Cuzco who offer trips to the Reserved Zone of Manu and end up halfway through the trip changing the route "due to emergencies", which, in reality means they have no permits to operate in the area. The following companies organize trips into the Multiple Use and Reserved Zones. Contact them for more details.

Amazon Trails Peru, C Tandapata 660, San Blas, Cuzco, T084-437499, or 974 1735 (mob), www.amazontrailsperu.com (owner Abraham Huamán and his German wife, Ulrike). Well-organized tours including visits to macaw and tapir licks, also trekking.

Expediciones Vilca, Plateros 363, Cuzco, T/F084-251872, www.cbc.org.pe/manuvilca/. Offers tours at economical prices.

InkaNatura, in Cuzco: C Plateros 361, T084-255255, in Lima: Manuel Bañón 461, San Isidro, T01-440 2022, in Chiclayo, T074-209948, www.inkanatura.com. Tours to Manu Wildlife Centre and Sandoval Lake Lodge (see above).

Manu Ecological Adventures, Plateros 356, Cuzco, T084-261640, www.manu adventures.com. This company operates one of the most physically active Manu programmes, with options for a mountain biking descent through the cloudforest and 3 hrs of white-water rafting on the way to **Erika Lodge** on the upper Río Madre de Dios.

Manu Expeditions, Humberto Vidal Unda G-5, p 2, Urb Magisterial, Cuzco, T084-226671, www.manuexpeditions.com. Owned by ornithologist, Barry Walker, 3 trips available to the reserve and Manu Wildlife Centre.

Manu Nature Tours, Av Pardo 1046, Cuzco, T084-252721, www.manuperu.com. Owned by Boris Gómez Luna, run lodge-based trips, owners of Manu Lodge and part owners of Manu Cloudforest Lodge; Manu is the only lodge in the Reserved Zone, open all year, situated on an ox-bow lake, providing access to the forest, US$130 per night including meals, guides available; activities include river-rafting and canopy-climbing, highly recommended for experiencing the jungle in comfort.

Oropéndola, Santa Teresa 379, interior 2do piso, T084-241428, www.oropendolaperu.org. Guide Walter Mancilla is an expert on flora and fauna. Uses lodges run by indigenous communities. Good reports of attention to detail and to the needs of clients.

Pantiacolla Tours SRL, Saphi 554, Cuzco, T084-238323, www.pantiacolla.com. Run by Marianne Von Vlaardingen and Gustavo Moscoso. They have tours to the Pantiacolla Lodge (see Sleeping, above) and also 8-day camping trips. Pantiacolla has started a community-based ecotourism project, called the Yine Project, with the people of Diamante in the Multiple Use Zone.

Puerto Maldonado *p1278*

Guides

All guides should have a carnet issued by the Ministry of Tourism (DIRCETUR), which also verifies them as suitable guides for trips to other places and confirms their identity. Check that the carnet has not expired. Reputable guides are **Hernán Llave Cortez**, **Romel Nacimiento** and the **Mejía** brothers, all of whom can be contacted on arrival at the airport, if available. Also recommended: **Víctor Yohamona**, T082-968 6279 (mob), victorguideperu@hotmail.com. Speaks English, French and German. Boat hire can be arranged through the Capitanía del Puerto (Río Madre de Dios), T573003. **Perú Tours**, Loreto 176, T082-573244, perutoursytravel@hotmail. com. Organize local trips. See also **Ceiba Tours**, under *Casa de hospedaje Mejía*, above.

⊙ Transport

To Puerto Maldonado: via Urcos and Mazuko *p1278*
Bus There are daily buses from the Terminal Terrestre in **Cuzco** with **Transportes Iguazú** and **Mendivil**. Both on Av Tambopata, blocks 3 and 5 in Puerto Maldonado. 19 hrs (potentially much longer in the wet), US$15, depart 1400 from Puerto Maldonado. Another option is to go from Cuzco to **Urcos**, 1 hr, US$2.25, then look for the **Transportes Juan Carlos** bus in Urcos' main plaza. This is a Volvo truck modified with seats and windows. In the dry season this takes 26 hrs to Puerto Maldonado, US$13; it leaves about 1500 and. There are also daily buses from **Mazuko** to Puerto Maldonado with **Transportes Bolpebra** and **Transportes Señor de la Cumbre**, 4 hrs, US$3.

To Puerto Maldonado: via Pilcopata and Itahuania *p1278*
Road From the Coliseo Cerrado in Cuzco 3 bus companies run to **Pilcopata** Mon, Wed, Fri, returning same night, US$10. They are fully booked even in low season. Trucks to Pilcopata run on same days, returning Tue, Thu, Sat, 10 hrs in wet season, less in the dry. Only basic supplies are available after leaving Cuzco, so take all your camping and food essentials, including insect repellent. Transport can be disrupted in the wet season because the road is in poor condition; paving is under way as part of the Carretera Interoceánica (tour companies have latest details). *Camioneta* service runs between Pilcopata and **Salvación** to connect with the buses, Mon, Wed, Fri. The same *camionetas* run **Itahuania-Shintuya-Salvacion** regularly, when sufficient passengers, probably once a day, and 2 trucks a day. On Sun, there is no traffic. To **Boca Manu** you can hire a boat in Atalaya, US$212 for a *peke peke*, or US$400 for a motor boat. It's cheaper to wait or hope for a boat going empty

1284

up to Boca Manu to pick up passengers, when the fare will be US$12.50 per passenger. Itahuania-Boca Manu in a shared boat with other passengers is US$6.25. A private, chartered boat would be US$105. From Itahuania, cargo boats leave for the gold mining centre of **Boca Colorado** on the Río Madre de Dios, via Boca Manu, but only when the boat is fully laden; about 6-8 a week, 9 hrs, US$15. From Boca Colorado colectivos leave from near football field for Puerto Carlos, 1 hr, US$5, ferry across river 10 mins, US$1.65; colectivo Puerto Carlos-Puerto Maldonado, 3 hrs, US$10, rough road, lots of stops (in Puerto Maldonado **Turismo Boca Colorado**, Tacna 342, T082-573435, leave when full). Tour companies usually use own vehicles for the overland trip from Cuzco to Manu.

Puerto Maldonado *p1278*
Air To **Lima**, daily with **Aerocóndor** and **Lan** via Cuzco. Moto-taxi from town to airport US$2, combi US$0.60, 8 km. **Airline offices** Lan, Av León Velarde y 2 de Mayo, T573677. **Aerocóndor**, Loreto 222, T571733. **Road and ferry** A standard journey by **moto-taxi** in town costs US$0.60, a ride on a **motorbike** US$0.30. Routes from Cuzco are given above. For **Boca Manu** and **Itahuania** take a colectivo to **Boca Colorado** (see above) and then take a cargo boat (no fixed schedule). From Itahuania there is transport to Pilcopata and Cuzco. To **Juliaca**, **Transportes Tahuamanu**, Fizcarrald 609, and **Transportes Madre de Dios**, Av Tambopata 1000, daily services via San Gabán, at 1900 and 1700 respectively, 18 hrs, US$15.

⊙ Directory

Puerto Maldonado *p1278*
Banks Open 0900-1300, 1700-1900. BCP, cash advances with Visa, ATM, no commission on TCs. **Banco de la Nación**, cash on Mastercard, quite good rates for TCs. The best rates for cash are at the *casas de cambio* on Puno 6th block, eg *Cárdenas Hnos*, Puno 605. **Consulates Bolivian Consulate**, on the north side of the plaza. **Internet** All over town. **Motorcycle hire** Scooters and mopeds can de hired from San Francisco and others, on the corner of Puno and G Prado for US$1.15 per hr or US$10 per day. Passport and driver's licence must be shown. **Post offices** Serpost: at Velarde 6th block, 0800-2000, 0800-1500 Sun. **Telephones** Telefónica, on west side of Plaza, next to Municipalidad; also on Plaza next to *El Hornito*, sells phone cards for national and international calls. **Useful addresses Peruvian immigration**, 26 de Diciembre 356, 1 block from Plaza, get your exit stamp here.

★ Don't miss ...

1 **Mercado del Puerto** Montevideo is a major port, as well as the capital. The 19th-century market building, near the docks, has been turned into a hive of restaurants serving one of Uruguay's staples – grilled meat. Lunchtimes are best, especially Saturday when you'll find live music, too, page 1298.

2 **Estancia tourism** Uruguay's agricultural heartland is ideal for estancia tourism (staying on a farm). Many welcome visitors, some for the day, others overnight. You can join in the work, or do absolutely nothing, but if you can do it on horseback, so much the better, page 1300

3 **Colonia del Sacramento** The only remnant of colonial architecture in this part of the continent, Colonia is a well-preserved historical gem on a small peninsula jutting into the Río de la Plata. The town also happens to be a short ferry ride from Buenos Aires, page 1305.

4 **Punta del Este** The premier South American beach resort, which bursts at the seams from December to February. There are quieter Atlantic beaches nearby and, out of season, you may have the coast pretty much to yourself, page 1315.

Essentials

Planning your trip

Where to go **Montevideo**, the capital, is the business heart of the country and has an interesting Ciudad Vieja (old city). The highlights are Mercado del Puerto, the former dockside market, which has become an emporium for traditional food and drink, and the magnificently restored Teatro Solís and the pedestrian Calle Sarandí. Within the city's limits are a number of beaches, which continue along the north shore of the Río de la Plata and on to the Atlantic seaboard. The most famous resort is **Punta del Este** which, in season (December-February), is packed with Argentines, Brazilians and locals taking their summer break. Beyond Punta del Este, there are quieter beaches with less infrastructure, but with sand dunes and other natural features. Along the coast, impressive villas and condominiums blend with their surroundings, a sort of museum of contemporary South American architecture under the open sky.

West of the capital is **Colonia del Sacramento**, a unique remnant of colonial building in this part of the continent. It is well preserved, standing on a small peninsula, and has one of the principal ferry ports for passenger traffic from Buenos Aires. Consequently it is a popular, but costly place, but well worth a visit. Continuing west you come to the confluence of the Río Uruguay with the Plata estuary. Up river are the last vestiges of the meat canning industry at **Fray Bentos**, which has a museum commemorating what used to be one of Uruguay's main businesses. Up river are towns such as **Paysandú** and the historic **Salto**, from which you can cross to Argentina, and the hot springs which have been developed into resorts.

The centre of the country is mainly agricultural land, used for livestock and crops. Many *estancias* (farms) accept visitors, some just for the day, others for longer stays. Daytrips out of Montevideo, Punta del Este, or Colonia, for instance, to an *estancia*, usually involve a meal, handicraft shopping and an educational element. Those ranches which offer lodging let you take part in the daily tasks, as these are working farms; you can do as much or as little as you like. Horse riding is the main activity and is usually suitable for all abilities.

When to go The climate is temperate, if somewhat damp and windy, and summer heat is tempered by Atlantic breezes. Winter (June-September) temperatures average 10-16°C, but can sometimes fall to below freezing. It is generally humid and hardly ever snows. Summer (December-March) temperatures average 21-27°C. There is always some wind and the nights are relatively cool. The rainfall, with prolonged wet periods in July and August, averages about 1,200 mm at Montevideo and some 250 more in the north, but the amount varies yearly.

Most tourists visit during the summer, which is also high season, when prices rise and hotels and transport need advance bookings. Seasonal variations for Montevideo and Punta del Este are given on pages 1296 and 1315. In the low season on the coast many places close.

Finding out more Ministry of Tourism ① *Edif Depósito Santos, Rambla 25 de Agosto y Yacaré, T02-188 5100, www.turismo.gub.uy and www.uruguaynatural.com.*

Websites

www.eltimon.com A good Uruguayan portal.
www.turismodeluruguay.com A tourism portal in English, Spanish and Portuguese.
www.turismoguambia.com.uy or
www.uruguayaltoque.com.uy Tourist information in Spanish with list of accommodation for all main towns in the country.

www.salimoshoy.com.uy Entertainment and cultural activities guide, also has some tourist information for the whole country, in Spanish.
www.brecha.com.uy *La Brecha*, a progressive weekly listing films, theatres and concerts in Montevideo and provinces, US$3. Recommended.

Maps **Automóvil Club del Uruguay** (see box page 1291), publishes road maps of the city and country, as do **Esso** and **Ancap**. A good road map of Uruguay and Montevideo (all in one) is published by **Silveira Mapas**, *Mapa de la República Oriental del Uruguay/Plano de la capital Montevideo*, US$6.40. **ITM** of Vancouver also publish a country map (1:800,000). Official maps are issued by **Instituto Geográfico Militar** ① *Abreu y 8 de Octubre, T801 6868, 0800-1230.*

Visas and immigration A passport is necessary for entry except for nationals of most Latin American countries and citizens of the USA, who can get in with national identity documents for stays of up to 90 days. Visas are not required for a stay of less than three months by nationals of all EU countries (except Bulgaria and Estonia), Argentina, Australia, Bahamas, Barbados, Belize, Bolivia, Brazil, Canada, Colombia, Costa Rica, Croatia, Chile, Dominican Republic, Ecuador, El Salvador, Guatemala, Honduras, Israel, Iceland, Jamaica, Japan, Liechtenstein, Malaysia, Mexico, New Zealand, Nicaragua, Norway, Panama, Paraguay, Peru, South Africa, Switzerland, Trinidad and Tobago, Turkey, USA, Venezuela. Visas cost £27 (or equivalent), and you need a passport photo and a ticket out of Uruguay. Visa processing may take 2-4 weeks. For those living in a country with no Uruguayan embassy, a visa can be applied for online and collected at any Uruguayan consulate before entering the country. Visas are valid for 90 days and usually single entry. Tourist cards (obligatory for all tourists, obtainable on entry) are valid for three months, extendable for a similar period at the **Migraciones office** ① *C Misiones 1513, T916 0471, www.dnm.minterior.gub.uy.*

Uruguayan embassies and consulates Visit www.mrree.gub.uy/mrree/Embajadas_y_Consulados/Misiones/misiones.htm for a complete list.

Money The currency is the *peso uruguayo*. Bank notes issued are for 5, 10, 20, 50, 100, 200, 500, 1,000 and 2,000 pesos uruguayos. Coins: 50 céntimos, 1, 2, 5 and 10 pesos. Any amount of currency can be taken in or out. Rates change often because of the floating **exchange rate** and inflation differentials against the \$US. Exchange rate in July 2007: US\$1=23.9, €1=32.53.

There is no restriction on foreign exchange transactions (so it is a good place to stock up with US\$ bills, though American Express and some banks refuse to do this for credit cards; most places charge 3% commission for such transactions). Those banks which give US\$ cash against a credit card are given in the text. Most ATMs in Montevideo can dispense both Uruguayan pesos and US\$. Dollars cash can be purchased when leaving the country. Changing Argentine pesos into Uruguayan pesos is usually a marginally worse rate than for dollars. Brazilian *reais* get a much worse rate. US\$ notes are accepted for some services, including most hotels and some restaurants.

Credit cards In some places there is a 10% charge to use a credit cards Visa and MasterCard. Most banks operate with **Banred** ATMs for Visa or MasterCard withdrawals. MasterCard emergency line call collect to USA, T1-636-722 7111. Visa emergency line, call collect T00-044-20-7937 8091. Most cheaper hotels outside major cities do not accept credit cards.

Cost of travelling Uruguay is comparatively inexpensive. Prices vary considerably between summer and winter, Punta del Este being one of the most expensive summer resort in Latin America. Someone staying in a cheap hotel, eating the *menú del día* and travelling by bus, should allow US\$40 per day. Internet price varies from US\$0.60 to US\$2 or more per hour.

Safety Personal security offers few problems in most of Uruguay. Be aware that gang robbery may occur in Montevideo (don't show any signs of obvious wealth). Adult and child beggars are often seen in restaurants, cafes, public places and buses, trying to sell small items or simply asking for money. They are not dangerous, but watch your belongings. The Policía Turística patrol the streets of the capital.

Getting around
Flight connections If flying from Uruguay to make an international connection in Buenos Aires, make sure your flight goes to Ezeiza International Airport (eg on United, American Airlines or TAM), not Aeroparque (almost all Aerolíneas Argentinas or Pluna flights). Luggage is not transferred automatically to Ezeiza and you will have to travel one hour between the airports by taxi or bus. If you need visa to enter Argentina, you must get a transit visa (takes up to four weeks to process in Montevideo), just to transfer between airports.

Bus and road All main cities and towns are served by good companies, but driving your own or a rented vehicle (see box, page 1291) is the best way to explore Uruguay, as it allows flexibility and access to many places not served by public transport. There are good services to neighbouring countries. Details are given in the text. A departure tax of US\$0.30-0.60 is charged with every bus ticket. **Hitching** is not easy.

Touching down

Airport tax US$16 on all air travellers leaving Uruguay for Buenos Aires, Aeroparque, but US$29 to Ezeiza and all other countries (payable in US$ or local currency), and a tax of 3% on all tickets issued and paid for in Uruguay.
Business hours Shops: Mon-Fri 1000-1900; Sat 1000-1300; **shopping malls**: daily 1000-2200. In small towns or non-tourist areas, there is a break for lunch and siesta, between 1300 and 1600. **Businesses**: 0830-1200, 1430-1830 or 1900. **Banks**: 1200-1700 in Montevideo (some till 1800); Mon-Fri 1300-1700 in Colonia; also in the afternoon in Punta del Este and elsewhere; banks close Sat. **Government offices**: Mon-Fri 1200-1800 in summer; Mon-Fri 1000-1700 (rest of the year).

In an emergency T911. Ambulance T105. Fire service T104. Road police T108. Tourist Police in Montevideo, at Colonia 1021 (on Plaza Fabini), T0800-8226. Road information, T1954.
International phone code +598. Ringing: long equal tones, long pauses. Engaged: short tones, short pauses.
Official time GMT -3 (Sep-Mar -2).
Tipping Restaurant and cafés usually include service, but an additional 10% is expected. Porters at the airport: US$1 per piece of luggage. Taxis: 5-10% of fare.
VAT/IVA 23%.
Voltage 220 volts 50 cycles AC. Various plugs used: round 2-pin or flat 2-pin (most common), oblique 2-pin with earth, 3 round pins in a line.
Weights and measures Metric.

Train The only passenger services are slow commuter services from Montevideo to Progreso, Canelones, Santa Lucía, 25 de Agosto and San José de Mayo; and from Montevideo to Pando and Sudriers.

Sleeping → *See page 58 for our hotel grade price guide.*
Camping There are lots of sites. Most towns have municipal sites (quality varies). Many sites along the Ruta Interbalnearia, but most of these close off season. The Tourist Office in Montevideo issues a good guide to campsites and youth hostels; see references in main text. The annual Guía de Verano is good for sites and prices, particularly at the beach resorts.

Youth hostels Red Uruguaya de Hostels ① *Paraguay 1212 (y Canelones), Montevideo, T900 5749, www.hosteluruguay.org,* operates 15 hostels (HI members) around Uruguay.

Eating → *See page 58 for our restaurant price guide.*
Eating out Dinner in 'top class restaurants' is served 2000-0100. In less formal restaurants service starts at 1930. Restaurants usually charge *cubierto* (bread), costing US$1-2, and more in Punta del Este. A *confitería* is an informal place which serves meals at any time, as opposed to a *restaurante*, which serves meals at set times. Many serve *preparación*, a collection of hors d'oeuvres. Uruguay does not have a great selection of international restaurants. Vegetarians may have to stick to salads, as even the dishes which are meatless elsewhere (*arroz a la cubana*, *tortilla española*) are served with bacon and sausages in Uruguay.

Food Beef is eaten at almost all meals. Most restaurants are *parrilladas* (grills) where the staple is beef. *Asado* (barbecued beef) is popular; the main cuts are *asado de tira* (ribs); *pulpa* (no bones), *lomo* (fillet steak) and entrecote. To get a lean piece of *asado*, ask for *asado flaco*. *Costilla* (chop) and *milanesa* (veal cutlet) are also popular; usually eaten with mixed salad or chips. *Chivitos* are Uruguayan steak burgers; *chivitos canadienses* are sandwiches filled with slices of meat, lettuce, tomato, etc (normally over US$3, very filling). Two other good local dishes are *puchero* (beef with vegetables, bacon, beans and sausages) and local varieties of pizza. Other specialities are barbecued pork, grilled chicken in wine, *cazuela* (or stew) usually with *mondongo* (tripe) or seafood (such as squid,

Driving in Uruguay

Road Driving is very expensive by South American standards: fuel costs are high and many roads have tolls (one-way tolls Montevideo-Colonia US$3.60, payable in UR$, AR$, US$ or Reais). Check at www.uruguaynatural.com for discounts and benefits for tourists driving a non-Uruguayan vehicle. Roads are generally in good condition; 23% are paved and a further 60% all-weather. In rural areas, motorists should drive with their headlights on even in daylight, especially on major roads. Uruguayans are polite drivers: outside Montevideo, trucks will move to the shoulder to let you pass and motorists will alert you of speed traps.

Documents 90-day temporary admission is usually given without any problems. Entry is easier and faster with a *carnet de passages*, but it is not essential. Without it you will be given a temporary import paper which must be surrendered on leaving the country. Insurance is required by law. For more information, see www.aduanas.gub.uy.

Organizations Automóvil Club del Uruguay, Av del Libertador 1532, T1707, www.acu.com.uy. Reciprocity with foreign automobile clubs is available; members do not have to pay for affiliation.

shark – *cazón*, mussels – *mejillones*). The sausages are very good and spicy (*chorizos*, *morcillas*, *salchichas*). *Morcilla dulce*, a sweet black sausage, made from blood, orange peel and walnuts, is tasty; so is the *morcilla salada*, which is savoury. For snacks, *media lunas mixtas* are a type of croissant filled with ham and cheese, either hot or cold; toasted sandwiches are readily available; *panchos* are hot dogs, *húngaras* are thin spicy sausage hot dogs. An excellent dessert is *chajá*, from Paysandú, a type of sponge-cake ball with cream and jam inside, also with peaches – very sweet; others are *massini* (a cream sponge), *Martín Fierro* (*dulce de membrillo* with cheese) and the common lemon pie. Pastries are very good indeed, and crystallized egg-yolks, known as *yemas*, are popular sweets. Ice cream is excellent everywhere.

Drink The beers are good. Local wines are very varied. 'Del museo' indicates the bodega's vintage reserve. *Uvita* is a sweet, potent liquor served in some old bars of Montevideo. The local spirits are *caña* and *grappa*. In the Mercado del Puerto, Montevideo, a *medio medio* is half still white wine, half sparkling white (elsewhere a *medio medio* is half *caña* and half whisky). *Espillinar* is a cross between whisky and rum. Try the *clérico*, a mixture of wine and fruit juices. Very good fresh orange and grapefruit juices (*exprimidos*). *Mate* is the favourite drink between meal hours. Coffee is good: a *cortado* is strong and white, *café con leche* is milk with a little coffee.

Festivals and events

Public holidays 1 Jan, 6 Jan; Carnival (see below); Easter week; 19 Apr; 1 May, 19 Jun; 18 Jul; 25 Aug (the night before is **Noche de la Nostalgia**, when people gather in *boliches* to dance to old-time songs); 12 Oct; 2 Nov; 25 Dec. 8 Dec is a religious holiday which also marks the official start of the summer holiday.

    Carnival week is officially the Monday and Tuesday preceding Ash Wednesday, but many firms close for the whole week. Business also comes to a standstill during **Holy Week**, which coincides with La Semana Criolla (horse-breaking, stunt riding by cowboys, dances and song). Department stores close only from Good Friday. Banks and offices close Thursday-Sunday. Easter Monday is not a holiday. A weekend of October is chosen annually for celebrating the **Día del Patrimonio** (Heritage Day) throughout the country: hundreds of buildings, both public or private, including embassies, are open to the public for that day only. Also special train services run. In mid-December there is a **Fireworks night** at Pocitos beach.

Montevideo → *Phone code: 02. Colour map 8, grid B6. Population: 1,311,976.*

Montevideo is many cities rolled into one. It is an international port at its western end and, in the east, a seaside resort with sandy streets and pine forests. In between are the faded Old City, the country's financial heart and the posh residential areas along the coast. Everything blends together: myriad architectural styles; café society and tango music; theatres; pizza, parrillada and wines; outdoor markets and indoor malls; agricultural fairs; football, vintage cars and traffic. This is where all the elements of Uruguay meet on the shores of the Río de la Plata.

Montevideo, the capital, was founded in 1726. The original site is on a promontory between the Río de la Plata and an inner bay, though the fortifications have been destroyed. In addition to some colonial Spanish and Italian architecture, French and art deco styles can be seen. The city not only dominates the country's commerce and culture: it accounts for 70% of industrial production and handles almost 90% of imports and exports. It is also a summer resort and the point of departure for a string of seaside resorts to the east. The city's population, indeed that of the entire country, is decreasing due to emigration and a very low birth-rate.

Ins and outs

Getting there Carrasco international **airport** is east of the centre, to which connections by bus or taxi are easy. It takes about 50 minutes by bus, 30 minutes by taxi, but there is a longer, more scenic route, by the coast, which may have fewer delays, but is more expensive (ask for the quick route if you want). Many arrive in Montevideo by boat from Buenos Aires. The **ferry terminal** is in the heart of the city, at the docks not far from the Mercado del Puerto. The **bus terminal**, Tres Cruces, is 10-15 minutes by city bus from the centre. It has good facilities and is used by bus companies. ▶ *For more detailed information, see Transport, page 1301.*

Montevideo Ciudad Vieja & Centre

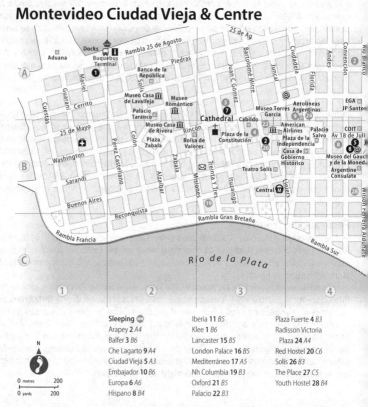

0 metres 200
0 yards 200

Sleeping ⬤
Arapey **2** A4
Balfer **3** B6
Che Lagarto **9** A4
Ciudad Vieja **5** A3
Embajador **10** B6
Europa **6** A6
Hispano **8** B4

Iberia **11** B5
Klee **1** B6
Lancaster **15** B5
London Palace **16** B5
Mediterráneo **17** A5
Nh Columbia **19** B3
Oxford **21** B5
Palacio **22** B3

Plaza Fuerte **4** B3
Radisson Victoria
 Plaza **24** A4
Red Hostel **20** C6
Solís **26** B3
The Place **27** C5
Youth Hostel **28** B4

Getting around The Ciudad Vieja can be explored on foot as it is not large. From there it is not far to Plazas de la Independencia, Fabini and Cagancha, but buses are plentiful along Avenida 18 de Julio, connecting all these places. To get to other parts of the city and the beach districts there are many buses, some running on express routes. There are two types of taxis, the ordinary ones, which are not expensive, but which charge more on Sunday and holidays, and *remises*, which operate out of offices and from the airport, and are more expensive. Full details are given in Local Transport, below. **Note** Some plazas and streets are known by two names: for instance, Plaza de la Constitución is also called Plaza Matriz. Streets whose names have been changed may not be marked as such on all maps: Michelini was Cuareim; Hector Gutiérrez Ruiz was Ibicuy; Convención was Latorre; Wilson Ferreira Aldunate was Río Branco.

Tourist offices Tourist information for the whole country is at the Tres Cruces bus terminal, daily 1000-2200 (T409 7399); at the Ministry of Tourism, Rambla 25 de Agosto y Yacaré (next to the port), T1885 ext 111, and at Carrasco international airport, T604 0386. For information on Montevideo, inside Palacio Municipal, 18 de Julio y Ejido, T1950 1830, daily 1000-1800, all helpful. Check at the municipal website for weekend tours, www.montevideo.gub.uy/culturo. For the Tourist Police, Colonia 1021 (north side of Plaza Fabini), T0800 8226. *Guía del Ocio* is recommended; it's sold at newsstands on Fridays (US$0.25) and has information on museums, cultural events and entertainment. Also check out: www.pimba.com.uy, www.montevideo .com.uy, www.cartelera.com.uy, www.salimoshoy.com.uy, www.aromperlanoche.com, www.bandajoven.com and www.eltimon.com.

Maps Best street maps of Montevideo are at the beginning of the *Guía Telefónica* (both white and yellow page volumes). Free maps can be obtained in all tourist offices and in some museums. The municipality's website, www.montevideo.gub.uy, has good maps. *Eureka Guía De Montevideo* is recommended for streets, with index and bus routes (US$5.20 from bookshops).

Sights

City centre

In the **Ciudad Vieja** is the oldest square in Montevideo: the **Plaza de la Constitución** or **Matriz**. On one side is the **Catedral** (1790-1804), with the historic **Cabildo** (1804) ① *JC Gómez 1362, T915 9685, Tue-Fri 1200-1700, Sat 1130-1630, Sun 1200-1700, free,* opposite. It contains the **Museo y Archivo Histórico Nacional**. The Cabildo has several exhibition halls. On the south side is the **Club Uruguay** (built in 1888, now crumbling), which is worth a look inside. See also the unusual fountain (1881), made by Italians who misspelt the Spanish inscription at the base.

Still further west along Calle Rincón is the small **Plaza Zabala**, with a monument to Bruno Mauricio de Zabala, founder of the city. North of this Plaza are: the **Banco de la República** ① *Cerrito y Zabala* and the **Aduana** ① *Rambla 25 de Agosto.* Several historic houses belong to the Museo Histórico Nacional: **Casa de Montero- Roosen, Museo Romántico** ① *25 de Mayo 428, T915 5361, Mon-Fri 1100-1700, free,* first built in 1728, rebuilt by Antonio Montero in 1831, contains late 19th, early 20th century furniture, furnishings and portraits. **Museo Casa de Rivera** ① *Rincón 437, T915 1051, Mon-Fri 1100-1700, free,* is an 1850 mansion of the

Eating ❼
Café Bacacay **2** *B3*
El Fogón **3** *B5*
Facal **4** *B6*
Gran China **6** *B5*
Il Mondo della Pizza **5** *B4, B5*
La Silenciosa **7** *A3*
Los Leños Uruguayos **8** *B5*

Mercado del Puerto **1** *A1*
Panini's **2** *B3*
Roma Amor **2** *B3*
Subte Pizzerías **9** *B6*
Tío Chef **10** *B6*
Vegetariana **11** *B6*
Viejo Sancho **12** *B6*

first president of the republic. Its rooms are dedicated to various stages of Uruguayan history. Another house belonging to the Museo Histórico Nacional in the Ciudad Vieja, **Museo Casa de Lavalleja** ① *Zabala 1469, Mon-Fri 1300-1700, free,* (1783) has historical mementoes and furniture. Also in the Ciudad Vieja is the **Palacio Taranco, Museo de Artes Decorativos** ① *25 de Mayo y 1 de Mayo, T915 1101, Tue-Sat 1215-1840, Sun 1400-1800, free,* whose garden overlooks Plaza Zabala, a palatial mansion in turn-of-the-20th-century French style, with sumptuously decorated rooms, and a museum of Islamic and Classical pottery and glass. It was first built as a theatre in 1793; in 1908 it was bought by the Ortiz de Taranco family.

Three blocks north of Plaza Zabala are the docks, while three blocks south is the Río de la Plata. The seafront road, the Rambla, has been opened round the point to the port. In the port (which can be visited Saturday 1300-sunset, Sunday 0800-sunset), the ship's bell of HMS *Ajax* has been set up to commemorate the scuttling of the *Graf Spee*; it is in an open-air museum on the opposite side of the road from the Port Administration, 50 m to the right next to a large military building (you may have to persuade the sailors to let you see it). The anchor of the *Graf Spee* was erected inside the port area in 1964 to commemorate the 25th anniversary of the battle.

In the Ciudad Vieja, many of the street names have descriptive plaques. Significant effort (some funds are coming from EU) is now being made to restore the old city to its former glory, but a lot of work is still needed. Areas for a pleasant walk are those around Plaza Matriz and Plaza Zabala, Peatonal Bacacay, the first blocks (closer to the centre) of Peatonal Sarandí, and Mercado del Puerto. Otherwise, a few buildings are worth seeing, but the general air is run down and dodgy (lonely, even, at weekends) and it feels unsafe the closer you get to the port.

Between the Ciudad Vieja and the new city is the largest of Montevideo's squares, **Plaza de la Independencia**, a short distance east of Plaza de la Constitución along the pedestrianized Calle Sarandí. New cafés and boutiques open by the month on Peatonal Sarandí, with shops and cafés, which has been extended to Alzaibar. Two small pedestrian zones full of cafés, live music (mostly after 2300) and restaurants, Peatonal Bacacay and Policia Vieja, lead off Sarandí. In the middle of Plaza de la Independencia is the subterranean marble mausoleum of Artigas, with his statue (1923) dominating the square above. Just west of the plaza is **Museo Torres García** ① *Sarandí 683, T916 2663, daily 0900-2000, bookshop, donation requested (US$2 or 5).* It has an exhibition of the paintings of Joaquín Torres García (1874-1949), one of Uruguay's foremost contributors to the modern art movements of the 20th century, and five floors dedicated to temporary exhibitions of contemporary Uruguayan and international artists. At the eastern end is the **Palacio Salvo** ① *Plaza Independencia 846-848*, built 1922-28. Architectural masterpiece for some, monstrosity for others, it was the first skyscraper in Uruguay. It houses an entire universe, with condominiums, art exhibitions, offices and dilapidated bars where couples dance tango between pool tables. On the southern side is the **Casa de Gobierno Histórico** ① *Palacio Estévez, Mon-Fri 1000-1500.* The modern block to the west of the Casa de Gobierno is the new Palacio de Justicia, still unfinished for lack of funds. The Casa de Gobierno, well-restored, is now used for ceremonial purposes only as the executive offices have been moved. Just off the plaza to the west is the splendid **Teatro Solís** (1842-69) ① *Reconquista y Bartolomé Mitre, T1950 3323, www.teatrosolis.org.uy. Guided visits on Wed, Fri, Sat and Sun 1100, 1200, 1600 (Sat also at 1300), Wed free, otherwise US$1.60 for tours in English.* It has been entirely restored to perfection, with added elevators, access for disabled people, marble flooring and impressive attention to detail. Built as an opera house, Teatro Solís is now used for many cultural events, including ballet, classical music, even the best tango performances. Check press for listings. Tickets are sold daily 1500-2000.

Avenida 18 de Julio runs east from Plaza de la Independencia. The **Museo de Arte Contemporaneo** ① *18 de Julio 965, T900 6662, daily 1400-2000 except Mon 1400-1830,* holds temporary exhibitions. The **Museo del Gaucho y de la Moneda** ① *Av 18 de Julio 998, Edif Banco de la República, T900 8764, Mon-Fri 1000-1700, free,* was renovated in 2003. Museo de la Moneda has a survey of Uruguayan currency and a collection of Roman coins; Museo del Gaucho is a fascinating history of the Uruguayan gaucho and is highly recommended. Between Julio Herrera and Río Negro is the **Plaza Fabini**, or **del Entrevero**, with a statue of a group of *gauchos* engaged in battle, the last big piece of work by sculptor José Belloni. Beneath the plaza is the **Salón Municipal de Exposiciones** ① *Tue-Sun 1500-2000, free,* temporary exhibitions of contemporary art, photography, etc. In the **Plaza Cagancha** (or Plaza Libertad) is a statue of Liberty. The restored **Mercado de la Abundancia** ① *San Jose 1312,* is an attractive old market with handicrafts shops, basic meat restaurants and tango on Saturday and Sunday evenings. The **Palacio Municipal** (La Intendencia) is on the south side of Avenida 18 de Julio, just before it bends north, at the statue of **El Gaucho**. It often has interesting art and photo exhibitions and there is a huge satellite image of the city displayed on the main hall's floor. The road which forks south from the Gaucho is Constituyente, and leads to the beach at Pocitos. **Museo de Historia del Arte** ① *Ejido 1326, T1950 2191, Tue-Sun 1430-2000* is also in the Palacio Municipal. **Centro Municipal de Fotografía** ① *Palacio Municipal (San José 1360, T1950 1113), Mon-Fri 1030-1900, Sat 0930-1430,* has temporary photography exhibitions.

The immense but dilapidated **Palacio Legislativo** ① *from Plaza Fabini head along Av del Libertador Brig Gen Juan Lavalleja (known as Av Libertador), 5 blocks east of Plaza de la Independencia (buses 150, 173, 175 from C Mercedes), guided visits hourly Mon-Fri 0900-1800, free,* , was built 1908-1925 from local marble: there are 55 colours of Uruguayan marble in the Salón de los Pasos Perdidos, 12 types of wood in the library. Other rooms are beautiful. Not far, and dramatically changing the city skyline, is the brand new 160-m high **Antel building** ① *Paraguay y Guatemala, Aguada, T928 0000, Mon, Wed, Fri 1530-1700; Tue, Thu 1030-1200,* with a terrace open to the public on the 26th floor for panoramic views over the bay.

Outside the centre

Museo Nacional de Antropología ① *Av de las Instrucciones 948, Prado, T359 3353, Mon-Fri 1300-1800, Sat, Sun and holidays 1000-1800, take bus 149 from Ejido,* has a modest but well-presented anthropological collection in the hall of a superb, late 19th century mansion, the ex-Quinta de Mendilaharsu (see, among other things, the Music Room with its huge Chinese silk tapestry). **Museo Municipal de Bellas Artes Juan Manuel Blanes** ① *Millán 4015, Prado, T336 2248, Tue-Sun 1215-1745, free, take buses 146, 148, 149, 150 from Mercedes,* in the ex-Quinta Raffo (a late 19th century mansion) dedicated to the work of the artist Blanes (1830-1901), plus a room of the works of Pedro Figari (1861-1938), a lawyer who painted strange, naive pictures of peasant life and negro ceremonies, also work by other Uruguayan artists; has a room with paintings by Courbet, Vlaminck, Utrillo, Dufy, etchings by Orozco and engravings by Goya; temporary exhibitions. **Museo Zoológico** ① *Rambla República de Chile 4215, Buceo, T622 0258, Tue-Sun 1300-1700, free, take bus 104 from 18 de Julio,* is well-displayed and arranged, recommended, great for children too.

Museo Naval ① *Rambla Costanera y Luis A de Herrera, Buceo, T622 1084, 0800-1200, 1400-1800, closed Thu, free,* has a small display of naval history from War of Independence onwards, documentation on Battle of the River Plate and sinking of the *Graf Spee*, and on the sailing ship *Capitán Miranda*, which circumnavigated the globe in 1937-8. This ship is now in the port (can be visited Saturday and Sunday), bus 104 from 18 de Julio.

In **Parque Batlle y Ordóñez** (reached eastwards of Avenida 18 de Julio), are several statues: the most interesting group is the very well-known **La Carreta** monument, by José Belloni, showing three yoke of oxen drawing a wagon. In the grounds is the **Estadio Centenario**, the national football stadium with a seating capacity of 70,000 and a football museum, an athletics field and a bicycle race-track (bus 107). The **Planetarium** ① *next to the Jardín Zoológico, free, gives good, 40-min shows on Thu at 1900, Fri at 2130, Sat and Sun at 1730 and 1830, free, www.montevideo.gub.uy/planetario/, getting there: bus 60 from Av 18 de Julio, or buses 141, 142 or 144 from San José,* is southeast of this park at Avenida Gral Rivera 3254.

From the Palacio Legislativo, Avenida Agraciada runs northwest to **Parque Prado**, the oldest of the city's many parks, about 5 km from Avenida 18 de Julio (bus 125 and others). Among fine lawns, trees and lakes is a rose garden planted with 850 varieties, the monument of **La Diligencia** (the stage coach), the Círculo de Tenis and the Sociedad Rural premises. Part of the park is the adjacent **Jardín Botánico**. ① *daily 0700-1900, guided tours, T336 4005. It is reached via Av 19 de Abril (bus 522 from Ejido next to Palacio Municipal), or via Av Dr LA de Herrera (bus 147 from Paysandú).* The largest and most popular park is **Parque Rodó**, on Rambla Presidente Wilson. Here are an open-air theatre, an amusement park, and a boating lake studded with islands. At the eastern end is the **Museo Nacional de Artes Visuales** ① *Tomás Giribaldi 2283, T711 6124, Wed-Sun 1500-1900, free,* a collection of contemporary plastic arts, plus a room devoted to Blanes. Recommended.

Among the main seaside residential areas are **Pocitos** and **Carrasco**, the city's poshest suburb and a delightful place behind the beach of the same name at the end of the Rambla Sur. It is backed by the forest of the **Parque Nacional Roosevelt**, a green belt stretching north to the marshes of Carrasco (which are being drained). The city itself is expanding beyond Roosevelt. The international airport is nearby. The express bus D1 runs every 30 minutes along Avenida 18 de Julio; this service, which costs slightly more (US$0.75) is about 30 minutes quicker to Carrasco.

At the western end of the bay is the **Cerro** ⓘ *getting there: bus from centre to Cerro: 125 'Cerro' from Mercedes, or boat Sat and Sun 1500-1900, US$5, T601 8601/2*, or hill, 139 m high (from which Montevideo gets its name), with the Fortaleza General Artigas, an old fort, on the top. It is now the **Museo Militar** ⓘ *T487 3121, Wed-Sun 1000-1700, US$0.40, getting there: bus from centre to Cerro: 125 'Cerro' from Mercedes, or boat Sat and Sun 1500-1900, US$5, T601 8601/2*. It houses historical momentos, documentation of War of Independence. The Cerro is surmounted by the oldest lighthouse in the country (1804).

Nine sandy bathing **beaches** stretch along almost the whole of the metropolitan water front, from Playa Ramírez in the west to Playa Carrasco in the east. Along the whole waterfront runs the Rambla Naciones Unidas, named along its several stretches in honour of various nations. Bus 104 from Aduana, which goes along Avenida 18 de Julio, gives a pleasant ride (further inland in winter) past Pocitos, Punta Gorda and all the beaches to Playa Miramar, beyond Carrasco, total journey time from Pocitos to Carrasco, 35 minutes. The seawater, despite its muddy colour (sediment stirred up by the Río de la Plata), is safe to bathe in and the beaches are clean. Lifeguards are on duty during the summer months.

⬤ Sleeping

Hotels may add 23% VAT, but it is usually included in the bill in cheaper and mid-range options; check when booking. High season is 15 Dec-15 Mar, book ahead; many beach hotels only offer full board during this time. After 1 Apr prices are reduced and some hotel dining rooms shut down. During Carnival, prices go up by 20%. The city is visited by Argentines at weekends: many hotels increase prices. Midweek prices may be lower than those posted. When not included, breakfast (*café completo*) costs US$2 or more. Most hotels above an **E** have cable TV and a mini bar or fridge.

The tourist office has information on the more expensive hotels. For more information and reservations contact **Asociación de Hoteles y Restaurantes del Uruguay**, Gutiérrez Ruiz 1213, T908 0141, ahru@montevideo.com.uy.

City centre *p1293, map p1292*
A Nh Columbia, Rambla Gran Bretaña 473, T916 0001, www.nh-hotels.com. 1st class. Rooms have IDD phone, minibar and TV. Breakfast, restaurant, sauna, music show.
A-B Plaza Fuerte, Bartolomé Mitre 1361, T915 6651, www.plazafuerte.com.uy. Restored 1913 building, historical monument, each room different, a/c, safe, internet, restaurant, pub.
D-E Palacio, Bartolomé Mitre 1364, T916 3612, www.hotelpalacio.com.uy. Well kept old hotel, rather gloomy though, safe, balconies, laundry service, stores luggage, no breakfast.
E Solís, Bartolomé Mitre 1314, T915 0279, hotelsolis@hotmail.com. Some rooms with bath and a/c, safe, bike rental, excursions, internet, bar, good value and location, but lots of street noise.
E Ciudad Vieja Hostel, Ituzaingó 1436, T915 6192, www.ciudadviejahostel.com. New hostel with lots of services (Spanish lessons, bike hire, city

tours, laundry, theatre tickets, football, massage), 2- to 6-bed rooms, free internet/Wi-Fi, safes, kitchen, airport transport, helpful staff. Recommended.

East of Ciudad Vieja
L-AL Radisson Victoria Plaza, Plaza Independencia 759, T902 0111, www.radisson.com/montevideouy. A/c, excellent restaurant (rooftop, fine views), less formal restaurant in lobby, luxurious casino in basement, new 5-star wing fully open, art gallery, business centre.
A Embajador, San José 1212, T902 0012, www.hotelembajador.com. Sauna, swimming pool in the summer, TV with BBC World, excellent. Recommended.
A-C Klee Internacional, San José 1303, T902 0606, www.multi.com.uy/hotelklee. Very comfortable, good value in standard rooms, spacious, includes internet use, breakfast, a/c, heater, minibar, good view, satellite TV. Highly recommended.
B Oxford, Paraguay 1286, T902 0046, www.hotel oxford.com.uy. Modern, with good breakfast, safes, laundry service, parking. Recommended.
B-C London Palace, Río Negro 1278, T902 0024, www.lphotel.biz/welcome.htm. Reliable, excellent breakfast, internet. Parking.
C Balfer, Z Michelini 1328, T902 0135, hotelbalfer@adinet.com.uy. Good, TV, safe deposit, excellent breakfast.
C Europa, Colonia 1341, T902 0045, www.hotel europa.com.uy. Comfortable, spacious rooms, a good choice, café, cybercafé, garage.
C Lancaster, Plaza Cagancha 1334, T902 1054, www.lancaster-hotel.com. One of the few relatively cheap options in the centre; despite needing a full renovation, rooms are yet quite acceptable with a/c, fridge, and some with nice views over Plaza Cagancha. With breakfast.

⬤ *For an explanation of the sleeping and eating price codes used in this guide, see page 58.*
⬤ *Other relevant information is found in Essentials page 1290.*

C Mediterráneo, Paraguay 1486, T900 5090, www.hotelmediterraneo.com.uy. With breakfast, TV, comfortable.

C-D Hispano, Convención 1317, T/F900 3816, www.hispanohotel.com. A/c, with breakfast, comfortable, laundry, parking.

C Red Hostel, San José 1406, T908 8514, www.redhostel.com. By the Intendencia, hostel with double rooms and dorms (**E** pp), all with shared bath, cheerful, cable TV, internet connection in rooms, computers, safe, breakfast, bike rental, roof terrace and kitchen.

D Iberia, Maldonado 1097, T901 3633, www.internet.com.uy/hoiberia. Modern, with TV, internet, fridge, parking, US$1 for breakfast.

D The Place, Maldonado 1080, T900 6047, F908 2198. This converted old house has large spotless rooms with TV, some with a/c. A good choice. Breakfast served in the new cafeteria.

E Arapey, Av Uruguay 925, near Convención, T900 7032, www.arapey.com.uy. Good location, on route to airport, variety of rooms with bath, TV, fan, heating, no breakfast.

E-F pp, Che Lagarto Hostel, Plaza Independencia 713, T903 0715, www.chelagarto.com. New hostel in a colonial building with terrace and views over the river and plaza. Excellent location. Dorms and doubles (**B-C**) including breakfast, most with private toilet. Restaurant/pub and common areas. Internet, 24-hr check in, credit cards welcome.

F Youth hostel (members only), Canelones 935, T908 1324, www.montevideohostel.com.uy. Open all year. US$10 pp (seasonal variations, breakfast included, towels US$1 extra), doors locked at 2400 (but security lax), clean, dormitory style, kitchen, lots of hot water, but shortage of bathrooms and noisy, bicycle hire US$1.

Outside the centre *p1295*
Near Tres Cruces bus terminal
A Days Inn, Acevedo Díaz 1821-23, T400 4840, www.daysinn.com.uy. A/c, breakfast, safe, coffee shop and health club, look for promotional offers.

C Royal Palace, Acevedo Díaz 1697, T401 0691, royalpalace@adinet.com.uy. 3-star, with TV, phone, 24-hr bar.

C Tres Cruces, Miguelete 2356 esq Acevedo Díaz, T402 3474, h3cruces@adinet.com.uy. A/c, TV, safe, coffee shop.

East of the centre
L Sheraton, Victor Solino 349, T710 2121, www.sheraton.com. Beside Shopping Punta Carretas, all facilities, good views, access to Golf Club. There is also a **Four Points Sheraton** at Ejido 1275, T901 7000, in the centre (**L-AL**).

A Pocitos Plaza, Benito Blanco 640, Pocitos, T712 3939, www.pocitosplazahotel.com.uy. Modern building in pleasant residential district, next to the river, with large functional rooms, gym and sauna.

C Oceanía, Mar Artico 1227, Playa Los Ingleses, Punta Gorda, T600 0444, www.hotelcasino oceania.com. In an attractive residential area on the coast, pleasant views, good restaurant and a night club *Makao* for the over 40s. Recommended.

Carrasco
LL-L Belmont House, Av Rivera 6512, T600 0430, www.belmonthouse.com.uy. 5-star, includes breakfast, small, beautifully furnished, top quality, excellent restaurant Allegro, pub/bar Memories, pool, 4 blocks from beach. Recommended.

AL Regency Suites, Gabriel Otero 6428, T600 1383, www.regency.com.uy. Good boutique-style hotel with all services, free internet, safety deposit, fitness centre, pool, restaurant *Tartufo* and pub, a couple of blocks from the beach.

A Cottage, Miraflores 1360, www.cottage.com.uy. In a beautiful location next to wide beaches and in quiet residential surroundings, very comfortable, simply furnished rooms with fridge and a/c, restaurant, pool in a lovely garden. Excellent value.

A Pedro Figari, Rambla Rep de México 6535, Carrasco, T600 8824, www.hotelpedrofigari.com. Best Western hotel. A/c, buffet, breakfast, cable TV, convenient for airport, very pleasant.

Camping Parque Roosevelt, near Carrasco, US$3 pp, free, hot showers, safe, no electricity, 15 km from centre, open all year. For vans and caravans only at Punta Ramírez on Rambla República Argentina, free for stays under 48 hrs, central, basic facilities, 24 hr security.

Eating

There is a 23% added tax on restaurant bills, plus a charge for bread and service (*cubierto*) that varies between US$1 to 2 pp. In Montevideo, expensive (♥♥♥) = over US$12, mid-range (♥♥) = US$7-12, cheap (♥) = under US$7.

City centre *p1293, map p1292*

♥♥♥ **La Silenciosa**, Ituzaingó 1426, T915 9409. In a converted Jesuit convent (18th-century), later a prestigious fashion house (19th-century), now a historical monument, excellent food, international and French, open Mon-Fri for lunch and Thu-Sat for dinner. Highly recommended.

♥♥♥ **Mercado del Puerto**, opposite the Aduana, Calle Piedras, between Maciel and Pérez Castellanos (take 'Aduana' bus). Don't miss eating at this 19th-century market building, closed Sun, delicious grills cooked on huge charcoal grates (menus are limited to beef, chicken and fish, including swordfish). It is best to go at lunchtime, especially Sat; the atmosphere is great, including buskers outside. Inside the Mercado del Puerto, those recommended are: **Roldós**, sandwiches, most people start with a *medio medio* (half still, half sparkling white wine). **La Estancia del Puerto, Cabaña Verónica, La Chacra del Puerto** (signed **Ottonello**). **Don Tiburón** has a bar inside and a more expensive and smart restaurant, **La Posada**, with tables outside.

♥♥♥ **Panini's**, Bacacay 1339 (also at 26 de Marzo 3586, Pocitos). Good Italian pasta. Large and lively.

♥♥♥ **Roma Amor**, Bacacay 1331. Lovely little Italian-style restaurant with delicious pasta, good desserts and local wines. Closed Sun lunch, great antipasti lunchtime buffet, US$8-10. Recommended.

♥ **Café Bacacay**, Bacacay 1310 y Buenos Aires. Good music and atmosphere, food served, try the specials. Recommended.

Plaza Cagancha

♥♥♥ **Facal Café Resto Bar**, 18 de Julio 1245, T908 7741. Good simple meals and café, open until early in the morning, tango performances in front; daily noon (see Tango a Cielo Abierto, below).

♥♥♥ **Los Leños Uruguayos**, San José 909. Good and smart *parrilla*, and also fish.

♥♥ **El Fogón**, San José 1080. Good value, very friendly, always full.

♥ **Gran China**, San José 1077. Good Chinese; set menus for US$5 pp.

♥♥♥ **Viejo Sancho**, San José 1229. Excellent, popular, complimentary sherry or vermouth to early arrivals; set menus for US$6 pp.

♥♥-♥ **Tío Chef**, Carlos Quijano 1334, T900-0130. Great authentic Chinese food.

Centro Cultural Mercado de la Abundancia, San Jose 1312 (see Sights, above) has good authentic local eateries, with lunch specials. Highly recommended.

♥ **Il Mondo della Pizza**, several locations, including 18 de Julio 1105, T900 0680, and 18 de Julio 922, T900 4416. Great pizza.

♥ **Subte Pizzerías**, Ejido 1327, T902 3050. An institution, cheap and good. Recommended.

♥ **Vegetariana**, Yí 1369. Closed Sun evening. Excellent, self-service buffet.

♥ Restaurant on 6th floor of YMCA building, Colonia 1870. Reasonable for lunch, with good views, ask for Asociación Cristiana de Jóvenes.

Outside the centre
Playa Ramírez (near Parque Rodó)

♥♥♥-♥♥ **'W' Lounge**, Rambla Wilson y Requena García. Fashionable place for young people with a range of foods and prices, Fri-Sat 2300, live music on Sat, rock, electronica, Latin.

In and around Pocitos

♥♥♥ **Che Montevideo**, Rambla Gandhi 630 (on the coast). A terrace on the river with a laid back atmosphere, serving fish, beef or chicken-based meals. Live music on Fri and Sat evenings.

♥♥♥ **Doña Flor**, Artigas 1034. Classy French restaurant, limited menu but good, moves to Punta del Este in summer.

♥♥♥ **El Entrevero**, 21 de Septiembre 2774. Excellent value, beef, take bus 522 from the centre.

♥♥♥ **El Viejo y el Mar**, Rambla Gandhi 400 block (on the coast), Punta Carretas. Fishing community atmosphere with a great location by the river.

♥♥♥ **La Spaghetteria 23**, Scosería 2584. Tue-Sun, very good Italian.

♥♥ **El Puesto de Joaquín**, Williman 637. Popular, good atmosphere, varied menu.

♥♥ **Pizza Trouville**, 21 de Septiembre y Francisco Vidal. A traditional pizza place with tables outside, next to the beach.

Carrasco

Several restaurants on Av Arocena close to the beach, packed Sun middle day.

♥♥♥ **Dackel**, Dr Gabriel Otero 6438, T600 6211. German/Swiss/Austrian food in a pleasant little place with tables outside, good prices.

♥♥♥ **Hacienda Las Palomas**, P Murillo 6566. Wed-Sat evenings, Sun lunchtime. A little away from Carrasco beach this good Mexican restaurant and tequila bar has an attractive terrace for eating outside.

La Pasiva, Av Arocena y Schroeder (and several others in most districts). This very popular local chain serves good simple meals and tasty sandwiches, including superb hot dogs known as *frankfurters*, or the spicier *húngaras*.

Confiterías Brasilero, Ituzaingó 1447, T915 8120, half a block from Plaza Matriz towards the port. Small entrance; easy to miss. A must, one of the oldest cafés in Montevideo and a permanent hangout of one of the greatest Latin American writers, Eduardo Galeano. Others include: **Café Iberia**, Uruguay esq Florida. Locals' bar. **Cake's**, José Ellauri 1067, Pocitos. Expensive. Recommended. **Conaprole Pocitos**, Rambla Gandhi y Solano Antuña. Ideal at sunset for riverviews, it serves very good strong coffee and quality Conaprole dairy products. A *completo* includes toasts, butter, jam, cheese, a slice of cake, biscuits, juice and coffee or tea, all for US$9. **Oro del Rhin**, Convención 1403. Mon-Sat 0830-2030, open since 1927 it retains the feel of an elegant *confitería* serving good cakes and sandwiches or vegetable pies for lunch. **La Pausa**, Sarandí 493, upstairs. Closed on Sun. Books and magazines on Uruguayan art and literature. **Bar Tasende**, Ciudadela y San José. A classic bar at the edge of Ciudad Vieja. Another bar with long history and loyal clientèle is **Mincho**, Yí 1369, Centro.

There are many good, cheap bakeries in Montevideo selling breads and a variety of sandwiches and local pastries.

Heladerías La Cigale, Av 18 de Julio on Plaza Cagancha and R Graseras 845 (Pocitos). **Las Delicias**, Schroeder 6454 y Av Arocena, Carrasco.

◑ Bars and clubs

Montevideo *p1292, map p1292*
Boliches
See www.aromperlanoche.com for latest events and recommendations. Head to Sarandí, Bacacay or Bartolomé Mitre in Ciudad Vieja, or to Pocitos and Punta Carretas. Discos charge around US$5. Bars/discos/pubs offering typical local nightlife: **30 y Pico**, 21 de Septiembre 2724, Pocitos. For the 30s crowd, Fri-Sat from 2200.
Almodobar, Rincón 626, Ciudad Vieja. Electronic and rock music, Fri, Sat 2230.
Amarcord, Julio Herrera y Obes 1231, Centro. Thu-Sat from 2100, traditional pop music. Live bands Fri.
Bancaria Jazz Club, Sarandí y Zabala p 5. Jazz sessions in the evenings.
Central, Rondeau 1383, Centro. Electronic and rock music on Sat from 2300.
Clyde's, Costa Rica y Rivera, Carrasco. Live music from 2000.
El Pony Pisador, Bartolomé Mitre 1326, Ciudad Vieja. Popular with the young crowd. Live music.
Fun-Fun, Ciudadela 1229, Ciudad Vieja, T915 8005. Hangout of local artists, founded in 1895,

used to be frequented by Carlos Gardel, where *uvita*, the drink, was born. Great music on Fri and Sat. Recommended.
Groove, Rambla República de Mexico 5521, Punta Gorda. Electronic music, Thu-Sat from 2400.
L.O.V.E., Mercedes y Ciudadela, Ciudad Vieja. Electronic music, Thu-Sat 2300.

◉ Entertainment

Montevideo *p1292, map p1292*
Cinema Very popular. During the week no cinemas open before 1730. Films are released quite soon after the UK and USA, and often before they get to Buenos Aires. Details in *Guía del Ocio* and monthly *Cinemateca Uruguaya* (free). At least half of Montevideo's cinemas show blue films – marked *sexo explícito*. **Cine Universitario**, 2 halls: Lumière and Chaplin, Canelones 1280, also for classic and serious films. **Cinemateca** film club has 4 separate cinemas: Cinemateca 18, 18 de Julio 1286, T900 9056; Cinemateca Salas 1 y 2, Dr L. Carnelli 1311, T418 2460; Linterna Mágica, Soriano 1227, T902 8290; and Cinemateca Sala Pocitos, A Chucarro 1036, T708 2957. The Cinemateca shows great films from all over the world and has an extended film archive. It organizes an international film festival, **Festival de invierno**. Entrance is US$2.50 for 6 months, which often admits 2.
Tanguerías El Milongón, Gaboto 1810, T929 0594, www.elmilongon.com.uy. A show that may include dinner beforehand, Mon-Sat. For tango, milonga, candombe and local folk music. **Joven Tango**, at Mercado de la Abundancia, Aquiles Lanza y San José, T901 5561. Cheap and atmospheric venue, Sun 2000. **Tabaris**, Tristán Narvaja 1518, T408 7856. Usually Fri, Sat 2200; check by phone. **Tango a Cielo Abierto**, Tango Under the Open Sky, in front of Café Facal, Paseo Yi and 18 de Julio, T908 7741 for information. Free and very good Uruguayan tango shows every day at noon on a wooden stage. Highly recommended. **La Escuela Universitaria de Música**, Sala Zitarrosa, 18 de Julio 1012. Good, free classical music concerts.
Theatres Montevideo has a vibrant theatre scene. Most performances are only on Fri, Sat and Sun, others also on Thu. Apart from **Teatro Solís** (see Sights, above), recommended are **Teatro del Centro Carlos E Sheck**, Plaza Cagancha 1162, T902 8915, and **Teatro Victoria**, Río Negro y Uruguay, T901 9971. See listings in the daily press and *La Brecha*. Prices are around US$4; performances are almost exclusively in Spanish starting at 2100 or at 1900 on Sun. **Teatro Millington-Drake** at the Anglo (see Cultural centres) puts on occasional productions, as do the theatres of the Alianza Uruguay-Estados Unidos and the Alianza Francesa (addresses below). Many theatres close Jan-Feb.

○ Shopping

Montevideo *p1292, map p1292*

The main shopping area is Av 18 de Julio. Many international newspapers can be bought on the east side of Plaza Independencia.

Bookshops The Sun market on Tristán Narvaja and nearby streets is good for second-hand books. Every December daily in the evening is a Book and Engraving Fair, at Plazoleta Florencio Sánchez (Parque Rodó), with readings and concerts. The following have a few English and American books, but selection in Montevideo is poor: **Bookshop SRL**, JE Rodó 1671 (at Minas y Constituyente), T401 1010, www.bookshop.com.uy, Cristina Mosca. With English stock, very friendly staff, also at Ellauri 363 and at both Montevideo and Portones Shopping Centers; specializes in travel. **El Galeón**, Juan Carlos Gómez 1327, Ciudad Vieja, elgaleon@netgate.com.uy. **Ibana**, International Book and News Agency, Convención 1485. Specializes in foreign publications. **El Libro Inglés**, Cerrito 483, Ciudad Vieja. **Plaza Libros**, Av 18 de Julio 1185. Has a wide range of international books, travel guides, and gay literature. **Puro Verso**, 18 de Julio 1199, T901 6429, puroverso@adinet.com.uy. Very good selection is in Spanish, small secondhand section in English, excellent café, chess tables. Others include: **Librería El Aleph**, Bartolomé Mitre 1358. Used and rare books in Spanish. **Librerías del Sur**, Av 18 de Julio 1578. Extensive stock. **Librería Oriente Occidente**, Rincón 609, Ciudad Vieja. Used and rare books, also has English books, exchange of books in perfect condition. **Linardi y Risso**, Juan Carlos Gómez 1435, Ciudad Vieja, lyrbooks@linardiyrisso.com. **Centro de la Cultura Uruguaya**, Plaza Fabini, T901 1714, www.corazonalsur.com.uy. For books on Uruguay in Spanish and Uruguayan music. **MVD bookstore**, Av 18 de Julio 1261. A small stock of English books.

Galleries There are many good art galleries. **Galería Latina**, Sarandí 671, T916 3737, is one of the best, with its own art publishing house. Several art galleries and shops lie along C Pérez Castellanos, near Mercado del Puerto.

Handicrafts Suede and leather are good buys. There are several shops and workshops around Plaza Independencia. Amethysts, topazes, agate and quartz are mined and polished in Uruguay and are also good buys. For authentic, fairly-priced crafts there is a marquee on Plaza Cagancha (No 1365), and at Mercado de la Abundancia, San José 1312, T901 0550, auda@minetuy.com. For leather goods, walk around C San José y W Ferreira Aldunate. **Montevideo Leather Factory**, Plaza Independencia 832, www.montevideoleatherfactory.com. Recommended. **Manos del Uruguay**, San José 1111, Sarandí y Bacacay, Ciudad Vieja, and at Shopping Centers, www.manos.com.uy.

A non-profit organization that sells very good quality, handwoven woollen clothing and a great range of crafts, made by independent craftsmen and women from all over Uruguay. **Mundo Mineral**, Sarandí 672. Recommended for amethysts, topazes, agate and quartz.

Markets Calle Tristán Narvaja (and nearby streets), opposite Facultad de Derecho on 18 de Julio. On Sun, 0800-1400, there is a large, crowded street market here, good for silver and copper, and all sorts of collectibles. **Plaza de la Constitución**, a small Sat morning market and a Sun antique fair are held here. **Villa Biarritz**, on Vásquez Ledesma near Parque Rodó, Pocitos. A big market selling fruit, vegetables, clothes and shoes (Tue and Sat 0900-1500, and Sun in Parque Rodó, 0800-1400).

Shopping malls The Montevideo Shopping Center, on the east edge of Pocitos (Herrera 1290 y Galanza, 1 block south of Rivera). Open daily 1000-2100 and has a self-service restaurant, a cinema and *confiterías*. It also has wide range of shops selling leather goods, Foto Martín, bookshop, supermarkets and more (bus 141 or 142 from San José). **Punta Carretas Shopping**, Ellauri 306, close to Playa Pocitos in the former prison. Open 0900-2200, is large, modern, with all types of shop, also cinema complex and good food patio, popular. Take bus 117 or 121 from Calle San José. Other shopping centres at Portones in Carrasco, the Tres Cruces bus station and Plaza Arozena Shopping Mall.

▲ Activities and tours

Montevideo *p1292, map p1292*

The **Asociación de Guías de Turismo de Montevideo**, T915 4857 or 099-417037 (mob), runs free historical and architecture tours of Ciudad Vieja leaving from the Cabildo every Sat 1200 and 1300, respectively. Check availability in English. Weekend tours of the city are organized by the **Municipalidad**, US$2.40, not every weekend, check at www.montevideo.gub.uy/cultura.

Day tours of Punta del Este are run by many travel agents and hotels, US$40-100 with meals.

Estancia tourism Information on *estancias* can be found at **Lares**, Wilson Ferreira 1341, T901 9120, www.lares.com.uy, an organization that represents 23 *estancias* and *posadas*; at the tourist offices in Montevideo; or general travel agencies and those that specialize in this field: **Estancias Gauchas**, Cecilia Regules Viajes, agent for an organization of 80 estancias offering lunch and/or lodging, English, French and Portuguese spoken. Full list of estancias at www.turismo.gub.uy (click on Operadores, then Estancias Turísticas). **Jetmar**, Plaza de la Independencia 725-7, T902 0793, info@jetmar.com.uy. A helpful tour operator. **Mundo Turismo Natural**, Colonia 971, T/F902 0862, www.mundoturismo.com.uy. Adventure and nature tourism specialists, mainly to Maldonado and Rocha departments.

Cecilia Regules Viajes, Bacacay 1334, T/F916 3011, T09-968 3608 (mob), regulesv@adinet.com.uy or uy21333@antel.com.uy, very good, knowledgeable, specialist in *estancia*, tango and railway tourism in Uruguay, and skiing in Argentina.

Rumbos, Galería del Libertador, Rio Branco 1377, p 7, T900 2407, fneffa@adinet.com.uy. Caters specifically for independent travellers, very helpful.

JP Santos, Colonia 951, T902 0300, fmaglione@jpsantos.com.uy. Helpful agency.

TransHotel, 8 de Octubre 2252, T402 9935, www.e-transhotel.com. Accommodation, eco-tourism, sightseeing and tailor-made itineraries.

Turisport Ltda, San José 930, T902 0829, www.turisport.com.uy. American Express for travel and mail services, good; sells Amex dollar TCs on Amex card and personal cheque at 1 commission.

Marian Whitaker, T700 6842, F701 5411. Bilingual tours of Montevideo/Uruguay, riding, hiking, fishing, visits to Santa Sofía *estancia* in Río Negro.

⊙ Transport

Montevideo *p1292, map p1292*
Air
The main airport is at Carrasco, 21 km outside the city, T601 1757; coffee shop and children's play area in departure lounge; left luggage US$1 per day per item; exchange facilities, but if closed, buses will accept US$ for fares to town. If making a hotel reservation, ask them to send a taxi to meet you; it's cheaper than taking an airport taxi. To Montevideo 30 mins by taxi or *remise* (US$12-20, depending on destination in the city – may be able to pay taxi driver in Argentine pesos or in US$, or charge it to hotel bill if without cash); about 50 mins by bus. Buses, Nos 700, 701, 704, 710 and 711, from Terminal Brum, Río Branco y Galicia, go to the airport US$1 (crowded before and after school hours); dark brown 'Copsa' bus terminates at the airport. COT buses connect airport and Punta del Este, US$5. **Pluna** runs a bus from *Hotel Victoria Plaza*, Plaza Independencia to airport at 30 mins past the hour (only for **Pluna** passengers). IBAT bus service T601 0209/0943 2373. **Concorde Travel** (Robert Mountford), Germán Barbato 1358, apto 1302, T902 6346/8, has a service from hotel to plane (almost) US$10-25.

Air services to **Argentina**: for the Puente Aéreo to Buenos Aires, check in at Montevideo airport, pay departure tax and go to immigration to fill in an Argentine entry form before going through Uruguayan immigration. Get your stamp out of Uruguay, surrender the tourist card you received on entry and get your stamp into Argentina. There are no immigration checks on arrival at Aeroparque, Buenos Aires.

Bus
Local City buses are comfortable and convenient. Pay your fare to the driver or to conductor in the centre of the bus, US$0.60; express buses D1 (see Sights Carrasco, above), D2, D3, 5, 8, 9, 10, 11 US$0.75. There are many buses to all parts from 18 de Julio; from other parts to the centre or old city, look for those marked 'Aduana'. For Pocitos from city centre take bus No 121 from Calle San José.

Remises: US$8 per hr; **Remises Carrasco**, T606 1412, www.remisescarrasco.com.uy; **Remises Montevideo**, Joaquín Requena 1303, F401 1149; **Libertad**, Plaza Cagancha 1126, T902 4393; **Juan Mastroianni**, T099-639865 (mob), good, safe, reasonably-priced; **Guillermo Muñoz**, Bartolito Mitre 2636, T707 3928.

Long distance During summer holidays buses are often full; it is advisable to book in advance (also for Fri and weekend travel all year round).

Buses within Uruguay: excellent terminal, Tres Cruces, Bulevar Artigas y Av Italia, T408 8710 (10-15 mins by bus from the centre, Nos 21, 64, 180, 187, 188 – in Ciudad Vieja from in front of Teatro Solís); it has a shopping mall, tourist office, internet café, restaurants, left luggage (free for 2 hrs at a time, if you have a ticket for that day, then US$0.70 up to 4 hrs, 24 hrs US$1.75), post and phone offices, toilets, good medical centre, **Banco de Montevideo** and **Indumex** cambio (accepts MasterCard). Visit www.trescruces.com.uy for bus schedules. Fares and journey times from the capital are given under destinations.

To Argentina (ferries and buses) You need a passport when buying international tickets. Direct to **Buenos Aires**: Buquebus, at the docks, in old customs hall, T130, Terminal Fluvio-Marítima, T916 8801, Terminal Tres Cruces, Local 28/29, T408 8120, in the Radisson, Colonia 751, T902 0526, and Punta Carretas Shopping, loc 219, T711 3893. 2-3 daily, 3 hrs, US$63 tourist class, US$75 1st class, plus a departure tax of US$1.50 pp. At Montevideo dock, go to Preembarque 30 mins before departure, present ticket and pay exit tax; then go to Migración for Uruguayan exit and Argentine entry formalities. The terminal is like an airport and the seats on the ferries are airplane seats. On board there is duty-free shopping, video and poor value food and drinks. Services via Colonia: bus/ ferry and catamaran services by Buquebus: 10 crossings daily from 45 mins to 3 hrs from Colonia, depending on vessel, fares: US$19.60 tourist, US$26 1st class on slowest *Eladia Isabel*, to US$34.50-45.20 on fast vessels. All have 2½-hr bus connection Montevideo-Colonia from Tres Cruces, US$7.30 extra. There are also bus connections to **Punta del Este** to/from Montevideo, 2 hrs. Cars are carried on either route, US$87-97 **Montevideo**, US$36-42 and 57-63 (depending on size of vehicle and boat) **Colonia**;

motorcycles US$68 Montevideo, US$23.60-35.60 Colonia. Schedules and fares can be checked on www.buquebus.com. Fares increase in high season, Dec-Jan, when there are more sailings. Check the website for promotional discounts that may offer up to almost half the price. If you want to break your journey in Colonia, you will have to buy your own bus ticket in another company to complete the trip to/from Montevideo. **Colonia Express**, W Ferreira Aldunate 1341, T901 9597; also at Tres Cruces bus terminal, CUT stand, www.colonia express.com, makes 2 crossings a day between Colonia and Buenos Aires in a fast catamaran (no vehicles) with bus connections to/from Montevideo, Punta del Este and other Uruguayan towns. Fares, including Montevideo-Colonia bus: US$33 (US$22 on Wed).

Services to **Carmelo** and **Tigre** (interesting trip): bus/ motor launch service by **Trans Uruguay/ Cacciola**, 3 a day, at Tres Cruces T402 5721, www.cacciolaviajes.com, US$22 (41 return); US$15 and 27 respectively Carmelo-Tigre. Bus service via **Fray Bentos**, **Bus de la Carrera** (Terminal Tres Cruces 25/26, T402 1313), 1000, 2200, 2230 (dormibus) and 2300 daily, US$21, 8 hrs. Bus services also nightly with **Cauvi** (T401 9196) and **Belgrano** (T401 4764). Advanced booking is advisable on all services at busy periods. On through buses to Brazil and Argentina, you can expect full luggage checks both by day and night. **To Paraguay, Brazil, Chile** If intending to travel through Uruguay to Brazil, do not forget to have Uruguayan entry stamped in your passport when crossing from Argentina. Without it you will not be able to cross the Brazilian border. To **Asunción**, Paraguay, US$52, 19 hrs: 3 a week each at 1300 with **EGA**, T402 5165 (and Río Branco 1417, T902 5335), and **Brújula**, T401 9198, both services recommended, meals served. Alternatively take bus to **Santa Fe**, Argentina (US$24), via Paysandú bridge, for easy access to Asunción. The through bus route is via Paysandú, Salto, Bella Unión, Uruguaiana, Paso de los Libres, Posadas, Encarnación, to Asunción (there are no passport or customs formalities except passport checks at Bella Unión and at Encarnación). There are very comfortable buses to **Porto Alegre** (US$30, 12 hrs, daily) and **São Paulo** (US$70, 30 hrs via Florianópolis, US$47, Camboriú, US$50, a good place to stop over, and Curitiba, US$57) with **EGA** and **TTL** (Tres Cruces or Río Branco 1375, T401 1410/901 9050, www.ttl.com.br), neither daily. A cheaper alternative route (which also avoids the risk of being stranded at the border by through-bus drivers) is to Chuy, **COT**, T409 4949, **Cynsa** T402 5363, or **Rutas del Sol**, T403 4657 (US$12.50, 5-6 hrs), then catch a bus to Porto Alegre (7½ hrs, US$13 if paid in reais), either direct or via Pelotas.

Taxi
The meter starts at US$1. In the central area fares are about US$2-4. Fares are shown on the meter by a number which determines the cost according to a table displayed by the passenger's seat; make sure the driver resets the meter, even in radio taxis. There is a small charge for each piece of luggage. Tipping is not expected but welcomed. Prices go up on Sat, Sun, holidays and late at night.

Train
Uruguayan railways, **AFE**, use outdated trains, but interesting rides for enthusiasts. The old train station has been abandoned, replaced by a small, glass and steel terminus known as **Nueva Estación Central** at Paraguay y Nicaragua (Aguada), T924 8080 or 924 9645, www.afe.com.uy. Passenger trains run Mon-Sat only along 2 lines, called 25 de Agosto and Sudriers. Most commuter trains run north between Montevideo and Progreso (about 7 a day), passing some of the most desperate neighbourhoods in Uruguay. Fewer services go beyond Progreso to 25 de Agosto (Florida), passing Canelones and Santa Lucía. Only once a day, a service goes as far as San José de Mayo on the same line. Another commuter line runs northeast from Montevideo to Sudriers, passing Pando. To Progreso (50 min, US$0.65), to Canelones (1 hr 20 min, US$0.80), to Santa Lucía (1 hr 40 min, US$1.20), to 25 de Agosto (1 hr 50 min, US$1.20), to San José de Mayo (almost 3 hrs, US$1.60), to Pando (1 hr, US$0.70). Occasionally, long distance services and a steam-engine run for special events, such as the 48-hr celebration of the Día del Patrimonio (Heritage Day) in Oct. More information, T903 3030 or 924 7328.

❶ Directory

Montevideo *p1292, map p1292*
Airline offices Aerolíneas Argentinas, Plaza Independencia 749 bis, T902 3691. **American Airlines**, Sarandí 699 bis y Plaza Independencia, T916 7138. **ASATEJ Uruguay**, Student Flight Centre, Río Negro 1354, p 2, of 1 y 2, T908 0509. **Gol**, T606 0901, www.voegol.com. **Iberia**, Colonia 973, T908 1032. **KLM**, Río Negro 1354, p 1, T902 5023. **LAN**, Colonia 993, p 4, T902 3881. **Pluna**, Colonia 1021, T902 1414, www.pluna.aero, Fast Track check-in and bus at *Victoria Plaza* hotel, Plaza Independencia, near the driveway off Florida. **Tam Mercosur**, Colonia 820, T901 8451. **United**, Plaza Independencia 831, p 5, T902 4630. For information on flight arrivals/departures, T601 1991, and www.aic.com.uy. **Banks** Don't trust the black market money changers offering temptingly good rates. **Casas de cambio** on Plaza Cagancha daily until 2200, including Sun; banks open 1200-1700 (some till 1800). Find most

banks along 25 de Mayo, Cerrito or Zabala, and on Plaza Matriz, in Ciudad Vieja, and in the centre along Av 18 de Julio. **Banred**, www.banred.com, is the largest ATM network from where you can withdraw US$ or pesos with a Visa or MasterCard. **ABN Amro, HSBC, Lloyds TSB, BBVA, Citibank** all have Banred ATMs. More ATMs in supermarkets. Airport bank daily 0700-2200. **American Express Bank**, Rincón 473, T916 0092/916 1162, does not change cash or TCs (see Turisport under Tour operators). **Western Union**, throughout the city in **Abitab** agencies, some exchange houses, and **Disco** or **Devoto** supermarkets. Exchange houses along 18 de Julio, eg **Bacacay**, at 853, **La Favorita** (Amex agents) at 1459, **Suizo** at 1190, **Regul**, at 1126, or in Ciudad Vieja, eg **Continental**, Misiones 1472, **Globus**, 25 de Mayo 466, but shop around for best rates (rates for cash are better than for TCs, but both are often better than in banks, and quicker service). **Brimar**, Misiones 1476, and **Delta**, Río Negro 1341, have been recommended. **Car hire** From US$36 to US$85 per 24 hrs (insurance included); guarantee of US$500 required. It is possible to negotiate small car for as little as US$39 per day, free mileage, including insurance and collision damage waiver, if you are hiring a car for at least 3 days (rates are lower out of season). Cheaper weekly rates available. Best to make reservations before arrival. It is wise to hire a small car (1.3 litre engine) as Uruguay is relatively flat and gas prices are high. **Punta Car**, Cerro Largo 1383, T900 2772, puntacar@ puntacar.com.uy, also at Aeropuerto Carrasco. **Snappy**, Andes 1363, T900 7728, www.snappy .com.uy. **Sudancar**, Acevedo Díaz 1813, T402 6620, www.sudancar.com.uy; many others. See Essentials, page 43 for international agencies. Most car companies don't allow their cars to be taken abroad. To travel to Argentina or Brazil, you can use **Maxicar** rentals in Salto, see page 1314.

Cultural centres Alianza Cultural Uruguay-Estados Unidos, Paraguay 1217, T902 5160, www.alianza.edu.uy, library Mon-Fri, 1400-2000, US publications (excellent selection), theatre, art gallery. **Instituto Cultural Anglo-Uruguayo** (known as the 'Anglo'), San José 1426, T902 3773, www.anglo.edu.uy (theatre, recommended, library Mon-Fri 0930-1200, 1430- 1930); café at No 1227. **Alliance Française**, Blvr Artigas 1229, T400 0505, www.alianzafrancesa. edu.uy (theatre, concerts, library, excellent bookshop). **Goethe Institut**, Canelones 1524, T400 5813, (Mon, Tue, Thu, Fri 1000-1300, 1600-1930). **Instituto Italiano de Cultura**, Paraguay 1177, T900 3354, iicmdeo@ adinet.com.uy. **Centro Cultural de España**, Rincón 627, Ciudad Vieja, T915 2250, www.cce.org.uy, Mon-Fri 1130-2000, Sat 1130-1800, has art exhibitions and a café. **Embassies and consulates** Argentine Consulate, Wilson Ferreira Aldunate 1281, T902 8623, www.consulado argentino.com.uy. Open 1400-1900, visa US$15, 1-day wait, English spoken. **Australian Consulate**, Cerro Largo 1000, T901 0743, payssed@ adinet.com.uy. **Belgian Consulate**, Rincón 625, of 26, T916 2719. **Brazilian Consulate**, Convención 1343, p 6, T901 2024, conbras@consbras.org.uy. Open 0930-1230, 1430-1730 (visas takes 24 hrs and the procedure is more complicated than Buenos Aires – need photo, onward ticket, entry ticket, proof of finances). **Canada**, Plaza Independencia 749, of 102, T902 2030, www.inter national.gc.ca/uruguay. **Chile**, 25 de Mayo 575, T916 4090. Open 0900- 1400, visa US$5, same day. **France**, Uruguay 853, T170-50000, www.amb-montevideo.fr. **Germany**, La Cumparsita 1417-35, T902 5222, www.monte video.diplo.de. Open 0930-1230. **Israel**, Blvd Gral Artigas 1585, T400 4164, ambassadorsec@montevideo.mfa.gov.il. **Italy**, JB Lamas 2857, T708 4916, www.amb italia.com.uy. **Netherlands**, Leyenda Patria 2880, Apt 202, T711 2956, www.holanda.org.uy. **New Zealand Consulate**, Miguel Grau 3789, T622 1543. **Paraguay**, Blvd Artigas 1256, T707 2138, embapur@ netgate.com.uy. Summer 0900-1200, winter 1400-1730. **Portugal**, Av Dr F Soca 1128, T708 4061, portmont@netgate.com.uy. **Spanish Consulate**, Libertad 2750, T708 0048, conespauy@netgate .com.uy. **Sweden**, Rambla 25 de Agosto 1825, No 508, of 107, T917 0289. **Switzerland**, Ing Federico Abadie 2934-40, T711 5545, www.eda.admin.ch/ montevideo. **UK**, Marco Bruto 1073, T622 3630, www.britishembassy.org.uy. **US Embassy** and **Consulate**, Lauro Muller 1776, T418 7777, http://uruguay.usembassy.gov. **Internet** Cyberi@, San José 933. Cyber Café, Plaza Cagancha 1340, US$0.60 per hr. **Millennium Café**, Paraguay 1325, local 53, in mall, US$0.60 per hr. **Cyber Café Nacho**, Av del Libertador 1607 y Cerro Largo, T903 9070. Open till 2200. **Cyber Café El Taller**, Juncal 1426. **Cyber Café Uruguay**, Colonia 1955. **Medical services** Hospital Británico, Av Italia 2420, T400 9011. Recommended. **Post offices** Misiones 1328 y Buenos Aires; 0800-1800 Mon-Fri, 0800-1300 Sat and holidays. **Poste restante** at main post office will keep mail for 1 month. Next to Pluna office on Av Libertador, next to Montevideo Shopping Center, 0800-1300, and under Intendencia at corner of Av 18 de Julio and Ejido, Mon-Fri 1000-2000, Sat 1700-2200. **Telephones** Antel, Fernández Crespo 1534 (headquarters) and at San José 1102 (Plaza), Arocena 1666 (Carrasco), Ariel 4914 (Sayago), Cádiz 3280 (Mercado Modelo), Garzón 1806 (Colón), José Belloni 4445 (Piedras Blancas); for international calls (including USA Direct Express), telex, fax, cables, daily 0800-2000. Long distance operator T120; for Latin America T0007, other countries T0008; special service T124. **Useful numbers** Information: T141.

Western Uruguay

West of Montevideo, Route 1, part of the Pan-American Highway, heads to the UNESCO World Heritage Site of Colonia del Sacramento and the tranquil town of Carmelo. Off the road are historic sites like the old British mining town of Conchillas and the Jesuit mission at Calera de las Huérfanas. Other roads lead to the Río Uruguay, Route 2 from Rosario to Fray Bentos, and Route 3 via San José de Mayo and Trinidad to the historic towns of Paysandú and Salto. The latter passes through farms and with cattle and sheep, man-made lakes and eventually the river itself. There are many hot-spring resorts in this part of Uruguay, some humble, others luxurious.

Colonias Valdense and Suiza

Route 1 to Colonia de Sacramento is being made into a four-lane highway. At Km 121 from Montevideo the road passes Colonia Valdense, a colony of Waldensians who still cling to some

Colonia del Sacramento

Sleeping ●
Blanca y Juan Carlos **3**
Casa Real **4**
Español **5**
Esperanza **6**
Hospedaje Colonial **7**
Hostal de los Poetas **2**
Italiano **8**

Leoncia **10**
Plaza Mayor **12**
Posada Casa Los Naranjos **9**
Posada de la Flor **11**
Posada del Angel **13**
Posada del Gobernador **14**
Posada del Río **15**
Posada del Virrey **16**

Posada Manuel
de Lobo **17**
Radisson Colonia
de Sacramento **1**
Romi **18**
Royal **19**

of the old customs of the Piedmontese Alps. Tourist information T055-88412. A road branches off north here to Colonia Suiza, a town of Swiss settlement also known as **Nueva Helvecia** (*Population 10,000, Phone code 0552*), with lovely parks, gardens and countryside. In the town is the Santuario de Nuestra Señora De Schonstatt, all walls are covered by plants, and the first steam mill in Uruguay (1875).The Swiss national day is celebrated with great enthusiasm.

The highway skirts **Rosario** (Phone code 052, 140 km from Montevideo, 60 before Colonia del Sacramento), called "the first Uruguayan Museum of Mural Art". There are dozens of impressive murals around the city, some depicting bullfights, others with abstract designs.

Colonia del Sacramento → *Phone code: 052, from Bs As: 022. Colour map 8, grid B5. Population 22,000.*

ⓘ *All museums Fri-Mon 1115-1645, closed either Tue, Wed or Thu, combined tickets US$0.40.*

Founded by Portuguese settlers from Brazil in 1680, Colonia del Sacramento was an important centre for smuggling British goods across the Río de la Plata into the Spanish colonies during the 17th century. The small historic section juts into the Río de la Plata, while the modern town extends around a bay. It is a lively place with streets lined with plane trees, a pleasant Plaza 25 de Agosto and a grand Intendencia Municipal (Méndez y Avenida Gen Flores – the main street). The town is kept very trim. The best beach is Playa Ferrando, 2 km to the east (buses from Gen Flores every two hours). There are regular connections by boat with Buenos Aires and a free port.

The **Barrio Histórico**, with its narrow streets (see Calle de los Suspiros), colonial buildings and reconstructed city walls, is charming because there are few such examples in this part of the continent. It has been declared Patrimonio Cultural de la Humanidad by UNESCO. The old town can be easily seen on foot in a day (wear comfortable shoes on the uneven cobbles), but spend one night there to experience the illuminations by nostalgic replica street lamps. The **Plaza Mayor** is especially picturesque and has parakeets in the palm trees. Grouped around it are the **Museo Municipal** in a mid-18th-century Portuguese residence of (with indigenous archaeology, historical items, paleontology, natural history), the **Casa Nacarello** next door (18th century; depicting colonial life), the **Casa del Virrey** (in ruins), the **Museo Portugués** (1720) with, downstairs, an exhibition of beautiful old maps, and the ruins of the Convento de San Francisco, to which is attached the **Faro** (lighthouse, entry US$0.60, daily till 1730 – on a clear day you can see Buenos Aires). At the eastern end is the **Puerta del Campo**, the restored city gate and drawbridge. Just north of the Plaza Mayor is the **Archivo Regional** (1750), collection of maps, police records 1876-1898 and 19th-century watercolours. The **Iglesia Matriz**, on Calle Vasconcellos (beside the Plaza de Armas/Manuel Lobo), is the oldest church in Uruguay. At the end of Calle Misiones de los Tapes, the Casa Portuguesa is now the tiny **Museo del Azulejo** (original floor, collection of French and Catalan tiles, plus the first Uruguayan tile from 1840). The house of Gen Mitre, Calles de San José y España, houses the **Museo Español**. At the north edge, the fortifications of the **Bastión del Carmen** can be seen; nearby is the Centro Cultural Bastión del Carmen, Rivadavia 223, in a 19th-century glue

To Real de San Carlos | **To 2**

Av Gen Artigas
Cnl Arroyo
Dr D Fosalba
Rivera
V García
To Playa Ferrando (2 km)

Intendencia
Municipal 🔟
🔟
Plaza de Deportes

Real de
an Carlos

Av General Flores

18 de Julio

Av E D Roosevelt

To Montevideo

@
🚌ℹ️
$

PUERTO

Punta Car
Europcar
Thrifty

To Buenos
Aires

Eating 🍴
Blanco y Negro 10
Club Colonia 2
El Asador 3
El Drugstore
  & Viejo Barrio 4
El Torreón 11
La Amistad 8

La Bodeguita 12
Lo de Renata 1
Mercosur 5
Mesón de la Plaza 9
Pulpería Los Faroles 6
Sacramento 13
Yacht Club 7

and soap factory, with frequent theatre productions (see www.cartelera.com.uy). In the third week of January, festivities mark the founding of Colonia, including a Funk and Jazz Festival held at Teatro Bastión del Carmen and at the Sheraton Colonia. The **Feria Artesanal** ① *Campus Municipal, Fosalba y Suárez*, is worth a visit.

Around the bay is **Real de San Carlos** ① *5 km, take 'Cotuc' or 'ABC' buses from Av Gral Flores, leaving Barrio Histórico, US$0.50*, an unusual, once grand but now sad tourist complex, built by Nicolás Mihanovic 1903-1912. The elegant bull-ring, in use for just two years, is falling apart (closed to visitors, bullfighting is banned in Uruguay). The casino, the nearest to Buenos Aires then (where gambling was prohibited), failed when a tax was imposed on Mihanovic's excursions; also disused is the huge Frontón court. Only the racecourse (Hipódromo) is still operational (men US$1, women free) and you can see the horses exercising on the beach.

Tourist offices ① *Flores y Rivera, T26141, daily 0900-2000 (closes at 1800 in winter), infoturismo@colonia.gub.uy, www.colonia.gub.uy*, good maps of the Barrio Histórico and the region. Also beside the **Old Gate** ① *Manuel Lobo e Ituzaingó, T28506, daily 0900-2000 (till 1800 in winter)*. Also an information desk at bus terminal. There is a **Ministry of Tourism** office at the passenger terminal at the dock, T24897. Visit www.guiacolonia.com.uy, www.en colonia.com, www.guear.com, www.colonianet.com.

Conchillas, 50 km from Colonia and 40 km from Carmelo, is a former British mining town from the late 19th century. It preserves dozens of buildings constructed by C H Walker and Co Ltd. The tourist office is open until 1700 and the police station is a good source of information. Direct buses from Colonia; road well marked on Route 21.

Carmelo → *Phone code 0542. Population 18,000.*

From Colonia, Route 21 heads northwest to Carmelo (74 km) on the banks of Arroyo Las Vacas. A fine avenue of trees leads to the river, crossed by the first swing bridge built 1912. Across the bridge is the Rambla de los Constituyentes and the Fuente de las Tentaciones. The church, museum and archive of El Carmen is on Plaza Artigas (named after the city's founder). In the Casa de Cultura Ignacio Barrios (IMC), 19 de Abril 246, is a tourist office and museum. Historically a mining centre, it is said that many luxurious buildings in Buenos Aires were made from they grey granite of Cerro Carmelo (mines flooded and used for watersports). It is one of the most important yachting centres on Río de la Plata and its microclimate produces much wine.

Calera de Las Huérfanas (Estancia de las Vacas) is the remains of one of the area's main Jesuit missions. Vines were introduced and lime was exported for the construction of Buenos Aires. After the expulsion of the Jesuits, it became an orphanage. It's in relatively good state and is best reached by car (exit from Route 21 clearly marked, some 10 km before Carmelo).

Mercedes → *Phone code: 0532. Colour map 8, grid B5. Population: 42,000.*

This livestock centre is best reached by Route 2 from the main Colonia-Montevideo highway. Founded in 1788, it is pleasant town on the Río Negro, a yachting and fishing centre during the season. Its charm (it is known as 'the city of flowers') derives from its Spanish-colonial appearance, though it is not as old as the older parts of Colonia. There is an attractive *costanera* (riverside drive). Some 4 km west of town is the Parque Mauá, dating from 1757. It has a mansion which contains the **Museum of Palaeontology** ① *daily 1100-1800, free*, on the ground floor. The building is worth wandering around to see the exterior, upper apartments and stable block. Camping is possible in season. It takes 45 minutes to walk to the park, a pleasant route passing Calera Real on the riverbank, dating back to 1722, the oldest industrial ruins in the country (lime kilns hewn out of the sandstone). **Tourist office**: At Colón, on the plaza, maps and hotel lists available. **Fray Bentos**: The tourist office is at Puente General San Martín, T28369.

Fray Bentos → *Phone code: 056. Colour map 8, grid B5. Population: 23,000.*

Route 2 continues westwards (34 km) to Fray Bentos, the main port on the east bank of Río Uruguay 193 km from Buenos Aires. Here in 1865 the Liebig company built its first factory producing meat extract. The original plant, much extended and known as **El Anglo**, has been restored as the **Museo de La Revolución Industrial** ① *Tue-Sun, entry by 1½-hr guided tour, US$1, 1000, 1430 (1000, 1130 and 1700 in summer), in Spanish, leaflet in English*. The office block in the factory has been preserved complete with its original fittings. Many machines can be seen. Within the complex is the Barrio Inglés, where workers were housed, and La Casa Grande, where the director lived. There are **beaches** to the northeast and southwest.

Crossing to Argentina

About 9 km upriver from Fray Bentos is the San Martín International Bridge, the most popular overland route with Argentina, toll US$4 per car (tourist office). Bicycles are not allowed to cross, but officials will give you a lift if there is no other traffic. Formalities are separate, at opposite ends of the bridge. The Argentine consulate is at Sarandí 3195, Fray Bentos. Tourist office at the bridge, T28369. **Note** This crossing was closed in 2007 owing to a long-running dispute between Argentina and Uruguay over a Uruguayan wood pulp mill. International buses were making a detour via Colón-Paysandú; otherwise take one of the crossings on the Río de la Plata.

Paysandú → *Phone code: 072. Colour map 8, grid A5. Population: 73,000.*

North of Fray Bentos, 130 km, is this undulating, historic city on the east bank of the Río Uruguay. Along Route 3, it's 380 km from Montevideo. Temperatures in summer can rise as high as 42°C. The **cathedral** ① *Mon-Fri 1100-1300, closed Tue; Sat-Sun 0800-1300*, is 19th-century. **Museo Histórico Municipal** ① *Zorilla y Leandro Gómez, Mon-Fri 0800-1645, Sat 0900- 0230*, has good collection of guns and furniture from the time of the Brazilian siege of 1864- 1865, well-documented. **Museo de la Tradición** ① *north of town at the Balneario Municipal, 0900-1800 daily, reached by bus to Zona Industrial*, gaucho articles, is also worth a visit. **Museo Salesiano** ① *Florida 1278, Mon-Fri 0830-1130* attached to Cathedral, interesting. **Tourist office** ① *Plaza de Constitución, 18 de Julio 1226, T26221, www.paysandu.com/turismo, Mon-Fri 0800-1900, Sat-Sun 0800-1800*, and at the Puente Gen Artigas, T27574.

Around Paysandú

The **Termas del Guaviyú** *US$0.50, getting there: 1½ hrs by bus, US$2, 4 a day*, thermal springs 50 km north, with four pools, restaurant, municipal motel (**C-E**) and private hotel (**C, Villagio**, www.villaggioguaviyu.com) and excellent cheap camping facilities. Along Route 90, 80 km east, are the **Termas de Almirón**, two pools, with camping and motels. The **Meseta de Artigas** ① *90 km north of Paysandú, 13 km off the highway to Salto, no public transport, free*, is 45 m above the Río Uruguay, which here narrows and forms whirlpools at the rapids of El Hervidero. It was used as a base by General Artigas during the struggle for independence. A terrace with a fine view, but the rapids are not visible from the Meseta. The statue, with Artigas' head topping a tall shaft, is very original.

Paysandú

Uruguay Western Uruguay

Sleeping	Gran Hotel	La Posada 6	Sarandí 11	Eating
Casa Grande 1	Paysandú 4	Lobato 7	Victoria 12	Artemio 1
Equinar 3	Hospedaje	Plaza 9		Los Tres Pinos 2
	Sosa 5	Rafaela 10		

⦂ Wreckers, revolutionaries and gauchos

Uruguay's passion for rural life began with Hernando Arias and the first shipment of cattle and horses to the Banda Oriental in 1603.

Today, a typical day on an *estancia* begins at the hearth, perhaps with a warming *mate*, before a horseride. The fireplace may be decorated with signs of present and past ownership, each brand burnt into the fireplace representing a personal history, but one element unites them all: the myth of the gaucho.

You might be forgiven for imagining yourself a latter-day gaucho as you put your foot in the *copa* (a cupped stirrup) and mount a sturdy Uruguayan horse, perhaps of the same breed as the one that Napoleon had shipped back to carry him around a wintry Europe. However, your thick poncho might well be the only piece of gaucho gear that you are wearing. Gauchos sometimes used ponchos as shields in knife fights, but on the ride you probably won't be needing a *facón* (a large dagger), nor a pair of *bombachas* (baggy trousers gathered at the ankle) or *culero* (an apron of soft leather tied around the waist, open on the left side) to avoid lacerations from

a lasso during branding and gelding. Horses on tourism estancias are used to novice riders, and *rebenques* (short whips) are best kept unused by your side. You'll find the Uruguayan horse a compliant platform for launching your *boleadoras* (three stones, covered with hide, on ropes tied at the middle, are used for entangling the legs of cattle). At this point you may learn whether your horse is a *pingo*, a gaucho's favourite horse, or *flete*, an ordinary cargo beast.

Riding along extensive *cuchillas* (ridges) and crossing rivers will bring to mind the nomadic gaucho lifestyle, and the revolutionary guerrilla bands, manned largely by gauchos. A *montonera* was a band of gauchos organized to drive the Brazilians and Argentinians out of Uruguay. Patriot leader Artigas was a gaucho-caudillo (boss).

Uruguayan life is built from livestock, sometimes quite literally. Houses were occasionally made from cattle hide. And cattle were put to other uses: coastal ranchers in Maldonado Department in the 19th century placed lights on the horns of their cows to lure ships onto the rocks for plunder.

Crossing to Argentina

The José Artigas international bridge connects with Colón, Argentina (US$4 per car), 8 km away. Immigration for both countries is on the Uruguayan side in the same office. Migración officials board the bus, but non-Argentine/Uruguayans should get off bus for stamp.

Salto → *Phone code: 073. Colour map 8, grid A5. Population: 99,000.*

A centre for cultivating and processing oranges and other citrus fruit, Salto is a beautifully kept town 120 km by paved road north of Paysandú. The town's commercial area is on Calle Uruguay, between Plazas Artigas and Treinta y Tres. There are lovely historic streets and walks along the river. Next to Club Uruguay, Calle Uruguay, is the *Farmacia Fénix*, "la más antigua de Salto", over 100 years old. See the beautiful but run-down **Parque Solari** (Ruta Gral Artigas, northeast of the centre) and the **Parque Harriague** (south of the centre) with an open-air theatre. The **Museo de Bellas Artes y Artes Decorativas** ① *Uruguay 1067, T29898*, in the French- style mansion of a rich *estanciero* (Palacio Gallino), well worth a visit. **Museo del Hombre y La Tecnología** ① *Brasil 510, T29898, ext 151, free*, is very interesting, with a small archaeological museum. There is a Shrove Tuesday carnival. **Tourist office** ① *Uruguay 1052, T34096, www.salto .gub.uy, 0800-2000, Sun 0800-1200*, free map; and at the international bridge, T28933.

The most popular tourist site in the area is the large **Presa de Salto Grande** dam and hydroelectric plant 20 km from Salto, built jointly by Argentina and Uruguay; taxi to dam US$5.50. A tour can be arranged with the tourist office in high season, US$2, minimum five people, every 30 minutes, 0700-1400; small visitors centre at the plant. A road runs along the top of the dam to Argentina. By launch to the **Salto Chico** beach, fishing, camping.

Near the dam (2 km north on the Route 3) is **Parque Acuático Termas de Salto Grande** ① *open all year 1000-1800, US$4.50, T30902, www.hotelhoracioquiroga.com/parque.htm*, (4 ha) in a natural setting. There are several pools, slides, hydro massages, water jets and man-made waterfalls.

Crossing to Argentina
North of the town, at the Salto Grande dam, there is an international bridge to Concordia, Argentina. **Immigration** is carried out on the bus. Immigration office on the Uruguayan side is often closed on Sunday and holidays, allowing free-flow of cars from both sides. A casino at the Uruguayan customs and immigration centre is only open late at night.

Termas del Daymán and other springs
About 10 km south of Salto on Route 3, reached by bus No 4 every 30 minutes from Calle Artigas, or from Avenida Sauzal at port then along Brasil, are **Termas del Daymán**, a small town built around curative hot springs. It is a nice place to spend a night; several restaurants around the beautifully laid out pools. **Complejo Médico Hidrotermal Daymán** ① *T69090, www.complejo medicohidrotermal.com.uy, therapeutical massage US$11.65 pesos for 20 mins, US$17.50 for 40 mins, full day water treatment from US$17.50*, has a spa and many specialized treatments in several separate pools (external and internal), showers, jacuzzis and rooms.

The road to **Termas del Arapey** branches off the partially paved Route 3 to Bella Unión, at 61 km north of Salto, and then runs 35 km east and then south. Pampa birds, rheas and metre-long lizards in evidence. Termas del Arapey is on the Arapey river south of Isla Cabellos (Baltazar Brum). The waters at these famous thermal baths (five pools) contain bicarbonated salts, calcium and magnesium.

To the Brazilian border: Artigas → *Phone code 0642. Colour map 8, grid A6.*
From near Bella Unión Route 30 runs east to Artigas, a frontier town in a cattle raising and agricultural area (excellent swimming upstream from the bridge). The town (*Population 40,000*) is known for its good quality amethysts. There is a bridge across the Río Cuaraim to the Brazilian town of Quaraí. The Brazilian consul is at Lecueder 432, T5414, vcartigas@mre.gov.br. Border crossing is straightforward, but you cannot get a Brazilian entry stamp in Quaraí. You have to get it at the airport in Porto Alegre (daily bus Quaraí-Porto Alegre at 2200).

● Sleeping

Nueva Helvecia *p1305*
L Nirvana, Av Batlle y Ordóñez, T44081, www.hotelnirvana.com. Restaurant (Swiss and traditional cuisine), dinner included mid-week off-season, sports facilities, gardens. Recommended.
D Del Prado, Av G Imhoff, T45812, www.hoteles colonia.com/prado/index2.htm. Open all year, huge buffet breakfast, TV, pool.
Camping Campsite in a park at the turnoff for Col Suiza, on main road, free, toilets, no showers.

Tourism farms
B pp Estancia Don Miguel, Ruta 1 Km 121 y Ruta 52, T0550-2041, esmiguel@adinet.com.uy. Book through **Cecilia Regules Viajes**. Rustic, working farm, full board, transport extra, good activities, little English spoken.
El Terruño, Ruta 1, Km 140, 35 km before Colonia, T/F0550-6004. Full day tours US$20, including rural safari, lunch.
Estancia Los Macachines, Km 93.5, Ruta 1, T0340-9074 (or Montevideo 600 1950, Nariño 1604, CP 11500), day visits with lunch, US$30, typical food, horse riding, sports, *estancia* tours.

Colonia del Sacramento *p1305, map p1304*
Choice is good including several recently renovated 19th-century posada hotels.

Barrio Histórico
AL Casa Real, Real 170, T20575, www.casareal-hotel.com. Cheaper Sun-Thu, historical building, 3 rooms, a/c, jacuzzi, patio, breakfast, *Parrilla del Barrio* restaurant at no 166; also 4-room section on Ruta 21, Km 180.9, a/c, restaurant. Cash only.
AL-A Plaza Mayor, Del Comercio 111, T23193, www.colonianet.com/plazamayor/. In a 19th-century house with patio gardens, lovely rooms with a/c or heating, *confitería*, English spoken.
AL-A Posada del Gobernador, 18 de Julio 205, T22918, 9150908 (mob), posadadelgobernador@adinet.com.uy. With breakfast, charming.

Centre
AL-A Esperanza, Gral Flores 237, T/F22922, www.hotelesperanzaspa.com. A charming place to stay with good restaurant.
AL-A Radisson Colonia de Sacramento, Washington Barbot 283, T30460,

www.radisson.com/coloniauy. Great location overlooking the bay, includes buffet breakfast, internet, 2 pools, 1 indoors, very good.

AL-B Posada del Virrey, España 217, T/F22223, www.posadadelvirrey.com. Large rooms, some with view over bay (cheaper with small bathroom and no balcony), with breakfast. Recommended.

A-B Italiano, Intendente Suárez y Manuel Lobo, T27878, www.hotelitaliano.com.uy. Open since 1928, it has been renovated with comfortable rooms with cheaper rates Mon-Thu. Large outdoor and indoor pools, gym, sauna and a good restaurant. Recommended.

A-B Posada Casa Los Naranjos, 18 de Julio y Ituzaingó, www.hotelescolonia.com/losnaranjos/index.htm. In an old house, a/c, small pool, family rooms US$5 more, comfortable, decent size rooms.

A-B Posada Manuel de Lobo, Ituzaingó 160, T22463, www.hotelescolonia.com/manueldelobo/manueldelobo.htm. Built in 1850. Large rooms, huge baths, parking, some smaller rooms, nice breakfast area inside and out.

B Leoncia, Rivera 214, T22369, www.hotelleoncia.com/.A/c, modern, good.

B Posada de la Flor, Ituzaingó 268, T24476, www.guiacolonia.com.uy/posadadelaflor. At the quiet end of C Ituzaingó, next to the river and to the Barrio Histórico, simply decorated rooms on a charming patio and roof terrace with river views.

B Posada del Angel, Washington Barbot 59, T/F24602, www.posadadelangel.net. Early 20th-century house, breakfast, pleasant and helpful, gym, sauna, pool.

B Royal, General Flores 340, T22169, www.guiacolonia.com.uy/ royal/index.htm. With breakfast, comfortable, good restaurant, pool, noisy a/c but recommended.

D Hostal de los Poetas, Mangarelli 677, T31643, www.hostaldelospoetas.com. Worth walking 15 min from the Barrio Histórico for one of the cheapest options in town with friendly owners, a few simple bedrooms and a lovely breakfast room across a tiny exuberant garden.

D Posada del Río, Washington Barbot 258, T/F23002, hdelrio@adinet.com.uy. A/c, small breakfast included, terrace overlooking bay.

D Romi, Rivera 236, T/F30456, hotelromicolonia@hotmail.com. With breakfast, old posada-style downstairs (19th-century), airy modernist upstairs with large glass roof. Recommended.

E Español, Lobo 377, T30759, www.guiacolonia.com.uy/espanol/index.htm. Good value, **F** pp with shared bath in dormitories, breakfast US$1.50, meals US$5. Recommended.

F pp **Hospedaje Colonial**, Flores 440, T/F30347. HI affiliated, hot showers, kitchen, restaurant below (ice cream parlour next door), free internet access and bicycle use (all ancient machines). Recommended.

Camping D Municipal site at Real de San Carlos, T24444, US$3.50 pp, in mini-cabañas, electric hook-ups, 100 m from beach, hot showers, open all year, safe, excellent. Recommended.

Family hospedajes These are good value: **E** pp 18 de Julio 481, T25813. With breakfast, bath, cable TV. **E** Domingo Baque 571, T26354, ter@adinet.com.uy. Includes breakfast, bath and cable TV, comfortable, nice family.

Carmelo p1306

LL Four Seasons, Ruta 21, Km 262, T9000, www.fourseasons.com/carmelo/. A luxurious resort between Carmelo and Nueva Palmira. Has a superb dining room, but if not a guest you will have to negotiate entry at the gate.

C Timabe, 19 de Abril y Solís, T5401, www.ciudadcarmelo.com/timabe. Near the swing bridge, with a/c or fan, TV, dining room, parking, good.

Camping At Playa Seré, hot showers.

Mercedes p1306

B Rambla Hotel, Av Asencio 728, T30696, www.mercedesramblahotel.com.uy. A 3-star hotel on the riverside with quite good rooms and Wi-Fi.

D Ito, Haedo 184, T24919, www.sorianototal.com/hotelito/mercedes.htm. Basic though decent rooms with cable TV in an old house.

F Hospedaje Mercedes, F Sánchez 614, T23804, opposite hospital. Shared bath, without breakfast, very helpful.

Camping **Club de Remeros**, De la Ribera y Gomensoro (on the riverside), T22534. Restaurant.

Tourism Farm A Estancia La Sirena Marinas del Río Negro, Ruta 14, Km 4, T0530-2726, www.lasirena.com.uy. *Estancia* dating from 1830, picturesque, on the river, birdwatching, fishing, waterskiing, accommodation, meals, price is per person, full board (**D** pp with breakfast) friendly owners Rodney, Lucia and Patricia Bruce. Warmly recommended.

Fray Bentos p1306

C Las Cañas, 8 km south, T22224, lascanas@adinet.com.uy. A tourist complex with a beach, entry US$1; pleasant, but crowded in summer. Accommodation in motel rooms with kitchenette and bath, cheaper without kitchen, all with a/c, TV, fridge. Camping US$8.50 per day minimum.

C Plaza, 18 de Julio y 25 de Mayo, T22363, www.grupocarminatti.com/hot1ha.html. Comfortable, a/c, TV, internet, with breakfast, on the Plaza Constitución.

E Colonial, 25 de Mayo 3293, T22260, hotelcol@adinet.com.uy. Attractive old building with patio.

Camping At the **Club Remeros**, near the river and at Colegio Laureles, 1 km from centre, T22236.

Paysandú *p1307, map p1307*

Book hotels in advance during Holy Week.

A Casa Grande, Florida 1221, Plaza Constitución, T24994, www.paysandu.com/ hotelcasagrande/. A/c, welcoming, parking, very good.

A Lobato, Gómez 1415, T22241, marioloba@ adinet.com.uy. With breakfast, a/c, modern, good.

D Plaza, Leandro Gómez 1211, T22022, hotelpla@ adinet.com.uy. A/c, balcony, breakfast, parking.

E Equinar, Sarandí 1192, T33060, oscarluisf@ yahoo.com. Nice communal area with open fire, parking, breakfast US$2.

E Sarandí, Sarandí 931, T23465. Good, comfortable.

F pp Victoria, 18 de Julio 979, T24320. Cheaper without bath, very helpful. Highly recommended.

G Hospedaje Sosa, Sarandí y Montevideo. Basic, family run.

Camping Balneario Municipal, 2 km north of centre, by the river, no facilities. **Camping Club de Pescadores**, Rambla Costanera Norte, T26220, US$2 per day, showers. Also at Parque Municipal.

Tourism farms **AL pp La Calera**, near Guichón, 89 km east of Paysandú, T409 7856, www.lacalera.com. 20 luxurious suites with fireplace, full board, dining room with home made food, swimming pool, riding, rodeo, conference facilities. Highly recommended.

Salto *p1308*

L-AL Hotel Horacio Quiroga, near Salto Chico, T34411, www.hotelhoracioquiroga.com. Best in town although some distance from centre, at the Termas complex, sports facilities, staffed by nearby catering school, special packages in season.

C Gran Hotel Salto, 25 de Agosto 5, T33250, saltotel@adinet.com.uy. With breakfast, a/c, good restaurant, reasonably priced. Recommended.

D Argentina, Uruguay 892, T29931, argentinahotel@adinet.com.uy. With breakfast, a/c, cafetería, comfortable.

E Concordia, Uruguay 749, T/F32735. Oldest hotel in Uruguay, founded 1860, Carlos Gardel stayed here, fine courtyard, pleasant breakfast room.

F Hostal del Jardín, Colón 47, T24274, hostalj@ adinet.com.uy. Comfortable, TV, fridge, very helpful, local breakfast, simple but spacious garden.

G Club Remeros de Salto, Rambla Gutiérrez y Belén (by the river) T33418, cremeros@ adinet.com.uy. Open all year, no cooking facilities, pool (US$4 per day), poor value.

Termas del Daymán *p1309*

B Hotel Termas Daymán, T69250, hterday@ adinet.com.uy, by the public spa. Recommended.

B La Posta del Daymán, Ruta 3, Km 487, T69801, www.lapostadeldayman.com. A/c, half-board or breakfast only (**C-D** low season, hostel accommodation about half price), thermal water in more expensive rooms, thermal swimming pool,

good restaurant, discounts for long stay, camping. Recommended. Slso has a hydrothermal complex.

D Estancia La Casona del Daymán, 3 km east of the bridge at Daymán, T073-02137. Well-preserved, but non-operational farm, horse riding.

E Bungalows El Puente, near the bridge over Río Dayman, T69271, includes entry to thermal baths.

E La Canela, Los Sauces entre Los Molles y Calle 1, T69121. Good value.

Camping Campsite at **Estancia San Niconor**, T/F0730-2209, 12 km from Termas de Daymán at the Termas de San Nicanor, Km 485, Route 3, good facilities; and *Cascadas*, US$3pp, T35245, Km 487, Route 3, closer to Daymán.

Termas del Arapey *p1309*

B-C Hotel Termas de Arapey, T0768-2441, www.hoteltermasdelarapey.com. Open all year, a/c, TV, safe, indoor/outdoor pool, restaurant.

Camping US$1 pp, good facilities

Artigas *p1309*

There are a few hotels in town and the **Club Deportivo Artigas**, Pte Berreta and LA de Herrera, 4 km from city, T0772-3860/2532, open all year, communal room, camping, restaurant, no cooking facilities, closes early.

Camping At Paseo 7 de Septiembre (by river), T2261, and at Club Zorrilla, T4341.

🍴 Eating

Nueva Helvecia *p1305*

♥♥-♥ Don Juan, main plaza. Snack bar/ restaurant excellent food, pastries and bread.

Colonia del Sacramento *p1305, map p1304*

♥♥♥ Blanco y Negro, Gen Flores 248, T22236, www.bynrestojazz.com.uy. Closed Wed. A smart place for a great range of meat dishes, hosts a jazz festival with live sessions every weekend of Feb. It is also one of the few places where you can try *ñandú* (rhea) meat. Cellar of local wines.

♥♥♥ El Drugstore, Vasconcellos 179, T25241. Very hip establishment, food is a fusion of Latin American, European and Asian (Japanese), good, creative and varied menú. Music and show.

♥♥♥ Lo de Renata, Flores 227, T31061. Open lunchtime daily and also Sat evenings. Good meat dishes from its *parrilla*, also a few Japanese dishes.

♥♥♥ Mesón de la Plaza, Vasconcellos 153, T24807. 140-year old house with a leafy courtyard, elegant dining, good traditional food.

♥♥♥ Sacramento, Del Comercio y De la Playa, T29245. Lunchtime; dinner, Fri-Sat only; closed Mon. Excellent food by local chef. Small, laid-back.

♥♥♥ Viejo Barrio (VB), Vasconcellos 169, T25399. Closed Wed. Very good for home-made pastas and fish, renowned live shows.

¶¶¶ **Yacht Club** (Puerto de Yates), T31354. Ideal at sunset with wonderful view of the bay. Good fish.
¶¶¶-¶¶ **Pulpería de los Faroles**, Misiones de los Tapes 101, T30271. Very inviting tables (candlelit at night) on the cobbled streets for a varied menú that includes tasty salads, seafood and local wines
¶¶ **Club Colonia**, Gen Flores 382, T22189. Good value, frequented by locals.
¶¶ **El Asador**, Ituzaingó 168. Good *parrillada* and pasta, nice atmosphere, value for money.
¶¶ **El Torreón**, end of Av Gen Flores. One of the best places to enjoy a sunset meal with views of the river. Slso a café serving toasties and cakes.
¶¶ **La Amistad**, 18 de Julio 448. Good local grill.
¶¶ **La Bodeguita**, Del Comercio 167. Tue-Sun evenings and Sat-Sun lunch. Its terrace on the river is the main attraction of this lively pizza place that serves also good *chivitos* and pasta.
¶¶ **Mercosur**, Flores y Ituzaingó, T24200. Popular, varied dishes. Also café serving homemade cakes.
Arcoiris, Av Gral Flores at Plaza 25 de Agosto. Very good ice cream.

Mercedes *p1306*
The following serve good food: **La Brasa**, Artigas 426. **Círculo Policial**, C 25 de Mayo. **El Emporio de los Panchos**, Roosevelt 711.

Fray Bentos *p1306*
¶¶ **Olla**, 18 de Julio near Plaza Constitución. Seafood and pasta, good value.
Several other cafés and pizzerías on 18 de Julio near Plaza Constitución.

Paysandú *p1307, map p1307*
¶¶ **Artemio**, 18 de Julio 1248. "best food in town"
¶¶ **Los Tres Pinos**, 19 Av España 1474. *Parrillada*, very good.

Salto *p1308*
¶¶ **La Caldera**, Uruguay 221, T24648. Good *parrillada*, also seafood, closed Mon lunchtime.
¶¶ **Pizzería La Farola**, Brasil 895 esq Soca.
¶¶-¶ **Don Diego**, Chiazzaro 20. Pasta.
¶ **Club de Uruguay**, Uruguay 754. Breakfast and good value meals.
Café Arabache, Uruguay 702. Daytime hangout.

Artigas *p1309*
¶¶-¶ **Donatello**, Lecueder. Good bar, pizza.
¶ **Deportivo**, Herrera. Good value.

Shopping

Colonia del Sacramento *p1305, map p1304*
Colonia has a large artist community, Uruguayan and international, with several good galleries, including **Galería del Bastión**, Rivadavia 214.
El Almacén, Real 150, is a good source of creative

1312

gifts. Decorative pottery by local artist Eduardo Acosta can be bought at **Paseo del Sol**, Del Comercio 158. **Oveja Negra**, De la Playa 114, is recommended for woollen and leather clothes. More leather shops on C Santa Rita, next to Yacht Club. **Afro**, 18 de Julio 246, specializes in *candombe* culture items from the local black community, also offers percussion lessons.

▲▲ Activities and tours

Colonia del Sacramento *p1305, map p1304*
City tours available with **Destino Viajes**, 18 de Julio 370, T25343, destinoviajes@adinet.com.uy, or **Guided Tours**, Av Flores y Rivera, T23148, sacratur@adinet.com.uy. **Asociación Guías de Colonia**, T22309/22796, asociacionguiascolonia@gmail.com, organizes walking tours (1½ hrs, US$4) in the Barrio Histórico, starting Mon-Sat 1500, Sun 1100 from tourist office next to Old Gate.

⊖ Transport

Nueva Helvecia *p1305*
Bus **Montevideo-Colonia Suiza**, frequent, with COT, 2-2½ hrs, US$5; **Turil**, goes to Colonia Suiza and Valdense; to **Colonia del Sacramento**, frequent, 1 hr, US$2.50. Local services between Colonia Valdense and Nueva Helvecia connect with Montevideo/ Colonia del Sacramento buses.

Colonia del Sacramento *p1305, map p1304*
Book in advance for all sailings in summer.
Road Roadworks on Route 1 west of Montevideo may delay traffic. There are plenty of filling stations. If driving north to Paysandú and Salto, especially on Route 3, fill up with fuel and drinking water at every opportunity, stations are few and far between. From Colonia to Punta del Este by passing Montevideo: take Ruta 11 at Ecilda Paullier, passing through San José de Mayo, Santa Lucía and Canelones, joiningthe Interbalnearia at Km 46.
Bus All leave from bus terminal between the ferry port and the petrol station (free luggage lockers, ATM, exchange, café and internet). To **Montevideo**, several services daily, 2¼-2¾ hrs, **COT**, T23121, **Chadre** and **Turil**, T25246, US$6.50. **Turil** to Col Valdense, US$2.50. **Chadre** to Conchillas, US$2. To **Carmelo**, 1½ hrs, **Chadre** and **Berrutti**, US$3. **Chadre** to Mercedes, US$6.50, Fray Bentos, US$8, Paysandú, US$11.50 and Salto, 8 hrs, US$16. **Turil** to Tacuarembó, US$13.50, Rivera, US$17.50, and Artigas, US$21.50. **Nossar**, T22934, to Durazno, US$7.50.
Ferry To **Buenos Aires**: 10 crossings daily, with **Buquebus** (T052-23030/22950), cars carried, fares and schedules given under Montevideo. **Colonia Express**, office at the port, T29676, www.colonia express.com, makes 2 crossings a day between Colonia and **Buenos Aires** (50 min) in a fast

catamaran (no vehicles carried) with bus connections to/from Montevideo, Punta del Este and Uruguayan towns: US$25 (US$14 on Wed).
Taxi A Méndez y Gral Flores, T22920; Av Flores y Suárez (on plaza), T22556.

Carmelo *p1306*
Bus To **Montevideo**, US$9, COT, Intertur, Chadre and Sabelín. To **Fray Bentos**, **Salto**, from main plaza 0710, 1540. To **Colonia**, see above. To **Argentina**: via Tigre, across the Paraná delta, an interesting bus/boat ride past innumerable islands: **Cacciola** 3 a day; office in Carmelo, Constituyente 263, T0542-8062, see under Montevideo page 1301.

Mercedes *p1306*
Bus To **Paysandú**, with Sabelín, Sánchez 782, T3937, 2½ hrs, US$3.85; also **Chadre** on the Montevideo-Bella Unión route. To **Montevideo**, US$10.15, CUT, Artigas (on plaza, also to **Argentina**), Agencia Central and Sabelín.

Fray Bentos *p1306*
Bus Terminal at 18 de Julio y Blanes, buses call here, but do not alight as buses also call at company offices around Plaza Constitución. To/from **Montevideo**, CUT, 4½ hrs, 6 a day, US$11.20, also Agencia Central. To **Mercedes**, ETA, US$0.65, frequent, 30 mins. To **Paysandú**, US$3.15.

Crossing to Argentina
Bus Note that the border was closed in 2007 (see page 1307). To **Gualeguaychú** (Argentina), ETA, 2 a day, 1 hr, US$3.15, passports inspected on bus. To **Buenos Aires**, 3½ hrs, US$12.

Paysandú *p1307, map p1307*
Bus It can be difficult to get a seat on long-distance buses going north. Terminal at Zorilla y Artigas, T23225. To/from **Montevideo**, US$13.60 (**Núñez**, Copay, T22094, 3 a day), 5-6 hrs, also Chadre, COT and Agencia Central. To **Salto** US$3.15, 6 a day. To **Rivera**, US$9.35, Copay, 0400 daily and Sun-Fri,1700 (Sat only as far as Tacuarembó). To **Fray Bentos**, 4 a day, 1½ hrs direct, 4 hrs via Young, US$3.15. To **Paso de los Toros** 1430 (return 0430), US$4, or by **Alonso** bus to **Guichón** at 0600, 1100, 1430 and change. To **Colonia** by **Chadre**, 1700, 6 hrs, US$11.50.

Fray Bentos: Crossing to Argentina *p1309*
Bus To **Colón** and **Concepción del Uruguay**, 3 a day (Copay 0815, 1645, Paccot 1445), 2 on Sun (Copay 1645), US$1.50 to Colón, US$2.50 to Concepción.

Salto *p1308*
Bus Terminal 15 blocks east of centre at Batlle y Blandengues, café/restaurant, shopping centre in same building with *casa de cambio*. Take taxi to centre. To/from **Montevideo**, 6-7¾ hrs, US$17.75-22 (**Norteño**, Núñez, Agencia Central and **Chadre**). To **Termas del Arapey**, 2 hrs, daily, US$3. **Paysandú** US$3.15, 2 hrs, 6 a day. To **Rivera**, US$10. To **Bella Unión**, 2 hrs, US$3.75, 6 a day. To **Colonia** by **Chadre**, 0555, 1555, 8 hrs, US$16; to **Fray Bentos**, same times, US$6.50.

Salto: Crossing to Argentina *p1308*
Bus To **Concordia**, **Chadre** (0800,1400, return 1200,1800) and **Flecha Bus**, 2 a day each, not Sun, US$3. To **Buenos Aires**, US$29, Flecha Bus. To **Posadas** night buses only, to **Puerto Iguazú**, 12 hrs, US$44.
Ferry To **Concordia**, Sanchristobal/Río Lago joint service, Mon-Sat several daily, fewer on Sun, US$2, depart port on C Brasil, 15 mins; immigration either side of river, quick and easy.

Artigas *p1309*
Bus To **Salto**, 225 km, Oribe 279, US$4.25. Turil and others from **Montevideo** via Durazno, Paso de los Toros and Tacuarembó, US$21.50.

❸ Directory

Colonia del Sacramento *p1305, map p1304*
Banks Banks open afternoon only. Most museums and restaurants accept Argentine pesos or US$, but rarely euros. Banco Crédit Uruguay, Flores y Barbot. Banco Comercial, on plaza, gives cash against Visa. HSBC, De Portugal y Vasconcellos (Barrio Histórico). Cambio Dromer, Flores 350, T22070, Mon-Fri 0900-2000, Sat 0900-1300, 1500-2000, Sun 1000-1300. Cambio Colonia and Western Union, Av Flores 401, T25032. **Car hire** Some near the gates to the port: Punta Car, T22353. Europcar and Thrifty, also at Flores 172, T22939, where there are bicycles (US$1.50 per hr), scooters (US$7 per hr) and electric cars (US$10-15 per hr) for hire. Motorcycle and bicycle hire also along Rivera near Av Flores, several shops, US$5 per hr, US$15 per day, recommended as traffic is slow. **Consulates** Argentine Consulate and Cultural Centre, Flores 209, T22086, open weekdays 1300-1800. **Internet** Inside mall at Av Flores 285, US$0.60 per hr. Bus terminal, US$2.70 per hr.
Post offices On main plaza. **Telephones** Telecentro Sacramento, Av Flores 172.

Carmelo *p1306*
Banks Banco de la República, Zorilla 361, for exchange and ATM.

Mercedes *p1306*
Banks Cambio Fagalde, Giménez 709. Banco Comercial on Colón (just off plaza) and Banco de la República, on plaza.

Fray Bentos *p1306*
Banks For exchange try **Cambio Fagalde**, Plaza Constitución, Mon-Fri 0800-1900, Sat 0800-1230.

Paysandú *p1307, map p1307*
Banks *Casas de cambio* on 18 de Julio: **Cambio Fagalde**, No 1004; **Cambio Bacacay**, No 1008; change TCs, Sat 0830-1230. **Banco de la República**, 18 de Julio y 19 de Abril. **Consulates** Argentina, Gómez 1034, T22253, Mon-Fri 1300-1800. **Internet** paysandu.com, 18 de Julio 1250, plaza, US$2 per hr. **Post offices** Montevideo y 18 de Julio. **Telephones** Antel, Montevideo 875, T22100.

Salto *p1308*
Banks Banco Pan de Azúcar does cash advances on Visa and MasterCard. **Banco de Crédito**. Both on Uruguay, several exchange houses on Uruguay. **Car hire** Maxicar, Paraguay 764, T35554, 099-73436 (mob), maxirent@adinet.com.uy. 24 hours, their cars are allowed to travel to Argentina and some to Brazil. **Consulates** Argentina, Artigas 1162, T32931, Mon-Fri 1300-1700. **Internet** Café Arabache, Uruguay 702 esq Sarandí, T32337. **Post offices** Treinta y Tres y Artigas. **Scooter hire** Agraciada 2019, T29967.

Eastern Uruguay

Resorts line the coast from Montevideo to Punta del Este, the ultimate magnet for summer holidaymakers, especially from Argentina. Out of season, it is quieter and you can have the beaches to yourself, which is pretty much the case the closer you get to Brazil year round. Inland are cattle ranches, some of which welcome visitors, and hills with expansive views.

East from Montevideo

This beautiful coast consists of an endless succession of small bays, beaches and promontories, set among hills and woods. The beach season is from December to the end of February. An excellent four-lane highway leads to Punta del Este and Rocha, and a good two-lane highway to Chuy. This route will give you a chance to see the most important Uruguayan beach resorts, as well as Parque Nacional Santa Teresa and other natural attractions. If driving there are three tolls each way (about US$2), but this route is the easiest and the most comfortable in Uruguay with sufficient service stations along the way.

Piriápolis → *Phone code: 043. Colour map 8, grid B6. Population: 6,000.*

This resort set among hills, 101 km from Montevideo, is laid out with an abundance of shady trees, and the district is rich in pine, eucalyptus and acacia woods. It has a good beach, a yacht harbour, a country club, a motor-racing track (street circuit) and is particularly popular with Argentines. It was, in fact, founded in the 1890s as a bathing resort for residents of Buenos Aires. Next to the marina is a small cable car (with seats for two) to the top of **Cerro San Antonio** ⓘ *US$2.50, 10 mins ride, free car park and toilets at lower station.* Magnificent views of Piriápolis and beaches, several restaurants. Recommended, but be careful when disembarking. North of the centre, at **Punta de Playa Colorada**, is a **marine rescue centre** ⓘ *T22960, sos-faunamarina@adinet.com.uy,* that looks after injured sea creatures before releasing them to the wild. **Tourist office**, Asociación de Turismo ⓘ *Rambla de los Argentinos 1348, 0900-2100 in summer, 1000-1800 in winter, T22560.*

About 6 km north on the R37 is **Cerro Pan de Azúcar** (Sugar Loaf Hill) ⓘ *getting there: take bus 'Cerro Pan de Azúcar' and get off after 6 km,* crowned by a tall cross with a circular stairway inside, fine coastal views. There is only a steep path, marked by red arrows, up to the cross. Just north of Piriápolis R 37 passes the La Cascada Municipal park (open all year) which contains the house of Francisco Piria, the founder of the resort, **Museo Castillo de Piria** ⓘ *open daily in summer, weekends in winter, 1200-2000.* About 4 km beyond Cerro Pan de Azúcar is the village of Pan de Azúcar, which has a **Museo al Aire Libre de Pintura** where the walls of the buildings have been decorated by Uruguayan and Argentine painters, designers and writers with humorous and tango themes (direct bus every hour from Piriápolis).

Portezuelo and Punta Ballena

R93 runs between the coast and the Laguna del Sauce to Portezuelo, which has good beaches. The **Arboreto Lussich** ⓘ *T78077, 1030-1630,* on the west slope of the Sierra de la Ballena (north of R93) contains a unique set of native and exotic trees. There are footpaths, or you can drive through; two *miradores*; worth a visit. From Portezuelo drive north towards the R9 by way of the R12 which then continues, unpaved, to Minas. Just off R12 is *El Sosiego* ① *1 km east from Solanas, then 4 km north*, T042-236288, *www.lapataia.com.uy/tambo/lapataia.htm*, a dairy farm open to the public, selling goats' cheese, ice cream, *dulce de leche*, homemade pizzas and pastas, and has an international jazz festival in January.

At Punta Ballena there is a wide crescent beach, calm water and very clean sand. The place is a residential resort but is still quiet. At the top of Punta Ballena there is a panoramic road 2½ km long with remarkable views of the coast. **Casa Pueblo**, the house and gallery of Uruguayan artist Carlos Páez Vilaro, is built in a Spanish-Moroccan style on a cliff over the sea; the gallery can be visited (US$5), there are paintings, collages and ceramics on display, and for sale; season: 1 November to 1 April. Walk downhill towards the sea for a good view of the house.

Maldonado → *Phone code: 042. Colour map 8, grid B6. Population: 55,000.*

The capital of Maldonado Department, 140 km E of Montevideo, is a peaceful town, sacked by the British in 1806. It has many colonial remains and the historic centre is being restored (2005). It is also a dormitory suburb of Punta del Este. Worth seeing is the **El Vigia watch tower** ① *Gorriti y Pérez del Puerto*; the Cathedral (started 1801, completed 1895), on Plaza San Fernando; the windmill; the **Cuartel de Dragones exhibition centre** ① *Pérez del Puerto y 18 de Julio, by Plaza San Fernando*, and the **Cachimba del Rey** ① *on the continuation of 3 de Febrero, almost Artigas*, an old well – legend claims that those who drink from it will never leave Maldonado. **Museo Mazzoni** ① *Ituzaingó 787, T21107, daily 1300-1830, Sun 1600- 2200* has regional items, indigenous, Spanish, Portuguese and English. **Museo de Arte Americano** ① *José Dodera 648 y Treinta y Tres, T22276, summer only 1800-2200*, a private museum of national and international art, interesting. **Tourist office** at the bus station, T225701. For information on concerts and exhibitions in summer T222276.

Punta del Este → *Phone code: 042. Colour map 8, grid B6.*

About 7 km from Maldonado and 139 km from Montevideo (a little less by dual carriageway), facing the bay on one side and the open waters of the Atlantic on the other, lies the largest and best known of the resorts, **Punta del Este**, which is particularly popular among Argentines and, recently, Brazilians. The narrow peninsula of Punta del Este has been entirely built over. On the land side, the city is flanked by large planted forests of eucalyptus, pine and mimosa. Two blocks from the sea, at the tip of the peninsula, is the historic monument of El Faro (lighthouse); in this part of the city no building may exceed its height. On the ocean side of the peninsula, at the end of Calle 25 (Arrecifes), is a shrine to the first mass said by the Conquistadores on this coast, 2 February 1515. Three blocks from the shrine is Plaza General Artigas, which has a *feria artesanal* (handicraft market); along its side runs Avenida Gorlero, the main street. There are two casinos, a golf course, and many beautiful holiday houses. **Museo Ralli of Contemporary Latin American Art** ① *Curupay y Los Arachanes, Barrio Beverly Hills, T483476, Tue-Sun 1700-2100 in Jan-Feb, Sat-Sun 1400-1800 rest of year, free*. Worth a visit but a car is needed.

Punta del Este has excellent bathing **beaches**, the calm *playa mansa* on the bay side, the rough *playa brava* on the ocean side. There are some small beaches hemmed in by rocks on this side of the peninsula, but most people go to where the extensive *playa brava* starts, opposite the *Hotel Playa*. Papa Charlie beach on the Atlantic (Parada 13) is preferred by families with small children as it is safe. Quieter beaches are at La Barra and beyond.

There is an excellent yacht marina, yacht and fishing clubs. There is good fishing both at sea and in three nearby lakes and the Río Maldonado. The *Muriel*, a late-19th-century yacht, makes three sailings daily, lasting three hours, US$35. **Tourist information** ① *Liga de Fomento, Parada 1, T45979, open 0800-2000; in bus station T494042; at Parada 24, Playa Las Delicias (Mansa side), T230050; and at airports*. See the websites www.puntaweb.com, www.puntadeleste.com and www.vivapunta.com.

Isla de Gorriti, visited by explorers including Solís, Magellan and Drake, was heavily fortified by the Spanish in the 1760's to keep the Portuguese out. The island, densely wooded and with superb beaches, is an ideal spot for campers (boats from 0800-1700, return 0915-1715, US$4.50, T441716; *Don Quico*, also does fishing trips, T448945). On **Isla de Lobos**, which is a government reserve within sight of the town, there is a huge sea-lion colony; excursions, US$30. Ticket should be booked in advance (T441716). See also Activities and tours, below.

Beaches east of Punta del Este

Between the Peninsula and the mouth of the Río Maldonado, a road runs along the coast, passing luxurious houses, dunes and pines. Some of the most renowned architects of Uruguay and Argentina design houses here. The river is crossed by a unique undulating bridge, like a shallow M, to **La Barra**, a fashionable place, especially for summer nightlife, with beaches, art galleries, bars and restaurants (bus from Punta del Este terminal; taxi US$15). The **Museo del Mar Sirenamis** ① *1 km off the coast road, watch for signs, T771817, 1600-2100 daily except Wed, US$2.50,* has an excellent collection on the subject of the sea, its life and history and on the first beach resorts (it claims to have 5,000 exhibits). The coast road climbs a headland here before descending to the beaches further north, Montoya and **Manantiales** (reached by Condesa bus; taxi US$23). Some 30 km from Punta del Este is the fishing village of **Faro José Ignacio** with a lighthouse ① *Fri-Sun 1700-1900,* a beach club and other new developments, now the road is paved. Coastal R10 runs some way east of José Ignacio, but there is no through connection to La Paloma as a new bridge across the mouth of the Lago Garzón is not operational. A car ferry sometimes runs; rowing boats will take pedestrians and cyclists across.

La Paloma and around → *Phone code: 0473. Colour map 8, grid B6. Population: 5,000.*

Protected by an island and a sandspit, this is a good port for yachts. The surrounding scenery is attractive, with extensive wetlands nearby. You can walk for miles along the beach. The pace here is more relaxed than Punta del Este. **Tourist office** is on Av Solari at entrance to town, very helpful, T96088.

Coastal R10 runs to Aguas Dulces (regular bus services along this route). About 10 km from La Paloma is **La Pedrera**, a beautiful village with sandy beaches. Beyond La Pedrera the road runs near pleasant fishing villages which are rapidly being developed with holiday homes, for example **Barra de Valizas**, 50 minutes north. At **Cabo Polonio** (permanent population 80), visits to the islands of Castillos and Wolf can be arranged to see sea lions and penguins. It has two great beaches: the north beach is more rugged, while the south is tamer by comparison. Both have lifeguards on duty (though their zone of protection only covers a tiny portion of the kilometres and kilometres of beach). The village is part of a nature reserve. This limits the number of people who are allowed to stay there since the number of lodgings is limited and camping is strictly forbidden (if you arrive with a tent, it may be confiscated). During January or February (and especially during Carnival), you **have** to reserve a room in one of the few posadas or hotels, or better yet, rent a house (see Sleeping, below). From Km 264 on the main road all-terrain vehicles run 8 km across the dunes to the village (several companies, US$2.50). Day visitors must leave just after sundown (see Transport, below). Ask locally in Valizas about walking there, 3-4 hours via the north beach (very interesting, but hot, unless you go early). There are also pine woods with paths leading to the beach or village.

The **Monte de Ombúes** ① *open in summer months, from Jan, free, basic restaurant with honest prices* is a wood containing a few *ombú* trees (Phytolacca dioica – the national tree), *coronilla* (Scutia buxifolia) and *canelón* (Rapanea laetevirens). It has a small circuit to follow and a good hide for birdwatching. To reach the woods from Km 264, go 2 km north along R10 to the bridge. Here take a boat with guide, 30 minutes along the river, US$5 including tour (*Monte Grande* recommended as they visit both sides of the river). You can also walk from Km 264 across the fields, but it's along way and the last 150 m are through thick brush. The bridge is 16 km from Castillos on R9 (see next paragraph): turn onto R16 towards Aguas Dulces, just before which you turn southwest onto R10.

From **Aguas Dulces** the road runs inland to the town of **Castillos** (easy bus connections to Chuy), where it rejoins R9. There is a tourist office at the Aguas Dulces/Castillos crossroads on R9 with details on hotels. At Km 298 there is a turning for **Punta del Diablo**, a fishing village in dramatic surroundings, again with fine beaches, popular with young people in high season.

Parque Nacional Santa Teresa

① *100 km from Rocha, 308 km from Montevideo, www.parquesantateresa.com.uy, 1000-1700 except Mon, US$1.20 (check opening times, maybe 1300 on weekdays).*

This park has curving, palm-lined avenues and plantations of many exotic trees. It also contains botanical gardens, fresh-water pools for bathing and beaches which stretch for many kilometres (the surf is too rough for swimming). It is the site of the impressive colonial fortress of Santa Teresa, begun by the Portuguese in 1762 and seized by the Spanish in 1793. The fortress houses a **museum** ① *Tue-Sun 1000-1700 (winter hours shorter), US$0.30, tickets from restaurant, La*

Posada del Viajero (opposite, recommended) of artefacts from the wars of independence. On the inland side of Route 9, the strange and gloomy Laguna Negra and the marshes of the Bañado de Santa Teresa support large numbers of wild birds. A road encirces the fortress; it's possible to drive or walk around even after closing. From there is a good view of Laguna Negra.

There are countless campsites (open all year), and a few cottages to let in the summer (usually snapped up quickly). At the *capatacia*, or administrative headquarters, campers pay US$2 pp for 3 nights (tickets are collected for each night stayed). Here there are also a small supermarket, greengrocer, butcher, bakery, medical clinic, petrol station, auto mechanic, post and telephone offices, and the *Club Santa Teresa*, where drinks and meals are available, but expensive. Practically every amenity is closed off-season. Tour by taxi (US$12, daily) can be made to Santa Teresa fortress, Laguna Negra, and the collection of native and exotic plants from the bathing resort of **La Coronilla** (10 km north of Santa Teresa, 20 south of Chuy; several hotels and restaurants most closed in winter). Montevideo-Chuy buses stop at La Coronilla.

Chuy → *Phone code: 0474. Colour map 7, inset. Population: 10,400. For details of Chuí in Brazil see page 456.*

At Chuy, 340 km from Montevideo, the Brazilian frontier runs along the main street, Avenida Internacional, which is called Avenida Brasil in Uruguay and Avenida Uruguaí in Brasil. The Uruguayan side has more services, including supermarkets, duty-free shops and a casino.

On the Uruguyan side, on a promontory overlooking Laguna Merín and the gaúcho landscape of southern Brazil, stands the restored fortress of **San Miguel** ① *US$0.40, closed Mon, bus from Chuy US$0.45, Rutas del Sol buses from Montevideo go here after passing through Chuy*, dating from 1734 and surrounded by a moat. It is set above a 1500-ha wetland park, which is good for birdwatching and is 7 km north of Chuy along Route 19 which is the border. There is a small museum of *criollo* and *indígena* culture, displaying, among other artefacts, old carriages and presses. Not always open in low season. A fine walk from here is 2 km to the Cerro Picudo. The path starts behind the museum, very apparent. Tours (US$9 from Chuy) end for the season after 31 March.

Border with Brazil → *From October to February, Uruguay is 1 hour behind Brazil.*

Uruguayan passport control is 2½ km before the border on Ruta 9 into Chuy, US$2 by taxi, 20 minutes' walk, or take a town bus; officials friendly and cooperative. Ministry of Tourism kiosk here is helpful, especially for motorists, T44599. Tourists may freely cross the border in either direction as long as they do not go beyond either country's border post. Taking a car into Brazil is no problem if the car is not registered in Brazil or Uruguay. (Uruguayan rental cars are not allowed out of the country. Although you can freely drive between Chuy and Chuí, if you break down/have an accident on the Brazilian side, car rental insurance will not cover it: park in Chuy, even if only one metre from Brazil, and walk.) From the border post, Ruta 9 bypasses the town, becoming BR-471 on the Brazilian side, leading to Brazilian immigration, also outside town. The Brazilian consulate is at Tito Fernández 147 esq Laguna Merín, T2049, Chuy. For buses to Brazilian destinations, go to the rodoviária in Chuí (details in the Brazil chapter, page 456). The bus companies that run from Chuy into Brazil ask for passports – make sure you get yours back before boarding the bus.

Entering Uruguay You must have a Brazilian exit stamp and a Uruguayan entry stamp (unless visiting only Chuí), otherwise you will be turned back at customs or other official posts. Those requiring a visa must have a medical examination before a visa can be issued in Chuí, cost about US$20 and US$10 respectively.

⬤ Sleeping

Piriápolis *p1314*
Many hotels along the sea front, most close end-Feb until mid-Dec. Reservation is advisable in high season. Many others than those listed in our price ranges E and up.
A-B Argentino, Rambla de los Argentinos y Armenia, T22791, www.argentinohotel.com.uy. A fine hotel and landmark designed by Piria with casino, 2 restaurants and medicinal springs, ice

rink and pool open to public for US$2.50 (in low season), also sauna.
D Centro, Sanabria 931, T/F22516. With breakfast, cafeteria, helpful about local sites.
D Danae, Rambla 1270 y Freire, T22594. **F** out of season, bath, breakfast, heating, very good.
D Rivadavia, Rambla 1208, T22532, rivacol@adinet.com.uy. Open all year (**F** in winter), hot water.

D-F pp **Youth hostel Albergue de Piriápolis**, behind Hotel Argentino, Simón del Pino 1106/1136, T20394, piriapolis@hosteluruguay.org. Rooms for 2-4 (open all year), 270 beds, hot showers, cooking facilities, student cards accepted.
E **Luján**, Sanabria 939, T22521. Simple rooms, family run, some rooms have balconies, homeopathist on top floor.
Camping International YMCA camp on the slope of Cerro del Toro, double rooms in bungalows, and tents. Site at Misiones y Niza, just behind bus station. Poor showers, smelly toilets, US$4.

Portezuelo and Punta Ballena *p1314*
LL-L **Hotel-Art Las Cumbres**, Ruta 12 Km 3.9, 4 km inland, T578689, www.cumbres.com.uy. Some rooms **AL** out of season, themed as an artist's house-studio, on a wooded hill with great views over Laguna del Sauce and the coast, pool, restaurant and tea room (expensive but popular).
L **Casa Pueblo**, T578611, www.clubhotel.com.ar. Highly recommended hotel and apartments, restaurant and, lower down the hill, a *parrillada*.
Campsite Near Arboreto Lussich, turn off at Km 128 on Interbalnearia, T427 8902/ 24181, or Montevideo 480 1662. US$5.60 for 2 with tent, many facilities, very clean.

Maldonado *p1315*
Hotel accommodation is scarce in summer; cheaper than Punta del Este, but you will have to commute to the beach. Basic 1-2 star places (**C-E**), open all year, include: **Catedral**, Florida 830 casi 18 de Julio, T242513, hotelcatedral@adinet.com.uy, central, and **Colonial**, 18 de Julio 841 y Florida, T223346, www.elhotelcolonial.com.
E **Celta**, Ituzaingó 839, T/F230139. Helpful, Irish owner, No 7 bus stop outside.
E **Hospedaje Isla de Gorriti**, Michelini 884, T245218. Nice courtyard. Recommended.
Camping Parque El Placer, T270034, free.

Punta del Este *p1315*
Note Streets on the peninsula have names and numbers; lowest numbers at the tip. Hotels are plentiful but expensive: we list only those that are recommended. Rates in the few hotels stilll open after the end of March are often halved. Visitors without a car have to take a hotel on the peninsula, unless they want to spend a fortune on taxis.

On the peninsula
L-AL **Remanso**, C 20 y 28, T447412, www.hotelremanso.com.uy. Some rooms **A** low season, comfortable, businesslike, pool, safe, open all year (also has suites in **LL** range). Recommended.
AL **Iberia**, C 24, No 685, T440405, iberiapunta@hotmail.com. **A** out of season, breakfast included, open all year, garage opposite.

AL-B **Palace**, Av Gorlero esq 11, T229596, www.visit-uruguay.com /es/palace.htm (closed in winter). 3-star. Breakfast only (expensive restaurant, *La Stampa*, in the hotel), well kept.
AL-B **Tánger**, C 31 entre 18 y 20, T441333, www.visit-uruguay.com /es/tanger.htm. Open all year, a/c, safe, disabled access, 2 pools.
A **Alhambra**, C 28, No 573, T440094, dirisuma@adinet.com.uy. Open all year, comfortable, TV, safe, parking, cafetería, continental breakfast. In same group is **A-B Príncipe**, C 20 No 938, T440351, smap65@hotmail.com.
C pp **Alicia Lorenzo**, Parada 5, T480781. Bed and breakfast room with bath, barbecue.
C **Embajador**, C Risso, parada 1, by bus terminal, T481008, F486750. 2-star. Good, closed in winter.
D **Youth hostel 1949**, C 30 y 18, info@1949hostel.com. 100 m from bus station, near the Information Centre. Small, **A** in double room, kitchen, bar, TV and DVD, close to beaches.
E pp **Youth hostel El Hostal**, C 25 No 544 y 24, T441632, elhostalpunta@yahoo.com. US$20 in dorm, includes breakfast, lockers, central, basic.

Beaches east of Punta del Este *p1316*
San Rafael (Parada 12)
L-AL **San Marcos**, Av Mar del Plata 191, T482 251, www.hotelsanmarcos.com. Pool (covered in winter), prices fall to **AL-B** in mid and low season, bicycle hire, internet US$4, very pleasant.
L-A **La Capilla**, Viña del Mar y Valparaíso, near San Marcos, T484059, www.lacapilla.com.uy. Open all year (suites rise to **LL** at Christmas), includes breakfast, kitchenette in some rooms, safes in rooms, gardens, pool, good, has been upgraded.
L-A **San Rafael**, Lorenzo Batlle y Pacheco, Parada 11 Brava, T482161, www.hotelsan rafael.com.uy. Large hotel, open all year, suites cost **LL** in high season, a/c, heating, safe, TV, spa.
Camping Camping San Rafael, T486715. Good facilities, US$7, bus 5 from Maldonado.

La Barra
LL-L **Mantra**, Ruta 10, Parada 48, T771000, www.mantraresort.com. Probably the best in town (5 star) , but you will still need a car to move around, although the place has everything. Open all year, great pool, casino, restaurants, concerts, even its own cinema and wine bar. Recommended.
L **La Posta del Cangrejo**, hotel/restaurant, Ruta 10 Km 160, T770021, alaposta@adinet.com.uy. Nice location, smart, if a bit old. Recommended.
L-AL **La Ballenera Bed and Breakfast**, Km 162, just off coast road ½ km east of the hilly promontory, behind Playa Montoya, T771079, T09-444 7935 (mob), http://laballenera.net/english/index.html. Half price in low season, big old wooden mansion, lovely breakfast terrace, kitchen and internet.

L-B Hostal de la Barra, Ruta 10, Km 161.300, T771521, www.hostaldelabarra.net. A small hotel, not a hostel, with sea view, forest view and loft rooms, open all year, neat, Christmas (**LL**), Carnaval and Semana Santa require 7 or 4-night stays.

D-E pp Backpacker de La Barra, C 9, No 2306, ½ km off main road, T/F772272, http://backpacker delabarra.com/espanol/index.html. Closed in low season, youth hostel style, price depends on dates and class of room, must stay 3 nights over New Year, café and restaurant, internet, laundry.

Camping There are 2 campsites after the bridge, the second is cheaper, US$9.75, good showers and toilets.

Manantiales

Resorts include: **LL-L Las Dunas**, Ruta 10, Km 163, T771211, lasdunas@adinet.com.uy, 5-star, opulent, and **L Las Olas**, Ruta 10, Km 162.5, T770466, www.lasolasresort.com.uy, 4-star.

D Manantiales Hostel, Ruta 10, Km 164, T774427, www.manantialeshostel.com. **C** end Dec to end Jan. Free pick-up from bus station, kitchen, bikes and surfboards for rent, lockers, DVDs, laundry, free internet, bar, open 1 Nov to 15 Apr.

La Paloma p1316

C Bahía, Av del Navio, between Solari and Del Sol, T/F0479-6029, www.elbahia.com.uy. Breakfast, rooms for 2-4, clean and simple, TV, Wi-Fi, laundry.

D Embeleco, De La Virgen, just off Solari, T0479-6108. Breakfast, half price in winter, welcoming.

Youth hostels **F** at Parque Andresito, T6396, lapaloma@hosteluruguay.org. 50 beds, US$10 pp, clean, friendly, good meals, kitchen, Nov-Apr.

Palma de Mallorca, on Playa La Aguada, in nearby La Aguada, luxury hotel, T0479-6739, www.hotelpalmademallorca.com. Right on the ocean. Family discounts and 7-day packages offered, heated pool.

Camping In Parque Andresito, T6107, US$11.75. Overpriced, thatched *cabañas* for rent, US$22-38 per day with maid and kitchen facilities, sleep 4-6. *Grill del Camping* for *parrillas*. La Aguada, T6239, 2 km east of town, 300 m from beach, US$5. Good, each site with BBQ, tap, sink, water and electricity.

Northeast of La Paloma

Ask around **Barra de Valizas** for cottage rental at US$25 per day, sleeps 4, fully equipped. At **Cabo Polonio** you cannot camp. There are posadas, some listed below, or you can rent a house; see www.cabopolonio.com for all options. Water is drawn from wells (*cachimba*) and there is no electricity (some houses have generators, some gas lamps, otherwise buy candles). There are 4 shops for supplies, largest is **El Templao**.

AL La Perla, Cabo Polonio, T0470-5125, T099-871017 (mob), www.mayoral.com.uy/laperla.htm.

Meals US$8-11. Houses or rooms to rent; no credit cards, horse riding, diving lessons, open all year.

AL-A Mariemar, Cabo Polonio, T0470-5164, 099-875260 (mob), mariemar@cabopolonio.com. Nice owners, own electricity generator, hot water, with breakfast, restaurant, check if open in winter. Recommended.

A Cabañas Buenavista, Punta del Diablo, 4 blocks from shore, T099-370807, mcontini@adinet.com.uy. 2 nice bungalows for 5, **C** in low season, equipped except for linen, terrace with ocean view, book in advance.

A Hostería del Pescador, Punta del Diablo, T0472-1611 LD17. Private house for 4, US$50 per day.

A Hotel La Pedrera, La Pedrera, T0479-2001, hpedrera@adinet.com.uy. Pool, tennis, good rooms.

A Posada Eirete, Barra de Valizas. Small, tasteful, good breakfasts, owned by painter María Beloso. Recommended.

D pp La Cañada, about 500 m outside Cabo Polonio, T099-550595 (mob), posadalacaniada@cabopolonio.com. Shared rooms, friendly, small restaurant. They also rent out a cabin.

D-E Hotel Gainford, Aguas Dulces, with restaurant, and others, including breakfast. Lots of cheap cabins for rent.

Reserva Ecológica La Laguna, about 2 km from Aguas Dulces, T099-602410/0475-2118. Private reserve on a 25 ha lake, with cabins for 4-6 (**B**), meals extra, open all year, many languages spoken, pick-up from bus stop in jeep or horse-drawn carriage, tours arranged, activities. (Rutas del Sol bus from Montevideo, US$10).

Youth hostels At La Pedrera: **Aguazul**, T0479-2847, aguazul@adinet.com.uy, US$30 pp. And **Casa de La Luna**, R10 Km 230, T0945-35928, ruta10km230@hotmail.com, US$21 pp. Both are HI hostels. **Barra de Valizas**, Calle Principal, T099-610267, www.valizashostel.com. US$7 pp, open Nov-Apr (all year for groups). 50 beds, kitchen for members, also has restaurant. Punta del Diablo Hostel, San Martín y Baldomir, T0477-2151, puntadeldiablouy@hotmail.com. US$5 pp.

Camping Camping Esmeralda, at Km 280.5, 17 km north of Castillos. **La Palomita**, 8 blocks from the sea, La Pedrera. Wooded, electricity, US$5, summer only.

Chuy p1317

All hotels are open the year round.

A-B Parador Fortín de San Miguel, Paraje 18 de Julio, near San Miguel fortress, T/F6607, www.el fortin.com. Excellent, full and half-board, colonial-style hotel. Beautiful rooms, gym, pool, difficult 9-hole golf course, fine food and service. Highly recommended. You don't have to go through Uruguayan formalities to get there from Brazil.

C Nuevo Hotel Plaza, Artigas y Arachanes, T/F2309, www.hotelplaza.chuynet.com. On

plaza, bath, good buffet breakfast, TV, very helpful, good, restaurant *El Mesón del Plaza*.
D Alerces, Laguna de Castillos 578, T/F2260, alerces@montevideo.com.uy. 4 blocks from border. Bath, TV, breakfast, heater, nice.
F Vittoria, Numancia 143, T2280. Price includes breakfast, simple and clean, parking.
Camping From Chuy buses run every 2 hrs to the Barra del Chuy campsite, Ruta 9 Km 331, turn right 13 km, T2425. Good bathing, many birds. *Cabañas* for up to 4 persons cost US$20 daily or less, depending on amenities.

🅞 Eating

Portezuelo and Punta Ballena *p1314*
ⵜⵜⵜ **Medio y Medio**, Cont Camino Lussich s/n, Punta Ballena, T578791. Jazz club and restaurant, music nightly and good food.
ⵜⵜⵜ-ⵜⵜ **Las Vertientes**, Camino de Los Ceibos, 2 km on the Route 9, T042-669997. Country restaurant, fresh food which all comes from own farm, good salads and sweets.

Maldonado *p1315*
Best ice cream at **Popy's**.
ⵜⵜⵜ-ⵜⵜ **Taberna Patxi**, Dodera 944, T238393. Very good Basque food with authentic recipes.
ⵜⵜⵜ-ⵜⵜ **Lo de Rubén**, Florida y Santa Teresa, T223059. *Parrillada*, best restaurant in town.
ⵜⵜ **Al Paso**, 18 de Julio 898, T222881. *Parrillada*, moderate prices.
ⵜⵜ **Piano-Bar JR Pizzetas**, Rincón y Gutiérrez Ruiz, T225215. Pizzas and pasta, under US$12 pp.

Punta del Este *p1315*
Many enticing ice cream parlours on Gorlero.
ⵜⵜⵜ **Blue Cheese**, Rambla y 23, T440354. For steaks and unlimited salads, good value.
ⵜⵜⵜ **Bungalow Suizo**, Av Roosevelt y Parada 8, T482358. Excellent Swiss, must book.
ⵜⵜⵜ **Cantón Chino**, C 28 y Gorlero, T441316. Creative Chinese food, good.
ⵜⵜⵜ **Company Bar**, C 29 entre 18 y 20, T440130. Live music in the evening, home made pasta, fish. Breakfast, lunch and dinner.
ⵜⵜⵜ **Daiquiri Fondue**, Rambla Williman y Parada 19, T226451, and C 9 entre 8 y 10, T488901. Good Swiss food including fondue.
ⵜⵜⵜ **Los Caracoles**, Calle 20 y 28, T440912. Excellent food (international, *parrilla*, seafood) at good prices.
ⵜⵜⵜ **El Ciclista**, Calle 20 y 27, T440007. Long-standing, with international cuisine, Italian, *parrilla* and seafood.
ⵜⵜⵜ **Gure-etxe** (also in La Coronilla), C 9 y 12. Seafood and Basque cuisine.
ⵜⵜⵜ **Kika's Café**, Rambla Artigas y C 28, T440951. Excellent fish, delicious Spanish dishes, sea view, but lunch specials are not a bargain.

ⵜⵜⵜ **Lo de Charlie**, 12 y La Salina, T444183. Fish.
ⵜⵜⵜ **Lo de Tere**, Rambla Artigas y 21, T440492, www.lodetere.com. Good local food, open all year but closed Wed in winter, 20% discount if eating lunch before 1300 or dinner before 2100.
ⵜⵜⵜ **La Tuttie**, C 9, No 607, T447044. Restaurant and fishmonger, fresh fish, popular with locals.
ⵜⵜⵜ **Solomio**, Rambla de Circunvalación y 8, T449298. Good fusion seafood.
ⵜⵜⵜ **Viejo Marino**, Calle 11 entre 14 y 12, Las Palmeras, T443565. Fish restaurant, busy, go early.
ⵜⵜⵜ **Virazón**, Rambla Artigas y C 28, T443924. Good food and great view, but expensive.
ⵜⵜⵜ **Yatch Club Uruguayo**, Gral Artigas y 8, T441056. Very good, fish, seafood, views over the port (not to be confused with the Yacht Club).
ⵜⵜ **Il Barreto**, C 9 y 10, T447243. Italian vegetarian, good value, live Italian and Latin music some evenings, open weekends only in low season.
ⵜ **Tutto Sapori**, Lenzina entre Yaro y Francia, T490 599. Italian specialities, terrace, accordion music.

Beaches east of Punta del Este *p1316*
La Barra
ⵜⵜⵜ **Deli Café Baby Gouda**, Ruta 10, Km 161, T771874. Alternative food, yoga and Arab dances.
ⵜⵜⵜ-ⵜⵜ **Bistro de Mar**, Ruta 10, Km 162, ½ km over the promontory, T771356. Old-style, Italian and French as well as local dishes, good wine selection. Claims to be the only "real" bistro in Punta del Este

Faro José Ignacio
ⵜⵜⵜ **121**, Los Teros and Zorzales, T0486-2009. Great location next to the lighthouse, good food and tranquil environment with private library which can be used by guests.
ⵜⵜⵜ **Parador Santa Teresita**, T0486-2004. Very popular, US$25 pp.

La Paloma *p1316*
ⵜⵜⵜ **Arrecife**, on main street. First class.
ⵜⵜ **Da Carlos**, Av Solari. Moderate prices, pizzas plus Uruguayan food.
ⵜⵜⵜ **La Marea**, near tourist office. Very popular, has outstanding seafood.

Northeast of La Paloma
In **Cabo Polonio**, there are a few restaurants, some with vegetarian options, so you don't have to bring any food with you. Fish is on the menu when the sea is calm enough for the fishermen to go out. The most expensive and fashionable is **La Puesta**, on the south beach. On weekends during the summer there are disc jockeys, dancing and live music. For self-catering, the stores sell fruit, vegetables, meat, etc. There are several restaurants in **Castillos** including ⵜⵜⵜ **La Strada**, 19 de Abril, and several restaurants in **Punta del Diablo**, eg ⵜⵜⵜ **La Posada**, highly recommended.

¶¶¶ **Chivito Veloz**, Aguas Dulces. Good, large portions for US$5.

Parque Nacional Santa Teresa *p1316*
¶¶ **La Ruta**, La Coronilla. This small round restaurant at the entrance to town may be your only option if you are driving in the evening and off season from Chuy to Punta or Montevideo. Good meat dishes. Off season, other restaurants in Coronilla are closed.

Chuy *p1317*
¶¶-¶ **Parrillada/Pizzería Javier**, Arachanes on plaza. Quite good.
¶¶-¶ **Restaurant Jesús**, Av Brasil y L Olivera. Good value and quality.

⦿ Bars and clubs

Punta del Este *p1315*
Sophia Caffe Concert, C 27 entre Gorlero y 24, T449505 to reserve. Can be packed in high season. Latin jazz, Bossa Nova, international music.

▲ Activities and tours

Punta del Este *p1315*
Diving Punta Divers, C 32, No 626, T482481, www.ssila.com. US$290 for 8 dives to caves at Punta Ballena and Gorriti, and to wrecks (eg HMS *Agamemon*, Nelson's favourite ship), courses offered. Trips include refreshments. Also offer dive in a gold mine near Minas. To see right whales at end-Aug to Nov, US$18.
Riding Nueva Escuela de Equitación, at Cantegril Country Club, Av Saravia, T223211. Classes, guided rides for all levels and ages.

⦿ Transport

Piriápolis *p1314*
Road Piriápolis may be reached either by following the very beautiful R10 from the end of the Interbalnearia, or by taking the original access road (R37) from Pan de Azúcar, which crosses the R93. The shortest route from Piriápolis to Punta del Este is by the Camino de las Bases which runs parallel to the R37 and joins the R93 some 4 km east of the R37 junction.
Bus Terminal on Misiones, 2 blocks from Hotel Argentino. To/from **Montevideo**, US$4, 1½ hrs. To **Punta del Este**, US$1.50, 50 mins. To **Maldonado**, US$1.20. For **Rocha**, **La Paloma** and **Chuy**, take bus to Pan de Azúcar and change.

Maldonado *p1315*
Bus Av Roosevelt y Sarandí, T225026. To/from **Montevideo**, US$5.50; to **Minas**, 2 hrs, 5 a day,

US$3. To **San Carlos** take a local bus 3 blocks from the main bus station, US$0.50.

Punta del Este *p1315*
Air Direct daily Boeing 737 flights from Buenos Aires to brand new Punta del Este airport during the high season. **Laguna del Sauce**, Capitán Curbelo (T559777), which handles flights to Buenos Aires, 40 mins. Airport tax US$20. Exchange facilities, tax-free shopping. Regular bus service to airport from Punta del Este (will deliver to and collect from private addresses and hotels), US$4, 90 mins before departure, also connects with arriving flights. Taxi US$25; *remise* US$18-US$38 depending on destination (T441269). El Jaguel airport is used by private planes.
Bus Local: Traffic is directed by a one-way system; town bus services start from C 5 (El Faro), near the lighthouse. www.puntaweb.com has details of bus routes. **Long distance**: terminal at Av Gorlero, Blvd Artigas and C 32, T486810 (served by local bus No 7); has toilets, newsagent, café and *Casa de Cambio Nelson*. To/from **Montevideo** via Carrasco airport, **COT** (T486810) or **Copsa** (T489 205), US$5.60, just over 2 hrs, many in the summer; 19 a day in winter. To **Piriápolis**, US$1.50. To **San Carlos** (US$1.45) for connections to Porto Alegre, Rocha, La Paloma, Chuy. Direct to **Chuy**, 4 hrs, US$5. Local bus fare about US$0.50. For transport Montevideo-Buenos Aires, **Buquebus** T484995/ 488380, at bus terminal, buses connect with ferries.

La Paloma *p1316*
Bus Frequent to and from **Rocha**, US$0.60, and to and from **the capital** (5 hrs, US$5.50). 4 buses daily to **Chuy**, US$3, 3½ hrs, 2 a day to San Carlos, Pan de Azúcar and Aguas Dulces, all with Rutas del Sol. Northeast of La Paloma, some Montevideo-Chuy buses go into **Punta del Diablo**, 4 km from the main road.
  To **Cabo Polonio**, Rutas del Sol from Montevideo, US$10.50, 4-5 hrs, and any of the coastal towns to Km 264, where you catch the truck to the village (see above). In Cabo Polonio, Rutas del Sol has an office next to El Templao, for arranging your return trip.

Chuy *p1317*
Bus To **Montevideo** (COT, Cynsa, Rutas del Sol) US$12.25, 4¾-6 hrs, may have to change buses in San Carlos; to **Maldonado** US$5. International buses which passing through en route from Montevideo to Brazil either stop in Chuy or at the border. Make sure the driver knows you need to stop at Uruguayan immigration. Sometimes everybody must get off for customs check. If looking for onward transport, if there is a free seat, most companies will let you pay on board.

⊙ Directory

Piriápolis *p1314*
Banks Banco de Uruguay on Rambla Argentinos changes TCs; **Casa de Cambio Monex**, Argentinos s/n, T25295. **Post offices** Av Piria y Tucumán.

Maldonado *p1315*
Banks Banco Pan de Azúcar, accepts Master-Card. **Cambio Bacacay**, Florida 803, good rates, TCs.

Punta del Este *p1315*
Airline offices Aerolíneas Argentinas, Galería Santos Dumont locales 2 y 3, T444343, Laguna del Sauce, T559777; **Pluna**, Av Roosevelt y Parada 9, T492050/490101. **Banks** Best rates of exchange from Banco de la República Oriental de Uruguay, which opens earlier and closes later than the other banks and accepts MasterCard, but no TCs. Many ATMs at banks on the peninsula and at Punta Shopping (Roosevelt). Also *casas de cambio*, eg **Indumex**, Av Gorlero y 28, **Brimar**, C 31 No 610. **Car hire** Punta Car, Continuación Gorlero s/n, *Hotel Playa*, T482112, puntacar@puntacar.com.uy. **Uno**, Gorlero y 21, T445018, unonobat@movinet.com.uy. And others. See Essentials, for international agencies. **Internet** Cybermix Café, Gorlero y 30, T447158, US$5 per hr. **Spot**, Gorlero y 30, T447290, open 0900-0200, US$6 per hr. **Post offices** Av Gorlero entre 31 y 32, 0900-1400, 1600-1900, daily (shorter hours out of season). **Scooter hire** US$10 per hr, US$25 per day,

with drivers licence (US$50 fine if caught without it) and ID documents, one place opposite bus terminal, others on same street as *Taller Los Angeles*, Parada 2 casi Blvr Artigas, T486732. **Los Angeles** rents scooters and bicycles (US$1.50-US$2.20 per hr, US$5.15-US$6 per day depending on number of gears, padlock and chain included, leave ID as deposit). **Telephones** telephone and fax on Calle 24 at Calle 25, by the plaza.

La Paloma *p1316*
Internet Arrecife, Solari, US$1.50 per hr, open 0900-1200, 1600 until late. **Useful services** Bike rental opposite the casino, US$3.50 a day; horses can be hired. One bank which changes TCs; also a supermarket and post office.

Chuy *p1317*
Banks Several *cambios* on Av Brasil, eg **Gales**, Artigas y Brasil, Mon-Fri 0830-1200, 1330-1800, Sat 0830-1200, and in World Trade Center, open 1000-2200; on either side of *Gales* are *Aces* and *Val*. All give similar rates, charging US$1 plus 1% commission on TCs, US$, pesos and reais. On Sun, try the casino, or look for someone on the street outside the *cambios*. Banco de la República Oriental Uruguay, Gen Artigas, changes TCs. No problem spending reais in Chuy or pesos in Chuí. **Internet** Nemar Informática, Numancia 139, T2980. US$3.50 per hr, open 0900-1200, 1500- 2100, Fri closes at 2000, Sat at 1300. **Post offices** On Gen Artigas. **Telephones** Antel, S Priliac almost Artigas, open 0700-2300.

Montevideo north to Brazil

Two roads run towards Melo, heart of cattle-ranching country: Route 8 and Route 7, the latter running for most of its length through the Cuchilla Grande, a range of hills with fine views. Route 8 via Minas and Treinta y Tres, is the more important of these two roads to the border and it is completely paved.

Minas and around → *Phone code: 0442. Colour map 8, grid B6. Population: 38,000.*
This picturesque small town, 120 km north of Montevideo, is set in wooded hills. Juan Lavalleja, the leader of the Thirty-Three who brought independence to the country, was born here, and there is an equestrian statue to Artigas, said to be the largest such in the world, on the Cerro Artigas just out of town. The church's portico and towers, some caves in the neighbourhood, and the countryside around are worth seeing. Good confectionery is made in Minas; the largest firm, opposite *Hotel Verdun*, shows tourists round its premises. Banks are open 1300-1700 Monday-Friday. There is a tourist office at the bus station.

The Parque Salus, on the slopes of Sierras de las Animas, is 8 km to the south and very attractive; take the town bus marked 'Cervecería Salus' from plaza to the Salus brewery, then walk two km to the mineral spring and bottling plant (**D** pp *Parador Salus*, half board, good). It is a lovely three-hour walk back to Minas from the springs. The Cascada de Agua del Penitente waterfall, 11 km east off Route 8, is interesting and you may see wild rheas nearby. Hard to get to in the off-season.

To the Brazilian Border

Route 8 continues north via **Treinta y Tres** (*Population 26,000*) to Melo (also reached by Route 7), near Aceguá close to the border. In **Melo** (*Population 51,000, Phone code 0462*), there are places to stay and exchange rates are usually better than at the frontier.

At 12 km southeast of Melo is the Posta del Chuy (2 km off Route 26). This house, bridge and toll gate (built 1851 by two Frenchmen) was once the only safe crossing place on the main road between Uruguay and Brazil. Nowadays it houses a display of gaucho paintings and artefacts relating to its history.

Río Branco was founded in 1914, on the Río Yaguarón. The 1 km-long Mauá bridge across the river leads to Jaguarão in Brazil. The Brazilian consulate is at 10 de Junio 379, T2003, bravcrb@adinet.com.uy. For road traffic, the frontier at Chuy is better than Río Branco or Aceguá. There is a toll 68 km north of Montevideo.

An alternative route to Brazil is via Route 5, the 509-km road from Montevideo to the border town of Rivera, which runs almost due north, bypassing Canelones and Florida before passing through Durazno. After crossing the Río Negro, it goes to Tacuarembó. South of the Río Negro is gently rolling cattle country, vineyards, orchards, orange, lemon and olive groves. North is hilly countryside with steep river valleys and cattle ranching. The road is dual carriageway as far as Canelones.

East of Florida, Route 56 traverses the countryside eastwards to **Cerro Colorado**, also known as Alejandro Gallinal, which has an unusual clock tower.

Durazno → *Phone code: 0362. Colour map 8, grid B6. Population: 34,000.*

On the Río Yí 182 km from Montevideo, Durazno is a friendly provincial town with tree-lined avenues and an airport. There is a good view of the river from the western bridge.

Dams on the Río Negro have created an extensive network of lakes near **Paso de los Toros** (*Population: 13,000; 66 km north of Durazno, bus from Montevideo US$6.50*), with camping and sports facilities. Some 43 km north of Paso de los Toros a 55-km road turns east to **San Gregorio de Polanco**, at the eastern end of Lago Rincón del Bonete. The beach by the lake is excellent, with opportunities for boat trips, horse riding and other sports.

Tacuarembó → *Phone code: 0632. Colour map 8, grid B6. Population: 51,000.*

This is an agro-industrial town and major route centre 390 km north of Montevideo. The nearby Valle Edén has good walking possibilities. Some 23 km west of Tacuarembó, along Route 26, is the **Carlos Gardel Museum** ⓘ *US$0.40*, a shrine to the great tango singer who was killed in an air crash in Medellín (Colombia). Uruguay, Argentina and France all claim him as a national son. The argument for his birth near here is convincing.

Brazilian border

Rivera (*Population 64,400, Phone code 0622*) is divided by a street from the Brazilian town of Santa Ana do Livramento. Points of interest are the park, the Plaza Internacional, and the dam of Cañapirú. Uruguayan immigration is in the Complejo Turístico at Sarandí y Viera, 14 blocks, 2 km, from the border (take bus along Agraciada). There is also a tourist office here, T5899. Luggage is inspected when boarding buses out of Rivera; there are also 3 checkpoints on the road out of town. The Brazilian consulate is at Ceballos 1159, T3278. Remember that you must have a Uruguayan exit stamp to enter Brazil and a Brazilian exit stamp to enter Uruguay.

● Sleeping

Minas *p1322*
E Ramos, 18 de Julio 833, near bus station. Basic (discount for HI members).
F Hostel de Villa Serrana, Calle Molle s/n off Route 8, Km 145, in small village of Villa Serrana, T02-901 3587, vserrana@hosteluruguay.org. US$6 pp a night (open all year), 28 km beyond Minas on road to Treinta y Tres. In a thatched house, kitchen for members, horses for hire, basic, take plenty of food and drink as there is no shop. Direct bus from

Montevideo or Minas, ask driver to set you down and walk 3 km to Villa Serrana; essential to book through Montevideo office.
Camping Arequita, T0440-2503, beautiful surroundings, cabañas with and without bath, camping US$6.
Tourism farm B pp **Posada El Abra**, Puntas de Santa Lucía, 25 km from Minas, T0440-2869, www.lavalleja.com/elabra. Small *estancia* in hills at the headwaters of the Río Santa Lucía, price is

full board, including transport, guides, horses for riding, good walking, remnant of native flora nearby, swimming in river, expansive views.

Treinta y Tres *p1323*

D pp Cañada del Brujo, Km 307.5, Ruta 8, Sierra del Yerbal, 34 km north of Treinta y Tres, T0452-2837, T099-297448 (mob), cdelbrujo@latin mail.com. An isolated hostel without electricity, basic but "fantastic", dormitory accommodation, local food, owner Pablo Rado drives you there, canoeing, trekking on foot or horseback, trips to Quebrada de los Cuervos. Recommended.

Melo *p1323*

A Virrey Pedro de Melo, J Muñiz 727, T22673, ximevito@adinet.com.uy. Better rooms in new part, 3-star, TV, minibar, café.

Cerro Colorado *p1323*

AL San Pedro de Timote, Km 142, R7, 14 km west of Cerro Colorado, T/F0598-310 8086, http://sanpedrodetimote.com.uy. A famous *estancia*, colonial-style, like a village with its own church, landscaped park, 3 pools, cinema, gym, horseriding, good restaurant, still a working ranch.
A Arteaga, 7 km off R7 north of Cerro Colorado, T02-707 4766, arteaga@paradaarteaga.com. Typical European *estancia*, famous, beautiful interior, pool.

Durazno *p1323*

There are a few hotels (**D-F**).
Camping At 33 Orientales, in park of same name by river, T2806, nice beach, hot showers, toilets, laundry sinks.
Tourism Farm Estancia Albergue El Silencio, Ruta 14 Km 166, 10 km west of Durazno, T2014 (or T0360-2270, HI member), silencio@adinet.com.uy. About 15 mins walk east of bridge over Río Yí where bus will stop: clean rooms, very friendly, riding, swimming, bird watching. Recommended.

Paso de los Toros *p1323*

E Sayonara, Sarandí y Barreto, T0664-2535/2743 2 blocks centre, renovated old residence, rooms with bath, a/c and cable TV. Includes breakfast.

San Gregoio de Polanco *p1323*

C Los Médanos, Arturo Mollo s/n, T0369-4013, www.losmedanos.com.uy. Good location, in a park by the lake, breakfast, well furnished rooms with a/c and TV, heated pool, jacuzzi, and a large restaurant (*parrilla*) across the road. Good value, cheaper off-season.

Tacuarembó *p1323*

C Tacuarembó, 18 de Julio 133, T22104, www.tacuarembohotel.com.uy. Breakfast,

central, TV, wireless internet, safe, restaurant, pool, parking.
E Plaza, 25 de Agosto 247, T27988. A/c, TV, small.
F Hospedaje 25, 25 de Mayo 358. Basic, garden.
Camping Campsites 1 km out of town in the Parque Laguna de las Lavanderas, T4761, and 7 km north on R26 at Balneario Iporá.

Rivera *p1323*

C Casablanca, Sarandí 484, T23221. Shower, breakfast, a/c, TV, comfortable, pleasant.
C-D Sarandí, Sarandí 777, T33963. Fan, good, **D** without bath.
Camping Municipal site near AFE station, and in the Parque Gran Bretaña 7 km south along R27.

🍴 Eating

Minas *p1322*

Recommended eating places are: **San Francisco**, 25 de Mayo 586, and **El Portal**, Aníbal del Campo 743, for *parrillada*.
Irisarri, C Treinta y Tres 618. The best pastry shop known for *yemas* (egg candy) and *damasquitos* (apricot sweets).

Tacuarembó *p1323*

Parrilla La Rueda, W Beltrán 251. Good.

🚌 Transport

Minas *p1322*

Bus To **Montevideo**, US$3.75, 5 companies, US$4.10, 2 hrs. To **Maldonado**, US$2.45, 5 a day, 2 hrs.

Melo *p1323*

Bus To **Montevideo** US$14, 5¼-6 hrs (Núñez, COTA). Several buses daily to Río Branco.

Durazno *p1323*

Bus To **Montevideo** US$6.65, 2½ hrs, many companies such as **Núñez**, **Turismar** and **Nossar**.

Tacuarembó *p1323*

Bus From **Montevideo**, US$14, 4-5 hrs (**Turil**, **Núñez** and others).

Rivera *p1323*

Bus Terminal at Uruguay y Viera (1½ km from the terminal in Santa Ana). To/from **Montevideo**, US$17.65, 5½-6¾ hrs (Agencia Central, Turil, Núñez). To **Paysandú**, Copay, T23733, at 0400, 1600, US$14. To **Tacuarembó**, US$3 (Núñez, Turil), no connections for Paysandú. To **Salto**, Mon and Fri 1630, 6 hrs, US$15. For **Artigas**, take bus from Livramento to Quaraí, then cross bridge.

Venezuela

Essentials	1328
Caracas	1334
Sights	1335
Around Caracas	1347
West from Caracas	1349
Maracay and around	1349
Valencia and around	1353
Coro and around	1357
From Maracaibo to Colombia	1360
Barquisimeto and around	1363
Valera to Mérida	1364
Mérida and around	1366
Mérida	1366
Sierra Nevada de Mérida	1372
Los Llanos and Amazonas	1378
Los Llanos	1379
Amazonas	1381
East coast	1383
Caracas to Puerto La Cruz	1384
Parque Nacional Mochima	1387
Cumaná	1389
Araya to Paria	1391
Isla de Margarita	1396
Los Roques	1403
Canaima and the Orinoco Delta	1404
Ciudad Bolívar	1405
Canaima and Angel Falls	1408
Ciudad Guayana and the Orinoco Delta	1411
Ciudad Guayana to Santa Elena de Uairén	1414
Mount Roraima	1421

� Footprint features

Don't miss …	1327
Touching down	1331
Driving in Venezuela	1332

Introduction

Venezuela is where the Andes meet the Caribbean. The Orinoco river separates great plains from the table-top mountains of the Gran Sabana, where waterfalls tumble in sheer drops into the forest and lost worlds are easy to imagine. More recent innovations – cable cars up to the high peaks, hang gliders for jumping off them – are now part of the scene at Mérida, capital of Venezuela's Andes. Lying at the heart of the country – geographically and spiritually – are the *llanos* (plains), a vast area of flat savannah the size of Italy and home to an immense variety of birds, exotic mammals and reptiles, such as caiman (alligators), giant anacondas, anteaters, pumas, jaguars and giant otters, to name but a few.

These plains flood seasonally, but when the waters retreat, the birds and animals share their territory with cattle and the *llanero* cowboys, renowned for their hospitality towards visitors who can stay at one of the many luxurious *hatos* – cattle ranches – or rough it on a budget tour from Mérida. If the sea is more to your taste, head for the country's seductive coastline – the longest in the Caribbean at over 2,500 km. Venezuela's waters play host to some of the best (and least known) diving in the region with three marine national parks. Pick of the bunch are Islas Los Roques, an archipelago of emerald and turquoise lagoons and dazzling white beaches. At the other end of the country, the Amazon is home to humid rainforests and rare plants and animals as well as over 20 different ethnic groups. This part of Venezuela is very much frontier territory and remains wild and untamed, as it was when the country received its first foreign visitor back in 1498. So overwhelmed was Columbus by what he saw that he described it as 'Paradise on Earth'.

★ Don't miss ...

1 **Henri Pittier National Park** This stunning landscape of tumbling mountain streams and steep rugged hills is a birdwatcher's heaven, page 1350.

2 **Sierra Nevada National Park** From the city of Mérida, the highest cable car in the world wings its way up to the summit of the Andes. There is great trekking in the *páramo* and agricultural highlands, page 1372.

3 **Los Llanos** Another excellent area for wildlife watching. The great plains of the Orinoco are cowboy country and many of the cattle ranches offer themselves as bases, page 1379.

4 **Mochima National Park** A string of beautiful beaches, sandy coves and islets, backed by lush, forested hills. This is one of the most accessible of Venezuela's protected areas, so hire a boat and spend a day snorkelling and sunbathing, page 1387.

5 **Los Roques** Emerald lagoons and dazzling sands surrounded by 20 km of coral reef make this Caribbean archipelago one of Venezuela's top attractions, page 1403.

6 **Angel Falls** From a table-top mountain, a waterfall tumbles for almost 1 km. It's an adventure to get to the base and a major expedition to get to the top, unless of course you just hop on a little plane and fly over, page 1408.

Essentials

Planning your trip

Caribbean coast Venezuela has the longest coastline in the Caribbean with numerous palm-fringed beaches of white sand. **Caracas** is hidden from the Caribbean by Monte Ávila, one of Venezuela's national parks, but you don't have to go too far beyond the mountain to find good beaches. Only a few hours west of the capital are some lovely little beaches. Further west is the Parque Nacional Morrocoy, with many islands close to the shore. North of Morrocoy is the historic town of Coro, surrounded by sand dunes, and the Paranaguá Peninsula. Parque Nacional Mochima, east of Caracas, has some excellent beaches and a multitude of islets to explore. Further east are unrivalled beaches on the Paria Peninsula, but they are harder to reach. Besides those islands already mentioned, there is Isla de Margarita, one of the country's principal destinations for local and foreign tourists. The Islas Los Roques, 166 km due north of the central coast, is a beautiful archipelago, still unspoilt despite the growth in tourist interest.

The Andes Venezuela's Andes have some gorgeous scenery, with snow-capped peaks and remote villages. The main centre is Mérida, in the Sierra Nevada of the same name. It has accommodation, other services and tour companies, which can arrange treks, climbing and other excursions. Two of its claims to fame are the highest cable car in the world, ascending the 4,776-m Pico Espejo, and the shop selling the largest number of ice cream flavours in the world.

The Llanos Life in the *llanos* revolves around the cycle of wet and dry seasons; the movement of cattle, the mainstay of the region's economy, depends on it. In the flat grasslands are slow running rivers which flood in the rainy season, creating a huge inland sea. When the rains cease, the whole area dries out completely. South of the cattle lands are forests and the tributaries of the Río Orinoco. Just after the May-November wet season, this is a paradise for nature lovers, with a spectacular variety of birds, monkeys, big cats, anaconda, river dolphins, caiman and capybara. Tours to the *llanos* are run from Mérida and there are ecotourism ranches which offer you the chance to get to know the lifestyle of the plains.

Guayana and the Orinoco Above the grasslands of the Gran Sabana rise *tepuis*, flat-topped mountains from which spring magnificent waterfalls and rivers. The Angel Falls, the highest in the world, are one such wonder, usually seen from a plane, but also reachable by a 2-3 day trip upriver. There are many other falls in the Gran Sabana and a few places to stay, the most popular being Canaima camp on a lagoon on the Río Carrao. Where Venezuela meets Brazil and Guyana is Mount Roraima; to reach its summit is one of the country's most adventurous excursions. The Orinoco delta is remote, but trips can be made from the small town of Tucupita. Amazonas too, is well off the beaten track, but here again trips can be made, from Puerto Ayacucho. Much of the rainforest is protected and you need permission from the authorities to visit areas beyond the reach of a tour company.

When to go The climate is tropical, with changes between the seasons being a matter of wet and dry, rather than hot and cold. Temperature is determined by altitude. The dry season in Caracas is December to April, with January and February the coolest months (there is a great difference between day and night temperatures at this time). The hottest months are July and August. The Caribbean coast is generally dry and rain is particularly infrequent in the states of Sucre, in the east, and Falcón, in the northwest. The lowlands of Maracaibo are very hot all year round; the least hot months are July to September. South of the Orinoco, in the Gran Sabana and Parque Nacional Canaima, the dry season is November to May. The same months are dry in the *llanos*, but the best time to visit is just after the rains, when the rivers and channels are still full of water and the humidity is not too high. In the Andes, the dry season is October to May, and this is the best time for climbing or hiking. The days are clear, but the nights are freezing cold. The rains usually begin in June, but in the mountains the weather can change from day to day. **High season,** when it is advisable to book in advance is: Carnaval, Easter, 15 July-15 September and Christmas to New Year.

Finding out more In charge of tourism is the **Ministerio del Poder Popular para el Turismo,** Av Francisco de Miranda con Av Principal de La Floresta, Edif Mintur (Frente al Colegio Universitario de Caracas), Chacao, Caracas, T0212-208 4511, www.mintur.gob.ve. At the same address are **Instituto Nacional de Promoción y Capacitación Turística – Inatur,**

To212-208 7918, www.inatur.gob.ve, which deals with tourism promotion, and **Venezolana de Turismo – Venetur**, www.venetur.gob.ve, which deals with marketing, the hotel sector, transport. For practical information, see www.venezuelavisitorsbureau.com and www.burode venezuela.com. Outside Venezuela, contact Venezuelan embassies and consulates. Read and heed the travel advice, which is regularly updated, at www.britain.org.ve and www .travel.state.gov (go to Consular Information Sheets under Travel Warnings).

National parks Venezuela has 43 national parks, 21 national monuments and various other refuges and reserves, some of which are mentioned in the text. A full list is published by the **Instituto Nacional de Parques** (Inparques), Salida del Distribuidor Santa Cecilia, Edificio Sur del Museo de Transporte, entre Avenida Francisco de Miranda y Autopista Francis Caracas, T273 2811 (Caracas), www.inparques.gob.ve. Each park has a regional director and its own guards (*guardaparques*). Permits (free) are required to stay in the parks (up to five), although this is not usually necessary for those parks visited frequently. For further information on the national parks system, visit the **Ministerio del Poder Popular para el Ambiente**, Centro Simón Bolívar, Torre Sul, Caracas 1010, T481 2209, www.marn.gov.ve. Ecotourism portal: **http://ecoportal .venezuela.com**, for ecotourism, sports, national parks and places to stay, lots of links and information in English, but confusing format. See also **www.parkswatch.org** for a good run down of the country's most important national parks.

Websites

Maps *Guía Vial de Venezuela*, edited by **Miro Popic** (Caracas 1999), US$25, is a motoring guide with road maps and tourist information. The best country map is the late Kevin Healey's, published by **International Travel Maps**, Vancouver, Canada; available at good travel agents.

Visas and immigration Entry is by passport and visa, or by passport and tourist card. Tourist cards (*tarjetas de ingreso*) are issued by airlines to visitors from all EU and other Western European countries, Australia, Canada, Japan, New Zealand, South Africa, USA and most South and Central American and Caribbean countries. To check if you need a visa, see www.mre.gov.ve/metadot/index.pl?iid=2871&isa=Category. Valid for 90 days, tourist cards cannot be extended. Overstaying your tourist card can lead to arrest and a fine when you try to depart. For a **tourist visa**, you need two passport photos, passport valid for six months, references from bank and employer, onward or return ticket and a completed and signed application form. The fee is £22 (or equivalent, costs vary from country to country). For a 90-day extension go to the Ministerio del Poder Popular para las Relaciones Interiores y

1329

Justicia, **ONIDEX** ① *Av Baralt on Plaza Miranda in Caracas, To800-664 3390 or 0212-483 2070, www.onidex.gov.ve; office at Plaza Caracas, Torre Norte (Centro CB), mezzanine, Mon-Fri 0700-1230 (Fri 0800)*, take passport, tourist visa, photographs and return ticket; passport with extension returned at end of day. ONIDEX offices in many cities do not offer extensions. Transit visas, valid for 72 hours are also available, mostly the same requirements and cost (inward and onward tickets needed). ONIDEX in Caracas will not exchange a transit for a tourist visa. In Manaus you also need a yellow fever inoculation certificate. Consuls may give a one-year visa if a valid reason can be given. To change a tourist visa to a business visa, to obtain or to extend the latter, costs £44 or equivalent.

Work visas also cost £44 and require authorization from the **Dirección General Sectorial de Identificación y Control de Extranjeros** in Caracas. Student visas require a letter of acceptance from the Venezuelan institution, references from bank and university, completed and signed application form, two passport photos, onward or return ticket, passport valid for six months and US$60. It generally takes two days to issue any visa.

Note If you are not eligible for a tourist card, you must get a consular visa in advance. Carry your passport with you at all times as the police do frequent spot checks and anyone found without ID is immediately detained (carrying a certified copy of your passport and entry stamp is permissible, though not always accepted by officials). You will also be asked to provide personal details (name, address, passport or ID number) eg in restaurants. There are many military checkpoints, especially in border areas, at which all transport is stopped. Have your documents ready and make sure you know what entry permits you need; the soldiers may be unfamiliar with regulations for foreigners. Border searches are very thorough. Business visitors on short visits are strongly advised to enter the country as tourists, otherwise they will have to obtain a tax clearance certificate (*solvencia*) before they can leave. Do not lose the carbon copy of your visa as this has to be surrendered when leaving the country.

Venezuelan embassies and consulates Visit www.mre.gov.ve.

Money The unit of currency is the bolívar. There are coins for 10, 20, 50, 100 and 500 bolívares, and notes for 1,000, 2,000, 5,000, 10,000, 20,000 and 50,000 bolívares. Have small coins and notes to hand, since in many shops and bars and on public transport large notes may be hard to change.

Venezuela has an exchange control regime for the bolívar. The government determines the 'official' rate, which has devalued slowly in relation to the dollar and other currencies since the measure was imposed in 2002. There is also a 'parallel' (ie black) market exchange of currencies. Any hard currency (eg dollar, euro – which is becoming popular) is difficult to buy officially. Even though changing bolívares for hard currency is punishable, it is common practice. If you do decide to change on the black market, a) find out what the unofficial rate is from as many sources as possible, and b) do the transaction with the most trusted person. Many travel agencies and hotels will not change on the black market openly. Banks and *casas de cambio* use the official rate; quoted rates in hotels tend to be worse than that, but they may be your best bet for changing on the black market. When goods and services are priced in dollars, check the exchange rate if you intend to pay in bolívares, it is usually unfavourable. The *Daily Journal* newspaper publishes the unofficial rate on its mast-head. The official bolívar **exchange rate** in July 2007 was US$: 2,147; euro: 2,916. In early 2007 the black market was offering anything between 300 and 1,000 bolívares above the official rate. Prices in this guide are calculated with the official exchange rate. **Note** In 2007, President Chávez announced that three zeros would be knocked off currency bills, making Bs 1,000 into Bs 1.

Plastic/TCs/banks (ATMs) Dollars cash and TCs can be changed in banks and *casas de cambio* at the official rate. To convert unused bolívares back into dollars upon leaving, you must present the original exchange receipt (up to 30% of original amount changed); only banks and authorized *casas de cambio* can legally sell bolívares. Some banks are reluctant to change either cash or TCs. *Casas de cambio* are a better bet, but their rates for TCs will be poor (because they use the official rate) and they insist on photocopying your passport, ask for proof of purchase of Tcs, ask you to sign a form saying where cash dollars came from and may even photograph you. Beware of forged Amex TCs and US$ notes.

You can also use Visa/Plus, MasterCard, Cirrus and Maestro for obtaining bolívares at the official rate. There are cash machines for Visa, Plus, MasterCard, Maestro and Cirrus at Simón

⦂ Touching down

Airport tax International passengers pay a combined airport and exit tax of around US$62 at the official exchange rate. It goes up every March. Many airlines collect some, if not all of the tax in the ticket price, but you have to check what has been paid. Children under two years do not pay tax. There is an 8% tax on the cost of all domestic flights, plus an airport tax of US$6.35-7.65, depending on airport. Exit stamps have to be paid by overland travellers, US$15. Correct taxes are not advertised and travellers have experienced overcharging.

Business hours Banks: 0830-1530 Mon-Fri only. **Government offices:** 0800-1200 are usual morning hours, although they vary. Officials have fixed hours, usually 0900-1000 or 1500-1600, for receiving visitors. **Businesses:** 0800-1800 with a midday break. **Shops:** 0900-1300, 1500-1900, Mon-Sat. Generally speaking, Venezuelans start work early, and by 0700 in the morning everything is in full swing. Most firms and offices close on Saturday.

In an emergency T171 for the integrated emergency system. CICPC (Cuerpo de Investigaciones Científicas, Penales y Criminalísticas), Av Urdaneta entre Pelota y Punceres; Edif Icauca, mezzanina 2, Caracas, T0212-564 7798, www.cicpc.gov.ve. For registering crimes, with agencies throughout the country.

International phone code +58. Ringing: long equal tones with equal long pauses. Engaged: short equal tones, with equal pauses.

Official time Four hours behind GMT, one hour ahead of EST.

Tipping Taxi drivers are not tipped if you have agreed the fare in advance. Usherettes are not tipped. Hotel porters, US$1; airport porters US$1 per piece of baggage. Restaurants 5-10% of bill.

VAT/IVA 11%.

Voltage 110 volts, 60 cycles. Plugs are 2-pin round and flat combined, 2-pin flat and 2-pin flat with optional D-shaped earth.

Weights and measures Metric.

Bolívar airport. You should be wary of using cash machines throughout the country; Visa and MasterCard transactions inside banks, although slower, are much safer. Queues at ATM machines attract thieves. In addition some ATMs require a Venezuelan ID number. *Corp Banca* is affiliated with American Express, no commission, some branches cash personal cheques from abroad on an Amex card; *American Express* travel services are handled by *Italcambio* and *Quo Vadis* agencies around the country. MasterCard assistance To800-1-002902. Visa assistance call collect +44-20-7937 8091 or F+44-17-3350 3670.

Cost of travelling On the cheapest possible budget you can get by on around US$25 pp per day, depending on which part of the country you visit. A less basic budget would be about US$50 per day, rising to US$100 and upwards for first class travel. The average cost for using the internet varies from US$0.50-0.80 outside Caracas to US$1-2 per hour in the capital.

Safety In Caracas and any popular tourist destination, especially on the coast, watch out for scams, cons and petty thieving. The beaches can be packed at weekends and, while empty on weekdays, the detritus left by the weekend crowds may not be cleared up. If you do find an isolated beach, it is wise to be on the lookout for unwanted attention from robbers. This may sound like a Catch-22, but there are quiet beaches where you will be undisturbed (simply make enquiries before setting out) and, in the main, Venezuelans are extremely hospitable.

Getting around

Air Most big places are served by **Aeropostal** *www.aeropostal.com*, **Aserca** *www.aserca airlines.com*, **Avior** *www.avior.com.ve*, **Conviasa** *www.conviasa.aero*, **Sol América, Láser** *www.laser.com.ve*, **Rutaca** *www.rutaca.com.ve*, **Santa Bárbara** *www.sbairlines.com*, **Lai, Transaven** and **Venezolana. Aereotuy/LTA** *www.lta.net.ve/Aereotuy.htm*, connects the

Driving in Venezuela

Road Roads are generally quite good, especially the four-lane *autopistas*. Quality varies throughout the country.

Safety Use private car parks whenever possible. If you have an accident and someone is injured, you will be detained as a matter of routine, even if you are not at fault. Carry a spare battery, water, fan belts, the obligatory breakdown triangle, a jack and spanners.

Documents Minimum driving age is 18. A valid driving licence from your own country, or international driving licence (preferred) is required. Neither a *carnet de passages*, nor a *libreta de pasos por aduana* is officially required, but is recommended. Before shipping your vehicle to Venezuela, go to a Venezuelan consul to obtain all necessary documentation. You must also go to a Venezuelan consul in the country in which you land your car if other than Venezuela. An entry permit for a car costs US$10 and requires one photograph (takes 24 hours).

Organizations Touring y Automóvil Club de Venezuela, Torre Phelps, p 15, of A y C, Plaza Venezuela, Caracas, T0212-781 9743, www.automovilclub venezuela.com. Issues *libreta de pasos por aduana*, see www.automovilclub venezuela.com/ doc_internacionales.htm.

Car hire Although expensive, it is a good idea to hire a car; many of the best places are off the beaten track. You need a credit card to rent a vehicle. Rates for a car range from US$55-100 per day, with insurance and unlimited mileage, plus government tax of 17%.

Fuel 91 and 95 octane, unleaded, cost US$0.15- 0.25 a litre; diesel, US$0.15 a litre. **Warning** There is a US$20 fine for running out of fuel.

coast, the Orinoco Delta and their camp in Canaima National Park, Arekuna. Apart from **Aserca**, which has been recommended, none is great. Lost luggage is a frequent problem. Internal airlines offer occasional family or student discounts, photocopies of ISIC card are useful. Beware of over-booking during holiday time, especially at Caracas airport; check in at least two hours before departure.

Bus and taxi Buses on most long-distance routes come in four standards, *normal*, *semi-ejecutivo*, *ejecutivo* and *bus-cama*. Fares are set by the authorities and you should see them posted on bus office windows. There are numerous services between the major cities and many services bypass Caracas, so you don't have to change buses in the capital. Buses stop frequently, but there may not always be a toilet at the stop. For journeys in a/c buses take a sleeping bag or similar because the temperature is set to freezing. This is most important on night journeys, which otherwise are fine. Also take earplugs against the loud stereo systems. The colectivo taxis and minibuses, known as *por puesto*, seem to monopolize transport to and from smaller towns and villages. For longer journeys they are normally twice as expensive as buses, but faster. They may be reluctant to take luggage and the ill-kempt. If first on board, wait for other passengers to arrive, do not take a *por puesto* on your own unless you want to pay for the whole vehicle. Outside Caracas, town taxis are relatively expensive.

Hitchhiking Hitchhiking (*cola*) is generally safe, as Venezuelans are usually friendly and helpful if you know some Spanish. The best places to try are Guardia Nacional posts outside cities. It is illegal on toll roads and, theoretically, for non-family members in the back of pick up trucks. Some drivers may ask for money for the lift, especially if on a bus route.

Sleeping → *See page 58 for our hotel grade price guide.*
Value for money is generally not very high, with one or two exceptions, but many foreign-run, no-frills places catering for backpackers are opening up. The major cities, Isla Margarita, Los Roques, Guayana and Amazonas have higher room rates (eg US$15 in Caracas for a decent room). Add 10-15% for air-conditioning. In the Andean region prices are lower at around US$8 per person. *Elizabeth Kline's Guide to Camps, Posadas and Cabins in Venezuela*, published

every 2 years or so, www.geocities.com/venezuelaposadasguide, is incredibly detailed and doesn't pull its punches. *La Guía Valentina Quintero* also covers whole country, suggesting routes, where to stay and eat, published biannually, www.valentinaquintero.com.ve. **Casa Tropical** (main office), Paseo Las Mercedes, Caracas, T212-715 6561, www.casatropical .com.ve, offers interesting accommodation options in the Andes, Ciudad Bolívar and Tacarigua National Park, among other places.

Camping Camping in Venezuela is a popular recreation, for spending a weekend at the beach, on the islands, in the Llanos and in the mountains. Camping, with or without a vehicle, is not possible at the roadside. If camping on the beach, for the sake of security, pitch your tent close to others, even though they play their radios loud.

Eating → *See page 58 for our restaurant price guide.*
Eating out Midday is the cheapest time to eat the main meal of the day and the best time to find fresh vegetables. Particularly good value is the three-course *menú ejecutivo* or *cubierto*. Minimum price for a meal is US$3-5, plus US$1 for drinks. Breakfast in your hotel is likely to be poor. It is better and cheaper in a *fuente de soda* and cheaper still in a *pastelería* or *arepería*.

Food There is excellent local fish (such as *pargo* or red snapper, *carite* or king fish), crayfish, small oysters and prawns. Although it is a protected species, turtle may appear on menus in the Península de Paraguaná as *ropa especial*. Of true Venezuelan food there is *sancocho* (a stew of vegetables, especially yuca, with meat, chicken or fish); *arepas*, white maize bread, very bland in flavour; toasted *arepas* served with various fillings or the local salty white cheese, are cheap, filling and nutritious; *cachapas*, a maize pancake wrapped around white cheese; *pabellón*, made of shredded meat, beans, rice and fried plantains; and *empanadas*, maize-flour pies containing cheese, meat or fish. At Christmas there are *hallacas*, maize pancakes stuffed with chicken, pork, olives, boiled in a plantain leaf. A *muchacho* (boy) on the menu is a cut of beef. *Ganso* is not goose but beef. *Solomo* and *lomito* are other cuts of beef. *Hervido* is chicken or beef with vegetables. *Contorno* with a meat or fish dish is a choice of fried chips, boiled potatoes, rice or yuca. *Caraotas* are beans; *cachitos* are filled *croissants*. *Pasticho* is what Venezuelans call Italian *lasagne*. The main fruits are bananas, oranges, grapefruit, mangoes, pineapple and pawpaws. Venezuelan names for fruit: *lechosa* is papaya, *patilla* water melon, *parchita* passion fruit, and *cambur* a small banana. Excellent strawberries are grown at Colonia Tovar, 90 minutes from Caracas, and in the Andes. Delicious sweets are *huevos chimbos* – egg yolk boiled and bottled in sugar syrup, and *quesillo* - made with milk, egg and caramel. The *Daily Journal* lists reliable restaurants in Caracas and Maracaibo. **Note** Venezuelans dine late!

Drink Venezuelan rum is very good; recommended brands are *Cacique, Pampero* and *Santa Teresa*. There are five good beers: *Polar* (the most popular, sold as Polar and Ice, and Solera and Solera Light), *Regional* (with a strong flavour of hops), *Cardenal* and *Nacional* (a *lisa* is a glass of keg beer; for a bottle of beer ask for a *tercio*); Brazilian *Brahma* beer (lighter than *Polar*) is now brewed in Venezuela. There are also mineral waters and gin. There is a good, local wine in Venezuela. The *Polar* brewery joined with Martell (France) to build a winery in Carora. Wines produced are 'Viña Altagracia' and 'Bodegas Pomar'. **Bodegas Pomar** (T0212-202 8924, bpventas@empresas-polar.com) also sells a champagne-style sparkling wine. Look out for Pomar wine festivals in March and September. Liqueurs are cheap, try the local *ponche crema*. Coffee is very cheap (*café con leche* is milky, *café marrón* much less so, *café negro* is black, which, though obvious, is not common in the rest of Latin America); it often has sugar already added, ask for "sin azúcar". Visitors should also try a *merengada*, a delicious drink made from fruit pulp, ice, milk and sugar; a *batido* is the same but with water and a little milk; *jugo* is the same but with water. A *plus-café* is an after-dinner liqueur. Water is free in restaurants even if no food is bought. Bottled water in *cervecerías* is often from the tap; no deception is intended, bottles are simply used as convenient jugs. Insist on seeing the bottle opened if you want mineral water. *Chicha de arroz* is a sweet drink made of milk, rice starch, sugar and vanilla. Fruit juices are very good, but ask for "jugo natural, preparado en el momento" for the freshest juice.

Festivals and events

National holidays include: 1 January, Carnival on the Monday-Tuesday before Ash Wednesday (everything shuts down Saturday-Tuesday; book accommodation in advance), Thursday-Saturday of Holy Week, 19 April, 1 May, 24 June (the feast day of San Juan Bautista, celebrated on the central coast where there were once large concentrations of plantation slaves who considered San Juan their special Saint; the best-known events are in villages such as Chuao, Cata and Ocumare de la Costa), 5 and 24 July, 24 September, 12 October, 2 November, 25 December. From 24 December-1 January, most restaurants close and there is no long-distance public transport. On New Year's Eve, everything closes and does not open for a least a day. Business travellers should not visit during Holy Week or Carnival. Extra holidays for banks: 19 March (San José), nearest Monday to 6 January, Ascension Day, 29 June, 15 August and 8 December. See *Atlas de tradiciones venezolanas*, Fundación Bigott/El Nacional (2005), a beautiful book with sections on festivals, gastronomy, music, *artesanías*, architecture and popular art. Also *Calendario de fiestas tradicionales venezolanas*, Cecilia Fuentes and Daría Hernández, Fundación Bigott (2003).

Caracas

→ *Phone code: 0212. Colour map 1, grid A6. Population: nearly 5 million (city 1,825,000). Altitude: 960 m.*

Caracas is not the gentlest of introductions to South America. Some enjoy its pleasant, year-round climate, its parks and cosmopolitan nightlife. Others are drawn to see firsthand the Chávez revolution in action. For others, it's more like a slap in the face from a garishly dressed, loud mestizo with a taste for all things American. Founded in 1567, it lies in a rift in thickly forested mountains which rise abruptly from a lush green coast to heights of 2,000 to 3,000 m. The small basin in which the capital lies runs some 24 km east and west. By way of escape, there are several nearby excursions to mountain towns, the Parque Nacional Monte Avila, beaches and Los Roques, a beautiful Caribbean atoll reached by a short flight.

Ins and outs

Getting there The **airport** is 28 km from Caracas, near the port of La Guaira: Maiquetía and Aeropuerto Auxiliar for national flights and Simón Bolívar for international flights. Both Maiquetía and Simón Bolívar have modern terminals. There are three main **bus terminals** in different parts of the city; where you arrive depends upon where you travelled from. ▶▶ *See also Transport, page 1343.*

Getting around The metro is a/c, clean, safe, comfortable and quicker than other city transport. Buses are overcrowded in rush hour and charge extra after 2100. Bus tickets cost US$0.35 around town and US$0.45 for suburban routes. On longer runs these buses are better for those with luggage than a *por puesto* minibus. Minibuses are known as *busetas*, *carmelitas* or *carritos*. *Por puestos* run on regular routes; fares depend on the distance travelled within the city and rise for journeys outside. Many *por puesto* services start in El Silencio.

Orientation In the centre, each street corner has a name: addresses are generally given as 'Santa Capilla a Mijares', rather than the official 'Calle Norte 2, No 26'. In the east, addresses are more obvious, 'y' or 'con' used for street intersections. Since the Second World War, older architecture has given way to modern multi-storeyed edifices and few colonial buildings remain intact. As such, many visitors find the city lacking in character. A 10-km strip from west to east, fragmented by traffic-laden arteries, contains several centres: Plaza Bolívar, Plaza Venezuela, Sabana Grande, Chacaíto, Altamira, La Floresta, Boleíta. The Avila mountain is always north.

Tourist offices Inatur, Av Francisco de Miranda con Av Principal de La Floresta, Edif Mintur (Frente al Colegio Universitario de Caracas), Chacao (see Finding out more, page 1328). There is a tourist office at the airport (see below).

Climate Maximum 32°C July-August, minimum 9°C January-February.

Security Safety in Caracas has deteriorated in recent years and crime rates have risen significantly. You should be on the lookout from the moment you arrive; there are many pirate taxis and rip-off merchants operating at the international airport. It is advisable not to arrive in Caracas at night and not to walk down narrow streets or in parks after dark. Avoid certain areas such as all western suburbs from the El Silencio monument to Propatria, the areas around the Nuevo Circo and La Bandera bus stations, the area around the *teleférico*, Chapellín near the Country Club, and Petare. Street crime is on the increase, even armed robbery in daylight. Even in a crowded place like Sabana Grande, bag slashing and mugging are not uncommon. Take care at all times and never carry valuables. Carry handbags, cameras etc on the side away from the road as motorcycle bag-snatchers are notorious. Car theft is common: always use car parks; never park on the street. Police searches are frequent and thorough, especially around Avenida Las Acacias after dark and in airports; always carry ID. If you have entered overland from Colombia, expect thorough investigation. Outside the capital, the atmosphere is much more relaxed, but as in any country you should be cautious at night, especially in the main cities.

Sights

Centre
ⓘ *Many museums close on Mon and at lunchtime.*
The shady **Plaza Bolívar**, with its fine equestrian statue of the Liberator and pleasant colonial cathedral, is still the official centre of the city, though no longer geographically so. Much of its colonial surroundings is being restored. In the **Capitolio Nacional** ⓘ *Tue-Sun, 0900-1200, 1400-1700,* the Elliptical Salon has some impressive paintings and murals by the Venezuelan artist Martín Tovar y Tovar and a bronze urn with the 1811 Declaration of Independence, which was signed here. The present **Cathedral** dating from 1674 has a beautiful façade, the Bolívar family chapel and paintings by Michelena, Murillo and an alleged Rubens 'Resurrection'. Bolívar was baptized in this Cathedral and the remains of his parents and wife are kept here.

The **Consejo Municipal** (City Hall) on Plaza Bolívar contains three **museums** ⓘ *all 3 open Tue-Fri 0930-1200, 1500-1800; Sat and Sun 0930-1800; informative guides are available*: a collection of the paintings of Emilio Boggio, a Venezuelan painter; the Raúl Santana Museum of the Creole Way of Life, a collection of miniature figures in costumes, all handmade by Raúl Santana; and the Sala de Arqueología Gaspar Marcano, exhibiting ceramics, mostly discovered on the coast.

Casa Natal del Libertador ⓘ *Sur 1 y Este 2, Jacinto a Traposos, opposite Plaza El Venezolano, T541 2563, Tue-Fri 1000- 1200, 1400-1700, Sun and holidays 1000-1300, 1400-1700*: a reconstruction of the house where Bolívar was born (24 July 1783). It contains interesting pictures and furniture and murals tell Bolívar's life story. The first house, of adobe, was destroyed by an earthquake. The second became a stable, and was later pulled down. **The Museo Bolivariano** is alongside the Casa Natal and contains the Liberator's war relics.

San Francisco ⓘ *Av Universidad y San Francisco (1 block southwest of Plaza Bolívar)*, should be seen for its colonial altars; it's oldest church in Caracas, rebuilt 1641. **Santa Teresa** ⓘ *between La Palma and Santa Teresa, just southeast of the Centro Simón Bolívar*, has good interior chapels and a supposedly miraculous portrait of Nazareno de San Pablo (popular and solemn devotions on Good Friday).

Panteón Nacional ① *Av Norte y Av Panteón, Tue-Sun 0900-1200,1400-1630.* The remains of Simón Bolívar, the Liberator, lie here in the Plaza Panteón. The tomb of Francisco Miranda (the Precursor of Independence), who died in a Spanish prison, has been left open to await the return of his body, likewise the tomb of Antonio José de Sucre, who was assassinated in Colombia. Every 25 years the President opens Bolívar's casket to verify that the remains are still there. Daniel O'Leary, Bolívar's Irish aide-de camp, is buried alongside.

Museo Histórico Fundación John Boulton ① *Torre El Chorro, 11th floor, Av Universidad y Sur 3, entre El Chorro y Dr Díaz, T564 4366, www.fundaboulton.org, Mon-Fri 0830-1130, 1330-1630, free, 2 tours a day by knowledgeable guides; underground parking on presentation of ID.* Previously in La Guaira, this museum contains many historical items, a small art collection and a library of 19th-century research, historical archives and commercial records of the Casa Boulton (easy access).

Museo de Arte Colonial ① *Quinta Anauco, Av Panteón, T551 8190, www.quintade anauco.org.ve, Mon-Fri 0900-1130, 1400-1630, Sat-Sun 1000-1600, US$2. Guided tour in Spanish available, getting there: take por puesto from Bellas Artes metro (at the same stop as the metro bus), those bound for San Bernardino go past Quinta Anauco.* This delightful house in the beautiful suburb of San Bernardino, was built in 1720 and was formerly the residence of the Marqués del Toro. The museum holds cultural events and chamber concerts most Saturdays and Sundays.

Sabana Grande and east of the centre

In the **Parque Central**, a concrete jungle complex between Avenida Lecuna (east end) and the elevated section of Avenida Bolívar, there are two, run-down octagonal towers (56 floors each – ask the security guard to let you go up to the roof, leave passport and they will guide you, not Monday) and four large, shabby apartment blocks with cafés, shops and Cantv centres below. Four museums are located here: **Museo de Arte Contemporáneo** ① *Parque Central, Cuadra Bolívar, T573 4602, www.maccsi.org entrance beside Anauco Hilton, Tue-Sun 1000-1800, free.* It has some 3,000 works on display, including modern sculptures and the works by, among others, Miró, Chagall and Matisse. There is a room devoted to Picasso. The **Museo de los Niños** ① *Parque Central, next to east Tower, Nivel Bolílovar, T575 4022, www.curiosikid .com, Mon-Fri 0900-1700, Sat-Sun 1000-1700, US$2, children US$1.50,* is an extremely

Caracas

▲ To Hotel Humboldt

To Simón Bolívar International Airport

PUERTA DE CARACAS

Gato Negro

Plaza Sucre Ⓜ

Propatria Ⓜ

CATIA

Pérez Bonalde Ⓜ

Av Sucre

Agua Salud

COTIZA

Quinta Anauco & Museo de Arte Colonial ▥

Maripérez Cable Railway Station

Av Fuerzas Armadas

Panteón Nacional & Biblioteca Nacional

SAN BERNARDINO   MARIPEREZ

23 DE ENERO

Caño Amarillo

Calvario Park

Capitolio Ⓜ

Av Urdaneta

Parque Carabobo

El Silencio   La Hoyada

Colegio de Ingenieros

A

To La Yaguara

Capuchinos Ⓜ

Av San Martín

Maternidad Ⓜ

QTA CRESPO

SAN AGUSTÍN

Bellas Artes

Av Bolívar

Plaza Venezuela

B

Artigas Ⓜ

La Paz Ⓜ

EL PARAISO

Autopista Fco Fajardo

CIUDAD UNIVERSITARIA

Sabana Grande

To La Yaguara

Cota 905

Ciudad Universitaria Ⓜ

CIUDAD UNIVERSITARIA

To Caricuao

EL CEMENTERIO

Los Símbolos

Autopista El Valle

SANTA MONICA

N

La Bandera Ⓜ

To Maracay & Valencia

El Valle Ⓜ

0 km   1
0 miles   1

Sleeping 🛏

Altamira **7**
CCCT Best Western **1**
Continental **2**

El Cid **3**
La Floresta **5**
Radisson Eurobuilding **4**
Residencia Montserrat **5**

popular and highly sophisticated interactive science museum. Also in the Parque Central complex, is the **Museo del Teclado** (Museum of Keyboard Instruments) ① *T572 0713, Mon-Fri 0900-1300, 1400-1600, Sat 1700-1900.*

Parque Los Caobos is peaceful, with fountains, and has a cafeteria in the middle. By the entrance in Avenida México is the cultural centre, **Ateneo de Caracas**, with a cinema, theatre, art gallery, concert room, bookshop and the imposing **Teresa Carreño theatre** complex. **Museo de Bellas Artes** ① *Plaza de los Museos in Parque Los Caobos free, Tue-Fri 0900-1700, Sat-Sun 1000-1700*, the oldest museum in Caracas, designed by Carlos Raúl Villanueva. It contains works by mainly Venezuelan and South American artists. Adjacent is the **Galería de Arte Nacional** ① *T578 1818, www.gan.org.ve, Tue-Fri 0900-1700, Sat-Sun 1000-1700*, displays the history of Venezuelan art and also houses the **Cinemateca Nacional** ① *Tue-Sun 1830 and 2130, Sun 1100 for children's films*. **Museo de Ciencias Naturales** ① *Plaza de los Museos, Los Caobos, T577 5094, Tue-Sun 1000-1700*, archaeological, particularly pre-Columbian, zoological and botanical exhibits, interesting temporary shows.

Jardín Botánico ① *near Plaza Venezuela, entrance by Ciudad Universitaria, Tue-Sun 0830-1630, guide US$1 in English*, is worth a visit. There are extensive plant collections and a small area of 'natural forest'. Here you can see the world's largest palm tree (*Corypha Sp*) and the Elephant Apple with its huge edible fruit. You need permission to take photographs.

Parque Nacional del Este ① *closed Mon, opens 0530 for joggers, 0830 for others, till 1700, reached from Parque del Este metro station*, is a popular place to relax, especially at weekends. There is a boating lake, a replica of Columbus' Santa María (being renovated since 1991), the Humboldt Planetarium ① *T234 9188, weekend shows, US$0.50*, a number of different sunken lakes featuring caiman and turtles, monkeys, a caged jaguar and a Harpy Eagle in an upsettingly small cage, many types of water birds, a terrarium ① *Sat-Sun, US$0.25*. **Museo de Transporte** ① *Parque Nacional del Este (to which it is connected by a pedestrian overpass), T234 1621, Sun 0900-1630, US$0.25*, has a large collection of locomotives and old cars.

Other parks

The densely wooded **Parque Caricuao** ① *Tue-Sun 0900-1630: take metro to Caricuao Zoológico, then 5 min walk up Av Principal La Hacienda*, is at the southwest end of the Metro line, and forms part of the Parque Nacional Macuro. A pleasant day out. At the foot of the Avila

Tamanaco **6**	Evio's Pizza **2**	Primi **3**
	Flor de Castilla **5**	Spizzico **4**
Eating ⑦	La Estancia **3**	
Chez Wong **1**	Miga's **6**	

Related maps
A Caracas centre, page 1338
B Sabana Grande, page 1340

mountain, the **Parque Los Chorros** ⓘ *Tue-Fri 0830-1630, Sat-Sun 0830-1800, take bus from Los Dos Caminos station to Lomas de Los Chorros* has impressive waterfalls and forest walks. **El Calvario**, west of El Silencio, with the Arch of Confederation at the entrance, has a good view of Centro Simón Bolívar, but muggings have been reported. It has a small Museo Ornitológico, botanical gardens and a picturesque chapel.

◉ Sleeping

Cheap *pensiones* are usually full of long-stay residents and have few rooms available for travellers. In the centre all cheap hotels take only short stay customers on Fri afternoon. The cheapest hotels are in the downtown area, but this is not a safe part of town at night, or even in the day with a backpack. Sabana Grande, which has a wide range of hotels, is not safe, either. If you don't want to stay in the suburbs or centre, spend a little more and go to the upmarket Chacao, Altamira, La Castellana districts (all easily reached by metro), where it is relatively safe to stroll around during the day. There are hotels on the coast, close to the airport, if you do not want to go into the city. Hotels in the following list are recommended, apart from any minor points mentioned. Some hotels listed below will charge an additional 17%

tax; others include it in their price. The airport tourist office is very helpful and will book hotel rooms. If you book from abroad, make sure you receive written confirmation before beginning your journey. For apartment rental, consult *El Universal* daily paper, small ads columns. The business anc commercial district is southeast of the centre, not on metro.

Central area *p1335, map p1338*
The cheapest hotels are around the Nuevo Circo bus terminal (not a safe area). Plaza Bolívar and its surrounding streets are busy by the day, but by night are deserted and unsafe.
L Caracas Hilton, Av Sur 25 with Av Mexico, T503 5012, www.hiltoncaracas.com.ve. Ageing luxury hotel, excellent business centre, spectacular city

Caracas centre

Sleeping ◉
Anauco Hilton 1
Ausonia 4
Avila 2

Caracas Hilton 3
Inter 6
Limón 7
Plaza Catedral 8

Renovación 9

Eating ◉
La Cocina Criolla de Francy 2

views, especially at night, noisy (traffic and a/c), useful long-term luggage deposit and good breakfast, nice pool, fax service open to non-residents, very helpful, good sushi bar.

C Plaza Catedral, Blvd Plaza Bolívar, next to Cathedral, T564 2111. Central location just off Plaza Bolívar, Amex accepted, a/c, English spoken, good restaurant, includes breakfast. Recommended.

D Inter, Animas a Calero, on corner of Av Urdaneta, near Nuevo Circo, T564 0251. Helpful, English spoken, very popular, poor restaurant, accepts credit cards.

D Limón, C Este 10, No 228, near metro Bellas Artes, T572 1968. Safe, parking, often recommended.

D-E Ausonia, Bolero a Pineda (next to Miraflores), T864 3931/3769. Its location right next to Miraflores (the presidential palace) makes this one of the safest options in the centre as soldiers are on guard nearby. Large hotel, a/c, TV, basic rooms, bit shabby but OK for the price.

E Renovación, Av Este 2 No 154, near Los Caobos and Bellas Artes metro, T571 0133, www.usuarios.lycos.es/hotelrenovacion. With a/c, modern, parking, lots of restaurants nearby.

San Bernardino *map p1338*

Residential area 2 km north of Bellas Artes metro.

A Avila, Av Jorge Washington, T555 3000, www.hotelavila.com.ve. Modern, medium-sized hotel, set in tranquil tropical gardens around 20 mins' drive from the centre, very pleasant, good service, most staff speak English and German, fans, mosquito screens, pool, Metrobus nearby, very good restaurant and poolside bar, travel agency, phones accept Visa/MasterCard.

Sabana Grande/Chacaíto *p1336, map p1340*

Many restaurants and shops here, but despite being well-placed for metro, safety has deteriorated greatly. Many hotels are in the Av Las Acacias/Av Casanova area, the majority are short stay.

L Gran Meliá, Av Casanova y El Recreo, T762 8111, gran.melia.caracas@solmelia.com. Top-ranking hotel with all facilities, business centre, generous gourmet buffets, restaurants (including Japanese and pizzería), gym, great pool area, piano bar.

AL Chacao Cumberland, Av Santa Lucía con Av Principal del Bosque, Chacaíto, T952 9833, www.hotelescumberland.com. 20 m from Chacaíto

Bars & clubs 🍸
Café Rajatabla **4**

metro, modern tower block, internet access in rooms, restaurant, good business facilities.

AL Coliseo, Av Casanova y Coromoto, T762 7916, www.hotelcoliseo.com.ve. 1970s high-rise, a/c, poor breakfast, more expensive rooms have internet connection, parking, taxi service, 100 m from Sabana Grande metro, overpriced.

AL Las Américas, C Los Cerritos, at the end of Av Casanova, T951 7133, www.hotellasamericas .com.ve. Modern tower blocks, tiny roof pool and restaurant, taxi service to airport, good value.

A Caracas Cumberland, 2da Av de las Delicias, T762 9961, www.hotelescumberland.com. Modern high-rise block, nice restaurant, taxi service to airport, travel agency.

B Savoy, Av Francisco Solano López y Av Las Delicias, T762 1971. Well-established large hotel, good food, efficient, terrace, secure car park, taxi service to airport.

C Crillón, Av Libertador, esq Av Las Acacias, T761 4411, www.hotelcrillon.com.ve. Near Plaza Venezuela metro. High-rise block, good service, comfortable, good bar.

C Plaza Palace, Av Los Mangos, Las Delicias, T762 4821, plaza_palace_hotel@hotmail.com. Good value if a bit tatty, a/c, TV, helpful, English spoken.

E Cristal, C Real de Sabana Grande, Pasaje Asunción, just off Av Abraham Lincoln, near Sabana Grande metro, T761 9131. Comfortable, a/c, safe, good value, restaurant, English spoken, helpful staff.

E pp Nuestro, C Colegio and Av Casanova, Sabana Grande. One of the cheapest options in town, basic rooms with bath and fan, terrace area, no dorms, secure (but the area is not), internet. Also known as **The Backpackers Hostel**. Works with recommended tour operator **Osprey**, T762 5975, www.ospreyvenezuela.com.

Chuao/Las Mercedes *map p1336*
An upmarket commercial district southeast of the centre and Sabana Grande, no metro station.

L Tamanaco Inter-Continental, Av Principal Las Mercedes, T909 7111, caracas@ interconti.com. The best hotel in Caracas, superb pool, luxury business hotel, normally fully booked (includes service, tax, rooms priced in US$), courteous staff, good facilities, excellent food.

AL CCCT Best Western, Torre D, Centro Ciudad Comercial Tamanaco (CCCT), Chuao, T700 8000, reservaciones@bwhotelcct.com. Large, smart business hotel with a pool terrace, tennis court, gym, internet connection in rooms, approached through shopping mall, not that easy to find.

AL Radisson Eurobuilding, Centro Ciudad Comercial Tamanaco (CCCT), Chuao, T902 1111, www.radisson.com. 5-star, modern, has all-suite wing, well-furnished, a/c, includes breakfast, efficient service, large pool, gym, restaurants, many services, weekend rates available.

Chacao, Altamira, La Castellana *map p1336*
These 3 districts, east of Gran Sabana and the centre, are adjacent to each other, and are a respectable commercial and residential zone.

Sabana Grande

Sleeping
Caracas
  Cumberland **10**
Coliseo **1**
Crillón **2**
Cristal **3**
Cumberland **4**
Gran Meliá **5**
Las Américas **6**
Nuestro **7**
Plaza Palace **8**
Savoy **9**

Bars & clubs
El Maní Es Así **1**

AL Continental, Av San Juan Bosco, Altamira, T261 0644, www.hotel-continental.org.ve. Smart, with breakfast, gardens and a good pool.
B Residencia Montserrat, Av Avila Sur, T263 3533, F261 1394. Near Plaza Altamira and Altamira metro station, pleasant, well-run, helpful, a/c, hot water, TV, parking. Recommended for long stays.
B-C El Cid, Av San Felipe, between 1a and 2a, La Castellana, T263 2611, cumarucidhotel@cantv.net. Spanish-style interior, large suites with living area, kitchenette en suite, a/c, good value, parking.
B-C La Floresta, Av Avila Sur, T263 1955, hotellafloresta@cantv.net. Near Altamira metro, hot water, cable TV, restaurant, bar, parking, modern, generally excellent but noisy a/c.
C Altamira, Av José Féliz Sosa, Altamira Sur, T267 4284 (do not confuse with **Altamira Suites Hotel**). The cheapest option in the area and close to Altamira metro. Safe, modern, comfortable, credit cards accepted, helpful and efficient staff, changes dollars, secure parking. Most rooms with balcony. Recommended.

Near airport
See Litoral Central, page 1348, below.

🍴 Eating

Central area *p1335, map p1338*
There are plenty of eating places around Plaza Bolívar and, better still, around Plaza La Candelaria.

🍴 **La Cocina Criolla de Francy**, Av Este 2 y Sur 11, La Candelaria. Good Spanish-Venezuelan food. Recommended.
🍴 The restaurant in the **Museo de Arte Contemporáneo** serves great food, good value.
🍴 **El Parador**, Av Urdaneta, esquina Ibarras a Maturín No 18. Great Spanish food and service.
🍴-🍴 **La Indicieta**, just off Plaza Bolívar. Good for breakfast, decent arepas, fresh juices and coffee.

Sabana Grande *p1336, map p1340*
This area is full of cafés, bars (*tascas*) and restaurants to suit all tastes and budgets, with lots of fast food outlets. There is a good selection of places in CC El Recreo. Waiters overcharge, check prices first. Arabic, Chinese and Hindu restaurants on C Villa Flor and all Arabic places have vegetarian options.
🍴 **Shorthorn**, Av Libertador y El Bosque. Very good, for meat dishes.
🍴-🍴 **El Caserío**, Fco Solano. Good national dishes.
🍴-🍴 **Urrutia**, Fco Solano y Los Mangos. Another good place for national dishes.
🍴 **El Arabito** C Villaflor, just off Av Abraham Lincoln between metro stations Sabana Grande and Plaza Venezuela. Arabic food.
🍴 **Arepería 24 Horas**, Av Casanova y Av Las Acacias. Busy, inexpensive and very popular.
🍴 **El Arepazo**, 1 block south of Chacaíto metro station. Every kind of arepa filling you could want.
🍴 **Arturo's**, is a chain of clean, modern, chicken-and-chips style restaurants in various locations.

Chuao/Las Mercedes
The area has a good selection of upmarket restaurants and US-style steak houses and chains.
🍴 **La Castañuela**, C Trinidad con C París. Live music at weekends, bar area, good Spanish food, generous portions, attentive service, popular.
🍴 **Nouveau Café**, Av Principal De Valle Arribe, cruce con Av Orinoco. Well-priced, tasty Mediterranean food, including pastas, nice décor and terrace. Open Sun.

Altamira, La Castellana *map p1336*
🍴 **Chez Wong**, on La Castellana roundabout. Reputed to be the best Chinese in town.
🍴 **Evio's Pizza**, Av 4 between Transversales 2 y 3, Los Palos Grandes, Altamira. Very good, live music from 2100.
🍴 **La Estancia**, Av Principal La Castellana, esq Urdaneta, near Altamira metro. Very good beef in traditional style and popular.
🍴 **Primi**, Av Principal La Castellana next door to *La Estancia*. Italian/Creole cuisine, quite chic, plenty of vegetarian dishes.
🍴 **Spizzico**, Av Principal La Castellana. Excellent Italian with fine service.
🍴-🍴 **Miga's**, opposite **Altamira Suites Hotel**, www.migas.com.ve. Busy café chain selling fresh

salads, sandwiches and meat dishes, some vegetarian options, open late.

†Flor de Castilla, Av Luis Roche, Sur Plaza Altamira, next to **Hotel Floresta**. Terrace, good pastries, coffee and snacks. Open late and on Sun.

⊕ Bars and clubs

Caracas *p1334, maps p1336, p1338 and p1340*
Check www.rumbacaracas.com to find out what's on. Caracas has a vibrant nightlife. *Caraqueños* dine at home around 2000, and in restaurants from 2100-2300, so clubs don't usually come to life until after 2300, and then go on to the early hours. Las Mercedes district is full of busy, trendy bars.

Bars
Café Rajatabla, in Ateneo cultural complex. Young crowd and often has live music.
El León, in La Castellana, opposite *Chez Wong*, T263 6014. Very popular café, open daily till 2400.
El Naturista, nearby, 2da Transversal, La Casteallana, T263 5350. Arepas by day, beer and bar at night, open daily, equally popular.
Centro Comercial San Ignacio, see Shopping, has many fashionable, though pricey bars and the occasional nightclubs. Try **Whisky Bar** (Nivel Blandín), usually packed, trendy and friendly crowd. Long bar with terrace area. Good.
La Suite bar, Centro Comercial Tolon Fashion Mall. Another popular bar, lavish décor, attracts weathly twenty-something crowd. Mix of music from house to 80s. Best nights Thu-Sat.
U-Bar, CC Macaracuay Plaza, Macaracuay. Popular, university bar, giant screen.

Clubs
La Belle Epoque, Av Leonardo da Vinci, Bello Monte, T753 1342, www.labelleepoque.net. Live music and house tunes, DJs, very hip.
El Maní es Así, C El Cristo, 1 block up from Av Fco Solano, Sabana Grande, T763 6671. Good for live salsa and dancing, open Tue-Sun till 0400/0500.

Discos
Most permit entry to couples only.
Extreme, Av Principal Las Mercedes. Popular disco.

⊕ Entertainment

Caracas *p1334, maps p1336, p1338 and p1340*
For details of cinemas and other events, see www.cantv.net or the newspapers, *El Universal* (the cinema page on www.el-universal.com has full listings), *El Nacional* and *Daily Journal*.

There are frequent Sun morning concerts in the **Teatro Municipal**, 1100. Concerts, ballet, theatre and film festivals at the **Ateneo de Caracas**, Paseo Colón, Plaza Morelos, and similar events, including foreign artists, at the **Complejo Cultural Teresa Carreño**, see page 1337. **Trasnocho Cultural**, Urb Las Mercedes, Centro Comercial Paseo Las Mercedes, Nivel Trasnocho, T993 1910, www.tras nochocultural.com. Has a theatre, cinemas, exhibition space, lounge bar with live DJs Thu-Sat, bookshop, café and a yoga centre.

⊛ Festivals and events

Caracas *p1334, maps p1336, p1338 and p1340*
3 May, Velorio de la Cruz de Mayo still celebrated with dances and parties in some districts. **18-25 Dec**, Yuletide masses at different churches leading up to Christmas. Traditional creole dishes served at breakfasts.

⊙ Shopping

Caracas *p1334, maps p1336, 1338 and p1340*
Bookshops American Bookshop, Nivel Jardín (bottom level) of CC Centro Plaza, Av Francisco de Miranda, Altamira metro, T286 2230/285 8779. Mon-Fri 0900-1830, Sat 0900-1730, good selection of second-hand English books.
Librería Alemana (Oscar Todtmann), Centro El Bosque, Av Libertador, T763 0881. For German books, closed Mon.
Librería Ecológica, Plaza Caracas, Centro Simón Bolívar, Edif Sur, El Silencio, near CANTV office. For environmental books, also has some maps.
Librería La France, Centro Comercial Chacaíto, local 4, sótano 1. French bookshop.
Tecni-ciencia libros, www.tecniciencia.com (online book catalogue). Branches across the city in most shopping centres; eg in CC Sambil, Nivel Acuario, T265 1765, CC San Ignacio. Good choice of foreign language books, including Footprint.
Handicrafts Good quality Sun craft market between Museo de Bellas Artes and Museo de Historia Natural (metro Bellas Artes).
Malls The CCCT shopping centre is worth a visit, as is the Centro Comercial Plaza Las Américas, mostly for fashion stores and beachwear. CC El Recreo in Sabana Grande has a good choice of shops and places to eat.
Centro Sambil, Av Libertador, 1 block south of Chacao Metro. One of the largest in South America, with every type of shop, internet cafés, bookshops, *cambio*, CANTV centres and cinema. Open Mon-Sun 1000-2100.

● *For an explanation of the sleeping and eating price codes used in this guide, see page 58. Other*
● *relevant information is found in Essentials pages 1332-1333.*

Always take identification when booking a long-distance journey. Times and fares of buses are given under destinations. Buses going west on the Panamericana route are not recommended because the old road suffers from many accidents.

Autoexpresos Ejecutivos, terminal at Av Principal de Bello Campo, Quinta Marluz (between Chacao and Altamira metro stops), T266 2321, www.aeroexpresos.com.ve, to **Maracay, Valencia, Barquisimeto, Maracaibo, Maturín** and **Puerto La Cruz**, reserve 2 days in advance, except for buses leaving on Fri (no left luggage). Fares are 3-4 times higher than other companies, but worth it. **Rodovias**, terminal at Av Libertador con Boulevard Amador Bendayan, between Plaza Venezuela and Colegio de Ingenieros metro, T577 7765/577 7011, www.rodovias.com.ve. Excellent long distance buses to Barquisimeto, Ciudad Bolívar, Ciudad Guayana, Maracaibo, Maturín, Carúpano, Cumaná, Puerto La Cruz and Valencia.

International buses Ormeño (T/F471 7205, www.grupo-ormeno.com) has 1 bus a week to **Cúcuta, Bogotá** (US$75), **Cali** (US$90), **Quito** (US$110), **Guayaquil** (US$140), **Lima** (US$180); Mon 1300, safe, comfortable, a/c, video, toilet; Terminal Camarqui at Final Av San Martín detras del Bloque de Armas, 10 mins from Metro La Paz. Accepts Mastercard and Maestro. Some destinations require a yellow fever certificate.

Car
Car hire Self-drive cars (Hertz, Avis, Budget, Dollar, ACO) are available at the airport (offices open 0700-2100, Avis till 2300, good service) and in town. They are cheaper than guided excursions for less than full loads. See rates on page 1332.

Metro
Operates 0530-2300, no smoking, luggage allowed only at off-peak times. There are 3 lines: Line 1 (west-east) from Propatria to Palo Verde; Line 2 (north-south), from El Silencio to Las Adjuntas, with connection to Caricuao Zoológico; Line 3, south from Plaza Venezuela via La Bandera to El Valle, plus metrobus El Valle-Los Teques; www.metrodecaracas.com.ve. New stations on Line 3 between El Valle and La Rinconada were under construction in 2007. Tickets cost US$0.50 per journey, slightly cheaper to buy return ticket; 10-journey tickets (Multi Abono) are available at US$2.10. Student discounts are available with ISIC card; apply at Parque del Este station. Metrobuses connect with the Metro system: get transfer tickets (*boleto integrado*, US$0.35) for services to southern districts, route maps displayed at stations; retain ticket after exit turnstile. Good selection of maps at shops in Altamira and La California stations.

Motorcycle
Motorcycles may not be ridden in Caracas between 2300 and 0500.

Taxi
Even though they are a legal requirement, meters are never used. Negotiate fares in advance; always offer 10% less than the driver's first quote and bargain hard. Most city trips are US$3.20 absolute minimum during the day (most fares US$5). Taxi drivers are authorized to charge an extra 20% on night trips after 1800, on Sun and all holidays, and US$1 for answering telephone calls. After 1800 drivers are selective about destinations. Beware of taxi drivers trying to renegotiate fixed rates because your destination is in 'a difficult area'. See warning above under Air about pirate taxis. See also under Air (or in Yellow Pages) for radio taxis. **Note** Never tell a driver it's your first visit to Caracas.

---

❶ Directory

Caracas *p1334, maps p1336, p1338 and p1340*
Airline offices Domestic: Aeropostal, main office: Av Paseo Colón, Torre Polar Oeste, p 22, Los Caobos, T708 6211. **Aereotuy**, Edif Gran Sabana, p 5, Av Lincoln y Blvd Sabana Grande, T761 6231. **Aserca**, Edif Taeca, C Guaicaipuro, El Rosal, T905 5333, also at Hotel Caracas Hilton and Hotel Intercontinental Tamanaco. **Avensa**, at international airport T355 1479. **Avior**, Torre Clemente, Av Venezuela, El Rosal, T955 3811, also at Hotel Caracas Hilton and CC Sambil. **El Sol de América**, flights from Caracas to Los Roques, T266 9059. **Láser**, T232 6533. **Rutaca**, Centro Seguros La Paz, Av Fco de Miranda, Nivel Mezzanina, loc C-12, La California Sur, T235-6035. **Santa Bárbara**, Av Fco de Miranda, Centro Lido, Nivel Miranda, loc M25, T952 9658, other offices in Caracas. See Getting around, page 1331 for websites. International: Aerolíneas Argentinas, Calle Guaicaipuro, Torre Hener p 1, of 1A, El Rosal, T951 6395, call centre 0800-1005655, closed at weekends. **Air France**, Edif Parque Cristal, Torre Este, p 2, Los Palos Grandes, T285 2843, www.airfrance.com.ve, T0800-100 4655. **Alitalia**, Edif Atlantic, p 5, Av Andrés Bello, Los Palos Grandes, T312 5000, www.ali talia.com.ve. **American**, Av Principal, La Castellana Centro Letonia, T209 8111, www.aa.com.ve, closed weekends, also in Tamanaco Intercontinental Hotel. **Avianca**, Av Tamanaco, Torre Norte del edif JW Marriott, loc 21 y 22, El Rosal, T200 5725. **British Airways**, Torre Copérnico (oeste), p 3, oficina 3-2-3-3, Centro San Ignacio, La Castellana, T266 0122. **Continental**, Centro Lido, Torre E, p 6, Av F de Miranda, T953 3107. **Cubana**, Edif Atlantic, p 4, of 5-6, Av Andrés Bello y 1ra Transversal, Los Palos Grandes, T286 9890. **Delta,**

Torre E, p 8, Centro Lido, Av Fco de Miranda, El Rosal, T0800-100 3453. **Iberia**, Av Fco de Miranda, edif Parque Cristal, Torre Este, p 9, Los Palos Grandes, T284 0020. **LAN**, Torre Kleper, of 3-1, Centro San Ignacio, Av Blandín, T267 9526. **Lufthansa**, Centro Torre Conaisa, p 1, of 16, Av San Felipe, La Castellana, T210 2100, closed Sat-Sun.

Banks See also Currency, page 1330. Plenty of ATMs around the city and most of the banks have branches in the major shopping centres (Sambil, San Igancio, El Tolón). Some ATMs, including at **Banco Unión**, provide bolívares with Cirrus/ Maestro though rates often poor. **Citibank** will exchange Citicorp cheques. **Unibanca** branches for Visa transactions. For cash advances on Visa go to **Banco Unión** or **Banco Provincial**. For Visa ATMs, branches of **Banco de Venezuela** (CC Sambil, Nivel Acuario) and **Banco Unión**. For cash advances on MasterCard and ATM go to branches of **Banco Mercantil**. For cash advance on American Express go to **Banco Consolidado**. To change American Express TCs, try **Corp Banca**, Av Principal de La Castellana, Plaza La Castellana, entre Blandín y Los Chaguaramas, Torre Corp Banca, Nivel E-3, La Castellana, T206 4521, mornings and afternoons. They ask for ID and proof of purchase. For money exchange and Amex travel services go to **Italcambio**, the official government exchange office and take ID. They also change Visa TCs, require proof of TC purchase, open Mon-Fri till 1630, Sat till 1200. Offices at Av Urdaneta, esq Animas a Platanal, Edif Camoruco, Nivel Pb, El Centro, T562 9555, or at Tamanaco Interncontinental Hotel, Las Mercedes. **Italcambio** also at national and international terminals at airport (may limit transaction to US$100, open public holidays). **La Moneda**, Centro Financiero Latino, Av Fco Solano, Edif San Germán, Sabana Grande, open Mon-Fri only. **Viajes Febres Parra**, Av. Libertador, Edif CC Libertador, PB, Loc 4 y 5, La Florida, and at airport. *Casa de cambio* also at CC Sambil shopping centre, Av Libertador, in Chacao.

Cultural centres British Council, Torre Credicard, p 3, Av Principal del Bosque, Chacaíto, T952 9965, www.britcoun.org/venezuela. Opposite Chacaíto metro, great internet café, magazines, newspapers, film library, courses. **El Centro Venezolano-Americano**, Av Principal José Martí, Las Mercedes, T993 7911, www.cva .org.ve. Good free library of books in English, cultural events and free concerts. Library Mon-Fri 0830-1830, Sat 0830-1200 and 1300-1530. Also Spanish courses, various levels, from US$65, highly recommended. **Asociación Cultural Humboldt (Goethe Institut)**, Av Jorge Washington con Juan Germán Roscio, San Bernardino, T552 7634, www.internet.ve/ asohum. Library, films, concerts, Spanish and German courses.

Embassies and consulates Many are open to the public only in the morning, some are closed on Fri. **Australia** has no embassy in Caracas, see www.venezuela.embassy.gov.au. **Austria**, Av La Estancia, Edif Torre las Mercedes, p 4, of 408, Chuao, T991 3863, www.austria.org.ve, Mon-Thu 0900-1200. **Belgium**, 10a Transversal con 9a Transversal, Altamira, T263 3334, www.diplomatie.be/caracas. **Brazil**, Edif 'Centro Gerencial Mohedano', p 6, between C Los Chaguaramas and Av Mohedano, La Castellana, T261 5505, www.embajada brasil.org.ve/, Mon-Fri 0900-1300. Visa (valid for 60 days, a photo, proof of funds and return airline ticket required) costs US$12, takes minimum 24 hrs but may take up to 5 working days. **Canada**, Av Sur Altamira near metro Altamira, T600 3000, www.dfait-maeci.gc.ca/ latin-america/caracas. Open Mon-Thu 0730-1630, Fri 0730-1300, consular services Mon-Fri 0800-1200. **Colombia**, 2da Calle de Campo Alegre, Torre Credival, p 11, Campo Alegre, T216 9596. **Denmark**, Av Fco de Miranda, Centro Seguros Sudamérica, p 10, of 10 D, El Rosal, T952 8255, www.dtccaracas.um.dk/da. Mon-Thu 0800-1600, Fri 0800-1300. **Finland**, C Sorocaima entre Av Venezuela y Av Tamanaco, Edif Atrium, p 1, El Rosal, T952 4111. **France**, C Madrid y Av Trinidad, Las Mercedes, T909 6500, www.francia.org.ve. Mon-Fri 0800-1200. **Germany**, Torre La Castellana, p 10, Av Eugenio Mendoza con C José Angel Lamas, La Castellana, T261 0181, www.caracas.diplo.de/es/Startseite.html, nearest metro Altamira. Mon-Wed 0900-1200. **Guyana**, Quinta Roraima, Av El Paseo, Prados del Este, T977 1158, www.guyana.org/spanish/ venezuela_embassy.html. Visas issued on the same day if you're early, need passport, return airline ticket, proof of funds, yellow fever certificate and 2 photos, US$19.55. **Israel**, Av Principal Los Ruices at Av Fco de Miranda, Centro Empresarial Miranda, p 4, of 4-D, T239 4511, http://caracas.mfa.gov.il. Mon-Fri 0900-1200. **Italy**, Edif Atrium, C Sorocaima entre Av Tamanaco y Venezuela, El Rosal, T952 7311, http://sedi.esteri.it/ambcaracas/. **Japan**, Av Principal con 2da Transversal, Edif Bancaracas, p 11, La Castellana, T261 8333, www.ve.emb-japan .go.jp, Mon-Fri 0900-1200, 1330-1700. **Netherlands**, Edif San Juan, p 9, San Juan Bosco and Av Transversal 2, Altamira, T276 9300, www.mfa.nl/car, Mon-Thu 0800-1100. **New Zealand** Consulate, Av Francisco de Miranda con Av Libertador, Torre KPMG, p 7, Chacao, T277 7965. **Spain**, Av Mohedano, entre 1 y 2 Transversal, Quinta Marmolejo, La Castellana, T263 2855, www.maec.es/embajadas/caracas/ es/home. **Sweden**, Torre Phelps, p 19, Plaza Venezuela, T781 6976. **Switzerland**, Av Eugenio Mendoza y San Felipe, Centro Letonia, Torre

ING-Bank, p 15, La Castellana, T261 2724, vertretung@car.rep.admin.ch. 0900-1200. **Suriname**, 4a Av de Altamira Norte, Quinta 41, Altamira, T263 8094, embsur1@cantv.net. **Trinidad**, beside the Suriname Embassy, Quinta Serrana, 4a Av de Altamira Norte, between 7a and 8a Transversal, Altamira, T261 5796. Visa costs US$20, you need 2 photos, it can take up to 1 week. **UK**, Torre La Castellana, p 11, Av Principal La Castellana, T263 8411, emergency mobile phone T0416-610 2118, www.britain.org.ve. Consular and visa section open Mon-Fri 0800-1200. **USA**, C F with C Suapure, Colinas de Valle Arriba, take metro to Chacaíto then taxi, T975 6411, http://caracas.usembassy.gov/.

Ferries Conferry office for tickets to **Isla de Margarita**, Plaza Venezuela, Av Casanova con Av Las Acacias, Torre Banhorient, PB, Sabana Grande, T0501-2663 3779. **Internet** Plenty of **CANTV** *centros de comunicaciones* and independent outlets around the city, eg Blvd Sabana Grande (Abraham Lincoln) with broadband, international faxes, and in shopping centres, eg CC Sambil,

Chacao. Average price US$1-2 per hr. **Ciber Catedral Internet café**, next door to Hotel Plaza Bolívar, just off the Plaza. Open Mon-Sat 0900-1900. See also **British Council**, above. **Medical services** Hospital de Clínicas, Av Panteón y Av Alameda, San Bernardino, T508 6111.

Post offices Ipostel main branch at Urdaneta y Norte 4, near Plaza Bolívar, for poste restante. Overseas package service; packages should be ready to send, also at airport. MRW, throughout the city, T0800-304 0000, see www.mrw.com.ve for branches. 24-hr service, more reliable than Ipostel. **Telephones** Public phones in Metro stations and along Blvd Sabana Grande (Abraham Lincoln). **Useful addresses** ONIDEX for visa renewal go to DIEX section, Av Baralt, Edif 1000, El Silencio, opposite Plaza Miranda, T483 2070/3581/2706. (Don't believe anyone who tells you visa extensions are not available.) **Touring y Automóvil Club de Venezuela**, Torre Phelps, p 15, of A y C, Plaza Venezuela, T781 9743, desiree@automovilclubvenezuela.com.

Around Caracas

Between the capital and the Caribbean coast is the national park of El Avila, not only a popular recreational area for caraqueños, but also a refuge for wildlife within earshot of the city and a good place for birdwatching and hiking. The coast itself is also a favourite weekend escape, although it can get busy. Nor, at weekends, can you expect to have Colonia Tovar to yourself, a German immigrant town to which city folk flock for the local produce and mild climate.

Monte Avila → *Colour map 1, grid A6.*

The 85,192-ha **Parque Nacional El Avila** forms the northern boundary of Caracas. The green slopes rise steeply from both the city and from the central Caribbean coast. Despite being so close to the capital, the fauna includes red howler monkeys, jaguar and puma. There are also several species of poisonous snake. Access to the park is from Caracas where there are several marked entrances along the Cota Mil (Avenida Boyacá), which are designed for hikers. Access from the old Caracas-La Guaira road which crosses the park from north to south on the western side was damaged by the heavy rains of December 1999. The Caribbean side of the park was worst affected, but all parts of the park are open. For information see www.el-avila.com.

A **cable railway** (*teleférico*) runs up Monte Avila ① *Sun-Tue 1030-1930, Wed-Sat 1030-2330, US$18 return, discount for over 65s, free for under 3s, Final Av Principal de Maripérez (Simón Rodríguez), take taxi from either Colegio de Ingenieros or Plaza Venezuela metro.* The *Humboldt Hotel* on the summit has been refurbished, but not reopened (a casino and nightclub may be built). Camping is possible with permission. A dirt road runs from La Puerta section of San Bernardino to the summit, 45 minutes by 4WD. A recommended trip is to ride up in a vehicle and hike back down (note that it is cold at the summit, around 13° C).

Listed below are three good places to start a hike in the park. Hikers should go in groups of at least three, for mountain and personal safety (Monte Avila is not a dangerous place, but the occasional thief lurks there). You should have a park permit from *Inparques* in Caracas to camp. Always take water and something for the cold at altitude. The unfit should not attempt any of the hikes. Full descriptions of the hiking routes are given in the *Footprint Venezuela.*

Pico Naiguatá (2,765 m) This is a very strenuous hike. Take the metro to La California, then a bus going up Avenida Sanz, ask for the Centro Comercial El Marqués. From there walk up Avenida Sanz towards Cota Mil (Avenida Boyacá), about four blocks. At the end of Avenida

Sanz, underneath the bridge, is the entrance to the Naiguatá trail. In about 40 minutes you reach La Julia *guardaparques* station, where you have to pay US$0.50 entrance.

Pico Oriental (2,600 m) From the Altamira metro station take a bus to 'La entrada de Sabas Nieves', where the *Tarzilandia* restaurant is. From here a dirt road leads up to the Sabas Nieves *guardaparques* station (about 40 minutes). The path to Pico Oriental starts at the back of Sabas Nieves and is extremely easy to follow. **Note** Paths beyond Sabas Nieves are shut in dry season (roughly February-June depending on the year) to prevent forest fires.

Hotel Humboldt (2,150 m) This is a relatively easy route of three hours. Take the metro bus from Bellas Artes station to El Avila stop, US$0.50; opposite is a grocery. Turn the corner and walk two blocks up towards the mountain. At the top of the street turn left; almost immediately on your right is the park entrance. **Note** This area is not safe before 0800 or after dark. Plenty of people take this route, starting 0830-0900, giving enough time to get up and down safely and in comfort.

Litoral Central

The Litoral Central is the name given to the stretch of Caribbean Coast directly north of Caracas. A paved road runs east from Catia La Mar, past the airport and then through the towns of Maiquetía, La Guaira and Macuto. This became the state of Vargas in January 1999 and in December that year was the focus of Venezuela's worst natural disaster of the 20th century. Prolonged heavy rains on deforested hillsides caused flash floods and landslides, killing and causing to disappear an estimated 30,000 people and leaving 400,000 homeless. It is planned to turn the whole area into a national park. From La Guaira a panoramic road runs to the beaches at Chichiriviche de la Costa, Puerto Cruz (nice beach, no shade, bars) and Puerto Maya (very nice beach with shade and services).

La Guaira, Venezuela's main port dates back to 1567. It achieved its greatest importance in the 18th century when the Basque Guipuzcoana Company held the royal trading monopoly. Much of the city was severely damaged in the 1999 floods.

Colonia Tovar and Guatopo → *Phone code: 0244. Population: 10,000. Altitude: 1,890 m.*

This picturesque mountain town was founded in 1843 by German immigrants from Kaiserstuhl in the Black Forest; a small **museum** ⓘ *1000-1800, Sat-Sun and holidays*, tells the history of the founding pioneers. They retained their customs and isolation until a paved road reached the settlement in 1963. It is now very touristy, attracting hordes of weekend visitors, but the blond hair, blue eyes and Schwartzwald-accented German of the inhabitants are still much in evidence. This *Tovarense* farming community make great bread, blackberry jam, bratwurst and beer. Colonia Tovar offers delightful landscapes, mild climate, old architecture and dignified hospitality. The surrounding countryside is good for horse riding.

From Colonia Tovar, Ruta 4 continues (paved but hair raising) south down the slopes for 34 km to La Victoria on the Caracas-Valencia Highway (see below); bus US$2; glorious scenery.

In **San Francisco de Yare** (*Phone code: 0239; 90 km from Caracas*), a celebration is held at Corpus Christi in early June (the eigth Thursday after Thursday of Semana Santa). Some 80 male 'Diablos' of all ages, dressed all in red and wearing horned masks, dance to the sound of their own drums and rattles. From Santa Teresa make a detour to the beautiful and little frequented **Parque Nacional Guatopo** on the road to Altagracia de Orituco (bus from Nuevo Circo marked 'El Popular', US$2.50). You must return to Santa Teresa to continue your journey to Yare. At the Parque Guatopo are various convenient places to picnic on the route through the forest and a number of good nature trails. Take insect repellent. Free camping at Hacienda La Elvira; take jeep from Altagracia de Orituco (US$1) and ask to be let off at the turn-off to the Hacienda. A permit must be obtained at the Inparques office, which has some accommodation, or baggage can be stored temporarily while walking in the park.

◉ Sleeping

Litoral Central *p1348*

If you're arriving or leaving the airport at odd times, there are some good choices in Catia La Mar and Macuto as an alternative to Caracas. These places often provide transfers, or a taxi costs about US$5, 5-20 mins depending on traffic.

L Eurobuilding Express Maiquetía, Av La Armada, T7000 700, maiquetia@eurobuilding .com.ve. Useful business hotel with pool, restaurant, tennis, cable TV, internet in rooms, airport transfers. **B Catimar**, Urb Puerto Viejo Av Principal, Catia La Mar, T351 7906, www.hotelcatimar.com. Price

includes transfers to and from airport (you may have to phone them from Asistencia al usuario desk), nice bar, restaurant, internet, basic rooms, expensive for what's offered. Near small Puerto Viejo beach, said to be safe, with a few restaurants (**Brisas del Mar, Puerto Mar**), snack bar.
B Posada Il Prezzano, Av Principal de Playa Grande c/c 5, Catia La Mar, T351 2626. Italian-run, spotless, pleasant, good value, a/c, restaurant.
B Santiago, Av La Playa, Urb Alamo, Macuto, T213 3500, www.hotelsantiago.com.ve. Comfortable, restaurant with live music, pool, secure parking, internet,15 mins' drive to airport.

Colonia Tovar p1348
There are many hotels, normally full at weekends. Rates, which are not below our **C** category, include good, German-style food. Half-board prices are usually **A**. Credit cards are widely accepted.

🍴 Eating

Colonia Tovar p1348
Many places serve German delicacies.
🍴 El Codazzi, in centre on C Codazzi. Traditional German and Hungarian dishes, strudel and biscuits, Wed-Sun 1100-1600. Recommended.
🍴 El Molino, C Molino next to the old mill, 5-min walk from main plaza. Great *jugo de fresas*, wide selection of German dishes, open 0900-1000, 1200-1600, 1800- 1900, Mon 0900-1400.
Café Munstall, opposite the church, interesting location in oldest house in Colonia Tovar. Excellent pastries and coffee at weekends.

Fruit, vegetables and flowers sold at **Frutería Bergman**, next to Lagoven station at east entrance to town; across the street is **Panadería Tovar** for delicious bread; many food stalls on weekends along Av Codazzi.

🔺 Activities and tours

Monte Avila p1347
Centro Excursionista Caracas, Av Santa Sofia Sur, Zona Polideportivo, Urb Santa Sofia. El Cafetal, Caracas, cecaracas@cantv.net. This hiking club meets Sat 1430, day and weekend hikes, very welcoming; some English and German spoken.

⊖ Transport

Colonia Tovar p1348
The 1½ hrs' windy drive up from Caracas on Ruta 4, through Antímano and El Junquito, is easy during the week, but murder (2½ hrs) on weekends – long traffic jams, difficult to find picnic spots or accommodation, definitely not recommended. It is generally easy to get a lift if there are no buses.
Bus From Av Sur 9 y El Rosario, next to Nuevo Circo, or, easier, from La Yaguara metro station, to El Junquito (1 hr, US$0.75), then change for Colonia Tovar (1 hr, US$1.45). *Por puesto* from Plaza Catia or O'Leary (more frequently), Caracas, 1 hr, US$2. Alternatively, take a *por puesto* from Plaza Capuchino to El Junquito, then one from there to Colonia Tovar, US$1.75. Last bus to Caracas 1800, later at weekends.

West from Caracas

The Central Highlands run through this varied region. North of the highlands is the Caribbean, with secluded coves and popular resorts such as Puerto Colombia. Straddling the mountains is the birders' paradise of Parque Nacional Henri Pittier. Two coastal national parks, Morrocoy, which lies offshore, and Los Médanos, around the old city of Coro, are further highlights of this area. West of Coro is the city and lake of Maracaibo, for most Venezuelans, a region summed up in three letters – oil. For others, it can be summed up in four letters – heat. Both are certainly true. To the south, though, are the eastern extremities of the Andean mountain chain, with quaint villages, lakes and high passes on the way to the Sierra Nevada de Mérida.

Maracay and around

Maracay is a hot, thriving industrial city and is the gateway to Henri Pittier national park. The city has some pleasant leafy residential neighbourhoods and is the centre of an important agricultural area. The great basin in which lies the Lago de Valencia and the industrial town of Valencia is 100 km west of Caracas. The basin, which is only 450 m above sea-level, receives plenty of rain and is one of the most important agricultural areas in the country.

Maracay → *Phone code: 0243. Colour map 1, grid A6. Population: 600,000. Altitude: 445 m.*

In its heyday Maracay was the favourite city of Gen Juan Vicente Gómez (dictator, 1909-1935) and some of his most fantastic whims are still there. **Jardín Las Delicias** (Avenida Las Delicias, en route to Choroní; take an Ocumare bus from terminal) with its beautiful zoological garden (closed Monday), park and fountain, built for his revels. The **Gómez mausoleum** (Calle Mariño) has a huge triumphal arch. The heart of the city is **Plaza Girardot**, on which stands the attractive, white **Cathedral**, dating back almost to the city's foundation in 1701. There is an interesting collection of prehispanic artefacts in the museum of the **Instituto de Antropología e Historia** ① *south side of the plaza, Tue-Sun 0800-1200, 1400-1800, free.* The opposite end of the same building has rooms dedicated to Gómez and Bolívar. At the rear of the building is the **Biblioteca de Historia** whose walls are lined with portraits of Bolívar. **Plaza Bolívar**, said to be the largest such-named plaza in Latin America, is 500 m east. On one side is the **Palacio del Gobierno**, originally the *Hotel Jardín*, built by Gómez in 1924. Also here are the **Palacio Legislativo** and the **opera house** (1973). The school and experimental stations of the Ministry of Agriculture are worth visiting. The San José festival is on 16-25 March.

Parque Nacional Henri Pittier

A land of steep, lush, rugged hills and tumbling mountain streams, the 107,800 ha park (US$1 pp), rises from sea-level in the north to 2,430 m at Pico Cenizo, descending to 450 m towards the Lago de Valencia. Named after Swiss conservationist and engineer Henri Pittier, the park was established in 1937 and is the oldest in the country. It has 578 bird species, including seven different eagles and eight kites. It contains 43% of all species in Venezuela. The park is also home to pumas and jaguars. It extends from the north of Maracay to the Caribbean, excluding the coastal towns of Ocumare, Cata and Choroní, and south to the valleys of Aragua and the villages of Vigírima, Mariara and Turmero. The dry season is December-March and the rainy season (although still agreeable) is April-November. The variation in altitude gives a great range of vegetation, including impressive lower and upper cloud forests and bamboo. See *Parque Nacional de Henri Pittier - Lista de Aves*, by Miguel Lentino and Mary Lou Goodwin, 1993.

Two paved roads cut through the Park. The Ocumare (western) road climbs to the 1,128 m high Portachuelo pass, guarded by twin peaks (38 km from Maracay). At the pass is Rancho Grande, the uncompleted palace/hotel Gómez was building when he died (in a state of disrepair). It is close to the bird migratory routes, September and October are the best months. There are many trails in the vicinity. Permits to visit the park and walk the trails near the Rancho Grande biological research station are available here.

Aragua Coast

To Cata and Cuyagua The road to the coast from Rancho Grande goes through **Ocumare de la Costa** (*Population: 6,140, 48 km from Maracay*), to La Boca de Ocumare and **El Playón** (hotels and restaurants at both places). The road is very busy at weekends. 20 minutes west by boat is **La Ciénaga**, a pretty place, but little shade. A few kilometres east is **Bahía de Cata**, now overdeveloped, particularly at the west end, while the smaller beach at **Catita** is reached by fishing boat ferries (10 minutes, US$1), or a 20-minute walk, tricky over rocks at the start. In Cata town (5 km inland, *population* of town and beach 3,120) is the small colonial church of San Francisco; devil dancers here fulfil an ancient vow by dancing non-stop through the morning of

Parque Nacional Henri Pittier

27 July each year. Cuyagua beach, unspoilt, is 23 km further on at the end of the road. Good surfing, dangerous rips for swimmers. Devil dancers here too, on movable date in July/August.

To Choroní The second twisty and narrow (eastern) road through the Parque Nacional Henri Pittier is spectacular and goes over a more easterly pass (1,830 m), to **Santa Clara de Choroní**, a small colonial town with attractive, pastel single-storey houses (no ATM). The Fiesta de San Juan on 31 May is worth seeing. Choroní is a good base for walking. There are many opportunities for exploring the unmarked trails, some originating in picturesque spots such as the river pools, 'pozos', of El Lajao (beware of the dangerous whirlpool), and Los Colores, 6 km above Choroní. Other recommended 'pozos' are La Virgen, 10 km from Choroní, and La Nevera, 11 km away.

Puerto Colombia and around → *Phone code: 0243. Colour map 1, grid A6. Population: 7,000.*

Just beyond Choroní is the popular fishing village of **Puerto Colombia**, a laid back place with several narrow streets lined with colonial buildings. During high season, its small main bay attracts arts and crafts sellers. It is a good place to stay and spend a couple of days beach hopping with boat rides to different bays. Five minutes' walk across the river lies Puerto Colombia's main attraction; the dazzling long stretch of white beach, Playa Grande, lined with palm trees beneath mountains. There is a row of good fish restaurants at the beach entrance. At weekends drummers drum and dancers gyrate and the beach gets crowded with campers and families. At other times it's more peaceful, with brightly painted fishing boats in the river and frigate birds wheeling overhead. If swimming, beware the strong undertow. There are public showers at the entrance. Many fishing boats are for hire in the harbour, US$55 for a day trip. A very bumpy, 30-minute ride east goes to **Cepe**, another beautiful long beach with good swimming, popular with campers. About US$23, boats usually take 6-10 people, or *por puesto* fishing boat from the port US$2.35 per person. From the beach, there is a delightful 25-minute walk to **Pueblo de Cepe** through the Henri Pittier park. Several places on the beach serve fish, salad and *tostones* for US$5-7. Most locals bring their own supplies in the obligatory beer cooler. From the beautiful unspoiled beach there are fishing and scuba diving trips. The latter, with guide and equipment, explore the only bit of coral on this stretch of the coast. At Cepe's west end, you can climb the hill and descend to **Playa Escondida**, a deserted but more rocky beach. Other beaches include: to the east, before Cepe, Valle Seco (boat US$31, some shade, natural pool protected by reef) and **Chuao**. To the west are: Diario (small, no shade), Aroa (lovely, with river and palms, rough sea but one safe bathing area, no services, take everything with you, 3 hours' hike from Choroní, go early) and Uricao (also isolated); boat to Uricao US$20.

● Sleeping

Maracay *p1350*
Budget hotels are in streets around Plaza Girardot.
A Italo, Av Las Delicias, Urb La Soledad, T232 1576, www.hotelitalo.com.ve. A/c, large, modern 4-star, on bus route, pleasant, small rooftop pool, good Italian restaurant, *El Fornaio*. Recommended.
C Posada El Limón, Calle de Pinal 64, El Limón suburb, near Parque Nacional Henri Pittier, T283 4925, T0414-444 1915 (mob), caribean@telcel .net.ve. Dutch owned, some way from centre, relaxed and pleasant, family atmosphere, spacious rooms with a/c and hot water, laundry, pool, good restaurant, internet, parking, trips to Parque with guide US$100, airport transfers.
C Princesa Plaza, Av Miranda Este entre Fuerzas Aéreas y Av Bermúdez, T232 2052. Large commercial hotel, 1 block east of Plaza Bolívar, convenient, a/c, inexpensive restaurant.
D Caroní, Ayacucho Norte 197, Bolívar, T554 4465. A/c, hot showers, comfortable. Recommended.
E Central, Av Santos Michelena 6, T245 2834. Safe and central, with fan.

E Sao Vicente, Av Bolívar 03. Decent budget option, a/c, central location, cable TV.

Parque Nacional Henri Pittier *p1350*
F pp Rancho Grande biological research station. Plenty of beds in basic dorms, US$7.50 pp per night, use of kitchen facilities, take warm sleeping bag, candles and food; nearest supplies at El Limón, 20 km before Rancho Grande.
F-G pp Campamento El Cocuy, Choroní (A full board), T243-991 1106, 0416-747 3833 (mob), www.cocuy.org.ve. Pleasant mountain refuge, beautiful views, sleeping in hammocks. Walking and bird-watching tours arranged with bi-lingual Spanish/English guides from US$25.

Aragua Coast *p1350*
Ocumare de la Costa
A De La Costa Eco-Lodge, California 23, T993 1986, 0414-460 0655 (mob), www.eco venezuela.com. Comfortable, upmarket lodge near beach, with outdoor bar serving food,

restaurant, roof terraces with good sea views, swimming pool, landscaped gardens, range of excursions, equipment hire, specialist bilingual guides. Price includes breakfast.
D Posada Mis Tres Tesoros, Anzoátegui 46, T993 1725, 0414-588 0149 (mob). 6 blocks from sea, a/c, cable TV, simple rooms, hot water, very good, helpful owners.

Choroní
A Hacienda El Portete, C El Cementerio, T991 1255, www.elportete.com. Restored cocoa plantation, colonial-style large grounds, restaurant, a/c, pool, many children's facilities, excursions.
B Hacienda La Aljorra, 1 km south in La Loma, T0212-252 0002(Caracas), 218 8841 (Choroní) laaljorra@hotmail.com. On roadside, out of town, **C** on weekdays, breakfast included, hot water, 300-year old cacao hacienda in 62 ha of wooded hillside. Large rooms, relaxing and peaceful.
B La Gran Posada, 5 km north of Choroní on a steep hillside above Maracay road, T217 0974. Small hotel right on the roadside with little open space. Neat, a/c pleasant bar and restaurant. Negotiate in low season.
D Posada Colonial El Picure, C Miranda No 34-A, T991 1296. Colonial house in centre of village, backs onto river. Popular with travellers, welcoming, dorms and private rooms, restaurant offering vegetarian options.

Puerto Colombia and around *p1351*
There are dozens of posadas for all budgets in town, but most are fully booked during high season when prices rise by around 40%.
A Hostal and Spa Casa Grande (also known as Coco's), Morillo 33, T991 1251, www.hostalcasa grande.com. One of the best in town, very attractive décor in colonial style, pool and nice gardens, parking. Excellent.
A Posada Xuchytlan, Av Principal, after Posada Cataquero, T991 1234. Charming, stylish colonial house with beautiful gardens, comfortable rooms, welcoming, a/c, parking, includes breakfast. Very pleasant.
B Posada El Malecón, El Malecón 1, T991 1107, www.geocities.com/posadaelmalecon. On seafront, a/c, hot water, less with fan, small, basic rooms. Discounts Mon-Thu (same owners as Vista Mar), secure parking.
B Posada Pittier, on road to Choroní, 10 min walk from Puerto Colombia, T/F991 1028, www .posadapittier.com. Small, immaculate rooms, a/c, good meals, helpful, garden. Recommended.
B-C La Posada de Choroní, Calle Principal, 2 blocks from Malecón, T991 1191, www.laposada dechoroni.3a2.com. Rooms with a/c and TV, cheaper without TV, cheaper with fan, hot water, colonial with rooms off central garden, parking.

C Brisas del Mar, C Principal at the port. Above a bar, noisy but comfortable, a/c, TV, bit overpriced.
C Hostal Vista Mar, C Colón at western end, T991 1250, www.hostalvistamar.com. On seafront, pleasant, terraces with hammocks and some rooms with sea view, some with a/c and TV, less with fan, helpful, secure parking.
D Costa Brava, Murillo 9, near Malecón, T991 1059, suarezjf@cantv.net. Cheaper without bath, basic, ceiling fans, laundry facilities, parking, good food, English spoken, family-run. Recommended.
D La Montañita, Murillo 6, T991 1132, choroni_ indio@hotmail.com. Popular, nice courtyard, charming owners, packages available (**B** full board).
D Posada Doña Enriqueta, Color 3, T991 1158, just off the seafront. Basic rooms, a/c, books tours, helpful, 40% discount Mon-Thu.
D Posada La Parchita, Trino Rangel, T991 1233, 0416-832 2790 (mob). Including breakfast, rooms set around a lovely patio, very nice. Recommended, book in advance.
D Posada Turpial, José Maitin 3, T991 1123, www.posadaturpial.com. **A** for full board room (2 sharing). Colonial house, a/c, well- organized, cosy, attractive, nice atmosphere, good restaurant, rooms around patio, TV, safety deposit box, German and English spoken. Book in advance. Owners run travel agency www.turpialtravel.com and organize local tours, dive trips. Recommended.
D Hostal Colonial, on Morillo, opposite bus stop, T218 5012, hcolonial@choroni.net. Popular hostel, good value, with fan, laundry, German owner. Also good tours in the Pittier park.
E Posada Alfonso, near checkpoint, T991 1037. German owner, quiet, hammocks, laundry facilities. Recommended.
E-F La Abuela, near bridge to Playa Grande. Basic, fan, shared bath.
F Casa Luna, next to Hostal Colonial, Morillo 35, no obvious sign, T951 5318, claudibeckmann@ web.de. Under new ownership. Colonial house, basic rooms, German and English spoken. Run travel agency including tours to Pittier park, diving trips and airport transfers, jungletrip@choroni.net.
Camping possible on Playa Grande, no permission needed and showers on beach; beware of theft. Gets crowded with campers during high season.

Cepe and Chuao
There are several *posadas* in the village of Chuao, but it is some distance from the beach (those listed below are closer to the sea). La Luzonera (**D**), on the plaza, is the best, but there are others (**F**), unsigned, basic. Camping is permitted on the Chuao and Cepe beaches.
B La Terraza del Morocho, Av Principal Las Tejerías 44, Chuao, T0414-450 3341. A/c, cable TV, helpful, ask about guides for trips to El Chorrerón waterfall and other sites.

B Posada Puerto Escondido, Cepe, T241 4645. Includes 3 meals, drinks and boat from Puerto Colombia, spacious rooms, with bath, hot water and fan, peaceful and homely atmosphere, tropical gardens and nice pool area, diving. Recommended.
E El Gran Cacao, 200 m up the hill from the port at Chuao, T218 3604. New, comfortable, with a/c, some rooms with TV. Recommended.
E Rincón del Marino, near El Gran Chaco in Chuao. Basic, with fan.

☢ Eating

Maracay *p1350*
Many excellent restaurants in the Av Las Delicias area (eg **Mansión Imperial**, also has internet, bakery and supermarket); many are American style drive-up, fast-food outlets. Many reliable Chinese restaurants and *loncherías*, *tascas* and inexpensive restaurants in the streets around Plazas Girardot and Bolívar.

Puerto Colombia *p1351*
††† ¶ **Mango**, Trino Rangel. Informal setting in patio, delicious catch of the day and pastas, generous portions. Recommended.
††† ¶ **Willy**, Vía Playa Grande 1, just after bridge along the river. Very popular, good seafood and meat dishes. In low season only opens Fri-Sun.
†† **Costa Café Terraza**, just before bridge to Playa Grande. Upstairs terrace looks onto river, excellent fresh fish and tasty dishes. Good service, accepts credit cards.
††-¶ **El Abuelo**, just before bridge to Playa Grande. Good food and value, accepts credit cards.

▲ Activities and tours

Puerto Colombia *p1351*
Claudia Beckmann and Emilio Espinoza, Unión 4, T951 5318, 0412-435 3056, jungletrip@ choroni.net. Good trips in the national park.

⊖ Transport

Maracay *p1350*
Bus The bus station is 2 km southeast of the centre, taxi US$3. *Por puesto* marked 'Terminal' for the bus station and 'Centro' for the centre (Plaza

Girardot). To **Maracaibo**, Expresos los Llanos, US$15. To **Valencia**, US$3.20, 1 hr, and **Caracas**, US$4 by *autobus*, 5 daily, US$5.50 by *microbus*, 1½-2 hrs, and US$5 by *por puesto*. **Barinas**, US$12, 7 hrs. **Mérida** US$19, 12 hrs; Ciudad Bolívar, US$17, 10 hrs. To **Coro**, US$12, 7¾ hrs.

Parque Nacional Henri Pittier *p1350*
Bus Depart from Maracay Terminal; pay full fare to **Ocumare** or hitch from the alcabala at El Limón. **Taxi** Can be hired at Maracay for a day's outing in the park for about US$55 (bargain hard).

Aragua Coast *p1350*
El Playón
Bus From **Maracay**, 2-2½ hours, US$2.50. To **Cata** from El Playón US$0.35 from plaza, from Ocumare de la Costa US$1.

Choroní
Bus **Maracay-Choroní**, beautiful journey Henri Pittier park, every 2 hrs from 0630-1700, more at the weekend, US$2.50, 2½-3 hrs. Taxi US$6.80. Road congested at holidays and weekends.

Puerto Colombia *p1351*
Bus From **Maracay** bus terminal leave from platform 5. Buses to Maracay depart from the park near the police checkpoint every hour or so from 0500, last one at 1700, US$4, 2-3 hrs.
Taxi From **Maracay** US$7 pp, 1-1½ hrs.

❶ Directory

Maracay *p1350*
Banks Italcambio (American Express), Av Aragua con C Bermúdez, C C Maracay Plaza, p 1, loc 110K, T235 6945, Mon-Fri 0830-1700, Sat 0830-1200. *Cambio* in **Air Mar** travel agency, ground floor of CADA Centro Comercial, Av 19 de Abril, Local 20, 2 blocks north of Plaza Girardot. 2.5 commission. **Internet** Several places around Plaza Bolívar and CC La Capilla, Av Santos Michelena.

Puerto Colombia *p1351*
Banks The nearest banks are in Maracay. Some *posadas* and restaurants change cash/TCs at poor rates, or give cash against credit cards (passport required). *Licorería San Sebastián*, by the bridge, changes cash and TCs and sells phone cards.

Valencia and around

Founded in 1555, Valencia is the capital of Carabobo State and Venezuela's third largest city. It's the centre of its most developed agricultural region and the most industrialized. Near the city are several groups of petroglyphs while the coast has some very popular beach areas. Best known of these is the Morrocoy national park, but you have to seek out the quiet spots.

Valencia → *Phone code: 0241. Colour map 1, grid A5. Population: 1,350,000. Altitude: 480 m.*

A road through low hills thickly planted with citrus, coffee and sugar runs 50 km west from Maracay to the valley in which Valencia lies. It is hot and humid with annual rainfall of 914 mm. Like its Spanish namesake, Valencia is famous for its oranges.

The **Cathedral** ① *daily 0630-1130, 1500-1830, Sun 0630-1200, 1500-1900*, built in 1580, is on the east side of **Plaza Bolívar**. The statue of the Virgen del Socorro (1550) in the left transept is the most valued treasure; on the second Sunday in November (during the Valencia Fair) it is paraded with a richly jewelled crown. See also **El Capitolio** ① *Páez, between Díaz Moreno y Montes de Oca*, the **Teatro Municipal** ① *Colombia y Av Carabobo*, the old **Carabobo University** building and the handsome **Plaza de Toros** ① *south end of Av Constitución beyond the ring road*, which is the second largest in Latin America after Mexico City. The magnificent former **residence of General Páez** (hero of the Carabobo battle) ① *Páez y Boyacá, Mon-Fri, free*, is now a museum. Equally attractive is the **Casa de los Celis** (1766) ① *Av Soublette y C Comercio, http://mipagina.cantv.net/casacelis, Tue-Sun 0800-1200, 1500-1700*. This well-restored colonial house and national monument served as a hospital for wounded soldiers during the Battle of Carabobo. It also houses the **Museo de Arte e Historia**, with pre-Columbian exhibits. Most of the interesting sights are closed on Monday.

Around Valencia

Most important of the region's petroglyphs can be found at the **Parque Nacional Piedras Pintadas**, where lines of prehispanic stone slabs, many bearing swirling glyphs, march up the ridges of Cerro Pintado. The new **Museo Parque Arqueológico Piedra Pintada** is at the foot of Cerro Las Rosas ① *Sector Tronconero, vía Vigirmia, Guacara, T041 571 596, Tue-Sat 0900-1700, Sun 1000-1600, free*, has 165 examples of rock art and menhirs (tours, parking, café).

Other extensive ancient petroglyphs have been discovered at **La Taimata** near Güigüe, 34 km east of Valencia on the lake's southern shore. There are more sites on rocks by the Río Chirgua, reached by a 10-km paved road from Highway 11, 50 km west of Valencia. About 5 km past Chirgua, at the Hacienda Cariaprima, is a remarkable 35 m-tall geoglyph, a humanoid figure carved into a steep mountain slope at the head of the valley.

At 30 km southwest of Valencia on the highway to San Carlos is the site of the **Carabobo** battlefield, an impressive historical monument surrounded by splendid gardens. The view over the field from the *mirador* where the Liberator directed the battle in 1814 is impressive. Historical explanations are given on Wednesday, weekends and holidays.

Coast north of Valencia

Puerto Cabello (*Colour map 1, grid A5, Phone code 0242, Population 185,000*), 55 km from Valencia, was one the most important ports in the colonial Americas, from which produce was transported to the Dutch possessions. Puerto Cabello has retained its maritime importance and is Venezuela's key port. Plaza Bolívar and the colonial part of town are by the waterfront promenade at Calle 24 de Julio. The **Museo de Antropología e Historia** ① *C Los Lanceros 43, Tue-Fri 0900-1600, Sat 0900-1230*, is in one of the few remaining colonial houses (1790), in the tangle of small streets between Plaza Bolívar and the sea. It displays the history of the region and has a room dedicated to Simón Bolívar.

To the east is **Bahía de Patanemo**, a beautiful, tranquil horseshoe-shaped beach shaded by palms. It has three main sectors, Santa Rita, Los Caneyes and Patanemo itself, with the village proper, further from the beach than the other two. All three have lodging, but it may be difficult to find meals midweek (try at posadas). Offshore is the lovely Isla Larga (no shade or facilities), best reached by boat from Quizandal, US$4.20, 15 minutes. There are several cafés along the beachfront. Nearby are two sunken wrecks that attract divers. From Puerto Cabello, take a *por puesto* from the terminal, 20 minutes, US$0.90, a taxi US$5.50.

Parque Nacional Morrocoy → *Colour map 1, grid A5.*

Palm-studded islets and larger islands (*cayos*) with secluded beaches make up Parque Nacional Morrocoy. The largest and most popular of the islands within the park is **Cayo Sombrero**, with two over-priced fish restaurants. No alcohol is sold on this or other islands; be aware of hidden extra costs and take your own supplies. It is very busy at weekends and during holidays and is generally dirty and noisy. But there are some deserted beaches, with trees on which to sling a hammock. For peace and quiet, take boats to the farthest cayos. **Playuela** is beautiful and is considered to have one of the nicest beaches of all. It has a small restaurant at

1354

weekends and there's a nice walk to Playuelita. **Boca Seca** is also pleasant, with shade and calm water suitable for children, but it can be windy. **Cayo Borracho**, one of the nicest islands, has become a turtle-nesting reserve, closed to visitors. **Playa Azul**, a nice small cayo, has shallow water. The water at **Pescadores** is very shallow. **Los Muertos** has two beaches with shade, mangroves and palms. **Mero**'s beach is beautiful, with palms, but is windy. With appropriate footwear it is possible to walk between some of the islands. Calm waters here are ideal for water-skiing while scuba diving is best suited to beginners. Two things to note, though: a chemical spill in the 1990s destroyed about 50% of the coral in the park, so snorkellers will see very little. Only by diving to deeper waters will you see coral, although in all locations there are still fish to watch. Secondly, take insect repellent against *puri puri* (tiny, vicious mosquitoes) and flies. A number of muggings have been reported around Playa Sur.

Adjoining the park to the north is a vast nesting area for scarlet ibis, flamingoes and herons, the **Cuare Wildlife Sanctuary**. Most of the flamingoes are in and around the estuary next to Chichiriviche, which is too shallow for boats but you can walk there or take a taxi. Birds are best watched early morning or late afternoon.

Tucacas and Chichiriviche → *Phone code 0259. Colour map 1, grid A5*

Tucacas is a hot, busy, dirty town, where bananas and other fruit are loaded for Curaçao and Aruba. This popular and expensive beach resort, with its garish high-rise blocks and casinos. Its port area is gaining a reputation for rip-offs and robberies. A few kilometres beyond Tucacas, towards Coro, is Chichiriviche (*Population 7,000*), smaller, more relaxed, but lined with tacky shops, also dirty and not that attractive. Both provide access to Parque Nacional Morrocoy, each town serving separate *cayos*, but only as far as Cayo Sombrero. Apart from this and the diving options, no one has a good word to say about Tucacas or Chichiriviche.

● Sleeping

Valencia *p1354*

There are many hotels across the price range on Av Bolívar, but it is a long avenue, so don't attempt to walk it.
A Don Pelayo, Av Díaz Moreno y Rondón, T857 8793, www.hoteldonpelayo.com. Central, modern block, restaurant, a/c, includes buffet breakfast.
C Marconi, Av Bolívar 141-65, T823 4843. Small, modern hotel, simple rooms, a/c, helpful, safe, laundry, recommended (next to a petrol station), take bus or colectivo from bus station to stop after 'El Elevado' bridge.
D Carabobo, C Libertad 100-37, esq Plaza Bolívar, T858 8860. Central, cold water, OK, with large a/c lobby.

Coast north of Valencia *p1354*

B-C Posada Santa Margarita, Bolívar 4-36, Puerto Cabello, T361 7113, www.ptocabello.com. Converted colonial house in historic part of town, 2 blocks from the waterfront promenade, organizes local day trips, attractively decorated rooms in colonial style, roof terrace, restaurant, breakfast included, small pool. Reserve in advance.
At **Patanemo** there are hotels and *posadas* in the village (eg **Patanemo**, **Chachita** and **Iliana**).
C-D Posada Edén, Final Av Principal Los Caneyes. The best posada in the region, small, comfortable, with a/c, TV, hot water, restaurant and pool.
D Posada Natal Mar, at entrance to Caneyes sector, 100 m from turn-off to Bahía de Patanemo. Small but clean rooms with a/c, TV, but no windows, restaurant upstairs.

Parque Nacional Morrocoy *p1354*

Camping is allowed at **Cayo Paiclás** and **Cayo Sol** but you must first make a reservation with **Inparques** (National Parks), T800 8487, Mon-Sun 0800-2000; reserve at least 8 working days in advance giving all details; US$2.50 pp per night, 7 nights maximum, pay in full in advance (very complicated procedure). Very few facilities and no fresh water at **Paiclás**. **Playa Azul** and **Paiclás** have ecological toilets. At weekends and holidays it is very crowded and litter-strewn (beware rats).
A pp **Villa Mangrovia** on the Lizardo Spit between Tucacas and Chichiriviche, the only place to stay in the park. 3 rooms, excellent food and service, charming owner. Book via **Last Frontiers**, T01296-653000, or **Journey Latin America**, T0161-832 1441.

Tucacas *p1355*

For a wider choice of budget accommodation stay at Chichiriviche rather than Tucacas. Most hotels and restaurants in Tucacas are on the long Av Libertador, the town's main street.
B Manaure, T812 0286. Modern, low-rise hotel, a/c, hot water, pool, good.
D-E Posada Amigos del Mar, C Nueva, near bus stop, beyond Hospital Viejo, T812 3962. Helpful staff, organizes trips to cayos and diving, use of kitchen, with fan. A good budget option.
Camping Gas in Tucacas or Puerto Cabello.

Chichiriviche p1355

There are plenty of posadas in town charging reasonable rates.

D-E Capri, Av Zamora, T818 6026. Near docks, basic rooms, a bit shabby, shower, fan or a/c, pleasant, Italian owner, good restaurant and supermarket.

C-D Posada Sol, Mar y Arena, Mariño y Partida, T815 0306, posadasolmaryarena@cantv.net. Small rooms with a/c, TV, welcoming, upstairs terrace with a grill, 1 block from sea, changes US$.

D Posada Villa Gregoria, C Mariño, 1 block north of bus stop behind the large water tank, T818 6359, www.villagregoria.com. Spanish-run, helpful, relaxing, good value, fan or a/c, laundry facilities, small rooms, hammocks, garden, secure parking. Tours to Coro and Choroní, English spoken.

E Posada Res Delia, C Mariño 30, 1 block from Gregoria, T818 6089. Including breakfast, **D** with a/c, shared bath, organizes tours.

F Morena's Place, Sector Playa Norte, 10 mins walk from the bus stop, T/F815 0936, posada morenas@hotmail.com. Beautifully decorated house, fan, hammocks, helpful hosts, English spoken. **F Posada Alemania**, Cementos Coro, T815 0912, posadaalemania@cantv.net. German-run, runs tours, rents snorkel gear, 200 m from Playa Sur, nice garden. **F Posada Tío José**, on street parallel to main avenue, 1 block off, T898 0215. More pricey in high season, a/c, TV, cosy atmosphere, pleasant decor. Recommended.

🍴 Eating

Valencia p1354

♥♥-♥ **La Rinconada**, Plaza Bolívar. Recommended, open Sun.

Chichiriviche p1355

Many fish restaurants along seafront, eg ♥♥ **Txalupa**. Good seafood and Spanish dishes, efficient service. And **Veracruz**. Good fish.

⛰ Activities and tours

Tucacas p1355

Bicycles can be hired in town.

Diving Equipment can be hired from near the harbour. There are several diving companies.

Submatur, C Ayacucho 6, near Plaza Bolívar, T812 0082, morrocoysubmatur1@cantv.net. Experienced owner, 4-day PADI course US$350, day trip 2 dives from US$65 (US$45 with own equipment); also rents rooms, **F**, fan and cooking facilities.

🚍 Transport

Valencia p1354

Air The airport is 6 km southeast of centre. Taxi airport-bus terminal US$4.65-7. **Aeropostal**

flights daily to **Barcelona, Caracas, Maracaibo, Miami** (daily), **Porlamar** and **San Antonio**. Santa Bárbara flies to **Barquisimeto, Mérida, San Antonio, Maracaibo** and **Aruba**. Dutch Antilles Express, www.flydae.com, to **Curaçao** 6 days a week.

Bus Terminal is 4 km east of centre, part of shopping mall *Big-Low* (24-hr restaurants). Entry to platforms by *ficha* (token), US$0.05. Left luggage. Minibus to centre, frequent and cheap, but slow and confusing route at peak times; taxi from bus station to centre, US$4 (official drivers wear ID badges). To **Caracas**, frequent buses with **Aeroexpresos Ejecutivos** from 0600-1900, 2½ hrs, US$5.50, *por puesto* US$6. To **Maracay**, US$3.20, 1hr. **Mérida**, 10-12 hrs, US$19; to **San Cristóbal**, 10 hrs, US$19. **Barquisimeto**, US$7, 3½ hrs. To **Maracaibo**, 2 evening buses with Aeroexpresos Ejecutivos, US$15, 8 hrs. **Puerto Cabello**, US$1.15, 1 hr. **Tucacas**, US$2.50, or US$5 by frequent *por puesto* service. To **Coro** US$7.25, 4½ hrs. To **Ciudad Bolívar**, US$15, 10 hrs.

Around Valencia p1354
Parque Nacional Piedras Pintadas
Bus To **Vigírima** 20 km northeast of Valencia at regular intervals (US$1), ask to get off at the 'Cerro Pintado' turnoff. Driving from Vigírima, turn left at a small blue 'Cadafe Tronconero' sign, then a further 3 km.

Carabobo
Bus To Carabobo leave from bottom of Av Bolívar Sur y C 75, or from Plaza 5 de Julio, Valencia, US$0.50, ask for Parque Carabobo (1¼ hrs).

Parque Nacional Morrocoy p1354
Ferry From **Tucacas**: prices per boat from US$20 return to **Paiclás** to US$40 return to **Cayo Sombrero** (max 7 per boat). Ticket office is left of the car entrance to the Park. Recommended boatmen are Orlando and Pepe. Boats to Boca Seca and Playuelita only leave from Tucacas.
From Chichiriviche: tickets can be bought per person or per boat and vary according to distance; US$20 per boat to **Los Muertos**, 10 min trip, US$32-68 to **Cayo Sombrero**. Prices are set for each cayo and there are long and short trips. There are 2 ports: one in the centre, one at Playa Sur. Ask for the ticket system to fix price and to ensure you'll be picked up on time for return trip.

Tucacas p1355
Bus Frequent *por puesto* from **Valencia**, US$5, bus US$2.50; to **Puerto Cabello**, take bus from the intersection of the coastal highway with the main avenue of Tucacas to **Morón** (35 mins, US$1.15), then from Morón to Puerto Cabello (15 mins, US$0.50); Tucacas-Morón bus goes on to

Puerto Cabello, if there are enough passengers. To **Coro**, US$5, 3 hrs.

Chichiriviche *p1355*

Bus To **Puerto Cabello**, frequent *por puestos* often via Valencia, 2 hrs, US$3.50; to **Barquisimeto** often via Morón, 3 hrs; to **Valera**, 9 hrs. To **Coro**, take a bus from the station on Av Zamora to **Sanare**, US$0.95, every 20 mins, then another to Coro, US$5.10, 3 hrs. Direct buses from **Valencia**, or take bus from Morón to Coro and get out at turnoff, 1½-2 hrs, US$4.

① Directory

Valencia *p1354*
Banks Corp Banca, Av Díaz Moreno, CC Colombia. Amex TCs changed. Italcambio, Av

Bolívar Norte, Edif Talia, loc 2, T821 8173. Amex travel services, Visa TCs, a long way north of centre in Urbanización Los Sauces, get off bus at junction with C 132; also at airport, Mon-Fri 0830-1700, Sat morning only.
Consulates British Honorary Consul, Dalca, Urb Industrial El Recreo, Calle B, Parcela 103, T878 3480, burguesdal@ cantv.net.ve.
Telephones CANTV, Plaza Bolívar, for international calls.

Tucacas *p1355*
Banks Banesco gives cash advance on credit cards. Hotels and travel agents will change money but at very low rates, if they have enough cash. In **Chichiriviche**, many hotels will change dollars and euros but at very low rates.

Venezuela Coro & around

Coro and around

The relaxed colonial city of Coro, with its sand-dune surroundings, sits at the foot of the arid, windswept Paranaguá Peninsula. Inland from Coro, the Sierra de San Luis is good walking country in fresher surroundings.

Coro → *Phone code: 0268. Colour map 1, grid A5. Population: 158,760. Mean temperature: 28°C.*

Coro, the capital of the Falcón state, is a UNESCO World Heritage Site. Founded in 1527, it became an important religious centre for Christians and Jews alike. The city, 177 km from Tucacas, is generally clean and well kept and its small colonial part has several shaded plazas and beautiful buildings, many of which date from the 18th century. Recently, efforts have been made to preserve and restore its colonial heritage. The **tourist office** is on Paseo Alameda, T251 5327, English spoken, helpful. See also www.coroweb.com (in English, French and Spanish).

The **Cathedral**, a national monument, was begun in 1583. **San Clemente** church has a wooden cross in the plaza in front, said to mark the site of the first mass said in Venezuela; it is believed to be the country's oldest such monument ① *Mass Mon-Sat 1930*. It is undergoing reconstruction. There are several interesting colonial houses: **Los Arcaya** ① *Zamora y Federación, Tue-Sat 0900- 1200,1500-1800, Sun 0900-1300, free*, one of the best examples of 18th-century architecture, houses the **Museo de Cerámica**, small but interesting, with a beautiful garden. **Los Senior** ① *Talavera y Hernández*, where Bolívar stayed in 1827, houses an extension of the **Museo de Arte** of the Universidad Francisco de Miranda, whose main branch is on Paseo Talavera entre Bolívar y Comercio. **Las Ventanas de Hierro** ① *Zamora y Colón, Tue-Sat 0900-1200, 1500-1800, Sun 0900-1300, US$0.20*, built 1764-1765, now the **Museo de Tradición Familiar**. Just beyond is the **Casa del Tesoro** ① *C Zamora, T252 8701, free*, an art gallery showing local artists' work. The **Jewish cemetery** ① *C 23 de Enero esq C Zamora*, is the oldest on the continent. It was founded by Jews who arrived from Curaçao at the beginning of the 19th century.

The **Museo de Coro 'Lucas Guillermo Castillo'** ① *C Zamora opposite Plaza San Clemente, T251 1298, Tue-Sat 0900-1200, 1500- 1800, Sun 0900-1330, US$0.25*, is in an old monastery, and has a good collection of church relics, recommended.

Coro is surrounded by sand dunes, **Los Médanos de Coro**, which form an impressive **national park** ① *www.losmedanos.com/; outside town on the main road to Punto Fijo: take bus marked 'Carabobo' from C35 Falcón y Av Miranda, or up Av Los Médanos and get off at the end, just after Plaza Concordia, from there walk 500 m to entrance, or take a taxi*. The place is guarded by police and is generally safe, but stay close to the entrance and on no account wander off across the dunes. Kiosk at entrance sells drinks and snacks; open till 2400.

On the road to the town's port, **La Vela de Coro**, near the turning, is the **Jardín Botánico Xerofito Dr León Croizat** ① *Sector Sabana Larga, T277 8451, Mon-Fri 0800-1200,*

1300-1600, Sat-Sun 0900-1700, free, getting there: take Vela bus from corner of C Falcón, opposite Banco Coro, and ask to be let off at Pasarela del Jardín Botánico – the bridge over the road. It is backed by UNESCO and has plants from Africa, Australia, etc. A very interesting place to visit, with tours in Spanish.

Paraguaná Peninsula → *Phone code: 0269. Colour map 1, grid A5. Population: 125,000.*

Punto Fijo and around This area is a must for windsurfers and is a great place for walking and flamingo spotting. The western side of the peninsula is industrialized, with oil refineries at Cardón and Amuay connected by pipeline to the Lago de Maracaibo oilfields. The main town is **Punto Fijo**, a busy, unappealing place, whose duty-free zone attracts shoppers with cheap electrical goods and alcohol. 5 km away is the residential area of **Judibana**, a much nicer place to stay, with shopping centre, cinema and restaurants.

Adícora A quiet if run-down little resort on the east side of the peninsula. The beaches are very windswept and not great but they are popular with wind- and kitesurfers. There are three windsurfing schools in town. Adícora is also a good base for exploring the beautiful, barren and wild peninsula where goats and wild donkeys roam.

Cerro Santa Ana (830 m) is the only hill on the peninsula and commands spectacular views. The entrance is at El Moruy; take bus to Pueblo Nuevo (0730-0800), then take one to Punto Fijo and ask to be dropped off at the entrance to Santa Ana. From the plaza walk back to the signpost for Pueblo Nuevo and take the dirt road going past a white building; 20 m to the left is Restaurant La Hija. Walk 1 km through scrubby vegetation (watch out for dogs) to the *Inparques* office (closed from Monday to Friday but busy at weekends). Register here before attempting the steep three-hour climb. It's safer to go on Saturday or Sunday. Some *posadas* in Coro arrange trips to the Peninsula.

Laguna Boca de Caño (also called Laguna Tiraya) is a nature reserve north of Adícora, inland from Supi, along a dirt track that is usually fit for all vehicles. There is abundant bird life, particularly flamingoes. It is the only mangrove zone on the east of the peninsula.

Sierra de San Luis

South of Coro, on the road to Barquisimeto, the Sierra includes the **Parque Nacional Juan C Falcón**, with tropical forest, caves and waterfalls. Visit it from the picturesque village of **Curimagua**; jeeps leave from Coro terminal, US$3.50, 1 hour. The lovely colonial town of **Cabure** is the capital of the Sierra. Jeeps leave from Coro terminal, 58 km, 1¼ hours, US$3. As well as hotels, Cabure has restaurants, bars, a bakery, supermarket and pharmacy. A few kilometres up the road is a series of beautiful waterfalls, called the Cataratas de Hueque. **The Spanish Road** is a fantastic three-hour walk through orange groves and tropical forest from Curimagua to Cabure. You will see many butterflies along the way. The path is not well marked, so it is best to hire a guide. Take water. It's very muddy in rains; take insect repellent and good shoes and be prepared to get wet. Ask at any of the hotels listed below. To walk the Spanish Road from Coro in one day, take

Coro

Callejón Aeropuerto
Av Josefa Camejo
C 23 Vuelvan Caras
C 25 Norte
C 25 Norte
C 27 Miranda
Av Miranda
C 58A Hernández
C 11 Miranda
To ①
C 31 Urdaneta
Casa del Tesoro
Museo de Cerámica
San Clemente
San Francisco
Museo de Coro ①
C 33 Zamora
Las Ventanas de Hierro
Paseo Alameda
Buses to Los Médanos
Plaza Falcón
C 35 Falcón
Casa de Los Senior
To Jewish Cemetery
C 39 Palmasola
Cathedral
Plaza Bolívar
Teatro de Loro
C 6 Federación
Paseo Talavera
Casa de las 100 Ventanas
C 58 Comercio
To Kuriana Travel &
C 58 Colón
C 41 Garcés
C 42 Amplies
To Bus Terminal (9 blocks)
C 45 Buchivacoa
To ④
To ⑧
N
0 metres 100
0 yards 100

Sleeping 🛏
El Gallo 2
Intercaribe 3
Miranda Cumberland 6
Posada Casa Tun Tun 1
Posada Don Antonio 7
Posada La Casa de los Pájaros 4
Taima Taima 5
Vila Antigua 8

Eating 🍴
Barra del Jacal 1
Dulzura y algo más 2
El Portón de Arturo 3
Mersi 5
Panadería Costa Nova 4
Posada Don Luis 6

transport to Cabure, ask to be dropped at the turn-off for the **Posada El Duende** (see below) and walk uphill 1 km to the Posada, where you begin the trek. The path eventually comes out to the Curimagua-Coro paved road, where you can take transport or hitch back to Coro.

☎ Sleeping

Coro *p1357, map p1358*
Coro has several excellent *posadas* catering for travellers; book well in advance, especially in Dec.
A-B Miranda Cumberland, Av Josefa Camejo, opposite old airport, T252 2422, www.hoteles cumberland.com. Large modern hotel, price includes breakfast, good value, restaurant, nice swimming pool area, travel agency.
D Intercaribe, Av Manaure entre Zamora y Urdaneta, T251 1844, intercaribe@cantv.net. Bland, modern, pool, a/c, small rooms.
D Taima Taima, C 35 Falcón (some distance from the centre), T252 1215, hospedajetaima taima@hotmail.com. Small rooms, a/c, TV, some hot water, parking.
D Villa Antigua, C 58 Comercio 46, T251 6479/ 0414-683 7433. Colonial style, a/c, TV, fountain in courtyard, restaurant, public phones.
D-E Posada Don Antonio, Paseo Talavera 11, T253 9578. Central, small rooms, a/c, internet, parking.
D-E Posada La Casa de los Pájaros, Monzón 74 entre Ampies y Comercio, T252 8215, www.casa delospajaros.com.ve. Colonial house 6 blocks from centre, being restored by the owners with local art and antiques, rooms with and without bath, camping US$4.50, tents for rent, hammock space US$5.50, breakfast US$2-4, 30 mins free internet, use of kitchen for small fee, laundry service, trips to local sights. Recommended.
E-F El Gallo, Federación 26, T252 9481, posada elgallo2001@hotmail.com. In colonial part, French/ Venezuelan owned, relaxed, spacious, internet, shared baths, courtyard with hammocks, dorms and private rooms, use of kitchen, some English spoken, see Eric for tours to Sierra San Luis, around $35 pp for a 1-day tour, includes lunch.
E-F Posada Casa Tun Tun, Zamora 92, entre Toledo y Hernández, T404 0347, www.casatuntun .over-blog.com. Run by knowledgeable and welcoming and Belgian couple. Restored colonial house with 3 attractive patios, kitchen facilities, laundry, relaxing hammock areas and dipping pool, dorms and rooms with bath and lovely décor. Good value, nice atmosphere, free morning coffee, changes US$. Highly recommended.
Camping About 30 km east of Coro at **La Cumara**, nice, good beach and dunes, US$2 pp.

Paraguaná Peninsula *p1358*
Punto Fijo
C Caraibi, Av Bolivia entre Peninsular y Ayacucho, T247 0227. With breakfast, good restaurant, parking, a/c, modern, accepts credit cards.

D Miami, C Falcón entre Av México y Bolivia, T245 8532. A/c, bit cheaper with fan, parking, restaurant. Recommended.

Judibana
C Jardín, on Av Mariscal y C Falcón, near airport, T246 1727. A/c, pool, restaurant, parking, accepts credit cards, changes US$ cash.
D Luigi, C Oeste, P PB, T246 0970. A/c, pleasant, good restaurant, accepts credit cards.

Adícora
C Hacienda La Pancha, Vía Pueblo Nuevo, 5 km from Adícora in the hills, T0414-969 2649, www .venaventours.com/haciendalapancha. Beautiful, old, colonial-style house set in countryside, nice owners, restaurant, pool, no children.
D Archie's Surf Posada, Playa Sur, T988 8285/ 415 7313, www.kitesurfing-venezuela.com. At entrance to Adícora, 5 mins' walk to centre. German-run, well established, organizes wind and kite surfing lessons. Also trips, horse riding and airport pick-ups. Furnished bungalows for 4-12, apartments for 2-4, hammocks. Good reports.
D-E Posada Kitzberger, C Comercio de Adícora, on Malecón, T988 8173. Fan and a/c, German owners, pleasant, cosy, no single rooms, good restaurant. Recommended.

Sierra de San Luís *p1358*
Curimagua
F-G Finca El Monte, Vía La Soledad, 5 km from the village, T404 0564, fincaelmonte@yahoo.com. Beautiful views, run by a Swiss couple on an ecological basis, hot water, meals, hammocks, colonial style, peaceful, Ernesto takes tours round the park, including birdwatching and cave tours. English, German and French spoken. Highly recommended.

Cabure
C-D Hotel El Duende, 20 mins uphill from village, T808 9066. A beautiful 19th-century posada and garden, price depends on size of room, fan, cold water, good restaurant, horse riding, walking, peaceful. Recommended.
In town are several budget options.

☎ Eating

Coro *p1357, map p1358*
♈ Barra del Jacal, Av Manaure y C 29 Unión. Outdoors, pizza and pasta.

¶ **Mersi**, C 56 Toledo y Zamora. Good pizzas and *empanadas*.

¶ **El Portón de Arturo**, C 56 Toledo, towards Plaza Falcón. All kinds of regional meat.

¶ **Posada Don Luis**, opposite airport. Serves local speciality, *chivo*, goat.

Cafés

Dulzura y algo más, on the corner of Paseo Alameda. Serves good ice cream and local sweets.

Panadería Costa Nova, Av Manaure, opposite *Hotel Intercaribe*. Good bread, sandwiches and pastries, open late.

Paraguaná Peninsula: Punto Fijo *p1358*
¶ **Colonial**, C Libertad entre Colombia y Ecuador. Cheap, recommended, lunch only.
¶ Good *panadería* opposite bus terminal.

Paraguaná Peninsula: Adícora *p1358*
Hotel Falcon III, C La Marina, Vía Las Cabanas, T697 9267. On beachfront, white hotel, serves excellent, good value seafood and fish soup. Also rents a/c, basic rooms (**B**).

⊛ Festivals and events

Coro *p1357, map p1358*
26 Jul, Coro Week. **9-12 Oct**, state fair. **24-25 Dec**, Tambor Coriano and Parranda de San Benito (Coro, La Vela and Puerto Cumarebo).

▲ Activities and tours

Coro *p1357, map p1358*
Contact *posadas* in town for tours, eg La Casa de los Párajos.

⊖ Transport

Coro *p1357, map p1358*
Air Airport open for domestic flights; see also Las Piedras, below, for flights.
Bus Terminal is on Av Los Médanos, entre Maparari y Libertad, buses go up C 35 Falcón, US$0.25, taxi US$2. To/from **Caracas** US$20, 6-8 hrs; **Maracaibo**, US$10, 4 hrs, *por puesto* US$12; **Tucacas**, every 20 mins, US$8, 3-4 hrs; **Punto Fijo**, *por puesto* US$2.

Paraguaná Peninsula *p1358*
Punto Fijo
Air Airport at **Las Piedras**: *por puestos* from C Garcés y Av Bolívar (don't believe taxis who say there are no *por puestos* from airport to town); taxi from Punto Fijo US$5, from bus terminal US$3. Several flights a day to **Aruba**, **Avensa** and **Santa Bárbara**, 2 a day to **Curaçao**, Dutch Caribbean Express. Domestic flights to **Caracas**, **Mérida** and **Maracaibo** with Santa Bárbara.
Bus Terminal on C Peninsular entre Colombia y Ecuador; *por puestos* to **Pueblo Nuevo, Adícora, Coro, Valencia** and **Maracaibo**. To **Maracay, Barquisimeto, Maracaibo** and **Caracas**: Expresos Occidente, on C Comercio entre Ecuador y Bolivia; to **Mérida, Barinas** and **Caracas**, Expresos San Cristóbal, C Carnevali behind Hotel América; Expresos Alianza, on Av Colombia between Carnevali and Democracia, to many destinations.

Adícora
Bus Several daily to and from **Coro**, from 0630-1700, US$2.30, 1 hr; to and from **Pueblo Nuevo** and **Punto Fijo**, several daily from 0600-1730.

⊙ Directory

Coro *p1357, map p1358*
Banks Banco Mercantil, C 35 Falcón y C 50 Colina, Edif Don Luis, ATM and cash on Mastercard or Visa. Banco Venezuela, Paseo Talavera. ATM and cash on Visa. Try hotels and travel agents for cash and TCs. **Internet** Falcontech, next door to Hotel Intercaribe, Av de Manaure. Also at CANTV Centro de Comunicaciones, Av Los Médanos, opposite bus terminal, also international calls.

Paraguaná Peninsula: Punto Fijo *p1358*
Banks Many banks on Av Bolívar y Comercio accept Visa, MasterCard and others, eg **Banco de Venezuela, Banesco**. Banco Mercantil, Av Bolívar y C Girardot. Changes Citicorp TCs. **Casa Fukayama**, Av Bolívar entre C Altagracia y Girardot. Changes US$ cash.
Consulates Dutch Consul in Punta Cardón, Judibana at Urb La Laguna, C Mucubaji 38, Roque Hernández, T240 7211. **Post offices** Ipostel at C Páez y Av Panamá, collection every 10 days.
Telephones CANTV at C Falcón y Av México.

From Maracaibo to Colombia

To the heart of Venezuela's oil business on the shores of Lake Maracaibo: not many tourists find their way here. Those that do are usually on their way to Colombia via the border crossing on the Guajira Peninsula to the north. If you've got the time to stop and can handle the heat, Maracaibo is the only town in Venezuela where occasionally you'll see indigenous people in traditional dress going about their business and nearby are reminders of prehispanic and oil-free customs.

Maracaibo → *Phone code: 0261. Colour map 1, grid A4. Population: 1,800,000.*
Maracaibo, capital of the State of Zulia, is Venezuela's second largest city and oil capital. The region is the economic powerhouse of the country with over 50% of the nation's oil production coming from the Lago de Maracaibo area and Zulia state. The lake is reputedly the largest fresh water reserve in South America. An long cement and steel bridge, Puente General Rafael Urdaneta, crosses Lago de Maracaibo, connecting the city with the rest of the country. Maracaibo is a sprawling modern city with wide, clean streets and, apart from the intense heat, is pleasant to walk around, especially around Plaza Bolívar (but it is not considered safe at night). The hottest months are July to September, but there is usually a sea breeze from 1500 until morning. Just north of the regional capital is a lagoon where you can still see the stilt houses that inspired the Spanish invaders to christen it 'Little Venice'. In the southwest is the **Catatumbo** delta, a huge swamp brimming with wildlife and one of the most fascinating trips in the whole country (best reached by tour from Mérida). Its nightly displays of lightning, best seen from May to November or December, have yet to be explained. The **tourist office** is Corzutur ① *T783 4928*. See www.zuliaturistica.com for more sights, events and advice.

Sights The traditional city centre is **Plaza Bolívar**, on which stand the **Cathedral** (at east end), the **Casa de Gobierno**, the **Asamblea Legislativa** and the **Casa de la Capitulación** (or Casa Morales) ① *Mon-Fri, 0800-1600, tour free,* a colonial building and national monument. The Casa has a large library dedicated to the Liberator. Next door is the 19th-century **Teatro Baralt**.

Running west of Plaza Bolívar is the **Paseo de las Ciencias**, a 1970s development which levelled all the old buildings in the area. Only the **Iglesia de Santa Bárbara** stands in the Paseo. **Calle Carabobo** (one block north of the Paseo de las Ciencias) is a very good example of a colourful, colonial Maracaibo street. One block south of the Paseo is **Plaza Baralt** ① *Av 6, stretching to C 100 and the old waterfront market* (**Mercado de Pulgas**). The **Centro de Arte de Maracaibo Lía Bermúdez** ① *in the 19th-century Mercado de Pulgas building, Mon-Fri 0800-1200, 1400-1600, Sat-Sun 0930-1700,* displays the work of national artists. It is a/c, a good place to escape the midday heat and makes a good starting place for a walking tour of the city centre. The Centro has a café, internet, bookshops, cinema and holds cultural events. The new part of the city round **Bella Vista** and towards the University is in vivid contrast with the small **old town** near the docks. The latter, with narrow streets and brightly-painted, colonial style adobe houses, has hardly changed from the 19th century, although many buildings are in an advanced state of decay. The buildings facing **Parque Urdaneta** (three blocks north of Paseo de las Ciencias) have been well-restored. Also well-preserved are the church of **Santa Lucía** and the streets around. This old residential area is a short ride (or long walk) north from the old centre. **Parque La Marina**, on the shores of the lake, contains sculptures by the Venezuelan artist, Jesús Soto (1923-2005). More of his work can be seen in the **Galería de Arte Brindhaven** (free), near Santa Lucía.

Paseo de Maracaibo, or del Lago, is a lakeside park near the *Hotel del Lago*. It offers walks along the shores of the lake at its narrowest point, stunning views of the Rafael Urdaneta bridge and of oil tankers sailing to the Caribbean. The park attracts a wide variety of birds. To get there take a 'Milagro' *por puesto* or a 'Norte' bus northbound and ask the driver to let you off at the entrance, which is well-marked. Opposite is the Mercado de los Indios Guajiros (see Shopping).

Maracaibo to Colombia
About one hour north is the Río Limón. Take a bus (US$0.70, from terminal or Avenida 15 entre C 76 y 77) to **El Moján**, riding with the Guajira Indians as they return to their homes on the peninsula. From El Moján, *por puestos* go to **Sinamaica** (US$1.40; taxi US$5). Beyond Sinamaica, a paved road passes the Sinamaica Lagoon and leads to the border with Colombia. Along the way you see Guajira Indians, the men with bare legs, on horseback; the women with long, black, tent-shaped dresses and painted faces, wearing the sandals with big wool pom-poms which they make and sell, more cheaply than in the tourist shops. The men do nothing: women do all the work, tending sheep and goats, selling slippers and raising very little on the dry, hot, scrubby Guajira Peninsula. Because of the proximity of the border, across which drug trafficking occurs, it is best not to stay in this area after 1600.

Border with Colombia → *Colombia is 1 hr behind Venezuela.*
The border operates 24 hours. You need an exit card and stamp, US$15, to leave Venezuela, payable in bolívares only. Ask for 90 days on entering Colombia and make sure you get an entry

stamp from the Colombian authorities (DAS). From the frontier to Macaio, it's a 15-minute drive. Check exchange rates as it may be better to change bolívares into Colombian pesos in Venezuela at the border rather than in Colombia. For entering Colombia, see page 836. To enter Venezuela by land a visa may be asked for, even for those who don't officially require one. Only 72-hour transit visas are issued at this border; *tarjetas de turismo* must be obtained from *ONIDEX* in Maracaibo (Edif Banco Maracaibo, Plaza Baralt, C Comercio, T721 1984), not an easy task. Get a visa in advance. Expect searches at the border and en route to Maracaibo.

● Sleeping

Maracaibo *p1361*
It is best to reserve well in advance.
A Kristoff, Av 8 Santa Rita entre C 68 y 69, T796 1000, www.hotelkristoff.com. In the north of the city some distance from centre. Smart, a/c, nice pool open to non-residents US$6, disco, laundry service, restaurant.
B Gran Hotel Delicias, Av 15 esq C 70, T797 6111, F797 3037. North of the city. Old-fashioned modern hotel, bland, a/c, restaurant, pool, disco, accepts credit cards.
D Doral, C 75 y Av 14A, T797 8385. North of the city. A/c, safe, decent rooms, with breakfast, helpful. Recommended.
D Paraíso, Av 93, No 82-70, sector Veritas, T797 6149. With small sitting room, a/c, cable.
E Acuario, C 78 (also known as Dr Portillo) No 9-43, Bella Vista, T797 1123. A/c, shower, safe, small rooms, safe parking, basic.
E San Martín, Av 3Y (San Martín) con C 80, T791 5095. A/c, restaurant next door, accepts credit cards.
F Victoria, Av 6-14, Plaza Baralt, T722 9466. Right in the centre, near Plaza Bolívar, unsafe area at night. Old building, basic, private and shared bath, no hot water, a/c.

● Eating

Maracaibo *p1361*
A range of US chain restaurants and Chinese restaurants in the north of town. Many places to eat and bars on Calle 72 and 5 de Julio. Most restaurants are closed on Sun. Many restaurants on *palafitos* (stilts) in Santa Rosa de Agua district, good for fish (*por puesto* US$0.35 to get there); best to go at lunchtime.
††† El Zaguán, on C Carabobo (see above). Serves traditional regional cooking, expensive and difficult to find at night.
††† El Carite, C 78, No 8-35, T71878. Excellent selection of fish and seafood, delicious and moderately-priced.
††† Mi Vaquita, Av 3H con C 76. Texan steak house, popular with wealthy locals, party atmosphere and bar area for dancing, pricey drinks. No sandals allowed.
††† Pizzería Napoletana, C 77 near Av 4. Excellent food but poor service, closed Tue.

† Bambi, Av 4, 78-70. Italian run with good cappuccino, pastries, recommended.
† Chips, Av 31 opposite Centro Comercial Salto Angel. Regional fast food, *tequeños* and *patacones*. Recommended. There are many other good restaurants around the Plaza de la República, C77/5 de Julio and Av 31, in Bella Vista.
† Kabuki, C 77 entre Av 12 y 13. Nice café with good food.
† La Friulana, C 95 con Av 3. Good cheap meal, closes 1900. Repeatedly recommended.

● Festivals and events

Maracaibo *p1361*
Virgen del Rosario, **5 Oct**; **24 Oct**; **18 Nov**, NS de Chiquimquira (La Chinita), processions, bullfights – the main regional religious festival.

● Shopping

Maracaibo *p1361*
Bookshops Librería Cultural, Av 5 de Julio. Best Spanish language bookstore in town. Librería Italiana, Av 5 de Julio, Ed Centro América. Postcards and foreign publications. Staff at the public library, Av 2, are helpful to tourists.
Handicrafts and markets El Mercado de los Indios Guajiros, open market at C 96 y Av 2 (El Milagro). A few crafts, some pottery, hammocks, etc. Las Pulgas, south side of C 100 entre Av 10 y 14. The outdoor market, enormous, mostly clothes, shoes, and general household goods. Most of the shops on **C Carabobo** sell regional crafts, eg *La Salita*.

● Transport

Maracaibo *p1361*
Air La Chinita airport is 25 km southwest of city centre. Taxis charge US$15, there are no *por puestos*. Good bookshop in arrivals sells city map; *Italcambio* for exchange, 0600-1800 daily, no commission; car hire offices outside. Frequent flights with **Aserca, Aeropostal, Avior, Láser** and **Santa Bárbara** to **Caracas, Valencia, Mérida, Barquisimeto, San Antonio, Barcelona, Las Piedras** and **Porlamar.** International flights to **Aruba** (*Santa Bárbara*) and **Miami** (*American, Aeropostal*).

Bus The bus station is 15 mins walk from centre, 1 km south of the old town. Ask for buses into town, local services are confusing. There are several fast and comfortable buses daily to **Valencia**, US$13, 8 hrs. **San Cristóbal**, US$18.25-20, 6-8 hrs, *por puesto*, US$23. **Barquisimeto**, 5½ hrs, US$10. **Coro** US$8, 4 hrs. **Caracas**, US$19, 10-13 hrs, *por puesto* US$40. **Mérida**, US$10.65-15, 5-7 hrs, or *por puesto*, US$12, 6½ hrs; **Aeroexpresos Ejecutivos** 6 a day from Av 15 con C 90 (Distribuidor las Delicias), T783 0620.

Local *Por puestos* go up and down Av 4 from the old centre to Bella Vista. Ruta 6 goes up and down C 67 (Cecilia Acosta). The San Jacinto bus goes along Av 15 (Las Delicias). Buses from Las Delicias also go to the centre and terminal. From C 76 to the centre *por puestos* marked 'Las Veritas' and buses marked 'Ziruma'. Look for the name of the route on the roof, or on the front window, passenger's side. A ride from downtown to Av 5 de Julio in a 'Bella Vista' *por puesto* costs US$0.35. Taxis minumum US$3.50.

Border with Colombia *p1361*
Maracaibo-Maicao
Bus Busven direct at 0400. Other buses operate during the morning, US$15. Or take a colectivo taxi from Maracaibo bus terminal (5 passengers), US$15 pp; shop around, plus US$1.50 road toll, 2-3 hrs. Lots of police checks, typically 6, en route. There are reports that border police are on the look out for bribes, so make sure your documents are in order. Some drivers are unwilling to stop for formalities; make sure the driver takes you all the way to Maicao and arrive before the last bus to Santa Marta or Cartagena (1630).

⊙ Directory

Maracaibo *p1361*
Banks Banco Mercantil, on corner of Plaza de la República. Cash advance on Visa and MasterCard. Branches of **Banco de Venezuela**, including at airport, for Visa ATMs. Best for dollars and TCs is **Casa de Cambio de Maracaibo**, C 78 con Av 9B. **Italcambio**, C C Montielco, loc PA 1-1, entre Av 20 y C 72, T7832682, Amex rep. **Citibank**, Av 15 (Las Delicias) con C 77 (5 de Julio) for Citicorp TCs. All banks shut at 1530, exchange morning only. *Cambio* at bus terminal will change Colombian pesos into bolívares at a poor rate. **Consulates** France, Edif Colegio Bellas Artes, Av 3F y C70, T791 2921. **Germany**, C77 No 3C-24, Edif Los Cerros p 9, Urb 5 de Julio, T791 2406. **Italy**, Av 17 entre C 71 y 55, Quinta La Querencia, Sector Baralt, T783 0834. **Netherlands**, Av 3C y C67, La Lago, Uni Centro Virginia, office 6, p 2, T791 7592. **Norway**, Auto Agro Maracaibo, CA; Av 4 (Bella Vista) No 85-150, T722 0922. **Spain**, C 70 con Av 15 (Las Delicias), Edif Consulado de España, Núm 1, parte Alta, Diagonal Gran Hotel Delicias, T759 1232. **UK**, Inspecciones CA, Av 9B con C 77 (5 de Julio), Edif Banco Industrial, T797 7003, alexp@inspecciones.com. **USA**, Centro Venezolano Americano del Zulia, C 63, No 3E-60, T718 0842. **Internet** Cyber Estudio, Av 10 No 66-110, 1100-2300, US$3 per hr. **Medical services** Hospital Coromoto, Av 3C, No 51, El Lago, T790 0017. **Post offices** Av Libertador y Av 3. **Telephones** CANTV, C 96, No 3-42, just off the main plaza. Centre for internet US$1.70 per hr and international calls.

Barquisimeto and around

→ *Phone code: 0251. Colour map 1, grid A5. Population: 900,000. Altitude: 565 m. Mean temperature: 25° C*

The arid, fruit-growing area around the city of Barquisimeto leads to the lush Andean foothills of Trujillo state. Venezuela's fourth largest city was largely destroyed by an earthquake in 1812, but is a nice enough place to spend a few days when visiting the area. For information: **División de Turismo y Recreación** ⓘ *Av Libertador, Edif Fundalara p 2, T255 9321/6580, dirtur@ cantv.net (take a No 12 bus)*. See also www.barquisimeto.com.

Many fascinating corners have been preserved and a law prohibiting demolition of older buildings means that some are being restored. The **Museo de Barquisimeto** ⓘ *Av 15 between C 25 and 26, Tue-Fri 0900-1700, Sat-Sun 1000-1700, free*, displays the town's history, also contemporary art. More old buildings are a block away around **Plaza Jacinto Lara**. The **San Francisco church** faces the plaza. On the opposite side is the small **Ateneo cultural centre** ⓘ *Cra 17 y C 23, Mon-Fri 0830-1200, 1500-1830, Sat 0900-1200, free*, which has temporary exhibitions in an 18th-century house. It also has a restaurant and occasional evening concerts. The **Cathedral** ⓘ *C 30 y Cra 26 (Venezuela)*, is a modern structure of reinforced concrete and glass. At the heart of the old city is **Plaza Bolívar**, with a statue of the Liberator and the white-painted **Iglesia Concepción** on the south side. Also on the plaza, the **Palacio Municipal** ⓘ *Cra 17 y C 25*, is an attractive modern building. **Parque Ayacucho** ⓘ *Cra 15 (Av Francisco de Miranda) between C 41-43*, has lush vegetation, paths, fountains and a bronze statue of Mariscal Sucre.

About 24 km southwest of Barquisimeto is the busy agricultural centre of **Quíbor** (*Phone code 0253, Population 53,525*). Festivals on 18 January (NS de Altagracia) and 12 June (San Antonio de Padua). The **Centro Antropológico de Quíbor** exhibits work of the *indígenas* who used to live in the region. South of Quíbor and 40 minutes from Barquisimeto is **Sanaré** (1,360 m), on the edge of the **Parque Nacional Yacambú**, where you can hike through tropical forest up the Fumerola, a sleeping volcano. About 60 km east of Barquisimeto is **Chivacoa** (*Population 40,400*). South of the town is the sacred mountain of the María-Lionza cult, practised throughout Venezuela. Celebrations are held there at weekends with 12 October (Día de la Raza) being the most important day. There is a Catholic festival, La Inmaculada Concepción, from 8-14 December.

● Sleeping

Barquisimeto *p1363*

C **Príncipe**, Av 18 entre C 22 y C 23, T231-2344. Pool, restaurant.

D **Hevelin**, Av Vargas entre 20 y 21. Hot water, a/c.

E **La Casona**, Av 17 con C 27 near Plaza Bolívar, T231 5311. A/c, hot water, restaurant.

E **Lido**, Av 15 entre C26 y 27. Hot water, a/c or fan.

Sanaré *p1364*

E **Posada Turística El Cerrito**, T0253-449 0011, manager speaks English, small restaurant and bar, tours to local sights and Yacambú, highly recommended.

● Eating

Barquisimeto *p1363*

¶ **Barquipán**, C 26 entre Cras 17 y 18. Good breakfasts, snacks.

¶ **Majestic**, Av 19 con C 31. Breakfast and vegetarian meals.

¶ **Sabor Vegetariano**, on C 24 entre Av 20 y 21, next to *El Rincón Griego* restaurant. Snacks.

● Festivals and events

Barquisimeto *p1363*

On **28 Dec** (morning) is the fiesta of La Zaragoza, when colourfully clad people pass through the streets accompanied by music and dancing. Huge crowds are attracted to the procession of La Divina Pastora in early **Jan**,

when an image of the Virgin Mary is carried from the shrine at Santa Rosa village into the city.

● Transport

Barquisimeto *p1363*

Air Jacinto Lara international airport is 8 km southwest of the centre, 10 mins, US$5 by taxi. Local buses outside, US$0.25. Flights to **Caracas**, **Maracaibo**, **Mérida**, **San Antonio** and **Valencia**.

Bus Terminal is on the edge of the city at Carrera 25 y C 44: to **Mérida**, 3-4 a day, at 1020 and several between 2000 and 0200, 8 hrs via Agua Viva and El Vigía, US$16 *bus cama*; to **Acarigua** (see page 1379), 1 hr, US$3. To **Barinas**, 5 hrs, US$9. To **Valera** *por puesto*, 3½ hrs, US$8.75. To **Tucacas** every 2 hrs; to **Coro** at 1200 and by night, 7 hrs, US$13. To **Caracas**, US$14, 5½ hrs.

● Directory

Barquisimeto *p1363*

Banks Banco Provincial, Av 20 entre C 31 y 32 and C 23 entre Avs 18 y 19, for Visa and MasterCard. Banco de Venezuela, Av 20 y C 31, No 31-08 (and other branches), Visa ATMs. Capital Express, Av Los Leones, Centro Comercial Paseo, next to C 90. Changes US$ cash at low rates. Italcambio, Av Los Leones, C C París, loc 1-40, T254 9790, and at airport for Amex. **Car hire** Volkswagen best at Av Pedro León Torres y C 56, also at airport. **Post offices** Av 17 con C 25. **Telephones** C 30 entre Avs 24 y 25.

Valera to Mérida

From the lowland heat of Valera, roads climb towards the mountains, passing colonial towns and entering an increasingly rugged landscape.

Valera → *Phone code: 0271. Colour map 1, grid A5. Population: 130,000.*

This is the most important town in Trujillo state. Here, you can choose between two roads over the Sierra, either via Timotes and Mucuchíes to Mérida, or via Boconó and down to the Llanos at Guanare. There are several upmarket business hotels, few decent budget ones, and lots of good Italian restaurants on the main street.

Trujillo → *Phone code: 0272. Colour map 1, grid A5. Population: 44,460. Altitude: 805 m.*

From Valera a road runs via the restored colonial village of **La Plazuela** to the state capital, Trujillo. This beautiful historic town consists of two streets running uphill from the Plaza Bolívar. It's a friendly place with a warm, subtropical climate. The **Centro de Historia de Trujillo**, on Avenida Independencia, is a restored colonial house, now a museum. Bolívar lived there and signed the 'proclamation of war to the death' in the house. A 47m-high monument to the **Virgen de la Paz** ① *0900-1700, US$1*, with lift, was built in 1983; it stands at 1,608 m, 2½ hours walk from town and gives good views to Lake Maracaibo but go early. Jeeps leave when full from opposite *Hotel Trujillo*, 20 minutes, US$1.40 per person. For **tourist information**, Av Principal La Plazuela, No 1-03, T236 1455, presidenciactt@hotmail.com.

Boconó and Niquitao

From Trujillo there is a high, winding, spectacular paved road to the town built on steep mountain sides and famed for its crafts. The **Centro de Acopio Artesanal Tiscachic** is highly recommended for *artesanía* (turn left just before bridge at entrance to town and walk 350 m).

Niquitao, a small town one hour southwest of Boconó, is still relatively unspoilt. Excursions can be made to the Teta de Niquitao (4,007 m), two hours by jeep, the waterfalls and pools known as Las Pailas, and a nearby lake. Southwest of Niquitao, by partly-paved road is **Las Mesitas**; continue up towards **Tuñame**, turn left on a good gravel road (no signs), cross pass and descend to **Pueblo Llano** (one basic hotel and restaurant), from where you can climb to the Parque Nacional Sierra Nevada at 3,600 m, passing Santo Domingo. Good hiking in the area; Johnny Olivo at the video shop on Plaza Bolívar is a knowledgeable guide.

Road to the high Andes

After **Timotes** the road climbs through increasingly wild, barren and rugged country and through the windy pass of **Pico El Aguila** (4,118 m) in the Sierra de la Culata, best seen early morning, otherwise frequently in the clouds. This is the way Bolívar went when crossing the Andes to liberate Colombia, and on the peak is the statue of a condor. At the pass is the tourist restaurant *Páramo Aguila*, reasonably priced with open fire. People stop for a hot chocolate or a *calentado*, a herb liquor drunk hot. There are also food stalls, souvenir sellers and horses for hire (high season and weekends). Across from the monument is a small chapel with fine views. A paved road leads from here 2 km to a *CANTV* microwave tower (4,318 m). Here are tall *frailejones* plants; nearby are large storage sheds for vegetables from Piñango cooperatives. Continuing north as a lonely track the road goes to the **Piñango lakes** (45 km) and the traditional village of **Piñango** (2,480 m), 1½ hours. Great views for miles around. Eventually the raod reaches the Panamerican and Lago de Maracaibo.

Santo Domingo (*Phone code 0274, Population 6,000, Altitude 2,178 m*), with good handicraft shops and fishing, is on the spectacular road up from Barinas to Mérida, before the Parque Nacional Sierra Nevada. Festival: 30 September, San Gerónimo. The tourist office is on the right leaving town, 10 minutes from the centre.

⬤ Sleeping

Trujillo *p1365*
E **Los Gallegos**, Av Independencia 5-65, T/F236 3193. With hot water, a/c or fan, with or without TV. As well as several other places.

Boconó *p1365*
D **Estancia de Mosquey**, Mosquey, 10 km from Boconó towards Biscucuy, T/F0272-652 1555, 0414-725 0073 (mob). Family run, great views, good beds, good restaurant, pool, recommended. There are 3 other basic hotels in town.

Niquitao *p1365*
E **Na Delia**, T0271-885 2113, on a hill 500 m out of town, both have restaurants.

E **Posada Turística de Niquitao**, T0271-885 2042/0414-723 3925/0416-771 7860.

Road to the high Andes *p1365*
Timotes
D **Las Truchas**, north entrance to town, T/F0271-828 9158, www.andes.net/lastruchas.
E **Carambay**, Av Bolívar 41, T0271-828 9261.

Santo Domingo
A **La Trucha Azul**, east end of town, T898 8111, 0416-674 8431 (mob). Rooms with open fireplace, expensive for what it offers.

A **Los Frailes**, between Santo Domingo and Laguna Mucubají at 3,700 m. T0274-417 3440 or

book through **Hoturvensa**, T/F0212-976
0530/976 4984, hoturvensa@cantv.net, but pay
at hotel. Cheaper in low season, includes
breakfast. Beautiful former monastery, specialises
in honeymoon packages, rooms are quite simple,
international menu and wines.Includes breakfast.
A-B **Moruco**, T898 8155, F898 8225, out of town.
Beautiful, good value, food good, bar.
C **Paso Real**, on the other side of the river from
Los Frailes, no phone. A good place to stay.

❶ Eating

Niquitao *p1365*
♍-♍ **La Estancia**, Plaza Bolívar. Owner Golfredo
Pérez, helpful, kind, knows area well, pizzas.

❷ Transport

Valera *p1364*
Bus The bus terminal on the edge of town. To
Boconó, US$6, 3 hrs; to **Trujillo**, *por puestos*, 30
mins, US$1; to **Caracas**, 9 hrs, US$18 (direct at 2230
with **Expresos Mérida**); to **Mérida**, 4 daily with

Trans Barinas, US$7, 4½ hrs; *por puestos* to
Mérida, 3 hrs, US$10, leave when full; to
Maracaibo, micros every 30 mins until 1730,
4 hrs, US$8.

Road to the high Andes *p1365*
Santo Domingo
Bus Buses or *busetas* pass through in either
direction at around 2 hr intervals all day.
Mérida 2 hrs, US$4 *por puesto*; **Barinas**
1½ hrs, US$4.25.

❸ Directory

Valera *p1364*
Banks Corp Banca, Av Bolívar con C 5, changes
Amex TCs, no commission. Banco de Venezuela,
C 7 con Av 10, cash on Visa and MasterCard, very
efficient and helpful.

Trujillo *p1365*
Banks Banco Provincial, on main plaza, cash
on Visa and MasterCard. Banco de Venezuela,
1 block down from cathedral, has ATM.

Mérida and around

*Venezuela's high Andes offer hiking and mountaineering, and fishing in lakes and rivers.
The main tourist centre is Mérida (674 km from Caracas), but there are many interesting
rural villages. The Transandean Highway runs through the Sierra to the border with
Colombia, while the Pan-American Highway runs along the foot of the Andes through El
Vigía and La Fría to join the Transandean at San Cristóbal.*

*The Sierra Nevada de Mérida, running from south of Maracaibo to the Colombian
frontier, is the only range in Venezuela where snow lies permanently on the higher peaks.
Several basins lying between the mountains are actively cultivated; the inhabitants are
concentrated mainly in valleys and basins at between 800 m and 1,300 m above sea level.
The towns of Mérida and San Cristóbal are in this zone.*

Mérida → *Phone code: 0274. Colour map 1, grid A4. Population: 300,000. Altitude: 1,640 m.*

Mérida stands on an alluvial terrace – a kind of giant shelf – 15 km long, 2½ km wide, within
sight of Pico Bolívar, the highest in Venezuela. The mountain is part of the Five White Eagles
group, visible from the city. The summits are at times covered in snow, but the glaciers and
snow are retreating. Founded in 1558, the capital of Mérida State retains some colonial
buildings but is mainly known for its 33 parks and many statues. For tourists, its claims to
fame are the great opportunities for doing adventure sports and the buzz from a massive
student population.

The heart of Venezuelan mountaineering and trekking is the Andes, with Mérida as the base,
and there are several important peaks and some superb hikes. Bear in mind that high altitudes
will be reached and acclimatization is essential. Suitable equipment is necessary and you may
consider bringing your own. In the Sierra Nevada is mountain biking, whitewater rafting, parapenting and horse riding. See also the companies listed in Activities and tours, page 1370.

Ins and outs
Getting around Mérida may seem a safe place, but theft and robbery does occur. Avoid the
Pueblo Nuevo area by the river at the stairs leading down from Avenida 2, as well as Avenida 2

itself. The **airport** is on the main highway, 5 km from the centre. *Por puesto* into town US$0.25, taxi US$2.75. The **bus terminal** is 3 km from the centre of town on the west side of the valley, linked by a frequent minibus service to Calle 25 entre Avenidas 2 y 3, US$0.25. City bus fares rise by 50 cents at weekends. A trolley bus system from the southern suburb of Ejido to La Hechicera in the north should be completed in 2007.▸▸ *For further details, see Transport, page 1377.*

Information **Tourist offices** Corporación Merideña de Turismo, Avenida Urdaneta y C 45, next to the airport, T263 4701 or 0800-637 4300, cormeturpromocion@hotmail.com. Low season 0800-1200, 1400-1800, high season 0800-1800, closed Sunday. They supply a useful map of the state and town. Also at the airport in the waiting lounge, very informative, same low season hours, 0730-1330 in high season; in the bus terminal, same hours, have a map of the city (free). At Parque Las Heroínas, and at Jardín Acuario, Avenida Andrés Bello, low season 0800-1200, 1400-1800, high season 0830- 1830. A good website for information on Mérida is www.andes.net (Spanish), www.andesholidays.com (English). **Inparques** (National Parks) Av Las Américas, C 2, sector Fondur, T262 1356, http://sierranevada.andigena.org. Map of Parque Nacional Sierra Nevada (mediocre) US$1; also, and easier, at Teleférico for permits.

Sights

In the city centre are **Plaza Bolívar**, on which stands the **cathedral**, dark and heavy inside, with **Museo Arquidiocesano** beside it, and **Plaza de Milla**, or **Sucre** ① *C 14 entre Avs 2 y 3*, always a hive of activity. The **Parque de las Cinco Repúblicas** ① *C 13, entre Avs 4 y 5, beside the barracks*, is renowned for having the first monument in the world to Bolívar (1842, replaced in 1988) and contains soil from each of the five countries he liberated (photography strictly prohibited). Three of the peaks known as the Five White Eagles (Bolívar, 5,007 m, La Silla del Toro, 4,755 m, and León 4,740 m) can be clearly seen from here. **Plaza Las Heroínas**, by the lowest station of the *teleférico* (see below) is busy till 2300, an outdoor party zone. Most tour operators have their offices here.

Less central parks include **Parque La Isla** ① *Prol Av Los Próceres*, which contains orchids, basketball and tennis courts, an amphitheatre and fountains. In the **Plaza Beethoven** ① *Santa María Norte*, a different melody from Beethoven's works is chimed every hour; *por puestos/busetas*, run along Avenida 5, marked 'Santa María' or 'Chorro de Milla', US$0.25. The **Jardín Botánico** ① *on the way to La Hechicera, open daily*, has the largest collection of bromeliads in South America; also a canopy walkway. The **Jardín Acuario**, beside the aquarium ① *high season daily 0800-1800, low season closed Mon, US$0.25; (busetas leave from Av 4 y C 25, US$0.25, passing airport)*, is an exhibition centre, mainly devoted to the way of life and the crafts of the Andean *campesinos*.

Mérida has several museums: **Museo de Arte Colonial** ① *Av 4, Casa 20-8, T252 7860, fundacolonial@latinmail.com, Tue-Fri 0900-1600, Sat-Sun 1400-1700 (1000-1700 high season)*, US$0.50. More interesting is the small **Museo Arqueológico** ① *Av 3, Edif del Rectorado de la Universidad de los Andes, just off Plaza Bolívar, T240 2344, museogrg@ula.ve, Tue-Sat 0800-1200, 1400-1800, Sun 1400-1800, US$0.50* with pre-Columbian exhibits from the Andes. **Museo de Arte Moderno** ① *Av 2 y C 21, Mon-Fri 0800-1600, Sat-Sun 0800-1300, free*, is in the Centro Cultural Don Tulio Febres Cordero; check here for cultural events. Roger Manrique has an impressive butterfly collection (over 10,000), also knowledgeable about Andean wildlife, contact **Arassari Trek**, see Tour operators, page 1370.

◉ Sleeping

Mérida *p1366, map p1368*
Book ahead in school holidays and Feria del Sol.
C **El Tisure**, Av 4 entre C 17 y 18, T252 6061. Modern, colonial-style, very pleasant, disco.
C **Encanto Andino**, C 24 No 6-53, entre Avs 6 y 7, T252 6929. D without bath, 5 rooms, easy going, kitchen with fridge and microwave, no breakfast.

C **La Montaña**, C 24 No 6-47 entre Av 6 y 7, T252 5977, www.posadalamontana.com. Hot water, TV, safe, fan, fridge, luggage store. Leafy corridor, very helpful, English spoken, excellent restaurant.
C **Mintoy**, C 25 (Ayacucho), No 8-130, T252 0340. 10% discount for cash, comfortably furnished, breakfast, good value, parking, suites with separate sitting area (sleeps 5).

● *For an explanation of the sleeping and eating price codes used in this guide, see page 58. Other*
● *relevant information is found in Essentials pages 1332-1333.*

C Posada Casa Sol, Av 4 entre C15 y C16, T252 4164, www.posadacasasol.com. Renovated colonial-era house with lovely rooms in distinctive, tasteful style, modern art on walls, hot water, garden, free internet, large breakfast US$6.35, very helpful, English, German and Italian spoken, limited parking. Highly recommended.
C Posada Doña Pumpa, Av 5 y C 14, T/F252 7286, www.donapumpa.com. Good showers, spacious rooms, cable TV, quiet, very comfortable, English-speaking owner, no breakfast, parking.
C Posada Luz Caraballo, Av 2 No 13-80, on Plaza de Milla, T252 5441, www.andes.net/luz

caraballo. Colonial-style old building, hot water, TV, excellent cheap restaurant, good bar, parking.
D Apart Hotel Central, Av 3, No 16-11, T252 7629, aparthotelcentral@hotmail.com. Good apartments for up to 12, TV, kitchen and parking.
D El Escalador, C 23 entre Avs 7 y 8, T252 2411, www.elescalador.com. Doubles or rooms with bed and bunks, hot water, TV, tourist information and tours, parapenting arranged, no breakfast.
D Los Bucares de Mérida, Av 4 No 15-5, T/F252 2841, www.losbucares.com. Cheaper in noisier rooms at front, hot showers, TV, family rooms **C**, nice patio with occasional live music, garage, safe, breakfast extra in *cafetín*.

Mérida

Sleeping
Apart Hotel Central 1 B5
El Escalador 21 C2
El Tisure 3 B5
Encanto Andino 4 C2
Italia 5 A4
Los Bucares de Mérida 9 B6
Luxemburgo 10 C2
Mintoy 11 D2
Montecarlo 12 C2
Mundo Mérida 15 D2

Nevada Palace 7 B2
Posada Alemania 16 A5
Posada Casa
  Alemana-Suiza 2 A1
Posada Casa Sol 17 B5
Posada Doña Pumpa 18 B6
Posada Familiar Mara 19 D2
Posada Guamanchi &
  Guamanchi Tours 22 D2
Posada Luz Caraballo 20 A6

Eating
Bimbo 13 B2
Buona Pizza 8 C2
Buona Pizza Express 21 C2
Café Atico 1 D2
Cheo's Pizzería 3 D2
Chipen 4 B2
El Museo 5 A6
El Sabor de los Quesos 6 A6
El Sano Glotón 7 B4
Espresso 22 B2

D **Luxemburgo**, C 24, between Avs 6-7, T252
6865, www.hotelluxemburgo.empate.com. Cold
water, safe, in same group as C **Nevada Palace**,
C 24, No 5-45, www.nevadapalace.andes.net,
with restaurant, modern, with **Palace Cyber**.
D **Montecarlo**, Av 7 entre C 24 y C 25, T252 5981,
F252 5910. Safe, parking, hot water, restaurant, ask
for a back room with mountain view.
D **Posada Casa Alemana-Suiza**, El Encanto, Av
2 No 38-120, T263 6503, info@casa-alemana.com.
Very nice, airport pick-up, parking, discount for
long stays, laundry, English and German spoken.
Also runs good tours and activities as **Carnaval
Tours**, T263 6503.

D **Posada Guamanchi**, C 24, No 8-86, T/F252
2080, www.guamanchi.com. Owned by tour
operator of same name, if on a tour you are
guaranteed a room. Rooms of varying size, some
with bath, some with good view, 2 kitchens, cable
TV room, terrace with hammocks, good, no parking.
D-E **Posada Alemania**, Av 2 entre C 17 y 18, No
17-76, T/F252 4067, www.colibri-tours.com.
E without bath, quiet, family atmosphere, leafy
patio, busy, breakfast US$4.55, laundry US$4.55,
kitchen, book exchange, tourist information,
English and German spoken, German owner.
Adventure tours with **Colibrí Tours**.
E **Italia**, C 19 entre Av 2 y 3, T252 5737. Hot
water, **F** in smaller rooms without bath, laundry
facilities, post box, **Ayary Tours** travel agency,
speak English, German and French, changes
dollars, Spanish lessons.
E **Mundo Mérida**, C 24 y Av 8, on Plaza las
Heroínas, T252 6844, jorgemda@hotmail.com.
Hot water, shared bath, opposite *Guamanchi
Tours*, luggage store, laundry, good.
E **Posada Familiar Mara**, C 24 No 8-215, T252
5507. Pleasant, hot water, luggage store, no TV,
no breakfast.

🍴 Eating

Mérida *p1366*
Many places offer student set lunches for US$1-1.50.
🍴🍴 **La Abadía**, Av 3 entre C 17 y 18, T251 0933,
www.grupoabadia.com. Excellent, varied menu,
including vegetarian, 30 mins free internet time
with each meal. Has other outlets including **La
Abadía del Angel**, C 21 entre Avs 5 y 6, café and
restaurant, with internet.
🍴🍴 **Chipen**, Av 5, No 23-67. Good meat.
🍴🍴 **El Museo**, Av 2, C12-13. Nice patio, lots of
graffiti, good food, pleasant place for a drink.
🍴🍴-🍴 **La Astilla**, C 14, No 2-20, Plaza de Milla.
Plants, nostalgic music, bar, varied menu
including pizza, frequented by locals and groups.
🍴🍴-🍴 **La Mamma**, Av 3 and C 19. Good pizza,
pasta, set lunches and salad bar, popular in the
evening, live music at weekends, local wine.
🍴 **Bimbo**, C 23, No 4-48. Clean, popular for lunch.
🍴 **Buona Pizza**, Av 7 entre C 24 y 25, T252 7639,
with Express branch opposite and 2 other
branches, open 1200-2300 daily, very good pizza.
🍴 **Café Atico**, C 25 near Plaza Las Heroínas.
Excellent lunch for US$4. Recommended.
🍴 **Cheo's Pizzería**, 3 separate restaurants on
Plaza Las Heroínas, one serves pizzas, another
chicken and meat, the third trout. Also has a
hotel on Plaza Las Heroínas.
🍴 **El Sabor de los Quesos**, on Plaza de Milla. Very
good and cheap pizzería, very busy, painted
green and white.
🍴 **El Tinajero**, C 29/Av 4. Clean, simple place.

Federico's **14** *D2*
El Tinajero **15** *B1*
Heladería Coromoto **9** *B1*
La Abadía **10** *B5*
La Abadía del Angel **23** *B3*
La Astilla **24** *A6*
La Esquina de
  Pajarito **11** *C2*
La Mamma **12** *B4*
T-Café **2** *B1*
Zanzibar **25** *B4*

Bars & clubs 🍸
Alfredo's **26** *B4*
Birosco Carioca **16** *A2*
Clover **17** *B6*
El Hoyo del
  Queque **18** *B4*
Kontiki **20** *A4*

Federico's, Pasaje Ayacucho No 25-24.
Vegetarian and pizza.
La Esquina de Pajarito, C 25 esquina Av 6.
Simple but good local food, cheap set lunch.
La Montaña, C 24 between Av 6 and 7 (next to *posada*). Good, cheap food, pleasant setting.
El Sano Glotón, Av 4 y C 18. Vegetarian.
Recommended. Next door but one is a great snack bar with excellent *empanadas*.
Zanzibar, Av 4 entre C 19 y 20. Very good value lunches under US$2, German chef.

Cafés
Espresso Café Cyber & Galería, Av 4, No 23-54, upstairs No 2A. With art gallery, good computers and TV, coffee and cakes.
Heladería La Coromoto, Av 3 y C 29, T523525, Tue-Sun 1415-2100, offers 750 flavours of ice cream, at least 60 choices daily, eg trout, avocado!
Reina de los Andes, Av 5 entre C 21 y 22. For arepas, juices and coffee.
T-Café, diagonally opposite **Heladería La Coromoto**. Homemade food, good lunches, juices, coffee and cakes.

🎵 Bars and clubs

Mérida *p1366, map1368*
There is no cover charge for nightclubs but always take your passport or a copy.
Alfredo's, C 19 y Av 4. Bar, popular, also vegetarian café (lunch US$1) and internet 0900-2300.
Birosca Carioca, Av 2 y C 24. Popular, with live music, take care outside.
Café Calypso, C 26, in Centro Comercial El Viaducto. Pop/rock music, a bit more pricey.
The Clover, Av 4 entre C 14 y 15. Irish bar with live music at weekends.
El Hoyo del Queque, across the road from *Alfredo's*. Usually packed, good meeting place.
Kontiki, Av 3 y C 19. Mérida's oldest club.

✳ Festivals and events

Mérida *p1366, map1368*
For 2 weeks leading up to Christmas there are daily song contests between local students on Plaza Bolívar, 1700-2200. **Feria del Sol**, held on the week preceding Ash Wednesday. This is also the peak bullfighting season. **1-2 Jan**, Paradura del Niño; **15 May**, San Isidro Labrador, a popular festival nationwide, but especially in Mérida.

🛒 Shopping

Mérida *p1366, map1368*
Bookshops Temas, Av 3, entre C31 y 32, No 31-24, T252 6068. Very good, amazing stock but hard to find things.

Camping shops 5007, Av 5 entre C 19 y 20, CC Mediterráneo, T252 6806. Recommended.
Cumbre Azul, C 24 opposite Plaza Las Heroínas, T416 3231, cumbreazul@hotmail.com. Rents and sells mountaineering equipment (also sells some fishing tackle). **Eco Bike**, Av 7 No 16-34. For mountain bikes and equipment. Many tour operators rent equipment.
Handicrafts Handicraft market on La Plaza de Las Heroínas, opposite *teleférico*. Mercado Principal on Av las Américas (buses for bus station pass by), has many small shops, top floor restaurant has regional *comida típica*, bargaining possible.

⛰ Activities and tours

Mérida *p1366, map1368*
Parapenting All agencies offer jumps. Conditions in Mérida are suitable for flying almost all year round. It takes on average 50 mins to get to a launch site and tandem jumps last 25 mins. There are 7 main sites. Price US$60. Can take own equipment and hire a guide. An experienced pilot is Oswaldo, T0414-717 5953.
Xtreme Adventours, Av 8, C24, Plaza Las Heroínas, T252 7241, www.xatours.com. Specializes in parapenting (latest equipment, safety) and many other adventure options, plus tours in the region. Also offers tours from Mérida to Canaima, Margarita and Los Roques.

Tour operators
Arassari Trek, C 24 No 8-301 (beside the teleférico), T/F252 5879, www.arassari.com. Run by Tom and Raquel Evenou, and Angel Barreto, English, French and German spoken, good tours with great guides at fair prices, very helpful and hospitable, highly recommended for trekking and climbing in the Sierra Nevada, horse riding, mountain biking, canyoning, caving, parapenting, rafting and canoeing. They also have a book exchange and cybercafé with excellent food. Their Llanos tour (US$130-140 for 4 days) is excellent with many different activities, have their own, superb purpose-built camp. English-speaking guide Alan Highton is highly recommended for the tours of the Llanos and the Río Catatumbo.
Fanny Tours, C 24, No 8-30, T252 2952, 0414-747 1349 (mob), www.fanny-tours.com. Patrizia Rossi, José Albarrán for parapenting (the first to do it), reliable. Apart from parapenting, specializes in mountain biking, US$30 half-day pp for 2, US$40 whole day without jeep support, US$58 with jeep, all inclusive; bike hire US$16. Also rafting US$140 pp for 4; Llanos, Catatumbo, canyoning, trekking to mountains and some climbing; also tours combining all types of sport; book and money exchange. Recommended.

Gravity Tours, C 24 entre Av 7 y 8, 1 block from cable car, T251 1279, 0414-737 7541 (mob), www.gravity-tours.com. Bilingual guides, natural history and adventure tours, some extreme, including rock climbing, rafting, biking, Llanos trips and Gran Sabana.

Guamanchi Tours, C 24, No 8-86, T/F252 2080, www.guamanchi.com. Owned by John and Joëlle Peña, with Volker on the team. German, French, Italian and English spoken, recommended for hiking, paragliding, horse riding, biking, birdwatching, equipment hire, exchange, information, mountain climbing, also tours to Llanos, Amazonia and Angel Falls, email service for customers, new 4WD jeeps, have a posada in town (see above) and another at Los Nevados (see below). Recommended.

Natoura Travel and Adventure Tours, C 24 No 8-237, near the teleférico, T252 4216, (in US 303-800 4639), www.natoura.com. Open daily 0830-1900, friendly company organizing tours throughout Venezuela, run by José Luis Troconis and Renate Reiners, English, French, German and Italian spoken, climbing, trekking, rafting, horse riding, mountain biking, birdwatching and equipment hire. Their self-drive option allows you to rent a car and they will reserve accommodation for your route. Repeatedly recommended.

Drivers Lucio (T252 8416) and Nicolás Savedra (T271 2618) and Juan Medina, *Yagrumo*, C 24, mostalla@hotmail.com.

❺ Transport

Mérida *p1366, map1368*

Air You can save a lot of time by checking in the day before flight. Daily flights to **Caracas** (1½ hrs direct), with **Santa Bárbara** (T263 2723); also to **Maracaibo, Barquisimeto, San Antonio** and **Valencia**. In the rainy season, especially on afternoon flights, planes may be diverted to San Antonio (3-5 hrs by road), or El Vigía (2½ hrs away). Airport tax US$6.35. *Casa de cambio* (see Banks below), various ATMs, shops, phones and a smart restaurant.

Bus The terminal has two levels, the upper one for small buses, minivans and cars to nearby destinations, the lower for interstate buses. Taxis line up outside the main entrance. A small exit tax of US$0.25 is charged for journeys in the the state, US$0.45 for long-distance, payable at one of two kiosks leading to buses. Make sure you pay, officials check buses before departure. On interstate buses, it is essential to book in advance; for buses within the state you pay on board. The terminal has a tourist office, phones, toilets, luggage store and places to eat. Fares: **Caracas**, US$15 (*normal*) to US$23.85 (*bus-cama*); **Maracay**, US$13.65-22; **Valencia**,

US$12.75-21.15; **Coro**, US$11.35-22; **Maracaibo**, US$10.75-16; **Barquisimeto**, US$16; **Puerto La Cruz**, US$33.75, **Cumaná**, US$37.25.

Bus companies: Expresos Occidente, T263 5844, daily direct to **Caracas**, 12 hrs, or via Valencia and Maracay; to **Coro/ Punto Fijo**, 12-14 hrs. Expresos San Cristóbal (T263 1881), daily direct to Caracas, 14 hrs, or via Valencia and Maracay; to **Maracaibo**, 8 hrs. Expresos Mérida (T263 3430), to Caracas hourly from 1800, some direct others via Valencia and Maracay; also to **Barquisimeto**, 8 hrs, **Maracaibo**, **Coro** and **Punto Fijo**. Transportes Barinas (T263 4651), to **Barinas** (US$5.75) via **Apartaderos** (US$2.60), to **Guanare** (US$7) and **Valera** (US$7). Expresos Los Llanos (T265 5927, www.expresoslosllanosca .com.ve), to Caracas at 1900. Expresos Coromoto, T417 1722, to **Maracaibo** 0845, 1345. From upper level of terminal: Táchira Mérida, to **San Cristóbal** (US$9, 6 hrs) and **San Antonio**. Also to Jaji, Chiguará, Apartaderos, Barinas (US$7.50, 4 hrs), El Vigía, Valera (US$10). **Líneas Unidas**, T263 8472, *por puesto* microbus with TV, and car, to **Maracaibo**, 1000, 2130; also **Fraternidad del Transporte**, T263 1187, 1000, 1400, 2145.

Taxi In town US$2.50-4.

❶ Directory

Mérida *p1366, map1368*

Banks Banco Mercantil, Av 5 y C 18. ATM takes Cirrus (commission lower than Visa). **Banco Provincial**, Av 4 y C 25, and **Banco de Venezuela**, Av 4 entre C 23 y 24, both ATM and cash advance on Visa and Mastercard at official rate. *Italcambio* at airport; this is often the easiest place to change cash and TCs. **Car hire** Several companies at the airport, including **Alquil Auto**, T263 1440, or **Dávila Tours**, Av Los Próceres opposite Urb la Trinidad, T266 0711, or airport T263 4510. **Consulates** Colombia, Av Andrés Bello, CC San Antonio, T266 2646, consulbia merida@yahoo.com, open 0800-1400. Visas take 10 min. **UK**, Professor Robert Kirby, honorary vice-Consul, Finca La Trinitaria, Santa Rosa, 10 mins from the town centre towards La Hechicera, T416 8496. **Internet** Places all over town, most with broadband, US$0.40-0.80 per hr. See *La Abadía* and *Arassari Trek* above. **CANTV Centro de Comunicaciones**, Av 7 entre C 25 y 26. Also at Av 6 y C 21, open Sun, has internet next to *Ipostel*. **Language schools** Iowa Institute, Av 4 y C 18, T252 6404, cathy@iowainstitute.com. Run by Cathy Jensen de Sánchez, competitive prices, fully qualified teachers, homestays arranged. Recommended. **Latinoamericano de Idiomas**, CC Mamayeya, p 4, of C-5-38, T/F244 7808. Contact Marinés Asprino, Conjunto Residencial Andrés Bello, Torre C, p 5, Apt 6-1,

T271 1209 for private lessons and cheap accommodation. Recommended. **Carolina Tenías**, 17 years' experience in private lessons for travellers, grammar and conversation, T252 4875, or 0416-971 1445 (mob). **Medical services** Doctors: **Dr Aldo Olivieri**, Av Principal La Llanita, La Otra Banda, Centro Profesional El Buho, 09, T244 0805, 0414-374 0356, aldrolia250@cantv.net, very good, gastroenterologist, speaks English and Italian. **Dr Giotto Guillén Echeverria**, Centro Médico La Trinidad, C 42 entre Avs Urdaneta y Gonzalo Picón, T263 9685, 0416-674 0707. Specialist in infections, speaks French. **Post offices** Ipostel, C 21 entre Avs 4 y 5, 0800-1900 daily. Post office also in bus terminal, 0800-1200, 1400-1700, weekdays only. **Telephones** CANTV, C 21 y Av 5, Mon-Sat 0800-1930.

Useful addresses Immigration office: ONIDEX, Av 4 y C 16, Mon-Thu 0800-1200, 1300-1630, Fri 0800-1500. Tourist police: The CICPC will provide a *constancia* reporting the crime and listing the losses. Their office is on Av Las Américas, at Viaducto Miranda, T262 0343. Open daily but they won't issue a *constancia* on Sun. To get there, take any bus marked 'Terminal Sur' or 'Mercado' leaving from C 25. You can also get a *constancia* from the *Prefectura Civil del Municipio Libertador*, but it can take all day and is only valid for a limited period of time; at Av 4 No 21-69, just off Plaza Bolívar; opening hours variable. The tourist offices are probably a better bet than the police if you need to register a theft for insurance purposes.

Sierra Nevada de Mérida

The Sierra is a mixture of the wild and isolated and the very touristy. In the latter group fall the cable car up Pico Espejo and villages designed to lure the shopper, but it is not difficult to escape the tour groups. There are routes from the mountains to the Llanos and to Colombia.

Parque Nacional Sierra Nevada (South)

Close to Mérida is the popular hiking area around Los Nevados, with the added attraction of the highest cable car in the world (if it's running). The further you go from Mérida, the greater the off-the-beaten-track possibilities for hiking and exploration that arise.

Since this is a national park, you need a permit from the *Inparques* (National Parks) offices in Mérida (see Ins and outs) to hike and camp overnight. Permits are not given to single hikers (except to Los Nevados), a minimum of two people is needed. Have your passport ready. Return permit after your hike; park guards will radio the start of trek to say you've reached the end. If camping, remember that the area is 3,500-4,200 m so acclimatization is necessary. Night temperatures can fall below freezing so a -12°C sleeping bag is necessary, plus good waterproofs. Conditions are much more severe than you'd think after balmy Mérida. Don't leave litter. Some treks are very difficult so check with the tourist office before leaving. Water purification is also recommended. See Mérida Tour operators and Parque Nacional Sierra Nevada (North) page 1373.

Pico Espejo The world's highest and longest aerial cableway (built by the French in 1957-60) runs to Pico Espejo (4,765 m) in four stages ① *T252 5080/1997, www.telefericode merida.com, 0700-1300 in high season, 0800-1130 low season, no service Mon and Tue, tickets, US$25, children US$17.25, senior citizens US$15, backpacks US$2.75. Buy in advance to avoid queues in high season; show passport when buying ticket; can pay by credit card. The ascent takes 1 hr.* When operating, its final station is at Pico Espejo, with a change of car at every station, all of which have cafés, toilets and advice. Beware altitude sickness: there is oxygen and a nursing station at higher points. The cars on each section are a different colour; each stage has recorded commentary. Barinas is the ground level station, Plaza de las Heroínas; you can hire, or buy, hats, gloves and scarves here, the Venezuelans all do. La Montaña (2,442 m) is the second station with a small Museo del Montañismo. You pass over various levels of forest. Next is La Aguada (3,452 m), then Loma Redonda (4,045 m). From here you can start the trek to Los Nevados (see below); you must inform Inparques if trekking to Los Nevados. Mules for hire US$7, and *arrieros* US$7, wait at Loma Redonda. You pause for 10 minutes at Loma Redonda before the final stage to Pico Espejo (US$6 if only taking this stage), where there is a statue of Nuestra Señora de las Nieves. Next door, so to speak, is Pico Bolívar (Mucumbari, where the sun sleeps) with Humboldt behind. It has remnants of a glacier. In the other direction, closest is La Silla del Toro and you can see a statue of Francisco Miranda with the Venezuelan flag on an outcrop. On a clear day you can see the blue haze of the Llanos to the east and west, as far as Sierra de Cocuy and Guicán in Colombia. Across Río Chama you can see Sierra de la Culata. It is recommended that you spend only 30 minutes at Pico Espejo. Apart from trek to Los Nevados, the only safe part to walk down is Loma Redonda to La Aguada; a rough but clear trail, two hours; wear boots, walk slowly, not for children or the elderly, take water.

Los Nevados From Los Nevados (*Altitude 2,711 m*), it is a very testing two-day trek to **Pico Espejo**, with a strong possibility of altitude sickness as the ascent is more than 1,600 m. It is best done November-June early in the morning (before 0830 ideally), before the clouds spoil the view. In summer the summit is clouded and covered with snow and there is no view. **Do not attempt Pico Espejo alone; go with a guide, it is easy to get lost**. Reputable trekking companies provide suitable clothing; temperatures can be 0° C. August is the coldest month.

From Los Nevados to **Loma Redonda** takes five to seven hours, four hours with mules (14 km). The hike is not too difficult; breathtaking views; be prepared for cold rain in the afternoon, start very early. The walk from Los Nevados to the village of **El Morro** (24 km) takes seven to nine hours (very steep in parts). (It's 47 km to Mérida; jeeps do the trip daily.) Sr Oviller Ruiz provides information on the history of the church and indigenous cemetery.

It is possible to hike from Pico Espejo to the cloud forest at La Mucuy (see page below), two to three days walking at over 4,000 m altitude, passing spectacular snow peaks and Lagos Verde and Coromoto. A tent and a warm sleeping bag are essential, as is a good map (local guides may lend theirs to photocopy). If you start at Pico Espejo you will be at the highest point first, so although you will be descending, you may have altitude sickness from the word go.

Parque Nacional Sierra Nevada (North) and Sierra de La Culata

The Transandean highway snakes its way through the rugged mountain landscape, past neat, little towns of red-tiled roofs, steep fields and terraces of maize and potatoes. The snow-tipped peaks of the high sierras watch over this bucolic scene, with Pico Bolívar lording it over them all. Throughout the park you will see a plant with felt-like leaves of pale grey-green, the *frailejón* (or great friar, *espeletia*), which blooms with yellow flowers from September to December. There are more than 130 species; tall ones grow at less than 1 cm a year.

Tabay The Plaza Bolívar in Tabay (10 km from Mérida, 30 minutes) is very nice, with its church, trees and plants. Around it are two minimercados, telecommunications, **Pizzería Valentina** (best in town), **Pastelitos** (at bus stop from Mérida, for empanadas etc in morning), all other transport stops, and other services. Jeeps run a regular service to **La Mucuy** cloud forest, 0600-2200, they are labelled (US$0.45 one way if five passengers, or US$2.25 for the whole vehicle). They drop you at the Guardaparques. There is nothing to pay for a day visit, but you pay per night if making the Travesía to Pico Espejo and the Teleférico down to Mérida. The distances on the park signs to Lagos Coromoto and Verde would appear to be very ambitious (eg Coromoto is not 3 hours, but an overnight trip if not continuing). When going back to Tabay, you may have to wait for a jeep; the driver will charge extra for backpacks. Jeeps also go to the **Aguas Termales** (from a different stop, just off Plaza Bolívar, US$0.70). It is possible to walk and there are signs. The water is 38°C, the pool man-made. Another excursion is to go horse riding at **Mano Poderosa** (see Sleeping, below). All Mérida agencies go here. It's also nice for walking.

Beyond Tabay the road goes through **Mucurubá** (2,400m) with a pleasant Plaza Bolívar and blue and white church, colonial buildings, handicrafts and Hospedaje Mococón, and passes the **Monumento al Perro Nevado**. It depicts Simón Bolívar, the Indian boy, Tinjaca, the Mucuchíes dog, Snowy, and the father and son who gave Bolívar the dog in 1813. According to legend, both Tinjaca and Nevado were devoted to Bolívar until their death on the same day at the Battle of Carabobo, 1821. At Mucuchíes (*Phone code: 0274, Population: 9,175, Altitude: 2,983 m*) the statue of the Liberator on Plaza Bolívar also features Tinjaca and Snowy. Also on the Plaza is a wooden statue of San Isidro, patron saint of farmers; all rural communities honour him on 15 May. The patron saint of Mucuchíes is San Benito; this festival (and several others) on 27-30 December is celebrated by participants wearing flower-decorated hats and firing blunderbusses. Tourist office on C 9 as you enter from Mérida, internet at C 9 Independencia.

The road leads up from Mucuchíes to **San Rafael de Mucuchíes** (*Altitude: 3,140 m. Fiesta 24 October*). You should visit the remarkable church, pieced together from thousands of stones, by the late Juan Félix Sánchez (born 1900), nationally renowned as a sculptor, philosopher and clown. The chapel is dedicated to the Virgen de Coromoto; it was blessed by Pope John Paul II. The tombs of Sánchez and is companion of 50 years, Epifania Gil, are inside. Next door is his house, now a museum with photos, weavings, sculptures (not always open). Opposite is the library given by him to the community. He built a similar chapel at El Tisure. The picturesque road continues to Apartaderos, two hours from Mérida. It follows the Río Chama valley in the heart of the cultivated highlands and the fields extend up to the edge of the *páramo*, clinging to the steepest slopes. Main crops are potatoes (4 harvests a year) onions, garlic and carrots. East of the Río Chama is the Sierra Nevada; to the west is the Sierra de La Culata. Handicrafts are on sale and there are cabins, *posadas* and eateries

Apartaderos (*Phone code 0274, Altitude 3,342 m*) is at the junction of Route 7 and the road over the Sierra Nevada to Barinas. About 3 km above Apartaderos, a narrow paved road (signposted) turns west off the highway at 'Escuela Estatal 121' and winds its way to **Llano del Hato** (3,510 m) and on to the four-domed **Centro de Investigaciones de Astronomía** (3,600 m) ① *the 4 telescopes and modern facilities are open Sat 1500-1900, during Carnaval, Semana Santa, August and year-end holidays, school holidays and some bank holidays at variable times (check website for details), US$3.65 for adults, US$2.25 under-18s, senior citizens free, www.cida.ve*. At least two viewing points on the way in give great views of the Lake Mucubají plateau. A good paved road descends 7 km from Llano del Hato to the Mérida highway at La Toma, just above Mucuchíes. Many prehispanic terraces and irrigation systems, adobe houses and ox-ploughed fields (*poyos*) are visible from the road.

Three kilometres beyond the junction of the roads from Barinas and Valera is the entrance to the **Parque Nacional Sierra Nevada** (*Línea Cultura* bus from Mérida ends at the junction, 2 hours; taxis run from bus stop to Park, US$2.25). At the turn-off to the park is a motel, restaurant (good coffee and *arepas*). Near the entrance is **Laguna Mucubají**, at 3,600 m, with free campsite (don't leave belongings unattended); visitors' centre, bookshop, good maps, interesting museum. A 2-2½-hour walk takes you to Laguna Negra and back (1½ hours on horseback, US$4.55-5.45 to hire a horse, guide US$4.55). A further 1½-hour walk from Laguna Negra is the beautiful Laguna Los Patos. There are many *frailejón* plants here. Guides (not always necessary) are at Laguna Mucubají or the hotels in Santo Domingo. *Páramo* tours to this area usually include Pico El Aguila (see Road to the high Andes section, page 1365).

From Mérida to the Panamericana

There are three routes from Mérida to the Panamericana which runs at the foot of the Andes near the border with Zulia state. The most northerly of them is the most interesting. This beautiful journey, starting in the highlands from Mérida, heads west. It passes La Chorrera waterfall on the way to La Encrucijada (restaurant and Trébol service station), where a side road leads to **Jají** (*Phone code: 0274*), a pretty colonial village with cobbled streets and arches on the exits to the plaza with its white and blue church. Most houses are given over to handicrafts shops. There are a few hotels and others in the hills, where there is good walking. *Buseta* from Mérida bus terminal, hourly, 50 minutes, US$1. From La Encrujidada the road passes dairy farms before its descent through cloud forest. Towns passed on the way are San Eusebio and Mirabel. This is prime birdwatching territory as the road, paved but rough in parts, twists down through several habitats. **La Azulita**, 73 km, 4 hours from Mérida, is the base for birdwatching tours, with several lodges nearby. A modern cathedral stands on the Plaza and, overall, it's a modern town. From La Azulita, the road meets the Panamericana at Caño Zancudo, passing en route the Cascada Palmita. Turn south for El Vigía, one of the hottest zones in South America, and routes to Lago de Maracaibo and Catatumbo.

El Vigía is where the second route from Mérida meets the Panamericana. Transandean Route 7 leaves Mérida and passes through the Chama valley, heading for Lagunillas and Tovar. Near Estanques, the main highway for bus and heavy traffic turns off Route 7. It descends from the grey, scarred mountains to go through two major tunnels before the thickly-wooded tropical hillsides above the plains. Buses between Mérida and San Crístobal then belt along the Panamericana to La Fría. The third route leaves the Transandean road at **Tovar** (*Phone code 0275, 96 km from Mérida*), passing through Zea, a pleasant town in the foothills.

From Mérida to Táchira

From Tovar the road continues to **Bailadores** (fiesta from Christmas to Candlemas, 2 February, bus US$1.25), and **La Grita**, a pleasant town in Táchira state (Sunday market, fiesta 6 August). This route takes the wild and beautiful old mountain road over Páramo de La Negra to San Cristóbal. No Mérida-San Cristóbal buses; by public transport change in Tovar and La Grita.

San Cristóbal → *Phone code: 0276. Colour map 1, grid B4. Population: 290,900. Altitude: 830 m.*

The capital of Táchira State was founded in 1561. Today it's a large, busy, but friendly place built over a series of hills and ravines, although a few blocks in historic centre, around cathedral, retain a colonial air. You need to know which district you are in for orientation, eg La Concordia for the bus station. The **Fiesta de San Sebastián** in second half of January is a major international event, with parades, trade shows, and much more; book ahead, prices rise. **Tourist office**: Cotatur, ⓘ *Av España con Av Carabobo, T357 9655, www.cotatur.gov.ve*. Helpful. **Inparques**, Parque Metropolitano, Avenida 19 de Abril, T346 6544.

On Sunday, take a taxi to **Peribeca** (US$11 one way), a tiny colonial village that comes alive with handicraft shops, restaurants and sellers of dairy products, fruit desserts and bewildering variety of liqueurs and infusions. The pretty handicraft alley is next to the modern church. There are two posadas, La Posada de la Abuela on the Plaza, and Posada Turística Doña Meche, just outside the village. Many restaurants open for Sunday lunch, the best is El Solar de Juancho. Alternatively, on Monday, go to the wholesale vegetable market of **Táriba**, just off highway going north. The town's huge white Basílica de la Virgen de la Consolación (1959) can be seen from the highway. Stained glass inside tells the story of the image. Her fiesta in August attracts great numbers of devotees. The market place is reached by a pedestrian suspension bridge goes from to plaza in front of the basilica. The town has colonial streets. There are other longer excursions to colonial villages, farming and handicraft-making communities, but public transport and car hire facilities are poor.

San Cristóbal to San Antonio → *Phone code: 0276. Colour map 1, grid B4. Population: 42,630.*

The border town of San Antonio is 55 km from San Cristóbal by a paved, congested road. At **Capacho** (25 km from San Antonio) is an interesting old Municipal Market building, with lions at the 4 corners. If travelling light and in no hurry, you can go via **Rubio** (45 minutes from San Cristóbal, US$1, Líneas Unidas). In coffee zone, it has a pleasant colonial centre, with an enormous brick church, Santa Bárbara, in neo-Gothic style (1934-71). It's a busy town with extensive modern outskirts. The roads to it are paved and quieter than the main road, with better scenery, too. Buses congregate around the market. Expreso La Moderna to San Antonio (70 minutes, US$1.15, to/from Av Venezuela in San Antonio) continues to Cúcuta (US$1.60).

San Antonio is connected by international bridge with Cúcuta on the Colombian side (about 16 km); continue by road or air to Bogotá. San Antonio has a colonial cathedral and some parks, but is not in the least tourist-orientated. Avenida Venezuela leads to Venezuelan customs. You can catch most transport here, to Cúcuta, San Cristóbal, Rubio, even some offices for Caracas, but the bus terminal is off the road to the airport: at the roundabout at end of Av Venezuela, turn left (C 11), take a Circunvalación combi marked Terminal (US$0.30). Also buses to airport. There is a festival on 13-20 May.

Border with Colombia   Get a Venezuelan exit stamp at **ONIDEX**. The Colombian consulate is at Centro Cívico San Antonio, loc 1-8, T771 5890, open 0800-1400; better to get a visa in Mérida. **Note**   Venezuelan time is one hour ahead of Colombian.

Entering Venezuela, go to **ONIDEX** for entry formalities then look for a bus to San Cristóbal on Av Venezuela, or go to the bus station (taxi from ONIDEX US$2). If Venezuelan customs is closed at weekends, it is not possible to cross from Cúcuta. There is a customs and Guardia Nacional post at Peracal outside San Antonio; be prepared for strip searches and for searches between San Cristóbal and Mérida, eg at La Jabonosa on the Panamericana.

If crossing by private vehicle, car documents must be stamped at the SENIAT office at the Puente Internacional, just before San Antonio. Two different stamps are needed at separate SENIAT buildings ⓘ *Mon-Fri 0800-1200, 1330-1700, Sat 0800-1200, T771 5411*. It's essential to have proof of car/motorbike ownership. You must check in advance if you need a visa and a *carnet de passages* (see page 43). See Cúcuta, Colombia, page 808, for details on exit formalities. Once in Venezuela, you may find police are ignorant of requirements for foreign cars.

⊜ Sleeping

Parque Nacional Sierra Nevada (South) *p1372*

Los Nevados

E pp **Posada Bella Vista**, behind church. Hot water, hammocks, great views, restaurant. Recommended.

E pp **Posada Guamanchi**, T252 2080, www .guamanchi.com. Owned by travel agency based in Mérida. Solar power, great views, cheaper without bath, 2 meals included. Recommended.

F pp **El Buen Jesús**, T252 5696. Hot water, Meals.

El Morro

E **Posada** run by Doña Chepa, as you enter from Los Nevados, warm. Recommended.

F pp **Posada El Orégano**, including meals, basic, good food. Recommended.

Parque Nacional Sierra Nevada (North) and Sierra de la Culata p1373

Tabay

D Casa Vieja, Transandina via Páramo, San Rafael de Tabay, inside the Parador Turístico El Paramito, T0274-417 1489, www.casa-vieja-merida.com. Plant-filled colonial house, German and Peruvian owners, good doubles, hot water, breakfast and dinner available, good food, relaxing, very helpful, lots of information on independent trips from Tabay and transport, English, French and German spoken. Travel agency, **Caiman Tours**, for Llanos, wildlife and adventure tours; see also www.birds-venezuela.de. From the bus terminal in Mérida take a bus via Mucuchíes or Apartaderos, 30 mins to Tabay, get off exactly 1.5 km after the gas station in Tabay village (just after you pass Plaza Bolivar); the bus stop is called "El Paramito". There is a sign on the road pointing left. Free pick up from the airport or terminal if you have a reservation. Warmly recommended.

D La Casona de Tabay, on the Mérida road 1½ km from the plaza, T0274-283 0089, posadala casona@cantv.net. A beautiful colonial-style hotel, surrounded by mountains, comfortable, home cooking, family-run. Take *por puesto*, 2 signposts.

F pp **Posada de la Mano Poderosa**, beyond San Rafael de Tabay on road to Mucuchíes, T0414-742 2862 (mob). Dorms, lovely, quiet, hot showers, good food, great value, get off at La Plazuela then walk 15 mins towards Vivero Fruti Flor.

Mucuchíes

B Los Conquistadores, Av Carabobo 14, T872 0350, www.andes.net/conquistadores. Nice decor, modern, breakfast, TV, heating, lots of facilities like pool tables and other games, garden, parking, restaurant 0800-2200, tasca, and bike hire. Arranges transport for tours, BBV Provincial and ATM.

E Posada Los Andes, Independencia 25, T872 0151, 0414-717 2313 (mob). Old house on street above plaza and a couple of blocks away, run by Las Hermanas Pironi Belli; 5 cosy rooms, hot water, shared bathrooms, TV in living room, excellent restaurant (breakfast extra, criollo and Italian food, 0800-2030). Internet available. Highly recommended.

Mucuposadas is a local network of basic lodgings, see www.andestropicales.org/Andes_Vzla.html.

San Rafael de Mucuchíes

C Posada San Rafael del Páramo, just outside San Rafael, 500m from the Capilla de Piedra, on road to Apartaderos, T872 0938. With breakfast, **D** without breakfast in low season. Charming

converted house with lots of interesting sculpture and paintings, hot water, heating, TV, also cabin with kitchenette, walking and riding tours (US$13.65 per day, guide extra). Recommended.

D Casa Sur, Independencia 72, T872 0342, 0416-275 1684 (mob), njespindola@yahoo.com. Hot water, heating, TV, breakfast extra, other meals on request.

E El Rosal, Bolívar 37, T872 0331, 0416-275 3254 (mob). Hot water, TV, good, also cabins with kitchenette (**B**), no breakfast, café nearby, restaurant for groups, tasca at weekends.

Apartaderos

B Hotel Parque Turístico, on main road, T888 0094, http://andes.net/hotelapartaderos. Cheaper in low season. Attractive modern chalet-style building, heating, very hot showers, helpful owner, expensive restaurant. Recommended.

C Hotel y Restaurante Mifafí, on main road, T888 0131, refugioturisticomifafi@hotmail.com. Cheaper without heating, pleasant rooms and cabins, hot water, TV, good food. A welcoming, reliable choice.

D Posada y Restaurant Juan Hilario, Mucuchíes side of town, T888 0145, 0414-747 3779 (mob). 9 big rooms with hot water, double bed and bunks, TV, cold but looks OK, all meals extra, parking.

E Posada Viejo Apartaderos, outside town, coming from Mucuchíes, T888 0003, posadaviejo apartaderos@cantv.net. Next to *bomba*, with **La Matica de Rosa** restaurant, T271 2209, Sra Marbeles. Open only in high season. Good value, good restaurant with reasonable prices.

From Mérida to the Panamericana:

Jají p1374

A pp **Estancia La Bravera**, 18 km from Jají towards La Azulita, T414 7144, 414-293 3306, www.estancialabravera.com. Cabins in beautiful flower gardens in the cloud forest, great for bird-watching, hot water, includes breakfast and dinner, lunch extra, much of the cooking uses home produce, holds an annual Estancia Musical (Aug).

B Hacienda La Carmen, Aldea La Playa, 2 km from Jají (there is public transport), T417 6010, www.haciendaelcarmen.com.ve. On a working dairy and coffee-processing farm, built 1863, fascinating buildings, lovely rooms, one with jacuzzi (**A**), some simpler rooms, breakfast included, owner Andrés Monzón.

D Posada Restaurant Aldea Vieja, C Principal, just off Plaza, T266 0072. Colonial style main building, also cabins for 4-8, lovely views, simple rooms, TV, hot water, meals extra (breakfast US$3.40), playground (watch out for the slides).

D-E Posada Turística Jají, beside the Prefectura, on the plaza, T416 6333. 4 rooms with hot water, no TV, historic, 2 fountains, restaurant 0800-2100, breakfast included if staying a few days.

From Mérida to the Panamericana:
La Azulita *p1374*
3 km before town is a turning left to San Luis and Saysayal Bajo. The sign mentions various *posadas*, but most not working. Recommended are:
B El Tao, on a side road beyond Remanso, 4-5 km, 6 mins in car from La Azulita, T0274-416 5333, 0416-175 0011 (mob), www.eltaomerida.com. Taoist owners and oriental-style spa with saunas, and natural therapies, many birds, favoured by birders and other groups, lovely gardens, very safe and peaceful, nice public areas. Cabins for 2-4, with breakfast, TV, hot water. Restaurant, boxed lunches and early breakfast for birding groups.
B-C Remanso del Quebradón, close to junction, T0416-775 7573, www.remanso.com.ve. 4 rooms with bath, on a small coffee farm with fruit trees in the gardens, restaurant, breakfast included, popular with birdwatchers.
E Posada Turística La Azulita, on Plaza Bolívar. Rooms around restaurant in courtyard, OK food. Some other lodgings in town.

San Cristóbal *p1374*
Cheapest hotels around the bus station, **B-C** business hotels in the centre (**El Faraón**, **Dinastía**) and more upmarket place in the north-western suburbs (eg **Castillo de la Fantasía**, **Los Pirineos**, **Posada Remanso de Pueblo Nuevo**).
B Del Rey, Av Ferrero Tamayo, Edif El Rey, T343 0561. Good showers, fridge, TV, Wi-Fi, kitchenette, laundry, no breakfast but *panadería* in building, pizzas. Recommended.
C Posada Rincón Tachirense, Av Ferrero Tamayo con C 3, N Ft-19, La Popita, T341 8573, www.posadarincontachirense.com. Not central, down hill from **Del Rey**, cheaper with shared bath, comfortable, a/c, TV, Wi-Fi and internet, breakfast and will ring out for pizza. Recommended.
D Posada Turística Don Manuel, Cra 10 No 1-104, just off Av 19 de Abril, Urb La Concordia, T347 8082. Rooms are across street; Sra Carmen will direct you. Hot water, family run, TV, fridge, fan, limited kitchen facilities, no breakfast, parking. Sleeps 8, always book in advance, convenient.
E Río de Janeiro, C 1, No 7-27, Urb Juan Maldonado, La Concordia, outside bus station, T347 7666. Big rooms, fan, hot shower, no breakfast.
F Tropical, Prol 5ta Av No 7472, T347 2932. Also opposite bus station, basic. Other cheapies in the area.

San Antonio *p1375*
Many hotels near town centre.
C-D Adriático, C6 y Cra 6, T771 3896. Not far from Av Venezuela, 3-star, functional.

F Neveri, C 3, No 3-13, esq Carrera 3, T771 5702. A/c, TV, safe, parking nearby, 1 block from Customs, opposite Guardia Nacional barracks. No food, dated. Internet next door.

🍴 Eating

San Cristóbal *p1374*
El Barrio Obrero has the main concentration of eateries, bars and discos. Try **Rocamar**, Cra 20 y C 14, for seafood. Also pizza places and *pastelerías*.
†††-†† La Olleta, Cra 21, no 10-171, just off plaza, Barrio Obrero, T356 6944. Smart, simple décor, Venezuelan and international with creative touches, well presented.
Around town there are many *panaderías* and *pastelerías* for snacks as well as bread and cakes, coffee and other drinks, eg **América**, Cra 8, Edif La Concordia, no 4-113, La Concordia (several on Cra 8 y C 4, La Concordia); also **Táchira** branches.

San Antonio *p1375*
† **Rosmar**, Cra 6 y C 6, opposite Hotel Adriático. Very popular for lunch, several choices, OK food.

🚌 Transport

Parque Nacional Sierra Nevada (South) *p1372*
Los Nevados
Jeep Los Nevados-**Mérida**, late afternoon (depart 0700 from Plaza Las Heroínas in Mérida), 5-6 hrs, US$10 pp, US$50 per jeep, very rough and narrow but spectacular.

Parque Nacional Sierra Nevada (North) *p1373*
Tabay
Regular *por puesto* service, buses from **Mérida** C 19 entre Avs 3 y 4, US$1.15. Gasoline in Tabay.

Apartaderos
Bus To **Mérida** from turn-off to Barinas; bus to **Barinas** on the road over the Sierra Nevada is unreliable, best to catch it in Mérida.

San Cristóbal *p1374*
Air Airport at Santo Domingo, 40 km away. Helpful tourist kiosk with leaflets, map of San Cristóbal US$0.45.Taxi to San Cristóbal US$22, can take as little as 35 mins, but normally much more, lots of traffic, nice scenery (tourist office says no other option). The highway is 30 mins' walk away; it may be possible to catch a bus, 1 hr, US$1. Daily flights to/from **Caracas** with Aserca and **Aeropostal**. Alternatively fly to San Antonio (see below) for better public transport links.
Bus Local: buses cost US$0.25. `Intercomunal' goes from Av Ferrero Tamayo (northwest) to Bus

Terminal. 'Tusca' from Av Ferrero Tamayo to centre. Taxis US$2.50 for a short run.

The **bus station** is in La Concordia, in the southeast. It is a bus terminal, shopping mall, market, phone exchange and food court all lumped together; the information booth has little useful information. Terminal tax US$0.10, paid on bus before departure. Company offices are grouped together: Expresos Mérida (not to Mérida), Aerobuses, Expresos Los Llanos (to San Fernando), Expresos Barinas (direct to San Fernando at 1700, and to Puerto Ayacuccho, T0276-414 6950), many others. Expresos Occicente have their own terminal nearby. To **Mérida**, US$9, 5 hrs, with **Táchira-Mérida** (buy ticket on bus); **Expreso Unido** to Mérida, 0530, 0830, plus *ejecutivos* 1130, 1430, 1730; also to Tovar 0930, 1430, 4 hrs, US$6.80. Buses to Mérida go via the Panamericana, not over the Páramo. National Guard Control at La Jabonesa, just before San Juan de Colón, be prepared for luggage search. To **Maracaibo**, 6-8 hrs, US$18.20-20. To **Caracas**, US$16-24, 15 hrs; **Valencia**, US$14-22. To **Barinas**, US$7.25-8.20. To **San Fernando de Apure** via **Guasdualito**, US$17.45-20. To **San Antonio**, 1¼ hrs (but San Cristóbal rush hour can add lots of time), US$1.60, **Línea San Antonio**, T347 0976 (San Antonio 771 2966) and **Unión de Conductores**, T346 0691 (San Antonio 771 1364). To **Cúcuta**, **Línea Venezuela**, T347 3086 (Cúcuta 0270-583 6413) and **Fronteras Unidas**, T347 7446 (Cúcuta 0270 583 5445) , US$4, Mon-Fri 0800-1200, 1400-1800. Opposite terminal on Rugeles, **Coop de Conductores Fronterizos** cars, T611 2256, to **San Antonio**.

San Antonio *p1375*

Air The airport has exchange facilities (mainly for Colombian pesos). Taxis run to ONIDEX (immigration) in town, and on to Cúcuta airport. Internal flights: to **Caracas**, Aeropostal, **Aserca** and **Rutaca**. Also flights to most parts of Venezuela.
Bus From terminal several companies to **Caracas**, via the Llanos, Valencia and Maracay. All *bus-cama*: Caracas US$26.50, Valencia US$21.35,

Maracay US$22. Expresos San Cristóbal have office on Av Venezuela, close to Customs, 1800 to Caracas, 13-14 hrs; Expresos Mérida, Av Venezuela, No 6-17, at 1900. Táchira-Mérida to **Mérida** and **Barquisimeto**, 1600; Expresos Unidos to Mérida 1200, 1700. To **San Cristóbal**, catch a bus on Av Venezuela.

Border with Colombia

Air It is cheaper, but slower, to fly **Caracas**-San Antonio, take a taxi to Cúcuta, then take an internal Colombian flight, than to fly direct Caracas-Colombia. The airport transfer at San Antonio is well-organized and taxi drivers make the 25-min trip with all stops. Air tickets out of Cúcuta can be reserved in a Venezuelan travel agency.
Bus On Av Venezuela por puestos/colectivos to **Cúcuta** charge US$1, and buses US$0.70 payable in bolívares or pesos, 30 mins. Some say to terminal, others to centre. Taxi to Cúcuta, US$12. On any transport that crosses the border, make sure the driver knows you need to stop to obtain stamps. *Por puesto* drivers may refuse to wait. Taxi drivers will stop at all the offices. Just to visit Cúcuta, no documents are needed.

❶ Directory

San Cristóbal *p1374*
Banks Plenty of ATMs in town. Major banks on Av 7 between Cs 9 and 10. Mon-Fri 0830-1530. TCs are difficult to change. **Consulates** German, Cra 3 con C 4,CC Dr Toto Gonzáles, p 1, of 7, T343 6218, kmargeit@ hotmail.com. UK, CC El Tama, loc 49, Altos de Pirineos, T356 6732, britcon-sc@cantv.net. **Telephones** Many CANTV offices and phones; also independent phone tables, with land lines and mobiles, everywhere.

San Antonio *p1375*
Banks Many *casas de cambio* on Av Venezuela near the international bridge will change Colombian pesos, but not all change cheques or even US$ cash. The exchange rate for bolívares to pesos is the same in San Antonio as in Cúcuta.

Los Llanos and Amazonas

A spectacular route descends from the Sierra Nevada to the flat llanos, one of the best places in the world to see birds and animals. This vast, sparsely populated wilderness of 300,000 sq km – one third of the country's area – lies between the Andes to the west and the Orinoco to the south and east. Southwest of the Guayana region, on the banks of the Orinoco, Puerto Ayacucho is the gateway to the jungles of Venezuela. Although it takes up about a fifth of the country, Amazonas and its tropical forests is for the most part unexplored and unspoilt.

Los Llanos

The *llanos* are veined by numerous slow-running rivers, forested along their banks. The flat plain is only varied here and there by *mesas*, or slight upthrusts of the land. About five million of the country's 6.4 million cattle are in the *llanos*, but only around 10% of the human population. When the whole plain is periodically under water, the *llaneros* drive their cattle into the hills or through the flood from one *mesa* to another. When the plain is parched by the sun and the savanna grasses become inedible they herd the cattle down to the damper region of the Apure and Orinoco. Finally they drive them into the valley of Valencia to be fattened.

In October and November, when the vast plains are still partially flooded, wildlife abounds. Animals include capybara, caiman, monkeys, anacondas, river dolphins, pumas and many varieties of birds. Though it's possible to explore this region independently, towns are few and far between and distances are great. It's better to visit the *llanos* as part of a tour from Mérida (see Tour operators, page 1370), or stay at one of the ecotourism *hatos*, or ranches (see below).

Guanare → *Phone code: 0257. Colour map 1, grid B5. Population: 32,500.*

An excellent road goes to the western *llanos* of Barinas from Valencia. It goes through San Carlos, Acarigua (an agricultural centre and the largest city in Portuguesa state) and Guanare, which is a national place of pilgrimage with an old parish church containing the much venerated relic of the Virgin of Coromoto. Pilgrimages to Coromoto are on 2 January and 11 September and Candlemas is 2 February.

Barinas → *Phone code: 0273. Colour map 1, grid A5. Population: 240,000.*

The road continues to Barinas, the hot, sticky capital of the cattle-raising and oil-rich state of Barinas. A couple of colonial buildings remain: the Palacio del Marqués on the west side of the plaza and the Casa de la Cultura on the north side. On the south side of the plaza is the beautifully restored, 19th-century Escuela de Música; the cathedral is to the east. The shady Parque Universitario, just outside the city on Avenida 23 de Enero, has a botanical garden open Monday to Friday. **Tourist office** ① *Av Insauste con Av Adonay Parra Jiménez, at entrance to La Ciudad Deportiva, T541 0522, corbatur@intercable.net.ve.* Helpful, maps, no English spoken; kiosks at airport and bus station.

San Fernando de Apure → *Phone code: 0247. Colour map 1, grid A6. Population: 135,000.*

At Lagua, 16 km east of Maracay, a good road leads south to San Fernando de Apure. It passes through San Juan de los Morros, which has natural hot springs; Ortiz, near the crossroads with the San Carlos-El Tigre road; the Guárico lake and Calabozo. Some 132 km south of Calabozo, San Fernando is the hot and sticky capital of the state of Apure and a fast-growing trade and transport hub for the region. There is *Corp Banca* for American Express, Avenida Miranda, Edif Chang, PB, and *Bancos Mercantil* (Paseo Libertador) and *Provincial* (Plaza Páez) with Visa and MasterCard ATM and cash advance. From San Fernando you can travel east to Ciudad Bolívar (see page 1405), or south to Puerto Ayacucho (see below).

San Fernando to Barinas

From San Fernando a road heads to head west to Barinas (468 km). It's a beautiful journey, but the road is in terrible condition between Manteca, La Ye junction and Bruzual, a town just south of the Puente Nutrias on the Río Apure. In the early morning, many animals and birds can be seen, and in the wet season caiman (alligators) cross the road. **Mantecal** is a friendly cattle-ranching town with hotels and restaurants. *Fiesta*, 23-26 February.

⬤ Sleeping

Guanare *p1379*
D **Italia**, Carrera 5, No 19-60. A/c, bar and restaurant, off-street parking.
E **Colina**, near the river at bottom of town. Motel-style, comfortable, restaurant.

Barinas *p1379*
C **Varyná**, Av 23 de Enero, near the airport, T553 3984. A/c, restaurant, parking. Recommended.
E **Internacional**, C Arzobispo Méndez on Plaza Zamora, T552 2343. A/c, safe, good restaurant.

E La Media Avenida, Av 23 de Enero, near the airport, T552 2278. Cold showers, bar, restaurant, parking. Recommended.

Opposite bus terminal
E Palacio. A/c, good value.
F pp Lisboa. Basic, fan.

Staying at a tourist ranch
An alternative to travelling independently or arranging a tour from Mérida is to stay at one of the tourist ranches. Most of these are in Apure state and can be reached from Barinas or San Fernando de Apure.
L pp Doña Bárbara ranch, book through *Doña Bárbara* travel agency, Paseo Libertador, Edif Hotel La Torraca, PB y Mezzanina, Apdo 55, San Fernando de Apure, T0247-341 3463, F341 2235, barbara@sfapure.c-com.net. Price includes 3 meals, 2 tours per day, bath, a/c or fan, clean, comfortable, or US$45 for a daytime visit.
LL-L pp Hato Piñero, T0212-991 8935, www.hato pinero.com. A safari- type lodge at a working ranch near El Baúl (turn off Tinaco-El Sombrero road at El Cantón). Fully inclusive price, per day, packages can include return overland or air transport from Caracas. Free drinks, good room, bi-lingual nature guide for excellent bird- and animal-watching trips. Highly recommended. No public transport to ranch but ask police in El Baúl for ride with Hato Piñero workers. From Caracas, 6 hrs; from Ciudad Bolívar, 9 hrs.
AL pp Hato El Cedral, about 30 mins by bus from Mantecal (see above). Address: Av La Salle, edif Pancho p 5, of 33, Los Caobos, Caracas, T0212- 781 8995, F793 6082, www.elcedral.com. A 53,000-ha ranch where hunting is banned. Fully inclusive price, tax extra (high season Dec to Apr), a/c, hot water, land and river safaris, guides, pool. Special offers at certain times of year.
AL pp Hato El Frío, office in Achaguas, T0240-808 3662/540 9420, www.elfrioeb.com. Biological station offering accommodation including 3 meals, 2 tours per day (price rises 15 Nov-30 Apr), with bath, a/c or fan, clean, comfortable, US$45 for a daytime visit.
A pp Reserva Privada de Flora y Fauna Mataclara, on the road to El Baúl at Km 93 (next to Hato Piñero turn off). Address: Prof Antonio González-Fernández, Universidad de Los Llanos 'Unellez', Mesa de Caracas, Guanare 3323, Estado de Portuguesa, T0241-867 7254, www.desarrollo ruralsostenible.net/mataclara.htm. Lodging with full board, horse riding, fishing and animal watching trips costs US$50 pp per day.

A-B pp Rancho Grande, close to Mantecal, T0416-873-1192 (mob), www.aventura sranchogrande.com. Run by very friendly and knowledgeable Ramón González. All inclusive, good wildlife spotting and horse riding trips.

San Fernando de Apure *p1379*
Most hotels are within 1 block of the intersection of Paseo Libertador and Av Miranda.
A Gran Hotel Plaza, C Bolívar, T342 1746, 2 blocks from the bus terminal. A/c, cable TV, safe, good.
D pp El Río, Av María Nieves, near the bus terminal, T341 1928. With a/c, good value.
D-E La Fuente, Miranda y Libertador, T342 3233. A/c, TV, phone, safe.
E La Torraca, Av Boulevard y Paseo Libertador by Plaza Bolívar, T342 2777. Excellent rooms, a/c, balcony overlooking centre of town. Recommended. **E Trinacria**, Av Miranda, near bus terminal, T342 3578. Huge rooms, a/c.

🍴 Eating

Guanare *p1379*
El Paisano, popular restaurant. **Restaurante Turístico La Casa Vieja**, good food and value.

Barinas *p1379*
† El Estribo, C Apure entre Av Garguera y Andrés Varela. Roast and barbecued local meat, good, open 1100-2400.
† Don Enrique, facing *Hotel Palacio*. Good, cheap.
† Yoanna, Av 7, 16-47, corner of Márques del Pumar. Arab owner, excellent.

San Fernando de Apure *p1379*
† Comedor in building beside CANTV. Has good *menú*, Mon-Fri, 1100-1200.
† Gran Imperio Romano, on Av Boulevard. Small, popular, good and cheap.
† Punto Criollo, Av Miranda. Good value.

🚌 Transport

Barinas *p1379*
Air Aeropuerto Nacional, Av 23 de Enero. Flights to **Caracas**.
Bus To **Mérida**, 6 a day with Transportes Barinas, US$5.75, spectacular ride through the mountains, 5-7 hrs (sit on right for best views); also to **Valera** at 0730, US$8.75, 7 hrs. To **Caracas**, US$14, 8 hrs, several companies go direct or via **Maracay** and **Valencia**, regularly 0730-2300. To **San Cristóbal**, several daily, US$7.25-8.20, 5 hrs; to **San Fernando de Apure**,

● *For an explanation of the sleeping and eating price codes used in this guide, see page 58. Other*
● *relevant information is found in Essentials pages 1332-1333.*

US$15.50, 9 hrs with **Expresos Los Llanos** at 0900, 2300; the same company also goes to **Maracaibo** (at 2000 and 2200, US$14, 8 hrs), **San Antonio** (at 2330) and **Puerto La Cruz** (3 a day, US$25, 16 hrs).

From Barinas there is a beautifully scenic road to Apartaderos, in the Sierra Nevada de Mérida (see page 1374). Motorists travelling east to Ciudad Bolívar can either go across the *llanos* or via San Carlos, Tinaco, El Sombrero, Chaguaramas, Valle de la Pascua (see below) and El Tigre. The latter route requires no ferry crossings and has more places with accommodation.

San Fernando de Apure *p1379*
Air Aeropuerto Las Flecheras, Av 1 de Mayo, T342 3356. Flights to **Caracas**.

Bus Terminal is modern and clean, not far from centre; US$2 taxi. To **Caracas**, US$16, 7 hrs; to **Barinas**, Expresos Zamora, 5 daily, 7 hrs (take food and drink), rough ride, day and night bus, US$15.50; to **Maracay**, US$12; to **Puerto Ayacucho**, US$15, 8 hrs; to **Calabozo**, 1½ hrs, US$3.

San Fernando to Barinas *p1379*
Bus San Fernando de Apure-Mantecal 3½ hrs, US$6; Mantecal-Barinas, 4 hrs, US$7.

❻ Directory

Barinas *p1379*
Banks Banco Mercantil, Av Marqués del Pumar y Bolívar, and Banco Provincial, Av Marqués del Pumar y Carvajal, for MasterCard or Visa cash withdrawals.

Amazonas

Much of Amazonas is stunningly beautiful and untouched, but access is only by river. The more easily accessible places lie on the course of the Orinoco and its tributaries. The best time to visit is October to December after the rains, but at any season, this is a remote part of the country. On arrival in Amazonas, you need to register at a Guardia Nacional checkpoint 20 km before Puerto Ayacucho. The national guard can be very strict and travellers are likely to be searched here.

San Fernando to Puerto Ayacucho

Due south of San Fernando de Apure is **Puerto Páez** (*Population 2,600, Phone code 0247*) at the confluence of the Meta and Orinoco rivers; here there is a crossing to El Burro west of the Caicara-Puerto Ayacucho road. Route 2 runs south from San Fernando to Puerto Páez, crossing several major rivers. Between the Capanaparo and Cinaruco rivers is the **Parque Nacional Cinaruco-Capanaparo** (also called **Santos Luzardo**), reached only from this road. If this road is closed, to get to Puerto Ayacucho from San Fernando involves a minimum 15-hour detour via the Caicara ferry.

From Caicara a new paved road runs 370 km southwest to Puerto Ayacucho. The turn off to **El Burro**, where the boat crosses the Orinoco to Puerto Páez (ferry US$1), is 88 km north of Puerto Ayacucho (*taxi* El Burro-Puerto Ayacucho, two hours US$8).

Puerto Ayacucho → *Phone code: 0248. Colour map 1, grid B6. Population: 73,660.*

The capital of the State of Amazonas, 800 km via Orinoco from Ciudad Bolívar, has an area of 175,000 sq km and a population of 80,000. At the end of the dry season (April), it is very hot and sticky. It is deep in the wild, but no direct boats do the five day journey up river. **Museo Etnológico Monseñor Enzo Ceccarelli** ⓘ *opposite church, Tue-Sat, Sun morning, US$1*, has a library and collection of regional exhibits, recommended. In front of the museum is a market, open every day, where *indígenas* sell handicrafts. One block away is the cathedral. The Salesian Mission House and boys' school on Plaza Bolívar may also be visited. Prices in Puerto Ayacucho are generally higher than north of the Orinoco. **Tourist office** is at the airport, amatuirismo@cantv.net. **Note** Malaria is prevalent in this area; take precautions.

Excursions Locals recommend October to December as the best time for trips, when the rivers are high but the worst of the rains has passed. In the low season, May-June, it may be difficult to organize tours for only a few days.

You can walk up **Cerro Perico** for good views of the town, or go to the Mirador, 1 km from centre, for good views of the Ature rapids. A recommended trip is to the village of Pintado (12 km south), where petroglyphs described by Humboldt can be seen on the huge rock **Cerro Pintado**. This is the most accessible petroglyph site of the hundreds scattered throughout Amazonas.

Some 35 km south on the road to Samariapo is the **Parque Tobogán de la Selva**, a pleasant picnic area with tables and refreshments based around a steeply inclined, smooth rock over which the Río Maripures cascades. This water-slide is great fun in the wet season; crowded on Sunday, take swimsuit, bathing shoes and food and drink (stick to the right to avoid crashing into the barrier, there are some painful rocks to the left near the bottom; few locals slide right from the top; also beware of broken glass). A small trail leads up from the slide to a natural jacuzzi after about 20 minutes. Taxi to Cerro Pintado and Parque Tobogán, US$15-20 return (be sure to organize your return with the driver, otherwise you may face a lengthy hike). Agencies in town arrange tours; easier but more expensive.

The well-paved road from Puerto Ayacucho to Samariapo (63 km) was built to bypass the rapids which here interrupt the Orinoco, dividing it into 'Upper' and 'Lower'; the powerful Maripures Rapids are very impressive.

Tours in Amazonas

For starting out, the best base is Puerto Ayacucho. Do not travel alone. By ascending the Autana or Sipapo rivers, for example, you can see **Autana-tepuy**, a 1,200 m-high soaring mass of rock which no-one has yet climbed from the base. There are other *tepuis* in the region, including the great mass of the Sierra de la Neblina on the Brazilian border.

San Juan de Manapiare (Population: 3,700) is the regional centre for the middle Ventuari. A beautiful track winds around the Cerro Guanay to get there. The road starts at Caicara and goes through Guaniamo and Sabana de Cardona.

⊜ Sleeping

Puerto Ayacucho *p1381*

B **Oriniquia Lodge**, on the Río Orinoco, 20 mins from airport, book through Cacao Travel, cacaotravel@cantv.net. Nice setting, comfortable.
D **City Center**, Av 23 de Enero, on roundabout at entrance to town, T521 0639. Pleasant, safe parking, takes credit cards.
E **Apure**, Av Orinoco 28, T521 0516, less than 1 km from centre. A/c, good restaurant. Recommended.
E **Guacharo's Amazonas Resort Hotel**, at end of Av Evelio Roa, 2 blocks from Av Río Negro, T521 0155. A/c, restaurant, attractive sitting room.
F **Res Internacional**, Av Aguerrevere 18, T521 0242. A/c (cheaper without), comfortable, shower, locked parking, safe but basic, not very clean, good place to find tour information and meet other travellers, if no room available you can sling up your hammock, bus drivers stay here and will drive you to the terminal for early morning journeys.
F **Tobogán**, Av Orinoco con Av Evelio Roa. With a/c, TV lounge, laundry facilities, helpful staff, English spoken, popular.
Private camps in Amazonas There are a number of private river camps on the upper Orinoco but they do not welcome casual guests.

Near Puerto Ayacucho

L pp **Jungle Camp Calypso**, run by *Calypso Tours*, T Caracas 0212-545 6009, F541 3036. In mixed jungle and dry forest setting, price is for 2 days including food, basic cabin accommodation, highly recommended, excursions in canoes.
B **Canturama Amazonas Resort**, T521 0266, or Caracas 0212-941 8813, F943 5160, 20 mins by vehicle south of town. On the banks of the Orinoco, 40 km from nearest jungle, highly recommended accommodation and food but beware biting insects by the river, day tours US$10.
C **Dantos Adventure**. Very basic jungle refuge, accommodation and canoe tours, probably cheapest option available, also space for camping, run by English-speaking guide Reni Barrio, recommended, ask at *Aguas Bravas* (see below).

Río Manapiare area

LL **Campamento Camani**, in a forest clearing on the banks of the Río Alto Ventuari, 2 hrs by launch from San Juan de Manapiare, T521 4553, www.camanicamp.com. From Puerto Ayacucho daily aerotaxi takes 50 mins. Maximum 26 at any one time, mosquito nets, all amenities, excursions available. Price is for 3 day/2 night package.
LL **Yutajé Camp**, on a tributary of Río Manapiare due east of Puerto Ayacucho. Restaurant and bar, full board (in theory), fishing, canoes, horses, air-boats, excursions to indigenous villages, expensive but professional, welcoming. Reached by plane from Puerto Ayacucho or boat up the Ríos Manapiare and Corocoro (take something soft to sit on). Price is for 3 day/2 night package.

🍴 Eating

Puerto Ayacucho *p1381*

 Cherazad, Aguerrevere y Av Orinoco. Arabic food, relatively expensive.
 El Padrino, in Urb Andrés Eloy Blanco on Av Belisio Pérez off Av 23 de Enero. Good Italian.
 El Espagetazo, Av Aguerrevere. Mainly pasta, most dishes US$3, popular with locals.

¶¶ **Las Palmeras**, Av 23 de Enero, 2 blocks from the Redoma. Pizzas and fast food.
¶ **Capi Fuente de Soda**, on Av Evelio Roa behind *gobernación*. Some vegetarian dishes.

⊙ Shopping

Puerto Ayacucho *p1381*
Handicrafts Good *artesanía* in the Plaza del Indio; also in **Artes Amazonas** on Av Evelio Roa, next to **Wayumi**, and in **Topocho** just up from Plaza del Indio. Vicente Barletta, **Típico El Casique**, Av Principal 583, Urb Andrés Eloy Blanco, has a good collection of masks (free); he also works as a guide, recommended, take own food and equipment.

▲ Activities and tours

Tours in Amazonas *p1382*
It is strongly recommended to go on tours organized by tour agents or guides registered in the **Asocación de Guías**, in the Cámara de Turismo de Puerto Ayacucho, Casa de la Piedra, on the Arteria Vial de la Av Orinoco with Av Principal (the house on top of the large rock). Some independent guides may not have permission to visit Amazonas. Tours cost US$50-120 pp per day. Those listed below will arrange permits and insurance but shop around.
Autana Aventura, Av Aguerrevere, 1 block from Av Orinoco. Owned by Julián Jaramillo.
Coyote Expediciones, Av Aguirrevere 75. Helpful, professional, English spoken, organizes trips staying in indigenous villages.
Expediciones Aguas Bravas Venezuela, Av Río Negro, No 32-2, in front of Plaza Rómulo Betancourt, T521 4458. Whitewater rafting, 2 daily from 0900-1200 and 1500-1800, 3-13 people per boat, reservations required at peak times, take insect repellent, sun protector, light shoes and swimsuit, US$35 pp.

Guaharibo CA, C Evelio Roa 39, in same building as *Wayumi*, T Caracas 952 6996, F953 0092. Manager Levis Olivo.
Tobogán Tours, Av 23 de Enero 24, near *Instituto del Menor*, T521 4865.
Yutajé Tours, in Urb Monte Bello, 1 block from Av Orinoco, past the Mercadito going out of town, T521 0664, turismoamazonas@cantv.net. Good value for money but the organization is erratic.

⊙ Transport

Puerto Ayacucho *p1381*
Air Airport 7 km southeast along Av Orinoco.
Bus Expresos del Valle to **Cuidad Bolívar** (US$17, 10 hrs; take something to eat, bus stops once for early lunch), **Caicara, Puerto Ordaz** and **San Félix**; Cooperativa Cacique to **San Fernando de Apure**, US$15, 8 hrs; both companies in bus terminal. Expresos La Prosperidad to **Caracas** and **Maracay** from Urb Alto Parima. Bus from **Caracas**, 2030, 2230 daily, US$28, 12 hrs (but much longer in wet season). *Por puesto* to Ciudad Bolívar, 3 daily, US$25, 10-12 hrs (Caicara Amazonas).
Ferry Ferry across the Orinoco, US$0.30. Boat to **Caicara**, 1½ days, US$18.75 including food, but bargain; repellent and hammock required.

⊙ Directory

Puerto Ayacucho *p1381*
Banks Unibanca, Av Orinoco No 37, has Visa ATM. Changing dollars is difficult; try *Hotel Tobogán*. **Internet** El Navegante, CC Maniglia, Av Orinoco, or on top floor of Biblioteca Pública Central, Av Río Negro. **Post offices** Ipostel on Av Aguerrevere 3 blocks up from Av Orinoco.
Telephones International calls from CANTV, on Av Orinoco next to *Hotel Apure*; also from *Las Churuatas* on Av Aguerrevere y C Amazonas, 1 block from Plaza del Indio.

East coast

Beautiful sandy bays, islands, forested slopes and a strong colonial influence all contribute to make this one of the most visited parts of the country. The western part, which is relatively dry, has most of the inhabitants and the two main cities, Barcelona and Cumaná, which is possibly the oldest Hispanic city on the South American mainland. In fact, the historical associations go back to the first arrival of the conquistadores. As you go east, you find some splendid beaches. Off shore are two of Venezuela's prime holiday attractions, Isla de Margarita, a mix of the overdeveloped and the quiet, and the island paradise of the Los Roques archipelago.

Caracas to Puerto La Cruz

Very much a holiday coastline, the first part takes its name from the sweeping Barlovento bay in Miranda state. Onshore trade winds give the seaboard a lusher aspect than the more arid landscape elsewhere. The neighbouring state is Anzoátegui, whose capital, Barcelona, is only 12 km from the more developed, more tourist-oriented Puerto La Cruz.

It is five hours from Caracas to Barcelona through Caucagua, from which there is a 58 km road northeast to **Higuerote** (*Phone code: 1234. Population: 13,700*). A coastal road from Los Caracas to Higuerote has many beaches and beautiful views. Parque Nacional Laguna de Tacarigua, reached 14 km before Higuerote on the Caucagua road, is an 18,400 ha park enclosing a lagoon, mangroves and many water birds, including flamingoes. Access and Inparques permits in the village of Tacarigua de la Laguna.

Parque Nacional Laguna de Tacarigua

At 14 km before Higuerote on the road from Caucagua is Tacarigua de Mamporal, where you can turn off to the **Parque Nacional Laguna de Tacarigua**. The 18,400 ha national park enclosing the lagoon is an important ecological reserve, with mangroves, good fishing and many water birds, including flamingoes (usually involving a day-long boat trip to see them, best time to see them 1700-1930; permit required from *Inparques* at the *muelle*, US$0.75). Boats leave from *Muelle Ciudad Tablita*; also from Inparques *muelle* (but overcharging is common here). Agencies have offices in Sector Belén in the fishing village of **Tacarigua de la Laguna**; fixed price of US$30 for two. Boats can be hired to anywhere in the Park and to *Club Miami* beach resort, **B**, includes two meals, on the Caribbean side of the eastern sandspit. Good fish dishes are served at *Bar-Restaurant Poleo Lebranche Asado*. The beaches beyond here are unspoilt and relaxing, but mosquitoes are a problem after sunset.

Barcelona → *Phone code: 0281. Colour map 2, grid A1. Population: 266,750. Mean temp: 27° C.*

Barcelona, founded in 1671, straddles the Río Neveri, 5 km from the sea. Its colonial streets and old buildings are pleasant if a little run down, and a more peaceful alternative to neighbouring Puerto La Cruz, 12 km away by 4-lane highway (Avenida Intercomunal), which has surpassed it touristically and commercially. Between the two towns is the residential resort of **Lechería**, which is the place for clubbing. ① *Take a* por puesto *to the beach, from Barcelona or Puerto La Cruz, or a taxi from either town.*

On **Plaza Boyacá** are the Palacio de Gobierno and San Cristóbal **Cathedral** ① *0600-1200, 1500-1930* (started 1748, rebuilt 1773), which contains the embalmed remains of the Italian martyr, San Celestino. Several blocks north on Avenida 5 de Julio are the twin **plazas of Bolívar** (with statue) and **Miranda**. Facing Plaza Bolívar are the ruins of the **Casa Fuerte**, a national monument, where 1600 of Bolívar's followers were massacred in 1817. Details of this and other historic epics can be found next door in the **public library**, weekdays only. **Museo de la Tradición** ① *C Juncal, Mon-Fri 0800-1200, 1400-1700, weekends 0900-1500*, in a 1671 building once the centre of the slave trade, houses a wide collection of indigenous and Spanish religious art. Next to the *por puesto* station on Avenida San Carlos, over 1 km south of Plaza Boyacá, is the **Mercado Libre**, for food and just about anything else. Tourist office: **Coranztur** ① *Palacio de Gobierno, Las Flores y Av 5 de Julio, T275 0474 or 0501-267 2698, www.fondoturismoanz.com.*

Puerto La Cruz and around → *Phone code: 0281. Colour map 2, grid A1.*

Originally a fishing village, Puerto La Cruz (*Population 220,000*) is now a major oil refining town and busy, modern holiday resort. (Tourist facilities are above average, if expensive and unhelpful and the sea is polluted.) The seafront avenue, Paseo Colón, extends to the eastern extremity of a broad bay. To the west the bay ends at the prominent El Morro headland. Most hotels, restaurants, bars and clubs are along Paseo Colón, from where you get excellent views of the Bahía de Pozuelas and the islands of the Parque Nacional Mochima (see below). Vendors of paintings, jewellery, leather and hammocks are on Paseo Colón in the evening, cheaper than the souvenir shops. The *Santa Cruz* festival is on 3 May, while 8 September is the *Virgen del Valle*, when boats cruise the harbour clad in palms and balloons; afternoon party at El Faro, Chimana, lots of salsa and beer. The main attractions of Puerto La Cruz lie offshore on the many islands of the beautiful Parque Nacional Mochima and in the surrounding waters. For details of how to get there, see below. The tourist office is **Coranztur** ⓘ *C Bolívar, Ed Araya, local 3 PB, T267 1632, www.fondoturismoanz.com, open Mon-Fri 0800-2100*. French, English, Italian and Dutch spoken, very helpful and friendly.

⊜ Sleeping

Parque Nacional Laguna de Tacarigua *p1384*
Tacarigua de la Laguna
C **Villa del Río**, about 3 km before the village on the road. Apart-hotel, price for 1-7 persons, bath, kitchen facilities, fan, connected with *Remigios Tours*, transfer to and from Tacarigua for US$20.
E **Casa de Ivan Pastuch**, 200 m from the Inparques *muelle*. Quiet, fan, use of cooker and fridge, German spoken. Recommended.

Barcelona *p1384*
D **Barcelona**, Av 5 de Julio, near Cathedral, T277 1065, F277 1076. TV, parking, 6th floor restaurant.
D **Neveri**, Av Fuerzas Armadas y Miranda, T277 2376. Similar, good restaurant *Castillo del Oriente*.
E **Madrid**, Juncal No 5-02, just behind cathedral, T274 4755. With restaurant.

E **Plaza**, Juncal No 4-07, opposite Cathedral, T277 2843. In a colonial building. Recommended.
E **Nueva Toledo**, Juncal No 5-61 y Av 5 de Julio, T274 3871. Basic, good value.

Puerto La Cruz *p1384, map p1385*
Newer, up-market hotels are at Lechería and El Morro; cheaper hotels are concentrated in the centre, though it's not easy to find a cheap hotel.
L **Gran Hotel Puerto La Cruz**, Paseo Colón, east edge of the centre, T500-3666, reservaciones. puertolacruz@hoteles premier.com. Best in this part of town, 5-star luxury hotel with all facilities.
B **Cristal Park**, Buenos Aires y Libertad, T267 3401, F265 3105. A/c, laundry, exchange at a good rate.
B **Rasil**, Paseo Colón y Monagas 6, T267 2422, rasil plc@hotmail.com. Rooms, suites and bungalows, 3 restaurants, bar, pool, gym, money exchange, car rental, convenient for ferries and buses.

Puerto La Cruz
To Cumaná & Parque Nacional Mochima

Marina

Paseo Colón
Flores
Av Alberto Ravel
Guaraguao
Plaza Colón
Carabobo
Av Municipal
Arismendi
Miranda
Freites
Paseo Colón
Ma-Ci-Te
Honduras
Av 5 de Julio
Girardot
C Maneiro
Bolívar
Libertad
Democracia
C Buenos Aires
C Sucre
Caribbean Sea
Plaza Bolívar
C Sucre
C Juncal
Por Puesto Terminal
Esperanza
C Providencia
Av Municipal
Boyacá
Anzoátegui
Por Puestos to Conferry Terminal
C S Rodríguez
Ricaurte
Venezuela
C Monagas
C Los Cocos
C Cementerio
To Car Ferry Terminal
To Caracas & Barcelona

0 metres 200
0 yards 200

Sleeping ⊜		Eating ⑦	
Caribbean Inn 1	Margelina 7	El Guatacarauzo 1	O Sole Mio 5
Comercio 2	Pippo 8	El Parador 2	Tío Pepe 6
Cristal Park 3	Rasil 9	El Teide 3	
Gaeta 4	Riviera 10	Heladería Tropic	
Gran Hotel	Senador 11	& Galería Colón 4	
Puerto La Cruz 5		La Colmena 7	

B **Senador**, Miranda y Bolívar, T267 3522, hotelsenadorplc@cantv.net. A/c, back rooms quieter, phone, restaurant with view, parking.

C **Caribbean Inn**, Freites, T267 4292, h-caribbean@convergence.com.ve. Big rooms, very well kept with quiet a/c, small pool, very good service.

C **Gaeta**, Paseo Colón y Maneiro, T265 0411, gaeta@telcel.net. Very modern, a/c, good location but very small rooms, restaurant, scooter rentals, *casa de cambio* (good rates).

C **Riviera**, Paseo Colón 33, T267 2111, hotelriviera@cantv.net. Seafront hotel, noisy a/c, some rooms have balcony, phone, bar, watersports, very good location, poor breakfast.

D **Comercio**, Maneiro y Libertad, T265 1429. Phones, cold water only, a/c, safe.

E **Margelina**, Paseo Colón 109, T268 7545. Large rooms, a bit tatty, a/c, TV.

F **Pippo**, Freites y Municipal, T268 8810. Cold water, some rooms with TV, very noisy.

🍴 Eating

Barcelona *p1384*
🍴 **Bueno Pollo**, Av Miranda y C 5 Maturín. Good grilled chicken, pleasant atmosphere.
🍴 **Lucky**, Av Miranda No 4-26, north of Plaza Bolívar. Chinese.

Puerto La Cruz *p1384, map p1385*
Many on Paseo Colón, eg **El Parador**, 2nd floor, excellent food and service. **Tío Pepe** and **Big Garden**, delicious sea food. **O Sole Mio**, cheap, excellent, wide variety.
🍴🍴 **El Guatacarauzo**, Paseo Colón near Pizza Hut. Live music, salsa, good atmosphere and value.
🍴🍴 **Maroco**, Av 5 de Julio 103. Good seafood.
🍴 **Celeri**, on Av Municipal, 1 block from Guamaché. Vegetarian, open weekdays 1130-1530. Recommended.
🍴 **El Farao**, east corner of main bus station. Excellent, authentic, spicy Arabic food.
🍴 **El Teide**, Av 5 de Julio No 153, near Plaza Bolívar. Good local food, closes at 2000.
🍴 **La Colmena**, next to *Hotel Riviera*. Vegetarian, worth trying.
🍴 **La Granela**, Miranda y Honduras. Another vegetarian option.
🍴 **La Taberna del Guácharo**, C Carabobo, east end of Paseo Colón. Excellent cheap Venezuelan cuisine, good service. Highly recommended.

Cafés
Heladería Tropic, Galería Colón on Paseo Colón. Good ice cream.
Sourdough Bakery and Grill, Paseo Colón. Indoor and outdoor seating, vegetarian options, excellent.

🍸 Bars and clubs

Puerto La Cruz *p1384, map p1385*
Most clubs have moved to El Morro and Lechería.
Casa Latina Av 5 de Julio. Good 1970s salsa.

⛰ Activities and tours

Puerto La Cruz *p1384, map p1385*
Diving Several companies, mostly on Paseo Colón, run diving courses. They're a bit more expensive than Santa Fe and Mochima. Hotels and travel agents also organize trips. The nearest recompression chamber is on Isla Margarita. We've received favourable reports on the following:
Aquatic Adventures (formerly Lolo's Diving Center), at end of Paseo Colón in the Marina, T0414-806 3744, or 0414-820 8758 (mob), www.aquatic adven.com. Very experienced, English spoken, collect you from hotel and provide lunch, US$50 for 2 dives, 2-3 person minimum, 4-day PADI course US$300, rents snorkelling equipment.
Explosub, *Gran Hotel Puerto La Cruz*, T267 3256. Efficient, helpful, will dive with 1 person, US$75 for 2 dives, good 4-island tour.
Kayaking Jakera, www.jakera.com. Sea kayaks for rent from their lodge at Playa Colorada (T0293-808 7057), trips to whole country arranged (lodge in Mérida too), Chris and Joanna helpful, English spoken.

Tour operators
Note Do not buy tours from wandering salespeople not affiliated with a registered tour company.
Ma-Ci-Te, CC Pasaje Colón, Paseo Colón, T268 8529, www.maciteturismo.com. Well organized, helpful, local and national tours, also diving, English and Italian spoken.

⊖ Transport

Barcelona *p1384*
Air The airport is 3 km south; also serves Puerto La Cruz. Many flights daily to Caracas, 40 mins, and daily flights to Porlamar, 30 mins, Maracaibo and Valencia (with **Aeropostal**, T286 4063, and **Aserca**). Oficambio exchange facilities (no TCs), *artesanía* shops, small museum, car rental agencies, Inatur booth (stays open late for some incoming flights, few handouts, friendly, cannot book hotels, a city map can be scrounged from **National Car Rental**). Taxi to airport from bus station US$3.50; taxi to Puerto La Cruz US$11.65.
Bus The Terminal de Pasajeros next to the Mercado Libre is used mostly by *por puestos*, with regular departures to Anaco, El Tigre, Maturín, Cumaná and other nearby destinations. Buses go to **Caracas** (5 hrs, 3 daily, US$8.75); **San Félix**

Mochima

C **Posada Gaby**, at end of road with its own pier next to sea, T431 0842/0414-773 1104. A/c or fan, breakfast available, lovely place, take guests to islands (included in the room price).

E **Posada Mochimero**, on main street in front of *Restaurant Mochimero*, T0414-773 8782. A/c or fan, rooms with bath, recently expanded.

E **Villa Vicenta**, Av Principal, T416 0916/0414-993 5877. Basic rooms with cold water and larger rooms with balcony, also cold water, dining room, owner Otilio is helpful.

Room to rent on the plaza from **José Cruz**, T416 6114 (his family also runs Posada Doña Cruz). A/c, TV, living room and bedroom. Recommended.

🍴 Eating

Parque Nacional Mochima *p1387*
Playa Colorada

† **Daniel's Barraca**, at east end of the beach, is good for cheap food.

Santa Fe

† **Club Naútico**, fish and Venezuelan dishes, open for lunch and dinner.

† **Los Molinos (Julios)**, opens all day from 0800, beach bar serves sandwiches, hamburgers and cocktails.

Mochima

† **El Mochimero**, on waterfront 5 mins from jetty. Highly recommended for lunch and dinner.

† **Il Forno de Mochima**, on the main street. Run by Roberto Iorio, for those who would like a change from seafood, homemade pastas and pizza.

† **Puerto Viejo**, on the plaza. Good food, if a bit pricey, good views.

▲▲ Activities and tours

Parque Nacional Mochima *p1387*
Mochima

Diving Francisco García, runs a diving school and shop (*Aquatics Diving Center*, T416 0009/0414-777 4894), C La Marina at Plaza Apolinar. Equipment hire, courses, trips.
Rodolfo Plaza runs a diving school (*La Posada de los Buzos*, T432 3416/0414-777 1949, mochima rafting@hotmail.com) and hires equipment, also walking and canoeing trips; contact him in Caracas (Los Palos Grandes, Av Andrés Bello entre 3a y 4a transversal, T0212-961 2531).

🚌 Transport

Parque Nacional Mochima *p1387*
Santa Fe

Getting there from **Cumaná**, take *por puesto* 1 block down from the Redonda del Indio, along Av Perimetral, US$1.75. It may be difficult to get a bus from **Puerto La Cruz** to stop at Santa Fe, take a *por puesto* (depart from terminal, US$3, 1 hr), or taxi, US$23 including wait.

Mochima

Bus From **Cumaná** to Mochima take a bus from outside the terminal and ask to be let off at the street where the transport goes to Mochima, US$1.50; change here to crowded bus or jeep (US$0.70). No buses between Santa Fe and Mochima, take a *por puesto*, bargain hard on the price, US$15-21 is reasonable. Bus to Cumaná, 1400, US$1.40.

Cumaná → *Phone code: 0293. Colour map 2, grid A1. Population: 280,000.*

Cumaná was founded in 1521 to exploit the nearby pearl fisheries. It straddles both banks of the Río Manzanares. Because of a succession of devastating earthquakes (the last in 1997), only a few historic sites remain. Cumaná is a charming place with its mixture of old and new, but the port area (1½ km from the centre) is not safe at night. Main festivals are 22 January, Santa Inés, a pre-Lenten carnival throughout the state of Sucre and 2 November, the Santos y Fideles Difuntos festival at El Tacal.

A long public beach, **San Luis**, is a short bus ride from the centre of town; take the 'San Luis/Los Chaimas' bus. The least spoilt part is the end by the *Hotel Los Bordones*.

The **Castillo de San Antonio de la Eminencia** (1686) has 16 mounted cannons, a drawbridge and dungeons from which there are said to be underground tunnels leading to the Santa Inés church. Restored in 1975, it is flood-lit at night (but don't go there after dark, it's not safe). The **Castillo de Santa María de la Cabeza** (1669) is a rectangular fortress with a panoramic view of San Antonio and the elegant homes below. **Convento de San Francisco**, the original Capuchin mission of 1514, was the first school on the continent; its remains are on the Plaza Badaracco Bermúdez facing the beach. The **Church of Santa Inés** (1637) was the base of the Franciscan missionaries; earthquakes have caused it to be rebuilt five times. A tiny 400-year-old statue of the Virgen de Candelaria is in the garden. The **home of Andrés Eloy Blanco**

(1896-1955) ⓘ *Mon-Fri 0800-1200, 1600-2000, Sat-Sun 0900-1200, 1600-2000, free,* one of Venezuela's greatest poets and politicians, on Plaza Bolívar, has been nicely restored to its turn-of-the-century elegance. On the opposite side of the plaza is **La Gobernación** around a courtyard lined by cannon from Santa María de la Cabeza; note the gargoyles and other colonial features. There are markets selling handicrafts and food on both sides of the river.

The **Museo Gran Mariscal de Ayacucho** ⓘ *Consejo Municipal in Parque Ayacucho, Tue-Fri 0845-1130, 1545-1830; free tours,* commemorates the battle of Ayacucho: with portraits, relics and letters of Bolívar and José Antonio Sucre (Bolívar's first lieutenant). **Museo del Mar** ⓘ *Av Universidad with Av Industrial, Tue-Sun 0830-1130, 1500-1800, US$0.75, getting there: take San Luis minibus from the cathedral,* has exhibits of tropical marine life, at the old airport.

For information contact **Dirección de Turismo** ⓘ *C Sucre 49, T431 6051, fonmitur@ venezuela.com.ve, open mornings only.* Very helpful, English spoken. Also **Fondoturismo de Sucre** ⓘ *Centro Profesional La Copita, edif A, p 4 of 43, T433 2584, procatur_sucre@ yahoo.com.* See also www.cumanaweb.com and www.sucreturistico.com.

◉ Sleeping

Cumaná *p1389*

A **Nueva Toledo Suites**, end of Av Universidad, close to San Luis beach, T451 8118, www.nueva toledo.com. A/c, hot water, TV, pool, beach bar, good value all-inclusive deals.

A **Los Bordones**, at end of Av Universidad on the beach, T451 3111. A/c, pool, restaurant, another hotel with all-inclusive options.

C **Bubulina's**, Callejón Santa Inés, half a block west of Santa Inés church, T451 2519, bubulinas@cantv.net. In the historic centre, beautifully restored colonial building, a/c, TV, hot water, good service, good restaurant with Venezuelan food. Recommended.

C **Gran Hotel**, Av Universidad near San Luis beach, T451 0671, F451 2677. A/c, pool, restaurant.

Cumaná

Sleeping 🛏
Astoria **1**
Bubulina's **2**
Gran **3**
Mariño **5**
Posada San Francisco **6**
Regina **7**

Eating 🍴
El Colmao **1**
El Mercadito **2**
Jardín de Sport **3**
La Casa Tomada **4**

D **Mariño**, Mariño y Junín, T432 0751. Central,
a/c, hot water, reasonable restaurant.
E **Posada San Francisco**, C Sucre 16, near
Santa Inés, T431 3926, posada_francisco@
cantv.com. Renovated colonial house,
courtyard, spacious rooms, hot water, a/c
(cheaper with fan), very helpful, bar,
restaurant. Recommended.
E **Regina**, Arismendi y Av Bermúdez, T431 1073.
Hot water, a/c, restaurant, helpful, safety deposit
box for valuables.
E-F **Astoria**, Sucre, T433 2708. A/c, shower,
basic, bar, restaurant with good food cooked
to order.

⊙ Eating

Cumaná *p1389*
All central restaurants close Sun lunchtime
₮₮ **El Colmao** on Plaza Pichincha, C Sucre. Very
good fish, charming service.
₮ **Ali Baba**, Av Bermúdez near corner of
C Castellón. Excellent middle eastern food.
Recommended.
₮ **El Mercadito** at Redoma del Indio. For
excellent cheap lunches, fish and seafood.
La Casa Tomada, just off Plaza Bolívar on Sucre.
A good *tasca* with reasonable prices.
Jardín de Sport, Plaza Bolívar. Outdoor café,
good food, noisy atmosphere. Recommended.

▲ Activities and tours

Cumaná *p1389*
Piel Rojo, Sr Nelson Castro, T432 5416/0414- 840
7694, or in *Posada San Francisco*. Local tours,
sailing, diving, many languages spoken.
Ya-Wei, in *Hotel Barceló* (see above), T451 9595,
yawei@telcel.net.ve. Organizes launches to Araya
Peninsula and beaches, diving, tours to Amazonas
and Gran Sabana.

⊙ Transport

Cumaná *p1389*
Bus Terminal 3 km northwest of the centre on
Av Las Palomas, just before the junction with the
peripheral road. Local bus into centre US$0.25,
taxi US$2.50. *Por puesto* to **Puerto La Cruz**,
US$7, bus US$3.50, 1½ hrs. To **Güiria**, US$10,
Expresos Los Llanos once a day, *por puesto*
US$15 (6-7 hrs), beware of overcharging, often
stop in Irapa. To **Carúpano**, US$3.50, 2-3 hrs. To
Caripe, you have to go to **Santa María**, south of
Cariaco, and change to *por puesto* there. To
Caracas, from US$12 depending on company (7-8
hrs), frequent service; many daily to **Ciudad
Guayana** and **Ciudad Bolívar**, US$12.50 and 12
respectively. **Caribe** runs all the way to **Boa Vista**
in Brazil. Also to Maturín and Barcelona.
Ferry For Ferries to **Araya Peninsula** and **Isla
Margarita**, see below and page 1402.

⊙ Directory

Cumaná *p1389*
Banks For cash advance on Visa and MasterCard
Banco Mercantil, Av Bermúdez, 2 blocks up from
Hotel Guaiqueri. ATM and cash advance on Visa
and Mastercard. Also **Banco Venezuela**, at Mariño
y Rojas. **Corp Banca**, Av Bermúdez y Av Perimetral,
edif Don Jesús No 21. Amex TCs changed at good
rates, no commission. **Oficambio**, Mariño y
Carabobo, Edif Funcal, 1 block from Plaza
Estudiante. Cash and TCs at official rate (take
passport and proof of purchase, may limit
exchange to US$200), open weekdays 0800-1130
and 1415-1730, Sat 0830-1130. **Internet** Centro
de Comunicaciones CANTV, CC San Onofre at the
end of Av Humboldt. **Comiti**, Edif Arismendi p2, Av
Arismendi. **Post offices** Ipostel, next to
Cathedral on C Paraíso. **Telephones** CANTV, on
C Montés con Boyacá, 2 blocks from Plaza Blanco.

Araya to Paria

This section is bounded by two peninsulas, Araya, which is an area of desert landscapes
and pink salt lakes, and Paria, a finger of land stretching out to the most easterly point on
Venezuela's Caribbean coast and a place of peaceful, coastal towns, beaches and forest.
The eastern mountains, rising to 2,000 m at their highest point, receive abundant rainfall in
their tropical forest.

Araya Peninsula

The main settlement is Araya which has an airport and a ferry dock. The major sight is the
Fortaleza de Santiago de León, built by Spain to protect the salt mines, but of which very
little now remains. Construction began in 1622 and it took 47 years to complete. Entry is
free, but the only facilities are a refreshment stand and a picnic area. Today the mines are
exploited by a Government-owned corporation, ENSAL. Windsurfing is excellent, but only for
the experienced.

Carúpano → *Phone code: 0294. Colour map 2, grid A1. Population: 120,000.*

This is a colonial town dating back to 1647, from which 70% of Venezuela's cocoa is shipped. The area around Plaza Santa Rosa has been declared a national and international heritage site by UNESCO. Buildings include the **Museo Histórico**, containing a comprehensive data base on the city, and the **Iglesia Santa Rosa**. The **Casa del Cable** ① *T331 3847/0414-780 0060, merle@telcel.net.ve*, location of the first telecommunications link with Europe, is the HQ of the Fundación Thomas Merle, run by Wilfried Merle, who has been instrumental in setting up ecotourism and economic development projects in the Paria Peninsula. Carúpano is famous throughout Venezuela as the last place still celebrating a traditional pre-Lenten Carnival: days of dancing, rum drinking, with completely masked women in black (*negritas*). Book well ahead for accommodation at this time (February). Other local festivals are 3 May, Velorios de la Cruz (street dances); 15 August, Asunción de la Virgen. On the outskirts of Carúpano is **Playa Copey** (ask the *por puesto*/bus to drop you at Playa Copey if arriving from Cumaná or other westerly points, or take a taxi from town, US$5).

Caripe → *Phone code: 0292. Population: 23,880.*

A paved road runs inland from Carúpano to Caripe via Cariaco and Santa María, two hours. Caripe is an attractive town set in gorgeous mountain scenery. There is a lively daily market. It is 12 km from the famous Cueva del Guácharo and a good place to escape from the beaches. It's especially good for walking and biking. At San Francisco, on the Maturín-Cumaná road (212 km, all paved but twisty; beautiful tropical mountain scenery), is a branch road running 22½ km northeast to Caripe. *Feria de las Flores* is on 2-12 August and *NS del Pilar* is 10-12 October. To get to Caripe from Caracas you must go to **Maturín**, the capital of Monagas state (*Phone code: 0291. Colour map 2, grid A1, relatively expensive accommodation*), then take a *por puesto*. Alternatively go to Cumaná and then to Santa María for *por puesto* services.

Cueva del Guácharo →

① *0800-1700, US$1.50 with compulsory guide in Spanish, US$4 with English speaking guide, last tour 1600, leave backpacks at the ticket office, cameras allowed but ask before using flash, to go further into the caves permits from Inparques in Caracas are needed.*

This remarkable cave was discovered by Humboldt and has since been penetrated 10½ km along a small, crystal-clear stream. In the first caves live around 18,000 *guácharos* (oil birds) with an in-built radar system for sightless flight. Their presence supports a variety of wildlife in the cave: blind mice, fish and crabs in the stream, yellow-green plants, crickets and ants. For two hours at dusk (about 1900) the birds pour out of the cave's mouth. Through a very narrow entrance is the *Cueva del Silencio* (Cave of Silence). About 2 km in is the *Pozo del Viento* (Well of the Wind).

Wear old clothes, stout shoes and be prepared to get wet. In the wet season it can be a bit slippery; tours into the cave may be shortened or even closed in August-September because of rising water level. There is a caving museum with a leaflet in English, US$0.80; good cafeteria. Opposite the road is a paved path to **Salto Paila**, a 25 m waterfall, about 30 minutes' walk, guides available. A beautiful path, built by Inparqes, starts at the caving museum, with some nice shelters for picnics. Camping is allowed by the cave for US$5, or you can sleep without a tent under the roof by the café for free.

Paria Peninsula

Río Caribe This lovely fishing village (*Phone code: 0294, Population: 25,100, 20 km E of Carúpano*) used to be a major cacao-exporting port. It is a good jumping-off point for the beautiful beaches of **Playa Medina** (in an old coconut plantation, 25 km east) and Pui Puy, both famous for their crystal-clear water and golden sands. Playa Medina is safe, has shade for rent and stalls selling food and drink; it is crowded at weekends and holidays. Cabins at the beach are very expensive (**A** per person). To get to Playa Medina, take a taxi with *Línea San Miguel* (Rivero y Mariño, T61107), departing in morning till 1000, returning around 1500, US$30-35 return trip per car, US$35-40 to Pui Puy. There are *camionetas* which go quite close to Medina and one which departs from opposite petrol station at exit to village (US$0.70, one hour), which drops you at entrance to beaches, but it's two hours walk from there (further to Pui Puy - take great care if walking as far as Pui Puy or beyond, armed robberies have been reported). Further east is the delightful village of **San Juan de las Galdonas** and some great beaches. There is a Banco Venezuela in Río Caribe for exchange. Near Chacaracual, 15 minutes' drive from Río Caribe is **Hacienda Bukare** ① T0294-416 7763, 808 1505, 0414-777 1147 (mob), www.bukare.com, a working cocoa hacienda which also sells chocolate and has an inn in beautiful surroundings.

Güiria At Bohordal, the paved road from Río Caribe across the mountains meets Route 9, which continues to the pleasant town of Irapa (*Population: 11,500; hotels, bus connections*). The paved highway continues 42 km to Güiria (*Phone code: 0294, Colour map 2, grid A2, Population: 30,000*), a friendly, peaceful town and a badly littered beach. Feria de la Pesca, 14 July. Gasoline is available.

Macuro A quiet town on the tip of the Peninsula, Macuro (*Population: 1,500*) is accessible by boat (two hours from Güiria) and by a new road from Güiria (20 km paved by May 2003, the remainder passable by 4WD). It was around here Columbus made the first recorded European landing on the continent on 5 August 1498. Locals like to believe the landing took place at Macuro, and the town's official new name is Puerto Colón. A big party is held here every year on 12 October to mark the official 'discovery' of America. Restaurants only open at weekends (good food at Sra Mercedes, on C Carabobo, round corner from *Posada Beatriz*, blue house). There are also a few basic shops and a pharmacy. The boat to Güiria leaves at 0500, arrive early, US$3-5 per person.

The beach is unattractive but the coast on the north side of the peninsula is truly wonderful; crystal-clear water and dazzling sands backed by dense jungle. A highly recommended trip for the adventurous is the hike to **Uquire** and **Don Pedro** on the north coast; 4-6 hours' walk, places to hang a hammock or pitch a tent. In Uquire ask for Nestor Mata, the Inparques guard, very helpful. **Note** This part of the peninsula is a national park; you need a permit from Inparques in Caracas.

⬤ Sleeping

Araya p1391
D Araya, difficult to get to without a car. A/c, hot water, with bath, good restaurant, offers tours to the Salinas and around Araya.
E Araya's Wind, beside the Fortaleza in front of beach, T0414-777 3682. Fan, some rooms with bath, cold water, good restaurantin high season.
E Posada Helen, behind *Araya's Wind*, T0414-775 4043. A/c, cheaper with fan, cold water.

Carúpano p1392
C Posada El Colibrí, at the 1st roundabout on entering town, follow the bypass to the right, then left into Av Sur, T332 3583. Cabins beside a pool, in tropical gardens, hot water, fan, TV, fully-equipped kitchen, various personal touches, restaurant service by arrangement, English, German and Dutch spoken, owners Polly and Gunter Hoffman. Recommended.
C Posada La Colina, on hill behind *Hotel Victoria*, F332 0527. A/c, TV, hot water, includes breakfast, pool, restaurant and bar, beautiful view. Recommended.
D Hotel Lilma, T331 1361, Av Independencia, 3 blocks from Plaza Colón, T331 1341. A/c, hot water in some, TV, restaurant, *tasca*, cinema.
E Bologna, Av Independencia, 1 block from Plaza Santa Rosa, T331 1241. Basic but clean, a/c,

F with fan, cheap restaurant.
E Centro, Carabobo, close to Iglesia Santa Catalina, T331 3673. A/c or fan, TV.
E Posada Zahuco, Av Perimetral. A/c, TV, hot water, use of kitchen and lounge.
E San Francisco, Av Juncal y Las Margaritas, T331 1074. A/c, no hot water, TV, parking, restaurant, *tasca*.
E Victoria, Av Perimetral next to *Posada Zahuco*, T331 1554. Safe but basic, some a/c.

Playa Copey
C Posada Nena, 1 block from the beach, T331 7297, www.posadanena.de. A/c, **D** with fan, hot water, games room, good restaurant, public phone, good service, German spoken, owner Volker Alsen offers day trips to Cueva del Guácharo, Mochima, Medina and other Venezuelan destinations. Recommended.
C-D Posada Casa Blanca, 5 mins from *Posada Nena*, T331 6896. Fan, hot water, safe, good family atmosphere, private stretch of beach illuminated at night, Spanish restaurant, German spoken, discounts for long stays.

Caripe p1392
D Finca Agroturística Campo Claro, at Teresén, T555 1013/0416-491 7654. Cabins with

⬤ *For an explanation of the sleeping and eating price codes used in this guide, see page 58. Other*
⬤ *relevant information is found in Essentials pages 1332-1333.*

cooking facilities and bath, also rooms (D), restaurant for residents, horse riding.
D Samán, Enrique Chaumer 29, T/F545 1183, www.hotelsaman.com. Also has more expensive suites, comfortable, pool, parking, not so welcoming to backpackers.
F Plaza Centro, opposite church on Plaza Bolívar, T545 1018. Hot water, not very clean.
F Venezia, Av Enrique Chaumer 118, 5 mins from centre, T545 10325, F545 1875. No sheets, poor water and electricity supply, restaurant, owner speaks English.

Paria Peninsula *p1392*
Río Caribe
As well as those listed, there are other *posadas* and private, unmarked pensions; ask around.
B Posada Caribana, Av Bermúdez 25, T646 1242, www.caribana.com.ve. Beautifully restored colonial house, tastefully decorated, some a/c, otherwise fans, with breakfast, restaurant, bar, excursions.
D La Posada de Arlet, 24 de Julio 22, T/F646 1290. Price (US$30) includes breakfast, a/c, laundry service, English and German spoken, bar, offers day trips to local beaches and rents mountain bikes (only place in town that does, check bike carefully). Recommended.
D Posada de Angel, 2 km away from the beach at Playa Medina, T577 4329. Nice place, private bathrooms, fan, mosquito netting on windows.
E Posada Vanexa, on right as you enter village, T646 1670. Basic but clean, use of cooker.
F Pensión Papagayo, 14 de Febrero, 1 block from police station, opposite *liceo*, T646 1868. Charming house and garden, fan, shared bath with hot water (single sex), use of kitchen, German spoken, nice atmosphere, owner Cristina Castillo leads tours in the area.

San Juan de las Galdonas
B Las Pioneras, T0416 694 0113/964 0843. 4 star overlooking the main beach, fan or a/c, hot water, bar/restaurant, swimming pool, jacuzzi, parking.
C pp Habitat Paria, T0414-779 7955, www.habitatparia.vzla.org. With breakfast and supper, huge, splendid, zodiac theme, fan, hot water in some rooms, bar/restaurant, terraces, garden. The *posada* is right behind Barlovento beach on the right hand side of San Juan. Also run day trips by boat US$30 pp, min 5 passengers, packed lunch included.
D Posada Las Tres Carabelas, T0416-894 0914 (mob), carabelas3@hotmail.com. Fans and mosquito nets, restaurant, bar, wonderful view, owner Javier knowledgeable about local area. Ask about new *posada* at Guariquen, as yet untouched by tourism.

Güiria
D Playa Paraíso, 10 mins from town on road to Las Salinas, T982 0350, F982 0451. A/c, hot water, pool, restaurant, OK (but has caged toucan), boat trips to Macuro and Trinidad.
E Miramar, Turiparin, close to Banco República, T982 0732. A/c, cheaper with fan.
F Plaza, esq Plaza Bolívar, T982 0022. Basic, restaurant, luggage store.
La Posada de Chuchu, C Bideau, 2 blocks from plaza, T982 1266. A/c, hot water, TV, fridge, good *creole* restaurant. Recommended.

Macuro
F Posada Beatriz, C Mariño y Carabobo. Basic, clean, with bath, fan.
G Posada Marlo, C Mariño. Shared bath, fan.

● Eating

Araya *p1391*
Eat early as most places close before 2000. Hamburger stalls around the dock and 2 *panaderías*.
† **El Delfín**, at the dock. Good food and service.
† **La Monaguense**, 2 blocks from dock. Good value Venezuelan food.
† **Parador Turístico Eugenía**, in front of *Posada Helen*. For good value meals.

Carúpano *p1392*
†† † **El Fogón de La Petaca**, Av Perimetral on the seafront. Traditional Venezuelan dishes, fish.
†† † **La Madriguera**, Av Independencia close to Plaza Santa Rosa. Good Italian food, some vegetarian dishes, Italian and English spoken.
† **Bam Bam**, kiosk at the end of Plaza Miranda, close to seafront. Tasty hotdogs and hamburgers.
† **La Flor de Oriente**, Av Libertad, 4 blocks from Plaza Colón. Open from 0800, arepas, fruit juice and main meals, good, large portions, good, food, reasonable prices, very busy at lunchtime.
† **El Oasis**, Juncal in front of Plaza Bolívar. Open from 1800, best Arabic food in Carúpano.

Other options include the **food stalls** in the market, especially the one next to the car park, and the *empanadas* in the Plaza Santa Rosa.

Caripe *p1392*
† **Tasca Restaurante Río Colorado**, G Blanco 77, T545 1243. Good, local food.
† **Trattoria de Stefano**, C Cabello. Wide variety of good food, popular with locals and tourists.

Paria Peninsula *P1392*
Río Caribe
† **Doña Eva**, Zea 46. Good food and is also a *posada*. † **Mi Cocina**, on the road parallel to Av Bermúdez, 3 mins' walk from Plaza Bolívar. Very good food, large portions.

Güiria

Everywhere is closed Sun, except for kiosks on Plaza Bolívar. Restaurants include:

♥ **El Limón**, C Piar, good value.

♥ **El Milagro**, corner of Plaza Bolívar. OK.

♥ **Rincón Güireño**, corner of Plaza Sucre. Good for breakfast (also rents rooms, **D-E**).

▲ Activities and tours

Carúpano p1392

Corpomedina, T331 5241, F331 3021, at the airport, associated with Fundación Thomas Merle (see Casa del Cable, page 1392), reservations for cabins at Medina or Pui Puy beach: at Medina US$143 for 2, US$250 for 4, including meals, but not alcoholic beverages or transport; at Pui Puy US$51 for 2, US$80 for 4, including breakfast. Transport from the airport to Medina and return for 2 people US$95, to Pui Puy US$110.

Mar y Luna, T/F332 2668, louisa@cantv.net. Offer day trips to Medina, Pui Puy, Caripe, El Pilar, Los Pozos, specialist surfing and diving packages, walking and hiking in the Paria Peninsula, reconfirmation of international flights, reservations for national flights, reservations for *posadas*, reception of fax and email, general information and advice, English, French, Portuguese and a little Italian spoken, very helpful.

Paria Peninsula: Macuro p1393

A highly recommended guide is Eduardo Rothe, who put together, and lives at, the Museo de Macuro on Calle Bolívar, 1 block from *Posada Beatriz*. He'll take you on walking tours to the north coast, US$10-15 pp per day, or boat trips (US$60 per boat), or fishing trips (US$30 pp per day, including mangroves).

⊖ Transport

Araya p1391

Ferry Cumaná-Araya ferry *la palita* shuttles back and forth from 0600 till 1700, US$1.85 pp, US$7.45 per car. At weekends it usually makes only 1 trip each way. Also **Naviarca** car ferry, 3 a day, T0800-227 2600/431 5577 or ferry terminal 433 3605. To get to ferry terminal take Conferry bus from **parador del centro**, just up from CANTV, in Cumaná (avoid walking; it can be dangerous). Alternatively, take a *tapadito* (passeger ferry in a converted fishing boat, leave when full, crowded, stuffy) to Manicuare and *camioneta* from there to Araya (15 mins). Return ferries from Araya depart from main wharf at end of Av Bermúdez. Ferries to **Isla de Margarita**, *tapaditos* depart from **Chacopata** (1 hr, US$10 one way). To get to Chacopata from Carúpano, take a *por puesto* at the stop diagonal to the

market entrance (where the fish is unloaded), US$5, 1½ hrs.

Carúpano p1392

Air The airport is 15 mins' walk from the centre, US$5 by taxi. **Avior** (T331 2867) flies daily to **Caracas** and **Porlamar**, and less frequently to **Barcelona**, **Güiria** and **Tucupita**.

Bus To **Caracas**, US$15, 8 hrs, *Rodovías* directly into central Caracas close to Metro Colegio de Ingenieros. Most other buses only go as far as Terminal de Oriente. To **Maracay**, **Valencia**, US$20, 10 hrs. For other destinations such as **Cumaná**, US$3.50, 2 hrs, **Puerto La Cruz**, US$7, 4 hrs (Mochima/Santa Fé), **Güiria**, US$5.15, 3 hrs *por puestos* are a better option. They run more frequently and make fewer stops. Buses do not go from Carúpano to Caripe, you have to take a *por puesto* to **Cariaco**, US$3, then another to **Santa María**, US$2.50, then another to Caripe, US$2.

Caripe p1392

Bus Terminal 1 block south of main plaza. For **Carúpano**, take *por puestos* to Santa María and Cariaco (see above), similarly for **Río Caribe**. To get to **Cumaná**, go to Santa María and catch transport from there. Bus to **Maturín** direct, 0600, 2½ hrs, US$4.25; Maturín-**Caracas** costs US$12, 7½ hrs. *Por puesto* to Ciudad Bolívar 1500, 1½ hrs, US$3.50.

Cueva del Guácharo p1392

Bus Frequent from **Caripe** to the caves. If staying in Caripe, take a *por puesto* (a jeep marked Santa María-Muelle), at 0800, see the caves and waterfall and catch the Cumaná bus which goes past the caves between 1200 and 1230. Taxis from Caripe (US$3, negotiate price), hitching possible. Bus from Cumaná direct to the Cueva del Guácharo leaves at 0715, US$3.50 and stops right in front of the caves. *Por puesto* from Cumaná US$12.50, 2 hrs. Private tours can be organized from Cumaná for about US$15 per person, with guide.

Paria Peninsula p1392

Río Caribe and San Juan de las Galdonas

Bus Direct from **Caracas** (Terminal del Oriente) to Río Caribe with **Cruceros Oriente Sur**, 10 hrs, and from **Maturín** with Expresos Maturín. *Por puesto* Carúpano-Río Caribe, US$1.50. Buses depart Río Caribe from the other Plaza Bolívar, 7 blocks up from pier. Jeep Carúpano-San Juan de las Galdonas 1100, 1½ hrs; *camioneta* from Río Caribe from stop near petrol station, 0600 till 1300.

Güiria

Bus Depart Plaza Sucre, at top end of C Bolívar: Expresos Maturín to **Maturín** (US$10, 6 hrs),

Caripito, San Félix, Cumaná, Puerto La Cruz and **Caracas**; also Expresos Los Llanos (recommended).

Ferry To **Macuro**: depart daily 1100-1200 from the Playita, US$3-5, return 0500, 2 hrs. **Travel to Trinidad** A ferry leaves every Wed at 1500 for Chaguaramas, Trinidad (leaves Trinidad at 0900, Wed), 3½ hrs, US$80 return (plus tax). There is a US$23 exit tax from Venezuela (US$12.10 from Trinidad). Talk to Siciliano Bottini at the *Agencia Naviera* for other ships to Trinidad. Don't take any old boat that's going; however safe it may appear you may come under suspicion for drug running.

⊙ Directory

Carúpano *p1392*
Banks It is not easy to change foreign currency in Carúpano. American Express TCs can be changed until 1400 at **Corp Banca**, C Güiria y C Carabobo. Cash advance on Visa or MasterCard at **Banco Caribe**, Av Independencia, 4 blocks from

Plaza Santa Rosa. ATMs are unreliable for European cards. Good rate at the casino on the waterfront near the bus station. It may be possible to change dollars in *Hotels Lilma, San Francisco* or *Victoria*, but rates are not good.
Internet Centro de Comunicaciones CANTV, C Juncal, opposite *Hotel San Francisco*, 0800-2000. **Cybercafé**, C Las Margaritas entre Juncal y Carabobo, same hours. **Ebenezer**, CC Sahara, C San Félix. **Post offices and telephones** Both **Ipostel** and **CANTV** are at the end of Carabobo, 1 block up from Plaza Santa Rosa.

Paria Peninsula: Güiria *p1393*
Useful services Immigration: visas can't be arranged in Güiria, should you need one; maximum length of stay 14 days (but check). For more than 14 days, get visa in Caracas. Remember to get exit stamp before leaving Venezuela. Officially, to enter Trinidad and Tobago you need a ticket to your home country, but a return to Venezuela is usually enough.

Isla de Margarita → *Colour map 2, grid A1*

Margarita is the country's main Caribbean holiday destination and is popular with both Venezuelans and foreign tourists. The island's reputation for picture-postcard, white-sand beaches is well-deserved. Some parts are crowded but there are undeveloped beaches and colonial villages. Porlamar is the most built up and commercial part of the island while Juan Griego and La Restinga are much quieter. If you book a place to stay in advance, it is possible to enjoy the island even on a budget during high season. If not, it is almost impossible to find accommodation for under US$23 per person a night. Despite the property boom and frenetic building on much of the coast and in Porlamar, much of the island has been given over to natural parks. Of these the most striking is the Laguna La Restinga.

The western part, the Peninsula de Macanao, is hotter and more barren, with scrub, sand dunes and marshes. Wild deer, goats and hares roam the interior, but 4WDs are needed to penetrate it. The entrance to the Peninsula de Macanao is a pair of hills known as **Las Tetas de María Guevara**, a national monument covering 1,670 ha. There are mangroves in the **Laguna de las Marites** natural monument, west of Porlamar. Other parks are **Cerro El Copey**, 7,130 ha, and **Cerro Matasiete y Guayamurí**, 1,672 ha (both reached from La Asunción). The climate is exceptionally good and dry. Roads are good and a bridge links the two parts. Nueva Esparta's population is over 250,000, of whom 85,000 live in Porlamar. The capital is La Asunción.

Ins and outs

Getting there and around There are many national, international and charter flights to Isla de Margarita. There also ferries from La Guaira (Caracas), Puerto La Cruz and Cumaná. Car hire is a good way of getting around (see Directory, below). Women should avoid walking alone at night on the island. ▸▸ *For more details, see Transport, page 1401.*

Information **Isla de Margarita**: The private **Cámara de Turismo** is at the seaward end of Avenida Santiago Mariño in Porlamar, T263 9024. They have free maps and are very helpful. A tourist information booth on Avenida 4 de Mayo, opposite the *Dugout* sports bar, has a good map, coupon booklet and *La Vista* tourist magazine. The **state tourism department** can be contacted on T262 2322, www.corpturmargarita.gov.ve. Travel agencies can also provide a tourist guide to Margarita. *MultiGuía de Margarita* (US$4) is published yearly and is a useful directory of tourist information and can be found in kiosks, *panaderías*, cafés and bookshops. The best map is available from *Corpoven*. **Websites**: www.islamargarita.com and www.margaritaonline.com. Many offices close for lunch.

Porlamar → *Phone code: 0295.*

Most of the island's high-rise hotels are at Porlamar which is 20 km from airport and 28 km from Punta de Piedra, where ferries dock. If you're seeking sun and sand, then head for the north coast towns where the beaches tend to be lined with low-rise hotels and thatched restaurants. Porlamar's beaches are nothing special, but it makes up for what it lacks in this department with its shops (see below). At Igualdad y Díaz is the **Museo de Arte Francisco Narváez**, displaying the work of this local sculptor. At night everything closes by 2300.

The **Bella Vista** beach is busy but clean and has lots of restaurants. **Playa Concorde** is small, sheltered and tucked by the marina. **Playa Morena** is a long, barren strip of sand for the Costa Azul hotel zone east of the city. **La Caracola** is a popular beach for a young crowd.

Ferries go from Punta de Piedra and *peñeros* from El Yaque and La Isleta to the **Isla de Coche** (11 km by 6), which has 4,500 inhabitants and one of the richest salt mines in the country (see Transport below). They also go, on hire only, to **Isla de Cubagua**, which is totally deserted, but you can visit the **ruins of Nueva Cádiz** (which have been excavated). Large private yachts and catamarans take tourists on day trips to Coche.

La Asunción → *Population: 30,000.*

The capital is a few kilometres inland from Porlamar. It has several **colonial buildings**, a **cathedral**, and the **fort of Santa Rosa** ① *Mon 0800-1500, other days 0800-1800*, with a famous bottle dungeon. There is a **museum** in the Casa Capitular, and a local **market**, good for handicrafts. Nearby is the **Cerro Matasiete** historical site, where the defeat of the Spanish on 31 July 1817 led to their evacuation of the island.

Pampatar → *Population: 25,000.*

For a more Venezuelan atmosphere go northeast to Pampatar, which is set around a bay favoured by yachtsmen as a summer anchorage. Pampatar has the island's largest fort, **San Carlos de Borromeo**, built in 1662 after the Dutch destroyed the original. Visit also the church of **Cristo del Buen Viaje**, the **Library/Museum** and the **customs house**. Jet skis can be hired on the clean and pretty beach. A fishing boat can be hired for US$20 for 2½ hours, 4-6 passengers; shop around for best price, good fun and fishing. There is a Spanish language school: **Centro de Linguística Aplicada** ① *Corocoro Qta, CELA Urb, Playa El Angel between Poralmar and Pampatar, T/F262 8198, http://cela-ve.com (useful website).*

Eastern and northern beaches.

Playa Guacuco, reached from La Asunción by a road through the Guayamurí reserve, is a popular local beach with a lot of surf, fairly shallow, palm trees, restaurants and car park; excellent horseriding here or up into the hills, US$30 for two hours, contact Harry Padrón at the ranch in Agua de Vaca, or phone travel agent on T261 1311. Playa Parguito further up the east coast is best for surfing (strong waves; full public services).

Playa El Agua has 4 km of white sand with many kiosks and shady restaurants. The sea is very rough in winter (dangerous for children), but fairly shallow; beware the strong cross current when you are about waist deep. This beach gets overcrowded at Venezuelan holiday times. The fashionable part is at the south end. The beach is 45 mins by bus from Porlamar (US$0.45). See also www.playaelagua.info.

Manzanillo (*population: 2,000*) is a picturesque bay between the mountains on the northeast point of the island with apartments (**A-B**), beach houses and good places to eat (cheaper than Playa El Agua). Playa Escondida is at the far end. Puerto Fermín/ El Tirano is where Lope de Aguirre, the infamous conquistador, landed in 1561 on his flight from Peru.

The coast road is interesting, with glimpses of the sea and beaches to one side. There are a number of clifftop look-out points. The road improves radically beyond Manzanillo, winding from one beach to the next. **Playa Puerto la Cruz** (wide and windy) adjoins **Pedro González** (population 3,700), with a broad sweeping beach, running from a promontory (easy to climb) to scrub and brush that reach down almost to the water's edge. **Playa Caribe** is a fantastic curve of white sand with moderate surf. Chairs and umbrellas can be hired from the many beach bars.

Further west is **Juan Griego** (*Population: 8,300*), a sleepy town whose picturesque bay is full of fishing boats. It's a good place for cheap shopping (quieter and safer than Porlamar). The little fort of La Galera is on a promontory at the northern side, beyond which is a bay of the same name with a narrow strip of beach and many seafront restaurants.

Playa El Yaque

Playa El Yaque on the south coast, near the airport, is a Mecca for wind- and kitesurfers. The winds are perfect from mid-June to mid-October and the water is shallow enough to stand when you fall off (see Activities and tours, below). Most come on package deals and therefore accommodation is expensive, but cheaper places can be found. There is no public transport; a taxi from Porlamar costs US$8. **Cholymar** travel agency will change money and there is *casa de cambio* in the Hotel California. A certified Spanish teacher, Mary Luz Jinete, offers lessons, T0416-797 8846 (mob), spanishwithmaryluz@yahoo.com, which cost from US$20-30 an hour depending on the size of the group.

La Restinga and around

This is the 22-km sandbar of broken seashells that joins the eastern and western parts of Margarita. Behind the *restinga* is the eponymous **national park**, designated a wetland of international importance. Over 100 species of birds live here, including the blue-crowned parakeet, which is endemic to Margarita. There are also marine turtles and other reptiles, dolphins, deer, ocelots, seahorses and oysters. *Lanchas* can be taken into the fascinating lagoon and mangrove swamps to the beach from landing stages at the eastern end (US$13-14 per person for an hour trip, plus US$0.35 entrance fee to park). Bus from Porlamar US$1. On La Restinga beach you can look for shellfish in the shallows (sun protection essential), the delicious oysters can be bought for around US$1 a dozen.

The **Península de Macanao**, over the road bridge from La Restinga is mountainous, arid, barely populated and a peaceful place to get away from the holidaymakers on the main part of Margarita. It also has some good beaches that are often deserted and is a good place for horseriding. Punta Arenas, a pleasant beach with calm water is the most popular and has some restaurants, chairs and sunshades. Further on is the wilder Playa Manzanillo. It's best visited in a hire car. **Boca del Río**, near the road bridge, has a **Museo Marino** ① *T291 3231, www.fpolar.org.ve/museomarino, US$2, US$1 children, daily 0900-1630, open until 1730 in high season*, which features collections of marine life, organized by ecosystem, and a small aquarium.

Isla de Margarita

😴 Sleeping

Porlamar p1397

Many luxury hotels are grouped in the Costa Azul suburb to the east of Porlamar, but they now pepper most of the northeast coast of the island. Most hotels and tour operators work on a high season/low season price system. High season prices (Christmas, Easter and Jun-Aug) can be as much as 35% higher. Flights and hotels are usually fully booked at this time. In low season, bargaining is possible. A good source of hotel information is www.elsoldemargarita. com.ve/margarita/hoteles.htm.

AL Bella Vista, Av Santiago Mariño, T261 7222, www.hbellavista.com. Large, luxury hotel with all expected services (but not overly helpful), good pool area with sea views, also beach, car hire, travel agency, French restaurant, and restaurant serving *comida criolla*.

B For You, Av Santiago Mariño, T263 8635, F261 8708. Modern, bland, large rooms, good service and roof restaurant, bar.

B Margarita Princess, Av 4 de Mayo, T263 5834. Large, comfortable rooms, balcony, restaurant, small pool.

B-C Posada Lutecia, Final C Campos Cedeño y Marcano, T/F263 8526. Lovely bright rooms with personal touch, a/c, hot water, TV, French-owned, café with outdoor seating near beach.

D Imperial, Av Raul Leoni, via El Morro, T261 6420, www.hotelimperial.com.ve. Modern hotel, best rooms in front have sea view, parking, balcony, safe, a/c, TV, restaurant, hot water, parking, English spoken.

D Tamaca, Prolongación de Marcano y Campos, near the sea, T261 1602. Popular, a/c, OK, E with fan, good atmosphere, German-run *tasca*.

La Asunción p1397

A Ciudad Colonial, C La Margarita, T242 3086. Upmarket hotel, swimming pool, a/c, accepts credit cards, restaurant.

B-C Posada Restaurant Ticino Da´Rocco, Crucero de Guacuco, vía Playa El Agua, C San Onofre, sector Camoruco, T242 2727. Pool, a/c, restaurant, accepts credit cards.

Playa Guacuco p1397

High season prices:

A Guacuco Resort, Vía Playa Guacuco, T242 3040, www.guacucoresort.com. Stylish, comfortable apartments for up to 4 people (prices quoted for 2) with balcony or terrace, 1 km from the beach and 300 m off the road, a/c, self-catering facilities, tranquil, beautiful tropical gardens with birds, pool and bar.

Playa El Agua p1397

Most *posadas* are along Calle Miragua, close to the beach.

A Coco Paraíso, Av Principal, T249 0117, cocoparaiso1@hotmail.com. Very pleasant, large rooms, a/c, pool, 3 mins from beach, German spoken.

B Chalets de Belén, Miragua 3, next to *El Agua*, T249 1707. 2 chalets for 4 and 6, kitchen facilities, good value, no towels provided, parking, laundry service, also 2 double rooms, **D** (discounts in low season).

B Costa Linda, C Miragua, T249 1303, www.hotelcostalinda.com. Very nice rooms in colonial-style house with a/c, relaxing, TV, safe, pool, restaurant and bar, includes breakfast, accepts credit cards, changes TCs and US$, English and German spoken.

B Doña Romelia, Av 31 de Julio (1 km before Playa Manzanillo), 10 min walk to Playa El Agua, T249 0238, www.hotelposadadonaromelia.com. Very attractive rustic style hotel, bright rooms with balconies and hammocks, nice pool area and garden. Well-run, helpful staff. Parking, breakfast included. Recommended.

B Trudel's Garden Vacation Homes, C Miragua, T249-0558, www.casatrudel.com (useful site). Six large, 2-bedroom houses set in a garden (US$65 for 3-6 people per house per night), 200 m from beach, full equipped kitchens, cable TV, good value, parking.

C Casa Trudel Bed & Breakfast, C Díaz Ordaz, T249-0558, www.casatrudel.com. Canadian run, small place, patio with hammocks, includes breakfast, 5 mins from beach, Wi-Fi, king size beds, hot water shower.

D Res Vacacional El Agua, C Miragua, T249 1975, T0414-797 3221 (mob). Fully equipped, self-catering bungalows for 4, 6 and 8 with fan, run down, but good value, 1 double room with fan, also **D**.

E Hostería El Agua, Av 31 de Julio vía Manzanillo, T249 1297, hosteriaelagua@ hotmail.com. One of the cheapest options, simple, a/c, hot water, safe, laundry facilities, restaurant/bar, on roadside 4 mins' walk from beach, English and Italian spoken.

Manzanillo and around *p1397*
Puerto Fermín

B-C Hostería Marymonte, Playa El Tirano, T234 8066. Beachfront, 8 cottages with hot water, mosquito net, fan or a/c, bar, pool, English spoken, price depends on season.

Playa Caribe

AL-A pp Posada Caracol formerly Casa Chiara. 8 private villas built with adobe and hardwood with small gardens that back on to a large pool, a huge *churuata* houses bar, restaurant and seating area, Italian owners, Paolo and Chiara, are great hosts, exceptional food. Highly recommended.

Juan Griego *p1397*
Many restaurants close out of season.

D Patrick's, El Fuerte, T/F253 6218. Good travellers hostel, a/c rooms with fine sunset views, excellent restaurant and bar, near beach, internet access. Recommended.

E Hotel Nuevo Juan Griego, next to beach, La Marina, Bvd Almte Brión, T253 2409. English spoken, fan, book exchange, popular. Recommended.

F La Posada de Clary, Los Mártires, T253 0037. Restaurant, also attractive apartments for 4, **E**, a/c, kitchen, parking. Recommended.

Playa El Yaque *p1398*

AL Hotel El Yaque Paradise, T263 9810, yaque@grupoparadise.com. Upmarket, pleasant, good rooms, a/c, pool, safety deposit box, bar, restaurant, English and German spoken, price includes breakfast.

C El Yaque Motion, T263 9742, www.elyaque motion.com. 400 m from beach. German run,

popular with wind- and kite surfers, well-established, a/c, kitchen, laundry, free internet and Wi-Fi connection, roof terrace, cheaper with fan and shared bath, rents 3 apartments for 4-6 people, English and German spoken, good. Enquire here for wind- and kite surfing lessons and equipment hire.

E-F Sail Fast Shop, T263 3449, herbert@sail-fast.com. Basic rooms 300 m from the beach, ask for Herbert Novak at the Sail Fast Shop opposite Hotel Yaque Paradise. Rooms with private bath, some with a/c, kitchen facilities.

La Restinga and around *p1398*
Península de Macanao

AL Makatao, T/F263 6647. Run by Dr Alexis Vásquez, price includes transfer, food, natural drinks and lodging in the singular rooms. The doctor runs health, 'eco-relax' and therapy programs, and there are mud baths at the *campamento*.

B Posada Río Grande, at *Cabatucan Ranch*, 2 km from Guayacancito on the road to Punta Arenas, T416 8111. Attractive rooms with a/c, hot water, full board available, charming, will also arrange all-inclusive scuba diving (US$57) and snorkelling trips (US$27) to Isla Cubagua.

C Auberge L'Oasis, Robledal, T291 5339 charles@enlared.net. A/c or fan, hot water, TV, sea view, garden, restaurant.

🍴 Eating

Porlamar *p1397*
The upmarket dining, such as Japanese food, is in Urb Costa Azul on Av Bolívar. Plenty of eating places on Campos and 4 de Mayo.

ⓣⓣ-ⓣ **Los 3 Delfines**, Cedeño 26-9. Good seafood.

ⓣⓣ-ⓣ **Rancho Grande**, C Guevara, near Playa El Agua bus stop. Colombian, good value.

ⓣ **Dino's Grill**, Igualdad y Martínez. Open 0700-1400, buffet lunch, indoor/outdoor seating, grill, home-made sausages, wood-fired pizza oven, cheap, good service.

ⓣ **Doña Martha**, Velázquez near Hernández. Colombian food, good, inexpensive.

ⓣ **Dragón Chino**, 4 de Mayo. Great Chinese.

ⓣ **La Isla**, Mariño y Cedeño. 8 fast food counters ranging from hamburgers to sausages from around the world.

ⓣ **El Pollo de Carlitos**, Marcano y Martínez. Pleasant location, live music most nights, good food and value.

ⓣ **El Punto Criollo**, Igualdad near **Hotel Porlamar**. Excellent value *comida margariteña*.

🔴 *For an explanation of the sleeping and eating price codes used in this guide, see page 58. Other* 🔴 *relevant information is found in Essentials pages 1332-1333.*

1400

Playa El Agua *p1397*

Several restaurants along C Miragua. Two good restaurants on beach in Playa Agua, ¶ **El Pacífico**, thatched roof, popular, good fish. Another beach restaurant ¶ (the one with blue and white seats) owned by friendly Italian, serves good, fresh Mediterranean-style food, pleasant terrace area and good service.
La Dorada, French owned by Gérard and Hilda, with beach view. Recommended as good value.

♫ Bars and clubs

Porlamar *p1397*

Several bars in the Centro Comercial Costal Azul.
Bahía, Av Raúl Leoni y Vía El Morro.
Bar-restaurant, excellent value, live music.
Dugout, Av 4 de Mayo. Popular sports bar.
Woody's Bar, Av 4 de Mayo. Spit and sawdust venue good for a drink and a dance.
Many hotels in Urb Costa Azul have relatively inexpensive **casinos**; the best are **Casino del Sol** at the *Hotel Marina Bay*, and **Gran Casino Hilton**.

Playa El Yaque *p1398*

Several beach bars; best bar is **Los Surf Piratas**, drinks and dancing from 2130.

✹ Festivals and events

Isla de Margarita *p1396, map p1398*

Many religious festivals on the island, including **19 Mar** at Paraguachí (*Feria de San José*, 10 days); **26 Jul** at Punta de Piedras; **31 Jul** (Batalla de Matasiete) and **15 Aug** (Asunción de la Virgen) at La Asunción; **1-8 Sep** at El Valle; **4-11 Nov** at Boca del Río, **4-30 Nov** at Boca del Pozo; **5-6 Dec** at Porlamar; **27 Dec-3 Jan** at Juan Griego See map for locations.

○ Shopping

Porlamar *p1397*

Margarita's status as a duty-free zone attracts Venezuelan shoppers, who go in droves for clothing, electronic goods and other items. Street sellers lay out their handicrafts on Av Santiago Mariño in the afternoon. When buying jewellery, bargain, don't pay by credit card (surcharges are imposed) and get a detailed guarantee of the item. Av Santiago Mariño and surroundings are the place for designer labels, but decent copies can be found on Blvds Guevara and Gómez and around Plaza Bolívar in the centre. For bargains on denims, t-shirts, shorts, swimming gear and bikinis, take a bus to Conejeros market (from Fraternidad, Igualdad a Velásquez).

▲ Activities and tours

Porlamar *p1397*

Diving Porlamar is a good place to book scuba diving and snorkelling trips: most go to Los Frailes, a small group of islands to the north of Playa Agua, and reputedly the best diving and snorkelling in Margarita, but it's also possible to dive at Parque Nacional La Restinga and Isla Cubagua. Prices from US$75 pp for an all-inclusive full day (2 dives), but bargaining is possible if you have a group of 4 or more. Snorkelling is always about half the price of scuba diving.
Aquanauts Diving, Urb Costa Azul, C Los Almendrones, Centro Comercial Bayside, local No 1-47, PB, T267 1645, www.aquanauts.com.ve. PADI school, scuba and snorkelling and fishing trips.
Natura Raid, Av 4 de Mayo con Av Santiago Mariño, of 41, p 4, Edif Silcat, T261 4419, www.naturaraid.com. Eco-tourism and adventure trips across Venezuela, including diving in Los Roques and sailing.
Sailing The private yachts **Viola Festival** and **Moon Dancer**, and the catamarans **Yemaya** and **Catatumbo** can be hired for mini cruises to the island of Coche or Isla Cubagua. Contact **Viola Turismo**, Caribbean Center Mall, Av Bolívar, opposite Hilton hotel. Expect to pay US$35-40 pp. They can also arrange fishing trips.

Playa El Yaque *p1398*

Sailboards, **kite surf** and **kayaks** can be hired on the beach from at least 5 well-equipped companies, who also offer lessons. Half day costs US$30, full day US$35-40 for sailboard; US$25 per hour for kite surf. English, German, French and Portuguese spoken. Enquire at **El Yaque Motion** (see Sleeping, above) for more information about wind and kite surfing. See also www.velawindsurf.com. A 5-min boat ride from **El Yaque Motion** hotel goes to Kitebeach, a designated area for kiters. A 20-min boat ride to Isla Coche leaves from **El Yaque Motion**, a recommended spot for advanced kiters. Rescue service available at the beach.

La Restinga and around *p1398*
Peninsula de Macanao
Horse riding You can ride on the peninsula at **Hato San Francisco Cabatucan**, T416 2000. Prices start at US$45pp.

⊖ Transport

Porlamar *p1397*

Air There are too many flight options to list here: check with local offices for details. **Gen Santiago Mariño Airport**, between Porlamar and

Punta de Piedras, has the international and national terminals at either end. Taxi from Porlamar US$13, 20-30 mins. There are scheduled flights to **Frankfurt** and internal flights to almost all Venezuela's airports. All national airlines have routes to **Margarita**. Many daily flights to/from **Caracas**, about US$100 return, with **Aeropostal, Láser, Santa Bárbara**, and **Aserca**, 45 mins flight; tickets are much cheaper if purchased in Venezuela. Reservations made from outside Venezuela are not always honoured. To **Canaima** and to **Los Roques** with **Aereotuy** and **Rutaca**.

Bus Local: *Por Puestos* serve most of the island, minimum fare US$0.75, few services at night and in low season: Airport, from Centro Comercial AB, Av Bolívar; La Asunción, from Fajardo, Igualdad a Marcano; Pampatar, from Fajardo y La Marina; La Restinga, from Mariño, La Marina a Maneiro; Playa El Agua, from Guevara, Marcano a Cedeño; Juan Griego, from Av Miranda, Igualdad a Marcano; Playa Guacuco, from Fraternidad, La Marina a Mérito (mornings), from Fajardo, Igualdad a Velásquez (afternoons).

Long distance: Several bus companies in Caracas sell through tickets from Caracas to Porlamar, arriving about midday. Buses return to Caracas from La Paralela bus station in Porlamar.

Ferry From **Puerto La Cruz** to Margarita (Punta de Piedras): **Conferry**, Los Cocos terminal, Puerto La Cruz, T0281-267 7847, www.conferry.com. Terminal has restaurant, CANTV and internet services. Price varies according to speed of ferry and class of seat, departs twice a day, night departures too (check times, extra ferries during high season). Slow ferry 5 hrs, passengers US$16-25 return, children 2-7 half price (proof of age required), cars US$40 return. Fast ferries, Conferry **Margarita Express** and **Cacique Express**, take 2-2½ hrs, US$18-27 one way. Also from Terminal Marítimo, La Guaira, near Caracas, T/F331 2053, US$37-51 one way. Ferries not always punctual. It is not uncommon for delays up to 6 hours during high season. It is most advisable to book in advance, especially if travelling with a car or motorbike during high season. Insist on a ticket even when you are told it is full. Don't believe taxi drivers at bus terminal who may tell you there's a ferry about to leave. To get to terminal in Puerto La Cruz, take 'Bello Monte' *por puesto* from Libertad y Anzoátegui, 2 blocks from Plaza Bolívar. From **Cumaná**, Conferry Terminal, Puerto Sucre, T0293-433 1903, twice a day (may wait until full of cars), US$10 one way for passengers. Conferry freefone

number for reservations 0501-2663 3779. **Gran Cacique II** is a passenger-only hydrofoil service that also runs from Puerto La Cruz (2 daily, US$20 one wa\y), and Cumaná (2 daily, US$16, 2 hrs). A ferry operated by **Conferry** from Punta de Piedras to Coche sails once a day, US$1.50, 1 hr.

Note Ferries are very busy at weekends and Mon. Conferry office in **Porlamar**, C Marcano entre Av Santiago Mariño y C Malaver, Mon-Fri 0800-1200, 1400-1730, Sat 0800, 1200.

Taxi To hire a taxi for a day costs US$15 per hr. Always fix fare in advance; 30% surcharge after 2100. Taxi from Playa El Agua to airport, US$16, from Restinga, US$22.

◉ Directory

Porlamar *p1397*

Airline offices Aeropostal, *Hotel Hilton*, Los Uveros, T264 5877, T0800-284 6637. Aereotuy, Edif Vista Bella, Av Santiago Mariño, T415 5778, emachado@lta.net.ve. Aserca, CC Provemed, local 5, Av Bolívar, Playa El Angel, T262 6677. Láser, T263 9195. Rutaca, Centro Comercial Jumbo, T263 9936. **Banks** National banks on Avs Santiago Mariño and 4 de Mayo. Banks are open 0830-1130, 1400-1630. **Casas de cambio:** Cambio Cussco at Velásquez y Av Santiago Mariño. Italcambio, CC Jumbo, Av 4 de Mayo, Nivel Ciudad, T265 9392. **Car hire** A cheap way of getting around the island; several offices at the airport, many offices at the entrance to *Hotel Bella Vista*, others on Av Santiago Mariño, average US$35 per day. Ramcar II, at airport and *Hotel Bella Vista*, recommended as cheap and reliable, non- deductible insurance. In all cases, check the brakes and bodywork and check conditions and terms of hire thoroughly. Scooters can also be hired. Motor cycles may not be ridden between 2000 and 0500. **Note** Make sure to fill up before leaving Porlamar as service stations become scarce the further away you get. Driving on Isla Margarita: the roads are generally good and most are paved. Signposts are often non-existent, confusing, or poorly-positioned. Although the free maps of the island are sometimes just as confusing, it is a good idea to have one with you before you start driving. It is best not to drive outside Porlamar after dark. Also beware of robbery of hired vehicles; park in private car parks whenever possible. **Internet** Several on Av Santiago Mariño. **Post offices** on Maneiro. **Telephones** Several on Av Santiago Mariño.

Los Roques

→ *Colour map 1, grid A6. Phone code: 0237. National park entry US$5, children 5-12 years, US$2.50.*

The turquoise and emerald lagoons and dazzling white sands of the Archipelago de Los Roques make up one of Venezuela's loveliest national parks. For lazing on an untouched beach, or for snorkelling and diving amid schools of fish and coral reefs, these islands cannot be beaten. Diving is best to the south of the archipelago. The islands tend to be very busy in July-August and at Christmas. Also look out for the excellent *Guía del Parque Nacional Archipiélago Los Roques* (Ecograph, 2004).

The islands of Los Roques, with long stretches of white beaches and over 20 km of coral reef in crystal-clear water, lie 166 km due north of La Guaira; the atoll, of about 340 islets and reefs, constitutes a national park of 225,153 ha. There are many bird nesting sites (eg the huge gull colonies on Francisqui and the pelicans, boobies and frigates on Selenqui); May is nesting time at the gull colonies. For more information write to La Fundación Científica Los Roques, Apdo No 1, Avenida Carmelitas, Caracas 1010. This is one of the least visited diving spots in the Caribbean; best visited midweek as Venezuelans swarm here on long weekends and at school holidays. (Low season is Easter to July.) Snorkelling is best at the southern part of the archipelago. There are at least seven main dive sites offering caves, cliffs, coral and, at Nordesqui, shipwrecks. There are many fish to be seen, including sharks at the caves of Olapa de Bavusqui. Prices are higher than the mainland and infrastructure is limited but the islands are beautiful and unspoiled. Camping is free, but campers need a permit from **Inparques** ① *T234 7331, F234 4238, or the office in Gran Roque, T0414-328 2121 (mob), Mon-Fri 0830-1200 and 1400-1800, weekends and holidays 0830-1200 and 1430-1730.* Average temperature 29° C with coolish nights. You will need strong sunblock as there is no shade.

Gran Roque (*Population 900*) is the main and only permanently inhabited island. The airport is here, as is the national guard, three grocery stores and a good craft shop, public phones, medical facilities, a few restaurants and accommodation. There is nowhere to change travellers' cheques. Park Headquarters are in the scattered fishing village. Tourist information is available free of charge from the very helpful *Oscar Shop*, directly in front as you leave the airstrip. Boat trips to other islands can be arranged here (round trip fares US$5-US$20, depending on distance, more for a tour).

You can negotiate with local fishermen for transport to other islands: you will need to take your own tent, food and (especially) water. **Madrisqui** has a good shallow beach and joins Pirata Cay by a sandspit. **Francisqui** is three islands joined by sandspits, with calm lagoon waters to the south and rolling surf to the north. You can walk with care from one cay to the other, maybe swimming at times. There's some shade in the mangrove near the bar at La Cueva. **Crasqui** has a 3-km beach with beautiful water and white sand. **Cayo de Agua** (1 hour by fast boat from Gran Roque) has an amazing sandspit joining its two parts and a nice walk to the lighthouse where you'll find two natural pools.

● Sleeping

In most places on Islas Los Roques, breakfast and dinner are included in the price.

Los Roques: Gran Roque *p1403*
There are over 60 *posadas* on Gran Roque (some bookable through **Aereotuy**), ranging from **D** to **L** In high season, Jul-Aug, Dec, prices are very high. Bargaining is advisable (especially in low season) if you intend to stay more than 2 nights.
AL pp **Piano y Papaya**, near Plaza Bolívar towards seafront, T0414-281 0104 (mob), www.piano ypapaya.com. Very tasteful, run by Italian artist, with fan, **AL** pp for bed and breakfast, credit cards and TCs accepted, Italian and English spoken.
AL pp **Posada Caracol**, on seafront near airstrip, T0414-313 0101 (mob), or Caracas T0212-267

5175, info@posadacaracol.com. Delightful, half-board and bed and breakfast options available, **A** pp, credit cards and TCs accepted, Italian and English spoken, good boats.
A-B pp **El Botuto**, on seafront near *Supermercado W Salazar*, T0416-621 0381 (mob), www.posadaelbotuto.com. Price for half board, depends on season, full board available, reservations must be made 50% in advance into an off-shore bank account. Nice airy rooms with fan, good simple food, locally-owned.
D pp **Posada Doña Magalis**, Plaza Bolívar, T0414-373 1993 (mob). Simple place, locally-owned, with fan, cheaper with shared bath, includes soft drinks, breakfast and dinner, delicious food.

D pp **Roquelusa**, behind *Supermercado W
Salazar*, T0414-369 6401 (mob). Probably the
cheapest option on Gran Roque, basic, with fan,
some with a/c.

Los Roques: Francisqui *p1403*
B There is one *posada*, T793 0694, F793 9579. Full
board including drinks, good food, friendly staff,
nice beach, snorkelling gear, water and light 24
hours, fan, bargaining possible if you stay for
several days; also hammock sites and camping.

▲▲ Activities and tours

Los Roques *p1403*
Diving Note For health reasons you must
allow 12 hrs to elapse between diving and flying
back to the mainland. All companies charge
US$85 for 2 dives including equipment, offering
pacjakes for 3 days or more.
Cayo de Agua and **Francisqui** recommended
for **snorkelling**. Boats can be arranged through
your posada, *Angel & Oscar Shop*, or with
independent fishermen.
Ecobuzos, 3 blocks from the airstrip, T221 1235 ,
T0414-793 1471 (mob), www.ecobuzos.com.
Very good, new equipment, modern boats,
experienced dive masters. PADI courses (US$350)
and beginner dives available.
Sesto Continente, past Inparques at the far end
of town, T/F9241853, scdrgerencia@telcel.net.ve.
Offer 2 dives for US$85. PADI courses and
beginner dives also available.
Sailing Fully equipped yachts can be chartered
for US$120 per day, all inclusive, highly
recommended as a worthwhile way of getting
some shade on the treeless beaches. Ask at

Angel & Oscar Shop, or **Posada Pez Ratón**,
pezratonfishing@cantv.net.
Ultralight flights Hernando Arnal, at the
airport and Plaza Bolívar, T0414-308 8622 (mob).
US$40 for 15 mins, US$70 for 30 mins, speaks
English, incredible views.
Windsurfing Happy Surf, Francisqui.
US$35.50 half day; US$50 full day, ask for Elías.

☉ Transport

Los Roques *p1403*
Air Flights from Maiquetía or Porlamar.
Aereotuy, Aeroejecutivos (T0414-939 7851),
Chapi Air, Sol de América (0212-266 9059) and
Transaven (T0212-355 1965) all fly from
Maiquetía (Aeropuerto Auxiliar) once a day, 40
mins, US$90-110. Some carriers charge more at
weekends. **Aereotuy** offer 1, 2 and 3-day
packages (return flight, accommodation, meals,
drinks, catamaran excursion with snorkelling and
diving equipment), from US$341.50 pp (1-day
from Margarita US$185), recommended. It's best
to buy a return to the mainland as buying and
confirming tickets and finding offices open on
the islands is difficult.

☉ Directory

Los Roques *p1403*
Banks Banesco, Plaza Bolívar, Mon-Fri
0830-1230, 1430-1700. Cash advances on Visa up
to US$500 per day. **Internet** Many posadas
have computers. If not, **Posada Acquamarina**
has a service for the public. **Public
telephones** Plaza Bolívar and Guardia National
on seafront.

Canaima and the Orinoco Delta

*In Parque Nacional Canaima, one of the largest national parks in the world, you'll find the
spectacular Angel Falls, the highest in the world, and the mysterious "Lost World" of
Roraima (described under South to Brazil). Canaima is the tourist centre for the park, but
indigenous communities are now accepting tourists. The historic Ciudad Bolívar on the Río
Orinoco is a good starting place for the superb landscapes further south. Further east,
beyond the industrial city of Ciudad Guayana, the Orinoco Delta is developing as a tourist
destination.*

    *Guayana, south of the Orinoco River, constitutes half of Venezuela, comprising rounded
forested hills and narrow valleys, rising to ancient flat-topped tablelands on the borders of
Brazil. These savannahs interspersed with semi-deciduous forest are sparsely populated.
So far, communications have been the main difficulty, but a road that leads to Manaus has
now been opened to Santa Elena de Uairén on the Brazilian frontier (see page 1416). The
area is Venezuela's largest gold and diamond source, but its immense reserves of iron ore,
manganese and bauxite are of far greater economic importance.*

Ciudad Bolívar → *Phone code: 0285. Colour map 2, grid A1, Population: 300,000.*

Ciudad Bolívar is on the narrows of the Orinoco, some 300 m wide, which gave the town its old name of Angostura, "The Narrows". It is 400 km from the Orinoco delta. It was here that Bolívar came after defeat to reorganize his forces, and the British Legionnaires joined him. At Angostura he was declared President of the Gran Colombia he had yet to build, and which was to fragment before his death.

At the Congress of Angostura, 15 February 1819, the representatives of the present day Venezuela, Colombia, Panama and Ecuador met to proclaim Gran Colombia. The building, on **Plaza Bolívar**, built 1766-76 by Manuel Centurión, the provincial governor, houses a museum, the **Casa del Congreso de Angostura**, with an ethnographic museum in the basement. Guides give tours in Spanish only. Also on this plaza is the **Cathedral** (which was completed in 1840), the **Casa de Los Gobernadores de la Colonia** (also built by Centurión in 1766), the **Real Intendencia**, and the **Casa de la Cultura**. Also on the north side of the plaza, at Bolívar 33, is the house where Gen Manuel Piar, the Liberator of Guayana from the Spanish, was held prisoner before being executed by Bolívar on 16 October 1817, for refusing to put himself under Bolívar's command. The restored **Plaza Miranda**, up C Carabobo, has an art centre. The present legislative assembly and **Consejo Municipal** are between Plaza Bolívar and Plaza Miranda. In 1824, when the town was still known as Angostura a Prussian physician to Bolívar's troops invented the bitters; the factory moved to Port of Spain in 1875.

Museum at **Casa del Correo del Orinoco** ⓘ *Paseo Orinoco y Carabobo, Mon-Fri 0930-1200, 1430-1700*, houses modern art and some exhibits of history of the city. **Museo Casa San Isidro** ⓘ *Av Táchira*, a mansion where Simón Bolívar stayed. **Museo Soto** ⓘ *Av Germania, 0930-1730, weekends and holidays 1000-1700, free, guide in Spanish only*, is

Ciudad Bolívar

Sleeping
- Amor Patria 1
- Colonial 3
- Da Gino 4
- Laja City 5
- Laja Real 6
- Posada Angostura 7
- Unión 2
- Universo 9
- Valentina 10

Eating
- Arabe-Venezolana 2
- Charly's 3
- Flamingo 1
- La Gran Fraternidad 4
- La Playa 5
- Lonchería Ché 6
- Lonchería Urica 7
- Pizzería La Casita 8
- Savoy 9

located some distance from the centre in pleasant gardens. It has works by Venezuela's Jesús Rafael Soto and other modern artists. Recommended.

Launches take passengers across the river, but there are no other passenger boat services. The Paseo Orinoco leading west out of town goes to the **Angostura Bridge**, which can be seen from town. This is the only bridge across the Orinoco, 1,668 m long (over a mile), opened in 1967 (toll US$0.80; cyclists and walkers are not allowed to cross, you must flag down a car or truck – another bridge is now being built in the Llanos). The **Zamuro hill fort**, dating from 1902 ① *entrance on Paseo Heres, closed 1200-1400*, is situated on another hill in the centre and dominates the city.

West of the centre is **El Zanjón**, an area of vegetation typical of the region. East is **Parque El Porvenir**, with botanical gardens. Outside the airport is the *Río Caroní* aeroplane, which Jimmy Angel landed on top of Auyán Tepuy (see page 1409).

The **tourist office** is **Dirección de Turismo** ① *Avenida Bolívar, Quinta Yeita 59, F632 2362, F632 2425, Mon-Fri 0800-1200, 1400-1730*. Helpful, English spoken. **Inparques** ① *Edif CVG Edelca, p 1, Av Germania con Calle 5 de Julio, T632 9908, drbolivar@ inparques.gov.ve, Mon-Fri 0800-1200, 1400-1730*, for camping permits and permission to climb Roraima.

To Ciudad Bolívar from the coast and the llanos Ciudad Bolívar can be reached easily by roads south from Caracas and Puerto La Cruz. The Caracas route, via Valle de la Pascua, and the Puerto La Cruz route, via Anaco, meet at El Tigre (*Population: 105,000*), which has good hotels and services. From the *llanos*, from **Chaguaramas** turn south through Las Mercedes (hotel **E**) to **Cabruta** (*Population: 4,300*), 179 km, road in extremely bad shape, daily bus to Caracas, US$11, basic hotel. Then take a ferry from opposite the airport to **Caicara** (ferry for cars 1½ hours, *lanchas* for pedestrians 25 minutes). Alternatively, from San Fernando de Apure take a bus to Calabozo and *por puesto* from there to El Sombrero (US$2), where you can catch the Ciudad Bolívar bus at 1700.

Tours can be made into the area south of the Río Orinoco from **Maripa** (*Colour map 2, grid A1*), travelling on the Río Caura. These include visits to indigenous villages, river bathing, jungle treks to waterfalls with explanations of wildlife and vegetation, usually starting from Ciudad Bolívar (see Activities and tours, below).

● Sleeping

Ciudad Bolívar *p1405*
Near airport
B Laja Real, Av Andrés Bello y Jesús Soto, opposite airport, T617 0100, www.lajareal.com. Comfortable rooms, also has suites, a/c, hot water, TV, fridge, pool open to non-residents for US$5 per day, excellent restaurant, sauna, gym, parking.
D Valentina, Av Maracay 55, T632 2145, F632 9311. Quiet, a/c, hot water, TV, comfortable, very good restaurant.
E Da Gino, Av Jesús Soto, opposite airport, T632 0313, F632 5454. A/c, hot water, TV, good service and restaurant, changes US$ cash.
D Laja City, Av Táchira y Av Bolívar, T/F632 9910, www.lajacity.com. Quiet, a/c, hot water, TV, restaurant.

In the centre
A Posada Casa Grande. C Boyacá 8, T632 4639, angostura@cacaotravel.com. Good hotel in colonial style, with breakfast, cable TV, a/c, hot water, restaurant, internet, pool.

C Posada Angostura, same contact details as *Posada Casa Grande* above, also on C Boyacá. Handsome rooms in old colonial house, a/c, fan, hot water, restaurant, and travel agency, good.
E Colonial, Paseo Orinoco, T632 4402, F632 3649. Has seen better days but good value, a/c, *Neckar* travel agency, nice restaurant on balcony overlooking river.
E Unión, Calle Urica, T632 3374. Clean, basic with fan, cable TV, helpful, filtered water, good value.
F Amor Patria, Amor Patria 30, T632 8819, plazabolivar@hotmail.com. Renovated colonial house, fan, shared bathrooms, kitchen, hammocks for hire (**G**). Run by Gerd Altmann, German and English spoken. Recommended.

Near the bus terminal
E Universo, Av República, 2 blocks left out of terminal, T654 3732. A/c, hot water, TV, restaurant, accepts credit cards.

● *For an explanation of the sleeping and eating price codes used in this guide, see page 58. Other*
● *relevant information is found in Essentials pages 1332-1333.*

Outside town

E Posada La Casita, Av Ligia Pulido, Urb 24 de Julio, PO Box 118, T632 3223, T0414-854 5146 (mob), reservation@gekkotours-venezuela.de. Very nice rooms, with cold water, fan, hammock with mosquito net can be rented, **G** space for tents, **G** Beautiful gardens (with small zoo), pool, laundry service, good food and drinks available, German and English spoken, helpful. Free pick up from airport or bus terminal (ring in advance). Free shuttle service into town. The owner runs **Gekko Tours** (see below).

✿ Eating

Ciudad Bolívar *p1405*

♯♯ Arabe-Venezolano, on Cumaná near Bolívar. Clean, a/c, good Arabic food, not cheap.

♯♯ Mirador Paseo Orinoco. *Comida criolla* with views over the river.

♯♯-♯ La Playa, C Urica entre Venezuela y Zea. Good for fish, reasonable prices.

♯ Flamingo, C Urica opposite Hotel Unión. Peruvian dishes, good value if they don't overcharge.

♯ La Carioca market, at the end of Paseo Orinoco, has series of small, cheap restaurants.

♯ Charly's, Venezuela. Good *fuente de soda*, cheap, fast service.

♯ Lonchería Ché, by *Hotel Colonial*. Good breakfast.

♯ Lonchería Urica, Urica, next to *Hotel Unión*. Good lunch for US$1.25, get there early.

♯ Mi Casa, C Venezuela. Open-air, good value.

♯ Pizzería La Casita Venezuela, opposite *La Casa de las Doce Ventanas*. Good value pizza and ice cream, views over Puente Angostura.

♯ Restaurant Vegetariano La Gran Fraternidad Amor Patria y Dalla Costa. Lunch only.

♯ Savoy, Venezuela y Dalla Costa. Good value breakfast.

❂ Shopping

Ciudad Bolívar *p1405*

Camping equipment White gas (stove fuel) is available at **Lubriven**, Av República 16, near the bus terminal.

Handicrafts Arts and crafts from Bolívar state, including basketry from the Orinoco Delta can be found in **La Carioca** market, at the end of Paseo Orinoco and **Tienda Artesanía Guayanesa** at the airport.

Jewellery There are many jewellers on Pasaje Guayana, which runs off Paseo Orinoco and near *Hotel Colonial*.

Supermarket Close to the Museo Soto on Av Germania, large and well-stocked.

▲▲ Activities and tours

Ciudad Bolívar *p1405*

Competition is stiff in Ciudad Bolívar, and among the genuine companies roam phoney salesmen. You are more than likely to have someone attempt to sell you a tour at the bus station. Do not pay any money to anyone in the bus station or on the street. Always ask to be taken to the office. Always ask for a receipt (and make sure that it comes on paper bearing the company logo). Be suspicious of people offering tours that start in another town or city. If you are unfortunate enough to fall prey to a con artist, be sure to make a *denuncio* at the police station and inform genuine travel agents.

Ciudad Bolívar is the best place to book a tour to Canaima, but you may pick up cheaper deals for trips to Roraima and the Gran Sabana from Santa Elena. There are 2 main tours operators in Canaima who offer tours at backpacker prices – *Bernal Tours* and *Tiuna Tours*. Most agents in Ciudad Bolívar sell one of these two options, but sometimes add commission. Always ask who will be running the actual tour; it may be cheaper to book from the tour operator directly. Service seems to change with the seasons. For 3 days/2 nights tours to Canaima expect to pay around US$190-230 pp; 4 days/3 nights to Gran Sabana US$250. 5 days/4 nights; Río Caura US$250-300.

Asociación Cooperativa Yajimadu, Servicios y Excursiones Ecoturísticas, T615 2354, dichenedu@hotmail.com, or Miguel Estaba, T0414-099 0568. US$275 for 5-day trip to Río Caura, 10 and 15-day trips also available, small groups catered for, guides are Ye'kwana from villages on the river, knowledgeable, Spanish spoken (some guides learning English), sleeping in hammocks, very good.

Expediciones Dearuna, C Libertad 16 (above Inversiones Ruiz), T632 4635. All usual tours at competitive prices, restructured in 2006.

Gekko Tours, run by Pieter Rothfuss at airport (also *Posada La Casita*), T632 3223, T0414-854 5146 (mob), www.gekkotours-venezuela.de. Gran Sabana, Canaima, Roraima, Orinoco Delta, rafting and river trips.

Miguel Gasca, T0414-923 5210/0166-629 4600 (mob), or find him at *Hotel Italia*. Recommended for tours to Roraima, Gran Sabana and Canaima.

Sapito Tours (Bernal Tours), at airport, T0414-854 8234 (mob), bernaltours@ terra.com.ve. Canaima tours slightly more expensive (and not always up-to-scratch, eg unplanned changes of itinerary, poor camping), *indígena* guides. Also offer tours to Roraima, Gran Sabana, Orinoco Delta, Kavác and Río Caura.

Soana Travel, run by Martin Haars at *Posada Don Carlos*, Boyacá 26, T0414 852 0373 (mob), soanatravel@gmx.de. Tours to Río Caura, Canaima and Gran Sabana, English and German spoken.

Tiuna Tours, at airport, T632 8697. Cheapest option for Canaima, have a camp that takes 180 people. Guides speak English, German and Italian.

Turi Express, at airport, T652 9764, T0414-893 9078 (mob), turiexpress@cantv.net. Range of tours plus Guri dam and fishing tours, good English.

---

❷ Transport

Air Minibuses and buses marked Terminal to town centre. Taxi to Paseo Orinoco US$2.25. To Caracas twice a week, 1½ hrs, **Aserca**. **Comeravia** and **Rutaca** (recommended for views) fly daily to **Canaima** and **Santa Elena**, US$55. Airport tax US$0.50. There are international phones at the airport, a good restaurant and car hire (Budget). Check where tours start from as some fly from Ciudad Guayana (**Turi Tours**), and charge passengers for taxi transfers.

Bus Terminal at junction of Av República and Av Sucre. To get there take bus marked Terminal going west along Paseo Orinoco (US$0.25). 10 daily to **Caracas** US$15 (student discount available, night bus $17.50), 8-9 hrs, with **Expresos Los Llanos**, **Rodovias**, and **Rápidos de Guayanesa**, *por puesto* US$40. 10 daily to **Puerto La Cruz**, US$8.50 (student discount available), 5 hrs, with **Caribe** and **Expresos San Cristobal**, *por puesto*, US$17.50. 1 daily to **Cumaná**, US$12, 7 hrs with **Caribe**. Several daily to **Maracay**, US$15, and **Valencia**, via Maracay, US$15, 8-9 hrs, with **Expresos Los Llanos** and Rodovias. **Tumeremo** US$9; Tumeremo bus through to El Dorado US$9.50, 3 daily. To **Santa Elena de Uairén** direct with **Caribe** US$26 (3 daily), **Expresos San Cristobal**, US$20 (2 daily), stopping en route with **Línea Orinoco**, **Transportes Mundial** (5 daily), spectacular views of Gran Sabana, 12-13 hrs. 1 daily to **Boa Vista** with **Caribe**, US$33, 20 hrs. To **Ciudad Guayana** hourly from 0700, US$3, 1½ hrs, *por puesto*, US$5.50, 1½ hrs. To **Ciudad Piar**, US$5, 3 hrs, and **La Paragua**, US$8, 4 hrs, with **Coop Gran Mcal Sucre**. 2 daily to **Caicara**, US$14 (including 2 ferry crossings), 7-8 hrs, with **Coop Gran Mcal Sucre**. To **Maturín** with **Unión Maturín**. 2 daily to **Puerto Ayacucho**, US$17, 10-12 hrs with **Coop Gran Mcal Sucre**, take food.

Taxi US$1.50 to virtually anywhere in town. US$2 from bus station to town centre.

❸ Directory

Ciudad Bolívar *p1405*
Banks Note TCs difficult to change. ATMs open only in banking hours. **Corp Banca**, Paseo Meneses, Edif Johanna. Amex TCs. **Banco de Venezuela**, near *Hotel Colonial*. Cash on Visa, ATM. **Banco Mercantil**, east end of Paseo Orinoco. Changes TCs, has ATM. **Banco Provincial**, west end of Av Jesús Soto, opposite Mobil petrol station. Cash on Visa, ATM.
Consulates Denmark, Av Táchira, Quinta Maninata 50, of 319, T632 3490, 0800-1200, 1500-1700. Italy, Av 17 de Diciembre, Edif Terepaima, Local 1, T/F654 4335.
Internet Places in the centre. Galaxia.com, C C Abboud Centre, Paseo Orinoco. **Galaxy Computer**, Av República y Jesús Soto, behind Mobil petrol station. **Post offices** Av Táchira, 15 mins walk from centre. **Telephones** CANTV, Av 5 de Julio, 100 m from Av Táchira (closed Sun).

Canaima and Angel Falls

→ *Colour map 2, grid B1. Park entry US$6 pp paid to Inparques on arrival in Canaima.*

At Canaima camp, the Río Carrao tumbles spectacularly over six waterfalls into the lagoon, which has beautiful tannin-stained water with soft beige beaches. It's a lovely spot, but it also has the air strip and is the centre of operations for river trips to Angel Falls. The Falls are named after Jimmie Angel, the US airman who first reported their existence in 1935. Two years later he returned and crash landed his plane, the *Río Caroní*, on top of Auyán Tepuy. The site is marked with a plaque. The sheer rock face was climbed in 1971 by three Americans and an Englishman, David Nott, who recounted the 10-day adventure in his book *Angels Four* (Prentice-Hall).

Canaima

There are several tourist lodges at Canaima and many package tours now visit on day trips. For good information on the region, see **www.thelostworld.org**. Do not forget swimwear, insect repellent and sun cream; waterproof clothing may be advisable. There are dangerous undercurrents in the lagoon; people have drowned while swimming near the falls. Do not walk barefoot as there are chiggers, or *niguas*, in the lagoon's sand beaches.

Trips to the Angel Falls

The Angel Falls, the highest in the world (979 m – its longest single drop is 807 m), 70 km downriver from Canaima, are best reached by plane to Canaima from Caracas, Ciudad Bolívar or Ciudad Guayana. Trips by boat upriver to the Angel Falls operate May-January, depending on the level of the water in the rivers. Even during the rainy season, you may have to get out and push. Most trips make an overnight stop on one of the islands, continuing to the Falls the next day. There are also bottom-numbing, 12-hour day trips which cost around US$150. More relaxing, with more stops are beauty spots, are 44-hour, 'three day' trips, US$260. If you have a *permiso de excursionistas* from *Inparques*, you may be able to go on one tour and come back with another, giving yourself more time at the Falls, but you may have to pay extra to do this, up to US$50 (take all food and gear). Trips can be arranged with agencies in Ciudad Bolívar (see above) or at Canaima airport. All *curiaras* (dugouts) must carry first aid, life jackets, etc. Take wet weather gear, swimwear, mosquito net for hammock and insect repellent, lots of film and a plastic bag to protect your camera/day bag. The light is best on the falls in the morning.

The cheapest way to fly over the falls is on scheduled flights from Ciudad Bolívar with Rutaca or Ciaca. From Canaima a 45-minute flight costs US$45 per person and does some circuits over and alongside the falls.

Kamarata

The largest of the tepuis, **Auyán Tepuy** (700 sq km) is also one of the more accessible. **Kamarata** is a friendly indigenous settlement with a Capuchin mission on the plain at the east foot of the tepuy. It has a well-stocked shop but no real hotels; basic rooms can be found for about US$6 per person, camping also possible at the mission (mosquito nets necessary and anti-malarial pills advised). Take food, although there is one place to eat, and locals may sell you dinner. The whole area is within the Parque Nacional Canaima.

Pemón families in Kamarata have formed co-operatives and can arrange *curiaras*, tents and porters for various excursions: see Activities and tours, below.

Kavác

About a two-hour walk northwest of Kamarata, this is a new indigenous-run resort consisting of a dozen thatched huts (*churuatas*) for guests, a small shop, and an excitingly short airstrip

Parque Nacional Canaima

serviced by Cessnas from Ciudad Bolívar, Santa Elena, and Isla Margarita; flights from the north provide excellent views of Angel Falls and Auyán Tepuy. There is a vehicle connection with Kamarata but it is expensive because all fuel has to be flown in. The prime local excursion is to **Kavác Canyon** and its waterfall known as La Cueva, which can be reached by joining a group or by setting out early west up the Río Kavác. A natural jacuzzi is encountered after a 30-minute wade along the sparkling stream, after which the gorge narrows dramatically until the falls are reached. Go in the morning to avoid groups of day-trippers from Porlamar. The sun's rays illuminate the vertical walls of the canyon only for a short time around 1100. Be prepared to get wet; swimwear and shoes with good grip, plus a dry change of clothing are recommended; also insect repellent, as there is a mosquito and midge invasion around dusk. Late afternoon winds off the savannah can make conditions chilly. It costs US$16 per person to stay at the camp (cheaper in hammocks), including a canyon tour. Take food with you.

Uruyén

South of Auyán Tepuy and west of Kamarata, **Uruyén** is similar to Kavác, only smaller and more intimate. It also has a beautiful canyon and is the starting point for treks up Auyán Tepuy. The camp is run by the Carvallo family. Charter flights can be arranged through **AmazonAir** ① *To212-283 6960, www.amazonair.com.*

⬤ Sleeping

Canaima *p1408*

LL Campamento Canaima, T0212-976 0530, www.hoturvensa.com.ve. Comfortable cabins, with shower and toilet. Meals are poor value, but drinks are at regular prices. Tours are well organized. 1 night, US$355 (high season price, 1 Dec-30 Apr), pp in double room, including transfers, meals, boat trip and flight over the Angel Falls, weather permitting. The airfare is not included. Although the quickest and most convenient way to visit Canaima is on a package tour, it is much cheaper to travel independently.

LL Campamiento Ucaima Jungle Rudy, T0286-962 2359, www.junglerudy.com. Run by the daughters of the late 'Jungle' Rudy Truffino, full board available, 1 hr walk from Canaima above Hacha Falls.

LL Wakü Lodge (Canaima Tours), T0286-962 0559, www.canaimatours.com. The best new option in Canaima, romantic, comfortable, right on lagoon, various packages. Recommended.

L Camp Wey Tüpü, in the village, T0414-884 0993 (mob). Ring direct to the camp if you wish to reserve lodgings only, *Roymar* in Caracas handle reservations of all-inclusive packages run from the camp, T/F0212-576 5655, roymar@cantv.net. Fan, shower, bar, price includes meals and flight over Falls.

L Parakaupa Lodge, 5 mins from airport, on southwestern side of lagoon, T0286-961 4963, parakaupa@etheron.net. Attractive rooms with bath, hammocks outside rooms, views over the lagoon and falls, restaurant, full board.

B Kusary, close to *Parakaupa Lodge*, near airport, T0286-962 0443. Basic but clean, with bath, fan, food available, ask for Claudio at *Tienda Canaima*.

E pp Kaikusé, next to *Kusary*, T0414-884 9031. Basic, clean with bath, hammocks.

Some families in the village rent hammocks for US$5-10 per person. Travel agencies also rent hammocks for US$3-5 per person a night; ask at the airport. Best place to rent a hammock or camp is at **Campamento Tomas Bernal** (*Bernal Tours*) on Anatoly Island, T0414-854-8234 (mob), bernaltours@terra.com.ve, or try at **Campamento Tiuna** (*Tiuna Tours*).

Camping Camp for free, but only around the *fuente de soda*; fires are not permitted. Ask *Inparques* at the airport. No tents available for hire.

❼ Eating

Canaima *p1408*

Food is expensive at the *Campamiento Canaima* restaurant. A cheaper option is *Simon's* restaurant in the village which is used by many of the agencies, US$4-5 pp, breakfast US$3. It is advisable to take food, though there are various stores, both on the west side, **Tienda Canaima**, or in the indian village, selling mainly canned foods. A *fuente de soda* overlooks the lagoon. There is an expensive snack bar at the airport; also souvenir shop.

⬛ Activities and tours

Canaima *p1408*

You can do walking expeditions into the jungle to indigenous villages with a guide, but bargain hard on the price. Other excursions are to the Mayupa Falls, including a canoe ride on the Río Carrao (US$50, half day), to Yuri Falls by jeep and boat (US$35, half day); to Isla Orquídea (US$75, full day, good boat ride, beach barbecue); to Saltos de Sapo and Sapito (3 hrs, US$25).

Guides in Canaima There is fierce competition at the airport but agencies pretty much offer the same thing at the same price. Some package tours to Canaima are listed under Caracas and Ciudad Bolívar Tour operators. Agents may tell you that guides speak English: some do, but many don't.

Bernal Tours (see above), with its own camp on Isla Anatoly in the lagoon, beds and hammocks, popular with travellers.

Kamaracoto Tours and **Tiuna Tours** for trips to Salto Sapo, Kavác, Salto Angel; they will also help with finding accommodation.

Kamarata *p1409*

Macunaima Tours (Tito Abati), **Excursiones Pemón** (Marino Sandoval), and **Jorge and Antonio Calcaño II** run local tours.

For details on climbing Auyán Tepuy, contact **Kamadac** in Santa Elena, run by Andreas Hauer (T0289-995 1408, T0414-886 6526 (mob), www.abenteuer-venezuela.de) or **Alechiven**, run by Edith Rogge, which has a base and radio at Kamarata, T0414-211828.

Alechiven and Pemón, co-operatives run 6-day river trips from Kamarata to Angel Falls (May-Dec), descending the **Río Akanán** to the Carrao by motorized dugout then turning south up the 'Devil's Canyon' to the Falls; the tours continue downriver to Canaima. It costs about US$450 for the *curiara* (minimum 4 persons), not including flights to Kamarata or food – supply your own food. River trips in this region are easier in the rainy season. Guides for Auyán Tepuy can be hired here for about US$25 per day, if you have your own equipment. Contact Andreas Hauer at *Kamadac*.

🚌 Transport

Canaima *p1408*

Air The return airfare from Caracas is US$300 with Avior, who fly daily from **Caracas**, 1 hr 40 mins direct. Do not rely on being able to change the return date on your flight and be even more wary of getting an open return. The airlines are quite happy to change your ticket, but the next available seat could be in 5 days time and Canaima is a very expensive place to kill time.

Arrangements are best made through travel agencies. **Aereotuy** runs 1 day excursions by 19-seat Dornier aircraft out of **Ciudad Bolívar**, landing at Canaima. There is a connecting **Aereotuy** flight from **Isla Margarita** (0900, returning 1500) and direct excursions from Margarita (0730 departure returning 1800). They have a new camp near the foot of Nonoy Tepuy, bookable only through **Aereotuy**, recommended (T0212-212 3110, www.lta.net.ve/canaima_ saltoangel.html). Other flights from Margarita with Rutaca. From **Ciudad Bolívar** and **Puerto Ordaz**, Canaima Tours (see above under Wakü Lodge) has daily flights, US$130 and US$180 respectively. Various companies offer day excursions in 5-seater Cessnas to Canaima from **Ciudad Bolívar**, book early, 0630-0700 at airport, US$180 pp, including flight over Angel Falls, boat across lagoon, lunch and trip to Salto Sapo; flight only, US$55 one way with **Rutaca**, **Comeravia** and **Ciaca**, 2 hrs. Reductions are available for parties. Note that you may not even see the falls from the air in the rainy season – the additional cost of a trip to the Angel Falls may well bring the cost of your journey up to that of a package. Flight to **Santa Elena** from Canaima costs US$55, one way. Tours can also be made to **Kavác** (see Kavác section).

Kamarata *p1409*

Air Aereotuy, Rutaca and Comeravia fly from **Ciudad Bolívar** (US$80 one way, 2 hrs), and Rutaca and Comeravia fly from **Santa Elena de Uairén** (US$140 one way).

Kavác *p1409*

Air A day excursion by light plane to Kavác from **Canaima** (45 mins' flight) can be made with any of the tour operators at the airport, and costs around US$130-140 per person depending on number of passengers. Flight only from **Ciudad Bolívar** to Kavác or Kamarata costs US$80 per person one way. Trips from Ciudad Bolívar can be arranged with tour agencies in town or at airport; around US$250 per person including flight via Angel Falls, meals, and 1 night's accommodation.

Ciudad Guayana and the Orinoco Delta

Ciudad Guayana → *Phone code: 0286. Colour map 2, grid A2. Population: 700,000.*

In an area rich in natural resources 105 km downriver from Ciudad Bolívar, an entirely new metropolis, known as Ciudad Guayana, is still being built on the south bank of the Orinoco and both sides of the Caroní River before it spills into the Orinoco. East of the Caroní is the commercial port of **San Félix** and the Palúa iron-ore terminal. Across the Caroní by the 470 m concrete bridge is **Puerto Ordaz** (airport), the iron-ore port connected by rail with the Cerro Bolívar open-cast iron mine. The iron-tinted waterfall in the pretty Parque Cachamay (20 minutes' walk from centre; closes 1700) is worth a visit.

Excursions Two hydroelectric plants can be visited: just up the Caroní at Macagua, with some truly beautiful cataracts called **Salto Llovizna** as you enter the grounds (known as Parque La Llovizna, taxi, US$5). A facility on the dam itself ① *Tue-Sun 0900-2100*, houses an archaeological museum, exhibits on the dam's construction (free), and a café. Higher up the river is the massive Guri dam ① *daily 0900-1030, 1415-1515*, take your passport; the area gets busy during holidays, Easter or carnival, powered by the world's second-largest reservoir, which is filled by the Paragua and Caroní rivers. The trip to Guri takes 90 minutes by taxi.

Los Castillos, supposedly where Sir Walter Raleigh's son was killed in the search for El Dorado, are two old forts down the Orinoco from San Félix (one hour by *por puesto*, US$2.50, or take a tour).

Tucupita → *Phone code: 0287, Colour map 2, grid A2, Population: 81,820.*

A worthwhile side trip along asphalted roads can be made to Tucupita (*Climate: very humid*), on the Orinoco delta. Though capital of Delta Amacuro state and the main commercial centre of the delta, there's a one-horse feel about it. There is a **tourist office** at Calle Dalla Costa beside Sonido Color 2000. Tourists should go there first for information on tours. **Note** Banks won't change travellers' cheques.

For a 3-4 day **trip to see the delta**, its fauna and the indigenous *Warao*, either arrange boats through the tourist office (see Ins and outs, above). Boats are not easy to come by and are expensive except for large groups. Bargain hard and never pay up front.

Excursions often only travel on the main river, not in the *caños* where wildlife is most often be seen. To avoid disappointment, be sure to determine where your guide intends to take you before you leave. If the river level rises after a downpour, arrangements may be cancelled. On all trips agree in advance exactly what is included, especially that there is enough food and water for you and your guide. Hammocks and mosquito repellents are essential.

Barrancas → *Colour map 2, grid A2. Population: 13,000.*

An interesting and friendly village, founded in 1530, Barrancas is one of the oldest villages in the Americas, but its precolonial past dates back to 1000 BC. Situated on the Orinoco, it can be reached by road from Tucupita (63 km), or from Maturín. It has two basic hotels (**D**). The village has a large community of Guyanese people who speak English. It is possible to take a boat to the *Warao* villages of **Curiapo** and **Amacuro** (near Guyana border), check at harbour.

It is possible to take a cargo boat to Mabaruma in Guyana from Curiapo. A trustworthy boatman is Bimbo, who lives at Wirma's guest house, where you can sleep if stuck in Curiapo (very likely). Contact Bimbo in advance through his sister in Tucupita; just ask for the "English woman" on Calle Amacuro – everyone knows her. In Curiapo, find Miss Teresa to get your exit stamp; she is rarely at home at the weekend. Take plenty of dollars cash, be prepared to wait for a boat and to cover yourself with a large plastic sheet once at sea (the mid part of the trip is on the open ocean). If thinking of taking this route, visit the Guyanese Embassy in Caracas first.

● Sleeping

Ciudad Guayana *p1411*
In Puerto Ordaz
C **Dos Ríos**, México esq Ecuador, T924 0679, F923 3092. New rooms have a/c, hot water, TV, pool, restaurant, *loncheria*, hairdresser, helpful.
D **Residencias Tore**, C San Cristóbal y Cra Los Andes, T923 0679, tore@cantv.net. Good rooms with a/c, hot water, TV, meals available. E in the house of Rolf and Rosa Kampen, C Surinam 03-07, Villa Antillana, 3 km from central Pto Ordaz, T/F923 0516. Room for 6 people, free pick up (best to contact by fax), breakfast US$4, dinner can be arranged. Rolf speaks English, German and Dutch. E with Wolfgang Löffler of *Lobo Tours*, C Zambia 2, Africana Manzana 39, T961 6286, F961 7708. Room for 8 people, free transfer from airport. 'El Lobo' speaks English and German. Recommended.

Tucupita *p1412*
D **Saxxi**, on main road into Tucupita, 10 mins from centre, T721 2112. Comfortable, hot water, a/c, bar/restaurant, disco Thu-Sat, pool. Also has camp *Mis Palafitos*, **AL**, T721 1733/ 0414-765 263, www.deltaorinocomispalafitos.com. All inclusive.
E **Gran Hotel Amacuro**, Bolívar 23, T721 0404. A/c, big rooms, dubious, **F** with fan.
E **Sans Souci**, Centurión 30, T721 0132, F721 6221. Safe, a/c, OK, **F** with fan. French spoken.
F **Residencias San Cristobal**, San Cristobal 50, T721 4529. Fan, parking.
G **Pequeño**, La Paz, T721 0523. Basic but clean, fan, good value, safe, stores luggage, orchid garden, popular with Israelis, closes at 2200.

🍴 Eating

Ciudad Guayana *p1411*
There are plenty of restaurants and cafés on Cras Tumeremo and Upata, off Av Las Américas. There is a very good *churrascaría* on Av Las Américas 15 mins walk from *Hotel Intercontinental Guyana* towards the airport, in an old hacienda building on the left, next to a *cervecería*, recommended. Fast food and upmarket eateries in Ciudad Comercial Altavista and surrounding streets.

Tucupita *p1412*
Capri, on Paseo Manamo. Very good.
Mi Tasca, C Dalla Costa. Popular, varied menu, large portions. Recommended.
Refresquería La Cascada, on Paseo Manamo. English spoken.

⛰️ Activities and tours

Ciudad Guayana *p1411*
Anaconda Tours, PB, loc 2, CC Anto, Av Las Américas, T923 7966, T/F922 6572, anaconda2@cantv.net. Trips to Castillos de Guayana (US$25 pp) and Guri dam (US$70 pp). Also organize tours to Orinoco Delta, Gran Sabana, Canaima, and Los Roques.
Bagheera Tours, p 2, of 86, C C Gran Sabana, Paseo Caroní, near airport, T952 9481, F952 8767, bagheera@telcel.net.ve. Tours to Gran Sabana, Angel Falls, Caura River and Orinoco Delta.
Lobo Tours, C Zambia No 2, Villa Africana Manzana 39, T961 6286, F961 7708. Wolfgang Löffler will tailor his tours to fit your demands. Trips generally organized to the Gran Sabana and Orinoco Delta, but will put together other excursions. Very helpful. US$70 pp per day all-inclusive, excellent cooking. English and German spoken. Recommended.
Piranha Tours, at *Hotel Intercontinental*, Av Guayana, Parque Punta Vista, Puerto Ordaz, T920 1111, F923 6487. River trips on the Caroní, to see the Cachamay Falls, and the confluence of the Caroní and Orinoco rivers, US$20-25 pp.
Sacoroco Tours, T961 5526, T0414-895 3948 (mob), sacoroco@cantv.net. Roger Ruffenach arranges tours to the less-visited southern parts of the Orinoco Delta (very basic facilities), leaving from Piacoa, cost US$250 pp. German spoken.
Recommended guide **Richard Brandt**, T/F922 4370 (or in Santa Elena de Uairén at *Cabañas Friedenau*), has his own car, speaks English and tailors trips to your requirements, including Roraima.

Tucupita *p1412*
Some boat owners visit hotels in the evenings looking for clients and may negotiate a price. Ask Pieter Rothfuss at *Gekko Tours/Posada La Casita* in Ciudad Bolívar and Roger Ruffenbach of *Sacoroco Tours* in Ciudad Guayana about a trip through the southern part of the delta and into the Sierra Imataca highlands. The following (and *Mis Palafitos* – see *Hotel Saxxi*) are registered with the tourist board and have insurance (this does not necessarily guarantee a good tour).
Aventura Turística, C Centurión 62, T/F721 0835, and at bus station, a_t_d_1973@ hotmail.com. Nicolás and Vidalig Montabric have 2 camps in the northern part of the delta, all-inclusive tours, English and French spoken.
Delta Sur, C Mariño and C Pativilca, T/F721 2666, oldest-established company, US$200-250 pp for 3 day tour, English spoken.
Tucupita Expeditions, opposite hospital, T721 0801, www.orinocodelta.com. US$255 pp for 3-day tour.

🚌 Transport

Ciudad Guayana *p1411*
Air Daily flights from Puerto Ordaz to **Caracas** and **Porlamar**. Walk 600 m to gas station on main road for buses to San Félix or Puerto Ordaz.
Bus Terminals at San Félix and close to Puerto Ordaz airport; long distance buses pass through both. Minibuses are fast, frequent and cheap; San Félix-Puerto Ordaz, US$1; buses run until 2100. Several buses daily to **Santa Elena de Uairén** (via El Callao), US$18, 10 hrs, with **Caribe** (T951 8385, recommended) and **Turgar** (or overnight bus, which misses the fine scenery, 9 hrs). **El Callao** (US$6.50), **Tumeremo** (US$8), **El Dorado** (US$9.50) and Km 88 with Turgar. **Ciudad Bolívar** US$3 (*por puesto* US$5.50), 1 hr. Bus to **Maturín** US$7, 2½ hrs. 8 daily to **Caracas**, US$17 (night bus US$20), 10 hrs, with **Rodovias** (T951 4630) and **Expresos Occidente** (T953 0624). 8 daily to **Barcelona** and **Puerto La Cruz**, US$13.50, 6 hrs, with **Caribe**. 2 daily to **Cumaná**, US$12.50, 8 hrs, with **Caribe**. 5 daily to **Valencia**, US$17, 10 hrs, with **Rodovias** and **Expresos Occidente**. To **Tucupita**, US$6, 3 hrs, leaving from San Félix bus terminal with **Expresos Guayanesa**, booking office opens 1 hr before departure, be there early, passport check just before Tucupita. San Félix bus terminal is not a safe place, especially at night.
International buses 1 bus daily to **Brazil**, US$33, 14 hrs including 3 refreshment stops, departs 2130, arrives Boa Vista 1130, with **Caribe** recommended, buses have a/c (take warm clothes), toilets and reclining seats.
Taxi San Félix-Puerto Ordaz US$2.50, Puerto Ordaz-airport US$3.25, airport-bus terminal US$12, San Félix bus terminal- Puerto Ordaz bus terminal US$5, bus terminal-town centre US$3, town centre-San Félix bus terminal US$3.50.

Tucupita *p1412*

Bus *Por puesto* from **Maturín** about US$10, 2-3 hrs; bus to Maturín, US$5, 3-4 hrs, with **Expresos Guayanesa**, US$6 with **Expresos Los Llanos** recommended. 2 daily to **San Félix**, US$6, 3 hrs, with **Expresos La Guayanesa**. 2 daily to **Caracas**, US$20, 12-13 hrs, with **Expresos Los Llanos** recommended. **Puerto La Cruz**, US$12, 7-8 hrs.

Barrancas *p1412*

Bus **Tucupita**-Barrancas, US$1.50, return at 0945 and 1700.

Directory

Ciudad Guayana *p1411*

Banks Corp Banca (American Express), Av Cuchivero y C Caruachi, Edif Seguros Orinoco, PB, Urb Alta Vista, and C Urbana, Edif Don Andrés, Puerto Ordaz. **Banco de Venezuela**, Av Las Américas y Av Monseñor Zabaleta. Banks will not exchange Brazilian currency. **Car hire** Many different agencies at the airport, Margarita

Rentals cars recommended, expect to pay US$50-60 per day; **Hertz**, Puerto Ordaz, rents 4WD vehicles. A car is very useful in this area, especially for visiting the Cerro Bolívar mine and Guri dam, or taking a road trip through the Gran Sabana to Brazil. **Consulates** Brazil, Av Las Américas, near CANTV, T962 4060, consbras@cantv.net, 0900-1700. Friendly, helpful, visa issued in 1 hr, no onward ticket requested (some nationalities have to pay, eg Australians), good information. **Internet** Planet Web Café, Carrera Tumeremo, **Cyberarepa**, an unanticipated fusion of global and Venezuelan culture, CC Altavista. **Medical services** Clinic Chilemex, Av Las Américas.

Tucupita *p1412*

Banks Unibanca C Petión, Delta a La Paz, cash advances against Visa. **Banco de Venezuela**, Paseo Manamo, Delta a La Paz, ATM and cash advances. **Internet** Compucenter.com, in the same Centro Comercial on Plaza Bolívar. **Delta Microsystems**, C Pativilca.

Ciudad Guayana to Santa Elena de Uairén

Travelling South from Ciudad Guayana to the Brazilian border is becoming an increasingly popular excursion for Venezuelan tourists, as well as for overland travellers heading into (or out of) Brazil via Boa Vista. The road to the border at Santa Elena de Uairén passes across the beautiful Gran Sabana and is completely paved, with all bridges in place.

Ins and outs

Getting around A 4WD is only necessary off the main road, particularly in the rainy season. You may need spare tanks of gasoline if you're planning to spend a lot of time away from the main road (eg in Kavanayen and El Paují) and have a gas-guzzling vehicle. It is also advisable to carry extra water and plenty of food. Small eating places may close out of season. There are Guardia Nacional checks at the Río Cuyuní (Km 8), at Km 126, and at San Ignacio de Yuruaní (Km 259), and a military checkpoint at Luepa (Km 143); all driving permits, car registration papers, and identification must be shown. ➤ *For further information, see Transport, page 1420.*

Advice Camping is possible but a good waterproof tent is essential. A small fee is payable to the *indígenas* living around Kaui, Kama and similar villages (see also under Parque Nacional Canaima). Insect repellent and long-sleeved/trousered clothes are needed against *puri-puri* (small, black, vicious biting insects) and mosquitoes (especially in El Dorado, at Km 88 and at Icabarú); or use baby oil mixed with vitamin B12. Arrange five-day/four-night tours of the Gran Sabana in Caracas or in Ciudad Bolívar (cheaper and easier). See www.lagransabana.com.

To Tumeremo

South from Ciudad Guayana Highway 10 is a four-lane *autopista* as far as **Upata** (*Phone code 0288, Population 51,500*). There's a good place to buy provisions opposite the petrol station. **Note** Water is rationed in Upata and hot water in hotels is rare south of Ciudad Guayana, except in the better hotels of Santa Elena. From Upata to Km 88, the road is partly resurfaced with occasional broad hard shoulders.

At 18 km beyond **Guasipati** is **El Callao** on the south bank of the Río Yuruari, off the highway, a small, clean, bright town (*Population 12,000*) whose pre-Lenten carnival has a touch of calypso from British Caribbean immigrants who came to mine gold at the end of the 19th century. The gold mine, 8 km away in El Perú, has a museum of geology and carnival (T762 0336). Sr Rafael, who lives opposite will show you the mine (T762 0662, evenings only).

The town has many jewellery shops and restaurants. You may be able to change US$ cash in *Banco de Venezuela* on main plaza, but not travellers' cheques. There is a chronic water shortage, check when it is available in your hotel. All prices rise for the carnival in February.

On another 41 km is **Tumeremo** (*Colour map 2, grid A2. Population: 25,000*), which is recommended as the best place to buy provisions. There is *Unibanca* (Visa), *Banco de Orinoco* (Amex, after 1500, US$5 commission), and gasoline (all grades) at a normal price (better than El Dorado). About 5 km from Tumeremo towards the Fuerte Tarabay is the beautiful artificial lake of San Pedro with free campsite.

El Dorado → *Phone code: 0288. Colour map 2, grid B2. Population: 4,000.*

This hot, dirty and very noisy miners' supply centre in dense forest is 76 km from Tumeremo, 278 km from Ciudad Guayana, and 7 km off the road on the Río Cuyuní. On an island in the river stands the regional prison made famous by Henri Charrière/Papillon's stay there in 1945, in use again after renovation. The local gold seams have been largely exhausted but mining still continues and the town's nightlife is entirely for the miners, violence is in the air at nightfall. El Dorado's other economic mainstay is its gas station (open 0800-1900, daily).

El Dorado to Santa Elena de Uairén

The turn-off to El Dorado is marked Km 0; distances are measured from here by green signs 2 km apart. About 3 km south of the turnoff to El Dorado, is the Río Cuyuní crossed by a bridge.

Las Claritas, a gold-miners' town at Km 85 has a couple of places to stay, a restaurant, a big market for food and gold, and safe parking at Las Hermanitas de las Pobres (Convent), which can be better reached by the track from Km 88. At **Km 88** (also called **San Isidro**), there is gasoline, a garage, one of the last reliable telephones before Santa Elena and Banco Guayana. Everything is expensive; better food shops at Km 85.

The wall of the Gran Sabana looms above Km 88 and the highway climbs steeply in sharp curves for 40 km before reaching the top. The road is in very good condition and presents no problem for conventional cars. 4WDs may be better in the wet season (May-October). At Km 100 the huge **Piedra de la Virgen** (sandy coloured with black streaks) is passed before the steepest climb (La Escalera) enters the beautiful **Parque Nacional Canaima** (see page 1408).

The landscape is essentially savannah, with clusters of trees, moriche palms and bromeliads. Characteristic of this area are the large abrupt *tepuis* (flat-topped mountains or mesas), hundreds of waterfalls, and the silence of one of the oldest plateaus on earth. At Km 119 (sign can only be seen going north) a short trail leads to the 40 m **Danto ('Tapir') Falls**, a powerful fall wreathed in mosses and mist. If you are paying for your ride, try to persuade the driver to make a short stop; the falls are close to the road (about five minutes slippery walk down on the left-hand side), but not visible from it. (Buses cannot be flagged down here because of dangerous bends.) The **Monumento al Soldado Pionero** (Km 137) commemorates the army engineers who built the road up from the lowlands, finally opened in 1973; barbecues, toilets, shelters are now almost all in ruins. Some 4 km beyond is **Luepa**; all travellers must stop at the *ciudadela* (military checkpoint) a little way south. There is a popular camping place at Luepa, on the right going south which belongs to a tour company. An informative guide on duty will rent you a tent or you can hang a hammock in an open-sided shelter (very cold at night, no water or facilities, possible to buy a meal from a tour group, but expensive). There is a breakfast place, US$4. The Inparques station at Luepa has some guestrooms which are intended for visitors of Inparques, but they may let you stay for a small fee. There is a kitchen at the station and a cafetería for employees of Inparques and Edelca. You can camp at a site right on the Río Aponwao on the left hand side of the road going south.

Some 8 km beyond Luepa, a poor, graded gravel road leads 70 km west to **Kavanayén** (little traffic, best to have your own vehicle with high clearance, especially during the wet season, take snacks; the road can be cycled but is slow, lots of soft, sandy places). Accommodation is at the Capuchin mission, **G**, very friendly, also in private homes. One of the two grocery stores will prepare food, or the restaurant opposite serves cheap breakfasts and dinners, order in advance. Medical post in front of the mission, where handicrafts are sold.

The settlement is surrounded by *tepuis*. Off the road to Kavanayén are the falls of **Torón Merú** and **Chinak-Merú** (also called Aponwao), 105 m high and very impressive. Neither is a straightforward detour, so get full instructions before setting out. Chinak-Merú is reached via the very friendly Pemón village of **Iboribó** (there is a small bakery near the junction to Torón). A day's walk west of Kavanayén are the lovely falls on the **Río Karuay**. Ask locals for details.

1415

For the remaining 180 km to Santa Elena de Uairén few people and only a handful of Pemón Indian villages are to be seen. San Juan and San Rafael de Kamoiran and **Rápidos de Kamoirán** are passed. The 5-m Kawí falls on the **Kaüi** River are at Km 195, while at Km 201.5 are the impressive 55 m high **Kama Merú** falls can be seen (nominal US$0.60 to walk to the bottom of the falls). Also a small lake, local handicrafts for sale, a small shop for supplies, canoe trips US$1.50 per hour per person. Cabins and *churuatas* can be rented for about US$3 pp, camping at US$2 per tent. *Puri-puri* flies descend at dusk. Buses can be flagged down going south or north three times a day; check times in advance.

At Km 237 the Río Arapán cascades over the charming **Quebrada Pacheco** ; pools nearby where you can swim. Tour groups often stop here. A path up the opposite side of the main falls leads to an isolated natural pool 20 minutes walk away, in the middle of the savannah. Nearby are more falls with waterslides and pools. **Warning**: Do not go beyond the red line at Pacheco: there is a hidden fall which has claimed lives. A new camp is being built between Kama Merú and Quebrada Pacheco. There are plans for lodging, a restaurant, an indigenous cultural centre, and to offer excursions in the savannah. Contact Oscar Romero on T0414-886 2034 (mob). Next is **Balneario Saro Wapo** on the Río Soruapé (Km 244), a good place for swimming and picnics, natural whirlpool, restaurant, 10 minutes downriver is a natural waterslide. Then, at Km 250, comes the Pemón village of Kumarakapai, San Francisco de Yuruaní (see page 1421), whose falls (Arapena-merú) can be seen from the road bridge, followed, 9 km of bends later, by the smaller village of **San Ignacio de Yuruaní** (strict military checkpoint; excellent regional food).

A trail at Km 275 leads to the **Quebrada de Jaspe** where a river cuts through striated cliffs and pieces of jasper glitter on the banks. Visit at midday when the sun shines best on the jasper, or at 1500 when the colour changes from red to orange, dazzlingly beautiful. Campsite beside the river, no facilities, bad drainage and exposed, not recommended.

Santa Elena de Uairén → *Phone code: 0289. Colour map 2, grid B2. Population: 15,000.*

This booming, pleasant frontier town was established by Capuchin Monks in 1931. Thanks to its relaxed atmosphere and plentiful supply of hotels, Santa Elena is an agreeable place in which to spend time. Gold is a better buy here than in Ciudad Bolívar. The local festival is on 9-19 August, featuring music, dance and handicrafts.

Border with Brazil

The 16 km road to the border is paved. The entire road links Caracas with Manaus in four days with hard driving; see Northern Brazil, page 556, for a description of the road from the border and Brazilian immigration formalities. New customs and immigration facilities are at the border, but your passport may require a stamp from the **ONIDEX** office behind the police station at the entrance of Santa Elena arriving from the north; open 0730-1230 and 1400-1800. All car documents must be stamped here on entry or exit. Staff at the Ministry of Justice and the Guardia Nacional headquarters (T960 3765/995 1189) have been recommended as helpful with entry and exit difficulties. The **Brazilian consulate** is at C Antonio José de Sucre 24 (opposite the petrol station), T995-1256, vcshubrcg@cantv.net; open 0800-1200, 1400-1800. You can get a visa here.

For entry to Venezuela, some nationalities who cross the border from Boa Vista, Brazil must have a visa, which costs US$75. It is not required by western Europeans, whose passport must be valid for one year, but check with a consulate before leaving home as rules do change. Venezuelan consulates are listed in directories in the Brazil chapter. A yellow fever vaccination certificate is required whichever direction you are going. Ask well in advance what other health requirements are in force (malaria test certificate may also be necessary). Entering by car, make sure to keep photocopies of your license, the Brazilian permission to leave and Venezuelan entry stamp. Allow two hours to undertake all formalities when crossing by private vehicle and don't cross during the lunch hour. In theory, fresh fruit and vegetables may not be brought into Venezuela. There are frequent road checks when heading north from Santa Elena. Seniat (the customs authority) has its Aduana Principal Ecológica outside the town and there may be up to eight more thorough searches, mainly for drugs. Your luggage will be searched and sealed before loading into the bus hold in Santa Elena and carry on luggage will be searched very thoroughly at checkpoints. These checks may make it inevitable that you arrive in Ciudad Bolívar after dark.

El Paují

A road leaves the highway 8 km south of Santa Elena and after passing through a tunnel of jungle vegetation emerges onto rolling savannah dotted with *tepuis*. The road has been considerably improved and has been paved for about 20 km. The rest is graded, but rapidly deteriorating. In 2005, it took 2-2½ hours to reach El Pauji. Take advice before setting out, as rain can rapidly degrade the quality of the road. At Km 58 is a Guardia Nacional checkpoint at Paraitepuí, waterfall nearby.

El Paují, 17 km further on, is an agricultural settlement with a growing number of foreign residents. It is a lovely area, with good walking. Excellent sights: **Chirica Tepuy**, huge, beautiful, jet black, set in rolling savannah; **Río Surucún**, where the largest diamond in Venezuela was found; **Salto Catedral** (61 km off the road), beautiful small hollow, lovely falls, bright red water below because of the tree roots, excellent for swimming (camping, shop, meals); **Salto La Gruta**, impressive falls, but very slippery; and **Pozo Esmeralda**, 1½ km outside El Paují towards Icabarú (400 m south of road), fine rapids, waterfall you can stand under and pools. At Los Saltos de Paují, there are many powerful falls; going from El Paují towards Santa Elena, before crossing the first bridge, take track on left for about 500 m. A good walk is to the small hill, 2 km from El Paují beyond the airfield; views from the crest over **El Abismo**, the plunging escarpment that marks the end of Gran Sabana highlands and the beginning of the Amazon rainforest. The jungle stretches as far as you can see. It takes an hour to reach the top, and the walk is highly recommended. Guides, though not necessary, can be found in the village. A recommended guide is German-speaking Marco. Small campsite (lovely in early morning or sunset).

Apiculture is the main activity of El Paují and there's an International Honey Festival every summer. The honey made in this area is delicious; buy it at the shop in El Paují or Salto Catedral. There is an InfoCentro project with computers and internet. See also www.elpauji.com.

Santa Elena de Uairén

Sleeping	Las 5 Jotas 8	Ya-Koo Ecological Camp 18
Augusta 19	Los Castaños 9	
Cabañas Friedenau 1	Lucrecia 10	**Eating**
Cabañas Roraima 2	Michelle 12	Alfredo's 2
Gran Sabana 4	Tavarúa 13	Café Goldrausch
Jaspe 5	Temiche Camp 14	& Tommy Town 3
Kiamantí 6	Tres Naciones 15	El Ranchón Criollo 1
La Posada Aventura	Villa Apoipó 16	Panadería Gran Café 4
& Adventure Tours 7	Villa Fairmont 17	Venezuela Primero 5

0 metres 50
0 yards 50

Sleeping

To El Callao p1414

Upata

D Andrea, Plaza Miranda, T221 3618, F221 3736. Decent rooms, a/c, hot water, TV, fridge in some rooms. Credit cards accepted, Chinese restaurant, safe parking, good.

E Yocoima, C Ayacucho, T221 1305. 25 rooms with a/c, TV, Italian restaurant, takes credit cards.

F Comercio, C Piar, T221 1156. Excellent.

Guasipati

D Hotel La Reina, Av Orinoco, T767 1357. A/c, hot water, cable TV, good.

E El Mery de Oro, Av Orinoco, T767 1287. Hot water, a/c, helpful if bland.

E Hotel Venezuela, C Roscio, close to Plaza Bolívar.

F Residencias El Agua, southern end of town. Basic, a/c, OK.

El Callao p1414

D New Millenium, Plaza Bolívar, T762 0448. Nice rooms, a/c, TV, laundry, parking, cheaper without hot water. Recommended.

D Arte Dorado, C Roscio 51, 5 mins from Plaza Bolívar, T762 0535. A/c, TV, parking.

E Isidora, on the road to El Perú but in town, T762 0290. A/c.

F Elvira, C Bolívar, 2 blocks from the plaza, T0416-788 7617 (mob). Shared bath, laundry facilities. Recommended.

G Italia Centro, C Ricuarte off Plaza Bolívar, T762 0770. Basic, a/c.

G Ritz, C Ricuarte, T762 0730. Basic, serves cold beer.

Tumeremo p1415

E Sinfontes, C El Dorado, 1 block down from *Leocar*, T771 0739. Good value, good beds, a/c, TV, bath, has seen better days.

D Miranda, Zea 33, T771 0202. Cable TV, a/c, parking, comfortable.

E La Francia, C Bolívar, T711 1477. Clean, a/c, **F** with fan, TV, basic.

F Pan-hoc, C Piar at Miranda, next to plaza Bolívar, T771 0264. Good value.

F Tumeremo City, on Zea, T771 0281, F771 0323. A/c, TV, parking. Recommended.

G Central, Piar y Miranda, T710 2064. Fan, OK, bakery and snackbar.

G Leocar, Dorado y Paez, next to the bus stop. Poor value, noisy, with fan or a/c, very basic.

El Dorado p1415

All hotels have problems with running water and there is lots of short-stay accommodation.

E El Encanto Cuyuní, a camp 3 km down the road at the Puente Río Cuyuní, T0288-808 3845. Bruno and Vanessa will pick you up from El Dorado, or buses will drop you at the bridge. Hammock space, camping, cabins under construction, guests can prepare food. Can arrange boat trips and tours.

E Universo, C Cuyuní, running parallel to the river, T991 1151. Clean, safe, a/c, geared towards tourists, some rooms have TV, safe parking. Recommended.

F Agua Selva, on right when entering town, T991 1093. Rustic camp, with shared bathrooms, fan, includes breakfast, dinner available at extra cost. Hammocks for rent, **G** including breakfast. Welcoming owner, tours. Recommended.

El Dorado to Santa Elena de Uairén p1415

A pp La Barquilla de Fresa, at Km 84.5. Run by Henry Cleve, English and German spoken. Book through Alba Betancourt in Caracas T0212-256 4162, T0416-709 7205 (mob), barquilladefresa@cantv.net. It specializes in bird watching tours and the inventory of bird species for the jungle here has reached more than 300 species. Full board lodging, reservations and deposit required.

A Campamento Turístico Anaconda, Las Claritas, T0286-923 7996, anaconda@cantv.net. Cabins with bath, fan, well-furnished, bar, including breakfast and dinner, reserved for tour groups (**C** in low season).

E El Parador del Viajero, Km 88. Restaurant.

E La Pilonera, opposite Vargas store, Km 88. With a/c and hot water, **G** with fan and cold water, safe parking, some rooms with bath, restaurant with good fruit drinks; good food next door at the El Tercer Mundo.

E Landolfi, Las Claritas, left turn in the centre of town towards the indigenous village of San Lucia de Inaway. A/c, **E** with fan, parking.

Rápidos de Kamoirán

E Campamento Rápidos de Kamoirán, Km 172, T0289-805 1505. Clean, with fan, well-kept, cold water, camping US$4, also restaurant, gasoline, and picnic spot by rapids.

Santa Elena de Uairén p1416, map p1417

B Gran Sabana, outside town, 10 km from border, T995 1810, www.hotelgransabana.com. Most luxurious in town, good service. Recommended.

B Ya-Koo Ecological Camp, 2 km on unpaved road to Sampai Indian community, up the mountain behind Santa Elena, T995 1742, www.ya-koo.com. *Cabañas* with all facilities in beautiful 10-ha site, full board, spacious rooms, hot water, natural swimming pool. **C** in low season. Recommended if you have a car.

D **Lucrecia**, Av Perimetral, T/F995 1105, near old terminal. A/c or fan, TV, restaurant, pool, parking, helpful, good.

D **Temiche Camp**, 5 mins from town on airport road, T962 2693/0414-886 2323. Nice rooms, hot water, meals and use of kitchen extra.

D **Villa Fairmont**, Urb Akurimá, T995 1022, at north edge of town. Large, comfortable rooms, a/c, hot water, TV, restaurant, small craft shop.

E **Augusta**, C Bolívar, next to Panadería Rico Pan, T995 1654. Hot water, fan, cable TV, spick and span, central location.

E pp **Cabañas Friedenau**, Av Ppal de Cielo Azul, off Av Perimetral, T995 1353, friedenau@ cantv.net. Self-contained chalets, price includes breakfast, pleasant grounds, caters for groups, vegetarian food, parking, transfer to Puerto Ordaz, bicycles and horseback trips, trips to Roraima (see below), English and German spoken. Recommended.

E **Cabañas Roraima**, up road behind bus terminal, near *Villa Fairmont*, T996 1164. A/c, hot water, fridge, also has cabins for up to 8, near supermarket. E **Los Castaños**, C Mcal Sucre, near old bus terminal, T995 1450. A/c, TV, **F** with fan only.

E pp **Kiamantí**, outside town near new bus terminal, T995 1952, kiamanti77@hotmail.com. Full board, fan, hot water, comfortable, parking, swimming pool.

E **Tavarúa**, near *Ya-Koo*, T04143-886 3899 or 0416-289 2600 (mob), robtavarua1@yahoo.com. Lovely rooms, hot water, meals available, pick-up from town, Roberto Campano is a guide.

E **Tres Naciones**, on C Zea, T995 1190. Basic, with a/c, hot water, restaurant, parking.

F **Jaspe**, on C Mcal Sucre, T995 1379, 150 m from old bus terminal on opposite side. Hot water, fan, TV, free coffee.

F **La Posada Aventura**, above *Adventure Tours* on Av Perimetral, T995 1574. Hot water, fan. Good.

F **Michelle**, C Urdaneta, next to *Café Goldrausch*, T995 1415, hotelmichelle@ cantv.net. Spotless, hot water, fan, helpful, laundry, good value. Credit cards accepted, cash advances on Visa if you are desperate.

F **Villa Apoipó**, on the road to the airport, turn left at the *Hotel Gran Sabana*, T492 2626, 0414-886 2049 (mob). Very nice rooms, hot water, fan. Set up to receive groups but will take independent travellers if you ring ahead. Use of kitchen or full board option. Bunk beds or hammocks available in large *churuata*.

G **Las 5 Jotas**, near *Cabañas Roraima*, T0414-886 1524. Comfortable, good value.

El Paují *p1417*

B pp **Campamento Amaribá**, 3½ km outside El Paují on road from Santa Elena, transport usually available from air strip, T0414-932 2169, reservations in Caracas T0212-753 9314, amariba@ cantv.net. Comfortable cabins with mosquito nets, separate bathrooms with good facilities, full board, kitchen, tours arranged, very hospitable.

D **Campamento El Paují**, 3½ km outside El Paují on road from Santa Elena, transport usually available from airstrip, T995 1431, or contact through Maripak. Beautiful cabins with spectacular views over the Gran Sabana, food available, camping US$6 per tent. Recommended.

D pp **Chimanta** and **Manoa**, T995 1431. Cosy rooms, restaurant serving vegan food.

D **Weimure**, 2 km out, outside El Paují on road from Santa Elena, pauji0@yahoo.com. Beautiful cabin close to river, dynamic architect owner.

E **Maripak**, near the airstrip and small store, T808 1033, maripaktepuy@hotmail.com, or reserve in Caracas T0212-234 3631. Run by Marielis Gil, cabins for 2/3 with bathroom, US$10 per meal, good food, organizes tours, camping US$6 per tent, has phone.

F **Canta Rana** tourist camp, 25 km from town. Basic accommodation, breakfast and dinner included in the price, owners, Alfonso and Barbara Borrero, speak German, English and Spanish, waterfall and lovely surroundings.

⑦ Eating

Tumeremo *p1415*

Restaurante Las Cuevas, near plaza. Popular, average food and prices, service slow, check your bill. **Restaurante Turístico**, expensive but OK.

El Dorado *p1415*

Archiven, Plaza Bolívar. Good, helpful owner. **El Caney**, on right just down from *Agua Selva*, good food. Recommended.
Restaurant by church serves delicious *criolla* food.

Santa Elena de Uairén *p1416, map p1417*
There are several restaurants on Mcal Sucre, one of these El Ranchón Criollo serves good *criolla* fare.
Alfredo's, Av Perimetral, at the end of C Urdaneta. Tasty pizzas at good prices.
Venezuela Primero, Av Perimetral. Chicken, meat, and seafood.

Cafés
On the Plaza is a pay-by-weight buffet restaurant serving very good local food. **Café Goldrausch**, C Urdaneta, next to *Tommy Town* Chinese restaurant. Makes good breakfasts, also dinners, and internet. Good place to form tour groups with other travellers. **Panadería Gran Café**, C Icabarú. Good breakfasts and coffee.

▲ Activities and tours

Santa Elena de Uairén *p1416, map p1417*
Santa Elena is becoming the most economical
place to book tours of the Gran Sabana, Roraima,
and other tepuis. The tours industry in Santa Elena
is burgeoning, with more and more operators
popping up every day, and freelance guides in the
street. Bargains are to be had if you shop around,
form larger groups, and haggle. Many tour
operators will tailor their tours to fit your needs,
contact by e-mail to discuss plans before arriving.
Adventure Tours, Av Perimetral at the end of
C Urdaneta, T/F995 1861 adventure3tours@
hotmail.com. Tours of Gran Sabana or El Paují,
US$25 pp/day guide and transport only, or US$50
pp/day all included, group discounts, 6 days to
Roraima US$236 per person all included
(minimum 4 persons). Sleeping bags and
camping mats available for hire.
Backpacker Tours, Urb Akurimá, T416 0602,
T0414-886 7227 (mob), www.venezuela-
tours.de. 1-5 day, all-inclusive jeep tours through
the Gran Sabana, visiting little-known falls in the
Kavanayen area, US$60 pp. Trekking to the
nearby Churikayen Tepuy, 3-4 days and to
Roraima, US$50 pp per day (minimum 4 persons).
German and English spoken. Recommended.
Kamadac, C Urdaneta, opposite *Café
Goldrausch*, T995 1408, T0414-886 6526 (mob),
www.abenteuer-venezuela.de. Run by Andreas
Hauer, tours of Gran Sabana, US$100 per day for
jeep (maximum 4 persons), El Paují area (includes
gold- washing), US$120, 2 days, all-inclusive
(minimum 4 persons), and Pemón-style fishing
trips. 6-day, all-inclusive tour to Roraima, US$250
pp (for 4-6 persons), sleeping bag and camping
mat US$25 extra, and also more adventurous
tours to; Auyán Tepuy from which Angel Falls
cascades (7-8 days, approximately US$70 pp per
day for 5-6 people), difficult; Acopan Tepuy,
virgin territory in the Chimantá massif (5-6 days,
approximately US$400 pp, groups of 3-4, or 7-8);
Kamarata Falls, from Kavác by *curiara* (4 days,
$400 pp for 4 persons). Recommended.
New Frontiers Adventure, also on C Urdaneta
next to *Tommy Town*, T995 1584, T0414-886
6040 (mob), www.newfrontiers adventures.com.
Affiliated to the International Ecotourism Society,
ecotours and tours for small groups. They offer all
the usual tours at standard prices, and 4-day,
all-inclusive walking tours at US$40 pp per day,
taking in the different ecosystems of the Gran
Sabana, and staying in Pemón villages. English,
French, and German spoken. Recommended.
Roberto's Mystic Tours, Ikabarú y Urdaneta,
mystic-tours@cantv.net. Roberto is very helpful
and knowledgeable about local culture (and
UFOs), great tours. Recommended.

Recommended guides **Rawllins** and
his brother, **Terry** (Guyanese) speak English,
excellent cooks, T0414-886 2669 (mob),
rawllins@yahoo.com, akawaio@hotmail.com.
Franklin Sierra, T995 1686, 0414-886 2448,
speaks English, Italian and other languages,
tailor-made tours, good service and value.

⊖ Transport

Tumeremo *p1415*
Bus To **Santa Elena**, US$15, 8-10 hrs, with
Líneas Orinoco, 2 blocks from plaza near
Leocar); **El Dorado**, US$2, 1½ hrs. Bus to
Ciudad Bolívar, US$11, 6 a day, 6½ hrs or *por
puesto* (via San Félix and Puerto Ordaz). Bus to
San Félix (Ciudad Guayana), US$3.60, *por puesto*
US$8.75. To **Caracas**, US$23, direct service at
1600, 14 hrs.

El Dorado *p1415*
Bus All buses stop on main plaza. From
Caracas, Expresos del Oriente, at 1830 daily,
US$24, 14½ hrs, return at 1400 (925 km). The
Orinoco bus line connects with **Ciudad Bolívar**
(6 hrs) and **Santa Elena**, as does Transmundial
(better buses, leaving 1100, US$9.50 to **Santa
Elena**, US$8 to San Félix, 4 hrs).

El Dorado to Santa Elena de Uairén *p1415*
Km 88 (San Isidro)
Bus Km 88-Caracas, US$24; to **Ciudad Bolívar**
wait at gas station for buses from Las Claritas
(depart 0900, 1100, 1500, 1800). Frequent *por
puestos* from **El Dorado** to Km 88, 1 hr, US$3.50.
Most non-luxury buses stop at the petrol station
to refuel. Alternatively get a ride with jeeps and
trucks (little passes after 1030).

Santa Elena de Uairén *p1416, map p1417*
Air Airport, 8 km from the centre. **Rutaca** is the
only company currently serving the airstrip in
Santa Elena. Their 5-seater Cessnas leave once or
twice a day for destinations that include **Ciudad
Bolívar, Canaima, Kavác, Kamarata**, and
Kavanayen (US$70 one way), **Wonken** (US$40
one way), and **El Paují** and **Icabarú** (US$25 one
way). To calculate the price of chartering an
airplane from Santa Elena to any destination, take
the cost per passenger and multiply by 5.
Bus The new bus terminal on the road to
Ciudad Bolívar is about 4 km from town, taxi
US$4-5. Get to the terminal 30 mins in advance
for the SENIAT baggage check for contraband.
From **Caracas** it is best to go to Ciudad Bolívar
and then take a bus direct to Boa Vista, or
Santa Elena. 10 buses daily from Santa Elena to
Ciudad Bolívar, US$17, with **Expresos Los
Llanos** (recommended), **San Cristobal**, and

Línea Orinoco, 10-12 hrs. 10 daily to **Ciudad Guayana** and **San Félix**, US$18, 10-11 hrs, with **Caribe** (recommended) and **Turgar**. 10 daily to **Puerto La Cruz**, US$23, 14 hrs, with **Caribe** (recommended), **Turgar**, and **Línea Orinoco**. **Expresos Maturín** goes to **Maturín** daily. **Expresos Los Llanos** go to **Maracay** and **Valencia** 3 times a day, US$30, 18-20 hrs. 3 buses daily to **Boa Vista**, US$8, 4 hrs, with **Eucatur**; at 0700 to **Manaus** about 15 hrs, US$31.50 (make sure ticket includes the exit tax). Take warm clothing for buses with a/c (the driver may even insist that the shades be closed throughout the journey, so as not to affect the a/c).

Hitchhiking North from Santa Elena is said to be easy. Stand at the roadside at the garage just opposite the terminal. Expect a charge of US$5.

Jeep To **El Paují** (see below), **Canta Rana** (US$15), and **Icabarú** (US$20) leave about 0700 from Plaza Bolívar. Can also be caught at *Panadería Gran Café*, C Icabarú. PDV gas station on road out of town, open 0800-1900.

El Paují *p1417*

Air El Paují to **Santa Elena** (see above).
Road To get further than El Paují – to Canta Rana and Icabarú – a 4WD vehicle is necessary. From Santa Elena, US$8-10 by jeep if full, more if not, daily at around 0600-0700 and 1500-1600 from Plaza Bolívar. Taxi US$10. **Hitching** from the airport is possible, but infrequent lifts. Jeep hire in El Paují, US$50 per day.

❶ Directory

El Dorado *p1415*

Banks There is a Banco de Venezuela, accepts Visa and MasterCard; exchange with the gold buyer on the main street, cash only, poor rates.

Santa Elena de Uairén *p1416, map p1417*

Banks ATMs are unlikely to accept non-Venezuelan cards. Banco Industrial C Bolívar. Cash advances on Visa. Try the shops in the centre for dollars cash, reais or TCs, eg *Casa de Los Cóchamos*, the gold shop south of main plaza, which changes TCs at lower rate than bank. Inversiones Fortaleza, C Urdaneta on plaza, cash dollars, TCs or Brazilian currency. La Boutique Zapatería also changes TCs and cash at reasonable rates. Also grocery store El Gordito, C Urdaneta, for Brazilian currency (English and French spoken). Try at border with Brazilians entering Venezuela. Generally the rates are poor; check with travellers going in opposite direction what rates should be. For better rates you must wait until Ciudad Guayana, or Boa Vista if going to Brazil (change some money into Brazilian currency before the bus leaves).
Internet Global de Communicaciones, C Icabarú y Urdaneta. Another place opposite Panadería Rico Pan on C Bolívar.
Telephones Global de Communicaciones, CANTV at the old bus terminal for international calls and faxes. It is cheaper to buy a card and call from a street phone for international calls.

Mount Roraima → *Altitude: 2,810 m.*

An exciting trek is to the summit of Mt Roraima, at one time believed to be the **'Lost World'** made famous by Arthur Conan Doyle's novel. 'Roroima' is a word in the Pemón Indian language meaning 'The great blue-green'. Owing to the tough terrain and extreme weather conditions, this hike is only suitable for the fit. Supplies for a week or more should be bought in Santa Elena. If your food is being supplied by a tour company, check what food you will be eating; often vegetarians go hungry.

San Francisco de Yuruaní

The starting point is this Pemón village, 9 km north of the San Ignacio military checkpoint (at which you must register). There are three small shops selling basic goods but not enough for Roraima hike. Meals are available and tents can be hired, US$3 each per day, quality of tents and stoves is poor; better equipment is available in Santa Elena.

Paraitepui

The road to Paraitepui (which is signposted), the nearest village to the mountain, leaves the highway 1 km south of San Francisco. It is in good condition, with three bridges; the full 25 km can be walked in seven hours. You can sleep for free in the village if hiring a guide; camping is permitted. Few supplies are available; a small shop sells basics. The villagers speak Tauripán, the local dialect of the Pemón linguistic group, but now most of them also speak Spanish.

Climbing Roraima

The foot trail winds back and forth on a more direct line than the little-used jeep track; it is comparatively straightforward and adequately marked descending from the heights just past Paraitepui across rolling hills and numerous clear streams. The goal, Roraima, is the mountain on the right, the other massive outcrop on the left is Mata Hui (known as Kukenán after the river which rises within it). If leaving the village early in the day, you may reach the Río Cuquenán crossing by early afternoon (good camping here). Three hours' walk brings you to a lovely bird-filled meadow below the foothills of the massif, another perfect camping spot known as *campamento base* (10 hours to base camp from Paraitepui). The footpath now climbs steadily upwards through the cloud forest at the mountain's base and becomes an arduous scramble over tree trunks and damp rocks until the cliff is reached. From here it is possible to ascend to the plateau along the 'easy' rock ledge which is the only route to the top. Walkers in good health should take about four hours from the meadow to the top. The summit is an eerie world of stone and water, difficult to move around easily. There are not many good spots to camp; but there are various overhanging ledges which are colourfully-known as 'hoteles' by the guides. Red painted arrows lead the way to the right after reaching the summit for the main group of these. A marked track leads to the survey pillar near the east cliff where Guyana, Brazil and Venezuela meet; allow a day as the track is very rough. Other sights include the Valley of the Crystals, La Laguna de Gladys and various sinkholes.

The whole trip can take anywhere between five days and two weeks. The dry season for trekking is November-May (with annual variations); June-August Roraima is usually enveloped in cloud. Do not remove crystals from the mountain; on-the-spot fines up to US$100 may be charged. Thorough searches are made on your return. Take your rubbish back down with you.

◉ Sleeping

San Francisco de Yuruaní *p1421*
F **El Caney de Yuruaní**, T995 1307. Clean, basic rooms, fan, restaurant.
F **Posada**, run by *Roraima Tours* (see below). Dormitories, usually full.
G **Arapena Posada**, T01414-890 3314 (mob). Run by Arepena Tours (see below), small, basic.
Sr Casilda Rodriguez has a *churuata* where you can sling a hammock.
Camping Permitted just about anywhere, free. Plenty of mosquitos at night.

Climbing Roraima *p1422*
Camping Full equipment including stove is essential (an igloo-type tent with a plastic sheet for the floor is best for the summit, where it can be wet), wear thick socks and boots to protect legs from snakes, warm clothes for the summit (much mist, rain squalls and lightning at night) and effective insect repellent – biting *plaga (blackflies)* infest the grasslands. The water on the summit and around the foot of Roraima is very pure, but as more do the trek, the waters are becoming dirtied. Bring bottled water or a purifier for the savannah. Fires must not be lit on top of Roraima, only gas or liquid fuel stoves. Litter is appearing along the trail; please take care of the environment.

▲ Activities and tours

Climbing Roraima *p1422*
Guides and tours The National Guard requires all visitors to have a guide beyond Paraitepui, otherwise you will be fined. It is not recommended to go alone; best to go with a guide or tour operator from Santa Elena (US$235-365, 6 days/5 nights) or from San Francisco; those hired on the street or in Paraitepui have no accident insurance cover. A guide can be of great assistance for the hike's final stages (it is very easy to get lost) and for knowing best places to camp. Guides in San Francisco de Yuruaní charge about US$35-40 a day, more if they carry your supplies. Check the camping gear for leaks, etc, and be clear about who is providing the guide's food.
Arapena Tours, T0414-890 3314 (mob), arapena tours@latinmail.com. Ovelio Rodriguez runs tours to Roraima and Kavurin, US$40 per day for guide.
Roraima Tours, T808 1037, T0414-886 3405 (mob), recommended, Ana Fernández is very helpful, all-inclusive tour (group rates can be arranged), or US$45 per day for guide only.
Guides available in Paraitepui cost US$23 a day, Spanish speaking guides available. The **Ayuso** brothers are the best-known guides. Ask for El Capitán, he is in charge of guides. To park at the Inparques office: US$9.50.

◉ Transport

San Francisco de Yuruaní *p1421*
Bus From **Santa Elena** will let you off here and pick up passengers en route northwards (no buses 1200-1900). Jeep to **Paraitepui** around US$100. Cheapest is Oscar Mejías Hernández, ask in village.

Guianas

Guyana	1426
Essentials	1426
Georgetown	1429
Outside Georgetown	1431
Suriname	1444
Essentials	1444
Paramaribo	1447
Outside Paramaribo	1449
Guyane	1456
Essentials	1456
Cayenne	1459
Outside Cayenne	1460

⁞ Footprint features

Don't miss …	1425
Touching down (Guyana)	1427
Driving in Guyana	1428
Touching down (Suriname)	1445
Driving in Suriname	1446
Touching down (Guyane)	1457
Driving in Guyane	1458

Introduction

Guyana's coastal region is dominated by a mixture of Calypso music, Dutch drainage systems, Hindu temples, rice and Demerara sugar. Leaving the sea behind, travelling by riverboat or by plane, it is a land of rainforests, which gives way to wildlife-rich savannahs and isolated ranches. Waterfalls tumble over jasper rocks, or, at Kaieteur, into a chasm almost five times the height of Niagara. Suriname, too, has the intriguing combination of Dutch, Asian and African, which influences the culture, food and street life. And, like its neighbour, when you head inland, you enter a different world of bronze-tinted rivers, jungles and Amerindian villages.

Despite having geographical features shared by other South American countries, Suriname and Guyana are classed as Caribbean states. Guyane, on the other hand, is an overseas department of France. It has a famous penal colony – now closed – circled by sharks, a European space programme whose launches can be witnessed and jungle adventure in the undeveloped interior. All this within the context of a corner of South America where coffee and croissants are served and the prices are more than Parisian.

★ Don't miss ...

1 **Kaieteur Falls (Guyana)** Water falls for 228 m over a massive fault in the bedrock deep in the rainforest, page 1433.

2 **Rupununi Savannah (Guyana)** Grasslands offer a real get-away-from-it-all experience. A handful of cattle ranches provide lodging and wildlife tours, page 1433.

3 **Iwokrama (Guyana)** With its canopy walkway, this is one of the best places to experience the rainforest, page 1434.

4 **Paramaribo (Suriname)** Hindu temples, mosques and synagogues sit alongside fine 18th- and 19th-century buildings in the capital, page 1447.

5 **Central Suriname Nature Reserve** Covering almost 10% of the country, this new park is a vast area of unspoilt rainforest, page 1450.

6 **Kourou (Guyane)** The European Space Agency launches its rockets here. Certainly not your everyday experience, page 1460.

7 **Iles du Salut (Guyane)** Once a notorious French convict settlement. Henri Charrière (Papillon) was here and escaped, page 1460.

Guyana

Essentials

Planning your trip

Where to go Despite being located on the Atlantic, **Georgetown**, capital of Guyana, is known as the 'Garden City of the Caribbean'. This gives some idea of the country's orientation, in trade and cultural terms. The coast, where most of the population live, is a mix of coconut palms and calypso music, Dutch place names and techniques for draining the land, Hindu temples and Islamic mosques, all of which reflect the chequered history of the country. The thinly populated interior is different again, with life revolving around the rivers in the tropical forest, or, further south, the scattered ranches of the Rupununi Savannah. The main tourist potential is in the largely untouched interior, where many places are best reached by river boat or plane. The improvement of the road from Georgetown to Lethem on the Brazilian border, with a regular bus service, opens up the interior for easier exploration. Highlights include the Kaieteur Falls, among the highest in the world, the Orinduik Falls on the border with Brazil and the Iwokrama Rain Forest Programme. Travelling on any of the rivers, many with excellent beaches, is the most interesting way to get around. On the coast there are no beaches for bathing, but in the far northwest is Shell Beach, a protected area for marine turtles and birdlife.

When to go Although hot, the climate is not unhealthy. Mean shade temperature throughout the year is 27° C; the mean maximum is about 31° C and the mean minimum 24° C. The heat is greatly tempered by cooling breezes from the sea and is most felt from August to October. There are two wet seasons in the north of the country, from May to June, and from December to the end of January, although they may extend into the months either side. The south and the Rupununi receive one wet season, May to July. Rainfall averages 2,300 mm a year in Georgetown. Note that the Republic Day celebrations (23 February) last about a week: during this time hotels in Georgetown are very full. Hotels are also very full during international cricket.

Finding out more Ministry of Tourism, Industry and Commerce ① *229 South Rd near Camp St, Georgetown, T226 2505, www.mintic.gov.gy*, formulates tourism policy. The **Guyana Tourism Authority** ① *National Exhibition Center, Sophia, Georgetown, T223 6351, www.guyana-tourism.com*, promotes the development of the tourism industry. **Tourism and Hospitality Association of Guyana** (THAG) ① *office and information desk at 157 Waterloo St, T225 0807, www.exploreguyana.com*. Private organization covering all areas of tourism. Produces a 80-page, full-colour magazine called *Explore Guyana*, which may be obtained from the Association at PO Box 101147, Georgetown, or phone the above number. **An online**

⁞ Touching down

Airport tax This is G$4,000 (US$20, £12, €14), payable in Guyanese dollars only at Cheddi Jagan International airport.
Business hours Banks 0800-1400 Mon-Thu Fri 0800-1430. **Shops** 0830-1600, Mon-Thu, 0830-1700 Fri, 0830-1200 Sat. **Markets** 0800-1600, Mon-Sat, except Wed 0900-1200, Sun 0800-1000.
In an emergency Police T911; Fire T912; Ambulance T226 9449.
International phone code +592.

Ringing: a double ring, repeated regularly. Engaged: equal tones, separated by equal pauses.
Official time Four hours behind GMT; one hour ahead of EST.
VAT 16%, introduced in January 2007.
Voltage 110 volts in Georgetown; 220 volts elsewhere, including some Georgetown suburbs. Plugs as in US.
Weights and measures Metric since 1982, but imperial is widely used.

tourist guide is www.turq.com/guyana. For news and information and lots of useful links, visit **www.guyana.org**. The government information agency's site is **www.gina.gov**.

Maps Maps of country and Georgetown (US$6) from **Department of Lands and Surveys**, Homestreet Ave, Durban Backland (take a taxi). T226 0524 in advance, poor stock. Rivers and islands change frequently, so maps can only give you a general direction. A local guide can be more reliable. Free country and city maps are available from most tour operators and hotels. Georgetown and Guyana maps in **Explore Guyana.** Guyana ITMB map is recommended.

Visas The following countries do not need a visa to visit Guyana: Australia, Canada, Japan, New Zealand, Norway, Switzerland, USA, EU countries (except Austria, Cyprus, Czech Republic, Estonia, Hungary, Latvia, Lithuania, Malta, Poland, Slovak Republic and Slovenia) and the Commonwealth countries. Visitors are advised to check with the nearest embassy, consulate or travel agent for changes to this list. All visitors require a passport with six months' validity and all nationalities, apart from those above, require visas. To obtain a visa, three photos, evidence of sufficient funds, a travel itinerary and, if coming from a country with yellow fever, a yellow fever certificate are required. If Guyana has no representation in your country, apply to the Guyana Embassy in Washington DC, or the Guyana Consulate General in New York. Tourist visas cost US$37, one-entry business visas US$37, multiple entry business visas US$46. Visitors from those countries where they are required arriving without visas are refused entry, unless a tour operator has obtained permission for the visitor to get a visa on arrival. To fly in to Guyana, an exit ticket is required, at land borders an onward ticket is usually not asked for.

Guyana's representation overseas

Belgium, 12 Avenue du Brésil, 1050 Brussels, T675 6216.
Brazil, SAS Q2 bl J, Ed Paulo Maurício, 13 andar, Brasília DF, T061-3224 9229.
Canada, High Commission: Burnside Building, 151 Slater St, suite 309, Ottawa, Ontario, K1P 5H3, 613-235 7249, guyanahcott@travelnet.com. Consulate-General: 505 Consumer's Rd, Suite 206, Willowdale, Toronto, Ontario, M2J 4X8, T416-494 6040, info@guyanaconsulate.com.

UK, High Commission, 3 Palace Ct, London, W2 4LP, T020-7229 7684, ghc.1@ic24.net.
USA, Embassy: 2490 Tracy Pl, NW, Washington DC 20008, T265 63834, guyanaembassy@hotmail.com. New York Consulate General: 866 United Nations Plaza, 3rd Fl, T212-527 3215-6.
Venezuela, Quinta Roraima, Av El Paseo, Prados del Este, Aptdo 51054, Caracas 1050, T978 2781.

Money The unit is the Guyanese dollar. There are notes for 20, 100, 500 and 1,000 dollars. Coins are for 1, 5 and 10 dollars. The official **exchange rate** is adjusted weekly in line with the rate offered by licensed exchange houses (*cambios*). In July 2007, this was G$190 = US$1, G$258 = €1. There are ATMs in Georgetown, see Directory, below. Also take cash dollars or euros. No *cambio* changes travellers' cheques. They only buy US or Canadian dollars, euros and pounds sterling. Most *cambios* accept drafts (subject to verification) and telegraphic

Driving in Guyana

Roads Most coastal towns are linked by a good 296-km road from Springlands in the east to Charity in the west; the Berbice and Essequibo rivers are crossed by ferries, the Demerara by a toll bridge, which, besides closing at high tide for ships to pass through (2-3 hours) is subject to frequent closures (when an alternative ferry service runs). Apart from a good road connecting Timehri and Linden, continuing as good dirt to Mabura Hill, and the new Georgetown-Lethem road, most other roads in the interior are very poor.

Safety Traffic drives on the left. There are shortages of car spares.

Documents No *carnet de passages* is required for driving a private vehicle.

Car hire Available from several firms, see under Georgetown.

Fuel Gasoline costs US$3-3.80 a gallon.

transfers, but not credit cards. Rates vary slightly between *cambios* and from day to day and some *cambios* offer better rates for changing over US$100. Rates for changing travellers' cheques are good on the black market. Banks in Georgetown which accept travellers' cheques are **Demerara Bank** (South Road and Camp Street), **Guyana Bank of Trade and Industry** (GBTI, 47 Water Street) and **National Bank of Industry and Commerce** (NBIC, 38-40 Water Street). All charge commission. **NBIC** and *cambios* accept euros at best rates. Note that to sell Guyanese dollars on leaving the country, you will need to produce your *cambio* receipt. The black market on America Street ('Wall Street') in Georgetown still operates, but the rates offered are not significantly better than the *cambio* rate. To avoid being robbed or cheated on the black market, or if you need to change money when *cambios* are closed, go by taxi and ask someone (preferably a friend) to negotiate for you. The black market also operates in Molson Creek/Springlands, the entry point from Suriname, and where the bus stops for the launches between Bonfim and Lethem at the Brazilian border.

Cost of travelling The devaluation means that, for foreigners, prices for food and drink are low at present. Even imported goods may be cheaper than elsewhere and locally produced goods such as fruit are very cheap. Hotels, tours and services in the interior are subject to electricity and fuel surcharges, which make them less cheap.

Getting around

Air Most flights to the interior leave from Ogle where a new municipal airport is under construction. It's about 15 minutes from Georgetown (taxi about US$6). For scheduled flights between Georgetown and Lethem see page 1443, and services to Kaieteur and Rupununi, see page 1442. Scheduled services to many parts of Guyana are offered by **Trans Guyana Airways**, **TGA**, Ogle, T222 2525, Monday to Saturday. Charter flights from Ogle are flown by **Roraima Airways**, **RAL**, T225 9648, www.roraimaairways.com, and **Air Services Ltd**, **ASL**, Wights Lane, Kingstown, T222 4357, asl@solutions2000.net. Domestic airlines are very strict on baggage allowance on internal flights: 20 lb pp (TGA and ASL) and 25 lb (Roraima).

Public road transport Minibuses and collective taxis, an H on their number plate, run between Georgetown and the entire coast from Charity to Corriverton; also to Linden. **Intraserv** bus service has a scheduled route from Georgetown to Lethem. All taxis also have an H on the number plate.

River There are over 960 km of navigable river, an important means of communication. Ferries and river boats are described here; also contact the Transport and Harbours Department, Water St, Georgetown. Six-seater river boats are called *ballahoos*, three- to four-seaters *corials*; they provide the transport in the forest. The ferry across the Corentyne to Suriname carries vehicles.

Sleeping → *See page 58 for our hotel grade price guide.*

The largest hotels in Georgetown have their own emergency electricity generators and water pumps to deal with any interruptions in supply. Other hotels usually provide a bucket of water in your room, fill this up when water is available. When booking an a/c room, ensure it also has natural ventilation.

Eating → *See page 58 for our eating price guide.*
Local food The blend of different influences – Indian, African, Chinese, Creole, English, Portuguese, Amerindian, North American – gives distinctive flavour to Guyanese cuisine. One well-known dish, traditional at Christmas, is pepper-pot: meat cooked in bitter cassava (casareep) juice with peppers and herbs. Seafood is plentiful and varied, as are tropical fruits and vegetables. The staple food is rice. In the interior wild meat is often available – try wild cow, or else *labba* (a small rodent).

Drink Rum is the most popular drink. There is a wide variety of brands, all cheap, including the best which are very good and cost US$3.50 a bottle. Demerara Distillers Ltd produces two prize-winning brands, the 12-year-old King of Diamonds premium rum, and the 15-year-old El Dorado (voted the best rum in the world in every year 1999-2005, US$45 in Georgetown, US$25 at duty free in the airport). Demerara Distillers, the makers of these rums, have a distillery tour and visit to their rum heritage, US$15. High wine is a strong local rum. There is also local brandy and whisky (Diamond Club), which are worth trying. D'Aguiar's Cream Liqueur, produced and bottled by Banks DIH Ltd, is excellent (and strong). The local beer, Banks, made partly from rice is good and cheap. There is a wide variety of fruit juices produced by Topico.

Festivals and events
Public holidays 1 January, New Years' Day; 23 February, Republic Day and Mashramani festival; Good Friday, Easter Monday; Labour Day, 1 May; Independence Day, 26 May (instigated in 1996); Caricom Day, first Monday in July; Freedom Day, first Monday in August; Christmas Day, 25 December, and Boxing Day, 26 December. Hindu and Muslim festivals follow a lunar calendar, and dates should be checked as required: Phagwah, usually March; Eid el Fitr, end of Ramadan; Eid el Azah; Youm un Nabi; Deepavali, usually November.

Georgetown → *Colour map 2, grid B3. Population: 200,000.*

Guyana's capital, and chief town and port, is on the east bank of the mouth of the Demerara river. The climate is tropical, with a mean temperature of 27° C, but the trade winds provide welcome relief. The city is built on a grid plan, with wide tree-lined streets and drainage canals following the layout of the old sugar estates. Parts of the city are very attractive, with white-painted wooden 19th century houses raised on stilts and a profusion of flowering trees. In the evening the sea wall is crowded with strollers and at Easter it is a mass of colourful kites.

Ins and outs
Getting there From the airport, take minibus No 42 to Georgetown US$1.50, one to hours hours (from Georgetown leaves from next to Parliament building); for a small charge they will take you to your hotel (similarly for groups going to the airport). A taxi costs US$20-25 (use approved airport taxis). Internal flights go from Ogle airstrip, 8 km from Georgetown; minibus from Market to Ogle US$0.50. ▶▶ *For more detailed information, see Transport, page 1441.*

Getting around Minibuses run regularly to most parts of the city, mostly from Stabroek market or Avenue of the Republic, standard fare G$40 (US$0.20) very crowded. It is difficult to get a seat during rush hours. Taxis: charge US$1.20 for short journeys, US$2.20 for longer runs, with higher rates at night (a safe option) and outside the city limits. Collective taxis ply set routes at a fixed fare; they stop at any point on request. Certain hand signals are used on some routes to indicate the final destination (ask). Special taxis at hotels and airports, marked 'special' on the windscreen, charge US$1.25 around town, stops and waiting time extra, or you can negotiate a 'by the hour' deal, usually US$6.

Security This is a beautiful city, but check with your hotel, tour operator, the police or government authorities about unsafe areas. Don't walk the streets at night: take a taxi, even for short hops, especially if going to Sheriff Street for the nightlife. At all times, avoid Albouystown (south of the centre) and the Tiger Bay area, just one block west of Main Street.

Georgetown

Atlantic Ocean

Seawall

Fort William Frederick

Umana Yana

Canadian High Commission

US Embassy

Carifesta Av

To 9 10 11 Kitty

Queen's College

Young St

Fort St

High St

Duke St

Parade St

Thomas Rd

To 9 & National Park

KINGSTON

Barrack St

Woolford Av

Cowan St

To 5 18 20 & Queenstown

Lamaha St

CUMMINGSBURG

New Market St

To 16 12

State House

UK High Commission

Walter Roth Museum

Promenade Gardens

To 9 & Queenstown

Main St

Carmichael St

Waterloo St

Camp St

Bentinck St

Middle St

Hope St

Independence Park

To 7 17 19
To 4

Creation Crafts

Holmes St

Quamina St

Guyana Stores

Library

The Bookseller

Church St

Astor Cinema

National Museum

Merrimans Mall

North Rd

To Cricket Ground

Hibiscus Craft Plaza

Bank of Guyana

St George's Anglican Cathedral

To Botanical Gardens & Zoo

Fogarty's Department Store

North St

Robb St

LACY TOWN

To 5

Demerara River

King St

High St

Wellington St

To National Art Collection

Regent St

City Hall

City Engineer's Office

To 3

To 13 & Bourda

Charlotte St

Avenue of the Republic

Victoria Law Courts

Speedboat to Parika Road

South Rd

To 16

To La Penitence

Stabroek

St Andrew's

Magistrates' Court

Roman Catholic Cathedral

To 15

Brickdam Parliament

Minibus to Airport
To Airport

To Charlestown & Albouystown

N

0 metres 200
0 yards 200

Sleeping
Ariantze & Sidewalk Café 1 B3
Brandsville's Apartments 20 B3
Cara Lodge & Bottle Bar & Restaurant 2 C3
Cara Suites, Bistro 176, Surinam Airways & Wilderness Explorers 3 B3

El Dorado Inn 17 C3
Emba-Sea 10 A3
Florentene's 12 C3
Friends 4 C3
Glow 9 B1
Grand Coastal Inn 5 B3
Grand Coastal Lodge 13 D3
Herdmanston Lodge 16 B3
Le Méridien Pegasus 6 A1
Melbourne Inn 18 B3
Regency Suites 15 D3
Rima Guest House 7 B2
Roraima Residence Inn 19 B3

Tower 8 C2
Waterchris 14 C3
Windjammer International Cuisine & Comfort Inn 11 A3
Woodbine 9 A3

Eating
Arawak Steak House 2 D1
Blue Iguana 14 C3
Brazil Churrascaria 3 D3
Coalpot 4 C2
Excellence 5 C3
Golden Coast 6 B2

Hack's Halal 7 D2
Jerries 8 B3
Juice Power 9 B3
KFC 15 C3
New Court Yard 1 B1
New Thriving 10 A3
Oasis Café 11 C2
Oasis Too 16 D2
Pizza Hut 17 B3
Popeye's 12 B3
Upscale 13 D2
Windies Sports Bar 18 B2

Leave your valuables in your hotel. These problems are restricted to Georgetown and nearby villages; the interior remains as safe as ever.

Sights

Although part of the old city centre was destroyed by fire in 1945, there are some fine 19th century buildings, particularly on or near High St and the Avenue of the Republic. **St George's Anglican Cathedral**, which dates from 1889 (consecrated 1894), is 44 m high and is reputed to be the tallest wooden building in the world (it was designed by Sir Arthur Blomfield). Above the altar is a chandelier given by Queen Victoria. The Gothic-style **City Hall** dates from 1888; its interior has been recently restored and may be viewed. Other fine buildings on High St are the City Engineer's Office, the Victoria Law Courts (1887) and the Magistrates' Court. The **Public Buildings**, on Brickdam, which house Parliament, are an impressive neo-classical structure built in 1839. Opposite, is **St Andrew's Presbytery** (18th century). **State House** on Main St is the residence of the president. Much of the city centre is dominated by the imposing tower above **Stabroek market** (1881). At the head of Brickdam is an aluminium arch commemorating independence. Nearby is a monument to the 1763 slave rebellion, surmounted by an impressive statue of Cuffy, its best-known leader. Near *Le Meridien Pegasus Hotel* on Seawall Rd is the **Umana Yana**, a conical thatched structure built by a group of Wai Wai Amerindians using traditional techniques for the 1972 conference of the Non-Aligned Movement.

The **National Museum** ⓘ *opposite the post office, Mon-Fri 0900-1700, Sat 0900-1200, free*, houses exhibits from Guyana and elsewhere, including a model of Georgetown before the 1945 fire and a good natural history section. The **Walter Roth Museum of Anthropology** ⓘ *Main St, Mon-Fri 0800-1300, 1400-1640, www.sdnp.org.gy/wrma/waiwai.htm*, has artefacts from Guyana's nine Amerindian tribes and serves as a research centre for the indigenous people.

The **Botanical Gardens** (20 minutes' walk from Anglican Cathedral, entry free), covering 50 ha, have Victorian bridges and pavilions, palms and lily ponds (undergoing continual improvements). The gardens are safe in daylight hours, but keep to the marked paths. Do not go to the gardens after dark. Near the southwest corner is the former residence of the president, Castellani House, which now houses the **National Art Collection** (open after extensive renovation), and there is also a large mausoleum containing the remains of the former president, Forbes Burnham, which is decorated with reliefs depicting scenes from his political career. Look out for the rare cannonball tree (*Couroupita Guianensis*), named after the appearance of its poisonous fruit. The Botanical Gardens offer great birdwatching. The city has 200 bird species from 39 families many of which can be seen in the gardens. Flycatchers, tanagers, hummingbirds and many migrating species such as Peregrine Falcons and warblers can be found around the capital, but the true stars are the Blood-coloured Woodpecker, which is endemic to the Guiana Shield, and Festive Parrot. Both are regularly spotted in the gardens. Tour operators offer birdwatching tours.

The **zoo** ⓘ *0800-1800, US$1.50 for adults, half price for children; to use personal video US$11*, is in very poor condition but is supposedly being upgraded. It carries the WWF logo and has educational programmes. It hss a collection of local animals including manatees, which usually surface around 1730. The zoo also boasts a breeding centre for endangered birds which are released into the wild. There are also beautiful tropical plants in the **Promenade Gardens** (frequently locked) on Middle St and in the **National Park** on Carifesta Avenue, which has a good public running track. Near the southeast corner of the Botanic Gardens is a well-equipped **National Sports Centre**. Nearby is the **Cultural Centre**, an impressive air-conditioned theatre with a large stage. Performances are also given at the **Playhouse Theatre** in Parade St.

The **Georgetown Cricket Club** at Bourda was one of the finest cricket grounds in the tropics. For the **ICC World Cup** in 2007, a new stadium was built at **Providence** on the east bank of Demerara right next to Buddy's International Hotel (8 km from the city on the airport road, take bus 42 or a taxi). It has fine modern stands but not enough protection from sun and rain. Guyana hosted six matches of the Super Eight series of the competition.

Outside Georgetown

The interior of Guyana is a land of great rivers, dramatic waterfalls, rainforests and savannahs. On the coast are turtle-nesting grounds and sea defences. You can stay at working ranches and secluded resorts. At all times, expect superb nature-watching.

Southeast to Suriname

Linden (*Population 60,000. 112 km south of Georgetown*). The second-largest town in Guyana, is a bauxite mining town on both banks of the Demerara River. The two towns are connected by a good road (slow for the first part to Timehri); the police checks are to stop drug and gun running. Linden is a company mining town. The opencast mine is 60-90 m deep and is said to have the world's longest boom walking dragline. The town is dominated by a disused alumina plant and scarred by old bauxite pits. In town, there is the lovely colonial guesthouse on the Demerara River, run by the mining company.

From Linden rough roads suitable for four-wheel drive vehicles run south to the bauxite mining towns of **Ituni** and **Kwakwani**. The road south to the logging centre at Mabura Hill is in excellent condition; from here a good road runs west to Mahdia, with a pontoon crossing of the Essequibo, and another road continues south from Mabura Hill to Kurupukari, but a four-wheel drive is needed. A good road goes west from Linden to Rockstone ferry on Essequibo River. From Rockstone roads run north to Bartica (bad) and southwest to Issano (being improved).

New Amsterdam (*Population 25,000. 104 km southeast of Georgetown*). On the east bank of the Berbice River, near its mouth, is the picturesque New Amsterdam. From Georgetown, take a minibus (44, or express No 50) or collective taxi to Rosignol on the west bank of the Berbice, US$1.10, then cross the river by the ferry, 15-minute crossing, but add another 45 minutes for unloading (US$0.30; also takes vehicles).

Corriverton (*Population 31,000*) The road continues east from New Amsterdam (minibus, No 50, US$1.75-2.50), to **Springlands** and **Skeldon** at the mouth of the Corentyne River. The two towns are officially known as **Corriverton** (Corentyne River Town). Springlands is 2 km long, so you need to know where you want to get off the bus. There are the *National Bank of Industry and Commerce* and the *Guyana National Commercial Bank*. Suriname dollars can officially be changed into Guyanese dollars. A ferry sails from Moleson, or Crabwood Creek, 13 km south of Springlands, to South Drain in Suriname, 40 km south of Nieuw-Nickerie (see Transport, below).

West from Georgetown

Travelling west from Georgetown, the road crosses the 2 km long floating Demerara bridge (opens often for shipping, US$0.25 toll, pedestrians free). Speedboats cross the Demerara from Stabroek market, US$0.30 every 30 minutes. The road continues 42 km, past rice paddies, *kokers* and through villages to **Parika**, a growing town on the east bank of the Essequibo River (minibus US$1). It has a Sunday market, 0600-1100, and three banks. From here ferries cross the river to **Adventure** on the west bank at 1700 daily and 0830 Wednesday and Friday, returning at 0300 daily and 1330 Wednesday and Friday; or speedboat US$2.40.

The northwest coastal area is mainly accessible by boat only. Speedboats cross from Parika to Supenaam, US$5.50 (can be very wet). From Supenaam minibuses or taxis (US$5.50 per person) go to Charity. From Adventure a road runs north through Anna Regina. Nearby there is a resort at **Lake Mainstay**. You can visit a hot and cold lake, which varies in temperature from one place to another, and the Wayaka Mainstay Amerindian Community, 13 km from Anna Regina. Mainstay is 2½ hours by road and ferry from Georgetown (depending on tides), 17 minutes by plane from Ogle (US$35). The road goes on to **Charity**, a pleasant little town with loud bars, two small hotels (eg **C** Xenon, comfortable) and a lively market on Monday (quiet at other times).

Border with Venezuela Near the border with Venezuela are the small ports of **Morawhanna** (Morajuana to the Venezuelans) and **Mabaruma**. Mabaruma has replaced Morawhanna as capital of the region since it is less at risk from flooding. If arriving from Venezuela, make sure that the official who stamps your passport is not an imposter. You may only be given a five-day temporary visa, to be renewed on arrival in Georgetown.

Shell Beach Part of a protected area of Atlantic coastline, Shell Beach is some 145 km long, from the Pomeroon River to the Venezuelan border. It safeguards the nesting grounds of leatherback, green, hawksbill and olive Ridley turtles. Nesting activity begins in late March and continues, with hatching, until mid-August. Former turtle hunters have been retrained to patrol and identify nest sites, which are logged using global positioning satellite equipment. The project receives support from WWF. The coast consists of areas of mangrove swamps with beaches formed entirely of eroded shell particles. There are large flocks of scarlet ibis. Other birds include Amazon parrots, macaws, toucans, woodpeckers and crab hawks. Iguanas are usually seen in the mangroves, with sightings of rare river dolphin on the narrower stretches of river.

The camp consists of a thatched dining area and huts for the staff and igloo-type tents for guests, with fly-sheets and mosquito netting (vital in the rainy season, when there are 'blizzards' of mosquitos). Showers and toilets are basic. Food is very good. An Arawak family runs the camp and offers daily activities of fishing and birdwatching. They are excellent English-speaking guides. Turtle watching is available in season.

Southwest from Georgetown: to Brazil

Fort Island and Bartica From Parika a vehicle ferry runs up the Essequibo River to Bartica on Monday, Thursday and Saturday, returning next day, US$1.60 one way. The 58 km journey takes six hours, stopping at **Fort Island**; boats come out from riverside settlements to load up with fruit. On Fort Island is a Dutch fort (built 1743, restored by Raleigh International in 1991) and the Dutch Court of Policy, built at the same time. There is also a small village; the rest of the island is dairy farms. River taxis run from Parika to Bartica all day, US$20 per person.

Bartica, at the junction of the Essequibo and Mazaruni rivers, is the 'take-off' town for the gold and diamond fields and the interior generally. Opposite Bartica, at the mouth of the Mazaruni, is Kaow Island, with a lumber mill. The *stelling* (wharf) and market in Bartica are very colourful. Bars flank the main street; *Crystal Crest* has a huge sound system and will play requests. Easter regatta, mostly power boats.

South of Bartica The Essequibo is navigable to large boats for some miles upstream Bartica. The Cuyuni flows into the Mazaruni three miles above Bartica, and above this confluence the Mazaruni is impeded for 190 km by thousands of islands, rapids and waterfalls. To avoid this stretch of treacherous river a road has been built from Bartica to Issano, where boats can be taken up the more tranquil upper Mazaruni. At the confluence of the Mazaruni and Cuyuni rivers are the ruins of the Dutch stronghold **Kyk-over-al**, once the seat of government for the Dutch county of Essequibo. Nearby are the **Marshall Falls** (30-60 minutes by boat from Bartica, US$50 per boat, return), which are beautiful, but too dangerous for swimming. You can swim in the nearby bay, part of the Rainbow River Marshall Falls property.

Kaieteur National Park ⓘ *Permission to enter park must be obtained from the National Parks Commission, Georgetown, T225 9142 (arranged by tour operators).* The **Kaieteur Falls**, on the Potaro River, nearly five times the height of Niagara, with a drop of 228 m, are almost 100 m wide. Ranking with the Niagara, Victoria, and Iguazú Falls in majesty and beauty, they have the added attraction of being surrounded by unspoilt forest. Lying within a national park, there is also plenty of wildlife: tapirs, ocelots, monkeys, armadillos, anteaters and birds. At the falls themselves, one can see the magnificent silver fox, the cock-of-the-rock and the Kaieteur swift, which lives behind the falls. At dusk the swifts swoop in and out of the gorge before passing through the deluge to roost behind the water. Tiny golden frogs live in the tank bromeliads. In the dry months, April and October, the flow of the falls is reduced; in January and June/July the flow is fullest. In the height of the wet season (June), the overland route is impassable.

The **Pakaraima Mountains** stretch from Kaieteur westwards to include the highest peak in Guyana, **Mount Roraima**, once believed to be the inspiration for Conan Doyle's *Lost World*. Roraima is very difficult to climb from the Guyanese side, but *Wilderness Explorers* offer trips via Brazil and Venezuela.

Orinduik Falls Orinduik Falls are on the Ireng River, which forms the border with Brazil; the river pours over steps and terraces of jasper, with a backdrop of the Pakaraima Mountains. There is good swimming at the falls which are a 25-minute flight from Kaieteur. Vincent and Rose Cheong run a tourist shelter and are full of information.

Rupununi Savannah This is an extensive area of dry grassland in the far southwest of Guyana, with scattered trees, termite mounds and wooded hills. The rivers, creeks and ponds, lined with Ite palms and other trees, are good for seeing wildlife. Among a wide variety of birds, look out for macaws, toucan, parrots, parakeets, osprey, hawks and jabiru storks (take binoculars). Many of the animals are nocturnal and seldom seen. The region is scattered with Amerindian villages and a few large cattle ranches which date from the late 19th century: the descendants of some of the Scots settlers still live here. Links with Brazil are much closer than with the Guyanese coast; many people speak Portuguese and most trade is with Brazil.

Avoid the Rupununi in the wet season (mid-May to August); much of the Savannah floods and malaria mosquitoes and *kabura*/sandflies are widespread. The best time is October to April. River bathing is good, but beware of dangerous stingrays and black caiman. Note that a permit from the Home Affairs Ministry is usually required to visit Rupununi, unless you go with a tour operator. Check in advance if your passport is sufficient. A separate permit to visit Amerindian villages is needed from the Minister of Amerindian Affairs, the President's office in Georgetown.

Lethem A small but scattered town on the Brazilian border (see below), this is the service centre for the Rupununi and for trade with Brazil. There are many small stores, a small hospital (T772 2006), a police station (T772 2011) and government offices. A big event at Easter is the rodeo, visited by cowboys from all over the Rupununi. Prices are about twice as high as in Georgetown. About 2½ km south of town at St Ignatius there is a Jesuit mission dating from 1911. In the nearby mountains there is good birdwatching and there are waterfalls to visit.

Border with Brazil The Tacutu River separates Lethem from Bonfim in Brazil. The crossing is about 1.6 km north of Lethem and 2½ km from Bonfim. Small boats ferry foot passengers, while vehicles cross by pontoon on demand (see Transport, below). A bridge is under construction. Formalities are tight on both sides of the border and it is important to observe them as people not having the correct papers and stamps will have problems further into either country. You must have a yellow fever certificate. All procedures for exit and entry are carried out at the Guyanese immigration office at the border. You are given a visa for the exact amount of time you stipulate staying. Immigration is supposedly open 24 hours, but officers usually go home at 1800. If arriving from Brazil, buy some Guyanese dollars in Boa Vista, or use the black market at the river, as there are no exchange facilities in Lethem.

Annai is a remote Amerindian village in the northern savannahs, south of the Iwokrama Rainforest Programme. It is possible to trek over the plains to the Rupununi River, or through dense jungle to the mountains. About 1-2 hours on foot are the villages of Kwatamang and Wowetta where Raleigh International built a health and community Centre in 1995. Some 25 km north of Annai is the Amerindian village of **Surama** which organizes its own ecotourism activities through the village council and can accommodate guests in the new Ecotourism Lodge 3 km from the river bank near a manakin lek; comfortable chalets (**C**), guided walks and river tours. The forest is beautiful, with many animals especially at dawn on the dirt road between Surama and the Lethem-Georgetown road. Birdwatching (US$6), night trekking (US$9), boating (US$30-60) and Land Rover trips (US$30) arranged; every visitor pays a village fee of US$3. Bookings are made via **Wilderness Explorers** in Georgetown, who have formed a partnership with Surama community to develop tourism, www.wilderness-explorers.com; through **The Rock View Lodge** (see Sleeping, below), or through Iwokrama. Transport to Surama can be arranged from Rock View, who can also organize transport from the Lethem-Guyana road.

Iwokrama Rainforest Programme ① *For information and prices, which change frequently, contact the administrator, Iwokrama International Centre for Rainforest Conservation and Development, 77 High St, Kingston, Georgetown, PO Box 10630, T225 1504, www.iwokrama .org.* This is a 360,000 ha project, set up by Guyana and the Commonwealth to conserve habitats such as primarily tropical forest. As well as conservation, the Programme will involve studies on the sustainable use of the rainforest and ecotourism. It is hoped that the results will provide a database for application worldwide. The Field Station is at Kurukupari, near the Arawak village of Fairview, on the northern boundary of the reserve. You can meet research teams, take boat trips and stay at satellite camps deep in the forest (Clearwater on the Burro-burro, Kabocalli and Turtle Mountain on the Essequibo). Fishing is good, especially for peacock bass. Well-trained rangers, who speak their native language and English, escort visitors through the forest on many trails. One goes to Turtle Mountain (45 minutes by boat, then 1½ hours walk), go early for great views of the forest canopy. Another trek is to the top of Mount Iwokrama, a difficult 20 km round trip; for the less fit there is a 10 km trail to the foot of the mountain to a pleasant stream and Amerindian petroglyphs. There are set rates for boat and Land Rover use and for field assistants to accompany you.

There is a 33-m high **Iwokrama Canopy Walkway,** managed by Wilderness Explorers, the Macushi community at Surama and Rock View Lodge, under the name of Community And Tourism Services (CATS); for information contact Wilderness Explorers (see Georgetown, Tour operators) ⓘ *US$ 20 pp for a day visit including entry to the walkway and qualified guide with good birding knowledge, www.iwokramacanopywalkway.com.* The walkway allows visitors to walk among the treetops and see the birds and monkeys of the upper canopy. Night excursions are available on the walkway. There is a library with birding books and a small arts and crafts shop. See Sleeping below, page 1438, **Atta Rainforest Lodge.**

● Sleeping

Georgetown *p1429, map p1430*

It's best to book in advance. There isn't much choice in the lower price categories and many small hotels and guesthouses are full of long-stay residents, while some are rented by the hour. If in doubt, go to a larger hotel for first night and look around next day in daylight. Many new hotels opened for the ICC World Cup. There are several business hotels (eg **B Regency Suites**, 98 Hadfield St, Werk-en-Rust, T225 4785) and apartments (eg **LL-L** Eddie Grant's **Blue Wave**, 8-9 North Road, Bourda, T227-8897, www.bluewave-gy.com; **AL-B Brandsville's Apartments**, 89 Pike St, Campbellville, T227 0989, bransville@gol.net.gy); **A M's Ville Apartments**, 230 Anaida Avenue, Eccles, East Bank Demerara, T233 2409, mvilleapartment@yahoo.com.

LL Buddy's International Hotel, Providence, East Bank Demerara, next to Cricket World Cup stadium, 15-20 mins drive out of the city, T265 7001, www.buddysguyana.com. 250 rooms all with a/c, huge pool with 2 poolside bars, creole restaurant and Chinese restaurant (**Buddy's Mei Tung**).
LL Le Méridien Pegasus, Seawall Rd, PO Box 101147, T225 2856, www.lemeridien-pegasus.com. Prices US$338-205, plus tax. Maintained to highest standard, very safe, a/c, comfortable, fridge, cable TV, lovely swimming pool, gym, tennis, business centre, massage and yoga 24-hr back up electricity.
L-AL Cara Suites, 176 Middle St, T226 1612/5, www.carahotels.com. Luxurious, secure, self-contained rooms with kitchen, grocery, shoeshine, laundry, internet access, airport pick-up.
L-AL Roraima Residence Inn, R8 Eping Avenue, Bel Air Park, T225 9648, www.roraimaairways.com. A small hotel with good standards, a/c and pool.
AL-A Cara Lodge, 294 Quamina St, T225 5301, www.carahotels.com. A Heritage House hotel, 150-year-old converted mansion, 36 rooms, broadband (DSL) internet in rooms, good service, superb, restaurant, bar, taxi service, laundry, business centre with internet, conference room.
AL-A Emba-Sea, 8 Pere St, Kitty, T225 0542. DSL internet ports in rooms, safety deposit bags, pool, craft shop, 24-hr café, mobile phones and car hire, beauty salon and business centre.
A El Dorado Inn, 295 Quamina and Thomas Sts, T225 3966, www.eldorado-inn.com. Good hotel

with nicely appointed rooms in central location. Also has **LL** suites.
A-B Tower, 74-75 Main St, T227 2015, hoteltower@solutions2000.net. A/c, old-fashioned and overpriced, lively bar, *Main Street Café*, swimming pool (member- ship for non-residents), gym, Muneshwer's travel agency.
A-B Ariantze, 176 Middle St, T227 0152, www.ariantzesidewalk.com. Fans, or a/c in deluxe rooms. Includes small breakfast, see Eating, below. Very good but can be noisy from music and nightclub next door.
A-C Grand Coastal Inn, 2 Area M Le Ressouvenir, 5 km out of city, T220 1091, www.grandcoastal.com. Three standards of room, with breakfast and drinking water, dining room, laundry, business centre with internet, car rental, tours, good.
A-C Grand Coastal Lodge, 144 W1/2 Regent St, Bourda, T231 7674, www.grandcoastal.com. Convenient location in central Georgetown, internet, rate includes light breakfast, safe deposit boxes, pure water system and back up generator.
A-C Windjammer International Cuisine and Comfort Inn, 27 Queen St, Kitty, T227 7478, www.windjammergy.com. 30 very comfy, rooms, a/c, hot water, 2 bridal suites.
A-C Woodbine, 41-42 New Market St, T225 9404, F225 8406, just off Main St. A/c or fan, bar, breakfast extra, restaurant, health club, overpriced and not a safe area.
B Herdmanston Lodge, 65 Peter Rose and Anira Sts, Queenstown, T225 0808, www.herdmanston lodge.com. In a lovely old house, pleasant district, with breakfast, restaurant, Wi-Fi throughout the hotel, very comfortable.
B-D Friends, 82 Robb St, T227 2383, F227 0762. Renovated with bath, a/c, TV, kitchenette, hot water, safe, cheaper without kitchen or a/c, mosquito net, bar, restaurant with Creole dishes, travel agency (domestic and international). Take care in this area.
B-D Sleepin Guesthouse, 24 Brickdam, Stabroek, T 223-0991 and 151 Church St., Alberttown, T231-7667, www.sleepinguesthouse.com. The Brickdam property is the better of the two. A/c, cheaper with fan, some rooms with kitchenette, Wi-Fi, meals served, also has car hire.

B-C **Waterchris**, 184 Waterloo St, T227 1980,
waterchris@mail.com. A/c, TV, hot water, phone
(D with fan), simple and rather run-down
wooden rooms, some with shared bath next to a
noisy TV lounge, good restaurant, breakfast extra.
C **Day Star**, 314 Sheriff St, Campbellville, T225
4425, F226 2665. Various rooms, bath, fan,
mosquito net, no restaurant but several nearby,
breakfast available, laundry, 15-20 mins from
centre. Recommended.
C-D **Melbourne Inn**, 29 Sherrif Street, Campbellville, T226 7050, www.melbourne inn.com. On this
famous street, rooms with and without a/c, some
with kitchen, all with bath, car hire.
C-E **Hotel Glow**, 23 Queen St, Kitty, T227 0863.
Clean, a/c or fan, some with TV, 24-hr restaurant,
breakfast extra, taxi or minibus to centre.
D **Rima Guest House**, 92 Middle St, T225 7401,
rima@networksgy.com. Good central area, well-
run, modern, popular with backpackers, no a/c,
hot, communal bath and toilets, good value,
internet, safe, mosquito nets, restaurant (breakfast
US$6, lunch/ dinner US$8). Mrs Nellie Singh is very
helpful. Highly recommended, book ahead.
E **Florentene's**, 3 North Rd, Lacytown, T226
2283. Central, very basic, friendly and safe, not
clean, neighbourhood is unsafe at night.
F-G **Tropicana**, Waterloo and Middle Sts.
Very basic, poor water pressure, some rooms
self-contained, use own lock on doors, noisy disco
on Sat night.

Resorts near Georgetown

AL pp **Timberhead**, operated by Tropical
Adventures Ltd, 10 Providence, East Bank
Demerara, T223-5108, geb@solutions 2000.net. In
the Santa Amerindian Reserve (founded 1858),
situated on a sandy hill overlooking Savannah and
the Pokerero Creek, 3 beautiful native lodges with
bath and kitchen facilities, well-run, good food,
lovely trip up the Kamuni River to get there, much
wildlife to be seen, 212 species of bird have been
recorded, activities include swimming, fishing,
jungle trails, visit to Santa Mission Arawak village,
volleyball, US$79 pp for a day trip (minimum
2 people), US$153 pp per night (including
transport, meals, bar, guide, accommodation).
Recommended.
AL **Emerald Tower Rainforest Lodge**, Madewini
on Demerara River, T227 2011, F225 6021, day tour
US$45, children US$25 (US$7 without meals,
children US$5), overnight stays US$120 double
(includes lodging, 3 meals, soft drinks), cabins for
day rental US$45 (weekends), meals cost US$10,
breakfast US$6, activities include swimming,

nature trails and birdwatching. Guests must
arrange own transport.
Arrowpoint Nature Resort, contact at R8 Eping
Av, Bel Air Park, Georgetown, T225 9648,
www.roraimaairways.com. In the heart of the
Santa Mission Amerindian reservation, offers a
"back to nature experience", with numerous
activities such as mountain biking, canoeing.

Linden p1432

C **Barrow's Dageraad Inn**, 82 Manni St, Mackenzie,
T444-6799, dunbarr@ networksgy.com. Breakfast,
US$3.50, all double/twin, hot water, a/c, TV, fridge.
C-D **Hotel Star Bonnett**, 671 Industrial Area,
1.5 km out of town on Georgetown Rd, T444
6505, F444 6829. Various standards of room, all
with a/c and TV, clean, breakfast US$4, good
lunches (US$4-5).
D-F **Summit Hotel**, 6 Industrial Area, McKenzie,
T444 6500. Cheaper shared rooms available,
breakfast extra.

New Amsterdam p1432

B **Little Rock Hotel**, 65 Vrymans Erven, T333 3758.
D without a/c, self-contained, hot water, a/c, TV,
phone, fridge, breakfast US$3-5, lunch/dinner
US$4-5. Also A-B **Little Rock Suites**, 10 Main and
Church Sts, T333 2727, irtvs@guyana.net.gy.
B-C **Church View Guest House**, 3 Main and
King Sts, T333 2880. Breakfast US$3-4.50, room
rate includes 1 hr in gym, a/c C without), phone,
TV, clean. Recommended.
C **Parkway**, 4 Main St, T333 6438, F333 2028.
Clean, a/c, safe, with bath, breakfast US$2.55- 4,
lunch/dinner US$4-5. Recommended.
D **Astor**, 7 Strand. All rooms self-contained,
breakfast US$2.45.

Berbice resorts

B pp **Dubalay Ranch**, a working ranch on the
Berbice River, 147 km from the river mouth, has
forest, savannah and swamp habitats, with some
300 bird species, deer, large cats, water buffalo and
Dutch colonial remains. Activities include boat
trips (US$25 with guide), riding (US$15 for first hr,
then US$10 per hr), bird- watching (US$15), jeep
tours (US$30), night time wildlife trips (US$50),
custom-made packages, or just relaxing. Price is
C for scientists or students, includes 3 meals and
soft drinks/juices, but not transport to the ranch
(US$230 return from/to Georgetown) or activities.
Small parties preferred; advance booking essential.
Contact **Shell Beach Adventures or Wilderness
Explorers**, see Tour operators, Georgetown.

Corriverton p1432

B Par Park, in Skeldon. With bath and a/c, hot water, TV, no meals available.

C Mahogony, in Skeldon. With bath, TV, fridge, hot water, clean, lunch/dinner US$2.60-3.25. Recommended.

F pp Swiss Guest House, Springlands, T339 2329. Pakistani run, with bath and fan, no meals, helpful, simple accommodation.

Others include **C Riverton Suites**, Lot 78 Springlands, T335 3039, F335 3056, and **D-E Paraton Inn**, K & L #78, Corriverton, T335 3025, F335 3093.

Lake Mainstay p1432

A Lake Mainstay Resort, T226 2975. 40 cabins with a/c, cheaper without lake view, also single rooms, beachfront on the lake, restaurant, bars, swimming, boating, other sports, birdwatching and nature trails, entertainment. Breakfast US$3.85, lunch and dinner US$7.20. Day trips for US$51 per person (1-7 passengers), US$31 (8 plus) including entry fees, road and boat transport, breakfast and lunch, but no drinks. Transport only is US$27.75 Georgetown-Parika return, US$83 return Parika-Supenaam in a regular speedboat, up to 10 people, US$33 return Supenaam-Lake Mainstay for up to 4.

Mabaruma p1432

There is a **Government Guest House**, 2 rooms with bath or shared bath, clean, book in advance. **E Kumaka Tourist Resort**, Maburuma, contact **Somwaru Travel Agency**, Georgetown, T225 9276. Meals, bath, run down; offers trips to Hosororo Falls, Babarima Amerindian settlement, rainforest, early examples of Amerindian art.

Bartica p1433

A-D Platinum Inn International, Lot 7, 1st Avenue, T455 3041, www.platinumparadise .bravehost.com. Range of rooms from suite with a/c, cable TV and fridge, to fan and TV, weekend packages available, internet, tours arranged, restaurant and bar.

B Marin Hotel, 19 Second Ave, T455 2243. **A** with a/c, with bath, TV, phone, fridge, meals available (breakfast US$2.75, lunch and dinner US$6).

C-D The New Modern Hotel & Nightclub, 9 First Ave, T/F455 2301, near ferry. 2 standards of room, with bath and fan. Recommended. Good food, best to book ahead.

Resorts near Bartica

L-A Baganara Island Resort, beautiful house on Baganara Island in Essequibo River a few miles south of Bartica, www.baganara.com. Price depends on season and standard of room, full board, private beach, watersports, airstrip; day trips

US$60 pp (minimum 10), with meals, bar and activities. Transport to resort US$30 pp return. **L-AL Baracara Island Resort**, 8 km up the Mazaruni at the Cuyuni and Mazaruni junction, T225 2281 (647-436-5502 Canada), www.enjoygt.com. Recently reopened timber lodge on an island, en suite rooms, lounge and deck, rainforest and river trips.

A Shanklands, booking office Middle and Camp Sts, Georgetown, T225 2678, www.shank lands.com. Dormitory accommodation available. On a cliff overlooking the Essequibo, 5 colonial style cottages. Activities include swimming, birdwatching, croquet, fishing, watersports, 1st class, US$60 pp for day trip (minimum 8 people), good food. **Shanklands** can be reached by boat from Parika or Bartica; the Baganara Island airstrip nearby; private transport by road can be arranged from **Timberhead** (see above).

C pp WilAmo Family House, 6½ km from Bartica, T226 5558, wilf@networksgy.com. A family house on the western bank of the Essequibo River. Maid service and cook available but need to bring own food.

South of Bartica p1433

B Rainbow River Safari, a 16,800 acre, independent conservation site on the Mazaruni River at Marshall Falls, very different from other jungle lodges (simple softwood cabins, basic bedding, pit latrines, washing in river), cooking over woodfire. Trails in unspoilt forest, waterfalls, wildlife watching, gold and diamond panning, swimming and other activities. Day trippers have to pay G$1,000. For prices and tours contact **Mr E** Sabat, tedsabat@aol.com or tedsabat@yahoo.com.

Kaieteur Falls p1433

F The rest house at the top of the Falls is open for guests, but is basic; enquire and pay first at the National Parks Commission, Georgetown, T225 9142 (if planning to stay overnight, you must be self-sufficient, whether the guest-house is open or not; take your own food and a hammock, it can be cold and damp at night; the warden is not allowed to collect money).

Resorts in the Rupununi p1433

For the first two ranches below, contact **Wilderness Explorers**. All transport is arranged. **L pp Dadanawa Ranch**, Duane and Sandy de Freitas, 96 km south of Lethem, one of the world's largest ranches, each bedroom has a verandah (being upgraded). They can organize trekking and horse riding trips, also camping with *vaqueros*. Tours also to the **Upper Rewa River**, minimum 14 day in conjunction with Wilderness Explorers: one of the most spectacular wildlife destinations in South America. Very remote and expensive but a high chance of seeing big cats, other large mammals and Harpy Eagle.

L pp Karanambu Ranch, Dianne McTurk, 96 km northeast of Lethem, on the Rupununi River, unique old home, cottages with bath, mosquito net, toiletries, good meals, fishing, excellent birdwatching and boat rides with guides. 24 km from Yupukari Amerindian village, trips possible. Dianne McTurk rears and rehabilitates orphaned giant river otters.

C pp Caiman House, Yupakari, www.rupununi learners.org. Price is full board at this field station where researchers study balck caiman. Rustic, airy rooms, relaxing, fresh fish, fruit and vegetables, homemade breads. The river trip to Yupukari offers ample opportunity for birdwatching.

Edwards Lodge, Rewa Village, North Rupununi, shirleyjmelville@yahoo.com. This lodge is on the Rewa River, 2-3 hrs by boat from Annai. 3 cabins with double bed, hammock accommodation available, outdoor toilet and bath, solar lighting. Packages include sport fishing in Bat Creek, Harpy eagle or wild cats viewing, Arapaima spotting; also excellent birdwatching.

Lethem *p1434*

A Maipaima Eco-Lodge, 56 km from Lethem in Nappi village, Kanuku Mountains, T772 2085, www.fosterparrots.com/etguyana.html. Two cabins and a large *benab* (dining hall), each cabin sleeps 4, buildings are elevated and connected by walkways. Hammock accommodation **F**.

B pp Manari Ranch Hotel, 11 km north of Lethem on a creek (good swimming). US$60 per day, can accommodate about 20 people, reserve through the Airport Shop.

C-D Takutu, T772 2034. Simple a/c and fan-cooled rooms, also hammock space (**F**), fridge, clean, breakfast US$3.25-3.80. Lunch/dinner US$3.95-4.20.

D Savannah Inn, T772 2035 (Georgetown T227 4938), savannahinn@futurenetgy.com, or book through **Wilderness Explorers**. Including breakfast, a/c cabins with bath (cheaper with fan), phone, TV, fridge, clean, bar, breakfast US$3.05-4.30, lunch or dinner US$4.30, changes reais into Guyanese dollars, tours arranged, will take you to airport.

E-F Cacique Guest House, T772 2083. With bath, fan, clean, breakfast US$3.25-3.80, lunch/dinner US$3.95-4.20.

Annai *p1434*

AL The Rock View Lodge, Annai, T226 5412, www.rockviewlodge.com, to book, or through **Wilderness Explorers**. Colin Edwards and family, guesthouse with 8 self-contained rooms, bars, zoo, natural rock swimming pool; in the Pakaraima foothills, where the savannah meets the Iwokrama Rainforest Programme (see below). Pony treks,

nature tours for painting, photography and fishing, regional Amerindian and other local cooking, full board. Recommended.

D The Oasis, Rock View's second facility on the Lethem-Georgetown road. With a bar, churrascaria restaurant, shop, accommodation in comfortable a/c rooms or hammock space (**G**). Onward air tickets and buses can be booked from here and tours from Rock View or for Surama/Iwokrama. Interesting nature trail in front of the Oasis up a forest-covered hill – sweeping views of the savannah – channel billed toucans very common.

Iwokrama *p1434*

A pp Atta Rainforest Lodge. For visits to the Iwokrama Canopy Walkway, guests stay overnight facilities in hammock with a bar, dining area and full bathroom facilities. Mosquito nets provided. New restaurant serves breakfast, lunch and dinner. The overnight trip rate includes entry to the Iwokrama Canopy Walkway, trained guide, hammock accommodation, 3 meals. Visitors can experience the dawn chorus and be on the walkway at dusk and into the night.

At **Iwokrama Field Station**, the rainforest lodge is one of the most comfortable in South America in a beautiful setting on the banks of the Essequibo, next to pristine forest, full of giant Moura trees and Kapoks. It has two types of accommodation, in free standing cabins or in a terrace of rooms. Tourists pay a fee for the bed and a user fee. The cabins are comfortable, with bath and veranda. Meals served in huge thatched dining research area with fine views of the river. All meals cost US$5 (take your own alcoholic drinks). Reservations for all Iwokrama lodges and information from **Wilderness Explorers**, see Georgetown, Tour operators, or from Rock View (see above).

Camps

Maparri Wilderness Camp. Contact **Wilderness Explorers** for rates and bookings. It is on the Maparri River, in the Kanuku Mountains, recognized by Conservation International as one of the few remaining pristine Amazonian areas, rich in flora and fauna. It is easy to watch macaws, herons, toucans, kingfisherm, maybe harpy eagles. With luck, you can see tayra, labba, ocelot, agouti, monkeys, tapir, even jaguar. Various treks are arranged. It can only be reached by air and river. **Maparri Camp** is built of wood, with open sides, and has hammocks with mosquito nets. The site overlooks a waterfall; the river water is crystal clear (unlike most rivers in Guyana) and the fall and surrounding pools are safe for swimming. The camp is merely a framework. Simple, nutritional meals, and fish from the river, are prepared over an open fire.

❼ Eating

Georgetown *p1429, map p1430*
A 10% service may be added to the bill. Many restaurants are closed on public holidays. Restaurants are categorized according to their most expensive dishes. All have much cheaper options on menus.

▦ **Bistro 176**, at *Cara Suites*, see above. Restaurant and bar offering local and international cuisine.

▦ **Bottle Bar and Restaurant** at *Cara Lodge*. Very good, pleasant surroundings, must book, also open for breakfast.

▦ **Golden Coast**, Main and Middle Sts. Chinese, good food, huge portions, classy.

▦-▥ **Arawak Steak House**, in roof garden, near Stabroek Market. Casual atmosphere, busy in evening, good value, closes 2200.

▦-▥ **Coalpot** in New Town. Good lunches starting at US$1.80, up to US$13.15 (no shorts allowed, cheaper cafetería).

▦-▥ **El Dorado**, at *Le Méridien* hotel. Good atmosphere, Caribbean, Continental, Guyanese.

▦-▥ **Excellence**, 82 Robb St, Bourda, T226 8782. Creole restaurant and night club (free entrance), which also has apartments (**A-B** per day) and a catering service.

▦-▥ **Hack's Halal**, 5 Commerce St, T225 6798. Specializing in West Indian food, with some vegetarian and sweet dishes.

▦-▥ **New Court Yard**, 35 Main St. Pleasant outdoor bar and restaurant.

▦-▥ **New Thriving**, Camp and Brickdam Sts. A/c, buffet restaurant with large, oily portions.

▦-▥ **Poolside**, at *Le Méridien*. BBQ, pizza, live bands.

▦-▥ **Sidewalk Café and Jazz Club** in *Ariantze Hotel*, Middle St. Buffet lunches Mon-Sat.

▦-▥ **Yue Yuan**, Robb St. Good Chinese.

▦ **Brazil Churrascaria**, 208 Alexander St, Lacytown. All you can eat for US$7.20. Great.

▦ **JR Burgers**, 3 Sandy Babb Str, Kitty. Popular.

▦ **Kamboat**, 51 Sheriff St, Campbellville. Recommended for Chinese.

▦ **Popeye's**, 1e Vissengen Rd and Duncan St, T223 6226. Serves chicken.

▦-▥ **Main Street Café**, at *Tower Hotel*. Good breakfast and other meals.

▥ **Jerries**, 228 Camp St near Middle St. Big portions, slow service, cheap beer. Also fresh daily baking.

▥ **Salt and Pepper Food Court**, 14-15 Croal and Longden Sts, T223 6172. Central, serves over 50 different Creole dishes (eg roti and curry, cook-up rice, pepper pot, etc).

▥ **Oasis Café**, 125 Carmichael Street, South Cummingsburg, T629 5414, wilwalker36@ gmail .com. Fashionable and safe, has Wi-Fi access, proprietor William Walker. A second branch at **Oasis**

Too, 216 South Road, Lacytown, T227 0121. Both serve creole food, mainly lunch. Recommended.

▥ **Upscale**, 32 Regent and Hing St, T225 4721. Popular, poetry night Tue, comedy night Fri.

▥ **Waterchris**, see Sleeping. Very good breakfast, also lunch and dinner.

Fast food: KFC, Vlissengen Road, T225 3909 and Mandela Avenue, T227 3110. **Pizza Hut**, Vissengen and Barima Avenue, T226 6888. Other chicken and pizza places.

Cafés

Juice Power, Middle St, past the hospital. Excellent fruit juices, also sells drinking water.

The Dutch Bottle Café, 10 North Road, Bourda, T231 6560. Serves a mix of Guyanese and international food, has Wi-Fi access.

The Original Dairy Bar, 42 Croal and United Nations Place, Stabroek, T225 5997, originaldairybar@yahoo.com.

Windies Sports Bar, 91 Middle St, T231 3624, dburgess@networksgy.com. Typical sports bar food of burgers, chips etc, popular hang out bar.

Corriverton *p1432*

Mansoor, in Skeldon. Good Indian food. Several good Chinese restaurants within a few blocks of Springlands town centre.

Bartica *p1433*

Riverview Beach Bar, at Goshan near Bartica (Camp Silo bible study centre). Popular hotel and bar, disco, nice beach, safe swimming.

Lethem *p1434*

The Airport Shop, good snacks, bar.

Foo Foods, T772 2010. Recommended for snacks.

❶ Bars and clubs

Georgetown *p1429, map p1430*
Surprisingly lively at night, mainly with gold miners, traders and overseas Guyanese throwing US$ around. Most nightclubs sell imported, as well as local Banks beer; many sell drinks by the bottle rather than shot, this works out cheaper. Don't walk home at night; take a taxi.

Blue Iguana, 71 5th St, Alberttown, T223 6266.

Club Elysium, 45 Main St, North Cummingsburg, T225 7775, albert16642004@yahoo.com.

El Club Latino, 57 Hadfield and Lime Sts, Werk-En-Rust, T227 4600.

Jazzy Jacks, Alexander St, near the Kitty Market (this area is unsafe unless you go with locals). Open till 0400 at weekends, US$3 entry.

Latino Bar, at *Le Méridien Pegasus*. Fri-Sat, Cuban theme, very popular, lively, no cover charge.

Sidewalk Café and Jazz Club in *Ariantze Hotel*, Middle St. US$3 on Thu, major international artists US$6-12.
Trump Card, Church St, near St George's. Sometimes has a live band.

Sheriff St is some way from the centre but is 'the street that never sleeps' full of late night Chinese restaurants (eg second branch of **Buddy's Mei Tung Restaurant**, No 137); and has some good bars including **Tennessee Lounge** (no cover charge), **Burns Beat** (US$5.50 for night club section), **Royal Castle** (Sheriff and Garnett Sts) for chicken burgers. Also **Cambo**, No 76 (also at 119 Regent Street, Lacytown); **VIP Kids Zone**, No 279 with John Smith St.

🎭 Entertainment

Georgetown *p1429, map p1430*
Cinema
Astor, Waterloo and Church Sts. US$1.05-2.65.
Strand, Charlotte St. US$1.60-2.65; 1 on Main St (poor sound quality, protect against mosquitoes). There are 2 theatres.

🛍 Shopping

Georgetown *p1429, map p1430*
The main shopping area is Regent St.
Bookshops The **Bookseller**, Church St. Wide selection. **Argosy** and **Kharg** both on Regent St. **Austin's Book Services**, 190 Church Street, Cummingsburg, T227 7395. **Dimension**, Cummings St. **GNTC**, Water St. **Universal Bookstore** on Water St, near Fogarty's. Good selection and cards.
Clothes Good T-shirts are sold at **Guyana Stores** (see below) and in the markets. **Tribal Vibes**, 92 Laluni Street, Queenstown, T225 7098. Locally designed T-shirts, shirts, vests and bags.
Crafts Items are a good buy: Amerindian

basketwork, hammocks, wood carvings, pottery, and small figures made out of Balata, a rubbery substance tapped from trees in the interior. Look for such items in the markets, or craft shops. **Creations Craft**, Water St; **Amerindian Hostel**, Princess St, **Hibiscus Craft Plaza**, outside General Post Office. Others are advertised in the papers.
Department stores and malls Guyana Stores, Church St, and **Fogarty's**, both of which stock a wide range of goods. The **City Mall**, Regent and Camp Streets, T225 6644, is a small mall with everything from food to jewellers.
Film Films over ASA400 are normally not available; bring your own stock.
Gold Gold is sold widely, often at good prices but make sure you know what you are buying. Do not buy it on the street.
Markets Most Guyanese do their regular shopping at the 4 big markets: **Stabroek** (don't take valuables), **Bourda**, **La Penitence** and **Kitty**.

🏃 Activities and tours

Georgetown *p1429, map p1430*
The tourism sector is promoting ecotourism in the form of environmentally friendly resorts and camps on Guyana's rivers and in the rainforest (see below). There is much tropical wildlife to be seen. See also **Birdwatching and nature tourism** in Planning your trip at the front of the book.
Dagron International, 35 Main St, T227-5525, www.sdnp.org.gy/guytrop/slothisland. Adventure and eco-tours within Guyana and in neighbouring countries and the Caribbean.
Earth Tours Ltd, 106 Lamaha St, North Cummingsburg, T223 7847, navindranarine@hotmail.com. Tours to Iwokrama, Kaieteur Falls and fishing trips to the east coast, Demerara River, Canal no 1 and Canal no 2.

Evergreen Adventures, 159 Charlotte St, T226 0605, www.evergreen-adventures.com. Tours on the Essequibo River to Baganara Island, bus tickets to Lethem.

Rainforest Tours, *Hotel Tower*, Main St, T227 2011 or 231 5661, www.rftours.com. Frank Singh, day and overland trips to Kaieteur, Santa Mission, Essequibo/Mazaruni; also Pakaraima Mountain hike, Kukubara to Orinduik, 5 days from one Amerindian village to another.

Roraima Airways, R8 Eping Av, Bel Air Park, T225 9648, F225 9646. Day trips to Kaieteur and Orinduik Falls.

Shanklands Rainforest Tour, Middle and Camp Sts, T225 2678, see page 1437. Custom-made itineraries, links to resorts, many options including birdwatching, river trips, safaris, hikes. They also run biology tours and school trips.

Shell Beach Adventures, office at *Le Méridien Pegasus*, T225 4483/4, (after hours T227 4732), www.sbadventures.com. Trips to Shell Beach in northwest Guyana, 2-day trip US$450 pp using light aircraft and camping on beach (minimum 2 people, cheaper rates for larger groups, ask about volunteering), day and overland trips to Kaieteur, trips to inland resorts and other locations.

Splashmin's, 48 High St, Werk-en-rust, Georgetown, T223 7301, www.splashmins.com. A water fun park on the Linden highway, 1 hr from the city, entrance and transportation from Georgetown: adult US$6, child US$5, with own transport, entry adult US$3.55, children over 7 US$2.50, children 6 and under free. Also has a resort hotel in **A** range.

Torong Guyana, 56 Coralita Av, Bel Air Park, T225 0876/226 5298, toronggy@networksgy.com. Air, land and river advice and logistical support to all destinations in Guyana, bespoke tours country-wide and excellent trips to Kaieteur.

Whitewater Adventure Tours, Lot no 3 Sandy Babb St, Kitty, T226 6614, F226 5225. Daytrips to Baracara Island on the Mazaruni River from US$60; trips to Marshall Falls (rapids) available, uses two jetboats for tours.

Wilderness Explorers, 176 Middle St, T227 7698, www.wilderness-explorers.com. (In London: c/o Claire Antell, 46 Melbourne Rd, London SW19 3BA, T020-8417 1585.) Offer ready-made or custom-designed itineraries. Tours to all of Guyana's interior resorts, day and overland tours to Kaieteur Falls, horse trekking, hiking and general tours in the Rupununi (agents for *Ranches of the Rupununi*) and rainforest (trips to Iwokrama Rain Forest Programme and joint managers of Iwokrama Canopy walkway, see page 1434). Tours also in Suriname, Guyane, Brazil, Venezuela, Barbados, Dominica, St Lucia and Trinidad and Tobago. Specialists in nature, adventure and birdwatching tours. Free tourism information,

booklet and advice available. Wilderness Explorers are general sales agents for Surinam Airways, Air Services Ltd and Trans Guyana Airways.

Wonderland Tours, 158 Waterloo St, T225 3122, T/F225 9795. (24 hrs), day trips to Kaieteur and Orinduik Falls, Santa Mission, Essequibo and Mazaruni rivers, city tours; special arrangements for overnight stays available, recommended.

Travel agents

Connections Travel, 6 Ave of the Republic.

Frandec Travel Service, Main St. Mr Mendoza. Repeatedly recommended (no tours to the interior).

H and R Ramdehol, 215 South Rd, Lacytown.

Bartica *p1433*

B Balkarran, 2 Triangle St, T455 2544. A good boatman and guide.

Essequibo Adventure Tours, 52 First Av, Bartica, T455 2441, sbell@gyananet.gy. Jet boat and tours on the Essequibo/ Mazaruni and Cuyuni Rivers.

⊖ Transport

Georgetown *p1429, map p1430*

Air Cheddi Jagan International Airport is at Timehri, 40 km south of Georgetown. Check in 3 hrs before most flights and you contact the airline the day before your flight to hear if it has been delayed, or brought forward. There are 3 duty-free shops. Some spirits are more expensive than downtown. There is also an exchange house, open usual banking hours; if closed, plenty of parallel traders outside (signboard in the exchange house says what the rate is). It is difficult to pay for flight tickets at the airport with credit cards or travellers' cheques. The exchange desk will change travellers' cheques for flight ticket purchases.

Flights are often booked up weeks in advance (especially at Christmas and in August) and are frequently overbooked, so it is essential to reconfirm your outward flight within 72 hrs of arrival, which can take some time, and difficult to change your travel plans at the last minute. A number of travel agents are now computerized, making the process easier. Check for special deals on flights to neighbouring countries. Foreigners must pay for airline tickets in US$ (most airlines do not accept US$100 bills), or other specified currencies. Luggage should be securely locked as theft from checked-in baggage is common.

Bus There are regular services by minibuses and collective taxis to most coastal towns from the Stabroek Market. Minibuses leave early; arrive before 0700. To **Moleson Creek** for the crossing to Suriname, No 65 from opposite the City Hall, Ave of the Republic between Regent and Charlotte Sts, leaves when full, US$8.25. This is not a safe area early in the morning, if there are no other passengers waiting take a taxi to Moleson Creek from Georgetown, US$30-35. **Avenish**, T642 5161, offers this service. Be sure he takes you to the legal ferry, via immigration and not the illegal crossing further north. If, by mistake, you get on a bus going only as far as **Springlands**, US$7, 15 mins before Moleson Creek, 3-4 hrs, the driver will probably take you for a little extra money (check with the driver in Georgetown where his bus is going); to **Rossignol**, US$3; to **Parika**, No 32, US$1.50; to **Linden**, No 43, US$3.Ask other passengers what the fare should be.

Note For visiting many parts of the interior, particularly Amerindian districts, permits are required in advance from the **Ministry of Home Affairs** and the **Minister of Amerindian Affairs** in the office of the president, New Garden St in Georgetown. If venturing out of Georgetown on your own, check beforehand whether you need a permit for where you intend to visit. Permits can be difficult to obtain and may require some time. Apply before arrival in Guyana. **Wilderness Explorers** offer a service for obtaining permits.

Georgetown to Suriname *p1432*
Boat To Suriname: a ferry from Moleson, or Crabwood Creek, 13 km south of Springlands, to South Drain (40 km south of Nieuw-Nickerie) runs daily at 1100, check-in 0930, US$10 single (US$15 return for 21 days), bicycles free, motorbikes US$5, cars US$15, 30-min crossing. Immigration forms are handed out on board. At the ferry point is a hut/bar where you can buy Suriname dollars.
Bus Direct buses **Georgetown- Moleson Creek**, 3-4 hrs, US$12.50 (US$10 to Springlands). Entering Guyana, you may be able to join a Paramaribo-Georgetown minibus at Immigration. Direct minibuses Georgetown- Paramaribo are operated by **Bobby's**, T226 8668, **Lambada**, US$22; they pick up and drop off at hotels. Also **Bin Laden**, T264 2993/624 2411 (mob). Check visa requirements for Suriname before travelling.

Mabaruma *p1432*
Air TGA flies from Georgetown Mon, Wed, Fri, US$78 one way, US$148 return.
Boat A ferry runs every other Tue from Georgetown at 1500 (US$8.35) to Mabaruma. The journey is surprisingly rough and 'you will have to fight for hammock space and watch your possessions like a hawk'. For assistance with transport contact Mr Prince through the Government Guest House. Boats also go from Charity (see page 1432) when there is demand. Ask for Peanut or Gavin. Boats go out to sea so you will get very wet, can be rough, 6 hrs, costs up to US$100 per boat.

Shell Beach *p1432*
Air/Boat Fly Georgetown-Mabaruma, then take a motorized canoe to Shell Beach, 1 hr (good trip in the early morning for birdwatching); the last 20 mins is from the mouth of the Waini River along coast to Shell Beach camp, which can be a jolting ride. Or from Georgetown by canoe along some very interesting waterways. Allow 3-4 days. For information, contact **Shell Beach Adventures** or **Wilderness Explorers**, see Activities and tours, Georgetown, above.

Kaieteur Falls and Orinduik *p1433*
Organized tours A trip to the Kaieteur Falls costs US$240 with most operators, minimum 5 people. The trip includes 2 hrs at Kaieteur Falls, 2 hrs at Orinduik Falls, lunch, drinks, park entrance fee and guide; sit on left for best views, take swimming gear. Trips depend on the charter plane being filled; there is normally at least 1 flight per week. Cancellations only occur in bad weather or if there are insufficient passengers. Operators offering this service are **Wilderness Explorers**, **Wonderland Tours** (Richard Ousman), **Torong Guyana**, **Shell Beach Adventures**, **Rainforest Tours**, and **Nature Tours**. Another option is Kaieteur Falls with **Baganara Island Resort** for US$190 pp. To charter a plane privately costs US$1,200 to Kaieteur and Orinduik. **Air Services Ltd** offer a Kaieteur only flight on Sat and Sun for US$190 (includes national park registration); flight must be full, last minute cancellations not uncommon. **Wilderness Explorers** and **Rainforest Tours** in Georgetown offer overland trips to Kaieteur for US$813 for groups of 3-5 people; rate includes all transport, meals, camping gear, guides and flight back to Georgetown. Minibuses run daily from Georgetown as far as Mahdia, via Mabura Hill.

On the Rupununi *p1433*
Transport around the Rupununi is difficult; there are a few 4WD vehicles, but ox-carts and bicycles are more common on the rough roads. From Lethem transport can be hired for day-trips to the Moco-Moco Falls and the Kumu Falls and to the Kanuku Mountains (4WD and driver to Moco-Moco US$72.50, long, rough ride and walk, but worth it). Trucks may also be hired to visit Annai, 130 km northeast (see below) along a poor road, 4 hrs journey, US$200. All trucks leaving town must check with the police.

Lethem *p1434*
The **Airport Shop** can arrange horse hire for US$8 per hr, and Land Rovers and trucks at US$3 per mile. **Savannah Inn** has good 4WD vehicles for hire with driver. For birdwatching trips and transport contact Loris Franklin, T772 2105, or

through the Airport Shop. Best time to ask about vehicle hire (with driver), or horse is when plane arrives, the only time when lots of people are around. Car hire is expensive.

Air TGA flies Georgetown-Lethem-Georgetown Mon, Wed, Fri, US$121 one way, US$227 return. Stops are available at Annai and Karanambu Ranch.

Road The road from Georgetown to Lethem via Mabura Hill and Kurupukari is now all-weather. It provides a through route from Georgetown to Boa Vista (Brazil). After Linden, it runs 100 km to Mabura Hill, then 50 km to Frenchman's Creek and on to the Essequibo. After the river and Iwokrama (see below) the road goes through jungle to **Rock View** (see Sleeping, above), the stop for Annai. Then the road crosses the Rupununi. **Intraserv**, 159 Charlotte St, Lacytown, Georgetown, T226 0605, Lethem T772 2202, have a scheduled bus service from Georgetown to Linden, Kurupukari, Mabura Hill, Rock View (for Annai) and Lethem every day. They leave Lethem at 0000, returning from Georgetown the following day. Baggage allowance: 75 lbs. Fares from Georgetown: Linden, Mabura Hill and Kurupukari US$25 (US$45.45 return); Annai US$30 (US$54.54 return); Lethem US$35 (US$64 return). Also minibuses which leave when full, US$40.

Border with Brazil *p1434*
From Lethem to the crossing (1.6 km), take a taxi, or pickup US$3-5.
Ferry for foot passengers US$1; vehicles pontoon US$4 return. It's then 2½ km to Bonfim.
Buses from Bonfim to Boa Vista (Brazil) 4-5 a day, 2½ hrs, US$5; colectivos charge US$18.

Annai *p1434*
Road TGA agent in Annai is Colin Edwards and the Rock View Lodge is beside the airstrip. Rock View-Georgetown by scheduled bus (see under Lethem), or Land Rover US$70 return. From **Karanambu** to **Rock View** by boat and jeep costs US$380 for up to 4 people, fascinating trip.

Iwokrama *p1434*
Road 1¼ hrs by road from Annai or Surama. Coming from Georgetown, you have to cross the Essequibo at Kurupukari; ferry runs 0800-1700, hoot for service, US$35 for a car, pick-up or small minibus, US$55 for 15-seat minibus, US$125 for truck.

❶ Directory

Georgetown *p1429, map p1430*
Airline offices International: **Caribbean Airlines**, 63 Robb Street, Robbstown, T1-800-538-2942, or 226-3661, www.caribbean-airlines.com (Caribbean, Miami, New York, Toronto, London - codeshare with BA). **Caribbean Star**,

Robb Street, T227 6770, www.flycaribbeanstar.com (within the Caribbean). **Meta**, 303 Church St, Queenstown, T225 5315, metageorgetown@hotmail.com (from Manaus and Boa Vista, Brazil, to Guyana and Suriname). **North American Airlines**, T227 5805 (flights to New York). **Surinam Airways**, 176 Middle St, T225 4894. **Travel Span GT Inc**, 69 Main Street, T227 1701, www.travelspangt.com (to New York, Fort Lauderdale and Trinidad). For domestic flights see Getting around, page 1428.

Banks Republic Bank, Guyana Bank of Trade and Industry (GBTI), Bank of Baroda, Bank of Nova Scotia (2 branches) will give cash advance on Visa card. ATMs at **Scotia Bank, Guyana Bank for Trade and Industry, Le Méridien Pegasus, City Mall** and **Buddy's International Mall**. Exchange houses: (*cambios*) in shops may be open longer. A good, safe *cambio* is **Kayman Sankar**, Lamaha St. There is a *cambio* next to *Rima Guest House*, Middle St. Roving *cambios* at entrance to Stabroek Market, take care. To buy Suriname dollars, go to **Swiss House**, a *cambio* in the unsafe market area around Water St and America St, known locally as 'Wall St'. There are others that will change Suriname dollars. **Car hire** Available through numerous companies (page 44 in the Guyana Telephone book lists some of them and the rest can be found in the yellow pages on page 24). Budget at *Ocean View Hotel*, US$105, plus US$250 deposit for minimum of 3 days. **Shivraj**, 98 Hadfield St, Werk-en-Rust, T226 0550/225 4785, carl@solution.com. US$54.65 plus US$220 deposit. A permit is needed from local police; rental agencies can advise. **Embassies and consulates** Brazilian Embassy, 308 Church St, Queenstown, T225 7970, bragetown@solutions2000.net. Visa issued next day, 90 days, 1 photo, US$12.75. Canadian High Commission, High and Young Sts, T227 2081-5, www.dfait-maeci.gc.ca/latin-america/guyana. French Consulate, 46 First Avenue, Subbryanville, T227 5435. Suriname Embassy, 171 Peter Rose and Crown St, Queenstown, T225 2846/2631, F225 0759. Consular section open Mon, Wed, Fri morning only, but visa application can be handed in at any time. UK High Commission, 44 Main St, T226 5881/4. US Embassy, 99-100 Young and Duke Sts, Kingston, T225 4900, www.usembguyana.com. Venezuelan Embassy, 296 Thomas St, South Cummingsburg, T226 6749/1534, F225 3241. **Internet** Byte 'N' Surf, 288 Middle St, South Cummingsburg, T225 6481, US$2.15 per hr. Internet World, 16 'B' Duncan St, Newton Kitty, T227 1051, US$1.90 per hr. Solutions 2000, 167 Waterloo St, South Cummingsburg, T225 2653/1436, US$2.15 per hr. The Computer Lab, 32-33 Regent & Hinck Streets, T223 3211. See Eating above for Wi-Fi at Oasis Café and

The Dutch Bottle Café. **Medical services** Well-equipped private hospitals include **St Joseph's**, Parade Street, Kingston; **Prashad's**, Thomas Street, doctor on call at weekends, 24-hour malaria clinic, T226 7214/9 (US$2 to US$8 per day; medical consultations cost US$2 to US$4). If admitted to hospital you are expected to provide sheets and food (St Joseph's provides these). The **Georgetown Hospital** remains understaffed even though facilities have improved. Recommended doctor, **Dr Clarence Charles**, 254 Thomas Street, surgery 1200-1400 hours. **Post offices** Main one on North St.

Suriname

Essentials

Planning your trip

Where to go Like its neighbours, Suriname has been influenced by a variety of cultures, African, Asian, European and Amerindian. Markets, customs, festivals and food all reflect this. In Paramaribo, the capital, there is some fine wooden architecture, dating from the Dutch colonial period, and important Jewish monuments. Colonial buildings can be seen elsewhere. Probably the main attraction is the tropical, Amazonian flora and fauna in this very sparsely populated country. Much of the interior is untouched and largely uninhabited. Infrastructure is limited, so tourist lodges, Amerindian and Maroon villages can only be reached by small boat or plane. The Maroons, descendants of escaped slaves, have maintained traditional African culture for centuries and, together with the Amerindians, have a special bond with the tropical rainforest and its biodiversity. Nature reserves, such as the Central Suriname Nature Reserve, formed by the Raleigh Falls, Eilerts de Haan mountain and Tafelberg reserves, Brownsberg, Wia-Wia and Galibi are given in the text below. Suriname is famous as nesting ground for marine turtles. There are no beaches to speak of; the sea and rivers around the coast are muddy, and mosquitoes can be a problem. Some recreational facilities have improvised beaches on the riverbanks (eg White Beach Resort, Overbridge, on the Suriname river).

When to go The climate is tropical and moist, but not very hot, since the northeast trade wind makes itself felt during the whole year. In the coastal area the temperature varies on an average from 23° to 31°C, during the day; the annual mean is 27°C, and the monthly mean ranges from 26° to 28°C. The mean annual rainfall is about 2,340 mm for Paramaribo and 1,930 mm for the western division. The seasons are: minor rainy season, November to February; minor dry season, February to April; main rainy season, April to August; main dry season, August to November. None of these seasons is, however, usually either very dry or very wet. The degree of cloudiness is fairly high and the average humidity is 82. The climate of the interior is similar but with higher rainfall. The high seasons, when everything is more expensive, are 15 March to 15 May, July to September and 15 December to 15 January.

Finding out more Suriname Tourism Foundation ① *Dr J F Nassylaan 2, T410357, www .suriname-tourism.org* (in English). Also try **Stinasu** or **NV Mets**, see Paramaribo Tour operators. The **Suriname Plan Atlas**, which has maps with natural environment and economic development topics, each with commentary in Dutch and English, is out of print, but it can be consulted at the **National Planning Office** on Dr Sophie Redmondstraat, www.planbureau.net.

Useful websites

http://lanic.utexas.edu/la/sa/suriname The University of Texas site, lots of links.
www.kabinet.sr.org Office of the President.
www.nickerie.com Marlon Romeo's web page on district of Nickerie in English.
www.ci-suriname.org Conservation International site. Information on Suriname, including the Central Suriname Nature Reserve.
www.stahm.com. The leading consultancy in ecotourism in the country with useful associations with a number of operators and NGOs. Helpful and informative.
www.nimos.org. NIMOS, a local organization, which acts as an advisory body to the Surinamese

Touching down

Airport tax Exit tax US$35.
**Business hours Shops and
businesses**: Mon-Fri 0900-1630,
Sat 0900-1300. **Government offices**:
Mon-Thu 0700-1500, Fri 0700-1430.
Banks: Mon-Fri 0900-1400 (airport
bank is open when flights operate).
In an emergency Police: Emergency
T115; Other police numbers T471111/
7777/3101. **First Aid centre**: Academic

Hospital, T442222. **Fire Brigade**:
T473333/ 491111/451111.
International phone code +597.
Ringing: equal tones and long pauses.
Engaged: equal tones with equal pauses.
Official time GMT -3.
Voltage 110/127 volts AC, 60 cycles.
Plug fittings: usually 2-pin round
(European continental type).
Weights and measures Metric.

government on all environmental issues.
whc.unesco.org/sites/940rev.htm. Information
about the Historic Inner City of Paramaribo and
the admission to the Unesco World Heritage list.

Visas and immigration Visitors must have a valid passport and a visa. Nationalities which
do not need a visa include: Israel, Japan, Switzerland and Caricom member states. To obtain a
visa in advance, you must apply to a Surinamese Embassy or Consulate at least two weeks
before your scheduled departure to Suriname. You need to fill an application with a copy of
your passport page, purpose of trip and flight number. You will then be issued a letter and
another form to be completed with a passport photo. Procedures at consulates vary. Visas
issued at the consulate in Cayenne normally take one day; two passport photos are required.
In Georgetown, visa applications can be given in at any time, but only collected when the
consular section is open on Monday, Wednesday and Friday morning. If applying when the
consulate is open, visas are usually processed on the same day. A visa costs US$30 for two
months (or €30 for one month; costs vary per nationality and where visa is bought). Make
sure your name on the visa agrees in detail with that on your passport. On entry to Suriname
(by land or air) your passport will be stamped by the military police indicating a brief period
(usually 7-10 days) for which you can remain in the country, regardless of the length of stay
authorized by your visa. If you are considering a longer visit, or want a multiple entry visa
(US$60-175 costs vary for length of stay), you should go as soon as possible to the Alien
Registration Office (Vreemdelingendienst) in Paramaribo to get a second stamp in your
passport: address, Mr J Lachmanstraat 167, at the Department of Civil Works building,
Paramaribo, T597 490666, Monday-Friday, 0700-1430. Allow 1½ hours for this. You must also
return here for any further extensions and for an exit authorization stamp (called 'stamp out')
two days before you leave the country. The final exit stamp is again given by the military police
at the airport or land border. Multiple entry visas may also be obtained at the Ministry of
Foreign Affairs, consular section, Henck Arronstraat 23-25 (opposite Surinaamsche Bank),
Paramaribo; passport and onward ticket required. These procedures are not usually
explained to visitors on arrival. **Note** Brazilians need a certificate of vaccination against
yellow fever to be allowed entry.

Suriname embassies and consulates See www.surinameembassy.org/embassy_
consulate.shtml for a list of Suriname's representation abroad. For visas and immigration, see
www.capitolvisa.com/Tourist/suriname.htm and **www.troon.org/suriname/travel.html**.

Money As of 1 January 2004, the unit of currency is the Suriname dollar (SRD, replacing the
Suriname guilder (Sf) at the rate of 1,000 to 1, divided into 100 cents. There are notes for 1, 2.50,
5, 10, 20, 50 and 100 dollars. Coins are for 1 and 2.50 dollars and 1, 5, 10 and 25 cents (the
25-cent coin is usually known as a *kwartje*, 10-cent *dubbeltje* and 5-cent *stuiver*). In July 2007
the **exchange rate** was SRD2.78 = US$1, SRD3.78 = €1. Euros are readily exchanged in banks
and with licensed money changers. On arrival at the Johan Adolf Pengel airport, you can change
a wide variety of currencies at the **de Surinaamsche Bank** into Surinamese dollars, including
reais, Trinidad and Tobago dollars, Barbados dollars. In Paramaribo *cambios* at various

Driving in Suriname

Roads 26% of roads are paved. East-west roads: From Albina to Paramaribo to Nieuw-Nickerie is paved. North-south roads: the road Paramaribo-Paranam-Afobaka-Pokigron is open. The road to the western interior, Zanderij-Apura, crosses the Coppename River; thereafter small bridges are in poor shape (take planks to bridge gaps). On the unpaved Moengo-Blakawatra road (eastern Suriname), the bridge across the Commewijne River is closed to traffic.

Road safety Driving is on the left, but many vehicles have left-hand drive. There is a 24 hour emergency service for motorists: **Wegenwacht**, Sr Winston Churchillweg 123, T484691/487540.

Documents All driving licences accepted, but you need a stamp from the local police and a deposit. To drive a foreign registered vehicle requires no *carnet* or other papers. People wishing to travel from Suriname to either Guyana or Guiane by car need special vehicle insurance, available from **Assuria Insurance Company**, Gravenstraat 5-7, Paramaribo. T473400, www.assuria.sr.

Note Although an international driver's license is accepted in both Suriname and Guyana, a special permit is required to drive a vehicle in the two countries for longer than one month.

Fuel Gasoline is sold as diesel, 'regular', unleaded, or super unleaded (more expensive): basic price SRD3 (US$1.10) per litre.

locations are open till late but only accept US dollars and euros. Officially visitors must declare foreign currency on arrival. When arriving by land, visitors' funds are rarely checked, but you should be prepared for it. If entering Suriname from Guyana, you can change money at one of several banks in Nieuw-Nickerie. If arriving via Albina, the nearest bank, *de Surinaamsche Bank* (www.dsbbank.sr), is in Moengo, otherwise *Hakrinbank* (www.hakrinbank.com) at Tamanredjo (Commewijne), or *Multitrack Money Exchange* not far from the Dr Jules Albert Wijdenbosch bridge in Meerzorg, Commewijne. On departure, you can change Suriname dollars into Guyanese or US$ at Corriverton or in Georgetown.

Confusingly, prices are quoted in three currencies: SRD for small items; US$ for most tourist items, sometimes euros; euros for books, upmarket clothing and real estate, but sometimes US$.

Safety Street crime in Paramaribo has been much reduced through intensive police surveillance. Although beggars and/or drug-addicts are a nuisance day or night, they are rarely dangerous. Generally, Paramaribo is much safer than Georgetown or Cayenne, but it's still wise to be cautious after dark and take care around the markets and docks. Do not photograph military installations. If in doubt, ask first. If travelling to the interior enquire at your hotel, the tourist information centre or any other tourist authority about the safety situation in the areas you plan to visit. Malaria exists at some places in the interior: contact the **Department of Public Health** ① *Rode Kruislaan 22, T499494, F491452*, for more information.

Getting around

Air Internal services are run by **Gum Air** (T498760, www.gumair.com) and **Blue Wing** (T434393, www.bluewingairlines.com), small air charter firms. **Hi Jet** is a helicopter charter company at Zorg en Hoop airport (T432577). There are no scheduled flights, only charters. The air companies fly to several Amerindian and Maroon villages. Most settlements have an airstrip, but internal air services are limited. These flights are on demand.

Road Details of buses and taxis are given in the text below. **Hitchhiking** is possible but neither common nor advisable.

Cycling Visit **Cardy Adventures and Bike Rental** ① *Cornelis Jongbawstraat 31, Paramaribo T422518, www.cardyadventures.com* for bikes. Recommended rides from Paramaribo include: to Nieuw-Amsterdam, Mariënburg, Alkmaar and back via Tamanredjo in the Javanese Commewijne district or from Rust en Werk to Spieringshoek to Reijnsdorp (3½ hours) and return to Leonsberg via ferry, whence it is a 30 minutes to Paramaribo.

Ferry The **Suriname Navigation Co** (SMS) has a daily service, leaving 0700, on Commewijne River (a nice four hour trip; you can get off at **De Nieuwe Grond**, a plantation owned by an English couple, and stay overnight). SMS ferry to Alliance/Reynsdorp leaves on Wednesday, Friday, Saturday or Sunday at 0700. **Note** It is advisable to check the weather conditions and probabilities of returning on schedule before you set out on a trip to the interior. Heavy rains can make it impossible for planes to land in some remote areas; little or no provision is made for such delays and it can be a long and hungry wait for better conditions.

Sleeping → *See page 58 for our hotel grade price guide.*
Hotels (and restaurants) are rare outside Paramaribo, but accommodation in the interior is excellent if organized through a tour operator. Many have their own resorts, such as the Mets' Awarradam complex near the Saramacca villages on Gran Rio. Going alone, you usually have to supply your own hammock and mosquito net, and food and drink. A tent is less useful in this climate. Do not travel independently without taking some local currency.

Eating → *See page 58 for our eating price guide.*
Surinamese cuisine is as rich and varied as the country's ethnic makeup. High-quality rice is the main staple. Cassava, sweet potatoes, plantain, and hot red peppers are widely used. *Pom* is a puree of the tayer root (a relative of cassava) tastily spiced and served with chicken. *Moksie Alesie* is rice mixed with meat, smoked chicken and fish, white beans, tomatoes, peppers and spices. *Pindasoep* (peanut soup with plantain dumplings or noodles) and *okersoep met tayerblad* (gumbo and cassava soup) are both worth a try. *Petjil* are vegetables cooked in peanut sauce. Well-known Indonesian dishes include *bami* (fried noodles) and *nasi goreng* (fried rice), both spicy and slightly sweet. Among the Hindustani dishes are *roti*, *somosa* and *phulawri* (fried chickpea balls). Among Suriname's many tropical fruit, palm nuts such as the orange-coloured awarra and the cone-shaped brown maripa are most popular.

Festivals and events
Public holidays 1 January, New Year; Holi Phagwa (Hindu spring festival, date varies each year, generally in March, very interesting but watch out for throwing of water, paint, talc and coloured powder); Good Friday; Easter (two days); 1 May (Labour Day); 1 July (Emancipation Day); Diwali (Hindu Festival of Light in October); 25 November (Independence Day); Christmas (two days). For Muslim holidays see note under Guyana.

Festivals **Avond Vierdaagse** starting on the first Wednesday after Easter is a carnival parade of the young and old dressed in traditional costume or simple clothes; it is organized by Bedrijven Vereniging Sport en Spel (BVVS), Johannes Mungrastraat 48, Paramaribo, T461020. **Surifesta** (www.surifesta.com) is a year-end festival, from mid- December to the first week of January, with shows, street parties, flower markets, culminating in **Het Vat** on 31 December. The **Suriname Jazz Festival**, www.surinamejazzfestival.com, is held annually in Paramaribo in October. Project manager: Ms Anne-Marie Hermelijn, an.hermelijn@surinamejazzfestival.com. **Nationale Kunstbeurs/National Art Fair/National Art Exhibition**, held in Vormingscentrum Ons Erf, Prins Hendrikstraat, Paramaribo, www.suriname-fvas.org/activities.html.

Paramaribo → *Colour map 2, grid B5. Population: 487,024 (2004).*

The capital and chief port, lies on the Suriname River, 12 km from the sea. There are many attractive colonial buildings. The **Governor's Mansion** (now the Presidential Palace) is on Onafhankelijkheidsplein (also called Eenheidsplein and, originally, Oranjeplein). Many beautiful 18th- and 19th-century buildings in Dutch (neo-Normanic) style are in the same area. A few have been restored, notably along the waterfront.

Ins and outs
Getting there The airport is 47 km south. There is no central bus station. ▸▸ *For more detailed information see Transport, page 1455.*

Getting around There are very few regular **buses**; the few services that are left leave from Heiligenweg. There are privately run 'wild buses', also known as 'numbered buses' which run on fixed routes around the city; they are minivans and are severely overcrowded. **Taxis** generally have no meters, average price US$2.50. The price should be agreed on beforehand to avoid trouble. Recommended is **Toutonne's Taxi**, T475734/425380, tourtaxi87@yahoo.com, reliable good value, will collect from airport with advance notice. If hiring a taxi for touring, beware of overcharging. If you're a hotel guest, let the hotel make arrangements.

Tourist information **Suriname Tourist Foundation**, main office JF Nassylaan 2, T410357, www.suriname-tourism.org. Monday-Friday 0730-1500. Branch office at the Zeelandia Complex, T479200, Monday-Friday 0900-1530. Or ask at operators like **Mets** or **Sun and Forest**.

Sights

Fort Zeelandia houses the Suriname Museum ① *T425871, Tue-Fri 0900-1400, Sun 1000-1400, US$2,* restored to this purpose after being repossessed by the military. The whole complex has been opened to the public again and its historic buildings can be visited. The fort itself now belongs to the Stichting (foundation) Surinaams Museum, and is generally in good condition. The old wooden officers' houses in the same complex have been restored with Dutch finance. Very few exhibits remain in the old museum in the residential suburb of Zorg en Hoop, Commewijnestraat. Look for Mr F H R Lim A Postraat if you wish to see what Paramaribo looked like only a comparatively short time ago. The 19th century **Roman Catholic St Peter and Paul Cathedral** (1885), built entirely of wood, is one of the largest wooden buildings in the Americas. This twin towered, neo-Gothic building with a rose window is both impressive and beautiful. Continuing restoration is due with funds from the European Union. Much of the old town, dating from the 19th century, and the churches have been restored. Other things to see are the colourful **market** and the waterfront, **Hindu temples** in Koningstraat and Wanicastraat (finally

Paramaribo

Sleeping
AaBéCé 13
Eco-Resort Inn 4
Fanna 5
Guest House 24 1
Guest House Albergo
Alberga 2
Guesthouse Centre 6

Guesthouse Sabana 6
Krasnapolsky 7
Queens Hotel & Casino 3
Residence Inn 8
Savoie 11
Torarica 9
YWCA Guesthouse 10

Zeelandia Suites &
Sun and Forest Tours 12

Eating
Bali 5
Café de Punt 1
Chi Min 6
Dumpling #1 7

completed after years of construction), one of the Caribbean's largest **mosques** at Keizerstraat (take a magnificent photo at sunset). There are two **synagogues**: one next to the mosque at Keizerstraat 88, the other (1854) on the corner of Klipstenstraat and Heerenstraat (closed, now houses an internet café and IT business unit). The new **Numismatich Museum** ① *Mr FHR Lim A Postraat 7, T520016, www.cbvs.sr daily 0800-1400*, displaying the history of Suriname's money, is operated by the Central Bank. A new harbour has been constructed about 1½ km upstream. Two pleasant parks are the **Palmentuin**, with a stage for concerts, and the **Cultuurtuin** (with poorly kept zoo owing to lack of funds, US$1.20, busy on Sunday), the latter is a 20-minute walk from the centre. National dress is normally only worn by the Asians on national holidays and at wedding parties, but some Javanese women still go about in sarong and klambi. A university (Anton de Kom Universiteit van Suriname) was opened in 1968. There is one public pool at Weidestraat, T475700, US$1.80 per person. There is an exotic Asian-flavour market area. There is a Sunday morning flea market on Tourtonnelaan.

An interesting custom throughout Suriname are birdsong competitions, held in parks and plazas on Sunday and holidays. People carrying their songbird (usually a small black tua-tua) in a cage are frequently seen; on their way to and from work or just taking their pet for a stroll.

Outside Paramaribo

Inland from Paramaribo

Accaribo resort, about one hour by car from the capital on the Suriname River, near the villages of La Vigilantia and Accaribo: seven rooms with bath, visit Amerindian settlement, pottery making, swimming in the river, Creole and Javanese cultures.

Powaka, about 90 minutes outside the capital, is a primitive village of thatched huts but with electric light and a small church. In the surrounding forest one can pick mangoes and other exotic fruit. An interesting excursion for a half or full day is to take minibus four, or taxi, to **Leonsberg** on the Suriname River (**Stardust Hotel**, with mid-priced restaurant, café, pool, games; restaurant **Rust Pelikan** on waterfront; at **Leonsberg** restaurant try *saoto* soup and other Javanese specialities, overlooking the river), then ferry to **Nieuw-Amsterdam**, the capital of the predominantly Javanese district of Commewijne. There is an open-air **museum** ① *open mornings only except Fri 1700-1900*, inside the old fortress that guarded the confluence of the Suriname and Commewijne rivers. There are some interesting plantation mansions left in the Commewijne district (some can be visited on tours). **Braamspunt**, a peninsula with nice beaches at the mouth of Suriname River, is 10 km from Paramaribo. Take a boat from the Leonsberg scaffold.

You can drive to **Jodensavanne** (Jews' Savannah, established 1639), which is south of Paramaribo on the opposite bank of the Suriname River, where a cemetery and the foundations of one of the oldest synagogues in the Western Hemisphere have been restored. You can also visit the healing well. There is no public transport and taxis won't go because of the bad road. It is still only 1½ hours with a suitable vehicle (see above for tours). There is a bridge across the Suriname River to Jodensavanne. **Blakawatra** is one of the most beautiful spots in Suriname (shame about the amount of rubbish strewn around).

Mambo **1**
Pannekoek en
  Poffertjes Café **8**
Power Smoothie **9**
Roopram Rotishop **10**
Spice Quest **11**
'T Lekkerbekje **1**
'T VAT' **2**

Uncle Ray & Warungs **3**
Zanzibar **1**

Bars & clubs 🎵
Broki **12**
Touché **4**

This was the scene of much fighting in the civil war. A full day trip to Jodensavanne and Blakawatra, returning to Paramaribo via Moengo, has been recommended if you can arrange the transport. Bus to Blakawatra at 0800, three hours, US$0.20. Some 5 km from the International Airport there is a resort called **Colakreek** *US$0.20*, so named for the colour of the water, but good for swimming (busy at weekends), lifeguards, water bicycles, children's village, restaurant, bar, tents or huts for overnight stay. The village of **Bersaba**, 40 km from Paramaribo close to the road to the airport, is popular area for the Coropinakreek. Many people go there and the neighbouring village of Republiek at weekends and on holidays.

Approximately 30 km southwest of Paramaribo, via **Lelydorp** (*Hotel De Lely*, Sastrodisomoweg 41; *The Lely Hills* casino), is the Bush Negro village of **Santigron**, on the east bank of the Saramacca River. Minibuses leave Paramaribo at 0530 and 1500, two hours, US$0.10. They return as soon as they drop off passengers in the village, so make sure you will have a bus to return on; there is no accommodation in Santigron. Nearby is the Amerindian village of **Pikin Poika**. The two make a good independent day trip. Tour agencies also visit the area about twice a month, including canoe rides on the Saramacca River and a Bush Negro dance performance.

By bus or car to **Afobakka**, where there is a large hydroelectric dam on the Suriname River. There is a government guest house (price includes three meals a day) in nearby **Brokopondo**. Victoria is an oil-palm plantation in the same area.

The hills of **Brownsberg National Park** ① *US$1.20*, an hour by car from Brokopondo, overlook the Professor Dr Ir van Blommensteinmeer reservoir. It features good walking, ample opportunities to see wildlife and three impressive waterfalls. Stinasu run all-inclusive tours from Paramaribo (one and three-day tours, price includes transport, accommodation, food, and guide). Independent visits are possible. Minibuses for Brownsweg leave Saramaccastraat in Paramaribo daily when full, be there 0800-0900, two hours, US$5.55. Trucks converted into buses do the trip for US$10. Go to Stinasu at least 24 hours in advance and pay for accommodation in their guest houses (US$35, or US$5 to camp) or to arrange for a vehicle to pick you up in Brownsweg (US$30). Take your own food. A fully organized day trip costs US$100.

Tukunari Island, in van Blommesteinmeer lake, is about three hours' drive from Paramaribo to Brokopondo then a two-hour canoe ride. The island is near the village of Lebi Doti, where Aucaner Maroons live. Tours with NV Mets include fishing, jungle treks and visits to villages.

Saramaka villages and **Awarradam**. There are many Saramaka villages along the Gran and Pikin Rios, both Suriname River tributaries. These are fascinating places, set up in the 17th and 18th centuries by escaped slaves, originally from Ghana, who preserve a ceremonial language, spirituality and traditions. NV Mets have a comfortable lodge on the Gran Rio at Awarradam, in front of a beautiful set of rapids in thick forest, and many other agencies, such as Sun and Forest, organize culturally sensitive tours to the villages. Independent visitors are not welcome.

Raleighvallen/Voltzberg Nature Reserve (78,170 ha) is a rainforest park, southwest of Paramaribo, on the Coppename River. It includes Foengoe Island in the river and Voltzberg peak; climbing the mountain at sunrise is unforgettable. The reserve can be reached by air, or by road (180 km) followed by a 3-4 hour boat ride. This reserve has been joined with Tafelberg and Eilerts de Haan reserves to create the **Central Suriname Nature Reserve** (1.592 million ha – 9.7% of Suriname's total land area). The Reserve is now part of the Unesco's World Heritage List (www.unesco.org). New tourist facilities have been opened. Stinasu does a US$10 tour, or can arrange all-inclusive tours with accommodation, transport, food and guides. **Stoelmanseiland**, on the Lawa River in the interior, and the Maroon villages and rapids in the area can be visited on an organized tour. Price US$170 per person for three days (five persons, minimum). They are, however, more easily reached by river from St-Laurent du Maroni and Maripasoula in Guyane.

Kasikasima and **Palumeu**, in the far south of Suriname, are a series of dramatic granite mountains rising out of pristine forest. The highest is Mount Kasikasima, near the Trio and Wajana Amerindian village of Palumeu. Mets have a comfortable river lodge here and organize trips up the mountain, as do other operators.

West of Paramaribo

A narrow but paved road leads through the citrus and vegetable growing areas of **Wanica** and **Saramaca**, linked by a bridge over the Saramaca River. At **Boskamp** (90 km from Paramaribo) is the Coppename River. The Coppename bridge crosses to **Jenny** on the west bank. The **Coppename Estuary** is a national park, protecting many bird colonies.

A further 50 km is **Totness**, where there was once a Scottish settlement. It is the largest village in the Coronie district, along the coast between Paramaribo and Nieuw-Nickerie on the

Guyanese border. There is a good government guesthouse. The road (bad, liable to flooding) leads through an extensive forest of coconut palms. Bus to Paramaribo at 0600. 40 km further west, 5 km south of the main road is **Wageningen**, a modern little town, the centre of the Suriname rice-growing area. The road from Nickerie has been renewed. One of the largest fully mechanized rice farms in the world is found here (*Hotel de Wereld*, T0251544). The **Bigi-Pan** area of mangroves is a birdwatchers' paradise; boats may be hired from local fishermen.

Nieuw-Nickerie (*Population over 8,000, district 45,000, mostly East Indian*) on the south bank of the Nickerie River 5 km from its mouth, opposite Guyana, is the main town and port of the Nickerie district and is distinguished for its rice fields. It is a clean and ordered town, but there are a lot of mosquitoes.

Border with Guyana

Ferry to Moleson Creek (for Springlands) From South Drain/Canawiama (Suriname, 40 km from Nieuw-Nickerie, road due to be paved) to Moleson/Crabwood Creek (Guyana), it's a 30-minute trip on the regular ferry. Immigration forms are handed out on the boat. See Transport below. The illegal 'Back Track' speedboat runs from a point 10 minutes from town, by a café on the beach. Seek local advice before using this route. **Note** Suriname is 1 hr ahead of Guyana.

Apura on the Corantijn can be reached by sea-going vessels (**C**) with three meals, advance booking from Paramaribo advisable, good). **Blanche Marie Falls**, 320 km from Paramaribo on the Apura road, is a popular destination. There is a guesthouse, Dubois, see Sleeping below. **Washabo** near Apura, which has an airstrip, is an Amerindian village. No public transport runs from Paramaribo to the Apura-Bakhuis area, but frequent charter flights go to the Washabo airstrip. Irregular small boats sail from Apura to Nieuw-Nickerie and to Springlands (Guyana).

East of Paramaribo to Guyane

Eastern Suriname was the area most severely damaged during the civil war. A paved road connects Meerzorg (bridge across the river) with Albina, passing through the districts of Commewijne and Marowijne. There is little population or agriculture left here. **Moengo**, 160 km up the Cottica River from Paramaribo, was a bauxite mining and loading centre for Suralco. It can be reached by medium draught ships and by cars. The new bauxite mining centre is at Coermotibo, not far from Moengo.

There are two **nature reserves** on the northeast coast of Suriname. Known primarily as a major nesting site for sea turtles (five species including the huge leatherback turtle come ashore to lay their eggs), **Wia-Wia Nature Reserve** (36,000 ha) also has nesting grounds for some magnificent birds. The nesting activity of sea turtles is best observed April-July (July is a good month to visit as you can see adults coming ashore to lay eggs and hatchlings rushing to the sea at high tide). Since the beaches and consequently the turtles have shifted westwards out of the reserve, accommodation is now at **Matapica** beach, not in the reserve itself. (After a visit to the reserves send any comments to Stinasu. Your support is needed to keep the reserves functioning.) The SMS riverboat from Paramaribo stops at Alliance on its journey up the Commewijne River. You then transfer to a Stinasu motorboat for a one hour ride to Matapica. The motorboat costs US$50 for four people, round trip; a guide is the same price. Suitable waterproof clothing should be worn. Fishermen make the crossing for US$3-4. Book a boat and accommodation through Stinasu or other agencies; keep your receipts or you will be refused entry. Early booking is essential. Stinasu has a lodge at Matapica. It can hold 8 people, facilities are basic and it costs US$53.

The **Galibi Nature Reserve** ⓘ *www.biotopic.demon.nl/suriname/suriname.htm*, where there are more turtle-nesting places, is near the mouth of the Marowijne River. There are Carib Indian villages. From Albina it is a three-hour (including 30 minutes on the open sea) boat trip to Galibi. There is new tourist lodge here: it has cooking facilities, a refrigerator, rooms with shower and toilet, powered mostly by solar energy. Make arrangements through Stinasu who run all-inclusive, four-day, three-night tours (you can save money by taking your own food and public transport to the river to meet the motorboat). Sun and Forest Tours also have tours here.

East of Moengo, the scars of war are most obvious. **Albina** is on the Marowijne River, the frontier with Guyane. Once a thriving, pleasant town and then a bombed-out wreck, it is now showing signs of recovery with shops, a market and restaurants (it's still not very inviting, though). *The Creek Hotel* (with eight rooms) is on the northern outskirts of town; the owner speaks English.

Border with Guyane

Customs and immigration on both sides close at 1900, but in Albina staff usually leave by 1700. Be wary of local information on exchange rates and transport to Paramaribo. Changing money on the Suriname side of the border is illegal; see Money, page 1445. Suriname dollars are not recognized in Guyane; when crossing to Suriname, pay for the boat in euros, or get the minivan driver to pay and he will stop at a cambio before reaching Paramaribo so you can change money and pay him. Immigration is at either end, next to the ferry terminal. Have your passport stamped before getting the boat. See Transport, 1455.

● Sleeping

Paramaribo *p1447, map p1448*
Service charge at hotels is 5-10%. Beware: many cheap hotels not listed are 'hot pillow' establishments. The Suriname Museum in Zorg-en-Hoop (see above) now has a good guest house; book in advance.

L Zeelandia Suites, Kleine Waterstraat 1a, T424631, www.zeelandiasuites.com. Smart, business-style suites with all mod cons next to a lively bar and restaurant area.

AL Krasnapolsky, Domineestraat 39, T475050, www.krasnapolsky.sr. A/c, central, travel agency, shopping centre, exhibition hall in the lobby, good breakfast and buffet, *Atrium* restaurant for local and international cuisine (mid-range), *Rumours Grand Café* (with jazz jam sessions on Tue and Fri), poolside bar, business centre with internet and conference facilities, takes Amex, swimming pool.

AL Torarica, Mr Rietbergplein, T471500, www.torarica.com. Best in town, very pleasant, book ahead, swimming pool and other sports facilities, sauna, casino, tropical gardens, a/c, central, 3 expensive restaurants (*Plantation Room*, European; *The Edge*, with live entertainment; good poolside buffet on Fri evening), superb breakfast, business centre with internet and conference facilities. A smart new hotel is being built next door. Has subsidiary *Tangelo Bar and Terrace*, at Mr Rietbergplein 1.

AL Queen's Hotel and Casino, Kleine Waterstraat 15, T474969, queenshotel@ parbo.net. Including breakfast, service charge and tax. A/c, TV with local and international channels, swimming pool, minibar, restaurant terrace, free entrance for hotel guests to *Starzz* disco.

A Eco-Resort Inn, Cornelis Jongbawstraat 16, PO Box 2998, T425522, www.ecoresortinn.com/ website/html/index.php. Use of *Torarica* facilities, good atmosphere and value, restaurant (mid-range), bar, Ms Maureen Libanon is very helpful, business centre, with internet and fax.

A-B De Luifel, Gondastraat 13 (about 15 mins from centre), T439933, F439930. A/c, warm water, cable TV, mid-priced European restaurant, special 'business-to-business' deal: 1 night with breakfast, laundry, airport transfer, car hire and taxes included, Amex accepted.

B Guesthouse Centre, Sommelsdijckstraat 4 (near *Hotel Torarica*), T426310, GuesthouseCentre@ mailandnews.com. A/c, TV, new, good value.

B Residence Inn, Anton Dragtenweg 7, T472387, www.surinamevacations.com. TV, minibar, laundry, including breakfast, credit cards accepted, in a residential area, pool, tennis court, a/c bar and *Atlantis* restaurant, European and Surinamese food (mid-range).

B Savoie, Johannes Mungrastraat 25, T432495, www.cq-link.sr/bedrijven/hotel-savoie. Breakfast extra.

B Shereday, Cornelis Prinsstraat 87, T434564, F463844, 5 km from centre. Exercise floor, swimming pool, restaurant/bar (mid-range).

B-C AaBéCé, Mahonielaan 55, T420851, www .hotelaabece.com. Small, simple, cosy and good, well-decorated, a/c, fridge, TV, kitchenette, safe.

C Guesthouse Amice, Gravenberchstraat 5 (10 mins from centre), T434289, www.guesthouse-amice.sr (in Netherlands, Robijndrift 47, 3436 BR Nieuwegein, T030-294 5229, amice@ worldonline.nl). Quiet neighbourhood, room with balcony more expensive, a/c, comfortable, internet, breakfast, airport transfer and tours available.

D-E Guest House Albergo Alberga, Lim A Po Straat 13b, T/F520050, 853 5741 (mob), www .guesthousealbergoalberga.com. Central, very pleasant, decorated with Amerindian costumes, terrace and TV area, spotless rooms with a/c or fan, breakfast extra, excellent value, book in advance.

C Guesthouse Sabana, Kleine Waterstraat 7, T424158, F310022, opposite *Torarica*. A/c, safe, helpful.

E YWCA Guesthouse (pronounced Why-Ka) at Heerenstraat 14-16, T476981. Destroyed by fire; new hostel to be built.

E-F Fanna, Prinsessestraat 31, T476789. From a/c with bath to basic, breakfast extra, safe, family run, English spoken.

● *For an explanation of the sleeping and eating price codes used in this guide, see page 58. Other*
● *relevant information is found in Essentials page 1447.*

F Guesthouse 24, Jesurunstraat 24. Simple but well-maintained apartments.

Inland from Paramaribo *p1449*

A Overbridge River Resort, 1 hr south of the capital, via Paranam (30 km), then 9.5 km to Powerline mast 20-21, then 7.5 km to resort, or 60 km by boat down Suriname River, www.over bridge.net. Reservations, Anton Dragtenweg 352, Paramaribo-Noord, T/F456440. Cabins by the river, price includes breakfast, weekend and other packages available.

A-C Hendrison Bungalows, Bersaba, contact address Andesietstraat 4, Paramaribo T/F457391 (Rodenryselaan 403, 3037 XG Rotterdam, T104-66414), www.hendrison.com. Fully-furnished.

B-C Residence Inn, R P Bharosstraat 84, Nieuw Nickerie, PO Box 4330, T0210950/1, www.suriname vacations.com. Best in town, prices higher at weekend, central, a/c, bath, hot water, TV, business centre with email (US$5 per hr), internet access (US$7 per hr), fax (US$0.35 national only), laundry, good restaurants (*De Palm* and *Café de Tropen*, both ▓), bar.

D Ameerali, Maynardstraat 32-36, Nieuw Nickerie, T0231212, F31066. A/c, good, restaurant (▓) and bar.

E Luxor, Gouverneurstraat, Nieuw Nickerie. Recently renovated, with mirror-glass frontage.

G Tropical, Gouverneurstraat 114, Nieuw Nickerie, T231796. Mostly short stay, noisy bar downstairs.

Hotel Frederiksdorp, T305003, frederiksdorp@ sr.net. Manager Mr Marcel Hagemeyer. In an old coffee plantation, apartments, bar, restaurant, museum, conference facilities and email.

Border with Guyana *p1451*

C Dubois, contact Eldoradolaan 22, Paramaribo T476904/2. Guesthouse near the Blanche Marie Falls, 320 km from Paramaribo on the Apura road.

🍴 Eating

Paramaribo *p1447, map p1448*
Meat and noodles from stalls in the market are very cheap. There are some good restaurants, mainly Indonesian and Chinese. Blauwgrond is the area for typical, cheap, Indonesian food, served in *warungs* (Indonesian for restaurants).

Indonesian

Try a *rijsttafel* in a restaurant such as **Sarinah** (open-air dining), Verlengde Gemenelandsweg 187. Javanese foodstalls on Waterkant are excellent and varied, lit at night by candles. Try *bami* (spicy noodles) and *petjil* (vegetables), recommended on Sun when the area is busiest. In restaurants a dish to try is *gadogado*, an Indonesian vegetable and peanut concoction.

▓ Bali, Ma Retraiteweg 3, T422325. Very good food, service and atmosphere, check bill.
▓ Jawa, Kasabaholoweg 7. Famous Indonesian restaurant.

Chinese

▓ Chi Min, Cornelis Jongbawstraat 83. For well-prepared Chinese food. Recommended.
▓ Dumpling #1, Dr JF Nassylaan 12, T477904. Open 1800-2300 daily, 0930-1500 Tue-Sat, 0800-1300 Sun. Simple, well-prepared Chinese dumplings and other such dishes. Generous portions, popular with children.

Others

▓ Spice Quest, Dr Nassylaan 107, T520747. Open 1100-1500, 1800-2300, closed Mon, same management as Dumpling #1. Creative menu, open-air and indoor seating, Japanese style setting. Recommended.
▓ Café De Punt, Kleine Waterstraat 17, opposite *Torarica*. Local and international cuisine, live entertainment at weekends.
▓ DOK 204, Anton Dragenweg 204, T311461. Surinamese dishes in an intimate restaurant decorated with a nautical theme.
▓ Mambo, opposite *Torarica*, next to Sabana Guesthouse. Local and international cuisine.
▓ 'T Lekkerbekje, Sommelsdijckstraat (near Guesthouse Centre). Specializes in fish.
▓ 'T VAT', opposite *Torarica*. A smart little square with lots of little bars and restaurants, popular after work for early evening meeting and drinking.
▓ Zanzibar, Sommelsdijckstraat 1, near Hotel Torarica, T471848. Surinamese and international cuisine, with entertainment, Tue-Sun 2000 till early morning.
▓-▓ Roopram Rotishop, Zwartenhovenbrug-straat 23, T478816. Rotis and accompanied fillings in an a/c fast-food style dining room, generous portions, *roti aard* particularly good.
▓ Pannekoek en Poffertjes Café, Sommelsdijckstraat 11, T422914. Specializes in 200 different sorts of pancakes. Open Thu, Sun 1000-2300, Fri-Sat 1000-0100.
▓ Power Smoothie, Zwartenhovenbrugstraat and Wilhelminastraat. Healthy fast food.
▓ Uncle Ray at Waterkant by the Javanese *warungs*, opposite Central Bank of Suriname. Local Creole food.

🍸 Bars and clubs

Paramaribo *p1447, map p1448*
All are liveliest Thu-Sat.
Ballrom Energy, L'Hermitageweg 25, T497534. Younger crowd.
Broki, Waterkant next to the Ferry Docks. Hammock bar, good food and atmosphere.

Don Julio Muziek Eetcafe, Wilhelminastraat 8 (near Torarica). Popular spot, live entertainment, Sun-Thu 1600-0100, Fri-Sat 1600- 0300.
El Molina, J A Pengelstraat, T478485. Fri-Sat opens 2300. Cosy disco, lots of soul music/ golden oldies.
Millennium, Petrus Dondersstraat 2, Rainville suburb. Popular with all ages but mostly the over-30s; **Grill** restaurant inside.
Rumors Grand Café, in the lobby of **Hotel Krasnapolsky**, T475050. Every Fri live entertainment (jamming) with "Time Out".
Starzz Disco, Kleine Waterstraat 5-7, T474993. Fri-Sat 2300.
The Jungle, Wilhelminastraat 60-62. For all ages.
Touché, Waaldijk/Dr Sophie Redmondstraat 60. Fri-Sat only 2300, small restaurant, the best disco.
Uptown Café, upstairs at Spanhoek Passage, T406181. Special entertainment programme every Fri-Sat.

Entertainment

Paramaribo *p1447, map p1448*
There are many **casinos** in the city, including at major hotels.

Shopping

Paramaribo *p1447, map p1448*
Arts and crafts Amerindian and Maroon carvings are better value at workshops on Nieuwe Domineestraat and Neumanpad. Many jewellers in the centre sell at reasonable prices. Local ceramics are sold on the road between the airport and Paranam, but they are rather brittle. Old Dutch bottles are sold. **Arts & Crafts**, Kersten Shopping Mall. Amerindian goods, batik prints, basketwork and drums. **Cultuurwinkel**, Anton de Komstraat. Bosneger carvings, also available at *Hotel Torarica*.
Bookshops Second-hand books, English and Dutch, are bought and sold in the market. Maps are hard to find, but try Vaco. The kiosk in Krasnapolsky Hotel sells books. **Boekhandel Univers NV**, Gravenstraat 61. Recommended for nature, linguistic and scholarly books on Suriname. **Hoeksteen**, Gravenstraat 17. **Kersten**, Domineestraat. One of 2 main bookshops in the city, selling English-language books. **Vaco**, opposite Krasnapolsky. The other main bookshop, also selling English books.
Film **Photo Max**, 37 Domineestraat, next to Krasnapolsky Hotel. Cheap film.
Music The following sell international and local music on CD (the latter is heavily influenced by Caribbean styles): **Beat Street** in Steenbakkerijstraat, near Krasnapolsky Hotel. **Boom Box**, Domineestraat, opposite Krasnapolsky Hotel. **Disco Amigo**, Wagenwegstraat, opposite Theater Star.

Shopping centre Hermitage Shopping **Mall**, Mauriciusstraat, 5 mins in taxi from centre. The only place open until 2100, with chemists, money exchange, top quality boutiques, coffee shops and music stores.
Supermarkets Many, well-stocked. **Choi's**, Johannes Mungrastraat, some way from centre. Excellent selections of Dutch and othe European goods, also Rossignol Deli in same complex.

▲ Activities and tours

Paramaribo *p1447, map p1448*
If intending to take a tour to the jungle and either Amerindian or Maroon villages, check how much time is spent in the jungle itself and on the conditions in the villages. One such trip is to Palumeu, an Amerindian village (Trio, Wajana and Akurio peoples) due south of Paramaribo, not far from the Brazilian border. Four-day, 3-night packages include flights, food, accommodation, jungle hikes and boat trips.
Access Suriname Travel, Prinsessestraat 37, T/F424522, www.surinametravel.com. Sells all major tours in Suriname and can supply general travel information on the country, manager Syrano Zalman is helpful.
Arinze Tours, Prinsessestraat 2c, T425960, www.arinzetours.com. Tours to Maroon villages of Santigron, manager George Lazo.
Cardy Adventures and Bike Rental, Cornelis Jongbawstraat 31 (near Eco Resort), T422518, www.cardyadventures.com. Bicycle rental (bikerental@cardyadventures.com) and tours to Commewijne district, and tours to Brownsberg, Raleigh Falls, Matapica and jungle survival trips, English spoken, very helpful and efficient, excellent food. Open Mon-Fri 0800-1600, Sat 0800-1300.
Danpaati Eco Lodges, Winchesterstraat 6, T/F401687, http://danpaati.net. Lodges in Upper Suriname (Boven Suriname) on Danpaati island.
Eagle Tours, Albatrosstraat 10, T311355 or 09-978850, www.eagletours.info. Tours of Paramaribo, Nickerie, Para, Commewijne and Jodensavanne; also fishing trips.
Ma-Ye-Du, Matoeliestraat 22, T410348, mayedu@sr.net. Tours to Maroon villages in Marowijne River.
Moonlight Jungle Tour, Julianastraat 36, T520709, www.surjungle.com. Jungle expeditions and cruises on Suriname River.
NV Mets (Movement for Eco-Tourism in Suriname), PO Box 9080, Dr JF Nassylaan 2, Paramaribo, T477088, F422322, www.suriname vacations.com. Also in Cayenne, 15 rue Louis Blanc, T317298, F305786; in Georgetown contact *Wilderness Explorers* (see page 1441). Trips to the interior, reasonable rates. Tours offered are City Tour, Rivercruise, Santigron (all day trips); 4/5 day trips to Tukunari Island; 4/5-day trips to Palumeu

(see below) staying in lodges; 8-day trip to Mount Kasikasima in remote southern Suriname (all transport, food and guides – good – included, US$625). Excellent lodge at Awarradam for the Saramaka maroon villages. Can be booked through any **Surinam Airways** outside Suriname.

Stinasu is the Foundation for Nature Preservation in Suriname, Cornelis Jongbawstraat 14, T476597, PO Box 12252, Paramaribo, www.stinasu.sr. It offers reasonably priced accommodation and provides tour guides on the extensive nature reserves throughout the country. One can see 'true wilderness and wildlife' with them.

Sun and Forest Tours, Kleine Waterstraat 1B, T478383, www.surinamesunforest.net. Excellent tours to the interior, including the Central Suriname Nature Reserve, to the turtle nesting beaches near Galibi and Amerindian villages. Onward transport to and trips within Guyane or Guyana with associated operators. Good, reliable service.

Suriname Safari Tours, Dr S S Kaffiludistraat 27, T400925, safaritours@sr.net. Excursions to the interior.

Tojo Adventures, Gravenstraat 73, T422654, www.surinamevakanties.com. Ecotours, helpful tour guides, art, stock for Mr Boyke Tojo. Or through **Mena-Eng**, www.mena-suriname.com.

Waldo's Travel Service, Heerenstraat 8, T422530, www.waldostravel.sr. For all tours within Suriname.

Nieuw Nickerie *p1451*
Manoetje Tours, Crownstraat 11, Nieuw-Nickerie, T231991 (Hans Overeem). Boat tours to, among other places, Apura, Orealla, Corantijn.

⊖ Transport

Paramaribo *p1447, map p1448*
Air Johan Pengel International Airport is 47 km south of Paramaribo. Minibus to town costs US$11 (eg **De Paarl**, T403610); bus costs US$11 with **Ashruf** taxi company, T454451 (it makes many stops), taxi proper costs US$30, but negotiate. *Hotels Krasnapolsky, Torarica, Eco Resort Inn* and *Residence Inn* offer free transfers to and from the international airport for guests with room reservation. There is a guest house near the airport. Internal flights leave from Zorg en Hoop airfield in a suburb of Paramaribo (take minibus 8 or 9 from Steenbakkerijstraat). See Getting there and Getting around in Essentials, above, for airline offices.

Bus To **Nickerie** from Dr Sophie Redmondstraat, near *Hotel Ambassador*, minibuses leave when full between 0500 and 1000, US$5, 3 hrs. There are also buses after 1200, but the price then depends on the driver, 4-5 hrs, extra for large bag. (Taxis from the same area are slightly faster.) Verify fares in advance and beware overcharging.

Minibus taxis to **Albina** US$7.40, 2-3 hrs from Paramaribo cross the new bridge; there is also a

bus from the station near the ferry services in Paramaribo at 0830, return 1300, US$1.65 (take an APB or PBA bus, which has a plainclothes policeman on board). **Taxis** are available, but dishonest (usually). There are irregular bus services to other towns. For full details ask drivers or enquire at the tourist office. There is much jostling in the queues and pure mayhem when boarding vehicles. They are all minivans and have no luggage space. Try to put bags under your seat or you will have to hold it in your lap.

Direct **buses** to **Georgetown** via South Drain (fare does not include ferry crossing), US$15-22: **Bobby's**, T498583 (very cramped), pick up and drop off at hotels; **Le Grand Baldew**, Tourtonnelaan 59, T474713, www.baldew.com (can organize trips through to Cayenne also), Master Card accepted. Also **Lambada Bus Service**, Keizerstraat 162. T411073, and **Bin Laden**, T0-210944/ 0-8809271 (mob).

Nieuw Nickerie *p1451*
Bus For bus services, see under Paramaribo. The bus station is next to the market on G G Maynardstraat.

Boat Ferry to Moleson Creek (for Springlands): from South Drain to Moleson/Crabwood Creek (Guyana), ferry at 1100 only, US$10, cars US$15, pick ups US$20. T472447 to check if ferry is running on holidays. Taxi bus from Nickerie market to South Drain at 0730, but can pick you up from your hotel. Bus Paramaribo-South Drain: US$5.55, eg with **Le Grand Baldew**. See under Transport, Paramaribo, for other companies.

Border with Guyane *p1452*
Boat Pirogues take people across the river to **St-Laurent du Maroni** for around US$3.50-4.75, in euros. The car ferry charges US$3.50 for foot passengers, US$25-30 per car, payable only in euros. If you don't want to take a shared minibus taxi (about US$12 pp) or a private taxi (US$50) from Paramaribo, ask to join a Stinasu tour to Galibi to get to Albina. Albina-Paramaribo: a scrum meets the boats from Guyane for the minibus taxis, 2-3 hrs. A bus leaves at 1300, US$1.65.

❸ Directory

Paramaribo *p1447, map p1448*
Airline offices Surinam Airways, Dr Sophie Redmondstraat 219, T432700, www.slm.firm.sr (to/from Amsterdam, joint operation with KLM, HK. Hof-en Burenstraat 1, T411811, Miami with Dutch Caribbean Airlines, www.flydca.net, and Caribbean). Caribbean Arilines, Wagenstraat 36, T520034 (to/from Port of Spain, www.caribbean-airlines.com). Meta, Henck Arronstraat 61, T597 520120, www.voemeta .com.br (Brazil via

Georgetown, schedules vary all the time). For **Air France** (flights between Cayenne and Europe), T473838. **Banks** Finabank, Dr Sophie Redmondstraat 61, opposite Ambassador Casino. **Hakrinbank**, Dr Sophie Redmondstraat 11-13, 0700-1400. **RBTT Bank**, Kerkplein 1, www.rbtt.com. Cash on Visa and Mastercard. ATMs issue Suriname dollars, foreign exchange desk inside bank. **De Surinaamsche Bank**, Gravenstraat 26-30, www.dsbbank.sr. Cash on Visa and Mastercard. **Surinaamse Postspaar Bank**, Heiligenweg near bus station. **Volks Crediet Bank**, Waterkant 104. **Landbouwbank**, Lim A Postraat 28-30, T475945, F410821. All banks except Finabank are closed on Sat. Amex agent is C Kersten and Co, NV, in Kersten Travel building opposite Hotel Krasnapolsky, T477148. Cambios for exchange, open evenings and on Sat: **De Vries**, Waterkant 92-94; **Dallex**, Keizerstraat 8; **Multitrack Money Exchange**, Mr Rietbergplein, opposite Torarica Hotel; **Surichange**, Dr Sophie Redmondstraat 71, **Yokohama Drive Through**, Saramaccastraat (open Sun), **Surora Drive Through**, Gravenstraat opposite 's Lands Hospitaal. **Bicycle hire** Fietsen in Suriname, FIS, Mijnhooplaan 21, T852 0021, info@fietsen -in-suriname.nl. **Koen's Verhuur Bedrijf**, Van Sommels- dijckstraat 6, T08-876106, open Mon-Sat 1000-1700, also rents scooters. See also **Cardy's** under Tour operators. **Car hire** Avis, Fred O'Kirkstraat, T450447, F456392; **Hertz at Real Car**, Van 't Hogerhuysstraat 19,T402833, ckcmotor@ sr.net; **SPAC**, Verl Gemenelandsweg 139A, T490877, www.spac .cq-link.sr. From US$30 per day, hotel delivery, drivers available. **U-Drive**, T490803, **Wheelz**, HD Benjaminstraat 20, T442929, 887 9366 (mob) or 8802361 after 1600 and at weekends, killit@ sr.net. Mastercard accepted, US$35-110 daily (tax not included). And other agencies include: **City Taxi, Purperhart, Kariem, Intercar. Embassies and consulates** Brazil, Maratakkastraat 2, T400200, brasaemb1@sr.net. **British Honorary Consul**, c/o VSH United Buildings, PO Box 1300, Van't Hogerhuysstraat 9-11, T402870, united@sr.net.

Canadian Honarary Consul, Wagen-wegstraat 50B, 1st floor, T424527, cantim@sr.net. **France**, 5-7 Henck Arronstraat, PO Box 2648, T475222. **German Honorary Consul**, Maagdenstraat 46, T474380. Guyana, Gravenstraat 82, T477985, guyembassy@sr.net. **Israeli Honorary Consul**, Klipstene- straat 2-10, T411998, F471154. **Netherlands**, Roseveltkade 5, T477211, nlgovprm@sr.net. **USA**, Dr Sophie Redmondstraat 129, PO Box 1821, T472900, consul T425788, consular parama@state.gov. **Venezuela**, Gravenstraat 23-25, T475401, resvensu@sr.net. **Internet** All Telesur Dienstencentrum offices offer email (about US$2 per hour), fax (send and receive), local and international phones and computer services. Eg **Paramaribo-West**, Zonnebloemstraat 50, T494555; **Paramaribo-Noord**, Hoek Jozel Israelstraat/ Kristalstraat, T550086; **Paramaribo-Zuid** (LATOUR), Latoruweg 57, T480093. **The Browser Internet Café**, Hoek Wilhelmina/HJ De Vriesstraat (opposite Pizza Hut), Paramaribo, T422977. Another important supplier of internet services is **Carib**, with branches in the synagogue at the Heerenstraat, the Hermitage Mall, Kwattaweg, also in Lelydorp and in Commewijne. Phone cards for cheap international calls are also available in newsagents, many shops and hotels throughout Paramaribo. These offer a far better deal than Telesur cards. These can be bought at **Telesur**, Heiligenweg 1, Paramaribo (near the fountain, downtown) and its branches, or in supermarkets nationwide, T474242, www.sr.net.

Nieuw Nickerie *p1451*
Banks There are 5 banks on the park, R P Bharosstraat with Landingstraat, and at the corner of Gouverneurstraat and Oost-Kanaalstraat. **Finabank** is in the Residence Inn Nickerie building. **Internet** At Surtel. Also Telesur Dienstencentrum, Oostkanaalstraat 3, T0-231391. **Post offices and telephones** Offices are on Oost- Kanaalstraat, between Gouverneurstraat and R P Bharosstraat. **Note** If phoning within town, omit 0 from prefix.

Guyane

Essentials

Planning your trip
Where to go Guyane is an Overseas Department of France, upon which it is heavily dependent. The capital, Cayenne, is on an island at the mouth of the river of the same name. Like its neighbours, Guyane has a populated coastal strip and much of the country remains sparsely populated and underdeveloped despite French aid. The department is known internationally for its space station at Kourou, home to the European Ariane space programme,

Touching down

Business hours Hours vary widely between different offices, shops and even between different branches of the same bank. There seem to be different business hours for every day of the week, but they are usually posted. Most shops and offices close for a few hours around midday.

International phone code +594. Ringing: equal tones with long pauses. Engaged: equal tones with equal pauses.
Official time GMT -3.
VAT 19.6%.
Voltage 220 volts. Plugs are the same as mainland Europe.
Weights and measures Metric.

where economic activity and investment is concentrated. The site has been used to launch over half the world's commercial satellites and over 20,000 foreigners are employed there. Tourism is slowly being developed and is increasing, as in all the Guianas, with adventure trips into the forests making up for the lack of good beaches. Almost all visitors are from France and Belgium. Over 10,000 tourists arrive annually, but their numbers are dwarfed by the 60,000 other visitors, businessmen and those who work in the space programme. An unusual attraction is the remains of the former penal colony, notably the Iles du Salut.

When to go The best months to visit are between August-November. The climate is tropical with heavy rainfall. Average temperature at sea level is fairly constant at 27°C. There is often a cool ocean breeze. Night and day temperatures vary more in the highlands. The rainy season is November-July, sometimes with a dry period in February and March. The great rains begin in May.

Finding out more The French Government tourist offices can usually provide leaflets on Guyane; also **Comité du Tourisme de la Guyane** ① *1 rue Clapeyron, 75008 Paris, T33-1-4294 1516, guyanaparis@wanadoo.fr*. In Guyane: **Comité du Tourisme de la Guyane** ① *12 rue Lallouette, BP 801, 97300 Cayenne, T05-94-296500, www.tourisme-guyane.com*. See also www.cr-guyane.fr. **Note** The Amerindian villages in the Haut-Maroni and Haut-Oyapock areas may only be visited with permission from the Préfecture in Cayenne *before* arrival in Guyane.

Visas and passports Passports are not required by nationals of France and most French-speaking African countries carrying identity cards. For EU visitors, documents are the same as for Metropolitan France (that is no visa, no exit ticket required – check with a consulate in advance). EU passports must be stamped; be sure to visit immigration if arriving from Suriname or Brazil, it is easy to miss. No visa required for most nationalities (except for those of Brazil, Guyana, Suriname, some Eastern European countries, and Asian – not Japan – and other African countries) for a stay of up to three months, but an exit ticket out of the country is essential (a ticket out of one of the other Guianas is not sufficient); a deposit is required otherwise. If you stay more than three months, income tax clearance is required before leaving the country. A visa costs €35, or equivalent (US$44).

Embassies and consulates A full list of France's overseas representation will be found at www.expatries.diplomatie.gouv.fr/annuaires/repdipet.asp

Money The currency is the euro. Take euros with you; many banks do not offer exchange facilities, but ATMs are common. Good rates can be obtained by using Visa or MasterCard (less common) to withdraw cash from any bank in Cayenne, Kourou and St-Laurent du Maroni. It is possible to pay for most hotels and restaurants with a Visa or MasterCard. American Express, Eurocard and Carte Bleue cards are also accepted.

Getting around

Air Internal air services are by **Air Guyane** (see Airline offices, Cayenne). These flights are always heavily booked, so be prepared to wait, or phone. There are daily connections to Maripasoula, at 0930 and 1430, Saül at 1200 and St-Georges at 0745 and 1430. Baggage allowance 10 kg. There are also helicopter companies with domestic services.

Driving in Guyane

Roads The main road, narrow, but now paved, runs for 130 km from Pointe Macouris, on the roadstead of Cayenne, to Iracoubo. Another 117 km takes it to Mana and St-Laurent. It also runs to Régina and St-Georges de l'Oyapock on the Brazilian border.

Documents There are no formalities for bringing a private car across the Guyane-Suriname border.

Car hire A convenient way to get around. There are 14 agencies in Cayenne; those at the airport open only for flight arrivals. **Avis**, **Budget** and **Hertz** have offices (see page 44 for websites). A local agency is **Jasmin**, T308490, www.jasminrent-a-car.gf. All types of car available, from economy to luxury to pick-ups and jeeps. Cheapest rates are about US$25 a day, km extra, US$290 per week including km, insurance extra. Check insurance details carefully; the excess is very high.

Motorcycle hire, also a good way to get around, at Ave Pasteur and Dr Gippet, from US$30-US$35 per day.

Fuel Gasoline/petrol costs about US$0.85 a litre; diesel US$0.55 a litre.

Road There are no railways, and about 1,000 km of road. It is now possible to travel overland to Cayenne from Suriname and onwards to Macapá in Brazil. The latter takes about 24 hours from Cayenne with half a day's waiting in St-Georges de l'Oyapock for the Brazilian bus to leave. The roads are much improved. Combis (minivans) ply the coastal roads between St-Laurent, Cayenne and St-Georges de l'Oyapock. Transport is expensive, around US$2 per 10 km. **Hitchhiking** is reported to be easy and widespread.

Boat 1-3 ton boats which can be hauled over the rapids are used by the gold-seekers, the forest workers, and the rosewood establishments. Ferries are free. Trips by motor-canoe (*pirogue*) up-river from Cayenne into the jungle can be arranged.

Sleeping → *See page 58 for our hotel grade price guide.*
There are no hotels under our **A** bracket and almost no restaurants under the ⫙⫙⫙ bracket. Accommodation in Guyane is more expensive than Paris, but food is better value. The Comité du Tourisme de la Guyane (see Finding out more above) has addresses of furnished apartments for rent (*Locations Clévacances*) and *Gîtes*, which are categorized as *Gîtes d'Amazonie*, with accommodation in hammocks or *carbets* (imitation Amerindian huts), *Carbets d'Hôtes*, which include breakfast, and *Gîtes Panda Tropiques Label*, which are approved by the WWF. **Ecotourisme Guyane Expedition** (EGE - see page 1465) can reserve hotels and private flats throughout the country for a small fee. Full details on their website, www.ecotourisme.fr, or contact the owner, Marc (through the site). He speaks English.

Festivals and events
Public holidays These are the same as in Metropolitan France, with the addition of **Slavery Day**, 10 June. **Carnaval** (February or March). Guyane's Carnaval is joyous and interesting. It is principally a Créole event, but there is some participation by all the different cultural groups in the department (best known are the contributions of the Brazilian and Haitian communities). Celebrations begin in January, with festivities every weekend, and culminate in colourful parades, music, and dance during the four days preceding Ash Wednesday. Each day has its own motif and the costumes are very elaborate. On Saturday night, a dance called 'Chez Nana – Au Soleil Levant' is held, for which the women disguise themselves beyond recognition as 'Touloulous', and ask the men to dance. They are not allowed to refuse. On Sunday there are parades in downtown Cayenne. Lundi Gras (Fat Monday) is the day to ridicule the institution of marriage, with mock wedding parties featuring men dressed as brides and women as grooms. 'Vaval', the devil and soul of Carnaval, appears on Mardi Gras (Fat Tuesday) with dancers sporting red costumes, horns, tails, pitch-forks, etc. He is burnt that night (in the form of a straw doll) on a large bonfire in the Place des Palmistes. Ash Wednesday is a time of sorrow, with participants in the final parades dressed in black and white.

Cayenne → *Population: 52,000-60,000 (est). Colour map 2, grid B6.*

The capital and the chief port of Guyane is on the island of Cayenne at the mouth of the Cayenne River. Founded by French traders in 16th-century, but taking its name from an Amerindian prince, Cayenne remained relatively isolated until after the Second World War when Guyane became part of metropolitan France and Rochambeau airport was constructed.

Ins and outs
Getting there Cayenne is 645 km from Georgetown (Guyana) and 420 km from Paramaribo (Suriname) by sea. ▶▶ *For detailed travel information see Transport, page 1465.*

Tourist offices Comité du Tourisme de la Guyane ① *12 rue Lallouette, BP 801, 97300 Cayenne, T296500, www.tourisme-guyane.com, 0800-1200, 1500-1800*, is helpful and has lots of brochures, but very little in English. There is also a **Cayenne municipal tourist office**, Place de Palmistes, next to the cinema. French only spoken. Useful city maps.

Sights
There is an interesting museum, the **Musée Départemental Franconie** ① *1 rue de Rémire, near the Place de Palmistes, T295913, Mon and Wed 0800-1300, Tue and Fri 1500-1800, Thu 1030-1330, Sat 0830-1200, US$2.25.* Its exhibits include pickled snakes and the trunk of the 'late beloved twin-trunked palm' of the Place de Palmistes. There is a good entomological collection and excellent paintings of convict life. Next door is the municipal library. **L'Orstom** (scientific research institute) ① *Route de Montabo, Mon and Fri 0700-1330, 1500-1800, Tue-Thu 0700-1300*, with a research library and permanent exhibits on Guyane's ecosystems and archaeological finds. Also worth a visit is **La Crique**, the colourful but dangerous area around the Canal Laussat (built by Malouet in 1777); the Jesuit-built residence (circa 1890) of the Prefect (**L'Hôtel-de-Ville**) in the Place de Grenoble; the **Place des Amandiers** (also known as the **Place Auguste-Horth**) by the sea; the Place des Palmistes, with assorted palms; a pool and

Cayenne

Sleeping 🛏
Best Western
 Amazonia **2**
Central **1**
Des Amandiers **3**
Ket Tai **4**

Eating 🍴
Bar des Palmistes **1**
Café de la Gare **2**
Crep'In **3**
Gloria Rotishop **4**
La Sarrasine **5**

Le Café Crème **6**
Le Paris-Dakar **7**
Le Patriarche **8**
Le Sandoucherie **9**
Paris Cayenne **10**
Porta Verde **11**

Bars & clubs 🍸
Harry's **12**

five cinemas. The **market** on Monday, Wednesday, Friday and Saturday mornings has a great Caribbean flavour, but is expensive. There are bathing beaches (water rather muddy) around the island, the best is Montjoly, but watch out for sharks. Minibuses run from the terminal to Rémire-Montjoly for beaches. They leave when full; check when the last one returns. There is a walking trail called **Rorota** which follows the coastline and can be reached from Montjoly or the Gosselin beaches. Another trail, **Habitation Vidal** in Rémire, passes through former sugar cane plantations and ends at the remains of 19th-century sugar mills.

Some 43 km southwest of Cayenne is **Montsinéry**, with a zoo featuring Amazonian flora and fauna (open daily 1000-1900), an orchid and a walking trail, Bagne des Annamites, through remains of a camp where prisoners from Indochina were interned in the 1930s.

Outside Cayenne

The European space centre at Kourou is one of the main attractions, especially when a rocket is being launched. In stark contrast are the abandoned penal settlements. Beyond is largely unexplored jungle. Also in this section are the routes to Suriname and Brazil.

West to Suriname

Kourou (*Population 20,000, 56 km west of Cayenne*) This is where the main French space centre (Centre Spatial Guyanais), used for the European Space Agency's Ariane programme, is located. It is referred to by the Guyanais as 'white city' because of the number of French families living there. Tourist attractions include bathing, fishing, sporting and aero club, and a variety of organized excursions. The tourist office is Syndicat d'Initiative de Kourou, T324884.

The **space centre** occupies an area of about 4 km deep along some 30 km of coast, bisected by the Kourou River. **Public guided tours** are given Monday to Thursday at 0745 and 1300 (Friday 0745 only). Tours are free and last 3½ hours; under eights are not admitted. Advance reservations must be made several days beforehand, T326123, F321745, Monday to Friday 0800-1200. No tours during a launch or on the days before or after. The **Musée de l'Espace** ① *T335384, Mon-Fri 0800-1800, Sat 1400-1800, US$7.15, no public transport, take a taxi or hitch*, can be visited without reservation. To watch a launch you must write to CNES at Centre Spatial Guyanais, Relations Publiques, BP 726, 97387 Kourou Cedex, T334200, F334719, saying you want to attend; phone or fax to find out when launches take place, or www.cnes.fr. Supply full names and ID; ask for your invitation from Centre d'acceuil du CSG, or Syndicat d'Initiative de Cayenne, 7 Avenue G Monnerville, 97300 Cayenne, T324884. Invitations must be collected two to three days before the launch; if you hear nothing, it's probably full, but you can try wait-listing (arrive early). There are five viewing sites: Toucan (for VIPs, but wait-listing, or enquiries, possible), Kikiwi, Colibri (both good), Agami (OK) and Ibis (not recommended). Alternatively, you can watch the launch for free, from 10 km, at Montagne Carapa at Pariacabo. Also see www.esa.int/education and www.arianespace.com.

Iles du Salut The Iles du Salut (many visitors at weekends), opposite Kourou, include the Ile Royale, the Ile Saint-Joseph, and the Ile du Diable. They were the scene of the notorious convict settlement built in 1852; the last prisoners left in 1953. One of their most famous residents was Henri Charrière, who made a miraculous escape to Venezuela. He later recounted the horrors of the penal colony and his hair-raising escape attempts in his book *Papillon*. There is a museum in the Commander's House on Ile Royale; brochures for sale. The Ile du Diable (Devil's Island), a rocky islet almost inaccessible from the sea, was where political prisoners, including Alfred Dreyfus and Henri Charrière, were held (access to this island is strictly forbidden). You can see monkeys, agoutis, turtles, hummingbirds and macaws, and there are many coconut palms. Take a torch for visiting the ruins. Paintings of prison life are on show in the tiny church. Visit the children's graveyard, hospital, mental asylum and death cells. These, and the church, are not always open. Conservation work is underway. Three guided tours in French are given weekly.

Sinnamary and St-Laurent du Maroni Between Kourou and Iracoubo, on the road west to St-Laurent, is **Sinnamary** (116 km from Cayenne), a pleasant town where Galibi Indians at a mission make artificial flowers, for sale to tourists. Carvings and jewellery are on sale here. There are three- to five-day excursions up the Sinnamary River. Scarlet ibis can be seen in numbers on the Sinnamary estuary at Iracoubo. (Tours at 1500, T345310, Amoida Georges, US$16.50.)

St-Laurent du Maroni (Population 25,000), formerly a penal transportation camp, is now a quiet colonial town 250 km from Cayenne on the river Maroni, bordering Suriname. It can be visited as a day tour from Cayenne if you hire a car, but note that everything closes for a long siesta. The old Camp de Transportation (the original penal centre) can be wandered round at will, but a guide is needed to enter the cells (an absolute must if visiting the country). **Guided tours** of Les Bagnes (prison camps) Monday-Saturday 0800, 0930, 1100, 1500, 1630, Sunday and holidays 0930-1100, chilling, buy tickets from tourist office here, US$4.65. Tourist office: **Office du Tourisme** ⓘ *1 esplanade Laurent Baudin, 97393 St-Laurent du Maroni, T342398, www.97320.com. Mon-Fri 0730-1800, Sat 0800-1300, 1500-1800, Sun 0900-1300.*

Border with Suriname Make sure you obtain proper entry stamps from immigration, not the police, to avoid problems when leaving. Customs and immigration, 2 km south of the centre, close at 1900. There are aggressive touts on the St-Laurent and Albina piers. It is best to change money in the Village Chinois in St-Laurent (dangerous area); although rates are lower than in Paramaribo, it is illegal to change money in Albina. Beware theft at St-Laurent's black market.

Around St-Laurent About 3 km from St-Laurent, along the Paul Isnard road, is Saint-Maurice, where the rum distillery of the same name can be visited, Monday to Friday 0730-1130. At Km 70 on the same dirt road is access to **Voltaire Falls**, 1½ hours walk from the road 7 km south of St-Laurent on the road to St-Jean du Maroni is the Amerindian village of **Terre Rouge**; canoes can be hired for day trips up the Maroni River (see Maripasoula below).

Some 40 km north of St-Laurent du Maroni is **Mana**, a delightful town with rustic architecture near the coast. 20 km west of Mana following the river along a single track access road is **Les Hattes**, or Yalimapo, an Amerindian village. About 4 km further on is Les Hattes beach where leatherback turtles lay their eggs at night; season April to August with May/June peak. No public transport to Les Hattes and its beach, but hitching possible at weekends; take food and water and mosquito repellent. Despite the dryish climate Mana is a malaria region. The freshwater of the Maroni and Mana rivers makes sea bathing pleasant. It is very quiet during the week.

Aouara, or Awala, an Amerindian village with hammock places, is 16 km west of Les Hattes. It also has a beach where leatherback turtles lay their eggs; they take about three hours over it. Take mosquito nets, hammock and insect repellent.

There are daily flights from Cayenne to **Maripasoula**; details in Air transport, page 1457, local office T372141. It is up the Maroni from St-Laurent (2-4 day journey up river in *pirogue*). There may be freight canoes which take passengers (US$40) or private boats (US$150) which leave from St-Laurent; 5-6 day tours and other options with *Takari Tour* or other operators in Cayenne.

South to Brazil

About 28 km southeast of Cayenne is the small town of **Roura**, which has an interesting church. An excursion may be made to the Fourgassier Falls several kilometres away (*L'Auberge des Cascades*, excellent restaurant). From Cayenne the road crosses a new bridge over the Comte River. Excursions can be arranged along the Comte River. Nearby is Dacca, a Laotian village, which has *La Crique Gabrielle*, T/F280104, a restaurant which also has rooms. For information about the area contact the **Syndicat D'Initiative de Roura**, T311104.

From Roura a paved road, RD06, runs southeast towards the village of **Kaw**, on an island amid swamps which are home to much rare wildlife including caimans. The village is reached from where the Roura road ends at the river at Approuague. Basic accommodation available; **Jacana Tour**, T380795, excursions by day or night on the river; take insect repellent.

At Km 53 on another road southeast to Régina is the turn-off to **Cacao** (a further 13 km), a small, quiet village, where Hmong refugees from Laos are settled; they are farmers and produce fine traditional handicrafts. The Sunday morning market has local produce, Laotian food and embroidery. Canoe/kayak rental behind *Degrad Cacao* restaurant, US$2.50 per hour, good wildlife trips upriver. Halfway along the side road is *Belle Vue* restaurant, open weekends, with superb view over the tropical forest. Ask the Comité du Tourisme de la Guyane for *gîtes* in the area.

Southwest of Kaw on the river Approuague is **Régina**, linked with Cayenne by a paved road. A good trip is on the river to Athanase with G Frétique, T304551. An unpaved road, runs from Régina to St-Georges de l'Oyapock (difficult during the rainy season).

Saül This remote gold-mining settlement in the 'massif central' is the geographical centre of Guyane. The main attractions are for the nature-loving tourist. Beautiful undisturbed tropical forests are accessible by a very well-maintained system of 90 km of marked trails, including several circular routes. There is running water, a radio telephone, and electricity. Ten-day expeditions are run by Christian Ball, '*Vie Sauvage*', 97314 Saül, US$86 (30% in advance) per day with meals, maps provided, own hammock and bedding useful but not essential. It can be cold at night. Another fascinating overland route goes from Roura (see below) up the Comte River to Belizon, followed by a 14-16-day trek through the jungle to Saül, visiting many villages en route, guide recommended. Meals from *Restaurant Pinot*. Two markets sell food.

Border with Brazil St-Georges de l'Oyapock, with its small detachment of the French Foreign Legion who parade on Bastille Day, is 15 minutes down river from Oiapoque in Brazil, US$4 per person by motorized canoe, bargain for a return fare. The tourist office is in the library to the left of the town hall. There are bars, restaurants, supermarkets with French specialities, a post office and public telephones which take phonecards. Thierry Beltran, Rue Henri Sulny, T370259, offers guided river and forest tours. A pleasant day trip is to the **Saut Maripa** rapids (not very impressive with high water), located about 30 minutes upstream along the Oiapock River, past the Brazilian towns of Oiapoque and Clevelândia do Norte. Hire a motorized *pirogue* (canoe) to take you to a landing downstream from the rapids. Then walk along the trolley track (used to move heavy goods around the rapids) for 20 minutes to the rundown huts by the rapids (popular and noisy at weekends). There are more rapids further upstream on the way to Camopi.

Immigration (*gendarmerie*) for entry/exit stamps at eastern end of town, follow signs, open daily 0700-1200, 1500-1800 (often not open after early morning on Sunday, in which case try the police at the airport); French, Portuguese and English spoken. One of the Livre Service supermarkets and *Hotel Chez Modestine* will sometimes change dollars cash into euros at poor rates; if entering the country here, change money before arriving in St-Georges. Brazilian currency is accepted in shops at poor rates.

● Sleeping

Cayenne *p1459, map p1459*
Most hotels are in the centre. A few of the better ones are in the suburb of Monjoly, next to a coarse sand beach and muddy sea, but the best district in Cayenne nonetheless. Hotels rarely add tax and service to their bill, but stick to prices posted outside or at the desk. B&B accommodation (gîte) is available for about US$60 a night (breakfast included) – contact the tourist office for details.
L-AL Novotel, Route de Montabo, Chemin St. Hilaire, T303838, www.accor-hotels.com. Beach-side hotel 3 km from the centre set in a tropical garden, pool, 2 tennis courts and a respectable French and Creole restaurant. Car hire available.
AL-A Best Western Amazonia, 28 Av Gen de Gaulle, T288300, www.bestwestern.com. A/c, luggage stored, pool, central location, good buffet breakfast extra.
A-B Hotel des Amandiers, Place Auguste-Horth, T289728. Pleasant, tranquil and breezy location next to a park on a little peninsula at the north end of town, a/c rooms.
B Central Hotel, corner rue Molé and rue Becker, T256565, www.centralhotel-cayenne.fr. Good location, 100m from the Place de Palmistes, a/c rooms and a terrace overlooking the street. Special prices for groups and business travellers. Book in advance through the net.
C Ket-Tai, Av de la Liberté corner Blvd Jubelin, T388777. The best cheapie in town at the very bottom end of this price range, simple a/c rooms

with en suites, look at a few before deciding. Chinese restaurant.

Around Rémire-Montjoly
A Motel du Lac, Chemin Poupon, Route de Montjoly, T380800, moteldulac@opensurf.net. In a protected area, very peaceful, garden, convenient for the airport, pool, bar, restaurant.

Near Matoury and the airport
B La Chaumiere, Chemin de la Chaumière (off the road to Kourou), 97351 Matoury, T255701, lachaumiere@wanadoo.fr. Set in gardens, thatched huts, restaurant, pool, at bottom end of this price band, good value, but cabs to town push up cost.

Apartment rentals
A good option, but what is on offer changes frequently. It's best to reserve through the tourist office who publish a brochure, *Locations de Vacances*, with full details including pictures. Contact them in advance through the website. Write in French if possible.

Kourou *p1460*
Hotels are overbooked and raise prices when there's an Ariane rocket launch (1 a month).
L Ariatel Kourou, Av de St-Exupéry, Lac Bois Diable, T328900, www.accor-hotels.com. Overlooking a lake, 9 hole golf course nearby, good restaurant and pool with snack bar.

AL **Mercure Inn**, near Lac Bois Diable, T321300, www.accor-hotels.com. A/c, modern, pool, good restaurant, best value for business visitors.

A **Hôtel des Roches**, Pointe des Roches, T320066, F320328. Fair, a/c, includes breakfast, pool with bar, beach, Le Paradisier restaurant, cybercafé.

A-B **Les Jardins D'Hermes**, 56 rue Duchesne, T320183. In heart of old Kourou, a/c, modern, good, restaurant.

B **Ballahou**, 2-3 rue Amet Martial, T220022, ballahou@ariasnet.fr. Small hotel with 14 rooms, some with cooking facilities, a/c, TV, nice, modern, good restaurant. Book ahead.

Camping
At Km 17.5 south of Kourou on the Saramaca road is **Les Maripas**, tourist camp, T325548, F323660. River and overland excursions, E for tent, book at Guyane Excursion, 7 quartier Simarouba, near *Restaurant Saramaca*.

Iles du Salut *p1460*
B **Auberge Iles du Salut**, on Ile Royale (postal address BP 324, 97378 Kourou, T321100, F324223). A 60-bed hotel (A full board), also hammock space US$20 per person; former guard's bungalow, main meals (excellent), minimum US$36, breakfast US$6; gift shop with high prices (especially when a cruise ship is in), good English guide book for sale.

Sinnamary *p1460*
A **Hôtel du Fleuve**, 11 rue Léon Mine, T345400, www.hoteldufleuve.com. Gardens, restaurant, internet access, pool, one of the grandest hotels west of Cayenne.

B **Chez Floria**, 14 rue Ronda Silva, Iracoubo, T346385, F326378. Very simple guest house with plain a/c rooms with en suites about 40 km from Sinnamary.

St-Laurent du Maroni *p1461*
A **Le Relais des 3 Lacs**, 19-23 Domaine du Lac Bleu, T340505, 23lacs@nplus.gf. A/c, cheaper with fan, shuttle to town centre, restaurant, gardens, pool.

B **La Tentiaire**, 12 Av Franklin Roosevelt, T342600, rioual.robert@wanadoo.fr. A/c, the best, breakfast extra, phone, pool, secure parking.

C **Chez Julienne**, rue Gaston Monnerville, 200 m past Texaco station, T341153. A/c, TV, a/c, shower, good value.

C **As**, 109 rue Thiers, T341084. A/c, pool, cheaper rooms poor value, run down, cheap restaurant.

Voltaire Falls *p1461*
B pp **Auberge des Chutes Voltaires**, T00-874-762-945-774 satellite 1300-1600, 1900-2200. Also hammock space US$11, meals extra.

Mana *p1461*
Nuns next to the church rent beds and hammocks, US$8, clean and simple, T348270, F348415, Communauté des Soeurs de St-Joseph de Cluny, 1 rue Bourguignon.

D **Le Bougainvillier**, 3 rue des Frères, T348062, F348295, a/c, D with shared bath.

Gîte Angoulême, Mme Maryse Buira, PK 206/207 RN1 Saut Sabbat, T346496, F348688. Beside the river Mana, hammock space US$7.15, gîte L for weekend, breakfast US$5.

Les Hattes *p1461*
Three *gîtes*, all D: Chez Jeanne, T342982, F342071; Chez Judith et Denis, T342438; Pointe les Hattes, chez Joseph, T343806.

Maripasoula *p1461*
A **Campement Touristique de Saut Sonnelle**, 48 rue Madame Payé, T314945. Full board.

D **Chez Dedè**, Av Leonard, T/F372074, US$4.50 for breakfast.

Roura *p1461*
D **Auberge du Camp Caïman**, RD06 29 km from Roura, T376034. Tourist camp (G to hang hammock), tours arranged to watch caiman in the swamps.

D **Hotel Relais de Patawa**, RD06 Km 36 from Cayenne, T280395. Rooms, or sling your hammock for US$4, cheaper rates for longer stays, highly recommended. The owners, M and Mme Baloup, who are entomologists, will show you their collection, take you on guided tours of local sights and introduce you to their pet anaconda.

Cacao *p1461*
D **Restaurant La Lan**, 1 room, good value, good food.

F **M Levessier**, T305122, has hammocks.

Régina *p1461*
F **Albergue de l'Approuague**, Lieu-dit Corossony, 97390 Régina. Price is for hammock space, meals expensive, great views of the forest.

Saül *p1461*
F pp **Larozaly**, a tourist camp in Saül, has running water, solar electricity, cooking facilities, and is a good place to stay.

Accommodation in Saul can be arranged through **Ecotourisme Guyane Expedition**, see Activities and tours, below.

St-Georges de l'Oyapock *p1462*
Accommodation is far cheaper on the Brazilian side.

C **Caz Cale**, rue E Elfort, 1 street back from the riverfront, just east of the main square, T/F370054. A/c, cheaper with fan.

C Chez Modestine, on the main square, T370013, F370214. A/c or fan, restaurant.
D Le Tamarin, rue Joseph Léandre, on the riverfront near the main square, T370884. With bath, fan, bar and restaurant.

⑦ Eating

Cayenne *p1459, map p1459*
There are, sadly, very few decent French *patisseries* and *boulangeries*. Many restaurants close on Sun. There are many small Chinese restaurants serving the same fare: noodles, rice, soups etc.
▼▼▼ Bar des Palmistes, Place des Palmistes. Good spot for people watching, opposite the Place des Palmistes. Simple French and Creole fare and cold, draft Abbaye beer.
▼▼▼ Cric-Crac at *Motel Beauregard*, Créole cooking, lovely atmosphere.
▼▼▼ La Baie des Iles, Km 10 Route des Plages, Rémire-Montjoly, T386020. On the beach, good value seafood, 1000-midnight, closed Mon evening and Tue.
▼▼▼ La Sarrasine, rue Lt Goinet 55, T317238. Good fish, salads, crêpes and quiches in an intimate little dining room. Good wine list and attentive service. At the bottom end of the price range.
▼▼▼ Le Kaz Kreol, 35 Av D'Estrées, T390697. Creole cooking served by waitresses in costume, delights include stuffed cassava, agouti stew and sauerkraut of papaya.
▼▼▼ Le Paris-Dakar, 103 rue Lt. Becker, T305517. Closed Sun, Mon lunch. African cooking from Senegal, Zaire, Benin and the Ivory Coast, like tropical fish slices on pureed aubergine, excellent vegetarian platter.
▼▼▼ Le Patriarche, rues Voltaire at Samuel Lubin, T317644. Excellent classical French and Creole cooking, one of the best in Guyane and very good value for this country. Reserve in advance.
▼▼▼-▼▼ Marveen Snack Bar, rue Christophe Colomb, near Canal de L'Est. Food and staff pleasant, the patrons are very helpful (the elder of the 2 is a pilot for the Guyane Flying Club).
▼▼▼ Paris-Cayenne, 59 rue de Lallouette, T317617. French cooking with tropical twist, nice decor.
▼▼▼ Porta Verde, 58 rue Lt Goinet, T291903. Brazilian buffet, US$12 per kg, lunchtime only. Recommended.
▼▼▼-▼▼ Crep'In, 5 rue Lt Becker, T 302806. Street stall and little café with sweet and savoury crêpes, breakfast specials, and a range of fresh fruit juices and sandwiches.
▼▼▼-▼▼ Le Café Crème, 42 rue Justin Catayée, T281256. Pastries, superior sandwiches, juices, breakfasts and excellent coffee.
▼▼▼-▼▼ Café de la Gare, 42 rue Léopold Hélder, T350799. Great little restaurant with club playing classy live music every Thu and weekend. Good

atmosphere, 20-40 something crowd.
▼▼▼ Gloria Rotishop, 14 rue Dr Barrat, T251643. Surinamese style rotis with excellent fillings and West Indian and Indian breads. English speaking.
▼▼▼ Le Sandouicherie, rue Félix Eboué at Lt Goinet, T289170. French bread sandwiches, snacks, juices and breakfasts, a/c.

Snacks
Vans around Place des Palmistes in evenings sell cheap, filling sandwiches. Along the Canal Laussant there are Javanese snack bars: try *bami* (spicy noodles) or *saté* (barbecued meat in a spicy peanut sauce). Also along the canal are small, cheap Créole restaurants, not very clean.

Kourou *p1460*
▼▼▼ Ballahou (see Sleeping). Best for fish and seafood (try *Guyabaisse*).
▼▼▼ Le Bistrot du Lac, Hotel Mercure Ariatel, T328900. Named chef, Dominique Pirou, has one of the best tables in Guyane, serving French Creole dishes like Grouper in wild mushroom sauce and Tiger prawns in citrus. The hotel's Le Ti-Gourmet (**▼▼▼-▼▼**) serves up-market snacks.
▼▼▼-▼▼ Le P'tit Café, 11 Place Monnerville, T228168. A good value set lunch and a respectable à la carte menu.
▼▼ Le Karting, Zone Portuaire de Pariacabo (at the entrance to Kourou), T320539 (closed Sat- Sun). Excellent lunch set meal with a big choice of starters and mains. Evening BBQ Tue and Fri.
▼ Many cheap Chinese (also takeaway), eg: **Le Chinatown**, rue Duchesne. Recommended. Many vans sell sandwiches filled with Créole food, good.
L'Hydromel, rue Raymond Cresson. Good pancakes. **Le Glacier des 2 Lacs**, 68 Ave des 2 Lacs. Ice cream, cakes, teas, very good.

St-Laurent du Maroni *p1461*
▼▼▼ La Goelette, Balaté Plage, 2.5 km from St-Laurent, T342897. Housed in a converted fishing boat on the river and serving fish and game. Nice atmosphere in the evenings. Closed Sun evening and Mon.
▼▼ Le Mambari, 7 rue Rousseau, T343590. Pizzas and light French food served in a large, upmarket *palapa*. Open until late.
▼ Many cheap Chinese restaurants.

⑥ Bars and clubs

Cayenne *p1459, map p1459*
Acropolys, Route de Cabassou, 3 km from town, T319781. Club music, Wed-Sat, 300-sq-m dance floor.
Harry's Bar, 20 rue Rouget de l'Isle, T292958.

Jazz, blues, Latin music and large selection of whiskies, also has English and Irish beer.

Kourou *p1460*
Clibertown, rue Guynemer, T323665; at the entrance to Kourou overlooking the lake. The most popular in town by far.

○ Shopping

Cayenne *p1459, map p1459*
Bookshops **Librairie AJC**, 31 Blvd Jubelin, has an excellent stock of books and maps on Guyane (in French). There is a branch in *Drugstore des Palmistes*, Place des Palmistes.

▲ Activities and tours

Cayenne *p1459, map p1459*
Look under Tours Opérateurs on www.tourisme-guyane.com for listings of French and local tour operators. Tours to the interior cost about US$80-100 pp per day. Pick-ups from the airport and accommodation in Cayenne for a night or two are usually part of the package. Full details on the company websites, some of it in English.
Ecotourisme Guyane Expedition (EGE), at **Takari Tour**, see below, www.ecotourisme.fr. Organize tours out of Cayenne, Kourou or St-Laurent du Maroni and book hotels throughout the country.
JAL Voyages, 26 Av Gen de Gaulle, T316820, www.jal-voyages.com. For a wide range of tours on the Mahury, Mana, Approuague rivers, on a houseboat on the Kaw marshes (US$85, very good accommodation, food and birdwatching) and to Devil's Island, a little English spoken. Recommended.
Takari Tour, 8 rue du Capitaine Bernard, BP 051397332, T311960, www.espace-amazonie. com. Recommended for inland tours, twinned with **Espace-Amazonie** in Kourou.
Thomas Cook, 2 Place du Marché, T255636. Flights, changes Thomas Cook traveller's cheques, English spoken.

Kourou *p1460*
Espace Amazonie, 7 Centre Commercial Simarouba, T323430, www.espace-amazonie.com.
Guyanespace Voyages, A Hector Berlioz, T223101, www.guyanespace.com.

St-Laurent du Maroni *p1461*
Ouest Guyane, 10 rue Féliz Eboué, T344444, ouestguyane@wanadoo.fr.
Youkaliba (Maroni) Expeditions, 3 rue Simon, T341645/312398. For canoe trips up the Maroni River. For example 1-night trip to Apatou, US$140; to Saut Anana on Mana River, 10 days, US$655.

⊖ Transport

Cayenne *p1459, map p1459*
Air Cayenne-Rochambeau Airport (T353882/89) is 16 km from Cayenne, 20 mins by taxi, and 67 km from Kourou (US$60-80). Cambio changes US$ and Brazilian reais, Cirrus and Visa Plus ATMs for withdrawing Euros. Only taxis (US$25 day, US$30 night, but you can bargain or share). The cheapest route to town is taxi to Matoury US$10, then bus to centre US$2. The cheapest method of return to airport is by collective taxi from corner of Av de la Liberté and rue Malouet to Matoury (10 km) for US$2.40, then hitch or walk.
Bus Terminal at corner of rue Molé and Av de la Liberté. Regular urban services run by **SMTC**, Place du Marché, T302100, Mon-Fri 0800-1200, 1500-1700. The only westbound bus is run by **Ruffinel & Cie**, 8 Av Galmot, T312666, as far as Kourou (US$12) leaves 0530 (not Sun). Minibuses to St-Laurent du Maroni leave when full from the terminal (can take up to 4 hrs waiting), 0400-1200, 2½ hrs, US$42-48. Service to **Mana** Mon and Thu only. To **Kaw**, Wed. To **Régina** US$25, and to **St-Georges del'Oyapock** US$45, 3 hrs, 4 daily. Arrive at the bus stop at 0700 to be sure of a seat. Be careful walking in this area – many drug addicts; take a cab to the bus stop.
Shared taxis (collectifs) Leave from the *gare routière* by the Canal Laussat early in the morning (Kourou US$12, St Laurent US$30-38). Other taxis can be found at the stand on Place des Palmistes, at the corner of Av Gen de Gaulle and Molé.

Kourou *p1460*
Taxi US$10, Lopez T320560, Gilles TT320307, Kourou T321444.
Bus To **Cayenne**, leaves Shell service station, corner Av de France, Av Vermont Polycarpe.
Share taxis To Cayenne 0600, 0630, 0700, 1330, US$12. Taxi to Cayenne or airport US$60 (US$85 at night). To St-Laurent du Maroni US$27 by *taxi collectif* (irregular) or by minibus from Shell station.

Iles du Salut *p1460*
Boat Ferry from Kourou's port at the end of Av Gen de Gaulle, 4 km from the old centre US$53 return (under 12s half price), leaves 0800 daily, returns at 1700 (book in advance, T320995), additional sailing Sat and high season, 1½-2 hr each way. Book in advance in Jul and Aug. Tickets may be obtained from **EGE, JAL, Takari**, see Activities and tours; **Air Guyane Voyages**, 2 rue Lalouette, T317200; in Kourou from au Carbet des Roches, cash only. Getting back to Cayenne late in the afternoon after the boat docks may be a problem if you lack your own transport: ask other tourists for a lift. There are no regular boats from Ile Royale to Ile Saint-Joseph, which is wilder and more beautiful,

with a small beach. You may be able to hire a
private boat at the ferry dock, or ask for James on
the Kourou-Ile Royale ferry. There are no sailings
between Ile Royale and Ile du Diable.

St-Laurent du Maroni p1461
Minibuses To Cayenne meet the ferry from
Suriname, leaving when full from rue du Port, 3 hrs
(not until 1830/1900), US$42-48. Ask the minibus at
rue du Port to pick up your luggage from your hotel.
Shared taxis To and from Cayenne, 8 people,
US$42-48 a head, 3½ hr trip. Bus to Cayenne at
0600, same price.
Freight pirogues Sometimes take passengers
inland along the Maroni River, but they can be
dangerous as they tend to be overladen, often
with dubious captains. Better to fly to Maripasoula
and return on a pirogue as they are empty going
down river. Alternatively, groups can hire a
pirogue for about US$200 a day.

Border with Suriname p1461
Boat Ferry for vehicles and passengers to Albina
Mon, Thu, 0700, 0900, 1400, 1600, Tue, Wed, Sat
0700, 0900, Sun, 1530, 1600, 30 mins. Passengers
US$4.40/€3.50 one-way, car US$25-30 one-way,
payable only in euros. Speedboats US$3.50-US$4.75.
Minibuses and **taxis** Transport to/from
Paramaribo meets the Albina ferry.

Cacao p1461
Minibus From **Cayenne**, Mon 1200;
Fri 1800, return Mon 0730, Fri 1400.

Saül p1461
Air Service with **Air Guyane** from Cayenne or via
Maripasoula (see above; local office T309111). Try
at airport even if flight said to be full. By *pirogue*
from Mana up Mana River, 9-12 days, then 1 day's
walk to Saül, or from St-Laurent via Maripasoula
along Moroni and Inini rivers, 15 days and 1 day's
walk to Saül, both routes expensive.

St-Georges de l'Oyapock p1462
Air Aside from minibus, flying is the only option.
For **Air Guyane** flights to Cayenne see Air
transport in Essentials. **Air Guyane** office at airport
open 0700-0730, 1400-1430 for check in, open
0800-1100 for reservations, T/F370360. Flights are
fully booked several days in advance; you must
check in at stated times. Extra flights are sometimes
added. The police check that those boarding
flights who have arrived from Brazil have obtained
their entry stamp; also thorough baggage search.
Minibuses To **Cayenne**, US$45, 3 hrs; US$20 on
unpaved road to Régina, then US$25 to Cayenne.

Onward buses to **Macapá** leave late afternoon,
10 hrs: book as soon as you arrive in Oiapoque
(Brazilian side). The road is generally good.

1466

ⓘ Directory

Cayenne p1459, map p1459
Airline offices Air Caraïbes, T293636, flies to
Pointe-à-Pitre, Fort-de-France, Port-au-Prince,
Macapá and Belém in Brazil and Dominican
Republic. **Air France**, 17-19 rue Lalouette, BP 33,
Cayenne, F298790. **Air Guyane**, 2 tte, 97300
Cayenne, T293630, F293631. **Surinam Airways**, 15
rue Louis Blanc, T293001, F305786. **TAF**, T303910,
French and Portuguese spoken, flights Cayenne-
Macapá-Belém-Fortaleza twice a week). Book at
least a week in advance through agents like EGE,
see page 1465). **Banks** Most banks have ATMs
for cash withdrawals on Visa, sometimes
MasterCard, never Amex. The Post Office
exchanges cash and TCs at good rates, but
complicated and time-consuming. Exchange
facility at the airport (see Airport information,
above). Central pharmacy may help when banks
are closed. Almost impossible to change dollars
outside Cayenne or Kourou. **Banque Nationale de
Paris-Guyane (BNPG)**, 2 Place Schoelcher; no
exchange facilities on Sat. **Banque Française
Commerciale (BFC)**, 2 Place des Palmistes (best
bank exchange rates). **Crédit Populaire Guyanais**,
93 rue Lalouette. **Banque Populaire**, 5 Av Gen de
Gaulle, Cirrus/ MasterCard ATM. **Crédit Mutuel**, 13
rue Léon Damas, Visa/Plus and Cirrus/ MasterCard
ATM. **Cambio Caraïbe**, Av Gen de Gaulle near
Catayée (best rates for US$). **Guyane Change**, Av
Gen de Gaulle near rue F Eboué. **Embassies and
consulates** British (Honorary), Mr Nouh-Chaia,
16 Ave Monnerville (BP 664, Cayenne 97300),
T311034, F304094. **Brazilian**, 444 chemin St
Antoine, T296010. **Dutch** (Honorary), Batiment
Sogudem, Port de Dégrad des Cannes, BP139,
Cayenne 97323, T354931, F354671. **Haitian**, 12 rue
L Héder, at corner of Place des Palmistes, T311858,
F312065, closed Sat. **Suriname**, 3 Ave L Héder,
T282160, F317645, Mon-Fri 0900-1200. English
spoken, visa takes 2 hrs, proof of travel out of
Venezuela or Guyana acceptable. For USA and
Canada, apply to embassies in Paramaribo.
Internet Cybercafé des Palmistes, 1 Av Gen de
Gaulle, US$15 per hr. **Post offices** Route de
Baduel, 2 km out from town (US$2.25 by taxi or 20
mins on foot), crowded. Poste Restante letters are
only kept for 2 weeks.

Kourou p1460
Banks Several in town, including **Banque
National de Paris Guyane**, near the Mairie.
Post offices Ave des Frères Kennedy.

St-Laurent du Maroni p1461
Banks BFC, 11 Av Félix Eboué, open Tue-Fri, Sat
morning. Cambio COP, 19 rue Montravel, near BNP,
T343823, changes euros and Suriname and US$.

Falkland Islands / Islas Malvinas

Essentials	1468
Stanley and around	1471
Beyond the Falklands	1477
South Georgia	1477
Antarctica	1478

⁞ Footprint features

Touching down	1470

Essentials → *Colour map 9, inset.*

Planning your trip

Where to go These remote South Atlantic outposts, where there are more penguins than people, are the only part of South America where UK sterling is the currency, and the British monarch's head appears on the stamps. Windswept they may be, but the islands are a haven for wildlife and a paradise for those who wish to see it: albatross nest in the tussac grass, sea lions breed on the beaches and Orca whales cruise off the coast. About 640 km (400 miles) east of the South American mainland, the Falklands Islands/Islas Malvinas are made up of two large islands and over 720 smaller ones. For anyone interested in marine mammals and birdlife, this is the place to go. The islands' remoteness adds to the charm of being able to see elephant seals, dolphins, whales, albatross and, above all, penguins at close range. Based on 2005/06 census figures from Falklands Conservation, there are 385,824 breeding pairs of five species of penguin (King, Magellanic, Macaroni, Gentoo, Rock Hopper) in the Islands. This constitutes 156 penguins per person (the Islands' human population in the 2006 census was 2,478). The capital, Stanley, is a small, modern town, with reminders of its seafaring past in the hulks of sailing ships in the bay. To visit the camp, as the land outside Stanley is known, 4WD vehicles make tours, or you can fly to farming outposts for warm hospitality, huge skies and unparalleled nature watching.

Note In accordance with the practice suggested by the UN, we are calling the islands by both their English and Spanish names.

When to go Best months to visit are Oct-Mar. Although the *Sunday Express* once referred to a mutton freezer in the Falklands as a Colonial Development project near the South Pole (8 March 1953), the Islands are in the same latitude south as London is north. The climate is cool and oceanic, dominated by persistent westerly winds which average 16 knots. Long periods of calm are rare except in winter. Though not always inclement, weather is very changeable but temperatures vary relatively little. At Stanley, the capital, the mean temperature in summer (January/February) is 15.4°C, but temperatures frequently exceed this on the islands. In winter (June/July/August) 4°C. Stanley's annual rainfall of about 600 mm is slightly higher than London's. In the drier camp, outside Stanley, summer drought sometimes threatens local water supplies. Snowfall is rare although a dusting may occur at any time of the year. Spring, autumn and winter clothing, as used in the UK, is suitable. Wind-protective clothing is recommended and sunblock is essential.

Finding out more The **Falkland Islands Tourist Board)** ① *PO Box 618, Stanley, F1QQ 1ZZ, T271019/22215, www.visitorfalklands.com,* runs the Jetty Visitor's Centre at the Public Jetty on Ross Road. It is open daily during summer and provides comprehensive local information on accommodation, tours, transport and activities. The **Falkland Islands Government London Office** (FIGO) ① *Falkland House, 14 Broadway, Westminster, London SW1H 0BH, T020-7222 2542, reception@falklands.gov.fk,* will answer enquiries. See also **Tourist offices**, under Stanley, Ins and outs, below. Also try: **www.falklandislands.com, www.falklands.info** (Falkland Islands information portal), **www.falklands.gov.fk** (the Falkland Islands Government page), **www.falklandnews.com** (Falkland Islands News Network), **www.falklands.com** (Merco Press, South Atlantic's News Agency) and **www.penguin-news.com** (*Penguin News* newspaper).

Before you travel

Getting in All travellers must have full, current passports to visit the Islands. Citizens of Britain, North America, Mercosur, Chile, and most Commonwealth countries and the European Union are permitted to visit the islands without a visa, as are holders of UN and International Committee of the Red Cross passports. Other nationals should apply for a visa from the Travel Coordinator at *Falkland House* in London (see above), the Immigration Department in Stanley (see Stanley, Useful addresses), or a British Embassy or Consulate. Visas cost £20. All visitors require a one month visitor permit, normally provided on arrival upon presentation of a return ticket. Proof of pre-booked accommodation and sufficient funds to cover the cost of your stay, and evidence of medical insurance (including cover for aero-medical evacuation) are also mandatory for all visitors. Work permits are not available. Do not stay beyond the valid period of your visa without applying to the Immigration Office for an extension.

Money

Currency The local pound (£) is on a par with sterling. Local notes and coins. UK notes and coins are also legal tender. Falkland Island pounds cannot be used outside the islands. Currency from Ascension Island, where the RAF Tri-Star stops for refuelling, or Saint Helena, is not accepted. Foreign currency (including US dollars and euros) and travellers' cheques can be changed at the *Standard Chartered Bank*, Ross Rd, Stanley. All establishments in the Islands accept pounds sterling, some also accept US dollars and euros (check when booking). Credit cards and TCs are only accepted by a handful of operators. Visitors are advised to take cash where possible, or discuss alternative payment methods with operators prior to arrival. There are currently no ATMs on the Islands.

Getting there

Air Flights from Santiago, via Puerto Montt and Punta Arenas with *LAN* (www.lan.com) go every Saturday morning and, once a month, stop at Río Gallegos in Argentina on both the outward and return flight. 2007 fares: return from Santiago £460, Puerto Montt £430, Punta Arenas £247. All fares include Chilean airport taxes, but exclude Falklands embarkation tax of £20 per person (payable at the airport on departure, cash only). Luggage allowances should be confirmed with your agent at the time of booking. Passengers should confirm flights 24 hours before scheduled departure. For more information, contact **International Tours and Travel Ltd** ① *PO Box 408, 1 Dean St, Stanley, FIQQ 1ZZ, T+500-22041, jf.itt@horizon.co.fk or visit www.falklandstravel.com.*

Touching down

Airport tax All departing passengers by air pay an embarkation tax of £20, payable is sterling, dollars or euros.

Business hours Office hours, including all government departments, Monday-Friday 0800-1200, 1300-1630. Banking hours: 0830-1500.

In an emergency T999. Stanley

Police Station T27222.
Hospital Reception T28000.

International phone code +500

Official time GMT -4 in winter (May-Aug), -3 in summer.

Voltage 220/ 240 volts at 50 cycles. Rectangular, three-blade plug as in the UK.

Weights and measures Metric.

The Ministry of Defence operates a charter flight to the Falkland Islands 6-7 times a month (flights approximately every five days). They depart from RAF Brize Norton, Oxfordshire, with a total flight time of 18 hours including a short stop-over in Ascension Island at the half way point (usually 1-2 hours in duration). The fare is £3,071 return, but there are also cheaper APEX (28 days or more in advance, £1,912) and group rates (£1,607 for six or more). Falkland Islands residents receive a discount (£1,198). As above, £20 exit tax is extra, confirm luggage allowance in advance and confirm the flight itself 24 hours before departure. Enquiries about flights can be addressed to the **Falkland Islands Government London Office** ① *Falkland House, 14 Broadway, Westminster, London SW1H oBH. T020-7222 2542, travel@falklands.gov.fk or visit www.falklands.gov.fk*, or to the **Falkland Islands Company Flights Department** ① *T27633, fic.travel@horizon.co.fk.*

Boat Cruise ships en-route to South Georgia and the Antarctic are also a popular way to see the Islands. Vessels typically visit between October and March each year. Passengers usually land for tours of Stanley and nearby sites, pub lunch, farmhouse tea, and call at outlying islands, such as West Point Island (owners Roddy and Lily Napier), or New Island (see below). Further details of companies that include the Falklands/Malvinas in their itineraries can be found on **www.visitorfalklands.com** and at **www.iaato.org**. Alternatively you can contact local port agents **Sulivan Shipping** ① *T 22626, sulivan@horizon.co.fk* and **Falkland Islands Company** (FIC) ① *T 27630, ficagents@horizon.co.fk.*

Airport information

Mount Pleasant airport, 35 miles from Stanley, is built to international specifications. Tax free shop does not take US$. **Falkland Islands Tours and Travel** ① *Andrew Williams, Lookout Industrial Estate, Stanley, T/F21775, fitt@horizon.co.fk,* transports passengers and luggage to and from the capital for £13 single. Departing passengers should make reservations. Also, **Bonner's Taxis** *T51126, abonner@horizon.co.fk,* for transport between Stanley and the airport.

Keeping in touch

Internet Internet is widely used and there is public internet access at the Jetty Visitor's Centre (Ross Road), **Zak's Computers** (Fitzroy Road) and various hotels and guest houses. **Post** Since the opening of Mount Pleasant, there is direct and dependable air mail service from the United Kingdom. Heavy parcels come by sea from the UK every month. There is also a weekly in and out-bound DHL service operated through the **Falkland Islands Chamber of Commerce** ① *PO Box 378, Stanley, T22264, commerce@horizon.co.fk.* Inter-island mail service is carried out by FIGAS. **Cable and Wireless,** the local phone operator, operates the local mobile phone network (www.cwfi.co.fk). International roaming is only available for T Mobile (UK), but other networks are planned to be added in the future. It is advisable to buy a local SIM card from Cable and Wireless for a small fee if you require mobile phone access. Handsets will generally need to be network 'unlocked' to accept the local SIM card.

Public holidays

1 January (New Year's day), Good Friday (Easter), 21 April (Queen's birthday), 14 June (Liberation Day), 1st Monday in October (Peat-cutting Day), 8 December (Battle Day), 25 December (Christmas day), 26-27 December (Stanley Races).

Stanley and around → *Population: 1,989.*

The capital, Stanley, on East Falkland, is the major population centre. Its residents live mostly in brightly-painted houses, many of which have corrugated iron roofs. Surrounded by rolling moorland, Stanley resembles parts of the Scottish Hebrides. The outer harbour of Port William is larger but less protected. East Cove, 30 miles southwest of the capital, is the principal port for the new military installations at Mount Pleasant.

Ins and outs

Getting around Outside Stanley, there is a major road to the airport at **Mount Pleasant**, but great care should nevertheless be taken on it. Roads connect Stanley with **San Carlos** (70 miles), **Port San Carlos** (75 miles) and **Goose Green** (64 miles). On **West Falkland** a new road connects most of the settlements. Elsewhere, tracks require 4WD or motorbikes. Remember to phone farms in the camp for permission to drive across private land. Off-road driving in the boggy terrain is a skill not easily learned by short-term visitors. Near Stanley and a few farm settlements there are still some clearly-marked and fenced minefields from the 1982 war. Visitors should *never* enter these areas and should report suspicious objects to the police or military authorities in Stanley. Free minefield maps are available from the Police Station, Ross Rd, Stanley, or Hillside Camp, West Hillside, Stanley. Ordnance Survey maps of the Islands are available from the Museum (see below), £2.50 each for the 1:50,000 sheets; there is also a two-sheet, 1:250,000 map suitable for most purposes. ▸▸ *For more detailed information see Transport, page 1477.*

Tourist offices The **Jetty Visitor's Centre**, at the head of the Public Jetty ① *Ross Rd, Stanley, T22281,* is the place to go for all information. See also above, under Finding our more. Available from the Jetty Visitor's Centre is *A Visitors' Guide to the Falklands* (2nd edition, £12.50).

For wildlife enthusiasts, especially ornithologists, the Islands are an exceptional destination. Make allowance for unpredictable weather. Always wear or carry waterproof clothing; wear good boots and a peaked hat to protect the eyes from rain or hail. For wildlife booklists, checlists and reports: **Falklands Conservation** ① *Jetty Visitors Centre, Ross Rd, PO Box 26, Stanley, T22247 (1 Princes Av, Finchley, London N3 2DA, T020 8343 0831), www.falklandsconservation.com.*

Sights

The **Museum** at Britannia House ① *Ross Rd West, T27428, Mon-Fri, 0930-1200, 1330-1600 (in summer, no lunch break), Sat-Sun, 1400-1600, £3, www.falklands-museum.com,* merits a visit. The manager is Mrs Leona Roberts. The ticket includes a visit to Cartmell Cottage, one of the original pioneer houses, whose interior reflects life in the late 19th century and the 1940s.

Falkland Islands/Islas Malvinas

Government House, the Anglican Cathedral (most southerly in the world, built in 1892), and monuments commemorating the naval battle of 1914 and the 1982 liberation are also worth seeing. At the public jetty, the **Jetty Visitors Centre** has permanent and temporary exhibitions, an information service, local produce and crafts, toilets, internet and phones. The public library has a good selection of books on travel and flora/fauna; in the same building is a public swimming pool. During the December holidays, the sports meeting at the race course attracts visitors from all over the Islands. The equally popular West and East Falkland sports, at the end of the shearing season in February/March rotate among the settlements.

Of particular interest are the hulks of **old sailing ships** at Stanley and Darwin. Examples at Stanley are the *Jhelum* (built in 1839 for the East India Company) near Government House, the *Charles Cooper* (the last US sailing packet to sail out of New York Harbour; in the Islands since 1866), and the iron-built *Lady Elizabeth* at the far end of the harbour (228 ft, with three masts still standing). A Maritime History Trail has been set up around Port Stanley (self-guided with interpretive panels; a book describing the Stanley wrecks is sold at the museum). At **Darwin** are the *Vicar of Bray* (last survivor of the California Gold Rush fleet), and another old iron ship, the *Garland*. There are interesting French buildings and ruins at Port Louis (the road between Stanley and Port Louis is a boulder-strewn clay track, tricky when wet).

From the Beaver hanger, Ross Rd West, walk past the various ships and monuments, along the harbour, up to the Falkland Islands Company offices. Here it is possible to walk onto the jetty and visit the after section of a 19th-century sailing vessel. Also below the jetty you will see a couple of 19th-century Welsh colliers. From here go east until you reach B slip, used by the British Forces during the 1982 conflict. Carry on east, past the floating harbour and around the head of the bay to the iron barque *Lady Elizabeth*. At low tide you can walk out to her. Follow the bay round and eventually you will come to various penguin rookeries and Gypsy Cove (see below).

Outside Stanley
Sparrow Cove, **Kidney Cove**, and adjacent areas, only a short distance from Stanley by boat, are good areas to see four species of penguin and other wildlife. 4WD tours to the site are also available with local operators. **Gypsy Cove**, within walking distance from Stanley for the fit, features a colony of burrowing Magellanic penguins, Black-crowned Night Herons and other shorebirds. Occasionally visitors can also spot orca, elephant seals, variable hawks and sea lions. **Note** Observe minefield fences which prevent

Stanley

To Government House, Cable & Wireless, Falkland Islands Museum & 8

Reservoir Rd

Stanley Harbour

Moody St
Allardyce St
St Mary's Walk
Thatcher Dr

Brandon Rd
King St

Cable St

Pioneer Row
Drury St

Dairy Paddock Rd

Barrack St

Ross Rd

St Mary's

Brisbane Rd

John St

Villiers St

FIC Store

Dean St

Beauchene Shopping Centre

Cathedral

Davis St

Philomel St

Fitzroy Rd

Crozier Place

Jetty Visitors Centre

Stanley Harbour

Hebe St

Fitzroy Rd East

Davis St East

Snake Hill

Ross Rd East

Snake Hill

To 7 3 & Airport

0 metres 100
0 yards 100

Eating
Deano's Bistro 1
Falklands Brasserie 2
Lighthouse Seaman's Centre 3
Woodbine Takeaway 4

Sleeping
Bennett House 8
Kay's B&B 3
Lafone Guest House 9
Malvina House 4
Millers 1
Shorty's Motel & Diner 10
Sue Binnie's 2
Upland Goose 6

Bars & clubs
Globe 5
Narrows 7
Stanley Arms 8
Victory 6

close inspection of the penguins (they are not unduly inhibiting, though). At **Cape Pembroke**, around the town airport and the renovated lighthouse you can see Gentoo penguins and ground-nesting birds such as dotterels, snipe, and Upland geese.

Volunteer Point, north of Stanley, is a wildlife sanctuary. It contains the only substantial nesting colony of King penguins outside of South Georgia (the most accessible site in the world). Gentoo penguins, Magellanic penguins, geese, ducks, and elephant seals are very tame and easily photographed. It is a private farm approximately 2½ hours drive from Stanley. The last part of the track is suitable for 4WDs only and is open from November to March, weather dependent. Visits can be arranged with a local guide.

Smaller islands: off East Falkland

Bleaker Island, hardly bleak, has a wonderful coastline with white sandy beaches and sheltered coves. Bird species include Rockhoppers, Magellanic and Gentoo penguins, waterfowl, ruddy-headed geese, Falkland Skuas and an impressive King Cormorant colony. The area north of the settlement was declared a National Nature Reserve in 1999. One of the key features of the island is Big Pond, where you can spot Chiloe Wigeon, Silvery and White-tufted Grebes, Speckled and Silver Teal and occasionally the rare Flying Steamer Duck. The island is owned and run by Phyll and Mike Rendell ① *T21355, mrendell@horizon.co.fk*; see Cobb's Cotage, below.

Sea Lion Island in the southeast, 35 minutes' flight from Stanley, is a delightful place to explore and relax. Throughout the austral summer the lodge accommodates a maximum of 23 visitors (see Sleeping). Many Southern Sea Lions breed on the beaches; Southern Elephant Seals also breed here. Up to three pods of orca whales are resident around the island and can be seen cruising the shore in search of elephant seal and sea lion pups risking their first swim (summer months). The island also has magnificent bird life: Gentoo, Magellanic and Rockhopper Penguins, Giant Petrels (known locally as stinkers), King Cormorants, the incredible flightless Steamer Duck, Black-crowned Night Herons, the friendly Tussac Bird, Oystercatcher (Magellanic and Black) and the rare Striated Caracara. Also on the island is the HMS *Sheffield* memorial.

Smaller islands: off West Falkland

Pebble Island is the third largest offshore island and is thought to be named after the unusual pebbles found on its beaches. The flight takes about 35 minutes from Stanley. Pebble is home to more than 40 species including Gentoo, Rockhopper, Macaroni and Magellanic penguins, King Cormorants, waterfowl, Falkland Skuas, Southern Giant Petrels, and Black-necked Swans. Southern sea lions can also be found on the coast. The eastern half of Pebble Island contains large ponds and wetlands with many waterfowl and wading birds. See Sleeping, below.

Saunders Island, besides a representative sample of wildlife, contains the ruins of the 18th century British outpost at Port Egmont. It is run by Suzan and David Pole-Evans. There is a small group of King Penguins at the Neck, a three-hour walk, 45 minutes by jeep from the settlement. Gentoo, Magellanic, Rockhoppers, King Cormorants and Black-browed Albatross can be seen here, as well as dolphins wave surfing and whales spouting. A further 1½-2 hours' walk goes to the point where elephant seals can be seen. Another good place is the bay just north of the Settlement with many Gentoo and Magellanic penguins. At a third site, the Rookery, you can see Gentoo, Magellanic, Rockhoppers, King Cormorants and Black-browed Albatross.

Carcass Island, taking it's name from HMS Carcass which visited in the late 18th century, is approximately 60 minutess by plane from Stanley. One of the most spectacular and attractive islands for wildlife and scenery, species include Striated Caracara, Gentoo and Magellanic penguins, abundant small birds such as Cobb's Wren. The island also has great examples of tussac grass. The island is cat, rat and mice free, allowing small bird species to flourish. Current owners and lodge proprietors are Rob and Lorraine McGill (see below).

New Island South, at the extreme west edge of the archipelago, is a nature reserve owned by the **New Island Conservation Trust** (www.newislandtrust.com). The aim of the project, begun in 1973 by Ian Strange, is to ensure that the island operates as a reserve in perpetuity. There is a fully-equipped field station in the settlement with accommodation for up to eight personnel who carry out scientific studies and field work usually during September-April. The recently refurbished Captain Charles Barnard Memorial Museum and Visitor Centre, at the head of the settlement harbour, is visited mostly by passengers on small adventure-cruise vessels. Limited accommodation is available from time to time to individual visitors who may access the island via FIGAS on flights limited to three passengers. Contact can be made through the Trust's website. New Island North owned by Tony Chater, has a small sheep farm.

● Sleeping

Stanley *p1471, map p1472*
Note: Advance reservation is essential. B&Bs cost £25 pp or less. See www.visitorfalklands.com.
AL pp Malvina House, 3 Ross Rd, T21355, malvina@horizon.co.fk. Very good, full board, power showers, hot drinks, central heating, TV, nice restaurant (open daily except Sun evening), bar, spa, laundry, Wi-Fi broadband for guests.
AL Upland Goose Hotel, 20-22 Ross Rd, T21455, fic@horizon.co.fk. Some cheaper rooms, full board, lounge bar. Restaurant for lunch and bar snacks Mon-Sat 1200-1330, dinner Mon-Sat 1730-1900, à la carte menu and desserts, Sun lunch, carvery 1200-1400, Sun bar snacks 1700-1900. Service with a sense of humour!
C Millers Hotel, Restaurant and Bar, 46 John St, T21572, millers@ horizon.co.fk. Extensive refurbishments in early 2007, 6 en suite rooms, satellite TV, coffee/tea facilities, room service, restaurant Wed-Mon. Sun/Mon evening bookings only. Thu pizza night, Sun lunch carvery.
D pp Kay's B&B, 14 Drury St, T/F21071, kay@horizon.co.fk. Excellent value, dinner, lunch and packed lunch available, good food. Camping £5 per tent per night, £2.50 for breakfast and shower in house for campers. Highly recommended.
Bennett House B&B, 14 Allardyce St, T21191, celiastewart@horizon.co.fk. Owned and run by Celia Stewart. Central, excellent home baking and breakfast, refurbished rooms, good views, welcoming. Camping £10 pp per night.
Sue Binnie's, Brandon Rd, T21051. Central B&B with 1 double room, shared bath, Spanish spoken.
Lafone Guest House, T22891, arlette@ horizon .co.fk. Owned and run by Arlette Betts, luxury B&B, good harbour views, evening meals on request.
Lookout Lodge, Keil Canal Rd, contact John Birmingham, T22834, lookout@horizon.co.fk. Over 50 single rooms. Originally built for contract workers, now offering simple accommodation and catering facilities for all meals.

Shorty's Diner & Motel, Snake Hill, T52854, www.shortys-diner.com. All rooms en suite, laundry, internet. The diner has good fast food, eat in or take away. Open 6 days (seasonal), weekdays 1030-2030, weekends 1030-2000.
The Waterfront, 36 Ross Rd, T21030, thewaterfront@horizon.co.fk. Very helpful, evening meals and snack lunches on request. Recommended.

Outside Stanley *p1472*
AL-A pp Sea Lion Lodge, Sea Lion Island, T32004, sealion_lodge @horizon.co.fk or www.sealion island.com. Seasonal prices, full board, some rooms en suite, modern, central heating, phone in rooms.
A Pebble Island Lodge, Pebble Island, T41093, pebblelodge@horizon.co.fk. This well-appointed lodge is run by Jacqui Jennings and Alan White. En suite rooms, central heating, full board, lounge, TV and DVD, phone and internet, island tours.
A pp Port Howard Lodge, Port Howard, West Falkland, T42187, porthowardlodge@horizon.co.fk. Prices seasonal, all rooms en suite, central heating, Land Rover hire. Excellent trout fishing, rod hire. Has an interesting war museum, and the chance to see the workings of a traditional large sheep station.
A pp Saunders Island, Suzan and David Pole-Evans, T41298, davidpe@horizon.co.fk. Self- catering Portakabin sleeping 8 at the Neck, transport £50. At the settlement are 2 self-catering cottages, for 10 and 6, **C** pp per night. A new self catering cottage at the Rookery is planned for late 2007/2008 (**A** pp, transport £20). Spectacular scenery and wildlife.
B Darwin House, Close to Goose Green, T32255, darwin.h@horizon.co.fk. Owners Bonnie and Ken Greenland. Close to the British and Argentine cemeteries and only 35 mins' drive from Mount Pleasant Airport, an excellent base for the start of a holiday. Fully-catered lodge, and 2 cottages for self-catering. Excellent home baking and evening meals. Battlefield tours available, also fishing, golf at nearby Goose Green, boat excursions.

C **Carcass Island Cottages**, owned and run by Rob and Lorraine McGill, Carcass Island, T41106, F41107. Rooms in main farmhouse, full board, good food, 1 self-catering cottage, summer only.

Cobbs Cottage, Bleaker Island, owned and run by Mike and Phyll Rendell, T21084 (Stanley), T32491 (Bleaker Island), mrendell@horizon.co.fk. 30-min flight south from Stanley, finished to a high standard throughout. Good wildlife.

Little Chartres Farm, West Falkland, F1ZZ 1QQ, T42215, www.littlechartres.horizon.co.fk. New, operated by Lesley and Jim Woodward, who are very accommodating and helpful. Excellent trout fishing. Tours available.

Port San Carlos Lodge, 2 hrs' drive from Stanley. Owned by Simon and Sandra Goss, T21315/41024, psclodge@horizon.co.fk. Tours and fishing.

Roy Cove, Crooked Inlet Farm, Danny and Joy Donnelly, T41102. A comfortable self-catering property, splendid sea views from the house overlooking the cove. Sea fishing nearby.

West Lagoons, Shelley and Peter Nightingale, adjacent Hill Cove settlement, West Falklands, T/F41194, sptk@horizon.co.fk. Full-board accommodation on a sheep farm.

Kingsford Valley Farm, San Carlos settlement, East Falklands, T/F32233, kvf@horizon.co.fk. Owned and run by Terence and Sheila McPhee.

2 self-catering cottages, one with 2-bedrooms, the other with 3, both include cots, children very welcome. Central heating, 24-hour power, TV, video, CD, enclosed gardens, close to trout fishing, San Carlos cemetry and museum. Terence McPhee offers wildlife and general tours on East Falklands.

🍴 Eating

Stanley *p1471, map p1472*

The Bread Shop. Open Mon-Sat. Wide range of breads, sandwiches, snacks, all freshly baked.

Deano's bistro, 40 John St, T21296. Bar snacks, including vegetarian menu.

Falklands Brasserie, Philomel St, central, near Public Jetty, T21159, brasserie@horizon.co.fk. Innovative cooking with local produce, from 1100.

Lighthouse Seamans' Centre, over the bridge next to FIPASS ('The Seaman's Mission'). Tea/coffee, snacks, home baking, lunches, open all day.

Michelle's Café, close to the Public Jetty. Open Mon-Sat, daytime and evening, home baking a speciality, all food cooked to order.

Stanley Arms Bar, 1 John Biscoe Rd, T22259. Good pub food, daily specials.

The Narrows Bar, 39 Ross Road East, T22272. Daily specials, good pub food, open daily 1200-1330, 1800-2000, Sun carvery 1200-1330.

Falkland Islands / Islas Malvinas Stanley & around Listings

Victory Bar, 1A Philomel St, T21199. Daily for specials, lunch, traditional English pub food, children welcome; evening meals Mon, Tue and Thu 1600-2030. Caters for cruise ships Oct-Mar.
Woodbine Takeaway, 29 Fitzroy Rd, T21102. Fish and chips and pizza. Closed Sun and Mon.

For groceries: **FIC West Store** (Ross Rd), **Kelper Family Stores** (4 locations), **Choice Fruits** (Industrial Lookout Estate), **Stanley Growers Garden Centre** (Stanley Airport Rd), **Seafish Chandlery** (Stanley Airport Rd), **Stanley Co-op** (Davis St), **Falklands Supplies** (Hebe St), **Stanley Services** (Stanley Airport Rd).

♪ Bars and clubs

Stanley *p1471, map p1472*
The pubs include: **Beagle Bar**, at Malvina House Hotel, **Narrows Bar**, see above, **Stanley Arms**, see above, **The Globe**, near the public jetty, **The Trough**, Airport Rd, BYO, check Penguin News for opening dates (usually Sat night), live music and funky chill-out lounge, and **The Victory**, see above.

▲▲ Activities and tours

Stanley *p1471, map p1472*
Fishing Superb for all levels of experience. The season runs 1 Sep-30 Apr (the fish depart late Nov and return early Mar). Note: a licence is not required for rod and line fishing; the daily limit is 6 brown/sea trout pp; mullet may be caught at any time; Falkland Islands Zebra Trout are protected and must never be caught; most land in the Falklands is privately owned, including rivers and streams, always seek permission from the owner. Ask travel agents about regulations for specific areas and changes to daily bag limits.

Tour operators
Also visit www.visitorfalklands.com.
Antarctic Cruises, Reservations: Vitacura 2771 of 904, Santiago, Chile, T236 5179, www.antarctic.cl.

Falkland Islands Company - Flights, T27633, fic.travel@horizon.co.fk. Local booking agent for the MoD charter flight via Brize Norton, UK.
Falkland Island Holidays (division of Stanley Services), Airport Rd, Stanley, T22622, www.falkandislandsholidays.com. Offer inbound tourist services, FIGAS flights, overland 4WD excursions from Stanley to various sights, bookings for lodgings and for fishing, riding and vehicle hire.
Golden Fleece Expedition Cruises, contact: Jerome Poncet, T42326, golden.fleece@horizon.co.fk. Specializes in film-work, scientific surveys or tourism around the Falklands, South Georgia or Antarctica.
International Tours and Travel Ltd, 1 Dean St, PO Box 408, Stanley, T22041, www.falklands travel.com. Handle inbound tourist bookings, book FIGAS flights, arrange tours etc and are the Falkland Island agents for **LAN**. Recommended.
Penguin Travel, Crozier Place, T27630, www.penguintravel-falklands.com. Wildlife tours on foot, or by 4WD, Stanley town tours on vintage double-decker Routemaster bus, battlesite tours.
South Atlantic Marine Services, Carol and Dave Eynon, PO Box 140, Stanley, T21145, dceynon@horizon.co.fk. Overland tours, boat trips, safaris and have a dive centre with deck recompression chamber (PADI courses).

Guided tours
Adventure Falklands, PO Box 223, T21383, pwatts@horizon.co.fk. Patrick Watts offers tours of battlefield and other historical sights, ornithological trips and more.
Cross Country Expeditions, T21494, scm@horizon.co.fk. Wildlife and fishing tours, airport transfers and lodging with Sam Miller.
Discovery Falklands, T21027, T51027 (mob), discovery@horizon.co.fk. Tony Smith specialises in battlefield tours, wildlife, general interest, historical, also provides logistical support and guidance for visiting TV Crews and media personnel. Highly recommended.

Dodo's Penguin Tours, contact Ian Doherty, T22327, T53398 (mob), idoherty@ horizon.co.fk. Driver guided tours to Volunteer Point, Gyspy Cove, Cape Bougainville, , Stanley town tours, Goose Green/San Carlos. Also tailor-made tours.
Falkland Frontiers, T21561, falklandfrontiers @horizon.co.fk. Neil Rowlands offers overland and boat tours, also fishing guide.
France's Falkland Forays, 7 Snake Hill, T21624, france@horizon.co.fk. Graham France's city, golf, penguin watching and historical tours.
Kidney Cove Safari Tours, T31001, allowe@ horizon.co.fk. Adrian and Lisa Lowe, offer overland 4WD tours to see 4 species of penguins at Kidney Cove, close to Stanley.

⊖ Transport

Falklands/Malvinas
Air The Falkland Islands Government Air Service (FIGAS, T27219, jross@figas.gov.fk) flies to farm settlements and settled outer islands according to bookings, seat availability, and weather. To book a seat, telephone FIGAS no later than the morning of the day before travelling; flight schedules are announced that evening on local radio (return airfares: Sea Lion Island £96, Pebble Island £108, Saunders Island £122, Carcass Island £145; luggage limit 14 kg/30 pounds). Services daily Oct-end Mar, 6 days a week otherwise; no flights on 1 Jan, Good Friday, 21 Apr, 14 Jun, 25 Dec. FIGAS tickets are also available from **Stanley Services Travel** and **International**

Tours and Travel Ltd, see Activities and tours, above. Flights leave from Stanley Airport, 3 miles east of town on the Cape Pembroke peninsula, 5 mins by car. Passengers arriving on **LAN** can fly with FIGAS directly to Port Howard or Pebble Island with prior arrangement.
Car rentals **Falklands Islands Company**, Travel Services, West Store, Stanley, T27678, www.the-falkland-islands-co.com. Contact Stephen Luxton. Rents Land Rover Defender, Discovery and Freelander. **Stanley Services Ltd**, Travel Division, Airport Rd, Stanley, T22622, info@falklandislands holidays.com. Rents Mitsubishi Pajeros.

❶ Directory

Stanley *p1471, map p1472*
Internet See Keeping in touch in Essentials.
Medical services Hospitals: Stanley has an excellent hospital, King Edward Memorial Hospital (KEMH), dental service included. T28000. Emergency T999. **Post offices** Philatelic Bureau (they sell stamps from South Georgia and the Antarctic Territories), T27180, www.falklands.gov. fk/pb.
Telephones Cable and Wireless, Ross Rd, overseas telephone, mobile, fax, telegraph and telex. The islands' telephone system has direct dialling worldwide. **Useful addresses** Immigration: Customs and Immigration Department, 3 H Jones Rd, Stanley, T27340, admin@customs.gov.fk. Library, T27147, is in the Community School and some other services are in Town Hall, Ross Rd. Other government offices are in the nearby Secretariat.

Beyond the Falklands

South Georgia

South Georgia, in latitude 54.5° south and longitude 36-38° west, has an area of 3,755 sq km, but no permanent residents. There are two British Antarctic Survey stations, King Edward Point and Bird Island, and a marine officer at the former is the government's representative and has responsibility for local administration. His duties include those of Harbour Master, Customs and Immigration Officer, Fisheries Officer and Postmaster. Visitors normally arrive by cruise ship from Ushuaia, Punta Arenas or Stanley. Intending visitors, who are not part of tour groups, must submit a request through the **Commissioner** ① *Government House, Stanley, Falkland Islands, South Atlantic, T500-27433, gov.house@horizon.co.fk*. There is a landing fee of £100.

South Georgia is a mass of high, snow-covered glaciated mountains. At King Edward Point, near sea level, snow falls on an average of nearly 200 days annually, but the coastal area is free from snow and partially covered by vegetation in summer. Wildlife consists of most of the same species found in the Falkland Islands/Islas Malvinas, but in much larger numbers. Reindeer, introduced by Norwegian whalers in 1909, have flourished. Other points of interest are seven abandoned whaling stations, the little white church, and several wrecks. A South Georgia Museum has been established at Grytviken. It has a display of artifacts, photographs and other items about the old Antarctic whaling and sealing industry with descriptions the history of the island and its wildlife. The island issues distinctive stamps, which are sold by the Post Office and museum. There is a **South Georgia website**: www.sgisland.org.

The Antarctic

Antarctica, the fifth largest continent, is 99.8% covered with perpetual ice. Although inaccessible, the number of tourists now exceeds the number of people on government research programmes. It is known for its extraordinary scenery, wildlife, scientific stations, and historic sites. The weather can be spectacularly severe, thus visits are confined to the brief summer. Presently 25 countries operate 60 scientific stations (44 remain open during winter). A winter population of about 1,200 lives in a continent larger than Europe. The Antarctic Heritage Trust and some other organizations maintain several historic huts where organized groups are admitted, and many current research stations allow visitors for a tour. Of the historic huts, the one at **Port Lockroy**, established in 1944 and now a museum, has become the most-visited site. The historic huts used by Scott, Shackleton, Mawson, and Borchgrevink during the 'heroic age' of exploration are on the Australian and New Zealand side of Antarctica thus very distant from South America.

Information The best single source of information is *Antarctica: great stories from the frozen continent* by Reader's Digest (first published Sydney 1985, with several later editions). General information can be found at **Scott Polar Research Institute** site, www.spri.cam.ac.uk. Also useful is the website of **International Association of Antarctica Tour Operators**, IAATO (see below).

Governance of Antarctica is principally through the Antarctic Treaty (1959) signed by all countries operating there (45 countries were parties to the Treaty in 2007). Most visitors will be affected by several provisions of the Treaty, in particular those of the Environmental Protocol of 1991. These provisions are aimed at the protection of wildlife (do not remove or interfere with animals or plants), respecting protected areas and research and keeping the environment pristine. Full details from www.iaato.org/docs/visitor_guidelines.pdf. Seven countries have claims over parts of Antarctica and three of these overlap (Antártida Argentina, British Antarctic Territory, and Territorio Chileno Antártico); the Treaty has neutralized these with provision of free access to citizens of contracting states. Some display of sovereignty is legitimate and many stations operate a Post Office where philatelic items and various souvenirs are sold.

The region south of South America is the most accessible part of the Antarctic and more than half the scientific stations are there or on adjacent islands. It is also one of the most spectacular areas with mountains, glaciers and fjords. Three ports are used: Stanley, Punta Arenas and Ushuaia, the latter is the major base for yachts. The South Shetland Islands and Antarctic Peninsula are most frequently visited, but ships also reach the South Orkney Islands and many call at South Georgia at the beginning or end of a voyage. Most vessels are booked well in advance by luxury class passengers but late vacancies are sometimes available from local agencies. Ships carrying 45-280 tourists land passengers at several sites during a two-week voyage. Some larger cruise vessels also visit; these generally do not land. During the 2006- 2007 austral summer 32,000 visitors arrived in Antarctica, of whom 24,000 landed on the continent.

Voyages from South America and the Falkland Islands/Islas Malvinas involve at least two days each way, crossing the Drake Passage where the sea may be very rough. No guarantee of landings, views or wildlife; and delays due to storms are not exceptional. Conversely, on a brilliant day, some of the most spectacular sights and wildlife anywhere can be seen. Visitors should be prepared for adverse conditions with warm clothing, windproofs and waterproofs, and boots for wet landings. Weather and state of the sea can change quickly without warning.

The **International Association of Antarctica Tour Operators** ① *PO Box 2178, Basalt, Colorado, US, CO 81621; T+1-970-704 1047, www.iaato.org*, represents the majority of companies offering Antarctic voyages. **Antarctic Logistics and Expeditions** (ALE) ① *4376 South 700 East, Suite 226, Salt Lake City, Utah 84107-3006, USA, T+1-801-266 4876, info@antarctic-logistics.com*, provides flights to Antarctica from Punta Arenas where there is a **local office** ① *Arauco 935, Punta Arenas, Chile, T+56-61-247735, chile@antarctic-logistics .com, Oct-Jan.* Wheeled aircraft fly as far as a summer camp at Patriot Hills (80° 19S, 81° 20W), the only land-based tourist facility, whence ski-aircraft proceed to the South Pole, vicinity of Vinson Massif (4,892 m, Antarctica's highest peak), and elsewhere. Some flights also go from Cape Town. 'Flightseeing' is made by Qantas from Australia aboard aircraft which do not land but spend about 4 hours over the continent (and about the same getting there and back).

Some private yachts carry passengers; enquire at Ushuaia, or the other ports listed. Travelling with the Argentine, Chilean, French or Russian supply ships may sometimes be arranged at departure ports. These are much cheaper than cruise ships but have limited itineraries.

Pre-independence history	1480
Post-independence history	1486
Government	1506
Culture	1508
People	1508
Music and dance	1513
Cinema/film	1522
Land and environment	1524
The Andean countries	1524
The Southern Cone	1527
Brazil and the north	1529

⁑ Footprint features

The Jesuits	1485
The Bandeirantes	1491
Ten of the best reads	1523

Pre-independence history

Earliest settlement

It is generally accepted that the earliest settlers in South America were related to people who had crossed the Bering Straits from Asia and drifted through the Americas from about 50,000 BC. Alternative theories of early migrations from across the Pacific and Atlantic have been rife since Thor Heyerdahl's raft expeditions in 1947 and 1969-1970. The earliest evidence of human presence has been found at various sites: in the Central Andes (with a radiocarbon date between 12000 and 9000 BC), northern Venezuela (11000 BC), southeast Brazil, south-central Chile and Argentine Patagonia (from at least 10000 BC). After the Pleistocene Ice Age, 8000-7000 BC, rising sea levels and climatic changes introduced new conditions as many mammal species became extinct and coastlands were drowned. A wide range of crops was brought into cultivation and camelids and guinea pigs were domesticated. It seems that people lived nomadically in small groups, mainly hunting and gathering but also cultivating some plants seasonally, until villages with effective agriculture began to appear between 2500-1500 BC. The earliest ceramic-making in the western hemisphere was thought to have come from what is now Colombia and Ecuador, around 4000 BC, but fragments of painted pottery were found near Santarém, Brazil, in 1991 with dates of 6000-5000 BC.

The coast of central Peru was where settled life began to develop most rapidly. The abundant wealth of marine life produced by the Humboldt Current, especially north of today's Lima, boosted population growth and settlement in this area. Around 2000 BC climatic change dried up the *lomas* ('fog meadows'), and drove sea shoals into deeper water. People turned more to farming and began to spread inland along river valleys. As sophisticated irrigation and canal systems were developed, farming productivity increased and communities had more time to devote to building and producing ceramics and textiles. The development of pottery also led to trade and cultural links with other communities.

The earliest buildings constructed by organized group labour were *huacas*, adobe platform mounds, centres of some cult or sacred power dating from the second millennium BC onwards. During this period, however, much more advanced architecture was being built at Kotosh, in the central Andes near Huánuco, now in Peru. Japanese archaeological excavations there in the 1960s revealed a temple with ornamental niches and friezes. Some of the earliest pottery was also found here, showing signs of influence from southern Ecuador and the tropical lowlands, adding weight to theories of Andean culture originating in the Amazon. Radiocarbon dates of some Kotosh remains are as early as 1850 BC.

Andean and Pacific coastal civilizations

Chavín and Sechín For the next 1,000 years or so up to c900 BC, communities grew and spread inland from the north coast and south along the north highlands. Farmers still lived in simple adobe or rough stone houses but built increasingly large and complex ceremonial centres. As farming became more productive and pottery more advanced, commerce grew and states began to develop throughout central and north-central Peru, with the associated signs of social structure and hierarchies.

Around 900 BC a new era was marked by the rise of two important centres; Chavín de Huántar in the central Andes and Sechín Alto, inland from Casma on the north coast, both now in Peru. The chief importance of Chavín de Huántar was not so much in its highly advanced architecture as in the influence of its cult, coupled with the artistic style of its ceramics and other artefacts. The founders of Chavín may have originated in the tropical lowlands, as some of its carved monoliths show representations of monkeys and felines.

The Chavín cult This was paralleled by the great advances made in this period in textile production and in some of the earliest examples of metallurgy. The origins of metallurgy have been attributed to some gold, silver and copper ornaments found in graves in Chongoyape, near Chiclayo, which show Chavín-style features. But earlier evidence has been discovered at Kuntur Wasi (some 120 km east of the coast at Pacasmayo) where 4,000-year old gold has been found, and in the Andahuaylas region, dating from 1800-900 BC. The religious symbolism of gold and other precious metals and stones is thought to have been an inspiration behind some of the beautiful artefacts found in the central Andean area.

The cultural brilliance of Chavín de Huántar was complemented by its contemporary, Sechín, with which may have combined forces, Sechín being the military power that spread the cultural word of Chavín. Their influence did not reach far to the south where the Paracas and Tiwanaku cultures held sway. The Chavín hegemony broke up around 500 BC, soon after which the Nazca culture began to bloom in southern Peru. This period, up to about AD 500, was a time of great social and cultural development. Sizable towns of 5-10,000 inhabitants grew on the south coast, populated by artisans, merchants and government and religious officials.

Paracas-Nazca Nazca origins are traced back to about the second century BC, to the Paracas Cavernas and Necropolis, on the coast in the national park near Pisco in Peru. The extreme dryness of the desert here has preserved remarkably the textiles and ceramics in the mummies' tombs excavated. The technical quality and stylistic variety in weaving and pottery rank them among the world's best, and many of the finest examples can be seen in the museums of Lima. The famous Nazca Lines are a feature of the region. Straight lines, abstract designs and outlines of animals are scratched in the dark desert surface forming a lighter contrast that can be seen clearly from the air. There are many theories of how and why the lines were made but no definitive explanation has yet been able to establish their place in South American history. There are similarities between the style of some of the line patterns and that of the pottery and textiles of the same period. In contrast to the quantity and quality of the Nazca artefacts found, relatively few major buildings belonging to this period have been uncovered in the southern desert. Alpaca hair found in Nazca textiles, however, indicates that there must have been strong trade links with highland people.

Moche culture Nazca's contemporaries on the north coast were the militaristic Moche who, from about AD 100-800, built up an empire whose traces stretch from Piura in the north to Huarmey, in the south. The Moche built their capital outside present day Trujillo. The huge pyramid temples of the Huaca del Sol and Huaca de la Luna mark the remains of this city. Moche roads and system of way stations are thought to have been an early inspiration for the Inca network. The Moche increased the coastal population with intensive irrigation projects. Skilful engineering works were carried out, such as the La Cumbre canal, still in use today, and the Ascope aqueduct, both on the Chicama River. The Moche's greatest achievement, however, was its artistic genius. Exquisite ornaments in gold, silver and precious stones were made by its craftsmen. Moche pottery progressed through five stylistic periods, most notable for the stunningly lifelike portrait vases. A wide variety of everyday scenes were created in naturalistic ceramics, telling us more about Moche life than is known about other earlier cultures, and perhaps used by them as 'visual aids' to compensate for the lack of a written language. A spectacular discovery of a Moche royal tomb at Sipán, made in February 1987 by Walter Alva, director of the Brüning Archaeological Museum, Lambayeque, included semi- precious stones brought from Chile and Argentina, and seashells from Ecuador. The Moche were great navigators.

The cause of the collapse of the Moche Empire around AD 600-700 is unknown, but it may have been started by a 30-year drought at the end of the sixth century, followed by one of the periodic El Niño flash floods (identified by meteorologists from ice thickness in the Andes) and finished by the encroaching forces of the Huari Empire. The decline of the Moche signalled a general tipping of the balance of power in Peru from the north coast to the south sierra.

Huari-Tiwanaku The ascendant Huari-Tiwanaku movement, from AD 600-1000, combined the religious cult of the Tiwanaku site in the Titicaca basin, with the military dynamism of the Huari, based in the central highlands. The two cultures developed independently but they are generally thought to have merged compatibly. Up until their own demise around AD 1440, the Huari-Tiwanaku had spread their empire and influence across much of south Peru, north Bolivia and Argentina. They made considerable gains in art and technology, building roads, terraces and irrigation canals across the country. The Huari-Tiwanaku ran their empire with efficient labour and administrative systems that were later adopted by the Incas. Labour tribute for state projects practised by the Moche were further developed. But the empire could not contain regional kingdoms who began to fight for land and power. As control broke down, rivalry and coalitions emerged, the system collapsed and the scene was set for the rise of the Incas.

Chachapoyas and Chimú cultures After the decline of the Huari Empire, the unity that had been imposed on the Andes was broken. A new stage of autonomous regional or local political organizations began. Among the cultures corresponding to this period were the Chachapoyas in northern highlands (see page 1158) and the Chimú. The Chachapoyas people were not so much an empire as a loose-knit 'confederation of ethnic groups with no recognized capital' (Morgan Davis 'Chachapoyas: The Cloud People', Ontario, 1988). But the culture did develop into an advanced society with great skill in road and monument building. Their fortress at Kuelap was known as the most impregnable in the Peruvian Andes. The Chimú culture had two centres. To the north was Lambayeque, near Chiclayo, while to the south, in the Moche valley near present-day Trujillo, was the great adobe walled city of Chan Chán. Covering 20 sq km, this was the largest pre-Hispanic Peruvian city. Chimú has been classified as a despotic state that based its power on wars of conquest. Rigid social stratification existed and power rested in the hands of the great lord *Siquic* and the lord *Alaec*. These lords were followed in social scale by a group of urban couriers who enjoyed a certain degree of economic power. At the bottom were the peasants and slaves. In 1450, the Chimú kingdom was conquered by the Inca Túpac Yupanqui, the son and heir of the Inca ruler Pachacuti Inca Yupanqui.

Cultures of the northern Andes What is today Ecuador was a densely populated region with a variety of peoples. One of the most important of these was the **Valdivia culture** (3500-1500 BC) on the coast, from which remains of buildings and earthenware figures have been found. A rich mosaic of cultures developed in the period 500 BC to AD 500, after which integration of groups occurred. In the mid-15th century, the relentless expansion of the Inca empire reached Ecuador. The **Cañaris** resisted until 1470 and the Quitu/Caras were defeated in 1492. Further north, most of the peoples who occupied Colombia were primitive hunters or nomad agriculturists, but one part of the country, the high basins of the Eastern Cordillera, was densely occupied by **Chibcha Indians** who had become sedentary farmers. Their staple foods were maize and the potato, and they had no domestic animal save the dog; the use they could make of the land was therefore limited. Other cultures present in Colombia in the pre-Columbian era were the **Tayrona, Quimbaya, Sinú** and **Calima**. Exhibits of theirs and the Chibcha (Muisca) Indians' goldwork can be seen at the Gold Museum in Bogotá and other cities.

Southern Andes Although there was some influence in southern Bolivia, northern Chile and northern Argentina from cultures such as Tiwanaku, most of the southern Andes was an area of autonomous peoples, probably living in fortified settlements by the time the Incas arrived in the mid-15th century. The conquerors from Peru moved south to the Río Maule in Chile where they encountered the fierce **Mapuches** (Araucanians) who halted their advance. Archaeological evidence from the Amazon basin and Brazil is more scanty than from the Andes or Pacific because the materials used for house building, clothing and decoration were perishable and did not survive the warm, humid conditions of the jungle. Ceramics have been found on Marajó island at the mouth of the Amazon while on the coast much evidence comes from huge shell mounds, called *sambaquis*. Although structured societies developed and population was large, no political groupings of the scale of those of the Andes formed. The Incas made few inroads into the Amazon so it was the arrival of the Portuguese in 1500 which initiated the greatest change on the Atlantic side of the continent.

The Inca Dynasty

The origins of the Inca Dynasty are shrouded in mythology and shaky evidence. The best known story reported by the Spanish chroniclers talks about Manco Cápac and his sister rising out of Lake Titicaca, created by the sun as divine founders of a chosen race. This was in approximately AD 1200. Over the next 300 years the small tribe grew to supremacy as leaders of the largest empire ever known in the Americas, the four territories of Tawantinsuyo, united by as the umbilicus of the Universe (the four quarters of Tawantinsuyo, all radiating out from Cuzco, were Chinchaysuyo, north and northwest; Cuntisuyo, south and west; Collasuyo, south and east; Antisuyo, east).

At its peak, just before the Spanish Conquest, the Inca Empire stretched from the Río Maule in central Chile, north to the present Ecuador-Colombia border, contained most of Ecuador, Peru, west Bolivia, north Chile and northwest Argentina. The area was roughly equivalent to France, Belgium, Holland, Luxembourg, Italy and Switzerland combined, 980,000 sq km. For a brief description of **Inca Society**, see under Cuzco. The first Inca ruler,

Manco Cápac, moved to the fertile Cuzco region, and established Cuzco as his capital. Successive generations of rulers were fully occupied with local conquests of rivals, such as the Colla and Lupaca to the south, and the Chanca to the northwest. At the end of Inca Viracocha's reign the hated Chanca were finally defeated, largely thanks to the heroism of one of his sons, Pachacuti Inca Yupanqui, who was subsequently crowned as the new ruler.

From the start of Pachacuti's own reign in 1438, imperial expansion grew in earnest. With the help of his son and heir, Topa Inca, territory was conquered from the Titicaca basin south into Chile, and all the north and central coast down to the Lurin Valley. In 1460-71, the Incas also laid siege to the Chimú. Typical of the Inca method of government, some of the Chimú skills were assimilated into their own political and administrative system, and some Chimú nobles were even given positions in Cuzco.

Perhaps the pivotal event in Inca history came in 1527 with the death of the ruler, Huayna Cápac. Civil war broke out in the confusion over his rightful successor. One of his legitimate sons, Huáscar, ruled the southern part of the empire from Cuzco. Atahualpa, Huáscar's half-brother, governed Quito, the capital of Chinchasuyo. In 1532, soon after Atahualpa had won the civil war, Francisco Pizarro arrived in Tumbes with 179 *conquistadores*, many on horseback. Atahualpa's army was marching south, probably for the first time, when he clashed with Pizarro at Cajamarca. **Francisco Pizarro**'s only chance against the formidable imperial army he encountered at Cajamarca was a bold stroke. He drew Atahualpa into an ambush, slaughtered his guards, promised him liberty if a certain room were filled with treasure, and finally killed him on the pretext that an Inca army was on its way to free him. Pushing on to Cuzco, he was at first hailed as the executioner of a traitor: Atahualpa had ordered the death of Huáscar in 1533, while himself captive of Pizarro, and his victorious generals were bringing the defeated Huáscar to see his half-brother. Panic followed when the *conquistadores* set about sacking the city, and they fought off with difficulty an attempt by Manco Inca to recapture Cuzco in 1536.

The Spanish conquest

Pizarro's arrival in Peru had been preceded by Columbus' landfall on the Paria Peninsula (Venezuela) on 5 August 1498 and Spanish reconaissance of the Pacific coast in 1522. Permanent Spanish settlement was established at Santa Marta (Colombia) in 1525 and Cartagena was founded in 1533. Gonzalo Jiménez de Quesada conquered the Chibcha kingdom and founded Bogotá in 1538. Pizarro's lieutenant, Sebastián de Belalcázar, was sent north through Ecuador; he captured Quito with Diego de Almagro in 1534. Gonzalo Pizarro, Francisco's brother, took over control of Quito in 1538 and, during his exploration of the Amazon lowlands, he sent Francisco de Orellana to prospect downriver. Orellana did not return, but drifted down the Amazon, finally reaching the river's mouth in 1542, the first European to cross the continent in this way. Belalcázar pushed north, founding Pasto, Cali and Popayán (Colombia) in 1536, arriving in Bogotá in 1538. Meanwhile, wishing to secure his communications with Spain, Pizarro founded Lima, near the ocean, as his capital in 1535. The same year Diego de Almagro set out to conquer Chile. Unsuccessful, he returned to Peru, quarrelled with Pizarro, and in 1538 fought a pitched battle with Pizarro's men at the Salt Pits, near Cuzco. He was defeated and put to death. Pizarro, who had not been at the battle, was assassinated in his palace in Lima by Almagro's son three years later. In 1541, Pedro de Valdivia founded Santiago de Chile after a renewed attempt to conquer Chile. Like the Incas before them, the Spaniards were unable to master the Mapuches; Valdivia was killed in 1553 and a defensive barrier along the Río Biobío had to be built in order to protect the colony.

Since 1516 European seafarers had visited the Río de la Plata, first Juan de Solís, then Sebastian Cabot and his rival Diego García in 1527. An expedition led by Pedro de Mendoza founded Buenos Aires in 1536, but it was abandoned in 1541. Mendoza sent Juan de Ayolas up the Río Paraná to reach Peru from the east. It is not known for certain what happened to Ayolas, but his lieutenant Domingo Martínez de Irala founded Asunción on the Paraguay in 1537. This was the base from which the Spaniards relaunched their conquest of the Río de la Plata and Buenos Aires was refounded in 1580.

Treasure hunt As Spanish colonization built itself around new cities, the *conquistadores* set about finding the wealth which had lured them to South America in the first place. The great prize came in 1545 when the hill of silver at Potosí (Bolivia) was discovered. Other

66 99 Given impetus by Napoleon's invasion of Spain in 1808, Simón Bolívar, El Libertador, led a revolution in the north and José de San Martín, with his Army of the Andes, led an uprising through Argentina and Chile. Both converged on Peru.

mining centres grew up and the trade routes to supply them and carry out the riches were established. The Spanish crown soon imposed political and administrative jurisdiction over its new empire, replacing the power of the *conquistadores* with that of governors and bureaucrats. The Viceroyalty of Peru became the major outlet for the wealth of the Americas, but each succeeding representative of the Kingdom of Spain was faced with the twofold threat of subduing the Inca successor state of Vilcabamba, north of Cuzco, and unifying the fierce Spanish factions. Francisco de Toledo (appointed 1568) solved both problems during his 14 years in office: Vilcabamba was crushed in 1572 and the last reigning Inca, Túpac Amaru, put to deCuscoath. For the next 200 years the Viceroys closely followed Toledo's system, if not his methods. The Major Government – the Viceroy, the *Audiencia* (High Court), and *corregidores* (administrators) – ruled through the Minor Government – Indian chiefs put in charge of large groups of natives: a rough approximation to the original Inca system.

Towards independence

The Indians of Peru rose in 1780, under the leadership of an Inca noble who called himself Túpac Amaru II. He and many of his lieutenants were captured and put to death under torture at Cuzco. Another Indian leader in revolt suffered the same fate in 1814, but this last flare-up had the sympathy of many of the locally born Spanish, who resented their status: inferior to the Spaniards born in Spain, the refusal to give them any but the lowest offices, the high taxation imposed by the home government, and the severe restrictions upon trade with any country but Spain. This was a complaint common to all parts of the Spanish empire and it fostered a twin-pronged independence movement. Given impetus by Napoleon's invasion of Spain in 1808, Simón Bolívar, El Libertador, led a revolution in the north and José de San Martín, with his Army of the Andes, led an uprising through Argentina and Chile. Both converged on Peru.

Bolívar, born in Venezuela in 1783, was involved in the early struggle to free the region from Spanish rule. In 1811 Venezuela declared itself an independent republic, only to be defeated by Spain in 1812. Bolívar led a new revolt in 1813, which was crushed in 1815. He went into exile in Jamaica and Haiti, to return in 1816 with a new army which, in a bold move, he led over the Andes from Venezuela to liberate Nueva Granada (as Colombia was called) at the Battle of Boyacá in 1819. He proclaimed a new republic, Gran Colombia, taking in Colombia, Venezuela and Ecuador. Venezuela was freed at the Battle of Carabobo in 1821.

San Martín's Argentine troops, convoyed from Chile under the protection of the English admiral, Lord Cochrane, landed in southern Peru on 7 September 1820. San Martín proclaimed Peruvian independence at Lima on 28 July 1821, though most of the country was still in the hands of the Viceroy, José de La Serna. Bolívar sent Antonio José de Sucre to Ecuador where, on 24 May 1822, he gained a victory over La Serna at Pichincha. San Martín, after a meeting with Bolívar at Guayaquil, left for Argentina and a self-imposed exile in France, while Bolívar and Sucre completed the conquest of Peru by defeating La Serna at the battle of Junín (6 August 1824) and the decisive battle of Ayacucho (9 December 1824). For over a year there was a last stand in the Real Felipe fortress at Callao by the Spanish troops under General Rodil before they capitulated on 22 January 1826. Bolívar was invited to stay in Peru, but in 1826 he left for Colombia where he tried to hold Gran Colombia together as a single state. He failed as internal divisions and political ambitions pulled the three new republics apart. While heading for exile, Bolívar died in 1830.

The Jesuits

Between 1609, when they built their first reducción or mission in the region of Guaíra in present day Brazil, and 1767, when they were expelled from Spanish America, the Jesuits founded about 50 missions around the upper reaches of the Ríos Paraná, Paraguay and Uruguay. In 1627, the northern missions around Guaíra were attacked by slave-hunting Bandeirantes from São Paulo, forcing them to flee southwards. Some 10,000 converts, led by their priests, floated 700 rafts down the Río Parapanema into the Paraná, only to find their route blocked by the Guaíra Falls. Pushing on for eight days through dense forest, they built new boats below the Falls and continued their journey to reestablish their missions 725 km from their original homes.

Efficiently organized and strictly laid out, the missions prospered, growing indigenous and European crops and herding cattle. Their success and economic power attracted many enemies, from the Spanish crown to local landowners. When, in 1750, Spain and Portugal settled their South American border dispute, seven missions were placed under Portuguese control. This the Jesuits resisted with arms, fuelling further the suspicion of the order's excessive power. Under highest secrecy, King Carlos III sent instructions to South America in 1767 to expel the Jesuits. 2,000 were shipped to Italy, their property was auctioned and their schools and colleges were taken over by the Franciscans and Dominicans. By the early 19th century, many of the missions had fallen into disrepair.

Only four missions show signs of their former splendour: San Ignacio Miní in Argentina; Jesús and Trinidad in Paraguay; and São Miguel in Brazil.

Brazil: from colony to independence

The Portuguese, Pedro Álvares Cabral, landed in Brazil on 22 April, 1500. He left after a week, shortly followed by Amérigo Vespucci who had been sent to explore further. The first system of government adopted by the Portuguese was a Capitania, a kind of feudal principality – there were 13 of them, but these were replaced in 1572 by a Viceroyalty. In the same year it was decided to divide the colony into two, north and south, with capitals at Salvador and Rio; it was not until 1763 that Rio became the sole capital.

Three centuries under the paternal eye of Portugal had ill-prepared the colonists for independent existence, except for the experience of Dutch invasion (1624 in Salvador, and 1630-1654 in Recife). The colonists ejected the Dutch from Brazil with little help from Portugal, and Brazilians date the birth of their national sentiment from these events. Growing resentment against Portuguese government and trade intervention led to the **Inconfidência**, the first revolution, masterminded by **Tiradentes** with 11 other citizens of Minas Gerais. They were unsuccessful (Tiradentes was executed), but when France invaded Portugal in 1807, King João VI was shipped to safety in Brazil, escorted by the British navy. Rio was temporarily declared the capital of the Portuguese Empire. The British, as a price for their assistance in the Portuguese war, forced the opening of Brazil's ports to non-Portuguese trade. King João VI returned to the mother country in 1821, leaving his son, the young Pedro, as Regent. Pedro refused to return control of Brazil to the Portuguese Côrtes (parliament), and on 13 May 1822, by popular request, he agreed to stay and assumed the title of 'Perpetual Defender and Protector of Brazil'. On 7 September he declared Brazil's independence with the cry 'Independence or Death' by the Rio Ipiranga; on 12 October he was proclaimed the constitutional emperor of Brazil, and on 1 December he was crowned in Rio.

Post-independence history

Argentina

Independence from Spain

In 1778, Spain finally permitted Buenos Aires to conduct overseas trade. Before that it was controlled by the Viceroy in Lima and was merely a military outpost for Spain to confront the Portuguese settlement at Colonia, across the estuary. Its population then was only 24,203 and its main activity was smuggling. Following Spain's alliance with Napoleon, Britain attacked Buenos Aires in 1806 and again in 1807. The defeat of these attacks, known as the Reconquista, greatly increased the confidence of the *porteños* (the name given to those born in Buenos Aires) to deal with all comers, including the mother-country. On 25 May 1810, the *cabildo* of Buenos Aires deposed the viceroy and announced that it was now governing on behalf of King Ferdinand VII, then a captive of Napoleon. Six years later, in July 1816, when Buenos Aires was threatened by invasion from Peru and blockaded by a Spanish fleet in the Río de la Plata, a national congress held at Tucumán declared independence. The declaration was given reality by José de San Martín, who marched an Argentine army across the Andes to free Chile and embarked his forces for Peru, where he captured Lima, the first step in the liberation of Peru.

The formation of the republic

When San Martín returned home, it was to find the country rent by conflict between the central government and the provinces. On the one hand stood the Unitarist party, bent on central control; on the other the Federalist party, insisting on local autonomy. The latter had for members the great *caudillos* (the large landowners backed by the *gauchos*) suspicious of the cities. One of their leaders, Juan Manuel de Rosas, took control in 1829. During his second term as Governor of Buenos Aires he asked for and was given extraordinary powers. The result was a 17-year reign of terror which became an international scandal. When he began a blockade of Asunción in 1845, Britain and France promptly countered with a three-year blockade of Buenos Aires. In 1851 Justo José de Urquiza, Governor of Entre Ríos, one of his old henchmen, organized a triple alliance of Brazil, Uruguay, and the Argentine opposition to overthrow him. He was defeated in 1852 at Caseros, a few kilometres from Buenos Aires, and fled to England. Rosas had started his career as a Federalist; once in power he was a Unitarist. His downfall meant the triumph of federalism. In 1853 a federal system was finally incorporated in the constitution, but Buenos Aires refused to join the new federation until the city, led by Bartolomé Mitre, was finally defeated by the federal forces in 1880. Buenos Aires was consequently made into a special federal territory. The conquest at about the same time of all the Indian tribes of the pampas and the south by a young colonel, Julio A Roca, was to make possible the final supremacy of Buenos Aires over all rivals.

20th century

From 1916 to 1930 the Unión Cívica Radical (founded in 1890) held power, under the leadership of Hipólito Yrigoyen and Marcelo T de Alvear, but lost it to the 1930 military uprising. Though seriously affected by the 1930s world depression, Argentina's rich soil and educated population had made it one of the world's 10 wealthiest countries, but this wealth was unevenly distributed, and political methods used by the conservatives and their military associates in the 1930s denied the middle and working classes any effective share in their own country's wealth and government.

Peronism and its legacy

A series of military coups in 1943-44 led to the rise of Col Juan Domingo Perón, basing his power on an alliance between the army and labour; his contacts with labour were greatly assisted by his charismatic wife Eva (since commemorated in the rock-opera and film *Evita*). In 1946 Perón was elected President. His government is chiefly remembered by many Argentines for improving the living conditions of the workers. Especially in its early years the government was strongly nationalistic, but also intolerant of opposition parties and independent newspapers. Although Perón was re-elected in 1951, his government soon ran into trouble: economic problems led to the introduction of a wage freeze, upsetting the labour unions, which were the heart of Peronist support; the death of Evita in 1952 was another blow. In September 1955 a military coup unseated

Perón, who went into exile. Perón's legacy dominated the period 1955-1973: society was bitterly divided between Peronists and anti-Peronists; the economy struggled; the armed forces, constantly involved in politics, were also divided. In a climate of tension and guerrilla-inspired violence, the military bowed out in 1973. Elections were won by the Peronist candidate, Hector Campora. Perón returned from exile in Madrid to resume as President in October 1973, but died on 1 July 1974, leaving the Presidency to his widow, Vice-President María Estela Martínez de Perón (his third wife). The subsequent chaotic political situation, including guerrilla warfare, led to her deposition by a military junta, led by Gen Jorge Videla in March 1976.

The Dirty War and after

Under the military, guerrilla warfare and the other features of dissidence were repressed with great brutality: about 9,000 people (although human rights organizations believe the total is at least double this) disappeared without trace during the so-called 'dirty war'. Confidence in the military ebbed when their economic policies began to go sour in 1980. In 1982-83 pressure for a democratic restoration grew particularly after the Falklands (Islas Malvinas) War with Great Britain in 1982, when Argentina invaded the South Atlantic islands run by the British, in an attempt to reclaim them. General elections on 30 October 1983 were won by the Unión Cívica Radical (UCR), with Dr Raúl Alfonsín as president. During 1985 Generals Videla, Viola and Galtieri were sentenced to long terms of imprisonment for their parts in the 'dirty war'.

Menem and his legacy

When Alfonsín was defeated by Dr Carlos Saúl Menem of the Partido Justicialista (Peronists) in May 1989, Alfonsín stepped down early because of economic instability. Strained relations between the Peronist Government and the military led to several rebellions, which President Menem attempted to appease by pardoning the imprisoned Generals. His popularity among civilians declined, but in 1991-92 the Economy Minister Domingo Cavallo succeeded in restoring confidence in the economy and government. The key was a Convertibility Law, passed in 1991, fixing the peso against the US dollar, and permitting the Central Bank to print local currency only when backed by gold or hard currency. This achieved price stability; the annual average growth of consumer prices fell from 3,080% in 1989 to 3.9% in 1994 and remained in single figures until 2001. Having succeeded in changing the constitution to permit the re-election of the president for a second term of four years, Menem was returned to office in 1995 by an electorate favouring stability. But his renewed popularity was short lived: unemployment remained high and corruption unrestrained. Menem failed to force another constitutional change to allow him to stand for a third term, but his rivalry with Peronist candidate, Eduardo Duhalde, was one of the factors behind the victory of Fernando de la Rúa of Alianza.

De la Rúa pledged to reduce joblessness, provide better healthcare and end corruption, but within a year was facing scandals and a series of economic crises. The peso became increasingly overvalued, but the government refused to modify the Convertibility Law. By the end of 2001, the country was in deep recession, unemployment was 20% and the government had practically run out of money to service its US$132 billion debt. As faith in the banking system and the government nosedived, Argentines started to take back their savings from banks; on 30 November 2001 alone, US$2 billion were withdrawn. The government imposed a US$250 weekly limit on cash withdrawals, leading to rioting, looting and 27 deaths, which eventually forced de la Rúa out of office. Three subsequent presidents resigned. On 2 January 2002, Eduardo Duhalde was sworn in as Argentina's fifth president in two weeks. The mammoth task of dragging the economy out of recession and restoring confidence could not be achieved before elections in April 2003, although positive steps were taken. The devaluation of the peso in 2002, which saw the real value of Argentines' savings plummet, did return the trade balance to surplus. Agriculture and tourism saw dramatic improvements and there was a slight fall in joblessness. Nevertheless, over half the population was living in poverty, desperate for work and food, many surviving thanks to barter clubs. Instead of a display of unity in the crisis, however, the Peronist party pulled itself apart prior to the elections, with the governor of Santa Cruz, Néstor Kirchner, running against ex-president Menem. In the first round, both polled more votes than liberal economist Ricardo López Murphy, but Menem, facing heavy defeat in the run-off, pulled out of the race at the last moment. This gave Kirchner the presidency but with the electoral support of just 22% of the vote from the first round (compared with 24% for Menem). By October 2005, Kirchner had gained sufficient popular support to win a substantial majority in mid-term congressional elections. At the same time, the economy recovered from a decline of 11% in 2002 to growth of an average of 9% between 2003 and 2006 (8.5% in that year). Symbolic of that upturn was the cancellation of its US$9.8 billion debt facility, thus severing all ties with the IMF. Stresses remained, however. Inflation, cut from 26% in 2002 to below 5% in 2004, increased again to 10% in 2005 and 2006. President Kirchner urged businesses not to increase prices. While unemployment had been reduced by late 2006 to under 10%, poverty and uneven distribution of wealth remained. Presidential elections were due on 28 October 2007. Kirchner decided not to run again but his wife, Cristina Fernández de Kirchner, was nominated as a candidate. Early indications were that she would win.

Bolivia

Coups, mines and wars

Bolivian politics have been the most turbulent in Latin America. Although in the 19th century the army was very small, officers were key figures in power-struggles, often backing different factions of the landowning elite. Between 1840 and 1849 there were 65 attempted *coups d'état*. The longest lasting government of the 19th century was that of Andrés Santa Cruz (1829-1839), but when he tried to unite Bolivia with Peru in 1836, Chile and Argentina intervened to overthrow him. After the War of the Pacific (1879-1883) there was greater stability, but opposition to the political dominance of the city of Sucre culminated in a revolt in 1899 led by business groups from La Paz and the tin-mining areas, as a result of which La Paz became the centre of government.

The Bolivian economy depended on tin exports during the 20th century. Railway construction and the demand for tin in Europe and the USA (particularly in wartime) led to a mining boom after 1900. By the 1920s the industry was dominated by three entrepreneurs, Simón Patiño, Mauricio Hochschild and the Aramayo family, who greatly influenced national politics. The importance of mining and the harsh conditions in the isolated mining camps of the Altiplano led to the rise of a militant miners movement.

Since independence Bolivia has suffered continual losses of territory, partly because of communications difficulties and the central government's inability to control distant provinces. The dispute between Chile and Peru over the nitrate-rich Atacama desert in 1879 soon dragged in Bolivia, which had signed a secret alliance with Peru in 1873. Following its rapid defeat in the War of the Pacific Bolivia lost her coastal provinces. As compensation Chile later agreed to build the railway between Arica and La Paz. When Brazil annexed the rich Acre Territory in 1903, Bolivia was compensated by another railway, but this Madeira-Mamoré line never reached its destination, Riberalta, and proved of little use; it was closed in 1972. There was not even an unbuilt railway to compensate Bolivia for its next loss. A long-running dispute with Paraguay over the Chaco erupted into war in 1932. Defeat in the so-called Chaco War (1932-1935) resulted in the loss of three quarters of the Chaco (see page 1497).

Modern Bolivia

The Chaco War was a turning point in Bolivian history, increasing the political influence of the army which in 1936 seized power for the first time since the War of the Pacific. Defeat bred nationalist resentment among junior army officers who had served in the Chaco and also led to the creation of a nationalist party, the Movimiento Nacionalista Revolucionario (MNR) led by Víctor Paz Estenssoro. Their anger was directed against the mine owners and the leaders who had controlled Bolivian politics. Between 1936 and 1946 a series of unstable military governments followed. This decade witnessed the apparent suicide in 1939 of one president (Germán Busch) and the public hanging in 1946 of another (Gualberto Villarroel). After a period of civilian government, the 1951 elections were won by the MNR but a coup prevented the party from taking office.

The 1952 revolution In April 1952 the military government was overthrown by a popular revolution in which armed miners and peasants played a major role. Paz Estenssoro became president and his MNR government nationalized the mines, introduced universal suffrage and began the break-up and redistribution of large estates. The economy, however, deteriorated, partly because of the hostility of the US government. Paz's successor, Hernán Siles Zuazo (president from 1956 to 1964), a hero of the 1952 revolution, was forced to take unpopular measures to stabilize the economy. Paz was re-elected president in 1960 and 1964, but shortly afterwards in November 1964 he was overthrown by his vice president, Gral René Barrientos, who relied on the support of the army and the peasants to defeat the miners.

Military rule in the 1970s The death of Barrientos in an air crash in 1969 was followed by three brief military governments. The third, led by Gral Torres, pursued left-wing policies which alarmed many army officers and business leaders. In August 1971 Torres was overthrown by Hugo Banzer, a right-wing colonel who outlawed political parties and trade unions. After Banzer was forced to call elections in 1978, a series of short-lived military governments overruled elections in 1978 and 1979 giving victories to Siles Zuazo. One of these, led by Gral García Meza (1980-1981) was notable for its brutal treatment of opponents and its links to the cocaine trade, which led to its isolation by the international community.

Return to democracy In August 1982 the military returned to barracks and Dr Siles Zuazo assumed the Presidency in a leftist coalition government with support from the communists and trade unions. Under this regime inflation spiralled out of control. The elections of 1985 were won again by Víctor Paz Estenssoro, who imposed a rigorous programme to stabilize the economy. In the elections of 1989, Gonzalo Sánchez de Lozada of the MNR (chief architect of the stabilization programme) failed to win enough votes to prevent Congress choosing Jaime Paz Zamora of the Movimiento de la Izquierda Revolucionaria (MIR), who came third in the elections, as president in August 1989. Paz had made an unlikely alliance with the former military dictator, Hugo Banzer (Acción Democrática Nacionalista).

Although Gonzalo Sánchez de Lozada just failed to gain the required 51% majority to win the presidency in the 1993 elections, the other candidates recognized his victory. The main element in his policies was the capitalization of state assets, in which investors agreed to inject fresh capital into a chosen state-owned company in return for a 50% controlling stake. The other 50% of the shares were distributed to all Bolivians over 18 via a private pension fund scheme. As the programme gained pace, so did opposition to it. In the elections of 1 June 1997, Banzer and the ADN secured 22% of the vote and ADN became the dominant party in a new coalition with three other parties. In his first two years in office, Banzer pursued economic austerity and the US-backed policy of eradicating coca production. In 2000, however, economic hardship in rural areas, together with unemployment and anger at both the coca eradication and a plan to raise water rates led to violent protests and road blocks in many parts of the country. With the country's economic and social problems still severe, President Banzer was forced to resign in August 2001 because of cancer. His replacement, Vice-President Jorge Quiroga, had just a year left of Banzer's term to serve before new elections were held, in which a coalition led by former president Sánchez de Lozada won an extremely narrow victory. The runner-up was Evo Morales, leader of the coca growers, who campaigned for a restoration of traditional coca production and an end to free market reforms.

From the outset, Sánchez de Lozada faced economic crisis. In February 2003, mass demonstrations turned into riots over tax increases and the president was forced to flee the presidential palace in an ambulance. A week later, the cabinet resigned, the tax hikes were cancelled, police were awarded a pay rise and Sánchez de Lozada vowed to forego his salary. This failed to ease tension and in September a protest over the sale of Bolivian gas to the US became a national uprising against Sánchez de Lozada's free-market policies. Weeks of violent street protests led to Sánchez de Lozada's resignation on 17 October 2003. Vice president Carlos Mesa took over the presidency, but he managed to survive only until June 2005, when Supreme Court President Eduardo Rodríguez was appointed interim president until new elections on 18 December 2005. Evo Morales of Movimiento al Socialismo (MAS), self-styled "United States' worst nightmare", managed to beat ex-president Quiroga by a clear majority.

Three main issues precipitated Mesa's demise: the continued opposition to gas sales abroad, linked with demands to renationalize the gas and oil industries; mass protests by the inhabitants of El Alto, calling for a more equal society and a new constituent assembly; and pressure from the business lobby in Santa Cruz for more autonomy for their region and a greater share of gas revenues. The first two, plus his support for coca growers, precipitated Morales' rise to power. Morales soon announced elections to a new constituent assembly and, in May 2006, sent troops into the gas fields. This latter move provoked foreign hydrocarbon companies to renegotiate their contracts with Bolivia, but progress in the constituent assembly was nothing like as speedy. From the outset, Morales' party and its allies disagreed with the opposition over the basic voting principles for approving each provision, making an August 2007 completion unlikely. This magnified Bolivia's basic division between the indigenous majority and the wealthy eastern lowlands. In late 2006 and early 2007, violent clashes occurred throughout the country over this issue and in Cochabamba campesinos confronted wealthy city dwellers and students over the position of the elected mayor, Manfred Reyes Villa's support for regional autonomy from the central government. Meanwhile, Morales' overall popularity remained unshaken.

Brazil

Imperial Brazil

Dom Pedro the First had the misfortune to be faced by a secession movement in the north, to lose the Banda Oriental (today Uruguay) and to get too involved in his complicated love life. Finally, he abdicated as the result of a military revolt in 1831, leaving his five-year-old son, Dom Pedro the Second, in the hands of a regent, as ruler. On 23 July 1840, the lad, though only 15, was proclaimed of age. Dom Pedro the Second, a strong liberal at heart, promoted education, increased communications, developed agriculture, stamped on corruption and encouraged immigration from Europe. Under his rule the war with the dictator López of Paraguay ended in Brazilian victory. Finally, he declared that he would rather lose his crown than allow slavery to continue, and on 13 May 1888, it was finally abolished by his daughter, Princess Isabel, who was acting as Regent during his temporary absence.

There is little doubt that it was this measure that cost him his throne. Many plantation owners, who had been given no compensation, turned against the Emperor; they were supported by elements in the army and navy, who felt that the Emperor had not given due heed to their interests since the Paraguayan War. On 15 November 1889, the Republic was proclaimed and the Emperor sailed for Europe. Two years later he died in a second-rate hotel in Paris, after steadfastly refusing a pension from the conscience-stricken revolutionaries. At the time of the first centenary of independence in 1922 the imperial family was allowed to return to Brazil, and the body of Dom Pedro was brought back and buried in the cathedral at Petrópolis.

From Republic to dictatorship

The history of the 'Old Republic' (1889-1930), apart from the first 10 years which saw several monarchist rebellions, was comparatively uneventful, a time of expansion and increasing prosperity. Brazil declared war on Germany during both wars and Brazilian troops fought in the Italian campaign in 1944-1945. In 1930 a revolution headed by Getúlio Vargas, Governor of Rio Grande do Sul, who was to become known as 'the Father of the Poor', deposed President Wáshington Luís. Vargas assumed executive power first as provisional president and then as dictator. He was forced to resign in October 1945. In 1946 a liberal republic was restored and the following 18 years saw considerable economic development and social advance.

An increase in government instability and corruption prompted the military to intervene in civil affairs. From March 1964 until March 1985, the military governed Brazil using political repression and torture, yet achieving great economic success (up to 1980). Between 1964 and 1974 average growth was 10% a year, but the divide between rich and poor widened. Labour leaders were oppressed, dissenters were jailed and *favelas* mushroomed. Political reform did not occur until 1980 and free elections were not held until 1989.

Return to democracy

In January 1985 a civilian, Tancredo Neves, representing a broad opposition to the military régime, was elected President by the electoral college introduced under the military's 1967 constitution. He was unable, because of illness, to take office: the vice-president elect, Sr José Sarney, was sworn in as acting President in March 1985, and in April became President on Sr Neves' death. After complete revision by a Constituent Assembly in 1987-1988, Brazil's new constitution of 1988 permitted direct presidential elections in November 1989. These were won by Fernando Collor de Melo, of the small Partido da Reconstrução Nacional, who narrowly defeated Luis Inácio da Silva (Lula), of the Workers Party (PT). Just over half-way through his five-year term, Collor was suspended from office after a landslide congressional vote to impeach him over his involvement in corruption. He avoided impeachment by resigning on 29 December 1992. Vice-president Itamar Franco took over, but had scant success in tackling poverty and inflation until the introduction of an anti-inflation package which introduced the real as the new currency.

Recent developments

The success of the **real** plan was the principal reason for its architect, finance minister Fernando Henrique Cardoso, defeating Lula in the presidential elections of October 1994. Throughout 1997 and 1998, the financial crisis in Asia threatened Brazil's currency and economic stability. Cardoso was therefore obliged to introduce policies which, at the cost of slowing down economic growth, would prevent an upsurge in inflation and a devaluation of the currency. At

The Bandeirantes

Reviled in some quarters for their appalling treatment of Indians, revered in others for their determination and willingness to withstand extreme hardship in the pursuit of their goals, the bandeirantes are an indispensible element in the formation of Brazil.

The Portuguese knew that South America held great riches; their Spanish rivals were shipping vast quantities back to Europe from Peru. Legends proliferated of mountains of precious stones, golden lakes and other marvels, also of terrifying places, all in the mysterious interior. Regardless of the number of expeditions sent into the sertão which returned empty-handed, or failed to return at all, there was always the promise of silver, emeralds or other jewels to lure the adventurous beyond the coast.

The one thing that Brazil had in abundance was Indians. Throughout the colony there was a demand for slaves to work the plantations and farms, especially in the early 17th century when Portugal temporarily lost its African possession of Angola.

The men who settled in São Paulo proved themselves expert at enslaving Indians. Without official sanction, and certainly not blessed by the Jesuits, these adventurers formed themselves into expeditions which would set out often for years at a time, to capture slaves for the internal market. The Guaraní Indians who had been organized into reducciones by the Jesuits around the Río Paraguay were the top prize and there developed an intense rivalry between the bandeirantes and the Jesuits. The priests regarded the Paulistas as murderous and inhumane; the slavers felt they had some justification in attacking the missions because they were in Spanish territory and, in the 17th century, the entire western boundary of Brazil was in dispute.

This was one side of the coin. The other was that the bandeirantes were incredibly resourceful, trekking for thousands of kilometres, withstanding great hardships, travelling light, inspired not just by the desire to get rich, but also by a fierce patriotism. To uncover the sertão's riches, they demystified it, trekking into Minas Gerais, Goiás and Mato Grosso looking for precious metals. Through their efforts, the Minas Gerais gold rush began. In the bandeirantes' footsteps came settlers and cattle herders who took over the lands that had been emptied of their Indian population. Although Indians were exploited as labour and became a source of income for the Paulistas, they also intermarried with the Europeans, hastening the miscegenation process which became so evident throughout Brazil.

the same time, the President was still faced with the social imbalances which his government had failed to redress: rising unemployment, unequal income distribution, crime, the low level of police pay, lamentable prison conditions, poor services in the state-run health and education services, land reform and the violence associated with landlessness. These issues notwithstanding, Cardoso again defeated Lula in presidential elections in October 1998. As the new administration battled to enforce greater budgetary discipline, the economy finally succumbed to internal and external pressures in early 1999. Brazil's decision in mid-January to devalue the real by 9% sent shockwaves through world financial markets as it implied that an IMF rescue package of November 1998 had failed. As capital continued to leave the country, the Government was soon forced to let the real float freely. In March 1999 the IMF resumed lending to Brazil, with support from the USA, and as early as May 1999 the economy showed signs of having confounded all the worst expectations. Despite further external shocks in 2001, such as 11 September and the economic crisis in Argentina, the economy remained stable thanks largely to the external sector.

The recession had lowered Cardoso's popularity and thus his influence over his coalition partners. At last the door was open for Lula, who in 2002, at the fourth attempt, won the presidency in the run-off vote against José Serra. Contrary to forecasts that he would lead Brazil down a left-wing path unacceptable to many outside agencies and governments, his first months in power met with approval at home and abroad. Although passionately committed to social reform, Lula did not abandon orthodox economic policies. This pragmatism has been slow to bring the benefits for which poor and dispossessed Brazilians were hoping.

The Workers Party's self-proclaimed uncorruptibility was dealt a severe blow when a number of voting and bribery scandals emerged in 2005. Many heads rolled in revelations of the scope of the *mensalão* (vote-buying) scandal. Lula himself did not escape untainted and doubts about his probity led to a second round in the October 2006 presidential elections. He eventually defeated Geraldo Alckmin of the Partido da Social Democracia Brasileira (PSDB) by a 61% to 39% majority. In Lula's first term, programmes aimed directly at alleviating poverty were boosted by low inflation (averaging 5.5% from 2004-2006) and a stable economy, as shown by the strong real against the dollar, but investment in health, education and other social areas remained low. The chief question for his second term would be whether tight controls would be kept on public spending, or whether Lula would allow some fiscal relaxation as a reward for those who supported him at the ballot box despite the *mensalão*.

Chile

Independence
In 1810 a group of Chilean patriots, including Bernardo O'Higgins – the illegitimate son of a Sligo-born Viceroy of Peru, Ambrosio O'Higgins, and a Chilean mother – revolted against Spain. This revolt led to seven years of war against the occupying troops of Spain – Lord Cochrane was in charge of the insurrectionist navy – and in 1817 Gen José de San Martín crossed the Andes with an army from Argentina and helped to gain a decisive victory. O'Higgins became the first head of state, but his liberal policies offended the dominant landed aristocracy, leading to his downfall in 1823. A period of anarchy followed, but in 1830 conservative forces led by Diego Portales restored order and introduced the authoritarian constitution of 1833. Under this charter, for almost a century, the country was ruled by a small oligarchy of landowners.

The War of the Pacific
During the 1870s disputes arose with Boliva and Peru over the northern deserts, which were rich in nitrates. Although most of the nitrates lay in Bolivia and Peru, much of the mining was carried out by Anglo-Chilean companies. In the ensuing War of the Pacific (1879-1883), Chile defeated its neighbours, gaining the Bolivian coastal region as well as the Peruvian provinces of Tarapacá and Arica. For the next 40 years it drew great wealth from the nitrate fields. In the south settlers began pushing across the Río Biobío in the 1860s, encouraged by government settlement schemes and helped by technological developments including repeating rifles, telegraph, railways and barbed wire. At the end of the War of the Pacific the large Chilean army was sent to subdue the Mapuches who were confined to ever-diminishing tribal lands. The territory was then settled by immigrants – particularly Germans – and by former peasants who had fought in the north.

The 20th century
The rule of the Right was challenged by the liberal regime of President Arturo Alessandri in 1920. Acute economic distress in 1924, linked to the replacement of Chilean nitrates with artificial fertilizers produced more cheaply in Europe, led to army intervention and some reforms were achieved. The inequalities in Chilean society grew ever sharper, despite the maintenance of political democracy, and gave rise to powerful socialist and communist parties. President Eduardo Frei's policy of 'revolution in freedom' (1964-1970) was the first concerted attempt at overall radical reform, but it raised hopes it could not satisfy. In 1970 a marxist coalition assumed office under Dr Salvador Allende; the frantic pace of change under his regime polarized the country into Left- and Right-wing camps. Increasing social and economic chaos formed the background for Allende's deposition by the army; he died on 11 September 1973. Chile was then ruled by a military president, Gen Augusto Pinochet Ugarte, and a four-man junta with absolute powers. In its early years particularly, the regime suppressed internal opposition by methods which were widely condemned. Despite economic prosperity and efforts to make the regime more popular, Pinochet's bid for a further eight years as president after 1989 was rejected by the electorate in a plebiscite in 1988.

Post-Pinochet

As a result, presidential and congressional elections were held in 1989. A Christian Democrat, Patricio Aylwin Azócar was elected President and took office in March 1990 in a peaceful transfer of power. While Aylwin's coalition held the Chamber of Deputies, the Senate majority was controlled by eight Pinochet appointees, who could block constitutional reform. Gen Pinochet remained as Army Commander although other armed forces chiefs were replaced. The new Congress set about revising many of the military's laws on civil liberties and the economy. In 1991 the National Commission for Truth and Reconciliation published a report with details of those who were killed under the military regime, but opposition by the armed forces prevented mass human rights trials. In December 1993 presidential elections were won by the Christian Democrat Eduardo Frei, son of the earlier president, but in Congress his party failed to achieve the required two-thirds majority to replace heads of the armed forces and end the system of designated senators. Oblivious to public sentiment, the military's position in the senate was strengthened when General Pinochet, who retired as army commander- in-chief in March 1998, took up a senate seat, as a former president who had held office for more than six years. Although ex-officio, Pinochet's presence, and therefore parliamentary immunity from prosecution for alleged crimes during his dictatorship, was offensive to parliamentarians who had suffered during his regime.

In October 1998, Pinochet's position came under threat from an unforeseen quarter when a Spanish magistrate filed for his extradition from London, where he was on a private visit, to face charges of torture against Spanish and Chilean citizens between 1973 and 1990. He was detained while the British judiciary deliberated and in March 1999 the Law Lords concluded that Pinochet should stand trial for criminal acts committed after 1988, the year Britain signed the international torture convention. In April, Home Secretary Jack Straw authorized the extradition, but throughout 1999 the process was subject to continuous legal disputes culminating in a health report which claimed that Pinochet was too ill to stand trial. On this evidence the Home Secretary was "minded" to allow Pinochet to return to Chile, which he did in January 2000. After arriving in Santiago apparently fully fit, Pinochet's health did decline, as did his seemingly untouchable status. Implications of his involvement in the torture and killings of the 1970s and 1980s began to surface and in June 2000 an appeals court stripped Pinochet of his immunity from trial.

Partly as a result of the Pinochet affair, but also because of economic recession, President Frei's standing suffered a sharp decline in 1999. The Concertación elected socialist Ricardo Lagos to be its December 1999 presidential candidate and he beat Joaquín Lavín only by the slimmest of majorities, thus becoming Chile's first socialist president since Salvador Allende. Despite positive economic results during his term, the main focus remained the legacy of Pinochet. While the former dictator enjoyed support from the military, the erosion of his position and image continued. Admissions by former military personnel that, under orders from above, they had committed human rights abuses in the 1970s and 1980s, a protracted process of indictments, house arrest on various charges and the freezing of his assets ensured that Pinochet's past remained in the spotlight until his death on 10 December 2006.

One of the leading contenders for the 2005 presidential election was Michelle Bachelet, who had survived torture while a political prisoner during the Pinochet regime. She was duly elected president in December 2005 and the Concertación coalition won majorities in both houses of congress. Bachelet had held the posts of health and defence minister under Lagos and she was intent upon following the main thrust of her predecessor's policies.

Colombia

Colombia's divided society

After the collapse of Simón Bolívar's Republic of Gran Colombia in 1829/30, what is now known as Colombia was called Nueva Granada until 1863. Almost from its inception the new country became the scene of strife between the centralizing pro-clerical Conservatives and the federalizing anti-clerical Liberals. From 1849 the Liberals were dominant during the next 30 years of insurrections and civil wars. In 1885 the Conservatives imposed a highly centralized constitution which was not modified for over 100 years. A Liberal revolt in 1899 turned into a civil war, 'the War of the Thousand Days'. The Liberals were finally defeated in 1902 after 100,000 people had died. It was in 1903 that Panama declared its independence from Colombia, following US pressure.

After 40 years of comparative peace, the strife between Conservatives and Liberals was reignited in a little-publicized but dreadfully bloody civil war known as *La Violencia* from 1948 to 1957 (some 300,000 people were killed). This was ended by a unique political truce, decided by plebiscite in 1957 under which the two political parties supported a single presidential candidate, divided all political offices equally between them, and thus maintained political stability for 16 years. The agreement was ended in 1978. Belisario Betancur, the Conservative president from 1982-1986, offered a general amnesty to guerrilla movements in an attempt to end violence in the country. Following an initial acceptance of the offer, only one of the four main guerrilla groups, the FARC, upheld the truce in 1985-1987. In May 1986, when the Liberal candidate, Sr Virgilio Barco, won the presidential elections, FARC's newly-formed political party, the Unión Patriótica (UP), won 10 seats in congress; the Liberal party took the majority. Right-wing groups refused to accept the UP and by the beginning of 1990, 1,040 party members had been killed in five years. During the campaign for the 1990 presidential both the Liberal Party and the UP presidential candidates, Luis Carlos Galán and Bernardo Jaramillo, were assassinated.

The narcotics trade
In Medellín and Cali, two cartels transformed Colombia's drugs industry into a major force in worldwide business and crime. Their methods were very different: Medellín being ostentatious and violent, Cali much more low-key. In 1986, President Barco instigated an international effort to bring them to justice, but opposition to extradition of suspects to the USA stymied progress. Pablo Escobar, the alleged leader of the Medillín drugs cartel, who had surrendered under secret terms in 1991, escaped from custody in July 1992. Despite a multi-million dollar reward offered for his recapture and renewed conditional offers of surrender, he remained at large until he was killed in December 1993.

Modern Colombia
Having won the presidential elections held on 27 May, 1990, César Gaviria Trujillo (Liberal), who took up the candidacy of the murdered Luis Carlos Galán, appointed a coalition government made up of Liberals from rival factions, Conservatives and the M-19 (Movimiento 19 de Abril).

The Gaviria government was unable to stem violence, whether perpetrated by drug traffickers, guerrillas or common criminals. Not surprisingly, this was one of the issues in the 1994 election campaign, in which Ernesto Samper (Liberal) defeated Andrés Pastrana (Conservative). The main thrust of Samper's programme was that Colombia's current economic strength should provide resources to tackle the social deprivation which causes drug use and insurgency. Most impetus was lost during 1995-1997, however, in the wake of revelations that Samper's election campaign had received about US$6 million from the Cali cartel. The debate over Samper's awareness of the funding lasted until June 1996, almost overshadowing the capture or surrender of most of the leading Cali drug lords.

In 1998, congressional and presidential elections were relatively peaceful and a welcome boost to confidence was given when the US withdrew its 'decertification' restrictions (in effect recognizing that Colombia was making progress against drug-trafficking, thus allowing US aid to flow). The new president, Andrés Pastrana, immediately devoted his efforts to bringing the guerrillas to the negotiating table. A stop-go process began with FARC in late 1998 and the insurgents were conceded a large demilitarized zone, based on San Vicente de Caguán in Caquetá. Not everyone was in favour of Pastrana's approach, especially since FARC violence and extortion did not cease. ELN, meanwhile, angry at being excluded from talks, stepped up its campaign, demanding similar treatment. Paramilitary groups, too, showed no signs of ending their activities. Pastrana also sought international aid for his Plan Colombia, aimed at combatting the drugs trade. The US$1.6 billion package, approved by the US Congress in May 2000, was to cover mainly military and anti-narcotics equipment, with the remainder destined for crop substitution and other sustainable agriculture projects. It has become clear that the policy of spraying drug crops has not achieved the desired result. Not only has the net area under cultivation increased, but the concentration on eradicating coca has permitted a dramatic expansion in the production of opium poppies. Furthermore, with both left-wing guerrillas and right-wing paramilitaries involved in the narcotics trade, the two fronts of fighting terrorism and drugs have become increasingly entangled.

Negotiations with the guerrilla groups continued unsuccessfully into 2002, but the terror campaigns of FARC and ELN increased the government's frustration and, with an eye on the approaching May 2002 elections, Pastrana abandoned his peace initative and sent in the Army. Strategic points in the demilitarized zone were quickly taken but the guerrillas melted away into the forests and countryside and the disruption and kidnapping continued.

The frontrunners for the 2002 presidential elections were both Liberals: Horacio Serpa was the official party candidate, while Alvaro Uribe Vélez left the Liberals to run under his own movement, Colombia First. The main thrust of Uribe's campaigning was that the time had come to stop pandering to the left-wing guerrillas and to use a firm hand to restore order and security. This struck a chord with many Colombians, not just those who supported Pastrana's later hard line, but also the illegal, right-wing paramilitary groups who are waging their own war against FARC and ELN. Consequently, Uribe won with over 50% of the vote in the first round. Despite (or maybe because of) Uribe's anti-guerrilla policies, and despite a decline in support for insurgents following numerous atrocities, violence continued, prompting a tough new anti-terrorism law. At the same time, and in the face of criticism, Uribe began peace talks with the AUC (United Self Defence Forces of Colombia), the paramilitary group implacably opposed to FARC and ELN and accused of some of the worst human rights abuses. Initially little progress was made, but in mid-2004, the AUC agreed to disarm. Uribe then launched Plan Patriota, a huge military offensive against FARC in southern Colombia. The strength of FARC's response to the Plan continued right up to national elections in 2006, but, having altered the constitution to permit a second presidential term, Uribe won the May 2006 elections with a 62% majority. In March 2006 his supporters won most seats in the senate and chamber of deputies.

In 2007, revelations about the complicity between elected politicians and paramilitary groups led to the arrest of 20 allies of President Urube, including congressmen and business leaders. The foreign minister, María Consuelo Araújo, resigned because of her family's involvement, but whether the President himself knew of these dealings was not revealed. 2006's election results not only demonstrated that public support for the hard-line approach had not dwindled, but also reassured foreign investors who were keen to support Colombia and its economy. But the impasse in the country's internal conflict seemed as intractable as ever. Demilitarised groups jostled for power, legitimate or otherwise, and some armed forces tried to negotiate peace deals with terms equal to or better than previous arrangements while the fiefdoms of guerrillas and drugs traffickers remained unchallenged. All the while many Colombians continued to face displacement, illegal expropriation of their land and violence.

Ecuador

After independence

Ecuador decided on complete independence from the Gran Colombia confederation in August 1830, under the presidency of Juan Flores.The country's 19th century history was a continuous struggle between pro-Church conservatives and anti-Church (but nonetheless devoutly Catholic) liberals. There were also long periods of military rule from 1895, when the liberal Gen Eloy Alfaro took power. During the late 1940s and the 1950s there was a prolonged period of prosperity (through bananas, largely) and constitutional rule, but the more typical pattern of alternating civilian and military governments was resumed in the 1960s and 1970s. Apart from the liberal- conservative struggles, there has been long-lasting rivalry between Quito and the Sierra on one hand and Guayaquil and the Costa on the other.

Return to democracy

Following seven years of military rule, the first presidential elections under a new constitution were held in 1979. The ensuing decades of democracy saw an oscillation of power between parties of the centre-right and centre-left. Governments of both political tendencies towed the international economic line and attempted to introduce neoliberal reforms. These measures were opposed by the country's labour organizations and by the indigenous movement, which gained considerable political power. Against a backdrop of this tug-of-war, disenchantment with the political process grew apace with bureaucratic corruption and the nation's economic woes. In 1996 the frustrated electorate swept a flamboyant populist named Abdalá Bucaram to power. His erratic administration lasted less than six months.

Following an interim government and the drafting of the country's 18th constitution, Ecuador elected Jamil Mahuad, a former mayor of Quito, to the presidency in 1998. Mahuad began his term by signing a peace treaty to end the decades-old and very emotional border dispute with Peru. This early success was his last, as a series of fraudulent bank failures sent the country into an economic and political tailspin. A freeze on bank accounts failed to stop landslide devaluation of the Sucre (Ecuador's currency since 1883) and Mahuad decreed the adoption of the US Dollar in a desperate bid for stability.

Less than a month later, on 21 January 2000, he was forced out of office by Ecuador's indigenous people and disgruntled members of the armed forces. The first overt military coup in South America in over two decades, it lasted barely three hours before power was handed to vice-president Gustavo Noboa. Significantly, all of the foregoing years of social unrest were never accompanied by serious bloodshed.

Noboa, a political outsider and academic, stepped into Mahuad's shoes with remarkable aplomb. With assistance from the USA and the International Monetary Fund, his government managed to flesh out and implement the dollarization scheme, thus achieving a measure of economic stability at the cost of deepening poverty. Social unrest diminished, and Ecuadoreans instead attempted to bring about change through the ballot box. In November 2002, Colonel Lucio Gutiérrez, leader of the January 2000 *coup*, was elected president by a comfortable majority. He had run on a populist platform in alliance with the indigenous movement and labour unions, but began to change his stripes soon after taking office. His administration was lacklustre and only constantly shifting allegiances and high petroleum revenues managed to keep him in power. In late 2004, the dismissal of all the supreme court judges by unconstitutional means – and tear gas – drew local and international criticism. Popular opposition in Quito grew, with peaceful, well-attended protests. The president's response, using heavy-handed police repression, led to mass demonstrations which swept Gutiérrez from office in April 2005. Vice-president Alfredo Palacio replaced him, but lacking a political party base, he found government no easy ride, having to face persistent strikes, especially in the Amazon region where protestors blocked oil pipelines to demand roads and other infrastructure projects promised by Gutiérrez. General elections, brought forward to November 2006, were won by Rafael Correa, leader of the Alianza País (AP) movement. He immediately called a national referendum to convene a constituent assembly to redraw the constitution and – if all goes the new president's way – shift the nation's foundations toward the political left, echoing processes already taking place in Venezuela and Bolivia. 80% of voters approved Correa's plans when the referendum was held in April 2007. Elections for the constituent assembly were due to take place in August or September 2007.

Paraguay

Independence and dictatorship

The disturbances in Buenos Aires in 1810-16, which led to independence from Spain, enabled creole leaders in Asunción to throw off the rule of Buenos Aires as well as Madrid. The new republic was, however, subject to pressure from both Argentina, which blocked Paraguayan trade on the Río de la Plata, and Brazil. Following independence Paraguay was ruled by a series of dictators, the first of whom, Dr Gaspar Rodríguez de Francia (1814-1840) known as 'El Supremo', imposed a policy of isolation and self-sufficiency. The opening of the Río de la Plata after the fall of the Argentine dictator Rosas enabled de Francia's successor, Carlos Antonio López (1840-1862) to import modern technology: in 1856 a railway line between Asunción and Villarrica was begun; an iron foundry and telegraph system were also developed. Carlos López was succeeded by his son, Francisco Solano López (López II), who saw himself as the Napoleon of South America. Believing Paraguay to be threatened by Brazil and Argentina, Solano López declared war on Brazil in 1865. When Argentina refused permission to send troops through Misiones to attack Brazil, López declared war on Argentina. With Uruguay supporting Brazil and Argentina, the ensuing War of the Triple Alliance was disastrous for the Paraguayan forces who held on against overwhelming odds until the death of López at the Battle of Cerro Corá on 1 March 1870. Of a pre-war population of 400,000, only 220,000 survived the war, 28,000 of them males, mostly either very young or very old. In the peace settlement Paraguay lost territory to Brazil and Argentina, although rivalry between these neighbours prevented a worse fate.

After the war, Paraguay experienced political instability as civilian factions competed for power, often appealing to the army officers for support. Although there were few policy differences between the two political parties (the National Republican Association, known as Colorados from its red banner, and the Liberal party who adopted the colour blue), rivalry was intense. Elections were held regularly, but whichever party was in government invariably intervened to fix the result and the opposition rarely participated.

The Chaco War

While Paraguayan leaders were absorbed with domestic disputes, Bolivia began occupying disputed parts of the Chaco in an attempt to gain access to the sea via the Río Paraguay. Although Bolivian moves started in the late 19th century, the dispute was given new intensity by the discovery of oil in the 1920s. In the five-year Chaco War (1932-1937) 56,000 Bolivians and 36,000 Paraguayans were killed. Despite general expectations Paraguayan troops under Mariscal Estigarribia pushed the Bolivian army out of most of the Chaco.

Victory in war only increased dissatisfaction in the army with the policies of pre-war governments. In February 1936 nationalist officers seized power and appointed the war hero, Colonel Rafael Franco as President. Although Franco was overthrown in a counter-coup in 1937, the so-called 'February Revolution' began major changes in Paraguay including the first serious attempt at land reform and legal recognition of the small labour movement. Between 1939 and 1954 Paraguayan politics were even more turbulent, as rival civilian factions and army officers vied for power. In 1946 civil war shook the country as army units based in Concepción fought to overthrow President Morínigo.

The Stroessner Years

A military coup in May 1954 led to General Alfredo Stroessner becoming President. Stroessner retained power for 34 years, the most durable dictator in Paraguayan history. His rule was based on control over the army and the Colorado party, both of which were purged of opponents. While a network of spies informed on dissidents, party membership was made compulsory for most official posts including teachers and doctors. In fraudulent elections Stroessner was re-elected eight times. Paraguay became a centre for smuggling, gambling and drug-running, much of it controlled by Stroessner's supporters. Meanwhile the government spent large amounts of money on transportation and infrastructure projects, including the giant hydroelectric dam at Itaipú. Although these projects brought employment, the completion of Itaipú in 1982 coincided with recession in Brazil and Argentina on whose economies Paraguay was heavily dependent. Meanwhile rivalry intensified within the regime over the succession, with Stroessner favouring his son, Gustavo. Opposition focussed around Gen Andrés Rodríguez, who was married to Stroessner's daughter. When Stroessner tried to force Rodríguez to retire, troops loyal to Rodríguez overthrew the 75-year old Stroessner, who left to live in Brazil.

Liberalization

Rodríguez, who became provisional president, easily won multi-party elections in May 1989. The commitment to greater democracy permitted opponents, who had previously boycotted, or been banned from elections, to gain an unprecedented number of seats in the legislative elections of the same date. Despite considerable scepticism over General Rodríguez's intentions, political liberalization became a reality. The presidential and congressional elections that he promised were held on 9 May 1993. The presidency was won by Juan Carlos Wasmosy of the Colorado Party and Domingo Laíno of the Authentic Radical Liberal Party came second.

The government's commitment to market reforms, privatization and to economic integration with Argentina and Brazil within Mercosur inspired protests from all quarters. 1994 saw the first general strike for 35 years. There were also demands for land reform. A worsening of relations between the military and the legislature in 1995 led to a critical few days in April 1996. Army commander General Lino Oviedo was dismissed for threatening a coup; Wasmosy offered him the defence ministry but then withdrew the offer after massive public protest. Oviedo was later arrested on charges of insurrection, but from jail he made many accusations about corruption at the highest level. To the dismay of the Colorado leadership, Oviedo was chosen as the party's candidate for the May 1998 presidential elections. This intensified the feud between Oviedo and Wasmosy who eventually succeeded in having Oviedo jailed by a military tribunal for 10 years for attempting a coup in 1996. A compromise ticket of Raúl Cubas Grau (Oviedo's running mate) and Luis María Argaña (Colorado party president and opponent of Wasmosy) won the election. Within a week of taking office in August 1998, Cubas released Oviedo from prison, provoking a constitutional crisis as the supreme court ruled that Oviedo should serve out his sentence. Matters came to a head when Vice President Argaña was shot in March 1999, just before the Senate was to vote on impeachment of Cubas. Intense diplomatic efforts, led by

1497

Paraguay's Mercosur partners, resulted in Cubas' resignation on 29 March. He was replaced by Luis González Macchi, the president of Congress. Cubas went into exile in Brazil, Oviedo in Argentina. In December 1999, Oviedo escaped from the Patagonian *estancia* where he was held and began verbal attacks on the government. Soldiers loyal to Oviedo staged an unsuccessful coup in May 2000. In the following month Oviedo was arrested in Brazil. The González Macchi administration, meanwhile, was facing economic recession, strikes and social discontent. The economic downturn and its repercussions worsened through 2002 as a result of Argentina's financial crisis. Unemployment stood at about 16% of the workforce and, according to the UN, one third of the population was living in poverty. In February 2003, González Macchi himself was discredited by, but avoided impeachment over, allegations of the misuse of state funds, fraud and the torture of leftwing militants (he was imprisoned for illegal enrichment in 2006). Nevertheless, in subsequent elections in April 2003, voters backed the Colorado Party and its candidate, Nicanor Duarte Frutos. Duarte's first act as president was to join other South American leaders in signing the Declaration of Asunción against drug trafficking. Since 2005, however, strain between Paraguay and its larger Mercosur partners has appeared, partly because of Paraguay's permission for US troops to conduct excercises in Paraguay, partly because of the tade imbalances between the smaller members and Argentina and Brazil. Over half of Paraguay's gdp comes from exports to its larger neighbours, a significant proportion of which is soybeans.

Peru

After independence
Important events following the ejection of the Spaniards were a temporary confederation between Peru and Bolivia in the 1830s; the Peruvian-Spanish War (1866); and the War of the Pacific (1879-1883), in which Peru and Bolivia were defeated by Chile and Peru lost its southern territory. The 19th and early 20th centuries were dominated by the traditional elites, with landowners holding great power over their workers. Political parties were slow to develop until the 1920s, when socialist thinkers Juan Carlos Mariátegui and Víctor Raúl Haya de la Torre began to call for change. Haya de la Torre formed the Alianza Popular Revolucionaria Americana (APRA), but in the 1930s and 40s he and his party were under threat from the military and the elilte.

To the Shining Path
A reformist military Junta took over control of the country in October 1968. Under its first leader, Gen Juan Velasco Alvarado, the Junta instituted a series of measures to raise the personal status and standard of living of the workers and the rural Indians, by land reform, worker participation in industrial management and ownership, and nationalization of basic industries, exhibiting an ideology perhaps best described as 'military socialism'. In view of his failing health Gen Velasco was replaced in 1975 by Gen Francisco Morales Bermúdez and policy (because of a mounting economic crisis and the consequent need to seek financial aid from abroad) swung to the Right. Presidential and congressional elections were held on 18 May 1980, and Fernando Belaúnde Terry was elected President for the second time. His term was marked by growing economic problems and the appearance of the Maoist terrorist movement Sendero Luminoso (Shining Path).

Initially conceived in the University of Ayacucho, the movement gained most support for its goal of overthrowing the whole system of Lima-based government from highland Indians and migrants to urban shanty towns. The activities of Sendero Luminoso and another terrorist group, Túpac Amaru (MRTA), frequently disrupted transport and electricity supplies, although their strategies had to be reconsidered after the arrest of both their leaders in 1992. Víctor Polay of MRTA was arrested in June and Abimael Guzmán of Sendero Luminoso was captured in September; he was sentenced to life imprisonment (although the sentence had to be reviewed in 2003 under legal reforms). Although Sendero did not capitulate, many of its members in 1994-1995 took advantage of the Law of Repentance, which guaranteed lighter sentences in return for surrender, and freedom in exchange for valuable information. Meanwhile, Túpac Amaru was thought to have ceased operations (see below).

The Fujimori years
The April 1985 elections were won by the APRA party leader Alán García Pérez. During his populist, left-wing presidency disastrous economic policies caused increasing poverty and

civil instability. In presidential elections held over two rounds in 1990, Alberto Fujimori of the Cambio 90 movement defeated the novelist Mario Vargas Llosa, who belonged to the Fredemo (Democratic Front) coalition. Fujimori, without an established political network behind him, failed to win a majority in either the senate or the lower house. Lack of congressional support was one of the reasons behind the dissolution of congress and the suspension of the constitution on 5 April 1992. With massive popular support, President Fujimori declared that he needed a freer hand to introduce free-market reforms, combat terrorism and drug trafficking, and root out corruption.

Elections to a new, 80-member Democratic Constituent Congress (CCD) in November 1992 and municipal elections in February 1993 showed that voters still had scant regard for mainstream political groups. A new constitution drawn up by the CCD was approved by a narrow majority of the electorate in October 1993. Among the new articles were the immediate re-election of the president (previously prohibited for one presidential term) and, as expected, Fujimori stood for re-election on 9 April 1995. He beat his independent opponent, the former UN General Secretary, Javier Pérez de Cuéllar, by a resounding margin. The coalition that supported him also won a majority in Congress.

The government's success in most economic areas did not accelerate the distribution of foreign funds for social projects. Furthermore, rising unemployment and the austerity imposed by economic policy continued to cause hardship for many. Dramatic events on 17 December 1996 thrust several of these issues into sharper focus. 14 Túpac Amaru terrorist infiltrated a reception at the Japanese Embassy in Lima, taking 490 hostages and demanding the release of their imprisoned colleagues and new measures to raise living standards. Most of the hostages were released and negotiations were pursued during a stalemate that lasted until 22 April 1997. The president took sole responsibility for the successful, but risky assault which freed all the hostages (one died of heart failure) and killed all the terrorists. By not yielding to Túpac Amaru, Fujimori regained much popularity. But this masked the fact that no concrete steps had been taken to ease poverty. It also deflected attention from Fujimori's plans to stand for a third term following his unpopular manipulation of the law to persuade Congress that the new constitution did not apply to his first period in office. Until the last month of campaigning for the 2000 presidential elections, Fujimori had a clear lead over his main rivals. His opponents insisted that Fujimori that should not stand and local and international observers voiced increasing concern over the state domination of the media. Meanwhile, the popularity of Alejandro Toledo, a centrist and former World Bank official of humble origins, surged to such an extent that he and Fujimori were neck-and neck in the first poll. Toledo and his supporters claimed that Fujimori's slim majority was the result of fraud, a view echoed in the pressure put on the president, by the US government among others, to allow a second ballot. The run-off election, on 28 May 2000, was also contentious since foreign observers, including the Organization of American States (OAS), said the electoral system was unprepared and flawed, proposing a postponement. The authorities refused to delay. Toledo boycotted the election and Fujimori was returned unopposed, but with minimal approval. Having won, he proposed to "strengthen democracy".

This pledge proved to be worthless following the airing of a secretly-shot video on 14 September 2000 of Fujimori's close aide and head of the National Intelligence Service (SIN), Vladimiro Montesinos, handing US$15,000 to a congressman, Alberto Kouri, to persuade him to switch allegiances to Fujimori's coalition. Fujimori's demise was swift. His initial reaction was to close down SIN and announce new elections, eventually set for 8 April 2001, at which he would not stand. Montesinos, declared a wanted man, fled to Panama, where he was denied asylum. He returned to Peru in October and Fujimori personally led the search parties to find his former ally. Peruvians watched in amazement as this game of cat-and-mouse was played out on their TV screens. While Montesinos himself successfully evaded capture, investigators began to uncover the extent of his empire, which held hundreds of senior figures in its web. Swiss bank accounts in his name were found to contain about US$70 million, while other millions were discovered in accounts in the Cayman Islands and elsewhere. As the search for him continued, Fujimori, apparently in pursuit of his presidential duties, made various overseas trips, including to Japan. Here, on 20 November, he sent Congress an email announcing his resignation. Congress rejected this, firing him instead on charges of being "morally unfit" to govern. An interim president, Valentín Paniagua, was sworn in, with ex-UN Secretary General Javier Pérez de Cuéllar as Prime Minister, and the government set about uncovering the depth of corruption associated with Montesinos and Fujimori. It also had to prepare for free and fair elections.

After Fujimori

In the run-up to the 2001 ballot, the front-runner was Alejandro Toledo, but with far from a clear majority. Ex-President Alan García emerged as Toledo's main opponent, forcing a run-off on 3 June. This was won by Toledo with 52% of the vote. He pledged to heal the wounds that had opened in Peru since his first electoral battle with the disgraced Fujimori, but his presidency was marked by slow progress on both the political and economic fronts. With the poverty levels still high, few jobs created and a variety of scandals, Toledo's popularity plummeted. A series of major confrontations and damaging strikes forced the president to declare a state of emergency in May 2003 to restore order. Nor could Toledo escape charges of corruption being laid at his own door; accusations that he and his sister orchestrated voter fraud in 2000 were upheld by a congressional commission in May 2005 (Toledo was formally charged in December 2006).

The April 2006 elections were contested by Alán García, the conservative Lourdes Flores and Ollanta Humala, a former military officer and unsuccessful coup leader who claimed support from Venezuela's Hugo Chávez and Evo Morales of Bolivia. García and Humala won through to the second round, which García won, in part because many were suspicious, even critical of the "Chávez factor" and the latter's interference in Peruvian affairs. García was anxious to overcome his past record as president and prior to taking office he pledged to rein in public spending and not squander the benefits of an economy growing consistently in 2005 and 2006, with further growth predicted for 2007. The Peruvian Congress approved a trade pact with the United States in 2006, García's support for this being an indication of his willingness to court orthodoxy, rather than the left-leaning model proposed by his Andean neighbours Hugo Chávez and Evo Morales.

All the while, the past continued to dog the present. Since 2002, Montesinos has been convicted of a number of crimes in a series trials and yet more prosecutions are in process. In 2004, prosecutors also sought to charge exiled Fujimori with ordering the deaths of 25 people in 1991 and 1992. This followed the Truth and Reconciliation Committee's report (2003) into the civil war of the 1980s-1990s, which stated that over 69,000 Peruvians had been killed. With attempts to extradite Fujimori from Japan coming to nothing, prosecution could not proceed. Meanwhile Fujimori himself declared that he would be exonerated and stand again for the presidency in 2006. To this end he flew to Chile in November 2005 with a view to entering Peru, but the Chilean authorities jailed him for seven months and then denied him exit from Chile, where he stayed on parole as an extradition request was heard in the courts. At the time of writing (June 2007), Fujimori was back under house arrest, pending the Chilean courts' ruling.

Uruguay

Struggle for independence

In 1808 Montevideo declared its independence from Buenos Aires. In 1811, the Brazilians attacked from the north, but the local patriot, José Gervasio Artigas, rose in arms against them. In the early stages he had some of the Argentine provinces as allies, but soon declared the independence of Uruguay from both Brazil and Argentina. Buenos Aires invaded again in 1812 and was able to enter Montevideo in June 1814. In January the following year the Orientales (Uruguayans) defeated the Argentines at Guayabos and regained Montevideo. The Portuguese then occupied all territory south of the Río Negro except Montevideo and Colonia. The struggle continued from 1814 to 1820, but Artigas had to flee to Paraguay when Brazil took Montevideo in 1820. In 1825 General Juan Lavalleja, at the head of 33 patriots (the Treinta y Tres Orientales), crossed the river and returned to Uruguay, with Argentine aid, to harass the invaders. After the defeat of the Brazilians at Ituzaingó on 20 February 1827, Britain intervened, both Argentina and Brazil relinquished their claims on the country, and independence was finally achieved in 1828.

19th-century upheavals

The early history of the republic was marked by a civil war (known as the Guerra Grande) which began as a conflict between two rival leaders, José Fructuoso Rivera with his Colorados and Manuel Oribe with his Blancos; these are still two of the three main parties today. Oribe was helped by the Argentine dictator, Juan Manuel de Rosas, but was overthrown in 1838. Blanco forces, backed by Rosas, besieged Montevideo between 1843 and 1851. Although Rosas fell from power in 1852, the contest between Colorados and Blancos continued. A Colorado, General Venancio Flores, helped by Argentina, became president and, in 1865, Uruguay was dragged into the war of the Triple Alliance against the Paraguayan dictator, López. Flores was assassinated in 1868 three days after his term as president ended.

Batlle y Ordoñez

The country, wracked by civil war, dictatorship and intrigue, only emerged from its long political turmoil in 1903, when another Colorado, a great but controversial man, José Batlle y Ordóñez was elected president. During Batlle y Ordóñez' two terms as president, 1903-1907 and 1911-1915, Uruguay became within a short space of time the only 'welfare state' in Latin America. Its workers' charter provides free medical service, old age and service pensions and unemployment pay. Education is free and compulsory, capital punishment abolished, and the church disestablished.

Guerrillas and military rule

As the country's former prosperity has ebbed away since the 1960s, the welfare state has become increasingly fictitious. The military promised to reduce bureaucracy and spend more on the poor and development after the turmoil of 1968-1973, the period in which the Tupamaros urban guerrilla movement was most active. In practice the military, which effectively wiped out the Tupamaros by 1972, expanded state spending by raising military and security programmes. Real wages fell to less than half their 1968 level and only the very wealthy benefited from the military regime's attempted neo-liberal economic policies. Less than 10% of the unemployed received social security payments. Montevideo began to sprout shanty towns, once unheard of in this corner of the hemisphere. Nevertheless, the country's middle class remains very large, if impoverished, and the return to democracy in 1985 raised hopes that the deterioration in the social structure would be halted. Almost 10% of the population emigrated for economic or political reasons during the 1960s and 1970s: the unemployed continue to leave, but the political and artistic exiles have returned.

Allying himself with the Armed Forces in 1973, the elected president, Juan M Bordaberry, dissolved Congress and stayed on to rule as the military's figurehead until 1976. Scheduled elections were cancelled in that year, and a further wave of political and trade union repression instituted. Unable to convince the population to vote for a new authoritarian constitution in 1980, the military became increasingly anxious to hand back power to conservative politicians.

Return to democracy

In August 1984 agreement was reached finally on the legalization of most of the banned leftist parties and elections were held in November. Under the moderate government of Julio María Sanguinetti (of the Colorado party) the process of national reconstruction and political reconciliation began with a widespread political amnesty. The moderate conservative Partido Nacional (Blancos) won November 1989 presidential and congressional elections and Luis Alberto Lacalle became president. There was considerable opposition to plans for wage restraint, spending cuts, social reforms and privatization. As a result, his Blanco Party lost the November 1994 elections: Colorado ex-president Sanguinetti was again victorious over the Blancos and the Frente Amplio, a broad left front. Each party won about a third of the seats in Congress. Soon after taking office in March 1995, President Sanguinetti managed to forge an alliance with the Blancos to introduce economic restructuring and steps towards implementing much needed social security reforms. While the coalition worked together to reduce the influence of the public sector, the Frente Amplio gained support for its aim of maintaining the welfare state.

In December 1996 a referendum approved constitutional reforms, including changes to the presidential selection process which restricted political parties to a single candidate for each election and introduced a second ballot for the presidency. The first elections under the new system were held at the end of 1999 and the Frente Amplio candidate, Tabaré Vásquez, was narrowly defeated in the second ballot by Jorge Batlle of the Colorados. In congress, however, the Frente Amplio, in coalition with Encuentro Progresista, was the single party with the largest number of seats.

After his predecessor had implemented essential reforms of the social security system, incoming president Jorge Batlle planned to bring new impetus to the economy through diversification away from wool and beef and opening new export markets. Unfortunately, the recession that began in 1999 persisted because of high international interest rates, rising oil prices and economic stagnation in Argentina, plus severe drought affecting domestic agriculture. Argentina's economic meltdown in 2001 ended any hope of improvement. In 2002 gdp fell by

20%, according to some estimates, unemployment stood at 20% of the workforce and the banking sector was in crisis. Financial collapse was averted in August 2002 only through an emergency loan of US$1.5 billion from the US. In this climate the ruling Colorado party lost to the Frente Amplio and its presidential candidate, Tabaré Vásquez, in the 31 October 2004 elections. Vásquez made his immediate priority the alleviation of poverty and this aim has been bolstered by a strong economy, fuelled mainly by increased exports, principally to the United States. In late 2006, Uruguay was able to pay off its total debt to the IMF. In a surprise move, Vásquez met President Bush in May 2006 to discuss a free trade pact. This might place Uruguay in opposition to the Mercosur agreement, but, like Paraguay, Uruguay does not feel supported by the larger members of the group. Moreover, it has been in dispute with Argentina over a wood pulp project on the Río Uruguay, which has led to border closures between the two countries.

Venezuela

After Independence
Despite being at the heart of Simón Bolívar's cherished Gran Colombia (together with Ecuador, Colombia and Panama), Venezuela under General Páez became an independent nation in 1830, before Bolívar's death. Páez was either president, or the power behind the presidency from 1831 to 1848, a time of stability and economic progress. In the second half of the 19th century, though, the rise of the Liberal Party in opposition to the ruling Conservatives led to conflicts and social upheaval. In 1870 a Liberal politician-general, Antonio Guzmán Blanco, came to power. Even though his term was peaceful, it marked the entry of the army into Venezuelan politics, a role which it did not relinquish for almost a century.

20th century
In the first half of the century presidents of note were Juan Vicente Gómez (1909-1935), a brutal but efficient dictator, and Isaías Medina Angarita, who introduced the oil laws. There was much material progress under the six-year dictatorship of Gen Marcos Pérez Jiménez (1952-1958), but his Gómez-like methods led to his overthrow in January 1958. A stable democracy has been created since, with presidential elections every five years. Carlos Andrés Pérez of the centre-left Democratic Action party (AD) took office in 1974, presiding over a period of rapid development following the first great oil-price rise, and was succeeded in 1979 by Luis Herrera Campins of the Christian Democratic party, Copei. Jaime Lusinchi of Democratic Action was elected president in 1983, to be followed by Carlos Andrés Pérez, who began his second term in 1989.

1990s: instability and economic crisis
Pérez' second term was marked by protests against economic adjustment and growing levels of poverty. In 1992 there were two unsuccessful coup attempts by military officers, including Colonel Hugo Chávez Frías, who became president by legitimate means in 1999. Among reforms designed to root out corruption, the Supreme Court and Central Bank were given greater independence. Both bodies were instrumental in the decision that Pérez himself be tried on corruption charges in 1993. The president was suspended from office, arrested and, after two years of house arrest, was found guilty in May 1996. An interim president, Senator Ramón José Velázquez, took office until the presidential elections of December 1993, in which Rafael Caldera, standing as an independent, was re-elected to office (as a member of Copei, he was president 1969-1974). Many of his aims, such as improvement in social conditions, tax reform and the control of inflation, had to be postponed, even reversed, in favour of solving an economic and financial crisis which began in 1994. This helped him to conclude an agreement with the IMF, but caused public protest at declining salaries and deteriorating public services.

Presidential elections in December 1998 were won by Hugo Chávez, by an overwhelming majority. On taking office in February 1999, Chávez called for a complete overhaul of Venezuela's political system in order to root out corruption and inefficiency. He obtained special powers from Congress to reduce the budget deficit and diversify the economy away from oil. These were first steps towards his aim of eradicating poverty and restoring real incomes, which had fallen by two thirds in 15 years. He set up a constituent assembly which drew up a new constitution and 70% of the electorate approved it in a plebiscite in December 1999. New elections, scheduled for May 2000 but postponed until end-July as the electoral commission failed to make the necessary preparations, were won comfortably by Chávez. Opposition parties did, however, increase their share of seats in Congress as the middle and upper classes supported Chávez' main challenger, Francisco Arias Calderón, while the president held on to his heartland in the poverty-stricken slums. The goals of the 'Chávez revolution' remained unchanged, but a referendum in late 2000 to reform labour unions and remove their supposedly corrupt leaders, while winning a majority, had very low voter turnout and was bitterly attacked at home and abroad.

The 2002 coup

Through 2001 and into 2002 Chávez succeeded in antagonizing dissident military officers, the business sector, the Roman Catholic Church and the press. The middle classes, office workers and trades unionists blamed him for mismanaging the economy. Pro- and anti-Chávez street demonstrations became a regular event in Caracas. When Chávez tried to reform PDVSA, the state oil company, replacing executives with his own allies, the value of the bolívar slumped against the dollar and oil workers went on strike. This led to a 48-hour general strike in early April and, during the protests, 16 people were killed. On 12 April it was announced that Chávez had been replaced as president after being arrested by the military high command. His successor was businessman Pedro Carmona, who dissolved Congress and cancelled the constitution, only to resign a day later in the face of pro-Chávez demonstrations equally as strong as those that had ousted the president. On 14 April, Chávez was restored to office, but society remained deeply polarised. The opposition coalition, made up of the business sector, the main trades union and the private media, kept up its pressure on Chávez. Calls for early elections were backed by the US, but the government insisted that the first poll to be held would a mid-term referendum in August 2003, as required by the constitution if sufficient voters requested it.

By end-2002, the political situation had deteriorated to such a degree that a general strike call was met with massive support. It lasted two months and cost Venezuela some US$6 billion as the oil industry was paralized, the banking sector shut down and the bolívar plummeted to record lows against the dollar. Chávez stood firm, the strike eventually ended, but the demand for a mid-term referendum did not evaporate. This was eventually held and Chávez won comfortably. Since then Chávez has continued to promote his model of 21st-century socialism, among whose aims is the removal of Latin America from the US sphere of influence. The chief motivation was to wrest power for the unrepresented people from the hands of the oligarchies that have controlled Latin America. The main methods included the supply of cheap oil, transcontinental infrastructure projects, forging ties with indigenous movements and oppostion parties in other countries and a continuing barrage of words against President Bush. Needless to say, relations with the US have been strained, but not so badly as to affect sales of Venezuelan oil. The inflamed rehetoric has been due on the one hand to US backing for the 2002 coup and, on the other, to Chávez' strong links with Fidel Castro and acceptance of practical aid from Cuba, and to Chávez' alleged moves towards authoritarianism (for instance not renewing the licence to broadcast of the opposition television channel, RCTV, in 2007). There was little danger, though, of Chávez losing the presidential elections of December 2006, which he won by a landslide. Opinion polls show that the majority of Venezuelans support the changes Chávez has instituted in political participation, economic benefits for the poor and social reform, despite the fierce debates within and outside Venezuela over the true meaning of Bolivarian democracy.

Guyana

The country was first partially settled between 1616 and 1621 by the Dutch West India Company, who erected a fort and depot at Fort Kyk-over-al (County of Essequibo). The first English attempt at settlement was made by Captain Leigh on the Oiapoque River (now French Guyane) in 1604, but he failed to establish a permanent settlement. Lord Willoughby, founded a settlement in 1663 at Suriname, which was captured by the Dutch in 1667 and ceded to them at the Peace of Breda in exchange for New York. The Dutch held the three colonies till 1796 when they were captured by a British fleet. The territory was restored to the Dutch in 1802, but in the following year was retaken by Great Britain, which finally gained it in 1814, when the counties of Essequibo, Berbice and Demerara were merged to form British Guiana.

During the 17th century the Dutch and English settlers established posts upriver, in the hills, mostly as trading points with the Amerindian natives. Plantations were laid out and worked by African slaves. Poor soil defeated this venture, and the settlers retreated with their slaves to the coastal area in mid-18th century: the old plantation sites can still be detected from the air. Coffee and cotton were the main crops until the late 18th century, but sugar had become the dominant crop by 1820. In 1834 slavery was abolished. Many slaves became small landholders, and settlers had to find another source of labour: indentured workers from India, a few Chinese, and some Portuguese labourers. At the end of their indentures many settled in Guyana.

The end of the colonial period was politically turbulent, with rioting between the mainly Indo-Guyanese People's Progressive Party (PPP), led by Dr Cheddi Jagan, and the mainly Afro-Guyanese People's National Congress (PNC), under Mr Forbes Burnham. The PNC, favoured over the PPP by the colonial authorities, formed a government in 1964 and retained office until 1992. Guyana is one of the few countries in the Caribbean where political parties have used race as an election issue. As a result, tension between the ethnic groups has manifested itself mainly at election time.

On 26 May 1966 Guyana gained independence, and on 23 February 1970 it became a co-operative republic within the Commonwealth, adopting a new constitution. Another new constitution was adopted in 1980; this declared Guyana to be in transition from capitalism to socialism. Many industries, including bauxite and sugar, were nationalized in the 1970s and close relations with the USSR and Eastern Europe were developed. Following the death of President Forbes Burnham in August 1985, Desmond Hoyte became president. Since then, relations with the United States have improved.

Regular elections to the National Assembly and to the presidency since independence were widely criticized as fraudulent. In October 1992 national assembly and presidential elections, declared free and fair by international observers, the PPP/Civic party, led by Dr Jagan, won power after 28 years in opposition. The installation of a government by democratic means was greeted with optimism and prompted foreign investors to study potential opportunities in Guyana. An economic recovery programme, which was part of an IMF Enhanced Structural Adjustment Facility, stimulated several years of positive gdp growth, but also seriously eroded workers' real income and hit the middle classes very hard.

In March 1997, President Jagan died after a heart attack. In new elections on 15 December 1997, the PPP/Civic alliance was re-elected. Jagan's widow, Janet, was elected as president. The PNC, led by Desmond Hoyte, disputed the results and a brief period of violent demonstrations was ended when a Caricom (Caribbean Common Market) mission agreed to mediate between the two sides. Even though the PPP/Civic was sworn in to office on 24 December 1997, agreeing to review the constitution and hold new elections within three years, Hoyte refused to recognize Jagan as president. In August 1999 President Jagan resigned because of ill health and Minister of Finance, Bharrat Jagdeo, was appointed in her place. New elections were eventually held in March 2001 and the PPP/Civic alliance and Jagdeo were returned to office. After the death of Desmond Hoyte in December 2002, Robert Corbin was elected leader of the opposition PNC/Reform. In May 2003, Jagdeo and Corbin agreed new terms for "constructive engagement", which included an end to the PNC/R's boycott of the National Assembly. New elections, held on 28 August 2006, again returned Jagdeo and the PPP/Civic to power, but this time without the inter-party violence that had marred previous polls. This, plus the good showing of the new Alliance for Change (AFC), which campaigned on a non-racial platform, raised hopes for better relations within Guyana's racially divided society. Whether Jagdeo would be prepared to work more closely with his rivals remained to be seen, but challenging tasks lay ahead, such as ending violent crime and raising Guyana from its Highly Indebted Poor Country status.

Suriname

Although Amsterdam merchants had been trading with the 'wild coast' of Guiana as early as 1613 (the name Parmurbo-Paramaribo was already known) it was not until 1630 that 60 English settlers came to Suriname under Captain Marshall and planted tobacco. The real founder of the colony was Lord Willoughby of Parham, governor of Barbados, who sent an expedition to Suriname in 1651 under Anthony Rowse to find a suitable place for settlement. Willoughbyland became an agricultural colony with 500 little sugar plantations, 1,000 white inhabitants and 2,000 African slaves. Jews from Holland and Italy joined them, as well as Dutch Jews ejected from Brazil after 1654. On 27 February 1667, Admiral Crynssen conquered the colony for the states of Zeeland and Willoughbyfort became the present Fort Zeelandia. By the Peace of Breda, 31 July 1667, it was agreed that Suriname should remain with the Netherlands, while Nieuw-Amsterdam (New York) should be given to England. The colony was subsequently reduced to four years. Congress is composed of a 120-seat Chamber of Deputies and a 38-seat Senate. The country is divided into 13 regions.

Colombia
Senators and Representatives are elected by popular vote. The Senate has 102 members, and the Chamber of Representatives has 166. The President is elected by direct vote for a term of four years and may stand for a second term. Every citizen over 18 can vote. The 1886 Constitution was reformed by a Constituent Assembly in 1991. Administratively the country is divided into 32 Departments and the Capital District of Bogotá.

Ecuador
There are 22 provinces, including the Galápagos Islands. Provinces are divided into *cantones* which are subdivided into *parroquias* for administration.

Under the 1998 constitution, all citizens over 18 are both entitled and required to vote. The president and vice-president are elected for a four-year term. The parliament (Congreso Nacional) has 100 members who are elected for a four-year term at the same time as the president.

Paraguay
A new Constitution was adopted in 1992. The country has 17 departments, with Asunción, the capital, as a separate entity. Executive power rests with the president, elected for five years. There is a two-chamber Congress (Senate 45 seats, Chamber of Deputies 80). Voting is secret and obligatory for all over 18.

Peru
Under the constitution of December 1993, there is a single chamber, 120-seat congress. Men and women over 18 are eligible to vote; registration and voting is compulsory until the age of 70. The President, to whom is entrusted the Executive Power, is elected for five years and may be re-elected for a second term. The country is divided into 25 regions, plus the province of Lima.

Uruguay
Uruguay is a republic with a bicameral legislature: a Senate with 30 seats and a Chamber of Representatives with 99 seats. The president, who is head of state and of the government, holds office for five years. The country is divided into 19 departments.

Venezuela
The Bolivarian Republic of Venezuela is a federal republic of 23 states, a Federal District and federal dependencies of over 70 islands. There is one legislative house, a chamber of deputies with 167 members who are elected every five years. Under the constitution of 30 December 1999, the president holds office for six years and may stand for immediate reelection.

Guyana
A Prime Minister and cabinet are responsible to the National Assembly, which has 65 members, elected for a maximum term of five years, with not more than 4 non-elected non-voting ministers and 2 non-elected non-voting parliamentary secretaries appointed by the president. The president is Head of State. The country is divided into 10 administrative regions.

Suriname
There is one legislative house, the National Assembly, which has 51 members, elected every five years. The President is both head of state and government. Suriname is divided into 10 districts, of which the capital is one.

Guyane
The head of state is the president of France; the local heads of government are Le Préfet (the Prefect), for France, and the presidents of the local General and Regional Councils. The General Council (19 members) and the Regional Council (34 members) are the two legislative houses. The main parties in the regional council are the Parti Socialiste Guyanais and the Front Democratique Guyanais. Guyane sends a representative to the French Senate and one to the National Assembly in Paris. The country is divided into two *arrondissements*, Cayenne and St-Laurent-du-Maroni.

Culture

People

Argentina → *Population in 2007 was 40.3 million. Population growth was 1.00%; infant mortality rate 14.3 per 1,000 live births; literacy rate 97.2% (2001); GDP per capita US$15,000 (2006).*

In the Federal Capital and Province of Buenos Aires, where about 45% of the population lives, the people are almost exclusively of European origin. In the far northern provinces, colonized from neighbouring countries, at least half the people are *mestizos* though they form about 15% of the population of the whole country. It is estimated that 12.8% are foreign born and generally of European origin, though there are also important communities of Syrians, Lebanese, Armenians, Japanese and Koreans. Not surprisingly, the traditional image of the Argentine is that of the *gaucho*; *gauchismo* has been a powerful influence in literature, sociology and folklore, and is celebrated each year in the week before the 'Day of Tradition', 10 November.

In the highlands of the northwest, in the Chaco, Misiones and in the southwest, there are still some **indigenous groups**. The total of the Indian population is unknown; estimates vary from 300,000 to 500,000. The pampas Indians were virtually exterminated in the 19th century; the Indians of Tierra del Fuego are extinct. Surviving peoples include the Wichi and others in Salta and Jujuy provinces (see page 143), various Chaco Indians (see page 167) and tribes related to the Mapuche and Tehuelche nations in the southwest.

Bolivia → *Population in 2007 was 9.12 million. Population growth was 1.42%; infant mortality rate 50.43 per 1,000 live births; literacy rate 86.7%; GDP per capita US$3,000 (2006).*

Of the total population, some two thirds are Indians, the remainder being *mestizos* (people of mixed Spanish and indigenous origin), Europeans and others. The racial composition varies from place to place: Indian around Lake Titicaca; more than half Indian in La Paz; three-quarters *mestizo* or European in the Yungas, Cochabamba, Santa Cruz and Tarija, the most European of all. There are also about 17,000 blacks, descendents of slaves brought from Peru and Buenos Aires in 16th century, who now live in the Yungas. Since the 1980s, regional tensions between the 'collas' (*altiplano* dwellers) and the 'cambas' (lowlanders) have become more marked. About two-thirds of the population lives in adobe huts. Under 40% of children of school age attend school even though it is theoretically compulsory between 7 and 14.

The most obdurate of Bolivian problems has always been that the main mass of population is, from a strictly economic viewpoint, in the wrong place, the poor Altiplano and not the potentially rich Oriente; and that the Indians live largely outside the monetary system on a self-sufficient basis. Since the land reform of 1952 isolated communities continue the old life but in the agricultural area around Lake Titicaca, the valleys of Cochabamba, the Yungas and the irrigated areas of the south, most peasants now own their land, however small the plot may be. Migration to the warmer and more fertile lands of the east region has been officially encouraged. At the same time roads are now integrating the food-producing eastern zones, with the bulk of the population living in the towns of the Altiplano or the west-facing slopes of the Eastern Cordillera.

The **highland Indians** are composed of two groups: those in La Paz and in the north of the Altiplano who speak the guttural Aymara (an estimated one million), and those elsewhere, who speak Quechua, the Inca tongue (three million – this includes the Indians in the northern Apolobamba region). Outside the big cities many of them speak no Spanish. In the lowlands are some 150,000 people in 30 groups, including the Ayoreo, Chiquitano, Chiriguano, Garavo, Chimane and Mojo. The **lowland Indians** are, in the main, Guaraní. About 70% of Bolivians are Aymara, Quechua or Tupi-Guaraní speakers. The first two are regarded as national languages, but were not, until very recently, taught in schools, a source of some resentment.

The Indian women retain their traditional costume, with bright petticoats (*polleras*), and in the highlands around La Paz wear, apparently from birth, a brown or grey bowler (locally called a *bombín*). Indians traditionally chew the coca leaf, which deadens hunger pains and gives a measure of oblivion. Efforts to control the cultivation of coca is one of many sources of friction between the indigenous population and the authorities; others include landlessness, and exploitation of labour. On feast days they drink with considerable application, wear the most sensational masks and dance till they drop.

Brazil → *Population in 2007 was 190.0 million. Population growth was 1.01%; infant mortality rate 27.62 per 1,000 live births; literacy rate 88.6%; GDP per capita US$8,600 (2006).*

At first the Portuguese colony grew slowly. From 1580 to 1640 the population was only about 50,000 apart from the million or so indigenous Indians. In 1700 there were some 750,000 non-indigenous people in Brazil. Early in the 19th century Humboldt computed there were about 920,000 whites, 1,960,000 Africans, and 1,120,000 Indians and *mestiços*: after three centuries of occupation a total of only four million, and over twice as many Africans as there were whites.

Modern immigration did not begin effectively until after 1850. Of the 4.6 million immigrants from Europe between 1884-1954, 32% were Italians, 30% Portuguese, 14% Spanish, 4% German. Since 1954 immigrants have averaged 50,000 a year. There are some one million Japanese-descended Brazilians; they grow a fifth of the coffee, 30% of the cotton, all the tea, and are very active in market gardening.

Today the whites and near-whites are about 54% of the population, people of mixed race about 40%, and Afro Brazilians 5%; the rest are Asians. There are large regional variations in the distribution of the races: the whites predominate in the south, which received the largest flood of European immigrants, and decrease more or less progressively towards the north.

Most of the German immigrants settled in the three southern states: Santa Catarina, Rio Grande do Sul, and Paraná. The Germans (and the Italians and Poles and other Slavs who followed them) did not in the main go as wage earners on the big estates, but as cultivators of their own small farms.

The arid wastes of the Sertão remain largely uncultivated. Its inhabitants are people of mixed Portuguese and Indian origin (*mestiço*); most live off the 'slash and burn' method of cultivation, which involves cutting down and burning the brushwood for a small patch of ground which is cultivated for a few years and then allowed to grow back.

Brazilian culture is rich in African influences. Those interested in the development of Afro-Brazilian music, dance, religion, arts and cuisine will find the whole country north of São Paulo fascinating, and especially the cities of Bahia and São Luís which retain the greatest African influences. Though there is no legal discrimination against black people, the economic and educational disparity – by default rather than intent of the Government – is such that successful Afro Brazilians are active almost exclusively in the worlds of sport, entertainment and arts. Black Pride movements are particularly strong in Bahia.

Rural and urban population The population has historically been heavily concentrated along the coastal strip where the original Portuguese settlers exploited the agricultural wealth, and further inland in the states of Minas Gerais and São Paulo where more recent development has followed the original search for gold, precious stones and slaves. Much of the interior of Pará, Amazonas, Goiás and the Mato Grosso has densities of one person per sq km or less. Internal migration has brought to the cities problems of unemployment, housing shortage, and extreme pressure on services; shanty towns – or *favelas, mocambos, alagados*, according to the region – are an integral part of the urban landscape. But while the northeast, because of its poverty, has lost many workers to the industries of the southeast, many rural workers from southern Brazil have moved north, drawn by the rapid development of Amazônia, creating unprecedented pressures on the environment.

Indigenous peoples It is estimated that, when the Portuguese arrived in Brazil, there were between three and five million Indians living in the area. Today there are only about 350,000. Tribal groups number 210; each has a unique dialect, but most languages belong to four main linguistic families, Tupi-Guarani, Ge, Carib and Arawak. A few tribes remain uncontacted, others are exclusively nomadic, others are semi-nomadic hunter-gatherers and farmers, while some are settled groups in close contact with non-Indian society. The struggle of groups such as the Yanomami to have their land demarcated in order to secure title is well-documented. The goal of the Statute of the Indian (Law 6.001/73), for demarcation of all Indian land by 1978, is largely unmet. It was feared that a new law introduced in January 1996 would slow the process even more. Funai, the National Foundation for the Support of the Indian, a part of the Interior Ministry, is charged with representing the Indians' interests, but lacks resources and support. There is no nationwide, representative body for indigenous people. Most of Brazil's indigenous people live in the Amazon region; they are affected by deforestation, encroachment from colonizers, small- and large-scale mining, and the construction of hydroelectric dams. Besides the Yanomami, other groups include the Xavante, Tukano, Kreen-Akrore, Kaiapó, Arawete and Arara.

Chile → *Population of Chile in 2007 was 16.3 million. Population growth was 0.91%; infant mortality rate 8.36 per 1,000 live births; literacy rate 95.7%; GDP per capita US$12,700 (2006).*

There is less racial diversity in Chile than in most Latin American countries. Over 90% of the population is *mestizo*. There has been much less immigration than in Argentina and Brazil. The German, French, Spanish, Italian and Swiss immigrants came mostly after 1846 as small farmers in the forest zone south of the Biobío. Between 1880 and 1900 gold-seeking Serbs and Croats settled in the far south, and the British took up sheep farming and commerce in the same region. The influence throughout Chile of the immigrants is out of proportion to their numbers: their signature on the land is seen, for instance, in the German appearance of Valdivia, Puerto Montt, Puerto Varas, Frutillar and Osorno.

The population is far from evenly distributed: Middle Chile (from Copiapó to Concepción), 18% of the country's area, contains 77% of the total population. The Metropolitan Region of Santiago contains, about 39% of the whole population. The rate of population growth per annum, at 1.5% (1993-98), is slightly under the average for Latin America. Many Chileans live in slum areas called *callampas* (mushrooms), or *tomas* on the outskirts of Santiago and around the factories. It is estimated that 22% of the population lives in acute poverty. Unemployment in 2002 was 8.8%.

There is disagreement over the number of **indigenous people** in Chile. The Mapuche nation, 95% of whom live in forest land around Temuco, between the Biobío and Toltén rivers, is put at one million by Survival International, but much less by others, including official, statistics. There are also 15,000-20,000 Aymara in the northern Chilean Andes and 2,000 Rapa Nui on Easter Island. A political party, the Party for Land and Identity, unites many Indian groupings, and legislation is proposed to restore indigenous people's rights.

Colombia → *Population in 2007 was 44.4 million. Population growth was 1.43%; infant mortality rate 20.13 per 1,000 live births; literacy rate 92.8%; GDP per capita US$8,400 (2006).*

The regions vary in their racial make-up: Antioquia and Caldas are largely of European descent, Pasto is Indian, the Cauca Valley and the rural area near the Caribbean are African or *mulato*. However, continual population migrations are evening out the differences. The birth and death rates vary greatly from one area to the other, but in general infant mortality is high. Hospitals and clinics are few in relation to the population. About 66% of the doctors are in the departmental capitals, which contain about half of the population, though all doctors have to spend a year in the country before they can get their final diploma. Education is free, and since 1927 theoretically compulsory, but many children, especially in rural areas, do not attend. There are high standards of secondary and university education, when it is available.

An estimated 400,000 **tribal peoples**, from 60 ethnic groups, live in Colombia. Groups include the Wayuú (in the Guajira), the Kogi and Arhauco (Sierra Nevada de Santa Marta), Amazonian indians such as the Witoto, the nomadic Nukak and the Ticuna, Andean indians and groups of the Llanos and in the Pacific Coast rain forest. The diversity and importance of indigenous peoples was recognized in the 1991 constitutional reforms when indians were granted the right to two senate seats; the National Colombian Indian Organization (ONIC) won a third seat in the October 1991 ballot. State recognition and the right to bilingual education has not, however, solved major problems of land rights, training and education, and justice.

Ecuador → *Population in 2007 was 13.8 million. Population growth was 1.55%; infant mortality rate 22.1 per 1,000 live births; literacy rate 91%; GDP per capita US$4,500 (2006).*

Roughly 50% of Ecuador's people live in the coastal region west of the Andes, 45% in the Andean Sierra and 5% in Oriente. Migration is occurring from the rural zones of both the coast and the highlands to the towns and cities, particularly Guayaquil and Quito, and agricultural colonization from other parts of the country is taking place in the Oriente. There has also been an important flux of mostly illegal migrants out of Ecuador, seeking opportunities in the USA and Spain; 380,000 people (3% of the population) left between 1995 and 2001. Ecuador's national average population density is the highest in South America. Average *per capita* income rose rapidly in the 1970s and 80s, like other oil-exporting countries, but the distribution has become increasingly skewed. A few Ecuadoreans are spectacularly wealthy, while more than 70% of the population lives in poverty. Dollarization, at turn of the millennium, accentuated this imbalance.

There are 2-3 million Quichua-speaking **highland Indians** and about 70,000 **lowland Indians**. The following indigenous groups maintain their distinct cultural identity: in the Oriente, Siona, Secoya, Cofán, Huaorani, Zápara, Quichua, Shiwiar, Achuar and Shuar; in the Sierra,

Otavalo, Salasaca, Puruhá, Cañari and Saraguro; on the coast, Chachi (Cayapa), Tsáchila (Colorado), Awa (Cuaiquer) and Epera. Many Amazonian Indian communities are fighting for land rights in the face of oil exploration and colonization.

Paraguay → *Population in 2007 was 6.7 million. Population growth was 2.42%; infant mortality rate 26.45 per 1,000 live births; literacy rate 94%; GDP per capita US$4,700 (2006).*

Since Spanish influence was less than in many other parts of South America, most people are bilingual, speaking both Spanish and Guaraní. Outside Asunción, most people speak Guaraní by preference. There is a Guaraní theatre, it is taught in private schools, and books and periodicals are published in that tongue, which has official status as the second national language. According to official figures, the **indigenous population** is about 39,000; non-government sources put it as high as 99,000 (see *Return of the Indian* by Phillip Wearne, London 1996, page 212). Two-thirds of them are in the Chaco, and one-third in the rest of the country. There are 17 distinct ethnic groups with five different languages, among which Guaraní predominates. The 1981 Law of Native Communities in theory guarantees Indian rights to ownership of their traditional lands and the maintenance of their culture. Contact Tierra Viva, Casilla de Correo 789, Asunción, T/F595-2185209.

Peru → *Population in 2007 was 28.7 million. Population growth was 1.29%; infant mortality rate 29.96 per 1,000 live births; literacy rate 87.7%; GDP per capita US$6,400 (2006).*

Peruvian society is a mixture of native Andean peoples, Afro-Peruvians, Spanish, immigrant Chinese, Japanese, Italians, Germans and, to a lesser extent, indigenous Amazon tribes. The first immigrants were the Spaniards who followed Pizarro's expeditionary force. Their effect, demographically, politically and culturally, has been enormous. Peru's black community is based on the coast, mainly in Chincha, south of Lima, and also in some working-class districts of the capital. Their forefathers were originally imported into Peru in the 16th century as slaves to work on the sugar and cotton plantations on the coast. Large numbers of poor Chinese labourers were brought to Peru in the mid-19th century to work in virtual slavery on the guano reserves on the Pacific coast and to build the railroads in the central Andes. The Japanese community, now numbering some 100,000, established itself in the first half of the 20th century. Like most of Latin America, Peru received many emigrés from Europe seeking land and opportunities in the late 19th century. The country's wealth and political power remains concentrated in the hands of this small and exclusive class of whites, which also consists of the descendants of the first Spanish families.

The **indigenous population** is put at about three million Quechua and Aymara Indians in the Andean region and 200,000-250,000 Amazonian Indians from 40-50 ethnic groups. In the Andes, there are 5,000 Indian communities but few densely populated settlements. Their literacy rate is the lowest of any comparable group in South America and their diet is 50% below acceptable levels. About two million Indians speak no Spanish, their main tongue being Quechua, the language of the Incas; they are largely outside the money economy. The conflict between Sendero Luminoso guerrillas and the security forces caused the death of thousands of highland Indians. Many Indian groups are under threat from colonization, development and road- building projects. Some have been dispossessed and exploited for their labour.

Uruguay → *Population in 2007 was 3.5 million. Population growth was 0.50%; infant mortality rate 12.02 per 1,000 live births; literacy rate 98%; GDP per capita US$10,700 (2006).*

Uruguayans are virtually all European, mostly of Spanish and Italian stock. A small percentage in parts of Montevideo and near the Brazilian border are of mixed African and European descent. Less than 10% are mestizos. There was little Spanish settlement in the early years and, for a long time, the area was inhabited mainly by groups of nomadic *gauchos* who trailed after the herds of cattle killing them for food and selling their hides only. Organized commerce began with the arrival of cattle buyers from Buenos Aires who found it profitable to hire herdsmen to look after cattle in defined areas around their headquarters. By about 1800 most of the land had been parcelled out into large *estancias*. The only commercial farming was around Montevideo, where small *chacras* grew vegetables, wheat and maize for the near-by town. Only after 1828 did immigration begin on any scale. Montevideo was then a small town of 20,000 inhabitants. Between 1836 and 1926 about 648,000 immigrants arrived in Uruguay, mostly from Italy and Spain, some into the towns, some to grow crops and vegetables round Montevideo. The native Uruguayans remained pastoralists, leaving commercial farming to the immigrants. More recent immigrants, however, Jewish, Armenian, Lebanese and others have chosen to enter the retail trades, textiles and leather production rather than farming.

Venezuela → *Population was 26.0 million in 2007. Population growth was 1.49%; infant mortality rate 22.52 per 1,000 live births; literacy rate 93%; GDP per capita US$6,900 (2006).*

A large number are of mixed Spanish and Indian origin. There are some pure Africans and a strong element of African descent along the coast, particularly at the ports. The arrival of 800,000 European immigrants, mostly in the 1950s, has greatly modified the racial make-up in Venezuela. One in six of all Venezuelans is foreign born. Venezuela, despite its wealth, still faces serious social problems. Many rural dwellers have drifted to the cities; one result of this exodus is that Venezuelan farmers do not provide all the food the nation needs and imports of foodstuffs are necessary, even for items such as beans and rice. A very small proportion of the population (150,000) is **Indian**. Among the best-known are the Yanomami, who live in Amazonas, and the Bari in the Sierra de Perijá (on the northwest border with Colombia). An Indian Reserve gives the Bari effective control of their own land, but this has not prevented infringement from mining, plantation or settlers. Other groups do not have title to their territory. These groups include the Wayuu (in the Guajira), the Panare and the Piaroa.

Guyana → *According to The World Factbook, population in 2007 was 796,095 (751,223 in the 2002). Population growth was 0.23%; infant mortality rate 31.35 per 1,000 live births; literacy rate 98.8%; GDP per capita US$4,700 (2006).*

Until the 1920s there was little natural increase in population, but the eradication of malaria and other diseases has since led to rapid expansion, particularly among the East Indians (Asian), who, according to most estimates, comprise about 50% of the population. The 2002 census showed the following ethnic distribution: East Indian 43.4%; black 30.2%; mixed 16.7%; Amerindian 9.2%; Chinese 0.2%; Portuguese 0.2%; white 0.1%. Descendants of the original **Amerindian inhabitants** are divided into nine ethnic groups, including the Akawaio, Makuxi and Pemon. Some have lost their isolation and moved to the urban areas, others keenly maintain aspects of their traditional culture and identity.

Suriname → *Population in 2007 was 470,784. Population growth was 1.10%; infant mortality rate 20.11 per 1,000 live births; literacy rate 89.6%; GDP per capita US$7,100 (2006).*

The estimated make-up of the population is: **Indo-Pakistanis** (known locally as Hindustanis), 37%; **Creoles** (European-African and other descent), 31%; **Javanese**, 15%; **Bush Negroes**, called 'Maroons' locally (retribalized descendants of slaves who escaped in the 17th century, living on the upper Saramacca, Suriname and Marowijne rivers), 10%; **Europeans, Chinese** and others, 3%; **Amerindians**, 3% (some sources say only 1%). About 90% of the existing population live in or around Paramaribo or in the coastal towns; the remainder, mostly Carib and Arawak Indians and Maroons, are widely scattered.The Asian people originally entered the country as contracted estate labourers, and settled in agriculture or commerce after completion of their term. They dominate the countryside, whereas Paramaribo is racially very mixed. Although some degree of racial tension exists between all the different groups, Creole-Hindustani rivalry is not as fundamental an issue as in Guyana, for example. Many Surinamese, of all backgrounds, pride themselves on their ability to get along with one another in such a heterogeneous country.

Guyane → *According to the French government, total population in 2006 was 202,000. UN statistics give population growth 2000-2005 as 2.59%; infant mortality rate 14 per 1,000 live births; GDP per capita (not PPP) US$9,705 (2003).*

There are widely divergent estimates for the ethnic composition of the population. Calculations vary according to the number included of illegal immigrants, attracted by social benefits and the high living standards. By some measures, over 40% of the population are Créoles, with correspondingly low figures for Europeans, Asians and Brazilians (around 17% in total). Other estimates put the Créole proportion at 36%, with Haitians 26%, Europeans 10% (of whom about 95% are from France), Brazilians 8%, Asians 4.7% (3.2% from Hong Kong, 1.5% from Laos), about 4% from Suriname and 2.5% from Guyana. The **Amerindian population** is put at 3.6% (over 4% by some estimates). The main groups are Galibis (1,700), Arawak (400), Wayanas (600), Palikours (500), Wayampis-Oyampis (600) and Emerillons (300). There are also bush negroes (Bonis, Saramacas, Djukas), who live mostly in the Maroni area, and others (Dominicans, St Lucians, etc) at 0.7%.

Music and dance

Argentina

Buenos Aires contains almost half of the country's population and its music is the **Tango**. Although also sung and played, the Tango was born as a dance just before the turn of the 20th century. The exact moment of the birth was not recorded by any contemporary observer and continues to be a matter of debate, though the roots can be traced. The name 'Tango' predates the dance and was given to the carnivals (and dances) of the black inhabitants of the Río de la Plata in the early l9th century. Elements of the black tradition were taken over by whites, as the black population declined into insignificance. However, the name 'Tango Americano' was also given to the Habanera (a Cuban descendant of the English Country Dance) which became the rage in Spain and bounced back into the Río de la Plata in the middle of the 19th century, not only as a fashionable dance, together with the polka, mazurka, waltz and cuadrille, but also as a song form in the very popular 'Zarzuelas', or Spanish operettas. However, the Habanera led not a double, but a triple life, by also infiltrating the lowest levels of society directly from Cuba via sailors who arrived in the ports of Montevideo and Buenos Aires. Here it encountered the Milonga, originally a Gaucho song style, but by 1880 a dance, especially popular with the so-called 'Compadritos' and 'Orilleros', who frequented the port area and its brothels, whence the Argentine Tango emerged around the turn of the century to dazzle the populace with its brilliant, personalized footwork, which could not be accomplished without the partners staying glued together. As a dance it became the rage and, as the infant recording industry grew by leaps and bounds, it also became popular as a song and an instrumental genre, with the original violins and flutes being eclipsed by the bandoneón button accordion, then being imported from Germany. In 1911 the new dance took Paris by storm and returned triumphant to Buenos Aires. It achieved both respectability and notoriety, becoming a global phenomenon after the First World War. The golden voice of the renowned Carlos Gardel soon gave a wholly new dimension to the music of the Tango until his death in 1935. After losing some popularity in Argentina, it came to the forefront again in the 1940s (1920-1950 is considered the real golden age). Its resurgence was assisted by Perón's decree that 50% of all music played on the radio must be Argentine, only to suffer a second, much more serious decline in the face of rock music over the past two decades. Fortunately, it has experienced another revival in recent years and the Tango and Milonga can once again be seen being danced in Buenos Aires. Apart from Carlos Gardel, other great names connected with the Tango are Francisco Canaro (Uruguayan), Osvaldo Pugliese and Astor Piazzolla, who has modernized it by fusion with jazz styles (nuevo tango).

If the Tango represents the soul of Buenos Aires, this is not the case in the rest of the country. The provinces have a very rich and attractive heritage of folk dances, mainly for couples, with arms held out and fingers clicked or handkerchiefs waved, with the 'Paso Valseado' as the basic step. Descended from the Zamacueca, and therefore a cousin of the Chilean Cueca and Peruvian Marinera, is the slow and stately Zamba, where the handkerchief is used to greatest effect. Equally popular throughout most of the country are the faster Gato, Chacarera and Escondido. These were the dances of the Gaucho and their rhythm evokes that of a cantering horse. Guitar and the bombo drum provide the accompaniment. Particularly spectacular is the Malambo, where the Gaucho shows off his dextrous footwork, the spurs of his boots adding a steely note to the rhythm.

Different regions of the country have their own specialities. The music of Cuyo in the west is sentimental and similar to that of neighbouring Chile, with its Cuecas for dance and Tonadas for song. The northwest on the other hand is Andean, with its musical culture closer to that of Bolivia, particularly on the Puna, where the Indians play the quena and charango and sound mournful notes on the great long erke. Here the dances are Bailecitos and Carnavalitos, while the songs are Vidalitas and the extraordinary high pitched Bagualas, the very essence of primeval pain. In the northeast provinces of Corrientes and Misiones, the music shares similarities with Paraguay. The Polca and Galopa are danced and the local Chamamé is sung, to the accordion or the harp, the style being sentimental. Santiago del Estero is the heartland of the Chacarera and the lyrics are often part Spanish and part Quichua, a local dialect of the Andean Quechua language. In the Province of Buenos Aires you are more likely to hear the Gauchos singing their Milongas, Estilos and Cifras and challenging each other to a Payada or rhymed duel. Argentina experienced a folk revival in the 50's and 60's and some of the most celebrated groups are still drawing enthusiastic audiences today. These groups include Los Chalchaleros and Los Fronterizos, the perennial virtuoso singer and guitarist, Eduardo Falú and, more recently, León Gieco from Santa Fe.

Bolivia

The heart of Bolivia is the Altiplano and it is the music of the Quechua and Aymara-speaking Indians of this area that provides the most distinctive Bolivian musical sound. Although there is much that is of Spanish colonial origin in the Indians' dances, the music itself has more Amerindian style and content than that of any other country in South America. It is rare to find an Indian who cannot play an instrument and it is these instruments, both wind and percussion, that are quintessentially Bolivian. The clear sounds of the quena and pinkullo, the deeper, breathier notes of the tarka, pututo and sicuri accompanied by huankaré, pululu and caja drums can be heard all over the Altiplano, the charango (a small, G-stringed guitar) being virtually the only instrument of European origin. The Indian dances are mainly collective and take place at religious fiestas. The dancers wear colourful costumes with elaborate, plumed headdresses and some of them still parody their ex-Spanish colonial masters.

The principal popular dances that can be regarded as 'national' in their countrywide appeal are the Cueca and Huayño. The Bolivian Cueca is a close relative of the Chilean national dance of the same name and they share a mutual origin in the Zamacueca, itself derived from the Spanish Fandango. The Huayño is of Indian origin and involves numerous couples, who whirl around or advance down the street, arm-in-arm, in a 'Pandilla'. Justly celebrated is the great carnival Diablada of Oruro, with its hordes of grotesquely masked devils, a spectacle comparable to those of Rio in Brazil and Barranquilla in Colombia. The region of Tarija near the Argentine border has a distinctive musical tradition of its own, based on religious processions that culminate with that of San Roque on the first Sunday in September. There are many professional folk groups on record, the best known being *Grupo Aymara, Los Runas, Los Laris, Los Masis, Kolla Marka* and *Bolivia Manta,* some of which have now established themselves in Europe and North America.

Brazil

Perhaps because of its sheer size, Brazil has a greater musical inventory than any other Latin American country, not only reflected in the immense regional spread of folk music but also in its successive waves of urban popular music. The Brazilian expresses themselves through music and dance to an extraordinary degree and the music covers the whole spectrum from the utmost rural simplicity to the ultimate state-of-the-art commercial sophistication.

The South In Paraná, Santa Catarina and Rio Grande do Sul, the music is strictly European in origin, rhythm and instrumentation. Rio Grande do Sul shares Gaucho dances such as the Pericom and song styles such as the Milonga, Trova and Pajada with neighbouring Uruguay and Argentina. The Chula is a competitive dance for men to show off (comparable to the Argentine Malambo), while the Pexinho is for men and women. The guitar and the accordion are favourite instruments, also true for Santa Catarina and Paraná, where the names of the dances denote their European origins: Mazurkas, Valsas, Chotes, Polquinhas and Rancheiras. The Chimarrita is a song style that came straight from the Azores. If you are feeling sentimental, you sing a Toada, if energetic, you stamp your feet to a Fandango. Except for the Batuque de Rio Grande do Sul in Porto Alegre, closely related to the Candombe of nearby Montevideo, there is no African influence in the music of this region and none of that classic Brazilian syncopation.

São Paulo, Rio de Janeiro, Minas Gerais Moving north into São Paulo, we enter an area rich in traditional folk dances and music, with the African admixture beginning to show up. At many religious festivals will be found the Congadas (European 'Moors and Christians', but danced by blacks) and Moçambique (a stick dance for men), while the Samba de Lenço, Fandango and Batuque are recreational dances for one or more couples. The instrumental accompaniment branches out into shakers (the ganzá), drums (caixas and tambores) and above all the guitar (viola). Try the great pilgrimage church at Aparecida do Norte on a Sunday. You might well see a group of religious dances. In the hinterland of Rio de Janeiro the Folias de Reis are out on the street from Christmas to Epiphany, singing from house to house, accompanying themselves on the caixa and adufe drums and the guitar, while in the old coastal towns of Paraty and Angra dos Reis are to be found the **Dança de Velhos** (the old men), performed to the accordion. The Jongo is a dance of African origin for men and women, naturally with a drum accompaniment. And there is hardly need to mention Rio at carnival and its Samba Schools. Further north again, we come to the states of Espíritu Santo, Minas Gerais and Goiás. In colonial Ouro Preto, in Minas, you can hear the old Modinha sung to the Portuguese guitar as a serenade and be transported into the past. Espíritu Santo is home to the Ticumbi, a kind of Congada, danced to the guitar and shakers (*chocalhos*). Goiás shares with Minas Gerais a very rich heritage of Portuguese derived religious folk song and dance, centred on Folias, Modas and Calangos.

Bahia Bahia is the heart of African Brazil and a very musical heart it is, born of the Yoruba religion that came with the slaves from what is now Nigeria. The resulting syncretic religion is known as Candomblé in Bahia and the gods or 'Orixás' are worshipped through song, dance and possession in the 'Terreiros', directed by the priests (Pais-de-Santo) and priestesses (Mães-de- Santo). The mainly female adepts, dressed entirely in white, circle gracefully to the background chant of 'Pontos' and the thunderous pounding of the atabaques, the tall drums. The two most revered priestesses are Mãe Olga de Alakêto and Mãe Menininha de Gantois. Similar syncretic African religions are found elsewhere in Brazil. Another vital African element in Bahian folk music is the spectacular dance-cum-martial arts form of Capoeira. Bodies whirl and cartwheel around to the sound of the berimbau (a one-stringed bow with resonator) and the accompanying chant. Related to the Capoeira is the stick dance Maculelê. Two of the best berimbau groups on record are *Camaféu de Oxóssi* and the *Cordão de Ouro*. Bahia has a carnival almost as celebrated as that of Rio and here you can see the Afoxé, a serious religious dance, performed to drums alone.

The North East North of Bahia is the Nordeste, with music that runs the whole gamut from black African to mediaeval Portuguese. In colonial times the church directed the peoples' musical energies into religious plays, songs and dances and a large number of these are still performed. The Bumba-Meu-Boi is a folk drama in the course of which a bull is killed and then brought back to life. Particularly popular in Piauí and Maranhão, its variants are found as far afield as Amazônia, where it is called the Boi-Bumbá, and Paraná in the far south, where it is known as Boi-Mamão. Also popular along the coast from Ceará to Paraíba is a nautical drama of Portuguese origin called Marujada or Nau Catarineta, a version of Moors and Christians, accompanied by Portuguese guitar (violão), drums and the ganzá scraper. In Alagoas, Sergipe and Pernambuco we find the sword dance called Reisado, danced after Christmas, the Caboclinhos, who are dressed like Indians and dance with bows and arrows, and the Guerreiros Alagoanos, a mixture of both. The last named are accompanied by the classical northeastern musical group called Terno de Pífanos, with the pífano vertical flute, accompanied by maracas and ganzá. The Banda de Pífanos of Caruaru in Pernambuco can be found on record. Recreational dance music in the Nordeste goes under the generic name of 'Forró', said to be derived from the expression 'For All', because the English companies operating at the turn of the century organized weekend dances for their workmen to which all comers were invited. Four very popular recreational folk dances of this region are the Ciranda (a round dance), the Coco, the Bate-Coxa (where the dancers bump bellies) and the Bambelô. Carnival in Recife, the largest city, is when and where to see the energetic and gymnastic Frevo, danced by young men with an umbrella in their hands, and the very stately and superbly costumed Maracatu dancers, with their queen and king. The Nordeste is equally rich in song styles, notably the Desafios, Emboladas, Cocos and Aboios. The Desafios are performed by so-called Repentistas or Violeiros, who accompany themselves on the Portuguese guitar and whose repertoire includes a large inventory of verse styles. They will sing about individual spectators, who then pay willingly for the compliment. The Emboladas and Cocos are similar, but faster and accompanied solely by tambourines, while the Aboios are songs related to cattle and cattlemen. Repentistas and Emboladores can be found at work in markets throughout the region. The premier Repentista is Otacílio Batista do Pajeú, who sang to the Pope during the latter's visit to Brazil. The music of the Nordeste has also been well propagated by more sophisticated groups that have based themselves on folk roots, such as the Quinteto Violado, Ariano Suassuna's Orchestra Armorial and Cussy de Almeida's Quinteto Armorial, not forgetting the veteran accordionist Luiz Gonzaga and Alceu Valença. As a result of the huge migration of nordestinos to the urban south, moreover, it is just as easy to hear this regional music in São Paulo as it is in Recife.

Pará and the Amazon Finally to Pará and the Amazon in the far north, where the music has been heavily influenced from the Caribbean. The most popular musical genre here is the Carimbó, danced to a Merengue-type rhythm and played on drums, wind or brass (usually the clarinet) and strings, particularly the banjo. Notable performers are Pinduca ('O Rei do Carimbó'), Veriquete and Vieira. It is the latter who thought up the term 'Lambada' for his particular version of the Carimbó, and the spectacular, thigh-entwining dance form introduced to the world in Paris by Karakos and Lorsac in 1988 had already been popular among young people at 'Forrós' throughout the region for some years. The very traditional island of Marajó in the mouth of the Amazon has preserved versions of 18th century dances, such as the Lundú and Chula.

Urban popular music The vast range of Brazilian regional folk music is only equalled by the chronological depth of its urban popular music, which surges like endless waves on a beach. For the origins we have to go back to Jesuit missions and Portuguese folk music, influenced and blended by African slaves, from which emerged the 19th century Lundús, Polcas and Maxixes that in turn gave way to the romantic and sentimental Choro song genre (from chorar, to weep), accompanied by guitar, flute and cavaquinho (small guitar), which became all the rage and indeed still has its adepts in Brazil today. A key figure in urban music was Ernesto Nazaré, composer and pianist, who occupied a special niche somewhere between popular and light classical, composing between 1880 and 1930 a vast number of Tangos Brasileiros (not to be confused with the Argentine variety), Mazurkas, Polcas, Waltzes and other popular songs.

Around the 1900s the instrumentation turned to brass and Rio's urban Samba was born, a birth that was announced by the recording in 1917 of Donga's 'Pelo Telefone'. Names from this early period are Pixinguinha, Sinhô, Heitor dos Prazeres, Ary Barroso, Noel Rosa and of course Carmen Miranda, who took the Samba to Hollywood and the rest of the world. It also became intimately connected with the carnival in the form of Marcha Ranchos and Sambas de Enredo as the first samba schools were formed, of which Salgueiro, Mangueira, Partido Alto, Portela, Mocidade Independente and Beija-Flor are some of the most famous. With the Escolas de Samba came the Batucada or percussion groups playing the pandeiro (tambourine), atabaque and tamborim (drum), agogô (cowbell), reco-reco, chocalho, afoxê and cuíca. This is the real engine room of Samba. Listen to Lúcio Perrone or Mocidade Independente de Padre Miguel. A new phase was ushered in with an invasion from Bahia and the Nordeste in the early 1950s. From Bahia came Dorival Caymmi, who dropped his fishermen's songs in favour of the Samba, and Luiz Gonzaga, who brought his accordion, zabumba drum and triangulo, with which to play his Baiãos (his 'Asa Branca' is a classic) and almost put the Samba itself into eclipse for several years. Almost, but not quite, for out of the ashes there soon arose Bossa Nova – white, middle class and silky smooth. Vinícius de Moraes and Tom Jobim were its heroes; 1958 to 1964 the years; Copacabana, Ipanema and Leblon the scene; 'Samba de uma Nota Só', 'A Garota de Ipanema' and 'Desafinado' the songs and Nara Leão, Baden Powell, Toquinho, João Gilberto, Luis Bonfá and Astrud Gilberto the main performers. Stan Getz, the American jazz saxophonist, helped export it to the world. What was now being called MPB (Música Popular Brasileira) then took off in several directions. Chico Buarque, Edu Lobo and Milton Nascimento were protest singers. Out of Bahia emerged 'Tropicalismo' in the persons of Gilberto Gil, Caetano Veloso and his sister Maria Bethânia, Gal Costa, João Gilberto and 'Som Livre'. The words were important, but the rhythm was still there. Brazilian rock also now appeared, with such stars as Roberto Carlos, Elis Regina, Rita Lee, and Ney Mattogrosso. Heavy metal is a popular genre that continues to evolve as exemplified by the band *Sepultura*. Recently, in turning towards international black consciousness, the Bahianos have mixed Reggae and Samba to produce 'axê'. Still, Samba has survived, although now called 'Pagode' and amazingly, 40% of all Brazilian records sold are of Música Sertaneja, a highly commercialized pseudo-folk genre which is closer to American Country and Western than to most other Brazilian music. Listen to the 'Duplas' of Tonico and Tinoco, Jacó e Jacozinho, Vieira and Vieirinha, or Leonardo and Leandro (who died in 1998) and you'll see. In the meantime a series of brilliant Brazilian instrumentalists have become international names and often live abroad – Sérgio Mendes, the guitarist Sebastião Tapajós, flautist Hermêto Paschoal, saxophonist Paulo Moura, accordionist Sivuca, percussionists Airto Moreira and Nana Vasconcelos, singer Flora Purim and all-rounder Egberto Gismonti are but a few. On the top of a huge recording industry, we're now a long way from the grassroots and the haunting flute music of the forest Indians.

Chile

At the very heart of Chilean music is the **Cueca**, a courting dance for couples, both of whom make great play with a handkerchief waved aloft in the right hand. The man's knees are slightly bent and his body arches back. It is lively and vigorous, seen to best advantage when performed by a Huaso wearing spurs. Guitar and harp are the accompanying instruments, while handclapping and shouts of encouragement add to the atmosphere. The dance has a common origin with the Argentine Zamba and Peruvian Marinera via the early 19th century Zamacueca, in turn descended from the Spanish Fandango. For singing only is the Tonada, with its variants the Glosa, Parabienes, Romance, Villancico (Christmas carol) and Esquinazo (serenade) and the Canto a lo Poeta, which can be in the form of a Contrapunto or Controversia, a musical duel. Among the most celebrated groups are Los Huasos Quincheros, Silvia Infante with Los Condores and the Conjunto Millaray. Famous folk singers in this genre are the Parra Family from Chillán, Hector Pávez and Margot Loyola. In the north of the country the music is Amerindian and closely related to that of Bolivia. Groups called 'Bailes' dance the Huayño, Taquirari, Cachimbo or Rueda at carnival and other festivities and precolumbian rites like the Cauzulor and Talatur. Instruments are largely wind and percussion, including zampoñas (pan pipes), lichiguayos, pututos (conch shells) and clarines. There are some notable religious festivals that attract large crowds of pilgrims and include numerous groups of costumed dancers. The most outstanding of these festivals are those of the Virgen de La Tirana near Iquique, San Pedro de Atacama, the Virgen de la Candelaria of Copiapó and the Virgen de Andacollo. In the south the Mapuche nation, the once greatly feared and admired 'Araucanos', who kept the Spaniards and Republicans at bay for 400 years, have their own songs, dance-songs and magic and collective dances, accompanied by wind instruments like the great long trutruca horn, the shorter pifilka and the kultrun drum. Further south still, the island of Chiloé, which remained in the hands of pro-Spanish loyalists after the rest of the country had become independent, has its own unique musical expression. Wakes and other religious social occasions include collective singing, while the dances, all of Spanish origin, such as the Vals, Pavo, Pericona and Nave have a heavier and less syncopated beat than in central Chile. Accompanying instruments here are the rabel (fiddle), guitar and accordion.

Colombia

No South American country has a greater variety of music than Colombia, strategically placed where the Andes meet the Caribbean. The four major musical areas are (a) the mountain heartland (b) the Pacific coast (c) the Caribbean coast and (d) the Llanos or eastern plains. The mountain heartland covers the Andean highlands and intervening valleys of the Cauca and Magdalena and includes the country's three largest cities, Bogotá, Cali and Medellín. It is relatively gentle and sentimental music, accompanied largely by string instruments, with an occasional flute and a chucho or carángano shaker to lay down the rhythm. The preferred instrument of the highlands and by extension Colombia's national instrument, is the tiple, a small 12-stringed guitar, most of which are manufactured at Chiquinquirá in Boyacá. The national dance is the Bambuco, whose lilting sounds are said to have inspired Colombian troops at the Battle of Ayacucho in 1824. It is to be found throughout the countrys heartland for dancing, singing and instrumentalizing and has long transcended its folk origins. The choreography is complex, including many figures, such as la Invitación, Los Ochos, Los Codos, Los Coqueteos, La Perseguida and La Arrodilla. Other related dances are the Torbellino, where the woman whirls like a top, the more stately Guabina, the Pasillo, Bunde, Sanjuanero and the picaresque Rajaleña. Particularly celebrated melodies are the 'Guabina Chiquinquireña' and the 'Bunde Tolimense'. The following fiestas, among others, provide a good opportunity of seeing the music and dance: La Fiesta del Campesino, ubiquitous on the first Sunday in June, the Fiesta del Bambuco in Neiva and Festival Folklórico Colombiano in Ibagué later in the month, the Fiesta Nacional de la Guabina y el Tiple, held in Vélez in early August, the Desfile de Silleteros in Medellín in the same month and Las Fiestas de Pubenza in Popayán just after the New Year, where the Conjuntos de Chirimía process through the streets.

On Colombia's tropical Pacific coast (and extending down into Esmeraldas, Ecuador) is to be found some of the most African sounding black music in all South America. The Currulao and its variants, the Berejú and Patacoré, are extremely energetic recreational dances and the vocals are typically African-style call- and-response. This is the home of the marimba and the music is very percussion driven, including the upright cununo drum plus bombos and redoblantes. Wakes are important in this region and at these the Bundes, Arrullos and Alabaos are sung. Best known is the 'Bunde de San Antonio'. The Jota Chocoana is a fine example of a Spanish dance taken by black people and turned into a satirical weapon against their masters. The regional fiestas are the Festival Folklórico del Litoral at Buenaventura in July and San Francisco de Asís at Quibdó on 4 August. Quibdó also features a Fiesta de los Indios at Easter.

The music of Colombia's Caribbean coast became popular for dancing throughout Latin America more than 30 years ago under the name of 'Música Tropical' and has much more recently become an integral part of the Salsa repertory. It can be very roughly divided into 'Cumbia' and 'Vallenato'. The Cumbia is a heavily black influenced dance form for several couples, the men forming an outer circle and the women an inner one. The men hold aloft a bottle of rum and the women a bundle of slim candles called 'espermas'. The dance probably originated in what is now Panama, moved east into Cartagena, where it is now centred and quite recently further east to Barranquilla and Santa Marta. The most celebrated Cumbias are those of Ciénaga, Mompós, Sampués, San Jacinto and Sincelejo. The instrumental accompaniment consists of gaitas or flautas de caña de millo, backed by drums. The gaitas ('male' and 'female') are vertical cactus flutes with beeswax heads, while the cañas de millo are smaller transverse flutes. The most famous conjuntos are the Gaiteros de San Jacinto, the Cumbia Soledeña and the Indios Selectos. Variants of the Cumbia are the Porro, Gaita, Puya, Bullerengue and Mapalé, these last two being much faster and more energetic. Lately Cumbia has also become very much part of the Vallenato repertoire and is therefore often played on the accordion. Vallenato music comes from Valledupar in the Department of César and is of relatively recent origin. It is built around one instrument, the accordion, albeit backed by guacharaca rasps and caja drums. The most popular rhythms are the Paseo and the Merengue, the latter having arrived from the Dominican Republic, where it is the national dance. Perhaps the first virtuoso accordionist was the legendary 'Francisco El Hombre', playing around the turn of the century. Today's best known names are those of Rafael Escalona, Alejandro Durán and Calixto Ochoa. In April the Festival de la Leyenda Vallenata is held in Valledupar and attended by thousands. Barranquilla is the scene of South America's second most celebrated Carnival, after that of Rio de Janeiro, with innumerable traditional masked groups, such as the Congos, Toros, Diablos and Caimanes. The Garabato is a dance in which death is defeated. Barranquilla's carnival is less commercialized and more traditional than that of Rio and should be a must for anyone with the opportunity to attend. Other important festivals in the region are the Corralejas de Sincelejo with its bullfights in January, La Candelaria in Cartagena on 2 February, the Festival de la Cumbia in El Banco in June, Fiesta del Caiman in Ciénaga in January and Festival del Porro in San Pelayo (Córdoba). To complete the music of the Caribbean region, the Colombian islands of San Andrés and Providencia, off the coast of Nicaragua, have a fascinating mix of mainland Colombian and Jamaican island music, with the Calypso naturally a prominent feature.

The fourth musical region is that of the great eastern plains, the so-called Llanos Orientales between the Ríos Arauca and Guaviare, a region where there is really no musical frontier between the two republics of Colombia and Venezuela. Here the Joropo reigns supreme as a dance, with its close relatives the Galerón, the slower and more romantic Pasaje and the breathlessly fast Corrido and Zumba que Zumba. These are dances for couples, with a lot of heel tapping, the arms hanging down loosely to the sides. Arnulfo Briceño and Pentagrama Llanera are the big names and the harp is the only instrument that matters, although normally backed by cuatro, guitar, tiple and maracas. The place to see and hear it all is at the Festival Nacional del Joropo at Villavicencio in December.

Ecuador

Culturally, ethnically and geographically, Ecuador is very much two countries – the Andean highlands with their centre at Quito and the Pacific lowlands behind Guayaquil. In spite of this, the music is relatively homogeneous and it is the Andean music that would be regarded as 'typically Ecuadorean'. The principal highland rhythms are the Sanjuanito, Cachullapi, Albaza, Yumbo and Danzante, danced by Indian and mestizo alike. These may be played by brass bands, guitar trios or groups of wind instruments, but it is the rondador, a small panpipe, that provides the classic Ecuadorean sound, although of late the Peruvian quena has been making heavy inroads via pan-Andean groups and has become a threat to the local instrument. The coastal region has its own song form, the Amorfino, but the most genuinely 'national' song and dance genres, both of European origin, are the Pasillo (shared with Colombia) in waltz time and the Pasacalle, similar to the Spanish Pasodoble. Of Ecuador's three best loved songs, 'El Chulla Quiteño', 'Romántico Quito' and 'Vasija de Barro', the first two are both Pasacalles. Even the Ecuadorean mestizo music has a melancholy quality not found in Peruvian 'Música Criolla', perhaps due to Quito being in the mountains, while Lima is on the coast. Music of the highland Indian communities is, as elsewhere in the region, related to religious feasts and ceremonies and geared to wind instruments such as the rondador, the pinqullo and pifano flutes and the great long guarumo horn with its mournful note. The guitar is also usually present and brass bands with well worn instruments can be found in even the smallest villages. Among the most outstanding traditional fiestas are Inti Raymi in Cayambe and Ingapirca, the Pase del Niño in Cuenca and other cities, the Mama Negra of Latacunga, carnival in Guaranda, the Yamor in Otavalo, the Fiesta de las Frutas y las Flores in Ambato, plus Corpus Cristi and the Feast of Saint John all over the highlands. Among the best known musical groups who have recorded are Los

Embajadores (whose 'Tormentos' is superb) and the Duo Benítez-Valencia for guitar. There is one totally different cultural area, that of the black inhabitants of the Province of Esmeraldas and the highland valley of the Río Chota in Imbabura. The former is a southern extension of the Colombian Pacific coast negro culture, centred round the marimba xylophone. The musical genres are also shared with black Colombians, including the Bunde, Bambuco, Caderona, Torbellino and Currulao dances and this music is some of the most African sounding in the whole of South America. The Chota Valley is an inverted oasis of desert in the Andes and here the black people dance the Bomba. It is also home to the unique Bandas Mochas, whose primitive instruments include leaves that are doubled over and blown through.

Paraguay

The music of Paraguay is a curiosity. Although this is the only South American country, the majority of whose population still speak the original native tongue, the music is totally European in origin. The 17th- and 18th-century Jesuits found the Guaraní people to be highly musical and when their missions were established, the natives were immediately and totally indoctrinated into European music, of which they became fine performers, albeit not composers or innovators. A good example is Cristóbal Pirioby (1764-94), who changed his name to José Antonio Ortiz and moved to Buenos Aires to perform. At his death he left a large collection of musical instruments and sheet music of works by Haydn, Boccherini, etc. After the disastrous War of the Triple Alliance there was an abandonment of things national and even the national anthem was composed by a Uruguayan. Although black slaves were introduced to the country, they became quickly absorbed and there is no trace of black influence in the music. Neither is there any Guaraní element, nor infusion from Brazil or Argentina. Virtually the only popular instruments are the guitar and harp and it is the latter in particular that has come to be the hallmark of all that is musically Paraguayan, with the assistance of such brilliant performers as Félix Pérez Cardoso and Digno García. Paraguayan songs are notably languid and extremely sentimental and the present repertoire is not 'traditional', but of 20th century origin and by known composers. Of the three principal musical genres, two are slow and for singing, while one is lively and purely for dancing. The two singing genres are the Canción Paraguaya (or Purajhéi) and the Guarania, the former being a slow polka, of which the earliest and most famous example is 'Campamento Cerro León' about the War of the Triple Alliance. The Guarania was developed by José Asunción Flores as recently as the 1920s and includes most of the country's best loved and oft-repeated songs, such as 'India', 'Mi Dicha Lejana' and 'Recuerdos de Ypacaraí'. Equally celebrated and far more vigorous is that favourite of harp virtuosos, the wordless but onomatopeic 'Pájaro Campana'.

For dancing there are the lively Polca Paraguaya and Polca Galopada, first mentioned in print in 1858. They have similarities with the Argentine 'Gato' for instance and are not a true polka nor a gallop, the names of these popular European dances having been attached to an existing Paraguayan dance of unknown name. The Polca is a dance for couples, whilst the even livelier Galopa is usually danced by groups of women, the so-called 'Galoperas', who swing round barefoot, balancing a bottle or jar on their heads. This in turn has developed into the 'Danza de la Botella' or bottle dance, a more recent variant for virtuoso individual performance. Other less well known dances are the Valseadas (a local variant of the waltz), the Chopi or Santa Fé (for three couples), the Taguato, Golondrina, Palomita and Solito, the last named a kind of 'musical chairs'. Paraguayan music first came to global attention soon after the second world war and a number of artists such as Luis Alberto del Paraná and Los Paraguayos have achieved world fame. At the other end of the spectrum the four barefoot old men of the Banda Peteke Peteke from Guajayvity near Yaguarón play their own traditional music on two mimby flutes and two little drums, a small idiosyncratic island in an ocean of harp music.

Peru

Peru is the Andean heartland. Its musicians, together with those of Bolivia, have appeared on the streets of cities all over Europe and North America. However, the costumes they wear, the instruments they play, notably the quena and charango, are not typical of Peru as a whole, only of the Cuzco region. Peruvian music divides at a very basic level into that of the highlands ('Andina') and that of the coast ('Criolla'). The highlands are immensely rich in terms of music and dance, with over 200 dances recorded. Every village has its fiestas and each fiesta has its communal and religious dances. Those of Paucartambo and Coylloriti (Q'olloriti) in the Cuzco region moreover attract innumerable groups of dancers from far and wide. The highlands themselves can be very roughly subdivided into some half dozen major musical regions, of

66 99 Peru is the Andean heartland. Its musicians have appeared on the streets of cities all over Europe and North America.

which perhaps the most characteristic are Ancash and the north, the Mantaro Valley, Cuzco, Puno and the Altiplano, Ayacucho and Parinacochas.

There is one recreational dance and musical genre, the Huayno, that is found throughout the whole of the Sierra, and has become ever more popular and commercialized to the point where it is in danger of swamping and indeed replacing the other more regional dances. Nevertheless, still very popular among Indians and/or Mestizos are the Marinera, Carnaval, Pasacalle, Chuscada (from Ancash), Huaylas, Santiago and Chonguinada (all from the Mantaro) and Huayllacha (from Parinacochas). For singing only are the mestizo Muliza, popular in the Central Region, and the soulful lament of the Yaravi, originally Indian, but taken up and developed early in the 19th century by the poet and hero of independence Mariano Melgar, from Arequipa.

The Peruvian Altiplano shares a common musical culture with that of Bolivia and dances such as the Auqui-Auqui and Sicuris, or Diabladas, can be found on either side of the border. The highland instrumentation varies from region to region, although the harp and violin are ubiquitous. In the Mantaro area the harp is backed by brass and wind instruments, notably the clarinet, in Cuzco it is the charango and quena and on the Altiplano the sicu panpipes. Two of the most spectacular dances to be seen are the Baile de las Tijeras ('scissor dance') from the Ayacucho/Huancavelica area, for men only and the pounding, stamping Huaylas for both sexes. Huaylas competitions are held annually in Lima and should not be missed. Indeed, owing to the overwhelming migration of peasants into the barrios of Lima, most types of Andean music and dance can be seen in the capital, notably on Sunday at the so-called 'Coliseos', which exist for that purpose. Were a Hall of Fame to be established, it would have to include the Ancashino singers La Pastorcita Huaracina and El Jilguero del Huascarán, the charango player Jaime Guardia, the guitar virtuoso Raul García from Ayacucho and the Lira Paucina trio from Parinacochas.

The flood of migration to the cities has meant that the distinct styles of regional and ethnic groups have become blurred. One example is Chicha, a hybrid of Huayno music and the Colombian Cumbia rhythm which comes from the pueblos jóvenes. More recent is Tecno-cumbia, which originated in the jungle region with groups such as Rossy War, from Puerto Maldonado, and Euforia, from Iquitos. It is a vibrant dance music which has gained much greater popularity across Peruvian society than chicha music ever managed.

The 'Música Criolla' from the coast could not be more different from that of the Sierra. Here the roots are Spanish and African. The popular Valsesito is a syncopated waltz that would certainly be looked at askance in Vienna; the Polca has also suffered an attractive sea change, but reigning over all is the Marinera, Peru's national dance, a rhythmic, graceful courting encounter, a close cousin of Chile's and Bolivia's Cueca and the Argentine Zamba, all of them descended from the Zamacueca. The Marinera has its 'Limeña' and 'Norteña' versions and a more syncopated relative, the Tondero, found in the north coastal regions, is said to have been influenced by slaves brought from Madagascar. All these dances are accompanied by guitars and frequently the *cajón*, a resonant wooden box on which the player sits, pounding it with his hands. Some of the great names of 'Música Criolla' are the singer/composers Chabuca Granda and Alicia Maguiña, the female singer Jesús Vásquez and the groups Los Morochucos and Hermanos Zañartu.

Also on the coast is to be found the music of the small black community, the 'Música Negroide' or 'Afro-Peruano', which had virtually died out when it was resuscitated in the 50s, but has since gone from strength to strength. It has all the qualities to be found in black music from the Caribbean – a powerful, charismatic beat, rhythmic and lively dancing, and strong percussion provided by the *cajón* and the *quijada de burro*, a donkey's jaw with the teeth loosened. Some of the classic dances in the black repertoire are the Festejo, Son del Diablo, Toro Mata, Landó and Alcatraz. In the Alcatraz one of the partners dances behind the other with a candle, trying to set light to a piece of paper tucked into the rear of the other partner's waist. Nicomedes and Victoria Santa Cruz have been largely responsible for popularizing this black music, and Peru Negro is another excellent professional group. The undoubted, internationally famous star, though, is Susana Baca. Finally, in the Peruvian Amazon region around Iquitos, local variants of the Huayno and Marinera are danced, as well as the Changanacui, accompanied by flute and drum.

Uruguay

Most musical influences came with the European immigrants who arrived after the disappearance of the Amerindian population. The folk songs and dances are very closely related to those of the Argentine pampas, except in the north, where they are shared with the neighbouring Brazilian state of Rio Grande do Sul. The major song genres are the Estilo, Cifra, Milonga and Vidalita, whilst the 'national' dance is the stately Pericón for six or more couples. The Milonga is also danced, as are the Tango, Cielito, Media Caña and Ranchera. The guitar is the instrument that accompanies most country music and as in Argentina, the gauchos like to engage in Payadas de Contrapunto, where two singers vie with each other, alternating improvised verses. 19th century Europe introduced other popular dances into Uruguay, such as the polca, waltz, chotis and mazurca, all of which were given a local touch. In the northern departments a number of dances are shared with Brazil, such as the Chimarrita, Carangueijo and Tirana, which are also sung, either in Spanish or Portuguese or a mixture of both. There were many black slaves in the Río de la Plata during colonial times and the African ritual of the Candombe was practised in Montevideo until late in the 19th century. Less than 3% of the population is black and the only musical remains of African origin are to be found in the presence during carnival of the Morenada groups of up to 50 Candomberos, who take part in the procession, playing their tamboril drums, while smaller groups take part in these so-called 'Llamadas' from December through to Holy Week. There are four sizes of drums – chico, repique, piano and bajo – and the complex polyrhythms produced by the mass of drummers advancing down the street is both unexpected and impressive.

Venezuela

Venezuelan music is more homogenous than that of some of the other republics. Its highly distinctive sound is based on an instrumental combination of harp, cuatro (a small, four stringed guitar) and maracas. Many of the rhythms have a very fast, almost headlong pace to them, stimulating both to the senses and to the feet, music here being almost inseparable from dance. The recipe for Venezuelan music is a classic European/African/Amerindian mix. The country's national dance is the Joropo, a name deriving from the Arab 'Xarop', meaning syrup and which originally meant a country dance. This is a dance for couples with several sequences, such as the Valseao, Zapatiao, Escobillao and Toriao. Closely related to the Joropo are the Corrido, with a ballad content, Galerón (slow for singing or fast for dancing), Pasaje (lyrical, very popular in the Llanos) and Golpe, from the State of Lara, to all of which styles the Joropo may be danced in different parts of the country. Note that the little cuatro is normally referred to as 'guitarra' while the Spanish guitar is called the 'guitarra grande'. Some of the dance rhythms have been imported from abroad or are shared with neighbouring countries, such as the urban Merengue (introduced into Caracas in the 1920s), the Jota and Malagueña of Anzoátegui State, the Pasillo (shared with Colombia and Ecuador), the Polo of the Oriente and Isla Margarita and the Bambuco, found in Lara and Táchira states near the border with Colombia.

There is a wealth of dances and musical forms found in particular towns or states at religious festivities. Outstanding among these is the Tamunangue of Lara State, danced in the second fortnight of June to the accompaniment of drums and small guitars and made up of seven individual dances, varying from the 'Batalla', where men battle with sticks, to the 'Bella', a flirtatious dance for couples. Corpus Cristi is the time to visit San Francisco de Yare in Miranda State, 90 km from Caracas, and see the 80 or so male 'Diablos' of all ages, dressed entirely in red and wearing large horned masks, who dance in the streets to the sound of their own drums and rattles. The Bailes de Tambor take place among the largely black people of the Barlovento coast during the feasts of San Juan and San Pedro and at Christmas. This is brilliant polyrhythm on huge drums (cumacos, minas and curvetas) held between the legs. Also in Barlovento, but in May, can be heard the Fulías, chant-and-response songs addressed to a venerated saint or cross, to the accompaniment of cuatro, tambora drum and maracas. Christmas is a great period for music from the Gaitas of Zulia to the ubiquitous Aguinaldos, both in Merengue rhythm, with solo verses responded to by a chorus and varied instrumental accompaniment. Notable in the eastern states are the folk theatre dances of the Pájaro Guarandol (a hunter shoots a large bird that is brought back to life), Carite (from Margarita, using a large model fish), Chiriguare (a monster that is duly despatched) and Burriquita (a hobby horse). More surprising is to find the

Calipso, played on steel bands by the black inhabitants of El Callao in the Orinoco region, whose ancestors came from Trinidad and who also perform the Limbo.

Venezuelans enjoy Salsa as much as other Hispanic peoples around the Caribbean, but they are also very keen on their own music, whether rustic 'folk' or urban 'popular'. The virtuoso harpist Juan Vicente Torrealba has performed with his group Los Torrealberos for more than three decades, usually with Mario Suárez as vocal soloist. Another famous singer is Simón Díaz. Outstanding among the folk groups who strive for authenticity are Un Solo Pueblo, Grupo Vera and Grupo Convenezuela. Choral and contrapuntal singing of native music in a more sophisticated style has also been perfected by Quinteto Contrapunto and Serenata Guayanesa.

Cinema/film

The cinema in South America has been largely dominated by Hollywood, in the films that are on offer to the public and what cinema-goers choose to see. The cinema also has to compete with television and the huge popularity of *telenovelas* (soap operas). Despite enthusiasm for film making since the beginnings of moving pictures, the industry in South America has been underfunded and has frequently had to confront repression and censorship. Individual countries can all claim a film industry at certain times and with certain motivations (eg in opposition to repression in Bolivia, Chilean cinema in exile after 1973), but Argentina and Brazil, together with Mexico, have been the leaders of film-making. Hugo Chávez, president of Venezuela, was intent in 2006 of overturning Hollywood's dominance of the Latin American cinema market. He launched a US$11 million Cinema Town studio with a view to producing films more representative of Latin America's own view of the continent, in parallel with the Telesur TV channel backed by Argentina, Cuba, Uruguay and Brazil, with Venezuela as major participant.

The earliest Argentine films were mostly silent documentaries, graduating into tango-led talkies in the 1930s. In the 1930s and 40s in Brazil, musicals were also the main box office draw. By the 1950s directors began to reject the old formulae and embraced 'new cinema' with its political and artistic messages. The chief exponents of this style in Argentina were Leopoldo Torre Nilsson (eg *La casa de ángel* – The House of the Angel – 1957) and Fernando Birri. One of the prominent directors in Brazil at this time was the neorrealist Nelson Perreira dos Santos (*Rio 40 Graus* – Rio 40°, 1955; *Vidas Secas* – Barren Lives, based on Graciliano Ramos' novel). *Cinema Novo* in Brazil reached its most fruitful period in the 1960s, especially in the work of Glauber Rocha (*O Cangaçeiro* – The Bandit, 1953, and *Deus e o Diabo no Terra do Sol* – God and the Devil in the Land of the Sun, 1963, both set in the Northeast; *O Barravento*). Before the descent into military dictatorship and censorship, 1966-68 saw production of the revolutionary four-hour documentary about Argentina, *La hora de los hornos* (The Hour of the Furnaces), directed by a group led by Fernando Solanas. This highly influential, politically-charged film confronted both Hollywood and the ideas of new cinema, but in the 1970s Solanas was forced into exile in France. The Radical government which took power after the demise of the Argentine generals in 1983 rejuvenated the National Film Institute, with the result that cinema flourished. Major films of this period were María Luisa Bemberg's *Camila* (1984), Luis Puenzo's *La historia oficial* (The Official Version , 1986 – the first Argentine film to win an Oscar) and Solanas' *Tangos, el exilio de Gardel* (Tangos the Exile of Gardel, 1985) and *Sur* (South, 1988). These and other films dealt, directly or by analogy, with the themes of the Dirty War, exile and the return to democracy. Recent successes from Argentina are Fabián Bielinsky's *Nueve Reinas* (Nine Queens, 2002), an award-winning tale of two small-time swindlers and their involvement in a once-in-a-lifetime scam, Carlos Sorín's *Bonbón el Perro* (2004), about a mechanic's attempts to overcome Argentina's economic collapse with a thoroughbred dog, and Solanas' 2005 film *La dignidad de los nadies* (The Dignity of the Nobodies), ten stories of people suffering in the economic collapse at the beginning of the 21st century. Lucrecia Martel's disturbing *La Ciénaga* (2001) is a vivid portrayal of a divided family's unhappy summer in their country house, rich in allegory and atmospheric detail. She followed this with *La Niña Santa* (The Holy Girl – 2004), an equally enigmatic, but also erotic film about a teenage girl who thinks she is a saint.

In 1981, Hector Babenco's *Pixote, a Lei do Mais Fraco* was released (Pixote), a harrowing tale of Brazil's homeless children, marking a resurgence in Brazilian cinema. International recognition came in the 1990s with works such as Fábio Barreto's *O Quatrilho* (The Quadrille) and Bruno Barreto's *O Que é Isso, Companheiro* (from Fernando Gabiera's book about the

❧ Ten of the best reads

Isabel Allende, *The House of the Spirits* (1982). A brilliant dynastic tale of 20th-century Chile, leading up to the events of 1973.

Jorge Amado, *Gabriela, Clove and Cinnamon* (1958). One of the Brazilian master storyteller's most popular books, set in Bahia.

Bruce Chatwin, *In Patagonia* (1977). A delightful, and not uncontroversial, mix of fact and fantasy.

Gabriel García Márquez, *One Hundred Years of Solitude* (1967). The Colombian novel which opened the world's eyes to South American magic realism.

John Hemming, *The Conquest of the Incas* (1970). A masterly account of the events that changed South America for ever.

Matthew Parris, *Inca Kola: A Traveller's Tale of Peru* (1993). A chronicle of Parris and three friends' bizarre adventures in Peru.

Mark J Plotkin, *Tales of a Shaman's Apprentice* (1993). An ethnobotanist's investigations into the ways of shamans in the northeastern Amazon rainforest.

Peter Robb, *A Death in Brazil: A Book of Omissions* (2003). Late 20th-century Brazil seen in the context of the rise and fall of Fernando Collor and PC Farias.

Harry Thompson, *This Thing of Darkness* (2005). An epic novel about the journeys of Fitzroy and Darwin on the *Beagle*.

Mario Vargas Llosa, *Conversation in the Cathedral* (1969). The Peruvian master's complex but compelling novel of life under the Odría dictatorship in 1950s Peru.

kidnapping of the US ambassador in 1969). This success was followed by Walter Salles' *Central do Brasil* (Central Station – 1988) and *Behind the Sun* (2001) and, in 2003, Fernando Meirelles' compelling, violent drama of the Rio favelas, *Cidade de Deus* (City of God) and Hector Babenco's drama about prison life in São Paulo, *Carandiru*. Salles' admirable film of Che Guevara's *The Motorcycle Diaries* was a huge international success. Two further successes of 2005 were Breno Silveira's *Os Dois Filhos de Francisco* (The Two Sons of Francisco), a dramatised biography of the *sertanejo* singers Zezé di Camargo and Luciano, and Sérgio Bianchi's *Quanto Vale ou É por Quilo?* (What is it Worth?), a lacerating critique of neoliberalism and consumerism which makes parallels with slavery.

Some films with a South American theme

1959 *Orfeu Negro* (Black Orpheus) (**Marcel Camus**). The Orpheus and Eurydice legend retold during Rio Carnaval; music by Antônio Carlos Jobim and Luiz Bonfa.

1972 *Aguirre Wrath of God* (**Werner Herzog**). About Lope de Aguirre, the murderous conquistador and his journey down the Amazon; Klaus Kinski stars.

1982 *Missing* (**Constantin Costa Gavras**). An American activist goes missing in an unspecified South American country. His wife, Sissy Spacek, and father, Jack Lemmon, set out to find him, despite the country's dictator and the US consul's opposition.

1982 *Fitzcarraldo* (**Werner Herzog**). The epic story of one man's obsession (Klaus Kinski again) to build an opera house in the Peruvian jungle; includes the remarkable attempt to haul a 300-ton ship over a mountain. See also *Burden of Dreams* (1982, Les Blank), which documents Herzog's obsession in making of *Fitzcarraldo*.

1985 *Kiss of the Spider Woman* (O Beijo da Mulher Aranha) (**Hector Babenco**). Based on the novel by Manuel Puig, a two-hander between a homosexual and a terrorist in a prison cell.

1986 *The Mission* (**Roland Joffé**). Robert de Niro and Jeremy Irons as Jesuit priests in the Missions in Argentina and Paraguay at the time of the expulsion of the order from South America accompanied by a beautiful Ennio Morricone score.

1994 *Death and the Maiden* (**Roman Polanski**). Taken from Ariel Dorfman's play of the same name, this is a grim story of a woman (Sigourney Weaver) taking revenge on the man (Ben Kingsley) who, she believes, was her torturer several years earlier (country unnamed).

1994 *The Postman* (Il Postino) (**Michael Radford**) Taken from Antonio Skármeta's novel,

El cartero de Neruda (originally called *Ardiente paciencia*); it weaves the story of a Chilean postman's love for a barmaid with the death of Pablo Neruda and the fall of Salvador Allende. **2002** *The Dancer Upstairs* (Pasos de baile)

(**John Malkovich**) Javier Bardem plays a detective seeking a guerrilla leader in an unnamed South American country in this adaptation of Nicholas Shakespeare's novel about the nature of corruption.

Land and environment

The dominant feature of South America's geography is the Andes mountain range which defines the western, Pacific, side of the continent from 12°N to 56°S, with tablelands and older mountains stretching east to the Atlantic Ocean. The highest peaks of the Andes have no rivals outside the Himalaya. Dominant to the east are the vast river basins of the Orinoco, the Paraná and above all the Amazon. At least part of every country (except Uruguay) is in the tropics, though the southernmost tips of Chile and Argentina are close to Antarctica. No wonder the variety of scenery, climate and vegetation is immense.

The Andean countries

Colombia → *Land area: 1,242,568 sq km.*

Four ranges of the Andes (*cordilleras*) run from north to south. Between the ranges run deep longitudinal valleys. Roughly half of Colombia consists of these deep north-south valleys of the Andes and the coastal fringes along the Pacific and Caribbean shorelines. The remaining 620,000 sq km east of the Andes consists of the hot plains (*llanos*) to the north, running down to the Orinoco River, and the Amazon forests to the south. Near the foot of the Andes, the *llanos* are used for cattle ranching, but beyond is jungle. Except for the northwest corner where oil has been found, islands of settlement are connected with the rest of the country only by air and river; the few roads are impassable most of the year. Almost all Colombians live in the western 50% of the country.

The **cordilleras**, the main Andes ranges, run northwards for 800 km from the borders of Ecuador to the Caribbean lowlands. A few peaks in the Western Cordillera are over 4,000 m but none reaches the snowline. The Central Cordillera, 50-65 km wide, is much higher; several of its peaks, snow clad, rise above 5,000 m and its highest, the volcano cone of Huila, is 5,750 m. The Eastern Cordillera extends north across the border into Venezuela (see below), and includes the spectacular Cucuy ranges. Apart from the peaks (a few are active volcanoes), there are large areas of high undulating plateaux, cold, treeless and inhospitable, dissected by deep river gorges. They have interesting flora and fauna and many of these regions are protected as national parks. In a high basin of the Eastern Cordillera, 160 km east of the Río Magdalena, the Spaniards in 1538 founded the city of Bogotá at 2,560 m, now the national capital. The great rural activity here is the growing of food: cattle, wheat, barley, maize and potatoes. The **valleys** between the Cordilleras are deep and dominated by the Magdalena and Cauca Rivers. The upper sections are filled with volcanic ash and are very fertile. With the tropical range of temperature and rainfall, this is very productive land. Coffee dominates but almost every known tropical fruit and vegetable grows here. In the upper parts of the valleys, the climate is more temperate, with another wide range of crops. There is cattle production everywhere; sugar, cotton, rice and tobacco are common.

The **Caribbean lowlands** include three centres of population, Cartagena, Barranquilla and Santa Marta, behind which lies a great lowland, the floodplain of the Magdalena, Cauca and their tributaries. During the dry season from October to March great herds of cattle are grazed there, but for the rest of the year much of it is a network of swamps and lagoons with very little land that can be cultivated except for a few ranges of low hills near the coast. The **northeast** includes one more mountain group in Colombia, the Sierra Nevada de Santa Marta, standing isolated from the other ranges on the shores of the Caribbean. This is the highest range of all: its snow-capped peaks rise to 5,800 m within 50 km of the coast. Further northeast, is La Guajira, a strange region of semi-desert, salt-pans, flamingos and unusual micro-climates. The **Pacific coast** stretches for 1,300 km. Along the coast north of Buenaventura runs the Serranía de Baudó, the shortest of the Cordilleras, thickly forested. East of it is a low trough before the land rises to the slopes of the Western Cordillera. The trough is drained southwards into the Pacific by the Río San Juan, and northwards into the Caribbean by the Río Atrato, both are partly navigable. The climate is hot and torrential rain falls daily. The inhabitants are mostly black. The 320 km south of the port of Buenaventura to the border with Ecuador is a wide, marshy, and sparsely inhabited coastal lowland.

Ecuador → *Land area: 272, 045 sq km.*

The Andes, running from north to south, form a mountainous backbone to the country. There are two main ranges, the Central Cordillera and the Western Cordillera, separated by a 400-km long Central Valley, whose rims are about 50 km apart. The rims are joined together, like the two sides of a ladder, by hilly rungs, and between each pair of rungs lies an intermont basin with a dense cluster of population. These basins are drained by rivers which cut through the rims to run either west to the Pacific or east to join the Amazon. Both rims of the Central Valley are lined with the cones of more than 50 volcanoes. Several of them have long been extinct, for example, Chimborazo, the highest (6,310 m). At least eight, however, are still active including Cotopaxi (5,897 m), which had several violent eruptions in the 19th century; Pichincha (4,794 m), which re-entered activity in 1998 and expelled a spectacular mushroom cloud in October 1999; and Sangay (5,230 m), one of the world's most active volcanoes, continuously emitting fumes and ash. Earthquakes too are common.

The **sierra**, as the central trough of the Andes is known, is home to about 47% of the people of Ecuador, the majority of whom are indigenous. Some of the land is still held in large private estates worked by the Indians, but a growing proportion is now made up of small family farms or is held by native communities, run as cooperatives. Some communities live at subsistence level, others have developed good markets for products using traditional skills in embroidery, pottery, jewellery, knitting, weaving, and carving. The **costa** is mostly lowland at an altitude of less than 300 m, apart from a belt of hilly land which runs northwest from Guayaquil to the coast, where it turns north and runs parallel to the shore to Esmeraldas. In the extreme north there is a typical tropical rain forest, severely endangered by uncontrolled logging. The forests thin out in the more southern lowlands and give way to tropical dry forest. The main agricultural exports come from the lowlands to the southeast and north of Guayaquil. The heavy rains, high temperature and humidity suit the growth of tropical crops. Bananas and mango are grown here while rice is farmed on the natural levees of this flood plain. The main crop comes from the alluvial fans at the foot of the mountains rising out of the plain. Coffee is grown on the higher ground. Shrimp farming was typical of the coast until this was damaged by disease in 1999. The Guayas lowland is also a great cattle-fattening area in the dry season. South of Guayaquil the rainfall is progressively less, mangroves disappear and by the border with Peru, it is semi-arid.

The **Oriente** is east of the Central Cordillera where the forest-clad mountains fall sharply to a chain of foothills (the Eastern Cordillera) and then the jungle through which meander the tributaries of the Amazon. This east lowland region makes up 36% of Ecuador's total territory, but is only sparsely populated by indigenous and agricultural colonists from the highlands. In total, the region has only 5% of the national population, but colonization is now proceeding rapidly owing to population pressure and in the wake of an oil boom in the northern Oriente. There is gold and other minerals in the south. The **Galápagos** are about 1,000 km west of Ecuador, on the Equator, and are not structuraly connected to the mainland. They mark the junction between two tectonic plates on the Pacific floor where basalt has escaped to form massive volcanoes, only the tips of which are above sea level. Several of the islands have volcanic activity today. Their isolation from any other land has led to the evolution of their unique flora and fauna.

Peru → *Land area: 1,285,216 sq km.*

The whole of Peru's west seaboard with the Pacific is desert on which rain seldom falls. From this coastal shelf the Andes rise to a high Sierra which is studded with groups of soaring mountains and gouged with deep canyons. The highland slopes more gradually east and is deeply forested and ravined. Eastward from these mountains lie the vast jungle lands of the Amazon basin.

The **Highlands** (or Sierra), at an average altitude of 3,000 m, cover 26% of the country and contain about 50% of the people, mostly Indian, an excessive density on such poor land. Here, high-level land of gentle slopes is surrounded by towering ranges of high peaks including the most spectacular range of the continent, the Cordillera Blanca. This has several ice peaks over 6,000 m; the highest, Huascarán, is 6,768 m and is a mecca for mountaineers. There are many volcanoes in the south. The north and east highlands are heavily forested up to a limit of 3,350 m: the grasslands are between the forest line and the snowline, which rises from 5,000 m in the latitude of Lima to 5,800 m in the south. Most of the Sierra is covered with grasses and shrubs, with Puna vegetation (bunch grass mixed with low, hairy-leaved plants) from north of Huaraz to the south. Here the indigenous graze llamas, alpacas and sheep providing meat, clothing, transport and even fuel from the animals' dung. Some potatoes and cereals (*quinua*, *kiwicha* and *kañiwa*) are grown at altitude, but the valley basins contain the best land for arable farming. Most of the rivers which rise in these mountains flow east to the Amazon and cut through the plateau in canyons, sometimes 1,500 m deep, in which the climate is tropical. A few go west to the Pacific including the Colca and Cotahuasi in the south, which have created canyons over 3,000 m deep.

The **coast**, a narrow ribbon of desert 2,250 km long, takes up 11% of the country and holds about 45% of the population. It is the economic heart of Peru, consuming most of the imports and supplying half of the exports. When irrigated, the river valleys are extremely fertile, creating oases which grow cotton throughout the country, sugar cane, rice and export crops such as asparagus in the north, grapes, fruit and olives in the south. At the same time, the coastal current teems with fish and Peru has in the past had the largest catch in the world. The **jungle** covers the forested eastern half of the Andes and the tropical forest beyond, altogether 62% of the country's area, but with only about 5% of the population who are crowded on the river banks in the cultivable land – a tiny part of the area. The few roads have to cope with dense forest, deep valleys, and sharp eastern slopes ranging from 2,150 m in the north to 5,800 m east of Lake Titicaca. Rivers are the main highways, though navigation is hazardous. The economic potential of the area includes reserves of timber, excellent land for rubber, jute, rice, tropical fruits and coffee and the breeding of cattle. The vast majority of Peru's oil and gas reserves are also east of the Andes.

Bolivia → *Land area: 1,098,581 sq km.*

A harsh, strange land, with a dreary grey solitude except for the bursts of green after rain, Bolivia is the only South American country with no coastline or navigable river to the sea. It is dominated by the Andes and has five distinct geographical areas. The **Andes** are at their widest in Bolivia, a maximum of 650 km. The Western Cordillera, which separates Bolivia from Chile, has high peaks of 5,800 m-6,500 m and a number of active volcanoes along its crest. The Eastern Cordillera also rises to giant massifs, with several peaks over 6,000 m in the Cordillera Real section to the north. The far sides of the Cordillera Real fall away very sharply to the northeast, towards the Amazon basin. The air is unbelievably clear – the whole landscape is a bowl of luminous light.

The **Altiplano** lies between the Cordilleras, a bleak, treeless, windswept plateau, much of it 4,000 m above sea-level. Its surface is by no means flat, and the Western Cordillera sends spurs dividing it into basins. The more fertile northern part has more inhabitants; the southern part is parched desert and almost unoccupied, save for a mining town here and there. Nearly 70% of the population lives on it; over half of the people in towns. **Lake Titicaca**, at the northern end of the Altiplano, is an inland sea of 8,965 sq km at 3,810 m, the highest navigable water in the world. Its depth, up to 280 m in some places, keeps the lake at an even all-year-round temperature of 10° C. This modifies the extremes of winter and night temperatures on the surrounding land, which supports a large Aymara indigenous population, tilling the fields and the hill terraces, growing potatoes and cereals, tending their sheep, alpaca and llamas, and using the resources of the lake. The **Yungas** and the **Puna** are to the east of the Altiplano. The heavily forested northeastern slopes of the Cordillera Real are deeply indented by the fertile valleys of the Yungas, drained into the Amazon lowlands by the Río Beni and its tributaries, where cacao, coffee, sugar, coca and tropical fruits are grown. Further south, from a point just north of Cochabamba, the Eastern Cordillera rises abruptly in sharp escarpments from the Altiplano and then flattens out to an easy slope east to the plains: an area known as the Puna. The streams which flow across the Puna cut increasingly deep incisions as they gather volume until the Puna is eroded to little more than a high remnant between the river valleys. In these valleys a variety of grain crops and fruits is grown.

The **tropical lowlands** stretch from the foothills of the Eastern Cordillera to the borders with Brazil, Paraguay and Argentina. They take up 70% of the total area of Bolivia, but contain only about 20% of its population. In the north and east the Oriente has dense tropical forest. Open plains covered with rough pasture, swamp and scrub occupy the centre. Before the expulsion of the Jesuits in 1767 this was a populous land of plenty; for 150 years Jesuit missionaries had controlled the area and guided it into a prosperous security. Decline followed but in recent years better times have returned. Meat is now shipped from Trinidad, capital of Beni Department, and from airstrips in the area, to the urban centres of La Paz, Oruro, and Cochabamba. Further south, the forests and plains beyond the Eastern Cordillera sweep down towards the Río Pilcomayo, which drains into the Río de la Plata, getting progressively less rain and merging into a comparatively dry land of scrub forest and arid savanna. The main city of this area is Santa Cruz de la Sierra, founded in the 16th century, now the second city of Bolivia and a large agricultural centre.

The Southern Cone

Chile → *Land area: 756, 626 sq km.*

Chile is a ribbon of land lying between the Andes and the Pacific. The Andes and a coastal range of highland take up from a third to a half of its width. There are wide variations of soil and vast differences of climate; these profoundly affect the density of population. Down virtually the whole length, between the Andes and the coastal ranges, is a longitudinal depression. For 1,050 km south of the capital Santiago this is a great valley stretching as far as Puerto Montt. South of Puerto Montt the sea has broken through the coastal range and drowned the valley, and there is a bewildering assortment of archipelagos and channels. The Andes, with many snow-capped peaks over 6,000 m, culminate near Santiago with several of almost 7,000 m. They diminish in height from Santiago southwards, but throughout the range are spectacular volcanoes right down to the southern seas, where the Strait of Magellan gives access to the Atlantic. Associated with the mountains are geological faults and earthquakes are common.

From north to south the country falls into five contrasted zones: The first 1,250 km from the Peruvian frontier to Copiapó is a rainless desert of hills and plains devoid of vegetation. Here lie nitrate deposits and several copper mines. There is almost no rain, just occasional mists. From Copiapó to Illapel (600 km) is semi-desert; there is a slight winter rainfall, but great tracts of land are without vegetation most of the year. Valley bottoms are cultivated under irrigation. From Illapel to Concepción is Chile's heartland, where the vast majority of its people live. Here there is abundant rainfall in the winter, but the summers are perfectly dry. Great farms and vineyards cover the country, which is exceptionally beautiful. The fourth zone, between Concepción and Puerto Montt, is a country of lakes and rivers, with heavy rainfall through much of the year. Cleared and cultivated land alternates with mountains and primeval forests. The fifth zone, from Puerto Montt to Cape Horn, stretches for 1,600 km. This is archipelagic Chile, a sparsely populated region of wild forests and mountains, glaciers, islands and channels. Rainfall is torrential, and the climate cold. South of Puerto Montt, the Camino Austral provides almost unbroken road access for more than 1,000 km. Chilean Patagonia is in the extreme south of this zone. A subdivision of the fifth zone is Atlantic Chile – that part which lies along the Magellan Strait to the east of the Andes, including the Chilean part of Tierra del Fuego island. There is a cluster of population here raising sheep and mining coal. Large offshore oilfields have been discovered in the far south.

Argentina → *Land area: 2, 780, 092 sq km.*

Argentina occupies most of the southern cone of the continent. There are four main physical areas: the Andes, the north and Mesopotamia, the Pampas, and Patagonia. Much of the country is comparatively flat which made modern communications easy. The **Andes** run the full length of Argentina, low and deeply glaciated in the Patagonian south, high and dry in the prolongation in northwest Argentina adjoining the Bolivian Altiplano. Though of modest height, Cerro Fitzroy and other peaks on the fringes of the Patagonia icecap are amongst the most dramatic on the continent, while many peaks in the north are over 6,000 m, including Aconcagua, the highest outside the Himalayas. To the east, in the shadow of the Andes, it is dry. Oases strung along the eastern foot of the Andes from Jujuy to San Rafael, including Tucumán and Mendoza, were the first places to be colonized by the Spaniards. Further south is the beautiful Lake District, with Bariloche at its heart. The mountain ridges and the many lakes created by the glaciers are now withdrawing under the impact of global warming. The **north** and **Mesopotamia** contains the vast plains of the Chaco and the floodplain lying between the rivers Paraná and Uruguay. Rice growing and ranching are widespread. The Province of Misiones in the northeast lies on the great Paraná plateau while the northwest Chaco has some of the highest temperatures in the continent.

The **Pampas** make up the heart of the country. These vast, rich plains lie south of the Chaco, and east of the Andes down to the Río Colorado. Buenos Aires lies on the northeast corner of the Pampas and is the only part of the country which has a dense population – about 40% of Argentines live in and around the capital. The Pampas stretch for hundreds of kilometres in almost unrelieved flatness, but get progressively wetter going east. Cattle and cereal growing dominate. **Patagonia** lies south of the Río Colorado – a land of arid, wind-swept plateaux cut across by ravines. In the deep south the wind is wilder and more continuous. There is no real summer, but the winters are rarely severe.

Uruguay → *Land area: 406,752 sq km.*

Unlike all other South American countries, Uruguay is compact (it's the smallest Hispanic country in South America), accessible and homogeneous. The **coast** along the Atlantic consists of bays, beaches and off-shore islands, lagoons and bars, the sand brought by currents north from the River Plate. Behind is a narrow plain which fringes most of the coast (but not near Montevideo). Behind is a line of mainly wooded hills (called *cuchillas*), the whole area extensively farmed with grain and cattle *estancias*. **Central Uruguay** up to the Brazilian border is pleasant, rolling country dissected by the Río Negro which rises in Brazil and on which a number of dams have been built. North of the river is agricultural and pasture country dominated by sheep. Near Minas there are stone quarries and other mining activity. **western Uruguay** is dominated by the River Plate from Montevideo round to Colonia, then north up the Río Uruguay which provides the frontier with Argentina. It consists of an alluvial flood plain stretching north to Fray Bentos where the first road crossing can be made. Thereafter, the general character of the land is undulating, with little forest except on the banks of its rivers and streams. The long grass slopes rise gently to far-off hills, but none of these is higher than 600 m. Five rivers flow westwards across the country to drain into the Río Uruguay, including the Río Negro. Cattle and wheat are the main traditional products.

Paraguay → *Land area: 406, 752 sq km.*

Paraguay is landlocked, divided into two distinct regions by the Río Paraguay. Eastern Paraguay combines habitats characteristic of three ecoregions: *cerrado* (a mosaic of dry forest and savanna habitats) in the north, humid Atlantic forest in the east, and natural grasslands and marshes in the south. West of the river lies the vast expanse of the Chaco, comprised of seasonally flooded palm-savannas in the south-east, semi-arid thorn scrub-forest to the west, and in the north, the Pantanal, part of the world's largest wetland. The Río Paraná forms part of the eastern and southern boundaries of the country but the rivers are so difficult to navigate that communication with Buenos Aires, 1,450 km from Asunción, has been mainly on land.

Eastern Paraguay is the 40% of the country east of the Río Paraguay, a rich land of rolling hills in which most of the population live. An escarpment runs north from the Río Alto Paraná, west of Encarnación, to the Brazilian border. East of this escarpment the Paraná Plateau extends across neighbouring parts of Argentina and Brazil. The Plateau, which is crossed by the Río Paraná, ranges from 300-600 m in height, was originally forest and enjoys relatively high levels of rainfall. West and south of the escarpment and stretching to the Río Paraguay lies a fertile plain with wooded hills, drained by several tributaries of the Río Paraná. Most of the population of Paraguay lives in these hilly lands, stretching southeast from the capital, to Encarnación. The area produces timber, cotton, hides and semi-tropical products. Closer to the rivers, much of the plain is flooded once a year; it is wet savanna, treeless, but covered with coarse grasses. The **Chaco**, about 60% of the country's area, is a flat, infertile plain stretching north along the west bank of the Río Paraguay. The marshy, unnavigable Río Pilcomayo, flowing southeast across the Chaco to join the Río Paraguay near Asunción, forms the frontier with Argentina. The landscape is dominated by the alluvial material brought down in the past by rivers from the Andes. As the rainfall diminishes westwards, the land can support little more than scrub and cacti. The arrival of the Mennonites has led to some intense production of fruit and other crops.

Brazil and the north

Brazil → *Land area: 8,547,404 sq km.*

Brazil is one of the largest countries of the world. It stretches over 4,300 km across the continent but is one of the few in South America that does not reach the Andes. The two great river basins, the Amazon and the River Plate, account for about three-fifths of Brazil's area.

The **Amazon Basin**, in northern and western Brazil, takes up more than a third of the whole country. The basin borders the Andes and funnels narrowly to the Atlantic, recalling the geological period, before the uplift of the Andes, when the Amazon flowed into the Pacific Ocean. Most of the drained area has an elevation of less than 250 m. The rainfall is heavy: some few places receive 3,750-5,000 mm a year, though over most of the area it is no more than from 1,500 to 2,500 mm. This heavy rain comes from the daily cycle of intense evaporation plus the saturated air brought by winds from the northeast and southeast, losing their moisture as they approach the Andes. Much of the basin suffers from annual floods. The region was covered by tropical forest, with little undergrowth except along the watercourses; it is now being rapidly cut down. The climate is hot and humidity high all year. The **Brazilian Highlands** lying southeast of the Amazon and northeast of the River Plate Basin form a tableland of from 300 to 900 m high, but here and there, mostly in southeast Brazil, mountain ranges rise from it. The highest temperature recorded was 42°C, in the dry northeastern states. The highest peak in southern Brazil, the Pico da Bandeira, northeast of Rio, is 2,898 m. The **Great Escarpment** is where the Brazilian Highlands cascade sharply down to the Atlantic, leaving a narrow coastal strip which is the economic heartland of the country. It runs from south of Salvador as far as Porto Alegre and in only a few places is this Escarpment breached by deeply cut river beds, for example those of the Rio Doce and the Rio Paraíba. Along most of its course, the Great Escarpment falls to the sea in parallel steps, each step separated by the trough of a valley. The few rivers rising on the Escarpment, which flow direct into the Atlantic are not navigable. Most of the rivers flow west, deep into the interior. Those in southern Brazil rise almost within sight of the sea, but run westward through the vast interior to join the Paraná, often with falls as they leave the Escarpment, including the spectacular Iguaçú. In the central area the Escarpment rivers run away from the sea to join the São Francisco river, which flows northwards parallel to the coast for 2,900 km, to tumble over the Paulo Afonso Falls on its eastward course to the Atlantic.

The **River Plate Basin**, in the southern part of Brazil, has a more varied surface and is less heavily forested than the Amazon Basin. The land is higher and the climate a little cooler. The **Guiana Highlands**, north of the Amazon, are ancient rock structures, some of the world's oldest. The area is part forest, part hot desert. Slopes facing northeast trade winds get heavy rainfall, but south it is drier. Brazil's highest peak, Pico da Neblina, 3,014 m, is on the Venezuelan border.

Guyane → *Land area: 83,900-86, 504 sq km (estimate).*

Guyane has its eastern frontier with Brazil formed partly by the river Oiapoque (Oyapock in French) and its southern, also with Brazil, formed by the Tumuc-Humac mountains (the only range of importance). The western frontier with Suriname is along the river Maroni-Litani. To the north is the Atlantic coastline of 320 km. The land rises gradually from a coastal strip some 15-40 km wide to the higher slopes and plains or savannahs, about 80 km inland. Forests cover the hills and valleys of the interior, and the territory is well watered, for over 20 rivers run to the Atlantic.

Suriname → *Land area: 163,820 sq km. (A large area in the southwest is in dispute with Guyana. There is a less serious border dispute with Guyane in the southeast.)*

Like its neighbours, Suriname has a coastline on the Atlantic to the north. The principal rivers are the Marowijne in the east, the Corantijn in the west, and the Suriname, Commewijne (with its tributary, the Cottica), Coppename, Saramacca and Nickerie. The country is divided into topographically quite diverse natural regions: the northern lowlands, 25 km wide in the east and 80 km wide in the west, have clay soil covered with swamps. There follows a region, 5-6 km wide, of a loamy and very white sandy soil, then an undulating region, about 30 km wide. It is mainly savanna, mostly covered with quartz sand, and overgrown with grass and shrubs. South of this lies the interior highland, almost entirely overgrown with dense tropical forest, intersected by streams. At the southern boundary with Brazil there are savannas.

Guyana → *Land area: 215,083 sq km.*

Guyana has an area of 215,083 sq km, nearly the size of Britain, but only about 2.5% is cultivated. About 90% of the population lives on the narrow coastal plain, either in Georgetown, the capital, or in villages along the main road running from Charity in the west to the Suriname border. The rivers give some access to the interior beyond which are the jungles and highlands towards the border with Brazil.

The **coastal plain** is mostly below sea level. Large wooden houses stand on stilts above ground level. A sea wall keeps out the Atlantic and the fertile clay soil is drained by a system of dykes; sluice gates, *kokers* are opened to let out water at low tide. Separate channels irrigate fields in dry weather. Most of the western third of the coastal plain is undrained and uninhabited. Four **major rivers** cross the coastal plain, from west to east they are the Essequibo, the Demerara, the Berbice, and the Corentyne. Only the Demerara is crossed by bridges. Elsewhere ferries must be used. At the mouth of the Essequibo River, 34 km wide, are islands the size of Barbados. The lower reaches of these rivers are navigable; but waterfalls and rapids prevent them being used by large boats to reach the interior. (The area west of the Essequibo River, about 70% of the national territory, is claimed by Venezuela.) The **jungles** and the **highlands** inland from the coastal plain, are thick rain forest, although in the east there is a large area of grassland. Towards Venezuela the rain forest rises in a series of steep escarpments, with spectacular waterfalls, the highest and best known of which are the Kaieteur Falls on the Potaro River. In the southwest is the Rupununi Savanna, an area of grassland more easily reached from Brazil than from Georgetown.

Venezuela → *Land area: 912, 050 sq km.*

Venezuela has 2,800 km of coastline on the Caribbean Sea and many islands. The Andes run up north-eastwards from Colombia, along the coast eastwards past Caracas, ending up as the north coast of the Caribbean island of Trinidad. In the northwest corner is the Maracaibo basin. South of the Andean spine is the vast plain of the Orinoco which reaches the sea near the Guyana border and to the southeast of that are the ancient rocks known as the Guayana Highlands.

The **Andes** are highest near the Colombian border where they are known as the Sierra Nevada de Mérida. Beyond they broaden out into the Segovia Highlands north of Barquisimeto, and then turn east in parallel ridges along the coast to form the Central Highlands, dipping into the Caribbean Sea only to rise again into the North Eastern Highlands of the peninsulas of Araya and Paria. This region has an agreeable climate and is well populated with most of the main towns. The **Maracaibo Lowlands** are around the fresh water lake of Maracaibo, the largest lake in South America, is 12,800 sq km. Considerable rainfall feeds the lake and many rivers flow through thick forest to create swamps on its southern shore. The area is dominated by the oil producing fields on both sides of the lake and beneath its surface. To the west, the Sierra de Perijá forms the boundary with Colombia and outside the lake to the east is the most northerly point of the country the peninsular of Paraguaná, virtually desert.

The **Llanos**, as the Orinoco plains are called, cover about one third of the country. They are almost flat and are a vast cattle range. The Orinoco river itself is part of Latin America's third largest river system. Many significant rivers flow from the Andes and Guayana Highlands to join the Orinoco, whose delta is made up of innumerable channels and thousands of forest-covered islands. The **Guayana Highlands**, which take up almost half the country, are south of the Orinoco. This is an area of ancient crystalline rocks that extend along the top of the continent towards the mouth of the Amazon and form the northern part of Brazil. In Venezuela they are noted for huge, precipitous granite blocks known as *tepuys*, many of which have their own unique flora, and create many high waterfalls including the Angel Falls, the world's highest.

Footnotes

Useful words and phrases	1532
Spanish and Portuguese pronunciation	1534
Index	1537
Advertisers' index	1547
Acknowledgements	1549
About the author	1551
Credits	1552
Map symbols	1553
Colour maps	1563

Useful words and phrases

Greetings & courtesies	Spanish	Portuguese
hello/good morning	*hola/buenos días*	*oi/bom dia*
good afternoon/evening/night	*buenas tardes/noches*	*boa tarde/boa noite*
goodbye	*adiós/chao*	*adeus/tchau*
see you later	*hasta luego*	*até logo*
how are you?	*¿cómo está/cómo estás?*	*como vai você?/tudo bem?*
		tudo bom?
I'm fine	*estoy bien*	*tudo bem /tudo bom*
pleased to meet you	*mucho gusto/encantado*	*um prazer*
please	*por favor*	*por favor/faz favor*
thank you (very much)	*(muchas) gracias*	*(muito) obrigado (man speaking)*
		/obrigada (woman speaking)
yes/no	*sí/no*	*sim/não*
excuse me/I beg your pardon	*permiso*	*com licença*
I don't understand	*no entiendo*	*não entendo*
please speak slowly	*hable despacio por favor*	*fale devagar por favor*
what's your name?/	*¿cómo se llama?/me llamo_*	*Qual é seu nome?/ O meu*
I'm called_		*nome é_*
Go away!	*¡Váyase!*	*Vai embora!*

Basic questions		
where is_?	*¿dónde está_?*	*onde está/onde fica?*
how much does it cost?	*¿cuánto cuesta?*	*quanto custa?*
when?	*¿cuándo?*	*quando?*
when does the bus leave/	*¿a qué hora sale/llega el*	*qa que hora sai/chega o*
arrive?	*autobus?*	*ônibus?*
why?	*¿por qué?*	*por que?*
how do I get to_?	*¿cómo llegar a_?*	*para chegar a_?*

Basics		
police (policeman)	*la policía (el policía)*	*a polícia (o polícia)*
hotel	*el hotel (la pensión, el*	*o hotel (a pensão,*
	residencial, el alojamiento)	*a hospedaria)*
room	*el cuarto/la habitación*	*o quarto*
single/double	*sencillo/doble*	*(quarto de) solteiro*
with two beds	*con dos camas*	*com duas camas*
bathroom/toilet	*el baño*	*o banheiro*
hot/cold water	*agua caliente/fría*	*água quente/fria*
toilet paper	*el papel higiénico*	*o papel higiênico*
restaurant	*el restaurante*	*o restaurante (o lanchonete)*
post office/telephone office	*el correo/el centro de llamadas*	*o correio/o centro telefônico*
supermarket/market	*el supermercado/el mercado*	*o supermercado/o mercado*
bank/exchange house	*el banco/la casa de cambio*	*o banco/a casa de câmbio*
exchange rate	*la tasa de cambio*	*a taxa de câmbio*
travellers' cheques	*los travelers/los cheques de*	*os travelers/os cheques de*
	viajero	*viagem*
cash	*el efectivo*	*o dinheiro*
breakfast/lunch	*el desayuno/el almuerzo*	*o café de manhã/o almoço*
dinner/supper	*la cena*	*o jantar*
meal/drink	*la comida/la bebida*	*a refeição/a bebida*
mineral water	*el agua mineral*	*a água mineral*
beer	*la cerveza*	*a cerveja*
without sugar/without meat	*sin azúcar/sin carne*	*sem açúcar/sem carne*

Getting around

on the left/right	*a la izquierda/derecha*	*á esquerda/á direita*
straight on	*derecho*	*direito*
bus station	*la terminal (terrestre)*	*a rodoviária*
bus stop	*la parada*	*a parada*
bus	*el bus/el autobus/la flota/ el colectivo/el micro*	*o ônibus*
train/train station	*el tren/la estación (de tren/ferrocarril)*	*o trem*
airport/aeroplane	*el aeropuerto/el avión*	*o aeroporto/o avião*
ticket/ticket office	*el boleto/la taquilla*	*o bilhete/a bilheteria*

Time

What time is it?	*¿Qué hora es?*	*Que horas são?*
at half past two/two thirty	*a las dos y media*	*as duas e meia*
it's one o'clock/ it's seven o'clock	*es la una/son las siete*	*é uma/são as sete*
ten minutes/five hours	*diez minutos/cinco horas*	*dez minutos/cinco horas*

Numbers

1	*uno/una*	*um/uma*
2	*dos*	*dois/duas*
3	*tres*	*três*
4	*cuatro*	*quatro*
5	*cinco*	*cinco*
6	*seis*	*seis*
7	*siete*	*sete*
8	*ocho*	*oito*
9	*nueve*	*nove*
10	*diez*	*dez*
11	*once*	*onze*
12	*doce*	*doze*
13	*trece*	*treze*
14	*catorce*	*catorze*
15	*quince*	*quinze*
16	*dieciseis*	*dezesseis*
17	*diecisiete*	*dezessete*
18	*dieciocho*	*dezoito*
19	*diecinueve*	*dezenove*
20	*veinte*	*vinte*
21	*veintiuno*	*vinte e um*
30	*treinte*	*trinta*
40	*cuarenta*	*quarenta*
50	*cincuenta*	*cinqüenta*
60	*sesenta*	*sessenta*
70	*setenta*	*setenta*
80	*ochenta*	*oitenta*
90	*noventa*	*noventa*
100	*cien, ciento*	*cem, cento*
1000	*mil*	*mil*

.

Spanish and Portuguese pronunciation

Spanish

The stress in a Spanish word conforms to one of three rules: 1) if the word ends in a vowel, or in n or **s**, the accent falls on the penultimate syllable (*ventana*, *ventanas*); 2) if the word ends in a consonant other than **n** or **s**, the accent falls on the last syllable (*hablar*); 3) if the word is to be stressed on a syllable contrary to either of the above rules, the acute accent on the relevant vowel indicates where the stress is to be placed (*pantalón*, *metáfora*). Note that adverbs such as *cuando*, 'when', take an accent when used interrogatively: ¿*cuándo*?, 'when?'

Vowels: **a** not quite as short as in English 'cat'; **e** as in English 'pay', but shorter in a syllable ending in a consonant; **i** as in English 'seek'; **o** as in English 'cot' (North American 'caught'), but more like 'pope' when the vowel ends a syllable; **u** as in English 'food'; after 'q' and in 'gue', 'gui', u is unpronounced; in 'güe' and 'güi' it is pronounced; **y** when a vowel, pronounced like 'i'; when a semiconsonant or consonant, it is pronounced like English 'yes'; **ai**, **ay** as in English 'write'; **ei**, **ey** as in English 'eight'; **oi**, **oy** as in English 'voice'

Unless listed below **consonants** can be pronounced in Spanish as they are in English. **b**, **v** have an interchangeable sound and both are a cross between the English 'b' and 'v', except at the beginning of a word or after 'm' or 'n' when it is like English 'b'; **c** like English 'k', except before 'e' or 'i' when it is as the 's' in English 'sip'; **g** before 'e' and 'i' it is the same as j; **h** when on its own, never pronounced; **j** as the 'ch' in the Scottish 'loch'; **ll** as the 'g' in English 'beige'; sometimes as the 'lli' in 'million'; **ñ** as the 'ni' in English 'onion'; **rr** trilled much more strongly than in English; **x** depending on its location, pronounced as in English 'fox', or 'sip', or like 'gs'; **z** as the 's' in English 'sip'.

Portuguese

There is no standard Portuguese and there are many differences between the Portuguese of Portugal and the Portuguese of Brazil. If learning Portuguese before you go, get lessons with a Brazilian, or from a language course which teaches Brazilian Portuguese. Within Brazil itself, there are variations in pronunciation, intonation, phraseology and slang. This makes for great richness and for the possibility of great enjoyment in the language. Describing the complex Portuguese vocalic system is best left to the experts; it would take up too much space here. A couple of points which the newcomer to the language will spot immediately, however, are: the use of the til (~) over **a** and **o**. This makes the vowel a nasal vowel. Vowels also become nasal when a word ends in **m** or **ns**, when a vowel is followed by **m** + consonant, or by **n** + consonant. Another important point of spelling is that words ending in **i** or **u** are accented on the last syllable, though unlike Spanish no accent is used there. This is especially important in place names: Buriti, Guarapari, Caxambu, Iguaçu. Note also the use of **ç**, which changes the pronunciation of **c** from hard [k] to soft [s].

Note: In conversation, most people refer to **you** as "*você*", although in the south and in Pará "*tu*" is more common. To be more polite, use "*O Senhor/A Senhora*". For **us**, "*a gente*" (people, folks) is very common when it includes **you** too.

Notes

Notes

Index → *Entries in bold refer to maps.*

A

Abancay 1261
Abra Pampa 156
Acandí 824
accommodation
  Argentina 68
  Brazil 345
  camping 58
  Chile 602
  Colombia 778
  Ecuador 890
  general 58
  Guyana 1428
  Guyane 1458
  Paraguay 1038
  Peru 1076
  Suriname 1447
  Uruguay 1290
  Venezuela 1332
  youth hostels 58
Aceguá 456
Achao 720
Acobamba 1262
Aconcagua 127
activities 20
Adícora 1358
Agua Blanca 989
Aguas Blancas 157
Aguas Calientes 1241
Aguas Dulces 1316
Aguaytía 1267
Alausí 954
Albina 1451
Alborada 977
Alcântara 526
Almofala 524
Alter do Chão 543
Alto Nangaritza 1012
Amaicha del Valle 139
Amaluza 971
Amantaní 1203
Ambato 943
Anchieta 427
Anco 1255
Ancoraimes 266
Ancud 719
Andahuaylas 1260
Andahuayllas 1233
Angel Falls 1408
Angol 681
Angra dos Reis 385
Annai 1434
Antarctica 1478
Anticura 703
Antofagasta 648, *650*
Antonina 438
Apartaderos 1374
Apolobamba 267
Apura 1451

Aquidaban 581
Aquiraz 523
Aquitania 804
Aracaju 505
Aracataca 830
Aracati 523
Aragua Coast 1350
Araya Peninsula 1391
Archidona 1010
Aregua 1050
Arequipa 1178, *1181*
  Centre *1184*
Argentina 61-232
Arica 665, *667*
Ariquemes 560
Ariri 409
Armenia 856
Armero 853
Arraial da Ajuda 482
Arrecifes 830
Artigas 1309
Assis Brasil 561
Asunción 1039, *1040*
Atacames 1000
Atalaya 1278
Auyán 1409
Ayabaca 1146
Ayacucho 1256, *1257*
Ayaviri 1205

B

Background 1479-1530
Baeza 1005
Bagua Grande 1166
Bahia 463
  carnival 476
Bahía Blanca 105
Bahía de Caráquez 994
Bahía Murta 738
Bahía Solano 850
Baixio 489
Ballestas Islands 1169
Balmaceda 732
Baños 946, *974*
Barão de Melgaço 589
Barcelona 1384
Barichara 806
Bariloche 185, *185*
  Road to Llao Llao *186*
  walks 188
Barinas 1379
Barquisimeto 1363
Barra 468
Barra da Lagoa 442
Barra da Tijuca 359
Barra de Santo Antônio 504
Barra de Valizas 1316
Barra do Quaraí 456

Barrancas (Col) 835
Barrancas (Ven) 1412
Barranco 1086
Barranquilla 827
Barreal 130
Barreirinhas 525
Barretos 410
Bartica 1433
Belém 535, *536*
Belén 134
Bella Vista 320
Belo Horizonte 411
  Centre *413*
  Pampulha *412*
Bento Gonçalves 454
Berlín 807
Bermejo 304
Bertioga 407
Birdwatching 20
Biribiri 430
Blakawatra 1449
Blanquillo 1278
Blumenau 443
Boa Vista 556
Boca Grande 877
Boca Manu 1278
Boconó 1365
Bogotá 780, *782*
  Centre *784*
Bolívar 930
Bolivia 233-336
Bonfim 557
Bonito 580
Borbón 1000
Bosque Protector
  Mindo-Nambillo 918
Boyuibe 328
BR-364 560
Braamspunt 1449
Brasiléia 561
Brasília 565, *564*
Brazil 337-336
Bucaramanga 806
Buenaventura 863
Buenos Aires 70
  Centre *74*
  Federal District *71*
  Recoleta & Palermo *77*
  San Telmo *83*
Búzios 379

C

Caacupé 1050
Cabanaconde 1189
Cabedelo 507
Cabo 495
Cabo Blanco 1147
Cabo de Vela 836

Cabo Frio 379
Cabo Polonio 1316
Cabruta 1406
Cabure 1358
Cacao 1461
Cáceres 589
Cachi 143
Cachoeira 478
Cachora 1247
Caeté 417
Cafayate 143
Cajamarca 1152, *1155*
Cajatambo 1123
Calama 652
Calca 1235
Caldera 645
Calderón 922
Calera de Las Huérfanas 1306
Caleta Olivia 210
Caleta Tortel 739
Cali *860*
Calingasta 130
Camarones 208
Camboriú 442
Camiña 663
camping 602
Campo Grande 579, *580*
Cananéia 409
Cañar 961
Cañaveral 830
Canela 453
Cañete 680
Cañete valley 1168
Canoa Quebrada 523
Cañón del Pato 1125
Capão 479
Capão da Canoa 449
Cape Horn 759
Capiatá 1050
Capilla del Monte 114
Capitán Badó 1051
Capitanejo 804
Capurganá 824
Carabuco 266
Caracaraí 556
Caracas 1334, *1336*
  Centre *1338*
  Sabana Grande *1340*
Caraíva 482
Caral 1124
Caranavi 275
Carapeguá 1056
Caravelas 483
Caraz 1118
Carhuaz 1119
Caripe 1392
Carlos Pellegrini 164
Carmelo 1306
Carmen de Patagones 201
carnet de passages 43
Carnival 372
Carnival in Bahia 476
Carolina 116
Cartagena (Arg) 634

Cartagena (Col) *814*
Cartago 857
Caruaru 500
Carúpano 1392
Casabindo 156
Cascavel 523
Casma 1125
Caspana 653
Cassino 455
Castillos 1316
Castro 720
Cata 1350
Catac 1116
Catacaos 1144
Catacocha 970
Catamarca 134
Catamarca Province 134
Catamayo 970
Catatumbo 1361
Cauca Valley 859
Caucasia 824
Caxias do Sul 454
Cayambe 922
Cayenne 1459, *1459*
Ceará 516
Celendín 1158
Cerro Castillo 732,749
Cerro Colorado (Arg) 115
Cerro Colorado (Uru) 1323
Cerro Corá 1061
Cerro de Pasco 1263
Cerro Perico 1381
Cerro Pintado 1381
Chacalluta-Tacna 666
Chacas 1117
Chachani 1180
Chachapoyas 1159, *1161*
Chachimbiro 930
Chaco (Arg) 167
Chaco (Par) 1063
Chaitén 727
Chala 1174
Chalalán 314
Chalhuanca 1174
Chan Chán 1129
Chanaballita 652
Chañaral 645
Chanchamayo 1262
Chapada dos Guimarães 590
Chapada dos Veadeiros 572
Chaparrí 1138
Charaña 249
Charazani 267
Charity 1432
Chavín de Huantar 1117
Chichiriviche 1355
Chiclayo 1137, *1139*
Chile 595-768
Chile Chico 738
Chilean Pacific Islands 761
Chilecito 133
Chillán 674, *675*
Chiloé 718, *721*
Chimborazo 953

Chimbote 1125
Chinchero 1236
Chipana-Río Loa 652
Chiquián 1123
Chiquinquirá 802
Chiuchín 1124
Chivacoa 1364
Chivay 1188
Chocó 849
Cholila 193
Chololó 1056
Chonchi 720
Choquequirao 1247
Chordeleg 961
Choro 249
Choroní 1351
Choshuenco 694
Chosica 1248
Chúa 264
Chugchilán 941
Chuí 456
Chulumani 275
Chungará 666
Chuquicamata 653
Churín 1124
Chuy 1317
Cidreira 450
Ciénaga 830
Ciudad Bolívar 1405, *1405*
Ciudad del Este 1052, *1052*
Ciudad Guayana 1411
Ciudad Perdida 831
climate
  Argentina 64
  Bolivia 236
  Brazil 340
  Chile 598
  Colombia 772
  Ecuador 886
  Falkland Islands 1468
  Guyana 1426
  Guyane 1457
  Paraguay 1036
  Peru 1070
  Suriname 1444
  Uruguay 1288
  Venezuela 1328
climbing 22
Clorinda 168
Cobija 318
Coca 1009
Cochabamba 306
Cochamó 708
Cochrane 738
Coconuco 871
Cocora 856
Coctaca 155
Cocuy 805
Colakreek 1450
Colca Canyon 1188
Colchane 662
Colombia 769-802
Colón 160
Colonia del Sacramento 1305, *1304*

Colonia Independencia 1052
Colonia Sarmiento 210
Colonia Suiza 1305
Colonia Tovar 1348
Colonia Volendam 1061
Colonias Valdense 1304
Comodoro Rivadavia 209
Comunidad Capirona 1010
Coñaripe 693
Conceição da Barra 427
Concepción (Bol) 331
Concepción (Chi) 678, *679*
Concepción (Par) 1061
Concepción (Per) 1249
Concepción del Uruguay 160
Conchi 653
Concón 634
Concordia 161
Conde 489
Confluencia 183
Congonhas 419
Conococha 1107
Constitución 674
Contulmo 680
Copacabana (Bol) 264, *265*
Copacabana (Bra) 358, *356*
Copiapó 644
Coquimbo 638
Cordilleras Huayhuash 1107
Córdoba 110, *111*
Corire 1192
Coro 1357, *1358*
Coroa Vermelha 482
Coroico 274
Coronel Oviedo 1051
Corral 702
Corrientes 164
Corriverton 1432
Corumbá 586
Cosquín 114
cost of travelling 19
Cotacachi 928
Cotahuasi 1192
Cotahuasi Canyon 1192
Coveñas 824
Coyhaique 730, *731*
Coyhaique Alto 731
credits 1539
Crucita 994
Cuchi Corral 114
Cúcuta 807, *809*
Cuenca 959, *962*
Cuestecita 835
Cueva de los Guácharos 870
Cueva del Guácharo 1392
Cuevas de las Manos 215
Cuiabá 588, *588*
Cumaná 1389, *1390*
Curacautín 687
Curicó 673
Curimagua 1358
Curitiba 432, *434*
Curvelo 430

Cuzco 1208, *1212*
  Around Plaza de Armas *1218*
cycling 44

D
Dalcahue 720
Darién 863
Darién Gap 824
Darwin, Charles 1017
Desaguadero (Bol) 265
Desaguadero (Per) 1206
Diamantina 430
Dolavon 207
drink
  Argentina 54
  Bolivia 241
  Brazil 347
  Chile 603
  Colombia 779
  Ecuador 892
  Paraguay 1038
  Peru 1078
  Uruguay 1291
  Venezuela 1333
Driving
  Argentina 68
  Bolivia 239
  Brazil 345
  Chile 603
  Colombia 777
  Guyana 1428
  Guyane 1458
  Ecuador 891
  Paraguay 1039
  Peru 1077
  Suriname 1446
  Uruguay 1291
  Venezuela 1332
drugs 56
Durazno 1323

E
Easter Island 762
eating 50
Ecuador 883-1032
Ekeko 247
El Altar 955
El Angel 930
El Bolsón 193
El Brujo 1129
El Burro 1381
El Calafate 217, *220*
El Cisne 970
El Colorado 623
El Dorado 800, 1415
El Fraile 731
El Maitén 738
El Misti 1180
El Moján 1361
El Mollar 139
El Morro 1373
El Palmar National Park 161
El Pauji 1417

El Peñol 848
El Playón 1350
El Progreso 1021
El Retiro 848
El Rey National Park 140
El Rodeo 134
El Tambo 964
El Tatio 657
El Valle 850
El Yaque 1398
embassies and consulates
  Argentina 66
  Bolivia 238
  Brazil 343
  Chile 601
  Colombia 774
  Ecuador 888
  Paraguay
  Peru 1072
  Uruguay 1289
  Venezuela 1330
Embu 399
Encarnación 1057, *1058*
Ensenada 707
Entre Lagos 703
Escoma 266
Esmeraldas 1000
Esperanza de El Tingo 941
Espíndola 1146
Espírito Santo 426
Esquel 194
Estância 505
events 20

F
Facatativá 797
Fachinal 738
Falkland Islands 1467-1478
Farellones 623
Faro José Ignacio 1316
Farol 444
Farroupilha 454
Fernando de Noronha 501
Ferreñafe 1140
festivals 20
Fiambalá 134
Fiesta de la Virgen de Urkupiña 311
Filadelfia 1065
Florencia 870
Florianópolis 440, *441*
food 50
food and drink
  Argentina 53
  Bolivia 240
  Brazil 346
  Chile 603
  Colombia 779
  Ecuador 891
  Guyana 1429
  Paraguay 1038
  Suriname 1447
  Uruguay 1290
  Venezuela 1333
Formosa 168

Fortaleza 516, *516*
Foz do Iguaçu 459, *458*
Francisqui 1403
Fray Bentos 1306
Frutillar 707
Fuerte Bulnes 744
Fundación 830
Futaleufú 729

G

Gaiman 207
Galápagos Islands 1017
Galerazamba 817
Garibáldi 454
Garzón 870
gauchos 1308
Genipabu 511
Georgetown 1429, *1430*
Girardot 796
Girón 807
Gobernador Costa 195
Gocta waterfall 1163
Goiânia 571
Goiás 571
Goiás Velho 571
Gonzanamá 970
Gorgona Island 864
government
  Argentina 1506
  Bolivia 1506
  Brazil 1506
  Chile 1506
  Colombia 1507
  Ecuador 1507
  Guyana 1507
  Guyane 1507
  Paraguay 1507
  Peru 1507
  Suriname 1507
  Uruguay 1507
  Venezuela 1507
Gramado 453
Guaduas 797
Guaíra 462
Guajará Mirim 560
Guajira Peninsula 835
Gualaceo 961
Gualeguaychú 160
Guamote 954
Guanare 1379
Guanay 275
Guane 806
Guanillos 652
Guanta 1387
Guaranda 953
Guarapari 427
Guarujá 407
Guasipati 1414
Guatapé 848
Guatavita 799
Guatavita Nueva 799
Guayaquil 976, *981*
Guayaramerín 317
Guicán 805

guide books 45
Güiria 1393
Guyana 1410-1444
Guyane 1456-1468

H

Hernandarias 1053
Higuera 327
Higuerote 1384
history
  Argentina 1486
  Bolivia 1488
  Brazil 1490
  Chile 1492
  Colombia 1493
  Ecuador 1495
  Guyana 1503
  Guyane 1506
  Paraguay 1496
  Peru 1498
  Suriname 1504
  Uruguay 1500
  Venezuela 1502
Hito Cajón 657
Hohenau 1058
holidays and festivals
  Argentina 70
  Bolivia 241
  Brazil 347
  Chile 604
  Colombia 780
  Ecuador 892
  Guyana 1429
  Guyane 1458
  Paraguay 1038
  Peru 1079
  Suriname 1447
  Uruguay 1291
  Venezuela 1334
Honda 797
Horcón 634
Hornopirén 727
Hotel Humboldt 1348
Huaca de la Luna 1128
Huacachina 1169
Hualahoyo 1250
Hualhuas 1250
Huallanca 1125
Huamachuco 1152
Huancacalle 1246
Huancas 1159
Huancavelica 1254
Huancayo 1250, *1251*
Huanchaco 1131
Huánuco 1263
Huaquillas 985
Huara 662
Huaraz 1107, *1109*
  Centre *1111*
Huari 1117
Huatajata 264
Huaura Valley 1124
Humahuaca 155

Humberstone 662

I

Ibagué 856
Ibarra 929
Iberá 164
Iberá Marshes 164
Ibibobo 328
Iboribó 1415
Ica 1169
Icho Cruz 115
Igarassu 500
Iguape 408
Iguazú Falls 173, *174*
Iles du Salut 1460
Ilha de Santa Catarina 442
Ilha do Marajó 537
Ilha do Mel 438
Ilha Grande 386
Ilhéus 481
Illampu 266
Imbassaí 489
Iñapari 1279
Inca Trail 1240
Inca Trail to Ingapirca 961
Ingapirca 961
internet 50
Inti Wara Yassi 308
Ipanema (Bra) 358, *359*
Ipiales 878
Iquique 660, *661*
Iquitos 1271, *1271*
Iriri 427
Irupana 275
Iruya 155
Ischigualasto Provincial Park 130
Isinliví 941
Isla de Coche 1397
Isla de Cubagua 1397
Isla de la Luna 265
Isla de Margarita 1396, *1398*
Isla del Sol 265
Isla Magdalena 744
Isla Malvinas 1467-1478
Isla Mancera 702
Isla Martín García 98
Isla Navarino 758
Isla Negra 634
Isla Tenglo 713
Islas Los Roques 1403
Isluga 662
Itá 1056
Itacaré 481
Itacuruçá 385
Itahuania 1278
Itaipú 1053
Itaipu Dam 459
Itanhaém 408
Itaparica 468
Itauguá 1050
Itaúnas 427
itineraries
  Brazil 340
  Colombia 772

Ecuador 886
Paraguay 1036
Peru 1070
Iturbe 155
Iwokrama 1434
Izcuchaca 1250

J

Jaén 1166
Jaguarão 456
Jaguaribe 469
Jají 1374
Jalapão 576
Jama 155
Jama Pass 154
Jardín 849
Jauja 1248
Jericó 849
Jericoacoara 525
Jesús 1058
Jesús María 115
Ji Paraná 560
Jijoca de Jericoacoara 524
Jimbura 971
Jipijapa 989
João Pesso 507
Jodensavanne 1449
Joinville 443
Juan C Falcón National Park 1358
Juan Fernández Islands 761
Juan Griego 1397
Juan López 649
Juanchaco 863
Judibana 1358
Jujuy 152
Juli 1197
Juliaca 1204
Junín 1263
Junín de los Andes 179

K

Kaieteur Falls 1433
Kaieteur National Park 1433
Kalahuta 264
Kamarata 1409
Kamoirán 1416
Kapawi Ecological Reserve 1014
Kavác 1409
Kavanayén 1415
Km 88 1415
Kourou 1460
Kuelap 1159
Kuntur Wasi 1154
Kyk-over-al 1433

L

La Arena 727
La Asunción 1397
La Azulita 1374
La Balsa 1166
La Barra 1316
La Boquilla 817
La Calera 1189

La Campana National Park 635
La Cumbre 114
La Cumbrecita 116
La Diablada festival 279
La Esperanza 929
La Falda 114
La Guaira 1348
La Herradura 638
La Junta 730
La Merced 1262
La Mucuy 1373
La Oroya 1248
La Paloma 1316
La Paz (Bol) 242, *244*
    Centre *246*
La Paz (Ecu) 930
La Pedrera 1316
La Pila 989
La Plata (Arg) 99
La Plata (Col) 870
La Portada 648
La Quiaca 156
La Quinua 1258
La Rioja 133
La Serena 638, *639*
La Tirana 662
La Tola 1000
La Toma (Arg) 116
La Toma (Ecu) 970
La Unión 1263
La Yunga 327
Ladrilleros 863
Lago Agrio 1006
Lago Calafquén 693
Lago Chungará 668
Lago de Janauri 548
Lago General Carrera 737
Lago Llanquihue 706
Lago Poopó 280
Lago Puyehue 703
Lago Ypacaraí 1050
Lagoinha 524
Lagos Fluminenses 379
Laguna 444
Laguna Colorada 284
Laguna Cuicocha 928
Laguna de los Cóndores 1158
Laguna de los Pozuelos 156
Lagunas 1269
Lagunilla 1169
Lagunillas 624
Lake District *177*
Lake Huiñamarca 264
Lake Titicaca (Bol) 264
Lake Titicaca (Per) 1203
Lambayeque 1137
Lampa 1205
Lamud 1159
language 52
language schools, Quito 915
Lanín National Park 179
Laquipampa 1140
Laraquete 680
Largo do Pelourinho 467

Las Cuevas 128
Las Grutas 201
Las Leñas 125
Las Pailas 143
Las Peñas 1000
Lasana 653
Lasso 936
Latacunga 936
Leblon 358
Lebu 680
Lechería 1384
Lelydorp 1450
Lençóis 478
Leonsberg 1449
Lérida 853
Les Hattes 1461
Lethem 1434
Leticia 880
Levanto 1159
Leymebamba 1158
Liberdade 397
Libertador Gen San Martín 157
Lican-Ray 693
Lima 1079, *1080*
Centre *1083*
Miraflores *1090*
Limones 1000
Linden 1432
Linhares 427
Llacanora 1153
Llachón 1198
Llano del Hato 1374
Llao Llao 186, *186*
Llapay 1168
Loja 969
Loma Plata 1066
Loreto 170
Los Andes 624
Los Angeles 680
Los Antiguos 215
Los Katíos National Park 825
Los Libertadores 624
Los Molles 125
Los Penitentes 126
Lota 680
Luepa 1415
Luicho 1192
Luján 98
Luque 1042
Luya 1159

M

Mabaruma 1432
Macapá 537
Macará 970
Macas 1012
Maceió 504
Machachi 935
Machala 984
Machalilla 993
Machu Picchu 1240
Macuro 1393
Madeira-Mamoré Railway 560
Madidi National Park 314

Magangué 823
Magdalena 319
Maicao 836
Maimará 155
Mairana 327
Maitencillo 634
Majorländia 523
Malagana 823
Malargüe 125
Maldonado 1315
Mana 1461
Manantiales 1316
Manaure 836
Manaus 545, *545*
Máncora 1147
Mangaratiba 385
Manglaralto 988
Mangue Seco 489
Manhumirim 425
Manizales 852
Manta 993
Mantecal 1379
Manu Biosphere Reserve 1277
Mapelo island 864
maps 45
Mar del Plata 104
Maracaibo 1361
Maracay 1350
Marajó 537
Maranhão 525
Marataízes 427
Marcahuasi 1248
Marechal Deodoro 504
Maresias 407
Mariana 418
Maripa 1406
Maripasoula 1461
Mariscal Estigarribia 1066
Mariscal Sucre 931
Marsella 855
Marshall Falls 1433
Mascarilla 930
Maturín 1392
Maullín 713
Mayocc 1255
Mbaracayú Forest Reserve 1051
Mbutuy 1051
Medellín 842, *843*
  Centre *844*
Mejillones 649
Melo 1323
Mendoza (Arg) 119, *120*
Mendoza (Per) 1159,
Mera 1011
Mercedes (Arg) 164
Mercedes (Uru) 1306
Mérida 1366, *1368*
Merlo 117
Milo Verde 430
Mina Clavero 115
Minas Gerais 411
Mindo 918
Miraflores 1086, *1090*
Miramar 104

Miranda 581
Misahuallí 1011
Mitad del Mundo 916
Mocha 944
Mochima 1388
Moengo 1451
Mompós 823
money
  Argentina 67
  Bolivia 238
  Brazil 343
  Chile 601
  Colombia 774
  credit cards 54
  Falkland Islands 1469
  Guyana 1427
  Guyane 1457
  Ecuador 888
  Paraguay 1037
  Peru 1072
  Suriname 1445
  travellers' cheques 55
  Uruguay 1289
  Venezuela 1330
Monguí 804
Monsefú 1137
Montañita 988
Monte Alegre 542
Monte Avila 1347
Monte Caseros 161
Monte Grande 640
Monteagudo 299
Montecristi 989
Montenegro 856
Montería 824
Montevideo 1292, *1292*
Montsinéry 1460
Moquegua 1193
Morawhanna 1432
Morretes 438
Morro de São Paulo 481
Morrocoy National Park 1354
Mórrope 1138
Mostardas 455
Mount Roraima 1421,1433
Moyobamba 1163
Mucuchíes 1373
Musichi 836

N
Nahuel Huapi National Park 182
Namballe 1166
Natal 509
National Vicuña Reserve 1188
Nazca 1172, *1175*
Nazca Lines 1173
Necochea 105
Neiva 872
Neu-Halbstadt 1066
Neuland 1066
Neuquén 177
New Amsterdam 1432
Niebla 702
Nieuw-Amsterdam 1449

Nieuw-Nickerie 1451
Niquitao 1365
Niterói 378
Nova 454
Nueva Germania 1051
Nuevo Rocafuerte 1006
Nuquí 850

O
O Aleijadinho 417
Óbidos 543
Ocongate 1233
Ocucaje 1169
Ocumare de la Costa 1350
Oiapoque 538
Old Patagonian Express 195
Olinda 499, *499*
Ollagüe 653
Ollantaytambo 1236
Olleros 1116
Olmos 1140
Olón 988
Oncol 702
Orán 157
Orinoco Delta 1411
Oruro 278
Osório 449
Osorno 702
Otavalo 923, *925*
Otway Sound 744
Ouro Preto 417
Ovalle 637

P
Pacasmayo 1152
Pachacámac 1087
Pachacuti Inca Yupanqui 1211
Paipa 804
Paita 1144
Pakaraima Mountains 1433
Palena 730
Palmas 576
Palmira 954
Palomino 831
Pampa Linda 193
Pampatar 1397
Pamplona 807
Panguipulli 694
Pantanal 577
Pântano do Sul 442
Papallacta 916
Papudo 634
Paracas 1168
Paracuru 524
Paraguaná 1358
Paraguarí 1056
Paraguay 1033-1066
Paráiba 507
Paraitepuí 1421
Paramaribo 1447, *1448*
Paramonga 1125
Paraná (Arg) 163
Paraná (Bra) 432

Paranaguá 437,438
Paraty 386
Paria Peninsula 1392
Parika 1432
Parinacota 668
Parintins 543
Pariti 264
Parnaíba 525
Parque Arqueológioco
  Tierradentro 866
Parque Manantial 1058
Parque Nacional Amacayacu 881
Parque Nacional Amboró 327
Parque Nacional Bernardo
  O'Higgins 749
Parque Nacional Cajas 961
Parque Nacional Calilegua 157
Parque Nacional Canaima 1409,
  1409
Parque Nacional Caparaó 419
Parque Nacional Chaco 168
Parque Nacional Chiloé 721
Parque Nacional Conguillio 687
Parque Nacional Cotopaxi 935
Parque Nacional de Aparados da
  Serra 454
Parque Nacional de Sete
  Cidades 531
Parque Nacional Ensenada de
  Utria 850
Parque Nacional Henri
  Pittier 1350, *1350*
Parque Nacional Iguazú 173
Parque Nacional Itatiaia 385
Parque Nacional Laguna de
  Tacarigua 1384
Parque Nacional Laguna San
  Rafael 739
Parque Nacional Lauca 668
Parque Nacional Lençóis 525
Parque Nacional Los Alerces 194
Parque Nacional Los Glaciares 217
Parque Nacional Marumbi 437
Parque Nacional Mburucuyá 164
Parque Nacional
  Mochima 1384,1387
Parque Nacional Monte
  Balmaceda 749
Parque Nacional Nahuelbuta 681
Parque Nacional Noel Kempff
  Mercado 332
Parque Nacional Pan de
  Azúcar 645
Parque Nacional Puracé 869
Parque Nacional Puyehue 703
Parque Nacional Quebrada del
  Condorito 115
Parque Nacional Sajama 280
Parque Nacional Sangay 1012
Parque Nacional Sierra
  Nevada 1372
Parque Nacional Tayrona 830
Parque Nacional Tijuca 360
Parque Nacional Torotoro 307

Parque Nacional Torres del
  Paine 753, *755*
Parque Nacional Vicente Pérez
  Rosales 707
Parque Pumalin 727
Parque Tobogán de la Selva 1382
Paso Agua Negra 640
Paso Carrirriñe 694
Paso Casas Viejas 749
Paso de Icalma 688
Paso de Jama 657
Paso de los Libres 161
Paso de los Toros 1323
Paso Huahum 694
Paso Pehuenche 674
Paso Pérez Rosales 708
Paso Pino Hachado 688
Paso Puyehue 703
Paso San Francisco 645
Paso Sico 657
Passo Fundo 455
Pasto 876
Patagonia 200
Patagonian Express 195
Patanemo 1354
Paucartambo 1232
Paute 961
Paysandú 1307, *1307*
Pedernales 995
Pedro González 1397
Pedro Juan Caballero 1061
Pedro Ruíz 1163
Pelechuco 267
Pelotas 455
Penedo 385,505
Península Valdés 202
Pereira 855
Peribeca 1375
Perito Moreno 215
Perito Moreno National Park 215
Pernambuco 490
Peru 1067-1284
Peruíbe 408
Petrohué 708
Petrópolis 380, *380*
Peulla 708
Pico El Aguila 1365
Pico Espejo 1372
Pico Naiguatá 1347
Pico Oriental 1348
Piedecuesta 807
Piedrabuena 210
Pikin Poika 1450
Pilaló 941
Pilcopata 1278
Pilón Lajas 314
Pimentel 1137
Pinamar 103
Piñán lakes 930
Piñango 1365
Piñas 985
Pinchollo 1189
Pirangi do Norte 511
Pirenópolis 572

Piriápolis 1314
Piribebuy 1051
Piripiri 532
Pisac 1234
Pisagua 663
Pisco 1168
Pisco Elqui 640
Piscobamba 1118
Pisimbalá 866
Pissis 134
Pitalito 870
Piúma 427
Piura 1143, *1144*
Playa Colorada 1388
Playa de Oro 1001
Playa El Agua 1397
Playa El Aguila 652
Playa Escondida 999
Playa Peruana 652
Playas 987
Pocitos 157
Pomabamba 1118
Pomaire 623
Pomerode 443
Ponta de Pedras 537
Ponta Negra *510*
Ponta Porã 581
Popayán 865, *866*
Porlamar 1397
Portezuelo 1314
Portillo 624
Porto Alegre 448, *450*
Porto Belo 442
Porto Seguro 482
Porto Velho 559
Portoviejo 994
Porvenir 758
Posadas 169
post 55
Potosí 292, *293*
Potrerillos 126
Powaka 1449
Pozo Almonte 662
Pozo Colorado 1065
Praia do Forte 488
Praia do Rosa 443
Praia Iguape 523
Prainha 523
Providencia 840
Pucallpa 1267
Pucón 691
Pueblito 830
Puelo 708
Puente del Inca 127
Puerto Acosta 266,1206
Puerto Aisén 731
Puerto Ayacucho 1381
Puerto Ayora 1020
Puerto Baquerizo Moreno 1021
Puerto Bermúdez 1263
Puerto Bertrand 738
Puerto Bolívar 984
Puerto Cabello 1354
Puerto Cayo 989

Puerto Chacabuco 732
Puerto Chicama 1131
Puerto Cisnes 730
Puerto Colombia (Col) 827
Puerto Colombia (Ven) 1351
Puerto Córdenas 729
Puerto Deseado 210
Puerto Eten 1137
Puerto Fuy 694
Puerto Guadal 738
Puerto Huacho 1124
Puerto Ibáñez 732
Puerto Iguazú 175, *173*
Puerto La Cruz 1384, *1385*
Puerto López 989
Puerto Madryn 202, *203*
Puerto Maldonado 1278
Puerto Montt 713, *714*
Puerto Nariño 881
Puerto Natales 748, *750*
Puerto Octay 706
Puerto Ordaz 1411
Puerto Páez 1381
Puerto Pérez 264
Puerto Pirehueico 694
Puerto Quito 918
Puerto Río Tranquilo 738
Puerto San Julián 210
Puerto Suárez 333
Puerto Varas 707
Puerto Villarroel 319
Puerto Williams 758
Pujilí 940
Pululahua 916
Puna West of Catamarca 134
Punata 307
Puno 1197, *1200*
Punta Arenas 742, *743*
Punta Ballena 1315
Punta Carnero 988
Punta de Piedra 1402
Punta del Diablo 1316
Punta del Este 1315
Punta Delgada 225, 759
Punta Rosa 103
Punta Sal Grande 1147
Punta Tombo 208
Punto Fijo 1358
Puquio 1174
Puracé 869
Purmamarca 155
Puruchuco 1087
Putre 668
Putumayo 877
Puyango 985
Puyo 1011
Puyuguapi 730

Q

Quaraí 456
Quebrada de Humahuaca 154
Quebrada de las Conchas 143
Quechualla 1192
Quellón 722

Quemchi 720
Quetena Chico 285
Quibdó 850
Quíbor 1364
Quichuas 1255
Quijarro 333
Quillacolla 307
Quillagua 652
Quilmes 139
Quilotoa 941
Quincemil 1278
Quinchamalí 676
Quinchao 720
Quintero 634
Quirusillas 327
Quito 893
  New city *898*
  Old city *897*

R

Ralún 708
Rancagua 673
Rapa Nui 762
Raqchi 1233
Ráquira 802
Raura 1107
Recife 490, *492*
  Boa Viagem *494*
  Orientation *491*
Recôncavo 478
Refugio de Vida Silvestre La Aurora
  del Palmar 161
Régina 1461
Reserva de la Biósfera del
  Chaco 1064
Reserva Eduardo Avaroa 284
Reserva Nacional Nalcas
  Malalcahuello 687
Resistencia 167
Riberalta 317
Río Blanco 624
Rio Branco (Bra) 561
Río Branco (Uru) 1323
Río Caribe 1392
Rio da Prata 581
Rio de Janeiro 348, *348*
  carnival 372
  Centre *351*
  Gloría, Santa Teresa, Catete,
  Flamengo *354*
  Ipanema & Leblon *359*
Río Gallegos 212, *213*
Río Grande (Arg) 225
Rio Grande (Bra) 455
Rio Grande do Sul 448
Río Mayo 215
Río Negro 727
Río Pilcomayo National Park 168
Río Turbio 219
Río Villegas 193
Riobamba 952, *956*
Riohacha 835
Rionegro 848
Riosucio 849

Rivera 1323
rodeo 410
Rondônia 559
Rosario 163
Rosario de la Frontera 139
Rumichaca 1255
Rurrenabaque 314
Ruta 40 215

S

Sabará 416
Sacred Valley, Peru *1234*
safety 56
  Bolivia 243
  Brazil 343
  Chile 601
  Colombia 776
  Ecuador 890
  Paraguay 1038
  Peru 1074
  Suriname 1446
  Venezuela 1331
  Uruguay 1289
Sajama 280
Salango 989
Salar de Atacama 657
Salar de Uyuni 284
Salento 856
Salinas 987
Salta 146, *147*
Salto 1308
Salto del Guaíra 1051
Salto El Laja 680
Salvador 463, *464*
  Centro Histórico *466*
Samaipata 326
Same 999
San Agustín 871
San Agustín de Cajas 1250
San Agustín del Valle Fértil 130
San Andrés 839, *839*
San Antonio (Chi) 634
San Antonio (Ven) 1375
San Antonio de Areco 99
San Antonio de Ibarra 929
San Antonio de los Cobres 146
San Antonio de Pichincha 918
San Antonio Oeste 201
San Bernardino 1050
San Borja 314
San Cipriano 863
San Clemente 994
San Clemente del Tuyú 103
San Cristóbal 1374
San Cristóbal (Bol) 284
San Félix 1411
San Fernando 673
San Fernando de Apure 1379
San Francisco de Yuruaní 1421
San Gabriel 930
San Gil 806
San Gregorio de Polanco 1323
San Ignacio 1166
San Ignacio de Moxos 319

San Ignacio de Velasco 331
San Ignacio de Yuruaní 1416
San Ignacio Guazú 1057
San Ignacio Miní 170
San Isidro 1415
San Jacinto (Col) 823
San Jacinto (Ecu) 994
San Javier 331
San Jerónimo 1250
San José de Chiquitos 332
San José de Jachal 130
San Juan 129, *130*
San Juan de Manapiare 1382
San Lázaro 298
San Lorenzo 1042
San Lorenzo (Bol) 304
San Lorenzo (Ecu) 1001
San Luis 1118
San Luis Province 116
San Marcos (Chi) 652
San Marcos (Per) 1117
San Martín de los Andes 179
San Matías 333
San Miguel 1001
San Miguel del Bala 314
San Pablo del Lago 924
San Pedro 1250
San Pedro de Atacama 656, *656*
San Pedro de Casta 1248
San Rafael 125
San Rafael de Mucuchíes 1373
San Ramón 1262
San Sebastián 758
San Vicente (Bol) 289
San Vicente (Ecu) 994
Sanaré 1364
Sandoná 877
Santa Ana 170
Santa Bárbara (Bra) 425
Santa Bárbara (Col) 848
Santa Catarina 440
Santa Cruz Cabrália 482
Santa Cruz de la Sierra 321, *322*
Santa Elena de Uairén 1416, *1417*
Santa Fe 163
Santa Fé de Antioquia 848
Santa María 1001
Santa María (Arg) 139
Santa María (Par) 1057
Santa María (Per) 1243
Santa Marta 829, *829*
Santa Rosa (Par) 1057
Santa Rosa (Per) 1137
Santa Rosa de Cabal 855
Santa Teresa (Bra) 353
Santa Teresa (Per) 1243
Santa Teresa National Park 1316
Santana do Livramento 456
Santarém 543
Santiago 605
   Bellavista and Lastarria *612*
   Centre *607*
   Orientation *605*
   Providencia *608*

West of centre *614*
Santiago del Estero 137
Santigron 1450
Santo Domingo 1365
Santo Domingo de los
   Colorados 995
Santos 406
São Cristóvão 505
São Félix 478
São Francisco do Sul 443
São Gonçalo do Rio das
   Pedras 430
São Gonçalo do Rio Preto 430
São João del Rei 420
São Joaquim 444
São José do Norte 455
São Lourenço do Sul 455
São Luis 525, *526*
São Miguel das Missões 455
São Paulo 391
Centre *394*
Jardins and Avenida Paulista *397*
São Pedro de Aldeia 379
São Sebastião 407
São Tomé das Letras 421
Sapecho 314
Saquarema 379
Saquisilí 941
Saraguro 968
Sarmiento 210
Sauces 977
Saül 1461
Saywite 1247
Sechín 1125
Serro 431
Shell 1011
shopping 57
Shuar Federation 1012
Sibambe 954
Sicán 1140
Sico 147
Sierra de la Ventana 105
Sierra de San Luis 1358
Sierra Nevada de Mérida 1366
Sierra Nevada de Santa Marta 831
Sierras de San Luis 116
Sigchos 941
Sígsig 961
Sihuas 1118
Silvia 866
Sinamaica 1361
Sincelejo 823
Sinnamary 1460
Sinsacate 115
Sipán 1138
Sítio do Conde 489
Socorro 806
Sogamoso 804
Soledad 827
Sorata 266, *269*
Soure 537
South American Explorer's 32
South Georgia 1477
sport 20

Stanley 1471, *1472*
St-Georges de l'Oyapock 1462
St-Laurent du Maroni 1461
Súa 999
Subaúma 489
Sucre 297, *299*
Sucúa 1012
Sullana 1146
Superagui National Park 438
Supía 849
Surama 1434
Suriname 1444-1456
Suriquí 264
Surire 668
Susques 155

T
Tabatinga 555
Tabay 1373
Tacna 1193, *1195*
Tacuarembó 1323
Tadó 850
Tafí del Valle 139
Taganga 830
Takesi Trail 249
Talampaya National Park 131
Talara 1147
Talca 674
Talcahuano 679
Taltal 645
Tandil 100
Tantauco 722
Tapay 1189
Taquile 1203
Tarabuco 298
Tarapaya 294
Tarapoto 1164
Tarija 303
Tarma 1262
Tarqui 993
Tastil 147
Tavares 455
telephone 59
Temuco 684, *686*
Tena 1010
Teresina 530
Termas de Pangui 693
Termas de Reyes 153
Termas de Río Hondo 137
Termas de San Luis 693
Terre Rouge 1461
Tiahuanaco 248
Tibau do Sul 511
Tierra del Fuego 225,758
Tierra del Fuego National Park 228
Tierradentro 866
Tigre 98
Tigua 940
Tilcara 155
Timaná 870
Tingo (Amazonas) 1158
Tingo (Arequipa) 1179
Tingo María 1266
Tinogasta 134

Tiquipaya 310
Tiradentes 420
Tobati 1051
Tocantins 576
Toconao 657
Toconce 653
Tocopilla 652
Tolú 823
Tópaga 804
Tornquist 105
Toro Muerto 1192
Totness 1450
tourist information
  Argentina 65
  Bolivia 236
  Brazil 341
  Chile 599
  Colombia 772
  Ecuador 887
  Guyane 1457
  Paraguay 1036
  Peru 1071
  Uruguay 1288
  Venezuela 1328
Train to the Clouds 148
train travel, Ecuador 954
Trancoso 482
transport
  river 44
transport, air
  air passes 37
  Argentina 67
  Bolivia 239
  Brazil 343
  Chile 601
  Ecuador 890
  Paraguay 1038
  Venezuela 1331
transport, bus
  Chile 602
transport, road
  Argentina 68
  Bolivia 239
  Brazil 344
  Colombia 778
  Ecuador 890
  motorcycling 44
  motoring 42
  shipping a vehicle 43
  Uruguay 1291
  Venezuela 1332
transport, train
  Bolivia 240
  Chile 602
Treinta y Tres 1323
Trelew 206, 207
Tren a las Nubes 148
Trindade 387
Trinidad (Bol) 319
Trinidad (Par) 1058
Trujillo (Per) 1127, *1130*
Trujillo (Ven) 1365
Tucacas 1355
Tucumán 138, *140*

Tucumé 1138
Tucupita 1412
Tulcán 931
Tumaco 877
Tumbes 1147, *1149*
Tumeremo 1415
Tunja 800
Tupiza 289
Túquerres 877
Turbaco 823
Turbo 824
Tutóia 525

U
Uaimiri Atroari Indian Reserve 556
Ubatuba 408
Ubu 427
Unduavi 274
Unguía 825
Urcos 1233
Urcuquí 930
Uribia 836
Uros 1203
Urubamba 1235
Uruguaiana 455
Uruguay 1285-1324
Ushuaia 226, *228*
Uspallata 126
Uyuni 283, *285*

V
Valdivia (Chi) 701, *701*
Valdivia (Ecu) 988
Valença 481
Valencia 1354
Valera 1364
Valle de la Luna 248
Valle de Lares 1235
Valle Nevado 623
Vallecito 129
Vallecitos 126
Valledupar 835
Vallegrande 327,330
Vallenar 644
Valles Calchaquíes 143
Valparaíso 625, *628*
  El Puerto, Cerros Alegre and
  Concepción *630*
vehicle documents 43
Venezuela 1325-1422
Viedma 201
Vila do Abraão 386
Vila Velha 433
Vilcabamba (Ecu) 974, *974*
Vilcabamba (Per) 1246
Vilches 674
Villa Albina 307
Villa Alpina 116
Villa Carlos Paz 114
Villa Cerro Castillo 732
Villa de Leiva 800, *801*
Villa Dorotea 749
Villa El Chocón 178

Villa Florida 1056
Villa General Belgrano 116
Villa Gesell 103
Villa La Angostura 183
Villa Mitre 104
Villa O'Higgins 739
Villa Rosario 807
Villa Traful 183
Villa Tunari 308
Villa Unión 133
Villamontes 328
Villarrica (Chi) 691
Villarrica (Par) 1052
Villavicencio 797
Villazón 290
Viña del Mar 625, *633*
Vinchina 133
Visviri 666
Vitória 426
Volcán Cayambe 922
Volcán Osorno 707
Voltaire Falls 1461

W
Wageningen 1451
Washabo 1451

X
Xapuri 561

Y
Yacambú 1364
Yacuiba 328
Yaguarón 1056
Yanama 1118
Yanque 1189
Yare 1348
Yarinacocha 1267
Yatasto 139
Yauyos 1168
Yavi 156
Ybycuí 1056
Yucay 1235
Yucumo 314
Yumina 1180
Yunga Cruz 250
Yungas 274
Yungay 1119
Yunguyo 1206
Yurimaguas 1269

Z
Zamora 970
Zapala 178
Zapallar 634
Zapiga 663
Zaruma 985
Zipaquirá 796
Zumba 975
Zumbahua 941
Zumbi 1012

Advertisers' index

A

Alpha Hostel, Brazil 361
Amauta Spanish School,
Peru 1231
Amazing Peru, UK 38
Amerispan, USA 53, Inside front
cover
Amigos Spanish School,
Peru 1231
Andando Tours-Angermeyer
Cruises, Ecuador 1030
Andean Travel Web, Peru 1210
Andes Explorer, Ecuador 1023
Andes Salt Expeditions,
Bolivia 287
AQP Servicios Integral de Viajes,
Peru 1101
Austral Tours, UK 40

B

Bala Tours, Bolivia 316
Bellavista Cloud Forest Reserve,
Ecuador 919
Biking Dutchman, Ecuador 908
Buena Vista Hostal, Peru 1182

C

Campo Aventura, Chile 709
Campus Trekking, Ecuador 932
Casa Mojanda, Ecuador 926
Casa Tropical (Cacao Travel
Group), Venezuela 1333
Casa Viena, Colombia 819
CEDEI (Centers for Interamerican
Studies), Ecuador 967
Che Lagarto Hostels (Argentina),
Argentina 81
Che Lagarto Hostels (Brazil),
Argentina 363, 388
Che Lagarto Hostels (Chile),
Argentina 611
Che Lagarto Hostels (Uruguay),
Argentina 1297
Class Adventure Travel, Peru 1100
Crillon Tours, Bolivia 271
Culturas Peru (A mi Manera),
Peru 1221

D

Domiruth Travel Service S.A.C.,
Peru 1209

E

El Misti Hostel, Brazil 362
Enchanted Expeditions,
Ecuador 1027
Enigma, Peru 1226

F

4starSouthAmerica.com, USA 40,
1557
Falkland Islands Tourist Board,
Falkland Islands 1469, 1559
Favela Tour, Brazil 374
Fertur Peru, Peru 1101

G

Galacruises Expeditions,
Ecuador 1029
Galapagos Classic Cruises, UK 39
Galápagos Tours, Ecuador 1031
Galextur-Hotel Silberstein
Galápagos, Ecuador 909
Gloria Tours/Hotel Gloria,
Bolivia 259

H

Hacienda Los Andes, Chile 642
Hostal Rio Amazonas, Chile 611
Hostel Manaus, Brazil 549
Hostelling International Argentina,
Argentina 1584
Hotel & Mirador Los Apus,
Peru 1217
Hotel Antumalal S.A, Chile 695
Hotel Esmeralda, Bolivia 275
Hotel Oberland, Bolivia 252
Hotel Rosario, Bolivia 251
Hotel Rosario del Lago,
Bolivia 267
Hotel Rumi Punku, Peru 1219
Hotel Sierra Madre, Ecuador 900
Hotel Westfalenhaus,
Paraguay 1043
Hoteles Libertador, Peru 1216

I

Iguana Tour, Brazil 553
Imbex Rent a Car, Bolivia 261
Inkaterra Urubamba Villas,
Peru 1237
International Bureau of Language,
Argentina 97
International Tours & Travel Ltd,
Falkland Islands 1476

J

Journey Latin America, UK 35,
1562
Joyeria King's Store, Bolivia 256

K

Kilca Hostel & Backpacker,
Argentina 82

L

Last Frontiers, UK 41
Latin American Travel Association,
UK 23
L'Auberge Inn, Ecuador 901
Little Chartres Farm, Falkland
Islands 1474

M

MAYUC, Peru 1227

N

Natoura C.A. Travel & Adventure
Tours, Venezuela 1329

Navimag, Chile Inside back cover

O

Oasis Overland, UK 36
Open Door Tour Operator, Brazil 578
Orient Express Hotels, Peru 1560

P

Pakacuna Backpackers, Peru 1092
Pantiacolla Tours SRL, Peru 1282
Peru For Less, Peru 1099
Peru Rail, Peru 1561
Peru Treks and Adventure, Peru 1226
Petita Rent A Car, Bolivia 260
Pousada Hibiscus Beach, Brazil 382

Q

Quilotoa Lodge, Ecuador 942
Quito Visitor's Bureau, Ecuador 893

R

Restaurant Vienna, Bolivia 254
Restaurant y Hostería jécole!,
Chile 696
Rio Flat Rental, Brazil 365

S

Safari Tours, Ecuador 910
San Antonio Abad Hotel, Peru 1089
Say Hueque, Argentina 67,91
Select Latin America, UK 37
Shorty's Diner & Motel, Falkland
Islands 1475
Sonesta Posadas del Inca, Peru 1217
South American Experience, UK 36
South American Explorers, Peru 1208
Stop & Drop, Peru 1091
Swallows And Amazons Tours, Brazil
552

T

Tambo Viejo, Peru 1182
Tangol, Argentina 90
Tierra de Fuego, Ecuador 911
Transturin, Bolivia 272
Trekking Chile, Chile 599
Trekking in Ecuador, Ecuador 889
Trips Worldwide, UK 37
Turisbus, Bolivia 257
Turismo Vida Sol e Mar Ltd, Brazil 444

W

Wasai Maldonado Ecolodge,
Peru 1283
Wilderness Explorers,
Guyana 1426,1440

Z

Zenith Travel, Ecuador 1557

Notes

Acknowledgements

For their assistance with the 2007 edition, the author wishes to thank all at Footprint, especially Nicola Gibbs, Felicity Laughton, Alan Murphy, Sarah Sorensen and Jo Williams.

In October-November 2006, the author was invited by PromPerú to join a birdwatching trip in southeast and northern Peru. Ben is most grateful to the following for a memorable journey: Christian Jara Amézaga and Guillermo Zariquiey Guillot of PromPerú; Beverley Mills of JCPR; the guides Matt Denton, Silverio Duri Valdivia and Fernando Angulo Pratalongo (of the Asociacón Cracidae Perú); Heinz Plenge of Chaparrí; Viajes Pacífico/Gray Line, especially Rocio Zavala; Rainforest Expeditions; Fernando Valdivia Gómez of TeleAndes; and Chris Harbard, Richard Thomas and Kevin Wilmot.

In January 2007, Ben visited Venezuela. For their help and hospitality in the Andes, he would like to thank: in Mérida: José Luis Troconis, Renate Reiners and all the staff at NAtourA Travel and Adventure Tours, Molina the driver, Ian and Mary Woodward; in San Rafael de Tabay: Joe Klaiber and the staff of Casa Vieja, Dirk Klaiber and Kai Putzka; also Steve Chew, Gillian Howe of Geodyssey and Jenny Hyden of JLA.

Huw Hennessy subedited large portions of the text for this edition; we are most grateful for his help on Argentina, Chile, Colombia, Venezuela, the Guianas, the Falklands and Essentials.

Argentina: Nicolás Kugler (Buenos Aires), and Christabelle Dilks (author of Footprint Argentina).
Bolivia: Geoffrey Groesberg (USA). Peter Hutchison (author of Footprint Mexico & Central America).
Brazil: Alex Robinson (author of Footprint Brazil). Peter Hutchison.
Chile: Janak Jani (author of Footprint Chile).
Colombia: Anastasia Moloney (Bogotá).
Ecuador: Robert and Daisy Kunstaetter (authors of Footprint Ecuador and the Galápagos); Jean Brown (Quito).
Paraguay: Hilary Wheat and Joe South (Asunción).
Peru: Heather MacBrayne, manager of South American Explorers, Cuzco, and Jennie Stephens-Romero, Assistant Manager at South American Explorers, Lima. Thanks are also due to all those who contributed to Footprint Peru, especially Steve Frankham, Robert and Daisy Kunstaetter, John Forrest and Julia Porturas and Walter Eberhart (full acknowledgements are given in the 6th edition). See also above.
Uruguay: Nicolás Kugler (Buenos Aires).
Venezuela: Anastasia Moloney (Bogotá); see also above.
Guyana: Tony Thorne and Teri O'Brien (Wilderness Explorers, Georgetown).
Suriname: Bryan J Soekra (Paramaribo), Jerry A-Kum, and Mark Wilson (Trinidad).
Falklands/Malvinas: Liz Dimmlich of the Falkland Islands Tourist Board.
Antarctica: Dr Robert Headland, Senior Associate at the Scott Polar Research Institute.
The Health section was written by Prof Larry Goodyer, head of the Leicester School of Pharmacy and director of Nomad Medical.

Travellers whose emails and letters have been used this year (in part of in full): Line Aagård Bersvendsen, Norway (Col); Greg Abbott, USA (Per); Monika Agoston, UK (Bol, Per); Danny Aisner, Israel (Arg, Chi); Eitan Almog, Israel (Bol); Guy Alon, Israel (Bol); Tomer Alpert, Israel (Bol, Per); Mike Anderson (Col); Carlos Andrés, Colombia (Col); Dafna Angel, Colombia (Col); Stephan Arsand, Germany (Per); Joanne Asquith (Chi); Julian Baggini, UK (Arg); Bruce A Bayle, USA (Bol, Chi, Col, Per); Beatrix and Peter, Switzerland (Chi); Alice Beckhan, USA (Bol); Uria Berchman, Israel (Bra); Martha Bernal, Colombia (Col); Gerhard Biebl, Germany (Per); Hanelore Bode, Germany (Per); Jane Bode, Australia (Bol); Peter Boers, Netherlands (Col, Guy, Ven); Jim Bray, USA (Chi); Tim Brignall, UK (Bol, Per); Alan Brown, UK (Ecu); Dan Buck, USA (Arg); Jeremy Cameron, UK (Guy); Jarrad Carley, Australia (Chi); Johan Carlstedt, UK (Col); Cathy, USA (Ecu); Stella Cederqvist, Sweden (Uru); Geri Clark Hellery, UK (Chi); Anna Coffin (Bol); Brendan Colleran, Ireland (Ecu); Stefan Cotting, Switzerland (Guy); Maureen Cox, UK (Bol, Ecu, Per); Marcel Daeppen, Switzerland (Chi); Paul Dalebout, Netherlands (Chi); Eli David, Israel (Arg, Bra, Col, Per, Uru); Manuel de Arpe, Spain (Chi); Johan de Bruin,

Netherlands (Per); Lina Duque, Colombia (Col); Reid Dusenberry, USA (Per); Sally Dutson (Chi); Patrick Eberhardt, Switzerland (Per); Zohar Ehrlich, Israel (Chi); Marianne Elfving, Chile (Chi); Conor Farrington, UK (Ecu); Julia Feuer, Germany (Per); Tom Fischer, Germany (Ecu); Natalia Franco, Colombia (Col); Sandro Franke, Germany (Ven); Barry Freeder, UK (Bol, Ecu); Reto Frei, Switzerland (Chi); Louise Fridman, Sweden (Ecu); Mary Fu, USA (Chi); Alla G, USA (Arg); Jeannette Van Der Gaag, Netherlands (Bol); Mario Gaetani, Italy (Per); Christian Gagiano, UK (Per); Danielle Gagnon, USA (Ecu); Alvaro García, Uruguay (Ven); Étienne Gauthier, Canada (Bol); Sandrine Genoud, Switzerland (Per); Rebecca Giles, UK (Per); Mauricio González, Colombia (Col); Skye Greer, USA (Ecu); Alan Grovalle, Ireland (Ecu); Thomas Gut, Switzerland (Bol, Bra, Chi, Col, Ecu, Per); Lucas Haenen, Netherlands (Chi); Shai Haim, Israel (Chi); Austin Harrison, UK (Ecu); Brenda Harrison (Bol); Caroline Hartung, Switzerland (Arg); Mark Heald, Australia (Arg); Matt Hellery (Per); Owen Henderson and friends, UK, Australia, New Zealand (Bol); Peter Hutchison, UK (Bol, Bra); Keith Hyams, UK (per); Alyssa Isbel, Australia (Chi); Martina Iseli, Switzerland (Bol, Chi, Ecu); Julian Jaccard (Col); Luc Jansen, Netherlands (Per); Joseph Janzen, USA (Par); Beat Joho, Switzerland (Per); Emily Jones, Australia (Chi); K Jorgensen, Denmark (Ecu); Julietta Juras, UK (Per); Nicole K and her dog, Switzerland (Arg); Mascha Kamphuis and Boudewijn Spiering, The Netherlands (Per); Yasmin Khan (Bol); Naomi Kirk-Lawlor (Chi); Jeppe Klode, Denmark (Per); Christian Koch, Germany (Bol); Doris Kramm, Germany (Chi); Brad Krupsaw and Miriam Posz, Argentina (Uru); Andreas Kubach, Germany (Arg); Samuel Kutter, Germany (Per); Ted Labbe, USA (Arg); Jasmin Lappalainen, Finland (Per); Gary Levy (Arg); Sandra Lew (Per); Ido Lippmann, Israel (Per); Vicky Locke, UK (Bol, Bra, Chi, Per); Henry Long (Bra, Per); Melissa Topacio Long, USA (Bol); Rachel Loong, Australia (Per); Mag Maaboud, France (Arg, Chi, Ecu, Uru); Isabel McClure, Canada (Per); Ciara Maguire, Eire (Arg, Bol, Chi, Ecu); Devin Malone, USA (Per); Shawn Malone, USA (Ven); Jan Martinkovic, Switzerland (Ecu, Per); Anna Maurer, Austria (Per); Nirva Mevlat, Turkey (Per); Alexamder Mliakoff; Jean Claude Moreno, France (Bol); Lilo Neugebauer (Arg, Col); Clare Newman, UK (Per); Jim O'Sullivan (Per); Janet Olss; Christina Peter, Switzerland (Bol); Patrick Öhrström, Sweden (Chi); Melanie Peterson, USA (Bol); Joachim Pietsch, Germany (Per); Julien Pilet, Switzerland (Per); Ronald Plant, UK (Arg, Bol, Bra, Chi, Ecu, Per, Uru, Ven, Guy, Fal); Karin Planta, Germany (Chi); Patricia Quigley, France (Arg, Bra, Uru); Stuart Rackham, UK (Ecu); Marc Redbarn, Australia (Per); Louisa Reynolds, UK (Ecu); Ashley Rhodes, Spain (Col); Volker Ridder, Germany (Bol); Carmen Rodríguez, Colombia (Col); Robert Roebuck, USA (Ven); Chris Rohner and Anita Dernbach, Germany (Per); Shirley Ross, UK (Ecu); Beatriz Ruiz Luque, Argentina (Per); Mark Riley, Australia (Per); Donna Sager, USA (Col); Guenther M Schilcher, Austria (Chi); Oliver Schütz (Arg); Klaus Schwab, Germany (Chi); Oliver Schwan, Germany (Col); Nadine and Oli Schwarz, Switzerland (Per); Colin Seftel, South Africa (Arg, Bol, Per); Rob Selder, Netherlands (Chi); Martin Sewell, UK (Arg); Brid Shaughnessy, Ireland (Ecu); Andre Siraa, USA (Arg, Fal); Craig and Georgina Smith, UK (Bra, Ven); Kathleen Stanford, Australia (Per); Wolf Staub, Chile (Chi); Martin Steer, Ireland (Bol, Per); Marieka Stenson (Bol); Ramon Stevens, Australia (Per); Sasha Swerdloff, USA (Per); Saar Szekely, Israel (Per); Lisa Tracey, UK (Ecu); Enrique Tuki, Easter Island (Chi); Stephane Vasseur, Canada (Col); Thomas Verroust, France (Col); Anne-Marie Vigeant, Canada (Per); Hansje Amélie Vos, Netherlands (Bra); Johan Wagemans, Belgium (Per); Janine Wagner, Switzerland (Per); Clive Walker, Costa Rica (Arg, Chi); Eva Wassertheurer, Austria (Ecu); Susanne Wernli, Germany (Bol, Chi); Philip Whitehead, Australia (Chi); Claire Williams, UK (Ecu); Graham Williams, UK (Arg, Bol, Bra, Chi); Nerys Williams, UK (Per); Sue Williams and family, Colombia (Col); Lorelei Wilmot-Smith, UK (Ecu); Ori Yekutiel, Israel (Arg, Chi).

We should also like to thank all those who contributed to Footprint's recent editions on Argentina, Brazil, Chile, Ecuador and the Galápagos and Peru.

Specialist contributors: Peter Pollard for Land and environment; Nigel Gallop for Music and dance; Katie Moore and Steve Frankham for Off the beaten track/Thirty ways to escape; Ashley Rawlings for Motorcycling; Hallam Murray for Cycling; Hilary Bradt for Hiking and trekking; Richard Robinson for World wide radio information; Mark Eckstein for Responsible travel.

About the author

One of the first assignments **Ben Box** took as a freelance writer in 1980 was sub-editing work on the *South American Handbook*. The plan then was to write about contemporary Iberian and Latin American affairs, but in no time at all the lands south of the Rio Grande took over, inspiring journeys to all corners of the sub-continent. Ben has contributed to newspapers, magazines and learned tomes, usually on the subject of travel, and became editor of the *South American Handbook* in 1989. He has also been involved in *Footprint Central America & Mexico*, *Footprint Caribbean Islands*, *Footprint Brazil* and *Footprint Peru* since their inception. In 2001 he wrote *Footprint Cuzco & the Inca Heartland*, on which he now collaborates with Steve Frankham. Having a doctorate in Spanish and Portuguese studies from London University, Ben maintains a strong interest in Latin American literature and as a cricketer he looks forward to the day his village side is invited to play anywhere in South America where there is a pitch.

Credits

Footprint credits

Editorial team: Sophie Blacksell, Nicola Gibbs,
Felicity Laughton, Alan Murphy, Jo Williams
Map editor: Sarah Sorensen
Picture editor: Kevin Feeney

Publisher: Patrick Dawson
Cartography: Kevin Feeney, John Higgins,
Robert Lunn, Sarah Sorensen
Design: Mytton Williams
Sales and marketing: Hannah Bonnell, Zoë
Jackson, Andy Riddle
Advertising: Debbie Wylde
Finance and administration:
Elizabeth Taylor

Photography credits

Front cover: Stone/Getty
Back cover: South American Handbook 1924
cover
Inside: Dan Bannister, Katarzyna Citko, Dario
Diament, Ricky Elrod, ene, Vladimir
Korostyscevskiy, Laura Lohrman Moore, Rene
Mally, Marc Pagani Photography, Lorenzo
Puricelli, rm, rsfatt, Vinicius
Tupinamba/Shutterstock, infocusphotos.com,
Pep Roig/Alamy, age footstock/Superstock

Print

Manufactured in Italy by LegoPrint
Pulp from sustainable forests

Footprint feedback

We try as hard as we can to make each
Footprint guide as up to date as possible but, of
course, things always change. If you want to let
us know about your experiences – good, bad or
ugly – then don't delay, go to
www.footprintbooks.com and send in your
comments.

Publishing information

South American Handbook
84th Edition
© Footprint Handbooks Ltd
September 2007

ISBN 978 1 904777 96 0
CIP DATA: A catalogue record for this book is
available from the British Library

® Footprint Handbooks and the Footprint mark
are a registered trademark of Footprint
Handbooks Ltd

Published by Footprint

6 Riverside Court
Lower Bristol Road
Bath BA2 3DZ, UK
T +44 (0)1225 469141
F +44 (0)1225 469461
discover@footprintbooks.com
www.footprintbooks.com

Map symbols

Administration

- □   Capital city
- ○   Other city, town
- ⌁   International border
- ⌁   Regional border
- ⌁   Disputed border

Roads and travel

- ▬   Motorway
- ▬   Main road (National highway)
- ▬   Minor road
- ----   Track
- ......   Footpath
- ▬   Railway with station
- ✈   Airport
- 🚌   Bus station
- Ⓜ   Metro station
- ----   Cable car
- ++++   Funicular
- ⛴   Ferry

Water features

- ▬   River, canal
- ◯   Lake, ocean
- ▾ᵥ▾   Seasonal marshland
- ░   Beach, sandbank
- 𝒲   Waterfall
- ⌁   Reef

Topographical features

- ◯   Contours (approx)
- ▲   Mountain, volcano
- ⇆   Mountain pass
- ⌁   Escarpment
- ⌁   Gorge
- ⌁   Glacier
- ▦   Salt flat
- ⌁   Rocks

Cities and towns

- ▬   Main through route
- ▬   Main street

Minor street

- ▬   Minor street
- ▦   Pedestrianized street
- Σ ⊏   Tunnel
- →   One-way street
- ‖‖‖‖‖   Steps
- ⋈   Bridge
- ▬   Fortified wall
- ▦   Park, garden, stadium
- ●   Sleeping
- ❷   Eating
- ❶   Bars & clubs
- ▦   Building
- ▪   Sight
- ✝ ✝   Cathedral, church
- ☗   Chinese temple
- 🛕   Hindu temple
- ⚲   Meru
- ☪   Mosque
- ⌂   Stupa
- ✡   Synagogue
- 🅷   Tourist office
- 🏛   Museum
- ✉   Post office
- Ⓟ   Police
- Ⓢ   Bank
- @   Internet
- ♪   Telephone
- ☎   Market
- ✚   Medical services
- 🅿   Parking
- ⛽   Petrol
- ⛳   Golf
- Ⓐ   Detail map
- ◁Ⓐ   Related map

Other symbols

- ∴   Archaeological site
- ♦   National park, wildlife reserve
- ✵   Viewing point
- Ⲗ   Campsite
- ⌂   Refuge, lodge
- 🏰   Castle, fort
- ⌁   Diving
- 🌲🌴   Deciduous, coniferous, palm trees
- ⌂   Hide
- ⌁   Vineyard, winery
- ⌁   Distillery
- ⌁   Shipwreck
- ✕   Historic battlefield

Complete title listing

Footprint publishes travel guides to over 150 destinations worldwide. Each guide is packed with practical, concise and colourful information for everybody from first-time travellers to travel aficionados. The list is growing fast and current titles are noted below. Available from all good bookshops and online www.footprintbooks.com

(P) denotes pocket guide

Latin America & Caribbean
Antigua & Leeward Islands (P)
Argentina
Barbados (P)
Bolivia
Brazil
Caribbean Islands
Mexico & Central America
Chile
Colombia
Costa Rica
Cuba
Cusco & the Inca heartland
Dominican Republic (P)
Ecuador & Galápagos
Havana (P)
Nicaragua
Patagonia
Peru
Peru, Bolivia & Ecuador
Rio de Janeiro (P)
South American Handbook

North America
Vancouver (P)
Discover Western Canada

Africa
Cape Town (P)
Egypt
Kenya
Morocco
Namibia
South Africa
Tanzania

Middle East
Dubai (P)
Jordan
Syria & Lebanon

Australasia
Australia
Discover East Coast Australia
New Zealand
Sydney (P)
West Coast Australia

Asia
Bali
Bangkok & the Beaches
Borneo
Cambodia
Goa
India
Indonesia
Laos
Malaysia & Singapore
Rajasthan
South India
Sri Lanka
Sumatra
Thailand
Vietnam
Vietnam, Cambodia & Laos

Europe
Andalucía
Barcelona (P)
Bilbao (P)
Bologna (P)
Britain
Cardiff (P)
Costa de la Luz (P)
Croatia
Dublin (P)
Edinburgh (P)
European City Breaks
Glasgow (P)
Lisbon (P)
London
London (P)
Madrid (P)
Naples & the Amalfi Coast (P)
Northern Spain
Reykjavík (P)
Scotland Highlands & Islands
Seville (P)

Siena & the heart of Tuscany (P)
Tallinn (P)
Turin (P)
Turkey
Valencia (P)
Verona (P)
Wales

Lifestyle guides
Body & Soul escapes
Diving the World
Snowboarding the World
Surfing Britain
Surfing Europe
Surfing the World
Travel with Kids
Wine Travel Guide to the World

Also available
Traveller's Handbook (WEXAS)
Traveller's Healthbook (WEXAS)
Traveller's Internet Guide (WEXAS)

The South American Handbook: 1924-2008

It was 1921

Ireland had just been partitioned, the British miners were striking for more pa
and the federation of British industry had an idea. Exports were booming in
South America – how about a Handbook for businessmen trading in that fa
away continent? The *Anglo-South American Handbook* was born that year,
written by W Koebel, the most prolific writer on Latin America of his day.

1924

Two editions later the book was 'privatized' and in 1924, in the hands of Roy
Mail, the steamship company for South America, became *The South America
Handbook*, subtitled 'South America in a nutshell'. This annual publication
became the 'bible' for generations of travellers to South America and remair
so to this day. In the early days travel was by sea and the Handbook gave all
the details needed for the long voyage from Europe. What to wear for dinne
how to arrange a cricket match with the Cable & Wireless staff on the Cape
Verde Islands and a full account of the journey from Liverpool up the Amazo
to Manaus: 5898 miles without changing cabin!

1939

As the continent opened up, *The South American Handbook* reported the nev
Pan Am flying boat services, and the fortnightly airship service from Rio to
Europe on the Graf Zeppelin. For reasons still unclear but with extraordinary
determination, the annual editions continued through the Second World Wa

1970s

From the 1970s, jet aircraft transformed travel. Many more people discovere
South America and the backpacking trail started to develop. All the while th
Handbook was gathering fans, including literary vagabonds such as Paul Therou
and Graham Greene (who once sent some updates addressed to **"The
publishers of the best travel guide in the world, Bath, England"**.)

1990s

During the 1990s Patrick and James Dawson, the publishers of *The South
American Handbook* set about developing a new travel guide series using th
legendary title as the flagship. By 1997 there were over a dozen guides in the
series and the Footprint imprint was launched.

2000s

In 2003, Footprint launched a new series of pocket guides focusing on short-brea
European cities. The series grew quickly and there were soon over 100 Footprint
travel guides covering more than 150 destinations. In January 2004, *The South
American Handbook* reached another milestone as it celebrated its 80th birthday.
Later that year, Footprint launched its first Activity guide: *Surfing Europe*, packed wit
colour photographs, maps and charts. This was followed by further thematic guide
such as *Surfing Britain, Surfing the World, Diving the World, Snowboarding the Worla
Body and Soul escapes, Wine Travel to the World and Travel with Kids.*

The future

There are many more guides in the pipeline. To keep up-to-date with new release
check out the Footprint website for all the latest news and information,
www.footprintbooks.com.

The Falkland Islands

Take the road less travelled
and discover the difference...

www.visitorfalklands.com

info@visitorfalklands.com

PERURAIL

Exploring the Land of the Incas

Cusco - Lake Titicaca

A stunning rail journey beginning in Cusco and running south to the historic city of Puno and the famed Lake Titicaca. The gentle climb is breathtaking, with the first half of the journey dominated by magnificent Andean mountains, which slowly give way to the gentler, rolling Andean plains with their herds of vicuña and alpaca. There is a scenic stop at La Raya, the highest point of the journey.

An extraordinary destination deserves an extraordinary passage of way
Welcome aboard the Perurail's train services

Cusco - Machu Picchu

"In the variety of its charms and the power of its spell, I know of no place in the world which can compare with it. Not only has it great snow peaks looming above the clouds... it has also in striking contrast, orchids and ferns, the delectable beauty of luxurious vegetation, and the mysterious witchery of the jungle..."
Hiram Bingham *("Machu Picchu, The Lost City of the Incas")*

reservas@perurail.com
Phone: 084-238722
Fax: 084-222114
www.perurail.com

1562

South America

1 Cartagena — CARACAS
VENEZUELA
GUYANA GEORGETOWN
PARAMARIBO
SURI- CAYENNE
NAME, GUYANE **2**
BOGOTA
Cali COLOMBIA

QUITO **11**
ECUADOR
aquil **4** Manaus *Amazon* Belém **5**

Trujillo PERU
BRAZIL Recife

LIMA
Cuzco
Salvador
3 Lake
Titicaca LA PAZ Santa Cruz
de la Sierra BRASÍLIA
6 BOLIVIA
PARAGUAY
São Paulo
Salta ASUNCION Rio de Janeiro
CHILE **7**

Pacific Ocean Córdoba *Atlantic Ocean*

SANTIAGO URUGUAY
BUENOS AIRES MONTEVIDEO
ARGENTINA
8

Puerto
Montt
9

9 inset
Río *Falkland*
Gallegos *Islands*
Punta
Arenas *Tierra del*
Fuego

N **10** ECUADOR
Galápagos
Islands
0 km 500
0 miles 500

	National highway including Pan-American Highway
	Paved road
	Unpaved all weather including unpaved Pan-American Highway
	Seasonal unpaved road, track
	Rail

	Altitude in metres
	4000
	3000
	2000
	1000
	500
	200
	0
	Neighbouring Country

Map 1

Atlantic Ocean

N

0 km 90
0 miles 90

A

New
Amsterdam

Nieuw
Nickerie

Corriverton

Nat Res
Coppename
Monding

Nat Res
Wia-Wia

NR
Galibi

PARAMARIBO

Paranam

Albina

Aouara

Mana

Iracouba

Sinnamary

Iles du Salut

NR
Brinckheuvel

Brokopondo

St-Laurent

Nat Park
Brownsweg

Prof Dr Ir W J van
Blommesteinmeer

Paul Isnard

Kourou

Montsinéry

CAYENNE

Roura

Central Suriname
Nature Reserve

Kaw

Cacao

SURINAME

Cottica

Maripasoula

Régina

PN de Cabo
Orange

B

Corantijn

St Georges

Oiapoque

Saül

GUYANE

AI Uaçá

Mont
St-Marcel

Calçoene

Lourenço

Serra de
Tumucumaque

EE de Maracá-
Japioca

Amapá

BRAZIL

Parque Indígena
Tumucumaque

AI Waiãpi

AI Uaçá

Araguari

Porto Grande

C

Abacate

Ilha Caviana

RB do Rio
Trombetas

Macapá

Arquipélago
Jurupari
I Queimada

Ilha
Mexicana

Map 4

Map 5

Monte Dorado

Ilha Grande
de Gurupá

I Mututi

Ilha de Marajó

Paru

Almeirim

Amazonas

EE do Marajó

Monte
Alegre

Prainha

Alter do Chão

Santarém

Pacoval

Xingu

Oeiras do
Pará

Belterra

4

5

6

Map 3

Map 4

Map 5

Ilha do Marajó

EE do Marajó ♦

Soure

Baía de Marajó

Curuçá

Salinópolis

Ponta de Pedras

Belém

Castanhal

Bragança

Viseu

Carutapera

Capanema

Oeiras do Para

I Siribuba

Abaetetuba

Acará

Irituia

Turiaçu

Cururupu

Abaetetuba-Miri

Concórdia do Pará

Sta Helena

Alcântara

Humb do Ca

A

Tomé-Açu

Paragominas

São Luís

Baía de São Marcos

Baía de São José

Icatu

PN do E Maran

Urba Santo

Goianésia

Represa de Tucuruí

Al Rio Pindaré ♦

Pindaré

Miranda do Norte

Chapadinha

RI Paracaná ♦

Santa Luzia

Bacabal

Timbír

Pedreiras

Peritoró

Açailândia

Arame

Presidente Dutra

Caxias

Marabá

Imperatriz

Map 4

Araguaia

Barro do Corda

Sá das Alpercatas

Colinas

Tucuma

Estreito

Pastos Bons

Xinguara

Araguaína

Carolina

Riachão

Represal de Boa Esperança

Floria

B

Balsas

Uruçuí

Bertolínia

Conceição do Araguaia

Al Kraós ♦

Itauei

Flores Piau

Elisau Martins

Canto Buri

Guaraí

RI Xerentes ♦

BRAZIL

Cristino Castro

PN Se Cap

Miranorte

Miracema do Tocantins

São Raim Nona

PN do Araguaia ♦

Santa Teresinha

Palmas

Gilbués

Ilha do Bananal ♦

Fatimá

Porto Nacional

São Félix do Araguaia

Santa Rita de Cássia

Barrage Sobrac

Gurupi

Dianópolis

Ibiraba

PI do Araguaia ♦

Peixe

Conceição do Tocantins

Espigão Mestre

Mimosa d'Oeste

Boqueirão

Barra

Xi X

C

Alvorada

Paranã

Taipas

Capi

Araguaçu

Arraias

Taguatinga

Barreiras

Pirajaba

Ibotirama

Br

São Miguel do Araguaia

Campos Belos

Roda Velha

Brejolândia

Mundo Novo

Teresina de Goiás

Nova Roma

São Domingos

Santana

São Francisco

Bom Jesus da Lapa

Crixás

PN Chapada dos Veadeiros ♦

Correntina

Santa Maria da Vitória

Mozorlândia

1

Niquelândia

Posse

2

Map 7

Coribe

3

Map 8

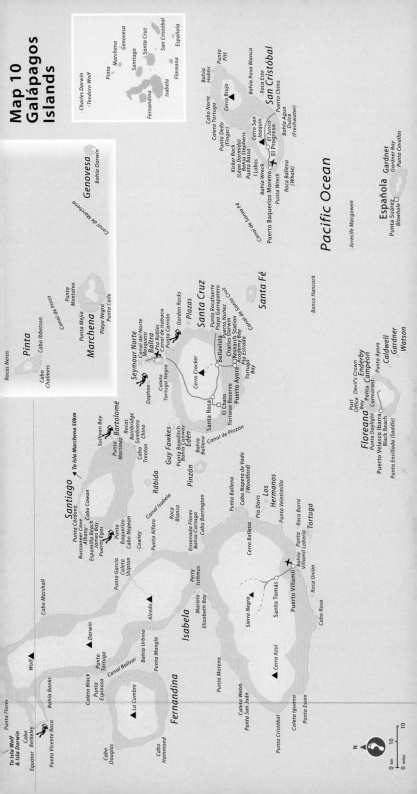

Map 10
Galápagos Islands

Pacific Ocean

Genovesa
Bahía Darwin
Canal de Marchena

Pinta
Cabo Nerus
Rocas Nerus
Cabo Chalmers
Cabo Ibbetson
Canal de Pinta
Punta Mejía
Punta Montalvo
Punta Calle
Playa Negra

Marchena

Santiago
Buccaneer Cove
Punta Córdova
Cabo Cowan
Albany
Espumilla Beach
James Bay
Puerto Egas
Punta Baquerizo
Cabo Nepean
Cowley
Punta Alfaro
To Isla Marchena 50km

Bartolomé
Punta Martínez
Rocas Bainbridge
Cabo Trenton
Sullivan Bay
Sombrero Chino

Seymour Norte
Baltra
Canal de Norte
Mosquera
Pta Robles
Punta Carrión
Canal de Itabaca
Caleta Tortuga Negra
Daphne

Santa Cruz
Punta de Norte
Punta Rocafuerte
Playa Garrapatero
Bellavista
Puerto Núñez
Charles Darwin Research Station
Academy Bay
Puerto Ayora
Punta Estrada
Tortuga Bay
El Chato Tortoise Reserve
Santa Rosa
Cerro Crocker
Gordon Rocks

Plazas
Santa Fé
Canal de Santa Cruz
Canal de Santa Fé

San Cristóbal
Punta Pitt
Bahía Rosa Blanca
Cabo Norte
Caleta Tortuga
Roca Este
Bahía Hobbs
Cerro Brujo
Punta Dedo (Finger)
Cerro San Joaquín
El Junco
El Progreso
Bahía Agua Dulce (Freshwater)
Kicker Rock (León Dormido)
Bahía Stephens
Punta Basso
I Lobos
Bahía Wreck
Puerto Baquerizo Moreno
Roca Ballena (Whale)
Punta Chino
Puerto Wreck
Punta Wreck

Guy Fawkes
Eden
Bahía Conway
Punta Bowditch

Pinzón
Bahía Ballena
Canal de Pinzón

Rábida
Roca Blanca
Canal Isabela

Los Hermanos
Punta Ballena
Cabo Ñapera de Vado (Woodford)
Ensenada Flores
Bahía Cartago
Cabo Barrington
Roca Barra
Punta Veintimilla

Tortuga
Cerro Ballena
Pta Davis
Roca Unión

Isabela
Cabo Marshall
Mariela
Elizabeth Bay
Perry Isthmus
Punta García
Caleta Shipton
Caleta Black
Punta San Juan
Coleta Webb
Punta Moreno
Cerro Azul
Punta Cristóbal
Coleta Iguana
Punta Essex
Cabo Rosa
Roca Rosa
Santo Tomás
Puerto Villamil
Bahía Villamil
Punta Lobería
Sierra Negra

Fernandina
Cabo Douglas
Cabo Hammond
Punta Mangle
Bahía Urbina
Canal Bolívar
La Cumbre
Caleta Black
Punta Espinosa
Bahía Banks
Darwin
Alcedo
Punta Tortuga
Cerro Ballena

To Isla Wolf & Isla Darwin
Wolf
Cabo Berkeley
Equator
Punta Vicente Roca
Punta Flores

Floreana
Post Office Bay
Devil's Crown
Punta Ayora
Cormorant
Punta Daylight
Punta Velasco Ibarra
Black Beach
Punta Ensillada (Saddle)
Enderby
Punta Campeón
Gardner
Caldwell
Watson

Española
Punta Suárez
Blowhole
Gardner
Gardner Bay
Punta Cevallos

Arrecife Macgowen
Banco Hancock

N
0 km   10
0 miles   10

Map 11 Ecuador

Footnotes